World Population

World Population
An Analysis of Vital Data

Nathan Keyfitz and Wilhelm Flieger

THE UNIVERSITY OF CHICAGO PRESS   CHICAGO & LONDON

Library of Congress Catalog Card Number: 68–14010

The University of Chicago Press, Chicago 60637
The University of Chicago Press, Ltd., London W. C. 1

Foreword

In this volume Professor Nathan Keyfitz, with the collaboration of his student Wilhelm Flieger, has demonstrated the power of the combination of demographic theory with the prodigious capabilities of the computer. They have, for the nations and subdivisions thereof for which basic population and vital statistics were available over time, caused the computer to apply techniques of analysis which set forth in comprehensive and voluminous form the meaning and implications of the data. In performing this task they have simultaneously facilitated the conduct of comparative demographic research and the testing and extension of demographic theory.

This volume is a product of a research program conducted at the Population Research and Training Center of the University of Chicago, initially made possible by a Ford Foundation grant, furthered in its experimental stages by a Population Council grant, and subsequently funded by a grant from the National Science Foundation. Earlier results of this research were reported in the volume *Comparative Demographic Computations* by Nathan Keyfitz and another of his students, Edmund M. Murphy, and in a number of articles in the technical journals. The investigations involved a highly interesting interplay of demographic theory and data which has led into various unexplored, or little explored, aspects of mathematical demography. Another offshoot of this research program will be the volume *Introduction to the Mathematics of Population* by Nathan Keyfitz, which will be published by Addison-Wesley in the series edited by Professor Frederick Mosteller.

Although the major bulk of this volume consists of computer output, it is more accurately described as a work of demographic analysis than as a compilation of data. Professional demographers as well as laymen in population matters would do well to read thoroughly the "Introduction" and to study carefully the "Tabular Summary" as a first step in the utilization of these materials. As the authors' introductory remarks and illustrative analytical observations indicate, this volume opens new vistas of opportunity for comparative demographic study. It permits, among other things, more careful examination of population dynamics—the interplay of fertility and mortality over time as it affects population growth and changes in the age structure. It affords a basis for evaluating the accuracy of vital statistics and census data, and the power of diverse techniques of population estimation.

The professional reader will find interesting the results of the application of principles and techniques, due to Thompson, Bourgeois-Pichat, and Coale, to relate births and age distribution; and he is likely to be grateful for the ready availability of such items as the a_x and other columns of the extensive life table; the comparison of observed and projected vital rates; the battery of standardized birth and death rates; the moments and cumulants of the principal distributions; the Leslie Matrix and its analysis; and the "miscellaneous results," including among other things an analysis of the contribution of the roots of the stable population equation to analysis of the age distribution. Also worthy of careful study are the tables using "male-dominant" as well as "female-dominant" models for the countries for which the data permit such calculations.

Although this volume is intended primarily to serve the professional demographer, the lay reader can use much of the information it contains and can profit greatly from a study of the data for the different countries over varying periods of time.

In the conduct of this program of study, Professor Keyfitz was able, in addition to adding to his basic contributions to demography, once more to demonstrate that the best way to train graduate students to do research is to provide them with opportunity to participate in research. This research program has provided a number of students with demographic apprenticeship training, including the co-author of this volume, Wilhelm Flieger; also, Rabindra Nath Bhattacharya, Susan Borker, Chen-Tung Chang, Prithwis Das Gupta, Rajinder P. Goyal, Jaya K. Misra, Edmund M. Murphy, Dhruva N. Nagnur, Mahendra K. Premi, Divakar Sharma, S. K. Sinha, Joseph Thomas, Andrea Tyree, and Dan D. Vandeportaele. It should be noted that by their labors these students have also made material contributions to demographic study and to future generations of students who will utilize these and subsequent findings in the classroom.

PHILIP M. HAUSER
Director
Population Research and Training Center
University of Chicago

Preface

The official position on population has changed from tribal to global in the past decade. Here is the first important matter on which local and national sovereignty has yielded to the interest of mankind. Throughout the span of human history, until about ten years ago, population was thought of in terms of the tribe, clan, culture group, religious group, or nation. The frame of reference was local, even though some localities were as big as the Augustinian Roman Empire, the France of Louis XIV, or Manchu China.

All these had in common a view that they needed more children. We cannot look back now and say that they were mistaken. For Rome more children meant more soldiers who could conquer fresh lands. Populous as the Empire was, the new children would be able to seize from barbarians the facilities for producing the food they needed. From the tribal viewpoint overpopulation is never a danger; new lands always exist to be conquered. Even within the tribe, to have more children is to increase one's standing and influence against less fertile neighbors.

The writers of civilized times who especially favored more people were those who identified with the autocratic ruler of a nation. To Süssmilch the divine order meant both that Frederick the Great should sit on the throne of Prussia and that Prussian women should bear more children who would grow up to serve in his armies. Süssmilch, an army chaplain, even called his book *Die Göttliche Ordnung*, to stress the high sanction given to the twin ideals of autocracy and population expansion.

By the time of Malthus, a generation or two later, the relation of rulers and ruled began to change drastically. From being stock, like cattle, and of similar usefulness to their proprietors, people were becoming, as the French Revolution showed, subjects for whom the ruler was forced to take responsibility. They were capable of riots that could threaten the whole civil order, a situation that has persisted from the storming of the Bastille in July, 1789, to the near-destruction of Detroit in July, 1967.

Docile subjects have largely disappeared today, along with the traditional absolute rulers whose property they were. Even where they remain, as in the Middle East, they cannot readily capture new lands in the face of resistance by small numbers of modernized people.

Moreover, the futility of breeding more and more subjects became apparent when human power began to be replaced by machine power. At the same time that men were making more demands on their rulers, they were becoming dispensable. In England, the leading country of the industrial revolution, excess population began to be seen as an obstacle to wealth and progress. The first writing of Malthus coincided with the first large-scale production of cotton textiles. While Malthus himself was oriented to the rural gentry, his ideas on population influenced others, notably Ricardo, who were concerned with industrial development and who saw how excess population can hold down wages.

The handicap that population increase imposes on the accumulation of capital has become especially clear in the presently underdeveloped countries, whether democratic or autocratic. A high burden of dependency, with 45 per cent and more of the population consisting of children under 15 years of age, absorbs the slender part of income that would otherwise be available for investment. Investment does not take place in sufficient amount, and when the children grow up they do not have the equipment that would enable them to be productive workers. Shortage of capital along with the shortage of land, which is a direct consequence of density, means that the new generation of workers either cannot find jobs at all, or else work unproductively. Either way they do not acquire enough of a stake in the system to motivate them to limit the numbers of their own children, and the pattern goes on repeating itself.

Among the facts that have led to the change in viewpoint is the sharp upturn of the curve of population. It took at least half a million years, up to 8000 B.C., to attain a population of five millions in the world. Growth sped with agriculture, and about the reign of Julius Caesar 300 million people, to within a hundred million either way, were dispersed over the planet. A similar pace of growth, neither faster nor slower as far as can be ascertained, continued through the Middle Ages and after, so that by 1750 A.D. the total was about 800 millions.

But now an acceleration started. The first billion was reached about 1825; the second billion about 1925; the third billion about 1960. The fourth billion will be reached in the mid-1970's. In the single month of September, 1967, the increase is more than in mankind's first half million years. If the present rate of somewhat over 2 per cent per year continues, without any further acceleration, the world population will be about 7 billion by the end of the century and about 14 billion by 2035, a year which 70 per cent of the children born in the United States in 1967 will live to see.

These numbers are due to death control's exceeding birth control. The death rate is still falling year by year at a fast pace, so that the 7 billions forecast by the year 2000 might even be criticized as conservative. To ascertain the trend in the birth rate is not easy; for all we know it may be rising at the present time. Some underdeveloped countries do indeed show a rise, not easily distinguished statistically from improved registration. If we are fortunate, the fall in the birth rate now seen in a few countries on the rim of Asia will spread rapidly elsewhere, but no one can yet judge the probability of this, nor its timing.

The initial upturn of world population came with the industrial revolution, occurring especially in Europe and America, which rapidly increased their proportion. Of the world growth from 1850 to 1900 some 56 per cent was in the presently developed countries, which contained about one third of the total. During 1900 to 1950 the developed and underdeveloped both grew at somewhat under one per cent per year, but recently the underdeveloped have sprung ahead. From 1950 to 1965 they increased at 2.1 per cent per year against the developed at 1.2 per cent. From 1965 to the end of the century, the underdeveloped could constitute 86 to 89 per cent of the growth, the developed countries only 11 to 14 per cent (Durand 1967, p. 7). These estimates are made by highly competent demographers, and they even assume some fall in fertility in Asia and Africa.

If from the tribal viewpoint overpopulation was never a danger, because the needed resources of land and food could always be obtained by conquest, from the world point of view overpopulation is plainly a danger. The crust of the planet contains a limited supply of minerals, especially of fossil fuels; it is overlaid with only so much soil from which food can be drawn; it has only so much air and water to absorb the pollutant by-products of human existence; ultimately it has only so much space on which humans can have elbow room. On the world scale all the rules of conduct change: having more children beyond a certain point does not increase total conquests or total influence; it only makes for deeper poverty in a deteriorating environment.

In the past ten years national policies have become oriented to this world point of view. Countries are prepared to yield national sovereignty in the field of population. No government today says what was the commonplace of Rome, of 17th century France, or of Germany under Hitler: we need more children *and* we will go out and conquer living room for them at the expense of less fertile peoples.

What we have called the tribal view of population is now untenable, because poor people cannot go out and conquer fertile lands for themselves, as they have done from biblical to mercantilist times; because even docile poor people are no longer of use to an autocrat; because in poor countries children compete with investment, and the latter offers a higher payoff in future income. In some countries one of these arguments prevails, and in others another, but among them they have very nearly driven out the tribal view from official circles.

That governments are coming to a world view is seen in many recent reports. Some 40 governments are providing assistance in family planning to their citizens. Three American presidents have frankly discussed the problem of overpopulation. The United Nations, the Catholic Church, and other international bodies have expressed their concern in a variety of ways (Hauser 1965, p. 3).

Such considerations have encouraged this assembly of material on world population. Data from many countries have become available through the leadership of the United Nations and other international agencies. Relatively precise official figures based on registration of births and deaths for nearly 30 per cent of humanity determine the limits of this volume.

To represent as much of the planet as is statistically covered and yet keep the bulk manageable, we have incorporated no subclasses other than age and sex, but on the other hand have subjected the data that are included to extensive computation. The meaning of death statistics is brought out by life tables. Birth data are better understood in terms of intrinsic rates. If births or deaths are to be compared among countries, standardization is needed. All these and many other derived numbers have been computed and printed out.

The figures, of which some 300,000 altogether are contained in these pages, are demographic analysis in the narrow sense (Hauser and Duncan 1959, p. 2). What form do actual age distributions have, and how are they changing? What are the trends in birth and death rates in America and in Asia? Do women in America have their children at younger ages than they used to? What are the ratios of men to women at various ages in Europe? For what countries is the birth rate falling, and how much of the fall is occurring at only the older ages of childbearing, how much through the span of reproductive life? Such are the questions directly answered by our numbers.

But taken in relation to other kinds of data, and to concepts and theories of economics, sociology, biology, and history, these numerical results provide a foundation for broad population studies. For what reasons lying in social structure do American women have children in a very narrow range of ages? What historical events of war and famine cause excess of one sex or the other at various ages today? What brought down the Swedish death rate so much earlier than the birth rate in the demographic transition of the 19th century, while in France births and deaths fell concurrently? Are we entering into a new phase of the demographic transition in the advanced countries, by which considerable oscillations in the birth rate about a mean of 18 or 20 per thousand will continue indefinitely? How long will it take for the fall in births, now statistically perceptible in half a dozen island and peninsular countries around the rim of Asia, to diffuse through the one and a half billion people on the continent proper?

While entirely clear-cut answers to such questions are not easily attained, data which follow can aid judgment and lend concreteness to theory.

NATHAN KEYFITZ
WILHELM FLIEGER, SVD

Contents

World Population

Introduction

The present report on a series of computations has seven objectives:

1. To present official data on births, deaths, and population, all by age and sex, for as many periods of time and countries as possible (Table 1).
2. To calculate life tables which conform to those data (Tables 2 and 3).
3. To facilitate comparisons of mortality and fertility among countries and moments of time (Tables 2, 3, and 6).
4. To establish a benchmark for work on future population, the benchmark taking the form of a projection with mortality and fertility fixed and zero migration (Tables 4 and 5).
5. To analyse age distributions (Tables 7, 9, and 10).
6. To infer birth rates from age distributions, and so check the birth rates as given in vital statistics (Table 8).
7. To work out such measures of the combined action of mortality and fertility as intrinsic rates of birth, death, and natural increase, and Gross and Net Reproduction Rates (Tables 4, 8, 9, and 10).

The ten tables are contained on a pair of facing pages produced by the computer. The first objective—assembly of data—is completed in Table 1, and the second—calculation of life tables—in Tables 2 and 3. In a number of instances several tables contribute to one objective; the life tables as well as the standardized rates facilitate comparisons of mortality (objective 3). The first eight tables will be easily read. Some of the measures of Tables 9 and 10, on the other hand, are more technical (for instance the complex roots of the projection matrix) and will be of interest only to specialists. We apologize to the general reader for the latter, and for the superfluous decimal places, especially for small countries, and plead computing convenience for both.

Comparisons among countries and points of time are tedious to make from the separate pages of the volume, and a combined summary and index shows a line for each population, on which 22 key figures are given along with a reference to the page on which more detailed information will be found.

The text below starts with a brief non-technical summary of the tables, including illustrations of their use.

A list of symbols and their definitions is presented for reference, arranged in the same sequence as the printout, sufficiently precise, it is hoped, to make the figures intelligible. For the reader who wants to go further on any point, detailed technical notes are available on request.

The main results, given on pages 54–577, are arranged by continents and, within continents, alphabetically by countries. It seemed more convenient to follow the United Nations (for example, in the *Demographic Yearbook*) than to innovate on arrangement. Territorial definitions of countries are in general those of the United Nations, except where the aim of historical comparability suggested a modification. For instance, Newfoundland, Yukon, and the Northwest Territories were omitted from Canada throughout the years 1931 to 1963.

We did not have the space to show all calculations for all countries and for all points of time, and were constrained to group calendar years; the Swedish and other long historical series are shown in five-year periods, and contemporary data often in three-year periods. The complete printout, Tables 1–10, spread over two facing pages, is shown at least once for all countries on which we had information, and at 25-year intervals where long sequences of years were available. For intermediate times within each interval, only the left-hand page, Tables 1–4, is given, providing data, life tables, and intrinsic rates. The summary, however, includes a line with 22 entries for each population whether printed in the body of the book as one page, two pages, or not at all.

Following the main set of tables are four subsidiary groups, largely experimental in character:

Pooled data. Advantage was taken of the capacity of the computer to add together data referring to different countries and then to work out life tables and other calculations for the aggregate, with the same program used for individual countries. The present volume makes only a small start in this by showing the Common Market countries and other groupings of Europe and then Europe as a whole. It also groups the states of the United States according to levels of mortality.

Cohorts. Most published demographic materials refer to cross sections of time—one-, three-, or five-year periods—showing different ages but making no attempt to follow the demographic careers of individuals. A few pages of this book are devoted to an experiment in following individuals and cohorts of individuals born in the same year. Data for persons under five years of age are taken at one point of time; for those five to nine years of age are taken five calendar years later, etc. In this way an approximation to cohorts has been made for the United States and Sweden.

Male-dominant tables. While in most of the volume births are associated with mothers, a mode of calculation known as female dominance and required by the nature of the data ordinarily published, seven countries do provide as well births by age of father, and so permit the alternative male-dominant computation. This does not affect mortality, and the left-hand page of the pair of facing pages, containing Tables 1–4, is not repeated.

Hypothetical materials. The partial or complete absence of birth and death information for much of the planet is the major defect of any such collection as the present one. Some guesses for missing territories are therefore attempted in the final section.

A NON-TECHNICAL ACCOUNT OF THE TABLES

We turn now to a discussion of the ways in which the ten tables shown on pairs of facing pages are intended to meet the seven objectives set for this volume.

1. *Official Data on Births, Deaths, and Population*

All the results of Tables 2–10 are based on the data of Table 1, and no other input was used. A statement of sources for any of the data is available on request to readers who wish to make use of it. The documentation that has been prepared turned out to be too bulky to print with each page of data, and its absence in the volume is regretted. We can only say here that the data comes from official national publications or through the reliable secondary source constituted by the United Nations *Demographic Yearbooks* from 1948 to 1966; a consolidated list of sources is included with the bibliography on pages 667–71.

Our aim was to incorporate whatever good data on birth and death by age and sex is extant, for all countries and as many years as possible. Even if we had been able to obtain all existing data, we would be considerably short of a complete picture of world mortality and fertility. Only 67 per cent of the world population is covered by a recent census (*United Nations*

Demographic Yearbook, 1963, p. 4), and the percentage is lower in earlier decades. The percentage comes down from 67 per cent to 62 per cent if we require that the census be by sex, and to 57 per cent if by age. The part of the world in which births and deaths are effectively registered is smaller yet. We restricted ourselves to countries in which births *and* deaths as well as population were available, all by age and sex.

The unevenness of coverage of the several continents is shown numerically by the populations in our collection as of 1965. The continental summary of Table A presents this along with the United Nations estimate of the population of the continent.

TABLE A

COVERAGE ATTAINED BY CONTINENTS, ABOUT 1965
(Population in Millions of Persons)

	Coverage of Present Compilation	*U. N. Estimate*
Africa	8	310
Northern America	214	214
Latin America	111	243
Asia	157	1,825
Europe	443	444
Oceania	14	18
USSR	0	231
TOTAL	947	3,285

Source: United Nations, *Demographic Yearbook*, 1965, Tables 1 and 4.

In all, some 947 million people, or 29 per cent of the world population, live in territories in which births and deaths are regularly registered with some claim to completeness and in which we were able to obtain data for at least one period.

The list of countries given as Table B is arranged by continents and alphabetically by countries within continents, as are the main results of this volume. The population shown is estimated to the nearest 100,000 in 1965. The code for quality of birth and death data is that used by the United Nations; C means that the registration is nationally estimated to be 90 per cent or more complete; U means that it is less than 90 per cent complete; • means that no information on quality of data is available.

TABLE B

LIST OF COUNTRIES INCLUDED IN PRESENT VOLUME,
INDICATION OF QUALITY OF STATISTICS,
AND 1965 POPULATION

Births[c]	Deaths[d]		Population in Millions[a] 1965
		Africa	
C	C†	Mauritius	0.7
C[e]	C[e]	Reunion	0.4
		South Africa	
C	C	Colored	1.8[b]
C	C	White	3.4[b]
·†	·	Togo	1.6
		Total Africa	7.9
		North America	
C†	C†	Barbados	0.2
C	C	Canada	19.6
C	C	Costa Rica	1.4
U†	U†	Dominican Republic	3.6
C	C	El Salvador	2.9
C†	C†	Grenada	0.1[b]
U†	U†	Honduras	2.3
C†	C†	Jamaica	1.8
C[e]	C[e]	Martinique	0.3
C†	C†	Mexico	40.9
C	U	Panama	1.2
C	C	Puerto Rico	2.6
C†	C†	St. Kitts	0.1[b]
C	C	Santa Lucia	0.1
C	C	Trinidad	1.0
C	C	United States	194.6
		Total North America	272.7
		South America	
C	C	Argentina	22.4
C†	C†	British Guiana	0.7[b]
C	C	Chile	8.6
U	U	French Guiana	0.04
U†	U†	Peru	11.7
U†	U	Venezuela	8.7
		Total South America	52.1

[a] Source: United Nations, *Demographic Yearbook*, 1965, Table 4.
[b] Extrapolated.
[c] Source: *Demographic Yearbook*, 1965, Table 11.
[d] Source: Same, Table 42.
[e] Includes children living to time of registration of birth.

TABLE B (continued)

Births[c]	Deaths[d]		Population in Millions[a] 1965
		Asia	
U†	U†	Ceylon	11.2
C†	C†	China (Taiwan)	12.4
·	·	Cyprus	0.6
C	U	Israel	2.6
C	C	Japan	98.0
C	C†	Singapore	1.9
U†	U†	Thailand	30.6
		Total Asia	157.3
		Europe	
C	C	Albania	1.9
C	C	Austria	7.3
C	C	Belgium	9.5
C	C	Bulgaria	8.2
C	C	Czechoslovakia	14.2
C	C	Denmark	4.8
C	C	Finland	4.6
C	C	France	48.9
C	C	East Germany	17.0
C	C	West Germany (incl. West Berlin)	59.0
U	U	Greece	8.5[b]
C	C	Hungary	10.1
C	C	Iceland	0.2[b]
C†	C†	Ireland	2.9
C	C	Italy	51.6
C	C	Luxemburg	0.3
C	C	Malta	0.3
C	C	Netherlands	12.3
C	C	Norway	3.7
C	C	Poland	31.4
C	C	Portugal	9.2
C	C	Romania	19.0
C	C	Spain	31.6
C	C	Sweden	7.7
C	C	Switzerland	5.9
		United Kingdom—	
C	C	England & Wales	47.8[b]
C	C†	Scotland	5.2[b]
C	C	Yugoslavia	19.5
		Total Europe	442.6

[a] Source: United Nations, *Demographic Yearbook*, 1965, Table 4.
[b] Extrapolated.
[c] Source: *Demographic Yearbook*, 1965, Table 11.
[d] Source: Same, Table 42.
[e] Includes children living to time of registration of birth.

TABLE B (continued)

Births[c]	Deaths[d]		Population in Millions[a] 1965
		Oceania	
C†	C†	Australia	11.4
C†	U†	Fiji Islands	.5
C†	C†	New Zealand	2.6
		Total Oceania	14.5
		GRAND TOTAL	947.1

Of the 947 million people who live in countries with some sort of registration system, about 83 million are in systems said to be incomplete either as to births or deaths. Many of the remainder tabulate births and deaths as of the time of registration, rather than by time of occurrence, which alone has demographic meaning; following the United Nations, a dagger (†) marks the tabulations by year of registration.

Estimates for eleven of the omitted territories, shown in the last section under the heading "Hypothetical Materials," point to a present population of about one and three-fourths billion persons. These include only countries of over 25 million persons. The fact that we had to resort to guesses in respect to more than half of the world's population again emphasizes the inadequacy of demographic coverage.

Africa is the continent about whose fertility and mortality least is known. The four representatives of Africa in this volume are Mauritius, an island in the Indian Ocean; Reunion, another island in the Indian Ocean east of Madagascar; South Africa; and Togo. Only the last named is on the mainland and provides statistics for a genuine African population, numbering about a million and a half showing a birth rate of 55 per thousand and a death rate of 29 per thousand. We regret especially, therefore, that an element of estimation exists in the birth and death data on Togo (*Demographic Yearbook*, 1965, pp. 267, 733).

Asia is better endowed with registration systems than Africa, and Latin America better yet. But even for Latin America considerably less than half of the population is included, and some of the statistics which exist show inadequacies, especially in respect to births.

Europe is almost completely covered in recent times, and it is the only continent for which we could usefully assemble population, births, and deaths, to provide a continental life table and other aggregate results. For the

United States a correction to registered births has been provided, and two sets of computations are printed out for Tables 5–10, based on the original and the corrected birth registrations.

The extension of demographic statistical coverage in Africa, Asia, and Latin America is an urgent necessity. Some material exists for individual countries concerning births, or concerning deaths, but not both; such fragments were not included here. For many countries neither births nor deaths are registered. The most immediate hope for these lies in sample surveys, where the need is for better techniques, statistical leadership, and operational skill.

In most instances we sent a copy of the data we had extracted from printed sources to the statistical authorities of the country, asking for corrections and, in particular, for estimates of underenumeration or registration. We received many modifications of the published national figures, and would like to thank the members of thirty-five statistical agencies, listed on page 671, that collaborated with us. Responsibility for errors in their reproduction, as in the computations made from them, is ours alone.

The data as set forth in each Table 1 of this volume are the same as those published or provided in correspondence by the national authorities, except for three kinds of minor adjustment performed by the computer:

a) Not-stated ages were distributed in proportion to the stated ages of each sex.

b) Population counts were adjusted to mid-period, generally by interpolating between successive censuses or estimates, age by age. In the few cases where a census or estimate for only one point of time was available, all ages were increased or diminished by a single ratio based on births minus deaths for that point of time.

c) Our main program required ages 0, 1–4, 5–9, . . ., 85+ for population and deaths. Where ages were missing or grouped, for instance 75+ being given as a single interval, we extrapolated by methods that suppose a stable distribution for the missing or grouped ages. In about a dozen cases the older ages appeared to be inaccurately given, as indicated for example by the age-specific death rates falling sharply towards the end of life. Such data were replaced by an extrapolation similar to that used where data were missing.

2. *Calculation of Life Tables*

Our printout shows for each of the 400 populations a life table containing ten columns in all. In some early work we graduated the population and deaths into single years of age, or fifths of a year of age, made the life table, and then condensed back to five-year age groups. This was abandoned in favor of an iterative process in which the life table was made to agree with the data in the five-year age groups given (Keyfitz 1966). The columns are discussed below and their use illustrated with the table based on average deaths of 1959–61 and the 1960 Census, for United States males (p. 152).

The column at the extreme right of Table 2 labelled $_nM_x$ exhibits the observed age-specific death rates. Each figure is the ratio of male deaths to population; $_1M_0$ is 63,477/2,091,000 or 0.030357; $_4M_1$ is 9,502/8,260,000 = 0.001150, etc. No data go into the table other than these deaths and population in the 19 ages shown. The life table method used agrees with data consisting of population estimates at mid-period and deaths. No use is made in Tables 2 and 3 of births to calculate q_0. An approximation to an alternative q_0, obtained by dividing deaths of the given year by births of the same year, is shown as column 13 of the Summary Table.

From the $_nM_x$ are calculated the probabilities, $_nq_x$, that a person alive at the beginning of the interval of n years will die during the interval. It suffices to say here that the $_nq_x$ is about n times the $_nM_x$.

The age-by-age probabilities of dying, $_nq_x$, permit construction of a hypothetical cohort of 100,000 boy babies just born, showing how many will survive to first birthday, fifth birthday, etc. Thus $l_0q_0 = 100,000 \times 0.029656 = 2,966$ or $_1d_0$ will be expected to die within the first year; this leaves $100,000 - 2,966 = 97,034$ or l_1 surviving to their first birthday; multiplying 97,034 by 0.004585 gives 445 or $_4d_1$ dying within the next four years; subtracting 445 from 97,034 gives 96,590 arriving at their fifth birthday, etc.

By completing the l_x and d_x to the end of life we have the story of the hypothetical cohort, and also the probabilities of surviving from any age to any other age. For instance, at the United States rates prevailing in 1959–61 the chance that a man of thirty survives to age seventy is $l_{70}/l_{30} = 52,189/93,779 = 0.55651$. In Sweden for 1778–82 the corresponding probability was quite different: $18,673/53.402 = 0.34967$ (p. 462).

The life table l_x may be thought of not only as the number of survivors of a cohort and as probabilities for any individual, but it also has a third meaning: the age distribution which could be existing at a moment of time, if the given mortality schedule prevailed and births were equal to deaths. The actual numbers that would be alive from ages x to $x + 4$ at last birthday, the area between x and $x + 5$ under the curve of l_x, is denoted $_nL_x$. With 100,000 births per year, subject to United States 1959–61 mortality, the number of persons living between ages 10 and 14 at last birthday would be $_5L_{10}$ or 481,026.

Reverting now to the probability viewpoint, $_5L_x$ is the expected number of years which will be lived in the interval by the l_x individuals who enter the age group. Thus the $l_{15} = 96,056$ boys of fifteen years of age will together live 478,868 years before the age of 20. Since the l_{20} who reach age 20 will have lived five years each in the preceding five years, or $5l_{20}$ in all, then the number of years lived by those $_5d_{15}$ who die in the interval must be the difference $_5L_{15} - 5l_{20}$, or an average of $(_5L_{15} - 5l_{20})/_5d_{15}$ or 2.6991 years. In general the average number of years lived in the interval by those dying in the interval is $_na_x = (_nL_x - nl_{x+5})/_nd_x$, and this is printed out as a separate column.

The column headed T_x is $_nL_x$ added up from the end of the table, and represents the total number of years in prospect for those who reach age x. Thus the 96,056 boys who reach age 15 have in prospect the sum of the L_x to the end of the table, which is $T_{15} = 5,235,792$. Hence the average in prospect for each, his expectation, is $T_{15}/l_{15} = 5,235,792/96,056 = 54.507$ years, and in general $\overset{\circ}{e}_x = T_x/l_x$. The expectation $\overset{\circ}{e}_x$ is of course a special case of $_na_x$ when n becomes large.

The column headed $_nm_x$ is the age-specific death rate in the hypothetical life table or stationary population. That population contains $_nL_x$ persons between ages x and $x + n$, $_nd_x$ of whom die during the year of time, so the age-specific death rate $_nm_x$ is $_nd_x/_nL_x$. Where the aggregate number is not stationary but increasing, the population is humped towards the lower end of each age group, and for those ages (beyond about 10) at which mortality is going up from age to age, the age-specific rate $_nM_x$ in the observed (increasing) population is less than $_nm_x$ in the stationary population. For example, at age 45 $_nM_x$ is 0.007461 while $_nm_x$ is 0.007477.

Our estimate of the rate of increase $_nr_x$ is made age by age; over 15-year sections of age corresponding to high birth rates or rapid immigration, the observed numbers will decrease more rapidly from age to age than the life table numbers. By comparing numbers in two age classes we infer a rate of increase for each five-year age group. These can be identified with the birth level at the time when the individuals were born; for the United States, rapid in the 1940's and 1950's (ages 5 to 20 in 1960) and slow in the 1930's (ages 20–30). Any negative values of r which appeared were replaced by zeros. The r's permitted calculating the $_nq_x$ with given $_nM_x$ by an iterative method (Keyfitz 1966).

Variation among life tables is suggested by the range of $\overset{\circ}{e}_0$ from 28.99 for Swedish males in 1808–12 to over 75.00 for females in several countries today.

Our computed life tables have been compared with those published by national statistical offices. A few such comparisons for $\overset{\circ}{e}_0$, shown in Table C, indicate the order of magnitude of the differences.

TABLE C

VALUES OF $\overset{\circ}{e}_0$ ON PRESENT COMPUTATION,
AND PUBLISHED OFFICIALLY,
FOR FIVE POPULATIONS.

	Present Computation	Official Figure[a]
UNITED STATES 1959–61		
Males	66.84	66.80
Females	73.40	73.24
ENGLAND AND WALES 1960–62		
Males	68.10	68.0
Females	73.97	74.0
SCOTLAND 1960–62		
Males	66.14	66.20
Females	71.91	71.87
CANADA 1960–62		
Males	68.41	68.35
Females	74.29	74.17
JAPAN 1962		
Males	66.26	66.24
Females	71.21	71.16

[a] Source: United Nations, *Demographic Yearbook*, 1963, Table 26.

3. *Comparisons of Mortality and Fertility*

Facilities for intercountry comparison are contained especially in Table 6, in which standardized rates by age and sex are shown with three different standards. But other material in the pair of facing pages, including crude rates and life tables, also contributes.

As an example of the sort of question for which the tables are designed to provide a convenient answer, consider the mortality of the United States against that of England and Wales, each in 1963.

The first observation seems to put England and Wales clearly ahead: for males the expectation of life at age zero was 67.869 (p. 538) against 66.677 in the United States (p. 160); for females England and Wales was 73.874 against 73.416 in the United States.

The age-weighting implicit in the $\overset{\circ}{e}_0$ is that of the stationary population. This suffers from two defects: the stationary population is not quite the same for the two populations being compared, and it is older on the whole than either one of two increasing populations. The latter point is of considerable effect in close comparisons; for United States males in 1963 the observed average age was 30.833 years, as against 36.231 years for the stationary population; for females the difference is greater, with 32.353 and 39.052. (These averages come from Table 7, discussed below.)

The crude death rates of Table 4 show the United States at 9.61 per thousand population, taking both sexes together, and England and Wales at 12.18. The difference for females is even more striking than for both sexes: 8.19 for the United States and 11.59 for England and Wales. We may want to know to what extent these differences are the result of irregularities in the age distribution, owing to different demographic histories, and to what extent they would persist if present birth and death rates in the two countries continued and irregularities were smoothed out. This is answered by the intrinsic death rate, which refers to the stable population, also shown in Table 4; for females the United States stands at 7.46 against 9.16 in England and Wales. But the stable population, even more than the stationary, is different between the two countries.

The comparison of two populations is best made with an age distribution that is the same for both and as similar as possible to those observed. Table 6 constitutes such a comparison for males, females, and total, using the United States 1960 as the standard, and England and Wales 1961 as the standard. England and Wales has higher mortality both when standardized on the United States (9.84 against 9.54) and on England and Wales (12.11 against 11.62).

Such a contradiction between the standardized rates on the one hand and the expectations of life on the other prompts us to look at the age-specific rates, $_nM_x$, given as the right-hand column of the life table. For males (Table 2) at all ages up to 60 the United States rates are higher; subsequently England and Wales is higher. For women the differentials are in the same direction, though somewhat less in amount, and the cross-over point is five years older.

The standardizations are useful for other kinds of analysis. The pace at which death rates were falling during the demographic transition in Sweden and elsewhere; the comparison of levels of fertility between the presently developing countries for which data are given in this volume and those of Europe when the latter were developing; the tendency toward a drop in fertility in certain countries on the rim of Asia; study of the countries of Western Europe to see if any meaningful differences appear; all these can be initiated with the materials of this volume.

4. A Projection Benchmark

Population projections as printed out in Tables 4 and 5 are to be thought of as interpretation of the present rather than prediction of future populations. If the observed rates of birth and death continue and immigration is zero, the figures shown will be attained; their meaning is conditional.

A use of our projections is to tie together the historical series. The 1808–12 data for Sweden project a total population 15 years later, in 1825, of 2,388,000. The projection to this same · date was 2,657,000 from the 1813–17 information; 2,692,000 from the 1818–22 information; 2,749,000 as actually observed in 1825. The steady rise in the prospects for 1825 as it was approached in time might have been due to immigration into Sweden, but in fact the cause was improvement in mortality and fertility over the fifteen-year period. The absolute number of deaths fell from 78,760 per year in 1808–12 to 59,350 per year in 1823–27; the number of births rose during the same period from 76,624 to 95,483.

In later years mortality and fertility changes were small compared with migration. For instance, the 1895 population was projected in 1880 at 5,485,000; in 1885 at 5,277,000; in 1890 at 5,053,000; and was counted at 4,896,000. The drop in the prospect as 1895 approached was due to emigration.

In a country with high immigration the differences are of course in the opposite direction. The projection of Canadian population from 1951 gave 16,049,000 for a date ten years later; the census count of 1961 was 17,769,-000 (after adjustment to July 1 for the same nine provinces). The difference of 1.7 million is due to immigration more than to any other factor.

5. *Analysis of Age Distributions*

Age distribution varies among countries in accord with their demographic history. High birth rates leave an age distribution which slopes sharply downwards; a wave of immigration leaves a hump which is seen in later censuses to travel through successive ages; a depression leaves a dip. We will exemplify some of the uses of the information on age distribution in the printout by comparing Canada and the United States for the year 1964 (pp. 89, 162–63).

Table 1 shows percentage age distribution to the right of the absolute numbers of each sex. On the male side we note that 2.4 per cent of Canadian males are under one year of age, against 2.2 per cent of United States males; the difference accords with the crude birth rates of the two countries as shown in Table 4. The difference in favor of Canada persists until age 40 for both sexes, after which the United States is ahead until the end of life. The country of higher birth rate has relatively more population below the average age.

A summary of the same percentage distributions is shown in Table 4, where, taking both sexes together, Canada has 33.41 per cent under age 15, while the United States has 31.08 per cent. Subsequent columns show how the figures will change, for males and females separately, when the populations are projected forward with the age-specific birth and death rates of 1964.

At the beginning of Table 10 is a decomposition of the female age distribution which, among other things, shows what sorts of cycles can be expected in the future. The contribution of the dominant root, shown in the second column of the table, is proportional to the female stable population that would result from continuance of 1964 age-specific birth and death rates. It falls far short of accounting for the observed age distribution. At ages 5–9, for example, the United States observed population is 677,000 above the stable age distribution; at ages 25–29, 1,123,000 below.

The nature of the indentations in the United States age distribution is not such that their movement with the passage of time will greatly alter the death rate. To see an example of change that does affect the death rate we turn to Japan females 1962. The stable component is below the observed for ages 10–19, and for all ages beyond 20 the stable is above the observed. The total of ages 55 and over is only 6,630,000 in the observed, and in the stable it is 21,293,000. This arises from the fact that the birth rates of Japan fell sharply in the twelve years before 1960. If we did not know this directly from vital statistics shown on other pages of the present volume, we could ascertain it from the calculations reported in Table 8 under "Thompson," where the intrinsic rate inferred from the children 10–14 is 17.47 per thousand, and that from the 0–5 is −1.72.

The population of Japan is bound to show higher average age with the passing of time, if the age-specific rates of 1962 persist. In Table 7 the average age of women in the observed population is 30.3 years; that in the stable is 40.0 years. The variance of ages in the observed female population is 401 and contrasts with the variance in the stable age distribution of 535. The rise in both mean and variance reflects a spread to the right in the age distribution, an aging which by itself would make for an increase in mortality. The crude death rate for females goes from the observed 6.82 per thousand to 15.77 per thousand in the stable population. On our assumptions the health condition of the population age for age does not change, and the rise from 6.82 to 15.77 is due entirely to the changed mix of ages.

The effect of the changed mix appears in various places in the printout for Japan. The proportion of females under 15 years of age (Table 4) drops from the observed 27.71 per cent to 18.26 per cent in the stable condition; the proportion over age 65 rises in about the same amount—from 6.54 per cent to 17.36 per cent. The projections show that the adjustment of the age proportions to the new birth levels is far more prompt for children than for old people. The dependency ratio (the ratio to those 15–64 of the number outside these ages) first falls—is as low as 43.20 by 1972—and then rises to 55.32 in the ultimate population, above its 1962 value.

Aside from the usual stable age distribution we have printed out the other real stable vector of the age distribution, which also appears in two forms. The Fisher reproductive value is the future girl children that will be born to a girl or woman now alive, on the given regime of mortality and fertility, if the children are discounted at the intrinsic rate. Then, considering a girl child just born (boy child in the male dominant tables) as having the value 1, we can find the total reproductive value of a population by multiplying the observed female age distribution by the column headed "Fisher," age for age, and this product is given in Table 9 of the printout. Its total is shown in column 21 of the summary table.

The total reproductive value for United States women stood at 53,996,-000 in 1959–61, and at 55,728,000 in 1964. The percentage increase over the three-year period is somewhat smaller than that of the population as a whole, owing to the fall in 1,000 r from 20.7 to 15.7.

With fixed age-specific rates, the reproductive value grows at the intrinsic rate. This property is not shared by numbers of individuals whose increase depends on their age distribution.

6. *Completeness of Birth Registration Estimated from Age Distribution*

Certain information has been incorporated in the printout to aid judgment on the quality of the statistics used, and in particular on the defect, which is both common and serious, of incomplete birth registrations. No examination for consistency could perceive an omission across the board (for instance the omission of an entire province of a country), but a substantial omission in the birth statistics when the deaths and population are complete can probably be detected.

We use as our illustration of this part of the analysis the printout for Panama 1962 (pp. 124–25), which shows (Table 4) an observed crude birth rate of 41.47 per thousand on the female side. The projections at the reported 1962 rates show a crude female birth rate of 41.06 for 1967; of 40.79 for 1972; of 40.64 for 1977; and 41.61 ultimately, the last being the intrinsic birth rate. That these do not change greatly in the projection shows that the population age distribution is nearly stable as observed in 1962, a point confirmed by the index of dissimilarity between observed and stable ages, Δ in Table 10, which is only 2.34, among the lowest of all the populations in the volume. This invites the use of the age distribution for the estimation of births.

The principal evidence on completeness of birth registrations appears in Table 8. Under "Thompson" is shown the Net Reproduction Rate (defined as the expected number of girl children that a girl child just born will bear under the given regime of mortality and fertility) worked out by the ratio of children to women in the census, and using the life table but disregarding altogether the birth registrations. The first figure of this part of the table tells us that the ratio of children 0–4 to women 15–44 estimates the NRR at 2.33. The observed NRR from vital statistics was 2.51. Using older children and older women results successively in 2.27, 2.26, and 2.23 for the estimate of the NRR. That the infant mortality was falling in the 20 years preceding 1962 would explain the rise in time of the NRR as obtained by this method, without the need to suppose that births were rising, although this is not excluded. The method seems relatively insensitive to migration from abroad.

These results can be converted into intrinsic rates of natural increase by noting that the time interval between the children and their mothers was 27.32 for the 0–4 and 15–44 calculation, and taking this root of the estimated NRR gives intrinsic rate of $\frac{\log_e 2.33}{27.32} = 31.0$ per thousand; the intrinsic rate of 34.65 of Table 4 is higher than this. The birth statistics come out well in this comparison; if anything is incomplete it must be the census at the younger ages.

A quite different way of using the age distribution to infer births appears under "Bourgeois-Pichat." Here we do not work with ages which represent successive generations (like 0–4 against 15–44) but with 25-year age intervals to which we fit a straight line in order to find its constants, ln b, the logarithm of the intrinsic birth rate, and r, the intrinsic rate of natural increase. Three successive 25-year stretches of the age distribution give for b the intrinsic birth rate 39.77; 38.84; 43.99 per thousand. Here again some confounding of the fall in infant deaths and the rise in births is inevitable, and again the registered births are substantially verified.

The reference is to time periods 5–29 years ago; 30–54 years ago; 55–79 years ago. The last, for instance, reflects the vital conditions of 1883–1907. The rate of natural increase r as here measured shows no systematic change over time. On the other hand the intrinsic death rate (obtained by subtraction as $d = b - r$) shows a steady rise as one goes backward in time—from 6.20 per thousand to 9.59 per thousand—which is at least in the right direction. The last line of this section prints out the age range that gave the best fit of all 25-year age ranges, which turned out to be 5–29 again for Panama 1962.

Another form of analysis appears under "Coale." Instead of assuming stability as in the previous calculation, the assumption was made that births might have been changing linearly or quadratically, and the program infers slope and curvature of the births through time as well as b, d, and r. We find an upward slope k_1 of 10.42 per thousand (or 0.01042) and a slight upward curvature k_2, along with $b = 39.70$; $d = 7.30$; $r = 32.41$, all per thousand population. The b, d, and r accord well enough with the observed intrinsic rates at the right of Table 4, b and r being only slightly low. Undoubtedly the positive slope k_1 is trying to tell us that infant deaths have gone down rather than that births have gone up. The program incorporated a test which automatically deleted this part of the printout where the constants did not provide a close reproduction of the observed ages (Keyfitz, Nagnur, and Sharma 1967).

Thus three somewhat different principles, designated Thompson, Burgeois-Pichat, and Coale, have been applied to estimate births from the age distribution. The conclusion for Panama is that births are more or less completely registered. In contrast to this we found, on applying the Bourgeois-Pichat method to the entire age distribution of the 1961 Census of India, an intrinsic birth rate of 42.90 per thousand, and natural increase of 23.00, both much higher than from vital statistics, and probably more accurate. Unfortunately, an age distribution such as that of the contemporary United States is too irregular to permit inference of this kind. The whole of Table 8 is suggestive only, intended to guide judgment on the published birth rates rather than to provide facts. In some instances, owing to immigration or other violation of the assumptions, figures in Table 8 are so clearly wrong that they cannot mislead anyone.

7. Combined Action of Mortality and Fertility

The rate of population increase through numerical excess of births over deaths is given in the first column of Table 4. For Finland 1964 the rate of natural increase by subtracting the death rate from the birth rate was $17.56 - 9.28 = 8.28$ per thousand (p. 309). This is shown separately for males and females for 1969, 1974, and 1979 on the projection, assuming the birth and death regime of 1964. Under the same assumption the birth rate would ultimately be 17.40, the death rate 10.93, and natural increase 6.47, all for females. This last is the intrinsic rate, not available for males in most populations. If it is assumed that the intrinsic rate of natural increase for males is the same as that for females, then the intrinsic or ultimate birth and death rates for males are available, and these are printed out as 18.97 and 12.49 per thousand, respectively, for Finland 1964. They are a rough estimate of the true rates for males.

Over-all rates of increase that would be shown by Finland, if its age-specific fertility and mortality were as observed, and its age distribution that of the standard population, are given in Table 6. There we see that with the age distribution of England and Wales 1961, Finland would show an increase of 2.52 per thousand; with that of the United States 1960 it would show 5.47; with that of Mexico 1960 it would show 13.32. Shifting to a younger age distribution raises the natural increase, other things being equal.

The Gross Reproduction Rate is the number of girl children that would be born to a woman at prevailing age-specific fertility rates if she were sure to live to the highest age of reproduction. It is shown in the first column of Table 8 as 1.235 for Finnish women, and is gross because it disregards deaths. If we think of a girl child just born, and consider the probability of her living to the age group 15–19, multiplied by the probability of her having a daughter if she does attain that age group, and add the corresponding product for all other age groups, then we arrive at the expected number of girl babies to which a girl child just born will give birth on the prevailing survivorship and fertility. This Net Reproduction Rate for Finland in 1964 was 1.198.

The length of generation T is defined (Lotka 1939, p. 69) as the number of years in which the female population would increase in the ratio of the Net Reproduction Rate if it were growing at r, the intrinsic rate of natural increase given at the right of our Table 4. This T is 27.925 years, as against the mean age of childbearing in the stationary population of 28.053 and in the stable population of 27.798, both printed out in the top row of Table 7. T is approximately equal to the arithmetic mean of the latter two figures.

We have presented a few instances of the demographic conclusions to which the printouts reproduced in this volume lend themselves. Many other examples would be as appropriate as those here given, and if the book is successful it will be because readers look at the tables and draw conclusions more extensive than we have found room to develop. In so doing they will see places where some other parameter than we have given could have been more usefully printed out, and where computations that did not occur to us could have been made. If the material is useful it will give rise to such complaints as that the nearly complete restriction to whole countries has been at the expense of more significant demographic units. Our hope is that with improved data, more effective techniques of computation, and more profound demographic questions to be answered, better books by other writers will follow this one.

In order to facilitate comparisons, especially of key items in historical series, a summary was prepared, showing a line for each population and giving the number of the page on which detail is to be found, immediately following this general introduction.

ADJUSTED BIRTHS FOR THE
UNITED STATES 1919–65

The United States was run twice, once with registered births and once with adjustment for underregistration. The adjusted births were kindly provided to us by the National Center for Health Statistics. The right-hand page only is shown for the adjusted (pp. 164–77), as no change is made in the life tables. The adjustment was small in recent years, amounting to about one per cent, but for the early period it was 10 per cent or higher. The number of births as adjusted is shown in Table D.

TABLE D

ADJUSTED BIRTHS BY AGE OF MOTHER,
UNITED STATES 1919–65

Age Last Birthday	1919–21	1924–26	1929–31	1934–36
10–14	3234	3819	3496	3587
15–19	295701	341170	317369	300731
20–24	816871	821075	760612	726926
25–29	774855	736148	643506	617561
30–34	533387	532978	440554	396055
35–39	354909	343094	288169	238596
40–44	118918	115593	96404	82708
45–49	17058	14756	11598	9882
M	1498158	1495526	1315558	1218827
F	1416775	1413107	1246150	1157219
Total	2914933	2908633	2561708	2376046

Age Last Birthday	1939–41	1944–46	1949–51	1954–56
10–14	3890	3896	5074	6123
15–19	335484	319880	445707	503432
20–24	809777	945233	1187300	1303571
25–29	697093	852139	1053762	1138244
30–34	431137	567347	618764	733375
35–39	223320	296196	306109	352913
40–44	67565	77989	78812	90244
45–49	7598	6491	5497	5440
M	1321999	1576914	1898430	2118240
F	1253865	1492257	1802595	2015102
Total	2575864	3069171	3701025	4133342

TABLE D (continued)

Age Last Birthday	1959–61	1960	1961	1962
10–14	6988	6764	7440	7284
15–19	594458	594710	609289	607573
20–24	1441469	1442138	1459963	1459692
25–29	1101886	1103104	1091636	1054471
30–34	696431	695439	684624	645245
35–39	365415	365667	361313	339858
40–44	93575	93360	95902	93200
45–49	5487	5445	5499	5310
M	2204821	2204678	2210522	2155631
F	2100888	2101949	2105144	2057002
Total	4305709	4306627	4315666	4212633

Age Last Birthday	1963	1964	1965
10–14	7478	8088	7703
15–19	593548	593818	598547
20–24	1468221	1452622	1350826
25–29	1032929	1016119	933943
30–34	616587	591163	535036
35–39	327022	314496	287277
40–44	90623	89254	83255
45–49	5152	4886	4829
M	2123961	2082135	1944519
F	2017599	1988311	1856897
Total	4141560	4070446	3801416

Source: National Center for Health Statistics.

Tabular Summary of Contents
with Page Listings

The 22 items of the summary are shown for all areas for which population, birth, and death data are available to us. Some of the numbers—for example, those concerned with individual states of the United States and provinces of Canada—are at no point shown in further detail. The majority will appear in the main body of the volume in the form of life tables for males and females, and intrinsic rates, provided on a single page of printing. Some two hundred will be given in the full detail of two pages, including the projection matrix and its analysis. A short account of the several columns of the summary follows. (For the few male dominant rows "female" is to be replaced by "male" in the description below.)

Column	Symbol	
1	$K/1000$	Population in thousands of persons as published or estimated to the middle of the year of observation given on the left.
2, 3		Projection with fixed age-specific rates to 5 and 10 years after the given year, also in thousands of persons; female dominant but showing total of both sexes.
4	$1000B/K$	Crude birth rate: 1000 times births divided by population.
5	$1000D/K$	Crude death rate.
6		Directly standardized birth rate, on the United States age-sex distribution of 1960: the birth rate that would exist if the age-sex-specific rates of the given population were applied to the age-sex distribution of the United States in 1960. The calculation is female dominant: births are associated with mothers.

7		Similarly standardized death rate.

Column	Symbol	
8, 9, 10	$1000b$ $1000d$ $1000r$	Female intrinsic rates of birth (8), death (9) and natural increase (10): these would apply if the age-specific birth and death rates observed were allowed to act for long enough that a stable age distribution was attained. Like other rates, multiplied by 1000 for ease in reading. r is the real root of the characteristic equation $$\int_0^\infty e^{-ra}p(a)m(a)da = 1.$$
11, 12	$\overset{\circ}{e}_0$	Expectation of life at birth for males (11) and females (12).
13	$1000M_0$	Infant mortality, measured by deaths under one year of age per thousand population.
14	GRR	Gross Reproduction Rate: the sum of the female age-specific fertility rates in five-year age groups, multiplied by five.
15	NRR R_0	Net Reproduction Rate: expected number of girl children that would be born to a girl child aged 0 on the female age-specific rates of birth and death prevailing in the given year. Hence the ratio of the number in one female generation to the preceding, again on the observed age-specific fertility rates and life table.
16	μ	The mean age at childbearing in the female stationary population.
17	σ^2	The variance of age at childbearing in the female stationary population.
18	r_2	The first complex root of the characteristic equation above, of which the real root appears in column 10. The symbol i, standing for $\sqrt{-1}$, is intended at the right, the second number being the imaginary term.
19	$\dfrac{100\,_{15}K_0}{K}$	Percentage of the population under 15 years of age at mid-period.
20	$\dfrac{100(_{15}K_0 + _{30}K_{65})}{_{50}K_{15}}$	100 times the dependency ratio: ratio of the population under 15 and 65 and over to those from 15 to 65.
21	V	Reproductive value: the expected future girl children who will be born to the existing female population on the observed regime of mortality and fertility, discounted at the intrinsic rate of natural increase.

				POPULATION (in 1000's)			VITAL RATES (Per 1000 Population)						
							BOTH SEXES COMBINED						
SER. NO.	AREA AND YEAR		PAGE	OBSERVED MID-PERIOD	PROJECTED		CRUDE		AGE-SEX STANDARDIZED ON U.S. 1960		FEMALE INTRINSIC		
					5 years	10 years	Birth	Death	Birth	Death	Birth	Death	Increase
				1	2	3	4	5	6	7	8	9	10
	AFRICA												
1	MAURITIUS	1955	54-55	551	634	727	41.69	12.86	37.71	19.47	41.61	11.18	30.43
2		1956-58	-	588	680	785	42.40	12.16	39.60	20.22	43.06	10.44	32.62
3		1959-61	56-57	639	735	849	39.31	10.70	37.43	17.71	41.19	9.78	31.40
4		1962	-	682	791	917	38.00	9.28	38.32	14.91	41.46	8.38	33.08
5		1963	58	701	819	966	40.14	9.56	40.99	16.15	43.84	8.56	35.28
6		1964	59	722	838	985	37.93	8.56	38.94	14.49	41.99	7.70	34.28
7		1965	60-61	741	854	994	35.39	8.55	36.00	14.24	39.22	8.07	31.15
8	REUNION	1961	62-63	346	403	470	43.94	11.56	42.55	16.61	43.87	10.80	33.08
9	SO. AFRICA	1957	64-65	1322	1542	1795	47.58	16.26	41.92	20.20	45.99	14.71	31.28
10	(Colored	1958	-	1363	1580	1831	46.95	16.86	41.42	21.26	45.61	15.27	30.34
11	Population)	1960	66-67	1549	1804	2108	45.19	15.09	41.24	18.14	45.12	13.07	32.05
12	SO. AFRICA	1950-52	68-69	2649	2864	3090	25.14	8.58	21.66	10.82	23.98	8.77	15.21
13	(White	1953-55	70	2801	3034	3277	24.79	8.41	22.00	10.46	24.52	8.19	16.32
14	Population)	1956-58	71	2954	3197	3459	24.72	8.58	22.31	10.48	25.03	7.89	17.14
15		1960	72-73	3129	3394	3688	24.38	8.56	22.41	10.43	25.30	7.55	17.75
16	TOGO	1961	74-75	1544	1731	1914	54.53	28.97	46.33	30.62	50.36	23.16	27.21
	NORTH AMERICA												
17	BARBADOS	1959-61	76-77	234	259	292	30.86	9.42	28.35	11.56	31.83	8.16	23.67
18		1962	78	233	255	290	29.48	9.07	26.47	11.41	30.11	7.60	22.51
19		1963	79	239	262	292	28.28	8.75	25.85	11.64	28.23	8.38	19.85
20		1965	80-81	244	269	299	26.08	7.81	23.80	10.23	26.02	7.93	18.09
21	CANADA	1930-32	82-83	10372	11062	11814	23.13	10.23	20.83	13.67	22.23	13.20	9.03
22		1940-42	84	11507	12243	13002	22.36	9.81	18.57	12.11	19.73	12.38	7.34
23		1950-52	85	13657	14875	16049	27.24	8.94	22.93	10.06	25.15	8.20	16.95
24		1960-62	86-87	17769	19413	21219	25.76	7.77	24.77	8.67	27.58	6.32	21.26
25		1963	88	18402	20008	21835	24.38	7.82	23.84	8.65	26.54	6.57	19.97
26		1964	89	18771	20343	22140	23.35	7.61	22.86	8.41	25.23	6.84	18.39
27		1965	90-91	19100	20490	22099	21.14	7.63	20.64	8.44	22.47	7.81	14.67
28	PR. EDWARD I.	1930-32	-	88	93	98	21.40	11.06	23.13	10.76	23.23	11.56	11.67
29		1940-42	-	95	101	109	22.04	11.08	21.57	10.97	23.06	10.88	12.19
30		1950-52	-	98	106	117	27.88	9.22	28.15	8.41	30.43	6.19	24.25
31		1960-62	-	105	118	131	26.65	9.53	31.05	8.22	33.40	5.01	28.39
32		1963	-	107	119	135	27.56	9.15	32.22	7.89	34.87	4.21	30.66
33		1964	-	107	121	133	25.49	9.17	30.06	8.14	31.87	4.88	26.99
34	NOVA SCOTIA	1930-32	-	513	543	576	22.46	11.90	22.05	12.91	23.39	12.59	10.80
35		1940-42	-	579	618	660	24.24	11.25	20.41	12.23	22.20	11.71	10.49
36		1950-52	-	643	704	763	27.12	9.14	24.46	9.48	26.89	7.40	19.49
37		1960-62	-	738	808	895	26.18	8.39	26.87	8.47	30.14	5.80	24.33
38		1963	-	756	825	917	25.09	8.42	25.82	8.45	28.77	5.90	22.87
39		1964	-	760	828	909	24.09	8.40	24.99	8.38	27.86	6.11	21.75
40	NEW BRUNSWICK	1930-32	-	409	443	476	26.22	11.57	25.89	13.67	27.74	11.83	15.91
41		1940-42	-	458	495	540	26.67	11.16	24.02	13.03	25.89	11.36	14.54
42		1950-52	-	516	575	642	31.73	9.31	29.15	10.27	32.01	7.02	24.99
43		1960-62	-	599	666	746	27.50	7.88	29.22	8.61	32.11	5.45	26.66
44		1963	-	614	675	758	25.68	7.84	27.43	8.53	29.99	5.72	24.27
45		1964	-	617	680	760	24.85	7.67	26.58	8.36	29.29	5.78	23.51
46	QUEBEC	1930-32	-	2878	3133	3423	28.89	11.99	26.05	16.03	27.43	13.87	13.55
47		1940-42	-	3338	3626	3937	26.77	10.08	22.15	13.74	23.63	12.05	11.58
48		1950-52	-	4066	4505	4945	30.04	8.47	24.75	11.24	26.80	8.47	18.33
49		1960-62	92	5270	5789	6364	25.94	6.91	23.84	9.42	25.95	7.19	18.76
50		1963	-	5476	5979	6545	24.41	6.98	22.53	9.40	24.68	7.60	17.08
51		1964	-	5570	6064	6624	23.49	6.74	21.68	9.01	23.45	7.75	15.71
52	ONTARIO	1930-32	-	3435	3596	3760	20.12	10.63	17.22	13.30	18.26	14.24	4.03
53		1940-42	-	3794	3959	4120	19.24	10.26	15.76	11.55	16.41	13.46	2.95
54		1950-52	-	4611	4948	5253	25.11	9.57	21.08	9.96	23.20	8.50	14.70
55		1960-62	93	6245	6777	7344	25.24	8.25	24.22	8.87	27.32	6.27	21.06
56		1963	-	6460	6981	7565	24.01	8.30	23.70	8.85	26.63	6.42	20.21
57		1964	-	6598	7122	7715	23.15	7.91	22.96	8.40	25.59	6.52	19.07
58	ALBERTA	1930-32	-	732	792	866	23.62	7.43	22.02	12.05	23.84	11.23	12.61
59		1940-42	-	797	857	916	22.15	7.81	18.74	11.00	20.12	11.44	8.69
60		1950-52	-	943	1042	1136	28.90	7.55	24.29	9.20	27.05	7.18	19.87
61		1960-62	-	1335	1489	1659	29.14	6.75	27.62	7.87	31.23	5.20	26.03
62		1963	-	1407	1560	1727	27.33	6.71	26.42	7.84	29.80	5.37	24.43
63		1964	-	1434	1576	1736	25.22	6.61	24.66	7.61	27.73	5.76	21.97

AGE   DISTRIBUTION

LIFE EXPECTANCY AT BIRTH $\overset{\circ}{e}_0$		INFANT MORTALITY RATE $1000 M_0$	REPRODUCTION RATES		NET MATERNITY FUNCTION		FIRST COMPLEX ROOT r_2	OBSERVED		REPRODUCTIVE VALUE (in 1000's) V	DISSIMILARITY OF OBSERVED FROM STABLE $\Delta\%$	SER. NO.
Males	Females		Gross	Net	Mean μ	Variance σ^2		Per cent Under 15	Dependency Ratio X 100			
11	12	13	14	15	16	17	18	19	20	21	22	
53.30	56.58	71.48	2.81	2.30	28.15	47.77	−0.0236+0.2199	41.85	81.84	284	4.41	1
53.82	57.48	74.31	2.95	2.45	28.24	47.42	−0.0206+0.2195	42.97	84.50	309	4.79	2
56.15	59.11	72.42	2.80	2.37	28.22	46.53	−0.0240+0.2235	44.30	90.03	329	3.96	3
58.83	62.35	67.28	2.87	2.50	28.46	45.25	−0.0187+0.2250	45.31	94.29	358	5.71	4
58.54	61.47	66.04	3.08	2.66	28.54	45.38	−0.0170+0.2246	45.36	94.58	385	6.36	5
60.13	63.72	59.35	2.94	2.60	28.63	43.86	−0.0147+0.2251	45.28	94.51	387	5.67	6
59.83	64.25	66.34	2.72	2.39	28.65	44.13	−0.0180+0.2226	44.89	93.31	387	3.97	7
52.21	60.01	126.77	3.21	2.63	30.01	46.06	−0.0106+0.2110	45.00	94.04	208	4.96	8
47.67	52.53	151.65	3.18	2.39	28.71	52.92	−0.0335+0.2244	43.88	89.11	811	1.98	9
46.87	51.73	155.35	3.13	2.33	28.71	53.48	−0.0364+0.2235	44.14	89.61	837	1.91	10
50.37	55.10	130.42	3.13	2.45	28.75	51.90	−0.0295+0.2236	45.10	93.20	939	1.75	11
64.50	70.15	35.87	1.63	1.53	28.25	38.13	−0.0261+0.2252	31.75	61.89	867	3.64	12
64.94	71.30	33.53	1.66	1.57	28.09	36.80	−0.0241+0.2281	31.87	62.61	919	3.43	13
64.80	71.57	31.29	1.69	1.60	27.85	35.43	−0.0222+0.2305	31.90	62.96	967	3.29	14
65.14	72.16	25.15	1.70	1.63	27.73	34.48	−0.0206+0.2329	32.40	64.15	1036	3.47	15
33.35	40.18	141.73	3.59	2.14	28.75	56.50	−0.0414+0.2155	47.94	7.15	1015	10.46	16
62.90	67.39	76.16	2.11	1.90	27.63	47.11	−0.0330+0.2218	38.06	79.44	98	6.85	17
63.11	69.32	59.26	2.00	1.84	27.73	46.24	−0.0306+0.2185	38.82	82.63	97	5.57	18
64.18	68.38	64.29	1.90	1.73	28.17	51.36	−0.0337+0.2115	40.53	87.53	101	5.64	19
66.92	71.08	40.00	1.75	1.65	28.05	50.00	−0.0354+0.2108	38.92	84.13	96	5.20	20
59.00	61.36	97.76	1.55	1.31	29.75	42.56	−0.0285+0.2058	31.59	59.12	3717	7.77	21
62.28	65.79	67.57	1.39	1.24	29.12	40.89	−0.0317+0.2112	27.81	52.67	3606	7.39	22
66.18	70.81	42.19	1.71	1.61	28.41	39.32	−0.0250+0.2217	30.14	61.12	4469	4.44	23
68.41	74.29	27.28	1.86	1.79	27.79	37.47	−0.0221+0.2319	33.74	70.71	6019	5.09	24
68.46	74.42	25.90	1.79	1.73	27.76	36.61	−0.0221+0.2317	33.65	70.48	6167	4.02	25
68.61	74.95	24.55	1.72	1.66	27.80	36.60	−0.0232+0.2307	33.41	69.76	6182	3.70	26
68.75	75.00	22.50	1.55	1.50	27.75	37.09	−0.0277+0.2288	33.07	68.80	5995	5.11	27
63.73	64.72	73.61	1.66	1.42	30.19	41.56	−0.0226+0.2028	31.92	71.84	31	4.93	28
64.13	66.17	73.97	1.62	1.43	29.60	43.57	−0.0280+0.2080	30.19	65.62	32	3.90	29
69.72	72.63	35.88	2.11	2.00	29.14	41.71	−0.0179+0.2168	33.41	76.31	37	7.21	30
68.93	74.70	31.81	2.30	2.21	28.54	41.21	−0.0175+0.2282	36.02	86.80	40	11.16	31
69.11	76.24	22.49	2.43	2.35	28.53	38.82	−0.0113+0.2268	35.68	85.31	43	11.64	32
68.28	76.03	25.58	2.22	2.15	28.86	39.02	−0.0129+0.2240	35.40	83.72	42	9.79	33
59.72	61.80	86.23	1.63	1.37	29.36	46.00	−0.0320+0.2065	32.54	67.96	182	5.68	34
61.12	64.86	73.35	1.53	1.34	28.49	43.01	−0.0345+0.2151	29.24	59.71	191	5.46	35
66.82	71.62	39.54	1.81	1.71	28.10	42.38	−0.0294+0.2232	32.62	69.98	220	3.91	36
68.44	74.24	30.67	2.02	1.93	27.58	39.95	−0.0248+0.2354	34.77	76.62	263	7.01	37
68.59	74.79	27.64	1.93	1.86	27.61	38.31	−0.0231+0.2329	34.52	75.74	266	5.84	38
68.77	74.87	24.10	1.88	1.81	27.84	38.96	−0.0230+0.2306	34.34	75.28	267	5.42	39
58.75	60.52	98.41	1.93	1.60	29.96	46.27	−0.0249+0.2044	35.42	72.78	169	4.21	40
60.42	62.80	90.99	1.79	1.52	29.38	45.38	−0.0283+0.2082	31.91	63.95	176	4.18	41
65.54	69.60	57.04	2.19	2.02	28.72	43.88	−0.0227+0.2202	35.69	76.23	209	5.03	42
68.51	73.89	29.64	2.18	2.08	28.05	40.37	−0.0202+0.2317	37.98	84.58	235	7.24	43
68.21	74.55	27.46	2.04	1.96	28.20	39.89	−0.0207+0.2281	37.36	82.44	238	5.99	44
68.76	74.81	24.45	2.00	1.92	28.17	38.71	−0.0193+0.2272	36.95	80.86	237	6.17	45
54.62	56.65	136.51	1.93	1.51	30.91	41.86	−0.0192+0.1998	35.55	67.68	1314	7.05	46
59.40	62.55	87.07	1.64	1.41	30.23	40.84	−0.0231+0.2048	31.92	59.24	1302	7.13	47
64.23	68.54	54.11	1.85	1.70	29.48	39.32	−0.0189+0.2137	33.70	65.09	1568	4.17	48
67.35	72.87	31.64	1.79	1.71	28.88	38.05	−0.0204+0.2207	35.40	70.13	1933	3.94	49
67.53	72.89	30.13	1.70	1.62	28.73	37.26	−0.0217+0.2217	34.84	68.82	1955	4.21	50
67.86	73.84	25.88	1.63	1.56	28.71	36.85	−0.0224+0.2216	34.46	67.86	1941	5.02	51
60.40	63.22	81.25	1.29	1.12	28.90	41.81	−0.0359+0.2100	27.92	53.26	1012	8.04	52
63.92	67.94	52.34	1.18	1.09	28.14	38.88	−0.0382+0.2178	24.43	47.91	968	7.13	53
66.69	71.77	34.65	1.57	1.49	27.64	37.80	−0.0288+0.2270	27.02	55.56	1304	6.09	54
68.32	74.47	23.58	1.82	1.76	27.23	35.90	−0.0225+0.2372	32.21	67.67	1966	7.59	55
68.21	74.67	22.78	1.78	1.72	27.27	34.95	−0.0217+0.2367	32.39	68.24	2034	6.53	56
68.84	75.45	20.28	1.72	1.67	27.32	35.04	−0.0224+0.2358	32.22	67.79	2054	5.36	57
62.26	64.41	72.89	1.65	1.44	29.20	42.29	−0.0288+0.2128	32.63	56.63	264	9.78	58
64.57	67.66	52.52	1.41	1.28	28.78	41.11	−0.0337+0.2159	28.71	51.31	251	10.24	59
67.85	72.06	34.79	1.83	1.73	27.96	38.53	−0.0241+0.2284	30.58	60.53	316	5.04	60
69.58	75.51	26.88	2.08	2.00	27.20	37.75	−0.0211+0.2411	35.25	73.12	478	6.01	61
69.77	75.64	23.64	1.98	1.92	27.15	37.42	−0.0228+0.2413	35.54	73.79	495	4.64	62
69.75	76.40	21.79	1.86	1.80	27.19	37.14	−0.0241+0.2404	35.58	73.92	492	4.44	63

			POPULATION (in 1000's)			VITAL RATES (Per 1000 Population)						
			OBSERVED MID-PERIOD	PROJECTED		BOTH SEXES COMBINED						
						CRUDE		AGE-SEX STANDARDIZED ON U.S. 1960		FEMALE INTRINSIC		
SER. NO.	AREA AND YEAR	PAGE	1	5 years 2	10 years 3	Birth 4	Death 5	Birth 6	Death 7	Birth 8	Death 9	Increase 10
64	SASKATCHEWAN 1930-32	–	922	1004	1101	23.22	6.66	22.80	11.11	24.28	10.64	13.64
65	1940-42	–	895	960	1034	20.84	7.12	18.50	10.06	19.21	11.54	7.68
66	1950-52	–	833	909	989	26.38	7.73	23.51	8.73	25.66	7.58	18.08
67	1960-62	–	926	1016	1119	25.72	7.55	27.18	7.30	30.25	5.28	24.97
68	1963	–	934	1024	1131	25.21	7.97	27.49	7.46	30.65	5.21	25.43
69	1964	–	944	1030	1136	24.03	7.81	26.39	7.22	29.33	5.44	23.89
70	MANITOBA 1930-32	–	700	745	799	20.42	7.78	18.27	11.81	19.27	13.02	6.25
71	1940-42	–	730	772	817	20.66	8.78	16.63	11.21	17.30	13.29	4.02
72	1950-52	–	778	841	898	25.71	8.53	21.48	9.26	23.26	8.52	14.74
73	1960-62	–	922	1002	1096	25.11	8.06	25.32	8.01	28.20	5.97	22.23
74	1963	–	951	1031	1123	23.93	8.34	24.54	8.14	27.63	6.21	21.42
75	1964	–	959	1034	1122	22.69	8.05	23.40	7.80	25.86	6.54	19.32
76	BR. COLUMBIA 1930-32	–	695	714	737	15.09	8.95	14.19	11.85	14.12	16.29	-2.17
77	1940-42	–	821	852	875	18.55	10.43	15.06	11.08	15.29	14.00	1.30
78	1950-52	–	1169	1242	1304	24.24	10.07	20.92	9.42	23.06	8.49	14.57
79	1960-62	–	1632	1756	1892	23.87	8.99	24.68	8.10	28.03	5.93	22.10
80	1963	–	1699	1816	1955	22.06	8.85	22.95	7.89	25.83	6.46	19.38
81	1964	–	1742	1850	1973	20.61	9.22	21.17	8.24	23.52	7.24	16.28
82	COSTA RICA 1960	94-95	1166	1455	1790	55.45	8.63	51.90	14.78	51.50	7.35	44.15
83	1963	96-97	1341	1640	2003	49.79	8.48	49.85	11.70	49.45	7.93	41.52
84	DOM. REP. 1960	98-99	3039	3498	4055	36.23	8.89	34.76	10.24	35.94	9.45	26.50
85	EL SALVADOR 1950	100-101	1858	2178	2531	48.73	14.77	39.85	17.92	43.17	15.09	28.08
86	GRENADA 1960	102-103	89	104	125	44.97	11.56	43.83	12.59	47.48	8.33	39.15
87	HONDURAS 1956-58	–	1768	2070	2422	42.38	10.58	38.72	12.63	40.47	10.54	29.93
88	1959-61	104-105	1940	2289	2702	42.42	9.26	39.62	12.26	41.12	9.08	32.04
89	1962	–	2068	2470	2946	44.55	9.02	42.17	13.62	43.42	8.70	34.73
90	1963	106	2137	2543	3033	43.83	9.13	41.72	14.68	43.18	8.66	34.52
91	1964	107	2209	2651	3177	45.52	9.30	43.71	14.78	44.63	8.92	35.71
92	1965	108-109	2284	2720	3248	43.03	8.60	41.76	14.89	42.49	8.43	34.06
93	JAMAICA 1951	110-111	1430	1593	1762	33.87	12.05	26.61	17.89	31.25	11.99	19.25
94	1952	–	1457	1626	1804	33.27	11.47	26.27	17.41	30.53	11.45	19.08
95	1956	112-113	1564	1792	2043	37.21	9.38	31.31	14.95	35.96	8.14	27.82
96	MARTINIQUE 1961	114-115	288	330	380	36.66	7.94	36.03	10.82	37.73	6.97	30.76
97	1963	116-117	308	348	395	33.20	8.17	33.36	11.77	35.09	6.80	28.29
98	MEXICO 1959-61	118-119	34997	41401	48866	46.14	11.32	42.33	15.12	44.14	11.19	32.95
99	1962	120-121	38543	45581	53854	44.25	10.46	41.99	14.29	43.26	9.61	33.65
100	PANAMA 1960	122-123	1000	1179	1389	41.25	8.39	37.31	11.11	41.77	8.08	33.69
101	1962	124-125	1075	1273	1508	41.54	7.32	37.51	10.30	41.61	6.97	34.65
102	PUERTO RICO 1960	126-127	2362	2700	3123	32.31	6.69	30.05	8.61	33.46	6.20	27.26
103	1963	128	2513	2840	3231	30.82	6.90	26.62	9.34	29.75	6.81	22.94
104	1964	129	2572	2902	3281	30.70	7.22	26.12	9.39	29.38	7.03	22.36
105	1965	130-131	2626	2961	3348	30.32	6.74	25.73	8.69	28.99	6.60	22.40
106	ST. KITTS 1960	132-133	57	64	75	42.53	13.39	44.35	14.70	46.71	9.67	37.04
107	SANTA LUCIA 1960	134-135	87	101	118	48.89	14.77	45.23	14.21	47.77	12.61	35.16
108	TRINIDAD 1954	136-137	698	818	948	41.93	9.76	37.74	14.27	43.37	8.07	35.30
109	1955	138	721	843	979	41.92	10.35	38.00	15.27	42.94	7.69	35.25
110	1956-58	139	765	880	1019	37.46	9.46	34.68	15.35	39.98	7.63	32.35
111	1959-61	140-141	831	966	1133	38.66	8.36	35.35	12.79	39.68	6.63	33.06
112	UNITED 1919-21	142-143	106630	112394	118083	23.42	12.49	18.91	16.90	20.75	16.06	4.70
113	STATES 1924-26	144	115829	121413	127018	21.36	11.84	17.36	17.03	18.93	15.69	3.24
114	1929-31	145	122988	127352	131600	18.56	11.43	14.84	15.39	15.55	17.17	-1.63
115	1934-36	146	127252	130790	134069	16.94	11.18	13.32	14.77	13.42	18.11	-4.70
116	1939-41	147	131684	136365	140496	18.07	10.64	13.91	13.06	14.16	16.14	-1.98
117	1944-46	148-149	131976	139210	145506	22.27	10.63	16.63	11.95	17.77	12.48	5.29
118	1949-51	150	151345	161450	170452	23.93	9.64	20.08	10.45	22.57	9.04	13.53
119	1954-56	151	164301	176635	188941	24.81	9.28	23.04	9.68	26.44	7.10	19.34
120	1959-61	152-153	179990	193305	208293	23.65	9.39	23.65	9.39	27.31	6.61	20.70
121	(Whites) 1959-61	154-155	159392	170319	182576	22.58	9.34	22.82	9.05	26.09	6.68	19.41
122	(Non-Whites) 1960	156-157	20599	22972	25734	31.90	10.04	29.60	12.54	35.82	6.84	28.98
123	UNITED 1962	158-159	185888	198762	213652	22.42	9.45	22.50	9.38	25.84	7.01	18.83
124	STATES 1963	160-161	188656	200956	215268	21.72	9.61	21.59	9.54	24.56	7.46	17.10
125	1964	162-163	191369	203484	217542	21.05	9.40	20.78	9.29	23.48	7.78	15.70

AGE　DISTRIBUTION

LIFE EXPECTANCY AT BIRTH ℓ_0		INFANT MORTALITY RATE	REPRODUCTION RATES		NET MATERNITY FUNCTION		FIRST COMPLEX ROOT	OBSERVED		REPRODUCTIVE VALUE (in 1000's)	DISSIMILARITY OF OBSERVED FROM STABLE	
Males 11	Females 12	$1000 M_0$ 13	Gross 14	Net 15	Mean μ 16	Variance σ^2 17	r_2 18	Per cent Under 15 19	Dependency Ratio X 100 20	V 21	$\Delta\%$ 22	SER. NO.
63.86	65.67	76.17	1.70	1.49	29.76	43.11	-0.0260+0.2080	35.38	63.29	358	11.83	64
66.18	68.75	53.07	1.38	1.25	29.56	41.37	-0.0301+0.2081	29.93	54.11	293	12.85	65
68.81	72.48	36.09	1.76	1.66	28.55	39.06	-0.0230+0.2224	30.72	63.43	279	3.53	66
70.59	76.23	26.81	2.05	1.97	27.70	37.86	-0.0197+0.2347	34.05	76.38	320	7.51	67
70.32	76.05	27.77	2.07	2.00	27.67	37.01	-0.0173+0.2356	34.31	77.42	329	8.03	68
70.82	76.36	24.68	1.99	1.92	27.78	36.88	-0.0179+0.2329	34.21	77.13	329	6.96	69
62.18	64.92	77.05	1.37	1.20	29.70	41.85	-0.0305+0.2060	31.22	55.63	238	13.42	70
64.12	66.98	60.42	1.25	1.12	29.03	40.23	-0.0343+0.2109	26.19	48.08	214	11.41	71
67.85	71.93	36.18	1.60	1.51	28.26	38.41	-0.0266+0.2226	28.72	59.12	238	4.81	72
69.53	75.27	28.03	1.90	1.83	27.59	36.91	-0.0209+0.2343	32.56	71.22	303	7.36	73
69.74	74.74	25.18	1.86	1.79	27.63	36.22	-0.0205+0.2330	32.54	71.20	312	7.01	74
69.90	75.53	23.95	1.76	1.69	27.61	36.62	-0.0232+0.2325	32.42	70.86	307	5.35	75
61.78	65.22	54.28	1.07	0.94	28.76	39.10	-0.0401+0.2118	24.64	43.18	167	15.90	76
63.13	68.67	44.66	1.13	1.04	27.89	36.10	-0.0379+0.2221	21.47	42.49	188	8.76	77
66.64	72.25	31.70	1.57	1.48	27.41	36.69	-0.0285+0.2310	26.18	58.73	312	7.92	78
68.88	75.43	24.21	1.86	1.80	26.97	35.12	-0.0213+0.2412	31.26	70.71	496	9.74	79
69.27	75.75	23.04	1.74	1.68	27.06	34.98	-0.0233+0.2388	31.30	70.19	508	7.08	80
68.63	75.59	20.48	1.59	1.55	27.09	35.49	-0.0273+0.2367	31.04	68.93	505	4.99	81
63.16	65.18	69.75	3.89	3.43	29.01	49.33	-0.0137+0.2237	46.36	96.46	739	7.47	82
62.64	65.24	88.15	3.70	3.23	29.23	48.80	-0.0122+0.2208	47.75	3.79	852	4.35	83
62.68	65.46	98.32	2.57	2.15	29.64	49.65	-0.0234+0.2084	47.29	1.03	1692	8.49	84
49.67	51.80	106.76	2.96	2.17	28.22	46.56	-0.0220+0.2279	41.16	78.95	1074	4.58	85
58.65	65.05	81.92	3.33	2.87	27.87	45.78	-0.0171+0.2314	47.67	12.15	52	9.04	86
58.35	60.08	56.50	2.82	2.30	28.60	50.29	-0.0253+0.2210	45.27	93.67	970	1.42	87
59.51	62.51	47.00	2.90	2.45	28.80	52.50	-0.0244+0.2178	47.34	99.97	1092	1.85	88
59.30	61.67	40.43	3.10	2.64	28.88	53.69	-0.0247+0.2157	48.72	4.40	1211	1.93	89
58.53	61.72	42.83	3.07	2.63	28.90	53.03	-0.0239+0.2148	49.41	6.70	1258	2.16	90
58.39	60.62	42.16	3.20	2.72	29.00	52.99	-0.0221+0.2145	50.10	9.04	1339	2.23	91
59.13	61.53	36.22	3.04	2.61	29.12	53.77	-0.0229+0.2112	50.79	11.44	1353	3.55	92
55.20	58.13	87.91	2.02	1.67	27.15	45.13	-0.0433+0.2333	36.15	66.51	597	3.50	93
58.16	59.59	79.52	1.99	1.67	27.23	45.68	-0.0432+0.2340	36.18	66.53	601	3.53	94
61.07	64.68	59.19	2.35	2.09	27.18	43.90	-0.0299+0.2390	38.01	72.18	688	5.75	95
63.09	68.21	56.43	2.75	2.48	30.29	44.50	-0.0091+0.2093	42.38	89.57	151	5.36	96
63.15	67.89	37.81	2.53	2.33	30.56	44.12	-0.0089+0.2058	42.16	89.12	154	4.41	97
55.64	58.61	102.00	3.14	2.54	29.06	46.26	-0.0172+0.2153	44.42	91.77	20819	2.47	98
58.27	61.12	76.70	3.10	2.59	29.14	46.48	-0.0169+0.2148	45.85	96.59	22343	1.55	99
62.74	65.23	57.47	2.82	2.45	27.43	45.23	-0.0244+0.2371	43.45	88.73	517	1.84	100
65.05	67.29	43.43	2.81	2.51	27.34	45.13	-0.0246+0.2381	43.35	88.55	547	2.34	101
67.41	72.03	43.75	2.26	2.10	27.86	47.20	-0.0372+0.2372	42.46	91.15	1084	4.08	102
66.54	72.02	47.19	1.98	1.85	27.38	46.65	-0.0490+0.2879	39.82	82.88	1047	3.56	103
66.32	71.77	53.01	1.95	1.81	27.14	46.33	-0.0636+0.2709	39.11	80.98	1050	3.10	104
67.72	73.18	42.93	1.92	1.81	26.98	45.56	-0.0500+0.2536	38.67	80.00	1044	2.70	105
56.57	61.26	101.36	3.23	2.72	27.91	48.31	-0.0263+0.2263	45.72	2.89	32	11.28	106
54.31	57.98	122.21	3.37	2.63	28.34	49.93	-0.0239+0.2258	44.26	96.25	52	7.85	107
59.85	62.08	72.58	2.83	2.50	26.75	44.79	-0.0338+0.2426	40.77	80.70	331	9.75	108
59.11	62.37	68.40	2.82	2.52	27.00	45.43	-0.0312+0.2394	41.45	82.52	346	8.83	109
60.13	63.20	64.90	2.59	2.34	26.99	43.21	-0.0295+0.2397	42.31	84.74	357	5.78	110
61.88	66.43	56.97	2.64	2.43	27.59	43.34	-0.0215+0.2335	42.36	87.24	410	4.40	111
54.49	56.41	88.79	1.41	1.14	28.56	43.79	-0.0396+0.2116	31.76	57.39	35692	9.62	112
56.34	59.01	73.90	1.29	1.10	28.30	44.18	-0.0430+0.2119	31.02	56.29	36169	10.42	113
57.27	60.67	68.06	1.10	0.96	27.87	44.30	-0.0496+0.2128	29.27	53.18	34225	14.12	114
58.53	62.58	63.74	0.99	0.88	27.56	43.11	-0.0536+0.2150	27.02	49.59	31894	15.53	115
61.14	65.58	54.48	1.04	0.95	27.15	39.72	-0.0494+0.2231	25.12	47.07	31840	12.46	116
62.26	68.11	43.18	1.24	1.15	27.44	38.71	-0.0394+0.2234	26.63	52.18	35897	6.29	117
65.28	70.86	33.91	1.50	1.43	26.55	37.07	-0.0358+0.2385	27.01	54.26	40653	6.04	118
66.45	72.61	29.73	1.73	1.66	26.47	35.88	-0.0291+0.2437	29.70	61.98	47574	9.32	119
66.84	73.40	26.83	1.78	1.71	26.37	34.51	-0.0251+0.2473	31.17	67.85	53996	9.62	120
67.58	74.33	23.57	1.72	1.66	26.45	33.61	-0.0243+0.2462	30.33	66.62	46037	9.29	121
61.23	66.69	45.72	2.24	2.08	25.94	39.82	-0.0327+0.2560	37.68	77.99	7972	10.38	122
66.93	73.52	25.36	1.70	1.63	26.41	34.16	-0.0259+0.2458	31.30	68.40	55340	7.90	123
66.68	73.42	25.27	1.62	1.56	26.47	34.13	-0.0273+0.2439	31.20	68.09	55462	6.36	124
66.90	73.72	24.64	1.57	1.51	26.53	34.26	-0.0287+0.2422	31.08	67.81	55728	5.09	125

POPULATION (in 1000's)   VITAL RATES (Per 1000 Population)

BOTH SEXES COMBINED

SER. NO.	AREA AND YEAR		PAGE	OBSERVED MID-PERIOD 1	PROJECTED 5 years 2	PROJECTED 10 years 3	CRUDE Birth 4	CRUDE Death 5	AGE-SEX STANDARDIZED ON U.S. 1960 Birth 6	AGE-SEX STANDARDIZED ON U.S. 1960 Death 7	FEMALE INTRINSIC Birth 8	FEMALE INTRINSIC Death 9	FEMALE INTRINSIC Increase 10
126	UNITED	1919-21	164	106630	114320	121973	27.34	12.49	22.11	16.90	24.67	14.43	10.23
127	STATES	1924-26	165	115829	123468	131185	25.11	11.84	20.42	17.03	22.81	13.77	9.04
128	(With	1929-31	166	122988	128673	134271	20.83	11.43	16.66	15.39	17.99	15.48	2.51
129	Adjusted	1934-36	167	127252	131841	136188	18.67	11.18	14.71	14.77	15.32	16.48	-1.16
130	Births)	1939-41	168	131684	137302	142370	19.56	10.64	15.08	13.06	15.78	14.84	0.94
131		1944-46	169	131976	139827	146727	23.26	10.63	17.37	11.95	18.77	11.89	6.88
132		1949-51	170	151345	161830	171206	24.45	9.64	20.53	10.45	23.17	8.80	14.37
133		1954-56	171	164301	176915	189512	25.16	9.28	23.37	9.68	26.86	6.98	19.88
134		1959-61	172	179990	193552	208810	23.92	9.39	23.92	9.39	27.65	6.52	21.13
135		1962	173	185888	198993	214142	22.66	9.45	22.74	9.38	26.15	6.91	19.24
136		1963	174	188656	201179	215740	21.95	9.61	21.82	9.54	24.85	7.36	17.50
137		1964	175	191369	203704	218011	21.27	9.40	21.00	9.29	23.77	7.67	16.10
138		1965	176-177	193818	204696	217455	19.61	9.43	19.20	9.30	21.29	8.64	12.65
139	ALABAMA	1959-61	-	3279	3563	3886	24.79	9.01	23.71	10.05	27.49	7.17	20.32
140	ALASKA	1959-61	-	228	257	289	31.35	5.47	29.76	10.44	34.73	5.69	29.04
141	ARIZONA	1959-61	-	1309	1446	1598	27.59	7.72	26.82	9.29	31.00	5.88	25.12
142	ARKANSAS	1959-61	-	1792	1926	2093	22.74	9.72	24.21	8.76	28.11	6.38	21.74
143	CALIFORNIA	1959-61	-	15776	16970	18261	23.51	8.48	23.36	8.83	27.08	6.40	20.68
144	COLORADO	1959-61	-	1761	1907	2070	24.53	8.58	23.76	8.63	27.39	6.38	21.01
145	CONNECTICUT	1959-61	-	2543	2704	2880	22.35	9.33	22.86	9.10	26.05	6.65	19.40
146	DELAWARE	1959-61	-	448	484	527	26.18	9.10	25.27	9.98	29.69	6.03	23.66
147	FLORIDA	1959-61	-	4968	5317	5693	23.15	9.48	23.73	8.78	27.57	6.59	20.98
148	GEORGIA	1959-61	-	3959	4309	4702	25.25	8.68	23.53	10.19	27.42	7.13	20.30
149	HAWAII	1959-61	-	636	707	781	27.20	5.40	25.05	8.15	28.65	6.00	22.65
150	IDAHO	1959-61	-	670	733	811	25.50	8.16	26.74	8.39	31.20	5.28	25.92
151	ILLINOIS	1959-61	-	10115	10801	11546	23.61	10.09	23.81	9.74	27.65	6.56	21.09
152	INDIANA	1959-61	-	4679	5033	5446	24.07	9.57	23.81	9.27	27.60	6.36	21.25
153	IOWA	1959-61	-	2766	2958	3191	23.17	10.28	24.78	8.33	28.57	5.72	22.85
154	KANSAS	1959-61	-	2186	2343	2529	23.36	9.57	24.17	8.20	27.90	5.91	21.99
155	KENTUCKY	1959-61	-	3049	3284	3563	23.78	9.65	23.96	9.38	27.47	6.66	20.81
156	LOUISIANA	1959-61	-	3272	3598	3977	27.52	8.84	26.42	10.17	31.01	6.19	24.82
157	MAINE	1959-61	-	972	1041	1128	23.95	11.09	25.18	9.51	29.38	5.99	23.39
158	MARYLAND	1959-61	-	3113	3367	3647	24.86	8.86	24.11	10.37	28.11	6.69	21.43
159	MASS.	1959-61	-	5163	5466	5800	22.33	10.82	23.15	9.44	26.19	6.70	19.50
160	MICHIGAN	1959-61	-	7855	8515	9252	24.91	8.59	24.75	9.41	28.68	6.13	22.55
161	MINNESOTA	1959-61	-	3428	3723	4066	25.49	9.11	26.94	8.32	30.57	5.24	25.33
162	MISSISSIPPI	1959-61	-	2187	2406	2673	27.35	9.73	28.05	10.14	32.76	6.27	26.49
163	MISSOURI	1959-61	-	4332	4598	4904	22.59	10.95	23.58	9.13	27.01	6.56	20.45
164	MONTANA	1959-61	-	677	735	805	25.82	9.59	27.31	9.32	31.71	5.45	26.26
165	NEBRASKA	1959-61	-	1416	1525	1647	24.22	9.87	25.53	8.21	29.35	5.52	23.83
166	NEVADA	1959-61	-	286	311	339	26.07	8.81	25.15	10.47	30.10	6.40	23.69
167	NEW HAMP.	1959-61	-	609	647	694	22.58	11.00	24.19	9.37	28.32	6.07	22.25
168	NEW JERSEY	1959-61	-	6085	6442	6810	21.84	9.78	22.23	9.84	25.53	7.22	18.31
169	NEW MEXICO	1959-61	-	957	1081	1226	31.64	6.64	29.15	9.00	34.05	5.36	28.69
170	NEW YORK	1959-61	-	16827	17716	18620	21.45	10.57	21.30	9.96	24.24	7.71	16.54
171	N. CAROLINA	1959-61	-	4574	4966	5413	24.23	8.12	22.26	9.99	25.52	7.53	17.99
172	N. DAKOTA	1959-61	-	635	698	774	26.33	8.41	28.42	8.21	32.15	5.00	27.15
173	OHIO	1959-61	-	9741	10451	11246	23.73	9.49	23.32	9.47	27.01	6.62	20.39
174	OKLAHOMA	1959-61	-	2335	2491	2671	21.89	9.69	22.23	8.59	25.59	6.83	18.76
175	OREGON	1959-61	-	1774	1887	2025	21.16	9.47	22.61	8.70	26.08	6.61	19.47
176	PENNSYLVANIA	1959-61	-	11349	11975	12669	21.40	10.61	21.77	10.07	24.99	7.45	17.54
177	RHODE ISLAND	1959-61	-	862	912	963	21.46	10.30	22.65	9.48	27.47	7.56	18.87
178	S. CAROLINA	1959-61	-	2392	2613	2868	25.08	8.46	23.46	11.01	27.47	7.56	19.91
179	S. DAKOTA	1959-61	-	683	746	822	25.98	9.36	28.36	8.51	32.29	5.08	27.21
180	TENNESSEE	1959-61	-	3579	3845	4148	23.04	9.07	21.78	9.51	24.91	7.59	17.31
181	TEXAS	1959-61	-	9622	10518	11521	25.80	7.87	24.61	8.77	28.55	6.19	22.36
182	UTAH	1959-61	-	896	1003	1126	29.21	6.70	27.78	8.35	31.50	5.13	26.37
183	VERMONT	1959-61	-	391	419	458	24.08	11.17	25.83	9.41	29.99	5.70	24.29
184	VIRGINIA	1959-61	-	3982	4306	4668	24.21	8.52	22.74	10.01	26.36	7.19	19.17
185	WASHINGTON	1959-61	-	2863	3071	3318	22.83	9.23	23.90	8.79	27.78	6.08	21.70
186	W. VIRGINIA	1959-61	-	1866	1990	2144	21.58	9.62	21.75	9.55	24.62	7.53	17.09
187	WISCONSIN	1959-61	-	3967	4287	4657	24.92	9.47	26.39	8.77	30.16	5.52	24.63
188	WYOMING	1959-61	-	331	361	395	25.43	8.11	25.49	8.96	29.50	5.87	23.63
189	WASH., D.C.	1959-61	-	767	819	867	26.23	11.49	22.97	11.39	26.89	7.90	18.99
190	CHICAGO	1959-61	-	3562	3794	4017	25.06	11.76	24.29	11.36	28.55	6.98	21.57
191	(White)	1959-61	-	843	953	1072	36.78	9.72	31.25	13.18	38.61	6.44	32.17
192	(Non-White)	1959-61	-	2719	2836	2955	21.42	12.40	21.93	10.83	25.08	7.50	17.58

SOUTH AMERICA

SER. NO.	AREA AND YEAR		PAGE	1	2	3	4	5	6	7	8	9	10
193	ARGENTINA	1961	178-179	21097	22575	24015	22.54	8.36	18.54	11.86	19.85	11.43	8.41
194	BR. GUIANA	1954	180-181	454	526	609	42.86	12.91	38.20	19.50	43.67	9.91	33.76
195		1955		467	543	636	43.22	11.90	39.06	18.83	44.07	9.22	34.86
196		1956	182-183	480	561	657	43.15	11.20	39.42	18.06	44.77	8.70	36.07

LIFE EXPECTANCY AT BIRTH ℓ_0		INFANT MORTALITY RATE	REPRODUCTION RATES		NET MATERNITY FUNCTION		FIRST COMPLEX ROOT	AGE DISTRIBUTION OBSERVED		REPRODUCTIVE VALUE (in 1000's)	DISSIMILARITY OF OBSERVED FROM STABLE	
Males	Females	$1000\,M_0$	Gross	Net	Mean μ	Variance σ^2	r_2	Per cent Under 15	Dependency Ratio X 100	V	$\Delta\%$	SER. NO.
11	12	13	14	15	16	17	18	19	20	21	22	
54.49	56.41	88.79	1.64	1.33	28.42	46.45	−0.0392+0.2131	31.76	57.39	38162	5.15	126
56.34	59.01	73.90	1.51	1.29	28.16	46.51	−0.0425+0.2136	31.02	56.29	38771	5.63	127
57.27	60.67	68.06	1.24	1.07	27.90	45.30	−0.0475+0.2138	29.27	53.18	36127	10.27	128
58.53	62.58	63.74	1.10	0.97	27.61	44.08	−0.0518+0.2157	27.02	49.59	33436	12.26	129
61.14	65.58	54.48	1.13	1.03	27.18	40.54	−0.0481+0.2240	25.12	47.07	33094	9.75	130
62.26	68.11	43.18	1.30	1.21	27.45	39.19	−0.0387+0.2238	26.63	52.18	36661	5.80	131
65.28	70.86	33.91	1.54	1.46	26.56	37.34	−0.0356+0.2388	27.01	54.26	41083	6.53	132
66.45	72.61	29.73	1.75	1.68	26.47	36.03	−0.0288+0.2440	29.70	61.98	47891	9.79	133
66.84	73.40	26.83	1.80	1.73	26.37	34.62	−0.0248+0.2475	31.17	67.85	54285	10.00	134
66.93	73.52	25.36	1.71	1.65	26.42	34.26	−0.0256+0.2460	31.30	68.40	55621	8.25	135
66.68	73.42	25.27	1.64	1.58	26.48	34.23	−0.0271+0.2441	31.20	68.09	55738	6.70	136
66.90	73.72	24.64	1.58	1.53	26.53	34.39	−0.0285+0.2423	31.08	67.81	56001	5.34	137
66.87	73.83	24.08	1.45	1.39	26.52	35.12	−0.0334+0.2402	30.91	67.44	54607	4.28	138
65.06	71.73	32.55	1.77	1.69	26.12	38.05	−0.0352+0.2516	33.93	72.20	1068	6.33	139
64.88	71.36	40.00	2.25	2.13	26.63	40.38	−0.0271+0.2537	35.51	61.01	81	10.23	140
65.38	73.72	33.16	2.01	1.91	26.26	36.15	−0.0231+0.2529	34.77	71.53	451	8.15	141
67.11	74.00	27.98	1.82	1.74	25.94	37.77	−0.0340+0.2589	31.89	74.74	547	10.75	142
67.62	74.48	24.51	1.75	1.69	25.85	33.28	−0.0255+0.2538	30.31	64.11	4493	10.08	143
67.71	74.49	27.80	1.79	1.72	26.11	34.40	−0.0254+0.2525	32.44	70.83	543	7.24	144
68.14	74.22	22.42	1.73	1.68	27.06	31.32	−0.0180+0.2388	29.48	64.06	721	11.45	145
66.38	72.77	25.86	1.90	1.84	26.18	34.06	−0.0223+0.2497	32.17	67.16	140	11.15	146
66.47	74.00	31.19	1.77	1.70	25.61	34.37	−0.0290+0.2570	29.62	68.90	1391	12.21	147
64.45	71.82	32.63	1.76	1.68	25.85	37.01	−0.0345+0.2541	33.57	69.33	1268	6.15	148
69.86	74.24	23.43	1.87	1.81	26.54	31.71	−0.0166+0.2455	34.41	64.00	213	6.22	149
68.06	75.14	23.29	2.02	1.94	26.12	34.22	−0.0182+0.2567	34.69	76.75	226	9.14	150
66.64	73.03	25.47	1.80	1.73	26.49	33.90	−0.0232+0.2452	29.77	65.13	2934	12.11	151
67.34	73.85	24.51	1.79	1.73	26.10	34.61	−0.0261+0.2525	31.78	70.45	1415	9.10	152
68.81	75.48	21.79	1.88	1.82	26.55	33.64	−0.0195+0.2485	31.11	75.42	838	12.38	153
68.79	75.48	22.84	1.82	1.76	26.08	33.85	−0.0230+0.2535	30.86	72.08	642	10.87	154
66.58	73.24	28.66	1.79	1.71	26.25	38.90	−0.0361+0.2517	32.25	72.03	944	8.09	155
64.97	71.86	32.38	1.99	1.89	26.19	36.31	−0.0255+0.2525	35.25	74.41	1140	8.52	156
66.83	73.61	26.93	1.90	1.83	26.29	33.42	−0.0204+0.2507	31.05	72.55	298	12.55	157
65.68	72.10	28.42	1.81	1.74	26.13	34.70	−0.0259+0.2496	32.01	64.79	954	9.46	158
67.46	73.87	22.57	1.75	1.69	27.40	32.50	−0.0180+0.2346	28.76	66.29	1478	12.90	159
67.36	73.49	24.53	1.87	1.81	26.60	33.87	−0.0210+0.2459	33.13	70.32	2509	9.02	160
68.86	75.39	21.93	2.04	1.98	27.35	35.04	−0.0162+0.2396	32.85	76.14	1146	11.93	161
64.75	71.04	41.03	2.11	1.99	26.48	39.78	−0.0305+0.2492	35.82	80.33	797	10.44	162
67.24	73.94	25.37	1.76	1.70	26.22	35.87	−0.0294+0.2491	29.28	69.31	1219	12.63	163
66.19	73.85	25.76	2.05	1.97	26.36	35.00	−0.0188+0.2540	33.67	76.57	225	10.72	164
68.82	75.59	23.47	1.92	1.86	26.48	33.55	−0.0187+0.2498	30.88	73.95	431	12.79	165
64.06	72.06	32.60	1.90	1.81	25.44	32.77	−0.0222+0.2617	30.58	58.61	85	10.87	166
67.13	74.18	23.74	1.85	1.79	26.52	33.12	−0.0199+0.2479	30.07	70.15	179	13.47	167
67.01	72.84	25.13	1.68	1.63	26.81	31.64	−0.0206+0.2408	28.83	61.45	1667	11.76	168
66.44	73.43	33.45	2.20	2.10	26.36	38.66	−0.0240+0.2565	37.93	76.42	371	6.14	169
66.68	72.71	25.20	1.61	1.55	26.89	32.22	−0.0230+0.2389	27.57	60.33	4475	11.07	170
64.91	72.41	32.83	1.66	1.59	25.98	36.49	−0.0345+0.2511	33.39	67.33	1443	4.04	171
68.98	75.27	24.26	2.14	2.07	27.27	35.95	−0.0165+0.2430	34.42	77.57	225	9.91	172
67.29	73.42	24.57	1.76	1.70	26.38	33.71	−0.0237+0.2472	31.72	69.37	2931	9.01	173
67.47	74.87	25.48	1.66	1.60	25.43	34.06	−0.0289+0.2632	29.97	68.50	648	8.78	174
67.51	74.88	24.56	1.70	1.64	25.87	31.90	−0.0225+0.2559	30.83	70.11	504	9.37	175
66.58	72.63	25.08	1.65	1.59	26.73	33.05	−0.0238+0.2411	29.11	64.15	3148	10.37	176
67.79	73.68	23.39	1.71	1.66	27.04	32.77	−0.0210+0.2390	28.37	63.36	238	12.31	177
63.13	70.36	33.99	1.76	1.67	26.01	37.10	−0.0337+0.2522	35.68	72.42	809	4.79	178
67.62	75.04	26.26	2.13	2.05	26.94	35.93	−0.0176+0.2468	33.57	78.84	233	12.13	179
66.41	72.83	30.64	1.63	1.56	25.95	36.73	−0.0358+0.2520	31.62	67.45	1064	5.32	180
67.11	74.32	29.34	1.84	1.77	25.91	35.70	−0.0286+0.2550	33.11	69.19	3065	7.56	181
68.70	75.08	20.42	2.09	2.02	27.08	36.70	−0.0197+0.2418	37.53	79.43	341	4.92	182
66.96	74.11	26.32	1.96	1.89	26.72	33.55	−0.0169+0.2465	31.45	74.41	124	13.35	183
65.62	72.42	30.74	1.71	1.63	26.01	35.85	−0.0314+0.2513	31.98	64.65	1213	5.74	184
67.73	74.83	24.07	1.80	1.74	26.01	31.98	−0.0201+0.2538	31.27	69.63	845	9.98	185
66.25	73.19	27.67	1.62	1.56	26.18	36.05	−0.0321+0.2525	32.17	70.77	555	6.26	186
68.38	74.52	23.25	2.00	1.93	27.20	34.14	−0.0165+0.2411	32.11	73.33	1282	12.48	187
66.56	74.30	27.85	1.90	1.82	25.80	33.72	−0.0212+0.2599	33.74	71.21	105	7.45	188
62.70	69.98	42.64	1.71	1.61	25.61	37.68	−0.0395+0.2494	25.35	52.44	205	13.89	189
64.09	70.67	30.60	1.83	1.75	26.33	34.78	−0.0255+0.2451	27.17	58.56	996	15.56	190
60.88	66.11	42.19	2.35	2.21	25.26	38.60	−0.0340+0.2688	36.49	70.17	322	14.22	191
65.27	72.23	24.65	1.65	1.59	26.78	32.63	−0.0234+0.2397	24.29	55.29	675	15.82	192
62.53	68.16	61.43	1.39	1.26	28.16	45.36	−0.0390+0.2174	29.87	53.96	6448	8.64	193
54.34	57.50	80.92	2.86	2.43	27.08	44.24	−0.0262+0.2378	42.37	84.85	228	7.16	194
56.00	58.76	75.38	2.91	2.51	27.21	44.57	−0.0253+0.2361	42.97	86.55	237	7.03	195
56.63	60.15	73.19	2.98	2.59	27.20	43.64	−0.0218+0.2374	43.59	88.48	248	6.96	196

			POPULATION (in 1000's)			VITAL RATES (Per 1000 Population)						
						BOTH SEXES COMBINED						
			OBSERVED MID-PERIOD	PROJECTED		CRUDE		AGE-SEX STANDARDIZED ON U.S. 1960		FEMALE INTRINSIC		
SER. NO.	AREA AND YEAR	PAGE	1	5 years 2	10 years 3	Birth 4	Death 5	Birth 6	Death 7	Birth 8	Death 9	Increase 10
197	CHILE 1953-55	184-185	6597	7281	8027	32.70	12.76	27.42	17.75	30.41	13.41	17.00
198	1959-61	186	7736	8632	9647	33.79	12.12	30.61	15.85	33.53	11.73	21.80
199	1962	187	8145	9107	10185	33.69	11.65	30.42	15.10	33.23	11.26	21.97
200	1964	188-189	8391	9364	10468	32.81	11.21	29.05	14.68	31.99	10.94	21.05
201	COLOMBIA 1964	190-191	17505	20196	23432	37.92	10.02	35.92	13.21	38.40	10.06	28.35
202	FR. GUIANA 1961	192-193	33	35	39	31.95	14.60	33.09	17.74	35.89	9.57	26.32
203	PERU 1961	194-195	9907	11239	12749	36.17	11.17	33.17	13.14	35.03	11.57	23.46
204	VENEZUELA 1963	196-197	8144	9732	11605	43.41	7.18	41.14	10.80	43.54	6.84	36.70
	ASIA											
205	CEYLON 1953	198-199	8162	9355	10663	39.35	10.90	34.41	14.32	37.47	11.83	25.64
206	1962	200-201	10444	11955	13656	35.50	8.51	32.53	13.55	34.80	8.40	26.40
207	CHINA 1956	202-203	9368	11188	13220	44.20	7.91	42.16	14.72	41.96	7.08	34.88
208	(TAIWAN) 1959-61	204	10612	12439	14483	39.62	6.96	37.66	13.45	38.94	6.84	32.10
209	1962	205	11330	13166	15261	37.37	6.44	35.58	12.94	37.59	6.53	31.06
210	1963	206	11698	13546	15677	36.27	6.13	34.66	12.51	36.85	6.37	30.49
211	1964	207	12070	13898	16032	34.54	5.74	32.90	11.87	35.47	6.18	29.29
212	1965	208-209	12443	14239	16385	32.68	5.46	31.06	11.33	34.13	6.15	27.98
213	CYPRUS 1950-52	210	502	555	611	28.07	7.91	24.79	10.39	26.01	8.86	17.14
214	1953-55	211	523	574	632	26.19	6.54	22.99	9.56	24.38	7.98	16.40
215	1956-58	212-213	546	598	659	25.82	6.21	22.52	9.26	24.45	7.62	16.83
216	1959	-	567	621	684	25.42	6.01	22.28	9.81	23.26	7.85	15.41
217	1960	214-215	573	633	698	25.31	5.58	22.80	7.46	23.98	7.15	16.83
218	ISRAEL 1949	-	919	1019	1110	29.35	6.70	21.50	11.72	23.64	9.91	13.72
219	(Jewish 1950-52	216-217	1304	1468	1616	31.89	6.44	25.56	10.15	28.28	7.78	20.50
220	Popu- 1953-55	218	1505	1666	1827	28.30	6.18	24.10	9.85	27.07	7.48	19.59
221	lation) 1956-58	219	1715	1879	2049	25.48	6.01	22.94	9.57	25.70	7.65	18.04
222	1960	220-221	1885	2059	2241	23.86	5.52	22.60	8.32	25.30	7.28	18.02
223	1963	222-223	2115	2294	2502	21.93	6.02	21.52	8.71	23.84	7.77	16.08
224	JAPAN 1939-41	224-225	72265	77047	82402	29.04	16.49	26.97	21.56	28.61	16.75	11.86
225	1950-52	226-227	84260	91250	98798	25.64	9.93	21.32	14.33	23.34	11.99	11.35
226	1953-55	228	87982	93482	99277	20.34	8.29	16.15	12.58	17.06	13.60	3.46
227	1956-58	229	90860	95506	100243	17.92	7.93	13.59	11.99	13.83	15.37	-1.54
228	1959-61	230-231	93224	97809	102554	17.24	7.48	12.77	10.98	12.71	15.60	-2.89
229	1962	-	94958	99501	104153	17.05	7.48	12.40	10.88	12.23	15.77	-3.54
230	1963	232-233	95912	100893	105927	17.30	6.99	12.56	9.96	12.38	15.15	-2.77
231	SINGAPORE 1957	234-235	1450	1723	2031	43.22	7.38	42.73	14.13	43.61	6.22	37.39
232	1962	236-237	1714	1972	2276	34.42	5.94	35.35	15.67	37.27	5.56	31.71
233	THAILAND 1960	238-239	26258	29866	33933	34.87	8.45	32.35	12.29	32.23	10.08	22.15
	EUROPE											
234	ALBANIA 1955	240-241	1381	1594	1832	44.39	15.02	45.79	14.40	44.74	15.35	29.39
235	AUSTRIA 1950-52	242-243	6933	7002	7030	15.08	12.37	13.47	12.10	13.17	16.02	-2.84
236	1953-55	244	6940	7022	7072	15.15	12.15	14.05	11.21	14.01	14.53	-0.52
237	1956-58	245	6966	7113	7238	16.95	12.54	16.42	10.92	17.28	11.80	5.48
238	1959-61	246-247	7048	7238	7414	18.06	12.45	17.63	10.35	18.73	10.52	8.21
239	1962	-	7130	7333	7523	18.69	12.74	18.15	10.29	19.56	9.90	9.67
240	1963	248	7172	7382	7575	18.80	12.77	18.23	10.22	19.83	9.70	10.13
241	1964	249	7215	7430	7618	18.55	12.35	17.97	9.77	19.37	9.75	9.62
242	1965	250-251	7255	7424	7578	17.91	12.99	17.44	10.18	18.71	10.17	8.55
243	BELGIUM 1900	252-253	6637	6992	7386	29.43	19.44	24.89	22.89	27.97	18.37	9.61
244	1903-07	-	7202	7582	7964	26.38	16.40	19.59	20.37	21.17	18.56	2.61
245	1908-12	254	7416	7718	8035	23.92	15.85	19.44	19.75	21.26	17.90	3.36
246	1919-21	255	7408	7635	7852	20.38	14.36	16.09	17.74	16.84	18.58	-1.74
247	1923-25	256	7752	7988	8176	19.69	13.25	15.41	15.99	15.94	17.49	-1.55
248	1928-32	257	8062	8230	8335	18.44	13.66	14.27	15.99	14.66	18.26	-3.60
249	1933-37	258-259	8279	8360	8377	15.83	12.82	12.72	14.60	12.46	19.11	-6.64
250	1938-42	260	8295	8252	8182	14.02	14.52	12.24	16.05	11.92	19.83	-7.91
251	1943-47	261	8370	8441	8482	16.21	14.06	14.72	14.87	14.77	16.56	-1.79
252	1948-52	262	8647	8817	8949	16.78	12.36	15.36	11.17	15.80	13.27	2.53
253	1953-57	263	8827	9007	9139	16.78	12.09	15.44	10.45	15.92	12.46	3.46

AGE   DISTRIBUTION

Life Expectancy at Birth $\overset{\circ}{e}_0$		Infant Mortality Rate $1000 M_0$	Reproduction Rates		Net Maternity Function		First Complex Root r_2	Observed		Reproductive Value (in 1000's) V	Dissimilarity of Observed from Stable $\Delta\%$	
Males	Females		Gross	Net	Mean μ	Variance σ^2		Per cent Under 15	Dependency Ratio X 100			SER. NO.
11	12	13	14	15	16	17	18	19	20	21	22	
52.04	56.56	148.15	2.07	1.64	29.44	51.09	-0.0303+0.2099	37.36	70.50	3103	4.84	197
54.17	59.19	135.43	2.30	1.87	29.30	47.25	-0.0218+0.2120	39.80	78.57	3788	2.31	198
54.76	60.36	129.99	2.28	1.88	29.26	46.95	-0.0217+0.2117	39.79	78.71	3955	2.29	199
55.70	61.29	119.28	2.18	1.82	29.08	48.62	-0.0268+0.2118	39.63	78.56	3976	3.01	200
58.23	61.56	89.20	2.71	2.27	29.60	50.90	-0.0208+0.2146	46.64	98.58	9980	4.46	201
54.31	61.52	70.65	2.42	2.08	28.52	49.47	-0.0326+0.2174	37.83	80.00	14	8.77	202
57.43	59.94	96.06	2.45	1.96	29.36	52.61	-0.0285+0.2135	43.33	89.88	5156	4.54	203
63.34	67.10	55.58	3.07	2.75	28.50	49.11	-0.0208+0.2270	45.17	92.51	4459	3.09	204
58.99	58.18	86.66	2.58	2.06	28.69	38.68	-0.0136+0.2204	39.70	76.08	4098	4.70	205
64.10	64.42	42.26	2.43	2.14	29.35	41.08	-0.0120+0.2127	40.68	78.99	4993	5.17	206
60.15	64.78	33.10	3.14	2.80	30.36	45.53	-0.0067+0.2123	44.18	87.40	5356	3.94	207
61.86	66.36	33.56	2.81	2.54	29.73	41.67	-0.0074+0.2183	45.13	90.85	5648	3.83	208
62.76	67.37	31.27	2.66	2.44	29.30	39.53	-0.0070+0.2228	45.92	93.82	5805	3.73	209
63.47	67.97	28.43	2.59	2.39	29.25	38.82	-0.0066+0.2235	45.90	93.88	5910	4.19	210
64.13	68.96	25.53	2.47	2.30	28.96	36.73	-0.0059+0.2266	45.64	93.10	5912	4.81	211
64.81	69.69	23.66	2.34	2.19	28.52	34.67	-0.0058+0.2304	45.17	91.52	5888	5.34	212
66.97	69.35	62.98	1.84	1.66	30.02	43.19	-0.0210+0.2087	34.64	68.79	199	3.59	213
69.94	72.77	45.55	1.73	1.62	29.69	42.93	-0.0234+0.2117	34.56	69.42	196	3.91	214
70.07	73.87	31.53	1.70	1.60	28.34	40.08	-0.0264+0.2274	34.45	70.16	192	3.31	215
70.58	74.38	33.70	1.63	1.55	28.73	39.95	-0.0262+0.2218	34.21	70.15	198	3.97	216
72.81	75.64	28.16	1.69	1.62	29.06	40.55	-0.0241+0.2184	36.71	74.25	213	6.53	217
64.90	67.52	54.99	1.60	1.47	28.17	35.34	-0.0237+0.2230	28.93	48.33	302	12.13	218
66.56	69.56	46.09	1.90	1.76	27.92	40.98	-0.0247+0.2258	30.40	52.43	454	9.32	219
68.02	70.83	35.13	1.80	1.70	27.53	38.93	-0.0254+0.2329	32.53	58.70	504	7.64	220
68.49	71.52	32.76	1.72	1.63	27.60	36.87	-0.0240+0.2318	34.53	64.19	569	6.68	221
70.50	73.31	27.90	1.71	1.64	27.79	35.74	-0.0210+0.2314	34.87	66.06	624	6.71	222
70.69	72.84	22.91	1.61	1.56	27.86	33.31	-0.0193+0.2309	33.77	64.74	688	5.89	223
47.71	50.54	98.14	2.02	1.43	30.66	38.09	-0.0189+0.2042	36.05	68.80	32715	3.37	224
59.42	62.75	55.95	1.60	1.39	29.42	31.27	-0.0172+0.2147	35.18	66.93	32647	7.33	225
62.54	66.49	44.56	1.22	1.10	28.98	27.44	-0.0223+0.2171	33.95	64.30	28985	15.11	226
63.83	68.21	38.36	1.03	0.96	28.43	23.41	-0.0245+0.2217	31.94	59.61	26405	19.12	227
65.50	70.34	31.01	0.98	0.92	27.88	19.69	-0.0229+0.2263	30.18	55.97	24950	19.83	228
66.26	71.21	26.44	0.95	0.91	27.74	17.56	-0.0216+0.2270	28.83	53.21	24237	19.77	229
67.29	72.43	23.79	0.96	0.93	27.78	16.96	-0.0202+0.2265	27.77	51.06	24333	19.17	230
60.20	66.46	44.49	3.17	2.90	29.34	43.33	-0.0065+0.2209	42.88	81.91	772	4.77	231
63.14	68.42	27.25	2.63	2.49	29.45	42.36	-0.0103+0.2187	45.96	93.05	843	4.65	232
58.39	63.76	51.32	2.33	1.94	30.60	49.73	-0.0204+0.2040	43.19	85.14	13575	8.03	233
54.55	55.40	117.16	3.43	2.43	31.16	59.44	-0.0203+0.2079	39.05	81.38	826	5.15	234
62.82	68.05	63.37	1.00	0.92	27.97	38.68	-0.0435+0.2166	22.91	50.39	1450	6.80	235
64.52	69.96	50.71	1.05	0.99	27.87	37.37	-0.0417+0.2200	22.88	51.83	1443	6.75	236
64.77	70.84	44.58	1.24	1.16	27.79	35.99	-0.0351+0.2238	21.77	50.37	1540	7.52	237
65.65	72.06	38.44	1.32	1.25	27.53	36.87	-0.0344+0.2271	22.04	52.13	1594	10.45	238
66.27	72.49	34.00	1.36	1.30	27.45	37.00	-0.0335+0.2282	22.62	54.37	1641	10.37	239
66.35	72.65	32.32	1.38	1.32	27.39	36.51	-0.0322+0.2284	22.77	55.14	1664	11.12	240
66.80	73.27	29.45	1.35	1.30	27.39	36.89	-0.0332+0.2282	22.99	56.19	1665	10.78	241
66.58	73.00	28.54	1.31	1.26	27.28	37.13	-0.0352+0.2284	23.27	57.40	1647	9.98	242
45.11	48.55	194.86	1.87	1.32	28.79	27.64	-0.0167+0.2157	31.87	61.51	2754	2.53	243
48.17	51.67	168.52	1.46	1.08	29.06	32.10	-0.0257+0.2078	30.37	57.15	2712	11.17	244
49.34	52.77	155.31	1.47	1.10	28.80	28.34	-0.0233+0.2136	30.52	58.42	2624	8.03	245
52.54	55.82	106.34	1.20	0.95	28.88	27.76	-0.0273+0.2121	25.55	47.13	2166	10.25	246
55.47	59.28	95.95	1.16	0.96	28.66	28.00	-0.0280+0.2137	23.28	43.37	2026	8.16	247
55.93	59.76	93.95	1.08	0.90	28.44	28.17	-0.0309+0.2148	22.99	43.93	1981	9.52	248
58.20	62.26	82.18	0.96	0.83	28.08	28.90	-0.0359+0.2168	23.74	47.15	1811	11.65	249
56.14	62.01	84.19	0.92	0.80	28.71	35.37	-0.0423+0.2117	22.34	45.84	1757	10.83	250
57.42	63.35	80.55	1.09	0.95	29.01	35.39	-0.0350+0.2119	21.02	44.85	1870	6.67	251
64.50	69.54	45.35	1.15	1.07	28.72	35.88	-0.0327+0.2149	20.94	47.13	1909	5.39	252
66.30	71.50	38.24	1.16	1.10	28.49	34.32	-0.0314+0.2184	21.63	49.43	1922	4.52	253

			POPULATION (in 1000's)			VITAL RATES (Per 1000 Population)							
						BOTH SEXES COMBINED							
			OBSERVED MID-PERIOD	PROJECTED		CRUDE		AGE-SEX STANDARDIZED ON U.S. 1960		FEMALE INTRINSIC			
				5 years	10 years	Birth	Death	Birth	Death	Birth	Death	Increase	
SER. NO.	AREA AND YEAR	PAGE	1	2	3	4	5	6	7	8	9	10	
254	BELGIUM 1958-62	264-265	9153	9359	9529	17.00	11.80	16.51	9.62	17.34	10.84	6.50	
255	1963	266-267	9290	9495	9696	17.14	12.56	17.22	10.01	18.42	10.33	8.08	
256	BULGARIA 1950-52	268-269	7284	7699	8066	22.39	10.79	16.93	12.84	17.44	15.04	2.40	
257	1953-55	270	7468	7859	8193	20.27	9.12	15.40	11.01	15.38	14.77	0.60	
258	1956-58	271	7651	8007	8316	18.61	8.61	14.75	10.38	14.76	14.40	0.36	
259	1959-61	272-273	7867	8207	8522	17.58	8.48	14.73	9.84	14.91	13.62	1.29	
260	1962	-	8013	8327	8624	16.74	8.69	14.36	9.71	14.50	13.57	0.93	
261	1963	274	8078	8405	8708	16.36	8.18	14.15	9.03	14.06	13.68	0.37	
262	1964	275	8144	8482	8786	16.08	7.92	14.02	8.61	13.70	13.61	0.09	
263	1965	276-277	8200	8503	8770	15.34	8.17	13.40	8.61	12.77	14.31	-1.55	
264	CZECHOSLO-VAKIA 1930	278-279	13964	14482	14894	21.78	13.92	15.90	17.28	16.43	18.74	-2.30	
265	1935	-	14339	14540	14650	17.03	13.30	12.59	16.73	12.21	21.15	-8.95	
266	1950-52	280-281	12532	13211	13808	22.75	11.19	19.54	12.51	21.42	11.23	10.19	
267	1953-55	282	12952	13585	14162	20.68	10.17	18.43	11.25	20.21	10.40	9.81	
268	1956-58	283	13358	13939	14512	18.71	9.65	17.55	10.40	19.16	10.36	8.80	
269	1959-61	284-285	13654	14109	14593	15.93	9.35	15.39	9.73	16.18	11.74	4.44	
270	1962	286	13860	14281	14767	15.69	10.01	15.03	10.44	15.83	12.03	3.80	
271	1963	287	13952	14497	15093	16.92	9.54	16.06	9.78	17.22	10.90	6.32	
272	1964	288-289	14058	14622	15239	17.16	9.59	16.12	9.63	17.25	10.80	6.45	
273	DENMARK 1950-52	290-291	4304	4483	4643	18.05	9.02	16.44	9.33	17.33	11.31	6.01	
274	1953-55	292	4407	4583	4759	17.51	8.93	16.59	8.86	17.49	10.89	6.60	
275	1956-58	293	4488	4660	4838	16.84	9.13	16.54	8.58	17.47	10.62	6.84	
276	1959-61	294-295	4581	4751	4937	16.48	9.40	16.25	8.47	17.22	10.68	6.54	
277	1962	296	4647	4822	5012	16.74	9.76	16.33	8.53	17.35	10.48	6.87	
278	1963	297	4684	4883	5093	17.60	9.77	16.94	8.43	18.16	9.96	8.20	
279	1964	298-299	4720	4916	5121	17.66	9.92	16.75	8.44	17.73	10.12	7.61	
280	FINLAND 1930	300-301	3654	3792	3917	20.59	13.20	16.97	15.58	17.28	17.13	0.15	
281	1950-52	302-303	4047	4312	4567	23.51	9.89	19.99	12.78	21.64	10.11	11.53	
282	1953-55	304	4187	4437	4677	21.53	9.35	19.07	12.22	20.72	9.96	10.76	
283	1956-58	305	4324	4551	4791	19.81	9.12	18.23	11.54	19.74	10.16	9.58	
284	1959-61	306-307	4430	4649	4890	18.62	8.97	17.60	11.01	19.02	10.18	8.85	
285	1962	-	4505	4711	4953	18.08	9.52	17.01	11.56	18.34	10.53	7.81	
286	1963	308	4543	4761	5014	18.11	9.25	17.02	11.09	18.29	10.42	7.87	
287	1964	309	4580	4792	5029	17.56	9.28	16.36	10.89	17.40	10.93	6.47	
288	1965	310-311	4612	4796	5013	16.89	9.64	15.52	11.42	16.25	11.70	4.55	
289	FRANCE 1851	312-313	35791	36406	36902	27.14	22.33	22.76	27.14	24.47	25.39	-0.92	
290	1854-58	-	36016	36090	36074	26.03	24.99	21.54	29.45	23.25	26.92	-3.67	
291	1861	314	37397	37964	38597	26.88	23.17	22.82	26.75	24.43	25.43	-0.99	
292	1864-68	315	38027	38477	38817	26.35	23.44	22.50	26.90	24.44	24.43	0.01	
293	1871	316	36731	35128	33665	22.49	31.95	19.52	34.91	20.94	31.63	-10.69	
294	1872	317	36106	36777	37333	26.75	21.96	22.93	24.97	24.94	23.23	1.71	
295	1874-78	318-319	36824	37415	37970	25.82	22.28	22.33	24.74	24.50	22.39	2.11	
296	1879-83	320	37541	37937	38297	24.86	22.41	21.89	24.91	24.12	23.12	0.99	
297	1884-88	321	37934	38209	38502	24.03	22.34	20.83	24.96	22.64	23.36	-0.72	
298	1889-93	322	38139	38146	38226	22.63	22.51	19.47	25.25	21.05	23.26	-2.21	
299	1894-98	323	38278	38495	38744	22.25	20.90	18.95	23.47	20.43	21.87	-1.44	
300	1899-1903	324-325	38473	38707	38948	21.86	20.63	18.48	23.13	20.11	20.83	-0.72	
301	1904-08	326	38868	39102	39326	20.57	19.80	17.56	22.29	18.88	19.64	-0.77	
302	1909-13	327	39215	39382	39522	19.29	18.51	16.22	20.77	17.32	19.69	-2.37	
303	1920-22	328	40228	40761	41118	19.93	17.00	16.09	17.97	16.92	18.13	-1.21	
304	1924-28	329	40295	40604	40775	18.78	17.13	15.13	18.09	15.84	18.36	-2.52	
305	1929-33	330-331	41225	41363	41249	17.54	16.43	14.38	17.20	14.93	18.12	-3.18	
306	1934-38	332	40957	40784	40465	15.53	15.73	13.42	15.96	13.65	18.07	-4.42	
307	1945-47	333	40282	41269	42185	19.28	13.98	17.88	13.88	18.84	13.81	5.03	
308	1949-53	334	42056	43473	44782	19.83	13.01	18.46	11.62	19.94	10.75	9.20	
309	1954-58	335	43843	45179	46315	18.40	11.88	17.38	10.30	18.52	10.50	8.02	
310	1959-63	336-337	46163	47647	49194	18.07	11.32	18.03	9.39	19.39	9.42	9.97	
311	1965	338-339	48919	50679	52687	17.63	11.05	18.10	8.66	19.42	9.03	10.39	
312	GERMANY (EAST) 1952	340-341	18328	18731	19085	16.70	12.09	15.42	11.34	15.91	13.68	2.23	
313	1953-55	342	18059	18458	18814	16.35	11.93	15.23	10.68	15.58	13.34	2.23	
314	1956-58	343	17517	17784	17940	15.72	12.54	14.55	10.35	14.65	13.70	0.95	
315	1959-61	344-345	17241	17523	17679	17.13	13.27	15.53	10.27	16.14	12.31	3.83	
316	1962	346	17102	17350	17505	17.42	13.68	16.05	10.21	16.93	11.55	5.38	
317	1963	347	17155	17468	17676	17.57	12.94	16.29	9.62	17.19	11.21	5.98	
318	1964	348-349	16992	17245	17420	17.18	13.31	16.21	9.76	17.17	11.16	6.01	
319	GERMANY (WEST) 1960	350-351	55585	57144	58389	17.43	11.57	15.55	10.51	16.05	12.24	3.81	
320	1961	352	56175	57947	59286	18.03	11.17	16.11	9.93	16.74	11.57	5.18	
321	1962	353	56938	58630	59875	17.89	11.32	15.94	9.92	16.52	11.59	4.93	
322	1963	354	57587	59299	60576	18.30	11.69	16.34	10.12	17.11	11.20	5.91	
323	1964	355	58266	60145	61501	18.29	11.05	16.43	9.45	17.08	10.96	6.12	
324	1965	356-357	59012	60623	61771	17.70	11.48	16.13	9.69	16.74	11.21	5.54	

AGE DISTRIBUTION

LIFE EXPECTANCY AT BIRTH $\dot{e}_0$		INFANT MORTALITY RATE $1000 M_0$	REPRODUCTION RATES		NET MATERNITY FUNCTION		FIRST COMPLEX ROOT r_2	OBSERVED		REPRODUCTIVE VALUE (in 1000's)	DISSIMILARITY OF OBSERVED FROM STABLE	
Males 11	Females 12	13	Gross 14	Net 15	Mean μ 16	Variance σ^2 17	18	Per cent Under 15 19	Dependency Ratio X 100 20	V 21	$\Delta\%$ 22	SER. NO.
67.70	73.40	25.60	1.24	1.20	28.01	33.57	−0.0297+0.2253	23.53	55.04	2025	6.25	254
66.87	72.97	28.02	1.30	1.25	27.78	32.21	−0.0276+0.2283	23.81	56.74	2117	6.83	255
58.78	62.72	103.94	1.27	1.07	26.67	35.98	−0.0430+0.2395	26.73	50.21	2027	11.40	256
62.68	66.56	88.58	1.15	1.02	26.19	35.05	−0.0460+0.2459	26.47	50.17	1878	13.69	257
65.11	68.68	66.09	1.11	1.01	25.65	32.28	−0.0429+0.2524	26.49	50.98	1787	11.94	258
66.90	70.44	47.80	1.11	1.03	25.09	29.95	−0.0394+0.2578	26.07	50.55	1729	10.69	259
67.79	71.47	37.89	1.08	1.02	25.13	29.49	−0.0394+0.2567	25.43	49.92	1705	9.77	260
68.67	72.18	36.44	1.06	1.01	25.03	28.44	−0.0391+0.2568	25.08	49.44	1687	10.81	261
69.34	73.27	33.61	1.05	1.00	24.87	28.14	−0.0396+0.2590	24.66	48.84	1665	11.57	262
69.39	73.66	31.73	1.00	0.96	24.91	28.06	−0.0411+0.2576	23.88	48.03	1618	12.50	263
52.40	55.97	153.21	1.19	0.94	28.59	39.17	−0.0421+0.2135	25.67	47.76	4177	13.18	264
54.59	58.25	126.60	0.95	0.77	28.37	37.81	−0.0485+0.2139	26.86	51.66	3558	17.35	265
62.03	66.63	74.30	1.46	1.32	27.38	37.30	−0.0353+0.2317	26.00	51.51	3404	6.46	266
65.29	69.97	40.13	1.38	1.30	27.20	35.85	−0.0350+0.2358	27.23	54.83	3351	6.46	267
66.67	71.61	31.40	1.32	1.26	26.69	33.24	−0.0345+0.2418	27.74	56.52	3310	5.37	268
67.58	72.97	24.51	1.16	1.12	26.00	29.56	−0.0342+0.2499	27.23	56.38	3096	7.02	269
67.13	72.81	23.17	1.14	1.10	25.87	28.17	−0.0329+0.2507	26.54	55.34	3102	6.09	270
67.46	73.40	23.42	1.22	1.18	25.94	27.87	−0.0299+0.2490	26.06	54.71	3223	6.07	271
67.73	73.65	22.08	1.22	1.18	26.03	28.09	−0.0300+0.2478	25.70	54.43	3253	6.41	272
69.42	71.99	30.09	1.23	1.18	27.65	36.28	−0.0356+0.2261	26.39	55.25	1039	5.42	273
70.05	72.92	26.97	1.24	1.20	27.38	34.67	−0.0342+0.2302	26.55	56.64	1051	4.78	274
70.37	73.78	23.60	1.24	1.20	27.09	33.14	−0.0329+0.2340	26.42	57.54	1052	4.79	275
70.56	74.09	22.25	1.23	1.19	26.95	31.69	−0.0313+0.2353	25.23	55.77	1059	4.75	276
70.32	74.46	20.26	1.24	1.20	26.88	31.21	−0.0305+0.2360	24.27	54.33	1073	4.54	277
70.43	74.53	19.84	1.28	1.24	26.85	31.23	−0.0293+0.2362	23.97	54.01	1096	5.03	278
70.31	74.83	18.98	1.26	1.22	26.73	31.02	−0.0300+0.2369	23.84	54.06	1091	4.56	279
53.87	58.20	75.14	1.26	1.00	30.59	45.04	−0.0354+0.1966	28.01	52.65	1164	9.99	280
62.28	68.78	37.76	1.50	1.40	29.32	41.26	−0.0287+0.2125	30.13	58.19	1272	4.48	281
63.72	70.29	32.29	1.43	1.36	28.94	40.57	−0.0312+0.2157	30.55	59.76	1264	4.62	282
64.70	71.15	25.97	1.37	1.31	28.59	39.74	−0.0335+0.2194	30.71	60.68	1257	4.31	283
65.38	72.19	22.54	1.33	1.28	28.33	38.33	−0.0336+0.2231	30.40	60.53	1248	4.93	284
65.11	72.26	20.82	1.29	1.24	28.16	37.15	−0.0337+0.2253	29.05	57.63	1239	4.63	285
65.53	72.68	18.61	1.29	1.25	28.11	37.27	−0.0335+0.2253	28.34	56.16	1246	4.80	286
65.64	72.81	17.44	1.23	1.20	28.05	37.74	−0.0360+0.2248	27.67	54.93	1227	5.20	287
65.32	72.83	17.61	1.17	1.14	28.03	38.15	−0.0375+0.2228	27.06	53.82	1200	5.82	288
38.34	39.65	237.84	1.70	0.97	29.68	37.34	−0.0325+0.2040	27.31	51.04	13941	4.43	289
35.91	38.17	223.07	1.61	0.90	29.29	38.45	−0.0371+0.2048	27.51	51.30	13455	4.81	290
38.29	39.60	234.52	1.70	0.97	29.27	38.84	−0.0353+0.2057	27.11	51.08	14264	3.91	291
39.30	40.93	216.59	1.68	1.00	29.14	39.06	−0.0354+0.2069	26.97	51.99	13934	2.47	292
28.61	33.71	244.77	1.46	0.73	28.68	38.63	−0.0476+0.2070	27.76	54.40	12847	6.98	293
40.04	42.40	209.78	1.72	1.05	28.99	38.16	−0.0344+0.2097	27.06	52.63	13271	2.38	294
41.33	43.72	200.65	1.67	1.06	28.94	38.13	−0.0343+0.2102	27.12	53.28	13192	1.86	295
40.22	42.85	222.54	1.66	1.03	28.99	38.12	−0.0348+0.2094	27.13	54.20	13677	3.00	296
40.40	43.12	218.52	1.56	0.98	29.10	38.06	−0.0355+0.2080	26.96	53.84	13443	4.21	297
40.90	44.09	217.43	1.46	0.94	29.28	39.14	−0.0371+0.2070	26.23	52.71	12941	4.57	298
43.03	46.59	208.69	1.43	0.96	29.42	40.74	−0.0375+0.2070	25.99	52.27	12698	4.59	299
45.02	48.53	172.58	1.39	0.98	29.09	40.67	−0.0393+0.2099	26.12	52.25	12139	3.28	300
48.07	51.61	136.52	1.32	0.98	29.90	44.60	−0.0385+0.2041	26.00	52.30	11829	3.33	301
49.18	53.14	126.90	1.22	0.93	28.55	39.05	−0.0422+0.2132	25.74	51.76	10888	5.22	302
52.88	56.61	109.09	1.21	0.97	28.72	37.85	−0.0386+0.2131	22.48	46.25	10450	5.34	303
53.37	57.67	90.83	1.14	0.93	28.33	37.77	−0.0418+0.2158	22.51	46.35	9962	5.81	304
54.85	59.64	79.84	1.09	0.91	27.99	37.98	−0.0448+0.2182	23.07	48.04	9572	6.01	305
56.27	62.14	68.33	1.02	0.88	27.86	36.87	−0.0452+0.2199	24.57	52.74	8958	6.84	306
57.90	63.69	106.44	1.35	1.16	28.89	35.19	−0.0296+0.2167	21.49	48.38	10248	6.50	307
63.88	69.63	47.94	1.39	1.30	28.55	34.44	−0.0258+0.2207	23.12	52.82	10594	8.23	308
66.03	72.43	32.47	1.32	1.25	28.40	33.72	−0.0275+0.2218	24.95	57.46	10697	6.44	309
67.46	74.23	23.23	1.37	1.32	28.10	33.30	−0.0259+0.2273	26.43	61.68	11445	6.80	310
68.27	75.48	18.25	1.37	1.33	27.81	32.53	−0.0250+0.2298	24.58	59.06	12023	7.45	311
64.28	68.32	61.76	1.15	1.06	27.17	34.02	−0.0388+0.2318	22.17	50.37	4008	8.32	312
65.68	69.83	52.73	1.14	1.06	26.95	33.95	−0.0407+0.2337	21.47	50.20	3850	8.68	313
66.19	70.79	46.70	1.09	1.03	26.67	32.64	−0.0413+0.2355	20.56	50.48	3527	7.53	314
66.69	71.51	39.21	1.16	1.11	26.30	33.23	−0.0404+0.2413	21.08	53.28	3491	8.90	315
67.25	72.07	32.21	1.20	1.15	26.02	33.25	−0.0408+0.2452	22.47	57.81	3463	9.36	316
67.73	72.65	32.09	1.22	1.17	26.00	33.08	−0.0402+0.2450	23.00	59.45	3513	9.60	317
67.79	72.77	28.89	1.22	1.17	26.13	32.70	−0.0386+0.2432	23.61	61.44	3499	9.83	318
66.47	71.84	35.08	1.17	1.12	28.83	33.44	−0.0287+0.2179	21.33	47.45	12587	7.07	319
66.91	72.43	33.48	1.21	1.16	28.65	33.36	−0.0279+0.2200	21.70	48.77	12720	7.40	320
67.10	72.77	30.14	1.20	1.15	28.54	32.87	−0.0277+0.2206	21.94	49.72	12727	6.39	321
67.04	72.74	28.13	1.23	1.18	28.51	32.33	−0.0259+0.2207	22.19	50.71	13002	7.06	322
67.59	73.58	26.00	1.24	1.19	28.54	32.42	−0.0253+0.2200	22.40	51.71	13160	7.71	323
67.61	73.44	24.17	1.21	1.17	28.47	32.89	−0.0264+0.2200	22.56	52.62	13124	7.31	324

POPULATION (in 1000's) — VITAL RATES (Per 1000 Population)

BOTH SEXES COMBINED

SER. NO.	AREA AND YEAR	PAGE	OBSERVED MID-PERIOD 1	PROJECTED 5 years 2	PROJECTED 10 years 3	CRUDE Birth 4	CRUDE Death 5	AGE-SEX STD Birth 6	AGE-SEX STD Death 7	FEMALE INTRINSIC Birth 8	Death 9	Increase 10
325	GREECE 1956-58	-	8096	8576	9031	19.33	7.38	14.70	8.51	14.24	13.41	0.83
326	1959-61	358-359	8327	8779	9172	18.74	7.42	14.24	8.35	13.69	13.59	0.10
327	1962	-	8451	8860	9216	18.01	7.88	14.12	7.96	13.60	13.53	0.07
328	1963	360	8480	8874	9222	17.48	7.88	13.86	8.12	13.20	13.89	-0.69
329	1964	361	8510	8913	9272	17.99	8.16	14.52	8.33	14.24	12.99	1.25
330	1965	362-363	8550	8951	9309	17.71	7.87	14.50	7.99	14.15	12.87	1.28
331	HUNGARY 1950-52	364-365	9423	9810	10147	20.24	11.47	16.52	13.23	17.43	13.96	3.47
332	1953-55	366	9706	10218	10684	22.00	10.87	18.43	12.34	20.06	11.50	8.56
333	1956-58	367	9839	10169	10450	17.56	10.36	15.32	11.39	15.75	13.60	2.15
334	1959-61	368-369	9984	10192	10368	14.62	10.08	13.02	10.76	12.42	15.89	-3.47
335	1962	-	10061	10158	10240	12.93	10.76	11.60	11.25	10.44	18.21	-7.77
336	1963	370	10088	10231	10345	13.12	9.90	11.72	10.15	10.52	17.63	-7.11
337	1964	371	10120	10258	10374	13.06	9.96	11.62	9.98	10.36	17.64	-7.28
338	1965	372-373	10148	10265	10365	13.11	10.65	11.63	10.47	10.51	17.59	-7.08
339	ICELAND 1920	374-375	94	100	107	27.90	14.44	25.87	16.29	25.84	14.35	11.49
340	1950	376	143	158	176	28.69	7.86	25.30	8.43	26.72	6.77	19.95
341	1955	-	158	177	193	28.48	6.95	26.29	7.41	29.02	5.48	23.54
342	1960	377	176	196	219	27.93	6.63	27.60	7.14	30.04	5.05	24.99
343	1962	378-379	182	203	222	25.82	6.77	25.99	7.25	28.61	5.39	23.22
344	IRELAND 1926	380-381	2976	3081	3197	20.55	14.02	20.66	14.82	21.49	15.08	6.41
345	1936	382	2972	3053	3149	19.55	14.33	19.68	14.64	20.64	14.61	6.02
346	1946	383	2961	3102	3251	22.94	14.00	22.15	13.35	22.96	11.75	11.21
347	1951	384	2958	3065	3190	21.26	14.33	21.48	13.22	22.59	10.62	11.97
348	1955-57	385	2895	3029	3178	21.14	12.09	22.69	10.71	23.61	8.76	14.85
349	1960-62	386-387	2815	2953	3132	21.59	11.99	25.40	10.02	26.34	7.23	19.11
350	ITALY 1931	388-389	41225	43392	45620	24.83	14.78	21.02	17.13	22.08	15.93	6.15
351	1936	390	42493	44362	46213	22.65	13.88	18.71	16.06	19.57	15.84	3.73
352	1950-52	391	47043	49053	51006	18.59	9.98	15.63	11.43	15.78	14.13	1.65
353	1960-62	392-393	50521	52627	54520	18.32	9.62	15.71	9.75	15.91	12.31	3.60
354	1964	394-395	52130	54668	56974	19.49	9.40	16.99	9.12	17.37	10.98	6.39
355	LUXEMBOURG 1903-07	-	245	259	274	30.57	18.95	28.82	22.24	30.73	17.39	13.33
356	1908-12	-	259	270	287	27.94	17.75	26.32	21.62	28.16	17.04	11.12
357	1913-17	-	260	270	276	22.26	17.28	20.37	21.43	21.93	18.66	3.28
358	1918-22	-	261	267	271	19.38	15.87	17.05	20.05	17.70	19.62	-1.92
359	1920-24	-	259	267	279	20.91	14.46	18.05	18.60	19.07	17.58	1.49
360	1923-27	-	274	284	290	20.44	13.75	17.12	17.52	18.33	17.02	1.30
361	1925-29	-	283	289	300	20.78	14.05	17.09	17.74	18.14	17.21	0.93
362	1928-32	-	298	308	318	20.15	13.34	16.07	16.76	16.78	17.09	-0.31
363	1933-37	-	297	300	302	15.55	12.57	12.23	15.51	11.88	20.23	-8.34
364	1938-42	-	295	298	294	14.72	12.94	12.01	15.04	11.51	20.18	-8.67
365	1943-47	-	292	292	292	14.54	13.26	12.41	14.51	11.91	19.40	-7.49
366	1945-49	-	290	291	289	14.55	12.65	12.67	13.54	12.22	18.26	-6.04
367	1948-52	-	297	300	301	14.99	12.00	12.97	12.22	12.69	16.80	-4.11
368	1953-57	-	309	314	316	15.90	11.91	13.64	11.06	13.70	14.80	-1.09
369	1958-62	396-397	318	321	323	15.80	11.63	14.38	10.30	14.71	13.23	1.48
370	1963	398-399	330	337	340	15.50	11.91	14.85	10.33	14.98	12.98	1.99
371	MALTA 1959-61	400-401	329	357	391	25.10	8.72	22.61	11.00	24.74	8.00	16.74
372	1962	-	329	355	388	22.84	8.63	20.95	10.87	22.56	8.92	13.64
373	1963	402	328	347	375	20.33	9.09	18.78	11.43	20.02	10.06	9.96
374	1964	403	324	344	367	19.76	8.52	18.04	10.47	19.35	10.37	8.98
375	1965	404-405	319	330	350	17.63	9.40	15.99	10.83	16.75	11.97	4.79
376	NETHERLANDS 1901	406-407	5166	5572	6024	32.60	17.42	30.61	20.14	31.41	16.63	14.78
377	1902	-	5234	5663	6137	32.24	16.47	30.14	19.46	30.75	15.67	15.08
378	1903-07	408	5461	5910	6399	31.31	15.48	28.98	18.30	29.85	14.92	14.93
379	1908-12	409	5860	6319	6818	28.95	13.95	26.63	16.98	27.66	13.94	13.72
380	1913-17	410	6337	6818	7339	27.25	12.77	24.87	15.88	25.94	13.29	12.64
381	1918-22	411	6790	7260	7755	26.41	13.19	23.82	16.44	24.79	14.24	10.55
382	1923-27	412	7307	7865	8472	24.61	9.95	22.05	12.96	22.89	11.75	11.14
383	1928-32	413	7856	8390	8954	22.77	9.64	19.90	12.69	20.63	12.26	8.37
384	1933-37	414-415	8387	8884	9392	20.41	8.71	17.29	11.48	17.73	12.85	4.89
385	1938-42	416	8856	9361	9871	20.69	9.33	17.37	11.71	18.02	12.46	5.56
386	1943-47	417	9218	9904	10576	25.83	10.82	22.14	12.85	23.01	10.91	12.10
387	1948-52	418	10114	10903	11670	23.23	7.56	20.77	8.83	21.41	8.95	12.46
388	1953-57	419	10751	11487	12205	21.43	7.60	19.89	8.33	20.64	8.81	11.83
389	1958-62	420-421	11487	12260	13075	21.07	7.64	20.43	7.85	21.53	7.99	13.54
390	1963	422	11966	12775	13671	20.88	8.00	20.56	7.93	21.78	7.77	14.01
391	1964	423	12127	12960	13873	20.69	7.70	20.35	7.56	21.52	7.77	13.75
392	1965	424-425	12295	13082	13953	19.94	7.97	19.56	7.73	20.68	8.16	12.52
393	NORWAY 1950-52	426-427	3296	3447	3568	18.76	8.68	16.40	8.07	16.43	11.28	5.15
394	1953-55	428	3394	3548	3683	18.59	8.51	17.48	7.66	18.08	9.87	8.20
395	1956-58	429	3492	3648	3789	18.16	8.80	18.48	7.66	19.49	8.98	10.51
396	1959-61	430-431	3581	3731	3892	17.45	9.09	18.71	7.61	19.83	8.68	11.15

AGE   DISTRIBUTION

LIFE EXPECTANCY AT BIRTH $\overset{\circ}{e}_0$		INFANT MORTALITY RATE	REPRODUCTION RATES		NET MATERNITY FUNCTION		FIRST COMPLEX ROOT	OBSERVED		REPRODUCTIVE VALUE (in 1000's)	DISSIMILARITY OF OBSERVED FROM STABLE	
Males	Females	$1000 M_0$	Gross	Net	Mean μ	Variance σ^2	r_2	Per cent Under 15	Dependency Ratio X 100	V	$\Delta\%$	SER. NO.
11	12	13	14	15	16	17	18	19	20	21	22	
69.54	72.56	41.04	1.09	1.02	29.20	33.37	-0.0286+0.2133	26.22	51.44	2179	12.72	325
70.09	73.33	39.67	1.06	1.00	28.73	31.47	-0.0287+0.2163	26.11	52.04	2100	12.76	326
70.11	73.72	40.64	1.06	1.00	28.59	31.49	-0.0299+0.2174	25.70	52.24	2089	12.47	327
70.20	73.72	38.55	1.04	0.98	28.47	31.63	-0.0311+0.2179	25.64	52.27	2066	13.17	328
69.87	73.75	36.32	1.09	1.04	28.21	31.55	-0.0300+0.2204	25.61	52.64	2081	10.64	329
70.57	74.32	34.04	1.09	1.04	28.09	32.16	-0.0307+0.2210	25.56	52.89	2057	10.45	330
60.58	65.09	80.03	1.23	1.10	27.11	37.97	-0.0450+0.2314	25.00	49.12	2382	5.58	331
63.52	67.43	63.76	1.37	1.26	27.20	36.88	-0.0377+0.2324	25.49	50.78	2545	5.94	332
64.26	68.79	60.30	1.14	1.06	26.28	34.50	-0.0465+0.2421	25.94	52.57	2265	5.35	333
65.87	70.30	49.17	0.97	0.91	25.78	32.30	-0.0498+0.2484	25.32	52.33	2047	10.34	334
65.66	70.16	47.95	0.87	0.82	25.69	31.16	-0.0523+0.2475	24.79	52.19	1919	12.71	335
66.60	71.28	42.91	0.88	0.83	25.80	30.00	-0.0488+0.2452	24.32	51.70	1921	12.96	336
67.03	71.86	41.30	0.87	0.83	25.73	28.78	-0.0466+0.2458	23.80	51.18	1889	13.17	337
66.71	71.56	40.37	0.88	0.83	25.65	28.13	-0.0456+0.2467	23.28	50.65	1872	11.96	338
53.31	56.72	88.56	1.88	1.43	31.16	40.57	-0.0193+0.1976	33.16	66.98	39	2.52	339
68.71	73.84	22.40	1.83	1.76	28.69	44.23	-0.0264+0.2155	30.56	61.58	49	4.40	340
70.81	76.32	23.19	1.97	1.91	27.98	43.66	-0.0291+0.2233	33.24	68.94	55	6.12	341
72.53	75.93	13.50	2.04	1.99	28.03	44.72	-0.0302+0.2249	34.80	75.02	63	6.74	342
71.45	76.53	17.24	1.94	1.89	28.02	44.21	-0.0306+0.2252	34.97	76.18	64	4.86	343
57.47	57.86	82.06	1.53	1.23	31.86	33.16	-0.0164+0.1937	29.20	62.19	1038	3.53	344
58.42	59.55	80.29	1.46	1.21	31.87	34.67	-0.0174+0.1927	27.64	59.48	975	3.31	345
.61.43	63.63	66.30	1.63	1.42	31.37	35.49	-0.0147+0.1970	27.85	62.57	992	3.59	346
63.58	66.18	45.37	1.59	1.45	31.48	34.15	-0.0130+0.1973	28.93	65.63	949	4.29	347
67.11	70.22	35.88	1.68	1.59	31.46	34.68	-0.0101+0.1981	30.09	69.57	946	6.09	348
68.12	71.88	28.64	1.89	1.80	31.23	34.42	-0.0070+0.2012	31.18	73.52	955	10.12	349
53.80	55.92	115.25	1.56	1.20	30.35	44.45	-0.0280+0.1990	29.79	58.98	15293	6.33	350
55.39	58.28	102.19	1.39	1.12	30.45	40.49	-0.0284+0.2002	30.98	62.64	14665	8.07	351
63.83	67.42	68.22	1.17	1.05	29.77	38.07	-0.0311+0.2059	26.38	52.89	13157	9.14	352
66.83	72.05	43.54	1.18	1.11	29.14	35.05	-0.0286+0.2128	24.78	52.00	12745	5.50	353
67.71	73.17	36.09	1.27	1.21	29.85	34.64	-0.0231+0.2094	24.24	51.42	13783	4.16	354
45.75	49.15	179.52	2.14	1.51	30.99	39.45	-0.0168+0.1998	32.48	62.38	110	1.97	355
46.64	50.52	173.54	1.94	1.40	30.49	40.61	-0.0217+0.2021	32.66	62.99	107	2.39	356
47.52	50.85	147.31	1.52	1.10	30.57	40.76	-0.0277+0.1982	30.41	57.54	94	5.92	357
50.08	52.86	118.96	1.25	0.94	30.47	39.55	-0.0322+0.1987	27.94	51.95	83	9.41	358
52.02	55.21	124.95	1.34	1.05	30.31	38.73	-0.0292+0.2020	26.95	49.85	84	7.05	359
53.51	57.12	120.35	1.29	1.04	29.93	38.96	-0.0313+0.2042	25.56	46.81	83	7.23	360
53.13	56.96	119.94	1.28	1.03	29.61	38.67	-0.0327+0.2061	24.72	45.02	83	7.32	361
55.20	58.93	97.34	1.19	0.99	29.27	38.67	-0.0354+0.2083	24.60	44.85	82	9.04	362
56.99	61.25	88.57	0.91	0.78	29.22	37.04	-0.0412+0.2067	24.56	46.33	69	15.30	363
57.83	62.31	80.91	0.89	0.77	29.22	34.95	-0.0384+0.2071	22.78	44.55	64	13.44	364
58.31	62.97	78.06	0.92	0.80	29.44	33.99	-0.0361+0.2058	20.80	42.46	62	10.97	365
60.82	64.91	65.93	0.94	0.84	29.07	32.15	-0.0351+0.2110	19.95	41.53	60	9.68	366
62.88	67.28	58.75	0.97	0.89	28.70	31.87	-0.0342+0.2145	19.34	41.03	60	8.27	367
64.79	69.99	43.42	1.03	0.97	28.16	31.37	-0.0334+0.2206	19.26	41.77	60	6.83	368
66.44	71.91	33.12	1.09	1.04	27.62	30.31	-0.0320+0.2275	20.74	45.83	62	5.69	369
66.87	71.99	28.76	1.10	1.06	27.42	29.60	-0.0312+0.2301	21.31	47.50	64	4.67	370
66.74	71.03	34.43	1.70	1.63	29.35	40.05	-0.0238+0.2152	36.66	78.18	124	3.83	371
67.07	70.92	35.77	1.55	1.48	29.15	39.30	-0.0268+0.2167	35.26	74.29	118	5.42	372
66.78	70.89	33.60	1.39	1.33	28.98	38.92	-0.0310+0.2168	34.40	72.21	111	8.06	373
67.97	71.21	34.62	1.36	1.30	29.09	38.70	-0.0308+0.2156	33.60	70.51	108	8.24	374
67.71	71.07	33.80	1.20	1.15	29.39	38.65	-0.0334+0.2103	32.91	71.82	100	10.41	375
47.40	50.66	115.82	2.27	1.59	31.88	37.40	-0.0120+0.1945	34.74	68.74	2595	1.51	376
49.54	52.23	94.90	2.22	1.61	31.91	37.41	-0.0117+0.1944	34.68	68.61	2572	1.61	377
51.18	53.81	96.16	2.15	1.60	31.88	37.33	-0.0118+0.1944	34.67	68.86	2615	1.36	378
54.09	56.30	102.34	1.97	1.54	31.84	37.58	-0.0133+0.1944	34.51	68.44	2646	2.39	379
56.29	58.29	93.84	1.84	1.49	31.73	38.08	-0.0150+0.1948	33.82	66.06	2708	3.07	380
55.31	57.00	86.94	1.76	1.39	31.61	38.18	-0.0172+0.1948	32.72	62.93	2790	3.46	381
62.22	63.66	48.24	1.63	1.42	31.77	37.86	-0.0160+0.1940	32.00	60.96	2830	4.53	382
63.28	64.71	53.37	1.47	1.30	31.81	37.65	-0.0180+0.1929	30.79	58.55	2844	6.40	383
65.76	67.19	41.94	1.28	1.17	31.72	39.27	-0.0223+0.1918	29.70	56.65	2747	9.38	384
64.90	67.72	39.89	1.29	1.19	30.81	36.58	-0.0225+0.2002	27.99	53.71	2745	7.32	385
60.48	65.64	53.66	1.63	1.45	31.02	35.32	-0.0146+0.2007	27.80	54.04	3195	3.77	386
70.07	72.54	26.61	1.54	1.47	30.94	36.31	-0.0152+0.2011	29.30	58.82	3304	4.04	387
71.03	74.02	20.42	1.48	1.43	30.41	35.46	-0.0170+0.2056	29.90	62.03	3337	3.67	388
71.39	75.43	16.72	1.53	1.49	29.75	34.07	-0.0162+0.2120	29.99	63.92	3529	3.82	389
71.01	75.80	16.13	1.54	1.50	29.36	33.36	-0.0163+0.2155	28.75	61.57	3649	3.73	390
71.31	76.28	15.07	1.53	1.49	29.21	32.96	-0.0166+0.2166	28.48	61.14	3665	3.69	391
71.14	76.17	14.48	1.47	1.43	28.98	32.82	-0.0184+0.2183	28.26	60.84	3620	3.26	392
70.59	73.98	26.57	1.22	1.16	29.65	39.36	-0.0299+0.2073	24.60	52.13	807	7.26	393
71.38	75.13	21.82	1.31	1.27	29.03	38.41	-0.0295+0.2144	25.46	55.05	829	6.39	394
71.33	75.48	20.93	1.39	1.35	28.59	37.20	-0.0283+0.2202	26.15	57.81	862	6.43	395
71.29	75.89	18.86	1.41	1.37	28.27	35.88	-0.0272+0.2240	25.92	58.62	883	7.12	396

			POPULATION (in 1000's)			VITAL RATES (Per 1000 Population)						
			OBSERVED MID-PERIOD	PROJECTED		CRUDE		AGE-SEX STANDARDIZED ON U.S. 1960		FEMALE INTRINSIC		
SER. NO.	AREA AND YEAR	PAGE		5 years	10 years	Birth	Death	Birth	Death	Birth	Death	Increase
			1	2	3	4	5	6	7	8	9	10
397	NORWAY 1962	–	3639	3789	3957	17.11	9.43	18.63	7.73	19.95	8.57	11.38
398	1963	432–433	3667	3812	3979	17.26	10.05	18.76	8.13	20.27	8.53	11.74
399	1964	434–435	3694	3858	4046	17.75	9.52	19.12	7.66	20.35	8.36	11.99
400	POLAND 1960	436–437	29577	31663	33734	22.35	7.58	19.30	10.22	20.77	10.10	10.67
401	1962	438–439	30324	32075	33891	19.77	7.89	17.46	10.78	18.50	11.18	7.32
402	PORTUGAL 1950–52	440–441	8459	8991	9545	24.60	12.17	20.91	14.94	21.54	13.87	7.67
403	1953–55	442	8570	9108	9674	23.71	11.36	20.18	13.69	20.90	13.03	7.87
404	1956–58	443	8680	9234	9801	24.06	11.54	20.45	13.64	21.51	12.51	9.00
405	1959–61	444–445	8865	9454	10057	24.23	10.99	20.69	12.64	21.64	11.88	9.76
406	1962	–	9008	9624	10254	24.44	10.75	20.98	12.14	21.89	11.31	10.58
407	1963	446	9074	9648	10242	23.38	10.80	20.18	12.20	21.02	11.33	9.69
408	1964	447	9143	9744	10360	23.75	10.60	20.58	11.78	21.40	11.05	10.35
409	1965	448–449	9234	9810	10400	22.77	10.31	19.84	11.37	20.64	10.86	9.77
410	ROMANIA 1956–58	–	17824	18962	19976	22.89	9.60	17.79	12.29	19.04	12.82	6.23
411	1959–61	450–451	18407	19237	19949	18.93	9.23	15.02	11.58	15.12	14.75	0.38
412	1962	–	18691	19290	19822	16.16	9.23	13.24	11.65	12.81	16.29	–3.48
413	1963	452	18813	19459	20034	15.67	8.28	13.05	10.25	12.30	16.20	–3.90
414	1964	453	18927	19559	20123	15.18	8.06	12.73	9.79	11.82	16.34	–4.52
415	1965	454–455	19027	19575	20080	14.63	8.59	12.36	10.26	11.96	16.24	–4.28
416	SPAIN 1950	456–457	27849	29119	30378	20.07	10.93	16.07	13.41	16.12	15.52	0.60
417	1960	458	30401	32307	34122	21.53	8.63	18.02	9.52	18.60	10.51	8.09
418	1962	459	30895	32749	34526	21.03	8.78	18.02	9.48	18.64	10.33	8.31
419	1963	460–461	31160	33061	34904	21.26	8.84	18.44	9..44	19.14	9.97	9.17
420	SWEDEN 1778–82	462–463	2104	2197	2292	34.51	25.92	29.88	29.00	31.16	25.26	5.90
421	1783–87	464	2147	2193	2238	31.60	27.26	26.92	31.24	28.57	27.17	1.40
422	1788–92	465	2161	2219	2272	33.64	27.71	28.71	31.52	30.61	26.25	4.36
423	1793–97	466	2274	2374	2470	33.97	24.88	29.57	28.94	31.40	23.82	7.58
424	1798–1802	467	2352	2414	2478	31.21	25.88	27.48	31.11	29.38	25.08	4.31
425	1803–07	468–469	2418	2497	2579	31.27	24.89	28.03	29.31	29.97	23.53	6.44
426	1808–12	470	2380	2371	2379	32.20	33.09	28.32	39.19	31.19	30.45	0.74
427	1813–17	471	2450	2553	2657	33.03	24.67	28.74	29.19	30.58	23.35	7.23
428	1818–22	472	2573	2692	2806	34.29	24.90	29.82	29.31	31.44	23.10	8.34
429	1823–27	473	2749	2931	3113	34.73	21.59	31.03	25.27	32.37	18.85	13.51
430	1828–32	474–475	2876	2980	3090	32.52	25.82	29.83	30.91	31.85	22.61	9.25
431	1833–37	476	3004	3166	3341	32.63	22.13	30.84	26.84	32.28	20.02	12.25
432	1838–42	477	3123	3267	3437	30.54	21.73	29.09	27.34	30.60	20.61	10.00
433	1843–47	478	3296	3471	3668	30.73	21.20	28.89	26.54	30.10	20.04	10.05
434	1848–52	479	3462	3662	3880	31.46	20.54	28.49	25.71	29.53	19.39	10.14
435	1853–57	480–481	3625	3795	3971	32.06	22.83	28.31	27.57	29.47	22.05	7.42
436	1858–62	482	3824	4094	4354	34.10	19.87	30.17	23.40	30.64	19.23	11.42
437	1863–67	483	4092	4356	4617	32.76	19.70	29.86	23.52	30.38	18.83	11.55
438	1868–72	484	4164	4363	4568	29.15	19.40	27.27	23.97	28.04	19.41	8.62
439	1873–77	485	4362	4621	4895	30.96	19.22	29.88	22.60	30.25	18.92	11.33
440	1878–82	486–487	4572	4856	5164	29.52	17.56	28.47	20.34	28.82	17.76	11.06
441	1883–87	488	4664	4962	5277	29.55	17.05	28.33	19.37	28.64	16.79	11.85
442	1888–92	489	4780	5053	5334	27.92	16.75	27.00	18.70	27.57	16.15	11.42
443	1893–97	490	4896	5175	5476	27.17	15.88	26.61	17.31	27.00	15.41	11.59
444	1898–1902	491	5117	5401	5707	26.79	16.19	26.20	17.38	26.81	15.33	11.48
445	1903–07	492–493	5278	5575	5902	25.68	15.00	24.92	15.82	25.58	14.27	11.31
446	1908–12	494	5499	5813	6151	24.72	14.11	23.47	14.84	24.23	13.56	10.66
447	1913–17	495	5696	5942	6218	21.95	13.83	20.23	14.71	20.84	14.57	6.27
448	1918–22	496	5876	6088	6314	20.99	14.19	18.68	14.97	19.15	15.80	3.35
449	1923–27	497	6045	6225	6414	17.50	11.91	15.06	12.63	15.01	16.19	–1.18
450	1928–32	498–499	6131	6232	6331	15.20	12.01	12.52	12.62	11.97	18.83	–6.87
451	1933–37	500	6242	6313	6367	13.95	11.62	11.12	11.90	10.15	20.17	–10.01
452	1938–42	501	6356	6490	6593	15.76	11.14	12.48	11.05	11.96	17.11	–5.15
453	1943–47	502–503	6636	6909	7128	19.81	10.69	16.43	10.10	17.00	12.19	4.81
454	1948–52	504	7017	7225	7379	16.64	9.85	15.05	9.12	15.23	12.51	2.71
455	1953–57	505	7262	7427	7568	14.81	9.65	14.58	8.52	14.58	12.54	2.04
456	1958–62	506–507	7480	7636	7791	14.02	9.82	14.39	8.01	14.29	12.43	1.85
457	1965	508–509	7734	7962	8177	15.88	10.11	15.63	7.63	16.01	10.83	5.17
458	SWITZERLAND 1950–52	510–511	4749	4904	5028	17.56	10.18	15.45	10.39	15.87	12.59	3.28
459	1953–55	512	4927	5081	5205	17.06	10.09	14.88	9.99	15.17	12.79	2.38
460	1956–58	513	5117	5298	5444	17.60	9.90	15.10	9.52	15.37	12.27	3.11
461	1959–61	514–515	5429	5643	5837	17.60	9.40	15.83	8.80	16.34	11.20	5.14
462	1962	516	5584	5825	6044	18.68	9.87	16.56	9.26	17.35	10.67	6.68
463	1963	517	5663	5924	6176	19.42	10.06	17.24	9.42	18.33	10.04	8.29
464	1964	518–519	5773	6069	6343	19.55	9.29	16.99	8.74	17.81	10.10	7.71
465	U.K. 1861	520–521	20132	21461	22853	34.59	21.61	29.74	25.35	31.73	21.53	10.20
466	(ENGLAND 1871	522	22794	24237	25781	34.98	22.59	30.69	26.38	33.03	21.78	11.25
467	AND 1881	523	26050	28084	30287	33.92	18.88	29.90	23.33	32.20	18.18	14.03
468	WALES) 1891	524	29091	30812	32770	31.42	20.21	26.77	26.33	29.71	19.70	10.01
469	1901	525	32616	34554	36574	28.51	16.91	22.56	22.09	24.76	18.61	6.15

AGE   DISTRIBUTION

Life Expectancy at Birth e_0		Infant Mortality Rate	Reproduction Rates		Net Maternity Function		First Complex Root	Observed		Reproductive Value (in 1000's)	Dissimilarity of Observed from Stable	
Males	Females	$1000 M_0$	Gross	Net	Mean μ	Variance σ^2	r_2	Per cent Under 15	Dependency Ratio X 100	V	$\Delta\%$	SER. NO.
11	12	13	14	15	16	17	18	19	20	21	22	
70.98	76.02	17.96	1.41	1.37	27.83	34.92	-0.0277+0.2283	25.25	57.93	890	7.13	397
70.83	75.47	17.27	1.42	1.38	27.81	34.58	-0.0269+0.2280	25.00	57.73	903	7.69	398
71.27	76.08	16.97	1.43	1.39	27.73	34.35	-0.0264+0.2290	24.84	57.78	914	7.88	399
64.85	70.69	60.87	1.44	1.34	27.47	37.38	-0.0351+0.2338	33.60	65.29	9036	7.55	400
64.56	70.68	54.85	1.30	1.22	27.33	35.59	-0.0365+0.2357	33.13	64.62	8759	8.67	401
55.86	60.95	109.97	1.55	1.26	30.38	43.13	-0.0286+0.2020	29.46	57.45	3071	5.10	402
58.34	63.47	103.05	1.50	1.27	30.19	42.79	-0.0292+0.2042	29.36	57.95	3004	4.64	403
58.87	64.05	99.44	1.53	1.30	29.72	42.58	-0.0299+0.2076	29.27	58.45	2988	2.95	404
60.16	65.57	97.67	1.54	1.33	29.57	41.58	-0.0292+0.2090	29.18	58.98	3008	2.69	405
60.95	66.69	90.81	1.56	1.36	29.55	42.18	-0.0293+0.2088	29.11	59.31	3031	2.44	406
61.71	67.41	80.68	1.50	1.33	29.66	42.36	-0.0294+0.2073	29.08	59.49	2979	2.61	407
62.10	67.71	77.17	1.52	1.36	29.65	42.74	-0.0295+0.2074	29.05	59.66	3003	2.63	408
63.12	68.95	69.50	1.47	1.33	29.61	43.05	-0.0308+0.2076	29.02	59.84	2942	2.88	409
62.12	65.73	81.10	1.33	1.18	27.21	38.94	-0.0431+0.2307	27.76	52.23	5117	7.31	410
63.26	67.06	76.36	1.12	1.01	26.43	38.54	-0.0558+0.2397	28.08	53.84	4617	11.65	411
64.44	68.21	60.80	0.99	0.91	26.06	36.91	-0.0591+0.2448	27.88	54.15	4257	14.41	412
65.91	69.73	55.98	0.97	0.90	25.92	36.78	-0.0602+0.2455	27.61	53.72	4171	15.15	413
66.69	70.66	49.42	0.95	0.89	25.90	35.26	-0.0560+0.2459	27.07	52.97	4088	15.98	414
66.57	70.60	44.62	0.95	0.89	25.99	34.80	-0.0539+0.2441	26.33	52.10	4064	14.88	415
58.68	63.44	87.88	1.20	1.02	30.63	36.58	-0.0277+0.2020	26.23	50.28	8617	10.56	416
67.91	72.38	36.99	1.35	1.27	29.97	33.27	-0.0201+0.2097	27.35	55.10	8907	4.22	417
68.18	72.77	32.86	1.35	1.28	29.88	33.04	-0.0193+0.2101	27.57	56.34	8983	3.32	418
68.14	73.01	32.45	1.38	1.31	30.01	32.09	-0.0175+0.2097	27.67	56.93	9179	2.90	419
36.00	38.52	211.62	2.21	1.21	32.24	43.29	-0.0216+0.1892	31.92	58.32	1114	3.09	420
33.58	36.56	231.45	2.00	1.05	32.05	42.50	-0.0256+0.1893	31.35	57.65	1078	3.94	421
33.34	37.32	255.30	2.12	1.15	32.15	42.48	-0.0226+0.1895	31.94	59.73	1100	2.08	422
37.45	40.18	194.30	2.19	1.27	32.19	41.75	-0.0195+0.1905	32.50	61.16	1163	2.30	423
35.99	38.89	248.96	2.03	1.15	32.18	41.84	-0.0224+0.1895	32.60	61.53	1171	2.16	424
37.81	40.59	223.07	2.08	1.23	32.19	42.10	-0.0210+0.1903	32.74	61.75	1184	1.63	425
28.99	32.76	260.08	2.10	1.02	31.92	40.76	-0.0259+0.1907	31.93	58.99	1231	1.80	426
37.33	40.76	216.98	2.13	1.26	32.23	40.64	-0.0191+0.1903	31.61	58.19	1235	1.94	427
37.42	40.90	206.69	2.20	1.31	32.35	41.08	-0.0182+0.1899	32.07	59.97	1312	2.75	428
41.96	46.40	178.35	2.30	1.54	32.28	41.21	-0.0140+0.1917	34.13	65.69	1382	4.33	429
36.77	41.27	203.99	2.21	1.35	32.32	40.08	-0.0171+0.1906	35.10	67.91	1468	2.97	430
40.25	44.67	185.99	2.28	1.48	32.44	39.70	-0.0139+0.1910	35.21	67.66	1542	2.83	431
39.97	44.21	184.61	2.16	1.38	32.62	38.15	-0.0144+0.1897	33.86	62.80	1585	2.21	432
40.78	45.20	174.16	2.13	1.39	32.83	37.82	-0.0135+0.1884	33.31	61.66	1677	2.17	433
41.54	46.28	165.60	2.10	1.39	32.97	37.88	-0.0131+0.1876	32.91	60.52	1740	2.02	434
38.75	42.60	164.80	2.09	1.28	33.04	38.20	-0.0156+0.1864	33.21	61.52	1851	2.15	435
43.07	46.54	150.76	2.23	1.46	33.13	39.25	-0.0124+0.1864	33.48	63.02	1960	2.31	436
43.35	47.18	148.04	2.20	1.46	33.02	39.85	-0.0130+0.1869	34.02	65.02	2053	2.21	437
43.11	46.87	157.70	2.01	1.33	32.96	39.15	-0.0152+0.1866	34.02	65.08	1991	2.87	438
43.64	47.22	155.36	2.20	1.44	32.70	41.34	-0.0150+0.1880	33.66	64.14	2153	2.90	439
46.58	49.53	131.33	2.10	1.43	32.47	41.50	-0.0159+0.1897	32.66	62.50	2164	2.52	440
48.08	51.13	121.69	2.09	1.46	32.36	41.89	-0.0156+0.1904	32.82	64.85	2148	2.16	441
49.78	52.44	115.87	2.00	1.44	32.22	42.29	-0.0167+0.1909	33.29	69.02	2101	2.22	442
51.51	54.09	106.93	1.96	1.44	32.02	42.31	-0.0173+0.1919	32.96	69.57	2092	2.44	443
51.53	54.26	106.84	1.94	1.43	31.68	42.79	-0.0188+0.1936	32.49	68.94	2140	2.36	444
54.28	56.77	90.16	1.84	1.42	31.43	42.96	-0.0200+0.1949	32.07	67.98	2105	2.06	445
56.35	58.95	69.78	1.73	1.39	31.15	43.73	-0.0220+0.1960	31.80	67.31	2095	1.57	446
56.98	59.58	51.40	1.50	1.21	31.00	44.27	-0.0267+0.1951	31.04	64.93	1997	4.18	447
55.96	58.71	46.42	1.38	1.11	30.64	44.00	-0.0308+0.1969	29.39	60.70	1923	5.49	448
61.46	63.77	42.01	1.12	0.96	30.53	44.37	-0.0350+0.1958	27.49	56.80	1735	10.84	449
62.02	64.11	42.55	0.93	0.81	29.99	44.35	-0.0418+0.1971	25.04	51.94	1524	14.85	450
63.75	66.15	37.26	0.83	0.74	29.61	42.75	-0.0450+0.1995	22.53	46.50	1358	16.88	451
65.62	68.42	31.31	0.93	0.86	29.18	40.38	-0.0412+0.2056	20.52	42.63	1361	11.53	452
67.63	70.16	23.71	1.22	1.15	28.87	39.28	-0.0326+0.2118	21.51	45.65	1547	6.51	453
70.04	72.76	18.92	1.12	1.08	28.16	39.77	-0.0391+0.2164	23.30	50.35	1506	6.73	454
70.94	74.18	16.27	1.09	1.06	27.66	36.86	-0.0395+0.2233	23.75	53.07	1488	6.11	455
71.55	75.22	15.57	1.08	1.05	27.45	33.87	-0.0360+0.2267	22.39	51.86	1499	5.51	456
71.75	76.14	13.51	1.18	1.15	27.08	33.03	-0.0325+0.2297	20.94	50.65	1587	5.83	457
66.78	71.20	30.98	1.16	1.10	29.30	33.15	-0.0268+0.2124	23.55	49.40	1122	5.29	458
67.40	72.15	28.75	1.12	1.07	29.15	33.11	-0.0282+0.2131	24.11	51.24	1155	5.22	459
68.03	73.17	24.33	1.14	1.09	28.95	33.33	-0.0286+0.2149	24.19	51.78	1204	4.48	460
68.83	74.32	23.91	1.20	1.16	28.68	31.54	-0.0256+0.2192	23.49	50.82	1294	3.42	461
68.44	73.91	24.76	1.25	1.21	28.45	31.83	-0.0254+0.2219	23.05	50.41	1350	3.28	462
68.18	74.03	25.18	1.31	1.26	28.35	31.03	-0.0230+0.2231	22.88	50.17	1398	3.79	463
68.92	74.85	23.64	1.29	1.24	28.38	31.18	-0.0234+0.2220	22.71	49.60	1431	4.36	464
40.51	43.03	178.12	2.21	1.37	30.78	42.03	-0.0224+0.1971	35.65	67.48	10369	3.11	465
39.22	42.43	182.43	2.29	1.41	30.80	41.75	-0.0213+0.1975	36.12	69.06	11946	1.70	466
44.18	47.38	145.84	2.23	1.54	30.89	40.62	-0.0179+0.1985	36.41	69.47	13234	1.43	467
41.94	45.64	176.72	2.00	1.36	30.90	39.14	-0.0203+0.1982	35.00	65.92	14283	3.84	468
45.40	49.39	176.56	1.69	1.21	30.85	36.48	-0.0226+0.1992	32.37	58.86	14415	7.81	469

			POPULATION (in 1000's)			VITAL RATES (Per 1000 Population)						
						BOTH SEXES COMBINED						
			OBSERVED MID-PERIOD	PROJECTED		CRUDE		AGE-SEX STANDARDIZED ON U.S. 1960		FEMALE INTRINSIC		
SER. NO.	AREA AND YEAR	PAGE	1	5 years 2	10 years 3	Birth 4	Death 5	Birth 6	Death 7	Birth 8	Death 9	Increase 10
470	U.K. 1911	526–527	36116	37861	39559	24.40	14.61	18.92	19.34	20.37	17.98	2.39
471	(ENGLAND 1921	528	37895	39800	41596	22.40	12.10	17.46	15.56	18.46	15.60	2.86
472	AND 1931	529	39993	40615	41033	15.80	12.29	12.21	14.96	11.86	19.74	-7.88
473	WALES) 1941	530–531	38743	38876	38713	14.95	13.54	11.23	13.82	10.32	20.51	-10.19
474	1945-47	532–533	40595	41880	42742	19.56	12.20	15.77	11.28	16.22	13.21	3.01
475	1950-52	534	43800	44454	44805	15.59	11.85	13.99	10.84	14.10	13.88	0.22
476	1955-57	535	44667	45432	46004	15.61	11.60	15.11	9.87	15.54	12.10	3.45
477	1960-62	536–537	46166	47478	48795	17.58	11.81	17.88	9.59	19.28	9.51	9.77
478	1963	538–539	47028	48486	50007	18.16	12.18	18.33	9.84	20.00	9.16	10.85
479	U.K. 1950-52	540–541	5100	5230	5344	17.88	12.50	15.63	12.30	16.44	13.12	3.31
480	(SCOTLAND) 1955-57	542	5145	5310	5465	18.52	11.96	16.96	11.21	18.27	11.01	7.25
481	1960-62	543	5184	5379	5593	19.73	12.15	18.96	10.93	20.92	9.31	11.61
482	1963	544–545	5205	5403	5619	19.73	12.59	19.40	11.20	21.63	8.97	12.67
483	YUGOSLAVIA 1950-52	546–547	16477	17902	19405	29.08	13.00	23.21	15.81	25.17	13.81	11.36
484	1953-55	548	17267	18765	20316	27.95	11.52	22.05	14.00	24.00	12.82	11.18
485	1956-58	549	18005	19265	20447	24.43	10.29	18.56	12.88	19.69	13.66	6.03
486	1961	550–551	18582	19818	21016	22.72	9.01	18.03	11.29	19.22	12.35	6.87
	OCEANIA											
487	AUSTRALIA 1911	552–553	4473	4862	5272	27.32	10.70	22.74	15.40	24.53	12.24	12.29
488	1921	554	5456	5862	6261	24.96	9.91	20.27	13.77	21.63	12.61	9.01
489	1933	555	6630	6886	7137	16.78	8.92	14.10	11.81	14.10	15.47	-1.37
490	1947	–	7579	8107	8582	24.06	9.69	19.95	10.43	21.75	9.31	12.44
491	1950-52	556–557	8422	8960	9430	23.18	9.56	19.97	10.57	21.99	8.94	13.05
492	1953-55	558	8987	9565	10102	22.71	9.05	20.78	9.90	23.13	8.15	14.98
493	1956-58	559	9640	10288	10948	22.65	8.81	21.84	9.68	24.40	7.46	16.94
494	1959-61	560–561	10275	10996	11788	22.62	8.65	22.44	9.52	25.28	7.01	18.27
495	1962	–	10705	11456	12293	22.15	8.70	22.04	9.32	24.74	7.10	17.64
496	1963	562	10916	11659	12497	21.59	8.69	21.48	9.30	24.03	7.36	16.67
497	1964	563	11136	11822	12604	20.58	9.03	20.30	9.69	22.38	8.09	14.29
498	1965	564–565	11360	12019	12767	19.62	8.78	19.13	9.46	20.94	8.64	12.29
499	FIJI IS. 1956	566	343	404	481	41.06	7.57	38.58	12.31	41.18	7.02	34.16
500	1963	567	435	511	602	38.01	5.78	33.84	9.93	36.77	6.06	30.71
501	1964	568–569	449	527	618	37.85	6.06	34.18	10.31	36.76	5.93	30.84
502	NEW ZEALAND 1951	570–571	1833	1960	2076	24.36	9.55	21.96	9.73	24.19	7.81	16.38
503	1952	–	1876	2010	2143	24.77	9.28	22.77	9.40	25.37	7.34	18.04
504	1953-55	572	1966	2115	2254	24.53	8.92	23.27	8.97	25.82	6.90	18.91
505	1956-58	573	2089	2254	2432	24.90	9.07	24.90	9.11	27.94	6.15	21.80
506	1959	–	2181	2359	2561	25.10	9.09	25.75	8.98	29.09	5.83	23.26
507	1961	574–575	2428	2617	2838	23.77	8.97	24.41	9.21	27.42	6.47	20.95
508	1963	–	2543	2773	3039	25.43	8.81	25.91	9.18	29.18	5.78	23.39
509	1965	576–577	2652	2855	3103	22.69	8.66	22.77	9.13	25.77	6.69	19.08
	POOLED DATA											
510	US Low Mort. 1959-61	582	58507	63161	68423	24.12	8.83	24.34	8.67	28.15	6.11	22.04
511	Med Mort. 1959-61	583	86634	92585	99171	23.19	9.76	23.16	9.61	26.66	6.81	19.84
512	Hi Mort. 1959-61	584	34815	37514	40576	24.20	9.45	23.55	10.24	27.38	7.03	20.35
513	EUROPE 1961	585	425406	443000	459400	18.61	10.01	16.82	9.71	17.58	11.16	6.42
514	COM. MARKET 1961	586	173941	180540	186405	18.33	10.30	16.72	9.37	17.40	10.86	6.54
515	EFTA 1961	587	88582	91568	94536	18.11	11.31	17.76	9.80	18.94	10.17	8.76
516	COMECON 1961	588	97475	101512	105318	17.95	9.21	15.75	10.17	16.28	12.44	3.84
	COHORTS											
517	UNITED 1910	592–593	155303	153341	151232	14.67	17.31	13.91	13.67	12.48	19.00	-6.52
518	STATES 1915	594	167208	165921	164472	15.04	16.57	14.47	12.50	13.44	16.96	-3.52
519	1920	595	172077	171806	171332	16.33	16.43	15.55	12.22	15.03	15.35	-0.33
520	1925	596–597	181415	183089	184400	18.16	15.92	17.19	11.33	17.56	12.78	4.78
521	1930	–	173702	177657	181159	20.70	15.47	19.53	10.99	21.23	10.65	10.57
522	UNITED 1910	598–599	155303	154510	153505	16.41	17.31	15.59	13.67	14.72	17.23	-2.50
523	STATES 1915	600	167208	166751	166101	16.16	16.57	15.54	12.50	14.89	15.85	-0.96
524	(With 1920	601	172077	172449	172596	17.16	16.43	16.35	12.22	16.11	14.63	1.48
525	Adjusted 1925	602–603	181415	183555	185320	18.73	15.92	17.74	11.33	18.30	12.38	5.92
526	Births) 1930	–	173702	177943	181722	21.06	15.47	19.88	10.99	21.71	10.46	11.25

AGE   DISTRIBUTION

LIFE EXPECTANCY AT BIRTH $\mathring{e}_0$		INFANT MORTALITY RATE	REPRODUCTION RATES		NET MATERNITY FUNCTION		FIRST COMPLEX ROOT	OBSERVED		REPRODUCTIVE VALUE (in 1000's)	DISSIMILARITY OF OBSERVED FROM STABLE	
Males	Females	$1000 M_0$	Gross	Net	Mean μ	Variance σ^2	r_2	Per cent Under 15	Dependency Ratio X 100	V	$\Delta\%$	SER. NO.
11	12	13	14	15	16	17	18	19	20	21	22	
49.36	53.33	146.54	1.42	1.07	30.37	35.96	−0.0266+0.2015	30.56	55.74	13569	10.29	470
55.98	59.94	88.40	1.31	1.09	29.67	34.90	−0.0279+0.2072	27.70	50.95	12128	8.16	471
58.15	62.34	70.11	0.92	0.79	29.02	34.74	−0.0399+0.2089	23.76	45.35	9516	13.61	472
58.54	64.63	63.05	0.84	0.74	28.63	36.37	−0.0464+0.2118	22.05	47.10	8268	13.19	473
63.97	68.94	48.67	1.18	1.09	28.81	34.51	−0.0309+0.2151	21.66	48.38	9545	5.66	474
66.44	71.50	29.47	1.05	1.01	28.09	33.28	−0.0351+0.2213	22.23	49.75	9008	4.80	475
67.71	73.29	24.56	1.14	1.10	27.67	32.17	−0.0325+0.2271	22.76	52.30	9235	4.62	476
68.10	73.97	22.38	1.35	1.30	27.42	31.91	−0.0262+0.2315	22.93	53.58	10305	9.27	477
67.87	73.87	21.68	1.38	1.34	27.36	31.64	−0.0250+0.2320	22.64	52.88	10766	9.80	478
64.39	68.65	38.75	1.17	1.10	28.60	34.12	−0.0309+0.2167	24.64	52.96	1240	2.90	479
65.91	71.10	30.32	1.28	1.22	28.08	32.72	−0.0280+0.2238	25.05	54.53	1261	3.93	480
66.14	71.91	27.71	1.43	1.38	27.72	32.39	−0.0243+0.2291	25.72	56.85	1322	7.98	481
65.82	71.89	26.32	1.47	1.41	27.63	31.42	−0.0220+0.2301	25.58	56.95	1345	9.31	482
55.28	58.19	117.68	1.73	1.38	28.92	44.79	−0.0339+0.2200	30.83	57.48	6419	6.97	483
58.76	61.13	109.62	1.64	1.37	28.63	43.56	−0.0351+0.2219	31.97	60.97	6524	6.34	484
60.53	63.14	103.25	1.39	1.18	27.99	42.07	−0.0426+0.2267	30.21	57.08	5847	9.99	485
63.55	66.82	83.71	1.35	1.21	27.43	42.39	−0.0439+0.2376	31.22	59.75	5626	9.48	486
57.35	61.11	71.96	1.70	1.45	30.31	42.51	−0.0228+0.2028	31.66	56.17	1744	7.33	487
59.05	63.06	66.94	1.51	1.31	29.79	41.82	−0.0277+0.2055	31.73	56.63	1912	8.42	488
63.55	67.33	41.74	1.05	0.96	29.14	41.02	−0.0385+0.2071	27.48	51.42	1758	14.46	489
66.35	70.98	28.26	1.50	1.42	28.46	35.69	−0.0245+0.2210	25.22	49.81	2127	6.03	490
66.28	71.68	25.07	1.50	1.44	28.02	35.32	−0.0255+0.2257	27.05	54.02	2313	5.96	491
67.06	72.70	23.68	1.57	1.51	27.77	34.42	−0.0238+0.2302	28.52	58.29	2513	5.96	492
67.50	73.35	21.92	1.65	1.59	27.59	33.52	−0.0211+0.2330	29.55	61.29	2769	6.87	493
67.67	73.87	21.10	1.70	1.64	27.49	32.79	−0.0189+0.2346	30.11	62.78	3042	7.28	494
67.80	74.20	20.66	1.67	1.62	27.51	32.54	−0.0190+0.2337	29.98	62.58	3184	6.23	495
67.86	74.17	19.96	1.63	1.57	27.49	32.94	−0.0205+0.2334	29.85	62.16	3222	5.36	496
67.46	73.82	19.07	1.52	1.48	27.51	33.40	−0.0233+0.2311	29.73	61.68	3207	3.56	497
67.75	74.13	18.62	1.44	1.40	27.39	33.31	−0.0255+0.2315	29.53	61.18	3186	3.55	498
63.49	64.91	46.01	2.88	2.59	28.66	49.69	−0.0238+0.2298	46.09	97.05	187	2.07	499
66.14	69.65	28.85	2.51	2.32	28.16	47.42	−0.0249+0.2397	44.79	92.35	217	3.66	500
64.97	70.10	31.82	2.55	2.38	28.76	46.18	−0.0202+0.2337	44.50	91.34	229	3.53	501
67.85	72.32	23.72	1.65	1.58	28.30	33.08	−0.0180+0.2255	28.48	61.44	534	7.19	502
68.51	72.61	22.68	1.72	1.65	28.26	33.24	−0.0170+0.2267	29.02	62.81	560	8.19	503
68.88	73.61	20.77	1.75	1.69	28.16	32.56	−0.0155+0.2285	29.90	65.07	594	8.46	504
68.88	73.97	20.28	1.88	1.82	27.85	31.77	−0.0127+0.2326	30.69	66.96	656	10.21	505
69.04	74.09	20.41	1.95	1.89	27.68	31.43	−0.0113+0.2344	31.43	68.46	703	10.86	506
68.25	73.55	24.47	1.84	1.77	27.71	32.37	−0.0146+0.2333	33.07	71.47	794	7.22	507
68.49	74.13	19.88	1.93	1.87	27.28	36.43	−0.0188+0.2338	32.94	70.44	850	8.72	508
68.44	74.29	17.88	1.72	1.67	27.17	34.32	−0.0212+0.2385	32.72	69.50	847	4.84	509
67.73	74.60	24.71	1.83	1.76	26.15	34.40	−0.0243+0.2520	31.52	69.53	17700	9.76	510
66.82	73.19	25.12	1.74	1.68	26.53	34.14	−0.0245+0.2447	30.44	66.35	25383	10.04	511
65.34	71.89	29.82	1.77	1.69	26.25	35.80	−0.0287+0.2481	32.08	67.66	10761	8.31	512
66.89	72.22	39.13	1.26	1.20	28.07	35.77	−0.0321+0.2239	25.79	55.39	1062	3.35	513
67.55	73.34	31.51	1.26	1.21	28.72	34.26	−0.0274+0.2189	24.47	54.16	42504	4.24	514
67.26	72.75	32.90	1.34	1.27	27.77	34.15	−0.0289+0.2273	23.80	54.13	21000	6.36	515
65.99	70.97	49.35	1.18	1.11	26.44	34.73	−0.0428+0.2433	27.99	57.43	23648	6.26	516
55.04	61.56	119.11	1.04	0.83	27.51	42.08	−0.0533+0.2126	20.66	55.61	32225	5.72	517
57.81	64.67	95.68	1.08	0.91	27.75	41.05	−0.0455+0.2131	20.54	55.86	34696	2.52	518
58.33	65.71	93.30	1.16	0.99	27.94	39.47	−0.0406+0.2142	20.79	57.09	37442	1.22	519
60.67	68.21	73.58	1.29	1.14	27.81	35.61	−0.0316+0.2197	20.57	56.77	40371	6.54	520
61.82	69.12	69.38	1.48	1.33	27.10	31.74	−0.0262+0.2335	20.08	55.11	39450	12.17	521
55.04	61.56	119.11	1.16	0.93	27.14	42.90	−0.0535+0.2157	20.66	55.61	33481	1.73	522
57.81	64.67	95.68	1.16	0.97	27.54	41.12	−0.0449+0.2157	20.54	55.86	35607	0.83	523
58.33	65.71	93.30	1.22	1.04	27.75	39.69	−0.0407+0.2162	20.79	57.09	38084	2.96	524
60.67	68.21	73.58	1.33	1.18	27.68	36.02	−0.0317+0.2207	20.57	56.77	40782	7.68	525
61.82	69.12	69.38	1.50	1.35	27.04	31.83	−0.0259+0.2342	20.08	55.11	39693	12.83	526

				POPULATION (in 1000's)			VITAL RATES (Per 1000 Population)						
							BOTH SEXES COMBINED						
				OBSERVED MID-PERIOD	PROJECTED		CRUDE		AGE-SEX STANDARDIZED ON U.S. 1960		FEMALE INTRINSIC		
SER. NO.	AREA AND YEAR		PAGE	1	5 years 2	10 years 3	Birth 4	Death 5	Birth 6	Death 7	Birth 8	Death 9	Increase 10
527	SWEDEN	1780	604-605	2426	2468	2510	32.91	28.53	28.88	30.70	30.43	25.81	4.62
528		1785	606	2435	2489	2540	33.85	27.81	29.46	30.60	30.96	25.87	5.09
529		1790	607	2545	2609	2666	34.24	27.21	29.93	29.57	31.30	25.25	6.04
530		1795	608	2815	2893	2960	33.93	26.46	30.07	28.20	31.24	24.13	7.12
531		1800	609	2851	2926	2993	33.97	26.35	30.44	28.22	31.64	24.55	7.09
532		1805	610-611	2858	2949	3034	33.95	25.69	30.50	26.69	31.51	23.06	8.45
533		1810	612	2793	2865	2924	33.85	26.86	30.68	27.87	31.73	25.01	6.71
534		1815	613	3165	3274	3366	32.70	24.15	29.93	24.41	30.60	21.78	8.82
535		1820	614	3564	3689	3806	32.23	23.16	29.94	23.17	30.25	20.81	9.43
536		1825	615	4136	4309	4467	31.37	21.44	29.32	20.90	29.24	18.70	10.55
537		1830	616-617	4086	4224	4354	30.81	22.52	28.74	21.96	28.75	20.17	8.58
538		1835	618	4173	4336	4499	30.62	21.52	28.78	20.51	28.68	18.68	9.99
539		1840	619	4091	4247	4399	30.15	21.54	28.34	20.53	28.27	18.88	9.39
540		1845	620	4319	4467	4610	28.55	21.13	26.99	20.01	26.89	18.90	7.99
541		1850	621	4346	4489	4646	28.61	21.46	27.52	20.01	27.49	18.77	8.72
542		1855	622-623	4589	4732	4884	28.02	21.56	27.08	20.11	27.20	19.31	7.89
543		1860	624	5029	5187	5363	26.87	20.81	26.19	19.20	26.44	18.43	8.01
544		1865	625	5291	5435	5605	25.62	20.50	25.44	18.84	25.69	18.33	7.36
545		1870	626	4940	5043	5169	24.33	20.52	24.45	18.79	24.72	18.75	5.97
546		1875	627	5335	5421	5518	23.11	20.52	23.44	18.20	23.64	18.82	4.83
547		1880	628-629	5862	5942	6035	21.75	19.48	21.80	16.95	22.01	18.07	3.94
548		1885	630	6119	6165	6227	20.00	18.94	19.92	16.10	19.95	17.90	2.05
549		1890	631	6567	6566	6582	17.77	18.21	17.51	15.19	17.06	18.37	-1.32
550		1895	632	6853	6796	6744	15.44	17.71	15.18	14.28	14.13	19.36	-5.22
551		1900	633	7355	7232	7112	13.30	17.34	13.18	13.65	11.51	20.93	-9.42
552		1905	634-635	7909	7749	7589	11.78	16.46	11.86	12.36	9.95	21.44	-11.49
553		1910	636	8464	8300	8136	11.63	15.91	11.90	11.50	10.05	20.43	-10.38
554		1915	637	8457	8325	8193	12.26	15.55	12.52	10.96	10.91	18.84	-7.93
555		1920	638	8114	8030	7941	13.09	15.30	13.13	10.48	11.94	17.14	-5.19
556		1925	639	8249	8178	8102	13.21	14.81	13.15	9.74	12.16	16.12	-3.96
	MALE DOMINANT												
557	UNITED STATES	1959-61	644	179990	192935	207070	23.65	9.39	23.65	9.39	27.48	6.57	20.92
558		1962	645	185888	198456	212769	22.42	9.45	22.85	9.38	26.59	6.77	19.81
559		1963	646	188656	200735	214695	21.72	9.61	22.12	9.54	25.74	7.06	18.68
560		1964	647	191369	203317	217197	21.05	9.40	21.44	9.29	24.78	7.31	17.48
561	CHILE	1964	648	8391	9366	10486	32.81	11.21	33.54	14.68	34.18	10.63	23.55
562	TRINIDAD	1956-58	649	765	876	1005	37.46	9.46	37.30	15.35	38.38	7.84	30.55
563	CYPRUS	1956-58	650	546	600	665	25.82	6.21	23.63	9.26	27.54	6.72	20.82
564	HUNGARY	1964	651	10120	10259	10380	13.06	9.96	11.76	9.98	12.39	15.34	-2.95
565	NORWAY	1963	652	3667	3803	3953	17.26	10.05	17.67	8.13	19.40	8.98	10.42
566	U.K. (ENG.,WALES)	1960-62	653	46166	47431	48643	17.58	11.81	16.91	9.59	19.14	9.59	9.55
	HYPOTHETICAL												
567	U.A.R.	1960	656	25984	29219	32555	46.54	19.30	43.68	25.06	43.24	16.92	26.31
568	BRAZIL	1950	657	51944	58368	65605	44.00	20.60	37.97	26.74	40.76	19.79	20.97
569	CHINA (MAINLAND)	1953	658	582800	640600	698400	41.59	20.99	39.17	24.71	42.09	20.09	22.00
570	INDIA	1961	659	439235	490700	546700	41.30	19.48	36.49	24.07	41.22	20.00	21.22
571	INDONESIA	1961	660	96319	107510	119335	45.00	21.40	37.25	26.50	41.71	21.54	20.17
572	IRAN	1956	661	19441	21926	24735	51.00	26.39	47.73	30.27	52.28	26.22	26.06
573	PAKISTAN	1961	662	93832	107358	122882	47.23	20.29	43.81	25.60	48.70	21.44	27.26
574	PHILIPPINES	1960	663	27420	32141	37729	43.48	10.87	40.44	14.76	41.66	11.10	30.56
575	REP. OF KOREA	1960	664	24989	28667	32712	40.60	12.20	37.13	17.31	39.56	12.30	27.26
576	TURKEY	1960	665	27506	31383	35591	45.71	16.55	42.05	21.50	44.59	16.56	28.04
577	U.S.S.R.	1959	666	208827	226757	243068	25.05	7.30	18.17	10.19	19.35	9.83	9.52

AGE   DISTRIBUTION

LIFE EXPECTANCY AT BIRTH $\overset{\circ}{e}_0$		INFANT MORTALITY RATE $1000 M_0$	REPRODUCTION RATES		NET MATERNITY FUNCTION		FIRST COMPLEX ROOT r_2	OBSERVED		REPRODUCTIVE VALUE (in 1000's) V	DISSIMILARITY OF OBSERVED FROM STABLE $\Delta\%$	SER. NO.
Males 11	Females 12	13	Gross 14	Net 15	Mean μ 16	Variance σ^2 17	18	Per cent Under 15 19	Dependency Ratio X 100 20	21	22	
34.36	37.89	211.62	2.14	1.16	32.29	42.31	−0.0221+0.1886	28.76	56.00	1162	4.26	527
34.23	37.79	231.45	2.18	1.18	32.31	41.96	−0.0214+0.1885	28.58	55.73	1185	4.66	528
34.78	38.52	255.30	2.21	1.21	32.38	41.12	−0.0198+0.1886	28.35	56.13	1234	5.68	529
35.86	39.92	238.48	2.22	1.26	32.40	40.73	−0.0187+0.1890	27.84	56.34	1328	6.65	530
35.52	39.43	248.96	2.25	1.26	32.25	40.07	−0.0189+0.1901	27.45	55.94	1346	6.63	531
36.84	41.32	223.07	2.26	1.31	32.25	40.98	−0.0183+0.1903	27.25	56.03	1326	7.48	532
34.78	39.02	260.08	2.27	1.24	32.34	40.68	−0.0195+0.1894	26.74	55.76	1341	5.86	533
39.08	43.32	216.98	2.21	1.33	32.55	40.98	−0.0173+0.1887	25.99	55.81	1424	7.98	534
40.76	44.75	206.69	2.21	1.36	32.92	40.51	−0.0154+0.1867	25.60	55.94	1579	8.60	535
44.24	48.03	178.35	2.16	1.41	33.12	39.05	−0.0130+0.1860	25.52	56.68	1760	9.28	536
42.11	46.10	203.99	2.11	1.33	33.02	37.86	−0.0141+0.1869	25.62	57.36	1770	7.16	537
44.43	48.38	185.99	2.12	1.39	33.08	38.85	−0.0137+0.1871	25.77	58.45	1781	7.87	538
44.20	48.20	184.61	2.09	1.36	32.86	38.73	−0.0146+0.1878	26.07	59.47	1746	6.98	539
44.85	48.59	174.16	1.99	1.30	32.74	39.20	−0.0163+0.1877	26.45	60.63	1797	5.21	540
44.90	48.61	165.60	2.03	1.33	32.53	37.51	−0.0154+0.1901	27.28	62.89	1827	5.44	541
44.72	47.93	164.80	2.00	1.29	32.22	38.52	−0.0178+0.1911	27.50	63.68	1919	4.35	542
46.52	49.54	150.76	1.93	1.29	32.00	39.05	−0.0186+0.1922	27.78	64.49	2048	4.21	543
47.09	49.98	148.04	1.88	1.26	31.80	39.14	−0.0196+0.1930	28.28	66.00	2108	3.50	544
47.03	49.67	157.70	1.81	1.21	31.49	38.49	−0.0213+0.1949	28.34	66.94	1903	2.86	545
47.76	50.05	155.36	1.74	1.16	31.18	37.98	−0.0231+0.1969	27.82	67.11	1943	2.28	546
49.78	52.25	131.33	1.62	1.13	30.65	37.98	−0.0259+0.2004	26.51	65.16	1956	1.84	547
51.27	53.99	121.69	1.48	1.06	30.15	37.86	−0.0293+0.2031	25.97	65.08	1883	1.65	548
52.80	55.80	120.73	1.31	0.96	29.57	37.04	−0.0336+0.2062	25.15	64.30	1822	3.14	549
54.49	57.70	106.93	1.13	0.86	29.07	36.47	−0.0388+0.2097	24.09	62.95	1688	6.13	550
55.67	59.25	106.84	0.99	0.76	28.83	38.34	−0.0465+0.2091	23.02	61.44	1627	9.87	551
58.96	62.35	90.16	0.88	0.71	29.32	41.93	−0.0480+0.2009	22.20	60.45	1624	11.63	552
61.24	64.66	69.78	0.88	0.73	29.75	40.32	−0.0412+0.1977	21.38	59.19	1689	10.19	553
62.67	66.23	51.40	0.93	0.79	29.48	34.35	−0.0349+0.2041	20.68	57.95	1665	7.49	554
63.85	67.87	46.42	0.99	0.86	28.70	30.87	−0.0337+0.2145	20.19	57.12	1571	4.60	555
65.95	70.12	42.01	0.99	0.89	27.96	32.45	−0.0385+0.2214	19.65	56.22	1520	3.14	556
66.84	73.40	26.83	1.96	1.84	29.55	46.23	−0.0170+0.2272	31.17	67.85	61599	10.28	557
66.93	73.52	25.36	1.90	1.78	29.53	45.62	−0.0171+0.2267	31.30	68.40	63189	9.01	558
66.68	73.42	25.24	1.84	1.72	29.58	45.22	−0.0177+0.2254	31.20	68.09	63635	7.98	559
66.90	73.72	24.64	1.78	1.67	29.62	45.02	−0.0191+0.2241	31.08	67.81	63896	6.67	560
55.70	61.29	114.30	2.75	2.17	33.66	70.58	−0.0328+0.2004	39.63	78.56	4805	2.03	561
60.13	63.20	61.04	3.06	2.66	33.05	63.75	−0.0173+0.2025	42.31	84.74	435	5.12	562
70.07	73.87	31.53	1.92	1.78	28.20	57.62	−0.0383+0.2353	34.45	70.16	199	3.07	563
67.03	71.86	40.00	0.99	0.92	29.73	38.72	−0.0327+0.2178	23.80	51.18	2306	9.53	564
70.83	75.47	16.87	1.45	1.38	31.45	45.48	−0.0228+0.2050	25.00	57.73	1009	6.15	565
68.10	73.97	21.64	1.41	1.34	30.52	42.22	−0.0227+0.2119	22.93	53.58	11630	7.20	566
40.42	48.46	173.49	3.14	2.18	30.15	35.35	−0.0024+0.2113	42.76	85.98	14985	6.19	567
41.15	44.13	183.34	2.80	1.83	29.42	49.66	−0.0260+0.2083	41.86	79.56	31221	3.39	568
43.55	44.01	176.52	2.91	1.88	29.36	49.61	−0.0268+0.2111	35.95	67.57	2957	7.97	569
46.02	44.03	165.64	2.69	1.77	27.58	51.35	−0.0444+0.2266	41.09	78.60	2323	1.88	570
41.70	42.09	190.35	2.76	1.74	28.08	47.94	−0.0368+0.2229	42.41	81.93	55294	4.61	571
37.35	37.55	232.27	3.53	2.03	27.79	46.76	−0.0332+0.2292	43.98	85.32	12607	3.83	572
44.38	42.45	177.80	3.25	2.08	27.55	51.20	−0.0401+0.2316	44.79	89.36	56178	0.15	573
55.40	58.68	104.36	3.00	2.43	29.82	45.96	−0.0141+0.2156	45.69	93.87	16470	3.82	574
54.80	55.69	99.24	2.75	2.18	29.18	47.51	−0.0215+0.2177	43.10	86.45	13233	3.41	575
48.27	48.72	140.97	3.11	2.20	28.89	51.29	−0.0279+0.2169	41.25	81.09	15112	7.43	576
67.73	72.87	30.71	1.36	1.31	28.49	39.04	−0.0320+0.2223	29.88	56.51	64374	7.62	577

Symbols Used and Their Definitions

Tables 1–10 for the United States 1965 (with adjusted births) are given below, with definitions required for reading the computer output. Where row and column headings are self-explanatory, discussion is omitted.

AGE AT LAST BIRTHDAY	BOTH SEXES	POPULATION MALES Number	%	FEMALES Number	%	BIRTHS BY AGE OF MOTHER	DEATHS BOTH SEXES	DEATHS MALES	FEMALES	AGE AT LAST BIRTHDAY
0	3857000	1969000	2.1	1888000	1.9	0	92894	53437	39457	0
1-4	16577000	8463000	8.9	8114000	8.2	0	15401	8531	6870	1-4
5-9	20518000	10426000	11.0	10092000	10.2	0	8957	5268	3689	5-9
10-14	18956000	9635000	10.1	9321000	9.4	7703	7724	4940	2784	10-14
15-19	16954000	8559000	9.0	8395000	8.5	598547	16129	11610	4519	15-19
20-24	13333000	6539000	6.9	6794000	6.9	1350826	16974	12152	4822	20-24
25-29	11205000	5508000	5.8	5697000	5.8	933943	15050	10138	4912	25-29
30-34	10948000	5378000	5.7	5570000	5.6	535036	18541	11470	7071	30-34
35-39	11920000	5828000	6.1	6092000	6.2	287277	28983	17645	11338	35-39
40-44	12411000	6033000	6.3	6378000	6.5	83255	45861	28054	17807	40-44
45-49	11449000	5570000	5.9	5879000	6.0	4829	66279	41422	24857	45-49
50-54	10570000	5146000	5.4	5424000	5.5	0	96619	62574	34045	50-54
55-59	9156000	4420000	4.6	4736000	4.8	0	126909	83466	43443	55-59
60-64	7809000	3710000	3.9	4099000	4.2	0	160645	104061	56584	60-64
65-69	6297000	2870000	3.0	3427000	3.5	0	199527	123021	76506	65-69
70-74	5189000	2283000	2.4	2906000	2.9		235995	137103	98892	70-74
75-79	3599000	1545000	1.6	2054000	2.1		245221	130538	114683	75-79
80-84	1995000	820000	0.9	1175000	1.2	1944519 M.	213218	101859	111359	80-84
85+	1075000	413000	0.4	662000	0.7	1856897 F.	217209	87911	129298	85+
TOTAL	193818000	95115000		98703000		3801416	1828136	1035200	792936	TOTAL

TABLE 1 DATA

POPULATION	Census or officially estimated populations by age at last birthday, adjusted by interpolation to mid-year, or to middle of three- or five-year period; not-stated ages distributed.
%	Percentage distribution of male and female numbers, rounded to one decimal place.
BIRTHS By Age of Mother	Registered births, where possible of residents of the country occurring in the given period, by age of mother, with not-stated ages distributed. Where a three- or five-year period is included, each figure shown is the average per year.
M. F.	Number of males and of females among the births registered.

DEACHS

DEATHS   Registered deaths by age at last birthday, also averaged where three- or five-year period is included.

x	$_nq_x$	l_x	$_nd_x$	$_nL_x$	$_nm_x$	$_na_x$	T_x	r_x	$\overset{\circ}{e}_x$	$_nM_x$	x
0	0.026580	100000	2658	97941	0.027139	0.2254	6686917	0.0000	66.869	0.027139	0
1	0.004020	97342	391	388227	0.001008	1.0844	6588976	0.0000	67.689	0.001008	1
5	0.002520	96951	244	484142	0.000505	2.5000	6200749	0.0073	63.958	0.000505	5
10	0.002578	96706	249	482994	0.000516	2.8451	5716607	0.0190	59.113	0.000513	10
15	0.006813	96457	657	480775	0.001367	2.7025	5233613	0.0375	54.259	0.001356	15
20	0.009271	95800	888	476823	0.001863	2.5499	4752838	0.0423	49.612	0.001858	20
25	0.009166	94912	870	472406	0.001842	2.5263	4276015	0.0176	45.053	0.001841	25
30	0.010610	94042	998	467824	0.002133	2.6104	3803609	0.0000	40.446	0.002133	30
35	0.015032	93044	1399	461954	0.003028	2.6654	3335785	0.0000	35.852	0.003028	35
40	0.023003	91645	2108	453348	0.004650	2.6858	2873831	0.0000	31.358	0.004650	40
45	0.036616	89537	3278	440115	0.007449	2.6907	2420483	0.0081	27.033	0.007437	45
50	0.059238	86259	5110	419367	0.012185	2.6660	1980368	0.0106	22.958	0.012160	50
55	0.090573	81149	7350	388331	0.018927	2.6307	1561000	0.0134	19.236	0.018884	55
60	0.131738	73799	9722	345754	0.028119	2.6095	1172670	0.0147	15.890	0.028049	60
65	0.194444	64077	12459	290025	0.042960	2.5633	826916	0.0147	12.905	0.042864	65
70	0.261705	51618	13509	224489	0.060175	2.5128	536891	0.0147	10.401	0.060054	70
75	0.348740	38109	13290	156960	0.084672	2.4730	312402	0.0147	8.198	0.084491	75
80	0.474815	24819	11784	94580	0.124597	2.4955	155441	0.0147	6.263	0.124218	80
85+	•1.000000	13034	13034	60862	0.214166	4.6693	60862	0.0147	4.669	0.212860	85+

TABLE 2 MALE LIFE TABLE

x Exact age with which interval begins; interval ends just below the value of x printed following. Thus 0 means "under 1 year of age"; 1 means "1 or more years of age and under 5."

$_nq_x$ Probability of dying, for an individual of exact age x, before reaching age $x + n$; n is 1 for the first line, 4 for the second, and 5 for all remaining lines up to the open interval 85+.

l_x Number surviving to exact age x out of 100,000 born, calculated as $l_x = l_{x-n}(1 - {_nq_{x-n}})$, $x = 1, 5, 10, \cdots, 85$.

$_nd_x$ Number dying between ages x and $x + n$ out of 100,000 born: $_nd_x = l_x {_nq_x}$.

$_nL_x$ Number of years lived between ages x and $x + n$ per 100,000 born: $_nL_x = \int_0^n l(x + t)dt$, which is the stationary age distribution.

$_nm_x$ Age-specific death rate in life table population for interval x to $x + n$: $_nm_x = \dfrac{_nd_x}{_nL_x}$.

$_na_x$ Average number of years lived in interval x to $x + n$ by those dying in interval.

T_x Total years lived beyond age x per 100,000 born.

r_x Increase from one annual cohort to the next as estimated from observed age distribution.

$\overset{\circ}{e}_x$ Expectation of life at age x, i.e., average number of years lived subsequent to age x by those reaching age x: $\overset{\circ}{e}_x = \dfrac{T_x}{l_x}$.

$_nM_x$ Observed age-specific death rate for the interval x to $x + n$, to which the life table has iterated.

	x	$_nq_x$	l_x	$_nd_x$	$_nL_x$	$_nm_x$	$_na_x$	T_x	r_x	$\overset{\circ}{e}_x$	$_nM_x$	x
	0	0.020570	100000	2057	98426	0.020899	0.2348	7382869	0.0000	73.829	0.020899	0
	1	0.003378	97943	331	390809	0.000847	1.0907	7284443	0.0000	74.374	0.000847	1
	5	0.001823	97612	178	487616	0.000365	2.5000	6893634	0.0066	70.623	0.000366	5
	10	0.001496	97434	146	486824	0.000299	2.6213	6406018	0.0180	65.747	0.000299	10
	15	0.002701	97288	263	485827	0.000541	2.6579	5919194	0.0311	60.842	0.000538	15
TABLE 3	20	0.003555	97026	345	484298	0.000712	2.5931	5433367	0.0381	55.999	0.000710	20
FEMALE	25	0.004313	96681	417	482416	0.000864	2.6320	4949069	0.0190	51.190	0.000862	25
LIFE	30	0.006329	96264	609	479893	0.001269	2.6605	4466654	0.0000	46.400	0.001269	30
TABLE	35	0.009265	95654	886	476203	0.001861	2.6658	3986761	0.0000	41.679	0.001861	35
	40	0.013871	94768	1315	470778	0.002792	2.6702	3510557	0.0007	37.044	0.002792	40
	45	0.020976	93454	1960	462685	0.004237	2.6618	3039779	0.0119	32.527	0.004228	45
	50	0.031003	91493	2837	450799	0.006292	2.6493	2577094	0.0152	28.167	0.006277	50
	55	0.045034	88657	3993	433897	0.009202	2.6487	2126295	0.0185	23.983	0.009173	55
	60	0.067170	84664	5687	410024	0.013870	2.6618	1692399	0.0246	19.990	0.013804	60
	65	0.106478	78977	8409	375002	0.022425	2.6355	1282375	0.0246	16.237	0.022324	65
	70	0.158070	70568	11155	326260	0.034190	2.6171	907372	0.0246	12.858	0.034030	70
	75	0.247088	59413	14680	261624	0.056112	2.5857	581112	0.0246	9.781	0.055834	75
	80	0.384378	44733	17194	180614	0.095199	2.6558	319488	0.0246	7.142	0.094774	80
	85+	1.000000	27539	27539	138874	0.198299	5.0429	138874	0.0246	5.043	0.195315	85+

Symbols of Table 3 are the same as those of Table 2.

		OBSERVED POPULATION			PROJECTED POPULATION						STABLE POPULATION	
					1970		1975		1980			
		BOTH SEXES	MALES	FEMALES	MALES	FEMALES	MALES	FEMALES	MALES	FEMALES	MALES	FEMALES
	RATES PER THOUSAND											
TABLE 4	Birth	19.61	20.44	18.81	22.12	20.26	23.68	21.65	24.38	22.29	22.77	21.29
OBSERVED	Death	9.43	10.88	8.03	11.02	8.62	10.96	8.95	10.72	9.06	10.12	8.64
AND	Increase	10.18	9.56	10.78	11.11	11.64	12.72	12.69	13.65	13.24		12.6505
PROJEC-												
TED	PERCENTAGE											
VITAL	under 15	30.91	32.06	29.80	30.84	28.48	30.04	27.63	30.26	27.87	30.15	28.39
RATES	15-64	59.72	59.60	59.84	60.79	60.62	61.66	61.17	61.51	60.68	62.44	61.01
	65 and over	9.37	8.34	10.36	8.37	10.89	8.30	11.20	8.24	11.45	7.41	10.60
	DEP. RATIO X 100	67.44	67.78	67.11	64.51	64.95	62.17	63.49	62.58	64.80	60.16	63.90

OBSERVED POPULATION; PROJECTED POPULATION; STABLE POPULATION

RATES PER THOUSAND

Birth }
Death }   Crude rates of birth and death per thousand population; i.e., deaths divided by population and births divided by population.

Increase   Difference between the rates of birth and death immediately above.

PERCENTAGE   The percentage under 15, 15–64, and 65 and over, all at last birthday.

DEP. RATIO × 100   The dependency ratio is defined as the total number under 15 and 65 and over, divided by the number 15–64.

PROJECTED POPULATION   Crude rates of birth, death, and natural increase per thousand population as they would occur in the years specified if the observed age-specific rates continued to hold.

STABLE POPULATION   Crude rates of birth, death, and natural increase, per thousand population, as they would stand ultimately if the observed age-specific rates applied; these are known as intrinsic rates *b*, *d*, and *r*. It is to be emphasized that our calculation in the main section of this book is female dominant. This means that essentially the female population is projected and male births are taken as female births multiplied by the observed ratio of males to females at birth. One aspect of this is that the female intrinsic rate of natural increase is applied to males as well.

AGE AT LAST BIRTHDAY	1970 BOTH SEXES	1970 MALES	FEMALES	1975 BOTH SEXES	1975 MALES	FEMALES	1980 BOTH SEXES	1980 MALES	FEMALES	AGE AT LAST BIRTHDAY	
0-4	19836	10115	9721	22572	11511	11061	25201	12851	12350	0-4	
5-9	20358	10389	9969	19761	10073	9688	22488	11463	11025	5-9	
10-14	20477	10401	10076	20317	10364	9953	19722	10049	9673	10-14	**TABLE 5**
15-19	18893	9591	9302	20408	10353	10055	20248	10316	9932	15-19	POPULATION
20-24	16858	8489	8369	18785	9512	9273	20291	10268	10023	20-24	PROJECTED
25-29	13246	6478	6768	16746	8410	8336	18661	9424	9237	25-29	WITH
30-34	11122	5455	5667	13148	6416	6732	16620	8328	8292	30-34	FIXED
35-39	10838	5311	5527	11010	5386	5624	13015	6335	6680	35-39	AGE—
40-44	11742	5719	6023	10676	5212	5464	10846	5286	5560	40-44	SPECIFIC
45-49	12125	5857	6268	11471	5552	5919	10429	5059	5370	45-49	BIRTH
50-54	11035	5307	5728	11688	5581	6107	11058	5291	5767	50-54	AND
55-59	9986	4765	5221	10428	4915	5513	11046	5168	5878	55-59	DEATH
60-64	8410	3935	4475	9176	4243	4933	9586	4376	5210	60-64	RATES
65-69	6861	3112	3749	7394	3301	4093	8071	3559	4512	65-69	(IN 1000's)
70-74	5203	2221	2982	5671	2409	3262	6116	2555	3561	70-74	
75-79	3926	1596	2330	3944	1553	2391	4299	1684	2615	75-79	
80-84	2349	931	1418	2571	962	1609	2587	936	1651	80-84	
85+	1431	528	903	1689	599	1090	1856	619	1237	85+	
TOTAL	204696	100200	104496	217455	106352	111103	232140	113567	118573	TOTAL	

Table 5 shows the projection from which the ratios of Table 4 have been derived; it is female dominant, in the sense that all births are imputed to mothers, except where otherwise stated. Males and females are both carried forward on the survivorship ratios $_5L_{x+5}/_5L_x$ of the male and female life tables, respectively. Births of female children are obtained by applying female age-specific birth rates (female children to women for each five-year age group) to the average of the female beginning and ending populations. Male births are obtained by multiplying female births by the observed sex ratio at birth. The process has a slight upward bias, but it is conveniently linear. To convert the figures of Table 5 into a prediction, one would need to superimpose a modification for the extent to which the birth and death rates are expected to change, and allowance would also have to be made for migration, which is disregarded here.

STANDARD COUNTRIES: STANDARDIZED RATES PER THOUSAND	ENGLAND AND WALES 1961 BOTH SEXES	MALES	FEMALES	UNITED STATES 1960 BOTH SEXES	MALES	FEMALES	MEXICO 1960 BOTH SEXES	MALES	FEMALES	TABLE 6
Birth	18.83	22.35*	17.83	19.20	20.67*	18.48	23.12	19.74*	22.53	STANDAR-
Death	11.32	12.22*	10.39	9.30	10.91*	7.73	4.98	8.74*	3.87	DIZED
Increase	7.52	10.14*	7.44	9.91	9.77*	10.75	18.14	11.00*	18.66	RATES

STANDARDIZED RATES PER THOUSAND

Directly standardized death rates are the application of the given age-specific rates to the standard age distribution and calculation of the overall death rate which results. Again, births are attributed to mothers in the female-dominant tables, and standardized like deaths.

ENGLAND AND WALES 1961 UNITED STATES 1960 MEXICO 1960

Three standard populations are available; any particular comparison desired will require choosing whichever of the three standards has an age distribution closest to that of the populations being compared. To compare Chile and Panama, for example, the Mexico 1960 standard will be most satisfactory; for comparing Canada and the United States, the United States 1960; for comparing European countries, England and Wales 1961. Indirect standardization, in which the age-specific rates of the standard country are applied to the age distribution of the given country, is signified in Table 6 by an asterisk, which appears on the male figures. We had no choice in respect to births, and have made births and deaths uniform. If the directly standardized male death rates are required, they may be found by subtracting the female standardized rate from the total, each weighted by its standard population.

	OBSERVED POP. MALES	OBSERVED POP. FEMALES	STATIONARY POP. MALES	STATIONARY POP. FEMALES	STABLE POP. MALES	STABLE POP. FEMALES	OBSERVED BIRTHS	NET MATERNITY FUNCTION	BIRTHS IN STABLE POP.	
μ	30.76966	32.45138	36.31209	39.22675	30.29530	32.41644	25.93169	26.52258	26.06189	TABLE 7
σ^2	483.0224	512.8470	498.7096	561.1014	447.6363	508.4277	37.05371	35.12088	33.54172	MOMENTS
κ_3	5238.099	5078.529	2772.020	2333.669	5079.454	5707.635	156.5260	123.9188	125.4173	AND
κ_4	-189976.	-232205.	-230914.	-325980.	-126455.	-192323.	-136.726	-191.354	-38.638	CUMULANTS
β_1	0.243470	0.191211	0.061951	0.030829	0.287646	0.247870	0.481591	0.354469	0.416829	
β_2	2.185739	2.117133	2.071557	1.964600	2.368917	2.256000	2.900416	2.844866	2.965656	
κ	-0.086601	-0.067774	-0.024074	-0.011307	-0.113253	-0.092642	-0.251036	-0.213634	-0.264917	

OBSERVED POP. STATIONARY POP. STABLE POP.

The numbers in Table 7 serve to describe age distribution of the observed, the stationary, and the stable populations, for males and females separately.

μ The first moment, or mean age.

σ^2 The second moment about the mean, called the variance; its square root, σ, is the standard deviation of the age distribution.

κ_3 The third cumulant, or third moment about the mean.

κ_4 The fourth cumulant, or fourth moment about the mean less three times the square of the variance.

β_1 The third cumulant squared divided by the variance cubed, or $\beta_1 = \kappa_3^2/\sigma^6$, a measure of skewness.

β_2 The fourth cumulant divided by the square of the variance plus three, $\beta_2 = \kappa_4/\sigma^4 + 3$, a measure of peakedness.

κ Indicator of which of the family of Pearson curves the given distribution falls into, defined as

$$\kappa = \frac{\beta_1(\beta_2 + 3)^2}{4(2\beta_2 - 3\beta_1 - 6)(4\beta_2 - 3\beta_1)}$$

In most of our observations the value of κ is between 0 and -1, within the range for Type I.

Similar parameters are calculated for the corresponding three distributions relating to births by age of mother:

OBSERVED BIRTHS   As reported for one, three, or five calendar years.

NET MATERNITY FUNCTION   The number of births that would occur at each age if the observed age-specific birth rates were applied to the number of women in the stationary age distribution.

BIRTHS IN STABLE POP.   The number of births that would occur at each age if the observed age-specific birth rates were applied to the number of women in the stable age distribution.

VITAL STATISTICS		THOMPSON				BOURGEOIS-PICHAT				COALE	TABLE 8
		AGE RANGE	NRR	1000r	INTERVAL	AGE RANGE	NRR	1000b	1000d	1000r		RATES FROM AGE DISTRI- BUTIONS AND VITAL STATISTICS (Females)
GRR	1.446										IBR	
NRR	1.395	0–4	1.51	15.38	27.41	5–29	2.17	27.19	−1.47	28.66	IDR	
TFR	2.960	5–9	1.62	17.92	27.37	30–54	0.97	12.00	13.30	−1.30	IRI	
GENERATION	26.291	10–14	1.54	15.67	27.31	55–79	1.46	24.42	10.43	13.99	K1	
SEX RATIO	104.719	15–19	1.41	12.03	27.22	*45–69	1.58	29.11	12.22	16.89	K2	

The purpose of Table 8 is to check the estimates of birth and natural increase as they are given by vital statistics. The means of checking is whatever inference could be drawn from the age distribution and the life table; except for the five figures on the left no use is made of birth statistics.

VITAL STATISTICS   Five figures calculated from birth and death registrations:

GRR   Gross Reproduction Rate, R_0, the sum of the age-specific female fertility rates (relating daughters to mothers) taken in five-year age groups and multiplied by five.

NRR   Net Reproduction Rate, the same as GRR except for a factor in each term from the female life table providing for the probability of surviving from age zero to the age group in question. The NRR is the number of girl children expected to be born to a girl child herself just born, and hence is the ratio of the number in one (female) generation to the number in the preceding generation, according to mortality and fertility in the given period.

TFR   Total Fertility Rate, same as GRR but for both sexes of children.

GENERATION   The number of years T which a population subject to the intrinsic rate r would take to increase in the ratio of the NRR, i.e., the solution in T of $e^{rT} = R_0$. The quantity T is a mean of the average age of childbearing in the stationary and in the stable populations.

SEX RATIO   The ratio of male to female births multiplied by 100.

THOMPSON

NRR   The ratio of children to women in the observed population, divided by the corresponding ratio from the life table, and with a small correction for variance; approximately

$$\frac{{}_5K_x}{{}_{30}K_{x+15}}\bigg/\frac{{}_5L_x}{{}_{30}L_{x+15}}, \quad x = 0, 5, 10, 15.$$

AGE RANGE
0–4   Children 0–4   referred to women 15–44; $x = 0$.
5–9   Children 5–9   referred to women 20–49; $x = 5$.
10–14   Children 10–14 referred to women 25–54; $x = 10$.
15–19   Children 15–19 referred to women 30–59; $x = 15$.
(Age taken at last birthday throughout.)

INTERVAL   In each instance number of years between the mean age of children x to $x + 4$, and of women $x + 15$ to $x + 44$, $x = 0, 5, 10, 15$.

1000r As here calculated, equal to the ratio of successive generations expressed as NRR, but reduced to an annual basis per thousand population:

$$r = \frac{\ln\left(\dfrac{{}_5K_x}{{}_{30}K_{x+15}}\bigg/\dfrac{{}_5L_x}{{}_{30}L_{x+15}}\right)}{\text{INTERVAL}}.$$

BOURGEOIS-PICHAT

1000b, 1000r Intrinsic rates of birth and natural increase inferred by least squares fitting of a straight line to the logarithm of the age distribution, per thousand population:

$$\ln\frac{{}_5K_x}{{}_5L_x} = \ln b - r(x + 2\tfrac{1}{2}) + \ln\frac{K}{l_0}$$

AGE RANGE
5–29 ⎫
30–54 ⎬   Intervals over which b and r were separately calculated, including finally the closest-fitting interval of 25 years after the computer had tried all such intervals, identified by asterisk *.
55–79 ⎭
1000d $d = b - r$ where b and r are obtained from straight-line fitting above. The departure of d from its value in Table 4 constitutes a check on the process.

NRR   Here calculated as 27th power of e^r, after r is inferred from age distribution.

COALE

IBR = 1000b ⎫
IDR = 1000d ⎬   Intrinsic rates of birth, death, and natural increase as inferred by a least squares fitting of a curve with constants b, r, k_1, and k_2 to the logarithm of age distribution from ages 5 to 74; shows blank where age distribution cannot be fitted by this model.
IRI = 1000r ⎭

K1 = 1000k_1 Linear component of inferred trend in births, or in births less infant deaths, multiplied by 1000.

K2 = 1000k_2 Quadratic component of inferred trend in births, or in births less infant deaths, multiplied by 1000.

Start of Age Interval	ORIGINAL MATRIX			FIRST STABLE MATRIX			SECOND STABLE MATRIX Z_2		
	SUB-DIAGONAL	ALTERNATIVE FIRST ROWS		% IN STABLE POPULATION	FISHER VALUES	REPRODUCTIVE VALUES	FIRST COLUMN	FIRST ROW	
		Projection	Integral						
0	0.99669	0.00000	0.00000	10.100	1.055	10549785	0.1748+0.0943	0.1748+0.0943	
5	0.99838	0.00099	0.00000	9.448	1.127	11378528	0.1872-0.1509	-0.0159+0.1632	
10	0.99795	0.08601	0.00204	8.854	1.202	11205023	-0.0808-0.2803	-0.1293+0.0400	
15	0.99685	0.32202	0.17586	8.294	1.192	10010789	-0.3513-0.0413	-0.0868-0.0937	
20	0.99611	0.43270	0.49042	7.760	0.934	6343797	-0.2109+0.3729	-0.0129-0.1264	
25	0.99477	0.31006	0.40436	7.255	0.541	3079232	0.3172+0.4102	0.0163-0.0913	
30	0.99231	0.17069	0.23693	6.774	0.250	1393118	0.6056-0.1615	0.3203-0.0462	
35	0.98861	0.07177	0.11632	6.310	0.087	530598	0.1033-0.7486	0.0118-0.0155	
40	0.98281	0.01656	0.03220	5.855	0.017	110296	-0.7809-0.4627	0.0030-0.0028	
45	0.97431	0.00098	0.00203	5.401	0.001	5714	-0.8706+0.6457	0.0002-0.0001	
50	0.96251	0.00000	0.00000	4.939	0.000	1	0.3055+1.2463	0.0000-0.0000	
55+	0.81532			19.010					

TABLE 9
LESLIE MATRIX AND ITS SPECTRAL COMPONENTS (Females)

ORIGINAL MATRIX	The female projection matrix. All elements but those of the first row and the subdiagonal are zero and are omitted to economize space in the printout.
SUBDIAGONAL	The elements of the subdiagonal shown are probabilities of surviving from the age group specified to the succeeding age group: $_5L_{x+5}/_5L_x$.

ALTERNATIVE FIRST ROWS

Projection	The first row of the usual projection matrix. The number opposite 15 is the factor by which the female population 15–19 is multiplied to obtain the contribution to the female children 0–4 alive at the end of the five-year period, etc. Used to obtain Tables 4 and 5.
Integral	An alternative first row that avoids the slight upward bias of the usual projection matrix for long-term projections and is consistent with the integral equation for r: $$\sum_{x=10}^{50} e^{-r(x+2.5)} {}_5L_x F_x = l_0.$$

FIRST STABLE MATRIX

% IN STABLE POP.	The percent distribution of the stable population, i.e., of any column of the first stable matrix obtained as a high power of the projection matrix.
FISHER VALUES	Numbers proportional to the rows of the first stable matrix; may be interpreted as index of reproductive value, i.e., the children expected to be born to a woman on the given fertility rates and life table, discounted at the intrinsic rate. Value is arbitrarily taken as unity at birth, and is necessarily zero at the end of the reproductive period.
REPRODUCTIVE VALUES	Fisher value multiplied by observed female population at each age.

SECOND STABLE MATRIX Z_2

FIRST COLUMN	Complex numbers for the first column of the second stable matrix, other columns being proportional to these numbers. The i's designating the imaginary parts have been omitted.
FIRST ROW	First row of the second stable matrix, also complex numbers (i's omitted).

Start of Age Interval	OBSERVED POPUL. (IN 100's)	CONTRIBUTIONS OF ROOTS (IN 100's) r_1	r_2, r_3	$r_4\text{-}r_{11}$	AGE-SP. BIRTH RATES	NET MATERNITY FUNCTION	COEFF. OF MATRIX EQUATION	PARAMETERS	INTEGRAL	MATRIX	EXP. INCREASE x	$e^{(x+8.5)r}$
0	100020	99629	-2694	3085	0.0000	0.0000	0.0003	L(1)	1.06530	1.06540	0	1.0321
5	100920	93204	8268	-552	0.0000	0.0000	0.0010	L(2)	0.30579	0.31879	50	1.9428
10	93210	87341	11727	-5858	0.0004	0.0020	0.0855		0.78901	0.75878	55	2.0697
15	83950	81812	-1145	3284	0.0348	0.1692	0.3198	R(1)	0.01265	0.01267	60	2.2048
20	67940	76548	-18297	9689	0.0971	0.4704	0.4283	R(2)	-0.03340	-0.03895	65	2.3488
25	56970	71570	-15476	876	0.0801	0.3863	0.3057		0.24021	0.23461	70	2.5022
30	55700	66825	12276	-23401	0.0469	0.2252	0.1674	C(1)		986452	75	2.6656
35	60920	62241	34018	-35339	0.0230	0.1097	0.0699	C(2)		423267	80	2.8396
40	63780	57755	13876	-7851	0.0064	0.0300	0.0159			2213743	85	3.0250
45	58790	53278	-35958	41471	0.0004	0.0019	0.0009	2P/Y	26.1568	26.7812	90	3.2226
50	54240	48723	-52592	58109	0.0000	0.0000	0.0000	DELTA	4.2768		95	3.4330
55+	190590	187526									100	3.6571

TABLE 10
AGE ANALYSIS AND MISCELLANEOUS RESULTS (Females)

OBSERVED POPUL. (in 100's) — Age distribution of females rounded to hundreds of persons, from Table 1.

CONTRIBUTIONS OF ROOTS (in 100's)

r_1 — The component of the age distribution that corresponds to the real root, proportional to the stable age distribution of Table 9. c_1 under MATRIX of second-to-last column of Table 10 multiplied by the percent distribution of the stable population of Table 9 gives the numbers under r_1 in Table 10.

r_2, r_3 — The component of the age distribution corresponding to the second and third roots. It is double the real part of the product of c_2 under MATRIX multiplied by the corresponding element of FIRST COLUMN under SECOND STABLE MATRIX Z_2 of Table 9. Describes any peculiarities of the observed age distribution that have periodicity of one generation.

$r_4\text{-}r_{11}$ — The remaining components of age distribution of all periodicities other than the generation.

AGE-SP. BIRTH RATES — Number of children born to women of age x to $x + 4$ at last birthday, divided by number of women in that age group and multiplied by the proportion of births that are female, designated $_5F_x$. The GRR of Table 8 is $5\Sigma_5F_x$.

NET MATERNITY FUNCTION — Age-specific birth rate multiplied by stationary population in the five-year age group: $_5L_x\,_5F_x$. The NRR of Table 8 is $\Sigma_5L_x\,_5F_x$.

COEFF. OF MATRIX EQUATION — Average of corresponding figure under NET MATERNITY FUNCTION and figure immediately below:
$$\tfrac{1}{2}(_5L_x\,_5F_x + {}_5L_{x+5}\,_5F_{x+5}).$$

PARAMETERS

$L(1) = \lambda_1$ — Ratio of increase per five-year period after stability is attained, if age-specific birth and death rates are held constant. Value under MATRIX is obtained as real root of polynomial equation whose coefficients are given in column headed COEFF. OF MATRIX EQUATION. Value under INTEGRAL obtained from intrinsic rate r_1 as $\lambda_1 = e^{5r_1}$. Numbers on same row in these two columns are different finite approximations to same parameter.

$L(2) = \lambda_2$ — Principal complex root of characteristic equation; value under MATRIX obtained as λ_2 from matrix equation; value under INTEGRAL obtained from integral equation as $\lambda_2 = e^{5r_2}$. The i's designating the imaginary parts have been omitted.

$R(1) = r_1$ — Intrinsic rate of natural increase obtained from characteristic equation of integral equation is r_1 under INTEGRAL; under MATRIX, $r_1 = 0.2 \ln \lambda_1$.

$R(2) = r_2$ — Second root of characteristic equation of integral equation under INTEGRAL, and $r_2 = 0.2 \ln \lambda_2$ under MATRIX. (The i's have been omitted.)

$C(1) = c_1$ — Factor to be applied to percent distribution of the stable population in order to obtain stable component in analysis of age distribution, as given in second column of Table 10 under r_1. $100c_1$ is the stable equivalent of the female population.

$C(2) = c_2$ — Factor to be multiplied by first column of second stable matrix to give the principal complex components of the age distribution, shown in third column of Table 10 under r_2, r_3. (The i's have been omitted.)

$2P/Y = 2\pi/y$ — If y is the imaginary part of the second complex root r_2 in the solution of the integral equation, then $2\pi/y$ is the wave length of the principal complex component. $2\pi/y$ is close to T, the length of generation in Table 8, and to the mean age of childbearing in Table 7.

$DELTA = \Delta$ — The index of dissimilarity between the observed age distribution and the stable component; when both are expressed as percentages, Δ is the sum of the positive differences.

EXP. INCREASE
$e^{(x+2\frac{1}{2})r}$ — Exponential function of the intrinsic rate r obtained from the integral equation, intended for ascertaining the stable age distribution beyond age 50 and other purposes.

Principal Results

Based on Official Data for Individual Countries
Periods of One, Three or Five Years
Applying Female-Dominant Computation

Africa
America
Asia
Europe
Oceania

TABLE 1 — DATA

AGE AT LAST BIRTHDAY	POPULATION BOTH SEXES	MALES Number	%	FEMALES Number	%	BIRTHS BY AGE OF MOTHER	DEATHS BOTH SEXES	MALES	FEMALES	AGE AT LAST BIRTHDAY
0	21587	10894	3.9	10693	3.9	0	1543	877	666	0
1-4	74324	37500	13.5	36824	13.5	0	1258	586	672	1-4
5-9	78214	39437	14.2	38777	14.2	0	178	79	99	5-9
10-14	56438	28117	10.1	28321	10.4	51	74	31	43	10-14
15-19	48115	23989	8.6	24126	8.8	3386	98	42	56	15-19
20-24	45379	22395	8.1	22984	8.4	6240	124	48	76	20-24
25-29	46333	23724	8.5	22609	8.3	5915	165	74	91	25-29
30-34	34907	18187	6.5	16720	6.1	4309	170	87	83	30-34
35-39	32955	17397	6.3	15558	5.7	2248	195	106	89	35-39
40-44	27125	14713	5.3	12412	4.5	745	260	169	91	40-44
45-49	22188	12126	4.4	10062	3.7	70	250	165	85	45-49
50-54	19331	10255	3.7	9076	3.3	6	360	239	121	50-54
55-59	14150	7114	2.6	7036	2.6	0	412	267	145	55-59
60-64	12523	5771	2.1	6752	2.5	0	457	257	200	60-64
65-69	8563	3337	1.2	5226	1.9	0	479	236	243	65-69
70-74	4614	1738	0.6	2876	1.1		412	181	231	70-74
75-79	2423	739	0.3	1684	0.6		322	114	208	75-79
80-84	1312	294	0.1	1018	0.4	11697 M.	217	59	158	80-84
85+	497	80	0.0	417	0.2	11273 F.	114	23	91	85+
TOTAL	550978	277807		273171		22970	7088	3640	3448	TOTAL

TABLE 2 — MALE LIFE TABLE

x	nq_x	l_x	nd_x	nL_x	nm_x	na_x	T_x	r_x	$\mathring{e}_x$	nM_x	x
0	0.076407	100000	7641	95369	0.080117	0.3939	5330470	0.0077	53.305	0.080503	0
1	0.059788	92359	5522	354613	0.015572	1.3155	5235101	0.0077	56.682	0.015627	1
5	0.009353	86837	812	432156	0.001879	2.5000	4880488	0.0495	56.203	0.002003	5
10	0.005491	86025	472	428931	0.001101	2.4716	4448332	0.0483	51.710	0.001103	10
15	0.008740	85553	748	425984	0.001755	2.6203	4019400	0.0211	46.982	0.001751	15
20	0.010662	84805	904	421880	0.002143	2.6279	3593416	0.0000	42.373	0.002143	20
25	0.015531	83901	1303	416466	0.003129	2.6688	3171536	0.0175	37.801	0.003119	25
30	0.023729	82598	1960	408324	0.004800	2.6198	2755070	0.0264	33.355	0.004784	30
35	0.030139	80638	2430	397619	0.006112	2.7080	2346746	0.0142	29.102	0.006093	35
40	0.056094	78207	4387	380581	0.011527	2.6165	1949127	0.0255	24.923	0.011486	40
45	0.066147	73820	4883	357576	0.013656	2.6396	1568547	0.0208	21.248	0.013607	45
50	0.111111	68937	7660	326720	0.023444	2.6543	1210971	0.0291	17.566	0.023306	50
55	0.172282	61278	10557	280529	0.037632	2.5505	884251	0.0217	14.430	0.037532	55
60	0.201503	50721	10220	228405	0.044747	2.5345	603721	0.0358	11.903	0.044533	60
65	0.302462	40500	12250	172179	0.071146	2.5246	375316	0.0358	9.267	0.070722	65
70	0.413065	28251	11669	111425	0.104728	2.4439	203137	0.0358	7.191	0.104143	70
75	0.549262	16581	9107	58713	0.155118	2.3436	91712	0.0358	5.531	0.154262	75
80	0.646441	7474	4831	23944	0.201780	2.2212	33000	0.0358	4.415	0.200681	80
85+	*1.000000	2642	2642	9056	0.291791	3.4271	9056	0.0358	3.427	0.287500	85+

TABLE 3 — FEMALE LIFE TABLE

x	nq_x	l_x	nd_x	nL_x	nm_x	na_x	T_x	r_x	$\mathring{e}_x$	nM_x	x
0	0.059901	100000	5990	96581	0.062022	0.4292	5658320	0.0077	56.583	0.062284	0
1	0.069549	94010	6538	359258	0.018199	1.4333	5561739	0.0077	59.161	0.018249	1
5	0.012025	87472	1052	434728	0.002419	2.5000	5202481	0.0460	59.476	0.002553	5
10	0.007558	86420	653	430454	0.001517	2.4812	4767753	0.0455	55.170	0.001518	10
15	0.011577	85767	993	426505	0.002328	2.6548	4337299	0.0185	50.571	0.002321	15
20	0.016409	84774	1391	420531	0.003308	2.6608	3910794	0.0032	46.132	0.003307	20
25	0.019977	83383	1666	412878	0.004035	2.5772	3490263	0.0277	41.858	0.004025	25
30	0.024580	81717	2009	403686	0.004976	2.5609	3077385	0.0325	37.659	0.004964	30
35	0.028268	79708	2253	393073	0.005732	2.5729	2673700	0.0239	33.544	0.005721	35
40	0.036115	77455	2797	380459	0.007353	2.5631	2280626	0.0364	29.444	0.007332	40
45	0.041536	74658	3101	365921	0.008474	2.6240	1900167	0.0221	25.452	0.008448	45
50	0.064895	71557	4644	346900	0.013386	2.6561	1534246	0.0220	21.441	0.013332	50
55	0.098351	66913	6581	318888	0.020637	2.6177	1187346	0.0087	17.745	0.020608	55
60	0.138600	60332	8362	281656	0.029689	2.6076	868457	0.0134	14.395	0.029621	60
65	0.209696	51970	10898	233737	0.046625	2.6038	586802	0.0134	11.291	0.046498	65
70	0.335783	41072	13791	171274	0.080522	2.5284	353065	0.0134	8.596	0.080320	70
75	0.468340	27281	12777	103238	0.123760	2.4042	181790	0.0134	6.664	0.123515	75
80	0.545598	14504	7913	50916	0.155422	2.3371	78552	0.0134	5.416	0.155206	80
85+	1.000000	6591	6591	27636	0.238479	4.1932	27636	0.0134	4.193	0.218226	85+

TABLE 4 — OBSERVED AND PROJECTED VITAL RATES

	OBSERVED POPULATION BOTH SEXES	MALES	FEMALES	PROJECTED 1960 MALES	FEMALES	1965 MALES	FEMALES	1970 MALES	FEMALES	STABLE POPULATION MALES	FEMALES
RATES PER THOUSAND											
Birth	41.69	42.10	41.27	40.46	39.68	40.13	39.34	41.08	40.21	42.43	41.61
Death	12.86	13.10	12.62	13.11	12.29	12.94	11.90	12.90	11.72	12.00	11.18
Increase	28.83	29.00	28.65	27.36	27.40	27.19	27.44	28.18	28.50		30.4332
PERCENTAGE											
under 15	41.85	41.74	41.96	44.11	43.86	44.08	43.62	43.84	43.25	44.75	44.25
15-64	54.99	56.04	53.94	53.44	52.15	53.52	52.81	53.71	53.38	53.45	53.06
65 and over	3.16	2.23	4.11	2.45	3.99	2.40	3.57	2.45	3.37	1.80	2.69
DEP. RATIO X 100	81.84	78.46	85.41	87.12	91.75	86.84	89.36	86.18	87.35	87.11	88.45

Excluding Rodrigues

TABLE 1 — DATA

AGE AT LAST BIRTHDAY	POPULATION BOTH SEXES	MALES Number	%	FEMALES Number	%	BIRTHS BY AGE OF MOTHER	DEATHS BOTH SEXES	MALES	FEMALES	AGE AT LAST BIRTHDAY
0	23320	11833	4.0	11487	4.0	0	1733	959	774	0
1-4	80752	40709	13.7	40043	13.8	0	939	445	494	1-4
5-9	84366	42687	14.3	41679	14.4	0	192	89	103	5-9
10-14	64176	32052	10.8	32124	11.1	57	80	36	44	10-14
15-19	49514	24855	8.4	24659	8.5	3570	110	41	69	15-19
20-24	50247	25175	8.5	25072	8.6	6881	156	63	93	20-24
25-29	44272	22818	7.7	21454	7.4	6040	181	72	109	25-29
30-34	38377	20009	6.7	18368	6.3	4886	196	91	105	30-34
35-39	33458	17753	6.0	15705	5.4	2628	206	117	89	35-39
40-44	29033	15571	5.2	13462	4.6	772	250	157	93	40-44
45-49	24887	13388	4.5	11499	4.0	88	298	199	99	45-49
50-54	20585	10769	3.6	9816	3.4	6	370	254	116	50-54
55-59	16282	8149	2.7	8133	2.8	0	437	289	148	55-59
60-64	11980	5530	1.9	6450	2.2	0	472	289	183	60-64
65-69	7834	3347	1.1	4487	1.5	0	501	279	222	65-69
70-74	5060	1996	0.7	3064	1.1		428	209	219	70-74
75-79	2458	753	0.3	1705	0.6		290	115	175	75-79
80-84	988	220	0.1	768	0.3	12675 M.	187	52	135	80-84
85+	283	42	0.0	241	0.1	12253 F.	122	17	105	85+
TOTAL	587872	297656		290216		24928	7148	3773	3375	TOTAL

TABLE 2 — MALE LIFE TABLE

x	$_nq_x$	l_x	$_nd_x$	$_nL_x$	$_nm_x$	$_na_x$	T_x	r_x	$\overset{\circ}{e}_x$	$_nM_x$	x
0	0.076592	100000	7659	95095	0.080542	0.3596	5382206	0.0092	53.822	0.081045	0
1	0.042232	92341	3900	358591	0.010875	1.2377	5287111	0.0092	57.256	0.010931	1
5	0.009990	88441	883	439997	0.002008	2.5000	4928520	0.0456	55.727	0.002085	5
10	0.005580	87558	489	436532	0.001119	2.4295	4488523	0.0526	51.264	0.001123	10
15	0.008248	87069	718	433672	0.001656	2.6701	4051991	0.0225	46.538	0.001650	15
20	0.012448	86351	1075	429196	0.002504	2.6203	3618319	0.0061	41.903	0.002502	20
25	0.015701	85276	1339	423203	0.003164	2.6275	3189122	0.0197	37.398	0.003155	25
30	0.022570	83937	1894	415227	0.004563	2.6464	2765919	0.0204	32.952	0.004548	30
35	0.032552	82043	2671	403958	0.006611	2.6580	2350693	0.0182	28.652	0.006590	35
40	0.049392	79372	3920	387636	0.010113	2.6471	1946734	0.0179	24.527	0.010083	40
45	0.072082	75452	5439	364481	0.014922	2.6506	1559098	0.0212	20.664	0.014864	45
50	0.112153	70013	7852	331426	0.023692	2.6263	1194618	0.0255	17.063	0.023586	50
55	0.164079	62161	10199	286194	0.035638	2.5871	863192	0.0302	13.886	0.035464	55
60	0.233197	51961	12117	230262	0.052624	2.5617	576998	0.0402	11.104	0.052260	60
65	0.346053	39844	13788	164467	0.083835	2.4795	346736	0.0402	8.702	0.083358	65
70	0.412897	26056	10758	102253	0.105214	2.3949	182269	0.0402	6.995	0.104709	70
75	0.546593	15298	8362	54381	0.153759	2.3561	80016	0.0402	5.231	0.152722	75
80	0.718369	6936	4983	20889	0.238534	2.2321	25635	0.0402	3.696	0.236364	80
85+	*1.000000	1953	1953	4747	0.411540	2.4299	4747	0.0402	2.430	0.404762	85+

TABLE 3 — FEMALE LIFE TABLE

x	$_nq_x$	l_x	$_nd_x$	$_nL_x$	$_nm_x$	$_na_x$	T_x	r_x	$\overset{\circ}{e}_x$	$_nM_x$	x
0	0.064408	100000	6441	96069	0.067043	0.3897	5747501	0.0078	57.475	0.067381	0
1	0.047596	93559	4453	362234	0.012293	1.3046	5651432	0.0078	60.405	0.012337	1
5	0.011878	89106	1058	442885	0.002390	2.5000	5289198	0.0429	59.358	0.002471	5
10	0.006846	88048	603	438765	0.001374	2.5559	4846313	0.0505	55.042	0.001370	10
15	0.013953	87445	1220	434379	0.002809	2.6681	4407548	0.0221	50.404	0.002798	15
20	0.018408	86225	1587	427345	0.003714	2.6192	3973168	0.0101	46.079	0.003709	20
25	0.025147	84638	2128	418021	0.005092	2.5724	3545823	0.0262	41.894	0.005081	25
30	0.028197	82509	2326	406754	0.005720	2.5103	3127802	0.0256	37.909	0.005716	30
35	0.027973	80183	2243	395374	0.005673	2.5304	2721048	0.0251	33.936	0.005667	35
40	0.034044	77940	2653	383261	0.006923	2.5738	2325674	0.0242	29.839	0.006908	40
45	0.042285	75286	3184	368787	0.008632	2.5986	1942413	0.0227	25.800	0.008609	45
50	0.057688	72103	4159	350692	0.011861	2.6387	1573627	0.0222	21.825	0.011817	50
55	0.087603	67943	5952	325695	0.018275	2.6442	1222934	0.0232	17.999	0.018197	55
60	0.133553	61991	8279	290499	0.028500	2.6498	897239	0.0212	14.474	0.028372	60
65	0.221641	53712	11905	239722	0.049661	2.5775	606740	0.0212	11.296	0.049476	65
70	0.303986	41807	12709	177260	0.071696	2.4996	367018	0.0212	8.779	0.071475	70
75	0.408257	29099	11880	115317	0.103018	2.4599	189758	0.0212	6.521	0.102639	75
80	0.605304	17219	10423	58979	0.176719	2.3984	74441	0.0212	4.323	0.175782	80
85+	*1.000000	6796	6796	15463	0.439525	2.2752	15463	0.0212	2.275	0.435685	85+

TABLE 4 — OBSERVED AND PROJECTED VITAL RATES

	OBSERVED POPULATION BOTH SEXES	MALES	FEMALES	PROJECTED POPULATION 1962 MALES	FEMALES	1967 MALES	FEMALES	1972 MALES	FEMALES	STABLE POPULATION MALES	FEMALES
RATES PER THOUSAND											
Birth	42.40	42.58	42.22	40.99	40.50	41.12	40.49	42.13	41.37	43.82	43.06
Death	12.16	12.68	11.63	12.62	11.36	12.46	11.17	12.33	11.09	11.21	10.44
Increase	30.24	29.91	30.59	28.37	29.14	28.67	29.32	29.80	30.28	32.6157	
PERCENTAGE											
under 15	42.97	42.76	43.19	44.75	44.65	44.95	44.64	44.89	44.41	46.17	45.71
15-64	54.20	55.10	53.28	53.09	51.88	52.86	51.94	52.92	52.26	52.34	51.82
65 and over	2.83	2.14	3.54	2.16	3.47	2.19	3.42	2.19	3.33	1.48	2.47
DEP. RATIO X 100	84.50	81.48	87.70	88.34	92.76	89.19	92.52	88.97	91.33	91.04	92.96

Excluding Rodrigues

TABLE 1 — DATA

AGE AT LAST BIRTHDAY	POPULATION BOTH SEXES	MALES Number	MALES %	FEMALES Number	FEMALES %	BIRTHS BY AGE OF MOTHER	DEATHS BOTH SEXES	DEATHS MALES	FEMALES	AGE AT LAST BIRTHDAY
0	22425	11350	3.5	11075	3.5	0	1624	905	719	0
1-4	88600	44800	13.9	43800	13.9	0	832	385	447	1-4
5-9	94000	47600	14.7	46400	14.7	0	179	75	104	5-9
10-14	77900	39400	12.2	38500	12.2	41	80	43	37	10-14
15-19	56100	28100	8.7	28000	8.9	3371	104	43	61	15-19
20-24	48600	24800	7.7	23800	7.5	6900	147	47	100	20-24
25-29	44400	22700	7.0	21700	6.9	6144	132	46	86	25-29
30-34	44400	22800	7.1	21600	6.8	4739	168	72	96	30-34
35-39	39400	20800	6.4	18600	5.9	3026	215	103	112	35-39
40-44	28100	14300	4.4	13800	4.4	789	203	120	83	40-44
45-49	27100	14200	4.4	12900	4.1	93	258	176	82	45-49
50-54	19600	10300	3.2	9300	2.9	4	351	240	111	50-54
55-59	16400	8300	2.6	8100	2.6	0	424	288	136	55-59
60-64	12000	5800	1.8	6200	2.0	0	495	303	192	60-64
65-69	8400	3700	1.1	4700	1.5	0	478	251	227	65-69
70-74	6229	2303	0.7	3926	1.2		428	198	230	70-74
75-79	3265	1111	0.3	2154	0.7		345	128	217	75-79
80-84	1378	425	0.1	953	0.3	12772 M.	225	69	156	80-84
85+	403	111	0.0	292	0.1	12335 F.	146	27	119	85+
TOTAL	638700	322900		315800		25107	6834	3519	3315	TOTAL

TABLE 2 — MALE LIFE TABLE

x	$_nq_x$	l_x	$_nd_x$	$_nL_x$	$_nm_x$	$_na_x$	T_x	r_x	$\mathring{e}_x$	$_nM_x$	x
0	0.075731	100000	7573	94977	0.079736	0.3368	5615483	0.0000	56.155	0.079736	0
1	0.033567	92427	3102	361016	0.008594	1.1986	5520506	0.0000	59.728	0.008594	1
5	0.007641	89324	683	444916	0.001534	2.5000	5159489	0.0323	57.761	0.001576	5
10	0.005442	88642	482	442002	0.001091	2.4969	4714574	0.0514	53.187	0.001091	10
15	0.007661	88159	675	439181	0.001538	2.6060	4272572	0.0448	48.464	0.001530	15
20	0.009442	87484	826	435397	0.001897	2.5502	3833391	0.0195	43.818	0.001895	20
25	0.010092	86658	875	431213	0.002028	2.6239	3397994	0.0062	39.211	0.002026	25
30	0.015692	85784	1346	425805	0.003161	2.6874	2966782	0.0055	34.584	0.003158	30
35	0.024700	84438	2086	417403	0.004997	2.7059	2540976	0.0413	30.093	0.004952	35
40	0.041371	82352	3407	403803	0.008437	2.6647	2123574	0.0298	25.787	0.008392	40
45	0.060528	78945	4778	383785	0.012451	2.7106	1719771	0.0189	21.784	0.012394	45
50	0.111072	74166	8238	351449	0.023440	2.6470	1335986	0.0304	18.013	0.023301	50
55	0.160629	65929	10590	304133	0.034821	2.5912	984538	0.0213	14.933	0.034699	55
60	0.232589	55339	12871	244879	0.052561	2.5283	680404	0.0458	12.295	0.052241	60
65	0.290538	42467	12338	181028	0.068157	2.4625	435525	0.0458	10.256	0.067838	65
70	0.353463	30129	10650	123257	0.086401	2.4282	254497	0.0458	8.447	0.085975	70
75	0.445029	19480	8669	74794	0.115905	2.3926	131240	0.0458	6.737	0.115211	75
80	0.571612	10811	6179	37763	0.163638	2.3639	56446	0.0458	5.221	0.162354	80
85+	*1.000000	4631	4631	18683	0.247880	4.0342	18683	0.0458	4.034	0.243243	85+

TABLE 3 — FEMALE LIFE TABLE

x	$_nq_x$	l_x	$_nd_x$	$_nL_x$	$_nm_x$	$_na_x$	T_x	r_x	$\mathring{e}_x$	$_nM_x$	x
0	0.062392	100000	6239	96104	0.064921	0.3756	5911437	0.0000	59.114	0.064921	0
1	0.039716	93761	3724	364880	0.010205	1.2706	5815333	0.0000	62.023	0.010205	1
5	0.010891	90037	981	447734	0.002190	2.5000	5450453	0.0317	60.536	0.002241	5
10	0.004794	89056	427	444214	0.000961	2.4969	5002719	0.0490	56.175	0.000961	10
15	0.010993	88630	974	441004	0.002209	2.7993	4558506	0.0457	51.433	0.002179	15
20	0.020837	87655	1826	433858	0.004210	2.5810	4117502	0.0218	46.974	0.004202	20
25	0.019623	85829	1684	424939	0.003963	2.5031	3683644	0.0056	42.919	0.003963	25
30	0.022009	84145	1852	416252	0.004449	2.5858	3258706	0.0107	38.727	0.004444	30
35	0.029732	82293	2447	412554	0.006035	2.5438	2842454	0.0391	34.541	0.006021	35
40	0.029638	79846	2366	393312	0.006017	2.4995	2437000	0.0306	30.521	0.006014	40
45	0.031506	77479	2441	381715	0.006395	2.6721	2043688	0.0320	26.377	0.006357	45
50	0.058412	75038	4383	364921	0.012011	2.6566	1661973	0.0350	22.148	0.011935	50
55	0.081181	70655	5736	339981	0.016871	2.6822	1297052	0.0218	18.357	0.016790	55
60	0.144767	64919	9398	302407	0.031078	2.6389	957071	0.0175	14.742	0.030968	60
65	0.216179	55521	12003	247966	0.048404	2.5305	654664	0.0175	11.791	0.048298	65
70	0.256345	43519	11156	189024	0.058738	2.5197	406698	0.0175	9.345	0.058584	70
75	0.403471	32363	13057	129165	0.101092	2.4996	216774	0.0175	6.698	0.100743	75
80	0.576424	19305	11128	67690	0.164398	2.4086	87610	0.0175	4.538	0.163693	80
85+	*1.000000	8177	8177	19920	0.410513	2.4360	19920	0.0175	2.436	0.407534	85+

TABLE 4 — OBSERVED AND PROJECTED VITAL RATES

	OBSERVED POPULATION BOTH SEXES	MALES	FEMALES	PROJECTED POPULATION 1965 MALES	FEMALES	1970 MALES	FEMALES	1975 MALES	FEMALES	STABLE POPULATION MALES	FEMALES
RATES PER THOUSAND											
Birth	39.31	39.55	39.06	38.93	38.43	40.07	39.51	41.46	40.83	41.77	41.19
Death	10.70	10.90	10.50	10.81	10.17	10.77	10.03	10.77	9.99	10.37	9.78
Increase	28.61	28.66	28.56	28.13	28.26	29.30	29.48	30.68	30.84		31.4038
PERCENTAGE											
under 15	44.30	44.33	44.26	44.16	43.98	43.66	43.40	43.57	43.25	44.79	44.50
15-64	52.62	53.30	51.93	53.43	52.51	53.92	53.27	54.10	53.64	53.33	52.74
65 and over	3.08	2.37	3.81	2.41	3.51	2.42	3.33	2.32	3.11	1.88	2.76
DEP. RATIO X 100	90.03	87.62	92.56	87.18	90.44	85.45	87.71	84.83	86.45	87.49	89.60

AGE AT LAST BIRTHDAY	1965 BOTH SEXES	MALES	FEMALES	1970 BOTH SEXES	MALES	FEMALES	1975 BOTH SEXES	MALES	FEMALES	AGE AT LAST BIRTHDAY	
0-4	123	62	61	142	72	70	170	86	84	0-4	
5-9	108	55	53	120	61	59	138	70	68	5-9	
10-14	93	47	46	107	54	53	118	60	58	10-14	TABLE 5
15-19	77	39	38	93	47	46	106	54	52	15-19	
20-24	56	28	28	77	39	38	92	47	45	20-24	POPULATION
25-29	48	25	23	55	28	27	75	38	37	25-29	PROJECTED
30-34	43	22	21	47	24	23	53	27	26	30-34	WITH
35-39	43	22	21	43	22	21	46	24	22	35-39	FIXED
40-44	38	20	18	42	22	20	41	21	20	40-44	AGE—
45-49	27	14	13	37	19	18	41	21	20	45-49	SPECIFIC
50-54	25	13	12	25	12	13	35	18	17	50-54	BIRTH
55-59	18	9	9	22	11	11	23	11	12	55-59	AND
60-64	14	7	7	15	7	8	19	9	10	60-64	DEATH
65-69	9	4	5	11	5	6	11	5	6	65-69	RATES
70-74	7	3	4	7	3	4	8	3	5	70-74	(IN 1000's)
75-79	4	1	3	4	2	2	5	2	3	75-79	
80-84	2	1	1	2	1	1	2	1	1	80-84	
85+	0	0	0	0	0	0	0	0	0	85+	
TOTAL	735	372	363	849	429	420	983	497	486	TOTAL	

STANDARD COUNTRIES:	ENGLAND AND WALES 1961 BOTH SEXES	MALES	FEMALES	UNITED STATES 1960 BOTH SEXES	MALES	FEMALES	MEXICO 1960 BOTH SEXES	MALES	FEMALES	
STANDARDIZED RATES PER THOUSAND										TABLE 6
Birth	36.70	38.42*	34.95	37.43	35.74*	36.23	42.05	36.09*	41.21	STANDARDIZED RATES
Death	20.96	28.16*	21.55	17.71	21.98*	17.01	11.10	11.40*	10.38	
Increase	15.74	10.26*	13.40	19.72	13.76*	19.22	30.94	24.68*	30.83	

	OBSERVED POP. MALES	FEMALES	STATIONARY POP. MALES	FEMALES	STABLE POP. MALES	FEMALES	OBSERVED BIRTHS	NET MATERNITY FUNCTION	BIRTHS IN STABLE POP.	
μ	22.90158	23.43787	33.32954	35.22849	21.68082	22.26756	27.45718	28.21644	26.75395	TABLE 7
σ^2	332.2353	367.0767	431.8682	481.6673	299.5194	328.2867	44.00258	46.53442	42.26782	MOMENTS
κ_3	4904.215	6301.344	2732.236	2705.384	4756.904	5689.461	114.0919	117.6464	150.5490	AND
κ_4	-17396.	3187.	-153254.	-222198.	18162.	25701.	-1181.378	-1373.657	-703.225	CUMULANTS
β_1	0.655846	0.802779	0.092679	0.065496	0.842120	0.914919	0.152783	0.137352	0.300141	
β_2	2.842402	3.023649	2.178306	2.042264	3.202451	3.238477	2.389856	2.365649	2.606382	
κ	-0.260763	-0.318417	-0.038334	-0.024724	-0.371251	-0.384490	-0.072631	-0.064989	-0.146716	

VITAL STATISTICS		THOMPSON AGE RANGE	NRR	1000r	INTERVAL	BOURGEOIS-PICHAT AGE RANGE	NRR	1000b	1000d	1000r	COALE		TABLE 8
GRR	2.804												RATES FROM AGE DISTRIBUTIONS AND VITAL STATISTICS (Females)
NRR	2.370	0-4	2.35	31.39	27.19	5-29	2.75	42.26	4.81	37.46	IBR	40.39	
TFR	5.707	5-9	2.26	30.75	27.13	30-54	2.54	51.26	16.70	34.55	IDR	8.30	
GENERATION	27.474	10-14	2.11	27.04	27.06	55-79	1.31	12.76	2.67	10.09	IRI	32.09	
SEX RATIO	103.543	15-19	1.73	16.00	26.94	*15-39	1.46	24.80	10.69	14.11	K1	6.40	
											K2	0.	

Start of Age Interval	ORIGINAL MATRIX SUB-DIAGONAL	ALTERNATIVE FIRST ROWS Projection	Integral	FIRST STABLE MATRIX % IN STABLE POPULATION	FISHER VALUES	REPRODUCTIVE VALUES	SECOND STABLE MATRIX Z₂ FIRST COLUMN	FIRST ROW	
0	0.97126	0.00000	0.00000	17.597	1.172	64323	0.1282+0.1005	0.1282+0.1005	TABLE 9
5	0.99214	0.00120	0.00000	14.599	1.413	65557	0.1649-0.0758	-0.0276+0.1436	LESLIE
10	0.99277	0.13655	0.00261	12.372	1.666	64131	0.0091-0.2064	-0.1235+0.0360	MATRIX
15	0.98380	0.45931	0.29494	10.492	1.803	50485	-0.2042-0.1167	-0.0953-0.0958	AND ITS
20	0.97944	0.64233	0.71023	8.817	1.598	38040	-0.2225+0.1447	-0.0230-0.1609	SPECTRAL
25	0.97956	0.56399	0.69361	7.376	1.142	24774	0.0303+0.2967	0.0339-0.1496	COMPONENTS
30	0.97406	0.42790	0.53748	6.172	0.690	14895	0.3120+0.1222	0.0584-0.0919	(Females)
35	0.97005	0.24703	0.39855	5.135	0.314	5837	0.2808-0.2475	0.0408-0.0353	
40	0.97051	0.07267	0.14006	4.255	0.080	1107	-0.1020-0.4038	0.0123-0.0075	
45	0.95600	0.00863	0.01766	3.528	0.009	117	-0.4518-0.1046	0.0015-0.0008	
50	0.93166	0.00049	0.00105	2.881	0.000	5	-0.3285+0.3881	0.0001-0.0000	
55+	0.77461			6.776					

Start of Age Interval	OBSERVED POPUL. (IN 100's)	CONTRIBUTIONS OF ROOTS (IN 100's) r_1	r_2, r_3	$r_4 \cdot r_{11}$	AGE-SP. BIRTH RATES	NET MATERNITY FUNCTION	COEFF. OF MATRIX EQUATION	PARAMETERS INTEGRAL	MATRIX	EXP. INCREASE x	$e^{(x+2\frac{1}{2})r}$	
0	549	529	15	5	0.0000	0.0000	0.0000	L(1) 1.17002	1.17070	0	1.0817	TABLE 10
5	464	439	28	-3	0.0000	0.0000	0.0012	L(2) 0.38828	0.39871	50	5.2002	
10	385	372	11	2	0.0005	0.0023	0.1315	0.79718	0.77530	55	6.0843	AGE ANALYSIS
15	280	315	-25	-10	0.0591	0.2608	0.4394	R(1) 0.03140	0.03152	60	7.1188	AND
20	238	265	-40	13	0.1424	0.6180	0.6045	R(2) -0.02405	-0.02744	65	8.3291	MISCELLANEOUS
25	217	222	-9	4	0.1391	0.5911	0.5199	0.22351	0.21916	70	9.7452	RESULTS
30	216	186	41	-11	0.1078	0.4487	0.3864	C(1)	3006	75	11.4020	(Females)
35	186	154	54	-22	0.0799	0.3241	0.2173	C(2)	7502	80	13.3406	
40	138	128	3	7	0.0281	0.1105	0.0620		2316	85	15.6087	
45	129	106	-63	86	0.0035	0.0135	0.0071	2P/Y 28.1115	28.6693	90	18.2625	
50	93	87	-67	74	0.0002	0.0008	0.0004	DELTA 3.9583		95	21.3674	
55+	263	204								100	25.0002	

TABLE 1 — DATA

AGE AT LAST BIRTHDAY	POPULATION BOTH SEXES	MALES Number	%	FEMALES Number	%	BIRTHS BY AGE OF MOTHER	DEATHS BOTH SEXES	MALES	FEMALES	AGE AT LAST BIRTHDAY
0	25150	12800	3.6	12350	3.5	0	1661	930	731	0
1-4	93100	47100	13.4	46000	13.2	0	757	372	385	1-4
5-9	103900	52350	14.9	51550	14.8	0	173	85	88	5-9
10-14	96000	48200	13.7	47800	13.7	34	106	63	43	10-14
15-19	69050	34550	9.8	34500	9.9	3754	125	50	75	15-19
20-24	46750	23350	6.6	23400	6.7	7559	119	39	80	20-24
25-29	45650	22700	6.4	22950	6.6	7064	130	49	81	25-29
30-34	38450	19400	5.5	19050	5.5	4960	134	53	81	30-34
35-39	42700	22050	6.3	20650	5.9	3606	169	77	92	35-39
40-44	32400	17000	4.8	15400	4.4	1071	190	106	84	40-44
45-49	28850	15250	4.3	13600	3.9	102	224	143	81	45-49
50-54	22700	12100	3.4	10600	3.0	6	329	215	114	50-54
55-59	18800	9500	2.7	9300	2.7	0	400	243	157	55-59
60-64	15150	7300	2.1	7850	2.2	0	510	299	211	60-64
65-69	10450	4400	1.2	6050	1.7	0	477	275	202	65-69
70-74	6750	2550	0.7	4200	1.2		468	204	264	70-74
75-79	3700	1250	0.4	2450	0.7		327	146	181	75-79
80-84	1500	400	0.1	1100	0.3	14291 M.	234	78	156	80-84
85+	400	100	0.0	300	0.1	13865 F.	176	30	146	85+
TOTAL	701450	352350		349100		28156	6709	3457	3252	TOTAL

TABLE 2 — MALE LIFE TABLE

x	nq_x	l_x	nd_x	nL_x	nm_x	na_x	T_x	r_x	$\dot{e}_x$	nM_x	x
0	0.069151	100000	6915	95424	0.072467	0.3382	5854177	0.0037	58.542	0.072656	0
1	0.030837	93085	2870	364305	0.007879	1.2008	5758753	0.0037	61.866	0.007898	1
5	0.007982	90215	720	449272	0.001603	2.5000	5394448	0.0187	59.796	0.001624	5
10	0.006507	89494	582	446000	0.001306	2.4726	4945176	0.0401	55.257	0.001307	10
15	0.007237	88912	643	442984	0.001453	2.5500	4499176	0.0710	50.603	0.001447	15
20	0.008347	88269	737	439563	0.001676	2.5842	4056192	0.0403	45.953	0.001670	20
25	0.010755	87532	941	435397	0.002162	2.5970	3616629	0.0164	41.318	0.002159	25
30	0.013571	86590	1175	430127	0.002732	2.5959	3181232	0.0002	36.739	0.002732	30
35	0.017354	85415	1482	423666	0.003499	2.6995	2751105	0.0093	32.209	0.003492	35
40	0.030915	83933	2595	413651	0.006273	2.6825	2327439	0.0307	27.730	0.006235	40
45	0.046168	81338	3755	398148	0.009432	2.7251	1913787	0.0235	23.529	0.009377	45
50	0.085743	77583	6652	372291	0.017868	2.6513	1515639	0.0298	19.536	0.017769	50
55	0.121038	70931	8585	334246	0.025686	2.6229	1143349	0.0233	16.119	0.025579	55
60	0.187952	62345	11718	283513	0.041331	2.5922	809103	0.0509	12.978	0.040959	60
65	0.272000	50627	13771	218835	0.062927	2.5090	525590	0.0509	10.382	0.062500	65
70	0.334094	36857	12314	152944	0.080511	2.4548	306755	0.0509	8.323	0.080000	70
75	0.452322	24543	11101	94210	0.117837	2.4322	153811	0.0509	6.267	0.116800	75
80	0.647364	13442	8702	44129	0.197187	2.3477	59601	0.0509	4.434	0.194999	80
85+	*1.000000	4740	4740	15472	0.306365	3.2641	15472	0.0509	3.264	0.300000	85+

TABLE 3 — FEMALE LIFE TABLE

x	nq_x	l_x	nd_x	nL_x	nm_x	na_x	T_x	r_x	$\dot{e}_x$	nM_x	x
0	0.056948	100000	5695	96388	0.059082	0.3658	6146903	0.0027	61.469	0.059190	0
1	0.032679	94305	3082	368745	0.008358	1.2499	6050515	0.0027	64.159	0.008370	1
5	0.008391	91223	765	454203	0.001685	2.5000	5681769	0.0169	62.284	0.001707	5
10	0.004509	90458	408	451317	0.000904	2.6148	5227566	0.0388	57.790	0.000900	10
15	0.010996	90050	990	448005	0.002210	2.7328	4776250	0.0693	53.040	0.002174	15
20	0.017005	89060	1514	441626	0.003429	2.5746	4328244	0.0376	48.599	0.003419	20
25	0.017509	87545	1533	433956	0.003532	2.5402	3886618	0.0169	44.395	0.003529	25
30	0.021046	86013	1810	425605	0.004253	2.5373	3452662	0.0064	40.141	0.004252	30
35	0.022055	84202	1857	416454	0.004459	2.5461	3027057	0.0166	35.950	0.004455	35
40	0.026970	82345	2221	406280	0.005466	2.5478	2610603	0.0365	31.703	0.005455	40
45	0.029531	80124	2366	395099	0.005989	2.6656	2204323	0.0305	27.511	0.005956	45
50	0.052755	77758	4102	379292	0.010815	2.6842	1809224	0.0271	23.267	0.010755	50
55	0.081379	73656	5994	354226	0.016921	2.6552	1429932	0.0123	19.414	0.016882	55
60	0.126637	67662	8569	317554	0.026983	2.5776	1075706	0.0295	15.898	0.026879	60
65	0.155445	59094	9186	273558	0.033579	2.6148	758152	0.0295	12.830	0.033388	65
70	0.273137	49908	13632	215910	0.063136	2.5331	484594	0.0295	9.710	0.062857	70
75	0.312873	36276	11350	152904	0.074228	2.4910	268684	0.0295	7.407	0.073878	75
80	0.527300	24926	13144	91863	0.143079	2.5069	115779	0.0295	4.645	0.141818	80
85+	*1.000000	11783	11783	23917	0.492651	2.0298	23917	0.0295	2.030	0.486667	85+

TABLE 4 — OBSERVED AND PROJECTED VITAL RATES

	OBSERVED POPULATION BOTH SEXES	MALES	FEMALES	PROJECTED POPULATION 1968 MALES	FEMALES	1973 MALES	FEMALES	1978 MALES	FEMALES	STABLE POPULATION MALES	FEMALES
RATES PER THOUSAND											
Birth	40.14	40.56	39.72	41.78	40.96	44.04	43.20	44.56	43.72	44.50	43.84
Death	9.56	9.81	9.32	10.02	9.34	10.10	9.37	10.06	9.28	9.22	8.56
Increase	30.58	30.75	30.40	31.76	31.62	33.94	33.83	34.50	34.44		35.2843
PERCENTAGE											
under 15	45.36	45.54	45.17	44.42	43.99	44.83	44.39	46.04	45.69	46.87	46.71
15-64	51.39	51.99	50.79	52.91	52.02	52.49	51.84	51.35	50.86	51.29	50.75
65 and over	3.25	2.47	4.04	2.67	3.99	2.68	3.77	2.61	3.44	1.84	2.54
DEP. RATIO X 100	94.58	92.33	96.90	88.99	92.23	90.51	92.88	94.74	96.60	94.97	97.05

Excluding Rodrigues

TABLE 1 — DATA

AGE AT LAST BIRTHDAY	POPULATION BOTH SEXES	MALES Number	%	FEMALES Number	%	BIRTHS BY AGE OF MOTHER	DEATHS BOTH SEXES	MALES	FEMALES	AGE AT LAST BIRTHDAY
0	26300	13250	3.7	13050	3.6	0	1561	880	681	0
1-4	94900	48100	13.3	46800	13.0	0	590	273	317	1-4
5-9	106000	53550	14.8	52450	14.6	0	154	82	72	5-9
10-14	99800	50100	13.8	49700	13.8	33	88	45	43	10-14
15-19	72600	36300	10.0	36300	10.1	3307	81	46	35	15-19
20-24	49650	24850	6.8	24800	6.9	7713	101	31	70	20-24
25-29	45600	22600	6.2	23000	6.4	6972	110	36	74	25-29
30-34	38800	19600	5.4	19200	5.3	4785	125	51	74	30-34
35-39	42450	21800	6.0	20650	5.7	3438	181	91	90	35-39
40-44	34600	18150	5.0	16450	4.6	1035	247	142	105	40-44
45-49	28400	15000	4.1	13400	3.7	98	228	146	82	45-49
50-54	24850	13200	3.6	11650	3.2	10	315	207	108	50-54
55-59	18900	9600	2.6	9300	2.6	0	369	242	127	55-59
60-64	15400	7450	2.1	7950	2.2	0	457	279	178	60-64
65-69	10950	4750	1.3	6200	1.7	0	426	221	205	65-69
70-74	6900	2600	0.7	4300	1.2		462	227	235	70-74
75-79	3950	1350	0.4	2600	0.7		335	145	190	75-79
80-84	1650	450	0.1	1200	0.3	13883 M.	209	71	138	80-84
85+	400	100	0.0	300	0.1	13508 F.	145	34	111	85+
TOTAL	722100	362800		359300		27391	6184	3249	2935	TOTAL

TABLE 2 — MALE LIFE TABLE

x	$_nq_x$	l_x	$_nd_x$	$_nL_x$	$_nm_x$	$_na_x$	T_x	r_x	$\mathring{e}_x$	$_nM_x$	x
0	0.063250	100000	6325	95656	0.066123	0.3132	6013219	0.0060	60.132	0.066415	0
1	0.022242	93675	2084	368794	0.005650	1.1655	5917563	0.0060	63.171	0.005676	1
5	0.007554	91591	692	456227	0.001517	2.5000	5548769	0.0179	60.582	0.001531	5
10	0.004471	90900	406	453457	0.000896	2.4395	5092542	0.0377	56.024	0.000898	10
15	0.006342	90493	574	451063	0.001272	2.5560	4639085	0.0690	51.264	0.001267	15
20	0.006234	89919	561	448224	0.001251	2.5513	4188022	0.0461	46.575	0.001247	20
25	0.007966	89359	712	445136	0.001599	2.6715	3739798	0.0220	41.852	0.001593	25
30	0.012935	88647	1147	440597	0.002603	2.6996	3294662	0.3009	37.166	0.002602	30
35	0.020693	87500	1811	433424	0.004178	2.7484	2854066	0.0030	32.618	0.004174	35
40	0.038577	85690	3306	420626	0.007859	2.6337	2420642	0.0300	28.249	0.007824	40
45	0.047736	82384	3933	402642	0.009767	2.6410	2000016	0.0212	24.277	0.009733	45
50	0.076051	78451	5966	378326	0.015770	2.6652	1597374	0.0283	20.361	0.015682	50
55	0.119526	72485	8664	341817	0.025346	2.6214	1219048	0.0313	16.818	0.025208	55
60	0.172585	63821	11015	292085	0.037710	2.5469	877231	0.0568	13.745	0.037450	60
65	0.211009	52806	11143	237016	0.047012	2.5754	585146	0.0568	11.081	0.046526	65
70	0.361107	41664	15045	170721	0.088127	2.5010	348130	0.0568	8.356	0.087308	70
75	0.421321	26619	11215	103731	0.108117	2.3818	177409	0.0568	6.665	0.107407	75
80	0.563770	15404	8684	54372	0.159718	2.3922	73678	0.0568	4.783	0.157778	80
85+	*1.000000	6720	6720	19307	0.348045	2.8732	19307	0.0568	2.873	0.340000	85+

TABLE 3 — FEMALE LIFE TABLE

x	$_nq_x$	l_x	$_nd_x$	$_nL_x$	$_nm_x$	$_na_x$	T_x	r_x	$\mathring{e}_x$	$_nM_x$	x
0	0.050248	100000	5025	96773	0.051923	0.3579	6372218	0.0072	63.722	0.052184	0
1	0.026490	94975	2516	372943	0.006746	1.2345	6275444	0.0072	66.075	0.006774	1
5	0.006759	92459	625	460735	0.001356	2.5000	5902501	0.0161	63.839	0.001373	5
10	0.004303	91834	395	458148	0.000862	2.4091	5441767	0.0358	59.256	0.000865	10
15	0.004950	91439	453	456250	0.000992	2.9094	4983618	0.0681	54.502	0.000964	15
20	0.014120	90987	1285	451926	0.002843	2.6591	4527368	0.0431	49.759	0.002823	20
25	0.015985	89702	1434	445009	0.003222	2.5583	4075442	0.0223	45.433	0.003217	25
30	0.019099	88268	1686	437217	0.003856	2.5539	3630433	0.0070	41.130	0.003854	30
35	0.021594	86582	1870	428442	0.004364	2.6094	3193217	0.0107	36.881	0.004358	35
40	0.031492	84713	2668	417021	0.006397	2.5477	2764775	0.0374	32.637	0.006383	40
45	0.030229	82045	2480	404223	0.006135	2.5804	2347754	0.0276	28.616	0.006119	45
50	0.045564	79565	3625	389295	0.009313	2.6475	1943531	0.0271	24.427	0.009270	50
55	0.066463	75939	5047	367904	0.013719	2.6635	1554236	0.0236	20.467	0.013656	55
60	0.107027	70892	7587	336476	0.022549	2.6296	1186332	0.0402	16.734	0.022390	60
65	0.154309	63305	9769	293224	0.033314	2.6148	849856	0.0402	13.425	0.033065	65
70	0.242250	53536	12969	235847	0.054990	2.5454	556632	0.0402	10.397	0.054651	70
75	0.310422	40567	12593	171289	0.073519	2.4949	320784	0.0402	7.907	0.073077	75
80	0.452564	27974	12660	108788	0.116374	2.5448	149495	0.0402	5.344	0.115001	80
85+	*1.000000	15314	15314	40707	0.376200	2.6582	40707	0.0402	2.658	0.370000	85+

TABLE 4 — OBSERVED AND PROJECTED VITAL RATES

	OBSERVED POPULATION BOTH SEXES	MALES	FEMALES	PROJECTED POPULATION 1969 MALES	FEMALES	1974 MALES	FEMALES	1979 MALES	FEMALES	STABLE POPULATION MALES	FEMALES
RATES PER THOUSAND											
Birth	37.93	38.27	37.60	40.00	39.27	42.68	41.88	43.27	42.44	42.77	41.99
Death	8.56	8.96	8.17	9.12	8.29	9.27	8.40	9.24	8.36	8.49	7.70
Increase	29.37	29.31	29.43	30.87	30.97	33.41	33.48	34.03	34.08	34.2828	
PERCENTAGE											
under 15	45.28	45.48	45.09	43.84	43.33	44.07	43.59	45.11	44.70	45.98	45.61
15-64	51.41	51.97	50.85	53.34	52.57	53.07	52.50	51.98	51.55	51.92	51.49
65 and over	3.30	2.55	4.06	2.82	4.10	2.86	3.91	2.92	3.75	2.10	2.90
DEP. RATIO X 100	94.51	92.42	96.66	87.48	90.23	88.43	90.49	92.39	94.00	92.59	94.23

TABLE 1 — DATA

AGE AT LAST BIRTHDAY	POPULATION BOTH SEXES	MALES Number	%	FEMALES Number	%	BIRTHS BY AGE OF MOTHER	DEATHS BOTH SEXES	MALES	FEMALES	AGE AT LAST BIRTHDAY
0	25400	12850	3.5	12550	3.4	0	1685	943	742	0
1-4	97700	49400	13.3	48300	13.1	0	702	353	349	1-4
5-9	109000	55200	14.8	53800	14.6	0	131	66	65	5-9
10-14	100550	50500	13.6	50050	13.6	41	78	42	36	10-14
15-19	77050	38550	10.4	38500	10.4	3245	98	45	53	15-19
20-24	52850	26450	7.1	26400	7.2	7682	106	39	67	20-24
25-29	46500	23050	6.2	23450	6.4	6400	117	46	71	25-29
30-34	39250	19700	5.3	19550	5.3	4557	91	30	61	30-34
35-39	41850	21350	5.7	20500	5.6	3171	142	69	73	35-39
40-44	37150	19400	5.2	17750	4.8	1030	194	125	69	40-44
45-49	27950	14650	3.9	13300	3.6	93	229	151	78	45-49
50-54	26100	13900	3.7	12200	3.3	4	323	215	108	50-54
55-59	18550	9450	2.5	9100	2.5	0	362	245	117	55-59
60-64	16100	7850	2.1	8250	2.2	0	452	273	179	60-64
65-69	11200	4950	1.3	6250	1.7	0	466	264	202	65-69
70-74	7550	2850	0.8	4700	1.3		414	214	200	70-74
75-79	4000	1350	0.4	2650	0.7		342	149	193	75-79
80-84	1850	550	0.1	1300	0.4	13291 M.	245	79	166	80-84
85+	450	100	0.0	350	0.1	12932 F.	160	40	120	85+
TOTAL	741050	372100		368950		26223	6337	3388	2949	TOTAL

TABLE 2 — MALE LIFE TABLE

x	$_nq_x$	l_x	$_nd_x$	$_nL_x$	$_nm_x$	$_na_x$	T_x	r_x	$\mathring{e}_x$	$_nM_x$	x
0	0.069930	100000	6993	95291	0.073385	0.3266	5982628	0.0000	59.826	0.073385	0
1	0.028019	93007	2606	364688	0.007146	1.1835	5887337	0.0000	63.300	0.007146	1
5	0.005862	90401	530	450681	0.001176	2.5000	5522648	0.0184	61.091	0.001196	5
10	0.004150	89871	373	448422	0.000832	2.4971	5071968	0.0349	56.436	0.000832	10
15	0.005863	89498	525	446238	0.001176	2.6129	4623546	0.0635	51.661	0.001167	15
20	0.007389	88973	657	443297	0.001483	2.6116	4177307	0.0499	46.950	0.001474	20
25	0.009930	88316	877	439389	0.001996	2.5016	3734010	0.0277	42.280	0.001996	25
30	0.007594	87439	664	435643	0.001524	2.6617	3294621	0.0057	37.679	0.001523	30
35	0.016046	86775	1392	430825	0.003232	2.8091	2858978	0.0000	32.947	0.003232	35
40	0.031970	85383	2730	420669	0.006489	2.7124	2428154	0.0311	28.438	0.006443	40
45	0.050523	82653	4176	403483	0.010350	2.6576	2007485	0.0228	24.288	0.010307	45
50	0.075041	78477	5889	378647	0.015553	2.6671	1604001	0.0272	20.439	0.015468	50
55	0.122612	72588	8900	341607	0.026054	2.6030	1225354	0.0317	16.881	0.025926	55
60	0.161573	63688	10290	293502	0.035060	2.5765	883747	0.0533	13.876	0.034777	60
65	0.237476	53398	12681	235840	0.053768	2.5436	590245	0.0533	11.054	0.053333	65
70	0.317945	40717	12946	171078	0.075672	2.4890	354405	0.0533	8.704	0.075088	70
75	0.432014	27771	11998	107895	0.111196	2.4194	183327	0.0533	6.601	0.110370	75
80	0.526473	15774	8304	57164	0.145274	2.3864	75432	0.0533	4.782	0.143636	80
85+	*1.000000	7469	7469	18268	0.408881	2.4457	18268	0.0533	2.446	0.400000	85+

TABLE 3 — FEMALE LIFE TABLE

x	$_nq_x$	l_x	$_nd_x$	$_nL_x$	$_nm_x$	$_na_x$	T_x	r_x	$\mathring{e}_x$	$_nM_x$	x
0	0.056939	100000	5694	96305	0.059124	0.3511	6424805	0.0000	64.248	0.059124	0
1	0.028334	94306	2672	369802	0.007226	1.2223	6328500	0.0000	67.106	0.007226	1
5	0.005928	91634	543	456812	0.001189	2.5000	5958698	0.0171	65.027	0.001208	5
10	0.003597	91091	328	454654	0.000721	2.5574	5501886	0.0325	60.400	0.000719	10
15	0.006980	90763	634	452402	0.001400	2.7684	5047232	0.0625	55.609	0.001377	15
20	0.012693	90130	1144	447935	0.002554	2.6284	4594830	0.0472	50.980	0.002538	20
25	0.015042	88986	1339	441626	0.003031	2.5332	4146895	0.0271	46.602	0.003028	25
30	0.015487	87647	1357	434880	0.003121	2.5284	3705269	0.0102	42.275	0.003120	30
35	0.017655	86290	1523	427698	0.003562	2.5387	3270389	0.0062	37.900	0.003561	35
40	0.019350	84766	1640	419917	0.003906	2.6136	2842691	0.0390	33.536	0.003887	40
45	0.029084	83126	2418	409977	0.005897	2.6616	2422774	0.0314	29.146	0.005865	45
50	0.043558	80708	3516	395258	0.008894	2.6437	2012797	0.0289	24.939	0.008852	50
55	0.062726	77193	4842	374693	0.012923	2.6721	1617539	0.0252	20.955	0.012857	55
60	0.103877	72351	7516	343990	0.021848	2.6363	1242846	0.0382	17.178	0.021697	60
65	0.150532	64835	9760	300438	0.032485	2.5677	898856	0.0382	13.864	0.032320	65
70	0.194057	55075	10688	249505	0.042836	2.5792	598418	0.0382	10.865	0.042553	70
75	0.311428	44388	13824	188267	0.073425	2.5642	348914	0.0382	7.861	0.072830	75
80	0.489134	30564	14950	115819	0.129081	2.5250	160647	0.0382	5.256	0.127692	80
85+	*1.000000	15614	15614	44828	0.348314	2.8710	44828	0.0382	2.871	0.342857	85+

TABLE 4 — OBSERVED AND PROJECTED VITAL RATES

	OBSERVED POPULATION BOTH SEXES	MALES	FEMALES	PROJECTED POPULATION 1970 MALES	FEMALES	1975 MALES	FEMALES	1980 MALES	FEMALES	STABLE POPULATION MALES	FEMALES
RATES PER THOUSAND											
Birth	35.39	35.72	35.05	38.05	37.26	40.70	39.78	41.52	40.52	40.28	39.22
Death	8.55	9.11	7.99	9.18	8.04	9.40	8.24	9.45	8.30	9.13	8.07
Increase	26.83	26.61	27.06	28.87	29.22	31.30	31.54	32.06	32.22		31.1491
PERCENTAGE											
under 15	44.89	45.14	44.64	43.02	42.43	42.53	42.03	43.09	42.63	43.77	43.20
15-64	51.73	52.23	51.23	54.03	53.32	54.54	53.92	53.85	53.39	53.74	53.22
65 and over	3.38	2.63	4.13	2.94	4.26	2.93	4.05	3.06	3.99	2.49	3.59
DEP. RATIO X 100	93.31	91.46	95.21	85.07	87.55	83.35	85.45	85.69	87.31	86.09	87.91

TABLE 5 — POPULATION PROJECTED WITH FIXED AGE—SPECIFIC BIRTH AND DEATH RATES (IN 1000's)

AGE AT LAST BIRTHDAY	1970 BOTH SEXES	MALES	FEMALES	1975 BOTH SEXES	MALES	FEMALES	1980 BOTH SEXES	MALES	FEMALES	AGE AT LAST BIRTHDAY
0-4	135	68	67	167	84	83	203	102	101	0-4
5-9	121	61	60	133	67	66	163	82	81	5-9
10-14	109	55	54	120	61	59	131	66	65	10-14
15-19	100	50	50	108	55	53	119	60	59	15-19
20-24	76	38	38	99	50	49	107	54	53	20-24
25-29	52	26	26	76	38	38	98	49	49	25-29
30-34	46	23	23	52	26	26	75	38	37	30-34
35-39	38	19	19	46	23	23	51	26	25	35-39
40-44	41	21	20	38	19	19	44	22	22	40-44
45-49	36	19	17	40	20	20	36	18	18	45-49
50-54	27	14	13	34	17	17	38	19	19	50-54
55-59	25	13	12	24	12	12	32	16	16	55-59
60-64	16	8	8	22	11	11	22	11	11	60-64
65-69	13	6	7	14	7	7	18	9	9	65-69
70-74	9	4	5	11	5	6	11	5	6	70-74
75-79	6	2	4	6	2	4	8	3	5	75-79
80-84	3	1	2	3	1	2	3	1	2	80-84
85+	1	0	1	1	0	1	1	0	1	85+
TOTAL	854	428	426	994	498	496	1160	581	579	TOTAL

TABLE 6 — STANDARDIZED RATES

STANDARD COUNTRIES:

STANDARDIZED RATES PER THOUSAND	ENGLAND AND WALES 1961 BOTH SEXES	MALES	FEMALES	UNITED STATES 1960 BOTH SEXES	MALES	FEMALES	MEXICO 1960 BOTH SEXES	MALES	FEMALES
Birth	35.36	39.55*	33.80	36.00	36.26*	34.98	40.03	36.59*	39.38
Death	16.63	22.47*	16.18	14.24	17.70*	12.79	8.87	9.57*	7.83
Increase	18.73	17.08*	17.62	21.77	18.56*	22.19	31.17	27.02*	31.56

TABLE 7 — MOMENTS AND CUMULANTS

	OBSERVED POP. MALES	FEMALES	STATIONARY POP. MALES	FEMALES	STABLE POP. MALES	FEMALES	OBSERVED BIRTHS	NET MATERNITY FUNCTION	BIRTHS IN STABLE POP.
μ	22.91857	23.49485	34.80340	37.06445	22.41222	23.15821	27.51640	28.64791	27.26640
σ^2	343.7780	375.7219	459.9971	518.6176	321.4291	354.6821	44.75505	44.12615	40.26492
κ_3	5467.353	6834.502	2506.688	2554.266	5248.452	6337.354	138.0212	108.5170	136.3877
κ_4	-18706.	6377.	-193404.	-269899.	15081.	25471.	-1152.358	-1175.517	-598.045
β_1	0.735733	0.880672	0.064556	0.046772	0.829482	0.900115	0.212503	0.137059	0.284951
β_2	2.841724	3.045176	2.085980	1.996526	3.145972	3.202469	2.424688	2.396278	2.631124
κ	-0.271528	-0.330567	-0.025336	-0.017328	-0.353241	-0.373058	-0.096487	-0.067195	-0.146684

TABLE 8 — RATES FROM AGE DISTRIBUTIONS AND VITAL STATISTICS (Females)

VITAL STATISTICS

		THOMPSON AGE RANGE	NRR	1000r	INTERVAL	BOURGEOIS-PICHAT AGE RANGE	NRR	1000b	1000d	1000r	COALE
GRR	2.718										
NRR	2.388	0-4	2.34	31.21	27.30	5-29	3.31	47.62	3.26	44.36	IBR
TFR	5.511	5-9	2.51	34.62	27.25	30-54	1.85	27.97	5.13	22.85	IDR
GENERATION	27.947	10-14	2.61	34.31	27.19	55-79	1.63	19.20	1.11	18.09	K1
SEX RATIO	102.776	15-19	2.27	30.23	27.09	*45-74	1.83	25.65	3.28	22.37	K2

TABLE 9 — LESLIE MATRIX AND ITS SPECTRAL COMPONENTS (Females)

Start of Age Interval	ORIGINAL MATRIX SUB-DIAGONAL	ALTERNATIVE FIRST ROWS Projection	Integral	FIRST STABLE MATRIX % IN STABLE POPULATION	FISHER VALUES	REPRODUCTIVE VALUES	SECOND STABLE MATRIX Z2 FIRST COLUMN	FIRST ROW
0	0.98006	0.00000	0.00000	16.955	1.159	70508	0.1404+0.0937	0.1404+0.0937
5	0.99528	0.00094	0.00000	14.212	1.382	74369	0.1616-0.0893	-0.0171+0.1533
10	0.99505	0.09733	0.00204	12.098	1.623	81220	-0.0056-0.2051	-0.1297+0.0496
15	0.99013	0.42800	0.20943	10.296	1.793	69047	-0.2053-0.3992	-0.1070-0.0924
20	0.98592	0.64369	0.72304	8.719	1.617	42685	-0.2016+0.1512	-0.0309-0.1649
25	0.98473	0.57748	0.67815	7.353	1.161	27223	0.0459+0.2736	0.0285-0.1549
30	0.98349	0.44274	0.57919	6.193	0.699	13662	0.2904+0.0934	0.0548-0.0967
35	0.98181	0.24326	0.38435	5.209	0.309	6338	0.2376-0.2361	0.0379-0.0383
40	0.97633	0.07454	0.14419	4.374	0.081	1439	-0.1103-0.3502	0.0122-0.0086
45	0.96410	0.00840	0.01737	3.653	0.009	115	-0.3943-0.0686	0.0014-0.0008
50	0.94797	0.00038	0.00081	3.012	0.000	5	-0.2606+0.3431	0.0001-0.0000
55+	0.80895			7.926				

TABLE 10 — AGE ANALYSIS AND MISCELLANEOUS RESULTS (Females)

Start of Age Interval	OBSERVED POPUL. (IN 100's)	CONTRIBUTIONS OF ROOTS (IN 100's) r_1	r_2, r_3	$r_4 \cdot r_{11}$	AGE-SP. BIRTH RATES	NET MATERNITY FUNCTION	COEFF. OF MATRIX EQUATION	PARAMETERS INTEGRAL	MATRIX	EXP. INCREASE x	$e^{(x+2\frac{1}{2})r}$
0	609	616	-21	13	0.0000	0.0000	0.0000	L(1) 1.16853	1.16918	0	1.0810
5	538	517	29	-8	0.0000	0.0000	0.0009	L(2) 0.40389	0.41146	50	5.1311
10	501	440	56	5	0.0004	0.0018	0.0949	0.81988	0.79554	55	5.9959
15	385	374	21	-10	0.0416	0.1880	0.4154	R(1) 0.03115	0.03126	60	7.0064
20	264	317	-47	-6	0.1435	0.6428	0.6186	R(2) -0.01799	-0.02204	65	8.1871
25	235	267	-73	40	0.1346	0.5944	0.5471	0.22262	0.21869	70	9.5669
30	196	225	-17	-13	0.1150	0.4999	0.4131	C(1)	3635	75	11.1792
35	205	189	71	-56	0.0763	0.3263	0.2232	C(2)	1520	80	13.0632
40	178	159	92	-73	0.0286	0.1202	0.0672		13575	85	15.2648
45	133	133	7	-6	0.0034	0.0141	0.0074	2P/Y 28.2244	28.7304	90	17.8373
50	122	109	-101	114	0.0002	0.0006	0.0003	DELTA 3.9748		95	20.8434
55+	326	288								100	24.3561

TABLE 1 — DATA

AGE AT LAST BIRTHDAY	POPULATION BOTH SEXES	MALES Number	%	FEMALES Number	%	BIRTHS BY AGE OF MOTHER	DEATHS BOTH SEXES	MALES	FEMALES	AGE AT LAST BIRTHDAY
0	10602	5326	3.2	5276	3.0	0	1344	728	616	0
1-4	48479	24304	14.4	24175	13.6	0	519	256	263	1-4
5-9	55667	28066	16.7	27601	15.6	0	69	43	26	5-9
10-14	40971	20697	12.3	20274	11.4	4	30	19	11	10-14
15-19	31196	15514	9.2	15682	8.8	1089	46	25	21	15-19
20-24	25278	11318	6.7	13960	7.9	3809	66	35	31	20-24
25-29	24017	11614	6.9	12403	7.0	4055	73	48	25	25-29
30-34	21020	10417	6.2	10603	6.0	3039	97	60	37	30-34
35-39	19913	9870	5.9	10043	5.7	2254	111	64	47	35-39
40-44	16097	7921	4.7	8176	4.6	866	143	88	55	40-44
45-49	14033	6938	4.1	7095	4.0	85	131	86	45	45-49
50-54	11490	5611	3.3	5879	3.3	4	169	108	61	50-54
55-59	8884	4105	2.4	4779	2.7	0	198	131	67	55-59
60-64	6390	2772	1.6	3618	2.0	0	208	128	80	60-64
65-69	4999	1931	1.1	3068	1.7	0	198	114	84	65-69
70-74	3389	1209	0.7	2180	1.2		199	102	97	70-74
75-79	2084	608	0.4	1476	0.8		174	71	103	75-79
80-84	1087	246	0.1	841	0.5	7697 M.	138	41	97	80-84
85+	415	68	0.0	347	0.2	7508 F.	88	17	71	85+
TOTAL	346011	168535		177476		15205	4001	2164	1837	TOTAL

TABLE 2 — MALE LIFE TABLE

x	$_nq_x$	l_x	$_nd_x$	$_nL_x$	$_nm_x$	$_na_x$	T_x	r_x	$\overset{\circ}{e}_x$	$_nM_x$	x
0	0.124721	100000	12472	91245	0.136688	0.2981	5220976	0.0000	52.210	0.136688	0
1	0.040904	87528	3580	339898	0.010533	1.1474	5129731	0.0000	58.607	0.010533	1
5	0.007368	83948	618	418192	0.001479	2.5000	4789833	0.0322	57.057	0.001532	5
10	0.004589	83329	382	415702	0.000920	2.5318	4371641	0.0581	52.462	0.000918	10
15	0.008160	82947	677	413226	0.001638	2.7727	3955939	0.0586	47.692	0.001611	15
20	0.015418	82270	1268	408383	0.003106	2.6612	3542713	0.0260	43.062	0.003092	20
25	0.020475	81002	1658	401067	0.004135	2.6240	3134329	0.0040	38.695	0.004133	25
30	0.028428	79343	2256	391245	0.005765	2.5749	2733262	0.0108	34.449	0.005760	30
35	0.032040	77087	2470	379636	0.006506	2.6512	2342017	0.0200	30.381	0.006484	35
40	0.054251	74618	4048	363340	0.011141	2.5921	1962381	0.0250	26.299	0.011110	40
45	0.060349	70569	4259	342637	0.012429	2.6026	1599041	0.0209	22.659	0.012396	45
50	0.092664	66311	6145	317174	0.019373	2.6598	1256404	0.0321	18.947	0.019248	50
55	0.149131	60166	8973	279339	0.032121	2.6047	939230	0.0382	15.611	0.031912	55
60	0.208137	51193	10655	229641	0.046400	2.5293	659891	0.0393	12.890	0.046176	60
65	0.258256	40538	10469	176485	0.059321	2.4969	430250	0.0393	10.613	0.059037	65
70	0.349118	30069	10498	123754	0.084827	2.4669	253765	0.0393	8.439	0.084367	70
75	0.449779	19571	8803	74967	0.117422	2.3997	130012	0.0393	6.643	0.116776	75
80	0.581284	10769	6260	37299	0.167821	2.3571	55045	0.0393	5.112	0.166666	80
85+	*1.000000	4509	4509	17745	0.254093	3.9356	17745	0.0393	3.936	0.250000	85+

TABLE 3 — FEMALE LIFE TABLE

x	$_nq_x$	l_x	$_nd_x$	$_nL_x$	$_nm_x$	$_na_x$	T_x	r_x	$\overset{\circ}{e}_x$	$_nM_x$	x
0	0.108158	100000	10816	92637	0.116755	0.3192	6001393	0.0000	60.014	0.116755	0
1	0.042218	89184	3765	346094	0.010879	1.1733	5908756	0.0000	66.253	0.010879	1
5	0.004400	85419	376	426155	0.000882	2.5000	5562662	0.0341	65.122	0.000942	5
10	0.002736	85043	233	424675	0.000548	2.6751	5136507	0.0557	60.399	0.000543	10
15	0.006738	84810	571	422769	0.001352	2.7548	4711832	0.0360	55.557	0.001339	15
20	0.011058	84239	932	418922	0.002224	2.5597	4289063	0.0215	50.915	0.002221	20
25	0.010063	83307	838	414546	0.002022	2.6242	3870141	0.0251	46.456	0.002016	25
30	0.017355	82469	1431	408985	0.003499	2.6518	3455595	0.0177	41.902	0.003490	30
35	0.023212	81038	1881	400736	0.004694	2.6320	3046610	0.0211	37.595	0.004680	35
40	0.033138	79157	2623	389335	0.006737	2.5410	2645874	0.0286	33.426	0.006727	40
45	0.031328	76534	2398	376914	0.006361	2.5997	2256540	0.0256	29.484	0.006342	45
50	0.050860	74136	3771	361755	0.010423	2.6328	1879626	0.0294	25.354	0.010376	50
55	0.068219	70366	4800	340481	0.014099	2.6361	1517871	0.0335	21.571	0.014020	55
60	0.105347	65565	6907	311136	0.022200	2.5835	1177390	0.0312	17.957	0.022112	60
65	0.129021	58658	7568	275082	0.027512	2.5940	866254	0.0312	14.768	0.027379	65
70	0.202012	51090	10321	230614	0.044754	2.5936	591172	0.0312	11.571	0.044495	70
75	0.299368	40769	12205	173876	0.070194	2.5444	360558	0.0312	8.844	0.069783	75
80	0.452473	28564	12925	111225	0.116201	2.5554	186681	0.0312	6.535	0.115339	80
85+	*1.000000	15640	15640	75456	0.207269	4.8246	75456	0.0312	4.825	0.204611	85+

TABLE 4 — OBSERVED AND PROJECTED VITAL RATES

	OBSERVED POPULATION BOTH SEXES	MALES	FEMALES	PROJECTED POPULATION 1966 MALES	FEMALES	1971 MALES	FEMALES	1976 MALES	FEMALES	STABLE POPULATION MALES	FEMALES
RATES PER THOUSAND											
Birth	43.94	45.67	42.30	44.10	40.95	44.58	41.49	46.31	43.20	46.39	43.87
Death	11.56	12.84	10.35	12.91	10.51	12.77	10.37	12.78	10.39	13.31	10.80
Increase	32.38	32.83	31.95	31.19	30.44	31.81	31.12	33.53	32.81		33.0756
PERCENTAGE											
under 15	45.00	46.51	43.57	46.74	44.11	45.18	42.88	45.58	43.34	46.33	44.66
15-64	51.54	51.08	51.97	50.90	51.57	52.45	52.89	52.02	52.50	51.84	52.04
65 and over	3.46	2.41	4.46	2.36	4.32	2.36	4.24	2.39	4.16	1.83	3.30
DEP. RATIO X 100	94.04	95.79	92.41	96.46	93.92	90.64	89.09	92.22	90.48	92.90	92.16

TABLE 5 — POPULATION PROJECTED WITH FIXED AGE—SPECIFIC BIRTH AND DEATH RATES (IN 1000's)

AGE AT LAST BIRTHDAY	1966 BOTH SEXES	MALES	FEMALES	1971 BOTH SEXES	MALES	FEMALES	1976 BOTH SEXES	MALES	FEMALES	AGE AT LAST BIRTHDAY
0-4	70	35	35	81	41	40	97	49	48	0-4
5-9	58	29	29	68	34	34	78	39	39	5-9
10-14	56	28	28	58	29	29	68	34	34	10-14
15-19	41	21	20	55	28	27	56	28	28	15-19
20-24	31	15	16	40	20	20	54	27	27	20-24
25-29	25	11	14	30	15	15	40	20	20	25-29
30-34	23	11	12	25	11	14	30	15	15	30-34
35-39	20	10	10	23	11	12	24	11	13	35-39
40-44	19	9	10	20	10	10	23	11	12	40-44
45-49	15	7	8	18	9	9	19	9	10	45-49
50-54	13	6	7	15	7	8	17	8	9	50-54
55-59	11	5	6	12	6	6	13	6	7	55-59
60-64	7	3	4	9	4	5	11	5	6	60-64
65-69	5	2	3	7	3	4	7	3	4	65-69
70-74	4	1	3	4	1	3	5	2	3	70-74
75-79	3	1	2	3	1	2	3	1	2	75-79
80-84	1	0	1	1	0	1	1	0	1	80-84
85+	1	0	1	1	0	1	1	0	1	85+
TOTAL	403	194	209	470	230	240	547	268	279	TOTAL

TABLE 6 — STANDARDIZED RATES

STANDARD COUNTRIES:

STANDARDIZED RATES PER THOUSAND	ENGLAND AND WALES 1961 BOTH SEXES	MALES	FEMALES	UNITED STATES 1960 BOTH SEXES	MALES	FEMALES	MEXICO 1960 BOTH SEXES	MALES	FEMALES
Birth	41.86	47.88*	40.07	42.55	44.58*	41.40	45.02	44.68*	44.35
Death	18.52	33.92*	16.08	16.61	26.63*	13.56	12.08	13.90*	9.98
Increase	23.34	13.96*	23.99	25.94	17.95*	27.84	32.95	30.78*	34.37

TABLE 7 — MOMENTS AND CUMULANTS

	OBSERVED POP. MALES	FEMALES	STATIONARY POP. MALES	FEMALES	STABLE POP. MALES	FEMALES	OBSERVED BIRTHS	NET MATERNITY FUNCTION	BIRTHS IN STABLE POP.
μ	22.31238	24.00187	33.30936	37.18144	21.02170	22.42315	28.98175	30.00581	28.46196
σ^2	332.8798	388.0286	440.7779	530.5063	291.9878	343.3002	44.24131	46.05790	42.89058
κ_3	5335.460	6932.702	2984.750	2995.539	4893.673	6434.042	101.2793	72.7730	115.7055
κ_4	-6724.	3122.	-161407.	-272900.	31952.	48344.	-1274.096	-1551.209	-1003.614
β_1	0.771759	0.822648	0.104029	0.060101	0.962001	1.023165	0.118456	0.054204	0.169677
β_2	2.939317	3.020737	2.169225	2.030334	3.374772	3.410201	2.349052	2.268756	2.454440
κ	-0.295828	-0.319543	-0.042094	-0.022588	-0.431031	-0.442072	-0.056552	-0.025972	-0.084725

TABLE 8 — RATES FROM AGE DISTRIBUTIONS AND VITAL STATISTICS (Females)

VITAL STATISTICS

		THOMPSON AGE RANGE	NRR	1000r	INTERVAL	BOURGEOIS-PICHAT AGE RANGE	NRR	1000b	1000d	1000r	COALE	
GRR	3.207										IBR	51.20
NRR	2.629	0-4	2.33	30.92	27.30	5-29	2.80	44.87	6.79	38.08	IDR	10.08
TFR	6.495	5-9	2.51	34.56	27.20	30-54	1.93	33.53	9.12	24.41	IRI	41.12
GENERATION	29.225	10-14	2.07	26.31	27.11	55-79	1.94	31.83	7.28	24.55	K1	45.24
SEX RATIO	102.517	15-19	1.81	16.08	26.98	*35-59	2.15	40.34	12.03	28.31	K2	0.51

TABLE 9 — LESLIE MATRIX AND ITS SPECTRAL COMPONENTS (Females)

Start of Age Interval	ORIGINAL MATRIX SUB-DIAGONAL	ALTERNATIVE FIRST ROWS Projection	Integral	FIRST STABLE MATRIX % IN STABLE POPULATION	FISHER VALUES	REPRODUCTIVE VALUES	SECOND STABLE MATRIX Z_2 FIRST COLUMN	FIRST ROW
0	0.97134	0.00000	0.00000	17.767	1.236	36413	0.1338+0.0780	0.1338+0.0780
5	0.99653	0.00021	0.00000	14.619	1.503	41476	0.1407-0.0793	0.0002+0.1485
10	0.99551	0.07510	0.00046	12.340	1.780	36087	0.0028-0.1729	-0.1197+0.0703
15	0.99090	0.36808	0.16341	10.406	2.018	31639	-0.1580-0.0959	-0.1234-0.0693
20	0.98955	0.64599	0.64206	8.734	1.944	27144	-0.1730+0.0935	-0.0520-0.1619
25	0.98659	0.66043	0.76933	7.321	1.513	18760	-0.0071+0.2088	0.0194-0.1702
30	0.97983	0.54866	0.67445	6.118	0.982	10415	0.1872+0.1183	0.0583-0.1175
35	0.97155	0.35457	0.52813	5.078	0.491	4933	0.2069-0.1071	0.0495-0.0523
40	0.96810	0.12729	0.24924	4.179	0.146	1190	0.0126-0.2427	0.0184-0.0128
45	0.95978	0.01368	0.02819	3.427	0.015	106	-0.2111-0.1387	0.0020-0.0012
50	0.94119	0.00074	0.00160	2.786	0.001	5	-0.2333+0.1156	0.0001-0.0001
55+	0.81760			7.225				

TABLE 10 — AGE ANALYSIS AND MISCELLANEOUS RESULTS (Females)

Start of Age Interval	OBSERVED POPUL. (IN 100's)	CONTRIBUTIONS OF ROOTS (IN 100's) r_1	r_2, r_3	$r_4 \cdot r_{11}$	AGE-SP. BIRTH RATES	NET MATERNITY FUNCTION	COEFF. OF MATRIX EQUATION	PARAMETERS	INTEGRAL	MATRIX	EXP. INCREASE x	$e^{(x+2\frac{1}{2})r}$
0	295	298	8	-11	0.0000	0.0000	0.0000	L(1)	1.17984	1.18055	0	1.0862
5	276	245	13	18	0.0000	0.0000	0.0002	L(2)	0.46783	0.47039	50	5.6773
10	203	207	5	-9	0.0001	0.0004	0.0727		0.82506	0.80370	55	6.6983
15	157	175	-9	-9	0.0343	0.1450	0.3547	R(1)	0.03308	0.03320	60	7.9029
20	140	146	-15	8	0.1347	0.5644	0.6168	R(2)	-0.01058	-0.01425	65	9.3241
25	124	123	-6	8	0.1614	0.6692	0.6240		0.21099	0.20825	70	11.0009
30	106	103	10	-7	0.1415	0.5788	0.5115	C(1)		1677	75	12.9793
35	100	85	18	-3	0.1108	0.4441	0.3239	C(2)		3678	80	15.3135
40	82	70	8	4	0.0523	0.2036	0.1130			1423	85	18.0675
45	71	57	-12	25	0.0059	0.0223	0.0118	2P/Y	29.7789	30.1707	90	21.3167
50	59	47	-20	33	0.0003	0.0012	0.0006	DELTA	4.9622		95	25.1503
55+	163	121									100	29.6733

TABLE 1 — DATA

AGE AT LAST BIRTHDAY	POPULATION BOTH SEXES	MALES Number	MALES %	FEMALES Number	FEMALES %	BIRTHS BY AGE OF MOTHER	DEATHS BOTH SEXES	DEATHS MALES	FEMALES	AGE AT LAST BIRTHDAY
0	52594	26255	4.0	26339	4.0	0	7976	4247	3729	0
1-4	182590	92151	14.0	90439	13.6	0	3893	1981	1912	1-4
5-9	189186	94414	14.3	94772	14.3	0	371	200	171	5-9
10-14	155973	78261	11.9	77712	11.7	50	195	116	79	10-14
15-19	136545	69206	10.5	67339	10.1	8038	341	185	156	15-19
20-24	118733	58408	8.9	60325	9.1	20387	465	267	198	20-24
25-29	101106	49007	7.4	52099	7.8	15782	426	234	192	25-29
30-34	82942	40757	6.2	42185	6.4	9654	475	271	204	30-34
35-39	66666	33619	5.1	33047	5.0	5963	474	263	211	35-39
40-44	56128	27966	4.2	28162	4.2	2406	565	338	227	40-44
45-49	50124	25182	3.8	24942	3.8	568	551	336	215	45-49
50-54	37569	18832	2.9	18737	2.8	76	691	423	268	50-54
55-59	31211	15749	2.4	15462	2.3	0	709	429	280	55-59
60-64	18281	8974	1.4	9307	1.4	0	829	460	369	60-64
65-69	16713	7558	1.1	9155	1.4	0	891	505	386	65-69
70-74	12474	5722	0.9	6752	1.0		828	459	369	70-74
75-79	7718	3510	0.5	4208	0.6		650	352	308	75-79
80-84	3328	1578	0.2	1750	0.3	31755 M.	539	261	278	80-84
85+	2580	1104	0.2	1476	0.2	31169 F.	628	298	330	85+
TOTAL	1322461	658253		664208		52924	21507	11625	9882	TOTAL

TABLE 2 — MALE LIFE TABLE

x	nq_x	l_x	nd_x	nL_x	nm_x	na_x	T_x	r_x	$\overset{o}{e}_x$	nM_x	x
0	0.146291	100000	14629	90520	0.161612	0.3520	4767311	0.0014	47.673	0.161760	0
1	0.081080	85371	6922	322267	0.021479	1.2238	4676791	0.0014	54.782	0.021497	1
5	0.009938	78449	780	390296	0.001998	2.5000	4354524	0.0349	55.508	0.002118	5
10	0.007405	77669	575	386961	0.001486	2.5909	3964228	0.0292	51.040	0.001482	10
15	0.013369	77094	1031	383134	0.002690	2.7323	3577267	0.0264	46.401	0.002673	15
20	0.022673	76064	1725	376158	0.004585	2.5880	3194133	0.0303	41.993	0.004571	20
25	0.023665	74339	1759	367434	0.004788	2.5778	2817975	0.0308	37.907	0.004775	25
30	0.032817	72580	2382	357141	0.006669	2.5828	2450542	0.0313	33.763	0.006649	30
35	0.038555	70198	2706	344554	0.007855	2.6222	2093400	0.0291	29.821	0.007823	35
40	0.058808	67491	3969	327829	0.012107	2.5743	1748847	0.0176	25.912	0.012086	40
45	0.064893	63522	4122	307802	0.013392	2.6203	1421017	0.0244	22.370	0.013343	45
50	0.106886	59400	6349	281695	0.022539	2.5892	1113215	0.0257	18.741	0.022462	50
55	0.128919	53051	6839	249032	0.027464	2.6278	831520	0.0425	15.674	0.027240	55
60	0.228169	46212	10544	205398	0.051335	2.5663	582489	0.0090	12.605	0.051259	60
65	0.285778	35668	10193	152424	0.066873	2.4576	377091	0.0090	10.572	0.066817	65
70	0.332430	25475	8469	105491	0.080277	2.4161	224667	0.0090	8.819	0.080217	70
75	0.398810	17006	6782	67546	0.100409	2.4220	119176	0.0090	7.008	0.100285	75
80	0.579926	10224	5929	35779	0.165717	2.4126	51630	0.0090	5.050	0.165399	80
85+	*1.000000	4295	4295	15851	0.270940	3.6909	15851	0.0090	3.691	0.269928	85+

TABLE 3 — FEMALE LIFE TABLE

x	nq_x	l_x	nd_x	nL_x	nm_x	na_x	T_x	r_x	$\overset{o}{e}_x$	nM_x	x
0	0.129567	100000	12957	91769	0.141188	0.3648	5253309	0.0043	52.533	0.141577	0
1	0.079731	87043	6940	329073	0.021090	1.2478	5161540	0.0043	59.299	0.021141	1
5	0.008384	80103	672	398837	0.001684	2.5000	4832467	0.0347	60.328	0.001804	5
10	0.005092	79432	404	396198	0.001021	2.6253	4433630	0.0327	55.817	0.001017	10
15	0.011576	79027	915	393030	0.002328	2.6981	4037432	0.0231	51.089	0.002317	15
20	0.016314	78112	1274	387479	0.003289	2.5805	3644402	0.0225	46.656	0.003282	20
25	0.018314	76838	1407	380784	0.003696	2.5795	3256924	0.0319	42.387	0.003685	25
30	0.024014	75431	1811	372817	0.004859	2.6053	2876140	0.0406	38.129	0.004836	30
35	0.031550	73619	2323	362501	0.006407	2.5906	2503323	0.0340	34.004	0.006385	35
40	0.039567	71297	2821	349553	0.008070	2.5430	2140822	0.0204	30.027	0.008061	40
45	0.042421	68476	2905	335478	0.008659	2.6244	1791269	0.0310	26.159	0.008620	45
50	0.069478	65571	4556	316979	0.014372	2.6127	1455791	0.0342	22.202	0.014303	50
55	0.087992	61015	5369	292806	0.018336	2.7145	1138813	0.0477	18.664	0.018109	55
60	0.181220	55646	10084	253713	0.039747	2.5686	846007	0.0178	15.203	0.039648	60
65	0.190698	45562	8689	205838	0.042211	2.4711	592294	0.0178	13.000	0.042163	65
70	0.240839	36873	8881	162172	0.054760	2.5006	386456	0.0178	10.481	0.054650	70
75	0.311334	27993	8715	118615	0.073474	2.5503	224285	0.0178	8.012	0.073194	75
80	0.569727	19278	10983	68844	0.159536	2.4920	105670	0.0178	5.481	0.158858	80
85+	*1.000000	8295	8295	36826	0.225238	4.4398	36826	0.0178	4.440	0.223577	85+

TABLE 4 — OBSERVED AND PROJECTED VITAL RATES

	OBSERVED POPULATION BOTH SEXES	MALES	FEMALES	PROJECTED POPULATION 1962 MALES	1962 FEMALES	1967 MALES	1967 FEMALES	1972 MALES	1972 FEMALES	STABLE POPULATION MALES	FEMALES
RATES PER THOUSAND											
Birth	47.58	48.24	46.93	47.62	46.03	47.20	45.41	47.29	45.36	48.26	45.99
Death	16.26	17.66	14.88	17.38	14.89	17.04	14.71	16.83	14.57	16.98	14.71
Increase	31.32	30.58	32.05	30.24	31.14	30.16	30.71	30.46	30.78	31.2807	
PERCENTAGE											
under 15	43.88	44.22	43.55	45.28	44.50	45.68	44.71	45.74	44.81	45.99	44.76
15-64	52.88	52.82	52.94	52.35	52.53	52.03	52.39	52.09	52.38	52.13	52.49
65 and over	3.24	2.96	3.51	2.37	2.97	2.29	2.90	2.17	2.81	1.89	2.75
DEP. RATIO X 100	89.11	89.32	88.91	91.01	90.38	92.21	90.89	91.98	90.91	91.83	90.52

South Africa 1957
Colored Population

TABLE 5 — POPULATION PROJECTED WITH FIXED AGE-SPECIFIC BIRTH AND DEATH RATES (IN 1000's)

AGE AT LAST BIRTHDAY	BOTH SEXES	1962 MALES	FEMALES	BOTH SEXES	1967 MALES	FEMALES	BOTH SEXES	1972 MALES	FEMALES	AGE AT LAST BIRTHDAY
0-4	282	141	141	324	162	162	374	187	187	0-4
5-9	223	112	111	266	133	133	306	153	153	5-9
10-14	188	94	94	221	111	110	265	132	133	10-14
15-19	154	77	77	186	93	93	219	110	109	15-19
20-24	134	68	66	152	76	76	183	91	92	20-24
25-29	116	57	59	131	66	65	149	74	75	25-29
30-34	99	48	51	113	55	58	129	65	64	30-34
35-39	80	39	41	96	46	50	110	54	56	35-39
40-44	64	32	32	77	37	40	92	44	48	40-44
45-49	53	26	27	61	30	31	73	35	38	45-49
50-54	47	23	24	50	24	26	56	27	29	50-54
55-59	34	17	17	42	20	22	45	21	24	55-59
60-64	26	13	13	29	14	15	36	17	19	60-64
65-69	15	7	8	21	10	11	22	10	12	65-69
70-74	12	5	7	11	5	6	16	7	9	70-74
75-79	9	4	5	8	3	5	7	3	4	75-79
80-84	4	2	2	5	2	3	5	2	3	80-84
85+	2	1	1	2	1	1	3	1	2	85+
TOTAL	1542	766	776	1795	888	907	2090	1033	1057	TOTAL

TABLE 6 — STANDARDIZED RATES

STANDARD COUNTRIES: STANDARDIZED RATES PER THOUSAND	ENGLAND AND WALES 1961 BOTH SEXES	MALES	FEMALES	UNITED STATES 1960 BOTH SEXES	MALES	FEMALES	MEXICO 1960 BOTH SEXES	MALES	FEMALES
Birth	41.31	47.08*	39.66	41.92	42.81*	40.92	46.50	45.84*	45.95
Death	22.24	39.75*	21.50	20.20	32.26*	18.38	15.62	16.91*	14.02
Increase	19.06	7.33*	18.16	21.72	10.56*	22.54	30.88	28.93*	31.92

TABLE 7 — MOMENTS AND CUMULANTS

	OBSERVED POP. MALES	FEMALES	STATIONARY POP. MALES	FEMALES	STABLE POP. MALES	FEMALES	OBSERVED BIRTHS	NET MATERNITY FUNCTION	BIRTHS IN STABLE POP.
μ	22.32862	22.71671	32.84582	35.14490	21.18928	22.12616	27.08974	28.71302	27.09494
σ^2	333.4445	344.8835	440.0420	491.3124	296.4330	327.9402	45.08204	52.91764	46.26158
κ_3	5943.011	6316.478	3214.844	3243.448	4953.394	5815.712	221.2740	199.5851	220.6604
κ_4	38743.	45177.	-155877.	-216142.	30551.	36483.	62.435	-1193.114	-176.852
β_1	0.952670	0.972596	0.121293	0.088703	0.941947	0.959007	0.534380	0.268816	0.491799
β_2	3.348458	3.379814	2.195005	2.104584	3.347673	3.339236	3.030720	2.573930	2.917364
κ	-0.421577	-0.432552	-0.049263	-0.034459	-0.421553	-0.418159	-0.299587	-0.132662	-0.257404

TABLE 8 — RATES FROM AGE DISTRIBUTIONS AND VITAL STATISTICS (Females)

VITAL STATISTICS		THOMPSON AGE RANGE	NRR	1000r	INTERVAL	BOURGEOIS-PICHAT AGE RANGE	NRR	1000b	1000d	1000r	COALE	
GRR	3.176										IBR	43.15
NRR	2.392	0-4	2.20	29.00	27.21	5-29	2.06	42.34	15.64	26.70	IDR	14.15
TFR	6.412	5-9	2.16	29.00	27.08	30-54	2.25	44.14	14.09	30.05	IRI	29.00
GENERATION	27.887	10-14	2.09	26.67	26.98	55-79	1.32	12.89	2.48	10.41	K1	0.
SEX RATIO	101.880	15-19	2.14	28.37	26.82	*20-44	2.54	51.74	17.27	34.47	K2	0.

TABLE 9 — LESLIE MATRIX AND ITS SPECTRAL COMPONENTS (Females)

Start of Age Interval	ORIGINAL MATRIX SUB-DIAGONAL	ALTERNATIVE FIRST ROWS Projection	Integral	FIRST STABLE MATRIX % IN STABLE POPULATION	FISHER VALUES	REPRODUCTIVE VALUES	SECOND STABLE MATRIX Z_2 FIRST COLUMN	FIRST ROW
0	0.94771	0.00000	0.00000	17.944	1.283	149779	0.1169+0.1342	0.1169+0.1342
5	0.99338	0.00067	0.00000	14.535	1.583	150060	0.1959-0.0477	-0.0577+0.1460
10	0.99201	0.12409	0.00145	12.341	1.864	144853	0.0566-0.2327	-0.1316+0.0133
15	0.98588	0.47169	0.26907	10.464	2.038	137231	-0.2143-0.1865	-0.0755-0.1102
20	0.98272	0.66253	0.76181	8.818	1.805	108874	-0.3114+0.1232	-0.0024-0.1640
25	0.97908	0.54928	0.68284	7.407	1.284	66892	-0.0396+0.3915	0.0443-0.1564
30	0.97233	0.42140	0.51587	6.198	0.815	34369	0.3858+0.2519	0.0705-0.1031
35	0.96428	0.27394	0.40674	5.151	0.424	14027	0.4663-0.2637	0.0560-0.0451
40	0.95974	0.11183	0.19258	4.246	0.151	4241	-0.0229-0.6172	0.0238-0.0130
45	0.94486	0.02773	0.05133	3.483	0.034	852	-0.6411-0.3022	0.0060-0.0024
50	0.92374	0.00423	0.00914	2.813	0.005	87	-0.6362+0.4863	0.0009-0.0002
55+	0.77637			6.601				

TABLE 10 — AGE ANALYSIS AND MISCELLANEOUS RESULTS (Females)

Start of Age Interval	OBSERVED POPUL. (IN 100's)	CONTRIBUTIONS OF ROOTS (IN 100's) r_1	r_2, r_3	r_4-r_{11}	AGE-SP. BIRTH RATES	NET MATERNITY FUNCTION	COEFF. OF MATRIX EQUATION	PARAMETERS		EXP. INCREASE	
										x	$e^{(x+2\frac{1}{2})r}$
0	1168	1176	14	-22	0.0000	0.0000	0.0000	L(1)	1.16930 INTEGRAL / 1.16996 MATRIX	0	1.0813
5	948	953	-17	12	0.0000	0.0000	0.0006	L(2)	0.36684 / 0.38444	50	5.1667
10	777	809	-37	5	0.0003	0.0013	0.1168		0.76223 / 0.74271	55	6.0414
15	673	686	-16	4	0.0591	0.2324	0.4405	R(1)	0.03128 / 0.03139	60	7.0642
20	603	578	34	-9	0.1674	0.6486	0.6100	R(2)	-0.03347 / -0.03575	65	8.2602
25	521	485	59	-24	0.1501	0.5714	0.4970		0.22445 / 0.21863	70	9.6586
30	422	406	17	-2	0.1134	0.4226	0.3733	C(1)	6554	75	11.2938
35	330	338	-62	55	0.0894	0.3240	0.2360	C(2)	-2546	80	13.2058
40	282	278	-89	93	0.0423	0.1479	0.0929		-7330	85	15.4415
45	249	228	-12	33	0.0113	0.0378	0.0221	2P/Y	27.9939 / 28.7387	90	18.0557
50	187	184	104	-101	0.0020	0.0064	0.0032	DELTA	1.9766	95	21.1125
55+	481	433								100	24.6868

TABLE 1 — DATA

AGE AT LAST BIRTHDAY	POPULATION BOTH SEXES	MALES Number	%	FEMALES Number	%	BIRTHS BY AGE OF MOTHER	DEATHS BOTH SEXES	MALES	FEMALES	AGE AT LAST BIRTHDAY
0	69030	34224	4.4	34806	4.5	0	9003	4795	4208	0
1-4	207092	102672	13.3	104420	13.4	0	4072	2091	1981	1-4
5-9	232284	115077	15.0	117207	15.0	0	409	215	194	5-9
10-14	190379	94366	12.3	96013	12.3	100	214	124	90	10-14
15-19	150258	74669	9.7	75589	9.7	8770	284	154	130	15-19
20-24	135692	67167	8.7	68525	8.8	22290	504	281	223	20-24
25-29	113991	55739	7.2	58252	7.5	17582	463	260	203	25-29
30-34	96291	48041	6.2	48250	6.2	11238	477	289	188	30-34
35-39	77362	39281	5.1	38081	4.9	6735	521	303	218	35-39
40-44	64856	33023	4.3	31833	4.1	2659	534	311	223	40-44
45-49	56609	28066	3.6	28543	3.7	580	636	353	283	45-49
50-54	46200	23465	3.1	22735	2.9	69	765	449	316	50-54
55-59	34890	18206	2.4	16684	2.1	0	730	451	279	55-59
60-64	25829	12354	1.6	13475	1.7	0	912	538	374	60-64
65-69	18897	8988	1.2	9909	1.3	0	919	504	415	65-69
70-74	13286	6159	0.8	7127	0.9		879	468	411	70-74
75-79	8861	4190	0.5	4671	0.6		768	397	371	75-79
80-84	4125	1921	0.2	2204	0.3	35239 M.	589	273	316	80-84
85+	3510	1526	0.2	1984	0.3	34784 F.	695	302	393	85+
TOTAL	1549442	769134		780308		70023	23374	12558	10816	TOTAL

TABLE 2 — MALE LIFE TABLE

x	nq_x	l_x	nd_x	nL_x	nm_x	na_x	T_x	r_x	$\dot{e}_x$	nM_x	x
0	0.127255	100000	12726	91887	0.138491	0.3625	5037326	0.0182	50.373	0.140106	0
1	0.076382	87274	6666	330722	0.020156	1.2433	4945439	0.0182	56.665	0.020366	1
5	0.008795	80608	709	401269	0.001767	2.5000	4614717	0.0313	57.249	0.001868	5
10	0.006562	79899	524	398210	0.001317	2.5450	4213448	0.0417	52.734	0.001314	10
15	0.010358	79375	822	395051	0.002081	2.7808	3815238	0.0316	48.066	0.002062	15
20	0.020780	78553	1632	388883	0.004197	2.6220	3420188	0.0254	43.540	0.004184	20
25	0.023114	76921	1778	380283	0.004675	2.5706	3031305	0.0286	39.408	0.004665	25
30	0.029738	75143	2235	370333	0.006034	2.5923	2651022	0.0289	35.280	0.006016	30
35	0.037962	72908	2768	357830	0.007735	2.5755	2280689	0.0298	31.282	0.007714	35
40	0.046156	70140	3237	342885	0.009442	2.5856	1922860	0.0239	27.414	0.009418	40
45	0.061259	66903	4098	324794	0.012618	2.6284	1579975	0.0209	23.616	0.012577	45
50	0.091751	62804	5762	300162	0.019198	2.5946	1255180	0.0245	19.986	0.019135	50
55	0.117742	57042	6716	269289	0.024941	2.6294	955019	0.0364	16.742	0.024772	55
60	0.197397	50326	9934	227467	0.043673	2.5678	685730	0.0187	13.626	0.043549	60
65	0.246301	40392	9948	177040	0.056193	2.4953	458263	0.0187	11.345	0.056075	65
70	0.318936	30443	9709	127517	0.076142	2.4562	281222	0.0187	9.238	0.075986	70
75	0.381363	20734	7907	83263	0.094965	2.4193	153705	0.0187	7.413	0.094749	75
80	0.518183	12827	6647	46641	0.142505	2.4459	70442	0.0187	5.492	0.142113	80
85+	1.000000	6180	6180	23801	0.259652	3.8513	23801	0.0187	3.851	0.197904	85+

TABLE 3 — FEMALE LIFE TABLE

x	nq_x	l_x	nd_x	nL_x	nm_x	na_x	T_x	r_x	$\dot{e}_x$	nM_x	x
0	0.111092	100000	11109	93015	0.119434	0.3713	5510235	0.0192	55.102	0.120899	0
1	0.071434	88891	6350	338173	0.018777	1.2613	5417220	0.0192	60.942	0.018971	1
5	0.007757	82541	640	411104	0.001557	2.5000	5079047	0.0318	61.534	0.001655	5
10	0.004684	81901	384	408558	0.000939	2.5349	4667943	0.0426	56.995	0.000937	10
15	0.008642	81517	705	406017	0.001735	2.7734	4259384	0.0318	52.251	0.001720	15
20	0.016188	80813	1308	400933	0.003263	2.6068	3853367	0.0231	47.683	0.003254	20
25	0.017297	79505	1375	394128	0.003489	2.5313	3452434	0.0316	43.424	0.003485	25
30	0.019389	78129	1515	387026	0.003914	2.6096	3058307	0.0383	39.144	0.003896	30
35	0.028349	76614	2172	377863	0.005748	2.6013	2671281	0.0360	34.867	0.005725	35
40	0.034538	74443	2571	366060	0.007024	2.6070	2293418	0.0215	30.808	0.007005	40
45	0.048592	71871	3492	351052	0.009948	2.6220	1927358	0.0235	26.817	0.009915	45
50	0.067500	68379	4616	330703	0.013957	2.5750	1576306	0.0401	23.052	0.013899	50
55	0.080839	63763	5155	306564	0.016814	2.6228	1245604	0.0338	19.535	0.016723	55
60	0.130599	58609	7654	274857	0.027848	2.6238	939040	0.0185	16.022	0.027755	60
65	0.190448	50955	9704	231089	0.041993	2.5594	664183	0.0185	13.035	0.041881	65
70	0.252674	41250	10423	180308	0.057806	2.5109	433094	0.0185	10.499	0.057668	70
75	0.332460	30827	10249	128610	0.079690	2.5093	252786	0.0185	8.200	0.079426	75
80	0.528641	20579	10879	75582	0.143932	2.4895	124176	0.0185	6.034	0.143376	80
85+	*1.000000	9700	9700	48594	0.199610	5.0098	48594	0.0185	5.010	0.198085	85+

TABLE 4 — OBSERVED AND PROJECTED VITAL RATES

	OBSERVED POPULATION BOTH SEXES	MALES	FEMALES	PROJECTED POPULATION 1965 MALES	FEMALES	1970 MALES	FEMALES	1975 MALES	FEMALES	STABLE POPULATION MALES	FEMALES
RATES PER THOUSAND											
Birth	45.19	45.82	44.58	45.77	44.27	46.54	44.81	47.21	45.31	47.27	45.12
Death	15.09	16.33	13.86	16.07	13.56	15.97	13.53	15.93	13.54	15.21	13.07
Increase	30.11	29.49	30.72	29.70	30.71	30.58	31.29	31.28	31.77	32.0535	
PERCENTAGE											
under 15	45.10	45.03	45.17	45.34	45.11	45.20	44.65	45.56	44.73	46.00	44.92
15-64	51.76	52.01	51.51	52.03	51.79	52.25	52.38	51.94	52.30	51.90	52.22
65 and over	3.14	2.96	3.32	2.62	3.11	2.55	2.97	2.51	2.97	2.10	2.85
DEP. RATIO X 100	93.20	92.28	94.12	92.19	93.11	91.40	90.91	92.53	91.21	92.68	91.49

Colored Population

TABLE 5 — POPULATION PROJECTED WITH FIXED AGE-SPECIFIC BIRTH AND DEATH RATES (IN 1000's)

AGE AT LAST BIRTHDAY	1965 BOTH SEXES	MALES	FEMALES	1970 BOTH SEXES	MALES	FEMALES	1975 BOTH SEXES	MALES	FEMALES	AGE AT LAST BIRTHDAY
0-4	323	161	162	379	189	190	449	224	225	0-4
5-9	263	130	133	307	153	154	360	179	181	5-9
10-14	230	114	116	261	129	132	305	152	153	10-14
15-19	189	94	95	229	113	116	259	128	131	15-19
20-24	149	74	75	186	92	94	226	112	114	20-24
25-29	133	66	67	145	72	73	183	90	93	25-29
30-34	111	54	57	130	64	66	142	70	72	30-34
35-39	93	46	47	108	52	56	127	62	65	35-39
40-44	75	38	37	90	44	46	104	50	54	40-44
45-49	62	31	31	71	36	35	86	42	44	45-49
50-54	53	26	27	58	29	29	66	33	33	50-54
55-59	42	21	21	48	23	25	53	26	27	55-59
60-64	30	15	15	37	18	19	42	20	22	60-64
65-69	21	10	11	25	12	13	30	14	16	65-69
70-74	14	6	8	16	7	9	19	9	10	70-74
75-79	9	4	5	10	4	6	11	5	6	75-79
80-84	5	2	3	5	2	3	5	2	3	80-84
85+	2	1	1	3	1	2	3	1	2	85+
TOTAL	1804	893	911	2108	1040	1068	2470	1219	1251	TOTAL

TABLE 6 — STANDARDIZED RATES

STANDARD COUNTRIES: STANDARDIZED RATES PER THOUSAND

	ENGLAND AND WALES 1961 BOTH SEXES	MALES	FEMALES	UNITED STATES 1960 BOTH SEXES	MALES	FEMALES	MEXICO 1960 BOTH SEXES	MALES	FEMALES
Birth	40.60	45.30*	39.09	41.24	41.28*	40.36	45.68	43.92*	45.26
Death	20.09	35.19*	19.90	18.14	28.60*	16.85	13.92	14.94*	12.56
Increase	20.51	10.11*	19.19	23.09	12.68*	23.51	31.75	28.98*	32.70

TABLE 7 — MOMENTS AND CUMULANTS

	OBSERVED POP. MALES	FEMALES	STATIONARY POP. MALES	FEMALES	STABLE POP. MALES	FEMALES	OBSERVED BIRTHS	NET MATERNITY FUNCTION	BIRTHS IN STABLE POP.
μ	22.37631	22.40063	33.67638	35.65914	21.30293	22.10904	27.15868	28.75028	27.11763
σ^2	339.8611	346.8092	458.5379	500.9717	303.3756	330.0609	44.70761	51.90395	45.66869
κ_3	6103.379	6539.638	3270.980	3189.836	5227.824	5951.627	204.1607	179.6341	204.2767
κ_4	36393.	50215.	-175154.	-229125.	36217.	40538.	-98.535	-1253.890	-296.532
β_1	0.948935	1.025264	0.110976	0.080928	0.978813	0.985120	0.466444	-0.230768	0.438109
β_2	3.315074	3.417492	2.166951	2.087052	3.393504	3.372115	2.950702	2.534566	2.857821
κ	-0.409863	-0.444667	-0.044455	-0.031225	-0.437473	-0.429364	-0.264976	-0.115258	-0.232371

TABLE 8 — RATES FROM AGE DISTRIBUTIONS AND VITAL STATISTICS (Females)

VITAL STATISTICS

GRR	3.132
NRR	2.447
TFR	6.304
GENERATION	27.917
SEX RATIO	101.308

THOMPSON

AGE RANGE	NRR	1000r	INTERVAL
0-4	2.35	31.35	27.24
5-9	2.37	32.57	27.12
10-14	2.28	29.76	27.01
15-19	2.12	27.99	26.84

BOURGEOIS-PICHAT

AGE RANGE	NRR	1000b	1000d	1000r
5-29	2.41	45.24	12.59	32.65
30-54	2.14	38.34	10.23	28.10
55-79	1.80	24.48	2.62	21.87
*20-44	2.55	48.47	13.79	34.69

COALE

IBR	46.81
IDR	12.62
IRI	34.19
K1	3.63
K2	0.

TABLE 9 — LESLIE MATRIX AND ITS SPECTRAL COMPONENTS (Females)

Start of Age Interval	SUB-DIAGONAL	ALTERNATIVE FIRST ROWS Projection	Integral	% IN STABLE POPULATION	FISHER VALUES	REPRODUCTIVE VALUES	SECOND STABLE MATRIX Z_2 FIRST COLUMN	FIRST ROW
0	0.95342	0.00000	0.00000	18.005	1.254	174648	0.1228+0.1240	0.1228+0.1240
5	0.99381	0.00111	0.00000	14.616	1.545	181123	0.1868-0.0579	-0.0477+0.1483
10	0.99378	0.12460	0.00242	12.367	1.825	175218	0.0406-0.2247	-0.1316+0.0222
15	0.98748	0.46826	0.26925	10.464	2.000	151146	-0.2110-0.1632	-0.0843-0.1067
20	0.98303	0.66613	0.75486	8.797	1.783	122213	-0.2810+0.1298	-0.0101-0.1657
25	0.98198	0.56819	0.70043	7.363	1.281	74614	-0.0167+0.3572	0.0400-0.1580
30	0.97632	0.43437	0.54050	6.156	0.806	38899	0.3569+0.2073	0.0664-0.1042
35	0.96876	0.27607	0.41043	5.117	0.412	15681	0.3999-0.2535	0.0526-0.0457
40	0.95900	0.11033	0.19384	4.221	0.142	4512	-0.0460-0.5371	0.0220-0.0129
45	0.94203	0.02482	0.04716	3.446	0.029	836	-0.5610-0.2333	0.0050-0.0022
50	0.92701	0.00325	0.00704	2.764	0.003	79	-0.5157+0.4319	0.0006-0.0002
55+	0.79118			6.684				

TABLE 10 — AGE ANALYSIS AND MISCELLANEOUS RESULTS (Females)

Start of Age Interval	OBSERVED POPUL. (IN 100's)	CONTRIBUTIONS OF ROOTS (IN 100's) r_1	r_2, r_3	r_4-r_{11}	AGE-SP. BIRTH RATES	NET MATERNITY FUNCTION	COEFF. OF MATRIX EQUATION	PARAMETERS INTEGRAL	MATRIX	EXP. INCREASE x	$e^{(x+2\frac{1}{2})r}$
0	1392	1391	4	-3	0.0000	0.0000	0.0000	L(1) 1.17382	1.17452	0	1.0834
5	1172	1129	20	23	0.0000	0.0000	0.0011	L(2) 0.37751	0.39258	50	5.3806
10	960	955	17	-12	0.0005	0.0021	0.1181	0.77584	0.75492	55	6.3159
15	756	808	-10	-43	0.0576	0.2340	0.4409	R(1) 0.03205	0.03217	60	7.4138
20	685	680	-33	39	0.1616	0.6478	0.6194	R(2) -0.02951	-0.03229	65	8.7025
25	583	569	-22	36	0.1499	0.5909	0.5194	0.22359	0.21825	70	10.2152
30	483	475	21	-14	0.1157	0.4478	0.3899	C(1)	7724	75	11.9909
35	381	395	51	-65	0.0879	0.3320	0.2419	C(2)	4540	80	14.0752
40	318	326	26	-34	0.0415	0.1519	0.0937		2855	85	16.5218
45	285	266	-38	57	0.0101	0.0354	0.0202	2P/Y 28.1016	28.7889	90	19.3937
50	227	213	-71	85	0.0015	0.0050	0.0025	DELTA 1.7492		95	22.7648
55+	561	516								100	26.7219

White Population

TABLE 1 — DATA

AGE AT LAST BIRTHDAY	POPULATION BOTH SEXES	MALES Number	%	FEMALES Number	%	BIRTHS BY AGE OF MOTHER	DEATHS BOTH SEXES	MALES	FEMALES	AGE AT LAST BIRTHDAY
0	63113	32198	2.4	30915	2.3	0	2264	1293	971	0
1-4	253385	129096	9.7	124289	9.4	0	580	329	251	1-4
5-9	277339	140930	10.6	136409	10.3	0	265	144	121	5-9
10-14	247197	125658	9.5	121539	9.2	10	153	80	73	10-14
15-19	214303	108833	8.2	105470	8.0	4343	254	171	83	15-19
20-24	207732	104291	7.9	103441	7.8	19714	335	218	117	20-24
25-29	197822	98609	7.4	99213	7.5	19602	350	214	136	25-29
30-34	193856	97195	7.3	96661	7.3	12700	418	255	163	30-34
35-39	192684	96317	7.3	96367	7.3	7445	577	333	244	35-39
40-44	183495	92419	7.0	91076	6.9	2529	791	487	304	40-44
45-49	146987	74052	5.6	72935	5.5	239	1005	611	394	45-49
50-54	112831	54855	4.1	57976	4.4	11	1211	731	480	50-54
55-59	102131	49422	3.7	52709	4.0	0	1600	1012	588	55-59
60-64	84517	40020	3.0	44497	3.4	0	1946	1188	758	60-64
65-69	66418	31684	2.4	34734	2.6	0	2334	1412	922	65-69
70-74	49864	24606	1.9	25258	1.9		2526	1491	1035	70-74
75-79	31595	15360	1.2	16235	1.2		2507	1367	1140	75-79
80-84	16224	7466	0.6	8758	0.7	34192 M.	2093	1036	1057	80-84
85+	7598	3193	0.2	4405	0.3	32401 F.	1521	657	864	85+
TOTAL	2649091	1326204		1322887		66593	22730	13029	9701	TOTAL

TABLE 2 — MALE LIFE TABLE

x	$_nq_x$	l_x	$_nd_x$	$_nL_x$	$_nm_x$	$_na_x$	T_x	r_x	$\mathring{e}_x$	$_nM_x$	x
0	).039033	100000	3903	97199	0.040158	0.2824	6450245	0.0000	64.502	0.040158	0
1	).010120	96097	972	381597	0.002548	1.1308	6353046	0.0000	66.111	0.002548	1
5	0.005057	95124	481	474419	0.001014	2.5000	5971450	0.0236	62.775	0.001022	5
10	0.003193	94643	302	472515	0.000640	2.6792	5497031	0.0249	58.082	0.000637	10
15	0.007853	94341	741	469993	0.001576	2.6888	5024517	0.0172	53.259	0.001571	15
20	0.010403	93600	974	465620	0.002091	2.5554	4554524	0.0079	48.659	0.002090	20
25	0.010796	92626	1000	460678	0.002171	2.5460	4088904	0.0048	44.144	0.002170	25
30	0.013036	91626	1194	455261	0.002624	2.5961	3628226	0.0000	39.598	0.002624	30
35	0.017151	90432	1551	448517	0.003458	2.6515	3172965	0.0014	35.087	0.003457	35
40	0.026131	88881	2323	439011	0.005290	2.6779	2724448	0.0208	30.653	0.005269	40
45	0.040826	86558	3534	424597	0.008323	2.6809	2285437	0.0435	26.403	0.008251	45
50	0.064924	83025	5390	402492	0.013392	2.6568	1860840	0.0267	22.413	0.013326	50
55	0.097786	77634	7592	370098	0.020512	2.6193	1458348	0.0107	18.785	0.020477	55
60	0.139006	70043	9736	326822	0.029791	2.5975	1088250	0.0222	15.537	0.029685	60
65	0.201469	60306	12150	271778	0.044705	2.5510	761427	0.0222	12.626	0.044565	65
70	0.264000	48157	12713	209160	0.060783	2.5127	489650	0.0222	10.168	0.060595	70
75	0.364601	35443	12923	144676	0.089321	2.4820	280489	0.0222	7.914	0.088997	75
80	0.514853	22521	11595	83200	0.139361	2.4641	135813	0.0222	6.031	0.138763	80
85+	*1.000000	10926	10926	52613	0.207664	4.8155	52613	0.0222	4.815	0.205763	85+

TABLE 3 — FEMALE LIFE TABLE

x	$_nq_x$	l_x	$_nd_x$	$_nL_x$	$_nm_x$	$_na_x$	T_x	r_x	$\mathring{e}_x$	$_nM_x$	x
0	0.030718	100000	3072	97801	0.031409	0.2843	7015055	0.0000	70.151	0.031409	0
1	0.008031	96928	778	385481	0.002019	1.1327	6917253	0.0000	71.365	0.002019	1
5	0.004396	96150	423	479692	0.000881	2.5000	6531773	0.0233	67.933	0.000887	5
10	0.002996	95727	287	477908	0.000600	2.4658	6052081	0.0250	63.222	0.000601	10
15	0.003936	95440	376	476314	0.000787	2.6385	5574173	0.0153	58.405	0.000787	15
20	0.005643	95065	536	474038	0.001132	2.6050	5097859	0.0050	53.625	0.001131	20
25	0.006834	94528	646	471078	0.001371	2.5813	4623821	0.0054	48.915	0.001371	25
30	0.008399	93882	789	467548	0.001687	2.6390	4152744	0.0011	44.234	0.001686	30
35	0.012590	93093	1172	462691	0.002533	2.6316	3685195	0.0035	39.586	0.002532	35
40	0.016632	91921	1529	456047	0.003352	2.6713	3222504	0.0243	35.057	0.003338	40
45	0.026873	90393	2429	446318	0.005443	2.6762	2766457	0.0396	30.605	0.005402	45
50	0.040737	87963	3583	431310	0.008308	2.6260	2320139	0.0242	26.376	0.008279	50
55	0.054469	84380	4596	411033	0.011182	2.6355	1888829	0.0147	22.385	0.011156	55
60	0.082371	79784	6572	383448	0.017139	2.6457	1477796	0.0334	18.522	0.017035	60
65	0.125554	73212	9192	344215	0.026704	2.6235	1094349	0.0334	14.948	0.026545	65
70	0.187770	64020	12021	291400	0.041253	2.6125	750134	0.0334	11.717	0.040977	70
75	0.301643	51999	15685	221820	0.070711	2.5662	458733	0.0334	8.822	0.070219	75
80	0.468248	36314	17004	139815	0.121617	2.5444	236913	0.0334	6.524	0.120690	80
85+	*1.000000	19310	19310	97099	0.198870	5.0284	97099	0.0334	5.028	0.196141	85+

TABLE 4 — OBSERVED AND PROJECTED VITAL RATES

	OBSERVED POPULATION BOTH SEXES	MALES	FEMALES	PROJECTED POPULATION 1956 MALES	FEMALES	1961 MALES	FEMALES	1966 MALES	FEMALES	STABLE POPULATION MALES	FEMALES
RATES PER THOUSAND											
Birth	25.14	25.78	24.49	24.60	23.24	24.37	22.94	24.85	23.34	25.34	23.98
Death	8.58	9.82	7.33	10.01	7.74	10.09	8.06	10.17	8.38	10.12	8.77
Increase	16.56	15.96	17.16	14.59	15.50	14.28	14.88	14.68	14.95		15.2126
PERCENTAGE											
under 15	31.75	32.26	31.23	32.57	31.26	32.36	30.84	31.72	30.10	32.30	30.90
15-64	61.77	61.53	62.01	61.26	61.43	61.53	61.44	62.32	62.00	61.39	60.62
65 and over	6.48	6.21	6.76	6.16	7.31	6.12	7.72	5.96	7.90	6.31	8.48
DEP. RATIO X 100	61.89	62.52	61.26	63.23	62.78	62.53	62.75	60.45	61.29	62.89	64.97

AGE AT LAST BIRTHDAY	1956 BOTH SEXES	MALES	FEMALES	1961 BOTH SEXES	MALES	FEMALES	1966 BOTH SEXES	MALES	FEMALES	AGE AT LAST BIRTHDAY	
0-4	325	166	159	341	174	167	368	188	180	0-4	
5-9	314	160	154	323	165	158	337	172	165	5-9	
10-14	276	140	136	312	159	153	321	164	157	10-14	
15-19	246	125	121	275	140	135	311	158	153	15-19	**TABLE 5**
20-24	213	108	105	245	124	121	273	138	135	20-24	POPULATION
25-29	206	103	103	211	107	104	243	123	120	25-29	PROJECTED
30-34	195	97	98	204	102	102	209	105	104	30-34	WITH
35-39	192	96	96	193	96	97	201	100	101	35-39	FIXED
40-44	189	94	95	188	94	94	190	94	96	40-44	AGE—
45-49	178	89	89	184	91	93	183	91	92	45-49	SPECIFIC
50-54	140	70	70	171	85	86	176	86	90	50-54	BIRTH
55-59	105	50	55	132	65	67	160	78	82	55-59	AND
60-64	93	44	49	97	45	52	120	57	63	60-64	DEATH
65-69	73	33	40	80	36	44	83	37	46	65-69	RATES
70-74	53	24	29	60	26	34	65	28	37	70-74	(IN 1000's)
75-79	36	17	19	39	17	22	44	18	26	75-79	
80-84	19	9	10	22	10	12	24	10	14	80-84	
85+	11	5	6	13	6	7	14	6	8	85+	
TOTAL	2864	1430	1434	3090	1542	1548	3322	1653	1669	TOTAL	

STANDARD COUNTRIES: STANDARDIZED RATES PER THOUSAND	ENGLAND AND WALES 1961 BOTH SEXES	MALES	FEMALES	UNITED STATES 1960 BOTH SEXES	MALES	FEMALES	MEXICO 1960 BOTH SEXES	MALES	FEMALES	
Birth	21.31	23.25*	20.10	21.66	21.77*	20.77	24.65	21.01*	23.93	**TABLE 6** STANDAR-
Death	13.07	14.17*	12.73	10.82	12.23*	9.62	6.21	8.84*	5.20	DIZED
Increase	8.24	9.08*	7.37	10.84	9.54*	11.14	18.44	12.17*	18.72	RATES

	OBSERVED POP. MALES	FEMALES	STATIONARY POP. MALES	FEMALES	STABLE POP. MALES	FEMALES	OBSERVED BIRTHS	NET MATERNITY FUNCTION	BIRTHS IN STABLE POP.	
μ	28.98589	29.72289	35.88959	38.15904	28.85231	30.40201	28.08249	28.25502	27.65795	**TABLE 7**
σ^2	421.8326	434.8136	491.7110	538.9473	427.1872	472.2224	37.56505	38.13038	36.18867	MOMENTS
κ_3	4779.211	4756.360	2843.915	2492.007	5314.259	5879.930	122.8914	125.0624	129.6550	AND
κ_4	-99976.	-115233.	-221448.	-292610.	-95541.	-137886.	-434.622	-408.720	-188.489	CUMULANTS
β_1	0.304293	0.275195	0.068030	0.039670	0.362269	0.328325	0.284899	0.282124	0.354699	
β_2	2.438154	2.390504	2.084092	1.992613	2.476457	2.381659	2.692005	2.718885	2.856074	
κ	-0.124967	-0.111918	-0.026552	-0.014756	-0.144337	-0.125273	-0.158279	-0.163286	-0.217112	

VITAL STATISTICS		THOMPSON AGE RANGE	NRR	1000r	INTERVAL	BOURGEOIS-PICHAT AGE RANGE	NRR	1000b	1000d	1000r	COALE		
GRR	1.628										IBR	22.75	**TABLE 8** RATES FROM AGE
NRR	1.530	0-4	1.52	15.66	27.38	5-29	1.50	23.25	8.18	15.07	IDR	10.59	DISTRI- BUTIONS
TFR	3.346	5-9	1.41	12.72	27.33	30-54	1.81	34.76	12.69	22.07	IRI	12.16	AND VITAL
GENERATION	27.954	10-14	1.35	10.98	27.25	55-79	2.03	44.61	18.31	26.30	K1	12.66	STATISTICS
SEX RATIO	105.528	15-19	1.27	8.46	27.14	*15-44	1.11	17.88	14.03	3.85	K2	0.29	(Females)

Start of Age Interval	ORIGINAL MATRIX SUB-DIAGONAL	ALTERNATIVE FIRST ROWS Projection	Integral	FIRST STABLE MATRIX % IN STABLE POPULATION	FISHER VALUES	REPRODUCTIVE VALUES	SECOND STABLE MATRIX Z2 FIRST COLUMN	FIRST ROW	
0	0.99257	0.00000	0.00000	11.166	1.075	166774	0.1625+0.0836	0.1625+0.0836	
5	0.99628	0.00010	0.00000	10.270	1.168	159366	0.1709-0.1246	-0.0015+0.1578	**TABLE 9**
10	0.99666	0.04835	0.00020	9.481	1.265	153795	-0.0403-0.2425	-0.1220+0.0598	LESLIE
15	0.99522	0.27141	0.10058	8.756	1.318	139012	-0.2729-0.0847	-0.1009-0.0747	MATRIX
20	0.99376	0.45491	0.46551	8.075	1.136	117526	-0.2300+0.2390	-0.0258-0.1294	AND ITS
25	0.99251	0.38561	0.48259	7.436	0.742	73609	0.1279+0.3626	0.0154-0.1082	SPECTRAL
30	0.98961	0.24436	0.32092	6.839	0.389	37623	0.4416+0.0561	0.0264-0.0626	COMPO-
35	0.98564	0.12301	0.18871	6.271	0.159	15334	0.2866-0.4265	0.0186-0.0245	NENTS
40	0.97867	0.03642	0.06783	5.728	0.040	3654	-0.2903-0.5145	0.0060-0.0056	(Females)
45	0.96637	0.00407	0.00800	5.194	0.004	310	-0.6735+0.0325	0.0007-0.0006	
50	0.95299	0.00022	0.00046	4.651	0.000	13	-0.3080+0.6949	0.0000-0.0000	
55+	0.80439			16.132					

Start of Age Interval	OBSERVED POPUL. (IN 100's)	CONTRIBUTIONS OF ROOTS (IN 100's) r_1	r_2, r_3	r_4-r_{11}	AGE-SP. BIRTH RATES	NET MATERNITY FUNCTION	COEFF. OF MATRIX EQUATION	PARAMETERS INTEGRAL	MATRIX	EXP. INCREASE x	$e^{(x+2\frac{1}{2})r}$	
0	1552	1464	67	21	0.0000	0.0000	0.0000	L(1) 1.07903	1.07917	0	1.0388	**TABLE 10**
5	1364	1346	51	-33	0.0000	0.0000	0.0001	L(2) 0.37763	0.38478	50	2.2226	AGE
10	1215	1243	-37	9	0.0000	0.0002	0.0478	0.79241	0.76613	55	2.3982	ANALYSIS
15	1055	1148	-107	14	0.0200	0.0954	0.2675	R(1) 0.01521	0.01524	60	2.5877	AND
20	1034	1059	-63	38	0.0927	0.4396	0.4462	R(2) -0.02607	-0.03079	65	2.7923	MISCEL-
25	992	975	79	-62	0.0961	0.4528	0.3759	0.22522	-0.22107	70	3.0129	LANEOUS
30	967	896	166	-96	0.0639	0.2989	0.2364	C(1)	13109	75	3.2510	RESULTS
35	964	822	66	75	0.0376	0.1739	0.1178	C(2)	18272	80	3.5080	(Females)
40	911	751	-152	312	0.0135	0.0616	0.0344		-4491	85	3.7852	
45	729	681	-243	292	0.0016	0.0071	0.0038	2P/Y 27.8985	28.4215	90	4.0844	
50	580	610	-50	20	0.0001	0.0004	0.0002	DELTA 3.6368		95	4.4071	
55+	1866	2115								100	4.7554	

White Population

TABLE 1 — DATA

AGE AT LAST BIRTHDAY	POPULATION BOTH SEXES	MALES Number	MALES %	FEMALES Number	FEMALES %	BIRTHS BY AGE OF MOTHER	DEATHS BOTH SEXES	DEATHS MALES	DEATHS FEMALES	AGE AT LAST BIRTHDAY
0	66128	33817	2.4	32311	2.3	0	2217	1248	969	0
1-4	256158	130609	9.3	125549	9.0	0	488	262	226	1-4
5-9	306693	156123	11.2	150570	10.7	0	220	126	94	5-9
10-14	263884	134242	9.6	129642	9.2	11	143	87	56	10-14
15-19	235643	119267	8.5	116376	8.3	4689	229	155	74	15-19
20-24	211941	107230	7.7	104711	7.5	21158	315	231	84	20-24
25-29	201988	100697	7.2	101291	7.2	20655	312	208	104	25-29
30-34	199534	99548	7.1	99986	7.1	13036	387	241	146	30-34
35-39	190062	94988	6.8	95074	6.8	7150	550	343	207	35-39
40-44	192032	96271	6.9	95761	6.8	2472	782	485	297	40-44
45-49	173415	86838	6.2	86577	6.2	250	1137	720	417	45-49
50-54	123155	60736	4.3	62419	4.5	11	1259	800	459	50-54
55-59	105416	50355	3.6	55061	3.9	0	1656	1061	595	55-59
60-64	89437	42240	3.0	47197	3.4	0	2053	1297	756	60-64
65-69	70662	32444	2.3	38218	2.7	0	2373	1403	970	65-69
70-74	53278	25070	1.8	28208	2.0		2664	1521	1143	70-74
75-79	34432	16347	1.2	18085	1.3		2715	1504	1211	75-79
80-84	18091	8482	0.6	9609	0.7	35548 M.	2188	1123	1065	80-84
85+	9222	3780	0.3	5442	0.4	33884 F.	1872	854	1018	85+
TOTAL	2801171	1399084		1402087		69432	23560	13669	9891	TOTAL

TABLE 2 — MALE LIFE TABLE

x	$_nq_x$	l_x	$_nd_x$	$_nL_x$	$_nm_x$	$_na_x$	T_x	r_x	$\overset{\circ}{e}_x$	$_nM_x$	x
0	0.035878	100000	3588	97365	0.036849	0.2656	6493808	0.0019	64.938	0.036905	0
1	0.007961	96412	768	383434	0.002002	1.1151	6396443	0.0019	66.345	0.002006	1
5	0.004005	95645	383	477266	0.000803	2.5000	6013009	0.0192	62.868	0.000807	5
10	0.003249	95262	310	475583	0.000651	2.6584	5535743	0.0261	58.111	0.000648	10
15	0.006512	94952	618	473361	0.001306	2.7367	5060160	0.0211	53.292	0.001300	15
20	0.010727	94334	1012	469210	0.002157	2.5702	4586799	0.0150	48.623	0.002154	20
25	0.010277	93322	959	464232	0.002066	2.5218	4117589	0.0053	44.122	0.002066	25
30	0.012041	92363	1112	459174	0.002422	2.6264	3653357	0.0033	39.554	0.002421	30
35	0.017903	91251	1634	452403	0.003611	2.6429	3194182	0.0000	35.004	0.003611	35
40	0.024915	89617	2233	442909	0.005041	2.6817	2741780	0.0036	30.594	0.005038	40
45	0.040979	87384	3581	428628	0.008354	2.6840	2298871	0.0375	26.308	0.008291	45
50	0.064389	83803	5396	406423	0.013277	2.6662	1870243	0.0407	22.317	0.013172	50
55	0.100570	78407	7885	373303	0.021123	2.6243	1463820	0.0149	18.669	0.021070	55
60	0.143250	70522	10101	328180	0.030778	2.5815	1090517	0.0163	15.464	0.030705	60
65	0.195889	60421	11836	273087	0.043341	2.5482	762337	0.0163	12.617	0.043244	65
70	0.264311	48585	12842	211141	0.060820	2.5249	489251	0.0163	10.070	0.060670	70
75	0.374019	35744	13369	144936	0.092240	2.4730	278109	0.0163	7.781	0.092005	75
80	0.496612	22375	11112	83656	0.132824	2.4605	133174	0.0163	5.952	0.132397	80
85+	*1.000000	11263	11263	49517	0.227460	4.3964	49517	0.0163	4.396	0.225926	85+

TABLE 3 — FEMALE LIFE TABLE

x	$_nq_x$	l_x	$_nd_x$	$_nL_x$	$_nm_x$	$_na_x$	T_x	r_x	$\overset{\circ}{e}_x$	$_nM_x$	x
0	0.029319	100000	2932	97880	0.029954	0.2768	7129853	0.0016	71.299	0.029990	0
1	0.007152	97068	694	386277	0.001797	1.1253	7031973	0.0016	72.444	0.001800	1
5	0.003094	96374	298	481124	0.000620	2.5000	6645696	0.0188	68.957	0.000624	5
10	0.002158	96076	207	479861	0.000432	2.5069	6164572	0.0252	64.164	0.000432	10
15	0.003183	95868	305	478615	0.000637	2.6200	5684711	0.0207	59.297	0.000636	15
20	0.004009	95563	383	476896	0.000803	2.5993	5206096	0.0131	54.478	0.000802	20
25	0.005124	95180	488	474745	0.001027	2.6309	4729199	0.0036	49.687	0.001027	25
30	0.007282	94692	690	471849	0.001461	2.6604	4254454	0.0048	44.929	0.001460	30
35	0.010834	94003	1018	467623	0.002178	2.6521	3782605	0.0021	40.239	0.002177	35
40	0.015413	92984	1433	461585	0.003105	2.6711	3314982	0.0061	35.651	0.003101	40
45	0.023979	91551	2195	452647	0.004850	2.6724	2853397	0.0378	31.167	0.004817	45
50	0.036368	89356	3250	439146	0.007400	2.6509	2400751	0.0377	26.867	0.007354	50
55	0.052830	86106	4549	419800	0.010836	2.6410	1961605	0.0168	22.781	0.010806	55
60	0.077606	81557	6329	392902	0.016109	2.6484	1541804	0.0309	18.905	0.016018	60
65	0.120394	75228	9057	354739	0.025531	2.6371	1148902	0.0309	15.272	0.025381	65
70	0.185744	66171	12291	301488	0.040767	2.6107	794163	0.0309	12.002	0.040520	70
75	0.289253	53880	15585	231341	0.067368	2.5579	492675	0.0309	9.144	0.066962	75
80	0.434147	38295	16626	149198	0.111434	2.5762	261334	0.0309	6.824	0.110834	80
85+	1.000000	21669	21669	112136	0.193243	5.1748	112136	0.0309	5.175	0.187063	85+

TABLE 4 — OBSERVED AND PROJECTED VITAL RATES

	OBSERVED POPULATION BOTH SEXES	MALES	FEMALES	PROJECTED 1959 MALES	1959 FEMALES	1964 MALES	1964 FEMALES	1969 MALES	1969 FEMALES	STABLE POPULATION MALES	FEMALES
RATES PER THOUSAND											
Birth	24.79	25.41	24.17	24.81	23.45	24.98	23.51	25.67	24.09	25.98	24.52
Death	8.41	9.77	7.05	9.90	7.49	9.95	7.83	10.02	8.11	9.65	8.19
Increase	16.38	15.64	17.11	14.91	15.96	15.03	15.68	15.66	15.98		16.3237
PERCENTAGE											
under 15	31.87	32.51	31.24	32.73	31.22	32.24	30.57	32.22	30.48	33.04	31.43
15-64	61.50	61.34	61.65	61.19	61.19	61.82	61.52	61.87	61.44	60.99	60.21
65 and over	6.63	6.16	7.10	6.08	7.59	5.94	7.91	5.90	8.08	5.97	8.36
DEP. RATIO X 100	62.61	63.03	62.19	63.43	63.42	61.76	62.55	61.62	62.77	63.95	66.10

TABLE 1 — DATA

AGE AT LAST BIRTHDAY	BOTH SEXES	POPULATION MALES Number	%	FEMALES Number	%	BIRTHS BY AGE OF MOTHER	DEATHS BOTH SEXES	MALES	FEMALES	AGE AT LAST BIRTHDAY
0	69508	35383	2.4	34125	2.3	0	2175	1249	926	0
1-4	266458	135997	9.2	130461	8.8	0	468	260	208	1-4
5-9	315494	160799	10.9	154695	10.4	0	227	135	92	5-9
10-14	290844	147780	10.0	143064	9.7	14	173	105	68	10-14
15-19	253417	128502	8.7	124915	8.4	5451	277	199	78	15-19
20-24	221230	112900	7.7	108330	7.3	22767	368	278	90	20-24
25-29	213629	107649	7.3	105980	7.2	22139	344	219	125	25-29
30-34	199260	98893	6.7	100367	6.8	13200	414	271	143	30-34
35-39	196931	98362	6.7	98569	6.7	7054	552	338	214	35-39
40-44	190555	94776	6.4	95779	6.5	2152	793	498	295	40-44
45-49	183354	91797	6.2	91557	6.2	223	1187	755	432	45-49
50-54	154052	76682	5.2	77370	5.2	12	1491	971	520	50-54
55-59	105318	50257	3.4	55061	3.7	0	1603	1033	570	55-59
60-64	95092	43969	3.0	51123	3.5	0	2212	1356	856	60-64
65-69	74986	33850	2.3	41136	2.8	0	2661	1593	1068	65-69
70-74	55124	24504	1.7	30620	2.1		2825	1553	1272	70-74
75-79	37341	17163	1.2	20178	1.4		2935	1592	1343	75-79
80-84	20444	9232	0.6	11212	0.8	37384 M.	2395	1210	1185	80-84
85+	11078	4647	0.3	6431	0.4	35628 F.	2236	992	1244	85+
TOTAL	2954115	1473142		1480973		73012	25336	14607	10729	TOTAL

TABLE 2 — MALE LIFE TABLE

x	$_nq_x$	l_x	$_nd_x$	$_nL_x$	$_nm_x$	$_na_x$	T_x	r_x	$\mathring{e}_x$	$_nM_x$	x
0	0.034342	100000	3434	97477	0.035231	0.2653	6479935	0.0025	64.799	0.035299	0
1	0.007585	96566	732	384150	0.001907	1.1148	6382458	0.0025	66.094	0.001912	1
5	0.004175	95833	400	478166	0.000837	2.5000	5998308	0.0137	62.591	0.000840	5
10	0.003563	95433	340	476387	0.000714	2.7071	5520142	0.0215	57.843	0.000711	10
15	0.007762	95093	738	473791	0.001558	2.7302	5043755	0.0253	53.040	0.001549	15
20	0.012245	94355	1155	468930	0.002464	2.5370	4569965	0.0155	48.434	0.002462	20
25	0.010124	93200	944	463661	0.002035	2.5224	4101035	0.0109	44.003	0.002034	25
30	0.013621	92256	1257	458266	0.002742	2.6007	3637374	0.0063	39.427	0.002740	30
35	0.017045	91000	1551	451342	0.003437	2.6431	3179108	0.0006	34.935	0.003436	35
40	0.025963	89448	2322	441847	0.005256	2.6770	2727766	0.0015	30.495	0.005254	40
45	0.040444	87126	3524	427418	0.008244	2.6694	2285919	0.0127	26.237	0.008225	45
50	0.062053	83602	5188	405919	0.012780	2.6689	1858501	0.0468	22.230	0.012663	50
55	0.098582	78415	7730	373785	0.020681	2.6342	1452582	0.0346	18.524	0.020554	55
60	0.143839	70684	10167	329057	0.030898	2.6036	1078797	0.0112	15.262	0.030840	60
65	0.211254	60517	12785	271231	0.047135	2.5474	749741	0.0112	12.389	0.047061	65
70	0.273963	47733	13077	206021	0.063474	2.5039	478510	0.0112	10.025	0.063377	70
75	0.375886	34656	13027	140206	0.092910	2.4612	272489	0.0112	7.863	0.092758	75
80	0.492424	21629	10651	81092	0.131340	2.4599	132282	0.0112	6.116	0.131065	80
85+	*1.000000	10978	10978	51190	0.214463	4.6628	51190	0.0112	4.663	0.213471	85+

TABLE 3 — FEMALE LIFE TABLE

x	$_nq_x$	l_x	$_nd_x$	$_nL_x$	$_nm_x$	$_na_x$	T_x	r_x	$\mathring{e}_x$	$_nM_x$	x
0	0.026545	100000	2654	98074	0.027066	0.2745	7157047	0.0033	71.570	0.027136	0
1	0.006327	97346	616	387610	0.001589	1.1232	7058972	0.0033	72.515	0.001594	1
5	0.002957	96730	286	482933	0.000592	2.5000	6671362	0.0132	68.969	0.000595	5
10	0.002374	96444	229	481649	0.000475	2.5136	6188429	0.0208	64.166	0.000475	10
15	0.003128	96215	301	480356	0.000626	2.6173	5706780	0.0272	59.313	0.000624	15
20	0.004155	95914	398	478627	0.000833	2.6365	5226424	0.0156	54.491	0.000831	20
25	0.005885	95515	562	476228	0.001180	2.6024	4747798	0.0065	49.707	0.001179	25
30	0.007106	94953	675	473174	0.001426	2.6410	4271569	0.0057	44.986	0.001425	30
35	0.010805	94278	1019	469002	0.002172	2.6538	3798396	0.0025	40.289	0.002171	35
40	0.015301	93260	1427	462967	0.003082	2.6650	3329393	0.0042	35.700	0.003080	40
45	0.023395	91833	2148	454118	0.004731	2.6515	2866427	0.0166	31.214	0.004718	45
50	0.033331	89684	2989	441419	0.006772	2.6574	2412308	0.0438	26.898	0.006721	50
55	0.050841	86695	4408	423221	0.010414	2.6735	1970889	0.0305	22.734	0.010352	55
60	0.080946	82287	6661	395803	0.016829	2.6528	1547668	0.0268	18.808	0.016744	60
65	0.122880	75627	9293	356135	0.026094	2.6329	1151865	0.0268	15.231	0.025963	65
70	0.189758	66334	12587	301480	0.041752	2.6017	795730	0.0268	11.996	0.041541	70
75	0.287271	53746	15440	230845	0.066884	2.5462	494249	0.0268	9.196	0.066558	75
80	0.417903	38307	16008	150800	0.106157	2.5893	263405	0.0268	6.876	0.105690	80
85+	1.000000	22298	22298	112605	0.198021	5.0500	112605	0.0268	5.050	0.193437	85+

TABLE 4 — OBSERVED AND PROJECTED VITAL RATES

	OBSERVED POPULATION BOTH SEXES	MALES	FEMALES	PROJECTED POPULATION 1962 MALES	FEMALES	1967 MALES	FEMALES	1972 MALES	FEMALES	STABLE POPULATION MALES	FEMALES
RATES PER THOUSAND											
Birth	24.72	25.38	24.06	25.20	23.75	25.76	24.19	26.20	24.54	26.60	25.03
Death	8.58	9.92	7.24	9.99	7.63	10.01	7.91	10.05	8.14	9.47	7.89
Increase	16.14	15.46	16.81	15.21	16.12	15.75	16.28	16.15	16.40	17.1352	
PERCENTAGE											
under 15	31.90	32.58	31.22	32.49	30.91	32.46	30.76	32.79	31.01	33.69	32.01
15-64	61.37	61.35	61.38	61.57	61.27	61.88	61.38	61.09	60.52	60.64	59.93
65 and over	6.74	6.07	7.40	5.93	7.82	5.67	7.86	6.12	8.46	5.67	8.06
DEP. RATIO X 100	62.96	63.00	62.91	62.41	63.22	61.61	62.92	63.69	65.23	64.91	66.86

White Population

TABLE 1 — DATA

AGE AT LAST BIRTHDAY	POPULATION BOTH SEXES	MALES Number	MALES %	FEMALES Number	FEMALES %	BIRTHS BY AGE OF MOTHER	DEATHS BOTH SEXES	DEATHS MALES	FEMALES	AGE AT LAST BIRTHDAY
0	89653	45364	2.9	44289	2.8	0	2255	1290	965	0
1-4	268957	136091	8.7	132866	8.5	0	463	253	210	1-4
5-9	334386	170597	10.9	163789	10.4	0	184	97	87	5-9
10-14	320722	164164	10.5	156558	10.0	22	157	94	63	10-14
15-19	282610	144275	9.3	138335	8.8	5889	288	195	93	15-19
20-24	238469	120020	7.7	118449	7.5	25594	388	307	81	20-24
25-29	207583	104477	6.7	103106	6.6	22365	339	242	97	25-29
30-34	210597	104505	6.7	106092	6.8	13401	442	298	144	30-34
35-39	196525	98721	6.3	97804	6.2	6759	564	363	201	35-39
40-44	187656	94053	6.0	93603	6.0	2052	806	515	291	40-44
45-49	185578	91879	5.9	93699	6.0	207	1232	762	470	45-49
50-54	172442	85998	5.5	86444	5.5	11	1740	1132	608	50-54
55-59	130605	64192	4.1	66413	4.2	0	1844	1164	680	55-59
60-64	94179	43731	2.8	50448	3.2	0	2240	1406	834	60-64
65-69	80037	35287	2.3	44750	2.8	0	2761	1653	1108	65-69
70-74	57113	24390	1.6	32723	2.1		3049	1720	1329	70-74
75-79	38644	16468	1.1	22176	1.4		3009	1559	1450	75-79
80-84	21750	9452	0.6	12298	0.8	39038 M.	2626	1280	1346	80-84
85+	11593	4617	0.3	6976	0.4	37262 F.	2402	1059	1343	85+
TOTAL	3129099	1558281		1570818		76300	26789	15389	11400	TOTAL

TABLE 2 — MALE LIFE TABLE

x	$_nq_x$	l_x	$_nd_x$	$_nL_x$	$_nm_x$	$_na_x$	T_x	r_x	$\dot{e}_x$	$_nM_x$	x
0	0.027306	100000	2731	98050	0.027849	0.2858	6514443	0.0275	65.144	0.028437	0
1	0.007212	97269	702	387067	0.001812	1.1342	6416394	0.0275	65.965	0.001859	1
5	0.002830	96568	273	482156	0.000567	2.5000	6029326	0.0091	62.436	0.000569	5
10	0.002873	96295	277	480861	0.000575	2.7859	5547170	0.0160	57.606	0.000573	10
15	0.006799	96018	653	478654	0.001364	2.7995	5066309	0.0299	52.764	0.001352	15
20	0.012741	95365	1215	473878	0.002564	2.5740	4587656	0.0300	48.106	0.002558	20
25	0.011519	94150	1084	468061	0.002317	2.5198	4113778	0.0113	43.694	0.002316	25
30	0.014164	93066	1318	462156	0.002852	2.5932	3645716	0.0028	39.174	0.002852	30
35	0.018245	91747	1674	454785	0.003681	2.6391	3183561	0.0067	34.699	0.003677	35
40	0.027039	90074	2436	444673	0.005477	2.6618	2728775	0.0016	30.295	0.005476	40
45	0.040684	87638	3565	429891	0.008294	2.6723	2284102	0.0002	26.063	0.008294	45
50	0.064045	84073	5384	407598	0.013210	2.6293	1854211	0.0228	22.055	0.013163	50
55	0.087787	78688	6908	377286	0.018309	2.6615	1446613	0.0475	18.384	0.018133	55
60	0.149596	71780	10738	333295	0.032218	2.6153	1069327	0.0115	14.897	0.032151	60
65	0.210544	61042	12852	273858	0.046930	2.5604	736032	0.0115	12.058	0.046844	65
70	0.300171	48190	14465	204789	0.070635	2.5001	462174	0.0115	9.591	0.070521	70
75	0.381312	33725	12860	135634	0.094811	2.4346	257385	0.0115	7.632	0.094668	75
80	0.499866	20865	10430	76892	0.135643	2.4516	121750	0.0115	5.835	0.135421	80
85+	1.000000	10435	10435	44859	0.232628	4.2987	44859	0.0115	4.299	0.229369	85+

TABLE 3 — FEMALE LIFE TABLE

x	$_nq_x$	l_x	$_nd_x$	$_nL_x$	$_nm_x$	$_na_x$	T_x	r_x	$\dot{e}_x$	$_nM_x$	x
0	0.021022	100000	2102	98524	0.021337	0.2978	7216477	0.0277	72.165	0.021789	0
1	0.006150	97898	602	389873	0.001544	1.1471	7117953	0.0277	72.708	0.001581	1
5	0.002641	97296	257	485836	0.000529	2.5000	6728080	0.0116	69.151	0.000531	5
10	0.002013	97039	195	484720	0.000403	2.5734	6242244	0.0164	64.327	0.000402	10
15	0.003364	96843	326	483431	0.000674	2.5863	5757524	0.0273	59.452	0.000672	15
20	0.003421	96518	330	481789	0.000685	2.5797	5274093	0.0287	54.644	0.000684	20
25	0.004701	96187	452	479873	0.000942	2.6465	4792304	0.0101	49.823	0.000941	25
30	0.006770	95735	648	477165	0.001358	2.6678	4312431	0.0039	45.045	0.001357	30
35	0.010245	95087	974	473168	0.002059	2.6721	3835266	0.0104	40.334	0.002055	35
40	0.015437	94113	1453	467209	0.003109	2.6898	3362098	0.0010	35.724	0.003109	40
45	0.024800	92660	2298	457907	0.005018	2.6529	2894890	0.0030	31.242	0.005016	45
50	0.034736	90362	3139	444401	0.007063	2.6392	2436982	0.0272	26.969	0.007033	50
55	0.050396	87223	4396	425853	0.010322	2.6650	1992581	0.0430	22.845	0.010239	55
60	0.079923	82828	6620	398539	0.016610	2.6435	1566728	0.0265	18.916	0.016532	60
65	0.117516	76208	8956	359877	0.024885	2.6369	1168189	0.0265	15.329	0.024760	65
70	0.185963	67252	12506	306359	0.040823	2.6091	808313	0.0265	12.019	0.040614	70
75	0.283180	54746	15503	235881	0.065723	2.5587	501953	0.0265	9.169	0.065386	75
80	0.429939	39243	16872	153428	0.109967	2.5848	266072	0.0265	6.780	0.109449	80
85+	1.000000	22371	22371	112644	0.198598	5.0353	112644	0.0265	5.035	0.192517	85+

TABLE 4 — OBSERVED AND PROJECTED VITAL RATES

	OBSERVED POPULATION BOTH SEXES	MALES	FEMALES	PROJECTED 1965 MALES	1965 FEMALES	1970 MALES	1970 FEMALES	1975 MALES	1975 FEMALES	STABLE POPULATION MALES	FEMALES
RATES PER THOUSAND											
Birth	24.38	25.05	23.72	25.69	24.19	26.51	24.88	26.74	25.06	26.87	25.30
Death	8.56	9.88	7.26	9.93	7.62	9.95	7.86	9.99	8.04	9.12	7.55
Increase	15.82	15.18	16.46	15.76	16.57	16.56	17.02	16.75	17.02		17.7537
PERCENTAGE											
under 15	32.40	33.13	31.67	32.65	31.12	32.87	31.23	33.48	31.60	34.16	32.41
15-64	60.92	61.08	60.76	61.81	61.13	61.36	60.63	60.20	59.57	60.45	59.70
65 and over	6.68	5.79	7.57	5.54	7.75	5.77	8.13	6.32	8.83	5.39	7.89
DEP. RATIO X 100	64.15	63.71	64.59	61.78	63.59	62.97	64.92	66.11	67.86	65.44	67.50

AGE AT LAST BIRTHDAY	1965 BOTH SEXES	1965 MALES	1965 FEMALES	1970 BOTH SEXES	1970 MALES	1970 FEMALES	1975 BOTH SEXES	1975 MALES	1975 FEMALES	AGE AT LAST BIRTHDAY	
0-4	392	200	192	437	223	214	484	247	237	0-4	**TABLE 5**
5-9	356	180	176	389	198	191	434	221	213	5-9	
10-14	333	170	163	356	180	176	388	198	190	10-14	POPULATION PROJECTED
15-19	319	163	156	332	169	163	354	179	175	15-19	WITH
20-24	281	143	138	318	162	156	330	168	162	20-24	FIXED
25-29	237	119	118	278	141	137	315	160	155	25-29	AGE—
30-34	206	103	103	234	117	117	276	139	137	30-34	SPECIFIC
35-39	208	103	105	204	102	102	231	115	116	35-39	BIRTH
40-44	194	97	97	205	101	104	199	99	100	40-44	AND
45-49	183	91	92	188	93	95	199	97	102	45-49	DEATH
50-54	178	87	91	175	86	89	180	88	92	50-54	RATES
55-59	163	80	83	168	81	87	165	80	85	55-59	(IN 1000's)
60-64	119	57	62	148	70	78	153	71	82	60-64	
65-69	82	36	46	103	47	56	128	58	70	65-69	
70-74	64	26	38	66	27	39	83	35	48	70-74	
75-79	41	16	25	46	17	29	48	18	30	75-79	
80-84	23	9	14	25	9	16	29	10	19	80-84	
85+	15	6	9	16	5	11	17	5	12	85+	
TOTAL	3394	1686	1708	3688	1828	1860	4013	1988	2025	TOTAL	

STANDARD COUNTRIES: STANDARDIZED RATES PER THOUSAND	ENGLAND AND WALES 1961 BOTH SEXES	MALES	FEMALES	UNITED STATES 1960 BOTH SEXES	MALES	FEMALES	MEXICO 1960 BOTH SEXES	MALES	FEMALES	
Birth	22.06	24.47*	20.88	22.41	22.68*	21.56	26.07	22.11*	25.39	**TABLE 6**
Death	12.67	14.13*	11.72	10.43	12.11*	8.73	5.66	8.57*	4.43	STANDARDIZED RATES
Increase	9.38	10.35*	9.16	11.98	10.58*	12.83	20.41	13.55*	20.96	

	OBSERVED POP. MALES	OBSERVED POP. FEMALES	STATIONARY POP. MALES	STATIONARY POP. FEMALES	STABLE POP. MALES	STABLE POP. FEMALES	OBSERVED BIRTHS	NET MATERNITY FUNCTION	BIRTHS IN STABLE POP.	
μ	28.79464	30.12361	35.64038	38.56467	27.65712	29.50142	27.27195	27.72906	27.09967	**TABLE 7**
σ^2	425.1310	458.9666	483.6295	545.7538	407.8769	463.7304	34.50948	34.47867	32.25638	MOMENTS
κ_3	4926.340	5178.038	2736.666	2403.875	5367.921	6262.629	130.2235	124.8233	124.9337	AND
κ_4	-108927.	-144232.	-214927.	-302469.	-73122.	-113882.	-60.949	-104.161	95.086	CUMULANTS
β_1	0.315850	0.277324	0.066207	0.035550	0.424644	0.393293	0.412632	0.380137	0.465064	
β_2	2.397313	2.315299	2.081108	1.984483	2.560466	2.470431	2.948821	2.912379	3.091387	
κ	-0.123637	-0.105560	-0.025824	-0.013190	-0.170001	-0.151019	-0.258001	-0.240269	-0.324349	

VITAL STATISTICS		AGE RANGE	THOMPSON NRR	1000r	INTERVAL	AGE RANGE	BOURGEOIS-PICHAT NRR	1000b	1000d	1000r	COALE		
GRR	1.698										IBR	24.23	**TABLE 8**
NRR	1.627	0-4	1.58	17.04	27.41	5-29	1.88	26.64	3.17	23.48	IDR	8.08	RATES FROM AGE DISTRIBUTIONS
TFR	3.477	5-9	1.56	16.46	27.36	30-54	1.16	16.56	11.01	5.55	IRI	16.15	AND VITAL STATISTICS
GENERATION	27.411	10-14	1.56	16.02	27.28	55-79	1.86	36.28	13.21	23.06	K1	0.	(Females)
SEX RATIO	104.766	15-19	1.44	12.94	27.18	*30-54	1.16	16.56	11.01	5.55	K2	0.	

Start of Age Interval	ORIGINAL MATRIX SUB-DIAGONAL	ALTERNATIVE FIRST ROWS Projection	ALTERNATIVE FIRST ROWS Integral	FIRST STABLE MATRIX % IN STABLE POPULATION	FISHER VALUES	REPRODUCTIVE VALUES	SECOND STABLE MATRIX Z₂ FIRST COLUMN	FIRST ROW	
0	0.99476	0.00000	0.00000	11.832	1.070	189567	0.1776+0.0793	0.1776+0.0793	**TABLE 9**
5	0.99770	0.00017	0.00000	10.769	1.176	192579	0.1655-0.1464	0.0011+0.1713	LESLIE MATRIX
10	0.99734	0.05080	0.00035	9.829	1.288	201636	-0.0739-0.2405	-0.1366+0.0630	AND ITS
15	0.99660	0.30758	0.10615	8.969	1.357	187720	-0.2841-0.0367	-0.1091-0.0904	SPECTRAL
20	0.99602	0.51534	0.53876	8.178	1.158	137168	-0.1716+0.2770	-0.0221-0.1446	COMPONENTS
25	0.99436	0.40847	0.54085	7.452	0.717	73944	0.2061+0.3080	0.0159-0.1114	(Females)
30	0.99162	0.23237	0.31495	6.779	0.349	37000	0.4150-0.0684	0.0222-0.0605	
35	0.98741	0.10823	0.17231	6.150	0.134	13074	0.1237-0.4598	0.0151-0.0229	
40	0.98009	0.02873	0.05466	5.556	0.031	2872	-0.4142-0.3413	0.0045-0.0049	
45	0.97050	0.00278	0.00551	4.982	0.003	268	-0.5394+0.2640	0.0005-0.0004	
50	0.95826	0.00015	0.00032	4.423	0.000	13	0.0192+0.6650	0.0000-0.0000	
55+	0.81194			15.080					

Start of Age Interval	OBSERVED POPUL. (IN 100's)	CONTRIBUTIONS OF ROOTS (IN 100's) r_1	r_2, r_3	r_4-r_{11}	AGE-SP. BIRTH RATES	NET MATERNITY FUNCTION	COEFF. OF MATRIX EQUATION	PARAMETERS	INTEGRAL	MATRIX	EXP. INCREASE x	$e^{(x+2\frac{1}{2})r}$	
0	1772	1793	-30	9	0.0000	0.0000	0.0000	L(1)	1.09283	1.09303	0	1.0454	**TABLE 10**
5	1638	1632	21	-16	0.0000	0.0000	0.0002	L(2)	0.35629	0.36225	50	2.5398	AGE ANALYSIS
10	1566	1490	59	16	0.0001	0.0003	0.0504		0.82869	0.79757	55	2.7755	AND MISCELLANEOUS
15	1383	1359	28	-5	0.0208	0.1005	0.3045	R(1)	0.01775	0.01779	60	3.0332	RESULTS
20	1184	1240	-50	-5	0.1055	0.5084	0.5084	R(2)	-0.02062	-0.02648	65	3.3147	(Females)
25	1031	1130	-84	-15	0.1059	0.5083	0.4013		0.23295	0.22889	70	3.6224	
30	1061	1028	-14	47	0.0617	0.2944	0.2270	C(1)		15157	75	3.9587	
35	978	932	95	-49	0.0337	0.1597	0.1049	C(2)		-3553	80	4.3262	
40	936	842	106	-12	0.0107	0.0500	0.0275			11248	85	4.7277	
45	937	755	-21	203	0.0011	0.0049	0.0026	2P/Y	26.9723	27.4504	90	5.1666	
50	864	670	-151	345	0.0001	0.0003	0.0001	DELTA	3.4711		95	5.6462	
55+	2358	2286									100	6.1703	

TABLE 1 — DATA

AGE AT LAST BIRTHDAY	POPULATION BOTH SEXES	MALES Number	%	FEMALES Number	%	BIRTHS BY AGE OF MOTHER	DEATHS BOTH SEXES	MALES	FEMALES	AGE AT LAST BIRTHDAY
0	76383	37048	5.1	39335	4.8	0	10826	5891	4935	0
1-4	251214	124586	17.1	126628	15.6	0	11424	5901	5523	1-4
5-9	280894	142427	19.5	138467	17.0	0	2979	1722	1257	5-9
10-14	131413	71260	9.8	60153	7.4	0	795	486	309	10-14
15-19	95907	47343	6.5	48564	6.0	7150	1024	446	578	15-19
20-24	106005	38909	5.3	67096	8.2	21910	1302	800	502	20-24
25-29	134217	53471	7.3	80746	9.9	25305	1839	805	1034	25-29
30-34	90403	36733	5.0	53670	6.6	14825	1221	562	659	30-34
35-39	95291	43316	5.9	51975	6.4	9935	1509	871	638	35-39
40-44	62522	30500	4.2	32022	3.9	3625	1216	775	441	40-44
45-49	62962	30655	4.2	32307	4.0	1420	1438	800	638	45-49
50-54	37031	16553	2.3	20478	2.5	0	1008	577	431	50-54
55-59	36301	16398	2.2	19903	2.4	0	1019	603	416	55-59
60-64	24501	11511	1.6	12990	1.6	0	1449	775	674	60-64
65-69	24946	11456	1.6	13490	1.7	0	1920	1302	618	65-69
70-74	12585	6598	0.9	5987	0.7		1022	591	431	70-74
75-79	13512	7560	1.0	5952	0.7		1449	805	644	75-79
80-84	5774	3090	0.4	2684	0.3	41315 M.	876	455	421	80-84
85+	1694	856	0.1	838	0.1	42855 F.	394	188	206	85+
TOTAL	1543555	730270		813285		84170	44710	24355	20355	TOTAL

TABLE 2 — MALE LIFE TABLE

x	nq_x	l_x	nd_x	nL_x	nm_x	na_x	T_x	r_x	$\dot{e}_x$	nM_x	x
0	0.145613	100000	14561	91575	0.159010	0.4214	3335404	0.0000	33.354	0.159010	0
1	0.168705	85439	14414	304316	0.047365	1.4026	3243829	0.0000	37.967	0.047365	1
5	0.056423	71025	4007	345105	0.011612	2.5000	2939513	0.0635	41.387	0.012090	5
10	0.033264	67017	2229	329310	0.006769	2.4087	2594407	0.1017	38.712	0.006820	10
15	0.046713	64788	3030	317159	0.009555	2.7622	2265098	0.0491	34.962	0.009421	15
20	0.097844	61758	6043	293891	0.020561	2.5346	1947939	0.0000	31.542	0.020561	20
25	0.072423	55715	4035	268023	0.015055	2.3848	1654047	0.0000	29.688	0.015055	25
30	0.073735	51680	3811	248989	0.015304	2.5302	1386024	0.0050	26.819	0.015300	30
35	0.095842	47869	4588	228161	0.020108	2.5619	1137035	0.0000	23.753	0.020108	35
40	0.119533	43282	5174	203493	0.025424	2.5037	908874	0.0102	20.999	0.025410	40
45	0.122773	38108	4679	178884	0.026155	2.5087	705381	0.0331	18.510	0.026097	45
50	0.160636	33429	5370	153733	0.034930	2.5022	526497	0.0297	15.750	0.034858	50
55	0.168735	28059	4735	128752	0.036773	2.5617	372764	0.0000	13.285	0.036773	55
60	0.290359	23325	6773	100221	0.067576	2.5780	244012	0.0173	10.461	0.067327	60
65	0.439314	16552	7272	63863	0.113863	2.4011	143791	0.0173	8.687	0.113652	65
70	0.357688	9281	3320	37107	0.089460	2.1995	79928	0.0173	8.612	0.089573	70
75	0.416683	5961	2484	23288	0.106660	2.3761	42821	0.0173	7.184	0.106481	75
80	0.529842	3477	1842	12482	0.147605	2.4040	19534	0.0173	5.618	0.147249	80
85+	1.000000	1635	1635	7052	0.231829	4.3135	7052	0.0173	4.314	0.219627	85+

TABLE 3 — FEMALE LIFE TABLE

x	nq_x	l_x	nd_x	nL_x	nm_x	na_x	T_x	r_x	$\dot{e}_x$	nM_x	x
0	0.116879	100000	11688	93403	0.125135	0.4355	4017924	0.0056	40.179	0.125461	0
1	0.156822	88312	13849	318077	0.043541	1.4604	3924522	0.0056	44.439	0.043616	1
5	0.041486	74463	3089	364591	0.008473	2.5000	3606445	0.0860	48.433	0.009078	5
10	0.025672	71374	1832	352481	0.005198	2.6058	3241854	0.0971	45.421	0.005137	10
15	0.057809	69541	4020	337775	0.011902	2.5297	2889373	0.0000	41.549	0.011902	15
20	0.036720	65521	2406	321570	0.007482	2.4915	2551598	0.0000	38.943	0.007482	20
25	0.062142	63115	3922	306003	0.012817	2.5594	2230028	0.0110	35.333	0.012806	25
30	0.059522	59193	3523	287031	0.012275	2.4643	1924024	0.0316	32.504	0.012279	30
35	0.059603	55670	3318	270049	0.012287	2.4986	1636993	0.0391	29.405	0.012275	35
40	0.066863	52352	3500	253276	0.013820	2.5769	1366945	0.0328	26.111	0.013772	40
45	0.094356	48851	4609	232925	0.019789	2.5417	1113668	0.0260	22.797	0.019748	45
50	0.099952	44242	4422	210025	0.021055	2.4707	880743	0.0280	19.907	0.021047	50
55	0.100146	39820	3988	189929	0.020996	2.7006	670719	0.0176	16.844	0.020901	55
60	0.230554	35832	8261	158855	0.052005	2.5421	480789	0.0176	13.418	0.051886	60
65	0.205215	27571	5658	123386	0.045856	2.4429	321934	0.0176	11.677	0.045812	65
70	0.306277	21913	6711	92952	0.072203	2.5247	198548	0.0176	9.061	0.071989	70
75	0.424566	15201	6454	59484	0.108500	2.4398	105597	0.0176	6.946	0.108199	75
80	0.554101	8747	4847	30817	0.157282	2.3902	46113	0.0176	5.272	0.156855	80
85+	1.000000	3900	3900	15296	0.254998	3.9216	15296	0.0176	3.922	0.245822	85+

TABLE 4 — OBSERVED AND PROJECTED VITAL RATES

RATES PER THOUSAND	OBSERVED POPULATION BOTH SEXES	MALES	FEMALES	PROJECTED 1966 MALES	FEMALES	1971 MALES	FEMALES	1976 MALES	FEMALES	STABLE MALES	FEMALES
Birth	54.53	56.57	52.69	49.02	44.87	48.45	43.89	53.32	47.94	56.49	50.36
Death	28.97	33.35	25.03	30.43	23.79	28.82	22.87	29.18	22.99	29.28	23.16
Increase	25.56	23.22	27.67	18.59	21.08	19.62	21.02	24.14	24.95		27.2050
PERCENTAGE											
under 15	47.94	51.39	44.83	53.92	49.40	49.14	46.24	47.01	44.52	50.08	47.01
15-64	48.27	44.56	51.61	43.13	47.50	48.50	50.77	51.20	52.77	48.78	50.75
65 and over	3.79	4.05	3.56	2.95	3.10	2.36	2.99	1.79	2.70	1.14	2.24
DEP. RATIO X 100	107.15	124.43	93.75	131.87	110.53	106.20	96.96	95.31	89.49	105.00	97.05

AGE AT LAST BIRTHDAY	BOTH SEXES	1966 MALES	FEMALES	BOTH SEXES	1971 MALES	FEMALES	BOTH SEXES	1976 MALES	FEMALES	AGE AT LAST BIRTHDAY	
0-4	333	160	173	341	164	177	395	190	205	0-4	
5-9	288	141	147	293	140	153	300	143	157	5-9	
10-14	270	136	134	276	134	142	281	133	148	10-14	**TABLE 5**
15-19	127	69	58	259	131	128	265	129	136	15-19	
20-24	90	44	46	119	64	55	243	121	122	20-24	POPULATION
25-29	99	35	64	84	40	44	110	58	52	25-29	PROJECTED
30-34	126	50	76	93	33	60	78	37	41	30-34	WITH
35-39	84	34	50	117	46	71	86	30	56	35-39	FIXED
40-44	88	39	49	77	30	47	108	41	67	40-44	AGE—
45-49	56	27	29	79	34	45	70	26	44	45-49	SPECIFIC
50-54	55	26	29	50	23	27	69	29	40	50-54	BIRTH
55-59	33	14	19	48	22	26	43	19	24	55-59	AND
60-64	30	13	17	26	11	15	39	17	22	60-64	DEATH
65-69	17	7	10	21	8	13	19	7	12	65-69	RATES
70-74	17	7	10	12	4	8	15	5	10	70-74	(IN 1000's)
75-79	8	4	4	11	4	7	8	3	5	75-79	
80-84	7	4	3	4	2	2	5	2	3	80-84	
85+	3	2	1	4	2	2	2	1	1	85+	
TOTAL	1731	812	919	1914	892	1022	2136	991	1145	TOTAL	

STANDARD COUNTRIES:	ENGLAND AND WALES 1961			UNITED STATES 1960			MEXICO 1960			
STANDARDIZED RATES PER THOUSAND	BOTH SEXES	MALES	FEMALES	BOTH SEXES	MALES	FEMALES	BOTH SEXES	MALES	FEMALES	**TABLE 6**
Birth	45.63	64.11*	45.03	46.33	60.56*	46.48	50.36	59.77*	51.15	STANDAR
Death	32.67	62.33*	30.16	30.62	52.15*	26.95	25.85	27.73*	22.51	DIZED
Increase	12.96	1.78*	14.87	15.71	8.41*	19.53	24.52	32.04*	28.65	RATES

	OBSERVED POP.		STATIONARY POP.		STABLE POP.		OBSERVED BIRTHS	NET MATERNITY FUNCTION	BIRTHS IN STABLE POP.	
	MALES	FEMALES	MALES	FEMALES	MALES	FEMALES				
μ	21.62884	22.73610	27.93698	31.46411	19.20856	21.03011	28.39343	28.74893	27.23431	**TABLE 7**
σ^2	386.0598	362.3528	383.6966	454.6171	257.6967	307.4068	44.76607	56.50317	50.52878	MOMENTS
κ_3	7790.865	6043.998	4302.313	4356.689	4419.343	5534.583	176.6009	200.3346	233.5959	AND
κ_4	36034.	9452.	-72926.	-154743.	44852.	44934.	-253.335	-1810.833	-650.867	CUMULANTS
β_1	1.054891	0.767810	0.327673	0.202011	1.141271	1.054458	0.347648	0.222481	0.422974	
β_2	3.241772	3.071989	2.504656	2.251279	3.675407	3.475493	2.873585	2.432805	2.745074	
κ	-0.390942	-0.328235	-0.139188	-0.078827	-0.543826	-0.465271	-0.221403	-0.100521	-0.202043	

VITAL STATISTICS			THOMPSON			BOURGEOIS-PICHAT					COALE		**TABLE 8**
		AGE RANGE	NRR	1000r	INTERVAL	AGE RANGE	NRR	1000b	1000d	1000r			RATES FROM AGE
GRR	3.594												DISTRI-
NRR	2.141	0-4	2.14	28.53	26.73	5-29	1.33	32.50	21.96	10.55	IBR		BUTIONS
TFR	7.058	5-9	2.00	26.51	26.57	30-54	2.41	70.67	38.07	32.60	IDR		AND VITAL
GENERATION	27.978	10-14	0.98	-0.72	26.44	55-79	1.88	49.58	26.19	23.39	IRI		STATISTICS
SEX RATIO	96.406	15-19	0.99	-0.52	26.31	*40-64	1.86	44.48	21.45	23.04	K1		(Females)
											K2		

Start of Age Interval	ORIGINAL MATRIX			FIRST STABLE MATRIX			SECOND STABLE MATRIX Z_2		
	SUB-DIAGONAL	ALTERNATIVE FIRST ROWS Projection	Integral	% IN STABLE POPULATION	FISHER VALUES	REPRODUCTIVE VALUES	FIRST COLUMN	FIRST ROW	
0	0.88605	0.00000	0.00000	19.399	1.298	215419	0.0927+0.1232	0.0927+0.1232	**TABLE 9**
5	0.96679	0.00000	0.00000	14.996	1.679	232499	0.1675-0.0215	-0.0559+0.1292	
10	0.95828	0.14779	0.00000	12.649	1.991	119747	0.0767-0.1867	-0.1171+0.0129	LESLIE
15	0.95202	0.47988	0.33016	10.575	2.181	105913	-0.1473-0.1883	-0.0726-0.0995	MATRIX
20	0.95159	0.65445	0.73228	8.784	1.971	132276	-0.2784+0.0411	-0.0037-0.1576	AND ITS
25	0.93800	0.59969	0.70277	7.292	1.482	119660	-0.1200+0.3085	0.0511-0.1538	SPECTRAL
30	0.94083	0.47774	0.61943	5.968	0.981	52651	0.2420+0.2979	0.0777-0.1061	COMPO-
35	0.93789	0.31145	0.42865	4.898	0.536	27862	0.4404-0.0734	0.0652-0.0496	NENTS
40	0.91965	0.16090	0.25386	4.008	0.224	7176	0.1786-0.4858	0.0342-0.0132	(Females)
45	0.90168	0.04606	0.09850	3.216	0.052	1686	-0.3796-0.4496	0.0087-0.0011	
50	0.90432	0.00005	0.00011	2.530	0.000	1	-0.6448+0.1200	0.0000-0.0000	
55+	0.74377			5.685					

Start of Age Interval	OBSERVED POPUL. (IN 100's)	CONTRIBUTIONS OF ROOTS (IN 100's)			AGE-SP. BIRTH RATES	NET MATERNITY FUNCTION	COEFF. OF MATRIX EQUATION	PARAMETERS		EXP. INCREASE		
		r_1	r_2, r_3	$r_4 \cdot r_{11}$				INTEGRAL	MATRIX	x	$e^{(x+2\frac{1}{2})r}$	
0	1660	1445	198	17	0.0000	0.0000	0.0000	L(1) 1.14571	1.14620	0	1.0704	**TABLE 10**
5	1385	1117	156	112	0.0000	0.0000	0.0000	L(2) 0.38491	0.40015	50	4.1715	
10	602	942	-75	-265	0.0000	0.0000	0.1266	0.71624	0.70308	55	4.7793	AGE
15	486	788	-309	7	0.0750	0.2532	0.3939	R(1) 0.02721	0.02729	60	5.4757	ANALYSIS
20	671	654	-255	271	0.1663	0.5346	0.5115	R(2) -0.04138	-0.04240	65	6.2735	AND
25	807	543	131	133	0.1596	0.4883	0.4460	0.21554	0.21068	70	7.1877	MISCEL-
30	537	444	498	-405	0.1406	0.4037	0.3332	C(1)	7448	75	8.2350	LANEOUS
35	520	365	396	-241	0.0973	0.2628	0.2044	C(2)	51851	80	9.4349	RESULTS
40	320	299	-217	239	0.0576	0.1460	0.0991		-41404	85	10.8097	(Females)
45	323	240	-766	849	0.0224	0.0521	0.0261	2P/Y 29.1515	29.8240	90	12.3847	
50	205	188	-569	586	0.0000	0.0000	0.0000	DELTA 10.4586		95	14.1893	
55+	618	423								100	16.2569	

TABLE 1 DATA

AGE AT LAST BIRTHDAY	POPULATION BOTH SEXES	MALES Number	MALES %	FEMALES Number	FEMALES %	BIRTHS BY AGE OF MOTHER	DEATHS BOTH SEXES	DEATHS MALES	FEMALES	AGE AT LAST BIRTHDAY
0	6788	3449	3.2	3339	2.6	0	517	279	238	0
1-4	25845	12881	12.1	12964	10.2	0	100	54	46	1-4
5-9	30698	15291	14.3	15407	12.1	0	20	11	9	5-9
10-14	25850	12824	12.0	13026	10.2	27	17	11	6	10-14
15-19	21489	10558	9.9	10931	8.6	1332	17	10	7	15-19
20-24	17494	8226	7.7	9268	7.3	2011	18	9	9	20-24
25-29	13472	5734	5.4	7738	6.1	1600	23	10	13	25-29
30-34	12788	5395	5.1	7393	5.8	1255	26	9	17	30-34
35-39	11840	4906	4.6	6934	5.4	707	29	14	15	35-39
40-44	12817	5613	5.3	7204	5.6	268	50	27	23	40-44
45-49	12104	5412	5.1	6692	5.2	29	86	43	43	45-49
50-54	11936	5498	5.2	6438	5.0	1	111	53	58	50-54
55-59	9445	4085	3.8	5360	4.2	0	129	67	62	55-59
60-64	7194	2771	2.6	4423	3.5	0	149	79	70	60-64
65-69	5444	1761	1.7	3683	2.9	0	153	71	82	65-69
70-74	3936	1034	1.0	2902	2.3		192	68	124	70-74
75-79	2713	680	0.6	2033	1.6		190	58	132	75-79
80-84	1515	338	0.3	1177	0.9	3693 M.	187	58	129	80-84
85+	938	187	0.2	751	0.6	3537 F.	193	48	145	85+
TOTAL	234306	106643		127663		7230	2207	979	1228	TOTAL

TABLE 2 MALE LIFE TABLE

x	$_nq_x$	l_x	$_nd_x$	$_nL_x$	$_nm_x$	$_na_x$	T_x	r_x	$\mathring{e}_x$	$_nM_x$	x
0	0.076120	100000	7612	94355	0.080674	0.2584	6290372	0.0036	62.904	0.080893	0
1	0.016498	92388	1524	365145	0.004174	1.1089	6196017	0.0036	67.065	0.004192	1
5	0.003529	90864	321	453517	0.000707	2.5000	5830872	0.0225	64.172	0.000719	5
10	0.004289	90543	388	451767	0.000860	2.5570	5377355	0.0362	59.390	0.000858	10
15	0.004736	90155	427	449729	0.000949	2.5516	4925588	0.0434	54.635	0.000947	15
20	0.005506	89728	494	447477	0.001104	2.6476	4475859	0.0598	49.883	0.001094	20
25	0.008707	89234	777	444277	0.001749	2.5650	4028382	0.0406	45.144	0.001744	25
30	0.008324	88457	736	440541	0.001671	2.6320	3584105	0.0137	40.518	0.001668	30
35	0.014176	87721	1244	435769	0.002854	2.7213	3143564	0.0000	35.836	0.002854	35
40	0.023789	86477	2057	427669	0.004810	2.7074	2707795	0.0000	31.312	0.004810	40
45	0.038987	84420	3291	414242	0.007945	2.6126	2280126	0.0000	27.009	0.007945	45
50	0.047279	81129	3836	396655	0.009670	2.6567	1865885	0.0174	22.999	0.009640	50
55	0.079912	77293	6177	372211	0.016594	2.6924	1469230	0.0510	19.009	0.016401	55
60	0.134133	71116	9539	332815	0.028662	2.6134	1097019	0.0311	15.426	0.028510	60
65	0.184619	61577	11368	280447	0.040536	2.5863	764203	0.0311	12.410	0.040318	65
70	0.283819	50209	14250	215695	0.066067	2.5194	483757	0.0311	9.635	0.065764	70
75	0.353043	35959	12695	147983	0.085787	2.4942	268061	0.0311	7.455	0.085294	75
80	0.597484	23264	13900	80417	0.172845	2.4501	120079	0.0311	5.162	0.171598	80
85+	1.000000	9364	9364	39662	0.236098	4.2355	39662	0.0311	4.236	0.256684	85+

TABLE 3 FEMALE LIFE TABLE

x	$_nq_x$	l_x	$_nd_x$	$_nL_x$	$_nm_x$	$_na_x$	T_x	r_x	$\mathring{e}_x$	$_nM_x$	x
0	0.067677	100000	6768	94956	0.071272	0.2547	6738776	0.0001	67.388	0.071279	0
1	0.014047	93232	1310	369139	0.003548	1.1058	6643820	0.0001	71.261	0.003548	1
5	0.002862	91923	263	458956	0.000573	2.5000	6274681	0.0211	68.260	0.000584	5
10	0.002303	91660	211	457777	0.000461	2.5306	5815725	0.0338	63.449	0.000461	10
15	0.003215	91449	294	456557	0.000644	2.6657	5357948	0.0334	58.590	0.000640	15
20	0.004881	91155	445	454758	0.000978	2.7189	4901392	0.0335	53.770	0.000971	20
25	0.008396	90710	762	451766	0.001686	2.6597	4446634	0.0209	49.021	0.001680	25
30	0.011437	89948	1029	447209	0.002300	2.5395	3994868	0.0088	44.413	0.002299	30
35	0.010760	88919	957	442281	0.002163	2.5796	3547659	0.0002	39.897	0.002163	35
40	0.015850	87963	1394	436699	0.003193	2.7669	3105378	0.0000	35.303	0.003193	40
45	0.031684	86568	2743	426465	0.006432	2.6753	2668679	0.0050	30.827	0.006426	45
50	0.044159	83825	3702	410244	0.009023	2.6001	2242213	0.0132	26.749	0.009009	50
55	0.056440	80124	4522	389746	0.011603	2.5957	1831970	0.0256	22.864	0.011567	55
60	0.076445	75602	5779	364164	0.015870	2.6046	1442224	0.0201	19.077	0.015826	60
65	0.106317	69822	7423	331878	0.022368	2.6786	1078060	0.0201	15.440	0.022264	65
70	0.194595	62399	12142	283034	0.042901	2.6149	746182	0.0201	11.958	0.042729	70
75	0.280999	50256	14122	216685	0.065173	2.5502	463148	0.0201	9.216	0.064929	75
80	0.430147	36134	15543	141302	0.109999	2.5867	246463	0.0201	6.821	0.109601	80
85+	1.000000	20591	20591	105161	0.195808	5.1070	105161	0.0201	5.107	0.193077	85+

TABLE 4 OBSERVED AND PROJECTED VITAL RATES

	OBSERVED POPULATION BOTH SEXES	MALES	FEMALES	PROJECTED POPULATION 1965 MALES	1965 FEMALES	1970 MALES	1970 FEMALES	1975 MALES	1975 FEMALES	STABLE POPULATION MALES	FEMALES
RATES PER THOUSAND											
Birth	30.86	34.63	27.71	34.64	28.68	35.46	30.24	35.80	31.31	32.93	31.83
Death	9.42	9.18	9.62	9.18	9.62	9.34	9.62	9.44	9.55	9.26	8.16
Increase	21.44	25.45	18.09	25.46	19.06	26.12	20.61	26.36	21.76	23.6720	
PERCENTAGE											
under 15	38.06	41.68	35.04	40.85	34.99	39.78	34.64	39.83	35.24	37.85	37.01
15-64	55.73	54.57	56.70	55.08	56.74	55.60	57.06	54.97	56.40	57.69	57.08
65 and over	6.21	3.75	8.26	4.07	8.28	4.62	8.30	5.21	8.36	4.46	5.92
DEP. RATIO X 100	79.44	83.24	76.38	81.56	76.25	79.86	75.26	81.93	77.31	73.34	75.20

AGE AT LAST BIRTHDAY	BOTH SEXES	1965 MALES	FEMALES	BOTH SEXES	1970 MALES	FEMALES	BOTH SEXES	1975 MALES	FEMALES	AGE AT LAST BIRTHDAY	
0-4	36	18	18	41	21	20	47	24	23	0-4	TABLE 5
5-9	32	16	16	35	18	17	41	21	20	5-9	
10-14	30	15	15	32	16	16	35	18	17	10-14	POPULATION
15-19	26	13	13	30	15	15	32	16	16	15-19	PROJECTED
20-24	22	11	11	26	13	13	30	15	16	20-24	WITH
25-29	17	8	9	21	10	11	26	13	13	25-29	FIXED
30-34	14	6	8	17	8	9	21	10	11	30-34	AGE—
35-39	12	5	7	14	6	8	17	8	9	35-39	SPECIFIC
40-44	12	5	7	12	5	7	13	6	7	40-44	BIRTH
45-49	12	5	7	12	5	7	12	5	7	45-49	AND
50-54	11	5	6	12	5	7	10	4	6	50-54	DEATH
55-59	11	5	6	11	5	6	11	5	6	55-59	RATES
60-64	9	4	5	11	5	6	10	4	6	60-64	(IN 1000's)
65-69	6	2	4	8	3	5	9	4	5	65-69	
70-74	4	1	3	5	2	3	6	2	4	70-74	
75-79	3	1	2	3	1	2	4	1	3	75-79	
80-84	1	0	1	1	0	1	3	1	2	80-84	
85+	1	0	1	1	0	1	1	0	1	85+	
TOTAL	259	120	139	292	138	154	328	157	171	TOTAL	

STANDARD COUNTRIES: STANDARDIZED RATES PER THOUSAND	ENGLAND AND WALES 1961 BOTH SEXES	MALES	FEMALES	UNITED STATES 1960 BOTH SEXES	MALES	FEMALES	MEXICO 1960 BOTH SEXES	MALES	FEMALES	
Birth	27.70	40.52*	26.26	28.35	36.58*	27.33	32.48	37.11*	31.69	TABLE 6
Death	13.40	17.07*	13.01	11.56	14.05*	10.33	7.49	8.70*	6.55	STANDARDIZED RATES
Increase	14.30	23.45*	13.26	16.79	22.53*	16.99	24.98	28.41*	25.14	

	OBSERVED POP. MALES	FEMALES	STATIONARY POP. MALES	FEMALES	STABLE POP MALES	FEMALES	OBSERVED BIRTHS	NET MATERNITY FUNCTION	BIRTHS IN STABLE POP.	
μ	25.18046	29.43607	36.25024	38.31312	25.71506	26.66665	26.69640	27.62591	26.49799	TABLE 7
σ^2	401.3686	491.2419	491.8871	545.4832	385.1432	421.8945	47.63743	47.11088	43.91202	
κ_3	5964.312	6518.100	2462.377	2594.036	5750.225	6770.128	167.6189	120.7124	147.6315	MOMENTS
κ_4	-75116.	-164908.	-231917.	-299702.	-35478.	-38406.	-1201.592	-1370.888	-885.539	AND
β_1	0.550162	0.358390	0.050946	0.041458	0.578766	0.610355	0.259897	0.139361	0.257399	CUMULANTS
β_2	2.533720	2.316639	2.041477	1.992774	2.760828	2.784227	2.470507	2.382326	2.540761	
κ	-0.192182	-0.126615	-0.019517	-0.015395	-0.232969	-0.242464	-0.116182	-0.066997	-0.124429	

VITAL STATISTICS		AGE RANGE	THOMPSON NRR	1000r	INTERVAL	BOURGEOIS-PICHAT AGE RANGE	NRR	1000b	1000d	1000r	COALE		TABLE 8
GRR	2.106										IBR	28.99	RATES FROM AGE DISTRIBUTIONS AND VITAL STATISTICS (Females)
NRR	1.897	0-4	1.91	24.34	27.38	5-29	2.48	33.86	0.27	33.59	IDR	6.28	
TFR	4.305	5-9	1.97	25.31	27.32	30-54	1.06	13.69	11.63	2.06	IRI	22.70	
GENERATION	27.056	10-14	1.75	20.31	27.24	55-79	1.69	32.51	13.08	19.42	K1	7.38	
SEX RATIO	104.411	15-19	1.53	14.84	27.11	* 5-29	2.48	33.86	0.27	33.59	K2	0.	

Start of Age Interval	ORIGINAL MATRIX SUB-DIAGONAL	ALTERNATIVE FIRST ROWS Projection	Integral	FIRST STABLE MATRIX % IN STABLE POPULATION	FISHER VALUES	REPRODUCTIVE VALUES	SECOND STABLE MATRIX Z_2 FIRST COLUMN	FIRST ROW	
0	0.98893	0.00000	0.00000	13.948	1.143	18628	0.1237+0.0930	0.1237+0.0930	TABLE 9
5	0.99743	0.00235	0.00000	12.250	1.301	20044	0.1655-0.0785	-0.0210+0.1291	
10	0.99733	0.14031	0.00499	10.851	1.466	19097	-0.0088-0.2185	-0.1042+0.0345	LESLIE
15	0.99606	0.38368	0.29353	9.611	1.494	16336	-0.2260-0.1304	-0.0835-0.0770	MATRIX
20	0.99342	0.47950	0.52267	8.502	1.249	11579	-0.2629+0.1663	-0.0231-0.1278	AND ITS
25	0.98991	0.42549	0.49808	7.500	0.865	6690	0.0299+0.3686	0.0265-0.1120	SPECTRAL
30	0.98898	0.30718	0.40891	6.594	0.492	3640	0.4032+0.1716	0.0409-0.0641	COMPONENTS
35	0.98738	0.15745	0.24561	5.791	0.206	1426	0.4016-0.3282	0.0256-0.0234	(Females)
40	0.97656	0.04704	0.08961	5.078	0.052	377	-0.1229-0.6004	0.0079-0.0049	
45	0.96196	0.00509	0.01044	4.404	0.005	36	-0.6881-0.1989	0.0009-0.0004	
50	0.95004	0.00018	0.00037	3.762	0.000	1	-0.5709+0.5951	0.0000-0.0000	
55+	0.82074			11.709					

Start of Age Interval	OBSERVED POPUL. (IN 100's)	CONTRIBUTIONS OF ROOTS (IN 100's) r_1	r_2, r_3	$r_4 \text{-} r_{11}$	AGE-SP. BIRTH RATES	NET MATERNITY FUNCTION	COEFF. OF MATRIX EQUATION	PARAMETERS INTEGRAL	MATRIX	EXP. INCREASE x	$e^{(x+2\frac{1}{2})r}$	
0	163	163	-1	1	0.0000	0.0000	0.0000	L(1) 1.12565	1.12602	0	1.0610	TABLE 10
5	154	143	8	4	0.0000	0.0000	0.0023	L(2) 0.37780	0.38826	50	3.4652	
10	130	126	10	-6	0.0010	0.0046	0.1384	0.75893	0.73988	55	3.9006	AGE
15	109	112	-0	-3	0.0596	0.2722	0.3774	R(1) 0.02367	0.02374	60	4.3907	ANALYSIS
20	93	99	-14	8	0.1062	0.4827	0.4699	R(2) -0.03333	-0.03593	65	4.9424	AND
25	77	87	-15	5	0.1012	0.4570	0.4142	0.22178	0.21751	70	5.5635	MISCELLANEOUS
30	74	77	3	-6	0.0830	0.3714	0.2960	C(1)	1165	75	6.2625	RESULTS
35	69	67	24	-23	0.0499	0.2206	0.1500	C(2)	1278	80	7.0494	(Females)
40	72	59	23	-10	0.0182	0.0795	0.0443		2158	85	7.9351	
45	67	51	-9	25	0.0021	0.0090	0.0047	2P/Y 28.3305	28.8873	90	8.9322	
50	64	44	-40	61	0.0001	0.0003	0.0002	DELTA 6.8509		95	10.0545	
55+	203	136								100	11.3178	

TABLE 1 — DATA

AGE AT LAST BIRTHDAY	POPULATION BOTH SEXES	MALES Number	%	FEMALES Number	%	BIRTHS BY AGE OF MOTHER	DEATHS BOTH SEXES	MALES	FEMALES	AGE AT LAST BIRTHDAY
0	6345	3196	3.1	3149	2.4	0	376	204	172	0
1-4	25914	12850	12.4	13064	10.0	0	87	55	32	1-4
5-9	31205	15493	15.0	15712	12.1	0	22	13	9	5-9
10-14	27162	13447	13.0	13715	10.5	22	17	10	7	10-14
15-19	22192	10722	10.4	11470	8.8	1305	16	8	8	15-19
20-24	16300	6890	6.7	9410	7.2	1813	21	12	9	20-24
25-29	12350	4455	4.3	7895	6.1	1546	20	7	13	25-29
30-34	11918	4435	4.3	7483	5.7	1217	18	12	6	30-34
35-39	11898	4720	4.6	7178	5.5	729	35	19	16	35-39
40-44	12430	5240	5.1	7190	5.5	233	38	21	17	40-44
45-49	11954	5229	5.1	6725	5.2	16	71	30	41	45-49
50-54	11655	5240	5.1	6415	4.9	0	115	66	49	50-54
55-59	9723	4220	4.1	5503	4.2	0	131	68	63	55-59
60-64	7389	2918	2.8	4471	3.4	0	175	85	90	60-64
65-69	5585	1868	1.8	3717	2.9	0	163	85	78	65-69
70-74	4072	1105	1.1	2967	2.3		190	78	112	70-74
75-79	2764	685	0.7	2079	1.6		185	68	117	75-79
80-84	1509	341	0.3	1168	0.9	3448 M.	197	63	134	80-84
85+	1057	216	0.2	841	0.6	3433 F.	239	58	181	85+
TOTAL	233422	103270		130152		6881	2116	962	1154	TOTAL

TABLE 2 — MALE LIFE TABLE

x	$_nq_x$	l_x	$_nd_x$	$_nL_x$	$_nm_x$	$_na_x$	T_x	r_x	$\mathring{e}_x$	$_nM_x$	x
0	0.061052	100000	6105	95648	0.063830	0.2872	6311215	0.0000	63.112	0.063830	0
1	0.016913	93895	1588	371030	0.004280	1.1356	6215566	0.0000	66.197	0.004280	1
5	0.004139	92307	382	460578	0.000830	2.5000	5844536	0.0160	63.316	0.000839	5
10	0.003709	91925	341	458764	0.000743	2.4788	5383958	0.0361	58.569	0.000744	10
15	0.003793	91584	347	457145	0.000760	2.7741	4925194	0.0659	53.778	0.000746	15
20	0.008746	91236	798	454261	0.001757	2.5951	4468049	0.0864	48.972	0.001742	20
25	0.007868	90438	712	450498	0.001579	2.6196	4013786	0.0422	44.381	0.001571	25
30	0.013444	89727	1206	445838	0.002706	2.6818	3563288	0.0000	39.713	0.002706	30
35	0.019931	88521	1764	438299	0.004025	2.5609	3117450	0.0000	35.217	0.004025	35
40	0.019846	86756	1722	429611	0.004008	2.5780	2679151	0.0000	30.881	0.004008	40
45	0.028327	85034	2409	419846	0.005737	2.7889	2249540	0.0000	26.454	0.005737	45
50	0.061269	82626	5062	401235	0.012617	2.6506	1829694	0.0098	22.144	0.012595	50
55	0.078251	77563	6069	373629	0.016245	2.6624	1428459	0.0403	18.417	0.016114	55
60	0.136997	71494	9794	334365	0.029293	2.6411	1054830	0.0278	14.754	0.029130	60
65	0.205867	61699	12702	277778	0.045727	2.5815	720465	0.0278	11.677	0.045503	65
70	0.301336	48998	14765	208271	0.070892	2.5132	442687	0.0278	9.035	0.070588	70
75	0.398388	34233	13638	136683	0.099778	2.4717	234416	0.0278	6.848	0.099270	75
80	0.626995	20595	12913	69451	0.185927	2.4039	97733	0.0278	4.746	0.184750	80
85+	*1.000000	7682	7682	28282	0.271624	3.6816	28282	0.0278	3.682	0.268519	85+

TABLE 3 — FEMALE LIFE TABLE

x	$_nq_x$	l_x	$_nd_x$	$_nL_x$	$_nm_x$	$_na_x$	T_x	r_x	$\mathring{e}_x$	$_nM_x$	x
0	0.052455	100000	5246	96036	0.054621	0.2442	6931971	0.0000	69.320	0.054621	0
1	0.009729	94754	922	376342	0.002449	1.0977	6835935	0.0000	72.144	0.002449	1
5	0.002834	93833	266	468498	0.000568	2.5000	6459593	0.0156	68.842	0.000573	5
10	0.002553	93567	239	467249	0.000511	2.5528	5991094	0.0309	64.030	0.000510	10
15	0.003499	93328	327	465866	0.000701	2.6328	5523846	0.0370	59.188	0.000697	15
20	0.004807	93001	447	463979	0.000964	2.7013	5057980	0.0363	54.386	0.000956	20
25	0.008196	92554	759	460858	0.001646	2.4782	4594001	0.0216	49.636	0.001647	25
30	0.004006	91796	368	458112	0.000803	2.6447	4133143	0.0082	45.025	0.000802	30
35	0.011090	91428	1014	454750	0.002230	2.6432	3675031	0.0022	40.196	0.002229	35
40	0.011775	90414	1065	449757	0.002367	2.8277	3220282	0.0033	35.617	0.002364	40
45	0.030088	89349	2688	440482	0.006103	2.6698	2770525	0.0059	31.008	0.006097	45
50	0.037575	86661	3256	425578	0.007652	2.6271	2330042	0.0120	26.887	0.007638	50
55	0.056048	83405	4675	406235	0.011507	2.6923	1904464	0.0235	22.834	0.011448	55
60	0.096154	78730	7570	375236	0.020174	2.5676	1498229	0.0211	19.030	0.020130	60
65	0.100210	71160	7131	338713	0.021053	2.6039	1122993	0.0211	15.781	0.020985	65
70	0.173776	64029	11127	293587	0.037899	2.6132	784280	0.0211	12.249	0.037749	70
75	0.249032	52902	13174	232963	0.056551	2.6053	490694	0.0211	9.275	0.056277	75
80	0.447746	39728	17788	154313	0.115272	2.6027	257731	0.0211	6.487	0.114726	80
85+	1.000000	21940	21940	103418	0.212148	4.7137	103418	0.0211	4.714	0.215221	85+

TABLE 4 — OBSERVED AND PROJECTED VITAL RATES

	OBSERVED POPULATION BOTH SEXES	MALES	FEMALES	1967 MALES	FEMALES	1972 MALES	FEMALES	1977 MALES	FEMALES	STABLE POPULATION MALES	FEMALES
RATES PER THOUSAND											
Birth	29.48	33.39	26.38	33.90	27.62	34.88	29.22	35.10	30.12	31.64	30.11
Death	9.07	9.32	8.87	9.04	8.72	9.16	8.81	9.19	8.75	9.13	7.60
Increase	20.41	24.07	17.51	24.86	18.91	25.72	20.40	25.91	21.37		22.5101
PERCENTAGE											
under 15	38.82	43.56	35.07	41.62	34.50	39.93	34.00	39.76	34.65	37.22	35.98
15-64	54.75	52.36	56.66	54.06	57.24	55.24	57.65	55.06	56.98	58.34	57.67
65 and over	6.42	4.08	8.28	4.32	8.26	4.83	8.35	5.18	8.37	4.43	6.35
DEP. RATIO X 100	82.63	91.00	76.50	84.96	74.70	81.01	73.45	81.63	75.49	71.41	73.39

TABLE 1 — DATA

AGE AT LAST BIRTHDAY	POPULATION BOTH SEXES	MALES Number	MALES %	FEMALES Number	FEMALES %	BIRTHS BY AGE OF MOTHER	DEATHS BOTH SEXES	DEATHS MALES	DEATHS FEMALES	AGE AT LAST BIRTHDAY
0	6502	3274	3.1	3228	2.4	0	418	228	190	0
1-4	26469	13365	12.6	13104	9.9	0	96	50	46	1-4
5-9	35524	17478	16.4	18046	13.6	0	22	9	13	5-9
10-14	28324	14488	13.6	13836	10.4	30	13	7	6	10-14
15-19	23674	11763	11.1	11911	9.0	1352	12	6	6	15-19
20-24	17068	7071	6.7	9997	7.5	1682	19	7	12	20-24
25-29	12346	4332	4.1	8014	6.0	1468	18	4	14	25-29
30-34	10871	3574	3.4	7297	5.5	1199	22	11	11	30-34
35-39	10653	3527	3.3	7126	5.4	724	29	13	16	35-39
40-44	10388	4293	4.0	6095	4.6	257	43	22	21	40-44
45-49	11533	4783	4.5	6750	5.1	42	58	33	25	45-49
50-54	11836	5226	4.9	6610	5.0	2	88	49	39	50-54
55-59	10740	4943	4.6	5797	4.4	0	121	66	55	55-59
60-64	8259	3469	3.3	4790	3.6	0	175	89	86	60-64
65-69	6199	2164	2.0	4035	3.0	0	161	81	80	65-69
70-74	3472	1281	1.2	2191	1.7		198	81	117	70-74
75-79	2680	687	0.6	1993	1.5		183	65	118	75-79
80-84	1703	465	0.4	1238	0.9	3471 M.	197	59	138	80-84
85+	617	122	0.1	495	0.4	3285 F.	217	54	163	85+
TOTAL	238858	106305		132553		6756	2090	934	1156	TOTAL

TABLE 2 — MALE LIFE TABLE

x	$_nq_x$	l_x	$_nd_x$	$_nL_x$	$_nm_x$	$_na_x$	T_x	r_x	$\mathring{e}_x$	$_nM_x$	x
0	0.066240	100000	6624	95118	0.069640	0.2629	6417924	0.0000	64.179	0.069640	0
1	0.014805	93376	1382	369513	0.003741	1.1127	6322807	0.0000	67.713	0.003741	1
5	0.002537	91994	233	459385	0.000508	2.5000	5953294	0.0125	64.714	0.000515	5
10	0.002413	91760	221	458248	0.000483	2.5030	5493909	0.0391	59.872	0.000483	10
15	0.002585	91539	237	457151	0.000518	2.7056	5035661	0.0711	55.011	0.000510	15
20	0.004983	91302	455	455414	0.000999	2.5893	4578510	0.0991	50.147	0.000990	20
25	0.004751	90847	432	453351	0.000952	2.9494	4123096	0.0668	45.385	0.000923	25
30	0.015330	90416	1386	448861	0.003088	2.6796	3669745	0.0179	40.588	0.003078	30
35	0.018268	89029	1626	441253	0.003686	2.6059	3220884	0.0000	36.178	0.003686	35
40	0.025314	87403	2213	431747	0.005125	2.6191	2779631	0.0000	31.802	0.005125	40
45	0.033938	85191	2891	419050	0.006899	2.6125	2347883	0.0000	27.560	0.006899	45
50	0.045859	82299	3774	402525	0.009376	2.6229	1928833	0.0000	23.437	0.009376	50
55	0.065174	78525	5118	380907	0.013436	2.7101	1526308	0.0258	19.437	0.013352	55
60	0.121727	73407	8936	345953	0.025829	2.6404	1145402	0.0350	15.603	0.025656	60
65	0.172817	64472	11142	295701	0.037679	2.6074	799449	0.0350	12.400	0.037431	65
70	0.275266	53330	14680	230711	0.063629	2.5519	503749	0.0350	9.446	0.063232	70
75	0.382832	38650	14796	155600	0.095093	2.4555	273037	0.0350	7.064	0.094614	75
80	0.482785	23854	11516	89965	0.128007	2.4555	117438	0.0350	4.923	0.126881	80
85+	*1.000000	12337	12337	27473	0.449076	2.2268	27473	0.0350	2.227	0.442623	85+

TABLE 3 — FEMALE LIFE TABLE

x	$_nq_x$	l_x	$_nd_x$	$_nL_x$	$_nm_x$	$_na_x$	T_x	r_x	$\mathring{e}_x$	$_nM_x$	x
0	0.056450	100000	5645	95906	0.058860	0.2747	6838119	0.0000	68.381	0.058860	0
1	0.013901	94355	1312	373647	0.003510	1.1234	6742213	0.0000	71.456	0.003510	1
5	0.003556	93043	331	464390	0.000712	2.5000	6368566	0.0152	68.447	0.000720	5
10	0.002157	92713	200	463043	0.000432	2.4003	5904177	0.0410	63.683	0.000434	10
15	0.002542	92513	235	462049	0.000509	2.8162	5441134	0.0319	58.815	0.000504	15
20	0.006035	92277	557	460112	0.001210	2.7108	4979085	0.0384	53.958	0.001200	20
25	0.008707	91721	799	456633	0.001749	2.5330	4518973	0.0299	49.269	0.001747	25
30	0.007515	90922	683	452946	0.001508	2.5646	4062340	0.0100	44.679	0.001507	30
35	0.011199	90239	1011	448842	0.002252	2.6735	3609394	0.0157	39.998	0.002245	35
40	0.017088	89228	1525	442453	0.003446	2.5819	3160552	0.0022	35.421	0.003445	40
45	0.018357	87703	1610	434697	0.003704	2.6275	2718099	0.0000	30.992	0.003704	45
50	0.029157	86093	2510	424669	0.005911	2.6903	2283402	0.0091	26.522	0.005900	50
55	0.046691	83583	3903	409068	0.009540	2.7330	1858733	0.0216	22.238	0.009488	55
60	0.086280	79681	6875	381852	0.018004	2.5926	1449665	0.0221	18.193	0.017954	60
65	0.095559	72806	6957	348458	0.019966	2.7620	1067813	0.0221	14.667	0.019827	65
70	0.237255	65848	15623	291444	0.053605	2.5806	719355	0.0221	10.924	0.053400	70
75	0.258798	50226	12998	218806	0.059405	2.5134	427911	0.0221	8.520	0.059207	75
80	0.442111	37227	16459	146609	0.112262	2.5984	209105	0.0221	5.617	0.111470	80
85+	*1.000000	20769	20769	62496	0.332319	3.0092	62496	0.0221	3.009	0.329293	85+

TABLE 4 — OBSERVED AND PROJECTED VITAL RATES

	OBSERVED POPULATION BOTH SEXES	OBSERVED MALES	OBSERVED FEMALES	PROJECTED 1968 MALES	1968 FEMALES	1973 MALES	1973 FEMALES	1978 MALES	1978 FEMALES	STABLE POPULATION MALES	STABLE FEMALES
RATES PER THOUSAND											
Birth	28.28	32.65	24.78	33.38	26.29	35.11	28.60	35.26	29.58	29.25	28.23
Death	8.75	8.79	8.72	8.69	8.71	8.78	8.75	8.85	8.74	9.40	8.38
Increase	19.53	23.87	16.06	24.70	17.58	26.33	19.84	26.40	20.84		19.8489
PERCENTAGE											
under 15	40.53	45.72	36.37	42.72	35.21	39.65	32.90	39.39	33.40	34.98	34.12
15-64	53.32	49.84	56.12	52.23	56.99	54.54	59.01	54.68	58.33	59.52	58.91
65 and over	6.14	4.44	7.51	5.05	7.81	5.81	8.09	5.93	8.26	5.50	6.97
DEP. RATIO X 100	87.53	100.65	78.19	91.46	75.48	83.35	69.46	82.89	71.43	68.00	69.74

TABLE 1 — DATA

AGE AT LAST BIRTHDAY	POPULATION BOTH SEXES	MALES Number	MALES %	FEMALES Number	FEMALES %	BIRTHS BY AGE OF MOTHER	DEATHS BOTH SEXES	MALES	FEMALES	AGE AT LAST BIRTHDAY
0	6250	3190	2.9	3060	2.3	0	250	127	123	0
1-4	25630	12985	11.9	12645	9.4	0	56	26	30	1-4
5-9	32555	16345	15.0	16210	12.0	0	17	7	10	5-9
10-14	30445	15160	13.9	15285	11.3	27	10	8	2	10-14
15-19	24790	12035	11.0	12755	9.5	1311	14	9	5	15-19
20-24	19135	9030	8.3	10105	7.5	1684	13	7	6	20-24
25-29	13035	4870	4.5	8165	6.1	1362	17	9	8	25-29
30-34	10780	3815	3.5	6965	5.2	980	16	7	9	30-34
35-39	11350	4280	3.9	7070	5.2	723	32	13	19	35-39
40-44	11515	4550	4.2	6965	5.2	246	47	18	29	40-44
45-49	11425	4685	4.3	6740	5.0	25	53	27	26	45-49
50-54	11100	4780	4.4	6320	4.7	0	71	40	31	50-54
55-59	10540	4510	4.1	6030	4.5	0	115	61	54	55-59
60-64	8740	3925	3.6	4815	3.6	0	189	97	92	60-64
65-69	6115	2265	2.1	3850	2.9	0	198	96	102	65-69
70-74	4605	1380	1.3	3225	2.4		207	84	123	70-74
75-79	3040	705	0.6	2335	1.7		183	64	119	75-79
80-84	1933	421	0.4	1512	1.1	3258 M.	213	64	149	80-84
85+	827	114	0.1	713	0.5	3100 F.	204	47	157	85+
TOTAL	243810	109045		134765		6358	1905	811	1094	TOTAL

TABLE 2 — MALE LIFE TABLE

x	nq_x	l_x	nd_x	nL_x	nm_x	na_x	T_x	r_x	$\mathring{e}_x$	nM_x	x
0	0.038668	100000	3867	97128	0.039812	0.2572	6691566	0.0000	66.916	0.039812	0
1	0.007963	96133	766	382319	0.002002	1.1079	6594439	0.0000	68.597	0.002002	1
5	0.002132	95368	203	476330	0.000427	2.5000	6212120	0.0056	65.139	0.000428	5
10	0.002645	95164	252	475224	0.000530	2.6260	5735790	0.0301	60.273	0.000528	10
15	0.003746	94913	356	473700	0.000751	2.5726	5260567	0.0511	55.425	0.000748	15
20	0.003972	94557	376	471954	0.000796	2.7881	4786867	0.0894	50.624	0.000775	20
25	0.009291	94181	875	468819	0.001867	2.6138	4314913	0.0846	45.815	0.001848	25
30	0.009147	93306	854	464506	0.001837	2.6267	3846094	0.0108	41.220	0.001835	30
35	0.015079	92453	1394	458973	0.003037	2.6391	3381588	0.0000	36.576	0.003037	35
40	0.019597	91059	1784	451071	0.003956	2.6336	2922616	0.0000	32.096	0.003956	40
45	0.028430	89274	2538	440396	0.005763	2.6457	2471545	0.0000	27.685	0.005763	45
50	0.041041	86736	3560	425391	0.008368	2.6712	2031149	0.0000	23.418	0.008368	50
55	0.065677	83176	5463	403391	0.013542	2.7134	1605758	0.0050	19.305	0.013525	55
60	0.117805	77714	9155	367305	0.024925	2.6774	1202367	0.0369	15.472	0.024713	60
65	0.193375	68559	13258	310805	0.042656	2.5871	835062	0.0369	12.180	0.042384	65
70	0.265813	55301	14700	240138	0.061214	2.5260	524258	0.0369	9.480	0.060870	70
75	0.371698	40601	15091	165146	0.091383	2.4912	284119	0.0369	6.998	0.090780	75
80	0.551303	25510	14064	91631	0.153482	2.4460	118974	0.0369	4.664	0.152018	80
85+	*1.000000	11446	11446	27343	0.418622	2.3888	27343	0.0369	2.389	0.412281	85+

TABLE 3 — FEMALE LIFE TABLE

x	nq_x	l_x	nd_x	nL_x	nm_x	na_x	T_x	r_x	$\mathring{e}_x$	nM_x	x
0	0.039057	100000	3906	97166	0.040196	0.2745	7108084	0.0000	71.081	0.040196	0
1	0.009426	96094	906	381771	0.002372	1.1232	7010918	0.0000	72.959	0.002372	1
5	0.003076	95189	293	475211	0.000616	2.5000	6629147	0.0017	69.642	0.000617	5
10	0.000649	94896	62	474303	0.000130	2.1438	6153936	0.0237	64.849	0.000131	10
15	0.001978	94834	188	473748	0.000396	2.7461	5679633	0.0410	59.890	0.000392	15
20	0.002992	94647	283	472582	0.000599	2.7031	5205885	0.0440	55.003	0.000594	20
25	0.004914	94363	464	470725	0.000985	2.6455	4733303	0.0363	50.160	0.000980	25
30	0.006465	93900	607	468144	0.001297	2.7685	4262578	0.0129	45.395	0.001292	30
35	0.013355	93293	1246	463617	0.002687	2.7157	3794434	0.0000	40.672	0.002687	35
40	0.020610	92047	1897	455590	0.004164	2.5524	3330816	0.0010	36.186	0.004164	40
45	0.019110	90150	1723	446494	0.003858	2.5302	2875226	0.0056	31.894	0.003858	45
50	0.024281	88427	2147	437201	0.004911	2.7024	2428732	0.0057	27.466	0.004905	50
55	0.044143	86280	3809	423008	0.009004	2.7967	1991531	0.0169	23.082	0.008955	55
60	0.091811	82471	7572	394582	0.019189	2.6526	1568523	0.0226	19.019	0.019107	60
65	0.124886	74899	9354	351923	0.026579	2.5867	1173942	0.0226	15.674	0.026494	65
70	0.174900	65545	11464	299686	0.038253	2.5540	822019	0.0226	12.541	0.038140	70
75	0.227880	54082	12324	240712	0.051199	2.5904	522332	0.0226	9.658	0.050964	75
80	0.402599	41757	16811	169388	0.099248	2.6564	281621	0.0226	6.744	0.098546	80
85+	*1.000000	24946	24946	112233	0.222270	4.4990	112233	0.0226	4.499	0.220196	85+

TABLE 4 — OBSERVED AND PROJECTED VITAL RATES

	OBSERVED POPULATION BOTH SEXES	MALES	FEMALES	PROJECTED POPULATION 1970 MALES	1970 FEMALES	1975 MALES	1975 FEMALES	1980 MALES	1980 FEMALES	STABLE POPULATION MALES	FEMALES
RATES PER THOUSAND											
Birth	26.08	29.88	23.00	31.46	25.11	32.73	27.03	32.50	27.64	26.79	26.02
Death	7.81	7.44	8.12	7.53	8.39	7.64	8.40	7.65	8.33	8.70	7.93
Increase	18.26	22.44	14.89	23.93	16.71	25.09	18.52	24.85	19.31		18.0947
PERCENTAGE											
under 15	38.92	43.73	35.02	40.36	32.86	38.35	31.82	38.25	32.47	33.58	32.55
15-64	54.31	51.80	56.34	54.30	58.36	55.95	59.26	56.16	58.77	60.45	59.51
65 and over	6.78	4.48	8.63	5.34	8.78	5.70	8.92	5.60	8.76	5.98	7.93
DEP. RATIO X 100	84.13	93.07	77.49	84.17	71.34	78.73	68.73	78.07	70.17	65.44	68.03

AGE AT LAST BIRTHDAY	1970 BOTH SEXES	1970 MALES	1970 FEMALES	1975 BOTH SEXES	1975 MALES	1975 FEMALES	1980 BOTH SEXES	1980 MALES	1980 FEMALES	AGE AT LAST BIRTHDAY	
0-4	33	17	16	39	20	19	45	23	22	0-4	
5-9	32	16	16	33	17	16	39	20	19	5-9	
10-14	32	16	16	32	16	16	33	17	16	10-14	
15-19	30	15	15	32	16	16	32	16	16	15-19	TABLE 5
20-24	25	12	13	30	15	15	32	16	16	20-24	POPULATION
25-29	19	9	10	25	12	13	30	15	15	25-29	PROJECTED
30-34	13	5	8	19	9	10	25	12	13	30-34	WITH
35-39	11	4	7	13	5	8	19	9	10	35-39	FIXED
40-44	11	4	7	11	4	7	13	5	8	40-44	AGE—
45-49	11	4	7	11	4	7	11	4	7	45-49	SPECIFIC
50-54	12	5	7	11	4	7	11	4	7	50-54	BIRTH
55-59	11	5	6	10	4	6	10	4	6	55-59	AND
60-64	10	4	6	10	4	6	10	4	6	60-64	DEATH
65-69	7	3	4	8	3	5	8	3	5	65-69	RATES
70-74	5	2	3	7	3	4	7	3	4	70-74	(IN 1000's)
75-79	4	1	3	4	1	3	5	2	3	75-79	
80-84	2	0	2	3	1	2	3	1	2	80-84	
85+	1	0	1	1	0	1	1	0	1	85+	
TOTAL	269	122	147	299	138	161	334	158	176	TOTAL	

STANDARD COUNTRIES: STANDARDIZED RATES PER THOUSAND	ENGLAND AND WALES 1961 BOTH SEXES	MALES	FEMALES	UNITED STATES 1960 BOTH SEXES	MALES	FEMALES	MEXICO 1960 BOTH SEXES	MALES	FEMALES	
Birth	23.25	40.19*	21.97	23.80	35.01*	22.86	26.84	37.91*	26.10	TABLE 6
Death	12.14	13.00*	11.60	10.23	10.91*	8.92	5.71	7.25*	4.95	STANDARDIZED RATES
Increase	11.11	27.18*	10.37	13.57	24.10*	13.94	21.13	30.66*	21.15	

	OBSERVED POP. MALES	FEMALES	STATIONARY POP. MALES	FEMALES	STABLE POP. MALES	FEMALES	OBSERVED BIRTHS	NET MATERNITY FUNCTION	BIRTHS IN STABLE POP.	
μ	24.83947	29.50399	36.54323	38.77222	28.19705	29.45977	26.61686	28.04662	27.12199	TABLE 7
σ^2	420.6228	495.8208	492.5244	551.1271	420.3540	466.0017	50.83679	50.00285	47.92979	MOMENTS
κ_3	7291.921	7025.689	2178.012	2395.679	5343.596	6397.589	182.2812	97.4586	130.5000	AND
κ_4	-72063.	-163800.	-241574.	-310653.	-94417.	-112345.	-1736.885	-2006.827	-1617.794	CUMULANTS
β_1	0.714505	0.404952	0.039704	0.034285	0.384434	0.404455	0.252930	0.075973	0.154669	
β_2	2.592690	2.333709	2.004147	1.977244	2.465656	2.482656	2.327929	2.197361	2.295774	
κ	-0.229570	-0.139234	-0.014911	-0.012661	-0.148361	-0.155098	-0.099788	-0.032689	-0.066423	

VITAL STATISTICS		AGE RANGE	THOMPSON NRR	1000r	INTERVAL	AGE RANGE	BOURGEOIS-PICHAT NRR	1000b	1000d	1000r	COALE	
GRR	1.755										IBR	TABLE 8
NRR	1.647	0-4	1.77	21.34	27.40	5-29	2.59	35.19	-0.06	35.26	IDR	RATES FROM AGE DISTRIBUTIONS
TFR	3.600	5-9	2.06	26.90	27.34	30-54	1.04	11.78	10.43	1.36	IRI	AND VITAL STATISTICS
GENERATION	27.582	10-14	2.09	26.49	27.28	55-79	1.67	30.63	11.58	19.05	K1	(Females)
SEX RATIO	105.097	15-19	1.81	15.96	27.21	*35-59	1.11	13.22	9.40	3.82	K2	

Start of Age Interval	ORIGINAL MATRIX SUB-DIAGONAL	ALTERNATIVE FIRST ROWS Projection	Integral	FIRST STABLE MATRIX % IN STABLE POPULATION	FISHER VALUES	REPRODUCTIVE VALUES	SECOND STABLE MATRIX Z_2 FIRST COLUMN	FIRST ROW	
0	0.99222	0.00000	0.00000	11.924	1.092	17151	0.1136+0.0755	0.1136+0.0755	TABLE 9
5	0.99809	0.00206	0.00000	10.806	1.205	19534	0.1471-0.3713	-0.0061+0.1137	LESLIE MATRIX
10	0.99883	0.12193	0.00432	9.850	1.320	20172	0.0162-0.1964	-0.0840+0.0434	AND ITS
15	0.99754	0.31411	0.25112	8.986	1.313	16752	-0.1941-0.1373	-0.0802-0.0509	SPECTRAL
20	0.99607	0.38858	0.40717	8.187	1.098	11092	-0.2613+0.1174	-0.0333-0.1026	COMPONENTS
25	0.99452	0.35815	0.40756	7.448	0.781	6373	-0.0382+0.3425	0.0151-0.0966	(Females)
30	0.99033	0.28253	0.34377	6.765	0.466	3246	0.3310+0.2486	0.0347-0.0573	
35	0.98269	0.15993	0.24985	6.119	0.204	1440	0.4574-0.1898	0.0236-0.0209	
40	0.98003	0.04531	0.08629	5.492	0.049	343	0.0819-0.5821	0.0068-0.0041	
45	0.97919	0.00434	0.00870	4.916	0.004	30	-0.5442-0.4338	0.0006-0.0003	
50	0.96753	0.00018	0.00039	4.396	0.000	1	-0.7689+0.2935	0.0000-0.0000	
55+	0.81344			15.112					

Start of Age Interval	OBSERVED POPUL. (IN 100's)	CONTRIBUTIONS OF ROOTS (IN 100's) r_1	r_2, r_3	$r_4 \cdot r_{11}$	AGE-SP. BIRTH RATES	NET MATERNITY FUNCTION	COEFF. OF MATRIX EQUATION	PARAMETERS INTEGRAL	MATRIX	EXP. INCREASE x	$e^{(x+2\frac{1}{2})r}$	
0	157	163	-7	2	0.0000	0.0000	0.0000	L(1) 1.09469	1.09490	0	1.0463	TABLE 10
5	162	148	9	6	0.0000	0.0000	0.0020	L(2) 0.41377	0.42081	50	2.5856	AGE
10	153	135	21	-3	0.0009	0.0041	0.1208	0.72846	0.71299	55	2.8305	ANALYSIS
15	128	123	14	-9	0.0501	0.2374	0.3107	R(1) 0.01809	0.01813	60	3.0985	AND
20	101	112	-14	4	0.0813	0.3840	0.3834	R(2) -0.03540	-0.03777	65	3.3919	MISCELLANEOUS
25	82	102	-37	17	0.0813	0.3829	0.3520	0.21085	0.20752	70	3.7131	RESULTS
30	70	92	-25	2	0.0686	0.3212	0.2762	C(1)	1367	75	4.0647	(Females)
35	71	84	23	-36	0.0499	0.2312	0.1548	C(2)	307	80	4.4496	
40	70	75	64	-69	0.0172	0.0785	0.0433		5428	85	4.8709	
45	67	67	44	-44	0.0018	0.0081	0.0040	2P/Y 29.7996	30.2772	90	5.3322	
50	63	60	-37	40	0.0000	0.0000	0.0000	DELTA 5.2039		95	5.8371	
55+	225	207								100	6.3898	

Excluding Yukon and Northwest Territories

TABLE 1 — DATA

AGE AT LAST BIRTHDAY	POPULATION BOTH SEXES	MALES Number	%	FEMALES Number	%	BIRTHS BY AGE OF MOTHER	DEATHS BOTH SEXES	MALES	FEMALES	AGE AT LAST BIRTHDAY
0	202571	102895	1.9	99676	2.0	0	19804	11287	8517	0
1-4	870340	439585	8.2	430755	8.6	0	5390	2893	2497	1-4
5-9	1130712	571588	10.6	559124	11.2	0	2249	1270	979	5-9
10-14	1073242	542568	10.1	530674	10.6	74	1672	861	811	10-14
15-19	1039394	525196	9.8	514198	10.3	15129	2537	1327	1210	15-19
20-24	911445	463796	8.6	447649	9.0	61110	3003	1536	1467	20-24
25-29	787072	410262	7.6	376810	7.5	65567	2833	1390	1443	25-29
30-34	709195	368281	6.9	340914	6.8	49290	2706	1305	1401	30-34
35-39	688426	359066	6.7	329360	6.6	33939	3146	1574	1572	35-39
40-44	645753	347427	6.5	298326	6.0	13342	3525	1894	1631	40-44
45-49	585095	321306	6.0	263789	5.3	1404	4118	2315	1803	45-49
50-54	489028	267396	5.0	221632	4.4	24	4888	2840	2048	50-54
55-59	367765	199492	3.7	168273	3.4	0	5400	3099	2301	55-59
60-64	295129	157119	2.9	138010	2.8	0	6427	3619	2808	60-64
65-69	231572	120880	2.3	110692	2.2	0	7860	4368	3492	65-69
70-74	171873	88685	1.7	83188	1.7		9204	5033	4171	70-74
75-79	98901	50135	0.9	48766	1.0		8679	4581	4098	75-79
80-84	49333	23950	0.4	25383	0.5	123186 M.	6770	3400	3370	80-84
85+	25379	11244	0.2	14135	0.3	116693 F.	5855	2672	3183	85+
TOTAL	10372225	5370871		5001354		239879	106066	57264	48802	TOTAL

TABLE 2 — MALE LIFE TABLE

x	nq_x	l_x	nd_x	nL_x	nm_x	na_x	T_x	r_x	$\mathring{e}_x$	nM_x	x
0	0.101591	100000	10159	92613	0.109694	0.2729	5899946	0.0000	58.999	0.109694	0
1	0.025835	89841	2321	352683	0.006581	1.1216	5807334	0.0000	64.640	0.006581	1
5	0.011048	87520	967	435182	0.002222	2.5000	5454651	0.0000	62.325	0.002222	5
10	0.007906	86553	684	431077	0.001587	2.5345	5019469	0.0065	57.993	0.001587	10
15	0.012582	85869	1080	426790	0.002531	2.6369	4588392	0.0132	53.435	0.002527	15
20	0.016445	84788	1394	420522	0.003316	2.5479	4161602	0.0215	49.082	0.003312	20
25	0.016803	83394	1401	413476	0.003389	2.5069	3741080	0.0197	44.860	0.003388	25
30	0.017575	81993	1441	406433	0.003545	2.5500	3327603	0.0096	40.584	0.003543	30
35	0.021691	80552	1747	398532	0.004384	2.5811	2921171	0.0014	36.265	0.004384	35
40	0.026921	78804	2121	388922	0.005455	2.5959	2522639	0.0055	32.011	0.005452	40
45	0.035517	76683	2724	376967	0.007225	2.6325	2133717	0.0186	27.825	0.007205	45
50	0.052106	73959	3854	360696	0.010684	2.6383	1756750	0.0368	23.753	0.010621	50
55	0.075348	70106	5282	338002	0.015628	2.6285	1396064	0.0371	19.914	0.015534	55
60	0.109731	64823	7113	307242	0.023152	2.6277	1058053	0.0288	16.322	0.023033	60
65	0.167099	57710	9643	265469	0.036325	2.6064	750810	0.0288	13.010	0.036135	65
70	0.250480	48067	12040	211028	0.057053	2.5659	485341	0.0288	10.097	0.056751	70
75	0.373337	36027	13450	146444	0.091845	2.4951	274313	0.0288	7.614	0.091373	75
80	0.519335	22577	11725	82201	0.142638	2.4538	127869	0.0288	5.664	0.141962	80
85+	1.000000	10852	10852	45668	0.237625	4.2083	45668	0.0288	4.208	0.237637	85+

TABLE 3 — FEMALE LIFE TABLE

x	nq_x	l_x	nd_x	nL_x	nm_x	na_x	T_x	r_x	$\mathring{e}_x$	nM_x	x
0	0.080542	100000	8054	94260	0.085447	0.2873	6135847	0.0000	61.358	0.085447	0
1	0.022808	91946	2097	361776	0.005797	1.1358	6041588	0.0000	65.708	0.005797	1
5	0.008717	89849	783	447285	0.001751	2.5000	5679811	0.0000	63.215	0.001751	5
10	0.007617	89065	678	443684	0.001529	2.5778	5232526	0.0066	58.749	0.001528	10
15	0.011728	88387	1037	439499	0.002359	2.6498	4788842	0.0146	54.180	0.002353	15
20	0.016299	87350	1424	433317	0.003286	2.5871	4349343	0.0279	49.792	0.003277	20
25	0.018989	85927	1632	425615	0.003834	2.5372	3916026	0.0235	45.574	0.003830	25
30	0.020351	84295	1715	417253	0.004111	2.5385	3490410	0.0093	41.407	0.004110	30
35	0.023600	82580	1949	408122	0.004775	2.5494	3073157	0.0086	37.214	0.004773	35
40	0.027012	80631	2178	397854	0.005474	2.5665	2665035	0.0166	33.052	0.005467	40
45	0.033710	78453	2645	385916	0.006853	2.5999	2267181	0.0227	28.899	0.006835	45
50	0.045451	75808	3446	370880	0.009290	2.6314	1881265	0.0353	24.816	0.009241	50
55	0.066583	72363	4818	350421	0.013750	2.6356	1510385	0.0333	20.872	0.013674	55
60	0.097442	67544	6582	322135	0.020431	2.6318	1159964	0.0238	17.173	0.020346	60
65	0.147313	60963	8981	283424	0.031686	2.6182	837829	0.0238	13.743	0.031547	65
70	0.224610	51982	11676	231782	0.050374	2.5908	554405	0.0238	10.665	0.050139	70
75	0.349028	40306	14068	166660	0.084412	2.5212	322624	0.0238	8.004	0.084034	75
80	0.499575	26238	13108	98226	0.133447	2.4851	155963	0.0238	5.944	0.132765	80
85+	*1.000000	13130	13130	57737	0.227417	4.3972	57737	0.0238	4.397	0.225186	85+

TABLE 4 — OBSERVED AND PROJECTED VITAL RATES

	OBSERVED POPULATION BOTH SEXES	MALES	FEMALES	PROJECTED POPULATION 1936 MALES	FEMALES	1941 MALES	FEMALES	1946 MALES	FEMALES	STABLE POPULATION MALES	FEMALES
RATES PER THOUSAND											
Birth	23.13	22.94	23.33	23.83	24.08	24.46	24.54	24.56	24.47	23.04	22.23
Death	10.23	10.66	9.76	11.14	10.04	11.66	10.42	12.13	10.78	14.00	13.20
Increase	12.90	12.27	13.57	12.69	14.04	12.79	14.11	12.43	13.70		9.0345
PERCENTAGE											
under 15	31.59	30.84	32.40	29.31	30.54	28.35	29.29	28.81	29.49	28.27	28.02
15-64	62.84	63.66	61.96	64.83	63.57	65.37	64.57	64.18	63.82	62.83	62.42
65 and over	5.56	5.49	5.64	5.86	5.89	6.28	6.15	7.01	6.69	8.90	9.56
DEP. RATIO X 100	59.12	57.07	61.39	54.26	57.31	52.98	54.87	55.81	56.69	59.15	60.21

Excluding Yukon and Northwest Territories

AGE AT LAST BIRTHDAY	1936 BOTH SEXES	1936 MALES	1936 FEMALES	1941 BOTH SEXES	1941 MALES	1941 FEMALES	1946 BOTH SEXES	1946 MALES	1946 FEMALES	AGE AT LAST BIRTHDAY	
0-4	1137	577	560	1249	634	615	1348	684	664	0-4	**TABLE 5**
5-9	1050	530	520	1113	564	549	1222	619	603	5-9	
10-14	1121	566	555	1041	525	516	1104	559	545	10-14	POPULATION
15-19	1063	537	526	1110	561	549	1031	520	511	15-19	PROJECTED
20-24	1024	517	507	1047	529	518	1094	552	542	20-24	WITH
25-29	896	456	440	1007	509	498	1029	520	509	25-29	FIXED
30-34	772	403	369	879	448	431	988	500	488	30-34	AGE—
35-39	694	361	333	756	395	361	862	440	422	35-39	SPECIFIC
40-44	671	350	321	677	352	325	738	386	352	40-44	BIRTH
45-49	626	337	289	651	340	311	657	342	315	45-49	AND
50-54	561	307	254	600	322	278	624	325	299	50-54	DEATH
55-59	460	251	209	528	288	240	565	302	263	55-59	RATES
60-64	336	181	155	421	228	193	482	262	220	60-64	(IN 1000's)
65-69	257	136	121	293	157	136	366	197	169	65-69	
70-74	187	96	91	207	108	99	236	125	111	70-74	
75-79	122	62	60	132	67	65	146	75	71	75-79	
80-84	57	28	29	70	35	35	75	37	38	80-84	
85+	28	13	15	33	16	17	40	19	21	85+	
TOTAL	11062	5708	5354	11814	6078	5736	12607	6464	6143	TOTAL	

STANDARD COUNTRIES: STANDARDIZED RATES PER THOUSAND	ENGLAND AND WALES 1961 BOTH SEXES	MALES	FEMALES	UNITED STATES 1960 BOTH SEXES	MALES	FEMALES	MEXICO 1960 BOTH SEXES	MALES	FEMALES	
Birth	20.48	20.61*	19.31	20.83	19.03*	19.96	22.25	18.88*	21.59	**TABLE 6**
Death	15.60	16.90*	16.75	13.67	14.35*	13.57	9.75	10.53*	9.12	STANDARDIZED RATES
Increase	4.89	3.71*	2.57	7.16	4.68*	6.39	12.50	8.36*	12.47	

	OBSERVED POP. MALES	OBSERVED POP. FEMALES	STATIONARY POP. MALES	STATIONARY POP. FEMALES	STABLE POP. MALES	STABLE POP. FEMALES	OBSERVED BIRTHS	NET MATERNITY FUNCTION	BIRTHS IN STABLE POP.	
μ	28.96603	28.15067	36.19811	36.67700	31.77412	32.13680	28.98700	29.75407	29.35422	**TABLE 7**
σ^2	399.2571	400.5000	505.5417	518.9255	470.9391	483.0880	42.65417	42.56005	41.77364	MOMENTS
κ_3	4472.649	5280.038	2820.376	2887.515	4723.299	4919.999	104.4555	82.1278	91.7695	AND
κ_4	-88159.	-62987.	-246400.	-263603.	-169608.	-180538.	-1078.751	-1125.530	-996.973	CUMULANTS
β_1	0.314320	0.433977	0.061566	0.059667	0.213598	0.214710	0.140598	0.087493	0.115529	
β_2	2.446952	2.607314	2.035889	2.021097	2.235254	2.226402	2.407077	2.378626	2.428681	
κ	-0.128640	-0.179055	-0.023211	-0.022263	-0.081247	-0.080990	-0.069432	-0.045438	-0.061011	

VITAL STATISTICS		THOMPSON AGE RANGE	NRR	1000r	INTERVAL	BOURGEOIS-PICHAT AGE RANGE	NRR	1000b	1000d	1000r	COALE	
GRR	1.551					5-29	1.57	29.44	12.71	16.73	IBR	**TABLE 8** RATES
NRR	1.306	0-4	1.27	8.91	27.23						IDR	FROM AGE DISTRIBUTIONS
TFR	3.189	5-9	1.50	15.08	27.17	30-54	1.53	28.46	12.62	15.83	IRI	AND VITAL
GENERATION	29.554	10-14	1.57	16.45	27.11	55-79	1.68	28.93	9.61	19.32	K1	STATISTICS
SEX RATIO	105.564	15-19	1.68	16.09	27.01	*25-49	1.39	24.69	12.63	12.06	K2	(Females)

Start of Age Interval	ORIGINAL MATRIX SUB-DIAGONAL	ALTERNATIVE FIRST ROWS Projection	ALTERNATIVE FIRST ROWS Integral	FIRST STABLE MATRIX % IN STABLE POPULATION	FISHER VALUES	REPRODUCTIVE VALUES	SECOND STABLE MATRIX Z2 FIRST COLUMN	FIRST ROW	
0	0.98081	0.00000	0.00000	9.916	1.121	594750	0.1378+0.0661	0.1378+0.0661	**TABLE 9**
5	0.99195	0.00015	0.00000	9.296	1.196	668752	0.1481-0.0943	0.0144+0.1322	LESLIE
10	0.99057	0.03248	0.00032	8.813	1.261	669380	-0.0022-0.2040	-0.0901+0.0706	MATRIX
15	0.98593	0.18193	0.06676	8.344	1.296	666153	-0.2024-0.1229	-0.0972-0.0360	AND ITS
20	0.98223	0.34101	0.30977	7.863	1.168	522799	-0.2439-0.1236	-0.0434-0.1001	SPECTRAL
25	0.98035	0.35024	0.39484	7.382	0.855	322072	-0.0274+0.3135	0.0061-0.1009	COMPONENTS
30	0.97812	0.27217	0.32808	6.917	0.512	174417	0.2891+0.2169	0.0282-0.0655	NENTS
35	0.97484	0.16266	0.23382	6.466	0.235	77482	0.3860-0.1501	0.0232-0.0277	(Females)
40	0.97000	0.05533	0.10148	6.025	0.065	19508	0.0872-0.4648	0.0083-0.0066	
45	0.96104	0.00602	0.01208	5.586	0.007	1733	-0.3963-0.3630	0.0009-0.0006	
50	0.94484	0.00012	0.00025	5.131	0.000	29	-0.5826+0.1630	0.0000-0.0000	
55+	0.78079			18.262					

Start of Age Interval	OBSERVED POPUL. (IN 100's)	CONTRIBUTIONS OF ROOTS (IN 100's) r_1	r_2, r_3	$r_4 \cdot r_{11}$	AGE-SP. BIRTH RATES	NET MATERNITY FUNCTION	COEFF. OF MATRIX EQUATION	PARAMETERS	INTEGRAL	MATRIX	EXP. INCREASE x	$e^{(x+2\frac{1}{2})r}$	
0	5304	5658	-275	-78	0.0000	0.0000	0.0000	L(1)	1.04621	1.04625	0	1.0228	**TABLE 10**
5	5591	5304	59	228	0.0000	0.0000	0.0002	L(2)	0.44715	0.45073	50	1.6069	AGE
10	5307	5028	440	-162	0.0001	0.0003	0.0316		0.74323	0.72491	55	1.6812	ANALYSIS
15	5142	4761	459	-78	0.0143	0.0629	0.1753	R(1)	0.00903	0.00904	60	1.7588	AND MISCEL-
20	4476	4486	-29	19	0.0664	0.2878	0.3243	R(2)	-0.02846	-0.03166	65	1.8401	LANEOUS
25	3768	4212	-646	202	0.0846	0.3603	0.3269		0.20584	0.20290	70	1.9251	RESULTS
30	3409	3947	-745	208	0.0703	0.2935	0.2490	C(1)		57057	75	2.0141	(Females)
35	3294	3690	-51	-345	0.0501	0.2046	0.1456	C(2)		-48364	80	2.1072	
40	2983	3438	913	-1368	0.0218	0.0866	0.0483			107291	85	2.2045	
45	2638	3187	1162	-1711	0.0026	0.0100	0.0051	2P/Y	30.5251	30.9664	90	2.3064	
50	2216	2928	214	-925	0.0001	0.0002	0.0001	DELTA	7.7676		95	2.4130	
55+	5884	10419									100	2.5245	

Excluding Yukon and Northwest Territories

TABLE 1 — DATA

AGE AT LAST BIRTHDAY	POPULATION BOTH SEXES	MALES Number	%	FEMALES Number	%	BIRTHS BY AGE OF MOTHER	DEATHS BOTH SEXES	MALES	FEMALES	AGE AT LAST BIRTHDAY
0	215532	109545	1.9	105987	1.9	0	14563	8346	6217	0
1-4	839289	425898	7.2	413391	7.4	0	3394	1854	1540	1-4
5-9	1046465	529475	9.0	516990	9.2	0	1470	829	641	5-9
10-14	1099278	555521	9.4	543757	9.7	74	1245	707	538	10-14
15-19	1117963	564142	9.6	553821	9.9	16925	1921	1110	811	15-19
20-24	1031228	517190	8.8	514038	9.2	71059	2376	1340	1036	20-24
25-29	966564	487820	8.3	478744	8.5	76815	2423	1241	1182	25-29
30-34	843819	431232	7.3	412587	7.4	51285	2323	1191	1132	30-34
35-39	760143	396444	6.7	363699	6.5	29512	2675	1422	1253	35-39
40-44	677047	348763	5.9	328284	5.9	10552	3110	1713	1397	40-44
45-49	635157	332402	5.6	302755	5.4	1071	4085	2335	1750	45-49
50-54	591494	315552	5.3	275942	4.9	21	5629	3370	2259	50-54
55-59	506776	274987	4.7	231789	4.1	0	7263	4402	2861	55-59
60-64	407363	218542	3.7	188821	3.4	0	8751	5303	3448	60-64
65-69	308305	162740	2.8	145565	2.6	0	10382	6056	4326	65-69
70-74	217584	111326	1.9	106258	1.9		11462	6473	4989	70-74
75-79	135962	67309	1.1	68653	1.2		11761	6280	5481	75-79
80-84	71640	34128	0.6	37512	0.7	132345 M.	9707	4955	4752	80-84
85+	35879	15986	0.3	19893	0.4	124969 F.	8309	3828	4481	85+
TOTAL	11507488	5899002		5608486		257314	112849	62755	50094	TOTAL

TABLE 2 — MALE LIFE TABLE

x	nq_x	l_x	nd_x	nL_x	nm_x	na_x	T_x	r_x	$\dot{e}_x$	nM_x	x
0	0.072170	100000	7217	94726	0.076188	0.2693	6228243	0.0000	62.282	0.076188	0
1	0.017197	92783	1596	366534	0.004353	1.1183	6133517	0.0000	66.106	0.004353	1
5	0.007798	91187	711	454159	0.001566	2.5000	5766983	0.0000	63.243	0.001566	5
10	0.006344	90476	574	450982	0.001273	2.5617	5312823	0.0000	58.721	0.001273	10
15	0.009799	89902	881	447429	0.001969	2.6354	4861841	0.0052	54.079	0.001968	15
20	0.012880	89021	1147	442288	0.002592	2.5418	4414412	0.0121	49.588	0.002591	20
25	0.012642	87875	1111	436606	0.002545	2.5085	3972124	0.0156	45.202	0.002544	25
30	0.013736	86764	1192	430926	0.002766	2.5724	3535518	0.0179	40.749	0.002762	30
35	0.017821	85572	1525	424225	0.003595	2.6164	3104592	0.0176	36.280	0.003587	35
40	0.024320	84047	2044	415398	0.004921	2.6335	2680367	0.0126	31.891	0.004912	40
45	0.034569	82003	2835	403363	0.007028	2.6533	2264968	0.0027	27.621	0.007025	45
50	0.052161	79168	4130	386137	0.010694	2.6499	1861606	0.0080	23.515	0.010680	50
55	0.077383	75039	5807	361478	0.016064	2.6380	1475469	0.0202	19.663	0.016008	55
60	0.115195	69232	7975	327202	0.024374	2.6228	1113990	0.0256	16.091	0.024265	60
65	0.171518	61257	10507	281059	0.037382	2.5991	786789	0.0256	12.844	0.037213	65
70	0.255662	50750	12975	222111	0.058416	2.5614	505729	0.0256	9.965	0.058145	70
75	0.379422	37775	14333	152917	0.093729	2.4911	283618	0.0256	7.508	0.093301	75
80	0.527417	23443	12364	84796	0.145808	2.4452	130701	0.0256	5.575	0.145189	80
85+	1.000000	11079	11079	45905	0.241336	4.1436	45905	0.0256	4.144	0.239460	85+

TABLE 3 — FEMALE LIFE TABLE

x	nq_x	l_x	nd_x	nL_x	nm_x	na_x	T_x	r_x	$\dot{e}_x$	nM_x	x
0	0.056286	100000	5629	95956	0.058658	0.2815	6578505	0.0000	65.785	0.058658	0
1	0.014744	94371	1391	373492	0.003725	1.1299	6482549	0.0000	68.692	0.003725	1
5	0.006180	92980	575	463464	0.001240	2.5000	6109056	0.0000	65.703	0.001240	5
10	0.004935	92405	456	460907	0.000989	2.5442	5645593	0.0000	61.096	0.000989	10
15	0.007301	91949	671	458164	0.001465	2.6429	5184686	0.0042	56.386	0.001464	15
20	0.010042	91278	917	454190	0.002018	2.5997	4726521	0.0126	51.782	0.002015	20
25	0.012286	90361	1110	449095	0.002472	2.5567	4272331	0.0196	47.280	0.002469	25
30	0.013652	89251	1218	443293	0.002749	2.5678	3823236	0.0246	42.837	0.002744	30
35	0.017114	88033	1507	436524	0.003451	2.5839	3379943	0.0194	38.394	0.003445	35
40	0.021096	86526	1825	428258	0.004262	2.6041	2943419	0.0139	34.018	0.004255	40
45	0.028556	84701	2419	417768	0.005790	2.6282	2515161	0.0114	29.695	0.005780	45
50	0.040277	82282	3314	403613	0.008211	2.6669	2097393	0.0182	25.490	0.008186	50
55	0.060216	78968	4755	383622	0.012395	2.6407	1693780	0.0253	21.449	0.012343	55
60	0.087944	74213	6527	355724	0.018347	2.6495	1310157	0.0250	17.654	0.018261	60
65	0.139430	67686	9438	316051	0.029861	2.6284	954433	0.0250	14.101	0.029719	65
70	0.211933	58249	12345	261618	0.047187	2.6001	638383	0.0250	10.960	0.046952	70
75	0.334827	45904	15370	191598	0.080220	2.5327	376764	0.0250	8.208	0.079836	75
80	0.483371	30534	14759	115857	0.127393	2.5057	185166	0.0250	6.064	0.126679	80
85+	*1.000000	15775	15775	69309	0.227600	4.3937	69309	0.0250	4.394	0.225255	85+

TABLE 4 — OBSERVED AND PROJECTED VITAL RATES

	OBSERVED POPULATION BOTH SEXES	MALES	FEMALES	PROJECTED POPULATION 1946 MALES	FEMALES	1951 MALES	FEMALES	1956 MALES	FEMALES	STABLE POPULATION MALES	FEMALES
RATES PER THOUSAND											
Birth	22.36	22.44	22.28	22.90	22.57	22.63	22.14	21.66	21.04	20.69	19.73
Death	9.81	10.64	8.93	11.23	9.38	11.60	9.71	11.91	10.03	13.34	12.38
Increase	12.55	11.80	13.35	11.67	13.18	11.03	12.43	9.75	11.01		7.3450
PERCENTAGE											
under 15	27.81	27.47	28.17	27.01	27.33	27.58	27.59	28.42	28.16	26.77	26.04
15-64	65.50	65.89	65.09	65.82	65.49	64.66	64.74	63.36	63.61	63.74	63.02
65 and over	6.69	6.64	6.74	7.18	7.18	7.76	7.67	8.22	8.23	9.49	10.93
DEP. RATIO X 100	52.67	51.76	53.64	51.94	52.70	54.67	54.47	57.83	57.21	56.88	58.67

Excluding Newfoundland, Yukon, and Northwest Territories

TABLE 1 — DATA

AGE AT LAST BIRTHDAY	POPULATION BOTH SEXES	MALES Number	MALES %	FEMALES Number	FEMALES %	BIRTHS BY AGE OF MOTHER	DEATHS BOTH SEXES	DEATHS MALES	FEMALES	AGE AT LAST BIRTHDAY
0	341783	174657	2.5	167126	2.5	0	14421	8270	6151	0
1-4	1322007	674640	9.8	647367	9.6	0	2456	1369	1087	1-4
5-9	1354259	691915	10.0	662344	9.8	0	1123	674	449	5-9
10-14	1098506	558781	8.1	539725	8.0	103	735	451	284	10-14
15-19	1028711	517411	7.5	511300	7.6	24593	1093	711	382	15-19
20-24	1060125	522880	7.6	537245	8.0	102514	1471	966	505	20-24
25-29	1104189	538796	7.8	565393	8.4	113305	1558	941	617	25-29
30-34	1018517	499921	7.2	518596	7.7	75714	1734	1002	732	30-34
35-39	976584	491583	7.1	485001	7.2	42069	2247	1258	989	35-39
40-44	850750	435889	6.3	414861	6.1	12750	2969	1728	1241	40-44
45-49	731037	380292	5.5	350745	5.2	1011	4025	2432	1593	45-49
50-54	650217	334038	4.8	316179	4.7	20	5516	3462	2054	50-54
55-59	559445	286799	4.2	272646	4.0	0	7395	4661	2734	55-59
60-64	496719	259197	3.8	237522	3.5	0	10180	6401	3779	60-64
65-69	424509	223186	3.2	201323	3.0	0	12942	7936	5006	65-69
70-74	308988	157119	2.3	151869	2.2		14770	8484	6286	70-74
75-79	184428	92052	1.3	92376	1.4		14401	7923	6478	75-79
80-84	94927	45049	0.7	49878	0.7	191510 M.	11833	6060	5773	80-84
85+	51545	22297	0.3	29248	0.4	180569 F.	11211	5109	6102	85+
TOTAL	13657246	6906502		6750744		372079	122080	69838	52242	TOTAL

TABLE 2 — MALE LIFE TABLE

x	nq_x	l_x	nd_x	nL_x	nm_x	na_x	T_x	r_x	$\mathring{e}_x$	nM_x	x
0	0.045643	100000	4564	96529	0.047284	0.2396	6617769	0.0018	66.178	0.047350	0
1	0.008051	95436	768	379510	0.002025	1.0942	6521240	0.0018	68.331	0.002029	1
5	0.004816	94667	456	472197	0.000966	2.5000	6141730	0.0406	64.877	0.000974	5
10	0.004040	94211	381	470145	0.000809	2.6025	5669533	0.0281	60.179	0.000807	10
15	0.006854	93831	643	467645	0.001375	2.6543	5199388	0.0053	55.412	0.001374	15
20	0.009195	93188	857	463829	0.001847	2.5388	4731743	0.0000	50.776	0.001847	20
25	0.008695	92331	803	459659	0.001747	2.5147	4267914	0.0027	46.224	0.001746	25
30	0.009979	91528	913	455430	0.002006	2.5802	3808255	0.0071	41.608	0.002004	30
35	0.012741	90615	1155	450364	0.002564	2.6536	3352826	0.0110	37.001	0.002559	35
40	0.019726	89460	1765	443226	0.003981	2.6912	2902462	0.0215	32.444	0.003964	40
45	0.031638	87695	2774	432071	0.006421	2.6912	2459236	0.0199	28.043	0.006395	45
50	0.050767	84921	4311	414565	0.010399	2.6712	2027165	0.0175	23.871	0.010364	50
55	0.078379	80610	6318	388166	0.016277	2.6444	1612600	0.0086	20.005	0.016252	55
60	0.116992	74292	8692	350658	0.024786	2.6069	1224434	0.0232	16.481	0.024696	60
65	0.164297	65600	10778	301980	0.035691	2.5858	873776	0.0232	13.320	0.035558	65
70	0.239469	54822	13128	242132	0.054219	2.5642	571797	0.0232	10.430	0.053997	70
75	0.355460	41694	14821	171481	0.086427	2.5042	329664	0.0232	7.907	0.086071	75
80	0.499657	26873	13427	99437	0.135035	2.4787	158183	0.0232	5.886	0.134520	80
85+	1.000000	13446	13446	58746	0.228882	4.3691	58746	0.0232	4.369	0.229135	85+

TABLE 3 — FEMALE LIFE TABLE

x	nq_x	l_x	nd_x	nL_x	nm_x	na_x	T_x	r_x	$\mathring{e}_x$	nM_x	x
0	0.035762	100000	3576	97306	0.036752	0.2467	7080770	0.0018	70.808	0.036805	0
1	0.006669	96424	643	383830	0.001675	1.0995	6983464	0.0018	72.425	0.001679	1
5	0.003344	95781	320	478103	0.000670	2.5000	6599634	0.0402	68.904	0.000678	5
10	0.002630	95460	251	476682	0.000527	2.5288	6121531	0.0253	64.126	0.000526	10
15	0.003729	95209	355	475200	0.000747	2.6137	5644849	0.0000	59.289	0.000747	15
20	0.004689	94854	445	473193	0.000940	2.5744	5169649	0.0000	54.501	0.000940	20
25	0.005443	94410	514	470809	0.001092	2.5880	4696456	0.0024	49.746	0.001091	25
30	0.007048	93896	662	467915	0.001414	2.6370	4225648	0.0139	45.004	0.001411	30
35	0.010180	93234	949	463946	0.002046	2.6571	3757733	0.0202	40.304	0.002039	35
40	0.014928	92285	1378	458209	0.003007	2.6665	3293786	0.0293	35.692	0.002991	40
45	0.022549	90907	2050	449718	0.004558	2.6498	2835577	0.0226	31.192	0.004542	45
50	0.032096	88857	2852	437610	0.006517	2.6591	2385859	0.0184	26.850	0.006496	50
55	0.049160	86005	4228	420175	0.010063	2.6700	1948249	0.0181	22.653	0.010028	55
60	0.077070	81777	6303	394106	0.015992	2.6548	1528073	0.0272	18.686	0.015910	60
65	0.118065	75475	8911	356410	0.025002	2.6474	1133967	0.0272	15.024	0.024866	65
70	0.189376	66564	12606	302830	0.041626	2.6209	777558	0.0272	11.681	0.041391	70
75	0.300750	53958	16228	230159	0.070508	2.5577	474728	0.0272	8.798	0.070126	75
80	0.453312	37730	17104	146809	0.116502	2.5536	244570	0.0272	6.482	0.115743	80
85+	*1.000000	20627	20627	97761	0.210992	4.7395	97761	0.0272	4.740	0.208630	85+

TABLE 4 — OBSERVED AND PROJECTED VITAL RATES

	OBSERVED POPULATION BOTH SEXES	MALES	FEMALES	PROJECTED POPULATION 1956 MALES	FEMALES	1961 MALES	FEMALES	1966 MALES	FEMALES	STABLE POPULATION MALES	FEMALES
RATES PER THOUSAND											
Birth	27.24	27.73	26.75	25.59	24.53	24.15	23.01	24.31	23.06	26.28	25.15
Death	8.94	10.11	7.74	10.27	7.97	10.33	8.20	10.37	8.43	9.33	8.20
Increase	18.31	17.62	19.01	15.32	16.55	13.82	14.82	13.94	14.63	16.9500	
PERCENTAGE											
under 15	30.14	30.41	29.87	32.59	31.71	33.03	31.93	32.13	30.86	32.92	31.89
15-64	62.06	61.78	62.36	59.49	60.25	59.22	59.84	60.23	60.71	60.48	60.00
65 and over	7.79	7.81	7.77	7.91	8.04	7.75	8.23	7.64	8.43	6.60	8.11
DEP. RATIO X 100	61.12	61.87	60.37	68.09	65.99	68.86	67.11	66.02	64.72	65.35	66.65

Excluding Newfoundland, Yukon, and Northwest Territories

TABLE 1 — DATA

AGE AT LAST BIRTHDAY	POPULATION BOTH SEXES	MALES Number	%	FEMALES Number	%	BIRTHS BY AGE OF MOTHER	DEATHS BOTH SEXES	MALES	FEMALES	AGE AT LAST BIRTHDAY
0	448929	229759	2.6	219170	2.5	0	12245	7048	5197	0
1-4	1735735	887878	9.9	847857	9.6	0	1932	1088	844	1-4
5-9	2012447	1029803	11.5	982644	11.2	0	1066	659	407	5-9
10-14	1797782	918594	10.2	879188	10.0	214	780	514	266	10-14
15-19	1392569	709148	7.9	683421	7.8	39110	1167	833	334	15-19
20-24	1152255	571012	6.4	581243	6.6	135694	1282	949	333	20-24
25-29	1177583	596857	6.6	580726	6.6	127276	1288	888	400	25-29
30-34	1241886	628717	7.0	613169	7.0	88618	1545	1001	544	30-34
35-39	1244326	617079	6.9	627247	7.1	50312	2265	1407	858	35-39
40-44	1094841	546795	6.1	548046	6.2	15384	2994	1861	1133	40-44
45-49	993351	503630	5.6	489721	5.6	1089	4579	2926	1653	45-49
50-54	846382	433483	4.8	412899	4.7	13	6254	4103	2151	50-54
55-59	693304	355398	4.0	337906	3.8	0	8224	5481	2743	55-59
60-64	572566	286870	3.2	285696	3.2	0	10592	6888	3704	60-64
65-69	477321	234650	2.6	242671	2.8	0	13419	8304	5115	65-69
70-74	394727	192143	2.1	202584	2.3		17354	10393	6961	70-74
75-79	269259	131452	1.5	137807	1.6		18865	10750	8115	75-79
80-84	144477	67812	0.8	76665	0.9	235040 M.	16206	8480	7726	80-84
85+	79548	34508	0.4	45040	0.5	222670 F.	15935	7252	8683	85+
TOTAL	17769288	8975588		8793700		457710	137992	80825	57167	TOTAL

TABLE 2 — MALE LIFE TABLE

x	nq_x	l_x	nd_x	nL_x	nm_x	na_x	T_x	r_x	$\mathring{e}_x$	nM_x	x
0	0.029915	100000	2992	97705	0.030618	0.2328	6840611	0.0024	68.406	0.030676	0
1	0.004868	97008	472	386659	0.001221	1.0893	6742906	0.0024	69.508	0.001225	1
5	0.003184	96536	307	481913	0.000638	2.5000	6356246	0.0188	65.843	0.000640	5
10	0.002815	96229	271	480521	0.000564	2.6998	5874334	0.0366	61.045	0.000560	10
15	0.005910	95958	567	478480	0.001185	2.6907	5393813	0.0464	56.210	0.001175	15
20	0.008281	95391	790	475007	0.001663	2.5353	4915332	0.0157	51.528	0.001662	20
25	0.007411	94601	701	471243	0.001488	2.4866	4440325	0.0000	46.937	0.001488	25
30	0.007930	93900	745	467712	0.001592	2.6000	3969082	0.0000	42.269	0.001592	30
35	0.011362	93155	1058	463300	0.002284	2.6606	3501370	0.0116	37.586	0.002280	35
40	0.016946	92097	1561	456904	0.003416	2.7064	3038071	0.0167	32.988	0.003403	40
45	0.028771	90536	2605	446696	0.005831	2.7025	2581166	0.0172	28.510	0.005810	45
50	0.046547	87931	4093	430187	0.009514	2.6865	2134470	0.0249	24.274	0.009465	50
55	0.074770	83838	6269	404508	0.015497	2.6575	1704283	0.0253	20.328	0.015422	55
60	0.113859	77570	8832	366804	0.024078	2.6172	1299775	0.0168	16.756	0.024011	60
65	0.163466	68738	11236	316627	0.035488	2.5915	932971	0.0168	13.573	0.035389	65
70	0.239451	57501	13769	253845	0.054241	2.5552	616345	0.0168	10.719	0.054090	70
75	0.340276	43733	14881	181464	0.082007	2.5002	362500	0.0168	8.289	0.081779	75
80	0.477755	28851	13784	109836	0.125495	2.5028	181037	0.0168	6.275	0.125051	80
85+	*1.000000	15068	15068	71200	0.211622	4.7254	71200	0.0168	4.725	0.210154	85+

TABLE 3 — FEMALE LIFE TABLE

x	nq_x	l_x	nd_x	nL_x	nm_x	na_x	T_x	r_x	$\mathring{e}_x$	nM_x	x
0	0.023246	100000	2325	98229	0.023666	0.2383	7429419	0.0025	74.294	0.023712	0
1	0.003957	97675	387	389578	0.000992	1.0933	7331189	0.0025	75.057	0.000995	1
5	0.002058	97289	200	485944	0.000412	2.5000	6941611	0.0188	71.351	0.000414	5
10	0.001515	97089	147	485084	0.000303	2.5532	6455668	0.0359	66.492	0.000303	10
15	0.002452	96942	238	484141	0.000491	2.6138	5970584	0.0409	61.589	0.000489	15
20	0.002864	96704	277	482847	0.000574	2.5706	5486443	0.0157	56.734	0.000573	20
25	0.003438	96427	332	481337	0.000689	2.5933	5003597	0.0000	51.890	0.000689	25
30	0.004427	96095	425	479481	0.000887	2.6576	4522260	0.0000	47.060	0.000887	30
35	0.006830	95670	653	476832	0.001370	2.6775	4042779	0.0098	42.258	0.001368	35
40	0.010335	95017	982	472822	0.002077	2.6971	3565947	0.0226	37.530	0.002067	40
45	0.016826	94035	1582	466512	0.003392	2.6858	3093125	0.0248	32.893	0.003375	45
50	0.025888	92452	2393	456700	0.005241	2.6763	2626614	0.0317	28.410	0.005210	50
55	0.040055	90059	3607	441917	0.008163	2.6776	2169913	0.0283	24.094	0.008118	55
60	0.063248	86452	5468	419540	0.013033	2.6740	1727996	0.0259	19.988	0.012965	60
65	0.100933	80984	8174	385768	0.021189	2.6570	1308456	0.0259	16.157	0.021078	65
70	0.159711	72810	11629	336577	0.034550	2.6635	922688	0.0259	12.673	0.034361	70
75	0.259037	61181	15848	267675	0.059207	2.5876	586110	0.0259	9.580	0.058887	75
80	0.403532	45333	18293	180668	0.101254	2.6275	318436	0.0259	7.024	0.100776	80
85+	1.000000	27040	27040	137768	0.196270	5.0950	137768	0.0259	5.095	0.192783	85+

TABLE 4 — OBSERVED AND PROJECTED VITAL RATES

	OBSERVED POPULATION BOTH SEXES	MALES	FEMALES	PROJECTED POPULATION 1966 MALES	FEMALES	1971 MALES	FEMALES	1976 MALES	FEMALES	STABLE POPULATION MALES	FEMALES
RATES PER THOUSAND											
Birth	25.76	26.19	25.32	25.64	24.61	26.87	25.66	28.17	26.81	28.83	27.58
Death	7.77	9.00	6.50	9.05	6.80	9.01	7.00	8.88	7.09	7.57	6.32
Increase	17.99	17.18	18.82	16.58	17.81	17.86	18.66	19.29	19.71		21.2615
PERCENTAGE											
under 15	33.74	34.16	33.31	33.93	32.83	33.59	32.35	33.79	32.42	35.71	34.45
15-64	58.58	58.48	58.68	58.94	59.00	59.40	59.40	59.20	59.11	58.67	58.16
65 and over	7.68	7.36	8.01	7.13	8.16	7.00	8.25	7.01	8.46	5.61	7.40
DEP. RATIO X 100	70.71	71.00	70.42	69.66	69.48	68.34	68.36	68.93	69.17	70.44	71.94

Excluding Newfoundland, Yukon, and Northwest Territories

AGE AT LAST BIRTHDAY	1966 BOTH SEXES	1966 MALES	1966 FEMALES	1971 BOTH SEXES	1971 MALES	1971 FEMALES	1976 BOTH SEXES	1976 MALES	1976 FEMALES	AGE AT LAST BIRTHDAY	
0-4	2298	1176	1122	2540	1300	1240	2913	1491	1422	0-4	**TABLE 5**
5-9	2175	1112	1063	2288	1170	1118	2528	1293	1235	5-9	
10-14	2008	1027	981	2170	1109	1061	2282	1166	1116	10-14	
15-19	1792	915	877	2001	1022	979	2163	1104	1059	15-19	POPULATION
20-24	1386	704	682	1783	908	875	1991	1015	976	20-24	PROJECTED
25-29	1145	566	579	1377	698	679	1773	901	872	25-29	WITH
30-34	1170	592	578	1139	562	577	1370	693	677	30-34	FIXED
35-39	1233	623	610	1162	587	575	1131	557	574	35-39	AGE-
40-44	1231	609	622	1219	614	605	1149	579	570	40-44	SPECIFIC
45-49	1076	535	541	1209	595	614	1197	600	597	45-49	BIRTH
50-54	964	485	479	1044	515	529	1174	573	601	50-54	AND
55-59	808	408	400	920	456	464	996	484	512	55-59	DEATH
60-64	643	322	321	749	370	379	854	414	440	60-64	RATES
65-69	511	248	263	573	278	295	668	319	349	65-69	(IN 1000's)
70-74	400	188	212	428	199	229	480	223	257	70-74	
75-79	298	137	161	302	134	168	324	142	182	75-79	
80-84	173	80	93	192	83	109	195	81	114	80-84	
85+	102	44	58	123	52	71	137	54	83	85+	
TOTAL	19413	9771	9642	21219	10652	10567	23325	11689	11636	TOTAL	

STANDARD COUNTRIES:	ENGLAND AND WALES 1961 BOTH SEXES	MALES	FEMALES	UNITED STATES 1960 BOTH SEXES	MALES	FEMALES	MEXICO 1960 BOTH SEXES	MALES	FEMALES	
STANDARDIZED RATES PER THOUSAND										**TABLE 6**
Birth	24.35	26.18*	22.96	24.77	24.74*	23.74	28.65	23.30*	27.81	STANDAR-
Death	10.56	11.16*	10.19	8.67	9.86*	7.56	4.71	7.37*	3.80	DIZED
Increase	13.79	15.02*	12.77	16.10	14.88*	16.19	23.94	15.93*	24.01	RATES

	OBSERVED POP. MALES	OBSERVED POP. FEMALES	STATIONARY POP. MALES	STATIONARY POP. FEMALES	STABLE POP. MALES	STABLE POP. FEMALES	OBSERVED BIRTHS	NET MATERNITY FUNCTION	BIRTHS IN STABLE POP.	
μ	29.42249	29.90782	37.12549	39.43402	27.12257	28.43062	27.77593	27.79003	26.97754	**TABLE 7**
σ^2	460.9939	470.5588	513.8104	561.4954	414.7202	456.7614	38.26629	37.46905	34.77164	
κ_3	5493.351	5642.264	2561.206	2132.751	6037.149	6819.864	109.5320	123.2984	129.3201	MOMENTS
κ_4	−139514.	−143022.	−255543.	−329741.	−58437.	−85951.	−641.430	−440.134	−124.885	AND
β_1	0.308027	0.305538	0.048359	0.025695	0.510973	0.488071	0.214108	0.288999	0.397792	CUMULANTS
β_2	2.343509	2.354084	2.032038	1.954123	2.660233	2.588025	2.561957	2.686498	2.896710	
κ	−0.116319	−0.116650	−0.018427	−0.009392	−0.203100	−0.187350	−0.113532	−0.158293	−0.237652	

VITAL STATISTICS		THOMPSON AGE RANGE	NRR	1000r	INTERVAL	BOURGEOIS-PICHAT AGE RANGE	NRR	1000b	1000d	1000r	COALE	
GRR	1.861										IBR	**TABLE 8**
NRR	1.790	0-4	1.73	20.53	27.44	5-29	2.18	28.20	−0.64	28.84	IDR	RATES FROM AGE DISTRI-
TFR	3.826	5-9	1.68	19.20	27.40	30-54	1.64	28.09	9.71	18.38	IRI	BUTIONS
GENERATION	27.379	10-14	1.57	16.27	27.35	55-79	1.54	21.36	5.42	15.95	K1	AND VITAL
SEX RATIO	105.555	15-19	1.30	9.38	27.27	*40-64	2.11	43.35	15.74	27.61	K2	STATISTICS (Females)

Start of Age Interval	ORIGINAL MATRIX SUB-DIAGONAL	ALTERNATIVE FIRST ROWS Projection	ALTERNATIVE FIRST ROWS Integral	FIRST STABLE MATRIX % IN STABLE POPULATION	FISHER VALUES	REPRODUCTIVE VALUES	SECOND STABLE MATRIX Z₂ FIRST COLUMN	SECOND STABLE MATRIX Z₂ FIRST ROW	
0	0.99618	0.00000	0.00000	12.776	1.081	1153206	0.1690+0.0905	0.1690+0.0905	**TABLE 9**
5	0.99823	0.00029	0.00000	11.441	1.207	1185967	0.1749−0.1319	−0.0097+0.1675	
10	0.99806	0.06806	0.00061	10.266	1.345	1182251	−0.0529−0.2452	−0.1364+0.0537	LESLIE
15	0.99733	0.34417	0.14322	9.210	1.425	973972	−0.2802−0.0629	−0.1041−0.0946	MATRIX
20	0.99687	0.53625	0.58426	8.257	1.217	707194	−0.1999+0.2607	−0.0215−0.1485	AND ITS
25	0.99614	0.43088	0.54850	7.399	0.776	450867	0.1745+0.3327	0.0191−0.1203	SPECTRAL
30	0.99448	0.26614	0.36170	6.626	0.400	244994	0.4287−0.0213	0.0294−0.0682	COMPO-
35	0.99159	0.12820	0.20074	5.923	0.158	98934	0.1833−0.4541	0.0199−0.0259	NENTS
40	0.98665	0.03591	0.07025	5.279	0.037	20399	−0.3812−0.4062	0.0062−0.0054	(Females)
45	0.97897	0.00268	0.00557	4.682	0.003	1288	−0.5983+0.1984	0.0005−0.0004	
50	0.96763	0.00004	0.00008	4.120	0.000	15	−0.0799+0.7034	0.0000−0.0000	
55+	0.82808			14.021					

Start of Age Interval	OBSERVED POPUL. (IN 100's)	CONTRIBUTIONS OF ROOTS (IN 100's) r_1	r_2, r_3	$r_4 \cdot r_{11}$	AGE-SP. BIRTH RATES	NET MATERNITY FUNCTION	COEFF. OF MATRIX EQUATION	PARAMETERS	INTEGRAL	MATRIX	x	EXP. INCREASE $e^{(x+8\frac{1}{2})r}$	
0	10670	10374	248	48	0.0000	0.0000	0.0000	L(1)	1.11216	1.11246	0	1.0546	**TABLE 10**
5	9826	9290	664	−127	0.0000	0.0000	0.0003	L(2)	0.35786	0.36611	50	3.0533	
10	8792	8336	314	142	0.0001	0.0006	0.0677			0.82096	0.79117	55	3.3958	AGE
15	6834	7479	−569	−75	0.0278	0.1348	0.3416	R(1)	0.02126	0.02131	60	3.7767	ANALYSIS
20	5812	6705	−958	65	0.1136	0.5484	0.5308	R(2)	−0.02206	−0.02745	65	4.2003	AND
25	5807	6008	−176	−25	0.1066	0.5132	0.4252			0.23195	0.22748	70	4.6714	MISCEL-
30	6132	5380	1083	−331	0.0703	0.3371	0.2616	C(1)		81199	75	5.1953	LANEOUS
35	6272	4809	1266	197	0.0390	0.1861	0.1253	C(2)		121793	80	5.7781	RESULTS
40	5480	4287	−195	1389	0.0137	0.0646	0.0348			90262	85	6.4262	(Females)
45	4897	3802	−1816	2911	0.0011	0.0050	0.0026	2P/Y	27.0891	27.6211	90	7.1469	
50	4129	3346	−1464	2248	0.0000	0.0001	0.0000	DELTA	5.0911		95	7.9486	
55+	13284	11385									100	8.8401	

88   Canada 1963

Excluding Newfoundland, Yukon, and Northwest Territories

	AGE AT LAST BIRTHDAY	POPULATION BOTH SEXES	MALES Number	%	FEMALES Number	%	BIRTHS BY AGE OF MOTHER	DEATHS BOTH SEXES	MALES	FEMALES	AGE AT LAST BIRTHDAY
	0	445625	227875	2.5	217750	2.4	0	11542	6620	4922	0
	1-4	1765133	902758	9.7	862375	9.5	0	1862	1085	777	1-4
	5-9	2079233	1063983	11.5	1015250	11.1	0	1160	708	452	5-9
	10-14	1902666	972958	10.5	929708	10.2	189	784	520	264	10-14
TABLE 1	15-19	1554309	793567	8.6	760742	8.3	40203	1320	895	425	15-19
DATA	20-24	1221466	608333	6.6	613133	6.7	139356	1456	1075	381	20-24
	25-29	1146608	575408	6.2	571200	6.3	121293	1283	882	401	25-29
	30-34	1214417	617250	6.7	597167	6.5	84121	1529	995	534	30-34
	35-39	1255050	626133	6.7	628917	6.9	47552	2239	1410	829	35-39
	40-44	1150525	570383	6.1	580142	6.4	14920	3116	1936	1180	40-44
	45-49	1022558	514283	5.5	508275	5.6	1020	4644	2957	1687	45-49
	50-54	896484	455717	4.9	440767	4.8	10	6551	4296	2255	50-54
	55-59	736016	375233	4.0	360783	4.0	0	8647	5800	2847	55-59
	60-64	596717	298817	3.2	297900	3.3	0	11158	7236	3922	60-64
	65-69	487492	237775	2.6	249717	2.7	0	13711	8531	5180	65-69
	70-74	397325	189875	2.0	207450	2.3		17385	10306	7079	70-74
	75-79	284950	135875	1.5	149075	1.6		19859	11220	8639	75-79
	80-84	157233	73750	0.8	83483	0.9	230055 M.	17785	9216	8569	80-84
	85+	88442	38767	0.4	49675	0.5	218609 F.	17806	8164	9642	85+
	TOTAL	18402249	9278740		9123509		448664	143837	83852	59985	TOTAL

	x	$_n q_x$	l_x	$_n d_x$	$_n L_x$	$_n m_x$	$_n a_x$	T_x	r_x	$\mathring{e}_x$	$_n M_x$	x
	0	0.028421	100000	2842	97831	0.029051	0.2367	6846132	0.0000	68.461	0.029051	0
	1	0.004791	97158	465	387278	0.001202	1.0921	6748302	0.0000	69.457	0.001202	1
	5	0.003313	96692	320	482661	0.000664	2.5000	6361024	0.0142	65.786	0.000665	5
	10	0.002683	96372	259	481261	0.000537	2.6820	5878362	0.0286	60.997	0.000534	10
TABLE 2	15	0.005683	96114	546	479324	0.001140	2.7225	5397101	0.0458	56.153	0.001128	15
	20	0.008810	95567	842	475768	0.001770	2.5438	4917778	0.0306	51.459	0.001767	20
MALE	25	0.007635	94725	723	471801	0.001533	2.4749	4442009	0.0000	46.894	0.001533	25
LIFE	30	0.008029	94002	755	468191	0.001612	2.5889	3970209	0.0000	42.235	0.001612	30
TABLE	35	0.011211	93247	1045	463791	0.002254	2.6601	3502018	0.0056	37.556	0.002252	35
	40	0.016897	92202	1558	457435	0.003406	2.7053	3038226	0.0161	32.952	0.003394	40
	45	0.028474	90644	2581	447094	0.005770	2.7036	2580791	0.0165	28.472	0.005750	45
	50	0.046336	88063	4080	430888	0.009470	2.6896	2133498	0.0216	24.227	0.009427	50
	55	0.074953	83983	6295	405183	0.015536	2.6600	1702610	0.0262	20.273	0.015457	55
	60	0.114740	77688	8914	367214	0.024274	2.6188	1297427	0.0143	16.701	0.024215	60
	65	0.165469	68774	11380	316434	0.035963	2.5891	930213	0.0143	13.526	0.035878	65
	70	0.240085	57394	13779	253266	0.054407	2.5540	613779	0.0143	10.694	0.054278	70
	75	0.342868	43615	14954	180666	0.082772	2.4986	360513	0.0143	8.266	0.082576	75
	80	0.477194	28661	13677	109117	0.125339	2.5005	179846	0.0143	6.275	0.124962	80
	85+	*1.000000	14984	14984	70729	0.211850	4.7203	70729	0.0143	4.720	0.210591	85+

	x	$_n q_x$	l_x	$_n d_x$	$_n L_x$	$_n m_x$	$_n a_x$	T_x	r_x	$\mathring{e}_x$	$_n M_x$	x
	0	0.022215	100000	2222	98296	0.022600	0.2330	7442124	0.0002	74.421	0.022604	0
	1	0.003594	97778	351	390091	0.000901	1.0895	7343828	0.0002	75.107	0.000901	1
	5	0.002216	97427	216	486596	0.000444	2.5000	6953736	0.0144	71.374	0.000445	5
	10	0.001422	97211	138	485722	0.000285	2.5849	6467141	0.0285	66.527	0.000284	10
	15	0.002804	97073	272	484718	0.000562	2.6243	5981418	0.0411	61.618	0.000559	15
TABLE 3	20	0.003106	96801	301	483266	0.000622	2.5457	5496700	0.0280	56.784	0.000621	20
	25	0.003505	96500	338	481682	0.000702	2.5791	5013434	0.0019	51.953	0.000702	25
FEMALE	30	0.004462	96162	429	479797	0.000894	2.6413	4531753	0.0000	47.126	0.000894	30
LIFE	35	0.006572	95733	629	477203	0.001318	2.6679	4051955	0.0015	42.326	0.001318	35
TABLE	40	0.010162	95104	966	473295	0.002042	2.7001	3574752	0.0192	37.588	0.002034	40
	45	0.016545	94137	1557	467081	0.003335	2.6854	3101457	0.0241	32.946	0.003319	45
	50	0.025414	92580	2353	457425	0.005144	2.6736	2634376	0.0290	28.455	0.005116	50
	55	0.038994	90227	3518	443008	0.007942	2.6901	2176951	0.0308	24.128	0.007891	55
	60	0.064169	86709	5564	420580	0.013229	2.6702	1733943	0.0244	19.997	0.013165	60
	65	0.099371	81145	8063	386820	0.020845	2.6558	1313364	0.0244	16.185	0.020743	65
	70	0.158641	73081	11594	338014	0.034299	2.6374	926543	0.0244	12.678	0.034124	70
	75	0.255489	61487	15709	269656	0.058257	2.5950	588529	0.0244	9.572	0.057951	75
	80	0.409668	45778	18754	181855	0.103125	2.6257	318873	0.0244	6.966	0.102644	80
	85+	1.000000	27024	27024	137018	0.197232	5.0702	137018	0.0244	5.070	0.194102	85+

		OBSERVED POPULATION BOTH SEXES	MALES	FEMALES	PROJECTED POPULATION 1968 MALES	FEMALES	1973 MALES	FEMALES	1978 MALES	FEMALES	STABLE POPULATION MALES	FEMALES
	RATES PER THOUSAND											
TABLE 4	Birth	24.38	24.79	23.96	25.18	24.16	26.68	25.47	27.77	26.42	27.80	26.54
OBSERVED	Death	7.82	9.04	6.57	9.04	6.85	8.98	7.04	8.85	7.09	7.83	6.57
AND	Increase	16.56	15.76	17.39	16.14	17.31	17.70	18.43	18.92	19.33		19.9707
PROJEC-												
TED	PERCENTAGE											
VITAL	under 15	33.65	34.14	33.16	33.40	32.25	32.99	31.73	33.31	31.95	34.81	33.50
RATES	15-64	58.66	58.58	58.74	59.50	59.50	59.97	59.86	59.59	59.36	59.26	58.64
	65 and over	7.69	7.29	8.10	7.09	8.25	7.04	8.41	7.10	8.69	5.93	7.86
	DEP. RATIO X 100	70.48	70.72	70.25	68.06	68.06	66.74	67.06	67.81	68.47	68.75	70.52

Excluding Newfoundland

TABLE 1 — DATA

AGE AT LAST BIRTHDAY	BOTH SEXES	MALES Number	%	FEMALES Number	%	BIRTHS BY AGE OF MOTHER	DEATHS BOTH SEXES	MALES	FEMALES	AGE AT LAST BIRTHDAY
0	436432	222479	2.4	213953	2.3	0	10714	6208	4506	0
1-4	1772668	907330	9.6	865338	9.3	0	1819	1028	791	1-4
5-9	2118550	1083975	11.5	1034575	11.1	0	1096	690	406	5-9
10-14	1944450	994858	10.5	949592	10.2	209	738	462	276	10-14
15-19	1645891	840258	8.9	805633	8.7	40418	1384	985	399	15-19
20-24	1279034	641642	6.8	637392	6.8	137329	1531	1153	378	20-24
25-29	1148034	573292	6.1	574742	6.2	118286	1211	844	367	25-29
30-34	1208209	614492	6.5	593717	6.4	80777	1582	1046	536	30-34
35-39	1256133	630125	6.7	626008	6.7	45164	2157	1368	789	35-39
40-44	1186541	587133	6.2	599408	6.4	14964	3330	2122	1208	40-44
45-49	1036475	519225	5.5	517250	5.6	1078	4631	2979	1652	45-49
50-54	922625	467208	4.9	455417	4.9	10	6758	4438	2320	50-54
55-59	762083	387133	4.1	374950	4.0	0	8709	5816	2893	55-59
60-64	612492	306575	3.2	305917	3.3	0	11579	7669	3910	60-64
65-69	496391	241133	2.5	255258	2.7	0	13722	8577	5145	65-69
70-74	397925	188800	2.0	209125	2.2		17129	10271	6858	70-74
75-79	291700	137258	1.5	154442	1.7		19573	11005	8568	75-79
80-84	163500	76575	0.8	86925	0.9	225272 M.	17655	9261	8394	80-84
85+	92284	40542	0.4	51742	0.6	212963 F.	17469	8049	9420	85+
TOTAL	18771417	9460033		9311384		438235	142787	83971	58816	TOTAL

TABLE 2 — MALE LIFE TABLE

x	nq_x	l_x	nd_x	nL_x	nm_x	na_x	T_x	r_x	$\overset{o}{e}_x$	nM_x	x
0	0.027320	100000	2732	97909	0.027904	0.2347	6861347	0.0000	68.613	0.027904	0
1	0.004517	97268	439	387794	0.001133	1.0907	6763438	0.0000	69.534	0.001133	1
5	0.003171	96829	307	483375	0.000635	2.5000	6375644	0.0120	65.845	0.000637	5
10	0.002334	96522	225	482099	0.000467	2.7419	5892269	0.0248	61.046	0.000464	10
15	0.005905	96296	569	480192	0.001184	2.7316	5410169	0.0427	56.182	0.001172	15
20	0.008956	95728	857	476522	0.001799	2.5309	4929978	0.0366	51.500	0.001797	20
25	0.007334	94870	696	472600	0.001472	2.4823	4453456	0.0027	46.943	0.001472	25
30	0.008476	94175	798	468943	0.001702	2.5817	3980855	0.0000	42.271	0.001702	30
35	0.010805	93376	1009	464539	0.002172	2.6781	3511913	0.0022	37.610	0.002171	35
40	0.017979	92367	1661	458013	0.003626	2.6967	3047373	0.0156	32.992	0.003614	40
45	0.028412	90707	2577	447602	0.005758	2.6981	2589361	0.0168	28.546	0.005737	45
50	0.046650	88130	4111	431110	0.009536	2.6800	2141759	0.0196	24.302	0.009499	50
55	0.072960	84018	6130	405830	0.015105	2.6734	1710648	0.0262	20.360	0.015023	55
60	0.118300	77889	9214	367478	0.025074	2.6612	1304818	0.0141	16.752	0.025015	60
65	0.164119	68674	11271	316151	0.035650	2.5849	937340	0.0141	13.649	0.035570	65
70	0.240497	57404	13805	253194	0.054525	2.5499	621189	0.0141	10.821	0.054401	70
75	0.334436	43598	14581	181452	0.080356	2.4940	367995	0.0141	8.441	0.080177	75
80	0.461352	29017	13387	110454	0.121202	2.5163	186543	0.0141	6.429	0.120940	80
85+	1.000000	15630	15630	76090	0.205418	4.8681	76090	0.0141	4.868	0.198536	85+

TABLE 3 — FEMALE LIFE TABLE

x	nq_x	l_x	nd_x	nL_x	nm_x	na_x	T_x	r_x	$\overset{o}{e}_x$	nM_x	x
0	0.020730	100000	2073	98429	0.021061	0.2421	7495001	0.0000	74.950	0.021061	0
1	0.003647	97927	357	390671	0.000914	1.0960	7396572	0.0000	75.531	0.000914	1
5	0.001954	97570	191	487373	0.000391	2.5000	7005901	0.0123	71.804	0.000392	5
10	0.001455	97379	142	486553	0.000291	2.5751	6518528	0.0247	66.940	0.000291	10
15	0.002486	97238	242	485614	0.000498	2.6258	6031975	0.0394	62.033	0.000495	15
20	0.002966	96996	288	484274	0.000594	2.5484	5546361	0.0332	57.181	0.000593	20
25	0.003190	96708	308	482800	0.000639	2.5990	5062087	0.0064	52.344	0.000639	25
30	0.004504	96400	434	480974	0.000903	2.6413	4579287	0.0000	47.503	0.000903	30
35	0.006283	95966	603	478430	0.001260	2.6816	4098312	0.0000	42.706	0.001260	35
40	0.010064	95363	960	474601	0.002022	2.6955	3619883	0.0170	37.959	0.002015	40
45	0.015928	94403	1504	468544	0.003209	2.6926	3145282	0.0241	33.318	0.003194	45
50	0.025297	92899	2350	459027	0.005120	2.6729	2676737	0.0270	28.813	0.005094	50
55	0.038142	90549	3454	444753	0.007765	2.6859	2217711	0.0316	24.492	0.007716	55
60	0.062374	87095	5432	422821	0.012848	2.6704	1772957	0.0264	20.357	0.012781	60
65	0.096712	81663	7898	389789	0.020262	2.6543	1350136	0.0264	16.533	0.020156	65
70	0.152958	73765	11283	342175	0.032974	2.6379	960347	0.0264	13.019	0.032794	70
75	0.245963	62482	15368	275472	0.055789	2.5964	618173	0.0264	9.894	0.055477	75
80	0.390447	47114	18395	189555	0.097045	2.6512	342701	0.0264	7.274	0.096566	80
85+	1.000000	28718	28718	153145	0.187524	5.3327	153145	0.0264	5.333	0.182058	85+

TABLE 4 — OBSERVED AND PROJECTED VITAL RATES

	OBSERVED POPULATION BOTH SEXES	MALES	FEMALES	PROJECTED 1969 MALES	FEMALES	1974 MALES	FEMALES	1979 MALES	FEMALES	STABLE POPULATION MALES	FEMALES
RATES PER THOUSAND											
Birth	23.35	23.81	22.87	24.60	23.46	26.12	24.79	27.10	25.64	26.55	25.23
Death	7.61	8.88	6.32	8.96	6.70	8.91	6.93	8.81	7.00	8.16	6.84
Increase	15.74	14.94	16.55	15.65	16.76	17.21	17.86	18.29	18.64	18.3938	
PERCENTAGE											
under 15	33.41	33.92	32.90	32.92	31.70	32.35	30.97	32.67	31.15	33.67	32.26
15-64	58.91	58.85	58.96	59.95	59.90	60.52	60.35	60.10	59.82	59.93	59.14
65 and over	7.68	7.23	8.14	7.13	8.40	7.13	8.67	7.24	9.02	6.40	8.61
DEP. RATIO X 100	69.76	69.93	69.59	66.81	66.94	65.24	65.69	66.40	67.16	66.87	69.10

AGE AT LAST BIRTHDAY	BOTH SEXES	POPULATION MALES Number	%	FEMALES Number	%	BIRTHS BY AGE OF MOTHER	DEATHS BOTH SEXES	MALES	FEMALES	AGE AT LAST BIRTHDAY
0	417893	214184	2.2	203709	2.1	0	9404	5391	4013	0
1-4	1767207	903725	9.4	863482	9.1	0	1699	940	759	1-4
5-9	2151550	1100475	11.4	1051075	11.1	0	1171	731	440	5-9
10-14	1979850	1013558	10.5	966292	10.2	196	789	490	299	10-14
15-19	1729791	882958	9.2	846833	8.9	41605	1460	1040	420	15-19
20-24	1343034	678142	7.0	664892	7.0	127479	1571	1187	384	20-24
25-29	1158034	576792	6.0	581242	6.1	107605	1299	917	382	25-29
30-34	1199909	610792	6.3	589117	6.2	71352	1541	1017	524	30-34
35-39	1252933	631625	6.6	621308	6.6	41158	2222	1405	817	35-39
40-44	1217041	601933	6.3	615108	6.5	13398	3347	2101	1246	40-44
45-49	1052975	525525	5.5	527450	5.6	1047	4668	2933	1735	45-49
50-54	945725	476908	5.0	468817	4.9	15	7139	4674	2465	50-54
55-59	787083	398333	4.1	388750	4.1	0	8970	6002	2968	55-59
60-64	629192	314675	3.3	314517	3.3	0	11512	7628	3884	60-64
65-69	505891	245133	2.5	260758	2.8	0	13944	8796	5148	65-69
70-74	400625	188800	2.0	211825	2.2		17439	10386	7053	70-74
75-79	297700	137958	1.4	159742	1.7		20000	11298	8702	75-79
80-84	169500	78675	0.8	90825	1.0	207552 M.	18468	9716	8752	80-84
85+	94484	41042	0.4	53442	0.6	196303 F.	19066	8660	10406	85+
TOTAL	19100417	9621233		9479184		403855	145709	85312	60397	TOTAL

TABLE 1 DATA

TABLE 2 MALE LIFE TABLE

x	$_nq_x$	l_x	$_nd_x$	$_nL_x$	$_nm_x$	$_na_x$	T_x	r_x	$\mathring{e}_x$	$_nM_x$	x
0	0.024695	100000	2470	98115	0.025170	0.2367	6875271	0.0000	68.753	0.025170	0
1	0.004148	97530	405	388945	0.001040	1.0921	6777156	0.0000	69.488	0.001040	1
5	0.003311	97126	322	484825	0.000663	2.5000	6388210	0.0091	65.772	0.000664	5
10	0.002426	96804	235	483486	0.000486	2.7222	5903385	0.0213	60.983	0.000483	10
15	0.005925	96569	572	481542	0.001188	2.7197	5419899	0.0390	56.124	0.001178	15
20	0.008732	95997	838	477929	0.001754	2.5450	4938356	0.0410	51.443	0.001750	20
25	0.007917	95159	753	473900	0.001590	2.4847	4460428	0.0088	46.873	0.001590	25
30	0.008292	94406	783	470130	0.001665	2.5752	3986527	0.0000	42.228	0.001665	30
35	0.011065	93623	1036	465697	0.002224	2.6659	3516397	0.0000	37.559	0.002224	35
40	0.017363	92587	1608	459225	0.003501	2.6919	3050700	0.0148	32.950	0.003490	40
45	0.027664	90979	2517	449156	0.005603	2.7190	2591476	0.0173	28.484	0.005581	45
50	0.048079	88463	4253	432438	0.009835	2.6783	2142320	0.0178	24.217	0.009801	50
55	0.073121	84209	6157	406635	0.015143	2.6594	1709881	0.0257	20.305	0.015068	55
60	0.114869	78052	8966	368945	0.024301	2.6226	1303246	0.0143	16.697	0.024241	60
65	0.165507	69086	11434	317895	0.035969	2.5918	934302	0.0143	13.524	0.035883	65
70	0.242896	57652	14003	253964	0.055139	2.5509	616407	0.0143	10.692	0.055011	70
75	0.340410	43648	14858	181017	0.082083	2.4946	362443	0.0143	8.304	0.081894	75
80	0.473120	28790	13621	109962	0.123871	2.5047	181426	0.0143	6.302	0.123496	80
85+	*1.000000	15169	15169	71463	0.212262	4.7112	71463	0.0143	4.711	0.211003	85+

TABLE 3 FEMALE LIFE TABLE

x	$_nq_x$	l_x	$_nd_x$	$_nL_x$	$_nm_x$	$_na_x$	T_x	r_x	$\mathring{e}_x$	$_nM_x$	x
0	0.019411	100000	1941	98535	0.019700	0.2451	7500153	0.0000	75.002	0.019700	0
1	0.003507	98059	344	391238	0.000879	1.0983	7401619	0.0000	75.481	0.000879	1
5	0.002086	97715	204	488065	0.000418	2.5000	7010381	0.0094	71.743	0.000419	5
10	0.001548	97511	151	487186	0.000310	2.5529	6522316	0.0212	66.888	0.000309	10
15	0.002487	97360	242	486223	0.000498	2.6116	6035129	0.0369	61.988	0.000496	15
20	0.002890	97118	281	484905	0.000579	2.5564	5548907	0.0371	57.136	0.000578	20
25	0.003285	96837	318	483423	0.000658	2.5967	5064002	0.0114	52.294	0.000657	25
30	0.004438	96519	428	481591	0.000889	2.5516	4580580	0.0000	47.458	0.000889	30
35	0.006555	96091	630	478992	0.001315	2.6776	4098989	0.0000	42.657	0.001315	35
40	0.010110	95461	965	475084	0.002032	2.6986	3619997	0.0142	37.921	0.002026	40
45	0.016402	94496	1550	468909	0.003305	2.6961	3144912	0.0237	33.281	0.003289	45
50	0.026081	92946	2424	459059	0.005281	2.6603	2676003	0.0252	28.791	0.005258	50
55	0.037731	90522	3415	444661	0.007681	2.6727	2216945	0.0318	24.491	0.007635	55
60	0.060326	87106	5255	423302	0.012414	2.6724	1772284	0.0262	20.346	0.012349	60
65	0.094865	81852	7765	391145	0.019852	2.6673	1348982	0.0262	16.481	0.019742	65
70	0.155090	74087	11490	343248	0.033475	2.6339	957837	0.0262	12.929	0.033296	70
75	0.242025	62597	15150	276570	0.054778	2.5965	614589	0.0262	9.818	0.054475	75
80	0.389999	47447	18504	191061	0.096850	2.6553	338019	0.0262	7.124	0.096361	80
85+	1.000000	28943	28943	146959	0.196944	5.0776	146959	0.0262	5.078	0.194715	85+

TABLE 4 OBSERVED AND PROJECTED VITAL RATES

RATES PER THOUSAND	OBSERVED POPULATION BOTH SEXES	MALES	FEMALES	PROJECTED POPULATION 1970 MALES	FEMALES	1975 MALES	FEMALES	1980 MALES	FEMALES	STABLE POPULATION MALES	FEMALES
Birth	21.14	21.57	20.71	22.78	21.71	24.34	23.08	25.27	23.89	23.76	22.47
Death	7.63	8.87	6.37	8.95	6.75	8.96	7.03	8.93	7.14	9.09	7.81
Increase	13.52	12.71	14.34	13.83	14.95	15.37	16.05	16.34	16.75		14.6668
PERCENTAGE											
under 15	33.07	33.59	32.54	31.95	30.72	30.79	29.43	30.75	29.26	31.04	29.55
15-64	59.24	59.22	59.27	60.89	60.75	61.94	61.65	61.81	61.37	61.44	60.33
65 and over	7.69	7.19	8.19	7.16	8.53	7.27	8.92	7.45	9.38	7.52	10.12
DEP. RATIO X 100	68.80	68.86	68.73	64.23	64.61	61.44	62.20	61.80	62.96	62.76	65.76

AGE AT LAST BIRTHDAY	1970 BOTH SEXES	MALES	FEMALES	1975 BOTH SEXES	MALES	FEMALES	1980 BOTH SEXES	MALES	FEMALES	AGE AT LAST BIRTHDAY	
0-4	2099	1076	1023	2392	1226	1166	2717	1393	1324	0-4	TABLE 5
5-9	2176	1113	1063	2091	1071	1020	2383	1221	1162	5-9	POPULATION
10-14	2146	1097	1049	2172	1110	1062	2086	1068	1018	10-14	PROJECTED
15-19	1973	1009	964	2140	1093	1047	2164	1105	1059	15-19	WITH
20-24	1721	876	845	1964	1002	962	2129	1085	1044	20-24	FIXED
25-29	1335	672	663	1711	869	842	1952	993	959	25-29	AGE—
30-34	1151	572	579	1327	667	660	1701	862	839	30-34	SPECIFIC
35-39	1191	605	586	1143	567	576	1318	661	657	35-39	BIRTH
40-44	1239	623	616	1178	597	581	1130	559	571	40-44	AND
45-49	1196	589	607	1217	609	608	1158	584	574	45-49	DEATH
50-54	1022	506	516	1161	567	594	1182	587	595	50-54	RATES
55-59	902	448	454	976	476	500	1109	533	576	55-59	(IN 1000's)
60-64	731	361	370	839	407	432	908	432	476	60-64	
65-69	562	271	291	653	311	342	750	351	399	65-69	
70-74	425	196	229	472	217	255	549	249	300	70-74	
75-79	306	135	171	324	140	184	359	154	205	75-79	
80-84	194	84	110	200	82	118	212	85	127	80-84	
85+	121	51	70	139	54	85	144	53	91	85+	
TOTAL	20490	10284	10206	22099	11065	11034	23951	11975	11976	TOTAL	

STANDARD COUNTRIES:

STANDARDIZED RATES PER THOUSAND	ENGLAND AND WALES 1961 BOTH SEXES	MALES	FEMALES	UNITED STATES 1960 BOTH SEXES	MALES	FEMALES	MEXICO 1960 BOTH SEXES	MALES	FEMALES	
Birth	20.28	22.44*	19.11	20.64	20.85*	19.76	23.90	19.98*	23.17	TABLE 6
Death	10.30	10.99*	9.75	8.44	9.74*	7.21	4.49	7.40*	3.55	STANDARDIZED
Increase	9.98	11.45*	9.36	12.20	11.12*	12.56	19.40	12.57*	19.62	RATES

	OBSERVED POP. MALES	FEMALES	STATIONARY POP. MALES	FEMALES	STABLE POP. MALES	FEMALES	OBSERVED BIRTHS	NET MATERNITY FUNCTION	BIRTHS IN STABLE POP.	
μ	29.41529	30.19143	37.09974	39.63027	29.96711	31.71228	27.33717	27.75320	27.19169	TABLE 7
σ^2	458.1626	475.1835	513.3014	566.3955	452.2777	503.6484	39.32557	37.08634	35.30559	MOMENTS
κ_3	5679.111	5807.260	2566.895	2115.915	5430.528	6041.798	133.4022	118.9577	123.3772	AND
κ_4	-133074.	-149209.	-254744.	-337408.	-124560.	-177723.	-568.172	-398.300	-197.493	CUMULANTS
β_1	0.335353	0.314310	0.048719	0.024640	0.318764	0.285726	0.292618	0.277424	0.345891	
β_2	2.366054	2.339198	2.033152	1.948242	2.391069	2.299369	2.632608	2.710410	2.841560	
κ	-0.125515	-0.117565	-0.018575	-0.008974	-0.123756	-0.106500	-0.149101	-0.160083	-0.210912	

VITAL STATISTICS

VITAL STATISTICS		THOMPSON AGE RANGE	NRR	1000r	INTERVAL	BOURGEOIS-PICHAT AGE RANGE	NRR	1000b	1000d	1000r	COALE		
GRR	1.549										IBR	24.72	TABLE 8
NRR	1.496	0-4	1.61	17.68	27.44	5-29	2.29	29.80	-0.89	30.70	IDR	7.08	RATES FROM AGE
TFR	3.187	5-9	1.72	20.04	27.41	30-54	1.31	19.22	9.15	10.07	IRI	17.64	DISTRIBUTIONS
GENERATION	27.470	10-14	1.66	18.24	27.36	55-79	1.86	33.97	10.91	23.07	K1	0.	AND VITAL
SEX RATIO	105.730	15-19	1.52	14.68	27.28	*40-69	2.07	43.19	16.23	26.96	K2	0.	STATISTICS (Females)

Start of Age Interval	ORIGINAL MATRIX SUB-DIAGONAL	ALTERNATIVE FIRST ROWS Projection	Integral	FIRST STABLE MATRIX % IN STABLE POPULATION	FISHER VALUES	REPRODUCTIVE VALUES	SECOND STABLE MATRIX Z₂ FIRST COLUMN	FIRST ROW	
0	0.99651	0.00000	0.00000	10.618	1.059	1130063	0.1642+0.0854	0.1642+0.0854	TABLE 9
5	0.99820	0.00024	0.00000	9.832	1.144	1202024	0.1738-0.1300	-0.0049+0.1577	LESLIE
10	0.99802	0.05861	0.00050	9.119	1.233	1191196	-0.0490-0.2503	-0.1228+0.0545	MATRIX
15	0.99729	0.28608	0.12133	8.456	1.267	1073073	-0.2898-0.0757	-0.0968-0.0791	AND ITS
20	0.99694	0.44791	0.47349	7.836	1.064	707243	-0.2276+0.2680	-0.0222-0.1280	SPECTRAL
25	0.99621	0.36399	0.45719	7.259	0.673	390903	0.1674+0.3771	0.0163-0.1028	COMPONENTS
30	0.99460	0.22260	0.29911	6.719	0.340	200094	0.4835+0.0150	0.0250-0.0567	(Females)
35	0.99184	0.10457	0.16359	6.210	0.131	81103	0.2614-0.5022	0.0162-0.0209	
40	0.98700	0.02826	0.05379	5.723	0.030	18454	-0.3958-0.5294	0.0048-0.0043	
45	0.97899	0.00240	0.00490	5.248	0.002	1264	-0.7535+0.1474	0.0004-0.0003	
50	0.96864	0.00004	0.00008	4.774	0.000	18	-0.2238+0.8559	0.0000-0.0000	
55+	0.82223			18.207					

Start of Age Interval	OBSERVED POPUL. (IN 100's)	CONTRIBUTIONS OF ROOTS (IN 100's) r_1	r_2, r_3	$r_4 \cdot r_{11}$	AGE-SP. BIRTH RATES	NET MATERNITY FUNCTION	COEFF. OF MATRIX EQUATION	PARAMETERS INTEGRAL	MATRIX	EXP. INCREASE x	$e^{(x+2\frac{1}{2})r}$	
0	10672	10447	-157	382	0.0000	0.0000	0.0000	L(1) 1.07609	1.07622	0	1.0373	TABLE 10
5	10511	9673	948	-110	0.0000	0.0000	0.0002	L(2) 0.36033	0.36869	50	2.1598	AGE
10	9663	8972	1182	-491	0.0001	0.0005	0.0583	0.79256	0.76550	55	2.3241	ANALYSIS
15	8468	8320	-103	251	0.0239	0.1161	0.2840	R(1) 0.01467	0.01469	60	2.5010	AND
20	6649	7710	-1734	674	0.0932	0.4519	0.4435	R(2) -0.02771	-0.03258	65	2.6913	MISCELLANEOUS
25	5812	7142	-1624	295	0.0900	0.4350	0.3593	0.22882	0.22439	70	2.8960	RESULTS
30	5891	6611	733	-1453	0.0589	0.2835	0.2189	C(1)	98386	75	3.1164	(Females)
35	6213	6109	2974	-2870	0.0322	0.1542	0.1023	C(2)	83669	80	3.3535	
40	6151	5630	2011	-1491	0.0106	0.0503	0.0274		252529	85	3.6087	
45	5275	5164	-2005	2116	0.0010	0.0045	0.0023	2P/Y 27.4594	28.0013	90	3.8833	
50	4688	4697	-4697	4688	0.0000	0.0001	0.0000	DELTA 5.1105		95	4.1788	
55+	14799	17913								100	4.4967	

TABLE 1 — DATA

AGE AT LAST BIRTHDAY	POPULATION BOTH SEXES	MALES Number	MALES %	FEMALES Number	FEMALES %	BIRTHS BY AGE OF MOTHER	DEATHS BOTH SEXES	DEATHS MALES	FEMALES	AGE AT LAST BIRTHDAY
0	134574	69021	2.6	65553	2.5	0	4258	2454	1804	0
1-4	536777	273646	10.4	263131	10.0	0	694	393	301	1-4
5-9	624785	319352	12.1	305433	11.6	0	398	252	146	5-9
10-14	569268	290288	11.0	278980	10.6	25	276	180	96	10-14
15-19	469307	236809	9.0	232498	8.8	7294	381	272	109	15-19
20-24	370847	181686	6.9	189161	7.2	37539	409	302	107	20-24
25-29	362412	180679	6.8	181733	6.9	39157	407	269	138	25-29
30-34	373228	185257	7.0	187971	7.1	29169	478	302	176	30-34
35-39	360021	179017	6.8	181004	6.9	17330	721	439	282	35-39
40-44	308810	152688	5.8	156122	5.9	5691	934	579	355	40-44
45-49	275535	137979	5.2	137556	5.2	464	1355	857	498	45-49
50-54	236838	118629	4.5	118209	4.5	7	1867	1206	661	50-54
55-59	190241	94434	3.6	95807	3.6	0	2478	1583	895	55-59
60-64	150292	73599	2.8	76693	2.9	0	3021	1881	1140	60-64
65-69	117146	56791	2.2	60355	2.3	0	3531	2113	1418	65-69
70-74	88386	41612	1.6	46774	1.8		4203	2362	1841	70-74
75-79	56076	26268	1.0	29808	1.1		4164	2223	1941	75-79
80-84	29701	13603	0.5	16098	0.6	70364 M.	3563	1777	1786	80-84
85+	15452	6701	0.3	8751	0.3	66312 F.	3294	1448	1846	85+
TOTAL	5269696	2638059		2631637		136676	36432	20892	15540	TOTAL

TABLE 2 — MALE LIFE TABLE

x	nq_x	l_x	nd_x	nL_x	nm_x	na_x	T_x	r_x	$\dot{e}_x$	nM_x	x
0	0.034612	100000	3461	97348	0.035554	0.2339	6735127	0.0000	67.351	0.035554	0
1	0.005721	96539	552	384548	0.001436	1.0901	6637778	0.0000	68.758	0.001436	1
5	0.003927	95987	377	478991	0.000787	2.5000	6253230	0.0156	65.147	0.000789	5
10	0.003107	95610	297	477342	0.000622	2.6218	5774240	0.0291	60.394	0.000620	10
15	0.005777	95313	551	475288	0.001159	2.6847	5296898	0.0457	55.574	0.001149	15
20	0.008286	94762	785	471877	0.001664	2.5388	4821610	0.0255	50.881	0.001662	20
25	0.007416	93977	697	468136	0.001489	2.4917	4349732	0.0000	46.285	0.001489	25
30	0.008119	93280	757	464596	0.001630	2.6195	3881597	0.0000	41.612	0.001630	30
35	0.012229	92522	1132	459985	0.002460	2.6783	3417001	0.0168	36.932	0.002452	35
40	0.018880	91391	1725	452979	0.003809	2.6962	2957016	0.0220	32.356	0.003792	40
45	0.030738	89665	2756	441982	0.006236	2.6977	2504036	0.0187	27.926	0.006211	45
50	0.049944	86909	4341	424516	0.010225	2.6890	2062055	0.0272	23.727	0.010166	50
55	0.081081	82569	6695	397113	0.016859	2.6503	1637539	0.0305	19.832	0.016763	55
60	0.120875	75874	9171	357428	0.025659	2.6075	1240426	0.0247	16.349	0.025557	60
65	0.171326	66703	11428	305912	0.037357	2.5847	882998	0.0247	13.238	0.037207	65
70	0.250000	55275	13819	242471	0.056991	2.5466	577086	0.0247	10.440	0.056762	70
75	0.350239	41456	14520	170873	0.084973	2.4925	334615	0.0247	8.072	0.084628	75
80	0.493604	26937	13296	101260	0.131306	2.4862	163742	0.0247	6.079	0.130632	80
85+	*1.000000	13641	13641	62483	0.218309	4.5807	62483	0.0247	4.581	0.216087	85+

TABLE 3 — FEMALE LIFE TABLE

x	nq_x	l_x	nd_x	nL_x	nm_x	na_x	T_x	r_x	$\dot{e}_x$	nM_x	x
0	0.026954	100000	2695	97944	0.027520	0.2372	7286679	0.0000	72.867	0.027520	0
1	0.004560	97305	444	387928	0.001144	1.0925	7188735	0.0000	73.879	0.001144	1
5	0.002376	96861	230	483729	0.000476	2.5000	6800807	0.0157	70.212	0.000478	5
10	0.001719	96631	166	482737	0.000344	2.4957	6317078	0.0269	65.373	0.000344	10
15	0.002350	96465	227	481778	0.000471	2.5978	5834340	0.0384	60.482	0.000469	15
20	0.002832	96238	273	480537	0.000567	2.6047	5352562	0.0240	55.618	0.000566	20
25	0.003790	95965	364	478954	0.000759	2.5997	4872026	0.0000	50.769	0.000759	25
30	0.004671	95602	447	476970	0.000936	2.6759	4393072	0.0000	45.952	0.000936	30
35	0.007785	95155	741	474054	0.001563	2.6761	3916102	0.0170	41.155	0.001558	35
40	0.011363	94414	1073	469585	0.002285	2.6830	3442048	0.0250	36.457	0.002274	40
45	0.018033	93341	1683	462806	0.003637	2.6823	2972463	0.0241	31.845	0.003620	45
50	0.027778	91658	2546	452430	0.005628	2.6979	2509657	0.0302	27.381	0.005592	50
55	0.046025	89112	4101	436056	0.009406	2.6827	2057227	0.0336	23.086	0.009342	55
60	0.072265	85011	6143	410682	0.014959	2.6605	1621171	0.0328	19.070	0.014864	60
65	0.112047	78867	8837	373607	0.023653	2.6541	1210489	0.0328	15.348	0.023494	65
70	0.181053	70031	12679	319992	0.039624	2.6212	836883	0.0328	11.950	0.039359	70
75	0.282523	57351	16215	247351	0.065553	2.5697	516891	0.0328	9.013	0.065117	75
80	0.440164	41137	18107	161837	0.111884	2.5784	269540	0.0328	6.552	0.110945	80
85+	*1.000000	23030	23030	107703	0.213827	4.6767	107703	0.0328	4.677	0.210947	85+

TABLE 4 — OBSERVED AND PROJECTED VITAL RATES

	OBSERVED POPULATION BOTH SEXES	MALES	FEMALES	PROJECTED POPULATION 1966 MALES	1966 FEMALES	1971 MALES	1971 FEMALES	1976 MALES	1976 FEMALES	STABLE POPULATION MALES	FEMALES
RATES PER THOUSAND											
Birth	25.94	26.67	25.20	26.40	24.88	27.24	25.64	28.06	26.39	27.20	25.95
Death	6.91	7.92	5.91	8.06	6.17	8.20	6.46	8.31	6.71	8.44	7.19
Increase	19.02	18.75	19.29	18.34	18.71	19.04	19.19	19.74	19.68	18.7584	
PERCENTAGE											
under 15	35.40	36.10	34.70	34.98	33.45	34.10	32.50	33.87	32.17	34.10	32.84
15-64	58.78	58.41	59.16	59.45	60.06	60.19	60.64	60.19	60.53	59.86	59.36
65 and over	5.82	5.50	6.15	5.57	6.49	5.71	6.86	5.94	7.30	6.04	7.80
DEP. RATIO X 100	70.13	71.22	69.05	68.21	66.49	66.13	64.92	66.14	65.21	67.05	68.47

TABLE 1 — DATA

AGE AT LAST BIRTHDAY	POPULATION BOTH SEXES	MALES Number	%	FEMALES Number	%	BIRTHS BY AGE OF MOTHER	DEATHS BOTH SEXES	MALES	FEMALES	AGE AT LAST BIRTHDAY
0	155382	79442	2.5	75940	2.4	0	3664	2099	1565	0
1-4	585904	300339	9.6	285565	9.2	0	563	321	242	1-4
5-9	675218	345641	11.0	329577	10.6	0	319	194	125	5-9
10-14	594918	304936	9.7	289982	9.3	76	245	162	83	10-14
15-19	439059	224229	7.1	214830	6.9	14626	343	249	94	15-19
20-24	387202	190504	6.1	196698	6.3	47381	394	295	99	20-24
25-29	421797	213080	6.8	208717	6.7	44463	432	288	144	25-29
30-34	459265	233586	7.4	225679	7.3	30323	523	335	188	30-34
35-39	469669	233041	7.4	236628	7.6	16215	808	505	303	35-39
40-44	398238	200400	6.4	197838	6.4	4316	1059	646	413	40-44
45-49	361187	184073	5.9	177114	5.7	249	1729	1116	613	45-49
50-54	310479	158170	5.0	152309	4.9	3	2389	1573	816	50-54
55-59	258867	131274	4.2	127593	4.1	0	3187	2155	1032	55-59
60-64	218827	107978	3.4	110849	3.6	0	4246	2804	1442	60-64
65-69	180249	85942	2.7	94307	3.0	0	5310	3265	2045	65-69
70-74	146429	66882	2.1	79547	2.6		6647	3894	2753	70-74
75-79	97981	44292	1.4	53689	1.7		7149	3893	3256	75-79
80-84	53619	22930	0.7	30689	1.0	80940 M.	6245	3026	3219	80-84
85+	30631	12005	0.4	18626	0.6	76712 F.	6290	2633	3657	85+
TOTAL	6244921	3138744		3106177		157652	51542	29453	22089	TOTAL

TABLE 2 — MALE LIFE TABLE

x	nq_x	l_x	nd_x	nL_x	nm_x	na_x	T_x	r_x	$\mathring{e}_x$	nM_x	x
0	0.025803	100000	2580	98024	0.026323	0.2341	6832004	0.0047	68.320	0.026422	0
1	0.004235	97420	413	388478	0.001062	1.0903	6733980	0.0047	69.123	0.001069	1
5	0.002793	97007	271	484358	0.000559	2.5000	6345502	0.0212	65.413	0.000561	5
10	0.002678	96736	259	483089	0.000536	2.7155	5861144	0.0426	60.589	0.000531	10
15	0.005586	96477	539	481139	0.001120	2.6859	5378054	0.0460	55.744	0.001110	15
20	0.007714	95938	740	477862	0.001549	2.5288	4896916	0.0037	51.042	0.001549	20
25	0.006735	95198	641	474374	0.001352	2.4791	4419054	0.0000	46.420	0.001352	25
30	0.007146	94557	676	471173	0.001434	2.6151	3944679	0.0000	41.717	0.001434	30
35	0.010805	93881	1014	467041	0.002172	2.6679	3473506	0.0131	36.999	0.002167	35
40	0.016081	92867	1493	460961	0.003240	2.7411	3006466	0.0200	32.374	0.003224	40
45	0.030018	91373	2743	450601	0.006087	2.7154	2545505	0.0174	27.858	0.006063	45
50	0.048844	88631	4329	433153	0.009994	2.6900	2094904	0.0233	23.636	0.009945	50
55	0.079363	84302	6690	405862	0.016484	2.6614	1661751	0.0212	19.712	0.016416	55
60	0.122558	77611	9512	365356	0.026035	2.6136	1255889	0.0152	16.182	0.025968	60
65	0.174391	68099	11876	311815	0.038086	2.5849	890532	0.0152	13.077	0.037991	65
70	0.255291	56223	14353	245905	0.058369	2.5468	578717	0.0152	10.293	0.058222	70
75	0.360645	41870	15100	171376	0.088112	2.4852	332812	0.0152	7.949	0.087894	75
80	0.496055	26770	13279	100315	0.132375	2.4747	161436	0.0152	6.031	0.131966	80
85+	*1.000000	13490	13490	61121	0.220718	4.5307	61121	0.0152	4.531	0.219325	85+

TABLE 3 — FEMALE LIFE TABLE

x	nq_x	l_x	nd_x	nL_x	nm_x	na_x	T_x	r_x	$\mathring{e}_x$	nM_x	x
0	0.020203	100000	2020	98457	0.020520	0.2360	7447169	0.0054	74.472	0.020608	0
1	0.003356	97980	329	390962	0.000841	1.0916	7348712	0.0054	75.002	0.000847	1
5	0.001884	97651	184	487794	0.000377	2.5000	6957750	0.0215	71.251	0.000379	5
10	0.001433	97467	140	486991	0.000287	2.5441	6469956	0.0425	66.381	0.000286	10
15	0.002194	97327	214	486124	0.000439	2.6019	5982965	0.0384	61.473	0.000438	15
20	0.002514	97114	244	484983	0.000503	2.6024	5496841	0.0024	56.602	0.000503	20
25	0.003444	96869	334	483546	0.000690	2.5981	5011858	0.0000	51.738	0.000690	25
30	0.004157	96536	401	481735	0.000833	2.6462	4528312	0.0000	46.908	0.000833	30
35	0.006399	96135	615	479259	0.001284	2.7021	4046577	0.0118	42.093	0.001280	35
40	0.010448	95519	998	475313	0.002100	2.7118	3567318	0.0268	37.347	0.002088	40
45	0.017243	94521	1630	468839	0.003476	2.6881	3092005	0.0226	32.712	0.003461	45
50	0.026584	92891	2469	458695	0.005384	2.6666	2623166	0.0273	28.239	0.005358	50
55	0.039871	90422	3605	443730	0.008125	2.6755	2164471	0.0233	23.937	0.008088	55
60	0.063427	86817	5507	421322	0.013070	2.6823	1720741	0.0221	19.820	0.013009	60
65	0.103607	81310	8424	386783	0.021780	2.6534	1299420	0.0221	15.981	0.021684	65
70	0.160675	72886	11711	336783	0.034773	2.6392	912636	0.0221	12.521	0.034608	70
75	0.265652	61175	16251	266702	0.060934	2.5895	575853	0.0221	9.413	0.060646	75
80	0.416149	44924	18695	177507	0.105319	2.6112	309151	0.0221	6.882	0.104891	80
85+	1.000000	26229	26229	131643	0.199241	5.0190	131643	0.0221	5.019	0.196339	85+

TABLE 4 — OBSERVED AND PROJECTED VITAL RATES

RATES PER THOUSAND	OBSERVED POPULATION BOTH SEXES	MALES	FEMALES	PROJECTED POPULATION 1966 MALES	FEMALES	1971 MALES	FEMALES	1976 MALES	FEMALES	STABLE POPULATION MALES	FEMALES
Birth	25.24	25.79	24.70	24.48	23.32	25.60	24.29	27.15	25.70	28.58	27.32
Death	8.25	9.38	7.11	9.39	7.37	9.39	7.54	9.33	7.63	7.53	6.27
Increase	16.99	16.40	17.59	15.08	15.94	16.21	16.75	17.82	18.07		21.0556
PERCENTAGE											
under 15	32.21	32.83	31.58	33.03	31.66	32.81	31.34	32.95	31.41	35.63	34.30
15-64	59.64	59.78	59.50	59.71	59.30	60.01	59.58	59.84	59.35	58.95	58.30
65 and over	8.15	7.39	8.91	7.26	9.04	7.18	9.08	7.21	9.23	5.42	7.40
DEP. RATIO X 100	67.67	67.28	68.06	67.48	68.63	66.65	67.85	67.11	68.49	69.63	71.53

TABLE 4 — OBSERVED AND PROJECTED VITAL RATES

TABLE 1 — DATA

AGE AT LAST BIRTHDAY	POPULATION BOTH SEXES	MALES Number	%	FEMALES Number	%	BIRTHS BY AGE OF MOTHER	DEATHS BOTH SEXES	MALES	FEMALES	AGE AT LAST BIRTHDAY
0	58441	29780	5.1	28661	4.9	0	4076	2242	1834	0
1-4	183692	93280	16.0	90412	15.5	0	1350	656	694	1-4
5-9	163928	83036	14.2	80892	13.9	0	278	142	136	5-9
10-14	134272	68192	11.7	66080	11.4	68	149	86	63	10-14
15-19	110687	55985	9.6	54702	9.4	7520	116	70	46	15-19
20-24	96265	48188	8.3	48077	8.3	18734	148	86	62	20-24
25-29	84327	40996	7.0	43331	7.5	16391	143	67	76	25-29
30-34	73308	35390	6.1	37918	6.5	11758	157	70	87	30-34
35-39	58270	28499	4.9	29771	5.1	7343	168	86	82	35-39
40-44	47162	23319	4.0	23843	4.1	2445	173	102	71	40-44
45-49	42628	21074	3.6	21554	3.7	374	234	133	101	45-49
50-54	34724	17231	3.0	17493	3.0	0	282	160	122	50-54
55-59	26163	13098	2.2	13065	2.2	0	314	176	138	55-59
60-64	19764	9858	1.7	9906	1.7	0	415	232	183	60-64
65-69	13620	6772	1.2	6848	1.2	0	444	246	198	65-69
70-74	9489	4747	0.8	4742	0.8		462	243	219	70-74
75-79	5697	2878	0.5	2819	0.5		412	220	192	75-79
80-84	2492	1250	0.2	1242	0.2	32859 M.	336	170	166	80-84
85+	673	457	0.1	216	0.0	31774 F.	406	155	251	85+
TOTAL	1165602	584030		581572		64633	10063	5342	4721	TOTAL

TABLE 2 — MALE LIFE TABLE

x	$_nq_x$	l_x	$_nd_x$	$_nL_x$	$_nm_x$	$_na_x$	T_x	r_x	$\dot{e}_x$	$_nM_x$	x
0	0.070653	100000	7065	95211	0.074207	0.3222	6315623	0.0201	63.156	0.075285	0
1	0.027195	92935	2527	364605	0.006932	1.1773	6220412	0.0201	66.933	0.007033	1
5	0.008243	90407	745	450174	0.001655	2.5000	5855807	0.0562	64.771	0.001710	5
10	0.006269	89662	562	446866	0.001258	2.4302	5405634	0.0381	60.289	0.001261	10
15	0.006251	89100	557	444154	0.001254	2.5844	4958768	0.0334	55.654	0.001250	15
20	0.008896	88543	788	440779	0.001787	2.5417	4514613	0.0295	50.988	0.001785	20
25	0.008144	87755	715	437005	0.001635	2.5214	4073835	0.0291	46.423	0.001634	25
30	0.009893	87041	861	433172	0.001988	2.6414	3636830	0.0342	41.783	0.001978	30
35	0.015077	86179	1299	427854	0.003037	2.6577	3203658	0.0386	37.174	0.003018	35
40	0.021733	84880	1845	420058	0.004392	2.6459	2775804	0.0257	32.703	0.004374	40
45	0.031211	83035	2592	409079	0.006335	2.6472	2355746	0.0237	28.370	0.006311	45
50	0.045702	80444	3676	393539	0.009342	2.6390	1946667	0.0381	24.199	0.009286	50
55	0.065708	76767	5044	372138	0.013555	2.6809	1553128	0.0411	20.232	0.013437	55
60	0.112320	71723	8056	339651	0.023718	2.6460	1180990	0.0398	16.466	0.023534	60
65	0.167891	63667	10689	292457	0.036549	2.5790	841338	0.0398	13.215	0.036326	65
70	0.228580	52978	12110	235144	0.051499	2.5437	548881	0.0398	10.361	0.051190	70
75	0.323636	40868	13226	171700	0.077033	2.5321	313737	0.0398	7.677	0.076442	75
80	0.511791	27642	14147	102898	0.137484	2.5040	142037	0.0398	5.138	0.136001	80
85+	*1.000000	13495	13495	39139	0.344795	2.9003	39139	0.0398	2.900	0.339168	85+

TABLE 3 — FEMALE LIFE TABLE

x	$_nq_x$	l_x	$_nd_x$	$_nL_x$	$_nm_x$	$_na_x$	T_x	r_x	$\dot{e}_x$	$_nM_x$	x
0	0.060637	100000	6064	96054	0.063128	0.3492	6517846	0.0194	65.178	0.063989	0
1	0.029723	93936	2792	367980	0.007587	1.2188	6421792	0.0194	68.363	0.007676	1
5	0.008052	91144	734	453887	0.001617	2.5000	6053812	0.0560	66.420	0.001681	5
10	0.004724	90410	427	450910	0.000947	2.3267	5599925	0.0380	61.939	0.000953	10
15	0.004207	89983	379	449001	0.000843	2.5830	5149016	0.0309	57.222	0.000841	15
20	0.006449	89605	578	446662	0.001294	2.6445	4700015	0.0220	52.453	0.001290	20
25	0.008756	89027	780	443275	0.001759	2.6155	4253353	0.0220	47.776	0.001754	25
30	0.011445	88247	1010	438798	0.002302	2.5859	3810078	0.0352	43.175	0.002294	30
35	0.013710	87237	1196	433252	0.002761	2.5465	3371280	0.0437	38.645	0.002754	35
40	0.014842	86041	1277	427175	0.002989	2.6268	2938028	0.0290	34.147	0.002978	40
45	0.023283	84764	1974	419217	0.004708	2.6673	2510853	0.0262	29.622	0.004686	45
50	0.034565	82791	2862	407255	0.007027	2.6593	2091636	0.0429	25.264	0.006974	50
55	0.052062	79929	4161	390053	0.010668	2.6950	1684381	0.0454	21.073	0.010563	55
60	0.089188	75768	6758	363036	0.018614	2.6614	1294328	0.0377	17.083	0.018474	60
65	0.136184	69010	9398	322742	0.029119	2.6262	931292	0.0377	13.495	0.028914	65
70	0.208852	59612	12450	267868	0.046479	2.5749	608550	0.0377	10.208	0.046183	70
75	0.294168	47162	13874	202051	0.068664	2.5667	340682	0.0377	7.224	0.068109	75
80	0.507433	33288	16892	124739	0.135416	2.5311	138631	0.0377	4.165	0.133656	80
85+	*1.000000	16397	16397	13892	1.180280	0.8473	13892	0.0377	0.847	1.162037	85+

TABLE 4 — OBSERVED AND PROJECTED VITAL RATES

	OBSERVED POPULATION BOTH SEXES	MALES	FEMALES	PROJECTED POPULATION 1965 MALES	FEMALES	1970 MALES	FEMALES	1975 MALES	FEMALES	STABLE POPULATION MALES	FEMALES
RATES PER THOUSAND											
Birth	55.45	56.26	54.63	51.71	50.32	48.85	47.63	48.35	47.22	52.25	51.50
Death	8.63	9.15	8.12	9.28	8.19	8.94	7.96	8.73	7.84	8.10	7.35
Increase	46.82	47.12	46.52	42.42	42.13	39.91	39.67	39.61	39.38		44.1538
PERCENTAGE											
under 15	46.36	46.96	45.75	49.99	48.93	51.86	50.90	51.38	50.63	51.89	51.60
15-64	50.90	50.28	51.53	47.33	48.32	45.49	46.31	45.96	46.50	46.35	46.47
65 and over	2.74	2.76	2.73	2.68	2.75	2.65	2.78	2.66	2.87	1.75	1.93
DEP. RATIO X 100	96.46	98.89	94.08	111.28	106.96	119.82	115.92	117.59	115.05	115.73	115.18

TABLE 5 — POPULATION PROJECTED WITH FIXED AGE-SPECIFIC BIRTH AND DEATH RATES (IN 1000's)

AGE AT LAST BIRTHDAY	1965 BOTH SEXES	MALES	FEMALES	1970 BOTH SEXES	MALES	FEMALES	1975 BOTH SEXES	MALES	FEMALES	AGE AT LAST BIRTHDAY
0-4	321	162	159	371	188	183	441	223	218	0-4
5-9	236	120	116	314	159	155	363	184	179	5-9
10-14	162	82	80	236	120	116	312	158	154	10-14
15-19	134	68	66	162	82	80	234	119	115	15-19
20-24	110	56	54	132	67	65	161	81	80	20-24
25-29	96	48	48	109	55	54	132	67	65	25-29
30-34	84	41	43	94	47	47	108	55	53	30-34
35-39	72	35	37	82	40	42	94	47	47	35-39
40-44	57	28	29	71	34	37	81	39	42	40-44
45-49	46	23	23	56	27	29	69	33	36	45-49
50-54	41	20	21	45	22	23	54	26	28	50-54
55-59	33	16	17	39	19	20	43	21	22	55-59
60-64	24	12	12	31	15	16	36	17	19	60-64
65-69	17	8	9	21	10	11	27	13	14	65-69
70-74	11	5	6	14	7	7	17	8	9	70-74
75-79	7	3	4	8	4	4	11	5	6	75-79
80-84	4	2	2	4	2	2	5	2	3	80-84
85+	0	0	0	1	1	0	1	1	0	85+
TOTAL	1455	729	726	1790	899	891	2189	1099	1090	TOTAL

TABLE 6 — STANDARDIZED RATES

STANDARD COUNTRIES: STANDARDIZED RATES PER THOUSAND	ENGLAND AND WALES 1961 BOTH SEXES	MALES	FEMALES	UNITED STATES 1960 BOTH SEXES	MALES	FEMALES	MEXICO 1960 BOTH SEXES	MALES	FEMALES
Birth	51.00	57.89*	48.59	51.90	52.83*	50.27	57.01	56.17*	55.91
Death	17.78	20.65*	22.43	14.78	16.47*	17.32	8.56	8.13*	8.70
Increase	33.22	37.24*	26.17	37.12	36.36*	32.95	48.45	48.04*	47.21

TABLE 7 — MOMENTS AND CUMULANTS

	OBSERVED POP. MALES	FEMALES	STATIONARY POP. MALES	FEMALES	STABLE POP. MALES	FEMALES	OBSERVED BIRTHS	NET MATERNITY FUNCTION	BIRTHS IN STABLE POP.
μ	21.59740	21.95667	36.81569	37.39506	19.07472	19.26828	27.60034	29.01456	26.87683
σ^2	338.7287	337.1363	508.3368	514.2026	274.9219	281.6785	43.75972	49.32730	42.94550
κ_3	6107.521	5759.132	2444.580	2002.892	5443.052	5631.060	140.3839	113.7690	166.8998
κ_4	29161.	17111.	-256221.	-278042.	76212.	76849.	-870.007	-1754.059	-626.376
β_1	0.959785	0.865561	0.045494	0.029506	1.425795	1.418794	0.235186	0.107841	0.351689
β_2	3.254152	3.150543	2.008458	1.948423	4.008335	3.968571	2.545668	2.279109	2.660375
κ	-0.390472	-0.356394	-0.017044	-0.010696	-0.658753	-0.639254	-0.118201	-0.048405	-0.169435

TABLE 8 — RATES FROM AGE DISTRIBUTIONS AND VITAL STATISTICS (Females)

VITAL STATISTICS			THOMPSON AGE RANGE	NRR	1000r	INTERVAL	BOURGEOIS-PICHAT AGE RANGE	NRR	1000b	1000d	1000r	COALE	
GRR	3.891												
NRR	3.431		0-4	2.85	38.25	27.37	5-29	2.26	37.14	6.94	30.20	IBR	41.44
TFR	7.915		5-9	2.27	30.68	27.32	30-54	2.49	42.80	9.04	33.76	IDR	6.80
GENERATION	27.922		10-14	2.16	27.70	27.26	55-79	3.22	69.41	26.12	43.29	IRI	34.63
SEX RATIO	103.415		15-19	2.13	27.89	27.17	*50-74	3.33	75.75	31.16	44.59	K1	0.
												K2	0.

TABLE 9 — LESLIE MATRIX AND ITS SPECTRAL COMPONENTS (Females)

Start of Age Interval	ORIGINAL MATRIX SUB-DIAGONAL	ALTERNATIVE FIRST ROWS Projection	Integral	FIRST STABLE MATRIX % IN STABLE POPULATION	FISHER VALUES	REPRODUCTIVE VALUES	SECOND STABLE MATRIX Z_2 FIRST COLUMN	FIRST ROW
0	0.97813	0.00000	0.00000	21.492	1.202	143099	0.1237+0.1109	0.1237+0.1109
5	0.99344	0.00117	0.00000	16.838	1.534	124081	0.1655-0.0634	-0.0395+0.1507
10	0.99577	0.15731	0.00262	13.399	1.926	127287	0.0207-0.1909	-0.1405+0.0309
15	0.99479	0.59894	0.35020	10.687	2.225	121724	-0.1741-0.1146	-0.1040-0.1197
20	0.99242	0.87265	0.99266	8.515	2.069	99476	-0.1969+0.1113	-0.0201-0.2024
25	0.98990	0.78158	0.96364	6.769	1.546	66997	0.0099+0.2445	0.0491-0.1994
30	0.98736	0.63147	0.78994	5.367	1.001	37962	0.2397+0.1110	0.0874-0.1314
35	0.98598	0.39666	0.62833	4.245	0.497	14806	0.2241-0.1751	0.0665-0.0544
40	0.98137	0.13634	0.26123	3.352	0.146	3487	-0.0575-0.3004	0.0235-0.0127
45	0.97146	0.01980	0.04408	2.635	0.019	412	-0.3141-0.0920	0.0034-0.0013
50	0.95776	0.00007	0.00015	2.050	0.000	1	-0.2386+0.2515	0.0000-0.0000
55+	0.82631			4.652				

TABLE 10 — AGE ANALYSIS AND MISCELLANEOUS RESULTS (Females)

Start of Age Interval	OBSERVED POPUL. (IN 100's)	CONTRIBUTIONS OF ROOTS (IN 100's) r_1	r_2, r_3	$r_4 - r_{11}$	AGE-SP. BIRTH RATES	NET MATERNITY FUNCTION	COEFF. OF MATRIX EQUATION	PARAMETERS	INTEGRAL	MATRIX	EXP. INCREASE x	$e^{(x+2\frac{1}{2})r}$
0	1191	1157	73	-39	0.0000	0.0000	0.0000	L(1)	1.24704	1.24846	0	1.1167
5	809	906	-48	-49	0.0000	0.0000	0.0011	L(2)	0.40815	0.41865	50	10.1561
10	661	721	-132	72	0.0005	0.0023	0.1529		0.83974	0.81590	55	12.6650
15	547	575	-74	46	0.0676	0.3034	0.5795	R(1)	0.04415	0.04438	60	15.7937
20	481	458	82	-60	0.1916	0.8556	0.8400	R(2)	-0.01373	-0.01732	65	19.6953
25	433	364	168	-99	0.1860	0.8243	0.7466		0.22368	0.21934	70	24.5607
30	379	289	70	20	0.1524	0.6689	0.5971	C(1)		5383	75	30.6281
35	298	228	-127	196	0.1213	0.5253	0.3703	C(2)		-1371	80	38.1943
40	238	180	-205	263	0.0504	0.2153	0.1256			-34458	85	47.6296
45	216	142	-55	129	0.0085	0.0358	0.0179	2P/Y	28.0907	28.6457	90	59.3958
50	175	110	180	-115	0.0000	0.0000	0.0000	DELTA	7.4661		95	74.0686
55+	388	250									100	92.3661

AGE AT LAST BIRTHDAY	POPULATION BOTH SEXES	MALES Number	%	FEMALES Number	%	BIRTHS BY AGE OF MOTHER	DEATHS BOTH SEXES	MALES	FEMALES	AGE AT LAST BIRTHDAY
0	51050	25917	3.9	25133	3.8	0	4500	2550	1950	0
1-4	198494	100738	15.0	97756	14.6	0	1491	722	769	1-4
5-9	219150	111278	16.6	107872	16.1	0	308	182	126	5-9
10-14	171751	86699	12.9	85052	12.7	68	134	80	54	10-14
15-19	130678	64243	9.6	66435	9.9	8261	139	78	61	15-19
20-24	103804	50646	7.5	53158	7.9	18740	168	105	63	20-24
25-29	84986	41382	6.2	43604	6.5	16485	178	98	80	25-29
30-34	77325	38637	5.8	38688	5.8	11940	162	79	83	30-34
35-39	67939	33509	5.0	34430	5.1	8094	188	100	88	35-39
40-44	53824	27032	4.0	26792	4.0	2795	230	130	100	40-44
45-49	45371	22841	3.4	22530	3.4	393	236	118	118	45-49
50-54	41714	21114	3.1	20600	3.1	0	309	186	123	50-54
55-59	26758	13413	2.0	13345	2.0	0	311	173	138	55-59
60-64	25690	12969	1.9	12721	1.9	0	454	221	233	60-64
65-69	15261	7379	1.1	7882	1.2	0	437	235	202	65-69
70-74	11957	6114	0.9	5843	0.9		572	295	277	70-74
75-79	9109	4424	0.7	4685	0.7		533	278	255	75-79
80-84	4615	2238	0.3	2377	0.4	34285 M.	466	232	234	80-84
85+	1674	810	0.1	864	0.1	32491 F.	560	250	310	85+
TOTAL	1341150	671383		669767		66776	11376	6112	5264	TOTAL

TABLE 1 DATA

TABLE 2 MALE LIFE TABLE

x	$_nq_x$	l_x	$_nd_x$	$_nL_x$	$_nm_x$	$_na_x$	T_x	r_x	$\mathring{e}_x$	$_nM_x$	x
0	0.092002	100000	9200	93507	0.098391	0.2942	6264322	0.0000	62.643	0.098391	0
1	0.028093	90800	2551	355912	0.007167	1.1431	6170816	0.0000	67.961	0.007167	1
5	0.007957	88249	702	439489	0.001598	2.5000	5814904	0.0350	65.892	0.001636	5
10	0.004582	87547	401	436696	0.000919	2.4122	5375415	0.0538	61.401	0.000923	10
15	0.006117	87146	533	434499	0.001227	2.6941	4938719	0.0524	56.672	0.001214	15
20	0.010365	86613	898	430918	0.002083	2.6104	4504220	0.0420	52.004	0.002073	20
25	0.011770	85715	1009	426045	0.002368	2.4928	4073302	0.0248	47.522	0.002368	25
30	0.010185	84706	863	421424	0.002047	2.5583	3647257	0.0188	43.058	0.002045	30
35	0.014911	83843	1250	416322	0.003003	2.6844	3225834	0.0325	38.475	0.002984	35
40	0.023846	82593	1969	408211	0.004825	2.5860	2809512	0.0339	34.016	0.004809	40
45	0.025596	80624	2064	398261	0.005182	2.6462	2401301	0.0188	29.784	0.005166	45
50	0.043499	78560	3417	384811	0.008880	2.6621	2003040	0.0443	25.497	0.008809	50
55	0.062847	75143	4723	364407	0.012959	2.6057	1618230	0.0359	21.535	0.012898	55
60	0.082554	70420	5813	338589	0.017170	2.6758	1253823	0.0349	17.805	0.017041	60
65	0.149019	64607	9628	300234	0.032067	2.6318	915234	0.0349	14.166	0.031847	65
70	0.216536	54979	11905	245579	0.048477	2.5374	615000	0.0349	11.186	0.048250	70
75	0.273143	43074	11765	186209	0.063184	2.5214	369422	0.0349	8.576	0.062839	75
80	0.418810	31309	13112	125103	0.104814	2.6022	183213	0.0349	5.852	0.103663	80
85+	*1.000000	18196	18196	58110	0.313135	3.1935	58110	0.0349	3.194	0.308642	85+

TABLE 3 FEMALE LIFE TABLE

x	$_nq_x$	l_x	$_nd_x$	$_nL_x$	$_nm_x$	$_na_x$	T_x	r_x	$\mathring{e}_x$	$_nM_x$	x
0	0.073756	100000	7376	95063	0.077587	0.3306	6523535	0.0000	65.235	0.077587	0
1	0.030785	92624	2851	362483	0.007867	1.1892	6428472	0.0000	69.404	0.007867	1
5	0.005613	89773	504	447605	0.001126	2.5000	6065990	0.0342	67.570	0.001168	5
10	0.003159	89269	282	445620	0.000633	2.4307	5618385	0.0477	62.938	0.000635	10
15	0.004608	88987	410	443961	0.000924	2.6244	5172765	0.0461	58.129	0.000918	15
20	0.005948	88577	527	441650	0.001193	2.6569	4728804	0.0408	53.386	0.001185	20
25	0.009163	88050	807	438318	0.001841	2.6047	4287154	0.0300	48.690	0.001835	25
30	0.010687	87243	932	433947	0.002149	2.5658	3848836	0.0215	44.116	0.002145	30
35	0.012758	86311	1101	428938	0.002567	2.6235	3414889	0.0340	39.565	0.002556	35
40	0.018605	85210	1585	422307	0.003754	2.6400	2985951	0.0386	35.042	0.003732	40
45	0.025909	83624	2167	412879	0.005248	2.5800	2563644	0.0213	30.657	0.005237	45
50	0.029676	81458	2417	401634	0.006019	2.6604	2150765	0.0456	26.403	0.005971	50
55	0.050956	79041	4028	386009	0.010434	2.7174	1749131	0.0371	22.130	0.010341	55
60	0.088256	75013	6620	359408	0.018420	2.6351	1363122	0.0328	18.172	0.018316	60
65	0.121680	68393	8322	322447	0.025809	2.6549	1003713	0.0328	14.676	0.025628	65
70	0.213236	60071	12809	268969	0.047624	2.5499	681266	0.0328	11.341	0.047407	70
75	0.240974	47261	11389	208181	0.054706	2.5304	412297	0.0328	8.724	0.054429	75
80	0.403392	35873	14471	145272	0.099611	2.6442	204116	0.0328	5.690	0.098443	80
85+	*1.000000	21402	21402	58844	0.363704	2.7495	58844	0.0328	2.749	0.358796	85+

TABLE 4 OBSERVED AND PROJECTED VITAL RATES

	OBSERVED POPULATION BOTH SEXES	MALES	FEMALES	PROJECTED POPULATION 1968 MALES	FEMALES	1973 MALES	FEMALES	1978 MALES	FEMALES	STABLE POPULATION MALES	FEMALES
RATES PER THOUSAND											
Birth	49.79	51.07	48.51	50.01	47.74	50.23	48.13	50.42	48.47	50.73	49.45
Death	8.48	9.10	7.86	9.45	8.10	9.32	8.05	9.19	7.91	9.21	7.93
Increase	41.31	41.96	40.65	40.57	39.64	40.91	40.08	41.23	40.56		41.5200
PERCENTAGE											
under 15	47.75	48.35	47.15	49.08	47.87	49.14	48.04	50.20	49.16	50.11	49.76
15-64	49.07	48.52	49.61	47.74	48.86	47.93	48.93	46.80	47.71	47.69	47.90
65 and over	3.18	3.12	3.23	3.18	3.27	2.93	3.03	3.01	3.12	2.20	2.35
DEP. RATIO X 100	103.79	106.08	101.55	109.48	104.69	108.62	104.38	113.70	109.58	109.67	108.78

AGE AT LAST BIRTHDAY	1968 BOTH SEXES	MALES	FEMALES	1973 BOTH SEXES	MALES	FEMALES	1978 BOTH SEXES	MALES	FEMALES	AGE AT LAST BIRTHDAY	
0-4	334	170	164	405	206	199	499	254	245	0-4	
5-9	244	124	120	326	166	160	397	202	195	5-9	
10-14	218	111	107	243	123	120	324	165	159	10-14	
15-19	171	86	85	217	110	107	241	122	119	15-19	**TABLE 5**
20-24	130	64	66	170	86	84	215	109	106	20-24	POPULATION
25-29	103	50	53	129	63	66	169	85	84	25-29	PROJECTED
30-34	84	41	43	102	50	52	127	62	65	30-34	WITH
35-39	76	38	38	83	40	43	101	49	52	35-39	FIXED
40-44	67	33	34	75	37	38	82	40	42	40-44	AGE—
45-49	52	26	26	65	32	33	74	37	37	45-49	SPECIFIC
50-54	44	22	22	50	25	25	63	31	32	50-54	BIRTH
55-59	40	20	20	42	21	21	48	24	24	55-59	AND
60-64	24	12	12	37	19	18	39	19	20	60-64	DEATH
65-69	22	11	11	22	11	11	33	16	17	65-69	RATES
70-74	13	6	7	19	9	10	18	9	9	70-74	(IN 1000's)
75-79	10	5	5	10	5	5	14	7	7	75-79	
80-84	6	3	3	6	3	3	7	3	4	80-84	
85+	2	1	1	2	1	1	2	1	1	85+	
TOTAL	1640	823	817	2003	1007	996	2453	1235	1218	TOTAL	

STANDARD COUNTRIES:	ENGLAND AND WALES 1961 BOTH SEXES	MALES	FEMALES	UNITED STATES 1960 BOTH SEXES	MALES	FEMALES	MEXICO 1960 BOTH SEXES	MALES	FEMALES	
STANDARDIZED RATES PER THOUSAND										**TABLE 6**
Birth	48.99	56.69*	46.20	49.85	51.79*	47.79	54.34	54.15*	52.75	STANDAR-DIZED
Death	13.29	19.75*	14.56	11.70	16.26*	11.81	8.17	8.78*	7.63	RATES
Increase	35.70	36.94*	31.64	38.15	35.54*	35.98	46.17	45.37*	45.12	

	OBSERVED POP. MALES	FEMALES	STATIONARY POP. MALES	FEMALES	STABLE POP. MALES	FEMALES	OBSERVED BIRTHS	NET MATERNITY FUNCTION	BIRTHS IN STABLE POP.	
μ	21.76313	21.98894	37.46366	37.99295	19.92249	20.12380	27.69610	29.23004	27.22487	**TABLE 7**
σ^2	349.4245	348.3176	527.6833	534.7263	295.5278	301.5078	45.85765	48.79827	43.28014	MOMENTS
κ_3	6865.587	6802.209	2567.025	2335.808	5910.239	6062.607	141.4694	104.8229	154.3365	AND
κ_4	48080.	50773.	-279330.	-293786.	77946.	78437.	-1163.265	-1653.729	-703.551	CUMULANTS
β_1	1.104829	1.094898	0.044848	0.035684	1.353366	1.340982	0.207534	0.094558	0.293813	
β_2	3.393788	3.418484	1.996839	1.972534	3.892474	3.862826	2.446835	2.305527	2.624406	
κ	-0.435498	-0.443437	-0.016652	-0.013109	-0.613801	-0.601407	-0.097145	-0.044508	-0.148004	

VITAL STATISTICS		THOMPSON AGE RANGE	NRR	1000r	INTERVAL	BOURGEOIS-PICHAT AGE RANGE	NRR	1000b	1000d	1000r	COALE		
GRR	3.701					5-29	3.34	49.70	5.09	44.61	IBR	43.91	**TABLE 8** RATES
NRR	3.226	0-4	2.66	35.79	27.37	30-54	2.24	35.12	5.28	29.83	IDR	7.69	FROM AGE DISTRI-
TFR	7.606	5-9	2.83	39.13	27.31	55-79	2.59	42.00	6.72	35.28	IRI	36.22	BUTIONS AND VITAL
GENERATION	28.208	10-14	2.60	34.06	27.25	* 5-29	3.34	49.70	5.09	44.61	K1	0.80	STATISTICS
SEX RATIO	105.522	15-19	2.38	31.89	27.17						K2	0.	(Females)

Start of Age Interval	ORIGINAL MATRIX SUB-DIAGONAL	ALTERNATIVE FIRST ROWS Projection	Integral	FIRST STABLE MATRIX % IN STABLE POPULATION	FISHER VALUES	REPRODUCTIVE VALUES	SECOND STABLE MATRIX Z₂ FIRST COLUMN	FIRST ROW	
0	0.97827	0.00000	0.00000	20.474	1.211	148798	0.1303+0.1009	0.1303+0.1009	
5	0.99557	0.00089	0.00000	16.258	1.525	164484	0.1590-0.0721	-0.0268+0.1532	**TABLE 9**
10	0.99628	0.13879	0.00197	13.139	1.886	160389	0.0113-0.1880	-0.1373+0.0443	LESLIE
15	0.99480	0.52879	0.30711	10.625	2.163	143711	-0.1737-0.1056	-0.1139-0.1074	MATRIX
20	0.99245	0.81007	0.87068	8.580	2.035	108190	-0.1880-0.1123	-0.0305-0.1936	AND ITS
25	0.99003	0.76094	0.93373	6.912	1.538	67066	0.0124+0.2351	0.0397-0.1916	SPECTRAL
30	0.98846	0.60220	0.76223	5.555	0.983	38040	0.2291+0.1060	0.0751-0.1283	COMPO-
35	0.98454	0.37601	0.58061	4.457	0.488	16794	0.2150-0.1639	0.0593-0.0554	NENTS
40	0.97767	0.13506	0.25765	3.562	0.148	3963	-0.0475-0.2844	0.0222-0.0136	(Females)
45	0.97276	0.01942	0.04297	2.827	0.019	431	-0.2898-0.0962	0.0032-0.0014	
50	0.96110	0.00005	0.00012	2.232	0.000	1	-0.2322+0.2227	0.0000-0.0000	
55+	0.83316			5.379					

Start of Age Interval	OBSERVED POPUL. (IN 100's)	CONTRIBUTIONS OF ROOTS (IN 100's) r_1	r_2, r_3	r_4-r_{11}	AGE-SP. BIRTH RATES	NET MATERNITY FUNCTION	COEFF. OF MATRIX EQUATION	PARAMETERS	INTEGRAL	MATRIX	EXP. INCREASE x	$e^{(x+2\frac{1}{2})r}$	
0	1229	1305	-8	-68	0.0000	0.0000	0.0000	L(1)	1.23072	1.23195	0	1.1094	**TABLE 10**
5	1079	1036	-11	53	0.0000	0.0000	0.0009	L(2)	0.42346	0.43118	50	8.8446	AGE
10	851	837	-2	15	0.0004	0.0017	0.1352		0.84029	0.81630	55	10.8852	ANALYSIS
15	664	677	11	-24	0.0605	0.2686	0.5131	R(1)	0.04152	0.04172	60	13.3966	AND
20	532	547	13	-28	0.1715	0.7576	0.7819	R(2)	-0.01217	-0.01599	65	16.4875	MISCEL-
25	436	441	0	-5	0.1840	0.8063	0.7290		0.22080	0.21697	70	20.2915	LANEOUS
30	387	354	-14	47	0.1502	0.6516	0.5711	C(1)		6374	75	24.9732	RESULTS
35	344	284	-15	75	0.1144	0.4906	0.3525	C(2)		-3245	80	30.7350	(Females)
40	268	227	2	39	0.0508	0.2144	0.1247			-221	85	37.8262	
45	225	180	18	27	0.0085	0.0350	0.0175	2P/Y	28.4564	28.9591	90	46.5535	
50	206	142	16	48	0.0000	0.0000	0.0000	DELTA	4.3549		95	57.2944	
55+	477	343									100	70.5134	

TABLE 1 — DATA

AGE AT LAST BIRTHDAY	POPULATION BOTH SEXES	MALES Number	MALES %	FEMALES Number	FEMALES %	BIRTHS BY AGE OF MOTHER	DEATHS BOTH SEXES	DEATHS MALES	DEATHS FEMALES	AGE AT LAST BIRTHDAY
0	112670	56768	3.7	55902	3.7	0	11078	6188	4890	0
1-4	445574	225535	14.7	220039	14.6	0	5241	2753	2488	1-4
5-9	486037	245971	16.1	240066	15.9	0	978	502	476	5-9
10-14	392794	202906	13.2	189888	12.6	12	440	262	178	10-14
15-19	285281	132804	8.7	152477	10.1	11929	427	215	212	15-19
20-24	256009	121085	7.9	134924	9.0	30796	540	273	267	20-24
25-29	212654	103712	6.8	108942	7.2	29685	540	264	276	25-29
30-34	186873	94477	6.2	92396	6.1	19778	624	318	306	30-34
35-39	150779	77293	5.0	73486	4.9	11220	430	227	203	35-39
40-44	123611	65694	4.3	57917	3.8	6579	495	261	234	40-44
45-49	96154	51522	3.4	44632	3.0	66	471	280	191	45-49
50-54	88803	46974	3.1	41829	2.8	37	592	310	282	50-54
55-59	50705	28843	1.9	21862	1.5	0	459	285	174	55-59
60-64	60848	32303	2.1	28545	1.9	0	803	447	356	60-64
65-69	26579	14212	0.9	12367	0.8	0	529	328	201	65-69
70-74	26888	14022	0.9	12866	0.9		868	477	391	70-74
75-79	20502	9973	0.7	10529	0.7		455	252	203	75-79
80-84	11480	5441	0.4	6039	0.4	56765 M.	676	358	318	30-84
85+	4739	2178	0.1	2561	0.2	53337 F.	1379	589	790	85+
TOTAL	3038980	1531713		1507267		110102	27025	14589	12436	TOTAL

TABLE 2 — MALE LIFE TABLE

x	$_nq_x$	l_x	$_nd_x$	$_nL_x$	$_nm_x$	$_na_x$	T_x	r_x	$\mathring{e}_x$	$_nM_x$	x
0	0.101676	100000	10168	93276	0.109005	0.3387	6267857	0.0000	62.679	0.109005	0
1	0.047213	89832	4241	347461	0.012207	1.2016	6174581	0.0000	68.734	0.012207	1
5	0.009885	85591	846	425840	0.001987	2.5000	5827120	0.0288	68.081	0.002041	5
10	0.006412	84745	543	422333	0.001287	2.4375	5401280	0.0601	63.736	0.001291	10
15	0.008114	84202	683	419383	0.001629	2.6204	4978947	0.0500	59.131	0.001619	15
20	0.011233	83518	938	415323	0.002259	2.5807	4559564	0.0226	54.593	0.002255	20
25	0.012675	82580	1047	410373	0.002551	2.5843	4144242	0.0221	50.184	0.002546	25
30	0.016701	81534	1362	404290	0.003368	2.5189	3733869	0.0263	45.795	0.003366	30
35	0.014599	80172	1170	397975	0.002941	2.5357	3329579	0.0331	41.531	0.002937	35
40	0.019772	79001	1562	391292	0.003992	2.6217	2931604	0.0365	37.108	0.003973	40
45	0.026898	77439	2083	382178	0.005450	2.5903	2540312	0.0282	32.804	0.005435	45
50	0.032712	75357	2465	370922	0.006646	2.6226	2158134	0.0509	28.639	0.006599	50
55	0.048473	72891	3533	356088	0.009923	2.6314	1787212	0.0275	24.519	0.009881	55
60	0.067672	69358	4694	335807	0.013977	2.6599	1431124	0.0523	20.634	0.013838	60
65	0.110357	64665	7136	306384	0.023292	2.6264	1095317	0.0523	16.938	0.023079	65
70	0.156847	57528	9023	264814	0.034073	2.4701	788933	0.0523	13.714	0.034018	70
75	0.120387	48505	5839	228681	0.025535	2.6290	524119	0.0523	10.805	0.025268	75
80	0.296229	42666	12639	186771	0.067670	2.8987	295438	0.0523	6.924	0.065796	80
85+	*1.000000	30027	30027	108667	0.276319	3.6190	108667	0.0523	3.619	0.270432	85-

TABLE 3 — FEMALE LIFE TABLE

x	$_nq_x$	l_x	$_nd_x$	$_nL_x$	$_nm_x$	$_na_x$	T_x	r_x	$\mathring{e}_x$	$_nM_x$	x
0	0.082801	100000	8280	94657	0.087475	0.3547	6546174	0.0000	65.462	0.087475	0
1	0.043854	91720	4022	355733	0.011307	1.2287	6451517	0.0000	70.339	0.011307	1
5	0.009567	87698	839	436391	0.001923	2.5000	6095784	0.0335	69.509	0.001983	5
10	0.004651	86859	404	433234	0.000932	2.3779	5659394	0.0441	65.156	0.000937	10
15	0.006965	86455	602	430860	0.001398	2.6639	5226160	0.0328	60.450	0.001397	15
20	0.009885	85852	849	427239	0.001986	2.6159	4795299	0.0316	55.855	0.001979	20
25	0.012639	85004	1074	422444	0.002543	2.6029	4368060	0.0352	51.387	0.002533	25
30	0.016433	83929	1379	416212	0.003314	2.5092	3945617	0.0364	47.011	0.003312	30
35	0.013751	82550	1135	409967	0.002769	2.5469	3529405	0.0435	42.755	0.002762	35
40	0.020078	81415	1635	403106	0.004055	2.5715	3119438	0.0461	38.315	0.004040	40
45	0.021257	79780	1696	394866	0.004295	2.6197	2716332	0.0277	34.048	0.004279	45
50	0.033416	78085	2609	384163	0.006792	2.6010	2321466	0.0650	29.730	0.006742	50
55	0.039222	75475	2960	370352	0.007993	2.6272	1937303	0.0295	25.668	0.007959	55
60	0.060915	72515	4417	352036	0.012548	2.6141	1566951	0.0436	21.609	0.012472	60
65	0.079003	68098	5380	327966	0.016404	2.6724	1214915	0.0436	17.841	0.016253	65
70	0.141425	62718	8870	291336	0.030445	2.4911	886949	0.0436	14.142	0.030390	70
75	0.092912	53848	5003	257382	0.019439	2.6299	595613	0.0436	11.061	0.019280	75
80	0.245452	48845	11989	220887	0.054277	3.0535	338232	0.0436	6.925	0.052658	80
85+	*1.000000	36856	36856	117344	0.314081	3.1839	117344	0.0436	3.184	0.308473	85+

TABLE 4 — OBSERVED AND PROJECTED VITAL RATES

	OBSERVED POPULATION BOTH SEXES	MALES	FEMALES	PROJECTED 1965 MALES	1965 FEMALES	1970 MALES	1970 FEMALES	1975 MALES	1975 FEMALES	STABLE POPULATION MALES	FEMALES
RATES PER THOUSAND											
Birth	36.23	37.06	35.39	38.20	36.53	39.47	37.80	40.72	39.03	37.11	35.94
Death	8.89	9.52	8.25	8.88	7.58	9.28	7.97	9.45	8.04	10.61	9.45
Increase	27.34	27.54	27.14	29.32	28.96	30.20	29.82	31.26	30.99		26.4959
PERCENTAGE											
under 15	47.29	47.74	46.83	44.76	44.30	42.12	41.53	40.72	39.96	39.53	39.21
15-64	49.74	49.27	50.22	51.55	52.18	54.19	55.12	55.22	56.30	54.86	54.79
65 and over	2.97	2.99	2.94	3.69	3.53	3.69	3.35	4.06	3.74	5.61	6.00
DEP. RATIO X 100	101.03	102.95	99.11	94.00	91.65	84.53	81.42	81.08	77.61	82.28	82.51

AGE AT LAST BIRTHDAY	1965 BOTH SEXES	1965 MALES	1965 FEMALES	1970 BOTH SEXES	1970 MALES	1970 FEMALES	1975 BOTH SEXES	1975 MALES	1975 FEMALES	AGE AT LAST BIRTHDAY	
0-4	537	274	263	641	327	314	768	392	376	0-4	
5-9	540	273	267	520	265	255	620	316	304	5-9	
10-14	482	244	238	536	271	265	515	262	253	10-14	**TABLE 5**
15-19	390	201	189	479	242	237	533	269	264	15-19	POPULATION
20-24	283	132	151	387	200	187	475	240	235	20-24	PROJECTED
25-29	253	120	133	279	130	149	382	197	185	25-29	WITH
30-34	209	102	107	249	118	131	275	128	147	30-34	FIXED
35-39	184	93	91	207	101	106	245	116	129	35-39	AGE—
40-44	148	76	72	180	91	89	203	99	104	40-44	SPECIFIC
45-49	121	64	57	145	74	71	177	89	88	45-49	BIRTH
50-54	93	50	43	117	62	55	141	72	69	50-54	AND
55-59	85	45	40	90	48	42	113	60	53	55-59	DEATH
60-64	48	27	21	81	43	38	85	45	40	60-64	RATES
65-69	56	29	27	44	25	19	75	39	36	65-69	(IN 1000's)
70-74	23	12	11	49	25	24	38	21	17	70-74	
75-79	23	12	11	21	11	10	43	22	21	75-79	
80-84	17	8	9	20	10	10	17	9	8	80-84	
85+	6	3	3	10	5	5	11	6	5	85+	
TOTAL	3498	1765	1733	4055	2048	2007	4716	2382	2334	TOTAL	

STANDARD COUNTRIES: STANDARDIZED RATES PER THOUSAND	ENGLAND AND WALES 1961 BOTH SEXES	MALES	FEMALES	UNITED STATES 1960 BOTH SEXES	MALES	FEMALES	MEXICO 1960 BOTH SEXES	MALES	FEMALES	
Birth	34.17	38.70*	32.08	34.76	35.52*	33.18	37.27	37.14*	36.01	**TABLE 6** STANDARDIZED RATES
Death	10.83	20.64*	11.37	10.24	17.03*	10.05	8.48	9.25*	7.84	
Increase	23.34	18.06*	20.71	24.52	18.49*	23.13	28.79	27.88*	28.18	

	OBSERVED POP. MALES	FEMALES	STATIONARY POP. MALES	FEMALES	STABLE POP. MALES	FEMALES	OBSERVED BIRTHS	NET MATERNITY FUNCTION	BIRTHS IN STABLE POP.	
μ	22.01898	21.52592	38.90231	39.49258	25.52549	25.81366	27.85031	29.64354	28.31044	**TABLE 7**
σ^2	347.2137	329.9941	572.4728	583.5988	416.4109	426.0956	44.22135	49.64505	46.60933	MOMENTS
κ_3	6654.568	6708.793	2747.964	2537.953	7445.087	7672.340	143.6927	89.7905	136.2107	AND
κ_4	46695.	83494.	-342207.	-365359.	-2348.	-6962.	-1015.301	-2088.147	-1379.944	CUMULANTS
β_1	1.057911	1.252479	0.040249	0.032406	0.767668	0.760912	0.238766	0.065892	0.183233	
β_2	3.387328	3.766732	1.955810	1.927267	2.986460	2.961653	2.480804	2.152755	2.364792	
κ	-0.433482	-0.570028	-0.014524	-0.011522	-0.306110	-0.299617	-0.110991	-0.027474	-0.081302	

VITAL STATISTICS		THOMPSON AGE RANGE	NRR	1000r	INTERVAL	BOURGEOIS-PICHAT AGE RANGE	NRR	1000b	1000d	1000r	COALE		**TABLE 8**
GRR	2.572										IBR	45.50	RATES FROM AGE
NRR	2.155	0-4	2.48	33.23	27.33	5-29	2.71	46.81	9.95	36.86	IDR	10.08	DISTRIBUTIONS
TFR	5.309	5-9	2.66	36.70	27.27	30-54	2.77	48.69	10.97	37.72	IRI	35.41	AND VITAL
GENERATION	28.970	10-14	2.54	33.35	27.23	55-79	2.42	29.58	-3.15	32.72	K1	-4.82	STATISTICS
SEX RATIO	106.427	15-19	2.53	34.23	27.17	*20-44	2.85	50.44	11.66	38.78	K2	0.	(Females)

Start of Age Interval	ORIGINAL MATRIX SUB-DIAGONAL	ALTERNATIVE FIRST ROWS Projection	Integral	FIRST STABLE MATRIX % IN STABLE POPULATION	FISHER VALUES	REPRODUCTIVE VALUES	SECOND STABLE MATRIX Z2 FIRST COLUMN	FIRST ROW	
0	0.96892	0.00000	0.00000	15.181	1.185	327036	0.1176+0.0857	0.1176+0.0857	
5	0.99277	0.00007	0.00000	12.879	1.397	335372	0.1482-0.0619	-0.0111+0.1314	**TABLE 9**
10	0.99452	0.08495	0.00015	11.195	1.607	305161	0.0271-0.1797	-0.1044+0.0518	LESLIE
15	0.99160	0.33225	0.18239	9.749	1.744	265966	-0.1582-0.1319	-0.0969-0.0624	MATRIX
20	0.98878	0.54292	0.53210	8.464	1.612	217489	-0.2201+0.0755	-0.0367-0.1307	AND ITS
25	0.98525	0.52733	0.63523	7.328	1.211	131944	-0.0558+0.2561	0.0177-0.1351	SPECTRAL
30	0.98499	0.39758	0.49902	6.321	0.770	71110	0.2133+0.2027	0.0481-0.0948	COMPONENTS
35	0.98326	0.28841	0.35594	5.452	0.414	30423	0.3187-0.0867	0.0470-0.0418	(Females)
40	0.97956	0.12550	0.26482	4.694	0.133	7717	0.1021-0.3557	0.0191-0.0086	
45	0.97290	0.00255	0.00345	4.026	0.004	156	-0.2803-0.3034	0.0004-0.0003	
50	0.96405	0.00096	0.00206	3.429	0.001	42	-0.4486+0.0912	0.0001-0.0001	
55+	0.84906			11.281					

Start of Age Interval	OBSERVED POPUL. (IN 100's)	CONTRIBUTIONS OF ROOTS (IN 100's) r_1	r_2, r_3	$r_4 \cdot r_{11}$	AGE-SP. BIRTH RATES	NET MATERNITY FUNCTION	COEFF. OF MATRIX EQUATION	PARAMETERS	INTEGRAL	MATRIX	EXP. INCREASE x	$e^{(x+2\frac{1}{2})r}$	
0	2759	2537	24	198	0.0000	0.0000	0.0000	L(1)	1.14166	1.14210	0	1.0685	**TABLE 10**
5	2401	2153	218	30	0.0000	0.0000	0.0001	L(2)	0.44891	0.45521	50	4.0190	
10	1899	1871	226	-198	0.0000	0.0001	0.0817		0.76797	0.75038	55	4.5883	AGE
15	1525	1629	-14	-91	0.0379	0.1633	0.3178	R(1)	0.02650	0.02657	60	5.2383	ANALYSIS
20	1349	1415	-305	240	0.1106	0.4724	0.5150	R(2)	-0.02341	-0.02610	65	5.9803	AND
25	1089	1225	-339	204	0.1320	0.5576	0.4946			0.20510	70	6.8275	MISCELLANEOUS
30	924	1056	-9	-123	0.1037	0.4316	0.3674	C(1)		16713	75	7.7946	RESULTS
35	735	911	417	-593	0.0740	0.3032	0.2625	C(2)		50405	80	8.8988	(Females)
40	579	784	496	-701	0.0550	0.2218	0.1123			55286	85	10.1593	
45	446	673	53	-279	0.0007	0.0028	0.0022	2P/Y	30.1548	30.6345	90	11.5984	
50	418	573	-553	398	0.0004	0.0016	0.0008	DELTA	8.4907		95	13.2414	
55+	948	1885									100	15.1172	

TABLE 1 — DATA

AGE AT LAST BIRTHDAY	BOTH SEXES	MALES Number	MALES %	FEMALES Number	FEMALES %	BIRTHS BY AGE OF MOTHER	DEATHS BOTH SEXES	DEATHS MALES	DEATHS FEMALES	AGE AT LAST BIRTHDAY
0	69268	35482	3.9	33786	3.6	0	7395	3989	3406	0
1-4	220347	110978	12.1	109369	11.7	0	5503	2817	2686	1-4
5-9	250663	126768	13.8	123895	13.2	0	1699	831	868	5-9
10-14	224606	116726	12.7	107880	11.5	0	525	277	248	10-14
15-19	199228	97285	10.6	101943	10.9	12646	819	434	385	15-19
20-24	177481	84016	9.1	93465	10.0	27847	1062	607	455	20-24
25-29	140595	66605	7.2	73990	7.9	23848	920	476	444	25-29
30-34	112647	55150	6.0	57497	6.1	14434	881	439	442	30-34
35-39	112145	54444	5.9	57701	6.1	8480	879	460	419	35-39
40-44	89704	44462	4.8	45242	4.8	2661	932	476	456	40-44
45-49	69315	34420	3.7	34895	3.7	496	769	434	335	45-49
50-54	63370	30987	3.4	32383	3.5	145	916	505	411	50-54
55-59	36108	17472	1.9	18636	2.0	0	606	318	288	55-59
60-64	37855	18758	2.0	19097	2.0	0	1028	476	552	60-64
65-69	20466	10258	1.1	10208	1.1	0	714	377	337	65-69
70-74	16617	7706	0.8	8911	0.9		871	411	460	70-74
75-79	10433	4800	0.5	5633	0.6		826	384	442	75-79
80-84	5435	2472	0.3	2963	0.3	46625 M.	678	308	370	80-84
85+	2022	906	0.1	1116	0.1	43932 F.	431	191	240	85+
TOTAL	1858305	919695		938610		90557	27454	14210	13244	TOTAL

TABLE 2 — MALE LIFE TABLE

x	nq_x	l_x	nd_x	nL_x	nm_x	na_x	T_x	r_x	$\mathring{e}_x$	nM_x	x
0	0.104603	100000	10460	93769	0.111555	0.4043	4967495	0.0135	49.675	0.112423	0
1	0.094665	89540	8476	335656	0.025253	1.3452	4873726	0.0135	54.431	0.025383	1
5	0.031987	81063	2593	398834	0.006501	2.5000	4538070	0.0130	55.982	0.006555	5
10	0.011740	78470	921	389867	0.002363	2.3033	4139236	0.0226	52.749	0.002373	10
15	0.022220	77549	1723	383808	0.004490	2.7149	3749369	0.0283	48.348	0.004461	15
20	0.035586	75826	2698	372560	0.007243	2.5653	3365561	0.0313	44.385	0.007225	20
25	0.035131	73128	2569	359227	0.007152	2.5046	2993001	0.0347	40.928	0.007147	25
30	0.039046	70559	2755	345955	0.007963	2.5181	2633774	0.0123	37.328	0.007960	30
35	0.041422	67804	2809	332131	0.008456	2.5478	2287819	0.0127	33.742	0.008449	35
40	0.052312	64995	3400	316676	0.010737	2.5592	1955688	0.0353	30.090	0.010706	40
45	0.061289	61595	3775	298776	0.012635	2.5633	1639012	0.0231	26.610	0.012609	45
50	0.078633	57820	4547	277916	0.016359	2.5403	1340236	0.0520	23.180	0.016297	50
55	0.087384	53273	4655	254999	0.018256	2.5582	1062320	0.0308	19.941	0.018201	55
60	0.120249	48618	5846	229017	0.025528	2.5927	807320	0.0407	16.605	0.025376	60
65	0.169670	42772	7257	196253	0.036978	2.5739	578303	0.0407	13.521	0.036752	65
70	0.237134	35515	8422	156900	0.053676	2.5452	382050	0.0407	10.758	0.053335	70
75	0.335341	27093	9085	112792	0.080550	2.5045	225150	0.0407	8.310	0.080000	75
80	0.478539	18008	8617	68558	0.125694	2.5074	112358	0.0407	6.239	0.124595	80
85+	*1.000000	9390	9390	43800	0.214392	4.6644	43800	0.0407	4.664	0.210817	85+

TABLE 3 — FEMALE LIFE TABLE

x	nq_x	l_x	nd_x	nL_x	nm_x	na_x	T_x	r_x	$\mathring{e}_x$	nM_x	x
0	0.094622	100000	9462	94431	0.100202	0.4115	5179677	0.0107	51.797	0.100811	0
1	0.091942	90538	8324	340241	0.024466	1.3679	5085245	0.0107	56.167	0.024559	1
5	0.034065	82214	2801	404066	0.006931	2.5000	4745004	0.0186	57.716	0.007006	5
10	0.011368	79413	903	394531	0.002288	2.1933	4340938	0.0157	54.663	0.002299	10
15	0.018745	78510	1472	389071	0.003782	2.6353	3946408	0.0108	50.266	0.003777	15
20	0.024120	77039	1858	380706	0.004881	2.5853	3557337	0.0272	46.176	0.004868	20
25	0.029695	75180	2232	370507	0.006025	2.5835	3176631	0.0424	42.253	0.006001	25
30	0.037741	72948	2753	357914	0.007692	2.5207	2806124	0.0177	38.467	0.007687	30
35	0.035709	70195	2507	344829	0.007269	2.5484	2448210	0.0159	34.877	0.007262	35
40	0.049274	67688	3335	330120	0.010100	2.5321	2103381	0.0410	31.075	0.010079	40
45	0.046946	64353	3021	314307	0.009612	2.5316	1773171	0.0230	27.554	0.009600	45
50	0.061855	61332	3794	297445	0.012754	2.5714	1458864	0.0503	23.786	0.012692	50
55	0.075089	57538	4320	277603	0.015564	2.6652	1161419	0.0349	20.185	0.015454	55
60	0.135666	53218	7220	248608	0.029041	2.5789	883815	0.0351	16.608	0.028905	60
65	0.153352	45998	7054	212721	0.033160	2.5519	635207	0.0351	13.810	0.033013	65
70	0.230527	38944	8978	172866	0.051934	2.5658	422487	0.0351	10.849	0.051622	70
75	0.329971	29966	9888	125246	0.078949	2.5135	249621	0.0351	8.330	0.078466	75
80	0.479221	20078	9622	76455	0.125851	2.5123	124375	0.0351	6.195	0.124873	80
85+	*1.000000	10456	10456	47920	0.218203	4.5829	47920	0.0351	4.583	0.215054	85+

TABLE 4 — OBSERVED AND PROJECTED VITAL RATES

	OBSERVED POPULATION BOTH SEXES	OBSERVED POPULATION MALES	OBSERVED POPULATION FEMALES	1955 MALES	1955 FEMALES	1960 MALES	1960 FEMALES	1965 MALES	1965 FEMALES	STABLE POPULATION MALES	STABLE POPULATION FEMALES
RATES PER THOUSAND											
Birth	48.73	50.70	46.81	48.56	45.29	46.15	43.38	43.81	41.44	44.36	43.17
Death	14.77	15.45	14.11	17.07	15.41	16.83	15.32	16.42	15.02	16.28	15.09
Increase	33.96	35.25	32.70	31.49	29.88	29.32	28.06	27.39	26.42		28.0790
PERCENTAGE											
under 15	41.16	42.40	39.95	43.61	41.73	45.03	43.11	46.45	44.47	44.30	43.65
15-64	55.88	54.76	56.98	53.22	54.95	52.01	53.77	50.29	52.05	52.45	52.88
65 and over	2.96	2.84	3.07	3.16	3.32	2.96	3.13	3.26	3.48	3.25	3.47
DEP. RATIO X 100	78.95	82.62	75.49	87.89	82.00	92.29	85.99	98.85	92.12	90.66	89.10

TABLE 5 — POPULATION PROJECTED WITH FIXED AGE—SPECIFIC BIRTH AND DEATH RATES (IN 1000's)

AGE AT LAST BIRTHDAY	1955 BOTH SEXES	1955 MALES	1955 FEMALES	1960 BOTH SEXES	1960 MALES	1960 FEMALES	1965 BOTH SEXES	1965 MALES	1965 FEMALES	AGE AT LAST BIRTHDAY
0-4	416	213	203	465	238	227	513	263	250	0-4
5-9	269	136	133	387	198	189	432	221	211	5-9
10-14	245	124	121	263	133	130	379	194	185	10-14
15-19	221	115	106	241	122	119	259	131	128	15-19
20-24	194	94	100	216	112	104	235	118	117	20-24
25-29	172	81	91	188	91	97	209	108	101	25-29
30-34	135	64	71	166	78	88	182	88	94	30-34
35-39	108	53	55	131	62	69	160	75	85	35-39
40-44	107	52	55	103	50	53	125	59	66	40-44
45-49	85	42	43	102	49	53	98	48	50	45-49
50-54	65	32	33	80	39	41	96	46	50	50-54
55-59	58	28	30	60	29	31	74	36	38	55-59
60-64	33	16	17	53	26	27	54	26	28	60-64
65-69	32	16	16	27	13	14	45	22	23	65-69
70-74	16	8	8	26	13	13	23	11	12	70-74
75-79	12	6	6	12	6	6	19	9	10	75-79
80-84	6	3	3	7	3	4	8	4	4	80-84
85+	4	2	2	4	2	2	4	2	2	85+
TOTAL	2178	1085	1093	2531	1264	1267	2915	1461	1454	TOTAL

TABLE 6 — STANDARDIZED RATES

STANDARD COUNTRIES: STANDARDIZED RATES PER THOUSAND	ENGLAND AND WALES 1961 BOTH SEXES	MALES	FEMALES	UNITED STATES 1960 BOTH SEXES	MALES	FEMALES	MEXICO 1960 BOTH SEXES	MALES	FEMALES
Birth	39.13	48.88*	36.79	39.85	44.37*	38.09	44.73	46.87*	43.29
Death	19.26	35.06*	20.30	17.92	28.23*	17.83	14.92	15.38*	14.31
Increase	19.87	13.82*	16.50	21.94	16.14*	20.26	29.81	31.49*	28.98

TABLE 7 — MOMENTS AND CUMULANTS

	OBSERVED POP. MALES	OBSERVED POP. FEMALES	STATIONARY POP. MALES	STATIONARY POP. FEMALES	STABLE POP. MALES	STABLE POP. FEMALES	OBSERVED BIRTHS	NET MATERNITY FUNCTION	BIRTHS IN STABLE POP.
μ	23.10957	23.69048	34.55753	35.20201	22.50170	22.89277	26.88972	28.21661	26.91735
σ^2	333.7787	336.8923	505.7884	512.7114	342.6755	351.8364	42.34888	46.55829	41.80527
κ_3	5531.591	5488.534	4034.959	3730.321	6288.606	6388.417	185.0669	167.1058	169.9743
κ_4	18634.	20509.	-223679.	-239460.	41963.	34416.	49.021	-259.283	53.566
β_1	0.822857	0.787843	0.125826	0.103246	0.982788	0.937053	0.450953	0.276689	0.395434
β_2	3.167255	3.180706	2.125646	2.089066	3.357357	3.278019	3.027334	2.880386	3.030650
κ	-0.359437	-0.362774	-0.047839	-0.038974	-0.424163	-0.397469	-0.293301	-0.209223	-0.292226

TABLE 8 — RATES FROM AGE DISTRIBUTIONS AND VITAL STATISTICS (Females)

VITAL STATISTICS		THOMPSON AGE RANGE	NRR	1000r	INTERVAL	BOURGEOIS-PICHAT AGE RANGE	NRR	1000b	1000d	1000r	COALE	
GRR	2.959	0-4	1.67	19.30	27.07	5-29	1.68	38.08	18.77	19.31	IBR	37.59
NRR	2.168	5-9	1.77	21.59	26.94	30-54	1.90	39.44	15.67	23.77	IDR	17.44
TFR	6.099	10-14	1.83	22.02	26.87	55-79	1.98	32.88	7.62	25.26	IRI	20.16
GENERATION	27.556	15-19	2.04	26.71	26.77	* 5-29	1.68	38.08	18.77	19.31	K1	-9.37
SEX RATIO	106.130										K2	0.

TABLE 9 — LESLIE MATRIX AND ITS SPECTRAL COMPONENTS (Females)

Start of Age Interval	ORIGINAL MATRIX SUB-DIAGONAL	ALTERNATIVE FIRST ROWS Projection	ALTERNATIVE FIRST ROWS Integral	FIRST STABLE MATRIX % IN STABLE POPULATION	FISHER VALUES	REPRODUCTIVE VALUES	SECOND STABLE MATRIX Z₂ FIRST COLUMN	FIRST ROW
0	0.92959	0.00000	0.00000	17.532	1.232	176396	0.1540+0.0923	0.1540+0.0923
5	0.97640	0.00000	0.00000	14.156	1.526	189068	0.1597-0.1042	-0.0147+0.1684
10	0.98616	0.12898	0.00000	12.006	1.799	194110	-0.0266-0.2110	-0.1415+0.0542
15	0.97850	0.43818	0.28061	10.284	1.939	197707	-0.2269-0.0771	-0.1184-0.1039
20	0.97321	0.64487	0.67396	8.741	1.730	161695	-0.1885+0.1903	-0.0317-0.1772
25	0.96601	0.59553	0.72910	7.389	1.230	91009	0.0986+0.2810	0.0288-0.1565
30	0.96344	0.41398	0.56787	6.200	0.706	40608	0.3265+0.0379	0.0440-0.0955
35	0.95761	0.21434	0.33245	5.189	0.314	18147	0.1947-0.3049	0.0293-0.0416
40	0.95184	0.07628	0.13305	4.316	0.102	4628	-0.2067-0.3375	0.0115-0.0132
45	0.94635	0.01945	0.03215	3.568	0.025	872	-0.4284+0.0415	0.0032-0.0032
50	0.93329	0.00472	0.01013	2.933	0.005	164	-0.1623+0.4361	0.0008-0.0005
55+	0.79497			7.684				

TABLE 10 — AGE ANALYSIS AND MISCELLANEOUS RESULTS (Females)

Start of Age Interval	OBSERVED POPUL. (IN 100's)	CONTRIBUTIONS OF ROOTS (IN 100's) r_1	r_2, r_3	r_4-r_{11}	AGE-SP. BIRTH RATES	NET MATERNITY FUNCTION	COEFF. OF MATRIX EQUATION	PARAMETERS	INTEGRAL	MATRIX	EXP. INCREASE x	$e^{(x+2\frac{1}{2})r}$
0	1432	1631	-61	-138	0.0000	0.0000	0.0000	L(1)	1.15073	1.15126	0	1.0727
5	1239	1317	-170	93	0.0000	0.0000	0.0000	L(2)	0.37458	0.38300	50	4.3673
10	1079	1117	-94	56	0.0000	0.0000	0.1171		0.81362	0.78706	55	5.0256
15	1019	956	122	-59	0.0602	0.2341	0.3922	R(1)	0.02808	0.02817	60	5.7831
20	935	813	237	-116	0.1445	0.5503	0.5648	R(2)	-0.02203	-0.02664	65	6.6548
25	740	687	80	-27	0.1564	0.5793	0.5076		0.22787	0.22358	70	7.6578
30	575	577	-214	212	0.1218	0.4359	0.3409	C(1)		9300	75	8.8121
35	577	483	-303	398	0.0713	0.2459	0.1700	C(2)		-35896	80	10.1403
40	452	401	-32	83	0.0285	0.0942	0.0579			-26783	85	11.6687
45	349	332	330	-313	0.0069	0.0217	0.0141	2P/Y	27.5738	28.1023	90	13.4275
50	324	273	350	-299	0.0022	0.0065	0.0032	DELTA	4.5781		95	15.4514
55+	666	715									100	17.7804

TABLE 1 — DATA

AGE AT LAST BIRTHDAY	POPULATION BOTH SEXES	MALES Number	MALES %	FEMALES Number	FEMALES %	BIRTHS BY AGE OF MOTHER	DEATHS BOTH SEXES	DEATHS MALES	FEMALES	AGE AT LAST BIRTHDAY
0	3821	1869	4.6	1952	4.0	0	313	170	143	0
1-4	13898	6924	16.9	6974	14.4	0	179	97	82	1-4
5-9	14041	7024	17.1	7017	14.5	0	5	3	2	5-9
10-14	10807	5391	13.2	5416	11.2	11	3	1	2	10-14
15-19	7849	3767	9.2	4082	8.4	651	8	4	4	15-19
20-24	6301	2771	6.8	3530	7.3	1220	14	6	8	20-24
25-29	5065	2068	5.0	2997	6.2	1002	16	8	8	25-29
30-34	4289	1885	4.6	2404	5.0	626	11	5	6	30-34
35-39	3787	1557	3.8	2230	4.6	388	16	9	7	35-39
40-44	3394	1432	3.5	1962	4.1	98	17	11	6	40-44
45-49	3387	1478	3.6	1909	4.0	16	14	8	6	45-49
50-54	3368	1451	3.5	1917	4.0	4	28	13	15	50-54
55-59	2412	997	2.4	1415	2.9	0	42	23	19	55-59
60-64	2240	820	2.0	1420	2.9	0	57	31	26	60-64
65-69	1541	567	1.4	974	2.0	0	48	22	26	65-69
70-74	1295	422	1.0	873	1.8		54	26	28	70-74
75-79	814	248	0.6	566	1.2		45	14	31	75-79
80-84	558	185	0.5	373	0.8	2015 M.	70	29	41	80-84
85+	431	116	0.3	315	0.7	2001 F.	92	30	62	85+
TOTAL	89298	40972		48326		4016	1032	510	522	TOTAL

TABLE 2 — MALE LIFE TABLE

x	$_nq_x$	l_x	$_nd_x$	$_nL_x$	$_nm_x$	$_na_x$	T_x	r_x	$\dot{e}_x$	$_nM_x$	x
0	0.086015	100000	8601	94595	0.090930	0.3716	5864802	0.0005	58.648	0.090958	0
1	0.053953	91399	4931	352092	0.014006	1.2619	5770207	0.0005	63.132	0.014009	1
5	0.001600	86467	138	431991	0.000320	2.5000	5418115	0.0455	62.661	0.000427	5
10	0.000977	86329	84	431503	0.000195	3.3160	4986125	0.0619	57.757	0.000185	10
15	0.005433	86245	469	430230	0.001089	2.8797	4554622	0.0655	52.811	0.001062	15
20	0.010938	85776	938	426776	0.002198	2.7572	4124393	0.0576	48.083	0.002165	20
25	0.019177	84838	1627	420156	0.003872	2.5208	3697617	0.0354	43.585	0.003868	25
30	0.013227	83211	1101	413454	0.002662	2.6370	3277461	0.0247	39.387	0.002653	30
35	0.028629	82110	2351	405071	0.005803	2.6688	2864008	0.0220	34.880	0.005780	35
40	0.037678	79759	3005	391222	0.007682	2.4791	2458936	0.0000	30.829	0.007682	40
45	0.026707	76754	2050	378712	0.005413	2.5319	2067715	0.0000	26.939	0.005413	45
50	0.044435	74704	3319	366439	0.009059	2.8661	1689002	0.0282	22.609	0.008959	50
55	0.110425	71385	7883	338816	0.023265	2.7028	1322564	0.0338	18.527	0.023069	55
60	0.173101	63502	10992	290326	0.037862	2.5269	983747	0.0153	15.492	0.037805	60
65	0.177177	52510	9304	239403	0.038861	2.5121	693421	0.0153	13.206	0.038801	65
70	0.266878	43206	11531	186907	0.061693	2.4742	454018	0.0153	10.508	0.061611	70
75	0.248647	31676	7876	139085	0.056627	2.5505	267111	0.0153	8.433	0.056452	75
80	0.564644	23800	13438	85379	0.157395	2.5385	128025	0.0153	5.379	0.156757	80
85+	1.000000	10361	10361	42646	0.242960	4.1159	42646	0.0153	4.116	0.258622	85+

TABLE 3 — FEMALE LIFE TABLE

x	$_nq_x$	l_x	$_nd_x$	$_nL_x$	$_nm_x$	$_na_x$	T_x	r_x	$\dot{e}_x$	$_nM_x$	x
0	0.069825	100000	6982	95650	0.073000	0.3770	6505475	0.0054	65.055	0.073258	0
1	0.045443	93018	4227	360546	0.011724	1.2738	6409826	0.0054	68.910	0.011758	1
5	0.000974	88791	87	443736	0.000195	2.5000	6049280	0.0471	68.130	0.000285	5
10	0.001890	88704	168	443175	0.000378	2.9395	5605543	0.0537	63.194	0.000369	10
15	0.004971	88536	440	441754	0.000996	2.8928	5162369	0.0417	58.308	0.000980	15
20	0.011321	88096	997	438137	0.002276	2.6494	4720614	0.0288	53.585	0.002266	20
25	0.013267	87099	1156	432620	0.002671	2.5126	4282478	0.0359	49.168	0.002669	25
30	0.012416	85943	1067	427084	0.002498	2.5326	3849857	0.0269	44.795	0.002496	30
35	0.015585	84876	1323	421116	0.003141	2.5316	3422774	0.0173	40.327	0.003139	35
40	0.015174	83554	1268	414590	0.003058	2.4937	3001657	0.0125	35.925	0.003058	40
45	0.015607	82286	1284	408606	0.003143	2.8025	2587067	0.0000	31.440	0.003143	45
50	0.038672	81001	3132	397967	0.007871	2.7525	2178461	0.0220	26.894	0.007825	50
55	0.065241	77869	5080	377324	0.013464	2.6339	1780494	0.0168	22.865	0.013428	55
60	0.087910	72789	6399	348624	0.018355	2.6059	1403169	0.0168	19.277	0.018310	60
65	0.125515	66390	8333	311589	0.026743	2.5566	1054546	0.0168	15.884	0.026694	65
70	0.149228	58057	8664	269393	0.032160	2.5886	742957	0.0168	12.797	0.032073	70
75	0.243284	49393	12017	218488	0.054999	2.6301	473564	0.0168	9.588	0.054770	75
80	0.432522	37377	16166	146550	0.110312	2.6185	255077	0.0168	6.824	0.109920	80
85+	1.000000	21210	21210	108527	0.195439	5.1167	108527	0.0168	5.117	0.196826	85+

TABLE 4 — OBSERVED AND PROJECTED VITAL RATES

RATES PER THOUSAND	OBSERVED POPULATION BOTH SEXES	MALES	FEMALES	PROJECTED 1965 MALES	1965 FEMALES	1970 MALES	1970 FEMALES	1975 MALES	1975 FEMALES	STABLE POPULATION MALES	STABLE FEMALES
Birth	44.97	49.18	41.41	48.41	41.91	49.46	43.81	50.96	46.02	49.54	47.48
Death	11.56	12.45	10.80	11.32	10.02	11.01	9.78	10.82	9.70	10.39	8.33
Increase	33.42	36.73	30.60	37.08	31.88	38.45	34.03	40.13	36.32		39.1496
PERCENTAGE											
under 15	47.67	51.76	44.20	51.45	45.40	50.27	45.65	49.49	45.80	49.16	48.29
15-64	47.14	44.48	49.39	45.14	48.45	46.65	48.79	47.48	48.90	48.88	48.97
65 and over	5.19	3.75	6.42	3.41	6.15	3.08	5.56	3.03	5.29	1.95	2.74
DEP. RATIO X 100	112.15	124.80	102.49	121.52	106.41	114.36	104.96	110.60	104.48	104.56	104.20

TABLE 5 — POPULATION PROJECTED WITH FIXED AGE—SPECIFIC BIRTH AND DEATH RATES (IN 1000's)

AGE AT LAST BIRTHDAY	1965 BOTH SEXES	1965 MALES	FEMALES	1970 BOTH SEXES	1970 MALES	FEMALES	1975 BOTH SEXES	1975 MALES	FEMALES	AGE AT LAST BIRTHDAY
0-4	20	10	10	24	12	12	30	15	15	0-4
5-9	18	9	9	20	10	10	24	12	12	5-9
10-14	14	7	7	17	8	9	19	9	10	10-14
15-19	10	5	5	14	7	7	17	8	9	15-19
20-24	8	4	4	10	5	5	14	7	7	20-24
25-29	6	3	3	8	4	4	10	5	5	25-29
30-34	5	2	3	6	3	3	8	4	4	30-34
35-39	4	2	2	5	2	3	6	3	3	35-39
40-44	4	2	2	4	2	2	5	2	3	40-44
45-49	3	1	2	3	1	2	4	2	2	45-49
50-54	3	1	2	3	1	2	3	1	2	50-54
55-59	3	1	2	3	1	2	3	1	2	55-59
60-64	2	1	1	3	1	2	3	1	2	60-64
65-69	2	1	1	2	1	1	3	1	2	65-69
70-74	1	0	1	2	1	1	2	1	1	70-74
75-79	1	0	1	1	0	1	1	0	1	75-79
80-84	0	0	0	0	0	0	0	0	0	80-84
85+	0	0	0	0	0	0	0	0	0	85+
TOTAL	104	49	55	125	59	66	152	72	80	TOTAL

TABLE 6 — STANDARDIZED RATES

STANDARD COUNTRIES:

STANDARDIZED RATES PER THOUSAND

	ENGLAND AND WALES 1961 BOTH SEXES	MALES	FEMALES	UNITED STATES 1960 BOTH SEXES	MALES	FEMALES	MEXICO 1960 BOTH SEXES	MALES	FEMALES
Birth	42.93	65.29*	41.46	43.83	58.91*	43.03	49.95	62.13*	49.64
Death	14.13	22.94*	13.22	12.59	19.32*	10.92	9.12	10.46*	7.73
Increase	28.80	42.35*	28.24	31.25	39.59*	32.12	40.83	51.67*	41.91

TABLE 7 — MOMENTS AND CUMULANTS

	OBSERVED POP. MALES	FEMALES	STATIONARY POP. MALES	FEMALES	STABLE POP. MALES	FEMALES	OBSERVED BIRTHS	NET MATERNITY FUNCTION	BIRTHS IN STABLE POP.
μ	21.37762	25.10684	35.77213	38.37457	20.10252	20.84321	26.53511	27.87013	26.10287
σ^2	384.0497	466.7684	495.0835	553.1281	290.0860	319.1248	42.67166	45.77882	40.17545
κ_3	8446.694	9081.889	2979.238	2710.951	5480.673	6466.904	167.0218	128.8549	153.5589
κ_4	61808.	-33342.	-224571.	-309428.	62944.	80381.	-335.066	-912.752	-329.356
β_1	1.259538	0.811051	0.073143	0.043428	1.230516	1.286801	0.359027	0.173065	0.363637
β_2	3.419054	2.846966	2.083787	1.988634	3.747994	3.789281	2.815986	2.564464	2.795947
κ	-0.445801	-0.282599	-0.028380	-0.016039	-0.564594	-0.575256	-0.206240	-0.098946	-0.201853

TABLE 8 — RATES FROM AGE DISTRIBUTIONS AND VITAL STATISTICS (Females)

VITAL STATISTICS		THOMPSON AGE RANGE	NRR	1000r	INTERVAL	BOURGEOIS-PICHAT AGE RANGE	NRR	1000b	1000d	1000r	COALE
GRR	3.329										
NRR	2.874	0-4	2.93	39.31	27.34	5-29	3.05	42.64	1.29	41.35	IBR
TFR	6.681	5-9	2.67	36.92	27.30	30-54	1.27	15.05	6.31	8.74	IDR
GENERATION	26.968	10-14	2.28	29.50	27.26	55-79	1.46	18.20	4.14	14.05	IRI
SEX RATIO	100.700	15-19	1.91	23.82	27.17	*15-39	2.21	31.97	2.53	29.44	K1
											K2

TABLE 9 — LESLIE MATRIX AND ITS SPECTRAL COMPONENTS (Females)

Start of Age Interval	ORIGINAL MATRIX SUB-DIAGONAL	ALTERNATIVE FIRST ROWS Projection	Integral	FIRST STABLE MATRIX % IN STABLE POPULATION	FISHER VALUES	REPRODUCTIVE VALUES	SECOND STABLE MATRIX Z₂ FIRST COLUMN	FIRST ROW
0	0.97269	0.00000	0.00000	19.715	1.207	10775	0.1384+0.1042	0.1384+0.1042
5	0.99873	0.00231	0.00000	15.753	1.511	10601	0.1656-0.0880	-0.0332+0.1566
10	0.99680	0.18298	0.00509	12.924	1.839	9958	-0.0107-0.2082	-0.1406+0.0323
15	0.99181	0.57082	0.39978	10.583	2.024	8262	-0.2143-0.0869	-0.1054-0.1216
20	0.98741	0.76798	0.86636	8.622	1.789	6317	-0.1870+0.1737	-0.0202-0.1931
25	0.98720	0.67214	0.83809	6.993	1.267	3798	0.0860+0.2670	0.0438-0.1721
30	0.98603	0.49093	0.65276	5.671	0.741	1781	0.3057+0.0385	0.0646-0.1011
35	0.98450	0.25363	0.43615	4.594	0.313	699	0.1802-0.2861	0.0395-0.0375
40	0.98557	0.06616	0.12521	3.715	0.077	150	-0.2005-0.3116	0.0106-0.0087
45	0.97396	0.01184	0.02101	3.008	0.014	26	-0.4027+0.0546	0.0020-0.0016
50	0.94813	0.00237	0.00523	2.406	0.002	5	-0.1310+0.4205	0.0004-0.0002
55+	0.83803			6.015				

TABLE 10 — AGE ANALYSIS AND MISCELLANEOUS RESULTS (Females)

Start of Age Interval	OBSERVED POPUL. (IN 100's)	CONTRIBUTIONS OF ROOTS (IN 100's) r_1	r_2, r_3	r_4-r_{11}	AGE-SP. BIRTH RATES	NET MATERNITY FUNCTION	COEFF. OF MATRIX EQUATION	PARAMETERS INTEGRAL	MATRIX	EXP. INCREASE x	$e(x+2\frac{1}{2})r$
0	89	84	3	3	0.0000	0.0000	0.0000	L(1) 1.21622	1.21735	0	1.1028
5	70	67	4	-1	0.0000	0.0000	0.0022	L(2) 0.36933	0.38019	50	7.8096
10	54	55	1	-2	0.0010	0.0045	0.1778	0.84055	0.81415	55	9.4982
15	41	45	-5	0	0.0795	0.3510	0.5528	R(1) 0.03915	0.03933	60	11.5519
20	35	37	-5	4	0.1722	0.7545	0.7376	R(2) -0.01709	-0.02140	65	14.0497
25	30	30	1	-0	0.1666	0.7207	0.6374	0.23136	-0.22678	70	17.0875
30	24	24	7	-7	0.1297	0.5541	0.4596	C(1)	426	75	20.7821
35	22	20	6	-3	0.0867	0.3651	0.2341	C(2)	1210	80	25.2756
40	20	16	-3	7	0.0249	0.1032	0.0601		266	85	30.7408
45	19	13	-10	16	0.0042	0.0171	0.0106	2P/Y 27.1576	27.7058	90	37.3875
50	19	10	-5	14	0.0010	0.0041	0.0021	DELTA 9.0355		95	45.4715
55+	59	26								100	55.3033

TABLE 1 — DATA

AGE AT LAST BIRTHDAY	POPULATION BOTH SEXES	MALES Number	%	FEMALES Number	%	BIRTHS BY AGE OF MOTHER	DEATHS BOTH SEXES	MALES	FEMALES	AGE AT LAST BIRTHDAY
0	90935	46231	4.8	44704	4.6	0	4274	2357	1917	0
1-4	272804	138693	14.3	134111	13.8	0	3722	1888	1834	1-4
5-9	311588	158703	16.4	152885	15.7	0	1059	539	520	5-9
10-14	243008	123818	12.8	119190	12.2	53	424	229	195	10-14
15-19	191790	94492	9.8	97298	10.0	12865	497	268	229	15-19
20-24	160939	77185	8.0	83754	8.6	22457	656	386	270	20-24
25-29	135455	65225	6.7	70230	7.2	20396	670	380	290	25-29
30-34	114702	56021	5.8	58681	6.0	14100	666	375	291	30-34
35-39	97356	47928	5.0	49428	5.1	8831	627	349	278	35-39
40-44	78847	39149	4.0	39698	4.1	2951	550	300	250	40-44
45-49	64307	32062	3.3	32245	3.3	524	546	307	239	45-49
50-54	51786	25593	2.6	26193	2.7	117	563	314	249	50-54
55-59	41271	20420	2.1	20851	2.1	0	556	288	268	55-59
60-64	33637	16756	1.7	16881	1.7	0	750	382	368	60-64
65-69	22221	11080	1.1	11141	1.1	0	545	285	260	65-69
70-74	12629	6149	0.6	6480	0.7		562	282	280	70-74
75-79	9703	4295	0.4	5408	0.6		453	243	210	75-79
80-84	5008	2232	0.2	2776	0.3	42674 M.	358	171	187	80-84
85+	1871	841	0.1	1030	0.1	39620 F.	476	202	274	85+
TOTAL	1939857	966873		972984		82294	17954	9545	8409	TOTAL

TABLE 2 — MALE LIFE TABLE

x	$_nq_x$	l_x	$_nd_x$	$_nL_x$	$_nm_x$	$_na_x$	T_x	r_x	$\mathring{e}_x$	$_nM_x$	x
0	0.048893	100000	4889	97181	0.050311	0.4235	5950861	0.0232	59.509	0.050983	0
1	0.052199	95111	4965	367587	0.013506	1.4104	5853679	0.0232	61.546	0.013613	1
5	0.016487	90146	1486	447015	0.003325	2.5000	5486093	0.0349	60.858	0.003396	5
10	0.009179	88660	814	441216	0.001844	2.4396	5039078	0.0494	56.836	0.001849	10
15	0.014233	87846	1250	436383	0.002865	2.7224	4597862	0.0442	52.340	0.002836	15
20	0.024808	86596	2148	427854	0.005021	2.6143	4161480	0.0324	48.056	0.005001	20
25	0.028764	84447	2429	416280	0.005835	2.5476	3733626	0.0262	44.212	0.005826	25
30	0.032961	82018	2703	403419	0.006701	2.5316	3317346	0.0242	40.446	0.006694	30
35	0.035789	79315	2839	389515	0.007288	2.5131	2913927	0.0286	36.739	0.007282	35
40	0.037680	76478	2882	375306	0.007678	2.5445	2524412	0.0322	33.009	0.007663	40
45	0.046940	73595	3455	359609	0.009606	2.5788	2149106	0.0328	29.202	0.009575	45
50	0.059706	70140	4188	340453	0.012301	2.5528	1789496	0.0331	25.513	0.012269	50
55	0.068484	65952	4517	318989	0.014159	2.6148	1449044	0.0266	21.971	0.014104	55
60	0.108678	61436	6677	290940	0.022949	2.5679	1130055	0.0588	18.394	0.022798	60
65	0.122250	54759	6694	257749	0.025972	2.6031	839115	0.0588	15.324	0.025722	65
70	0.207820	48065	9989	215933	0.046259	2.5582	581365	0.0588	12.095	0.045861	70
75	0.249077	38076	9484	166566	0.056938	2.4890	365433	0.0588	9.597	0.056578	75
80	0.331903	28592	9490	121240	0.078273	2.7112	198867	0.0588	6.955	0.076612	80
85+	*1.000000	19102	19102	77627	0.246077	4.0638	77627	0.0588	4.064	0.240190	85+

TABLE 3 — FEMALE LIFE TABLE

x	$_nq_x$	l_x	$_nd_x$	$_nL_x$	$_nm_x$	$_na_x$	T_x	r_x	$\mathring{e}_x$	$_nM_x$	x
0	0.041362	100000	4136	97673	0.042347	0.4375	6251466	0.0235	62.515	0.042882	0
1	0.052504	95864	5033	370718	0.013577	1.4695	6153793	0.0235	64.193	0.013675	1
5	0.016496	90831	1498	450407	0.003327	2.5000	5783075	0.0354	63.669	0.003401	5
10	0.008101	89332	724	444757	0.001627	2.3685	5332668	0.0430	59.695	0.001636	10
15	0.011757	88608	1042	440580	0.002365	2.6363	4887911	0.0329	55.163	0.002354	15
20	0.016049	87567	1405	434471	0.003235	2.6074	4447331	0.0294	50.788	0.003224	20
25	0.020498	86161	1766	426530	0.004141	2.5786	4012860	0.0315	46.574	0.004129	25
30	0.024544	84395	2071	416906	0.004968	2.5524	3586330	0.0302	42.494	0.004959	30
35	0.027783	82324	2287	405988	0.005634	2.5379	3169423	0.0335	38.499	0.005624	35
40	0.031074	80037	2487	394079	0.006311	2.5456	2763435	0.0363	34.527	0.006298	40
45	0.036514	77550	2832	380877	0.007435	2.5735	2369356	0.0340	30.553	0.007412	45
50	0.046653	74718	3486	365216	0.009545	2.5978	1988479	0.0339	26.613	0.009506	50
55	0.062735	71232	4469	345711	0.012926	2.6615	1623262	0.0297	22.788	0.012853	55
60	0.104091	66763	6949	316902	0.021929	2.5659	1277552	0.0553	19.136	0.021800	60
65	0.111481	59814	6668	283122	0.023552	2.6084	960650	0.0553	16.061	0.023337	65
70	0.196062	53146	10420	239873	0.043439	2.5186	677528	0.0553	12.748	0.043210	70
75	0.177873	42726	7600	194661	0.039041	2.5040	437655	0.0553	10.243	0.038831	75
80	0.300810	35126	10566	152748	0.069175	2.8344	242994	0.0553	6.918	0.067363	80
85+	*1.000000	24560	24560	90246	0.272144	3.6745	90246	0.0553	3.675	0.266019	85+

TABLE 4 — OBSERVED AND PROJECTED VITAL RATES

	OBSERVED POPULATION BOTH SEXES	MALES	FEMALES	PROJECTED POPULATION 1965 MALES	FEMALES	1970 MALES	FEMALES	1975 MALES	FEMALES	STABLE POPULATION MALES	FEMALES
RATES PER THOUSAND											
Birth	42.42	44.14	40.72	43.53	40.56	43.76	41.11	44.08	41.70	42.16	41.12
Death	9.26	9.87	8.64	9.94	8.70	10.05	8.88	10.12	8.91	10.12	9.08
Increase	33.17	34.26	32.08	33.59	31.86	33.70	32.23	33.96	32.79		32.0381
PERCENTAGE											
under 15	47.34	48.35	46.34	47.92	45.86	45.84	44.76	46.66	44.48	45.40	44.61
15-64	50.01	49.11	50.90	49.17	51.02	50.10	51.95	50.23	52.13	51.31	51.74
65 and over	2.65	2.54	2.76	2.91	3.12	3.06	3.29	3.11	3.39	3.29	3.65
DEP. RATIO X 100	99.97	103.62	96.46	103.37	96.02	99.60	92.48	99.10	91.83	94.88	93.27

TABLE 5 — POPULATION PROJECTED WITH FIXED AGE-SPECIFIC BIRTH AND DEATH RATES (IN 1000's)

AGE AT LAST BIRTHDAY	1965 BOTH SEXES	MALES	FEMALES	1970 BOTH SEXES	MALES	FEMALES	1975 BOTH SEXES	MALES	FEMALES	AGE AT LAST BIRTHDAY
0-4	416	215	201	492	254	238	587	303	284	0-4
5-9	350	178	172	401	207	194	474	245	229	5-9
10-14	308	157	151	346	176	170	395	204	191	10-14
15-19	240	122	118	305	155	150	342	174	168	15-19
20-24	189	93	96	236	120	116	299	152	147	20-24
25-29	157	75	82	184	90	94	231	117	114	25-29
30-34	132	63	69	153	73	80	179	87	92	30-34
35-39	111	54	57	128	61	67	148	70	78	35-39
40-44	94	46	48	107	52	55	124	59	65	40-44
45-49	76	38	38	90	44	46	104	50	54	45-49
50-54	61	30	31	73	36	37	86	42	44	50-54
55-59	49	24	25	57	28	29	68	33	35	55-59
60-64	38	19	19	45	22	23	53	26	27	60-64
65-69	30	15	15	33	16	17	39	19	20	65-69
70-74	18	9	9	25	12	13	28	14	14	70-74
75-79	10	5	5	15	7	8	20	10	10	75-79
80-84	7	3	4	7	3	4	11	5	6	80-84
85+	3	1	2	5	2	3	4	2	2	85+
TOTAL	2289	1147	1142	2702	1358	1344	3192	1612	1580	TOTAL

TABLE 6 — STANDARDIZED RATES

STANDARD COUNTRIES: STANDARDIZED RATES PER THOUSAND	ENGLAND AND WALES 1961 BOTH SEXES	MALES	FEMALES	UNITED STATES 1960 BOTH SEXES	MALES	FEMALES	MEXICO 1960 BOTH SEXES	MALES	FEMALES
Birth	38.90	46.85*	36.29	39.62	42.72*	37.58	43.56	45.35*	41.83
Death	13.63	23.41*	14.18	12.26	18.66*	12.00	9.14	9.23*	8.55
Increase	25.26	23.45*	22.12	27.36	24.07*	25.58	34.41	36.12*	33.28

TABLE 7 — MOMENTS AND CUMULANTS

	OBSERVED POP. MALES	FEMALES	STATIONARY POP. MALES	FEMALES	STABLE POP. MALES	FEMALES	OBSERVED BIRTHS	NET MATERNITY FUNCTION	BIRTHS IN STABLE POP.
μ	21.21813	21.73561	36.40419	37.41082	22.10408	22.60815	27.19317	28.80195	27.13597
σ^2	325.7308	330.1008	537.3973	551.3615	340.6363	354.4642	46.94093	52.50227	47.16281
κ_3	6108.558	6129.529	3767.722	3381.425	6625.662	6884.551	175.4468	149.1811	180.6409
κ_4	44292.	47003.	-272230.	-299203.	62478.	57166.	-681.130	-1295.781	-644.883
β_1	1.079695	1.044514	0.091468	0.068217	1.110672	1.064227	0.297632	0.153778	0.311052
β_2	3.417457	3.431350	2.057362	2.015778	3.538448	3.454978	2.690880	2.529916	2.710078
κ	-0.443289	-0.449055	-0.034043	-0.025124	-0.486415	-0.456973	-0.161551	-0.086851	-0.169149

TABLE 8 — RATES FROM AGE DISTRIBUTIONS AND VITAL STATISTICS (Females)

VITAL STATISTICS		THOMPSON AGE RANGE	NRR	1000r	INTERVAL	BOURGEOIS-PICHAT AGE RANGE	NRR	1000b	1000d	1000r	COALE	
GRR	2.901										IBR	45.14
NRR	2.449	0-4	2.41	32.33	27.20	5-29	2.61	43.94	8.41	35.53	IDR	9.62
TFR	6.026	5-9	2.50	34.55	27.12	30-54	2.52	44.45	10.22	34.24	IRI	35.52
GENERATION	27.955	10-14	2.32	30.30	27.05	55-79	4.33	150.19	95.94	54.25	K1	0.
SEX RATIO	107.708	15-19	2.25	29.99	26.97	*15-39	2.25	38.67	8.56	30.11	K2	0.

TABLE 9 — LESLIE MATRIX AND ITS SPECTRAL COMPONENTS (Females)

Start of Age Interval	ORIGINAL MATRIX SUB-DIAGONAL	ALTERNATIVE FIRST ROWS Projection	Integral	FIRST STABLE MATRIX % IN STABLE POPULATION	FISHER VALUES	REPRODUCTIVE VALUES	SECOND STABLE MATRIX Z_2 FIRST COLUMN	FIRST ROW
0	0.96160	0.00000	0.00000	17.822	1.155	206607	0.1236+0.0944	0.1236+0.0944
5	0.98746	0.00050	0.00000	14.593	1.411	215744	0.1569-0.0695	-0.0213+0.1393
10	0.99061	0.14819	0.00109	12.269	1.678	199975	0.0163-0.1937	-0.1169+0.0426
15	0.98613	0.44722	0.32303	10.349	1.816	176720	-0.1843-0.1220	-0.1007-0.0863
20	0.98172	0.62379	0.65507	8.690	1.639	137281	-0.2213+0.1166	-0.0319-0.1575
25	0.97744	0.59226	0.70952	7.264	1.227	86151	-0.0045+0.2817	0.0305-0.1520
30	0.97381	0.46710	0.58703	6.045	0.774	45408	0.2747+0.1562	0.0570-0.0984
35	0.97067	0.28281	0.43649	5.013	0.379	18734	0.3006-0.1854	0.0425-0.0428
40	0.96650	0.10152	0.18161	4.143	0.122	4841	-0.0203-0.3928	0.0160-0.0125
45	0.95888	0.02315	0.03970	3.409	0.027	865	-0.3929-0.1895	0.0039-0.0027
50	0.94659	0.00504	0.01091	2.784	0.005	130	-0.3906+0.2790	0.0008-0.0004
55+	0.82859			7.619				

TABLE 10 — AGE ANALYSIS AND MISCELLANEOUS RESULTS (Females)

Start of Age Interval	OBSERVED POPUL. (IN 100's)	CONTRIBUTIONS OF ROOTS (IN 100's) r_1	r_2, r_3	$r_4 \cdot r_{11}$	AGE-SP. BIRTH RATES	NET MATERNITY FUNCTION	COEFF. OF MATRIX EQUATION	PARAMETERS	INTEGRAL	MATRIX	EXP. INCREASE x	$e^{(x+2\frac{1}{2})r}$
0	1788	1756	16	16	0.0000	0.0000	0.0000	L(1)	1.17373	1.17443	0	1.0834
5	1529	1437	57	34	0.0000	0.0000	0.0005	L(2)	0.40985	0.41859	50	5.3763
10	1192	1209	42	-58	0.0002	0.0010	0.1407		0.78430	0.76433	55	6.3103
15	973	1019	-28	-18	0.0637	0.2805	0.4207	R(1)	0.03204	0.03216	60	7.4067
20	838	856	-84	66	0.1291	0.5609	0.5786	R(2)	-0.02445	-0.02752	65	8.6935
25	702	715	-55	42	0.1398	0.5964	0.5393		0.21785	0.21395	70	10.2038
30	587	595	47	-55	0.1157	0.4823	0.4158	C(1)		9850	75	11.9766
35	494	494	119	-119	0.0860	0.3492	0.2451	C(2)		13953	80	14.0573
40	397	408	70	-81	0.0358	0.1410	0.0854			9599	85	16.4996
45	322	336	-73	60	0.0078	0.0298	0.0188	2P/Y	28.8417	29.3674	90	19.3661
50	262	274	-163	150	0.0022	0.0079	0.0039	DELTA	1.8518		95	22.7307
55+	646	750									100	26.6798

TABLE 1 — DATA

AGE AT LAST BIRTHDAY	POPULATION BOTH SEXES	MALES Number	%	FEMALES Number	%	BIRTHS BY AGE OF MOTHER	DEATHS BOTH SEXES	MALES	FEMALES	AGE AT LAST BIRTHDAY
0	104866	53233	5.0	51633	4.8	0	4491	2447	2044	0
1-4	314600	159700	15.0	154900	14.4	0	4066	2089	1977	1-4
5-9	362917	184648	17.4	178269	16.6	0	1204	659	545	5-9
10-14	273440	138957	13.1	134483	12.5	139	456	253	203	10-14
15-19	208686	101995	9.6	106691	9.9	14851	516	265	251	15-19
20-24	173182	82217	7.7	90965	8.5	25862	704	431	273	20-24
25-29	146386	69967	6.6	76419	7.1	22123	641	395	246	25-29
30-34	124492	60557	5.7	63935	6.0	16207	678	395	283	30-34
35-39	103940	51061	4.8	52879	4.9	10263	610	340	270	35-39
40-44	82461	40907	3.8	41554	3.9	3597	590	293	297	40-44
45-49	66527	33282	3.1	33245	3.1	572	527	287	240	45-49
50-54	52596	26243	2.5	26353	2.5	35	609	332	277	50-54
55-59	41475	20682	1.9	20793	1.9	0	613	327	286	55-59
60-64	34038	17013	1.6	17025	1.6	0	831	422	409	60-64
65-69	21975	11069	1.0	10906	1.0	0	668	358	310	65-69
70-74	11785	5838	0.5	5947	0.6		707	381	326	70-74
75-79	8515	3863	0.4	4652	0.4		592	308	284	75-79
80-84	3746	1624	0.2	2122	0.2	48241 M.	467	220	247	80-84
85+	1165	478	0.0	687	0.1	45408 F.	540	231	309	85+
TOTAL	2136792	1063334		1073458		93649	19510	10433	9077	TOTAL

TABLE 2 — MALE LIFE TABLE

x	nq_x	l_x	nd_x	nL_x	nm_x	na_x	T_x	r_x	e_x	nM_x	x
0	0.044220	100000	4422	97474	0.045365	0.4289	5852815	0.0235	58.528	0.045968	0
1	0.050254	95578	4803	369976	0.012982	1.4317	5755341	0.0235	60.216	0.013081	1
5	0.017324	90775	1573	449943	0.003495	2.5000	5385365	0.0375	59.327	0.003569	5
10	0.009008	89202	804	443916	0.001810	2.3923	4935422	0.0570	55.328	0.001821	10
15	0.013090	88399	1157	439406	0.002633	2.7636	4491506	0.0495	50.810	0.002598	15
20	0.025989	87242	2267	430792	0.005263	2.6113	4052100	0.0329	46.447	0.005242	20
25	0.027871	84974	2368	419031	0.005652	2.5340	3621307	0.0248	42.616	0.005646	25
30	0.032121	82606	2653	406449	0.006528	2.5198	3202276	0.0251	38.766	0.006523	30
35	0.032770	79953	2620	393228	0.006663	2.5059	2795827	0.0325	34.969	0.006659	35
40	0.035263	77333	2727	379959	0.007177	2.5417	2402599	0.0355	31.068	0.007163	40
45	0.042435	74606	3166	365462	0.008663	2.6103	2022641	0.0352	27.111	0.008623	45
50	0.061635	71440	4403	346599	0.012704	2.5928	1657179	0.0352	23.197	0.012651	50
55	0.076478	67036	5127	322966	0.015874	2.6172	1310580	0.0262	19.550	0.015811	55
60	0.117706	61910	7287	291988	0.024957	2.5902	987614	0.0437	15.953	0.024805	60
65	0.151645	54622	8283	253618	0.032660	2.6466	695626	0.0437	12.735	0.032343	65
70	0.282998	46339	13114	199494	0.065736	2.5444	442008	0.0437	9.539	0.065262	70
75	0.333378	33225	11077	138059	0.080231	2.4660	242514	0.0437	7.299	0.079731	75
80	0.510554	22149	11308	82424	0.137194	2.4957	104455	0.0437	4.716	0.135469	80
85+	*1.000000	10841	10841	22031	0.492061	2.0323	22031	0.0437	2.032	0.483264	85+

TABLE 3 — FEMALE LIFE TABLE

x	nq_x	l_x	nd_x	nL_x	nm_x	na_x	T_x	r_x	e_x	nM_x	x
0	0.038247	100000	3825	97853	0.039086	0.4386	6172024	0.0239	61.720	0.039587	0
1	0.049108	96175	4723	372773	0.012670	1.4745	6074171	0.0239	63.157	0.012763	1
5	0.014801	91452	1354	453878	0.002982	2.5000	5701398	0.0381	62.343	0.003057	5
10	0.007485	90099	674	448744	0.001503	2.4066	5247520	0.0493	58.242	0.001509	10
15	0.011755	89424	1051	444628	0.002364	2.6277	4798776	0.0368	53.663	0.002353	15
20	0.014924	88373	1319	438640	0.003007	2.5542	4354148	0.0305	49.270	0.003001	20
25	0.016017	87054	1394	431903	0.003228	2.5840	3915508	0.0318	44.978	0.003219	25
30	0.021961	85660	1881	423748	0.004439	2.5805	3483605	0.0325	40.668	0.004426	30
35	0.025323	83779	2122	413797	0.005127	2.5976	3059857	0.0376	36.523	0.005106	35
40	0.035209	81657	2875	401241	0.007165	2.5495	2646060	0.0397	32.404	0.007147	40
45	0.035598	78782	2805	387116	0.007245	2.5771	2244819	0.0376	28.494	0.007219	45
50	0.051504	75978	3913	370527	0.010561	2.6077	1857703	0.0366	24.451	0.010511	50
55	0.066987	72065	4827	349038	0.013830	2.6623	1487177	0.0283	20.637	0.013755	55
60	0.114139	67237	7674	317659	0.024159	2.5859	1138139	0.0426	16.927	0.024023	60
65	0.134179	59563	7992	278844	0.028661	2.6264	820480	0.0426	13.775	0.028425	65
70	0.242802	51571	12521	227053	0.055148	2.5402	541636	0.0426	10.503	0.054818	70
75	0.266529	39049	10408	169358	0.061454	2.5126	314583	0.0426	8.056	0.061049	75
80	0.459187	28641	13152	111387	0.118073	2.5805	145225	0.0426	5.070	0.116400	80
85+	*1.000000	15490	15490	33838	0.457759	2.1846	33838	0.0426	2.185	0.449782	85+

TABLE 4 — OBSERVED AND PROJECTED VITAL RATES

	OBSERVED POPULATION BOTH SEXES	MALES	FEMALES	PROJECTED POPULATION 1968 MALES	FEMALES	1973 MALES	FEMALES	1978 MALES	FEMALES	STABLE POPULATION MALES	FEMALES
RATES PER THOUSAND											
Birth	43.83	45.37	42.30	44.94	42.23	45.58	43.11	46.20	43.92	44.34	43.18
Death	9.13	9.81	8.46	9.68	8.33	9.78	8.45	9.86	8.54	9.82	8.66
Increase	34.70	35.56	33.84	35.25	33.90	35.80	34.66	36.33	35.39	34.5212	
PERCENTAGE											
under 15	49.41	50.46	48.37	49.83	47.82	48.33	46.40	48.11	46.13	47.23	46.38
15-64	48.38	47.39	49.36	47.79	49.67	49.24	51.01	49.46	51.23	50.28	50.79
65 and over	2.21	2.15	2.27	2.38	2.51	2.43	2.59	2.43	2.64	2.50	2.83
DEP. RATIO X 100	106.70	111.01	102.59	109.27	101.32	103.08	96.04	102.16	95.21	98.91	96.90

TABLE 1 — DATA

AGE AT LAST BIRTHDAY	POPULATION BOTH SEXES	MALES Number	%	FEMALES Number	%	BIRTHS BY AGE OF MOTHER	DEATHS BOTH SEXES	MALES	FEMALES	AGE AT LAST BIRTHDAY
0	110017	55819	5.1	54198	4.9	0	4638	2557	2081	0
1-4	330049	167457	15.2	162592	14.6	0	4541	2330	2211	1-4
5-9	381913	194242	17.7	187671	16.9	0	1510	753	757	5-9
10-14	284624	144523	13.2	140101	12.6	199	458	240	218	10-14
15-19	214817	104712	9.5	110105	9.9	15493	537	288	249	15-19
20-24	177590	84016	7.6	93574	8.4	27841	634	369	265	20-24
25-29	150333	71668	6.5	78665	7.1	23297	636	376	260	25-29
30-34	128042	62199	5.7	65843	5.9	18126	659	352	307	30-34
35-39	106311	52191	4.8	54120	4.9	11002	608	328	280	35-39
40-44	83710	41513	3.8	42197	3.8	3893	570	296	274	40-44
45-49	67285	33703	3.1	33582	3.0	664	557	297	260	45-49
50-54	52830	26453	2.4	26377	2.4	16	634	332	302	50-54
55-59	41511	20762	1.9	20749	1.9	0	638	341	297	55-59
60-64	34156	17093	1.6	17063	1.5	0	907	475	432	60-64
65-69	21853	11051	1.0	10802	1.0	0	721	363	358	65-69
70-74	11451	5712	0.5	5739	0.5		678	344	334	70-74
75-79	7722	3441	0.3	4281	0.4		806	380	426	75-79
80-84	3406	1509	0.1	1897	0.2	51970 M.	539	252	287	80-84
85+	1059	466	0.0	593	0.1	48561 F.	275	127	148	85+
TOTAL	2208679	1098530		1110149		130531	20546	10800	9746	TOTAL

TABLE 2 — MALE LIFE TABLE

x	$_nq_x$	l_x	$_nd_x$	$_nL_x$	$_nm_x$	$_na_x$	T_x	r_x	$\overset{\circ}{e}_x$	$_nM_x$	x
0	0.044101	100000	4410	97503	0.045230	0.4337	5839489	0.0233	58.395	0.045809	0
1	0.053380	95590	5103	369360	0.013815	1.4524	5741986	0.0233	60.069	0.013914	1
5	0.018794	90487	1701	448185	0.003794	2.5000	5372626	0.0380	59.374	0.003877	5
10	0.008202	88787	728	442012	0.001648	2.3614	4924440	0.0594	55.464	0.001661	10
15	0.013811	88058	1216	437495	0.002780	2.6998	4482428	0.0514	50.903	0.002750	15
20	0.021817	86842	1895	429681	0.004409	2.6085	4044933	0.0337	46.578	0.004392	20
25	0.025930	84948	2203	419319	0.005253	2.5394	3615253	0.0249	42.559	0.005246	25
30	0.027933	82745	2311	408007	0.005665	2.5262	3195934	0.0260	38.624	0.005659	30
35	0.030995	80434	2493	396025	0.006295	2.5357	2787927	0.0341	34.661	0.006285	35
40	0.035134	77941	2738	383017	0.007149	2.5583	2391902	0.0364	30.689	0.007130	40
45	0.043342	75202	3259	368210	0.008852	2.6063	2008884	0.0358	26.713	0.008812	45
50	0.061186	71943	4402	349148	0.012607	2.5996	1640675	0.0360	22.805	0.012551	50
55	0.079419	67541	5364	325074	0.016501	2.6452	1291526	0.0255	19.122	0.016424	55
60	0.130903	62177	8139	291147	0.027956	2.5749	966452	0.0463	15.544	0.027789	60
65	0.153409	54038	8290	250302	0.033120	2.6009	675306	0.0463	12.497	0.032848	65
70	0.265717	45748	12156	199669	0.060881	2.6085	425004	0.0463	9.290	0.060224	70
75	0.435247	33592	14621	131184	0.111453	2.4847	225335	0.0463	6.708	0.110433	75
80	0.584120	18971	11081	65750	0.168539	2.3735	94151	0.0463	4.963	0.166997	80
85+	*1.000000	7890	7890	28401	0.277795	3.5998	28401	0.0463	3.600	0.272532	85+

TABLE 3 — FEMALE LIFE TABLE

x	$_nq_x$	l_x	$_nd_x$	$_nL_x$	$_nm_x$	$_na_x$	T_x	r_x	$\overset{\circ}{e}_x$	$_nM_x$	x
0	0.037154	100000	3715	97939	0.037936	0.4453	6061841	0.0238	60.618	0.038396	0
1	0.052277	96285	5033	372591	0.013509	1.5073	5963902	0.0238	61.940	0.013598	1
5	0.019567	91251	1785	451792	0.003952	2.5000	5591310	0.0382	61.274	0.004034	5
10	0.007656	89466	685	445453	0.001538	2.2620	5139519	0.0510	57.447	0.001556	10
15	0.011298	88781	1003	441511	0.002272	2.6147	4694066	0.0382	52.873	0.002261	15
20	0.014096	87778	1237	435882	0.002839	2.5709	4252556	0.0308	48.447	0.002832	20
25	0.016455	86540	1424	429293	0.003317	2.6068	3816673	0.0316	44.103	0.003305	25
30	0.023116	85116	1968	420809	0.004676	2.5748	3387380	0.0329	39.797	0.004663	30
35	0.025618	83149	2130	410550	0.005188	2.5617	2966571	0.0391	35.678	0.005174	35
40	0.032070	81019	2598	398777	0.006516	2.5694	2556021	0.0413	31.549	0.006493	40
45	0.038197	78420	2995	384951	0.007781	2.6128	2157244	0.0387	27.509	0.007742	45
50	0.055955	75425	4220	366982	0.011500	2.5968	1772293	0.0370	23.497	0.011449	50
55	0.069598	71204	4956	344411	0.014389	2.6571	1405311	0.0274	19.736	0.014314	55
60	0.120114	66249	7957	312196	0.025488	2.6063	1060900	0.0429	16.014	0.025318	60
65	0.154670	58291	9016	269900	0.033405	2.6091	748704	0.0429	12.844	0.033142	65
70	0.257287	49275	12678	215858	0.058733	2.5928	478804	0.0429	9.717	0.058198	70
75	0.400633	36597	14662	146173	0.100307	2.4892	262945	0.0429	7.185	0.099509	75
80	0.543252	21935	11916	78210	0.152364	2.4188	116772	0.0429	5.323	0.151291	80
85+	1.000000	10019	10019	38562	0.259816	3.8489	38562	0.0429	3.849	0.249579	85+

TABLE 4 — OBSERVED AND PROJECTED VITAL RATES

RATES PER THOUSAND	OBSERVED POPULATION BOTH SEXES	MALES	FEMALES	1969 MALES	FEMALES	1974 MALES	FEMALES	1979 MALES	FEMALES	STABLE POPULATION MALES	FEMALES
Birth	45.52	47.31	43.74	46.60	43.57	47.13	44.47	47.61	45.26	45.51	44.63
Death	9.30	9.83	8.78	9.77	8.69	9.83	8.77	9.90	8.86	9.81	8.92
Increase	36.21	37.48	34.96	36.84	34.88	37.30	35.70	37.70	36.39	35.7088	
PERCENTAGE											
under 15	50.10	51.16	49.05	50.68	48.59	49.23	47.20	49.17	47.11	47.94	47.38
15-64	47.84	46.82	48.85	47.08	49.11	48.51	50.45	48.60	50.54	49.76	50.15
65 and over	2.06	2.02	2.10	2.24	2.30	2.26	2.35	2.24	2.35	2.29	2.47
DEP. RATIO X 100	109.04	113.59	104.72	112.41	103.64	106.13	98.23	105.77	97.86	100.96	99.40

TABLE 1 — DATA

AGE AT LAST BIRTHDAY	BOTH SEXES	POPULATION MALES Number	%	FEMALES Number	%	BIRTHS BY AGE OF MOTHER	DEATHS BOTH SEXES	MALES	FEMALES	AGE AT LAST BIRTHDAY
0	115438	58541	5.2	56897	5.0	0	4181	2360	1821	0
1-4	346313	175621	15.5	170692	14.9	0	4189	2138	2051	1-4
5-9	401935	204358	18.0	197577	17.2	0	1444	758	686	5-9
10-14	296377	150359	13.2	146018	12.7	169	519	280	239	10-14
15-19	221230	107544	9.5	113686	9.9	15276	613	292	321	15-19
20-24	182177	85881	7.6	96296	8.4	26889	656	396	260	20-24
25-29	154445	73448	6.5	80997	7.1	22466	630	381	249	25-29
30-34	131746	63911	5.6	67835	5.9	17692	641	342	299	30-34
35-39	108759	53352	4.7	55407	4.8	11213	622	317	305	35-39
40-44	85009	42145	3.7	42864	3.7	3917	535	296	239	40-44
45-49	68036	34130	3.0	33906	3.0	660	540	274	266	45-49
50-54	53042	26659	2.3	26383	2.3	8	587	314	273	50-54
55-59	41509	20823	1.8	20686	1.8	0	617	332	285	55-59
60-64	34246	17167	1.5	17079	1.5	0	809	417	392	60-64
65-69	21706	11024	1.0	10682	0.9	0	758	384	374	65-69
70-74	11088	5575	0.5	5513	0.5		681	356	325	70-74
75-79	6987	3133	0.3	3854	0.3		823	403	420	75-79
80-84	3005	1323	0.1	1682	0.1	51162 M.	532	254	278	80-84
85+	909	392	0.0	517	0.0	47128 F.	262	122	140	85+
TOTAL	2283957	1135386		1148571		98290	19639	10416	9223	TOTAL

TABLE 2 — MALE LIFE TABLE

x	$_nq_x$	l_x	$_nd_x$	$_nL_x$	$_nm_x$	$_na_x$	T_x	r_x	$\overset{\circ}{e}_x$	$_nM_x$	x
0	0.038909	100000	3891	97797	0.039786	0.4338	5912956	0.0240	59.130	0.040314	0
1	0.046901	96109	4508	372955	0.012086	1.4528	5815159	0.0240	60.506	0.012174	1
5	0.018026	91601	1651	453879	0.003638	2.5000	5442205	0.0393	59.412	0.003709	5
10	0.009207	89950	828	447590	0.001850	2.3905	4988325	0.0617	55.456	0.001862	10
15	0.013642	89122	1216	442818	0.002746	2.7029	4540735	0.0531	50.950	0.002715	15
20	0.022888	87906	2012	434707	0.004628	2.6020	4097918	0.0338	46.617	0.004611	20
25	0.025625	85894	2201	424010	0.005191	2.5189	3663211	0.0244	42.648	0.005187	25
30	0.026425	83693	2212	412976	0.005355	2.5179	3239201	0.0265	38.703	0.005351	30
35	0.029341	81482	2391	401540	0.005954	2.5458	2826224	0.0356	34.685	0.005942	35
40	0.034602	79091	2737	388743	0.007040	2.5479	2424684	0.0377	30.657	0.007023	40
45	0.039556	76354	3020	374529	0.008064	2.6025	2035941	0.0372	26.664	0.008028	45
50	0.057574	73334	4222	356595	0.011840	2.6140	1661411	0.0376	22.655	0.011778	50
55	0.077126	69112	5330	332888	0.016012	2.6229	1304816	0.0272	18.880	0.015944	55
60	0.115503	63781	7367	301285	0.024452	2.6080	971929	0.0416	15.238	0.024291	60
65	0.162212	56414	9151	260414	0.035141	2.6332	670643	0.0416	11.888	0.034833	65
70	0.279678	47263	13219	204830	0.064534	2.6180	410230	0.0416	8.680	0.063857	70
75	0.488656	34045	16636	128187	0.129781	2.4732	205400	0.0416	6.033	0.128631	75
80	0.636185	17409	11075	57209	0.193590	2.3062	77213	0.0416	4.435	0.191989	80
85+	*1.000000	6334	6334	20004	0.316618	3.1584	20004	0.0416	3.158	0.311224	85+

TABLE 3 — FEMALE LIFE TABLE

x	$_nq_x$	l_x	$_nd_x$	$_nL_x$	$_nm_x$	$_na_x$	T_x	r_x	$\overset{\circ}{e}_x$	$_nM_x$	x
0	0.031081	100000	3108	98290	0.031621	0.4497	6153070	0.0244	61.531	0.032005	0
1	0.046380	96892	4494	376474	0.011937	1.5313	6054780	0.0244	62.490	0.012016	1
5	0.016856	92398	1557	458097	0.003400	2.5000	5678307	0.0395	61.455	0.003472	5
10	0.008117	90841	737	452299	0.001630	2.4180	5220210	0.0529	57.466	0.001637	10
15	0.014066	90103	1267	447943	0.002832	2.5747	4767911	0.0391	52.916	0.002824	15
20	0.013418	88836	1192	441215	0.002702	2.5131	4320468	0.0311	48.634	0.002700	20
25	0.015314	87644	1342	435009	0.003085	2.6082	3879253	0.0318	44.262	0.003074	25
30	0.021892	86302	1889	426984	0.004425	2.6052	3444244	0.0336	39.909	0.004408	30
35	0.027204	84412	2296	416400	0.005515	2.5343	3017259	0.0406	35.744	0.005505	35
40	0.027607	82116	2267	405078	0.005596	2.5729	2600860	0.0430	31.673	0.005576	40
45	0.038698	79849	3090	391859	0.007886	2.6096	2195781	0.0407	27.499	0.007845	45
50	0.050709	76759	3892	374439	0.010395	2.5962	1803923	0.0389	23.501	0.010348	50
55	0.067067	72867	4887	352859	0.013850	2.6520	1429484	0.0285	19.618	0.013777	55
60	0.109704	67980	7458	322290	0.023140	2.6389	1076625	0.0434	15.837	0.022952	60
65	0.162884	60522	9858	279160	0.035313	2.6212	754335	0.0434	12.464	0.035012	65
70	0.260428	50664	13194	221643	0.059530	2.5992	475175	0.0434	9.379	0.058952	70
75	0.430750	37470	16140	146827	0.109926	2.4894	253532	0.0434	6.766	0.108978	75
80	0.580099	21330	12373	74218	0.166715	2.3790	106705	0.0434	5.003	0.165279	80
85+	*1.000000	8956	8956	32487	0.275693	3.6272	32487	0.0434	3.627	0.270793	85+

TABLE 4 — OBSERVED AND PROJECTED VITAL RATES

	OBSERVED POPULATION BOTH SEXES	MALES	FEMALES	PROJECTED POPULATION 1970 MALES	FEMALES	1975 MALES	FEMALES	1980 MALES	FEMALES	STABLE POPULATION MALES	FEMALES
RATES PER THOUSAND											
Birth	43.03	45.06	41.03	44.82	41.35	45.75	42.67	46.57	43.84	43.43	42.49
Death	8.60	9.17	8.03	8.98	7.84	9.10	7.98	9.24	8.14	9.37	8.43
Increase	34.44	35.89	33.00	35.84	33.52	36.65	34.70	37.32	35.70		34.0591
PERCENTAGE											
under 15	50.79	51.87	49.73	50.81	48.59	48.78	46.52	48.31	45.90	46.76	46.18
15-64	47.30	46.25	48.33	47.07	49.23	49.05	51.23	49.53	51.81	50.76	51.12
65 and over	1.91	1.89	1.94	2.12	2.18	2.17	2.26	2.16	2.29	2.48	2.69
DEP. RATIO X 100	111.44	116.24	106.90	112.47	103.11	103.86	95.22	101.91	93.01	97.01	95.61

AGE AT LAST BIRTHDAY	1970 BOTH SEXES	MALES	FEMALES	1975 BOTH SEXES	MALES	FEMALES	1980 BOTH SEXES	MALES	FEMALES	AGE AT LAST BIRTHDAY	
0-4	509	264	245	616	319	297	755	391	364	0-4	
5-9	446	226	220	491	254	237	594	308	286	5-9	
10-14	397	202	195	440	223	217	485	251	234	10-14	
15-19	293	149	144	392	199	193	434	220	214	15-19	TABLE 5
20-24	218	106	112	288	146	142	386	196	190	20-24	POPULATION
25-29	179	84	95	214	103	111	282	142	140	25-29	PROJECTED
30-34	152	72	80	175	82	93	208	100	108	30-34	WITH
35-39	128	62	66	148	70	78	170	79	91	35-39	FIXED
40-44	106	52	54	124	60	64	142	67	75	40-44	AGE—
45-49	82	41	41	102	50	52	120	58	62	45-49	SPECIFIC
50-54	64	32	32	79	39	40	97	47	50	50-54	BIRTH
55-59	50	25	25	61	30	31	73	36	37	55-59	AND
60-64	38	19	19	46	23	23	55	27	28	60-64	DEATH
65-69	30	15	15	32	16	16	39	19	20	65-69	RATES
70-74	17	9	8	24	12	12	26	13	13	70-74	(IN 1000's)
75-79	7	3	4	11	5	6	15	7	8	75-79	
80-84	3	1	2	4	2	2	5	2	3	80-84	
85+	1	0	1	1	0	1	2	1	1	85+	
TOTAL	2720	1362	1358	3248	1633	1615	3888	1964	1924	TOTAL	

STANDARD COUNTRIES:

STANDARDIZED RATES PER THOUSAND	ENGLAND AND WALES 1961 BOTH SEXES	MALES	FEMALES	UNITED STATES 1960 BOTH SEXES	MALES	FEMALES	MEXICO 1960 BOTH SEXES	MALES	FEMALES	
Birth	40.98	50.06*	38.08	41.76	45.69*	39.45	45.31	48.67*	43.34	TABLE 6
Death	17.47	25.27*	18.89	14.89	19.48*	14.84	9.66	8.72*	9.12	STANDARDIZED RATES
Increase	23.51	24.79*	19.19	26.87	26.21*	24.61	35.65	39.95*	34.22	

	OBSERVED POP. MALES	FEMALES	STATIONARY POP. MALES	FEMALES	STABLE POP. MALES	FEMALES	OBSERVED BIRTHS	NET MATERNITY FUNCTION	BIRTHS IN STABLE POP.	
μ	19.81444	20.19137	35.12181	35.86131	21.26160	21.60581	27.32709	29.12427	27.29694	TABLE 7
σ^2	297.8518	295.6331	484.5896	497.1272	312.9714	322.0930	48.26600	53.77032	49.01874	MOMENTS
κ_3	5653.133	5490.557	2747.962	2675.068	5685.381	5878.153	156.7753	106.4278	167.4859	AND
κ_4	49508.	52291.	-229641.	-242490.	42136.	41777.	-1311.408	-2208.328	-1316.712	CUMULANTS
β_1	1.209422	1.166739	0.066359	0.058246	1.054400	1.034042	0.218591	0.072859	0.238161	
β_2	3.558054	3.598298	2.022084	2.018796	3.430174	3.402692	2.437069	2.236202	2.452018	
κ	-0.488150	-0.506081	-0.024612	-0.021723	-0.448295	-0.439081	-0.099724	-0.032775	-0.107499	

VITAL STATISTICS		THOMPSON AGE RANGE	NRR	1000r	INTERVAL	BOURGEOIS-PICHAT AGE RANGE	NRR	1000b	1000d	1000r	COALE		TABLE 8
GRR	3.036										IBR	42.95	RATES FROM AGE DISTRIBUTIONS AND VITAL STATISTICS (Females)
NRR	2.613	0-4	2.70	36.44	27.23	5-29	3.06	48.56	7.13	41.43	IDR	8.62	
TFR	6.332	5-9	2.88	38.91	27.16	30-54	3.04	53.20	12.07	41.13	IRI	34.32	
GENERATION	28.197	10-14	2.57	33.97	27.07	55-79	4.78	156.14	98.19	57.95	K1	-5.68	
SEX RATIO	108.560	15-19	2.43	33.00	26.96	*15-39	2.39	39.13	6.90	32.22	K2	0.	

Start of Age Interval	ORIGINAL MATRIX SUB-DIAGONAL	ALTERNATIVE FIRST ROWS Projection	Integral	FIRST STABLE MATRIX % IN STABLE POPULATION	FISHER VALUES	REPRODUCTIVE VALUES	SECOND STABLE MATRIX Z_2 FIRST COLUMN	FIRST ROW	
0	0.96489	0.00000	0.00000	18.579	1.146	260761	0.1094+0.0862	0.1094+0.0862	
5	0.98734	0.00130	0.00000	15.110	1.409	278353	0.1422-0.0556	-0.0173+0.1259	TABLE 9
10	0.98926	0.15261	0.00287	12.574	1.691	246979	0.0270-0.1690	-0.1048+0.0435	LESLIE
15	0.98608	0.46634	0.33306	10.484	1.852	210525	-0.1484-0.1223	-0.0975-0.0741	MATRIX
20	0.98593	0.62908	0.69214	8.714	1.686	162378	-0.2023+0.0739	-0.0387-0.1494	AND ITS
25	0.98155	0.60707	0.68752	7.241	1.298	105144	-0.0433+0.2373	0.0277-0.1524	SPECTRAL
30	0.97521	0.52148	0.64647	5.991	0.860	58370	0.2036+0.1756	0.0628-0.1011	COMPONENTS
35	0.97281	0.33153	0.50163	4.924	0.434	24056	0.2819-0.0960	0.0489-0.0435	(Females)
40	0.96737	0.12544	0.22651	4.037	0.139	5961	0.0662-0.3223	0.0191-0.0111	
45	0.95554	0.02249	0.04825	3.292	0.022	745	-0.2685-0.2420	0.0033-0.0014	
50	0.94237	0.00035	0.00075	2.651	0.000	9	-0.3740+0.1183	0.0001-0.0000	
55+	0.79622			6.403					

Start of Age Interval	OBSERVED POPUL. (IN 100's)	CONTRIBUTIONS OF ROOTS (IN 100's) r_1	r_2, r_3	$r_4 \cdot r_{11}$	AGE-SP. BIRTH RATES	NET MATERNITY FUNCTION	COEFF. OF MATRIX EQUATION	PARAMETERS INTEGRAL	MATRIX	EXP. INCREASE x	$e^{(x+2\frac{1}{2})r}$	
0	2276	2181	30	64	0.0000	0.0000	0.0000	L(1) 1.18566	1.18645	0	1.0889	TABLE 10
5	1976	1774	128	74	0.0000	0.0000	0.0013	L(2) 0.43887	0.44585	50	5.9781	AGE
10	1460	1476	109	-125	0.0006	0.0025	0.1454	0.77626	0.75927	55	7.0880	ANALYSIS
15	1137	1231	-38	-56	0.0644	0.2883	0.4395	R(1) 0.03406	0.03419	60	8.4039	AND
20	963	1023	-180	120	0.1339	0.5907	0.5846	R(2) -0.02292	-0.02545	65	9.9641	MISCELLANEOUS
25	810	850	-156	116	0.1330	0.5785	0.5562	-0.21125	0.20797	70	11.8140	RESULTS
30	678	703	48	-73	0.1251	0.5340	0.4690	C(1)	11739	75	14.0073	(Females)
35	554	578	247	-271	0.0970	0.4041	0.2908	C(2)	34799	80	16.6079	
40	429	474	217	-263	0.0438	0.1775	0.1070		26566	85	19.6912	
45	339	386	-58	11	0.0093	0.0366	0.0186	2P/Y 29.7436	30.2125	90	23.3470	
50	264	311	-323	276	0.0001	0.0005	0.0003	DELTA 3.5459		95	27.6815	
55+	600	752								100	32.8207	

TABLE 1 — DATA

AGE AT LAST BIRTHDAY	POPULATION BOTH SEXES	MALES Number	MALES %	FEMALES Number	FEMALES %	BIRTHS BY AGE OF MOTHER	DEATHS BOTH SEXES	DEATHS MALES	DEATHS FEMALES	AGE AT LAST BIRTHDAY
0	44750	22500	3.2	22250	3.0	0	3934	2122	1812	0
1-4	152550	76600	11.0	75950	10.3	0	1708	924	784	1-4
5-9	168700	84400	12.1	84300	11.5	0	454	233	221	5-9
10-14	151100	75650	10.9	75450	10.3	54	218	101	117	10-14
15-19	143150	72200	10.4	70950	9.7	7758	323	132	191	15-19
20-24	126500	62700	9.0	63800	8.7	15143	472	203	269	20-24
25-29	108250	50850	7.3	57400	7.8	11589	501	222	279	25-29
30-34	104000	47900	6.9	56100	7.6	7586	511	252	259	30-34
35-39	100600	47850	6.9	52750	7.2	4729	542	248	294	35-39
40-44	79400	38200	5.5	41200	5.6	1370	672	359	313	40-44
45-49	73700	36300	5.2	37400	5.1	202	696	374	322	45-49
50-54	54300	26750	3.8	27550	3.8	10	864	480	384	50-54
55-59	40450	19000	2.7	21450	2.9	0	626	336	290	55-59
60-64	28650	12650	1.8	16000	2.2	0	901	469	432	60-64
65-69	24000	10400	1.5	13600	1.9	0	742	366	376	65-69
70-74	14400	6050	0.9	8350	1.1		1098	562	536	70-74
75-79	8800	3550	0.5	5250	0.7		843	438	405	75-79
80-84	3900	1250	0.2	2650	0.4	24378 M.	942	399	543	80-84
85+	3150	900	0.1	2250	0.3	24063 F.	1186	431	755	85+
TOTAL	1430350	695700		734650		48441	17233	8651	8582	TOTAL

TABLE 2 — MALE LIFE TABLE

x	nq_x	l_x	nd_x	nL_x	nm_x	na_x	T_x	r_x	$\overset{\circ}{e}_x$	nM_x	x
0	0.088353	100000	8835	94286	0.093707	0.3533	5519538	0.0095	55.195	0.094311	0
1	0.046443	91165	4234	352914	0.011997	1.2262	5425252	0.0095	59.510	0.012063	1
5	0.013502	86931	1174	431719	0.002719	2.5000	5072338	0.0224	58.349	0.002761	5
10	0.006639	85757	569	427279	0.001332	2.3553	4640618	0.0138	54.114	0.001335	10
15	0.009136	85188	778	424158	0.001835	2.7125	4213339	0.0168	49.460	0.001828	15
20	0.016149	84409	1363	418851	0.003254	2.6558	3789181	0.0319	44.891	0.003238	20
25	0.021648	83046	1798	410892	0.004375	2.5865	3370330	0.0226	40.584	0.004366	25
30	0.025967	81248	2110	401016	0.005261	2.5231	2959438	0.0011	36.425	0.005261	30
35	0.025669	79139	2031	390915	0.005197	2.6478	2558422	0.0165	32.328	0.005183	35
40	0.046053	77107	3551	377009	0.009419	2.5987	2167507	0.0191	28.110	0.009398	40
45	0.050483	73556	3713	359014	0.010343	2.6391	1790498	0.0237	24.342	0.010303	45
50	0.086335	69843	6030	334506	0.018026	2.5607	1431484	0.0488	20.496	0.017944	50
55	0.085730	63813	5471	306201	0.017866	2.6485	1096978	0.0525	17.191	0.017684	55
60	0.170238	58342	9932	267386	0.037145	2.5508	790777	0.0163	13.554	0.037075	60
65	0.163015	48410	7894	223449	0.035330	2.6437	523390	0.0163	10.812	0.035192	65
70	0.379524	40516	15377	164952	0.093219	2.5530	299941	0.0163	7.403	0.092893	70
75	0.469697	25139	11808	95368	0.123812	2.4316	134989	0.0163	5.370	0.123380	75
80	0.862722	13331	11501	35825	0.321040	2.3193	39621	0.0163	2.972	0.319199	80
85+	*1.000000	1830	1830	3796	0.482143	2.0741	3796	0.0163	2.074	0.478889	85+

TABLE 3 — FEMALE LIFE TABLE

x	nq_x	l_x	nd_x	nL_x	nm_x	na_x	T_x	r_x	$\overset{\circ}{e}_x$	nM_x	x
0	0.076855	100000	7685	95030	0.080874	0.3534	5812979	0.0101	58.130	0.081438	0
1	0.039916	92315	3685	359037	0.010263	1.2263	5717948	0.0101	61.940	0.010323	1
5	0.012856	88630	1139	440300	0.002588	2.5000	5358911	0.0222	60.464	0.002622	5
10	0.007725	87490	676	435767	0.001551	2.5078	4918612	0.0152	56.219	0.001551	10
15	0.013416	86814	1165	431392	0.002700	2.6994	4482845	0.0140	51.637	0.002692	15
20	0.020908	85650	1791	423948	0.004224	2.5988	4051453	0.0171	47.303	0.004216	20
25	0.024016	83859	2014	414276	0.004861	2.5080	3627504	0.0082	43.257	0.004861	25
30	0.022825	81845	1868	404594	0.004617	2.5213	3213229	0.0036	39.260	0.004617	30
35	0.027574	79977	2205	394587	0.005589	2.5982	2808634	0.0251	35.118	0.005573	35
40	0.037381	77772	2907	381791	0.007615	2.5693	2414047	0.0271	31.040	0.007597	40
45	0.042374	74864	3172	366795	0.008649	2.6274	2032256	0.0306	27.146	0.008610	45
50	0.067616	71692	4848	346599	0.013986	2.5531	1665460	0.0431	23.231	0.013938	50
55	0.065946	66845	4408	323845	0.013612	2.6456	1318861	0.0375	19.730	0.013520	55
60	0.126986	62436	7929	292923	0.027067	2.5709	995016	0.0208	15.936	0.027000	60
65	0.130392	54508	7107	255869	0.027778	2.6545	702093	0.0208	12.881	0.027647	65
70	0.278439	47401	13198	204847	0.064429	2.5636	446224	0.0208	9.414	0.064192	70
75	0.325609	34202	11137	143668	0.077516	2.5446	241377	0.0208	7.057	0.077143	75
80	0.675655	23066	15585	75606	0.206128	2.4511	97710	0.0208	4.236	0.204905	80
85+	*1.000000	7481	7481	22104	0.338459	2.9546	22104	0.0208	2.955	0.335556	85+

TABLE 4 — OBSERVED AND PROJECTED VITAL RATES

RATES PER THOUSAND	OBSERVED POPULATION BOTH SEXES	OBSERVED MALES	OBSERVED FEMALES	PROJECTED 1956 MALES	1956 FEMALES	1961 MALES	1961 FEMALES	1966 MALES	1966 FEMALES	STABLE POPULATION MALES	STABLE FEMALES
Birth	33.87	35.04	32.75	33.54	31.57	32.36	30.61	31.90	30.30	32.24	31.25
Death	12.05	12.43	11.68	12.17	11.28	12.14	11.31	12.37	11.55	12.99	11.99
Increase	21.82	22.61	21.07	21.37	20.30	20.22	19.30	19.52	18.75		19.2548
PERCENTAGE											
under 15	36.15	37.25	35.11	37.58	35.81	37.59	36.09	37.21	35.99	36.63	36.14
15-64	60.06	59.57	60.52	59.43	59.99	59.21	59.50	59.18	59.29	59.14	58.47
65 and over	3.79	3.18	4.37	2.99	4.21	3.20	4.41	3.61	4.71	4.23	5.38
DEP. RATIO X 100	66.51	67.88	65.24	68.27	66.70	68.89	68.07	68.98	68.66	69.09	71.01

AGE AT LAST BIRTHDAY	1956 BOTH SEXES	1956 MALES	1956 FEMALES	1961 BOTH SEXES	1961 MALES	1961 FEMALES	1966 BOTH SEXES	1966 MALES	1966 FEMALES	AGE AT LAST BIRTHDAY	
0-4	226	113	113	242	121	121	261	130	131	0-4	
5-9	191	96	95	219	109	110	233	116	117	5-9	
10-14	167	84	83	189	95	94	216	108	108	10-14	
15-19	150	75	75	166	83	83	187	94	93	15-19	**TABLE 5**
20-24	141	71	70	147	74	73	163	82	81	20-24	POPULATION
25-29	124	62	62	138	70	68	145	73	72	25-29	PROJECTED
30-34	106	50	56	121	60	61	135	68	67	30-34	WITH
35-39	102	47	55	103	48	55	118	59	59	35-39	FIXED
40-44	97	46	51	98	45	53	100	47	53	40-44	AGE—
45-49	76	36	40	93	44	49	94	43	51	45-49	SPECIFIC
50-54	69	34	35	71	34	37	87	41	46	50-54	BIRTH
55-59	50	24	26	64	31	33	66	31	35	55-59	AND
60-64	36	17	19	44	21	23	57	27	30	60-64	DEATH
65-69	25	11	14	31	14	17	38	18	20	65-69	RATES
70-74	19	8	11	19	8	11	24	10	14	70-74	(IN 1000's)
75-79	9	3	6	12	4	8	13	5	8	75-79	
80-84	4	1	3	4	1	3	6	2	4	80-84	
85+	1	0	1	1	0	1	1	0	1	85+	
TOTAL	1593	778	815	1762	862	900	1944	954	990	TOTAL	

STANDARD COUNTRIES: STANDARDIZED RATES PER THOUSAND	ENGLAND AND WALES 1961 BOTH SEXES	MALES	FEMALES	UNITED STATES 1960 BOTH SEXES	MALES	FEMALES	MEXICO 1960 BOTH SEXES	MALES	FEMALES	
Birth	26.08	31.85*	25.11	26.61	29.24*	26.04	31.04	29.71*	30.76	**TABLE 6**
Death	20.54	27.37*	20.52	17.89	21.91*	16.51	11.99	12.61*	10.90	STANDARDIZED RATES
Increase	5.54	4.48*	4.59	8.72	7.33*	9.53	19.05	17.10*	19.85	

	OBSERVED POP. MALES	OBSERVED POP. FEMALES	STATIONARY POP. MALES	STATIONARY POP. FEMALES	STABLE POP. MALES	STABLE POP. FEMALES	OBSERVED BIRTHS	NET MATERNITY FUNCTION	BIRTHS IN STABLE POP.	
μ	25.12045	26.44028	34.09705	35.52457	26.03049	26.75963	26.59075	27.14647	26.27054	**TABLE 7**
σ^2	346.7172	374.7522	453.6278	495.2953	376.1805	405.6185	43.00919	45.12942	41.65964	MOMENTS
κ_3	4543.488	5065.486	2540.225	2889.615	5040.087	5834.670	169.9973	175.1004	183.8113	AND
κ_4	-31020.	-30354.	-196947.	-238439.	-55880.	-59378.	-593.804	-685.597	-220.442	CUMULANTS
β_1	0.495282	0.487539	0.069127	0.068721	0.477185	0.510128	0.363246	0.333576	0.467302	
β_2	2.741955	2.783862	2.042917	2.028038	2.605121	2.639097	2.678989	2.663373	2.872982	
κ	-0.215062	-0.222457	-0.026011	-0.025551	-0.187706	-0.199498	-0.175687	-0.165532	-0.241167	

VITAL STATISTICS		THOMPSON AGE RANGE	NRR	1000r	INTERVAL	BOURGEOIS-PICHAT AGE RANGE	NRR	1000b	1000d	1000r	COALE	
GRR	2.020										IBR	**TABLE 8**
NRR	1.672	0-4	1.55	16.44	27.17	5-29	1.53	29.15	13.41	15.74	IDR	RATES FROM AGE DISTRIBUTIONS
TFR	4.066	5-9	1.48	14.62	27.09	30-54	2.11	48.60	20.93	27.67	IRI	AND VITAL
GENERATION	26.703	10-14	1.47	14.04	27.00	55-79	2.23	49.56	19.89	29.67	K1	STATISTICS
SEX RATIO	101.309	15-19	1.54	15.30	26.87	* 5-29	1.53	29.15	13.41	15.74	K2	(Females)

Start of Age Interval	ORIGINAL MATRIX SUB-DIAGONAL	ALTERNATIVE FIRST ROWS Projection	ALTERNATIVE FIRST ROWS Integral	FIRST STABLE MATRIX % IN STABLE POPULATION	FISHER VALUES	REPRODUCTIVE VALUES	SECOND STABLE MATRIX Z_2 FIRST COLUMN	FIRST ROW	
0	0.96968	0.00000	0.00000	13.537	1.155	113406	0.1358+0.1311	0.1358+0.1311	**TABLE 9**
5	0.98970	0.00080	0.00000	11.919	1.312	110569	0.2153-0.0823	-0.0501+0.1463	LESLIE
10	0.98996	0.12289	0.00169	10.711	1.459	110049	0.0210-0.2864	-0.1235+0.0133	MATRIX
15	0.98274	0.38638	0.25880	9.628	1.479	104954	-0.3122-0.1751	-0.0686-0.1015	AND ITS
20	0.97718	0.49019	0.56176	8.592	1.204	76795	-0.3600+0.2579	-0.0026-0.1365	SPECTRAL
25	0.97663	0.37664	0.47786	7.623	0.777	44615	0.0995-0.5357	0.0314-0.1148	COMPONENTS
30	0.97527	0.25111	0.32005	6.760	0.431	24186	0.6483+0.1686	0.0430-0.0670	(Females)
35	0.96757	0.13739	0.21218	5.987	0.189	9996	0.5251-0.6330	0.0293-0.0252	
40	0.96072	0.04335	0.07870	5.260	0.052	2130	-0.4270-0.9064	0.0096-0.0056	
45	0.94494	0.00648	0.01278	4.588	0.007	268	-1.2118+0.0026	0.0014-0.0007	
50	0.93435	0.00041	0.00086	3.937	0.000	12	-0.6087+1.3069	0.0001-0.0000	
55+	0.78025			11.457					

Start of Age Interval	OBSERVED POPUL. (IN 100's)	CONTRIBUTIONS OF ROOTS (IN 100's) r_1	r_2, r_3	r_4-r_{11}	AGE-SP. BIRTH RATES	NET MATERNITY FUNCTION	COEFF. OF MATRIX EQUATION	PARAMETERS		EXP. INCREASE x	$e^{(x+2\frac{1}{2})r}$	
0	982	988	20	-26	0.0000	0.0000	0.0000	L(1) INTEGRAL 1.10106	MATRIX 1.10130	0	1.0493	**TABLE 10**
5	843	870	-26	-2	0.0000	0.0000	0.0008	L(2) 0.31692	0.33692	50	2.7480	AGE
10	755	782	-57	30	0.0004	0.0015	0.1179	0.74041	0.71930	55	3.0257	ANALYSIS
15	710	703	-20	27	0.0543	0.2343	0.3671	R(1) 0.01925	0.01930	60	3.3315	AND
20	638	627	67	-56	0.1179	0.4999	0.4577	R(2) -0.04329	-0.04606	65	3.6682	MISCELLANEOUS
25	574	557	101	-83	0.1003	0.4155	0.3436	0.23327	0.22655	70	4.0389	RESULTS
30	561	494	4	63	0.0672	0.2718	0.2237	C(1)	7302	75	4.4471	(Females)
35	528	437	-148	238	0.0445	0.1757	0.1194	C(2)	-2236	80	4.8965	
40	412	384	-159	187	0.0165	0.0631	0.0365		-9826	85	5.3914	
45	374	335	55	-16	0.0027	0.0098	0.0052	2P/Y 26.9349	27.7344	90	5.9362	
50	276	287	284	-296	0.0002	0.0006	0.0003	DELTA 3.4950		95	6.5361	
55+	696	837								100	7.1967	

TABLE 1 — DATA

Age at last birthday	Population Both Sexes	Males Number	Males %	Females Number	Females %	Births by age of mother	Deaths Both Sexes	Deaths Males	Females	Age at last birthday
0	54600	27700	3.6	26900	3.3	0	3232	1788	1444	0
1-4	186100	93600	12.3	92500	11.5	0	1372	756	616	1-4
5-9	188400	94600	12.5	93800	11.7	0	283	144	139	5-9
10-14	165300	82700	10.9	82600	10.3	80	136	65	71	10-14
15-19	149500	75400	9.9	74100	9.2	9516	191	93	98	15-19
20-24	132200	66400	8.7	65800	8.2	18040	255	116	139	20-24
25-29	111300	53500	7.0	57800	7.2	14268	283	120	163	25-29
30-34	98900	44800	5.9	54100	6.7	9044	308	149	159	30-34
35-39	100300	45900	6.0	54400	6.8	5286	355	157	198	35-39
40-44	86300	40200	5.3	46100	5.7	1687	458	249	209	40-44
45-49	78300	37400	4.9	40900	5.1	242	597	343	254	45-49
50-54	66000	32100	4.2	33900	4.2	14	769	423	346	50-54
55-59	50700	24500	3.2	26200	3.3	0	655	390	265	55-59
60-64	34600	15900	2.1	18700	2.3	0	838	441	397	60-64
65-69	27200	11800	1.6	15400	1.9	0	732	394	308	65-69
70-74	16491	6391	0.8	10100	1.3		1042	520	522	70-74
75-79	10226	3826	0.5	6400	0.8		872	426	446	75-79
80-84	4304	1904	0.3	2400	0.3	29602 M.	883	365	518	80-84
85+	2879	679	0.1	2200	0.3	28575 F.	1439	514	925	85+
TOTAL	1563600	759300		804300		58177	14670	7453	7217	TOTAL

TABLE 2 — MALE LIFE TABLE

x	$_nq_x$	l_x	$_nd_x$	$_nL_x$	$_nm_x$	$_na_x$	T_x	r_x	$\dot{e}_x$	$_nM_x$	x
0	0.061453	100000	6145	96026	0.063996	0.3533	6107322	0.0124	61.073	0.064549	0
1	0.031376	93855	2945	367250	0.008018	1.2262	6011296	0.0124	64.049	0.008077	1
5	0.007362	90910	669	452876	0.001478	2.5000	5644045	0.0355	62.084	0.001522	5
10	0.003916	90241	353	450296	0.000785	2.4324	5191169	0.0216	57.526	0.000786	10
15	0.006170	89887	555	448138	0.001238	2.6603	4740873	0.0207	52.742	0.001233	15
20	0.008733	89333	780	444804	0.001754	2.6171	4292735	0.0326	48.053	0.001747	20
25	0.011216	88552	993	440418	0.002255	2.6396	3847931	0.0370	43.454	0.002243	25
30	0.016511	87559	1446	434280	0.003329	2.5677	3407513	0.0123	38.917	0.003326	30
35	0.016987	86114	1463	427150	0.003424	2.6632	2973233	0.0068	34.527	0.003420	35
40	0.030614	84651	2592	417239	0.006211	2.6791	2546083	0.0143	30.077	0.006194	40
45	0.044973	82059	3690	401576	0.009190	2.6371	2128844	0.0131	25.943	0.009171	45
50	0.064053	78369	5020	379709	0.013220	2.5824	1727268	0.0295	22.040	0.013178	50
55	0.077397	73349	5677	353346	0.016066	2.6396	1347559	0.0522	18.372	0.015918	55
60	0.130403	67672	8825	317029	0.027835	2.5827	994213	0.0264	14.692	0.027736	60
65	0.155991	58847	9180	272979	0.033628	2.6842	677185	0.0264	11.507	0.033390	65
70	0.341044	49668	16939	207039	0.081815	2.5619	404206	0.0264	8.138	0.081364	70
75	0.434046	32729	14209	127062	0.111828	2.4254	197167	0.0264	6.024	0.111343	75
80	0.640041	18520	11853	61394	0.193072	2.3674	70104	0.0264	3.785	0.191703	80
85+	*1.000000	6666	6666	8711	0.765319	1.3066	8711	0.0264	1.307	0.756996	85+

TABLE 3 — FEMALE LIFE TABLE

x	$_nq_x$	l_x	$_nd_x$	$_nL_x$	$_nm_x$	$_na_x$	T_x	r_x	$\dot{e}_x$	$_nM_x$	x
0	0.051480	100000	5148	96670	0.053253	0.3532	6468098	0.0114	64.681	0.053680	0
1	0.025985	94852	2465	372571	0.006616	1.2260	6371428	0.0114	67.172	0.006659	1
5	0.007213	92387	666	460270	0.001448	2.5000	5998857	0.0343	64.932	0.001482	5
10	0.004286	91721	393	457609	0.000859	2.4673	5538587	0.0225	60.385	0.000860	10
15	0.006620	91328	605	455245	0.001328	2.6942	5080978	0.0214	55.635	0.001323	15
20	0.010545	90723	957	451360	0.002120	2.6424	4625734	0.0227	50.987	0.002112	20
25	0.014018	89766	1258	445756	0.002823	2.5554	4174373	0.0169	46.503	0.002820	25
30	0.014592	88508	1292	439378	0.002940	2.5511	3728617	0.0030	42.127	0.002939	30
35	0.018060	87217	1575	432277	0.003644	2.5839	3289239	0.0123	37.713	0.003640	35
40	0.022487	85641	1926	423601	0.004546	2.6080	2856962	0.0239	33.360	0.004534	40
45	0.030744	83716	2574	412587	0.006238	2.6721	2433362	0.0240	29.067	0.006210	45
50	0.049941	81142	4052	395843	0.010237	2.5654	2020775	0.0354	24.904	0.010206	50
55	0.049889	77090	3846	376534	0.010214	2.6823	1624932	0.0467	21.078	0.010114	55
60	0.101271	73244	7417	348195	0.021303	2.5702	1248398	0.0318	17.044	0.021230	60
65	0.096390	65826	6345	314590	0.020169	2.7083	900202	0.0318	13.675	0.020000	65
70	0.231382	59481	13763	264549	0.052024	2.6126	585612	0.0318	9.845	0.051683	70
75	0.301546	45718	13786	195926	0.070364	2.6306	321063	0.0318	7.023	0.069688	75
80	0.701566	31932	22403	102768	0.217992	2.4604	125137	0.0318	3.919	0.215833	80
85+	*1.000000	9530	9530	22369	0.426022	2.3473	22369	0.0318	2.347	0.420455	85+

TABLE 4 — OBSERVED AND PROJECTED VITAL RATES

	Observed Population Both Sexes	Males	Females	Projected 1961 Males	Females	1966 Males	Females	1971 Males	Females	Stable Population Males	Females
RATES PER THOUSAND											
Birth	37.21	38.99	35.53	37.05	34.16	35.87	33.35	35.81	33.54	36.98	35.96
Death	9.38	9.82	8.97	9.53	8.42	9.49	8.53	9.60	8.70	9.16	8.14
Increase	27.82	29.17	26.55	27.53	25.73	26.38	24.82	26.20	24.85	27.8203	
PERCENTAGE											
under 15	38.01	39.33	36.78	40.70	38.27	41.58	39.32	41.33	39.29	41.35	40.81
15-64	58.08	57.43	58.68	56.02	57.23	54.73	55.85	54.59	55.47	55.28	54.94
65 and over	3.91	3.24	4.54	3.28	4.49	3.69	4.84	4.08	5.24	3.36	4.25
DEP. RATIO X 100	72.18	74.11	70.40	78.51	74.72	82.71	79.06	83.19	80.28	80.89	82.03

AGE AT LAST BIRTHDAY	1961 BOTH SEXES	1961 MALES	1961 FEMALES	1966 BOTH SEXES	1966 MALES	1966 FEMALES	1971 BOTH SEXES	1971 MALES	1971 FEMALES	AGE AT LAST BIRTHDAY	
0-4	285	144	141	313	158	155	352	178	174	0-4	
5-9	236	119	117	278	140	138	307	155	152	5-9	**TABLE 5**
10-14	187	94	93	234	118	116	277	140	137	10-14	POPULATION
15-19	164	82	82	187	94	93	233	117	116	15-19	PROJECTED
20-24	148	75	73	163	82	81	185	93	92	20-24	WITH
25-29	131	66	65	147	74	73	161	81	80	25-29	FIXED
30-34	110	53	57	129	65	64	145	73	72	30-34	AGE-
35-39	97	44	53	108	52	56	127	64	63	35-39	SPECIFIC
40-44	98	45	53	95	43	52	106	51	55	40-44	BIRTH
45-49	84	39	45	95	43	52	92	41	51	45-49	AND
50-54	74	35	39	80	37	43	91	41	50	50-54	DEATH
55-59	62	30	32	70	33	37	75	34	41	55-59	RATES
60-64	46	22	24	57	27	30	65	30	35	60-64	(IN 1000's)
65-69	31	14	17	41	19	22	50	23	27	65-69	
70-74	22	9	13	24	10	14	32	14	18	70-74	
75-79	11	4	7	15	5	10	17	6	11	75-79	
80-84	5	2	3	6	2	4	8	3	5	80-84	
85+	1	0	1	1	0	1	1	0	1	85+	
TOTAL	1792	877	915	2043	1002	1041	2324	1144	1180	TOTAL	

STANDARD COUNTRIES:	ENGLAND AND WALES 1961 BOTH SEXES	MALES	FEMALES	UNITED STATES 1960 BOTH SEXES	MALES	FEMALES	MEXICO 1960 BOTH SEXES	MALES	FEMALES	
STANDARDIZED RATES PER THOUSAND										**TABLE 6**
Birth	30.67	38.08*	29.20	31.31	34.71*	30.30	36.59	35.67*	35.85	STANDARDIZED
Death	17.57	20.62*	17.81	14.95	16.54*	13.73	8.91	9.50*	7.95	RATES
Increase	13.10	17.47*	11.38	16.36	18.17*	16.57	27.69	26.18*	27.90	

	OBSERVED POP. MALES	FEMALES	STATIONARY POP. MALES	FEMALES	STABLE POP. MALES	FEMALES	OBSERVED BIRTHS	NET MATERNITY FUNCTION	BIRTHS IN STABLE POP.	
μ	24.81958	26.36728	35.40899	36.95664	23.75365	24.37709	26.50330	27.17793	25.96302	**TABLE 7**
σ^2	365.4216	393.8005	473.0947	511.3109	349.6467	374.4613	42.65310	43.89586	39.24093	MOMENTS
κ_3	5024.216	5270.991	2287.375	2279.468	5541.839	6259.816	172.9825	162.1351	170.1025	AND
κ_4	-46634.	-57852.	-221185.	-270648.	-6681.	-5679.	-444.375	-550.783	-33.395	CUMULANTS
β_1	0.517314	0.454942	0.049412	0.038870	0.718488	0.746281	0.385614	0.310802	0.478854	
β_2	2.650767	2.626952	2.011767	1.964776	2.945349	2.959499	2.755742	2.714153	2.978312	
κ	-0.202743	-0.186587	-0.018488	-0.014145	-0.291238	-0.297557	-0.196738	-0.169963	-0.275952	

VITAL STATISTICS		AGE RANGE	THOMPSON NRR	1000r	INTERVAL	AGE RANGE	BOURGEOIS-PICHAT NRR	1000b	1000d	1000r	COALE		**TABLE 8**
GRR	2.352					5-29	1.83	29.87	7.51	22.36	IBR	31.00	RATES FROM AGE
NRR	2.094	0-4	1.91	24.47	27.31	30-54	1.68	30.33	11.04	19.30	IDR	9.22	DISTRIBUTIONS
TFR	4.788	5-9	1.66	18.93	27.24	55-79	2.78	74.92	37.05	37.87	IRI	21.78	AND VITAL
GENERATION	26.560	10-14	1.60	17.11	27.17	* 5-29	1.83	29.87	7.51	22.36	K1	31.97	STATISTICS
SEX RATIO	103.594	15-19	1.58	15.98	27.06						K2	0.56	(Females)

Start of Age Interval	ORIGINAL MATRIX SUB-DIAGONAL	ALTERNATIVE FIRST ROWS Projection	Integral	FIRST STABLE MATRIX % IN STABLE POPULATION	FISHER VALUES	REPRODUCTIVE VALUES	SECOND STABLE MATRIX Z₂ FIRST COLUMN	FIRST ROW	
0	0.98088	0.00000	0.00000	15.774	1.142	136310	0.1591+0.1218	0.1591+0.1218	
5	0.99422	0.00111	0.00000	13.457	1.338	125523	0.2039-0.1141	-0.0418+0.1666	**TABLE 9**
10	0.99483	0.14834	0.00239	11.636	1.546	127725	-0.0284-0.2749	-0.1436+0.0232	LESLIE
15	0.99147	0.46124	0.31730	10.068	1.617	119814	-0.3119-0.0980	-0.0898-0.1218	MATRIX
20	0.98758	0.59688	0.67740	8.682	1.344	88435	-0.2517+0.2919	-0.0093-0.1675	AND ITS
25	0.98569	0.47436	0.60992	7.457	0.875	50561	0.1977+0.4073	0.0316-0.1374	SPECTRAL
30	0.98384	0.30282	0.41305	6.393	0.471	25479	0.5301-0.0236	0.0417-0.0802	COMPONENTS
35	0.97993	0.15330	0.24008	5.470	0.199	10827	0.2203-0.5805	0.0281-0.0319	(Females)
40	0.97400	0.04881	0.09042	4.662	0.055	2532	-0.5194-0.5037	0.0098-0.0077	
45	0.95942	0.00728	0.01462	3.949	0.008	312	-0.7741+0.3213	0.0015-0.0010	
50	0.95122	0.00048	0.00102	3.296	0.000	16	-0.0132+0.9562	0.0001-0.0001	
55+	0.80736			9.155					

Start of Age Interval	OBSERVED POPUL. (IN 100's)	CONTRIBUTIONS OF ROOTS (IN 100's) r_1	r_2, r_3	r_4-r_{11}	AGE-SP. BIRTH RATES	NET MATERNITY FUNCTION	COEFF. OF MATRIX EQUATION	PARAMETERS	INTEGRAL	MATRIX	EXP. INCREASE x	$e^{(x+2\frac{1}{2})r}$	
0	1194	1168	42	-15	0.0000	0.0000	0.0000	L(1)	1.14924	1.14978	0	1.0720	**TABLE 10**
5	938	996	-32	-27	0.0000	0.0000	0.0011	L(2)	0.31604	0.33310	50	4.3084	AGE
10	826	861	-87	52	0.0005	0.0022	0.1447			0.80124	0.77209	55	4.9514	ANALYSIS
15	741	745	-37	33	0.0631	0.2872	0.4475	R(1)	0.02782	0.02791	60	5.6903	AND
20	658	643	87	-72	0.1347	0.6078	0.5741	R(2)	-0.02986	-0.03466	65	6.5396	MISCELLANEOUS
25	578	552	132	-106	0.1212	0.5405	0.4506			0.23902	-0.23270	70	7.5155	RESULTS
30	541	473	4	64	0.0821	0.3608	0.2835	C(1)		7403	75	8.6372	(Females)
35	544	405	-178	317	0.0477	0.2063	0.1412	C(2)		1033	80	9.9262	
40	461	345	-169	285	0.0180	0.0761	0.0441			-15751	85	11.4076	
45	409	292	85	31	0.0029	0.0120	0.0064	2P/Y	26.2874	27.0014	90	13.1101	
50	339	244	301	-206	0.0002	0.0008	0.0004	DELTA	5.7530		95	15.0666	
55+	814	678									100	17.3152	

TABLE 1 — DATA

AGE AT LAST BIRTHDAY	POPULATION BOTH SEXES	MALES Number	%	FEMALES Number	%	BIRTHS BY AGE OF MOTHER	DEATHS BOTH SEXES	MALES	FEMALES	AGE AT LAST BIRTHDAY
0	7638	3880	2.8	3758	2.5	0	431	247	184	0
1-4	37150	18714	13.5	18436	12.3	0	229	121	108	1-4
5-9	42423	21372	15.4	21051	14.1	0	24	10	14	5-9
10-14	35022	17614	12.7	17408	11.6	11	9	4	5	10-14
15-19	26648	13148	9.5	13500	9.0	652	22	15	7	15-19
20-24	19188	8229	5.9	10959	7.3	2365	28	16	12	20-24
25-29	18415	8476	6.1	9939	6.6	2881	33	14	19	25-29
30-34	17352	8180	5.9	9172	6.1	2324	45	19	26	30-34
35-39	16057	7700	5.5	8357	5.6	1573	63	26	37	35-39
40-44	14345	6928	5.0	7417	5.0	694	84	52	32	40-44
45-49	12957	6395	4.6	6562	4.4	70	133	67	66	45-49
50-54	11344	5497	4.0	5847	3.9	3	128	74	54	50-54
55-59	8915	4192	3.0	4723	3.2	0	146	83	63	55-59
60-64	6932	3085	2.2	3847	2.6	0	147	89	58	60-64
65-69	5076	2108	1.5	2968	2.0	0	143	73	70	65-69
70-74	3861	1585	1.1	2276	1.5		163	79	84	70-74
75-79	2695	1044	0.8	1651	1.1		143	72	71	75-79
80-84	1471	504	0.4	967	0.6	5299 M.	153	57	96	80-84
85+	950	246	0.2	704	0.5	5274 F.	165	50	115	85+
TOTAL	288439	138897		149542		10573	2289	1168	1121	TOTAL

TABLE 2 — MALE LIFE TABLE

x	nq_x	l_x	nd_x	nL_x	nm_x	na_x	T_x	r_x	$\mathring{e}_x$	nM_x	x
0	0.061062	100000	6106	95919	0.063660	0.3317	6309156	0.0000	63.092	0.063660	0
1	0.025402	93894	2385	368875	0.006466	1.1908	6213237	0.0000	66.173	0.006466	1
5	0.002215	91509	203	457037	0.000444	2.5000	5844362	0.0231	63.867	0.000468	5
10	0.001171	91306	107	456331	0.000234	3.1397	5387325	0.0481	59.003	0.000227	10
15	0.005823	91199	531	454829	0.001168	2.8030	4930994	0.0750	54.068	0.001141	15
20	0.009697	90668	879	451185	0.001949	2.5492	4476165	0.0422	49.369	0.001944	20
25	0.008225	89789	739	447129	0.001652	2.5425	4024980	0.0000	44.827	0.001652	25
30	0.011564	89050	1030	442832	0.002325	2.6502	3577850	0.0073	40.178	0.002323	30
35	0.016825	88021	1481	436852	0.003390	2.8052	3135018	0.0126	35.617	0.003377	35
40	0.036968	86540	3199	425280	0.007523	2.6813	2698166	0.0114	31.178	0.007506	40
45	0.051173	83340	4265	406452	0.010493	2.5966	2272886	0.0127	27.272	0.010477	45
50	0.065462	79076	5176	383012	0.013515	2.6111	1866434	0.0281	23.603	0.013462	50
55	0.095064	73899	7025	352739	0.019916	2.6148	1483421	0.0373	20.074	0.019800	55
60	0.135271	66874	9046	312222	0.028973	2.5516	1130682	0.0392	16.908	0.028849	60
65	0.160226	57828	9266	266348	0.034787	2.5401	818460	0.0392	14.153	0.034630	65
70	0.223037	48562	10831	216131	0.050114	2.5367	552112	0.0392	11.369	0.049842	70
75	0.296082	37731	11172	160941	0.069414	2.5192	335981	0.0392	8.905	0.068965	75
80	0.446551	26560	11860	103883	0.114170	2.5620	175040	0.0392	6.590	0.113096	80
85+	*1.000000	14699	14699	71157	0.206576	4.8408	71157	0.0392	4.841	0.203252	85+

TABLE 3 — FEMALE LIFE TABLE

x	nq_x	l_x	nd_x	nL_x	nm_x	na_x	T_x	r_x	$\mathring{e}_x$	nM_x	x
0	0.047451	100000	4745	96914	0.048962	0.3497	6821256	0.0000	68.213	0.048962	0
1	0.023057	95255	2196	374913	0.005858	1.2198	6724342	0.0000	70.593	0.005858	1
5	0.003213	93059	299	464545	0.000644	2.5000	6349429	0.0225	68.230	0.000665	5
10	0.001430	92760	133	463455	0.000286	2.4127	5884883	0.0440	63.442	0.000287	10
15	0.002628	92627	243	462604	0.000526	2.8215	5421429	0.0457	58.530	0.000519	15
20	0.005504	92384	508	460778	0.001104	2.7595	4958824	0.0295	53.677	0.001095	20
25	0.009545	91875	877	457345	0.001917	2.6844	4498046	0.0159	48.958	0.001912	25
30	0.014118	90998	1285	452006	0.002842	2.6768	4040701	0.0143	44.404	0.002835	30
35	0.021928	89713	1967	443774	0.004433	2.5634	3588695	0.0173	40.002	0.004427	35
40	0.021467	87746	1884	434492	0.004335	2.7494	3144921	0.0185	35.841	0.004314	40
45	0.049177	85863	4223	419133	0.010074	2.5892	2710430	0.0153	31.567	0.010058	45
50	0.045222	81640	3692	399143	0.009250	2.5466	2291296	0.0224	28.066	0.009236	50
55	0.064770	77948	5049	377459	0.013375	2.5673	1892154	0.0292	24.275	0.013339	55
60	0.073014	72899	5323	351719	0.015133	2.5993	1514695	0.0280	20.778	0.015077	60
65	0.112237	67577	7585	319934	0.023707	2.6335	1162976	0.0280	17.210	0.023585	65
70	0.169709	59992	10181	274964	0.037027	2.5448	843042	0.0280	14.053	0.036907	70
75	0.196255	49811	9776	225846	0.043285	2.6258	568078	0.0280	11.405	0.043004	75
80	0.401773	40035	16085	160910	0.099964	2.6836	342232	0.0280	8.548	0.099276	80
85+	1.000000	23950	23950	181323	0.132086	7.5708	181323	0.0280	7.571	0.163353	85+

TABLE 4 — OBSERVED AND PROJECTED VITAL RATES

RATES PER THOUSAND	OBSERVED POPULATION BOTH SEXES	MALES	FEMALES	PROJECTED POPULATION 1966 MALES	FEMALES	1971 MALES	FEMALES	1976 MALES	FEMALES	STABLE POPULATION MALES	FEMALES
Birth	36.66	38.15	35.27	37.28	34.70	38.08	35.68	39.28	37.03	39.00	37.73
Death	7.94	8.41	7.50	8.51	7.80	8.51	7.80	8.43	7.75	8.24	6.97
Increase	28.72	29.74	27.77	28.77	26.90	29.57	27.88	30.85	29.28		30.7621
PERCENTAGE											
under 15	42.38	44.34	40.56	43.49	40.42	42.23	39.88	42.57	40.76	43.07	42.32
15-64	52.75	51.71	53.71	52.44	53.65	53.56	54.15	53.09	53.26	53.64	53.32
65 and over	4.87	3.95	5.73	4.08	5.94	4.21	5.98	4.34	5.98	3.30	4.36
DEP. RATIO X 100	89.57	93.37	86.18	90.71	86.40	86.71	84.68	88.34	87.76	86.44	87.54

AGE AT LAST BIRTHDAY	BOTH SEXES	1966 MALES	FEMALES	BOTH SEXES	1971 MALES	FEMALES	BOTH SEXES	1976 MALES	FEMALES	AGE AT LAST BIRTHDAY	
0-4	52	26	26	61	30	31	72	36	36	0-4	
5-9	44	22	22	52	26	26	60	30	30	5-9	
10-14	42	21	21	44	22	22	52	26	26	10-14	
15-19	35	18	17	42	21	21	44	22	22	15-19	**TABLE 5**
20-24	26	13	13	34	17	17	42	21	21	20-24	POPULATION
25-29	19	8	11	26	13	13	34	17	17	25-29	PROJECTED
30-34	18	8	10	19	8	11	26	13	13	30-34	WITH
35-39	17	8	9	18	8	10	19	8	11	35-39	FIXED
40-44	15	7	8	17	8	9	17	8	9	40-44	AGE—
45-49	14	7	7	15	7	8	17	8	9	45-49	SPECIFIC
50-54	12	6	6	13	6	7	15	7	8	50-54	BIRTH
55-59	11	5	6	12	6	6	12	6	6	55-59	AND
60-64	8	4	4	9	4	5	11	5	6	60-64	DEATH
65-69	6	3	3	7	3	4	9	4	5	65-69	RATES
70-74	5	2	3	5	2	3	6	3	3	70-74	(IN 1000's)
75-79	3	1	2	3	1	2	4	2	2	75-79	
80-84	2	1	1	2	1	1	2	1	1	80-84	
85+	1	0	1	1	0	1	3	1	2	85+	
TOTAL	330	160	170	380	183	197	445	218	227	TOTAL	

STANDARD COUNTRIES:	ENGLAND AND WALES 1961			UNITED STATES 1960			MEXICO 1960			
STANDARDIZED RATES PER THOUSAND	BOTH SEXES	MALES	FEMALES	BOTH SEXES	MALES	FEMALES	BOTH SEXES	MALES	FEMALES	**TABLE 6**
Birth	35.45	43.27*	34.28	36.03	40.39*	35.41	37.78	39.40*	37.60	STANDAR-
Death	12.53	16.14*	12.16	10.82	13.51*	9.78	7.10	8.30*	6.22	DIZED
Increase	22.93	27.13*	22.12	25.21	26.88*	25.63	30.68	31.10*	31.37	RATES

	OBSERVED POP. MALES	FEMALES	STATIONARY POP. MALES	FEMALES	STABLE POP. MALES	FEMALES	OBSERVED BIRTHS	NET MATERNITY FUNCTION	BIRTHS IN STABLE POP.	
μ	24.21467	25.95172	36.40275	38.70439	23.00835	23.78431	29.46018	30.28557	28.89039	**TABLE 7**
σ^2	390.7671	430.1770	510.7605	571.9162	345.2092	378.1804	44.03416	44.50320	41.86015	MOMENTS
κ_3	6516.596	7354.211	3177.567	3310.187	6122.131	7259.471	83.3149	67.4872	102.0259	AND
κ_4	-29971.	-36671.	-237264.	-322292.	33386.	49033.	-1179.085	-1333.091	-882.326	CUMULANTS
β_1	0.711685	0.679408	0.075777	0.058574	0.911084	0.974345	0.081297	0.051674	0.141912	
β_2	2.803723	2.801833	2.090510	2.014664	3.280155	3.342838	2.391913	2.326904	2.496468	
κ	-0.261128	-0.256126	-0.029491	-0.021764	-0.398002	-0.419216	-0.043405	-0.026679	-0.078249	

VITAL STATISTICS			THOMPSON			BOURGEOIS-PICHAT					COALE	
		AGE RANGE	NRR	1000r	INTERVAL	AGE RANGE	NRR	1000b	1000d	1000r		**TABLE 8**
GRR	2.746										IBR	RATES FROM AGE DISTRI-
NRR	2.484	0-4	2.15	27.99	27.33	5-29	2.83	39.81	1.28	38.53	IDR	BUTIONS
TFR	5.505	5-9	2.31	31.34	27.23	30-54	1.57	23.39	6.66	16.73	IRI	AND VITAL
GENERATION	29.581	10-14	2.07	26.26	27.12	55-79	2.13	42.02	13.94	28.09	K1	STATISTICS
SEX RATIO	100.474	15-19	1.75	16.22	26.98	*20-44	1.55	22.83	6.70	16.13	K2	(Females)

Start of Age Interval	ORIGINAL MATRIX SUB-DIAGONAL	ALTERNATIVE FIRST ROWS Projection	Integral	FIRST STABLE MATRIX % IN STABLE POPULATION	FISHER VALUES	REPRODUCTIVE VALUES	SECOND STABLE MATRIX Z₂ FIRST COLUMN	FIRST ROW	
0	0.98457	0.00000	0.00000	16.523	1.144	25383	0.1391+0.0725	0.1391+0.0725	**TABLE 9**
5	0.99765	0.00074	0.00000	13.942	1.355	28533	0.1402-0.0867	0.0084+0.1491	LESLIE
10	0.99817	0.05747	0.00161	11.920	1.584	27583	-0.0030-0.1754	-0.1165+0.0783	MATRIX
15	0.99605	0.30979	0.12275	10.197	1.786	24117	-0.1622-0.0927	-0.1271-0.0606	AND ITS
20	0.99255	0.59252	0.54851	8.704	1.737	19037	-0.1728+0.0977	-0.0554-0.1545	SPECTRAL
25	0.98833	0.63580	0.73676	7.404	1.359	13512	-0.0046+0.2101	0.0156-0.1629	COMPO-
30	0.98179	0.51564	0.64402	6.271	0.869	7973	0.1880+0.1174	0.0508-0.1129	NENTS
35	0.97908	0.32931	0.47841	5.276	0.433	3615	0.2063-0.1064	0.0444-0.0515	(Females)
40	0.96465	0.12222	0.23782	4.427	0.131	970	0.0147-0.2420	0.0173-0.0131	
45	0.95230	0.01313	0.02711	3.660	0.013	88	-0.2064-0.1403	0.0019-0.0013	
50	0.94567	0.00060	0.00130	2.987	0.001	3	-0.2297+0.1073	0.0001-0.0001	
55+	0.84181			8.689					

Start of Age Interval	OBSERVED POPUL. (IN 100's)	CONTRIBUTIONS OF ROOTS (IN 100's) r_1	r_2, r_3	r_4-r_{11}	AGE-SP. BIRTH RATES	NET MATERNITY FUNCTION	COEFF. OF MATRIX EQUATION	PARAMETERS	INTEGRAL	MATRIX	EXP. INCREASE x	$e^{(x+2\frac{1}{2})r}$	
0	222	230	1	-9	0.0000	0.0000	0.0000	L(1)	1.16627	1.16687	0	1.0799	**TABLE 10**
5	211	194	8	9	0.0000	0.0000	0.0007	L(2)	0.47814	0.47916	50	5.0279	AGE
10	174	166	8	1	0.0003	0.0015	0.0565		0.82711	0.80558	55	5.8639	ANALYSIS
15	135	142	-1	-6	0.0241	0.1114	0.3037	R(1)	0.03076	0.03087	60	6.8389	AND
20	110	121	-9	-2	0.1076	0.4960	0.5786	R(2)	-0.00913	-0.01295	65	7.9760	MISCEL-
25	99	103	-9	6	0.1446	0.6613	0.6163			0.20933	0.20684	70	9.3022	LANEOUS
30	92	87	0	4	0.1264	0.5713	0.4940	C(1)		1391	75	10.8489	RESULTS
35	84	73	11	-1	0.0939	0.4167	0.3097	C(2)		1465	80	12.6527	(Females)
40	74	62	11	2	0.0467	0.2028	0.1125			2188	85	14.7565	
45	66	51	0	15	0.0053	0.0223	0.0117	2P/Y	30.0159	30.3767	90	17.2100	
50	58	42	-11	28	0.0003	0.0010	0.0005	DELTA	5.3574		95	20.0716	
55+	171	121									100	23.4088	

TABLE 1 — DATA

AGE AT LAST BIRTHDAY	POPULATION BOTH SEXES	MALES Number	%	FEMALES Number	%	BIRTHS BY AGE OF MOTHER	DEATHS BOTH SEXES	MALES	FEMALES	AGE AT LAST BIRTHDAY
0	10474	5403	3.6	5071	3.2	0	396	227	169	0
1-4	40365	20668	13.9	19697	12.4	0	196	100	96	1-4
5-9	40584	20501	13.8	20083	12.7	0	28	18	10	5-9
10-14	38323	19118	12.8	19205	12.1	11	27	19	8	10-14
15-19	30327	15082	10.1	15245	9.6	658	20	11	9	15-19
20-24	20846	9393	6.3	11453	7.2	2096	33	23	10	20-24
25-29	19675	9091	6.1	10584	6.7	2777	39	16	23	25-29
30-34	17319	8025	5.4	9294	5.9	2284	49	22	27	30-34
35-39	16971	8113	5.4	8858	5.6	1622	89	42	47	35-39
40-44	15135	7194	4.8	7941	5.0	690	80	38	42	40-44
45-49	13097	6586	4.4	6511	4.1	78	126	65	61	45-49
50-54	12115	5848	3.9	6267	3.9	1	153	95	58	50-54
55-59	9860	4683	3.1	5177	3.3	0	159	79	80	55-59
60-64	7384	3353	2.2	4031	2.5	0	194	119	75	60-64
65-69	5717	2419	1.6	3298	2.1	0	187	115	72	65-69
70-74	4455	1904	1.3	2551	1.6		181	95	86	70-74
75-79	2878	1064	0.7	1814	1.1		213	102	111	75-79
80-84	1582	484	0.3	1098	0.7	5130 M.	164	54	110	80-84
85+	642	154	0.1	488	0.3	5087 F.	180	59	121	85+
TOTAL	307749	149083		158666		10217	2514	1299	1215	TOTAL

TABLE 2 — MALE LIFE TABLE

x	$_nq_x$	l_x	$_nd_x$	$_nL_x$	$_nm_x$	$_na_x$	T_x	r_x	$\dot{e}_x$	$_nM_x$	x
0	0.040843	100000	4084	97330	0.041964	0.3463	6314989	0.0017	63.150	0.042014	0
1	0.019077	95916	1830	378565	0.004833	1.2139	6217659	0.0017	64.824	0.004838	1
5	0.004287	94086	403	469421	0.000859	2.5000	5839094	0.0292	62.061	0.000878	5
10	0.004953	93683	464	467241	0.000993	2.4757	5369673	0.0298	57.318	0.000994	10
15	0.003746	93218	349	465359	0.000750	2.9003	4902432	0.0699	52.591	0.000729	15
20	0.012223	92869	1135	461603	0.002459	2.5835	4437072	0.0487	47.778	0.002449	20
25	0.008766	91734	804	456683	0.001761	2.5275	3975469	0.0136	43.337	0.001760	25
30	0.013652	90930	1241	451857	0.002747	2.7501	3518787	0.0083	38.698	0.002741	30
35	0.025583	89689	2294	442925	0.005180	2.5948	3066930	0.0064	34.195	0.005177	35
40	0.026157	87394	2286	431635	0.005296	2.6660	2624005	0.0146	30.025	0.005282	40
45	0.048366	85108	4116	416095	0.009893	2.7052	2192370	0.0104	25.760	0.009869	45
50	0.078273	80992	6340	389524	0.016275	2.5652	1776275	0.0194	21.932	0.016245	50
55	0.081731	74652	6101	359036	0.016994	2.6685	1386751	0.0347	18.576	0.016870	55
60	0.164459	68551	11274	315837	0.035695	2.6124	1027715	0.0317	14.992	0.035491	60
65	0.212704	57277	12183	255674	0.047651	2.4792	711878	0.0317	12.429	0.047540	65
70	0.223028	45094	10057	200621	0.050131	2.5292	456203	0.0317	10.117	0.049895	70
75	0.387960	35037	13593	141061	0.096362	2.4896	255582	0.0317	7.295	0.095865	75
80	0.437490	21444	9382	83447	0.112425	2.4660	114521	0.0317	5.341	0.111571	80
85+	*1.000000	12062	12062	31074	0.388178	2.5761	31074	0.0317	2.576	0.383117	85+

TABLE 3 — FEMALE LIFE TABLE

x	$_nq_x$	l_x	$_nd_x$	$_nL_x$	$_nm_x$	$_na_x$	T_x	r_x	$\dot{e}_x$	$_nM_x$	x
0	0.032634	100000	3263	97947	0.033318	0.3710	6789424	0.0004	67.894	0.033327	0
1	0.019235	96737	1861	381849	0.004873	1.2608	6691477	0.0004	69.172	0.004874	1
5	0.002397	94876	227	473811	0.000480	2.5000	6309628	0.0240	66.504	0.000498	5
10	0.002084	94648	197	472760	0.000417	2.5564	5835817	0.0271	61.658	0.000417	10
15	0.002973	94451	281	471600	0.000595	2.6622	5363057	0.0511	56.781	0.000590	15
20	0.004415	94170	416	469966	0.000885	2.8693	4891457	0.0354	51.943	0.000873	20
25	0.010851	93755	1017	466423	0.002181	2.6898	4421491	0.0189	47.160	0.002173	25
30	0.014476	92737	1342	460618	0.002914	2.7140	3955068	0.0145	42.648	0.002905	30
35	0.026222	91395	2397	451190	0.005312	2.5861	3494450	0.0110	38.235	0.005306	35
40	0.026217	88998	2333	439488	0.005309	2.6409	3043260	0.0245	34.195	0.005289	40
45	0.045866	86665	3975	423683	0.009382	2.5742	2603773	0.0154	30.044	0.009369	45
50	0.045341	82690	3749	404479	0.009269	2.6071	2180089	0.0122	26.365	0.009255	50
55	0.074770	78941	5902	380523	0.015511	2.5974	1775610	0.0294	22.493	0.015453	55
60	0.089108	73038	6508	349134	0.018641	2.5326	1395087	0.0268	19.101	0.018606	60
65	0.104047	66530	6922	315939	0.021910	2.5858	1045953	0.0268	15.721	0.021831	65
70	0.157020	59608	9360	276002	0.033911	2.6455	730014	0.0268	12.247	0.033712	70
75	0.267894	50248	13461	218757	0.061535	2.5869	454012	0.0268	9.035	0.061191	75
80	0.406991	36787	14972	148245	0.100995	2.6162	235254	0.0268	6.395	0.100182	80
85+	*1.000000	21815	21815	87009	0.250722	3.9885	87009	0.0268	3.988	0.247951	85+

TABLE 4 — OBSERVED AND PROJECTED VITAL RATES

	OBSERVED POPULATION BOTH SEXES	MALES	FEMALES	PROJECTED POPULATION 1968 MALES	FEMALES	1973 MALES	FEMALES	1978 MALES	FEMALES	STABLE POPULATION MALES	FEMALES
RATES PER THOUSAND											
Birth	33.20	34.41	32.06	34.55	32.40	35.81	33.77	36.77	34.85	36.19	35.09
Death	8.17	8.71	7.66	8.50	7.61	8.48	7.54	8.35	7.46	7.89	6.80
Increase	25.03	25.70	24.40	26.06	24.79	27.33	26.23	28.42	27.39		28.2939
PERCENTAGE											
under 15	42.16	44.06	40.37	42.59	39.36	42.22	39.57	41.17	39.40	41.67	40.80
15-64	52.88	51.90	53.80	53.43	54.83	53.74	54.61	54.77	54.80	55.07	54.70
65 and over	4.96	4.04	5.83	3.98	5.81	4.04	5.82	4.05	5.80	3.26	4.51
DEP. RATIO X 100	89.12	92.69	85.88	87.17	82.38	86.07	83.11	82.57	82.48	81.58	82.82

AGE AT LAST BIRTHDAY	BOTH SEXES	1968 MALES	FEMALES	BOTH SEXES	1973 MALES	FEMALES	BOTH SEXES	1978 MALES	FEMALES	AGE AT LAST BIRTHDAY	
0-4	52	26	26	60	30	30	72	36	36	0-4	**TABLE 5**
5-9	50	26	24	52	26	26	60	30	30	5-9	
10-14	40	20	20	50	26	24	52	26	26	10-14	
15-19	38	19	19	40	20	20	49	25	24	15-19	POPULATION
20-24	30	15	15	38	19	19	40	20	20	20-24	PROJECTED
25-29	20	9	11	30	15	15	38	19	19	25-29	WITH
30-34	19	9	10	20	9	11	30	15	15	30-34	FIXED
35-39	17	8	9	19	9	10	20	9	11	35-39	AGE—
40-44	17	8	9	17	8	9	19	9	10	40-44	SPECIFIC
45-49	15	7	8	16	8	8	16	7	9	45-49	BIRTH
50-54	12	6	6	13	6	7	15	7	8	50-54	AND
55-59	11	5	6	12	6	6	13	6	7	55-59	DEATH
60-64	9	4	5	10	5	5	10	5	5	60-64	RATES
65-69	7	3	4	7	3	4	9	4	5	65-69	(IN 1000's)
70-74	5	2	3	5	2	3	7	3	4	70-74	
75-79	3	1	2	3	1	2	4	1	3	75-79	
80-84	2	1	1	2	1	1	3	1	2	80-84	
85+	1	0	1	1	0	1	1	0	1	85+	
TOTAL	348	169	179	395	194	201	458	223	235	TOTAL	

STANDARD COUNTRIES:	ENGLAND AND WALES 1961			UNITED STATES 1960			MEXICO 1960			
STANDARDIZED RATES PER THOUSAND	BOTH SEXES	MALES	FEMALES	BOTH SEXES	MALES	FEMALES	BOTH SEXES	MALES	FEMALES	**TABLE 6**
Birth	32.81	39.53*	31.66	33.36	36.53*	32.72	34.55	36.33*	34.31	STANDAR-DIZED RATES
Death	13.90	16.55*	13.33	11.77	13.71*	10.41	6.94	8.16*	5.98	
Increase	18.90	22.98*	18.32	21.59	22.82*	22.31	27.61	28.17*	28.34	

	OBSERVED POP. MALES	FEMALES	STATIONARY POP. MALES	FEMALES	STABLE POP. MALES	FEMALES	OBSERVED BIRTHS	NET MATERNITY FUNCTION	BIRTHS IN STABLE POP.	
μ	24.07646	25.89661	35.50461	37.71656	23.56955	24.42721	29.68753	30.55550	29.27300	**TABLE 7**
σ^2	392.3249	430.8193	482.8907	540.2038	347.1225	381.1825	44.71697	44.12009	42.21676	MOMENTS
κ_3	6535.870	7283.423	2798.653	2946.569	5697.081	6771.299	65.9527	50.4403	82.6272	AND
κ_4	-35009.	-44200.	-214530.	-288829.	8193.	16871.	-1276.632	-1278.072	-967.447	CUMULANTS
β_1	0.707407	0.663416	0.069559	0.055076	0.775991	0.827838	0.048646	0.029624	0.090738	
β_2	2.772549	2.761861	2.079994	2.010251	3.067999	3.116113	2.361559	2.343428	2.457178	
κ	-0.254985	-0.246474	-0.027005	-0.020462	-0.327710	-0.344535	-0.026419	-0.016244	-0.052061	

VITAL STATISTICS		THOMPSON AGE RANGE	NRR	1000r	INTERVAL	BOURGEOIS-PICHAT AGE RANGE	NRR	1000b	1000d	1000r	COALE	
GRR	2.532										IBR	**TABLE 8**
NRR	2.331	0-4	2.25	29.66	27.31	5-29	2.59	36.71	1.50	35.21	IDR	RATES FROM AGE DISTRI-BUTIONS
TFR	5.085	5-9	2.10	27.85	27.20	30-54	1.52	21.44	5.98	15.46	IRI	AND VITAL STATISTICS
GENERATION	29.910	10-14	2.17	28.01	27.09	55-79	1.98	36.01	10.79	25.21	K1	(Females)
SEX RATIO	100.845	15-19	1.88	23.39	26.96	*50-74	2.02	37.88	11.92	25.96	K2	

Start of Age Interval	ORIGINAL MATRIX SUB-DIAGONAL	ALTERNATIVE FIRST ROWS Projection	Integral	FIRST STABLE MATRIX % IN STABLE POPULATION	FISHER VALUES	REPRODUCTIVE VALUES	SECOND STABLE MATRIX Z₂ FIRST COLUMN	FIRST ROW	
0	0.98752	0.00000	0.00000	15.720	1.118	27689	0.1381+0.0650	0.1381+0.0650	**TABLE 9**
5	0.99778	0.00068	0.00000	13.470	1.305	26201	0.1345-0.0878	0.0163+0.1442	
10	0.99755	0.05211	0.00147	11.662	1.506	28925	-0.0044-0.1706	-0.1076+0.0843	LESLIE
15	0.99654	0.26939	0.11067	10.094	1.682	25637	-0.1568-0.0912	-0.1278-0.0479	MATRIX
20	0.99246	0.52963	0.46923	8.729	1.643	18812	-0.1697+0.0909	-0.0621-0.1438	AND ITS
25	0.98755	0.60328	0.67273	7.517	1.311	13873	-0.0124+0.2031	0.0112-0.1561	SPECTRAL
30	0.97953	0.50777	0.63010	6.441	0.847	7869	0.1750+0.1232	0.0475-0.1085	COMPO-NENTS
35	0.97406	0.31981	0.46949	5.475	0.417	3691	0.2053-0.0879	0.0408-0.0495	(Females)
40	0.96404	0.11758	0.22279	4.627	0.126	1000	0.0341-0.2291	0.0159-0.0129	
45	0.95467	0.01449	0.03072	3.871	0.014	93	-0.1819-0.1533	0.0020-0.0013	
50	0.94077	0.00019	0.00041	3.206	0.000	1	-0.2298+0.0756	0.0000-0.0000	
55+	0.82415			9.188					

Start of Age Interval	OBSERVED POPUL. (IN 100's)	CONTRIBUTIONS OF ROOTS (IN 100's) r_1	r_2, r_3	$r_4 \cdot r_{11}$	AGE-SP. BIRTH RATES	NET MATERNITY FUNCTION	COEFF. OF MATRIX EQUATION	PARAMETERS INTEGRAL	MATRIX	EXP. INCREASE x	$e^{(x+\frac{5}{2})r}$	
0	248	236	2	10	0.0000	0.0000	0.0000	L(1) 1.15197	1.15246	0	1.0733	**TABLE 10**
5	201	203	11	-12	0.0000	0.0000	0.0007	L(2) 0.49298	0.49275	50	4.4169	
10	192	175	10	7	0.0003	0.0013	0.0513	0.81937	0.79915	55	5.0881	AGE
15	152	152	-1	2	0.0215	0.1013	0.2648	R(1) 0.02829	0.02838	60	5.8613	ANALYSIS
20	115	131	-12	-5	0.0911	0.4282	0.5188	R(2) -0.00895	-0.01262	65	6.7520	AND
25	106	113	-12	5	0.1306	0.6093	0.5865	0.20583	0.20365	70	7.7781	MISCEL-LANEOUS
30	93	97	-0	-4	0.1224	0.5636	0.4875	C(1)	1504	75	8.9601	RESULTS
35	89	82	13	-7	0.0912	0.4114	0.3007	C(2)	2002	80	10.3217	(Females)
40	79	70	15	-5	0.0433	0.1901	0.1077		2944	85	11.8902	
45	65	58	2	5	0.0060	0.0253	0.0128	2P/Y 30.5258	30.8526	90	13.6971	
50	63	48	-14	28	0.0001	0.0003	0.0002	DELTA 4.4065		95	15.7786	
55+	185	138								100	18.1764	

118   Mexico 1959–61

TABLE 1 — DATA

AGE AT LAST BIRTHDAY	POPULATION BOTH SEXES	MALES Number	%	FEMALES Number	%	BIRTHS BY AGE OF MOTHER	DEATHS BOTH SEXES	MALES	FEMALES	AGE AT LAST BIRTHDAY
0	1156283	592447	3.4	563836	3.2	0	117937	64716	53221	0
1-4	4667265	2369673	13.6	2297592	13.1	0	66022	32730	33292	1-4
5-9	5343878	2721158	15.6	2622720	14.9	0	14157	7285	6872	5-9
10-14	4379517	2245726	12.9	2133791	12.2	1465	6258	3488	2770	10-14
15-19	3552962	1749121	10.0	1803841	10.3	189086	7727	4308	3419	15-19
20-24	2961491	1413552	8.1	1547939	8.8	463709	10094	5455	4639	20-24
25-29	2516666	1202742	6.9	1313924	7.5	417450	10572	5865	4707	25-29
30-34	2063003	1014869	5.8	1048134	6.0	282044	10102	5667	4435	30-34
35-39	1927193	962313	5.5	964880	5.5	193272	12072	6890	5182	35-39
40-44	1370581	678762	3.9	691819	3.9	67903	9848	5633	4215	40-44
45-49	1239104	613088	3.5	626016	3.6	0	11512	6648	4864	45-49
50-54	1067747	529654	3.0	538093	3.1	0	12223	6969	5254	50-54
55-59	804810	407779	2.3	397031	2.3	0	13667	7776	5891	55-59
60-64	746238	372857	2.1	373381	2.1	0	16173	8662	7511	60-64
65-69	417420	205085	1.2	212335	1.2	0	14226	7404	6822	65-69
70-74	375805	182586	1.0	193219	1.1		17604	8786	8818	70-74
75-79	236669	112898	0.6	123771	0.7		15650	7599	8051	75-79
80-84	124054	57843	0.3	66211	0.4	828503 M.	13578	6097	7481	80-84
85+	46317	20996	0.1	25321	0.1	786426 F.	16688	6931	9757	85+
TOTAL	34997003	17453149		17543854		1614929	396110	208909	187201	TOTAL

TABLE 2 — MALE LIFE TABLE

x	nq_x	l_x	nd_x	nL_x	nm_x	na_x	T_x	r_x	$\dot{e}_x$	nM_x	x
0	0.102003	100000	10200	93379	0.109235	0.3510	5564010	0.0000	55.640	0.109235	0
1	0.053207	89800	4778	345925	0.013812	1.2219	5470631	0.0000	60.920	0.013812	1
5	0.013058	85022	1110	422333	0.002629	2.5000	5124706	0.0227	60.275	0.002677	5
10	0.007728	83912	648	417919	0.001552	2.4737	4702372	0.0422	56.040	0.001553	10
15	0.012349	83263	1028	413938	0.002484	2.6886	4284453	0.0437	51.457	0.002463	15
20	0.019203	82235	1579	407418	0.003876	2.6213	3870515	0.0337	47.067	0.003859	20
25	0.024145	80656	1947	398533	0.004887	2.5633	3463097	0.0283	42.937	0.004876	25
30	0.027584	78708	2171	388270	0.005592	2.5722	3064564	0.0165	38.936	0.005584	30
35	0.035277	76537	2700	376111	0.007179	2.5650	2676294	0.0332	34.967	0.007160	35
40	0.040807	73837	3013	361871	0.008326	2.5723	2300183	0.0365	31.152	0.008299	40
45	0.052894	70824	3746	345021	0.010858	2.5711	1938312	0.0141	27.368	0.010843	45
50	0.063980	67078	4292	325074	0.013202	2.5964	1593291	0.0268	23.753	0.013158	50
55	0.091290	62786	5732	300022	0.019104	2.5732	1268217	0.0166	20.199	0.019069	55
60	0.110528	57055	6306	270076	0.023349	2.5902	968195	0.0357	16.970	0.023231	60
65	0.166726	50748	8461	233178	0.036286	2.5695	698119	0.0357	13.756	0.036102	65
70	0.215877	42287	9129	188854	0.048338	2.5262	464942	0.0357	10.995	0.048120	70
75	0.289776	33158	9609	141948	0.067690	2.5184	276088	0.0357	8.326	0.067309	75
80	0.423709	23550	9978	93630	0.106572	2.5827	134140	0.0357	5.696	0.105405	80
85+	*1.000000	13572	13572	40510	0.335015	2.9849	40510	0.0357	2.985	0.330110	85+

TABLE 3 — FEMALE LIFE TABLE

x	nq_x	l_x	nd_x	nL_x	nm_x	na_x	T_x	r_x	$\dot{e}_x$	nM_x	x
0	0.089101	100000	8910	94395	0.094391	0.3710	5861297	0.0000	58.613	0.094391	0
1	0.055747	91090	5078	350449	0.014490	1.2607	5766902	0.0000	63.310	0.014490	1
5	0.012739	86012	1096	427320	0.002564	2.5000	5416453	0.0243	62.973	0.002620	5
10	0.006444	84916	547	423151	0.001293	2.3876	4989132	0.0357	58.754	0.001298	10
15	0.009489	84369	801	419990	0.001906	2.6822	4565981	0.0301	54.119	0.001895	15
20	0.014928	83568	1248	414862	0.003007	2.6110	4145991	0.0288	49.612	0.002997	20
25	0.017802	82321	1465	408035	0.003591	2.5639	3731129	0.0354	45.324	0.003582	25
30	0.020990	80856	1697	400168	0.004241	2.5783	3323094	0.0265	41.099	0.004231	30
35	0.026575	79158	2104	390662	0.005385	2.5617	2922927	0.0363	36.925	0.005371	35
40	0.030107	77055	2320	379630	0.006111	2.5674	2532265	0.0370	32.863	0.006093	40
45	0.038197	74735	2855	366772	0.007783	2.5823	2152634	0.0173	28.804	0.007770	45
50	0.047955	71880	3447	351214	0.009815	2.6247	1785862	0.0351	24.845	0.009764	50
55	0.071868	68433	4918	330428	0.014884	2.6134	1434648	0.0218	20.964	0.014838	55
60	0.096414	63515	6124	303031	0.020208	2.6250	1104220	0.0270	17.385	0.020116	60
65	0.149723	57391	8593	266292	0.032268	2.5952	801188	0.0270	13.960	0.032128	65
70	0.205934	48799	10049	219353	0.045813	2.5481	534896	0.0270	10.961	0.045637	70
75	0.281657	38749	10914	166957	0.065370	2.5454	315543	0.0270	8.143	0.065048	75
80	0.446456	27835	12427	109044	0.113965	2.5753	148587	0.0270	5.338	0.112988	80
85+	*1.000000	15408	15408	39542	0.389662	2.5663	39542	0.0270	2.566	0.385332	85+

TABLE 4 — OBSERVED AND PROJECTED VITAL RATES

	OBSERVED POPULATION BOTH SEXES	MALES	FEMALES	PROJECTED POPULATION 1965 MALES	FEMALES	1970 MALES	FEMALES	1975 MALES	FEMALES	STABLE POPULATION MALES	FEMALES
RATES PER THOUSAND											
Birth	46.14	47.47	44.83	46.72	44.34	46.25	44.07	45.74	43.73	45.40	44.14
Death	11.32	11.97	10.67	12.52	11.06	12.40	10.99	12.23	10.88	12.45	11.19
Increase	34.83	35.50	34.16	34.20	33.28	33.85	33.08	33.51	32.85		32.9511
PERCENTAGE											
under 15	44.42	45.43	43.42	45.82	44.14	45.84	44.27	46.97	45.46	45.94	45.21
15-64	52.15	51.25	53.04	50.68	52.22	50.79	52.25	49.73	51.06	51.24	51.64
65 and over	3.43	3.32	3.54	3.50	3.65	3.37	3.48	3.30	3.48	2.82	3.15
DEP. RATIO X 100	91.77	95.12	88.54	97.32	91.51	96.88	91.39	101.10	95.85	95.16	93.65

TABLE 5 — POPULATION PROJECTED WITH FIXED AGE-SPECIFIC BIRTH AND DEATH RATES (IN 1000's)

AGE AT LAST BIRTHDAY	1965 BOTH SEXES	1965 MALES	1965 FEMALES	1970 BOTH SEXES	1970 MALES	1970 FEMALES	1975 BOTH SEXES	1975 MALES	1975 FEMALES	AGE AT LAST BIRTHDAY
0-4	7735	3944	3791	9043	4611	4432	10571	5390	5181	0-4
5-9	5597	2848	2749	7434	3792	3642	8691	4433	4258	5-9
10-14	5290	2693	2597	5540	2818	2722	7358	3752	3606	10-14
15-19	4342	2224	2118	5245	2667	2578	5493	2791	2702	15-19
20-24	3504	1722	1782	4281	2189	2092	5171	2625	2546	20-24
25-29	2905	1383	1522	3436	1684	1752	4200	2142	2058	25-29
30-34	2461	1172	1289	2840	1347	1493	3360	1641	1719	30-34
35-39	2006	983	1023	2393	1135	1258	2763	1305	1458	35-39
40-44	1864	926	938	1940	946	994	2314	1092	1222	40-44
45-49	1315	647	668	1789	883	906	1863	902	961	45-49
50-54	1177	578	599	1250	610	640	1699	832	867	50-54
55-59	995	489	506	1097	533	564	1165	563	602	55-59
60-64	731	367	364	904	440	464	997	480	517	60-64
65-69	650	322	328	637	317	320	788	380	408	65-69
70-74	341	166	175	531	261	270	521	257	264	70-74
75-79	284	137	147	258	125	133	402	196	206	75-79
80-84	155	74	81	187	91	96	169	82	87	80-84
85+	49	25	24	61	32	29	74	39	35	85+
TOTAL	41401	20700	20701	48866	24481	24385	57599	28902	28697	TOTAL

TABLE 6 — STANDARDIZED RATES

STANDARD COUNTRIES: STANDARDIZED RATES PER THOUSAND	ENGLAND AND WALES 1961 BOTH SEXES	MALES	FEMALES	UNITED STATES 1960 BOTH SEXES	MALES	FEMALES	MEXICO 1960 BOTH SEXES	MALES	FEMALES
Birth	41.53	49.22*	39.19	42.33	44.92*	40.62	46.14	47.47*	44.83
Death	16.82	25.49*	17.98	15.12	21.08*	15.09	11.32	11.97*	10.67
Increase	24.70	23.73*	21.21	27.21	23.84*	25.52	34.83	35.50*	34.16

TABLE 7 — MOMENTS AND CUMULANTS

	OBSERVED POP. MALES	OBSERVED POP. FEMALES	STATIONARY POP. MALES	STATIONARY POP. FEMALES	STABLE POP. MALES	STABLE POP. FEMALES	OBSERVED BIRTHS	NET MATERNITY FUNCTION	BIRTHS IN STABLE POP.
μ	22.65561	23.11113	35.62830	36.57213	21.66655	22.15118	27.58056	29.06081	27.51677
σ^2	352.5852	354.0937	509.1437	519.4135	324.3205	337.6606	42.79600	46.25635	43.01138
κ_3	6601.935	6551.424	3436.868	2913.471	6075.455	6292.189	116.5303	70.8103	122.2549
κ_4	34596.	37019.	−240034.	−266065.	53701.	45626.	−1245.737	−1890.598	−1187.465
β_1	0.994375	0.966756	0.089496	0.060573	1.082018	1.028400	0.173248	0.050662	0.187838
β_2	3.278288	3.295247	2.074042	2.013810	3.510543	3.400177	2.319826	2.116398	2.358120
κ	−0.398633	−0.403357	−0.033841	−0.022445	−0.477329	−0.438328	−0.074429	−0.020780	−0.082289

TABLE 8 — RATES FROM AGE DISTRIBUTIONS AND VITAL STATISTICS (Females)

VITAL STATISTICS		THOMPSON AGE RANGE	NRR	1000r	INTERVAL	BOURGEOIS-PICHAT AGE RANGE	NRR	1000b	1000d	1000r	COALE	
GRR	3.142										IBR	42.34
NRR	2.539	0-4	2.11	28.31	27.24	5-29	2.36	43.49	11.67	31.82	IDR	11.57
TFR	6.452	5-9	2.34	31.98	27.14	30-54	2.18	38.55	9.71	28.84	IRI	30.77
GENERATION	28.280	10-14	2.23	29.01	27.07	55-79	2.09	34.02	6.68	27.33	K1	0.
SEX RATIO	105.350	15-19	2.23	29.81	26.96	* 5-29	2.36	43.49	11.67	31.82	K2	0.

TABLE 9 — LESLIE MATRIX AND ITS SPECTRAL COMPONENTS (Females)

Start of Age Interval	ORIGINAL MATRIX SUB-DIAGONAL	ALTERNATIVE FIRST ROWS Projection	ALTERNATIVE FIRST ROWS Integral	FIRST STABLE MATRIX % IN STABLE POPULATION	FISHER VALUES	REPRODUCTIVE VALUES	SECOND STABLE MATRIX Z_2 FIRST COLUMN	SECOND STABLE MATRIX Z_2 FIRST ROW
0	0.96061	0.00000	0.00000	18.131	1.219	3487907	0.1245+0.0870	0.1245+0.0870
5	0.99024	0.00074	0.00000	14.762	1.497	3926548	0.1455−0.0703	−0.0141+0.1420
10	0.99253	0.11343	0.00162	12.390	1.783	3804255	0.0108−0.1770	−0.1192+0.0520
15	0.98779	0.43405	0.24658	10.423	1.980	3571627	−0.1639−0.1056	−0.1085−0.0814
20	0.98354	0.66293	0.70466	8.726	1.829	2831717	−0.1885+0.1000	−0.0383−0.1611
25	0.98072	0.62997	0.74735	7.274	1.373	1803817	−0.0055+0.2325	0.0278−0.1616
30	0.97625	0.50327	0.63298	6.047	0.869	910397	0.2174−0.1287	0.0623−0.1063
35	0.97176	0.32027	0.47118	5.003	0.421	406549	0.2365−0.1370	0.0497−0.0426
40	0.96613	0.10631	0.23087	4.121	0.110	75988	−0.0042−0.2942	0.0161−0.0078
45	0.95758	0.00000	0.00000	3.374	0.000	3	−0.2769−0.1501	0.0000−0.0000
50	0.94082	0.00000	0.00000	2.739	0.000	1	−0.2826+0.1783	0.0000−0.0000
55+	0.81228			7.010				

TABLE 10 — AGE ANALYSIS AND MISCELLANEOUS RESULTS (Females)

Start of Age Interval	OBSERVED POPUL. (IN 100's)	CONTRIBUTIONS OF ROOTS (IN 100's) r_1	r_2, r_3	$r_4 \cdot r_{11}$	AGE-SP. BIRTH RATES	NET MATERNITY FUNCTION	COEFF. OF MATRIX EQUATION	PARAMETERS	INTEGRAL	MATRIX	EXP. INCREASE x	$e^{(x+2\frac{1}{2})r}$
0	28614	31275	−587	−2074	0.0000	0.0000	0.0000	L(1)	1.17910	1.17984	0	1.0859
5	26227	25464	−939	1702	0.0000	0.0000	0.0007	L(2)	0.43531	0.44143	50	5.6403
10	21338	21372	−323	288	0.0003	0.0014	0.1079		0.80777	0.78725	55	6.6505
15	18038	17979	786	−727	0.0510	0.2144	0.4098	R(1)	0.03295	0.03308	60	7.8416
20	15479	15053	1230	−803	0.1459	0.6052	0.6183	R(2)	−0.01720	−0.02050	65	9.2461
25	13139	12548	373	218	0.1547	0.6313	0.5778		0.21530	0.21195	70	10.9021
30	10481	10430	−1060	1110	0.1310	0.5244	0.4527	C(1)		172499	75	12.8547
35	9649	8631	−1560	2578	0.0975	0.3811	0.2813	C(2)		−287201	80	15.1570
40	6918	7109	−409	218	0.0478	0.1815	0.0907			−73524	85	17.8717
45	6260	5821	1370	−930	0.0000	0.0000	0.0000	2P/Y	29.1830	29.6444	90	21.0726
50	5381	4724	1885	−1229	0.0000	0.0000	0.0000	DELTA	2.4664		95	24.8468
55+	13913	12093									100	29.2970

TABLE 1 — DATA

AGE AT LAST BIRTHDAY	POPULATION BOTH SEXES	MALES Number	%	FEMALES Number	%	BIRTHS BY AGE OF MOTHER	DEATHS BOTH SEXES	MALES	FEMALES	AGE AT LAST BIRTHDAY
0	1557000	796000	4.1	761000	3.9	0	119430	65558	53872	0
1-4	5606000	2876000	14.9	2730000	14.2	0	67413	33566	33847	1-4
5-9	5797000	2969000	15.4	2828000	14.7	0	13577	6962	6615	5-9
10-14	4712000	2385000	12.4	2327000	12.1	1456	6253	3430	2823	10-14
15-19	3850000	1932000	10.0	1918000	10.0	194026	7518	4142	3376	15-19
20-24	3195000	1579000	8.2	1616000	8.4	479981	9757	5376	4381	20-24
25-29	2692000	1313000	6.8	1379000	7.2	440632	10385	5748	4637	25-29
30-34	2288000	1111000	5.8	1177000	6.1	299377	10099	5643	4456	30-34
35-39	1939000	943000	4.9	996000	5.2	209080	11906	6531	5375	35-39
40-44	1602000	772000	4.0	830000	4.3	80929	10097	5778	4319	40-44
45-49	1310000	629000	3.3	681000	3.5	0	10842	6181	4661	45-49
50-54	1112000	547000	2.8	565000	2.9	0	12318	7054	5264	50-54
55-59	915000	459000	2.4	456000	2.4	0	13337	7510	5827	55-59
60-64	703000	348000	1.8	355000	1.8	0	18281	9799	8482	60-64
65-69	509000	247000	1.3	262000	1.4	0	14348	7517	6831	65-69
70-74	349000	168000	0.9	181000	0.9		17286	8743	8543	70-74
75-79	220000	106000	0.6	114000	0.6		14212	7163	7049	75-79
80-84	135439	64945	0.3	70494	0.4	880648 M.	13932	6268	7664	80-84
85+	51561	24055	0.1	27506	0.1	824833 F.	22055	9149	12906	85+
TOTAL	38543000	19269000		19274000		1705481	403046	212118	190928	TOTAL

TABLE 2 — MALE LIFE TABLE

x	$_nq_x$	l_x	$_nd_x$	$_nL_x$	$_nm_x$	$_na_x$	T_x	r_x	$\mathring{e}_x$	$_nM_x$	x
0	0.078063	100000	7806	95037	0.082140	0.3643	5827484	0.0040	58.275	0.082359	0
1	0.045137	92194	4161	357318	0.011646	1.2469	5732447	0.0040	62.178	0.011671	1
5	0.011316	88032	996	437671	0.002276	2.5000	5375129	0.0389	61.059	0.002345	5
10	0.007159	87036	623	433609	0.001437	2.4774	4937458	0.0412	56.729	0.001438	10
15	0.010746	86413	929	429916	0.002160	2.6856	4503849	0.3390	52.120	0.002144	15
20	0.016968	85484	1450	423983	0.003421	2.6287	4073933	0.3353	47.657	0.003405	20
25	0.021711	84034	1824	415738	0.004389	2.5706	3649950	0.0308	43.434	0.004378	25
30	0.025160	82210	2068	406066	0.005094	2.5917	3234213	0.0277	39.341	0.005079	30
35	0.034127	80141	2735	394031	0.006941	2.5597	2828146	0.3298	35.290	0.006926	35
40	0.036845	77406	2852	380079	0.007504	2.5623	2434115	0.3326	31.446	0.007484	40
45	0.048128	74554	3588	364132	0.009854	2.5925	2054036	0.0245	27.551	0.009827	45
50	0.062646	70966	4446	344065	0.012921	2.5786	1689904	0.0187	23.813	0.012896	50
55	0.079145	66520	5265	320200	0.016442	2.6444	1345839	0.3269	20.232	0.016362	55
60	0.132149	61256	8095	286519	0.028253	2.5591	1025639	0.3299	16.744	0.028158	60
65	0.142230	53161	7561	247415	0.030560	2.5681	739120	0.0299	13.904	0.030433	65
70	0.231726	45600	10567	202121	0.052279	2.5510	491705	0.0299	10.783	0.052042	70
75	0.289725	35033	10150	149637	0.067830	2.4849	289584	0.3299	8.266	0.067575	75
80	0.395099	24883	9831	100858	0.097476	2.6039	139947	0.0299	5.624	0.096512	80
85+	*1.000000	15052	15052	39089	0.385067	2.5969	39089	0.0299	2.597	0.380337	85+

TABLE 3 — FEMALE LIFE TABLE

x	$_nq_x$	l_x	$_nd_x$	$_nL_x$	$_nm_x$	$_na_x$	T_x	r_x	$\mathring{e}_x$	$_nM_x$	x
0	0.067636	100000	6764	95843	0.070570	0.3853	6111654	0.0048	61.117	0.070791	0
1	0.047878	93236	4464	360864	0.012370	1.2935	6015811	0.0048	64.522	0.012398	1
5	0.011280	88772	1001	441359	0.002269	2.5000	5654948	0.0363	63.702	0.002339	5
10	0.006027	87771	529	437485	0.001209	2.4086	5213589	0.0372	59.400	0.001213	10
15	0.008819	87242	769	434420	0.001771	2.6733	4776105	0.0346	54.745	0.001760	15
20	0.013518	86473	1169	429578	0.002721	2.6169	4341684	0.0303	50.209	0.002711	20
25	0.016707	85304	1425	423041	0.003369	2.5599	3912106	0.0284	45.861	0.003363	25
30	0.018818	83879	1578	415607	0.003798	2.6016	3489065	0.0285	41.597	0.003786	30
35	0.026675	82300	2195	406113	0.005406	2.5459	3073458	0.0300	37.344	0.005397	35
40	0.025736	80105	2062	395462	0.005213	2.5447	2667345	0.0324	33.298	0.005204	40
45	0.033801	78043	2638	383911	0.006871	2.6096	2271882	0.0315	29.111	0.006844	45
50	0.045751	75405	3450	368789	0.009355	2.6123	1887972	0.0307	25.038	0.009317	50
55	0.062498	71955	4497	349408	0.012870	2.6942	1519183	0.0319	21.113	0.012779	55
60	0.113286	67458	7642	318785	0.023973	2.5783	1169775	0.0270	17.341	0.023893	60
65	0.123188	59816	7369	281390	0.026187	2.5991	850990	0.0270	14.227	0.026073	65
70	0.212544	52448	11147	235152	0.047405	2.5702	569600	0.0270	10.860	0.047199	70
75	0.269381	41300	11126	179094	0.062121	2.5365	334447	0.0270	8.098	0.061833	75
80	0.434103	30175	13099	119366	0.109738	2.5946	155353	0.0270	5.148	0.108718	80
85+	*1.000000	17076	17076	35987	0.474494	2.1075	35987	0.0270	2.108	0.469207	85+

TABLE 4 — OBSERVED AND PROJECTED VITAL RATES

	OBSERVED POPULATION BOTH SEXES	MALES	FEMALES	PROJECTED POPULATION 1967 MALES	FEMALES	1972 MALES	FEMALES	1977 MALES	FEMALES	STABLE POPULATION MALES	FEMALES
RATES PER THOUSAND											
Birth	44.25	45.70	42.80	44.88	42.34	44.65	42.38	44.80	42.75	44.28	43.26
Death	10.46	11.01	9.91	10.82	9.62	10.68	9.57	10.62	9.59	10.63	9.61
Increase	33.79	34.69	32.89	34.06	32.72	33.97	32.81	34.18	33.16	33.6501	
PERCENTAGE											
under 15	45.85	46.84	44.86	47.25	45.16	47.05	45.13	46.76	45.02	46.11	45.45
15-64	50.87	49.99	51.74	49.59	51.46	49.78	51.47	50.14	51.57	51.12	51.44
65 and over	3.28	3.17	3.40	3.16	3.38	3.18	3.40	3.11	3.41	2.77	3.12
DEP. RATIO X 100	96.59	100.03	93.26	101.67	94.34	100.90	94.29	99.45	93.91	95.61	94.41

AGE AT LAST BIRTHDAY	1967 BOTH SEXES	1967 MALES	1967 FEMALES	1972 BOTH SEXES	1972 MALES	1972 FEMALES	1977 BOTH SEXES	1977 MALES	1977 FEMALES	AGE AT LAST BIRTHDAY	
0-4	8393	4314	4079	9843	5059	4784	11662	5994	5668	0-4	**TABLE 5**
5-9	6927	3553	3374	8116	4174	3942	9518	4895	4623	5-9	POPULATION
10-14	5744	2941	2803	6864	3520	3344	8042	4135	3907	10-14	PROJECTED
15-19	4676	2365	2311	5700	2916	2784	6811	3490	3321	15-19	WITH
20-24	3802	1905	1897	4617	2332	2285	5629	2876	2753	20-24	FIXED
25-29	3139	1548	1591	3736	1868	1868	4537	2287	2250	25-29	AGE—
30-34	2637	1282	1355	3075	1512	1563	3660	1825	1835	30-34	SPECIFIC
35-39	2228	1078	1150	2568	1244	1324	2995	1467	1528	35-39	BIRTH
40-44	1880	910	970	2160	1040	1120	2489	1200	1289	40-44	AND
45-49	1546	740	806	1813	871	942	2083	996	1087	45-49	DEATH
50-54	1248	594	654	1473	699	774	1727	823	904	50-54	RATES
55-59	1044	509	535	1173	553	620	1383	650	733	55-59	(IN 1000's)
60-64	827	411	416	944	456	488	1060	495	565	60-64	
65-69	614	301	313	722	355	367	824	393	431	65-69	
70-74	421	202	219	507	245	262	597	290	307	70-74	
75-79	262	124	138	316	149	167	381	182	199	75-79	
80-84	147	71	76	176	84	92	212	101	111	80-84	
85+	46	25	21	51	28	23	60	32	28	85+	
TOTAL	45581	22873	22708	53854	27105	26749	63670	32131	31539	TOTAL	

STANDARD COUNTRIES: STANDARDIZED RATES PER THOUSAND	ENGLAND AND WALES 1961 BOTH SEXES	MALES	FEMALES	UNITED STATES 1960 BOTH SEXES	MALES	FEMALES	MEXICO 1960 BOTH SEXES	MALES	FEMALES	
Birth	41.22	48.14*	38.63	41.99	43.78*	40.02	45.72	46.77*	44.11	**TABLE 6** STANDAR-
Death	16.24	23.77*	17.64	14.29	19.47*	14.45	10.00	10.37*	9.48	DIZED
Increase	24.98	24.37*	21.00	27.70	24.31*	25.57	35.71	36.40*	34.63	RATES

	OBSERVED POP. MALES	OBSERVED POP. FEMALES	STATIONARY POP. MALES	STATIONARY POP. FEMALES	STABLE POP. MALES	STABLE POP. FEMALES	OBSERVED BIRTHS	NET MATERNITY FUNCTION	BIRTHS IN STABLE POP.	
μ	21.90559	22.61469	35.83288	36.79615	21.59254	22.05574	27.75777	29.13638	27.55340	**TABLE 7**
σ^2	346.2836	352.2877	508.8543	520.5257	322.5252	336.1051	43.77930	46.47720	43.13488	MOMENTS
κ_3	6664.344	6483.932	3269.508	2759.572	6039.326	6290.816	117.3774	69.9606	124.4381	AND
κ_4	46324.	34900.	-243195.	-271271.	53521.	46882.	-1349.556	-1970.269	-1218.441	CUMULANTS
β_1	1.069594	0.961577	0.081131	0.053995	1.087141	1.042290	0.164196	0.048751	0.192939	
β_2	3.386313	3.281211	2.060778	1.998803	3.514514	3.415008	2.295869	2.087893	2.345142	
κ	-0.433094	-0.398828	-0.030604	-0.019895	-0.478554	-0.443232	-0.069689	-0.019514	-0.082906	

VITAL STATISTICS		AGE RANGE	THOMPSON NRR	1000r	INTERVAL	AGE RANGE	BOURGEOIS-PICHAT NRR	1000b	1000d	1000r	COALE		
GRR	3.096										IBR	44.51	**TABLE 8** RATES
NRR	2.595	0-4	2.42	32.40	27.25	5-29	2.50	42.30	8.34	33.96	IDR	9.21	FROM AGE DISTRI-
TFR	6.401	5-9	2.35	32.19	27.17	30-54	2.31	40.53	9.48	31.05	IRI	35.30	BUTIONS AND VITAL
GENERATION	28.335	10-14	2.26	29.40	27.11	55-79	2.59	51.86	16.60	35.26	K1	17.69	STATISTICS
SEX RATIO	106.767	15-19	2.18	28.79	27.01	*35-64	2.34	41.49	9.95	31.54	K2	0.23	(Females)

Start of Age Interval	ORIGINAL MATRIX SUB-DIAGONAL	ALTERNATIVE FIRST ROWS Projection	ALTERNATIVE FIRST ROWS Integral	FIRST STABLE MATRIX % IN STABLE POPULATION	FISHER VALUES	REPRODUCTIVE VALUES	SECOND STABLE MATRIX Z_2 FIRST COLUMN	SECOND STABLE MATRIX Z_2 FIRST ROW	
0	0.96640	0.00000	0.00000	18.212	1.190	4152752	0.1223+0.0878	0.1223+0.0878	**TABLE 9**
5	0.99122	0.00068	0.00000	14.865	1.457	4121561	0.1459-0.0678	-0.0153+0.1400	LESLIE
10	0.99300	0.11163	0.00150	12.445	1.740	4049055	0.0138-0.1759	-0.1182+0.0505	MATRIX
15	0.98885	0.43609	0.24305	10.437	1.941	3722837	-0.1608-0.1081	-0.1067-0.0810	AND ITS
20	0.98478	0.67555	0.71363	8.717	1.799	2907898	-0.1894+0.0951	-0.0373-0.1600	SPECTRAL
25	0.98243	0.62886	0.76772	7.250	1.347	1858117	-0.0111+0.2306	0.0273-0.1622	COMPO-
30	0.97716	0.50745	0.61113	6.016	0.862	1015103	0.2123+0.1335	0.0641-0.1077	NENTS
35	0.97377	0.33669	0.50436	4.965	0.427	425548	0.2384-0.1290	0.0524-0.0429	(Females)
40	0.97079	0.10768	0.23426	4.083	0.108	89800	0.0051-0.2919	0.0163-0.0076	
45	0.96061	0.00000	0.00000	3.348	0.000	3	-0.2703-0.1587	0.0000-0.0000	
50	0.94745	0.00000	0.00000	2.716	0.000	1	-0.2880+0.1674	0.0000-0.0000	
55+	0.81348			6.946					

Start of Age Interval	OBSERVED POPUL. (IN 100's)	CONTRIBUTIONS OF ROOTS (IN 100's) r_1	r_2, r_3	r_4-r_{11}	AGE-SP. BIRTH RATES	NET MATERNITY FUNCTION	COEFF. OF MATRIX EQUATION	PARAMETERS	PARAMETERS INTEGRAL	PARAMETERS MATRIX	EXP. INCREASE x	EXP. INCREASE $e^{(x+2\frac{1}{2})r}$	
0	34910	34353	448	108	0.0000	0.0000	0.0000	L(1)	1.18323	1.18400	0	1.0878	**TABLE 10**
5	28280	28040	356	-115	0.0000	0.0000	0.0007	L(2)	0.43784	0.44407	50	5.8511	AGE
10	23270	23474	-142	-62	0.0003	0.0013	0.1069		0.80778	0.78756	55	6.9232	ANALYSIS
15	19180	19687	-582	74	0.0489	0.2125	0.4148	R(1)	0.03365	0.03378	60	8.1918	AND
20	16160	16443	-454	172	0.1436	0.6171	0.6354	R(2)	-0.01693	-0.02016	65	9.6928	MISCEL-
25	13790	13676	207	-93	0.1545	0.6538	0.5825		0.21482	0.21148	70	11.4688	LANEOUS
30	11770	11348	759	-336	0.1230	0.5113	0.4618	C(1)		188631	75	13.5703	RESULTS
35	9960	9365	562	33	0.1015	0.4123	0.2994	C(2)		146008	80	16.0569	(Females)
40	8300	7702	-288	886	0.0472	0.1865	0.0932			-51960	85	18.9990	
45	6810	6315	-954	1449	0.0000	0.0000	0.0000	2P/Y	29.2488	29.7112	90	22.4802	
50	5650	5124	-667	1193	0.0000	0.0000	0.0000	DELTA	1.5478		95	26.5994	
55+	14660	13102									100	31.4733	

Panama 1960
Excluding Canal Zone and Tribal Indian Population

TABLE 1 — DATA

AGE AT LAST BIRTHDAY	POPULATION BOTH SEXES	MALES Number	MALES %	FEMALES Number	FEMALES %	BIRTHS BY AGE OF MOTHER	DEATHS BOTH SEXES	DEATHS MALES	DEATHS FEMALES	AGE AT LAST BIRTHDAY
0	38100	19500	3.8	18600	3.8	0	2371	1302	1069	0
1-4	134500	68200	13.4	66300	13.5	0	1275	653	622	1-4
5-9	140697	71199	14.0	69498	14.2	0	295	155	140	5-9
10-14	121200	61600	12.1	59600	12.1	123	148	84	64	10-14
15-19	100300	49800	9.8	50500	10.3	7438	158	81	77	15-19
20-24	83800	42100	8.3	41700	8.5	13015	223	116	107	20-24
25-29	69500	35100	6.9	34400	7.0	10100	200	96	104	25-29
30-34	60800	31100	6.1	29700	6.0	5988	179	91	88	30-34
35-39	54500	28000	5.5	26500	5.4	3486	190	91	99	35-39
40-44	47400	25000	4.9	22400	4.6	938	222	122	100	40-44
45-49	40900	21600	4.2	19300	3.9	149	264	139	125	45-49
50-54	29900	15900	3.1	14000	2.9	21	251	139	112	50-54
55-59	23000	11700	2.3	11300	2.3	0	307	173	134	55-59
60-64	19800	10200	2.0	9600	2.0	0	353	204	149	60-64
65-69	13732	7170	1.4	6562	1.3	0	369	215	154	65-69
70-74	10056	5110	1.0	4946	1.0		428	253	175	70-74
75-79	6666	3277	0.6	3389	0.7		446	252	194	75-79
80-84	3730	1761	0.3	1969	0.4	20832 M.	410	220	190	80-84
85+	1519	683	0.1	836	0.2	20426 F.	298	150	148	85+
TOTAL	1000100	509000		491100		41258	8387	4536	3851	TOTAL

TABLE 2 — MALE LIFE TABLE

x	nq_x	l_x	nd_x	nL_x	nm_x	na_x	T_x	r_x	$\mathring{e}_x$	nM_x
0	0.063713	100000	6371	95965	0.066392	0.3667	6273820	0.0084	62.738	0.066769
1	0.037158	93629	3479	364954	0.009533	1.2518	6177855	0.0084	65.982	0.009575
5	0.010604	90150	956	448358	0.002132	2.5000	5812901	0.0317	64.481	0.002177
10	0.006776	89194	604	444409	0.001360	2.4195	5364543	0.0342	60.145	0.001364
15	0.008154	88589	722	441266	0.001637	2.6734	4920134	0.0362	55.539	0.001626
20	0.013723	87867	1206	436415	0.002763	2.5786	4478869	0.0325	50.973	0.002755
25	0.013587	86661	1177	430370	0.002736	2.5065	4042454	0.0275	46.647	0.002735
30	0.014536	85484	1243	424350	0.002928	2.5308	3612084	0.0197	42.255	0.002926
35	0.016161	84241	1361	417961	0.003257	2.6166	3187734	0.0183	37.841	0.003250
40	0.024189	82880	2005	409639	0.004894	2.6261	2769774	0.0211	33.419	0.004880
45	0.031841	80875	2575	398224	0.006467	2.6118	2360135	0.0387	29.183	0.006435
50	0.043260	78300	3387	383614	0.008830	2.6722	1961911	0.0517	25.056	0.008742
55	0.071751	74912	5375	361809	0.014856	2.6273	1578297	0.0299	21.069	0.014786
60	0.095933	69537	6671	331735	0.020109	2.6087	1216488	0.0358	17.494	0.020000
65	0.140861	62866	8855	293306	0.030192	2.6257	884754	0.0358	14.074	0.029986
70	0.222407	54011	12012	241021	0.049840	2.5830	591447	0.0358	10.950	0.049511
75	0.324780	41999	13640	176224	0.077403	2.5243	350426	0.0358	8.344	0.076900
80	0.479740	28358	13605	108012	0.125955	2.5170	174202	0.0358	6.143	0.124929
85+	*1.000000	14754	14754	66190	0.222898	4.4864	66190	0.0358	4.486	0.219619

TABLE 3 — FEMALE LIFE TABLE

x	nq_x	l_x	nd_x	nL_x	nm_x	na_x	T_x	r_x	$\mathring{e}_x$	nM_x
0	0.055253	100000	5525	96574	0.057214	0.3799	6523351	0.0068	65.234	0.057473
1	0.036476	94475	3446	368527	0.009351	1.2804	6426778	0.0068	68.026	0.009382
5	0.009794	91029	892	452914	0.001969	2.5000	6058251	0.0320	66.553	0.002014
10	0.005340	90137	481	449439	0.001071	2.4110	5605337	0.0306	62.187	0.001074
15	0.007650	89656	686	446701	0.001535	2.6999	5155898	0.0341	57.508	0.001525
20	0.012807	88970	1139	442132	0.002577	2.6157	4709197	0.0359	52.930	0.002566
25	0.015016	87830	1319	435883	0.003026	2.5212	4267065	0.0310	48.583	0.003023
30	0.014724	86511	1274	429427	0.002966	2.5429	3831182	0.0229	44.285	0.002963
35	0.018550	85238	1581	422356	0.003744	2.5764	3401755	0.0245	39.909	0.003736
40	0.022161	83657	1854	413646	0.004480	2.6168	2979398	0.0269	35.615	0.004464
45	0.032035	81803	2621	402727	0.006507	2.6012	2565534	0.0407	31.362	0.006477
50	0.039490	79182	3127	388464	0.008049	2.6185	2162807	0.0450	27.314	0.008000
55	0.057848	76055	4400	369749	0.011899	2.6073	1774343	0.0260	23.330	0.011858
60	0.075270	71656	5394	345421	0.015614	2.6163	1404594	0.0399	19.602	0.015521
65	0.111850	66262	7411	313671	0.023628	2.6201	1059173	0.0399	15.985	0.023468
70	0.164219	58851	9664	271142	0.035643	2.6086	745502	0.0399	12.668	0.035382
75	0.253127	49186	12450	215782	0.057699	2.5785	474360	0.0399	9.644	0.057244
80	0.390760	36736	14355	147681	0.097202	2.6441	258578	0.0399	7.039	0.096496
85+	1.000000	22381	22381	110897	0.201818	4.9550	110897	0.0399	4.955	0.177033

TABLE 4 — OBSERVED AND PROJECTED VITAL RATES

	OBSERVED POPULATION BOTH SEXES	MALES	FEMALES	PROJECTED POPULATION 1965 MALES	FEMALES	1970 MALES	FEMALES	1975 MALES	FEMALES	STABLE POPULATION MALES	FEMALES
RATES PER THOUSAND											
Birth	41.25	40.93	41.59	40.98	41.34	41.05	41.17	41.09	41.03	42.47	41.7
Death	8.39	8.91	7.84	9.05	8.08	9.05	8.08	9.04	8.07	8.78	8.0
Increase	32.87	32.02	33.75	31.93	33.26	32.00	33.09	32.05	32.95		33.686
PERCENTAGE											
under 15	43.45	43.32	43.58	43.57	43.90	44.05	44.36	44.26	44.63	45.20	44.9
15-64	52.98	53.14	52.82	52.79	52.29	52.42	51.84	52.16	51.57	51.65	51.4
65 and over	3.57	3.54	3.60	3.64	3.81	3.53	3.80	3.57	3.80	3.15	3.6
DEP. RATIO X 100	88.73	88.17	89.32	89.41	91.24	90.75	92.92	91.70	93.91	93.62	94.2

Panama 1960

Excluding Canal Zone and Tribal Indian Population

AGE AT LAST BIRTHDAY	1965 BOTH SEXES	1965 MALES	1965 FEMALES	1970 BOTH SEXES	1970 MALES	1970 FEMALES	1975 BOTH SEXES	1975 MALES	1975 FEMALES	AGE AT LAST BIRTHDAY	
0-4	207	104	103	244	123	121	287	144	143	0-4	TABLE 5
5-9	168	85	83	203	102	101	237	119	118	5-9	
10-14	140	71	69	167	85	82	201	101	100	10-14	
15-19	120	61	59	139	70	69	166	84	82	15-19	POPULATION
20-24	99	49	50	119	60	59	137	69	68	20-24	PROJECTED
25-29	83	42	41	98	49	49	118	60	58	25-29	WITH
30-34	69	35	34	82	41	41	97	48	49	30-34	FIXED
35-39	60	31	29	67	34	33	80	40	40	35-39	AGE—
40-44	53	27	26	59	30	29	66	33	33	40-44	SPECIFIC
45-49	46	24	22	52	27	25	57	29	28	45-49	BIRTH
50-54	40	21	19	44	23	21	50	26	24	50-54	AND
55-59	28	15	13	38	20	18	42	22	20	55-59	DEATH
60-64	22	11	11	26	14	12	35	18	17	60-64	RATES
65-69	18	9	9	19	9	10	23	12	11	65-69	(IN 1000's)
70-74	12	6	6	15	7	8	16	8	8	70-74	
75-79	8	4	4	9	4	5	11	5	6	75-79	
80-84	4	2	2	5	2	3	6	3	3	80-84	
85+	2	1	1	3	1	2	3	1	2	85+	
TOTAL	1179	598	581	1389	701	688	1632	822	810	TOTAL	

STANDARD COUNTRIES:	ENGLAND AND WALES 1961 BOTH SEXES	MALES	FEMALES	UNITED STATES 1960 BOTH SEXES	MALES	FEMALES	MEXICO 1960 BOTH SEXES	MALES	FEMALES	
STANDARDIZED RATES PER THOUSAND										TABLE 6
Birth	36.55	41.26*	35.07	37.31	37.74*	36.39	43.20	39.11*	42.66	STANDAR-
Death	12.53	18.16*	12.86	11.11	14.95*	10.63	7.98	8.43*	7.45	DIZED
Increase	24.02	23.09*	22.21	26.20	22.79*	25.76	35.22	30.68*	35.22	RATES

	OBSERVED POP. MALES	OBSERVED POP. FEMALES	STATIONARY POP. MALES	STATIONARY POP. FEMALES	STABLE POP. MALES	STABLE POP. FEMALES	OBSERVED BIRTHS	NET MATERNITY FUNCTION	BIRTHS IN STABLE POP.	
μ	23.39893	23.12094	37.06463	38.18878	22.19847	22.50800	26.07179	27.42616	25.92427	TABLE 7
σ^2	360.6423	358.4320	524.0850	555.9368	338.8856	353.1750	41.41775	45.23476	39.70578	
κ_3	6168.240	6511.676	2770.481	2915.283	6324.288	6886.956	175.7350	157.0526	168.0458	MOMENTS
κ_4	9767.	31336.	-270015.	-312274.	45985.	58073.	-190.303	-610.169	-49.699	AND
β_1	0.811134	0.920800	0.053322	0.049464	1.027694	1.076675	0.434667	0.266485	0.451122	CUMULANTS
β_2	3.075093	3.243911	2.016932	1.989618	3.400414	3.465582	2.889064	2.701801	2.968476	
κ	-0.332206	-0.386326	-0.019956	-0.018172	-0.438429	-0.460362	-0.240908	-0.155046	-0.269608	

VITAL STATISTICS			THOMPSON AGE RANGE	NRR	1000r	INTERVAL	BOURGEOIS-PICHAT AGE RANGE	NRR	1000b	1000d	1000r	COALE		TABLE 8
GRR	2.820													RATES FROM AGE
NRR	2.455		0-4	2.30	30.58	27.30	5-29	2.46	40.69	7.28	33.41	IBR	40.97	DISTRI-
TFR	5.697		5-9	2.25	30.31	27.23	30-54	2.34	40.85	9.39	31.46	IDR	8.40	BUTIONS
GENERATION	26.660		10-14	2.26	29.30	27.17	55-79	2.69	52.59	15.95	36.64	IRI	32.58	AND VITAL
SEX RATIO	101.988		15-19	2.23	29.57	27.08	*25-49	1.96	31.87	7.01	24.86	K1	13.08	STATISTICS
												K2	0.21	(Females)

Start of Age Interval	ORIGINAL MATRIX SUB-DIAGONAL	ALTERNATIVE FIRST ROWS Projection	Integral	FIRST STABLE MATRIX % IN STABLE POPULATION	FISHER VALUES	REPRODUCTIVE VALUES	SECOND STABLE MATRIX Z_2 FIRST COLUMN	FIRST ROW	
0	0.97380	0.00000	0.00000	17.912	1.168	99201	0.1503+0.1175	0.1503+0.1175	
5	0.99233	0.00236	0.00000	14.729	1.421	98755	0.1891-0.1018	-0.0418+0.1642	TABLE 9
10	0.99391	0.17092	0.00517	12.342	1.693	100906	-0.0197-0.2456	-0.1461+0.0239	
15	0.98977	0.52523	0.36879	10.358	1.816	91727	-0.2675-0.0928	-0.0960-0.1282	LESLIE
20	0.98586	0.69259	0.78182	8.657	1.553	64771	-0.2203+0.2376	-0.0109-0.1842	MATRIX
25	0.98519	0.56671	0.73546	7.206	1.045	35947	0.1470+0.3388	0.0385-0.1562	AND ITS
30	0.98353	0.38108	0.50504	5.995	0.584	17345	0.4207+0.0018	0.0527-0.0918	SPECTRAL
35	0.97989	0.19869	0.32952	4.979	0.250	6638	0.1942-0.4371	0.0343-0.0355	COMPO-
40	0.97309	0.05686	0.10489	4.120	0.066	1474	-0.3650-0.4006	0.0104-0.0087	NENTS
45	0.96458	0.01055	0.01934	3.385	0.012	228	-0.5777+0.1947	0.0020-0.0015	(Females)
50	0.95182	0.00173	0.00376	2.757	0.002	24	-0.0602+0.6772	0.0003-0.0002	
55+	0.83719			7.561					

Start Age Interval	OBSERVED POPUL. (IN 100's)	CONTRIBUTIONS OF ROOTS (IN 100's) r_1	r_2, r_3	$r_4 \cdot r_{11}$	AGE-SP. BIRTH RATES	NET MATERNITY FUNCTION	COEFF. OF MATRIX EQUATION	PARAMETERS			EXP. INCREASE		
									INTEGRAL	MATRIX	x	$e^{(x+2\frac{1}{2})r}$	
0	849	861	-2	-10	0.0000	0.0000	0.0000	L(1)	1.18345	1.18426	0	1.0879	TABLE 10
5	695	708	-13	1	0.0000	0.0000	0.0023	L(2)	0.33256	0.34777	50	5.8623	
10	596	593	-10	13	0.0010	0.0046	0.1652		0.82045	0.79196	55	6.9378	AGE
15	505	498	8	-1	0.0729	0.3257	0.5045	R(1)	0.03369	0.03382	60	8.2105	ANALYSIS
20	417	416	21	-20	0.1545	0.6832	0.6584	R(2)	-0.02437	-0.02902	65	9.7167	AND
25	344	346	9	-11	0.1454	0.6336	0.5311		0.23714	0.23140	70	11.4992	MISCEL-
30	297	288	-19	28	0.0998	0.4286	0.3519	C(1)		4805	75	13.6088	LANEOUS
35	265	239	-29	55	0.0651	0.2751	0.1804	C(2)		-2311	80	16.1053	RESULTS
40	224	198	-2	28	0.0207	0.0858	0.0506			-2302	85	19.0598	(Females)
45	193	163	36	-5	0.0038	0.0154	0.0091	2P/Y	26.4958	27.1524	90	22.5563	
50	140	132	34	-26	0.0007	0.0029	0.0014	DELTA	1.8415		95	26.6942	
55+	386	363									100	31.5912	

Excluding Canal Zone and Tribal Indian Population

TABLE 1 — DATA

AGE AT LAST BIRTHDAY	POPULATION BOTH SEXES	MALES Number	%	FEMALES Number	%	BIRTHS BY AGE OF MOTHER	DEATHS BOTH SEXES	MALES	FEMALES	AGE AT LAST BIRTHDAY
0	40058	20267	3.7	19791	3.7	0	1940	1075	865	0
1-4	144188	72813	13.3	71375	13.5	0	1091	539	552	1-4
5-9	152083	77249	14.1	74834	14.2	0	255	142	113	5-9
10-14	129861	66125	12.1	63736	12.1	141	120	66	54	10-14
15-19	107441	53427	9.8	54014	10.2	8252	170	93	77	15-19
20-24	89977	45261	8.3	44716	8.5	14155	200	91	109	20-24
25-29	75006	37952	6.9	37054	7.0	10810	173	85	88	25-29
30-34	65531	33520	6.1	32011	6.1	6463	183	104	79	30-34
35-39	58477	30221	5.5	28256	5.4	3678	210	113	97	35-39
40-44	51356	26877	4.9	24479	4.6	1010	224	120	104	40-44
45-49	43564	23277	4.3	20287	3.8	146	244	136	108	45-49
50-54	32874	17281	3.2	15593	3.0	19	297	180	117	50-54
55-59	25009	12705	2.3	12304	2.3	0	278	150	128	55-59
60-64	21143	11151	2.0	9992	1.9	0	410	230	180	60-64
65-69	14617	7356	1.3	7261	1.4	0	418	234	184	65-69
70-74	11318	6007	1.1	5311	1.0		480	278	202	70-74
75-79	7560	3617	0.7	3943	0.7		438	254	184	75-79
80-84	3423	1530	0.3	1893	0.4	22778 M.	319	153	166	80-84
85+	1938	834	0.2	1104	0.2	21896 F.	421	185	236	85+
TOTAL	1075424	547470		527954		44674	7871	4228	3643	TOTAL

TABLE 2 — MALE LIFE TABLE

x	nq_x	l_x	nd_x	nL_x	nm_x	na_x	T_x	r_x	$\mathring{e}_x$	nM_x	x
0	0.051083	100000	5108	96756	0.052795	0.3650	6504622	0.0068	65.046	0.053042	0
1	0.028918	94892	2744	372016	0.007376	1.2484	6407866	0.0068	67.528	0.007403	1
5	0.008977	92148	827	458670	0.001804	2.5000	6035849	0.0313	65.502	0.001838	5
10	0.004976	91320	454	455459	0.000998	2.4834	5577179	0.0355	61.073	0.000998	10
15	0.008705	90866	791	452446	0.001748	2.6180	5121720	0.0363	56.366	0.001741	15
20	0.010020	90075	903	448162	0.002014	2.5473	4669274	0.0322	51.838	0.002011	20
25	0.011169	89172	996	443468	0.002246	2.5958	4221112	0.0276	47.336	0.002240	25
30	0.015429	88176	1360	437609	0.003109	2.5941	3777644	0.0197	42.842	0.003103	30
35	0.018553	86816	1611	430163	0.003744	2.5680	3340035	0.0183	38.473	0.003739	35
40	0.022133	85205	1886	421481	0.004474	2.5894	2909872	0.0216	34.151	0.004465	40
45	0.029048	83320	2420	411016	0.005889	2.6936	2488391	0.0376	29.866	0.005843	45
50	0.051119	80899	4135	394577	0.010481	2.6013	2077375	0.0509	25.679	0.010416	50
55	0.057725	76764	4431	373375	0.011868	2.6431	1682798	0.0303	21.922	0.011806	55
60	0.099255	72233	7179	344812	0.020821	2.6528	1309423	0.0479	18.103	0.020626	60
65	0.148820	65153	9696	302449	0.032059	2.5952	964612	0.0479	14.805	0.031811	65
70	0.209382	55457	11612	248983	0.046636	2.5626	662162	0.0479	11.940	0.046279	70
75	0.300736	43845	13186	186398	0.070741	2.5103	413179	0.0479	9.424	0.070224	75
80	0.399920	30660	12261	121815	0.100656	2.5886	226781	0.0479	7.397	0.100001	80
85+	1.000000	18398	18398	104966	0.175277	5.7053	104966	0.0479	5.705	0.221823	85+

TABLE 3 — FEMALE LIFE TABLE

x	nq_x	l_x	nd_x	nL_x	nm_x	na_x	T_x	r_x	$\mathring{e}_x$	nM_x	x
0	0.042389	100000	4239	97408	0.043517	0.3885	6729113	0.0066	67.291	0.043707	0
1	0.030213	95761	2893	375237	0.007710	1.3014	6631705	0.0066	69.253	0.007734	1
5	0.007327	92868	680	462638	0.001471	2.5000	6256468	0.0331	67.370	0.001510	5
10	0.004226	92187	390	459958	0.000847	2.4876	5793831	0.0315	62.848	0.000847	10
15	0.007161	91798	657	457495	0.001437	2.7275	5333873	0.0339	58.105	0.001426	15
20	0.012151	91140	1107	453018	0.002445	2.5763	4876378	0.0355	53.504	0.002438	20
25	0.011805	90033	1063	447505	0.002375	2.4973	4423360	0.0310	49.130	0.002375	25
30	0.012293	88970	1094	442207	0.002473	2.5832	3975855	0.0245	44.688	0.002468	30
35	0.017067	87876	1500	435784	0.003442	2.6010	3533647	0.0234	40.212	0.003433	35
40	0.021083	86377	1821	427483	0.004260	2.5839	3097863	0.0288	35.865	0.004249	40
45	0.026415	84556	2234	417451	0.005350	2.6148	2670380	0.0395	31.581	0.005324	45
50	0.037076	82322	3052	404359	0.007548	2.6242	2252930	0.0424	27.367	0.007503	50
55	0.051124	79270	4053	386945	0.010473	2.6794	1848571	0.0331	23.320	0.010403	55
60	0.086980	75217	6542	360605	0.018143	2.6338	1461626	0.0416	19.432	0.018014	60
65	0.120177	68675	8253	323578	0.025506	2.6013	1101020	0.0416	16.032	0.025341	65
70	0.174727	60422	10557	276189	0.038225	2.5448	777443	0.0416	12.867	0.038034	70
75	0.211085	49866	10526	223835	0.047024	2.5786	501254	0.0416	10.052	0.046665	75
80	0.369370	39339	14531	163343	0.088957	2.7048	277419	0.0416	7.052	0.087692	80
85+	*1.000000	24808	24808	114076	0.217471	4.5983	114076	0.0416	4.598	0.213768	85+

TABLE 4 — OBSERVED AND PROJECTED VITAL RATES

	OBSERVED POPULATION BOTH SEXES	MALES	FEMALES	PROJECTED POPULATION 1967 MALES	FEMALES	1972 MALES	FEMALES	1977 MALES	FEMALES	STABLE POPULATION MALES	FEMALES
RATES PER THOUSAND											
Birth	41.54	41.61	41.47	41.31	41.06	41.15	40.79	41.09	40.64	42.25	41.61
Death	7.32	7.72	6.90	8.04	7.06	8.13	7.14	8.11	7.08	7.61	6.97
Increase	34.22	33.88	34.57	33.28	34.00	33.02	33.65	32.98	33.56		34.6460
PERCENTAGE											
under 15	43.35	43.19	43.51	43.82	44.07	44.49	44.61	45.06	44.96	45.61	45.31
15-64	53.04	53.28	52.79	52.48	52.15	51.87	51.60	51.26	51.24	51.25	51.20
65 and over	3.61	3.53	3.70	3.71	3.78	3.64	3.79	3.68	3.79	3.13	3.49
DEP. RATIO X 100	88.55	87.70	89.43	90.56	91.74	92.78	93.79	95.09	95.15	95.10	95.31

Panama 1962
Excluding Canal Zone and Tribal Indian Population

TABLE 5 — POPULATION PROJECTED WITH FIXED AGE—SPECIFIC BIRTH AND DEATH RATES (IN 1000's)

AGE AT LAST BIRTHDAY	BOTH SEXES	1967 MALES	FEMALES	BOTH SEXES	1972 MALES	FEMALES	BOTH SEXES	1977 MALES	FEMALES	AGE AT LAST BIRTHDAY
0-4	229	116	113	269	137	132	317	161	156	0-4
5-9	180	91	89	224	114	110	264	134	130	5-9
10-14	151	77	74	179	90	89	223	113	110	10-14
15-19	129	66	63	150	76	74	178	90	88	15-19
20-24	106	53	53	128	65	63	148	75	73	20-24
25-29	89	45	44	105	52	53	126	64	62	25-29
30-34	74	37	37	88	44	44	104	52	52	30-34
35-39	65	33	32	73	37	36	86	43	43	35-39
40-44	58	30	28	63	32	31	71	36	35	40-44
45-49	50	26	24	56	29	27	61	31	30	45-49
50-54	42	22	20	48	25	23	54	28	26	50-54
55-59	31	16	15	40	21	19	46	24	22	55-59
60-64	23	12	11	29	15	14	38	20	18	60-64
65-69	19	10	9	20	10	10	25	13	12	65-69
70-74	12	6	6	16	8	8	17	8	9	70-74
75-79	8	4	4	10	5	5	12	6	6	75-79
80-84	5	2	3	6	3	3	7	3	4	80-84
85+	2	1	1	4	2	2	5	3	2	85+
TOTAL	1273	647	626	1508	765	743	1782	904	878	TOTAL

TABLE 6 — STANDARDIZED RATES

STANDARD COUNTRIES: STANDARDIZED RATES PER THOUSAND	ENGLAND AND WALES 1961 BOTH SEXES	MALES	FEMALES	UNITED STATES 1960 BOTH SEXES	MALES	FEMALES	MEXICO 1960 BOTH SEXES	MALES	FEMALES
Birth	36.73	41.83*	34.89	37.51	38.28*	36.23	43.56	39.66*	42.59
Death	11.82	15.81*	12.36	10.30	13.01*	10.01	6.97	7.36*	6.52
Increase	24.91	26.03*	22.53	27.22	25.27*	26.22	36.59	32.30*	36.07

TABLE 7 — MOMENTS AND CUMULANTS

	OBSERVED POP. MALES	FEMALES	STATIONARY POP. MALES	FEMALES	STABLE POP. MALES	FEMALES	OBSERVED BIRTHS	NET MATERNITY FUNCTION	BIRTHS IN STABLE POP.
μ	23.46873	23.18459	37.53729	38.38478	22.02737	22.30238	25.98301	27.34259	25.80344
σ^2	360.8523	360.7710	538.0208	556.7606	337.7101	348.8636	41.22807	45.12949	39.48020
κ_3	6142.049	6576.532	2992.053	2816.396	6476.751	6843.757	175.1320	154.8987	167.7255
κ_4	7829.	31824.	-280388.	-313995.	57702.	61681.	-210.785	-675.150	-73.588
β_1	0.802856	0.921084	0.057483	0.045960	1.089136	1.103119	0.437676	0.261044	0.457151
β_2	3.060126	3.244511	2.031364	1.987055	3.505944	3.506802	2.875991	2.668503	2.952788
κ	-0.327632	-0.386520	-0.021682	-0.016909	-0.475040	-0.474531	-0.237479	-0.146605	-0.264640

TABLE 8 — RATES FROM AGE DISTRIBUTIONS AND VITAL STATISTICS (Females)

VITAL STATISTICS		THOMPSON AGE RANGE	NRR	1000r	INTERVAL	BOURGEOIS-PICHAT AGE RANGE	NRR	1000b	1000d	1000r	COALE	
GRR	2.806	0-4	2.33	30.95	27.32	5-29	2.48	39.77	6.20	33.57	IBR	39.70
NRR	2.510	5-9	2.27	30.71	27.27	30-54	2.31	38.84	7.88	30.96	IDR	7.30
TFR	5.725	10-14	2.26	29.31	27.21	55-79	2.53	43.99	9.59	34.40	IRI	32.41
GENERATION	26.557	15-19	2.23	29.62	27.12	* 5-29	2.48	39.77	6.20	33.57	K1	10.42
SEX RATIO	104.028										K2	0.17

TABLE 9 — LESLIE MATRIX AND ITS SPECTRAL COMPONENTS (Females)

Start of Age Interval	ORIGINAL MATRIX SUB-DIAGONAL	ALTERNATIVE FIRST ROWS Projection	Integral	% IN STABLE POPULATION	FISHER VALUES	REPRODUCTIVE VALUES	SECOND STABLE MATRIX Z₂ FIRST COLUMN	FIRST ROW
0	0.97883	0.00000	0.00000	18.092	1.153	105085	0.1488+0.1207	0.1488+0.1207
5	0.99424	0.00255	0.00000	14.881	1.401	104870	0.1925-0.1002	-0.0454+0.1630
10	0.99466	0.17857	0.00559	12.433	1.674	106716	-0.0175-0.2490	-0.1461+0.0199
15	0.99018	0.54001	0.38592	10.392	1.796	97023	-0.2709-0.0956	-0.0931-0.1312
20	0.98779	0.70045	0.79967	8.647	1.530	68421	-0.2241+0.2411	-0.0085-0.1860
25	0.98815	0.56899	0.73697	7.178	1.026	38018	0.1507+0.3446	0.0408-0.1572
30	0.98544	0.38243	0.51002	5.960	0.572	18306	0.4301-0.0012	0.0546-0.0915
35	0.98088	0.19766	0.32883	4.936	0.243	6874	0.1941-0.4503	0.0350-0.0349
40	0.97642	0.05595	0.10424	4.068	0.063	1539	-0.3811-0.4056	0.0105-0.0083
45	0.96865	0.00973	0.01820	3.338	0.011	214	-0.5917+0.2124	0.0019-0.0014
50	0.95708	0.00143	0.00312	2.717	0.001	22	-0.0457+0.7031	0.0003-0.0001
55+	0.83656			7.357				

TABLE 10 — AGE ANALYSIS AND MISCELLANEOUS RESULTS (Females)

Start of Age Interval	OBSERVED POPUL. (IN 100's)	r_1	r_2, r_3	$r_4 \cdot r_{11}$	AGE-SP. BIRTH RATES	NET MATERNITY FUNCTION	COEFF. OF MATRIX EQUATION	PARAMETERS INTEGRAL	MATRIX	x	EXP. INCREASE $e(x+2\frac{1}{2})r$
0	912	928	-0	-16	0.0000	0.0000	0.0000	L(1) 1.18914	1.19001	0	1.0905
5	748	763	-19	4	0.0000	0.0000	0.0025	L(2) 0.32806	0.34420	50	6.1652
10	637	638	-17	17	0.0011	0.0050	0.1738	0.82132	0.79279	55	7.3312
15	540	533	9	-2	0.0749	0.3426	0.5227	R(1) 0.03465	0.03479	60	8.7178
20	447	443	31	-27	0.1552	0.7029	0.6714	R(2) -0.02457	-0.02917	65	10.3667
25	371	368	16	-14	0.1430	0.6399	0.5387	0.23816	0.23224	70	12.3275
30	320	306	-26	40	0.0990	0.4376	0.3578	C(1)	5128	75	14.6591
35	283	253	-45	74	0.0638	0.2780	0.1822	C(2)	-3000	80	17.4317
40	245	209	-7	43	0.0202	0.0864	0.0506		-3671	85	20.7287
45	203	171	51	-19	0.0035	0.0147	0.0086	2P/Y 26.3826	27.0548	90	24.6494
50	156	139	54	-38	0.0006	0.0024	0.0012	DELTA 2.3416		95	29.3115
55+	418	377								100	34.8555

TABLE 1 — DATA

AGE AT LAST BIRTHDAY	BOTH SEXES	POPULATION MALES Number	%	FEMALES Number	%	BIRTHS BY AGE OF MOTHER	DEATHS BOTH SEXES	MALES	FEMALES	AGE AT LAST BIRTHDAY
0	75674	38242	3.3	37432	3.1	0	3311	1874	1437	0
1-4	278673	141398	12.1	137275	11.5	0	857	412	445	1-4
5-9	327565	165966	14.2	161599	13.5	0	285	158	127	5-9
10-14	321030	162187	13.9	158843	13.3	108	193	121	72	10-14
15-19	247424	122817	10.5	124607	10.4	11907	261	165	96	15-19
20-24	174168	81385	7.0	92783	7.8	25704	274	167	107	20-24
25-29	138737	63158	5.4	75579	6.3	17439	235	121	114	25-29
30-34	128342	59167	5.1	69175	5.8	10538	290	172	118	30-34
35-39	130866	61546	5.3	69320	5.8	7424	381	216	165	35-39
40-44	108710	53734	4.6	54976	4.6	2726	431	260	171	40-44
45-49	106135	53867	4.6	52268	4.4	451	526	320	206	45-49
50-54	76761	40499	3.5	36262	3.0	17	664	400	264	50-54
55-59	66336	34581	3.0	31755	2.7	0	662	419	243	55-59
60-64	58250	29142	2.5	29108	2.4	0	962	572	390	60-64
65-69	48350	24631	2.1	23719	2.0	0	1133	693	440	65-69
70-74	31981	16580	1.4	15401	1.3		1232	722	510	70-74
75-79	21455	10402	0.9	11053	0.9		993	553	440	75-79
80-84	10387	4772	0.4	5615	0.5	38944 M.	1022	511	511	80-84
85+	11272	4323	0.4	6949	0.6	37370 F.	2079	822	1257	85+
TOTAL	2362116	1168397		1193719		76314	15791	8678	7113	TOTAL

TABLE 2 — MALE LIFE TABLE

x	$_nq_x$	l_x	$_nd_x$	$_nL_x$	$_nm_x$	$_na_x$	T_x	r_x	$\mathring{e}_x$	$_nM_x$
0	0.047123	100000	4712	96582	0.048791	0.2747	6740741	0.0057	67.407	0.049004
1	0.011492	95288	1095	378001	0.002897	1.1234	6644159	0.0057	69.727	0.002914
5	0.004733	94193	446	469848	0.000949	2.5000	6266158	0.0088	66.525	0.000952
10	0.003736	93747	350	467898	0.000749	2.6120	5796310	0.0292	61.829	0.000746
15	0.006788	93397	634	465523	0.001362	2.6972	5328412	0.0676	57.051	0.001343
20	0.010246	92763	950	461488	0.002060	2.5534	4862889	0.0646	52.423	0.002052
25	0.009561	91812	878	456941	0.001921	2.5859	4401402	0.0297	47.939	0.001916
30	0.014435	90934	1313	451532	0.002907	2.6084	3944460	0.0000	43.377	0.002907
35	0.017413	89622	1561	444373	0.003512	2.6062	3492928	0.0060	38.974	0.003510
40	0.023936	88061	2108	435237	0.004843	2.5956	3048555	0.0086	34.619	0.004839
45	0.029404	85953	2527	423851	0.005963	2.6595	2613318	0.0217	30.404	0.005941
50	0.048462	83426	4043	407472	0.009922	2.6114	2189468	0.0349	26.244	0.009877
55	0.059074	79383	4689	385815	0.012155	2.6332	1781995	0.0196	22.448	0.012116
60	0.094282	74693	7042	356751	0.019740	2.6264	1396180	0.0340	18.692	0.019628
65	0.132498	67651	8964	316793	0.028295	2.6056	1039429	0.0340	15.365	0.028135
70	0.197415	58687	11586	264929	0.043732	2.5394	722636	0.0340	12.313	0.043546
75	0.236814	47102	11154	208430	0.053516	2.5723	457706	0.0340	9.717	0.053163
80	0.430057	35947	15459	143033	0.108083	2.6258	249277	0.0340	6.935	0.107082
85+	*1.000000	20488	20488	106244	0.192838	5.1857	106244	0.0340	5.186	0.190146

TABLE 3 — FEMALE LIFE TABLE

x	$_nq_x$	l_x	$_nd_x$	$_nL_x$	$_nm_x$	$_na_x$	T_x	r_x	$\mathring{e}_x$	$_nM_x$
0	0.037226	100000	3723	97445	0.038202	0.3136	7203378	0.0066	72.034	0.038390
1	0.012784	96277	1231	381621	0.003225	1.1660	7105933	0.0066	73.807	0.003242
5	0.003902	95047	371	474306	0.000782	2.5000	6724312	0.0082	70.748	0.000786
10	0.002264	94676	214	472842	0.000453	2.4961	6250007	0.0254	66.015	0.000453
15	0.003884	94461	367	471458	0.000778	2.6875	5777165	0.0530	61.159	0.000770
20	0.005787	94094	545	469181	0.001161	2.6291	5305707	0.0488	56.387	0.001153
25	0.007530	93550	704	466039	0.001512	2.5724	4836526	0.0279	51.700	0.001508
30	0.008500	92845	789	462335	0.001707	2.6023	4370486	0.0068	47.073	0.001706
35	0.011864	92056	1092	457680	0.002386	2.6180	3908151	0.0206	42.454	0.002380
40	0.015478	90964	1408	451440	0.003119	2.5993	3450472	0.0251	37.932	0.003110
45	0.019686	89556	1763	443737	0.003973	2.7065	2999032	0.0371	33.488	0.003941
50	0.035940	87793	3155	431374	0.007314	2.5941	2555295	0.0433	29.106	0.007280
55	0.037661	84638	3188	415671	0.007668	2.6413	2123920	0.0131	25.094	0.007652
60	0.065276	81450	5317	394715	0.013470	2.5420	1708249	0.0314	20.973	0.013398
65	0.089455	76134	6811	364757	0.018671	2.6637	1313535	0.0314	17.253	0.018551
70	0.153901	69323	10669	320764	0.033261	2.5769	948778	0.0314	13.686	0.033115
75	0.183259	58654	10749	267968	0.040113	2.6002	628014	0.0314	10.707	0.039808
80	0.379979	47905	18203	197968	0.091949	2.7169	360046	0.0314	7.516	0.091007
85+	*1.000000	29702	29702	162078	0.183259	5.4568	162078	0.0314	5.457	0.180889

TABLE 4 — OBSERVED AND PROJECTED VITAL RATES

	OBSERVED POPULATION BOTH SEXES	MALES	FEMALES	PROJECTED POPULATION 1965 MALES	FEMALES	1970 MALES	FEMALES	1975 MALES	FEMALES	STABLE POPULATION MALES	FEMALES
RATES PER THOUSAND											
Birth	32.31	33.33	31.31	35.66	33.59	37.37	35.28	36.82	34.84	34.57	33.46
Death	6.69	7.43	5.96	7.38	5.72	7.57	5.98	7.55	6.07	7.31	6.20
Increase	25.62	25.90	25.35	28.28	27.87	29.80	29.29	29.27	28.77		27.255
PERCENTAGE											
under 15	42.46	43.46	41.48	41.01	39.12	40.77	38.90	41.49	39.65	40.07	39.17
15-64	52.31	51.34	53.26	53.74	55.49	54.03	55.69	53.49	55.10	55.19	55.12
65 and over	5.23	5.20	5.26	5.25	5.38	5.20	5.41	5.02	5.25	4.74	5.71
DEP. RATIO X 100	91.15	94.77	87.74	86.08	80.21	85.08	79.57	86.95	81.48	81.21	81.43

TABLE 5 — POPULATION PROJECTED WITH FIXED AGE-SPECIFIC BIRTH AND DEATH RATES (IN 1000's)

AGE AT LAST BIRTHDAY	1965 BOTH SEXES	MALES	FEMALES	1970 BOTH SEXES	MALES	FEMALES	1975 BOTH SEXES	MALES	FEMALES	AGE AT LAST BIRTHDAY
0-4	405	206	199	494	251	243	579	294	285	0-4
5-9	351	178	173	401	204	197	488	248	240	5-9
10-14	326	165	161	349	177	172	400	203	197	10-14
15-19	319	161	158	325	164	161	348	176	172	15-19
20-24	246	122	124	318	160	158	323	163	160	20-24
25-29	173	81	92	244	121	123	315	158	157	25-29
30-34	137	62	75	171	80	91	241	119	122	30-34
35-39	126	58	68	135	61	74	169	78	91	35-39
40-44	128	60	68	125	57	68	133	60	73	40-44
45-49	106	52	54	126	59	67	122	56	66	45-49
50-54	103	52	51	103	50	53	121	56	65	50-54
55-59	73	38	35	98	49	49	99	48	51	55-59
60-64	62	32	30	68	35	33	91	45	46	60-64
65-69	53	26	27	56	28	28	62	31	31	65-69
70-74	42	21	21	46	22	24	49	24	25	70-74
75-79	26	13	13	33	16	17	37	17	20	75-79
80-84	15	7	8	19	9	10	24	11	13	80-84
85+	9	4	5	12	5	7	15	7	8	85+
TOTAL	2700	1338	1362	3123	1548	1575	3616	1794	1822	TOTAL

TABLE 6 — STANDARDIZED RATES

STANDARD COUNTRIES: STANDARDIZED RATES PER THOUSAND

	ENGLAND AND WALES 1961 BOTH SEXES	MALES	FEMALES	UNITED STATES 1960 BOTH SEXES	MALES	FEMALES	MEXICO 1960 BOTH SEXES	MALES	FEMALES
Birth	29.55	39.73*	28.04	30.05	36.17*	28.99	34.54	36.66*	33.74
Death	10.08	11.93*	10.06	8.61	10.27*	7.91	5.49	6.53*	4.78
Increase	19.47	27.80*	17.98	21.44	25.90*	21.08	29.05	30.13*	28.96

TABLE 7 — MOMENTS AND CUMULANTS

	OBSERVED POP. MALES	FEMALES	STATIONARY POP. MALES	FEMALES	STABLE POP. MALES	FEMALES	OBSERVED BIRTHS	NET MATERNITY FUNCTION	BIRTHS IN STABLE POP.
μ	24.72166	24.99419	37.87930	39.58049	24.89811	25.71072	26.55725	27.86035	26.59021
σ^2	413.6607	406.2612	543.5792	576.5197	391.1754	418.4211	45.09017	47.19536	41.79091
κ_3	7553.666	7569.352	2923.471	2475.864	6835.931	7461.267	217.2113	191.0578	201.8225
κ_4	-18442.	13055.	-290947.	-348163.	6505.	-3278.	-361.557	-813.451	-2.890
β_1	0.806089	0.854479	0.053202	0.031990	0.780694	0.759949	0.514658	0.347242	0.558076
β_2	2.892226	3.079101	2.015335	1.952499	3.042509	2.981277	2.822167	2.634798	2.998346
κ	-0.290299	-0.336532	-0.019888	-0.011606	-0.321254	-0.304101	-0.235607	-0.163767	-0.289988

TABLE 8 — RATES FROM AGE DISTRIBUTIONS AND VITAL STATISTICS (Females)

VITAL STATISTICS

		THOMPSON AGE RANGE	NRR	1000r	INTERVAL	BOURGEOIS-PICHAT AGE RANGE	NRR	1000b	1000d	1000r	COALE	
GRR	2.258											
NRR	2.100	0-4	2.08	27.71	27.38	5-29	2.97	42.33	2.04	40.29	IBR	35.12
TFR	4.611	5-9	2.26	30.48	27.34	30-54	2.13	33.80	5.71	28.09	IDR	6.15
GENERATION	27.213	10-14	2.55	33.39	27.28	55-79	2.27	39.09	8.71	30.38	IRI	28.97
SEX RATIO	104.212	15-19	2.24	29.69	27.20	*25-49	1.58	22.02	5.11	16.91	K1	0.
											K2	0.

TABLE 9 — LESLIE MATRIX AND ITS SPECTRAL COMPONENTS (Females)

Start of Age Interval	SUB-DIAGONAL	ALTERNATIVE FIRST ROWS Projection	Integral	% IN STABLE POPULATION	FISHER VALUES	REPRODUCTIVE VALUES	SECOND STABLE MATRIX Z_2 FIRST COLUMN	FIRST ROW
0	0.99006	0.00000	0.00000	15.005	1.117	195121	0.1446+0.1658	0.1446+0.1658
5	0.99691	0.00080	0.00000	12.958	1.293	209000	0.2557-0.0764	-0.0751+0.1651
10	0.99707	0.11255	0.00171	11.267	1.487	236121	0.0443-0.3228	-0.1487-0.0002
15	0.99517	0.43546	0.23998	9.799	1.583	197279	-0.3364-0.2124	-0.0666-0.1296
20	0.99330	0.59379	0.69573	8.505	1.335	123889	-0.4055+0.2661	0.0109-0.1663
25	0.99205	0.44791	0.57947	7.369	0.874	66023	0.0906+0.5831	0.0417-0.1475
30	0.98993	0.30304	0.38257	6.376	0.505	34954	0.6906+0.1931	0.0595-0.0939
35	0.98637	0.18299	0.26896	5.505	0.243	16868	0.5597-0.6653	0.0465-0.0382
40	0.98294	0.06811	0.12453	4.736	0.076	4158	-0.4519-0.9483	0.0179-0.0088
45	0.97214	0.01066	0.02167	4.061	0.011	565	-1.2645+0.0227	0.0028-0.0010
50	0.96360	0.00055	0.00118	3.443	0.001	19	-0.5987+1.3819	0.0001-0.0000
55+	0.84424			10.976				

TABLE 10 — AGE ANALYSIS AND MISCELLANEOUS RESULTS (Females)

CONTRIBUTIONS OF ROOTS (IN 100's)

Start of Age Interval	OBSERVED POPUL. (IN 100's)	r_1	r_2, r_3	r_4-r_{11}	AGE-SP. BIRTH RATES	NET MATERNITY FUNCTION	COEFF. OF MATRIX EQUATION	PARAMETERS INTEGRAL	MATRIX	EXP. INCREASE x	$e^{(x+2\frac{1}{2})r}$
0	1747	1837	-123	33	0.0000	0.0000	0.0000	L(1) 1.14600	1.14650	0	1.0705
5	1616	1586	9	20	0.0000	0.0000	0.0008	L(2) 0.31145	0.33792	50	4.1826
10	1588	1379	-192	17	0.0003	0.0016	0.1111	0.76951	0.74320	55	4.7932
15	1246	1200	180	-134	0.0468	0.2206	0.4285	R(1) 0.02726	0.02734	60	5.4931
20	928	1041	-104	-10	0.1357	0.6365	0.5815	R(2) -0.03723	-0.04057	65	6.2951
25	756	902	-372	225	0.1130	0.5266	0.4357	0.23724	0.22881	70	7.2141
30	692	781	-220	132	0.0746	0.3449	0.2925			75	8.2674
35	693	674	327	-307	0.0524	0.2400	0.1748	C(1)	12243	80	9.4745
40	550	580	649	-680	0.0243	0.1096	0.0642	C(2)	-7366	85	10.8578
45	523	497	172	-147	0.0042	0.0187	0.0099		30733	90	12.4430
50	363	422	-761	702	0.0002	0.0010	0.0005	2P/Y 26.4842	27.4602	95	14.2597
55+	1236	1344						DELTA 4.0753		100	16.3416

TABLE 1 — DATA

AGE AT LAST BIRTHDAY	POPULATION BOTH SEXES	MALES Number	%	FEMALES Number	%	BIRTHS BY AGE OF MOTHER	DEATHS BOTH SEXES	MALES	FEMALES	AGE AT LAST BIRTHDAY
0	73200	38500	3.1	34700	2.7	0	3454	1999	1455	0
1-4	280500	141400	11.4	139100	10.9	0	653	314	339	1-4
5-9	327999	166400	13.5	161599	12.7	0	211	123	88	5-9
10-14	318900	161500	13.1	157400	12.3	132	170	110	60	10-14
15-19	254200	125400	10.1	128800	10.1	13054	280	178	102	15-19
20-24	204200	100500	8.1	103700	8.1	26744	287	188	99	20-24
25-29	169300	77400	6.3	91900	7.2	17584	252	160	92	25-29
30-34	147700	64500	5.2	83200	6.5	10054	305	195	110	30-34
35-39	133300	61000	4.9	72300	5.7	6864	402	263	139	35-39
40-44	125000	61500	5.0	63500	5.0	3008	448	276	172	40-44
45-49	112700	54900	4.4	57800	4.5	0	555	347	208	45-49
50-54	95400	48500	3.9	46900	3.7	0	751	468	283	50-54
55-59	71900	36700	3.0	35200	2.8	0	801	536	265	55-59
60-64	60400	29700	2.4	30700	2.4	0	1083	649	434	60-64
65-69	51300	25900	2.1	25400	2.0	0	1306	775	531	65-69
70-74	37700	19100	1.5	18600	1.5		1384	844	540	70-74
75-79	26187	12708	1.0	13479	1.1		1285	728	557	75-79
80-84	15967	7340	0.6	8627	0.7	39772 M.	1277	634	643	80-84
85+	7147	3052	0.2	4095	0.3	37668 F.	2446	1061	1385	85+
TOTAL	2513000	1236000		1277000		77440	17350	9848	7502	TOTAL

TABLE 2 — MALE LIFE TABLE

x	$_nq_x$	l_x	$_nd_x$	$_nL_x$	$_nm_x$	$_na_x$	T_x	r_x	$\mathring{e}_x$	$_nM_x$	x
0	0.049699	100000	4970	96217	0.051653	0.2389	6653833	0.0067	66.538	0.051922	0
1	0.008747	95030	831	377705	0.002201	1.0937	6557616	0.0067	69.006	0.002221	1
5	0.003677	94199	346	470129	0.000737	2.5000	6179911	0.0096	65.605	0.000739	5
10	0.003420	93853	321	468527	0.000685	2.7081	5709782	0.0274	60.838	0.000681	10
15	0.007131	93532	667	466104	0.001431	2.6707	5241255	0.0461	56.037	0.001419	15
20	0.009342	92865	868	462213	0.001877	2.5682	4775151	0.0464	51.421	0.001871	20
25	0.010335	91997	951	457713	0.002077	2.6103	4312938	0.0421	46.881	0.002067	25
30	0.015057	91046	1371	452005	0.003033	2.6463	3855224	0.0207	42.344	0.003023	30
35	0.021334	89675	1913	443715	0.004312	2.5630	3403219	0.0007	37.950	0.004311	35
40	0.022210	87762	1949	434098	0.004490	2.5820	2959505	-0.0057	33.722	0.004488	40
45	0.031230	85813	2680	422781	0.006339	2.6550	2525406	-0.0172	29.429	0.006321	45
50	0.047427	83133	3943	406421	0.009701	2.6554	2102626	-0.0303	25.292	0.009649	50
55	0.070982	79190	5621	382674	0.014689	2.6378	1696204	-0.0339	21.419	0.014605	55
60	0.104139	73569	7661	349443	0.021925	2.5980	1313530	-0.0233	17.854	0.021852	60
65	0.139967	65908	9225	307240	0.030025	2.5828	964087	-0.0233	14.628	0.029923	65
70	0.199821	56683	11326	255553	0.044321	2.5401	656847	-0.0233	11.588	0.044188	70
75	0.251479	45356	11406	198469	0.057471	2.5178	401294	-0.0233	8.848	0.057287	75
80	0.362244	33950	12298	141140	0.087135	2.6736	202825	-0.0233	5.974	0.086376	80
85+	*1.000000	21652	21652	61685	0.351009	2.8489	61685	-0.0233	2.849	0.347641	85+

TABLE 3 — FEMALE LIFE TABLE

x	$_nq_x$	l_x	$_nd_x$	$_nL_x$	$_nm_x$	$_na_x$	T_x	r_x	$\mathring{e}_x$	$_nM_x$	x
0	0.040690	100000	4069	97041	0.041931	0.2727	7201820	0.0000	72.018	0.041931	0
1	0.009680	95931	929	381051	0.002437	1.1215	7104779	0.0000	74.061	0.002437	1
5	0.002704	95002	257	474370	0.000541	2.5000	6723728	0.0089	70.774	0.000545	5
10	0.001910	94745	181	473300	0.000382	2.6372	6249359	0.0222	65.959	0.000381	10
15	0.003977	94565	376	471938	0.000797	2.6486	5776059	0.0410	61.081	0.000792	15
20	0.004769	94188	449	469839	0.000956	2.5430	5304121	0.0328	56.314	0.000955	20
25	0.005001	93739	469	467559	0.001003	2.5744	4834282	0.0210	51.572	0.001001	25
30	0.006612	93270	617	464898	0.001326	2.6423	4366723	0.0226	46.818	0.001322	30
35	0.009605	92654	890	461173	0.001930	2.6454	3901825	0.0251	42.112	0.001923	35
40	0.013491	91764	1238	455877	0.002716	2.6234	3440651	0.0197	37.495	0.002709	40
45	0.017934	90526	1623	448867	0.003617	2.6825	2984774	0.0263	32.972	0.003599	45
50	0.029921	88902	2660	438193	0.006070	2.6246	2535908	0.0439	28.525	0.006034	50
55	0.037267	86242	3214	423812	0.007583	2.6976	2097714	0.0337	24.323	0.007528	55
60	0.068759	83028	5709	401809	0.014208	2.6646	1673902	0.0260	20.161	0.014137	60
65	0.099894	77319	7724	368071	0.020984	2.6015	1272093	0.0260	16.452	0.020906	65
70	0.136096	69596	9472	325057	0.029139	2.5800	904022	0.0260	12.990	0.029032	70
75	0.188993	60124	11363	273522	0.041543	2.6153	578965	0.0260	9.630	0.041324	75
80	0.323204	48761	15760	208913	0.075437	2.7860	305443	0.0260	6.264	0.074533	80
85+	*1.000000	33001	33001	96530	0.341875	2.9250	96530	0.0260	2.925	0.338217	85+

TABLE 4 — OBSERVED AND PROJECTED VITAL RATES

	OBSERVED POPULATION BOTH SEXES	MALES	FEMALES	PROJECTED POPULATION 1968 MALES	FEMALES	1973 MALES	FEMALES	1978 MALES	FEMALES	STABLE POPULATION MALES	FEMALES
RATES PER THOUSAND											
Birth	30.82	32.18	29.50	33.43	30.75	34.17	31.54	33.37	30.91	31.06	29.75
Death	6.90	7.97	5.87	7.92	5.81	7.96	5.96	7.88	6.06	8.13	6.81
Increase	23.91	24.21	23.62	25.51	24.93	26.21	25.57	25.49	24.85	22.9353	
PERCENTAGE											
under 15	39.82	41.08	38.59	39.25	36.74	38.99	36.43	39.33	36.77	37.13	35.89
15-64	54.68	53.41	55.91	55.42	57.67	55.84	58.00	55.45	57.45	57.38	57.25
65 and over	5.50	5.51	5.50	5.34	5.58	5.17	5.56	5.21	5.78	5.49	6.86
DEP. RATIO X 100	82.88	87.24	78.85	80.45	73.39	79.08	72.41	80.33	74.07	74.28	74.67

129   Puerto Rico 1964

TABLE 1 — DATA

AGE AT LAST BIRTHDAY	POPULATION BOTH SEXES	MALES Number	%	FEMALES Number	%	BIRTHS BY AGE OF MOTHER	DEATHS BOTH SEXES	MALES	FEMALES	AGE AT LAST BIRTHDAY
0	77000	39000	3.1	38000	2.9	0	4082	2375	1707	0
1-4	280300	142200	11.3	138100	10.6	0	748	361	387	1-4
5-9	330601	166701	13.2	163900	12.5	0	222	134	88	5-9
10-14	318200	161100	12.8	157100	12.0	122	170	105	65	10-14
15-19	252400	123200	9.8	129200	9.9	13512	282	179	103	15-19
20-24	210700	103000	8.2	107700	8.2	27694	281	190	91	20-24
25-29	175700	81200	6.4	94500	7.2	18254	285	170	115	25-29
30-34	155000	68400	5.4	86600	6.6	10010	310	193	117	30-34
35-39	139600	63400	5.0	76200	5.8	6700	379	227	152	35-39
40-44	130000	63800	5.0	66200	5.1	2272	457	296	161	40-44
45-49	117500	58400	4.6	59100	4.5	392	574	368	206	45-49
50-54	100700	51100	4.0	49600	3.8	0	760	481	279	50-54
55-59	76400	39000	3.1	37400	2.9	0	803	520	283	55-59
60-64	63300	31500	2.5	31800	2.4	0	1064	625	439	60-64
65-69	52500	26500	2.1	26000	2.0	0	1375	820	555	65-69
70-74	40000	20200	1.6	19800	1.5		1382	820	562	70-74
75-79	27540	13448	1.1	14092	1.1		1342	773	569	75-79
80-84	17018	7948	0.6	9070	0.7	40490 M.	1366	689	677	80-84
85+	7741	3403	0.3	4338	0.3	38466 F.	2684	1120	1564	85+
TOTAL	2572200	1263500		1308700		78956	18566	10446	8120	TOTAL

TABLE 2 — MALE LIFE TABLE

x	nq_x	l_x	nd_x	nL_x	nm_x	na_x	T_x	r_x	$\mathring{e}_x$	nM_x	x
0	0.057883	100000	5788	95577	0.060562	0.2358	6632124	0.0071	66.321	0.060897	0
1	0.009981	94212	940	374112	0.002514	1.0915	6536547	0.0071	69.381	0.002539	1
5	0.003995	93271	373	465425	0.000801	2.5000	6162435	0.0105	66.070	0.000804	5
10	0.003274	92899	304	463797	0.000656	2.7074	5697010	0.0294	61.325	0.000652	10
15	0.007294	92595	675	461398	0.001464	2.6673	5233213	0.0434	56.517	0.001453	15
20	0.009208	91919	846	457538	0.001850	2.5681	4771816	0.0399	51.913	0.001845	20
25	0.010454	91073	952	453071	0.002101	2.5918	4314278	0.0387	47.372	0.002094	25
30	0.014047	90121	1266	447569	0.002828	2.6030	3861206	0.0219	42.845	0.002822	30
35	0.017756	88855	1578	440484	0.003582	2.5974	3413637	0.0033	38.418	0.003580	35
40	0.022953	87277	2003	431602	0.004641	2.6119	2973154	0.0035	34.066	0.004639	40
45	0.031121	85274	2654	420114	0.006317	2.6427	2541552	0.0156	29.805	0.006301	45
50	0.046254	82620	3822	404060	0.009458	2.6344	2121438	0.0308	25.677	0.009413	50
55	0.064968	78799	5119	381859	0.013407	2.6297	1717378	0.0345	21.795	0.013333	55
60	0.095139	73679	7010	351810	0.019925	2.6339	1335519	0.0238	18.126	0.019841	60
65	0.144368	66669	9625	310024	0.031046	2.5768	983709	0.0238	14.755	0.030943	65
70	0.185063	57044	10557	259271	0.040717	2.5418	673685	0.0238	11.810	0.040594	70
75	0.252567	46488	11741	203515	0.057692	2.5367	414414	0.0238	8.915	0.057481	75
80	0.363286	34746	12623	144338	0.087454	2.6714	210899	0.0238	6.070	0.086689	80
85+	*1.000000	22124	22124	66561	0.332380	3.0086	66561	0.0238	3.009	0.329121	85+

TABLE 3 — FEMALE LIFE TABLE

x	nq_x	l_x	nd_x	nL_x	nm_x	na_x	T_x	r_x	$\mathring{e}_x$	nM_x	x
0	0.043272	100000	4327	96885	0.044663	0.2801	7177027	0.0075	71.770	0.044921	0
1	0.011036	95673	1056	379659	0.002781	1.1285	7080143	0.0075	74.004	0.002802	1
5	0.002660	94617	252	472455	0.000533	2.5000	6700483	0.0103	70.817	0.000537	5
10	0.002073	94365	196	471363	0.000415	2.6326	6228028	0.0233	65.999	0.000414	10
15	0.003995	94170	376	469949	0.000801	2.6113	5756665	0.0370	61.131	0.000797	15
20	0.004229	93793	397	468015	0.000848	2.6005	5286716	0.0303	56.366	0.000845	20
25	0.006078	93397	568	465612	0.001219	2.5844	4818702	0.0207	51.594	0.001217	25
30	0.006750	92829	627	462652	0.001354	2.6164	4353090	0.0201	46.894	0.001351	30
35	0.009954	92202	918	458818	0.002000	2.6090	3890438	0.0249	42.195	0.001995	35
40	0.012125	91285	1107	453791	0.002439	2.6221	3431620	0.0229	37.593	0.002432	40
45	0.017371	90178	1566	447258	0.003502	2.6819	2977829	0.0251	33.022	0.003486	45
50	0.027924	88611	2474	437217	0.005659	2.6399	2530571	0.0402	28.558	0.005625	50
55	0.037475	86137	3228	423260	0.007626	2.6999	2093354	0.0360	24.303	0.007567	55
60	0.067204	82909	5572	401584	0.013875	2.6739	1670094	0.0247	20.144	0.013805	60
65	0.101861	77337	7878	367758	0.021421	2.5973	1268510	0.0247	16.402	0.021346	65
70	0.133185	69460	9251	324851	0.028478	2.5736	900752	0.0247	12.968	0.028384	70
75	0.185094	60209	11144	274562	0.040589	2.6238	575901	0.0247	9.565	0.040378	75
80	0.323573	49064	15876	210224	0.075519	2.7893	301339	0.0247	6.142	0.074641	80
85+	*1.000000	33188	33188	91115	0.364248	2.7454	91115	0.0247	2.745	0.360535	85+

TABLE 4 — OBSERVED AND PROJECTED VITAL RATES

	OBSERVED POPULATION BOTH SEXES	MALES	FEMALES	PROJECTED POPULATION 1969 MALES	FEMALES	1974 MALES	FEMALES	1979 MALES	FEMALES	STABLE POPULATION MALES	FEMALES
RATES PER THOUSAND											
Birth	30.70	32.05	29.39	32.96	30.32	33.59	30.97	32.95	30.47	30.80	29.38
Death	7.22	8.27	6.20	8.24	6.07	8.29	6.23	8.25	6.35	8.44	7.03
Increase	23.48	23.78	23.19	24.72	24.25	25.30	24.74	24.70	24.12	22.3583	
PERCENTAGE											
under 15	39.11	40.29	37.98	38.63	36.38	38.38	36.01	38.64	36.28	36.61	35.46
15-64	55.26	54.06	56.41	55.83	57.95	56.19	58.28	55.82	57.74	57.60	57.48
65 and over	5.63	5.66	5.60	5.54	5.67	5.44	5.71	5.53	5.98	5.79	7.06
DEP. RATIO X 100	80.98	84.99	77.26	79.11	72.56	77.98	71.58	79.14	73.18	73.61	73.97

TABLE 1 — DATA

AGE AT LAST BIRTHDAY	POPULATION BOTH SEXES	MALES Number	MALES %	FEMALES Number	FEMALES %	BIRTHS BY AGE OF MOTHER	DEATHS BOTH SEXES	MALES	FEMALES	AGE AT LAST BIRTHDAY
0	79400	40400	3.1	39000	2.9	0	3409	1958	1451	0
1-4	284700	144200	11.2	140500	10.5	0	523	239	284	1-4
5-9	333400	168200	13.1	165200	12.3	0	198	117	81	5-9
10-14	317800	160800	12.5	157000	11.7	108	162	107	55	10-14
15-19	249100	120400	9.4	128700	9.6	13780	266	172	94	15-19
20-24	209000	99100	7.7	109900	8.2	28060	288	192	96	20-24
25-29	178900	82100	6.4	96800	7.2	18578	274	172	102	25-29
30-34	160200	71600	5.6	88600	6.6	10040	261	169	92	30-34
35-39	144400	66500	5.2	77900	5.8	6370	371	218	153	35-39
40-44	138800	67400	5.2	71400	5.3	2282	452	299	153	40-44
45-49	122500	61500	4.8	61000	4.6	390	587	348	239	45-49
50-54	107000	54800	4.3	52200	3.9	0	788	523	265	50-54
55-59	82000	42100	3.3	39900	3.0	0	853	565	288	55-59
60-64	66800	33200	2.6	33600	2.5	0	1081	672	409	60-64
65-69	53700	27000	2.1	26700	2.0	0	1375	822	553	65-69
70-74	42100	21100	1.6	21000	1.6		1436	862	544	70-74
75-79	29363	14541	1.1	14822	1.1		1369	749	620	75-79
80-84	18145	8479	0.7	9666	0.7	40824 M.	1355	695	660	80-84
85+	8292	3580	0.3	4712	0.4	38784 F.	2668	1164	1504	85+
TOTAL	2625600	1287000		1338600		79608	17686	10043	7643	TOTAL

TABLE 2 — MALE LIFE TABLE

x	nq_x	l_x	nd_x	nL_x	nm_x	na_x	T_x	r_x	$\mathring{e}_x$	nM_x	x
0	0.046340	100000	4634	96364	0.048089	0.2153	6771844	0.0099	67.718	0.048465	0
1	0.006492	95366	619	379655	0.001631	1.0779	6675480	0.0099	69.999	0.001657	1
5	0.003462	94747	328	472914	0.000694	2.5000	6295825	0.0128	66.449	0.000696	5
10	0.003347	94419	316	471377	0.000670	2.7293	5822911	0.0326	61.671	0.000665	10
15	0.007181	94103	676	468947	0.001441	2.6810	5351534	0.0470	56.869	0.001429	15
20	0.009667	93427	903	464938	0.001942	2.5668	4882587	0.0364	52.261	0.001937	20
25	0.010434	92524	965	460242	0.002098	2.5374	4417649	0.0304	47.746	0.002095	25
30	0.011758	91559	1077	455207	0.002365	2.5981	3957407	0.0186	43.223	0.002360	30
35	0.016270	90482	1472	448913	0.003279	2.6242	3502200	0.0027	38.706	0.003278	35
40	0.021956	89010	1954	440365	0.004438	2.6029	3053287	0.0034	34.303	0.004436	40
45	0.027999	87056	2437	429604	0.005674	2.6721	2612923	0.0145	30.014	0.005659	45
50	0.046891	84618	3968	413762	0.009590	2.6490	2183319	0.0284	25.802	0.009544	50
55	0.065403	80650	5275	390760	0.013499	2.6320	1769557	0.0361	21.941	0.013420	55
60	0.096972	75375	7309	359522	0.020331	2.6256	1378797	0.0262	18.292	0.020241	60
65	0.142243	68066	9682	316865	0.030555	2.5764	1019274	0.0262	14.975	0.030444	65
70	0.185969	58384	10858	265031	0.040968	2.5234	702409	0.0262	12.031	0.040853	70
75	0.229322	47527	10899	210780	0.051707	2.5362	437379	0.0262	9.203	0.051510	75
80	0.348165	36628	12752	153961	0.082830	2.7120	226598	0.0262	6.187	0.081966	80
85+	*1.000000	23875	23875	72638	0.328689	3.0424	72638	0.0262	3.042	0.325140	85+

TABLE 3 — FEMALE LIFE TABLE

x	nq_x	l_x	nd_x	nL_x	nm_x	na_x	T_x	r_x	$\mathring{e}_x$	nM_x	x
0	0.035973	100000	3597	97357	0.036950	0.2653	7317714	0.0089	73.177	0.037205	0
1	0.007960	96403	767	383397	0.002001	1.1148	7220356	0.0089	74.898	0.002021	1
5	0.002431	95635	232	477595	0.000487	2.5000	6836960	0.0125	71.490	0.000490	5
10	0.001756	95403	168	476620	0.000352	2.6449	6359364	0.0245	66.658	0.000350	10
15	0.003665	95235	349	475355	0.000734	2.6474	5882745	0.0350	61.771	0.000730	15
20	0.004368	94886	414	473426	0.000875	2.5743	5407389	0.0276	56.988	0.000874	20
25	0.005258	94472	497	471133	0.001054	2.5311	4933963	0.0205	52.227	0.001054	25
30	0.005199	93975	489	468741	0.001042	2.6787	4462830	0.0205	47.490	0.001038	30
35	0.009797	93487	916	465248	0.001969	2.6143	3994089	0.0198	42.724	0.001964	35
40	0.010705	92571	991	460557	0.002152	2.6828	3528842	0.0219	38.121	0.002143	40
45	0.019495	91580	1785	453700	0.003935	2.6485	3068285	0.0276	33.504	0.003918	45
50	0.025205	89794	2263	443593	0.005102	2.6237	2614585	0.0372	29.117	0.005077	50
55	0.035752	87531	3129	430407	0.007271	2.6840	2170991	0.0363	24.803	0.007218	55
60	0.059566	84402	5027	410425	0.012249	2.6960	1740584	0.0282	20.623	0.012173	60
65	0.099023	79374	7860	377998	0.020793	2.5988	1330159	0.0282	16.758	0.020712	65
70	0.122443	71514	8756	336542	0.026019	2.5984	952161	0.0282	13.314	0.025905	70
75	0.191130	62758	11995	285158	0.042064	2.6131	615619	0.0282	9.809	0.041830	75
80	0.300755	50763	15267	220543	0.069226	2.8207	330461	0.0282	6.510	0.068280	80
85+	*1.000000	35496	35496	109918	0.322929	3.0967	109918	0.0282	3.097	0.319185	85+

TABLE 4 — OBSERVED AND PROJECTED VITAL RATES

RATES PER THOUSAND	OBSERVED POPULATION BOTH SEXES	MALES	FEMALES	1970 MALES	1970 FEMALES	1975 MALES	1975 FEMALES	1980 MALES	1980 FEMALES	STABLE POPULATION MALES	STABLE POPULATION FEMALES
Birth	30.32	31.72	28.97	32.33	29.62	32.87	30.21	32.36	29.84	30.28	28.99
Death	6.74	7.80	5.71	7.82	5.70	7.90	5.86	7.84	6.00	7.88	6.60
Increase	23.58	23.92	23.26	24.51	23.92	24.97	24.35	24.52	23.84		22.3987
PERCENTAGE											
under 15	38.67	39.91	37.48	38.54	36.09	38.35	35.75	38.55	35.92	36.53	35.34
15-64	55.56	54.29	56.78	55.73	58.02	55.95	58.24	55.60	57.75	57.60	57.41
65 and over	5.77	5.80	5.74	5.73	5.89	5.70	6.01	5.85	6.33	5.87	7.25
DEP. RATIO X 100	80.00	84.20	76.13	79.42	72.35	78.74	71.71	79.86	73.17	73.60	74.19

TABLE 5 — POPULATION PROJECTED WITH FIXED AGE—SPECIFIC BIRTH AND DEATH RATES (IN 1000's)

AGE AT LAST BIRTHDAY	1970 BOTH SEXES	1970 MALES	1970 FEMALES	1975 BOTH SEXES	1975 MALES	1975 FEMALES	1980 BOTH SEXES	1980 MALES	1980 FEMALES	AGE AT LAST BIRTHDAY
0-4	410	209	201	472	241	231	533	272	261	0-4
5-9	361	183	178	407	208	199	468	239	229	5-9
10-14	333	168	165	361	183	178	406	207	199	10-14
15-19	317	160	157	331	167	164	359	182	177	15-19
20-24	247	119	128	315	159	156	329	165	164	20-24
25-29	207	98	109	246	118	128	312	157	155	25-29
30-34	177	81	96	206	97	109	244	117	127	30-34
35-39	159	71	88	176	80	96	204	96	108	35-39
40-44	142	65	77	156	69	87	174	79	95	40-44
45-49	136	66	70	140	64	76	154	68	86	45-49
50-54	119	59	60	132	63	69	135	61	74	50-54
55-59	103	52	51	114	56	58	127	60	67	55-59
60-64	77	39	38	96	48	48	106	51	55	60-64
65-69	60	29	31	69	34	35	86	42	44	65-69
70-74	47	23	24	52	24	28	60	29	31	70-74
75-79	35	17	18	38	18	20	42	19	23	75-79
80-84	22	11	11	26	12	14	29	13	16	80-84
85+	9	4	5	11	5	6	13	6	7	85+
TOTAL	2961	1454	1507	3348	1646	1702	3781	1863	1918	TOTAL

TABLE 6 — STANDARDIZED RATES

STANDARD COUNTRIES:

STANDARDIZED RATES PER THOUSAND	ENGLAND AND WALES 1961 BOTH SEXES	MALES	FEMALES	UNITED STATES 1960 BOTH SEXES	MALES	FEMALES	MEXICO 1960 BOTH SEXES	MALES	FEMALES
Birth	25.26	34.13*	23.85	25.73	31.20*	24.70	30.45	31.68*	29.60
Death	10.24	11.49*	10.20	8.69	9.98*	7.91	5.17	6.80*	4.33
Increase	15.02	22.64*	13.65	17.04	21.22*	16.79	25.28	24.89*	25.27

TABLE 7 — MOMENTS AND CUMULANTS

	OBSERVED POP. MALES	OBSERVED POP. FEMALES	STATIONARY POP. MALES	STATIONARY POP. FEMALES	STABLE POP. MALES	STABLE POP. FEMALES	OBSERVED BIRTHS	NET MATERNITY FUNCTION	BIRTHS IN STABLE POP.
μ	26.25485	26.58016	37.70881	39.62795	26.84860	27.97380	25.94501	26.97904	25.96528
σ^2	430.3199	416.3483	534.8416	567.8252	420.4333	453.8664	41.48964	45.55735	40.78726
κ_3	6991.462	6696.439	2721.668	2055.594	6563.474	7062.585	217.0105	210.4855	212.9760
κ_4	-58864.	-33563.	-285128.	-345275.	-45391.	-74578.	155.176	-452.877	206.487
β_1	0.613425	0.621323	0.048417	0.023080	0.579664	0.533511	0.659390	0.468564	0.668479
β_2	2.682117	2.806380	2.003244	1.929132	2.743210	2.637961	3.090146	2.781795	3.124121
κ	-0.224984	-0.248488	-0.018006	-0.008291	-0.229808	-0.203747	-0.327551	-0.218669	-0.339998

TABLE 8 — RATES FROM AGE DISTRIBUTIONS AND VITAL STATISTICS (Females)

VITAL STATISTICS		THOMPSON AGE RANGE	NRR	1000r	INTERVAL	BOURGEOIS-PICHAT AGE RANGE	NRR	1000b	1000d	1000r	COALE	
GRR	1.921										IBR	30.27
NRR	1.809	0-4	1.83	22.73	27.42	5-29	2.12	32.99	5.16	27.83	IDR	7.56
TFR	3.942	5-9	1.91	24.03	27.38	30-54	1.88	30.36	7.01	23.34	IRI	22.71
GENERATION	26.463	10-14	2.03	25.42	27.33	55-79	2.06	32.23	5.53	26.70	K1	-3.86
SEX RATIO	105.260	15-19	1.88	16.74	27.26	*20-44	1.73	27.10	6.85	20.24	K2	0.

TABLE 9 — LESLIE MATRIX AND ITS SPECTRAL COMPONENTS (Females)

Start of Age Interval	ORIGINAL MATRIX SUB-DIAGONAL	ALTERNATIVE FIRST ROWS Projection	ALTERNATIVE FIRST ROWS Integral	FIRST STABLE MATRIX % IN STABLE POPULATION	FISHER VALUES	REPRODUCTIVE VALUES	SECOND STABLE MATRIX Z₂ FIRST COLUMN	SECOND STABLE MATRIX Z₂ FIRST ROW
0	0.99343	0.00000	0.00000	13.201	1.100	197389	0.1545+0.2430	0.1545+0.2430
5	0.99796	0.00080	0.00000	11.721	1.238	204598	0.3678-0.0685	-0.1292+0.1801
10	0.99735	0.12586	0.00170	10.455	1.388	217857	0.0962-0.4787	-0.1651-0.0405
15	0.99594	0.42318	0.26522	9.320	1.418	182483	-0.5325-0.3494	-0.0379-0.1597
20	0.99516	0.52267	0.63245	8.296	1.126	123705	-0.6810+0.4736	0.0372-0.1760
25	0.99492	0.35679	0.47540	7.379	0.688	66594	0.2411+1.0523	0.0550-0.1515
30	0.99255	0.22775	0.28070	6.561	0.379	33606	1.3875+0.2198	0.0684-0.0914
35	0.98992	0.13281	0.20255	5.821	0.175	13651	0.9369-1.5645	0.0495-0.0331
40	0.98511	0.04479	0.07917	5.150	0.051	3607	-1.4265-1.8810	0.0173-0.0067
45	0.97772	0.00749	0.01580	4.534	0.007	450	-2.9344+0.8010	0.0028-0.0005
50	0.97027	0.00002	0.00005	3.963	0.000	1	-0.4500+3.8633	0.0000-0.0000
55+	0.83612			13.599				

TABLE 10 — AGE ANALYSIS AND MISCELLANEOUS RESULTS (Females)

Start of Age Interval	OBSERVED POPUL. (IN 100's)	CONTRIBUTIONS OF ROOTS (IN 100's) r_1	r_2, r_3	$r_4 \cdot r_{11}$	AGE-SP. BIRTH RATES	NET MATERNITY FUNCTION	COEFF. OF MATRIX EQUATION	PARAMETERS	INTEGRAL	MATRIX	EXP. INCREASE x	$e^{(x+2\frac{1}{2})r}$
0	1795	1838	-73	30	0.0000	0.0000	0.0000	L(1)	1.11851	1.11884	0	1.0576
5	1652	1632	-5	25	0.0000	0.0000	0.0008	L(2)	0.23230	0.28531	50	3.2412
10	1570	1456	119	-5	0.0003	0.0016	0.1248		0.74321	0.70944	55	3.6253
15	1287	1298	125	-135	0.0522	0.2480	0.4184	R(1)	0.02240	0.02246	60	4.0549
20	1099	1155	-82	26	0.1244	0.5889	0.5147	R(2)	-0.05003	-0.05367	65	4.5354
25	968	1027	-291	231	0.0935	0.4405	0.3495		0.25357	0.23768	70	5.0729
30	886	914	-144	116	0.0552	0.2588	0.2221	C(1)		13924	75	5.6740
35	779	811	352	-383	0.0398	0.1853	0.1285	C(2)		-3102	80	6.3464
40	714	717	581	-585	0.0156	0.0717	0.0429			13102	85	7.0985
45	610	631	-28	6	0.0031	0.0141	0.0071	2P/Y	24.7787	26.4350	90	7.9397
50	522	552	-984	955	0.0000	0.0000	0.0000	DELTA	2.6976		95	8.8806
55+	1504	1894									100	9.9330

TABLE 1 — DATA

AGE AT LAST BIRTHDAY	POPULATION BOTH SEXES	MALES Number	MALES %	FEMALES Number	FEMALES %	BIRTHS BY AGE OF MOTHER	DEATHS BOTH SEXES	DEATHS MALES	FEMALES	AGE AT LAST BIRTHDAY
0	2358	1172	4.5	1186	3.9	0	239	131	108	0
1-4	8494	4102	15.6	4392	14.3	0	118	66	52	1-4
5-9	8739	4360	16.6	4379	14.3	0	5	5	0	5-9
10-14	6489	3263	12.4	3226	10.5	8	4	1	3	10-14
15-19	5079	2390	9.1	2689	8.8	464	5	3	2	15-19
20-24	3442	1536	5.8	1906	6.2	655	8	2	6	20-24
25-29	2879	1241	4.7	1638	5.3	521	7	3	4	25-29
30-34	2766	1203	4.6	1563	5.1	401	16	8	8	30-34
35-39	2683	1206	4.6	1477	4.8	258	9	6	3	35-39
40-44	2649	1168	4.4	1481	4.8	112	15	6	9	40-44
45-49	2846	1296	4.9	1550	5.0	7	17	9	8	45-49
50-54	2487	1131	4.3	1356	4.4	0	24	14	10	50-54
55-59	1771	758	2.9	1013	3.3	0	34	24	10	55-59
60-64	1512	599	2.3	913	3.0	0	36	11	25	60-64
65-69	924	314	1.2	610	2.0	0	26	14	12	65-69
70-74	804	280	1.1	524	1.7		56	13	43	70-74
75-79	548	174	0.7	374	1.2		41	15	26	75-79
80-84	335	96	0.4	239	0.8	1264 M.	45	17	28	80-84
85+	235	46	0.2	189	0.6	1162 F.	59	17	42	85+
TOTAL	57040	26335		30705		2426	764	365	399	TOTAL

TABLE 2 — MALE LIFE TABLE

x	$_nq_x$	l_x	$_nd_x$	$_nL_x$	$_nm_x$	$_na_x$	T_x	r_x	$\mathring{e}_x$	$_nM_x$	x
0	0.104040	100000	10404	93378	0.111417	0.3635	5657215	0.0049	56.572	0.111775	0
1	0.061462	89596	5507	343215	0.016045	1.2454	5563837	0.0049	62.099	0.016090	1
5	0.005129	84089	431	419368	0.001028	2.5000	5220621	0.0437	62.084	0.001147	5
10	0.001546	83658	129	417987	0.000309	2.6577	4801253	0.0594	57.391	0.000306	10
15	0.006336	83529	529	416407	0.001271	2.6637	4383266	0.0743	52.476	0.001255	15
20	0.006568	82999	545	413733	0.001318	2.6804	3966859	0.0640	47.794	0.001302	20
25	0.012142	82454	1001	410210	0.002441	2.9412	3553127	0.0213	43.092	0.002417	25
30	0.032722	81453	2665	400797	0.006650	2.5730	3142916	0.0000	38.586	0.006650	30
35	0.024561	78788	1935	388952	0.004975	2.4229	2742119	0.0000	34.804	0.004975	35
40	0.025368	76853	1950	379520	0.005137	2.5668	2353167	0.0000	30.619	0.005137	40
45	0.034177	74903	2560	368631	0.006944	2.7013	1973647	0.0000	26.349	0.006944	45
50	0.061148	72343	4424	352205	0.012560	2.8500	1605016	0.0378	22.186	0.012378	50
55	0.147104	67920	9991	314760	0.031742	2.5140	1252810	0.0396	18.446	0.031662	55
60	0.087996	57928	5097	277037	0.018400	2.5274	938050	0.0230	16.193	0.018364	60
65	0.201784	52831	10660	238276	0.044740	2.5725	661013	0.0230	12.512	0.044586	65
70	0.208873	42170	8808	189100	0.046580	2.5305	422737	0.0230	10.024	0.046429	70
75	0.358204	33362	11950	137830	0.086705	2.5749	233636	0.0230	7.003	0.086207	75
80	0.611994	21412	13104	73540	0.178186	2.4421	95807	0.0230	4.475	0.177084	80
85+	*1.000000	8308	8308	22267	0.373108	2.6802	22267	0.0230	2.680	0.369565	85+

TABLE 3 — FEMALE LIFE TABLE

x	$_nq_x$	l_x	$_nd_x$	$_nL_x$	$_nm_x$	$_na_x$	T_x	r_x	$\mathring{e}_x$	$_nM_x$	x
0	0.085945	100000	8594	94457	0.090988	0.3551	6126355	0.0012	61.264	0.091062	0
1	0.045821	91406	4188	354018	0.011831	1.2293	6031897	0.0012	65.991	0.011840	1
5	0.	87217	0	436086	0.	-0.	5677880	0.0517	65.100	0.	5
10	0.004678	87217	408	435135	0.000938	2.6698	5241794	0.0482	60.100	0.000930	10
15	0.003831	86809	333	433413	0.000767	3.0952	4806659	0.0512	55.370	0.000744	15
20	0.015705	86477	1358	429134	0.003165	2.6079	4373246	0.0472	50.571	0.003148	20
25	0.012173	85119	1036	423162	0.002449	2.6540	3944112	0.0165	46.337	0.002442	25
30	0.025264	84082	2124	415058	0.005118	2.4796	3520950	0.0066	41.875	0.005118	30
35	0.010107	81958	828	407783	0.002031	2.5768	3105892	0.0016	37.896	0.002031	35
40	0.029948	81130	2430	399820	0.006077	2.6010	2698108	0.0000	33.257	0.006077	40
45	0.025486	78700	2006	388562	0.005162	2.5377	2298288	0.0029	29.203	0.005161	45
50	0.036407	76694	2792	376825	0.007410	2.6195	1909727	0.0354	24.901	0.007375	50
55	0.048820	73902	3608	361790	0.009972	2.8600	1532902	0.0261	20.742	0.009872	55
60	0.128419	70294	9027	329361	0.027408	2.5507	1171113	0.0100	16.660	0.027382	60
65	0.094770	61267	5806	293893	0.019756	2.8571	841752	0.0100	13.739	0.019672	65
70	0.342226	55461	18980	230877	0.082209	2.5539	547858	0.0100	9.878	0.082061	70
75	0.293775	36481	10717	154106	0.069544	2.3596	316982	0.0100	8.689	0.069519	75
80	0.456359	25764	11757	100109	0.117446	2.5583	162876	0.0100	6.322	0.117155	80
85+	*1.000000	14006	14006	62766	0.223147	4.4814	62766	0.0100	4.481	0.222222	85+

TABLE 4 — OBSERVED AND PROJECTED VITAL RATES

	OBSERVED POPULATION BOTH SEXES	MALES	FEMALES	1965 MALES	1965 FEMALES	1970 MALES	1970 FEMALES	1975 MALES	1975 FEMALES	STABLE POPULATION MALES	STABLE POPULATION FEMALES
RATES PER THOUSAND											
Birth	42.53	48.00	37.84	47.87	39.30	49.62	42.08	52.12	45.46	48.91	46.71
Death	13.39	13.86	12.99	13.10	11.44	12.87	11.36	12.86	11.16	11.88	9.67
Increase	29.14	34.14	24.85	34.77	27.86	36.75	30.72	39.26	34.29		37.0359
PERCENTAGE											
under 15	45.72	48.97	42.93	49.35	44.20	48.55	44.06	48.65	43.91	47.91	47.35
15-64	49.29	47.57	50.76	47.16	49.98	47.97	50.61	47.70	50.88	49.91	50.05
65 and over	4.99	3.46	6.31	3.49	5.81	3.48	5.33	3.65	5.21	2.18	2.61
DEP. RATIO X 100	102.89	110.21	97.00	112.03	100.06	108.48	97.59	109.64	96.53	100.38	99.82

AGE AT LAST BIRTHDAY	1965 BOTH SEXES	MALES	FEMALES	1970 BOTH SEXES	MALES	FEMALES	1975 BOTH SEXES	MALES	FEMALES	AGE AT LAST BIRTHDAY	
0-4	12	6	6	14	7	7	18	9	9	0-4	
5-9	10	5	5	12	6	6	14	7	7	5-9	
10-14	8	4	4	10	5	5	12	6	6	10-14	
15-19	6	3	3	8	4	4	10	5	5	15-19	**TABLE 5**
20-24	5	2	3	6	3	3	8	4	4	20-24	POPULATION
25-29	4	2	2	5	2	3	6	3	3	25-29	PROJECTED
30-34	3	1	2	3	1	2	5	2	3	30-34	WITH
35-39	3	1	2	3	1	2	3	1	2	35-39	FIXED
40-44	2	1	1	3	1	2	3	1	2	40-44	AGE—
45-49	2	1	1	2	1	1	2	1	1	45-49	SPECIFIC
50-54	3	1	2	2	1	1	2	1	1	50-54	BIRTH
55-59	2	1	1	2	1	1	2	1	1	55-59	AND
60-64	2	1	1	2	1	1	2	1	1	60-64	DEATH
65-69	2	1	1	2	1	1	2	1	1	65-69	RATES
70-74	0	0	0	1	0	1	1	0	1	70-74	(IN 1000's)
75-79	0	0	0	0	0	0	0	0	0	75-79	
80-84	0	0	0	0	0	0	0	0	0	80-84	
85+	0	0	0	0	0	0	0	0	0	85+	
TOTAL	64	30	34	75	35	40	90	43	47	TOTAL	

STANDARD COUNTRIES: STANDARDIZED RATES PER THOUSAND	ENGLAND AND WALES 1961 BOTH SEXES	MALES	FEMALES	UNITED STATES 1960 BOTH SEXES	MALES	FEMALES	MEXICO 1960 BOTH SEXES	MALES	FEMALES	
Birth	43.39	64.97*	40.28	44.35	59.47*	41.85	50.26	58.52*	48.02	**TABLE 6**
Death	16.56	26.12*	16.63	14.70	21.57*	13.62	10.60	11.99*	9.40	STANDARDIZED RATES
Increase	26.83	38.85*	23.65	29.64	37.90*	28.23	39.66	46.53*	38.63	

	OBSERVED POP. MALES	FEMALES	STATIONARY POP. MALES	FEMALES	STABLE POP. MALES	FEMALES	OBSERVED BIRTHS	NET MATERNITY FUNCTION	BIRTHS IN STABLE POP.	
μ	22.77348	25.91049	35.52445	36.94995	20.64291	21.11773	26.82811	27.90863	26.13788	**TABLE 7**
σ^2	398.6705	475.8317	487.7830	518.0268	299.6563	316.6854	50.39186	48.30729	42.86803	MOMENTS
κ_3	7311.169	8268.834	2798.404	2671.750	5525.363	6050.894	175.8407	120.9561	166.5754	AND
κ_4	-22807.	-85187.	-224652.	-263271.	53115.	59074.	-1711.554	-1721.214	-725.699	CUMULANTS
β_1	0.843590	0.634641	0.067475	0.051349	1.134623	1.152803	0.241634	0.129783	0.352226	
β_2	2.856502	2.623760	2.055815	2.018932	3.591518	3.589033	2.325985	2.262419	2.605098	
κ	-0.288593	-0.219876	-0.025712	-0.019290	-0.506231	-0.503504	-0.096355	-0.055645	-0.160005	

VITAL STATISTICS		THOMPSON AGE RANGE	NRR	1000r	INTERVAL	BOURGEOIS-PICHAT AGE RANGE	NRR	1000b	1000d	1000r	COALE	**TABLE 8**
GRR	3.229										IBR	RATES FROM AGE DISTRIBUTIONS AND VITAL STATISTICS (Females)
NRR	2.719	0-4	2.90	39.03	27.29	5-29	3.69	45.76	-2.62	48.38	IDR	
TFR	6.741	5-9	2.57	35.55	27.22	30-54	1.00	12.10	12.21	-0.11	IRI	
GENERATION	27.007	10-14	1.97	24.50	27.17	55-79	1.64	26.46	8.07	18.39	K1	
SEX RATIO	108.778	15-19	1.73	15.86	27.11	*25-49	0.98	11.94	12.81	-0.87	K2	

Start of Age Interval	ORIGINAL MATRIX SUB-DIAGONAL	ALTERNATIVE FIRST ROWS Projection	Integral	FIRST STABLE MATRIX % IN STABLE POPULATION	FISHER VALUES	REPRODUCTIVE VALUES	SECOND STABLE MATRIX Z2 FIRST COLUMN	FIRST ROW	
0	0.97238	0.00000	0.00000	19.160	1.221	6813	0.1135+0.1123	0.1135+0.1123	**TABLE 9**
5	0.99782	0.00266	0.00000	15.468	1.513	6625	0.1700-0.0577	-0.0442+0.1350	LESLIE MATRIX
10	0.99604	0.18726	0.00584	12.815	1.823	5881	0.0281-0.2052	-0.1221+0.0177	AND ITS
15	0.99013	0.55079	0.40662	10.598	1.975	5310	-0.1970-0.1346	-0.0825-0.1091	SPECTRAL
20	0.98608	0.70597	0.80981	8.712	1.723	3283	-0.2386+0.1329	-0.0101-0.1696	COMPONENTS
25	0.98085	0.61190	0.74953	7.133	1.230	2014	0.0139+0.3111	0.0478-0.1548	(Females)
30	0.98247	0.45988	0.60457	5.809	0.748	1169	0.3226+0.1436	0.0701-0.0934	
35	0.98047	0.26725	0.41163	4.738	0.345	510	0.3097-0.2549	0.0480-0.0341	
40	0.97184	0.08526	0.17821	3.857	0.091	135	-0.1016-0.4432	0.0149-0.0062	
45	0.96979	0.00493	0.00912	3.112	0.006	9	-0.4965-0.1205	0.0009-0.0005	
50	0.96010	0.00079	0.00174	2.506	0.001	1	-0.3696+0.4376	0.0001-0.0000	
55+	0.80947			6.092					

Start of Age Interval	OBSERVED POPUL. (IN 100's)	CONTRIBUTIONS OF ROOTS (IN 100's) r_1	r_2, r_3	$r_4 \cdot r_{11}$	AGE-SP. BIRTH RATES	NET MATERNITY FUNCTION	COEFF. OF MATRIX EQUATION	PARAMETERS INTEGRAL	MATRIX	EXP. INCREASE x	$e^{(x+2\frac{1}{2})r}$	
0	56	50	2	4	0.0000	0.0000	0.0000	L(1) 1.20343	1.20443	0	1.0970	**TABLE 10**
5	44	41	5	-2	0.0000	0.0000	0.0026	L(2) 0.37288	0.38660	50	5.9893	AGE ANALYSIS
10	32	34	3	-4	0.0012	0.0052	0.1817	0.79373	0.77370	55	8.4112	AND
15	27	28	-4	3	0.0826	0.3582	0.5323	R(1) 0.03704	0.03720	60	10.1223	MISCELLANEOUS
20	19	23	-7	4	0.1646	0.7064	0.6755	R(2) -0.02626	-0.02902	65	12.1815	RESULTS
25	16	19	-3	0	0.1523	0.6447	0.5774	0.22632	0.22148	70	14.6597	(Females)
30	16	15	7	-6	0.1229	0.5100	0.4256	C(1)	262	75	17.6419	
35	15	12	10	-8	0.0837	0.3412	0.2430	C(2)	1261	80	21.2309	
40	15	10	2	3	0.0362	0.1448	0.0766		500	85	25.5500	
45	16	8	-11	19	0.0022	0.0084	0.0042	2P/Y 27.7621	28.3689	90	30.7478	
50	14	7	-14	21	0.0000	0.0000	0.0000	DELTA 11.2791		95	37.0029	
55+	39	16								100	44.5306	

TABLE 1 — DATA

AGE AT LAST BIRTHDAY	BOTH SEXES	POPULATION MALES Number	%	FEMALES Number	%	BIRTHS BY AGE OF MOTHER	DEATHS BOTH SEXES	MALES	FEMALES	AGE AT LAST BIRTHDAY
0	3715	1879	4.6	1836	4.0	0	454	233	221	0
1-4	11772	5904	14.4	5868	12.8	0	254	149	105	1-4
5-9	12255	6162	15.0	6093	13.3	0	26	16	10	5-9
10-14	10643	5474	13.3	5169	11.3	5	18	10	8	10-14
15-19	8509	4165	10.2	4344	9.5	671	19	8	11	15-19
20-24	6675	3061	7.5	3614	7.9	1231	19	6	13	20-24
25-29	5258	2284	5.6	2974	6.5	985	21	10	11	25-29
30-34	4491	1966	4.8	2525	5.5	688	24	10	14	30-34
35-39	4475	1937	4.7	2538	5.6	468	19	9	10	35-39
40-44	3951	1865	4.5	2086	4.6	160	30	17	13	40-44
45-49	3537	1708	4.2	1829	4.0	27	25	11	14	45-49
50-54	3009	1356	3.3	1653	3.6	5	33	19	14	50-54
55-59	2170	969	2.4	1201	2.6	0	32	19	13	55-59
60-64	2116	818	2.0	1298	2.8	0	58	28	30	60-64
65-69	1400	538	1.3	862	1.9	0	34	16	18	65-69
70-74	1124	389	0.9	735	1.6		44	15	29	70-74
75-79	637	213	0.5	424	0.9		23	5	18	75-79
80-84	538	181	0.4	357	0.8	2165 M.	57	20	37	80-84
85+	452	144	0.4	308	0.7	2075 F.	91	32	59	85+
TOTAL	86727	41013		45714		4240	1281	633	648	TOTAL

TABLE 2 — MALE LIFE TABLE

x	nq_x	l_x	nd_x	nL_x	nm_x	na_x	T_x	r_x	$\mathring{e}_x$	nM_x	x
0	0.114544	100000	11454	93064	0.123081	0.3944	5430960	0.0126	54.310	0.124002	0
1	0.094041	88546	8327	331841	0.025093	1.3169	5337896	0.0126	60.284	0.025237	1
5	0.012344	80219	990	398618	0.002484	2.5000	5006056	0.0277	62.405	0.002597	5
10	0.009070	79228	719	394296	0.001822	2.4307	4607438	0.0372	58.154	0.001827	10
15	0.009568	78510	751	390682	0.001923	2.5143	4213142	0.0563	53.664	0.001921	15
20	0.009903	77759	770	387062	0.001989	2.7508	3822459	0.0576	49.158	0.001960	20
25	0.021796	76989	1678	380982	0.004404	2.6392	3435398	0.0403	44.622	0.004378	25
30	0.025116	75311	1892	371826	0.005087	2.5010	3054416	0.0117	40.558	0.005086	30
35	0.022982	73419	1687	363150	0.004646	2.6613	2682590	0.0000	36.538	0.004646	35
40	0.044585	71732	3198	350767	0.009118	2.5322	2319440	0.0053	32.335	0.009115	40
45	0.031823	68534	2181	337495	0.006462	2.6280	1968674	0.0231	28.726	0.006440	45
50	0.068400	66353	4539	321177	0.014131	2.6673	1631178	0.0434	24.583	0.014012	50
55	0.094241	61814	5825	295406	0.019720	2.6543	1310002	0.0286	21.193	0.019608	55
60	0.158106	55989	8852	257957	0.034316	2.5163	1014596	0.0324	18.121	0.034230	60
65	0.138256	47137	6517	219030	0.029754	2.4446	756638	0.0324	16.052	0.029740	65
70	0.175294	40620	7120	184729	0.038545	2.4202	537608	0.0324	13.235	0.038560	70
75	0.113130	33499	3790	159267	0.023795	2.8286	352879	0.0324	10.534	0.023474	75
80	0.440845	29710	13097	117354	0.111605	2.7040	193612	0.0324	6.517	0.110497	80
85+	1.000000	16612	16612	76258	0.217842	4.5905	76258	0.0324	4.590	0.222221	85+

TABLE 3 — FEMALE LIFE TABLE

x	nq_x	l_x	nd_x	nL_x	nm_x	na_x	T_x	r_x	$\mathring{e}_x$	nM_x	x
0	0.110957	100000	11096	92966	0.119351	0.3661	5798414	0.0132	57.984	0.120370	0
1	0.067743	88904	6023	339058	0.017763	1.2505	5705448	0.0132	64.175	0.017894	1
5	0.007697	82882	638	412814	0.001545	2.5000	5366390	0.0346	64.748	0.001641	5
10	0.007743	82244	637	409709	0.001554	2.6292	4953576	0.0321	60.230	0.001548	10
15	0.012657	81607	1033	405620	0.002546	2.6620	4543867	0.0332	55.680	0.002532	15
20	0.017871	80574	1440	399359	0.003606	2.5611	4138246	0.0345	51.359	0.003597	20
25	0.018392	79134	1455	392175	0.003711	2.5980	3738888	0.0317	47.247	0.003699	25
30	0.027348	77679	2124	383087	0.005545	2.5019	3346713	0.0111	43.084	0.005545	30
35	0.019519	75554	1475	374118	0.003942	2.5223	2963626	0.0142	39.225	0.003940	35
40	0.030804	74080	2282	364949	0.006253	2.6118	2589508	0.0268	34.956	0.006232	40
45	0.037602	71798	2700	352363	0.007662	2.5457	2224559	0.0157	30.984	0.007654	45
50	0.041594	69098	2874	338473	0.008491	2.5586	1872197	0.0334	27.095	0.008469	50
55	0.052979	66224	3508	323182	0.010856	2.7375	1533723	0.0110	23.160	0.010824	55
60	0.109607	62715	6874	296820	0.023159	2.5623	1210542	0.0196	19.302	0.023112	60
65	0.099641	55841	5564	265754	0.020937	2.5821	913721	0.0196	16.363	0.020882	65
70	0.180334	50277	9067	229223	0.039554	2.5555	647968	0.0196	12.888	0.039456	70
75	0.193605	41211	7979	187090	0.042646	2.6233	418745	0.0196	10.161	0.042453	75
80	0.414886	33232	13788	132405	0.104131	2.6733	231655	0.0196	6.971	0.103641	80
85+	1.000000	19445	19445	99250	0.195915	5.1042	99250	0.0196	5.104	0.191559	85+

TABLE 4 — OBSERVED AND PROJECTED VITAL RATES

	OBSERVED POPULATION BOTH SEXES	MALES	FEMALES	PROJECTED POPULATION 1965 MALES	FEMALES	1970 MALES	FEMALES	1975 MALES	FEMALES	STABLE POPULATION MALES	FEMALES
RATES PER THOUSAND											
Birth	48.89	52.79	45.39	50.89	44.92	49.92	44.95	49.51	45.27	49.67	47.77
Death	14.77	15.43	14.18	15.52	14.00	15.19	13.71	15.08	13.61	14.50	12.61
Increase	34.12	37.35	31.22	35.37	30.92	34.73	31.24	34.42	31.66		35.1625
PERCENTAGE											
under 15	44.26	47.35	41.49	47.41	43.21	47.85	44.51	48.11	45.26	47.20	46.70
15-64	50.95	49.08	52.64	49.01	51.03	48.67	50.29	48.33	49.66	50.06	50.11
65 and over	4.79	3.57	5.88	3.58	5.76	3.49	5.20	3.56	5.08	2.74	3.19
DEP. RATIO X 100	96.25	103.75	89.98	104.04	95.97	105.48	98.85	106.89	101.36	99.77	99.55

AGE AT LAST BIRTHDAY	1965 BOTH SEXES	MALES	FEMALES	1970 BOTH SEXES	MALES	FEMALES	1975 BOTH SEXES	MALES	FEMALES	AGE AT LAST BIRTHDAY	
0-4	20	10	10	23	12	11	27	14	13	0-4	**TABLE 5**
5-9	14	7	7	18	9	9	22	11	11	5-9	
10-14	12	6	6	14	7	7	18	9	9	10-14	
15-19	10	5	5	12	6	6	14	7	7	15-19	POPULATION
20-24	8	4	4	10	5	5	12	6	6	20-24	PROJECTED
25-29	7	3	4	8	4	4	10	5	5	25-29	WITH
30-34	5	2	3	6	3	3	8	4	4	30-34	FIXED
35-39	4	2	2	5	2	3	6	3	3	35-39	AGE—
40-44	4	2	2	4	2	2	5	2	3	40-44	SPECIFIC
45-49	4	2	2	4	2	2	4	2	2	45-49	BIRTH
50-54	4	2	2	4	2	2	4	2	2	50-54	AND
55-59	3	1	2	3	1	2	4	2	2	55-59	DEATH
60-64	2	1	1	2	1	1	3	1	2	60-64	RATES
65-69	2	1	1	2	1	1	2	1	1	65-69	(IN 1000's)
70-74	1	0	1	2	1	1	2	1	1	70-74	
75-79	1	0	1	1	0	1	2	1	1	75-79	
80-84	0	0	0	0	0	0	0	0	0	80-84	
85+	0	0	0	0	0	0	0	0	0	85+	
TOTAL	101	48	53	118	58	60	143	71	72	TOTAL	

STANDARD COUNTRIES: STANDARDIZED RATES PER THOUSAND	ENGLAND AND WALES 1961 BOTH SEXES	MALES	FEMALES	UNITED STATES 1960 BOTH SEXES	MALES	FEMALES	MEXICO 1960 BOTH SEXES	MALES	FEMALES	
Birth	44.38	63.03*	42.09	45.23	56.92*	43.62	50.59	59.19*	49.39	**TABLE 6**
Death	15.05	28.36*	15.17	14.21	23.77*	13.51	12.21	12.95*	11.22	STANDARDIZED RATES
Increase	29.33	34.67*	26.93	31.02	33.15*	30.10	38.38	46.24*	38.17	

	OBSERVED POP. MALES	FEMALES	STATIONARY POP. MALES	FEMALES	STABLE POP. MALES	FEMALES	OBSERVED BIRTHS	NET MATERNITY FUNCTION	BIRTHS IN STABLE POP.	
μ	22.46547	25.34064	36.54402	37.67331	21.19421	21.61610	27.08608	28.33616	26.60960	**TABLE 7**
σ^2	374.9514	439.9260	536.5653	557.0535	322.2911	336.9139	47.96350	49.92837	43.95235	MOMENTS
κ_3	7403.818	8243.041	3747.258	3331.993	6342.491	6781.351	191.0784	154.3252	181.1272	AND
κ_4	40013.	-7825.	-263907.	-307603.	73449.	75156.	-825.183	-1136.811	-381.512	CUMULANTS
β_1	1.039888	0.798061	0.090899	0.064227	1.201641	1.202474	0.330895	0.191351	0.386385	
β_2	3.284614	2.959566	2.083344	2.008719	3.707116	3.662104	2.641302	2.543970	2.802511	
κ	-0.401841	-0.303153	-0.034591	-0.023614	-0.549636	-0.529278	-0.160822	-0.103040	-0.208209	

VITAL STATISTICS		THOMPSON AGE RANGE	NRR	1000r	INTERVAL	BOURGEOIS-PICHAT AGE RANGE	NRR	1000b	1000d	1000r	COALE	
GRR	3.373										IBR	**TABLE 8**
NRR	2.626	0-4	2.29	30.39	27.23	5-29	2.46	41.70	8.42	33.28	IDR	RATES FROM AGE DISTRIBUTIONS AND VITAL STATISTICS (Females)
TFR	6.893	5-9	2.15	28.73	27.14	30-54	1.60	26.45	9.10	17.35	IRI	
GENERATION	27.455	10-14	2.04	25.87	27.08	55-79	1.49	20.68	5.85	14.83	K1	
SEX RATIO	104.337	15-19	1.93	24.41	27.01	* 5-29	2.46	41.70	8.42	33.28	K2	

Start of Age Interval	ORIGINAL MATRIX SUB-DIAGONAL	ALTERNATIVE FIRST ROWS Projection	Integral	FIRST STABLE MATRIX % IN STABLE POPULATION	FISHER VALUES	REPRODUCTIVE VALUES	SECOND STABLE MATRIX Z₂ FIRST COLUMN	FIRST ROW	
0	0.95553	0.00000	0.00000	18.961	1.262	9719	0.1293+0.1090	0.1293+0.1090	**TABLE 9**
5	0.99248	0.00101	0.00000	15.186	1.575	9598	0.1703-0.0730	-0.0359+0.1501	LESLIE MATRIX
10	0.99002	0.16268	0.00223	12.632	1.892	9782	0.0127-0.2105	-0.1322+0.0309	AND ITS
15	0.98456	0.51781	0.35659	10.482	2.073	9006	-0.2070-0.1201	-0.0979-0.1098	SPECTRAL
20	0.98201	0.70391	0.78634	8.650	1.849	6681	-0.2260+0.1480	-0.0200-0.1784	COMPONENTS
25	0.97683	0.63150	0.76460	7.120	1.342	3991	0.0347+0.3022	0.0409-0.1651	(Females)
30	0.97659	0.47841	0.62902	5.829	0.823	2079	0.3199+0.1172	0.0645-0.1040	
35	0.97549	0.27403	0.42569	4.772	0.388	984	0.2780-0.2612	0.0455-0.0435	
40	0.96551	0.09615	0.17707	3.901	0.120	250	-0.1215-0.4090	0.0167-0.0117	
45	0.96058	0.01868	0.03408	3.157	0.022	41	-0.4649-0.0830	0.0034-0.0021	
50	0.95482	0.00320	0.00698	2.542	0.003	6	-0.3115+0.4165	0.0006-0.0002	
55+	0.83445			6.768					

Start of Age Interval	OBSERVED POPUL. (IN 100's)	CONTRIBUTIONS OF ROOTS (IN 100's) r_1	r_2, r_3	r_4-r_{11}	AGE-SP. BIRTH RATES	NET MATERNITY FUNCTION	COEFF. OF MATRIX EQUATION	PARAMETERS INTEGRAL	MATRIX	EXP. INCREASE x	$e^{(x+2\frac{1}{2})r}$	
0	77	78	1	-2	0.0000	0.0000	0.0000	L(1) 1.19221	1.19309	0	1.0919	**TABLE 10**
5	61	63	-2	-0	0.0000	0.0000	0.0010	L(2) 0.37940	0.39145	50	6.3346	AGE
10	52	52	-3	2	0.0005	0.0019	0.1543	0.80221	0.77941	55	7.5522	ANALYSIS
15	43	43	-1	1	0.0756	0.3066	0.4862	R(1) 0.03516	0.03531	60	9.0039	AND
20	36	36	3	-2	0.1667	0.6657	0.6507	R(2) -0.02389	-0.02735	65	10.7346	MISCELLANEOUS
25	30	29	3	-3	0.1621	0.6357	0.5732	0.22581	0.22107	70	12.7979	RESULTS
30	25	24	0	1	0.1333	0.5108	0.4242	C(1)	413	75	15.2579	(Females)
35	25	20	-4	10	0.0902	0.3376	0.2373	C(2)	-207	80	18.1906	
40	21	16	-4	9	0.0375	0.1370	0.0812		-602	85	21.6872	
45	18	13	1	4	0.0072	0.0255	0.0152	2P/Y 27.8257	28.4216	90	25.8557	
50	17	10	6	-0	0.0015	0.0050	0.0025	DELTA 7.8521		95	30.8256	
55+	52	28								100	36.7507	

TABLE 1 — DATA

AGE AT LAST BIRTHDAY	POPULATION BOTH SEXES	MALES Number	MALES %	FEMALES Number	FEMALES %	BIRTHS BY AGE OF MOTHER	DEATHS BOTH SEXES	DEATHS MALES	DEATHS FEMALES	AGE AT LAST BIRTHDAY
0	24400	12300	3.5	12100	3.5	0	1771	964	807	0
1-4	85450	43050	12.3	42400	12.2	0	350	190	160	1-4
5-9	97750	49150	14.1	48600	14.0	0	94	55	39	5-9
10-14	76800	38900	11.1	37900	10.9	89	65	35	30	10-14
15-19	59650	30100	8.6	29550	8.5	5423	89	33	56	15-19
20-24	50200	24550	7.0	25650	7.4	8562	135	54	81	20-24
25-29	51050	24950	7.1	26100	7.5	6912	156	73	83	25-29
30-34	48400	24250	6.9	24150	6.9	4725	195	78	117	30-34
35-39	44300	22400	6.4	21900	6.3	2745	228	107	121	35-39
40-44	39400	20000	5.7	19400	5.6	714	259	142	117	40-44
45-49	33200	17100	4.9	16100	4.6	76	339	193	146	45-49
50-54	26550	13650	3.9	12900	3.7	7	374	190	184	50-54
55-59	19700	9950	2.8	9750	2.8	0	327	195	132	55-59
60-64	13600	7050	2.0	6550	1.9	0	449	257	192	60-64
65-69	10200	5050	1.4	5150	1.5	0	606	344	262	65-69
70-74	8300	3750	1.1	4550	1.3		490	253	237	70-74
75-79	5250	2150	0.6	3100	0.9		320	177	143	75-79
80-84	2300	950	0.3	1350	0.4	14843 M.	275	120	155	80-84
85+	1100	400	0.1	700	0.2	14410 F.	285	99	186	85+
TOTAL	697600	349700		347900		29253	6807	3559	3248	TOTAL

TABLE 2 — MALE LIFE TABLE

x	n_{q_x}	l_x	n_{d_x}	n_{L_x}	n_{m_x}	n_{a_x}	T_x	r_x	$\mathring{e}_x$	n_{M_x}	x
0	0.073588	100000	7359	94608	0.077782	0.2673	5984759	0.0100	59.848	0.078374	0
1	0.017245	92641	1598	365958	0.004365	1.1165	5890151	0.0100	63.580	0.004413	1
5	0.005482	91044	499	453970	0.001099	2.5000	5524193	0.0333	60.676	0.001119	5
10	0.004489	90545	406	451706	0.000900	2.4996	5070223	0.0481	55.997	0.000900	10
15	0.005528	90138	498	449565	0.001108	2.7413	4618516	0.0447	51.238	0.001096	15
20	0.010973	89640	984	445904	0.002206	2.6672	4168952	0.0166	46.508	0.002200	20
25	0.014526	88656	1288	440147	0.002926	2.5666	3723047	0.0000	41.994	0.002926	25
30	0.015974	87368	1396	433508	0.003219	2.6116	3282900	0.0073	37.575	0.003216	30
35	0.023676	85973	2036	425097	0.004788	2.6583	2849392	0.0144	33.143	0.004777	35
40	0.035049	83937	2942	412838	0.007126	2.6721	2424295	0.0195	28.882	0.007100	40
45	0.055133	80995	4466	394279	0.011326	2.6043	2011457	0.0273	24.834	0.011287	45
50	0.067656	76530	5178	370181	0.013987	2.5920	1617179	0.0397	21.131	0.013919	50
55	0.094612	71352	6751	341082	0.019792	2.6776	1246998	0.0442	17.477	0.019598	55
60	0.169229	64601	10932	297534	0.036743	2.6700	905916	0.0317	14.023	0.036454	60
65	0.292001	53669	15671	229159	0.068386	2.4996	608382	0.0317	11.336	0.068119	65
70	0.286837	37998	10899	161401	0.067528	2.3772	379223	0.0317	9.980	0.067467	70
75	0.341223	27098	9247	111883	0.082646	2.4467	217821	0.0317	8.038	0.082326	75
80	0.477971	17852	8533	67198	0.126979	2.5018	105939	0.0317	5.934	0.126316	80
85+	1.000000	9319	9319	38741	0.240551	4.1571	38741	0.0317	4.157	0.247499	85+

TABLE 3 — FEMALE LIFE TABLE

x	n_{q_x}	l_x	n_{d_x}	n_{L_x}	n_{m_x}	n_{a_x}	T_x	r_x	$\mathring{e}_x$	n_{M_x}	x
0	0.063114	100000	6311	95382	0.066170	0.2683	6208415	0.0104	62.084	0.066694	0
1	0.014765	93689	1383	370767	0.003731	1.1174	6113033	0.0104	65.248	0.003774	1
5	0.003919	92305	362	460622	0.000785	2.5000	5742266	0.0348	62.209	0.000802	5
10	0.004008	91944	368	458903	0.000803	2.7886	5281644	0.0487	57.444	0.000792	10
15	0.009525	91575	872	455914	0.001913	2.7517	4822741	0.0371	52.664	0.001895	15
20	0.015682	90703	1422	450070	0.003160	2.5786	4366827	0.0095	48.144	0.003158	20
25	0.015784	89280	1409	443021	0.003181	2.6012	3916758	0.0025	43.870	0.003180	25
30	0.023975	87871	2107	434282	0.004851	2.5920	3473736	0.0129	39.532	0.004845	30
35	0.027274	85764	2339	423053	0.005529	2.5339	3039454	0.0164	35.440	0.005525	35
40	0.029811	83425	2487	411174	0.006049	2.6068	2616401	0.0242	31.362	0.006031	40
45	0.044653	80938	3614	396251	0.009121	2.6646	2205226	0.0312	27.246	0.009068	45
50	0.069084	77324	5342	373507	0.014302	2.5452	1808976	0.0374	23.395	0.014264	50
55	0.066299	71982	4772	348802	0.013682	2.6722	1435469	0.0506	19.942	0.013538	55
60	0.138167	67210	9286	314573	0.029520	2.6872	1086667	0.0283	16.168	0.029313	60
65	0.226455	57924	13117	257030	0.051034	2.5155	772094	0.0283	13.329	0.050874	65
70	0.229092	44807	10265	197137	0.052069	2.3798	515065	0.0283	11.495	0.052088	70
75	0.208305	34542	7195	155172	0.046369	2.5627	317927	0.0283	9.204	0.046129	75
80	0.454506	27347	12429	107269	0.115869	2.6294	162756	0.0283	5.952	0.114815	80
85+	*1.000000	14917	14917	55487	0.268845	3.7196	55487	0.0283	3.720	0.265714	85+

TABLE 4 — OBSERVED AND PROJECTED VITAL RATES

	OBSERVED POPULATION BOTH SEXES	MALES	FEMALES	PROJECTED POPULATION 1959 MALES	FEMALES	1964 MALES	FEMALES	1969 MALES	FEMALES	STABLE POPULATION MALES	FEMALES
RATES PER THOUSAND											
Birth	41.93	42.44	41.42	40.14	39.18	40.51	39.56	41.28	40.33	44.05	43.37
Death	9.76	10.18	9.34	10.43	9.47	10.30	9.48	10.22	9.35	8.75	8.07
Increase	32.18	32.27	32.08	29.71	29.72	30.20	30.08	31.06	30.99		35.2966
PERCENTAGE											
under 15	40.77	41.01	40.53	42.97	42.61	43.65	43.25	44.85	44.44	46.74	46.66
15-64	55.34	55.48	55.20	53.74	53.52	53.12	52.94	51.87	51.74	51.22	50.85
65 and over	3.89	3.52	4.27	3.29	3.87	3.22	3.81	3.29	3.83	2.04	2.49
DEP. RATIO X 100	80.70	80.26	81.15	86.08	86.86	88.24	88.91	92.81	93.29	95.23	96.66

TABLE 5 — POPULATION PROJECTED WITH FIXED AGE-SPECIFIC BIRTH AND DEATH RATES (IN 1000's)

AGE AT LAST BIRTHDAY	1959 BOTH SEXES	1959 MALES	1959 FEMALES	1964 BOTH SEXES	1964 MALES	1964 FEMALES	1969 BOTH SEXES	1969 MALES	1969 FEMALES	AGE AT LAST BIRTHDAY
0-4	143	72	71	163	82	81	192	97	95	0-4
5-9	109	55	54	141	71	70	161	81	80	5-9
10-14	97	49	48	108	54	54	141	71	70	10-14
15-19	77	39	38	97	49	48	107	54	53	15-19
20-24	59	30	29	75	38	37	95	48	47	20-24
25-29	49	24	25	58	29	29	75	38	37	25-29
30-34	51	25	26	49	24	25	57	29	28	30-34
35-39	48	24	24	49	24	25	47	23	24	35-39
40-44	43	22	21	46	23	23	47	23	24	40-44
45-49	38	19	19	42	21	21	44	22	22	45-49
50-54	31	16	15	36	18	18	39	20	19	50-54
55-59	25	13	12	29	15	14	33	17	16	55-59
60-64	18	9	9	22	11	11	26	13	13	60-64
65-69	10	5	5	14	7	7	17	8	9	65-69
70-74	8	4	4	8	4	4	11	5	6	70-74
75-79	7	3	4	5	2	3	6	3	3	75-79
80-84	3	1	2	4	2	2	3	1	2	80-84
85+	2	1	1	2	1	1	2	1	1	85+
TOTAL	818	411	407	948	475	473	1103	554	549	TOTAL

TABLE 6 — STANDARDIZED RATES

STANDARD COUNTRIES: STANDARDIZED RATES PER THOUSAND	ENGLAND AND WALES 1961 BOTH SEXES	MALES	FEMALES	UNITED STATES 1960 BOTH SEXES	MALES	FEMALES	MEXICO 1960 BOTH SEXES	MALES	FEMALES
Birth	36.88	41.41*	35.21	37.74	38.80*	36.63	44.44	37.92*	43.67
Death	16.68	20.75*	17.24	14.27	16.88*	13.76	9.00	9.81*	8.42
Increase	20.19	20.66*	17.97	23.47	21.92*	22.87	35.45	28.11*	35.25

TABLE 7 — MOMENTS AND CUMULANTS

	OBSERVED POP. MALES	OBSERVED POP. FEMALES	STATIONARY POP. MALES	STATIONARY POP. FEMALES	STABLE POP. MALES	STABLE POP. FEMALES	OBSERVED BIRTHS	NET MATERNITY FUNCTION	BIRTHS IN STABLE POP.
μ	24.78675	25.05461	34.90893	36.01775	21.05317	21.28161	26.30713	26.75233	25.20180
σ^2	371.5772	385.2323	471.5558	506.6528	300.1379	313.5048	43.13595	44.78936	38.79219
κ_3	5215.530	5891.021	2943.707	3242.050	5295.416	5875.817	152.2087	158.2955	176.8981
κ_4	-43000.	-25150.	-193658.	-234623.	42501.	57275.	-816.077	-924.170	-142.970
β_1	0.530212	0.607034	0.082640	0.080818	1.037140	1.120480	0.288643	0.278877	0.536060
β_2	2.688565	2.830530	2.129099	2.085991	3.471799	3.582740	2.561416	2.539317	2.904993
κ	-0.211469	-0.251383	-0.033037	-0.031158	-0.464895	-0.503901	-0.136508	-0.130557	-0.259564

TABLE 8 — RATES FROM AGE DISTRIBUTIONS AND VITAL STATISTICS (Females)

VITAL STATISTICS		THOMPSON AGE RANGE	NRR	1000r	INTERVAL	BOURGEOIS-PICHAT AGE RANGE	NRR	1000b	1000d	1000r	COALE
GRR	2.826										IBR
NRR	2.500	0-4	2.09	27.95	27.21	5-29	2.29	35.29	4.56	30.73	IDR
TFR	5.738	5-9	2.02	26.47	27.13	30-54	1.91	35.94	12.05	23.90	IRI
GENERATION	25.959	10-14	1.70	19.33	27.02	55-79	1.39	14.53	2.27	12.26	K1
SEX RATIO	103.005	15-19	1.48	14.01	26.88	*25-49	1.63	28.61	10.46	18.15	K2

TABLE 9 — LESLIE MATRIX AND ITS SPECTRAL COMPONENTS (Females)

Start of Age Interval	ORIGINAL MATRIX SUB-DIAGONAL	ALTERNATIVE FIRST ROWS Projection	ALTERNATIVE FIRST ROWS Integral	FIRST STABLE MATRIX % IN STABLE POPULATION	FISHER VALUES	REPRODUCTIVE VALUES	SECOND STABLE MATRIX Z2 FIRST COLUMN	SECOND STABLE MATRIX Z2 FIRST ROW
0	0.98814	0.00000	0.00000	18.567	1.171	63808	0.1260+0.1442	0.1260+0.1442
5	0.99627	0.00269	0.00000	15.367	1.415	68751	0.2157-0.0723	-0.0713+0.1446
10	0.99349	0.21203	0.00589	12.822	1.692	64132	0.0194-0.2718	-0.1346-0.0089
15	0.98718	0.58903	0.46028	10.670	1.784	52709	-0.2908-0.1462	-0.0633-0.1377
20	0.98434	0.68254	0.83720	8.822	1.459	37416	-0.2928+0.2519	0.0114-0.1799
25	0.98027	0.52426	0.66421	7.273	0.958	24991	0.1420+0.4345	0.0567-0.1495
30	0.97414	0.36482	0.49071	5.972	0.540	13043	0.5371+0.0424	0.0682-0.0815
35	0.97192	0.18498	0.31437	4.872	0.223	4894	0.2876-0.5616	0.0394-0.0270
40	0.96370	0.04748	0.09231	3.966	0.052	1003	-0.4766-0.5625	0.0103-0.0052
45	0.94260	0.00601	0.01184	3.201	0.006	103	-0.8140+0.2592	0.0013-0.0006
50	0.93386	0.00062	0.00136	2.527	0.001	8	-0.0834+0.9645	0.0001-0.0000
55+	0.79662			5.940				

TABLE 10 — AGE ANALYSIS AND MISCELLANEOUS RESULTS (Females)

Start of Age Interval	OBSERVED POPUL. (IN 100's)	CONTRIBUTIONS OF ROOTS (IN 100's) r_1	r_2, r_3	$r_4 \cdot r_{11}$	AGE-SP. BIRTH RATES	NET MATERNITY FUNCTION	COEFF. OF MATRIX EQUATION	PARAMETERS	INTEGRAL	MATRIX	EXP. INCREASE x	$e^{(x+2\frac{1}{2})r}$
0	545	566	19	-39	0.0000	0.0000	0.0000	L(1)	1.19301	1.19394	0	1.0923
5	486	468	-7	25	0.0000	0.0000	0.0027	L(2)	0.29564	0.31976	50	6.3794
10	379	391	-33	21	0.0012	0.0053	0.2087			0.79100	0.76785	55	7.6107
15	296	325	-20	-9	0.0904	0.4122	0.5761	R(1)	0.03530	0.03545	60	9.0797
20	257	269	28	-41	0.1644	0.7401	0.6590	R(2)	-0.03381	-0.03684	65	10.8322
25	261	222	54	-15	0.1305	0.5779	0.4982			0.24262	0.23524	70	12.9229
30	242	182	10	50	0.0964	0.4186	0.3399	C(1)		3047	75	15.4173
35	219	148	-66	137	0.0617	0.2612	0.1679	C(2)		426	80	18.3930
40	194	121	-73	146	0.0181	0.0745	0.0419			-6113	85	21.9431
45	161	98	25	39	0.0023	0.0092	0.0051	2P/Y	25.8969	26.7096	90	26.1784
50	129	77	117	-65	0.0003	0.0010	0.0005	DELTA	9.7496		95	31.2313
55+	312	181									100	37.2593

TABLE 1 — DATA

AGE AT LAST BIRTHDAY	POPULATION BOTH SEXES	MALES Number	%	FEMALES Number	%	BIRTHS BY AGE OF MOTHER	DEATHS BOTH SEXES	MALES	FEMALES	AGE AT LAST BIRTHDAY
0	30000	15250	4.2	14750	4.1	0	2052	1176	876	0
1-4	87750	44250	12.2	43500	12.1	0	354	197	157	1-4
5-9	99150	50300	13.9	48850	13.6	0	90	43	47	5-9
10-14	81900	41150	11.4	40750	11.3	59	63	26	37	10-14
15-19	62000	31150	8.6	30850	8.6	5520	113	58	55	15-19
20-24	53300	26150	7.2	27150	7.6	8725	138	62	76	20-24
25-29	51350	25050	6.9	26300	7.3	7280	153	71	82	25-29
30-34	48150	24050	6.7	24100	6.7	4850	178	82	96	30-34
35-39	45000	22700	6.3	22300	6.2	2884	205	98	107	35-39
40-44	39650	20150	5.6	19500	5.4	790	264	143	121	40-44
45-49	34100	17500	4.8	16600	4.6	108	337	193	144	45-49
50-54	27150	14000	3.9	13150	3.7	0	386	209	177	50-54
55-59	20300	10250	2.8	10050	2.8	0	410	267	143	55-59
60-64	13950	7200	2.0	6750	1.9	0	436	248	188	60-64
65-69	9900	4950	1.4	4950	1.4	0	712	390	322	65-69
70-74	8150	3700	1.0	4450	1.2		536	304	232	70-74
75-79	5500	2250	0.6	3250	0.9		402	221	181	75-79
80-84	2450	1000	0.3	1450	0.4	15476 M.	294	129	165	80-84
85+	1100	400	0.1	700	0.2	14740 F.	339	111	228	85+
TOTAL	720850	361450		359400		30216	7462	4028	3434	TOTAL

TABLE 2 — MALE LIFE TABLE

x	nq_x	l_x	nd_x	nL_x	nm_x	na_x	T_x	r_x	$\dot{e}_x$	nM_x	x
0	0.071519	100000	7152	94775	0.075462	0.2694	5911142	0.0288	59.111	0.077115	0
1	0.017051	92848	1583	366831	0.004316	1.1184	5816367	0.0288	62.644	0.004452	1
5	0.004156	91265	379	455377	0.000833	2.5000	5449537	0.0352	59.711	0.000855	5
10	0.003205	90886	291	453798	0.000642	2.8344	4994160	0.0470	54.950	0.000632	10
15	0.009348	90594	847	451015	0.001878	2.6890	4540362	0.0436	50.117	0.001862	15
20	0.011806	89747	1060	446172	0.002375	2.5790	4089348	0.0194	45.565	0.002371	20
25	0.014081	88688	1249	440405	0.002836	2.5700	3643175	0.0055	41.079	0.002834	25
30	0.016918	87439	1479	433621	0.003412	2.5834	3202770	0.0064	36.629	0.003410	30
35	0.021419	85960	1841	425502	0.004327	2.6661	2769149	0.0130	32.214	0.004317	35
40	0.035034	84119	2947	413754	0.007123	2.6793	2343648	0.0187	27.861	0.007097	40
45	0.053933	81172	4378	395462	0.011070	2.6252	1929893	0.0255	23.775	0.011029	45
50	0.072642	76794	5578	370941	0.015039	2.6646	1534432	0.0369	19.981	0.014929	50
55	0.123350	71215	8784	335040	0.026219	2.6053	1163491	0.0415	16.338	0.026049	55
60	0.160461	62431	10018	288891	0.034676	2.6778	828451	0.0256	13.270	0.034444	60
65	0.330722	52413	17334	219112	0.079111	2.5220	539560	0.0256	10.294	0.078788	65
70	0.337747	35079	11848	144059	0.082243	2.3551	320448	0.0256	9.135	0.082162	70
75	0.391457	23231	9094	92371	0.098451	2.3846	176389	0.0256	7.593	0.098222	75
80	0.481643	14137	6809	52631	0.129373	2.4460	84018	0.0256	5.943	0.129000	80
85+	1.000000	7328	7328	31387	0.233479	4.2830	31387	0.0256	4.283	0.277501	85+

TABLE 3 — FEMALE LIFE TABLE

x	nq_x	l_x	nd_x	nL_x	nm_x	na_x	T_x	r_x	$\dot{e}_x$	nM_x	x
0	0.055805	100000	5580	95960	0.058154	0.2760	6237099	0.0279	62.371	0.059390	0
1	0.013897	94420	1312	373905	0.003509	1.1246	6141139	0.0279	65.041	0.003609	1
5	0.004725	93107	440	464437	0.000947	2.5000	5767234	0.0341	61.942	0.000962	5
10	0.004570	92667	423	462359	0.000916	2.6899	5302797	0.0449	57.224	0.000908	10
15	0.008953	92244	826	459332	0.001798	2.7142	4840438	0.0388	52.474	0.001783	15
20	0.013921	91418	1273	454028	0.002803	2.5933	4381106	0.0133	47.924	0.002799	20
25	0.015453	90145	1396	447338	0.003120	2.5717	3927079	0.0087	43.564	0.003118	25
30	0.019748	88750	1753	439507	0.003988	2.5797	3479741	0.0125	39.208	0.003983	30
35	0.023753	86997	2066	429997	0.004806	2.5859	3040234	0.0163	34.946	0.004798	35
40	0.030664	84931	2604	418445	0.006224	2.6161	2610237	0.0231	30.734	0.006205	40
45	0.042722	82326	3517	403370	0.008719	2.6509	2191792	0.0302	26.623	0.008675	45
50	0.065381	78809	5153	381498	0.013506	2.5648	1788423	0.0378	22.693	0.013460	50
55	0.069498	73657	5119	356297	0.014367	2.6586	1406924	0.0499	19.101	0.014229	55
60	0.132044	68538	9050	322474	0.028064	2.7664	1050627	0.0229	15.329	0.027852	60
65	0.280554	59488	16689	255866	0.065228	2.5091	728153	0.0229	12.240	0.065051	65
70	0.228414	42798	9776	187765	0.052064	2.3172	472288	0.0229	11.035	0.052135	70
75	0.245687	33022	8113	145126	0.055904	2.5366	284523	0.0229	8.616	0.055692	75
80	0.449690	24909	11201	97708	0.114642	2.6041	139397	0.0229	5.596	0.113794	80
85+	*1.000000	13708	13708	41688	0.328816	3.0412	41688	0.0229	3.041	0.325714	85+

TABLE 4 — OBSERVED AND PROJECTED VITAL RATES

	OBSERVED POPULATION BOTH SEXES	MALES	FEMALES	PROJECTED POPULATION 1960 MALES	FEMALES	1965 MALES	FEMALES	1970 MALES	FEMALES	STABLE POPULATION MALES	FEMALES
RATES PER THOUSAND											
Birth	41.92	42.82	41.01	40.94	39.27	41.12	39.48	41.78	40.18	44.03	42.94
Death	10.35	11.14	9.55	11.23	9.47	10.98	9.44	10.79	9.25	8.78	7.69
Increase	31.57	31.67	31.46	29.71	29.80	30.13	30.05	30.99	30.93	35.2518	
PERCENTAGE											
under 15	41.45	41.76	41.14	43.66	42.80	44.63	43.78	45.53	44.61	46.88	46.58
15-64	54.79	54.83	54.74	53.27	53.57	52.43	52.70	51.52	51.88	51.28	51.06
65 and over	3.76	3.40	4.12	3.07	3.63	2.94	3.52	2.95	3.51	1.84	2.36
DEP. RATIO X 100	82.52	82.37	82.67	87.74	86.67	90.74	89.76	94.08	92.77	95.02	95.86

TABLE 1 — DATA

AGE AT LAST BIRTHDAY	POPULATION BOTH SEXES	MALES Number	%	FEMALES Number	%	BIRTHS BY AGE OF MOTHER	DEATHS BOTH SEXES	MALES	FEMALES	AGE AT LAST BIRTHDAY
0	26950	13850	3.6	13100	3.4	0	1749	986	763	0
1-4	100800	50950	13.3	49850	13.1	0	394	213	181	1-4
5-9	106700	53750	14.0	52950	13.9	0	96	48	48	5-9
10-14	89200	44900	11.7	44300	11.6	54	81	48	33	10-14
15-19	67800	34350	8.9	33450	8.8	5034	80	44	36	15-19
20-24	55650	27550	7.2	28100	7.4	8820	104	52	52	20-24
25-29	52100	25400	6.6	26700	7.0	6737	110	51	59	25-29
30-34	49050	24350	6.3	24700	6.5	4635	142	65	77	30-34
35-39	46000	23150	6.0	22850	6.0	2596	184	95	89	35-39
40-44	41200	20900	5.4	20300	5.3	707	238	124	114	40-44
45-49	35850	18300	4.8	17550	4.6	72	300	179	121	45-49
50-54	29100	15000	3.9	14100	3.7	0	381	208	173	50-54
55-59	22100	11150	2.9	10950	2.9	0	439	255	184	55-59
60-64	15250	7800	2.0	7450	2.0	0	472	271	201	60-64
65-69	9850	4950	1.3	4900	1.3	0	691	392	299	65-69
70-74	7900	3650	1.0	4250	1.1		560	295	265	70-74
75-79	5650	2300	0.6	3350	0.9		441	225	216	75-79
80-84	2750	1100	0.3	1650	0.4	14616 M.	343	152	191	80-84
85+	1100	400	0.1	700	0.2	14039 F.	431	153	278	85+
TOTAL	765000	383800		381200		28655	7236	3856	3380	TOTAL

TABLE 2 — MALE LIFE TABLE

x	nq_x	l_x	nd_x	nL_x	nm_x	na_x	T_x	r_x	$\dot{e}_x$	nM_x	x
0	0.067430	100000	6743	95093	0.070909	0.2723	6013393	0.0052	60.134	0.071191	
1	0.016433	93257	1532	368616	0.004157	1.1211	5918300	0.0052	63.462	0.004181	0
5	0.004367	91725	401	457621	0.000875	2.5000	5549684	0.0349	60.504	0.000893	1
10	0.005350	91324	489	455437	0.001073	2.5781	5092062	0.0437	55.758	0.001069	5
15	0.006425	90835	584	452793	0.001289	2.6289	4636625	0.0475	51.044	0.001281	10
20	0.009416	90252	850	449199	0.001892	2.5761	4183832	0.0284	46.357	0.001887	15
25	0.009999	89402	894	444843	0.002010	2.5758	3734633	0.0102	41.773	0.002008	20
30	0.013278	88508	1175	439787	0.002672	2.6567	3289790	0.0065	37.169	0.002669	25
35	0.020360	87333	1778	432498	0.004111	2.6566	2850003	0.0111	32.634	0.004104	30
40	0.029360	85555	2512	421954	0.005953	2.6831	2417506	0.0171	28.257	0.005933	35
45	0.047992	83043	3985	405841	0.009820	2.6480	1995552	0.0234	24.030	0.009781	40
50	0.067582	79057	5343	382778	0.013958	2.6587	1589711	0.0346	20.108	0.013867	45
55	0.109288	73715	8056	349529	0.023049	2.6361	1206933	0.0423	16.373	0.022870	50
60	0.161569	65658	10604	303906	0.034894	2.7004	857404	0.0152	13.059	0.034744	55
65	0.331598	55054	18256	229974	0.079382	2.5188	553498	0.0152	10.054	0.079192	60
70	0.333026	36798	12255	151547	0.080864	2.3525	323523	0.0152	8.792	0.080822	65
75	0.390447	24543	9583	97802	0.097983	2.4000	171976	0.0152	7.007	0.097826	70
80	0.511623	14961	7654	55193	0.138680	2.4380	74174	0.0152	4.958	0.138182	75
85+	*1.000000	7306	7306	18981	0.384930	2.5979	18981	0.0152	2.598	0.382500	80
											85+

TABLE 3 — FEMALE LIFE TABLE

x	nq_x	l_x	nd_x	nL_x	nm_x	na_x	T_x	r_x	$\dot{e}_x$	nM_x	x
0	0.055804	100000	5580	95979	0.058142	0.2795	6320304	0.0023	63.203	0.058244	0
1	0.014341	94420	1354	373789	0.003623	1.1279	6224325	0.0023	65.922	0.003631	1
5	0.004441	93066	413	464294	0.000890	2.5000	5850535	0.0336	62.865	0.000907	5
10	0.003727	92652	345	462416	0.000747	2.5524	5386241	0.0451	58.134	0.000745	10
15	0.005419	92307	500	460389	0.001086	2.7094	4923825	0.0443	53.342	0.001076	15
20	0.009236	91807	848	457018	0.001855	2.6230	4463436	0.0208	48.618	0.001851	20
25	0.011004	90959	1001	452405	0.002213	2.6136	4006418	0.0106	44.047	0.002210	25
30	0.015493	89958	1394	446453	0.003122	2.6064	3554013	0.0125	39.508	0.003117	30
35	0.019336	88564	1712	438752	0.003903	2.6239	3107559	0.0155	35.088	0.003117	35
40	0.027770	86852	2412	428472	0.005629	2.6009	2668808	0.0209	30.728	0.003895	40
45	0.034118	84440	2881	415513	0.006933	2.6793	2240336	0.0286	26.532	0.005616	45
50	0.059968	81559	4891	396268	0.012342	2.6432	1824823	0.0352	22.374	0.006895	50
55	0.081434	76668	6243	368586	0.016939	2.6369	1428555	0.0460	18.633	0.012269	55
60	0.127712	70425	8994	331739	0.027112	2.7336	1059969	0.0164	15.051	0.016804	60
65	0.265829	61431	16330	266972	0.061168	2.5394	728230	0.0164	11.855	0.026980	65
70	0.267977	45100	12086	193790	0.062364	2.3765	461258	0.0164	10.227	0.061020	70
75	0.277658	33015	9167	141893	0.064604	2.4713	267463	0.0164	8.101	0.062353	75
80	0.453748	23848	10821	92991	0.116365	2.5743	125571	0.0164	5.265	0.064478	80
85+	*1.000000	13027	13027	32579	0.399851	2.5009	32579	0.0164	2.501	0.115758	85+
										0.397143	

TABLE 4 — OBSERVED AND PROJECTED VITAL RATES

	OBSERVED POPULATION BOTH SEXES	MALES	FEMALES	PROJECTED 1962 MALES	FEMALES	1967 MALES	FEMALES	1972 MALES	FEMALES	STABLE POPULATION MALES	FEMALES
RATES PER THOUSAND											
Birth	37.46	38.08	36.83	37.77	36.54	39.04	37.78	40.29	39.01	40.95	39.98
Death	9.46	10.05	8.87	9.75	8.50	9.69	8.50	9.63	8.38	8.60	7.63
Increase	28.00	28.04	27.96	28.03	28.04	29.36	29.28	30.67	30.63	32.3512	
PERCENTAGE											
under 15	42.31	42.59	42.03	43.03	42.32	43.17	42.35	43.30	42.51	44.68	44.24
15-64	54.13	54.18	54.08	53.98	54.16	53.87	54.15	53.66	53.94	53.14	53.01
65 and over	3.56	3.23	3.90	2.99	3.52	2.96	3.50	3.04	3.55	2.18	2.74
DEP. RATIO X 100	84.74	84.56	84.91	85.24	84.65	85.65	84.67	86.35	85.40	88.19	88.63

TABLE 1 DATA

AGE AT LAST BIRTHDAY	POPULATION BOTH SEXES	MALES Number	%	FEMALES Number	%	BIRTHS BY AGE OF MOTHER	DEATHS BOTH SEXES	MALES	FEMALES	AGE AT LAST BIRTHDAY
0	28365	14301	3.5	14064	3.4	0	1616	903	713	0
1-4	101644	51161	12.4	50483	12.1	0	317	178	139	1-4
5-9	118810	59385	14.4	59425	14.2	0	76	45	31	5-9
10-14	103020	51714	12.6	51306	12.3	55	63	41	22	10-14
15-19	82273	39750	9.7	42523	10.2	5490	94	59	35	15-19
20-24	66616	32688	7.9	33928	8.1	10082	91	46	45	20-24
25-29	52404	25136	6.1	27268	6.5	7548	110	57	53	25-29
30-34	48685	23979	5.8	24706	5.9	5074	118	59	59	30-34
35-39	46446	22771	5.5	23675	5.7	2948	151	79	72	35-39
40-44	41479	21575	5.2	19904	4.8	807	213	120	93	40-44
45-49	37880	19544	4.7	18336	4.4	106	304	171	133	45-49
50-54	29374	15491	3.8	13883	3.3	0	397	238	159	50-54
55-59	22407	11619	2.8	10788	2.6	0	426	251	175	55-59
60-64	16082	7966	1.9	8116	1.9	0	471	276	195	60-64
65-69	15792	6801	1.7	8991	2.1	0	646	352	294	65-69
70-74	8981	3878	0.9	5103	1.2		559	305	254	70-74
75-79	5149	2240	0.5	2909	0.7		458	239	219	75-79
80-84	2756	1045	0.3	1711	0.4	16401 M.	364	152	212	80-84
85+	2499	856	0.2	1643	0.4	15709 F.	470	176	294	85+
TOTAL	830662	411900		418762		32110	6944	3747	3197	TOTAL

TABLE 2 MALE LIFE TABLE

x	$_nq_x$	l_x	$_nd_x$	$_nL_x$	$_nm_x$	$_na_x$	T_x	r_x	$\mathring{e}_x$	$_nM_x$	x
0	0.059971	100000	5997	95596	0.062734	0.2656	6187876	0.0085	61.879	0.063142	
1	0.013650	94003	1283	372310	0.003446	1.1151	6092280	0.0085	64.809	0.003479	1
5	0.003733	92720	346	462734	0.000748	2.5000	5719970	0.0221	61.691	0.000758	5
10	0.003987	92374	368	461018	0.000799	2.6906	5257236	0.0392	56.913	0.000793	10
15	0.007423	92005	683	458377	0.001490	2.5840	4796218	0.0446	52.130	0.001484	15
20	0.007048	91322	644	455074	0.001414	2.6108	4337842	0.0442	47.500	0.001407	20
25	0.011308	90679	1025	450925	0.002274	2.5922	3882767	0.0289	42.819	0.002268	25
30	0.012239	89653	1097	445628	0.002462	2.5950	3431843	0.0073	38.279	0.002460	30
35	0.017230	88556	1526	439236	0.003474	2.6771	2986215	0.0069	33.721	0.003469	35
40	0.027507	87030	2394	429609	0.005572	2.6848	2546979	0.0096	29.265	0.005562	40
45	0.043115	84636	3649	414818	0.008797	2.7082	2117370	0.0236	25.017	0.008749	45
50	0.074591	80987	6041	390689	0.015462	2.6416	1702552	0.0368	21.022	0.015364	50
55	0.103491	74946	7756	356328	0.021767	2.6272	1311863	0.0434	17.504	0.021603	55
60	0.160413	67190	10778	310096	0.034757	2.6012	955535	0.0184	14.221	0.034647	60
65	0.230344	56412	12994	250306	0.051913	2.5563	645439	0.0184	11.442	0.051757	65
70	0.329110	43418	14289	181200	0.078859	2.4884	395133	0.0184	9.101	0.078649	70
75	0.418708	29129	12196	114041	0.106947	2.4089	213934	0.0184	7.344	0.106696	75
80	0.528914	16932	8956	61393	0.145875	2.4018	99893	0.0184	5.900	0.145454	80
85+	*1.000000	7977	7977	38500	0.207181	4.8267	38500	0.0184	4.827	0.205607	85

TABLE 3 FEMALE LIFE TABLE

x	$_nq_x$	l_x	$_nd_x$	$_nL_x$	$_nm_x$	$_na_x$	T_x	r_x	$\mathring{e}_x$	$_nM_x$	x
0	0.048560	100000	4856	96429	0.050359	0.2646	6643206	0.0087	66.432	0.050697	0
1	0.010820	95144	1029	377605	0.002726	1.1142	6546777	0.0087	68.809	0.002753	1
5	0.002563	94114	241	469969	0.000513	2.5000	6169172	0.0219	65.550	0.000522	5
10	0.002153	93873	202	468892	0.000431	2.6517	5699203	0.0329	60.712	0.000429	10
15	0.004146	93671	388	467473	0.000831	2.7249	5230311	0.0405	55.837	0.000823	15
20	0.006661	93283	621	464967	0.001336	2.6713	4762838	0.0431	51.058	0.001326	20
25	0.009706	92662	899	461157	0.001950	2.6087	4297871	0.0298	46.382	0.001944	25
30	0.011885	91762	1091	456183	0.002391	2.5904	3836714	0.0117	41.812	0.002388	30
35	0.015141	90672	1373	450130	0.003050	2.6489	3380531	0.0184	37.283	0.003041	35
40	0.023200	89299	2072	441680	0.004691	2.6765	2930401	0.0207	32.816	0.004672	40
45	0.035859	87227	3128	428867	0.007293	2.6764	2488722	0.0284	28.532	0.007253	45
50	0.056120	84099	4720	409343	0.011530	2.6371	2059855	0.0415	24.493	0.011453	50
55	0.078526	79379	6233	382066	0.016315	2.6206	1650512	0.0368	20.793	0.016222	55
60	0.113869	73146	8329	345661	0.024096	2.5905	1268446	0.0206	17.341	0.024027	60
65	0.151963	64817	9850	300275	0.032803	2.5827	922785	0.0206	14.237	0.032699	65
70	0.222639	54967	12238	245022	0.049946	2.5638	622510	0.0206	11.325	0.049775	70
75	0.318242	42729	13598	179961	0.075562	2.5228	377488	0.0206	8.834	0.075284	75
80	0.471190	29131	13726	110389	0.124344	2.5274	197527	0.0206	6.781	0.123904	80
85+	1.000000	15405	15405	87137	0.176788	5.6565	87137	0.0206	5.656	0.178941	85

TABLE 4 OBSERVED AND PROJECTED VITAL RATES

	OBSERVED POPULATION BOTH SEXES	MALES	FEMALES	PROJECTED POPULATION 1965 MALES	FEMALES	1970 MALES	FEMALES	1975 MALES	FEMALES	STABLE POPULATION MALES	FEMALES
RATES PER THOUSAND											
Birth	38.66	39.82	37.51	40.54	38.33	41.33	39.20	41.19	39.18	40.93	39.6
Death	8.36	9.10	7.63	9.08	7.53	8.95	7.46	8.78	7.38	7.87	6.63
Increase	30.30	30.72	29.88	31.46	30.80	32.38	31.75	32.41	31.80		33.0584
PERCENTAGE											
under 15	42.36	42.87	41.86	43.22	42.03	43.89	42.43	45.24	43.68	44.91	44.20
15-64	53.41	53.54	53.28	53.53	53.61	52.93	53.47	51.55	52.36	52.70	52.6
65 and over	4.23	3.60	4.86	3.25	4.37	3.19	4.09	3.20	3.96	2.39	3.19
DEP. RATIO X 100	87.24	86.79	87.68	86.82	86.54	88.94	87.01	93.97	90.98	89.76	90.09

AGE AT LAST BIRTHDAY	1965 BOTH SEXES	MALES	FEMALES	1970 BOTH SEXES	MALES	FEMALES	1975 BOTH SEXES	MALES	FEMALES	AGE AT LAST BIRTHDAY	
0-4	166	84	82	197	100	97	234	119	115	0-4	
5-9	129	65	64	164	83	81	195	99	96	5-9	
10-14	118	59	59	128	64	64	164	83	81	10-14	TABLE 5
15-19	102	51	51	118	59	59	128	64	64	15-19	POPULATION
20-24	81	39	42	102	51	51	117	58	59	20-24	PROJECTED
25-29	66	32	34	81	39	42	101	51	50	25-29	WITH
30-34	52	25	27	65	32	33	80	39	41	30-34	FIXED
35-39	48	24	24	51	24	27	65	32	33	35-39	AGE—
40-44	45	22	23	47	23	24	50	24	26	40-44	SPECIFIC
45-49	40	21	19	45	22	23	45	22	23	45-49	BIRTH
50-54	36	18	18	38	20	18	42	20	22	50-54	AND
55-59	27	14	13	33	17	16	35	18	17	55-59	DEATH
60-64	20	10	10	24	12	12	30	15	15	60-64	RATES
65-69	13	6	7	16	8	8	20	10	10	65-69	(IN 1000's)
70-74	12	5	7	11	5	6	13	6	7	70-74	
75-79	6	2	4	8	3	5	7	3	4	75-79	
80-84	3	1	2	3	1	2	5	2	3	80-84	
85+	2	1	1	2	1	1	3	1	2	85+	
TOTAL	966	479	487	1133	564	569	1334	666	668	TOTAL	

STANDARD COUNTRIES:	ENGLAND AND WALES 1961 BOTH SEXES	MALES	FEMALES	UNITED STATES 1960 BOTH SEXES	MALES	FEMALES	MEXICO 1960 BOTH SEXES	MALES	FEMALES	
STANDARDIZED RATES PER THOUSAND										TABLE 6
Birth	34.62	42.40*	32.83	35.35	38.72*	34.07	40.74	39.31*	39.76	STANDAR-DIZED
Death	15.26	18.40*	15.04	12.79	15.08*	11.58	7.66	8.69*	6.65	RATES
Increase	19.36	24.01*	17.79	22.56	23.64*	22.49	33.08	30.62*	33.11	

	OBSERVED POP. MALES	FEMALES	STATIONARY POP. MALES	FEMALES	STABLE POP. MALES	FEMALES	OBSERVED BIRTHS	NET MATERNITY FUNCTION	BIRTHS IN STABLE POP.	
μ	24.05312	24.48689	35.17542	37.10769	21.92966	22.56415	26.34584	27.59102	26.16287	TABLE 7
σ^2	370.1044	390.1403	470.9041	520.8636	315.7415	340.9108	42.02370	43.34059	38.77994	MOMENTS
κ_3	5937.327	6958.908	2678.928	2896.859	5379.840	6233.716	161.0460	125.9044	146.7718	AND
κ_4	-19547.	6668.	-199264.	-256926.	28208.	42052.	-631.825	-923.629	-338.453	CUMULANTS
β_1	0.695359	0.815492	0.068727	0.059386	0.919483	0.980780	0.349476	0.194714	0.369372	
β_2	2.857301	3.043809	2.101406	2.052978	3.282949	3.361832	2.642226	2.508291	2.774947	
κ	-0.269174	-0.324505	-0.027221	-0.022770	-0.398972	-0.425781	-0.165618	-0.099715	-0.197803	

VITAL STATISTICS		THOMPSON AGE RANGE	NRR	1000r	INTERVAL	BOURGEOIS-PICHAT AGE RANGE	NRR	1000b	1000d	1000r	COALE	TABLE 8
GRR	2.643											RATES FROM AGE DISTRI-BUTIONS AND VITAL STATISTICS (Females)
NRR	2.430	0-4	2.17	28.34	27.35	5-29	2.83	41.46	2.96	38.51	IBR	
TFR	5.402	5-9	2.31	31.38	27.27	30-54	1.85	28.45	5.58	22.86	IDR	
GENERATION	26.864	10-14	2.27	29.42	27.17	55-79	1.44	14.47	1.07	13.40	IRI	
SEX RATIO	104.405	15-19	2.10	27.46	27.01	* 5-29	2.83	41.46	2.96	38.51	K1	
											K2	

Start of Age Interval	ORIGINAL MATRIX SUB-DIAGONAL	ALTERNATIVE FIRST ROWS Projection	Integral	FIRST STABLE MATRIX % IN STABLE POPULATION	FISHER VALUES	REPRODUCTIVE VALUES	SECOND STABLE MATRIX Z2 FIRST COLUMN	FIRST ROW	
0	0.99143	0.00000	0.00000	17.368	1.145	73910	0.1475+0.1074	0.1475+0.1074	TABLE 9
5	0.99771	0.00124	0.00000	14.586	1.363	81023	0.1796-0.1011	-0.0322+0.1583	LESLIE
10	0.99697	0.15049	0.00270	12.327	1.612	82697	-0.0197-0.2335	-0.1386+0.0319	MATRIX
15	0.99464	0.49243	0.32521	10.411	1.736	73808	-0.2506-0.0899	-0.0986-0.1155	AND ITS
20	0.99180	0.66291	0.74851	8.772	1.493	50661	-0.2107+0.2160	-0.0165-0.1747	SPECTRAL
25	0.98921	0.55654	0.69725	7.369	1.012	27594	0.1230+0.3180	0.0359-0.1493	COMPO-
30	0.98673	0.38061	0.51732	6.175	0.563	13920	0.3836+0.0229	0.0507-0.0865	NENTS
35	0.98123	0.19052	0.31365	5.162	0.232	5502	0.2026-0.3816	0.0318-0.0324	(Females)
40	0.97099	0.05346	0.10213	4.290	0.057	1140	-0.2939-0.3834	0.0095-0.0070	
45	0.95448	0.00672	0.01442	3.529	0.007	121	-0.5209+0.1195	0.0012-0.0007	
50	0.93336	0.00008	0.00018	2.853	0.000	1	-0.1173+0.5693	0.0000-0.0000	
55+	0.80846			7.158					

Start of Age Interval	OBSERVED POPUL. (IN 100's)	CONTRIBUTIONS OF ROOTS (IN 100's) r_1	r_2, r_3	r_4-r_{11}	AGE-SP. BIRTH RATES	NET MATERNITY FUNCTION	COEFF. OF MATRIX EQUATION	PARAMETERS INTEGRAL	MATRIX	EXP. INCREASE x	$e^{(x+2\frac{1}{2})r}$	
0	645	691	-21	-24	0.0000	0.0000	0.0000	L(1) 1.17974	1.18051	0	1.0862	TABLE 10
5	594	580	-10	24	0.0000	0.0000	0.0012	L(2) 0.35251	0.36475	50	5.6721	AGE
10	513	490	18	5	0.0005	0.0025	0.1489	0.82579	0.79825	55	6.6916	ANALYSIS
15	425	414	29	-18	0.0632	0.2953	0.4856	R(1) 0.03306	0.03319	60	7.8944	AND
20	339	349	4	-14	0.1454	0.6760	0.6502	R(2) -0.02154	-0.02610	65	9.3133	MISCEL-
25	273	293	-34	13	0.1354	0.6245	0.5414	0.23347	0.22844	70	10.9872	LANEOUS
30	247	246	-37	39	0.1005	0.4583	0.3663	C(1)	3976	75	12.9620	RESULTS
35	237	205	8	24	0.0609	0.2742	0.1809	C(2)	-4632	80	15.2918	(Females)
40	199	171	54	-25	0.0198	0.0876	0.0499		3479	85	18.0403	
45	183	140	40	3	0.0028	0.0121	0.0061	2P/Y 26.9125	27.5049	90	21.2828	
50	139	113	-29	54	0.0000	0.0000	0.0000	DELTA 4.4032		95	25.1081	
55+	393	285								100	29.6209	

TABLE 1 — DATA

AGE AT LAST BIRTHDAY	BOTH SEXES	POPULATION MALES Number	%	FEMALES Number	%	BIRTHS BY AGE OF MOTHER	DEATHS BOTH SEXES	MALES	FEMALES	AGE AT LAST BIRTHDAY
0	2278571	1153736	2.1	1124835	2.2	0	202321	114840	87481	0
1-4	9376978	4749510	8.7	4627468	8.9	0	82595	43770	38825	1-4
5-9	11475275	5794759	10.7	5680516	10.9	0	32468	17447	15021	5-9
10-14	10735265	5415431	10.0	5319834	10.2	1651	23338	12439	10899	10-14
15-19	9565595	4743236	8.7	4822359	9.2	217140	36731	18635	18096	15-19
20-24	9346053	4570144	8.4	4775909	9.1	693321	51019	23878	27141	20-24
25-29	9122027	4555060	8.4	4566967	8.7	694796	57132	26967	30165	25-29
30-34	8199612	4190557	7.7	4009055	7.7	477171	56772	28622	28150	30-34
35-39	7812641	4086903	7.5	3725738	7.1	302165	60287	32221	28066	35-39
40-44	6458663	3349013	6.2	3109650	5.9	100476	56448	30615	25833	40-44
45-49	5820232	3137574	5.8	2682658	5.1	10372	62278	34603	27675	45-49
50-54	4784838	2559656	4.7	2225182	4.3	293	68721	37961	30760	50-54
55-59	3627609	1922191	3.5	1705418	3.3	0	72858	40252	32606	55-59
60-64	3010081	1593300	2.9	1416781	2.7	0	86224	47396	38828	60-64
65-69	2113732	1102528	2.0	1011204	1.9	0	90389	48579	41810	65-69
70-74	1417089	717927	1.3	699162	1.3		93387	48729	44658	70-74
75-79	873118	427883	0.8	445235	0.9		86124	43339	42785	75-79
80-84	408518	188852	0.3	219666	0.4	1283556 M.	62015	29417	32598	80-84
85+	204581	88770	0.2	115811	0.2	1213829 F.	50294	22038	28256	85+
TOTAL	106630478	54347030		52283448		2497385	1331401	701748	629653	TOTAL

TABLE 2 — MALE LIFE TABLE

x	nq_x	l_x	nd_x	nL_x	nm_x	na_x	T_x	r_x	$\mathring{e}_x$	nM_x	x
0	0.093224	100000	9322	93657	0.099537	0.3196	5448768	0.0000	54.488	0.099537	0
1	0.035927	90678	3258	353503	0.009216	1.1739	5355111	0.0000	59.057	0.009216	1
5	0.014916	87420	1304	433839	0.003006	2.5000	5001607	0.0043	57.214	0.003011	5
10	0.011437	86116	985	428191	0.002300	2.5754	4567768	0.0172	53.042	0.002297	10
15	0.019503	85131	1660	421747	0.003937	2.6466	4139577	0.0131	48.626	0.003929	15
20	0.025796	83471	2153	412118	0.005225	2.5689	3717830	0.0000	44.541	0.005225	20
25	0.029181	81317	2373	400758	0.005921	2.5438	3305712	0.0027	40.652	0.005920	25
30	0.033595	78944	2652	388213	0.006832	2.5456	2904954	0.0040	36.797	0.006830	30
35	0.038705	76292	2953	374210	0.007891	2.5445	2516741	0.0145	32.988	0.007884	35
40	0.044760	73339	3283	358660	0.009153	2.5518	2142531	0.0172	29.214	0.009141	40
45	0.053796	70057	3769	341141	0.011047	2.5821	1783870	0.0155	25.463	0.011029	45
50	0.071926	66288	4768	320017	0.014899	2.6043	1442700	0.0337	21.764	0.014831	50
55	0.100048	61520	6155	292827	0.021019	2.5998	1122683	0.0260	18.249	0.020941	55
60	0.139364	55365	7716	258238	0.029879	2.5910	829856	0.0288	14.989	0.029747	60
65	0.199902	47649	9525	215143	0.044274	2.5745	571618	0.0288	11.996	0.044061	65
70	0.291756	38124	11123	163102	0.068196	2.5260	356475	0.0288	9.350	0.067875	70
75	0.404246	27001	10915	107256	0.101767	2.4577	193373	0.0288	7.162	0.101287	75
80	0.553579	16086	8905	56893	0.156520	2.4126	86117	0.0288	5.354	0.155768	80
85+	1.000000	7181	7181	29224	0.245726	4.0696	29224	0.0288	4.070	0.248259	85+

TABLE 3 — FEMALE LIFE TABLE

x	nq_x	l_x	nd_x	nL_x	nm_x	na_x	T_x	r_x	$\mathring{e}_x$	nM_x	x
0	0.073959	100000	7396	95097	0.077772	0.3370	5641109	0.0000	56.411	0.077772	0
1	0.032790	92604	3036	361911	0.008390	1.1989	5546013	0.0000	59.889	0.008390	1
5	0.013113	89568	1175	444902	0.002640	2.5000	5184102	0.0040	57.879	0.002644	5
10	0.010209	88393	902	439804	0.002052	2.6051	4739200	0.0138	53.615	0.002049	10
15	0.018627	87491	1630	433693	0.003758	2.6923	4299395	0.0070	49.141	0.003753	15
20	0.028031	85861	2407	423514	0.005683	2.5938	3865703	0.0000	45.023	0.005683	20
25	0.032510	83454	2713	410567	0.006608	2.5292	3442189	0.0110	41.246	0.006605	25
30	0.034518	80741	2787	396774	0.007024	2.5128	3031622	0.0133	37.547	0.007022	30
35	0.036997	77954	2884	382617	0.007538	2.5198	2634848	0.0178	33.800	0.007533	35
40	0.040775	75070	3061	367853	0.008321	2.5510	2252231	0.0243	30.002	0.008307	40
45	0.050452	72009	3633	351281	0.010342	2.5878	1884378	0.0229	26.169	0.010316	45
50	0.067162	68376	4592	330861	0.013880	2.6006	1533096	0.0311	22.422	0.013824	50
55	0.091725	63784	5851	304892	0.019189	2.6025	1202235	0.0255	18.849	0.019119	55
60	0.128975	57933	7472	271749	0.027496	2.6022	897343	0.0204	15.489	0.027406	60
65	0.188559	50461	9515	229323	0.041491	2.5845	625594	0.0204	12.398	0.041347	65
70	0.276751	40946	11332	176811	0.064091	2.5361	396271	0.0204	9.678	0.063874	70
75	0.387528	29614	11478	119038	0.096422	2.4705	219460	0.0204	7.411	0.096095	75
80	0.535061	18136	9704	65172	0.148901	2.4346	100422	0.0204	5.537	0.148398	80
85+	1.000000	8432	8432	35250	0.239214	4.1804	35250	0.0204	4.180	0.243984	85+

TABLE 4 — OBSERVED AND PROJECTED VITAL RATES

	OBSERVED POPULATION BOTH SEXES	MALES	FEMALES	PROJECTED POPULATION 1925 MALES	FEMALES	1930 MALES	FEMALES	1935 MALES	FEMALES	STABLE POPULATION MALES	FEMALES
RATES PER THOUSAND											
Birth	23.42	23.62	23.22	23.29	22.83	23.13	22.60	23.02	22.41	21.45	20.75
Death	12.49	12.91	12.04	13.24	12.20	13.75	12.58	14.26	13.01	16.76	16.06
Increase	10.93	10.71	11.17	10.05	10.63	9.38	10.02	8.76	9.40		4.6961
PERCENTAGE											
under 15	31.76	31.49	32.04	30.24	30.56	29.02	29.13	28.43	28.36	27.13	26.90
15-64	63.53	63.86	63.19	64.59	64.35	65.43	65.50	65.39	65.77	64.18	63.91
65 and over	4.71	4.65	4.76	5.17	5.09	5.56	5.37	6.18	5.87	8.69	9.20
DEP. RATIO X 100	57.39	56.59	58.24	54.82	55.41	52.85	52.66	52.92	52.06	55.82	56.48

AGE AT LAST BIRTHDAY	1925 BOTH SEXES	MALES	FEMALES	1930 BOTH SEXES	MALES	FEMALES	1935 BOTH SEXES	MALES	FEMALES	AGE AT LAST BIRTHDAY	
0-4	11502	5849	5653	11961	6082	5879	12452	6332	6120	0-4	TABLE 5
5-9	11327	5727	5600	11177	5674	5503	11624	5901	5723	5-9	POPULATION
10-14	11334	5719	5615	11189	5653	5536	11041	5601	5440	10-14	PROJECTED
15-19	10580	5334	5246	11170	5633	5537	11027	5558	5459	15-19	WITH
20-24	9344	4635	4709	10335	5212	5123	10912	5505	5407	20-24	FIXED
25-29	9074	4444	4630	9072	4507	4565	10034	5068	4966	25-29	AGE—
30-34	8826	4412	4414	8779	4305	4474	8778	4366	4412	30-34	SPECIFIC
35-39	7905	4039	3866	8509	4253	4256	8465	4150	4315	35-39	BIRTH
40-44	7499	3917	3582	7589	3872	3717	8169	4077	4092	40-44	AND
45-49	6156	3186	2970	7147	3726	3421	7232	3683	3549	45-49	DEATH
50-54	5470	2943	2527	5785	2988	2797	6717	3495	3222	50-54	RATES
55-59	4393	2342	2051	5021	2693	2328	5311	2734	2577	55-59	(IN 1000's)
60-64	3215	1695	1520	3894	2066	1828	4450	2375	2075	60-64	
65-69	2523	1327	1196	2695	1412	1283	3263	1721	1542	65-69	
70-74	1616	836	780	1928	1006	922	2060	1071	989	70-74	
75-79	943	472	471	1075	550	525	1283	662	621	75-79	
80-84	471	227	244	508	250	258	579	292	287	80-84	
85+	216	97	119	249	117	132	268	129	139	85+	
TOTAL	112394	57201	55193	118083	59999	58084	123665	62730	60935	TOTAL	

STANDARD COUNTRIES: STANDARDIZED RATES PER THOUSAND	ENGLAND AND WALES 1961 BOTH SEXES	MALES	FEMALES	UNITED STATES 1960 BOTH SEXES	MALES	FEMALES	MEXICO 1960 BOTH SEXES	MALES	FEMALES	
Birth	18.57	19.93*	17.50	18.91	18.64*	18.11	20.98	18.34*	20.34	TABLE 6
Death	19.40	22.60*	20.94	16.90	18.82*	17.00	11.93	13.08*	11.39	STANDARDIZED RATES
Increase	-0.83	-2.66*	-3.44	2.01	-0.18*	1.11	9.06	5.26*	8.96	

	OBSERVED POP. MALES	FEMALES	STATIONARY POP. MALES	FEMALES	STABLE POP. MALES	FEMALES	OBSERVED BIRTHS	NET MATERNITY FUNCTION	BIRTHS IN STABLE POP.	
μ	28.43515	27.84290	34.35172	34.71130	32.14164	32.45787	28.08727	28.55565	28.34148	TABLE 7
σ²	381.8306	378.6519	479.2225	488.5965	461.3252	470.3747	41.01854	43.78932	43.24895	MOMENTS
κ3	4057.570	4667.052	3358.735	3402.639	4234.058	4326.836	115.6987	112.6163	117.4521	AND
κ4	-76291.	-49547.	-204568.	-215877.	-167100.	-176496.	-776.309	-1067.492	-981.354	CUMULANTS
β1	0.295747	0.401204	0.102504	0.099261	0.182596	0.179891	0.193962	0.151042	0.170528	
β2	2.476721	2.654429	2.109233	2.095715	2.214832	2.202287	2.538604	2.443291	2.475344	
κ	-0.127145	-0.179784	-0.039390	-0.037837	-0.070515	-0.068935	-0.103273	-0.076630	-0.087202	

VITAL STATISTICS		THOMPSON AGE RANGE	NRR	1000r	INTERVAL	BOURGEOIS-PICHAT AGE RANGE	NRR	1000b	1000d	1000r	COALE	
GRR	1.407					5-29	1.21	25.17	18.25	6.92	IBR	TABLE 8
NRR	1.143	0-4	1.22	7.28	27.04	30-54	1.77	39.63	18.48	21.14	IDR	RATES FROM AGE
TFR	2.895	5-9	1.30	9.86	26.96	55-79	1.92	43.67	19.51	24.16	IRI	DISTRIBUTIONS
GENERATION	28.448	10-14	1.33	10.61	26.89	*35-74	2.01	49.27	23.34	25.93	K1	AND VITAL
SEX RATIO	105.744	15-19	1.36	11.04	26.76						K2	STATISTICS (Females)

Start Age Interval	ORIGINAL MATRIX SUB-DIAGONAL	ALTERNATIVE FIRST ROWS Projection	Integral	FIRST STABLE MATRIX % IN STABLE POPULATION	FISHER VALUES	REPRODUCTIVE VALUES	SECOND STABLE MATRIX Z2 FIRST COLUMN	FIRST ROW	
0	0.97351	0.00000	0.00000	9.375	1.107	6367124	0.1342+0.0773	0.1342+0.0773	TABLE 9
5	0.98854	0.00034	0.00000	8.915	1.164	6612284	0.1621-0.0921	0.0012+0.1286	LESLIE
10	0.98610	0.04966	0.00070	8.608	1.205	6411090	0.0035-0.2279	-0.0902+0.0541	MATRIX
15	0.97653	0.20745	0.10120	8.291	1.195	5764759	-0.2374-0.1446	-0.0825-0.0451	AND ITS
20	0.96943	0.32503	0.32627	7.909	1.018	4862390	-0.2959+0.1586	-0.0309-0.0943	SPECTRAL
25	0.96640	0.29671	0.34192	7.489	0.704	3215431	-0.0161+0.4022	0.0097-0.0880	COMPONENTS
30	0.96432	0.21905	0.26750	7.069	0.406	1627730	0.4046+0.2604	0.0264-0.0541	(Females)
35	0.96141	0.12457	0.18227	6.659	0.180	669183	0.5123-0.2585	0.0198-0.0215	
40	0.95495	0.03999	0.07262	6.253	0.048	148757	0.0440-0.6809	0.0066-0.0048	
45	0.94187	0.00443	0.00869	5.833	0.005	13244	-0.6668-0.4526	0.0007-0.0005	
50	0.92151	0.00015	0.00030	5.366	0.000	352	-0.8483+0.4021	0.0000-0.0000	
55+	0.75254			18.232					

Start Age Interval	OBSERVED POPUL. (IN 100's)	CONTRIBUTIONS OF ROOTS (IN 100's) r1	r2, r3	r4-r11	AGE-SP. BIRTH RATES	NET MATERNITY FUNCTION	COEFF. OF MATRIX EQUATION	PARAMETERS INTEGRAL	MATRIX	EXP. INCREASE x	e(x+2½)r	
0	57523	56947	-11	587	0.0000	0.0000	0.0000	L(1) 1.02376	1.02377	0	1.0118	TABLE 10
5	56805	54152	1658	995	0.0000	0.0000	0.0003	L(2) 0.40248	0.41000	50	1.2796	AGE
10	53198	52288	2072	-1162	0.0002	0.0007	0.0478	0.71462	0.69688	55	1.3100	ANALYSIS
15	48224	50364	90	-2231	0.0219	0.0949	0.1969	R(1) 0.00470	0.00470	60	1.3411	AND
20	47759	48040	-2942	2661	0.0706	0.2988	0.3012	R(2) -0.03965	-0.04250	65	1.3730	MISCELLANEOUS
25	45670	45490	-3708	3887	0.0739	0.3036	0.2666	0.21157	0.20780	70	1.4056	RESULTS
30	40091	42941	-279	-2572	0.0579	0.2295	0.1902			75	1.4390	(Females)
35	37257	40448	4948	-8139	0.0394	0.1508	0.1043	C(1)	607429	80	1.4732	
40	31097	37984	6363	-13250	0.0157	0.0578	0.0322	C(2)	255542	85	1.5082	
45	26827	35431	672	-9276	0.0019	0.0066	0.0034	2P/Y 29.6975	450686	90	1.5440	
50	22252	32596	-7960	-2384	0.0001	0.0002	0.0001	DELTA 9.6154	30.2367	95	1.5807	
55+	56133	110747								100	1.6183	

TABLE 1 — DATA

AGE AT LAST BIRTHDAY	POPULATION BOTH SEXES	MALES Number	%	FEMALES Number	%	BIRTHS BY AGE OF MOTHER	DEATHS BOTH SEXES	MALES	FEMALES	AGE AT LAST BIRTHDAY
0	2460000	1252000	2.1	1208000	2.1	0	181784	103453	78331	0
1-4	9856000	5008000	8.5	4848000	8.5	0	66670	35762	30908	1-4
5-9	12086998	6112999	10.4	5973999	10.5	0	25653	14099	11554	5-9
10-14	11527000	5784000	9.8	5743000	10.1	2244	20145	11141	9004	10-14
15-19	10784000	5357000	9.1	5427000	9.5	254830	33399	16863	16536	15-19
20-24	9907000	4923000	8.4	4984000	8.7	691395	44194	21678	22516	20-24
25-29	9350000	4645000	7.9	4705000	8.3	654513	45282	22273	23009	25-29
30-34	9370000	4717000	8.0	4653000	8.2	473844	47512	24728	22784	30-34
35-39	8076000	4142000	7.0	3934000	6.9	291163	55922	30250	25672	35-39
40-44	7500000	3927000	6.7	3573000	6.3	96784	60316	33858	26458	40-44
45-49	6304000	3284000	5.6	3020000	5.3	9223	67823	38452	29371	45-49
50-54	5217000	2757000	4.7	2460000	4.3	195	78890	44914	33976	50-54
55-59	4362000	2311000	3.9	2051000	3.6	0	84826	48391	36435	55-59
60-64	3243000	1681000	2.9	1562000	2.7	0	99605	55653	43952	60-64
65-69	2537000	1311000	2.2	1226000	2.2	0	112246	62221	50025	65-69
70-74	1618000	822000	1.4	796000	1.4		111360	59911	51449	70-74
75-79	1026743	499812	0.8	526931	0.9		100425	52061	48364	75-79
80-84	460368	215136	0.4	245232	0.4	1272149 M.	76007	36869	39138	80-84
85+	143891	64053	0.1	79838	0.1	1202042 F.	59865	26132	33733	85+
TOTAL	115829000	58813000		57016000		2474191	1371924	738709	633215	TOTAL

TABLE 2 — MALE LIFE TABLE

x	$_nq_x$	l_x	$_nd_x$	$_nL_x$	$_nm_x$	$_na_x$	T_x	r_x	$\mathring{e}_x$	$_nM_x$
0	0.078194	100000	7819	94631	0.082630	0.3134	5633668	0.0000	56.337	0.082630
1	0.027997	92181	2581	361408	0.007141	1.1657	5539037	0.0000	60.089	0.007141
5	0.011446	89600	1026	445435	0.002302	2.5000	5177629	0.0045	57.786	0.002306
10	0.009596	88574	850	440819	0.001928	2.5853	4732194	0.0109	53.426	0.001926
15	0.015657	87724	1373	435403	0.003155	2.6566	4291375	0.0130	48.919	0.003148
20	0.021801	86351	1883	427179	0.004407	2.5695	3855972	0.0100	44.655	0.004403
25	0.023694	84468	2001	417391	0.004795	2.5264	3428794	0.0000	40.593	0.004795
30	0.025899	82467	2136	407179	0.005245	2.5862	3011403	0.0059	36.517	0.005242
35	0.035921	80331	2886	394679	0.007311	2.5823	2604224	0.0112	32.419	0.007303
40	0.042292	77446	3275	379321	0.008635	2.5860	2209545	0.0142	28.530	0.008622
45	0.057124	74170	4237	360721	0.011746	2.6090	1830224	0.0234	24.676	0.011709
50	0.078538	69933	5492	336397	0.016327	2.5840	1469503	0.0189	21.013	0.016291
55	0.100111	64441	6451	306790	0.021028	2.6107	1133106	0.0269	17.584	0.020939
60	0.153808	57990	8919	268487	0.033220	2.5938	826316	0.0211	14.249	0.033107
65	0.213322	49070	10468	219812	0.047622	2.5601	557829	0.0211	11.368	0.047461
70	0.309293	38603	11940	163276	0.073125	2.5093	338017	0.0211	8.756	0.072884
75	0.412661	26663	11003	105261	0.104529	2.4502	174741	0.0211	6.554	0.104161
80	0.594570	15660	9311	54054	0.172256	2.3959	69481	0.0211	4.437	0.171376
85+	*1.000000	6349	6349	15427	0.411570	2.4297	15427	0.0211	2.430	0.407975

TABLE 3 — FEMALE LIFE TABLE

x	$_nq_x$	l_x	$_nd_x$	$_nL_x$	$_nm_x$	$_na_x$	T_x	r_x	$\mathring{e}_x$	$_nM_x$
0	0.062137	100000	6214	95826	0.064844	0.3282	5900680	0.0000	59.007	0.064844
1	0.025052	93786	2350	368533	0.006375	1.1857	5804854	0.0000	61.894	0.006375
5	0.009614	91437	879	454986	0.001932	2.5000	5436321	0.0024	59.454	0.001934
10	0.007819	90558	708	451119	0.001570	2.6422	4981335	0.0076	55.007	0.001568
15	0.015162	89850	1362	446107	0.003054	2.6943	4530216	0.0111	50.420	0.003047
20	0.022363	88487	1979	437641	0.004522	2.5766	4084108	0.0100	46.155	0.004518
25	0.024158	86509	2090	427332	0.004890	2.5065	3646467	0.0021	42.152	0.004890
30	0.024214	84419	2044	417100	0.004901	2.5571	3219136	0.0126	38.133	0.004897
35	0.032170	82375	2650	405427	0.006536	2.5676	2802036	0.0201	34.016	0.006526
40	0.036431	79725	2904	391573	0.007417	2.5727	2396609	0.0187	30.061	0.007405
45	0.047695	76820	3664	375357	0.009761	2.6137	2005036	0.0272	26.100	0.009725
50	0.067030	73156	4904	353975	0.013853	2.5924	1629679	0.0250	22.277	0.013811
55	0.085561	68252	5840	327360	0.017839	2.6194	1275704	0.0263	18.691	0.017765
60	0.132183	62413	8250	292324	0.028222	2.6072	948344	0.0179	15.195	0.028138
65	0.186227	54163	10087	246444	0.040928	2.5839	656020	0.0179	12.112	0.040803
70	0.279371	44076	12314	189969	0.064819	2.5302	409576	0.0179	9.292	0.064634
75	0.373732	31763	11871	128926	0.092074	2.4823	219607	0.0179	6.914	0.091784
80	0.568370	19892	11306	70510	0.160345	2.4395	90681	0.0179	4.559	0.159597
85+	*1.000000	8586	8586	20170	0.425673	2.3492	20170	0.0179	2.349	0.422518

TABLE 4 — OBSERVED AND PROJECTED VITAL RATES

	OBSERVED POPULATION BOTH SEXES	MALES	FEMALES	PROJECTED POPULATION 1930 MALES	FEMALES	1935 MALES	FEMALES	1940 MALES	FEMALES	STABLE POPULATION MALES	FEMALES
RATES PER THOUSAND											
Birth	21.36	21.63	21.08	21.74	21.09	21.76	21.02	21.67	20.84	19.78	18.9
Death	11.84	12.56	11.11	12.80	11.25	13.30	11.70	13.78	12.17	16.54	15.6
Increase	9.52	9.07	9.98	8.94	9.84	8.46	9.32	7.90	8.68		3.240
PERCENTAGE											
under 15	31.02	30.87	31.17	29.45	29.35	28.19	27.84	27.42	26.92	25.92	25.3
15-64	63.98	64.18	63.79	65.35	65.38	66.13	66.46	66.46	66.95	65.36	64.8
65 and over	5.00	4.95	5.04	5.20	5.28	5.69	5.70	6.12	6.13	8.72	9.8
DEP. RATIO X 100	56.29	55.82	56.77	53.02	52.96	51.22	50.47	50.47	49.37	53.00	54.1

TABLE 1 — DATA

AGE AT LAST BIRTHDAY	POPULATION BOTH SEXES	MALES Number	%	FEMALES Number	%	BIRTHS BY AGE OF MOTHER	DEATHS BOTH SEXES	MALES	FEMALES	AGE AT LAST BIRTHDAY
0	2181019	1107380	1.8	1073639	1.8	0	148439	84233	64206	0
1-4	9211088	4672067	7.5	4539021	7.5	0	53051	28632	24419	1-4
5-9	12577837	6368321	10.2	6209516	10.2	0	24268	13474	10794	5-9
10-14	12033597	6082707	9.8	5950890	9.8	2842	18706	10533	8173	10-14
15-19	11572958	5768600	9.3	5804358	9.6	277920	32447	17108	15339	15-19
20-24	10899558	5353542	8.6	5546016	9.1	680272	43644	22180	21464	20-24
25-29	9875265	4880558	7.8	4994707	8.2	581320	44134	22521	21613	25-29
30-34	9155480	4577613	7.4	4577867	7.5	395806	46431	24451	21980	30-34
35-39	9204195	4675110	7.5	4529085	7.5	252959	56723	31153	25570	35-39
40-44	8031696	4154677	6.7	3877019	6.4	83891	64419	36889	27530	40-44
45-49	7078705	3689846	5.9	3388859	5.6	8062	74909	43549	31360	45-49
50-54	6005617	3146008	5.1	2859609	4.7	152	87315	50942	36373	50-54
55-59	4686474	2445968	3.9	2240506	3.7	0	95623	55581	40042	55-59
60-64	3780478	1955503	3.1	1824975	3.0	0	110550	63002	47548	60-64
65-69	2795219	1429757	2.3	1365462	2.2	0	121292	67757	53535	65-69
70-74	1963142	997262	1.6	965880	1.6		128190	70121	58069	70-74
75-79	1123428	555479	0.9	567949	0.9		110697	58212	52485	75-79
80-84	542238	254440	0.4	287798	0.5	1172543 M.	80928	40059	40869	80-84
85+	270244	116239	0.2	154005	0.3	1110681 F.	64394	28675	35719	85+
TOTAL	122988238	62231077		60757161		2283224	1406160	769072	637088	TOTAL

TABLE 2 — MALE LIFE TABLE

x	$_nq_x$	l_x	$_nd_x$	$_nL_x$	$_nm_x$	$_na_x$	T_x	r_x	$\mathring{e}_x$	$_nM_x$	x
0	0.072253	100000	7225	94988	0.076065	0.3063	5727445	0.0000	57.274	0.076065	0
1	0.024094	92775	2235	364744	0.006128	1.1570	5632457	0.0000	60.711	0.006128	1
5	0.010523	90539	953	450315	0.002116	2.5000	5267713	0.0000	58.181	0.002116	5
10	0.008629	89587	773	446075	0.001733	2.5963	4817398	0.0078	53.774	0.001732	10
15	0.014751	88814	1310	441006	0.002971	2.6628	4371322	0.0098	49.219	0.002966	15
20	0.020531	87504	1797	433161	0.004147	2.5750	3930316	0.0127	44.916	0.004143	20
25	0.022827	85707	1956	423730	0.004617	2.5438	3497155	0.0110	40.804	0.004614	25
30	0.026365	83751	2208	413383	0.005341	2.5678	3073425	0.0000	36.697	0.005341	30
35	0.032803	81543	2675	401281	0.006666	2.5955	2660042	0.0029	32.622	0.006664	35
40	0.043543	78868	3434	386100	0.008895	2.6009	2258761	0.0147	28.640	0.008879	40
45	0.057499	75434	4337	366767	0.011826	2.6021	1872661	0.0157	24.825	0.011802	45
50	0.078191	71096	5559	342155	0.016247	2.6029	1505894	0.0245	21.181	0.016193	50
55	0.108081	65537	7083	310645	0.022802	2.5943	1163738	0.0243	17.757	0.022724	55
60	0.149934	58454	8764	271088	0.032330	2.5833	853093	0.0229	14.594	0.032218	60
65	0.213065	49690	10587	222600	0.047561	2.5585	582005	0.0229	11.713	0.047391	65
70	0.300169	39102	11737	166327	0.070568	2.5135	359405	0.0229	9.191	0.070314	70
75	0.414627	27365	11346	107872	0.105183	2.4482	193078	0.0229	7.056	0.104796	75
80	0.556591	16019	8916	56422	0.158023	2.4008	85206	0.0229	5.319	0.157440	80
85+	1.000000	7103	7103	28785	0.246760	4.0525	28785	0.0229	4.053	0.246691	85+

TABLE 3 — FEMALE LIFE TABLE

x	$_nq_x$	l_x	$_nd_x$	$_nL_x$	$_nm_x$	$_na_x$	T_x	r_x	$\mathring{e}_x$	$_nM_x$	x
0	0.057462	100000	5746	96087	0.059802	0.3191	6066840	0.0000	60.668	0.059802	0
1	0.021197	94254	1998	371367	0.005380	1.1731	5970752	0.0000	63.348	0.005380	1
5	0.008654	92256	798	459284	0.001738	2.5000	5599385	0.0000	60.694	0.001738	5
10	0.006849	91458	626	455804	0.001374	2.6316	5140101	0.0050	56.202	0.001373	10
15	0.013145	90831	1194	451398	0.002645	2.6909	4684298	0.0044	51.572	0.002643	15
20	0.019191	89637	1720	444029	0.003874	2.5835	4232899	0.0113	47.223	0.003870	20
25	0.021422	87917	1883	434943	0.004330	2.5356	3788870	0.0148	43.096	0.004327	25
30	0.023734	86034	2042	425158	0.004803	2.5467	3353927	0.0049	38.984	0.004801	30
35	0.027872	83992	2341	414275	0.005651	2.5725	2928769	0.0109	34.870	0.005646	35
40	0.034985	81651	2857	401369	0.007117	2.5901	2514493	0.0218	30.796	0.007101	40
45	0.045382	78794	3576	385406	0.009278	2.6051	2113124	0.0209	26.818	0.009254	45
50	0.061959	75218	4660	364960	0.012770	2.6115	1727718	0.0283	22.969	0.012720	50
55	0.086030	70558	6070	338296	0.017943	2.6124	1362758	0.0265	19.314	0.017872	55
60	0.123059	64488	7936	303452	0.026152	2.6075	1024462	0.0230	15.886	0.026054	60
65	0.179730	56552	10164	258236	0.039360	2.5873	721010	0.0230	12.750	0.039207	65
70	0.262847	46388	12193	202018	0.060355	2.5460	462774	0.0230	9.976	0.060120	70
75	0.376015	34195	12858	138597	0.092771	2.4818	260756	0.0230	7.626	0.092411	75
80	0.518883	21337	11071	77675	0.142535	2.4512	122159	0.0230	5.725	0.142006	80
85+	1.000000	10266	10266	44484	0.230774	4.3332	44484	0.0230	4.333	0.231933	85+

TABLE 4 — OBSERVED AND PROJECTED VITAL RATES

	OBSERVED POPULATION BOTH SEXES	MALES	FEMALES	PROJECTED POPULATION 1935 MALES	FEMALES	1940 MALES	FEMALES	1945 MALES	FEMALES	STABLE POPULATION MALES	FEMALES
RATES PER THOUSAND											
Birth	18.56	18.84	18.28	19.13	18.44	19.29	18.48	19.12	18.22	16.50	15.55
Death	11.43	12.36	10.49	12.83	10.90	13.44	11.49	14.03	12.11	18.13	17.17
Increase	7.13	6.48	7.79	6.31	7.55	5.85	6.99	5.10	6.11		-1.6285
PERCENTAGE											
under 15	29.27	29.29	29.25	27.23	26.92	25.35	24.83	24.89	24.17	22.65	21.76
15-64	65.28	65.32	65.25	66.95	67.11	68.41	68.74	68.24	68.70	66.53	65.61
65 and over	5.44	5.39	5.50	5.82	5.97	6.24	6.44	6.87	7.13	10.82	12.64
DEP. RATIO X 100	53.18	53.10	53.26	49.37	49.01	46.18	45.48	46.55	45.57	50.30	52.43

TABLE 1 — DATA

AGE AT LAST BIRTHDAY	POPULATION Both Sexes	MALES Number	%	FEMALES Number	%	BIRTHS BY AGE OF MOTHER	DEATHS Both Sexes	MALES	FEMALES	AGE AT LAST BIRTHDAY
0	1952000	993000	1.5	959000	1.5	0	124414	70916	53498	0
1-4	8219000	4155000	6.5	4064000	6.4	0	38798	20970	17828	1-4
5-9	11789000	6006000	9.4	5783000	9.2	0	19230	10720	8510	5-9
10-14	12424000	6260000	9.8	6164000	9.8	3010	17105	9755	7350	10-14
15-19	11813000	5888000	9.2	5925000	9.4	269352	27284	15001	12283	15-19
20-24	11317000	5599000	8.7	5718000	9.1	663227	37032	19742	17290	20-24
25-29	10558000	5207000	8.1	5351000	8.5	566678	39761	20713	19048	25-29
30-34	9717000	4818000	7.5	4899000	7.8	361146	42009	22597	19412	30-34
35-39	8974000	4502000	7.0	4472000	7.1	212551	51545	28733	22812	35-39
40-44	8739000	4450000	6.9	4289000	6.8	72716	62304	36280	26024	40-44
45-49	7699000	3987000	6.2	3712000	5.9	7020	76707	45663	31044	45-49
50-54	6510000	3381000	5.3	3129000	5.0	145	91972	54947	37025	50-54
55-59	5431000	2805000	4.4	2626000	4.2	0	102603	61052	41551	55-59
60-64	4308000	2203000	3.4	2105000	3.3	0	120715	70163	50552	60-64
65-69	3245000	1645000	2.6	1600000	2.5	0	134652	76125	58527	65-69
70-74	2196000	1093000	1.7	1103000	1.7		139310	76108	63202	70-74
75-79	1447263	703847	1.1	743416	1.2		131180	69465	61715	75-79
80-84	685338	316292	0.5	369046	0.6	1105887 M.	92728	46498	46230	80-84
85+	228399	98861	0.2	129538	0.2	1049958 F.	73612	33003	40609	85+
TOTAL	127252000	64111000		63141000		2155845	1422961	788451	634510	TOTAL

TABLE 2 — MALE LIFE TABLE

x	$_nq_x$	l_x	$_nd_x$	$_nL_x$	$_nm_x$	$_na_x$	T_x	r_x	$\dot{e}_x$	$_nM_x$	x
0	0.067981	100000	6798	95190	0.071416	0.2924	5853401	0.0000	58.534	0.071416	0
1	0.019901	93202	1855	367505	0.005047	1.1412	5758211	0.0000	61.782	0.005047	1
5	0.008885	91347	812	454707	0.001785	2.5000	5390706	0.0000	59.013	0.001785	5
10	0.007763	90536	703	450989	0.001558	2.5971	4935999	0.0002	54.520	0.001558	10
15	0.012680	89833	1139	446493	0.002551	2.6552	4485011	0.0086	49.926	0.002548	15
20	0.017494	88694	1552	439710	0.003529	2.5777	4038518	0.0089	45.533	0.003526	20
25	0.019711	87142	1718	431506	0.003981	2.5523	3598808	0.0110	41.298	0.003978	25
30	0.023212	85424	1983	422353	0.004695	2.5951	3167302	0.0097	37.077	0.004690	30
35	0.031435	83442	2623	410910	0.006383	2.5993	2744949	0.0016	32.897	0.006382	35
40	0.040004	80818	3233	396367	0.008157	2.6103	2334038	0.0037	28.880	0.008153	40
45	0.055870	77585	4335	377613	0.011479	2.6206	1937672	0.0157	24.975	0.011453	45
50	0.078389	73251	5742	352454	0.016292	2.5967	1560058	0.0188	21.297	0.016252	50
55	0.103700	67509	7001	320716	0.021828	2.5963	1207604	0.0201	17.888	0.021765	55
60	0.148386	60508	8979	280875	0.031966	2.5870	886888	0.0240	14.657	0.031849	60
65	0.208627	51530	10750	231430	0.046452	2.5612	606013	0.0240	11.760	0.046277	65
70	0.297626	40779	12137	173672	0.069884	2.5098	374583	0.0240	9.186	0.069632	70
75	0.395296	28642	11322	114309	0.099048	2.4473	200911	0.0240	7.015	0.098693	75
80	0.535389	17320	9273	62736	0.147810	2.4264	86602	0.0240	5.000	0.147009	80
85+	*1.000000	8047	8047	23867	0.337169	2.9659	23867	0.0240	2.966	0.333832	85+

TABLE 3 — FEMALE LIFE TABLE

x	$_nq_x$	l_x	$_nd_x$	$_nL_x$	$_nm_x$	$_na_x$	T_x	r_x	$\dot{e}_x$	$_nM_x$	x
0	0.053703	100000	5370	96267	0.055785	0.3049	6257926	0.0000	62.579	0.055785	0
1	0.017331	94630	1640	373853	0.004387	1.1553	6161659	0.0000	65.113	0.004387	1
5	0.007331	92990	682	463244	0.001472	2.5000	5787805	0.0000	62.241	0.001472	5
10	0.005945	92308	549	460224	0.001192	2.6009	5324561	0.0000	57.683	0.001192	10
15	0.010326	91759	948	456597	0.002075	2.6793	4864338	0.0054	53.012	0.002073	15
20	0.015021	90812	1364	450780	0.003026	2.5965	4407740	0.0072	48.537	0.003024	20
25	0.017656	89448	1579	443365	0.003562	2.5478	3956960	0.0119	44.238	0.003560	25
30	0.019645	87868	1726	435150	0.003967	2.5715	3513595	0.0138	39.987	0.003962	30
35	0.025212	86142	2172	425446	0.005105	2.5756	3078445	0.0083	35.737	0.005101	35
40	0.029942	83970	2514	413812	0.006076	2.5977	2652999	0.0123	31.594	0.006068	40
45	0.041132	81456	3350	399320	0.008390	2.6239	2239187	0.0229	27.489	0.008363	45
50	0.057700	78106	4507	379737	0.011868	2.6054	1839868	0.0227	23.556	0.011833	50
55	0.076505	73599	5631	354595	0.015879	2.6202	1460131	0.0230	19.839	0.015823	55
60	0.114091	67968	7755	321400	0.024127	2.6219	1105536	0.0270	16.265	0.024015	60
65	0.168874	60214	10169	276661	0.036754	2.5996	784136	0.0270	13.023	0.036579	65
70	0.252129	50045	12618	219250	0.057550	2.5451	507475	0.0270	10.140	0.057300	70
75	0.344609	37427	12898	154713	0.083366	2.4861	288225	0.0270	7.701	0.083015	75
80	0.479353	24530	11758	93226	0.126128	2.4978	133512	0.0270	5.443	0.125268	80
85+	*1.000000	12771	12771	40286	0.317015	3.1544	40286	0.0270	3.154	0.313491	85+

TABLE 4 — OBSERVED AND PROJECTED VITAL RATES

	OBSERVED POPULATION Both Sexes	Males	Females	PROJECTED POPULATION 1940 Males	Females	1945 Males	Females	1950 Males	Females	STABLE POPULATION Males	Females
RATES PER THOUSAND											
Birth	16.94	17.25	16.63	17.60	16.83	17.67	16.78	17.10	16.13	14.45	13.42
Death	11.18	12.30	10.05	12.97	10.70	13.63	11.38	14.19	11.99	19.14	18.11
Increase	5.76	4.95	6.58	4.63	6.13	4.04	5.40	2.90	4.13		-4.6962
PERCENTAGE											
under 15	27.02	27.16	26.88	24.75	24.16	23.23	22.54	23.26	22.34	20.48	19.37
15-64	66.85	66.82	66.88	68.73	68.99	69.70	69.94	69.07	69.42	67.18	65.76
65 and over	6.13	6.02	6.25	6.51	6.85	7.07	7.52	7.67	8.25	12.35	14.88
DEP. RATIO X 100	49.59	49.65	49.53	45.49	44.95	43.47	42.98	44.78	44.06	48.86	52.07

TABLE 1 — DATA

Age at last birthday	Population Both Sexes	Males Number	%	Females Number	%	Births by age of mother	Deaths Both Sexes	Deaths Males	Deaths Females	Age at last birthday
0	2044253	1039294	1.6	1004959	1.5	0	111364	63577	47787	0
1-4	8621337	4379653	6.6	4241684	6.4	0	25312	13786	11526	1-4
5-9	10716170	5435888	8.3	5280282	8.0	0	11620	6653	4967	5-9
10-14	11693715	5925992	9.0	5767723	8.8	3353	11759	6907	4852	10-14
15-19	12261267	6126813	9.3	6134454	9.3	304821	21345	11989	9356	15-19
20-24	11465777	5560455	8.4	5905322	9.0	750282	27946	15550	12396	20-24
25-29	10997943	5341558	8.1	5656385	8.6	651361	30735	16692	14043	25-29
30-34	10245043	5051936	7.7	5193107	7.9	400965	34488	18851	15637	30-34
35-39	9555901	4740378	7.2	4815523	7.3	202889	41820	23289	18531	35-39
40-44	8813287	4427045	6.7	4386242	6.7	60482	53564	30859	22705	40-44
45-49	8267463	4210577	6.4	4056886	6.2	5479	71448	42610	28838	45-49
50-54	7286053	3762788	5.7	3523265	5.4	172	92077	56047	36030	50-54
55-59	5888607	3032235	4.6	2856372	4.3	0	107544	65570	41974	55-59
60-64	4755781	2411041	3.7	2344740	3.6	0	125338	74263	51075	60-64
65-69	3819239	1901337	2.9	1917902	2.9	0	147238	84231	63007	65-69
70-74	2588234	1278226	1.9	1310008	2.0		153386	84460	68926	70-74
75-79	1517858	729655	1.1	788203	1.2		140086	73624	66462	75-79
80-84	778288	360522	0.5	417766	0.6	1221339 M.	110151	55000	55151	80-84
85+	367653	157594	0.2	210059	0.3	1158465 F.	83714	37681	46033	85+
TOTAL	131683869	65872987		65810882		2379804	1400935	781639	619296	TOTAL

TABLE 2 — MALE LIFE TABLE

x	$_nq_x$	l_x	$_nd_x$	$_nL_x$	$_nm_x$	$_na_x$	T_x	r_x	$\overset{\circ}{e}_x$	$_nM_x$	x
0	0.058519	100000	5852	95662	0.061173	0.2587	6113748	0.0000	61.137	0.061173	0
1	0.012477	94148	1175	373196	0.003148	1.1091	6018086	0.0000	63.922	0.003148	1
5	0.006101	92973	567	463449	0.001224	2.5000	5644890	0.0000	60.715	0.001224	5
10	0.005812	92406	537	460756	0.001166	2.6273	5181441	0.0000	56.072	0.001166	10
15	0.009747	91869	895	457258	0.001958	2.6693	4720685	0.0044	51.385	0.001957	15
20	0.013902	90974	1265	451810	0.002797	2.5818	4263427	0.0110	46.864	0.002797	20
25	0.015512	89709	1392	445143	0.003126	2.5553	3811617	0.0064	42.489	0.003125	25
30	0.018506	88317	1634	437650	0.003734	2.5912	3366474	0.0081	38.118	0.003731	30
35	0.024308	86683	2107	428411	0.004918	2.6253	2928825	0.0081	33.788	0.004913	35
40	0.034313	84576	2902	416027	0.006976	2.6388	2500414	0.0047	29.564	0.006971	40
45	0.049463	81674	4040	398831	0.010129	2.6391	2084387	0.0058	25.521	0.010120	45
50	0.072125	77634	5599	374877	0.014936	2.6261	1685555	0.0176	21.712	0.014895	50
55	0.103121	72035	7428	342371	0.021697	2.6034	1310678	0.0224	18.195	0.021624	55
60	0.143743	64606	9287	300578	0.030896	2.5822	968307	0.0210	14.988	0.030801	60
65	0.200501	55320	11092	249559	0.044445	2.5622	667729	0.0210	12.070	0.044301	65
70	0.284818	44228	12597	189991	0.066303	2.5273	418170	0.0210	9.455	0.066076	70
75	0.402777	31631	12740	125825	0.101254	2.4623	228179	0.0210	7.214	0.100902	75
80	0.544838	18891	10292	67239	0.153073	2.4162	102355	0.0210	5.418	0.152557	80
85+	1.000000	8598	8598	35116	0.244856	4.0840	35116	0.0210	4.084	0.239101	85+

TABLE 3 — FEMALE LIFE TABLE

x	$_nq_x$	l_x	$_nd_x$	$_nL_x$	$_nm_x$	$_na_x$	T_x	r_x	$\overset{\circ}{e}_x$	$_nM_x$	x
0	0.045957	100000	4596	96648	0.047551	0.2706	6557563	0.0000	65.576	0.047551	0
1	0.010785	95404	1029	378653	0.002717	1.1196	6460915	0.0000	67.721	0.002717	1
5	0.004692	94375	443	470770	0.000941	2.5000	6082261	0.0000	64.448	0.000941	5
10	0.004198	93933	394	468733	0.000841	2.6416	5611492	0.0000	59.740	0.000841	10
15	0.007599	93538	711	466034	0.001525	2.6687	5142759	0.0000	54.980	0.001525	15
20	0.010449	92827	970	461800	0.002100	2.5910	4676725	0.0061	50.381	0.002099	20
25	0.012349	91857	1134	456532	0.002485	2.5712	4214925	0.0103	45.885	0.002483	25
30	0.014965	90723	1358	450341	0.003015	2.5878	3758393	0.0130	41.427	0.003011	30
35	0.019094	89365	1706	442746	0.003854	2.6083	3308052	0.0129	37.017	0.003848	35
40	0.025606	87659	2245	432952	0.005184	2.6193	2865305	0.0119	32.687	0.005176	40
45	0.035027	85415	2992	419986	0.007124	2.6313	2432354	0.0146	28.477	0.007108	45
50	0.050105	82423	4130	402328	0.010265	2.6306	2012368	0.0246	24.415	0.010226	50
55	0.071280	78293	5581	378228	0.014755	2.6281	1610039	0.0255	20.564	0.014695	55
60	0.103987	72712	7561	345572	0.021880	2.6209	1231812	0.0266	16.941	0.021783	60
65	0.153000	65151	9968	301954	0.033012	2.6123	886240	0.0266	13.603	0.032852	65
70	0.234364	55183	12933	244585	0.052877	2.5775	584285	0.0266	10.588	0.052615	70
75	0.349837	42250	14781	174452	0.084726	2.5104	339700	0.0266	8.040	0.084321	75
80	0.497638	27469	13670	102968	0.132758	2.4850	165248	0.0266	6.016	0.132013	80
85+	*1.000000	13800	13800	62280	0.221574	4.5132	62280	0.0266	4.513	0.219143	85+

TABLE 4 — OBSERVED AND PROJECTED VITAL RATES

	Observed Population Both Sexes	Males	Females	Projected 1945 Males	Females	1950 Males	Females	1955 Males	Females	Stable Population Males	Females
RATES PER THOUSAND											
Birth	18.07	18.54	17.60	18.50	17.43	17.85	16.71	16.87	15.70	15.24	14.16
Death	10.64	11.87	9.41	12.50	10.08	13.03	10.70	13.55	11.35	17.22	16.14
Increase	7.43	6.67	8.19	5.99	7.35	4.82	6.02	3.32	4.35	-1.9803	
PERCENTAGE											
under 15	25.12	25.47	24.76	24.38	23.45	24.27	23.12	24.22	22.90	21.55	20.34
15-64	67.99	67.80	68.18	68.44	68.87	68.07	68.56	67.43	67.92	66.68	65.13
65 and over	6.89	6.72	7.06	7.17	7.68	7.66	8.32	8.35	9.18	11.77	14.53
DEP. RATIO X 100	47.07	47.48	46.66	46.10	45.20	46.91	45.86	48.31	47.23	49.97	53.54

TABLE 1 — DATA

AGE AT LAST BIRTHDAY	POPULATION BOTH SEXES	MALES Number	%	FEMALES Number	%	BIRTHS BY AGE OF MOTHER	DEATHS BOTH SEXES	MALES	FEMALES	AGE AT LAST BIRTHDAY
0	2525835	1289170	2.1	1236665	1.8	0	109060	62473	46587	0
1-4	10621075	5412547	8.7	5208528	7.5	0	21467	11776	9691	1-4
5-9	11347130	5777183	9.3	5569947	8.0	0	10048	5938	4110	5-9
10-14	10649314	5399248	8.7	5250066	7.5	3541	9217	5646	3571	10-14
15-19	10816157	5060021	8.1	5756136	8.2	302146	16407	9960	6447	15-19
20-24	9024615	2921712	4.7	6102903	8.7	906983	23423	13712	9711	20-24
25-29	9024061	3159487	5.1	5864574	8.4	822057	23947	13241	10706	25-29
30-34	10298147	4684422	7.5	5613725	8.0	545583	28740	15606	13134	30-34
35-39	9766381	4634766	7.5	5131615	7.3	280768	37341	20736	16605	35-39
40-44	9322149	4585236	7.4	4736913	6.8	73100	49069	28593	20476	40-44
45-49	8512209	4236729	6.8	4275480	6.1	5260	66420	39991	26429	45-49
50-54	7870197	3963555	6.4	3906642	5.6	204	91050	56358	34692	50-54
55-59	6783447	3449657	5.6	3333790	4.8	0	112321	69990	42331	55-59
60-64	5304616	2675547	4.3	2629069	3.8	0	131632	80014	51618	60-64
65-69	4070875	2006320	3.2	2064555	3.0	0	151133	87544	63589	65-69
70-74	2962283	1423405	2.3	1538878	2.2		161906	89083	72823	70-74
75-79	1795375	849158	1.4	946217	1.4		150144	78626	71518	75-79
80-84	856232	390738	0.6	465494	0.7	1510369 M.	114041	56060	57981	80-84
85+	425676	182003	0.3	243673	0.3	1429273 F.	95524	42523	53001	85+
TOTAL	131975774	62100904		69874870		2939642	1402890	787870	615020	TOTAL

TABLE 2 — MALE LIFE TABLE

x	nq_x	l_x	nd_x	nL_x	nm_x	na_x	T_x	r_x	$\dot{e}_x$	nM_x	x
0	0.046749	100000	4675	96469	0.048460	0.2446	6225624	0.0000	62.256	0.048460	0
1	0.008648	95325	824	378908	0.002176	1.0979	6129155	0.0000	64.297	0.002176	1
5	0.005107	94501	483	471297	0.001024	2.5000	5750247	0.0203	60.849	0.001028	5
10	0.005228	94018	492	468957	0.001048	2.6927	5278950	0.0120	56.148	0.001046	10
15	0.010022	93527	937	465637	0.002013	2.8703	4809993	0.0590	51.429	0.001968	15
20	0.023301	92589	2157	457748	0.004713	2.5905	4344357	0.0431	46.921	0.004693	20
25	0.020730	90432	1875	447328	0.004191	2.4228	3886609	0.0000	42.978	0.004191	25
30	0.016520	88557	1463	439139	0.003331	2.5076	3439281	0.0000	38.837	0.003331	30
35	0.022135	87094	1928	430892	0.004474	2.6248	3000142	0.0000	34.447	0.004474	35
40	0.030741	85166	2618	419679	0.006238	2.6501	2569250	0.0025	30.167	0.006236	40
45	0.046211	82548	3815	403788	0.009447	2.6530	2149570	0.0048	26.040	0.009439	45
50	0.068838	78734	5420	380805	0.014233	2.6268	1745782	0.0061	22.173	0.014219	50
55	0.097022	73314	7113	349588	0.020347	2.6128	1364977	0.0183	18.618	0.020289	55
60	0.140035	66201	9270	308692	0.030031	2.5933	1015389	0.0268	15.338	0.029906	60
65	0.197874	56930	11265	257144	0.043808	2.5581	706697	0.0268	12.413	0.043634	65
70	0.271844	45665	12414	197553	0.062838	2.5211	449553	0.0268	9.845	0.062584	70
75	0.376541	33251	12521	134629	0.093000	2.4739	252000	0.0268	7.579	0.092593	75
80	0.523159	20731	10846	75257	0.144114	2.4494	117371	0.0268	5.662	0.143472	80
85+	1.000000	9885	9885	42114	0.234726	4.2603	42114	0.0268	4.260	0.233640	85+

TABLE 3 — FEMALE LIFE TABLE

x	nq_x	l_x	nd_x	nL_x	nm_x	na_x	T_x	r_x	$\dot{e}_x$	nM_x	x
0	0.036643	100000	3664	97271	0.037671	0.2553	6810989	0.0000	68.110	0.037671	0
1	0.007403	96336	713	383279	0.001861	1.1063	6713718	0.0000	69.691	0.001861	1
5	0.003663	95623	350	477237	0.000734	2.5000	6330439	0.0195	66.202	0.000738	5
10	0.003395	95272	323	475590	0.000680	2.6160	5853202	0.0000	61.437	0.000680	10
15	0.005586	94949	530	473506	0.001120	2.6669	5377612	0.0000	56.637	0.001120	15
20	0.007926	94418	748	470288	0.001591	2.5895	4904106	0.0000	51.940	0.001591	20
25	0.009093	93670	852	466290	0.001827	2.5814	4433818	0.0065	47.334	0.001826	25
30	0.011649	92818	1081	461519	0.002343	2.6202	3967528	0.0109	42.745	0.002340	30
35	0.016083	91737	1475	455175	0.003241	2.6205	3506009	0.0137	38.218	0.003236	35
40	0.021435	90262	1935	446726	0.004331	2.6314	3050834	0.0138	33.800	0.004323	40
45	0.030522	88327	2696	435269	0.006194	2.6389	2604109	0.0129	29.483	0.006182	45
50	0.043589	85631	3733	419318	0.008902	2.6326	2168839	0.0158	25.328	0.008880	50
55	0.061916	81898	5071	397547	0.012755	2.6445	1749521	0.0263	21.362	0.012698	55
60	0.094355	76828	7249	367049	0.019749	2.6426	1351974	0.0318	17.598	0.019634	60
65	0.144216	69579	10034	323944	0.030975	2.6133	984925	0.0318	14.156	0.030800	65
70	0.213409	59544	12707	266987	0.047595	2.5814	660981	0.0318	11.101	0.047322	70
75	0.320189	46837	14997	197220	0.076040	2.5352	393994	0.0318	8.412	0.075583	75
80	0.478567	31840	15238	121442	0.125473	2.5220	196774	0.0318	6.180	0.124558	80
85+	*1.000000	16603	16603	75332	0.220393	4.5374	75332	0.0318	4.537	0.217509	85

TABLE 4 — OBSERVED AND PROJECTED VITAL RATES

RATES PER THOUSAND	OBSERVED POPULATION BOTH SEXES	MALES	FEMALES	PROJECTED POPULATION 1950 MALES	FEMALES	1955 MALES	FEMALES	1960 MALES	FEMALES	STABLE POPULATION MALES	FEMALES
Birth	22.27	24.32	20.45	22.96	19.30	21.37	17.95	20.54	17.25	19.23	17.77
Death	10.63	12.69	8.80	13.18	9.41	13.52	10.00	13.73	10.57	13.95	12.48
Increase	11.64	11.63	11.65	9.78	9.89	7.85	7.95	6.81	6.69		5.2856
PERCENTAGE											
under 15	26.63	28.79	24.71	29.86	25.51	30.35	25.85	29.59	25.16	26.18	24.48
15-64	65.71	63.40	67.77	61.84	66.31	60.72	65.14	60.99	64.99	64.60	63.69
65 and over	7.66	7.81	7.53	8.30	8.18	8.93	9.01	9.42	9.85	9.22	11.83
DEP. RATIO X 100	52.18	57.73	47.57	61.71	50.80	64.68	53.52	63.96	53.88	54.79	57.01

TABLE 5 — POPULATION PROJECTED WITH FIXED AGE—SPECIFIC BIRTH AND DEATH RATES (IN 1000's)

AGE AT LAST BIRTHDAY	1950 BOTH SEXES	MALES	FEMALES	1955 BOTH SEXES	MALES	FEMALES	1960 BOTH SEXES	MALES	FEMALES	AGE AT LAST BIRTHDAY
0-4	14017	7164	6853	13794	7050	6744	13579	6940	6639	0-4
5-9	13045	6644	6401	13909	7103	6806	13686	6989	6697	5-9
10-14	11299	5748	5551	12990	6611	6379	13849	7067	6782	10-14
15-19	10588	5361	5227	11234	5708	5526	12915	6564	6351	15-19
20-24	10691	4974	5717	10462	5270	5192	11100	5611	5489	20-24
25-29	8906	2855	6051	10529	4861	5668	10297	5150	5147	25-29
30-34	8907	3102	5805	8792	2803	5989	10382	4772	5610	30-34
35-39	10133	4596	5537	8768	3043	5725	8657	2750	5907	35-39
40-44	9550	4514	5036	9911	4477	5434	8583	2964	5619	40-44
45-49	9027	4412	4615	9250	4343	4907	9601	4307	5294	45-49
50-54	8115	3996	4119	8607	4161	4446	8823	4096	4727	50-54
55-59	7343	3639	3704	7573	3668	3905	8034	3819	4215	55-59
60-64	6124	3046	3078	6633	3213	3420	6844	3239	3605	60-64
65-69	4549	2229	2320	5254	2537	2717	5694	2676	3018	65-69
70-74	3243	1541	1702	3624	1712	1912	4188	1949	2239	70-74
75-79	2107	970	1137	2307	1050	1257	2580	1167	1413	75-79
80-84	1058	475	583	1242	542	700	1361	587	774	80-84
85+	508	219	289	627	266	361	737	303	434	85+
TOTAL	139210	65485	73725	145506	68418	77088	150910	70950	79960	TOTAL

TABLE 6 — STANDARDIZED RATES

STANDARD COUNTRIES:

STANDARDIZED RATES PER THOUSAND

	ENGLAND AND WALES 1961 BOTH SEXES	MALES	FEMALES	UNITED STATES 1960 BOTH SEXES	MALES	FEMALES	MEXICO 1960 BOTH SEXES	MALES	FEMALES
Birth	16.30	26.22*	15.36	16.63	25.29*	15.93	19.33	21.77*	18.75
Death	14.37	14.98*	14.26	11.95	13.04*	10.84	7.06	10.44*	5.94
Increase	1.93	11.24*	1.10	4.68	12.24*	5.08	12.27	11.33*	12.81

TABLE 7 — MOMENTS AND CUMULANTS

	OBSERVED POP. MALES	FEMALES	STATIONARY POP. MALES	FEMALES	STABLE POP. MALES	FEMALES	OBSERVED BIRTHS	NET MATERNITY FUNCTION	BIRTHS IN STABLE POP.
μ	32.48421	32.16241	35.36545	37.45044	32.83772	34.71873	27.20503	27.43753	27.22342
σ^2	466.4942	426.6055	487.1412	524.9403	468.3896	507.5197	36.63754	38.71311	38.13632
κ_3	2854.275	3531.374	3007.505	2609.061	4052.978	3945.860	106.9095	107.5023	110.6831
κ_4	-209598.	-126559.	-216695.	-272406.	-177225.	-230767.	-461.746	-632.749	-560.503
β_1	0.080251	0.160623	0.078243	0.047059	0.159855	0.119104	0.232409	0.199187	0.220875
β_2	2.036850	2.304591	2.086855	2.011455	2.192186	2.104081	2.656007	2.577803	2.614610
κ	-0.029706	-0.069064	-0.030272	-0.017646	-0.062034	-0.044787	-0.135172	-0.110610	-0.123970

TABLE 8 — RATES FROM AGE DISTRIBUTIONS AND VITAL STATISTICS (Females)

VITAL STATISTICS		THOMPSON AGE RANGE	NRR	1000r	INTERVAL	BOURGEOIS-PICHAT AGE RANGE	NRR	1000b	1000d	1000r	COALE
GRR	1.241	0-4	1.12	4.18	27.34	5-29	0.85	15.48	21.71	-6.22	IBR
NRR	1.155	5-9	1.01	0.23	27.28	30-54	1.44	26.81	13.38	13.42	IDR
TFR	2.553	10-14	1.00	0.13	27.20	55-79	1.96	49.27	24.44	24.83	IRI
GENERATION	27.330	15-19	1.18	5.92	27.08	*30-54	1.44	26.81	13.38	13.42	K1
SEX RATIO	105.674										K2

TABLE 9 — LESLIE MATRIX AND ITS SPECTRAL COMPONENTS (Females)

Start of Age Interval	ORIGINAL MATRIX SUB-DIAGONAL	ALTERNATIVE FIRST ROWS Projection	Integral	FIRST STABLE MATRIX % IN STABLE POPULATION	FISHER VALUES	REPRODUCTIVE VALUES	SECOND STABLE MATRIX Z₂ FIRST COLUMN	FIRST ROW
0	0.99311	0.00000	0.00000	8.427	1.054	6795000	0.1481+0.0821	0.1481+0.0821
5	0.99655	0.00079	0.00000	8.150	1.090	6071470	0.1735-0.1158	-0.0041+0.1374
10	0.99562	0.06184	0.00160	7.910	1.122	5892127	-0.0288-0.2563	-0.1004+0.0479
15	0.99320	0.23376	0.12428	7.670	1.092	6285449	-0.2976-0.1135	-0.0809-0.0595
20	0.99150	0.33598	0.35185	7.419	0.881	5375179	-0.2925+0.2618	-0.0220-0.0999
25	0.98977	0.27613	0.33187	7.164	0.555	3254022	0.1212+0.4674	0.0137-0.0810
30	0.98625	0.17658	0.23010	6.905	0.281	1580222	0.5782+0.1309	0.0224-0.0432
35	0.98144	0.08161	0.12954	6.633	0.104	535274	0.4667-0.5553	0.0133-0.0146
40	0.97435	0.01943	0.03654	6.340	0.021	101663	-0.3403-0.8150	0.0033-0.0026
45	0.96335	0.00150	0.00291	6.016	0.002	6819	-1.0641-0.0862	0.0003-0.0002
50	0.94808	0.00006	0.00012	5.644	0.000	245	-0.6747+1.0829	0.0000-0.0000
55+	0.78045			21.722				

TABLE 10 — AGE ANALYSIS AND MISCELLANEOUS RESULTS (Females)

Start of Age Interval	OBSERVED POPUL. (IN 100's)	CONTRIBUTIONS OF ROOTS (IN 100's) r_1	r_2, r_3	r_4-r_{11}	AGE-SP. BIRTH RATES	NET MATERNITY FUNCTION	COEFF. OF MATRIX EQUATION	PARAMETERS		EXP. INCREASE	
									INTEGRAL	MATRIX	x	$e^{(x+2\frac{1}{2})r}$

Start of Age Interval	OBSERVED POPUL. (IN 100's)	r_1	r_2, r_3	r_4-r_{11}	AGE-SP. BIRTH RATES	NET MATERNITY FUNCTION	COEFF. OF MATRIX EQUATION		INTEGRAL	MATRIX	x	$e^{(x+2\frac{1}{2})r}$
0	64452	62613	1911	-73	0.0000	0.0000	0.0000	L(1)	1.02678	1.02680	0	1.0133
5	55699	60559	-3557	-1302	0.0000	0.0000	0.0008	L(2)	0.35999	0.36960	50	1.3198
10	52501	58775	-6944	670	0.0003	0.0016	0.0612		0.73786	0.71633	55	1.3552
15	57561	56990	-2434	3005	0.0255	0.1208	0.2303	R(1)	0.00529	0.00529	60	1.3915
20	61029	55126	7819	-1916	0.0723	0.3398	0.3288	R(2)	-0.03945	-0.04312	65	1.4287
25	58646	53231	12508	-7093	0.0682	0.3178	0.2679			0.22338	0.21889	70	1.4670
30	56137	51311	2275	2551	0.0473	0.2181	0.1696	C(1)		743046	75	1.5063
35	51316	49285	-16239	18271	0.0266	0.1211	0.0773	C(2)		-112824	80	1.5466
40	47369	47108	-21522	21784	0.0075	0.0335	0.0181			-1367461	85	1.5880
45	42755	44702	43	-1990	0.0000	0.0026	0.0014	2P/Y	28.1280	28.7044	90	1.6306
50	39066	41940	31140	-34013	0.0000	0.0001	0.0001	DELTA	6.2924		95	1.6742
55+	112217	161407									100	1.7191

TABLE 1 — DATA

AGE AT LAST BIRTHDAY	POPULATION BOTH SEXES	MALES Number	%	FEMALES Number	%	BIRTHS BY AGE OF MOTHER	DEATHS BOTH SEXES	MALES	FEMALES	AGE AT LAST BIRTHDAY
0	3169046	1613408	2.1	1555638	2.0	0	107453	61848	45605	0
1-4	13096498	6674558	8.9	6421940	8.4	0	18665	10317	8348	1-4
5-9	13387843	6812195	9.1	6575648	8.6	0	8437	4965	3472	5-9
10-14	11225160	5714047	7.6	5511113	7.2	5050	6639	4168	2471	10-14
15-19	10636236	5321421	7.1	5314815	7.0	432870	11620	7549	4071	15-19
20-24	11426026	5574612	7.4	5851414	7.7	1163622	16794	10853	5941	20-24
25-29	12211629	5957170	7.9	6254459	8.2	1035567	19579	11836	7743	25-29
30-34	11554959	5642117	7.5	5912842	7.8	606481	23073	13375	9698	30-34
35-39	11260606	5522804	7.4	5737802	7.5	297021	32209	18749	13460	35-39
40-44	10251022	5089590	6.8	5161432	6.8	75903	45294	27148	18146	40-44
45-49	9118777	4547968	6.1	4570809	6.0	4844	62282	38313	23969	45-49
50-54	8297893	4139093	5.5	4158800	5.5	152	87025	54730	32295	50-54
55-59	7264543	3640330	4.8	3624213	4.8	0	113972	72755	41217	55-59
60-64	6089691	3048322	4.1	3041369	4.0	0	141064	88232	52832	60-64
65-69	5019415	2432058	3.2	2587357	3.4	0	166750	99766	66984	65-69
70-74	3443141	1641170	2.2	1801971	2.4		175546	98474	77072	70-74
75-79	2171149	1008855	1.3	1162294	1.5		170733	90325	80408	75-79
80-84	1134852	508627	0.7	626225	0.8	1857643 M.	135543	66857	68686	80-84
85+	586667	241074	0.3	345593	0.5	1763867 F.	116708	51164	65544	85+
TOTAL	151345153	75129419		76215734		3621510	1459386	831424	627962	TOTAL

TABLE 2 — MALE LIFE TABLE

x	$_nq_x$	l_x	$_nd_x$	$_nL_x$	$_nm_x$	$_na_x$	T_x	r_x	$\mathring{e}_x$	$_nM_x$	x
0	0.037240	100000	3724	97146	0.038334	0.2336	6527936	0.0000	65.279	0.038334	0
1	0.006155	96276	593	383380	0.001546	1.0899	6430790	0.0000	66.795	0.001546	1
5	0.003613	95683	346	477553	0.000724	2.5000	6047411	0.0362	63.202	0.000729	5
10	0.003658	95338	349	475885	0.000733	2.6947	5569858	0.0238	58.422	0.000729	10
15	0.007071	94989	672	473383	0.001419	2.6752	5093973	0.0011	53.627	0.001419	15
20	0.009688	94317	914	469354	0.001947	2.5574	4620590	0.0000	48.990	0.001947	20
25	0.009886	93404	923	464746	0.001987	2.5399	4151236	0.0000	44.444	0.001987	25
30	0.011794	92480	1091	459803	0.002372	2.6180	3686490	0.0051	39.863	0.002371	30
35	0.016862	91389	1541	453362	0.003399	2.6734	3226687	0.0068	35.307	0.003395	35
40	0.026415	89848	2373	443743	0.005348	2.6827	2773325	0.0139	30.867	0.005334	40
45	0.041404	87475	3622	428949	0.008443	2.6732	2329583	0.0119	26.631	0.008424	45
50	0.064217	83853	5385	406612	0.013243	2.6499	1900634	0.0087	22.666	0.013223	50
55	0.095537	78469	7497	374486	0.020018	2.6181	1494022	0.0102	19.040	0.019986	55
60	0.135739	70972	9634	331604	0.029052	2.5861	1119536	0.0252	15.774	0.028944	60
65	0.187097	61338	11476	278717	0.041175	2.5625	787931	0.0252	12.846	0.041021	65
70	0.262209	49862	13074	217041	0.060239	2.5319	509214	0.0252	10.212	0.060002	70
75	0.366333	36788	13477	149927	0.089887	2.4763	292173	0.0252	7.942	0.089532	75
80	0.494993	23311	11539	87354	0.132094	2.4692	142245	0.0252	6.102	0.131445	80
85+	*1.000000	11772	11772	54892	0.214465	4.6628	54892	0.0252	4.663	0.212234	85+

TABLE 3 — FEMALE LIFE TABLE

x	$_nq_x$	l_x	$_nd_x$	$_nL_x$	$_nm_x$	$_na_x$	T_x	r_x	$\mathring{e}_x$	$_nM_x$	x
0	0.028680	100000	2868	97832	0.029316	0.2440	7086299	0.0000	70.863	0.029316	0
1	0.005180	97132	503	387067	0.001300	1.0975	6988467	0.0000	71.948	0.001300	1
5	0.002610	96629	252	482513	0.000523	2.5000	6601400	0.0363	68.317	0.000528	5
10	0.002245	96377	216	481366	0.000449	2.6111	6118886	0.0208	63.489	0.000449	10
15	0.003823	96160	368	479938	0.000766	2.6523	5637520	0.0000	58.626	0.000766	15
20	0.005064	95793	485	477796	0.001015	2.5947	5157582	0.0000	53.841	0.001015	20
25	0.006172	95308	588	475127	0.001238	2.6025	4679786	0.0000	49.102	0.001238	25
30	0.008177	94719	775	471766	0.001642	2.6371	4204659	0.0069	44.391	0.001640	30
35	0.011687	93945	1098	467156	0.002350	2.6612	3732892	0.0112	39.735	0.002346	35
40	0.017492	92847	1624	460439	0.003527	2.6631	3265736	0.0191	35.173	0.003516	40
45	0.025971	91223	2369	450560	0.005258	2.6558	2805297	0.0162	30.752	0.005244	45
50	0.038223	88854	3396	436273	0.007785	2.6459	2354737	0.0153	26.501	0.007765	50
55	0.055563	85457	4748	416118	0.011411	2.6479	1918464	0.0194	22.449	0.011373	55
60	0.083837	80709	6766	387530	0.017460	2.6330	1502345	0.0302	18.614	0.017371	60
65	0.122644	73943	9069	348268	0.026039	2.6532	1114816	0.0302	15.077	0.025889	65
70	0.195032	64874	12653	294081	0.043024	2.6061	766547	0.0302	11.816	0.042771	70
75	0.297036	52222	15512	222982	0.069565	2.5421	472466	0.0302	9.047	0.069180	75
80	0.430105	36710	15789	143242	0.110227	2.5714	249484	0.0302	6.796	0.109683	80
85+	1.000000	20921	20921	106242	0.196917	5.0783	106242	0.0302	5.078	0.189656	85+

TABLE 4 — OBSERVED AND PROJECTED VITAL RATES

	OBSERVED POPULATION BOTH SEXES	MALES	FEMALES	PROJECTED POPULATION 1955 MALES	FEMALES	1960 MALES	FEMALES	1965 MALES	FEMALES	STABLE POPULATION MALES	FEMALES
RATES PER THOUSAND											
Birth	23.93	24.73	23.14	22.45	20.89	21.34	19.76	21.89	20.21	23.88	22.57
Death	9.64	11.07	8.24	11.41	8.80	11.60	9.24	11.75	9.65	10.35	9.04
Increase	14.29	13.66	14.90	11.05	12.09	9.74	10.52	10.13	10.55		13.5318
PERCENTAGE											
under 15	27.01	27.70	26.33	29.78	28.09	30.36	28.45	29.65	27.66	30.99	29.60
15-64	64.83	64.53	65.12	62.08	62.72	61.27	61.78	61.86	62.07	62.05	61.20
65 and over	8.16	7.76	8.56	8.13	9.19	8.37	9.77	8.48	10.28	6.95	9.20
DEP. RATIO X 100	54.26	54.96	53.57	61.07	59.44	63.21	61.86	61.65	61.12	61.15	63.39

TABLE 1 — DATA

AGE AT LAST BIRTHDAY	POPULATION BOTH SEXES	MALES Number	%	FEMALES Number	%	BIRTHS BY AGE OF MOTHER	DEATHS BOTH SEXES	MALES	FEMALES	AGE AT LAST BIRTHDAY
0	3611000	1839000	2.3	1772000	2.1	0	107366	61771	45595	0
1-4	14694000	7485000	9.2	7209000	8.7	0	16751	9236	7515	1-4
5-9	17151000	8765000	10.8	8386000	10.1	0	8443	4987	3456	5-9
10-14	13343000	6787000	8.4	6556000	7.9	6105	6339	4049	2290	10-14
15-19	11029000	5523000	6.8	5506000	6.6	494610	10560	7351	3209	15-19
20-24	10310000	4941000	6.1	5369000	6.4	1286729	13641	9576	4065	20-24
25-29	11599000	5659000	7.0	5940000	7.1	1125315	15754	10266	5488	25-29
30-34	12314000	5990000	7.4	6324000	7.6	723730	20272	12285	7987	30-34
35-39	11545000	5628000	6.9	5917000	7.1	346188	27867	16562	11305	35-39
40-44	11192000	5476000	6.8	5716000	6.9	88114	41785	25341	16444	40-44
45-49	10085000	4980000	6.1	5105000	6.1	5009	60298	37909	22389	45-49
50-54	8812000	4348000	5.4	4464000	5.4	115	82669	52936	29733	50-54
55-59	7853000	3846000	4.7	4007000	4.8	0	109682	70748	38934	55-59
60-64	6694000	3258000	4.0	3436000	4.1	0	143797	91427	52370	60-64
65-69	5349000	2582000	3.2	2767000	3.3	0	179096	108913	70183	65-69
70-74	4067000	1888000	2.3	2179000	2.6		192958	110275	82683	70-74
75-79	2546000	1150000	1.4	1396000	1.7		187264	99190	88074	75-79
80-84	1325000	582000	0.7	743000	0.9	2088791 M.	156381	76235	80146	80-84
85+	782000	326000	0.4	456000	0.5	1987124 F.	143841	61649	82192	85+
TOTAL	164301000	81053000		83248000		4075915	1524764	870706	654058	TOTAL

TABLE 2 — MALE LIFE TABLE

x	$_nq_x$	l_x	$_nd_x$	$_nL_x$	$_nm_x$	$_na_x$	T_x	r_x	$\mathring{e}_x$	$_nM_x$	x
0	0.032736	100000	3274	97460	0.033589	0.2240	6644963	0.0000	66.450	0.033589	0
1	0.004918	96726	476	385518	0.001234	1.0835	6547503	0.0000	67.691	0.001234	1
5	0.002825	96251	272	480574	0.000566	2.5000	6161985	0.0310	64.020	0.000569	5
10	0.003015	95979	289	479247	0.000604	2.7642	5681411	0.0454	59.194	0.000597	10
15	0.006677	95689	639	476980	0.001339	2.7046	5202164	0.0304	54.365	0.001331	15
20	0.009645	95051	917	473005	0.001938	2.5480	4725184	0.0000	49.712	0.001938	20
25	0.009030	94134	850	468551	0.001814	2.5086	4252179	0.0000	45.172	0.001814	25
30	0.010205	93284	952	464143	0.002051	2.6096	3783628	0.0000	40.560	0.002051	30
35	0.014629	92332	1351	458519	0.002946	2.6749	3319485	0.0059	35.952	0.002943	35
40	0.022929	90981	2086	450104	0.004635	2.6982	2860966	0.0074	31.446	0.004628	40
45	0.037516	88895	3335	436760	0.007636	2.6868	2410862	0.0152	27.120	0.007612	45
50	0.059323	85560	5076	415896	0.012204	2.6548	1974102	0.0134	23.073	0.012175	50
55	0.088286	80484	7106	385616	0.018427	2.6350	1558206	0.0098	19.360	0.018395	55
60	0.131908	73379	9679	343759	0.028157	2.6099	1172590	0.0200	15.980	0.028062	60
65	0.191727	63699	12213	288692	0.042304	2.5595	828830	0.0200	13.012	0.042182	65
70	0.255761	51486	13168	224804	0.058577	2.5222	540139	0.0200	10.491	0.058408	70
75	0.355277	38318	13614	157333	0.086527	2.4835	315335	0.0200	8.229	0.086252	75
80	0.489425	24705	12091	92022	0.131393	2.4828	158003	0.0200	6.396	0.130988	80
85+	1.000000	12614	12614	65981	0.191171	5.2309	65981	0.0200	5.231	0.189108	85+

TABLE 3 — FEMALE LIFE TABLE

x	$_nq_x$	l_x	$_nd_x$	$_nL_x$	$_nm_x$	$_na_x$	T_x	r_x	$\mathring{e}_x$	$_nM_x$	x
0	0.025234	100000	2523	98069	0.025731	0.2346	7261399	0.0000	72.614	0.025731	0
1	0.004157	97477	405	388728	0.001042	1.0906	7163331	0.0000	73.488	0.001042	1
5	0.002040	97071	198	484862	0.000408	2.5000	6774603	0.0309	69.790	0.000412	5
10	0.001753	96873	170	483960	0.000351	2.6033	6289741	0.0417	64.927	0.000349	10
15	0.002918	96704	282	482853	0.000584	2.6436	5805782	0.0194	60.037	0.000583	15
20	0.003779	96421	364	481229	0.000757	2.5918	5322929	0.0000	55.205	0.000757	20
25	0.004609	96057	443	479228	0.000924	2.6118	4841700	0.0000	50.404	0.000924	25
30	0.006296	95614	602	476662	0.001263	2.6599	4362472	0.0000	45.626	0.001263	30
35	0.009524	95012	905	472954	0.001913	2.6716	3885810	0.0081	40.898	0.001911	35
40	0.014318	94107	1347	467400	0.002883	2.6725	3412856	0.0118	36.266	0.002877	40
45	0.021784	92760	2021	459088	0.004402	2.6687	2945455	0.0202	31.754	0.004386	45
50	0.032883	90739	2984	446686	0.006680	2.6508	2486367	0.0174	27.401	0.006661	50
55	0.047637	87755	4180	428993	0.009745	2.6597	2039681	0.0160	23.243	0.009716	55
60	0.074035	83575	6187	403474	0.015335	2.6725	1610688	0.0298	19.272	0.015242	60
65	0.120233	77388	9305	364867	0.025501	2.6280	1207214	0.0298	15.600	0.025364	65
70	0.174837	68083	11903	311937	0.038160	2.6076	842347	0.0298	12.372	0.037945	70
75	0.275011	56180	15450	243404	0.063475	2.5732	530410	0.0298	9.441	0.063090	75
80	0.425553	40730	17333	159817	0.108453	2.5955	287006	0.0298	7.047	0.107868	80
85+	1.000000	23397	23397	127190	0.183953	5.4362	127190	0.0298	5.436	0.180246	85+

TABLE 4 — OBSERVED AND PROJECTED VITAL RATES

	OBSERVED POPULATION BOTH SEXES	MALES	FEMALES	PROJECTED POPULATION 1960 MALES	FEMALES	1965 MALES	FEMALES	1970 MALES	FEMALES	STABLE POPULATION MALES	FEMALES
RATES PER THOUSAND											
Birth	24.81	25.77	23.87	23.95	22.08	24.33	22.37	26.01	23.90	27.81	26.44
Death	9.28	10.74	7.86	10.96	8.37	11.01	8.76	10.97	9.04	8.48	7.10
Increase	15.53	15.03	16.01	12.99	13.71	13.32	13.61	15.04	14.86	19.3365	
PERCENTAGE											
under 15	29.70	30.69	28.74	32.31	30.07	32.05	29.77	32.24	29.89	34.83	33.40
15-64	61.74	61.25	62.20	59.46	60.25	59.69	60.08	59.60	59.72	59.62	59.04
65 and over	8.56	8.05	9.06	8.23	9.68	8.26	10.15	8.15	10.40	5.55	7.56
DEP. RATIO X 100	61.98	63.25	60.76	68.19	65.97	67.53	66.45	67.77	67.46	67.74	69.39

TABLE 1 — DATA

AGE AT LAST BIRTHDAY	POPULATION BOTH SEXES	MALES Number	MALES %	FEMALES Number	FEMALES %	BIRTHS BY AGE OF MOTHER	DEATHS BOTH SEXES	DEATHS MALES	FEMALES	AGE AT LAST BIRTHDAY
0	4112000	2091000	2.4	2021000	2.2	0	110325	63477	46848	0
1-4	16252000	8260000	9.3	7992000	8.7	0	17150	9502	7648	1-4
5-9	18826000	9572000	10.8	9254000	10.1	0	8995	5269	3726	5-9
10-14	16909000	8595000	9.7	8314000	9.1	7007	7416	4751	2665	10-14
15-19	13351000	6700000	7.6	6651000	7.3	586680	12052	8516	3536	15-19
20-24	10850000	5295000	6.0	5555000	6.1	1426306	13394	9527	3867	20-24
25-29	10822000	5312000	6.0	5510000	6.0	1091598	13959	9109	4850	25-29
30-34	11900000	5823000	6.6	6077000	6.7	688729	19213	11731	7482	30-34
35-39	12481000	6079000	6.9	6402000	7.0	359657	28757	17333	11424	35-39
40-44	11641000	5693000	6.4	5948000	6.5	91784	42349	26034	16315	40-44
45-49	10912000	5371000	6.1	5541000	6.1	5114	63232	40074	23158	45-49
50-54	9650000	4754000	5.4	4896000	5.4	115	89394	58276	31118	50-54
55-59	8464000	4142000	4.7	4322000	4.7	0	115328	75555	39773	55-59
60-64	7162000	3418000	3.9	3744000	4.1	0	151005	96180	54825	60-64
65-69	6264000	2929000	3.3	3335000	3.7	0	194440	119799	74641	65-69
70-74	4769000	2195000	2.5	2574000	2.8		219736	127145	92591	70-74
75-79	3084000	1372000	1.5	1712000	1.9		217286	115507	101779	75-79
80-84	1601000	674000	0.8	927000	1.0	2179873 M.	183278	87929	95349	80-84
85+	940000	367000	0.4	573000	0.6	2077117 F.	182797	76140	106657	85+
TOTAL	179990000	88642000		91348000		4256990	1690106	961854	728252	TOTAL

TABLE 2 — MALE LIFE TABLE

x	nq_x	l_x	nd_x	nL_x	nm_x	na_x	T_x	r_x	$\overset{\circ}{e}_x$	nM_x
0	0.029656	100000	2966	97709	0.030352	0.2274	6683654	0.0002	66.837	0.030357
1	0.004585	97034	445	386841	0.001150	1.0857	6585945	0.0002	67.872	0.001150
5	0.002740	96590	265	482286	0.000549	2.5000	6199104	0.0179	64.180	0.000550
10	0.002787	96325	268	481026	0.000558	2.7715	5716818	0.0350	59.349	0.000553
15	0.006397	96056	615	478868	0.001283	2.6991	5235792	0.0472	54.507	0.001271
20	0.008966	95442	856	475110	0.001801	2.5470	4756924	0.0215	49.841	0.001799
25	0.008538	94586	808	470929	0.001715	2.5218	4281814	0.0000	45.269	0.001715
30	0.010025	93779	940	466648	0.002015	2.6124	3810885	0.0000	40.637	0.002015
35	0.014163	92838	1315	461141	0.002851	2.6797	3344236	0.0000	36.022	0.002851
40	0.022662	91524	2074	452844	0.004580	2.6981	2883095	0.0076	31.501	0.004573
45	0.036753	89449	3288	439669	0.007477	2.6946	2430251	0.0102	27.169	0.007461
50	0.059720	86162	5146	418740	0.012288	2.6544	1990582	0.0136	23.103	0.012258
55	0.087640	81016	7100	388295	0.018286	2.6357	1571842	0.0140	19.402	0.018241
60	0.132179	73916	9770	346167	0.028224	2.6036	1183548	0.0185	16.012	0.028139
65	0.186407	64146	11957	291562	0.041011	2.5606	837380	0.0185	13.054	0.040901
70	0.253907	52189	13251	228150	0.058080	2.5252	545819	0.0185	10.459	0.057925
75	0.348328	38938	13563	160625	0.084440	2.4885	317668	0.0185	8.158	0.084189
80	0.492710	25375	12502	95473	0.130951	2.4885	157044	0.0185	6.189	0.130458
85+	*1.000000	12872	12872	61570	0.209065	4.7832	61570	0.0185	4.783	0.207466

TABLE 3 — FEMALE LIFE TABLE

x	nq_x	l_x	nd_x	nL_x	nm_x	na_x	T_x	r_x	$\overset{\circ}{e}_x$	nM_x
0	0.022772	100000	2277	98262	0.023175	0.2366	7339633	0.0003	73.396	0.023181
1	0.003816	97723	373	389807	0.000957	1.0921	7241372	0.0003	74.101	0.000957
5	0.002001	97350	195	486263	0.000401	2.5000	6851565	0.0180	70.381	0.000403
10	0.001606	97155	156	485399	0.000321	2.5857	6365302	0.0326	65.517	0.000321
15	0.002670	96999	259	484385	0.000535	2.6454	5879903	0.0398	60.618	0.000532
20	0.003481	96740	337	482892	0.000697	2.6017	5395518	0.0181	55.773	0.000696
25	0.004392	96403	423	481010	0.000880	2.6242	4912625	0.0000	50.959	0.000880
30	0.006138	95980	589	478515	0.001231	2.6500	4431615	0.0000	46.172	0.001231
35	0.008886	95391	848	474981	0.001785	2.6725	3953100	0.0003	41.441	0.001784
40	0.013656	94543	1291	469714	0.002749	2.6755	3478120	0.0116	36.789	0.002743
45	0.020751	93252	1935	461751	0.004191	2.6697	3008405	0.0151	32.261	0.004179
50	0.031404	91317	2868	449845	0.006375	2.6497	2546655	0.0184	27.888	0.006356
55	0.045183	88449	3996	432909	0.009231	2.6636	2096810	0.0171	23.706	0.009202
60	0.071121	84453	6006	408161	0.014716	2.6520	1663901	0.0269	19.702	0.014643
65	0.106807	78446	8379	372465	0.022495	2.6407	1255740	0.0269	16.008	0.022381
70	0.166508	70068	11667	322604	0.036165	2.6227	883276	0.0269	12.606	0.035972
75	0.261162	58401	15252	255131	0.059781	2.5824	560672	0.0269	9.600	0.059450
80	0.410211	43149	17700	171227	0.103373	2.6200	305541	0.0269	7.081	0.102858
85+	1.000000	25449	25449	134314	0.189471	5.2779	134314	0.0269	5.278	0.186139

TABLE 4 — OBSERVED AND PROJECTED VITAL RATES

RATES PER THOUSAND	OBSERVED POPULATION BOTH SEXES	MALES	FEMALES	PROJECTED POPULATION 1965 MALES	1965 FEMALES	1970 MALES	1970 FEMALES	1975 MALES	1975 FEMALES	STABLE POPULATION MALES	FEMALES
Birth	23.65	24.59	22.74	24.81	22.84	26.44	24.30	27.77	25.54	28.72	27.31
Death	9.39	10.85	7.97	10.95	8.44	10.91	8.77	10.65	8.88	8.02	6.61
Increase	14.26	13.74	14.77	13.86	14.40	15.54	15.54	17.12	16.66	20.6979	
PERCENTAGE											
under 15	31.17	32.17	30.19	32.47	30.27	32.73	30.40	33.46	31.02	35.74	34.27
15-64	59.58	59.33	59.82	59.15	59.34	59.03	59.01	58.54	58.35	59.02	58.40
65 and over	9.25	8.50	9.98	8.39	10.39	8.23	10.59	8.00	10.63	5.25	7.33
DEP. RATIO X 100	67.85	68.56	67.16	69.07	68.53	69.40	69.47	70.82	71.38	69.45	71.22

TABLE 5 — POPULATION PROJECTED WITH FIXED AGE—SPECIFIC BIRTH AND DEATH RATES (IN 1000's)

AGE AT LAST BIRTHDAY	1965 BOTH SEXES	1965 MALES	1965 FEMALES	1970 BOTH SEXES	1970 MALES	1970 FEMALES	1975 BOTH SEXES	1975 MALES	1975 FEMALES	AGE AT LAST BIRTHDAY
0-4	21538	10990	10548	24029	12261	11768	27470	14017	13453	0-4
5-9	20279	10303	9976	21448	10939	10509	23927	12203	11724	5-9
10-14	18785	9547	9238	20234	10276	9958	21400	10910	10490	10-14
15-19	16853	8556	8297	18722	9504	9218	20167	10230	9937	15-19
20-24	13278	6647	6631	16760	8489	8271	18620	9430	9190	20-24
25-29	10781	5248	5533	13194	6589	6605	16654	8415	8239	25-29
30-34	10745	5264	5481	10706	5201	5505	13099	6529	6570	30-34
35-39	11786	5754	6032	10643	5202	5441	10603	5139	5464	35-39
40-44	12301	5970	6331	11616	5651	5965	10489	5108	5381	40-44
45-49	11374	5527	5847	12020	5796	6224	11350	5486	5864	45-49
50-54	10513	5115	5398	10960	5264	5696	11583	5520	6063	50-54
55-59	9120	4408	4712	9938	4743	5195	10364	4882	5482	55-59
60-64	7768	3693	4075	8372	3930	4442	9127	4229	4898	60-64
65-69	6296	2879	3417	6829	3110	3719	7364	3310	4054	65-69
70-74	5181	2292	2889	5212	2253	2959	5655	2434	3221	70-74
75-79	3581	1545	2036	3898	1614	2284	3926	1586	2340	75-79
80-84	1964	815	1149	2285	919	1366	2492	959	1533	80-84
85+	1162	435	727	1427	526	901	1664	592	1072	85+
TOTAL	193305	94988	98317	208293	102267	106026	225954	110979	114975	TOTAL

TABLE 6 — STANDARDIZED RATES

STANDARD COUNTRIES:
STANDARDIZED RATES PER THOUSAND

	ENGLAND AND WALES 1961 BOTH SEXES	MALES	FEMALES	UNITED STATES 1960 BOTH SEXES	MALES	FEMALES	MEXICO 1960 BOTH SEXES	MALES	FEMALES
Birth	23.21	26.01*	21.94	23.65	24.59*	22.74	28.66	22.64*	27.89
Death	11.44	12.22*	10.72	9.39	10.85*	7.97	5.10	8.52*	4.04
Increase	11.77	13.78*	11.23	14.26	13.74*	14.77	23.56	14.12*	23.85

TABLE 7 — MOMENTS AND CUMULANTS

	OBSERVED POP. MALES	OBSERVED POP. FEMALES	STATIONARY POP. MALES	STATIONARY POP. FEMALES	STABLE POP. MALES	STABLE POP. FEMALES	OBSERVED BIRTHS	NET MATERNITY FUNCTION	BIRTHS IN STABLE POP.
μ	31.06962	32.35280	36.40658	39.09770	26.92328	28.46219	26.42382	26.36661	25.63734
σ^2	484.0616	504.3773	500.5406	557.4892	405.1716	454.8091	37.12857	34.51203	31.79151
κ_3	4658.402	4568.530	2753.278	2330.219	5819.511	6747.221	130.1019	131.2802	130.7706
κ_4	-201102.	-224021.	-233772.	-320384.	-53123.	-84596.	-410.135	-95.878	144.145
β_1	0.191325	0.162662	0.060448	0.031339	0.509162	0.483908	0.330706	0.419264	0.532215
β_2	2.141749	2.119401	2.066930	1.969144	2.676405	2.591029	2.702484	2.919503	3.142619
κ	-0.069071	-0.059308	-0.023434	-0.011531	-0.205491	-0.186952	-0.172535	-0.248430	-0.348850

TABLE 8 — RATES FROM AGE DISTRIBUTIONS AND VITAL STATISTICS (Females)

VITAL STATISTICS		THOMPSON AGE RANGE	NRR	1000r	INTERVAL	BOURGEOIS-PICHAT AGE RANGE	NRR	1000b	1000d	1000r	COALE
GRR	1.780										
NRR	1.713	0-4	1.63	18.23	27.42	5-29	2.15	25.60	-2.66	28.27	IBR
TFR	3.649	5-9	1.55	16.13	27.37	30-54	1.26	19.34	10.85	8.50	IDR
GENERATION	25.997	10-14	1.40	12.28	27.31	55-79	1.46	24.35	10.42	13.93	IRI
SEX RATIO	104.947	15-19	1.15	4.90	27.22	*40-64	1.56	28.40	11.82	16.58	K1
											K2

TABLE 9 — LESLIE MATRIX AND ITS SPECTRAL COMPONENTS (Females)

Start of Age Interval	ORIGINAL MATRIX SUB-DIAGONAL	ALTERNATIVE FIRST ROWS Projection	Integral	FIRST STABLE MATRIX % IN STABLE POPULATION	FISHER VALUES	REPRODUCTIVE VALUES	SECOND STABLE MATRIX Z_2 FIRST COLUMN	FIRST ROW
0	0.99630	0.00000	0.00000	12.676	1.079	10800848	0.1886+0.0973	0.1886+0.0973
5	0.99822	0.00100	0.00000	11.384	1.201	11114551	0.1845-0.1658	-0.0206+0.1804
10	0.99791	0.10582	0.00211	10.244	1.334	11087943	-0.1049-0.2709	-0.1505+0.0381
15	0.99692	0.40982	0.22122	9.215	1.368	9099645	-0.3401+0.0023	-0.0960-0.1189
20	0.99610	0.54071	0.64393	8.281	1.079	5993823	-0.1385+0.3728	-0.0116-0.1528
25	0.99481	0.37014	0.49685	7.436	0.616	3394755	0.3499+0.3059	0.0164-0.1085
30	0.99261	0.20135	0.28423	6.669	0.286	1736066	0.4787-0.2552	0.0217-0.0560
35	0.98891	0.08506	0.14089	5.967	0.100	643154	-0.0801-0.6266	0.0133-0.0194
40	0.98305	0.01945	0.03870	5.319	0.020	118416	-0.7126-0.1709	0.0035-0.0035
45	0.97422	0.00113	0.00231	4.714	0.001	6200	-0.4758+0.6985	0.0002-0.0002
50	0.96235	0.00003	0.00006	4.140	0.000	133	0.5535+0.7916	0.0000-0.0000
55+	0.82386			13.955				

TABLE 10 — AGE ANALYSIS AND MISCELLANEOUS RESULTS (Females)

Start Age Interval	OBSERVED POPUL. (IN 100's)	CONTRIBUTIONS OF ROOTS (IN 100's) r_1	r_2, r_3	r_4-r_{11}	AGE-SP. BIRTH RATES	NET MATERNITY FUNCTION	COEFF. OF MATRIX EQUATION	PARAMETERS	INTEGRAL	MATRIX	EXP. INCREASE x	$e(x+2\frac{1}{2})r$
0	100130	98128	1473	530	0.0000	0.0000	0.0000	L(1)	1.10903	1.10932	0	1.0531
5	92540	88130	5769	-1359	0.0000	0.0000	0.0010	L(2)	0.28957	0.30236	50	2.9643
10	83140	79303	2777	1059	0.0004	0.0020	0.1052		0.83333	0.79698	55	3.2875
15	66510	71339	-5603	774	0.0430	0.2085	0.4067	R(1)	0.02070	0.02075	60	3.6460
20	55550	64110	-8451	-109	0.1253	0.6050	0.5350	R(2)	-0.02507	-0.03194	65	4.0435
25	55100	57567	651	-3118	0.0967	0.4650	0.3648			0.24727	0.24164	70	4.4844
30	60770	51624	12065	-2919	0.0553	0.2646	0.1974	C(1)		774147	75	4.9733
35	64020	46193	9082	8745	0.0274	0.1302	0.0828	C(2)		818042	80	5.5156
40	59480	41179	-8824	27125	0.0075	0.0354	0.0187			829379	85	6.1170
45	55410	36491	-19371	38289	0.0005	0.0021	0.0011	2P/Y	25.4100	26.0025	90	6.7839
50	48960	32047	-4075	20988	0.0000	0.0001	0.0000	DELTA	9.6211		95	7.5236
55+	171870	108036									100	8.3439

White Population

TABLE 1 — DATA

AGE AT LAST BIRTHDAY	BOTH SEXES	POPULATION MALES Number	%	FEMALES Number	%	BIRTHS BY AGE OF MOTHER	DEATHS BOTH SEXES	MALES	FEMALES	AGE AT LAST BIRTHDAY
0	3491000	1782000	2.3	1709000	2.1	0	82275	47874	34401	0
1-4	13894000	7081000	9.0	6813000	8.4	0	12871	7183	5688	1-4
5-9	16200000	8259000	10.5	7941000	9.8	0	7322	4348	2974	5-9
10-14	14752000	7516000	9.6	7236000	9.0	2635	6136	3936	2200	10-14
15-19	11722000	5894000	7.5	5828000	7.2	458457	10073	7217	2856	15-19
20-24	9517000	4668000	5.9	4849000	6.0	1219278	10688	7795	2893	20-24
25-29	9514000	4703000	6.0	4811000	6.0	939959	10480	7027	3453	25-29
30-34	10542000	5197000	6.6	5345000	6.6	589746	14280	9012	5268	30-34
35-39	11137000	5445000	6.9	5692000	7.0	307004	21912	13587	8325	35-39
40-44	10457000	5131000	6.5	5326000	6.6	78302	33458	21171	12287	40-44
45-49	9814000	4840000	6.2	4974000	6.2	4223	51785	33678	18107	45-49
50-54	8734000	4304000	5.5	4430000	5.5	74	74609	49955	24654	50-54
55-59	7657000	3742000	4.8	3915000	4.8	0	97738	65716	32022	55-59
60-64	6566000	3128000	4.0	3438000	4.3	0	130866	84998	45868	60-64
65-69	5746000	2683000	3.4	3063000	3.8	0	172850	107433	65417	65-69
70-74	4418000	2027000	2.6	2391000	3.0		200818	116661	84157	70-74
75-79	2864000	1267000	1.6	1597000	2.0		203045	107828	95217	75-79
80-84	1498000	626000	0.8	872000	1.1	1847741 M.	173913	83077	90836	80-84
85+	869000	336000	0.4	533000	0.7	1751937 F.	173050	71529	101521	85+
TOTAL	159392000	78629000		80763000		3599678	1488169	850025	638144	TOTAL

TABLE 2 — MALE LIFE TABLE

x	$_nq_x$	l_x	$_nd_x$	$_nL_x$	$_nm_x$	$_na_x$	T_x	r_x	$\dot{e}_x$	$_nM_x$	x
0	0.026319	100000	2632	97966	0.026865	0.2271	6758225	0.0000	67.582	0.026865	
1	0.004046	97368	394	388324	0.001014	1.0855	6660259	0.0000	68.403	0.001014	
5	0.002622	96974	254	484235	0.000525	2.5000	6271935	0.0158	64.676	0.000526	
10	0.002640	96720	255	483032	0.000529	2.7774	5787700	0.0331	59.840	0.000524	10
15	0.006160	96465	594	480950	0.001236	2.6902	5304668	0.0465	54.991	0.001224	15
20	0.008321	95870	798	477381	0.001671	2.5296	4823717	0.0210	50.315	0.001670	20
25	0.007443	95073	708	473598	0.001494	2.5050	4346336	0.0000	45.716	0.001494	25
30	0.008635	94365	815	469882	0.001734	2.6158	3872739	0.0000	41.040	0.001734	30
35	0.012405	93550	1161	465074	0.002495	2.6933	3402856	0.0000	36.375	0.002495	35
40	0.020471	92390	1891	457625	0.004133	2.7143	2937782	0.0074	31.798	0.004126	40
45	0.034321	90498	3106	445364	0.006974	2.7052	2480157	0.0103	27.406	0.006958	45
50	0.056644	87392	4950	425391	0.011637	2.6625	2034793	0.0139	23.283	0.011607	50
55	0.084512	82442	6967	395772	0.017604	2.6407	1609402	0.0136	19.522	0.017562	55
60	0.127924	75475	9655	354292	0.027252	2.6094	1213630	0.0173	16.080	0.027173	60
65	0.182879	65820	12037	299824	0.040147	2.5680	859338	0.0173	13.056	0.040042	65
70	0.252556	53783	13583	235392	0.057704	2.5321	559513	0.0173	10.403	0.057554	70
75	0.351489	40200	14130	165552	0.085349	2.4914	324122	0.0173	8.063	0.085105	75
80	0.498731	26070	13002	97623	0.133184	2.4830	158569	0.0173	6.082	0.132710	80
85+	*1.000000	13068	13068	60946	0.214421	4.6637	60946	0.0173	4.664	0.212884	85

TABLE 3 — FEMALE LIFE TABLE

x	$_nq_x$	l_x	$_nd_x$	$_nL_x$	$_nm_x$	$_na_x$	T_x	r_x	$\dot{e}_x$	$_nM_x$	x
0	0.019825	100000	1982	98488	0.020129	0.2373	7432845	0.0000	74.328	0.020129	
1	0.003331	98018	327	391121	0.000835	1.0925	7334357	0.0000	74.827	0.000835	1
5	0.001864	97691	182	488000	0.000373	2.5000	6943236	0.0159	71.073	0.000375	5
10	0.001523	97509	148	487185	0.000305	2.5805	6455236	0.0306	66.202	0.000304	10
15	0.002459	97360	239	486233	0.000492	2.6229	5968051	0.0396	61.299	0.000490	15
20	0.002983	97121	290	484903	0.000597	2.5773	5481818	0.0186	56.443	0.000597	20
25	0.003583	96831	347	483327	0.000718	2.6109	4996915	0.0000	51.604	0.000718	25
30	0.004917	96484	474	481309	0.000986	2.6550	4513588	0.0000	46.781	0.000986	30
35	0.007288	96010	700	478430	0.001463	2.6851	4032279	0.0000	41.999	0.001463	35
40	0.011499	95310	1096	474021	0.002312	2.6911	3553849	0.0111	37.287	0.002307	40
45	0.018098	94214	1705	467111	0.003650	2.6775	3079828	0.0147	32.690	0.003640	45
50	0.027552	92509	2549	456573	0.005582	2.6567	2612717	0.0183	28.243	0.005565	50
55	0.040262	89960	3622	441386	0.008206	2.6763	2156143	0.0167	23.968	0.008179	55
60	0.065025	86338	5614	418621	0.013411	2.6718	1714757	0.0260	19.861	0.013340	60
65	0.102209	80724	8251	384290	0.021470	2.6570	1296136	0.0260	16.056	0.021357	65
70	0.163276	72474	11833	334374	0.035389	2.6343	911846	0.0260	12.582	0.035197	70
75	0.261890	60640	15881	264897	0.059952	2.5880	577472	0.0260	9.523	0.059622	75
80	0.414311	44759	18544	177154	0.104679	2.6161	312575	0.0260	6.983	0.104170	80
85+	1.000000	26215	26215	135421	0.193582	5.1658	135421	0.0260	5.166	0.190470	85

TABLE 4 — OBSERVED AND PROJECTED VITAL RATES

	OBSERVED POPULATION BOTH SEXES	MALES	FEMALES	PROJECTED POPULATION 1965 MALES	FEMALES	1970 MALES	FEMALES	1975 MALES	FEMALES	STABLE POPULATION MALES	FEMALES
RATES PER THOUSAND											
Birth	22.58	23.50	21.69	23.76	21.83	25.38	23.27	26.62	24.43	27.50	26.0
Death	9.34	10.81	7.90	10.93	8.40	10.92	8.76	10.69	8.90	8.09	6.6
Increase	13.25	12.69	13.79	12.82	13.43	14.46	14.51	15.94	15.52	19.409	
PERCENTAGE											
under 15	30.33	31.33	29.34	31.49	29.29	31.73	29.38	32.44	29.99	34.67	33.1
15-64	60.02	59.84	60.19	59.78	59.79	59.69	59.47	59.18	58.78	59.66	58.9
65 and over	9.66	8.82	10.47	8.73	10.92	8.58	11.15	8.38	11.24	5.67	7.9
DEP. RATIO X 100	66.62	67.11	66.15	67.29	67.26	67.53	68.16	68.98	70.14	67.63	69.7

White Population

AGE AT LAST BIRTHDAY	1965 BOTH SEXES	MALES	FEMALES	1970 BOTH SEXES	MALES	FEMALES	1975 BOTH SEXES	MALES	FEMALES	AGE AT LAST BIRTHDAY	
0-4	18245	9334	8911	20291	10381	9910	23084	11810	11274	0-4	**TABLE 5**
5-9	17320	8826	8494	18177	9295	8882	20215	10337	9878	5-9	POPULATION
10-14	16166	8238	7928	17284	8804	8480	18139	9272	8867	10-14	PROJECTED
15-19	14706	7484	7222	16115	8203	7912	17229	8766	8463	15-19	WITH
20-24	11662	5850	5812	14630	7428	7202	16033	8142	7891	20-24	FIXED
25-29	9464	4631	4833	11597	5804	5793	14548	7369	7179	25-29	AGE—
30-34	9457	4666	4791	9408	4595	4813	11527	5758	5769	30-34	SPECIFIC
35-39	10457	5144	5313	9380	4618	4762	9332	4548	4784	35-39	BIRTH
40-44	10998	5358	5640	10325	5061	5264	9262	4544	4718	40-44	AND
45-49	10242	4994	5248	10771	5214	5557	10113	4926	5187	45-49	DEATH
50-54	9485	4623	4862	9900	4770	5130	10412	4980	5432	50-54	RATES
55-59	8287	4004	4283	9001	4301	4700	9396	4437	4959	55-59	(IN 1000's)
60-64	7063	3350	3713	7647	3585	4062	8308	3850	4458	60-64	
65-69	5803	2647	3156	6244	2835	3409	6763	3034	3729	65-69	
70-74	4771	2106	2665	4824	2078	2746	5192	2226	2966	70-74	
75-79	3320	1426	1894	3592	1481	2111	3638	1462	2176	75-79	
80-84	1815	747	1068	2108	841	1267	2286	874	1412	80-84	
85+	1058	391	667	1282	466	816	1493	525	968	85+	
TOTAL	170319	83819	86500	182576	89760	92816	196970	96860	100110	TOTAL	

STANDARD COUNTRIES: STANDARDIZED RATES PER THOUSAND	ENGLAND AND WALES 1961 BOTH SEXES	MALES	FEMALES	UNITED STATES 1960 BOTH SEXES	MALES	FEMALES	MEXICO 1960 BOTH SEXES	MALES	FEMALES	
Birth	22.41	24.79*	21.14	22.82	23.46*	21.88	27.63	21.51*	26.83	**TABLE 6** STANDARDIZED RATES
Death	11.08	11.84*	10.32	9.05	10.54*	7.61	4.80	8.41*	3.74	
Increase	11.33	12.94*	10.82	13.77	12.92*	14.27	22.83	13.10*	23.09	

	OBSERVED POP. MALES	FEMALES	STATIONARY POP. MALES	FEMALES	STABLE POP. MALES	FEMALES	OBSERVED BIRTHS	NET MATERNITY FUNCTION	BIRTHS IN STABLE POP.	
μ	31.54706	32.92951	36.56801	39.32412	27.57208	29.21862	26.54412	26.44871	25.78010	**TABLE 7**
σ^2	486.9085	509.5066	501.8501	559.5917	415.0630	467.1681	36.37258	33.61501	31.11529	MOMENTS
κ_3	4437.153	4318.767	2649.323	2174.322	5731.214	6617.051	127.8675	128.8964	127.9875	AND
κ_4	-208742.	-235992.	-237821.	-326348.	-68842.	-107635.	-379.538	-59.533	153.778	CUMULANTS
β_1	0.170556	0.141017	0.055533	0.026979	0.459358	0.429447	0.339780	0.437403	0.543768	
β_2	2.119528	2.090929	2.055717	1.957832	2.600397	2.506820	2.713116	2.947314	3.158835	
κ	-0.061727	-0.051341	-0.021432	-0.009879	-0.183332	-0.163783	-0.176989	-0.260421	-0.356718	

VITAL STATISTICS		THOMPSON AGE RANGE	NRR	1000r	INTERVAL	BOURGEOIS-PICHAT AGE RANGE	NRR	1000b	1000d	1000r	COALE	
GRR	1.717										IBR	**TABLE 8** RATES FROM AGE DISTRIBUTIONS AND VITAL STATISTICS (Females)
NRR	1.660	0-4	1.58	16.99	27.43	5-29	2.11	24.79	-2.78	27.57	IDR	
TFR	3.528	5-9	1.51	15.11	27.40	30-54	1.23	18.64	11.03	7.62	IRI	
GENERATION	26.110	10-14	1.38	11.66	27.34	55-79	1.44	23.94	10.42	13.53	K1	
SEX RATIO	105.468	15-19	1.13	4.43	27.26	*40-64	1.55	28.02	11.82	16.19	K2	

Start Age Interval	ORIGINAL MATRIX SUB-DIAGONAL	ALTERNATIVE FIRST ROWS Projection	Integral	FIRST STABLE MATRIX % IN STABLE POPULATION	FISHER VALUES	REPRODUCTIVE VALUES	SECOND STABLE MATRIX Z_2 FIRST COLUMN	FIRST ROW	
0	0.99671	0.00000	0.00000	12.184	1.072	9134366	0.1891+0.0925	0.1891+0.0925	**TABLE 9**
5	0.99833	0.00043	0.00000	11.018	1.185	9412148	0.1796-0.1671	-0.0160+0.1800	LESLIE
10	0.99805	0.09398	0.00091	9.980	1.308	9465214	-0.1069-0.2656	-0.1490+0.0425	MATRIX
15	0.99726	0.39249	0.19677	9.037	1.344	7830576	-0.3339+0.0053	-0.0976-0.1149	AND ITS
20	0.99675	0.53161	0.62897	8.177	1.063	5154956	-0.1338+0.3656	-0.0125-0.1499	SPECTRAL
25	0.99582	0.36369	0.48871	7.395	0.604	2905167	0.3418+0.2982	0.0154-0.1054	COMPONENTS
30	0.99402	0.19534	0.27599	6.681	0.277	1479948	0.4667-0.2470	0.0202-0.0539	(Females)
35	0.99078	0.08162	0.13491	6.026	0.096	548576	-0.0735-0.6091	0.0124-0.0186	
40	0.98542	0.01851	0.03677	5.417	0.019	100746	-0.6891-0.1734	0.0032-0.0034	
45	0.97744	0.00103	0.00212	4.843	0.001	5073	-0.4710+0.6695	0.0002-0.0002	
50	0.96674	0.00002	0.00004	4.295	0.000	86	0.5212+0.7766	0.0000-0.0000	
55+	0.82438			14.947					

Start Age Interval	OBSERVED POPUL. (IN 100's)	CONTRIBUTIONS OF ROOTS (IN 100's) r_1	r_2, r_3	$r_4 \cdot r_{11}$	AGE-SP. BIRTH RATES	NET MATERNITY FUNCTION	COEFF. OF MATRIX EQUATION	PARAMETERS	INTEGRAL	MATRIX	EXP. INCREASE x	$e^{(x+2\frac{1}{2})r}$	
0	85220	83701	975	544	0.0000	0.0000	0.0000	L(1)	1.10191	1.10217	0	1.0497	**TABLE 10**
5	79410	75693	4957	-1240	0.0000	0.0000	0.0004	L(2)	0.29518	0.30666	50	2.7705	AGE
10	72360	68562	2822	977	0.0002	0.0009	0.0935		0.83477	0.79862	55	3.0528	ANALYSIS
15	58280	62085	-4389	584	0.0383	0.1862	0.3898	R(1)	0.01941	0.01946	60	3.3639	AND
20	48490	56176	-7506	-180	0.1224	0.5934	0.5265	R(2)	-0.02434	-0.03122	65	3.7068	MISCELLANEOUS
25	48110	50803	-308	-2384	0.0951	0.4596	0.3590		0.24618	0.24083	70	4.0845	RESULTS
30	53450	45901	9923	-2374	0.0537	0.2585	0.1920	C(1)		686996	75	4.5008	(Females)
35	56920	41397	8683	6840	0.0263	0.1256	0.0798	C(2)		644640	80	4.9595	
40	53260	37214	-6143	22190	0.0072	0.0339	0.0179			790592	85	5.4649	
45	49740	33272	-16658	33126	0.0004	0.0019	0.0010	2P/Y	25.5225	26.0894	90	6.0219	
50	44300	29507	-5560	20353	0.0000	0.0000	0.0000	DELTA	9.2935		95	6.6356	
55+	158090	102687									100	7.3118	

Non-White Population—With Adjusted Deaths

TABLE 1 — DATA

AGE AT LAST BIRTHDAY	POPULATION BOTH SEXES	MALES Number	%	FEMALES Number	%	BIRTHS BY AGE OF MOTHER	DEATHS BOTH SEXES	MALES	FEMALES	AGE AT LAST BIRTHDAY
0	621000	309000	3.1	312000	2.9	0	28394	15873	12521	0
1-4	2358000	1179000	11.8	1179000	11.1	0	4542	2495	2047	1-4
5-9	2625000	1312000	13.1	1313000	12.4	0	1741	927	814	5-9
10-14	2158000	1080000	10.8	1078000	10.2	4256	1405	901	504	10-14
15-19	1629000	806000	8.0	823000	7.8	128836	2010	1294	716	15-19
20-24	1334000	628000	6.3	706000	6.7	206950	2936	1822	1114	20-24
25-29	1307000	608000	6.1	699000	6.6	150704	3798	2322	1476	25-29
30-34	1359000	627000	6.3	732000	6.9	99320	5317	2761	2556	30-34
35-39	1344000	634000	6.3	710000	6.7	52482	7222	4161	3061	35-39
40-44	1183000	562000	5.6	621000	5.9	13588	9014	4968	4046	40-44
45-49	1098000	531000	5.3	567000	5.4	916	10948	6216	4732	45-49
50-54	916000	450000	4.5	466000	4.4	54	13143	7941	5202	50-54
55-59	807000	400000	4.0	407000	3.8	0	15664	9021	6643	55-59
60-64	596000	290000	2.9	306000	2.9	0	17043	9891	7152	60-64
65-69	519000	247000	2.5	272000	2.6	0	20935	11606	9329	65-69
70-74	351000	168000	1.7	183000	1.7		22036	11816	10220	70-74
75-79	220000	105000	1.0	115000	1.1		17043	9216	7827	75-79
80-84	103000	48000	0.5	55000	0.5	331516 M.	11566	6155	5411	80-84
85+	71000	31000	0.3	40000	0.4	325590 F.	11980	5730	6250	85+
TOTAL	20599000	10015000		10584000		657106	206737	115116	91621	TOTAL

TABLE 2 — MALE LIFE TABLE

x	$_nq_x$	l_x	$_nd_x$	$_nL_x$	$_nm_x$	$_na_x$	T_x	r_x	$\dot{e}_x$	$_nM_x$	x
0	0.049319	100000	4932	96228	0.051252	0.2352	6122822	0.0029	61.228	0.051369	0
1	0.008379	95068	797	377955	0.002108	1.0911	6026594	0.0029	63.392	0.002116	1
5	0.003495	94272	329	470534	0.000700	2.5000	5648639	0.0309	59.919	0.000707	5
10	0.004209	93942	395	468811	0.000843	2.7261	5178105	0.0478	55.120	0.000834	10
15	0.008110	93547	759	466034	0.001628	2.7600	4709294	0.0525	50.342	0.001605	15
20	0.014465	92788	1342	460787	0.002913	2.6508	4243260	0.0254	45.731	0.002901	20
25	0.018920	91446	1730	453031	0.003819	2.5738	3782474	0.0000	41.363	0.003819	25
30	0.021789	89716	1955	443921	0.004404	2.6180	3329443	0.0000	37.111	0.004404	30
35	0.032332	87761	2837	432069	0.006567	2.6266	2885521	0.0044	32.879	0.006563	35
40	0.043327	84923	3679	415792	0.008849	2.6017	2453452	0.0088	28.890	0.008840	40
45	0.057032	81244	4633	395222	0.011724	2.6265	2037660	0.0099	25.081	0.011706	45
50	0.084753	76610	6493	367421	0.017672	2.5926	1642438	0.0110	21.439	0.017647	50
55	0.107249	70117	7520	332494	0.022617	2.5941	1275018	0.0199	18.184	0.022552	55
60	0.157975	62597	9889	289018	0.034215	2.5762	942523	0.0218	15.057	0.034107	60
65	0.211274	52709	11136	236237	0.047139	2.5480	653505	0.0218	12.398	0.046988	65
70	0.299578	41573	12454	176585	0.070528	2.4885	417268	0.0218	10.037	0.070333	70
75	0.358906	29118	10451	118760	0.087999	2.4326	240683	0.0218	8.266	0.087771	75
80	0.486002	18668	9072	70478	0.128727	2.4804	121923	0.0218	6.531	0.128229	80
85+	*1.000000	9595	9595	51444	0.186514	5.3615	51444	0.0218	5.362	0.184839	85

TABLE 3 — FEMALE LIFE TABLE

x	$_nq_x$	l_x	$_nd_x$	$_nL_x$	$_nm_x$	$_na_x$	T_x	r_x	$\dot{e}_x$	$_nM_x$	x
0	0.038820	100000	3882	97053	0.039999	0.2407	6669263	0.0042	66.693	0.040131	0
1	0.006871	96118	660	382553	0.001726	1.0951	6572211	0.0042	68.376	0.001736	1
5	0.003061	95458	292	476557	0.000613	2.5000	6189657	0.0315	64.842	0.000620	5
10	0.002348	95165	223	475294	0.000470	2.6161	5713100	0.0461	60.033	0.000468	10
15	0.004389	94942	417	473776	0.000880	2.7607	5237806	0.0414	55.169	0.000870	15
20	0.007879	94525	745	470883	0.001582	2.6590	4764029	0.0148	50.400	0.001578	20
25	0.010507	93780	985	466618	0.002112	2.6823	4293147	0.0000	45.779	0.002112	25
30	0.017315	92795	1607	460159	0.003492	2.6250	3826529	0.0000	41.236	0.003492	30
35	0.021375	91188	1949	451332	0.004319	2.6349	3366369	0.0118	36.917	0.004311	35
40	0.032144	89239	2868	439356	0.006529	2.6156	2915038	0.0161	32.665	0.006515	40
45	0.041001	86371	3541	423344	0.008365	2.5970	2475681	0.0202	28.663	0.008346	45
50	0.054538	82829	4517	403402	0.011198	2.6215	2052337	0.0215	24.778	0.011163	50
55	0.078850	78312	6175	376854	0.016385	2.6183	1648935	0.0254	21.056	0.016322	55
60	0.111233	72137	8024	341469	0.023499	2.6050	1272082	0.0347	17.634	0.023373	60
65	0.159407	64113	10220	296110	0.034515	2.6071	930613	0.0347	14.515	0.034298	65
70	0.246333	53893	13276	236611	0.056107	2.5552	634503	0.0347	11.773	0.055847	70
75	0.291224	40617	11829	173116	0.068328	2.4663	397892	0.0347	9.796	0.068061	75
80	0.394652	28789	11361	114911	0.098872	2.6027	224776	0.0347	7.808	0.098382	80
85+	1.000000	17427	17427	109864	0.158624	6.3042	109864	0.0347	6.304	0.156251	85

TABLE 4 — OBSERVED AND PROJECTED VITAL RATES

	OBSERVED POPULATION BOTH SEXES	MALES	FEMALES	PROJECTED POPULATION 1965 MALES	FEMALES	1970 MALES	FEMALES	1975 MALES	FEMALES	STABLE POPULATION MALES	FEMALES
RATES PER THOUSAND											
Birth	31.90	33.10	30.76	32.86	30.48	34.63	32.13	36.36	33.82	37.32	35.82
Death	10.04	11.49	8.66	11.25	8.81	10.96	8.89	10.57	8.81	8.34	6.84
Increase	21.86	21.61	22.11	21.61	21.67	23.67	23.24	25.78	25.01		28.9776
PERCENTAGE											
under 15	37.68	38.74	36.68	39.78	37.54	40.07	37.75	40.74	38.37	42.78	41.5
15-64	56.18	55.28	57.04	54.55	56.15	54.35	55.81	54.01	55.31	54.31	54.5
65 and over	6.14	5.98	6.28	5.66	6.31	5.58	6.44	5.26	6.32	2.92	3.8
DEP. RATIO X 100	77.99	80.91	75.32	83.31	78.10	84.01	79.19	85.16	80.80	84.14	83.3

Non-White Population—With Adjusted Deaths

AGE AT LAST BIRTHDAY	1965 BOTH SEXES	1965 MALES	1965 FEMALES	1970 BOTH SEXES	1970 MALES	1970 FEMALES	1975 BOTH SEXES	1975 MALES	1975 FEMALES	AGE AT LAST BIRTHDAY	
0-4	3299	1655	1644	3779	1896	1883	4477	2246	2231	0-4	
5-9	2959	1477	1482	3277	1643	1634	3752	1881	1871	5-9	
10-14	2617	1307	1310	2949	1471	1478	3267	1637	1630	10-14	
15-19	2149	1074	1075	2604	1299	1305	2935	1462	1473	15-19	TABLE 5
20-24	1615	797	818	2130	1062	1068	2582	1285	1297	20-24	POPULATION
25-29	1317	617	700	1595	784	811	2102	1044	1058	25-29	PROJECTED
30-34	1285	596	689	1295	605	690	1567	768	799	30-34	WITH
35-39	1328	610	718	1256	580	676	1266	589	677	35-39	FIXED
40-44	1301	610	691	1286	587	699	1216	558	658	40-44	AGE—
45-49	1132	534	598	1246	580	666	1231	558	673	45-49	SPECIFIC
50-54	1034	494	540	1067	497	570	1174	539	635	50-54	BIRTH
55-59	842	407	435	952	447	505	982	449	533	55-59	AND
60-64	717	348	369	748	354	394	845	388	457	60-64	DEATH
65-69	502	237	265	604	284	320	631	289	342	65-69	RATES
70-74	402	185	217	389	177	212	468	212	256	70-74	(IN 1000's)
75-79	247	113	134	283	124	159	274	119	155	75-79	
80-84	138	62	76	156	67	89	180	74	106	80-84	
85+	88	35	53	118	45	73	134	49	85	85+	
TOTAL	22972	11158	11814	25734	12502	13232	29083	14147	14936	TOTAL	

STANDARD COUNTRIES: STANDARDIZED RATES PER THOUSAND	ENGLAND AND WALES 1961 BOTH SEXES	MALES	FEMALES	UNITED STATES 1960 BOTH SEXES	MALES	FEMALES	MEXICO 1960 BOTH SEXES	MALES	FEMALES	
Birth	28.91	35.77*	27.76	29.60	33.54*	28.90	35.93	31.95*	35.52	TABLE 6
Death	15.00	16.64*	14.63	12.54	14.33*	11.31	7.47	9.73*	6.37	STANDARDIZED RATES
Increase	13.91	19.12*	13.13	17.06	19.22*	17.59	28.46	22.22*	29.15	

	OBSERVED POP. MALES	OBSERVED POP. FEMALES	STATIONARY POP. MALES	STATIONARY POP. FEMALES	STABLE POP. MALES	STABLE POP. FEMALES	OBSERVED BIRTHS	NET MATERNITY FUNCTION	BIRTHS IN STABLE POP.	
μ	27.32491	27.95120	34.84779	37.02540	22.90837	23.87582	25.76202	25.94322	24.79581	TABLE 7
σ^2	445.9185	443.3638	479.8447	527.0770	333.2870	365.1607	40.86065	39.81760	35.19402	MOMENTS
κ_3	5985.608	5686.596	3354.820	3268.285	5650.682	6472.656	152.8527	156.8326	159.8840	AND
κ_4	-119566.	-113775.	-194874.	-255958.	25242.	26219.	-571.617	-361.762	133.769	CUMULANTS
β_1	0.404064	0.371043	0.101868	0.072949	0.862475	0.860425	0.342476	0.389625	0.586413	
β_2	2.398690	2.421205	2.153645	2.078659	3.227245	3.196628	2.657631	2.771823	3.107998	
κ	-0.145448	-0.140064	-0.040738	-0.028184	-0.379801	-0.369905	-0.166679	-0.201306	-0.332071	

VITAL STATISTICS		THOMPSON AGE RANGE	NRR	1000r	INTERVAL	BOURGEOIS-PICHAT AGE RANGE	NRR	1000b	1000d	1000r	COALE	TABLE 8
GRR	2.236										IBR	RATES FROM AGE DISTRIBUTIONS AND VITAL STATISTICS (Females)
NRR	2.085	0-4	2.00	26.25	27.29	5-29	2.41	31.69	-0.96	32.65	IDR	
TFR	4.512	5-9	1.85	23.01	27.20	30-54	1.54	26.22	10.20	16.02	IRI	
GENERATION	25.358	10-14	1.58	16.67	27.09	55-79	1.69	30.64	11.10	19.54	K1	
SEX RATIO	101.820	15-19	1.27	8.53	26.94	*35-59	1.67	30.40	11.33	19.08	K2	

Start Age Interval	ORIGINAL MATRIX SUB-DIAGONAL	ALTERNATIVE FIRST ROWS Projection	Integral	FIRST STABLE MATRIX % IN STABLE POPULATION	FISHER VALUES	REPRODUCTIVE VALUES	SECOND STABLE MATRIX Z₂ FIRST COLUMN	FIRST ROW	
0	0.99364	0.00000	0.00000	16.015	1.120	1670622	0.1823+0.1476	0.1823+0.1476	TABLE 9
5	0.99735	0.00468	0.00000	13.760	1.304	1712341	0.2409-0.1495	-0.0657+0.1826	LESLIE MATRIX AND ITS SPECTRAL COMPONENTS (Females)
10	0.99681	0.19010	0.01009	11.866	1.507	1624576	-0.0753-0.3356	-0.1608-0.0024	
15	0.99389	0.53218	0.39996	10.227	1.535	1263150	-0.4143-0.0476	-0.0765-0.1540	
20	0.99094	0.60215	0.74893	8.789	1.186	837320	-0.2190+0.4542	0.0019-0.1807	
25	0.98616	0.41516	0.55085	7.531	0.703	491620	0.4303+0.4292	0.0313-0.1374	
30	0.98082	0.24736	0.34666	6.421	0.353	258482	0.6559-0.3182	0.0400-0.0752	
35	0.97347	0.11314	0.18886	5.446	0.134	94992	-0.1013-0.8638	0.0245-0.0262	
40	0.96355	0.02785	0.05590	4.584	0.029	17840	-1.0055-0.2229	0.0065-0.0049	
45	0.95290	0.00205	0.00413	3.819	0.002	1189	-0.6341+1.0271	0.0005-0.0004	
50	0.93419	0.00014	0.00030	3.147	0.000	62	0.8828+1.0855	0.0000-0.0000	
55+	0.80636			8.395					

Start Age Interval	OBSERVED POPUL. (IN 100's)	CONTRIBUTIONS OF ROOTS (IN 100's) r_1	r_2, r_3	$r_4 \cdot r_{11}$	AGE-SP. BIRTH RATES	NET MATERNITY FUNCTION	COEFF. OF MATRIX EQUATION	PARAMETERS INTEGRAL	MATRIX	EXP. INCREASE x	$e^{(x+2\frac{1}{2})r}$	
0	14910	14455	471	-16	0.0000	0.0000	0.0000	L(1) 1.15591	1.15653	0	1.0751	TABLE 10
5	13130	12419	870	-160	0.0000	0.0000	0.0046	L(2) 0.24346	0.27023	50	4.5783	AGE ANALYSIS AND MISCELLANEOUS RESULTS (Females)
10	10780	10710	4	66	0.0020	0.0093	0.1884	0.81341	0.77642	55	5.2921	
15	8230	9231	-1277	276	0.0776	0.3675	0.5257	R(1) 0.02898	0.02908	60	6.1172	
20	7060	7933	-1021	148	0.1452	0.6839	0.5912	R(2) -0.03272	-0.03918	65	7.0709	
25	6990	6797	1052	-859	0.1068	0.4985	0.4039	0.25599	0.24717	70	8.1733	
30	7320	5796	2305	-781	0.0672	0.3094	0.2373	C(1) 90259		75	9.4476	
35	7100	4915	303	1882	0.0366	0.1653	0.1065	C(2) 158237		80	10.9206	
40	6210	4137	-3021	5094	0.0108	0.0476	0.0255	36097		85	12.6232	
45	5670	3447	-2748	4971	0.0008	0.0034	0.0018	2P/Y 24.5443	25.4201	90	14.5913	
50	4660	2840	2010	-190	0.0001	0.0002	0.0001	DELTA 10.3831		95	16.8662	
55+	13780	7577								100	19.4959	

TABLE 1 — DATA

AGE AT LAST BIRTHDAY	POPULATION BOTH SEXES	MALES Number	MALES %	FEMALES Number	FEMALES %	BIRTHS BY AGE OF MOTHER	DEATHS BOTH SEXES	MALES	FEMALES	AGE AT LAST BIRTHDAY
0	4161000	2124000	2.3	2037000	2.2	0	105513	60959	44554	0
1-4	16585000	8437000	9.2	8148000	8.6	0	16259	8839	7420	1-4
5-9	19735000	10030000	11.0	9705000	10.3	0	8963	5147	3816	5-9
10-14	17709000	9007000	9.9	8702000	9.2	7340	7453	4775	2678	10-14
15-19	14860000	7466000	8.2	7394000	7.8	600298	13002	9127	3875	15-19
20-24	11582000	5652000	6.2	5930000	6.3	1444978	14351	10153	4198	20-24
25-29	10730000	5279000	5.8	5451000	5.8	1045086	13779	8925	4854	25-29
30-34	11501000	5639000	6.2	5862000	6.2	638382	18527	11361	7166	30-34
35-39	12407000	6051000	6.6	6356000	6.7	334708	29326	17606	11720	35-39
40-44	12018000	5854000	6.4	6164000	6.5	91490	43535	26606	16929	40-44
45-49	11128000	5454000	6.0	5674000	6.0	4970	64151	40447	23704	45-49
50-54	10042000	4923000	5.4	5119000	5.4	110	92841	60396	32445	50-54
55-59	8736000	4257000	4.7	4479000	4.7	0	118808	78004	40804	55-59
60-64	7384000	3520000	3.9	3864000	4.1	0	154155	98184	55971	60-64
65-69	6267000	2893000	3.2	3374000	3.6	0	199130	123004	76126	65-69
70-74	5000000	2264000	2.5	2736000	2.9		229051	132005	97046	70-74
75-79	3308000	1456000	1.6	1852000	2.0		230909	122771	108138	75-79
80-84	1753000	732000	0.8	1021000	1.1	2132466 M.	195698	93224	102474	80-84
85+	982000	380000	0.4	602000	0.6	2034896 F.	201269	83256	118013	85+
TOTAL	185888000	91418000		94470000		4167362	1756720	994789	761931	TOTAL

TABLE 2 — MALE LIFE TABLE

x	$_nq_x$	l_x	$_nd_x$	$_nL_x$	$_nm_x$	$_na_x$	T_x	r_x	$\dot{e}_x$	$_nM_x$	x
0	0.028074	100000	2807	97820	0.028700	0.2235	6693302	0.0000	66.933	0.028700	
1	0.004178	97193	406	387586	0.001048	1.0831	6595482	0.0000	67.860	0.001048	
5	0.002556	96787	247	483314	0.000512	2.5000	6207896	0.0152	64.140	0.000513	
10	0.002669	96539	258	482123	0.000534	2.7791	5724582	0.0288	59.298	0.000530	10
15	0.006155	96281	593	480051	0.001234	2.7108	5242459	0.0454	54.449	0.001222	15
20	0.008958	95689	857	476344	0.001800	2.5500	4762408	0.0330	49.770	0.001796	20
25	0.008418	94832	798	472180	0.001691	2.5223	4286064	0.0000	45.197	0.001691	25
30	0.010026	94033	943	467924	0.002015	2.6209	3813884	0.0000	40.559	0.002015	30
35	0.014450	93091	1345	462324	0.002910	2.6739	3345960	0.0000	35.943	0.002910	35
40	0.022515	91745	2066	453965	0.004550	2.6947	2883636	0.0056	31.431	0.004545	40
45	0.036530	89680	3276	440854	0.007431	2.6970	2429671	0.0095	27.093	0.007416	45
50	0.059757	86404	5163	419918	0.012296	2.6563	1988817	0.0123	23.018	0.012268	50
55	0.088020	81241	7151	389274	0.018370	2.6326	1568899	0.0145	19.312	0.018324	55
60	0.131104	74090	9713	347264	0.027971	2.6131	1179625	0.0163	15.922	0.027893	60
65	0.193017	64376	12426	291555	0.042619	2.5594	832360	0.0163	12.930	0.042518	65
70	0.255159	51951	13256	226835	0.058437	2.5167	540805	0.0163	10.410	0.058306	70
75	0.348534	38695	13486	159538	0.084535	2.4837	313970	0.0163	8.114	0.084321	75
80	0.483874	25208	12198	95449	0.127793	2.4919	154432	0.0163	6.126	0.127355	80
85+	*1.000000	13011	13011	58984	0.220582	4.5335	58984	0.0163	4.533	0.219095	85

TABLE 3 — FEMALE LIFE TABLE

x	$_nq_x$	l_x	$_nd_x$	$_nL_x$	$_nm_x$	$_na_x$	T_x	r_x	$\dot{e}_x$	$_nM_x$	x
0	0.021514	100000	2151	98360	0.021872	0.2376	7352068	0.0000	73.521	0.021872	
1	0.003633	97849	355	390361	0.000911	1.0928	7253708	0.0000	74.132	0.000911	
5	0.001956	97493	191	486989	0.000392	2.5000	6863347	0.0152	70.398	0.000393	
10	0.001541	97302	150	486151	0.000308	2.5904	6376358	0.0268	65.531	0.000308	10
15	0.002633	97152	256	485163	0.000527	2.6575	5890207	0.0378	60.628	0.000524	15
20	0.003545	96897	343	483661	0.000710	2.6050	5405044	0.0298	55.782	0.000708	20
25	0.004443	96553	429	481744	0.000891	2.6177	4921383	0.0002	50.971	0.000890	25
30	0.006095	96124	586	479250	0.001222	2.6593	4439639	0.0000	46.186	0.001222	30
35	0.009180	95538	877	475646	0.001844	2.6681	3960390	0.0000	41.453	0.001844	35
40	0.013665	94661	1294	470293	0.002751	2.6706	3484743	0.0085	36.813	0.002746	40
45	0.020739	93368	1936	462325	0.004188	2.6688	3014450	0.0143	32.286	0.004178	45
50	0.031311	91431	2863	450422	0.006356	2.6475	2552126	0.0172	27.913	0.006338	50
55	0.044748	88569	3963	433579	0.009141	2.6625	2101704	0.0185	23.730	0.009110	55
60	0.070376	84605	5954	409078	0.014555	2.6574	1668125	0.0255	19.717	0.014485	60
65	0.107585	78651	8462	373263	0.022670	2.6373	1259047	0.0255	16.008	0.022563	65
70	0.164293	70189	11532	323496	0.035647	2.6195	885784	0.0255	12.620	0.035470	70
75	0.257016	58658	15076	256849	0.058696	2.5829	562288	0.0255	9.586	0.058390	75
80	0.402317	43582	17534	173875	0.100841	2.6304	305439	0.0255	7.008	0.100366	80
85+	1.000000	26048	26048	131564	0.197989	5.0508	131564	0.0255	5.051	0.196034	85

TABLE 4 — OBSERVED AND PROJECTED VITAL RATES

	OBSERVED POPULATION BOTH SEXES	MALES	FEMALES	PROJECTED POPULATION 1967 MALES	1967 FEMALES	1972 MALES	1972 FEMALES	1977 MALES	1977 FEMALES	STABLE POPULATION MALES	FEMALES
RATES PER THOUSAND											
Birth	22.42	23.33	21.54	24.33	22.37	26.00	23.88	27.15	24.96	27.24	25.8
Death	9.45	10.88	8.07	10.94	8.54	10.86	8.84	10.57	8.91	8.40	7.0
Increase	12.97	12.44	13.47	13.39	13.83	15.14	15.05	16.58	16.05	18.832	
PERCENTAGE											
under 15	31.30	32.38	30.27	32.25	29.98	32.21	29.84	32.85	30.43	34.42	32.9
15-64	59.38	59.17	59.59	59.43	59.50	59.62	59.46	59.17	58.78	59.90	59.1
65 and over	9.31	8.45	10.15	8.33	10.52	8.17	10.70	7.98	10.78	5.67	7.9
DEP. RATIO X 100	68.40	69.00	67.82	68.28	68.06	67.73	68.19	69.02	70.12	66.93	69.1

TABLE 5 — POPULATION PROJECTED WITH FIXED AGE—SPECIFIC BIRTH AND DEATH RATES (IN 1000's)

AGE AT LAST BIRTHDAY	1967 BOTH SEXES	1967 MALES	1967 FEMALES	1972 BOTH SEXES	1972 MALES	1972 FEMALES	1977 BOTH SEXES	1977 MALES	1977 FEMALES	AGE AT LAST BIRTHDAY
0-4	21441	10935	10506	24260	12373	11887	27622	14087	13535	0-4
5-9	20664	10515	10149	21357	10888	10469	24164	12319	11845	5-9
10-14	19693	10005	9688	20621	10490	10131	21312	10861	10451	10-14
15-19	17652	8968	8684	19631	9962	9669	20555	10444	10111	15-19
20-24	14779	7408	7371	17556	8899	8657	19524	9885	9639	20-24
25-29	11509	5603	5906	14686	7344	7342	17444	8821	8623	25-29
30-34	10654	5231	5423	11428	5552	5876	14581	7277	7304	30-34
35-39	11390	5572	5818	10551	5169	5382	11318	5486	5832	35-39
40-44	12226	5942	6284	11223	5471	5752	10396	5075	5321	40-44
45-49	11745	5685	6060	11948	5770	6178	10968	5313	5655	45-49
50-54	10723	5195	5528	11319	5415	5904	11515	5496	6019	50-54
55-59	9492	4564	4928	10137	4816	5321	10703	5020	5683	55-59
60-64	8024	3798	4226	8720	4071	4649	9317	4296	5021	60-64
65-69	6481	2955	3526	7044	3188	3856	7660	3418	4242	65-69
70-74	5175	2251	2924	5355	2299	3056	5823	2481	3342	70-74
75-79	3764	1592	2172	3905	1583	2322	4043	1617	2426	75-79
80-84	2125	871	1254	2424	953	1471	2519	947	1572	80-84
85+	1225	452	773	1487	538	949	1702	589	1113	85+
TOTAL	198762	97542	101220	213652	104781	108871	231166	113432	117734	TOTAL

TABLE 6 — STANDARDIZED RATES

STANDARD COUNTRIES:

STANDARDIZED RATES PER THOUSAND

	ENGLAND AND WALES 1961 BOTH SEXES	MALES	FEMALES	UNITED STATES 1960 BOTH SEXES	MALES	FEMALES	MEXICO 1960 BOTH SEXES	MALES	FEMALES
Birth	22.08	25.30*	20.89	22.50	23.74*	21.64	27.23	22.06*	26.53
Death	11.44	12.22*	10.68	9.38	10.87*	7.94	27.23	22.06*	26.53
Increase	10.64	13.08*	10.21	13.11	12.87*	13.71	5.04	8.58*	3.98

(Mexico: Death 22.20, 13.47, 22.55; Increase 22.20)*

Note — Mexico column: Birth 27.23 / 22.06* / 26.53; Death 5.04 / 8.58* / 3.98; Increase 22.20 / 13.47* / 22.55

TABLE 7 — MOMENTS AND CUMULANTS

	OBSERVED POP. MALES	OBSERVED POP. FEMALES	STATIONARY POP. MALES	STATIONARY POP. FEMALES	STABLE POP. MALES	STABLE POP. FEMALES	OBSERVED BIRTHS	NET MATERNITY FUNCTION	BIRTHS IN STABLE POP.
μ	30.89496	32.33227	36.36526	39.10285	27.67187	29.32691	26.22234	26.40979	25.75016
σ^2	485.5304	509.4157	499.0043	557.4209	414.9491	467.3276	37.04819	34.15743	31.73142
κ_3	4921.490	4796.752	2731.324	2316.254	5672.331	6564.318	142.2548	128.8390	128.1503
κ_4	-199490.	-229917.	-232436.	-320893.	-70070.	-108741.	-289.741	-66.979	141.354
β_1	0.211614	0.174051	0.060039	0.030976	0.450338	0.422197	0.397954	0.416523	0.514009
β_2	2.153771	2.114015	2.066543	1.967254	2.593051	2.502091	2.788906	2.942593	3.140387
κ	-0.075660	-0.062523	-0.023277	-0.011384	-0.180332	-0.161562	-0.207098	-0.256180	-0.348608

TABLE 8 — RATES FROM AGE DISTRIBUTIONS AND VITAL STATISTICS (Females)

VITAL STATISTICS

		THOMPSON AGE RANGE	NRR	1000r	INTERVAL	BOURGEOIS-PICHAT AGE RANGE	NRR	1000b	1000d	1000r	COALE	
GRR	1.696					5-29	2.26	26.90	-3.31	30.21	IBR	
NRR	1.634	0-4	1.61	17.83	27.42	30-54	1.13	16.05	11.41	4.64	IDR	
TFR	3.474	5-9	1.60	17.48	27.37	55-79	1.42	22.72	9.84	12.88	IRI	
GENERATION	26.076	10-14	1.46	13.64	27.31	*40-64	1.56	28.33	11.78	16.55	K1	
SEX RATIO	104.795	15-19	1.26	8.12	27.22						K2	

TABLE 9 — LESLIE MATRIX AND ITS SPECTRAL COMPONENTS (Females)

Start of Age Interval	SUB-DIAGONAL	ORIGINAL MATRIX ALTERNATIVE FIRST ROWS Projection	Integral	% IN STABLE POPULATION	FISHER VALUES	REPRODUCTIVE VALUES	SECOND STABLE MATRIX Z_2 FIRST COLUMN	FIRST ROW
0	0.99646	0.00000	0.00000	12.061	1.072	10920931	0.1872+0.0937	0.1872+0.0937
5	0.99828	0.00100	0.00000	10.936	1.183	11476876	0.1816-0.1651	-0.0169+0.1777
10	0.99797	0.09768	0.00211	9.934	1.301	11319386	-0.1040-0.2689	-0.1464+0.0410
15	0.99690	0.38672	0.20308	9.021	1.327	9815396	-0.3386-0.0000	-0.0958-0.1129
20	0.99604	0.51861	0.60953	8.183	1.047	6211367	-0.1433+0.3705	-0.0123-0.1472
25	0.99482	0.35803	0.47958	7.417	0.597	3256607	0.3445+0.3133	0.0159-0.1039
30	0.99248	0.19230	0.27241	6.714	0.274	1606492	0.4875-0.2439	0.0203-0.0530
35	0.98875	0.08034	0.13173	6.063	0.096	608256	-0.0603-0.6338	0.0123-0.0183
40	0.98306	0.01874	0.03711	5.455	0.019	118570	-0.7132-0.2005	0.0033-0.0034
45	0.97426	0.00107	0.00219	4.880	0.001	6050	-0.5139+0.6859	0.0002-0.0002
50	0.96261	0.00003	0.00005	4.326	0.000	128	0.5211+0.8332	0.0000-0.0000
55+	0.82160			15.012				

TABLE 10 — AGE ANALYSIS AND MISCELLANEOUS RESULTS (Females)

Start of Age Interval	OBSERVED POPUL. (IN 100's)	CONTRIBUTIONS OF ROOTS (IN 100's) r_1	r_2, r_3	$r_4 \cdot r_{11}$	AGE-SP. BIRTH RATES	NET MATERNITY FUNCTION	COEFF. OF MATRIX EQUATION	PARAMETERS	INTEGRAL	MATRIX	EXP. INCREASE x	$e^{(x+2\frac{1}{2})r}$
0	101850	100681	-173	1342	0.0000	0.0000	0.0000	L(1)	1.09874	1.09897	0	1.0482
5	97050	91289	6749	-987	0.0000	0.0000	0.0013	L(2)	0.29438	0.30644	50	2.6877
10	87020	82924	5957	-1861	0.0004	0.0020	0.0972		0.82794	0.79256	55	2.9531
15	73940	75303	-4265	2903	0.0396	0.1923	0.3839	R(1)	0.01883	0.01888	60	3.2447
20	59300	68309	-11816	2808	0.1190	0.5755	0.5132	R(2)	-0.02586	-0.03256	65	3.5651
25	54510	61910	-4124	-3276	0.0936	0.4510	0.3529			0.24584	70	3.9171
30	58620	56043	12733	-10156	0.0532	0.2548	0.1886	C(1)		834766	75	4.3038
35	63560	50612	16366	-3418	0.0257	0.1223	0.0782	C(2)		629970	80	4.7288
40	61640	45536	-3569	19673	0.0072	0.0341	0.0180			1350998	85	5.1957
45	56740	40733	-25009	41016	0.0004	0.0020	0.0013				90	5.7087
50	51190	36110	-15947	31027	0.0000	0.0000	0.0000	2P/Y	25.5585	26.1396	95	6.2723
55+	179280	125315						DELTA	7.8997		100	6.8917

TABLE 1 — DATA

AGE AT LAST BIRTHDAY	POPULATION BOTH SEXES	MALES Number	%	FEMALES Number	%	BIRTHS BY AGE OF MOTHER	DEATHS BOTH SEXES	MALES	FEMALES	AGE AT LAST BIRTHDAY
0	4092000	2090000	2.3	2002000	2.1	0	103426	59756	43670	0
1-4	16657000	8482000	9.1	8175000	8.5	0	16576	9143	7433	1-4
5-9	20075000	10203000	11.0	9872000	10.3	0	9054	5273	3781	5-9
10-14	18036000	9170000	9.9	8866000	9.2	7594	7476	4686	2790	10-14
15-19	15467000	7790000	8.4	7677000	8.0	586461	13954	9774	4180	15-19
20-24	12304000	6015000	6.5	6289000	6.6	1453757	15377	10914	4463	20-24
25-29	10840000	5328000	5.7	5512000	5.7	1023954	14365	9421	4944	25-29
30-34	11285000	5538000	6.0	5747000	6.0	610203	18525	11427	7098	30-34
35-39	12281000	5996000	6.5	6285000	6.6	322186	29601	17813	11788	35-39
40-44	12213000	5943000	6.4	6270000	6.5	88983	44702	27256	17446	40-44
45-49	11212000	5481000	5.9	5731000	6.0	4800	65596	41358	24238	45-49
50-54	10240000	5008000	5.4	5232000	5.5	82	94889	61584	33305	50-54
55-59	8862000	4305000	4.6	4557000	4.7	0	124590	81854	42736	55-59
60-64	7529000	3587000	3.9	3942000	4.1	0	158468	101261	57207	60-64
65-69	6242000	2865000	3.1	3377000	3.5	0	202063	125133	76930	65-69
70-74	5088000	2282000	2.5	2806000	2.9		238454	138194	100260	70-74
75-79	3405000	1488000	1.6	1917000	2.0		240425	128201	112224	75-79
80-84	1827000	759000	0.8	1068000	1.1	2101632 M.	205395	98135	107260	80-84
85+	1001000	385000	0.4	616000	0.6	1996388 F.	210613	86503	124110	85+
TOTAL	188656000	92715000		95941000		4098020	1813549	1027686	785863	TOTAL

TABLE 2 — MALE LIFE TABLE

x	$_nq_x$	l_x	$_nd_x$	$_nL_x$	$_nm_x$	$_na_x$	T_x	r_x	$\overset{\circ}{e}_x$	$_nM_x$	x
0	0.027973	100000	2797	97837	0.028591	0.2269	6667716	0.0000	66.677	0.028591	0
1	0.004298	97203	418	387593	0.001078	1.0854	6569879	0.0000	67.589	0.001078	1
5	0.002574	96785	249	483302	0.000516	2.5000	6182286	0.0135	63.877	0.000517	5
10	0.002573	96536	248	482132	0.000515	2.8007	5698984	0.0263	59.035	0.000511	10
15	0.006311	96287	608	480046	0.001266	2.7118	5216852	0.0409	54.180	0.001255	15
20	0.009051	95680	866	476281	0.001818	2.5546	4736805	0.0363	49.507	0.001814	20
25	0.008804	94814	835	472002	0.001769	2.5247	4260525	0.0064	44.936	0.001768	25
30	0.010266	93979	965	467595	0.002063	2.6160	3788522	0.0000	40.312	0.002063	30
35	0.014752	93014	1372	461873	0.002971	2.6695	3320928	0.0000	35.703	0.002971	35
40	0.022711	91642	2081	453414	0.004590	2.6957	2859055	0.0042	31.198	0.004586	40
45	0.037154	89561	3328	440127	0.007560	2.6931	2405640	0.0092	26.860	0.007546	45
50	0.059896	86233	5165	419100	0.012324	2.6639	1965513	0.0115	22.793	0.012297	50
55	0.091175	81068	7391	387821	0.019059	2.6296	1546413	0.0139	19.075	0.019014	55
60	0.132534	73677	9765	345066	0.028298	2.6119	1158592	0.0140	15.725	0.028230	60
65	0.197740	63912	12638	288747	0.043768	2.5618	813526	0.0140	12.729	0.043676	65
70	0.263574	51274	13515	222740	0.060674	2.5115	524778	0.0140	10.235	0.060558	70
75	0.354431	37760	13383	155007	0.086339	2.4751	302038	0.0140	7.999	0.086157	75
80	0.488866	24376	11917	91898	0.129675	2.4839	147031	0.0140	6.032	0.129294	80
85+	*1.000000	12460	12460	55133	0.225992	4.4249	55133	0.0140	4.425	0.224683	85+

TABLE 3 — FEMALE LIFE TABLE

x	$_nq_x$	l_x	$_nd_x$	$_nL_x$	$_nm_x$	$_na_x$	T_x	r_x	$\overset{\circ}{e}_x$	$_nM_x$	x
0	0.021456	100000	2146	98364	0.021813	0.2377	7341647	0.0000	73.416	0.021813	0
1	0.003627	97854	355	390386	0.000909	1.0929	7243283	0.0000	74.021	0.000909	1
5	0.001906	97499	186	487032	0.000382	2.5000	6852897	0.0133	70.287	0.000383	5
10	0.001576	97314	153	486201	0.000316	2.6082	6365865	0.0248	65.416	0.000315	10
15	0.002733	97160	266	485177	0.000547	2.6498	5879664	0.0338	60.515	0.000544	15
20	0.003554	96895	344	483647	0.000712	2.6010	5394488	0.0324	55.674	0.000710	20
25	0.004480	96550	433	481721	0.000898	2.6192	4910841	0.0081	50.863	0.000897	25
30	0.006158	96118	592	479205	0.001235	2.6617	4429120	0.0000	46.080	0.001235	30
35	0.009337	95526	892	475549	0.001876	2.6676	3949915	0.0000	41.349	0.001876	35
40	0.013838	94634	1310	470118	0.002786	2.6697	3474366	0.0063	36.714	0.002782	40
45	0.020990	93324	1959	462050	0.004239	2.6663	3004248	0.0137	32.191	0.004229	45
50	0.031445	91366	2873	450086	0.006383	2.6533	2542197	0.0164	27.824	0.006366	50
55	0.046031	88493	4073	432921	0.009409	2.6574	2092112	0.0185	23.642	0.009378	55
60	0.070484	84419	5950	408146	0.014579	2.6556	1659191	0.0244	19.654	0.014512	60
65	0.108553	78469	8518	372220	0.022884	2.6374	1251045	0.0244	15.943	0.022781	65
70	0.165355	69951	11567	322196	0.035902	2.6174	878825	0.0244	12.563	0.035731	70
75	0.257525	58384	15035	255557	0.058834	2.5815	556629	0.0244	9.534	0.058541	75
80	0.402444	43349	17445	172925	0.100885	2.6298	301072	0.0244	6.945	0.100431	80
85+	1.000000	25903	25903	128147	0.202137	4.9471	128147	0.0244	4.947	0.201478	85+

TABLE 4 — OBSERVED AND PROJECTED VITAL RATES

	OBSERVED POPULATION BOTH SEXES	MALES	FEMALES	PROJECTED POPULATION 1968 MALES	FEMALES	1973 MALES	FEMALES	1978 MALES	FEMALES	STABLE POPULATION MALES	FEMALES
RATES PER THOUSAND											
Birth	21.72	22.67	20.81	23.86	21.81	25.47	23.26	26.50	24.24	25.99	24.5
Death	9.61	11.08	8.19	11.09	8.66	10.97	8.95	10.67	9.02	8.90	7.4
Increase	12.11	11.58	12.62	12.76	13.15	14.50	14.31	15.83	15.22		17.095
PERCENTAGE											
under 15	31.20	32.30	30.14	31.97	29.62	31.74	29.27	32.29	29.76	33.27	31.6
15-64	59.49	59.31	59.66	59.77	59.80	60.18	59.97	59.79	59.35	60.72	59.1
65 and over	9.31	8.39	10.20	8.26	10.58	8.08	10.77	7.92	10.89	6.02	8.5
DEP. RATIO X 100	68.09	68.60	67.61	67.31	67.22	66.17	66.76	67.24	68.49	64.70	67.3

AGE AT LAST BIRTHDAY	1968 BOTH SEXES	MALES	FEMALES	1973 BOTH SEXES	MALES	FEMALES	1978 BOTH SEXES	MALES	FEMALES	AGE AT LAST BIRTHDAY	
0-4	21145	10808	10337	23927	12230	11697	27085	13844	13241	0-4	
5-9	20667	10526	10141	21062	10761	10301	23832	12176	11656	5-9	
10-14	20033	10178	9855	20624	10500	10124	21018	10735	10283	10-14	
15-19	17977	9130	8847	19968	10134	9834	20558	10455	10103	15-19	**TABLE 5**
20-24	15382	7729	7653	17878	9059	8819	19858	10055	9803	20-24	POPULATION
25-29	12225	5961	6264	15281	7659	7622	17761	8977	8784	25-29	PROJECTED
30-34	10761	5278	5483	12136	5905	6231	15171	7588	7583	30-34	WITH
35-39	11173	5470	5703	10655	5214	5441	12017	5833	6184	35-39	FIXED
40-44	12099	5886	6213	11008	5370	5638	10497	5118	5379	40-44	AGE—
45-49	11931	5769	6162	11821	5714	6107	10754	5213	5541	45-49	SPECIFIC
50-54	10802	5219	5583	11496	5493	6003	11389	5441	5948	50-54	BIRTH
55-59	9666	4634	5032	10200	4830	5370	10857	5083	5774	55-59	AND
60-64	8126	3830	4296	8867	4123	4744	9359	4297	5062	60-64	DEATH
65-69	6597	3002	3595	7123	3205	3918	7777	3450	4327	65-69	RATES
70-74	5133	2210	2923	5427	2315	3112	5864	2473	3391	70-74	(IN 1000's)
75-79	3814	1588	2226	3857	1538	2319	4079	1611	2468	75-79	
80-84	2179	882	1297	2448	942	1506	2481	912	1569	80-84	
85+	1246	455	791	1490	529	961	1681	565	1116	85+	
TOTAL	200956	98555	102401	215268	105521	109747	232038	113826	118212	TOTAL	

STANDARD COUNTRIES: STANDARDIZED RATES PER THOUSAND	ENGLAND AND WALES 1961 BOTH SEXES	MALES	FEMALES	UNITED STATES 1960 BOTH SEXES	MALES	FEMALES	MEXICO 1960 BOTH SEXES	MALES	FEMALES	
Birth	21.18	24.65*	20.00	21.59	23.00*	20.72	26.08	21.58*	25.34	**TABLE 6**
Death	11.62	12.47*	10.78	9.54	11.10*	8.02	5.11	8.80*	4.01	STANDAR-DIZED RATES
Increase	9.56	12.18*	9.22	12.05	11.90*	12.70	20.97	12.78*	21.33	

	OBSERVED POP. MALES	FEMALES	STATIONARY POP. MALES	FEMALES	STABLE POP. MALES	FEMALES	OBSERVED BIRTHS	NET MATERNITY FUNCTION	BIRTHS IN STABLE POP.	
μ	30.83302	32.35349	36.23137	39.05196	28.32123	30.11712	26.14773	26.47319	25.87248	**TABLE 7**
σ^2	484.6250	510.4885	495.5256	556.2088	421.9453	477.5099	36.63560	34.12644	31.98213	MOMENTS
κ_3	5025.263	4887.649	2713.646	2318.496	5476.272	6336.438	146.0418	125.1370	125.1836	AND
κ_4	-196345.	-230630.	-228634.	-319253.	-85067.	-130666.	-210.115	-95.280	93.204	CUMULANTS
β_1	0.221871	0.179573	0.060521	0.031239	0.399210	0.368760	0.433755	0.394002	0.479041	
β_2	2.163996	2.114999	2.068872	1.968048	2.522196	2.426941	2.843451	2.918187	3.091122	
κ	-0.079190	-0.064225	-0.023500	-0.011485	-0.158970	-0.140144	-0.227711	-0.244390	-0.324033	

VITAL STATISTICS		THOMPSON AGE RANGE	NRR	1000r	INTERVAL	BOURGEOIS-PICHAT AGE RANGE	NRR	1000b	1000d	1000r	COALE	
GRR	1.624					5-29	2.23	26.99	-2.65	29.64	IBR	**TABLE 8** RATES FROM AGE DISTRI-BUTIONS AND VITAL STATISTICS (Females)
NRR	1.564	0-4	1.58	17.16	27.41	5-29	2.23	26.99	-2.65	29.64	IDR	
TFR	3.333	5-9	1.61	17.69	27.37	30-54	1.07	14.50	11.98	2.52	IRI	
GENERATION	26.170	10-14	1.48	14.14	27.31	55-79	1.41	22.41	9.79	12.62	K1	
SEX RATIO	105.272	15-19	1.30	9.23	27.21	*40-69	1.53	27.44	11.58	15.86	K2	

Start Age Interval	ORIGINAL MATRIX SUB-DIAGONAL	ALTERNATIVE FIRST ROWS Projection	Integral	FIRST STABLE MATRIX % IN STABLE POPULATION	FISHER VALUES	REPRODUCTIVE VALUES	SECOND STABLE MATRIX Z_2 FIRST COLUMN	FIRST ROW	
0	0.99649	0.00000	0.00000	11.511	1.068	10864633	0.1835+0.0923	0.1835+0.0923	**TABLE 9**
5	0.99829	0.00102	0.00000	10.529	1.167	11522043	0.1811-0.1610	-0.0152+0.1735	LESLIE
10	0.99789	0.09177	0.00213	9.648	1.273	11282960	-0.0977-0.2691	-0.1414+0.0422	MATRIX
15	0.99685	0.36527	0.18983	8.837	1.291	9912300	-0.3379-0.0102	-0.0943-0.1066	AND ITS
20	0.99602	0.49547	0.57442	8.086	1.020	6414186	-0.1584+0.3660	-0.0128-0.1415	SPECTRAL
25	0.99478	0.34690	0.46163	7.393	0.584	3221753	0.3320+0.3329	0.0162-0.1003	COMPO-NENTS
30	0.99237	0.18697	0.26385	6.750	0.268	1539226	0.5086-0.2185	0.0203-0.0509	(Females)
35	0.98858	0.07773	0.12739	6.149	0.093	583834	-0.0178-0.6498	0.0121-0.0173	
40	0.98284	0.01788	0.03527	5.580	0.018	115549	-0.7142-0.2615	0.0031-0.0032	
45	0.97411	0.00102	0.00208	5.034	0.001	5795	-0.5895+0.6597	0.0002-0.0002	
50	0.96186	0.00002	0.00004	4.501	0.000	96	0.4557+0.9124	0.0000-0.0000	
55+	0.81855			15.982					

Start Age Interval	OBSERVED POPUL. (IN 100's)	CONTRIBUTIONS OF ROOTS (IN 100's) r_1	r_2, r_3	$r_4 \cdot r_{11}$	AGE-SP. BIRTH RATES	NET MATERNITY FUNCTION	COEFF. OF MATRIX EQUATION	PARAMETERS INTEGRAL	MATRIX	EXP. INCREASE x	$e^{(x+2\frac{1}{2})r}$	
0	101770	100822	-773	1721	0.0000	0.0000	0.0000	L(1) 1.08924	1.08943	0	1.0437	**TABLE 10**
5	98720	92220	7182	-682	0.0000	0.0000	0.0010	L(2) 0.30025	0.31210	50	2.4535	AGE
10	88660	84505	7345	-3191	0.0004	0.0020	0.0913	0.81908	0.78520	55	2.6725	ANALYSIS
15	76770	77405	-3613	2978	0.0372	0.1806	0.3626	R(1) 0.01710	0.01713	60	2.9110	AND
20	62890	70827	-13383	5446	0.1126	0.5446	0.4903	R(2) -0.02731	-0.03369	65	3.1708	MISCEL-LANEOUS
25	55120	64754	-6630	-3004	0.0905	0.4360	0.3419	0.24389	-0.23849	70	3.4537	RESULTS
30	57470	59127	12807	-14464	0.0517	0.2479	0.1833	C(1)	875899	75	3.7619	(Females)
35	62850	53860	20279	-11288	0.0250	0.1188	0.0756	C(2)	582011	80	4.0976	
40	62700	48874	-71	13897	0.0069	0.0325	0.0172		1576283	85	4.4633	
45	57310	44092	-27658	40876	0.0004	0.0019	0.0010	2P/Y 25.7627	26.3454	90	4.8616	
50	52320	39424	-23460	36356	0.0000	0.0000	0.0000	DELTA 6.3552		95	5.2954	
55+	182830	139989								100	5.7680	

TABLE 1 — DATA

AGE AT LAST BIRTHDAY	POPULATION BOTH SEXES	MALES Number	%	FEMALES Number	%	BIRTHS BY AGE OF MOTHER	DEATHS BOTH SEXES	MALES	FEMALES	AGE AT LAST BIRTHDAY
0	4051000	2069000	2.2	1982000	2.0	0	99816	57368	42448	0
1-4	16640000	8486000	9.0	8154000	8.4	0	15981	8881	7100	1-4
5-9	20347000	10341000	11.0	10006000	10.3	0	9036	5314	3722	5-9
10-14	18436000	9371000	10.0	9065000	9.3	7816	7720	4926	2794	10-14
15-19	16233000	8188000	8.7	8045000	8.3	585710	15182	10792	4390	15-19
20-24	12825000	6279000	6.7	6546000	6.7	1439486	16305	11614	4691	20-24
25-29	11046000	5432000	5.8	5614000	5.8	1007362	14736	9799	4937	25-29
30-34	11066000	5434000	5.8	5632000	5.8	585006	18914	11754	7160	30-34
35-39	12109000	5916000	6.3	6193000	6.4	309814	29366	17804	11562	35-39
40-44	12352000	6007000	6.4	6345000	6.5	87626	45544	28027	17517	40-44
45-49	11313000	5517000	5.9	5796000	6.0	4670	65303	41098	24205	45-49
50-54	10420000	5084000	5.4	5336000	5.5	0	95402	61328	34074	50-54
55-59	9000000	4358000	4.6	4642000	4.8	0	124478	81835	42643	55-59
60-64	7675000	3653000	3.9	4022000	4.1	0	158668	102084	56584	60-64
65-69	6251000	2857000	3.0	3394000	3.5	0	196788	121225	75563	65-69
70-74	5154000	2289000	2.4	2865000	2.9		234254	135642	98612	70-74
75-79	3505000	1520000	1.6	1985000	2.0		238069	126801	111268	75-79
80-84	1911000	791000	0.8	1120000	1.2	2060162 M.	205208	97707	107501	80-84
85+	1035000	398000	0.4	637000	0.7	1967328 F.	207281	83779	123502	85+
TOTAL	191369000	93990000		97379000		4027490	1798051	1017778	780273	TOTAL

TABLE 2 — MALE LIFE TABLE

x	nq_x	l_x	nd_x	nL_x	nm_x	na_x	T_x	r_x	$\dot{e}_x$	nM_x
0	0.027146	100000	2715	97902	0.027727	0.2270	6690031	0.0000	66.900	0.027727
1	0.004173	97285	406	387958	0.001047	1.0855	6592130	0.0000	67.761	0.001047
5	0.002561	96879	248	483777	0.000513	2.5000	6204171	0.0112	64.040	0.000514
10	0.002644	96631	256	482599	0.000529	2.8181	5720394	0.0226	59.198	0.000526
15	0.006623	96376	638	480414	0.001329	2.7049	5237796	0.0388	54.348	0.001318
20	0.009226	95737	883	476523	0.001854	2.5504	4757382	0.0393	49.692	0.001850
25	0.008984	94854	852	472167	0.001805	2.5313	4280859	0.0126	45.131	0.001804
30	0.010760	94002	1011	467593	0.002163	2.6107	3808692	0.0000	40.517	0.002163
35	0.014942	92991	1389	461709	0.003009	2.6655	3341098	0.0000	35.929	0.003009
40	0.023089	91601	2115	453112	0.004668	2.6865	2879389	0.0021	31.434	0.004666
45	0.036681	89486	3282	439839	0.007463	2.6874	2426277	0.0089	27.113	0.007449
50	0.058784	86204	5067	419189	0.012089	2.6656	1986438	0.0111	23.044	0.012063
55	0.090098	81136	7310	388369	0.018823	2.6319	1567249	0.0139	19.316	0.018778
60	0.131311	73826	9694	345946	0.028022	2.6085	1178880	0.0164	15.968	0.027945
65	0.192694	64132	12358	290536	0.042535	2.5624	832933	0.0164	12.988	0.042431
70	0.258748	51774	13396	225565	0.059391	2.5139	542397	0.0164	10.476	0.059258
75	0.345253	38378	13250	158449	0.083623	2.4763	316833	0.0164	8.256	0.083422
80	0.473113	25128	11888	95915	0.123945	2.4998	158384	0.0164	6.303	0.123523
85+	*1.000000	13239	13239	62468	0.211938	4.7184	62468	0.0164	4.718	0.210500

TABLE 3 — FEMALE LIFE TABLE

x	nq_x	l_x	nd_x	nL_x	nm_x	na_x	T_x	r_x	$\dot{e}_x$	nM_x
0	0.021072	100000	2107	98388	0.021417	0.2351	7372302	0.0000	73.723	0.021417
1	0.003474	97893	340	390582	0.000871	1.0910	7273914	0.0000	74.305	0.000871
5	0.001853	97553	181	487312	0.000371	2.5000	6883332	0.0107	70.560	0.000372
10	0.001544	97372	150	486502	0.000309	2.6185	6396020	0.0214	65.686	0.000308
15	0.002739	97222	266	485484	0.000548	2.6547	5909518	0.0320	60.784	0.000546
20	0.003589	96955	348	483940	0.000719	2.5949	5424034	0.0353	55.944	0.000717
25	0.004396	96607	425	482030	0.000881	2.6283	4940094	0.0141	51.136	0.000879
30	0.006338	96183	610	479486	0.001271	2.6584	4458065	0.0000	46.350	0.001271
35	0.009294	95573	888	475789	0.001867	2.6618	3978578	0.0000	41.629	0.001867
40	0.013724	94685	1299	470394	0.002763	2.6679	3502789	0.0038	36.994	0.002761
45	0.020727	93385	1936	462418	0.004186	2.6705	3032396	0.0130	32.472	0.004176
50	0.031535	91450	2884	450468	0.006402	2.6487	2569978	0.0157	28.103	0.006386
55	0.045103	88566	3995	433447	0.009216	2.6513	2119510	0.0187	23.931	0.009186
60	0.068413	84571	5786	409303	0.014136	2.6575	1686062	0.0252	19.937	0.014069
65	0.106218	78786	8368	374145	0.022367	2.6360	1276759	0.0252	16.206	0.022264
70	0.159757	70417	11250	325274	0.034585	2.6167	902614	0.0252	12.818	0.034420
75	0.247749	59167	14672	260413	0.056342	2.5856	577340	0.0252	9.758	0.056054
80	0.388389	44495	17281	179209	0.096432	2.6512	316927	0.0252	7.123	0.095983
85+	1.000000	27214	27214	137718	0.197605	5.0606	137718	0.0252	5.061	0.193881

TABLE 4 — OBSERVED AND PROJECTED VITAL RATES

	OBSERVED POPULATION BOTH SEXES	MALES	FEMALES	PROJECTED POPULATION 1969 MALES	FEMALES	1974 MALES	FEMALES	1979 MALES	FEMALES	STABLE POPULATION MALES	FEMALES
RATES PER THOUSAND											
Birth	21.05	21.92	20.20	23.34	21.42	24.89	22.80	25.74	23.61	24.93	23.4
Death	9.40	10.83	8.01	10.96	8.56	10.88	8.87	10.61	8.96	9.23	7.7
Increase	11.65	11.09	12.19	12.38	12.85	14.00	13.93	15.13	14.65	15.703	
PERCENTAGE											
under 15	31.08	32.20	29.99	31.57	29.23	31.16	28.75	31.63	29.22	32.26	30.6
15-64	59.59	59.44	59.74	60.07	60.02	60.61	60.27	60.25	59.62	61.21	60.1
65 and over	9.33	8.36	10.27	8.35	10.74	8.23	10.98	8.12	11.16	6.53	9.2
DEP. RATIO X 100	67.81	68.24	67.40	66.46	66.60	64.99	65.93	55.97	67.73	63.37	66.3

AGE AT LAST BIRTHDAY	1969 BOTH SEXES	MALES	FEMALES	1974 BOTH SEXES	MALES	FEMALES	1979 BOTH SEXES	MALES	FEMALES	AGE AT LAST BIRTHDAY	
0-4	20903	10659	10244	23717	12094	11623	26680	13605	13075	0-4	**TABLE 5**
5-9	20612	10510	10102	20822	10613	10209	23626	12042	11584	5-9	POPULATION
10-14	20305	10316	9989	20569	10484	10085	20779	10587	10192	10-14	PROJECTED
15-19	18375	9329	9046	20237	10269	9968	20501	10437	10064	15-19	WITH
20-24	16141	8122	8019	18270	9253	9017	20123	10186	9937	20-24	FIXED
25-29	12742	6222	6520	16035	8047	7988	18150	9168	8982	25-29	AGE—
30-34	10963	5379	5584	12647	6161	6486	15915	7969	7946	30-34	SPECIFIC
35-39	10955	5366	5589	10853	5312	5541	12520	6084	6436	35-39	BIRTH
40-44	11929	5806	6123	10791	5266	5525	10691	5213	5478	40-44	AND
45-49	12068	5831	6237	11655	5636	6019	10543	5111	5432	45-49	DEATH
50-54	10904	5258	5646	11633	5557	6076	11234	5371	5863	50-54	RATES
55-59	9844	4710	5134	10304	4871	5433	10996	5149	5847	55-59	(IN 1000's)
60-64	8265	3882	4383	9044	4196	4848	9469	4339	5130	60-64	
65-69	6745	3068	3677	7267	3260	4007	7956	3524	4432	65-69	
70-74	5169	2218	2951	5578	2382	3196	6015	2531	3484	70-74	
75-79	3902	1608	2294	3920	1558	2362	4232	1673	2559	75-79	
80-84	2286	920	1366	2551	973	1578	2569	943	1626	80-84	
85+	1376	515	861	1649	599	1050	1847	634	1213	85+	
TOTAL	203484	99719	103765	217542	106531	111011	233846	114566	119280	TOTAL	

STANDARD COUNTRIES: STANDARDIZED RATES PER THOUSAND	ENGLAND AND WALES 1961 BOTH SEXES	MALES	FEMALES	UNITED STATES 1960 BOTH SEXES	MALES	FEMALES	MEXICO 1960 BOTH SEXES	MALES	FEMALES	
Birth	20.39	23.92*	19.30	20.78	22.21*	20.00	25.05	21.03*	24.41	**TABLE 6** STANDAR-DIZED RATES
Death	11.31	12.16*	10.44	9.29	10.84*	7.78	5.00	8.63*	3.91	
Increase	9.08	11.76*	8.86	11.49	11.37*	12.22	20.05	12.40*	20.50	

	OBSERVED POP. MALES	FEMALES	STATIONARY POP. MALES	FEMALES	STABLE POP. MALES	FEMALES	OBSERVED BIRTHS	NET MATERNITY FUNCTION	BIRTHS IN STABLE POP.	
μ	30.78450	32.38614	36.35730	39.19914	28.97963	30.87416	26.07459	26.52993	25.97443	**TABLE 7**
σ^2	484.1064	511.8785	500.0399	560.4503	432.5926	489.5886	36.48266	34.25606	32.32419	MOMENTS
κ_3	5141.085	4987.929	2785.031	2336.559	5446.570	6222.088	148.9456	122.4203	123.1643	AND
κ_4	-193333.	-231648.	-232216.	-324939.	-97737.	-150774.	-158.928	-133.165	43.186	CUMULANTS
β_1	0.232963	0.185498	0.062036	0.031013	0.366445	0.329897	0.456874	0.372816	0.449145	
β_2	2.175057	2.115913	2.071284	1.965507	2.477722	2.370980	2.880594	2.886521	3.041332	
κ	-0.082995	-0.066031	-0.024099	-0.011381	-0.145510	-0.124611	-0.241749	-0.230204	-0.299528	

VITAL STATISTICS		THOMPSON AGE RANGE	NRR	1000r	INTERVAL	BOURGEOIS-PICHAT AGE RANGE	NRR	1000b	1000d	1000r	COALE	
GRR	1.567											**TABLE 8** RATES FROM AGE DISTRI-BUTIONS AND VITAL STATISTICS (Females)
NRR	1.510	0-4	1.55	16.42	27.41	5-29	2.19	27.07	-2.02	29.09	IBR	
TFR	3.208	5-9	1.62	17.89	27.37	30-54	1.01	13.07	12.66	0.42	IDR	
GENERATION	26.250	10-14	1.51	14.79	27.31	55-79	1.43	23.39	10.06	13.33	K1	
SEX RATIO	104.719	15-19	1.35	10.72	27.22	*45-69	1.57	28.72	12.05	16.67	K2	

Start of Age Interval	ORIGINAL MATRIX SUB-DIAGONAL	ALTERNATIVE FIRST ROWS Projection	Integral	FIRST STABLE MATRIX % IN STABLE POPULATION	FISHER VALUES	REPRODUCTIVE VALUES	SECOND STABLE MATRIX Z₂ FIRST COLUMN	FIRST ROW	
0	0.99661	0.00000	0.00000	11.049	1.063	10778563	0.1803+0.0917	0.1803+0.0917	**TABLE 9** LESLIE MATRIX AND ITS SPECTRAL COMPO-NENTS (Females)
5	0.99834	0.00103	0.00000	10.178	1.154	11550323	0.1813-0.1571	-0.0143+0.1700	
10	0.99791	0.08779	0.00214	9.393	1.250	11329413	-0.0917-0.2699	-0.1372+0.0427	
15	0.99682	0.34873	0.18086	8.664	1.261	10147666	-0.3380-0.0199	-0.0927-0.1015	
20	0.99605	0.47607	0.54627	7.983	0.997	6525890	-0.1731+0.3625	-0.0133-0.1367	
25	0.99472	0.33769	0.44575	7.350	0.575	3225470	0.3207+0.3520	0.0164-0.0977	
30	0.99229	0.18333	0.25803	6.758	0.264	1486058	0.5291-0.1946	0.0204-0.0494	
35	0.98866	0.07605	0.12427	6.199	0.091	564823	0.0227-0.6654	0.0119-0.0167	
40	0.98304	0.01744	0.03431	5.665	0.018	114215	-0.7151-0.3199	0.0031-0.0030	
45	0.97416	0.00096	0.00200	5.147	0.001	5483	-0.6620+0.6338	0.0002-0.0002	
50	0.96222	0.00000	0.00000	4.635	0.000	1	0.3913+0.9878	0.0000-0.0000	
55+	0.81919			16.980					

Start of Age Interval	OBSERVED POPUL. (IN 100's)	CONTRIBUTIONS OF ROOTS (IN 100's) r_1	r_2, r_3	$r_4 \cdot r_{11}$	AGE-SP. BIRTH RATES	NET MATERNITY FUNCTION	COEFF. OF MATRIX EQUATION	PARAMETERS		INTEGRAL	MATRIX	EXP. INCREASE x	$e^{(x+2\frac{1}{2})r}$	
0	101360	101267	-1801	1894	0.0000	0.0000	0.0000	L(1)		1.08168	1.08184	0	1.0400	**TABLE 10**
5	100060	93288	7005	-234	0.0000	0.0000	0.0010	L(2)		0.30492	0.31672	50	2.2806	AGE ANALYSIS
10	90650	86088	8813	-4250	0.0004	0.0020	0.0874			0.81086	0.77826	55	2.4668	AND
15	80450	79408	-1995	3037	0.0356	0.1727	0.3462	R(1)		0.01570	0.01573	60	2.6683	MISCEL-LANEOUS
20	65460	73168	-14201	6493	0.1074	0.5198	0.4712	R(2)		-0.02870	-0.03481	65	2.8863	RESULTS
25	56140	67366	-9885	-1340	0.0877	0.4225	0.3329			0.24222	0.23686	70	3.1220	(Females)
30	56320	61941	11107	-16728	0.0507	0.2433	0.1798					75	3.3771	
35	61930	56813	23709	-18592	0.0244	0.1163	0.0740	C(1)			916549	80	3.6529	
40	63450	51920	5597	5933	0.0067	0.0317	0.0168	C(2)			399461	85	3.9513	
45	57960	47178	-27701	38482	0.0004	0.0018	0.0009				1768014	90	4.2740	
50	53360	42482	-31804	42681	0.0000	0.0000	0.0000	2P/Y		25.9398	26.5269	95	4.6231	
55+	186650	155630						DELTA		5.0924		100	5.0007	

With Adjusted Births

TABLE 5 — POPULATION PROJECTED WITH FIXED AGE—SPECIFIC BIRTH AND DEATH RATES (IN 1000's)

AGE AT LAST BIRTHDAY	1925 BOTH SEXES	MALES	FEMALES	1930 BOTH SEXES	MALES	FEMALES	1935 BOTH SEXES	MALES	FEMALES	AGE AT LAST BIRTHDAY
0-4	13428	6828	6600	13978	7108	6870	14556	7402	7154	0-4
5-9	11327	5727	5600	13050	6625	6425	13584	6896	6688	5-9
10-14	11334	5719	5615	11189	5653	5536	12890	6539	6351	10-14
15-19	10580	5334	5246	11170	5633	5537	11027	5568	5459	15-19
20-24	9344	4635	4709	10335	5212	5123	10912	5505	5407	20-24
25-29	9074	4444	4630	9072	4507	4565	10034	5068	4966	25-29
30-34	8826	4412	4414	8779	4305	4474	8778	4366	4412	30-34
35-39	7905	4039	3866	8509	4253	4256	8465	4150	4315	35-39
40-44	7499	3917	3582	7589	3872	3717	8169	4077	4092	40-44
45-49	6156	3186	2970	7147	3726	3421	7232	3683	3549	45-49
50-54	5470	2943	2527	5785	2988	2797	6717	3495	3222	50-54
55-59	4393	2342	2051	5021	2693	2328	5311	2734	2577	55-59
60-64	3215	1695	1520	3894	2066	1828	4450	2375	2075	60-64
65-69	2523	1327	1196	2695	1412	1283	3263	1721	1542	65-69
70-74	1616	836	780	1928	1006	922	2060	1071	989	70-74
75-79	943	472	471	1075	550	525	1283	662	621	75-79
80-84	471	227	244	508	250	258	579	292	287	80-84
85+	216	97	119	249	117	132	268	129	139	85+
TOTAL	114320	58180	56140	121973	61976	59997	129578	65733	63845	TOTAL

TABLE 6 — STANDARDIZED RATES

STANDARD COUNTRIES: STANDARDIZED RATES PER THOUSAND

	ENGLAND AND WALES 1961 BOTH SEXES	MALES	FEMALES	UNITED STATES 1960 BOTH SEXES	MALES	FEMALES	MEXICO 1960 BOTH SEXES	MALES	FEMALES
Birth	21.71	23.27*	20.45	22.11	21.76*	21.17	24.61	21.41*	23.86
Death	19.40	22.60*	20.94	16.90	18.82*	17.00	11.93	13.08*	11.39
Increase	2.31	0.67*	-0.49	5.20	2.94*	4.17	12.69	8.33*	12.48

TABLE 7 — MOMENTS AND CUMULANTS

	OBSERVED POP. MALES	FEMALES	STATIONARY POP. MALES	FEMALES	STABLE POP. MALES	FEMALES	OBSERVED BIRTHS	NET MATERNITY FUNCTION	BIRTHS IN STABLE POP.
μ	28.43515	27.84290	34.35172	34.71130	29.65638	29.92417	27.92920	28.41794	27.92815
σ^2	381.8306	378.6519	479.2225	488.5965	435.5680	443.9739	43.40241	46.45033	45.08604
κ_3	4057.570	4667.052	3358.735	3402.639	5022.661	5159.730	130.2674	127.2984	138.9343
κ_4	-76291.	-49547.	-204568.	-215877.	-117176.	-123710.	-896.315	-1247.366	-1015.389
β_1	0.295747	0.401204	0.102504	0.099261	0.305281	0.304216	0.207553	0.161689	0.210617
β_2	2.476721	2.654429	2.109233	2.095715	2.382373	2.372388	2.524190	2.421882	2.500485
κ	-0.127145	-0.179784	-0.039390	-0.037837	-0.119327	-0.118057	-0.106166	-0.078673	-0.104248

TABLE 8 — RATES FROM AGE DISTRIBUTIONS AND VITAL STATISTICS (Females)

VITAL STATISTICS		THOMPSON AGE RANGE	NRR	1000r	INTERVAL	BOURGEOIS-PICHAT AGE RANGE	NRR	1000b	1000d	1000r	COALE
GRR	1.642	0-4	1.22	7.28	27.04						IBR
NRR	1.334	5-9	1.30	9.86	26.96	5-29	1.21	25.17	18.25	6.92	IDR
TFR	3.378	10-14	1.33	10.61	26.89	30-54	1.77	39.63	18.48	21.14	IRI
GENERATION	28.172	15-19	1.36	11.04	26.76	55-79	1.92	43.67	19.51	24.16	K1
SEX RATIO	105.744					*35-74	2.01	49.27	23.34	25.93	K2

TABLE 9 — LESLIE MATRIX AND ITS SPECTRAL COMPONENTS (Females)

Start of Age Interval	ORIGINAL MATRIX SUB-DIAGONAL	ALTERNATIVE FIRST ROWS Projection	Integral	FIRST STABLE MATRIX % IN STABLE POPULATION	FISHER VALUES	REPRODUCTIVE VALUES	SECOND STABLE MATRIX Z2 FIRST COLUMN	FIRST ROW
0	0.97351	0.00000	0.00000	10.992	1.122	6455030	0.1277+0.0853	0.1277+0.0853
5	0.98854	0.00067	0.00000	10.166	1.213	6892094	0.1654-0.0812	-0.0081+0.1277
10	0.98610	0.06783	0.00139	9.548	1.291	6868452	0.0154-0.2240	-0.0941+0.0467
15	0.97653	0.25360	0.13973	8.945	1.301	6273534	-0.2262-0.1527	-0.0809-0.0536
20	0.96943	0.37263	0.38977	8.299	1.111	5305034	-0.2955+0.1433	-0.0283-0.1026
25	0.96640	0.33123	0.38663	7.643	0.775	3538029	-0.0289+0.3914	0.0133-0.0964
30	0.96432	0.24978	0.30318	7.018	0.459	1840749	0.3861+0.2636	0.0318-0.0601
35	0.96141	0.14663	0.21708	6.429	0.210	784236	0.5012-0.2400	0.0241-0.0243
40	0.95495	0.04922	0.08715	5.873	0.059	184406	0.0518-0.6565	0.0085-0.0057
45	0.94187	0.00706	0.01449	5.328	0.008	20199	-0.6379-0.4403	0.0012-0.0006
50	0.92151	0.00000	0.00000	4.768	0.000	1	-0.8136+0.3844	0.0000-0.0000
55+	0.75950			14.992				

TABLE 10 — AGE ANALYSIS AND MISCELLANEOUS RESULTS (Females)

Start of Age Interval	OBSERVED POPUL. (IN 100's)	CONTRIBUTIONS OF ROOTS (IN 100's) r_1	r_2, r_3	r_4-r_{11}	AGE-SP. BIRTH RATES	NET MATERNITY FUNCTION	COEFF. OF MATRIX EQUATION
0	57523	61025	-598	-2904	0.0000	0.0000	0.0000
5	56805	56441	-1909	2273	0.0000	0.0000	0.0006
10	53198	53009	-1460	1649	0.0003	0.0013	0.0653
15	48224	49662	1049	-2487	0.0298	0.1293	0.2407
20	47759	46074	3401	-1717	0.0831	0.3521	0.3453
25	45670	42435	2568	666	0.0825	0.3386	0.2976
30	40091	38962	-1773	2902	0.0647	0.2566	0.2169
35	37257	35696	-5750	7312	0.0463	0.1772	0.1228
40	31097	32604	-4336	2828	0.0186	0.0684	0.0396
45	26827	29581	2902	-5656	0.0031	0.0109	0.0054
50	22252	26470	9304	-13522	0.0000	0.0000	0.0000
55+	56133	83232					

PARAMETERS

	INTEGRAL	MATRIX
L(1)	1.05250	1.05256
L(2)	0.39802	0.40684
	-0.71925	0.70192
R(1)	0.01023	0.01025
R(2)	-0.03920	-0.04182
	0.21307	0.20910
C(1)		555190
C(2)		-431810
		-296140
2P/Y	29.4887	30.0486
DELTA	5.1544	

EXP. INCREASE

x	$e^{(x+2\frac{1}{2})r}$
0	1.0259
50	1.7113
55	1.8012
60	1.8957
65	1.9952
70	2.1000
75	2.2102
80	2.3263
85	2.4484
90	2.5769
95	2.7122
100	2.8546

With Adjusted Births

TABLE 5 — POPULATION PROJECTED WITH FIXED AGE-SPECIFIC BIRTH AND DEATH RATES (IN 1000's)

AGE AT LAST BIRTHDAY	1930 BOTH SEXES	1930 MALES	1930 FEMALES	1935 BOTH SEXES	1935 MALES	1935 FEMALES	1940 BOTH SEXES	1940 MALES	1940 FEMALES	AGE AT LAST BIRTHDAY
0-4	13729	6997	6732	14390	7334	7056	14971	7630	7341	0-4
5-9	12048	6114	5934	13430	6834	6596	14077	7163	6914	5-9
10-14	11973	6050	5923	11934	6051	5883	13304	6764	6540	10-14
15-19	11392	5713	5679	11832	5975	5857	11795	5977	5818	15-19
20-24	10580	5256	5324	11176	5605	5571	11608	5862	5746	20-24
25-29	9677	4810	4867	10334	5135	5199	10917	5477	5440	25-29
30-34	9123	4531	4592	9443	4693	4750	10084	5010	5074	30-34
35-39	9095	4572	4523	8856	4392	4464	9165	4548	4617	35-39
40-44	7781	3981	3800	8762	4394	4368	8532	4221	4311	40-44
45-49	7159	3734	3425	7428	3786	3642	8366	4179	4187	45-49
50-54	5911	3063	2848	6713	3483	3230	6965	3530	3435	50-54
55-59	4789	2514	2275	5427	2793	2634	6163	3176	2987	55-59
60-64	3853	2022	1831	4232	2200	2032	4796	2444	2352	60-64
65-69	2693	1376	1317	3200	1656	1544	3515	1802	1713	65-69
70-74	1919	974	945	2037	1022	1015	2420	1230	1190	70-74
75-79	1070	530	540	1269	628	641	1348	659	689	75-79
80-84	545	257	288	567	272	295	673	322	351	80-84
85+	131	61	70	155	73	82	163	78	85	85+
TOTAL	123468	62555	60913	131185	66326	64859	138862	70072	68790	TOTAL

TABLE 6 — STANDARDIZED RATES

STANDARD COUNTRIES: STANDARDIZED RATES PER THOUSAND	ENGLAND AND WALES 1961 BOTH SEXES	MALES	FEMALES	UNITED STATES 1960 BOTH SEXES	MALES	FEMALES	MEXICO 1960 BOTH SEXES	MALES	FEMALES
Birth	20.04	21.79*	18.87	20.42	20.36*	19.54	23.00	19.94*	22.29
Death	19.99	21.57*	21.57	17.03	17.99*	17.01	10.92	12.77*	10.26
Increase	0.06	0.21*	-2.70	3.38	2.38*	2.53	12.09	7.17*	12.04

TABLE 7 — MOMENTS AND CUMULANTS

	OBSERVED POP. MALES	OBSERVED POP. FEMALES	STATIONARY POP. MALES	STATIONARY POP. FEMALES	STABLE POP. MALES	STABLE POP. FEMALES	OBSERVED BIRTHS	NET MATERNITY FUNCTION	BIRTHS IN STABLE POP.
μ	28.74243	28.33446	34.20587	34.99589	30.14328	30.77896	27.68926	28.15574	27.72224
σ^2	386.2744	383.0256	465.6349	482.8190	431.3440	448.0443	44.31084	46.51126	45.25786
κ_3	3999.814	4444.906	3000.234	2957.495	4486.639	4628.090	132.2132	133.1849	143.9088
κ_4	-85338.	-64744.	-196965.	-219682.	-128877.	-146107.	-1028.546	-1292.563	-1069.953
β_1	0.277582	0.351594	0.089161	0.077713	0.250825	0.238145	0.200918	0.176293	0.223405
β_2	2.428063	2.558689	2.091558	2.057622	2.307329	2.272170	2.476154	2.402503	2.477632
κ	-0.116496	-0.152709	-0.034231	-0.029341	-0.097467	-0.091062	-0.098116	-0.082171	-0.105750

TABLE 8 — RATES FROM AGE DISTRIBUTIONS AND VITAL STATISTICS (Females)

VITAL STATISTICS		THOMPSON AGE RANGE	NRR	1000r	INTERVAL	BOURGEOIS-PICHAT AGE RANGE	NRR	1000b	1000d	1000r	COALE
GRR	1.515										IBR
NRR	1.287	0-4	1.21	7.01	27.14	5-29	1.28	24.88	15.60	9.27	IDR
TFR	3.119	5-9	1.30	9.64	27.06	30-54	1.84	40.83	18.15	22.68	IRI
GENERATION	27.938	10-14	1.35	11.05	26.97	55-79	1.99	47.50	21.93	25.57	K1
SEX RATIO	105.832	15-19	1.40	12.11	26.82	* 5-29	1.28	24.88	15.60	9.27	K2

TABLE 9 — LESLIE MATRIX AND ITS SPECTRAL COMPONENTS (Females)

Start Age Interval	ORIGINAL MATRIX SUB-DIAGONAL	ALTERNATIVE FIRST ROWS Projection	ALTERNATIVE FIRST ROWS Integral	FIRST STABLE MATRIX % IN STABLE POPULATION	FISHER VALUES	REPRODUCTIVE VALUES	SECOND STABLE MATRIX Z_2 FIRST COLUMN	SECOND STABLE MATRIX Z_2 FIRST ROW
0	0.97982	0.00000	0.00000	10.357	1.101	6668714	0.1233+0.0877	0.1233+0.0877
5	0.99150	0.00074	0.00000	9.699	1.176	7024536	0.1687-0.0772	-0.0117+0.1229
10	0.98889	0.07087	0.00153	9.191	1.240	7121149	0.0216-0.2291	-0.0906+0.0413
15	0.98102	0.25321	0.14506	8.687	1.233	6691430	-0.2322-0.1649	-0.0743-0.0531
20	0.97644	0.35816	0.38015	8.145	1.031	5137298	-0.3177+0.1457	-0.0247-0.0967
25	0.97606	0.30260	0.36104	7.602	0.701	3296092	-0.0398+0.4252	0.0132-0.0892
30	0.97201	0.22483	0.26432	7.092	0.410	1905636	0.4255+0.3016	0.0304-0.0543
35	0.96583	0.13362	0.20125	6.589	0.186	732233	0.5763-0.2650	0.0227-0.0209
40	0.95859	0.04178	0.07465	6.082	0.049	176090	0.0707-0.7632	0.0073-0.0045
45	0.94303	0.00551	0.01127	5.572	0.006	17520	-0.7505-0.5309	0.0009-0.0004
50	0.92481	0.00000	0.00000	5.023	0.000	1	-0.9852+0.4540	0.0000-0.0000
55+	0.75526			15.962				

TABLE 10 — AGE ANALYSIS AND MISCELLANEOUS RESULTS (Females)

Start Age Interval	OBSERVED POPUL. (IN 100's)	CONTRIBUTIONS OF ROOTS (IN 100's) r_1	r_2, r_3	$r_4 \cdot r_{11}$	AGE-SP. BIRTH RATES	NET MATERNITY FUNCTION	COEFF. OF MATRIX EQUATION	PARAMETERS	INTEGRAL	MATRIX	EXP. INCREASE x	$e^{(x+8\frac{1}{2})r}$
0	60560	63633	-952	-2121	0.0000	0.0000	0.0000	L(1)	1.04622	1.04626	0	1.0228
5	59740	59592	-1427	1575	0.0000	0.0000	-0.0007	L(2)	0.38970	0.39941	50	1.6070
10	57430	56473	-322	1279	0.0003	0.0015	0.0689		0.70865	0.69227	55	1.6813
15	54270	53376	1792	-898	0.0305	0.1362	0.2433	R(1)	0.00904	0.00904	60	1.7590
20	49840	50048	2687	-2895	0.0800	0.3503	0.3376	R(2)	-0.04246	-0.04482	65	1.8403
25	47050	46708	594	-251	0.0760	0.3248	0.2785		0.21350	0.20950	70	1.9253
30	46530	43574	-3285	6241	0.0556	0.2321	0.2019	C(1)		614421	75	2.0143
35	39340	40481	-4875	3733	0.0424	0.1718	0.1167	C(2)		-408393	80	2.1074
40	35730	37369	-1060	-579	0.0157	0.0615	0.0352			-31624	85	2.2048
45	30200	34238	5794	-9832	0.0024	0.0089	0.0045	2P/Y	29.4151	29.9916	90	2.3067
50	24600	30860	8334	-14594	0.0000	0.0000	0.0000	DELTA	5.6310		95	2.4133
55+	64870	98071									100	2.5248

With Adjusted Births

AGE AT LAST BIRTHDAY	1935 BOTH SEXES	1935 MALES	1935 FEMALES	1940 BOTH SEXES	1940 MALES	1940 FEMALES	1945 BOTH SEXES	1945 MALES	1945 FEMALES	AGE AT LAST BIRTHDAY	
0-4	12158	6193	5965	12682	6460	6222	13040	6642	6398	0-4	**TABLE 5**
5-9	11176	5661	5515	11926	6066	5860	12441	6328	6113	5-9	POPULATI*
10-14	12470	6308	6162	11081	5608	5473	11825	6009	5816	10-14	PROJECTE
15-19	11907	6014	5893	12340	6237	6103	10964	5544	5420	15-19	WITH
20-24	11376	5666	5710	11704	5907	5797	12129	6126	6003	20-24	FIXED
25-29	10670	5237	5433	11136	5543	5593	11457	5778	5679	25-29	AGE—
30-34	9643	4761	4882	10419	5109	5310	10874	5407	5467	30-34	SPECIFIC
35-39	8905	4444	4461	9379	4622	4757	10134	4960	5174	35-39	BIRTH
40-44	8886	4498	4388	8597	4275	4322	9056	4447	4609	40-44	AND
45-49	7670	3947	3723	8486	4273	4213	8211	4061	4150	45-49	DEATH
50-54	6651	3442	3209	7207	3682	3525	7976	3986	3990	50-54	RATES
55-59	5507	2856	2651	6100	3125	2975	6611	3343	3268	55-59	(IN 1000's)
60-64	4145	2135	2010	4871	2493	2378	5395	2727	2668	60-64	
65-69	3159	1606	1553	3463	1753	1710	4070	2047	2023	65-69	
70-74	2136	1068	1068	2415	1200	1215	2648	1310	1338	70-74	
75-79	1310	647	663	1426	693	733	1612	778	834	75-79	
80-84	609	291	318	709	338	371	773	362	411	80-84	
85+	295	130	165	330	148	182	386	173	213	85+	
TOTAL	128673	64904	63769	134271	67532	66739	139602	70028	69574	TOTAL	

STANDARD COUNTRIES:

STANDARDIZED RATES PER THOUSAND	ENGLAND AND WALES 1961 BOTH SEXES	MALES	FEMALES	UNITED STATES 1960 BOTH SEXES	MALES	FEMALES	MEXICO 1960 BOTH SEXES	MALES	FEMALES	
Birth	16.34	18.26*	15.41	16.66	16.98*	15.97	18.95	16.63*	18.39	**TABLE 6**
Death	18.06	19.81*	18.82	15.39	16.73*	14.87	10.03	12.43*	9.21	STANDAR-DIZED RATES
Increase	-1.71	-1.55*	-3.41	1.27	0.25*	1.10	8.92	4.20*	9.18	

	OBSERVED POP. MALES	FEMALES	STATIONARY POP. MALES	FEMALES	STABLE POP. MALES	FEMALES	OBSERVED BIRTHS	NET MATERNITY FUNCTION	BIRTHS IN STABLE POP.	
μ	29.58275	29.29107	34.38025	35.53259	33.20750	34.29773	27.39589	27.90341	27.78486	**TABLE 7**
σ^2	392.2170	389.6533	471.2374	495.9271	462.6904	487.4361	43.85160	45.30408	44.96069	MOMENTS*
κ_3	3946.491	4354.501	3164.924	3102.909	3635.624	3652.504	145.9566	135.4179	138.0756	AND
κ_4	-91458.	-71945.	-196012.	-228063.	-178563.	-209238.	-911.549	-1081.837	-1024.667	CUMULAN*
β_1	0.258133	0.320510	0.095721	0.078938	0.133440	0.115194	0.252634	0.197215	0.209766	
β_2	2.405475	2.526148	2.117320	2.072701	2.165914	2.119346	2.525967	2.472907	2.493106	
κ	-0.108545	-0.140177	-0.037315	-0.030148	-0.052085	-0.044052	-0.120963	-0.096483	-0.103076	

VITAL STATISTICS		THOMPSON AGE RANGE	NRR	1000r	INTERVAL	BOURGEOIS-PICHAT AGE RANGE	NRR	1000b	1000d	1000r	COALE	
GRR	1.239										IBR	**TABLE 8** RATES FROM AGE DISTRI-BUTIONS AND VITAL STATISTICS (Females)
NRR	1.072	0-4	1.05	1.89	27.17	5-29	1.22	23.73	16.31	7.42	IDR	
TFR	2.547	5-9	1.26	8.54	27.10	30-54	1.59	32.38	15.31	17.07	IRI	
GENERATION	27.844	10-14	1.31	9.85	27.00	55-79	1.82	39.06	16.94	22.13	K1	
SEX RATIO	105.570	15-19	1.39	11.90	26.86	*45-69	2.00	48.85	23.22	25.63	K2	

Start of Age Interval	ORIGINAL MATRIX SUB-DIAGONAL	ALTERNATIVE FIRST ROWS Projection	Integral	% IN STABLE POPULATION	FISHER VALUES	REPRODUCTIVE VALUES	SECOND STABLE MATRIX Z2 FIRST COLUMN	FIRST ROW	
0	0.98252	0.00000	0.00000	8.359	1.076	6041012	0.1275+0.0856	0.1275+0.0856	**TABLE 9**
5	0.99242	0.00066	0.00000	8.110	1.109	6888287	0.1738-0.0854	-0.0083+0.1215	LESLIE
10	0.99033	0.06223	0.00134	7.948	1.131	6731568	0.0164-0.2461	-0.0860+0.0419	MATRIX
15	0.98367	0.21555	0.12512	7.773	1.089	6321083	-0.2606-0.1743	-0.0704-0.0475	AND ITS
20	0.97954	0.29942	0.31383	7.551	0.885	4909532	-0.3549+0.1751	-0.0232-0.0859	SPECTRAL
25	0.97750	0.25344	0.29481	7.304	0.586	2927630	-0.0321+0.4964	0.0110-0.0763	COMPO-NENTS
30	0.97440	0.17991	0.22021	7.051	0.328	1502242	0.5194+0.3459	0.0240-0.0450	(Females)
35	0.96885	0.09973	0.14559	6.784	0.142	644514	0.6991-0.3467	0.0172-0.0171	
40	0.96023	0.03201	0.05690	6.491	0.038	147104	0.0607-0.9684	0.0057-0.0037	
45	0.94695	0.00389	0.00783	6.155	0.004	14017	-0.9965-0.6608	0.0007-0.0003	
50	0.92694	0.00000	0.00000	5.756	0.000	1	-1.3005+0.6481	0.0000-0.0000	
55+	0.75513			20.719					

CONTRIBUTIONS OF ROOTS (IN 100's)

Start of Age Interval	OBSERVED POPUL. (IN 100's)	r_1	r_2, r_3	$r_4 \cdot r_{11}$	AGE-SP. BIRTH RATES	NET MATERNITY FUNCTION	COEFF. OF MATRIX EQUATION	PARAMETERS INTEGRAL	MATRIX	EXP. INCREASE x	$e^{(x+2\frac{1}{2})r}$	
0	56127	60436	-2357	-1953	0.0000	0.0000	0.0000	L(1) 1.01263	1.01264	0	1.0063	**TABLE 10**
5	62095	58639	-336	3793	0.0000	0.0000	0.0007	L(2) 0.37913	0.38917	50	1.1409	AGE ANALYSIS
10	59509	57468	3357	-1317	0.0003	0.0013	0.0607	0.69126	0.67508	55	1.1553	AND
15	58044	56203	4806	-2965	0.0266	0.1201	0.2081	R(1) 0.00251	0.00251	60	1.1699	MISCEL-LANEOUS
20	55460	54595	674	190	0.0667	0.2962	0.2844	R(2) -0.04755	-0.04989	65	1.1847	RESULTS
25	49947	52811	-6780	3917	0.0627	0.2726	0.2358	0.21383	0.20957	70	1.1997	(Females)
30	45779	50978	-9560	4360	0.0468	0.1990	0.1636	C(1)	723043	75	1.2148	
35	45291	49054	-1305	-2458	0.0310	0.1282	0.0884	C(2)	-446249	80	1.2302	
40	38770	46932	13243	-21405	0.0121	0.0485	0.0275		711746	85	1.2457	
45	33889	44503	18300	-28915	0.0017	0.0064	0.0032	2P/Y 29.3844	29.9814	90	1.2614	
50	28596	41616	2382	-15402	0.0000	0.0000	0.0000	DELTA 10.2652		95	1.2774	
55+	74066	149807								100	1.2935	

With Adjusted Births

AGE AT LAST BIRTHDAY	1940 BOTH SEXES	MALES	FEMALES	1945 BOTH SEXES	MALES	FEMALES	1950 BOTH SEXES	MALES	FEMALES	AGE AT LAST BIRTHDAY	
0-4	11326	5765	5561	11719	5965	5754	11772	5992	5780	0-4	**TABLE 5**
5-9	10009	5059	4950	11145	5665	5480	11532	5862	5670	5-9	POPULATION
10-14	11702	5957	5745	9935	5018	4917	11063	5619	5444	10-14	PROJECTED
15-19	12313	6198	6115	11598	5898	5700	9847	4968	4879	15-19	WITH
20-24	11649	5799	5850	12141	6103	6038	11435	5808	5627	20-24	FIXED
25-29	11119	5495	5624	11443	5690	5753	11928	5990	5938	25-29	AGE—
30-34	10349	5097	5252	10898	5378	5520	11217	5570	5647	30-34	SPECIFIC
35-39	9477	4687	4790	10093	4958	5135	10629	5232	5397	35-39	BIRTH
40-44	8693	4343	4350	9181	4522	4659	9777	4783	4994	40-44	AND
45-49	8378	4239	4139	8334	4137	4197	8804	4308	4496	45-49	DEATH
50-54	7251	3721	3530	7893	3957	3936	7854	3862	3992	50-54	RATES
55-59	5999	3077	2922	6682	3386	3296	7276	3601	3675	55-59	(IN 1000's)
60-64	4837	2457	2380	5342	2694	2648	5954	2966	2988	60-64	
65-69	3627	1815	1812	4073	2024	2049	4500	2220	2280	65-69	
70-74	2502	1234	1268	2798	1362	1436	3143	1519	1624	70-74	
75-79	1497	719	778	1708	813	895	1910	897	1013	75-79	
80-84	834	386	448	864	395	469	985	446	539	80-84	
85+	279	120	159	341	147	194	353	150	203	85+	
TOTAL	131841	66168	65673	136188	68112	68076	139979	69793	70186	TOTAL	

STANDARD COUNTRIES: STANDARDIZED RATES PER THOUSAND	ENGLAND AND WALES 1961 BOTH SEXES	MALES	FEMALES	UNITED STATES 1960 BOTH SEXES	MALES	FEMALES	MEXICO 1960 BOTH SEXES	MALES	FEMALES	
Birth	14.42	16.18*	13.61	14.71	15.04*	14.11	16.93	14.77*	16.45	**TABLE 6**
Death	17.38	18.35*	17.91	14.77	15.64*	14.06	9.29	12.33*	8.35	STANDARDIZED RATES
Increase	-2.96	-2.17*	-4.30	-0.06	-0.60*	0.05	7.64	2.43*	8.10	

	OBSERVED POP. MALES	FEMALES	STATIONARY POP. MALES	FEMALES	STABLE POP. MALES	FEMALES	OBSERVED BIRTHS	NET MATERNITY FUNCTION	BIRTHS IN STABLE POP.	
μ	30.70353	30.60297	34.59946	36.04440	35.14934	36.62892	27.12490	27.60832	27.66201	**TABLE 7**
σ^2	398.0641	397.8096	471.9101	501.8267	475.2811	505.0073	42.12544	44.07524	44.23991	MOMENTS
κ_3	3713.684	4061.719	3021.170	2880.877	2784.269	2596.759	151.9012	142.3629	141.2982	AND
κ_4	-103923.	-89554.	-200480.	-240997.	-207513.	-248301.	-598.149	-898.508	-924.915	CUMULANTS
β_1	0.218651	0.262056	0.086851	0.065673	0.072206	0.052356	0.308666	0.236706	0.230585	
β_2	2.344151	2.434104	2.099770	2.043018	2.081361	2.026395	2.662930	2.537478	2.527422	
κ	-0.090981	-0.112698	-0.033666	-0.024802	-0.027986	-0.019771	-0.159013	-0.117557	-0.114245	

VITAL STATISTICS		THOMPSON AGE RANGE	NRR	1000r	INTERVAL	BOURGEOIS-PICHAT AGE RANGE	NRR	1000b	1000d	1000r	COALE	
GRR	1.096										IBR	**TABLE 8**
NRR	0.968	0-4	0.91	-3.25	27.23	5-29	1.07	21.01	18.57	2.44	IDR	RATES FROM AGE
TFR	2.250	5-9	1.13	4.42	27.15	30-54	1.50	29.52	14.57	14.94	IRI	DISTRIBUTIONS
GENERATION	27.635	10-14	1.29	9.44	27.06	55-79	2.00	51.55	25.86	25.69	K1	AND VITAL STATISTICS
SEX RATIO	105.324	15-19	1.35	10.77	26.92	*40-64	1.86	43.56	20.65	22.91	K2	(Females)

Start Age Interval	ORIGINAL MATRIX SUB-DIAGONAL	ALTERNATIVE FIRST ROWS Projection	Integral	FIRST STABLE MATRIX % IN STABLE POPULATION	FISHER VALUES	REPRODUCTIVE VALUES	SECOND STABLE MATRIX Z_2 FIRST COLUMN	FIRST ROW	
0	0.98537	0.00000	0.00000	7.223	1.060	5326836	0.1293+0.0885	0.1293+0.0885	**TABLE 9**
5	0.99348	0.00066	0.00000	7.159	1.070	6187819	0.1817-0.0890	-0.0103+0.1209	LESLIE
10	0.99212	0.05832	0.00133	7.154	1.070	6596004	0.0158-0.2628	-0.0848+0.0389	MATRIX
15	0.98726	0.20179	0.11588	7.138	1.010	5984291	-0.2872-0.1862	-0.0658-0.0472	AND ITS
20	0.98355	0.27549	0.29024	7.089	0.800	4576445	-0.3927+0.2045	-0.0197-0.0803	SPECTRAL
25	0.98147	0.22296	0.26348	7.013	0.512	2739658	-0.0201+0.5702	0.0105-0.0688	COMPONENTS
30	0.97770	0.15227	0.18457	6.923	0.278	1360570	0.6253+0.3838	0.0212-0.0394	(Females)
35	0.97266	0.08255	0.12181	6.808	0.117	524342	0.8226-0.4547	0.0148-0.0145	
40	0.96498	0.02502	0.04403	6.660	0.030	127987	0.0125-1.1978	0.0047-0.0030	
45	0.95096	0.00305	0.00608	6.464	0.003	12069	-1.3100-0.7601	0.0006-0.0003	
50	0.93379	0.00000	0.00000	6.183	0.000	1	-1.6285+0.9535	0.0000-0.0000	
55+	0.75551			24.187					

Start Age Interval	OBSERVED POPUL. (IN 100's)	CONTRIBUTIONS OF ROOTS (IN 100's) r_1	r_2, r_3	$r_4 \cdot r_{11}$	AGE-SP. BIRTH RATES	NET MATERNITY FUNCTION	COEFF. OF MATRIX EQUATION	PARAMETERS INTEGRAL	MATRIX	EXP. INCREASE x	$e^{(x+2\frac{1}{2})r}$	
0	50230	56975	-3739	-3005	0.0000	0.0000	0.0000	L(1) 0.99421	0.99421	0	0.9971	**TABLE 10**
5	57830	56468	-2292	3654	0.0000	0.0000	0.0007	L(2) 0.36496	0.37614	50	0.9409	AGE
10	61640	56426	3344	1870	0.0003	0.0013	0.0571	0.68011	0.66409	55	0.9354	ANALYSIS
15	59250	56308	8163	-5220	0.0247	0.1129	0.1960	R(1) -0.00116	-0.00116	60	0.9300	AND
20	57180	55914	4785	-3519	0.0619	0.2791	0.2642	R(2) -0.05179	-0.05404	65	0.9246	MISCELLANEOUS
25	53510	55314	-7530	5725	0.0562	0.2492	0.2103	0.21566	0.21109	70	0.9193	RESULTS
30	48990	54605	-17474	11858	0.0394	0.1713	0.1409	C(1)	788790	75	0.9139	(Females)
35	44720	53698	-9659	681	0.0260	0.1106	0.0747	C(2)	-970935	80	0.9087	
40	42890	52534	16394	-26038	0.0094	0.0389	0.0220		694431	85	0.9034	
45	37120	50989	35994	-49864	0.0013	0.0052	0.0026	2P/Y 29.1352	29.7653	90	0.8982	
50	31290	48771	18380	-35861	0.0000	0.0000	0.0000	DELTA 12.2596		95	0.8930	
55+	86760	190787								100	0.8878	

With Adjusted Births

AGE AT LAST BIRTHDAY	BOTH SEXES	1945 MALES	FEMALES	BOTH SEXES	1950 MALES	FEMALES	BOTH SEXES	1955 MALES	FEMALES	AGE AT LAST BIRTHDAY	
0-4	12334	6288	6046	12455	6350	6105	12181	6210	5971	0-4	**TABLE 5**
5-9	10553	5356	5197	12205	6216	5989	12324	6277	6047	5-9	
10-14	10661	5404	5257	10499	5325	5174	12143	6180	5963	10-14	POPULATI●
15-19	11616	5881	5735	10590	5363	5227	10429	5285	5144	15-19	PROJECTE●
20-24	12133	6054	6079	11493	5811	5682	10479	5299	5180	20-24	WITH
25-29	11316	5478	5838	11973	5964	6009	11343	5725	5618	25-29	FIXED
30-34	10832	5252	5580	11145	5386	5759	11792	5864	5928	30-34	AGE—
35-39	10051	4945	5106	10627	5141	5486	10934	5272	5662	35-39	SPECIFIC
40-44	9312	4603	4709	9795	4802	4993	10356	4992	5364	40-44	BIRTH
45-49	8499	4244	4255	8981	4413	4568	9447	4604	4843	45-49	AND
50-54	7844	3958	3886	8065	3989	4076	8524	4148	4376	50-54	DEATH
55-59	6749	3437	3312	7269	3615	3654	7475	3643	3832	55-59	RATES
60-64	5272	2662	2610	6043	3017	3026	6511	3173	3338	60-64	(IN 1000's)
65-69	4051	2002	2049	4490	2210	2280	5149	2505	2644	65-69	
70-74	3002	1448	1554	3184	1524	1660	3530	1683	1847	70-74	
75-79	1781	847	934	2067	959	1108	2193	1009	1184	75-79	
80-84	855	390	465	1004	452	552	1166	512	654	80-84	
85+	441	188	253	485	204	281	570	236	334	85+	
TOTAL	137302	68437	68865	142370	70741	71629	146546	72617	73929	TOTAL	

STANDARD COUNTRIES:	ENGLAND AND WALES 1961 BOTH SEXES	MALES	FEMALES	UNITED STATES 1960 BOTH SEXES	MALES	FEMALES	MEXICO 1960 BOTH SEXES	MALES	FEMALES	
STANDARDIZED RATES PER THOUSAND										**TABLE 6**
Birth	14.77	17.09*	13.94	15.08	15.94*	14.46	17.66	15.54*	17.14	STANDAR-
Death	15.59	16.23*	15.84	13.06	13.96*	12.20	7.93	11.15*	7.00	DIZED
Increase	-0.81	0.86*	-1.90	2.02	1.97*	2.26	9.72	4.38*	10.14	RATES

	OBSERVED POP. MALES	FEMALES	STATIONARY POP. MALES	FEMALES	STABLE POP. MALES	FEMALES	OBSERVED BIRTHS	NET MATERNITY FUNCTION	BIRTHS IN STABLE POP.	
μ	31.59886	31.65585	35.14553	36.79890	34.69482	36.31532	26.75937	27.17640	27.13623	**TABLE 7**
σ^2	409.3749	408.6099	478.9875	513.7564	476.1473	511.0474	38.52707	40.54183	40.41502	MOMENTS
κ_3	3493.385	3802.147	2912.079	2750.871	3105.945	2989.281	135.7462	134.1113	134.6197	AND
κ_4	-117810.	-103040.	-208355.	-255743.	-202433.	-249418.	-327.440	-541.708	-525.455	CUMULAN●
β_1	0.177881	0.211900	0.077167	0.055804	0.089364	0.066950	0.322224	0.269911	0.274529	
β_2	2.297026	2.382855	2.091854	2.031078	2.107108	2.044993	2.779403	2.670422	2.678301	
κ	-0.074333	-0.092273	-0.030022	-0.021081	-0.034767	-0.025293	-0.188276	-0.149623	-0.152532	

VITAL STATISTICS		THOMPSON AGE RANGE	NRR	1000r	INTERVAL	BOURGEOIS-PICHAT AGE RANGE	NRR	1000b	1000d	1000r	COALE	
GRR	1.125										IBR	**TABLE 8**
NRR	1.026	0-4	0.93	-2.56	27.30	5-29	0.88	17.28	22.03	-4.75	IDR	RATES FROM AGE
TFR	2.312	5-9	1.00	-0.16	27.23	30-54	1.44	27.22	13.84	13.38	IRI	DISTRI- BUTIONS
GENERATION	27.156	10-14	1.16	5.44	27.14	55-79	1.81	40.86	18.92	21.94	K1	AND VITAL
SEX RATIO	105.434	15-19	1.34	10.44	27.01	*25-49	1.40	26.45	13.90	12.55	K2	STATISTIC● (Females)

Start of Age Interval	ORIGINAL MATRIX SUB-DIAGONAL	ALTERNATIVE FIRST ROWS Projection	Integral	% IN STABLE POPULATION	FISHER VALUES	REPRODUCTIVE VALUES	SECOND STABLE MATRIX Z₂ FIRST COLUMN	FIRST ROW	
0	0.99047	0.00000	0.00000	7.485	1.054	5532273	0.1454+0.0913	0.1454+0.0913	**TABLE 9**
5	0.99567	0.00078	0.00000	7.379	1.070	5647930	0.1891-0.1117	-0.0113+0.1336	LESLIE
10	0.99424	0.06368	0.00156	7.312	1.079	6220685	-0.0161-0.2821	-0.0964+0.0398	MATRIX
15	0.99092	0.22046	0.12683	7.236	1.022	6271707	-0.3316-0.1478	-0.0713-0.0584	AND ITS
20	0.98859	0.29957	0.31801	7.136	0.802	4736300	-0.3629+0.2905	-0.0174-0.0907	SPECTRA●
25	0.98644	0.23730	0.28581	7.022	0.496	2803340	0.1171+0.5821	0.0128-0.0723	COMPO-
30	0.98314	0.14878	0.19253	6.894	0.251	1304159	0.7278+0.2077	0.0200-0.0391	NENTS
35	0.97788	0.07107	0.10755	6.746	0.097	467463	0.6585-0.7005	0.0126-0.0139	(Females)
40	0.97005	0.01992	0.03572	6.565	0.023	101332	-0.4049-1.1454	0.0038-0.0028	
45	0.95796	0.00217	0.00434	6.339	0.002	9226	-1.5085-0.2075	0.0004-0.0002	
50	0.94010	0.00000	0.00000	6.044	0.000	1	-1.0846+1.5414	0.0000-0.0000	
55+	0.76644			23.843					

Start of Age Interval	OBSERVED POPUL. (IN 100's)	CONTRIBUTIONS OF ROOTS (IN 100's) r_1	r_2, r_3	$r_4 \cdot r_{11}$	AGE-SP. BIRTH RATES	NET MATERNITY FUNCTION	COEFF. OF MATRIX EQUATION	PARAMETERS INTEGRAL	MATRIX	EXP. INCREASE x	$e^{(x+2\frac{1}{2})r}$	
0	52466	57843	-2756	-2620	0.0000	0.0000	0.0000	L(1) 1.00473	1.00473	0	1.0024	**TABLE 1●**
5	52803	57021	-5520	1302	0.0000	0.0000	0.0008	L(2) 0.34261	0.35497	50	1.0508	AGE
10	57677	56507	-1977	3147	0.0003	0.0015	0.0628	0.70760	0.68772	55	1.0558	ANALYSIS
15	61345	55917	6794	-1367	0.0266	0.1241	0.2162	R(1) 0.00094	0.00094	60	1.0608	AND
20	59053	55149	11231	-7326	0.0667	0.3083	0.2911	R(2) -0.04811	-0.05126	65	1.0658	MISCEL-
25	56564	54263	2048	253	0.0600	0.2739	0.2279	0.22398	-0.21886	70	1.0708	LANEOUS
30	51931	53275	-15890	14547	0.0404	0.1820	0.1410	C(1)	772789	75	1.0759	RESULTS
35	48155	52130	-21834	17859	0.0226	0.0999	0.0662	C(2)	-1211466	80	1.0810	(Females)●
40	43862	50737	199	-7073	0.0075	0.0325	0.0181		-419529	85	1.0861	
45	40569	48986	34808	-43224	0.0009	0.0038	0.0019	2P/Y 28.0529	28.7084	90	1.0912	
50	35233	46705	39213	-50686	0.0000	0.0000	0.0000	DELTA 9.7479		95	1.0964	
55+	98451	184256								100	1.1016	

United States 1944–46
With Adjusted Births

AGE AT LAST BIRTHDAY	BOTH SEXES	1950 MALES	FEMALES	BOTH SEXES	1955 MALES	FEMALES	BOTH SEXES	1960 MALES	FEMALES	AGE AT LAST BIRTHDAY	
0-4	14634	7479	7155	14403	7361	7042	14186	7250	6936	0-4	
5-9	13045	6644	6401	14521	7415	7106	14291	7298	6993	5-9	
10-14	11299	5748	5551	12990	6611	6379	14459	7378	7081	10-14	
15-19	10588	5361	5227	11234	5708	5526	12915	6564	6351	15-19	TABLE 5
20-24	10691	4974	5717	10462	5270	5192	11100	5611	5489	20-24	POPULATION
25-29	8906	2855	6051	10529	4861	5668	10297	5150	5147	25-29	PROJECTED
30-34	8907	3102	5805	8792	2803	5989	10382	4772	5610	30-34	WITH
35-39	10133	4596	5537	8768	3043	5725	8657	2750	5907	35-39	FIXED
40-44	9550	4514	5036	9911	4477	5434	8583	2964	5619	40-44	AGE—
45-49	9027	4412	4615	9250	4343	4907	9601	4307	5294	45-49	SPECIFIC
50-54	8115	3996	4119	8607	4161	4446	8823	4096	4727	50-54	BIRTH
55-59	7343	3639	3704	7573	3668	3905	8034	3819	4215	55-59	AND
60-64	6124	3046	3078	6633	3213	3420	6844	3239	3605	60-64	DEATH
65-69	4549	2229	2320	5254	2537	2717	5694	2676	3018	65-69	RATES
70-74	3243	1541	1702	3624	1712	1912	4188	1949	2239	70-74	(IN 1000's)
75-79	2107	970	1137	2307	1050	1257	2580	1167	1413	75-79	
80-84	1058	475	583	1242	542	700	1361	587	774	80-84	
85+	508	219	289	627	266	361	737	303	434	85+	
TOTAL	139827	65800	74027	146727	69041	77686	152732	71880	80852	TOTAL	

STANDARD COUNTRIES: STANDARDIZED RATES PER THOUSAND	ENGLAND AND WALES 1961 BOTH SEXES	MALES	FEMALES	UNITED STATES 1960 BOTH SEXES	MALES	FEMALES	MEXICO 1960 BOTH SEXES	MALES	FEMALES	
Birth	17.03	27.37*	16.05	17.37	26.40*	16.64	20.19	22.73*	19.58	TABLE 6
Death	14.37	14.98*	14.26	11.95	13.04*	10.84	7.06	10.44*	5.94	STANDARDIZED RATES
Increase	2.66	12.39*	1.79	5.43	13.35*	5.80	13.13	12.29*	13.64	

	OBSERVED POP. MALES	FEMALES	STATIONARY POP. MALES	FEMALES	STABLE POP. MALES	FEMALES	OBSERVED BIRTHS	NET MATERNITY FUNCTION	BIRTHS IN STABLE POP.	
μ	32.48421	32.16241	35.36545	37.45044	32.09544	33.91389	27.21163	27.44703	27.16564	TABLE 7
σ^2	466.4942	426.6055	487.1412	524.9403	461.7009	500.9345	37.07623	39.18973	38.41963	MOMENTS
κ_3	2854.275	3531.374	3007.505	2609.061	4325.060	4302.066	109.1894	109.7160	113.9835	AND
κ_4	-209598.	-126559.	-216695.	-272406.	-163628.	-215425.	-484.429	-664.740	-565.250	CUMULANTS
β_1	0.080251	0.160623	0.078243	0.047059	0.190065	0.147235	0.233924	0.199997	0.229100	
β_2	2.036850	2.304591	2.086855	2.011455	2.232397	2.141511	2.647598	2.567180	2.617057	
κ	-0.029706	-0.069064	-0.030272	-0.017646	-0.073915	-0.355482	-0.134104	-0.109355	-0.127140	

VITAL STATISTICS		THOMPSON AGE RANGE	NRR	1000r	INTERVAL	BOURGEOIS-PICHAT AGE RANGE	NRR	1000b	1000d	1000r	COALE	
GRR	1.296										IBR	TABLE 8
NRR	1.207	0-4	1.12	4.18	27.34	5-29	0.85	15.48	21.71	-6.22	IDR	RATES FROM AGE DISTRIBUTIONS
TFR	2.666	5-9	1.01	0.23	27.28	30-54	1.44	26.81	13.38	13.42	IRI	AND VITAL
GENERATION	27.306	10-14	1.00	0.13	27.20	55-79	1.96	49.27	24.44	24.83	K1	STATISTICS
SEX RATIO	105.673	15-19	1.18	5.92	27.08	*30-54	1.44	26.81	13.38	13.42	K2	(Females)

Start Age Interval	ORIGINAL MATRIX SUB-DIAGONAL	ALTERNATIVE FIRST ROWS Projection	Integral	FIRST STABLE MATRIX % IN STABLE POPULATION	FISHER VALUES	REPRODUCTIVE VALUES	SECOND STABLE MATRIX Z_2 FIRST COLUMN	FIRST ROW	
0	0.99311	0.00000	0.00000	8.866	1.058	6822072	0.1475+0.0840	0.1475+0.0840	TABLE 9
5	0.99655	0.00086	0.00000	8.507	1.103	6144567	0.1745-0.1140	-0.0060+0.1382	LESLIE
10	0.99562	0.06550	0.00176	8.191	1.145	6010541	-0.0267-0.2554	-0.1021+0.0469	MATRIX
15	0.99320	0.24463	0.13210	7.879	1.121	6449956	-0.2946-0.1144	-0.0815-0.0619	AND ITS
20	0.99150	0.34924	0.36816	7.560	0.907	5535473	-0.2902+0.2575	-0.0218-0.1028	SPECTRAL
25	0.98977	0.28661	0.34539	7.242	0.574	3366344	0.1182+0.4606	0.0145-0.0837	COMPONENTS
30	0.98625	0.18457	0.24023	6.926	0.294	1649111	0.5673+0.1289	0.0236-0.0451	(Females)
35	0.98144	0.08631	0.13720	6.599	0.110	565544	0.4558-0.5434	0.0141-0.0154	
40	0.97435	0.02096	0.03914	6.257	0.023	109632	-0.3337-0.7931	0.0036-0.0029	
45	0.96335	0.00177	0.00361	5.891	0.002	7756	-1.0333-0.0789	0.0003-0.0002	
50	0.94808	0.00000	0.00000	5.483	0.000	1	-0.6458+1.0516	0.0000-0.0000	
55+	0.78270			20.600					

Start Age Interval	OBSERVED POPUL. (IN 100's)	CONTRIBUTIONS OF ROOTS (IN 100's) r_1	r_2, r_3	r_4-r_{11}	AGE-SP. BIRTH RATES	NET MATERNITY FUNCTION	COEFF. OF MATRIX EQUATION	PARAMETERS INTEGRAL	MATRIX	EXP. INCREASE x	$e^{(x+2\frac{1}{2})r}$	
0	64452	63851	1755	-1154	0.0000	0.0000	0.0000	L(1) 1.03501	1.03504	0	1.0174	TABLE 10
5	55699	61264	-4783	-782	0.0000	0.0000	0.0009	L(2) 0.35981	0.36966	50	1.4352	AGE
10	52501	58986	-8038	1552	0.0004	0.0017	0.0648	0.74126	0.71959	55	1.4854	ANALYSIS
15	57561	56740	-1789	2611	0.0270	0.1279	0.2410	R(1) 0.00688	0.00689	60	1.5374	AND
20	61029	54447	10137	-3555	0.0753	0.3542	0.3418	R(2) -0.03872	-0.04240	65	1.5912	MISCELLANEOUS
25	58646	52156	14047	-7558	0.0706	0.3294	0.2781	0.22378	0.21925	70	1.6469	RESULTS
30	56137	49875	505	5757	0.0491	0.2268	0.1773	C(1)	720164	75	1.7046	(Females)
35	51316	47525	-20389	24181	0.0281	0.1277	0.0817	C(2)	-320595	80	1.7643	
40	47369	45064	-23352	25658	0.0080	0.0358	0.0195		-1607198	85	1.8260	
45	42755	42422	4089	-3756	0.0007	0.0032	0.0016	2P/Y 28.0777	28.6577	90	1.8900	
50	39066	39484	37943	-38360	0.0000	0.0000	0.0000	DELTA 5.8035		95	1.9561	
55+	112217	148351								100	2.0246	

AGE AT LAST BIRTHDAY	BOTH SEXES	1955 MALES	FEMALES	BOTH SEXES	1960 MALES	FEMALES	BOTH SEXES	1965 MALES	FEMALES	AGE AT LAST BIRTHDAY	
0-4	17561	8968	8593	17267	8818	8449	17952	9168	8784	0-4	**TABLE 5**
5-9	16175	8237	7938	17462	8912	8550	17172	8764	8408	5-9	
10-14	13348	6788	6560	16127	8208	7919	17411	8881	8530	10-14	
15-19	11179	5684	5495	13294	6753	6541	16061	8165	7896	15-19	POPULATION
20-24	10567	5276	5291	11106	5636	5470	13206	6695	6511	20-24	PROJECTED
25-29	11339	5520	5819	10486	5224	5262	11020	5580	5440	25-29	WITH
30-34	12104	5894	6210	11239	5461	5778	10393	5169	5224	30-34	FIXED
35-39	11418	5563	5855	11961	5811	6150	11106	5385	5721	35-39	AGE—
40-44	11061	5406	5655	11216	5445	5771	11749	5688	6061	40-44	SPECIFIC
45-49	9971	4920	5051	10759	5225	5534	10911	5264	5647	45-49	BIRTH
50-54	8737	4311	4426	9555	4664	4891	10311	4953	5358	50-54	AND
55-59	7779	3812	3967	8192	3971	4221	8960	4295	4665	55-59	DEATH
60-64	6598	3223	3375	7070	3376	3694	7447	3516	3931	60-64	RATES
65-69	5295	2562	2733	5742	2709	3033	6157	2837	3320	65-69	(IN 1000's)
70-74	4079	1894	2185	4303	1995	2308	4671	2110	2561	70-74	
75-79	2500	1134	1366	2965	1308	1657	3128	1378	1750	75-79	
80-84	1335	588	747	1539	661	878	1826	762	1064	80-84	
85+	784	320	464	923	369	554	1066	415	651	85+	
TOTAL	161830	80100	81730	171206	84546	86660	180547	89025	91522	TOTAL	

STANDARD COUNTRIES: STANDARDIZED RATES PER THOUSAND	ENGLAND AND WALES 1961 BOTH SEXES	MALES	FEMALES	UNITED STATES 1960 BOTH SEXES	MALES	FEMALES	MEXICO 1960 BOTH SEXES	MALES	FEMALES	
Birth	20.11	22.39*	18.98	20.53	21.14*	19.71	24.61	20.12*	23.91	**TABLE 6**
Death	12.68	13.34*	12.36	10.45	11.66*	9.29	5.87	9.15*	4.89	STANDARDIZED RATES
Increase	7.43	9.05*	6.63	10.09	9.48*	10.42	18.74	10.97*	19.02	

	OBSERVED POP. MALES	FEMALES	STATIONARY POP. MALES	FEMALES	STABLE POP. MALES	FEMALES	OBSERVED BIRTHS	NET MATERNITY FUNCTION	BIRTHS IN STABLE POP.	
μ	31.81264	32.44485	36.04757	38.26510	29.32933	30.87917	26.68329	26.56025	26.00719	**TABLE 7**
σ^2	450.7643	456.6536	494.6343	541.0309	434.3504	478.8078	35.45700	37.33796	35.44547	
κ_3	3561.340	3670.938	2831.622	2510.802	5264.878	5792.156	114.7269	129.6424	133.2170	MOMENTS
κ_4	-163652.	-159722.	-225407.	-294037.	-105418.	-148405.	-277.058	-345.873	-145.326	AND
β_1	0.138477	0.141512	0.066255	0.039807	0.338264	0.305631	0.295273	0.322881	0.398508	CUMULANTS
β_2	2.194581	2.234068	2.078704	1.995482	2.441227	2.352671	2.779623	2.751906	2.884330	
κ	-0.055127	-0.058202	-0.025787	-0.014840	-0.134190	-0.116541	-0.181653	-0.181605	-0.233772	

VITAL STATISTICS		THOMPSON AGE RANGE	NRR	1000r	INTERVAL	BOURGEOIS-PICHAT AGE RANGE	NRR	1000b	1000d	1000r	COALE	
GRR	1.536										IBR	**TABLE 8**
NRR	1.459	0-4	1.36	11.42	27.39	5-29	1.00	16.11	16.08	0.04	IDR	RATES FROM AGE DISTRIBUTIONS AND VITAL STATISTICS (Females)
TFR	3.153	5-9	1.14	4.83	27.34	30-54	1.49	27.23	12.46	14.77	IRI	
GENERATION	26.281	10-14	0.99	-0.21	27.26	55-79	1.82	41.47	19.28	22.20	K1	
SEX RATIO	105.317	15-19	1.03	0.94	27.15	*35-59	1.58	30.29	13.30	16.99	K2	

Start of Age Interval	ORIGINAL MATRIX SUB-DIAGONAL	ALTERNATIVE FIRST ROWS Projection	Integral	FIRST STABLE MATRIX % IN STABLE POPULATION	FISHER VALUES	REPRODUCTIVE VALUES	SECOND STABLE MATRIX Z₂ FIRST COLUMN	FIRST ROW	
0	0.99508	0.00000	0.00000	10.846	1.069	8526066	0.1661+0.1015	0.1661+0.1015	**TABLE 9**
5	0.99762	0.00108	0.00000	10.043	1.154	7589673	0.1936-0.1371	-0.0227+0.1581	
10	0.99703	0.09982	0.00225	9.323	1.242	6845678	-0.0606-0.2835	-0.1264+0.0339	LESLIE
15	0.99554	0.33756	0.20530	8.650	1.232	6547046	-0.3472-0.0688	-0.0830-0.0943	MATRIX
20	0.99441	0.43745	0.49674	8.013	0.967	5660320	-0.2442+0.3559	-0.0122-0.1275	AND ITS
25	0.99293	0.32165	0.41246	7.415	0.575	3597804	0.2808+0.4444	0.0192-0.0952	SPECTRAL
30	0.99023	0.18596	0.25619	6.851	0.276	1634097	0.6313-0.1003	0.0243-0.0493	COMPONENTS
35	0.98562	0.08077	0.13061	6.313	0.099	569310	0.1906-0.7515	0.0141-0.0167	(Females)
40	0.97855	0.01942	0.03738	5.790	0.021	106327	-0.7426-0.5696	0.0037-0.0031	
45	0.96829	0.00142	0.00294	5.272	0.001	6457	-0.9786+0.5481	0.0003-0.0002	
50	0.95380	0.00000	0.00000	4.750	0.000	1	0.1389+1.3229	0.0000-0.0000	
55+	0.80385			16.732					

Start of Age Interval	OBSERVED POPUL. (IN 100's)	CONTRIBUTIONS OF ROOTS (IN 100's) r_1	r_2, r_3	$r_4 \cdot r_{11}$	AGE-SP. BIRTH RATES	NET MATERNITY FUNCTION	COEFF. OF MATRIX EQUATION	PARAMETERS INTEGRAL	MATRIX	EXP. INCREASE x	$e^{(x+2\frac{1}{2})r}$	
0	79776	74162	6632	-1018	0.0000	0.0000	0.0000	L(1) 1.07451	1.07464	0	1.0366	**TABLE 10**
5	65756	68671	-1515	-1399	0.0000	0.0000	0.0011	L(2) 0.30785	0.32241	50	2.1267	
10	55111	63749	-11338	2700	0.0004	0.0022	0.0991	0.77834	0.75014	55	2.2852	AGE
15	53148	59145	-8673	2676	0.0408	0.1960	0.3341	R(1) 0.01437	0.01440	60	2.4555	ANALYSIS
20	58514	54791	8530	-4807	0.0988	0.4722	0.4310	R(2) -0.03558	-0.04055	65	2.6384	AND
25	62545	50701	21084	-9240	0.0821	0.3899	0.3152	0.23883	0.23297	70	2.8350	MISCELLANEOUS
30	59128	46845	7615	4668	0.0510	0.2405	0.1809	C(1)	683759	75	3.0462	RESULTS
35	57378	43165	-23802	38015	0.0260	0.1214	0.0778	C(2)	890504	80	3.2732	(Females)
40	51614	39590	-33840	45865	0.0074	0.0342	0.0184		-1809526	85	3.5171	
45	45708	36049	2406	7252	0.0006	0.0026	0.0013	2P/Y 26.3081	26.9695	90	3.7792	
50	41588	32482	50350	-41244	0.0000	0.0000	0.0000	DELTA 6.5268		95	4.0608	
55+	131890	114409								100	4.3633	

With Adjusted Births

AGE AT LAST BIRTHDAY	BOTH SEXES	1960 MALES	FEMALES	BOTH SEXES	1965 MALES	FEMALES	BOTH SEXES	1970 MALES	FEMALES	AGE AT LAST BIRTHDAY	
0-4	20009	10215	9794	20830	10634	10196	23281	11885	11396	0-4	
5-9	18223	9278	8945	19919	10164	9755	20737	10581	10156	5-9	
10-14	17111	8741	8370	18181	9252	8929	19873	10136	9737	10-14	
15-19	13296	6755	6541	17050	8699	8351	18116	9208	8908	15-19	**TABLE 5**
20-24	10964	5477	5487	13218	6699	6519	16950	8627	8323	20-24	POPULATION
25-29	10241	4894	5347	10890	5425	5465	13128	6636	6492	25-29	PROJECTED
30-34	11514	5606	5908	10166	4848	5318	10809	5374	5435	30-34	WITH
35-39	12192	5917	6275	11400	5538	5862	10067	4790	5277	35-39	FIXED
40-44	11373	5525	5848	12010	5809	6201	11229	5436	5793	40-44	AGE—
45-49	10928	5314	5614	11105	5361	5744	11728	5637	6091	45-49	SPECIFIC
50-54	9709	4742	4967	10523	5060	5463	10693	5105	5588	50-54	BIRTH
55-59	8318	4031	4287	9167	4397	4770	9937	4691	5246	55-59	AND
60-64	7198	3429	3769	7626	3594	4032	8407	3920	4487	60-64	DEATH
65-69	5843	2736	3107	6287	2879	3408	6664	3018	3646	65-69	RATES
70-74	4377	2011	2366	4787	2131	2656	5156	2242	2914	70-74	(IN 1000's)
75-79	3021	1321	1700	3253	1407	1846	3564	1491	2073	75-79	
80-84	1590	673	917	1889	773	1116	2035	823	1212	80-84	
85+	1008	417	591	1211	482	729	1442	554	888	85+	
TOTAL	176915	87082	89833	189512	93152	96360	203816	100154	103662	TOTAL	

STANDARD COUNTRIES: STANDARDIZED RATES PER THOUSAND	ENGLAND AND WALES 1961 BOTH SEXES	MALES	FEMALES	UNITED STATES 1960 BOTH SEXES	MALES	FEMALES	MEXICO 1960 BOTH SEXES	MALES	FEMALES	
Birth	22.91	25.34*	21.65	23.37	24.16*	22.45	28.15	22.29*	27.38	**TABLE 6**
Death	11.79	12.47*	11.26	9.68	10.99*	8.39	5.32	8.57*	4.30	STANDAR-DIZED
Increase	11.12	12.87*	10.39	13.70	13.16*	14.06	22.83	13.72*	23.08	RATES

	OBSERVED POP. MALES	FEMALES	STATIONARY POP. MALES	FEMALES	STABLE POP. MALES	FEMALES	OBSERVED BIRTHS	NET MATERNITY FUNCTION	BIRTHS IN STABLE POP.	
μ	31.36555	32.36535	36.36823	38.83728	27.22318	28.68788	26.77769	26.47419	25.74241	**TABLE 7**
σ^2	471.3140	481.2710	500.7301	551.8880	409.4717	455.2883	36.20535	36.02680	33.42597	MOMENTS
κ_3	4087.738	4008.460	2802.939	2385.658	5787.983	6580.502	108.9026	128.9754	131.8407	AND
κ_4	-187227.	-192664.	-232305.	-310814.	-58827.	-91026.	-427.664	-275.179	-11.828	CUMULANTS
β_1	0.159601	0.144140	0.062577	0.033858	0.487958	0.458837	0.249895	0.355743	0.465422	
β_2	2.157153	2.168196	2.073488	1.979534	2.649145	2.560872	2.673745	2.787986	2.989414	
κ	-0.060158	-0.055726	-0.024342	-0.012533	-0.196840	-0.177422	-0.144215	-0.198114	-0.278824	

VITAL STATISTICS		THOMPSON AGE RANGE	NRR	1000r	INTERVAL	BOURGEOIS-PICHAT AGE RANGE	NRR	1000b	1000d	1000r	COALE	**TABLE 8**
GRR	1.753	0-4	1.52	15.52	27.41	5-29	1.59	21.08	3.87	17.21	IBR	RATES FROM AGE DISTRI-BUTIONS
NRR	1.680	5-9	1.43	13.12	27.37	30-54	1.45	25.29	11.60	13.69	IDR	AND VITAL
TFR	3.596	10-14	1.13	4.60	27.30	55-79	1.70	34.94	15.19	19.75	IRI	STATISTICS
GENERATION	26.104	15-19	1.00	-0.18	27.20	*40-64	1.62	31.33	13.37	17.96	K1	(Females)
SEX RATIO	105.118										K2	

Start of Age Interval	ORIGINAL MATRIX SUB-DIAGONAL	ALTERNATIVE FIRST ROWS Projection	Integral	FIRST STABLE MATRIX % IN STABLE POPULATION	FISHER VALUES	REPRODUCTIVE VALUES	SECOND STABLE MATRIX Z_2 FIRST COLUMN	FIRST ROW	
0	0.99603	0.00000	0.00000	12.456	1.079	9693093	0.1774+0.1033	0.1774+0.1033	**TABLE 9**
5	0.99814	0.00111	0.00000	11.230	1.197	10038970	0.1918-0.1498	-0.0254+0.1713	LESLIE
10	0.99771	0.10936	0.00233	10.146	1.324	8678753	-0.0807-0.2776	-0.1420+0.0336	MATRIX
15	0.99664	0.39564	0.22805	9.163	1.348	7419451	-0.3417-0.0334	-0.0901-0.1119	AND ITS
20	0.99584	0.51455	0.60557	8.266	1.065	5719397	-0.1872+0.3616	-0.0110-0.1465	SPECTRAL
25	0.99465	0.36426	0.47794	7.451	0.624	3707219	0.3157+0.3651	0.0197-0.1079	COMPO-NENTS
30	0.99222	0.20783	0.28924	6.708	0.298	1884224	0.5401-0.1866	0.0259-0.0562	(Females)
35	0.98826	0.08929	0.14876	6.025	0.106	625255	0.0321-0.6740	0.0152-0.0190	
40	0.98222	0.01998	0.03938	5.390	0.021	117830	-0.7221-0.3293	0.0037-0.0034	
45	0.97299	0.00126	0.00266	4.792	0.001	6308	-0.6708+0.6410	0.0002-0.0002	
50	0.96039	0.00000	0.00000	4.220	0.000	1	0.4009+0.9968	0.0000-0.0000	
55+	0.81839			14.154					

Start of Age Interval	OBSERVED POPUL. (IN 100's)	CONTRIBUTIONS OF ROOTS (IN 100's) r_1	r_2, r_3	r_4-r_{11}	AGE-SP. BIRTH RATES	NET MATERNITY FUNCTION	COEFF. OF MATRIX EQUATION	PARAMETERS INTEGRAL	MATRIX	EXP. INCREASE x	$e^{(x+2\frac{1}{2})r}$	
0	89810	86610	5739	-2538	0.0000	0.0000	0.0000	L(1) 1.10449	1.10476	0	1.0509	**TABLE 10**
5	83860	78085	3685	2089	0.0000	0.0000	0.0011	L(2) 0.29749	0.31185	50	2.8393	AGE
10	65560	70549	-4832	-157	0.0005	0.0022	0.1087	0.81309	0.78019	55	3.1360	ANALYSIS
15	55060	63713	-9458	805	0.0446	0.2152	0.3924	R(1) 0.01988	0.01993	60	3.4637	AND
20	53690	57478	-1522	-2266	0.1184	0.5696	0.5087	R(2) -0.02882	-0.03482	65	3.8256	MISCEL-LANEOUS
25	59400	51811	11958	-4369	0.0934	0.4477	0.3586	0.24401	0.23811	70	4.2254	RESULTS
30	63240	46647	12644	3949	0.0565	0.2695	0.2035	C(1)	695348	75	4.6669	(Females)
35	59170	41895	-5634	22908	0.0291	0.1375	0.0868	C(2)	1337002	80	5.1545	
40	57160	37477	-22481	42164	0.0077	0.0360	0.0192		-481656	85	5.6931	
45	51050	33320	-11762	29492	0.0005	0.0024	0.0012	2P/Y 25.7496	26.3879	90	6.2880	
50	44640	29346	20323	-5029	0.0000	0.0000	0.0000	DELTA 9.7861		95	6.9451	
55+	149840	98417								100	7.6708	

With Adjusted Births

TABLE 5 — POPULATION PROJECTED WITH FIXED AGE-SPECIFIC BIRTH AND DEATH RATES (IN 1000's)

AGE AT LAST BIRTHDAY	1965 BOTH SEXES	1965 MALES	1965 FEMALES	1970 BOTH SEXES	1970 MALES	1970 FEMALES	1975 BOTH SEXES	1975 MALES	1975 FEMALES	AGE AT LAST BIRTHDAY
0-4	21785	11116	10669	24301	12400	11901	27779	14175	13604	0-4
5-9	20279	10303	9976	21693	11064	10629	24199	12342	11857	5-9
10-14	18785	9547	9238	20234	10276	9958	21645	11035	10610	10-14
15-19	16853	8556	8297	18722	9504	9218	20167	10230	9937	15-19
20-24	13278	6647	6631	16760	8489	8271	18620	9430	9190	20-24
25-29	10781	5248	5533	13194	6589	6605	16654	8415	8239	25-29
30-34	10745	5264	5481	10706	5201	5505	13099	6529	6570	30-34
35-39	11786	5754	6032	10643	5202	5441	10603	5139	5464	35-39
40-44	12301	5970	6331	11616	5651	5965	10489	5108	5381	40-44
45-49	11374	5527	5847	12020	5796	6224	11350	5486	5864	45-49
50-54	10513	5115	5398	10960	5264	5696	11583	5520	6063	50-54
55-59	9120	4408	4712	9938	4743	5195	10364	4882	5482	55-59
60-64	7768	3693	4075	8372	3930	4442	9127	4229	4898	60-64
65-69	6296	2879	3417	6829	3110	3719	7364	3310	4054	65-69
70-74	5181	2292	2889	5212	2253	2959	5655	2434	3221	70-74
75-79	3581	1545	2036	3898	1614	2284	3926	1586	2340	75-79
80-84	1964	815	1149	2285	919	1366	2492	959	1533	80-84
85+	1162	435	727	1427	526	901	1664	592	1072	85+
TOTAL	193552	95114	98438	208810	102531	106279	226780	111401	115379	TOTAL

TABLE 6 — STANDARDIZED RATES

STANDARD COUNTRIES:

STANDARDIZED RATES PER THOUSAND	ENGLAND AND WALES 1961 BOTH SEXES	MALES	FEMALES	UNITED STATES 1960 BOTH SEXES	MALES	FEMALES	MEXICO 1960 BOTH SEXES	MALES	FEMALES
Birth	23.47	26.31*	22.20	23.92	24.87*	23.00	28.98	22.90*	28.21
Death	11.44	12.22*	10.72	9.39	10.85*	7.97	5.10	8.52*	4.04
Increase	12.03	14.08*	11.48	14.53	14.02*	15.03	23.88	14.38*	24.17

TABLE 7 — MOMENTS AND CUMULANTS

	OBSERVED POP. MALES	OBSERVED POP. FEMALES	STATIONARY POP. MALES	STATIONARY POP. FEMALES	STABLE POP. MALES	STABLE POP. FEMALES	OBSERVED BIRTHS	NET MATERNITY FUNCTION	BIRTHS IN STABLE POP.
μ	31.06962	32.35280	36.40658	39.09770	26.74729	28.26466	26.43001	26.37240	25.62621
σ^2	484.0616	504.3773	500.5406	557.4892	402.6310	451.8613	37.24276	34.62152	31.82977
κ_3	4658.402	4568.530	2753.278	2330.219	5841.824	6782.903	130.7018	131.8810	131.4391
κ_4	-201102.	-224021.	-233772.	-320384.	-49306.	-79195.	-420.558	-104.829	144.884
β_1	0.191325	0.162662	0.060448	0.031339	0.522848	0.498673	0.330703	0.419108	0.535733
β_2	2.141749	2.119401	2.066930	1.969144	2.695853	2.612127	2.696791	2.912544	3.143006
κ	-0.069071	-0.059308	-0.023434	-0.011531	-0.211406	-0.193065	-0.171361	-0.246074	-0.348886

TABLE 8 — RATES FROM AGE DISTRIBUTIONS AND VITAL STATISTICS (Females)

VITAL STATISTICS		THOMPSON AGE RANGE	NRR	1000r	INTERVAL	BOURGEOIS-PICHAT AGE RANGE	NRR	1000b	1000d	1000r	COALE
GRR	1.801										IBR
NRR	1.732	0-4	1.63	18.23	27.42	5-29	2.15	25.60	-2.66	28.27	IDR
TFR	3.690	5-9	1.55	16.13	27.37	30-54	1.26	19.34	10.85	8.50	IRI
GENERATION	25.994	10-14	1.40	12.28	27.31	55-79	1.46	24.35	10.42	13.93	K1
SEX RATIO	104.947	15-19	1.15	4.90	27.22	*40-64	1.56	28.40	11.82	16.58	K2

TABLE 9 — LESLIE MATRIX AND ITS SPECTRAL COMPONENTS (Females)

Start of Age Interval	ORIGINAL MATRIX SUB-DIAGONAL	ALTERNATIVE FIRST ROWS Projection	ALTERNATIVE FIRST ROWS Integral	FIRST STABLE MATRIX % IN STABLE POPULATION	FISHER VALUES	REPRODUCTIVE VALUES	SECOND STABLE MATRIX Z2 FIRST COLUMN	FIRST ROW
0	0.99630	0.00000	0.00000	12.820	1.080	10812564	0.1891+0.0979	0.1891+0.0979
5	0.99822	0.00100	0.00000	11.489	1.205	11151001	0.1850-0.1660	-0.0211+0.1811
10	0.99791	0.10720	0.00211	10.315	1.341	11148759	-0.1051-0.2711	-0.1514+0.0378
15	0.99692	0.41445	0.22440	9.259	1.378	9164657	-0.3400+0.0028	-0.0964-0.1202
20	0.99610	0.54617	0.65149	8.303	1.088	6042371	-0.1375+0.3726	-0.0116-0.1542
25	0.99481	0.37387	0.50208	7.439	0.622	3426876	0.3500+0.3040	0.0164-0.1097
30	0.99261	0.20392	0.28772	6.656	0.289	1757595	-0.4758-0.2562	0.0219-0.0569
35	0.98891	0.08649	0.14330	5.943	0.102	653605	-0.0830-0.6230	0.0136-0.0198
40	0.98305	0.01989	0.03950	5.286	0.020	120944	-0.7093-0.1655	0.0036-0.0036
45	0.97422	0.00118	0.00249	4.674	0.001	6347	-0.4675+0.6967	0.0002-0.0002
50	0.96235	0.00000	0.00000	4.096	0.000	1	0.5551+0.7806	0.0000-0.0000
55+	0.82444			13.719				

TABLE 10 — AGE ANALYSIS AND MISCELLANEOUS RESULTS (Females)

Start of Age Interval	OBSERVED POPUL. (IN 100's)	CONTRIBUTIONS OF ROOTS (IN 100's) r_1	r_2, r_3	$r_4 \cdot r_{11}$	AGE-SP. BIRTH RATES	NET MATERNITY FUNCTION	COEFF. OF MATRIX EQUATION	PARAMETERS	INTEGRAL	MATRIX	EXP. INCREASE x	$e^{(x+8\frac{1}{2})r}$
0	100130	98600	1340	189	0.0000	0.0000	0.0000	L(1)	1.11145	1.11176	0	1.0543
5	92540	88361	5249	-1070	0.0000	0.0000	0.0010	L(2)	0.28909	0.30195	50	3.0329
10	83140	79337	2514	1289	0.0004	0.0020	0.1066		0.83475	0.79818	55	3.3709
15	66510	71213	-5099	396	0.0436	0.2112	0.4113	R(1)	0.02113	0.02119	60	3.7466
20	55550	63857	-7650	-657	0.1266	0.6114	0.5404	R(2)	-0.02480	-0.03171	65	4.1642
25	55100	57214	634	-2748	0.0976	0.4694	0.3685			0.24748	0.24183	70	4.6283
30	60770	51196	10932	-1358	0.0559	0.2676	0.1999	C(1)		769120	75	5.1441
35	64020	45709	8138	10172	0.0279	0.1323	0.0842	C(2)		743788	80	5.7174
40	59480	40659	-8061	26883	0.0077	0.0361	0.0191			752146	85	6.3547
45	55410	35951	-17435	36893	0.0005	0.0022	0.0011	2P/Y	25.3887	25.9821	90	7.0629
50	48960	31504	-3484	20940	0.0000	0.0000	0.0000	DELTA	9.9953		95	7.8501
55+	171870	105519									100	8.7250

With Adjusted Births

AGE AT LAST BIRTHDAY	BOTH SEXES	1967 MALES	FEMALES	BOTH SEXES	1972 MALES	FEMALES	BOTH SEXES	1977 MALES	FEMALES	AGE AT LAST BIRTHDAY	
0-4	21672	11053	10619	24519	12505	12014	27915	14237	13678	0-4	
5-9	20664	10515	10149	21588	11006	10582	24423	12451	11972	5-9	
10-14	19693	10005	9688	20621	10490	10131	21542	10978	10564	10-14	
15-19	17652	8968	8684	19631	9962	9669	20555	10444	10111	15-19	**TABLE 5**
20-24	14779	7408	7371	17556	8899	8657	19524	9885	9639	20-24	POPULATION
25-29	11509	5603	5906	14686	7344	7342	17444	8821	8623	25-29	PROJECTED
30-34	10654	5231	5423	11428	5552	5876	14581	7277	7304	30-34	WITH
35-39	11390	5572	5818	10551	5169	5382	11318	5486	5832	35-39	FIXED
40-44	12226	5942	6284	11223	5471	5752	10396	5075	5321	40-44	AGE—
45-49	11745	5685	6060	11948	5770	6178	10968	5313	5655	45-49	SPECIFIC
50-54	10723	5195	5528	11319	5415	5904	11515	5496	6019	50-54	BIRTH
55-59	9492	4564	4928	10137	4816	5321	10703	5020	5683	55-59	AND
60-64	8024	3798	4226	8720	4071	4649	9317	4296	5021	60-64	DEATH
65-69	6481	2955	3526	7044	3188	3856	7660	3418	4242	65-69	RATES
70-74	5175	2251	2924	5355	2299	3056	5823	2481	3342	70-74	(IN 1000's)
75-79	3764	1592	2172	3905	1583	2322	4043	1617	2426	75-79	
80-84	2125	871	1254	2424	953	1471	2519	947	1572	80-84	
85+	1225	452	773	1487	538	949	1702	589	1113	85+	
TOTAL	198993	97660	101333	214142	105031	109111	231948	113831	118117	TOTAL	

STANDARD COUNTRIES:	ENGLAND AND WALES 1961			UNITED STATES 1960			MEXICO 1960			
STANDARDIZED RATES PER THOUSAND	BOTH SEXES	MALES	FEMALES	BOTH SEXES	MALES	FEMALES	BOTH SEXES	MALES	FEMALES	**TABLE 6**
Birth	22.32	25.57*	21.12	22.74	24.00*	21.88	27.52	22.30*	26.81	STANDAR-DIZED
Death	11.44	12.22*	10.68	9.38	10.87*	7.94	5.04	8.58*	3.98	RATES
Increase	10.88	13.35*	10.44	13.36	13.12*	13.94	22.49	13.71*	22.83	

	OBSERVED POP. MALES	FEMALES	STATIONARY POP. MALES	FEMALES	STABLE POP. MALES	FEMALES	OBSERVED BIRTHS	NET MATERNITY FUNCTION	BIRTHS IN STABLE POP.	
μ	30.89496	32.33227	36.36526	39.10285	27.50160	29.13516	26.22896	26.41608	25.74072	**TABLE 7**
σ^2	485.5304	509.4157	499.0043	557.4209	412.6091	464.6173	37.15428	34.25769	31.76694	MOMENTS
κ_3	4921.490	4796.752	2731.324	2316.254	5700.396	6607.975	142.8710	129.3970	128.7688	AND
κ_4	-199490.	-229917.	-232436.	-320893.	-66341.	-103449.	-299.578	-75.524	141.429	CUMULANTS
β_1	0.211614	0.174051	0.060039	0.030976	0.462587	0.435362	0.397980	0.416461	0.517243	
β_2	2.153771	2.114015	2.066543	1.967254	2.610322	2.520778	2.782984	2.935647	3.140148	
κ	-0.075660	-0.062523	-0.023277	-0.011384	-0.185528	-0.166904	-0.205665	-0.253668	-0.348302	

VITAL STATISTICS		THOMPSON AGE RANGE	NRR	1000r	INTERVAL	BOURGEOIS-PICHAT AGE RANGE	NRR	1000b	1000d	1000r	COALE	**TABLE 8**
GRR	1.714											RATES FROM AGE
NRR	1.652	0-4	1.61	17.83	27.42	5-29	2.26	26.90	-3.31	30.21	IBR	DISTRIBUTIONS
TFR	3.511	5-9	1.60	17.48	27.37	30-54	1.13	16.05	11.41	4.64	IDR	AND VITAL
GENERATION	26.074	10-14	1.46	13.64	27.31	55-79	1.42	22.72	9.84	12.88	IRI	STATISTICS
SEX RATIO	104.795	15-19	1.26	8.12	27.22	*40-64	1.56	28.33	11.78	16.55	K1	(Females)
											K2	

Start of Age Interval	ORIGINAL MATRIX SUB-DIAGONAL	ALTERNATIVE FIRST ROWS Projection	Integral	FIRST STABLE MATRIX % IN STABLE POPULATION	FISHER VALUES	REPRODUCTIVE VALUES	SECOND STABLE MATRIX Z₂ FIRST COLUMN	FIRST ROW	
0	0.99646	0.00000	0.00000	12.195	1.073	10932123	0.1875+0.0942	0.1875+0.0942	
5	0.99828	0.00100	0.00000	11.034	1.186	11512411	0.1820-0.1652	-0.0174+0.1783	**TABLE 9**
10	0.99797	0.09885	0.00210	10.003	1.308	11378041	-0.1041-0.2690	-0.1473+0.0407	LESLIE
15	0.99690	0.39085	0.20576	9.065	1.337	9882257	-0.3383+0.0003	-0.0962-0.1140	MATRIX
20	0.99604	0.52361	0.61637	8.206	1.056	6259860	-0.1423+0.3701	-0.0123-0.1485	AND ITS
25	0.99482	0.36148	0.48439	7.422	0.603	3286086	0.3443+0.3114	0.0160-0.1050	SPECTRAL
30	0.99248	0.19466	0.27562	6.705	0.277	1625656	0.4846-0.2446	0.0205-0.0538	COMPONENTS
35	0.98875	0.08164	0.13389	6.042	0.097	617751	-0.0528-0.6302	0.0126-0.0187	(Females)
40	0.98306	0.01914	0.03786	5.425	0.020	120973	-0.7096-0.1955	0.0034-0.0035	
45	0.97426	0.00112	0.00234	4.843	0.001	6177	-0.5059+0.6838	0.0002-0.0002	
50	0.96261	0.00000	0.00000	4.284	0.000	1	0.5222+0.8224	0.0000-0.0000	
55+	0.82215			14.777					

Start of Age Interval	OBSERVED POPUL. (IN 100's)	r_1	r_2, r_3	$r_4 \cdot r_{11}$	AGE-SP. BIRTH RATES	NET MATERNITY FUNCTION	COEFF. OF MATRIX EQUATION	PARAMETERS	INTEGRAL	MATRIX	EXP. INCREASE x	$e^{(x+2\frac{1}{2})r}$	
0	101850	101137	-313	1027	0.0000	0.0000	0.0000	L(1)	1.10100	1.10125	0	1.0493	**TABLE 10**
5	97050	91513	6262	-725	0.0000	0.0000	0.0010	L(2)	0.29403	0.30614	50	2.7464	AGE
10	87020	82956	5720	-1656	0.0004	0.0020	0.0983		0.82929	0.79372	55	3.0238	ANALYSIS
15	73940	75176	-3792	2556	0.0401	0.1947	0.3880	R(1)	0.01924	0.01929	60	3.3292	AND
20	59300	68053	-11061	2308	0.1202	0.5813	0.5182	R(2)	-0.02560	-0.03234	65	3.6655	MISCELLANEOUS
25	54510	61551	-4118	-2923	0.0945	0.4550	0.3563			0.24601	70	4.0357	RESULTS
30	58620	55603	11678	-8661	0.0537	0.2576	0.1909	C(1)		829334	75	4.4433	(Females)
35	63560	50111	15424	-1975	0.0261	0.1242	0.0795	C(2)		559052	80	4.8921	
40	61640	44992	-2932	19580	0.0074	0.0347	0.0184			1279420	85	5.3862	
45	56740	40163	-23154	39731	0.0005	0.0021	0.0011	2P/Y	25.5400	26.1217	90	5.9302	
50	51190	35531	-15205	30863	0.0000	0.0000	0.0000	DELTA	8.2468		95	6.5291	
55+	179280	122548									100	7.1886	

174 United States 1963
With Adjusted Births

AGE AT LAST BIRTHDAY	BOTH SEXES	1968 MALES	FEMALES	BOTH SEXES	1973 MALES	FEMALES	BOTH SEXES	1978 MALES	FEMALES	AGE AT LAST BIRTHDAY	
0-4	21368	10922	10446	24177	12358	11819	27366	13988	13378	0-4	**TABLE 5**
5-9	20667	10526	10141	21284	10874	10410	24082	12304	11778	5-9	POPULATION
10-14	20033	10178	9855	20624	10500	10124	21240	10848	10392	10-14	PROJECTED
15-19	17977	9130	8847	19968	10134	9834	20558	10455	10103	15-19	WITH
20-24	15382	7729	7653	17878	9059	8819	19858	10055	9803	20-24	FIXED
25-29	12225	5961	6264	15281	7659	7622	17761	8977	8784	25-29	AGE-
30-34	10761	5278	5483	12136	5905	6231	15171	7588	7583	30-34	SPECIFIC
35-39	11173	5470	5703	10655	5214	5441	12017	5833	6184	35-39	BIRTH
40-44	12099	5886	6213	11008	5370	5638	10497	5118	5379	40-44	AND
45-49	11931	5769	6162	11821	5714	6107	10754	5213	5541	45-49	DEATH
50-54	10802	5219	5583	11496	5493	6003	11389	5441	5948	50-54	RATES
55-59	9666	4634	5032	10200	4830	5370	10857	5083	5774	55-59	(IN 1000's)
60-64	8126	3830	4296	8867	4123	4744	9359	4297	5062	60-64	
65-69	6597	3002	3595	7123	3205	3918	7777	3450	4327	65-69	
70-74	5133	2210	2923	5427	2315	3112	5864	2473	3391	70-74	
75-79	3814	1588	2226	3857	1538	2319	4079	1611	2468	75-79	
80-84	2179	882	1297	2448	942	1506	2481	912	1569	80-84	
85+	1246	455	791	1490	529	961	1681	565	1116	85+	
TOTAL	201179	98669	102510	215740	105762	109978	232791	114211	118580	TOTAL	

STANDARD COUNTRIES: STANDARDIZED RATES PER THOUSAND	ENGLAND AND WALES 1961 BOTH SEXES	MALES	FEMALES	UNITED STATES 1960 BOTH SEXES	MALES	FEMALES	MEXICO 1960 BOTH SEXES	MALES	FEMALES	
Birth	21.41	24.91*	20.21	21.82	23.24*	20.94	26.35	21.81*	25.60	**TABLE 6** STANDAR-
Death	11.62	12.47*	10.78	9.54	11.10*	8.02	5.11	8.80*	4.01	DIZED RATES
Increase	9.79	12.44*	9.43	12.28	12.14*	12.92	21.24	13.01*	21.60	

	OBSERVED POP. MALES	FEMALES	STATIONARY POP. MALES	FEMALES	STABLE POP. MALES	FEMALES	OBSERVED BIRTHS	NET MATERNITY FUNCTION	BIRTHS IN STABLE POP.	
μ	30.83302	32.35349	36.23137	39.05196	28.15239	29.92606	26.15432	26.47961	25.86352	**TABLE 7**
σ^2	484.6250	510.4885	495.5256	556.2088	419.7415	474.9574	36.74526	34.23110	32.02358	MOMENTS
κ_3	5025.263	4887.649	2713.646	2318.496	5509.663	6387.810	146.8391	125.8386	125.9204	AND
κ_4	-196345.	-230630.	-228606.	-319253.	-81401.	-125431.	-216.967	-101.207	94.740	CUMULANTS
β_1	0.221871	0.179573	0.060521	0.031239	0.410492	0.380838	0.434590	0.394789	0.482817	
β_2	2.163996	2.114999	2.068872	1.968048	2.537973	2.443973	2.839309	2.913629	3.092383	
κ	-0.079190	-0.064225	-0.023500	-0.011485	-0.163684	-0.144967	-0.226742	-0.242910	-0.324633	

VITAL STATISTICS		THOMPSON AGE RANGE	NRR	1000r	INTERVAL	BOURGEOIS-PICHAT AGE RANGE	NRR	1000b	1000d	1000r	COALE	
GRR	1.641										IBR	**TABLE 8** RATES
NRR	1.581	0-4	1.58	17.16	27.41	5-29	2.23	26.99	-2.65	29.64	IDR	FROM AGE DISTRI-
TFR	3.368	5-9	1.61	17.69	27.37	30-54	1.07	14.50	11.98	2.52	IRI	BUTIONS
GENERATION	26.168	10-14	1.48	14.14	27.31	55-79	1.41	22.41	9.79	12.62	K1	AND VITAL
SEX RATIO	105.272	15-19	1.30	9.23	27.21	*40-69	1.53	27.44	11.58	15.86	K2	STATISTICS (Females)

Start of Age Interval	ORIGINAL MATRIX SUB-DIAGONAL	ALTERNATIVE FIRST ROWS Projection	Integral	FIRST STABLE MATRIX % IN STABLE POPULATION	FISHER VALUES	REPRODUCTIVE VALUES	SECOND STABLE MATRIX Z₂ FIRST COLUMN	FIRST ROW	
0	0.99649	0.00000	0.00000	11.639	1.069	10875491	0.1839+0.0928	0.1839+0.0928	**TABLE 9**
5	0.99829	0.00100	0.00000	10.625	1.171	11556815	0.1815-0.1610	-0.0157+0.1741	LESLIE
10	0.99789	0.09285	0.00210	9.716	1.279	11340017	-0.0977-0.2691	-0.1422+0.0419	MATRIX
15	0.99685	0.36910	0.19232	8.882	1.300	9978212	-0.3376-0.0099	-0.0946-0.1076	AND ITS
20	0.99602	0.50014	0.58072	8.111	1.028	6462940	-0.1575+0.3656	-0.0128-0.1426	SPECTRAL
25	0.99478	0.35015	0.46614	7.400	0.590	3250049	0.3318+0.3311	0.0163-0.1014	COMPO-
30	0.99237	0.18920	0.26688	6.744	0.271	1557250	0.5058-0.2191	0.0205-0.0516	NENTS
35	0.98858	0.07895	0.12943	6.131	0.094	592877	-0.0202-0.6464	0.0123-0.0177	(Females)
40	0.98284	0.01826	0.03595	5.552	0.019	117984	-0.7109-0.2565	0.0032-0.0032	
45	0.97411	0.00107	0.00224	4.999	0.001	6005	-0.5816+0.6580	0.0002-0.0002	
50	0.96186	0.00000	0.00000	4.460	0.000	1	0.4575+0.9019	0.0000-0.0000	
55+	0.81910			15.743					

Start of Age Interval	OBSERVED POPUL. (IN 100's)	CONTRIBUTIONS OF ROOTS (IN 100's) r_1	r_2, r_3	$r_4 \cdot r_{11}$	AGE-SP. BIRTH RATES	NET MATERNITY FUNCTION	COEFF. OF MATRIX EQUATION	PARAMETERS	INTEGRAL	MATRIX	EXP. INCREASE x	$e^{(x+2\frac{1}{2})r}$	
0	101770	101267	-912	1414	0.0000	0.0000	0.0000	L(1)	1.09143	1.09163	0	1.0447	**TABLE 10**
5	98720	92441	6716	-437	0.0000	0.0000	0.0010	L(2)	0.29994	0.31184	50	2.5058	AGE
10	88660	84537	7112	-2989	0.0004	0.0020	0.0924		0.82035	0.78630	55	2.7349	ANALYSIS
15	76770	77278	-3165	2656	0.0377	0.1827	0.3664	R(1)	0.01750	0.01753	60	2.9849	AND
20	62890	70569	-12637	4958	0.1137	0.5501	0.4949	R(2)	-0.02706	-0.03348	65	3.2578	MISCEL-
25	55120	64388	-6580	-2688	0.0913	0.4398	0.3451		0.24406	0.23865	70	3.5556	LANEOUS
30	57470	58675	11794	-12999	0.0523	0.2505	0.1855	C(1)		870071	75	3.8807	RESULTS
35	62850	53340	19280	-9770	0.0253	0.1205	0.0768	C(2)		512781	80	4.2355	(Females)
40	62700	48305	442	13953	0.0070	0.0331	0.0176			1507444	85	4.6227	
45	57310	43491	-25802	39621	0.0004	0.0020	0.0010	2P/Y	25.7449	26.3284	90	5.0454	
50	52320	38809	-22499	36011	0.0000	0.0000	0.0000	DELTA	6.7001		95	5.5067	
55+	182830	136972									100	6.0101	

With Adjusted Births

TABLE 5 — POPULATION PROJECTED WITH FIXED AGE-SPECIFIC BIRTH AND DEATH RATES (IN 1000's)

AGE AT LAST BIRTHDAY	1969 BOTH SEXES	MALES	FEMALES	1974 BOTH SEXES	MALES	FEMALES	1979 BOTH SEXES	MALES	FEMALES	AGE AT LAST BIRTHDAY
0-4	21123	10771	10352	23966	12221	11745	26957	13746	13211	0-4
5-9	20612	10510	10102	21042	10725	10317	23873	12168	11705	5-9
10-14	20305	10316	9989	20569	10484	10085	20999	10699	10300	10-14
15-19	18375	9329	9046	20237	10269	9968	20501	10437	10064	15-19
20-24	16141	8122	8019	18270	9253	9017	20123	10186	9937	20-24
25-29	12742	6222	6520	16035	8047	7988	18150	9168	8982	25-29
30-34	10963	5379	5584	12647	6161	6486	15915	7969	7946	30-34
35-39	10955	5366	5589	10853	5312	5541	12520	6084	6436	35-39
40-44	11929	5806	6123	10791	5266	5525	10691	5213	5478	40-44
45-49	12068	5831	6237	11655	5636	6019	10543	5111	5432	45-49
50-54	10904	5258	5646	11633	5557	6076	11234	5371	5863	50-54
55-59	9844	4710	5134	10304	4871	5433	10996	5149	5847	55-59
60-64	8265	3882	4383	9044	4196	4848	9469	4339	5130	60-64
65-69	6745	3068	3677	7267	3260	4007	7956	3524	4432	65-69
70-74	5169	2218	2951	5578	2382	3196	6015	2531	3484	70-74
75-79	3902	1608	2294	3920	1558	2362	4232	1673	2559	75-79
80-84	2286	920	1366	2551	973	1578	2569	943	1626	80-84
85+	1376	515	861	1649	599	1050	1847	634	1213	85+
TOTAL	203704	99831	103873	218011	106770	111241	234590	114945	119645	TOTAL

TABLE 6 — STANDARDIZED RATES

STANDARD COUNTRIES: STANDARDIZED RATES PER THOUSAND	ENGLAND AND WALES 1961 BOTH SEXES	MALES	FEMALES	UNITED STATES 1960 BOTH SEXES	MALES	FEMALES	MEXICO 1960 BOTH SEXES	MALES	FEMALES
Birth	20.60	24.17*	19.51	21.00	22.45*	20.21	25.31	21.26*	24.66
Death	11.31	12.16*	10.44	9.29	10.84*	7.78	5.00	8.63*	3.91
Increase	9.30	12.01*	9.06	11.71	11.61*	12.43	20.31	12.63*	20.75

TABLE 7 — MOMENTS AND CUMULANTS

	OBSERVED POP. MALES	FEMALES	STATIONARY POP. MALES	FEMALES	STABLE POP. MALES	FEMALES	OBSERVED BIRTHS	NET MATERNITY FUNCTION	BIRTHS IN STABLE POP.
μ	30.78450	32.38614	36.35730	39.19914	28.80698	30.67877	26.07870	26.53491	25.96361
σ^2	484.1064	511.8785	500.0399	560.4503	430.4057	487.0871	36.62489	34.38895	32.39684
κ_3	5141.085	4987.929	2785.031	2336.559	5484.917	6281.338	149.7434	123.0778	123.8468
κ_4	-193333.	-231648.	-232216.	-324939.	-93947.	-145399.	-163.676	-136.761	45.686
β_1	0.232963	0.185498	0.062036	0.031013	0.377317	0.341416	0.456422	0.372480	0.451088
β_2	2.175057	2.115913	2.071284	1.965507	2.492862	2.387160	2.877979	2.884355	3.043529
κ	-0.082995	-0.066031	-0.024099	-0.011381	-0.150017	-0.129155	-0.240932	-0.229429	-0.300619

TABLE 8 — RATES FROM AGE DISTRIBUTIONS AND VITAL STATISTICS (Females)

VITAL STATISTICS		THOMPSON AGE RANGE	NRR	1000r	INTERVAL	BOURGEOIS-PICHAT AGE RANGE	NRR	1000b	1000d	1000r	COALE
GRR	1.583										IBR
NRR	1.526	0-4	1.55	16.42	27.41	5-29	2.19	27.07	-2.02	29.09	IDR
TFR	3.241	5-9	1.62	17.89	27.37	30-54	1.01	13.07	12.66	0.42	IRI
GENERATION	26.247	10-14	1.51	14.79	27.31	55-79	1.43	23.39	10.06	13.33	K1
SEX RATIO	104.719	15-19	1.35	10.72	27.22	*45-69	1.57	28.72	12.05	16.67	K2

TABLE 9 — LESLIE MATRIX AND ITS SPECTRAL COMPONENTS (Females)

Start Age Interval	ORIGINAL MATRIX SUB-DIAGONAL	ALTERNATIVE FIRST ROWS Projection	Integral	% IN STABLE POPULATION	FISHER VALUES	REPRODUCTIVE VALUES	SECOND STABLE MATRIX Z2 FIRST COLUMN	FIRST ROW
0	0.99661	0.00000	0.00000	11.175	1.064	10789309	0.1804+0.0922	0.1804+0.0922
5	0.99834	0.00106	0.00000	10.274	1.158	11585082	0.1817-0.1570	-0.0148+0.1704
10	0.99791	0.08903	0.00222	9.462	1.256	11386046	-0.0914-0.2699	-0.1378+0.0424
15	0.99682	0.35232	0.18354	8.710	1.269	10212813	-0.3376-0.0201	-0.0929-0.1024
20	0.99605	0.48032	0.55180	8.010	1.004	6574011	-0.1726+0.3617	-0.0133-0.1378
25	0.99472	0.34085	0.45007	7.360	0.580	3254249	0.3199+0.3507	0.0165-0.0986
30	0.99229	0.18553	0.26101	6.753	0.267	1503515	0.5266-0.1944	0.0207-0.0500
35	0.98866	0.07726	0.12628	6.182	0.093	573537	0.0214-0.6620	0.0121-0.0170
40	0.98304	0.01779	0.03498	5.638	0.018	116522	-0.7115-0.3162	0.0032-0.0031
45	0.97416	0.00101	0.00210	5.113	0.001	5731	-0.6554+0.6313	0.0002-0.0002
50	0.96222	0.00000	0.00000	4.595	0.000	1	0.3917+0.9786	0.0000-0.0000
55+	0.81975			16.730				

TABLE 10 — AGE ANALYSIS AND MISCELLANEOUS RESULTS (Females)

Start Age Interval	OBSERVED POPUL. (IN 100's)	CONTRIBUTIONS OF ROOTS (IN 100's) r_1	r_2, r_3	$r_4\text{-}r_{11}$	AGE-SP. BIRTH RATES	NET MATERNITY FUNCTION	COEFF. OF MATRIX EQUATION
0	101360	101714	-1943	1590	0.0000	0.0000	0.0000
5	100060	93512	6538	10	0.0000	0.0000	0.0011
10	90650	86121	8576	-4047	0.0004	0.0021	0.0886
15	80450	79280	-1548	2718	0.0361	0.1750	0.3498
20	65460	72903	-13441	5998	0.1084	0.5246	0.4754
25	56140	66987	-9811	-1036	0.0884	0.4262	0.3360
30	56320	61469	10090	-15239	0.0513	0.2458	0.1819
35	61930	56268	22653	-16991	0.0248	0.1180	0.0752
40	63450	51318	6053	6079	0.0069	0.0323	0.0171
45	57960	46538	-25798	37220	0.0004	0.0019	0.0010
50	53360	41822	-30690	42229	0.0000	0.0000	0.0000
55+	186650	152273					

PARAMETERS	INTEGRAL	MATRIX
L(1)	1.08385	1.08402
L(2)	0.30472	0.31659
	0.81810	0.77919
R(1)	0.01610	0.01613
R(2)	-0.02850	-0.03462
	0.24235	0.23697
C(1)		910204
C(2)		330241
		1700311
2P/Y	25.9262	26.5143
DELTA	5.3445	

EXP. INCREASE x	$e^{(x+2\frac{1}{2})r}$
0	1.0411
50	2.3290
55	2.5243
60	2.7359
65	2.9653
70	3.2139
75	3.4834
80	3.7755
85	4.0920
90	4.4352
95	4.8070
100	5.2101

TABLE 1 — DATA

AGE AT LAST BIRTHDAY	BOTH SEXES	POPULATION MALES Number	%	FEMALES Number	%	BIRTHS BY AGE OF MOTHER	DEATHS BOTH SEXES	MALES	FEMALES	AGE AT LAST BIRTHDAY
0	3857000	1969000	2.1	1888000	1.9	0	92894	53437	39457	0
1-4	16577000	8463000	8.9	8114000	8.2	0	15401	8531	6870	1-4
5-9	20518000	10426000	11.0	10092000	10.2	0	8957	5268	3689	5-9
10-14	18956000	9635000	10.1	9321000	9.4	7703	7724	4940	2784	10-14
15-19	16954000	8559000	9.0	8395000	8.5	598547	16129	11610	4519	15-19
20-24	13333000	6539000	6.9	6794000	6.9	1350826	16974	12152	4822	20-24
25-29	11205000	5508000	5.8	5697000	5.8	933943	15050	10138	4912	25-29
30-34	10948000	5378000	5.7	5570000	5.6	535036	18541	11470	7071	30-34
35-39	11920000	5828000	6.1	6092000	6.2	287277	28983	17645	11338	35-39
40-44	12411000	6033000	6.3	6378000	6.5	83255	45861	28054	17807	40-44
45-49	11449000	5570000	5.9	5879000	6.0	4829	66279	41422	24857	45-49
50-54	10570000	5146000	5.4	5424000	5.5	0	96619	62574	34045	50-54
55-59	9156000	4420000	4.6	4736000	4.8	0	126909	83466	43443	55-59
60-64	7809000	3710000	3.9	4099000	4.2	0	160645	104061	56584	60-64
65-69	6297000	2870000	3.0	3427000	3.5	0	199527	123021	76506	65-69
70-74	5189000	2283000	2.4	2906000	2.9		235995	137103	98892	70-74
75-79	3599000	1545000	1.6	2054000	2.1		245221	130538	114683	75-79
80-84	1995000	820000	0.9	1175000	1.2	1944519 M.	213218	101859	111359	80-84
85+	1075000	413000	0.4	662000	0.7	1856897 F.	217209	87911	129298	85+
TOTAL	193818000	95115000		98703000		3801416	1828136	1035200	792936	TOTAL

TABLE 2 — MALE LIFE TABLE

x	nq_x	l_x	nd_x	nL_x	nm_x	na_x	T_x	r_x	$\overset{\circ}{e}_x$	nM_x	x
0	0.026580	100000	2658	97941	0.027139	0.2254	6686917	0.0000	66.869	0.027139	0
1	0.004020	97342	391	388227	0.001008	1.0844	6588976	0.0000	67.689	0.001008	1
5	0.002520	96951	244	484142	0.000505	2.5000	6200749	0.0073	63.958	0.000505	5
10	0.002578	96706	249	482994	0.000516	2.8451	5716607	0.0190	59.113	0.000513	10
15	0.006813	96457	657	480775	0.001367	2.7025	5233613	0.0375	54.259	0.001356	15
20	0.009271	95800	888	476823	0.001863	2.5499	4752838	0.0423	49.612	0.001858	20
25	0.009166	94912	870	472406	0.001842	2.5263	4276015	0.0176	45.053	0.001841	25
30	0.010610	94042	998	467824	0.002133	2.6104	3803609	0.0000	40.446	0.002133	30
35	0.015032	93044	1399	461954	0.003028	2.6654	3335785	0.0000	35.852	0.003028	35
40	0.023003	91645	2108	453348	0.004650	2.6858	2873831	0.0000	31.358	0.004650	40
45	0.036616	89537	3278	440115	0.007449	2.6907	2420483	0.0081	27.033	0.007437	45
50	0.059238	86259	5110	419367	0.012185	2.6660	1980368	0.0106	22.958	0.012160	50
55	0.090573	81149	7350	388331	0.018927	2.6307	1561000	0.0134	19.236	0.018884	55
60	0.131738	73799	9722	345754	0.028119	2.6095	1172670	0.0147	15.890	0.028049	60
65	0.194444	64077	12459	290025	0.042960	2.5633	826916	0.0147	12.905	0.042864	65
70	0.261705	51618	13509	224489	0.060175	2.5128	536891	0.0147	10.401	0.060054	70
75	0.348740	38109	13290	156960	0.084672	2.4730	312402	0.0147	8.198	0.084491	75
80	0.474815	24819	11784	94580	0.124597	2.4955	155441	0.0147	6.263	0.124218	80
85+	*1.000000	13034	13034	60862	0.214166	4.6693	60862	0.0147	4.669	0.212860	85+

TABLE 3 — FEMALE LIFE TABLE

x	nq_x	l_x	nd_x	nL_x	nm_x	na_x	T_x	r_x	$\overset{\circ}{e}_x$	nM_x	x
0	0.020570	100000	2057	98426	0.020899	0.2348	7382869	0.0000	73.829	0.020899	0
1	0.003378	97943	331	390809	0.000847	1.0907	7284443	0.0000	74.374	0.000847	1
5	0.001823	97612	178	487616	0.000365	2.5000	6893634	0.0066	70.623	0.000366	5
10	0.001496	97434	146	486824	0.000299	2.6213	6406018	0.0180	65.747	0.000299	10
15	0.002701	97288	263	485827	0.000541	2.6579	5919194	0.0311	60.842	0.000538	15
20	0.003555	97026	345	484298	0.000712	2.5931	5433367	0.0381	55.999	0.000710	20
25	0.004313	96681	417	482416	0.000864	2.6320	4949069	0.0190	51.190	0.000862	25
30	0.006329	96264	609	479893	0.001269	2.6605	4466654	0.0000	46.400	0.001269	30
35	0.009265	95654	886	476203	0.001861	2.6658	3986761	0.0000	41.679	0.001861	35
40	0.013871	94768	1315	470778	0.002792	2.6702	3510557	0.0007	37.044	0.002792	40
45	0.020976	93454	1960	462685	0.004237	2.6618	3039779	0.0119	32.527	0.004228	45
50	0.031003	91493	2837	450799	0.006292	2.6493	2577094	0.0152	28.167	0.006277	50
55	0.045034	88657	3993	433897	0.009202	2.6487	2126295	0.0185	23.983	0.009173	55
60	0.067170	84664	5687	410024	0.013870	2.6618	1692399	0.0246	19.990	0.013804	60
65	0.106478	78977	8409	375002	0.022425	2.6355	1282375	0.0246	16.237	0.022324	65
70	0.158070	70568	11155	326260	0.034190	2.6171	907372	0.0246	12.858	0.034030	70
75	0.247088	59413	14680	261624	0.056112	2.5857	581112	0.0246	9.781	0.055834	75
80	0.384378	44733	17194	180614	0.095199	2.6558	319488	0.0246	7.142	0.094774	80
85+	1.000000	27539	27539	138874	0.198299	5.0429	138874	0.0246	5.043	0.195315	85+

TABLE 4 — OBSERVED AND PROJECTED VITAL RATES

RATES PER THOUSAND	OBSERVED POPULATION BOTH SEXES	MALES	FEMALES	PROJECTED 1970 MALES	FEMALES	1975 MALES	FEMALES	1980 MALES	FEMALES	STABLE POPULATION MALES	FEMALES
Birth	19.61	20.44	18.81	22.12	20.26	23.68	21.65	24.38	22.29	22.77	21.29
Death	9.43	10.88	8.03	11.02	8.62	10.96	8.95	10.72	9.06	10.12	8.64
Increase	10.18	9.56	10.78	11.11	11.64	12.72	12.69	13.65	13.24	12.6505	
PERCENTAGE											
under 15	30.91	32.06	29.80	30.84	28.48	30.04	27.63	30.26	27.87	30.15	28.39
15-64	59.72	59.60	59.84	60.79	60.62	61.66	61.17	61.51	60.68	62.44	61.01
65 and over	9.37	8.34	10.36	8.37	10.89	8.30	11.20	8.24	11.45	7.41	10.60
DEP. RATIO X 100	67.44	67.78	67.11	64.51	64.95	62.17	63.49	62.58	64.80	60.16	63.90

With Adjusted Births

TABLE 5 — POPULATION PROJECTED WITH FIXED AGE-SPECIFIC BIRTH AND DEATH RATES (IN 1000's)

AGE AT LAST BIRTHDAY	1970 BOTH SEXES	1970 MALES	1970 FEMALES	1975 BOTH SEXES	1975 MALES	1975 FEMALES	1980 BOTH SEXES	1980 MALES	1980 FEMALES	AGE AT LAST BIRTHDAY
0-4	19836	10115	9721	22572	11511	11061	25201	12851	12350	0-4
5-9	20358	10389	9969	19761	10073	9688	22488	11463	11025	5-9
10-14	20477	10401	10076	20317	10364	9953	19722	10049	9673	10-14
15-19	18893	9591	9302	20408	10353	10055	20248	10316	9932	15-19
20-24	16858	8489	8369	18785	9512	9273	20291	10268	10023	20-24
25-29	13246	6478	6768	16746	8410	8336	18661	9424	9237	25-29
30-34	11122	5455	5667	13148	6416	6732	16620	8328	8292	30-34
35-39	10838	5311	5527	11010	5386	5624	13015	6335	6680	35-39
40-44	11742	5719	6023	10676	5212	5464	10846	5286	5560	40-44
45-49	12125	5857	6268	11471	5552	5919	10429	5059	5370	45-49
50-54	11035	5307	5728	11688	5581	6107	11058	5291	5767	50-54
55-59	9986	4765	5221	10428	4915	5513	11046	5168	5878	55-59
60-64	8410	3935	4475	9176	4243	4933	9586	4376	5210	60-64
65-69	6861	3112	3749	7394	3301	4093	8071	3559	4512	65-69
70-74	5203	2221	2982	5671	2409	3262	6116	2555	3561	70-74
75-79	3926	1596	2330	3944	1553	2391	4299	1684	2615	75-79
80-84	2349	931	1418	2571	962	1609	2587	936	1651	80-84
85+	1431	528	903	1689	599	1090	1856	619	1237	85+
TOTAL	204696	100200	104496	217455	106352	111103	232140	113567	118573	TOTAL

TABLE 6 — STANDARDIZED RATES

STANDARD COUNTRIES:

STANDARDIZED RATES PER THOUSAND	ENGLAND AND WALES 1961 BOTH SEXES	MALES	FEMALES	UNITED STATES 1960 BOTH SEXES	MALES	FEMALES	MEXICO 1960 BOTH SEXES	MALES	FEMALES
Birth	18.83	22.35*	17.83	19.20	20.67*	18.48	23.12	19.74*	22.53
Death	11.32	12.22*	10.39	9.30	10.91*	7.73	4.98	8.74*	3.87
Increase	7.52	10.14*	7.44	9.91	9.77*	10.75	18.14	11.00*	18.66

TABLE 7 — MOMENTS AND CUMULANTS

	OBSERVED POP. MALES	FEMALES	STATIONARY POP. MALES	FEMALES	STABLE POP. MALES	FEMALES	OBSERVED BIRTHS	NET MATERNITY FUNCTION	BIRTHS IN STABLE POP.
μ	30.76966	32.45138	36.31209	39.22675	30.29530	32.41644	25.93169	26.52258	26.06189
σ^2	483.0224	512.8470	498.7096	561.1014	447.6363	508.4277	156.5260	123.9188	125.4173
κ_3	5238.099	5078.529	2772.020	2333.669	5079.454	5707.635	37.05371	35.12088	33.54172
κ_4	-189976.	-232205.	-230914.	-325980.	-126455.	-192323.	-136.726	-191.354	-38.638
β_1	0.243470	0.191211	0.061951	0.030829	0.287646	0.247870	0.481591	0.354469	0.416829
β_2	2.185739	2.117133	2.071557	1.964600	2.368917	2.256000	2.900416	2.844866	2.965656
κ	-0.086601	-0.067774	-0.024074	-0.011307	-0.113253	-0.092642	-0.251036	-0.213634	-0.264917

TABLE 8 — RATES FROM AGE DISTRIBUTIONS AND VITAL STATISTICS (Females)

VITAL STATISTICS		THOMPSON AGE RANGE	NRR	1000r	INTERVAL	BOURGEOIS-PICHAT AGE RANGE	NRR	1000b	1000d	1000r	COALE	
GRR	1.446											
NRR	1.395	0-4	1.51	15.38	27.41	5-29	2.17	27.19	-1.47	28.66	IBR	
TFR	2.960	5-9	1.62	17.92	27.37	30-54	0.97	12.00	13.30	-1.30	IDR	
GENERATION	26.291	10-14	1.54	15.67	27.31	55-79	1.46	24.42	10.43	13.99	IRI	
SEX RATIO	104.719	15-19	1.41	12.03	27.22	*45-69	1.58	29.11	12.22	16.89	K1	
											K2	

TABLE 9 — LESLIE MATRIX AND ITS SPECTRAL COMPONENTS (Females)

Start of Age Interval	ORIGINAL MATRIX SUB-DIAGONAL	ALTERNATIVE FIRST ROWS Projection	Integral	FIRST STABLE MATRIX % IN STABLE POPULATION	FISHER VALUES	REPRODUCTIVE VALUES	SECOND STABLE MATRIX Z_2 FIRST COLUMN	FIRST ROW
0	0.99669	0.00000	0.00000	10.100	1.055	10549785	0.1748+0.0943	0.1748+0.0943
5	0.99838	0.00099	0.00000	9.448	1.127	11378528	0.1872-0.1509	-0.0159+0.1632
10	0.99795	0.08601	0.00204	8.854	1.202	11205023	-0.0808-0.2803	-0.1293+0.0400
15	0.99685	0.32202	0.17586	8.294	1.192	10010789	-0.3513-0.0413	-0.0868-0.0937
20	0.99611	0.43270	0.49042	7.760	0.934	6343797	-0.2109+0.3729	-0.0129-0.1264
25	0.99477	0.31006	0.40436	7.255	0.541	3079232	0.3172+0.4102	0.0163-0.0913
30	0.99231	0.17069	0.23693	6.774	0.250	1393118	0.6056-0.1615	0.0203-0.0462
35	0.98861	0.07177	0.11632	6.310	0.087	530598	0.1033-0.7486	0.0118-0.0155
40	0.98281	0.01656	0.03220	5.855	0.017	110296	-0.7809-0.4627	0.0030-0.0028
45	0.97431	0.00098	0.00203	5.401	0.001	5714	-0.8706+0.6457	0.0002-0.0001
50	0.96251	0.00000	0.00000	4.939	0.000	1	0.3055+1.2463	0.0000-0.0000
55+	0.81532			19.010				

TABLE 10 — AGE ANALYSIS AND MISCELLANEOUS RESULTS (Females)

Start of Age Interval	OBSERVED POPUL. (IN 100's)	CONTRIBUTIONS OF ROOTS (IN 100's) r_1	r_2, r_3	$r_4 \text{-} r_{11}$	AGE-SP. BIRTH RATES	NET MATERNITY FUNCTION	COEFF. OF MATRIX EQUATION	PARAMETERS	INTEGRAL	MATRIX	EXP. INCREASE x	$e^{(x+2\frac{1}{2})r}$
0	100020	99629	-2694	3085	0.0000	0.0000	0.0000	L(1)	1.06530	1.06540	0	1.0321
5	100920	93204	8268	-552	0.0000	0.0000	0.0010	L(2)	0.30579	0.31879	50	1.9428
10	93210	87341	11727	-5858	0.0004	0.0020	0.0855		0.78901	0.75878	55	2.0697
15	83950	81812	-1145	3284	0.0348	0.1692	0.3198	R(1)	0.01265	0.01267	60	2.2048
20	67940	76548	-18297	9689	0.0971	0.4704	0.4283	R(2)	-0.03340	-0.03895	65	2.3488
25	56970	71570	-15476	876	0.0801	0.3863	0.3057			0.24021	0.23461	70	2.5022
30	55700	66825	12276	-23401	0.0469	0.2252	0.1674	C(1)		986452	75	2.6656
35	60920	62241	34018	-35339	0.0230	0.1197	0.0699	C(2)		423267	80	2.8396
40	63780	57755	13876	-7851	0.0064	0.0300	0.0159			2213743	85	3.0250
45	58790	53278	-35958	41471	0.0004	0.0019	0.0009	2P/Y	26.1568	26.7812	90	3.2226
50	54240	48723	-52592	58109	0.0000	0.0000	0.0000	DELTA	4.2768		95	3.4330
55+	190590	187526									100	3.6571

TABLE 1 — DATA

AGE AT LAST BIRTHDAY	POPULATION BOTH SEXES	MALES Number	%	FEMALES Number	%	BIRTHS BY AGE OF MOTHER	DEATHS BOTH SEXES	MALES	FEMALES	AGE AT LAST BIRTHDAY
0	462442	235259	2.2	227183	2.2	0	28406	15590	12816	0
1-4	1739664	885022	8.3	854642	8.2	0	6224	3171	3053	1-4
5-9	2127925	1083485	10.1	1044440	10.0	0	1878	1084	794	5-9
10-14	1972062	996424	9.3	975638	9.4	1157	1421	850	571	10-14
15-19	1781393	901628	8.4	879765	8.5	48692	2185	1280	905	15-19
20-24	1737593	882372	8.2	855221	8.2	128955	2787	1630	1157	20-24
25-29	1794116	904932	8.5	889184	8.6	131402	3151	1864	1287	25-29
30-34	1693921	852403	8.0	841518	8.1	94538	3789	2243	1546	30-34
35-39	1444477	719997	6.7	724480	7.0	50768	4394	2641	1753	35-39
40-44	1357335	680407	6.4	676928	6.5	16590	5301	3317	1984	40-44
45-49	1258707	642821	6.0	615886	5.9	2611	7515	4791	2724	45-49
50-54	1085068	574383	5.4	510685	4.9	726	10418	6967	3451	50-54
55-59	883557	460009	4.3	423548	4.1	0	13232	8995	4237	55-59
60-64	667171	352786	3.3	314385	3.0	0	15929	10570	5359	60-64
65-69	512404	263423	2.5	248981	2.4	0	16895	10943	5952	65-69
70-74	272882	133810	1.3	139072	1.3		15734	9473	6261	70-74
75-79	175271	80801	0.8	94470	0.9		15296	8406	6890	75-79
80-84	94480	40072	0.4	54408	0.5	242494 M.	13061	6371	6690	80-84
85+	36935	14047	0.1	22888	0.2	232945 F.	3861	3695	5166	85+
TOTAL	21097403	10704081		10393322		475439	176477	103881	72596	TOTAL

TABLE 2 — MALE LIFE TABLE

x	$_nq_x$	l_x	$_nd_x$	$_nL_x$	$_nm_x$	$_na_x$	T_x	r_x	$\dot{e}_x$	$_nM_x$	x
0	0.063030	100000	6303	95359	0.066097	0.2636	6253240	0.0034	62.532	0.066267	0
1	0.014132	93697	1324	370966	0.003569	1.1133	6157881	0.0034	65.721	0.003583	1
5	0.004967	92373	459	460717	0.000996	2.5000	5786916	0.0101	62.647	0.001000	5
10	0.004264	91914	392	458630	0.000855	2.6008	5326198	0.0174	57.948	0.000853	10
15	0.007086	91522	648	456082	0.001422	2.6425	4867569	0.0108	53.185	0.001420	15
20	0.009195	90874	836	452336	0.001847	2.5684	4411487	0.0000	48.545	0.001847	20
25	0.010249	90038	923	447952	0.002060	2.5751	3959150	0.0013	43.972	0.002060	25
30	0.013108	89115	1168	442797	0.002638	2.6213	3511198	0.0201	39.401	0.002631	30
35	0.018225	87947	1603	435919	0.003677	2.6189	3068401	0.0189	34.889	0.003668	35
40	0.024123	86344	2083	426825	0.004880	2.6490	2632482	0.0062	30.488	0.004875	40
45	0.036699	84261	3092	414144	0.007467	2.6836	2205657	0.0091	26.176	0.007453	45
50	0.059229	81169	4808	394677	0.012181	2.6768	1791513	0.0208	22.071	0.012130	50
55	0.093932	76362	7173	364898	0.019657	2.6425	1396836	0.0286	18.292	0.019554	55
60	0.140384	69189	9713	322520	0.030116	2.5884	1031938	0.0343	14.915	0.029962	60
65	0.189877	59476	11293	270164	0.041801	2.5901	709418	0.0343	11.928	0.041542	65
70	0.302973	48183	14598	204954	0.071226	2.5367	439254	0.0343	9.116	0.070794	70
75	0.412844	33585	13865	132541	0.104611	2.4481	234300	0.0343	6.976	0.104033	75
80	0.565262	19719	11147	69628	0.160089	2.4011	101759	0.0343	5.160	0.158990	80
85+	*1.000000	8573	8573	32131	0.266806	3.7480	32131	0.0343	3.748	0.263045	85+

TABLE 3 — FEMALE LIFE TABLE

x	$_nq_x$	l_x	$_nd_x$	$_nL_x$	$_nm_x$	$_na_x$	T_x	r_x	$\dot{e}_x$	$_nM_x$	x
0	0.054075	100000	5408	96113	0.056262	0.2813	6816375	0.0035	68.164	0.056413	0
1	0.014095	94592	1333	374543	0.003560	1.1297	6720261	0.0035	71.044	0.003572	1
5	0.003772	93259	352	465417	0.000756	2.5000	6345718	0.0089	68.044	0.000760	5
10	0.002927	92907	272	463883	0.000586	2.5954	5880302	0.0164	63.292	0.000585	10
15	0.005141	92636	476	462060	0.001031	2.6529	5416418	0.0122	58.470	0.001029	15
20	0.006742	92159	621	459282	0.001353	2.5617	4954358	0.0000	53.759	0.001353	20
25	0.007212	91538	660	456084	0.001447	2.5667	4495077	0.0001	49.106	0.001447	25
30	0.009164	90878	833	452396	0.001841	2.6063	4038993	0.0186	44.444	0.001837	30
35	0.012050	90045	1085	447609	0.002424	2.5891	3586597	0.0194	39.831	0.002420	35
40	0.014580	88960	1297	441733	0.002936	2.6352	3138988	0.0131	35.285	0.002931	40
45	0.021981	87663	1927	433824	0.004442	2.6697	2697256	0.0236	30.769	0.004423	45
50	0.033433	85736	2866	421963	0.006793	2.6567	2263432	0.0305	26.400	0.006758	50
55	0.049262	82870	4082	404898	0.010082	2.6852	1841469	0.0377	22.221	0.010004	55
60	0.082440	78787	6495	378567	0.017157	2.6337	1436571	0.0386	18.234	0.017046	60
65	0.114240	72292	8251	342211	0.024112	2.6672	1058004	0.0386	14.635	0.023905	65
70	0.204835	64041	13118	288992	0.045391	2.6207	715793	0.0386	11.177	0.045020	70
75	0.311263	50923	15850	215691	0.073486	2.5444	426802	0.0386	8.381	0.072933	75
80	0.470275	35072	16494	133192	0.123834	2.5345	211110	0.0386	6.019	0.122960	80
85+	1.000000	18579	18579	77918	0.238439	4.1939	77918	0.0386	4.194	0.225707	85+

TABLE 4 — OBSERVED AND PROJECTED VITAL RATES

	OBSERVED POPULATION BOTH SEXES	MALES	FEMALES	PROJECTED POPULATION 1966 MALES	FEMALES	1971 MALES	FEMALES	1976 MALES	FEMALES	STABLE POPULATION MALES	FEMALES
RATES PER THOUSAND											
Birth	22.54	22.65	22.41	22.00	21.50	21.70	20.98	21.61	20.69	21.23	19.85
Death	8.36	9.70	6.98	10.27	7.48	10.83	7.98	11.38	8.62	12.82	11.43
Increase	14.17	12.95	15.43	11.72	14.02	10.87	12.99	10.23	12.07		8.4115
PERCENTAGE											
under 15	29.87	29.90	29.85	29.29	28.83	28.48	27.78	28.03	27.11	27.65	26.11
15-64	64.95	65.13	64.77	65.07	65.02	65.22	65.09	65.00	64.81	64.21	62.64
65 and over	5.18	4.97	5.39	5.65	6.15	6.30	7.13	6.97	8.09	8.15	11.26
DEP. RATIO X 100	53.96	53.54	54.40	53.69	53.79	53.33	53.64	53.85	54.31	55.75	59.65

AGE AT LAST BIRTHDAY	BOTH SEXES	1966 MALES	FEMALES	BOTH SEXES	1971 MALES	FEMALES	BOTH SEXES	1976 MALES	FEMALES	AGE AT LAST BIRTHDAY	
0-4	2263	1149	1114	2350	1193	1157	2460	1249	1211	0-4	
5-9	2177	1107	1070	2238	1136	1102	2323	1179	1144	5-9	
10-14	2120	1079	1041	2168	1102	1066	2228	1130	1098	10-14	
15-19	1963	991	972	2110	1073	1037	2158	1096	1062	15-19	**TABLE 5**
20-24	1768	894	874	1949	983	966	2095	1064	1031	20-24	POPULATION
25-29	1723	874	849	1754	886	868	1932	973	959	25-29	PROJECTED
30-34	1777	895	882	1706	864	842	1736	875	861	30-34	WITH
35-39	1672	839	833	1754	881	873	1683	850	833	35-39	FIXED
40-44	1420	705	715	1644	822	822	1723	862	861	40-44	AGE—
45-49	1325	660	665	1386	684	702	1604	797	807	45-49	SPECIFIC
50-54	1212	613	599	1276	629	647	1335	652	683	50-54	BIRTH
55-59	1021	531	490	1141	566	575	1202	582	620	55-59	AND
60-64	803	407	396	927	469	458	1038	501	537	60-64	DEATH
65-69	580	296	284	699	341	358	807	393	414	65-69	RATES
70-74	410	200	210	464	224	240	560	258	302	70-74	(IN 1000's)
75-79	191	87	104	286	129	157	324	145	179	75-79	
80-84	100	42	58	109	45	64	165	68	97	80-84	
85+	50	18	32	54	20	34	58	21	37	85+	
TOTAL	22575	11387	11188	24015	12047	11968	25431	12695	12736	TOTAL	

STANDARD COUNTRIES:	ENGLAND AND WALES 1961			UNITED STATES 1960			MEXICO 1960			
STANDARDIZED RATES PER THOUSAND	BOTH SEXES	MALES	FEMALES	BOTH SEXES	MALES	FEMALES	BOTH SEXES	MALES	FEMALES	**TABLE 6**
Birth	18.20	19.20*	17.28	18.54	17.98*	17.90	21.02	17.64*	20.55	STANDAR-
Death	13.97	16.14*	13.38	11.86	13.40*	10.39	7.32	9.59*	6.20	DIZED
Increase	4.23	3.05*	3.90	6.68	4.58*	7.51	13.70	8.05*	14.34	RATES

	OBSERVED POP.		STATIONARY POP.		STABLE POP.		OBSERVED BIRTHS	NET MATERNITY FUNCTION	BIRTHS IN STABLE POP.	
	MALES	FEMALES	MALES	FEMALES	MALES	FEMALES				
μ	29.42430	29.42797	35.68692	38.13758	31.74903	33.74437	27.81663	28.16489	27.77102	**TABLE 7**
σ^2	393.1057	397.1226	481.1782	535.1880	452.8642	506.2953	42.03775	45.36233	44.11675	MOMENTS
κ_3	3604.580	4014.708	2517.069	2285.258	4132.865	4484.380	130.7233	146.1551	149.8513	AND
κ_4	-105335.	-89407.	-219203.	-293411.	-160844.	-222435.	-276.277	-490.001	-378.383	CUMULANTS
β_1	0.213886	0.257356	0.056869	0.034068	0.183907	0.154951	0.230032	0.228845	0.261523	
β_2	2.318364	2.433077	2.053250	1.975612	2.215726	2.132250	2.843661	2.761874	2.805587	
κ	-0.087393	-0.111210	-0.021869	-0.012567	-0.070976	-0.057504	-0.183290	-0.157655	-0.179925	

VITAL STATISTICS		THOMPSON				BOURGEOIS-PICHAT				COALE		**TABLE 8**
		AGE RANGE	NRR	1000r	INTERVAL	AGE RANGE	NRR	1000b	1000d	1000r			RATES
GRR	1.391										IBR		FROM AGE
NRR	1.265	0-4	1.28	9.24	27.38	5-29	1.24	22.24	14.18	8.06	IDR		DISTRI-
TFR	2.838	5-9	1.31	10.00	27.34	30-54	1.71	33.79	13.98	19.81	IRI		BUTIONS
GENERATION	27.967	10-14	1.31	9.83	27.28	55-79	3.78	175.31	126.07	49.23	K1		AND VITAL
SEX RATIO	104.099	15-19	1.31	9.52	27.19	*25-49	1.56	29.80	13.24	16.56	K2		STATISTICS (Females)

Start of Age Interval	ORIGINAL MATRIX			FIRST STABLE MATRIX			SECOND STABLE MATRIX Z_2		
	SUB-DIAGONAL	ALTERNATIVE FIRST ROWS Projection	Integral	% IN STABLE POPULATION	FISHER VALUES	REPRODUCTIVE VALUES	FIRST COLUMN	FIRST ROW	
0	0.98887	0.00000	0.00000	9.149	1.085	1173573	0.1404+0.0828	0.1404+0.0828	
5	0.99671	0.00136	0.00000	8.674	1.144	1195037	0.1714-0.1012	-0.0037+0.1334	**TABLE 9**
10	0.99607	0.06493	0.00279	8.289	1.196	1166712	-0.0070-0.2450	-0.0965+0.0496	LESLIE
15	0.99309	0.23663	0.13034	7.916	1.181	1039414	-0.2680-0.1382	-0.0824-0.0545	MATRIX
20	0.99304	0.34306	0.35510	7.544	0.981	839377	-0.3076-0.2060	-0.0270-0.0999	AND ITS
25	0.99191	0.29887	0.34802	7.183	0.656	583381	0.0387+0.4524	0.0122-0.0873	SPECTRAL
30	0.98942	0.20947	0.26457	6.831	0.363	305479	0.5080+0.2265	0.0248-0.0507	COMPO-
35	0.98687	0.10868	0.16503	6.480	0.153	110844	0.5425-0.4096	0.0164-0.0198	NENTS
40	0.98210	0.03306	0.05772	6.131	0.042	28586	-0.1172-0.8203	0.0053-0.0052	(Females)
45	0.97266	0.00648	0.00998	5.773	0.008	5132	-0.9397-0.3567	0.0011-0.0011	
50	0.95956	0.00164	0.00335	5.384	0.002	871	-0.9210+0.7809	0.0003-0.0002	
55+	0.79279			20.648					

Start of Age Interval	OBSERVED POPUL. (IN 100's)	CONTRIBUTIONS OF ROOTS (IN 100's)			AGE-SP. BIRTH RATES	NET MATERNITY FUNCTION	COEFF. OF MATRIX EQUATION	PARAMETERS			EXP. INCREASE		
		r_1	r_2, r_3	r_4-r_{11}					INTEGRAL	MATRIX	x	$e^{(x+2\frac{1}{2})r}$	
0	10818	10723	125	-30	0.0000	0.0000	0.0000	L(1)	1.04295	1.04300	0	1.0213	**TABLE 10**
5	10444	10166	181	97	0.0000	0.0000	0.0013	L(2)	0.38269	0.39151	50	1.5552	AGE
10	9756	9715	27	14	0.0006	0.0027	0.0640		0.72826	0.70867	55	1.6220	ANALYSIS
15	8798	9278	-242	-238	0.0271	0.1253	0.2323	R(1)	0.00841	0.00842	60	1.6917	AND
20	8552	8842	-329	39	0.0739	0.3393	0.3348	R(2)	-0.03904	-0.04224	65	1.7643	MISCEL-
25	8892	8418	-25	498	0.0724	0.3302	0.2896		0.21739	0.21321	70	1.8401	LANEOUS
30	8415	8006	464	-55	0.0550	0.2490	0.2013	C(1)		117207	75	1.9192	RESULTS
35	7245	7595	586	-936	0.0343	0.1537	0.1034	C(2)		48779	80	2.0016	(Females)
40	6769	7186	-1	-416	0.0120	0.0530	0.0310			6938	85	2.0876	
45	6159	6767	-867	259	0.0021	0.0090	0.0060	2P/Y	28.9025	29.4690	90	2.1772	
50	5107	6310	-1007	-197	0.0007	0.0029	0.0015	DELTA	8.6376		95	2.2708	
55+	12978	24201									100	2.3683	

TABLE 1 — DATA

AGE AT LAST BIRTHDAY	POPULATION BOTH SEXES	MALES Number	%	FEMALES Number	%	BIRTHS BY AGE OF MOTHER	DEATHS BOTH SEXES	MALES	FEMALES	AGE AT LAST BIRTHDAY
0	18375	9420	4.2	8955	3.9	0	1487	852	635	0
1-4	63575	32285	14.3	31290	13.7	0	576	305	271	1-4
5-9	61300	31035	13.7	30265	13.3	0	108	62	46	5-9
10-14	49030	24800	11.0	24230	10.6	145	56	31	25	10-14
15-19	41770	21005	9.3	20765	9.1	3308	99	45	54	15-19
20-24	37960	18865	8.3	19095	8.4	6185	109	39	70	20-24
25-29	31770	15480	6.8	16290	7.2	4697	116	42	74	25-29
30-34	27835	13745	6.1	14090	6.2	2998	129	62	67	30-34
35-39	25225	12545	5.5	12680	5.6	1588	146	70	76	35-39
40-44	22320	11170	4.9	11150	4.9	480	216	119	97	40-44
45-49	20700	10565	4.7	10135	4.5	43	238	134	104	45-49
50-54	16235	8185	3.6	8050	3.5	5	376	217	159	50-54
55-59	12690	6285	2.8	6405	2.8	0	323	183	140	55-59
60-64	8985	4290	1.9	4695	2.1	0	332	191	141	60-64
65-69	6825	2875	1.3	3950	1.7	0	478	259	219	65-69
70-74	4760	1910	0.8	2850	1.3		350	171	179	70-74
75-79	2770	1005	0.4	1765	0.8		309	131	178	75-79
80-84	1145	450	0.2	695	0.3	9899 M.	216	85	131	80-84
85+	520	195	0.1	325	0.1	9550 F.	193	56	137	85+
TOTAL	453790	226110		227680		19449	5857	3054	2803	TOTAL

TABLE 2 — MALE LIFE TABLE

x	nq_x	l_x	nd_x	nL_x	nm_x	na_x	T_x	r_x	$\dot{e}_x$	nM_x	x
0	0.084746	100000	8475	94347	0.089824	0.3329	5433932	0.0098	54.339	0.090446	0
1	0.036576	91525	3348	356704	0.009385	1.1926	5339585	0.0098	58.340	0.009447	1
5	0.009603	88178	847	438772	0.001930	2.5000	4982881	0.0484	56.509	0.001998	5
10	0.006239	87331	545	435310	0.001252	2.5306	4544109	0.0374	52.033	0.001250	10
15	0.010678	86786	927	431685	0.002147	2.5764	4108799	0.0255	47.344	0.002142	15
20	0.010301	85860	884	427133	0.002071	2.5530	3677114	0.0283	42.827	0.002067	20
25	0.013553	84975	1152	422202	0.002728	2.6791	3249981	0.0287	38.246	0.002713	25
30	0.022364	83823	1875	414662	0.004521	2.6237	2827778	0.0168	33.735	0.004511	30
35	0.027634	81949	2265	404556	0.005598	2.7088	2413116	0.0142	29.447	0.005580	35
40	0.052004	79684	4144	388563	0.010665	2.6211	2008560	0.0074	25.206	0.010654	40
45	0.061855	75540	4673	367003	0.012732	2.7104	1619997	0.0157	21.445	0.012683	45
50	0.125050	70868	8862	332972	0.026615	2.5889	1252994	0.0281	17.681	0.026512	50
55	0.136356	62006	8455	289297	0.029226	2.5480	920022	0.0328	14.838	0.029117	55
60	0.201857	53551	10810	242243	0.044623	2.6399	630725	0.0095	11.778	0.044522	60
65	0.367680	42741	15715	174204	0.090211	2.4863	388481	0.0095	9.089	0.090087	65
70	0.361801	27026	9778	109162	0.089574	2.3442	214278	0.0095	7.929	0.089529	70
75	0.487065	17248	8401	64356	0.130538	2.3950	105116	0.0095	6.094	0.130348	75
80	0.626846	8847	5546	29309	0.189219	2.3084	40759	0.0095	4.607	0.188890	80
85+	*1.000000	3301	3301	11451	0.288311	3.4685	11451	0.0095	3.468	0.287179	85+

TABLE 3 — FEMALE LIFE TABLE

x	nq_x	l_x	nd_x	nL_x	nm_x	na_x	T_x	r_x	$\dot{e}_x$	nM_x	x
0	0.067399	100000	6740	95621	0.070485	0.3503	5749520	0.0087	57.495	0.070910	0
1	0.033657	93260	3139	364317	0.008616	1.2209	5653898	0.0087	60.625	0.008661	1
5	0.007264	90121	655	448970	0.001458	2.5000	5289581	0.0477	58.694	0.001520	5
10	0.005190	89467	464	446277	0.001040	2.7248	4840612	0.0362	54.105	0.001032	10
15	0.012983	89002	1156	442359	0.002612	2.7047	4394335	0.0213	49.373	0.002601	15
20	0.018211	87847	1600	435398	0.003674	2.6021	3951975	0.0206	44.987	0.003666	20
25	0.022492	86247	1940	426466	0.004549	2.5413	3516577	0.0260	40.773	0.004543	25
30	0.023531	84307	1984	416680	0.004761	2.5523	3090112	0.0201	36.653	0.004755	30
35	0.029615	82323	2438	405819	0.006008	2.6217	2673431	0.0171	32.475	0.005994	35
40	0.042664	79885	3408	391200	0.008712	2.5863	2267613	0.0141	28.386	0.008700	40
45	0.050332	76477	3849	373484	0.010306	2.6874	1876412	0.0205	24.536	0.010261	45
50	0.094593	72628	6870	346587	0.019822	2.5906	1502928	0.0279	20.694	0.019752	50
55	0.103995	65758	6838	311987	0.021919	2.5430	1156341	0.0308	17.585	0.021858	55
60	0.140534	58919	8280	275048	0.030105	2.6391	844354	0.0117	14.331	0.030032	60
65	0.244237	50639	12368	222715	0.055533	2.5355	569306	0.0117	11.242	0.055443	65
70	0.271412	38271	10387	165156	0.062894	2.4776	346591	0.0117	9.056	0.062807	70
75	0.403585	27884	11254	111317	0.101095	2.5028	181436	0.0117	6.507	0.100850	75
80	0.633612	16630	10537	55734	0.189063	2.3980	70119	0.0117	4.216	0.188490	80
85+	*1.000000	6093	6093	14385	0.423587	2.3608	14385	0.0117	2.361	0.421538	85+

TABLE 4 — OBSERVED AND PROJECTED VITAL RATES

	OBSERVED POPULATION BOTH SEXES	MALES	FEMALES	PROJECTED POPULATION 1959 MALES	FEMALES	1964 MALES	FEMALES	1969 MALES	FEMALES	STABLE POPULATION MALES	FEMALES
RATES PER THOUSAND											
Birth	42.86	43.78	41.94	42.09	40.44	41.66	40.11	42.85	41.32	44.89	43.67
Death	12.91	13.51	12.31	12.96	11.68	12.53	11.31	12.27	11.04	11.13	9.91
Increase	29.95	30.27	29.63	29.13	28.76	29.14	28.80	30.58	30.28		33.7591
PERCENTAGE											
under 15	42.37	43.14	41.61	45.19	43.96	45.97	45.00	45.40	44.76	46.74	46.48
15-64	54.10	54.02	54.18	52.28	52.36	51.57	51.53	52.20	51.92	51.72	51.36
65 and over	3.53	2.85	4.21	2.53	3.69	2.46	3.47	2.40	3.31	1.54	2.16
DEP. RATIO X 100	84.85	85.13	84.57	91.29	91.00	93.91	94.05	91.57	92.60	93.35	94.71

AGE AT LAST BIRTHDAY	1959 BOTH SEXES	1959 MALES	FEMALES	1964 BOTH SEXES	1964 MALES	FEMALES	1969 BOTH SEXES	1969 MALES	FEMALES	AGE AT LAST BIRTHDAY	
0-4	93	47	46	106	53	53	125	63	62	0-4	
5-9	80	41	39	91	46	45	103	52	51	5-9	TABLE 5
10-14	61	31	30	79	40	39	91	46	45	10-14	
15-19	49	25	24	61	31	30	79	40	39	15-19	POPULATION
20-24	41	21	20	48	24	24	59	30	29	20-24	PROJECTED
25-29	38	19	19	41	21	20	47	24	23	25-29	WITH
30-34	31	15	16	36	18	18	40	20	20	30-34	FIXED
35-39	27	13	14	31	15	16	36	18	18	35-39	AGE—
40-44	24	12	12	26	13	13	29	14	15	40-44	SPECIFIC
45-49	22	11	11	23	11	12	25	12	13	45-49	BIRTH
50-54	19	10	9	20	10	10	21	10	11	50-54	AND
55-59	14	7	7	16	8	8	17	8	9	55-59	DEATH
60-64	11	5	6	12	6	6	14	7	7	60-64	RATES
65-69	7	3	4	9	4	5	9	4	5	65-69	(IN 1000's)
70-74	5	2	3	5	2	3	5	2	3	70-74	
75-79	3	1	2	3	1	2	3	1	2	75-79	
80-84	1	0	1	2	1	1	1	0	1	80-84	
85+	0	0	0	0	0	0	0	0	0	85+	
TOTAL	526	263	263	609	304	305	704	351	353	TOTAL	

STANDARD COUNTRIES:	ENGLAND AND WALES 1961 BOTH SEXES	MALES	FEMALES	UNITED STATES 1960 BOTH SEXES	MALES	FEMALES	MEXICO 1960 BOTH SEXES	MALES	FEMALES	
STANDARDIZED RATES PER THOUSAND										TABLE 6
Birth	37.34	44.09*	35.53	38.20	40.33*	36.95	44.49	41.55*	43.58	STANDAR-
Death	23.04	30.14*	23.87	19.50	23.98*	18.75	12.11	12.72*	11.15	DIZED
Increase	14.30	13.95*	11.66	18.70	16.35*	18.20	32.38	28.82*	32.42	RATES

	OBSERVED POP. MALES	FEMALES	STATIONARY POP. MALES	FEMALES	STABLE POP. MALES	FEMALES	OBSERVED BIRTHS	NET MATERNITY FUNCTION	BIRTHS IN STABLE POP.	
μ	23.34982	24.32399	32.85932	34.31508	20.77038	21.16171	26.10533	27.07862	25.59593	TABLE 7
σ^2	355.2523	384.8878	422.3350	464.1570	283.0663	302.0949	41.22452	44.24022	39.33174	
κ_3	5392.889	6196.914	2630.264	2918.433	4583.163	5291.734	154.8313	134.6986	152.6225	MOMENTS
κ_4	-23963.	-22682.	-150087.	-195511.	25112.	38373.	-373.491	-839.615	-225.386	AND
β_1	0.648683	0.673517	0.091839	0.085174	0.926117	1.015701	0.342177	0.209543	0.382832	CUMULANTS
β_2	2.810129	2.846887	2.158547	2.092511	3.313405	3.420474	2.780230	2.571012	2.854306	
κ	-0.253250	-0.264109	-0.037323	-0.032868	-0.409466	-0.446144	-0.193128	-0.113270	-0.221848	

VITAL STATISTICS		AGE RANGE	THOMPSON NRR	1000r	INTERVAL	AGE RANGE	BOURGEOIS-PICHAT NRR	1000b	1000d	1000r	COALE		TABLE 8
GRR	2.856												RATES FROM AGE
NRR	2.432	0-4	2.34	31.33	27.17	5-29	2.07	34.64	7.65	26.99	IBR	34.78	DISTRI-
TFR	5.817	5-9	1.98	25.66	27.06	30-54	1.62	26.77	8.93	17.84	IDR	8.59	BUTIONS
GENERATION	26.323	10-14	1.77	20.85	26.92	55-79	1.30	14.89	5.23	9.66	IRI	26.19	AND VITAL
SEX RATIO	103.654	15-19	1.69	16.31	26.70	*10-34	1.86	31.62	8.56	23.06	K1	5.33	STATISTICS
											K2	0.	(Females)

Start of Age Interval	ORIGINAL MATRIX SUB-DIAGONAL	ALTERNATIVE FIRST ROWS Projection	Integral	FIRST STABLE MATRIX % IN STABLE POPULATION	FISHER VALUES	REPRODUCTIVE VALUES	SECOND STABLE MATRIX Z2 FIRST COLUMN	FIRST ROW	
0	0.97615	0.00000	0.00000	18.512	1.182	47559	0.1439+0.1186	0.1439+0.1186	TABLE 9
5	0.99400	0.00672	0.00000	15.253	1.434	43407	0.1889-0.0961	-0.0451+0.1577	
10	0.99122	0.18507	0.01471	12.798	1.701	41225	-0.0147-0.2449	-0.1414+0.0179	LESLIE
15	0.98426	0.53989	0.39147	10.708	1.813	37644	-0.2260-0.0974	-0.0900-0.1282	MATRIX
20	0.97948	0.68467	0.79594	8.896	1.534	29289	-0.2241+0.2350	-0.0077-0.1817	AND ITS
25	0.97705	0.56035	0.70853	7.355	1.029	16765	0.1436+0.3414	0.0428-0.1527	SPECTRAL
30	0.97393	0.37800	0.52285	6.066	0.570	8034	0.4214+0.0053	0.0555-0.0871	COMPO-
35	0.96398	0.18828	0.30774	4.987	0.235	2978	0.1964-0.4359	0.0341-0.0318	NENTS
40	0.95471	0.05319	0.10579	4.058	0.058	645	-0.3606-0.3976	0.0100-0.0066	(Females)
45	0.92798	0.00544	0.01043	3.270	0.006	61	-0.5654+0.1910	0.0010-0.0007	
50	0.90017	0.00070	0.00153	2.561	0.001	6	-0.0548+0.6426	0.0001-0.0001	
55+	0.76836			5.538					

Start of Age Interval	OBSERVED POPUL. (IN 100's)	CONTRIBUTIONS OF ROOTS (IN 100's) r_1	r_2, r_3	r_4-r_{11}	AGE-SP. BIRTH RATES	NET MATERNITY FUNCTION	COEFF. OF MATRIX EQUATION	PARAMETERS INTEGRAL	MATRIX	EXP. INCREASE x	$e^{(x+2\frac{1}{2})r}$	
0	402	379	20	3	0.0000	0.0000	0.0000	L(1) 1.18388	1.18471	0	1.0881	TABLE 10
5	303	313	2	-12	0.0000	0.0000	0.0066	L(2) 0.32668	0.34290	50	5.8847	
10	242	262	-25	5	0.0029	0.0131	0.1796	0.81429	0.78720	55	6.9667	AGE
15	208	219	-26	14	0.0782	0.3460	0.5193	R(1) 0.03376	0.03390	60	8.2478	ANALYSIS
20	191	182	10	-1	0.1590	0.6925	0.6481	R(2) -0.02616	-0.03048	65	9.7644	AND
25	163	151	42	-30	0.1416	0.6038	0.5196	0.23785	0.23200	70	11.5598	MISCEL-
30	141	124	26	-9	0.1045	0.4353	0.3424	C(1)	2050	75	13.6854	LANEOUS
35	127	102	-31	56	0.0615	0.2496	0.1661	C(2)	3008	80	16.2019	RESULTS
40	112	83	-61	89	0.0211	0.0827	0.0452		-4945	85	19.1810	(Females)
45	101	67	-15	49	0.0021	0.0078	0.0044	2P/Y 26.4161	27.0829	90	22.7080	
50	81	53	60	-32	0.0003	0.0011	0.0005	DELTA 7.1645		95	26.8835	
55+	207	114								100	31.8268	

TABLE 1 — DATA

AGE AT LAST BIRTHDAY	POPULATION BOTH SEXES	MALES Number	%	FEMALES Number	%	BIRTHS BY AGE OF MOTHER	DEATHS BOTH SEXES	MALES	FEMALES	AGE AT LAST BIRTHDAY
0	19430	9830	4.1	9600	4.0	0	1422	777	645	0
1-4	68880	34995	14.6	33885	14.1	0	484	253	231	1-4
5-9	67985	34255	14.3	33730	14.0	0	88	50	38	5-9
10-14	53130	26910	11.2	26220	10.9	229	37	22	15	10-14
15-19	43965	22080	9.2	21885	9.1	3278	83	37	46	15-19
20-24	39230	19635	8.2	19595	8.1	6699	106	47	59	20-24
25-29	33385	16385	6.8	17000	7.1	4989	119	59	60	25-29
30-34	28765	14170	5.9	14595	6.1	3356	112	45	67	30-34
35-39	25510	12870	5.4	12640	5.2	1625	135	65	70	35-39
40-44	22805	11390	4.8	11415	4.7	524	162	85	77	40-44
45-49	21285	10855	4.5	10430	4.3	29	211	123	88	45-49
50-54	17070	8560	3.6	8510	3.5	4	292	177	115	50-54
55-59	13410	6665	2.8	6745	2.8	0	358	217	141	55-59
60-64	9505	4560	1.9	4945	2.1	0	332	214	118	60-64
65-69	6790	2905	1.2	3885	1.6	0	402	196	206	65-69
70-74	4830	1925	0.8	2905	1.2		354	183	171	70-74
75-79	2895	1025	0.4	1870	0.8		274	121	153	75-79
80-84	1205	455	0.2	750	0.3	10461 M.	217	86	131	80-84
85+	415	170	0.1	245	0.1	10272 F.	192	59	133	85+
TOTAL	480490	239640		240850		20733	5380	2816	2564	TOTAL

TABLE 2 — MALE LIFE TABLE

x	$_nq_x$	l_x	$_nd_x$	$_nL_x$	$_nm_x$	$_na_x$	T_x	r_x	$\mathring{e}_x$	$_nM_x$	x
0	0.074646	100000	7465	94921	0.078640	0.3196	5662850	0.0071	56.628	0.079044	0
1	0.028193	92535	2609	362769	0.007191	1.1739	5567929	0.0071	60.171	0.007230	1
5	0.007008	89927	630	448057	0.001407	2.5000	5205160	0.0483	57.882	0.001460	5
10	0.004092	89296	365	445592	0.000820	2.5664	4757103	0.0428	53.273	0.000818	10
15	0.008395	88931	747	442932	0.001686	2.6922	4311510	0.0299	48.482	0.001676	15
20	0.011955	88184	1054	438455	0.002405	2.6601	3868579	0.0273	43.869	0.002394	20
25	0.017870	87130	1557	431820	0.003606	2.5397	3430124	0.0294	39.368	0.003601	25
30	0.015787	85573	1351	424602	0.003182	2.5850	2998304	0.0205	35.038	0.003176	30
35	0.025031	84222	2108	416187	0.005065	2.6646	2573702	0.0167	30.559	0.005051	35
40	0.036731	82114	3016	403503	0.007475	2.6572	2157515	0.0094	26.275	0.007463	40
45	0.055426	79098	4384	385444	0.011374	2.7087	1754012	0.0161	22.175	0.011331	45
50	0.099164	74714	7409	356259	0.020796	2.6637	1368568	0.0276	18.317	0.020678	50
55	0.151647	67305	10207	311973	0.032716	2.5946	1012308	0.0299	15.041	0.032558	55
60	0.210883	57098	12041	255978	0.047039	2.5489	700335	0.0160	12.265	0.046930	60
65	0.289273	45057	13034	192745	0.067622	2.5034	444358	0.0160	9.862	0.067470	65
70	0.382589	32023	12252	128631	0.095248	2.4301	251612	0.0160	7.857	0.095065	70
75	0.451273	19772	8922	75426	0.118293	2.3738	122982	0.0160	6.220	0.118049	75
80	0.631163	10849	6848	36102	0.189675	2.3503	47556	0.0160	4.383	0.189012	80
85+	*1.000000	4002	4002	11454	0.349368	2.8623	11454	0.0160	2.862	0.347059	85+

TABLE 3 — FEMALE LIFE TABLE

x	$_nq_x$	l_x	$_nd_x$	$_nL_x$	$_nm_x$	$_na_x$	T_x	r_x	$\mathring{e}_x$	$_nM_x$	x
0	0.063930	100000	6393	95726	0.066785	0.3314	6014934	0.0084	60.149	0.067187	0
1	0.026604	93607	2490	367431	0.006778	1.1904	5919208	0.0084	63.235	0.006817	1
5	0.005362	91117	489	454362	0.001075	2.5000	5551777	0.0483	60.930	0.001127	5
10	0.002902	90628	263	452579	0.000581	2.8666	5097415	0.0422	56.245	0.000572	10
15	0.010528	90365	951	449671	0.002116	2.7357	4644836	0.0272	51.401	0.002102	15
20	0.014979	89414	1339	443844	0.003018	2.5923	4195164	0.0223	46.919	0.003011	20
25	0.017539	88074	1545	436641	0.003538	2.5849	3751320	0.0258	42.593	0.003529	25
30	0.022752	86530	1969	427886	0.004601	2.5814	3314679	0.0251	38.307	0.004591	30
35	0.027363	84561	2314	417179	0.005546	2.5688	2886793	0.0190	34.139	0.005538	35
40	0.033221	82247	2732	404610	0.006753	2.5752	2469614	0.0124	30.027	0.006746	40
45	0.041498	79515	3300	389800	0.008465	2.6443	2065004	0.0202	25.970	0.008437	45
50	0.065847	76215	5019	369322	0.013588	2.6580	1675204	0.0295	21.980	0.013514	50
55	0.099812	71196	7106	338686	0.020982	2.5661	1305882	0.0347	18.342	0.020904	55
60	0.113478	64090	7273	303573	0.023957	2.6794	967196	0.0165	15.091	0.023862	60
65	0.235287	56817	13368	251471	0.053161	2.5602	663623	0.0165	11.680	0.053024	65
70	0.256305	43449	11136	188917	0.058947	2.4563	412152	0.0165	9.486	0.058864	70
75	0.341396	32313	11031	134355	0.082107	2.5335	223235	0.0165	6.909	0.081818	75
80	0.606773	21281	12913	73569	0.175520	2.4570	88879	0.0165	4.176	0.174667	80
85+	*1.000000	8368	8368	15310	0.546598	1.8295	15310	0.0165	1.829	0.542857	85+

TABLE 4 — OBSERVED AND PROJECTED VITAL RATES

	OBSERVED POPULATION BOTH SEXES	MALES	FEMALES	PROJECTED POPULATION 1961 MALES	FEMALES	1966 MALES	FEMALES	1971 MALES	FEMALES	STABLE POPULATION MALES	FEMALES
RATES PER THOUSAND											
Birth	43.15	43.65	42.65	42.27	41.27	42.33	41.31	43.72	42.65	45.79	44.77
Death	11.20	11.75	10.65	11.30	10.18	10.99	9.94	10.79	9.73	9.73	8.70
Increase	31.95	31.90	32.00	30.97	31.09	31.34	31.37	32.93	32.92	36.0682	
PERCENTAGE											
under 15	43.59	44.23	42.95	46.00	45.03	45.53	45.71	46.13	45.62	47.83	47.40
15-64	53.06	53.07	53.05	51.45	51.34	50.96	50.80	51.42	50.99	50.65	50.43
65 and over	3.36	2.70	4.01	2.54	3.64	2.51	3.49	2.45	3.38	1.52	2.17
DEP. RATIO X 100	88.48	88.44	88.52	94.35	94.79	96.23	96.85	94.49	96.11	97.45	98.31

TABLE 5 — POPULATION PROJECTED WITH FIXED AGE—SPECIFIC BIRTH AND DEATH RATES (IN 1000's)

AGE AT LAST BIRTHDAY	1961 BOTH SEXES	1961 MALES	1961 FEMALES	1966 BOTH SEXES	1966 MALES	1966 FEMALES	1971 BOTH SEXES	1971 MALES	1971 FEMALES	AGE AT LAST BIRTHDAY
0-4	102	51	51	118	59	59	140	70	70	0-4
5-9	87	44	43	100	50	50	115	58	57	5-9
10-14	68	34	34	86	44	42	100	50	50	10-14
15-19	53	27	26	67	34	33	85	43	42	15-19
20-24	44	22	22	52	26	26	67	34	33	20-24
25-29	38	19	19	43	22	21	51	26	25	25-29
30-34	33	16	17	38	19	19	42	21	21	30-34
35-39	28	14	14	32	16	16	37	19	18	35-39
40-44	24	12	12	27	13	14	31	15	16	40-44
45-49	22	11	11	24	12	12	26	13	13	45-49
50-54	20	10	10	20	10	10	22	11	11	50-54
55-59	15	7	8	18	9	9	19	9	10	55-59
60-64	11	5	6	13	6	7	15	7	8	60-64
65-69	7	3	4	9	4	5	11	5	6	65-69
70-74	5	2	3	5	2	3	7	3	4	70-74
75-79	3	1	2	3	1	2	3	1	2	75-79
80-84	1	0	1	2	1	1	2	1	1	80-84
85+	0	0	0	0	0	0	0	0	0	85+
TOTAL	561	278	283	657	328	329	773	386	387	TOTAL

TABLE 6 — STANDARDIZED RATES

STANDARD COUNTRIES:

STANDARDIZED RATES PER THOUSAND	ENGLAND AND WALES 1961 BOTH SEXES	MALES	FEMALES	UNITED STATES 1960 BOTH SEXES	MALES	FEMALES	MEXICO 1960 BOTH SEXES	MALES	FEMALES
Birth	38.54	44.72*	37.01	39.42	40.89*	38.49	45.79	42.29*	45.25
Death	21.50	26.98*	22.36	18.06	21.39*	17.44	10.81	11.24*	9.89
Increase	17.04	17.74*	14.65	21.36	19.49*	21.05	34.97	31.05*	35.37

TABLE 7 — MOMENTS AND CUMULANTS

	OBSERVED POP. MALES	OBSERVED POP. FEMALES	STATIONARY POP. MALES	STATIONARY POP. FEMALES	STABLE POP. MALES	STABLE POP. FEMALES	OBSERVED BIRTHS	NET MATERNITY FUNCTION	BIRTHS IN STABLE POP.
μ	22.99256	23.88299	33.41508	35.19075	20.36947	20.84936	26.14274	27.19672	25.63063
σ^2	351.9286	381.9691	431.8742	478.7351	279.1101	300.6379	40.69903	43.63812	38.91176
κ_3	5491.005	6344.456	2558.016	2727.713	4672.400	5449.343	139.0429	118.7503	139.4793
κ_4	-19393.	-17168.	-162107.	-217534.	32514.	46998.	-401.434	-893.801	-257.245
β_1	0.691735	0.722278	0.081233	0.067813	1.004045	1.092841	0.286778	0.169696	0.330200
β_2	2.843424	2.882328	2.130867	2.050846	3.417369	3.519989	2.757649	2.530637	2.830103
κ	-0.265891	-0.277809	-0.032579	-0.025722	-0.445472	-0.480334	-0.173744	-0.093233	-0.204172

TABLE 8 — RATES FROM AGE DISTRIBUTIONS AND VITAL STATISTICS (Females)

VITAL STATISTICS		THOMPSON AGE RANGE	NRR	1000r	INTERVAL	BOURGEOIS-PICHAT AGE RANGE	NRR	1000b	1000d	1000r	COALE	
GRR	2.976										IBR	39.63
NRR	2.591	0-4	2.49	33.58	27.21	5-29	2.33	36.90	5.64	31.25	IDR	6.71
TFR	6.008	5-9	2.18	29.36	27.13	30-54	1.63	25.39	7.21	18.18	IRI	32.93
GENERATION	26.399	10-14	1.90	23.29	27.03	55-79	1.56	20.32	3.74	16.58	K1	23.91
SEX RATIO	101.840	15-19	1.78	16.57	26.86	*15-39	1.92	31.16	7.05	24.12	K2	0.24

TABLE 9 — LESLIE MATRIX AND ITS SPECTRAL COMPONENTS (Females)

Start of Age Interval	ORIGINAL MATRIX SUB-DIAGONAL	ALTERNATIVE FIRST ROWS Projection	ALTERNATIVE FIRST ROWS Integral	FIRST STABLE MATRIX % IN STABLE POPULATION	FISHER VALUES	REPRODUCTIVE VALUES	SECOND STABLE MATRIX Z_2 FIRST COLUMN	SECOND STABLE MATRIX Z_2 FIRST ROW
0	0.98101	0.00000	0.00000	19.008	1.180	51328	0.1463+0.1143	0.1463+0.1143
5	0.99608	0.00998	0.00000	15.558	1.442	48644	0.1829-0.0990	-0.0413+0.1606
10	0.99357	0.18077	0.02193	12.929	1.724	45191	-0.0200-0.2355	-0.1455+0.0220
15	0.98704	0.55901	0.37613	10.718	1.864	40802	-0.2539-0.0861	-0.0957-0.1306
20	0.98377	0.72349	0.85851	8.826	1.595	31263	-0.2033+0.2234	-0.0106-0.1890
25	0.97995	0.59524	0.73696	7.244	1.076	18288	0.1387+0.3095	0.0429-0.1600
30	0.97498	0.40763	0.57743	5.923	0.599	8739	0.3793-0.0037	0.0576-0.0915
35	0.96987	0.19858	0.32284	4.818	0.243	3067	0.1650-0.3886	0.0349-0.0333
40	0.96340	0.05574	0.11528	3.899	0.058	664	-0.3212-0.3395	0.0102-0.0065
45	0.94746	0.00370	0.00698	3.134	0.004	42	-0.4834+0.1744	0.0007-0.0005
50	0.91705	0.00054	0.00118	2.477	0.001	5	-0.0362+0.5546	0.0001-0.0001
55+	0.78297			5.466				

TABLE 10 — AGE ANALYSIS AND MISCELLANEOUS RESULTS (Females)

Start of Age Interval	OBSERVED POPUL. (IN 100's)	CONTRIBUTIONS OF ROOTS (IN 100's) r_1	r_2, r_3	$r_4 \cdot r_{11}$	AGE-SP. BIRTH RATES	NET MATERNITY FUNCTION	COEFF. OF MATRIX EQUATION	PARAMETERS	INTEGRAL	MATRIX	EXP. INCREASE x	$e^{(x+2\frac{1}{2})r}$
0	435	414	20	1	0.0000	0.0000	0.0000	L(1)	1.19763	1.19858	0	1.0944
5	337	339	6	-7	0.0000	0.0000	0.0098	L(2)	0.33591	0.35036	50	6.6431
10	262	281	-20	1	0.0043	0.0196	0.1766		0.83135	0.80300	55	7.9559
15	219	233	-25	11	0.0742	0.3337	0.5427	R(1)	0.03607	0.03623	60	9.5282
20	196	192	3	1	0.1694	0.7518	0.6933	R(2)	-0.02182	-0.02645	65	11.4113
25	170	158	34	-22	0.1454	0.6349	0.5612		0.23736	0.23188	70	13.6664
30	146	129	28	-11	0.1139	0.4875	0.3766	C(1)		2176	75	16.3672
35	126	105	-18	40	0.0637	0.2657	0.1789	C(2)		3683	80	19.6018
40	114	85	-50	80	0.0227	0.0920	0.0487			-3917	85	23.4756
45	104	68	-22	58	0.0014	0.0054	0.0031	2P/Y	26.4712	27.0972	90	28.1150
50	85	54	41	-10	0.0002	0.0009	0.0004	DELTA	6.9622		95	33.6713
55+	213	119									100	40.3256

TABLE 1
DATA

AGE AT LAST BIRTHDAY	POPULATION BOTH SEXES	MALES Number	%	FEMALES Number	%	BIRTHS BY AGE OF MOTHER	DEATHS BOTH SEXES	MALES	FEMALES	AGE AT LAST BIRTHDAY
0	183227	92639	2.9	90588	2.7	0	27145	14740	12405	0
1-4	686214	344909	10.6	341305	10.2	0	7171	3589	3582	1-4
5-9	869260	437730	13.5	431530	12.9	0	1399	752	647	5-9
10-14	725862	365773	11.3	360089	10.7	539	971	522	449	10-14
15-19	638152	313843	9.7	324309	9.7	21544	1434	769	665	15-19
20-24	639396	306355	9.5	333041	9.9	58365	1922	1034	888	20-24
25-29	498211	237044	7.3	261167	7.8	56892	2054	1098	956	25-29
30-34	424043	206628	6.4	217415	6.5	38918	2126	1164	962	30-34
35-39	419251	199487	6.2	219764	6.5	25789	2350	1313	1037	35-39
40-44	359356	182321	5.6	177035	5.3	11294	2789	1672	1117	40-44
45-49	290432	142034	4.4	148398	4.4	1903	2989	1793	1196	45-49
50-54	257288	127693	3.9	129595	3.9	449	3490	2052	1438	50-54
55-59	179122	88170	2.7	90952	2.7	0	3773	2234	1539	55-59
60-64	163974	76758	2.4	87216	2.6	0	4484	2547	1937	60-64
65-69	103548	49477	1.5	54071	1.6	0	4766	2616	2150	65-69
70-74	80842	36296	1.1	44546	1.3		5069	2623	2446	70-74
75-79	47758	20132	0.6	27626	0.8		4193	1984	2209	75-79
80-84	23153	9033	0.3	14120	0.4	109234 M.	3146	1327	1819	80-84
85+	7939	2819	0.1	5120	0.2	106459 F.	2876	1013	1863	85+
TOTAL	6597028	3239141		3357887		215693	84147	44842	39305	TOTAL

TABLE 2
MALE LIFE TABLE

x	$_nq_x$	l_x	$_nd_x$	$_nL_x$	$_nm_x$	$_na_x$	T_x	r_x	$\mathring{e}_x$	$_nM_x$	x
0	0.142748	100000	14275	89715	0.159112	0.2795	5204031	0.0000	52.040	0.159112	0
1	0.040415	85725	3465	332950	0.010406	1.1280	5114316	0.0000	59.659	0.010406	1
5	0.008447	82261	695	409566	0.001697	2.5000	4781365	0.0140	58.125	0.001718	5
10	0.007136	81566	582	406435	0.001432	2.6053	4371799	0.0316	53.598	0.001427	10
15	0.012212	80984	989	402605	0.002456	2.6604	3965364	0.0153	48.965	0.002450	15
20	0.016797	79995	1344	396785	0.003386	2.6269	3562759	0.0246	44.537	0.003375	20
25	0.022985	78651	1808	388901	0.004648	2.5914	3165974	0.0348	40.253	0.004632	25
30	0.027807	76843	2137	379003	0.005638	2.5599	2777073	0.0116	36.139	0.005633	30
35	0.032417	74707	2422	367711	0.006586	2.5961	2398070	0.0056	32.100	0.006582	35
40	0.045019	72285	3254	353667	0.009201	2.6163	2030359	0.0246	28.088	0.009171	40
45	0.061409	69031	4239	334926	0.012657	2.5876	1676692	0.0231	24.289	0.012624	45
50	0.077745	64791	5037	311972	0.016146	2.6208	1341766	0.0303	20.709	0.016070	50
55	0.119807	59754	7159	281514	0.025430	2.5894	1029794	0.0261	17.234	0.025337	55
60	0.154187	52595	8110	243387	0.033319	2.5845	748280	0.0262	14.227	0.033182	60
65	0.234833	44486	10447	196796	0.053084	2.5463	504893	0.0262	11.350	0.052873	65
70	0.306476	34039	10432	143879	0.072506	2.4774	308097	0.0262	9.051	0.072267	70
75	0.394581	23607	9315	94168	0.098917	2.4378	164218	0.0262	6.956	0.098550	75
80	0.535414	14292	7652	51772	0.147803	2.4272	70050	0.0262	4.901	0.146905	80
85+	*1.000000	6640	6640	18278	0.363274	2.7527	18278	0.0262	2.753	0.359347	85+

TABLE 3
FEMALE LIFE TABLE

x	$_nq_x$	l_x	$_nd_x$	$_nL_x$	$_nm_x$	$_na_x$	T_x	r_x	$\mathring{e}_x$	$_nM_x$	x
0	0.124921	100000	12492	91224	0.136939	0.2975	5656022	0.0000	56.560	0.136939	0
1	0.040759	87508	3567	339855	0.010495	1.1467	5564799	0.0000	63.592	0.010495	1
5	0.007356	83941	617	418162	0.001477	2.5000	5224944	0.0145	62.245	0.001499	5
10	0.006232	83324	519	415368	0.001250	2.5915	4806782	0.0271	57.688	0.001247	10
15	0.010212	82804	846	412027	0.002052	2.6402	4391414	0.0058	53.034	0.002051	15
20	0.013279	81959	1088	407204	0.002673	2.6201	3979387	0.0189	48.553	0.002666	20
25	0.018213	80871	1473	400806	0.003675	2.5920	3572183	0.0390	44.172	0.003660	25
30	0.021899	79398	1739	392712	0.004428	2.5408	3171377	0.0129	39.943	0.004425	30
35	0.023356	77659	1814	383891	0.004725	2.5720	2778664	0.0155	35.780	0.004719	35
40	0.031187	75845	2365	373541	0.006332	2.5968	2394774	0.0330	31.575	0.006309	40
45	0.039643	73480	2913	360423	0.008082	2.6053	2021233	0.0229	27.507	0.008059	45
50	0.054382	70567	3838	343767	0.011163	2.6373	1660810	0.0372	23.535	0.011096	50
55	0.081551	66729	5442	320595	0.016974	2.6018	1317043	0.0230	19.737	0.016921	55
60	0.105985	61287	6496	291143	0.022310	2.6455	996448	0.0231	16.259	0.022209	60
65	0.182087	54792	9977	249927	0.039919	2.5912	705305	0.0231	12.872	0.039763	65
70	0.242413	44815	10864	197202	0.055089	2.5264	455378	0.0231	10.161	0.054910	70
75	0.334367	33951	11352	141418	0.080274	2.5037	258176	0.0231	7.604	0.079961	75
80	0.489695	22599	11067	85366	0.129637	2.5034	116758	0.0231	5.166	0.128824	80
85+	*1.000000	11532	11532	31391	0.367376	2.7220	31391	0.0231	2.722	0.363867	85+

TABLE 4
OBSERVED AND PROJECTED VITAL RATES

	OBSERVED POPULATION BOTH SEXES	MALES	FEMALES	PROJECTED POPULATION 1959 MALES	FEMALES	1964 MALES	FEMALES	1969 MALES	FEMALES	STABLE POPULATION MALES	FEMALES
RATES PER THOUSAND											
Birth	32.70	33.72	31.70	33.88	31.83	33.78	31.72	33.68	31.61	32.20	30.41
Death	12.76	13.84	11.71	14.05	11.89	14.18	12.04	14.29	12.19	15.20	13.41
Increase	19.94	19.88	20.00	19.83	19.94	19.60	19.68	19.38	19.42	16.9999	
PERCENTAGE											
under 15	37.36	38.31	36.44	37.64	35.92	36.29	34.72	36.39	34.87	35.24	33.98
15-64	58.65	58.05	59.23	58.54	59.46	59.96	60.74	59.63	60.29	60.04	59.85
65 and over	3.99	3.64	4.33	3.81	4.62	3.75	4.55	3.99	4.84	4.72	6.17
DEP. RATIO X 100	70.50	72.26	68.83	70.82	68.19	66.77	64.65	67.71	65.86	66.55	67.08

185   Chile 1953–55

TABLE 5 — POPULATION PROJECTED WITH FIXED AGE-SPECIFIC BIRTH AND DEATH RATES (IN 1000's)

AGE AT LAST BIRTHDAY	1959 BOTH SEXES	MALES	FEMALES	1964 BOTH SEXES	MALES	FEMALES	1969 BOTH SEXES	MALES	FEMALES	AGE AT LAST BIRTHDAY
0-4	971	487	484	1071	537	534	1176	590	586	0-4
5-9	843	424	419	941	472	469	1038	520	518	5-9
10-14	863	434	429	837	421	416	934	468	466	10-14
15-19	719	362	357	855	430	425	830	417	413	15-19
20-24	630	309	321	710	357	353	844	424	420	20-24
25-29	628	300	328	618	303	315	697	350	347	25-29
30-34	487	231	256	614	293	321	604	295	309	30-34
35-39	413	200	213	474	224	250	598	284	314	35-39
40-44	406	192	214	400	193	207	459	216	243	40-44
45-49	344	173	171	388	182	206	383	183	200	45-49
50-54	274	132	142	324	161	163	366	169	197	50-54
55-59	236	115	121	251	119	132	297	145	152	55-59
60-64	159	76	83	210	100	110	223	103	120	60-64
65-69	137	62	75	133	62	71	175	81	94	65-69
70-74	79	36	43	104	45	59	101	45	56	70-74
75-79	56	24	32	55	24	31	72	30	42	75-79
80-84	28	11	17	32	13	19	31	13	18	80-84
85+	8	3	5	10	4	6	12	5	7	85+
TOTAL	7281	3571	3710	8027	3940	4087	8840	4338	4502	TOTAL

TABLE 6 — STANDARDIZED RATES

STANDARD COUNTRIES:

STANDARDIZED RATES PER THOUSAND	ENGLAND AND WALES 1961 BOTH SEXES	MALES	FEMALES	UNITED STATES 1960 BOTH SEXES	MALES	FEMALES	MEXICO 1960 BOTH SEXES	MALES	FEMALES
Birth	26.97	31.29*	25.80	27.42	28.50*	26.66	29.59	29.54*	29.13
Death	19.82	28.62*	19.94	17.75	23.39*	16.66	13.05	14.42*	11.79
Increase	7.15	2.67*	5.86	9.66	5.12*	10.00	16.54	15.12*	17.34

TABLE 7 — MOMENTS AND CUMULANTS

	OBSERVED POP. MALES	FEMALES	STATIONARY POP. MALES	FEMALES	STABLE POP. MALES	FEMALES	OBSERVED BIRTHS	NET MATERNITY FUNCTION	BIRTHS IN STABLE POP.
μ	25.19985	25.95546	34.12187	35.98604	26.81501	28.04346	28.22244	29.43513	28.55218
σ^2	361.3513	375.3884	463.6528	501.3711	389.9125	424.9028	47.78871	51.09362	48.57721
κ_3	5210.643	5568.115	3080.402	2839.436	5216.865	5702.148	171.3390	140.7162	154.4346
κ_4	-29127.	-24041.	-189103.	-242216.	-58139.	-85020.	-629.584	-960.647	-643.185
β_1	0.575432	0.586103	0.095200	0.063971	0.459111	0.423846	0.268990	0.148453	0.208061
β_2	2.776935	2.829394	2.120345	2.036429	2.617585	2.527979	2.724321	2.632015	2.727435
κ	-0.235567	-0.248094	-0.037231	-0.024069	-0.185950	-0.165319	-0.160774	-0.098834	-0.141871

TABLE 8 — RATES FROM AGE DISTRIBUTIONS AND VITAL STATISTICS (Females)

VITAL STATISTICS		THOMPSON AGE RANGE	NRR	1000r	INTERVAL	BOURGEOIS-PICHAT AGE RANGE	NRR	1000b	1000d	1000r	COALE	
GRR	2.067				27.24	5-29	1.70	34.47	14.91	19.56	IBR	34.38
NRR	1.637	0-4	1.55	16.40	27.15	30-54	1.81	35.71	13.75	21.96	IDR	14.32
TFR	4.187	5-9	1.76	21.20	27.06	55-79	1.72	28.07	7.89	20.18	IRI	20.06
GENERATION	28.990	10-14	1.70	19.19	26.93	*35-59	2.42	57.96	25.30	32.66	K1	-4.17
SEX RATIO	102.607	15-19	1.74	16.10							K2	0.

TABLE 9 — LESLIE MATRIX AND ITS SPECTRAL COMPONENTS (Females)

Start of Age Interval	SUB-DIAGONAL	ALTERNATIVE FIRST ROWS Projection	Integral	FIRST STABLE MATRIX % IN STABLE POPULATION	FISHER VALUES	REPRODUCTIVE VALUES	SECOND STABLE MATRIX Z2 FIRST COLUMN	FIRST ROW
0	0.97004	0.00000	0.00000	12.576	1.210	522397	0.1343+0.0820	0.1343+0.0820
5	0.99332	0.00158	0.00000	11.203	1.358	585910	0.1596-0.0838	-0.0013+0.1373
10	0.99196	0.07169	0.00332	10.220	1.486	535257	0.0117-0.2112	-0.1012+0.0590
15	0.98830	0.25492	0.14748	9.310	1.544	500828	-0.2054-0.1388	-0.0972-0.0542
20	0.98429	0.41454	0.38906	8.450	1.389	462755	-0.2622+0.1226	-0.0375-0.1165
25	0.97981	0.41833	0.48361	7.638	1.028	268411	-0.0341+0.3348	0.0128-0.1137
30	0.97754	0.31246	0.39739	6.873	0.626	136045	0.3123+0.2328	0.0326-0.0759
35	0.97304	0.19088	0.26052	6.170	0.310	68213	0.4158-0.1715	0.0280-0.0357
40	0.96488	0.08103	0.14163	5.514	0.110	19487	0.0761-0.5114	0.0128-0.0111
45	0.95379	0.01716	0.02847	4.886	0.023	3360	-0.4557-0.3737	0.0029-0.0023
50	0.93260	0.00369	0.00769	4.280	0.004	531	-0.6249+0.2246	0.0006-0.0003
55+	0.77905			12.881				

TABLE 10 — AGE ANALYSIS AND MISCELLANEOUS RESULTS (Females)

Start of Age Interval	OBSERVED POPUL. (IN 100's)	CONTRIBUTIONS OF ROOTS (IN 100's) r_1	r_2, r_3	r_4-r_{11}	AGE-SP. BIRTH RATES	NET MATERNITY FUNCTION	COEFF. OF MATRIX EQUATION	PARAMETERS INTEGRAL	MATRIX	EXP. INCREASE x	$e^{(x+2\frac{1}{2})r}$
0	4319	4510	-73	-118	0.0000	0.0000	0.0000	L(1) 1.08872	1.08889	0	1.0434
5	4315	4018	19	278	0.0000	0.0000	0.0015	L(2) 0.42809	0.43450	50	2.4412
10	3601	3665	122	-186	0.0007	0.0031	0.0691	0.74539	0.72651	55	2.6578
15	3243	3339	120	-215	0.0328	0.1351	0.2437	R(1) 0.01700	0.01703	60	2.8936
20	3330	3030	-23	323	0.0865	0.3522	0.3916	R(2) -0.03026	-0.03332	65	3.1503
25	2612	2739	-190	63	0.1075	0.4309	0.3889	0.20990	0.20636	70	3.4298
30	2174	2465	-195	-96	0.0884	0.3470	0.2847	C(1)	35862	75	3.7340
35	2198	2213	23	-38	0.0579	0.2223	0.1700	C(2)	-9343	80	4.0653
40	1770	1977	286	-493	0.0315	0.1176	0.0702		29342	85	4.4260
45	1484	1752	304	-573	0.0063	0.0228	0.0143	2P/Y 29.9348	30.4475	90	4.8186
50	1296	1535	-15	-224	0.0017	0.0059	0.0029	DELTA 4.8447		95	5.2461
55+	3237	4619								100	5.7115

AGE AT LAST BIRTHDAY	POPULATION BOTH SEXES	MALES Number	%	FEMALES Number	%	BIRTHS BY AGE OF MOTHER	DEATHS BOTH SEXES	MALES	FEMALES	AGE AT LAST BIRTHDAY
0	239818	122787	3.2	117031	3.0	0	32478	17646	14832	0
1-4	928329	468806	12.3	459523	11.7	0	7741	3906	3835	1-4
5-9	1036634	522463	13.8	514171	13.1	0	1514	834	680	5-9
10-14	874177	437963	11.5	436214	11.1	626	952	540	412	10-14
15-19	750399	366945	9.7	383454	9.7	27593	1332	734	598	15-19
20-24	642094	311416	8.2	330678	8.4	66091	1725	977	748	20-24
25-29	556998	270144	7.1	286854	7.3	67899	1964	1112	852	25-29
30-34	487373	235401	6.2	251972	6.4	54431	2336	1334	1002	30-34
35-39	433220	207946	5.5	225274	5.7	30836	2399	1383	1016	35-39
40-44	386804	186053	4.9	200751	5.1	11679	2732	1663	1069	40-44
45-49	355860	173660	4.6	182200	4.6	1851	3219	1963	1256	45-49
50-54	301707	146931	3.9	154776	3.9	394	3681	2244	1437	50-54
55-59	224346	111949	2.9	112397	2.9	0	4203	2482	1721	55-59
60-64	193402	88578	2.3	104824	2.7	0	4944	2830	2114	60-64
65-69	130902	61864	1.6	69038	1.8	0	5133	2855	2278	65-69
70-74	92702	41885	1.1	50817	1.3		5467	2897	2570	70-74
75-79	58675	25016	0.7	33659	0.9		4789	2342	2447	75-79
80-84	30926	12245	0.3	18681	0.5	132819 M.	3561	1567	1994	80-84
85+	11710	4228	0.1	7482	0.2	128581 F.	3604	1241	2363	85+
TOTAL	7736076	3796280		3939796		261400	93774	50550	43224	TOTAL

TABLE 1 DATA

TABLE 2 — MALE LIFE TABLE

x	$_nq_x$	l_x	$_nd_x$	$_nL_x$	$_nm_x$	$_na_x$	T_x	r_x	$\mathring{e}_x$	$_nM_x$	x
0	0.130026	100000	13003	90477	0.143712	0.2675	5417016	0.0000	54.170	0.143712	0
1	0.032545	86997	2831	339826	0.008332	1.1168	5326539	0.0000	61.226	0.008332	1
5	0.007789	84166	656	419191	0.001564	2.5000	4986713	0.0268	59.249	0.001596	5
10	0.006162	83510	515	416302	0.001236	2.5712	4567522	0.0339	54.694	0.001233	10
15	0.010019	82996	831	413061	0.002013	2.6928	4151219	0.0320	50.017	0.002000	15
20	0.015630	82164	1284	407782	0.003149	2.6333	3738158	0.0275	45.496	0.003137	20
25	0.020443	80880	1653	400462	0.004129	2.6177	3330376	0.0237	41.177	0.004116	25
30	0.028005	79227	2219	390768	0.005678	2.5818	2929914	0.0206	36.981	0.005667	30
35	0.032782	77008	2524	378946	0.006662	2.5861	2539146	0.0166	32.973	0.006651	35
40	0.043791	74483	3262	364555	0.008947	2.5894	2160200	0.0091	29.002	0.008938	40
45	0.055094	71222	3924	346657	0.011319	2.5911	1795645	0.0120	25.212	0.011304	45
50	0.073963	67298	4978	324600	0.015334	2.6114	1448989	0.0280	21.531	0.015272	50
55	0.105689	62320	6587	295827	0.022265	2.6051	1124389	0.0279	18.042	0.022171	55
60	0.148911	55734	8299	258606	0.032093	2.5826	828561	0.0299	14.866	0.031949	60
65	0.208262	47434	9879	213062	0.046366	2.5594	569955	0.0299	12.016	0.046150	65
70	0.295954	37556	11115	160019	0.069459	2.5025	356894	0.0299	9.503	0.069166	70
75	0.378604	26441	10011	106523	0.093976	2.4346	196875	0.0299	7.446	0.093620	75
80	0.485283	16430	7973	61894	0.128822	2.4594	90352	0.0299	5.499	0.127970	80
85+	*1.000000	8457	8457	28457	0.297179	3.3650	28457	0.0299	3.365	0.293519	85+

TABLE 3 — FEMALE LIFE TABLE

x	$_nq_x$	l_x	$_nd_x$	$_nL_x$	$_nm_x$	$_na_x$	T_x	r_x	$\mathring{e}_x$	$_nM_x$	x
0	0.116164	100000	11616	91659	0.126736	0.2819	5919359	0.0000	59.194	0.126736	0
1	0.032602	88384	2881	345266	0.008346	1.1303	5827701	0.0000	65.936	0.008346	1
5	0.006435	85502	550	426135	0.001291	2.5000	5482435	0.0248	64.120	0.001323	5
10	0.004719	84952	401	423780	0.000946	2.5570	5056300	0.0282	59.520	0.000944	10
15	0.007805	84551	660	421219	0.001567	2.6724	4632520	0.0261	54.790	0.001560	15
20	0.011289	83891	947	417206	0.002270	2.6247	4211301	0.0268	50.200	0.002262	20
25	0.014788	82944	1227	411792	0.002979	2.6129	3794095	0.0241	45.743	0.002970	25
30	0.019725	81717	1612	404675	0.003983	2.5726	3382303	0.0203	41.390	0.003977	30
35	0.022329	80106	1789	396150	0.004515	2.5524	2977628	0.0182	37.171	0.004510	35
40	0.026324	78317	2062	386598	0.005333	2.5811	2581479	0.0158	32.962	0.005325	40
45	0.033984	76255	2591	375070	0.006909	2.6052	2194881	0.0190	28.783	0.006894	45
50	0.045748	73664	3370	360440	0.009350	2.6619	1819811	0.0382	24.704	0.009284	50
55	0.074117	70294	5210	339053	0.015366	2.6168	1459371	0.0241	20.761	0.015312	55
60	0.096675	65084	6292	310486	0.020265	2.6266	1120318	0.0281	17.213	0.020167	60
65	0.153672	58792	9035	272404	0.033167	2.6141	809832	0.0281	13.775	0.032996	65
70	0.225903	49757	11240	221280	0.050797	2.5529	537429	0.0281	10.801	0.050574	70
75	0.308733	38517	11891	162878	0.073008	2.5019	316149	0.0281	8.208	0.072700	75
80	0.426239	26625	11349	105460	0.107612	2.5621	153270	0.0281	5.757	0.106739	80
85+	*1.000000	15277	15277	47810	0.319528	3.1296	47810	0.0281	3.130	0.315825	85+

TABLE 4 — OBSERVED AND PROJECTED VITAL RATES

	OBSERVED POPULATION BOTH SEXES	MALES	FEMALES	1965 MALES	FEMALES	1970 MALES	FEMALES	1975 MALES	FEMALES	STABLE POPULATION MALES	FEMALES
RATES PER THOUSAND											
Birth	33.79	34.99	32.64	35.38	33.02	36.00	33.63	36.63	34.27	35.34	33.53
Death	12.12	13.32	10.97	13.00	10.78	13.11	10.96	13.19	11.12	13.54	11.73
Increase	21.67	21.67	21.67	22.38	22.24	22.89	22.67	23.43	23.14		21.7963
PERCENTAGE											
under 15	39.80	40.88	38.76	40.21	38.04	39.14	37.08	38.51	36.62	38.19	36.84
15-64	56.00	55.29	56.68	55.84	57.05	56.87	58.03	57.37	58.23	57.71	57.70
65 and over	4.20	3.83	4.56	3.95	4.91	3.99	4.90	4.12	5.15	4.10	5.46
DEP. RATIO X 100	78.57	80.86	76.42	79.08	75.29	75.84	72.33	74.31	71.75	73.29	73.30

TABLE 1 — DATA

AGE AT LAST BIRTHDAY	POPULATION BOTH SEXES	MALES Number	%	FEMALES Number	%	BIRTHS BY AGE OF MOTHER	DEATHS BOTH SEXES	MALES	FEMALES	AGE AT LAST BIRTHDAY
0	255009	130651	3.3	124358	3.0	0	33149	18119	15030	0
1-4	977079	493453	12.3	483626	11.7	0	7385	3721	3664	1-4
5-9	1088073	548672	13.7	539401	13.0	0	1457	776	681	5-9
10-14	920643	461094	11.5	459549	11.1	616	887	514	373	10-14
15-19	788335	385772	9.7	402563	9.7	29191	1288	754	534	15-19
20-24	678555	328895	8.2	349660	8.4	70682	1732	1006	726	20-24
25-29	587440	284718	7.1	302722	7.3	69162	1769	990	779	25-29
30-34	514880	248604	6.2	266276	6.4	58333	2598	1502	1096	30-34
35-39	458224	219889	5.5	238335	5.7	32138	2554	1526	1028	35-39
40-44	407088	195702	4.9	211386	5.1	12213	2974	1810	1164	40-44
45-49	373183	182008	4.6	191175	4.6	1799	3497	2230	1267	45-49
50-54	314318	153183	3.8	161135	3.9	306	4068	2529	1539	50-54
55-59	234137	116737	2.9	117400	2.8	0	4192	2474	1718	55-59
60-64	201667	92329	2.3	109338	2.6	0	5134	2987	2147	60-64
65-69	140289	66685	1.7	73604	1.8	0	5112	2864	2248	65-69
70-74	98946	44739	1.1	54207	1.3		5237	2822	2415	70-74
75-79	62359	26424	0.7	35935	0.9		4749	2381	2368	75-79
80-84	32733	12764	0.3	19969	0.5	139715 M.	3634	1570	2064	80-84
85+	12350	4339	0.1	8011	0.2	134725 F.	3458	1221	2237	85+
TOTAL	8145308	3996658		4148650		274440	94874	51796	43078	TOTAL

TABLE 2 — MALE LIFE TABLE

x	$_nq_x$	l_x	$_nd_x$	$_nL_x$	$_nm_x$	$_na_x$	T_x	r_x	$\mathring{e}_x$	$_nM_x$	x
0	0.125791	100000	12579	90705	0.138682	0.2610	5476106	0.0000	54.761	0.138682	0
1	0.029520	87421	2581	342228	0.007541	1.1111	5385401	0.0000	61.603	0.007541	1
5	0.006899	84840	585	422738	0.001385	2.5000	5043173	0.0273	59.443	0.001414	5
10	0.005579	84255	470	420148	0.001119	2.6042	4620435	0.0339	54.839	0.001115	10
15	0.009793	83785	820	417038	0.001967	2.7014	4200287	0.0318	50.132	0.001955	15
20	0.015225	82964	1263	411788	0.003068	2.5980	3783248	0.0275	45.601	0.003059	20
25	0.017318	81701	1415	405205	0.003492	2.6669	3371460	0.0240	41.266	0.003477	25
30	0.029850	80286	2397	395700	0.006056	2.6084	2966255	0.0202	36.946	0.006042	30
35	0.034179	77890	2662	383004	0.006951	2.5791	2570555	0.0167	33.000	0.006940	35
40	0.045289	75228	3407	367958	0.009259	2.5989	2187551	0.0096	29.079	0.009249	40
45	0.059593	71821	4280	348814	0.012270	2.5959	1819593	0.0120	25.335	0.012252	45
50	0.079614	67541	5377	324680	0.016561	2.5780	1470780	0.0279	21.776	0.016510	50
55	0.101234	62163	6293	295718	0.021280	2.6006	1146100	0.0280	18.437	0.021193	55
60	0.150650	55870	8417	258928	0.032507	2.5734	850382	0.0344	15.221	0.032352	60
65	0.195099	47454	9258	214548	0.043152	2.5460	591454	0.0344	12.464	0.042948	65
70	0.273905	38195	10462	165019	0.063398	2.5188	376906	0.0344	9.868	0.063077	70
75	0.367912	27733	10203	112703	0.090534	2.4554	211887	0.0344	7.640	0.090108	75
80	0.472103	17530	8276	66762	0.123962	2.4761	99183	0.0344	5.658	0.123002	80
85+	*1.000000	9254	9254	32421	0.285433	3.5035	32421	0.0344	3.503	0.281401	85+

TABLE 3 — FEMALE LIFE TABLE

x	$_nq_x$	l_x	$_nd_x$	$_nL_x$	$_nm_x$	$_na_x$	T_x	r_x	$\mathring{e}_x$	$_nM_x$	x
0	0.111148	100000	11115	91964	0.120861	0.2770	6035712	0.0000	60.357	0.120861	0
1	0.029659	88885	2636	347963	0.007576	1.1255	5943749	0.0000	66.870	0.007576	1
5	0.006148	86249	530	429919	0.001233	2.5000	5595786	0.0252	64.879	0.001263	5
10	0.004053	85719	347	427733	0.000812	2.5223	5165866	0.0282	60.265	0.000812	10
15	0.006646	85371	567	425549	0.001333	2.6952	4738134	0.0260	55.500	0.001326	15
20	0.010365	84804	879	421928	0.002083	2.6209	4312585	0.0265	50.854	0.002076	20
25	0.012840	83925	1078	417100	0.002584	2.6670	3890657	0.0244	46.359	0.002573	25
30	0.020413	82847	1691	410145	0.004123	2.5809	3473557	0.0201	41.927	0.004116	30
35	0.021367	81156	1734	401543	0.004319	2.5564	3063412	0.0185	37.747	0.004313	35
40	0.027209	79422	2161	391873	0.005515	2.5764	2661868	0.0166	33.515	0.005507	40
45	0.032703	77261	2527	380270	0.006644	2.6115	2269995	0.0202	29.381	0.006627	45
50	0.047010	74734	3513	365415	0.009614	2.6498	1889725	0.0387	25.286	0.009551	50
55	0.070935	71221	5052	344043	0.014684	2.6124	1524310	0.0242	21.402	0.014634	55
60	0.094275	66169	6238	315983	0.019742	2.6175	1180267	0.0333	17.837	0.019636	60
65	0.143007	59931	8571	279089	0.030709	2.6004	864284	0.0333	14.421	0.030542	65
70	0.201876	51360	10368	231528	0.044783	2.5624	585195	0.0333	11.394	0.044551	70
75	0.284789	40992	11674	176162	0.066269	2.5332	353667	0.0333	8.628	0.065897	75
80	0.417117	29318	12229	117145	0.104392	2.5922	177505	0.0333	6.054	0.103360	80
85+	*1.000000	17089	17089	60360	0.283118	3.5321	60360	0.0333	3.532	0.279241	85+

TABLE 4 — OBSERVED AND PROJECTED VITAL RATES

	OBSERVED POPULATION BOTH SEXES	MALES	FEMALES	PROJECTED POPULATION 1967 MALES	FEMALES	1972 MALES	FEMALES	1977 MALES	FEMALES	STABLE POPULATION MALES	FEMALES
RATES PER THOUSAND											
Birth	33.69	34.96	32.47	35.28	32.79	35.85	33.34	36.45	33.94	35.16	33.23
Death	11.65	12.96	10.38	12.71	10.29	12.82	10.49	12.91	10.67	13.19	11.26
Increase	22.05	22.00	22.09	22.58	22.49	23.03	22.85	23.55	23.27	21.9661	
PERCENTAGE											
under 15	39.79	40.88	38.73	40.26	38.00	39.26	37.06	38.62	36.57	38.25	36.76
15-64	55.96	55.24	56.64	55.71	56.98	56.66	57.90	57.17	58.13	57.58	57.57
65 and over	4.26	3.88	4.62	4.03	5.03	4.08	5.04	4.21	5.30	4.17	5.67
DEP. RATIO X 100	78.71	81.02	76.54	79.50	75.51	76.50	72.72	74.92	72.03	73.66	73.69

TABLE 1 — DATA

AGE AT LAST BIRTHDAY	BOTH SEXES	POPULATION MALES Number	%	FEMALES Number	%	BIRTHS BY AGE OF MOTHER	DEATHS BOTH SEXES	MALES	FEMALES	AGE AT LAST BIRTHDAY
0	263828	134425	3.3	129403	3.0	0	31469	17065	14404	0
1-4	991665	500664	12.2	491001	11.5	0	7161	3600	3561	1-4
5-9	1089003	545235	13.3	543768	12.7	0	1392	734	658	5-9
10-14	980663	491191	11.9	489472	11.4	700	922	505	417	10-14
15-19	831439	414979	10.1	416460	9.7	30837	1270	722	548	15-19
20-24	719297	349607	8.5	369690	8.6	76506	1685	994	691	20-24
25-29	595227	285211	6.9	310016	7.2	66990	1776	1036	740	25-29
30-34	538585	256831	6.2	281754	6.6	52759	2318	1343	975	30-34
35-39	486944	235410	5.7	251534	5.9	33592	2691	1599	1092	35-39
40-44	412458	197574	4.8	214884	5.0	12097	2835	1823	1012	40-44
45-49	350089	169816	4.1	180273	4.2	1558	3135	1988	1147	45-49
50-54	314010	150564	3.7	163446	3.8	284	4043	2476	1567	50-54
55-59	250813	122047	3.0	128766	3.0	0	4332	2629	1703	55-59
60-64	200646	94663	2.3	105983	2.5	0	5235	3008	2227	60-64
65-69	145934	67873	1.7	78061	1.8	0	5511	3075	2436	65-69
70-74	104702	46942	1.1	57760	1.3		5711	3074	2637	70-74
75-79	66967	28605	0.7	38362	0.9		5043	2541	2502	75-79
80-84	35557	14268	0.3	21289	0.5	139853 M.	3956	1769	2187	80-84
85+	13514	5013	0.1	8501	0.2	135470 F.	3573	1214	2359	85+
TOTAL	8391341	4110918		4280423		275323	94058	51195	42863	TOTAL

TABLE 2 — MALE LIFE TABLE

x	$n q_x$	l_x	$n d_x$	$n L_x$	$n m_x$	$n a_x$	T_x	r_x	$\mathring{e}_x$	$n M_x$	x
0	0.115994	100000	11599	91484	0.126792	0.2659	5569713	0.0017	55.697	0.126948	0
1	0.028126	88401	2486	346430	0.007177	1.1153	5478229	0.0017	61.971	0.007190	1
5	0.006590	85914	566	428156	0.001322	2.5000	5131799	0.0229	59.732	0.001346	5
10	0.005139	85348	439	425680	0.001030	2.5830	4703644	0.0261	55.111	0.001028	10
15	0.008725	84909	741	422853	0.001752	2.7125	4277963	0.0322	50.383	0.001740	15
20	0.014189	84169	1194	418015	0.002857	2.6323	3855111	0.0347	45.802	0.002843	20
25	0.018072	82974	1500	411313	0.003646	2.6269	3437095	0.0270	41.424	0.003632	25
30	0.025868	81475	2108	402347	0.005238	2.6146	3025782	0.0140	37.138	0.005229	30
35	0.033496	79367	2658	390474	0.006808	2.6068	2623435	0.0192	33.054	0.006792	35
40	0.045246	76709	3471	375183	0.009251	2.5912	2232961	0.0235	29.110	0.009227	40
45	0.057038	73238	4177	356164	0.011729	2.5998	1857778	0.0150	25.366	0.011707	45
50	0.079246	69061	5473	332112	0.016479	2.5896	1501614	0.0166	21.743	0.016445	50
55	0.102729	63588	6532	302231	0.021614	2.5952	1169502	0.0238	18.392	0.021541	55
60	0.148233	57056	8458	264847	0.031934	2.5842	867272	0.0329	15.200	0.031776	60
65	0.204791	48598	9952	218622	0.045524	2.5515	602425	0.0329	12.396	0.045305	65
70	0.282479	38646	10917	165962	0.065777	2.5023	383803	0.0329	9.931	0.065485	70
75	0.363330	27729	10075	112931	0.089212	2.4476	217841	0.0329	7.856	0.088831	75
80	0.474862	17654	8383	67146	0.124853	2.4800	104910	0.0329	5.942	0.123983	80
85+	*1.000000	9271	9271	37765	0.245493	4.0734	37765	0.0329	4.073	0.242170	85+

TABLE 3 — FEMALE LIFE TABLE

x	$n q_x$	l_x	$n d_x$	$n L_x$	$n m_x$	$n a_x$	T_x	r_x	$\mathring{e}_x$	$n M_x$	x
0	0.103067	100000	10307	92596	0.111308	0.2816	6128515	0.0000	61.285	0.111311	0
1	0.028418	89693	2549	351458	0.007252	1.1300	6035920	0.0000	67.295	0.007253	1
5	0.005918	87144	516	434433	0.001187	2.5000	5684462	0.0210	65.230	0.001210	5
10	0.004254	86629	369	432233	0.000853	2.5297	5250029	0.0256	60.604	0.000852	10
15	0.006587	86260	568	429970	0.001322	2.6582	4817796	0.0267	55.852	0.001316	15
20	0.009335	85692	800	426552	0.001875	2.6153	4387826	0.0277	51.205	0.001869	20
25	0.011908	84892	1011	422067	0.002395	2.6324	3961273	0.0246	46.662	0.002387	25
30	0.017195	83881	1442	415959	0.003468	2.6101	3539207	0.0175	42.193	0.003460	30
35	0.021508	82439	1773	407853	0.004347	2.5517	3123248	0.0229	37.886	0.004341	35
40	0.023340	80666	1883	398768	0.004721	2.5779	2715395	0.0283	33.662	0.004710	40
45	0.031444	78783	2477	388077	0.006383	2.6435	2316627	0.0207	29.405	0.006363	45
50	0.047034	76306	3589	373016	0.009622	2.6282	1928550	0.0240	25.274	0.009587	50
55	0.064447	72717	4686	352546	0.013293	2.6447	1555533	0.0292	21.392	0.013226	55
60	0.100602	68030	6844	323923	0.021129	2.6289	1202988	0.0320	17.683	0.021013	60
65	0.145806	61186	8921	284446	0.031364	2.5919	879064	0.0320	14.367	0.031206	65
70	0.206215	52265	10778	234959	0.045871	2.5538	594618	0.0320	11.377	0.045654	70
75	0.282099	41487	11703	178507	0.065563	2.5282	359659	0.0320	8.669	0.065221	75
80	0.415104	29784	12363	119201	0.103718	2.5963	181152	0.0320	6.082	0.102729	80
85+	*1.000000	17420	17420	61952	0.281191	3.5563	61952	0.0320	3.556	0.277497	85+

TABLE 4 — OBSERVED AND PROJECTED VITAL RATES

	OBSERVED POPULATION BOTH SEXES	MALES	FEMALES	PROJECTED POPULATION 1969 MALES	FEMALES	1974 MALES	FEMALES	1979 MALES	FEMALES	STABLE POPULATION MALES	FEMALES
RATES PER THOUSAND											
Birth	32.81	34.02	31.65	34.47	32.09	35.05	32.65	35.42	33.03	33.82	31.99
Death	11.21	12.45	10.01	12.22	9.92	12.30	10.12	12.34	10.26	12.77	10.94
Increase	21.60	21.57	21.64	22.25	22.16	22.75	22.54	23.07	22.77		21.0531
PERCENTAGE											
under 15	39.63	40.66	38.63	39.57	37.46	38.89	36.69	38.22	36.17	37.50	35.98
15-64	56.00	55.38	56.60	56.37	57.56	57.00	58.21	57.64	58.52	58.15	58.09
65 and over	4.37	3.96	4.77	4.07	4.99	4.12	5.10	4.14	5.30	4.36	5.93
DEP. RATIO X 100	78.56	80.56	76.67	77.41	73.75	75.45	71.81	73.49	70.87	71.97	72.15

AGE AT LAST BIRTHDAY	1969 BOTH SEXES	1969 MALES	1969 FEMALES	1974 BOTH SEXES	1974 MALES	1974 FEMALES	1979 BOTH SEXES	1979 MALES	1979 FEMALES	AGE AT LAST BIRTHDAY	
0-4	1294	653	641	1467	740	727	1665	840	825	0-4	
5-9	1228	621	607	1265	638	627	1435	724	711	5-9	
10-14	1083	542	541	1221	617	604	1258	634	624	10-14	**TABLE 5**
15-19	975	488	487	1076	538	538	1214	613	601	15-19	POPULATION
20-24	823	410	413	965	482	483	1066	532	534	20-24	PROJECTED
25-29	710	344	366	813	404	409	953	475	478	25-29	WITH
30-34	585	279	306	698	337	361	798	395	403	30-34	FIXED
35-39	525	249	276	571	271	300	680	327	353	35-39	AGE—
40-44	472	226	246	509	239	270	553	260	293	40-44	SPECIFIC
45-49	397	188	209	454	215	239	490	227	263	45-49	BIRTH
50-54	331	158	173	376	175	201	430	200	230	50-54	AND
55-59	291	137	154	308	144	164	349	159	190	55-59	DEATH
60-64	225	107	118	262	120	142	276	126	150	60-64	RATES
65-69	171	78	93	192	88	104	224	99	125	65-69	(IN 1000's)
70-74	116	52	64	136	59	77	153	67	86	70-74	
75-79	76	32	44	84	35	49	98	40	58	75-79	
80-84	43	17	26	48	19	29	54	21	33	80-84	
85+	19	8	11	23	10	13	26	11	15	85+	
TOTAL	9364	4589	4775	10468	5131	5337	11722	5750	5972	TOTAL	

STANDARD COUNTRIES: STANDARDIZED RATES PER THOUSAND	ENGLAND AND WALES 1961 BOTH SEXES	MALES	FEMALES	UNITED STATES 1960 BOTH SEXES	MALES	FEMALES	MEXICO 1960 BOTH SEXES	MALES	FEMALES	
Birth	28.53	33.67*	27.21	29.05	30.77*	28.16	31.75	31.93*	31.17	**TABLE 6** STANDARDIZED RATES
Death	16.49	24.14*	16.01	14.68	20.00*	13.31	10.61	12.14*	9.32	
Increase	12.04	9.54*	11.20	14.37	10.76*	14.85	21.14	19.79*	21.85	

	OBSERVED POP. MALES	OBSERVED POP. FEMALES	STATIONARY POP. MALES	STATIONARY POP. FEMALES	STABLE POP. MALES	STABLE POP. FEMALES	OBSERVED BIRTHS	NET MATERNITY FUNCTION	BIRTHS IN STABLE POP.	
μ	24.58431	25.62592	34.84345	37.22088	25.68552	27.10126	27.92870	29.07828	28.03750	**TABLE 7**
σ^2	374.8664	393.8508	481.4115	526.7484	380.0820	421.9397	46.23791	48.62033	46.00174	MOMENTS
κ_3	6019.962	6245.943	3287.880	2791.400	5704.966	6373.515	138.0969	111.9601	135.5266	AND
κ_4	-18260.	-26678.	-201832.	-273275.	-26262.	-55241.	-994.787	-1289.955	-927.924	CUMULANTS
β_1	0.687952	0.638558	0.096891	0.053313	0.592754	0.540763	0.192918	0.109062	0.188680	
β_2	2.870061	2.828015	2.129122	2.015096	2.818209	2.689716	2.534699	2.454319	2.561506	
κ	-0.270840	-0.255377	-0.038117	-0.019923	-0.246678	-0.213571	-0.102388	-0.060253	-0.104448	

VITAL STATISTICS		AGE RANGE	THOMPSON NRR	1000r	INTERVAL	AGE RANGE	BOURGEOIS-PICHAT NRR	1000b	1000d	1000r	COALE		
GRR	2.180										IBR	35.48	**TABLE 8** RATES
NRR	1.824	0-4	1.89	24.11	27.30	5-29	2.05	36.27	9.60	26.67	IDR	10.68	FROM AGE DISTRIBUTIONS
TFR	4.430	5-9	1.91	24.24	27.23	30-54	1.87	33.65	10.55	23.09	IRI	24.80	AND VITAL
GENERATION	28.553	10-14	1.94	24.00	27.15	55-79	2.09	41.21	13.94	27.27	K1	0.	STATISTICS
SEX RATIO	103.235	15-19	1.85	16.48	27.04	* 5-29	2.05	36.27	9.60	26.67	K2	0.	(Females)

Start Age Interval	ORIGINAL MATRIX SUB-DIAGONAL	ALTERNATIVE FIRST ROWS Projection	ALTERNATIVE FIRST ROWS Integral	FIRST STABLE MATRIX % IN STABLE POPULATION	FISHER VALUES	REPRODUCTIVE VALUES	SECOND STABLE MATRIX Z_2 FIRST COLUMN	FIRST ROW	
0	0.97833	0.00000	0.00000	13.494	1.186	735911	0.1290+0.0800	0.1290+0.0800	**TABLE 9**
5	0.99494	0.00155	0.00000	11.880	1.347	732657	0.1525-0.0807	-0.0035+0.1336	LESLIE
10	0.99476	0.08203	0.00329	10.636	1.503	735713	0.0084-0.1991	-0.1016+0.0556	MATRIX
15	0.99205	0.30518	0.17053	9.521	1.581	658554	-0.1937-0.1245	-0.0965-0.0582	AND ITS
20	0.98948	0.45966	0.47660	8.499	1.406	519959	-0.2365+0.1203	-0.0383-0.1224	SPECTRAL
25	0.98553	0.43767	0.49765	7.568	1.029	318870	-0.0177+0.3044	0.0152-0.1197	COMPONENTS
30	0.98051	0.34762	0.43124	6.711	0.633	178357	0.2905+0.1933	0.0398-0.0768	(Females)
35	0.97773	0.20603	0.30756	5.922	0.297	74684	0.3570-0.1745	0.0301-0.0323	
40	0.97319	0.07069	0.12965	5.210	0.088	18806	0.0334-0.4499	0.0108-0.0083	
45	0.96119	0.01127	0.01990	4.563	0.014	2484	-0.4200-0.2892	0.0018-0.0013	
50	0.94512	0.00190	0.00400	3.946	0.002	331	-0.5153+0.2419	0.0003-0.0002	
55+	0.80178			12.051					

Start Age Interval	OBSERVED POPUL. (IN 100's)	CONTRIBUTIONS OF ROOTS (IN 100's) r_1	r_2, r_3	$r_4 \cdot r_{11}$	AGE-SP BIRTH RATES	NET MATERNITY FUNCTION	COEFF. OF MATRIX EQUATION	PARAMETERS INTEGRAL	PARAMETERS MATRIX	EXP. INCREASE x	$e^{(x+2\frac{1}{2})r}$	
0	6204	6007	5	193	0.0000	0.0000	0.0000	L(1) 1.11101	1.11128	0	1.0540	**TABLE 10**
5	5438	5288	219	-70	0.0000	0.0000	0.0015	L(2) 0.42840	0.43447	50	3.0201	AGE
10	4895	4735	250	-89	0.0007	0.0030	0.0798	0.76228	0.74341	55	3.3553	ANALYSIS
15	4165	4238	-2	-72	0.0364	0.1567	0.2955	R(1) 0.02105	0.02110	60	3.7278	AND
20	3697	3783	-334	248	0.1018	0.4343	0.4415	R(2) -0.02684	-0.02992	65	4.1416	MISCELLANEOUS
25	3100	3369	-385	117	0.1063	0.4488	0.4160	0.21176	0.20838	70	4.6013	RESULTS
30	2818	2988	-6	-164	0.0921	0.3832	0.3256	C(1)	44515	75	5.1121	(Females)
35	2515	2636	496	-616	0.0657	0.2680	0.1892	C(2)	39622	80	5.6796	
40	2149	2319	575	-746	0.0277	0.1105	0.0635		60981	85	6.3101	
45	1803	2031	20	-248	0.0043	0.0165	0.0098	2P/Y 29.6716	30.1524	90	7.0105	
50	1634	1757	-703	581	0.0009	0.0032	0.0016	DELTA 3.0073		95	7.7887	
55+	4387	5364								100	8.6533	

TABLE 1 — DATA

AGE AT LAST BIRTHDAY	POPULATION BOTH SEXES	MALES Number	%	FEMALES Number	%	BIRTHS BY AGE OF MOTHER	DEATHS BOTH SEXES	MALES	FEMALES	AGE AT LAST BIRTHDAY
0	631218	319140	3.7	312078	3.5	0	56306	30882	25424	0
1-4	2458072	1244934	14.4	1213138	13.7	0	30485	15357	15128	1-4
5-9	2803955	1420171	16.5	1383784	15.6	0	6166	3370	2796	5-9
10-14	2271648	1149829	13.3	1121819	12.6	425	2579	1503	1076	10-14
15-19	1768066	837256	9.7	930810	10.5	70986	3216	1814	1402	15-19
20-24	1419002	672053	7.8	746949	8.4	184021	3812	2299	1513	20-24
25-29	1167157	550306	6.4	616851	6.9	172261	3613	2035	1578	25-29
30-34	1031481	500799	5.8	530682	6.0	115998	3824	2004	1820	30-34
35-39	925476	443678	5.1	481798	5.4	87160	4418	2170	2248	35-39
40-44	719504	360355	4.2	359149	4.0	25387	3960	1987	1973	40-44
45-49	592904	291590	3.4	301314	3.4	6202	4363	2385	1978	45-49
50-54	518893	262556	3.0	256337	2.9	1376	5569	3075	2494	50-54
55-59	331982	167321	1.9	164661	1.9	0	5257	2936	2321	55-59
60-64	340051	164008	1.9	176349	2.0	0	8169	4430	3739	60-64
65-69	189766	92318	1.1	97448	1.1	0	6735	3672	3063	65-69
70-74	149157	68375	0.8	80782	0.9		7530	3835	3695	70-74
75-79	83793	39430	0.5	44363	0.5		6281	3186	3095	75-79
80-84	57198	23680	0.3	33518	0.4	335998 M.	5436	2368	3068	80-84
85+	44948	16870	0.2	28078	0.3	327818 F.	7630	2819	4811	85+
TOTAL	17504577	8624669		8879908		663816	175349	92127	83222	TOTAL

TABLE 2 — MALE LIFE TABLE

x	nq_x	l_x	nd_x	nL_x	nm_x	na_x	T_x	r_x	$\mathring{e}_x$	nM_x	x
0	0.091062	100000	9106	94105	0.096766	0.3527	5822669	0.0000	58.227	0.096766	0
1	0.047709	90894	4336	351541	0.012336	1.2250	5728564	0.0000	63.025	0.012336	1
5	0.011546	86557	999	430288	0.002323	2.5000	5377023	0.0263	62.121	0.002373	5
10	0.006506	85558	557	426383	0.001306	2.4725	4946735	0.0511	57.817	0.001307	10
15	0.010892	85001	926	422874	0.002189	2.6968	4520352	0.0515	53.180	0.002167	15
20	0.017025	84075	1431	416922	0.003433	2.5858	4097478	0.0387	48.736	0.003421	20
25	0.018337	82644	1515	409469	0.003701	2.5244	3680556	0.0257	44.535	0.003698	25
30	0.019835	81129	1609	401706	0.004006	2.5530	3271087	0.0174	40.320	0.004002	30
35	0.024210	79519	1925	392891	0.004900	2.5553	2869381	0.0281	36.084	0.004891	35
40	0.027330	77594	2121	382902	0.005538	2.6094	2476490	0.0360	31.916	0.005514	40
45	0.040266	75474	3039	370195	0.008209	2.6395	2093588	0.0233	27.739	0.008179	45
50	0.057357	72435	4156	352354	0.011795	2.6374	1723393	0.0434	23.792	0.011712	50
55	0.084652	68279	5780	327737	0.017636	2.6373	1371039	0.0288	20.080	0.017547	55
60	0.127461	62499	7966	293443	0.027147	2.6085	1043301	0.0305	16.693	0.027011	60
65	0.182051	54533	9928	248481	0.039954	2.5642	749859	0.0305	13.751	0.039776	65
70	0.247203	44605	11026	195742	0.056332	2.5257	501377	0.0305	11.240	0.056088	70
75	0.336231	33578	11290	139213	0.081100	2.4598	305635	0.0305	9.102	0.080801	75
80	0.396968	22288	8848	88245	0.100264	2.5506	166422	0.0305	7.467	0.100000	80
85+	1.000000	13441	13441	78177	0.171925	5.8165	78177	0.0305	5.817	0.167102	85

TABLE 3 — FEMALE LIFE TABLE

x	nq_x	l_x	nd_x	nL_x	nm_x	na_x	T_x	r_x	$\mathring{e}_x$	nM_x	x
0	0.077500	100000	7750	95131	0.081467	0.3717	6156316	0.0000	61.563	0.081467	0
1	0.048234	92250	4450	356818	0.012470	1.2623	6061185	0.0000	65.704	0.012470	1
5	0.009789	87800	860	436853	0.001967	2.5000	5704367	0.0266	64.970	0.002021	5
10	0.004765	86941	414	433626	0.000955	2.3962	5267514	0.0383	60.587	0.000959	10
15	0.007548	86527	653	431095	0.001515	2.6451	4833888	0.0392	55.866	0.001506	15
20	0.010121	85873	869	427284	0.002034	2.6034	4402793	0.0391	51.271	0.002026	20
25	0.012758	85004	1085	422427	0.002567	2.6080	3975509	0.0316	46.768	0.002558	25
30	0.017055	83920	1431	416193	0.003439	2.6200	3553081	0.0212	42.339	0.003430	30
35	0.023142	82489	1909	407829	0.004681	2.5829	3136888	0.0345	38.028	0.004666	35
40	0.027184	80580	2190	397554	0.005510	2.5602	2729060	0.0414	33.868	0.005494	40
45	0.032431	78389	2542	385891	0.006588	2.6184	2331506	0.0267	29.743	0.006565	45
50	0.047928	75847	3635	370647	0.009808	2.6376	1945614	0.0505	25.652	0.009729	50
55	0.068451	72212	4943	349364	0.014148	2.6340	1574968	0.0227	21.810	0.014096	55
60	0.101319	67269	6816	320122	0.021291	2.6199	1225604	0.0252	18.220	0.021202	60
65	0.146630	60453	8864	280905	0.031556	2.5902	905482	0.0252	14.978	0.031432	65
70	0.206538	51589	10655	232001	0.045927	2.5651	624577	0.0252	12.107	0.045740	70
75	0.297912	40934	12195	174184	0.070010	2.5001	392576	0.0252	9.591	0.069765	75
80	0.370955	28739	10661	116164	0.091775	2.6150	218392	0.0252	7.599	0.091533	80
85+	1.000000	18078	18078	102228	0.176841	5.6548	102228	0.0252	5.655	0.171345	85

TABLE 4 — OBSERVED AND PROJECTED VITAL RATES

RATES PER THOUSAND	OBSERVED POPULATION BOTH SEXES	MALES	FEMALES	PROJECTED POPULATION 1969 MALES	1969 FEMALES	1974 MALES	1974 FEMALES	1979 MALES	1979 FEMALES	STABLE POPULATION MALES	FEMALES
Birth	37.92	38.96	36.92	40.01	38.05	41.32	39.41	42.26	40.39	39.67	38.4
Death	10.02	10.68	9.37	10.28	9.01	10.45	9.10	10.65	9.34	11.32	10.0
Increase	27.91	28.28	27.54	29.73	29.04	30.86	30.30	31.61	31.05		28.347
PERCENTAGE											
under 15	46.64	47.93	45.39	45.69	43.69	43.44	41.89	42.84	41.58	42.16	41.4
15-64	50.36	49.28	51.41	51.24	52.84	53.61	54.84	54.03	54.98	54.18	54.3
65 and over	3.00	2.79	3.20	3.07	3.47	2.94	3.27	3.13	3.44	3.66	4.2
DEP. RATIO X 100	98.58	102.94	94.53	95.17	89.24	86.53	82.35	85.09	81.90	84.55	84.0

AGE AT LAST BIRTHDAY	1969 BOTH SEXES	1969 MALES	1969 FEMALES	1974 BOTH SEXES	1974 MALES	1974 FEMALES	1979 BOTH SEXES	1979 MALES	1979 FEMALES	AGE AT LAST BIRTHDAY	
0-4	3257	1637	1620	3889	1955	1934	4655	2340	2315	0-4	**TABLE 5**
5-9	2984	1510	1474	3147	1581	1566	3758	1888	1870	5-9	POPULATION
10-14	2781	1407	1374	2959	1496	1463	3121	1567	1554	10-14	PROJECTED
15-19	2255	1140	1115	2762	1396	1366	2939	1484	1455	15-19	WITH
20-24	1748	825	923	2229	1124	1105	2729	1376	1353	20-24	FIXED
25-29	1398	660	738	1723	811	912	2197	1104	1093	25-29	AGE—
30-34	1148	540	608	1376	648	728	1694	795	899	30-34	SPECIFIC
35-39	1010	490	520	1124	528	596	1346	633	713	35-39	BIRTH
40-44	902	432	470	984	477	507	1096	515	581	40-44	AND
45-49	697	348	349	874	418	456	954	462	492	45-49	DEATH
50-54	567	278	289	667	332	335	836	398	438	50-54	RATES
55-59	486	244	242	531	258	273	624	308	316	55-59	(IN 1000's)
60-64	301	150	151	440	219	221	481	231	250	60-64	
65-69	294	139	155	259	127	132	379	185	194	65-69	
70-74	153	73	80	237	109	128	209	100	109	70-74	
75-79	110	49	61	112	52	60	174	78	96	75-79	
80-84	55	25	30	71	31	40	73	33	40	80-84	
85+	50	21	29	48	22	26	63	27	36	85+	
TOTAL	20196	9968	10228	23432	11584	11848	27328	13524	13804	TOTAL	

STANDARD COUNTRIES: STANDARDIZED RATES PER THOUSAND	ENGLAND AND WALES 1961 BOTH SEXES	MALES	FEMALES	UNITED STATES 1960 BOTH SEXES	MALES	FEMALES	MEXICO 1960 BOTH SEXES	MALES	FEMALES	
Birth	35.41	42.12*	33.90	35.92	38.46*	34.95	38.72	40.31*	38.14	**TABLE 6** STANDAR-
Death	14.74	24.29*	15.14	13.21	19.84*	12.69	9.92	10.45*	9.15	DIZED
Increase	20.68	17.83*	18.76	22.71	18.62*	22.26	28.80	29.86*	29.00	RATES

	OBSERVED POP. MALES	OBSERVED POP. FEMALES	STATIONARY POP. MALES	STATIONARY POP. FEMALES	STABLE POP. MALES	STABLE POP. FEMALES	OBSERVED BIRTHS	NET MATERNITY FUNCTION	BIRTHS IN STABLE POP.	
μ	21.70918	22.31875	36.22113	37.35987	23.59595	24.13319	28.03403	29.60257	28.16538	**TABLE 7**
σ^2	336.8618	344.0440	516.2734	539.0370	360.4742	377.3498	46.53596	50.90012	46.23966	MOMENTS
κ_3	6464.357	6737.262	3340.732	3169.911	6333.319	6745.649	167.5568	153.2429	173.0253	AND
κ_4	49370.	65019.	-242604.	-278252.	∠3328.	21310.	-589.538	-961.196	-424.522	CUMULANTS
β_1	1.093189	1.114615	0.081104	0.064156	0.856328	0.846867	0.278585	0.178076	0.302813	
β_2	3.435071	3.549301	2.089796	2.042362	3.179525	3.149656	2.727771	2.629000	2.801450	
κ	-0.449022	-0.490487	-0.031362	-0.024254	-0.364488	-0.355178	-0.164310	-0.110731	-0.189527	

VITAL STATISTICS		THOMPSON AGE RANGE	NRR	1000r	INTERVAL	BOURGEOIS-PICHAT AGE RANGE	NRR	1000b	1000d	1000r	COALE		
GRR	2.712	0-4	2.30	30.57	27.29	5-29	2.85	47.59	8.78	38.81	IBR	44.31	**TABLE 8** RATES FROM AGE DISTRI-
NRR	2.267	5-9	2.56	35.41	27.20	30-54	2.42	42.60	9.84	32.75	IDR	10.14	BUTIONS
TFR	5.492	10-14	2.44	32.04	27.12	55-79	2.10	28.16	0.74	27.41	IRI	34.18	AND VITAL
GENERATION	28.873	15-19	2.40	32.41	27.01	* 5-29	2.85	47.59	8.78	38.81	K1	0.	STATISTICS
SEX RATIO	102.495										K2	0.	(Females)

Start of Age Interval	ORIGINAL MATRIX SUB-DIAGONAL	ALTERNATIVE FIRST ROWS Projection	ALTERNATIVE FIRST ROWS Integral	FIRST STABLE MATRIX % IN STABLE POPULATION	FISHER VALUES	REPRODUCTIVE VALUES	SECOND STABLE MATRIX Z₂ FIRST COLUMN	FIRST ROW	
0	0.96660	0.00000	0.00000	16.203	1.186	1809581	0.1362+0.0891	0.1362+0.0891	**TABLE 9**
5	0.99261	0.00042	0.00000	13.586	1.415	1958025	0.1579-0.0814	-0.0095+0.1488	LESLIE
10	0.99416	0.08503	0.00091	11.699	1.643	1842936	0.0078-0.1990	-0.1198+0.0580	MATRIX
15	0.99116	0.35760	0.18271	10.089	1.803	1678673	-0.1900-0.1178	-0.1092-0.0750	AND ITS
20	0.98863	0.58303	0.59024	8.674	1.669	1247017	-0.2195+0.1201	-0.0390-0.1500	SPECTRAL
25	0.98524	0.55197	0.66905	7.439	1.247	769218	-0.0042-0.2793	0.0194-0.1492	COMPO-
30	0.97990	0.44175	0.52368	6.358	0.794	421566	0.2681+0.1572	0.0489-0.1008	NENTS
35	0.97481	0.27878	0.43342	5.404	0.400	192563	0.2976-0.1724	0.0397-0.0466	(Females)
40	0.97066	0.10118	0.16935	4.570	0.133	47892	-0.0036-0.3786	0.0156-0.0150	
45	0.96050	0.02872	0.04931	3.848	0.035	10455	-0.3630-0.2011	0.0047-0.0036	
50	0.94258	0.00599	0.01286	3.206	0.006	1580	-0.3838+0.2351	0.0010-0.0005	
55+	0.81410			8.923					

Start of Age Interval	OBSERVED POPUL. (IN 100's)	CONTRIBUTIONS OF ROOTS (IN 100's) r_1	r_2, r_3	$r_4 \cdot r_{11}$	AGE-SP. BIRTH RATES	NET MATERNITY FUNCTION	COEFF. OF MATRIX EQUATION	PARAMETERS INTEGRAL	PARAMETERS MATRIX	EXP. INCREASE x	$e^{(x+2\frac{1}{2})r}$	
0	15252	15029	-123	346	0.0000	0.0000	0.0000	L(1) 1.15227	1.15279	0	1.0734	**TABLE 10**
5	13838	12602	893	343	0.0000	0.0000	0.0004	L(2) 0.43018	0.43650	50	4.4292	AGE
10	11218	10851	1137	-770	0.0002	0.0008	0.0816	0.79206	0.77050	55	5.1037	ANALYSIS
15	9308	9358	135	-184	0.0377	0.1624	0.3411	R(1) 0.02835	0.02844	60	5.8808	AND
20	7469	8046	-1280	704	0.1217	0.5199	0.5512	R(2) -0.02077	-0.02431	65	6.7763	MISCEL-
25	6169	6900	-1577	846	0.1379	0.5826	0.5159	0.21465	0.21107	70	7.8081	LANEOUS
30	5307	5897	-140	-450	0.1079	0.4493	0.4068	C(1)	92752	75	8.9971	RESULTS
35	4818	5013	1789	-1984	0.0893	0.3643	0.2516	C(2)	138206	80	0.3671	(Females)
40	3591	4239	2112	-2759	0.0349	0.1388	0.0890		280289	85	1.9457	
45	3013	3569	124	-680	0.0102	0.0392	0.0245	2P/Y 29.2718	29.7679	90	3.7647	
50	2563	2974	-2379	1968	0.0027	0.0098	0.0049	DELTA 4.4615		95	5.8606	
55+	6252	8276								100	8.2758	

TABLE 1 — DATA

AGE AT LAST BIRTHDAY	POPULATION BOTH SEXES	MALES Number	%	FEMALES Number	%	BIRTHS BY AGE OF MOTHER	DEATHS BOTH SEXES	MALES	FEMALES	AGE AT LAST BIRTHDAY
0	821	421	2.5	400	2.4	0	58	29	29	0
1-4	3945	1979	11.7	1966	12.0	0	36	24	12	1-4
5-9	4481	2213	13.0	2268	13.8	0	7	3	4	5-9
10-14	3376	1668	9.8	1708	10.4	4	3	1	2	10-14
15-19	2308	1126	6.6	1182	7.2	118	6	3	3	15-19
20-24	1992	924	5.4	1068	6.5	271	3	2	1	20-24
25-29	2100	1045	6.2	1055	6.4	262	9	5	4	25-29
30-34	2168	1147	6.8	1021	6.2	194	13	4	9	30-34
35-39	2202	1151	6.8	1051	6.4	136	12	11	1	35-39
40-44	2027	1085	6.4	942	5.7	79	16	10	6	40-44
45-49	1804	980	5.8	824	5.0	2	22	14	8	45-49
50-54	1576	866	5.1	710	4.3	0	25	18	7	50-54
55-59	1253	703	4.1	550	3.4	0	27	16	11	55-59
60-64	1107	589	3.5	518	3.2	0	44	35	9	60-64
65-69	951	540	3.2	411	2.5	0	63	49	14	65-69
70-74	625	307	1.8	318	1.9		53	37	16	70-74
75-79	371	148	0.9	223	1.4		41	23	18	75-79
80-84	188	57	0.3	131	0.8	555 M.	30	12	18	80-84
85+	72	15	0.1	57	0.3	511 F.	19	5	14	85+
TOTAL	33367	16964		16403		1066	487	301	186	TOTAL

TABLE 2 — MALE LIFE TABLE

x	nq_x	l_x	nd_x	nL_x	nm_x	na_x	T_x	r_x	$\mathring{e}_x$	nM_x	x
0	0.066088	100000	6609	95941	0.068884	0.3859	5431090	0.0000	54.311	0.068884	0
1	0.046968	93391	4386	361699	0.012127	1.2948	5335149	0.0000	57.127	0.012127	1
5	0.006432	89005	573	443593	0.001291	2.5000	4973450	0.0328	55.878	0.001356	5
10	0.003088	88432	273	441604	0.000618	2.9597	4529858	0.0663	51.224	0.000600	10
15	0.013330	88159	1175	437996	0.002683	2.6178	4088254	0.0570	46.374	0.002664	15
20	0.010778	86984	938	432755	0.002166	2.6910	3650257	0.0045	41.965	0.002164	20
25	0.023647	86046	2035	425253	0.004785	2.5528	3217502	0.0000	37.393	0.004785	25
30	0.017302	84012	1454	416805	0.003487	2.7612	2792249	0.0000	33.236	0.003487	30
35	0.046719	82558	3857	403585	0.009557	2.6132	2375445	0.0000	28.773	0.009557	35
40	0.045102	78701	3550	384912	0.009222	2.5788	1971859	0.0056	25.055	0.009217	40
45	0.069183	75152	5199	363463	0.014305	2.6353	1586948	0.0080	21.117	0.014286	45
50	0.099006	69952	6926	332789	0.020811	2.5493	1223484	0.0139	17.490	0.020785	50
55	0.108475	63027	6837	299651	0.022816	2.7354	890695	0.0084	14.132	0.022760	55
60	0.260751	56190	14652	246091	0.059537	2.6208	591044	0.0083	10.519	0.059423	60
65	0.369188	41538	15335	168800	0.090850	2.4639	344953	0.0083	8.304	0.090741	65
70	0.457855	26203	11997	99447	0.120639	2.3687	176153	0.0083	6.723	0.120521	70
75	0.547342	14206	7775	49982	0.155564	2.2932	76707	0.0083	5.400	0.155405	75
80	0.665155	6430	4277	20288	0.210828	2.2262	26725	0.0083	4.156	0.210526	80
85+	*1.000000	2153	2153	6437	0.334485	2.9897	6437	0.0083	2.990	0.333333	85+

TABLE 3 — FEMALE LIFE TABLE

x	nq_x	l_x	nd_x	nL_x	nm_x	na_x	T_x	r_x	$\mathring{e}_x$	nM_x	x
0	0.069052	100000	6905	95244	0.072500	0.3112	6152264	0.0000	61.523	0.072500	0
1	0.023999	93095	2234	366041	0.006104	1.1630	6057020	0.0000	65.063	0.006104	1
5	0.008653	90861	786	452337	0.001738	2.5000	5690979	0.0299	62.634	0.001764	5
10	0.005890	90074	531	449117	0.001181	2.6343	5238642	0.0635	58.159	0.001171	10
15	0.012600	89544	1128	444874	0.002536	2.4785	4789525	0.0452	53.488	0.002538	15
20	0.004684	88416	414	441152	0.000939	2.7651	4344651	0.0095	49.139	0.000936	20
25	0.018810	88001	1655	436558	0.003792	2.9162	3903499	0.0001	44.357	0.003791	25
30	0.043098	86346	3721	422164	0.008815	2.4292	3466941	0.0000	40.152	0.008815	30
35	0.004732	82625	391	411912	0.000949	1.9003	3044777	0.0040	36.851	0.000951	35
40	0.031566	82234	2596	405386	0.006403	2.7722	2632864	0.0186	32.017	0.006369	40
45	0.047490	79638	3782	388960	0.009723	2.5595	2227478	0.0193	27.970	0.009709	45
50	0.048460	75856	3676	370738	0.009915	2.6761	1838518	0.0282	24.237	0.009859	50
55	0.095454	72180	6890	344046	0.020026	2.5537	1467780	0.0147	20.335	0.020000	55
60	0.083510	65290	5452	313353	0.017400	2.5977	1123734	0.0103	17.211	0.017375	60
65	0.157885	59838	9448	276791	0.034132	2.6292	810382	0.0103	13.543	0.034063	65
70	0.224510	50390	11313	224444	0.050405	2.5686	533590	0.0103	10.589	0.050314	70
75	0.337043	39077	13171	162844	0.080879	2.5292	309146	0.0103	7.911	0.080717	75
80	0.508032	25906	13161	95601	0.137669	2.4933	146302	0.0103	5.647	0.137405	80
85+	1.000000	12745	12745	50701	0.251381	3.9780	50701	0.0103	3.978	0.245613	85+

TABLE 4 — OBSERVED AND PROJECTED VITAL RATES

	OBSERVED POPULATION BOTH SEXES	MALES	FEMALES	PROJECTED POPULATION 1966 MALES	FEMALES	1971 MALES	FEMALES	1976 MALES	FEMALES	STABLE POPULATION MALES	FEMALES
RATES PER THOUSAND											
Birth	31.95	32.72	31.15	32.59	30.41	35.14	32.39	38.22	35.02	37.88	35.89
Death	14.60	17.74	11.34	16.45	11.04	15.36	10.75	14.50	10.60	11.56	9.57
Increase	17.35	14.97	19.81	16.14	19.37	19.77	21.65	23.72	24.43		26.3188
PERCENTAGE											
under 15	37.83	37.03	38.66	39.14	38.86	39.22	37.36	40.34	37.50	42.08	40.43
15-64	55.55	56.68	54.39	55.65	54.38	56.40	56.33	55.72	56.37	55.92	55.36
65 and over	6.61	6.29	6.95	5.21	6.77	4.38	6.31	3.94	6.14	2.00	4.21
DEP. RATIO X 100	80.00	76.41	83.87	79.70	83.90	77.31	77.52	79.48	77.41	78.81	80.65

TABLE 5 — POPULATION PROJECTED WITH FIXED AGE-SPECIFIC BIRTH AND DEATH RATES (IN 1000's)

AGE AT LAST BIRTHDAY	1966 BOTH SEXES	1966 MALES	1966 FEMALES	1971 BOTH SEXES	1971 MALES	1971 FEMALES	1976 BOTH SEXES	1976 MALES	1976 FEMALES	AGE AT LAST BIRTHDAY
0-4	5	3	2	6	3	3	7	4	3	0-4
5-9	4	2	2	5	3	2	6	3	3	5-9
10-14	4	2	2	4	2	2	5	3	2	10-14
15-19	4	2	2	4	2	2	4	2	2	15-19
20-24	2	1	1	4	2	2	4	2	2	20-24
25-29	2	1	1	2	1	1	4	2	2	25-29
30-34	2	1	1	2	1	1	2	1	1	30-34
35-39	2	1	1	2	1	1	2	1	1	35-39
40-44	2	1	1	2	1	1	2	1	1	40-44
45-49	2	1	1	2	1	1	2	1	1	45-49
50-54	2	1	1	2	1	1	2	1	1	50-54
55-59	2	1	1	2	1	1	2	1	1	55-59
60-64	2	1	1	2	1	1	2	1	1	60-64
65-69	0	0	0	0	0	0	1	0	1	65-69
70-74	0	0	0	0	0	0	0	0	0	70-74
75-79	0	0	0	0	0	0	0	0	0	75-79
80-84	0	0	0	0	0	0	0	0	0	80-84
85+	0	0	0	0	0	0	0	0	0	85+
TOTAL	35	18	17	39	20	19	45	23	22	TOTAL

TABLE 6 — STANDARDIZED RATES

STANDARD COUNTRIES:

STANDARDIZED RATES PER THOUSAND

	ENGLAND AND WALES 1961 BOTH SEXES	MALES	FEMALES	UNITED STATES 1960 BOTH SEXES	MALES	FEMALES	MEXICO 1960 BOTH SEXES	MALES	FEMALES
Birth	32.47	34.77*	30.17	33.09	33.19*	31.26	36.79	30.25*	35.18
Death	20.45	27.09*	17.26	17.74	22.87*	13.85	11.18	16.35*	8.87
Increase	12.02	7.68*	12.91	15.35	10.32*	17.41	25.61	13.90*	26.31

TABLE 7 — MOMENTS AND CUMULANTS

	OBSERVED POP. MALES	OBSERVED POP. FEMALES	STATIONARY POP. MALES	STATIONARY POP. FEMALES	STABLE POP. MALES	STABLE POP. FEMALES	OBSERVED BIRTHS	NET MATERNITY FUNCTION	BIRTHS IN STABLE POP.
μ	28.57949	27.74526	32.43857	36.32333	22.81559	24.47621	28.40056	28.52086	27.21271
σ^2	449.6999	464.1288	410.3916	511.6218	311.6777	374.1807	50.10753	49.46516	45.61164
κ_3	4576.098	6630.220	2387.636	2991.597	4479.880	6292.421	118.5851	125.8318	163.2201
κ_4	-176580.	-118811.	-148236.	-251376.	-8943.	1316.	-1950.966	-1843.597	-985.263
β_1	0.230262	0.439684	0.082479	0.066828	0.662850	0.755773	0.111777	0.130822	0.280750
β_2	2.126834	2.448456	2.119847	2.039660	2.907935	3.009396	2.222959	2.246528	2.526412
κ	-0.079427	-0.158965	-0.032703	-0.025137	-0.276064	-0.310591	-0.047152	-0.055153	-0.129319

TABLE 8 — RATES FROM AGE DISTRIBUTIONS AND VITAL STATISTICS (Females)

VITAL STATISTICS

		THOMPSON AGE RANGE	NRR	1000r	INTERVAL	BOURGEOIS-PICHAT AGE RANGE	NRR	1000b	1000d	1000r	COALE
GRR	2.421										
NRR	2.082	0-4	2.08	27.82	27.22	5-29	2.81	37.15	-1.07	38.23	IBR
TFR	5.050	5-9	2.11	28.01	27.14	30-54	1.42	23.93	10.88	13.05	IDR
GENERATION	27.859	10-14	1.65	18.31	27.05	55-79	1.29	17.23	7.84	9.39	IRI
SEX RATIO	108.611	15-19	1.22	7.24	26.93	*35-59	1.84	36.95	14.38	22.57	K1
											K2

TABLE 9 — LESLIE MATRIX AND ITS SPECTRAL COMPONENTS (Females)

Start of Age Interval	ORIGINAL MATRIX SUB-DIAGONAL	ALTERNATIVE FIRST ROWS Projection	Integral	FIRST STABLE MATRIX % IN STABLE POPULATION	FISHER VALUES	REPRODUCTIVE VALUES	SECOND STABLE MATRIX Z₂ FIRST COLUMN	FIRST ROW
0	0.98060	0.00000	0.00000	15.528	1.157	2737	0.1122+0.1062	0.1122+0.1062
5	0.99288	0.00257	0.00000	13.344	1.346	3053	0.1718-0.0545	-0.0330+0.1281
10	0.99055	0.11192	0.00553	11.611	1.544	2638	0.0421-0.2089	-0.1087+0.0278
15	0.99163	0.38857	0.23576	10.079	1.648	1948	-0.1914-0.1627	-0.0780-0.0812
20	0.98959	0.55225	0.59925	8.759	1.443	1542	-0.2775+0.1045	-0.0158-0.1327
25	0.96703	0.47772	0.58648	7.596	1.019	1075	-0.0507+0.3456	0.0295-0.1256
30	0.97572	0.34967	0.44873	6.437	0.631	644	0.3197+0.2437	0.0524-0.0829
35	0.98416	0.23432	0.30559	5.504	0.323	339	0.4276-0.1877	0.0441-0.0332
40	0.95948	0.09401	0.19805	4.747	0.099	93	0.0504-0.5446	0.0163-0.0060
45	0.95315	0.00283	0.00287	3.992	0.004	3	-0.5162-0.3518	0.0006-0.0005
50	0.92800	0.00156	0.00333	3.334	0.002	1	-0.6329+0.3189	0.0003-0.0001
55+	0.79993			9.069				

TABLE 10 — AGE ANALYSIS AND MISCELLANEOUS RESULTS (Females)

Start of Age Interval	OBSERVED POPUL. (IN 100's)	CONTRIBUTIONS OF ROOTS (IN 100's) r₁	r₂,r₃	r₄-r₁₁	AGE-SP. BIRTH RATES	NET MATERNITY FUNCTION	COEFF. OF MATRIX EQUATION	PARAMETERS INTEGRAL	MATRIX	EXP. INCREASE x	$e^{(x+2\frac{1}{2})r}$
0	24	22	1	0	0.0000	0.0000	0.0000	L(1) 1.14064	1.14110	0	1.0680
5	23	19	2	1	0.0000	0.0000	0.0025	L(2) 0.39513	0.40705	50	3.9818
10	17	17	2	-1	0.0011	0.0050	0.1090	0.75220	0.73488	55	4.5418
15	12	15	-2	-1	0.0479	0.2129	0.3747	R(1) 0.02632	0.02640	60	5.1806
20	11	13	-4	2	0.1216	0.5366	0.5282	R(2) -0.03258	-0.03485	65	5.9092
25	11	11	-2	2	0.1190	0.5197	0.4521	0.21742	0.21299	70	6.7403
30	10	9	3	-2	0.0911	0.3845	0.3200	C(1)	145	75	7.6883
35	11	8	6	-4	0.0620	0.2555	0.2092	C(2)	617	80	8.7697
40	9	7	3	-1	0.0402	0.1630	0.0837		249	85	10.0031
45	8	6	-5	7	0.0012	0.0045	0.0023	2P/Y 28.8984	29.4996	90	11.4099
50	7	5	-9	12	0.0000	0.0000	0.0000	DELTA 8.7653		95	13.0147
55+	22	13								100	14.8452

TABLE 1 — DATA

AGE AT LAST BIRTHDAY	POPULATION BOTH SEXES	MALES Number	MALES %	FEMALES Number	FEMALES %	BIRTHS BY AGE OF MOTHER	DEATHS BOTH SEXES	MALES	FEMALES	AGE AT LAST BIRTHDAY
0	350228	175115	3.6	175113	3.5	0	33642	18130	15512	0
1-4	1322141	665509	13.5	656632	13.2	0	21782	10764	11018	1-4
5-9	1467099	739198	15.0	727901	14.6	0	3547	1864	1683	5-9
10-14	1152776	594996	12.1	557780	11.2	466	1949	1016	933	10-14
15-19	974206	494224	10.0	479982	9.6	38070	2346	1240	1106	15-19
20-24	848618	420771	8.5	427847	8.6	100210	3004	1468	1536	20-24
25-29	741643	360031	7.3	381612	7.7	94573	2904	1389	1515	25-29
30-34	620325	311700	6.3	308625	6.2	62822	2825	1390	1435	30-34
35-39	540228	260692	5.3	279536	5.6	43192	2818	1420	1398	35-39
40-44	420541	209151	4.2	211390	4.2	14745	2729	1494	1235	40-44
45-49	364814	177404	3.6	187410	3-8	3394	2884	1553	1331	45-49
50-54	292013	143055	2.9	148958	3.0	846	2845	1581	1264	50-54
55-59	225556	110147	2.2	115409	2.3	0	2768	1621	1147	55-59
60-64	189405	88297	1.8	101108	2.0	0	3287	1770	1517	60-64
65-69	150015	68602	1.4	81413	1.6	0	3965	2049	1916	65-69
70-74	111650	49761	1.0	61889	1.2		4559	2245	2314	70-74
75-79	75168	32384	0.7	42784	0.9		4851	2256	2595	75-79
80-84	42689	17601	0.4	25088	0.5	184751 M.	4540	1971	2569	80-84
85+	17631	6880	0.1	10751	0.2	173567 F.	3368	1344	2024	85+
TOTAL	9906746	4925518		4981228		358318	110613	56565	54048	TOTAL

TABLE 2 — MALE LIFE TABLE

x	$_nq_x$	l_x	$_nd_x$	$_nL_x$	$_nm_x$	$_na_x$	T_x	r_x	$\mathring{e}_x$	$_nM_x$
0	0.097211	100000	9721	93895	0.103532	0.3719	5742911	0.0000	57.429	0.103532
1	0.061953	90279	5593	345806	0.016174	1.2627	5649017	0.0000	62.573	0.016174
5	0.012169	84686	1031	420853	0.002449	2.5000	5303211	0.0291	62.622	0.002522
10	0.008504	83655	711	416500	0.001708	2.5026	4882358	0.0382	58.363	0.001708
15	0.012530	82944	1039	412269	0.002521	2.6420	4465859	0.0321	53.842	0.002509
20	0.017337	81905	1420	406077	0.003497	2.5735	4053590	0.0283	49.492	0.003489
25	0.019135	80485	1540	398641	0.003863	2.5440	3647513	0.0261	45.319	0.003858
30	0.022103	78945	1745	390474	0.004469	2.5648	3248872	0.0278	41.154	0.004459
35	0.026975	77200	2082	380980	0.005466	2.5901	2858398	0.0343	37.026	0.005447
40	0.035214	75117	2645	369188	0.007165	2.5813	2477419	0.0314	32.981	0.007143
45	0.042973	72472	3114	354804	0.008778	2.5738	2108231	0.0291	29.090	0.008754
50	0.054035	69358	3748	337746	0.011096	2.5871	1753426	0.0363	25.281	0.011052
55	0.071353	65610	4681	316786	0.014778	2.5940	1415680	0.0332	21.577	0.014717
60	0.096175	60929	5860	290626	0.020163	2.6080	1098894	0.0383	18.036	0.020046
65	0.140195	55069	7720	256840	0.030059	2.6032	808268	0.0383	14.677	0.029868
70	0.204546	47348	9685	213268	0.045412	2.5762	551428	0.0383	11.646	0.045116
75	0.299067	37663	11264	160576	0.070147	2.5371	338160	0.0383	8.978	0.069664
80	0.442915	26400	11693	103483	0.112992	2.5613	177585	0.0383	6.727	0.111983
85+	*1.000000	14707	14707	74101	0.198468	5.0386	74101	0.0383	5.039	0.195349

TABLE 3 — FEMALE LIFE TABLE

x	$_nq_x$	l_x	$_nd_x$	$_nL_x$	$_nm_x$	$_na_x$	T_x	r_x	$\mathring{e}_x$	$_nM_x$
0	0.084048	100000	8405	94881	0.088583	0.3909	5993829	0.0000	59.938	0.088583
1	0.064217	91595	5882	350544	0.016780	1.3075	5898948	0.0000	64.402	0.016780
5	0.011049	85713	947	426199	0.002222	2.5000	5548405	0.0346	64.732	0.002312
10	0.008332	84766	706	422070	0.001673	2.5060	5122206	0.0397	60.427	0.001673
15	0.011507	84060	967	418043	0.002314	2.6670	4700136	0.0241	55.914	0.002304
20	0.017830	83093	1482	411893	0.003597	2.5899	4282093	0.0195	51.534	0.003590
25	0.019689	81611	1607	404113	0.003976	2.5466	3870200	0.0286	47.422	0.003970
30	0.023013	80004	1841	395487	0.004655	2.5370	3466087	0.0266	43.324	0.004650
35	0.024741	78163	1934	386056	0.005009	2.5388	3070600	0.0327	39.285	0.005001
40	0.028873	76229	2201	375781	0.005857	2.5621	2684544	0.0341	35.217	0.005842
45	0.034980	74028	2590	363829	0.007117	2.5625	2308764	0.0279	31.188	0.007102
50	0.041679	71439	2977	349905	0.008509	2.5522	1944935	0.0400	27.225	0.008486
55	0.048717	68461	3335	334336	0.009976	2.6103	1595029	0.0281	23.298	0.009939
60	0.072842	65126	4744	314485	0.015085	2.6507	1260693	0.0294	19.358	0.015004
65	0.112065	60382	6767	285932	0.023666	2.6387	946207	0.0294	15.670	0.023534
70	0.172522	53615	9250	245998	0.037601	2.6131	660275	0.0294	12.315	0.037390
75	0.265683	44366	11787	193207	0.061008	2.5719	414277	0.0294	9.338	0.060654
80	0.408771	32578	13317	129354	0.102951	2.6169	221069	0.0294	6.786	0.102400
85+	1.000000	19261	19261	91715	0.210011	4.7617	91715	0.0294	4.762	0.188261

TABLE 4 — OBSERVED AND PROJECTED VITAL RATES

	OBSERVED POPULATION BOTH SEXES	MALES	FEMALES	PROJECTED POPULATION 1966 MALES	1966 FEMALES	1971 MALES	1971 FEMALES	1976 MALES	1976 FEMALES	STABLE POPULATION MALES	FEMALES
RATES PER THOUSAND											
Birth	36.17	37.51	34.84	37.26	34.92	37.61	35.50	38.55	36.61	35.92	35.0
Death	11.17	11.48	10.85	11.19	10.46	11.29	10.54	11.45	10.70	12.46	11.5
Increase	25.00	26.02	23.99	26.07	24.46	26.32	24.95	27.10	25.91	23.455	
PERCENTAGE											
under 15	43.33	44.15	42.51	42.81	41.61	40.89	39.57	39.92	38.41	38.75	38.2
15-64	52.66	52.29	53.04	53.52	53.82	55.42	55.93	56.29	57.03	56.14	55.9
65 and over	4.01	3.56	4.46	3.67	4.57	3.69	4.49	3.79	4.55	5.11	5.8
DEP. RATIO X 100	89.88	91.25	88.55	86.83	85.80	80.46	78.78	77.66	75.33	78.11	78.8

TABLE 5 — POPULATION PROJECTED WITH FIXED AGE—SPECIFIC BIRTH AND DEATH RATES (IN 1000's)

AGE AT LAST BIRTHDAY	1966 BOTH SEXES	MALES	FEMALES	1971 BOTH SEXES	MALES	FEMALES	1976 BOTH SEXES	MALES	FEMALES	AGE AT LAST BIRTHDAY
0-4	1690	866	824	1928	988	940	2238	1147	1091	0-4
5-9	1601	805	796	1617	829	788	1846	946	900	5-9
10-14	1453	732	721	1584	796	788	1601	820	781	10-14
15-19	1141	589	552	1438	724	714	1569	788	781	15-19
20-24	960	487	473	1124	580	544	1416	713	703	20-24
25-29	833	413	420	942	478	464	1103	569	534	25-29
30-34	726	353	373	816	405	411	922	468	454	30-34
35-39	605	304	301	709	344	365	796	395	401	35-39
40-44	525	253	272	588	295	293	688	333	355	40-44
45-49	406	201	205	506	243	263	567	283	284	45-49
50-54	349	169	180	388	191	197	484	231	253	50-54
55-59	276	134	142	330	158	172	367	179	188	55-59
60-64	210	101	109	257	123	134	307	145	162	60-64
65-69	170	78	92	188	89	99	231	109	122	65-69
70-74	127	57	70	144	65	79	159	74	85	70-74
75-79	86	37	49	98	43	55	111	49	62	75-79
80-84	50	21	29	57	24	33	65	28	37	80-84
85+	31	13	18	35	15	20	40	17	23	85+
TOTAL	11239	5613	5626	12749	6390	6359	14510	7294	7216	TOTAL

TABLE 6 — STANDARDIZED RATES

STANDARD COUNTRIES: STANDARDIZED RATES PER THOUSAND

	ENGLAND AND WALES 1961 BOTH SEXES	MALES	FEMALES	UNITED STATES 1960 BOTH SEXES	MALES	FEMALES	MEXICO 1960 BOTH SEXES	MALES	FEMALES
Birth	32.69	36.93*	30.69	33.17	33.74*	31.66	35.95	35.77*	34.74
Death	14.21	24.02*	14.60	13.14	19.89*	12.72	10.66	11.22*	10.07
Increase	18.48	12.91*	16.08	20.03	13.85*	18.94	25.29	24.55*	24.67

TABLE 7 — MOMENTS AND CUMULANTS

	OBSERVED POP. MALES	FEMALES	STATIONARY POP. MALES	FEMALES	STABLE POP. MALES	FEMALES	OBSERVED BIRTHS	NET MATERNITY FUNCTION	BIRTHS IN STABLE POP.
μ	22.83394	23.78783	36.68128	37.68981	25.57779	26.08743	27.96745	29.36245	28.12840
σ^2	350.7194	378.3554	531.8668	553.6223	401.7741	420.0224	46.56767	52.60963	48.38174
κ_3	6453.466	7007.249	3347.863	3117.254	6703.284	7107.730	180.0855	170.6631	187.7984
κ_4	37725.	29566.	−270089.	−309099.	−13744.	−23092.	−356.970	−987.401	−466.210
β_1	0.965399	0.906557	0.074495	0.057267	0.692835	0.681780	0.321147	0.200025	0.311415
β_2	3.306697	3.206533	2.045225	1.991514	2.914857	2.869106	2.835388	2.643251	2.800832
κ	−0.407059	−0.374508	−0.027929	−0.020909	−0.281256	−0.269833	−0.203788	−0.121564	−0.191441

TABLE 8 — RATES FROM AGE DISTRIBUTIONS AND VITAL STATISTICS (Females)

VITAL STATISTICS

GRR	2.455
NRR	1.962
TFR	5.069
GENERATION	28.737
SEX RATIO	106.444

THOMPSON

AGE RANGE	NRR	1000r	INTERVAL
0-4	2.14	27.91	27.22
5-9	2.22	30.01	27.14
10-14	1.98	24.74	27.09
15-19	2.02	26.09	27.02

BOURGEOIS-PICHAT

AGE RANGE	NRR	1000b	1000d	1000r
5-29	2.16	39.85	11.33	28.52
30-54	2.31	44.10	13.05	31.05
55-79	1.78	24.10	2.70	21.41
*10-39	1.93	35.86	11.50	24.35

COALE

IBR	40.39
IDR	11.19
IRI	29.20
K1	0.
K2	0.

TABLE 9 — LESLIE MATRIX AND ITS SPECTRAL COMPONENTS (Females)

Start of Age interval	SUB-DIAGONAL	ALTERNATIVE FIRST ROWS Projection	Integral	% IN STABLE POPULATION	FISHER VALUES	REPRODUCTIVE VALUES	SECOND STABLE MATRIX Z2 FIRST COLUMN	FIRST ROW
0	0.95684	0.00000	0.00000	14.737	1.189	989145	0.1309+0.0925	0.1309+0.0925
5	0.99031	0.00089	0.00000	12.537	1.398	1017584	0.1629−0.0753	−0.0132+0.1424
10	0.99046	0.08565	0.00191	11.038	1.587	885037	0.0185−0.2073	−0.1123+0.0513
15	0.98529	0.33452	0.18147	9.720	1.699	815513	−0.1975−0.1386	−0.0980−0.0698
20	0.98111	0.51498	0.53587	8.515	1.536	657093	−0.2522+0.1177	−0.0344−0.1352
25	0.97865	0.48226	0.56700	7.427	1.136	433692	−0.0274+0.3185	0.0184−0.1332
30	0.97615	0.38231	0.46571	6.462	0.720	222249	0.3005+0.2093	0.0443−0.0897
35	0.97338	0.23994	0.35351	5.608	0.364	101752	0.3786−0.1783	0.0361−0.0418
40	0.96820	0.09417	0.15959	4.853	0.127	26947	0.0392−0.4753	0.0153−0.0136
45	0.96173	0.02543	0.04143	4.178	0.032	6077	−0.4446−0.3073	0.0044−0.0033
50	0.95550	0.00613	0.01299	3.572	0.006	965	−0.5497+0.2611	0.0010−0.0005
55+	0.82410			11.352				

TABLE 10 — AGE ANALYSIS AND MISCELLANEOUS RESULTS (Females)

CONTRIBUTIONS OF ROOTS (IN 100's)

Start of Age interval	OBSERVED POPUL. (IN 100's)	r_1	r_2, r_3	$r_4 \cdot r_{11}$	AGE-SP. BIRTH RATES	NET MATERNITY FUNCTION	COEFF. OF MATRIX EQUATION
0	8317	7748	197	372	0.0000	0.0000	0.0000
5	7279	6591	578	110	0.0000	0.0000	0.0009
10	5578	5803	413	−638	0.0004	0.0017	0.0812
15	4800	5110	−299	−11	0.0384	0.1606	0.3140
20	4278	4477	−896	698	0.1135	0.4673	0.4762
25	3816	3905	−631	542	0.1200	0.4851	0.4375
30	3086	3397	458	−769	0.0986	0.3900	0.3394
35	2795	2949	1348	−1501	0.0748	0.2889	0.2280
40	2114	2552	937	−1375	0.0338	0.1270	0.0794
45	1874	2196	−681	359	0.0088	0.0319	0.0208
50	1490	1878	−1961	1573	0.0028	0.0096	0.0048
55+	4384	5968					

PARAMETERS

	INTEGRAL	MATRIX
L(1)	1.12443	1.12478
L(2)	0.41813	0.42626
	0.75988	0.74025
R(1)	0.02346	0.02352
R(2)	−0.02847	−0.03152
	0.21355	0.20967
C(1)		52574
C(2)		136916
		87287
2P/Y	29.4224	29.9672
DELTA	4.5435	

EXP. INCREASE

x	$e^{(x+2\frac{1}{2})r}$
0	1.0604
50	3.4261
55	3.8524
60	4.3317
65	4.8707
70	5.4768
75	6.1583
80	6.9246
85	7.7862
90	8.7550
95	9.8444
100	1.0694

TABLE 1 — DATA

AGE AT LAST BIRTHDAY	POPULATION BOTH SEXES	MALES Number	MALES %	FEMALES Number	FEMALES %	BIRTHS BY AGE OF MOTHER	DEATHS BOTH SEXES	DEATHS MALES	DEATHS FEMALES	AGE AT LAST BIRTHDAY
0	308530	157153	3.8	151377	3.8	0	17149	9479	7670	0
1-4	1160664	591196	14.3	569468	14.2	0	7134	3494	3640	1-4
5-9	1208414	618523	14.9	589891	14.7	0	1935	1009	926	5-9
10-14	1000882	511336	12.4	489546	12.2	796	890	591	299	10-14
15-19	786112	393575	9.5	392537	9.8	49162	956	622	334	15-19
20-24	649686	324789	7.8	324897	8.1	104087	1438	873	565	20-24
25-29	578311	296656	7.2	281655	7.0	88138	1381	809	572	25-29
30-34	526524	273309	6.6	253215	6.3	59394	1447	782	665	30-34
35-39	448326	234048	5.7	214278	5.3	38580	1430	793	637	35-39
40-44	358923	188792	4.6	170131	4.2	10870	1881	1080	801	40-44
45-49	306536	159959	3.9	146577	3.7	2251	1969	1149	820	45-49
50-54	246926	125617	3.0	121309	3.0	268	2578	1580	998	50-54
55-59	184296	93512	2.3	90784	2.3	0	2726	1594	1132	55-59
60-64	144672	70544	1.7	74128	1.9	0	3920	2109	1811	60-64
65-69	98049	45087	1.1	52962	1.3	0	2317	1210	1107	65-69
70-74	60930	24901	0.6	36029	0.9		2885	1381	1504	70-74
75-79	41521	16147	0.4	25374	0.6		1946	891	1055	75-79
80-84	24078	8816	0.2	15262	0.4	180683 M.	2222	877	1345	80-84
85+	10249	3492	0.1	6757	0.2	172863 F.	2270	858	1412	85+
TOTAL	8143629	4137452		4006177		353546	58474	31181	27293	TOTAL

TABLE 2 — MALE LIFE TABLE

x	nq_x	l_x	nd_x	nL_x	nm_x	na_x	T_x	r_x	$\dot{e}_x$	nM_x	x
0	0.057867	100000	5787	96112	0.060208	0.3281	6334491	0.0025	63.345	0.060317	0
1	0.023214	94213	2187	370698	0.005900	1.1857	6238378	0.0025	66.215	0.005910	1
5	0.007979	92026	734	458295	0.001602	2.5000	5867681	0.0356	63.761	0.001631	5
10	0.005762	91292	526	455141	0.001156	2.4947	5409386	0.0439	59.254	0.001156	10
15	0.007942	90766	721	452169	0.001594	2.6963	4954044	0.0437	54.583	0.001580	15
20	0.013383	90045	1205	447313	0.002694	2.5834	4502076	0.0258	49.998	0.002688	20
25	0.013546	88840	1203	441199	0.002728	2.5071	4054763	0.0145	45.641	0.002727	25
30	0.014221	87636	1246	435120	0.002864	2.5430	3613564	0.0208	41.234	0.002861	30
35	0.016905	86390	1460	428542	0.003408	2.6657	3178443	0.0332	36.792	0.003388	35
40	0.028346	84930	2407	418937	0.005747	2.6275	2749901	0.0326	32.379	0.005721	40
45	0.035546	82522	2933	405796	0.007229	2.6765	2330964	0.0327	28.246	0.007183	45
50	0.061478	79589	4893	386386	0.012663	2.6377	1925168	0.0414	24.189	0.012578	50
55	0.082562	74696	6167	359039	0.017177	2.6583	1538782	0.0385	20.601	0.017046	55
60	0.139789	68529	9580	318971	0.030033	2.5287	1179743	0.0550	17.215	0.029896	60
65	0.127034	58949	7489	276661	0.027068	2.5849	860772	0.0550	14.602	0.026837	65
70	0.245470	51461	12632	226135	0.055861	2.5325	584110	0.0550	11.351	0.055460	70
75	0.243676	38829	9462	170357	0.055540	2.4860	357976	0.0550	9.219	0.055181	75
80	0.408426	29367	11994	118498	0.101220	2.6374	187619	0.0550	6.389	0.099478	80
85+	*1.000000	17373	17373	69121	0.251340	3.9787	69121	0.0550	3.979	0.245704	85+

TABLE 3 — FEMALE LIFE TABLE

x	nq_x	l_x	nd_x	nL_x	nm_x	na_x	T_x	r_x	$\dot{e}_x$	nM_x	x
0	0.048979	100000	4898	96841	0.050577	0.3550	6710064	0.0026	67.101	0.050668	0
1	0.025087	95102	2386	373798	0.006383	1.2292	6613223	0.0026	69.538	0.006392	1
5	0.007637	92716	708	461811	0.001533	2.5000	6239425	0.0363	67.296	0.001570	5
10	0.003021	92008	278	459281	0.000605	2.2645	5777614	0.0399	62.795	0.000611	10
15	0.004294	91730	394	457775	0.000860	2.7732	5318333	0.0400	57.978	0.000851	15
20	0.008698	91336	794	454805	0.001747	2.6371	4860558	0.0316	53.216	0.001739	20
25	0.010125	90542	917	450497	0.002035	2.5857	4405753	0.0228	48.660	0.002031	25
30	0.013072	89625	1172	445280	0.002631	2.5704	3955256	0.0248	44.131	0.002626	30
35	0.014838	88454	1312	439167	0.002988	2.6373	3509976	0.0365	39.682	0.002973	35
40	0.023368	87141	2036	430833	0.004727	2.6069	3070809	0.0335	35.239	0.004708	40
45	0.027702	85105	2358	419907	0.005615	2.6171	2639976	0.0278	31.020	0.005594	45
50	0.040627	82747	3362	405852	0.008283	2.6548	2220070	0.0395	26.830	0.008227	50
55	0.061155	79386	4855	385886	0.012581	2.7256	1814217	0.0349	22.853	0.012469	55
60	0.115643	74531	8619	351469	0.024523	2.5421	1428332	0.0441	19.164	0.024431	60
65	0.100070	65912	6596	313625	0.021031	2.5842	1076863	0.0441	16.338	0.020902	65
70	0.190254	59316	11285	268896	0.041968	2.5469	763238	0.0441	12.867	0.041744	70
75	0.190165	48031	9134	217981	0.041902	2.5724	494343	0.0441	10.292	0.041578	75
80	0.371722	38897	14459	161527	0.089514	2.7205	276361	0.0441	7.105	0.088128	80
85+	*1.000000	24438	24438	114835	0.212812	4.6990	114835	0.0441	4.699	0.208968	85+

TABLE 4 — OBSERVED AND PROJECTED VITAL RATES

	OBSERVED POPULATION BOTH SEXES	MALES	FEMALES	PROJECTED POPULATION 1968 MALES	1968 FEMALES	1973 MALES	1973 FEMALES	1978 MALES	1978 FEMALES	STABLE POPULATION MALES	FEMALES
RATES PER THOUSAND											
Birth	43.41	43.67	43.15	42.85	42.27	42.87	42.24	43.20	42.50	44.54	43.54
Death	7.18	7.54	6.81	7.77	6.99	7.86	6.99	7.93	6.97	7.84	6.84
Increase	36.23	36.13	36.34	35.08	35.28	35.01	35.25	35.26	35.53		36.6998
PERCENTAGE											
under 15	45.17	45.40	44.94	45.84	45.44	46.07	45.75	46.36	45.99	47.30	46.63
15-64	51.95	52.23	51.66	51.47	51.00	51.05	50.71	50.59	50.41	50.14	50.31
65 and over	2.88	2.38	3.40	2.70	3.56	2.88	3.54	3.04	3.60	2.56	3.06
DEP. RATIO X 100	92.51	91.48	93.58	94.29	96.08	95.89	97.21	97.66	98.38	99.45	98.75

TABLE 5 — POPULATION PROJECTED WITH FIXED AGE-SPECIFIC BIRTH AND DEATH RATES (IN 1000's)

AGE LAST BIRTHDAY	1968 BOTH SEXES	1968 MALES	1968 FEMALES	1973 BOTH SEXES	1973 MALES	1973 FEMALES	1978 BOTH SEXES	1978 MALES	1978 FEMALES	AGE AT LAST BIRTHDAY
0-4	1799	916	883	2128	1083	1045	2546	1296	1250	0-4
5-9	1442	735	707	1766	899	867	2088	1063	1025	5-9
10-14	1201	614	587	1433	730	703	1755	893	862	10-14
15-19	996	508	488	1195	610	585	1426	725	701	15-19
20-24	779	389	390	988	503	485	1185	604	581	20-24
25-29	642	320	322	770	384	386	976	496	480	25-29
30-34	571	293	278	634	316	318	761	379	382	30-34
35-39	519	269	250	563	288	275	625	311	314	35-39
40-44	439	229	210	508	263	245	551	282	269	40-44
45-49	349	183	166	427	222	205	494	255	239	45-49
50-54	294	152	142	334	174	160	409	211	198	50-54
55-59	232	117	115	277	142	135	314	162	152	55-59
60-64	166	83	83	209	104	105	249	126	123	60-64
65-69	127	61	66	146	72	74	184	90	94	65-69
70-74	82	37	45	107	50	57	122	59	63	70-74
75-79	48	19	29	65	28	37	84	38	46	75-79
80-84	30	11	19	35	13	22	46	19	27	80-84
85+	16	5	11	20	7	13	23	8	15	85+
TOTAL	9732	4941	4791	11605	5888	5717	13838	7017	6821	TOTAL

TABLE 6 — STANDARDIZED RATES

STANDARD COUNTRIES: STANDARDIZED RATES PER THOUSAND	ENGLAND AND WALES 1961 BOTH SEXES	MALES	FEMALES	UNITED STATES 1960 BOTH SEXES	MALES	FEMALES	MEXICO 1960 BOTH SEXES	MALES	FEMALES
Birth	40.42	43.25*	38.30	41.14	39.93*	39.63	46.03	41.16*	44.90
Death	12.46	18.86*	12.61	10.80	14.91*	10.17	7.25	7.61*	6.57
Increase	27.96	24.40*	25.69	30.34	25.02*	29.46	38.78	33.56*	38.33

TABLE 7 — MOMENTS AND CUMULANTS

	OBSERVED POP. MALES	OBSERVED POP. FEMALES	STATIONARY POP. MALES	STATIONARY POP. FEMALES	STABLE POP. MALES	STABLE POP. FEMALES	OBSERVED BIRTHS	NET MATERNITY FUNCTION	BIRTHS IN STABLE POP.
	22.24340	22.69901	36.72764	38.24079	21.09735	21.59249	27.14232	28.50180	26.73229
$_2$	327.0127	353.9388	520.1311	553.0227	314.4670	332.5292	44.61142	49.11167	43.00052
$_3$	5349.487	6506.942	3088.376	2919.565	6030.328	6607.039	163.3653	151.5559	176.5968
$_4$	11793.	35289.	−254970.	−304242.	63718.	72066.	−582.057	−1078.596	−286.084
$_1$	0.818334	0.954925	0.067783	0.050397	1.169383	1.187202	0.300595	0.193906	0.392233
$_2$	3.110283	3.281700	2.057538	2.005205	3.644336	3.651737	2.707535	2.552813	2.845280
$_x$	−0.342317	−0.398881	−0.025859	−0.018735	−0.525331	−0.526510	−0.165849	−0.105157	−0.220926

TABLE 8 — RATES FROM AGE DISTRIBUTIONS AND VITAL STATISTICS (Females)

VITAL STATISTICS		AGE RANGE	THOMPSON NRR	1000r	INTERVAL	AGE RANGE	BOURGEOIS-PICHAT NRR	1000b	1000d	1000r	COALE	
R	3.071											
R	2.753	0-4	2.51	33.61	27.34	5-29	2.69	41.57	4.98	36.58	IBR	44.16
R	6.281	5-9	2.43	33.20	27.27	30-54	2.40	40.49	8.07	32.42	IDR	6.69
NERATION	27.598	10-14	2.33	30.30	27.20	55-79	2.81	54.80	16.58	38.22	IRI	37.47
X RATIO	104.524	15-19	2.17	28.67	27.10	*30-54	2.40	40.49	8.07	32.42	K1	26.82
											K2	0.37

TABLE 9 — LESLIE MATRIX AND ITS SPECTRAL COMPONENTS (Females)

ORIGINAL MATRIX SUB-DIAGONAL	ALTERNATIVE FIRST ROWS Projection	ALTERNATIVE FIRST ROWS Integral	FIRST STABLE MATRIX % IN STABLE POPULATION	FISHER VALUES	REPRODUCTIVE VALUES	SECOND STABLE MATRIX Z_2 FIRST COLUMN	SECOND STABLE MATRIX Z_2 FIRST ROW
0.98124	0.00000	0.00000	18.756	1.163	838697	0.1349+0.1118	0.1349+0.1118
0.99452	0.00186	0.00000	15.307	1.426	840999	0.1777−0.0791	−0.0364+0.1537
0.99672	0.14550	0.00410	12.661	1.721	842736	0.0090−0.2185	−0.1371+0.0315
0.99351	0.51032	0.31589	10.495	1.907	748490	−0.2162−0.1184	−0.0987−0.1129
0.99053	0.72524	0.80806	8.672	1.710	555580	−0.2270+0.1587	−0.0182−0.1808
0.98842	0.62680	0.78929	7.144	1.224	344703	0.0464+0.3067	0.0386−0.1681
0.98627	0.47419	0.59162	5.873	0.751	190148	0.3303+0.1056	0.0645−0.1067
0.98102	0.27927	0.45412	4.818	0.356	76298	0.2691−0.2778	0.0466−0.0444
0.97464	0.09073	0.16115	3.931	0.105	17896	−0.1437−0.4043	0.0161−0.0120
0.96653	0.02013	0.03873	3.186	0.021	3144	−0.4696−0.0558	0.0037−0.0022
0.95080	0.00254	0.00557	2.561	0.002	298	−0.2825+0.4329	0.0005−0.0002
0.83308			6.595				

TABLE 10 — AGE ANALYSIS AND MISCELLANEOUS RESULTS (Females)

OBSERVED POPUL. (IN 100's)	CONTRIBUTIONS OF ROOTS (IN 100's) r_1	r_2, r_3	$r_4 \cdot r_{11}$	AGE-SP. BIRTH RATES	NET MATERNITY FUNCTION	COEFF. OF MATRIX EQUATION	PARAMETERS	PARAMETERS INTEGRAL	PARAMETERS MATRIX	EXP. INCREASE x	$e^{(x+2\frac{1}{2})r}$
7208	7232	91	−115	0.0000	0.0000	0.0000	L(1)	1.20141	1.20237	0	1.0961
5899	5902	−7	4	0.0000	0.0000	0.0018	L(2)	0.38048	0.39245	50	6.8671
4895	4882	−121	135	0.0008	0.0037	0.1420		0.81714	0.79243	55	8.2502
3925	4047	−112	−9	0.0612	0.2803	0.4964	R(1)	0.03670	0.03686	60	9.9119
3249	3344	42	−137	0.1566	0.7124	0.7008	R(2)	−0.02077	−0.02459	65	11.9083
2817	2755	182	−121	0.1530	0.6893	0.6000		0.22701	0.22219	70	14.3069
2532	2265	129	139	0.1147	0.5107	0.4486	C(1)		38559	75	17.1885
2143	1858	−100	385	0.0880	0.3866	0.2606	C(2)		10509	80	20.6505
1701	1516	−258	443	0.0312	0.1346	0.0831			−28145	85	24.8097
1466	1229	−130	367	0.0075	0.0315	0.0180	2P/Y	27.6785	28.2783	90	29.8068
1213	988	184	41	0.0011	0.0044	0.0022	DELTA	3.0913		95	35.8103
3013	2543									100	43.0230

TABLE 1 — DATA

AGE AT LAST BIRTHDAY	POPULATION BOTH SEXES	MALES Number	%	FEMALES Number	%	BIRTHS BY AGE OF MOTHER	DEATHS BOTH SEXES	MALES	FEMALES	AGE AT BIRTH
0	263880	132096	3.1	131784	3.4	0	22869	12626	10243	0
1-4	954552	481598	11.2	472954	12.3	0	17118	7827	9291	1-
5-9	1094540	554244	12.9	540296	14.0	0	3611	1677	1934	5-
10-14	927491	478383	11.1	449108	11.6	187	1280	635	645	10-
15-19	709430	367229	8.5	342201	8.9	23154	1413	625	788	15-
20-24	773564	398198	9.3	375366	9.7	96544	2149	805	1344	20-
25-29	714495	374054	8.7	340441	8.8	99643	2390	904	1486	25-
30-34	524910	287493	6.7	237417	6.1	57922	1876	817	1059	30-
35-39	539833	294380	6.8	245453	6.4	36532	2446	1126	1320	35-
40-44	374983	212181	4.9	162802	4.2	6156	1858	1013	845	40-
45-49	373244	212979	5.0	160265	4.2	1079	2590	1502	1088	45-
50-54	280354	160890	3.7	119464	3.1	0	2496	1474	1022	50-
55-59	190116	109780	2.6	80336	2.1	0	2591	1595	996	55-
60-64	154663	84602	2.0	70061	1.8	0	3099	1828	1271	60-
65-69	113590	62571	1.5	51019	1.3	0	3652	2057	1595	65-
70-74	76509	40808	0.9	35701	0.9		4000	2143	1857	70-
75-79	44881	22995	0.5	21886	0.6		3466	1806	1660	75-
80-84	29251	15686	0.4	13565	0.4	163888 M.	3837	1982	1855	80-
85+	21840	11326	0.3	10514	0.3	157329 F.	6262	3032	3230	85-
TOTAL	8162126	4301493		3860633		321217	89003	45474	43529	TOT

TABLE 2 — MALE LIFE TABLE

x	n_{q_x}	l_x	n_{d_x}	n_{L_x}	n_{m_x}	n_{a_x}	T_x	r_x	$\dot{e}_x$	n_{M_x}
0	0.090171	100000	9017	94414	0.095506	0.3805	5899277	0.0012	58.993	0.095582
1	0.062222	90983	5661	348544	0.016242	1.2819	5804863	0.0012	63.802	0.016252
5	0.014766	85322	1260	423459	0.002975	2.5000	5456319	0.0193	63.950	0.003026
10	0.006561	84062	551	418816	0.001317	2.2918	5032860	0.0393	59.871	0.001327
15	0.008487	83510	709	415838	0.001704	2.5827	4614044	0.0167	55.251	0.001702
20	0.010059	82802	833	411984	0.002022	2.5696	4198206	0.0000	50.702	0.002022
25	0.012039	81969	987	407442	0.002422	2.5660	3786042	0.0302	46.191	0.002417
30	0.014143	80982	1145	402157	0.002848	2.5965	3378781	0.0210	41.723	0.002842
35	0.019004	79837	1517	395538	0.003836	2.5975	2976624	0.0266	37.284	0.003825
40	0.023693	78319	1856	387196	0.004792	2.6282	2581086	0.0273	32.956	0.004774
45	0.034771	76464	2659	375982	0.007071	2.6163	2193890	0.0207	28.692	0.007052
50	0.045255	73805	3340	361161	0.009248	2.6455	1817908	0.0564	24.631	0.009162
55	0.070825	70465	4991	340560	0.014654	2.6426	1456747	0.0494	20.673	0.014529
60	0.103194	65474	6757	311313	0.021703	2.6233	1116187	0.0263	17.048	0.021607
65	0.153093	58718	8989	272129	0.033033	2.6128	804874	0.0263	13.708	0.032875
70	0.233242	49729	11623	220331	0.052751	2.5641	532744	0.0263	10.713	0.052514
75	0.329700	38106	12564	159242	0.078896	2.5097	312414	0.0263	8.199	0.078539
80	0.477931	25542	12207	96197	0.126901	2.5132	153172	0.0263	5.997	0.126355
85+	1.000000	13335	13335	56975	0.234048	4.2726	56975	0.0263	4.273	0.267702

TABLE 3 — FEMALE LIFE TABLE

x	n_{q_x}	l_x	n_{d_x}	n_{L_x}	n_{m_x}	n_{a_x}	T_x	r_x	$\dot{e}_x$	n_{M_x}
0	0.074249	100000	7425	95666	0.077612	0.4163	5818125	0.0026	58.181	0.077726
1	0.074670	92575	6913	352219	0.019626	1.3843	5722459	0.0026	61.814	0.019645
5	0.017373	85663	1488	424592	0.003505	2.5000	5370240	0.0232	62.691	0.003580
10	0.007098	84174	597	419268	0.001425	2.3158	4945648	0.0435	58.755	0.001436
15	0.011487	83577	960	415665	0.002310	2.6886	4526381	0.0156	54.158	0.002303
20	0.017751	82617	1467	409583	0.003581	2.6130	4110716	0.0000	49.756	0.003581
25	0.021630	81150	1755	401423	0.004373	2.5341	3701132	0.0416	45.608	0.004365
30	0.022088	79395	1754	392654	0.004466	2.5365	3299710	0.0280	41.561	0.004460
35	0.026560	77641	2062	383090	0.005383	2.5189	2907055	0.0326	37.442	0.005378
40	0.025677	75579	1941	373128	0.005201	2.5433	2523966	0.0370	33.395	0.005190
45	0.033480	73638	2465	362251	0.006806	2.5901	2150838	0.0242	29.208	0.006789
50	0.042252	71173	3007	348694	0.008624	2.6154	1788587	0.0601	25.130	0.008555
55	0.060596	68166	4131	331042	0.012477	2.6306	1439893	0.0407	21.123	0.012398
60	0.087384	64035	5596	307106	0.018221	2.6643	1108852	0.0213	17.316	0.018141
65	0.146208	58440	8544	272079	0.031404	2.6453	801745	0.0213	13.719	0.031263
70	0.231617	49895	11557	221364	0.052206	2.5675	529667	0.0213	10.616	0.052015
75	0.320457	38339	12286	161327	0.076155	2.5284	308302	0.0213	8.042	0.075848
80	0.507813	26053	13230	96345	0.137318	2.5085	146975	0.0213	5.641	0.136749
85+	1.000000	12823	12823	50630	0.253265	3.9484	50630	0.0213	3.948	0.307210

TABLE 4 — OBSERVED AND PROJECTED VITAL RATES

	OBSERVED POPULATION			PROJECTED POPULATION 1958		1963		1968		STABLE POPULATION	
RATES PER THOUSAND	BOTH SEXES	MALES	FEMALES	MALES	FEMALES	MALES	FEMALES	MALES	FEMALES	MALES	FEMA
Birth	39.35	38.10	40.75	36.45	38.61	35.91	37.69	35.82	37.30	37.16	37.
Death	10.90	10.57	11.28	10.83	11.16	10.85	11.03	11.07	11.09	11.51	11.
Increase	28.45	27.53	29.48	25.62	27.45	25.05	26.65	24.76	26.21		25.64
PERCENTAGE											
under 15	39.70	38.27	41.29	38.60	41.45	38.52	40.82	39.06	40.89	39.73	40.
15-64	56.79	58.16	55.27	57.79	55.18	57.70	55.85	56.69	55.50	55.74	55.
65 and over	3.50	3.57	3.44	3.61	3.37	3.78	3.32	4.25	3.61	4.53	4.
DEP. RATIO X 100	76.08	71.94	80.93	73.05	81.22	73.31	79.04	76.41	80.20	79.41	81.

TABLE 5 — POPULATION PROJECTED WITH FIXED AGE-SPECIFIC BIRTH AND DEATH RATES (IN 1000's)

AGE AT LAST BIRTHDAY	1958 BOTH SEXES	1958 MALES	1958 FEMALES	1963 BOTH SEXES	1963 MALES	1963 FEMALES	1968 BOTH SEXES	1968 MALES	1968 FEMALES	AGE AT LAST BIRTHDAY
0-4	1496	759	737	1653	839	814	1858	943	915	0-4
5-9	1160	587	573	1425	726	699	1574	802	772	5-9
10-14	1082	548	534	1146	580	566	1408	718	690	10-14
15-19	920	475	445	1073	544	529	1137	576	561	15-19
20-24	701	364	337	910	471	439	1060	539	521	20-24
25-29	762	394	368	690	360	330	895	465	430	25-29
30-34	702	369	333	749	389	360	678	355	323	30-34
35-39	515	283	232	688	363	325	733	382	351	35-39
40-44	527	288	239	503	277	226	671	355	316	40-44
45-49	364	206	158	512	280	232	488	269	219	45-49
50-54	359	205	154	350	198	152	492	269	223	50-54
55-59	265	152	113	339	193	146	331	187	144	55-59
60-64	175	100	75	244	139	105	312	176	136	60-64
65-69	136	74	62	154	88	66	214	121	93	65-69
70-74	93	51	42	111	60	51	125	71	54	70-74
75-79	55	29	26	67	37	30	80	43	37	75-79
80-84	27	14	13	34	18	16	40	22	18	80-84
85+	16	9	7	15	8	7	19	11	8	85+
TOTAL	9355	4907	4448	10663	5570	5093	12115	6304	5811	TOTAL

TABLE 6 — STANDARDIZED RATES

STANDARD COUNTRIES:

STANDARDIZED RATES PER THOUSAND	ENGLAND AND WALES 1961 BOTH SEXES	MALES	FEMALES	UNITED STATES 1960 BOTH SEXES	MALES	FEMALES	MEXICO 1960 BOTH SEXES	MALES	FEMALES
Birth	33.76	32.94*	32.05	34.41	30.36*	33.20	38.16	31.39*	37.28
Death	15.92	20.92*	17.98	14.32	17.29*	15.14	10.86	10.24*	11.04
Increase	17.84	12.02*	14.07	20.09	13.07*	18.07	27.30	21.15*	26.24

TABLE 7 — MOMENTS AND CUMULANTS

	OBSERVED POP. MALES	OBSERVED POP. FEMALES	STATIONARY POP. MALES	STATIONARY POP. FEMALES	STABLE POP. MALES	STABLE POP. FEMALES	OBSERVED BIRTHS	NET MATERNITY FUNCTION	BIRTHS IN STABLE POP.
μ	25.13846	23.68440	36.79754	36.62378	24.98311	24.75663	27.66121	28.68662	27.66863
μ_2	357.6466	346.0729	518.7208	522.9334	387.1837	386.9825	34.28048	38.67798	36.47954
κ_3	5188.195	5869.511	2764.607	2891.316	6373.067	6527.940	98.6155	77.3373	93.1551
κ_4	-9918.	31606.	-262491.	-271415.	-12132.	-7161.	-335.232	-721.259	-496.971
β_1	0.588397	0.831191	0.054760	0.058459	0.699755	0.735323	0.241407	0.103368	0.178758
β_2	2.922465	3.263898	2.024455	2.007476	2.919070	2.952181	2.714733	2.517871	2.626550
κ	-0.270732	-0.392689	-0.020594	-0.021596	-0.283034	-0.294675	-0.150204	-0.063251	-0.110589

TABLE 8 — RATES FROM AGE DISTRIBUTIONS AND VITAL STATISTICS (Females)

VITAL STATISTICS

		THOMPSON AGE RANGE	NRR	1000r	INTERVAL	BOURGEOIS-PICHAT AGE RANGE	NRR	1000b	1000d	1000r	COALE	
GRR	2.584										IBR	36.23
NRR	2.060	0-4	1.88	23.94	27.22	5-29	1.69	35.36	16.01	19.35	IDR	13.81
TFR	5.277	5-9	1.94	24.86	27.14	30-54	2.26	44.79	14.66	30.13	IRI	22.42
GENERATION	28.173	10-14	1.91	23.49	27.10	55-79	2.16	33.27	4.83	28.44	K1	-9.72
SEX RATIO	104.169	15-19	1.79	15.84	27.02	*50-74	2.59	52.86	17.56	35.30	K2	0.

TABLE 9 — LESLIE MATRIX AND ITS SPECTRAL COMPONENTS (Females)

ORIGINAL MATRIX SUB-DIAGONAL	ALTERNATIVE FIRST ROWS Projection	ALTERNATIVE FIRST ROWS Integral	FIRST STABLE MATRIX % IN STABLE POPULATION	FIRST STABLE MATRIX FISHER VALUES	FIRST STABLE MATRIX REPRODUCTIVE VALUES	SECOND STABLE MATRIX Z2 FIRST COLUMN	SECOND STABLE MATRIX Z2 FIRST ROW
0.94799	0.00000	0.00000	15.770	1.189	719056	0.1511+0.0717	0.1511+0.0717
0.98746	0.00045	0.00000	13.146	1.426	770674	0.1388-0.1043	0.0065+0.1610
0.99141	0.07403	0.00097	11.415	1.642	737523	-0.0301-0.1854	-0.1291+0.0745
0.98537	0.35220	0.15826	9.951	1.795	614234	-0.1934-0.0646	-0.1272-0.0787
0.98008	0.59675	0.60158	8.622	1.647	618075	-0.1588+0.1524	-0.0442-0.1639
0.97816	0.58279	0.68458	7.431	1.187	403982	0.0656+0.2269	0.0241-0.1511
0.97564	0.42687	0.57063	6.391	0.671	159354	0.2479+0.0507	0.0453-0.0884
0.97400	0.20365	0.34812	5.483	0.262	64341	0.1711-0.2094	0.0268-0.0323
0.97085	0.04864	0.08844	4.696	0.057	9354	-0.1129-0.2655	0.0069-0.0068
0.96258	0.00739	0.01573	4.009	0.008	1239	-0.3057-0.0249	0.0011-0.0008
0.94938	0.00001	0.00002	3.393	0.000	1	-0.1730+0.2732	0.0000-0.0000
0.80480			9.691				

TABLE 10 — AGE ANALYSIS AND MISCELLANEOUS RESULTS (Females)

OBSERVED POPUL. (IN 100's)	CONTRIBUTIONS OF ROOTS (IN 100's) r_1	r_2, r_3	r_4-r_{11}	AGE-SP. BIRTH RATES	NET MATERNITY FUNCTION	COEFF. OF MATRIX EQUATION	PARAMETERS	INTEGRAL	MATRIX	EXP. INCREASE x	$e^{(x+2\frac{1}{2})r}$
6047	6265	72	-290	0.0000	0.0000	0.0000	L(1)	1.13681	1.13723	0	1.0662
5403	5222	-81	261	0.0000	0.0000	0.0004	L(2)	0.42181	0.42438	50	3.8434
4491	4535	-162	119	0.0002	0.0009	0.0693		0.83334	0.80844	55	4.3692
3422	3953	-69	-462	0.0331	0.1378	0.3269	R(1)	0.02564	0.02572	60	4.9669
3754	3425	121	207	0.1260	0.5160	0.5457	R(2)	-0.01365	-0.01819	65	5.6464
3404	2952	201	252	0.1434	0.5755	0.5223		0.22044	0.21748	70	6.4189
2374	2539	61	-226	0.1195	0.4692	0.3742	C(1)		39726	75	7.2970
2455	2178	-169	446	0.0729	0.2793	0.1742	C(2)		3423	80	8.2953
1628	1866	-237	-0	0.0185	0.0691	0.0405			-43267	85	9.4301
1603	1593	-42	52	0.0033	0.0119	0.0060	2P/Y	28.5023	28.8909	90	10.7203
1195	1348	225	-378	0.0000	0.0000	0.0000	DELTA	4.6973		95	12.1869
2831	3850									100	13.8541

TABLE 1 — DATA

AGE AT LAST BIRTHDAY	POPULATION BOTH SEXES	MALES Number	MALES %	FEMALES Number	FEMALES %	BIRTHS BY AGE OF MOTHER	DEATHS BOTH SEXES	DEATHS MALES	DEATHS FEMALES	AGE AT LAST BIRTHDAY
0	453000	229000	4.2	224000	4.5	0	19142	10561	8581	0
1-4	1251000	634000	11.5	617000	12.5	0	11383	5318	6065	1-4
5-9	1378000	698000	12.7	680000	13.8	0	3073	1461	1612	5-9
10-14	1167000	602000	10.9	565000	11.4	160	1450	755	695	10-14
15-19	893000	462000	8.4	431000	8.7	26849	1447	687	760	15-19
20-24	973000	501000	9.1	472000	9.6	102594	1938	805	1133	20-24
25-29	899000	471000	8.6	428000	8.7	105267	1995	838	1157	25-29
30-34	661000	362000	6.6	299000	6.1	76788	1865	827	1038	30-34
35-39	680000	371000	6.7	309000	6.3	48026	2361	1112	1249	35-39
40-44	472000	267000	4.8	205000	4.2	9747	1861	1068	793	40-44
45-49	470000	268000	4.9	202000	4.1	1331	2705	1597	1108	45-49
50-54	353000	203000	3.7	150000	3.0	0	2794	1695	1099	50-54
55-59	239000	138000	2.5	101000	2.0	0	3377	2152	1225	55-59
60-64	195000	107000	1.9	88000	1.8	0	4280	2594	1686	60-64
65-69	142000	78000	1.4	64000	1.3	0	4926	2859	2067	65-69
70-74	97000	52000	0.9	45000	0.9		5511	3112	2399	70-74
75-79	57000	29000	0.5	28000	0.6		4557	2490	2067	75-79
80-84	48195	26024	0.5	22171	0.4	188938 M.	4915	2574	2341	80-84
85+	15805	7976	0.1	7829	0.2	181824 F.	9336	4547	4789	85+
TOTAL	10444000	5506000		4938000		370762	88916	47052	41864	TOTAL

TABLE 2 — MALE LIFE TABLE

x	nq_x	l_x	nd_x	nL_x	nm_x	na_x	T_x	r_x	$\mathring{e}_x$	nM_x
0	0.043942	100000	4394	97326	0.045149	0.3915	6410471	0.0328	64.105	0.046118
1	0.032360	95606	3094	374098	0.008270	1.3090	6313145	0.0328	66.033	0.008388
5	0.010213	92512	945	460198	0.002053	2.5000	5939047	0.0328	64.198	0.002093
10	0.006227	91567	570	456354	0.001249	2.4013	5478849	0.0398	59.834	0.001254
15	0.007414	90997	675	453330	0.001488	2.5471	5022495	0.0169	55.194	0.001487
20	0.008002	90322	723	449830	0.001607	2.5348	4569165	0.0000	50.587	0.001607
25	0.008879	89599	796	446069	0.001784	2.5755	4119336	0.0306	45.975	0.001779
30	0.011388	88804	1011	441599	0.002290	2.6061	3673267	0.0215	41.364	0.002285
35	0.014928	87793	1311	435835	0.003007	2.6128	3231668	0.0274	36.810	0.002997
40	0.019898	86482	1721	428356	0.004017	2.6438	2795834	0.0283	32.328	0.004000
45	0.029477	84761	2499	417912	0.005979	2.6412	2367478	0.0214	27.931	0.005959
50	0.041506	82263	3414	403505	0.008462	2.7130	1949566	0.0569	23.699	0.008350
55	0.075965	78848	5990	380301	0.015750	2.6727	1546061	0.0482	19.608	0.015594
60	0.115000	72859	8379	344370	0.024331	2.6222	1165760	0.0208	16.000	0.024243
65	0.169096	64480	10903	296317	0.036796	2.6078	821390	0.0208	12.739	0.036654
70	0.261686	53577	14020	233467	0.060052	2.5453	525073	0.0208	9.800	0.059846
75	0.352703	39556	13952	162112	0.086061	2.4434	291606	0.0208	7.372	0.085862
80	0.399438	25605	10227	102752	0.099536	2.5290	129494	0.0208	5.057	0.098908
85+	*1.000000	15377	15377	26742	0.575027	1.7390	26742	0.0208	1.739	0.570085

TABLE 3 — FEMALE LIFE TABLE

x	nq_x	l_x	nd_x	nL_x	nm_x	na_x	T_x	r_x	$\mathring{e}_x$	nM_x
0	0.036769	100000	3677	97874	0.037568	0.4217	6442486	0.0332	64.425	0.038308
1	0.037911	96323	3652	375811	0.009717	1.4036	6344613	0.0332	65.868	0.009830
5	0.011519	92671	1067	460688	0.002317	2.5000	5968801	0.0361	64.408	0.002371
10	0.006105	91604	559	456566	0.001225	2.4008	5508113	0.0440	60.130	0.001230
15	0.008800	91045	801	453328	0.001767	2.6346	5051547	0.0162	55.484	0.001763
20	0.011933	90244	1077	448609	0.002400	2.5775	4598219	0.0000	50.953	0.002400
25	0.013476	89167	1202	442921	0.002713	2.5764	4149610	0.0428	46.538	0.002703
30	0.017253	87965	1518	436142	0.003480	2.5727	3706689	0.0291	42.138	0.003472
35	0.020024	86447	1731	427933	0.004045	2.5133	3270547	0.0339	37.833	0.004042
40	0.019217	84716	1628	419622	0.003880	2.5673	2842614	0.0382	33.554	0.003868
45	0.027164	83089	2257	410074	0.005504	2.6215	2422992	0.0258	29.162	0.005485
50	0.036423	80831	2944	397291	0.007410	2.6679	2012918	0.0613	24.903	0.007327
55	0.059441	77887	4630	378653	0.012227	2.6709	1615626	0.0408	20.743	0.012129
60	0.092019	73258	6741	350557	0.019230	2.6664	1236973	0.0176	16.885	0.019159
65	0.150544	66517	10014	308927	0.032414	2.6376	886416	0.0176	13.326	0.032297
70	0.236393	56503	13357	249840	0.053462	2.5538	577489	0.0176	10.221	0.053311
75	0.311903	43146	13461	181903	0.074002	2.4871	327648	0.0176	7.594	0.073821
80	0.421816	29685	12522	117892	0.106212	2.5616	145745	0.0176	4.910	0.105588
85+	*1.000000	17163	17163	27854	0.616195	1.6229	27854	0.0176	1.623	0.611700

TABLE 4 — OBSERVED AND PROJECTED VITAL RATES

	OBSERVED POPULATION BOTH SEXES	MALES	FEMALES	PROJECTED POPULATION 1967 MALES	1967 FEMALES	1972 MALES	1972 FEMALES	1977 MALES	1977 FEMALES	STABLE POPULATION MALES	FEMA
RATES PER THOUSAND											
Birth	35.50	34.31	36.82	33.50	35.51	33.21	34.81	33.23	34.51	34.78	34.
Death	8.51	8.55	8.48	8.23	7.83	8.17	7.70	8.39	7.79	8.38	8.
Increase	26.99	25.77	28.34	25.27	27.68	25.03	27.11	24.85	26.72		26.39
PERCENTAGE											
under 15	40.68	39.28	42.24	39.49	42.19	39.41	41.50	38.72	40.29	39.91	40.
15-64	55.87	57.21	54.37	57.08	54.55	57.07	55.31	57.35	56.25	55.94	55.
65 and over	3.45	3.51	3.38	3.43	3.26	3.52	3.19	3.93	3.45	4.16	4.
DEP. RATIO X 100	78.99	74.79	83.91	75.19	83.33	75.21	80.80	74.36	77.76	78.78	80.

AGE AT LAST BIRTHDAY	1967 BOTH SEXES	1967 MALES	1967 FEMALES	1972 BOTH SEXES	1972 MALES	1972 FEMALES	1977 BOTH SEXES	1977 MALES	1977 FEMALES	AGE AT LAST BIRTHDAY	
0-4	1849	940	909	2069	1052	1017	2341	1190	1151	0-4	
5-9	1660	842	818	1802	918	884	2016	1027	989	5-9	
10-14	1366	692	674	1646	835	811	1786	910	876	10-14	
15-19	1159	598	561	1357	688	669	1635	830	805	15-19	**TABLE 5**
20-24	885	458	427	1148	593	555	1344	682	662	20-24	POPULATION
25-29	963	497	466	876	455	421	1136	588	548	25-29	PROJECTED
30-34	887	466	421	951	492	459	865	450	415	30-34	WITH
35-39	650	357	293	874	460	414	935	485	450	35-39	FIXED
40-44	668	365	303	639	351	288	857	452	405	40-44	AGE—
45-49	460	260	200	652	356	296	624	343	281	45-49	SPECIFIC
50-54	455	259	196	446	252	194	630	343	287	50-54	BIRTH
55-59	334	191	143	431	244	187	422	237	185	55-59	AND
60-64	219	125	94	305	173	132	394	221	173	60-64	DEATH
65-69	170	92	78	190	108	82	266	149	117	65-69	RATES
70-74	113	61	52	136	73	63	152	85	67	70-74	(IN 1000's)
75-79	69	36	33	81	43	38	96	50	46	75-79	
80-84	36	18	18	44	23	21	51	27	24	80-84	
85+	12	7	5	9	5	4	11	6	5	85+	
TOTAL	11955	6264	5691	13656	7121	6535	15561	8075	7486	TOTAL	

STANDARD COUNTRIES:	ENGLAND AND WALES 1961 BOTH SEXES	MALES	FEMALES	UNITED STATES 1960 BOTH SEXES	MALES	FEMALES	MEXICO 1960 BOTH SEXES	MALES	FEMALES	
STANDARDIZED RATES PER THOUSAND										**TABLE 6**
Birth	31.88	30.16*	30.30	32.53	27.80*	31.43	35.11	28.74*	34.35	STANDARDIZED
Death	15.96	16.68*	18.24	13.55	13.65*	14.32	8.05	7.79*	8.08	RATES
Increase	15.92	13.48*	12.07	18.98	14.15*	17.11	27.06	20.95*	26.26	

	OBSERVED POP. MALES	OBSERVED POP. FEMALES	STATIONARY POP. MALES	STATIONARY POP. FEMALES	STABLE POP. MALES	STABLE POP. FEMALES	OBSERVED BIRTHS	NET MATERNITY FUNCTION	BIRTHS IN STABLE POP.	
μ	24.74553	23.31301	36.54688	36.91857	24.76366	24.84063	28.18282	29.35000	28.23070	**TABLE 7**
σ^2	360.4633	347.8401	500.4164	514.0103	376.1086	383.7276	37.18892	41.08263	39.43667	MOMENTS
κ_3	5248.642	5911.797	2345.000	2391.402	6000.313	6299.124	83.6393	49.0587	74.9068	AND
κ_4	-13375.	29129.	-249357.	-270037.	-17236.	-15139.	-711.250	-1048.972	-882.392	CUMULANTS
β_1	0.588181	0.830425	0.043882	0.042110	0.676718	0.702249	0.136013	0.034710	0.091483	
β_2	2.897063	3.240753	2.004231	1.977934	2.878152	2.897189	2.485725	2.378491	2.432637	
κ	-0.264173	-0.384193	-0.016410	-0.015438	-0.271111	-0.278461	-0.074704	-0.019803	-0.050655	

VITAL STATISTICS		THOMPSON AGE RANGE	NRR	1000r	INTERVAL	BOURGEOIS-PICHAT AGE RANGE	NRR	1000b	1000d	1000r	COALE	
GRR	2.433										IBR	**TABLE 8** RATES FROM AGE DISTRIBUTIONS AND VITAL STATISTICS (Females)
RR	2.138	0-4	2.18	28.50	27.29	5-29	1.72	32.31	12.12	20.19	IDR	
TFR	4.961	5-9	1.99	25.76	27.24	30-54	2.34	41.56	10.05	31.51	IRI	
GENERATION	28.787	10-14	1.97	24.42	27.19	55-79	2.10	26.88	-0.52	27.40	K1	
SEX RATIO	103.913	15-19	1.85	16.47	27.11	*50-74	2.55	43.87	9.21	34.66	K2	

Start Age Interval	ORIGINAL MATRIX SUB-DIAGONAL	ALTERNATIVE FIRST ROWS Projection	Integral	% IN STABLE POPULATION	FISHER VALUES	REPRODUCTIVE VALUES	SECOND STABLE MATRIX Z_2 FIRST COLUMN	FIRST ROW	
0	0.97256	0.00000	0.00000	15.461	1.127	947707	0.1412+0.0645	0.1412+0.0645	
5	0.99105	0.00033	0.00000	13.172	1.323	899417	0.1328-0.0953	0.0134+0.1468	**TABLE 9**
10	0.99291	0.07217	0.00070	11.436	1.523	860579	-0.0181-0.1745	-0.1125+0.0787	LESLIE
15	0.98959	0.32219	0.15458	9.947	1.669	719446	-0.1725-0.0763	-0.1258-0.0592	MATRIX
20	0.98732	0.53451	0.53937	8.623	1.559	735695	-0.1627+0.1198	-0.0563-0.1503	AND ITS
25	0.98469	0.57939	0.61032	7.458	1.192	510210	0.0248+0.2146	0.0194-0.1505	SPECTRAL
30	0.98118	0.47541	0.63728	6.433	0.719	214952	0.2117+0.0907	0.0485-0.0922	COMPONENTS
35	0.98058	0.23468	0.38568	5.529	0.290	89730	0.1953-0.1474	0.0296-0.0347	(Females)
40	0.97725	0.06270	0.11798	4.750	0.068	14015	-0.0329-0.2578	-0.0084-0.0075	
45	0.96883	0.00765	0.01634	4.066	0.008	1528	-0.2540-0.1053	0.0010-0.0008	
50	0.95309	0.00001	0.00002	3.451	0.000	1	-0.2282+0.1765	0.0000-0.0000	
55+	0.80153			9.673					

Start Age Interval	OBSERVED POPUL. (IN 100's)	CONTRIBUTIONS OF ROOTS (IN 100's) r_1	r_2, r_3	$r_4 \cdot r_{11}$	AGE-SP. BIRTH RATES	NET MATERNITY FUNCTION	COEFF. OF MATRIX EQUATION	PARAMETERS	INTEGRAL	MATRIX	EXP. INCREASE x	$e^{(x+2\frac{1}{2})r}$	
0	8410	7895	347	168	0.0000	0.0000	0.0000	L(1)	1.14110	1.14154	0	1.0682	**TABLE 10**
5	6800	6726	139	-65	0.0000	0.0000	0.0003	L(2)	0.45774	0.45859	50	3.9985	AGE
10	5650	5840	-244	54	0.0001	0.0006	0.0696		0.82325	0.80160	55	4.5627	ANALYSIS
15	4310	5079	-421	-348	0.0305	0.1385	0.3083	R(1)	0.02640	0.02648	60	5.2065	AND
20	4720	4403	-167	484	0.1066	0.4782	0.5062	R(2)	-0.01196	-0.01592	65	5.9411	MISCELLANEOUS
25	4280	3808	305	167	0.1206	0.5342	0.5418		0.21267	0.21023	70	6.7794	RESULTS
30	2990	3285	513	-808	0.1259	0.5493	0.4377	C(1)		51064	75	7.7360	(Females)
35	3090	2824	196	70	0.0762	0.3262	0.2120	C(2)		95472	80	8.8275	
40	2050	2425	-372	-3	0.0233	0.0978	0.0555			-60037	85	10.0731	
45	2020	2076	-611	555	0.0032	0.0133	0.0066	2P/Y	29.5443	29.8872	90	11.4944	
50	1500	1762	-224	-38	0.0000	0.0000	0.0000	DELTA	5.1733		95	13.1162	
55+	3560	4940									100	14.9669	

TABLE 1 — DATA

AGE AT LAST BIRTHDAY	POPULATION BOTH SEXES	MALES Number	%	FEMALES Number	%	BIRTHS BY AGE OF MOTHER	DEATHS BOTH SEXES	MALES	FEMALES
0	414108	211611	4.4	202497	4.4	0	13708	7350	6358
1-4	1447016	742672	15.6	704344	15.3	0	14049	6939	7110
5-9	1348300	693171	14.5	655129	14.3	0	2049	1143	906
10-14	929012	480254	10.1	448758	9.8	61	915	545	370
15-19	951247	488192	10.2	463055	10.1	23210	1261	705	556
20-24	712920	308880	6.5	404040	8.8	106179	1624	878	746
25-29	725197	368182	7.7	357015	7.8	120231	1760	940	820
30-34	625372	328542	6.9	296830	6.5	86987	1987	1088	899
35-39	519116	281441	5.9	237675	5.2	52064	2168	1252	916
40-44	457547	255882	5.4	201665	4.4	21324	2598	1584	1014
45-49	373828	199671	4.2	174157	3.8	3980	2905	1867	1038
50-54	281491	148830	3.1	132661	2.9	0	3500	2217	1283
55-59	209070	105287	2.2	103783	2.3	0	3788	2459	1329
60-64	142982	68713	1.4	74269	1.6	0	4138	2576	1562
65-69	102594	45179	0.9	57415	1.2	0	4582	2598	1984
70-74	70346	27600	0.6	42746	0.9		5128	2665	2463
75-79	37619	12528	0.3	25091	0.5		3980	1748	2232
80-84	15402	4500	0.1	10902	0.2	212554 M.	2850	1117	1733
85+	4494	1001	0.0	3493	0.1	201482 F.	1085	231	854
TOTAL	9367661	4772136		4595525		414036	74075	39902	34173

TABLE 2 — MALE LIFE TABLE

x	$_nq_x$	l_x	$_nd_x$	$_nL_x$	$_nm_x$	$_na_x$	T_x	r_x	$\mathring{e}_x$	$_nM_x$
0	0.033874	100000	3387	98053	0.034547	0.4252	6015149	0.0092	60.151	0.034734
1	0.036375	96613	3514	377373	0.009312	1.4171	5917096	0.0092	61.246	0.009343
5	0.007755	93098	722	463687	0.001557	2.5000	5539722	0.0655	59.504	0.001649
10	0.005654	92376	522	460565	0.001134	2.4784	5076036	0.0338	54.950	0.001135
15	0.007272	91854	668	457760	0.001459	2.7394	4615471	0.0424	50.248	0.001444
20	0.014145	91186	1290	452804	0.002848	2.5763	4157711	0.0258	45.596	0.002843
25	0.012685	89896	1140	446666	0.002553	2.5315	3704907	0.0000	41.213	0.002553
30	0.016474	88756	1462	440288	0.003321	2.6120	3258241	0.0235	36.710	0.003312
35	0.022070	87294	1927	431893	0.004461	2.6248	2817953	0.0204	32.281	0.004449
40	0.030646	85367	2616	420689	0.006219	2.6506	2386061	0.0279	27.951	0.006190
45	0.046136	82751	3818	404859	0.009430	2.6700	1965372	0.0443	23.750	0.009350
50	0.072618	78933	5732	381245	0.015035	2.6585	1560512	0.0485	19.770	0.014896
55	0.111741	73201	8180	346708	0.023592	2.6407	1179268	0.0527	16.110	0.023355
60	0.173104	65022	11256	298109	0.037756	2.6013	832560	0.0395	12.804	0.037489
65	0.253898	53766	13651	235622	0.057936	2.5674	534451	0.0395	9.940	0.057505
70	0.390641	40115	15671	161172	0.097229	2.4855	298829	0.0395	7.449	0.096558
75	0.513917	24444	12562	89394	0.140528	2.3868	137657	0.0395	5.631	0.139527
80	0.744367	11882	8845	35314	0.250453	2.2756	48263	0.0395	4.062	0.248221
85+	*1.000000	3037	3037	12949	0.234572	4.2631	12949	0.0395	4.263	0.230769

TABLE 3 — FEMALE LIFE TABLE

x	$_nq_x$	l_x	$_nd_x$	$_nL_x$	$_nm_x$	$_na_x$	T_x	r_x	$\mathring{e}_x$	$_nM_x$
0	0.030689	100000	3069	98278	0.031227	0.4389	6478104	0.0101	64.781	0.031398
1	0.039245	96931	3804	378122	0.010060	1.4758	6379826	0.0101	65.818	0.010094
5	0.006362	93127	592	464154	0.001276	2.5000	6001703	0.0672	64.446	0.001383
10	0.004111	92535	380	461714	0.000824	2.4782	5537549	0.0337	59.843	0.000824
15	0.005997	92154	553	459486	0.001203	2.6749	5075836	0.0093	55.080	0.001201
20	0.009219	91602	844	455998	0.001852	2.6202	4616350	0.0242	50.396	0.001846
25	0.011456	90757	1040	451292	0.002304	2.6021	4160351	0.0285	45.841	0.002297
30	0.015094	89717	1354	445338	0.003041	2.6006	3709059	0.0376	41.342	0.003029
35	0.019164	88363	1693	437750	0.003868	2.5988	3263722	0.0347	36.935	0.003854
40	0.024895	86670	2158	428122	0.005040	2.5776	2825972	0.0262	32.606	0.005028
45	0.029552	84512	2497	416680	0.005994	2.6454	2397849	0.0353	28.373	0.005960
50	0.047562	82015	3901	400820	0.009732	2.6279	1981169	0.0423	24.156	0.009671
55	0.062632	78114	4892	379066	0.012906	2.6487	1580349	0.0441	20.231	0.012806
60	0.100968	73221	7393	348811	0.021195	2.6605	1201283	0.0375	16.406	0.021032
65	0.160841	65828	10588	304058	0.034822	2.6308	852472	0.0375	12.950	0.034555
70	0.254209	55241	14043	242035	0.058019	2.5668	548414	0.0375	9.928	0.057619
75	0.366360	41198	15093	168423	0.089615	2.5111	306379	0.0375	7.437	0.088956
80	0.568678	26105	14845	92612	0.160295	2.4462	137956	0.0375	5.285	0.158962
85+	*1.000000	11259	11259	45344	0.248312	4.0272	45344	0.0375	4.027	0.244489

TABLE 4 — OBSERVED AND PROJECTED VITAL RATES

	OBSERVED POPULATION BOTH SEXES	MALES	FEMALES	PROJECTED POPULATION 1961 MALES	FEMALES	1966 MALES	FEMALES	1971 MALES	FEMALES	STABLE POPULATION MALES	FEMAL
RATES PER THOUSAND											
Birth	44.20	44.54	43.84	42.74	42.02	40.39	39.63	40.27	39.45	42.85	41.
Death	7.91	8.36	7.44	8.29	7.31	8.25	7.17	8.31	7.11	7.97	7.
Increase	36.29	36.18	36.41	34.45	34.71	32.14	32.47	31.96	32.34		34.87
PERCENTAGE											
under 15	44.18	44.59	43.75	47.47	46.70	47.67	46.87	46.17	45.30	46.75	45.
15-64	53.36	53.51	53.21	50.65	50.39	50.35	50.21	51.68	51.71	51.38	51.
65 and over	2.46	1.90	3.04	1.88	2.90	1.99	2.92	2.16	2.99	1.88	2.
DEP. RATIO X 100	87.40	86.88	87.94	97.43	98.44	98.62	99.17	93.51	93.38	94.64	94.

TABLE 5 — POPULATION PROJECTED WITH FIXED AGE—SPECIFIC BIRTH AND DEATH RATES (IN 1000's)

AGE AT LAST BIRTHDAY	1961 BOTH SEXES	1961 MALES	1961 FEMALES	1966 BOTH SEXES	1966 MALES	1966 FEMALES	1971 BOTH SEXES	1971 MALES	1971 FEMALES	AGE AT LAST BIRTHDAY
0-4	2114	1084	1030	2387	1224	1163	2733	1402	1331	0-4
5-9	1815	931	884	2060	1057	1003	2327	1194	1133	5-9
10-14	1341	689	652	1803	924	879	2048	1050	998	10-14
15-19	924	477	447	1333	684	649	1794	919	875	15-19
20-24	943	483	460	915	472	443	1321	677	644	20-24
25-29	705	305	400	931	476	455	905	466	439	25-29
30-34	715	363	352	695	300	395	919	470	449	30-34
35-39	614	322	292	702	356	346	683	295	388	35-39
40-44	506	274	232	599	314	285	686	347	339	40-44
45-49	442	246	196	490	264	226	580	302	278	45-49
50-54	356	188	168	421	232	189	466	248	218	50-54
55-59	260	135	125	329	171	158	390	211	179	55-59
60-64	186	91	95	231	116	115	293	147	146	60-64
65-69	119	54	65	155	72	83	193	92	101	65-69
70-74	77	31	46	89	37	52	115	49	66	70-74
75-79	45	15	30	49	17	32	57	21	36	75-79
80-84	19	5	14	22	6	16	24	7	17	80-84
85+	7	2	5	9	2	7	10	2	8	85+
TOTAL	11188	5695	5493	13220	6724	6496	15544	7899	7645	TOTAL

TABLE 6 — STANDARDIZED RATES

STANDARD COUNTRIES:

STANDARDIZED RATES PER THOUSAND	ENGLAND AND WALES 1961 BOTH SEXES	MALES	FEMALES	UNITED STATES 1960 BOTH SEXES	MALES	FEMALES	MEXICO 1960 BOTH SEXES	MALES	FEMALES
Birth	41.56	43.57*	39.20	42.16	40.93*	40.43	44.17	40.65*	42.88
Death	17.52	22.91*	16.79	14.72	17.44*	12.98	8.73	8.18*	7.57
Increase	24.04	20.66*	22.41	27.44	23.49*	27.45	35.45	32.47*	35.31

TABLE 7 — MOMENTS AND CUMULANTS

	OBSERVED POP. MALES	OBSERVED POP. FEMALES	STATIONARY POP. MALES	STATIONARY POP. FEMALES	STABLE POP. MALES	STABLE POP. FEMALES	OBSERVED BIRTHS	NET MATERNITY FUNCTION	BIRTHS IN STABLE POP.
μ	22.08391	22.38063	34.19039	36.64599	20.99827	21.77564	28.92771	30.36500	28.76912
σ^2	319.4369	341.5541	445.7976	506.5610	295.4279	326.1711	41.18879	45.53132	41.60901
κ_3	4522.536	5830.083	2323.701	2503.331	4974.182	5985.628	125.8707	93.0938	128.0966
κ_4	-18778.	20940.	-186290.	-253600.	27625.	43240.	-601.972	-1311.365	-675.395
β_1	0.627493	0.853043	0.060946	0.048210	0.959597	1.032484	0.226732	0.091814	0.227779
β_2	2.815975	3.179499	2.062624	2.011706	3.316514	3.406440	2.645172	2.367438	2.609894
κ	-0.251328	-0.364354	-0.023525	-0.018060	-0.410316	-0.440447	-0.131275	-0.046686	-0.125508

TABLE 8 — RATES FROM AGE DISTRIBUTIONS AND VITAL STATISTICS (Females)

VITAL STATISTICS		THOMPSON AGE RANGE	NRR	1000r	INTERVAL	BOURGEOIS-PICHAT AGE RANGE	NRR	1000b	1000d	1000r	COALE	
GRR	3.140										IBR	38.49
NRR	2.803	0-4	2.60	34.99	27.31	5-29	1.96	33.50	8.49	25.01	IDR	6.34
TFR	6.453	5-9	2.23	29.96	27.24	30-54	2.45	42.23	8.99	33.23	IRI	32.16
GENERATION	29.556	10-14	1.79	21.09	27.16	55-79	2.17	29.52	0.82	28.71	K1	0.
SEX RATIO	105.495	15-19	2.20	29.21	27.05	*20-44	2.42	41.31	8.51	32.80	K2	0.

TABLE 9 — LESLIE MATRIX AND ITS SPECTRAL COMPONENTS (Females)

Start Age Interval	ORIGINAL MATRIX SUB-DIAGONAL	ALTERNATIVE FIRST ROWS Projection	ALTERNATIVE FIRST ROWS Integral	FIRST STABLE MATRIX % IN STABLE POPULATION	FISHER VALUES	REPRODUCTIVE VALUES	SECOND STABLE MATRIX Z₂ FIRST COLUMN	SECOND STABLE MATRIX Z₂ FIRST ROW
0	0.97429	0.00000	0.00000	18.370	1.144	1037591	0.1433+0.0798	0.1433+0.0798
5	0.99474	0.00016	0.00000	15.023	1.399	916554	0.1447-0.0867	0.0024+0.1595
10	0.99518	0.05798	0.00034	12.544	1.675	751818	-0.0031-0.1770	-0.1305+0.0778
15	0.99241	0.36041	0.12679	10.479	1.939	897800	-0.1627-0.0901	-0.1346-0.0753
20	0.98968	0.69095	0.66474	8.729	1.912	772500	-0.1669+0.1005	-0.0539-0.1762
25	0.98680	0.72558	0.85186	7.252	1.503	536469	0.0040+0.2034	0.0203-0.1846
30	0.98296	0.58929	0.74129	6.007	0.973	288750	0.1856+0.1022	0.0580-0.1303
35	0.97801	0.37379	0.55411	4.956	0.493	117182	0.1881-0.1139	0.0508-0.0621
40	0.97327	0.14834	0.26747	4.069	0.163	32925	-0.0049-0.2269	0.0219-0.0179
45	0.96194	0.02649	0.05779	3.324	0.025	4432	-0.2045-0.1120	0.0039-0.0024
50	0.94573	0.00001	0.00002	2.684	0.000	1	-0.2022+0.1231	0.0000-0.0000
55+	0.80446			6.562				

TABLE 10 — AGE ANALYSIS AND MISCELLANEOUS RESULTS (Females)

Start Age Interval	OBSERVED POPUL. (IN 100's)	CONTRIBUTIONS OF ROOTS (IN 100's) r_1	r_2, r_3	$r_4 \cdot r_{11}$	AGE-SP. BIRTH RATES	NET MATERNITY FUNCTION	COEFF. OF MATRIX EQUATION	PARAMETERS	INTEGRAL	MATRIX	EXP. INCREASE x	$e^{(x+2\frac{1}{2})r}$
0	9068	8199	610	259	0.0000	0.0000	0.0000	L(1)	1.19052	1.19131	0	1.0911
5	6551	6706	-2	-152	0.0000	0.0000	0.0002	L(2)	0.47167	0.47313	50	6.2409
10	4488	5599	-661	-451	0.0001	0.0003	0.0562		0.84436	0.82089	55	7.4299
15	4631	4677	-691	644	0.0244	0.1121	0.3476	R(1)	0.03488	0.03501	60	8.8455
20	4040	3896	4	140	0.1279	0.5831	0.6614	R(2)	-0.00668	-0.01079	65	10.5307
25	3570	3237	760	-427	0.1639	0.7396	0.6873			0.21227	0.20959	70	12.5371
30	2968	2681	786	-499	0.1426	0.6351	0.5509	C(1)		44636	75	14.9257
35	2377	2212	-7	172	0.1066	0.4666	0.3435	C(2)		109978	80	17.7694
40	2017	1816	-849	1049	0.0515	0.2203	0.1333			-184708	85	21.1548
45	1742	1484	-863	1121	0.0111	0.0463	0.0232	2P/Y	29.5996	29.9787	90	25.1853
50	1327	1198	10	119	0.0000	0.0000	0.0000	DELTA	3.9435		95	29.9837
55+	3177	2929									100	35.6963

AGE AT LAST BIRTHDAY	POPULATION BOTH SEXES	MALES Number	%	FEMALES Number	%	BIRTHS BY AGE OF MOTHER	DEATHS BOTH SEXES	MALES	FEMALES	AGE AT LAST BIRTHDAY
0	394548	202952	3.7	191596	3.7	0	13241	7137	6104	0
1-4	1525877	782294	14.4	743583	14.4	0	12187	5951	6236	1-4
5-9	1721206	882946	16.3	838260	16.2	0	2026	1122	904	5-9
10-14	1147853	591090	10.9	556763	10.7	58	920	542	378	10-14
15-19	958739	494218	9.1	464521	9.0	21623	1268	707	561	15-19
20-24	763954	322212	5.9	441742	8.5	112156	1749	986	763	20-24
25-29	785742	396921	7.3	388821	7.5	131093	1726	971	755	25-29
30-34	724109	384010	7.1	340099	6.6	87402	1967	1145	822	30-34
35-39	617765	336856	6.2	280909	5.4	48200	2200	1338	862	35-39
40-44	493241	273655	5.0	219586	4.2	17394	2457	1576	881	40-44
45-49	448541	251651	4.6	196890	3.8	2461	2964	1959	1005	45-49
50-54	342394	184926	3.4	157468	3.0	0	3671	2416	1255	50-54
55-59	250001	130966	2.4	119035	2.3	0	4244	2757	1487	55-59
60-64	175766	87107	1.6	88659	1.7	0	4574	2827	1747	60-64
65-69	114623	53077	1.0	61546	1.2	0	4631	2699	1932	65-69
70-74	76863	32001	0.6	44862	0.9		4784	2493	2291	70-74
75-79	46317	16845	0.3	29472	0.6		4480	1994	2486	75-79
80-84	19005	5938	0.1	13067	0.3	216587 M.	3347	1274	2073	80-84
85+	5228	1144	0.0	4084	0.1	203800 F.	1428	367	1061	85+
TOTAL	10611772	5430809		5180963		420387	73864	40261	33603	TOTAL

TABLE 1 DATA

TABLE 2 MALE LIFE TABLE

x	$_nq_x$	l_x	$_nd_x$	$_nL_x$	$_nm_x$	$_na_x$	T_x	r_x	$\dot{e}_x$	$_nM_x$	x
0	0.034442	100000	3444	97958	0.035160	0.4071	6186421	0.0003	61.864	0.035166	
1	0.029825	96556	2880	378603	0.007606	1.3537	6088464	0.0003	63.056	0.007607	
5	0.006059	93676	568	466961	0.001215	2.5000	5709861	0.0485	60.953	0.001271	
10	0.004588	93109	427	464496	0.000920	2.5514	5242900	0.0569	56.310	0.000917	1
15	0.007260	92681	673	461927	0.001457	2.8009	4778403	0.0590	51.557	0.001431	1
20	0.015207	92008	1399	456633	0.003064	2.5638	4316477	0.0194	46.914	0.003060	2
25	0.012157	90609	1102	450277	0.002446	2.4863	3859843	0.0000	42.599	0.002446	2
30	0.014824	89508	1327	444355	0.002986	2.6006	3409566	0.0134	38.092	0.002982	3
35	0.019759	88181	1742	436785	0.003989	2.6359	2965212	0.0297	33.626	0.003972	3
40	0.028498	86438	2463	426344	0.005778	2.6257	2528427	0.0234	29.251	0.005759	4
45	0.038454	83975	3229	412367	0.007831	2.6748	2102083	0.0307	25.032	0.007785	4
50	0.064062	80746	5173	391719	0.013205	2.6780	1689716	0.0517	20.926	0.013065	5
55	0.101226	75573	7650	359812	0.021261	2.6400	1297987	0.0535	17.175	0.021051	5
60	0.151850	67923	10314	314974	0.032746	2.6108	938185	0.0496	13.812	0.032454	6
65	0.228015	57609	13136	256101	0.051291	2.5681	623211	0.0496	10.818	0.050851	6
70	0.328459	44473	14608	185960	0.078553	2.5077	367111	0.0496	8.255	0.077904	7
75	0.457876	29866	13675	114419	0.119515	2.4472	181151	0.0496	6.066	0.118373	7
80	0.688060	16191	11140	51307	0.217130	2.3387	66732	0.0496	4.122	0.214550	8
85+	*1.000000	5051	5051	15424	0.327440	3.0540	15424	0.0496	3.054	0.320804	8

TABLE 3 FEMALE LIFE TABLE

x	$_nq_x$	l_x	$_nd_x$	$_nL_x$	$_nm_x$	$_na_x$	T_x	r_x	$\dot{e}_x$	$_nM_x$	x
0	0.031284	100000	3128	98197	0.031859	0.4236	6636335	0.0000	66.363	0.031859	
1	0.032833	96872	3181	379251	0.008386	1.4108	6538139	0.0000	67.493	0.008386	
5	0.005055	93691	474	467271	0.001014	2.5000	6158888	0.0493	65.736	0.001078	
10	0.003401	93217	317	465313	0.000681	2.5578	5691617	0.0582	61.057	0.000679	1
15	0.006045	92900	562	463198	0.001212	2.6774	5226304	0.0219	56.257	0.001208	1
20	0.008613	92339	795	459773	0.001730	2.5850	4763106	0.0161	51.583	0.001727	2
25	0.009680	91543	886	455564	0.001945	2.5699	4303333	0.0241	47.009	0.001942	2
30	0.012050	90657	1092	450656	0.002424	2.5923	3847769	0.0301	42.443	0.002417	3
35	0.015297	89565	1370	444538	0.003082	2.6012	3397113	0.0406	37.929	0.003069	3
40	0.019935	88195	1758	436749	0.004025	2.5971	2952575	0.0315	33.478	0.004012	4
45	0.025331	86437	2189	427035	0.005127	2.6488	2515826	0.0278	29.106	0.005104	4
50	0.039434	84247	3322	413506	0.008034	2.6732	2088790	0.0420	24.794	0.007970	5
55	0.061191	80925	4952	393054	0.012598	2.6632	1675285	0.0444	20.702	0.012492	5
60	0.094800	75973	7202	362935	0.019844	2.6493	1282231	0.0368	16.877	0.019705	6
65	0.147059	68771	10113	319867	0.031618	2.6281	919295	0.0368	13.368	0.031391	6
70	0.228825	58657	13422	260939	0.051439	2.5899	599429	0.0368	10.219	0.051068	7
75	0.351638	45235	15906	187071	0.085029	2.5415	338490	0.0368	7.483	0.084351	7
80	0.565813	29329	16595	103770	0.159917	2.4602	151419	0.0368	5.163	0.158644	8
85+	1.000000	12734	12734	47649	0.267249	3.7418	47649	0.0368	3.742	0.259795	8

TABLE 4 OBSERVED AND PROJECTED VITAL RATES

	OBSERVED POPULATION BOTH SEXES	MALES	FEMALES	PROJECTED POPULATION 1965 MALES	FEMALES	1970 MALES	FEMALES	1975 MALES	FEMALES	STABLE POPULATION MALES	FEMALES
RATES PER THOUSAND											
Birth	39.62	39.88	39.34	38.21	37.60	37.51	36.81	39.37	38.52	39.85	38.9
Death	6.96	7.41	6.49	7.53	6.43	7.69	6.44	7.93	6.54	7.75	6.8
Increase	32.65	32.47	32.85	30.68	31.17	29.82	30.38	31.44	31.99	32.095	
PERCENTAGE											
under 15	45.13	45.28	44.98	46.22	45.77	44.27	43.59	43.53	42.66	44.56	43.6
15-64	52.40	52.71	52.07	51.60	51.23	53.31	53.28	53.76	54.03	52.99	52.9
65 and over	2.47	2.01	2.95	2.18	3.01	2.43	3.13	2.71	3.31	2.45	3.4
DEP. RATIO X 100	90.85	89.72	92.05	93.80	95.21	87.60	87.69	86.02	85.08	88.73	88.7

TABLE 1 — DATA

AGE AT LAST BIRTHDAY	POPULATION BOTH SEXES	MALES Number	%	FEMALES Number	%	BIRTHS BY AGE OF MOTHER	DEATHS BOTH SEXES	MALES	FEMALES	AGE AT LAST BIRTHDAY
0	394222	203125	3.5	191097	3.5	0	12329	6569	5760	0
1-4	1561005	801135	13.8	759870	13.8	0	9955	5032	4923	1-4
5-9	1808124	927609	16.0	880515	15.9	0	1991	1103	888	5-9
10-14	1439166	739745	12.7	699421	12.7	76	1019	605	414	10-14
15-19	931596	479631	8.3	451965	8.2	20549	1246	717	529	15-19
20-24	778108	316999	5.5	461109	8.4	117903	1816	1026	790	20-24
25-29	832882	426086	7.3	406796	7.4	138077	1609	961	648	25-29
30-34	769468	408706	7.0	360762	6.5	85200	1993	1203	790	30-34
35-39	665605	365203	6.3	300402	5.4	43759	2244	1439	805	35-39
40-44	551019	306967	5.3	244052	4.4	15961	2514	1571	943	40-44
45-49	464797	262846	4.5	201951	3.7	1944	3010	1986	1024	45-49
50-54	378910	207068	3.6	171842	3.1	0	3824	2563	1261	50-54
55-59	276570	146262	2.5	130308	2.4	0	4428	2854	1574	55-59
60-64	196929	98363	1.7	98566	1.8	0	4950	3072	1878	60-64
65-69	125444	59028	1.0	66416	1.2	0	4884	2865	2019	65-69
70-74	79950	33963	0.6	45987	0.8		4987	2661	2326	70-74
75-79	49128	18139	0.3	30989	0.6		4707	2082	2625	75-79
80-84	21483	6597	0.1	14886	0.3	218332 M.	3784	1376	2408	80-84
85+	6028	1369	0.0	4659	0.1	205137 F.	1631	420	1211	85+
TOTAL	11330434	5808841		5521593		423469	72921	40105	32816	TOTAL

TABLE 2 — MALE LIFE TABLE

x	$_nq_x$	l_x	$_nd_x$	$_nL_x$	$_nm_x$	$_na_x$	T_x	r_x	$\mathring{e}_x$	$_nM_x$	x
0	0.031722	100000	3172	98090	0.032340	0.3978	6276280	0.0000	62.763	0.032340	0
1	0.024709	96828	2393	380914	0.006281	1.3263	6178190	0.0000	63.806	0.006281	1
5	0.005796	94435	547	470808	0.001163	2.5000	5797276	0.0284	61.389	0.001189	5
10	0.004106	93888	386	468511	0.000823	2.5911	5326468	0.0649	56.732	0.000818	10
15	0.007656	93502	716	465952	0.001536	2.8215	4857957	0.0830	51.955	0.001495	15
20	0.016062	92787	1490	460271	0.003238	2.5430	4392005	0.0092	47.335	0.003237	20
25	0.011213	91296	1024	453886	0.002255	2.4656	3931734	0.0000	43.066	0.002255	25
30	0.014636	90272	1321	448208	0.002948	2.6131	3477848	0.0124	38.526	0.002943	30
35	0.019572	88951	1741	440589	0.003951	2.6068	3029640	0.0247	34.060	0.003940	35
40	0.025384	87210	2214	430815	0.005138	2.6350	2589050	0.0275	29.687	0.005118	40
45	0.037355	84996	3175	417618	0.007603	2.6806	2158235	0.0313	25.392	0.007556	45
50	0.060685	81821	4965	397541	0.012490	2.6706	1740617	0.0458	21.273	0.012378	50
55	0.094224	76856	7242	367268	0.019718	2.6508	1343076	0.0539	17.475	0.019513	55
60	0.146639	69614	10208	323754	0.031531	2.6178	975808	0.0518	14.017	0.031231	60
65	0.219058	59406	13013	265563	0.049003	2.5819	652054	0.0518	10.976	0.048536	65
70	0.330255	46393	15321	193843	0.079040	2.5119	386491	0.0518	8.331	0.078350	70
75	0.447078	31071	13891	119860	0.115897	2.4447	192648	0.0518	6.200	0.114780	75
80	0.677023	17180	11631	55084	0.211156	2.3506	72788	0.0518	4.237	0.208579	80
85+	*1.000000	5549	5549	17704	0.313418	3.1906	17704	0.0518	3.191	0.306793	85+

TABLE 3 — FEMALE LIFE TABLE

x	$_nq_x$	l_x	$_nd_x$	$_nL_x$	$_nm_x$	$_na_x$	T_x	r_x	$\mathring{e}_x$	$_nM_x$	x
0	0.029612	100000	2961	98244	0.030142	0.4069	6737002	0.0000	67.370	0.030142	0
1	0.025478	97039	2472	381611	0.006479	1.3533	6638758	0.0000	68.413	0.006479	1
5	0.004886	94566	462	471677	0.000980	2.5000	6257147	0.0286	66.167	0.001008	5
10	0.002969	94104	279	469842	0.000595	2.5670	5785470	0.0659	61.479	0.000592	10
15	0.005883	93825	552	467852	0.001180	2.6950	5315628	0.0405	56.655	0.001170	15
20	0.008534	93273	796	464413	0.001714	2.5478	4847776	0.0090	51.974	0.001713	20
25	0.007945	92477	735	460591	0.001595	2.5584	4383364	0.0228	47.400	0.001593	25
30	0.010924	91742	1002	456305	0.002196	2.5995	3922773	0.0282	42.759	0.002190	30
35	0.013376	90740	1214	450816	0.002692	2.6235	3466468	0.0362	38.202	0.002680	35
40	0.019231	89526	1722	443534	0.003882	2.6204	3015652	0.0359	33.685	0.003864	40
45	0.025157	87805	2209	433790	0.005092	2.6309	2572118	0.0298	29.294	0.005071	45
50	0.036328	85596	3109	420762	0.007390	2.6793	2138329	0.0360	24.982	0.007338	50
55	0.059231	82486	4886	401052	0.012182	2.6711	1717566	0.0431	20.822	0.012079	55
60	0.091774	77600	7122	371276	0.019182	2.6514	1316514	0.0349	16.965	0.019053	60
65	0.142742	70479	10060	328615	0.030614	2.6364	945238	0.0349	13.412	0.030399	65
70	0.226926	60418	13711	269154	0.050939	2.5976	616623	0.0349	10.206	0.050580	70
75	0.352899	46708	16483	193086	0.085367	2.5458	347469	0.0349	7.439	0.084707	75
80	0.573410	30225	17331	106321	0.163007	2.4569	154383	0.0349	5.108	0.161763	80
85+	1.000000	12894	12894	48062	0.268269	3.7276	48062	0.0349	3.728	0.259928	85+

TABLE 4 — OBSERVED AND PROJECTED VITAL RATES

	OBSERVED POPULATION BOTH SEXES	MALES	FEMALES	PROJECTED POPULATION 1967 MALES	FEMALES	1972 MALES	FEMALES	1977 MALES	FEMALES	STABLE POPULATION MALES	FEMALES
RATES PER THOUSAND											
Birth	37.37	37.59	37.15	35.99	35.46	36.92	36.25	39.42	38.57	38.56	37.59
Death	6.44	6.90	5.94	7.10	5.92	7.39	6.00	7.67	6.15	7.50	6.53
Increase	30.94	30.68	31.21	28.89	29.54	29.53	30.25	31.75	32.41	31.0596	
PERCENTAGE											
under 15	45.92	45.99	45.84	44.72	44.37	42.80	42.19	42.64	41.81	43.74	42.73
15-64	51.59	51.96	51.21	52.97	52.55	54.59	54.55	54.41	54.73	53.59	53.61
65 and over	2.49	2.05	2.95	2.30	3.09	2.61	3.26	2.94	3.47	2.67	3.66
DEP. RATIO X 100	93.82	92.46	95.26	88.78	90.31	83.20	83.31	83.77	82.73	86.60	86.54

TABLE 1 — DATA

AGE AT LAST BIRTHDAY	POPULATION BOTH SEXES	MALES Number	%	FEMALES Number	%	BIRTHS BY AGE OF MOTHER	DEATHS BOTH SEXES	MALES	FEMALES	AGE AT LAST BIRTHDAY
0	393333	202452	3.4	190881	3.4	0	11181	5977	5204	0
1-4	1583905	813306	13.6	770599	13.5	0	9381	4751	4630	1-4
5-9	1841078	944273	15.7	896805	15.7	0	1848	1039	809	5-9
10-14	1551163	796411	13.3	754752	13.2	69	1095	634	461	10-14
15-19	967257	497319	8.3	469938	8.2	20045	1154	672	482	15-19
20-24	786557	319048	5.3	467509	8.2	117498	1655	951	704	20-24
25-29	854143	435895	7.3	418248	7.3	140691	1717	1010	707	25-29
30-34	786062	416829	6.9	369233	6.5	85150	1951	1179	772	30-34
35-39	693695	381338	6.4	312357	5.5	43346	2248	1355	893	35-39
40-44	575825	321177	5.4	254648	4.5	15438	2595	1694	901	40-44
45-49	470041	264819	4.4	205222	3.6	2013	3199	2109	1090	45-49
50-54	403465	223909	3.7	179556	3.2	0	3766	2448	1318	50-54
55-59	290713	154282	2.6	136431	2.4	0	4432	2909	1523	55-59
60-64	205797	103695	1.7	102102	1.8	0	5063	3180	1883	60-64
65-69	132771	62564	1.0	70207	1.2	0	5006	2932	2074	65-69
70-74	81725	34895	0.6	46830	0.8		5023	2647	2376	70-74
75-79	50623	19016	0.3	31607	0.6		4667	2139	2528	75-79
80-84	22854	7179	0.1	15675	0.3	218523 M.	3957	1412	2545	80-84
85+	6619	1519	0.0	5100	0.1	205727 F.	1796	441	1355	85+
TOTAL	11697626	5999926		5697700		424250	71734	39479	32255	TOTAL

TABLE 2 — MALE LIFE TABLE

x	$_nq_x$	l_x	$_nd_x$	$_nL_x$	$_nm_x$	$_na_x$	T_x	r_x	$\dot{e}_x$	$_nM_x$	x
0	0.029009	100000	2901	98259	0.029523	0.3997	6346996	0.0000	63.470	0.029523	0
1	0.023008	97099	2234	382435	0.005842	1.3317	6248738	0.0000	64.354	0.005842	1
5	0.005391	94865	511	473047	0.001081	2.5000	5866302	0.0223	61.838	0.001100	5
10	0.003993	94354	377	470856	0.000800	2.5777	5393256	0.0631	57.160	0.000796	10
15	0.006938	93977	652	468464	0.001392	2.8211	4922400	0.0898	52.379	0.001351	15
20	0.014807	93325	1382	463255	0.002983	2.5614	4453936	0.0107	47.725	0.002981	20
25	0.011518	91943	1059	457046	0.002317	2.4795	3990682	0.0000	43.404	0.002317	25
30	0.014060	90884	1278	451335	0.002831	2.5855	3533636	0.0105	38.881	0.002828	30
35	0.017674	89606	1584	444286	0.003565	2.6351	3082301	0.0223	34.398	0.003553	35
40	0.026188	88022	2305	434720	0.005303	2.6609	2638015	0.0310	29.970	0.005274	40
45	0.039243	85717	3364	420619	0.007997	2.6314	2203295	0.0281	25.704	0.007964	45
50	0.053755	82354	4427	401483	0.011026	2.6767	1782676	0.0420	21.647	0.010933	50
55	0.091356	77927	7119	373041	0.019084	2.6693	1381193	0.0573	17.724	0.018855	55
60	0.144224	70808	10212	329705	0.030973	2.6173	1008152	0.0546	14.238	0.030667	60
65	0.212380	60595	12869	271875	0.047335	2.5833	678446	0.0546	11.196	0.046864	65
70	0.321731	47726	15355	200532	0.076571	2.5188	406571	0.0546	8.519	0.075856	70
75	0.440410	32371	14257	125478	0.113618	2.4483	206039	0.0546	6.365	0.112484	75
80	0.652533	18115	11820	59363	0.199120	2.3597	80561	0.0546	4.447	0.196684	80
85+	*1.000000	6294	6294	21198	0.296930	3.3678	21198	0.0546	3.368	0.290323	85+

TABLE 3 — FEMALE LIFE TABLE

x	$_nq_x$	l_x	$_nd_x$	$_nL_x$	$_nm_x$	$_na_x$	T_x	r_x	$\dot{e}_x$	$_nM_x$	x
0	0.026831	100000	2683	98415	0.027263	0.4093	6796950	0.0000	67.970	0.027263	0
1	0.023658	97317	2302	383191	0.006008	1.3609	6698535	0.0000	68.832	0.006008	1
5	0.004398	95015	418	474028	0.000882	2.5000	6315344	0.0223	66.467	0.000902	5
10	0.003059	94597	289	472274	0.000613	2.5494	5841316	0.0639	61.750	0.000611	10
15	0.005160	94307	487	470406	0.001034	2.6777	5369042	0.0469	56.931	0.001026	15
20	0.007509	93821	704	467404	0.001507	2.5883	4898636	0.0102	52.213	0.001506	20
25	0.008431	93116	785	463672	0.001693	2.5687	4431231	0.0219	47.588	0.001690	25
30	0.010435	92331	963	459355	0.002097	2.6118	3967559	0.0270	42.971	0.002091	30
35	0.014249	91368	1302	453714	0.002869	2.6001	3508205	0.0343	38.397	0.002859	35
40	0.017640	90066	1589	446572	0.003558	2.6349	3054491	0.0382	33.914	0.003538	40
45	0.026342	88477	2331	436879	0.005335	2.6373	2607919	0.0296	29.476	0.005311	45
50	0.036273	86146	3125	423384	0.007381	2.6484	2171040	0.0331	25.202	0.007340	50
55	0.054883	83022	4557	404521	0.011264	2.6764	1747657	0.0446	21.051	0.011163	55
60	0.088988	78465	6982	375991	0.018571	2.6605	1343136	0.0346	17.118	0.018442	60
65	0.139054	71483	9940	334025	0.029758	2.6470	967145	0.0346	13.530	0.029541	65
70	0.227403	61543	13995	273990	0.051078	2.5903	633120	0.0346	10.287	0.050737	70
75	0.336679	47548	16008	198587	0.080611	2.5543	359130	0.0346	7.553	0.079982	75
80	0.576059	31539	18169	111011	0.163665	2.4698	160542	0.0346	5.090	0.162360	80
85+	1.000000	13371	13371	49531	0.269948	3.7044	49531	0.0346	3.704	0.265685	85+

TABLE 4 — OBSERVED AND PROJECTED VITAL RATES

RATES PER THOUSAND	OBSERVED POPULATION BOTH SEXES	MALES	FEMALES	PROJECTED POPULATION 1968 MALES	FEMALES	1973 MALES	FEMALES	1978 MALES	FEMALES	STABLE POPULATION MALES	FEMALES
Birth	36.27	36.42	36.11	35.11	34.68	36.59	36.00	39.09	38.31	37.79	36.85
Death	6.13	6.58	5.66	6.82	5.67	7.15	5.77	7.45	5.94	7.31	6.37
Increase	30.14	29.84	30.45	28.29	29.02	29.43	30.23	31.64	32.37		30.4867
PERCENTAGE											
under 15	45.90	45.94	45.86	43.97	43.68	42.16	41.62	42.20	41.45	43.23	42.25
15-64	51.58	51.97	51.17	53.65	53.19	55.12	55.05	54.68	54.99	53.95	53.93
65 and over	2.52	2.09	2.97	2.38	3.13	2.72	3.34	3.12	3.57	2.83	3.83
DEP. RATIO X 100	93.88	92.41	95.45	86.41	88.02	81.41	81.67	82.88	81.87	85.37	85.44

TABLE 1 — DATA

AGE AT LAST BIRTHDAY	POPULATION BOTH SEXES	MALES Number	MALES %	FEMALES Number	FEMALES %	BIRTHS BY AGE OF MOTHER	DEATHS BOTH SEXES	DEATHS MALES	FEMALES	AGE AT LAST BIRTHDAY
0	389831	200794	3.2	189037	3.2	0	9952	5434	4518	0
1-4	1597724	821207	13.3	776517	13.2	0	7889	3883	4006	1-4
5-9	1881225	964956	15.6	916269	15.6	0	1476	834	642	5-9
10-14	1640345	841146	13.6	799199	13.6	99	1050	620	430	10-14
15-19	1034519	531428	8.6	503091	8.6	18591	1193	702	491	15-19
20-24	788979	318826	5.1	470153	8.0	119329	1721	1044	677	20-24
25-29	874291	445106	7.2	429185	7.3	143520	1693	981	712	25-29
30-34	800932	423287	6.8	377645	6.4	80859	1865	1116	749	30-34
35-39	726344	400660	6.5	325684	5.5	39020	2336	1507	829	35-39
40-44	601833	336099	5.4	265734	4.5	13801	2673	1732	941	40-44
45-49	479417	270331	4.4	209086	3.6	1707	3053	2090	963	45-49
50-54	423222	236988	3.8	186234	3.2	0	3925	2660	1265	50-54
55-59	306874	163501	2.6	143373	2.4	0	4623	3032	1591	55-59
60-64	214322	108910	1.8	105412	1.8	0	5235	3300	1935	60-64
65-69	142067	67351	1.1	74716	1.3	0	5244	3051	2193	65-69
70-74	84887	36587	0.6	48300	0.8		5069	2724	2345	70-74
75-79	51469	19571	0.3	31898	0.5		4641	2102	2539	75-79
80-84	24643	7796	0.1	16847	0.3	215119 M.	3862	1445	2417	80-84
85+	7179	1741	0.0	5438	0.1	201807 F.	1761	483	1278	85+
TOTAL	12070103	6196285		5873818		416926	69261	38740	30521	TOTAL

TABLE 2 — MALE LIFE TABLE

x	$_nq_x$	l_x	$_nd_x$	$_nL_x$	$_nm_x$	$_na_x$	T_x	r_x	$\mathring{e}_x$	$_nM_x$	x
0	0.026622	100000	2662	98372	0.027063	0.3886	6413188	0.0000	64.132	0.027063	0
1	0.018675	97338	1818	384446	0.004728	1.3015	6314816	0.0000	64.875	0.004728	1
5	0.004252	95520	406	476584	0.000852	2.5000	5930370	0.0178	62.085	0.000864	5
10	0.003710	95114	353	474737	0.000743	2.6425	5453785	0.0588	57.340	0.000737	10
15	0.006835	94761	648	472430	0.001371	2.8786	4979048	0.0953	52.543	0.001321	15
20	0.016256	94113	1530	466818	0.003277	2.5500	4506618	0.0151	47.885	0.003275	20
25	0.010958	92583	1015	460312	0.002204	2.4324	4039800	0.0000	43.634	0.002204	25
30	0.013113	91569	1201	454983	0.002639	2.6170	3579489	0.0078	39.091	0.002637	30
35	0.018690	90368	1689	447841	0.003771	2.6318	3124506	0.0193	34.575	0.003761	35
40	0.025594	88679	2270	438056	0.005181	2.6474	2676665	0.0339	30.184	0.005153	40
45	0.038130	86409	3295	424291	0.007765	2.6460	2238609	0.0271	25.907	0.007731	45
50	0.055094	83115	4579	404910	0.011309	2.6713	1814318	0.0383	21.829	0.011224	50
55	0.089905	78536	7061	376196	0.018769	2.6657	1409408	0.0582	17.946	0.018544	55
60	0.142621	71475	10194	333050	0.030607	2.6138	1033212	0.0568	14.456	0.030300	60
65	0.206103	61281	12630	275917	0.045775	2.5861	700162	0.0568	11.425	0.045300	65
70	0.316802	48651	15413	205033	0.075172	2.5202	424245	0.0568	8.720	0.074453	70
75	0.424891	33238	14123	130178	0.108487	2.4500	219212	0.0568	6.595	0.107404	75
80	0.628930	19116	12022	64058	0.187680	2.3782	89034	0.0568	4.658	0.185351	80
85+	*1.000000	7093	7093	24976	0.283997	3.5212	24976	0.0568	3.521	0.277427	85+

TABLE 3 — FEMALE LIFE TABLE

x	$_nq_x$	l_x	$_nd_x$	$_nL_x$	$_nm_x$	$_na_x$	T_x	r_x	$\mathring{e}_x$	$_nM_x$	x
0	0.023567	100000	2357	98604	0.023900	0.4078	6895521	0.0000	68.955	0.023900	0
1	0.020358	97643	1988	385318	0.005159	1.3561	6796917	0.0000	69.610	0.005159	1
5	0.003430	95656	328	477457	0.000687	2.5000	6411599	0.0173	67.028	0.000701	5
10	0.002705	95327	258	476021	0.000542	2.6126	5934142	0.0593	62.250	0.000538	10
15	0.004917	95070	467	474267	0.000986	2.6880	5458120	0.0521	57.412	0.000976	15
20	0.007185	94602	680	471375	0.001442	2.5949	4983853	0.0145	52.682	0.001440	20
25	0.008273	93922	777	467720	0.001661	2.5648	4512478	0.0202	48.045	0.001659	25
30	0.009893	93145	921	463505	0.001988	2.5892	4044758	0.0256	43.424	0.001985	30
35	0.012703	92224	1171	458333	0.002556	2.6218	3581253	0.0325	38.832	0.002545	35
40	0.017644	91052	1606	451428	0.003559	2.6135	3122920	0.0408	34.298	0.003541	40
45	0.022882	89446	2047	442390	0.004626	2.6357	2671492	0.0307	29.867	0.004606	45
50	0.033635	87399	2940	430181	0.006834	2.6818	2229102	0.0305	25.505	0.006793	50
55	0.054604	84459	4612	411630	0.011204	2.6870	1798921	0.0452	21.299	0.011097	55
60	0.088650	79848	7078	382677	0.018497	2.6603	1387291	0.0382	17.374	0.018357	60
65	0.138228	72769	10059	340084	0.029577	2.6377	1004614	0.0382	13.805	0.029351	65
70	0.218861	62710	13725	280565	0.048919	2.5965	664530	0.0382	10.597	0.048551	70
75	0.335128	48986	16416	204603	0.080236	2.5436	383965	0.0382	7.838	0.079597	75
80	0.526944	32569	17162	118701	0.144583	2.4877	179362	0.0382	5.507	0.143468	80
85+	1.000000	15407	15407	60662	0.253983	3.9373	60662	0.0382	3.937	0.235014	85+

TABLE 4 — OBSERVED AND PROJECTED VITAL RATES

	OBSERVED POPULATION BOTH SEXES	MALES	FEMALES	PROJECTED POPULATION 1969 MALES	1969 FEMALES	1974 MALES	1974 FEMALES	1979 MALES	1979 FEMALES	STABLE POPULATION MALES	FEMALES
RATES PER THOUSAND											
Birth	34.54	34.72	34.36	33.84	33.36	35.98	35.31	38.53	37.66	36.47	35.47
Death	5.74	6.25	5.20	6.56	5.27	6.94	5.42	7.23	5.61	7.18	6.18
Increase	28.80	28.47	29.16	27.28	28.09	29.04	29.90	31.30	32.06		29.2897
PERCENTAGE											
under 15	45.64	45.64	45.64	43.13	42.82	41.30	40.69	41.53	40.68	42.34	41.27
15-64	51.79	52.21	51.34	54.40	53.97	55.85	55.86	55.19	55.62	54.60	54.58
65 and over	2.57	2.15	3.02	2.47	3.21	2.85	3.45	3.29	3.69	3.06	4.15
DEP. RATIO X 100	93.10	91.53	94.78	83.83	85.28	79.07	79.02	81.21	79.78	83.14	83.21

TABLE 1 — DATA

AGE AT LAST BIRTHDAY	POPULATION BOTH SEXES	MALES Number	%	FEMALES Number	%	BIRTHS BY AGE OF MOTHER	DEATHS BOTH SEXES	MALES	FEMALES	AGE AT LAST BIRTHDAY
0	381211	196410	3.1	184801	3.1	0	9020	4881	4139	0
1-4	1606979	826603	12.9	780376	12.9	0	7558	3930	3628	1-4
5-9	1912245	980979	15.3	931266	15.4	0	1430	821	609	5-9
10-14	1719559	881597	13.8	837962	13.9	127	1051	642	409	10-14
15-19	1137819	582253	9.1	555566	9.2	20422	1215	707	508	15-19
20-24	777031	315178	4.9	461853	7.6	120475	1545	924	621	20-24
25-29	894615	453271	7.1	441344	7.3	143235	1674	1018	656	25-29
30-34	814948	427463	6.7	387485	6.4	75735	1829	1086	743	30-34
35-39	756621	418474	6.5	338147	5.6	33798	2173	1417	756	35-39
40-44	631222	353886	5.5	277336	4.6	11442	2588	1705	883	40-44
45-49	495993	280270	4.4	215723	3.6	1370	3076	2090	986	45-49
50-54	439094	247632	3.9	191462	3.2	0	3940	2663	1277	50-54
55-59	322744	172597	2.7	150147	2.5	0	4729	3174	1555	55-59
60-64	226489	115706	1.8	110783	1.8	0	5380	3422	1958	60-64
65-69	150355	71755	1.1	78600	1.3	0	5300	3119	2181	65-69
70-74	89487	38976	0.6	50511	0.8		5157	2717	2440	70-74
75-79	52225	19977	0.3	32248	0.5		4499	2029	2470	75-79
80-84	26064	8259	0.1	17805	0.3	209793 M.	3873	1424	2449	80-84
85+	7814	1951	0.0	5863	0.1	196811 F.	1850	512	1338	85+
TOTAL	12442515	6393237		6049278		406604	67887	38281	29606	TOTAL

TABLE 2 — MALE LIFE TABLE

x	nq_x	l_x	nd_x	nL_x	nm_x	na_x	T_x	r_x	$\dot{e}_x$	nM_x	x
0	0.024484	100000	2448	98524	0.024851	0.3971	6480725	0.0000	64.807	0.024851	0
1	0.018779	97552	1832	385305	0.004754	1.3242	6382201	0.0000	65.424	0.004754	1
5	0.004131	95720	395	477610	0.000828	2.5000	5996896	0.0132	62.651	0.000837	5
10	0.003658	95324	349	475792	0.000733	2.6204	5519287	0.0513	57.900	0.000728	10
15	0.006285	94976	597	473600	0.001260	2.8585	5043495	0.1013	53.103	0.001214	15
20	0.014578	94379	1376	468546	0.002936	2.5669	4569896	0.0226	48.421	0.002932	20
25	0.011166	93003	1038	462373	0.002246	2.4570	4101350	0.0000	44.099	0.002246	25
30	0.012632	91964	1162	457020	0.002542	2.5879	3638977	0.0054	39.569	0.002541	30
35	0.016832	90803	1528	450396	0.003393	2.6333	3181958	0.0154	35.043	0.003386	35
40	0.023966	89274	2140	441372	0.004847	2.6635	2731562	0.0350	30.597	0.004818	40
45	0.036811	87135	3208	428133	0.007492	2.6491	2290189	0.0282	26.283	0.007457	45
50	0.052853	83927	4436	409355	0.010836	2.6822	1862056	0.0368	22.187	0.010754	50
55	0.089164	79491	7088	380916	0.018607	2.6663	1452701	0.0569	18.275	0.018390	55
60	0.139389	72404	10092	337888	0.029869	2.6090	1071785	0.0578	14.803	0.029575	60
65	0.198481	62311	12368	281654	0.043911	2.5822	733898	0.0578	11.778	0.043467	65
70	0.299730	49944	14970	212684	0.070385	2.5260	452244	0.0578	9.055	0.069710	70
75	0.407035	34974	14236	138744	0.102604	2.4623	239560	0.0578	6.850	0.101567	75
80	0.597453	20738	12390	71032	0.174433	2.4010	100816	0.0578	4.861	0.172418	80
85+	1.000000	8348	8348	29784	0.280292	3.5677	29784	0.0578	3.568	0.262429	85+

TABLE 3 — FEMALE LIFE TABLE

x	nq_x	l_x	nd_x	nL_x	nm_x	na_x	T_x	r_x	$\dot{e}_x$	nM_x	x
0	0.022102	100000	2210	98684	0.022397	0.4046	6969340	0.0000	69.693	0.022397	0
1	0.018370	97790	1796	386392	0.004649	1.3460	6870656	0.0000	70.259	0.004649	1
5	0.003220	95993	309	479194	0.000645	2.5000	6484264	0.0126	67.549	0.000654	5
10	0.002452	95684	235	477862	0.000491	2.6165	6005070	0.0510	62.759	0.000488	10
15	0.004614	95450	440	476231	0.000925	2.6907	5527208	0.0587	57.907	0.000914	15
20	0.006714	95009	638	473505	0.001347	2.5847	5050977	0.0217	53.163	0.001345	20
25	0.007415	94371	700	470161	0.001488	2.5768	4577471	0.0160	48.505	0.001486	25
30	0.009562	93672	896	466189	0.001921	2.5781	4107310	0.0248	43.848	0.001917	30
35	0.011160	92776	1035	461408	0.002244	2.6133	3641121	0.0311	39.246	0.002236	35
40	0.015901	91741	1459	455267	0.003204	2.6451	3179713	0.0417	34.660	0.003184	40
45	0.022725	90282	2052	446583	0.004594	2.6476	2724446	0.0324	30.177	0.004571	45
50	0.033008	88230	2912	434530	0.006705	2.6647	2277863	0.0293	25.817	0.006670	50
55	0.051040	85318	4355	416538	0.010454	2.6919	1843513	0.0436	21.608	0.010357	55
60	0.085511	80963	6923	388626	0.017815	2.6615	1426975	0.0397	17.625	0.017674	60
65	0.131294	74040	9721	347375	0.027984	2.6520	1038349	0.0397	14.024	0.027748	65
70	0.217946	64319	14018	287625	0.048686	2.5981	690974	0.0397	10.743	0.048306	70
75	0.324514	50301	16323	211396	0.077217	2.5429	403049	0.0397	8.013	0.076594	75
80	0.511468	33978	17378	125342	0.138648	2.5033	191653	0.0397	5.641	0.137546	80
85+	1.000000	16599	16599	66311	0.250321	3.9949	66311	0.0397	3.995	0.228212	85+

TABLE 4 — OBSERVED AND PROJECTED VITAL RATES

	OBSERVED POPULATION BOTH SEXES	MALES	FEMALES	PROJECTED POPULATION 1970 MALES	FEMALES	1975 MALES	FEMALES	1980 MALES	FEMALES	STABLE POPULATION MALES	FEMALES
RATES PER THOUSAND											
Birth	32.68	32.81	32.53	32.73	32.30	35.62	34.99	37.86	37.02	35.18	34.13
Death	5.46	5.99	4.89	6.35	5.01	6.78	5.20	7.09	5.40	7.19	6.15
Increase	27.22	26.83	27.64	26.38	27.29	28.84	29.79	30.77	31.62	27.9810	
PERCENTAGE											
under 15	45.17	45.14	45.20	42.08	41.84	40.30	39.76	40.75	39.98	41.30	40.20
15-64	52.21	52.66	51.74	55.32	54.85	56.68	56.65	55.77	56.19	55.32	55.26
65 and over	2.62	2.20	3.06	2.60	3.31	3.02	3.59	3.47	3.83	3.38	4.53
DEP. RATIO X 100	91.52	89.89	93.28	80.78	82.31	76.43	76.51	79.30	77.96	80.75	80.95

AGE AT LAST BIRTHDAY	BOTH SEXES	1970 MALES	FEMALES	BOTH SEXES	1975 MALES	FEMALES	BOTH SEXES	1980 MALES	FEMALES	AGE AT LAST BIRTHDAY	
0-4	2107	1086	1021	2523	1300	1223	3130	1613	1517	0-4	
5-9	1963	1010	953	2081	1072	1009	2492	1284	1208	5-9	
10-14	1906	977	929	1957	1006	951	2074	1068	1006	10-14	TABLE 5
15-19	1713	878	835	1899	973	926	1949	1001	948	15-19	POPULATION
20-24	1128	576	552	1698	868	830	1882	962	920	20-24	PROJECTED
25-29	770	311	459	1116	568	548	1681	857	824	25-29	WITH
30-34	886	448	438	762	307	455	1106	562	544	30-34	FIXED
35-39	805	421	384	875	442	433	753	303	450	35-39	AGE—
40-44	744	410	334	791	413	378	860	433	427	40-44	SPECIFIC
45-49	615	343	272	725	398	327	771	400	371	45-49	BIRTH
50-54	478	268	210	593	328	265	698	380	318	50-54	AND
55-59	414	230	184	450	249	201	559	305	254	55-59	DEATH
60-64	293	153	140	375	204	171	409	221	188	60-64	RATES
65-69	195	96	99	253	128	125	323	170	153	65-69	(IN 1000's)
70-74	119	54	65	155	73	82	200	96	104	70-74	
75-79	62	25	37	83	35	48	108	48	60	75-79	
80-84	29	10	19	35	13	22	46	18	28	80-84	
85+	12	3	9	14	4	10	17	5	12	85+	
TOTAL	14239	7299	6940	16385	8381	8004	19058	9726	9332	TOTAL	

STANDARD COUNTRIES:	ENGLAND AND WALES 1961			UNITED STATES 1960			MEXICO 1960			
STANDARDIZED RATES PER THOUSAND	BOTH SEXES	MALES	FEMALES	BOTH SEXES	MALES	FEMALES	BOTH SEXES	MALES	FEMALES	TABLE 6
Birth	30.61	34.38*	28.72	31.06	32.87*	29.63	35.16	30.98*	33.95	STANDAR-
Death	13.75	15.96*	13.64	11.33	12.37*	10.23	6.29	6.59*	5.41	DIZED
Increase	16.86	18.42*	15.08	19.74	20.50*	19.40	28.87	24.39*	28.55	RATES

	OBSERVED POP. MALES	FEMALES	STATIONARY POP. MALES	FEMALES	STABLE POP. MALES	FEMALES	OBSERVED BIRTHS	NET MATERNITY FUNCTION	BIRTHS IN STABLE POP.	
μ	23.28486	22.89676	35.68732	37.82288	23.82435	24.79475	27.76361	28.51985	27.54208	TABLE 7
σ^2	336.9832	342.0964	480.7721	526.0706	352.1826	385.2197	30.99558	34.67493	31.06693	
κ_3	4706.636	5934.564	2459.738	2235.478	5659.537	6473.455	113.8392	130.4333	126.1061	MOMENTS
κ_4	-38466.	18456.	-221280.	-282403.	-2601.	-7465.	203.333	3.596	293.211	AND
β_1	0.578891	0.879695	0.054445	0.034325	0.733260	0.733072	0.435196	0.408066	0.530368	CUMULANTS
β_2	2.661264	3.157702	2.042664	1.979575	2.979026	2.949692	3.211645	3.002991	3.303797	
κ	-0.215676	-0.359164	-0.020801	-0.012700	-0.300867	-0.293852	-0.412269	-0.279737	-0.460877	

VITAL STATISTICS		THOMPSON				BOURGEOIS-PICHAT				COALE		TABLE 8
		AGE RANGE	NRR	1000r	INTERVAL	AGE RANGE	NRR	1000b	1000d	1000r		RATES
GRR	2.336											FROM AGE
NRR	2.190	0-4	2.27	29.87	27.38	5-29	3.01	43.74	2.90	40.84	IBR 36.74	DISTRI-
TFR	4.827	5-9	2.54	34.89	27.33	30-54	2.48	41.68	7.98	33.71	IDR 6.84	BUTIONS
GENERATION	28.023	10-14	2.59	33.95	27.28	55-79	3.64	93.56	45.73	47.83	IRI 29.91	AND VITAL
SEX RATIO	106.596	15-19	2.00	25.57	27.18	*50-74	3.48	83.63	37.47	46.17	K1 -4.92	STATISTICS
											K2 0.	(Females)

Start of Age Interval	ORIGINAL MATRIX SUB-DIAGONAL	ALTERNATIVE FIRST ROWS Projection	Integral	FIRST STABLE MATRIX % IN STABLE POPULATION	FISHER VALUES	REPRODUCTIVE VALUES	SECOND STABLE MATRIX Z₂ FIRST COLUMN	FIRST ROW	
0	0.98788	0.00000	0.00000	15.471	1.105	1066508	0.1813+0.0684	0.1813+0.0684	
5	0.99722	0.00018	0.00000	13.282	1.287	1198623	0.1450-0.1427	0.0132+0.1842	TABLE 9
10	0.99659	0.04318	0.00038	11.510	1.485	1244338	-0.0729-0.2028	-0.1527+0.0842	LESLIE
15	0.99428	0.34763	0.09256	9.969	1.667	925950	-0.2273-0.3199	-0.1405-0.1006	MATRIX
20	0.99294	0.68454	0.65684	8.614	1.543	712413	-0.1197+0.2091	-0.0327-0.1846	AND ITS
25	0.99155	0.60852	0.81722	7.433	1.026	452716	0.1474+0.2071	0.0209-0.1486	SPECTRAL
30	0.98975	0.34559	0.49216	6.405	0.512	198489	0.2631-0.0495	0.0251-0.0831	COMPO-
35	0.98669	0.16513	0.25168	5.509	0.210	70913	0.0687-0.2730	0.0185-0.0353	NENTS
40	0.98092	0.05574	0.10389	4.724	0.060	16539	-0.2297-0.1853	0.0076-0.0096	(Females)
45	0.97261	0.00746	0.01598	4.027	0.007	1546	-0.2756+0.1364	0.0011-0.0011	
50	0.95899	0.00001	0.00001	3.404	0.000	1	0.0086+0.3176	0.0000-0.0000	
55+	0.81240			9.650					

Start of Age Interval	OBSERVED POPUL. (IN 100's)	CONTRIBUTIONS OF ROOTS (IN 100's) r_1	r_2, r_3	$r_4 \cdot r_{11}$	AGE-SP. BIRTH RATES	NET MATERNITY FUNCTION	COEFF. OF MATRIX EQUATION	PARAMETERS INTEGRAL	MATRIX	EXP. INCREASE x	$e^{(x+8\frac{1}{2})r}$	
0	9652	9737	-124	39	0.0000	0.0000	0.0000	L(1) 1.15016	1.15068	0	1.0725	
5	9313	8359	981	-28	0.0000	0.0000	0.0002	L(2) 0.39496	0.39448	50	4.3449	TABLE 10
10	8380	7244	1009	126	0.0001	0.0000	0.0425	0.88747	0.85466	55	4.9973	AGE
15	5556	6274	-205	-513	0.0178	0.0847	0.3413	R(1) 0.02798	0.02807	60	5.7478	ANALYSIS
20	4619	5421	-1310	507	0.1263	0.5979	0.6682	R(2) -0.00581	-0.01210	65	6.6109	AND
25	4413	4678	-930	665	0.1571	0.7396	0.5898	0.23041	0.22767	70	7.6036	MISCEL-
30	3875	4031	635	-791	0.0946	0.4410	0.3321	C(1)	62935	75	8.7454	LANEOUS
35	3381	3467	1589	-1675	0.0484	0.2232	0.1571	C(2)	69117	80	10.0586	RESULTS
40	2773	2973	697	-897	0.0200	0.0909	0.0523		273689	85	11.5691	(Females)
45	2157	2535	-1128	750	0.0031	0.0137	0.0069	2P/Y 27.2691	27.5974	90	13.3064	
50	1915	2142	-1727	1499	0.0000	0.0000	0.0000	DELTA 5.3385		95	15.3045	
55+	4460	6073								100	17.6027	

TABLE 1 — DATA

AGE AT LAST BIRTHDAY	BOTH SEXES	POPULATION MALES Number	%	FEMALES Number	%	BIRTHS BY AGE OF MOTHER	DEATHS BOTH SEXES	MALES	FEMALES	AGE AT LAST BIRTHDAY
0	13640	7108	2.8	6532	2.6	0	859	447	412	0
1-4	54688	28553	11.4	26135	10.4	0	299	159	140	1-4
5-9	54092	27962	11.1	26130	10.4	64	64	38	26	5-9
10-14	51464	26623	10.6	24841	9.9	0	28	17	11	10-14
15-19	45979	23413	9.3	22566	9.0	669	34	20	14	15-19
20-24	41801	20098	8.0	21703	8.6	3521	45	27	18	20-24
25-29	37140	17742	7.1	19398	7.7	4179	46	25	21	25-29
30-34	33152	15858	6.3	17294	6.9	2852	42	25	17	30-34
35-39	30733	15062	6.0	15671	6.2	2012	63	33	30	35-39
40-44	28572	13844	5.5	14728	5.9	725	67	34	33	40-44
45-49	24368	12031	4.8	12337	4.9	123	87	51	36	45-49
50-54	22519	11089	4.4	11430	4.6	12	118	69	49	50-54
55-59	17819	8909	3.5	8910	3.5	0	141	89	52	55-59
60-64	15331	7641	3.0	7690	3.1	0	208	117	91	60-64
65-69	12491	6229	2.5	6262	2.5	0	227	138	89	65-69
70-74	8949	4423	1.8	4526	1.8		375	196	179	70-74
75-79	5508	2620	1.0	2888	1.2		348	189	159	75-79
80-84	2424	1186	0.5	1238	0.5	7257 M.	426	213	213	80-84
85+	1330	607	0.2	723	0.3	6836 F.	495	225	270	85+
TOTAL	502000	250998		251002		14093	3972	2112	1860	TOTAL

TABLE 2 — MALE LIFE TABLE

x	$_nq_x$	l_x	$_nd_x$	$_nL_x$	$_nm_x$	$_na_x$	T_x	r_x	$\dot{e}_x$	$_nM_x$	x
0	0.060298	100000	6030	95883	0.062887	0.3172	6696878	0.0000	66.969	0.062887	
1	0.021929	93970	2061	370051	0.005569	1.1707	6600996	0.0000	70.246	0.005569	
5	0.006657	91910	612	458018	0.001336	2.5000	6230945	0.0270	67.794	0.001359	
10	0.003179	91298	290	455717	0.000637	2.3406	5772927	0.0169	63.232	0.000639	10
15	0.004283	91008	390	454129	0.000858	2.6699	5317210	0.0272	58.426	0.000854	15
20	0.006711	90618	608	451619	0.001346	2.5831	4863081	0.0265	53.666	0.001343	20
25	0.007026	90010	632	448487	0.001416	2.5312	4411462	0.0223	49.011	0.001409	25
30	0.007865	89377	703	445199	0.001579	2.5992	3962975	0.0147	44.340	0.001576	30
35	0.010907	88674	967	441031	0.002193	2.5800	3517776	0.0115	39.671	0.002191	35
40	0.012251	87707	1074	436028	0.002464	2.6662	3076745	0.0197	35.080	0.002456	40
45	0.021058	86633	1824	428923	0.004253	2.6756	2640718	0.0180	30.482	0.004239	45
50	0.030804	84808	2612	417971	0.006250	2.6760	2211795	0.0235	26.080	0.006222	50
55	0.049051	82196	4032	401564	0.010040	2.6647	1793824	0.0269	21.824	0.009990	55
60	0.074197	78164	5800	377081	0.015380	2.6309	1392260	0.0272	17.812	0.015312	60
65	0.106074	72365	7676	344142	0.022305	2.6966	1015179	0.0272	14.029	0.022154	65
70	0.201633	64689	13043	292569	0.044582	2.6330	671037	0.0272	10.373	0.044314	70
75	0.309818	51645	16001	220121	0.072690	2.6185	378468	0.0272	7.328	0.072137	75
80	0.621287	35645	22146	122338	0.181019	2.4765	158347	0.0272	4.442	0.179595	80
85+	*1.000000	13499	13499	36009	0.374876	2.6675	36009	0.0272	2.668	0.370675	85

TABLE 3 — FEMALE LIFE TABLE

x	$_nq_x$	l_x	$_nd_x$	$_nL_x$	$_nm_x$	$_na_x$	T_x	r_x	$\dot{e}_x$	$_nM_x$	x
0	0.060453	100000	6045	95845	0.063074	0.3127	6934870	0.0000	69.349	0.063074	
1	0.021107	93955	1983	370196	0.005357	1.1649	6839025	0.0000	72.791	0.005357	
5	0.004855	91972	447	458741	0.000973	2.5000	6468828	0.0254	70.335	0.000995	
10	0.002206	91525	202	457086	0.000442	2.3316	6010087	0.0141	65.666	0.000443	10
15	0.003103	91323	283	455944	0.000621	2.6290	5553001	0.0129	60.806	0.000620	15
20	0.004146	91040	377	454298	0.000831	2.6139	5097057	0.0143	55.987	0.000829	20
25	0.005402	90662	490	452101	0.001083	2.5282	4642759	0.0217	51.209	0.001083	25
30	0.004921	90173	444	449830	0.000986	2.6723	4190658	0.0201	46.474	0.000983	30
35	0.009547	89729	857	446617	0.001918	2.6334	3740828	0.0143	41.690	0.001914	35
40	0.011165	88872	992	441968	0.002245	2.5884	3294211	0.0216	37.067	0.002241	40
45	0.014537	87880	1278	436383	0.002928	2.6391	2852244	0.0223	32.456	0.002918	45
50	0.021305	86602	1845	428646	0.004304	2.6337	2415861	0.0283	27.896	0.004287	50
55	0.029047	84757	2462	418239	0.005886	2.7465	1987215	0.0328	23.446	0.005836	55
60	0.057814	82295	4758	400195	0.011889	2.6288	1568976	0.0308	19.065	0.011834	60
65	0.069683	77538	5403	375924	0.014373	2.8228	1168781	0.0308	15.074	0.014213	65
70	0.182012	72135	13129	329755	0.039815	2.6451	792856	0.0308	10.991	0.039549	70
75	0.246590	59005	14550	261539	0.055633	2.6985	463101	0.0308	7.848	0.055055	75
80	0.607221	44455	26994	155397	0.173710	2.5225	201562	0.0308	4.534	0.172052	80
85+	*1.000000	17461	17461	46165	0.378229	2.6439	46165	0.0308	2.644	0.373444	85

TABLE 4 — OBSERVED AND PROJECTED VITAL RATES

	OBSERVED POPULATION BOTH SEXES	MALES	FEMALES	PROJECTED POPULATION 1956 MALES	FEMALES	1961 MALES	FEMALES	1966 MALES	FEMALES	STABLE POPULATION MALES	FEMALES
RATES PER THOUSAND											
Birth	28.07	28.91	27.23	28.43	26.87	27.85	26.41	27.39	26.05	26.56	26.01
Death	7.91	8.41	7.41	8.03	7.08	8.28	7.46	8.46	7.74	9.41	8.8
Increase	20.16	20.50	19.82	20.40	19.79	19.58	18.94	18.93	18.30	17.144	
PERCENTAGE											
under 15	34.64	35.95	33.32	35.33	33.02	35.16	33.08	33.66	32.06	32.32	31.7
15-64	59.25	58.04	60.45	58.41	60.35	58.38	59.92	59.58	60.38	60.01	59.7
65 and over	6.12	6.00	6.23	6.26	6.64	6.46	7.00	6.76	7.56	7.67	8.6
DEP. RATIO X 100	68.79	72.29	65.43	71.20	65.71	71.28	66.88	67.84	65.61	66.64	67.5

TABLE 1 — DATA

AGE AT LAST BIRTHDAY	POPULATION BOTH SEXES	MALES Number	MALES %	FEMALES Number	FEMALES %	BIRTHS BY AGE OF MOTHER	DEATHS BOTH SEXES	DEATHS MALES	DEATHS FEMALES	AGE AT LAST BIRTHDAY
0	13085	6637	2.6	6448	2.5	0	596	312	284	0
1-4	52574	27424	10.5	25150	9.6	0	156	93	63	1-4
5-9	62964	32914	12.7	30050	11.4	0	40	23	17	5-9
10-14	52132	26734	10.3	25398	9.7	0	14	9	5	10-14
15-19	47042	23931	9.2	23111	8.8	685	27	18	9	15-19
20-24	41833	20182	7.8	21651	8.2	3556	38	28	10	20-24
25-29	38608	18033	6.9	20575	7.8	4108	33	20	13	25-29
30-34	34807	16476	6.3	18331	7.0	2774	35	20	15	30-34
35-39	31309	14928	5.7	16381	6.2	1784	42	22	20	35-39
40-44	29607	14423	5.5	15184	5.8	668	65	39	26	40-44
45-49	26332	12746	4.9	13586	5.2	111	76	47	29	45-49
50-54	23100	11381	4.4	11719	4.5	10	102	63	39	50-54
55-59	20430	9995	3.8	10435	4.0	0	134	81	53	55-59
60-64	15633	7830	3.0	7803	3.0	0	188	105	83	60-64
65-69	13881	6809	2.6	7072	2.7	0	228	129	99	65-69
70-74	9626	4788	1.8	4838	1.8		331	180	151	70-74
75-79	6404	3052	1.2	3352	1.3		373	207	166	75-79
80-84	2597	1241	0.5	1356	0.5	7001 M.	432	193	239	80-84
85+	1037	477	0.2	560	0.2	6695 F.	508	233	275	85+
TOTAL	523001	260001		263000		13696	3418	1822	1596	TOTAL

TABLE 2 — MALE LIFE TABLE

x	$_nq_x$	l_x	$_nd_x$	$_nL_x$	$_nm_x$	$_na_x$	T_x	r_x	$\mathring{e}_x$	$_nM_x$	x
0	0.045503	100000	4550	96797	0.047009	0.2960	6994143	0.0000	69.941	0.047009	0
1	0.013435	95450	1282	378138	0.003391	1.1451	6897346	0.0000	72.262	0.003391	1
5	0.003428	94167	323	470030	0.000687	2.5000	6519208	0.0229	69.230	0.000699	5
10	0.001684	93845	158	468834	0.000337	2.5419	6049179	0.0314	64.460	0.000337	10
15	0.003784	93686	355	467648	0.000758	2.7868	5580345	0.0273	59.564	0.000752	15
20	0.006923	93332	646	465077	0.001389	2.5508	5112697	0.0271	54.780	0.001387	20
25	0.005526	92686	512	462130	0.001108	2.4643	4647620	0.0191	50.144	0.001109	25
30	0.006058	92174	558	459506	0.001215	2.5605	4185489	0.0177	45.409	0.001214	30
35	0.007362	91615	674	456528	0.001477	2.7058	3725984	0.0116	40.670	0.001474	35
40	0.013465	90941	1225	451844	0.002710	2.6651	3269455	0.0132	35.952	0.002704	40
45	0.018336	89716	1645	444716	0.003699	2.6506	2817611	0.0198	31.406	0.003687	45
50	0.027406	88071	2414	434692	0.005553	2.6537	2372895	0.0187	26.943	0.005536	50
55	0.039995	85657	3426	420338	0.008150	2.6798	1938203	0.0287	22.627	0.008104	55
60	0.065310	82232	5371	398481	0.013477	2.6397	1517864	0.0300	18.458	0.013410	60
65	0.091418	76861	7026	368152	0.019086	2.7011	1119383	0.0300	14.564	0.018946	65
70	0.174027	69835	12153	320863	0.037876	2.6706	751231	0.0300	10.757	0.037594	70
75	0.294327	57681	16977	248216	0.068397	2.6326	430368	0.0300	7.461	0.067824	75
80	0.564108	40704	22962	146277	0.156974	2.5069	182152	0.0300	4.475	0.155520	80
85+	*1.000000	17743	17743	35875	0.494573	2.0219	35875	0.0300	2.022	0.488470	85+

TABLE 3 — FEMALE LIFE TABLE

x	$_nq_x$	l_x	$_nd_x$	$_nL_x$	$_nm_x$	$_na_x$	T_x	r_x	$\mathring{e}_x$	$_nM_x$	x
0	0.042654	100000	4265	96887	0.044024	0.2703	7277367	0.0006	72.774	0.044045	0
1	0.009942	95735	952	380197	0.002503	1.1192	7180480	0.0006	75.004	0.002505	1
5	0.002783	94783	264	473255	0.000557	2.5000	6800283	0.0208	71.746	0.000566	5
10	0.000979	94519	93	472347	0.000196	2.3207	6327029	0.0259	66.939	0.000197	10
15	0.001950	94427	184	471698	0.000390	2.6416	5854681	0.0156	62.003	0.000389	15
20	0.002310	94242	218	470691	0.000462	2.6082	5382983	0.0111	57.118	0.000389	20
25	0.003160	94025	297	469416	0.000633	2.6166	4912291	0.0160	52.245	0.000632	25
30	0.004097	93728	384	467735	0.000821	2.6479	4442876	0.0219	47.402	0.000818	30
35	0.006103	93344	570	465379	0.001224	2.6494	3975141	0.0176	42.586	0.001221	35
40	0.008543	92774	793	461974	0.001716	2.6080	3509762	0.0170	37.831	0.001712	40
45	0.010659	91981	980	457605	0.002142	2.6522	3047789	0.0236	33.135	0.002135	45
50	0.016582	91001	1509	451501	0.003342	2.6780	2590184	0.0230	28.463	0.003328	50
55	0.025366	89492	2270	442418	0.005131	2.7792	2138683	0.0347	23.898	0.005079	55
60	0.052177	87222	4551	425438	0.010697	2.6552	1696265	0.0321	19.448	0.010637	60
65	0.068456	82671	5659	400608	0.014127	2.7477	1270827	0.0321	15.372	0.013999	65
70	0.146485	77012	11281	358768	0.031444	2.6696	870219	0.0321	11.300	0.031211	70
75	0.225810	65731	14843	295754	0.050186	2.7835	511451	0.0321	7.781	0.049523	75
80	0.618590	50888	31479	176694	0.178154	2.5302	215697	0.0321	4.239	0.176255	80
85+	*1.000000	19409	19409	39003	0.497636	2.0095	39003	0.0321	2.010	0.491071	85+

TABLE 4 — OBSERVED AND PROJECTED VITAL RATES

RATES PER THOUSAND	OBSERVED POPULATION BOTH SEXES	MALES	FEMALES	PROJECTED 1959 MALES	1959 FEMALES	1964 MALES	1964 FEMALES	1969 MALES	1969 FEMALES	STABLE POPULATION MALES	FEMALES
Birth	26.19	26.93	25.46	26.36	24.97	26.03	24.70	26.19	24.91	25.05	24.38
Death	6.54	7.01	6.07	6.92	5.97	7.29	6.40	7.55	6.80	8.65	7.98
Increase	19.65	19.92	19.39	19.44	19.00	18.73	18.31	18.64	18.11		16.4026
PERCENTAGE											
under 15	34.56	36.04	33.10	35.25	32.66	33.39	31.54	32.43	31.04	31.40	30.76
15-64	59.02	57.66	60.37	58.13	60.44	59.55	60.88	60.24	60.93	60.19	59.99
65 and over	6.41	6.29	6.53	6.62	6.90	7.06	7.58	7.34	8.03	8.40	9.25
DEP. RATIO X 100	69.42	73.42	65.64	72.03	65.45	67.93	64.26	66.01	64.11	66.13	66.69

TABLE 1 — DATA

AGE AT LAST BIRTHDAY	POPULATION BOTH SEXES	MALES Number	%	FEMALES Number	%	BIRTHS BY AGE OF MOTHER	DEATHS BOTH SEXES	MALES	FEMALES	AGE AT LAST BIRTHDAY
0	13794	7120	2.6	6674	2.4	0	435	212	223	0
1-4	52251	27074	10.0	25177	9.2	0	129	55	74	1-4
5-9	65819	34309	12.7	31510	11.5	0	60	37	23	5-9
10-14	56209	29086	10.7	27123	9.9	0	28	13	15	10-14
15-19	48658	24830	9.2	23828	8.7	987	40	31	9	15-19
20-24	42338	20958	7.7	21380	7.8	4360	59	45	14	20-24
25-29	38988	18037	6.7	20951	7.6	4237	88	68	20	25-29
30-34	36297	16920	6.2	19377	7.0	2546	66	49	17	30-34
35-39	32785	15389	5.7	17396	6.3	1418	65	50	15	35-39
40-44	30043	14459	5.3	15584	5.7	452	75	51	24	40-44
45-49	28305	13682	5.0	14623	5.3	92	83	48	35	45-49
50-54	24063	11734	4.3	12329	4.5	6	116	72	44	50-54
55-59	21874	10670	3.9	11204	4.1	0	155	100	55	55-59
60-64	17528	8620	3.2	8908	3.2	0	225	141	84	60-64
65-69	14038	6949	2.6	7089	2.6	0	208	133	75	65-69
70-74	11388	5570	2.1	5818	2.1		330	157	173	70-74
75-79	7039	3423	1.3	3616	1.3		369	197	172	75-79
80-84	3761	1796	0.7	1965	0.7	7212 M.	365	153	212	80-84
85+	820	372	0.1	448	0.2	6886 F.	493	221	272	85+
TOTAL	545998	270998		275000		14098	3389	1833	1556	TOTAL

TABLE 2 — MALE LIFE TABLE

x	$_nq_x$	l_x	$_nd_x$	$_nL_x$	$_nm_x$	$_na_x$	T_x	r_x	$\dot e_x$	$_nM_x$
0	0.029081	100000	2908	97938	0.029693	0.2909	7007142	0.0036	70.071	0.029775
1	0.008054	97092	782	386131	0.002025	1.1395	6909204	0.0036	71.161	0.002031
5	0.005356	96310	516	480260	0.001074	2.5000	6523073	0.0150	67.730	0.001078
10	0.002238	95794	214	478452	0.000448	2.5821	6042813	0.0316	63.081	0.000447
15	0.006281	95580	600	476566	0.001260	2.7802	5564361	0.0315	58.217	0.001248
20	0.010760	94979	1022	472582	0.002163	2.7356	5087796	0.0296	53.567	0.002147
25	0.018691	93957	1756	465459	0.003773	2.5359	4615214	0.0182	49.120	0.003770
30	0.014367	92201	1325	457634	0.002895	2.4543	4149754	0.0127	45.008	0.002896
35	0.016124	90877	1465	450769	0.003251	2.5339	3692121	0.0125	40.628	0.003249
40	0.017485	89411	1563	443162	0.003528	2.5089	3241352	0.0083	36.252	0.003527
45	0.017442	87848	1532	435629	0.003517	2.6438	2798190	0.0168	31.853	0.003508
50	0.030361	86316	2621	425511	0.006159	2.6848	2362561	0.0187	27.371	0.006136
55	0.046076	83695	3856	409604	0.009415	2.6995	1937050	0.0206	23.144	0.009372
60	0.079077	79839	6313	384014	0.016440	2.5957	1527447	0.0397	19.132	0.016357
65	0.091888	73525	6756	351279	0.019233	2.5803	1143433	0.0397	15.552	0.019139
70	0.133556	66769	8917	313213	0.028471	2.6862	792154	0.0397	11.864	0.028187
75	0.254564	57852	14727	253822	0.058021	2.5937	478941	0.0397	8.279	0.057552
80	0.360399	43125	15542	179447	0.086611	2.6723	225119	0.0397	5.220	0.085190
85+	*1.000000	27583	27583	45673	0.603922	1.6558	45673	0.0397	1.656	0.594086

TABLE 3 — FEMALE LIFE TABLE

x	$_nq_x$	l_x	$_nd_x$	$_nL_x$	$_nm_x$	$_na_x$	T_x	r_x	$\dot e_x$	$_nM_x$
0	0.032575	100000	3257	97779	0.033315	0.3183	7386646	0.0040	73.866	0.033413
1	0.011626	96743	1125	383790	0.002931	1.1721	7288866	0.0040	75.343	0.002939
5	0.003613	95618	345	477225	0.000724	2.5000	6905077	0.0148	72.215	0.000730
10	0.002751	95272	262	475672	0.000551	2.3681	6427852	0.0274	67.468	0.000553
15	0.001889	95010	180	474612	0.000378	2.5564	5952180	0.0233	62.648	0.000378
20	0.003276	94831	311	473433	0.000656	2.6815	5477568	0.0122	57.762	0.000655
25	0.004764	94520	450	471495	0.000955	2.5467	5004134	0.0090	52.943	0.000955
30	0.004375	94070	412	469310	0.000877	2.4767	4532639	0.0177	48.184	0.000877
35	0.004317	93658	404	467344	0.000865	2.6578	4063329	0.0208	43.385	0.000862
40	0.007698	93254	718	464620	0.001545	2.7034	3595986	0.0158	38.561	0.001540
45	0.011945	92536	1105	460105	0.002402	2.6707	3131365	0.0210	33.839	0.002393
50	0.017755	91431	1623	453321	0.003581	2.6397	2671260	0.0231	29.216	0.003569
55	0.024432	89807	2194	444058	0.004941	2.7312	2217939	0.0268	24.697	0.004909
60	0.046326	87613	4059	428374	0.009475	2.6121	1773881	0.0367	20.247	0.009430
65	0.052440	83554	4378	408295	0.010724	2.8356	1345507	0.0367	16.103	0.010580
70	0.140347	79176	11112	370252	0.030012	2.6937	937212	0.0367	11.837	0.029735
75	0.216108	68064	14709	306065	0.048059	2.6713	566960	0.0367	8.330	0.047566
80	0.434888	53355	23203	211982	0.109459	2.6386	260895	0.0367	4.890	0.107888
85+	*1.000000	30151	30151	48913	0.616434	1.6222	48913	0.0367	1.622	0.607143

TABLE 4 — OBSERVED AND PROJECTED VITAL RATES

	OBSERVED POPULATION BOTH SEXES	MALES	FEMALES	1962 MALES	FEMALES	1967 MALES	FEMALES	1972 MALES	FEMALES	STABLE POPULATION MALES	FEMALES
RATES PER THOUSAND											
Birth	25.82	26.61	25.04	26.04	24.54	26.13	24.66	26.54	25.08	25.26	24.4
Death	6.21	6.76	5.66	7.12	5.87	7.52	6.29	7.82	6.69	8.43	7.6
Increase	19.61	19.85	19.38	18.92	18.67	18.62	18.36	18.72	18.38		16.826
PERCENTAGE											
under 15	34.45	36.01	32.90	34.97	32.22	33.36	31.11	33.06	31.06	32.21	31.0
15-64	58.77	57.31	60.21	57.84	60.28	59.01	60.68	59.18	60.33	59.47	59.5
65 and over	6.79	6.68	6.89	7.19	7.50	7.63	8.21	7.76	8.60	8.32	9.4
DEP. RATIO X 100	70.16	74.50	66.08	72.89	65.89	69.46	64.79	68.99	65.74	68.15	68.0

AGE AT LAST BIRTHDAY	BOTH SEXES	1962 MALES	FEMALES	BOTH SEXES	1967 MALES	FEMALES	BOTH SEXES	1972 MALES	FEMALES	AGE AT LAST BIRTHDAY	
0-4	70	36	34	78	40	38	86	44	42	0-4	**TABLE 5**
5-9	66	34	32	70	36	34	76	39	37	5-9	POPULATION
10-14	65	34	31	65	34	31	70	36	34	10-14	PROJECTED
15-19	56	29	27	65	34	31	65	34	31	15-19	WITH
20-24	49	25	24	56	29	27	65	34	31	20-24	FIXED
25-29	42	21	21	48	24	24	55	28	27	25-29	AGE—
30-34	39	18	21	41	20	21	48	24	24	30-34	SPECIFIC
35-39	36	17	19	38	17	21	41	20	21	35-39	BIRTH
40-44	32	15	17	35	16	19	38	17	21	40-44	AND
45-49	29	14	15	32	15	17	35	16	19	45-49	DEATH
50-54	27	13	14	29	14	15	32	15	17	50-54	RATES
55-59	23	11	12	27	13	14	28	13	15	55-59	(IN 1000's)
60-64	21	10	11	23	11	12	26	12	14	60-64	
65-69	16	8	8	19	9	10	21	10	11	65-69	
70-74	12	6	6	15	7	8	17	8	9	70-74	
75-79	10	5	5	10	5	5	12	6	6	75-79	
80-84	5	2	3	6	3	3	8	4	4	80-84	
85+	0	0	0	2	1	1	2	1	1	85+	
TOTAL	598	298	300	659	328	331	725	361	364	TOTAL	

STANDARD COUNTRIES:	ENGLAND AND WALES 1961			UNITED STATES 1960			MEXICO 1960			
STANDARDIZED RATES PER THOUSAND	BOTH SEXES	MALES	FEMALES	BOTH SEXES	MALES	FEMALES	BOTH SEXES	MALES	FEMALES	**TABLE 6**
Birth	22.19	27.14*	21.00	22.52	25.00*	21.67	25.62	25.08*	24.97	STANDAR-
Death	11.15	9.46*	12.51	9.26	8.23*	9.44	4.93	6.11*	4.55	DIZED
Increase	11.03	17.67*	8.49	13.25	16.77*	12.23	20.69	18.97*	20.42	RATES

	OBSERVED POP.		STATIONARY POP.		STABLE POP.		OBSERVED BIRTHS	NET MATERNITY FUNCTION	BIRTHS IN STABLE POP.	
	MALES	FEMALES	MALES	FEMALES	MALES	FEMALES				
μ	27.99414	29.08202	38.33950	39.66975	29.72206	30.76822	27.78444	28.34014	27.65279	**TABLE 7**
σ^2	444.8809	439.6926	544.1142	555.7586	469.0180	489.3398	37.23142	40.08416	37.44334	MOMENTS
κ_3	6121.717	5379.387	2230.200	1415.988	6168.283	5981.114	147.9798	155.8873	157.2506	AND
κ_4	-114666.	-117911.	-315858.	-343336.	-132601.	-170902.	26.349	-213.409	53.713	CUMULANTS
β_1	0.425613	0.340422	0.030876	0.011680	0.368774	0.305304	0.424303	0.377314	0.471043	
β_2	2.420642	2.390106	1.933130	1.888404	2.397206	2.286283	3.019009	2.867179	3.038311	
κ	-0.152716	-0.129207	-0.011044	-0.004110	-0.136944	-0.110606	-0.288063	-0.224770	-0.299124	

VITAL STATISTICS		AGE RANGE	THOMPSON NRR	1000r	INTERVAL	AGE RANGE	BOURGEOIS-PICHAT NRR	1000b	1000d	1000r	COALE	**TABLE 8**
GRR	1.700											RATES FROM AGE
NRR	1.602	0-4	1.57	16.88	27.45	5-29	1.74	27.06	6.55	20.51	IBR	DISTRI-
TFR	3.481	5-9	1.70	19.50	27.42	30-54	1.71	28.64	8.78	19.86	IDR	BUTIONS
GENERATION	27.993	10-14	1.58	16.58	27.39	55-79	2.37	56.69	24.67	32.02	IRI	AND VITAL
SEX RATIO	104.734	15-19	1.53	14.79	27.34	*25-49	1.61	26.25	8.69	17.56	K1	STATISTICS
											K2	(Females)

Start of Age Interval	ORIGINAL MATRIX SUB-DIAGONAL	ALTERNATIVE FIRST ROWS Projection	Integral	FIRST STABLE MATRIX % IN STABLE POPULATION	FISHER VALUES	REPRODUCTIVE VALUES	SECOND STABLE MATRIX Z₂ FIRST COLUMN	FIRST ROW	
0	0.99098	0.00000	0.00000	11.299	1.083	34484	0.1681+0.0903	0.1681+0.0903	**TABLE 9**
5	0.99674	0.00000	0.00000	10.292	1.189	37453	0.1800-0.1288	-0.0060+0.1645	LESLIE
10	0.99777	0.04861	0.00000	9.429	1.297	35189	-0.0423-0.2546	-0.1289+0.0576	MATRIX
15	0.99752	0.28796	0.10162	8.647	1.362	32451	-0.2885-0.3867	-0.1011-0.0818	AND ITS
20	0.99591	0.47671	0.50028	7.929	1.173	25075	-0.2392+0.2577	-0.0238-0.1348	SPECTRAL
25	0.99537	0.39166	0.49612	7.258	0.763	15985	0.1466+0.3826	0.0143-0.1126	COMPO-
30	0.99581	0.24999	0.32234	6.640	0.408	7904	0.4752+0.0432	0.0260-0.0672	NENTS
35	0.99417	0.12978	0.19997	6.078	0.174	3024	0.2892-0.4747	0.0194-0.0280	(Females)
40	0.99028	0.04144	0.07115	5.554	0.049	762	-0.3474-0.5453	0.0070-0.0075	
45	0.98526	0.00796	0.01543	5.055	0.008	123	-0.7445+0.0827	0.0014-0.0012	
50	0.97957	0.00057	0.00119	4.578	0.001	7	-0.2927+0.8124	0.0001-0.0001	
55+	0.82783			17.241					

Start of Age Interval	OBSERVED POPUL. (IN 100's)	CONTRIBUTIONS OF ROOTS (IN 100's) r₁	r₂, r₃	r₄-r₁₁	AGE-SP. BIRTH RATES	NET MATERNITY FUNCTION	COEFF. OF MATRIX EQUATION	PARAMETERS	INTEGRAL	MATRIX	EXP. INCREASE x	$e^{(x+2\frac{1}{2})r}$	
0	319	323	0	-5	0.0000	0.0000	0.0000	L(1)	1.08777	1.08795	0	1.0430	**TABLE 10**
5	315	294	11	10	0.0000	0.0000	0.0000	L(2)	0.36843	0.37679	50	2.4191	AGE
10	271	269	11	-9	0.0000	0.0000	0.0480		0.79496	0.76719	55	2.6314	ANALYSIS
15	238	247	-4	-5	0.0202	0.0960	0.2838	R(1)	0.01683	0.01686	60	2.8624	AND
20	214	226	-18	6	0.0996	0.4716	0.4687	R(2)	-0.02643	-0.03140	65	3.1136	MISCEL-
25	210	207	-14	16	0.0988	0.4657	0.3835		0.22736	0.22285	70	3.3869	LANEOUS
30	194	190	11	-7	0.0642	0.3012	0.2436	C(1)		2856	75	3.6842	RESULTS
35	174	174	30	-29	0.0398	0.1861	0.1259	C(2)		1373	80	4.0076	(Females)
40	156	159	16	-18	0.0142	0.0658	0.0400			2302	85	4.3593	
45	146	144	-24	26	0.0031	0.0141	0.0076	2P/Y	27.6352	28.1941	90	4.7420	
50	123	131	-45	38	0.0002	0.0011	0.0005	DELTA	3.3114		95	5.1582	
55+	390	492									100	5.6109	

TABLE 1 — DATA

AGE AT LAST BIRTHDAY	POPULATION BOTH SEXES	MALES Number	%	FEMALES Number	%	BIRTHS BY AGE OF MOTHER	DEATHS BOTH SEXES	MALES	FEMALES	AGE AT LAST BIRTHDAY
0	15374	7837	2.8	7537	2.6	0	433	221	212	0
1-4	59913	30567	10.8	29346	10.1	0	100	53	47	1-4
5-9	67986	34876	12.4	33110	11.4	0	14	6	8	5-9
10-14	67050	34268	12.2	32782	11.3	0	16	8	8	10-14
15-19	47619	23452	8.3	24167	8.3	771	17	8	9	15-19
20-24	47043	22645	8.0	24398	8.4	4465	15	9	6	20-24
25-29	38207	17801	6.3	20406	7.0	4290	28	19	9	25-29
30-34	37283	16964	6.0	20319	7.0	2707	28	17	11	30-34
35-39	30779	15470	5.5	15309	5.3	1621	36	23	13	35-39
40-44	32050	14877	5.3	17173	5.9	549	41	28	13	40-44
45-49	27546	13991	5.0	13555	4.7	89	89	61	28	45-49
50-54	28259	13030	4.6	15229	5.2	8	96	53	43	50-54
55-59	19283	10206	3.6	9077	3.1	0	119	85	34	55-59
60-64	20766	9369	3.3	11397	3.9	0	217	121	96	60-64
65-69	11162	5914	2.1	5248	1.8	0	222	132	90	65-69
70-74	11472	5229	1.9	6243	2.1		343	193	150	70-74
75-79	4686	2561	0.9	2125	0.7		337	183	154	75-79
80-84	4660	2127	0.8	2533	0.9	7526 M.	450	221	229	80-84
85+	1862	816	0.3	1046	0.4	6974 F.	599	285	314	85+
TOTAL	573000	282000		291000		14500	3200	1726	1474	TOTAL

TABLE 2 — MALE LIFE TABLE

x	nq_x	l_x	nd_x	nL_x	nm_x	na_x	T_x	r_x	$\dot{e}_x$	nM_x	x
0	0.027612	100000	2761	98011	0.028173	0.2795	7281333	0.0012	72.813	0.028200	0
1	0.006892	97239	670	387030	0.001732	1.1280	7183322	0.0012	73.873	0.001734	1
5	0.000846	96569	82	482638	0.000169	2.5000	6796292	0.0108	70.378	0.000172	5
10	0.001174	96487	113	482168	0.000235	2.6530	6313654	0.0394	65.435	0.000233	10
15	0.001711	96374	165	481472	0.000343	2.6007	5831486	0.0411	60.509	0.000341	15
20	0.002006	96209	193	480633	0.000402	2.8755	5350013	0.0270	55.608	0.000397	20
25	0.005341	96016	513	478856	0.001071	2.6158	4869380	0.0280	50.714	0.001067	25
30	0.005004	95503	478	476360	0.001003	2.5838	4390525	0.0129	45.973	0.001002	30
35	0.007418	95025	705	473448	0.001489	2.6206	3914165	0.0117	41.191	0.001487	35
40	0.009394	94320	886	469659	0.001887	2.8087	3440717	0.0077	36.479	0.001882	40
45	0.021596	93434	2018	462326	0.004364	2.5997	2971059	0.0096	31.798	0.004360	45
50	0.020253	91416	1851	452798	0.004089	2.6869	2508733	0.0265	27.443	0.004068	50
55	0.041078	89565	3679	439369	0.008374	2.7019	2055934	0.0247	22.955	0.008328	55
60	0.063072	85886	5417	416907	0.012993	2.6886	1616566	0.0278	18.822	0.012915	60
65	0.106677	80469	8584	382314	0.022453	2.6668	1199659	0.0278	14.908	0.022320	65
70	0.170962	71884	12289	330704	0.037162	2.6632	817344	0.0278	11.370	0.036910	70
75	0.305581	59595	18211	253487	0.071842	2.5571	486640	0.0278	8.166	0.071457	75
80	0.417632	41384	17283	164938	0.104786	2.5710	233153	0.0278	5.634	0.103902	80
85+	*1.000000	24101	24101	68215	0.353304	2.8304	68215	0.0278	2.830	0.349265	85+

TABLE 3 — FEMALE LIFE TABLE

x	nq_x	l_x	nd_x	nL_x	nm_x	na_x	T_x	r_x	$\dot{e}_x$	nM_x	x
0	0.027532	100000	2753	97993	0.028096	0.2711	7563683	0.0015	75.637	0.028128	0
1	0.006367	97247	619	387204	0.001599	1.1200	7465690	0.0015	76.771	0.001602	1
5	0.001195	96628	115	482850	0.000239	2.5000	7078486	0.0112	73.255	0.000242	5
10	0.001224	96512	118	482279	0.000245	2.5127	6595636	0.0312	68.340	0.000244	10
15	0.001860	96394	179	481522	0.000372	2.5003	6113357	0.0292	63.420	0.000372	15
20	0.001230	96215	118	480785	0.000246	2.5579	5631835	0.0166	58.534	0.000246	20
25	0.002208	96096	212	479981	0.000442	2.6394	5151050	0.0179	53.603	0.000441	25
30	0.002715	95884	260	478810	0.000544	2.6547	4671069	0.0281	48.716	0.000541	30
35	0.004241	95624	406	477126	0.000850	2.5518	4192258	0.0161	43.841	0.000849	35
40	0.003793	95218	361	475308	0.000760	2.8298	3715132	0.0111	39.017	0.000757	40
45	0.010301	94857	977	472043	0.002070	2.7050	3239824	0.0101	34.155	0.002066	45
50	0.014089	93880	1323	466251	0.002837	2.6189	2767781	0.0373	29.482	0.002824	50
55	0.018715	92557	1732	458972	0.003774	2.7976	2301530	0.0245	24.866	0.003746	55
60	0.041804	90825	3797	445777	0.008517	2.8011	1842558	0.0345	20.287	0.008423	60
65	0.082958	87028	7220	418225	0.017263	2.6569	1396781	0.0345	16.050	0.017149	65
70	0.115690	79809	9233	379019	0.024360	2.8313	978555	0.0345	12.261	0.024027	70
75	0.310311	70576	21900	300002	0.073001	2.5856	599537	0.0345	8.495	0.072470	75
80	0.374616	48675	18235	199569	0.091369	2.5976	299535	0.0345	6.154	0.090407	80
85+	*1.000000	30441	30441	99966	0.304512	3.2839	99966	0.0345	3.284	0.300191	85+

TABLE 4 — OBSERVED AND PROJECTED VITAL RATES

	OBSERVED POPULATION BOTH SEXES	MALES	FEMALES	PROJECTED POPULATION 1965 MALES	FEMALES	1970 MALES	FEMALES	1975 MALES	FEMALES	STABLE POPULATION MALES	FEMALES
RATES PER THOUSAND											
Birth	25.31	26.69	23.97	26.64	24.13	27.29	24.91	27.73	25.51	24.50	23.98
Death	5.58	6.12	5.07	6.09	5.33	6.08	5.06	6.50	6.09	7.67	7.15
Increase	19.72	20.57	18.90	20.55	18.80	21.21	19.85	21.24	19.42	16.8330	
PERCENTAGE											
under 15	36.71	38.14	35.32	35.68	32.96	34.47	31.84	33.72	31.03	31.40	30.74
15-64	57.39	55.96	58.77	57.84	59.82	58.75	60.85	59.02	60.49	60.13	59.67
65 and over	5.91	5.90	5.91	6.48	7.21	6.78	7.30	7.26	8.49	8.48	9.60
DEP. RATIO X 100	74.25	78.70	70.15	72.89	67.16	70.23	64.33	69.43	65.33	66.31	67.59

TABLE 5 POPULATION PROJECTED WITH FIXED AGE—SPECIFIC BIRTH AND DEATH RATES (IN 1000's)

AGE AT LAST BIRTHDAY	1965 BOTH SEXES	1965 MALES	1965 FEMALES	1970 BOTH SEXES	1970 MALES	1970 FEMALES	1975 BOTH SEXES	1975 MALES	1975 FEMALES	AGE AT LAST BIRTHDAY
0-4	74	38	36	83	43	40	94	49	45	0-4
5-9	75	38	37	73	38	35	83	43	40	5-9
10-14	68	35	33	75	38	37	73	38	35	10-14
15-19	67	34	33	68	35	33	75	38	37	15-19
20-24	47	23	24	67	34	33	68	35	33	20-24
25-29	47	23	24	47	23	24	67	34	33	25-29
30-34	38	18	20	46	22	24	47	23	24	30-34
35-39	37	17	20	38	18	20	46	22	24	35-39
40-44	30	15	15	37	17	20	37	17	20	40-44
45-49	32	15	17	30	15	15	36	16	20	45-49
50-54	27	14	13	31	14	17	30	15	15	50-54
55-59	28	13	15	26	13	13	31	14	17	55-59
60-64	19	10	9	27	12	15	26	13	13	60-64
65-69	20	9	11	17	9	8	25	11	14	65-69
70-74	10	5	5	17	7	10	15	8	7	70-74
75-79	9	4	5	8	4	4	14	6	8	75-79
80-84	3	2	1	6	3	3	6	3	3	80-84
85+	2	1	1	2	1	1	3	1	2	85+
TOTAL	633	314	319	698	346	352	776	386	390	TOTAL

TABLE 6 STANDARDIZED RATES

STANDARD COUNTRIES: STANDARDIZED RATES PER THOUSAND	ENGLAND AND WALES 1961 BOTH SEXES	MALES	FEMALES	UNITED STATES 1960 BOTH SEXES	MALES	FEMALES	MEXICO 1960 BOTH SEXES	MALES	FEMALES
Birth	22.48	27.86*	20.95	22.80	25.54*	21.61	25.30	25.73*	24.27
Death	9.09	8.69*	9.84	7.46	7.55*	7.28	3.89	5.34*	3.56
Increase	13.38	19.17*	11.11	15.34	17.98*	14.32	21.41	20.39*	20.71

TABLE 7 MOMENTS AND CUMULANTS

	OBSERVED POP. MALES	OBSERVED POP. FEMALES	STATIONARY POP. MALES	STATIONARY POP. FEMALES	STABLE POP. MALES	STABLE POP. FEMALES	OBSERVED BIRTHS	NET MATERNITY FUNCTION	BIRTHS IN STABLE POP.
μ	27.31711	28.16812	38.80038	39.96482	30.19064	30.97402	28.18448	29.06223	28.36327
σ^2	440.3191	437.7284	540.3217	561.4661	471.3225	493.7906	37.62918	40.54914	38.30805
κ_3	6415.734	5964.352	1862.412	1480.703	5859.593	6059.520	147.1059	128.7383	136.7683
κ_4	-94974.	-95533.	-309215.	-344498.	-143898.	-171021.	-167.518	-609.554	-336.173
β_1	0.482159	0.424143	0.021988	0.012387	0.327929	0.304964	0.406149	0.248583	0.332737
β_2	2.510142	2.501410	1.940855	1.907203	2.352235	2.298602	2.881693	2.629278	2.770922
κ	-0.175522	-0.161911	-0.007982	-0.004419	-0.122295	-0.111545	-0.234186	-0.135517	-0.188610

TABLE 8 RATES FROM AGE DISTRIBUTIONS AND VITAL STATISTICS (Females)

VITAL STATISTICS		THOMPSON AGE RANGE	NRR	1000r	INTERVAL	BOURGEOIS-PICHAT AGE RANGE	NRR	1000b	1000d	1000r	COALE
GRR	1.691										IBR
NRR	1.621	0-4	1.79	21.85	27.47	5-29	1.96	29.27	4.31	24.97	IDR
TFR	3.517	5-9	1.77	21.03	27.45	30-54	1.41	20.10	7.41	12.69	IRI
GENERATION	28.710	10-14	1.90	22.96	27.42	55-79	1.98	31.80	6.60	25.21	K1
SEX RATIO	107.915	15-19	1.57	15.53	27.38	* 5-29	1.96	29.27	4.31	24.97	K2

TABLE 9 LESLIE MATRIX AND ITS SPECTRAL COMPONENTS (Females)

Start of Age Interval	ORIGINAL MATRIX SUB-DIAGONAL	ALTERNATIVE FIRST ROWS Projection	ALTERNATIVE FIRST ROWS Integral	FIRST STABLE MATRIX % IN STABLE POPULATION	FISHER VALUES	REPRODUCTIVE VALUES	SECOND STABLE MATRIX Z_2 FIRST COLUMN	FIRST ROW
0	0.99516	0.00000	0.00000	11.166	1.075	39636	0.1531+0.0821	0.1531+0.0821
5	0.99882	0.00000	0.00000	10.214	1.175	38900	0.1664-0.1093	0.0008+0.1515
10	0.99843	0.03717	0.00000	9.377	1.280	41953	-0.0191-0.2282	-0.1154+0.0635
15	0.99847	0.25043	0.07765	8.605	1.355	32735	-0.2411-0.1059	-0.1021-0.0649
20	0.99833	0.45843	0.44543	7.897	1.206	29434	-0.2394+0.1856	-0.0311-0.1255
25	0.99756	0.40037	0.51169	7.246	0.821	16759	0.0562+0.3437	0.0127-0.1136
30	0.99648	0.27856	0.32426	6.644	0.464	9436	0.3779+0.1317	0.0307-0.0704
35	0.99619	0.16071	0.25772	6.085	0.207	3163	0.3398-0.3090	0.0239-0.0287
40	0.99313	0.04491	0.07781	5.572	0.052	898	-0.1255-0.5119	0.0072-0.0069
45	0.98773	0.00827	0.01598	5.086	0.009	118	-0.5831-0.1532	0.0014-0.0010
50	0.98439	0.00061	0.00128	4.617	0.001	9	-0.4697+0.4997	0.0001-0.0001
55+	0.82812			17.492				

TABLE 10 AGE ANALYSIS AND MISCELLANEOUS RESULTS (Females)

Start of Age Interval	OBSERVED POPUL. (IN 100's)	CONTRIBUTIONS OF ROOTS (IN 100's) r_1	r_2, r_3	r_4-r_{11}	AGE-SP. BIRTH RATES	NET MATERNITY FUNCTION	COEFF. OF MATRIX EQUATION
0	369	351	1	17	0.0000	0.0000	0.0000
5	331	321	24	-14	0.0000	0.0000	0.0000
10	328	295	25	8	0.0000	0.0000	0.0369
15	242	270	-4	-24	0.0153	0.0739	0.2485
20	244	248	-38	34	0.0880	0.4232	0.4543
25	204	228	-36	12	0.1011	0.4853	0.3961
30	203	209	11	-16	0.0641	0.3068	0.2749
35	153	191	59	-98	0.0509	0.2430	0.1580
40	172	175	51	-54	0.0154	0.0731	0.0440
45	136	160	-23	-2	0.0032	0.0149	0.0080
50	152	145	-91	98	0.0003	0.0012	0.0006
55+	377	550					

PARAMETERS	INTEGRAL	MATRIX
L(1)	1.08781	1.08798
L(2)	0.40848	0.41431
	0.78676	0.76297
R(1)	0.01683	0.01686
R(2)	-0.02410	-0.02827
	0.21838	0.21467
C(1)		3142
C(2)		3469
		5800
2P/Y	28.7715	29.2697
DELTA	6.5348	

EXP. INCREASE x	$e^{(x+2\frac{1}{2})r}$
0	1.0430
50	2.4199
55	2.6324
60	2.8635
65	3.1150
70	3.3885
75	3.6860
80	4.0097
85	4.3618
90	4.7448
95	5.1614
100	5.6146

TABLE 1 — DATA

AGE AT LAST BIRTHDAY	POPULATION BOTH SEXES	MALES Number	MALES %	FEMALES Number	FEMALES %	BIRTHS BY AGE OF MOTHER	DEATHS BOTH SEXES	DEATHS MALES	DEATHS FEMALES	AGE AT LAST BIRTHDAY
0	37097	19118	2.9	17979	2.8	0	1710	944	766	0
1-4	139549	71916	10.8	67633	10.6	0	470	248	222	1-4
5-9	118798	61012	9.2	57786	9.1	0	112	67	45	5-9
10-14	100909	51902	7.8	49007	7.7	24	67	37	30	10-14
15-19	109730	57122	8.6	52608	8.3	3906	137	95	42	15-19
20-24	109198	54931	8.2	54267	8.5	11730	186	125	61	20-24
25-29	115283	58062	8.7	57221	9.0	12036	164	102	62	25-29
30-34	94312	48036	7.2	46276	7.3	7493	156	83	73	30-34
35-39	106724	52030	7.8	54694	8.6	4914	217	110	107	35-39
40-44	104163	54649	8.2	49514	7.8	1295	266	138	128	40-44
45-49	77957	42350	6.4	35607	5.6	150	344	200	144	45-49
50-54	63883	33379	5.0	30504	4.8	31	448	271	177	50-54
55-59	40445	21501	3.2	18944	3.0	0	437	262	175	55-59
60-64	33581	16047	2.4	17534	2.8	0	673	377	296	60-64
65-69	22531	10546	1.6	11985	1.9	0	715	377	338	65-69
70-74	15838	7361	1.1	8477	1.3		838	419	419	70-74
75-79	8053	3813	0.6	4240	0.7		642	325	317	75-79
80-84	4129	1867	0.3	2262	0.4	21481 M.	503	238	265	80-84
85+	1522	653	0.1	869	0.1	20098 F.	308	135	173	85+
TOTAL	1303702	666295		637407		41579	8393	4553	3840	TOTAL

TABLE 2 — MALE LIFE TABLE

x	$_nq_x$	l_x	$_nd_x$	$_nL_x$	$_nm_x$	$_na_x$	T_x	r_x	$\mathring{e}_x$	$_nM_x$	x
0	0.047581	100000	4758	96633	0.049239	0.2923	6655902	0.0037	66.559	0.049378	0
1	0.013615	95242	1297	377260	0.003437	1.1411	6559269	0.0037	68.870	0.003448	1
5	0.005348	93945	502	468470	0.001072	2.5000	6182009	0.0546	65.804	0.001098	5
10	0.003562	93443	333	466438	0.000714	2.6683	5713539	0.0056	61.145	0.000713	10
15	0.008284	93110	771	463770	0.001663	2.6923	5247101	0.0000	56.354	0.001663	15
20	0.011314	92339	1045	459087	0.002276	2.5053	4783331	0.0000	51.802	0.002276	20
25	0.008738	91294	798	454420	0.001755	2.4306	4324244	0.0115	47.366	0.001757	25
30	0.008606	90496	779	450565	0.001729	2.5390	3869824	0.0092	42.762	0.001728	30
35	0.010517	89717	944	446299	0.002114	2.5750	3419259	0.0000	38.111	0.002114	35
40	0.012601	88774	1119	441308	0.002535	2.7098	2972960	0.0177	33.489	0.002525	40
45	0.023616	87655	2070	433586	0.004774	2.7344	2531652	0.0443	28.882	0.004723	45
50	0.040290	85585	3448	419903	0.008212	2.6734	2098066	0.0596	24.514	0.008119	50
55	0.060147	82137	4940	399424	0.012368	2.7207	1678163	0.0594	20.431	0.012185	55
60	0.112468	77197	8682	365619	0.023746	2.6545	1278739	0.0526	16.565	0.023493	60
65	0.166094	68514	11380	315311	0.036091	2.6044	913119	0.0526	13.327	0.035748	65
70	0.251803	57135	14387	250483	0.057436	2.5540	597808	0.0526	10.463	0.056922	70
75	0.353448	42748	15109	175771	0.085959	2.4871	347325	0.0526	8.125	0.085235	75
80	0.486551	27639	13448	104383	0.128830	2.4858	171554	0.0526	6.207	0.127477	80
85+	*1.000000	14191	14191	67170	0.211271	4.7333	67170	0.0526	4.733	0.206738	85+

TABLE 3 — FEMALE LIFE TABLE

x	$_nq_x$	l_x	$_nd_x$	$_nL_x$	$_nm_x$	$_na_x$	T_x	r_x	$\mathring{e}_x$	$_nM_x$	x
0	0.041259	100000	4126	97126	0.042480	0.3034	6956242	0.0039	69.562	0.042605	0
1	0.012966	95874	1243	379958	0.003272	1.1535	6859116	0.0039	71.543	0.003282	1
5	0.003764	94631	356	472264	0.000754	2.5000	6479158	0.0544	68.468	0.000779	5
10	0.003057	94275	288	470657	0.000612	2.5132	6006894	0.0087	63.717	0.000612	10
15	0.003984	93987	374	469046	0.000798	2.6316	5536236	0.0000	58.904	0.000798	15
20	0.005605	93612	525	466776	0.001124	2.5513	5067190	0.0000	54.130	0.001124	20
25	0.005410	93088	504	464221	0.001085	2.5840	4600414	0.0147	49.420	0.001084	25
30	0.007861	92584	728	461181	0.001578	2.6118	4136193	0.0030	44.675	0.001577	30
35	0.009736	91856	894	457138	0.001956	2.6046	3675012	0.0000	40.008	0.001956	35
40	0.012935	90962	1177	452059	0.002603	2.6624	3217873	0.0402	35.376	0.002585	40
45	0.020178	89785	1812	444682	0.004074	2.6573	2765815	0.0443	30.805	0.004044	45
50	0.028925	87974	2545	433942	0.005864	2.6715	2321133	0.0570	26.384	0.005803	50
55	0.045727	85429	3906	418243	0.009340	2.7214	1887190	0.0452	22.091	0.009238	55
60	0.082149	81522	6697	392140	0.017078	2.6897	1468947	0.0510	18.019	0.016881	60
65	0.133706	74825	10005	350728	0.028525	2.6611	1076807	0.0510	14.391	0.028202	65
70	0.222692	64821	14435	289266	0.049902	2.5866	726079	0.0510	11.201	0.049428	70
75	0.317629	50386	16004	212196	0.075421	2.5173	436813	0.0510	8.669	0.074764	75
80	0.458493	34382	15764	133044	0.118486	2.5345	224618	0.0510	6.533	0.117154	80
85+	*1.000000	18618	18618	91574	0.203311	4.9186	91574	0.0510	4.919	0.199079	85+

TABLE 4 — OBSERVED AND PROJECTED VITAL RATES

	OBSERVED POPULATION BOTH SEXES	MALES	FEMALES	PROJECTED POPULATION 1956 MALES	FEMALES	1961 MALES	FEMALES	1966 MALES	FEMALES	STABLE POPULATION MALES	FEMALES
RATES PER THOUSAND											
Birth	31.89	32.24	31.53	28.52	27.87	25.65	25.04	25.07	24.42	29.06	28.28
Death	6.44	6.83	6.02	7.34	6.51	7.74	6.83	8.33	7.32	8.56	7.78
Increase	25.46	25.41	25.51	21.17	21.35	17.91	18.20	16.74	17.10	20.5011	
PERCENTAGE											
under 15	30.40	30.61	30.19	33.70	33.20	35.22	34.63	33.67	33.07	35.25	34.57
15-64	65.60	65.75	65.45	62.17	61.77	60.13	60.08	60.58	60.63	58.88	58.74
65 and over	3.99	3.64	4.37	4.12	5.02	4.65	5.29	5.75	6.30	5.87	6.68
DEP. RATIO X 100	52.43	52.08	52.79	60.84	61.89	66.32	66.44	65.08	64.93	69.84	70.23

Jewish Population

TABLE 5 — POPULATION PROJECTED WITH FIXED AGE-SPECIFIC BIRTH AND DEATH RATES (IN 1000's)

AGE AT LAST BIRTHDAY	1956 BOTH SEXES	1956 MALES	1956 FEMALES	1961 BOTH SEXES	1961 MALES	1961 FEMALES	1966 BOTH SEXES	1966 MALES	1966 FEMALES	AGE AT LAST BIRTHDAY
0-4	197	101	96	196	101	95	202	104	98	0-4
5-9	175	90	85	195	100	95	194	100	94	5-9
10-14	119	61	58	174	90	84	194	100	94	10-14
15-19	101	52	49	117	60	57	173	89	84	15-19
20-24	109	57	52	100	51	49	117	60	57	20-24
25-29	108	54	54	108	56	52	99	51	48	25-29
30-34	115	58	57	108	54	54	107	55	52	30-34
35-39	94	48	46	113	57	56	106	53	53	35-39
40-44	105	51	54	92	47	45	112	56	56	40-44
45-49	103	54	49	104	51	53	91	46	45	45-49
50-54	76	41	35	100	52	48	101	49	52	50-54
55-59	61	32	29	72	39	33	95	49	46	55-59
60-64	38	20	18	57	29	28	67	36	31	60-64
65-69	30	14	16	33	17	16	50	25	25	65-69
70-74	18	8	10	24	11	13	26	13	13	70-74
75-79	11	5	6	13	6	7	17	8	9	75-79
80-84	5	2	3	7	3	4	8	3	5	80-84
85+	3	1	2	3	1	2	5	2	3	85+
TOTAL	1468	749	719	1616	825	791	1764	899	865	TOTAL

TABLE 6 — STANDARDIZED RATES

STANDARD COUNTRIES: STANDARDIZED RATES PER THOUSAND	ENGLAND AND WALES 1961 BOTH SEXES	MALES	FEMALES	UNITED STATES 1960 BOTH SEXES	MALES	FEMALES	MEXICO 1960 BOTH SEXES	MALES	FEMALES
Birth	25.07	26.76*	23.49	25.56	25.08*	24.34	29.25	24.05*	28.20
Death	12.16	13.32*	12.98	10.15	10.70*	9.91	6.11	6.70*	5.59
Increase	12.91	13.44*	10.50	15.41	14.38*	14.43	23.14	17.35*	22.61

TABLE 7 — MOMENTS AND CUMULANTS

	OBSERVED POP. MALES	OBSERVED POP. FEMALES	STATIONARY POP. MALES	STATIONARY POP. FEMALES	STABLE POP. MALES	STABLE POP. FEMALES	OBSERVED BIRTHS	NET MATERNITY FUNCTION	BIRTHS IN STABLE POP.
μ	28.14715	28.43584	37.20224	38.23560	27.47433	28.09287	27.78223	27.92297	27.06628
σ^2	367.4268	377.1844	514.9864	535.4757	421.7664	440.0650	39.65439	40.97531	38.40857
κ_3	3014.791	3411.935	2432.903	2265.863	5990.585	6305.775	119.8216	121.2833	128.4527
κ_4	-83168.	-76855.	-260969.	-291229.	-71044.	-83220.	-491.498	-441.058	-247.067
β_1	0.183232	0.216940	0.043337	0.033439	0.478324	0.466580	0.230248	0.213814	0.291207
β_2	2.383953	2.459789	2.015995	1.984325	2.600624	2.570270	2.687436	2.737305	2.832522
κ	-0.082931	-0.101634	-0.016376	-0.012432	-0.187255	-0.180379	-0.140670	-0.146291	-0.195973

TABLE 8 — RATES FROM AGE DISTRIBUTIONS AND VITAL STATISTICS (Females)

VITAL STATISTICS		THOMPSON AGE RANGE	NRR	1000r	INTERVAL	BOURGEOIS-PICHAT AGE RANGE	NRR	1000b	1000d	1000r	COALE
GRR	1.896										
NRR	1.757	0-4	1.58	17.06	27.40	5-29	0.93				IBR
TFR	3.922	5-9	1.13	4.45	27.36	30-54	1.82	17.33	19.83	-2.50	IDR
GENERATION	27.490	10-14	1.03	1.14	27.31	55-79	2.34	38.06	15.79	22.27	IRI
SEX RATIO	106.881	15-19	1.27	8.53	27.23	* 5-29	0.93	45.88	14.38	31.50	K1
								17.33	19.83	-2.50	K2

TABLE 9 — LESLIE MATRIX AND ITS SPECTRAL COMPONENTS (Females)

Start of Age Interval	ORIGINAL MATRIX SUB-DIAGONAL	ALTERNATIVE FIRST ROWS Projection	ALTERNATIVE FIRST ROWS Integral	FIRST STABLE MATRIX % IN STABLE POPULATION	FIRST STABLE MATRIX FISHER VALUES	FIRST STABLE MATRIX REPRODUCTIVE VALUES	SECOND STABLE MATRIX Z_2 FIRST COLUMN	SECOND STABLE MATRIX Z_2 FIRST ROW
0	0.98990	0.00000	0.00000	12.833	1.103	94417	0.1518+0.0830	0.1518+0.0830
5	0.99660	0.00056	0.00000	11.463	1.235	71346	0.1626-0.1133	-0.0058+0.1510
10	0.99658	0.08588	0.00119	10.308	1.372	67253	-0.0334-0.2260	-0.1196+0.0538
15	0.99516	0.33364	0.18022	9.270	1.431	75282	-0.2503-0.0816	-0.1011-0.0792
20	0.99453	0.49044	0.52468	8.324	1.224	66413	-0.2125+0.2161	-0.0284-0.1372
25	0.99345	0.42801	0.51057	7.470	0.820	46914	0.1135+0.3296	0.0208-0.1162
30	0.99123	0.28939	0.39304	6.697	0.439	20336	0.3972-0.0520	0.0332-0.0646
35	0.98889	0.13342	0.21809	5.990	0.169	9262	0.2564-0.3811	0.0190-0.0234
40	0.98368	0.03493	0.06349	5.345	0.041	2029	-0.2596-0.4568	0.0053-0.0054
45	0.97585	0.00600	0.01023	4.744	0.007	249	-0.5968+0.0328	0.0009-0.0009
50	0.96382	0.00117	0.00247	4.178	0.001	36	-0.2671+0.6196	0.0002-0.0001
55+	0.80722			13.377				

TABLE 10 — AGE ANALYSIS AND MISCELLANEOUS RESULTS (Females)

Start of Age Interval	OBSERVED POPUL. (IN 100's)	CONTRIBUTIONS OF ROOTS (IN 100's) r_1	r_2, r_3	$r_4 - r_{11}$	AGE-SP. BIRTH RATES	NET MATERNITY FUNCTION	COEFF. OF MATRIX EQUATION	PARAMETERS		EXP. INCREASE x	$e^{(x+8\frac{1}{3})r}$
0	856	763	80	13	0.0000	0.0000	0.0000	L(1) 1.10794	MATRIX 1.10821	0	1.0526
5	578	682	-49	-55	0.0000	0.0000	0.0006	L(2) 0.37796	0.38530	50	2.9338
10	490	613	-156	33	0.0002	0.0011	0.0847	0.79893	0.77395	55	3.2505
15	526	551	-95	70	0.0359	0.1683	0.3280	R(1) 0.02050	0.02055	60	3.6014
20	543	495	109	-61	0.1045	0.4877	0.4798	R(2) -0.02470	-0.02911	65	3.9901
25	572	444	238	-110	0.1017	0.4720	0.4165	0.22578	0.22178	70	4.4208
30	463	398	100	-35	0.0783	0.3610	0.2797	C(1)	5948	75	4.8980
35	547	356	-211	402	0.0434	0.1985	0.1278	C(2)	8210	80	5.4267
40	495	318	-346	524	0.0126	0.0571	0.0331		-33248	85	6.0125
45	356	282	-76	150	0.0020	0.0091	0.0056	2P/Y 27.8284	28.3312	90	6.6615
50	305	249	368	-312	0.0005	0.0021	0.0011	DELTA 9.3204		95	7.3806
55+	643	796								100	8.1773

218   Israel 1953–55
Jewish Population

TABLE 1 — DATA

AGE AT LAST BIRTHDAY	POPULATION BOTH SEXES	MALES Number	MALES %	FEMALES Number	FEMALES %	BIRTHS BY AGE OF MOTHER	DEATHS BOTH SEXES	DEATHS MALES	DEATHS FEMALES	AGE AT LAST BIRTHDAY
0	41679	21478	2.8	20201	2.7	0	1464	794	670	0
1-4	166675	85665	11.2	81010	10.9	0	371	196	175	1-4
5-9	168654	86794	11.4	81860	11.1	0	93	62	31	5-9
10-14	112545	57974	7.6	54571	7.4	7	54	35	19	10-14
15-19	118709	61726	8.1	56983	7.7	3890	133	97	36	15-19
20-24	119521	60857	8.0	58664	7.9	13429	159	111	48	20-24
25-29	116746	56824	7.4	59922	8.1	12095	141	81	60	25-29
30-34	116360	59639	7.8	56721	7.7	8090	144	80	64	30-34
35-39	92731	44810	5.9	47921	6.5	3558	160	74	86	35-39
40-44	117385	58254	7.6	59131	8.0	1288	299	139	160	40-44
45-49	96060	50906	6.7	45154	6.1	201	380	214	166	45-49
50-54	76951	39891	5.2	37060	5.0	25	549	324	225	50-54
55-59	55243	29003	3.8	26240	3.5	0	625	378	247	55-59
60-64	38492	19436	2.5	19056	2.6	0	753	435	318	60-64
65-69	29532	13655	1.8	15877	2.1	0	927	502	425	65-69
70-74	19430	8911	1.2	10519	1.4		1022	507	515	70-74
75-79	10919	5146	0.7	5773	0.8		912	458	454	75-79
80-84	5341	2387	0.3	2954	0.4	21954 M.	695	323	372	80-84
85+	1860	783	0.1	1077	0.1	20629 F.	412	175	237	85+
TOTAL	1504833	764139		740694		42583	9293	4985	4308	TOTAL

TABLE 2 — MALE LIFE TABLE

x	$_nq_x$	l_x	$_nd_x$	$_nL_x$	$_nm_x$	$_na_x$	T_x	r_x	$\dot{e}_x$	$_nM_x$	x
0	0.036009	100000	3601	97407	0.036968	0.2798	6801971	0.0000	68.020	0.036968	0
1	0.009092	96399	876	383079	0.002288	1.1283	6704564	0.0000	69.550	0.002288	1
5	0.003480	95523	332	476782	0.000697	2.5000	6321485	0.0603	66.178	0.000714	5
10	0.003045	95190	290	475312	0.000610	2.7951	5844703	0.0332	61.400	0.000604	10
15	0.007828	94900	743	472762	0.001571	2.6584	5369391	0.0000	56.579	0.001571	15
20	0.009077	94157	855	468634	0.001824	2.4804	4896629	0.0066	52.005	0.001824	20
25	0.007101	93303	663	464809	0.001425	2.4261	4427995	0.0005	47.458	0.001425	25
30	0.006690	92640	620	461671	0.001342	2.5317	3963186	0.0223	42.780	0.001341	30
35	0.008226	92020	757	458306	0.001652	2.6275	3501515	0.0006	38.051	0.001651	35
40	0.011866	91264	1083	453848	0.002386	2.7190	3043209	0.0000	33.345	0.002386	40
45	0.021019	90181	1895	446680	0.004244	2.7720	2589361	0.0332	28.713	0.004204	45
50	0.040293	88285	3557	433268	0.008210	2.7068	2142681	0.0480	24.270	0.008122	50
55	0.064049	84728	5427	411105	0.013200	2.6902	1709413	0.0579	20.175	0.013033	55
60	0.107350	79301	8513	376604	0.022604	2.6622	1298308	0.0471	16.372	0.022381	60
65	0.170319	70788	12057	325104	0.037085	2.6082	921704	0.0471	13.021	0.036763	65
70	0.251581	58732	14776	257560	0.057368	2.5569	596600	0.0471	10.158	0.056896	70
75	0.366143	43956	16094	179384	0.089719	2.4901	339041	0.0471	7.713	0.089001	75
80	0.502797	27862	14009	102742	0.136349	2.4667	159656	0.0471	5.730	0.135316	80
85+	1.000000	13853	13853	56914	0.243400	4.1085	56914	0.0471	4.108	0.223500	85+

TABLE 3 — FEMALE LIFE TABLE

x	$_nq_x$	l_x	$_nd_x$	$_nL_x$	$_nm_x$	$_na_x$	T_x	r_x	$\dot{e}_x$	$_nM_x$	x
0	0.032399	100000	3240	97685	0.033167	0.2856	7083262	0.0000	70.833	0.033167	0
1	0.008588	96760	831	384659	0.002160	1.1340	6985577	0.0000	72.195	0.002160	1
5	0.001799	95929	173	479214	0.000360	2.5000	6600918	0.0609	68.810	0.000379	5
10	0.001750	95757	168	478391	0.000350	2.6603	6121704	0.0358	63.930	0.000348	10
15	0.003154	95589	302	477237	0.000632	2.6531	5643313	0.0000	59.037	0.000632	15
20	0.004083	95287	389	475501	0.000818	2.5924	5166076	0.0000	54.216	0.000818	20
25	0.004995	94898	474	473337	0.001001	2.5632	4690575	0.0024	49.427	0.001001	25
30	0.005644	94424	533	470866	0.001132	2.6427	4217238	0.0211	44.663	0.001128	30
35	0.008936	93891	839	467510	0.001795	2.6784	3746373	0.0000	39.901	0.001795	35
40	0.013450	93052	1252	462310	0.002707	2.6411	3278863	0.0033	35.237	0.002706	40
45	0.018374	91801	1687	455094	0.003706	2.6817	2816553	0.0427	30.681	0.003676	45
50	0.030215	90114	2723	444262	0.006129	2.6829	2361459	0.0480	26.205	0.006071	50
55	0.046654	87391	4077	427604	0.009535	2.7060	1917197	0.0562	21.938	0.009413	55
60	0.081072	83314	6754	400865	0.016850	2.6747	1489594	0.0459	17.879	0.016668	60
65	0.127253	76560	9742	360111	0.027054	2.6713	1088729	0.0459	14.221	0.026768	65
70	0.220976	66817	14765	298738	0.049425	2.6060	728618	0.0459	10.905	0.048959	70
75	0.331483	52052	17254	217551	0.079312	2.5247	429879	0.0459	8.259	0.078642	75
80	0.483068	34798	16810	132117	0.127233	2.5091	212328	0.0459	6.102	0.125930	80
85+	*1.000000	17988	17988	80211	0.224260	4.4591	80211	0.0459	4.459	0.220056	85+

TABLE 4 — OBSERVED AND PROJECTED VITAL RATES

	OBSERVED POPULATION BOTH SEXES	MALES	FEMALES	PROJECTED POPULATION 1959 MALES	1959 FEMALES	1964 MALES	1964 FEMALES	1969 MALES	1969 FEMALES	STABLE POPULATION MALES	FEMALES
RATES PER THOUSAND											
Birth	28.30	28.73	27.85	25.89	25.10	24.26	23.52	25.67	24.86	27.74	27.07
Death	6.18	6.52	5.82	6.94	6.22	7.46	6.64	8.08	7.18	8.15	7.48
Increase	22.12	22.21	22.03	18.94	18.89	16.80	16.88	17.59	17.68		19.5919
PERCENTAGE											
under 15	32.53	32.97	32.08	35.23	34.34	34.27	33.41	32.35	31.49	34.44	33.77
15-64	63.01	62.99	63.03	60.28	60.39	60.44	60.71	61.34	61.62	59.49	59.28
65 and over	4.46	4.04	4.89	4.50	5.27	5.29	5.87	6.31	6.89	6.07	6.94
DEP. RATIO X 100	58.70	58.75	58.66	65.90	65.58	65.46	64.71	63.02	62.29	68.08	68.68

Jewish Population

TABLE 1 — DATA

AGE AT LAST BIRTHDAY	POPULATION BOTH SEXES	MALES Number	%	FEMALES Number	%	BIRTHS BY AGE OF MOTHER	DEATHS BOTH SEXES	MALES	FEMALES	AGE AT LAST BIRTHDAY
0	45110	23159	2.7	21951	2.6	0	1478	807	671	0
1-4	176200	90717	10.4	85483	10.1	0	290	147	143	1-4
5-9	210905	108567	12.5	102338	12.1	0	103	60	43	5-9
10-14	159930	82120	9.4	77810	9.2	7	77	48	29	10-14
15-19	122573	63335	7.3	59238	7.0	3438	146	114	32	15-19
20-24	131360	67886	7.8	63474	7.5	13762	177	135	42	20-24
25-29	123900	61577	7.1	62323	7.4	12698	136	88	48	25-29
30-34	124730	60792	7.0	63938	7.6	8593	149	85	64	30-34
35-39	109862	56107	6.4	53755	6.4	3904	177	93	84	35-39
40-44	108378	51673	5.9	56705	6.7	1052	265	127	138	40-44
45-49	116604	59277	6.8	57327	6.8	246	421	222	199	45-49
50-54	89212	47610	5.5	41602	4.9	0	582	342	240	50-54
55-59	71661	36738	4.2	34923	4.1	0	814	468	346	55-59
60-64	46293	24182	2.8	22111	2.6	0	894	523	371	60-64
65-69	34731	16417	1.9	18314	2.2	0	1102	597	505	65-69
70-74	21828	10027	1.2	11801	1.4		1111	570	541	70-74
75-79	13182	6284	0.7	6898	0.8		1060	548	512	75-79
80-84	6410	2815	0.3	3595	0.4	22499 M.	825	386	439	80-84
85+	2238	891	0.1	1347	0.2	21201 F.	505	209	296	85+
TOTAL	1715107	870174		844933		43700	10312	5569	4743	TOTAL

TABLE 2 — MALE LIFE TABLE

x	$_nq_x$	l_x	$_nd_x$	$_nL_x$	$_nm_x$	$_na_x$	T_x	r_x	$\mathring{e}_x$	$_nM_x$	x
0	0.033938	100000	3394	97451	0.034825	0.2489	6849207	0.0008	68.492	0.034846	0
1	0.006445	96606	623	384620	0.001619	1.1012	6751756	0.0008	69.889	0.001620	1
5	0.002733	95984	262	479262	0.000547	2.5000	6367136	0.0318	66.336	0.000553	5
10	0.002988	95721	286	478015	0.000598	2.9337	5887874	0.0530	61.511	0.000585	10
15	0.008987	95435	858	475167	0.001805	2.6578	5409859	0.0175	56.686	0.001800	15
20	0.009893	94578	936	470509	0.001989	2.4573	4934691	0.0010	52.176	0.001989	20
25	0.007113	93642	666	466485	0.001428	2.4100	4464182	0.0095	47.673	0.001429	25
30	0.006969	92976	648	463280	0.001399	2.5314	3997698	0.0079	42.997	0.001398	30
35	0.008271	92328	764	459828	0.001661	2.6285	3534418	0.0145	38.281	0.001658	35
40	0.012219	91564	1119	455121	0.002458	2.6709	3074590	0.0000	33.578	0.002458	40
45	0.018589	90445	1681	448451	0.003749	2.7541	2619374	0.0040	28.961	0.003745	45
50	0.035708	88764	3170	436664	0.007259	2.7419	2170923	0.0402	24.457	0.007183	50
55	0.062638	85595	5361	415648	0.012899	2.7011	1734260	0.0543	20.261	0.012739	55
60	0.104024	80233	8346	381711	0.021865	2.6691	1318612	0.0504	16.435	0.021628	60
65	0.168799	71887	12134	330490	0.036716	2.6147	936901	0.0504	13.033	0.036365	65
70	0.251468	59753	15026	262028	0.057344	2.5552	606410	0.0504	10.149	0.056847	70
75	0.360390	44727	16119	183237	0.087969	2.4938	344382	0.0504	7.700	0.087206	75
80	0.508597	28608	14550	105192	0.138316	2.4705	161145	0.0504	5.633	0.137123	80
85+	1.000000	14058	14058	55953	0.251245	3.9802	55953	0.0504	3.980	0.234567	85+

TABLE 3 — FEMALE LIFE TABLE

x	$_nq_x$	l_x	$_nd_x$	$_nL_x$	$_nm_x$	$_na_x$	T_x	r_x	$\mathring{e}_x$	$_nM_x$	x
0	0.029867	100000	2987	97810	0.030535	0.2667	7151666	0.0014	71.517	0.030568	0
1	0.006649	97013	645	386193	0.001670	1.1160	7053856	0.0014	72.710	0.001673	1
5	0.002064	96368	199	481344	0.000413	2.5000	6667663	0.0315	69.189	0.000420	5
10	0.001869	96169	180	480410	0.000374	2.5702	6186319	0.0543	64.327	0.000373	10
15	0.002703	95990	259	479328	0.000541	2.6096	5705909	0.0198	59.443	0.000540	15
20	0.003303	95730	316	477882	0.000662	2.5707	5226581	0.0000	54.597	0.000662	20
25	0.003844	95414	367	476186	0.000770	2.5905	4748699	0.0000	49.769	0.000770	25
30	0.005004	95047	476	474124	0.001003	2.6625	4272513	0.0137	44.952	0.001001	30
35	0.007800	94571	738	471151	0.001566	2.6863	3798389	0.0104	40.164	0.001563	35
40	0.012099	93834	1135	466511	0.002434	2.6591	3327239	0.0000	35.459	0.002434	40
45	0.017312	92698	1605	459789	0.003490	2.6926	2860727	0.0273	30.861	0.003471	45
50	0.028753	91094	2619	449489	0.005827	2.7172	2400938	0.0434	26.357	0.005769	50
55	0.049005	88474	4336	432416	0.010027	2.7038	1951449	0.0527	22.057	0.009908	55
60	0.081541	84139	6861	404742	0.016951	2.6750	1519033	0.0481	18.054	0.016779	60
65	0.130687	77278	10099	362627	0.027850	2.6471	1114290	0.0481	14.419	0.027575	65
70	0.208260	67179	13991	302317	0.046278	2.6001	751663	0.0481	11.189	0.045844	70
75	0.316273	53188	16822	224555	0.074912	2.5398	449346	0.0481	8.448	0.074224	75
80	0.473098	36366	17205	139306	0.123503	2.5283	224791	0.0481	6.181	0.122115	80
85+	*1.000000	19161	19161	85485	0.224150	4.4613	85485	0.0481	4.461	0.219748	85+

TABLE 4 — OBSERVED AND PROJECTED VITAL RATES

	OBSERVED POPULATION BOTH SEXES	MALES	FEMALES	PROJECTED 1962 MALES	FEMALES	1967 MALES	FEMALES	1972 MALES	FEMALES	STABLE POPULATION MALES	FEMALES
RATES PER THOUSAND											
Birth	25.48	25.86	25.09	23.97	23.25	24.34	23.59	26.28	25.44	26.40	25.70
Death	6.01	6.40	5.61	6.93	6.10	7.56	6.63	8.19	7.22	8.36	7.65
Increase	19.47	19.46	19.48	17.05	17.15	16.78	16.96	18.09	18.22	18.0449	
PERCENTAGE											
under 15	34.53	35.00	34.04	34.70	33.73	32.54	31.65	31.48	30.61	33.29	32.55
15-64	60.90	60.81	61.00	60.46	60.83	61.59	61.89	61.61	62.07	60.13	59.91
65 and over	4.57	4.19	4.97	4.83	5.43	5.87	6.47	6.91	7.32	6.58	7.54
DEP. RATIO X 100	64.19	64.44	63.94	65.39	64.38	62.37	61.58	62.32	61.10	66.31	66.92

TABLE 1 — DATA

AGE AT LAST BIRTHDAY	POPULATION BOTH SEXES	MALES Number	MALES %	FEMALES Number	FEMALES %	BIRTHS BY AGE OF MOTHER	DEATHS BOTH SEXES	DEATHS MALES	FEMALES	AGE AT LAST BIRTHDAY
0	44235	22720	2.4	21515	2.3	0	1234	685	549	0
1-4	175738	90436	9.5	85302	9.2	0	261	141	120	1-4
5-9	233901	120339	12.6	113562	12.2	0	125	74	51	5-9
10-14	203446	104678	11.0	98768	10.6	17	78	50	28	10-14
15-19	136732	70458	7.4	66274	7.1	3150	103	71	32	15-19
20-24	133677	68875	7.2	64802	7.0	13659	106	71	35	20-24
25-29	131385	66871	7.0	64514	6.9	13729	124	68	56	25-29
30-34	124851	60656	6.3	64195	6.9	8636	121	63	58	30-34
35-39	128539	64436	6.7	64103	6.9	4445	191	103	88	35-39
40-44	102451	50162	5.2	52289	5.6	1077	214	114	100	40-44
45-49	124689	61118	6.4	63571	6.8	268	418	210	208	45-49
50-54	109341	56784	5.9	52557	5.7	0	671	388	283	50-54
55-59	81482	42522	4.5	38960	4.2	0	849	507	342	55-59
60-64	61972	31660	3.3	30312	3.3	0	1051	628	423	60-64
65-69	37826	19151	2.0	18675	2.0	0	1135	626	509	65-69
70-74	27864	12565	1.3	15299	1.6		1216	611	605	70-74
75-79	15879	7376	0.8	8503	0.9		1039	533	506	75-79
80-84	8057	3512	0.4	4545	0.5	22979 M.	879	417	462	80-84
85+	2961	1196	0.1	1765	0.2	22002 F.	589	254	335	85+
TOTAL	1885026	955515		929511		44981	10404	5614	4790	TOTAL

TABLE 2 — MALE LIFE TABLE

x	nq_x	l_x	nd_x	nL_x	nm_x	na_x	T_x	r_x	$\dot{e}_x$	nM_x	x
0	0.029492	100000	2949	97819	0.030150	0.2606	7049866	0.0000	70.499	0.030150	0
1	0.006208	97051	603	386462	0.001559	1.1107	6952046	0.0000	71.633	0.001559	1
5	0.003063	96448	295	481503	0.000614	2.5000	6565584	0.0069	68.074	0.000615	5
10	0.002407	96153	231	480225	0.000482	2.6700	6084082	0.3529	63.275	0.000478	10
15	0.005050	95921	484	478450	0.001012	2.6115	5603857	0.0410	58.421	0.001008	15
20	0.005141	95437	491	475957	0.001031	2.4988	5125408	0.0042	53.705	0.001031	20
25	0.005072	94946	482	473527	0.001017	2.4995	4649450	0.0117	48.969	0.001017	25
30	0.005182	94465	490	471156	0.001039	2.6144	4175923	0.0026	44.206	0.001039	30
35	0.007985	93975	750	468118	0.001603	2.6568	3704767	0.0174	39.423	0.001598	35
40	0.011309	93225	1054	463660	0.002274	2.6623	3236649	0.0030	34.719	0.002273	40
45	0.017049	92171	1571	457345	0.003436	2.7673	2772990	0.0000	30.085	0.003436	45
50	0.033894	90599	3071	446060	0.006884	2.7414	2315645	0.0291	25.559	0.006833	50
55	0.058604	87528	5130	425826	0.012046	2.6964	1869585	0.0459	21.360	0.011923	55
60	0.095960	82399	7907	393534	0.020092	2.6654	1443759	0.0614	17.522	0.019836	60
65	0.153118	74492	11406	345178	0.033044	2.6082	1050225	0.0614	14.099	0.032688	65
70	0.219236	63086	13831	281651	0.049106	2.5577	705047	0.0614	11.176	0.048627	70
75	0.309384	49255	15239	208590	0.073066	2.5270	423396	0.0614	8.596	0.072261	75
80	0.464609	34016	15804	131190	0.120469	2.5392	214806	0.0614	6.315	0.118736	80
85+	*1.000000	18212	18212	83616	0.217806	4.5912	83616	0.0614	4.591	0.212375	85+

TABLE 3 — FEMALE LIFE TABLE

x	nq_x	l_x	nd_x	nL_x	nm_x	na_x	T_x	r_x	$\dot{e}_x$	nM_x	x
0	0.025049	100000	2505	98166	0.025517	0.2678	7331322	0.0000	73.313	0.025517	0
1	0.005604	97495	546	388405	0.001407	1.1170	7233156	0.0000	74.190	0.001407	1
5	0.002236	96949	217	484202	0.000448	2.5000	6844751	0.0072	70.602	0.000449	5
10	0.001419	96732	137	483320	0.000284	2.5262	6360550	0.3535	65.754	0.000283	10
15	0.002423	96595	234	482414	0.000485	2.6093	5877230	0.0417	60.844	0.000483	15
20	0.002698	96361	260	481192	0.000540	2.6460	5394816	0.0021	55.986	0.000540	20
25	0.004331	96101	416	479499	0.000868	2.5858	4913624	0.0001	51.130	0.000868	25
30	0.004508	95684	431	477394	0.000903	2.6147	4434125	0.0000	46.341	0.000903	30
35	0.006862	95253	654	474730	0.001377	2.6496	3956732	0.0192	41.539	0.001373	35
40	0.009520	94600	901	470927	0.001912	2.7008	3482002	0.0000	36.808	0.001912	40
45	0.016238	93699	1522	465019	0.003272	2.7154	3011075	0.0000	32.136	0.003272	45
50	0.026837	92177	2474	455197	0.005434	2.6998	2546056	0.0433	27.621	0.005385	50
55	0.043410	89704	3894	439495	0.008860	2.6827	2090859	0.0460	23.309	0.008778	55
60	0.068623	85810	5889	415670	0.014166	2.7280	1651365	0.0574	19.245	0.013955	60
65	0.129363	79921	10339	375169	0.027558	2.6364	1235695	0.0574	15.461	0.027256	65
70	0.181942	69582	12660	317220	0.039909	2.5757	860526	0.0574	12.367	0.039545	70
75	0.262404	56922	14937	248255	0.060167	2.5659	543306	0.0574	9.545	0.059508	75
80	0.414119	41986	17387	168474	0.103203	2.6158	295051	0.0574	7.027	0.101650	80
85+	*1.000000	24599	24599	126577	0.194337	5.1457	126577	0.0574	5.146	0.189802	85+

TABLE 4 — OBSERVED AND PROJECTED VITAL RATES

	OBSERVED POPULATION BOTH SEXES	MALES	FEMALES	PROJECTED 1965 MALES	FEMALES	1970 MALES	FEMALES	1975 MALES	FEMALES	STABLE POPULATION MALES	FEMALES
RATES PER THOUSAND											
Birth	23.86	24.05	23.67	23.03	22.62	24.68	24.20	26.56	25.99	25.90	25.30
Death	5.52	5.88	5.15	6.61	5.86	7.28	6.46	7.87	7.06	7.88	7.28
Increase	18.34	18.17	18.52	16.42	16.76	17.40	17.74	18.69	18.92	18.0173	
PERCENTAGE											
under 15	34.87	35.39	34.33	33.23	32.40	30.97	30.35	31.07	30.56	32.81	32.23
15-64	60.22	60.02	60.42	61.05	61.27	62.19	62.32	60.88	60.87	60.01	59.61
65 and over	4.91	4.58	5.25	5.72	6.33	6.84	7.33	8.05	8.57	7.18	8.17
DEP. RATIO X 100	66.06	66.60	65.52	63.80	63.21	60.79	60.46	64.25	64.28	66.64	67.77

Jewish Population

TABLE 5 — POPULATION PROJECTED WITH FIXED AGE-SPECIFIC BIRTH AND DEATH RATES (IN 1000's)

AGE AT LAST BIRTHDAY	1965 BOTH SEXES	MALES	FEMALES	1970 BOTH SEXES	MALES	FEMALES	1975 BOTH SEXES	MALES	FEMALES	AGE AT LAST BIRTHDAY
0-4	223	114	109	247	126	121	290	148	142	0-4
5-9	219	113	106	222	113	109	246	125	121	5-9
10-14	233	120	113	218	112	106	222	113	109	10-14
15-19	203	104	99	233	120	113	218	112	106	15-19
20-24	136	70	66	202	104	98	232	119	113	20-24
25-29	134	69	65	136	70	66	201	103	98	25-29
30-34	131	67	64	132	68	64	135	69	66	30-34
35-39	124	60	64	130	66	64	132	68	64	35-39
40-44	128	64	64	123	60	63	128	65	63	40-44
45-49	101	49	52	126	63	63	122	59	63	45-49
50-54	122	60	62	99	48	51	122	61	61	50-54
55-59	105	54	51	117	57	60	95	46	49	55-59
60-64	76	39	37	98	50	48	110	53	57	60-64
65-69	55	28	27	67	34	33	87	44	43	65-69
70-74	32	16	16	46	23	23	56	28	28	70-74
75-79	21	9	12	24	12	12	35	17	18	75-79
80-84	11	5	6	14	6	8	15	7	8	80-84
85+	5	2	3	7	3	4	10	4	6	85+
TOTAL	2059	1043	1016	2241	1135	1106	2456	1241	1215	TOTAL

TABLE 6 — STANDARDIZED RATES

STANDARD COUNTRIES:

STANDARDIZED RATES PER THOUSAND	ENGLAND AND WALES 1961 BOTH SEXES	MALES	FEMALES	UNITED STATES 1960 BOTH SEXES	MALES	FEMALES	MEXICO 1960 BOTH SEXES	MALES	FEMALES
Birth	22.23	23.81*	21.08	22.60	22.23*	21.78	26.20	21.46*	25.56
Death	10.19	9.87*	10.86	8.32	8.19*	8.08	4.51	5.74*	4.09
Increase	12.04	13.95*	10.22	14.28	14.04*	13.70	21.69	15.72*	21.47

TABLE 7 — MOMENTS AND CUMULANTS

	OBSERVED POP. MALES	FEMALES	STATIONARY POP. MALES	FEMALES	STABLE POP. MALES	FEMALES	OBSERVED BIRTHS	NET MATERNITY FUNCTION	BIRTHS IN STABLE POP.
μ	28.37487	28.97128	37.97891	39.07179	29.07746	29.73493	27.70220	27.79031	27.12931
σ^2	414.7121	423.0648	527.8801	553.0917	449.1951	470.8217	35.00757	35.74486	33.46359
κ_3	4233.757	4289.033	2281.749	2202.283	5922.184	6332.681	119.5222	126.5328	126.1644
κ_4	-133542.	-131692.	-279327.	-315072.	-107448.	-121882.	-44.930	-66.603	111.081
β_1	0.251311	0.242939	0.035394	0.028665	0.386954	0.384243	0.332975	0.350563	0.424772
β_2	2.223533	2.264223	1.997597	1.970052	2.467488	2.450171	2.963339	2.947872	3.099196
κ	-0.091290	-0.091847	-0.013278	-0.010584	-0.149176	-0.146491	-0.254348	-0.249745	-0.330110

TABLE 8 — RATES FROM AGE DISTRIBUTIONS AND VITAL STATISTICS (Females)

VITAL STATISTICS		THOMPSON AGE RANGE	NRR	1000r	INTERVAL	BOURGEOIS-PICHAT AGE RANGE	NRR	1000b	1000d	1000r	COALE
GRR	1.712										
NRR	1.640	0-4	1.67	19.20	27.44	5-29	2.28	30.16	-0.41	30.57	IBR
TFR	3.500	5-9	1.79	21.54	27.40	30-54	1.17	17.39	11.54	5.85	IDR
GENERATION	27.456	10-14	1.60	16.88	27.36	55-79	3.29	119.14	74.98	44.16	IRI
SEX RATIO	104.441	15-19	1.14	4.70	27.27	*15-39	1.02	14.84	14.12	0.72	K1
											K2

TABLE 9 — LESLIE MATRIX AND ITS SPECTRAL COMPONENTS (Females)

Start of Age Interval	ORIGINAL MATRIX SUB-DIAGONAL	ALTERNATIVE FIRST ROWS Projection	Integral	FIRST STABLE MATRIX % IN STABLE POPULATION	FISHER VALUES	REPRODUCTIVE VALUES	SECOND STABLE MATRIX Z₂ FIRST COLUMN	FIRST ROW
0	0.99513	0.00000	0.00000	11.778	1.075	114805	0.1734+0.0776	0.1734+0.0776
5	0.99818	0.00020	0.00000	10.709	1.182	134239	0.1628-0.1419	0.0021+0.1671
10	0.99813	0.05666	0.00043	9.767	1.296	127993	-0.0689-0.2364	-0.1323+0.0632
15	0.99747	0.30676	0.11833	8.907	1.360	90131	-0.2775-0.0418	-0.1089-0.0865
20	0.99648	0.50318	0.52477	8.118	1.162	75281	-0.1760+0.2670	-0.0246-0.1425
25	0.99561	0.41263	0.52982	7.391	0.733	47303	0.1917+0.3093	0.0170-0.1113
30	0.99442	0.24215	0.33493	6.723	0.361	23149	0.4108-0.0502	0.0232-0.0597
35	0.99199	0.10683	0.17264	6.109	0.135	8664	0.1442-0.4474	0.0141-0.0224
40	0.98745	0.02945	0.05128	5.537	0.033	1746	-0.3915-0.3610	0.0045-0.0054
45	0.97888	0.00502	0.01046	4.995	0.005	315	-0.5549+0.2298	0.0008-0.0007
50	0.96550	0.00002	0.00005	4.468	0.000	1	-0.0273+0.6710	0.0000-0.0000
55+	0.81617			15.499				

TABLE 10 — AGE ANALYSIS AND MISCELLANEOUS RESULTS (Females)

Start Age Interval	OBSERVED POPUL. (IN 100's)	CONTRIBUTIONS OF ROOTS (IN 100's) r_1	r_2, r_3	r_4-r_{11}	AGE-SP. BIRTH RATES	NET MATERNITY FUNCTION	COEFF. OF MATRIX EQUATION	PARAMETERS INTEGRAL	MATRIX	EXP. INCREASE x	$e^{(x+2\frac{1}{2})r}$
0	1068	1074	13	-19	0.0000	0.0000	0.0000	L(1) 1.09427	1.09447	0	1.0461
5	1136	976	125	34	0.0000	0.0000	0.0002	L(2) 0.36185	0.36756	50	2.5752
10	988	891	103	-6	0.0001	0.0004	0.0563	0.82456	0.79464	55	2.8179
15	663	812	-64	-85	0.0232	0.1122	0.3041	R(1) 0.01802	0.01805	60	3.0835
20	648	740	-195	103	0.1031	0.4961	0.4976	R(2) -0.02097	-0.02659	65	3.3742
25	645	674	-103	74	0.1041	0.4991	0.4066	0.23145	0.22751	70	3.6923
30	642	613	154	-125	0.0658	0.3141	0.2376	C(1)	9118	75	4.0404
35	641	557	280	-196	0.0339	0.1610	0.1042	C(2)	15580	80	4.4213
40	523	505	68	-50	0.0101	0.0474	0.0285		26305	85	4.8381
45	636	455	-294	474	0.0021	0.0096	0.0048	2P/Y 27.1467	27.6171	90	5.2941
50	526	407	-362	480	0.0000	0.0000	0.0000	DELTA 6.7083		95	5.7932
55+	1181	1413								100	6.3393

Jewish Population

TABLE 1 — DATA

AGE AT LAST BIRTHDAY	BOTH SEXES	POPULATION MALES Number	%	FEMALES Number	%	BIRTHS BY AGE OF MOTHER	DEATHS BOTH SEXES	MALES	FEMALES	AGE AT LAST BIRTHDAY
0	46004	23697	2.2	22307	2.1	0	1054	598	456	0
1-4	184798	94673	8.8	90125	8.6	0	178	83	95	1-4
5-9	237904	122509	11.5	115395	11.0	0	95	64	31	5-9
10-14	245448	126359	11.8	119089	11.4	0	80	50	30	10-14
15-19	201609	104714	9.8	96895	9.3	3409	160	110	50	15-19
20-24	137031	70014	6.5	67017	6.4	13846	121	81	40	20-24
25-29	137027	68490	6.4	68537	6.6	14263	106	66	40	25-29
30-34	131627	63877	6.0	67750	6.5	9180	140	80	60	30-34
35-39	133004	62860	5.9	70144	6.7	4272	207	109	98	35-39
40-44	129060	65104	6.1	63956	6.1	1189	267	142	125	40-44
45-49	113133	54618	5.1	58515	5.6	225	403	208	195	45-49
50-54	126557	64497	6.0	62060	5.9	0	802	436	366	50-54
55-59	98636	52649	4.9	45987	4.4	0	1080	636	444	55-59
60-64	76085	38959	3.6	37126	3.6	0	1442	812	630	60-64
65-69	49940	25340	2.4	24600	2.4	0	1538	860	678	65-69
70-74	32975	16048	1.5	16927	1.6		1627	856	771	70-74
75-79	20312	9426	0.9	10886	1.0		1524	723	801	75-79
80-84	10083	4482	0.4	5601	0.5	23998 M.	1190	534	656	80-84
85+	3597	1519	0.1	2078	0.2	22386 F.	723	304	419	85+
TOTAL	2114830	1069835		1044995		46384	12737	6752	5985	TOTAL

TABLE 2 — MALE LIFE TABLE

x	nq_x	l_x	nd_x	nL_x	nm_x	na_x	T_x	r_x	$\mathring{e}_x$	nM_x
0	0.024747	100000	2475	98066	0.025235	0.2185	7068600	0.0000	70.686	0.025235
1	0.003498	97525	341	389105	0.000877	1.0799	6970534	0.0000	71.474	0.000877
5	0.002609	97184	254	485287	0.000522	2.5000	6581429	0.0000	67.721	0.000522
10	0.001985	96931	192	484226	0.000397	2.7791	6096142	0.0151	62.892	0.000396
15	0.005285	96738	511	482488	0.001060	2.6476	5611916	0.0581	58.011	0.001050
20	0.005764	96227	555	479737	0.001156	2.4807	5129428	0.0414	53.306	0.001157
25	0.004808	95672	460	477220	0.000964	2.5183	4649691	0.0081	48.600	0.000964
30	0.006249	95212	595	474649	0.001254	2.6250	4172471	0.0073	43.823	0.001252
35	0.008634	94617	817	471133	0.001734	2.6084	3697822	0.0000	39.082	0.001734
40	0.010876	93800	1020	466646	0.002186	2.6909	3226689	0.0117	34.400	0.002181
45	0.018879	92780	1752	459941	0.003808	2.7391	2760043	0.0000	29.748	0.003808
50	0.033291	91029	3030	448289	0.006760	2.7383	2300102	0.0000	25.268	0.006760
55	0.059291	87998	5217	428050	0.012189	2.7114	1851813	0.0376	21.044	0.012080
60	0.100560	82781	8324	394466	0.021103	2.6650	1423762	0.0590	17.199	0.020842
65	0.158612	74456	11810	344128	0.034318	2.6160	1029296	0.0590	13.824	0.033938
70	0.237877	62647	14902	276744	0.053848	2.5514	685169	0.0590	10.937	0.053340
75	0.324400	47744	15488	200019	0.077434	2.5011	408425	0.0590	8.554	0.076703
80	0.464612	32256	14987	124185	0.120679	2.5248	208406	0.0590	6.461	0.119144
85+	*1.000000	17270	17270	84220	0.205053	4.8768	84220	0.0590	4.877	0.200132

TABLE 3 — FEMALE LIFE TABLE

x	nq_x	l_x	nd_x	nL_x	nm_x	na_x	T_x	r_x	$\mathring{e}_x$	nM_x
0	0.020138	100000	2014	98511	0.020442	0.2607	7284344	0.0000	72.843	0.020442
1	0.004204	97986	412	390755	0.001054	1.1108	7185832	0.0000	73.335	0.001054
5	0.001342	97574	131	487544	0.000269	2.5000	6795078	0.0000	69.640	0.000269
10	0.001263	97443	123	486934	0.000253	2.7061	6307533	0.0172	64.730	0.000252
15	0.002597	97320	253	486004	0.000520	2.6371	5820599	0.0570	59.809	0.000516
20	0.002982	97067	289	484620	0.000597	2.5210	5334595	0.0340	54.958	0.000597
25	0.002914	96778	282	483214	0.000584	2.6012	4849975	0.0000	50.114	0.000584
30	0.004419	96496	426	481495	0.000886	2.6893	4366762	0.0000	45.253	0.000886
35	0.006968	96070	669	478780	0.001398	2.6571	3885267	0.0044	40.442	0.001397
40	0.009760	95400	931	474859	0.001961	2.6998	3406487	0.0160	35.707	0.001954
45	0.016538	94469	1562	468811	0.003332	2.7377	2931628	0.0000	31.033	0.003332
50	0.029210	92907	2714	458320	0.005921	2.7102	2462817	0.0180	26.508	0.005898
55	0.047676	90193	4300	441124	0.009748	2.7116	2004498	0.0410	22.225	0.009655
60	0.082454	85893	7082	413007	0.017148	2.6763	1563373	0.0491	18.201	0.016969
65	0.130622	78811	10294	369797	0.027838	2.5438	1150366	0.0491	14.597	0.027561
70	0.207069	68516	14188	308520	0.045986	2.5992	780568	0.0491	11.392	0.045549
75	0.313834	54329	17050	229623	0.074253	2.5355	472049	0.0491	8.689	0.073581
80	0.458485	37278	17092	144317	0.118431	2.5382	242426	0.0491	6.503	0.117122
85+	*1.000000	20187	20187	98109	0.205759	4.8600	98109	0.0491	4.860	0.201636

TABLE 4 — OBSERVED AND PROJECTED VITAL RATES

	OBSERVED POPULATION BOTH SEXES	MALES	FEMALES	PROJECTED POPULATION 1968 MALES	FEMALES	1973 MALES	FEMALES	1978 MALES	FEMALES	STABLE POPULATION MALES	FEMALES
RATES PER THOUSAND											
Birth	21.93	22.43	21.42	23.59	22.57	25.85	24.76	26.41	25.34	24.34	23.84
Death	6.02	6.31	5.73	7.13	6.43	7.74	6.97	8.14	7.41	8.26	7.77
Increase	15.91	16.12	15.69	16.46	16.13	18.11	17.79	18.26	17.93		16.078
PERCENTAGE											
under 15	33.77	34.33	33.20	31.46	30.43	30.71	29.69	31.68	30.54	31.50	31.01
15-64	60.70	60.36	61.05	62.09	62.77	61.75	62.68	59.86	60.71	60.87	60.66
65 and over	5.53	5.31	5.75	6.45	6.80	7.55	7.64	8.46	8.75	7.63	8.33
DEP. RATIO X 100	64.74	65.67	63.80	61.06	59.32	61.96	59.55	67.06	64.71	64.29	64.8

Jewish Population

TABLE 5 — POPULATION PROJECTED WITH FIXED AGE-SPECIFIC BIRTH AND DEATH RATES (IN 1000's)

AGE AT LAST BIRTHDAY	1968 BOTH SEXES	MALES	FEMALES	1973 BOTH SEXES	MALES	FEMALES	1978 BOTH SEXES	MALES	FEMALES	AGE AT LAST BIRTHDAY
0-4	242	125	117	283	146	137	327	169	158	0-4
5-9	230	118	112	242	125	117	283	146	137	5-9
10-14	237	122	115	230	118	112	241	124	117	10-14
15-19	245	126	119	237	122	115	229	117	112	15-19
20-24	201	104	97	244	125	119	236	121	115	20-24
25-29	137	70	67	200	104	96	243	125	118	25-29
30-34	136	68	68	136	69	67	199	103	96	30-34
35-39	130	63	67	136	68	68	135	69	66	35-39
40-44	132	62	70	130	63	67	134	67	67	40-44
45-49	127	64	63	130	61	69	128	62	66	45-49
50-54	110	53	57	125	63	62	127	60	67	50-54
55-59	122	62	60	106	51	55	119	60	59	55-59
60-64	92	49	43	113	57	56	99	47	52	60-64
65-69	67	34	33	81	42	39	100	50	50	65-69
70-74	41	20	21	55	27	28	66	34	32	70-74
75-79	25	12	13	30	15	15	41	20	21	75-79
80-84	13	6	7	15	7	8	19	9	10	80-84
85+	7	3	4	9	4	5	10	5	5	85+
TOTAL	2294	1161	1133	2502	1267	1235	2736	1388	1348	TOTAL

TABLE 6 — STANDARDIZED RATES

STANDARD COUNTRIES:	ENGLAND AND WALES 1961 BOTH SEXES	MALES	FEMALES	UNITED STATES 1960 BOTH SEXES	MALES	FEMALES	MEXICO 1960 BOTH SEXES	MALES	FEMALES
STANDARDIZED RATES PER THOUSAND									
Birth	21.19	23.88*	19.82	21.52	22.21*	20.47	24.94	21.37*	24.01
Death	10.87	9.81*	12.03	8.71	8.27*	8.78	4.48	6.10*	4.19
Increase	10.32	14.07*	7.79	12.81	13.94*	11.68	20.45	15.27*	19.82

TABLE 7 — MOMENTS AND CUMULANTS

	OBSERVED POP. MALES	FEMALES	STATIONARY POP. MALES	FEMALES	STABLE POP. MALES	FEMALES	OBSERVED BIRTHS	NET MATERNITY FUNCTION	BIRTHS IN STABLE POP.
μ	28.82263	29.33205	37.80862	38.51684	29.85191	30.34254	27.66460	27.85520	27.30190
σ^2	427.4658	429.2894	523.9658	536.9693	456.7753	469.9952	34.56763	33.31345	31.34949
κ_3	4643.326	4552.364	2314.752	2136.846	5639.587	5770.909	113.2487	123.0593	120.9063
κ_4	−144376.	−136523.	−272823.	−294115.	−125592.	−139875.	−65.129	75.799	197.455
β_1	0.276029	0.261953	0.037248	0.029492	0.333724	0.320781	0.310497	0.409610	0.474467
β_2	2.209879	2.259191	2.006253	1.979958	2.398054	2.366782	2.945495	3.068301	3.200912
κ	−0.097079	−0.096818	−0.014049	−0.010969	−0.128332	−0.121856	−0.243042	−0.312601	−0.392315

TABLE 8 — RATES FROM AGE DISTRIBUTIONS AND VITAL STATISTICS (Females)

VITAL STATISTICS		THOMPSON AGE RANGE	NRR	1000r	INTERVAL	BOURGEOIS-PICHAT AGE RANGE	NRR	1000b	1000d	1000r	COALE
GRR	1.614										IBR
NRR	1.558	0-4	1.53	15.77	27.44	5-29	2.37	31.20	−0.68	31.89	IDR
TFR	3.344	5-9	1.72	19.99	27.41	30-54	1.14	15.95	11.21	4.74	IRI
GENERATION	27.576	10-14	1.78	20.73	27.35	55-79	3.33	132.31	87.78	44.54	K1
SEX RATIO	107.201	15-19	1.52	14.55	27.26	*20-44	1.01	13.61	13.20	0.41	K2

TABLE 9 — LESLIE MATRIX AND ITS SPECTRAL COMPONENTS (Females)

Start Age Interval	ORIGINAL MATRIX SUB-DIAGONAL	ALTERNATIVE FIRST ROWS Projection	Integral	FIRST STABLE MATRIX % IN STABLE POPULATION	FISHER VALUES	REPRODUCTIVE VALUES	SECOND STABLE MATRIX Z₂ FIRST COLUMN	FIRST ROW
0	0.99648	0.00000	0.00000	11.216	1.064	119598	0.1757+0.0701	0.1757+0.0701
5	0.99875	0.00000	0.00000	10.312	1.157	133515	0.1552−0.1467	0.0092+0.1672
0	0.99809	0.04146	0.00000	9.502	1.256	149533	−0.0767−0.2293	−0.1306+0.0695
5	0.99715	0.28477	0.08648	8.750	1.319	127841	−0.2718−0.0304	−0.1116−0.0818
0	0.99710	0.48892	0.50787	8.050	1.130	75752	−0.1604+0.2642	−0.0260−0.1401
5	0.99644	0.40511	0.51156	7.405	0.707	48464	0.1946+0.2900	0.0166−0.1074
0	0.99436	0.23148	0.33308	6.808	0.337	22811	0.3896−0.0616	0.0210−0.0551
5	0.99181	0.09368	0.14971	6.246	0.119	8374	0.1217−0.4275	0.0114−0.0200
0	0.98726	0.02641	0.04570	5.715	0.030	1918	−0.3783−0.3263	0.0038−0.0049
5	0.97762	0.00454	0.00941	5.206	0.004	262	−0.5093+0.2304	0.0007−0.0007
0	0.96248	0.00002	0.00004	4.696	0.000	1	−0.0057+0.6193	0.0000−0.0000
5+	0.80306			16.094				

TABLE 10 — AGE ANALYSIS AND MISCELLANEOUS RESULTS (Females)

Start Age Interval	OBSERVED POPUL. (IN 100's)	CONTRIBUTIONS OF ROOTS (IN 100's) r₁	r₂, r₃	r₄-r₁₁	AGE-SP. BIRTH RATES	NET MATERNITY FUNCTION	COEFF. OF MATRIX EQUATION	PARAMETERS	INTEGRAL	MATRIX	EXP. INCREASE x	$e^{(x+2\frac{1}{2})r}$
0	1124	1189	−73	9	0.0000	0.0000	0.0000	L(1)	1.08371	1.08387	0	1.0410
5	1154	1093	73	−13	0.0000	0.0000	0.0000	L(2)	0.36725	0.37120	50	2.3260
0	1191	1007	164	20	0.0000	0.0000	0.0413			0.83055	0.80048	55	2.5207
5	969	928	62	−20	0.0170	0.0825	0.2829	R(1)	0.01608	0.01611	60	2.7317
0	670	853	−150	−33	0.0997	0.4832	0.4843	R(2)	−0.01928	−0.02503	65	2.9604
5	685	785	−222	122	0.1004	0.4853	0.4001			0.23089	0.22732	70	3.2082
0	678	722	−19	−25	0.0654	0.3149	0.2278	C(1)		10601	75	3.4768
5	701	662	265	−225	0.0294	0.1407	0.0917	C(2)		−7641	80	3.7678
0	640	606	274	−240	0.0090	0.0426	0.0257			33121	85	4.0832
5	585	552	−75	108	0.0019	0.0087	0.0044	2P/Y	27.2125	27.6406	90	4.4251
0	621	498	−409	532	0.0000	0.0000	0.0000	DELTA	5.8904		95	4.7955
5+	1432	1706									100	5.1970

224 Japan 1939–41

TABLE 1 — DATA

AGE AT LAST BIRTHDAY	POPULATION BOTH SEXES	MALES Number	%	FEMALES Number	%	BIRTHS BY AGE OF MOTHER	BOTH SEXES	DEATHS MALES	FEMALES	AGE AT LAST BIRTHDAY
0	1976310	1002198	2.8	974112	2.7	0	193962	105854	88108	0
1-4	7040661	3560861	9.9	3479800	9.6	0	143581	73392	70189	1-4
5-9	8726954	4409497	12.2	4317457	12.0	0	34837	17581	17256	5-9
10-14	8306208	4190675	11.6	4115533	11.4	194	24636	10824	13812	10-14
15-19	7340636	3682703	10.2	3657933	10.1	42173	59697	29499	30198	15-19
20-24	6047488	3030013	8.4	3017475	8.4	431847	56009	28379	27630	20-24
25-29	5602895	2813826	7.8	2789069	7.7	664110	46899	23508	23391	25-29
30-34	4900522	2485963	6.9	2414559	6.7	507298	37657	18815	18842	30-34
35-39	4377728	2240113	6.2	2137615	5.9	315626	35683	18026	17657	35-39
40-44	3793397	1957943	5.4	1835454	5.1	122438	35360	19061	16299	40-44
45-49	3168412	1631437	4.5	1536975	4.3	12552	37657	21920	15737	45-49
50-54	2853094	1441031	4.0	1412063	3.9	2003	47876	28331	19545	50-54
55-59	2527994	1226108	3.4	1301886	3.6	0	60384	35766	24618	55-59
60-64	2199353	1036577	2.9	1162776	3.2	0	76428	44660	31768	60-64
65-69	1533161	693141	1.9	840020	2.3	0	78655	43510	35145	65-69
70-74	979414	415195	1.1	564219	1.6		80250	40599	39651	70-74
75-79	538315	213252	0.6	325063	0.9		66062	30277	35785	75-79
80-84	250338	89562	0.2	160776	0.4	1074488 M.	47710	19228	28482	80-84
85+	101716	30726	0.1	70990	0.2	1023753 F.	28474	9501	18973	85+
TOTAL	72264596	36150821		36113775		2098241	1191817	618731	573086	TOTAL

TABLE 2 — MALE LIFE TABLE

x	$_nq_x$	l_x	$_nd_x$	$_nL_x$	$_nm_x$	$_na_x$	T_x	r_x	$\dot{e}_x$	$_nM_x$
0	0.099123	100000	9912	93975	0.105478	0.3921	4771219	0.0022	47.712	0.105622
1	0.078041	90088	7031	341444	0.020591	1.3108	4677245	0.0022	51.919	0.020611
5	0.019720	83057	1638	411191	0.003983	2.5000	4335800	0.0012	52.203	0.003987
10	0.012897	81419	1050	404791	0.002594	2.8047	3924609	0.0138	48.202	0.002583
15	0.039489	80369	3174	394429	0.008046	2.6630	3519818	0.0253	43.796	0.008010
20	0.045762	77196	3533	377112	0.009367	2.4904	3125389	0.0179	40.487	0.009366
25	0.040876	73663	3011	360597	0.008350	2.4371	2748276	0.0114	37.309	0.008354
30	0.037127	70652	2623	346634	0.007567	2.4742	2387679	0.0150	33.795	0.007568
35	0.039486	68029	2686	333531	0.008054	2.5382	2041045	0.0156	30.003	0.008047
40	0.047675	65343	3115	319211	0.009759	2.5919	1707514	0.0216	26.132	0.009735
45	0.065257	62227	4061	301475	0.013470	2.6208	1388303	0.0168	22.310	0.013436
50	0.094025	58167	5469	277811	0.019687	2.6191	1086828	0.0083	18.685	0.019660
55	0.136367	52697	7186	246234	0.029184	2.5992	809017	0.0030	15.352	0.029170
60	0.195318	45511	8889	205913	0.043170	2.5653	562783	0.0128	12.366	0.043084
65	0.272267	36622	9971	158511	0.062904	2.5329	356870	0.0128	9.745	0.062772
70	0.392557	26651	10462	106769	0.097988	2.4684	198359	0.0128	7.443	0.097783
75	0.517748	16189	8382	58913	0.142274	2.3715	91590	0.0128	5.658	0.141977
80	0.677791	7807	5292	24585	0.215241	2.2690	32677	0.0128	4.185	0.214690
85+	*1.000000	2516	2516	8092	0.310872	3.2168	8092	0.0128	3.217	0.309217

TABLE 3 — FEMALE LIFE TABLE

x	$_nq_x$	l_x	$_nd_x$	$_nL_x$	$_nm_x$	$_na_x$	T_x	r_x	$\dot{e}_x$	$_nM_x$
0	0.085715	100000	8572	94899	0.090323	0.4049	5053806	0.0024	50.538	0.090450
1	0.076515	91428	6996	347155	0.020151	1.3471	4958907	0.0024	54.238	0.020170
5	0.019778	84433	1670	417989	0.003995	2.5000	4611752	0.0005	54.620	0.003997
10	0.016705	82763	1383	410699	0.003366	2.7466	4193762	0.0119	50.672	0.003356
15	0.040626	81380	3306	399076	0.008285	2.6331	3783064	0.0237	46.486	0.008255
20	0.044756	78074	3494	381584	0.009157	2.4853	3383988	0.0182	43.343	0.009157
25	0.041036	74580	3060	365090	0.008383	2.4484	3002404	0.0139	40.258	0.008387
30	0.038262	71519	2736	350698	0.007803	2.4790	2637314	0.0186	36.876	0.007803
35	0.040489	68783	2785	336980	0.008264	2.5100	2286615	0.0192	33.244	0.008260
40	0.043493	65998	2870	322892	0.008890	2.5271	1949635	0.0240	29.541	0.008880
45	0.050029	63128	3158	307981	0.010255	2.5757	1626743	0.0155	25.769	0.010239
50	0.067002	59969	4018	290198	0.013846	2.5986	1318762	0.0026	21.991	0.013841
55	0.090449	55951	5061	267630	0.018909	2.6039	1028565	0.0000	18.383	0.018909
60	0.128532	50891	6541	238807	0.027391	2.6081	760935	0.0154	14.952	0.027321
65	0.190650	44349	8455	201493	0.041963	2.6045	522127	0.0154	11.773	0.041838
70	0.300425	35894	10784	153006	0.070478	2.5457	320634	0.0154	8.933	0.070276
75	0.431020	25111	10823	98044	0.110392	2.4583	167629	0.0154	6.676	0.110086
80	0.602949	14287	8615	48490	0.177659	2.3754	69585	0.0154	4.870	0.177153
85+	1.000000	5673	5673	21095	0.268915	3.7186	21095	0.0154	3.719	0.267262

TABLE 4 — OBSERVED AND PROJECTED VITAL RATES

	OBSERVED POPULATION BOTH SEXES	MALES	FEMALES	PROJECTED POPULATION 1945 MALES	FEMALES	1950 MALES	FEMALES	1955 MALES	FEMALES	STABLE POPULATION MALES	FEMAL
RATES PER THOUSAND											
Birth	29.04	29.72	28.35	30.45	29.06	31.30	29.89	31.66	30.26	29.81	28.6
Death	16.49	17.12	15.87	17.21	15.95	17.38	16.15	17.43	16.23	17.94	16.7
Increase	12.54	12.61	12.48	13.24	13.11	13.92	13.74	14.23	14.03		11.864
PERCENTAGE											
under 15	36.05	36.41	35.68	35.13	34.26	34.50	33.55	34.99	33.96	34.22	33.3
15-64	59.24	59.60	58.89	60.69	59.99	61.35	60.66	60.97	60.41	61.25	60.3
65 and over	4.71	3.99	5.43	4.18	5.74	4.14	5.79	4.04	5.63	4.53	6.2
DEP. RATIO X 100	68.80	67.79	69.82	64.78	66.68	62.99	64.85	64.03	65.53	63.27	65.7

AGE AT LAST BIRTHDAY	1945 BOTH SEXES	MALES	FEMALES	1950 BOTH SEXES	MALES	FEMALES	1955 BOTH SEXES	MALES	FEMALES	AGE AT LAST BIRTHDAY	
0-4	9630	4895	4735	10558	5367	5191	11528	5860	5668	0-4	
5-9	8520	4309	4211	9101	4623	4478	9977	5068	4909	5-9	
10-14	8583	4341	4242	8380	4242	4138	8950	4551	4399	10-14	
15-19	8082	4083	3999	8352	4230	4122	8154	4133	4021	15-19	TABLE 5
20-24	7019	3521	3498	7728	3904	3824	7985	4044	3941	20-24	POPULATION
25-29	5784	2897	2887	6713	3367	3346	7391	3733	3658	25-29	PROJECTED
30-34	5384	2705	2679	5558	2785	2773	6451	3236	3215	30-34	WITH
35-39	4712	2392	2320	5177	2603	2574	5345	2680	2665	35-39	FIXED
40-44	4192	2144	2048	4512	2289	2223	4958	2491	2467	40-44	AGE—
45-49	3600	1849	1751	3979	2025	1954	4282	2162	2120	45-49	SPECIFIC
50-54	2951	1503	1448	3354	1704	1650	3707	1866	1841	50-54	BIRTH
55-59	2579	1277	1302	2668	1332	1336	3031	1510	1521	55-59	AND
60-64	2187	1025	1162	2230	1068	1162	2306	1114	1192	60-64	DEATH
65-69	1779	798	981	1769	789	980	1802	822	980	65-69	RATES
70-74	1105	467	638	1282	537	745	1276	532	744	70-74	(IN 1000's)
75-79	591	229	362	667	258	409	774	297	477	75-79	
80-84	250	89	161	275	96	179	310	108	202	80-84	
85+	99	29	70	99	29	70	109	31	78	85+	
TOTAL	77047	38553	38494	82402	41248	41154	88336	44238	44098	TOTAL	

STANDARD COUNTRIES:	ENGLAND AND WALES 1961 BOTH SEXES	MALES	FEMALES	UNITED STATES 1960 BOTH SEXES	MALES	FEMALES	MEXICO 1960 BOTH SEXES	MALES	FEMALES	TABLE 6
STANDARDIZED RATES PER THOUSAND										STANDAR-DIZED
Birth	26.57	27.31*	25.13	26.97	25.21*	25.93	27.72	25.70*	26.98	RATES
Death	24.18	33.56*	24.11	21.56	27.48*	20.24	16.09	17.63*	15.02	
Increase	2.40	-6.25*	1.01	5.41	-2.26*	5.69	11.62	8.07*	11.96	

	OBSERVED POP. MALES	FEMALES	STATIONARY POP. MALES	FEMALES	STABLE POP. MALES	FEMALES	OBSERVED BIRTHS	NET MATERNITY FUNCTION	BIRTHS IN STABLE POP.	TABLE 7
μ	26.18418	27.05187	32.17921	33.84406	27.28055	28.42503	30.00046	30.66357	30.19314	MOMENTS
σ^2	372.7114	407.2548	435.0972	482.0639	387.7625	427.6605	36.04603	38.09115	37.02465	AND
κ_3	4989.119	5893.959	3177.702	3530.733	4635.615	5418.505	92.5650	85.9954	93.5448	CUMULANTS
κ_4	-54248.	-63591.	-163165.	-212584.	-80132.	-101827.	-477.822	-689.719	-571.083	
β_1	0.480762	0.514299	0.122593	0.111280	0.368568	0.375372	0.182945	0.133807	0.172412	
β_2	2.609487	2.616588	2.138104	2.085212	2.467067	2.443242	2.632251	2.524638	2.583402	
κ	-0.189096	-0.196792	-0.047265	-0.041530	-0.144731	-0.143576	-0.113190	-0.077868	-0.101363	

VITAL STATISTICS		THOMPSON AGE RANGE	NRR	1000r	INTERVAL	BOURGEOIS-PICHAT AGE RANGE	NRR	1000b	1000d	1000r	COALE		TABLE 8
GRR	2.017										IBR	32.06	RATES FROM AGE DISTRI-BUTIONS
NRR	1.435	0-4	1.37	11.89	26.92	5-29	1.57	33.24	16.44	16.80	IDR	16.47	AND VITAL STATISTICS
TFR	4.134	5-9	1.55	16.58	26.88	30-54	1.66	34.93	16.25	18.68	IRI	15.59	(Females)
GENERATION	30.427	10-14	1.63	17.96	26.85	55-79	1.70	43.60	23.87	19.72	K1	0.	
SEX RATIO	104.956	15-19	1.62	16.01	26.74	*25-49	1.76	37.79	16.92	20.86	K2	0.	

Start of Age Interval	ORIGINAL MATRIX SUB-DIAGONAL	ALTERNATIVE FIRST ROWS Projection	Integral	FIRST STABLE MATRIX % IN STABLE POPULATION	FISHER VALUES	REPRODUCTIVE VALUES	SECOND STABLE MATRIX Z₂ FIRST COLUMN	FIRST ROW	TABLE 9
0	0.94556	0.00000	0.00000	12.283	1.165	5186948	0.1470+0.0578	0.1470+0.0578	LESLIE
5	0.98256	0.00005	0.00000	10.945	1.307	5642932	0.1347-0.0991	0.0277+0.1467	MATRIX
10	0.97170	0.01213	0.00010	10.134	1.412	5809277	-0.0134-0.1834	-0.0994+0.0923	AND ITS
15	0.95617	0.16001	0.02562	9.279	1.527	5585724	-0.1766-0.0939	-0.1224-0.0329	SPECTRAL
20	0.95678	0.40002	0.31797	8.361	1.500	4525809	-0.1857+0.1065	-0.0595-0.1228	COMPO-NENTS
25	0.96058	0.47443	0.52903	7.538	1.177	3281769	-0.0094+0.2291	0.0060-0.1322	(Females)
30	0.96088	0.37958	0.46679	6.823	0.725	1749882	0.2032+0.1397	0.0345-0.0893	
35	0.95819	0.22816	0.32805	6.178	0.340	727506	0.2436-0.1049	0.0293-0.0399	
40	0.95382	0.08034	0.14821	5.579	0.100	182837	0.0439-0.2811	0.0110-0.0105	
45	0.94226	0.01025	0.01814	5.014	0.013	19577	-0.2291-0.1995	0.0014-0.0014	
50	0.92223	0.00153	0.00315	4.452	0.002	2371	-0.3067+0.0925	0.0002-0.0002	
55+	0.75507			13.413					

Start Age Interval	OBSERVED POPUL. (IN 100's)	CONTRIBUTIONS OF ROOTS (IN 100's) r_1	r_2, r_3	$r_4\cdot r_{11}$	AGE-SP. BIRTH RATES	NET MATERNITY FUNCTION	COEFF. OF MATRIX EQUATION	PARAMETERS INTEGRAL	MATRIX	EXP. INCREASE x	$e^{(x+8\frac12)r}$	TABLE 10
0	44539	46635	-1530	-566	0.0000	0.0000	0.0000	L(1) 1.06112	1.06120	0	1.0301	AGE ANALYSIS
5	43175	41553	722	900	0.0000	0.0000	0.0000	L(2) 0.47542	0.47572	50	1.8643	AND MISCEL-LANEOUS
10	41155	38474	2626	55	0.0000	0.0001	0.0113	0.77583	0.75614	55	1.9783	RESULTS (Females)
15	36579	35229	2179	-829	0.0056	0.0224	0.1444	R(1) 0.01186	0.01188	60	2.0992	
20	30175	31743	-574	-994	0.0698	0.2665	0.3453	R(2) -0.01888	-0.02256	65	2.2275	
25	27891	28619	-3152	2424	0.1162	0.4242	0.3918	0.20421	0.20184	70	2.3636	
30	24146	25906	-2949	1189	0.1025	0.3595	0.3011	C(1)	379657	75	2.5081	
35	21376	23457	267	-2348	0.0720	0.2428	0.1739	C(2)	-245712	80	2.6614	
40	18355	21180	3708	-6533	0.0325	0.1051	0.0587		697943	85	2.8240	
45	15370	19037	3910	-7577	0.0040	0.0123	0.0071	2P/Y 30.7689	31.1288	90	2.9966	
50	14121	16903	217	-2999	0.0007	0.0020	0.0010	DELTA 3.3671		95	3.1798	
55+	44257	50922								100	3.3741	

TABLE 1 — DATA

AGE AT LAST BIRTHDAY	POPULATION BOTH SEXES	MALES Number	%	FEMALES Number	%	BIRTHS BY AGE OF MOTHER	DEATHS BOTH SEXES	MALES	FEMALES	AGE AT LAST BIRTHDAY
0	2183417	1115917	2.7	1067500	2.5	0	120856	65737	55119	0
1-4	9677833	4933583	11.9	4744250	11.1	0	73831	37792	36039	1-4
5-9	8983084	4554917	11.0	4428167	10.3	0	17228	9267	7961	5-9
10-14	8797917	4446500	10.8	4351417	10.1	29	9038	4585	4453	10-14
15-19	8683583	4383583	10.6	4300000	10.0	46721	17278	8932	8346	15-19
20-24	7833833	3889250	9.4	3944583	9.2	569236	28536	14991	13545	20-24
25-29	6444000	2989167	7.2	3454833	8.0	760788	27354	13370	13984	25-29
30-34	5176250	2318917	5.6	2857333	6.7	467296	22481	10479	12002	30-34
35-39	5106500	2394500	5.8	2712000	6.3	243287	24126	11854	12272	35-39
40-44	4644000	2255083	5.5	2388917	5.6	69241	26807	14220	12587	40-44
45-49	3944500	1994667	4.8	1949833	4.5	3286	31264	17647	13617	45-49
50-54	3480583	1763833	4.3	1716750	4.0	206	38800	22447	16353	50-54
55-59	2823917	1418417	3.4	1405500	3.3	31	47220	27895	19325	55-59
60-64	2338666	1130833	2.7	1207833	2.8	0	59579	34390	25189	60-64
65-69	1740333	783833	1.9	956500	2.2	0	73140	39834	33306	65-69
70-74	1280834	541167	1.3	739667	1.7		82545	41594	40951	70-74
75-79	737500	288667	0.7	448833	1.0		69704	31685	38019	75-79
80-84	294884	106018	0.3	188866	0.4	1108606 M.	42027	16723	25304	80-84
85+	88200	25899	0.1	62301	0.1	1051515 F.	24502	8166	16336	85+
TOTAL	84259834	41334751		42925083		2160121	836316	431608	404708	TOTAL

TABLE 2 — MALE LIFE TABLE

x	$_nq_x$	l_x	$_nd_x$	$_nL_x$	$_nm_x$	$_na_x$	T_x	r_x	$\mathring{e}_x$	$_nM_x$	x
0	0.056760	100000	5676	96353	0.058908	0.3574	5941733	0.0000	59.417	0.058908	0
1	0.030005	94324	2830	369467	0.007660	1.2337	5845380	0.0000	61.971	0.007660	1
5	0.009962	91494	911	455190	0.002002	2.5000	5475913	0.0277	59.850	0.002035	5
10	0.005143	90582	466	451748	0.001031	2.5024	5020723	0.0024	55.427	0.001031	10
15	0.010175	90117	917	448550	0.002044	2.7830	4568975	0.0112	50.701	0.002038	15
20	0.019184	89200	1711	441933	0.003872	2.6243	4120425	0.0347	46.193	0.003854	20
25	0.022151	87488	1938	432639	0.004479	2.5216	3678492	0.0473	42.046	0.004473	25
30	0.022352	85550	1912	422994	0.004521	2.5117	3245854	0.0176	37.941	0.004519	30
35	0.024458	83638	2046	413208	0.004951	2.5637	2822860	0.0000	33.751	0.004951	35
40	0.031107	81593	2538	401907	0.006315	2.6139	2409652	0.0118	29.533	0.006306	40
45	0.043426	79055	3433	387138	0.008868	2.6305	2007745	0.0155	25.397	0.008847	45
50	0.061995	75622	4688	367067	0.012772	2.6449	1620607	0.0208	21.430	0.012726	50
55	0.094364	70933	6694	338869	0.019753	2.6398	1253540	0.0241	17.672	0.019666	55
60	0.142914	64240	9181	299465	0.030657	2.6326	914672	0.0405	14.238	0.030411	60
65	0.227709	55059	12537	244909	0.051192	2.5764	615207	0.0405	11.174	0.050820	65
70	0.323984	42522	13776	178129	0.077339	2.4972	370298	0.0405	8.708	0.076860	70
75	0.429797	28745	12355	111887	0.110420	2.4229	192169	0.0405	6.685	0.109763	75
80	0.561531	16391	9204	57867	0.159052	2.3830	80282	0.0405	4.898	0.157738	80
85+	*1.000000	7187	7187	22415	0.320628	3.1189	22415	0.0405	3.119	0.315302	85

TABLE 3 — FEMALE LIFE TABLE

x	$_nq_x$	l_x	$_nd_x$	$_nL_x$	$_nm_x$	$_na_x$	T_x	r_x	$\mathring{e}_x$	$_nM_x$	x
0	0.050008	100000	5001	96851	0.051634	0.3702	6274724	0.0000	62.747	0.051634	0
1	0.029766	94999	2828	372246	0.007596	1.2590	6177873	0.0000	65.031	0.007596	1
5	0.008802	92172	811	458829	0.001768	2.5000	5805627	0.0260	62.987	0.001798	5
10	0.005104	91360	466	455650	0.001023	2.5307	5346797	0.0015	58.524	0.001023	10
15	0.009682	90894	880	452493	0.001945	2.7534	4891148	0.0078	53.812	0.001941	15
20	0.017070	90014	1537	446415	0.003442	2.6213	4438655	0.0186	49.311	0.003434	20
25	0.020060	88477	1775	438005	0.004052	2.5313	3992240	0.0283	45.122	0.004048	25
30	0.020795	86702	1803	429031	0.004202	2.5146	3554235	0.0200	40.993	0.004200	30
35	0.022391	84900	1901	419820	0.004528	2.5397	3125204	0.0133	36.811	0.004525	35
40	0.026082	82999	2165	409765	0.005283	2.5851	2705384	0.0275	32.596	0.005269	40
45	0.034456	80834	2785	397515	0.007006	2.6109	2295619	0.0259	28.399	0.006984	45
50	0.046726	78049	3647	381581	0.009557	2.6249	1898104	0.0229	24.320	0.009526	50
55	0.066812	74402	4971	360269	0.013798	2.6383	1516523	0.0209	20.383	0.013750	55
60	0.100067	69431	6948	330855	0.020999	2.6541	1156254	0.0345	16.653	0.020855	60
65	0.161787	62483	10109	288371	0.035055	2.6215	825399	0.0345	13.210	0.034821	65
70	0.245193	52374	12842	230553	0.055700	2.5613	537029	0.0345	10.254	0.055364	70
75	0.351283	39532	13887	162961	0.085217	2.5012	306476	0.0345	7.753	0.084706	75
80	0.503868	25645	12922	95679	0.135053	2.4812	143515	0.0345	5.596	0.133979	80
85+	*1.000000	12723	12723	47836	0.265983	3.7596	47836	0.0345	3.760	0.262211	85

TABLE 4 — OBSERVED AND PROJECTED VITAL RATES

	OBSERVED POPULATION BOTH SEXES	MALES	FEMALES	PROJECTED POPULATION 1956 MALES	FEMALES	1961 MALES	FEMALES	1966 MALES	FEMALES	STABLE POPULATION MALES	FEMALES
RATES PER THOUSAND											
Birth	25.64	26.82	24.50	27.39	25.17	27.15	25.10	26.28	24.42	24.26	23.3
Death	9.93	10.44	9.43	10.46	9.54	10.70	9.81	10.84	9.95	12.91	11.9
Increase	15.71	16.38	15.07	16.93	15.63	16.46	15.29	15.45	14.47		11.346.
PERCENTAGE											
under 15	35.18	36.41	33.99	35.36	32.98	35.15	32.81	33.00	30.90	30.64	29.7
15-64	59.90	59.36	60.43	60.13	61.20	60.16	61.30	62.07	63.04	62.82	61.9
65 and over	4.92	4.22	5.58	4.51	5.82	4.70	5.89	4.93	6.06	6.54	8.3
DEP. RATIO X 100	66.93	68.45	65.49	66.30	63.41	66.23	63.13	61.10	58.63	59.18	61.4

AGE AT LAST BIRTHDAY	BOTH SEXES	1956 MALES	FEMALES	BOTH SEXES	1961 MALES	FEMALES	BOTH SEXES	1966 MALES	FEMALES	AGE AT LAST BIRTHDAY	
0-4	10650	5447	5203	11631	5949	5682	12345	6314	6031	0-4	
5-9	11596	5911	5685	10411	5322	5089	11371	5813	5558	5-9	
10-14	8917	4520	4397	11512	5867	5645	10335	5282	5053	10-14	
15-19	8736	4415	4321	8855	4488	4367	11431	5825	5606	15-19	**TABLE 5**
20-24	8561	4319	4242	8613	4350	4263	8730	4422	4308	20-24	POPULATION
25-29	7677	3807	3870	8390	4228	4162	8441	4258	4183	25-29	PROJECTED
30-34	6307	2923	3384	7514	3723	3791	8211	4134	4077	30-34	WITH
35-39	5061	2265	2796	6166	2855	3311	7346	3636	3710	35-39	FIXED
40-44	4976	2329	2647	4932	2203	2729	6009	2777	3232	40-44	AGE—
45-49	4489	2172	2317	4811	2243	2568	4769	2122	2647	45-49	SPECIFIC
50-54	3763	1891	1872	4285	2060	2225	4592	2127	2465	50-54	BIRTH
55-59	3249	1628	1621	3513	1746	1767	4001	1901	2100	55-59	AND
60-64	2544	1253	1291	2928	1439	1489	3166	1543	1623	60-64	DEATH
65-69	1978	925	1053	2150	1025	1125	2474	1177	1297	65-69	RATES
70-74	1335	570	765	1515	673	842	1645	746	899	70-74	(IN 1000's)
75-79	863	340	523	899	358	541	1018	423	595	75-79	
80-84	413	149	264	483	176	307	502	185	317	80-84	
85+	135	41	94	190	58	132	221	68	153	85+	
TOTAL	91250	44905	46345	98798	48763	50035	106607	52753	53854	TOTAL	

STANDARD COUNTRIES:	ENGLAND AND WALES 1961			UNITED STATES 1960			MEXICO 1960			
STANDARDIZED RATES PER THOUSAND	BOTH SEXES	MALES	FEMALES	BOTH SEXES	MALES	FEMALES	BOTH SEXES	MALES	FEMALES	**TABLE 6**
Birth	20.97	25.82*	19.78	21.32	23.33*	20.45	23.19	24.42*	22.52	STANDAR-
Death	16.76	19.97*	17.03	14.33	16.43*	13.48	9.14	10.58*	8.37	DIZED
Increase	4.21	5.86*	2.75	6.99	6.91*	6.97	14.05	13.83*	14.15	RATES

	OBSERVED POP.		STATIONARY POP.		STABLE POP.		OBSERVED BIRTHS	NET MATERNITY FUNCTION	BIRTHS IN STABLE POP.	
	MALES	FEMALES	MALES	FEMALES	MALES	FEMALES				
μ	26.07094	27.26921	34.82915	36.43339	29.70509	30.87462	28.68787	29.41828	29.04509	**TABLE 7**
σ^2	384.6889	403.6359	471.0603	510.7781	428.5453	464.6011	29.82363	31.26814	30.34039	MOMENTS
κ_3	5246.100	5572.549	2713.890	2794.124	4619.595	5148.236	91.9037	79.9044	83.4633	AND
κ_4	-63053.	-60760.	-207530.	-255240.	-123199.	-152047.	-199.599	-352.608	-264.570	CUMULANTS
β_1	0.483442	0.472214	0.070462	0.058586	0.271155	0.264287	0.318408	0.208851	0.249418	
β_2	2.573926	2.627064	2.065652	2.021673	2.329170	2.295602	2.775593	2.639348	2.712593	
κ	-0.184372	-0.190126	-0.026991	-0.021894	-0.105056	-0.100313	-0.186378	-0.124052	-0.152244	

VITAL STATISTICS		THOMPSON				BOURGEOIS-PICHAT				COALE		**TABLE 8**
		AGE RANGE	NRR	1000r	INTERVAL	AGE RANGE	NRR	1000b	1000d	1000r		RATES FROM AGE DISTRI-
GRR	1.605											BUTIONS
NRR	1.393	0-4	1.64	18.50	27.22	5-29	1.30	24.98	15.35	9.62	IBR 27.17	AND VITAL
TFR	3.297	5-9	1.42	12.94	27.17	30-54	1.77	32.15	10.95	21.20	IDR 11.35	STATISTICS
GENERATION	29.231	10-14	1.57	16.37	27.11	55-79	1.45	19.85	6.20	13.65	IRI 15.82	(Females)
SEX RATIO	105.429	15-19	1.75	16.17	27.01	*45-69	1.71	29.25	9.42	19.83	K1 -3.64	
											K2 0.	

Start Age Interval	ORIGINAL MATRIX			FIRST STABLE MATRIX			SECOND STABLE MATRIX Z_2		
	SUB-DIAGONAL	ALTERNATIVE FIRST ROWS Projection	Integral	% IN STABLE POPULATION	FISHER VALUES	REPRODUCTIVE VALUES	FIRST COLUMN	FIRST ROW	
0	0.97811	0.00000	0.00000	10.646	1.096	6371489	0.1603+0.0564	0.1603+0.0564	**TABLE 9**
5	0.99307	0.00001	0.00000	9.838	1.186	5253407	0.1390-0.1226	0.0266+0.1535	LESLIE
10	0.99307	0.01233	0.00002	9.230	1.264	5502216	-0.0433-0.2006	-0.1093+0.0886	MATRIX
15	0.98657	0.17496	0.02552	8.660	1.334	5736646	-0.2174-0.0666	-0.1200-0.0478	AND ITS
20	0.98116	0.41145	0.33901	8.072	1.237	4879054	-0.1806+0.1730	-0.0437-0.1264	SPECTRAL
25	0.97951	0.43432	0.51731	7.482	0.875	3021566	-0.0688+0.2649	0.0141-0.1149	COMPO-
30	0.97853	0.28695	0.38419	6.924	0.459	1311404	0.2892+0.0756	0.0270-0.0651	NENTS
35	0.97605	0.13472	0.21074	6.401	0.175	474499	0.2261-0.2352	0.0172-0.0240	(Females)
40	0.97010	0.03496	0.06809	5.903	0.038	91753	-0.1033-0.3397	0.0048-0.0048	
45	0.95992	0.00207	0.00396	5.410	0.002	4680	-0.3753-0.0818	0.0003-0.0003	
50	0.94415	0.00018	0.00032	4.907	0.000	474	-0.2725+0.3080	0.0000-0.0000	
55+	0.77818			16.528					

Start Age Interval	OBSERVED POPUL. (IN 100's)	CONTRIBUTIONS OF ROOTS (IN 100's)			AGE-SP. BIRTH RATES	NET MATERNITY FUNCTION	COEFF. OF MATRIX EQUATION	PARAMETERS			EXP. INCREASE		
		r_1	r_2, r_3	r_4-r_{11}					INTEGRAL	MATRIX	x	$e^{(x+2\frac{1}{2})r}$	
0	58118	51388	1399	5330	0.0000	0.0000	0.0000	L(1)	1.05837	1.05845	0	1.0288	**TABLE 10**
5	44282	47488	1294	-4500	0.0000	0.0000	0.0000	L(2)	0.43751	0.43762	50	1.8143	AGE
10	43514	44554	-291	-749	0.0000	0.0000	0.0120		0.80631	0.78267	55	1.9202	ANALYSIS
15	43000	41802	-1902	3100	0.0053	0.0239	0.1688	R(1)	0.01135	0.01136	60	2.0322	AND
20	39446	38963	-1688	2171	0.0702	0.3136	0.3916	R(2)	-0.01725	-0.02180	65	2.1509	MISCEL-
25	34548	36118	487	-2056	0.1072	0.4695	0.4055			0.21473	70	2.2764	LANEOUS
30	28573	33424	2537	-7387	0.0796	0.3416	0.2624	C(1)		482718	75	2.4093	RESULTS
35	27120	30900	2121	-5902	0.0437	0.1833	0.1206	C(2)		444722	80	2.5499	(Females)
40	23889	28495	-759	-3846	0.0141	0.0578	0.0305			23550	85	2.6988	
45	19498	26116	-3300	-3318	0.0008	0.0033	0.0017	2P/Y	29.2610	29.6107	90	2.8563	
50	17168	23685	-2569	-3949	0.0001	0.0002	0.0001	DELTA	7.3345		95	3.0230	
55+	50095	79786									100	3.1995	

TABLE 1 — DATA

AGE AT LAST BIRTHDAY	POPULATION BOTH SEXES	MALES Number	MALES %	FEMALES Number	FEMALES %	BIRTHS BY AGE OF MOTHER	DEATHS BOTH SEXES	DEATHS MALES	DEATHS FEMALES	AGE AT LAST BIRTHDAY
0	1758417	900917	2.1	857500	1.9	0	79731	43551	36180	0
1-4	8215833	4194583	9.7	4021250	9.0	0	40788	21090	19698	1-4
5-9	10290084	5239917	12.1	5050167	11.3	0	15041	8309	6732	5-9
10-14	9602917	4860500	11.2	4742417	10.6	18	6866	3752	3114	10-14
15-19	8640583	4364583	10.1	4276000	9.6	28157	11849	6737	5112	15-19
20-24	8315833	4174250	9.7	4141583	9.3	479585	20720	11832	8888	20-24
25-29	7368000	3611167	8.4	3756833	8.4	694634	20710	11183	9527	25-29
30-34	5833250	2607917	6.0	3225333	7.2	389813	17466	8339	9127	30-34
35-39	4992500	2292500	5.3	2700000	6.0	155970	17606	8609	8997	35-39
40-44	4884000	2314083	5.4	2569917	5.7	39226	21886	11474	10412	40-44
45-49	4226500	2082667	4.8	2143833	4.8	1881	27437	15489	11948	45-49
50-54	3773583	1897833	4.4	1875750	4.2	128	37214	21822	15392	50-54
55-59	3076917	1545417	3.6	1531500	3.4	24	46295	27919	18376	55-59
60-64	2438666	1192833	2.8	1245833	2.8	0	56894	33848	23046	60-64
65-69	1904333	881833	2.0	1022500	2.3	0	70980	39886	31094	65-69
70-74	1354834	575167	1.3	779667	1.7		82416	42239	40177	70-74
75-79	839500	328667	0.8	510833	1.1		78097	36112	41985	75-79
80-84	354032	125360	0.3	228672	0.5	919467 M.	47966	19573	28393	80-84
85+	112052	31557	0.1	80495	0.2	869969 F.	29226	9823	19403	85+
TOTAL	87981834	43221751		44760083		1789436	729188	381587	347601	TOTAL

TABLE 2 — MALE LIFE TABLE

x	nq_x	l_x	nd_x	nL_x	nm_x	na_x	T_x	r_x	$\mathring{e}_x$	nM_x	x
0	0.046836	100000	4684	96886	0.048341	0.3352	6253749	0.0000	62.537	0.048341	0
1	0.019832	95316	1890	375966	0.005028	1.1961	6156863	0.0000	64.594	0.005028	1
5	0.007888	93426	737	465288	0.001584	2.5000	5780897	0.0025	61.877	0.001586	5
10	0.003851	92689	357	462548	0.000772	2.4859	5315609	0.0172	57.349	0.000772	10
15	0.007720	92332	713	460074	0.001549	2.7733	4853061	0.0136	52.561	0.001544	15
20	0.014103	91619	1292	455007	0.002840	2.6091	4392987	0.0163	47.948	0.002835	20
25	0.015382	90327	1389	448188	0.003100	2.5182	3937980	0.0440	43.597	0.003097	25
30	0.015891	88938	1413	441206	0.003203	2.5354	3489792	0.0422	39.239	0.003198	30
35	0.018622	87524	1630	433692	0.003758	2.5886	3048586	0.0081	34.831	0.003755	35
40	0.024522	85895	2106	424507	0.004962	2.6424	2614894	0.0044	30.443	0.004958	40
45	0.036630	83788	3069	411774	0.007453	2.6648	2190387	0.0121	26.142	0.007437	45
50	0.056172	80719	4534	393003	0.011537	2.6638	1778613	0.0179	22.035	0.011498	50
55	0.087085	76185	6635	365333	0.018160	2.6499	1385610	0.0276	18.187	0.018066	55
60	0.133849	69550	9309	325674	0.028585	2.6283	1020276	0.0387	14.670	0.028376	60
65	0.205329	60241	12369	271460	0.045566	2.5952	694603	0.0387	11.530	0.045231	65
70	0.312483	47872	14959	202337	0.073932	2.5251	423143	0.0387	8.839	0.073438	70
75	0.430544	32913	14170	128198	0.110536	2.4336	220806	0.0387	6.709	0.109874	75
80	0.557297	18742	10445	66376	0.157363	2.3829	92608	0.0387	4.941	0.156135	80
85+	*1.000000	8297	8297	26232	0.316299	3.1616	26232	0.0387	3.162	0.311278	85

TABLE 3 — FEMALE LIFE TABLE

x	nq_x	l_x	nd_x	nL_x	nm_x	na_x	T_x	r_x	$\mathring{e}_x$	nM_x	x
0	0.041061	100000	4106	97319	0.042192	0.3471	6649152	0.0000	66.492	0.042192	0
1	0.019330	95894	1854	378414	0.004898	1.2153	6551833	0.0000	68.324	0.004898	1
5	0.006640	94040	624	468640	0.001332	2.5000	6173420	0.0008	65.647	0.001333	5
10	0.003275	93416	306	466300	0.000656	2.4540	5704780	0.0157	61.069	0.000657	10
15	0.005980	93110	557	464299	0.001199	2.7557	5238480	0.0123	56.261	0.001196	15
20	0.010691	92553	989	460416	0.002149	2.6260	4774181	0.0109	51.583	0.002146	20
25	0.012617	91564	1155	454988	0.002539	2.5511	4313765	0.0225	47.112	0.002536	25
30	0.014076	90408	1273	448926	0.002835	2.5524	3858776	0.0302	42.682	0.002830	30
35	0.016551	89136	1475	442092	0.003337	2.5692	3409850	0.0194	38.255	0.003332	35
40	0.020106	87660	1762	434082	0.004060	2.6060	2967758	0.0189	33.855	0.004051	40
45	0.027612	85898	2372	423896	0.005595	2.6417	2533676	0.0257	29.496	0.005573	45
50	0.040412	83526	3375	409676	0.008239	2.6436	2109781	0.0252	25.259	0.008206	50
55	0.058630	80151	4699	389704	0.012058	2.6488	1700104	0.0284	21.211	0.011999	55
60	0.089224	75451	6732	361492	0.018623	2.6583	1310400	0.0337	17.367	0.018498	60
65	0.142833	68719	9815	320484	0.030627	2.6453	948908	0.0337	13.808	0.030410	65
70	0.230504	58904	13578	261766	0.051869	2.5877	628424	0.0337	10.669	0.051531	70
75	0.342694	45326	15533	187896	0.082668	2.5063	366658	0.0337	8.089	0.082189	75
80	0.471459	29793	14046	112538	0.124813	2.5032	178761	0.0337	6.000	0.124165	80
85+	1.000000	15747	15747	66223	0.237787	4.2054	66223	0.0337	4.205	0.241047	85

TABLE 4 — OBSERVED AND PROJECTED VITAL RATES

	OBSERVED POPULATION BOTH SEXES	MALES	FEMALES	PROJECTED POPULATION 1959 MALES	1959 FEMALES	1964 MALES	1964 FEMALES	1969 MALES	1969 FEMALES	STABLE POPULATION MALES	FEMALES
RATES PER THOUSAND											
Birth	20.34	21.27	19.44	21.82	20.00	22.03	20.27	22.21	20.50	18.03	17.06
Death	8.29	8.83	7.77	9.13	8.17	9.56	8.60	9.91	8.93	14.57	13.60
Increase	12.05	12.44	11.67	12.69	11.83	12.47	11.67	12.30	11.57		3.4577
PERCENTAGE											
under 15	33.95	35.16	32.78	32.10	29.82	29.38	27.28	28.01	26.05	24.61	23.4.
15-64	60.86	60.35	61.36	63.04	63.98	65.39	66.21	66.36	67.01	65.66	64.0
65 and over	5.19	4.49	5.86	4.86	6.19	5.23	6.51	5.63	6.94	9.73	12.5.
DEP. RATIO X 100	64.30	65.71	62.96	58.64	56.29	52.94	51.04	50.68	49.22	52.30	56.2

TABLE 1 — DATA

AGE AT LAST BIRTHDAY	POPULATION BOTH SEXES	MALES Number	%	FEMALES Number	%	BIRTHS BY AGE OF MOTHER	DEATHS BOTH SEXES	MALES	FEMALES	AGE AT LAST BIRTHDAY
0	1569044	804245	1.8	764799	1.7	0	62476	34605	27871	0
1-4	6902809	3529802	7.9	3373007	7.3	0	23638	12510	11128	1-4
5-9	11145338	5687694	12.7	5457644	11.8	0	12292	7013	5279	5-9
10-14	9403864	4774856	10.7	4629008	10.0	13	5773	3275	2498	10-14
15-19	8962825	4525676	10.1	4437149	9.6	19967	10388	6078	4310	15-19
20-24	8583290	4292307	9.6	4290983	9.3	446504	17946	10512	7434	20-24
25-29	7880550	3924677	8.8	3955873	8.6	698471	18032	10157	7875	25-29
30-34	6712873	3200408	7.2	3512465	7.6	329265	16793	8692	8101	30-34
35-39	5281272	2351440	5.3	2929832	6.3	109475	15945	7880	8065	35-39
40-44	4973923	2316222	5.2	2657701	5.8	23476	19733	10406	9327	40-44
45-49	4599777	2205067	4.9	2394710	5.2	1217	27538	15469	12069	45-49
50-54	3877065	1929908	4.3	1947157	4.2	82	36068	21446	14622	50-54
55-59	3401068	1700715	3.8	1700353	3.7	17	49178	30166	19012	55-59
60-64	2651827	1303976	2.9	1347851	2.9	0	60146	36635	23511	60-64
65-69	2036130	958383	2.1	1077747	2.3	0	74347	42977	31370	65-69
70-74	1406960	606223	1.4	800737	1.7		85793	44921	40872	70-74
75-79	902214	352508	0.8	549706	1.2		86955	40755	46200	75-79
80-84	419974	147024	0.3	272950	0.6	836679 M.	62263	25630	36633	80-84
85+	148890	44335	0.1	104555	0.2	791808 F.	35060	11720	23340	85+
TOTAL	90859693	44655466		46204227		1628487	720364	380847	339517	TOTAL

TABLE 2 — MALE LIFE TABLE

x	nq_x	l_x	nd_x	nL_x	nm_x	na_x	T_x	r_x	$\overset{\circ}{e}_x$	nM_x	x
0	0.041788	100000	4179	97119	0.043028	0.3106	6383225	0.0000	63.832	0.043028	0
1	0.014035	95821	1345	379468	0.003544	1.1623	6286106	0.0000	65.602	0.003544	1
5	0.006146	94476	581	470930	0.001233	2.5000	5906638	0.0000	62.520	0.001233	5
10	0.003426	93896	322	468684	0.000686	2.5307	5435708	0.0219	57.891	0.000686	10
15	0.006712	93574	628	466469	0.001346	2.7691	4967024	0.0092	53.081	0.001343	15
20	0.012189	92946	1133	462012	0.002452	2.6017	4500556	0.0120	48.421	0.002449	20
25	0.012865	91813	1181	456131	0.002589	2.5164	4038543	0.0268	43.987	0.002588	25
30	0.013528	90632	1226	450158	0.002724	2.5526	3582412	0.0484	39.527	0.002716	30
35	0.016674	89406	1491	443454	0.003362	2.6018	3132254	0.0289	35.034	0.003351	35
40	0.022236	87915	1955	434997	0.004494	2.6580	2688800	0.0017	30.584	0.004493	40
45	0.034586	85960	2973	422900	0.007030	2.6788	2253804	0.0110	26.219	0.007015	45
50	0.054311	82987	4507	404446	0.011144	2.6726	1830904	0.0144	22.063	0.011112	50
55	0.085474	78480	6708	376671	0.017809	2.6553	1426458	0.0208	18.176	0.017737	55
60	0.132457	71772	9507	336336	0.028265	2.6308	1049787	0.0318	14.627	0.028095	60
65	0.203568	62265	12675	280910	0.045122	2.6003	713451	0.0318	11.458	0.044843	65
70	0.314805	49590	15611	209453	0.074533	2.5440	432541	0.0318	8.722	0.074100	70
75	0.447942	33979	15221	130932	0.116247	2.4402	223088	0.0318	6.566	0.115614	75
80	0.599201	18758	11240	64087	0.175387	2.3572	92156	0.0318	4.913	0.174326	80
85+	*1.000000	7518	7518	28069	0.267850	3.7334	28069	0.0318	3.733	0.264351	85+

TABLE 3 — FEMALE LIFE TABLE

x	nq_x	l_x	nd_x	nL_x	nm_x	na_x	T_x	r_x	$\overset{\circ}{e}_x$	nM_x	x
0	0.035563	100000	3556	97586	0.036442	0.3212	6821320	0.0000	68.213	0.036442	0
1	0.013075	96444	1261	382214	0.003299	1.1760	6723734	0.0000	69.717	0.003299	1
5	0.004825	95183	459	474766	0.000967	2.5000	6341520	0.0000	66.625	0.000967	5
10	0.002695	94724	255	472979	0.000540	2.4995	5866754	0.0200	61.936	0.000540	10
15	0.004854	94468	459	471311	0.000973	2.7529	5393774	0.0065	57.096	0.000971	15
20	0.008637	94010	812	468116	0.001735	2.6195	4922463	0.0099	52.361	0.001732	20
25	0.009916	93198	924	463730	0.001993	2.5559	4454348	0.0180	47.795	0.001991	25
30	0.011489	92274	1060	458785	0.002311	2.5640	3990618	0.0277	43.248	0.002306	30
35	0.013704	91213	1250	453048	0.002759	2.5848	3531832	0.0251	38.721	0.002753	35
40	0.017441	89963	1569	446095	0.003517	2.6276	3078784	0.0165	34.223	0.003509	40
45	0.025010	88394	2211	436784	0.005061	2.6531	2632689	0.0259	29.783	0.005040	45
50	0.037059	86184	3194	423420	0.007543	2.6520	2195905	0.0265	25.479	0.007509	50
55	0.054721	82990	4541	404308	0.011232	2.6567	1772485	0.0251	21.358	0.011181	55
60	0.084245	78449	6609	376825	0.017538	2.6671	1368178	0.0265	17.440	0.017443	60
65	0.137009	71840	9843	336166	0.029279	2.6599	991353	0.0265	13.800	0.029107	65
70	0.228477	61997	14165	276001	0.051322	2.6008	655187	0.0265	10.568	0.051043	70
75	0.349105	47832	16698	197704	0.084462	2.5173	379186	0.0265	7.927	0.084045	75
80	0.499516	31134	15552	115349	0.134824	2.4850	181482	0.0265	5.829	0.134211	80
85+	1.000000	15582	15582	66133	0.235614	4.2442	66133	0.0265	4.244	0.223231	85+

TABLE 4 — OBSERVED, PROJECTED, AND STABLE RATES

	OBSERVED POPULATION BOTH SEXES	MALES	FEMALES	PROJECTED POPULATION 1962 MALES	FEMALES	1967 MALES	FEMALES	1972 MALES	FEMALES	STABLE POPULATION MALES	FEMALES
RATES PER THOUSAND											
Birth	17.92	18.74	17.14	19.17	17.57	19.17	17.61	19.59	18.02	14.82	13.83
Death	7.93	8.53	7.35	8.95	7.80	9.42	8.23	9.87	8.66	16.36	15.37
Increase	9.99	10.21	9.79	10.22	9.77	9.75	9.38	9.72	9.36	-1.5433	
PERCENTAGE											
under 15	31.94	33.14	30.79	29.97	27.77	25.84	23.93	25.28	23.44	21.23	19.97
15-64	62.65	62.14	63.14	64.88	65.76	68.51	69.08	68.75	69.10	66.94	64.67
65 and over	5.41	4.72	6.07	5.15	6.47	5.65	6.98	5.97	7.46	11.83	15.36
DEP. RATIO X 100	59.61	60.92	58.37	54.14	52.07	45.96	44.75	45.46	44.72	49.40	54.63

TABLE 1 — DATA

AGE AT LAST BIRTHDAY	POPULATION BOTH SEXES	MALES Number	%	FEMALES Number	%	BIRTHS BY AGE OF MOTHER	DEATHS BOTH SEXES	MALES	FEMALES	AGE AT LAST BIRTHDAY
0	1574587	806692	1.8	767895	1.6	0	49844	28086	21758	0
1-4	6312894	3227991	7.1	3084903	6.5	0	15539	8585	6954	1-4
5-9	9367582	4785053	10.5	4582529	9.7	0	8378	4928	3450	5-9
10-14	10881827	5549521	12.1	5332306	11.2	9	5702	3377	2325	10-14
15-19	9283743	4667283	10.2	4616460	9.7	19348	9627	5987	3640	15-19
20-24	8342662	4140327	9.0	4202335	8.9	443279	14458	8825	5633	20-24
25-29	8185247	4082268	8.9	4102979	8.6	745329	15665	9254	6411	25-29
30-34	7457822	3706157	8.1	3751665	7.9	303853	15800	8903	6897	30-34
35-39	5976944	2729274	6.0	3247670	6.8	79776	15500	8128	7372	35-39
40-44	5015703	2277732	5.0	2737971	5.8	14644	17424	9225	8199	40-44
45-49	4801262	2253320	4.9	2547942	5.4	858	25354	14139	11215	45-49
50-54	4174691	2031451	4.4	2143240	4.5	58	34853	20510	14343	50-54
55-59	3623524	1794834	3.9	1828690	3.9	12	48284	29899	18385	55-59
60-64	2910149	1427360	3.1	1482789	3.1	0	60776	37473	23303	60-64
65-69	2150869	1021744	2.2	1129125	2.4	0	73346	43309	30037	65-69
70-74	1550904	686436	1.5	864468	1.8		87179	47216	39963	70-74
75-79	950622	374814	0.8	575808	1.2		87657	41425	46232	75-79
80-84	478181	167465	0.4	310716	0.7	826060 M.	69318	28674	40644	80-84
85+	184917	55499	0.1	129418	0.3	781106 F.	42695	14374	28321	85+
TOTAL	93224130	45785221		47438909		1607166	697399	372317	325082	TOTAL

TABLE 2 — MALE LIFE TABLE

x	nq_x	l_x	nd_x	nL_x	nm_x	na_x	T_x	r_x	$\mathring{e}_x$	nM_x
0	0.033991	100000	3399	97631	0.034816	0.3029	6549795	0.0000	65.498	0.034816
1	0.010558	96601	1020	383500	0.002660	1.1530	6452164	0.0000	66.792	0.002660
5	0.005136	95581	491	476677	0.001030	2.5000	6068665	0.0000	63.492	0.001030
10	0.003039	95090	289	474753	0.000609	2.5862	5591987	0.0016	58.807	0.000609
15	0.006439	94801	610	472627	0.001292	2.7426	5117235	0.0280	53.979	0.001283
20	0.010614	94191	1000	468545	0.002134	2.5917	4644608	0.0114	49.311	0.002131
25	0.011274	93191	1051	463349	0.002267	2.5204	4176062	0.0088	44.812	0.002267
30	0.011969	92140	1103	458007	0.002408	2.5571	3712713	0.0378	40.294	0.002402
35	0.014862	91037	1353	451951	0.002994	2.6079	3254706	0.0456	35.751	0.002978
40	0.020110	89684	1804	444198	0.004060	2.6579	2802765	0.0149	31.251	0.004050
45	0.030954	87881	2720	433105	0.006281	2.6844	2358557	0.0049	26.838	0.006275
50	0.049452	85161	4211	416065	0.010122	2.6876	1925452	0.0121	22.610	0.010096
55	0.080644	80949	6512	389517	0.016718	2.6613	1509387	0.0181	18.646	0.016658
60	0.124310	74437	9253	350324	0.026414	2.6373	1119870	0.0314	15.044	0.026253
65	0.193459	65184	12610	295706	0.042645	2.6040	769546	0.0314	11.806	0.042387
70	0.295734	52574	15548	224715	0.069189	2.5460	473841	0.0314	9.013	0.068784
75	0.433379	37026	16046	144367	0.111149	2.4597	249126	0.0314	6.728	0.110521
80	0.593110	20980	12443	72225	0.172283	2.3743	104759	0.0314	4.993	0.171224
85+	*1.000000	8536	8536	32534	0.262385	3.8112	32534	0.0314	3.811	0.258996

TABLE 3 — FEMALE LIFE TABLE

x	nq_x	l_x	nd_x	nL_x	nm_x	na_x	T_x	r_x	$\mathring{e}_x$	nM_x
0	0.027790	100000	2779	98076	0.028335	0.3077	7034306	0.0000	70.343	0.028335
1	0.008959	97221	871	386409	0.002254	1.1587	6936229	0.0000	71.345	0.002254
5	0.003757	96350	362	480845	0.000753	2.5000	6549820	0.0000	67.979	0.000753
10	0.002178	95988	209	479421	0.000436	2.5169	6068975	0.0000	63.226	0.000436
15	0.003957	95779	379	478037	0.000793	2.7359	5589554	0.0230	58.359	0.000788
20	0.006689	95400	638	475479	0.001342	2.6172	5111518	0.0105	53.580	0.001340
25	0.007788	94762	738	472011	0.001564	2.5632	4636038	0.0098	48.923	0.001563
30	0.009167	94024	862	468030	0.001842	2.5766	4164028	0.0215	44.287	0.001838
35	0.011323	93162	1055	463279	0.002277	2.6011	3695998	0.0292	39.673	0.002270
40	0.014914	92107	1374	457294	0.003004	2.6408	3232719	0.0211	35.097	0.002995
45	0.021859	90733	1983	449034	0.004417	2.6642	2775425	0.0199	30.589	0.004402
50	0.033094	88750	2937	436876	0.006723	2.6597	2326390	0.0263	26.213	0.006692
55	0.049346	85813	4235	419162	0.010102	2.6616	1889514	0.0264	22.019	0.010054
60	0.076256	81578	6221	393436	0.015812	2.6762	1470352	0.0288	18.024	0.015716
65	0.125998	75358	9495	354628	0.026774	2.6662	1076916	0.0288	14.291	0.026602
70	0.209432	65863	13794	296504	0.046521	2.6215	722288	0.0288	10.967	0.046228
75	0.336837	52069	17539	217186	0.080754	2.5392	425784	0.0288	8.177	0.080291
80	0.495158	34530	17098	129884	0.131640	2.4987	208598	0.0288	6.041	0.130807
85+	*1.000000	17432	17432	78714	0.221464	4.5154	78714	0.0288	4.515	0.218834

TABLE 4 — OBSERVED AND PROJECTED VITAL RATES

	OBSERVED POPULATION BOTH SEXES	MALES	FEMALES	PROJECTED POPULATION 1965 MALES	FEMALES	1970 MALES	FEMALES	1975 MALES	FEMALES	STABLE POPULATION MALES	FEMA
RATES PER THOUSAND											
Birth	17.24	18.04	16.47	18.21	16.64	18.95	17.34	18.83	17.25	13.73	12.
Death	7.48	8.13	6.85	8.67	7.41	9.18	7.88	9.65	8.39	16.62	15.
Increase	9.76	9.91	9.61	9.55	9.23	9.77	9.46	9.18	8.86		-2.89
PERCENTAGE											
under 15	30.18	31.38	29.02	26.75	24.71	24.67	22.78	24.78	22.89	20.10	18.
15-64	64.12	63.58	64.63	67.66	68.37	69.22	69.65	68.76	68.87	66.85	64.
65 and over	5.70	5.04	6.34	5.59	6.93	6.11	7.57	6.46	8.24	13.05	16.
DEP. RATIO X 100	55.97	57.28	54.72	47.79	46.27	44.47	43.57	45.43	45.20	49.60	55.

AGE LAST BIRTHDAY	1965 BOTH SEXES	1965 MALES	1965 FEMALES	1970 BOTH SEXES	1970 MALES	1970 FEMALES	1975 BOTH SEXES	1975 MALES	1975 FEMALES	AGE AT LAST BIRTHDAY	
0-4	7991	4093	3898	8601	4406	4195	9164	4694	4470	0-4	**TABLE 5**
5-9	7821	3997	3824	7923	4055	3868	8528	4365	4163	5-9	POPULATION
10-14	9335	4766	4569	7794	3981	3813	7896	4039	3857	10-14	PROJECTED
15-19	10842	5525	5317	9300	4744	4556	7765	3963	3802	15-19	WITH
20-24	9219	4627	4592	10765	5477	5288	9234	4703	4531	20-24	FIXED
25-29	8266	4094	4172	9134	4576	4558	10666	5416	5250	25-29	AGE—
30-34	8103	4035	4068	8184	4047	4137	9043	4523	4520	30-34	SPECIFIC
35-39	7371	3657	3714	8009	3982	4027	8089	3994	4095	35-39	BIRTH
40-44	5888	2682	3206	7260	3594	3666	7889	3914	3975	40-44	AND
45-49	4910	2221	2689	5763	2615	3148	7104	3505	3599	45-49	DEATH
50-54	4644	2165	2479	4749	2133	2616	5576	2513	3063	50-54	RATES
55-59	3958	1902	2056	4405	2027	2378	4507	1997	2510	55-59	(IN 1000's)
60-64	3330	1614	1716	3640	1710	1930	4055	1823	2232	60-64	
65-69	2542	1205	1337	2910	1363	1547	3184	1444	1740	65-69	
70-74	1720	776	944	2033	916	1117	2329	1035	1294	70-74	
75-79	1074	441	633	1191	499	692	1407	588	819	75-79	
80-84	532	188	344	600	221	379	664	250	414	80-84	
85+	263	75	188	293	84	209	328	99	229	85+	
TOTAL	97809	48063	49746	102554	50430	52124	107428	52865	54563	TOTAL	

STANDARD COUNTRIES:	ENGLAND AND WALES 1961 BOTH SEXES	MALES	FEMALES	UNITED STATES 1960 BOTH SEXES	MALES	FEMALES	MEXICO 1960 BOTH SEXES	MALES	FEMALES	
STANDARDIZED RATES PER THOUSAND										**TABLE 6**
Birth	12.59	15.03*	11.86	12.77	13.93*	12.23	14.92	14.37*	14.46	STANDARDIZED
Death	13.33	14.08*	13.21	10.98	11.85*	9.87	6.08	8.75*	5.17	RATES
Increase	-0.74	0.95*	-1.36	1.79	2.08*	2.35	8.84	5.62*	9.29	

	OBSERVED POP. MALES	FEMALES	STATIONARY POP. MALES	FEMALES	STABLE POP. MALES	FEMALES	OBSERVED BIRTHS	NET MATERNITY FUNCTION	BIRTHS IN STABLE POP.	
μ	28.27537	29.73843	36.02097	38.05578	37.43204	39.60105	27.59062	27.88249	27.94574	**TABLE 7**
μ_2	378.1179	401.1754	484.9855	531.5934	490.7374	536.8768	17.99218	19.69194	19.88824	MOMENTS
κ_3	4785.722	4929.062	2326.887	2251.711	1645.984	1396.816	57.0658	67.5069	68.2768	AND
κ_4	-60569.	-70001.	-229099.	-288826.	-241105.	-301396.	248.890	271.536	271.407	CUMULANTS
β_1	0.423656	0.376293	0.047464	0.033751	0.022925	0.012608	0.559115	0.596802	0.592593	
β_2	2.576360	2.565052	2.025984	1.977939	1.998832	1.954347	3.768848	3.700246	3.686166	
κ	-0.172098	-0.159627	-0.018010	-0.012478	-0.008724	-0.004671	-3.422877	-1.320344	-1.259736	

VITAL STATISTICS		THOMPSON AGE RANGE	NRR	1000r	INTERVAL	BOURGEOIS-PICHAT AGE RANGE	NRR	1000b	1000d	1000r	COALE	
RR	0.978										IBR	**TABLE 8**
NRR	0.922	0-4	0.99	-0.45	27.38	5-29	1.25	23.22	14.94	8.28	IDR	RATES FROM AGE
GFR	2.013	5-9	1.29	9.35	27.34	30-54	1.90	36.20	12.33	23.87	IRI	DISTRIBUTIONS
GENERATION	27.914	10-14	1.65	18.05	27.28	55-79	2.10	44.43	16.87	27.56	K1	AND VITAL
SEX RATIO	105.755	15-19	1.60	16.34	27.19	*45-69	2.15	46.28	17.90	28.39	K2	STATISTICS (Females)

ORIGINAL MATRIX SUB-DIAGONAL	ALTERNATIVE FIRST ROWS Projection	Integral	% IN STABLE POPULATION	FISHER VALUES	REPRODUCTIVE VALUES	SECOND STABLE MATRIX Z_2 FIRST COLUMN	FIRST ROW	
0.99249	0.00000	0.00000	6.201	1.025	3947603	0.1764+0.0408	0.1764+0.0408	**TABLE 9**
0.99704	0.00000	0.00000	6.244	1.018	4663002	0.1304-0.1611	0.0353+0.1542	LESLIE
0.99711	0.00492	0.00000	6.316	1.006	5364014	-0.1010-0.2159	-0.1071+0.0863	MATRIX
0.99465	0.12846	0.00980	6.390	0.989	4567211	-0.2741-0.0041	-0.1091-0.0512	AND ITS
0.99270	0.33650	0.24659	6.448	0.848	3563847	-0.1418+0.2807	-0.0243-0.1103	SPECTRAL
0.99157	0.30842	0.42466	6.494	0.495	2029868	0.2180+0.2865	0.0176-0.0751	COMPONENTS
0.98985	0.12398	0.18933	6.533	0.173	649356	0.4037-0.0808	0.0109-0.0276	(Females)
0.98708	0.03514	0.05742	6.561	0.044	142961	0.1187-0.4548	0.0038-0.0071	
0.98194	0.00669	0.01250	6.570	0.007	20489	-0.4065-0.3480	0.0008-0.0012	
0.97292	0.00043	0.00079	6.545	0.001	1357	-0.5558+0.2416	0.0001-0.0001	
0.95945	0.00005	0.00008	6.461	0.000	180	-0.0291+0.6794	0.0000-0.0000	
+ 0.77363			29.236					

OBSERVED POPUL. (IN 100's)	CONTRIBUTIONS OF ROOTS (IN 100's) r_1	r_2, r_3	$r_4 \cdot r_{11}$	AGE-SP. BIRTH RATES	NET MATERNITY FUNCTION	COEFF. OF MATRIX EQUATION	PARAMETERS INTEGRAL	MATRIX	EXP. INCREASE x	$e^{(x+8\frac{1}{2})r}$	
38528	43538	-4157	-853	0.0000	0.0000	0.0000	L(1) 0.98565	0.98565	0	0.9928	**TABLE 10**
45825	43840	1752	234	0.0000	0.0000	0.0000	L(2) 0.37942	0.37929	50	0.8592	AGE
53323	44346	7234	1743	0.0000	0.0000	0.0049	0.80698	0.77969	55	0.8468	ANALYSIS
46165	44861	4963	-3659	0.0020	0.0097	0.1267	R(1) -0.00289	-0.00289	60	0.8347	AND
42023	45270	-4563	1316	0.0513	0.2438	0.3302	R(2) -0.02292	-0.02853	65	0.8227	MISCELLANEOUS
41030	45594	-11088	6524	0.0883	0.4167	0.3005	0.22626	0.22361	70	0.8109	RESULTS
37517	45867	-5120	-3231	0.0394	0.1842	0.1198	C(1)	702077	75	0.7992	(Females)
32477	46062	9363	-22948	0.0119	0.0553	0.0336	C(2)	-886367	80	0.7878	
27380	46128	15980	-34729	0.0026	0.0119	0.0063		1260665	85	0.7765	
25479	45954	3762	-24237	0.0002	0.0007	0.0004	2P/Y 27.7698	28.0992	90	0.7653	
21432	45360	-16614	-7314	0.0000	0.0001	0.0000	DELTA 19.8299		95	0.7543	
+ 63210	205257								100	0.7435	

TABLE 1 — DATA

AGE AT LAST BIRTHDAY	POPULATION BOTH SEXES	MALES Number	MALES %	FEMALES Number	FEMALES %	BIRTHS BY AGE OF MOTHER	DEATHS BOTH SEXES	DEATHS MALES	DEATHS FEMALES	AGE AT LAST BIRTHDAY
0	1615750	829250	1.8	786500	1.6	0	38434	21758	16676	0
1-4	6253250	3202250	6.8	3051000	6.3	0	10098	5798	4300	1-4
5-9	8119250	4149500	8.8	3969750	8.1	0	5243	3254	1989	5-9
10-14	10642000	5427500	11.5	5214500	10.7	10	4332	2728	1604	10-14
15-19	9703750	4922250	10.4	4781500	9.8	18204	7370	4838	2532	15-19
20-24	8905500	4442000	9.4	4463500	9.1	440368	11494	7255	4239	20-24
25-29	8319250	4123000	8.8	4196250	8.6	801237	12688	7732	4956	25-29
30-34	7920250	3957250	8.4	3963000	8.1	321554	14084	8494	5590	30-34
35-39	6948000	3383500	7.2	3564500	7.3	67132	16021	9380	6641	35-39
40-44	5366750	2375500	5.0	2991250	6.1	10461	16835	9127	7708	40-44
45-49	4846000	2233750	4.7	2612250	5.4	541	23248	13078	10170	45-49
50-54	4531250	2139500	4.5	2391750	4.9	14	33718	19714	14004	50-54
55-59	3718000	1816750	3.9	1901250	3.9	0	44995	27862	17133	55-59
60-64	3234750	1578000	3.3	1656750	3.4	0	62311	39074	23237	60-64
65-69	2398000	1139250	2.4	1258750	2.6	0	75969	45473	30496	65-69
70-74	1657250	741250	1.6	916000	1.9		86946	48158	38788	70-74
75-79	998750	403250	0.9	595500	1.2		87259	42406	44853	75-79
80-84	511250	180250	0.4	331000	0.7	852561 M.	70858	29138	41720	80-84
85+	223250	65250	0.1	158000	0.3	806960 F.	48650	16051	32599	85+
TOTAL	95912250	47109250		48803000		1659521	670553	361318	309235	TOTAL

TABLE 2 — MALE LIFE TABLE

x	nq_x	l_x	nd_x	nL_x	nm_x	na_x	T_x	r_x	$\mathring{e}_x$	nM_x
0	0.025717	100000	2572	98180	0.026193	0.2923	6728652	0.0022	67.287	0.026238
1	0.007191	97428	701	387710	0.001807	1.1410	6630472	0.0022	68.055	0.001811
5	0.003913	96728	379	482692	0.000784	2.5000	6242762	0.0000	64.540	0.000784
10	0.002510	96349	242	481161	0.000503	2.5817	5760070	0.0000	59.783	0.000503
15	0.004926	96107	473	479465	0.000987	2.7365	5278909	0.0190	54.927	0.000983
20	0.008150	95634	779	476307	0.001636	2.6102	4799444	0.0162	50.186	0.001633
25	0.009339	94855	886	472105	0.001876	2.5530	4323137	0.0097	45.576	0.001875
30	0.010693	93969	1005	467415	0.002150	2.5834	3851032	0.0176	40.982	0.002146
35	0.013855	92964	1288	461756	0.002789	2.6215	3383617	0.0482	36.397	0.002772
40	0.019156	91676	1756	454262	0.003866	2.6555	2921861	0.0375	31.872	0.003842
45	0.028904	89920	2599	443558	0.005860	2.6757	2467599	0.0044	27.442	0.005855
50	0.045213	87321	3948	427482	0.009235	2.6895	2024041	0.0109	23.179	0.009214
55	0.074252	83373	6191	402457	0.015382	2.6729	1596560	0.0145	19.150	0.015336
60	0.117731	77182	9087	364504	0.024929	2.6442	1194102	0.0341	15.471	0.024762
65	0.183299	68095	12482	310645	0.040180	2.6100	829598	0.0341	12.183	0.039915
70	0.281891	55614	15677	239747	0.065389	2.5556	518953	0.0341	9.331	0.064969
75	0.417332	39937	16667	157520	0.105807	2.4702	279206	0.0341	6.991	0.105160
80	0.571421	23270	13297	81712	0.162728	2.3951	121686	0.0341	5.229	0.161654
85+	*1.000000	9973	9973	39974	0.249489	4.0082	39974	0.0341	4.008	0.245992

TABLE 3 — FEMALE LIFE TABLE

x	nq_x	l_x	nd_x	nL_x	nm_x	na_x	T_x	r_x	$\mathring{e}_x$	nM_x
0	0.020855	100000	2086	98516	0.021169	0.2884	7243017	0.0021	72.430	0.021203
1	0.005604	97914	549	390087	0.001407	1.1369	7144501	0.0021	72.967	0.001409
5	0.002502	97366	244	486220	0.000501	2.5000	6754414	0.0000	69.372	0.000501
10	0.001537	97122	149	485240	0.000308	2.5193	6268194	0.0000	64.539	0.000308
15	0.002655	96973	257	484285	0.000532	2.7507	5782954	0.0150	59.635	0.000530
20	0.004746	96715	459	482494	0.000951	2.6406	5298669	0.0121	54.786	0.000950
25	0.005894	96256	567	479908	0.001182	2.5788	4816175	0.0107	50.035	0.001181
30	0.007039	95689	674	476828	0.001413	2.5980	4336266	0.0149	45.316	0.001411
35	0.009306	95016	884	472979	0.001869	2.6266	3859439	0.0262	40.619	0.001863
40	0.012866	94131	1211	467819	0.002589	2.6572	3386460	0.0284	35.976	0.002577
45	0.019352	92920	1798	460404	0.003906	2.6660	2918641	0.0184	31.410	0.003893
50	0.029014	91122	2644	449443	0.005882	2.6675	2458237	0.0257	26.977	0.005855
55	0.044350	88478	3924	433235	0.009058	2.6666	2008794	0.0274	22.704	0.009011
60	0.068371	84554	5781	409395	0.014121	2.6863	1575559	0.0311	18.634	0.014026
65	0.115458	78773	9095	372736	0.024401	2.6767	1166164	0.0311	14.804	0.024227
70	0.193704	69678	13497	316490	0.042645	2.6370	793428	0.0311	11.387	0.042345
75	0.319824	56181	17968	237017	0.075809	2.5574	476931	0.0311	8.489	0.075320
80	0.482689	38213	18445	145328	0.126920	2.5203	239915	0.0311	6.278	0.126042
85+	*1.000000	19768	19768	94587	0.208994	4.7848	94587	0.0311	4.785	0.206323

TABLE 4 — OBSERVED AND PROJECTED VITAL RATES

	OBSERVED POPULATION BOTH SEXES	MALES	FEMALES	PROJECTED 1968 MALES	1968 FEMALES	1973 MALES	1973 FEMALES	1978 MALES	1978 FEMALES	STABLE POPULATION MALES	FEMALES
RATES PER THOUSAND											
Birth	17.30	18.10	16.54	18.27	16.70	18.56	16.99	17.61	16.14	13.41	12.3
Death	6.99	7.67	6.34	8.29	6.95	8.83	7.48	9.31	8.08	16.18	15.1
Increase	10.31	10.43	10.20	9.98	9.76	9.73	9.51	8.30	8.06	-2.769	
PERCENTAGE											
under 15	27.77	28.89	26.68	25.04	23.08	24.55	22.63	24.65	22.74	19.85	18.4
15-64	66.20	65.74	66.64	68.89	69.43	68.97	69.25	58.48	68.20	66.52	63.8
65 and over	6.04	5.37	6.68	6.07	7.49	6.48	8.12	6.87	9.06	13.63	17.7
DEP. RATIO X 100	51.06	52.11	50.06	45.15	44.04	44.99	44.41	46.03	46.63	50.33	56.7

TABLE 5 — POPULATION PROJECTED WITH FIXED AGE—SPECIFIC BIRTH AND DEATH RATES (IN 1000's)

AGE AT LAST BIRTHDAY	BOTH SEXES (1968)	MALES (1968)	FEMALES (1968)	BOTH SEXES (1973)	MALES (1973)	FEMALES (1973)	BOTH SEXES (1978)	MALES (1978)	FEMALES (1978)	AGE AT LAST BIRTHDAY
0-4	8337	4271	4066	8877	4548	4329	9132	4679	4453	0-4
5-9	7824	4005	3819	8289	4243	4046	8827	4519	4308	5-9
10-14	8098	4136	3962	7803	3992	3811	8268	4230	4038	10-14
15-19	10612	5408	5204	8076	4122	3954	7782	3978	3804	15-19
20-24	9654	4890	4764	10558	5373	5185	8034	4095	3939	20-24
25-29	8843	4403	4440	9585	4847	4738	10482	5325	5157	25-29
30-34	8251	4082	4169	8770	4359	4411	9507	4799	4708	30-34
35-39	7840	3909	3931	8169	4033	4136	8681	4306	4375	35-39
40-44	6855	3329	3526	7734	3846	3888	8058	3967	4091	40-44
45-49	5264	2320	2944	6720	3250	3470	7581	3755	3826	45-49
50-54	4703	2153	2550	5109	2235	2874	6519	3132	3387	50-54
55-59	4319	2014	2305	4485	2027	2458	4875	2105	2770	55-59
60-64	3442	1645	1797	4003	1824	2179	4159	1836	2323	60-64
65-69	2853	1345	1508	3038	1402	1636	3539	1555	1984	65-69
70-74	1948	879	1069	2319	1038	1281	2471	1082	1389	70-74
75-79	1173	487	686	1378	578	800	1641	682	959	75-79
80-84	574	209	365	674	253	421	791	300	491	80-84
85+	303	88	215	340	102	238	398	124	274	85+
TOTAL	100893	49573	51320	105927	52072	53855	110745	54469	56276	TOTAL

TABLE 6 — STANDARDIZED RATES

STANDARD COUNTRIES: STANDARDIZED RATES PER THOUSAND	ENGLAND AND WALES 1961 BOTH SEXES	MALES	FEMALES	UNITED STATES 1960 BOTH SEXES	MALES	FEMALES	MEXICO 1960 BOTH SEXES	MALES	FEMALES
Birth	12.38	14.59*	11.67	12.56	13.54*	12.04	14.75	13.86*	14.31
Death	12.21	12.72*	12.02	9.96	10.74*	8.84	5.26	8.05*	4.38
Increase	0.17	1.88*	-0.35	2.60	2.79*	3.19	9.49	5.81*	9.93

TABLE 7 — MOMENTS AND CUMULANTS

	OBSERVED POP. MALES	FEMALES	STATIONARY POP. MALES	FEMALES	STABLE POP. MALES	FEMALES	OBSERVED BIRTHS	NET MATERNITY FUNCTION	BIRTHS IN STABLE POP.
μ	29.05779	30.62873	36.40876	38.55848	37.77980	40.06245	27.53805	27.77610	27.82902
σ^2	377.4059	401.9130	492.2628	540.5611	497.7082	545.3378	16.09081	16.95977	17.09534
κ_3	4482.738	4545.041	2300.965	2149.056	1626.794	1295.707	42.4534	48.6568	49.2638
κ_4	-62817.	-77265.	-237324.	-301853.	-248859.	-313408.	183.743	223.466	225.394
β_1	0.373818	0.318185	0.044384	0.029239	0.021465	0.010352	0.432604	0.485319	0.485762
β_2	2.558981	2.521682	2.020626	1.966987	1.995376	1.946149	3.709670	3.776910	3.771236
κ	-0.158151	-0.138958	-0.016819	-0.010762	-0.008157	-0.003818	2.958767	4.170865	4.796261

TABLE 8 — RATES FROM AGE DISTRIBUTIONS AND VITAL STATISTICS (Females)

VITAL STATISTICS		THOMPSON AGE RANGE	NRR	1000r	INTERVAL	BOURGEOIS-PICHAT AGE RANGE	NRR	1000b	1000d	1000r	COALE
GRR	0.965										IBR
NRR	0.926	0-4	0.94	-2.29	27.40	5-29	1.01	19.17	18.91	0.25	IDR
TFR	1.985	5-9	1.06	2.28	27.37	30-54	1.89	36.48	12.97	23.51	IRI
GENERATION	27.802	10-14	1.53	15.37	27.32	55-79	2.16	47.72	19.12	28.60	K1
SEX RATIO	105.651	15-19	1.56	15.57	27.23	*10-34	1.41	25.49	12.78	12.71	K2

TABLE 9 — LESLIE MATRIX AND ITS SPECTRAL COMPONENTS (Females)

Start Age Interval	ORIGINAL MATRIX SUB-DIAGONAL	ALTERNATIVE FIRST ROWS Projection	Integral	FIRST STABLE MATRIX % IN STABLE POPULATION	FISHER VALUES	REPRODUCTIVE VALUES	SECOND STABLE MATRIX Z₂ FIRST COLUMN	FIRST ROW
0	0.99512	0.00000	0.00000	6.092	1.016	3899960	0.1760+0.0363	0.1760+0.0363
5	0.99799	0.00000	0.00000	6.147	1.007	3998412	0.1237-0.1616	0.0387+0.1539
0	0.99803	0.00452	0.00000	6.220	0.995	5190399	-0.1024-0.2063	-0.1072+0.0896
5	0.99630	0.12129	0.00898	6.295	0.979	4681249	-0.2625+0.0047	-0.1129-0.0508
0	0.99464	0.34281	0.23279	6.359	0.845	3773611	-0.1247+0.2703	-0.0243-0.1136
5	0.99358	0.32260	0.45052	6.413	0.488	2047933	0.2142+0.2601	0.0203-0.0755
0	0.99193	0.11858	0.19145	6.460	0.154	612184	0.3702-0.3902	0.0108-0.0246
5	0.98909	0.02648	0.04444	6.498	0.032	114419	0.0901-0.4206	0.0028-0.0052
0	0.98415	0.00440	0.00825	6.516	0.005	14350	-0.3822-0.2971	0.0005-0.0008
5	0.97619	0.00025	0.00049	6.502	0.000	699	-0.4858+0.2408	0.0000-0.0000
0	0.96394	0.00001	0.00001	6.436	0.000	17	0.0062+0.6024	0.0000-0.0000
5+	0.77989			30.062				

TABLE 10 — AGE ANALYSIS AND MISCELLANEOUS RESULTS (Females)

Start Age Interval	OBSERVED POPUL. (IN 100's)	CONTRIBUTIONS OF ROOTS (IN 100's) r_1	r_2,r_3	r_4-r_{11}	AGE-SP. BIRTH RATES	NET MATERNITY FUNCTION	COEFF. OF MATRIX EQUATION	PARAMETERS INTEGRAL	MATRIX	EXP. INCREASE x	$e^{(x+2\frac{1}{2})r}$
0	38375	42992	-4772	155	0.0000	0.0000	0.0000	L(1) 0.98625	0.98625	0	0.9931
5	39698	43379	-1696	-1986	0.0000	0.0000	0.0000	L(2) 0.38352	0.38210	50	0.8647
0	52145	43895	4463	3787	0.0000	0.0000	0.0045	0.81871	0.79128	55	0.8528
5	47815	44419	6596	-3200	0.0019	0.0090	0.1202	R(1) -0.00277	-0.00277	60	0.8411
0	44635	44871	757	-993	0.0480	0.2315	0.3385	R(2) -0.02017	-0.02586	65	0.8295
5	41963	45253	-7720	4430	0.0928	0.4456	0.3169	0.22654	0.22419	70	0.8181
0	39630	45589	-8560	2601	0.0395	0.1881	0.1157	C(1)	705677	75	0.8069
5	35645	45851	1450	-11656	0.0092	0.0433	0.0256	C(2)	-1264121	80	0.7958
0	29913	45983	12297	-28367	0.0017	0.0080	0.0042		443055	85	0.7848
5	26123	45885	10150	-29912	0.0001	0.0005	0.0002	2P/Y 27.7352	28.0267	90	0.7740
0	23918	45417	-5494	-16006	0.0000	0.0000	0.0000	DELTA 19.1658		95	0.7634
5+	68173	212141								100	0.7529

TABLE 1 — DATA

AGE AT LAST BIRTHDAY	POPULATION BOTH SEXES	MALES Number	%	FEMALES Number	%	BIRTHS BY AGE OF MOTHER	DEATHS BOTH SEXES	MALES	FEMALES	AGE AT LAST BIRTHDAY
0	57903	29900	3.9	28003	4.1	0	2576	1456	1120	0
1-4	207580	107183	14.0	100397	14.6	0	958	489	469	1-4
5-9	218797	112402	14.7	106395	15.5	0	305	167	138	5-9
10-14	137589	71868	9.4	65721	9.6	20	122	71	51	10-14
15-19	135679	70148	9.2	65531	9.6	5090	133	81	52	15-19
20-24	119536	61401	8.0	58135	8.5	17551	165	95	70	20-24
25-29	111848	59799	7.8	52049	7.6	18419	183	91	92	25-29
30-34	90282	50305	6.6	39977	5.8	11514	223	133	90	30-34
35-39	82800	46550	6.1	36250	5.3	7052	302	178	124	35-39
40-44	76284	43075	5.6	33209	4.8	2698	435	257	178	40-44
45-49	66827	37829	4.9	28998	4.2	341	627	416	211	45-49
50-54	51981	29354	3.8	22627	3.3	0	746	519	227	50-54
55-59	37621	20643	2.7	16978	2.5	0	841	572	269	55-59
60-64	24412	12100	1.6	12312	1.8	0	871	600	271	60-64
65-69	14300	6531	0.9	7769	1.1	0	702	453	249	65-69
70-74	8877	3509	0.5	5368	0.8		584	325	259	70-74
75-79	4920	1619	0.2	3301	0.5		451	205	246	75-79
80-84	2299	596	0.1	1703	0.2	32283 M.	310	107	203	80-84
85+	782	151	0.0	631	0.1	30402 F.	172	42	130	85+
TOTAL	1450317	764963		685354		62685	10706	6257	4449	TOTAL

TABLE 2 — MALE LIFE TABLE

x	$_nq_x$	l_x	$_nd_x$	$_nL_x$	$_nm_x$	$_na_x$	T_x	r_x	$\overset{\circ}{e}_x$	$_nM_x$	x
0	0.046874	100000	4687	96832	0.048408	0.3242	6019764	0.0081	60.198	0.048696	0
1	0.017918	95313	1708	376434	0.004537	1.1801	5922932	0.0081	62.142	0.004562	1
5	0.007210	93605	675	466337	0.001447	2.5000	5546497	0.0625	59.254	0.001486	5
10	0.004913	92930	457	463478	0.000985	2.4353	5080161	0.0460	54.667	0.000988	10
15	0.005766	92473	533	461086	0.001156	2.5987	4616682	0.0145	49.924	0.001155	15
20	0.007712	91940	709	457961	0.001548	2.5471	4155596	0.0145	45.199	0.001547	20
25	0.007602	91231	694	454522	0.001526	2.6458	3697635	0.0182	40.530	0.001522	25
30	0.013192	90537	1194	449910	0.002655	2.6750	3243113	0.0224	35.821	0.002644	30
35	0.018989	89343	1697	442765	0.003832	2.6712	2793202	0.0115	31.264	0.003824	35
40	0.029535	87647	2589	432363	0.005987	2.7327	2350438	0.0142	26.817	0.005966	40
45	0.053936	85058	4588	414715	0.011062	2.6951	1918074	0.0271	22.550	0.010997	45
50	0.085549	80470	6884	386204	0.017825	2.6544	1503359	0.0422	18.682	0.017681	50
55	0.131687	73586	9690	345242	0.028068	2.6587	1117155	0.0582	15.182	0.027709	55
60	0.223257	63896	14265	284869	0.050076	2.5738	771913	0.0569	12.081	0.049587	60
65	0.297090	49631	14745	211053	0.069863	2.4839	487045	0.0569	9.813	0.069362	65
70	0.376211	34886	13124	140713	0.093271	2.4311	275991	0.0569	7.911	0.092619	70
75	0.478028	21761	10403	81510	0.127622	2.3760	135278	0.0569	6.216	0.126621	75
80	0.610255	11359	6932	38220	0.181366	2.3204	53768	0.0569	4.734	0.179531	80
85+	*1.000000	4427	4427	15548	0.284735	3.5120	15548	0.0569	3.512	0.278146	85

TABLE 3 — FEMALE LIFE TABLE

x	$_nq_x$	l_x	$_nd_x$	$_nL_x$	$_nm_x$	$_na_x$	T_x	r_x	$\overset{\circ}{e}_x$	$_nM_x$	x
0	0.038755	100000	3876	97473	0.039760	0.3480	6645720	0.0083	66.457	0.039996	0
1	0.018357	96124	1765	379587	0.004649	1.2168	6548247	0.0083	68.123	0.004671	1
5	0.006248	94360	590	470326	0.001253	2.5000	6168661	0.0650	65.374	0.001297	5
10	0.003849	93770	361	467904	0.000771	2.3735	5698335	0.0476	60.769	0.000776	10
15	0.003965	93409	370	466163	0.000795	2.6123	5230431	0.0114	55.995	0.000794	15
20	0.006026	93039	561	463887	0.001209	2.6661	4764269	0.0218	51.207	0.001204	20
25	0.008840	92478	817	460446	0.001775	2.6200	4300382	0.0357	46.501	0.001768	25
30	0.011254	91661	1032	455877	0.002263	2.6464	3839936	0.0338	41.893	0.002251	30
35	0.017016	90629	1542	449569	0.003430	2.6799	3384060	0.0150	37.340	0.003421	35
40	0.026532	89087	2364	439854	0.005374	2.6385	2934491	0.0170	32.940	0.005360	40
45	0.035908	86724	3114	426200	0.007307	2.6180	2494637	0.0309	28.765	0.007276	45
50	0.049364	83609	4127	408353	0.010107	2.6512	2068437	0.0428	24.739	0.010032	50
55	0.076862	79482	6109	382888	0.015955	2.6227	1660084	0.0450	20.886	0.015844	55
60	0.105291	73373	7726	348329	0.022179	2.6007	1277196	0.0513	17.407	0.022011	60
65	0.149927	65647	9842	304552	0.032317	2.5935	928867	0.0513	14.149	0.032050	65
70	0.217605	55805	12144	249500	0.048671	2.5686	624315	0.0513	11.187	0.048249	70
75	0.317050	43662	13843	184058	0.075210	2.5258	374815	0.0513	8.585	0.074523	75
80	0.464667	29819	13856	114896	0.120594	2.5319	190757	0.0513	6.397	0.119202	80
85+	*1.000000	15963	15963	75861	0.210424	4.7523	75861	0.0513	4.752	0.206022	85

TABLE 4 — OBSERVED AND PROJECTED VITAL RATES

	OBSERVED POPULATION BOTH SEXES	MALES	FEMALES	PROJECTED POPULATION 1962 MALES	FEMALES	1967 MALES	FEMALES	1972 MALES	FEMALES	STABLE POPULATION MALES	FEMALES
RATES PER THOUSAND											
Birth	43.22	42.20	44.36	40.53	41.85	39.37	40.05	40.95	41.12	44.84	43.6
Death	7.38	8.18	6.49	8.49	6.62	8.64	6.58	8.76	6.62	7.45	6.2
Increase	35.84	34.02	37.87	32.04	35.23	30.73	33.46	32.19	34.50	37.389	
PERCENTAGE											
under 15	42.88	42.01	43.85	45.41	47.05	45.44	46.45	45.30	45.88	48.17	47.2
15-64	54.97	56.37	53.41	52.77	50.00	52.44	50.39	52.32	50.75	50.34	50.1
65 and over	2.15	1.62	2.74	1.81	2.95	2.12	3.16	2.39	3.37	1.48	2.5
DEP. RATIO X 100	81.91	77.40	87.22	89.49	99.98	90.71	98.44	91.15	97.04	98.65	99.3

TABLE 5 — POPULATION PROJECTED WITH FIXED AGE-SPECIFIC BIRTH AND DEATH RATES (IN 1000's)

AGE LAST BIRTHDAY	BOTH SEXES	1962 MALES	FEMALES	BOTH SEXES	1967 MALES	FEMALES	BOTH SEXES	1972 MALES	FEMALES	AGE AT LAST BIRTHDAY
0-4	318	163	155	360	185	175	425	218	207	0-4
5-9	262	135	127	313	161	152	355	182	173	5-9
10-14	218	112	106	260	134	126	312	160	152	10-14
15-19	136	71	65	216	111	105	259	134	125	15-19
20-24	135	70	65	136	71	65	215	110	105	20-24
25-29	119	61	58	134	69	65	135	70	65	25-29
30-34	111	59	52	117	60	57	132	68	64	30-34
35-39	89	50	39	109	58	51	115	59	56	35-39
40-44	80	45	35	87	48	39	107	57	50	40-44
45-49	73	41	32	78	44	34	83	46	37	45-49
50-54	63	35	28	69	38	31	74	41	33	50-54
55-59	47	26	21	57	31	26	63	34	29	55-59
60-64	32	17	15	41	22	19	50	26	24	60-64
65-69	20	9	11	27	13	14	33	16	17	65-69
70-74	10	4	6	15	6	9	19	8	11	70-74
75-79	6	2	4	8	3	5	10	3	7	75-79
80-84	3	1	2	3	1	2	4	1	3	80-84
85+	1	0	1	1	0	1	2	0	2	85+
TOTAL	1723	901	822	2031	1055	976	2393	1233	1160	TOTAL

TABLE 6 — STANDARDIZED RATES

STANDARD COUNTRIES:	ENGLAND AND WALES 1961			UNITED STATES 1960			MEXICO 1960		
STANDARDIZED RATES PER THOUSAND	BOTH SEXES	MALES	FEMALES	BOTH SEXES	MALES	FEMALES	BOTH SEXES	MALES	FEMALES
Birth	42.00	39.52*	39.48	42.73	36.60*	40.83	46.47	36.94*	44.96
Death	16.79	22.96*	14.90	14.13	17.23*	11.53	8.18	8.40*	6.63
Increase	25.21	16.56*	24.58	28.60	19.37*	29.30	38.29	28.54*	38.33

TABLE 7 — MOMENTS AND CUMULANTS

	OBSERVED POP. MALES	FEMALES	STATIONARY POP. MALES	FEMALES	STABLE POP. MALES	FEMALES	OBSERVED BIRTHS	NET MATERNITY FUNCTION	BIRTHS IN STABLE POP.
μ	23.14747	22.71386	33.86366	37.11965	20.26601	21.12957	28.08108	29.34169	27.71774
σ^2	323.8792	346.5448	435.0481	520.8158	278.2127	315.1473	40.47245	43.33133	39.18327
κ_3	3949.669	5625.882	2371.853	2801.907	4681.920	6027.757	132.5842	94.1385	124.0012
κ_4	-47034.	86.	-167561.	-261127.	33227.	62027.	-530.027	-1091.134	-494.232
β_1	0.459168	0.760506	0.068322	0.055572	1.017928	1.160836	0.265158	0.108925	0.255593
β_2	2.551621	3.000714	2.114682	2.037315	3.429276	3.624532	2.676422	2.418869	2.678094
κ	-0.176198	-0.308866	-0.027402	-0.021109	-0.449374	-0.517651	-0.149402	-0.057442	-0.146846

TABLE 8 — RATES FROM AGE DISTRIBUTIONS AND VITAL STATISTICS (Females)

VITAL STATISTICS		THOMPSON				BOURGEOIS-PICHAT					COALE	
		AGE RANGE	NRR	1000r	INTERVAL	AGE RANGE	NRR	1000b	1000d	1000r		
GRR	3.175										IBR	
NRR	2.904	0-4	2.58	34.69	27.35	5-29	2.25	35.69	5.66	30.03	IDR	
TFR	6.547	5-9	2.45	33.65	27.26	30-54	1.80	26.70	4.94	21.76	IRI	
GENERATION	28.517	10-14	1.74	20.07	27.16	55-79	3.85	113.96	64.05	49.91	K1	
SEX RATIO	106.187	15-19	2.02	26.09	27.01	*50-74	3.74	106.41	57.51	48.90	K2	

TABLE 9 — LESLIE MATRIX AND ITS SPECTRAL COMPONENTS (Females)

Part Age Interval	ORIGINAL MATRIX SUBDIAGONAL	ALTERNATIVE FIRST ROWS Projection	Integral	FIRST STABLE MATRIX % IN STABLE POPULATION	FISHER VALUES	REPRODUCTIVE VALUES	SECOND STABLE MATRIX Z₂ FIRST COLUMN	FIRST ROW
	0.98588	0.00000	0.00000	19.007	1.150	147651	0.1496+0.0854	0.1496+0.0854
	0.99485	0.00035	0.00000	15.531	1.407	149727	0.1512-0.0970	-0.0061+0.1651
	0.99628	0.08987	0.00077	12.806	1.706	112139	-0.0167-0.1883	-0.1417+0.0676
	0.99512	0.43741	0.19732	10.575	1.963	128613	-0.1840-0.0764	-0.1327-0.0972
	0.99258	0.75561	0.76696	8.722	1.874	108951	-0.1610+0.1344	-0.0424-0.1920
	0.99008	0.73928	0.89900	7.175	1.403	73007	0.0467+0.2152	0.0294-0.1855
	0.98616	0.55513	0.73168	5.888	0.851	34007	0.2224+0.0611	0.0583-0.1210
	0.97839	0.31701	0.49421	4.813	0.393	14261	0.1640-0.1760	0.0444-0.0523
	0.96896	0.10713	0.20639	3.903	0.113	3738	-0.0827-0.2348	0.0162-0.0131
	0.95813	0.01361	0.02979	3.134	0.013	377	-0.2526-0.0364	0.0021-0.0013
	0.93764	0.00005	0.00011	2.489	0.000	1	-0.1513+0.2097	0.0000-0.0000
5+	0.81478			5.958				

TABLE 10 — AGE ANALYSIS AND MISCELLANEOUS RESULTS (Females)

Part Age Interval	OBSERVED POPUL. (IN 100's)	CONTRIBUTIONS OF ROOTS (IN 100's) r₁	r₂, r₃	r₄·r₁₁	AGE-SP. BIRTH RATES	NET MATERNITY FUNCTION	COEFF. OF MATRIX EQUATION	PARAMETERS	INTEGRAL	MATRIX	EXP. INCREASE x	$e^{(x+2\frac{1}{2})r}$
	1284	1222	83	-22	0.0000	0.0000	0.0000	L(1)	1.20556	1.20652	0	1.0980
	1064	999	14	51	0.0000	0.0000	0.0003	L(2)	0.43517	0.43813	50	7.1202
	657	824	-78	-89	0.0001	0.0007	0.0881		0.86443	0.83773	55	8.5838
	655	680	-91	67	0.0377	0.1756	0.4274	R(1)	0.03739	0.03755	60	10.3483
	581	561	-3	23	0.1464	0.6792	0.7347	R(2)	-0.00655	-0.01123	65	12.4756
	520	461	98	-39	0.1716	0.7903	0.7135			0.22088	0.21778	70	15.0401
	400	379	99	-78	0.1397	0.6368	0.5305	C(1)		6431	75	18.1318
	363	310	-12	65	0.0944	0.4242	0.2987	C(2)		16912	80	21.8590
	332	251	-118	199	0.0394	0.1733	0.0988			-19140	85	26.3523
	290	202	-99	188	0.0057	0.0243	0.0122	2P/Y	28.4456	28.8506	90	31.7694
	226	160	29	37	0.0000	0.0000	0.0000	DELTA	4.7717		95	38.3000
5+	481	383									100	46.1730

TABLE 1 — DATA

AGE AT LAST BIRTHDAY	POPULATION BOTH SEXES	MALES Number	%	FEMALES Number	%	BIRTHS BY AGE OF MOTHER	DEATHS BOTH SEXES	MALES	FEMALES	AGE AT LAST BIRTHDAY
0	67786	34745	3.9	33041	4.0	0	1847	1106	741	0
1-4	243014	124555	13.9	118459	14.5	0	630	311	319	1-4
5-9	260800	134700	15.0	126100	15.4	0	203	113	90	5-9
10-14	216100	110800	12.4	105300	12.9	33	128	66	62	10-14
15-19	135700	70800	7.9	64900	7.9	3489	115	70	45	15-19
20-24	135700	70200	7.8	65500	8.0	16719	164	93	71	20-24
25-29	119200	61200	6.8	58000	7.1	17408	149	92	57	25-29
30-34	111700	59700	6.7	52000	6.4	12290	200	109	91	30-34
35-39	88300	49200	5.5	39100	4.8	6348	241	153	88	35-39
40-44	80300	45100	5.0	35200	4.3	2385	343	224	119	40-44
45-49	73500	41200	4.6	32300	4.0	305	536	352	184	45-49
50-54	63200	35400	3.9	27800	3.4	0	796	535	261	50-54
55-59	47500	26200	2.9	21300	2.6	0	896	615	281	55-59
60-64	32600	17200	1.9	15400	1.9	0	1097	745	352	60-64
65-69	19900	9200	1.0	10700	1.3	0	864	562	302	65-69
70-74	11600	4600	0.5	7000	0.9		819	434	385	70-74
75-79	4874	1704	0.2	3170	0.4		536	234	302	75-79
80-84	1509	476	0.1	1033	0.1	30388 M.	367	124	243	80-84
85+	417	120	0.0	297	0.0	28589 F.	247	66	181	85+
TOTAL	1713700	897100		816600		58977	10178	6004	4174	TOTAL

TABLE 2 — MALE LIFE TABLE

x	nq_x	l_x	nd_x	nL_x	nm_x	na_x	T_x	r_x	$\mathring{e}_x$	nM_x
0	0.030932	100000	3093	97853	0.031610	0.3060	6314121	0.0093	63.141	0.031832
1	0.009845	96907	954	384915	0.002479	1.1565	6216268	0.0093	64.147	0.002497
5	0.004129	95953	396	478773	0.000828	2.5000	5831354	0.0351	60.773	0.000839
10	0.002985	95557	285	477086	0.000598	2.5562	5352580	0.0636	56.015	0.000596
15	0.004966	95271	473	475245	0.000995	2.6503	4875494	0.0447	51.175	0.000989
20	0.006610	94798	627	472473	0.001326	2.5774	4400249	0.0133	46.417	0.001325
25	0.007497	94172	706	469141	0.001505	2.5667	3927776	0.0147	41.709	0.001503
30	0.009123	93466	853	465349	0.001832	2.6787	3458635	0.0198	37.004	0.001826
35	0.015518	92613	1437	459762	0.003126	2.7018	2993286	0.0249	32.320	0.003110
40	0.024623	91176	2245	450746	0.004981	2.7137	2533524	0.0125	27.787	0.004967
45	0.042054	88931	3740	436140	0.008575	2.7234	2082778	0.0151	23.420	0.008544
50	0.073425	85191	6255	411386	0.015205	2.6710	1646639	0.0299	19.329	0.015113
55	0.112438	78936	8875	374075	0.023726	2.6786	1235252	0.0461	15.649	0.023473
60	0.197879	70060	13863	316924	0.043744	2.5924	861177	0.0552	12.292	0.043314
65	0.267344	56197	15024	243827	0.061617	2.5268	544253	0.0552	9.685	0.061087
70	0.383670	41173	15797	165939	0.095197	2.4725	300426	0.0552	7.297	0.094348
75	0.509891	25376	12939	93236	0.138778	2.3998	134487	0.0552	5.300	0.137324
80	0.769592	12437	9571	36158	0.264712	2.2807	41251	0.0552	3.317	0.260505
85+	*1.000000	2866	2866	5093	0.562650	1.7773	5093	0.0552	1.777	0.550000

TABLE 3 — FEMALE LIFE TABLE

x	nq_x	l_x	nd_x	nL_x	nm_x	na_x	T_x	r_x	$\mathring{e}_x$	nM_x
0	0.021958	100000	2196	98577	0.022275	0.3521	6842453	0.0094	68.425	0.022427
1	0.010634	97804	1040	388329	0.002678	1.2240	6743876	0.0094	68.953	0.002693
5	0.003500	96764	339	482974	0.000700	2.5000	6355547	0.0352	65.681	0.000714
10	0.002939	96425	283	481418	0.000589	2.4974	5872573	0.0658	60.903	0.000589
15	0.003485	96142	335	479921	0.000698	2.6460	5391155	0.0467	56.075	0.000693
20	0.005409	95807	518	477767	0.001085	2.5537	4911234	0.0103	51.262	0.001084
25	0.004918	95289	469	475337	0.000986	2.6391	4433467	0.0219	46.527	0.000983
30	0.008764	94820	831	472146	0.001760	2.6477	3958130	0.0378	41.744	0.001750
35	0.011255	93989	1058	467454	0.002263	2.6443	3485984	0.0366	37.089	0.002251
40	0.016828	92931	1564	461064	0.003392	2.7026	3018530	0.0155	32.481	0.003381
45	0.028222	91367	2579	450919	0.005718	2.7049	2557467	0.0176	27.991	0.005697
50	0.046170	88789	4099	434298	0.009439	2.6468	2106547	0.0323	23.725	0.009388
55	0.064563	84690	5468	410723	0.013313	2.6729	1672249	0.0445	19.746	0.013192
60	0.109012	79222	8636	375343	0.023009	2.5955	1261526	0.0471	15.924	0.022857
65	0.133534	70586	9426	330693	0.028502	2.6410	886183	0.0471	12.555	0.028224
70	0.245515	61160	15016	270053	0.055603	2.6194	555490	0.0471	9.083	0.055000
75	0.390695	46144	18028	186833	0.096495	2.5656	285437	0.0471	6.186	0.095268
80	0.735820	28116	20688	86651	0.238755	2.3933	98604	0.0471	3.507	0.235236
85+	*1.000000	7428	7428	11954	0.621379	1.6093	11954	0.0471	1.609	0.609428

TABLE 4 — OBSERVED AND PROJECTED VITAL RATES

	OBSERVED POPULATION BOTH SEXES	MALES	FEMALES	PROJECTED POPULATION 1967 MALES	FEMALES	1972 MALES	FEMALES	1977 MALES	FEMALES	STABLE POPULATION MALES	FEMALE
RATES PER THOUSAND											
Birth	34.42	33.87	35.01	33.45	34.13	35.49	35.78	38.09	38.01	38.41	37.2
Death	5.94	6.69	5.11	6.90	5.08	7.27	5.35	7.48	5.52	6.70	5.5
Increase	28.48	27.18	29.90	26.55	29.05	28.22	30.43	30.61	32.49	31.710	
PERCENTAGE											
under 15	45.96	45.12	46.89	43.69	44.81	42.13	42.88	41.26	41.53	43.97	43.0
15-64	51.80	53.08	50.39	54.09	52.15	55.26	53.78	55.87	54.90	53.87	53.6
65 and over	2.23	1.79	2.72	2.22	3.04	2.61	3.34	2.87	3.57	2.16	3.3
DEP. RATIO X 100	93.05	88.39	98.44	84.87	91.75	80.96	85.95	78.98	82.14	85.65	86.4

TABLE 5 — POPULATION PROJECTED WITH FIXED AGE-SPECIFIC BIRTH AND DEATH RATES (IN 1000's)

AGE AT LAST BIRTHDAY	1967 BOTH SEXES	MALES	FEMALES	1972 BOTH SEXES	MALES	FEMALES	1977 BOTH SEXES	MALES	FEMALES	AGE AT LAST BIRTHDAY
0-4	304	156	148	358	184	174	441	226	215	0-4
5-9	308	158	150	302	155	147	355	182	173	5-9
10-14	260	134	126	307	157	150	301	154	147	10-14
15-19	215	110	105	259	134	125	306	157	149	15-19
20-24	135	70	65	215	110	105	258	133	125	20-24
25-29	135	70	65	134	70	64	213	109	104	25-29
30-34	119	61	58	134	69	65	133	69	64	30-34
35-39	110	59	51	117	60	57	132	68	64	35-39
40-44	87	48	39	109	58	51	115	59	56	40-44
45-49	78	44	34	85	47	38	106	56	50	45-49
50-54	70	39	31	74	41	33	80	44	36	50-54
55-59	58	32	26	64	35	29	68	37	31	55-59
60-64	41	22	19	51	27	24	57	30	27	60-64
65-69	27	13	14	34	17	17	42	21	21	65-69
70-74	15	6	9	20	9	11	26	12	14	70-74
75-79	8	3	5	10	4	6	13	5	8	75-79
80-84	2	1	1	3	1	2	4	1	3	80-84
85+	0	0	0	0	0	0	0	0	0	85+
TOTAL	1972	1026	946	2276	1178	1098	2650	1363	1287	TOTAL

TABLE 6 — STANDARDIZED RATES

STANDARD COUNTRIES: STANDARDIZED RATES PER THOUSAND

	ENGLAND AND WALES 1961 BOTH SEXES	MALES	FEMALES	UNITED STATES 1960 BOTH SEXES	MALES	FEMALES	MEXICO 1960 BOTH SEXES	MALES	FEMALES
Birth	34.78	34.04*	32.68	35.35	31.49*	33.77	38.41	31.80*	37.14
Death	19.47	18.34*	19.98	15.67	13.87*	14.51	7.63	6.91*	6.52
Increase	15.32	15.69*	12.70	19.68	17.62*	19.25	30.78	24.89*	30.63

TABLE 7 — MOMENTS AND CUMULANTS

	OBSERVED POP. MALES	FEMALES	STATIONARY POP. MALES	FEMALES	STABLE POP. MALES	FEMALES	OBSERVED BIRTHS	NET MATERNITY FUNCTION	BIRTHS IN STABLE POP.
μ	22.87718	22.35891	34.35210	36.74318	22.21570	23.10782	28.31091	29.44841	28.09337
σ^2	332.7931	343.7944	438.1554	493.0315	312.0246	345.9808	37.52860	42.36083	38.80638
κ_3	4508.800	5705.035	2007.859	1922.402	4887.132	5868.773	118.1580	98.4776	122.8889
κ_4	-46221.	-5631.	-183684.	-251494.	5734.	10831.	-363.715	-1029.453	-499.918
β_1	0.551568	0.800978	0.047927	0.030836	0.786215	0.831646	0.264143	0.127580	0.258414
β_2	2.582662	2.952359	2.043212	1.965386	3.058895	3.090485	2.741753	2.426309	2.668035
κ	-0.198982	-0.301912	-0.018449	-0.011317	-0.326011	-0.337784	-0.163470	-0.065837	-0.145717

TABLE 8 — RATES FROM AGE DISTRIBUTIONS AND VITAL STATISTICS (Females)

VITAL STATISTICS
GRR	2.631
NRR	2.489
TFR	5.427
GENERATION	28.762
SEX RATIO	106.293

THOMPSON
AGE RANGE	NRR	1000r	INTERVAL
0-4	2.80	37.61	27.39
5-9	2.60	35.72	27.34
10-14	2.47	32.35	27.25
15-19	1.76	16.23	27.11

BOURGEOIS-PICHAT
AGE RANGE	NRR	1000b	1000d	1000r
5-29	2.93	40.97	1.20	39.77
30-54	1.95	28.03	3.22	24.81
55-79	3.50	91.11	44.75	46.36
*50-74	3.42	86.53	40.93	45.60

COALE: IBR, IDR, IRI, K1, K2

TABLE 9 — LESLIE MATRIX AND ITS SPECTRAL COMPONENTS (Females)

Start of Age Interval	ORIGINAL MATRIX SUB-DIAGONAL	ALTERNATIVE FIRST ROWS Projection	Integral	FIRST STABLE MATRIX % IN STABLE POPULATION	FISHER VALUES	REPRODUCTIVE VALUES	SECOND STABLE MATRIX Z_2 FIRST COLUMN	FIRST ROW
0	0.99192	0.00000	0.00000	16.806	1.111	168336	0.1503+0.0828	0.1503+0.0828
5	0.99678	0.00037	0.00000	14.218	1.313	165618	0.1539-0.0996	-0.0017+0.1606
10	0.99689	0.06362	0.00080	12.087	1.544	162633	-0.0161-0.1961	-0.1326+0.0694
15	0.99551	0.36332	0.13736	10.277	1.746	113289	-0.1937-0.0844	-0.1250-0.0836
20	0.99491	0.65363	0.65217	8.726	1.650	108100	-0.1780+0.1401	-0.0413-0.1698
25	0.99329	0.63125	0.76685	7.405	1.215	70466	0.0420+0.2390	0.0226-0.1633
30	0.99006	0.46862	0.60387	6.273	0.728	37854	0.2465+0.0814	0.0490-0.1063
35	0.98633	0.27047	0.41481	5.297	0.336	13144	0.2008-0.1906	0.0384-0.0459
40	0.97800	0.09082	0.17312	4.456	0.095	3341	-0.0774-0.2837	0.0139-0.0113
45	0.96314	0.01115	0.02405	3.717	0.011	342	-0.3018-0.0695	0.0017-0.0011
50	0.94572	0.00004	0.00009	3.053	0.000	1	-0.2116+0.2417	0.0000-0.0000
55+	0.79670			7.684				

TABLE 10 — AGE ANALYSIS AND MISCELLANEOUS RESULTS (Females)

Start of Age Interval	OBSERVED POPUL. (IN 100's)	CONTRIBUTIONS OF ROOTS (IN 100's) r_1	r_2, r_3	$r_4\text{-}r_{11}$	AGE-SP. BIRTH RATES	NET MATERNITY FUNCTION	COEFF. OF MATRIX EQUATION
0	1515	1360	74	81	0.0000	0.0000	0.0000
5	1261	1151	156	-46	0.0000	0.0000	0.0004
10	1053	978	75	0	0.0002	0.0007	0.0629
15	649	832	-105	-78	0.0261	0.1251	0.3581
20	655	706	-192	140	0.1237	0.5912	0.6414
25	580	599	-74	55	0.1455	0.6916	0.6163
30	520	508	145	-132	0.1146	0.5409	0.4544
35	391	429	231	-268	0.0787	0.3679	0.2597
40	352	361	68	-77	0.0328	0.1514	0.0860
45	323	301	-190	212	0.0046	0.0206	0.0103
50	278	247	-261	292	0.0000	0.0000	0.0000
55+	589	622					

PARAMETERS
	INTEGRAL	MATRIX
L(1)	1.17181	1.17247
L(2)	0.43619	0.43930
	0.84362	0.81806
R(1)	0.03171	0.03182
R(2)	-0.01032	-0.01483
	0.21872	0.21560
C(1)		8094
C(2)		36573
		21989
2P/Y	28.7268	29.1433
DELTA	4.6536	

EXP. INCREASE
x	$e^{(x+2\frac{1}{2})r}$
0	1.0825
50	5.2847
55	6.1927
60	7.2567
65	8.5035
70	9.9645
75	11.6766
80	13.6828
85	16.0337
90	18.7885
95	22.0166
100	25.7994

TABLE 1 — DATA

AGE AT LAST BIRTHDAY	POPULATION BOTH SEXES	MALES Number	%	FEMALES Number	%	BIRTHS BY AGE OF MOTHER	DEATHS BOTH SEXES	MALES	FEMALES	AGE AT LAST BIRTHDAY
0	611636	305452	2.3	306184	2.3	0	46989	26919	20070	0
1-4	3635149	1836112	14.0	1799037	13.7	0	39694	20939	18755	1-4
5-9	3999174	2016270	15.3	1982904	15.1	0	13253	6982	6271	5-9
10-14	3093646	1565892	11.9	1527754	11.7	250	6115	3415	2700	10-14
15-19	2503381	1265155	9.6	1238226	9.4	50247	5281	2814	2467	15-19
20-24	2420394	1214359	9.2	1206035	9.2	241585	7156	3540	3616	20-24
25-29	2074755	1026656	7.8	1048099	8.0	254252	6991	3286	3705	25-29
30-34	1756918	885683	6.7	871235	6.6	185721	7273	3586	3687	30-34
35-39	1374451	693449	5.3	681002	5.2	121568	7722	3947	3775	35-39
40-44	1134443	569750	4.3	564693	4.3	50040	8006	4309	3697	40-44
45-49	978413	494692	3.8	483721	3.7	10501	8522	5112	3410	45-49
50-54	813420	402425	3.1	410995	3.1	1374	9133	5479	3654	50-54
55-59	651814	322259	2.4	329555	2.5	0	9367	5700	3667	55-59
60-64	474391	229019	1.7	245372	1.9	0	10109	6009	4100	60-64
65-69	313148	149292	1.1	163856	1.3	0	8942	5171	3771	65-69
70-74	198262	87986	0.7	110276	0.8		8690	4627	4063	70-74
75-79	117319	49285	0.4	68034	0.5		7008	3536	3472	75-79
80-84	62086	24307	0.2	37779	0.3	484031 M.	5741	2665	3076	80-84
85+	45116	16106	0.1	29010	0.2	431507 F.	5860	2382	3478	85+
TOTAL	26257916	13154149		13103767		915538	221852	120418	101434	TOTAL

TABLE 2 — MALE LIFE TABLE

x	$_nq_x$	l_x	$_nd_x$	$_nL_x$	$_nm_x$	$_na_x$	T_x	r_x	$\dot{e}_x$	$_nM_x$	x
0	0.083387	100000	8339	94620	0.088128	0.3548	5838546	0.0000	58.385	0.088128	0
1	0.044219	91661	4053	355413	0.011404	1.2288	5743926	0.0000	62.665	0.011404	1
5	0.016956	87608	1485	434327	0.003420	2.5000	5388513	0.0263	61.507	0.003463	5
10	0.010787	86123	929	428178	0.002170	2.3785	4954186	0.0441	57.525	0.002181	10
15	0.011079	85194	944	423669	0.002228	2.5644	4526008	0.0231	53.126	0.002224	15
20	0.014491	84250	1221	418275	0.002919	2.5644	4102339	0.0181	48.693	0.002915	20
25	0.015913	83029	1321	411930	0.003207	2.5670	3684063	0.0282	44.371	0.003201	25
30	0.020140	81708	1646	404620	0.004067	2.6187	3272133	0.0350	40.047	0.004049	30
35	0.028214	80062	2259	394924	0.005720	2.6156	2867514	0.0384	35.816	0.005692	35
40	0.037263	77803	2899	382086	0.007588	2.6098	2472589	0.0260	31.780	0.007563	40
45	0.050563	74904	3787	365427	0.010364	2.5992	2090503	0.0243	27.909	0.010334	45
50	0.066114	71117	4702	344220	0.013659	2.5832	1725075	0.0291	24.257	0.013615	50
55	0.085284	66415	5664	318506	0.017783	2.6045	1380856	0.0377	20.791	0.017688	55
60	0.124183	60751	7544	285496	0.026425	2.5800	1062350	0.0530	17.487	0.026238	60
65	0.160892	53206	8561	245239	0.034907	2.5711	776853	0.0530	14.601	0.034637	65
70	0.234381	44646	10464	197466	0.052992	2.5379	531614	0.0530	11.907	0.052588	70
75	0.306091	34182	10463	144699	0.072307	2.4950	334148	0.0530	9.776	0.071746	75
80	0.430516	23719	10211	92389	0.110527	2.5621	189448	0.0530	7.987	0.109639	80
85+	1.000000	13508	13508	97059	0.139169	7.1855	97059	0.0530	7.186	0.147895	85+

TABLE 3 — FEMALE LIFE TABLE

x	$_nq_x$	l_x	$_nd_x$	$_nL_x$	$_nm_x$	$_na_x$	T_x	r_x	$\dot{e}_x$	$_nM_x$	x
0	0.062976	100000	6298	96074	0.065549	0.3766	6375645	0.0000	63.756	0.065549	0
1	0.040547	93702	3799	364449	0.010425	1.2730	6279571	0.0000	67.016	0.010425	1
5	0.015481	89903	1392	446036	0.003120	2.5000	5915122	0.0276	65.794	0.003163	5
10	0.008742	88511	774	440513	0.001757	2.3601	5469087	0.0450	61.790	0.001767	10
15	0.009942	87737	872	436615	0.001998	2.6244	5028573	0.0215	57.314	0.001992	15
20	0.014906	86865	1295	431220	0.003003	2.6014	4591958	0.0138	52.863	0.002998	20
25	0.017561	85570	1503	424193	0.003542	2.5655	4160739	0.0289	48.624	0.003535	25
30	0.021025	84068	1768	416077	0.004248	2.5890	3736545	0.0387	44.447	0.004232	30
35	0.027438	82300	2258	406025	0.005562	2.5751	3320469	0.0379	40.346	0.005543	35
40	0.032257	80042	2582	393845	0.006556	2.5347	2914444	0.0278	36.411	0.006547	40
45	0.034706	77460	2688	380721	0.007061	2.5528	2520600	0.0244	32.541	0.007050	45
50	0.043636	74772	3263	365953	0.008916	2.5772	2139879	0.0295	28.619	0.008891	50
55	0.054500	71509	3897	348262	0.011190	2.6181	1773925	0.0397	24.807	0.011127	55
60	0.080936	67612	5472	324990	0.016838	2.6119	1425663	0.0522	21.086	0.016709	60
65	0.110027	62139	6837	294428	0.023221	2.6204	1100673	0.0522	17.713	0.023014	65
70	0.170410	55302	9424	253712	0.037145	2.5807	806245	0.0522	14.579	0.036844	70
75	0.228546	45878	10485	203727	0.051468	2.5523	552533	0.0522	12.043	0.051033	75
80	0.340616	35393	12055	146816	0.082112	2.7221	348806	0.0522	9.855	0.081421	80
85+	1.000000	23338	23338	201989	0.115539	8.6551	201989	0.0522	8.655	0.119890	85+

TABLE 4 — OBSERVED AND PROJECTED VITAL RATES

	OBSERVED POPULATION BOTH SEXES	MALES	FEMALES	PROJECTED POPULATION 1965 MALES	FEMALES	1970 MALES	FEMALES	1975 MALES	FEMALES	STABLE POPULATION MALES	FEMALES
RATES PER THOUSAND											
Birth	34.87	36.80	32.93	36.50	32.94	35.60	33.29	37.36	34.21	33.92	32.23
Death	8.45	9.15	7.74	9.29	7.80	9.54	8.08	9.81	8.40	11.78	10.08
Increase	26.42	27.64	25.19	27.21	25.14	27.06	25.21	27.55	25.81		22.1485
PERCENTAGE											
under 15	43.19	43.51	42.86	42.44	41.21	40.41	38.58	39.98	37.56	37.95	37.00
15-64	54.01	54.00	54.02	54.64	55.06	56.27	57.17	56.43	57.75	56.98	56.36
65 and over	2.80	2.49	3.12	2.92	3.73	3.32	4.26	3.59	4.70	5.07	6.65
DEP. RATIO X 100	85.14	85.18	85.11	83.02	81.62	77.72	74.93	77.20	73.17	75.50	77.45

TABLE 5 — POPULATION PROJECTED WITH FIXED AGE—SPECIFIC BIRTH AND DEATH RATES (IN 1000's)

AGE AT LAST BIRTHDAY	1965 BOTH SEXES	1965 MALES	1965 FEMALES	1970 BOTH SEXES	1970 MALES	1970 FEMALES	1975 BOTH SEXES	1975 MALES	1975 FEMALES	AGE AT LAST BIRTHDAY
0-4	4442	2323	2119	5058	2645	2413	5842	3055	2787	0-4
5-9	4106	2067	2039	4295	2242	2053	4890	2553	2337	5-9
10-14	3946	1988	1958	4052	2038	2014	4237	2210	2027	10-14
15-19	3063	1549	1514	3908	1967	1941	4012	2016	1996	15-19
20-24	2472	1249	1223	3026	1530	1496	3859	1942	1917	20-24
25-29	2382	1196	1186	2433	1230	1203	2977	1506	1471	25-29
30-34	2036	1008	1028	2339	1175	1164	2388	1208	1180	30-34
35-39	1714	864	850	1987	984	1003	2283	1147	1136	35-39
40-44	1332	671	661	1661	836	825	1925	952	973	40-44
45-49	1091	545	546	1281	642	639	1597	800	797	45-49
50-54	931	466	465	1038	513	525	1218	604	614	50-54
55-59	763	372	391	873	431	442	974	475	499	55-59
60-64	597	289	308	699	334	365	799	386	413	60-64
65-69	419	197	222	527	248	279	618	287	331	65-69
70-74	261	120	141	350	158	192	440	200	240	70-74
75-79	153	64	89	201	88	113	270	116	154	75-79
80-84	80	31	49	105	41	64	138	56	82	80-84
85+	78	26	52	100	33	67	131	43	88	85+
TOTAL	29866	15025	14841	33933	17135	16798	38598	19556	19042	TOTAL

TABLE 6 — STANDARDIZED RATES

STANDARD COUNTRIES: STANDARDIZED RATES PER THOUSAND	ENGLAND AND WALES 1961 BOTH SEXES	MALES	FEMALES	UNITED STATES 1960 BOTH SEXES	MALES	FEMALES	MEXICO 1960 BOTH SEXES	MALES	FEMALES
Birth	31.95	34.24*	29.19	32.35	31.26*	30.04	33.57	33.37*	31.56
Death	13.50	23.99*	12.83	12.29	19.19*	11.01	9.48	10.49*	8.37
Increase	18.46	10.24*	16.36	20.06	12.07*	19.03	24.09	22.88*	23.19

TABLE 7 — MOMENTS AND CUMULANTS

	OBSERVED POP. MALES	OBSERVED POP. FEMALES	STATIONARY POP. MALES	STATIONARY POP. FEMALES	STABLE POP. MALES	STABLE POP. FEMALES	OBSERVED BIRTHS	NET MATERNITY FUNCTION	BIRTHS IN STABLE POP.
μ	22.67084	23.18576	36.28662	38.57891	25.88994	26.99317	29.05658	30.59600	29.47870
σ^2	322.7240	342.5596	525.9206	585.9545	402.2720	445.2923	43.81345	49.73219	46.89198
κ_3	5312.809	5971.961	3700.191	3723.546	6580.374	7763.252	150.9267	113.9081	140.9511
κ_4	18053.	28831.	-246476.	-338670.	-14388.	-22083.	-556.600	-1427.154	-992.342
β_1	0.839759	0.887208	0.094121	0.068916	0.665184	0.682577	0.270838	0.105486	0.192682
β_2	3.173337	3.245687	2.108883	2.013608	2.911086	2.888633	2.710047	2.422974	2.548701
κ	-0.361959	-0.386268	-0.036485	-0.025320	-0.277082	-0.274139	-0.158110	-0.056254	-0.104156

TABLE 8 — RATES FROM AGE DISTRIBUTIONS AND VITAL STATISTICS (Females)

VITAL STATISTICS		THOMPSON AGE RANGE	NRR	1000r	INTERVAL	BOURGEOIS-PICHAT AGE RANGE	NRR	1000b	1000d	1000r	COALE	
GRR	2.331	0-4	2.04	27.14	27.22	5-29	2.12	38.90	11.10	27.80	IBR	44.83
NRR	1.945	5-9	2.25	30.42	27.14	30-54	2.28	41.34	10.86	30.47	IDR	10.68
TFR	4.945	10-14	2.04	25.77	27.07	55-79	4.16	152.04	99.26	52.78	IRI	34.15
GENERATION	30.032	15-19	1.96	24.96	26.99	*35-59	2.12	36.14	8.36	27.78	K1	32.46
SEX RATIO	112.172										K2	0.52

TABLE 9 — LESLIE MATRIX AND ITS SPECTRAL COMPONENTS (Females)

Start of Age Interval	ORIGINAL MATRIX SUB-DIAGONAL	ALTERNATIVE FIRST ROWS Projection	ALTERNATIVE FIRST ROWS Integral	FIRST STABLE MATRIX % IN STABLE POPULATION	FISHER VALUES	REPRODUCTIVE VALUES	SECOND STABLE MATRIX Z_2 FIRST COLUMN	SECOND STABLE MATRIX Z_2 FIRST ROW
0	0.96854	0.00000	0.00000	14.064	1.147	2414356	0.1306+0.0749	0.1306+0.0749
5	0.98762	0.00017	0.00000	12.190	1.323	2623600	0.1451-0.0764	0.0061+0.1381
10	0.99115	0.04383	0.00037	10.774	1.497	2286696	0.0146-0.1816	-0.1021+0.0712
15	0.98764	0.25874	0.09309	9.557	1.637	2026618	-0.1622-0.1221	-0.1088-0.0465
20	0.98370	0.47637	0.45954	8.447	1.551	1870908	-0.2110+0.0796	-0.0513-0.1248
25	0.98087	0.49018	0.55651	7.437	1.207	1264788	-0.0506+0.2443	0.0072-0.1358
30	0.97584	0.42040	0.48903	6.528	0.802	698377	0.1977+0.1914	0.0422-0.0979
35	0.97000	0.28702	0.40953	5.701	0.424	288616	0.2935-0.0707	0.0397-0.0475
40	0.96668	0.11894	0.20329	4.949	0.149	84061	0.1063-0.3118	0.0176-0.0148
45	0.96121	0.02705	0.04980	4.281	0.031	14977	-0.2244-0.2790	0.0041-0.0028
50	0.95166	0.00363	0.00767	3.683	0.004	1530	-0.3846+0.0434	0.0005-0.0003
55+	0.83449			12.389				

TABLE 10 — AGE ANALYSIS AND MISCELLANEOUS RESULTS (Females)

Start of Age Interval	OBSERVED POPUL. (IN 100's)	CONTRIBUTIONS OF ROOTS (IN 100's) r_1	r_2, r_3	$r_4 \cdot r_{11}$	AGE-SP. BIRTH RATES	NET MATERNITY FUNCTION	COEFF. OF MATRIX EQUATION	PARAMETERS	INTEGRAL	MATRIX	EXP. INCREASE x	$e^{(x+2\frac{1}{2})r}$
0	21052	20173	359	520	0.0000	0.0000	0.0000	L(1)	1.11711	1.11740	0	1.0569
5	19829	17485	1360	984	0.0000	0.0000	0.0002	L(2)	0.47277	0.47611	50	3.1989
10	15278	15455	1182	-1359	0.0001	0.0003	0.0419		0.76942	0.75105	55	3.5735
15	12382	13708	-272	-1054	0.0191	0.0835	0.2453	R(1)	0.02215	0.02220	60	3.9920
20	12060	12117	-1787	1731	0.0944	0.4071	0.4461	R(2)	-0.02039	-0.02348	65	4.4595
25	10481	10667	-1783	1597	0.1143	0.4850	0.4515			0.20396	0.20116	70	4.9817
30	8712	9363	75	-726	0.1005	0.4180	0.3798	C(1)		143438	75	5.5651
35	6810	8177	2246	-3613	0.0841	0.3416	0.2531	C(2)		310097	80	6.2168
40	5647	7099	2534	-3986	0.0418	0.1645	0.1017			300684	85	6.9448
45	4837	6141	286	-1590	0.0102	0.0390	0.0224	2P/Y	30.8054	31.2348	90	7.7581
50	4110	5283	-2646	1473	0.0016	0.0058	0.0029	DELTA	8.0279		95	8.6667
55+	9839	17770									100	9.6816

TABLE 1 DATA

AGE AT LAST BIRTHDAY	BOTH SEXES	POPULATION MALES Number	%	FEMALES Number	%	BIRTHS BY AGE OF MOTHER	DEATHS BOTH SEXES	MALES	FEMALES	AGE AT LAST BIRTHDAY
0	54439	27869	3.9	26570	3.9	0	6378	3228	3150	0
1-4	166655	86536	12.2	80119	11.9	0	5832	2719	3113	1-4
5-9	168451	87823	12.4	80628	12.0	0	696	364	332	5-9
10-14	149721	79835	11.3	69886	10.4	11	253	141	112	10-14
15-19	140337	75386	10.6	64951	9.6	4040	264	120	144	15-19
20-24	116851	62529	8.8	54322	8.1	14659	288	129	159	20-24
25-29	103097	55257	7.8	47840	7.1	16156	297	176	121	25-29
30-34	79901	39588	5.6	40313	6.0	11611	287	136	151	30-34
35-39	72786	37345	5.3	35441	5.3	8707	262	135	127	35-39
40-44	66809	34237	4.8	32572	4.8	3985	293	162	131	40-44
45-49	58103	28473	4.0	29630	4.4	1604	357	211	146	45-49
50-54	44154	21947	3.1	22207	3.3	527	394	248	146	50-54
55-59	43297	19908	2.8	23389	3.5	0	491	269	222	55-59
60-64	36078	16713	2.4	19365	2.9	0	574	333	241	60-64
65-69	29314	13191	1.9	16123	2.4	0	713	396	317	65-69
70-74	22432	9745	1.4	12687	1.9		850	448	402	70-74
75-79	15569	6478	0.9	9091	1.4		928	463	465	75-79
80-84	9142	3607	0.5	5535	0.8	31347 M.	900	419	481	80-84
85+	3917	1450	0.2	2467	0.4	29953 F.	693	297	396	85+
TOTAL	1381053	707917		673136		61300	20750	10394	10356	TOTAL

TABLE 2 MALE LIFE TABLE

x	nq_x	l_x	nd_x	nL_x	nm_x	na_x	T_x	r_x	$\mathring{e}_x$	nM_x	x
0	0.107843	100000	10784	93730	0.115057	0.4186	5454597	0.0125	54.546	0.115828	
1	0.115663	89216	10319	329955	0.031274	1.3924	5360866	0.0125	60.089	0.031420	
5	0.019832	78897	1565	390572	0.004006	2.5000	5030911	0.0263	63.766	0.004145	
10	0.008755	77332	677	384769	0.001760	2.2057	4640339	0.0130	60.005	0.001766	10
15	0.007935	76655	608	381777	0.001593	2.5367	4255571	0.0228	55.516	0.001592	15
20	0.010313	76047	784	378395	0.002073	2.6556	3873794	0.0289	50.940	0.002063	20
25	0.015864	75263	1194	373427	0.003197	2.5835	3495398	0.0427	46.443	0.003185	25
30	0.017047	74069	1263	367209	0.003439	2.5184	3121971	0.0358	42.150	0.003435	30
35	0.017931	72806	1306	360852	0.003618	2.5665	2754762	0.0107	37.837	0.003615	35
40	0.023484	71500	1679	353565	0.004749	2.6556	2393909	0.0221	33.481	0.004732	40
45	0.036663	69821	2560	343130	0.007460	2.6653	2040344	0.0368	29.222	0.007411	45
50	0.055153	67261	3710	327368	0.011332	2.5902	1697214	0.0249	25.233	0.011300	50
55	0.065542	63552	4165	307756	0.013534	2.5984	1369846	0.0128	21.555	0.013512	55
60	0.095602	59386	5677	283446	0.020030	2.6246	1062091	0.0316	17.884	0.019925	60
65	0.140756	53709	7560	250461	0.030184	2.6079	778645	0.0316	14.497	0.030020	65
70	0.207862	46149	9593	207515	0.046226	2.5782	528184	0.0316	11.445	0.045972	70
75	0.305360	36556	11163	155282	0.071888	2.5365	320669	0.0316	8.772	0.071473	75
80	0.454690	25394	11546	98662	0.117028	2.5484	165387	0.0316	6.513	0.116163	80
85+	*1.000000	13847	13847	66725	0.207528	4.8186	66725	0.0316	4.819	0.204828	85

TABLE 3 FEMALE LIFE TABLE

x	nq_x	l_x	nd_x	nL_x	nm_x	na_x	T_x	r_x	$\mathring{e}_x$	nM_x	x
0	0.110397	100000	11040	93732	0.117780	0.4322	5540030	0.0136	55.400	0.118555	
1	0.140791	88960	12525	323851	0.038675	1.4459	5446298	0.0136	61.222	0.038855	
5	0.019363	76435	1480	378477	0.003910	2.5000	5122447	0.0311	67.017	0.004118	5
10	0.007944	74955	595	373152	0.001596	2.2699	4743969	0.0193	63.291	0.001603	10
15	0.011059	74360	822	369843	0.002223	2.6200	4370818	0.0230	58.779	0.002217	15
20	0.014539	73538	1069	365034	0.002929	2.5176	4000975	0.0279	54.407	0.002927	20
25	0.012591	72469	912	360116	0.002534	2.5596	3635941	0.0269	50.173	0.002529	25
30	0.018587	71556	1330	354525	0.003752	2.5525	3275825	0.0266	45.780	0.003746	30
35	0.017763	70226	1247	348021	0.003583	2.5075	2921299	0.0176	41.599	0.003583	35
40	0.019933	68979	1375	341349	0.004026	2.5613	2573278	0.0138	37.305	0.004022	40
45	0.024435	67604	1652	334048	0.004945	2.5965	2231738	0.0332	33.012	0.004927	45
50	0.032444	65952	2140	324683	0.006590	2.6275	1897690	0.0168	28.774	0.006574	50
55	0.046430	63812	2963	311978	0.009497	2.6095	1573007	0.0043	24.651	0.009492	55
60	0.060757	60849	3697	295512	0.012510	2.6375	1261030	0.0317	20.724	0.012445	60
65	0.094529	57152	5403	273082	0.019784	2.6532	965518	0.0317	16.894	0.019661	65
70	0.148200	51750	7669	240553	0.031882	2.6275	692435	0.0317	13.380	0.031686	70
75	0.229014	44080	10095	196109	0.051477	2.5935	451882	0.0317	10.251	0.051149	75
80	0.359014	33985	12201	139582	0.087413	2.6996	255774	0.0317	7.526	0.086902	80
85+	1.000000	21784	21784	116192	0.187484	5.3338	116192	0.0317	5.334	0.160518	85

TABLE 4 OBSERVED AND PROJECTED VITAL RATES

	OBSERVED POPULATION BOTH SEXES	MALES	FEMALES	PROJECTED POPULATION 1960 MALES	FEMALES	1965 MALES	FEMALES	1970 MALES	FEMALES	STABLE POPULATION MALES	FEMALES
RATES PER THOUSAND											
Birth	44.39	44.28	44.50	43.54	43.88	42.70	43.19	41.99	42.61	44.00	44.74
Death	15.02	14.68	15.38	15.38	16.45	15.17	16.27	14.92	16.02	14.61	15.3
Increase	29.36	29.60	29.11	28.16	27.43	27.53	26.92	27.08	26.59	29.386	
PERCENTAGE											
under 15	39.05	39.84	38.21	40.80	39.93	41.99	41.35	42.42	41.99	42.87	42.5
15-64	55.13	55.29	54.97	54.36	53.17	53.33	51.85	53.17	51.72	53.22	52.6
65 and over	5.82	4.87	6.82	4.83	6.90	4.68	6.81	4.42	6.28	3.91	4.8
DEP. RATIO X 100	81.38	80.88	81.91	83.94	88.07	87.51	92.88	88.08	93.35	87.90	89.9

TABLE 5 — POPULATION PROJECTED WITH FIXED AGE—SPECIFIC BIRTH AND DEATH RATES (IN 1000's)

AGE AT LAST BIRTHDAY	1960 BOTH SEXES	MALES	FEMALES	1965 BOTH SEXES	MALES	FEMALES	1970 BOTH SEXES	MALES	FEMALES	AGE AT LAST BIRTHDAY
0-4	276	142	134	312	161	151	352	181	171	0-4
5-9	202	105	97	252	131	121	285	148	137	5-9
10-14	166	87	79	199	104	95	248	129	119	10-14
15-19	148	79	69	165	86	79	197	103	94	15-19
20-24	139	75	64	147	79	68	163	85	78	20-24
25-29	116	62	54	137	74	63	144	77	67	25-29
30-34	101	54	47	114	61	53	135	73	62	30-34
35-39	79	39	40	99	53	46	112	60	52	35-39
40-44	72	37	35	77	38	39	97	52	45	40-44
45-49	65	33	32	70	36	34	75	37	38	45-49
50-54	56	27	29	63	32	31	67	34	33	50-54
55-59	42	21	21	54	26	28	60	30	30	55-59
60-64	40	18	22	39	19	20	50	24	26	60-64
65-69	33	15	18	36	16	20	36	17	19	65-69
70-74	25	11	14	28	12	16	31	13	18	70-74
75-79	17	7	10	20	8	12	22	9	13	75-79
80-84	10	4	6	12	5	7	13	5	8	80-84
85+	7	2	5	8	3	5	9	3	6	85+
TOTAL	1594	818	776	1832	944	888	2096	1080	1016	TOTAL

TABLE 6 — STANDARDIZED RATES

STANDARD COUNTRIES: STANDARDIZED RATES PER THOUSAND	ENGLAND AND WALES 1961 BOTH SEXES	MALES	FEMALES	UNITED STATES 1960 BOTH SEXES	MALES	FEMALES	MEXICO 1960 BOTH SEXES	MALES	FEMALES
Birth	45.51	43.03*	43.10	45.79	39.08*	44.09	46.98	41.61*	45.79
Death	14.50	24.47*	14.45	14.40	20.81*	13.91	13.40	12.84*	13.33
Increase	31.01	18.56*	28.65	31.39	18.26*	30.18	33.58	28.77*	32.47

TABLE 7 — MOMENTS AND CUMULANTS

	OBSERVED POP. MALES	FEMALES	STATIONARY POP. MALES	FEMALES	STABLE POP. MALES	FEMALES	OBSERVED BIRTHS	NET MATERNITY FUNCTION	BIRTHS IN STABLE POP.
μ	24.77036	26.65668	36.95833	38.67734	23.45700	24.01861	29.72341	31.15830	29.44754
σ^2	393.0808	453.1554	533.0466	578.8307	368.1407	396.0235	54.98820	59.43777	52.73854
κ_3	6857.685	7565.491	3012.628	2895.443	6643.368	7557.986	240.7039	216.5910	234.5933
κ_4	-371.	-63154.	-277111.	-349149.	25255.	31230.	-432.000	-1113.566	-145.853
β_1	0.774300	0.615082	0.059923	0.043229	0.884576	0.919707	0.348464	0.223405	0.375186
β_2	2.997598	2.692458	2.024733	1.957904	3.186343	3.199124	2.857129	2.684797	2.947561
κ	-0.309430	-0.226930	-0.022420	-0.015580	-0.367661	-0.372870	-0.216231	-0.137825	-0.252847

TABLE 8 — RATES FROM AGE DISTRIBUTIONS AND VITAL STATISTICS (Females)

VITAL STATISTICS		THOMPSON AGE RANGE	NRR	1000r	INTERVAL	BOURGEOIS-PICHAT AGE RANGE	NRR	1000b	1000d	1000r	COALE	
GRR	3.430										IBR	39.45
NRR	2.435	0-4	1.98	25.88	27.33	5-29	1.89	37.91	14.42	23.49	IDR	13.79
TFR	7.019	5-9	1.87	23.26	27.24	30-54	1.87	36.59	13.50	23.10	IRI	25.66
GENERATION	30.286	10-14	1.86	22.35	27.20	55-79	1.87	41.94	18.75	23.19	K1	4.35
SEX RATIO	104.654	15-19	1.93	24.18	27.14	*15-39	2.08	41.43	14.25	27.18	K2	0.

TABLE 9 — LESLIE MATRIX AND ITS SPECTRAL COMPONENTS (Females)

Start of Age Interval	ORIGINAL MATRIX SUB-DIAGONAL	ALTERNATIVE FIRST ROWS Projection	Integral	FIRST STABLE MATRIX % IN STABLE POPULATION	FISHER VALUES	REPRODUCTIVE VALUES	SECOND STABLE MATRIX Z$_2$ FIRST COLUMN	FIRST ROW
0	0.90635	0.00000	0.00000	17.399	1.286	137202	0.1397+0.0961	0.1397+0.0961
5	0.98593	0.00016	0.00000	13.609	1.644	132570	0.1580-0.0704	-0.0089+0.1659
10	0.99113	0.06306	0.00035	11.578	1.932	135042	0.0249-0.1904	-0.1317+0.0711
15	0.98700	0.33519	0.13659	9.903	2.177	141425	-0.1668-0.1345	-0.1249-0.0735
20	0.98653	0.61520	0.59259	8.435	2.120	115147	-0.2242+0.0801	-0.0496-0.1630
25	0.98448	0.63382	0.74160	7.181	1.688	80750	-0.0541+0.2588	0.0148-0.1746
30	0.98165	0.53989	0.63249	6.100	1.159	46718	0.2134+0.2009	0.0514-0.1327
35	0.98138	0.37314	0.53950	5.168	0.661	23418	0.3125-0.0854	0.0499-0.0758
40	0.97806	0.17884	0.26867	4.377	0.291	9487	0.0997-0.3437	0.0290-0.0338
45	0.97196	0.07876	0.11888	3.694	0.110	3258	-0.2655-0.2911	0.0144-0.0111
50	0.96087	0.02421	0.05211	3.098	0.027	597	-0.4234+0.0816	0.0042-0.0019
55+	0.84403			9.457				

TABLE 10 — AGE ANALYSIS AND MISCELLANEOUS RESULTS (Females)

Start of Age Interval	OBSERVED POPUL. (IN 100's)	CONTRIBUTIONS OF ROOTS (IN 100's) r_1	r_2, r_3	r_4-r_{11}	AGE-SP. BIRTH RATES	NET MATERNITY FUNCTION	COEFF. OF MATRIX EQUATION	PARAMETERS	INTEGRAL	MATRIX	EXP. INCREASE x	$e^{(x+2\frac{1}{2})r}$
0	1067	1097	4	-34	0.0000	0.0000	0.0000	L(1)	1.15828	1.15881	0	1.0762
5	806	858	-48	-3	0.0000	0.0000	0.0001	L(2)	0.45766	0.46352	50	4.6777
10	699	730	-60	29	0.0001	0.0003	0.0563		0.77889	0.75770	55	5.4180
15	650	624	-10	35	0.0304	0.1124	0.2969	R(1)	0.02939	0.02948	60	6.2756
20	543	532	63	-51	0.1319	0.4813	0.5378	R(2)	-0.02032	-0.02370	65	7.2689
25	478	453	86	-60	0.1650	0.5942	0.5466		0.20791	0.20436	70	8.4194
30	403	385	22	-3	0.1407	0.4989	0.4584	C(1)		6305	75	9.7520
35	354	326	-80	108	0.1200	0.4178	0.3110	C(2)		-8765	80	11.2955
40	326	276	-118	168	0.0598	0.2042	0.1463			-14694	85	13.0833
45	296	233	-39	102	0.0265	0.0884	0.0630	2P/Y	30.2205	30.7463	90	15.1541
50	222	195	98	-71	0.0116	0.0376	0.0188	DELTA	5.1548		95	17.5526
55+	887	596									100	20.3308

TABLE 1 — DATA

AGE AT LAST BIRTHDAY	POPULATION BOTH SEXES	MALES Number	MALES %	FEMALES Number	FEMALES %	BIRTHS BY AGE OF MOTHER	DEATHS BOTH SEXES	MALES	FEMALES	AGE AT LAST BIRTHDAY
0	98741	50348	1.6	48393	1.3	0	6257	3620	2637	0
1-4	430002	219991	6.8	210011	5.7	0	1048	566	482	1-4
5-9	512812	260844	8.1	251968	6.8	0	405	237	168	5-9
10-14	546666	277775	8.6	268891	7.2	16	345	210	135	10-14
15-19	439242	223370	6.9	215872	5.8	7416	547	352	195	15-19
20-24	485730	243483	7.6	242247	6.5	28231	837	531	306	20-24
25-29	516505	223669	7.0	292836	7.9	33336	893	476	417	25-29
30-34	376415	160586	5.0	215829	5.8	19083	757	374	383	30-34
35-39	459232	201186	6.3	258046	6.9	11350	1194	624	570	35-39
40-44	536323	241299	7.5	295024	7.9	4722	1993	1041	952	40-44
45-49	541426	254165	7.9	287261	7.7	379	3195	1834	1361	45-49
50-54	494557	227478	7.1	267079	7.2	12	4625	2758	1867	50-54
55-59	410868	177295	5.5	233573	6.3	0	5606	3243	2363	55-59
60-64	350037	149119	4.6	200918	5.4	0	7453	4116	3337	60-64
65-69	292559	123809	3.8	168750	4.5	0	10082	5271	4811	65-69
70-74	220522	92134	2.9	128388	3.5		12500	6142	6358	70-74
75-79	136643	56347	1.8	80296	2.2		12719	5809	6910	75-79
80-84	61587	25162	0.8	36425	1.0	53840 M.	9318	4123	5195	80-84
85+	23566	8987	0.3	14579	0.4	50705 F.	6002	2409	3593	85+
TOTAL	6933433	3217047		3716386		104545	85776	43736	42040	TOTAL

TABLE 2 — MALE LIFE TABLE

x	nq_x	l_x	nd_x	nL_x	nm_x	na_x	T_x	r_x	$\dot{e}_x$	nM_x	x
0	0.068081	100000	6808	94690	0.071900	0.2200	6281601	0.0000	62.816	0.071900	
1	0.010215	93192	952	369989	0.002573	1.0809	6186912	0.0000	66.389	0.002573	
5	0.004533	92240	418	460154	0.000909	2.5000	5816923	0.0000	63.063	0.000909	
10	0.003783	91822	347	458304	0.000758	2.6809	5356769	0.0145	58.339	0.000756	10
15	0.007868	91474	720	455706	0.001579	2.6844	4898465	0.0116	53.550	0.001576	15
20	0.010846	90755	984	451361	0.002181	2.5489	4442759	0.0000	48.953	0.002181	20
25	0.010591	89770	951	446484	0.002129	2.5098	3991399	0.0394	44.462	0.002128	25
30	0.011588	88820	1029	441609	0.002331	2.5811	3544914	0.0082	39.911	0.002329	30
35	0.015395	87790	1352	435744	0.003102	2.6259	3103305	0.0000	35.349	0.003102	35
40	0.021358	86439	1846	427923	0.004314	2.6863	2667562	0.0000	30.861	0.004314	40
45	0.035492	84593	3002	416080	0.007216	2.7071	2239638	0.0000	26.476	0.007216	45
50	0.059205	81590	4831	396658	0.012178	2.6618	1823558	0.0237	22.350	0.012124	50
55	0.087994	76760	6754	367801	0.018364	2.6314	1426901	0.0233	18.589	0.018292	55
60	0.129839	70005	9089	328353	0.027682	2.6154	1059100	0.0166	15.129	0.027602	60
65	0.193565	60916	11791	276146	0.042699	2.5885	730747	0.0166	11.996	0.042574	65
70	0.287032	49125	14100	210906	0.066856	2.5378	454601	0.0166	9.254	0.066664	70
75	0.409722	35024	14350	138790	0.103395	2.4682	243695	0.0166	6.958	0.103093	75
80	0.576066	20674	11910	72433	0.164424	2.4023	104905	0.0166	5.074	0.163858	80
85+	*1.000000	8764	8764	32472	0.269907	3.7050	32472	0.0166	3.705	0.268054	85

TABLE 3 — FEMALE LIFE TABLE

x	nq_x	l_x	nd_x	nL_x	nm_x	na_x	T_x	r_x	$\dot{e}_x$	nM_x	x
0	0.052318	100000	5232	96011	0.054491	0.2376	6804776	0.0000	68.048	0.054491	0
1	0.009120	94768	864	376560	0.002295	1.0928	6708765	0.0000	70.791	0.002295	1
5	0.003328	93904	313	468739	0.000667	2.5000	6332204	0.0000	67.433	0.000667	5
10	0.002511	93591	235	467392	0.000503	2.5966	5863466	0.0148	62.650	0.000502	10
15	0.004515	93356	421	465801	0.000905	2.6731	5396074	0.0095	57.801	0.000903	15
20	0.006297	92935	585	463261	0.001263	2.5834	4930272	0.0000	53.051	0.001263	20
25	0.007101	92350	656	460157	0.001425	2.5717	4467012	0.0101	48.371	0.001424	25
30	0.008844	91694	811	456514	0.001776	2.5881	4006855	0.0109	43.698	0.001775	30
35	0.010987	90883	999	452050	0.002209	2.6311	3550341	0.0000	39.065	0.002209	35
40	0.016013	89885	1439	446049	0.003227	2.6556	3098291	0.0000	34.470	0.003227	40
45	0.023448	88445	2074	437362	0.004742	2.6544	2652242	0.0051	29.987	0.004738	45
50	0.034459	86371	2976	424845	0.007006	2.6443	2214881	0.0136	25.644	0.006990	50
55	0.049585	83395	4135	407346	0.010152	2.6713	1790035	0.0177	21.465	0.010117	55
60	0.080440	79260	6376	381540	0.016710	2.6850	1382690	0.0275	17.445	0.016609	60
65	0.134421	72884	9797	341526	0.028686	2.6631	1001150	0.0275	13.736	0.028510	65
70	0.222633	63087	14045	281923	0.049819	2.6140	659624	0.0275	10.456	0.049522	70
75	0.356459	49042	17481	202014	0.086536	2.5291	377701	0.0275	7.702	0.086057	75
80	0.522310	31560	16484	115002	0.143340	2.4696	175687	0.0275	5.567	0.142622	80
85+	1.000000	15076	15076	60685	0.248432	4.0253	60685	0.0275	4.025	0.246450	85

TABLE 4 — OBSERVED AND PROJECTED VITAL RATES

	OBSERVED POPULATION BOTH SEXES	MALES	FEMALES	PROJECTED POPULATION 1956 MALES	1956 FEMALES	1961 MALES	1961 FEMALES	1966 MALES	1966 FEMALES	STABLE POPULATION MALES	FEMALES
RATES PER THOUSAND											
Birth	15.08	16.74	13.64	16.00	13.11	15.92	13.13	15.92	13.23	14.35	13.17
Death	12.37	13.60	11.31	14.17	12.43	14.68	13.47	15.07	14.35	17.19	16.02
Increase	2.71	3.14	2.33	1.84	0.67	1.25	-0.34	0.85	-1.12		-2.8445
PERCENTAGE											
under 15	22.91	25.15	20.97	23.76	19.85	22.95	19.26	22.03	18.66	20.27	18.96
15-64	66.49	65.33	67.50	66.38	67.44	65.81	66.85	66.75	66.15	66.82	64.77
65 and over	10.60	9.53	11.53	9.87	12.71	10.24	13.89	11.22	15.19	12.91	16.27
DEP. RATIO X 100	50.39	53.07	48.14	50.65	48.29	49.68	49.58	49.81	51.17	49.66	54.39

AGE AT LAST BIRTHDAY	1956 BOTH SEXES	MALES	FEMALES	1961 BOTH SEXES	MALES	FEMALES	1966 BOTH SEXES	MALES	FEMALES	AGE AT LAST BIRTHDAY	
0-4	482	246	236	474	242	232	476	243	233	0-4	
5-9	524	268	256	478	244	234	470	240	230	5-9	
10-14	511	260	251	523	267	256	476	243	233	10-14	
15-19	544	276	268	508	258	250	520	265	255	15-19	**TABLE 5**
20-24	436	221	215	541	274	267	505	256	249	20-24	POPULATION
25-29	482	241	241	432	219	213	536	271	265	25-29	PROJECTED
30-34	512	221	291	477	238	239	428	216	212	30-34	WITH
35-39	372	158	214	506	218	288	471	235	236	35-39	FIXED
40-44	453	198	255	367	156	211	498	214	284	40-44	AGE—
45-49	524	235	289	442	192	250	358	151	207	45-49	SPECIFIC
50-54	521	242	279	505	224	281	426	183	243	50-54	BIRTH
55-59	467	211	256	493	225	268	476	207	269	55-59	AND
60-64	377	158	219	428	188	240	452	201	251	60-64	DEATH
65-69	305	125	180	329	133	196	373	158	215	65-69	RATES
70-74	234	95	139	244	96	148	264	102	162	70-74	(IN 1000's)
75-79	153	61	92	162	62	100	169	63	106	75-79	
80-84	75	29	46	84	32	52	89	32	57	80-84	
85+	30	11	19	37	13	24	42	14	28	85+	
TOTAL	7002	3256	3746	7030	3281	3749	7029	3294	3735	TOTAL	

STANDARD COUNTRIES:	ENGLAND AND WALES 1961 BOTH SEXES	MALES	FEMALES	UNITED STATES 1960 BOTH SEXES	MALES	FEMALES	MEXICO 1960 BOTH SEXES	MALES	FEMALES	
STANDARDIZED RATES PER THOUSAND										**TABLE 6**
Birth	13.22	16.99*	12.43	13.47	15.69*	12.88	15.40	14.81*	14.90	STANDAR-DIZED
Death	14.44	14.28*	14.56	12.10	12.62*	11.09	7.29	11.04*	6.24	RATES
Increase	-1.22	2.71*	-2.13	1.37	3.06*	1.78	8.11	3.77*	8.67	

	OBSERVED POP. MALES	FEMALES	STATIONARY POP. MALES	FEMALES	STABLE POP. MALES	FEMALES	OBSERVED BIRTHS	NET MATERNITY FUNCTION	BIRTHS IN STABLE POP.	
μ	34.33783	36.93720	35.88069	37.73882	37.26838	39.23204	28.18937	27.96948	28.08586	**TABLE 7**
σ^2	470.0278	470.4650	484.6457	522.2274	490.7326	527.2737	38.42474	38.68006	38.97850	MOMENTS
κ_3	2406.830	1233.345	2466.326	2176.644	1807.334	1365.888	125.3073	105.8053	104.0095	AND
κ_4	-219492.	-216794.	-224934.	-278653.	-237675.	-290366.	-381.683	-607.867	-644.331	CUMULANTS
β_1	0.055785	0.014608	0.053435	0.033266	0.027640	0.012727	0.276770	0.193443	0.182672	
β_2	2.006493	2.020526	2.042352	1.978251	2.013052	1.955585	2.741488	2.593712	2.575909	
κ	-0.020647	-0.005718	-0.020432	-0.012308	-0.010594	-0.004719	-0.167025	-0.110915	-0.104242	

VITAL STATISTICS		THOMPSON AGE RANGE	NRR	1000r	INTERVAL	BOURGEOIS-PICHAT AGE RANGE	NRR	1000b	1000d	1000r	COALE	**TABLE 8**
GRR	1.005										IBR	RATES FROM AGE DISTRI-
NRR	0.923	0-4	0.99	-0.47	27.38	5-29	0.88	13.45	18.29	-4.84	IDR	BUTIONS
TFR	2.073	5-9	0.92	-3.15	27.34	30-54	0.68	8.73	22.94	-14.20	IRI	AND VITAL
GENERATION	28.028	10-14	0.95	-1.77	27.28	55-79	1.50	36.65	21.56	15.10	K1	STATISTICS
SEX RATIO	106.183	15-19	0.78	-9.35	27.18	*50-74	1.54	38.62	22.75	15.87	K2	(Females)

Start Age Interval	ORIGINAL MATRIX SUB-DIAGONAL	ALTERNATIVE FIRST ROWS Projection	Integral	FIRST STABLE MATRIX % IN STABLE POPULATION	FISHER VALUES	REPRODUCTIVE VALUES	SECOND STABLE MATRIX Z₂ FIRST COLUMN	FIRST ROW	
0	0.99189	0.00000	0.00000	6.269	1.051	271470	0.1467+0.0730	0.1467+0.0730	**TABLE 9**
5	0.99713	0.00007	0.00000	6.307	1.044	263106	0.1694-0.1162	0.0061+0.1306	LESLIE
0	0.99660	0.03930	0.00014	6.379	1.032	277591	-0.0240-0.2577	-0.0882+0.0547	MATRIX
5	0.99455	0.17219	0.07818	6.449	0.980	211517	-0.2983-0.1315	-0.0778-0.0429	AND ITS
0	0.99330	0.26314	0.26521	6.505	0.789	191229	-0.3267+0.2471	-0.0257-0.0833	SPECTRAL
5	0.99208	0.23098	0.25907	6.554	0.505	147939	0.0714+0.5092	0.0092-0.0695	COMPO-
0	0.99022	0.15124	0.20122	6.596	0.257	55563	0.6013+0.2325	0.0178-0.0376	NENTS
5	0.98672	0.06850	0.10010	6.625	0.096	24735	0.6203-0.5158	0.0107-0.0133	(Females)
0	0.98052	0.01982	0.03642	6.630	0.023	6737	-0.1855-0.9886	0.0033-0.0027	
5	0.97138	0.00156	0.00300	6.594	0.002	494	-1.1820-0.3952	0.0003-0.0002	
0	0.95881	0.00005	0.00010	6.497	0.000	15	-1.1299+1.0315	0.0000-0.0000	
5+	0.76802			28.594					

Start Age Interval	OBSERVED POPUL. (IN 100's)	CONTRIBUTIONS OF ROOTS (IN 100's) r_1	r_2, r_3	r_4-r_{11}	AGE-SP. BIRTH RATES	NET MATERNITY FUNCTION	COEFF. OF MATRIX EQUATION	PARAMETERS	INTEGRAL	MATRIX	EXP. INCREASE x	$e^{(x+2\frac{1}{2})r}$	
0	2584	2456	62	66	0.0000	0.0000	0.0000	L(1)	0.98588	0.98588	0	0.9929	**TABLE 10**
5	2520	2471	131	-82	0.0000	0.0000	0.0001	L(2)	0.37736	0.38505	50	0.8613	AGE
0	2689	2499	62	127	0.0000	0.0001	0.0389		0.71085	0.69133	55	0.8491	ANALYSIS
5	2159	2527	-131	-237	0.0167	0.0776	0.1697	R(1)	-0.00284	-0.00284	60	0.8371	AND
0	2422	2549	-259	133	0.0565	0.2618	0.2580	R(2)	-0.04347	-0.04681	65	0.8253	MISCEL-
5	2928	2568	-110	470	0.0552	0.2541	0.2249		0.21662	0.21252	70	0.8136	LANEOUS
0	2158	2584	274	-699	0.0429	0.1958	0.1461	C(1)		39179	75	0.8022	RESULTS
5	2580	2595	506	-521	0.0213	0.0964	0.0655	C(2)		28472	80	0.7908	(Females)
0	2950	2598	187	166	0.0078	0.0346	0.0187			14780	85	0.7797	
5	2873	2584	-556	845	0.0006	0.0028	0.0014	2P/Y	29.0057	29.5648	90	0.7687	
0	2671	2546	-948	1074	0.0000	0.0001	0.0000	DELTA	6.8031		95	0.7578	
5+	8629	11203									100	0.7471	

TABLE 1 — DATA

AGE AT LAST BIRTHDAY	POPULATION BOTH SEXES	MALES Number	%	FEMALES Number	%	BIRTHS BY AGE OF MOTHER	DEATHS BOTH SEXES	MALES	FEMALES	AGE AT LAST BIRTHDAY
0	99280	50725	1.6	48555	1.3	0	5035	2931	2104	0
1-4	390079	199098	6.2	190981	5.1	0	724	399	325	1-4
5-9	500751	255749	7.9	245002	6.6	0	350	206	144	5-9
10-14	597756	304597	9.4	293159	7.9	13	310	182	128	10-14
15-19	441607	224826	7.0	216781	5.8	7106	435	289	146	15-19
20-24	452707	230580	7.2	222127	6.0	28480	685	477	208	20-24
25-29	483826	229276	7.1	254550	6.8	31471	736	469	267	25-29
30-34	499528	211083	6.5	288445	7.8	24482	845	438	407	30-34
35-39	328558	141154	4.4	187404	5.0	8888	792	384	408	35-39
40-44	512297	226499	7.0	285798	7.7	4342	1652	856	796	40-44
45-49	529429	241937	7.5	287492	7.7	357	2680	1488	1192	45-49
50-54	518848	242293	7.5	276555	7.4	4	4396	2650	1746	50-54
55-59	444674	196142	6.1	248532	6.7	0	5752	3447	2305	55-59
60-64	359678	151468	4.7	208210	5.6	0	7291	4118	3173	60-64
65-69	304694	125735	3.9	178959	4.8	0	9989	5328	4661	65-69
70-74	229373	94156	2.9	135217	3.6		12257	5969	6288	70-74
75-79	150376	60334	1.9	90042	2.4		13444	6135	7309	75-79
80-84	69749	27578	0.9	42171	1.1	54004 M.	10199	4448	5751	80-84
85+	26998	10120	0.3	16878	0.5	51139 F.	6770	2724	4046	85+
TOTAL	6940208	3223350		3716858		105143	84342	42938	41404	TOTAL

TABLE 2 — MALE LIFE TABLE

x	nq_x	l_x	nd_x	nL_x	nm_x	na_x	T_x	r_x	$\mathring{e}_x$	nM_x	x
0	0.055280	100000	5528	95673	0.057780	0.2173	6452393	0.0000	64.524	0.057782	
1	0.007969	94472	753	375689	0.002004	1.0792	6356720	0.0000	67.287	0.002004	
5	0.004019	93719	377	467654	0.000805	2.5000	5981031	0.3000	63.819	0.000805	
10	0.002989	93342	279	466061	0.000599	2.6668	5513377	0.0121	59.066	0.000598	1
15	0.006449	93063	600	463957	0.001294	2.7335	5047315	0.0265	54.235	0.001285	1
20	0.010292	92463	952	460006	0.002069	2.5725	4583359	0.0000	49.569	0.002069	2
25	0.010176	91512	931	455227	0.002046	2.4969	4123352	0.0068	45.058	0.002046	2
30	0.010355	90580	938	450616	0.002081	2.5623	3668125	0.0463	40.496	0.002075	3
35	0.013515	89643	1212	445334	0.002720	2.6236	3217509	0.0000	35.893	0.002720	3
40	0.018732	88431	1656	438310	0.003779	2.6786	2772175	0.0000	31.348	0.003779	4
45	0.030327	86775	2632	427885	0.006150	2.7249	2333866	0.0000	26.896	0.006150	4
50	0.053448	84143	4497	410330	0.010960	2.6910	1905980	0.0097	22.652	0.010937	5
55	0.084821	79646	6756	382346	0.017669	2.6641	1495650	0.0288	18.779	0.017574	5
60	0.128032	72890	9332	342263	0.027266	2.6225	1113303	0.0161	15.274	0.027187	6
65	0.192651	63558	12244	288172	0.042490	2.5812	771040	0.0161	12.131	0.042375	6
70	0.274907	51313	14106	221894	0.063573	2.5421	482868	0.0161	9.410	0.063395	7
75	0.405638	37207	15093	147991	0.101983	2.4793	260974	0.0161	7.014	0.101684	7
80	0.570031	22114	12606	77894	0.161834	2.4077	112984	0.0161	5.109	0.161289	8
85+	*1.000000	9508	9508	35090	0.270977	3.6903	35090	0.0161	3.690	0.269170	8

TABLE 3 — FEMALE LIFE TABLE

x	nq_x	l_x	nd_x	nL_x	nm_x	na_x	T_x	r_x	$\mathring{e}_x$	nM_x	x
0	0.041928	100000	4193	96774	0.043326	0.2306	6996208	0.0002	69.962	0.043332	
1	0.006772	95807	649	381339	0.001701	1.0879	6899434	0.0002	72.014	0.001702	
5	0.002934	95158	279	475094	0.000588	2.5000	6518095	0.0000	68.497	0.000588	
10	0.002182	94879	207	473887	0.000437	2.5407	6043001	0.0117	63.692	0.000437	1
15	0.003376	94672	320	472610	0.000676	2.6524	5569114	0.0271	58.825	0.000673	1
20	0.004671	94353	441	470696	0.000936	2.5811	5096504	0.0000	54.016	0.000936	2
25	0.005231	93912	491	468376	0.001049	2.5930	4625808	0.0000	49.257	0.001049	2
30	0.007066	93420	660	465559	0.001418	2.6623	4157431	0.0291	44.502	0.001411	3
35	0.010830	92760	1005	461417	0.002177	2.6264	3691872	0.0000	39.800	0.002177	3
40	0.013835	91756	1269	455783	0.002785	2.6400	3230455	0.0000	35.207	0.002785	4
45	0.020532	90486	1858	448098	0.004146	2.6672	2774672	0.0000	30.664	0.004146	4
50	0.031149	88628	2761	436669	0.006322	2.6550	2326574	0.0081	26.251	0.006313	5
55	0.045556	85868	3912	420248	0.009308	2.6761	1889905	0.0185	22.009	0.009274	5
60	0.074031	81956	6067	395750	0.015331	2.6876	1469657	0.0271	17.932	0.015239	6
65	0.123528	75889	9374	357661	0.026210	2.6764	1073907	0.0271	14.151	0.026045	6
70	0.210543	66514	14004	299327	0.046785	2.6261	716245	0.0271	10.768	0.046503	7
75	0.339911	52510	17849	218667	0.081626	2.5413	416919	0.0271	7.940	0.081173	7
80	0.506202	34661	17546	128017	0.137057	2.4913	198252	0.0271	5.720	0.136373	8
85+	1.000000	17116	17116	70234	0.243694	4.1035	70234	0.0271	4.104	0.239721	8

TABLE 4 — OBSERVED AND PROJECTED VITAL RATES

	OBSERVED POPULATION BOTH SEXES	MALES	FEMALES	PROJECTED POPULATION 1959 MALES	FEMALES	1964 MALES	FEMALES	1969 MALES	FEMALES	STABLE POPULATION MALES	FEMALES
RATES PER THOUSAND											
Birth	15.15	16.75	13.76	16.15	13.33	16.62	13.82	16.51	13.85	15.21	14.0
Death	12.15	13.32	11.14	13.96	12.37	14.42	13.37	14.72	14.16	15.73	14.5
Increase	3.00	3.43	2.62	2.20	0.96	2.20	0.44	1.79	-0.30		-0.517
PERCENTAGE											
under 15	22.88	25.13	20.92	23.08	19.30	22.71	19.16	22.78	19.41	21.45	20.0
15-64	65.86	65.00	66.61	66.79	67.03	66.46	65.83	65.29	64.27	66.37	64.2
65 and over	11.26	9.86	12.46	10.14	13.66	10.83	15.01	11.94	16.31	12.18	15.6
DEP. RATIO X 100	51.83	53.84	50.12	49.73	49.18	50.47	51.91	53.17	55.58	50.68	55.5

TABLE 1 — DATA

AGE AT LAST BIRTHDAY	POPULATION BOTH SEXES	MALES Number	%	FEMALES Number	%	BIRTHS BY AGE OF MOTHER	DEATHS BOTH SEXES	MALES	FEMALES	AGE AT LAST BIRTHDAY
0	113162	57812	1.8	55350	1.5	0	5045	2891	2154	0
1-4	401225	204631	6.3	196594	5.3	0	674	372	302	1-4
5-9	501981	256277	7.9	245704	6.6	0	306	189	117	5-9
10-14	500315	255137	7.9	245178	6.6	28	258	155	103	10-14
15-19	572726	293277	9.1	279449	7.5	10168	606	440	166	15-19
20-24	406092	206315	6.4	199777	5.4	30680	707	544	163	20-24
25-29	460222	232656	7.2	227566	6.1	33495	793	550	243	25-29
30-34	488866	215821	6.7	273045	7.3	26638	874	502	372	30-34
35-39	410601	173410	5.4	237191	6.4	13273	886	473	413	35-39
40-44	398773	172606	5.3	226167	6.1	3483	1269	677	592	40-44
45-49	513634	228743	7.1	284891	7.6	333	2562	1418	1144	45-49
50-54	516726	238278	7.4	278448	7.5	1	4172	2515	1657	50-54
55-59	477383	217122	6.7	260261	7.0	0	6239	3915	2324	55-59
60-64	387586	162674	5.0	224912	6.0	0	7806	4527	3279	60-64
65-69	308709	125603	3.9	183106	4.9	0	9923	5308	4615	65-69
70-74	240178	95669	3.0	144509	3.9		12685	6222	6463	70-74
75-79	157151	61396	1.9	95755	2.6		13781	6250	7531	75-79
80-84	79786	30373	0.9	49413	1.3	60580 M.	11283	4817	6466	80-84
85+	30745	11192	0.3	19553	0.5	57519 F.	7496	2919	4577	85+
TOTAL	6965861	3238992		3726869		118099	87365	44684	42681	TOTAL

TABLE 2 — MALE LIFE TABLE

x	$_nq_x$	l_x	$_nd_x$	$_nL_x$	$_nm_x$	$_na_x$	T_x	r_x	$\mathring{e}_x$	$_nM_x$	x
0	0.047748	100000	4775	96283	0.049591	0.2215	6477015	0.0106	64.770	0.050007	0
1	0.007116	95225	678	378923	0.001788	1.0819	6380732	0.0106	67.007	0.001818	1
5	0.003679	94548	348	471868	0.000737	2.5000	6001809	0.0018	63.479	0.000737	5
10	0.003033	94200	286	470359	0.000608	2.7612	5529940	0.0000	58.704	0.000608	10
15	0.007518	93914	706	468000	0.001509	2.7765	5059581	0.0197	53.875	0.001500	15
20	0.013118	93208	1223	463061	0.002641	2.5639	4591581	0.0208	49.262	0.002637	20
25	0.011750	91985	1081	457189	0.002364	2.4671	4128520	0.0000	44.882	0.002364	25
30	0.011574	90904	1052	451921	0.002328	2.5276	3671331	0.0270	40.387	0.002326	30
35	0.013582	89852	1220	446351	0.002734	2.6144	3219410	0.0195	35.830	0.002728	35
40	0.019434	88632	1722	439153	0.003922	2.6736	2773059	0.0000	31.287	0.003922	40
45	0.030561	86910	2656	428453	0.006199	2.7054	2333906	0.0000	26.854	0.006199	45
50	0.051527	84254	4341	411307	0.010555	2.7055	1905452	0.0000	22.616	0.010555	50
55	0.086820	79912	6938	383301	0.018101	2.6563	1494146	0.0197	18.697	0.018031	55
60	0.130826	72974	9547	342098	0.027907	2.6146	1110845	0.0162	15.222	0.027829	60
65	0.192201	63427	12191	287670	0.042378	2.5829	768746	0.0162	12.120	0.042260	65
70	0.281012	51237	14398	220762	0.065220	2.5399	481076	0.0162	9.389	0.065037	70
75	0.405705	36838	14946	146398	0.102088	2.4712	260314	0.0162	7.066	0.101798	75
80	0.563352	21893	12333	77509	0.159122	2.4090	113916	0.0162	5.203	0.158596	80
85+	*1.000000	9560	9560	36407	0.262575	3.8084	36407	0.0162	3.808	0.260811	85+

TABLE 3 — FEMALE LIFE TABLE

x	$_nq_x$	l_x	$_nd_x$	$_nL_x$	$_nm_x$	$_na_x$	T_x	r_x	$\mathring{e}_x$	$_nM_x$	x
0	0.037481	100000	3748	97116	0.038594	0.2306	7083614	0.0105	70.836	0.038916	0
1	0.006024	96252	580	383319	0.001513	1.0879	6986498	0.0105	72.586	0.001536	1
5	0.002376	95672	227	477792	0.000476	2.5000	6603179	0.0019	69.019	0.000476	5
10	0.002098	95445	200	476734	0.000420	2.5582	6125387	0.0000	64.177	0.000420	10
15	0.002974	95244	283	475553	0.000596	2.6377	5648653	0.0199	59.307	0.000594	15
20	0.004081	94961	388	473883	0.000818	2.6185	5173100	0.0197	54.476	0.000816	20
25	0.005325	94574	504	471661	0.001068	2.6039	4699217	0.0000	49.688	0.001068	25
30	0.006790	94070	639	468817	0.001362	2.6006	4227556	0.0000	44.941	0.001362	30
35	0.008692	93431	812	465244	0.001746	2.6652	3758739	0.0170	40.230	0.001741	35
40	0.013008	92619	1205	460293	0.002618	2.6740	3293496	0.0000	35.560	0.002618	40
45	0.019891	91414	1818	452822	0.004016	2.6633	2833203	0.0000	30.993	0.004016	45
50	0.029360	89596	2631	441819	0.005954	2.6580	2380381	0.0029	26.568	0.005951	50
55	0.043842	86965	3813	425975	0.008951	2.6784	1938562	0.0119	22.291	0.008929	55
60	0.070908	83153	5896	402155	0.014661	2.6921	1512587	0.0251	18.190	0.014579	60
65	0.119715	77256	9249	364812	0.025352	2.6785	1110432	0.0251	14.373	0.025204	65
70	0.203232	68008	13821	307296	0.044977	2.6310	745620	0.0251	10.964	0.044724	70
75	0.331050	54186	17938	226915	0.079054	2.5462	438325	0.0251	8.089	0.078649	75
80	0.491041	36248	17799	135407	0.131450	2.5060	211410	0.0251	5.832	0.130856	80
85+	1.000000	18449	18449	76004	0.242735	4.1197	76004	0.0251	4.120	0.234083	85+

TABLE 4 — OBSERVED AND PROJECTED VITAL RATES

	OBSERVED POPULATION BOTH SEXES	MALES	FEMALES	PROJECTED POPULATION 1962 MALES	FEMALES	1967 MALES	FEMALES	1972 MALES	FEMALES	STABLE POPULATION MALES	FEMALES
RATES PER THOUSAND											
Birth	16.95	18.70	15.43	18.87	15.67	18.66	15.63	18.35	15.53	18.68	17.28
Death	12.54	13.80	11.45	14.33	12.61	14.51	13.38	14.55	14.00	13.20	11.80
Increase	4.41	4.91	3.98	4.54	3.05	4.16	2.25	3.80	1.53		5.4788
PERCENTAGE											
under 15	21.77	23.89	19.93	24.38	20.47	25.05	21.23	25.67	21.99	25.42	23.80
15-64	66.50	66.10	66.86	65.27	65.04	63.72	63.05	62.46	61.32	64.97	63.40
65 and over	11.72	10.01	13.21	10.35	14.49	11.23	15.71	11.88	16.70	9.61	12.79
DEP. RATIO X 100	50.37	51.29	49.57	53.21	53.74	56.93	58.60	60.11	63.09	53.92	57.72

TABLE 1 — DATA

AGE AT LAST BIRTHDAY	POPULATION BOTH SEXES	MALES Number	%	FEMALES Number	%	BIRTHS BY AGE OF MOTHER	DEATHS BOTH SEXES	MALES	FEMALES	AGE AT LAST BIRTHDAY
0	121216	62205	1.9	59011	1.6	0	4660	2672	1988	0
1-4	449048	229240	7.0	219808	5.8	0	675	389	286	1-4
5-9	482310	246001	7.5	236309	6.3	0	270	157	113	5-9
10-14	500936	256177	7.8	244759	6.5	31	206	131	75	10-14
15-19	553726	281998	8.6	271728	7.2	13277	569	414	155	15-19
20-24	480216	245961	7.5	234255	6.2	37741	666	509	157	20-24
25-29	420668	213070	6.5	207598	5.5	33106	627	444	183	25-29
30-34	464265	226195	6.9	238070	6.3	24202	775	495	280	30-34
35-39	495321	209636	6.4	285685	7.6	15323	1041	577	464	35-39
40-44	324295	137725	4.2	186570	5.0	3329	980	518	462	40-44
45-49	474617	206998	6.3	267619	7.1	283	2198	1238	960	45-49
50-54	507285	226896	6.9	280389	7.4	1	3857	2332	1525	50-54
55-59	492308	225772	6.9	266536	7.1	0	6204	3948	2256	55-59
60-64	419872	181285	5.5	238587	6.3	0	8373	5102	3271	60-64
65-69	323909	129503	3.9	194406	5.2	0	9929	5470	4459	65-69
70-74	247889	95784	2.9	152105	4.0		12542	6188	6354	70-74
75-79	165468	63002	1.9	102466	2.7		13803	6207	7596	75-79
80-84	87800	32279	1.0	55521	1.5	65562 M.	11944	5005	6939	80-84
85+	36390	12680	0.4	23710	0.6	61731 F.	8431	3225	5206	85+
TOTAL	7047539	3282407		3765132		127293	87750	45021	42729	TOTAL

TABLE 2 — MALE LIFE TABLE

x	$_nq_x$	l_x	$_nd_x$	$_nL_x$	$_nm_x$	$_na_x$	T_x	r_x	$\dot{e}_x$	$_nM_x$	x
0	0.041369	100000	4137	96818	0.042728	0.2308	6564829	0.0067	65.648	0.042955	0
1	0.006689	95863	641	381585	0.001681	1.0880	6468011	0.0067	67.471	0.001697	1
5	0.003174	95222	302	475354	0.000636	2.5000	6086426	0.0120	63.918	0.000638	5
10	0.002554	94920	242	474074	0.000511	2.8359	5611072	0.0000	59.114	0.000511	10
15	0.007320	94677	693	471805	0.001469	2.7185	5136999	0.0027	54.258	0.001468	15
20	0.010312	93984	969	467554	0.002073	2.5583	4665194	0.0261	49.638	0.002069	20
25	0.010366	93015	964	462671	0.002084	2.5071	4197640	0.0063	45.129	0.002084	25
30	0.010884	92051	1002	457809	0.002188	2.5598	3734969	0.0000	40.575	0.002188	30
35	0.013747	91049	1252	452256	0.002768	2.6119	3277159	0.0468	35.993	0.002752	35
40	0.018642	89797	1674	445082	0.003761	2.6678	2824904	0.0000	31.459	0.003761	40
45	0.029500	88123	2600	434663	0.005981	2.7099	2379822	0.0000	27.006	0.005981	45
50	0.050205	85524	4294	417765	0.010278	2.7053	1945159	0.0000	22.744	0.010278	50
55	0.084081	81230	6830	390230	0.017502	2.6692	1527394	0.0043	18.803	0.017487	55
60	0.132254	74400	9840	348562	0.028229	2.6180	1137163	0.0173	15.284	0.028144	60
65	0.192106	64560	12402	292781	0.042361	2.5795	788602	0.0173	12.215	0.042238	65
70	0.279342	52158	14570	224877	0.064790	2.5351	495821	0.0173	9.506	0.064604	70
75	0.395338	37588	14860	150384	0.098814	2.4727	270944	0.0173	7.208	0.098521	75
80	0.555255	22728	12620	81101	0.155607	2.4215	120560	0.0173	5.304	0.155055	80
85+	*1.000000	10108	10108	39460	0.256166	3.9037	39460	0.0173	3.904	0.254338	85+

TABLE 3 — FEMALE LIFE TABLE

x	$_nq_x$	l_x	$_nd_x$	$_nL_x$	$_nm_x$	$_na_x$	T_x	r_x	$\dot{e}_x$	$_nM_x$	x
0	0.032685	100000	3268	97479	0.033530	0.2288	7205948	0.0060	72.059	0.033689	0
1	0.005140	96732	497	385478	0.001290	1.0867	7108469	0.0060	73.487	0.001301	1
5	0.002378	96234	229	480600	0.000476	2.5000	6722991	0.0123	69.861	0.000478	5
10	0.001531	96006	147	479670	0.000306	2.5629	6242391	0.0000	65.021	0.000306	10
15	0.002850	95859	273	478646	0.000571	2.6324	5762721	0.0039	60.117	0.000570	15
20	0.003354	95585	321	477156	0.000672	2.5948	5284075	0.0262	55.281	0.000670	20
25	0.004398	95265	419	475326	0.000882	2.6171	4806919	0.0000	50.458	0.000882	25
30	0.005864	94846	556	472911	0.001176	2.6299	4331594	0.0000	45.670	0.001176	30
35	0.008120	94290	766	469658	0.001630	2.6621	3858683	0.0227	40.924	0.001624	35
40	0.012318	93524	1152	464922	0.002478	2.6587	3389025	0.0040	36.237	0.002476	40
45	0.017787	92372	1643	458020	0.003587	2.6629	2924103	0.0000	31.656	0.003587	45
50	0.026855	90729	2436	447976	0.005439	2.6733	2466083	0.0000	27.181	0.005439	50
55	0.041566	88292	3670	432957	0.008477	2.6826	2018107	0.0073	22.857	0.008464	55
60	0.066803	84622	5653	410017	0.013787	2.6836	1585150	0.0263	18.732	0.013710	60
65	0.109558	78969	8652	374841	0.023081	2.6875	1175133	0.0263	14.881	0.022937	65
70	0.191213	70318	13446	319909	0.042030	2.6438	800292	0.0263	11.381	0.041774	70
75	0.315368	56872	17936	240610	0.074542	2.5607	480383	0.0263	8.447	0.074132	75
80	0.479568	38936	18673	148485	0.125754	2.5260	239773	0.0263	6.158	0.124979	80
85+	*1.000000	20264	20264	91287	0.221978	4.5050	91287	0.0263	4.505	0.219570	85+

TABLE 4 — OBSERVED AND PROJECTED VITAL RATES

	OBSERVED POPULATION BOTH SEXES	MALES	FEMALES	PROJECTED POPULATION 1965 MALES	FEMALES	1970 MALES	FEMALES	1975 MALES	FEMALES	STABLE POPULATION MALES	FEMALES
RATES PER THOUSAND											
Birth	18.06	19.97	16.40	20.04	16.57	19.64	16.40	19.22	16.25	20.17	18.73
Death	12.45	13.72	11.35	14.07	12.50	14.09	13.19	13.97	13.73	11.96	10.52
Increase	5.61	6.26	5.05	5.97	4.07	5.55	3.22	5.25	2.52		8.2117
PERCENTAGE											
under 15	22.04	24.18	20.18	25.23	21.18	26.75	22.62	27.05	23.12	27.10	25.43
15-64	65.73	65.67	65.79	63.97	63.37	61.66	60.80	61.21	59.51	64.18	62.60
65 and over	12.22	10.15	14.03	10.80	15.45	11.59	16.58	11.73	17.36	8.72	11.97
DEP. RATIO X 100	52.13	52.28	52.00	56.32	57.81	62.18	64.48	63.37	68.03	55.82	59.75

AGE AT LAST BIRTHDAY	1965 BOTH SEXES	MALES	FEMALES	1970 BOTH SEXES	MALES	FEMALES	1975 BOTH SEXES	MALES	FEMALES	AGE AT LAST BIRTHDAY	
0-4	622	319	303	636	326	310	640	328	312	0-4	**TABLE 5**
5-9	567	290	277	619	317	302	632	324	308	5-9	POPULATION
10-14	481	245	236	566	289	277	617	316	301	10-14	PROJECTED
15-19	499	255	244	479	244	235	563	287	276	15-19	WITH
20-24	550	279	271	496	253	243	477	242	235	20-24	FIXED
25-29	476	243	233	547	277	270	493	250	243	25-29	AGE—
30-34	418	211	207	473	241	232	542	274	268	30-34	SPECIFIC
35-39	459	223	236	413	208	205	469	238	231	35-39	BIRTH
40-44	489	206	283	454	220	234	408	205	203	40-44	AND
45-49	319	135	184	480	201	279	446	215	231	45-49	DEATH
50-54	461	199	262	309	129	180	466	194	272	50-54	RATES
55-59	483	212	271	439	186	253	295	121	174	55-59	(IN 1000's)
60-64	454	202	252	446	189	257	406	166	240	60-64	
65-69	370	152	218	400	169	231	394	159	235	65-69	
70-74	265	99	166	303	117	186	327	130	197	70-74	
75-79	178	64	114	192	67	125	218	78	140	75-79	
80-84	97	34	63	106	35	71	113	36	77	80-84	
85+	50	16	34	56	17	39	60	17	43	85+	
TOTAL	7238	3384	3854	7414	3485	3929	7566	3580	3986	TOTAL	

STANDARD COUNTRIES: STANDARDIZED RATES PER THOUSAND	ENGLAND AND WALES 1961 BOTH SEXES	MALES	FEMALES	UNITED STATES 1960 BOTH SEXES	MALES	FEMALES	MEXICO 1960 BOTH SEXES	MALES	FEMALES	
Birth	17.30	19.98*	16.26	17.63	18.55*	16.84	20.53	18.17*	19.86	**TABLE 6** STANDARDIZED RATES
Death	12.53	13.04*	12.01	10.35	11.68*	8.95	5.76	10.26*	4.63	
Increase	4.77	6.94*	4.25	7.28	6.86*	7.90	14.77	7.92*	15.23	

	OBSERVED POP. MALES	FEMALES	STATIONARY POP. MALES	FEMALES	STABLE POP. MALES	FEMALES	OBSERVED BIRTHS	NET MATERNITY FUNCTION	BIRTHS IN STABLE POP.	
μ	34.59600	38.25933	36.19373	38.70500	32.27245	34.35309	27.56222	27.52823	27.21220	**TABLE 7**
σ^2	492.7807	515.5712	489.9250	541.6490	462.8186	515.1734	39.37933	36.86856	35.93118	MOMENTS
κ_3	2871.724	957.076	2420.972	2045.767	4101.892	4310.985	100.3890	112.5002	115.6514	AND
κ_4	-250176.	-286001.	-231175.	-305316.	-173744.	-238896.	-932.205	-434.129	-323.878	CUMULANTS
β_1	0.068917	0.006684	0.049841	0.026337	0.169721	0.135923	0.165032	0.252545	0.288328	
β_2	1.969759	1.924054	2.036877	1.959328	2.188872	2.099876	2.398861	2.680621	2.749136	
κ	-0.024463	-0.002430	-0.019041	-0.009662	-0.064997	-0.050085	-0.077853	-0.146417	-0.172059	

VITAL STATISTICS		THOMPSON AGE RANGE	NRR	1000r	INTERVAL	BOURGEOIS-PICHAT AGE RANGE	NRR	1000b	1000d	1000r	COALE	
GRR	1.319										IBR	**TABLE 8** RATES FROM AGE DISTRIBUTIONS AND VITAL STATISTICS (Females)
NRR	1.252	0-4	1.15	5.16	27.42	5-29	1.16	14.56	9.05	5.51	IDR	
TFR	2.719	5-9	0.98	-0.89	27.38	30-54	0.81	10.20	18.11	-7.91	IRI	
GENERATION	27.370	10-14	0.97	-1.09	27.33	55-79	1.62	46.06	28.25	17.80	K1	
SEX RATIO	106.206	15-19	1.02	0.81	27.25	*50-74	1.48	36.67	22.24	14.42	K2	

Start of Age Interval	ORIGINAL MATRIX SUB-DIAGONAL	ALTERNATIVE FIRST ROWS Projection	Integral	FIRST STABLE MATRIX % IN STABLE POPULATION	FISHER VALUES	REPRODUCTIVE VALUES	SECOND STABLE MATRIX Z_2 FIRST COLUMN	FIRST ROW	
0	0.99512	0.00000	0.00000	8.864	1.057	294630	0.1599+0.0833	0.1599+0.0833	**TABLE 9** LESLIE MATRIX AND ITS SPECTRAL COMPONENTS (Females)
5	0.99806	0.00015	0.00000	8.465	1.106	261462	0.1758-0.1288	-0.0033+0.1492	
10	0.99787	0.05725	0.00030	8.109	1.155	282681	-0.0458-0.2601	-0.1116+0.0520	
15	0.99689	0.24530	0.11681	7.766	1.145	311222	-0.3072-0.0896	-0.0884-0.0684	
20	0.99616	0.37470	0.38517	7.430	0.937	219520	-0.2617+0.2856	-0.0209-0.1110	
25	0.99492	0.30519	0.38125	7.103	0.583	120967	0.1698+0.4367	0.0145-0.0874	
30	0.99312	0.18143	0.24304	6.783	0.286	68111	0.5640+0.0494	0.0212-0.0468	
35	0.98992	0.08350	0.12823	6.465	0.107	30603	0.3542-0.5837	0.0134-0.0166	
40	0.98515	0.02212	0.04266	6.142	0.024	4407	-0.4410-0.6921	0.0038-0.0032	
45	0.97807	0.00124	0.00253	5.807	0.001	338	-0.9759+0.1069	0.0002-0.0002	
50	0.96648	0.00000	0.00001	5.451	0.000	1	-0.3987+1.0957	0.0000-0.0000	
55+	0.79822			21.616					

Start of Age Interval	OBSERVED POPUL. (IN 100's)	CONTRIBUTIONS OF ROOTS (IN 100's) r_1	r_2, r_3	$r_4 \cdot r_{11}$	AGE-SP. BIRTH RATES	NET MATERNITY FUNCTION	COEFF. OF MATRIX EQUATION	PARAMETERS	INTEGRAL	MATRIX	EXP. INCREASE x	$e^{(x+2\frac{1}{2})r}$	
0	2788	2777	4	7	0.0000	0.0000	0.0000	L(1)	1.04191	1.04195	0	1.0207	**TABLE 10** AGE ANALYSIS AND MISCELLANEOUS RESULTS (Females)
5	2363	2652	-173	-116	0.0000	0.0000	0.0001	L(2)	0.35496	0.36420	50	1.5390	
10	2448	2540	-191	99	0.0001	0.0003	0.0569		0.76340	0.73860	55	1.6035	
15	2717	2433	49	235	0.0237	0.1134	0.2431	R(1)	0.00821	0.00822	60	1.6707	
20	2343	2328	333	-318	0.0781	0.3728	0.3702	R(2)	-0.03442	-0.03884	65	1.7407	
25	2076	2225	285	-434	0.0773	0.3676	0.3004		0.22711	0.22254	70	1.8137	
30	2381	2125	-183	439	0.0493	0.2331	0.1777	C(1)		31328	75	1.8897	
35	2857	2025	-610	1441	0.0260	0.1222	0.0812	C(2)		-19729	80	1.9689	
40	1866	1924	-383	325	0.0087	0.0402	0.0213			-40259	85	2.0514	
45	2676	1819	471	386	0.0005	0.0023	0.0012	2P/Y	27.6656	28.2344	90	2.1374	
50	2804	1708	1040	57	0.0000	0.0000	0.0000	DELTA	10.4456		95	2.2270	
55+	10333	6772									100	2.3203	

TABLE 1 — DATA

AGE AT LAST BIRTHDAY	POPULATION BOTH SEXES	MALES Number	%	FEMALES Number	%	BIRTHS BY AGE OF MOTHER	DEATHS BOTH SEXES	MALES	FEMALES	AGE AT LAST BIRTHDAY
0	130482	66516	2.0	63966	1.7	0	4217	2391	1826	0
1-4	489286	250379	7.5	238907	6.2	0	645	375	270	1-4
5-9	527809	268997	8.0	258812	6.8	0	250	157	93	5-9
10-14	485252	247513	7.4	237739	6.2	38	192	113	79	10-14
15-19	499125	254542	7.6	244583	6.4	13465	449	335	114	15-19
20-24	590272	301299	9.0	288973	7.6	47457	690	517	173	20-24
25-29	397143	201850	6.0	195293	5.1	32315	496	359	137	25-29
30-34	444126	224866	6.7	219260	5.7	23294	698	467	231	30-34
35-39	472460	215067	6.4	257393	6.7	13589	1017	583	434	35-39
40-44	448887	188087	5.6	260800	6.8	4486	1297	721	576	40-44
45-49	343477	146919	4.4	196558	5.1	163	1557	833	724	45-49
50-54	492365	216068	6.5	276297	7.2	2	3506	2066	1440	50-54
55-59	487677	218727	6.5	268950	7.0	0	5851	3609	2242	55-59
60-64	447341	197981	5.9	249360	6.5	0	8988	5611	3377	60-64
65-69	350858	140915	4.2	209943	5.5	0	11181	6273	4908	65-69
70-74	255282	96654	2.9	158628	4.1		12937	6430	6507	70-74
75-79	175298	64096	1.9	111202	2.9		14696	6565	8131	75-79
80-84	92569	32905	1.0	59664	1.6	68759 M.	12804	5130	7674	80-84
85+	42359	14043	0.4	28316	0.7	66050 F.	10108	3815	6293	85+
TOTAL	7172068	3347424		3824644		134809	91579	46350	45229	TOTAL

TABLE 2 — MALE LIFE TABLE

x	nq_x	l_x	nd_x	nL_x	nm_x	na_x	T_x	r_x	$\overset{\circ}{e}_x$	nM_x	x
0	0.034858	100000	3486	97340	0.035811	0.2369	6635185	0.0048	66.352	0.035946	0
1	0.005926	96514	572	384394	0.001488	1.0922	6537845	0.0048	67.740	0.001498	1
5	0.002893	95942	278	479017	0.000579	2.5000	6153451	0.0239	64.137	0.000584	5
10	0.002284	95665	219	477850	0.000457	2.8324	5674434	0.0048	59.316	0.000457	10
15	0.006561	95446	626	475789	0.001316	2.6972	5196584	0.0000	54.445	0.001316	15
20	0.008554	94820	811	472115	0.001718	2.5532	4720796	0.0215	49.787	0.001716	20
25	0.008864	94009	833	467993	0.001781	2.5379	4248680	0.0274	45.194	0.001779	25
30	0.010332	93176	963	463557	0.002077	2.5890	3780688	0.0000	40.576	0.002077	30
35	0.013495	92213	1244	458115	0.002716	2.6297	3317131	0.0151	35.973	0.002711	35
40	0.019098	90968	1737	450760	0.003854	2.6502	2859016	0.0342	31.429	0.003833	40
45	0.027983	89231	2497	440397	0.005670	2.6936	2408256	0.0000	26.989	0.005670	45
50	0.046784	86734	4058	424375	0.009562	2.7091	1967859	0.0000	22.688	0.009562	50
55	0.079474	82676	6571	398221	0.016500	2.6926	1543484	0.0000	18.669	0.016500	55
60	0.133131	76106	10132	356597	0.028413	2.6380	1145263	0.0129	15.048	0.028341	60
65	0.201311	65974	13281	297696	0.044613	2.5776	788666	0.0129	11.954	0.044516	65
70	0.286179	52692	15079	226188	0.066668	2.5281	490970	0.0129	9.318	0.066526	70
75	0.407218	37613	15317	149216	0.102648	2.4636	264783	0.0129	7.040	0.102424	75
80	0.556277	22296	12403	79344	0.156318	2.4089	115567	0.0129	5.183	0.155904	80
85+	*1.000000	9893	9893	36223	0.273127	3.6613	36223	0.0129	3.661	0.271666	85+

TABLE 3 — FEMALE LIFE TABLE

x	nq_x	l_x	nd_x	nL_x	nm_x	na_x	T_x	r_x	$\overset{\circ}{e}_x$	nM_x	x
0	0.027807	100000	2781	97863	0.028414	0.2315	7265170	0.0059	72.652	0.028546	0
1	0.004468	97219	434	387613	0.001121	1.0886	7167306	0.0059	73.723	0.001130	1
5	0.001779	96785	172	483494	0.000356	2.5000	6779694	0.0236	70.049	0.000359	5
10	0.001661	96613	160	482673	0.000332	2.5679	6296199	0.0053	65.169	0.000332	10
15	0.002328	96452	225	481727	0.000466	2.6185	5813526	0.0000	60.274	0.000466	15
20	0.002994	96228	288	480442	0.000600	2.5814	5331799	0.0219	55.408	0.000599	20
25	0.003514	95940	337	478900	0.000704	2.6324	4851358	0.0269	50.567	0.000702	25
30	0.005255	95602	502	476852	0.001054	2.6913	4372458	0.0000	45.736	0.001054	30
35	0.008397	95100	799	473616	0.001686	2.6405	3895606	0.0000	40.963	0.001686	35
40	0.011037	94301	1041	469094	0.002219	2.6810	3421990	0.0246	36.288	0.002209	40
45	0.018260	93261	1703	462320	0.003683	2.6611	2952896	0.0000	31.663	0.003683	45
50	0.025747	91558	2357	452301	0.005212	2.6720	2490576	0.0000	27.202	0.005212	50
55	0.040905	89200	3649	437565	0.008339	2.6876	2038275	0.0016	22.850	0.008336	55
60	0.065958	85552	5643	414746	0.013605	2.6939	1600710	0.0206	18.710	0.013543	60
65	0.111378	79909	8900	378897	0.023489	2.6801	1185964	0.0206	14.841	0.023378	65
70	0.187818	71009	13337	323592	0.041215	2.6417	807067	0.0206	11.366	0.041020	70
75	0.311601	57672	17971	244671	0.073449	2.5688	483475	0.0206	8.383	0.073119	75
80	0.485447	39701	19273	149251	0.129131	2.5266	238804	0.0206	6.015	0.128620	80
85+	1.000000	20428	20428	89553	0.228115	4.3838	89553	0.0206	4.384	0.222241	85+

TABLE 4 — OBSERVED AND PROJECTED VITAL RATES

RATES PER THOUSAND	OBSERVED POPULATION BOTH SEXES	MALES	FEMALES	PROJECTED POPULATION 1968 MALES	FEMALES	1973 MALES	FEMALES	1978 MALES	FEMALES	STABLE POPULATION MALES	FEMALES
Birth	18.80	20.54	17.27	20.29	17.18	19.72	16.88	19.71	17.08	21.22	19.83
Death	12.77	13.85	11.83	13.89	12.69	13.76	13.25	13.46	13.58	11.09	9.70
Increase	6.03	6.69	5.44	6.40	4.49	5.96	3.63	6.25	3.50		10.1319
PERCENTAGE											
under 15	22.77	24.90	20.90	26.54	22.54	27.63	23.76	27.53	24.08	28.32	26.71
15-64	64.46	64.69	64.25	62.32	61.39	60.90	59.33	61.27	58.64	63.70	62.20
65 and over	12.78	10.41	14.84	11.14	16.08	11.47	16.91	11.19	17.28	7.98	11.10
DEP. RATIO X 100	55.14	54.59	55.63	60.47	62.90	64.20	68.55	63.21	70.53	57.00	60.78

TABLE 1 — DATA

AGE AT LAST BIRTHDAY	POPULATION BOTH SEXES	MALES Number	MALES %	FEMALES Number	FEMALES %	BIRTHS BY AGE OF MOTHER	DEATHS BOTH SEXES	DEATHS MALES	DEATHS FEMALES	AGE AT LAST BIRTHDAY
0	132860	67857	2.0	65003	1.7	0	3913	2265	1648	0
1-4	499809	255272	7.6	244537	6.4	0	636	346	290	1-4
5-9	547759	279224	8.3	268535	7.0	0	285	168	117	5-9
10-14	478652	244122	7.2	234530	6.1	34	204	128	76	10-14
15-19	494854	252522	7.5	242332	6.3	13310	430	314	116	15-19
20-24	588565	299727	8.9	288838	7.5	46755	711	536	175	20-24
25-29	424046	216119	6.4	207927	5.4	33717	540	388	152	25-29
30-34	431647	218519	6.5	213128	5.5	22245	647	439	208	30-34
35-39	465552	219520	6.5	246032	6.4	12798	971	581	390	35-39
40-44	480054	201018	6.0	279036	7.3	4786	1301	706	595	40-44
45-49	314035	133612	4.0	180423	4.7	196	1417	801	616	45-49
50-54	483154	210419	6.2	272735	7.1	0	3482	2027	1455	50-54
55-59	485554	215819	6.4	269735	7.0	0	5577	3475	2102	55-59
60-64	452051	200518	6.0	251533	6.5	0	8895	5605	3290	60-64
65-69	360241	146113	4.3	214128	5.6	0	11145	6271	4874	65-69
70-74	259530	97509	2.9	162021	4.2		12670	6256	6414	70-74
75-79	178221	64206	1.9	114015	3.0		14031	6228	7803	75-79
80-84	94511	33303	1.0	61208	1.6	68366 M.	12473	5017	7456	80-84
85+	44305	14501	0.4	29804	0.8	65475 F.	9753	3487	6266	85+
TOTAL	7215400	3369900		3845500		133841	89081	45038	44043	TOTAL

TABLE 2 — MALE LIFE TABLE

x	nq_x	l_x	nd_x	nL_x	nm_x	na_x	T_x	r_x	$\dot{e}_x$	nM_x	x
0	0.032423	100000	3242	97517	0.033249	0.2342	6680321	0.0050	66.803	0.033379	0
1	0.005363	96758	519	385521	0.001346	1.0904	6582804	0.0050	68.034	0.001355	1
5	0.002985	96239	287	480476	0.000598	2.5000	6197283	0.0272	64.395	0.000602	5
10	0.002625	95951	252	479192	0.000526	2.7532	5716808	0.0094	59.580	0.000524	10
15	0.006200	95700	593	477139	0.001243	2.7091	5237616	0.0000	54.730	0.001243	15
20	0.008911	95106	847	473465	0.001790	2.5614	4760477	0.0139	50.054	0.001788	20
25	0.008943	94259	843	469205	0.001797	2.5213	4287012	0.0298	45.481	0.001795	25
30	0.009996	93416	934	464823	0.002009	2.5834	3817807	0.0000	40.869	0.002009	30
35	0.013159	92482	1217	459507	0.002648	2.6147	3352985	0.0057	36.256	0.002647	35
40	0.017574	91265	1604	452614	0.003544	2.6863	2893477	0.0458	31.704	0.003512	40
45	0.029566	89661	2651	442198	0.005995	2.6961	2440863	0.0000	27.223	0.005995	45
50	0.047118	87010	4100	425590	0.009633	2.6923	1998665	0.0000	22.970	0.009633	50
55	0.077624	82910	6436	399703	0.016101	2.6928	1573075	0.0000	18.973	0.016101	55
60	0.131478	76475	10055	358592	0.028040	2.6348	1173372	0.0161	15.343	0.027953	60
65	0.194852	66420	12942	300741	0.043034	2.5771	814780	0.0161	12.267	0.042919	65
70	0.277534	53478	14842	230730	0.064326	2.5300	514039	0.0161	9.612	0.064158	70
75	0.390305	38636	15080	155041	0.097263	2.4709	283309	0.0161	7.333	0.097000	75
80	0.540528	23556	12733	84291	0.151057	2.4304	128269	0.0161	5.445	0.150647	80
85+	1.000000	10823	10823	43977	0.246112	4.0632	43977	0.0161	4.063	0.240467	85+

TABLE 3 — FEMALE LIFE TABLE

x	nq_x	l_x	nd_x	nL_x	nm_x	na_x	T_x	r_x	$\dot{e}_x$	nM_x	x
0	0.024781	100000	2478	98141	0.025250	0.2497	7326989	0.0052	73.270	0.025353	0
1	0.004697	97522	458	388760	0.001178	1.1018	7228849	0.0052	74.125	0.001186	1
5	0.002156	97064	209	484796	0.000432	2.5000	6840089	0.0271	70.470	0.000436	5
10	0.001619	96855	157	483885	0.000324	2.5291	6355293	0.0099	65.617	0.000324	10
15	0.002391	96698	231	482939	0.000479	2.6220	5871408	0.0000	60.719	0.000479	15
20	0.003029	96467	292	481627	0.000607	2.5862	5388469	0.0147	55.858	0.000606	20
25	0.003660	96174	352	480028	0.000733	2.6032	4906842	0.0296	51.020	0.000731	25
30	0.004869	95822	467	478029	0.000976	2.6791	4426814	0.0000	46.198	0.000976	30
35	0.007896	95356	753	475010	0.001585	2.6500	3948785	0.0000	41.411	0.001585	35
40	0.010663	94603	1009	470666	0.002143	2.6719	3473776	0.0287	36.720	0.002132	40
45	0.016937	93594	1585	464302	0.003414	2.6860	3003110	0.0000	32.087	0.003414	45
50	0.026345	92009	2424	454368	0.005335	2.6584	2538808	0.0000	27.593	0.005335	50
55	0.038274	89585	3429	439993	0.007793	2.6869	2084439	0.0000	23.268	0.007793	55
60	0.063837	86156	5500	418142	0.013153	2.7021	1644446	0.0243	19.087	0.013080	60
65	0.108675	80656	8765	382946	0.022889	2.6801	1226304	0.0243	15.204	0.022762	65
70	0.181889	71891	13076	328551	0.039800	2.6367	843358	0.0243	11.731	0.039587	70
75	0.294864	58815	17342	252064	0.068801	2.5777	514807	0.0243	8.753	0.068438	75
80	0.471162	41472	19540	159468	0.122534	2.5489	262743	0.0243	6.335	0.121815	80
85+	*1.000000	21932	21932	103276	0.212365	4.7089	103276	0.0243	4.709	0.210240	85+

TABLE 4 — OBSERVED AND PROJECTED VITAL RATES

	OBSERVED POPULATION BOTH SEXES	MALES	FEMALES	PROJECTED POPULATION 1969 MALES	FEMALES	1974 MALES	FEMALES	1979 MALES	FEMALES	STABLE POPULATION MALES	FEMALES
RATES PER THOUSAND											
Birth	18.55	20.29	17.03	19.91	16.84	19.35	16.53	19.51	16.89	20.77	19.37
Death	12.35	13.36	11.45	13.57	12.47	13.50	13.13	13.23	13.47	11.15	9.75
Increase	6.20	6.92	5.57	6.34	4.37	5.85	3.41	6.28	3.42		9.6205
PERCENTAGE											
under 15	22.99	25.12	21.13	26.77	22.74	27.48	23.63	27.18	23.73	27.90	26.25
15-64	64.02	64.33	63.76	61.81	60.78	60.81	59.02	61.49	58.62	63.74	62.13
65 and over	12.98	10.55	15.11	11.43	16.48	11.71	17.36	11.33	17.65	8.36	11.62
DEP. RATIO X 100	56.19	55.45	56.85	61.80	64.52	64.45	69.44	62.63	70.60	56.90	60.94

TABLE 1 — DATA

AGE AT LAST BIRTHDAY	POPULATION BOTH SEXES	MALES Number	%	FEMALES Number	%	BIRTHS BY AGE OF MOTHER	DEATHS BOTH SEXES	MALES	FEMALES	AGE AT LAST BIRTHDAY
0	128690	65607	1.9	63083	1.6	0	3673	2056	1617	0
1-4	510975	260762	7.7	250213	6.5	0	625	360	265	1-4
5-9	568153	289935	8.6	278218	7.2	0	278	165	113	5-9
10-14	480081	244757	7.2	235324	6.1	21	199	119	80	10-14
15-19	499160	255006	7.5	244154	6.3	13817	413	298	115	15-19
20-24	550132	279364	8.2	270768	7.0	42944	555	421	134	20-24
25-29	476600	243458	7.2	233142	6.0	36008	518	376	142	25-29
30-34	417187	210830	6.2	206357	5.3	20641	680	474	206	30-34
35-39	459716	223466	6.6	236250	6.1	11892	996	658	338	35-39
40-44	488993	206224	6.1	282769	7.3	4370	1444	820	624	40-44
45-49	318276	134485	4.0	183791	4.8	231	1428	810	618	45-49
50-54	461045	199338	5.9	261707	6.8	0	3215	1824	1391	50-54
55-59	483871	212657	6.3	271214	7.0	0	5823	3569	2254	55-59
60-64	454329	201700	5.9	252629	6.5	0	9189	5822	3367	60-64
65-69	369927	151752	4.5	218175	5.6	0	12096	6948	5148	65-69
70-74	265727	99096	2.9	166631	4.3		13553	6758	6795	70-74
75-79	179298	63798	1.9	115500	3.0		15163	6710	8453	75-79
80-84	96677	33656	1.0	63021	1.6	66365 M.	13406	5317	8089	80-84
85+	46149	14931	0.4	31218	0.8	63559 F.	11019	3910	7109	85+
TOTAL	7254986	3390822		3864164		129924	94273	47415	46858	TOTAL

TABLE 2 — MALE LIFE TABLE

x	nq_x	l_x	nd_x	nL_x	nm_x	na_x	T_x	r_x	$\dot{e}_x$	nM_x	x
0	0.030612	100000	3061	97683	0.031338	0.2433	6657756	0.0000	66.578	0.031338	0
1	0.005500	96939	533	386207	0.001381	1.0969	6560072	0.0000	67.672	0.001381	1
5	0.002820	96406	272	481348	0.000565	2.5000	6173865	0.0280	64.041	0.000569	5
10	0.002436	96134	234	480143	0.000488	2.7553	5692517	0.0122	59.215	0.000486	10
15	0.005827	95900	559	478201	0.001169	2.6796	5212374	0.0000	54.352	0.001169	15
20	0.007509	95341	716	474950	0.001507	2.5498	4734173	0.0032	49.655	0.001507	20
25	0.007714	94625	730	471369	0.001548	2.5956	4259224	0.0265	45.012	0.001544	25
30	0.011191	93895	1051	466979	0.002250	2.6244	3787854	0.0063	40.341	0.002248	30
35	0.014620	92844	1357	460987	0.002945	2.6173	3320876	0.0000	35.768	0.002945	35
40	0.019842	91487	1815	453168	0.004006	2.6498	2859889	0.0466	31.260	0.003976	40
45	0.029697	89671	2663	442134	0.006023	2.6630	2406721	0.0000	26.839	0.006023	45
50	0.044815	87009	3899	426139	0.009150	2.7165	1964587	0.0000	22.579	0.009150	50
55	0.080796	83109	6715	400101	0.016783	2.6999	1538449	0.0000	18.511	0.016783	55
60	0.135375	76394	10342	357558	0.028924	2.6393	1138347	0.0102	14.901	0.028865	60
65	0.206379	66052	13632	297219	0.045865	2.5760	780789	0.0102	11.821	0.045785	65
70	0.292149	52421	15315	224188	0.068311	2.5243	483570	0.0102	9.225	0.068196	70
75	0.415480	37106	15417	146331	0.105356	2.4574	259382	0.0102	6.990	0.105176	75
80	0.560667	21689	12160	76818	0.158301	2.3991	113051	0.0102	5.212	0.157981	80
85+	*1.000000	9529	9529	36233	0.262987	3.8025	36233	0.0102	3.802	0.261871	85+

TABLE 3 — FEMALE LIFE TABLE

x	nq_x	l_x	nd_x	nL_x	nm_x	na_x	T_x	r_x	$\dot{e}_x$	nM_x	x
0	0.025141	100000	2514	98081	0.025633	0.2367	7299506	0.0000	72.995	0.025633	0
1	0.004223	97486	412	388746	0.001059	1.0921	7201425	0.0000	73.871	0.001059	1
5	0.002012	97074	195	484883	0.000403	2.5000	6812679	0.0280	70.180	0.000406	5
10	0.001699	96879	165	483990	0.000340	2.5408	6327796	0.0127	65.317	0.000340	10
15	0.002352	96714	228	483018	0.000471	2.5677	5843806	0.0000	60.423	0.000471	15
20	0.002472	96487	239	481851	0.000495	2.5581	5360788	0.0041	55.560	0.000495	20
25	0.003055	96248	294	480556	0.000612	2.6695	4878937	0.0265	50.691	0.000609	25
30	0.004980	95954	478	478657	0.000998	2.6686	4398381	0.0000	45.838	0.000998	30
35	0.007130	95476	681	475798	0.001431	2.6736	3919724	0.0000	41.054	0.001431	35
40	0.011023	94796	1045	471509	0.002216	2.6764	3443925	0.0228	36.330	0.002207	40
45	0.016696	93751	1565	465127	0.003365	2.6830	2972375	0.0042	31.705	0.003363	45
50	0.026252	92186	2420	455314	0.005315	2.6803	2507248	0.0000	27.198	0.005315	50
55	0.040768	89765	3660	440339	0.008311	2.6805	2051934	0.0000	22.859	0.008311	55
60	0.064924	86106	5590	417675	0.013384	2.7006	1611595	0.0184	18.716	0.013328	60
65	0.112300	80516	9042	381589	0.023695	2.6787	1193920	0.0184	14.828	0.023596	65
70	0.186720	71474	13346	325896	0.040950	2.6417	812331	0.0184	11.365	0.040779	70
75	0.311726	58128	18120	246598	0.073480	2.5694	486435	0.0184	8.368	0.073186	75
80	0.484497	40008	19384	150489	0.128805	2.5269	239837	0.0184	5.995	0.128354	80
85+	1.000000	20624	20624	89348	0.230832	4.3322	89348	0.0184	4.332	0.227720	85+

TABLE 4 — OBSERVED AND PROJECTED VITAL RATES

	OBSERVED POPULATION BOTH SEXES	MALES	FEMALES	PROJECTED POPULATION 1970 MALES	FEMALES	1975 MALES	FEMALES	1980 MALES	FEMALES	STABLE POPULATION MALES	FEMALES
RATES PER THOUSAND											
Birth	17.91	19.57	16.45	19.23	16.28	18.91	16.18	19.32	16.75	20.10	18.71
Death	12.99	13.98	12.13	13.95	12.89	13.74	13.43	13.37	13.72	11.55	10.17
Increase	4.91	5.59	4.32	5.28	3.39	5.17	2.75	5.95	3.02		8.5456
PERCENTAGE											
under 15	23.27	25.39	21.40	26.88	22.85	27.14	23.36	26.65	23.27	27.27	25.57
15-64	63.53	63.89	63.22	61.75	60.62	61.42	59.35	62.58	59.47	64.33	62.58
65 and over	13.20	10.71	15.39	11.37	16.52	11.44	17.29	10.77	17.26	8.40	11.86
DEP. RATIO X 100	57.40	56.51	58.19	61.95	64.95	62.81	68.49	59.80	68.15	55.45	59.80

AGE AT LAST BIRTHDAY	1970				1975			1980			AGE AT LAST BIRTHDAY	
	BOTH SEXES	MALES	FEMALES	BOTH SEXES	MALES	FEMALES		BOTH SEXES	MALES	FEMALES		
0-4	634	323	311	640	326	314		658	335	323	0-4	
5-9	637	325	312	631	321	310		637	324	313	5-9	
10-14	567	289	278	635	324	311		629	320	309	10-14	
15-19	479	244	235	565	288	277		634	323	311	15-19	**TABLE 5**
20-24	497	253	244	476	242	234		562	286	276	20-24	POPULATION
25-29	547	277	270	494	251	243		474	240	234	25-29	PROJECTED
30-34	473	241	232	544	275	269		491	249	242	30-34	WITH
35-39	413	208	205	469	238	231		538	271	267	35-39	FIXED
40-44	454	220	234	408	205	203		463	234	229	40-44	AGE—
45-49	480	201	279	445	214	231		401	200	201	45-49	SPECIFIC
50-54	310	130	180	467	194	273		433	207	226	50-54	BIRTH
55-59	440	187	253	296	122	174		446	182	264	55-59	AND
60-64	447	190	257	407	167	240		274	109	165	60-64	DEATH
65-69	399	168	231	393	158	235		358	139	219	65-69	RATES
70-74	300	114	186	323	126	197		320	119	201	70-74	(IN 1000's)
75-79	191	65	126	216	75	141		232	83	149	75-79	
80-84	103	33	70	111	34	77		125	39	86	80-84	
85+	53	16	37	58	16	42		62	16	46	85+	
TOTAL	7424	3484	3940	7578	3576	4002		7737	3676	4061	TOTAL	

STANDARD COUNTRIES:	ENGLAND AND WALES 1961			UNITED STATES 1960			MEXICO 1960				
STANDARDIZED RATES PER THOUSAND	BOTH SEXES	MALES	FEMALES	BOTH SEXES	MALES	FEMALES	BOTH SEXES	MALES	FEMALES		**TABLE 6**
Birth	17.10	18.81*	16.21	17.44	17.39*	16.81	20.45	17.28*	19.95		STANDAR-
Death	12.45	13.07*	11.83	10.18	11.79*	8.68	5.35	10.25*	4.25		DIZED
Increase	4.65	5.75*	4.38	7.26	5.60*	8.12	15.09	7.02*	15.71		RATES

	OBSERVED POP.		STATIONARY POP.		STABLE POP.		OBSERVED BIRTHS	NET MATERNITY FUNCTION	BIRTHS IN STABLE POP.	
	MALES	FEMALES	MALES	FEMALES	MALES	FEMALES				
μ	34.10128	38.22659	36.11602	38.77006	32.07925	34.24922	27.03119	27.28190	26.95089	**TABLE 7**
σ^2	504.1602	545.6088	484.8859	540.9937	457.4222	513.6914	38.03508	37.13342	36.16425	MOMENTS
κ_3	3443.281	1270.526	2315.072	1968.867	4030.331	4322.789	147.4495	111.7081	114.9666	AND
κ_4	-257996.	-334706.	-227010.	-305593.	-169676.	-237196.	-319.622	-428.084	-324.974	CUMULANTS
β_1	0.092521	0.009939	0.047012	0.024483	0.169719	0.137855	0.395124	0.243711	0.279451	
β_2	1.984976	1.875653	2.034469	1.955859	2.189067	2.101116	2.779063	2.689544	2.751521	
κ	-0.032507	-0.003469	-0.017977	-0.008973	-0.065007	-0.050751	-0.204149	-0.145481	-0.170218	

VITAL STATISTICS		THOMPSON				BOURGEOIS-PICHAT				COALE	**TABLE 8**
		AGE RANGE	NRR	1000r	INTERVAL	AGE RANGE	NRR	1000b	1000d	1000r	RATES
GRR	1.313									IBR	FROM AGE
NRR	1.261	0-4	1.25	8.34	27.44	5-29	1.11	14.42	10.60	3.82 IDR	DISTRI-
TFR	2.684	5-9	1.16	5.40	27.40	30-54	0.83	9.50	16.44	-6.94 IRI	BUTIONS
GENERATION	27.116	10-14	0.98	-0.78	27.35	55-79	1.39	33.06	20.76	12.29 K1	AND VITAL
SEX RATIO	104.415	15-19	0.98	-0.86	27.27	*50-74	1.18	21.86	15.69	6.17 K2	STATISTICS (Females)

Start of Age Interval	ORIGINAL MATRIX			FIRST STABLE MATRIX			SECOND STABLE MATRIX Z2			
	SUB-DIAGONAL	ALTERNATIVE FIRST ROWS		% IN STABLE POPULATION	FISHER VALUES	REPRODUCTIVE VALUES	FIRST COLUMN	FIRST ROW		
		Projection	Integral							
0	0.99601	0.00000	0.00000	8.920	1.049	328706	0.1587+0.0832	0.1587+0.0832		**TABLE 9**
5	0.99816	0.00011	0.00000	8.512	1.099	305880	0.1750-0.1292	-0.0045+0.1475		LESLIE
10	0.99799	0.06736	0.00022	8.141	1.149	270499	-0.0484-0.2601	-0.1107+0.0496		MATRIX
15	0.99758	0.25579	0.13769	7.784	1.131	276212	-0.3103-0.3853	-0.0872-0.0697		AND ITS
20	0.99731	0.37228	0.38587	7.440	0.915	247638	-0.2580+0.2941	-0.0204-0.1109		SPECTRAL
25	0.99605	0.30255	0.37577	7.110	0.565	131836	0.1846+0.4383	0.0155-0.0860		COMPO-
30	0.99403	0.17869	0.24336	6.785	0.274	56508	0.5765+0.0309	0.0211-0.0448		NENTS
35	0.99107	0.07818	0.12247	6.462	0.099	23368	0.3387-0.6119	0.0123-0.0154		(Females)
40	0.98638	0.01987	0.03760	6.136	0.021	6052	-0.4861-0.6908	0.0034-0.0030		
45	0.97890	0.00149	0.00304	5.799	0.002	277	-1.0023+0.1629	0.0003-0.0002		
50	0.96711	0.00000	0.00001	5.439	0.000	1	-0.3475+1.1606	0.0000-0.0000		
55+	0.79871			21.472						

Start of Age Interval	OBSERVED POPUL. (IN 100's)	CONTRIBUTIONS OF ROOTS (IN 100's)			AGE-SP. BIRTH RATES	NET MATERNITY FUNCTION	COEFF. OF MATRIX EQUATION	PARAMETERS		EXP. INCREASE		
		r_1	r_2, r_3	$r_4 - r_{11}$				INTEGRAL	MATRIX	x	$e(x+2\frac{1}{2})r$	
0	3133	2918	149	66	0.0000	0.0000	0.0000	L(1) 1.04365	1.04370	0	1.0216	**TABLE 10**
5	2782	2785	34	-37	0.0000	0.0000	0.0001	L(2) 0.34879	0.35842	50	1.5662	AGE
10	2353	2663	-184	-126	0.0000	0.0002	0.0670	0.76280	0.73810	55	1.6346	ANALYSIS
15	2442	2547	-246	141	0.0277	0.1337	0.2538	R(1) 0.00855	0.00855	60	1.7059	AND
20	2708	2434	11	263	0.0776	0.3739	0.3685	R(2) -0.03517	-0.03956	65	1.7804	MISCEL-
25	2331	2326	375	-370	0.0756	0.3631	0.2987	0.22839	0.22375	70	1.8581	LANEOUS
30	2064	2220	382	-538	0.0489	0.2342	0.1757	C(1)	32715	75	1.9392	RESULTS
35	2363	2114	-148	396	0.0246	0.1172	0.0764	C(2)	31553	80	2.0239	(Females)
40	2828	2007	-715	1535	0.0076	0.0357	0.0193		-29539	85	2.1122	
45	1838	1897	-536	477	0.0006	0.0029	0.0014	2P/Y 27.5112	28.0815	90	2.2044	
50	2617	1779	466	371	0.0000	0.0000	0.0000	DELTA 9.9785		95	2.3007	
55+	11184	7025								100	2.4011	

TABLE 1 — DATA

AGE AT LAST BIRTHDAY	POPULATION BOTH SEXES	MALES Number	%	FEMALES Number	%	BIRTHS BY AGE OF MOTHER	DEATHS BOTH SEXES	MALES	FEMALES	AGE AT LAST BIRTHDAY
0	170646	86331	2.6	84315	2.5	0	33253	18488	14765	0
1-4	614109	308339	9.3	305770	9.2	0	11405	5918	5487	1-4
5-9	688110	344921	10.4	343189	10.3	0	2781	1395	1386	5-9
10-14	642409	322282	9.7	320127	9.6	0	1515	705	810	10-14
15-19	642672	322774	9.8	319898	9.6	8056	2550	1223	1327	15-19
20-24	604102	304044	9.2	300058	9.0	49710	3419	1732	1687	20-24
25-29	528186	275036	8.3	253150	7.6	65881	3448	1668	1780	25-29
30-34	478368	239924	7.3	238444	7.2	47064	3199	1617	1582	30-34
35-39	416781	208382	6.3	208399	6.3	22882	3428	1794	1634	35-39
40-44	370853	184280	5.6	186573	5.6	1761	3571	2027	1544	40-44
45-49	311828	153998	4.7	157830	4.7	0	3827	2230	1597	45-49
50-54	273950	133532	4.0	140418	4.2	0	4547	2653	1894	50-54
55-59	263325	128041	3.9	135284	4.1	0	6023	3362	2661	55-59
60-64	219374	105437	3.2	113937	3.4	0	7311	3936	3375	60-64
65-69	167143	78874	2.4	88269	2.7	0	8500	4479	4021	65-69
70-74	120870	56274	1.7	64596	1.9		9884	4983	4901	70-74
75-79	77086	34797	1.1	42289	1.3		9659	4606	5053	75-79
80-84	33621	14437	0.4	19184	0.6	100176 M.	6544	2980	3564	80-84
85+	13594	5324	0.2	8270	0.2	95178 F.	4182	1724	2458	85+
TOTAL	6637027	3307027		3330000		195354	129046	67520	61526	TOTAL

TABLE 2 — MALE LIFE TABLE

x	$_nq_x$	l_x	$_nd_x$	$_nL_x$	$_nm_x$	$_na_x$	T_x	r_x	$\dot{e}_x$	$_nM_x$	x
0	0.186552	100000	18655	87112	0.214153	0.3091	4511363	0.0000	45.114	0.214153	0
1	0.072805	81345	5922	308562	0.019193	1.1604	4424251	0.0000	54.389	0.019193	1
5	0.019831	75423	1496	373373	0.004006	2.5000	4115689	0.0129	54.568	0.004044	5
10	0.010876	73927	804	367599	0.002187	2.4684	3742316	0.0037	50.622	0.002188	10
15	0.018788	73123	1374	362432	0.003790	2.6840	3374717	0.0020	46.151	0.003789	15
20	0.028119	71749	2018	353849	0.005702	2.5734	3012285	0.0106	41.984	0.005697	20
25	0.029893	69731	2084	343494	0.006068	2.5229	2658436	0.0175	38.124	0.006065	25
30	0.033206	67647	2246	332760	0.006750	2.5629	2314942	0.0208	34.221	0.006740	30
35	0.042244	65401	2763	320329	0.008625	2.5842	1982182	0.0177	30.308	0.008609	35
40	0.053684	62638	3363	305073	0.011023	2.5863	1661853	0.0190	26.531	0.011000	40
45	0.070111	59275	4156	286374	0.014512	2.5933	1356780	0.0174	22.889	0.014481	45
50	0.094782	55119	5224	262953	0.019868	2.5799	1070405	0.0000	19.420	0.019868	50
55	0.123432	49895	6159	234551	0.026257	2.5766	807452	0.0000	16.183	0.026257	55
60	0.171255	43736	7490	200557	0.037346	2.5802	572901	0.0027	13.099	0.037330	60
65	0.249414	36246	9040	159124	0.056813	2.5546	372344	0.0027	10.273	0.056787	65
70	0.362357	27206	9858	111281	0.088589	2.4896	213220	0.0027	7.837	0.088549	70
75	0.492645	17348	8546	64535	0.132429	2.4019	101939	0.0027	5.876	0.132368	75
80	0.663031	8801	5836	28256	0.206530	2.3008	37404	0.0027	4.250	0.206413	80
85+	*1.000000	2966	2966	9149	0.324182	3.0847	9149	0.0027	3.085	0.323817	85+

TABLE 3 — FEMALE LIFE TABLE

x	$_nq_x$	l_x	$_nd_x$	$_nL_x$	$_nm_x$	$_na_x$	T_x	r_x	$\dot{e}_x$	$_nM_x$	x
0	0.156611	100000	15661	89432	0.175117	0.3252	4855186	0.0000	48.552	0.175117	0
1	0.068324	84339	5762	321115	0.017945	1.1815	4765753	0.0000	56.507	0.017945	1
5	0.019823	78577	1558	388989	0.004004	2.5000	4444639	0.0127	56.564	0.004039	5
10	0.012572	77019	968	382675	0.002530	2.5011	4055650	0.0038	52.658	0.002530	10
15	0.020548	76051	1563	376576	0.004150	2.6469	3672976	0.0024	48.296	0.004148	15
20	0.027788	74488	2070	367461	0.005633	2.5947	3296400	0.0177	44.254	0.005622	20
25	0.034571	72418	2504	355876	0.007035	2.5177	2928939	0.0164	40.445	0.007031	25
30	0.032644	69914	2282	343887	0.006637	2.5091	2573063	0.0124	36.803	0.006635	30
35	0.038487	67632	2603	331728	0.007847	2.5286	2229176	0.0169	32.960	0.007841	35
40	0.040595	65029	2640	318647	0.008284	2.5382	1897448	0.0192	29.178	0.008276	40
45	0.049476	62389	3087	304488	0.010138	2.5834	1578801	0.0181	25.306	0.010118	45
50	0.065352	59303	3876	287266	0.013491	2.6140	1274313	0.0014	21.488	0.013488	50
55	0.093965	55427	5208	264756	0.019672	2.6230	987047	0.0006	17.808	0.019670	55
60	0.138409	50219	6951	234484	0.029643	2.6103	722291	0.0041	14.383	0.029622	60
65	0.205424	43268	8888	194962	0.045590	2.5948	487807	0.0041	11.274	0.045554	65
70	0.319783	34380	10994	144792	0.075930	2.5344	292844	0.0041	8.518	0.075872	70
75	0.457736	23386	10705	89521	0.119575	2.4396	148052	0.0041	6.331	0.119487	75
80	0.622327	12681	7892	42444	0.185936	2.3438	58530	0.0041	4.616	0.185779	80
85+	*1.000000	4789	4789	16086	0.297730	3.3587	16086	0.0041	3.359	0.297219	85+

TABLE 4 — OBSERVED AND PROJECTED VITAL RATES

	OBSERVED POPULATION BOTH SEXES	MALES	FEMALES	PROJECTED POPULATION 1905 MALES	FEMALES	1910 MALES	FEMALES	1915 MALES	FEMALES	STABLE POPULATION MALES	FEMALES
RATES PER THOUSAND											
Birth	29.43	30.29	28.58	31.03	29.25	30.88	29.08	30.36	28.58	29.80	27.97
Death	19.44	20.42	18.48	19.99	18.08	19.80	17.93	19.56	17.74	20.19	18.37
Increase	9.99	9.87	10.11	11.03	11.16	11.08	11.16	10.80	10.85		9.6064
PERCENTAGE											
under 15	31.87	32.11	31.63	32.28	31.72	32.47	31.83	32.32	31.64	31.58	30.83
15-64	61.92	62.15	61.68	62.23	61.80	62.19	61.78	62.68	62.25	62.88	62.38
65 and over	6.21	5.74	6.68	5.50	6.48	5.35	6.39	5.00	6.11	5.54	6.79
DEP. RATIO X 100	61.51	60.89	62.12	60.70	61.82	60.81	61.87	59.53	60.65	59.04	60.32

AGE LAST BIRTHDAY	1905 BOTH SEXES	1905 MALES	1905 FEMALES	1910 BOTH SEXES	1910 MALES	1910 FEMALES	1915 BOTH SEXES	1915 MALES	1915 FEMALES	AGE AT LAST BIRTHDAY	
0-4	818	412	406	870	438	432	909	458	451	0-4	**TABLE 5**
5-9	742	372	370	774	389	385	823	414	409	5-9	
10-14	678	340	338	731	367	364	762	383	379	10-14	
15-19	633	318	315	667	335	332	720	362	358	15-19	POPULATION
20-24	627	315	312	617	310	307	651	327	324	20-24	PROJECTED
25-29	586	295	291	608	306	302	599	301	298	25-29	WITH
30-34	511	266	245	567	286	281	588	296	292	30-34	FIXED
35-39	461	231	230	492	256	236	546	275	271	35-39	AGE—
40-44	398	198	200	441	220	221	471	244	227	40-44	SPECIFIC
45-49	351	173	178	377	186	191	417	206	211	45-49	BIRTH
50-54	290	141	149	327	159	168	351	171	180	50-54	AND
55-59	248	119	129	263	126	137	297	142	155	55-59	DEATH
60-64	229	109	120	217	102	115	230	108	122	60-64	RATES
65-69	179	84	95	187	87	100	176	81	95	65-69	(IN 1000's)
70-74	121	55	66	129	59	70	135	61	74	70-74	
75-79	73	33	40	73	32	41	77	34	43	75-79	
80-84	35	15	20	33	14	19	33	14	19	80-84	
85+	12	5	7	13	5	8	12	5	7	85+	
TOTAL	6992	3481	3511	7386	3677	3709	7797	3882	3915	TOTAL	

STANDARD COUNTRIES: STANDARDIZED RATES PER THOUSAND	ENGLAND AND WALES 1961 BOTH SEXES	MALES	FEMALES	UNITED STATES 1960 BOTH SEXES	MALES	FEMALES	MEXICO 1960 BOTH SEXES	MALES	FEMALES	
Birth	24.40	26.23*	23.04	24.89	24.18*	23.90	27.52	24.86*	26.75	**TABLE 6**
Death	25.13	31.60*	25.80	22.89	26.95*	21.95	18.04	19.14*	16.70	STANDARDIZED RATES
Increase	-0.73	-5.36*	-2.76	2.00	-2.78*	1.94	9.48	5.72*	10.04	

	OBSERVED POP. MALES	OBSERVED POP. FEMALES	STATIONARY POP. MALES	STATIONARY POP. FEMALES	STABLE POP. MALES	STABLE POP. FEMALES	OBSERVED BIRTHS	NET MATERNITY FUNCTION	BIRTHS IN STABLE POP.	
μ	28.15684	28.92904	32.86779	34.07490	28.77454	29.71074	28.32642	28.79315	28.50873	**TABLE 7**
σ^2	406.6149	430.4997	443.3773	472.1092	406.6871	433.8749	27.48326	27.64204	27.39812	MOMENTS
κ_3	5183.413	5455.498	3102.476	3104.656	4428.100	4730.001	30.7556	22.9869	27.7432	AND
κ_4	-77221.	-100050.	-170346.	-206283.	-103266.	-128450.	-490.983	-505.987	-473.144	CUMULANTS
β_1	0.399652	0.373036	0.110432	0.091601	0.291510	0.273923	0.045566	0.025018	0.037424	
β_2	2.532946	2.460151	2.133467	2.074496	2.375639	2.317652	2.349976	2.337784	2.369693	
κ	-0.160525	-0.144985	-0.042966	-0.034574	-0.114958	-0.104826	-0.024499	-0.013727	-0.020979	

VITAL STATISTICS		THOMPSON AGE RANGE	NRR	1000r	INTERVAL	BOURGEOIS-PICHAT AGE RANGE	NRR	1000b	1000d	1000r	COALE		
GRR	1.870										IBR	26.33	**TABLE 8**
NRR	1.317	0-4	1.32	10.42	27.06	5-29	1.28	28.77	19.67	9.10	IDR	19.96	RATES FROM AGE DISTRIBUTIONS
TFR	3.839	5-9	1.33	10.57	26.96	30-54	1.62	37.04	19.21	17.83	IRI	6.37	AND VITAL
GENERATION	28.651	10-14	1.37	11.63	26.89	55-79	1.29	26.45	16.89	9.56	K1	-29.19	STATISTICS
SEX RATIO	105.251	15-19	1.47	13.81	26.77	*30-54	1.62	37.04	19.21	17.83	K2	-0.39	(Females)

Start Age Interval	ORIGINAL MATRIX SUB-DIAGONAL	ALTERNATIVE FIRST ROWS Projection	Integral	FIRST STABLE MATRIX % IN STABLE POPULATION	FISHER VALUES	REPRODUCTIVE VALUES	SECOND STABLE MATRIX Z₂ FIRST COLUMN	FIRST ROW	
0	0.94749	0.00000	0.00000	11.215	1.247	486407	0.1566+0.0493	0.1566+0.0493	**TABLE 9**
5	0.98377	0.00000	0.00000	10.127	1.381	473895	0.1251-0.1195	0.0308+0.1528	
10	0.98406	0.02478	0.00000	9.495	1.473	471476	-0.0484-0.1830	-0.1088+0.0920	LESLIE
15	0.97580	0.18686	0.05160	8.905	1.539	492307	-0.2009-0.0502	-0.1256-0.0477	MATRIX
20	0.96847	0.41775	0.33943	8.282	1.416	424890	-0.1529-0.1647	-0.0473-0.1320	AND ITS
25	0.96631	0.45102	0.53320	7.644	0.996	252208	0.0759+0.2298	0.0186-0.1189	SPECTRAL
30	0.96464	0.30333	0.40440	7.040	0.500	119174	0.2556+0.0477	0.0322-0.0612	COMPONENTS
35	0.96057	0.11887	0.22496	6.472	0.152	31582	0.1771-0.2154	0.0152-0.0168	(Females)
40	0.95556	0.00944	0.01932	5.925	0.011	2096	-0.1102-0.2767	0.0012-0.0012	
45	0.94344	0.00001	0.00001	5.396	0.000	4	-0.3141-0.0393	0.0000-0.0000	
50	0.92164	0.00001	0.00001	4.852	0.000	1	-0.1951+0.2687	0.0000-0.0000	
55+	0.74397			14.647					

Start Age Interval	OBSERVED POPUL. (IN 100's)	CONTRIBUTIONS OF ROOTS (IN 100's) r_1	r_2, r_3	r_4-r_{11}	AGE-SP. BIRTH RATES	NET MATERNITY FUNCTION	COEFF. OF MATRIX EQUATION	PARAMETERS INTEGRAL	MATRIX	EXP. INCREASE x	$e^{(x+2\frac{1}{2})r}$	
0	3901	3882	-35	54	0.0000	0.0000	0.0000	L(1) 1.04920	1.04926	0	1.0243	**TABLE 10**
5	3432	3505	-58	-16	0.0000	0.0000	0.0000	L(2) 0.43458	0.43396	50	1.6559	
10	3201	3287	-21	-64	0.0000	0.0000	0.0231	0.81078	0.78769	55	1.7374	AGE
15	3199	3082	47	69	0.0123	0.0462	0.1714	R(1) 0.00961	0.00962	60	1.8229	ANALYSIS
20	3001	2867	74	60	0.0807	0.2966	0.3739	R(2) -0.01670	-0.02122	65	1.9125	AND
25	2532	2646	22	-136	0.1268	0.4512	0.3910	0.21575	0.21345	70	2.0066	MISCELLANEOUS
30	2384	2437	-63	11	0.0962	0.3307	0.2541	C(1)	34613	75	2.1054	RESULTS
35	2084	2240	-91	-66	0.0535	0.1775	0.0961	C(2)	-14094	80	2.2090	(Females)
40	1866	2051	-21	-164	0.0046	0.0147	0.0073		-9459	85	2.3177	
45	1578	1868	81	-371	0.0000	0.0000	0.0000	2P/Y 29.1223	29.4365	90	2.4317	
50	1404	1679	106	-381	0.0000	0.0000	0.0000	DELTA 2.5269		95	2.5514	
55+	4718	5070								100	2.6769	

254 Belgium 1908–12

TABLE 1 — DATA

AGE AT LAST BIRTHDAY	POPULATION BOTH SEXES	MALES Number	%	FEMALES Number	%	BIRTHS BY AGE OF MOTHER	DEATHS BOTH SEXES	MALES	FEMALES	AGE AT LAST BIRTHDAY
0	159857	80878	2.2	78979	2.1	0	24827	13778	11049	0
1-4	600280	301237	8.2	299043	8.0	0	9709	5027	4682	1-4
5-9	763191	382850	10.4	380341	10.2	0	2514	1282	1232	5-9
10-14	740081	371253	10.1	368828	9.9	0	1525	733	792	10-14
15-19	685868	343895	9.4	341973	9.1	6726	2318	1155	1163	15-19
20-24	631774	316504	8.6	315270	8.4	43543	2889	1478	1411	20-24
25-29	614739	303802	8.3	310937	8.3	59344	2874	1393	1481	25-29
30-34	561432	281092	7.7	280340	7.5	43974	3060	1492	1568	30-34
35-39	512431	256464	7.0	255967	6.8	22155	3248	1662	1586	35-39
40-44	449328	224392	6.1	224936	6.0	1609	3444	1867	1577	40-44
45-49	387094	191959	5.2	195135	5.2	0	3953	2251	1702	45-49
50-54	337877	165172	4.5	172705	4.6	0	4702	2670	2032	50-54
55-59	273819	131440	3.6	142379	3.8	0	5640	3221	2419	55-59
60-64	226663	107008	2.9	119655	3.2	0	6995	3803	3192	60-64
65-69	196291	91836	2.5	104455	2.8	0	9049	4774	4275	65-69
70-74	138709	63512	1.7	75197	2.0		10160	5126	5034	70-74
75-79	81146	35987	1.0	45159	1.2		9223	4442	4781	75-79
80-84	38774	16391	0.4	22383	0.6	90598 M.	6871	3136	3735	80-84
85+	16180	6224	0.2	9956	0.3	86753 F.	4516	1859	2657	85+
TOTAL	7415534	3671896		3743638		177351	117517	61149	56368	TOTAL

TABLE 2 — MALE LIFE TABLE

x	$_nq_x$	l_x	$_nd_x$	$_nL_x$	$_nm_x$	$_na_x$	T_x	r_x	$\dot{e}_x$	$_nM_x$
0	0.152692	100000	15269	89632	0.170355	0.3210	4933798	0.0000	49.338	0.170355
1	0.063747	84731	5401	323668	0.016688	1.1757	4844167	0.0000	57.171	0.016688
5	0.016604	79329	1317	393354	0.003349	2.5000	4520499	0.0000	56.984	0.003349
10	0.009823	78012	766	388140	0.001974	2.4925	4127144	0.0081	52.904	0.001974
15	0.016697	77246	1290	383211	0.003366	2.6596	3739005	0.0126	48.404	0.003359
20	0.023095	75956	1754	375477	0.004672	2.5466	3355793	0.0080	44.181	0.004670
25	0.022673	74202	1682	366835	0.004586	2.5183	2980316	0.0071	40.165	0.004585
30	0.026223	72520	1902	357964	0.005312	2.5629	2613481	0.0116	36.038	0.005308
35	0.031951	70618	2256	347636	0.006490	2.5826	2255518	0.0159	31.940	0.006480
40	0.040896	68362	2796	335130	0.008342	2.6112	1907882	0.0203	27.909	0.008320
45	0.057179	65566	3749	318881	0.011757	2.6129	1572752	0.0188	23.987	0.011726
50	0.078084	61817	4827	297615	0.016219	2.6237	1253871	0.0209	20.284	0.016165
55	0.116063	56990	6614	269127	0.024577	2.6077	956257	0.0185	16.779	0.024505
60	0.163704	50376	8247	231909	0.035560	2.5785	687130	0.0038	13.640	0.035539
65	0.230757	42129	9722	186892	0.052017	2.5567	455221	0.0038	10.805	0.051984
70	0.336129	32407	10893	134879	0.080762	2.5069	268329	0.0038	8.280	0.080709
75	0.468533	21514	10080	81611	0.123515	2.4246	133450	0.0038	6.203	0.123433
80	0.633551	11434	7244	37833	0.191474	2.3306	51839	0.0038	4.534	0.191325
85+	*1.000000	4190	4190	14006	0.299159	3.3427	14006	0.0038	3.343	0.298683

TABLE 3 — FEMALE LIFE TABLE

x	$_nq_x$	l_x	$_nd_x$	$_nL_x$	$_nm_x$	$_na_x$	T_x	r_x	$\dot{e}_x$	$_nM_x$
0	0.128016	100000	12802	91507	0.139898	0.3365	5277458	0.0000	52.775	0.139898
1	0.059995	87198	5231	334136	0.015657	1.1982	5185951	0.0000	59.473	0.015657
5	0.016066	81967	1317	406543	0.003239	2.5000	4851815	0.0000	59.192	0.003239
10	0.010681	80650	861	401104	0.002148	2.5076	4445272	0.0079	55.118	0.002147
15	0.016898	79789	1348	395755	0.003407	2.6353	4044169	0.0124	50.686	0.003401
20	0.022143	78440	1737	387955	0.004477	2.5549	3648413	0.0052	46.512	0.004476
25	0.023547	76704	1806	379071	0.004765	2.5382	3260458	0.0068	42.507	0.004763
30	0.027607	74897	2068	369405	0.005597	2.5421	2881387	0.0139	38.471	0.005593
35	0.030537	72830	2224	358666	0.006201	2.5346	2511982	0.0158	34.491	0.006196
40	0.034515	70606	2437	347081	0.007021	2.5593	2153316	0.0200	30.498	0.007011
45	0.042796	68169	2917	333823	0.008739	2.5933	1806236	0.0175	26.497	0.008722
50	0.057380	65251	3744	317339	0.011798	2.6181	1472413	0.0194	22.565	0.011766
55	0.081932	61507	5039	295635	0.017046	2.6384	1155074	0.0189	18.779	0.016990
60	0.125592	56468	7092	265479	0.026714	2.6226	859438	0.0077	15.220	0.026677
65	0.186585	49376	9213	224779	0.040986	2.6011	593959	0.0077	12.029	0.040927
70	0.287900	40163	11563	172479	0.067040	2.5493	369180	0.0077	9.192	0.066944
75	0.417883	28600	11952	112732	0.106017	2.4674	196701	0.0077	6.878	0.105870
80	0.582026	16649	9690	57978	0.167131	2.3927	83969	0.0077	5.044	0.166867
85+	*1.000000	6959	6959	25991	0.267735	3.7350	25991	0.0077	3.735	0.266874

TABLE 4 — OBSERVED AND PROJECTED VITAL RATES

	OBSERVED POPULATION BOTH SEXES	MALES	FEMALES	PROJECTED 1915 MALES	FEMALES	1920 MALES	FEMALES	1925 MALES	FEMALES	STABLE POPULATION MALES	FEMALES
RATES PER THOUSAND											
Birth	23.92	24.67	23.17	24.74	23.23	24.84	23.32	24.79	23.28	22.65	21.2
Death	15.85	16.65	15.06	16.50	15.00	16.63	15.17	16.82	15.37	19.29	17.9
Increase	8.07	8.02	8.12	8.24	8.23	8.21	8.15	7.97	7.91	3.363	
PERCENTAGE											
under 15	30.52	30.94	30.11	29.41	28.57	28.21	27.37	27.92	27.06	26.40	25.5
15-64	63.12	63.23	63.02	65.00	64.66	66.32	65.88	66.47	65.96	65.52	64.5
65 and over	6.35	5.83	6.87	5.59	6.77	5.47	6.75	5.61	6.97	8.08	9.8
DEP. RATIO X 100	58.42	58.15	58.68	53.84	54.65	50.78	51.80	50.45	51.60	52.62	54.9

TABLE 1 — DATA

AGE AT LAST BIRTHDAY	POPULATION BOTH SEXES	MALES Number	%	FEMALES Number	%	BIRTHS BY AGE OF MOTHER	DEATHS BOTH SEXES	MALES	FEMALES	AGE AT LAST BIRTHDAY
0	152072	77276	2.1	74796	2.0	0	16171	9265	6906	0
1-4	386799	195201	5.4	191598	5.1	0	5289	2801	2488	1-4
5-9	652082	327088	9.0	324994	8.6	0	2187	1088	1099	5-9
10-14	701924	351928	9.6	349996	9.3	0	1600	763	837	10-14
15-19	724203	362518	9.9	361685	9.6	4958	2805	1456	1349	15-19
20-24	681733	339661	9.3	342072	9.1	38691	3964	2213	1751	20-24
25-29	601631	293564	8.0	308067	8.2	49173	3623	1898	1725	25-29
30-34	555064	272813	7.5	282251	7.5	36928	3408	1717	1691	30-34
35-39	536664	266702	7.3	269962	7.2	19740	3426	1740	1686	35-39
40-44	499949	248213	6.8	251736	6.7	1464	3605	1868	1737	40-44
45-49	453132	224347	6.1	228785	6.1	0	3993	2116	1877	45-49
50-54	390612	192045	5.3	198567	5.3	0	4843	2590	2253	50-54
55-59	324968	157588	4.3	167380	4.5	0	5890	3173	2717	55-59
60-64	267128	126382	3.5	140746	3.7	0	7337	3895	3442	60-64
65-69	197913	90645	2.5	107268	2.9	0	8513	4268	4245	65-69
70-74	138670	61955	1.7	76715	2.0		9462	4531	4931	70-74
75-79	89218	38812	1.1	50406	1.3		9640	4499	5141	75-79
80-84	39429	16106	0.4	23323	0.6	77698 M.	6730	2915	3815	80-84
85+	14857	5723	0.2	9134	0.2	73256 F.	3896	1544	2352	85+
TOTAL	7408048	3648567		3759481		150954	106382	54340	52042	TOTAL

TABLE 2 — MALE LIFE TABLE

x	nq_x	l_x	nd_x	nL_x	nm_x	na_x	T_x	r_x	$\mathring{e}_x$	nM_x	x
0	0.108575	100000	10858	92890	0.116886	0.3452	5253672	0.0380	52.537	0.119895	0
1	0.053991	89142	4813	343152	0.014026	1.2120	5160782	0.0380	57.894	0.014349	1
5	0.016494	84330	1391	418170	0.003326	2.5000	4817630	0.0000	57.129	0.003326	5
10	0.010783	82939	894	412507	0.002168	2.5563	4399460	0.0000	53.045	0.002168	10
15	0.019899	82044	1633	406491	0.004016	2.7153	3986952	0.0000	48.595	0.004016	15
20	0.032107	80412	2582	395779	0.006523	2.5680	3580461	0.0151	44.527	0.006515	20
25	0.031805	77830	2475	382909	0.006465	2.4792	3184682	0.0154	40.918	0.006465	25
30	0.030979	75355	2334	370909	0.006294	2.4883	2801772	0.0032	37.181	0.006294	30
35	0.032106	73020	2344	359298	0.006525	2.5248	2430863	0.0028	33.290	0.006524	35
40	0.036979	70676	2614	347012	0.007532	2.5638	2071565	0.0096	29.311	0.007526	40
45	0.046211	68062	3145	332790	0.009451	2.6088	1724554	0.0158	25.338	0.009432	45
50	0.065564	64917	4256	314507	0.013533	2.6323	1391764	0.0214	21.439	0.013486	50
55	0.096420	60661	5849	289439	0.020208	2.6295	1077256	0.0209	17.759	0.020135	55
60	0.143993	54812	7893	255181	0.030929	2.6081	787817	0.0206	14.373	0.030819	60
65	0.211976	46919	9946	210481	0.047253	2.5752	532636	0.0206	11.352	0.047085	65
70	0.310616	36974	11485	156466	0.073400	2.5270	322155	0.0206	8.713	0.073134	70
75	0.448545	25489	11433	98267	0.116346	2.4479	165689	0.0206	6.500	0.115918	75
80	0.613668	14056	8626	47465	0.181727	2.3550	67422	0.0206	4.797	0.180988	80
85+	*1.000000	5430	5430	19957	0.272099	3.6751	19957	0.0206	3.675	0.269789	85+

TABLE 3 — FEMALE LIFE TABLE

x	nq_x	l_x	nd_x	nL_x	nm_x	na_x	T_x	r_x	$\mathring{e}_x$	nM_x	x
0	0.085173	100000	8517	94578	0.090056	0.3634	5582313	0.0378	55.823	0.092331	0
1	0.049205	91483	4501	353530	0.012733	1.2451	5487735	0.0378	59.987	0.012986	1
5	0.016766	86981	1458	431261	0.003382	2.5000	5134205	0.0000	59.027	0.003382	5
10	0.011887	85523	1017	425095	0.002391	2.5213	4702944	0.0000	54.990	0.002391	10
15	0.018486	84506	1562	418852	0.003730	2.6443	4277850	0.0000	50.622	0.003730	15
20	0.025301	82944	2099	409614	0.005123	2.5666	3858998	0.0111	46.525	0.005119	20
25	0.027626	80846	2233	398691	0.005602	2.5207	3449384	0.0136	42.666	0.005599	25
30	0.029520	78612	2321	387283	0.005992	2.5101	3050693	0.0072	38.807	0.005991	30
35	0.030754	76292	2346	375631	0.006246	2.5168	2663410	0.0051	34.911	0.006245	35
40	0.033944	73945	2510	363562	0.006904	2.5442	2287779	0.0096	30.939	0.006900	40
45	0.040293	71435	2878	350248	0.008218	2.5932	1924217	0.0152	26.937	0.008204	45
50	0.055393	68557	3798	333748	0.011379	2.6205	1573969	0.0196	22.959	0.011346	50
55	0.078370	64759	5075	311759	0.016279	2.6282	1240221	0.0176	19.151	0.016233	55
60	0.115966	59684	6921	282053	0.024539	2.6353	928461	0.0182	15.556	0.024455	60
65	0.181364	52763	9569	240495	0.039714	2.6112	646408	0.0182	12.251	0.039574	65
70	0.278525	43194	12030	186538	0.064493	2.5537	405453	0.0182	9.387	0.064277	70
75	0.406669	31163	12673	123844	0.102331	2.4772	218915	0.0182	7.025	0.101992	75
80	0.575696	18490	10645	64833	0.164186	2.4055	95071	0.0182	5.142	0.163572	80
85+	*1.000000	7845	7845	30238	0.259452	3.8543	30238	0.0182	3.854	0.257499	85+

TABLE 4 — OBSERVED AND PROJECTED VITAL RATES

RATES PER THOUSAND	OBSERVED POPULATION BOTH SEXES	MALES	FEMALES	PROJECTED POPULATION 1925 MALES	FEMALES	1930 MALES	FEMALES	1935 MALES	FEMALES	STABLE POPULATION MALES	FEMALES
Birth	20.38	21.30	19.49	21.66	19.89	21.55	19.85	20.58	19.00	17.92	16.84
Death	14.36	14.89	13.84	16.12	14.83	16.65	15.30	17.03	15.67	19.66	18.58
Increase	6.02	6.40	5.64	5.54	5.07	4.90	4.55	3.54	3.33	-1.7389	
PERCENTAGE											
under 15	25.55	26.08	25.04	24.72	23.61	24.51	23.30	26.01	24.74	23.00	22.25
15-64	67.97	68.08	67.86	69.02	68.85	68.77	68.73	66.68	66.73	66.17	65.39
65 and over	6.48	5.84	7.10	6.27	7.54	6.73	7.97	7.31	8.53	10.84	12.36
DEP. RATIO X 100	47.13	46.89	47.36	44.89	45.24	45.42	45.50	49.97	49.87	51.13	52.94

TABLE 1 — DATA

AGE AT LAST BIRTHDAY	POPULATION BOTH SEXES	MALES Number	%	FEMALES Number	%	BIRTHS BY AGE OF MOTHER	DEATHS BOTH SEXES	MALES	FEMALES	AGE AT LAST BIRTHDAY
0	147073	74664	2.0	72409	1.8	0	14111	8030	6081	0
1-4	435938	219541	5.8	216397	5.5	0	4738	2510	2228	1-4
5-9	622058	333190	8.8	288868	7.3	0	1043	558	485	5-9
10-14	599458	305740	8.0	293718	7.4	0	1039	490	549	10-14
15-19	692740	347244	9.1	345496	8.8	5453	2245	1110	1135	15-19
20-24	694333	348775	9.2	345558	8.8	39223	3353	1868	1485	20-24
25-29	654541	325522	8.6	329019	8.3	50861	3099	1653	1446	25-29
30-34	606729	300519	7.9	306210	7.8	37116	2742	1415	1327	30-34
35-39	560659	276002	7.3	284657	7.2	18640	2823	1437	1386	35-39
40-44	519029	256073	6.7	262956	6.7	1370	3281	1780	1501	40-44
45-49	485757	240152	6.3	245605	6.2	0	4008	2198	1810	45-49
50-54	431293	212350	5.6	218943	5.5	0	5021	2761	2260	50-54
55-59	369635	180143	4.7	189492	4.8	0	6135	3361	2774	55-59
60-64	392524	144754	3.8	247770	6.3	0	7709	4135	3574	60-64
65-69	226135	105062	2.8	121073	3.1	0	9191	4772	4419	65-69
70-74	158495	71446	1.9	87049	2.2		10175	5037	5138	70-74
75-79	95587	41278	1.1	54309	1.4		9597	4564	5033	75-79
80-84	43160	17537	0.5	25623	0.6	78126 M.	7627	3404	4223	80-84
85+	17290	6425	0.2	10865	0.3	74537 F.	4749	1922	2827	85+
TOTAL	7752434	3806417		3946017		152663	102686	53005	49681	TOTAL

TABLE 2 — MALE LIFE TABLE

x	nq_x	l_x	nd_x	nL_x	nm_x	na_x	T_x	r_x	$\dot{e}_x$	nM_x	x
0	0.098810	100000	9881	93416	0.105775	0.3336	5546819	0.0241	55.468	0.107548	0
1	0.043612	90119	3930	349447	0.011247	1.1938	5453404	0.0241	60.513	0.011433	1
5	0.008339	86189	719	429147	0.001675	2.5000	5103957	0.0000	59.218	0.001675	5
10	0.007984	85470	682	425774	0.001603	2.6913	4674811	0.0000	54.695	0.001603	10
15	0.015868	84788	1345	420892	0.003197	2.7359	4249036	0.0000	50.114	0.003197	15
20	0.026438	83442	2206	411840	0.005357	2.5652	3828145	0.0016	45.878	0.005356	20
25	0.025061	81236	2036	401015	0.005077	2.4628	3416305	0.0098	42.054	0.005078	25
30	0.023269	79200	1843	391385	0.004709	2.4949	3015290	0.0116	38.072	0.004709	30
35	0.025732	77357	1991	381964	0.005211	2.5770	2623905	0.0106	33.919	0.005206	35
40	0.034213	75367	2579	370653	0.006957	2.6029	2241942	0.0069	29.747	0.006951	40
45	0.044840	72788	3264	356160	0.009164	2.6159	1871289	0.0093	25.709	0.009153	45
50	0.063202	69524	4394	337173	0.013032	2.6219	1515129	0.0155	21.793	0.013002	50
55	0.089603	65130	5836	311804	0.018716	2.6272	1177956	0.0189	18.086	0.018657	55
60	0.134213	59294	7958	277557	0.028672	2.6232	866152	0.0202	14.608	0.028566	60
65	0.205328	51336	10541	231231	0.045586	2.5855	588595	0.0202	11.465	0.045421	65
70	0.301141	40796	12285	173642	0.070750	2.5307	357364	0.0202	8.760	0.070501	70
75	0.433255	28510	12352	111280	0.111001	2.4684	183722	0.0202	6.444	0.110567	75
80	0.644292	16158	10411	53388	0.194997	2.3678	72441	0.0202	4.483	0.194103	80
85+	*1.000000	5748	5748	19053	0.301659	3.3150	19053	0.0202	3.315	0.299144	85+

TABLE 3 — FEMALE LIFE TABLE

x	nq_x	l_x	nd_x	nL_x	nm_x	na_x	T_x	r_x	$\dot{e}_x$	nM_x	x
0	0.078431	100000	7843	94902	0.082644	0.3500	5928279	0.0234	59.283	0.083981	0
1	0.039491	92157	3639	358511	0.010151	1.2202	5833377	0.0234	63.298	0.010296	1
5	0.008360	88518	740	440738	0.001679	2.5000	5474866	0.0000	61.851	0.001679	5
10	0.009305	87778	817	436987	0.001869	2.6728	5034129	0.0000	57.351	0.001869	10
15	0.016300	86961	1417	431469	0.003285	2.6473	4597142	0.0000	52.865	0.003285	15
20	0.021264	85543	1819	423253	0.004298	2.5461	4165673	0.0008	48.697	0.004297	20
25	0.021735	83724	1820	414059	0.004395	2.4928	3742420	0.0077	44.699	0.004395	25
30	0.021442	81905	1756	405155	0.004335	2.5130	3328360	0.0100	40.637	0.004334	30
35	0.024072	80148	1929	396012	0.004872	2.5483	2923205	0.0103	36.472	0.004869	35
40	0.028174	78219	2204	385758	0.005713	2.5782	2527193	0.0089	32.309	0.005708	40
45	0.036260	76015	2756	373497	0.007380	2.6130	2141435	0.0107	28.171	0.007370	45
50	0.050483	73259	3698	357499	0.010345	2.6216	1767938	0.0153	24.133	0.010322	50
55	0.070648	69561	4914	335696	0.014639	2.5363	1410439	0.0000	20.276	0.014639	55
60	0.070445	64646	4554	312944	0.014552	2.7408	1074743	0.0313	16.625	0.014425	60
65	0.169381	60092	10179	276762	0.036778	2.6717	761800	0.0313	12.677	0.036499	65
70	0.259279	49914	12942	218007	0.059363	2.5613	485038	0.0313	9.718	0.059024	70
75	0.378286	36972	13986	149985	0.093249	2.5065	267031	0.0313	7.223	0.092673	75
80	0.581861	22986	13375	80582	0.165976	2.4319	117046	0.0313	5.092	0.164812	80
85+	*1.000000	9611	9611	36464	0.263585	3.7938	36464	0.0313	3.794	0.260193	85

TABLE 4 — OBSERVED AND PROJECTED VITAL RATES

	OBSERVED POPULATION BOTH SEXES	MALES	FEMALES	PROJECTED POPULATION 1930 MALES	FEMALES	1935 MALES	FEMALES	1940 MALES	FEMALES	STABLE POPULATION MALES	FEMALES
RATES PER THOUSAND											
Birth	19.69	20.52	18.89	20.25	18.68	19.10	17.68	17.63	16.39	17.07	15.9
Death	13.25	13.93	12.59	14.82	13.79	15.30	14.52	15.76	15.14	18.62	17.4
Increase	6.45	6.60	6.30	5.43	4.89	3.79	3.16	1.87	1.24	-1.550	
PERCENTAGE											
under 15	23.28	24.51	22.08	24.57	22.36	24.03	22.85	24.47	23.33	22.41	21.4
15-64	69.75	69.13	70.34	68.52	67.41	68.43	66.54	67.32	65.69	66.34	64.9
65 and over	6.97	6.35	7.58	6.91	10.22	7.54	10.60	8.21	10.98	11.25	13.6
DEP. RATIO X 100	43.37	44.65	42.16	45.94	48.34	46.14	50.28	48.55	52.23	50.75	54.0

TABLE 1

AGE AT LAST BIRTHDAY	POPULATION BOTH SEXES	MALES Number	%	FEMALES Number	%	BIRTHS BY AGE OF MOTHER	DEATHS BOTH SEXES	MALES	FEMALES	AGE AT LAST BIRTHDAY
0	142580	72262	1.8	70318	1.7	0	13396	7678	5718	0
1-4	517227	259822	6.5	257405	6.3	0	4109	2208	1901	1-4
5-9	684195	347264	8.7	336931	8.3	0	1517	809	708	5-9
10-14	509209	257272	6.4	251937	6.2	0	829	420	409	10-14
15-19	653802	328370	8.2	325432	8.0	5381	2025	1040	985	15-19
20-24	702809	356396	8.9	346413	8.5	38162	2877	1509	1368	20-24
25-29	714399	362649	9.1	351750	8.6	50513	2979	1547	1432	25-29
30-34	665657	332699	8.3	332958	8.2	36057	2993	1562	1431	30-34
35-39	585079	285461	7.2	299618	7.4	17339	3023	1596	1427	35-39
40-44	534617	262216	6.6	272401	6.7	1228	3478	1909	1569	40-44
45-49	513911	254039	6.4	259872	6.4	0	4362	2465	1897	45-49
50-54	470517	231868	5.8	238649	5.9	0	5616	3168	2448	50-54
55-59	413248	202115	5.1	211133	5.2	0	7103	4001	3102	55-59
60-64	347113	162899	4.1	184214	4.5	0	8867	4817	4050	60-64
65-69	257616	121349	3.0	136267	3.3	0	10671	5571	5100	65-69
70-74	180701	82262	2.1	98439	2.4		11813	5893	5920	70-74
75-79	101758	43710	1.1	58048	1.4		10995	5161	5834	75-79
80-84	47275	19183	0.5	28092	0.7	76002 M.	7958	3513	4445	80-84
85+	20181	7276	0.2	12905	0.3	72678 F.	5489	2167	3322	85+
TOTAL	8061894	3989112		4072782		148680	110100	57034	53066	TOTAL

TABLE 2

x	nq_x	l_x	nd_x	nL_x	nm_x	na_x	T_x	r_x	$\dot{e}_x$	nM_x	x
0	0.098600	100000	9860	93135	0.105868	0.3037	5593431	0.0050	55.934	0.106252	0
1	0.033057	90140	2980	352079	0.008463	1.1539	5500296	0.0050	61.019	0.008498	1
5	0.011453	87160	998	433306	0.002304	2.5000	5148216	0.0218	59.066	0.002330	5
10	0.008134	86162	701	429130	0.001633	2.6026	4714911	0.0035	54.721	0.001633	10
15	0.015720	85461	1343	424169	0.003167	2.6646	4285781	0.0000	50.149	0.003167	15
20	0.020953	84118	1762	416265	0.004234	2.5467	3861612	0.0000	45.907	0.004234	20
25	0.021106	82355	1738	407454	0.004266	2.5132	3445348	0.0025	41.835	0.004266	25
30	0.023233	80617	1873	398494	0.004700	2.5486	3037894	0.0192	37.683	0.004695	30
35	0.027629	78744	2176	388462	0.005601	2.5831	2639400	0.0181	33.519	0.005591	35
40	0.035794	76568	2741	376267	0.007284	2.6008	2250938	0.0043	29.398	0.007280	40
45	0.047433	73828	3502	360784	0.009706	2.6141	1874671	0.0023	25.392	0.009703	45
50	0.066250	70326	4659	340548	0.013681	2.6216	1513887	0.0088	21.527	0.013663	50
55	0.094742	65667	6221	313526	0.019843	2.6198	1173339	0.0148	17.868	0.019796	55
60	0.138553	59445	8236	277552	0.029675	2.6111	859813	0.0203	14.464	0.029570	60
65	0.207276	51209	10614	230377	0.046074	2.5817	582262	0.0203	11.370	0.045909	65
70	0.305443	40595	12399	172437	0.071906	2.5373	351885	0.0203	8.668	0.071637	70
75	0.455181	28195	12834	108286	0.118519	2.4528	179447	0.0203	6.364	0.118074	75
80	0.617985	15361	9493	51623	0.183893	2.3471	71161	0.0203	4.632	0.183130	80
85+	*1.000000	5868	5868	19538	0.300346	3.3295	19538	0.0203	3.329	0.297828	85+

TABLE 3

x	nq_x	l_x	nd_x	nL_x	nm_x	na_x	T_x	r_x	$\dot{e}_x$	nM_x	x
0	0.076828	100000	7683	94766	0.081071	0.3188	5975658	0.0042	59.757	0.081316	0
1	0.028850	92317	2663	361739	0.007363	1.1727	5880891	0.0042	63.703	0.007385	1
5	0.010339	89654	927	445952	0.002079	2.5000	5519153	0.0231	61.561	0.002101	5
10	0.008087	88727	718	441923	0.001624	2.6149	5073201	0.0014	57.178	0.001623	10
15	0.015027	88009	1323	436944	0.003027	2.6540	4631278	0.0000	52.623	0.003027	15
20	0.019556	86687	1695	429277	0.003949	2.5479	4194334	0.0000	48.385	0.003949	20
25	0.020151	84992	1713	420692	0.004071	2.5093	3765056	0.0000	44.299	0.004071	25
30	0.021271	83279	1771	412009	0.004300	2.5244	3344364	0.0117	40.159	0.004298	30
35	0.023562	81507	1920	402839	0.004767	2.5532	2932355	0.0152	35.977	0.004763	35
40	0.028425	79587	2262	392458	0.005764	2.5788	2529516	0.0084	31.783	0.005760	40
45	0.035898	77325	2776	379992	0.007305	2.6108	2137058	0.0057	27.637	0.007300	45
50	0.050144	74549	3738	363870	0.010273	2.6259	1757067	0.0103	23.569	0.010258	50
55	0.071109	70811	5035	342125	0.014718	2.6310	1393197	0.0107	19.675	0.014692	55
60	0.104962	65775	6904	312684	0.022080	2.6545	1051071	0.0211	15.980	0.021985	60
65	0.172500	58872	10155	270203	0.037584	2.6215	738887	0.0211	12.542	0.037427	65
70	0.263291	48716	12827	212408	0.060386	2.5697	468184	0.0211	9.610	0.060139	70
75	0.402491	35890	14445	143162	0.100901	2.4880	255776	0.0211	7.127	0.100503	75
80	0.559412	21444	11996	75540	0.158807	2.4132	112613	0.0211	5.251	0.158230	80
85+	1.000000	9448	9448	37074	0.254847	3.9239	37074	0.0211	3.924	0.257420	85+

TABLE 4

	OBSERVED POPULATION BOTH SEXES	MALES	FEMALES	PROJECTED POPULATION 1935 MALES	FEMALES	1940 MALES	FEMALES	1945 MALES	FEMALES	STABLE POPULATION MALES	FEMALES
RATES PER THOUSAND											
Birth	18.44	19.05	17.84	18.27	17.11	16.66	15.59	15.93	14.89	15.73	14.66
Death	13.66	14.30	13.03	14.85	13.57	15.41	14.14	16.02	14.79	19.33	18.26
Increase	4.79	4.75	4.82	3.43	3.54	1.26	1.44	-0.09	0.09		-3.5998
PERCENTAGE											
under 15	22.99	23.48	22.51	24.60	23.62	23.40	22.55	22.54	21.66	21.13	20.24
15-64	69.48	69.66	69.30	67.89	67.32	68.37	67.62	68.56	67.75	66.96	65.66
65 and over	7.54	6.86	8.19	7.51	9.07	8.23	9.83	8.90	10.59	11.91	14.10
DEP. RATIO X 100	43.93	43.56	44.30	47.30	48.55	46.26	47.89	45.86	47.59	49.34	52.30

TABLE 1 — DATA

AGE AT LAST BIRTHDAY	POPULATION BOTH SEXES	MALES Number	%	FEMALES Number	%	BIRTHS BY AGE OF MOTHER	DEATHS BOTH SEXES	MALES	FEMALES
0	123932	62909	1.5	61023	1.5	0	10185	5833	4352
1-4	511678	258049	6.3	253629	6.1	0	2981	1607	1374
5-9	659107	330667	8.1	328440	7.8	0	1279	696	583
10-14	670962	337861	8.3	333101	8.0	0	972	509	463
15-19	513904	258719	6.3	255185	6.1	4731	1245	649	596
20-24	649456	326017	8.0	323439	7.7	34385	2083	1125	958
25-29	697820	353627	8.6	344193	8.2	44024	2406	1279	1127
30-34	707025	358232	8.8	348793	8.3	30818	2695	1470	1225
35-39	653406	325342	7.9	328064	7.8	15928	3044	1666	1378
40-44	571618	277727	6.8	293891	7.0	1144	3346	1848	1498
45-49	520318	253819	6.2	266499	6.4	0	4185	2356	1829
50-54	493168	241758	5.9	251410	6.0	0	5484	3157	2327
55-59	443158	215916	5.3	227242	5.4	0	7203	4089	3114
60-64	376357	181723	4.4	194634	4.7	0	9190	5049	4141
65-69	289366	137167	3.4	152199	3.6	0	11072	5865	5207
70-74	202452	92734	2.3	109718	2.6		12518	6356	6162
75-79	121070	52871	1.3	68199	1.6		11982	5779	6203
80-84	52576	21168	0.5	31408	0.8	67172 M.	8499	3818	4681
85+	21776	7652	0.2	14124	0.3	63858 F.	5764	2253	3511
TOTAL	8279149	4093958		4185191		131030	106133	55404	50729

TABLE 2 — MALE LIFE TABLE

x	$_nq_x$	l_x	$_nd_x$	$_nL_x$	$_nm_x$	$_na_x$	T_x	r_x	$\mathring{e}_x$	$_nM_x$
0	0.086963	100000	8696	93789	0.092721	0.2858	5820256	0.0000	58.203	0.092721
1	0.024473	91304	2234	358811	0.006227	1.1342	5726467	0.0000	62.719	0.006227
5	0.010469	89069	932	443015	0.002105	2.5000	5367656	0.0000	60.264	0.002105
10	0.007514	88137	662	439061	0.001508	2.5498	4924641	0.0227	55.875	0.001507
15	0.012471	87474	1091	434815	0.002509	2.6558	4485579	0.0011	51.279	0.002509
20	0.017110	86384	1478	428313	0.003451	2.5607	4050764	0.0000	46.893	0.003451
25	0.017924	84906	1522	420768	0.003617	2.5296	3622452	0.0000	42.664	0.003617
30	0.020321	83384	1694	412797	0.004105	2.5674	3201684	0.0041	38.397	0.004103
35	0.025344	81689	2070	403462	0.005131	2.5925	2788887	0.0202	34.140	0.005121
40	0.032824	79619	2613	391859	0.006669	2.6139	2385425	0.0180	29.961	0.006654
45	0.045436	77005	3499	376706	0.009288	2.6217	1993566	0.0044	25.889	0.009282
50	0.063352	73507	4657	356464	0.013064	2.6229	1616860	0.3027	21.996	0.013059
55	0.090727	68850	6247	329368	0.018965	2.6178	1260397	0.0091	18.306	0.018938
60	0.130787	62603	8188	293453	0.027901	2.6105	931028	0.0248	14.872	0.027784
65	0.194638	54416	10591	246582	0.042953	2.5928	637576	0.0248	11.717	0.042758
70	0.294460	43824	12904	187421	0.068853	2.5435	390993	0.0248	8.922	0.068540
75	0.429601	30920	13283	120960	0.109815	2.4675	203572	0.0248	6.584	0.109304
80	0.614319	17637	10835	59747	0.181341	2.3754	82613	0.0248	4.684	0.180366
85+	*1.000000	6802	6802	22866	0.297478	3.3616	22866	0.0248	3.362	0.294433

TABLE 3 — FEMALE LIFE TABLE

x	$_nq_x$	l_x	$_nd_x$	$_nL_x$	$_nm_x$	$_na_x$	T_x	r_x	$\mathring{e}_x$	$_nM_x$
0	0.067927	100000	6793	95247	0.071317	0.3002	6225637	0.0000	62.256	0.071317
1	0.021340	93207	1989	367160	0.005417	1.1499	6130390	0.0000	65.772	0.005417
5	0.008836	91218	806	454076	0.001775	2.5000	5763230	0.0000	63.181	0.001775
10	0.006940	90412	627	450542	0.001393	2.5786	5309154	0.0235	58.722	0.001390
15	0.011615	89785	1043	446458	0.002336	2.6353	4858613	0.0007	54.114	0.002336
20	0.014703	88742	1305	440526	0.002962	2.5602	4412155	0.0000	49.719	0.002962
25	0.016240	87437	1420	433676	0.003274	2.5283	3971629	0.0000	45.423	0.003274
30	0.017412	86017	1498	426412	0.003512	2.5471	3537953	0.0012	41.131	0.003512
35	0.020811	84519	1759	418323	0.004205	2.5598	3111541	0.0129	36.815	0.004200
40	0.025219	82761	2087	408786	0.005106	2.5966	2693218	0.0155	32.542	0.005097
45	0.033798	80673	2727	396852	0.006871	2.6105	2284432	0.0087	28.317	0.006863
50	0.045328	77947	3533	381364	0.009265	2.6311	1887580	0.0063	24.216	0.009256
55	0.066509	74414	4949	360432	0.013731	2.6489	1506216	0.0113	20.241	0.013703
60	0.101774	69464	7070	330683	0.021379	2.6464	1145784	0.0252	16.495	0.021276
65	0.158935	62395	9917	288423	0.034383	2.6251	815101	0.0252	13.064	0.034212
70	0.248218	52478	13026	230817	0.056434	2.5762	526678	0.0252	10.036	0.056162
75	0.372078	39452	14679	160626	0.091387	2.5044	295861	0.0252	7.499	0.090954
80	0.538253	24773	13334	89059	0.149721	2.4494	135234	0.0252	5.459	0.149038
85+	1.000000	11439	11439	46175	0.247725	4.0367	46175	0.0252	4.037	0.248583

TABLE 4 — OBSERVED AND PROJECTED VITAL RATES

	OBSERVED POPULATION BOTH SEXES	MALES	FEMALES	PROJECTED POPULATION 1940 MALES	FEMALES	1945 MALES	FEMALES	1950 MALES	FEMALES	STABLE POPULATION MALES	FEMA
RATES PER THOUSAND											
Birth	15.83	16.41	15.26	15.06	13.98	14.56	13.49	14.72	13.62	13.46	12.
Death	12.82	13.53	12.12	14.19	12.83	14.99	13.66	15.77	14.47	20.11	19.
Increase	3.01	2.87	3.14	0.87	1.15	-0.44	-0.17	-1.05	-0.85		-6.64
PERCENTAGE											
under 15	23.74	24.17	23.32	22.62	21.73	21.16	20.16	20.12	19.08	18.89	17.
15-64	67.96	68.22	67.70	68.88	68.29	69.54	68.89	69.93	69.12	67.17	65.
65 and over	8.30	7.61	8.98	8.50	9.98	9.30	10.95	9.95	11.80	13.95	16.
DEP. RATIO X 100	47.15	46.59	47.71	45.18	46.43	43.81	45.16	43.00	44.67	48.89	52.

TABLE 5 — POPULATION PROJECTED WITH FIXED AGE-SPECIFIC BIRTH AND DEATH RATES (IN 1000's)

AGE LAST BIRTHDAY	1940 BOTH SEXES	MALES	FEMALES	1945 BOTH SEXES	MALES	FEMALES	1950 BOTH SEXES	MALES	FEMALES	AGE AT LAST BIRTHDAY
0-4	577	293	284	546	277	269	538	273	265	0-4
5-9	623	314	309	566	287	279	535	271	264	5-9
10-14	654	328	326	618	311	307	561	284	277	10-14
15-19	665	335	330	648	325	323	612	308	304	15-19
20-24	507	255	252	656	330	326	639	320	319	20-24
25-29	638	320	318	498	250	248	645	324	321	25-29
30-34	685	347	338	627	314	313	490	246	244	30-34
35-39	692	350	342	671	339	332	614	307	307	35-39
40-44	637	316	321	674	340	334	653	329	324	40-44
45-49	552	267	285	615	304	311	652	327	325	45-49
50-54	496	240	256	527	253	274	586	287	299	50-54
55-59	461	223	238	464	222	242	492	233	259	55-59
60-64	400	192	208	417	199	218	420	198	222	60-64
65-69	323	153	170	344	162	182	357	167	190	65-69
70-74	226	104	122	252	116	136	269	123	146	70-74
75-79	136	60	76	152	67	85	170	75	95	75-79
80-84	64	26	38	72	30	42	80	33	47	80-84
85+	24	8	16	30	10	20	33	11	22	85+
TOTAL	8360	4131	4229	8377	4136	4241	8346	4116	4230	TOTAL

TABLE 6 — STANDARDIZED RATES

STANDARD COUNTRIES: STANDARDIZED RATES PER THOUSAND	ENGLAND AND WALES 1961 BOTH SEXES	MALES	FEMALES	UNITED STATES 1960 BOTH SEXES	MALES	FEMALES	MEXICO 1960 BOTH SEXES	MALES	FEMALES
Birth	12.49	13.28*	11.80	12.72	12.60*	12.21	14.52	12.00*	14.12
Death	16.96	17.09*	17.44	14.60	14.77*	13.81	9.71	12.29*	8.71
Increase	-4.47	-3.82*	-5.64	-1.88	-2.17*	-1.59	4.81	-0.29*	5.41

TABLE 7 — MOMENTS AND CUMULANTS

	OBSERVED POP. MALES	FEMALES	STATIONARY POP. MALES	FEMALES	STABLE POP. MALES	FEMALES	OBSERVED BIRTHS	NET MATERNITY FUNCTION	BIRTHS IN STABLE POP.
μ_1	33.16101	34.21220	35.11448	36.47176	38.34152	39.89465	28.34939	28.07839	28.28513
μ_2	419.2555	440.7144	478.3638	508.2994	491.4706	520.2198	27.36674	28.90315	29.16649
μ_3	2622.965	2642.359	2729.729	2675.762	1185.792	883.507	35.8612	41.5926	37.6477
μ_4	-142194.	-161305.	-216679.	-253939.	-244103.	-280502.	-516.882	-569.921	-606.943
β_1	0.093357	0.081567	0.068071	0.054518	0.011845	0.005544	0.062745	0.071647	0.057125
β_2	2.191048	2.169511	2.053110	2.017144	1.989403	1.963517	2.309847	2.317780	2.286523
κ	-0.039057	-0.033908	-0.025863	-0.020382	-0.004524	-0.002085	-0.031152	-0.035413	-0.027824

TABLE 8 — RATES FROM AGE DISTRIBUTIONS AND VITAL STATISTICS (Females)

VITAL STATISTICS		THOMPSON AGE RANGE	NRR	1000r	INTERVAL	BOURGEOIS-PICHAT AGE RANGE	NRR	1000b	1000d	1000r	COALE
R	0.959										IBR
NRR	0.829	0-4	0.93	-2.85	27.26	5-29	0.91	15.90	19.47	-3.57	IDR
GRR	1.968	5-9	0.96	-1.55	27.20	30-54	1.37	28.63	16.90	11.73	IRI
GENERATION	28.182	10-14	0.99	-0.20	27.14	55-79	1.68	45.76	26.63	19.13	K1
SEX RATIO	105.190	15-19	0.80	-8.63	27.03	*40-64	1.28	25.35	16.09	9.26	K2

TABLE 9 — LESLIE MATRIX AND ITS SPECTRAL COMPONENTS (Females)

SUB-DIAGONAL	ALTERNATIVE FIRST ROWS Projection	Integral	% IN STABLE POPULATION	FISHER VALUES	REPRODUCTIVE VALUES	SECOND STABLE MATRIX Z_2 FIRST COLUMN	FIRST ROW
0.98198	0.00000	0.00000	5.861	1.064	334659	0.1542+0.0538	0.1542+0.0538
0.99222	0.00000	0.00000	5.950	1.048	344119	0.1457-0.1308	0.0227+0.1343
0.99094	0.02070	0.00000	6.103	1.021	340257	-0.0536-0.2310	-0.0881+0.0699
0.98671	0.13909	0.04109	6.252	0.975	248974	-0.2760-0.0780	-0.0890-0.0370
0.98445	0.26167	0.23563	6.377	0.806	260661	-0.2427+0.2459	-0.0304-0.0871
0.98325	0.24201	0.28349	6.489	0.509	175265	0.1182+0.3981	0.0103-0.0715
0.98103	0.15323	0.19584	6.596	0.239	83428	0.4870+0.1062	0.0183-0.0345
0.97720	0.05899	0.10761	6.689	0.070	22878	0.3928-0.4495	0.0085-0.0089
0.97080	0.00438	0.00861	6.757	0.005	1420	-0.2436-0.6691	0.0006-0.0006
0.96097	0.00001	0.00001	6.781	0.000	4	-0.8339-0.1296	0.0000-0.0000
0.94511	0.00000	0.00001	6.737	0.000	1	-0.6051+0.7836	0.0000-0.0000
0.75084			29.408				

TABLE 10 — AGE ANALYSIS AND MISCELLANEOUS RESULTS (Females)

OBSERVED POPUL. (IN 100's)	CONTRIBUTIONS OF ROOTS (IN 100's) r_1	r_2, r_3	r_4-r_{11}	AGE-SP. BIRTH RATES	NET MATERNITY FUNCTION	COEFF. OF MATRIX EQUATION	PARAMETERS		INTEGRAL	MATRIX	EXP. INCREASE x	$e^{(x+2\frac{1}{2})r}$
3147	3006	140	0	0.0000	0.0000	0.0000	L(1)		0.96733	0.96735	0	0.9835
3284	3052	228	4	0.0000	0.0000	0.0000	L(2)		0.39108	0.39518	50	0.7056
3331	3130	63	137	0.0000	0.0000	0.0202			0.73866	0.71753	55	0.6825
2552	3207	-261	-394	0.0090	0.0403	0.1343	R(1)		-0.00664	-0.00664	60	0.6602
3234	3271	-395	359	0.0518	0.2282	0.2493	R(2)		-0.03587	-0.03990	65	0.6386
3442	3329	-81	195	0.0623	0.2703	0.2270			0.21677	0.21348	70	0.6178
3488	3383	476	-371	0.0431	0.1836	0.1413	C(1)			51292	75	0.5976
3281	3431	667	-817	0.0237	0.0990	0.0534	C(2)			54653	80	0.5781
2939	3466	87	-614	0.0019	0.0078	0.0039				26428	85	0.5592
2665	3478	-843	30	0.0000	0.0000	0.0000	2P/Y		28.9849	29.4327	90	0.5409
2514	3455	-1076	134	0.0000	0.0000	0.0000	DELTA	11.6536			95	0.5232
7975	15084										100	0.5062

TABLE 1 — DATA

AGE AT LAST BIRTHDAY	POPULATION BOTH SEXES	MALES Number	MALES %	FEMALES Number	FEMALES %	BIRTHS BY AGE OF MOTHER	DEATHS BOTH SEXES	DEATHS MALES	DEATHS FEMALES	AGE AT LAST BIRTHDAY
0	107662	54753	1.3	52909	1.3	0	9064	5232	3832	0
1-4	474215	239207	5.8	235008	5.6	0	2426	1318	1108	1-4
5-9	619653	312164	7.6	307489	7.3	0	1217	673	544	5-9
10-14	651245	326413	8.0	324832	7.7	18	1004	546	458	10-14
15-19	656164	330138	8.1	326026	7.8	4953	1700	971	729	15-19
20-24	505540	253112	6.2	252428	6.0	25390	2193	1415	778	20-24
25-29	634611	317218	7.8	317393	7.5	36067	2753	1728	1025	25-29
30-34	681064	343936	8.4	337128	8.0	27913	2879	1744	1135	30-34
35-39	686953	346889	8.5	340064	8.1	16759	3360	2020	1340	35-39
40-44	630632	312408	7.6	318224	7.6	4818	4066	2442	1624	40-44
45-49	547412	264213	6.5	283199	6.7	370	4769	2811	1958	45-49
50-54	492347	238112	5.8	254235	6.0	4	6219	3550	2669	50-54
55-59	456638	220909	5.4	235729	5.6	0	7938	4643	3295	55-59
60-64	396674	190087	4.6	206587	4.9	0	10435	5916	4519	60-64
65-69	317475	149591	3.7	167884	4.0	0	12972	7105	5867	65-69
70-74	222339	102214	2.5	120125	2.9		14731	7766	6965	70-74
75-79	133117	58186	1.4	74931	1.8		14641	7331	7310	75-79
80-84	60845	24605	0.6	36240	0.9	59640 M.	10987	5094	5893	80-84
85+	20749	6936	0.2	13813	0.3	56652 F.	7116	2790	4326	85+
TOTAL	8295335	4091091		4204244		116292	120470	65095	55375	TOT.

TABLE 2 — MALE LIFE TABLE

x	$_nq_x$	l_x	$_nd_x$	$_nL_x$	$_nm_x$	$_na_x$	T_x	r_x	$\mathring{e}_x$	$_nM_x$
0	0.089320	100000	8932	93473	0.095556	0.2693	5614262	0.0000	56.143	0.095556
1	0.021695	91068	1976	358579	0.005510	1.1184	5520788	0.0000	60.623	0.005510
5	0.010722	89092	955	443073	0.002156	2.5000	5162209	0.0000	57.942	0.002156
10	0.008330	88137	734	438918	0.001673	2.5935	4719136	0.0000	53.543	0.001673
15	0.014698	87403	1285	434144	0.002959	2.7661	4280218	0.0222	48.971	0.002941
20	0.027580	86118	2375	424854	0.005590	2.5847	3846073	0.0000	44.660	0.005590
25	0.026866	83743	2250	413021	0.005447	2.4690	3421219	0.0000	40.854	0.005447
30	0.025037	81493	2040	402372	0.005071	2.5033	3008198	0.0000	36.913	0.005071
35	0.028722	79453	2282	391753	0.005825	2.5847	2605826	0.0036	32.797	0.005823
40	0.038459	77171	2968	378763	0.007836	2.6106	2214074	0.0193	28.691	0.007817
45	0.051990	74203	3858	361807	0.010663	2.6133	1835311	0.0162	24.734	0.010639
50	0.072006	70345	5065	339619	0.014915	2.6100	1473504	0.0027	20.947	0.014909
55	0.100074	65280	6533	310786	0.021020	2.6101	1133885	0.0008	17.370	0.021018
60	0.145014	58747	8519	273308	0.031170	2.6023	823098	0.0092	14.011	0.031123
65	0.213318	50228	10715	225216	0.047574	2.5805	549790	0.0092	10.946	0.047496
70	0.320624	39513	12661	166352	0.076110	2.5346	324574	0.0092	8.214	0.075978
75	0.477258	26852	12815	101534	0.126218	2.4463	158223	0.0092	5.892	0.125993
80	0.666579	14037	9357	45098	0.207475	2.3189	56688	0.0092	4.039	0.207030
85+	*1.000000	4680	4680	11591	0.403785	2.4766	11591	0.0092	2.477	0.402249

TABLE 3 — FEMALE LIFE TABLE

x	$_nq_x$	l_x	$_nd_x$	$_nL_x$	$_nm_x$	$_na_x$	T_x	r_x	$\mathring{e}_x$	$_nM_x$
0	0.068853	100000	6885	95067	0.072426	0.2835	6200945	0.0000	62.009	0.072426
1	0.018607	93115	1733	367489	0.004715	1.1319	6105878	0.0000	65.574	0.004715
5	0.008807	91382	805	454898	0.001769	2.5000	5738389	0.0000	62.796	0.001769
10	0.007026	90577	636	451337	0.001410	2.5652	5283490	0.0000	58.331	0.001410
15	0.011161	89941	1004	447346	0.002244	2.6502	4832154	0.0230	53.726	0.002236
20	0.015295	88937	1360	441368	0.003082	2.5611	4384808	0.0000	49.302	0.003082
25	0.016018	87577	1403	434393	0.003229	2.5116	3943440	0.0000	45.028	0.003229
30	0.016695	86174	1439	427325	0.003367	2.5364	3509048	0.0000	40.721	0.003367
35	0.019519	84735	1654	419678	0.003941	2.5830	3081723	0.0017	36.369	0.003940
40	0.025249	83081	2098	410393	0.005111	2.6100	2662044	0.0131	32.041	0.005103
45	0.034096	80984	2761	398413	0.006931	2.6443	2251651	0.0152	27.804	0.006914
50	0.051265	78222	4010	381558	0.010510	2.6176	1853238	0.0080	23.692	0.010498
55	0.067715	74212	5025	359166	0.013991	2.6329	1471681	0.0059	19.831	0.013978
60	0.104307	69187	7217	328935	0.021939	2.6444	1112515	0.0155	16.080	0.021875
65	0.161805	61970	10027	286039	0.035055	2.6252	783580	0.0155	12.644	0.034947
70	0.254953	51943	13243	227690	0.058163	2.5817	497540	0.0155	9.579	0.057981
75	0.393213	38700	15217	155507	0.097856	2.5033	269851	0.0155	6.973	0.097556
80	0.574167	23483	13483	82619	0.163195	2.4194	114343	0.0155	4.869	0.162610
85+	*1.000000	10000	10000	31724	0.315208	3.1725	31724	0.0155	3.173	0.313183

TABLE 4 — OBSERVED AND PROJECTED VITAL RATES

	OBSERVED POPULATION BOTH SEXES	MALES	FEMALES	PROJECTED POPULATION 1945 MALES	1945 FEMALES	1950 MALES	1950 FEMALES	1955 MALES	1955 FEMALES	STABLE POPULATION MALES	FEMAL
RATES PER THOUSAND											
Birth	14.02	14.58	13.47	14.31	13.12	14.50	13.21	14.60	13.23	13.39	11.
Death	14.52	15.91	13.17	16.37	13.78	17.07	14.59	17.74	15.39	21.30	19.
Increase	-0.50	-1.33	0.30	-2.07	-0.65	-2.58	-1.38	-3.14	-2.15	-7.91	
PERCENTAGE											
under 15	22.34	22.79	21.89	21.29	20.16	20.18	18.92	19.69	18.30	18.96	17.
15-64	68.57	68.86	68.29	69.79	69.14	70.39	69.56	70.58	69.54	67.97	65.
65 and over	9.10	8.35	9.82	8.92	10.69	9.43	11.52	9.73	12.16	13.08	16.
DEP. RATIO X 100	45.84	45.23	46.44	43.29	44.63	42.07	43.76	41.67	43.80	47.13	51.

TABLE 1 — DATA

AGE AT LAST BIRTHDAY	POPULATION BOTH SEXES	MALES Number	%	FEMALES Number	%	BIRTHS BY AGE OF MOTHER	DEATHS BOTH SEXES	MALES	FEMALES	AGE AT LAST BIRTHDAY
0	121013	61736	1.5	59277	1.4	0	9748	5579	4169	0
1-4	440627	239502	5.8	201125	4.7	0	2033	1105	928	1-4
5-9	574388	289076	7.0	285312	6.7	0	1114	629	485	5-9
10-14	623688	313491	7.6	310197	7.3	12	1024	568	456	10-14
15-19	645014	322100	7.8	322914	7.6	5857	1729	1027	702	15-19
20-24	676423	338452	8.2	337971	8.0	35800	2513	1582	931	20-24
25-29	464325	231059	5.6	233266	5.5	34168	1907	1134	773	25-29
30-34	632033	313884	7.6	318149	7.5	31977	2597	1556	1041	30-34
35-39	670885	336936	8.2	333949	7.9	20347	3116	1914	1202	35-39
40-44	676551	339357	8.2	337194	7.9	7012	3977	2466	1511	40-44
45-49	613916	300061	7.3	313225	7.4	501	4990	3063	1927	45-49
50-54	522903	248273	6.0	274630	6.5	6	5921	3610	2311	50-54
55-59	461973	219012	5.3	242961	5.7	0	7417	4396	3021	55-59
60-64	414462	195520	4.7	218942	5.2	0	9782	5586	4196	60-64
65-69	344711	160024	3.9	184687	4.3	0	12532	6806	5726	65-69
70-74	249597	112813	2.7	136784	3.2		14724	7574	7150	70-74
75-79	148938	64341	1.6	84597	2.0		14630	7137	7493	75-79
80-84	68149	26960	0.7	41189	1.0	70380 M.	10950	4893	6057	80-84
85+	20621	5838	0.1	14783	0.3	65300 F.	6942	2655	4287	85+
TOTAL	8370217	4119065		4251152		135680	117646	63280	54366	TOTAL

TABLE 2 — MALE LIFE TABLE

x	$_nq_x$	l_x	$_nd_x$	$_nL_x$	$_nm_x$	$_na_x$	T_x	r_x	$\mathring{e}_x$	$_nM_x$	x
0	0.084679	100000	8468	93704	0.090369	0.2565	5741744	0.0000	57.417	0.090369	0
1	0.018212	91532	1667	361306	0.004614	1.1073	5648039	0.0000	61.706	0.004614	1
5	0.010821	89865	972	446894	0.002176	2.5000	5286733	0.0000	58.830	0.002176	5
10	0.009020	88893	802	442547	0.001812	2.6096	4839839	0.0000	54.446	0.001812	10
15	0.015825	88091	1394	437220	0.003188	2.6802	4397292	0.0000	49.918	0.003188	15
20	0.023160	86697	2008	428602	0.004685	2.5684	3960072	0.0288	45.677	0.004674	20
25	0.024243	84689	2053	418315	0.004908	2.5016	3531470	0.0026	41.699	0.004908	25
30	0.024485	82636	2023	408164	0.004957	2.5211	3113155	0.0000	37.673	0.004957	30
35	0.028017	80612	2258	397578	0.005681	2.5716	2704991	0.0000	33.555	0.005681	35
40	0.035731	78354	2800	385085	0.007270	2.6124	2307413	0.0039	29.449	0.007267	40
45	0.049878	75554	3768	368820	0.010218	2.6247	1922328	0.0208	25.443	0.010187	45
50	0.070419	71786	5055	346838	0.014575	2.6081	1553508	0.0170	21.641	0.014540	50
55	0.095788	66731	6392	318306	0.020081	2.5988	1206670	0.0033	18.083	0.020072	55
60	0.134023	60339	8087	282251	0.028651	2.5957	888364	0.0182	14.723	0.028570	60
65	0.193398	52252	10105	236850	0.042666	2.5845	606113	0.0182	11.600	0.042531	65
70	0.289114	42147	12185	180876	0.067342	2.5497	369263	0.0182	8.761	0.067138	70
75	0.434347	29961	13014	116910	0.111314	2.4721	188387	0.0182	6.288	0.110925	75
80	0.616112	16948	10442	57279	0.182297	2.3702	71477	0.0182	4.217	0.181490	80
85+	*1.000000	6506	6506	14198	0.458223	2.1823	14198	0.0182	2.182	0.454779	85+

TABLE 3 — FEMALE LIFE TABLE

x	$_nq_x$	l_x	$_nd_x$	$_nL_x$	$_nm_x$	$_na_x$	T_x	r_x	$\mathring{e}_x$	$_nM_x$	x
0	0.066334	100000	6633	95252	0.069640	0.2843	6334857	0.0132	63.349	0.070331	0
1	0.017998	93367	1680	368648	0.004558	1.1327	6239605	0.0132	66.829	0.004614	1
5	0.008463	91686	776	456491	0.001700	2.5000	5870956	0.0000	64.033	0.001700	5
10	0.007324	90910	666	452928	0.001470	2.5625	5414465	0.0000	59.558	0.001470	10
15	0.010814	90244	976	448899	0.002174	2.6193	4961537	0.0000	54.979	0.002174	15
20	0.013717	89269	1224	443380	0.002762	2.5802	4512638	0.0298	50.551	0.002755	20
25	0.016436	88044	1447	436640	0.003314	2.5260	4069259	0.0029	46.218	0.003314	25
30	0.016228	86597	1405	429487	0.003272	2.5108	3632618	0.0000	41.949	0.003272	30
35	0.017840	85192	1520	422252	0.003599	2.5617	3203132	0.0000	37.599	0.003599	35
40	0.022173	83672	1855	413922	0.004482	2.6084	2780879	0.0018	33.236	0.004481	40
45	0.030373	81817	2485	403167	0.006164	2.6195	2366957	0.0143	28.930	0.006152	45
50	0.041357	79332	3281	388897	0.008436	2.6344	1963790	0.0167	24.754	0.008415	50
55	0.060506	76051	4602	369437	0.012455	2.6493	1574893	0.0098	20.708	0.012434	55
60	0.092065	71449	6578	341803	0.019245	2.6523	1205457	0.0215	16.872	0.019165	60
65	0.145053	64871	9410	302155	0.031142	2.6406	863654	0.0215	13.313	0.031004	65
70	0.233127	55461	12930	246252	0.052505	2.5981	561499	0.0215	10.124	0.052272	70
75	0.364416	42532	15499	174243	0.088953	2.5214	315247	0.0215	7.412	0.088573	75
80	0.537132	27033	14520	98241	0.147801	2.4571	141004	0.0215	5.216	0.147053	80
85+	*1.000000	12513	12513	42764	0.292595	3.4177	42764	0.0215	3.418	0.289995	85+

TABLE 4 — OBSERVED AND PROJECTED VITAL RATES

	OBSERVED POPULATION BOTH SEXES	MALES	FEMALES	PROJECTED POPULATION 1950 MALES	FEMALES	1955 MALES	FEMALES	1960 MALES	FEMALES	STABLE POPULATION MALES	FEMALES
RATES PER THOUSAND											
Birth	16.21	17.09	15.36	17.22	15.41	17.07	15.24	16.68	14.86	16.35	14.77
Death	14.06	15.36	12.79	16.21	13.87	16.84	14.66	17.29	15.32	18.15	16.56
Increase	2.15	1.72	2.57	1.00	1.54	0.24	0.58	-0.62	-0.47	-1.7923	
PERCENTAGE											
under 15	21.02	21.94	20.13	21.82	19.66	22.46	19.92	22.90	20.83	22.28	20.55
15-64	69.04	69.08	69.00	68.59	68.55	67.66	67.62	66.92	65.97	66.42	64.90
65 and over	9.94	8.98	10.87	9.59	11.79	9.88	12.46	10.18	13.20	11.29	14.55
DEP. RATIO X 100	44.85	44.77	44.93	45.79	45.87	47.80	47.88	49.42	51.59	50.55	54.09

TABLE 1 DATA

AGE AT LAST BIRTHDAY	POPULATION BOTH SEXES	MALES Number	%	FEMALES Number	%	BIRTHS BY AGE OF MOTHER	DEATHS BOTH SEXES	MALES	FEMALES	AGE AT LAST BIRTHDAY
0	140020	71435	1.7	68585	1.6	0	6350	3671	2679	0
1-4	556896	283427	6.7	273469	6.2	0	1121	618	503	1-4
5-9	546208	277381	6.5	268827	6.1	0	402	229	173	5-9
10-14	567869	285840	6.7	282029	6.4	10	335	187	148	10-14
15-19	618032	310675	7.3	307357	7.0	6648	631	376	255	15-19
20-24	654120	330675	7.8	323445	7.4	40302	1039	641	398	20-24
25-29	693742	354402	8.3	339340	7.7	47589	1247	751	496	25-29
30-34	479884	243329	5.7	236555	5.4	25485	1066	627	439	30-34
35-39	620729	311632	7.3	309097	7.0	18042	1678	993	685	35-39
40-44	651505	325168	7.6	326337	7.4	6469	2585	1587	998	40-44
45-49	651777	322867	7.6	328910	7.5	506	4002	2509	1493	45-49
50-54	588609	283676	6.7	304933	6.9	0	5536	3431	2105	50-54
55-59	494794	230441	5.4	264353	6.0	0	6982	4207	2775	55-59
60-64	423604	196191	4.6	227413	5.2	0	9139	5320	3819	60-64
65-69	366540	168775	4.0	197765	4.5	0	12140	6646	5494	65-69
70-74	281826	127810	3.0	154016	3.5		15356	7934	7422	70-74
75-79	182903	80355	1.9	102548	2.3		16054	7835	8219	75-79
80-84	89074	37248	0.9	51826	1.2	74548 M.	12514	5718	6796	80-84
85+	38380	13987	0.3	24393	0.6	70503 F.	8670	3394	5276	85+
TOTAL	8646512	4255314		4391198		145051	106847	56674	50173	TOTAL

TABLE 2 MALE LIFE TABLE

x	nq_x	l_x	nd_x	nL_x	nm_x	na_x	T_x	r_x	$\dot{e}_x$	nM_x
0	0.049454	100000	4945	96234	0.051389	0.2385	6450035	0.0000	64.500	0.051389
1	0.008667	95055	824	377824	0.002180	1.0934	6353801	0.0000	66.844	0.002180
5	0.004093	94231	386	470190	0.000820	2.5000	5975977	0.0204	63.419	0.000826
10	0.003266	93845	306	468497	0.000654	2.6215	5505787	0.0000	58.669	0.000654
15	0.006035	93539	564	466405	0.001210	2.7179	5037291	0.0000	53.853	0.001210
20	0.009647	92974	897	462713	0.001938	2.5947	4570886	0.0000	49.163	0.001938
25	0.010559	92077	972	458012	0.002123	2.5580	4108173	0.0285	44.617	0.002119
30	0.012815	91105	1168	452699	0.002579	2.5803	3650161	0.3103	40.065	0.002577
35	0.015813	89937	1422	446333	0.003186	2.6418	3197462	0.0000	35.552	0.003186
40	0.024130	88515	2136	437627	0.004881	2.6832	2751129	0.0000	31.081	0.004881
45	0.038206	86379	3300	424223	0.007779	2.6747	2313501	0.0056	26.783	0.007771
50	0.059019	83079	4903	403879	0.012140	2.6512	1889279	0.0213	22.741	0.012095
55	0.087744	78176	6859	374604	0.018311	2.6274	1485400	0.0181	19.001	0.018256
60	0.127586	71316	9099	334741	0.027182	2.5997	1110796	0.0155	15.576	0.027116
65	0.180237	62217	11214	284026	0.039482	2.5869	776054	0.0155	12.473	0.039378
70	0.270073	51004	13775	221287	0.062248	2.5512	492028	0.0155	9.647	0.062077
75	0.392232	37229	14602	149351	0.097772	2.4803	270741	0.0155	7.272	0.097505
80	0.547820	22626	12395	80529	0.153924	2.4265	121390	0.0155	5.365	0.153512
85+	1.000000	10231	10231	40862	0.250388	3.9938	40862	0.0155	3.994	0.242655

TABLE 3 FEMALE LIFE TABLE

x	nq_x	l_x	nd_x	nL_x	nm_x	na_x	T_x	r_x	$\dot{e}_x$	nM_x
0	0.037949	100000	3795	97154	0.039061	0.2501	6954263	0.0000	69.543	0.039061
1	0.007318	96205	704	382780	0.001839	1.1022	6857109	0.0000	71.276	0.001839
5	0.003192	95501	305	476743	0.000639	2.5000	6474329	0.0183	67.793	0.000644
10	0.002621	95196	249	475376	0.000525	2.5737	5997586	0.0000	63.002	0.000525
15	0.004140	94947	393	473820	0.000830	2.6752	5522211	0.0000	58.161	0.000830
20	0.006134	94554	580	471379	0.001231	2.6053	5048391	0.0000	53.392	0.001231
25	0.007302	93974	686	468211	0.001466	2.5857	4577012	0.0298	48.705	0.001462
30	0.009243	93287	862	464350	0.001857	2.5803	4108801	0.0075	44.045	0.001856
35	0.011022	92425	1019	459688	0.002216	2.6075	3644451	0.0000	39.431	0.002216
40	0.015182	91406	1388	453772	0.003058	2.6507	3184763	0.0000	34.842	0.003058
45	0.022466	90019	2022	445372	0.004541	2.6658	2730991	0.0021	30.338	0.004539
50	0.034056	87996	2997	432978	0.006921	2.6632	2285619	0.0147	25.974	0.006903
55	0.051409	84999	4370	414812	0.010534	2.6691	1852641	0.0183	21.796	0.010497
60	0.081148	80630	6543	387903	0.016867	2.6699	1437829	0.0213	17.832	0.016793
65	0.130996	74087	9705	347717	0.027911	2.6593	1049926	0.0213	14.172	0.027780
70	0.216902	64382	13965	288502	0.048404	2.6077	702209	0.0213	10.907	0.048190
75	0.335727	50417	16926	210318	0.080480	2.5324	413707	0.0213	8.206	0.080148
80	0.495499	33491	16595	125961	0.131744	2.4996	203390	0.0213	6.073	0.131130
85+	*1.000000	16896	16896	77429	0.218216	4.5826	77429	0.0213	4.583	0.216292

TABLE 4 OBSERVED AND PROJECTED VITAL RATES

	OBSERVED POPULATION BOTH SEXES	MALES	FEMALES	PROJECTED POPULATION 1955 MALES	FEMALES	1960 MALES	FEMALES	1965 MALES	FEMALES	STABLE POPULATION MALES	FEMALES
RATES PER THOUSAND											
Birth	16.78	17.52	16.06	17.27	15.80	16.60	15.17	15.89	14.52	16.96	15.8
Death	12.36	13.32	11.43	13.94	12.28	14.31	12.91	14.58	13.41	14.43	13.2
Increase	4.42	4.20	4.63	3.33	3.52	2.29	2.26	1.30	1.11		2.527
PERCENTAGE											
under 15	20.94	21.57	20.33	22.66	21.12	23.94	22.22	23.39	21.68	23.51	22.3
15-64	67.97	68.36	67.58	67.05	66.09	65.57	64.25	65.46	63.83	65.56	64.2
65 and over	11.09	10.06	12.08	10.30	12.79	10.50	13.52	11.15	14.49	10.93	13.
DEP. RATIO X 100	47.13	46.28	47.96	49.15	51.31	52.52	55.63	52.77	56.66	52.53	56.

TABLE 1 — DATA

AGE AT LAST BIRTHDAY	POPULATION BOTH SEXES	MALES Number	%	FEMALES Number	%	BIRTHS BY AGE OF MOTHER	DEATHS BOTH SEXES	MALES	FEMALES	AGE AT LAST BIRTHDAY
0	142312	72749	1.7	69563	1.6	0	5442	3139	2303	0
1-4	555597	283628	6.5	271969	6.1	0	814	463	351	1-4
5-9	670180	341164	7.9	329016	7.3	0	381	225	156	5-9
10-14	541432	274107	6.3	267325	6.0	11	251	150	101	10-14
15-19	574649	289476	6.7	285173	6.4	6060	377	249	128	15-19
20-24	631929	317444	7.3	314485	7.0	41192	649	434	215	20-24
25-29	665013	337510	7.8	327508	7.3	48404	802	518	284	25-29
30-34	645581	329369	7.6	316212	7.1	32734	979	591	388	30-34
35-39	504870	255153	5.9	249717	5.6	13842	1005	588	417	35-39
40-44	624828	312788	7.2	312040	7.0	5449	1892	1148	744	40-44
45-49	643924	319592	7.4	324332	7.2	418	3260	2057	1203	45-49
50-54	624000	305021	7.0	318979	7.1	0	5128	3287	1841	50-54
55-59	545333	257119	5.9	288214	6.4	0	7225	4565	2660	55-59
60-64	447108	204134	4.7	242974	5.4	0	9096	5434	3662	60-64
65-69	372222	168207	3.9	204015	4.6	0	11852	6616	5236	65-69
70-74	295191	131722	3.0	163469	3.6		15265	7934	7331	70-74
75-79	198339	86267	2.0	112072	2.5		17269	8480	8789	75-79
80-84	100351	41527	1.0	58824	1.3	76051 M.	14481	6690	7791	80-84
85+	44091	16211	0.4	27880	0.6	72059 F.	10574	4230	6344	85+
TOTAL	8826955	4343188		4483767		148110	106742	56798	49944	TOTAL

TABLE 2 — MALE LIFE TABLE

x	$_nq_x$	l_x	$_nd_x$	$_nL_x$	$_nm_x$	$_na_x$	T_x	r_x	$\dot{e}_x$	$_nM_x$	x
0	0.041720	100000	4172	96774	0.043111	0.2267	6630100	0.0011	66.301	0.043148	0
1	0.006488	95828	622	381500	0.001630	1.0852	6533327	0.0011	68.178	0.001632	1
5	0.003269	95206	311	475253	0.000655	2.5000	6151827	0.0253	64.616	0.000660	5
10	0.002736	94895	260	473846	0.000548	2.5762	5676573	0.0158	59.819	0.000547	10
15	0.004292	94635	406	472241	0.000860	2.6961	5202727	0.0000	54.977	0.000860	15
20	0.006813	94229	642	469606	0.001367	2.6004	4730486	0.0000	50.202	0.001367	20
25	0.007645	93587	715	466187	0.001535	2.5552	4260880	0.0000	45.528	0.001535	25
30	0.008954	92872	832	462351	0.001799	2.5851	3794693	0.0261	40.860	0.001794	30
35	0.011466	92040	1055	457734	0.002306	2.6627	3332342	0.0027	36.205	0.002304	35
40	0.018199	90985	1656	451155	0.003670	2.7237	2874608	0.0000	31.594	0.003670	40
45	0.031715	89329	2833	440167	0.006436	2.7134	2423453	0.0000	27.130	0.006436	45
50	0.052688	86496	4557	421956	0.010800	2.6909	1983286	0.0105	22.929	0.010776	50
55	0.085535	81939	7009	393179	0.017826	2.6438	1561330	0.0221	19.055	0.017754	55
60	0.125366	74930	9394	352162	0.026674	2.6061	1168151	0.0126	15.590	0.026620	60
65	0.179939	65536	11793	299189	0.039415	2.5838	815988	0.0126	12.451	0.039332	65
70	0.263056	53744	14138	234178	0.060371	2.5568	516800	0.0126	9.616	0.060233	70
75	0.395099	39606	15648	158809	0.098536	2.4936	282622	0.0126	7.136	0.098299	75
80	0.569982	23958	13656	84536	0.161534	2.4184	123812	0.0126	5.168	0.161101	80
85+	*1.000000	10302	10302	39276	0.262306	3.8123	39276	0.0126	3.812	0.260934	85+

TABLE 3 — FEMALE LIFE TABLE

x	$_nq_x$	l_x	$_nd_x$	$_nL_x$	$_nm_x$	$_na_x$	T_x	r_x	$\dot{e}_x$	$_nM_x$	x
0	0.032255	100000	3226	97517	0.033077	0.2302	7150207	0.0011	71.502	0.033107	0
1	0.005134	96774	497	385651	0.001288	1.0876	7052690	0.0011	72.878	0.001291	1
5	0.002349	96278	226	480822	0.000470	2.5000	6667040	0.0238	69.248	0.000474	5
10	0.001887	96051	181	479801	0.000378	2.4871	6186217	0.0139	64.405	0.000378	10
15	0.002242	95870	215	478844	0.000449	2.6407	5706416	0.0000	59.522	0.000449	15
20	0.003413	95655	326	477501	0.000684	2.6261	5227572	0.0000	54.650	0.000684	20
25	0.004327	95329	412	475666	0.000867	2.6294	4750071	0.0000	49.828	0.000867	25
30	0.006139	94916	583	473202	0.001231	2.6330	4274405	0.0259	45.033	0.001227	30
35	0.008317	94334	785	469816	0.001670	2.6398	3801203	0.0000	40.295	0.001670	35
40	0.011856	93549	1109	465163	0.002384	2.6719	3331387	0.0000	35.611	0.002384	40
45	0.018388	92440	1700	458258	0.003709	2.6811	2866223	0.0000	31.006	0.003709	45
50	0.028509	90740	2587	447712	0.005778	2.6850	2407965	0.0058	26.537	0.005772	50
55	0.045342	88153	3997	431517	0.009263	2.6859	1960253	0.0176	22.237	0.009229	55
60	0.073111	84156	6153	406542	0.015134	2.6858	1528736	0.0190	18.165	0.015072	60
65	0.121579	78003	9484	367931	0.025775	2.6711	1122194	0.0190	14.386	0.025665	65
70	0.203440	68520	13940	309527	0.045036	2.6274	754263	0.0190	11.008	0.044846	70
75	0.329962	54580	18009	228746	0.078731	2.5482	444736	0.0190	8.148	0.078423	75
80	0.495159	36571	18108	136247	0.132908	2.5052	215990	0.0190	5.906	0.132446	80
85+	1.000000	18462	18462	79743	0.231525	4.3192	79743	0.0190	4.319	0.227546	85+

TABLE 4 — OBSERVED, PROJECTED, STABLE RATES

	OBSERVED POPULATION BOTH SEXES	MALES	FEMALES	PROJECTED POPULATION 1960 MALES	FEMALES	1965 MALES	FEMALES	1970 MALES	FEMALES	STABLE POPULATION MALES	FEMALES
RATES PER THOUSAND											
Birth	16.78	17.51	16.07	16.82	15.41	15.97	14.62	16.02	14.67	17.06	15.92
Death	12.09	13.08	11.14	13.52	11.89	13.81	12.46	14.09	12.98	13.60	12.46
Increase	4.69	4.43	4.93	3.31	3.52	2.15	2.15	1.93	1.69		3.4598
PERCENTAGE											
under 15	21.63	22.37	20.92	23.81	22.11	23.62	21.88	23.13	21.43	23.73	22.40
15-64	66.92	67.41	66.45	65.81	64.50	65.48	63.74	65.16	63.15	65.48	63.77
65 and over	11.44	10.22	12.63	10.38	13.39	10.90	14.39	11.71	15.41	10.80	13.83
DEP. RATIO X 100	49.43	48.35	50.48	51.94	55.04	52.73	56.90	53.48	58.35	52.73	56.81

TABLE 1 — DATA

AGE AT LAST BIRTHDAY	POPULATION BOTH SEXES	MALES Number	MALES %	FEMALES Number	FEMALES %	BIRTHS BY AGE OF MOTHER	DEATHS BOTH SEXES	DEATHS MALES	FEMALES	AGE AT LAST BIRTHDAY
0	154050	78750	1.8	75300	1.6	0	3943	2278	1665	0
1-4	595850	304400	6.8	291450	6.2	0	662	369	293	1-4
5-9	709950	361300	8.1	348650	7.5	0	358	206	152	5-9
10-14	694150	351800	7.8	342350	7.3	15	272	167	105	10-14
15-19	544700	275750	6.1	268950	5.8	7215	394	270	124	15-19
20-24	571750	286650	6.4	285100	6.1	43155	603	434	169	20-24
25-29	622250	311100	6.9	311150	6.7	50753	694	469	225	25-29
30-34	652250	328700	7.3	323550	6.9	32982	876	553	323	30-34
35-39	690000	351200	7.8	338800	7.3	17037	1214	731	483	35-39
40-44	465650	234700	5.2	230950	5.0	4125	1354	838	516	40-44
45-49	612350	304600	6.8	307750	6.6	332	2769	1748	1021	45-49
50-54	624750	306800	6.8	317950	6.8	1	4738	3106	1632	50-54
55-59	603550	290550	6.5	313000	6.7	0	7402	4860	2542	55-59
60-64	516700	237500	5.3	279200	6.0	0	9988	6228	3760	60-64
65-69	404700	177150	3.9	227550	4.9	0	12192	6989	5203	65-69
70-74	307650	131850	2.9	175800	3.8		15015	7808	7207	70-74
75-79	214450	89950	2.0	124500	2.7		17462	8479	8983	75-79
80-84	115050	46100	1.0	68950	1.5	80013 M.	15509	7070	8439	80-84
85+	53450	18800	0.4	34650	0.7	75602 F.	12591	5092	7499	85+
TOTAL	9153250	4487650		4665600		155615	108036	57695	50341	TOTAL

TABLE 2 — MALE LIFE TABLE

x	$_nq_x$	l_x	$_nd_x$	$_nL_x$	$_nm_x$	$_na_x$	T_x	r_x	$\mathring{e}_x$	$_nM_x$
0	0.028251	100000	2825	97847	0.028873	0.2379	6769920	0.0024	67.699	0.028927
1	0.004817	97175	468	387339	0.001208	1.0930	6672073	0.0024	68.660	0.001212
5	0.002842	96707	275	482847	0.000569	2.5000	6284734	0.0078	64.987	0.000570
10	0.002382	96432	230	481627	0.000477	2.6788	5801887	0.0264	60.166	0.000475
15	0.004906	96202	472	479934	0.000983	2.7173	5320260	0.0195	55.303	0.000979
20	0.007542	95730	722	476897	0.001514	2.5697	4840326	0.0000	50.562	0.001514
25	0.007510	95008	713	473272	0.001508	2.5198	4363429	0.0000	45.927	0.001508
30	0.008378	94295	790	469554	0.001682	2.5687	3890157	0.0000	41.255	0.001682
35	0.010418	93505	974	465267	0.002094	2.6822	3420603	0.0314	36.582	0.002081
40	0.017747	92531	1642	458882	0.003578	2.7030	2955337	0.0106	31.939	0.003571
45	0.028323	90889	2574	448576	0.005739	2.7207	2496455	0.0000	27.467	0.005739
50	0.049467	88314	4369	431524	0.010124	2.6999	2047879	0.0000	23.189	0.010124
55	0.080610	83946	6767	403890	0.016754	2.6594	1616356	0.0084	19.255	0.016727
60	0.123704	77179	9547	363159	0.026290	2.6187	1212465	0.0146	15.710	0.026223
65	0.180479	67632	12206	308646	0.039547	2.5822	849306	0.0146	12.558	0.039452
70	0.259158	55425	14364	241944	0.059369	2.5505	540660	0.0146	9.755	0.059219
75	0.382120	41062	15690	166005	0.094518	2.4951	298717	0.0146	7.275	0.094263
80	0.551644	25371	13996	90967	0.153856	2.4358	132712	0.0146	5.231	0.153363
85+	*1.000000	11375	11375	41745	0.272497	3.6698	41745	0.0146	3.670	0.270851

TABLE 3 — FEMALE LIFE TABLE

x	$_nq_x$	l_x	$_nd_x$	$_nL_x$	$_nm_x$	$_na_x$	T_x	r_x	$\mathring{e}_x$	$_nM_x$
0	0.021708	100000	2171	98365	0.022069	0.2469	7339770	0.0025	73.398	0.022112
1	0.003997	97829	391	390183	0.001002	1.0997	7241405	0.0025	74.021	0.001005
5	0.002174	97438	212	486661	0.000435	2.5000	6851222	0.0063	70.314	0.000436
10	0.001513	97226	149	485762	0.000307	2.5171	6364561	0.0256	65.461	0.000307
15	0.002308	97077	224	484855	0.000462	2.6279	5878799	0.0178	60.558	0.000461
20	0.002960	96853	287	483575	0.000593	2.5905	5393944	0.0000	55.692	0.000593
25	0.003609	96567	349	482002	0.000723	2.6151	4910369	0.0000	50.850	0.000723
30	0.004980	96218	479	479962	0.000998	2.6459	4428367	0.0000	46.024	0.000998
35	0.007146	95739	684	477105	0.001434	2.6762	3948405	0.0322	41.241	0.001426
40	0.011128	95055	1058	472809	0.002237	2.6700	3471301	0.0073	36.519	0.002234
45	0.016461	93997	1547	466385	0.003318	2.6733	2998491	0.0000	31.900	0.003318
50	0.025363	92450	2345	456813	0.005133	2.6819	2532106	0.0000	27.389	0.005133
55	0.039897	90105	3595	442232	0.008129	2.6931	2075293	0.0045	23.032	0.008121
60	0.065616	86510	5676	419448	0.013533	2.6918	1633061	0.0221	18.877	0.013467
65	0.109118	80834	8820	383751	0.022985	2.6853	1213614	0.0221	15.014	0.022865
70	0.187769	72013	13522	328177	0.041203	2.6417	829862	0.0221	11.524	0.040995
75	0.308058	58491	18019	248573	0.072489	2.5646	501685	0.0221	8.577	0.072153
80	0.472103	40473	19107	155292	0.123041	2.5365	253111	0.0221	6.254	0.122394
85+	*1.000000	21365	21365	97819	0.218417	4.5784	97819	0.0221	4.578	0.216421

TABLE 4 — OBSERVED AND PROJECTED VITAL RATES

	OBSERVED POPULATION BOTH SEXES	MALES	FEMALES	PROJECTED POPULATION 1965 MALES	1965 FEMALES	1970 MALES	1970 FEMALES	1975 MALES	1975 FEMALES	STABLE POPULATION MALES	FEMALES
RATES PER THOUSAND											
Birth	17.00	17.83	16.20	16.84	15.27	17.06	15.48	17.80	16.18	18.54	17.3
Death	11.80	12.86	10.79	13.21	11.60	13.48	12.20	13.68	12.67	12.04	10.8
Increase	5.20	4.97	5.41	3.62	3.68	3.58	3.28	4.12	3.52		6.495
PERCENTAGE											
under 15	23.53	24.43	22.67	24.49	22.53	24.43	22.38	24.29	22.26	25.61	24.
15-64	64.50	65.24	63.79	64.57	62.72	63.84	61.78	63.58	61.37	64.62	62.8
65 and over	11.97	10.34	13.53	10.94	14.75	11.73	15.83	12.13	16.37	9.78	12.9
DEP. RATIO X 100	55.04	53.29	56.75	54.88	59.45	56.64	61.86	57.28	62.95	54.76	59.0

AGE AT LAST BIRTHDAY	1965 BOTH SEXES	MALES	FEMALES	1970 BOTH SEXES	MALES	FEMALES	1975 BOTH SEXES	MALES	FEMALES	AGE AT LAST BIRTHDAY	
0-4	744	381	363	743	381	362	778	399	379	0-4	**TABLE 5**
5-9	746	381	365	741	380	361	740	379	361	5-9	POPULATION
10-14	708	360	348	745	380	365	740	379	361	10-14	PROJECTED
15-19	693	351	342	706	359	347	743	379	364	15-19	WITH
20-24	542	274	268	689	348	341	703	357	346	20-24	FIXED
25-29	568	284	284	539	272	267	686	346	340	25-29	AGE—
30-34	619	309	310	565	282	283	536	270	266	30-34	SPECIFIC
35-39	648	326	322	614	306	308	561	280	281	35-39	BIRTH
40-44	682	346	336	640	321	319	607	302	305	40-44	AND
45-49	457	229	228	670	339	331	628	314	314	45-49	DEATH
50-54	594	293	301	444	221	223	650	326	324	50-54	RATES
55-59	595	287	308	566	274	292	423	207	216	55-59	(IN 1000's)
60-64	558	261	297	550	258	292	524	247	277	60-64	
65-69	457	202	255	494	222	272	486	219	267	65-69	
70-74	334	139	195	376	158	218	406	174	232	70-74	
75-79	223	90	133	242	95	147	274	109	165	75-79	
80-84	127	49	78	133	50	83	144	52	92	80-84	
85+	64	21	43	72	23	49	75	23	52	85+	
TOTAL	9359	4583	4776	9529	4669	4860	9704	4762	4942	TOTAL	

STANDARD COUNTRIES: STANDARDIZED RATES PER THOUSAND	ENGLAND AND WALES 1961 BOTH SEXES	MALES	FEMALES	UNITED STATES 1960 BOTH SEXES	MALES	FEMALES	MEXICO 1960 BOTH SEXES	MALES	FEMALES	
Birth	16.25	17.13*	15.30	16.51	16.30*	15.81	19.02	15.11*	18.43	**TABLE 6**
Death	11.82	12.09*	11.51	9.62	10.86*	8.43	5.02	9.55*	4.08	STANDARDIZED RATES
Increase	4.43	5.04*	3.79	6.90	5.44*	7.38	14.00	5.56*	14.35	

	OBSERVED POP. MALES	FEMALES	STATIONARY POP. MALES	FEMALES	STABLE POP. MALES	FEMALES	OBSERVED BIRTHS	NET MATERNITY FUNCTION	BIRTHS IN STABLE POP.	
μ	35.15867	37.24111	36.55699	38.86468	33.39957	35.38588	28.24331	28.00643	27.77716	**TABLE 7**
σ^2	485.7615	523.3502	495.3051	544.2083	475.3802	524.9553	32.02373	33.57215	32.85648	MOMENTS
κ_3	2284.398	1805.978	2332.849	2005.319	3755.273	3869.949	84.7852	109.5646	110.7222	AND
κ_4	-232995.	-289432.	-239068.	-308939.	-195696.	-260113.	-295.175	-210.789	-136.032	CUMULANTS
β_1	0.045528	0.022753	0.044787	0.024950	0.131268	0.103525	0.218889	0.317251	0.345626	
β_2	2.012584	1.943276	2.025514	1.956859	2.134037	2.056120	2.712171	2.812980	2.873992	
κ	-0.017115	-0.008269	-0.017036	-0.009147	-0.049976	-0.038031	-0.142161	-0.196255	-0.221158	

VITAL STATISTICS		THOMPSON AGE RANGE	NRR	1000r	INTERVAL	BOURGEOIS-PICHAT AGE RANGE	NRR	1000b	1000d	1000r	COALE	
GRR	1.245					5-29	1.23	15.68	7.95	7.74	IBR	**TABLE 8**
NRR	1.199	0-4	1.23	7.61	27.43	30-54	1.01	13.83	13.64	0.19	IDR	RATES FROM AGE DISTRIBUTIONS
TFR	2.563	5-9	1.14	4.82	27.40	55-79	1.67	45.92	26.89	19.03	IRI	AND VITAL STATISTICS
GENERATION	27.891	10-14	1.09	3.20	27.35	*15-39	0.71	9.59	22.15	-12.56	K1	(Females)
SEX RATIO	105.835	15-19	0.85	-6.24	27.27						K2	

Start Age Interval	ORIGINAL MATRIX SUB-DIAGONAL	ALTERNATIVE FIRST ROWS Projection	Integral	FIRST STABLE MATRIX % IN STABLE POPULATION	FISHER VALUES	REPRODUCTIVE VALUES	SECOND STABLE MATRIX Z₂ FIRST COLUMN	FIRST ROW	
0	0.99614	0.00000	0.00000	8.336	1.040	381480	0.1678+0.0725	0.1678+0.0725	**TABLE 9**
5	0.99815	0.00005	0.00000	8.038	1.079	376085	0.1657-0.1393	0.0087+0.1541	LESLIE
10	0.99813	0.03183	0.00011	7.766	1.116	382074	-0.0598-0.2497	-0.1129+0.0647	MATRIX
15	0.99736	0.21100	0.06472	7.504	1.122	301815	-0.2967-0.0691	-0.0967-0.0630	AND ITS
20	0.99675	0.37258	0.36515	7.245	0.942	268644	-0.2307+0.2778	-0.0244-0.1121	SPECTRAL
25	0.99577	0.31404	0.39349	6.990	0.588	182886	0.1721+0.3917	0.0126-0.0879	COMPONENTS
30	0.99405	0.18030	0.24591	6.738	0.282	91155	0.5057+0.0253	0.0183-0.0465	(Females)
35	0.99100	0.08068	0.12131	6.484	0.104	35276	0.2942-0.5210	0.0117-0.0170	
40	0.98641	0.02246	0.04309	6.220	0.024	5509	-0.3938-0.5845	0.0037-0.0035	
45	0.97948	0.00128	0.00260	5.939	0.001	399	-0.8195+0.1062	0.0002-0.0002	
50	0.96808	0.00000	0.00001	5.631	0.000	1	-0.3164+0.9085	0.0000-0.0000	
55+	0.79710			23.107					

Start Age Interval	CONTRIBUTIONS OF ROOTS (IN 100's) OBSERVED POPUL. (IN 100's)	r_1	r_2, r_3	$r_4 \cdot r_{11}$	AGE-SP. BIRTH RATES	NET MATERNITY FUNCTION	COEFF. OF MATRIX EQUATION	PARAMETERS	INTEGRAL	MATRIX	EXP. INCREASE x	$e^{(x+2\frac{1}{2})r}$	
0	3668	3510	153	4	0.0000	0.0000	0.0000	L(1)	1.03301	1.03303	0	1.0164	**TABLE 10**
5	3487	3385	178	-76	0.0000	0.0000	0.0001	L(2)	0.37032	0.37649	50	1.4064	AGE ANALYSIS
10	3424	3271	-26	179	0.0000	0.0001	0.0316		0.77844	0.75237	55	1.4528	AND
15	2690	3160	-278	-193	0.0130	0.0632	0.2094	R(1)	0.00650	0.00650	60	1.5007	MISCELLANEOUS
20	2851	3051	-258	58	0.0735	0.3556	0.3688	R(2)	-0.02969	-0.03456	65	1.5503	RESULTS
25	3112	2944	117	51	0.0792	0.3820	0.3098		0.22535	0.22137	70	1.6014	(Females)
30	3236	2838	485	-87	0.0495	0.2377	0.1771	C(1)		42111	75	1.6543	
35	3388	2730	350	308	0.0244	0.1166	0.0788	C(2)		48289	80	1.7089	
40	2310	2619	-307	-3	0.0087	0.0410	0.0217			6307	85	1.7653	
45	3078	2501	-805	1381	0.0005	0.0024	0.0012	2P/Y	27.8817	28.3837	90	1.8236	
50	3180	2371	-420	1228	0.0000	0.0000	0.0000	DELTA	6.2457		95	1.8838	
55+	12237	9731									100	1.9460	

TABLE 1 — DATA

AGE AT LAST BIRTHDAY	POPULATION BOTH SEXES	MALES Number	%	FEMALES Number	%	BIRTHS BY AGE OF MOTHER	DEATHS BOTH SEXES	MALES	FEMALES	AGE AT LAST BIRTHD.
0	154458	79284	1.7	75174	1.6	0	4328	2480	1848	0
1-4	614918	314901	6.9	300017	6.3	0	684	397	287	1-4
5-9	739408	377626	8.3	361782	7.6	0	296	186	110	5-9
10-14	702749	358739	7.9	344010	7.3	20	309	198	111	10-14
15-19	661587	336883	7.4	324704	6.9	9013	507	368	139	15-19
20-24	542165	274549	6.0	267616	5.6	44646	555	428	127	20-24
25-29	595328	300310	6.6	295018	6.2	50156	605	405	200	25-29
30-34	654689	329102	7.2	325587	6.9	33638	883	564	319	30-34
35-39	660201	330672	7.3	329529	7.0	16684	1297	816	481	35-39
40-44	610737	303862	6.7	306875	6.5	4833	1696	1019	677	40-44
45-49	475965	235271	5.2	240694	5.1	197	2503	1585	918	45-49
50-54	598865	292859	6.4	306006	6.5	5	4904	3262	1642	50-54
55-59	589477	282946	6.2	306531	6.5	0	7751	5125	2626	55-59
60-64	537818	249677	5.5	288141	6.1	0	11269	7217	4052	60-64
65-69	431403	189076	4.2	242327	5.1	0	14032	8052	5980	65-69
70-74	317018	132880	2.9	184138	3.9		16087	8296	7791	70-74
75-79	218707	90059	2.0	128648	2.7		18523	8890	9633	75-79
80-84	123949	49646	1.1	74303	1.6	81874 M.	16945	7680	9265	80-84
85+	60328	21973	0.5	38355	0.8	77318 F.	13544	5405	8139	85+
TOTAL	9289770	4550315		4739455		159192	116718	62373	54345	TOTAL

TABLE 2 — MALE LIFE TABLE

x	$n q_x$	l_x	$n d_x$	$n L_x$	$n m_x$	$n a_x$	T_x	r_x	$\dot{e}_x$	$n M_x$
0	0.030548	100000	3055	97659	0.031280	0.2338	6687046	0.0000	66.870	0.031280
1	0.005024	96945	487	386363	0.001261	1.0901	6589386	0.0000	67.970	0.001261
5	0.002455	96458	237	481699	0.000492	2.5000	6203023	0.0087	64.308	0.000493
10	0.002763	96221	266	480502	0.000553	2.7261	5721324	0.0108	59.460	0.000552
15	0.005475	95955	525	478563	0.001098	2.6885	5240822	0.0257	54.617	0.001092
20	0.007767	95430	741	475321	0.001559	2.5312	4762259	0.0101	49.903	0.001559
25	0.006721	94689	636	471866	0.001349	2.5201	4286938	0.0000	45.274	0.001349
30	0.008534	94053	803	468362	0.001714	2.6320	3815072	0.0000	40.563	0.001714
35	0.012276	93250	1145	463542	0.002470	2.6351	3346710	0.0055	35.890	0.002468
40	0.016772	92105	1545	457051	0.003380	2.7508	2883168	0.0302	31.303	0.003353
45	0.033176	90560	3004	445959	0.006737	2.7225	2426117	0.0000	26.790	0.006737
50	0.054292	87556	4754	426769	0.011138	2.6836	1980157	0.0000	22.616	0.011138
55	0.086881	82802	7194	397169	0.018113	2.6588	1553389	0.0000	18.760	0.018113
60	0.135388	75608	10236	353583	0.028951	2.6106	1156219	0.0092	15.292	0.028905
65	0.193188	65372	12629	296132	0.042647	2.5669	802636	0.0092	12.278	0.042586
70	0.270930	52743	14290	228530	0.062529	2.5377	506504	0.0092	9.603	0.062432
75	0.395742	38453	15218	153908	0.098874	2.4794	277975	0.0092	7.229	0.098713
80	0.550119	23236	12782	82500	0.154939	2.4223	124066	0.0092	5.339	0.154695
85+	1.000000	10453	10453	41567	0.251481	3.9764	41567	0.0092	3.976	0.245985

TABLE 3 — FEMALE LIFE TABLE

x	$n q_x$	l_x	$n d_x$	$n L_x$	$n m_x$	$n a_x$	T_x	r_x	$\dot{e}_x$	$n M_x$
0	0.024126	100000	2413	98143	0.024583	0.2304	7296729	0.0000	72.967	0.024583
1	0.003816	97587	372	389265	0.000957	1.0877	7198586	0.0000	73.766	0.000957
5	0.001515	97215	147	485707	0.000303	2.5000	6809321	0.0082	70.044	0.000304
10	0.001613	97068	157	484960	0.000323	2.5803	6323615	0.0105	65.146	0.000323
15	0.002142	96911	208	484052	0.000429	2.5731	5838655	0.0247	60.248	0.000428
20	0.002372	96704	229	482969	0.000475	2.6080	5354604	0.0091	55.371	0.000475
25	0.003384	96474	326	481604	0.000678	2.6535	4871635	0.0000	50.497	0.000678
30	0.004888	96148	470	479640	0.000980	2.6640	4390031	0.0000	45.659	0.000980
35	0.007279	95678	696	476768	0.001461	2.6732	3910390	0.0044	40.870	0.001460
40	0.011045	94981	1049	472508	0.002220	2.7143	3433623	0.0290	36.151	0.002206
45	0.018901	93932	1775	465512	0.003814	2.6634	2961115	0.0000	31.524	0.003814
50	0.026498	92157	2442	455093	0.005366	2.6700	2495603	0.0000	27.080	0.005366
55	0.042003	89715	3768	439868	0.008567	2.6899	2040509	0.0000	22.744	0.008567
60	0.068376	85946	5877	416209	0.014120	2.6989	1600641	0.0176	18.624	0.014063
65	0.117123	80070	9378	378521	0.024775	2.6725	1184432	0.0176	14.793	0.024677
70	0.192985	70692	13642	321172	0.042477	2.6334	805911	0.0176	11.400	0.042311
75	0.317474	57049	18112	241002	0.075152	2.5571	484739	0.0176	8.497	0.074879
80	0.477887	38938	18608	148631	0.125195	2.5248	243737	0.0176	6.260	0.124692
85+	*1.000000	20330	20330	95107	0.213758	4.6782	95107	0.0176	4.678	0.212202

TABLE 4 — OBSERVED AND PROJECTED VITAL RATES

	OBSERVED POPULATION BOTH SEXES	MALES	FEMALES	1968 MALES	FEMALES	1973 MALES	FEMALES	1978 MALES	FEMALES	STABLE POPULATION MALES	FEMAL
RATES PER THOUSAND											
Birth	17.14	17.99	16.31	17.84	16.14	18.39	16.65	19.02	17.28	19.73	18.4
Death	12.56	13.71	11.47	13.82	12.14	13.78	12.52	13.69	12.76	11.65	10.3
Increase	4.57	4.29	4.85	4.02	4.00	4.61	4.13	5.33	4.52		8.083
PERCENTAGE											
under 15	23.81	24.85	22.81	25.13	22.98	25.28	23.09	25.51	23.36	26.88	25.2
15-64	63.80	64.53	63.10	63.72	61.91	63.28	61.22	63.15	60.92	64.37	62.7
65 and over	12.39	10.63	14.09	11.15	15.11	11.44	15.69	11.34	15.72	8.76	11.9
DEP. RATIO X 100	56.74	54.98	58.47	56.93	61.53	58.03	63.35	58.35	64.14	55.36	59.3

TABLE 5 — POPULATION PROJECTED WITH FIXED AGE-SPECIFIC BIRTH AND DEATH RATES (IN 1000's)

AGE AT LAST BIRTHDAY	1968 BOTH SEXES	1968 MALES	1968 FEMALES	1973 BOTH SEXES	1973 MALES	1973 FEMALES	1978 BOTH SEXES	1978 MALES	1978 FEMALES	AGE AT LAST BIRTHDAY
0-4	778	399	379	804	412	392	849	435	414	0-4
5-9	766	392	374	775	397	378	800	410	390	5-9
10-14	738	377	361	764	391	373	773	396	377	10-14
15-19	700	357	343	736	375	361	763	390	373	15-19
20-24	659	335	324	698	355	343	733	373	360	20-24
25-29	540	273	267	655	332	323	694	352	342	25-29
30-34	592	298	294	537	271	266	652	330	322	30-34
35-39	650	326	324	587	295	292	532	268	264	35-39
40-44	653	326	327	642	321	321	580	291	289	40-44
45-49	598	296	302	640	318	322	629	313	316	45-49
50-54	460	225	235	580	284	296	619	304	315	50-54
55-59	569	273	296	437	210	227	550	264	286	55-59
60-64	542	252	290	523	243	280	402	187	215	60-64
65-69	471	209	262	475	211	264	458	203	255	65-69
70-74	352	146	206	383	161	222	387	163	224	70-74
75-79	227	89	138	252	98	154	276	109	167	75-79
80-84	127	48	79	133	48	85	148	53	95	80-84
85+	73	25	48	75	24	51	79	24	55	85+
TOTAL	9495	4646	4849	9696	4746	4950	9924	4865	5059	TOTAL

TABLE 6 — STANDARDIZED RATES

STANDARD COUNTRIES: STANDARDIZED RATES PER THOUSAND	ENGLAND AND WALES 1961 BOTH SEXES	MALES	FEMALES	UNITED STATES 1960 BOTH SEXES	MALES	FEMALES	MEXICO 1960 BOTH SEXES	MALES	FEMALES
Birth	16.95	17.81*	15.95	17.22	16.95*	16.48	20.01	15.59*	19.39
Death	12.30	12.66*	11.86	10.01	11.43*	8.69	5.26	10.04*	4.23
Increase	4.65	5.15*	4.09	7.21	5.51*	7.78	14.76	5.55*	15.16

TABLE 7 — MOMENTS AND CUMULANTS

	OBSERVED POP. MALES	OBSERVED POP. FEMALES	STATIONARY POP. MALES	STATIONARY POP. FEMALES	STABLE POP. MALES	STABLE POP. FEMALES	OBSERVED BIRTHS	NET MATERNITY FUNCTION	BIRTHS IN STABLE POP.
μ	34.82426	37.14454	36.24249	38.71029	32.38739	34.43204	28.11517	27.77555	27.50184
σ^2	494.1158	533.1627	488.9608	540.6473	462.5999	514.8239	33.34813	32.21180	31.33719
κ_3	2788.215	2128.973	2402.005	2042.215	4044.866	4259.452	86.3519	107.6214	108.6479
κ_4	-241301.	-304102.	-228755.	-302830.	-173400.	-238519.	-378.891	-165.013	-79.625
β_1	0.064442	0.029906	0.049354	0.026391	0.165269	0.132963	0.201062	0.346539	0.383586
β_2	2.011670	1.930209	2.043199	1.963974	2.189716	2.100076	2.659301	2.840966	2.918917
κ	-0.023744	-0.010683	-0.018968	-0.009718	-0.063633	-0.049146	-0.124899	-0.210865	-0.243125

TABLE 8 — RATES FROM AGE DISTRIBUTIONS AND VITAL STATISTICS (Females)

VITAL STATISTICS		THOMPSON AGE RANGE	NRR	1000r	INTERVAL	BOURGEOIS-PICHAT AGE RANGE	NRR	1000b	1000d	1000r	COALE
GRR	1.300										
NRR	1.250	0-4	1.20	6.63	27.44	5-29	1.41	17.27	4.51	12.76	IBR
TFR	2.676	5-9	1.21	6.88	27.40	30-54	1.18	17.52	11.33	6.18	IDR
GENERATION	27.638	10-14	1.11	3.92	27.34	55-79	1.43	32.43	19.16	13.27	IRI
SEX RATIO	105.893	15-19	1.03	1.11	27.26	*50-74	1.24	22.83	14.76	8.07	K1
											K2

TABLE 9 — LESLIE MATRIX AND ITS SPECTRAL COMPONENTS (Females)

Start of Age Interval	ORIGINAL MATRIX SUB-DIAGONAL	ALTERNATIVE FIRST ROWS Projection	Integral	FIRST STABLE MATRIX % IN STABLE POPULATION	FISHER VALUES	REPRODUCTIVE VALUES	SECOND STABLE MATRIX Z_2 FIRST COLUMN	FIRST ROW
0	0.99651	0.00000	0.00000	8.799	1.047	392725	0.1713+0.0723	0.1713+0.0723
5	0.99846	0.00007	0.00000	8.420	1.094	395705	0.1639-0.1443	0.0079+0.1582
10	0.99813	0.03286	0.00014	8.074	1.141	392380	-0.0692-0.2474	-0.1182+0.0644
15	0.99776	0.22988	0.06705	7.740	1.155	375183	-0.2974-0.0530	-0.0986-0.0692
20	0.99717	0.39813	0.40299	7.416	0.965	258170	-0.2080+0.2878	-0.0229-0.1178
25	0.99592	0.32302	0.41068	7.102	0.589	173902	0.1984+0.3670	0.0134-0.0900
30	0.99401	0.18186	0.24957	6.792	0.277	90126	0.4890-0.0227	0.0185-0.0465
35	0.99107	0.07840	0.12230	6.484	0.098	32449	0.2247-0.5274	0.0112-0.0162
40	0.98519	0.01960	0.03804	6.171	0.021	6338	-0.4408-0.5038	0.0031-0.0031
45	0.97762	0.00099	0.00198	5.839	0.001	243	-0.7490+0.2069	0.0002-0.0001
50	0.96654	0.00002	0.00004	5.482	0.000	6	-0.1600+0.8806	0.0000-0.0000
55+	0.79689			21.680				

TABLE 10 — AGE ANALYSIS AND MISCELLANEOUS RESULTS (Females)

Start Age Interval	OBSERVED POPUL. (IN 100's)	CONTRIBUTIONS OF ROOTS (IN 100's) r_1	r_2, r_3	r_4-r_{11}	AGE-SP. BIRTH RATES	NET MATERNITY FUNCTION	COEFF. OF MATRIX EQUATION	PARAMETERS INTEGRAL	PARAMETERS MATRIX	EXP. INCREASE x	$e^{(x+2\frac{1}{2})r}$
0	3752	3684	60	8	0.0000	0.0000	0.0000	L(1) 1.04125	1.04129	0	1.0204
5	3618	3526	127	-35	0.0000	0.0000	0.0001	L(2) 0.36257	0.36861	50	1.5287
10	3440	3381	47	12	0.0000	0.0001	0.0327	0.79209	0.76453	55	1.5917
15	3247	3241	-127	134	0.0135	0.0653	0.2283	R(1) 0.00808	0.00809	60	1.6574
20	2676	3105	-195	-234	0.0810	0.3913	0.3945	R(2) -0.02759	-0.03280	65	1.7257
25	2950	2974	-23	-1	0.0826	0.3977	0.3192	0.22831	0.22431	70	1.7969
30	3256	2844	245	167	0.0502	0.2407	0.1790			75	1.8710
35	3295	2715	281	299	0.0246	0.1172	0.0767	C(1)	41871	80	1.9482
40	3069	2584	-50	535	0.0076	0.0361	0.0190	C(2)	24307	85	2.0286
45	2407	2445	-431	394	0.0004	0.0019	0.0009	2P/Y 27.5209	16273 / 28.0114	90	2.1123
50	3060	2295	-364	1129	0.0000	0.0000	0.0000	DELTA 6.8286		95	2.1994
55+	12624	9078								100	2.2901

TABLE 1 — DATA

AGE AT LAST BIRTHDAY	BOTH SEXES	MALES Number	%	FEMALES Number	%	BIRTHS BY AGE OF MOTHER	DEATHS BOTH SEXES	MALES	FEMALES	AGE AT LAST BIRTHDAY
0	156976	79227	2.2	77749	2.1	0	16316	9068	7248	0
1-4	587976	301421	8.3	286555	7.9	0	5113	2632	2481	1-4
5-9	612959	312041	8.6	300918	8.3	0	992	518	474	5-9
10-14	588868	299819	8.2	289049	7.9	0	774	407	367	10-14
15-19	677180	345235	9.5	331945	9.1	18087	1604	820	784	15-19
20-24	683005	346305	9.5	336700	9.2	61927	2361	1264	1097	20-24
25-29	694161	348722	9.6	345439	9.5	49509	2163	1158	1005	25-29
30-34	449651	223861	6.1	225790	6.2	19308	1412	755	657	30-34
35-39	512040	257436	7.1	254604	7.0	10152	1629	891	738	35-39
40-44	515635	261211	7.2	254424	7.0	3457	2130	1201	929	40-44
45-49	449444	227590	6.2	221854	6.1	689	2534	1474	1060	45-49
50-54	365053	182552	5.0	182501	5.0	0	3054	1807	1247	50-54
55-59	266258	129045	3.5	137213	3.8	0	3429	1969	1460	55-59
60-64	236966	112431	3.1	124535	3.4	0	5211	2722	2489	60-64
65-69	186055	86021	2.4	100034	2.7	0	6947	3620	3327	65-69
70-74	137353	61482	1.7	75871	2.1		7128	3533	3595	70-74
75-79	91793	39454	1.1	52339	1.4		5965	2874	3091	75-79
80-84	51795	21162	0.6	30633	0.8	84209 M.	4927	2424	2503	80-84
85+	21276	8170	0.2	13106	0.4	78920 F.	4895	2398	2497	85+
TOTAL	7284444	3643185		3641259		163129	78584	41535	37049	TOTAL

TABLE 2 — MALE LIFE TABLE

x	nq_x	l_x	nd_x	nL_x	nm_x	na_x	T_x	r_x	$\mathring{e}_x$	nM_x	x
0	0.105946	100000	10595	92565	0.114456	0.2983	5877770	0.0000	58.778	0.114456	0
1	0.034079	89405	3047	348931	0.008732	1.1475	5785204	0.0000	64.708	0.008732	1
5	0.008138	86359	703	430036	0.001634	2.5000	5436274	0.0205	62.950	0.001660	5
10	0.006765	85656	580	426893	0.001357	2.6086	5006238	0.0000	58.446	0.001357	10
15	0.011811	85076	1005	423065	0.002375	2.6951	4579346	0.0000	53.826	0.002375	15
20	0.018088	84071	1521	416629	0.003650	2.5484	4156281	0.0000	49.438	0.003650	20
25	0.016454	82551	1358	409324	0.003318	2.4751	3739652	0.0402	45.301	0.003321	25
30	0.016726	81192	1358	402569	0.003373	2.5018	3330328	0.0270	41.018	0.003373	30
35	0.017161	79834	1370	395836	0.003461	2.5651	2927759	0.0000	36.673	0.003461	35
40	0.022764	78464	1786	388083	0.004603	2.6269	2531923	0.0076	32.268	0.004598	40
45	0.032054	76678	2458	377628	0.006509	2.6554	2143840	0.0290	27.959	0.006477	45
50	0.048773	74220	3620	362630	0.009982	2.6596	1766212	0.0465	23.797	0.009899	50
55	0.074095	70600	5231	340738	0.015352	2.6556	1403582	0.0325	19.881	0.015258	55
60	0.115141	65369	7527	309250	0.024339	2.6621	1062844	0.0245	16.259	0.024210	60
65	0.191659	57843	11086	262382	0.042252	2.5798	753595	0.0245	13.028	0.042083	65
70	0.251760	46757	11772	204293	0.057622	2.4949	491212	0.0245	10.506	0.057464	70
75	0.308663	34985	10798	147740	0.073091	2.4826	286919	0.0245	8.201	0.072844	75
80	0.449510	24186	10872	94276	0.115321	2.5482	139179	0.0245	5.754	0.114545	80
85+	*1.000000	13314	13314	44903	0.296510	3.3726	44903	0.0245	3.373	0.293513	85-

TABLE 3 — FEMALE LIFE TABLE

x	nq_x	l_x	nd_x	nL_x	nm_x	na_x	T_x	r_x	$\mathring{e}_x$	nM_x	x
0	0.087507	100000	8751	94053	0.093040	0.3204	6271644	0.0027	62.716	0.093223	0
1	0.033738	91249	3079	356300	0.008640	1.1749	6177591	0.0027	67.700	0.008658	1
5	0.007721	88171	681	439152	0.001550	2.5000	5821291	0.0199	66.023	0.001575	5
10	0.006329	87490	554	436137	0.001270	2.6280	5382139	0.0000	61.517	0.001270	10
15	0.011745	86936	1021	432303	0.002362	2.6703	4946002	0.0000	56.892	0.002362	15
20	0.016160	85915	1388	426147	0.003258	2.5298	4513699	0.0000	52.537	0.003258	20
25	0.014427	84527	1219	419547	0.002907	2.4684	4087553	0.0370	48.358	0.002909	25
30	0.014443	83307	1203	413521	0.002910	2.4934	3668006	0.0276	44.030	0.002910	30
35	0.014391	82104	1182	407622	0.002899	2.5464	3254485	0.0000	39.638	0.002899	35
40	0.018118	80923	1466	401094	0.003655	2.5998	2846863	0.0101	35.180	0.003651	40
45	0.023714	79456	1884	392814	0.004797	2.6284	2445769	0.0283	30.781	0.004778	45
50	0.033867	77572	2627	381717	0.006882	2.6613	2052956	0.0409	26.465	0.006833	50
55	0.052278	74945	3918	365806	0.010711	2.7235	1671238	0.0264	22.299	0.010640	55
60	0.096174	71027	6831	339312	0.020132	2.6835	1305432	0.0320	18.379	0.019986	60
65	0.154760	64196	9935	297125	0.033437	2.5988	966120	0.0320	15.050	0.033259	65
70	0.212701	54261	11541	242678	0.047558	2.5196	668996	0.0320	12.329	0.047383	70
75	0.257966	42720	11020	185931	0.059270	2.4894	426317	0.0320	9.979	0.059057	75
80	0.346379	31700	10980	133068	0.082514	2.6840	240386	0.0320	7.583	0.081708	80
85+	*1.000000	20719	20719	107318	0.193067	5.1796	107318	0.0320	5.180	0.190523	85-

TABLE 4 — OBSERVED AND PROJECTED VITAL RATES

	OBSERVED POPULATION BOTH SEXES	MALES	FEMALES	PROJECTED POPULATION 1956 MALES	FEMALES	1961 MALES	FEMALES	1966 MALES	FEMALES	STABLE POPULATION MALES	FEMALES
RATES PER THOUSAND											
Birth	22.39	23.11	21.67	22.18	20.80	20.37	19.13	19.41	18.25	18.54	17.44
Death	10.79	11.40	10.17	11.66	10.79	11.97	11.11	12.40	11.46	16.14	15.04
Increase	11.61	11.71	11.50	10.52	10.01	8.40	8.02	7.01	6.79		2.4010
PERCENTAGE											
under 15	26.73	27.24	26.21	27.39	26.30	27.32	26.20	25.83	24.79	23.65	22.7
15-64	66.57	66.82	66.32	66.32	65.62	66.18	65.49	66.84	66.13	64.65	63.2
65 and over	6.70	5.94	7.47	6.29	8.08	6.50	8.31	7.33	9.08	11.70	14.0
DEP. RATIO X 100	50.21	49.66	50.78	50.78	52.39	51.10	52.71	49.62	51.22	54.67	58.1

TABLE 5 — POPULATION PROJECTED WITH FIXED AGE—SPECIFIC BIRTH AND DEATH RATES (IN 1000's)

AGE AT LAST BIRTHDAY	1956 BOTH SEXES	1956 MALES	1956 FEMALES	1961 BOTH SEXES	1961 MALES	1961 FEMALES	1966 BOTH SEXES	1966 MALES	1966 FEMALES	AGE AT LAST BIRTHDAY
0-4	732	374	358	724	370	354	706	361	345	0-4
5-9	726	371	355	714	365	349	705	360	345	5-9
10-14	609	310	299	721	368	353	709	362	347	10-14
15-19	584	297	287	603	307	296	715	365	350	15-19
20-24	667	340	327	575	293	282	594	302	292	20-24
25-29	671	340	331	656	334	322	565	287	278	25-29
30-34	683	343	340	662	335	327	647	329	318	30-34
35-39	443	220	223	673	337	336	651	329	322	35-39
40-44	503	252	251	435	216	219	661	331	330	40-44
45-49	503	254	249	491	246	245	424	210	214	45-49
50-54	435	219	216	486	244	242	474	236	238	50-54
55-59	347	172	175	412	205	207	461	229	232	55-59
60-64	244	117	127	318	156	162	378	186	192	60-64
65-69	204	95	109	210	99	111	274	132	142	65-69
70-74	149	67	82	163	74	89	168	77	91	70-74
75-79	102	44	58	111	48	63	122	54	68	75-79
80-84	62	25	37	70	28	42	76	31	45	80-84
85+	35	10	25	42	12	30	48	14	34	85+
TOTAL	7699	3850	3849	8066	4037	4029	8378	4195	4183	TOTAL

TABLE 6 — STANDARDIZED RATES

STANDARD COUNTRIES: STANDARDIZED RATES PER THOUSAND	ENGLAND AND WALES 1961 BOTH SEXES	MALES	FEMALES	UNITED STATES 1960 BOTH SEXES	MALES	FEMALES	MEXICO 1960 BOTH SEXES	MALES	FEMALES
Birth	16.64	18.94*	15.60	16.93	17.44*	16.14	20.31	17.61*	19.60
Death	14.22	16.77*	14.20	12.84	14.34*	11.93	9.62	10.60*	8.72
Increase	2.42	2.18*	1.40	4.09	3.10*	4.20	10.69	7.01*	10.88

TABLE 7 — MOMENTS AND CUMULANTS

	OBSERVED POP. MALES	OBSERVED POP. FEMALES	STATIONARY POP. MALES	STATIONARY POP. FEMALES	STABLE POP. MALES	STABLE POP. FEMALES	OBSERVED BIRTHS	NET MATERNITY FUNCTION	BIRTHS IN STABLE POP.
μ	29.94903	31.06824	36.35464	37.89948	35.14323	36.59379	26.10963	26.67423	26.58331
σ^2	399.5402	428.6777	508.1377	547.5903	500.7230	539.7568	32.20149	35.98502	35.58955
κ_3	4071.476	4454.996	2795.858	2914.069	3373.683	3603.184	169.7054	165.0942	164.3193
κ_4	-84460.	-105192.	-248896.	-296594.	-231910.	-276754.	812.216	313.881	341.893
β_1	0.259910	0.251943	0.059578	0.051717	0.090660	0.082562	0.862509	0.584923	0.598976
β_2	2.470912	2.427571	2.036047	2.010876	2.075036	2.050058	3.783285	3.242394	3.269926
κ	-0.116233	-0.109019	-0.022512	-0.019290	-0.034268	-0.030822	-0.774612	-0.400085	-0.415047

TABLE 8 — RATES FROM AGE DISTRIBUTIONS AND VITAL STATISTICS (Females)

VITAL STATISTICS		THOMPSON AGE RANGE	NRR	1000r	INTERVAL	BOURGEOIS-PICHAT AGE RANGE	NRR	1000b	1000d	1000r	COALE
GRR	1.267										IBR
NRR	1.066	0-4	1.16	5.36	27.30	5-29	0.75	16.88	27.74	-10.86	IDR
TFR	2.619	5-9	1.03	1.05	27.27	30-54	1.22	21.25	13.92	7.33	IRI
GENERATION	26.628	10-14	1.08	2.77	27.23	55-79	1.41	21.69	9.03	12.65	K1
SEX RATIO	106.702	15-19	1.42	12.41	27.16	* 5-29	0.75	16.88	27.74	-10.86	K2

TABLE 9 — LESLIE MATRIX AND ITS SPECTRAL COMPONENTS (Females)

Start Age Interval	ORIGINAL MATRIX SUB-DIAGONAL	ALTERNATIVE FIRST ROWS Projection	ALTERNATIVE FIRST ROWS Integral	FIRST STABLE MATRIX % IN STABLE POPULATION	FISHER VALUES	REPRODUCTIVE VALUES	SECOND STABLE MATRIX Z_2 FIRST COLUMN	FIRST ROW
0	0.97513	0.00000	0.00000	7.806	1.117	406878	0.1857+0.0924	0.1857+0.0924
5	0.99313	0.00000	0.00000	7.521	1.159	348820	0.1964-0.1671	-0.0096+0.1666
10	0.99121	0.05884	0.00000	7.380	1.181	341454	-0.0968-0.3117	-0.1240+0.0448
15	0.98576	0.25687	0.11943	7.228	1.140	378378	-0.4102-0.0424	-0.0822-0.0818
20	0.98451	0.35408	0.40314	7.040	0.879	296056	-0.2516+0.4529	-0.0143-0.1098
25	0.98564	0.24795	0.31414	6.848	0.502	173491	0.3984+0.5137	0.0092-0.0781
30	0.98573	0.13597	0.18743	6.669	0.235	53003	0.7903-0.2065	0.0133-0.0409
35	0.98399	0.05800	0.08740	6.495	0.087	22140	0.1518-1.0150	0.0085-0.0158
40	0.97936	0.01811	0.02978	6.315	0.024	6006	-1.0956-0.6755	0.0033-0.0042
45	0.97175	0.00338	0.00680	6.111	0.004	830	-1.3130+0.9260	0.0007-0.0006
50	0.95832	0.00001	0.00001	5.867	0.000	1	0.4152+1.9463	0.0000-0.0000
55+	0.78462			24.720				

TABLE 10 — AGE ANALYSIS AND MISCELLANEOUS RESULTS (Females)

Start Age Interval	OBSERVED POPUL. (IN 100's)	CONTRIBUTIONS OF ROOTS (IN 100's) r_1	r_2, r_3	r_4-r_{11}	AGE-SP. BIRTH RATES	NET MATERNITY FUNCTION	COEFF. OF MATRIX EQUATION	PARAMETERS	INTEGRAL	MATRIX	EXP. INCREASE x	$e^{(x+2\frac{1}{2})r}$
0	3643	3416	124	104	0.0000	0.0000	0.0000	L(1)	1.01208	1.01208	0	1.0060
5	3009	3291	-141	-141	0.0000	0.0000	0.0000	L(2)	0.29423	0.30845	50	1.1343
10	2890	3229	-335	-4	0.0000	0.0000	0.0570		0.75096	0.72137	55	1.1480
15	3319	3163	-107	264	0.0264	0.1140	0.2466	R(1)	0.00240	0.00240	60	1.1619
20	3367	3080	426	-140	0.0890	0.3792	0.3350	R(2)	-0.04300	-0.04853	65	1.1759
25	3454	2997	590	-132	0.0693	0.2909	0.2310		0.23948	0.23335	70	1.1901
30	2258	2918	-90	-571	0.0414	0.1711	0.1249	C(1)		43758	75	1.2045
35	2546	2842	-1019	723	0.0193	0.0786	0.0525	C(2)		7755	80	1.2191
40	2544	2763	-864	645	0.0066	0.0264	0.0161			-51369	85	1.2338
45	2219	2674	748	-1203	0.0015	0.0059	0.0030	2P/Y	26.2372	26.9262	90	1.2487
50	1825	2567	2064	-2806	0.0000	0.0000	0.0000	DELTA	11.4043		95	1.2638
55+	5337	10817									100	1.2790

TABLE 1 — DATA

AGE AT LAST BIRTHDAY	POPULATION BOTH SEXES	MALES Number	MALES %	FEMALES Number	FEMALES %	BIRTHS BY AGE OF MOTHER	DEATHS BOTH SEXES	DEATHS MALES	DEATHS FEMALES	AGE AT LAST BIRTHDAY
0	142236	73074	2.0	69162	1.9	0	12599	7075	5524	0
1-4	575784	294716	7.9	281068	7.5	0	3263	1654	1609	1-4
5-9	671513	342003	9.2	329510	8.8	0	702	395	307	5-9
10-14	587153	298629	8.0	288524	7.7	0	519	301	218	10-14
15-19	610087	310758	8.3	299329	8.0	17800	858	486	372	15-19
20-24	678392	345838	9.3	332554	8.9	57797	1237	692	545	20-24
25-29	691705	351401	9.4	340304	9.1	44421	1327	706	621	25-29
30-34	639321	317080	8.5	322241	8.6	21264	1277	698	579	30-34
35-39	406281	202532	5.4	203749	5.5	6776	987	548	439	35-39
40-44	510434	257499	6.9	252935	6.8	2811	1650	937	713	40-44
45-49	486896	245726	6.6	241170	6.5	498	2278	1314	964	45-49
50-54	407979	204365	5.5	203614	5.5	0	2941	1755	1186	50-54
55-59	310534	153716	4.1	156818	4.2	0	3599	2118	1481	55-59
60-64	231191	108497	2.9	122694	3.3	0	4264	2281	1983	60-64
65-69	188323	86602	2.3	101721	2.7	0	6797	3426	3371	65-69
70-74	144482	64702	1.7	79780	2.1		7624	3854	3770	70-74
75-79	100549	43504	1.2	57045	1.5		6510	3085	3425	75-79
80-84	59218	24515	0.7	34703	0.9	78044 M.	4840	2363	2477	80-84
85+	25447	9971	0.3	15476	0.4	73323 F.	4863	2370	2493	85+
TOTAL	7467525	3735128		3732397		151367	68135	36058	32077	TOTAL

TABLE 2 — MALE LIFE TABLE

x	nq_x	l_x	nd_x	nL_x	nm_x	na_x	T_x	r_x	$\mathring{e}_x$	nM_x	x
0	0.090427	100000	9043	93397	0.096820	0.2698	6268486	0.0000	62.685	0.096820	
1	0.022092	90957	2009	358040	0.005612	1.1188	6175089	0.0000	67.890	0.005612	
5	0.005686	88948	506	443475	0.001141	2.5000	5817049	0.0185	65.398	0.001155	
10	0.005031	88442	445	441136	0.001009	2.5842	5373574	0.0084	60.758	0.001008	10
15	0.007791	87997	686	438360	0.001564	2.6289	4932438	0.0000	56.052	0.001564	15
20	0.009956	87312	869	434422	0.002001	2.5428	4494078	0.0000	51.472	0.002001	20
25	0.009997	86442	864	430066	0.002009	2.5171	4059655	0.0066	46.964	0.002009	25
30	0.010986	85578	940	425598	0.002209	2.5611	3629589	0.0528	42.413	0.002201	30
35	0.013468	84638	1140	420458	0.002711	2.6035	3203991	0.0180	37.855	0.002706	35
40	0.018040	83498	1506	413940	0.003639	2.6428	2783533	0.0000	33.336	0.003639	40
45	0.026497	81992	2173	404920	0.005365	2.6802	2369593	0.0175	28.900	0.005347	45
50	0.042418	79819	3386	391252	0.008654	2.6829	1964673	0.0379	24.614	0.008588	50
55	0.067324	76434	5146	370096	0.013904	2.6541	1573422	0.0492	20.585	0.013779	55
60	0.100889	71288	7192	339812	0.021165	2.6882	1203325	0.0284	16.880	0.021024	60
65	0.181667	64096	11644	292710	0.039780	2.6153	863513	0.0284	13.472	0.039560	65
70	0.259989	52452	13637	228173	0.059765	2.5006	570803	0.0284	10.882	0.059565	70
75	0.300922	38815	11680	164258	0.071109	2.4473	342629	0.0284	8.827	0.070913	75
80	0.393670	27135	10682	109962	0.097143	2.5931	178372	0.0284	6.574	0.096391	80
85+	*1.000000	16452	16452	68410	0.240498	4.1580	68410	0.0284	4.158	0.237689	85

TABLE 3 — FEMALE LIFE TABLE

x	nq_x	l_x	nd_x	nL_x	nm_x	na_x	T_x	r_x	$\mathring{e}_x$	nM_x	x
0	0.075604	100000	7560	94659	0.079870	0.2935	6656495	0.0000	66.565	0.079870	
1	0.022530	92440	2083	363807	0.005725	1.1423	6561837	0.0000	70.985	0.005725	
5	0.004575	90357	413	450751	0.000917	2.5000	6198030	0.0173	68.595	0.000932	
10	0.003774	89944	339	448899	0.000756	2.5870	5747279	0.0087	63.899	0.000756	10
15	0.006196	89604	555	446713	0.001243	2.6654	5298381	0.0000	59.131	0.001243	15
20	0.008162	89049	727	443479	0.001639	2.5708	4851667	0.0000	54.483	0.001639	20
25	0.009083	88322	802	439617	0.001825	2.5149	4408188	0.0014	49.910	0.001825	25
30	0.008961	87520	784	435666	0.001800	2.5344	3968571	0.0494	45.345	0.001797	30
35	0.010740	86736	932	431436	0.002159	2.5933	3532906	0.0220	40.732	0.002155	35
40	0.014001	85804	1201	426173	0.002819	2.6297	3101470	0.0000	36.146	0.002819	40
45	0.019854	84603	1680	419064	0.004008	2.5486	2675297	0.0176	31.622	0.003997	45
50	0.028939	82923	2400	409048	0.005866	2.6802	2256234	0.0369	27.209	0.005825	50
55	0.046630	80523	3755	393987	0.009530	2.7017	1847186	0.0407	22.940	0.009444	55
60	0.078602	76769	6034	370251	0.016297	2.7475	1453199	0.0291	18.930	0.016162	60
65	0.154419	70734	10923	327752	0.033326	2.6270	1082949	0.0291	15.310	0.033140	65
70	0.212171	59812	12690	267620	0.047419	2.5227	755197	0.0291	12.626	0.047255	70
75	0.261093	47121	12303	204399	0.060192	2.4634	487577	0.0291	10.347	0.060040	75
80	0.302376	34818	10528	147125	0.071559	2.7372	283178	0.0291	8.133	0.071377	80
85+	1.000000	24290	24290	136053	0.178534	5.6012	136053	0.0291	5.601	0.161088	85

TABLE 4 — OBSERVED AND PROJECTED VITAL RATES

	OBSERVED POPULATION BOTH SEXES	MALES	FEMALES	PROJECTED POPULATION 1959 MALES	FEMALES	1964 MALES	FEMALES	1969 MALES	FEMALES	STABLE POPULATION MALES	FEMALES
RATES PER THOUSAND											
Birth	20.27	20.89	19.65	19.32	18.17	18.10	17.05	17.94	16.92	16.31	15.38
Death	9.12	9.65	8.59	10.07	9.29	10.53	9.69	11.13	10.17	15.71	14.77
Increase	11.15	11.24	11.05	9.25	8.88	7.57	7.36	6.81	6.74		0.6030
PERCENTAGE											
under 15	26.47	27.00	25.94	26.68	25.56	25.36	24.26	23.83	22.84	21.70	20.79
15-64	66.59	66.86	66.32	66.91	66.15	67.51	66.83	67.89	67.16	64.83	63.30
65 and over	6.94	6.14	7.74	6.41	8.29	7.13	8.91	8.29	10.01	13.47	15.91
DEP. RATIO X 100	50.17	49.56	50.78	49.45	51.17	48.13	49.64	47.30	48.90	54.24	57.98

TABLE 1 — DATA

AGE AT LAST BIRTHDAY	POPULATION BOTH SEXES	MALES Number	%	FEMALES Number	%	BIRTHS BY AGE OF MOTHER	DEATHS BOTH SEXES	MALES	FEMALES	AGE AT LAST BIRTHDAY
0	137282	70139	1.8	67143	1.8	0	9073	5084	3989	0
1-4	541700	276566	7.2	265134	6.9	0	2558	1321	1237	1-4
5-9	713814	363775	9.5	350039	9.1	0	589	333	256	5-9
10-14	634056	322250	8.4	311806	8.1	40	395	228	167	10-14
15-19	570977	288615	7.6	282362	7.4	17733	576	347	229	15-19
20-24	641127	320729	8.4	320398	8.4	57370	842	507	335	20-24
25-29	651652	328330	8.6	323322	8.4	39345	964	555	409	25-29
30-34	674826	338397	8.9	336429	8.8	19149	1105	635	470	30-34
35-39	504258	252519	6.6	251739	6.6	6540	1062	592	470	35-39
40-44	449368	226176	5.9	223192	5.8	1862	1319	740	579	40-44
45-49	503708	255786	6.7	247922	6.5	358	2150	1247	903	45-49
50-54	448934	227456	6.0	221478	5.8	16	3004	1790	1214	50-54
55-59	355477	174419	4.6	181058	4.7	0	3936	2353	1583	55-59
60-64	267342	126588	3.3	140754	3.7	0	4914	2779	2135	60-64
65-69	209086	91282	2.4	117804	3.1	0	6369	3199	3170	65-69
70-74	174262	77823	2.0	96439	2.5		8833	4279	4554	70-74
75-79	101355	45369	1.2	55986	1.5		7819	3734	4085	75-79
80-84	43341	19091	0.5	24250	0.6	73188 M.	5323	2465	2858	80-84
85+	28688	12874	0.3	15814	0.4	69225 F.	5067	2393	2674	85+
TOTAL	7651253	3818184		3833069		142413	65898	34581	31317	TOTAL

TABLE 2 — MALE LIFE TABLE

x	nq_x	l_x	nd_x	nL_x	nm_x	na_x	T_x	r_x	$\overset{\circ}{e}_x$	nM_x	x
0	0.068912	100000	6891	95072	0.072485	0.2848	6511260	0.0000	65.113	0.072485	0
1	0.018848	93109	1755	367404	0.004776	1.1332	6416189	0.0000	68.911	0.004776	1
5	0.004548	91354	415	455731	0.000912	2.5000	6048785	0.0054	66.213	0.000915	5
10	0.003538	90938	322	453914	0.000709	2.5827	5593054	0.0223	61.504	0.000708	10
15	0.005995	90617	543	451806	0.001202	2.6486	5139139	0.0000	56.713	0.001202	15
20	0.007874	90073	709	448638	0.001581	2.5614	4687333	0.0000	52.039	0.001581	20
25	0.008417	89364	752	444966	0.001690	2.5332	4238696	0.0000	47.432	0.001690	25
30	0.009356	88612	829	441045	0.001880	2.5693	3793730	0.0243	42.813	0.001876	30
35	0.011711	87783	1028	436466	0.002355	2.6174	3352685	0.0379	38.193	0.002344	35
40	0.016234	86755	1408	430468	0.003272	2.6522	2916219	0.0000	33.614	0.003272	40
45	0.024104	85347	2057	421972	0.004875	2.6855	2485750	0.0000	29.125	0.004875	45
50	0.038908	83289	3241	409018	0.007923	2.7074	2063779	0.0299	24.778	0.007870	50
55	0.066007	80049	5284	387995	0.013618	2.6818	1654761	0.0445	20.672	0.013490	55
60	0.105022	74765	7852	355361	0.022096	2.6485	1266766	0.0331	16.943	0.021953	60
65	0.162603	66913	10880	308572	0.035260	2.6109	911405	0.0331	13.621	0.035045	65
70	0.243542	56033	13646	246809	0.055291	2.5558	602833	0.0331	10.759	0.054984	70
75	0.342877	42386	14533	175600	0.082764	2.5001	356024	0.0331	8.399	0.082303	75
80	0.490156	27853	13652	105065	0.129942	2.4949	180424	0.0331	6.478	0.129118	80
85+	*1.000000	14201	14201	75359	0.188441	5.3067	75359	0.0331	5.307	0.185879	85+

TABLE 3 — FEMALE LIFE TABLE

x	nq_x	l_x	nd_x	nL_x	nm_x	na_x	T_x	r_x	$\overset{\circ}{e}_x$	nM_x	x
0	0.057053	100000	5705	96032	0.059411	0.3045	6868174	0.0000	68.682	0.059411	0
1	0.018418	94295	1737	372238	0.004666	1.1548	6772142	0.0000	71.819	0.004666	1
5	0.003634	92558	336	461949	0.000728	2.5000	6399905	0.0047	69.145	0.000731	5
10	0.002676	92222	247	460499	0.000536	2.5303	5937955	0.0208	64.388	0.000536	10
15	0.004047	91975	372	458992	0.000811	2.6292	5477457	0.0000	59.554	0.000811	15
20	0.005215	91603	478	456861	0.001046	2.5882	5018465	0.0000	54.785	0.001046	20
25	0.006305	91125	575	454220	0.001265	2.5559	4561604	0.0000	50.059	0.001265	25
30	0.006977	90550	632	451228	0.001400	2.5875	4107384	0.0236	45.360	0.001397	30
35	0.009342	89919	840	447601	0.001877	2.6281	3656156	0.0391	40.661	0.001867	35
40	0.012892	89079	1148	442678	0.002594	2.6357	3208556	0.0000	36.019	0.002594	40
45	0.018057	87930	1588	435932	0.003642	2.6574	2765878	0.0000	31.455	0.003642	45
50	0.027196	86342	2348	426267	0.005509	2.6811	2329946	0.0257	26.985	0.005481	50
55	0.043200	83994	3629	411649	0.008815	2.7063	1903679	0.0360	22.664	0.008743	55
60	0.073927	80366	5941	388199	0.015304	2.7059	1492031	0.0372	18.566	0.015168	60
65	0.127653	74425	9501	350020	0.027143	2.6735	1103832	0.0372	14.832	0.026909	65
70	0.213403	64924	13855	291311	0.047561	2.5958	753811	0.0372	11.611	0.047222	70
75	0.310835	51069	15874	216108	0.073454	2.5282	462501	0.0372	9.056	0.072965	75
80	0.454785	35195	16006	134958	0.118601	2.5431	246393	0.0372	7.001	0.117856	80
85+	1.000000	19189	19189	111435	0.172198	5.8073	111435	0.0372	5.807	0.169091	85+

TABLE 4 — OBSERVED AND PROJECTED VITAL RATES

	OBSERVED POPULATION BOTH SEXES	MALES	FEMALES	PROJECTED POPULATION 1962 MALES	FEMALES	1967 MALES	FEMALES	1972 MALES	FEMALES	STABLE POPULATION MALES	FEMALES
RATES PER THOUSAND											
Birth	18.61	19.17	18.06	17.75	16.74	17.41	16.43	17.57	16.60	15.56	14.76
Death	8.61	9.06	8.17	9.57	8.85	10.30	9.61	10.99	10.29	15.21	14.40
Increase	10.00	10.11	9.89	8.18	7.89	7.11	6.82	6.58	6.31	0.3592	
PERCENTAGE											
under 15	26.49	27.05	25.94	25.95	24.84	24.07	23.04	23.15	22.17	21.30	20.48
15-64	66.23	66.50	65.97	67.06	66.39	67.96	67.21	67.55	66.89	64.89	63.66
65 and over	7.28	6.45	8.10	6.98	8.77	7.97	9.75	9.30	10.94	13.81	15.86
DEP. RATIO X 100	50.98	50.38	51.59	49.12	50.63	47.15	48.78	48.05	49.49	54.11	57.08

TABLE 1 — DATA

AGE AT LAST BIRTHDAY	POPULATION BOTH SEXES	MALES Number	MALES %	FEMALES Number	FEMALES %	BIRTHS BY AGE OF MOTHER	DEATHS BOTH SEXES	DEATHS MALES	DEATHS FEMALES	AGE AT LAST BIRTHDAY
0	133811	68746	1.8	65065	1.7	0	6396	3545	2851	0
1-4	525684	268544	6.8	257140	6.5	0	1553	810	743	1-4
5-9	688407	351119	8.9	337288	8.6	0	470	271	199	5-9
10-14	702999	357669	9.1	345330	8.8	129	416	257	159	10-14
15-19	590813	299928	7.6	290885	7.4	21189	533	351	182	15-19
20-24	579338	290778	7.4	288560	7.3	53469	668	405	263	20-24
25-29	656626	329610	8.4	327016	8.3	38584	869	509	360	25-29
30-34	662879	333775	8.5	329104	8.4	16856	1063	641	422	30-34
35-39	649564	324290	8.3	325274	8.3	6433	1313	745	568	35-39
40-44	394158	196952	5.0	197206	5.0	1340	1137	637	500	40-44
45-49	506050	256138	6.5	249912	6.3	240	2054	1195	859	45-49
50-54	479792	242349	6.2	237443	6.0	37	3206	1927	1279	50-54
55-59	400446	200101	5.1	200345	5.1	0	4329	2623	1706	55-59
60-64	305960	146332	3.7	159628	4.1	0	5701	3295	2406	60-64
65-69	213805	96799	2.5	117006	3.0	0	6419	3407	3012	65-69
70-74	175873	75303	1.9	100570	2.6		9197	4357	4840	70-74
75-79	119143	53540	1.4	65603	1.7		9550	4495	5055	75-79
80-84	53356	22908	0.6	30448	0.8	71089 M.	6524	2969	3555	80-84
85+	28670	12675	0.3	15995	0.4	67188 F.	5296	2489	2807	85+
TOTAL	7867374	3927556		3939818		138277	66694	34928	31766	TOTAL

TABLE 2 — MALE LIFE TABLE

x	$_nq_x$	l_x	$_nd_x$	$_nL_x$	$_nm_x$	$_na_x$	T_x	r_x	$\mathring{e}_x$	$_nM_x$
0	0.049700	100000	4970	96387	0.051563	0.2730	6690067	0.0001	66.901	0.051567
1	0.011960	95030	1137	376849	0.003016	1.1217	6593680	0.0001	69.385	0.003016
5	0.003852	93893	362	468563	0.000772	2.5000	6216832	0.0000	66.212	0.000772
10	0.003593	93532	336	466857	0.000720	2.6137	5748269	0.0149	61.458	0.000719
15	0.005849	93196	545	464680	0.001173	2.6173	5281412	0.0196	56.670	0.001170
20	0.006940	92651	643	461680	0.001393	2.5527	4816732	0.0000	51.988	0.001393
25	0.007692	92008	708	458317	0.001544	2.5676	4355052	0.0000	47.334	0.001544
30	0.009558	91300	873	454387	0.001920	2.5791	3896736	0.0000	42.681	0.001920
35	0.011492	90427	1039	449656	0.002311	2.6135	3442349	0.0503	38.068	0.002297
40	0.016098	89388	1439	443549	0.003244	2.6434	2992693	0.0203	33.480	0.003234
45	0.023079	87949	2030	435072	0.004665	2.6978	2549144	0.0000	28.984	0.004665
50	0.039182	85919	3366	421860	0.007980	2.7020	2114071	0.0164	24.605	0.007951
55	0.064126	82553	5294	400560	0.013216	2.6947	1692211	0.0365	20.499	0.013108
60	0.107594	77259	8313	366757	0.022665	2.6496	1291651	0.0332	16.718	0.022517
65	0.163335	68946	11261	317907	0.035423	2.6180	924894	0.0332	13.415	0.035197
70	0.254662	57685	14690	252472	0.058185	2.5526	606987	0.0332	10.522	0.057860
75	0.348174	42995	14970	177358	0.084404	2.4872	354515	0.0332	8.246	0.083956
80	0.491334	28025	13770	105553	0.130454	2.4892	177157	0.0332	6.321	0.129605
85+	*1.000000	14255	14255	71604	0.199087	5.0229	71604	0.0332	5.023	0.196371

TABLE 3 — FEMALE LIFE TABLE

x	$_nq_x$	l_x	$_nd_x$	$_nL_x$	$_nm_x$	$_na_x$	T_x	r_x	$\mathring{e}_x$	$_nM_x$
0	0.042489	100000	4249	96968	0.043818	0.2864	7044015	0.0000	70.440	0.043818
1	0.011463	95751	1098	379860	0.002889	1.1348	6947047	0.0000	72.553	0.002889
5	0.002946	94653	279	472570	0.000590	2.5000	6567188	0.0000	69.381	0.000590
10	0.002300	94375	217	471334	0.000461	2.5154	6094617	0.0143	64.579	0.000460
15	0.003132	94158	295	470094	0.000627	2.6482	5623283	0.0173	59.722	0.000626
20	0.004547	93863	427	468292	0.000911	2.6064	5153189	0.0000	54.901	0.000911
25	0.005490	93436	513	465932	0.001101	2.5679	4684897	0.0000	50.140	0.001101
30	0.006392	92923	594	463192	0.001282	2.6038	4218965	0.0000	45.403	0.001282
35	0.008759	92329	809	459741	0.001759	2.6451	3755774	0.0494	40.678	0.001746
40	0.012642	91520	1157	454861	0.002544	2.6318	3296033	0.0238	36.014	0.002535
45	0.017049	90363	1541	448217	0.003437	2.6641	2841172	0.0000	31.442	0.003437
50	0.026686	88823	2370	438624	0.005404	2.6841	2392954	0.0165	26.941	0.005387
55	0.042054	86452	3636	423944	0.008576	2.7124	1954331	0.0305	22.606	0.008515
60	0.073372	82817	6076	400092	0.015188	2.6975	1530386	0.0330	18.479	0.015073
65	0.122423	76740	9395	361995	0.025953	2.6895	1130295	0.0330	14.729	0.025742
70	0.217140	67345	14623	301780	0.048457	2.6102	768300	0.0330	11.408	0.048126
75	0.324952	52722	17132	221072	0.077496	2.5171	466519	0.0330	8.849	0.077054
80	0.450302	35590	16026	136578	0.117341	2.5316	245447	0.0330	6.897	0.116756
85+	1.000000	19564	19564	108869	0.179699	5.5649	108869	0.0330	5.565	0.175493

TABLE 4 — OBSERVED AND PROJECTED VITAL RATES

	OBSERVED POPULATION BOTH SEXES	OBSERVED MALES	OBSERVED FEMALES	PROJECTED 1965 MALES	1965 FEMALES	1970 MALES	1970 FEMALES	1975 MALES	1975 FEMALES	STABLE MALES	STABLE FEMALES
RATES PER THOUSAND											
Birth	17.58	18.10	17.05	17.35	16.36	17.59	16.60	17.30	16.34	15.68	14.9
Death	8.48	8.89	8.06	9.54	8.86	10.27	9.54	10.87	10.12	14.39	13.6
Increase	9.10	9.21	8.99	7.81	7.50	7.32	7.06	6.43	6.22		1.290
PERCENTAGE											
under 15	26.07	26.63	25.50	24.89	23.76	23.75	22.63	23.41	22.30	21.87	20.9
15-64	66.42	66.71	66.13	67.69	66.98	67.64	67.03	66.76	66.19	64.95	63.7
65 and over	7.51	6.65	8.37	7.42	9.26	8.61	10.34	9.83	11.50	13.18	15.3
DEP. RATIO X 100	50.55	49.89	51.22	47.73	49.29	47.83	49.18	49.79	51.08	53.97	56.9

AGE AT LAST BIRTHDAY	1965 BOTH SEXES	1965 MALES	1965 FEMALES	1970 BOTH SEXES	1970 MALES	1970 FEMALES	1975 BOTH SEXES	1975 MALES	1975 FEMALES	AGE AT LAST BIRTHDAY	
0-4	656	336	320	674	345	329	699	358	341	0-4	**TABLE 5**
5-9	653	334	319	651	333	318	668	342	326	5-9	
10-14	686	350	336	651	333	318	649	332	317	10-14	POPULATION
15-19	700	356	344	684	348	336	649	331	318	15-19	PROJECTED
20-24	588	298	290	697	354	343	680	346	334	20-24	WITH
25-29	576	289	287	584	296	288	692	351	341	25-29	FIXED
30-34	652	327	325	571	286	285	580	293	287	30-34	AGE—
35-39	657	330	327	646	323	323	566	283	283	35-39	SPECIFIC
40-44	642	320	322	649	326	323	638	319	319	40-44	BIRTH
45-49	387	193	194	631	314	317	638	320	318	45-49	AND
50-54	493	248	245	377	187	190	614	304	310	50-54	DEATH
55-59	459	230	229	472	236	236	362	178	184	55-59	RATES
60-64	372	183	189	428	211	217	439	216	223	60-64	(IN 1000's)
65-69	271	127	144	330	159	171	379	183	196	65-69	
70-74	175	77	98	221	101	120	269	126	143	70-74	
75-79	127	53	74	125	54	71	159	71	88	75-79	
80-84	73	32	41	77	31	46	76	32	44	80-84	
85+	40	16	24	54	22	32	57	21	36	85+	
TOTAL	8207	4099	4108	8522	4259	4263	8814	4406	4408	TOTAL	

STANDARD COUNTRIES:	ENGLAND AND WALES 1961 BOTH SEXES	MALES	FEMALES	UNITED STATES 1960 BOTH SEXES	MALES	FEMALES	MEXICO 1960 BOTH SEXES	MALES	FEMALES	
STANDARDIZED RATES PER THOUSAND										**TABLE 6**
Birth	14.46	15.18*	13.61	14.73	14.42*	14.10	18.64	13.81*	18.06	STANDARDIZED RATES
Death	11.79	11.54*	12.36	9.84	10.01*	9.41	5.90	7.93*	5.31	
Increase	2.66	3.64*	1.25	4.89	4.40*	4.70	12.74	5.88*	12.75	

	OBSERVED POP. MALES	FEMALES	STATIONARY POP. MALES	FEMALES	STABLE POP. MALES	FEMALES	OBSERVED BIRTHS	NET MATERNITY FUNCTION	BIRTHS IN STABLE POP.	
μ	31.79126	32.87444	37.27651	38.58128	36.61294	37.88337	25.28174	25.08804	25.04684	**TABLE 7**
σ^2	420.5341	444.3869	515.9112	542.3851	512.5333	539.2715	28.93813	29.94933	29.74628	MOMENTS
κ_3	3466.184	3623.326	2451.107	2220.700	2782.853	2603.658	125.1697	157.9241	156.7827	AND
κ_4	-125942.	-149772.	-260869.	-300522.	-253153.	-292830.	524.249	889.711	889.753	CUMULANTS
β_1	0.161547	0.149600	0.043752	0.030907	0.057519	0.043226	0.646527	0.928401	0.933895	
β_2	2.287856	2.241585	2.019896	1.978447	2.036306	1.993068	3.626031	3.991916	4.005551	
κ	-0.068258	-0.061373	-0.016581	-0.011464	-0.021785	-0.016026	-0.821491	-1.074084	-1.096292	

VITAL STATISTICS		THOMPSON AGE RANGE	NRR	1000r	INTERVAL	BOURGEOIS-PICHAT AGE RANGE	NRR	1000b	1000d	1000r	COALE	
GRR	1.106										IBR	**TABLE 8**
NRR	1.033	0-4	1.07	2.45	27.41	5-29	1.12	18.41	14.28	4.13	IDR	RATES FROM AGE DISTRIBUTIONS AND VITAL STATISTICS (Females)
TFR	2.277	5-9	1.15	5.04	27.38	30-54	1.53	28.63	12.99	15.64	IRI	
GENERATION	25.067	10-14	1.20	6.66	27.33	55-79	1.97	49.20	24.03	25.17	K1	
SEX RATIO	105.806	15-19	1.08	2.82	27.25	*15-39	0.80	13.56	21.77	-8.21	K2	

Start of Age Interval	ORIGINAL MATRIX SUB-DIAGONAL	ALTERNATIVE FIRST ROWS Projection	Integral	FIRST STABLE MATRIX % IN STABLE POPULATION	FISHER VALUES	REPRODUCTIVE VALUES	SECOND STABLE MATRIX Z₂ FIRST COLUMN	FIRST ROW	
0	0.99107	0.00000	0.00000	7.089	1.052	338951	0.2064+0.0744	0.2064+0.0744	**TABLE 9**
5	0.99738	0.00043	0.00000	6.980	1.068	360332	0.1687-0.2177	-0.0058+0.1747	LESLIE
10	0.99737	0.08460	0.00087	6.917	1.078	372129	-0.1960-0.2874	-0.1331+0.0382	MATRIX
15	0.99617	0.29822	0.16931	6.855	0.998	290365	-0.4216+0.1238	-0.0787-0.0973	AND ITS
20	0.99496	0.35065	0.43070	6.784	0.694	200151	-0.0152-0.5542	-0.0077-0.1054	SPECTRAL
25	0.99412	0.19567	0.27425	6.707	0.331	108211	0.6585+0.2333	0.0050-0.0578	COMPONENTS
30	0.99255	0.08207	0.11905	6.625	0.128	42114	0.5348-0.6983	0.0043-0.0250	(Females)
35	0.98939	0.03070	0.04597	6.533	0.043	13913	-0.6281-0.9099	0.0029-0.0091	
40	0.98539	0.00897	0.01579	6.422	0.011	2144	-1.3270+0.3976	0.0012-0.0023	
45	0.97860	0.00129	0.00223	6.287	0.002	383	-0.0379+1.7284	0.0002-0.0003	
50	0.96653	0.00018	0.00036	6.113	0.000	45	2.0236+0.7044	0.0000-0.0000	
55+	0.78507			26.688					

Start of Age Interval	OBSERVED POPUL. (IN 100's)	CONTRIBUTIONS OF ROOTS (IN 100's) r₁	r₂,r₃	r₄-r₁₁	AGE-SP. BIRTH RATES	NET MATERNITY FUNCTION	COEFF. OF MATRIX EQUATION	PARAMETERS	INTEGRAL	MATRIX	EXP. INCREASE x	e^(x+2½)r	
0	3222	3282	-45	-14	0.0000	0.0000	0.0000	L(1)	1.00647	1.00647	0	1.0032	**TABLE 10**
5	3373	3231	144	-3	0.0000	0.0000	0.0004	L(2)	0.22838	0.24316	50	1.0701	AGE
10	3453	3202	184	67	0.0002	0.0009	0.0836		0.78892	0.75122	55	1.0770	ANALYSIS
15	2909	3173	-87	-177	0.0354	0.1664	0.2940	R(1)	0.00129	0.00129	60	1.0840	AND
20	2886	3141	-361	106	0.0900	0.4216	0.3444	R(2)	-0.03937	-0.04725	65	1.0910	MISCELLANEOUS
25	3270	3105	-142	307	0.0573	0.2671	0.1912		0.25780	0.25155	70	1.0981	RESULTS
30	3291	3067	463	-238	0.0249	0.1153	0.0797	C(1)		46293	75	1.1052	(Females)
35	3253	3024	582	-354	0.0096	0.0442	0.0296	C(2)		779	80	1.1123	
40	1972	2973	-279	-721	0.0033	0.0150	0.0086			32526	85	1.1195	
45	2499	2911	-1125	713	0.0005	0.0021	0.0012	2P/Y	24.3721	24.9778	90	1.1268	
50	2374	2830	-427	-29	0.0001	0.0003	0.0002	DELTA	10.6878		95	1.1341	
55+	6896	12355									100	1.1414	

TABLE 1 — DATA

AGE AT LAST BIRTHDAY	POPULATION BOTH SEXES	MALES Number	MALES %	FEMALES Number	FEMALES %	BIRTHS BY AGE OF MOTHER	DEATHS BOTH SEXES	DEATHS MALES	FEMALES	AGE AT LAST BIRTHDAY
0	129432	66336	1.6	63096	1.6	0	4717	2648	2069	0
1-4	523778	268783	6.7	254995	6.3	0	1050	530	520	1-4
5-9	658471	336073	8.3	322398	8.0	0	426	232	194	5-9
10-14	714468	364055	9.0	350413	8.7	143	384	245	139	10-14
15-19	652076	331234	8.2	320842	7.9	21823	566	357	209	15-19
20-24	570523	288270	7.1	282253	7.0	51304	568	382	186	20-24
25-29	617053	308307	7.6	308746	7.6	35054	724	463	261	25-29
30-34	648228	325999	8.1	322229	8.0	16077	919	553	366	30-34
35-39	670645	336744	8.3	333901	8.3	6046	1241	754	487	35-39
40-44	568312	283649	7.0	284663	7.0	1536	1407	831	576	40-44
45-49	405674	203392	5.0	202282	5.0	127	1600	933	667	45-49
50-54	486071	245131	6.1	240940	6.0	33	2942	1796	1146	50-54
55-59	442530	222209	5.5	220321	5.4	0	4513	2699	1814	55-59
60-64	344661	167577	4.2	177084	4.4	0	5945	3428	2517	60-64
65-69	250428	116476	2.9	133952	3.3	0	7140	3859	3281	65-69
70-74	170256	72820	1.8	97436	2.4		8022	3769	4253	70-74
75-79	126981	54888	1.4	72093	1.8		10187	4596	5591	75-79
80-84	65112	28637	0.7	36475	0.9	57907 M.	7901	3592	4309	80-84
85+	33446	13962	0.3	19484	0.5	64236 F.	5805	2598	3207	85+
TOTAL	8078145	4034542		4043603		132143	66057	34265	31792	TOTAL

TABLE 2 — MALE LIFE TABLE

x	nq_x	l_x	nd_x	nL_x	nm_x	na_x	T_x	r_x	$\overset{\circ}{e}_x$	nM_x	x
0	0.038765	100000	3877	97113	0.039918	0.2552	6867459	0.0000	68.675	0.039918	0
1	0.007843	96123	754	382312	0.001972	1.1062	6770346	0.0000	70.434	0.001972	1
5	0.003446	95370	329	476026	0.000690	2.5000	6388034	0.0000	66.982	0.000690	5
10	0.003360	95041	319	474444	0.000673	2.6187	5912008	0.0007	62.205	0.000673	10
15	0.005390	94722	511	472395	0.001081	2.6237	5437563	0.0223	57.406	0.001078	15
20	0.006607	94211	622	469539	0.001326	2.5635	4965168	0.0059	52.703	0.001325	20
25	0.007481	93589	700	466227	0.001502	2.5483	4495630	0.0000	48.036	0.001502	25
30	0.008447	92888	785	462549	0.001696	2.5868	4029403	0.0000	43.379	0.001696	30
35	0.011151	92104	1027	458066	0.002242	2.6117	3566854	0.0117	38.726	0.002239	35
40	0.014662	91077	1335	452257	0.002953	2.6581	3108788	0.0473	34.134	0.002930	40
45	0.022739	89741	2041	443986	0.004596	2.6862	2656531	0.0098	29.602	0.004587	45
50	0.036025	87701	3159	431227	0.007327	2.6965	2212545	0.0000	25.228	0.007327	50
55	0.059395	84541	5021	411123	0.012214	2.6930	1781319	0.0252	21.070	0.012146	55
60	0.098225	79520	7811	379333	0.020591	2.6614	1370196	0.0320	17.231	0.020456	60
65	0.154383	71709	11071	332162	0.033329	2.6168	990863	0.0320	13.818	0.033131	65
70	0.231157	60638	14017	269223	0.052065	2.5765	658701	0.0320	10.863	0.051758	70
75	0.347913	46621	16220	192643	0.084199	2.5053	389478	0.0320	8.354	0.083734	75
80	0.474596	30401	14428	114478	0.126035	2.4964	196835	0.0320	6.475	0.125432	80
85+	1.000000	15973	15973	82357	0.193947	5.1560	82357	0.0320	5.156	0.186077	85+

TABLE 3 — FEMALE LIFE TABLE

x	nq_x	l_x	nd_x	nL_x	nm_x	na_x	T_x	r_x	$\overset{\circ}{e}_x$	nM_x	x
0	0.032036	100000	3204	97695	0.032791	0.2806	7218341	0.0000	72.183	0.032791	0
1	0.008110	96796	785	384932	0.002039	1.1290	7120645	0.0000	73.563	0.002039	1
5	0.003004	96011	288	479336	0.000602	2.5000	6735713	0.0000	70.155	0.000602	5
10	0.001981	95723	190	478146	0.000397	2.5250	6256377	0.0000	65.359	0.000397	10
15	0.003258	95533	311	476915	0.000653	2.5828	5778231	0.0210	60.484	0.000651	15
20	0.003290	95222	313	475346	0.000659	2.5593	5301317	0.0031	55.673	0.000659	20
25	0.004218	94909	400	473590	0.000845	2.6155	4825971	0.0000	50.848	0.000845	25
30	0.005664	94508	535	471263	0.001136	2.6104	4352381	0.0000	46.053	0.001136	30
35	0.007278	93973	684	468242	0.001461	2.6257	3881118	0.0109	41.300	0.001459	35
40	0.010161	93289	948	464250	0.002042	2.6825	3412876	0.0479	36.584	0.002023	40
45	0.016398	92341	1514	458169	0.003305	2.6636	2948626	0.0134	31.932	0.003297	45
50	0.023525	90827	2137	449229	0.004756	2.7035	2490457	0.0000	27.420	0.004756	50
55	0.040615	88691	3602	435230	0.008276	2.7174	2041228	0.0221	23.015	0.008233	55
60	0.069280	85088	5895	411879	0.014312	2.6992	1605998	0.0300	18.874	0.014214	60
65	0.116662	79193	9239	374543	0.024667	2.6811	1194119	0.0300	15.079	0.024494	65
70	0.199065	69955	13926	316853	0.043949	2.6360	819576	0.0300	11.716	0.043649	70
75	0.327169	56029	18328	234990	0.077996	2.5363	502724	0.0300	8.973	0.077553	75
80	0.454029	37701	17117	144246	0.118667	2.5275	267734	0.0300	7.102	0.118136	80
85+	1.000000	20584	20584	123488	0.166685	5.9993	123488	0.0300	5.999	0.164597	85+

TABLE 4 — OBSERVED AND PROJECTED VITAL RATES

	OBSERVED POPULATION BOTH SEXES	MALES	FEMALES	PROJECTED POPULATION 1968 MALES	FEMALES	1973 MALES	FEMALES	1978 MALES	FEMALES	STABLE POPULATION MALES	FEMALES
RATES PER THOUSAND											
Birth	16.36	16.83	15.89	16.77	15.84	16.87	15.95	16.23	15.36	14.77	14.06
Death	8.18	8.49	7.86	9.25	8.72	9.95	9.37	10.63	9.93	14.39	13.68
Increase	8.18	8.34	8.02	7.52	7.13	6.91	6.58	5.60	5.43		0.3743
PERCENTAGE											
under 15	25.08	25.66	24.51	23.80	22.67	23.10	21.98	22.75	21.69	21.06	20.19
15-64	66.92	67.23	66.61	67.95	67.30	67.24	66.72	66.51	66.01	64.71	63.49
65 and over	8.00	7.11	8.89	8.25	10.04	9.66	11.30	10.73	12.30	14.23	16.32
DEP. RATIO X 100	49.44	48.74	50.14	47.16	48.60	48.72	49.88	50.34	51.49	54.53	57.50

TABLE 1 — DATA

AGE AT LAST BIRTHDAY	POPULATION BOTH SEXES	MALES Number	%	FEMALES Number	%	BIRTHS BY AGE OF MOTHER	DEATHS BOTH SEXES	MALES	FEMALES	AGE AT LAST BIRTHDAY
0	128129	65808	1.6	62321	1.5	0	4306	2407	1899	0
1-4	522175	268003	6.6	254172	6.2	0	898	475	423	1-4
5-9	652694	333270	8.2	319424	7.8	0	369	216	153	5-9
10-14	705720	359765	8.8	345955	8.5	151	320	195	125	10-14
15-19	676016	343425	8.4	332591	8.2	23414	518	331	187	15-19
20-24	577399	292300	7.2	285099	7.0	52446	568	385	183	20-24
25-29	593895	297045	7.3	296850	7.3	31970	594	366	228	25-29
30-34	652160	327595	8.1	324565	8.0	15646	820	496	324	30-34
35-39	666755	335195	8.2	331560	8.1	5615	1138	681	457	35-39
40-44	617450	307642	7.6	309808	7.6	1553	1593	953	640	40-44
45-49	390784	195397	4.8	195387	4.8	142	1507	928	579	45-49
50-54	484026	244146	6.0	239880	5.9	21	2830	1744	1086	50-54
55-59	451398	226272	5.6	225126	5.5	0	4373	2643	1730	55-59
60-64	361816	177187	4.4	184629	4.5	0	5849	3491	2358	60-64
65-69	260036	121227	3.0	138809	3.4	0	7281	3993	3288	65-69
70-74	171161	74104	1.8	97057	2.4		7877	3809	4068	70-74
75-79	129357	55225	1.4	74132	1.8		9868	4443	5425	75-79
80-84	68502	30251	0.7	38251	0.9	67447 M.	8112	3705	4407	80-84
85+	34866	14351	0.4	20515	0.5	63511 F.	5658	2562	3096	85+
TOTAL	8144339	4068208		4076131		130958	64479	33823	30656	TOTAL

TABLE 2 — MALE LIFE TABLE

x	nq_x	l_x	nd_x	nL_x	nm_x	na_x	T_x	r_x	$\dot{e}_x$	nM_x	x
0	0.035604	100000	3560	97341	0.036576	0.2533	6933536	0.0000	69.335	0.036576	0
1	0.007053	96440	680	383789	0.001772	1.1047	6836194	0.0000	70.886	0.001772	1
5	0.003235	95759	310	478023	0.000648	2.5000	6452405	0.0000	67.381	0.000648	5
10	0.002707	95450	258	476633	0.000542	2.6205	5974383	0.0000	62.592	0.000542	10
15	0.004824	95191	459	474884	0.000967	2.6651	5497749	0.0198	57.755	0.000964	15
20	0.006568	94732	622	472129	0.001318	2.5398	5022866	0.0133	53.022	0.001317	20
25	0.006142	94110	578	469121	0.001232	2.5300	4550736	0.0000	48.356	0.001232	25
30	0.007543	93532	706	465970	0.001514	2.6066	4081615	0.0000	43.639	0.001514	30
35	0.010117	92826	939	461934	0.002033	2.6598	3615644	0.0041	38.951	0.002032	35
40	0.015519	91887	1426	456119	0.003126	2.6742	3153711	0.0508	34.322	0.003098	40
45	0.023560	90461	2131	447327	0.004764	2.6640	2697592	0.0183	29.820	0.004749	45
50	0.035135	88330	3103	434461	0.007143	2.6837	2250265	0.0000	25.476	0.007143	50
55	0.057111	85226	4867	414905	0.011731	2.6933	1815804	0.0197	21.306	0.011681	55
60	0.094826	80359	7620	384009	0.019841	2.6724	1400900	0.0326	17.433	0.019702	60
65	0.153607	72739	11173	337120	0.033143	2.6215	1016841	0.0326	13.979	0.032938	65
70	0.229651	61566	14139	273480	0.051699	2.5706	679721	0.0326	11.041	0.051401	70
75	0.336614	47427	15965	197337	0.080900	2.5071	406241	0.0326	8.566	0.080453	75
80	0.466655	31462	14682	119280	0.123089	2.5116	208904	0.0326	6.640	0.122475	80
85+	1.000000	16780	16780	89623	0.187232	5.3410	89623	0.0326	5.341	0.178525	85+

TABLE 3 — FEMALE LIFE TABLE

x	nq_x	l_x	nd_x	nL_x	nm_x	na_x	T_x	r_x	$\dot{e}_x$	nM_x	x
0	0.029805	100000	2981	97814	0.030471	0.2665	7327265	0.0000	73.273	0.030471	0
1	0.006625	97019	643	386224	0.001664	1.1159	7229451	0.0000	74.515	0.001664	1
5	0.002392	96377	231	481307	0.000479	2.5000	6843227	0.0000	71.005	0.000479	5
10	0.001805	96146	174	480305	0.000361	2.5473	6361920	0.0000	66.169	0.000361	10
15	0.002813	95973	270	479216	0.000563	2.6029	5881615	0.0188	61.284	0.000562	15
20	0.003207	95703	307	477766	0.000642	2.5650	5402399	0.0107	56.450	0.000642	20
25	0.003833	95396	366	476099	0.000768	2.5948	4924633	0.0000	51.623	0.000768	25
30	0.004979	95030	473	474027	0.000998	2.6251	4448533	0.0000	46.812	0.000998	30
35	0.006873	94557	650	471264	0.001379	2.6603	3974507	0.0032	42.033	0.001378	35
40	0.010362	93907	973	467253	0.002083	2.6547	3503243	0.0508	37.305	0.002066	40
45	0.014771	92934	1373	461462	0.002975	2.6636	3035990	0.0225	32.668	0.002963	45
50	0.022404	91561	2051	453098	0.004527	2.7052	2574528	0.0000	28.118	0.004527	50
55	0.037907	89510	3393	439761	0.007716	2.7047	2121429	0.0182	23.701	0.007685	55
60	0.062531	86117	5385	418317	0.012873	2.7220	1681668	0.0314	19.528	0.012772	60
65	0.113106	80732	9131	382572	0.023868	2.6906	1263351	0.0314	15.649	0.023687	65
70	0.191893	71601	13740	325510	0.042210	2.6351	880779	0.0314	12.301	0.041914	70
75	0.311805	57861	18041	245039	0.073626	2.5464	555269	0.0314	9.597	0.073180	75
80	0.446058	39820	17762	153415	0.115776	2.5471	310230	0.0314	7.791	0.115213	80
85+	1.000000	22058	22058	156814	0.140661	7.1093	156814	0.0314	7.109	0.150914	85+

TABLE 4 — OBSERVED AND PROJECTED VITAL RATES

	OBSERVED POPULATION BOTH SEXES	MALES	FEMALES	PROJECTED POPULATION 1969 MALES	FEMALES	1974 MALES	FEMALES	1979 MALES	FEMALES	STABLE POPULATION MALES	FEMALES
RATES PER THOUSAND											
Birth	16.08	16.58	15.58	16.74	15.72	16.65	15.64	15.92	14.97	14.47	13.70
Death	7.92	8.31	7.52	9.17	8.59	9.87	9.29	10.56	9.87	14.38	13.61
Increase	8.16	8.27	8.06	7.57	7.13	6.78	6.36	5.37	5.10		0.0898
PERCENTAGE											
under 15	24.66	25.24	24.09	23.53	22.34	22.96	21.72	22.62	21.42	20.76	19.79
15-64	67.18	67.50	66.86	67.89	67.17	67.05	66.42	66.39	65.78	64.62	63.03
65 and over	8.15	7.26	9.05	8.58	10.49	9.99	11.86	10.99	12.80	14.62	17.19
DEP. RATIO X 100	48.84	48.14	49.56	47.31	48.88	49.13	50.56	50.62	52.02	54.75	58.66

TABLE 1 — DATA

AGE AT LAST BIRTHDAY	POPULATION BOTH SEXES	MALES Number	%	FEMALES Number	%	BIRTHS BY AGE OF MOTHER	DEATHS BOTH SEXES	MALES	FEMALES	AGE AT LAST BIRTHDAY
0	122337	62873	1.5	59464	1.4	0	3882	2216	1666	0
1-4	511464	262544	6.4	248920	6.1	0	759	408	351	1-4
5-9	652587	333926	8.1	318661	7.8	0	367	231	136	5-9
10-14	671892	342634	8.4	329258	8.0	167	305	198	107	10-14
15-19	711013	361863	8.8	349150	8.5	23268	552	378	174	15-19
20-24	590144	299167	7.3	290977	7.1	50658	540	380	160	20-24
25-29	570340	286290	7.0	284050	6.9	29999	594	382	212	25-29
30-34	644008	322712	7.9	321296	7.8	14664	833	524	309	30-34
35-39	653147	328198	8.0	324949	7.9	5437	1145	696	449	35-39
40-44	644613	321733	7.9	322880	7.9	1429	1525	924	601	40-44
45-49	394234	196136	4.8	198098	4.8	138	1421	833	588	45-49
50-54	491193	247319	6.0	243874	5.9	31	2964	1769	1195	50-54
55-59	465904	233415	5.7	232489	5.7	0	4320	2594	1726	55-59
60-64	374965	185872	4.5	189093	4.6	0	6147	3689	2458	60-64
65-69	283330	132650	3.2	150680	3.7	0	7948	4413	3535	65-69
70-74	179110	80054	2.0	99056	2.4		8323	4115	4208	70-74
75-79	127634	52615	1.3	75019	1.8		10030	4502	5528	75-79
80-84	72837	32121	0.8	40716	1.0	64818 M.	8951	4060	4891	80-84
85+	39344	15958	0.4	23386	0.6	60973 F.	6364	2833	3531	85+
TOTAL	8200096	4098080		4102016		125791	66970	35145	31825	TOTAL

TABLE 2 — MALE LIFE TABLE

x	$_nq_x$	l_x	$_nd_x$	$_nL_x$	$_nm_x$	$_na_x$	T_x	r_x	$\overset{\circ}{e}_x$	$_nM_x$	x
0	0.034330	100000	3433	97402	0.035246	0.2432	6939050	0.0000	69.390	0.035246	0
1	0.006188	96567	598	384533	0.001554	1.0969	6841648	0.0000	70.849	0.001554	1
5	0.003453	95969	331	479019	0.000692	2.5000	6457115	0.0000	67.283	0.000692	5
10	0.002885	95638	276	477535	0.000578	2.6256	5978096	0.0000	62.507	0.000578	10
15	0.005219	95362	498	475634	0.001046	2.6362	5500561	0.0126	57.681	0.001045	15
20	0.006338	94864	601	472846	0.001272	2.5447	5024927	0.0222	52.970	0.001270	20
25	0.006650	94263	627	469781	0.001334	2.5519	4552081	0.0000	48.291	0.001334	25
30	0.008087	93636	757	466362	0.001624	2.5971	4082300	0.0000	43.597	0.001624	30
35	0.010550	92879	980	462063	0.002121	2.6198	3615938	0.0000	38.932	0.002121	35
40	0.014370	91899	1321	456389	0.002893	2.6473	3153875	0.0485	34.319	0.002872	40
45	0.021123	90579	1913	448485	0.004266	2.6959	2697486	0.0218	29.781	0.004247	45
50	0.035180	88665	3119	436099	0.007153	2.6830	2249001	0.0000	25.365	0.007153	50
55	0.054387	85546	4653	417057	0.011156	2.7061	1812902	0.0165	21.192	0.011113	55
60	0.095446	80893	7721	386557	0.019974	2.6803	1395845	0.0285	17.255	0.019847	60
65	0.154901	73173	11334	338877	0.033447	2.6192	1009288	0.0285	13.793	0.033268	65
70	0.229694	61838	14204	274833	0.051682	2.5811	670411	0.0285	10.841	0.051403	70
75	0.354032	47634	16864	196107	0.085994	2.5057	395578	0.0285	8.305	0.085565	75
80	0.476664	30770	14667	115567	0.126914	2.4892	199471	0.0285	6.483	0.126397	80
85+	1.000000	16103	16103	83904	0.191923	5.2104	83904	0.0285	5.210	0.177529	85-

TABLE 3 — FEMALE LIFE TABLE

x	$_nq_x$	l_x	$_nd_x$	$_nL_x$	$_nm_x$	$_na_x$	T_x	r_x	$\overset{\circ}{e}_x$	$_nM_x$	x
0	0.027446	100000	2745	97963	0.028017	0.2577	7365753	0.0000	73.658	0.028017	0
1	0.005617	97255	546	387442	0.001410	1.1083	7267790	0.0000	74.729	0.001410	1
5	0.002132	96709	206	483030	0.000427	2.5000	6880348	0.0000	71.145	0.000427	5
10	0.001624	96503	157	482130	0.000325	2.5451	6397318	0.0000	66.291	0.000325	10
15	0.002492	96346	240	481153	0.000499	2.5935	5915189	0.0119	61.395	0.000498	15
20	0.002751	96106	264	479894	0.000551	2.5922	5434035	0.0201	56.542	0.000550	20
25	0.003725	95842	357	478357	0.000746	2.6131	4954141	0.0000	51.691	0.000746	25
30	0.004798	95485	458	476341	0.000962	2.6352	4475784	0.0000	46.874	0.000962	30
35	0.006886	95027	654	473586	0.001382	2.6349	3999444	0.0000	42.088	0.001382	35
40	0.009345	94372	882	469809	0.001877	2.6727	3525858	0.0475	37.361	0.001861	40
45	0.014817	93490	1385	464270	0.002984	2.7029	3056049	0.0249	32.688	0.002968	45
50	0.024225	92105	2231	455345	0.004900	2.6781	2591779	0.0000	28.139	0.004900	50
55	0.036639	89874	3293	441818	0.007453	2.7069	2136435	0.0174	23.771	0.007424	55
60	0.063546	86581	5502	420356	0.013089	2.7192	1694616	0.0277	19.573	0.012999	60
65	0.112003	81079	9081	384458	0.023620	2.6944	1274260	0.0277	15.716	0.023460	65
70	0.194151	71998	13976	326949	0.042746	2.6358	889802	0.0277	12.359	0.042481	70
75	0.313553	58022	18193	245537	0.074095	2.5500	562853	0.0277	9.701	0.073688	75
80	0.460446	39829	18339	151983	0.120666	2.5375	317316	0.0277	7.967	0.120125	80
85+	1.000000	21490	21490	165333	0.129979	7.6935	165333	0.0277	7.694	0.150987	85-

TABLE 4 — OBSERVED AND PROJECTED VITAL RATES

	OBSERVED POPULATION BOTH SEXES	MALES	FEMALES	PROJECTED POPULATION 1970 MALES	FEMALES	1975 MALES	FEMALES	1980 MALES	FEMALES	STABLE POPULATION MALES	FEMALES
RATES PER THOUSAND											
Birth	15.34	15.82	14.86	16.17	15.17	15.84	14.86	15.18	14.25	13.59	12.77
Death	8.17	8.58	7.76	9.38	8.90	10.09	9.61	10.89	10.26	15.13	14.31
Increase	7.17	7.24	7.11	6.79	6.27	5.75	5.25	4.29	3.99	-1.5469	
PERCENTAGE											
under 15	23.88	24.45	23.31	23.03	21.83	22.26	21.06	21.85	20.68	19.77	18.73
15-64	67.55	67.90	67.21	67.97	67.22	67.35	66.60	66.78	66.02	64.85	62.99
65 and over	8.56	7.65	9.48	9.00	10.95	10.39	12.35	11.37	13.30	15.38	18.27
DEP. RATIO X 100	48.03	47.27	48.79	47.12	48.76	48.48	50.16	49.74	51.46	54.20	58.75

AGE AT LAST BIRTHDAY	1970 BOTH SEXES	MALES	FEMALES	1975 BOTH SEXES	MALES	FEMALES	1980 BOTH SEXES	MALES	FEMALES	AGE AT LAST BIRTHDAY	
0-4	627	322	305	648	333	315	645	331	314	0-4	
5-9	630	323	307	623	320	303	645	331	314	5-9	
10-14	651	333	318	628	322	306	622	319	303	10-14	
15-19	670	341	329	649	332	317	627	321	306	15-19	TABLE 5
20-24	708	360	348	667	339	328	647	330	317	20-24	POPULATION
25-29	587	297	290	704	357	347	664	337	327	25-29	PROJECTED
30-34	567	284	283	584	295	289	701	355	346	30-34	WITH
35-39	639	320	319	563	282	281	579	292	287	35-39	FIXED
40-44	646	324	322	633	316	317	557	278	279	40-44	AGE—
45-49	635	316	319	638	319	319	623	310	313	45-49	SPECIFIC
50-54	385	191	194	620	307	313	622	310	312	50-54	BIRTH
55-59	474	237	237	371	182	189	598	294	304	55-59	AND
60-64	437	216	221	444	219	225	348	169	179	60-64	DEATH
65-69	336	163	173	392	190	202	398	192	206	65-69	RATES
70-74	236	108	128	279	132	147	326	154	172	70-74	(IN 1000's)
75-79	131	57	74	173	77	96	204	94	110	75-79	
80-84	77	31	46	80	34	46	105	45	60	80-84	
85+	67	23	44	74	23	51	74	24	50	85+	
TOTAL	8503	4246	4257	8770	4379	4391	8985	4486	4499	TOTAL	

STANDARD COUNTRIES:	ENGLAND AND WALES 1961 BOTH SEXES	MALES	FEMALES	UNITED STATES 1960 BOTH SEXES	MALES	FEMALES	MEXICO 1960 BOTH SEXES	MALES	FEMALES	TABLE 6
STANDARDIZED RATES PER THOUSAND										STANDAR-
Birth	13.15	14.17*	12.35	13.40	13.38*	12.80	17.06	12.50*	16.50	DIZED
Death	10.54	10.08*	11.02	8.61	8.85*	8.14	4.78	7.31*	4.19	RATES
Increase	2.61	4.09*	1.33	4.79	4.53*	4.66	12.28	5.19*	12.30	

	OBSERVED POP. MALES	FEMALES	STATIONARY POP. MALES	FEMALES	STABLE POP. MALES	FEMALES	OBSERVED BIRTHS	NET MATERNITY FUNCTION	BIRTHS IN STABLE POP.	TABLE 7
μ	32.99919	34.14711	37.71972	39.33949	38.53326	40.20870	24.83037	24.90551	24.95231	MOMENTS
σ^2	433.9591	457.7141	524.2175	560.3143	527.5455	563.3938	30.03919	28.05895	28.27694	AND
κ_3	3163.771	3311.744	2365.024	2242.280	1935.897	1737.354	145.2598	140.3241	141.5337	CUMULANTS
κ_4	-149120.	-169964.	-273440.	-322356.	-281113.	-330114.	557.025	786.398	787.952	
β_1	0.122480	0.114375	0.038827	0.028581	0.025526	0.016879	0.778442	0.891354	0.885977	
β_2	2.208161	2.188725	2.004965	1.973231	1.989908	1.959984	3.617303	3.998849	3.985450	
κ	-0.050287	-0.046558	-0.014605	-0.010581	-0.009613	-0.006255	-0.638045	-1.211475	-1.184270	

VITAL STATISTICS			THOMPSON AGE RANGE	NRR	1000r	INTERVAL	BOURGEOIS-PICHAT AGE RANGE	NRR	1000b	1000d	1000r	COALE	TABLE 8
GRR	1.005											IBR	RATES FROM AGE DISTRI-
NRR	0.962		0-4	0.96	-1.51	27.44	5-29	1.19	17.83	11.24	6.59	IDR	BUTIONS
TFR	2.072		5-9	1.08	2.69	27.41	30-54	1.66	31.98	13.26	18.73	IRI	AND VITAL
GENERATION	2.072		10-14	1.14	4.62	27.36	55-79	2.63	102.82	66.94	35.88	K1	STATISTICS
SEX RATIO	106.306		15-19	1.23	7.34	27.29	*20-44	0.81	12.22	20.13	-7.90	K2	(Females)

Note: GENERATION value reads 24.929 and SEX RATIO 106.306.

Start Age Interval	ORIGINAL MATRIX SUB-DIAGONAL	ALTERNATIVE FIRST ROWS Projection	Integral	FIRST STABLE MATRIX % IN STABLE POPULATION	FISHER VALUES	REPRODUCTIVE VALUES	SECOND STABLE MATRIX Z₂ FIRST COLUMN	FIRST ROW	TABLE 9
0	0.99511	0.00000	0.00000	6.221	1.026	316433	0.2030+0.0746	0.2030+0.0746	LESLIE
5	0.99814	0.00060	0.00000	6.238	1.023	326054	0.1699-0.2157	-0.0064+0.1702	MATRIX
10	0.99797	0.07884	0.00119	6.275	1.017	334725	-0.1943-0.2908	-0.1287+0.0365	AND ITS
15	0.99738	0.28267	0.15619	6.311	0.930	324626	-0.4287+0.1206	-0.0746-0.0931	SPECTRAL
20	0.99680	0.32866	0.40804	6.343	0.634	184540	-0.0229+0.5664	-0.0061-0.0995	COMPO-
25	0.99579	0.17771	0.24753	6.372	0.293	83235	0.6760+0.2507	0.0060-0.0534	NENTS
30	0.99422	0.07326	0.10697	6.395	0.109	34984	0.5687-0.7182	0.0052-0.0218	(Females)
35	0.99203	0.02485	0.03922	6.407	0.033	10743	-0.6431-0.9681	0.0027-0.0069	
40	0.98821	0.00602	0.01037	6.405	0.007	2379	-1.4173+0.3947	0.0008-0.0016	
45	0.98078	0.00097	0.00163	6.379	0.001	228	-0.0799+1.8535	0.0001-0.0003	
50	0.97029	0.00015	0.00030	6.305	0.000	38	2.1748+0.8131	0.0000-0.0000	
55+	0.79072			30.348					

Start Age Interval	OBSERVED POPUL. (IN 100's)	CONTRIBUTIONS OF ROOTS (IN 100's) r_1	r_2, r_3	r_4-r_{11}	AGE-SP. BIRTH RATES	NET MATERNITY FUNCTION	COEFF. OF MATRIX EQUATION	PARAMETERS	INTEGRAL	MATRIX	EXP. INCREASE x	$e^{(x+2\frac12)r}$	TABLE 10
0	3084	3158	-103	28	0.0000	0.0000	0.0000	L(1)	0.99230	0.99230	0	0.9961	AGE
5	3187	3167	27	-8	0.0000	0.0000	0.0006	L(2)	0.22736	0.24257	50	0.9220	ANALYSIS
10	3293	3186	187	-81	0.0002	0.0012	0.0783		0.78181	0.74519	55	0.9149	AND
15	3492	3204	103	184	0.0323	0.1554	0.2802	R(1)	-0.00155	-0.00155	60	0.9078	MISCEL-
20	2910	3221	-222	-89	0.0844	0.4050	0.3249	R(2)	-0.04111	-0.04875	65	0.9009	LANEOUS
25	2841	3235	-342	-52	0.0512	0.2449	0.1751		0.25756	0.25122	70	0.8939	RESULTS
30	3213	3247	90	-123	0.0221	0.1054	0.0719	C(1)		50772	75	0.8870	(Females)
35	3249	3253	623	-626	0.0081	0.0384	0.0242	C(2)		-17792	80	0.8802	
40	3229	3252	344	-367	0.0021	0.0101	0.0058			20336	85	0.8734	
45	1981	3239	-725	-532	0.0003	0.0016	0.0009	2P/Y	24.3951	25.0107	90	0.8667	
50	2439	3201	-1105	342	0.0001	0.0003	0.0001	DELTA	12.5005		95	0.8600	
55+	8104	15408									100	0.8534	

TABLE 1 — DATA

AGE AT LAST BIRTHDAY	POPULATION BOTH SEXES	MALES Number	MALES %	FEMALES Number	FEMALES %	BIRTHS BY AGE OF MOTHER	DEATHS BOTH SEXES	DEATHS MALES	DEATHS FEMALES	AGE AT LAST BIRTHDAY
0	266979	135749	2.0	131230	1.8	-0	40904	22882	18022	0
1-4	1044350	527402	7.8	516948	7.2	-0	8980	4614	4366	1
5-9	1418676	716429	10.6	702247	9.8	-0	4196	2125	2071	5
10-14	854402	432394	6.4	422008	5.9	-0	1577	801	776	10
15-19	1337355	670220	9.9	667135	9.3	17614	4192	2138	2054	15
20-24	1390894	699430	10.3	691464	9.6	91918	5864	3136	2728	20
25-29	1296947	641802	9.5	655145	9.1	91937	5615	2840	2775	25
30-34	1130134	539395	8.0	590739	8.2	59696	5249	2690	2559	30
35-39	922585	426274	6.3	496311	6.9	31352	5136	2536	2600	35
40-44	816772	375692	5.6	441080	6.1	10463	5428	2904	2524	40
45-49	744791	345121	5.1	399670	5.6	1070	6398	3455	2943	45
50-54	683961	318825	4.7	365136	5.1	72	8415	4671	3744	50
55-59	613072	287701	4.3	325371	4.5	-0	10861	5934	4927	55
60-64	513441	239635	3.5	273806	3.8	-0	13728	7185	6543	60
65-69	389151	177860	2.6	211291	2.9	-0	16073	7905	8168	65
70-74	281418	125202	1.9	156216	2.2		18232	8491	9741	70
75-79	163915	70480	1.0	93435	1.3		16471	7466	9005	75
80-84	68744	28118	0.4	40626	0.6	156158 M.	10790	4768	6022	80
85+	25929	9829	0.1	16100	0.2	147964 F.	6318	2484	3834	85
TOTAL	13963516	6767558		7195958		304122	194427	99025	95402	TO

TABLE 2 — MALE LIFE TABLE

x	nq_x	l_x	nd_x	nL_x	nm_x	na_x	T_x	r_x	$\dot{e}_x$	nM_x
0	0.149751	100000	14975	88841	0.168561	0.2548	5239763	0.0000	52.398	0.168561
1	0.034130	85025	2902	331701	0.008749	1.1059	5150922	0.0000	60.581	0.008749
5	0.014492	82123	1190	407639	0.002920	2.5000	4819220	0.0385	58.683	0.002966
10	0.009221	80933	746	402815	0.001853	2.5222	4411581	0.0043	54.509	0.001852
15	0.015832	80187	1270	397968	0.003190	2.6647	4008766	0.0000	49.993	0.003190
20	0.022175	78917	1750	390298	0.004484	2.5500	3610798	0.0001	45.754	0.004484
25	0.021895	77167	1690	381635	0.004427	2.5140	3220501	0.0214	41.734	0.004425
30	0.024690	75477	1864	372827	0.004998	2.5531	2838866	0.0359	37.612	0.004987
35	0.029407	73614	2165	362835	0.005966	2.5819	2466039	0.0301	33.500	0.005949
40	0.037996	71449	2715	350708	0.007741	2.5920	2103204	0.0133	29.436	0.007730
45	0.048929	68734	3363	335643	0.010019	2.6186	1752496	0.0059	25.497	0.010011
50	0.070817	65371	4629	315827	0.014658	2.6176	1416833	0.0034	21.674	0.014651
55	0.098380	60742	5976	289408	0.020648	2.6068	1101006	0.0073	18.126	0.020626
60	0.140457	54766	7692	255331	0.030127	2.5950	811598	0.0302	14.819	0.029983
65	0.201484	47074	9485	212340	0.044667	2.5719	556267	0.0302	11.817	0.044445
70	0.291763	37589	10967	160878	0.068171	2.5319	343928	0.0302	9.150	0.067818
75	0.419340	26622	11164	104817	0.106507	2.4656	183050	0.0302	6.876	0.105931
80	0.590190	15458	9123	53477	0.170603	2.3897	78233	0.0302	5.061	0.169570
85+	*1.000000	6335	6335	24756	0.255901	3.9078	24756	0.0302	3.908	0.252722

TABLE 3 — FEMALE LIFE TABLE

x	nq_x	l_x	nd_x	nL_x	nm_x	na_x	T_x	r_x	$\dot{e}_x$	nM_x
0	0.124883	100000	12488	90935	0.137331	0.2741	5596534	0.0000	55.965	0.137331
1	0.032981	87512	2886	341743	0.008446	1.1228	5505599	0.0000	62.913	0.008446
5	0.014416	84625	1220	420077	0.002904	2.5000	5163857	0.0388	61.020	0.002949
10	0.009153	83405	763	415128	0.001839	2.5117	4743779	0.0028	56.876	0.001839
15	0.015283	82642	1263	410225	0.003079	2.6363	4328651	0.0000	52.378	0.003079
20	0.019538	81379	1590	403006	0.003945	2.5537	3918426	0.0000	48.150	0.003945
25	0.020962	79789	1673	394782	0.004237	2.5107	3515420	0.0116	44.059	0.004236
30	0.021454	78117	1676	386457	0.004337	2.5381	3120638	0.0232	39.948	0.004332
35	0.025895	76441	1979	377344	0.005246	2.5450	2734181	0.0241	35.769	0.005239
40	0.028251	74461	2104	367181	0.005729	2.5636	2356837	0.0157	31.652	0.005722
45	0.036232	72358	2622	355524	0.007374	2.6106	1989657	0.0113	27.498	0.007364
50	0.050129	69736	3496	340405	0.010270	2.6330	1634133	0.0100	23.433	0.010254
55	0.073278	66240	4854	319791	0.015178	2.6495	1293728	0.0129	19.531	0.015143
60	0.113686	61386	6979	290488	0.024024	2.6439	973937	0.0273	15.866	0.023896
65	0.177803	54407	9674	248930	0.038861	2.6114	683449	0.0273	12.562	0.038658
70	0.271629	44734	12151	193916	0.062661	2.5515	434518	0.0273	9.713	0.062356
75	0.389033	32583	12676	130911	0.096827	2.4753	240602	0.0273	7.384	0.096377
80	0.535007	19907	10650	71526	0.148902	2.4331	109691	0.0273	5.510	0.148230
85+	1.000000	9257	9257	38165	0.242541	4.1230	38165	0.0273	4.123	0.238137

TABLE 4 — OBSERVED AND PROJECTED VITAL RATES

	OBSERVED POPULATION BOTH SEXES	MALES	FEMALES	PROJECTED POPULATION 1935 MALES	1935 FEMALES	1940 MALES	1940 FEMALES	1945 MALES	1945 FEMALES	STABLE POPULATION MALES	FEM
RATES PER THOUSAND											
Birth	21.78	23.07	20.56	22.41	20.07	20.09	18.09	19.55	17.68	17.60	16
Death	13.92	14.63	13.26	14.97	13.73	15.20	14.11	15.45	14.46	19.90	18
Increase	7.86	8.44	7.30	7.43	6.34	4.88	3.98	4.10	3.22	-2.3	
PERCENTAGE											
under 15	25.67	26.77	24.63	28.57	26.42	26.36	24.47	25.10	23.38	22.04	21
15-64	67.68	67.15	68.18	64.83	65.82	66.63	67.25	67.67	67.88	66.38	65
65 and over	6.65	6.08	7.19	6.60	7.76	7.00	8.28	7.23	8.74	11.59	13
DEP. RATIO X 100	47.76	48.93	46.68	54.25	51.93	50.08	48.69	47.78	47.31	50.65	52

AGE AT LAST BIRTHDAY	1935 BOTH SEXES	1935 MALES	1935 FEMALES	1940 BOTH SEXES	1940 MALES	1940 FEMALES	1945 BOTH SEXES	1945 MALES	1945 FEMALES	AGE AT LAST BIRTHDAY	
0-4	1303	660	643	1260	638	622	1208	612	596	0-4	**TABLE 5**
5-9	1272	643	629	1265	640	625	1222	618	604	5-9	
10-14	1402	708	694	1257	635	622	1249	632	617	10-14	
15-19	844	427	417	1385	699	686	1243	628	615	15-19	POPULATION
20-24	1312	657	655	829	419	410	1360	686	674	20-24	PROJECTED
25-29	1361	684	677	1285	643	642	811	410	401	25-29	WITH
30-34	1268	627	641	1331	668	663	1256	628	628	30-34	FIXED
35-39	1102	525	577	1236	610	626	1297	650	647	35-39	AGE—
40-44	895	412	483	1068	507	561	1199	590	609	40-44	SPECIFIC
45-49	787	360	427	862	394	468	1029	486	543	45-49	BIRTH
50-54	708	325	383	747	338	409	819	371	448	50-54	AND
55-59	635	292	343	658	298	360	694	310	384	55-59	DEATH
60-64	550	254	296	570	258	312	590	263	327	60-64	RATES
65-69	434	199	235	464	211	253	481	214	267	65-69	(IN 1000's)
70-74	300	135	165	334	151	183	357	160	197	70-74	
75-79	187	82	105	199	88	111	221	98	123	75-79	
80-84	87	36	51	100	42	58	106	45	61	80-84	
85+	35	13	22	44	17	27	50	19	31	85+	
TOTAL	14482	7039	7443	14894	7256	7638	15192	7420	7772	TOTAL	

STANDARD COUNTRIES:	ENGLAND AND WALES 1961 BOTH SEXES	MALES	FEMALES	UNITED STATES 1960 BOTH SEXES	MALES	FEMALES	MEXICO 1960 BOTH SEXES	MALES	FEMALES	
STANDARDIZED RATES PER THOUSAND										**TABLE 6**
Birth	15.65	18.12*	14.76	15.90	16.68*	15.25	17.80	17.39*	17.27	STANDAR-DIZED
Death	19.27	22.03*	19.98	17.28	18.77*	16.66	13.16	14.19*	12.10	RATES
Increase	-3.62	-3.91*	-5.22	-1.38	-2.10*	-1.41	4.64	3.21*	5.17	

	OBSERVED POP. MALES	FEMALES	STATIONARY POP. MALES	FEMALES	STABLE POP. MALES	FEMALES	OBSERVED BIRTHS	NET MATERNITY FUNCTION	BIRTHS IN STABLE POP.	
μ	29.76000	31.34112	34.70067	35.80407	35.80848	36.96281	28.01432	28.58524	28.68056	**TABLE 7**
σ^2	401.1089	418.0758	477.7511	500.0725	484.1477	506.0322	35.51236	39.17085	39.44641	
κ_3	4298.564	3905.438	3023.825	2870.184	2526.124	2300.387	121.7436	120.3603	118.9377	MOMENTS
κ_4	-91179.	-114176.	-209106.	-240421.	-222720.	-253906.	-226.528	-594.147	-630.869	AND
β_1	0.286325	0.208725	0.083851	0.065875	0.056231	0.040838	0.330943	0.241034	0.230471	CUMULANTS
β_2	2.433279	2.346769	2.083856	2.038597	2.049826	2.008447	2.820377	2.612771	2.594562	
κ	-0.119514	-0.088105	-0.032163	-0.024781	-0.021575	-0.015374	-0.201481	-0.130306	-0.123923	

VITAL STATISTICS		THOMPSON AGE RANGE	NRR	1000r	INTERVAL	BOURGEOIS-PICHAT AGE RANGE	NRR	1000b	1000d	1000r	COALE	
GRR	1.193											**TABLE 8**
NRR	0.936	0-4	0.99	-0.40	27.20	5-29	0.76	17.57	27.75	-10.18	IBR	RATES FROM AGE
TFR	2.452	5-9	1.17	5.69	27.14	30-54	1.60	35.91	18.60	17.31	IDR	DISTRI-BUTIONS
GENERATION	28.633	10-14	0.77	-9.92	27.08	55-79	1.54	35.62	19.52	16.10	IRI	AND VITAL
SEX RATIO	105.538	15-19	1.33	10.30	26.97	*40-64	1.37	27.42	15.73	11.70	K1	STATISTICS
											K2	(Females)

Start of Age interval	ORIGINAL MATRIX SUB-DIAGONAL	ALTERNATIVE FIRST ROWS Projection	Integral	FIRST STABLE MATRIX % IN STABLE POPULATION	FISHER VALUES	REPRODUCTIVE VALUES	SECOND STABLE MATRIX Z_2 FIRST COLUMN	FIRST ROW	
0	0.97088	0.00000	0.00000	7.151	1.149	744773	0.1460+0.0748	0.1460+0.0748	
5	0.98822	0.00000	0.00000	7.023	1.170	821591	0.1678-0.1085	0.0066+0.1345	**TABLE 9**
10	0.98819	0.02746	0.00000	7.021	1.170	493895	-0.0126-0.2474	-0.0913+0.0588	
15	0.98240	0.16525	0.05526	7.018	1.139	759763	-0.2735-0.1397	-0.0819-0.0422	LESLIE
20	0.97959	0.28461	0.27823	6.974	0.953	658761	-0.3176+0.2061	-0.0281-0.0873	MATRIX
25	0.97891	0.25183	0.29371	6.911	0.628	411158	0.0244+0.4647	0.0077-0.0770	AND ITS
30	0.97642	0.17129	0.21151	6.844	0.338	199774	0.5094+0.2591	0.0199-0.0452	SPECTRAL
35	0.97307	0.09079	0.13222	6.760	0.141	69888	0.5867-0.3821	0.0145-0.0175	COMPO-NENTS
40	0.96825	0.02770	0.04965	6.654	0.036	15815	-0.0463-0.8535	0.0047-0.0039	(Females)
45	0.95747	0.00302	0.00560	6.517	0.004	1495	-0.9263-0.4693	0.0005-0.0004	
50	0.93944	0.00021	0.00041	6.312	0.000	88	-1.0443+0.6824	0.0000-0.0000	
55+	0.74958			24.814					

Start of Age interval	OBSERVED POPUL. (IN 100's)	CONTRIBUTIONS OF ROOTS (IN 100's) r_1	r_2, r_3	r_4-r_{11}	AGE-SP. BIRTH RATES	NET MATERNITY FUNCTION	COEFF. OF MATRIX EQUATION	PARAMETERS INTEGRAL	MATRIX	EXP. INCREASE x	$e^{(x+2\frac{1}{2})r}$	
0	6482	6334	258	-110	0.0000	0.0000	0.0000	L(1) 0.98855	0.98855	0	0.9943	**TABLE 10**
5	7022	6221	-20	822	0.0000	0.0000	0.0000	L(2) 0.39051	0.39814	50	0.8861	
10	4220	6219	-414	-1585	0.0000	0.0000	0.0263	0.70963	0.69046	55	0.8760	AGE
15	6671	6217	-482	937	0.0128	0.0527	0.1567	R(1) -0.00230	-0.00230	60	0.8659	ANALYSIS
20	6915	6178	40	697	0.0647	0.2606	0.2651	R(2) -0.04215	-0.04537	65	0.8560	AND
25	6551	6122	779	-349	0.0683	0.2695	0.2298	0.21354	0.20955	70	0.8462	MISCEL-LANEOUS
30	5907	6062	896	-1051	0.0492	0.1900	0.1530			75	0.8365	RESULTS
35	4963	5988	-76	-949	0.0307	0.1160	0.0792	C(1)	88580	80	0.8270	(Females)
40	4411	5894	-1432	-51	0.0115	0.0424	0.0235	C(2)	46537	85	0.8175	
45	3997	5773	-1626	-151	0.0013	0.0046	0.0025		-81352	90	0.8081	
50	3651	5591	138	-2078	0.0001	0.0003	0.0002	2P/Y 29.4233	29.9845	95	0.7989	
55+	11168	21980						DELTA 13.1764		100	0.7897	

TABLE 1 — DATA

AGE AT LAST BIRTHDAY	POPULATION BOTH SEXES	MALES Number	%	FEMALES Number	%	BIRTHS BY AGE OF MOTHER	DEATHS BOTH SEXES	MALES	FEMALES	AGE AT LAST BIRTHDAY
0	265568	136257	2.2	129311	2.0	0	19733	11190	8543	0
1-4	1031035	526879	8.7	504156	7.8	0	2929	1554	1375	1-4
5-9	1078691	545830	9.0	532861	8.3	0	845	500	345	5-9
10-14	883154	446670	7.3	436484	6.8	58	660	390	270	10-14
15-19	889362	448375	7.4	440987	6.8	22884	1239	756	483	15-19
20-24	995631	496087	8.1	499544	7.8	97524	1898	1146	752	20-24
25-29	1043452	509383	8.4	534069	8.3	89361	2147	1256	891	25-29
30-34	696462	341246	5.6	355216	5.5	38480	1615	927	688	30-34
35-39	860470	420622	6.9	439848	6.8	25785	2435	1338	1097	35-39
40-44	980579	480226	7.9	500353	7.8	10169	3757	2160	1597	40-44
45-49	902786	439496	7.2	463290	7.2	795	5221	3097	2124	45-49
50-54	792565	372551	6.1	420014	6.5	32	7236	4334	2902	50-54
55-59	618469	277979	4.6	340490	5.3	0	8700	5012	3688	55-59
60-64	491324	216192	3.6	275132	4.3	0	10992	6069	4923	60-64
65-69	401932	173739	2.9	228193	3.5	0	14003	7218	6785	65-69
70-74	288989	126295	2.1	162694	2.5		16890	8174	8716	70-74
75-79	184553	77923	1.3	106630	1.7		17571	8028	9543	75-79
80-84	91499	39004	0.6	52495	0.8	147363 M.	13437	6006	7431	80-84
85+	35347	14015	0.2	21332	0.3	137725 F.	8908	3594	5314	85+
TOTAL	12531868	6088769		6443099		285088	140216	72749	67467	TOTAL

TABLE 2 — MALE LIFE TABLE

x	$_nq_x$	l_x	$_nd_x$	$_nL_x$	$_nm_x$	$_na_x$	T_x	r_x	$\mathring{e}_x$	$_nM_x$	x
0	C.077140	100000	7714	93983	0.082079	0.2200	6203216	0.0007	62.032	0.082124	
1	0.011684	92286	1078	365996	0.002946	1.0809	6109234	0.0007	66.199	0.002949	
5	0.004504	91208	411	455012	0.000903	2.5000	5743237	0.0380	62.969	0.000916	
10	0.004372	90797	397	453065	0.000876	2.6828	5288225	0.0186	58.242	0.000873	10
15	0.008397	90400	759	450234	0.001686	2.6736	4835160	0.0000	53.486	0.001686	15
20	0.011486	89641	1030	445699	0.002310	2.5664	4384926	0.0000	48.917	0.002310	20
25	0.012269	88611	1087	440370	0.002469	2.5292	3939228	0.0349	44.455	0.002466	25
30	0.013505	87524	1182	434723	0.002719	2.5486	3498857	0.0164	39.976	0.002717	30
35	0.015785	86342	1363	428451	0.003181	2.6084	3064134	0.0000	35.488	0.003181	35
40	0.022256	84979	1891	420486	0.004498	2.6684	2635683	0.0000	31.016	0.004498	40
45	0.034798	83088	2891	408770	0.007073	2.6931	2215197	0.0179	26.661	0.007047	45
50	0.056992	80197	4571	390325	0.011710	2.6682	1806427	0.0338	22.525	0.011633	50
55	0.087018	75626	6581	362623	0.018148	2.6436	1416101	0.0356	18.725	0.018030	55
60	0.131911	69045	9108	323449	0.028158	2.6090	1053478	0.0183	15.258	0.028072	60
65	0.189302	59937	11346	272259	0.041674	2.5826	730029	0.0183	12.180	0.041545	65
70	0.280038	48591	13607	209559	0.064933	2.5457	457770	0.0183	9.421	0.064721	70
75	0.409566	34984	14328	138638	0.103350	2.4678	248211	0.0183	7.095	0.103025	75
80	0.551669	20656	11395	73735	0.154542	2.4073	109573	0.0183	5.305	0.153985	80
85+	*1.000000	9261	9261	35839	0.258394	3.8701	35839	0.0183	3.870	0.256440	85

TABLE 3 — FEMALE LIFE TABLE

x	$_nq_x$	l_x	$_nd_x$	$_nL_x$	$_nm_x$	$_na_x$	T_x	r_x	$\mathring{e}_x$	$_nM_x$	x
0	0.062878	100000	6288	95190	0.066055	0.2350	6663435	0.0002	66.634	0.066066	0
1	0.010820	93712	1014	371899	0.002727	1.0909	6568245	0.0002	70.090	0.002727	1
5	0.003169	92698	294	462757	0.000635	2.5000	6196346	0.0360	66.844	0.000647	5
10	0.003097	92405	286	461351	0.000620	2.6525	5733589	0.0182	62.049	0.000619	10
15	0.005462	92118	503	459417	0.001095	2.6660	5272238	0.0000	57.233	0.001095	15
20	0.007500	91615	687	456411	0.001505	2.5769	4812821	0.0000	52.533	0.001505	20
25	0.008322	90928	757	452787	0.001671	2.5505	4356410	0.0324	47.910	0.001668	25
30	0.009654	90171	871	448754	0.001940	2.5838	3903623	0.0174	43.291	0.001937	30
35	0.012396	89301	1107	443847	0.002494	2.5991	3454870	0.0000	38.688	0.002494	35
40	0.015839	88194	1397	437658	0.003192	2.6291	3011023	0.0000	34.141	0.003192	40
45	0.022728	86797	1973	429366	0.004594	2.6584	2573365	0.0128	29.648	0.004585	45
50	0.034147	84824	2897	417377	0.006940	2.6714	2144000	0.0236	25.276	0.006909	50
55	0.053159	81928	4355	399542	0.010901	2.6817	1726623	0.0309	21.075	0.010831	55
60	0.086318	77573	6696	372279	0.017986	2.6727	1327081	0.0245	17.108	0.017893	60
65	0.139751	70877	9905	331255	0.029902	2.6650	954802	0.0245	13.471	0.029734	65
70	0.238471	60972	14540	269997	0.053852	2.6024	623547	0.0245	10.227	0.053573	70
75	0.367242	46432	17053	189669	0.089909	2.5084	353549	0.0245	7.614	0.089496	75
80	0.518426	29379	15231	107147	0.142147	2.4603	163880	0.0245	5.578	0.141556	80
85+	1.000000	14148	14148	56733	C.249378	4.0100	56733	0.0245	4.010	0.249110	85

TABLE 4 — OBSERVED AND PROJECTED VITAL RATES

	OBSERVED POPULATION BOTH SEXES	MALES	FEMALES	PROJECTED POPULATION 1956 MALES	FEMALES	1961 MALES	FEMALES	1966 MALES	FEMALES	STABLE POPULATION MALES	FEMALES
RATES PER THOUSAND											
Birth	22.75	24.20	21.38	22.37	19.88	21.15	18.91	21.47	19.32	22.68	21.42
Death	11.19	11.95	10.47	12.22	10.97	12.41	11.39	12.75	11.88	12.49	11.23
Increase	11.56	12.25	10.90	10.15	8.92	8.74	7.52	8.72	7.44		10.1900
PERCENTAGE											
under 15	26.00	27.19	24.88	29.03	26.51	29.27	26.67	28.21	25.82	28.77	27.64
15-64	66.00	65.73	66.26	63.83	64.14	63.30	63.28	63.53	63.10	63.37	62.70
65 and over	8.00	7.08	8.87	7.14	9.35	7.43	10.05	8.25	11.08	7.86	9.66
DEP. RATIO X 100	51.51	52.14	50.93	56.67	55.90	57.98	58.03	57.39	58.47	57.80	59.54

TABLE 5 — POPULATION PROJECTED WITH FIXED AGE-SPECIFIC BIRTH AND DEATH RATES (IN 1000's)

AGE AT LAST BIRTHDAY	1956 BOTH SEXES	1956 MALES	1956 FEMALES	1961 BOTH SEXES	1961 MALES	1961 FEMALES	1966 BOTH SEXES	1966 MALES	1966 FEMALES	AGE AT LAST BIRTHDAY
0-4	1306	670	636	1286	660	626	1319	677	642	0-4
5-9	1284	656	628	1293	663	630	1273	653	620	5-9
10-14	1074	543	531	1279	653	626	1288	660	628	10-14
15-19	879	444	435	1069	540	529	1272	649	623	15-19
20-24	882	444	438	871	439	432	1061	535	526	20-24
25-29	986	490	496	874	439	435	862	434	428	25-29
30-34	1032	503	529	975	484	491	864	433	431	30-34
35-39	687	336	351	1020	496	524	963	477	486	35-39
40-44	847	413	434	676	330	346	1002	486	516	40-44
45-49	958	467	491	826	401	425	661	321	340	45-49
50-54	870	420	450	923	446	477	797	383	414	50-54
55-59	748	346	402	821	390	431	871	414	457	55-59
60-64	565	248	317	684	309	375	750	348	402	60-64
65-69	427	182	245	491	209	282	593	260	333	65-69
70-74	320	134	186	340	140	200	391	161	230	70-74
75-79	198	84	114	219	88	131	233	93	140	75-79
80-84	101	41	60	109	44	65	121	47	74	80-84
85+	47	19	28	52	20	32	56	22	34	85+
TOTAL	13211	6440	6771	13808	6751	7057	14377	7053	7324	TOTAL

TABLE 6 — STANDARDIZED RATES

STANDARD COUNTRIES: STANDARDIZED RATES PER THOUSAND	ENGLAND AND WALES 1961 BOTH SEXES	MALES	FEMALES	UNITED STATES 1960 BOTH SEXES	MALES	FEMALES	MEXICO 1960 BOTH SEXES	MALES	FEMALES
Birth	19.21	21.86*	17.98	19.54	20.29*	18.60	22.89	19.52*	22.06
Death	14.83	15.34*	15.28	12.51	13.23*	11.77	7.81	10.24*	6.88
Increase	4.38	6.52*	2.71	7.03	7.06*	6.83	15.08	9.27*	15.18

TABLE 7 — MOMENTS AND CUMULANTS

	OBSERVED POP. MALES	OBSERVED POP. FEMALES	STATIONARY POP. MALES	STATIONARY POP. FEMALES	STABLE POP. MALES	STABLE POP. FEMALES	OBSERVED BIRTHS	NET MATERNITY FUNCTION	BIRTHS IN STABLE POP.
μ	31.68351	33.59685	35.91902	37.51468	31.11792	32.39552	27.15679	27.38050	26.98628
σ^2	437.5893	462.3251	487.7521	518.0782	451.2293	482.5697	36.05399	37.30230	35.90149
κ_3	3183.008	2698.790	2540.793	2213.163	4497.227	4614.621	167.3564	136.1517	138.5160
κ_4	-155090.	-191680.	-227111.	-272622.	-151018.	-190088.	156.049	-307.952	-148.127
β_1	0.120914	0.073705	0.055634	0.035224	0.220139	0.189492	0.597619	0.357141	0.414632
β_2	2.190065	2.103226	2.045359	1.984288	2.258292	2.183727	3.120048	2.778684	2.885076
κ	-0.048907	-0.029077	-0.021278	-0.013071	-0.084775	-0.070821	-0.337209	-0.196074	-0.236592

TABLE 8 — RATES FROM AGE DISTRIBUTIONS AND VITAL STATISTICS (Females)

VITAL STATISTICS		THOMPSON AGE RANGE	NRR	1000r	INTERVAL	BOURGEOIS-PICHAT AGE RANGE	NRR	1000b	1000d	1000r	COALE
GRR	1.458										IBR
NRR	1.319	0-4	1.32	10.32	27.37	5-29	0.90	15.40	19.28	-3.88	IDR
TFR	3.018	5-9	1.10	3.52	27.33	30-54	0.74	9.55	20.85	-11.30	IRI
GENERATION	27.182	10-14	0.92	-3.18	27.27	55-79	1.82	46.99	24.79	22.20	K1
SEX RATIO	106.998	15-19	0.98	-0.68	27.18	*45-74	1.91	52.97	29.01	23.96	K2

TABLE 9 — LESLIE MATRIX AND ITS SPECTRAL COMPONENTS (Females)

Start Age Interval	ORIGINAL MATRIX SUB-DIAGONAL	ALTERNATIVE FIRST ROWS Projection	ALTERNATIVE FIRST ROWS Integral	FIRST STABLE MATRIX % IN STABLE POPULATION	FISHER VALUES	REPRODUCTIVE VALUES	SECOND STABLE MATRIX Z_2 FIRST COLUMN	SECOND STABLE MATRIX Z_2 FIRST ROW
0	0.99072	0.00000	0.00000	9.758	1.098	695514	0.1662+0.0950	0.1662+0.0950
5	0.99696	0.00015	0.00000	9.187	1.166	621436	0.1895-0.1332	-0.0127+0.1577
10	0.99581	0.05845	0.00031	8.703	1.231	537239	-0.0487-0.2778	-0.1216+0.0456
15	0.99346	0.27737	0.12012	8.236	1.236	545171	-0.3311-0.0899	-0.0862-0.0802
20	0.99206	0.40754	0.45189	7.775	1.003	501030	-0.2695+0.3173	-0.0168-0.1189
25	0.99109	0.30991	0.38730	7.330	0.613	327315	0.2093+0.4591	0.0147-0.0932
30	0.98907	0.18764	0.25075	6.903	0.307	109199	0.6107+0.0068	0.0229-0.0515
35	0.98606	0.08875	0.13569	6.488	0.119	52247	0.3210-0.6644	0.0151-0.0190
40	0.98105	0.02483	0.04704	6.079	0.028	13984	-0.5600-0.6901	0.0046-0.0039
45	0.97208	0.00202	0.00397	5.668	0.002	1015	-1.0337+0.2561	0.0004-0.0003
50	0.95727	0.00009	0.00018	5.235	0.000	38	-0.2464+1.2403	0.0000-0.0000
55+	0.78343			18.638				

TABLE 10 — AGE ANALYSIS AND MISCELLANEOUS RESULTS (Females)

Start Age Interval	OBSERVED POPUL. (IN 100's)	CONTRIBUTIONS OF ROOTS (IN 100's) r_1	r_2, r_3	$r_4 \cdot r_{11}$	AGE-SP. BIRTH RATES	NET MATERNITY FUNCTION	COEFF. OF MATRIX EQUATION	PARAMETERS INTEGRAL	PARAMETERS MATRIX	x	EXP. INCREASE $e^{(x+2\frac{1}{2})r}$
0	6335	5758	483	94	0.0000	0.0000	0.0000	L(1) 1.05227	1.05233	0	1.0258
5	5329	5421	47	-140	0.0000	0.0000	0.0001	L(2) 0.33604	0.34791	50	1.7074
10	4365	5136	-663	-108	0.0001	0.0003	0.0577	0.76787	0.74108	55	1.7967
15	4410	4860	-755	304	0.0251	0.1152	0.2728	R(1) 0.01019	0.01020	60	1.8906
20	4995	4588	200	208	0.0943	0.4305	0.3982	R(2) -0.03530	-0.04001	65	1.9894
25	5341	4325	1315	-300	0.0808	0.3660	0.3004	0.23166	0.22638	70	2.0934
30	3552	4074	1060	-1582	0.0523	0.2348	0.1803	C(1)	59011	75	2.2028
35	4398	3829	-835	1405	0.0283	0.1257	0.0843	C(2)	85645	80	2.3179
40	5004	3588	-2398	3814	0.0098	0.0430	0.0233		-104228	85	2.4391
45	4633	3345	-1237	2525	0.0008	0.0036	0.0019	2P/Y 27.1230	27.7556	90	2.5666
50	4200	3089	2164	-1053	0.0000	0.0002	0.0001	DELTA 6.4581		95	2.7007
55+	11870	10998								100	2.8419

TABLE 1 — DATA

AGE AT LAST BIRTHDAY	POPULATION BOTH SEXES	MALES Number	%	FEMALES Number	%	BIRTHS BY AGE OF MOTHER	DEATHS BOTH SEXES	MALES	FEMALES	AGE AT LAST BIRTHDAY
0	259929	133662	2.1	126267	1.9	0	10432	5918	4514	0
1-4	1038715	532623	8.4	506092	7.6	0	2085	1126	959	1-4
5-9	1223417	622020	9.9	601397	9.0	0	709	433	276	5-9
10-14	1005161	509441	8.1	495720	7.5	59	540	337	203	10-14
15-19	839647	423671	6.7	415976	6.3	19257	838	563	275	15-19
20-24	946534	474880	7.5	471654	7.1	92887	1305	886	419	20-24
25-29	992833	489500	7.8	503333	7.6	80356	1454	904	550	25-29
30-34	1017940	497128	7.9	520812	7.8	49852	1798	1070	728	30-34
35-39	588073	286299	4.5	301774	4.5	16057	1418	801	617	35-39
40-44	968376	474565	7.5	493811	7.4	8689	3147	1819	1328	40-44
45-49	934838	454144	7.2	480694	7.2	674	4870	2881	1989	45-49
50-54	861717	416314	6.6	445403	6.7	24	7289	4496	2793	50-54
55-59	693766	313657	5.0	380109	5.7	0	9363	5642	3721	55-59
60-64	521764	230045	3.6	291719	4.4	0	11254	6445	4809	60-64
65-69	419784	178393	2.8	241391	3.6	0	14744	7706	7038	65-69
70-74	308993	131720	2.1	177273	2.7		17598	8527	9071	70-74
75-79	191119	80380	1.3	110739	1.7		18244	8309	9935	75-79
80-84	98996	40724	0.6	58272	0.9	138172 M.	14787	6569	8218	80-84
85+	40452	16614	0.3	23838	0.4	129683 F.	9842	3910	5932	85+
TOTAL	12952054	6305780		6646274		267855	131717	68342	63375	TOTAL

TABLE 2 — MALE LIFE TABLE

x	$_nq_x$	l_x	$_nd_x$	$_nL_x$	$_nm_x$	$_na_x$	T_x	r_x	$\mathring{e}_x$	$_nM_x$	x
0	0.042855	100000	4286	96792	0.044276	0.2514	6529158	0.0000	65.292	0.044276	0
1	0.008405	95714	804	380527	0.002114	1.1032	6432367	0.0000	67.204	0.002114	1
5	0.003443	94910	327	473733	0.000690	2.5000	6051839	0.0258	63.764	0.000696	5
10	0.003327	94583	315	472191	0.000666	2.6975	5578106	0.0376	58.976	0.000662	10
15	0.006631	94268	625	469895	0.001330	2.6849	5105915	0.0057	54.164	0.001329	15
20	0.009286	93643	870	466090	0.001866	2.5545	4636020	0.0000	49.507	0.001866	20
25	0.009192	92774	853	461762	0.001847	2.5291	4169929	0.0000	44.947	0.001847	25
30	0.010756	91921	989	457219	0.002163	2.5866	3708168	0.0514	40.341	0.002152	30
35	0.013899	90932	1264	451650	0.002798	2.6178	3250949	0.0018	35.751	0.002798	35
40	0.018996	89668	1703	444394	0.003833	2.6823	2799298	0.0000	31.218	0.003833	40
45	0.031310	87965	2754	433525	0.006353	2.7126	2354904	0.0064	26.771	0.006344	45
50	0.052979	85211	4514	415656	0.010861	2.6967	1921379	0.0257	22.549	0.010800	50
55	0.086950	80696	7017	387021	0.018130	2.6540	1505723	0.0408	18.659	0.017988	55
60	0.131658	73680	9701	345299	0.028093	2.6186	1118702	0.0154	15.183	0.028016	60
65	0.195985	63979	12539	289527	0.043308	2.5780	773403	0.0154	12.088	0.043197	65
70	0.279838	51440	14395	221772	0.064909	2.5387	483876	0.0154	9.407	0.064736	70
75	0.410676	37045	15214	146769	0.103657	2.4721	262105	0.0154	7.075	0.103371	75
80	0.566122	21832	12359	76419	0.161733	2.4032	115336	0.0154	5.283	0.161305	80
85+	1.000000	9472	9472	38917	0.243397	4.1085	38917	0.0154	4.109	0.235343	85+

TABLE 3 — FEMALE LIFE TABLE

x	$_nq_x$	l_x	$_nd_x$	$_nL_x$	$_nm_x$	$_na_x$	T_x	r_x	$\mathring{e}_x$	$_nM_x$	x
0	0.034832	100000	3483	97433	0.035750	0.2630	6997262	0.0000	69.973	0.035750	0
1	0.007538	96517	728	383967	0.001895	1.1128	6899829	0.0000	71.488	0.001895	1
5	0.002263	95789	217	478404	0.000453	2.5000	6515862	0.0235	68.023	0.000459	5
10	0.002053	95572	196	477392	0.000411	2.6043	6037458	0.0364	63.172	0.000409	10
15	0.003302	95376	315	476141	0.000662	2.6489	5560066	0.0043	58.296	0.000661	15
20	0.004432	95061	421	474295	0.000888	2.5993	5083925	0.0000	53.481	0.000888	20
25	0.005449	94640	516	471960	0.001093	2.5965	4609631	0.0000	48.707	0.001093	25
30	0.007015	94124	660	469061	0.001408	2.6374	4137671	0.0497	43.960	0.001398	30
35	0.010178	93464	951	465061	0.002045	2.6261	3668610	0.0033	39.252	0.002045	35
40	0.013362	92513	1236	459665	0.002689	2.6552	3203548	0.0000	34.628	0.002689	40
45	0.020514	91276	1872	452021	0.004142	2.6708	2743884	0.0061	30.061	0.004138	45
50	0.030999	89404	2771	440571	0.006291	2.6730	2291863	0.0170	25.635	0.006271	50
55	0.048183	86633	4174	423522	0.009856	2.6903	1851291	0.0319	21.369	0.009789	55
60	0.079844	82458	6584	397132	0.016578	2.6974	1427769	0.0242	17.315	0.016485	60
65	0.137215	75875	10411	355098	0.029319	2.6684	1030638	0.0242	13.583	0.029156	65
70	0.229090	65463	14997	291527	0.051443	2.6135	675540	0.0242	10.319	0.051170	70
75	0.368253	50466	18584	206179	0.090137	2.5166	384013	0.0242	7.609	0.089715	75
80	0.516822	31882	16477	116368	0.141597	2.4598	177833	0.0242	5.578	0.141028	80
85+	1.000000	15405	15405	61466	0.250623	3.9901	61466	0.0242	3.990	0.248847	85+

TABLE 4 — OBSERVED AND PROJECTED VITAL RATES

	OBSERVED POPULATION BOTH SEXES	MALES	FEMALES	PROJECTED POPULATION 1959 MALES	FEMALES	1964 MALES	FEMALES	1969 MALES	FEMALES	STABLE POPULATION MALES	FEMALES
RATES PER THOUSAND											
Birth	20.68	21.91	19.51	20.28	18.16	20.17	18.15	21.19	19.18	21.33	20.21
Death	10.17	10.84	9.54	11.13	10.08	11.46	10.57	11.85	11.14	11.52	10.40
Increase	10.51	11.07	9.98	9.15	8.08	8.71	7.58	9.34	8.04		9.8136
PERCENTAGE											
under 15	27.23	28.51	26.02	29.13	26.53	28.27	25.71	27.50	25.14	28.23	27.02
15-64	64.59	64.39	64.78	63.64	63.73	63.95	63.54	63.71	63.04	63.72	62.87
65 and over	8.18	7.10	9.20	7.23	9.75	7.78	10.74	8.79	11.82	8.05	10.12
DEP. RATIO X 100	54.83	55.31	54.37	57.13	56.91	56.37	57.37	56.97	58.63	56.94	59.06

TABLE 1 DATA

AGE AT LAST BIRTHDAY	POPULATION BOTH SEXES	MALES Number	%	FEMALES Number	%	BIRTHS BY AGE OF MOTHER	DEATHS BOTH SEXES	MALES	FEMALES	AGE AT LAST BIRTHDAY
0	250831	128814	2.0	122017	1.8	0	7876	4531	3345	0
1-4	1028489	528019	8.1	500470	7.3	0	1549	845	704	1-4
5-9	1291003	660750	10.1	630253	9.2	0	723	453	270	5-9
10-14	1135145	575007	8.8	560138	8.2	59	556	356	200	10-14
15-19	913104	461361	7.1	451743	6.6	21365	828	580	248	15-19
20-24	855482	430542	6.6	424940	6.2	87082	1082	749	333	20-24
25-29	980277	488580	7.5	491697	7.2	73381	1281	847	434	25-29
30-34	1017383	496508	7.6	520875	7.6	44153	1568	952	616	30-34
35-39	806551	394448	6.1	412103	6.0	18700	1617	946	671	35-39
40-44	749400	365035	5.6	384365	5.6	4672	2221	1275	946	40-44
45-49	962108	470086	7.2	492022	7.2	493	4426	2658	1768	45-49
50-54	881870	424844	6.5	457026	6.7	11	6927	4289	2638	50-54
55-59	775705	363384	5.6	412321	6.0	0	9910	6206	3704	55-59
60-64	592331	258315	4.0	334016	4.9	0	12136	7049	5087	60-64
65-69	436178	185758	2.9	250420	3.7	0	14602	7796	6806	65-69
70-74	325774	133621	2.1	192153	2.8		17799	8713	9086	70-74
75-79	207602	87102	1.3	120500	1.8		18266	8358	9908	75-79
80-84	100691	40343	0.6	60348	0.9	128631 M.	14998	6540	8458	80-84
85+	48111	19963	0.3	28148	0.4	121285 F.	10498	4301	6197	85+
TOTAL	13358035	6512480		6845555		249916	128863	67444	61419	TOTAL

TABLE 2 MALE LIFE TABLE

x	$_nq_x$	l_x	$_nd_x$	$_nL_x$	$_nm_x$	$_na_x$	T_x	r_x	$\mathring{e}_x$	$_nM_x$	x
0	0.034267	100000	3427	97418	0.035175	0.2466	6666897	0.0000	66.669	0.035175	0
1	0.006372	96573	615	384509	0.001600	1.0994	6569479	0.0000	68.026	0.001600	1
5	0.003412	95958	327	478972	0.000684	2.5000	6184970	0.0124	64.455	0.000686	5
10	0.003112	95631	298	477466	0.000623	2.6912	5705999	0.0351	59.667	0.000619	10
15	0.006299	95333	601	475272	0.001264	2.6814	5228533	0.0277	54.845	0.001257	15
20	0.008661	94732	821	471655	0.001740	2.5533	4753261	0.0000	50.176	0.001740	20
25	0.008631	93912	811	467548	0.001734	2.5178	4281606	0.0000	45.592	0.001734	25
30	0.009556	93101	890	463344	0.001920	2.5686	3814059	0.0194	40.967	0.001917	30
35	0.011969	92212	1104	458443	0.002407	2.6300	3350715	0.0283	36.337	0.002398	35
40	0.017324	91108	1578	451885	0.003493	2.6842	2892272	0.0000	31.746	0.003493	40
45	0.027913	89530	2499	441970	0.005654	2.7276	2440387	0.0000	27.258	0.005654	45
50	0.049507	87031	4309	425285	0.010131	2.7097	1998418	0.0152	22.962	0.010095	50
55	0.082683	82722	6836	397657	0.017190	2.6661	1573133	0.0320	19.017	0.017078	55
60	0.128598	75886	9759	356245	0.027394	2.6240	1175476	0.0212	15.490	0.027288	60
65	0.191194	66128	12643	300135	0.042125	2.5874	819231	0.0212	12.389	0.041969	65
70	0.281661	53484	15064	230228	0.065433	2.5310	519096	0.0212	9.706	0.065207	70
75	0.387435	38420	14885	154545	0.096317	2.4770	288868	0.0212	7.519	0.095956	75
80	0.570346	23535	13423	82468	0.162766	2.4259	134323	0.0212	5.707	0.162110	80
85+	1.000000	10112	10112	51856	0.194998	5.1283	51856	0.0212	5.128	0.215448	85+

TABLE 3 FEMALE LIFE TABLE

x	$_nq_x$	l_x	$_nd_x$	$_nL_x$	$_nm_x$	$_na_x$	T_x	r_x	$\mathring{e}_x$	$_nM_x$	x
0	0.026869	100000	2687	98011	0.027414	0.2599	7161242	0.0000	71.612	0.027414	0
1	0.005604	97313	545	387676	0.001407	1.1101	7063231	0.0000	72.583	0.001407	1
5	0.002131	96768	206	483323	0.000427	2.5000	6675555	0.0099	68.985	0.000428	5
10	0.001788	96562	173	482388	0.000358	2.5714	6192231	0.0329	64.127	0.000357	10
15	0.002753	96389	265	481323	0.000551	2.6596	5709843	0.0271	59.238	0.000549	15
20	0.003911	96124	376	479710	0.000784	2.5866	5228520	0.0000	54.394	0.000784	20
25	0.004404	95748	422	477723	0.000883	2.5926	4748809	0.0000	49.597	0.000883	25
30	0.005909	95326	563	475294	0.001185	2.6296	4271087	0.0165	44.805	0.001183	30
35	0.008148	94763	772	472005	0.001636	2.6583	3795792	0.0287	40.056	0.001628	35
40	0.012236	93990	1150	467261	0.002461	2.6598	3323787	0.0000	35.363	0.002461	40
45	0.017818	92840	1654	460369	0.003593	2.6830	2856526	0.0000	30.768	0.003593	45
50	0.028543	91186	2603	449895	0.005785	2.6810	2396157	0.0117	26.278	0.005772	50
55	0.044208	88583	3916	433891	0.009026	2.6951	1946262	0.0218	21.971	0.008983	55
60	0.074063	84667	6271	408944	0.015334	2.7048	1512371	0.0285	17.863	0.015230	60
65	0.128599	78397	10082	368514	0.027358	2.6721	1103426	0.0285	14.075	0.027178	65
70	0.213702	68315	14599	306822	0.047581	2.6196	734913	0.0285	10.758	0.047285	70
75	0.343654	53716	18460	223182	0.082711	2.5407	428090	0.0285	7.970	0.082224	75
80	0.516398	35256	18206	129213	0.140901	2.4839	204909	0.0285	5.812	0.140154	80
85+	1.000000	17050	17050	75696	0.225242	4.4397	75696	0.0285	4.440	0.220158	85+

TABLE 4 OBSERVED AND PROJECTED VITAL RATES

RATES PER THOUSAND	OBSERVED POPULATION BOTH SEXES	MALES	FEMALES	PROJECTED POPULATION 1962 MALES	FEMALES	1967 MALES	FEMALES	1972 MALES	FEMALES	STABLE POPULATION MALES	FEMALES
Birth	18.71	19.75	17.72	19.06	17.17	19.94	18.03	21.02	19.11	20.28	19.16
Death	9.65	10.36	8.97	10.86	9.66	11.35	10.33	11.73	10.94	11.48	10.36
Increase	9.06	9.40	8.75	8.20	7.50	8.59	7.70	9.29	8.17		8.8010
PERCENTAGE											
under 15	27.74	29.06	26.48	28.41	25.81	27.08	24.69	26.71	24.50	27.33	26.06
15-64	63.89	63.77	64.00	63.93	63.61	64.28	63.50	63.82	62.73	63.96	62.91
65 and over	8.37	7.17	9.52	7.66	10.58	8.64	11.80	9.47	12.76	8.71	11.04
DEP. RATIO X 100	56.52	56.81	56.25	56.41	57.21	55.57	57.47	56.69	59.41	56.34	58.96

TABLE 1 — DATA

AGE AT LAST BIRTHDAY	POPULATION BOTH SEXES	MALES Number	%	FEMALES Number	%	BIRTHS BY AGE OF MOTHER	DEATHS BOTH SEXES	MALES	FEMALES	AGE AT LAST BIRTHDAY
0	212784	109415	1.6	103369	1.5	0	5216	3007	2209	0
1-4	957006	490828	7.4	466178	6.7	0	1221	686	535	1-4
5-9	1292648	663153	10.0	629495	9.0	0	605	379	226	5-9
10-14	1255967	640099	9.6	615868	8.8	42	496	325	171	10-14
15-19	1034916	523018	7.9	511898	7.3	23468	901	660	241	15-19
20-24	848956	427532	6.4	421424	6.0	84134	1015	758	257	20-24
25-29	911738	457327	6.9	454411	6.5	59663	1106	766	340	25-29
30-34	983434	486496	7.3	496938	7.1	31951	1416	936	480	30-34
35-39	1030590	500951	7.5	529639	7.6	15363	1940	1211	729	35-39
40-44	596738	290464	4.4	306274	4.4	2666	1702	1031	671	40-44
45-49	910961	443654	6.7	467307	6.7	251	3980	2374	1606	45-49
50-54	923414	446100	6.7	477314	6.8	10	6688	4158	2530	50-54
55-59	825515	392836	5.9	432679	6.2	0	10084	6398	3686	55-59
60-64	665255	294962	4.4	370293	5.3	0	13133	7983	5150	60-64
65-69	476565	201883	3.0	274682	3.9	0	15209	8341	6868	65-69
70-74	340437	137413	2.1	203024	2.9		17826	8731	9095	70-74
75-79	223375	89782	1.3	133593	1.9		18602	8344	10258	75-79
80-84	109393	44394	0.7	64999	0.9	111997 M.	15257	6503	8754	80-84
85+	54396	21468	0.3	32928	0.5	105551 F.	11296	4488	6808	85+
TOTAL	13654088	6661775		6992313		217548	127693	67079	60614	TOTAL

TABLE 2 — MALE LIFE TABLE

x	nq_x	l_x	nd_x	nL_x	nm_x	na_x	T_x	r_x	$\mathring{e}_x$	nM_x	x
0	0.026934	100000	2693	98004	0.027483	0.2589	6757656	0.0000	67.577	0.027483	0
1	0.005568	97307	542	387660	0.001398	1.1093	6659652	0.0000	68.440	0.001398	1
5	0.002853	96765	276	483134	0.000572	2.5000	6271992	0.0000	64.817	0.000572	5
10	0.002553	96489	246	481897	0.000511	2.7828	5788859	0.0230	59.995	0.000508	10
15	0.006342	96242	610	479811	0.001272	2.7042	5306961	0.0391	55.142	0.001262	15
20	0.008831	95632	845	476086	0.001774	2.5444	4827151	0.0118	50.476	0.001773	20
25	0.008340	94787	791	471972	0.001675	2.5146	4351065	0.0000	45.903	0.001675	25
30	0.009575	93997	900	467804	0.001924	2.5778	3879093	0.0000	41.268	0.001924	30
35	0.012100	93097	1126	462818	0.002434	2.6334	3411288	0.0490	36.642	0.002417	35
40	0.017627	91970	1621	456062	0.003555	2.6621	2948470	0.0085	32.059	0.003549	40
45	0.026431	90349	2388	446275	0.005351	2.7089	2492408	0.0000	27.586	0.005351	45
50	0.045659	87961	4016	430648	0.009326	2.7196	2046133	0.0023	23.262	0.009321	50
55	0.078879	83945	6622	404392	0.016374	2.6844	1615486	0.0243	19.245	0.016287	55
60	0.127731	77323	9877	363196	0.027194	2.6286	1211093	0.0257	15.663	0.027065	60
65	0.188595	67447	12720	306519	0.041499	2.5853	847897	0.0257	12.571	0.041316	65
70	0.275591	54727	15082	236397	0.063800	2.5311	541378	0.0257	9.892	0.063538	70
75	0.377577	39645	14969	160388	0.093329	2.4724	304982	0.0257	7.693	0.092956	75
80	0.530987	24676	13102	89058	0.147122	2.4460	144593	0.0257	5.860	0.146484	80
85+	1.000000	11573	11573	55535	0.208395	4.7986	55535	0.0257	4.799	0.209056	85+

TABLE 3 — FEMALE LIFE TABLE

x	nq_x	l_x	nd_x	nL_x	nm_x	na_x	T_x	r_x	$\mathring{e}_x$	nM_x	x
0	0.021040	100000	2104	98454	0.021370	0.2651	7297146	0.0000	72.971	0.021370	0
1	0.004575	97896	448	390292	0.001148	1.1146	7198693	0.0000	73.534	0.001148	1
5	0.001793	97448	175	486804	0.000359	2.5000	6808401	0.0000	69.867	0.000359	5
10	0.001390	97273	135	486040	0.000278	2.5846	6321597	0.0203	64.988	0.000278	10
15	0.002364	97138	230	485150	0.000473	2.6453	5835557	0.0375	60.075	0.000471	15
20	0.003048	96909	295	483831	0.000610	2.5925	5350407	0.0113	55.211	0.000610	20
25	0.003734	96613	361	482199	0.000748	2.5973	4866576	0.0000	50.372	0.000748	25
30	0.004819	96252	464	480165	0.000966	2.6357	4384377	0.0000	45.551	0.000966	30
35	0.006920	95789	663	477405	0.001388	2.6807	3904212	0.0469	40.759	0.001376	35
40	0.010921	95126	1039	473228	0.002195	2.6887	3426806	0.0103	36.024	0.002191	40
45	0.017048	94087	1604	466713	0.003437	2.6797	2953579	0.0000	31.392	0.003437	45
50	0.026193	92483	2422	466811	0.005303	2.6867	2486866	0.0022	26.890	0.005300	50
55	0.041914	90061	3775	441581	0.008548	2.6896	2030055	0.0165	22.541	0.008519	55
60	0.067880	86286	5857	417994	0.014012	2.7063	1588474	0.0314	18.409	0.013908	60
65	0.119032	80429	9574	379997	0.025194	2.6867	1170480	0.0314	14.553	0.025003	65
70	0.203731	70855	14435	320013	0.045109	2.6265	790483	0.0314	11.156	0.044798	70
75	0.325019	56420	18337	237235	0.077297	2.5535	470469	0.0314	8.339	0.076785	75
80	0.502598	38082	19140	141262	0.135493	2.5066	233234	0.0314	6.124	0.134679	80
85+	1.000000	18942	18942	91972	0.205957	4.8554	91972	0.0314	4.855	0.206755	85+

TABLE 4 — OBSERVED AND PROJECTED VITAL RATES

	OBSERVED POPULATION BOTH SEXES	MALES	FEMALES	PROJECTED POPULATION 1965 MALES	FEMALES	1970 MALES	FEMALES	1975 MALES	FEMALES	STABLE POPULATION MALES	FEMALES
RATES PER THOUSAND											
Birth	15.93	16.81	15.10	17.44	15.69	18.93	17.08	19.44	17.62	17.32	16.18
Death	9.35	10.07	8.67	10.77	9.56	11.36	10.39	11.77	11.05	12.88	11.74
Increase	6.58	6.74	6.43	6.68	6.13	7.57	6.69	7.66	6.57		4.4432
PERCENTAGE											
under 15	27.23	28.57	25.96	26.45	23.97	24.89	22.63	25.02	22.85	24.31	22.88
15-64	63.95	64.00	63.90	65.20	64.38	65.61	64.38	64.62	63.12	65.09	63.49
65 and over	8.82	7.43	10.14	8.35	11.64	9.50	12.99	10.37	14.03	10.59	13.62
DEP. RATIO X 100	56.38	56.26	56.49	53.37	55.32	52.41	55.33	54.75	58.42	53.62	57.50

AGE AT LAST BIRTHDAY	1965 BOTH SEXES	MALES	FEMALES	1970 BOTH SEXES	MALES	FEMALES	1975 BOTH SEXES	MALES	FEMALES	AGE AT LAST BIRTHDAY	
0-4	1099	564	535	1208	620	588	1321	678	643	0-4	**TABLE 5**
5-9	1164	597	567	1094	561	533	1203	617	586	5-9	
10-14	1290	661	629	1162	596	566	1091	559	532	10-14	
15-19	1252	637	615	1286	659	627	1158	593	565	15-19	POPULATION
20-24	1030	519	511	1245	632	613	1279	653	626	20-24	PROJECTED
25-29	844	424	420	1023	514	509	1238	627	611	25-29	WITH
30-34	905	453	452	838	420	418	1017	510	507	30-34	FIXED
35-39	975	481	494	898	448	450	832	416	416	35-39	AGE—
40-44	1019	494	525	964	474	490	888	442	446	40-44	SPECIFIC
45-49	586	284	302	1001	483	518	947	464	483	45-49	BIRTH
50-54	885	428	457	570	274	296	973	466	507	50-54	AND
55-59	880	419	461	844	402	442	544	258	286	55-59	DEATH
60-64	763	353	410	813	376	437	780	361	419	60-64	RATES
65-69	586	249	337	670	298	372	715	318	397	65-69	(IN 1000's)
70-74	387	156	231	475	192	283	544	230	314	70-74	
75-79	244	93	151	277	106	171	340	130	210	75-79	
80-84	130	50	80	142	52	90	161	59	102	80-84	
85+	70	28	42	83	31	52	90	32	58	85+	
TOTAL	14109	6890	7219	14593	7138	7455	15121	7413	7708	TOTAL	

STANDARD COUNTRIES: STANDARDIZED RATES PER THOUSAND	ENGLAND AND WALES 1961 BOTH SEXES	MALES	FEMALES	UNITED STATES 1960 BOTH SEXES	MALES	FEMALES	MEXICO 1960 BOTH SEXES	MALES	FEMALES	
Birth	15.16	16.38*	14.25	15.39	15.51*	14.71	19.03	14.65*	18.42	**TABLE 6**
Death	12.04	12.11*	12.08	9.73	10.58*	8.80	5.09	8.68*	4.22	STANDARDIZED RATES
Increase	3.12	4.28*	2.18	5.65	4.93*	5.91	13.94	5.96*	14.20	

	OBSERVED POP. MALES	FEMALES	STATIONARY POP. MALES	FEMALES	STABLE POP. MALES	FEMALES	OBSERVED BIRTHS	NET MATERNITY FUNCTION	BIRTHS IN STABLE POP.	
μ	32.18331	34.46223	36.56799	38.61904	34.38204	36.25388	26.13324	26.00399	25.86479	**TABLE 7**
σ^2	455.8265	490.6331	498.1884	537.7408	485.0169	525.9354	30.52919	29.56036	28.93150	MOMENTS
κ_3	3488.640	2932.120	2454.425	2010.680	3453.257	3281.468	119.6901	142.4983	140.5383	AND
κ_4	-189097.	-242251.	-238238.	-299447.	-209757.	-270143.	50.984	427.428	464.516	CUMULANTS
β_1	0.128503	0.072794	0.048721	0.026000	0.104517	0.074018	0.503466	0.786122	0.815598	
β_2	2.089908	1.993644	2.040103	1.964442	2.108331	2.023372	3.054702	3.489152	3.554956	
κ	-0.047320	-0.026224	-0.018688	-0.009581	-0.040047	-0.027271	-0.307563	-0.517029	-0.556640	

VITAL STATISTICS		THOMPSON AGE RANGE	NRR	1000r	INTERVAL	BOURGEOIS-PICHAT AGE RANGE	NRR	1000b	1000d	1000r	COALE	
GRR	1.163					5-29	1.72	21.82	1.67	20.15	IBR	**TABLE 8**
NRR	1.122	0-4	1.23	7.75	27.43	5-29	1.72	21.82	1.67	20.15	IDR	RATES
TFR	2.397	5-9	1.38	11.95	27.40	30-54	1.05	14.60	12.93	1.67	IRI	FROM AGE
GENERATION	25.934	10-14	1.32	9.95	27.35	55-79	2.26	80.62	50.47	30.15	K1	DISTRIBUTIONS
SEX RATIO	106.107	15-19	1.09	3.08	27.27	*50-74	2.02	61.10	35.06	26.04	K2	AND VITAL STATISTICS (Females)

Start of Age Interval	ORIGINAL MATRIX SUB-DIAGONAL	ALTERNATIVE FIRST ROWS Projection	Integral	FIRST STABLE MATRIX % IN STABLE POPULATION	FISHER VALUES	REPRODUCTIVE VALUES	SECOND STABLE MATRIX Z₂ FIRST COLUMN	FIRST ROW	
0	0.99603	0.00000	0.00000	7.823	1.034	589159	0.2050+0.0796	0.2050+0.0796	**TABLE 9**
5	0.99843	0.00008	0.00000	7.621	1.062	668463	0.1780-0.2027	-0.0037+0.1792	LESLIE
10	0.99817	0.05434	0.00016	7.441	1.087	669691	-0.1592-0.2912	-0.1379+0.0471	MATRIX
15	0.99728	0.29042	0.10993	7.264	1.058	541364	-0.4035+0.0610	-0.0856-0.0965	AND ITS
20	0.99663	0.39186	0.47870	7.085	0.783	329992	-0.0996+0.4914	-0.0098-0.1156	SPECTRAL
25	0.99578	0.23159	0.31483	6.906	0.397	180233	0.5248+0.3217	0.0051-0.0711	COMPONENTS
30	0.99425	0.11043	0.15417	6.726	0.167	82834	0.5915-0.4694	0.0082-0.0345	(Females)
35	0.99125	0.04462	0.06955	6.540	0.057	29941	-0.2916-0.8778	0.0060-0.0122	
40	0.98623	0.01095	0.02087	6.341	0.012	3597	-1.1290-0.0331	0.0018-0.0024	
45	0.97878	0.00066	0.00129	6.116	0.001	324	-0.5082+1.2748	0.0001-0.0001	
50	0.96666	0.00002	0.00005	5.855	0.000	12	1.2338+1.1027	0.0000-0.0000	
55+	0.78940			24.281					

Start of Age Interval	OBSERVED POPUL. (IN 100's)	CONTRIBUTIONS OF ROOTS (IN 100's) r_1	r_2, r_3	r_4-r_{11}	AGE-SP. BIRTH RATES	NET MATERNITY FUNCTION	COEFF. OF MATRIX EQUATION	PARAMETERS INTEGRAL	MATRIX	EXP. INCREASE x	$e^{(x+2\frac{1}{2})r}$	
0	5695	5791	-165	69	0.0000	0.0000	0.0000	L(1) 1.02246	1.02248	0	1.0112	**TABLE 10**
5	6295	5641	676	-22	0.0000	0.0000	0.0001	L(2) 0.26613	0.27838	50	1.2627	AGE
10	6159	5509	820	-170	0.0000	0.0002	0.0540	0.79947	0.76251	55	1.2911	ANALYSIS
15	5119	5378	-331	72	0.0222	0.1079	0.2883	R(1) 0.00444	0.00445	60	1.3201	AND
20	4214	5245	-1517	486	0.0969	0.4687	0.3879	R(2) -0.03425	-0.04172	65	1.3497	MISCELLANEOUS
25	4544	5113	-778	210	0.0637	0.3072	0.2285	0.24989	0.24415	70	1.3801	RESULTS
30	4969	4979	1630	-1640	0.0312	0.1498	0.1085	C(1)	74029	75	1.4111	(Females)
35	5296	4842	2539	-2085	0.0141	0.0672	0.0436	C(2)	18230	80	1.4428	
40	3063	4694	-312	-1319	0.0042	0.0200	0.0106		150694	85	1.4752	
45	4673	4527	-4027	4173	0.0003	0.0012	0.0006	2P/Y 25.1438	25.7349	90	1.5083	
50	4773	4334	-2874	3313	0.0000	0.0000	0.0000	DELTA 7.0182		95	1.5422	
55+	15122	17975								100	1.5769	

TABLE 1 — DATA

AGE AT LAST BIRTHDAY	POPULATION BOTH SEXES	MALES Number	%	FEMALES Number	%	BIRTHS BY AGE OF MOTHER	DEATHS BOTH SEXES	MALES	FEMALES	AGE AT LAST BIRTHDAY
0	213779	109508	1.6	104271	1.5	0	4954	2858	2096	0
1-4	882182	451695	6.7	430487	6.1	0	1002	566	436	1-4
5-9	1278115	653370	9.7	624745	8.8	0	650	408	242	5-9
10-14	1304815	666010	9.8	638805	9.0	45	483	297	186	10-14
15-19	1141729	579190	8.6	562539	7.9	25283	896	662	234	15-19
20-24	919505	465766	6.9	453739	6.4	90014	1026	784	242	20-24
25-29	859947	431832	6.4	428115	6.0	56008	990	708	282	25-29
30-34	964301	479341	7.1	484960	6.8	29495	1363	898	465	30-34
35-39	1005891	491008	7.3	514883	7.3	13297	1971	1195	776	35-39
40-44	788882	383105	5.7	405777	5.7	3177	2073	1250	823	40-44
45-49	745523	361949	5.4	383574	5.4	132	3229	1970	1259	45-49
50-54	942749	459129	6.8	483620	6.8	5	6777	4297	2480	50-54
55-59	841569	402073	5.9	439496	6.2	0	10362	6718	3644	55-59
60-64	712363	324230	4.8	388133	5.5	0	14792	9161	5631	60-64
65-69	518970	216840	3.2	302130	4.3	0	17034	9433	7601	65-69
70-74	349757	139324	2.1	210433	3.0		19418	9682	9736	70-74
75-79	225336	86714	1.3	138622	2.0		21143	9617	11526	75-79
80-84	114103	42837	0.6	71266	1.0	111719 M.	17255	7170	10085	80-84
85+	50348	18052	0.3	32296	0.5	105737 F.	13298	5243	8055	85+
TOTAL	13859864	6761973		7097891		217456	138716	72917	65799	TOTAL

TABLE 2 — MALE LIFE TABLE

x	$_nq_x$	l_x	$_nd_x$	$_nL_x$	$_nm_x$	$_na_x$	T_x	r_x	$\mathring{e}_x$	$_nM_x$	x
0	0.025599	100000	2560	98087	0.026099	0.2527	6713188	0.0000	67.132	0.026099	0
1	0.004994	97440	487	388351	0.001253	1.1042	6615101	0.0000	67.889	0.001253	1
5	0.003117	96953	302	484012	0.000624	2.5000	6226750	0.0000	64.224	0.000624	5
10	0.002234	96651	216	482769	0.000447	2.7429	5742738	0.0114	59.417	0.000446	10
15	0.005744	96435	554	480914	0.001152	2.7216	5259969	0.0347	54.544	0.001143	15
20	0.008396	95881	805	477440	0.001686	2.5575	4779055	0.0278	49.843	0.001683	20
25	0.008164	95076	776	473457	0.001640	2.5199	4301615	0.0000	45.244	0.001640	25
30	0.009325	94300	879	469376	0.001873	2.5845	3828158	0.0000	40.595	0.001873	30
35	0.012127	93421	1133	464401	0.002440	2.6145	3358782	0.0199	35.953	0.002434	35
40	0.016274	92288	1502	457957	0.003279	2.6814	2894381	0.0270	31.363	0.003263	40
45	0.026880	90786	2440	448359	0.005443	2.7174	2436424	0.0000	26.837	0.005443	45
50	0.045819	88346	4048	432518	0.009359	2.7247	1988065	0.0000	22.503	0.009359	50
55	0.080744	84298	6807	405774	0.016774	2.6912	1555547	0.0173	18.453	0.016708	55
60	0.132864	77491	10296	363063	0.028358	2.6308	1149773	0.0193	14.837	0.028255	60
65	0.197499	67195	13271	303998	0.043655	2.5903	786710	0.0193	11.708	0.043502	65
70	0.297646	53924	16050	230152	0.069738	2.5409	482712	0.0193	8.952	0.069493	70
75	0.433603	37874	16422	147576	0.111280	2.4551	252560	0.0193	6.668	0.110905	75
80	0.583039	21452	12507	74433	0.168034	2.3754	104984	0.0193	4.894	0.167378	80
85+	*1.000000	8945	8945	30551	0.292773	3.4156	30551	0.0193	3.416	0.290439	85

TABLE 3 — FEMALE LIFE TABLE

x	$_nq_x$	l_x	$_nd_x$	$_nL_x$	$_nm_x$	$_na_x$	T_x	r_x	$\mathring{e}_x$	$_nM_x$	x
0	0.019806	100000	1981	98531	0.020101	0.2582	7281445	0.0000	72.814	0.020101	0
1	0.004039	98019	396	390933	0.001013	1.1087	7182914	0.0000	73.281	0.001013	1
5	0.001935	97623	189	487645	0.000387	2.5000	6791981	0.0000	69.573	0.000387	5
10	0.001455	97435	142	486821	0.000291	2.5207	6304336	0.0101	64.703	0.000291	10
15	0.002086	97293	203	485981	0.000418	2.6205	5817515	0.0338	59.794	0.000416	15
20	0.002670	97090	259	484825	0.000535	2.5928	5331534	0.0268	54.913	0.000533	20
25	0.003288	96831	318	483399	0.000659	2.6325	4846709	0.0000	50.054	0.000659	25
30	0.004784	96512	462	481491	0.000959	2.6826	4363310	0.0000	45.210	0.000959	30
35	0.007527	96050	723	478550	0.001511	2.6456	3881820	0.0163	40.414	0.001507	35
40	0.010143	95327	967	474390	0.002038	2.6754	3403270	0.0273	35.701	0.002028	40
45	0.016288	94361	1537	468249	0.003282	2.6878	2928880	0.0000	31.039	0.003282	45
50	0.025340	92824	2352	458687	0.005128	2.6909	2460631	0.0000	26.509	0.005128	50
55	0.040807	90471	3692	443915	0.008317	2.7131	2001944	0.0131	22.128	0.008291	55
60	0.070626	86780	6129	419817	0.014599	2.7024	1558030	0.0267	17.954	0.014508	60
65	0.119616	80651	9647	380961	0.025323	2.6892	1138213	0.0267	14.113	0.025158	65
70	0.209718	71004	14891	319836	0.046557	2.6373	757252	0.0267	10.665	0.046267	70
75	0.346870	56113	19464	232771	0.083618	2.5445	437416	0.0267	7.795	0.083147	75
80	0.519819	36649	19051	133952	0.142221	2.4796	204644	0.0267	5.584	0.141512	80
85+	1.000000	17598	17598	70692	0.248940	4.0170	70692	0.0267	4.017	0.249411	85

TABLE 4 — OBSERVED AND PROJECTED VITAL RATES

	OBSERVED POPULATION BOTH SEXES	MALES	FEMALES	PROJECTED 1967 MALES	FEMALES	1972 MALES	FEMALES	1977 MALES	FEMALES	STABLE POPULATION MALES	FEMALES
RATES PER THOUSAND											
Birth	15.69	16.52	14.90	17.81	16.08	19.20	17.38	19.16	17.42	17.03	15.83
Death	10.01	10.78	9.27	11.24	10.01	11.76	10.71	12.11	11.30	13.23	12.03
Increase	5.68	5.74	5.63	6.57	6.07	7.44	6.67	7.05	6.12		3.7952
PERCENTAGE											
under 15	26.54	27.81	25.34	25.59	23.30	24.48	22.33	25.28	23.14	24.05	22.53
15-64	64.38	64.74	64.03	66.00	64.71	66.17	64.58	64.64	62.91	65.79	63.86
65 and over	9.08	7.45	10.63	8.41	11.99	9.35	13.09	10.08	13.95	10.16	13.61
DEP. RATIO X 100	55.34	54.47	56.17	51.51	54.53	51.13	54.85	54.69	58.96	52.00	56.58

TABLE 1 — DATA

AGE AT LAST BIRTHDAY	POPULATION BOTH SEXES	MALES Number	%	FEMALES Number	%	BIRTHS BY AGE OF MOTHER	DEATHS BOTH SEXES	MALES	FEMALES	AGE AT LAST BIRTHDAY
0	222469	114010	1.7	108459	1.5	0	5211	3013	2198	0
1-4	858134	439431	6.5	418703	5.9	0	957	552	405	1-4
5-9	1252178	639915	9.4	612263	8.6	0	584	352	232	5-9
10-14	1303650	665832	9.8	637818	8.9	53	526	347	179	10-14
15-19	1194121	606348	8.9	587773	8.2	27779	997	712	285	15-19
20-24	960499	486976	7.2	473523	6.6	97934	1129	888	241	20-24
25-29	843725	423938	6.2	419787	5.9	59843	997	697	300	25-29
30-34	954001	475657	7.0	478344	6.7	32645	1370	920	450	30-34
35-39	986491	482398	7.1	504093	7.1	14153	1825	1186	639	35-39
40-44	908205	440816	6.5	467389	6.5	3474	2586	1582	1004	40-44
45-49	641453	311033	4.6	330420	4.6	111	2777	1712	1065	45-49
50-54	942697	458297	6.7	484480	6.8	6	6669	4219	2450	50-54
55-59	853033	408151	6.0	444882	6.2	0	10001	6555	3446	55-59
60-64	733932	336756	4.9	397176	5.6	0	14576	9134	5442	60-64
65-69	541093	227085	3.3	314008	4.4	0	17139	9542	7597	65-69
70-74	357541	141456	2.1	216085	3.0		18320	9239	9081	70-74
75-79	229537	87437	1.3	142100	2.0		19354	8611	10743	75-79
80-84	117262	43632	0.6	73630	1.0	121243 M.	16092	6607	9485	80-84
85+	51585	18147	0.3	33438	0.5	114755 F.	11997	4602	7395	85+
TOTAL	13951606	6807315		7144291		235998	133107	70470	62637	TOTAL

TABLE 2 — MALE LIFE TABLE

x	nq_x	l_x	nd_x	nL_x	nm_x	na_x	T_x	r_x	$\dot{e}_x$	nM_x	x
0	0.025861	100000	2586	98064	0.026372	0.2515	6746106	0.0027	67.461	0.026427	0
1	0.004990	97414	486	388247	0.001252	1.1033	6648042	0.0027	68.245	0.001256	1
5	0.002747	96928	266	483973	0.000550	2.5000	6259794	0.0000	64.582	0.000550	5
10	0.002606	96661	252	482741	0.000522	2.7500	5775821	0.0047	59.753	0.000521	10
15	0.005896	96410	568	480756	0.001182	2.7271	5293081	0.0301	54.902	0.001174	15
20	0.009093	95841	872	477071	0.001827	2.5500	4812325	0.0341	50.211	0.001823	20
25	0.008187	94970	778	472912	0.001644	2.5094	4335254	0.0006	45.649	0.001644	25
30	0.009626	94192	907	468770	0.001934	2.5835	3862343	0.0000	41.005	0.001934	30
35	0.012230	93285	1141	463730	0.002460	2.6359	3393573	0.0050	36.378	0.002459	35
40	0.017919	92145	1651	456869	0.003614	2.6663	2929843	0.0402	31.796	0.003589	40
45	0.027177	90493	2459	446801	0.005504	2.6963	2472974	0.0000	27.328	0.005504	45
50	0.045080	88034	3969	431097	0.009206	2.7136	2026173	0.0000	23.016	0.009206	50
55	0.077664	84065	6529	405248	0.016111	2.6903	1595076	0.0140	18.974	0.016060	55
60	0.128101	77537	9933	364191	0.027273	2.6348	1189828	0.0286	15.345	0.027123	60
65	0.191645	67604	12956	306777	0.042232	2.5885	825637	0.0286	12.213	0.042020	65
70	0.282440	54648	15435	235186	0.065628	2.5345	518860	0.0286	9.495	0.065314	70
75	0.395558	39213	15511	156754	0.098952	2.4656	283674	0.0286	7.234	0.098482	75
80	0.543011	23702	12871	84592	0.152149	2.4243	126920	0.0286	5.355	0.151426	80
85+	1.000000	10832	10832	42328	0.255896	3.9078	42328	0.0286	3.908	0.253597	85+

TABLE 3 — FEMALE LIFE TABLE

x	nq_x	l_x	nd_x	nL_x	nm_x	na_x	T_x	r_x	$\dot{e}_x$	nM_x	x
0	0.019921	100000	1992	98510	0.020222	0.2522	7340350	0.0028	73.404	0.020266	0
1	0.003846	98008	377	390940	0.000964	1.1038	7241840	0.0028	73.890	0.000967	1
5	0.001893	97631	185	487693	0.000379	2.5000	6850900	0.0000	70.171	0.000379	5
10	0.001403	97446	137	486900	0.000281	2.5785	6363206	0.0037	65.300	0.000281	10
15	0.002429	97310	236	485980	0.000486	2.5977	5876306	0.0293	60.388	0.000485	15
20	0.002549	97073	247	484770	0.000511	2.5918	5390326	0.0331	55.528	0.000509	20
25	0.003567	96826	345	483308	0.000715	2.6238	4905556	0.0000	50.664	0.000715	25
30	0.004693	96480	453	481324	0.000941	2.6204	4422248	0.0000	45.836	0.000941	30
35	0.006321	96028	607	478740	0.001268	2.6972	3940924	0.0009	41.040	0.001268	35
40	0.010768	95421	1027	474722	0.002164	2.6831	3462184	0.0401	36.283	0.002148	40
45	0.015996	94393	1510	468460	0.003223	2.6786	2987461	0.0000	31.649	0.003223	45
50	0.024995	92883	2322	459017	0.005058	2.6746	2519001	0.0000	27.120	0.005058	50
55	0.038153	90562	3455	444900	0.007766	2.7115	2059984	0.0115	22.747	0.007746	55
60	0.066916	87106	5829	422192	0.013806	2.7115	1615083	0.0313	18.542	0.013702	60
65	0.115319	81278	9373	384623	0.024369	2.6780	1192891	0.0313	14.677	0.024194	65
70	0.192415	71905	13836	326864	0.042328	2.6395	808268	0.0313	11.241	0.042025	70
75	0.320929	58069	18636	244867	0.076107	2.5597	481403	0.0313	8.290	0.075602	75
80	0.486200	39433	19172	147972	0.129567	2.5177	236536	0.0313	5.998	0.128820	80
85+	1.000000	20261	20261	88564	0.228768	4.3712	88564	0.0313	4.371	0.221155	85+

TABLE 4 — OBSERVED AND PROJECTED VITAL RATES

	OBSERVED POPULATION BOTH SEXES	MALES	FEMALES	PROJECTED POPULATION 1968 MALES	FEMALES	1973 MALES	FEMALES	1978 MALES	FEMALES	STABLE POPULATION MALES	FEMALES
RATES PER THOUSAND											
Birth	16.92	17.81	16.06	19.20	17.34	20.26	18.35	19.84	18.04	18.48	17.22
Death	9.54	10.35	8.77	11.06	9.69	11.57	10.42	11.86	10.97	12.16	10.90
Increase	7.37	7.46	7.30	8.14	7.64	8.69	7.92	7.97	7.07		6.3192
PERCENTAGE											
under 15	26.06	27.31	24.88	25.63	23.35	25.28	23.07	26.59	24.37	25.62	24.05
15-64	64.64	65.08	64.22	65.59	64.24	65.01	63.43	63.06	61.36	64.78	63.10
65 and over	9.30	7.61	10.91	8.77	12.41	9.71	13.50	10.35	14.27	9.60	12.86
DEP. RATIO X 100	54.71	53.65	55.72	52.46	55.66	53.82	57.65	58.58	62.97	54.36	58.49

TABLE 1 — DATA

AGE AT LAST BIRTHDAY	POPULATION BOTH SEXES	MALES Number	%	FEMALES Number	%	BIRTHS BY AGE OF MOTHER	DEATHS BOTH SEXES	MALES	FEMALES	AGE AT LAST BIRTHDAY
0	234336	120206	1.8	114130	1.6	0	5175	2995	2180	0
1-4	859097	440142	6.4	418955	5.8	0	953	550	403	1-4
5-9	1214260	620363	9.0	593897	8.3	0	580	370	210	5-9
10-14	1305583	667159	9.7	638424	8.9	58	446	295	151	10-14
15-19	1227549	623831	9.1	603718	8.4	28043	961	695	266	15-19
20-24	1007905	511470	7.5	496435	6.9	101688	1139	892	247	20-24
25-29	841203	422571	6.2	418632	5.8	60274	947	694	253	25-29
30-34	935299	467498	6.8	467801	6.5	33004	1301	851	450	30-34
35-39	971311	476347	6.9	494964	6.9	14278	1763	1158	605	35-39
40-44	989144	480179	7.0	508965	7.1	3838	2799	1756	1043	40-44
45-49	575208	278616	4.1	296592	4.1	111	2420	1455	965	45-49
50-54	934350	453187	6.6	481163	6.7	4	6413	3942	2471	50-54
55-59	869772	416965	6.1	452807	6.3	0	10262	6576	3686	55-59
60-64	751581	346650	5.1	404625	5.6	0	14905	9363	5542	60-64
65-69	561649	237214	3.5	324435	4.5	0	17843	10167	7676	65-69
70-74	369545	145605	2.1	223940	3.1		19046	9492	9554	70-74
75-79	235327	88885	1.3	146442	2.0		19520	8693	10827	75-79
80-84	120697	44416	0.6	76281	1.1	124179 M.	16344	6705	9639	80-84
85+	54152	18834	0.3	35318	0.5	117119 F.	12042	4591	7451	85+
TOTAL	14057968	6860444		7197524		241298	134859	71240	63619	TOTAL

TABLE 2 — MALE LIFE TABLE

x	$_nq_x$	l_x	$_nd_x$	$_nL_x$	$_nm_x$	$_na_x$	T_x	r_x	$\mathring{e}_x$	$_nM_x$	x
0	0.024316	100000	2432	98194	0.024763	0.2572	6772864	0.0078	67.729	0.024916	
1	0.004937	97568	482	388881	0.001239	1.1079	6674670	0.0078	68.410	0.001250	
5	0.002978	97087	289	484711	0.000596	2.5000	6285790	0.0000	64.744	0.000596	5
10	0.002209	96798	214	483506	0.000442	2.7445	5801079	0.0000	59.930	0.000442	10
15	0.005591	96584	540	481699	0.001121	2.7400	5317573	0.0255	55.057	0.001114	15
20	0.008703	96044	836	478179	0.001748	2.5595	4835874	0.0374	50.351	0.001744	20
25	0.008179	95208	779	474097	0.001642	2.5053	4357695	0.0073	45.770	0.001642	25
30	0.009062	94429	856	470081	0.001820	2.5858	3883598	0.0000	41.127	0.001820	30
35	0.012086	93574	1131	465214	0.002431	2.6535	3413517	0.0000	36.479	0.002431	35
40	0.018271	92443	1689	458243	0.003686	2.6493	2948303	0.0499	31.893	0.003657	40
45	0.025800	90754	2341	448348	0.005222	2.6852	2490060	0.0002	27.438	0.005222	45
50	0.042649	88412	3771	433491	0.008698	2.7273	2041712	0.0000	23.093	0.008698	50
55	0.076271	84641	6456	408360	0.015989	2.7001	1608221	0.0102	19.000	0.015771	55
60	0.127550	78186	9973	367425	0.027142	2.6432	1199861	0.0288	15.346	0.026986	60
65	0.195096	68213	13308	308942	0.043076	2.5862	832436	0.0288	12.203	0.042860	65
70	0.281697	54905	15476	236293	0.065497	2.5297	523493	0.0288	9.535	0.065190	70
75	0.393390	39429	15511	157842	0.098268	2.4662	287200	0.0288	7.284	0.097801	75
80	0.541964	23918	12963	85456	0.151687	2.4268	129358	0.0288	5.408	0.150959	80
85+	1.000000	10955	10955	43902	0.249539	4.0074	43902	0.0288	4.007	0.243760	85

TABLE 3 — FEMALE LIFE TABLE

x	$_nq_x$	l_x	$_nd_x$	$_nL_x$	$_nm_x$	$_na_x$	T_x	r_x	$\mathring{e}_x$	$_nM_x$	x
0	0.018721	100000	1872	98611	0.018984	0.2579	7364905	0.0078	73.649	0.019101	0
1	0.003803	98128	373	391433	0.000953	1.1085	7266295	0.0078	74.049	0.000962	1
5	0.001766	97755	173	488342	0.000354	2.5000	6874862	0.0000	70.328	0.000354	5
10	0.001182	97582	115	487631	0.000237	2.5767	6386520	0.0000	65.448	0.000237	10
15	0.002207	97467	215	486822	0.000442	2.6229	5898889	0.0248	60.522	0.000441	15
20	0.002491	97252	242	485669	0.000499	2.5669	5412066	0.0361	55.650	0.000498	20
25	0.003020	97009	293	484361	0.000605	2.6578	4926398	0.0053	50.783	0.000604	25
30	0.004799	96716	464	482483	0.000962	2.6318	4442037	0.0000	45.928	0.000962	30
35	0.006094	96252	587	479904	0.001222	2.6851	3959554	0.0000	41.137	0.001222	35
40	0.010301	95666	985	476061	0.002070	2.6993	3479651	0.0491	36.373	0.002049	40
45	0.016154	94680	1529	469865	0.003255	2.6878	3003589	0.0022	31.724	0.003254	45
50	0.025376	93151	2364	460283	0.005135	2.6855	2533725	0.0000	27.200	0.005135	50
55	0.040027	90787	3634	445572	0.008156	2.6987	2073441	0.0087	22.839	0.008140	55
60	0.066885	87153	5829	422350	0.013802	2.6986	1627869	0.0334	18.678	0.013697	60
65	0.113012	81324	9191	385360	0.023849	2.6869	1205519	0.0334	14.824	0.023660	65
70	0.195087	72133	14072	327381	0.042984	2.6347	820159	0.0334	11.370	0.042663	70
75	0.315011	58061	18290	245659	0.074452	2.5590	492778	0.0334	8.487	0.073934	75
80	0.484062	39771	19252	151191	0.127334	2.5241	247118	0.0334	6.214	0.126361	80
85+	*1.000000	20519	20519	95928	0.213906	4.6750	95928	0.0334	4.675	0.210969	85-

TABLE 4 — OBSERVED AND PROJECTED VITAL RATES

	OBSERVED POPULATION BOTH SEXES	MALES	FEMALES	PROJECTED POPULATION 1969 MALES	FEMALES	1974 MALES	FEMALES	1979 MALES	FEMALES	STABLE POPULATION MALES	FEMALES
RATES PER THOUSAND											
Birth	17.16	18.10	16.27	19.53	17.59	20.34	18.38	19.64	17.83	18.49	17.25
Death	9.59	10.38	8.84	11.09	9.82	11.56	10.54	11.80	11.05	12.04	10.80
Increase	7.57	7.72	7.43	8.43	7.77	8.79	7.85	7.84	6.78		6.4485
PERCENTAGE											
under 15	25.70	26.94	24.53	25.46	23.17	25.54	23.27	26.82	24.53	25.65	24.10
15-64	64.76	65.27	64.27	65.56	64.11	64.57	62.94	62.81	61.05	64.76	63.02
65 and over	9.54	7.80	11.20	8.98	12.72	9.89	13.79	10.37	14.42	9.59	12.88
DEP. RATIO X 100	54.43	53.22	55.60	52.53	55.98	54.86	58.87	59.21	63.80	54.42	58.68

AGE AT LAST BIRTHDAY	1969 BOTH SEXES	MALES	FEMALES	1974 BOTH SEXES	MALES	FEMALES	1979 BOTH SEXES	MALES	FEMALES	AGE AT LAST BIRTHDAY	
0-4	1251	642	609	1382	709	673	1444	741	703	0-4	
5-9	1089	558	531	1246	639	607	1376	706	670	5-9	
10-14	1212	619	593	1086	556	530	1243	637	606	10-14	
15-19	1302	665	637	1209	617	592	1084	554	530	15-19	TABLE 5
20-24	1221	619	602	1296	660	636	1203	612	591	20-24	POPULATION
25-29	1002	507	495	1215	614	601	1288	654	634	25-29	PROJECTED
30-34	836	419	417	996	503	493	1207	609	598	30-34	WITH
35-39	928	463	465	830	415	415	989	498	491	35-39	FIXED
40-44	960	469	491	918	456	462	819	408	411	40-44	AGE—
45-49	972	470	502	944	459	485	902	446	456	45-49	SPECIFIC
50-54	560	269	291	946	454	492	919	444	475	50-54	BIRTH
55-59	893	427	466	535	254	281	904	428	476	55-59	AND
60-64	804	375	429	826	384	442	495	228	267	60-64	DEATH
65-69	661	292	369	707	315	392	726	323	403	65-69	RATES
70-74	457	181	276	537	223	314	574	241	333	70-74	(IN 1000's)
75-79	265	97	168	328	121	207	384	149	235	75-79	
80-84	138	48	90	156	53	103	193	66	127	80-84	
85+	71	23	48	82	25	57	93	27	66	85+	
TOTAL	14622	7143	7479	15239	7457	7782	15843	7771	8072	TOTAL	

STANDARD COUNTRIES: STANDARDIZED RATES PER THOUSAND	ENGLAND AND WALES 1961 BOTH SEXES	MALES	FEMALES	UNITED STATES 1960 BOTH SEXES	MALES	FEMALES	MEXICO 1960 BOTH SEXES	MALES	FEMALES	
Birth	15.88	17.91*	14.93	16.12	16.67*	15.42	19.93	15.91*	19.30	TABLE 6
Death	11.89	12.27*	11.59	9.63	10.72*	8.42	4.94	8.97*	3.97	STANDARDIZED RATES
Increase	3.99	5.64*	3.34	6.49	5.95*	6.99	14.99	6.94*	15.33	

	OBSERVED POP. MALES	FEMALES	STATIONARY POP. MALES	FEMALES	STABLE POP. MALES	FEMALES	OBSERVED BIRTHS	NET MATERNITY FUNCTION	BIRTHS IN STABLE POP.	
μ	32.55458	35.00284	36.45851	38.80719	33.33912	35.36917	25.75092	26.02949	25.83745	TABLE 7
σ^2	453.4810	497.1621	492.7720	541.5747	473.1978	522.7475	30.17843	28.08760	30.30450	MOMENTS
κ_3	3471.335	3052.372	2314.590	1978.113	3710.978	3810.102	138.8197	121.8378	119.7221	AND
κ_4	-191463.	-253179.	-235974.	-305249.	-193965.	-257978.	252.656	311.704	353.842	CUMULANTS
β_1	0.129216	0.075819	0.044772	0.024634	0.129972	0.101624	0.701152	0.669915	0.703802	
β_2	2.068966	1.975690	2.028212	1.959273	2.133763	2.055943	3.277419	3.395106	3.474472	
κ	-0.046772	-0.026862	-0.017070	-0.009052	-0.049538	-0.037397	-0.405258	-0.485403	-0.538315	

VITAL STATISTICS		THOMPSON AGE RANGE	NRR	1000r	INTERVAL	BOURGEOIS-PICHAT AGE RANGE	NRR	1000b	1000d	1000r	COALE	
GRR	1.220										IBR	TABLE 8
NRR	1.182	0-4	1.05	1.89	27.44	5-29	1.65	21.51	2.90	18.61	IDR	RATES FROM AGE DISTRIBUTIONS
TFR	2.513	5-9	1.30	9.76	27.41	30-54	1.20	17.31	10.50	6.81	IRI	AND VITAL
GENERATION	25.933	10-14	1.40	12.18	27.36	55-79	2.04	66.59	40.26	26.34	K1	STATISTICS
SEX RATIO	106.028	15-19	1.29	9.09	27.28	*50-74	1.75	45.61	24.88	20.73	K2	(Females)

Start Age Interval	ORIGINAL MATRIX SUB-DIAGONAL	ALTERNATIVE FIRST ROWS Projection	Integral	FIRST STABLE MATRIX % IN STABLE POPULATION	FISHER VALUES	REPRODUCTIVE VALUES	SECOND STABLE MATRIX Z_2 FIRST COLUMN	FIRST ROW	
0	0.99653	0.00000	0.00000	8.317	1.037	552740	0.1967+0.0744	0.1967+0.0744	
5	0.99854	0.00011	0.00000	8.025	1.075	638204	0.1662-0.1899	-0.0007+0.1753	TABLE 9
10	0.99834	0.05526	0.00022	7.759	1.111	709514	-0.1441-0.2671	-0.1368+0.0504	LESLIE
15	0.99763	0.29827	0.11228	7.500	1.092	659449	-0.3614+0.0499	-0.0900-0.0960	MATRIX
20	0.99731	0.41437	0.49513	7.245	0.821	407480	-0.0957+0.4277	-0.0101-0.1204	AND ITS
25	0.99612	0.25481	0.34802	6.996	0.419	175495	0.4410+0.2873	0.0092-0.0739	SPECTRAL
30	0.99465	0.11803	0.17054	6.748	0.169	79251	0.5078-0.3750	0.0100-0.0334	COMPONENTS
35	0.99199	0.04320	0.06973	6.498	0.053	26170	-0.2080-0.7270	0.0057-0.0107	(Females)
40	0.98698	0.00941	0.01823	6.242	0.010	5034	-0.9004-0.0710	0.0015-0.0019	
45	0.97961	0.00045	0.00090	5.965	0.000	138	-0.4533+0.9730	0.0001-0.0001	
50	0.96804	0.00001	0.00002	5.658	0.000	5	0.8882+0.9025	0.0000-0.0000	
55+	0.79517			23.048					

Start Age Interval	OBSERVED POPUL. (IN 100's)	CONTRIBUTIONS OF ROOTS (IN 100's) r_1	r_2, r_3	$r_4 \cdot r_{11}$	AGE-SP. BIRTH RATES	NET MATERNITY FUNCTION	COEFF. OF MATRIX EQUATION	PARAMETERS INTEGRAL	MATRIX	EXP. INCREASE x	$e^{(x+2\frac{1}{2})r}$	
0	5331	6082	-601	-150	0.0000	0.0000	0.0000	L(1) 1.03277	1.03279	0	1.0163	TABLE 10
5	5939	5868	-132	203	0.0000	0.0000	0.0001	L(2) 0.28050	0.29048	50	1.4029	AGE
10	6384	5674	757	-46	0.0000	0.0000	0.0002	0.0550	0.81391	0.77799	55	1.4489	ANALYSIS
15	6037	5484	827	-274	0.0225	0.1098	0.2963	R(1) 0.00645	0.00645	60	1.4964	AND
20	4964	5298	-398	64	0.0994	0.4829	0.4107	R(2) -0.02996	-0.03716	65	1.5454	MISCELLANEOUS
25	4186	5116	-1527	598	0.0699	0.3385	0.2519	0.24778	0.24269	70	1.5960	RESULTS
30	4678	4934	-709	453	0.0342	0.1652	0.1162	C(1)	73122	75	1.6483	(Females)
35	4950	4752	1600	-1402	0.0140	0.0672	0.0423	C(2)	-124713	80	1.7023	
40	5090	4564	2351	-1826	0.0037	0.0174	0.0091		74381	85	1.7581	
45	2966	4362	-317	-1079	0.0002	0.0009	0.0004	2P/Y 25.3577	25.8898	90	1.8157	
50	4812	4137	-3558	4233	0.0000	0.0000	0.0000	DELTA 6.4119		95	1.8752	
55+	16638	16853								100	1.9367	

TABLE 1 — DATA

AGE AT LAST BIRTHDAY	POPULATION BOTH SEXES	MALES Number	%	FEMALES Number	%	BIRTHS BY AGE OF MOTHER	DEATHS BOTH SEXES	MALES	FEMALES	AGE AT LAST BIRTHDAY
0	76200	39100	1.8	37100	1.7	0	2293	1340	953	0
1-4	330600	169400	7.9	161200	7.4	0	444	260	184	1-4
5-9	409800	209300	9.8	200500	9.2	0	198	123	75	5-9
10-14	319200	162100	7.6	157100	7.2	1	137	84	53	10-14
15-19	293600	149200	7.0	144400	6.7	5757	201	125	76	15-19
20-24	291200	146400	6.9	144800	6.7	22283	280	180	100	20-24
25-29	310700	153200	7.2	157500	7.3	23531	359	221	138	25-29
30-34	315200	155900	7.3	159300	7.3	15177	432	237	195	30-34
35-39	314100	155900	7.3	158200	7.3	8157	585	313	272	35-39
40-44	310300	153800	7.2	156500	7.2	2613	836	439	397	40-44
45-49	281100	137900	6.5	143200	6.6	165	1268	682	586	45-49
50-54	253100	122200	5.7	130900	6.0	3	1708	921	787	50-54
55-59	218500	105000	4.9	113500	5.2	0	2252	1253	999	55-59
60-64	184300	88200	4.1	96100	4.4	0	3150	1680	1470	60-64
65-69	153700	73100	3.4	80600	3.7	0	4200	2168	2032	65-69
70-74	115100	55000	2.6	60100	2.8		5496	2781	2715	70-74
75-79	72700	34400	1.6	38300	1.8		5937	2883	3054	75-79
80-84	37400	17100	0.8	20300	0.9	39992 M.	4906	2293	2613	80-84
85+	16820	7020	0.3	9800	0.5	37695 F.	4127	1774	2353	85+
TOTAL	4303620	2134220		2169400		77687	38809	19757	19052	TOTAL

TABLE 2 — MALE LIFE TABLE

x	$_nq_x$	l_x	$_nd_x$	$_nL_x$	$_nm_x$	$_na_x$	T_x	r_x	$\overset{\circ}{e}_x$	$_nM_x$	x
0	0.033407	100000	3341	97478	0.034271	0.2449	6941668	0.0000	69.417	0.034271	0
1	0.006112	96659	591	384923	0.001535	1.0982	6844191	0.0000	70.807	0.001535	1
5	0.002913	96069	280	479643	0.000583	2.5000	6459268	0.0243	67.236	0.000588	5
10	0.002597	95789	249	478347	0.000520	2.6007	5979625	0.0332	62.425	0.000518	10
15	0.004188	95540	400	476769	0.000839	2.6741	5501278	0.0093	57.581	0.000838	15
20	0.006129	95140	583	474300	0.001230	2.5999	5024509	0.0000	52.812	0.001230	20
25	0.007187	94557	680	471111	0.001443	2.5392	4550209	0.0000	48.121	0.001443	25
30	0.007573	93877	711	467660	0.001520	2.5736	4079098	0.0000	43.451	0.001520	30
35	0.009991	93166	931	463629	0.002008	2.6342	3611438	0.0000	38.763	0.002008	35
40	0.014207	92235	1310	458172	0.002860	2.7067	3147809	0.0092	34.128	0.002854	40
45	0.024534	90925	2231	449462	0.004963	2.6855	2689637	0.0180	29.581	0.004946	45
50	0.037169	88694	3297	435802	0.007565	2.6735	2240176	0.0194	25.257	0.007537	50
55	0.058277	85398	4977	415394	0.011981	2.6703	1804374	0.0202	21.129	0.011933	55
60	0.091578	80421	7365	384776	0.019141	2.6471	1388980	0.0259	17.271	0.019048	60
65	0.139284	73056	10176	341275	0.029816	2.6408	1004205	0.0259	13.746	0.029658	65
70	0.226511	62881	14243	280205	0.050831	2.5990	662930	0.0259	10.543	0.050564	70
75	0.348323	48637	16942	201162	0.084218	2.5194	382725	0.0259	7.869	0.083808	75
80	0.499106	31696	15820	117455	0.134687	2.4860	181564	0.0259	5.728	0.134094	80
85+	1.000000	15876	15876	64109	0.247645	4.0380	64109	0.0259	4.038	0.252708	85

TABLE 3 — FEMALE LIFE TABLE

x	$_nq_x$	l_x	$_nd_x$	$_nL_x$	$_nm_x$	$_na_x$	T_x	r_x	$\overset{\circ}{e}_x$	$_nM_x$	x
0	0.025198	100000	2520	98096	0.025687	0.2444	7199098	0.0000	71.991	0.025687	
1	0.004551	97480	444	388633	0.001141	1.0978	7101002	0.0000	72.846	0.001141	
5	0.001853	97037	180	484733	0.000371	2.5000	6712369	0.0227	69.174	0.000374	
10	0.001691	96857	164	483890	0.000338	2.5949	6227635	0.0324	64.297	0.000337	10
15	0.002631	96693	254	482864	0.000527	2.6381	5743746	0.0076	59.402	0.000526	15
20	0.003447	96439	332	481396	0.000691	2.6039	5260882	0.0000	54.552	0.000691	20
25	0.004372	96106	420	479533	0.000876	2.6247	4779485	0.0000	49.731	0.000876	25
30	0.006103	95686	584	477052	0.001224	2.6406	4299953	0.0000	44.938	0.001224	30
35	0.008562	95102	814	473601	0.001719	2.6552	3822901	0.0073	40.198	0.001719	35
40	0.012627	94288	1191	468686	0.002540	2.6885	3349300	0.0137	35.522	0.002537	40
45	0.020316	93097	1891	461074	0.004102	2.6675	2880614	0.0171	30.942	0.004092	45
50	0.029723	91206	2711	449656	0.006029	2.6493	2419540	0.0214	26.528	0.006012	50
55	0.043327	88495	3834	433633	0.008842	2.6942	1969884	0.0246	22.260	0.008802	55
60	0.074248	84661	6286	408744	0.015378	2.6839	1536251	0.0246	18.146	0.015297	60
65	0.119713	78375	9382	370055	0.025354	2.6746	1127507	0.0246	14.386	0.025211	65
70	0.205080	68992	14149	311458	0.045428	2.6321	757452	0.0246	10.979	0.045175	70
75	0.334686	54843	18355	229064	0.080132	2.5401	445994	0.0246	8.132	0.079739	
80	0.484543	36488	17680	136780	0.129259	2.5053	216930	0.0246	5.945	0.128719	
85+	1.000000	18808	18808	80150	0.234659	4.2615	80150	0.0246	4.261	0.240103	

TABLE 4 — OBSERVED AND PROJECTED VITAL RATES

	OBSERVED POPULATION BOTH SEXES	MALES	FEMALES	PROJECTED POPULATION 1956 MALES	FEMALES	1961 MALES	FEMALES	1966 MALES	FEMALES	STABLE POPULATION MALES	FEMALES
RATES PER THOUSAND											
Birth	18.05	18.74	17.38	17.52	16.31	17.35	16.22	18.35	17.21	17.90	17.
Death	9.02	9.26	8.78	9.83	9.38	10.35	9.96	10.83	10.55	11.88	11.
Increase	9.03	9.48	8.59	7.68	6.94	7.00	6.25	7.52	6.66		6.01
PERCENTAGE											
under 15	26.39	27.17	25.62	27.23	25.66	25.40	23.98	24.27	23.00	24.65	24.
15-64	64.41	64.08	64.74	63.48	63.97	64.75	64.88	65.29	65.03	63.82	63.
65 and over	9.20	8.74	9.64	9.30	10.36	9.85	11.14	10.45	11.97	11.53	12.
DEP. RATIO X 100	55.25	56.04	54.47	57.54	56.31	54.43	54.14	53.17	53.77	56.69	57.

TABLE 5 — POPULATION PROJECTED WITH FIXED AGE—SPECIFIC BIRTH AND DEATH RATES (IN 1000's)

AGE AT LAST BIRTHDAY	1956 BOTH SEXES	MALES	FEMALES	1961 BOTH SEXES	MALES	FEMALES	1966 BOTH SEXES	MALES	FEMALES	AGE AT LAST BIRTHDAY
0-4	372	191	181	373	191	182	396	203	193	0-4
5-9	404	207	197	371	190	181	371	190	181	5-9
10-14	409	209	200	404	207	197	369	189	180	10-14
15-19	319	162	157	408	208	200	403	206	197	15-19
20-24	292	148	144	317	161	156	406	207	199	20-24
25-29	289	145	144	290	147	143	316	160	156	25-29
30-34	309	152	157	287	144	143	289	146	143	30-34
35-39	313	155	158	307	151	156	285	143	142	35-39
40-44	311	154	157	310	153	157	303	149	154	40-44
45-49	305	151	154	305	151	154	304	150	154	45-49
50-54	274	134	140	296	146	150	297	147	150	50-54
55-59	242	116	126	262	127	135	284	139	145	55-59
60-64	204	97	107	227	108	119	245	118	127	60-64
65-69	165	78	87	183	86	97	204	96	108	65-69
70-74	128	60	68	137	64	73	153	71	82	70-74
75-79	83	39	44	93	43	50	100	46	54	75-79
80-84	43	20	23	49	23	26	55	25	30	80-84
85+	21	9	12	24	11	13	28	13	15	85+
TOTAL	4483	2227	2256	4643	2311	2332	4808	2398	2410	TOTAL

TABLE 6 — STANDARDIZED RATES

STANDARD COUNTRIES: STANDARDIZED RATES PER THOUSAND	ENGLAND AND WALES 1961 BOTH SEXES	MALES	FEMALES	UNITED STATES 1960 BOTH SEXES	MALES	FEMALES	MEXICO 1960 BOTH SEXES	MALES	FEMALES
Birth	16.15	17.47*	15.19	16.44	16.53*	15.71	19.10	15.37*	18.48
Death	11.52	10.33*	12.72	9.33	9.14*	9.35	4.98	7.56*	4.57
Increase	4.63	7.14*	2.47	7.11	7.39*	6.36	14.12	7.81*	13.91

TABLE 7 — MOMENTS AND CUMULANTS

	OBSERVED POP. MALES	FEMALES	STATIONARY POP. MALES	FEMALES	STABLE POP. MALES	FEMALES	OBSERVED BIRTHS	NET MATERNITY FUNCTION	BIRTHS IN STABLE POP.
μ	32.71441	33.81207	37.62948	38.35881	34.55205	35.20011	27.89936	27.65109	27.42247
σ^2	464.0740	473.8914	520.0235	533.1144	501.7860	515.5964	36.16676	36.27826	35.57503
κ_3	3387.278	3036.793	2249.748	2067.683	3771.433	3714.172	104.6385	115.8280	117.9361
κ_4	-185541.	-199605.	-272781.	-293293.	-229690.	-250149.	-437.046	-386.639	-304.497
β_1	0.114799	0.086655	0.035991	0.028217	0.112579	0.100645	0.231448	0.280988	0.308928
β_2	2.138479	2.111178	1.991286	1.968044	2.087770	2.059022	2.665875	2.706227	2.759402
κ	-0.044648	-0.033935	-0.013423	-0.010406	-0.042048	-0.037165	-0.136742	-0.160184	-0.179957

TABLE 8 — RATES FROM AGE DISTRIBUTIONS AND VITAL STATISTICS (Females)

VITAL STATISTICS		THOMPSON AGE RANGE	NRR	1000r	INTERVAL	BOURGEOIS-PICHAT AGE RANGE	NRR	1000b	1000d	1000r	COALE	
GRR	1.232										IBR	20.82
NRR	1.180	0-4	1.27	8.73	27.42	5-29	1.34	18.41	7.66	10.75	IDR	7.75
TFR	2.539	5-9	1.28	9.02	27.38	30-54	1.21	19.83	12.88	6.94	IRI	13.07
GENERATION	27.536	10-14	1.01	0.26	27.32	55-79	1.71	37.70	17.88	19.82	K1	50.43
SEX RATIO	106.094	15-19	0.96	-1.54	27.23	*50-74	1.72	38.48	18.36	20.12	K2	0.75

TABLE 9 — LESLIE MATRIX AND ITS SPECTRAL COMPONENTS (Females)

Start Age Interval	ORIGINAL MATRIX SUB-DIAGONAL	ALTERNATIVE FIRST ROWS Projection	Integral	FIRST STABLE MATRIX % IN STABLE POPULATION	FISHER VALUES	REPRODUCTIVE VALUES	SECOND STABLE MATRIX Z₂ FIRST COLUMN	FIRST ROW
0	0.99590	0.00000	0.00000	8.310	1.043	206786	0.1605+0.0823	0.1605+0.0823
5	0.99826	0.00001	0.00000	8.030	1.079	216355	0.1767-0.1299	-0.0016+0.1484
10	0.99788	0.04699	0.00002	7.779	1.114	175006	-0.0454-0.2634	-0.1095+0.0532
15	0.99696	0.22824	0.09558	7.532	1.101	159034	-0.3118-0.0939	-0.0868-0.0647
20	0.99613	0.35746	0.36894	7.287	0.900	130279	-0.2719+0.2885	-0.0210-0.1064
25	0.99483	0.28834	0.35819	7.043	0.557	87665	0.1661+0.4526	0.0129-0.0841
30	0.99277	0.17295	0.22841	6.799	0.274	43703	0.5819+0.0651	0.0202-0.0453
35	0.98962	0.08040	0.12362	6.550	0.103	16314	0.3858-0.5957	0.0129-0.0161
40	0.98376	0.02105	0.04003	6.290	0.023	3548	-0.4356-0.7386	0.0037-0.0031
45	0.97524	0.00139	0.00276	6.004	0.001	205	-1.0274+0.0717	0.0002-0.0002
50	0.96437	0.00003	0.00005	5.682	0.000	4	-0.4703+1.1325	0.0000-0.0000
55+	0.78912			22.695				

TABLE 10 — AGE ANALYSIS AND MISCELLANEOUS RESULTS (Females)

Start Age Interval	OBSERVED POPUL. (IN 100's)	CONTRIBUTIONS OF ROOTS (IN 100's) r_1	r_2, r_3	$r_4 \cdot r_{11}$	AGE-SP. BIRTH RATES	NET MATERNITY FUNCTION	COEFF. OF MATRIX EQUATION	PARAMETERS	INTEGRAL	MATRIX	EXP. INCREASE x	$e^{(x+2\frac{1}{2})r}$
0	1983	1819	133	31	0.0000	0.0000	0.0000	L(1)	1.03053	1.03055	0	1.0151
5	2005	1758	206	41	0.0000	0.0000	0.0000	L(2)	0.35687	0.36599	50	1.3713
10	1571	1703	28	-159	0.0000	0.0000	0.0467		0.75724	0.73276	55	1.4132
15	1444	1649	-276	71	0.0193	0.0934	0.2264	R(1)	0.00601	0.00602	60	1.4563
20	1448	1595	-341	194	0.0747	0.3595	0.3535	R(2)	-0.03556	-0.03992	65	1.5008
25	1575	1542	38	-5	0.0725	0.3476	0.2841		0.22608	0.22151	70	1.5466
30	1593	1488	545	-440	0.0462	0.2205	0.1695	C(1)		21890	75	1.5938
35	1582	1434	534	-386	0.0250	0.1185	0.0782	C(2)		48316	80	1.6425
40	1565	1377	-221	409	0.0081	0.0380	0.0203			13552	85	1.6926
45	1432	1314	-1012	1130	0.0006	0.0026	0.0013	2P/Y	27.7921	28.3646	90	1.7443
50	1309	1244	-761	827	0.0000	0.0001	0.0000	DELTA	5.4208		95	1.7975
55+	4187	4968									100	1.8524

TABLE 1 — DATA

AGE AT LAST BIRTHDAY	POPULATION BOTH SEXES	MALES Number	%	FEMALES Number	%	BIRTHS BY AGE OF MOTHER	DEATHS BOTH SEXES	MALES	FEMALES	AGE AT LAST BIRTHDAY
0	75600	38900	1.8	36700	1.7	0	2039	1195	844	0
1-4	301900	154600	7.1	147300	6.6	0	343	204	139	1-4
5-9	431200	220900	10.1	210300	9.5	0	175	109	66	5-9
10-14	361200	184000	8.4	177200	8.0	2	112	68	44	10-14
15-19	306500	155400	7.1	151100	6.8	6169	195	133	62	15-19
20-24	287300	144400	6.6	142900	6.4	23390	268	192	76	20-24
25-29	296800	147200	6.7	149600	6.7	22880	307	184	123	25-29
30-34	319100	157800	7.2	161300	7.3	15010	405	225	180	30-34
35-39	301600	149700	6.8	151900	6.8	7215	500	264	236	35-39
40-44	314500	156100	7.1	158400	7.1	2341	794	422	372	40-44
45-49	295000	145300	6.6	149700	6.7	149	1216	653	563	45-49
50-54	264000	128400	5.9	135700	6.1	1	1707	967	740	50-54
55-59	234900	112600	5.1	122300	5.5	0	2406	1348	1058	55-59
60-64	193500	92200	4.2	101300	4.6	0	3154	1747	1407	60-64
65-69	161900	76500	3.5	85400	3.8	0	4342	2280	2062	65-69
70-74	121800	57500	2.6	64300	2.9		5561	2813	2748	70-74
75-79	80800	38500	1.8	42300	1.9		6267	3088	3179	75-79
80-84	40200	18600	0.9	21600	1.0	39844 M.	5245	2513	2732	80-84
85+	18760	8220	0.4	10540	0.5	37313 F.	4306	1938	2368	85+
TOTAL	4406560	2186720		2219840		77157	39342	20343	18999	TOTAL

TABLE 2 — MALE LIFE TABLE

x	$_nq_x$	l_x	$_nd_x$	$_nL_x$	$_nm_x$	$_na_x$	T_x	r_x	$\mathring{e}_x$	$_nM_x$	x
0	0.030019	100000	3002	97720	0.030720	0.2406	7005212	0.0000	70.052	0.030720	0
1	0.005258	96998	510	386511	0.001320	1.0949	6907492	0.0000	71.213	0.001320	1
5	0.002461	96488	237	481847	0.000493	2.5000	6520981	0.0043	67.583	0.000493	5
10	0.001859	96251	179	480842	0.000372	2.7039	6039135	0.0347	62.744	0.000370	10
15	0.004294	96072	413	479422	0.000861	2.7298	5558293	0.0234	57.856	0.000856	15
20	0.006628	95659	634	476748	0.001330	2.5590	5078871	0.0042	53.093	0.001330	20
25	0.006231	95025	592	473653	0.001250	2.5130	4602123	0.0000	48.431	0.001250	25
30	0.007105	94433	671	470536	0.001426	2.5718	4128471	0.0000	43.719	0.001426	30
35	0.008781	93762	823	466872	0.001764	2.6462	3657935	0.0000	39.013	0.001764	35
40	0.013434	92939	1249	461827	0.002703	2.7040	3191063	0.0001	34.335	0.002703	40
45	0.022315	91690	2046	453770	0.004509	2.7122	2729236	0.0149	29.766	0.004494	45
50	0.037171	89644	3332	440515	0.007564	2.6875	2275466	0.0177	25.383	0.007537	50
55	0.058459	86312	5046	419794	0.012020	2.6681	1834951	0.0206	21.260	0.011972	55
60	0.091108	81266	7404	388922	0.019037	2.6486	1415158	0.0248	17.414	0.018948	60
65	0.139832	73862	10328	344857	0.029950	2.6324	1026236	0.0248	13.894	0.029804	65
70	0.219810	63534	13965	284075	0.049161	2.5945	681379	0.0248	10.725	0.048922	70
75	0.336140	49568	16662	206725	0.080600	2.5322	397304	0.0248	8.015	0.080208	75
80	0.502761	32907	16544	121889	0.135731	2.4962	190579	0.0248	5.792	0.135108	80
85+	1.000000	16362	16362	68690	0.238207	4.1980	68690	0.0248	4.198	0.235765	85

TABLE 3 — FEMALE LIFE TABLE

x	$_nq_x$	l_x	$_nd_x$	$_nL_x$	$_nm_x$	$_na_x$	T_x	r_x	$\mathring{e}_x$	$_nM_x$	x
0	0.022600	100000	2260	98273	0.022997	0.2360	7291574	0.0000	72.916	0.022997	0
1	0.003764	97740	368	389890	0.000944	1.0916	7193301	0.0000	73.596	0.000944	1
5	0.001566	97372	152	486479	0.000313	2.5000	6803411	0.0033	69.870	0.000314	5
10	0.001244	97220	121	485805	0.000249	2.5812	6316932	0.0328	64.976	0.000248	10
15	0.002056	97099	200	485022	0.000412	2.6424	5831127	0.0211	60.054	0.000410	15
20	0.002656	96899	257	483893	0.000532	2.6594	5346104	0.0004	55.172	0.000532	20
25	0.004103	96642	397	482275	0.000822	2.6462	4862212	0.0000	50.312	0.000822	25
30	0.005565	96245	536	479958	0.001116	2.6339	4379937	0.0000	45.508	0.001116	30
35	0.007740	95710	741	476815	0.001554	2.6613	3899979	0.0002	40.748	0.001554	35
40	0.011679	94969	1109	472281	0.002348	2.6901	3423164	0.0000	36.045	0.002348	40
45	0.018678	93860	1753	465202	0.003768	2.6637	2950882	0.0117	31.439	0.003761	45
50	0.026996	92106	2486	454746	0.005468	2.6728	2485681	0.0145	26.987	0.005453	50
55	0.042573	89620	3815	439254	0.008686	2.6814	2030935	0.0202	22.662	0.008651	55
60	0.067692	85805	5808	415624	0.013975	2.6932	1591681	0.0273	18.550	0.013989	60
65	0.115019	79996	9201	378647	0.024300	2.6813	1176057	0.0273	14.701	0.024145	65
70	0.195162	70795	13817	321305	0.043001	2.6353	797409	0.0273	11.264	0.042737	70
75	0.319002	56979	18176	240485	0.075582	2.5568	476105	0.0273	8.356	0.075154	75
80	0.483787	38802	18772	147468	0.127296	2.5206	235620	0.0273	6.072	0.126481	80
85+	*1.000000	20030	20030	88152	0.227225	4.4009	88152	0.0273	4.401	0.224668	85

TABLE 4 — OBSERVED AND PROJECTED VITAL RATES

	OBSERVED POPULATION BOTH SEXES	MALES	FEMALES	PROJECTED POPULATION 1959 MALES	FEMALES	1964 MALES	FEMALES	1969 MALES	FEMALES	STABLE POPULATION MALES	FEMALES
RATES PER THOUSAND											
Birth	17.51	18.22	16.81	17.56	16.25	18.12	16.83	19.17	17.88	18.11	17.4
Death	8.93	9.30	8.56	9.92	9.27	10.44	9.92	10.82	10.46	11.51	10.8
Increase	8.58	8.92	8.25	7.65	6.99	7.68	6.91	8.35	7.42		6.598
PERCENTAGE											
under 15	26.55	27.37	25.75	26.60	24.97	24.71	23.22	24.75	23.30	24.95	24.3
15-64	63.84	63.52	64.16	63.76	64.12	65.02	64.93	64.43	64.10	63.64	63.0
65 and over	9.61	9.12	10.10	9.64	10.91	10.26	11.85	10.81	12.60	11.41	12.6
DEP. RATIO X 100	56.64	57.43	55.87	56.85	55.97	53.80	54.02	55.20	56.01	57.14	58.5

3 Denmark 1956–58

TABLE 1 / A

AGE AT LAST BIRTHDAY	POPULATION BOTH SEXES	MALES Number	%	FEMALES Number	%	BIRTHS BY AGE OF MOTHER	DEATHS BOTH SEXES	MALES	FEMALES	AGE AT LAST BIRTHDAY
0	75501	38788	1.7	36713	1.6	0	1782	1066	716	0
1-4	297506	152850	6.9	144656	6.4	0	282	161	121	1-4
5-9	387470	198057	8.9	189413	8.4	0	144	93	51	5-9
10-14	425337	217591	9.8	207746	9.2	5	141	90	51	10-14
15-19	324425	165321	7.4	159104	7.0	6672	199	132	67	15-19
20-24	286540	143655	6.5	142885	6.3	24512	230	163	67	20-24
25-29	281519	139318	6.3	142201	6.3	21826	261	160	101	25-29
30-34	300597	147825	6.6	152772	6.8	13693	347	189	158	30-34
35-39	312593	154538	6.9	158055	7.0	6762	497	264	233	35-39
40-44	302958	149822	6.7	153136	6.8	1947	727	397	330	40-44
45-49	307436	152216	6.8	155220	6.9	139	1183	645	538	45-49
50-54	276528	135245	6.1	141283	6.2	1	1787	1035	752	50-54
55-59	245967	118006	5.3	127961	5.7	0	2529	1484	1045	55-59
60-64	210117	99736	4.5	110381	4.9	0	3367	1926	1441	60-64
65-69	168104	78962	3.5	89142	3.9	0	4455	2441	2014	65-69
70-74	131446	61449	2.8	69997	3.1		5836	3050	2786	70-74
75-79	86468	40478	1.8	45990	2.0		6553	3232	3321	75-79
80-84	45971	21415	1.0	24556	1.1	38972 M.	5809	2872	2937	80-84
85+	21348	9363	0.4	11985	0.5	36585 F.	4831	2186	2645	85+
TOTAL	4487831	2224635		2263196		75557	40960	21586	19374	TOTAL

TABLE 2 / MALE

x	nq_x	l_x	nd_x	nL_x	nm_x	na_x	T_x	r_x	$\mathring{e}_x$	nM_x	x
0	0.026901	100000	2690	97925	0.027471	0.2286	7036829	0.0006	70.368	0.027483	0
1	0.004197	97310	408	388050	0.001052	1.0865	6938904	0.0006	71.307	0.001053	1
5	0.002345	96902	227	483940	0.000470	2.5000	6550854	0.0000	67.603	0.000470	5
10	0.002072	96674	200	482904	0.000415	2.6665	6066914	0.0176	62.756	0.000414	10
15	0.004015	96474	387	481473	0.000805	2.6849	5584010	0.0407	57.881	0.000798	15
20	0.005663	96087	544	479106	0.001136	2.5611	5102537	0.0160	53.104	0.001135	20
25	0.005726	95542	547	476357	0.001148	2.5233	4623432	0.0000	48.391	0.001148	25
30	0.006373	94995	605	473517	0.001279	2.5881	4147075	0.0000	43.656	0.001279	30
35	0.008508	94390	803	470073	0.001708	2.6627	3673558	0.0000	38.919	0.001708	35
40	0.013169	93587	1232	465091	0.002650	2.6923	3203485	0.0000	34.230	0.002650	40
45	0.021014	92354	1941	457375	0.004243	2.7341	2738395	0.0056	29.651	0.004237	45
50	0.037749	90414	3413	444242	0.007683	2.7070	2281020	0.0175	25.229	0.007653	50
55	0.061280	87001	5331	422541	0.012618	2.6625	1836777	0.0176	21.112	0.012576	55
60	0.092713	81669	7572	390538	0.019388	2.6480	1414236	0.0210	17.317	0.019311	60
65	0.144547	74097	10711	345000	0.031039	2.6269	1023699	0.0210	13.816	0.030914	65
70	0.222398	63387	14097	282896	0.049832	2.5854	678628	0.0210	10.706	0.049635	70
75	0.334570	49290	16491	205700	0.080170	2.5290	395732	0.0210	8.029	0.079846	75
80	0.499780	32799	16392	121757	0.134631	2.4989	190032	0.0210	5.794	0.134112	80
85+	1.000000	16407	16407	68275	0.240302	4.1614	68275	0.0210	4.161	0.233471	85+

TABLE 3 / FEMALE

x	nq_x	l_x	nd_x	nL_x	nm_x	na_x	T_x	r_x	$\mathring{e}_x$	nM_x	x
0	0.019206	100000	1921	98542	0.019490	0.2408	7377683	0.0008	73.777	0.019503	0
1	0.003334	98079	327	391368	0.000836	1.0951	7279141	0.0008	74.217	0.000836	1
5	0.001345	97752	132	488433	0.000269	2.5000	6887773	0.0000	70.461	0.000269	5
10	0.001229	97621	120	487820	0.000246	2.6292	6399340	0.0171	65.553	0.000245	10
15	0.002112	97501	206	487012	0.000423	2.6094	5911521	0.0370	60.630	0.000421	15
20	0.002345	97295	228	485933	0.000470	2.6262	5424509	0.0107	55.753	0.000469	20
25	0.003545	97067	344	484530	0.000710	2.6639	4938576	0.0000	50.878	0.000710	25
30	0.005159	96723	499	482441	0.001034	2.6514	4454046	0.0000	46.050	0.001034	30
35	0.007345	96224	707	479461	0.001474	2.6548	3971605	0.0000	41.275	0.001474	35
40	0.010721	95517	1024	475215	0.002155	2.6870	3492145	0.0000	36.561	0.002155	40
45	0.017207	94493	1626	468696	0.003469	2.6824	3016929	0.0045	31.928	0.003466	45
50	0.026353	92867	2447	458634	0.005336	2.6710	2548234	0.0138	27.440	0.005323	50
55	0.040196	90420	3635	443654	0.008192	2.6768	2089599	0.0162	23.110	0.008167	55
60	0.063749	86785	5532	421165	0.013136	2.6936	1645945	0.0279	18.966	0.013055	60
65	0.108012	81253	8776	385934	0.022740	2.6836	1224780	0.0279	15.074	0.022593	65
70	0.183071	72476	13268	331189	0.040063	2.6491	838847	0.0279	11.574	0.039802	70
75	0.308603	59208	18272	251558	0.072634	2.5655	507658	0.0279	8.574	0.072211	75
80	0.464479	40936	19014	157907	0.120413	2.5400	256100	0.0279	6.256	0.119605	80
85+	*1.000000	21922	21922	98194	0.223255	4.4792	98194	0.0279	4.479	0.220693	85+

TABLE 4 / OBSERVED, PROJECTED

	OBSERVED POPULATION BOTH SEXES	MALES	FEMALES	PROJECTED POPULATION 1962 MALES	FEMALES	1967 MALES	FEMALES	1972 MALES	FEMALES	STABLE POPULATION MALES	FEMALES
RATES PER THOUSAND											
Birth	16.84	17.52	16.17	17.66	16.31	19.00	17.59	19.28	17.92	18.18	17.47
Death	9.13	9.70	8.56	10.29	9.34	10.70	9.98	11.01	10.51	11.33	10.62
Increase	7.71	7.82	7.60	7.37	6.97	8.30	7.61	8.27	7.42		6.8419
PERCENTAGE											
under 15	26.42	27.30	25.56	25.20	23.57	24.70	23.08	25.16	23.60	25.10	24.34
15-64	63.48	63.19	63.76	64.70	64.72	64.67	64.29	63.69	63.06	63.68	62.80
65 and over	10.10	9.51	10.68	10.10	11.71	10.63	12.62	11.15	13.34	11.22	12.87
DEP. RATIO X 100	57.54	58.26	56.84	54.56	54.51	54.64	55.54	57.01	58.58	57.04	59.24

TABLE 1 — DATA

AGE AT LAST BIRTHDAY	POPULATION BOTH SEXES	MALES Number	%	FEMALES Number	%	BIRTHS BY AGE OF MOTHER	DEATHS BOTH SEXES	MALES	FEMALES	AGE AT LAST BIRTHDAY
0	74323	38107	1.7	36216	1.6	0	1654	960	694	0
1-4	293908	150918	6.6	142990	6.2	0	271	157	114	1-4
5-9	370803	190218	8.4	180585	7.8	0	163	100	63	5-9
10-14	416672	213036	9.4	203636	8.8	9	120	76	44	10-1
15-19	380931	194715	8.6	186216	8.1	7751	222	158	64	15-1
20-24	303081	153404	6.8	149677	6.5	25391	232	169	63	20-2
25-29	278808	138853	6.1	139955	6.1	21839	249	158	91	25-2
30-34	286888	141925	6.2	144963	6.3	12575	332	187	145	30-3
35-39	311401	153348	6.7	158053	6.8	6105	495	253	242	35-3
40-44	299707	148419	6.5	151288	6.6	1703	731	394	337	40-4
45-49	305734	151273	6.7	154461	6.7	109	1139	645	494	45-4
50-54	292554	143807	6.3	148747	6.4	0	1807	1056	751	50-5
55-59	257805	124502	5.5	133303	5.8	0	2581	1544	1037	55-5
60-64	223895	105755	4.7	118140	5.1	0	3526	2055	1471	60-6
65-69	179318	83840	3.7	95478	4.1	0	4622	2603	2019	65-6
70-74	137447	63361	2.8	74086	3.2		6041	3132	2909	70-7
75-79	93681	43006	1.9	50675	2.2		7076	3530	3546	75-7
80-84	50368	23298	1.0	27070	1.2	38707 M.	6413	3088	3325	80-8
85+	23647	10478	0.5	13169	0.6	36775 F.	5375	2459	2916	85+
TOTAL	4580971	2272263		2308708		75482	43049	22724	20325	TOT

TABLE 2 — MALE LIFE TABLE

x	$_nq_x$	l_x	$_nd_x$	$_nL_x$	$_nm_x$	$_na_x$	T_x	r_x	$\mathring{e}_x$	$_nM_x$
0	0.024715	100000	2472	98113	0.025190	0.2366	7055831	0.0001	70.558	0.025192
1	0.004148	97528	405	388938	0.001040	1.0921	6957718	0.0001	71.340	0.001040
5	0.002625	97124	255	484982	0.000526	2.5000	6568780	0.0000	67.633	0.000526
10	0.001782	96869	173	483942	0.000357	2.6678	6083798	0.0000	62.804	0.000357
15	0.004074	96696	394	482571	0.000816	2.6890	5599856	0.0321	57.912	0.000811
20	0.005505	96302	530	480218	0.001104	2.5588	5117285	0.0328	53.138	0.001102
25	0.005675	95772	544	477522	0.001138	2.5365	4637067	0.0066	48.418	0.001138
30	0.006567	95229	625	474629	0.001318	2.5779	4159545	0.0000	43.680	0.001318
35	0.008218	94603	777	471201	0.001650	2.6641	3684916	0.0000	38.951	0.001650
40	0.013193	93826	1238	466281	0.002655	2.6982	3213715	0.0000	34.252	0.002655
45	0.021114	92588	1955	458479	0.004264	2.7178	2747435	0.0000	29.674	0.004264
50	0.036204	90633	3281	445656	0.007363	2.7113	2288955	0.0118	25.255	0.007343
55	0.060477	87352	5283	424464	0.012446	2.6724	1843299	0.0180	21.102	0.012401
60	0.093249	82069	7653	392362	0.019505	2.6501	1418836	0.0195	17.288	0.019432
65	0.145073	74416	10796	346435	0.031163	2.6244	1026474	0.0195	13.794	0.031047
70	0.221605	63620	14099	284137	0.049619	2.5909	680039	0.0195	10.689	0.049431
75	0.342161	49522	16944	205669	0.082387	2.5248	395902	0.0195	7.995	0.082082
80	0.494743	32577	16117	121191	0.132992	2.4937	190234	0.0195	5.839	0.132544
85+	1.000000	16460	16460	69043	0.238402	4.1946	69043	0.0195	4.195	0.234681

TABLE 3 — FEMALE LIFE TABLE

x	$_nq_x$	l_x	$_nd_x$	$_nL_x$	$_nm_x$	$_na_x$	T_x	r_x	$\mathring{e}_x$	$_nM_x$
0	0.018878	100000	1888	98561	0.019153	0.2376	7408572	0.0006	74.086	0.019163
1	0.003179	98112	312	391542	0.000797	1.0928	7310011	0.0006	74.507	0.000797
5	0.001743	97800	170	488575	0.000349	2.5000	6918469	0.0000	70.741	0.000349
10	0.001080	97630	105	487885	0.000216	2.4953	6429893	0.0000	65.860	0.000216
15	0.001724	97524	168	487223	0.000345	2.6241	5942008	0.0305	60.928	0.000344
20	0.002111	97356	206	486299	0.000423	2.6494	5454785	0.0281	56.029	0.000421
25	0.003243	97151	316	485023	0.000651	2.6833	4968487	0.0025	51.142	0.000650
30	0.004990	96835	483	483056	0.001000	2.6809	4483464	0.0000	46.300	0.001000
35	0.007628	96352	735	480043	0.001531	2.6633	4000408	0.0000	41.519	0.001531
40	0.011080	95617	1059	475597	0.002228	2.6506	3520365	0.0000	36.817	0.002228
45	0.015873	94558	1501	469300	0.003198	2.6758	3044768	0.0000	32.200	0.003198
50	0.024996	93057	2326	459880	0.005058	2.6769	2575468	0.0095	27.676	0.005049
55	0.038316	90731	3476	445584	0.007802	2.6788	2115588	0.0149	23.317	0.007779
60	0.060858	87254	5310	424464	0.012524	2.6860	1670004	0.0266	19.140	0.012451
65	0.101465	81944	8314	390602	0.021286	2.7005	1246000	0.0266	15.205	0.021146
70	0.180805	73630	13313	336913	0.039514	2.6537	855398	0.0266	11.618	0.039265
75	0.300648	60317	18134	257643	0.070385	2.5768	518485	0.0266	8.596	0.069975
80	0.474115	42183	20000	161759	0.123638	2.5422	260842	0.0266	6.184	0.122831
85+	*1.000000	22183	22183	99083	0.223887	4.4665	99083	0.0266	4.467	0.221429

TABLE 4 — OBSERVED AND PROJECTED VITAL RATES

	OBSERVED POPULATION BOTH SEXES	MALES	FEMALES	PROJECTED POPULATION 1965 MALES	FEMALES	1970 MALES	FEMALES	1975 MALES	FEMALES	STABLE POPULATION MALES	FEMA
RATES PER THOUSAND											
Birth	16.48	17.03	15.93	18.02	16.85	19.01	17.80	18.70	17.55	17.94	17.
Death	9.40	10.00	8.80	10.56	9.58	10.91	10.18	11.18	10.66	11.40	10.
Increase	7.08	7.03	7.13	7.46	7.28	8.10	7.62	7.52	6.89		6.53
PERCENTAGE											
under 15	25.23	26.07	24.40	24.43	22.89	24.55	23.10	25.19	23.82	24.88	24.
15-64	64.20	64.08	64.31	65.11	64.74	64.45	63.68	63.21	62.20	63.76	62.
65 and over	10.58	9.86	11.28	10.46	12.37	11.00	13.23	11.59	13.97	11.36	13.
DEP. RATIO X 100	55.77	56.06	55.49	53.59	54.46	55.15	57.04	58.20	60.77	56.84	59.

TABLE 5 — POPULATION PROJECTED WITH FIXED AGE-SPECIFIC BIRTH AND DEATH RATES (IN 1000's)

AGE LAST BIRTHDAY	1965 BOTH SEXES	MALES	FEMALES	1970 BOTH SEXES	MALES	FEMALES	1975 BOTH SEXES	MALES	FEMALES	AGE AT LAST BIRTHDAY
0-4	387	198	189	424	217	207	448	229	219	0-4
5-9	367	188	179	385	197	188	423	216	207	5-9
10-14	370	190	180	366	188	178	384	196	188	10-14
15-19	415	212	203	369	189	180	365	187	178	15-19
20-24	380	194	186	414	211	203	368	188	180	20-24
25-29	302	153	149	378	193	185	412	210	202	25-29
30-34	277	138	139	301	152	149	377	192	185	30-34
35-39	285	141	144	276	137	139	299	151	148	35-39
40-44	309	152	157	282	139	143	273	136	137	40-44
45-49	295	146	149	304	149	155	278	137	141	45-49
50-54	298	147	151	288	142	146	296	145	151	50-54
55-59	281	137	144	287	140	147	277	135	142	55-59
60-64	242	115	127	264	127	137	269	129	140	60-64
65-69	202	93	109	219	102	117	238	112	126	65-69
70-74	151	69	82	171	77	94	184	83	101	70-74
75-79	103	46	57	113	50	63	127	55	72	75-79
80-84	57	25	32	63	27	36	69	29	40	80-84
85+	30	13	17	33	14	19	37	15	22	85+
TOTAL	4751	2357	2394	4937	2451	2486	5124	2545	2579	TOTAL

TABLE 6 — STANDARDIZED RATES

STANDARD COUNTRIES: STANDARDIZED RATES PER THOUSAND

	ENGLAND AND WALES 1961 BOTH SEXES	MALES	FEMALES	UNITED STATES 1960 BOTH SEXES	MALES	FEMALES	MEXICO 1960 BOTH SEXES	MALES	FEMALES
Birth	15.98	17.64*	15.09	16.25	16.47*	15.60	19.41	15.40*	18.86
Death	10.52	9.87*	11.16	8.47	8.87*	8.13	4.34	7.69*	3.83
Increase	5.46	7.77*	3.93	7.78	7.59*	7.47	15.07	7.71*	15.04

TABLE 7 — MOMENTS AND CUMULANTS

	OBSERVED POP. MALES	FEMALES	STATIONARY POP. MALES	FEMALES	STABLE POP. MALES	FEMALES	OBSERVED BIRTHS	NET MATERNITY FUNCTION	BIRTHS IN STABLE POP.
	33.81585	35.17720	37.73669	39.01395	34.39155	35.49666	26.79851	26.95329	26.73498
	482.9919	497.3601	521.0207	546.7721	500.9405	527.5875	34.03661	31.68845	30.95618
	3471.638	2950.544	2224.305	1954.928	3869.444	3862.550	120.6243	112.1062	111.9367
	-218563.	-244256.	-273295.	-313863.	-226062.	-264637.	-147.862	2.137	59.298
	0.106967	0.070761	0.034980	0.023380	0.119107	0.101593	0.369003	0.394963	0.422379
	2.063093	2.012575	1.993251	1.950151	2.099143	2.049261	2.872367	3.002128	3.061879
	-0.039381	-0.025928	-0.013081	-0.008539	-0.044606	-0.037188	-0.224922	-0.278368	-0.309065

TABLE 8 — RATES FROM AGE DISTRIBUTIONS AND VITAL STATISTICS (Females)

VITAL STATISTICS		THOMPSON AGE RANGE	NRR	1000r	INTERVAL	BOURGEOIS-PICHAT AGE RANGE	NRR	1000b	1000d	1000r	COALE
R	1.229										IBR
R	1.192	0-4	1.14	4.77	27.43	5-29	1.54	20.05	4.05	16.00	IDR
R	2.523	5-9	1.18	6.21	27.40	30-54	0.92	12.20	15.19	-2.99	IRI
GENERATION	26.844	10-14	1.33	10.25	27.35	55-79	1.77	44.13	23.05	21.09	K1
SEX RATIO	105.254	15-19	1.21	6.75	27.27	*50-74	1.69	39.58	20.11	19.48	K2

TABLE 9 — LESLIE MATRIX AND ITS SPECTRAL COMPONENTS (Females)

ORIGINAL MATRIX SUB-DIAGONAL	ALTERNATIVE FIRST ROWS Projection	Integral	FIRST STABLE MATRIX % IN STABLE POPULATION	FISHER VALUES	REPRODUCTIVE VALUES	SECOND STABLE MATRIX Z_2 FIRST COLUMN	FIRST ROW
0.99688	0.00000	0.00000	8.303	1.037	185831	0.1776+0.0754	0.1776+0.0754
0.99859	0.00005	0.00000	8.011	1.075	194091	0.1690-0.1581	0.0025+0.1609
0.99864	0.04968	0.00011	7.742	1.112	226450	-0.0914-0.2624	-0.1217+0.0562
0.99810	0.25184	0.10103	7.483	1.099	204646	-0.3326-0.0273	-0.0926-0.0774
0.99738	0.38834	0.41173	7.228	0.876	131119	-0.1917+0.3518	-0.0171-0.1157
0.99594	0.28945	0.37874	6.978	0.504	70503	0.2927+0.3812	0.0133-0.0815
0.99376	0.14939	0.21054	6.726	0.221	32073	0.5596-0.1356	0.0150-0.0394
0.99074	0.05943	0.09375	6.469	0.074	11720	0.1227-0.6771	0.0085-0.0132
0.98676	0.01426	0.02732	6.203	0.015	2289	-0.6785-0.4605	0.0023-0.0025
0.97993	0.00084	0.00170	5.924	0.001	132	-0.8259+0.5148	0.0001-0.0001
0.96891	0.00001	0.00002	5.618	0.000	1	0.1605+1.1357	0.0000-0.0000
0.79979			23.316				

TABLE 10 — AGE ANALYSIS AND MISCELLANEOUS RESULTS (Females)

OBSERVED POPUL. (IN 100's)	CONTRIBUTIONS OF ROOTS (IN 100's) r_1	r_2, r_3	r_4-r_{11}	AGE-SP. BIRTH RATES	NET MATERNITY FUNCTION	COEFF. OF MATRIX EQUATION	PARAMETERS INTEGRAL	MATRIX	EXP. INCREASE x	$e^{(x+2\frac{1}{2})r}$
1792	1913	-131	10	0.0000	0.0000	0.0000	L(1) 1.03321	1.03324	0	1.0165
1806	1845	-5	-35	0.0000	0.0000	0.0001	L(2) 0.32837	0.33678	50	1.4093
2036	1783	184	69	0.0000	0.0001	0.0495	0.78971	0.76018	55	1.4561
1862	1724	186	-47	0.0203	0.0988	0.2504	R(1) 0.00654	0.00654	60	1.5045
1497	1665	-85	-83	0.0826	0.4019	0.3853	R(2) -0.03127	-0.03692	65	1.5544
1400	1607	-350	142	0.0760	0.3687	0.2864	0.23535	-0.23075	70	1.6061
1450	1549	-218	118	0.0423	0.2042	0.1472	C(1)	23035	75	1.6594
1581	1490	290	-200	0.0188	0.0903	0.0582	C(2)	-25784	80	1.7145
1513	1429	590	-506	0.0055	0.0261	0.0138		26114	85	1.7715
1545	1365	157	23	0.0003	0.0016	0.0008	2P/Y 26.6976	27.2292	90	1.8303
1487	1294	-676	869	0.0000	0.0000	0.0000	DELTA 4.7507		95	1.8911
5119	5371								100	1.9539

TABLE 1 DATA

AGE AT LAST BIRTHDAY	POPULATION BOTH SEXES	MALES Number	%	FEMALES Number	%	BIRTHS BY AGE OF MOTHER	DEATHS BOTH SEXES	MALES	FEMALES	AGE AT L. BIRTH
0	77038	39294	1.7	37744	1.6	0	1561	909	652	0
1-4	293413	149943	6.5	143470	6.1	0	247	128	119	1-
5-9	370888	190179	8.3	180709	7.7	0	161	106	55	5-9
10-14	386606	197635	8.6	188971	8.1	4	134	91	43	10-1
15-19	422439	216521	9.4	205918	8.8	8765	230	148	82	15-1
20-24	319097	162041	7.0	157056	6.7	26929	259	186	73	20-2
25-29	284226	142323	6.2	141903	6.1	22342	218	145	73	25-2
30-34	280999	139478	6.1	141521	6.0	12292	311	174	137	30-3
35-39	299557	147848	6.4	151709	6.5	5718	444	265	179	35-3
40-44	310294	153516	6.7	156778	6.7	1661	747	417	330	40-4
45-49	298361	147373	6.4	150988	6.4	96	1154	661	493	45-4
50-54	299863	147951	6.4	151912	6.5	1	1859	1148	711	50-5
55-59	265544	128861	5.6	136683	5.8	0	2734	1695	1039	55-5
60-64	230550	108937	4.7	121613	5.2	0	3766	2274	1492	60-6
65-69	189719	87958	3.8	101761	4.3	0	5054	2874	2180	65-6
70-74	141673	64703	2.8	76970	3.3		6364	3383	2981	70-7
75-79	98173	44563	1.9	53610	2.3		7424	3737	3687	75-7
80-84	52768	23873	1.0	28895	1.2	39849 M.	6788	3300	3488	80-8
85+	25691	11184	0.5	14507	0.6	37959 F.	5879	2719	3160	85-
TOTAL	4646899	2304181		2342718		77808	45334	24360	20974	TOT

TABLE 2 MALE LIFE TABLE

x	$_nq_x$	l_x	$_nd_x$	$_nL_x$	$_nm_x$	$_na_x$	T_x	r_x	$\mathring{e}_x$	$_nM_x$
0	0.022656	100000	2266	98243	0.023061	0.2246	7032018	0.0039	70.320	0.023133
1	0.003387	97734	331	389972	0.000849	1.0838	6933775	0.0039	70.945	0.000854
5	0.002783	97403	271	486339	0.000557	2.5000	6543802	0.0000	67.182	0.000557
10	0.002300	97132	223	485116	0.000460	2.5568	6057463	0.0000	62.363	0.000460
15	0.003426	96909	332	483784	0.000686	2.7075	5572347	0.0191	57.501	0.000684
20	0.005737	96577	554	481532	0.001151	2.5587	5088563	0.0409	52.689	0.001148
25	0.005083	96023	488	478903	0.001019	2.5171	4607031	0.0139	47.978	0.001019
30	0.006219	95535	594	476264	0.001248	2.6260	4128128	0.0000	43.211	0.001248
35	0.008925	94941	847	472726	0.001792	2.6662	3651865	0.0000	38.465	0.001792
40	0.013497	94093	1270	467545	0.002716	2.6990	3179139	0.0000	33.787	0.002716
45	0.022199	92823	2061	459422	0.004485	2.7218	2711594	0.0000	29.212	0.004485
50	0.038165	90763	3464	445889	0.007769	2.7123	2252172	0.0053	24.814	0.007759
55	0.064031	87299	5590	423496	0.013199	2.6747	1806282	0.0170	20.691	0.013154
60	0.099774	81709	8152	389329	0.020940	2.6429	1382786	0.0167	16.923	0.020874
65	0.152019	73556	11182	341153	0.032777	2.6185	993458	0.0167	13.506	0.032675
70	0.232689	62374	14514	276728	0.052448	2.5785	652305	0.0167	10.458	0.052285
75	0.347951	47861	16653	197963	0.084123	2.5176	375578	0.0167	7.847	0.083859
80	0.510088	31207	15919	114814	0.138646	2.4821	177615	0.0167	5.691	0.138231
85+	1.000000	15289	15289	62801	0.243452	4.1076	62801	0.0167	4.108	0.243116

TABLE 3 FEMALE LIFE TABLE

x	$_nq_x$	l_x	$_nd_x$	$_nL_x$	$_nm_x$	$_na_x$	T_x	r_x	$\mathring{e}_x$	$_nM_x$
0	0.016996	100000	1700	98730	0.017214	0.2529	7445914	0.0044	74.459	0.017274
1	0.003292	98300	324	392265	0.000825	1.1044	7347184	0.0044	74.742	0.000829
5	0.001521	97977	149	489512	0.000304	2.5000	6954919	0.0000	70.985	0.000304
10	0.001137	97828	111	488870	0.000228	2.5858	6465408	0.0000	66.090	0.000228
15	0.001994	97717	195	488120	0.000399	2.6236	5976537	0.0181	61.162	0.000398
20	0.002326	97522	227	487053	0.000466	2.5511	5488417	0.0368	56.279	0.000465
25	0.002574	97295	250	485899	0.000515	2.7012	5001364	0.0098	51.404	0.000514
30	0.004829	97044	469	484117	0.000968	2.6412	4515465	0.0000	46.530	0.000968
35	0.005883	96576	568	481570	0.001180	2.6969	4031348	0.0000	41.743	0.001180
40	0.010474	96008	1006	477726	0.002105	2.7012	3549778	0.0000	36.974	0.002105
45	0.016202	95002	1539	471404	0.003265	2.6570	3072051	0.0000	32.337	0.003265
50	0.023172	93463	2166	462292	0.004685	2.6809	2600647	0.0050	27.825	0.004680
55	0.037460	91297	3420	448583	0.007624	2.6892	2138356	0.0144	23.422	0.007602
60	0.059996	87877	5272	427259	0.012340	2.7000	1689773	0.0255	19.229	0.012268
65	0.102677	82605	8482	393477	0.021556	2.6954	1262514	0.0255	15.284	0.021423
70	0.178462	74123	13228	339536	0.038960	2.6505	869036	0.0255	11.724	0.038729
75	0.296199	60895	18037	260805	0.069159	2.5789	529500	0.0255	8.695	0.068774
80	0.468051	42858	20060	165132	0.121477	2.5494	268695	0.0255	6.269	0.120714
85+	*1.000000	22798	22798	103563	0.220139	4.5426	103563	0.0255	4.543	0.217826

TABLE 4 OBSERVED AND PROJECTED VITAL RATES

	OBSERVED POPULATION BOTH SEXES	MALES	FEMALES	PROJECTED POPULATION 1967 MALES	FEMALES	1972 MALES	FEMALES	1977 MALES	FEMALES	STABLE POPULATION MALES	FEMA
RATES PER THOUSAND											
Birth	16.74	17.29	16.20	18.69	17.48	19.10	17.87	18.52	17.35	18.18	17.
Death	9.76	10.57	8.95	11.00	9.71	11.26	10.28	11.44	10.70	11.31	10.
Increase	6.99	6.72	7.25	7.70	7.77	7.85	7.59	7.08	6.64		6.86
PERCENTAGE											
under 15	24.27	25.04	23.52	24.46	22.96	24.89	23.44	25.65	24.19	25.22	24.
15-64	64.79	64.88	64.71	64.99	64.26	64.11	63.02	62.83	61.58	63.90	62.
65 and over	10.93	10.08	11.77	10.55	12.78	11.00	13.55	11.52	14.23	10.88	13.
DEP. RATIO X 100	54.33	54.14	54.52	53.87	55.62	55.99	58.69	59.16	62.40	56.49	59.

TABLE 1 — DATA

AGE AT LAST BIRTHDAY	POPULATION BOTH SEXES	MALES Number	%	FEMALES Number	%	BIRTHS BY AGE OF MOTHER	DEATHS BOTH SEXES	MALES	FEMALES	AGE AT LAST BIRTHDAY
0	79414	40570	1.7	38844	1.6	0	1576	941	635	0
1-4	295795	151015	6.5	144780	6.1	0	271	148	123	1-4
5-9	369595	189479	8.2	180116	7.6	0	157	107	50	5-9
10-14	377780	193215	8.3	184565	7.8	0	108	66	42	10-14
15-19	429158	220164	9.5	208994	8.9	9712	252	171	81	15-19
20-24	334212	170106	7.3	164106	7.0	28764	234	161	73	20-24
25-29	289926	145438	6.3	144488	6.1	23708	253	166	87	25-29
30-34	279046	138606	6.0	140440	5.9	12585	302	155	147	30-34
35-39	295806	146231	6.3	149575	6.3	5923	491	262	229	35-39
40-44	311290	153913	6.6	157377	6.7	1625	788	441	347	40-44
45-49	295526	145946	6.3	149580	6.3	96	1117	634	483	45-49
50-54	301896	149081	6.4	152815	6.5	0	1844	1111	733	50-54
55-59	270011	131120	5.6	138891	5.9	0	2823	1749	1074	55-59
60-64	234309	110785	4.8	123524	5.2	0	3802	2275	1527	60-64
65-69	194529	90102	3.9	104427	4.4	0	5216	2973	2243	65-69
70-74	144192	65584	2.8	78608	3.3		6260	3367	2893	70-74
75-79	100211	45148	1.9	55063	2.3		7449	3715	3734	75-79
80-84	54032	24159	1.0	29873	1.3	42286 M.	6741	3286	3455	80-84
85+	26851	11700	0.5	15151	0.6	40127 F.	6089	2807	3282	85+
TOTAL	4683579	2322362		2361217		82413	45773	24535	21238	TOTAL

TABLE 2 — MALE LIFE TABLE

x	$_nq_x$	l_x	$_nd_x$	$_nL_x$	$_nm_x$	$_na_x$	T_x	r_x	$\mathring{e}_x$	$_nM_x$	x
0	0.022680	100000	2268	98274	0.023078	0.2388	7042749	0.0064	70.427	0.023194	0
1	0.003877	97732	379	389827	0.000972	1.0936	6944476	0.0064	71.056	0.000980	1
5	0.002820	97353	274	486079	0.000565	2.5000	6554649	0.0000	67.329	0.000565	5
10	0.001707	97079	166	485000	0.000342	2.6282	6068570	0.0000	62.512	0.000342	10
15	0.003884	96913	376	483684	0.000778	2.6614	5583570	0.0120	57.614	0.000777	15
20	0.004737	96537	457	481575	0.000950	2.5778	5099885	0.0405	52.829	0.000946	20
25	0.005694	96079	547	479044	0.001142	2.5287	4618310	0.0194	48.068	0.001141	25
30	0.005577	95532	533	476392	0.001118	2.6175	4139266	0.0000	43.329	0.001118	30
35	0.008922	94999	848	473046	0.001792	2.6984	3662874	0.0000	38.557	0.001792	35
40	0.014232	94152	1340	467649	0.002865	2.6786	3189828	0.0000	33.880	0.002865	40
45	0.021506	92812	1996	459484	0.004344	2.7077	2722179	0.0000	29.330	0.004344	45
50	0.036666	90816	3330	446522	0.007457	2.7303	2262695	0.0027	24.915	0.007452	50
55	0.064891	87486	5677	424218	0.013382	2.6728	1816173	0.0162	20.760	0.013339	55
60	0.098253	81809	8038	390125	0.020604	2.6462	1391955	0.0174	17.015	0.020535	60
65	0.153401	73771	11317	341868	0.033102	2.6152	1001830	0.0174	13.580	0.032996	65
70	0.228927	62454	14298	277609	0.051502	2.5755	659962	0.0174	10.567	0.051339	70
75	0.342656	48157	16501	199879	0.082556	2.5211	382354	0.0174	7.940	0.082285	75
80	0.504330	31656	15965	117008	0.136443	2.4894	182475	0.0174	5.764	0.136016	80
85+	1.000000	15691	15691	65467	0.239676	4.1723	65467	0.0174	4.172	0.239915	85+

TABLE 3 — MALE LIFE TABLE

x	$_nq_x$	l_x	$_nd_x$	$_nL_x$	$_nm_x$	$_na_x$	T_x	r_x	$\mathring{e}_x$	$_nM_x$	x
0	0.016073	100000	1607	98813	0.016266	0.2615	7452722	0.0064	74.527	0.016347	0
1	0.003366	98393	331	392614	0.000843	1.1115	7353909	0.0064	74.740	0.000850	1
5	0.001387	98062	136	489968	0.000278	2.5000	6961295	0.0000	70.989	0.000278	5
10	0.001137	97926	111	489361	0.000228	2.6003	6471327	0.0000	66.084	0.000228	10
15	0.001939	97814	190	488619	0.000388	2.6168	5981966	0.0114	61.156	0.000388	15
20	0.002230	97625	218	487600	0.000446	2.5996	5493347	0.0364	56.270	0.000445	20
25	0.003016	97407	294	486360	0.000604	2.7052	5005747	0.0149	51.390	0.000602	25
30	0.005221	97113	507	484390	0.001047	2.6821	4519387	0.0000	46.537	0.001047	30
35	0.007628	96606	737	481302	0.001531	2.6539	4034996	0.0000	41.768	0.001531	35
40	0.010968	95869	1051	476880	0.002205	2.6650	3553695	0.0000	37.068	0.002205	40
45	0.016024	94818	1519	470533	0.003229	2.6594	3076814	0.0000	32.450	0.003229	45
50	0.023730	93298	2214	461363	0.004799	2.6834	2606282	0.0024	27.935	0.004797	50
55	0.038063	91084	3469	447392	0.007753	2.6851	2144919	0.0133	23.549	0.007733	55
60	0.060441	87616	5296	425880	0.012434	2.6967	1697527	0.0260	19.375	0.012362	60
65	0.102870	82320	8468	391947	0.021606	2.6793	1271647	0.0260	15.448	0.021479	65
70	0.170367	73852	12582	339776	0.037030	2.6568	879699	0.0260	11.912	0.036803	70
75	0.292725	61270	17935	262983	0.068199	2.5821	539923	0.0260	8.812	0.067813	75
80	0.453355	43335	19646	168757	0.116416	2.5610	276941	0.0260	6.391	0.115657	80
85+	*1.000000	23689	23689	108184	0.218967	4.5669	108184	0.0260	4.567	0.216619	85+

TABLE 4 — OBSERVED AND PROJECTED VITAL RATES

	OBSERVED POPULATION BOTH SEXES	MALES	FEMALES	PROJECTED POPULATION 1968 MALES	FEMALES	1973 MALES	FEMALES	1978 MALES	FEMALES	STABLE POPULATION MALES	FEMALES
RATES PER THOUSAND											
Birth	17.60	18.21	16.99	19.52	18.20	19.62	18.31	18.86	17.64	18.99	18.16
Death	9.77	10.56	8.99	10.98	9.76	11.21	10.31	11.36	10.70	10.79	9.96
Increase	7.82	7.64	8.00	8.55	8.44	8.41	8.00	7.50	6.94		8.1989
PERCENTAGE											
under 15	23.97	24.73	23.22	24.73	23.22	25.51	24.02	26.42	24.91	26.08	25.13
15-64	64.93	65.08	64.79	64.62	63.80	63.41	62.26	62.04	60.77	63.53	62.32
65 and over	11.10	10.19	11.99	10.64	12.98	11.08	13.72	11.54	14.32	10.39	12.55
DEP. RATIO X 100	54.01	53.66	54.35	54.74	56.75	57.71	60.62	61.17	64.56	57.41	60.46

AGE AT LAST BIRTHDAY	BOTH SEXES	POPULATION MALES Number	%	FEMALES Number	%	BIRTHS BY AGE OF MOTHER	DEATHS BOTH SEXES	MALES	FEMALES	AGE AT LAST BIRTHDAY
0	82202	42162	1.8	40040	1.7	0	1560	915	645	0
1-4	301330	153779	6.6	147551	6.2	0	244	145	99	1-4
5-9	368168	188702	8.1	179466	7.5	0	153	93	60	5-9
10-14	373625	191161	8.2	182464	7.7	0	123	84	39	10-14
15-19	425908	218557	9.3	207351	8.7	10042	277	201	76	15-19
20-24	353065	179822	7.7	173243	7.3	30222	243	173	70	20-24
25-29	295360	148467	6.3	146893	6.2	23779	261	159	102	25-29
30-34	277837	138175	5.9	139662	5.9	12142	281	178	103	30-34
35-39	290719	143901	6.2	146818	6.2	5571	460	255	205	35-39
40-44	312688	154296	6.6	158392	6.7	1511	691	379	312	40-44
45-49	293345	145119	6.2	148226	6.2	89	1153	678	475	45-49
50-54	301183	148600	6.4	152583	6.4	0	1852	1123	729	50-54
55-59	275851	134081	5.7	141770	6.0	0	2805	1789	1016	55-59
60-64	237886	112638	4.8	125248	5.3	0	4005	2495	1510	60-64
65-69	198272	91422	3.9	106850	4.5	0	5354	3101	2253	65-69
70-74	147445	66804	2.9	80641	3.4		6505	3501	3004	70-74
75-79	101826	45539	1.9	56287	2.4		7579	3885	3694	75-79
80-84	55657	24597	1.1	31060	1.3	43006 M.	6983	3303	3680	80-84
85+	27804	12007	0.5	15797	0.7	40350 F.	6282	2895	3387	85+
TOTAL	4720171	2339829		2380342		83356	46811	25352	21459	TOTAL

TABLE 1 — DATA

TABLE 2 — MALE LIFE TABLE

x	nq_x	l_x	nd_x	nL_x	nm_x	na_x	T_x	r_x	$\overset{\circ}{e}_x$	nM_x	x
0	0.021211	100000	2121	98392	0.021558	0.2417	7030715	0.0084	70.307	0.021702	
1	0.003721	97879	364	390458	0.000933	1.0958	6932324	0.0084	70.826	0.000943	
5	0.002460	97515	240	486973	0.000493	2.5000	6541866	0.0019	67.086	0.000493	
10	0.002195	97275	214	485883	0.000439	2.7007	6054893	0.0000	62.245	0.000439	10
15	0.004591	97061	446	484244	0.000920	2.6172	5569010	0.0053	57.376	0.000920	15
20	0.004805	96616	464	481932	0.000963	2.5308	5084766	0.0377	52.629	0.000962	20
25	0.005349	96151	514	479502	0.001073	2.5608	4602834	0.0253	47.871	0.001071	25
30	0.006423	95637	614	476717	0.001288	2.6099	4123332	0.0018	43.114	0.001288	30
35	0.008823	95023	838	473130	0.001772	2.6332	3646615	0.0000	38.376	0.001772	35
40	0.012214	94184	1150	468319	0.002456	2.7376	3173486	0.0000	33.694	0.002456	40
45	0.023113	93034	2150	460258	0.004672	2.7156	2705166	0.0000	29.077	0.004672	45
50	0.037145	90884	3376	446714	0.007557	2.7179	2244908	0.0000	24.701	0.007557	50
55	0.064914	87508	5680	424434	0.013384	2.6930	1798194	0.0138	20.549	0.013343	55
60	0.105565	81827	8638	388756	0.022220	2.6406	1373760	0.0167	16.789	0.022151	60
65	0.157274	73189	11511	338365	0.034019	2.6039	985004	0.0167	13.458	0.033902	65
70	0.233123	61678	14379	273523	0.052568	2.5750	646639	0.0167	10.484	0.052407	70
75	0.352733	47300	16684	194974	0.085571	2.5111	373116	0.0167	7.888	0.085311	75
80	0.498761	30616	15270	113398	0.134657	2.4817	178142	0.0167	5.819	0.134285	80
85+	1.000000	15346	15346	64744	0.237023	4.2190	64744	0.0167	4.219	0.241108	85

TABLE 3 — FEMALE LIFE TABLE

x	nq_x	l_x	nd_x	nL_x	nm_x	na_x	T_x	r_x	$\overset{\circ}{e}_x$	nM_x	x
0	0.015819	100000	1582	98794	0.016012	0.2374	7482799	0.0076	74.828	0.016109	
1	0.002652	98418	261	392914	0.000664	1.0926	7384006	0.0076	75.027	0.000671	
5	0.001669	98157	164	490376	0.000334	2.5000	6991092	0.0024	71.223	0.000334	
10	0.001068	97993	105	489708	0.000214	2.5308	6500716	0.0000	66.338	0.000214	
15	0.001832	97889	179	489014	0.000367	2.6088	6011008	0.0049	61.407	0.000367	
20	0.002030	97709	198	488084	0.000406	2.6674	5521993	0.0340	56.515	0.000404	2
25	0.003473	97511	339	486741	0.000696	2.5980	5033909	0.0209	51.624	0.000694	2
30	0.003681	97172	358	485037	0.000737	2.6951	4547168	0.0000	46.795	0.000737	3
35	0.006959	96815	674	482510	0.001396	2.6809	4062131	0.0000	41.958	0.001396	3
40	0.009804	96141	943	478523	0.001970	2.6858	3579621	0.0000	37.233	0.001970	4
45	0.015906	95198	1514	472470	0.003205	2.6748	3101098	0.0005	32.575	0.003205	4
50	0.023625	93684	2213	463245	0.004778	2.6617	2628628	0.0000	28.058	0.004778	5
55	0.035338	91471	3232	449896	0.007185	2.6929	2165383	0.0121	23.673	0.007167	5
60	0.058998	88238	5206	429253	0.012128	2.7066	1715487	0.0254	19.441	0.012056	6
65	0.101106	83033	8395	395767	0.021212	2.6897	1286234	0.0254	15.491	0.021086	6
70	0.172174	74637	12851	342976	0.037468	2.6491	890466	0.0254	11.931	0.037252	
75	0.284718	61787	17592	266531	0.066003	2.5896	547490	0.0254	8.861	0.065628	
80	0.461981	44195	20417	171220	0.119245	2.5631	280959	0.0254	6.357	0.118481	
85+	*1.000000	23778	23778	109739	0.216676	4.6152	109739	0.0254	4.615	0.214408	

TABLE 4 — OBSERVED AND PROJECTED VITAL RATES

	OBSERVED POPULATION BOTH SEXES	MALES	FEMALES	PROJECTED POPULATION 1969 MALES	FEMALES	1974 MALES	FEMALES	1979 MALES	FEMALES	STABLE POPULATION MALES	FEMA
RATES PER THOUSAND											
Birth	17.66	18.38	16.95	19.57	18.03	19.45	17.94	18.66	17.26	18.64	17.
Death	9.92	10.83	9.02	11.22	9.77	11.40	10.31	11.51	10.71	11.03	10.
Increase	7.74	7.54	7.94	8.35	8.26	8.05	7.64	7.15	6.55		7.61
PERCENTAGE											
under 15	23.84	24.61	23.09	24.84	23.20	25.71	23.98	26.45	24.63	25.75	24.
15-64	64.91	65.12	64.70	64.48	63.62	63.19	62.07	62.10	60.86	63.78	62.
65 and over	11.25	10.27	12.21	10.68	13.18	11.10	13.95	11.45	14.51	10.47	12.
DEP. RATIO X 100	54.06	53.57	54.55	55.08	57.18	58.25	61.12	61.02	64.30	56.80	60.

AGE LAST BIRTHDAY	1969 BOTH SEXES	MALES	FEMALES	1974 BOTH SEXES	MALES	FEMALES	1979 BOTH SEXES	MALES	FEMALES	AGE AT LAST BIRTHDAY	
0-4	431	222	209	461	237	224	468	241	227	0-4	**TABLE 5**
5-9	382	195	187	430	221	209	459	236	223	5-9	POPULATION
10-14	367	188	179	382	195	187	428	220	208	10-14	PROJECTED
15-19	373	191	182	367	188	179	381	194	187	15-19	WITH
20-24	425	218	207	372	190	182	366	187	179	20-24	FIXED
25-29	352	179	173	422	216	206	370	189	181	25-29	AGE—
30-34	294	148	146	350	178	172	421	215	206	30-34	SPECIFIC
35-39	276	137	139	292	146	146	348	177	171	35-39	BIRTH
40-44	288	142	146	274	136	138	289	145	144	40-44	AND
45-49	308	152	156	284	140	144	269	133	136	45-49	DEATH
50-54	286	141	145	300	147	153	277	136	141	50-54	RATES
55-59	289	141	148	275	134	141	289	140	149	55-59	(IN 1000's)
60-64	258	123	135	270	129	141	258	123	135	60-64	
65-69	213	98	115	232	107	125	243	113	130	65-69	
70-74	167	74	93	179	79	100	194	86	108	70-74	
75-79	111	48	63	125	53	72	134	56	78	75-79	
80-84	62	26	36	68	28	40	77	31	46	80-84	
85+	34	14	20	38	15	23	42	16	26	85+	
TOTAL	4916	2437	2479	5121	2539	2582	5313	2638	2675	TOTAL	

STANDARD COUNTRIES: STANDARDIZED RATES PER THOUSAND	ENGLAND AND WALES 1961 BOTH SEXES	MALES	FEMALES	UNITED STATES 1960 BOTH SEXES	MALES	FEMALES	MEXICO 1960 BOTH SEXES	MALES	FEMALES	
Birth	16.46	18.75*	15.44	16.75	17.26*	15.97	20.14	16.69*	19.45	**TABLE 6**
Death	10.47	10.31*	10.64	8.44	9.30*	7.72	4.24	8.06*	3.57	STANDARDIZED RATES
Increase	5.99	8.45*	4.80	8.31	7.96*	8.26	15.89	8.63*	15.88	

	OBSERVED POP. MALES	FEMALES	STATIONARY POP. MALES	FEMALES	STABLE POP. MALES	FEMALES	OBSERVED BIRTHS	NET MATERNITY FUNCTION	BIRTHS IN STABLE POP.	
μ	34.08494	35.63726	37.46527	39.23284	33.63337	35.11173	26.17238	26.73115	26.48225	**TABLE 7**
σ^2	487.8975	509.7328	514.5165	551.8806	490.1996	528.3011	32.09602	31.01868	30.22573	MOMENTS
κ_3	3514.659	2994.582	2253.521	1941.317	4066.080	4177.438	127.4420	104.2025	104.1131	AND
κ_4	-225428.	-262452.	-263433.	-320765.	-207860.	-259682.	91.944	-11.571	44.534	CUMULANTS
β_1	0.106361	0.067709	0.037284	0.022421	0.140357	0.118352	0.491215	0.363820	0.392537	
β_2	2.053001	1.989899	2.004891	1.946835	2.134984	2.069581	3.089253	2.987974	3.048746	
κ	-0.038867	-0.024440	-0.014046	-0.008174	-0.052978	-0.043312	-0.323043	-0.269194	-0.301718	

VITAL STATISTICS		THOMPSON AGE RANGE	NRR	1000r	INTERVAL	BOURGEOIS-PICHAT AGE RANGE	NRR	1000b	1000d	1000r	COALE		
GRR	1.258					5-29	1.26	17.69	9.01	8.68	IBR	20.19	**TABLE 8**
NRR	1.224	0-4	1.14	4.86	27.44	30-54	0.85	10.19	16.18	-5.99	IDR	6.12	RATES FROM AGE DISTRIBUTIONS
TFR	2.599	5-9	1.16	5.42	27.41	55-79	1.68	40.25	21.12	19.12	IRI	14.07	AND VITAL STATISTICS
GENERATION	26.606	10-14	1.20	6.55	27.36	*50-74	1.56	33.89	17.31	16.58	K1	39.85	(Females)
SEX RATIO	106.582	15-19	1.35	10.68	27.29						K2	0.52	

Start age interval	ORIGINAL MATRIX SUB-DIAGONAL	ALTERNATIVE FIRST ROWS Projection	Integral	FIRST STABLE MATRIX % IN STABLE POPULATION	FISHER VALUES	REPRODUCTIVE VALUES	SECOND STABLE MATRIX Z_2 FIRST COLUMN	FIRST ROW	
	0.99729	0.00000	0.00000	8.556	1.036	194413	0.1774+0.0741	0.1774+0.0741	**TABLE 9**
	0.99864	0.00000	0.00000	8.214	1.080	193737	0.1652-0.1590	0.0021+0.1612	LESLIE
	0.99858	0.05755	0.00000	7.897	1.123	204900	-0.0959-0.2566	-0.1231+0.0552	MATRIX
	0.99810	0.26485	0.11749	7.591	1.108	229843	-0.3268-0.0167	-0.0936-0.0805	AND ITS
	0.99725	0.39973	0.42320	7.293	0.879	152228	-0.1734+0.3500	-0.0164-0.1184	SPECTRAL
	0.99650	0.29576	0.39271	7.001	0.500	73433	0.3009+0.3557	0.0145-0.0818	COMPONENTS
	0.99479	0.14839	0.21091	6.716	0.214	29825	0.5316-0.1606	0.0152-0.0381	(Females)
	0.99174	0.05642	0.09205	6.431	0.068	10045	0.0761-0.6563	0.0080-0.0121	
	0.98735	0.01205	0.02314	6.140	0.013	2013	-0.6786-0.3923	0.0019-0.0021	
	0.98047	0.00071	0.00144	5.836	0.001	107	-0.7436+0.5512	0.0001-0.0001	
	0.97118	0.00001	0.00002	5.508	0.000	1	0.2466+1.0571	0.0000-0.0000	
+	0.80438			22.817					

Start age interval	OBSERVED POPUL. (IN 100's)	CONTRIBUTIONS OF ROOTS (IN 100's) r_1	r_2, r_3	$r_4 \cdot r_{11}$	AGE-SP. BIRTH RATES	NET MATERNITY FUNCTION	COEFF. OF MATRIX EQUATION	PARAMETERS INTEGRAL	MATRIX	EXP. INCREASE x	$e^{(x+2\frac{1}{2})r}$	
	1876	1990	-106	-8	0.0000	0.0000	0.0000	L(1) 1.03879	1.03882	0	1.0192	**TABLE 10**
	1795	1911	-133	16	0.0000	0.0000	0.0000	L(2) 0.32407	0.33230	50	1.4911	AGE
	1825	1837	26	-38	0.0000	0.0000	0.0573	0.79723	0.76718	55	1.5490	ANALYSIS
	2074	1766	214	94	0.0234	0.1146	0.2634	R(1) 0.00761	0.00762	60	1.6091	AND
	1732	1697	166	-130	0.0844	0.4122	0.3968	R(2) -0.03003	-0.03581	65	1.6715	MISCELLANEOUS
	1469	1629	-147	-13	0.0784	0.3814	0.2928	0.23694	0.23241	70	1.7363	RESULTS
	1397	1562	-375	209	0.0421	0.2041	0.1464	C(1)	23262	75	1.8036	(Females)
	1468	1496	-147	119	0.0184	0.0886	0.0554	C(2)	-33051	80	1.8736	
	1584	1428	391	-235	0.0046	0.0221	0.0117		-7350	85	1.9463	
	1482	1357	573	-448	0.0003	0.0014	0.0007	2P/Y 26.5178	27.0350	90	2.0217	
	1526	1281	-8	252	0.0000	0.0000	0.0000	DELTA 4.5554		95	2.1002	
+	5577	5308								100	2.1816	

TABLE 1 — DATA

AGE AT LAST BIRTHDAY	POPULATION BOTH SEXES	MALES Number	MALES %	FEMALES Number	FEMALES %	BIRTHS BY AGE OF MOTHER	DEATHS BOTH SEXES	DEATHS MALES	DEATHS FEMALES	AGE AT LAST BIRTHDAY
0	74804	38315	2.1	36489	2.0	0	5653	3183	2470	0
1-4	271388	137761	7.6	133627	7.2	0	2400	1255	1145	1-4
5-9	354132	180027	10.0	174105	9.4	0	1107	621	486	5-9
10-14	323032	164234	9.1	158798	8.6	4	1055	505	550	10-14
15-19	349726	178074	9.9	171652	9.3	2666	2032	1047	985	15-19
20-24	352883	178235	9.9	174648	9.4	17493	2624	1492	1132	20-24
25-29	308317	154371	8.6	153946	8.3	20960	2160	1161	999	25-29
30-34	271790	133386	7.4	138404	7.5	16370	1871	978	893	30-34
35-39	238691	116878	6.5	121813	6.6	10988	1676	903	773	35-39
40-44	227325	111237	6.2	116088	6.3	5925	1829	1050	779	40-44
45-49	205428	100653	5.6	104775	5.7	814	1909	1147	762	45-49
50-54	179065	86610	4.8	92455	5.0	15	2375	1423	952	50-54
55-59	152977	72061	4.0	80916	4.4	1	2815	1699	1116	55-59
60-64	107247	49665	2.8	57582	3.1	0	2765	1554	1211	60-64
65-69	94688	41756	2.3	52932	2.9	0	3800	2006	1794	65-69
70-74	66476	27999	1.6	38477	2.1		3853	1786	2067	70-74
75-79	43694	18099	1.0	25595	1.4		3917	1696	2221	75-79
80-84	21669	8778	0.5	12891	0.7	38588 M.	2615	1022	1593	80-84
85+	10215	4210	0.2	6005	0.3	36648 F.	1784	647	1137	85+
TOTAL	3653547	1802349		1851198		75236	48240	25175	23065	TOTAL

TABLE 2 — MALE LIFE TABLE

x	nq_x	l_x	nd_x	nL_x	nm_x	na_x	T_x	r_x	$\mathring{e}_x$	nM_x
0	0.078469	100000	7847	94809	0.082765	0.3384	5386563	0.0053	53.866	0.083075
1	0.035423	92153	3264	359476	0.009081	1.2011	5291754	0.0053	57.423	0.009110
5	0.017088	88889	1519	440646	0.003447	2.5000	4932278	0.0023	55.488	0.003449
10	0.015264	87370	1334	433718	0.003075	2.6525	4491632	0.0000	51.409	0.003075
15	0.029001	86036	2495	424379	0.005880	2.6748	4057913	0.0000	47.165	0.005880
20	0.041018	83541	3427	409234	0.008373	2.5279	3633534	0.0066	43.494	0.008371
25	0.036875	80114	2954	393051	0.007516	2.4542	3224300	0.0213	40.246	0.007521
30	0.036002	77160	2778	378828	0.007333	2.4900	2831249	0.0204	36.693	0.007332
35	0.037930	74382	2821	364967	0.007730	2.5388	2452421	0.0102	32.971	0.007726
40	0.046155	71561	3303	349749	0.009444	2.5612	2087454	0.0055	29.170	0.009439
45	0.055548	68258	3792	332187	0.011414	2.5992	1737704	0.0130	25.458	0.011396
50	0.079245	64466	5109	310155	0.016471	2.6164	1405517	0.0166	21.802	0.016430
55	0.111965	59358	6646	280713	0.023675	2.5811	1095362	0.0320	18.454	0.023577
60	0.145974	52712	7695	244960	0.031412	2.5828	814649	0.0258	15.455	0.031290
65	0.215551	45017	9704	201254	0.048215	2.5540	569690	0.0258	12.655	0.048041
70	0.275894	35314	9743	152209	0.064010	2.4997	368435	0.0258	10.433	0.063788
75	0.378967	25571	9691	103072	0.094017	2.4426	216227	0.0258	8.456	0.093707
80	0.445420	15880	7073	60616	0.116693	2.4740	113155	0.0258	7.125	0.116427
85+	1.000000	8807	8807	52539	0.167627	5.9656	52539	0.0258	5.966	0.153681

TABLE 3 — FEMALE LIFE TABLE

x	nq_x	l_x	nd_x	nL_x	nm_x	na_x	T_x	r_x	$\mathring{e}_x$	nM_x
0	0.064682	100000	6468	95823	0.067501	0.3542	5819690	0.0041	58.197	0.067692
1	0.033406	93532	3125	365465	0.008550	1.2277	5723868	0.0041	61.197	0.008569
5	0.013849	90407	1252	448906	0.002789	2.5000	5358404	0.0027	59.270	0.002791
10	0.017179	89155	1532	442203	0.003464	2.6670	4909497	0.0000	55.067	0.003464
15	0.028302	87624	2480	432165	0.005738	2.5995	4467294	0.0000	50.983	0.005738
20	0.031897	85144	2716	418960	0.006482	2.5116	4035129	0.0045	47.392	0.006482
25	0.031925	82428	2632	405522	0.006489	2.4855	3616168	0.0168	43.871	0.006489
30	0.031742	79796	2533	392604	0.006452	2.4821	3210646	0.0170	40.235	0.006452
35	0.031235	77263	2413	380271	0.006346	2.4946	2818042	0.0111	36.473	0.006346
40	0.033010	74850	2471	368110	0.006712	2.5149	2437771	0.0084	32.569	0.006710
45	0.035788	72379	2590	355638	0.007284	2.5839	2069661	0.0150	28.595	0.007273
50	0.050348	69789	3514	340547	0.010318	2.6101	1714023	0.0155	24.560	0.010297
55	0.067109	66275	4448	320821	0.013863	2.6267	1373476	0.0328	20.724	0.013792
60	0.100592	61828	6219	294486	0.021119	2.6442	1052655	0.0221	17.026	0.021031
65	0.157412	55608	8753	257190	0.034035	2.6180	758169	0.0221	13.634	0.033893
70	0.238507	46855	11175	207169	0.053942	2.5746	500979	0.0221	10.692	0.053720
75	0.357412	35680	12752	146425	0.087091	2.4927	293809	0.0221	8.235	0.086775
80	0.468045	22927	10731	86578	0.123946	2.4892	147385	0.0221	6.428	0.123575
85+	1.000000	12196	12196	60806	0.200576	4.9856	60806	0.0221	4.986	0.189343

TABLE 4 — OBSERVED AND PROJECTED VITAL RATES

	OBSERVED POPULATION BOTH SEXES	MALES	FEMALES	PROJECTED POPULATION 1935 MALES	1935 FEMALES	1940 MALES	1940 FEMALES	1945 MALES	1945 FEMALES	STABLE POPULATION MALES	FEMALES
RATES PER THOUSAND											
Birth	20.59	21.41	19.80	21.58	19.97	21.09	19.52	20.48	18.96	18.66	17.2
Death	13.20	13.97	12.46	14.53	13.00	14.97	13.38	15.32	13.70	18.51	17.1
Increase	7.39	7.44	7.34	7.05	6.98	6.12	6.14	5.16	5.26		0.151
PERCENTAGE											
under 15	28.01	28.87	27.17	28.19	26.57	27.22	25.66	26.91	25.35	24.77	23.3
15-64	65.51	65.54	65.49	65.95	65.92	66.35	66.16	66.13	65.84	64.72	63.7
65 and over	6.48	5.60	7.34	5.86	7.52	6.43	8.18	6.96	8.81	10.51	12.9
DEP. RATIO X 100	52.65	52.59	52.70	51.62	51.71	50.71	51.15	51.21	51.87	54.51	56.9

AGE AT LAST BIRTHDAY	BOTH SEXES	1935 MALES	FEMALES	BOTH SEXES	1940 MALES	FEMALES	BOTH SEXES	1945 MALES	FEMALES	AGE AT LAST BIRTHDAY	
0-4	352	179	173	362	184	178	364	185	179	0-4	TABLE 5
5-9	337	171	166	342	174	168	352	179	173	5-9	
10-14	349	177	172	331	168	163	337	171	166	10-14	
15-19	316	161	155	341	173	168	323	164	159	15-19	POPULATION
20-24	338	172	166	305	155	150	329	167	162	20-24	PROJECTED
25-29	340	171	169	326	165	161	295	149	146	25-29	WITH
30-34	298	149	149	329	165	164	315	159	156	30-34	FIXED
35-39	263	129	134	287	143	144	318	159	159	35-39	AGE—
40-44	230	112	118	253	123	130	277	137	140	40-44	SPECIFIC
45-49	218	106	112	220	106	114	242	117	125	45-49	BIRTH
50-54	194	94	100	206	99	107	208	99	109	50-54	AND
55-59	165	78	87	180	85	95	190	89	101	55-59	DEATH
60-64	137	63	74	148	68	80	161	74	87	60-64	RATES
65-69	91	41	50	117	52	65	126	56	70	65-69	(IN 1000's)
70-74	75	32	43	72	31	41	91	39	52	70-74	
75-79	46	19	27	51	21	30	50	21	29	75-79	
80-84	26	11	15	27	11	16	31	13	18	80-84	
85+	17	8	9	20	9	11	21	10	11	85+	
TOTAL	3792	1873	1919	3917	1932	1985	4030	1988	2042	TOTAL	

STANDARD COUNTRIES:	ENGLAND AND WALES 1961			UNITED STATES 1960			MEXICO 1960			
STANDARDIZED RATES PER THOUSAND	BOTH SEXES	MALES	FEMALES	BOTH SEXES	MALES	FEMALES	BOTH SEXES	MALES	FEMALES	TABLE 6
Birth	16.73	17.75*	15.80	16.97	16.31*	16.28	17.52	16.70*	17.03	STANDAR-DIZED RATES
Death	17.68	21.63*	17.77	15.58	18.42*	14.69	11.49	13.44*	10.47	
Increase	-0.95	-3.87*	-1.97	1.38	-2.11*	1.60	6.03	3.26*	6.56	

	OBSERVED POP. MALES	FEMALES	STATIONARY POP. MALES	FEMALES	STABLE POP. MALES	FEMALES	OBSERVED BIRTHS	NET MATERNITY FUNCTION	BIRTHS IN STABLE POP.	
μ	29.16871	30.73364	34.13621	35.85412	34.06200	35.77527	29.93374	30.58692	30.57978	TABLE 7
σ^2	392.5060	424.7962	489.8665	520.4648	489.2587	519.9365	43.58954	45.04023	45.02661	MOMENTS
κ_3	4479.521	4594.599	3995.451	3466.134	4025.460	3505.130	116.5005	89.8003	90.0156	AND
κ_4	-72294.	-105553.	-198630.	-257916.	-197337.	-256633.	-1139.805	-1416.118	-1413.482	CUMULANTS
β_1	0.331837	0.275393	0.135800	0.085215	0.138362	0.087409	0.163873	0.088258	0.088762	
β_2	2.530743	2.415064	2.172268	2.047871	2.175612	2.050681	2.400118	2.301931	2.302809	
κ	-0.143754	-0.114490	-0.053163	-0.031670	-0.054173	-0.032488	-0.077544	-0.041758	-0.042007	

VITAL STATISTICS		THOMPSON AGE RANGE	NRR	1000r	INTERVAL	BOURGEOIS-PICHAT AGE RANGE	NRR	1000b	1000d	1000r	COALE	TABLE 8
GRR	1.265					5-29	0.94	20.18	22.30	-2.13	IBR	RATES FROM AGE DISTRI-BUTIONS
NRR	1.005	0-4	1.01	0.32	27.05	30-54	1.39	28.00	15.88	12.12	IDR	AND VITAL
TFR	2.597	5-9	1.11	3.93	27.02	55-79	1.60	34.73	17.40	17.34	IRI	STATISTICS
GENERATION	30.585	10-14	1.11	3.76	27.00	*25-59	1.42	29.17	16.08	13.09	K1	(Females)
SEX RATIO	105.294	15-19	1.31	9.69	26.93						K2	

Start Age Interval	ORIGINAL MATRIX SUB-DIAGONAL	ALTERNATIVE FIRST ROWS Projection	Integral	FIRST STABLE MATRIX % IN STABLE POPULATION	FISHER VALUES	REPRODUCTIVE VALUES	SECOND STABLE MATRIX Z2 FIRST COLUMN	FIRST ROW	
0	0.97316	0.00000	0.00000	7.967	1.084	184462	0.1299+0.0611	0.1299+0.0611	TABLE 9
5	0.98507	0.00003	0.00000	7.747	1.115	194143	0.1457-0.0853	0.0197+0.1204	LESLIE
10	0.97730	0.01708	0.00006	7.626	1.133	179892	0.0144-0.2006	-0.0740+0.0708	MATRIX
15	0.96945	0.12654	0.03491	7.447	1.141	195870	-0.1857-0.1482	-0.0871-0.0187	AND ITS
20	0.96792	0.26059	0.22514	7.214	1.036	181007	-0.2664+0.0812	-0.0458-0.0783	SPECTRAL
25	0.96814	0.28161	0.30604	6.977	0.780	120023	-0.0981+0.3108	-0.0020-0.0866	COMPO-NENTS
30	0.96859	0.23104	0.26586	6.750	0.491	67888	0.2349+0.3006	0.0223-0.0610	(Females)
35	0.96802	0.15685	0.20276	6.533	0.248	30229	0.4459-0.0276	0.0227-0.0284	
40	0.96612	0.06577	0.11473	6.319	0.081	9386	0.2687-0.4485	0.0099-0.0076	
45	0.95757	0.00891	0.01746	6.100	0.010	1041	-0.2543-0.5553	0.0013-0.0008	
50	0.94207	0.00021	0.00039	5.837	0.000	26	-0.6966-0.1212	0.0000-0.0000	
55+	0.76664			23.485					

Start Age Interval	OBSERVED POPUL. (IN 100's)	CONTRIBUTIONS OF ROOTS (IN 100's) r_1	r_2, r_3	$r_4 \cdot r_{11}$	AGE-SP. BIRTH RATES	NET MATERNITY FUNCTION	COEFF. OF MATRIX EQUATION	PARAMETERS	INTEGRAL	MATRIX	EXP. INCREASE x	$e^{(x+2\frac{1}{2})r}$	
0	1701	1755	-47	-7	0.0000	0.0000	0.0000	L(1)	1.00076	1.00076	0	1.0004	TABLE 10
5	1741	1707	-41	75	0.0000	0.0000	0.0000	L(2)	0.46466	0.46811	50	1.0080	AGE ANALYSIS
10	1588	1680	10	-102	0.0000	0.0001	0.0164			0.69710	0.68190	55	1.0088	AND MISCEL-LANEOUS
15	1717	1641	71	4	0.0076	0.0327	0.1186	R(1)	0.00015	0.00015	60	1.0095	RESULTS
20	1746	1589	81	77	0.0488	0.2044	0.2367	R(2)	-0.03540	-0.03796	65	1.0103	(Females)
25	1539	1537	9	-6	0.0663	0.2689	0.2476			0.19657	0.19384	70	1.0110	
30	1384	1487	-99	-4	0.0576	0.2262	0.1966	C(1)		22030	75	1.0118	
35	1218	1439	-143	-78	0.0439	0.1671	0.1293	C(2)		-16253	80	1.0126	
40	1161	1392	-54	-177	0.0249	0.0915	0.0525			3744	85	1.0134	
45	1048	1344	124	-420	0.0038	0.0135	0.0069	2P/Y	31.9636	32.4144	90	1.0141	
50	925	1286	236	-597	0.0001	0.0003	0.0001	DELTA	9.9945		95	1.0149	
55+	2744	5174									100	1.0157	

TABLE 1 — DATA

AGE AT LAST BIRTHDAY	POPULATION BOTH SEXES	MALES Number	%	FEMALES Number	%	BIRTHS BY AGE OF MOTHER	DEATHS BOTH SEXES	MALES	FEMALES	AGE AT LAST BIRTHDAY
0	93226	47628	2.5	45598	2.2	0	3520	1980	1540	0
1-4	402376	205438	10.6	196938	9.3	0	833	477	356	1-4
5-9	385224	196965	10.2	188259	8.9	0	322	198	124	5-9
10-14	338638	171988	8.9	166650	7.9	4	240	140	100	10-14
15-19	309949	157126	8.1	152823	7.2	4008	402	240	162	15-19
20-24	325342	164533	8.5	160809	7.6	24891	670	428	242	20-24
25-29	308233	148612	7.7	159621	7.6	27292	771	475	296	25-29
30-34	270653	125290	6.5	145363	6.9	19306	732	433	299	30-34
35-39	282883	132448	6.8	150435	7.1	13171	953	591	362	35-39
40-44	290594	137555	7.1	153039	7.2	5845	1310	850	460	40-44
45-49	249378	116779	6.0	132599	6.3	620	1701	1111	590	45-49
50-54	211366	95800	5.0	115566	5.5	10	2278	1456	822	50-54
55-59	168096	74312	3.8	93784	4.4	0	2718	1719	999	55-59
60-64	141948	59510	3.1	82438	3.9	0	3553	2054	1499	60-64
65-69	110972	43867	2.3	67105	3.2	0	4408	2282	2126	65-69
70-74	78535	29468	1.5	49067	2.3		4914	2213	2701	70-74
75-79	49008	17298	0.9	31710	1.5		4944	1959	2985	75-79
80-84	21569	7296	0.4	14273	0.7	48813 M.	3323	1212	2111	80-84
85+	9275	2708	0.1	6567	0.3	46334 F.	2440	737	1703	85+
TOTAL	4047265	1934621		2112644		95147	40032	20555	19477	TOTAL

TABLE 2 — MALE LIFE TABLE

x	nq_x	l_x	nd_x	nL_x	nm_x	na_x	T_x	r_x	$\mathring{e}_x$	nM_x
0	0.040345	100000	4035	97048	0.041572	0.2684	6227617	0.0000	62.276	0.041572
1	0.009226	95965	885	381310	0.002322	1.1176	6130569	0.0000	63.883	0.002322
5	0.004966	95080	472	474220	0.000996	2.5000	5749259	0.0373	60.468	0.001005
10	0.004074	94608	385	472128	0.000816	2.6327	5275039	0.0216	55.757	0.000814
15	0.007616	94223	718	469490	0.001528	2.7392	4802911	0.0028	50.974	0.001527
20	0.012932	93505	1209	464658	0.002602	2.6289	4333421	0.0031	46.344	0.002601
25	0.015878	92296	1465	457887	0.003201	2.5495	3868763	0.0241	41.917	0.003196
30	0.017146	90830	1557	450363	0.003458	2.5676	3410876	0.0079	37.552	0.003456
35	0.022076	89273	1971	441667	0.004462	2.6167	2960513	0.0000	33.163	0.004462
40	0.030487	87302	2662	430271	0.006186	2.6556	2518845	0.0061	28.852	0.006179
45	0.046770	84641	3959	413991	0.009562	2.6731	2088575	0.0262	24.676	0.009514
50	0.073752	80682	5950	389422	0.015280	2.6693	1674583	0.0296	20.755	0.015198
55	0.110037	74731	8223	354074	0.023225	2.6186	1285162	0.0238	17.197	0.023132
60	0.159865	66508	10632	306940	0.034640	2.5922	931087	0.0219	14.000	0.034515
65	0.231373	55876	12928	247680	0.052197	2.5481	624147	0.0219	11.170	0.052021
70	0.317031	42948	13616	180694	0.075353	2.4996	376467	0.0219	8.766	0.075098
75	0.439944	29332	12904	113546	0.113649	2.4339	195772	0.0219	6.674	0.113250
80	0.579643	16428	9522	57083	0.166813	2.3687	82227	0.0219	5.005	0.166118
85+	*1.000000	6905	6905	25144	0.274635	3.6412	25144	0.0219	3.641	0.272157

TABLE 3 — FEMALE LIFE TABLE

x	nq_x	l_x	nd_x	nL_x	nm_x	na_x	T_x	r_x	$\mathring{e}_x$	nM_x
0	0.032954	100000	3295	97575	0.033773	0.2642	6878253	0.0000	68.783	0.033773
1	0.007193	96705	696	384811	0.001808	1.1138	6780678	0.0000	70.117	0.001808
5	0.003251	96009	312	479264	0.000651	2.5000	6395867	0.0366	66.617	0.000659
10	0.003005	95697	288	477805	0.000602	2.6395	5916603	0.0201	61.827	0.000600
15	0.005290	95409	505	475873	0.001061	2.6750	5438797	0.0025	57.005	0.001060
20	0.007497	94905	712	472820	0.001505	2.6069	4962924	0.0000	52.294	0.001505
25	0.009235	94193	870	468842	0.001855	2.5584	4490104	0.0083	47.669	0.001854
30	0.010235	93323	955	464277	0.002057	2.5513	4021262	0.0038	43.090	0.002057
35	0.011962	92368	1105	459163	0.002406	2.5770	3556985	0.0000	38.509	0.002406
40	0.014943	91263	1364	453090	0.003010	2.6350	3097822	0.0095	33.944	0.003006
45	0.022118	89899	1988	444886	0.004469	2.6809	2644732	0.0234	29.419	0.004450
50	0.035153	87911	3090	432338	0.007148	2.6645	2199846	0.0274	25.024	0.007113
55	0.052219	84821	4429	413855	0.010702	2.6863	1767508	0.0224	20.838	0.010652
60	0.087701	80391	7050	385673	0.018281	2.6903	1353653	0.0232	16.838	0.018183
65	0.148182	73341	10868	341245	0.031848	2.6572	967980	0.0232	13.198	0.031682
70	0.244157	62473	15253	275732	0.055319	2.5982	626735	0.0232	10.032	0.055047
75	0.382483	47220	18061	191016	0.094552	2.5038	351004	0.0232	7.433	0.094134
80	0.534260	29159	15579	104918	0.148483	2.4401	159988	0.0232	5.487	0.147902
85+	1.000000	13581	13581	55070	0.246604	4.0551	55070	0.0232	4.055	0.259328

TABLE 4 — OBSERVED AND PROJECTED VITAL RATES

	OBSERVED POPULATION BOTH SEXES	MALES	FEMALES	PROJECTED POPULATION 1956 MALES	FEMALES	1961 MALES	FEMALES	1966 MALES	FEMALES	STABLE POPULATION MALES	FEMALES
RATES PER THOUSAND											
Birth	23.51	25.23	21.93	23.55	20.65	22.60	19.95	22.67	20.16	23.27	21.6
Death	9.89	10.62	9.22	10.72	9.45	10.94	9.78	11.19	10.07	11.74	10.1
Increase	13.62	14.61	12.71	12.83	11.19	11.66	10.17	11.48	10.08		11.531
PERCENTAGE											
under 15	30.13	32.15	28.28	32.85	29.07	32.57	29.07	30.43	27.33	30.45	28.6
15-64	63.21	62.65	63.73	61.82	62.63	61.97	62.41	63.78	63.63	63.27	62.4
65 and over	6.66	5.20	7.99	5.33	8.30	5.46	8.52	5.79	9.04	6.28	8.9
DEP. RATIO X 100	58.19	59.63	56.90	61.76	59.67	61.37	60.23	56.80	57.16	58.04	60.2

AGE AT LAST BIRTHDAY	1956 BOTH SEXES	MALES	FEMALES	1961 BOTH SEXES	MALES	FEMALES	1966 BOTH SEXES	MALES	FEMALES	AGE AT LAST BIRTHDAY	
0-4	456	233	223	462	236	226	480	245	235	0-4	TABLE 5
5-9	492	251	241	453	231	222	458	234	224	5-9	POPULATION
10-14	384	196	188	490	250	240	451	230	221	10-14	PROJECTED
15-19	337	171	166	382	195	187	487	248	239	15-19	WITH
20-24	308	156	152	334	169	165	379	193	186	20-24	FIXED
25-29	321	162	159	304	153	151	331	167	164	25-29	AGE—
30-34	304	146	158	317	159	158	300	151	149	30-34	SPECIFIC
35-39	267	123	144	299	143	156	312	156	156	35-39	BIRTH
40-44	277	129	148	262	120	142	294	140	154	40-44	AND
45-49	282	132	150	270	124	146	254	115	139	45-49	DEATH
50-54	239	110	129	270	124	146	259	117	142	50-54	RATES
55-59	198	87	111	223	100	123	253	113	140	55-59	(IN 1000's)
60-64	151	64	87	179	76	103	202	87	115	60-64	
65-69	121	48	73	129	52	77	152	61	91	65-69	
70-74	86	32	54	94	35	59	100	38	62	70-74	
75-79	53	19	34	58	20	38	63	22	41	75-79	
80-84	26	9	17	28	9	19	31	10	21	80-84	
85+	10	3	7	13	4	9	14	4	10	85+	
TOTAL	4312	2071	2241	4567	2200	2367	4820	2331	2489	TOTAL	

STANDARD COUNTRIES:

STANDARDIZED RATES PER THOUSAND	ENGLAND AND WALES 1961 BOTH SEXES	MALES	FEMALES	UNITED STATES 1960 BOTH SEXES	MALES	FEMALES	MEXICO 1960 BOTH SEXES	MALES	FEMALES	
Birth	19.68	22.87*	18.58	19.99	21.17*	19.18	21.85	20.74*	21.23	TABLE 6
Death	15.58	17.25*	15.19	12.78	14.44*	11.31	7.09	10.04*	5.84	STANDARDIZED RATES
Increase	4.11	5.62*	3.39	7.21	6.73*	7.87	14.76	10.70*	15.39	

	OBSERVED POP. MALES	FEMALES	STATIONARY POP. MALES	FEMALES	STABLE POP. MALES	FEMALES	OBSERVED BIRTHS	NET MATERNITY FUNCTION	BIRTHS IN STABLE POP.	
μ	28.70655	31.65127	34.77727	37.39718	29.64985	31.67631	29.22333	29.31636	28.82432	TABLE 7
σ^2	408.9411	456.1775	463.9733	514.2367	421.8074	472.9627	41.11850	41.25548	39.89932	MOMENTS
κ_3	4081.210	3764.313	2664.107	2182.822	4493.938	4792.617	121.4554	112.6472	122.1626	AND
κ_4	-112329.	-167370.	-196154.	-268335.	-116142.	-174135.	-918.284	-925.219	-714.561	CUMULANTS
β_1	0.243554	0.149269	0.071060	0.035039	0.269099	0.217103	0.212188	0.180716	0.234953	
β_2	2.328307	2.195716	2.088806	1.985269	2.347226	2.221546	2.456871	2.456397	2.551143	
κ	-0.097113	-0.058775	-0.027757	-0.013015	-0.106090	-0.081378	-0.099758	-0.088925	-0.118893	

VITAL STATISTICS		THOMPSON AGE RANGE	NRR	1000r	INTERVAL	BOURGEOIS-PICHAT AGE RANGE	NRR	1000b	1000d	1000r	COALE		
GRR	1.498	0-4	1.52	15.69	27.36	5-29	1.18	18.36	12.14	6.22	IBR	18.58	TABLE 8
NRR	1.398	5-9	1.20	6.81	27.33	30-54	1.25	20.66	12.44	8.22	IDR	12.73	RATES FROM AGE DISTRIBUTIONS
TFR	3.077	10-14	1.11	3.77	27.27	55-79	1.55	27.48	11.31	16.17	IRI	5.85	AND VITAL STATISTICS
GENERATION	29.069	15-19	1.08	2.92	27.18	*40-64	1.90	43.70	19.91	23.78	K1	13.33	(Females)
SEX RATIO	105.350										K2	0.30	

Start of Age interval	ORIGINAL MATRIX SUB-DIAGONAL	ALTERNATIVE FIRST ROWS Projection	Integral	FIRST STABLE MATRIX % IN STABLE POPULATION	FISHER VALUES	REPRODUCTIVE VALUES	SECOND STABLE MATRIX Z_2 FIRST COLUMN	FIRST ROW	
0	0.99353	0.00000	0.00000	10.147	1.067	258720	0.1443+0.0771	0.1443+0.0771	TABLE 9
5	0.99696	0.00003	0.00000	9.516	1.137	214141	0.1624-0.1004	0.0049+0.1401	LESLIE
10	0.99596	0.03071	0.00000	8.955	1.209	201434	-0.0062-0.2236	-0.1013+0.0637	MATRIX
15	0.99358	0.21144	0.06341	8.418	1.253	191467	-0.2299-0.1251	-0.0950-0.0499	AND ITS
20	0.99158	0.38094	0.37424	7.895	1.109	178319	-0.2610+0.1588	-0.0346-0.1083	SPECTRAL
25	0.99026	0.35530	0.41339	7.390	0.775	123698	0.0073+0.3558	0.0100-0.1020	COMPONENTS
30	0.98898	0.25770	0.32111	6.907	0.446	64882	0.3623+0.2005	0.0284-0.0642	(Females)
35	0.98677	0.14710	0.21168	6.448	0.200	30114	0.4128-0.2471	0.0224-0.0267	
40	0.98189	0.05025	0.09234	6.006	0.056	8555	-0.0074-0.5577	0.0082-0.0063	
45	0.97179	0.00559	0.01130	5.566	0.006	759	-0.5607-0.3156	0.0009-0.0006	
50	0.95725	0.00010	0.00021	5.106	0.000	12	-0.6330+0.3726	0.0000-0.0000	
55+	0.78245			17.646					

Start of Age interval	OBSERVED POPUL. (IN 100's)	CONTRIBUTIONS OF ROOTS (IN 100's) r_1	r_2, r_3	$r_4 \cdot r_{11}$	AGE-SP. BIRTH RATES	NET MATERNITY FUNCTION	COEFF. OF MATRIX EQUATION	PARAMETERS INTEGRAL	MATRIX	EXP. INCREASE x	$e^{(x+8\frac{1}{3})r}$	
0	2425	2074	189	163	0.0000	0.0000	0.0000	L(1) 1.05935	1.05943	0	1.0292	TABLE 10
5	1883	1945	110	-172	0.0000	0.0000	0.0000	L(2) 0.42182	0.42738	50	1.8320	AGE
10	1667	1830	-129	-35	0.0000	0.0001	0.0304	0.75677	0.73611	55	1.9407	ANALYSIS
15	1528	1721	-302	110	0.0128	0.0608	0.2086	R(1) 0.01153	0.01155	60	2.0559	AND
20	1608	1614	-178	173	0.0754	0.3564	0.3734	R(2) -0.02868	-0.03223	65	2.1779	MISCELLANEOUS
25	1596	1510	202	-116	0.0833	0.3904	0.3453	0.21246	0.20895	70	2.3072	RESULTS
30	1454	1412	477	-436	0.0647	0.3003	0.2480	C(1)	20438	75	2.4441	(Females)
35	1504	1318	284	-97	0.0426	0.1958	0.1400	C(2)	50763	80	2.5891	
40	1530	1227	-313	616	0.0186	0.0843	0.0472		-27350	85	2.7428	
45	1326	1138	-742	930	0.0023	0.0101	0.0052	2P/Y 29.5738	30.0696	90	2.9056	
50	1156	1044	-439	551	0.0000	0.0002	0.0001	DELTA 4.4843		95	3.0781	
55+	3449	3606								100	3.2607	

TABLE 1 — DATA

AGE AT LAST BIRTHDAY	POPULATION BOTH SEXES	MALES Number	%	FEMALES Number	%	BIRTHS BY AGE OF MOTHER	DEATHS BOTH SEXES	MALES	FEMALES	AGE AT LAST BIRTHDAY
0	87970	44784	2.2	43186	2.0	0	2841	1649	1192	0
1-4	367505	187678	9.4	179827	8.2	0	643	383	260	1-4
5-9	480996	245603	12.2	235393	10.8	0	330	208	122	5-9
10-14	342545	174454	8.7	168091	7.7	4	199	126	73	10-14
15-19	323891	164649	8.2	159242	7.3	4420	300	199	101	15-19
20-24	309714	156849	7.8	152865	7.0	24402	444	298	146	20-24
25-29	314127	156667	7.8	157460	7.2	25881	548	361	187	25-29
30-34	292464	137039	6.8	155425	7.1	18727	635	384	251	30-34
35-39	261201	120488	6.0	140713	6.5	11095	750	460	290	35-39
40-44	288937	135869	6.8	153068	7.0	5134	1165	736	429	40-44
45-49	271367	126841	6.3	144526	6.6	482	1670	1087	583	45-49
50-54	227964	104981	5.2	122983	5.6	6	2212	1428	784	50-54
55-59	186773	82182	4.1	104591	4.8	0	2823	1783	1040	55-59
60-64	144340	61217	3.1	83123	3.8	0	3453	2041	1412	60-64
65-69	118814	47005	2.3	71809	3.3	0	4478	2364	2114	65-69
70-74	82908	30798	1.5	52110	2.4		5020	2280	2740	70-74
75-79	51411	18117	0.9	33294	1.5		5209	2105	3104	75-79
80-84	25234	8343	0.4	16891	0.8	46145 M.	3982	1443	2539	80-84
85+	8739	2640	0.1	6099	0.3	44006 F.	2462	761	1701	85+
TOTAL	4186900	2006204		2180696		90151	39164	20096	19068	TOTAL

TABLE 2 — MALE LIFE TABLE

x	nq_x	l_x	nd_x	nL_x	nm_x	na_x	T_x	r_x	$\dot{e}_x$	nM_x	x
0	0.035855	100000	3585	97375	0.036821	0.2678	6372403	0.0000	63.724	0.036821	0
1	0.008115	96415	782	383402	0.002041	1.1170	6275028	0.0000	65.084	0.002041	1
5	0.004195	95632	401	477158	0.000841	2.5000	5891626	0.0276	61.607	0.000847	5
10	0.003620	95231	345	475329	0.000725	2.6038	5414468	0.0391	56.856	0.000722	10
15	0.006038	94886	573	473113	0.001211	2.6991	4939139	0.0094	52.053	0.001209	15
20	0.009460	94313	892	469440	0.001901	2.6164	4466026	0.0031	47.353	0.001900	20
25	0.011468	93421	1071	464510	0.002306	2.5771	3996587	0.0112	42.780	0.002304	25
30	0.013953	92350	1289	458663	0.002809	2.6053	3532077	0.0234	38.247	0.002802	30
35	0.018918	91061	1723	451229	0.003818	2.6331	3073414	0.0000	33.751	0.003818	35
40	0.026747	89338	2390	441123	0.005417	2.6693	2622185	0.0000	29.351	0.005417	40
45	0.042150	86949	3665	426235	0.008598	2.6780	2181062	0.0169	25.084	0.008570	45
50	0.066286	83284	5521	403536	0.013680	2.6662	1754827	0.0292	21.070	0.013602	50
55	0.103752	77763	8068	369745	0.021821	2.6361	1351291	0.0315	17.377	0.021696	55
60	0.154840	69695	10792	322073	0.033465	2.5996	981546	0.0202	14.083	0.033340	60
65	0.224575	58904	13228	262182	0.050455	2.5555	658973	0.0202	11.187	0.050293	65
70	0.313473	45675	14318	192759	0.074279	2.5124	396791	0.0202	8.687	0.074031	70
75	0.448969	31357	14078	120750	0.116592	2.4403	204032	0.0202	6.507	0.116189	75
80	0.595080	17279	10282	59213	0.173649	2.3565	83282	0.0202	4.820	0.172960	80
85+	*1.000000	6997	6997	24069	0.290690	3.4401	24069	0.0202	3.440	0.288258	85+

TABLE 3 — FEMALE LIFE TABLE

x	nq_x	l_x	nd_x	nL_x	nm_x	na_x	T_x	r_x	$\dot{e}_x$	nM_x	x
0	0.027051	100000	2705	98004	0.027602	0.2621	7029451	0.0000	70.295	0.027602	0
1	0.005759	97295	560	387561	0.001446	1.1120	6931447	0.0000	71.242	0.001446	1
5	0.002564	96735	248	483053	0.000514	2.5000	6543886	0.0275	67.648	0.000518	5
10	0.002174	96487	210	481920	0.000435	2.5569	6060833	0.0386	62.815	0.000434	10
15	0.003171	96277	305	480672	0.000635	2.6689	5578913	0.0088	57.947	0.000634	15
20	0.004765	95971	457	478768	0.000955	2.6186	5098241	0.0002	53.122	0.000955	20
25	0.005921	95514	566	476221	0.001188	2.6132	4619473	0.0000	48.364	0.001188	25
30	0.008052	94949	765	472915	0.001617	2.6091	4143252	0.0096	43.637	0.001615	30
35	0.010254	94184	966	468617	0.002061	2.6150	3670337	0.0000	38.970	0.002061	35
40	0.013921	93218	1298	463030	0.002803	2.6408	3201720	0.0000	34.346	0.002803	40
45	0.020046	91921	1843	455318	0.004047	2.6747	2738691	0.0176	29.794	0.004034	45
50	0.031562	90078	2843	443786	0.006406	2.6775	2283373	0.0258	25.349	0.006375	50
55	0.048897	87235	4266	426337	0.010005	2.6939	1839586	0.0286	21.088	0.009943	55
60	0.082106	82969	6812	399122	0.017068	2.6918	1413250	0.0208	17.033	0.016987	60
65	0.138374	76157	10538	356227	0.029583	2.6696	1014127	0.0208	13.316	0.029439	65
70	0.234591	65619	15394	291389	0.052828	2.6156	657900	0.0208	10.026	0.052581	70
75	0.379816	50225	19076	203762	0.093621	2.5171	366511	0.0208	7.297	0.093230	75
80	0.544560	31149	16962	112320	0.151019	2.4399	162748	0.0208	5.225	0.150316	80
85+	*1.000000	14186	14186	50429	0.281319	3.5547	50429	0.0208	3.555	0.278898	85+

TABLE 4 — OBSERVED AND PROJECTED VITAL RATES

	OBSERVED POPULATION BOTH SEXES	MALES	FEMALES	PROJECTED POPULATION 1959 MALES	FEMALES	1964 MALES	FEMALES	1969 MALES	FEMALES	STABLE POPULATION MALES	FEMALES
RATES PER THOUSAND											
Birth	21.53	23.00	20.18	21.87	19.32	21.56	19.18	22.91	20.51	22.30	20.72
Death	9.35	10.02	8.74	10.24	9.08	10.53	9.40	10.85	9.76	11.54	9.96
Increase	12.18	12.98	11.44	11.63	10.24	11.04	9.78	12.07	10.75		10.7635
PERCENTAGE											
under 15	30.55	32.53	28.73	32.74	29.17	30.15	27.10	29.14	26.40	29.52	27.76
15-64	62.59	62.15	63.01	61.82	62.34	64.11	63.91	64.65	64.01	63.75	62.71
65 and over	6.86	5.33	8.26	5.43	8.48	5.74	8.99	6.21	9.59	6.72	9.54
DEP. RATIO X 100	59.76	60.91	58.71	61.75	60.40	55.98	56.46	54.69	56.22	56.85	59.47

TABLE 1 — DATA

AGE AT LAST BIRTHDAY	POPULATION BOTH SEXES	MALES Number	%	FEMALES Number	%	BIRTHS BY AGE OF MOTHER	DEATHS BOTH SEXES	MALES	FEMALES	AGE AT LAST BIRTHDAY
0	85984	43997	2.1	41987	1.9	0	2233	1258	975	0
1-4	349486	178168	8.6	171318	7.6	0	605	331	274	1-4
5-9	478538	244181	11.8	234357	10.4	0	297	187	110	5-9
10-14	414043	211262	10.2	202781	9.0	4	199	120	79	10-14
15-19	339600	172575	8.3	167025	7.4	4870	282	189	93	15-19
20-24	300531	152932	7.4	147599	6.6	23911	368	257	111	20-24
25-29	314361	158784	7.6	155577	6.9	24857	517	359	158	25-29
30-34	303987	148227	7.1	155760	6.9	17150	633	417	216	30-34
35-39	271156	125145	6.0	146011	6.5	10257	758	466	292	35-39
40-44	269069	124345	6.0	144724	6.4	4177	1117	710	407	40-44
45-49	284499	133410	6.4	151089	6.7	445	1678	1096	582	45-49
50-54	246003	113105	5.4	132898	5.9	6	2316	1527	789	50-54
55-59	205348	91281	4.4	114067	5.1	0	3008	1918	1090	55-59
60-64	156580	66443	3.2	90137	4.0	0	3573	2177	1396	60-64
65-69	123551	49266	2.4	74285	3.3	0	4470	2357	2113	65-69
70-74	90016	33286	1.6	56730	2.5		5323	2471	2852	70-74
75-79	53608	18670	0.9	34938	1.6		5226	2070	3156	75-79
80-84	26676	8730	0.4	17946	0.8	43873 M.	4145	1497	2648	80-84
85+	10975	3708	0.2	7267	0.3	41804 F.	2681	834	1847	85+
TOTAL	4324011	2077515		2246496		85677	39429	20241	19188	TOTAL

TABLE 2 — MALE LIFE TABLE

x	nq_x	l_x	nd_x	nL_x	nm_x	na_x	T_x	r_x	$\mathring{e}_x$	nM_x	x
0	0.028020	100000	2802	97998	0.028593	0.2856	6470414	0.0000	64.704	0.028593	0
1	0.007392	97198	718	386733	0.001858	1.1340	6372416	0.0000	65.561	0.001858	1
5	0.003817	96479	368	481477	0.000765	2.5000	5985683	0.0040	62.041	0.000766	5
10	0.002848	96111	274	479905	0.000570	2.6207	5504207	0.0340	57.269	0.000568	10
15	0.005498	95837	527	477979	0.001102	2.7075	5024302	0.0312	52.425	0.001095	15
20	0.008377	95311	798	474668	0.001682	2.6398	4546323	0.0066	47.700	0.001680	20
25	0.011245	94512	1063	470010	0.002261	2.6000	4071655	0.0009	43.081	0.002261	25
30	0.014003	93449	1309	464109	0.002820	2.6021	3601645	0.0209	38.541	0.002813	30
35	0.018497	92141	1704	456701	0.003732	2.6515	3137536	0.0136	34.052	0.003724	35
40	0.028172	90436	2548	446196	0.005710	2.6504	2680835	0.0000	29.643	0.005710	40
45	0.040312	87889	3543	431210	0.008216	2.6762	2234639	0.0007	25.426	0.008215	45
50	0.065737	84346	5545	408781	0.013564	2.6649	1803429	0.0241	21.381	0.013501	50
55	0.100640	78801	7931	375273	0.021133	2.6379	1394649	0.0313	17.698	0.021012	55
60	0.152328	70870	10796	328401	0.032873	2.5961	1019376	0.0201	14.384	0.032765	60
65	0.214892	60075	12910	268939	0.048002	2.5650	690975	0.0201	11.502	0.047842	65
70	0.314258	47165	14822	198999	0.074483	2.5154	422036	0.0201	8.948	0.074235	70
75	0.432941	32343	14003	125874	0.111244	2.4403	223037	0.0201	6.896	0.110873	75
80	0.589442	18341	10811	62828	0.172068	2.3753	97163	0.0201	5.298	0.171478	80
85+	1.000000	7530	7530	34336	0.219301	4.5599	34336	0.0201	4.560	0.224920	85+

TABLE 3 — FEMALE LIFE TABLE

x	nq_x	l_x	nd_x	nL_x	nm_x	na_x	T_x	r_x	$\mathring{e}_x$	nM_x	x
0	0.022846	100000	2285	98383	0.023221	0.2923	7114544	0.0000	71.145	0.023221	0
1	0.006368	97715	622	389082	0.001599	1.1410	7016161	0.0000	71.802	0.001599	1
5	0.002340	97093	227	484898	0.000468	2.5000	6627079	0.0043	68.255	0.000469	5
10	0.001949	96866	189	483867	0.000390	2.5472	6142181	0.0334	63.409	0.000390	10
15	0.002792	96677	270	482747	0.000559	2.6338	5658315	0.0312	58.528	0.000557	15
20	0.003756	96407	362	481176	0.000753	2.6246	5175568	0.0063	53.684	0.000752	20
25	0.005066	96045	487	479071	0.001016	2.6279	4694392	0.0000	48.877	0.001016	25
30	0.006916	95559	661	476236	0.001388	2.6446	4215321	0.0049	44.112	0.001387	30
35	0.009960	94898	945	472261	0.002001	2.6436	3739085	0.0053	39.401	0.002000	35
40	0.013968	93952	1312	466653	0.002812	2.6309	3266824	0.0000	34.771	0.002812	40
45	0.019102	92640	1770	459060	0.003855	2.6601	2800171	0.0045	30.226	0.003852	45
50	0.029408	90870	2672	448167	0.005963	2.6853	2341111	0.0219	25.763	0.005937	50
55	0.047015	88198	4147	431384	0.009612	2.6833	1892945	0.0289	21.462	0.009556	55
60	0.075189	84052	6320	405766	0.015575	2.7069	1461561	0.0232	17.389	0.015488	60
65	0.134102	77732	10424	364446	0.028602	2.6772	1055795	0.0232	13.583	0.028444	65
70	0.225588	67308	15184	300432	0.050540	2.6220	691349	0.0232	10.271	0.050273	70
75	0.370613	52124	19318	212840	0.090762	2.5266	390917	0.0232	7.500	0.090331	75
80	0.538105	32806	17653	119030	0.148308	2.4508	178078	0.0232	5.428	0.147553	80
85+	*1.000000	15153	15153	59048	0.256624	3.8968	59048	0.0232	3.897	0.254163	85+

TABLE 4 — OBSERVED AND PROJECTED VITAL RATES

	OBSERVED POPULATION BOTH SEXES	MALES	FEMALES	PROJECTED POPULATION 1962 MALES	FEMALES	1967 MALES	FEMALES	1972 MALES	FEMALES	STABLE POPULATION MALES	FEMALES
RATES PER THOUSAND											
Birth	19.81	21.12	18.61	20.72	18.37	21.58	19.25	22.75	20.43	21.22	19.74
Death	9.12	9.74	8.54	10.12	8.98	10.49	9.40	10.81	9.82	11.64	10.16
Increase	10.70	11.38	10.07	10.60	9.39	11.09	9.86	11.94	10.62		9.5829
PERCENTAGE											
under 15	30.71	32.62	28.95	31.01	27.71	28.76	25.86	28.55	25.82	28.59	26.78
15-64	62.24	61.91	62.54	63.25	63.35	65.01	64.50	64.70	63.81	64.12	62.92
65 and over	7.05	5.47	8.51	5.74	8.94	6.23	9.64	6.74	10.37	7.29	10.30
DEP. RATIO X 100	60.68	61.52	59.91	58.09	57.85	53.82	55.05	54.55	56.72	55.96	58.93

TABLE 1 — DATA

AGE AT LAST BIRTHDAY	POPULATION BOTH SEXES	MALES Number	%	FEMALES Number	%	BIRTHS BY AGE OF MOTHER	DEATHS BOTH SEXES	MALES	FEMALES	AGE AT LAST BIRTHDAY
0	80290	40971	1.9	39319	1.7	0	1810	1045	765	0
1-4	332195	169657	8.0	162538	7.1	0	396	225	171	1-4
5-9	443422	225946	10.6	217476	9.5	0	241	153	88	5-9
10-14	490905	250391	11.7	240514	10.5	6	202	131	71	10-14
15-19	356621	181335	8.5	175286	7.6	5047	301	217	84	15-19
20-24	314909	160427	7.5	154482	6.7	25071	353	258	95	20-24
25-29	292305	149102	7.0	143203	6.2	22811	420	299	121	25-29
30-34	308289	154702	7.3	153587	6.7	15978	571	404	167	30-34
35-39	294154	138956	6.5	155198	6.8	9642	757	492	265	35-39
40-44	252967	115990	5.4	136977	6.0	3533	967	616	351	40-44
45-49	276435	128307	6.0	148128	6.5	366	1585	1049	536	45-49
50-54	267371	123363	5.8	144008	6.3	5	2443	1638	805	50-54
55-59	220362	99293	4.7	121069	5.3	0	3116	2041	1075	55-59
60-64	175911	74448	3.5	101463	4.4	0	3948	2400	1548	60-64
65-69	128966	52006	2.4	76960	3.4	0	4563	2484	2079	65-69
70-74	95391	35360	1.7	60031	2.6		5520	2524	2996	70-74
75-79	58542	20243	0.9	38299	1.7		5508	2151	3357	75-79
80-84	28417	9305	0.4	19112	0.8	42183 M.	4286	1487	2799	80-84
85+	12182	3662	0.2	8520	0.4	40276 F.	2761	868	1893	85+
TOTAL	4429634	2133464		2296170		82459	39748	20482	19266	TOTAL

TABLE 2 — MALE LIFE TABLE

x	nq_x	l_x	nd_x	nL_x	nm_x	na_x	T_x	r_x	$\mathring{e}_x$	nM_x	x
0	0.025034	100000	2503	98151	0.025506	0.2614	6537730	0.0000	65.377	0.025506	
1	0.005285	97497	515	388498	0.001326	1.1114	6439579	0.0000	66.049	0.001326	
5	0.003380	96981	328	484087	0.000677	2.5000	6051081	0.0000	62.394	0.000677	
10	0.002624	96654	254	482686	0.000526	2.7071	5566994	0.0213	57.597	0.000523	10
15	0.006016	96400	580	480657	0.001206	2.6851	5084308	0.0434	52.742	0.001197	15
20	0.008025	95820	769	477254	0.001611	2.5999	4603651	0.0180	48.045	0.001608	20
25	0.009980	95051	949	472978	0.002006	2.5994	4126396	0.0016	43.412	0.002005	25
30	0.012984	94102	1222	467601	0.002613	2.6174	3653418	0.0044	38.824	0.002611	30
35	0.017626	92881	1637	460554	0.003555	2.6492	3185818	0.0251	34.300	0.003541	35
40	0.026241	91243	2394	450633	0.005313	2.6677	2725263	0.0025	29.868	0.005311	40
45	0.040118	88849	3564	435983	0.008176	2.6817	2274630	0.0000	25.601	0.008176	45
50	0.064534	85285	5504	413559	0.013308	2.6626	1838647	0.0120	21.559	0.013278	50
55	0.098525	79781	7860	380358	0.020666	2.6405	1425088	0.0290	17.863	0.020555	55
60	0.150239	71920	10805	333685	0.032382	2.6014	1044730	0.0265	14.526	0.032237	60
65	0.214705	61115	13122	273562	0.047966	2.5602	711045	0.0265	11.634	0.047764	65
70	0.304169	47994	14598	203656	0.071681	2.5126	437483	0.0265	9.115	0.071380	70
75	0.419258	33395	14001	131205	0.106713	2.4451	233827	0.0265	7.002	0.106259	75
80	0.562457	19394	10908	67966	0.160496	2.3947	102622	0.0265	5.291	0.159807	80
85+	1.000000	8486	8486	34656	0.244859	4.0840	34656	0.0265	4.084	0.237030	85

TABLE 3 — FEMALE LIFE TABLE

x	nq_x	l_x	nd_x	nL_x	nm_x	na_x	T_x	r_x	$\mathring{e}_x$	nM_x	x
0	0.019182	100000	1918	98592	0.019456	0.2659	7219133	0.0000	72.191	0.019456	0
1	0.004196	98082	412	391140	0.001052	1.1153	7120541	0.0000	72.598	0.001052	1
5	0.002021	97670	197	487858	0.000405	2.5000	6729401	0.0000	68.899	0.000405	5
10	0.001477	97473	144	487012	0.000296	2.5535	6241543	0.0212	64.034	0.000295	10
15	0.002408	97329	234	486091	0.000482	2.6377	5754531	0.0438	59.125	0.000479	15
20	0.003078	97095	299	484762	0.000616	2.6211	5268440	0.0196	54.261	0.000615	20
25	0.004216	96796	408	483005	0.000845	2.6143	4783678	0.0000	49.420	0.000845	25
30	0.005423	96388	523	480716	0.001087	2.6628	4300673	0.0000	44.619	0.001087	30
35	0.008518	95865	817	477426	0.001710	2.6756	3819957	0.0097	39.847	0.001707	35
40	0.012740	95048	1211	472395	0.002563	2.6492	3342530	0.0021	35.167	0.002562	40
45	0.017941	93837	1684	465257	0.003618	2.6657	2870135	0.0000	30.586	0.003618	45
50	0.027669	92154	2550	454861	0.005606	2.6828	2404878	0.0144	26.096	0.005590	50
55	0.043751	89604	3920	439011	0.008930	2.7020	1950017	0.0256	21.763	0.008879	55
60	0.074110	85684	6350	413840	0.015344	2.7041	1511006	0.0240	17.635	0.015257	60
65	0.127843	79334	10142	373222	0.027175	2.6882	1097166	0.0240	13.830	0.027014	65
70	0.224185	69191	15512	309110	0.050182	2.6246	723944	0.0240	10.463	0.049908	70
75	0.361699	53680	19416	220424	0.088084	2.5291	414834	0.0240	7.728	0.087652	75
80	0.531894	34264	18225	123896	0.147097	2.4614	194410	0.0240	5.674	0.146453	80
85+	1.000000	16039	16039	70514	0.227461	4.3964	70514	0.0240	4.396	0.222182	85

TABLE 4 — OBSERVED AND PROJECTED VITAL RATES

	OBSERVED POPULATION BOTH SEXES	MALES	FEMALES	PROJECTED POPULATION 1965 MALES	FEMALES	1970 MALES	FEMALES	1975 MALES	FEMALES	STABLE POPULATION MALES	FEMALES
RATES PER THOUSAND											
Birth	18.62	19.77	17.54	20.16	17.97	22.01	19.72	22.50	20.28	20.55	19.02
Death	8.97	9.60	8.39	10.10	8.95	10.51	9.40	10.78	9.80	11.71	10.18
Increase	9.64	10.17	9.15	10.05	9.02	11.50	10.32	11.72	10.48		8.8453
PERCENTAGE											
under 15	30.40	32.20	28.74	28.86	25.90	27.76	25.05	28.33	25.74	27.98	26.09
15-64	62.29	62.15	62.43	65.00	64.51	65.52	64.62	64.37	63.10	64.36	63.04
65 and over	7.30	5.65	8.84	6.14	9.59	6.71	10.33	7.30	11.17	7.66	10.87
DEP. RATIO X 100	60.53	60.90	60.19	53.84	55.02	52.62	54.75	55.35	58.49	55.37	58.64

TABLE 5 — POPULATION PROJECTED WITH FIXED AGE-SPECIFIC BIRTH AND DEATH RATES (IN 1000's)

AGE AT LAST BIRTHDAY	1965 BOTH SEXES	MALES	FEMALES	1970 BOTH SEXES	MALES	FEMALES	1975 BOTH SEXES	MALES	FEMALES	AGE AT LAST BIRTHDAY
0-4	417	213	204	465	237	228	518	264	254	0-4
5-9	411	210	201	416	212	204	463	236	227	5-9
10-14	442	225	217	410	209	201	414	211	203	10-14
15-19	489	249	240	441	224	217	408	208	200	15-19
20-24	355	180	175	487	248	239	439	223	216	20-24
25-29	313	159	154	352	178	174	484	245	239	25-29
30-34	290	147	143	310	157	153	349	176	173	30-34
35-39	305	152	153	287	145	142	307	155	152	35-39
40-44	290	136	154	300	149	151	282	142	140	40-44
45-49	247	112	135	283	132	151	293	144	149	45-49
50-54	267	122	145	238	106	132	273	125	148	50-54
55-59	252	113	139	252	112	140	225	98	127	55-59
60-64	201	87	114	231	100	131	230	98	132	60-64
65-69	153	61	92	174	71	103	200	82	118	65-69
70-74	103	39	64	121	45	76	138	53	85	70-74
75-79	66	23	43	70	25	45	83	29	54	75-79
80-84	32	10	22	36	12	24	39	13	26	80-84
85+	16	5	11	17	5	12	20	6	14	85+
TOTAL	4649	2243	2406	4890	2367	2523	5165	2508	2657	TOTAL

TABLE 6 — STANDARDIZED RATES

STANDARD COUNTRIES: STANDARDIZED RATES PER THOUSAND

	ENGLAND AND WALES 1961 BOTH SEXES	MALES	FEMALES	UNITED STATES 1960 BOTH SEXES	MALES	FEMALES	MEXICO 1960 BOTH SEXES	MALES	FEMALES
Birth	17.34	18.84*	16.41	17.60	17.59*	16.94	20.03	17.10*	19.51
Death	13.65	14.60*	13.18	11.01	12.39*	9.55	5.65	9.36*	4.48
Increase	3.69	4.23*	3.23	6.59	5.20*	7.39	14.38	7.74*	15.03

TABLE 7 — MOMENTS AND CUMULANTS

	OBSERVED POP. MALES	FEMALES	STATIONARY POP. MALES	FEMALES	STABLE POP. MALES	FEMALES	OBSERVED BIRTHS	NET MATERNITY FUNCTION	BIRTHS IN STABLE POP.
μ	29.56219	32.66138	35.46194	38.15341	31.38468	33.61318	28.23776	28.33501	27.98296
σ^2	417.6739	474.3446	474.7989	525.5578	444.7310	497.6792	39.10129	38.32771	37.10314
κ_3	4269.917	3833.823	2553.658	1971.822	4156.179	4232.653	131.1999	136.5613	140.0765
κ_4	-129065.	-205736.	-209034.	-285089.	-149207.	-218372.	-606.186	-476.419	-309.739
β_1	0.250223	0.137715	0.060925	0.026784	0.196380	0.145337	0.287934	0.331220	0.384148
β_2	2.260169	2.085629	2.072750	1.967859	2.245614	2.118347	2.603518	2.675688	2.775004
κ	-0.093614	-0.050091	-0.023727	-0.009890	-0.076720	-0.053849	-0.142849	-0.167289	-0.200930

TABLE 8 — RATES FROM AGE DISTRIBUTIONS AND VITAL STATISTICS (Females)

VITAL STATISTICS

		THOMPSON AGE RANGE	NRR	1000r	INTERVAL	BOURGEOIS-PICHAT AGE RANGE	NRR	1000b	1000d	1000r	COALE
GRR	1.331										
NRR	1.283	0-4	1.29	9.51	27.42	5-29	1.97	25.39	0.31	25.07	IBR
TFR	2.724	5-9	1.43	13.23	27.38	30-54	1.02	14.12	13.34	0.78	IDR
GENERATION	28.158	10-14	1.59	16.70	27.33	55-79	1.94	48.85	24.34	24.50	IRI
SEX RATIO	104.735	15-19	1.17	5.69	27.25	*50-74	1.98	51.77	26.40	25.36	K1
											K2

TABLE 9 — LESLIE MATRIX AND ITS SPECTRAL COMPONENTS (Females)

Start of Age interval	ORIGINAL MATRIX SUB-DIAGONAL	ALTERNATIVE FIRST ROWS Projection	Integral	FIRST STABLE MATRIX % IN STABLE POPULATION	FISHER VALUES	REPRODUCTIVE VALUES	SECOND STABLE MATRIX Z_2 FIRST COLUMN	FIRST ROW
0	0.99617	0.00000	0.00000	9.115	1.044	210687	0.1598+0.0892	0.1598+0.0892
5	0.99827	0.00003	0.00000	8.687	1.095	238176	0.1838-0.1213	-0.0047+0.1520
10	0.99811	0.03440	0.00006	8.296	1.147	275800	-0.0278-0.2642	-0.1136+0.0545
15	0.99727	0.22801	0.07041	7.922	1.165	204193	-0.2983-0.1169	-0.0890-0.0659
20	0.99638	0.38393	0.39688	7.558	0.982	151755	-0.2905+0.2543	-0.0220-0.1112
25	0.99526	0.31435	0.38955	7.205	0.628	89985	0.1108+0.4513	0.0120-0.0931
30	0.99316	0.19822	0.25441	6.860	0.330	50726	0.5432+0.1316	0.0229-0.0549
35	0.98946	0.10483	0.15193	6.518	0.139	21617	0.4402-0.5060	0.0175-0.0220
40	0.98489	0.03376	0.06308	6.170	0.037	5009	-0.2948-0.7456	0.0061-0.0049
45	0.97765	0.00300	0.00604	5.814	0.003	449	-0.9491-0.0970	0.0006-0.0004
50	0.96516	0.00004	0.00008	5.438	0.000	6	-0.6178+0.9426	0.0000-0.0000
55+	0.78822			20.417				

TABLE 10 — AGE ANALYSIS AND MISCELLANEOUS RESULTS (Females)

Start of Age interval	OBSERVED POPUL. (IN 100's)	CONTRIBUTIONS OF ROOTS (IN 100's) r_1	r_2, r_3	r_4-r_{11}	AGE-SP. BIRTH RATES	NET MATERNITY FUNCTION	COEFF. OF MATRIX EQUATION	PARAMETERS	INTEGRAL	MATRIX	EXP. INCREASE x	$e^{(x+2\frac{1}{2})r}$
0	2019	2141	-125	2	0.0000	0.0000	0.0000	L(1)	1.04522	1.04527	0	1.0224
5	2175	2041	135	-1	0.0000	0.0000	0.0000	L(2)	0.37174	0.38097	50	1.5910
10	2405	1949	331	125	0.0000	0.0001	0.0342		0.75913	0.73475	55	1.6630
15	1753	1861	171	-279	0.0141	0.0684	0.2263	R(1)	0.00885	0.00885	60	1.7382
20	1545	1776	-291	60	0.0793	0.3843	0.3800	R(2)	-0.03362	-0.03784	65	1.8168
25	1432	1693	-570	310	0.0778	0.3758	0.3100		0.22309	0.21849	70	1.8989
30	1536	1612	-210	134	0.0508	0.2443	0.1946	C(1)		23493	75	1.9848
35	1552	1531	590	-570	0.0303	0.1449	0.1022	C(2)		-4314	80	2.0745
40	1370	1450	952	-1031	0.0126	0.0595	0.0326			62105	85	2.1684
45	1481	1366	202	-87	0.0012	0.0056	0.0028	2P/Y	28.1650	28.7572	90	2.2664
50	1440	1277	-1117	1280	0.0000	0.0001	0.0000	DELTA	4.9275		95	2.3689
55+	4255	4797									100	2.4760

TABLE 1 — DATA

AGE AT LAST BIRTHDAY	POPULATION BOTH SEXES	MALES Number	%	FEMALES Number	%	BIRTHS BY AGE OF MOTHER	DEATHS BOTH SEXES	MALES	FEMALES	AGE AT LAST BIRTHDAY
0	80400	41100	1.9	39300	1.7	0	1496	837	659	0
1-4	318400	162300	7.4	156100	6.6	0	331	194	137	1-4
5-9	424400	216400	9.9	208000	8.8	0	211	138	73	5-9
10-14	464100	236800	10.8	227300	9.7	3	188	128	60	10-14
15-19	449000	228600	10.4	220400	9.4	6671	304	227	77	15-19
20-24	330700	167800	7.7	162900	6.9	25936	350	249	101	20-24
25-29	296100	151300	6.9	144800	6.2	22736	391	276	115	25-29
30-34	300000	152200	6.9	147800	6.3	14851	556	407	149	30-34
35-39	300000	147800	6.7	152200	6.5	8430	756	551	205	35-39
40-44	271200	125100	5.7	146100	6.2	3302	1000	668	332	40-44
45-49	256700	117000	5.3	139700	5.9	313	1517	1005	512	45-49
50-54	273600	126100	5.8	147500	6.3	9	2658	1798	860	50-54
55-59	239600	107500	4.9	132100	5.6	0	3411	2299	1112	55-59
60-64	192100	82600	3.8	109500	4.7	0	4279	2668	1611	60-64
65-69	141300	56500	2.6	84800	3.6	0	5103	2814	2289	65-69
70-74	98400	36900	1.7	61500	2.6		5718	2682	3036	70-74
75-79	63700	21900	1.0	41800	1.8		5881	2350	3531	75-79
80-84	30000	9700	0.4	20300	0.9	42130 M.	4511	1569	2942	80-84
85+	13000	4000	0.2	9000	0.4	40121 F.	3349	1079	2270	85+
TOTAL	4542700	2191600		2351100		82251	42010	21939	20071	TOTAL

TABLE 2 — MALE LIFE TABLE

x	$_nq_x$	l_x	$_nd_x$	$_nL_x$	$_nm_x$	$_na_x$	T_x	r_x	$\mathring{e}_x$	$_nM_x$	x
0	0.020063	100000	2006	98545	0.020359	0.2749	6553043	0.0004	65.530	0.020365	0
1	0.004763	97994	467	390632	0.001195	1.1235	6454498	0.0004	65.866	0.001195	1
5	0.003183	97527	310	486859	0.000638	2.5000	6063866	0.0000	62.176	0.000638	5
10	0.002699	97216	262	485462	0.000541	2.6373	5577007	0.0000	57.367	0.000541	10
15	0.004987	96954	483	483656	0.001000	2.6957	5091545	0.0334	52.515	0.000993	15
20	0.007427	96471	717	480642	0.001491	2.6125	4607888	0.0398	47.765	0.001484	20
25	0.009091	95754	871	476707	0.001826	2.6302	4127246	0.0078	43.103	0.001824	25
30	0.013287	94884	1261	471446	0.002674	2.6427	3650538	0.0000	38.474	0.002674	30
35	0.018521	93623	1734	464023	0.003737	2.6406	3179092	0.0158	33.956	0.003728	35
40	0.026457	91889	2431	453790	0.005357	2.6743	2715069	0.0177	29.547	0.005340	40
45	0.042114	89458	3767	438595	0.008590	2.6925	2261279	0.0000	25.278	0.008590	45
50	0.068985	85690	5911	414585	0.014259	2.6543	1822684	0.0000	21.271	0.014259	50
55	0.102094	79779	8145	379548	0.021460	2.6247	1408098	0.0202	17.650	0.021386	55
60	0.150555	71634	10785	332337	0.032452	2.6047	1028550	0.0270	14.358	0.032300	60
65	0.222888	60849	13563	271134	0.050022	2.5585	696214	0.0270	11.442	0.049805	65
70	0.308676	47287	14596	199994	0.072983	2.5035	425080	0.0270	8.989	0.072683	70
75	0.422380	32690	13808	128123	0.107770	2.4414	225087	0.0270	6.885	0.107306	75
80	0.567154	18883	10709	65915	0.162471	2.3904	96964	0.0270	5.135	0.161753	80
85+	1.000000	8173	8173	31048	0.263242	3.7988	31048	0.0270	3.799	0.269751	85+

TABLE 3 — FEMALE LIFE TABLE

x	$_nq_x$	l_x	$_nd_x$	$_nL_x$	$_nm_x$	$_na_x$	T_x	r_x	$\mathring{e}_x$	$_nM_x$	x
0	0.016564	100000	1656	98778	0.016768	0.2625	7267998	0.0000	72.680	0.016768	0
1	0.003502	98344	344	392380	0.000878	1.1123	7169219	0.0000	72.900	0.000878	1
5	0.001753	97999	172	489567	0.000351	2.5000	6776839	0.0000	69.152	0.000351	5
10	0.001319	97827	129	488815	0.000264	2.4999	6287273	0.0000	64.269	0.000264	10
15	0.001758	97698	172	488099	0.000352	2.7120	5798458	0.0329	59.351	0.000349	15
20	0.003115	97527	304	486919	0.000624	2.6467	5310359	0.0414	54.450	0.000620	20
25	0.003967	97223	386	485189	0.000795	2.5990	4823440	0.0089	49.612	0.000794	25
30	0.005028	96837	487	483023	0.001008	2.6117	4338251	0.0000	44.799	0.001008	30
35	0.006714	96350	647	480259	0.001347	2.6920	3855228	0.0000	40.013	0.001347	35
40	0.011318	95703	1083	476033	0.002275	2.7063	3374969	0.0062	35.265	0.002272	40
45	0.018171	94620	1719	469134	0.003665	2.6925	2898937	0.0000	30.638	0.003665	45
50	0.028760	92901	2672	458246	0.005831	2.6577	2429803	0.0000	26.155	0.005831	50
55	0.041469	90229	3742	442525	0.008455	2.6962	1971557	0.0207	21.851	0.008418	55
60	0.071631	86487	6195	418307	0.014810	2.7193	1529031	0.0263	17.679	0.014712	60
65	0.127825	80292	10263	377751	0.027170	2.6898	1110724	0.0263	13.834	0.026993	65
70	0.222015	70029	15547	313122	0.049653	2.6188	732973	0.0263	10.467	0.049366	70
75	0.351125	54481	19130	225238	0.084931	2.5343	419851	0.0263	7.706	0.084474	75
80	0.528834	35352	18695	128351	0.145656	2.4724	194613	0.0263	5.505	0.144926	80
85+	1.000000	16656	16656	66262	0.251374	3.9781	66262	0.0263	3.978	0.252221	85+

TABLE 4 — OBSERVED AND PROJECTED VITAL RATES

	OBSERVED POPULATION BOTH SEXES	MALES	FEMALES	PROJECTED POPULATION 1968 MALES	FEMALES	1973 MALES	FEMALES	1978 MALES	FEMALES	STABLE POPULATION MALES	FEMALES
RATES PER THOUSAND											
Birth	18.11	19.22	17.06	20.86	18.59	22.04	19.73	21.67	19.52	19.86	18.29
Death	9.25	10.01	8.54	10.46	9.08	10.79	9.57	10.97	9.95	11.99	10.42
Increase	8.86	9.21	8.53	10.40	9.50	11.25	10.16	10.71	9.57		7.8695
PERCENTAGE											
under 15	28.34	29.96	26.83	27.75	24.93	27.56	24.85	28.56	25.86	27.38	25.35
15-64	64.04	64.15	63.93	65.80	65.00	65.41	64.21	64.02	62.51	64.83	63.27
65 and over	7.63	5.89	9.25	6.45	10.07	7.02	10.94	7.42	11.64	7.79	11.37
DEP. RATIO X 100	56.16	55.87	56.43	51.98	53.85	52.87	55.74	56.20	59.98	54.25	58.04

TABLE 1 — DATA

AGE AT LAST BIRTHDAY	POPULATION BOTH SEXES	MALES Number	%	FEMALES Number	%	BIRTHS BY AGE OF MOTHER	DEATHS BOTH SEXES	MALES	FEMALES	AGE AT LAST BIRTHDAY
0	80024	40905	1.9	39119	1.7	0	1396	824	572	0
1-4	318717	162535	7.4	156182	6.6	0	320	187	133	1-4
5-9	416806	212592	9.6	204214	8.6	0	214	144	70	5-9
10-14	451836	230339	10.4	221497	9.3	3	174	113	61	10-14
15-19	475753	242343	11.0	233410	9.9	7364	404	263	141	15-19
20-24	334981	169874	7.7	165107	7.0	25215	371	270	101	20-24
25-29	306390	156417	7.1	149973	6.3	22485	402	300	102	25-29
30-34	292700	148823	6.7	143877	6.1	13664	478	317	161	30-34
35-39	301998	150099	6.8	151899	6.4	8087	738	509	229	35-39
40-44	281606	130818	5.9	150788	6.4	3342	1066	749	317	40-44
45-49	249379	113356	5.1	136023	5.7	265	1465	976	489	45-49
50-54	270858	124263	5.6	146595	6.2	3	2515	1715	800	50-54
55-59	246220	110455	5.0	135765	5.7		3584	2410	1174	55-59
60-64	196213	84733	3.8	111480	4.7	0	4554	2829	1725	60-64
65-69	147775	58975	2.7	88800	3.7	0	5223	2855	2368	65-69
70-74	99521	37470	1.7	62051	2.6	0	5878	2723	3155	70-74
75-79	64889	22311	1.0	42578	1.8		6307	2513	3794	75-79
80-84	31086	10047	0.5	21039	0.9	41209 M.	4843	1699	3144	80-84
85+	13166	4051	0.2	9115	0.4	39219 F.	2580	832	1748	85+
TOTAL	4579918	2210406		2369512		80428	42512	22228	20284	TOTAL

TABLE 2 — MALE LIFE TABLE

x	nq_x	l_x	nd_x	nL_x	nm_x	na_x	T_x	r_x	$\overset{\circ}{e}_x$	nM_x	x
0	0.019853	100000	1985	98554	0.020144	0.2719	6564421	0.0000	65.644	0.020144	0
1	0.004587	98015	450	390764	0.001151	1.1207	6465866	0.0000	65.968	0.001151	1
5	0.003381	97565	330	487001	0.000677	2.5000	6075102	0.0000	62.267	0.000677	5
10	0.002450	97235	238	485622	0.000491	2.6735	5588101	0.0000	57.470	0.000491	10
15	0.005446	96997	528	483775	0.001092	2.7086	5102479	0.0294	52.605	0.001085	15
20	0.007953	96469	767	480506	0.001597	2.6048	4618705	0.0422	47.878	0.001589	20
25	0.009551	95701	914	476272	0.001919	2.5541	4138199	0.0114	43.241	0.001918	25
30	0.010600	94787	1005	471564	0.002131	2.6383	3661927	0.0018	38.633	0.002130	30
35	0.016859	93783	1581	465296	0.003398	2.7123	3190363	0.0093	34.019	0.003391	35
40	0.028368	92202	2616	454927	0.005749	2.6752	2725066	0.0223	29.556	0.005726	40
45	0.042204	89586	3781	439128	0.008610	2.6720	2270139	0.0000	25.340	0.008610	45
50	0.066853	85805	5736	415632	0.013801	2.6652	1831011	0.0000	21.339	0.013801	50
55	0.104023	80069	8329	380644	0.021881	2.6348	1415379	0.0158	17.677	0.021819	55
60	0.155072	71740	11125	331895	0.033519	2.5906	1034735	0.0247	14.423	0.033387	60
65	0.217194	60615	13165	270898	0.048598	2.5559	702840	0.0247	11.595	0.048410	65
70	0.308897	47450	14657	200860	0.072972	2.5173	431943	0.0247	9.103	0.072671	70
75	0.438673	32793	14385	127184	0.113106	2.4432	231082	0.0247	7.047	0.112635	75
80	0.583316	18407	10737	63246	0.169772	2.3697	103899	0.0247	5.644	0.169105	80
85+	1.000000	7670	7670	40653	0.188672	5.3002	40653	0.0247	5.300	0.205382	85+

TABLE 3 — FEMALE LIFE TABLE

x	nq_x	l_x	nd_x	nL_x	nm_x	na_x	T_x	r_x	$\overset{\circ}{e}_x$	nM_x	x
0	0.014469	100000	1447	98950	0.014622	0.2743	7281496	0.0000	72.815	0.014622	0
1	0.003398	98553	335	393249	0.000852	1.1229	7182546	0.0000	72.880	0.000852	1
5	0.001712	98218	168	490671	0.000343	2.5000	6789297	0.0000	69.125	0.000343	5
10	0.001376	98050	135	489940	0.000275	2.6978	6298626	0.0000	64.239	0.000275	10
15	0.003026	97915	296	488869	0.000606	2.6150	5808686	0.0289	59.324	0.000604	15
20	0.003057	97619	298	487355	0.000612	2.5243	5319817	0.0436	54.496	0.000612	20
25	0.003402	97320	331	485825	0.000681	2.6528	4832462	0.0130	49.655	0.000680	25
30	0.005580	96989	541	483675	0.001119	2.6514	4346637	0.0000	44.816	0.001119	30
35	0.007511	96448	724	480525	0.001508	2.6328	3862962	0.0000	40.052	0.001508	35
40	0.010480	95724	1003	476311	0.002106	2.7002	3382437	0.0088	35.335	0.002102	40
45	0.017827	94720	1689	469694	0.003595	2.6855	2906126	0.0000	30.681	0.003595	45
50	0.026945	93032	2507	459344	0.005457	2.6800	2436431	0.0000	26.189	0.005457	50
55	0.042577	90525	3854	443826	0.008684	2.7168	1977087	0.0180	21.840	0.008647	55
60	0.075205	86671	6518	418368	0.015580	2.7009	1533262	0.0291	17.691	0.015474	60
65	0.126488	80153	10138	377389	0.026864	2.6944	1114893	0.0291	13.910	0.026667	65
70	0.228214	70014	15978	312145	0.051189	2.6263	737504	0.0291	10.534	0.050845	70
75	0.366689	54036	19825	221162	0.089642	2.5274	425359	0.0291	7.872	0.089107	75
80	0.543343	34211	18588	123708	0.150259	2.4529	204197	0.0291	5.969	0.149436	80
85+	*1.000000	15623	15623	80489	0.194097	5.1521	80489	0.0291	5.152	0.191772	85+

TABLE 4 — OBSERVED AND PROJECTED VITAL RATES

	OBSERVED POPULATION BOTH SEXES	MALES	FEMALES	PROJECTED POPULATION 1969 MALES	FEMALES	1974 MALES	FEMALES	1979 MALES	FEMALES	STABLE POPULATION MALES	FEMALES
RATES PER THOUSAND											
Birth	17.56	18.64	16.55	20.49	18.25	21.39	19.15	20.82	18.74	18.97	17.40
Death	9.28	10.06	8.56	10.62	9.27	10.93	9.72	11.10	10.09	12.49	10.93
Increase	8.28	8.59	7.99	9.86	8.98	10.46	9.43	9.72	8.65		6.4716
PERCENTAGE											
under 15	27.67	29.24	26.21	27.26	24.50	27.14	24.49	27.92	25.32	26.43	24.42
15-64	64.54	64.75	64.36	66.09	65.17	65.62	64.28	64.54	62.87	65.27	63.55
65 and over	7.78	6.01	9.44	6.66	10.33	7.24	11.22	7.53	11.81	8.30	12.03
DEP. RATIO X 100	54.93	54.45	55.39	51.32	53.44	52.39	55.56	54.93	59.06	53.21	57.35

TABLE 1 — DATA

AGE AT LAST BIRTHDAY	BOTH SEXES	MALES Number	%	FEMALES Number	%	BIRTHS BY AGE OF MOTHER	DEATHS BOTH SEXES	MALES	FEMALES	AGE AT LAST BIRTHDAY
0	77863	39776	1.8	38087	1.6	0	1371	806	565	0
1-4	318652	162592	7.3	156060	6.5	0	291	175	116	1-4
5-9	409532	209008	9.4	200524	8.4	0	254	155	99	5-9
10-14	442065	225152	10.1	216913	9.1	4	177	115	62	10-14
15-19	488616	249038	11.2	239578	10.0	8074	340	235	105	15-19
20-24	353220	179289	8.1	173931	7.3	24173	359	279	80	20-24
25-29	309861	157756	7.1	152105	6.4	21762	397	301	96	25-29
30-34	287701	146722	6.6	140979	5.9	12740	475	337	138	30-34
35-39	303778	151888	6.8	151890	6.4	7882	783	593	190	35-39
40-44	288866	135529	6.1	153337	6.4	2943	1126	773	353	40-44
45-49	246631	111905	5.0	134726	5.6	299	1426	966	460	45-49
50-54	265973	121394	5.5	144579	6.1	8	2479	1732	747	50-54
55-59	252251	113221	5.1	139010	5.8	0	3634	2485	1149	55-59
60-64	201180	86859	3.9	114321	4.8	0	4471	2853	1618	60-64
65-69	152608	60959	2.7	91649	3.8	0	5479	3002	2477	65-69
70-74	102526	38558	1.7	63968	2.7		6041	2956	3085	70-74
75-79	65393	22549	1.0	42844	1.8		6423	2498	3925	75-79
80-84	31771	10221	0.5	21550	0.9	39906 M.	5192	1819	3373	80-84
85+	13235	4054	0.2	9181	0.4	37979 F.	3755	1181	2574	85+
TOTAL	4611702	2226470		2385232		77885	44473	23261	21212	TOTAL

TABLE 2 — MALE LIFE TABLE

x	$_nq_x$	l_x	$_nd_x$	$_nL_x$	$_nm_x$	$_na_x$	T_x	r_x	$\overset{\circ}{e}_x$	$_nM_x$	x
0	0.019966	100000	1997	98530	0.020263	0.2640	6531564	0.0000	65.316	0.020263	0
1	0.004292	98003	421	390800	0.001076	1.1136	6433034	0.0000	65.641	0.001076	1
5	0.003701	97583	361	487011	0.000742	2.5000	6042234	0.0000	51.919	0.000742	5
10	0.002551	97222	248	485509	0.000511	2.5821	5555223	0.0000	57.140	0.000511	10
15	0.004732	96974	459	483826	0.000948	2.7290	5069715	0.0218	52.279	0.000944	15
20	0.007796	96515	752	480787	0.001565	2.6251	4585888	0.0442	47.515	0.001556	20
25	0.009510	95762	911	476604	0.001911	2.5758	4105101	0.0181	42.868	0.001908	25
30	0.011426	94852	1084	471737	0.002297	2.6739	3628497	0.0012	38.254	0.002297	30
35	0.019359	93768	1815	464617	0.003907	2.6738	3156760	0.0040	33.666	0.003904	35
40	0.028259	91953	2598	453677	0.005728	2.6577	2692143	0.0247	29.277	0.005704	40
45	0.042331	89354	3782	438004	0.008636	2.6822	2238466	0.0019	25.052	0.008632	45
50	0.069033	85572	5907	414037	0.014268	2.6602	1800462	0.0000	21.040	0.014268	50
55	0.104489	79664	8324	378551	0.021989	2.6248	1386425	0.0109	17.403	0.021948	55
60	0.152698	71340	10894	330512	0.032960	2.5958	1007875	0.0209	14.128	0.032846	60
65	0.220589	60447	13334	269797	0.049422	2.5673	677363	0.0209	11.206	0.049246	65
70	0.322707	47113	15204	197653	0.076921	2.5064	407566	0.0209	8.651	0.076664	70
75	0.432566	31909	13803	124166	0.111165	2.4367	209912	0.0209	6.578	0.110781	75
80	0.608184	18106	11012	61604	0.178754	2.3731	85747	0.0209	4.736	0.177966	80
85+	*1.000000	7094	7094	24142	0.293856	3.4030	24142	0.0209	3.403	0.291317	85+

TABLE 3 — FEMALE LIFE TABLE

x	$_nq_x$	l_x	$_nd_x$	$_nL_x$	$_nm_x$	$_na_x$	T_x	r_x	$\overset{\circ}{e}_x$	$_nM_x$	x
0	0.014673	100000	1467	98911	0.014834	0.2578	7283177	0.0000	72.832	0.014834	0
1	0.002967	98533	292	393286	0.000743	1.1084	7184266	0.0000	72.912	0.000743	1
5	0.002465	98240	242	490596	0.000494	2.5000	6790981	0.0000	69.126	0.000494	5
10	0.001428	97998	140	489635	0.000286	2.4589	6300384	0.0000	64.291	0.000286	10
15	0.002193	97858	215	488772	0.000439	2.5827	5810749	0.0217	59.379	0.000438	15
20	0.002306	97644	225	487675	0.000462	2.5864	5321977	0.0449	54.504	0.000460	20
25	0.003162	97418	308	486374	0.000633	2.6684	4834302	0.0203	49.624	0.000631	25
30	0.004883	97110	474	484428	0.000979	2.6295	4347928	0.0000	44.773	0.000979	30
35	0.006237	96636	603	481805	0.001251	2.7169	3863501	0.0000	39.980	0.001251	35
40	0.011471	96033	1102	477623	0.002306	2.6902	3381696	0.0097	35.214	0.002302	40
45	0.016944	94932	1608	470905	0.003416	2.6659	2904073	0.0024	30.591	0.003414	45
50	0.025528	93323	2382	461097	0.005167	2.6829	2433168	0.0000	26.072	0.005167	50
55	0.040689	90941	3700	446211	0.008293	2.7045	1972071	0.0148	21.685	0.008266	55
60	0.068933	87241	6014	422561	0.014232	2.7315	1525860	0.0210	17.490	0.014153	60
65	0.127809	81227	10382	382138	0.027167	2.6885	1103299	0.0210	13.583	0.027027	65
70	0.217500	70845	15409	317675	0.048475	2.6409	721161	0.0210	10.179	0.048227	70
75	0.375227	55437	20801	226015	0.092035	2.5402	403286	0.0210	7.275	0.091611	75
80	0.560661	34635	19419	123466	0.157279	2.4401	177271	0.0210	5.118	0.156520	80
85+	*1.000000	15217	15217	53805	0.282812	3.5359	53805	0.0210	3.536	0.280362	85+

TABLE 4 — OBSERVED AND PROJECTED VITAL RATES

	OBSERVED POPULATION BOTH SEXES	MALES	FEMALES	PROJECTED POPULATION 1970 MALES	FEMALES	1975 MALES	FEMALES	1980 MALES	FEMALES	STABLE POPULATION MALES	FEMALES
RATES PER THOUSAND											
Birth	16.89	17.92	15.92	19.78	17.62	20.53	18.35	19.89	17.86	17.88	16.25
Death	9.64	10.45	8.89	10.80	9.28	11.12	9.76	11.32	10.22	13.33	11.70
Increase	7.25	7.48	7.03	8.98	8.34	9.41	8.59	8.57	7.64		4.5477
PERCENTAGE											
under 15	27.06	28.59	25.64	26.71	23.99	26.52	23.89	27.05	24.46	25.27	23.12
15-64	65.01	65.29	64.75	66.61	65.60	66.19	64.73	65.48	63.63	66.03	64.05
65 and over	7.93	6.12	9.61	6.68	10.41	7.29	11.38	7.46	11.90	8.70	12.83
DEP. RATIO X 100	53.82	53.17	54.44	50.14	52.43	51.08	54.50	52.71	57.15	51.44	56.13

AGE AT LAST BIRTHDAY	1970 BOTH SEXES	1970 MALES	1970 FEMALES	1975 BOTH SEXES	1975 MALES	1975 FEMALES	1980 BOTH SEXES	1980 MALES	1980 FEMALES	AGE AT LAST BIRTHDAY	
0-4	411	210	201	458	234	224	481	246	235	0-4	
5-9	395	201	194	409	209	200	456	233	223	5-9	
10-14	408	208	200	394	201	193	456	233	223	10-14	
15-19	441	224	217	408	208	200	408	208	200	15-19	**TABLE 5**
20-24	486	247	239	439	223	216	393	200	193	20-24	POPULATION
25-29	351	178	173	483	245	238	405	206	199	25-29	PROJECTED
30-34	307	156	151	349	176	173	436	221	215	30-34	WITH
35-39	285	145	140	305	154	151	480	243	237	35-39	FIXED
40-44	299	148	151	280	141	139	345	173	172	40-44	AGE—
45-49	282	131	151	291	143	148	299	150	149	45-49	SPECIFIC
50-54	238	106	132	272	124	148	273	136	137	50-54	BIRTH
55-59	251	111	140	225	97	128	280	135	145	55-59	AND
60-64	231	99	132	229	97	132	256	113	143	60-64	DEATH
65-69	174	71	103	200	81	119	205	84	121	65-69	RATES
70-74	121	45	76	138	52	86	199	79	120	70-74	(IN 1000's)
75-79	69	24	45	82	28	54	158	59	99	75-79	
80-84	34	11	23	37	12	25	94	33	61	80-84	
85+	13	4	9	14	4	10	44	14	30	85+	
							16	5	11		
TOTAL	4796	2319	2477	5013	2429	2584	5228	2538	2690	TOTAL	

STANDARD COUNTRIES:	ENGLAND AND WALES 1961 BOTH SEXES	MALES	FEMALES	UNITED STATES 1960 BOTH SEXES	MALES	FEMALES	MEXICO 1960 BOTH SEXES	MALES	FEMALES	
STANDARDIZED RATES PER THOUSAND										**TABLE 6**
Birth	15.26	16.92*	14.42	15.52	15.61*	14.91	17.81	15.46*	17.33	STANDAR-DIZED
Death	14.24	15.13*	13.59	11.42	12.93*	9.73	5.61	10.10*	4.30	RATES
Increase	1.03	1.80*	0.83	4.10	2.68*	5.17	12.20	5.37*	13.03	

	OBSERVED POP. MALES	FEMALES	STATIONARY POP. MALES	FEMALES	STABLE POP. MALES	FEMALES	OBSERVED BIRTHS	NET MATERNITY FUNCTION	BIRTHS IN STABLE POP.	
μ	30.23961	33.38864	35.16690	38.16114	33.07698	35.81194	27.38676	28.03340	27.85178	**TABLE 7**
σ^2	417.3940	478.0221	465.7998	521.5739	452.6547	510.6178	40.35232	38.14924	37.55650	MOMENTS
κ_3	4244.120	3783.837	2449.135	1778.208	3311.915	3019.964	153.2768	129.5646	131.0614	AND
κ_4	-128015.	-215206.	-202197.	-285093.	-175976.	-258613.	-416.203	-359.700	-288.609	CUMULANTS
β_1	0.247706	0.131075	0.059351	0.022285	0.118265	0.068504	0.357559	0.302353	0.324261	
β_2	2.265203	2.058203	2.068085	1.952016	2.141148	2.008120	2.744396	2.752845	2.795384	
κ	-0.093278	-0.046971	-0.023059	-0.008160	-0.045929	-0.025068	-0.188019	-0.176669	-0.192981	

VITAL STATISTICS		AGE RANGE	THOMPSON NRR	1000r	INTERVAL	AGE RANGE	BOURGEOIS-PICHAT NRR	1000b	1000d	1000r	COALE	
GRR	1.169										IBR	**TABLE 8** RATES FROM AGE DISTRI-BUTIONS
NRR	1.136	0-4	1.13	4.58	27.44	5-29	1.50	21.67	6.63	15.05	IDR	
TFR	2.398	5-9	1.30	9.69	27.40	30-54	0.97	12.24	13.28	-1.04	IRI	AND VITAL
GENERATION	27.942	10-14	1.44	13.31	27.35	55-79	2.17	68.09	39.45	28.63	K1	STATISTICS
SEX RATIO	105.074	15-19	1.60	16.30	27.27	*25-59	0.99	12.72	13.01	-0.29	K2	(Females)

Start of Age Interval	ORIGINAL MATRIX SUB-DIAGONAL	ALTERNATIVE FIRST ROWS Projection	Integral	FIRST STABLE MATRIX % IN STABLE POPULATION	FISHER VALUES	REPRODUCTIVE VALUES	SECOND STABLE MATRIX Z_2 FIRST COLUMN	FIRST ROW	
0	0.99675	0.00000	0.00000	7.906	1.027	199477	0.1585+0.0837	0.1585+0.0837	**TABLE 9**
5	0.99804	0.00002	0.00000	7.703	1.055	211458	0.1809-0.1251	-0.0009+0.1461	LESLIE
10	0.99824	0.04039	0.00004	7.515	1.081	234458	-0.0338-0.2681	-0.1059+0.0542	MATRIX
15	0.99775	0.20685	0.08181	7.333	1.066	255422	-0.3114-0.1151	-0.0853-0.0595	AND ITS
20	0.99733	0.33802	0.33738	7.152	0.880	153079	-0.3019+0.2741	-0.0220-0.1013	SPECTRAL
25	0.99600	0.27971	0.34731	6.972	0.555	84349	0.1274+0.4841	0.0112-0.0823	COMPO-NENTS
30	0.99459	0.17038	0.21937	6.788	0.281	39622	0.5986-0.1352	0.0193-0.0464	(Females)
35	0.99132	0.08511	0.12597	6.600	0.113	17174	0.4850-0.5737	0.0137-0.0178	
40	0.98593	0.02566	0.04659	6.395	0.028	4366	-0.3479-0.8481	0.0045-0.0040	
45	0.97917	0.00273	0.00539	6.164	0.003	378	-1.1079-0.1004	0.0005-0.0004	
50	0.96772	0.00007	0.00013	5.899	0.000	10	-0.7235+1.1288	0.0000-0.0000	
55+	0.78082			23.572					

Start of Age Interval	OBSERVED POPUL. (IN 100's)	CONTRIBUTIONS OF ROOTS (IN 100's) r_1	r_2, r_3	$r_4 \cdot r_{11}$	AGE-SP. BIRTH RATES	NET MATERNITY FUNCTION	COEFF. OF MATRIX EQUATION	PARAMETERS		INTEGRAL	MATRIX	EXP. INCREASE x	$e^{(x+2\frac{1}{2})r}$	
0	1941	2098	-187	30	0.0000	0.0000	0.0000	L(1)		1.02300	1.02301	0	1.0114	**TABLE 10**
5	2005	2045	-40	1	0.0000	0.0000	0.0000	L(2)		0.36575	0.37490	50	1.2697	AGE
10	2169	1995	236	-62	0.0000	0.0000	0.0402			0.74406	0.72075	55	1.2989	ANALYSIS
15	2396	1946	329	121	0.0164	0.0803	0.2054	R(1)		0.00455	0.00455	60	1.3287	AND
20	1739	1898	16	-175	0.0678	0.3305	0.3349	R(2)		-0.03748	-0.04155	65	1.3593	MISCEL-LANEOUS
25	1521	1851	-478	148	0.0698	0.3393	0.2764			0.22278	0.21823	70	1.3906	RESULTS
30	1410	1802	-564	172	0.0441	0.2135	0.1677	C(1)			26543	75	1.4225	(Females)
35	1519	1752	79	-312	0.0253	0.1219	0.0833	C(2)			-38270	80	1.4553	
40	1533	1698	932	-1096	0.0094	0.0447	0.0249				39254	85	1.4887	
45	1347	1636	927	-1216	0.0011	0.0051	0.0026	2P/Y		28.2030	28.7915	90	1.5230	
50	1446	1566	-332	212	0.0000	0.0001	0.0001	DELTA		5.8181		95	1.5580	
55+	4825	6257										100	1.5938	

Excluding Nice and La Savoie

TABLE 1 — DATA

AGE AT LAST BIRTHDAY	POPULATION BOTH SEXES	MALES Number	%	FEMALES Number	%	BIRTHS BY AGE OF MOTHER	DEATHS BOTH SEXES	MALES	FEMALES	AGE AT LAST BIRTHDAY
0	658642	334714	1.9	323928	1.8	0	156654	86002	70652	0
1-4	2669917	1351996	7.6	1317921	7.3	0	99567	50327	49240	1-4
5-9	3297524	1677508	9.4	1620016	9.0	0	33805	16643	17162	5-9
10-14	3149963	1604424	9.0	1545539	8.6	0	16587	7645	8942	10-14
15-19	3148249	1593753	9.0	1554496	8.6	39394	19903	9357	10546	15-19
20-24	2977094	1452286	8.2	1524808	8.5	212385	26923	14373	12550	20-24
25-29	2871096	1435706	8.1	1435390	8.0	282691	24892	12422	12470	25-29
30-34	2707846	1354797	7.6	1353049	7.5	234996	23618	11268	12350	30-34
35-39	2573434	1296267	7.3	1277167	7.1	147438	24295	11785	12510	35-39
40-44	2361601	1186930	6.7	1174671	6.5	54367	25330	12980	12350	40-44
45-49	2102634	1056072	5.9	1046562	5.8	0	26965	14214	12751	45-49
50-54	2063948	1037999	5.8	1025949	5.7	0	33395	17917	15478	50-54
55-59	1576527	742864	4.2	833663	4.6	0	35285	17081	18204	55-59
60-64	1314332	592910	3.3	721422	4.0	0	42687	19430	23257	60-64
65-69	996309	469563	2.6	526746	2.9	0	49954	23690	26264	65-69
70-74	697895	333678	1.9	364217	2.0		57227	27314	29913	70-74
75-79	380407	171491	1.0	208916	1.2		46925	21142	25783	75-79
80-84	171413	73349	0.4	98064	0.5	496606 M.	34335	15289	19046	80-84
85+	71909	30708	0.2	41201	0.2	474665 F.	20785	9277	11508	85+
TOTAL	35790740	17797015		17993725		971271	799132	398156	400976	TOTAL

TABLE 2 — MALE LIFE TABLE

x	$_nq_x$	l_x	$_nd_x$	$_nL_x$	$_nm_x$	$_na_x$	T_x	r_x	$\mathring{e}_x$	$_nM_x$	x
0	0.220315	100000	22031	85745	0.256942	0.3530	3833599	0.0000	38.336	0.256942	0
1	0.134959	77969	10523	282680	0.037224	1.2255	3747854	0.0000	48.069	0.037224	1
5	0.048406	67446	3265	329068	0.009921	2.5000	3465174	0.0000	51.377	0.009921	5
10	0.023522	64181	1510	316830	0.004765	2.3001	3136106	0.0000	48.863	0.004765	10
15	0.028976	62672	1816	309116	0.005875	2.6641	2819276	0.0035	44.985	0.005871	15
20	0.048315	60856	2940	297059	0.009898	2.5450	2510161	0.0017	41.248	0.009897	20
25	0.042324	57915	2451	283307	0.008652	2.4421	2213101	0.0000	38.213	0.008652	25
30	0.040737	55464	2259	271654	0.008317	2.4922	1929795	0.0017	34.794	0.008317	30
35	0.044473	53205	2366	260202	0.009094	2.5396	1658141	0.0039	31.165	0.009091	35
40	0.053298	50838	2710	247579	0.010944	2.5592	1397939	0.0095	27.498	0.010936	40
45	0.065164	48129	3136	233017	0.013459	2.5681	1150360	0.0000	23.902	0.013459	45
50	0.082999	44993	3734	215914	0.017295	2.5768	917343	0.0176	20.389	0.017261	50
55	0.109370	41258	4512	195397	0.023093	2.5857	701429	0.0323	17.001	0.022993	55
60	0.152125	36746	5590	170276	0.032829	2.5933	506032	0.0109	13.771	0.032771	60
65	0.225191	31156	7016	138788	0.050552	2.5781	335755	0.0109	10.777	0.050451	65
70	0.340556	24140	8221	100240	0.082013	2.5113	196967	0.0109	8.159	0.081857	70
75	0.468753	15919	7462	60408	0.123527	2.4288	96727	0.0109	6.076	0.123283	75
80	0.670446	8457	5670	27136	0.208945	2.3282	36319	0.0109	4.295	0.208441	80
85+	*1.000000	2787	2787	9184	0.303477	3.2951	9184	0.0109	3.295	0.302104	85+

TABLE 3 — FEMALE LIFE TABLE

x	$_nq_x$	l_x	$_nd_x$	$_nL_x$	$_nm_x$	$_na_x$	T_x	r_x	$\mathring{e}_x$	$_nM_x$	x
0	0.191806	100000	19181	87940	0.218110	0.3712	3964674	0.0000	39.647	0.218110	0
1	0.135575	80819	10957	293268	0.037362	1.2612	3876735	0.0000	47.968	0.037362	1
5	0.051602	69862	3605	340299	0.010594	2.5000	3583466	0.0000	51.293	0.010594	5
10	0.028490	66257	1888	326264	0.005786	2.3392	3243167	0.0000	48.948	0.005786	10
15	0.033369	64370	2148	316608	0.006784	2.5603	2916903	0.0000	45.315	0.006784	15
20	0.040334	62222	2510	304916	0.008231	2.5325	2600295	0.0000	41.791	0.008231	20
25	0.042518	59712	2539	292222	0.008688	2.5034	2295379	0.0032	38.441	0.008688	25
30	0.044625	57173	2551	279503	0.009128	2.5060	2003157	0.0025	35.037	0.009128	30
35	0.047815	54622	2612	266604	0.009796	2.5091	1723653	0.0044	31.556	0.009795	35
40	0.051256	52010	2666	253450	0.010518	2.5240	1457049	0.0092	28.015	0.010514	40
45	0.059159	49344	2919	239573	0.012185	2.5511	1203599	0.0012	24.392	0.012184	45
50	0.072855	46425	3382	223994	0.015100	2.5958	964026	0.0069	20.765	0.015087	50
55	0.103968	43043	4475	204526	0.021880	2.6115	740031	0.0128	17.193	0.021836	55
60	0.149813	38568	5778	178984	0.032282	2.6021	535505	0.0081	13.885	0.032238	60
65	0.222796	32790	7305	146295	0.049937	2.5833	356521	0.0081	10.873	0.049861	65
70	0.341410	25484	8701	105787	0.082247	2.5134	210227	0.0081	8.249	0.082130	70
75	0.468565	16784	7864	63635	0.123584	2.4208	104440	0.0081	6.223	0.123413	75
80	0.640179	8920	5710	29353	0.194534	2.3302	40804	0.0081	4.575	0.194219	80
85+	*1.000000	3209	3209	11452	0.280254	3.5682	11452	0.0081	3.568	0.279314	85+

TABLE 4 — OBSERVED AND PROJECTED VITAL RATES

	OBSERVED POPULATION BOTH SEXES	MALES	FEMALES	PROJECTED POPULATION 1856 MALES	FEMALES	1861 MALES	FEMALES	1866 MALES	FEMALES	STABLE POPULATION MALES	FEMALES
RATES PER THOUSAND											
Birth	27.14	27.90	26.38	27.54	26.19	26.96	25.76	26.29	25.22	25.31	24.47
Death	22.33	22.37	22.28	23.10	22.99	23.46	23.29	23.78	23.54	26.23	25.39
Increase	4.81	5.53	4.10	4.44	3.20	3.50	2.47	2.50	1.67	-0.9218	
PERCENTAGE											
under 15	27.31	27.92	26.72	27.31	26.49	26.71	26.25	27.01	26.76	25.84	25.81
15-64	66.21	66.02	66.40	66.49	66.25	66.80	66.22	65.59	65.15	65.07	64.86
65 and over	6.48	6.06	6.89	6.20	7.26	6.49	7.54	7.40	8.08	9.09	9.33
DEP. RATIO X 100	51.04	51.47	50.61	50.39	50.94	49.71	51.01	52.46	53.49	53.67	54.17

Excluding Nice and La Savoie

AGE AT LAST BIRTHDAY	1856 BOTH SEXES	MALES	FEMALES	1861 BOTH SEXES	MALES	FEMALES	1866 BOTH SEXES	MALES	FEMALES	AGE AT LAST BIRTHDAY	
0-4	3652	1836	1816	3654	1837	1817	3620	1820	1800	0-4	
5-9	2973	1507	1466	3261	1640	1621	3263	1641	1622	5-9	
10-14	3168	1615	1553	2856	1451	1405	3133	1579	1554	10-14	
15-19	3065	1565	1500	3083	1576	1507	2779	1415	1364	15-19	TABLE 5
20-24	3029	1532	1497	2948	1504	1444	2966	1514	1452	20-24	POPULATION
25-29	2846	1385	1461	2896	1461	1435	2819	1435	1384	25-29	PROJECTED
30-34	2750	1377	1373	2726	1328	1398	2773	1401	1372	30-34	WITH
35-39	2589	1298	1291	2629	1319	1310	2605	1272	1333	35-39	FIXED
40-44	2447	1233	1214	2462	1235	1227	2500	1255	1245	40-44	AGE—
45-49	2227	1117	1110	2309	1161	1148	2322	1162	1160	45-49	SPECIFIC
50-54	1958	979	979	2073	1035	1038	2149	1076	1073	50-54	BIRTH
55-59	1876	939	937	1779	886	893	1885	937	948	55-59	AND
60-64	1377	647	730	1639	819	820	1554	772	782	60-64	DEATH
65-69	1073	483	590	1124	528	596	1337	667	670	65-69	RATES
70-74	720	339	381	775	349	426	812	381	431	70-74	(IN 1000's)
75-79	420	201	219	433	204	229	466	210	256	75-79	
80-84	173	77	96	191	90	101	198	92	106	80-84	
85+	63	25	38	64	26	38	70	31	39	85+	
TOTAL	36406	18155	18251	36902	18449	18453	37251	18660	18591	TOTAL	

STANDARD COUNTRIES: STANDARDIZED RATES PER THOUSAND	ENGLAND AND WALES 1961 BOTH SEXES	MALES	FEMALES	UNITED STATES 1960 BOTH SEXES	MALES	FEMALES	MEXICO 1960 BOTH SEXES	MALES	FEMALES		
Birth	22.35	24.02*	21.17	22.76	22.47*	21.92	24.16	21.82*	23.55	TABLE 6	
Death	28.42	33.47*	30.28	27.14	28.38*	27.26	24.11	21.58*	23.36	STANDAR-DIZED RATES	
Increase	-6.07	-9.45*	-9.11	-4.37	-5.91*	-5.34	0.05	0.23*	0.20		

	OBSERVED POP. MALES	FEMALES	STATIONARY POP. MALES	FEMALES	STABLE POP. MALES	FEMALES	OBSERVED BIRTHS	NET MATERNITY FUNCTION	BIRTHS IN STABLE POP.		
μ	30.47366	31.38913	32.59415	32.74690	33.02035	33.17785	29.56842	29.67913	29.71549	TABLE 7	
σ^2	405.1596	423.0198	460.7380	465.8725	463.9321	469.0951	36.98386	37.34134	37.38595	MOMENTS	
κ_3	3622.702	3664.493	3552.054	3585.539	3376.983	3405.094	51.7937	48.8631	47.9214	AND	
κ_4	-114210.	-133449.	-186540.	-192293.	-193251.	-199155.	-978.018	-1012.183	-1020.585	CUMULANTS	
β_1	0.197327	0.177397	0.129002	0.127147	0.114207	0.112325	0.053030	0.045856	0.043947		
β_2	2.304253	2.254247	2.121252	2.114009	2.102130	2.094956	2.284973	2.274096	2.269816		
κ	-0.081131	-0.071305	-0.048706	-0.047810	-0.043093	-0.042213	-0.025946	-0.022395	-0.021417		

VITAL STATISTICS		THOMPSON AGE RANGE	NRR	1000r	INTERVAL	BOURGEOIS-PICHAT AGE RANGE	NRR	1000b	1000d	1000r	COALE	TABLE 8
GRR	1.703					5-29	0.94	25.94	28.28	-2.34	IBR	RATES FROM AGE DISTRI-BUTIONS
NRR	0.973	0-4	0.89	-4.43	26.93	30-54	1.12	30.64	26.58	4.06	IDR	AND VITAL
TFR	3.485	5-9	1.00	-0.11	26.80	55-79	1.40	46.96	34.58	12.39	IRI	STATISTICS
GENERATION	29.697	10-14	1.01	0.28	26.74	*20-44	1.10	30.14	26.60	3.54	K1	(Females)
SEX RATIO	104.622	15-19	1.07	2.65	26.62						K2	

Start of Age Interval	ORIGINAL MATRIX SUB-DIAGONAL	ALTERNATIVE FIRST ROWS Projection	Integral	FIRST STABLE MATRIX % IN STABLE POPULATION	FISHER VALUES	REPRODUCTIVE VALUES	SECOND STABLE MATRIX Z_2 FIRST COLUMN	FIRST ROW		
0	0.89269	0.00000	0.00000	9.349	1.309	2148675	0.1408+0.0552	0.1408+0.0552	TABLE 9	
5	0.95876	0.00000	0.00000	8.384	1.459	2364049	0.1302-0.0954	0.0269+0.1391	LESLIE	
10	0.97040	0.02291	0.00000	8.075	1.515	2341572	-0.0125-0.1845	-0.0900+0.0848	MATRIX	
15	0.96307	0.14856	0.04710	7.873	1.523	2367787	-0.1886-0.1023	-0.1066-0.0277	AND ITS	
20	0.95837	0.30556	0.25889	7.617	1.372	2092720	-0.2156+0.1204	-0.0510-0.0996	SPECTRAL	
25	0.95647	0.33819	0.36606	7.334	1.008	1447203	-0.0157+0.2825	0.0048-0.1017	COMPO-NENTS	
30	0.95385	0.26435	0.32282	7.047	0.587	793612	0.2632+0.1880	0.0276-0.0636	(Females)	
35	0.95066	0.14852	0.21457	6.753	0.249	318519	0.3417-0.1388	0.0211-0.0247		
40	0.94525	0.04311	0.08602	6.449	0.057	66584	0.0746-0.4124	0.0063-0.0046		
45	0.93497	0.00000	0.00000	6.124	0.000	4	-0.3485-0.3206	0.0000-0.0000		
50	0.91308	0.00000	0.00000	5.752	0.000	1	-0.5111+0.1373	0.0000-0.0000		
55+	0.72245			19.243						

Start of Age Interval	OBSERVED POPUL. (IN 100's)	CONTRIBUTIONS OF ROOTS (IN 100's) r_1	r_2, r_3	$r_4 \cdot r_{11}$	AGE-SP. BIRTH RATES	NET MATERNITY FUNCTION	COEFF. OF MATRIX EQUATION	PARAMETERS INTEGRAL	MATRIX	EXP. INCREASE x	$e^{(x+2\frac{1}{2})r}$	
0	16418	17921	-585	-917	0.0000	0.0000	0.0000	L(1) 0.99540	0.99540	0	0.9977	TABLE 10
5	16200	16071	-638	767	0.0000	0.0000	0.0000	L(2) 0.44502	0.44772	50	0.9528	AGE
10	15455	15480	-67	43	0.0000	0.0000	0.0196	0.72432	0.70669	55	0.9484	ANALYSIS
15	15545	15091	765	-311	0.0124	0.0392	0.1234	R(1) -0.00092	-0.00092	60	0.9440	AND
20	15248	14601	1032	-385	0.0681	0.2076	0.2444	R(2) -0.03248	-0.03569	65	0.9397	MISCEL-LANEOUS
25	14354	14058	257	40	0.0962	0.2813	0.2592	0.20397	0.20122	70	0.9354	RESULTS
30	13530	13508	-1038	1061	0.0849	0.2372	0.1938	C(1)	191687	75	0.9311	(Females)
35	12772	12944	-1602	1429	0.0564	0.1504	0.1039	C(2)	-220871	80	0.9268	
40	11747	12362	-603	-12	0.0226	0.0573	0.0287		-33158	85	0.9225	
45	10466	11739	1327	-2601	0.0000	0.0000	0.0000	2P/Y 30.8041	31.2262	90	0.9183	
50	10259	11027	2349	-3116	0.0000	0.0000	0.0000	DELTA 4.4257		95	0.9140	
55+	27942	36887								100	0.9098	

TABLE 1 — DATA

AGE AT LAST BIRTHDAY	POPULATION BOTH SEXES	MALES Number	%	FEMALES Number	%	BIRTHS BY AGE OF MOTHER	DEATHS BOTH SEXES	MALES	FEMALES	AGE AT LAST BIRTHDAY
0	812194	413347	2.2	398847	2.1	0	190480	105012	85468	0
1-4	2807316	1415885	7.6	1391431	7.4	0	112360	57034	55326	1-4
5-9	3279221	1652499	8.9	1626722	8.7	0	28335	13975	14360	5-9
10-14	3239448	1641655	8.8	1597793	8.5	0	17628	8098	9530	10-14
15-19	3252596	1634660	8.8	1617936	8.6	55168	23349	11145	12204	15-19
20-24	3080588	1502701	8.1	1577887	8.4	236008	29514	15586	13928	20-24
25-29	2938286	1463324	7.8	1474962	7.9	287297	25383	11886	13497	25-29
30-34	2774659	1401860	7.5	1372799	7.3	228181	24342	11233	13109	30-34
35-39	2654069	1341357	7.2	1312712	7.0	144462	24087	11668	12419	35-39
40-44	2476855	1251698	6.7	1225157	6.5	53962	25651	12887	12764	40-44
45-49	2302129	1156720	6.2	1145409	6.1	0	27648	14237	13411	45-49
50-54	2013209	1010796	5.4	1002413	5.3	0	32677	17067	15610	50-54
55-59	1705539	845847	4.5	859692	4.6	0	36835	18982	17853	55-59
60-64	1554458	771093	4.1	783365	4.2	0	53132	27733	25399	60-64
65-69	1101910	512689	2.7	589221	3.1	0	52759	24816	27943	65-69
70-74	726675	326997	1.8	399678	2.1		56907	25687	31220	70-74
75-79	419967	194114	1.0	225853	1.2		50593	23771	26822	75-79
80-84	183255	83331	0.4	99924	0.5	514735 M.	35645	16413	19232	80-84
85+	74452	30957	0.2	43495	0.2	490343 F.	19266	8141	11125	85+
TOTAL	37396826	18651530		18745296		1005078	866591	435371	431220	TOTAL

TABLE 2 — MALE LIFE TABLE

x	nq_x	l_x	nd_x	nL_x	nm_x	na_x	T_x	r_x	$\dot{e}_x$	nM_x	x
0	0.218590	100000	21859	86041	0.254053	0.3614	3829026	0.0000	38.290	0.254053	0
1	0.145012	78141	11331	281304	0.040282	1.2413	3742985	0.0000	47.900	0.040282	1
5	0.041409	66810	2767	327132	0.008457	2.5000	3461681	0.0000	51.814	0.008457	5
10	0.024353	64043	1560	316177	0.004933	2.4106	3134549	0.0000	48.944	0.004933	10
15	0.033561	62483	2097	307486	0.006820	2.6484	2818372	0.0017	45.106	0.006818	15
20	0.050559	60386	3053	294338	0.010373	2.5125	2510886	0.0020	41.580	0.010372	20
25	0.039779	57333	2281	280780	0.008123	2.4186	2216548	0.0000	38.661	0.008123	25
30	0.039277	55053	2162	269852	0.008013	2.4973	1935768	0.0006	35.162	0.008013	30
35	0.042586	52890	2252	258901	0.008700	2.5353	1665916	0.0025	31.498	0.008699	35
40	0.050228	50638	2543	246962	0.010299	2.5511	1407016	0.0045	27.786	0.010296	40
45	0.059816	48095	2877	233517	0.012319	2.5819	1160054	0.0085	24.120	0.012308	45
50	0.081218	45218	3674	217226	0.016915	2.5879	926538	0.0144	20.491	0.016885	50
55	0.106560	41543	4427	197167	0.022452	2.6167	709312	0.0029	17.074	0.022441	55
60	0.165830	37117	6155	170673	0.036063	2.5776	512145	0.0181	13.798	0.035966	60
65	0.216993	30962	6718	138395	0.048546	2.5570	341472	0.0181	11.029	0.048404	65
70	0.329690	24243	7993	101415	0.078812	2.5227	203077	0.0181	8.377	0.078554	70
75	0.467080	16250	7590	61779	0.122862	2.4344	101662	0.0181	6.256	0.122459	75
80	0.647060	8660	5604	28347	0.197679	2.3314	39883	0.0181	4.605	0.196962	80
85+	*1.000000	3057	3057	11536	0.264964	3.7741	11536	0.0181	3.774	0.262978	85+

TABLE 3 — FEMALE LIFE TABLE

x	nq_x	l_x	nd_x	nL_x	nm_x	na_x	T_x	r_x	$\dot{e}_x$	nM_x	x
0	0.189105	100000	18911	88248	0.214288	0.3786	3960399	0.0000	39.604	0.214288	0
1	0.143512	81089	11637	292674	0.039762	1.2774	3872151	0.0000	47.752	0.039762	1
5	0.043185	69452	2999	339763	0.008828	2.5000	3579477	0.0000	51.539	0.008828	5
10	0.029373	66453	1952	327257	0.005964	2.4348	3239714	0.0000	48.752	0.005964	10
15	0.037034	64501	2389	316685	0.007543	2.5637	2912457	0.0000	45.154	0.007543	15
20	0.043191	62112	2683	303911	0.008827	2.5209	2595772	0.0006	41.792	0.008827	20
25	0.044733	59430	2658	290494	0.009151	2.4972	2291861	0.0047	38.564	0.009151	25
30	0.046628	56771	2647	277205	0.009549	2.4876	2001367	0.0022	35.253	0.009549	30
35	0.046210	54124	2501	264362	0.009461	2.4979	1724162	0.0017	31.856	0.009461	35
40	0.050788	51623	2622	251620	0.010420	2.5230	1459800	0.0032	28.278	0.010418	40
45	0.056957	49001	2791	238205	0.011717	2.5635	1208180	0.0078	24.656	0.011708	45
50	0.075153	46210	3473	222668	0.015596	2.5863	969975	0.0130	20.991	0.015572	50
55	0.098972	42737	4230	203597	0.020775	2.6147	747306	0.0026	17.486	0.020767	55
60	0.150666	38507	5802	178604	0.032484	2.5984	543709	0.0114	14.120	0.032423	60
65	0.213086	32706	6969	146655	0.047521	2.5788	365106	0.0114	11.163	0.047424	65
70	0.327797	25737	8436	107783	0.078272	2.5227	218451	0.0114	8.488	0.078113	70
75	0.455883	17300	7887	66277	0.118998	2.4357	110668	0.0114	6.397	0.118759	75
80	0.637811	9413	6004	31124	0.192903	2.3446	44391	0.0114	4.716	0.192466	80
85+	*1.000000	3409	3409	13267	0.256991	3.8912	13267	0.0114	3.891	0.255777	85+

TABLE 4 — OBSERVED AND PROJECTED VITAL RATES

	OBSERVED POPULATION BOTH SEXES	MALES	FEMALES	PROJECTED POPULATION 1866 MALES	FEMALES	1871 MALES	FEMALES	1876 MALES	FEMALES	STABLE POPULATION MALES	FEMALES
RATES PER THOUSAND											
Birth	26.88	27.60	26.16	27.30	26.00	26.75	25.57	26.07	24.99	25.27	24.43
Death	23.17	23.34	23.00	23.97	23.57	24.38	23.88	24.69	24.09	26.27	25.43
Increase	3.70	4.26	3.15	3.33	2.43	2.37	1.69	1.37	0.90		-0.9946
PERCENTAGE											
under 15	27.11	27.47	26.75	26.99	26.54	26.83	26.52	26.78	26.62	25.73	25.79
15-64	66.19	66.38	66.00	66.04	65.71	65.85	65.55	65.48	65.18	64.99	64.62
65 and over	6.70	6.16	7.25	6.97	7.75	7.32	7.93	7.73	8.20	9.28	9.59
DEP. RATIO X 100	51.08	50.66	51.51	51.43	52.17	51.86	52.56	52.71	53.43	53.86	54.75

TABLE 1 DATA

AGE AT LAST BIRTHDAY	POPULATION BOTH SEXES	MALES Number	%	FEMALES Number	%	BIRTHS BY AGE OF MOTHER	DEATHS BOTH SEXES	MALES	FEMALES	AGE AT LAST BIRTHDAY
0	822828	417584	2.2	405244	2.1	0	178215	97991	80224	0
1-4	2897941	1467869	7.7	1430072	7.5	0	100541	50798	49743	1-4
5-9	3359332	1701578	8.9	1657754	8.7	0	25878	12808	13070	5-9
10-14	3176604	1612861	8.5	1563743	8.2	0	15411	7099	8312	10-14
15-19	3231813	1626736	8.5	1605077	8.4	56494	22393	10646	11747	15-19
20-24	3143910	1549074	8.1	1594836	8.4	242874	29589	15468	14121	20-24
25-29	2989718	1496226	7.9	1493492	7.9	284946	27266	13270	13996	25-29
30-34	2782451	1398306	7.3	1384145	7.3	223273	26424	12612	13812	30-34
35-39	2684185	1356155	7.1	1328030	7.0	141690	26272	13073	13199	35-39
40-44	2485297	1253424	6.6	1231873	6.5	52681	28961	15365	13596	40-44
45-49	2349371	1176533	6.2	1172838	6.2	0	30729	16854	13875	45-49
50-54	2082212	1042248	5.5	1039964	5.5	0	36098	19687	16411	50-54
55-59	1768098	882348	4.6	885750	4.7	0	40800	21910	18890	55-59
60-64	1501985	753153	4.0	748832	3.9	0	52973	27779	25194	60-64
65-69	1251788	616033	3.2	635755	3.3	0	65735	33964	31771	65-69
70-74	803476	372645	2.0	430831	2.3		67170	31586	35584	70-74
75-79	433029	189418	1.0	243611	1.3		55321	24392	30929	75-79
80-84	191741	84704	0.4	107037	0.6	513103 M.	39532	18169	21363	80-84
85+	71566	29688	0.2	41878	0.2	488855 F.	22036	9605	12431	85+
TOTAL	38027345	19026583		19000762		1001958	891344	453076	438268	TOTAL

TABLE 2 MALE LIFE TABLE

x	$_nq_x$	l_x	$_nd_x$	$_nL_x$	$_nm_x$	$_na_x$	T_x	r_x	$\dot{e}_x$	$_nM_x$	x
0	0.203868	100000	20387	86878	0.234662	0.3563	3929913	0.0000	39.299	0.234662	0
1	0.126324	79613	10057	290611	0.034607	1.2316	3843036	0.0000	48.271	0.034607	1
5	0.036874	69556	2565	341368	0.007513	2.5000	3552425	0.0025	51.073	0.007527	5
10	0.021762	66991	1458	331217	0.004401	2.4353	3211056	0.0000	47.932	0.004401	10
15	0.032229	65533	2112	322727	0.006544	2.6610	2879839	0.0000	43.945	0.006544	15
20	0.048727	63421	3090	309486	0.009985	2.5340	2557112	0.0000	40.319	0.009985	20
25	0.043366	60331	2616	295001	0.008869	2.4566	2247626	0.0010	37.255	0.008869	25
30	0.044103	57715	2545	282206	0.009020	2.4985	1952625	0.0008	33.832	0.009019	30
35	0.047088	55169	2598	269474	0.009640	2.5468	1670418	0.0009	30.278	0.009640	35
40	0.059518	52572	3129	255207	0.012261	2.5549	1400945	0.0022	26.648	0.012258	40
45	0.069232	49443	3423	238870	0.014330	2.5628	1145737	0.0036	23.173	0.014325	45
50	0.090403	46020	4160	220006	0.018910	2.5744	906867	0.0097	19.706	0.018889	50
55	0.117248	41859	4908	197466	0.024854	2.5895	686861	0.0065	16.409	0.024831	55
60	0.169619	36951	6268	169620	0.036951	2.5850	489395	0.0113	13.244	0.036884	60
65	0.243288	30684	7465	135144	0.055237	2.5520	319775	0.0113	10.422	0.055133	65
70	0.350148	23219	8130	95735	0.084922	2.4959	184631	0.0113	7.952	0.084762	70
75	0.484013	15089	7303	56597	0.129038	2.4194	88896	0.0113	5.892	0.128773	75
80	0.681240	7786	5304	24664	0.215046	2.3106	32299	0.0113	4.149	0.214501	80
85+	*1.000000	2482	2482	7635	0.325057	3.0764	7635	0.0113	3.076	0.323531	85+

TABLE 3 FEMALE LIFE TABLE

x	$_nq_x$	l_x	$_nd_x$	$_nL_x$	$_nm_x$	$_na_x$	T_x	r_x	$\dot{e}_x$	$_nM_x$	x
0	0.176172	100000	17617	88992	0.197965	0.3751	4092851	0.0000	40.929	0.197965	0
1	0.127067	82383	10468	300950	0.034784	1.2697	4003859	0.0000	48.601	0.034784	1
5	0.038592	71915	2775	352635	0.007870	2.5000	3702909	0.0026	51.490	0.007884	5
10	0.026223	69139	1813	341090	0.005315	2.4593	3350274	0.0000	48.457	0.005315	10
15	0.035958	67326	2421	330787	0.007319	2.5860	3009184	0.0000	44.695	0.007319	15
20	0.043324	64905	2812	317585	0.008854	2.5313	2678396	0.0000	41.266	0.008854	20
25	0.045791	62093	2843	303374	0.009372	2.5053	2360811	0.0047	38.020	0.009371	25
30	0.048677	59250	2884	289017	0.009979	2.4920	2057437	0.0019	34.725	0.009979	30
35	0.048490	56366	2733	274996	0.009939	2.4997	1768420	0.0015	31.374	0.009939	35
40	0.053713	53633	2881	261001	0.011037	2.5134	1493424	0.0015	27.845	0.011037	40
45	0.057508	50752	2919	246622	0.011835	2.5543	1232423	0.0045	24.283	0.011830	45
50	0.076120	47833	3641	230392	0.015804	2.5900	985801	0.0121	20.609	0.015780	50
55	0.101639	44192	4492	210262	0.021362	2.6179	755409	0.0102	17.094	0.021327	55
60	0.155763	39701	6184	183665	0.033669	2.6005	545147	0.0044	13.731	0.033644	60
65	0.223035	33517	7475	149467	0.050014	2.5765	361482	0.0044	10.785	0.049974	65
70	0.342906	26041	8930	108031	0.082659	2.5166	212015	0.0044	8.141	0.082594	70
75	0.478473	17112	8187	64438	0.127059	2.4205	103985	0.0044	6.077	0.126961	75
80	0.650384	8924	5804	29055	0.199765	2.3181	39546	0.0044	4.431	0.199586	80
85+	*1.000000	3120	3120	10492	0.297381	3.3627	10492	0.0044	3.363	0.296838	85+

TABLE 4 OBSERVED AND PROJECTED VITAL RATES

	OBSERVED POPULATION BOTH SEXES	MALES	FEMALES	PROJECTED POPULATION 1871 MALES	FEMALES	1876 MALES	FEMALES	1881 MALES	FEMALES	STABLE POPULATION MALES	FEMALES
RATES PER THOUSAND											
Birth	26.35	26.97	25.73	26.65	25.47	26.05	24.92	25.56	24.45	25.45	24.44
Death	23.44	23.81	23.07	24.21	23.36	24.45	23.44	24.61	23.52	25.44	24.43
Increase	2.91	3.15	2.66	2.43	2.11	1.61	1.47	0.95	0.93		0.0084
PERCENTAGE											
under 15	26.97	27.33	26.61	27.47	26.92	27.42	26.97	27.31	26.96	26.73	26.48
15-64	65.79	65.88	65.71	65.44	65.41	65.34	65.28	65.21	65.04	65.14	64.69
65 and over	7.24	6.79	7.68	7.09	7.68	7.24	7.74	7.47	8.00	8.13	8.83
DEP. RATIO X 100	51.99	51.80	52.19	52.81	52.89	53.05	53.18	53.34	53.75	53.52	54.59

Excluding L'Alsace-Lorraine

TABLE 1 — DATA

AGE AT LAST BIRTHDAY	POPULATION BOTH SEXES	MALES Number	%	FEMALES Number	%	BIRTHS BY AGE OF MOTHER	DEATHS BOTH SEXES	MALES	FEMALES	AGE AT LAST BIRTHDAY
0	741238	373147	2.0	368091	2.0	0	181433	98699	82734	0
1-4	2916393	1467584	8.0	1448809	7.9	0	131745	68212	63533	1-4
5-9	3346717	1691963	9.2	1654754	9.0	0	44955	22640	22315	5-9
10-14	3192182	1612925	8.8	1579257	8.6	0	25496	12089	13407	10-14
15-19	3043483	1531911	8.3	1511572	8.2	45038	35213	17820	17393	15-19
20-24	3034718	1504748	8.2	1529970	8.3	224022	74799	53609	21190	20-24
25-29	2791771	1410530	7.7	1381241	7.5	227329	56310	35468	20842	25-29
30-34	2681389	1346927	7.3	1334462	7.3	175756	47516	27361	20155	30-34
35-39	2505097	1265691	6.9	1239406	6.8	112152	44412	24641	19771	35-39
40-44	2333445	1178488	6.4	1154957	6.3	41824	44072	24411	19661	40-44
45-49	2176003	1094061	5.9	1081942	5.9	0	44246	24840	19406	45-49
50-54	1981644	991305	5.4	990339	5.4	0	48412	26643	21769	50-54
55-59	1757380	890463	4.8	866917	4.7	0	52723	28830	23893	55-59
60-64	1484925	745385	4.0	739540	4.0	0	62033	33090	28943	60-64
65-69	1139264	556342	3.0	582922	3.2	0	66815	35040	31775	65-69
70-74	843384	406879	2.2	436505	2.4		83351	43488	39863	70-74
75-79	479979	219079	1.2	260900	1.4		65000	30432	34568	75-79
80-84	201962	84951	0.5	117011	0.6	422879 M.	41501	18043	23458	80-84
85+	80134	32373	0.2	47761	0.3	403242 F.	23584	10093	13491	85+
TOTAL	36731108	18404752		18326356		826121	1173616	635449	538167	TOTAL

TABLE 2 — MALE LIFE TABLE

x	nq_x	l_x	nd_x	nL_x	nm_x	na_x	T_x	r_x	$\overset{\circ}{e}_x$	nM_x	x
0	0.226707	100000	22671	85710	0.264504	0.3697	2860774	0.0000	28.608	0.264504	0
1	0.164900	77329	12752	274351	0.046479	1.2579	2775064	0.0000	35.886	0.046479	1
5	0.064739	64578	4181	312437	0.013381	2.5000	2500713	0.0000	38.724	0.013381	5
10	0.036763	60397	2220	296252	0.007495	2.4177	2188276	0.0004	36.232	0.007495	10
15	0.056793	58177	3304	284033	0.011633	2.9268	1892025	0.0000	32.522	0.011633	15
20	0.163825	54873	8990	252326	0.035627	2.5486	1607991	0.0000	29.304	0.035627	20
25	0.117744	45883	5402	214850	0.025145	2.3039	1355665	0.0000	29.546	0.025145	25
30	0.096460	40481	3905	192223	0.020314	2.3928	1140815	0.0000	28.182	0.020314	30
35	0.092757	36576	3393	174265	0.019468	2.4608	948592	0.0000	25.935	0.019468	35
40	0.098448	33183	3267	157712	0.020714	2.4886	774327	0.0000	23.335	0.020714	40
45	0.107439	29916	3214	141567	0.022704	2.5063	616615	0.0000	20.611	0.022704	45
50	0.125978	26702	3364	125161	0.026877	2.5176	475048	0.0000	17.791	0.026877	50
55	0.149923	23338	3499	108071	0.032376	2.5362	349888	0.0000	14.992	0.032376	55
60	0.200197	19839	3972	89440	0.044407	2.5435	241817	0.0023	12.189	0.044393	60
65	0.272798	15868	4329	68700	0.063008	2.5423	152376	0.0023	9.603	0.062983	65
70	0.420421	11539	4851	45372	0.106922	2.4598	83677	0.0023	7.252	0.106882	70
75	0.507185	6688	3392	24411	0.138952	2.3384	38305	0.0023	5.728	0.138909	75
80	0.673545	3296	2220	10447	0.212492	2.2826	13895	0.0023	4.216	0.212394	80
85+	*1.000000	1076	1076	3448	0.312071	3.2044	3448	0.0023	3.204	0.311772	85

TABLE 3 — FEMALE LIFE TABLE

x	nq_x	l_x	nd_x	nL_x	nm_x	na_x	T_x	r_x	$\overset{\circ}{e}_x$	nM_x	x
0	0.197352	100000	19735	87804	0.224765	0.3820	3371187	0.0000	33.712	0.224765	0
1	0.156748	80265	12581	286906	0.043852	1.2854	3283383	0.0000	40.907	0.043852	1
5	0.065228	67683	4415	327380	0.013485	2.5000	2996477	0.0000	44.272	0.013485	5
10	0.041537	63269	2628	309560	0.008489	2.4191	2669097	0.0000	42.187	0.008489	10
15	0.055970	60641	3394	294969	0.011507	2.5740	2359537	0.0000	38.910	0.011507	15
20	0.066956	57247	3833	276752	0.013850	2.5266	2064568	0.0000	36.065	0.013850	20
25	0.072691	53414	3883	257313	0.015089	2.4877	1787816	0.0000	33.471	0.015089	25
30	0.072748	49531	3603	238571	0.015103	2.4792	1530503	0.0000	30.900	0.015103	30
35	0.076691	45928	3522	220803	0.015952	2.4916	1291932	0.0000	28.130	0.015952	35
40	0.081627	42405	3461	203336	0.017023	2.4892	1071129	0.0000	25.259	0.017023	40
45	0.085856	38944	3344	186413	0.017936	2.5156	867794	0.0000	22.283	0.017936	45
50	0.104276	35600	3712	168883	0.021981	2.5435	681381	0.0000	19.140	0.021981	50
55	0.129139	31888	4118	149405	0.027563	2.5631	512498	0.0005	16.072	0.027561	55
60	0.178610	27770	4960	126736	0.039137	2.5575	363093	0.0000	13.075	0.039136	60
65	0.240511	22810	5486	100643	0.054510	2.5561	236357	0.0000	10.362	0.054510	65
70	0.371631	17324	6438	70498	0.091324	2.4959	135714	0.0000	7.834	0.091323	70
75	0.492227	10886	5358	40441	0.132496	2.3895	65216	0.0000	5.991	0.132495	75
80	0.650484	5528	3596	17935	0.200479	2.3015	24774	0.0000	4.482	0.200478	80
85+	*1.000000	1932	1932	6839	0.282473	3.5402	6839	0.0000	3.540	0.282469	85

TABLE 4 — OBSERVED AND PROJECTED VITAL RATES

	OBSERVED POPULATION BOTH SEXES	MALES	FEMALES	PROJECTED POPULATION 1876 MALES	FEMALES	1881 MALES	FEMALES	1886 MALES	FEMALES	STABLE POPULATION MALES	FEMALES
RATES PER THOUSAND											
Birth	22.49	22.98	22.00	23.75	22.28	24.47	22.52	25.26	22.81	25.40	20.94
Death	31.95	34.53	29.37	33.67	28.45	34.29	28.65	34.96	28.98	36.09	31.6
Increase	-9.46	-11.55	-7.36	-9.92	-6.16	-9.82	-6.13	-9.70	-6.17	-10.690	
PERCENTAGE											
under 15	27.76	27.96	27.56	27.02	26.24	25.97	24.92	25.23	23.79	26.58	22.8
15-64	64.77	64.98	64.55	65.63	65.81	66.37	67.00	66.89	67.88	65.05	66.3
65 and over	7.47	7.06	7.89	7.35	7.94	7.66	8.08	7.88	8.33	8.37	10.7
DEP. RATIO X 100	54.40	53.89	54.91	52.37	51.94	50.68	49.25	49.50	47.32	53.74	50.6

Excluding L'Alsace-Lorraine

TABLE 1 — DATA

AGE AT LAST BIRTHDAY	POPULATION BOTH SEXES	MALES Number	%	FEMALES Number	%	BIRTHS BY AGE OF MOTHER	DEATHS BOTH SEXES	MALES	FEMALES	AGE AT LAST BIRTHDAY
0	699913	355036	2.0	344877	1.9	0	146828	81453	65375	0
1-4	2661044	1346326	7.5	1314718	7.3	0	82420	41449	40971	1-4
5-9	3265528	1657091	9.2	1608437	8.9	0	25210	12182	13028	5-9
10-14	3143264	1598911	8.9	1544353	8.5	0	15029	7010	8019	10-14
15-19	3051914	1532303	8.5	1519611	8.4	52426	19168	8845	10323	15-19
20-24	3174625	1511050	8.4	1663575	9.2	268461	28960	15906	13054	20-24
25-29	2605143	1291886	7.2	1313257	7.2	263656	27399	14294	13105	25-29
30-34	2544454	1278002	7.1	1266452	7.0	203180	26116	13167	12949	30-34
35-39	2486476	1249275	6.9	1237201	6.8	129825	25496	12880	12616	35-39
40-44	2330478	1170132	6.5	1160346	6.4	48452	27176	14529	12647	40-44
45-49	2197124	1097812	6.1	1099312	6.1	0	28807	15638	13169	45-49
50-54	1975896	984030	5.5	991866	5.5	0	32696	17919	14777	50-54
55-59	1786256	888897	4.9	897359	5.0	0	38702	20675	18027	55-59
60-64	1504213	747989	4.2	756224	4.2	0	47733	25335	22398	60-64
65-69	1104036	535128	3.0	568908	3.1	0	52534	27400	25134	65-69
70-74	836712	406234	2.3	430478	2.4	0	64331	33407	30924	70-74
75-79	470068	218545	1.2	251523	1.4	0	53572	26208	27364	75-79
80-84	191671	82290	0.5	109381	0.6	494481 M.	32876	14104	18772	80-84
85+	77362	31365	0.2	45997	0.3	471519 F.	18011	7410	10601	85+
TOTAL	36106177	17982302		18123875		966000	793064	409811	383253	TOTAL

TABLE 2 — MALE LIFE TABLE

x	$n q_x$	l_x	$n d_x$	$n L_x$	$n m_x$	$n a_x$	T_x	r_x	$\mathring{e}_x$	$n M_x$	x
0	0.199565	100000	19957	86986	0.229422	0.3479	4003739	0.0000	40.037	0.229422	0
1	0.113427	80043	9079	294904	0.030787	1.2167	3916753	0.0000	48.933	0.030787	1
5	0.036094	70964	2561	348418	0.007351	2.5000	3621849	0.0000	51.038	0.007351	5
10	0.021671	68403	1482	338172	0.004383	2.4079	3273431	0.0025	47.855	0.004384	10
15	0.028484	66921	1906	330225	0.005772	2.7030	2935259	0.0000	43.862	0.005772	15
20	0.051370	65014	3340	317017	0.010535	2.5881	2605034	0.0075	40.069	0.010526	20
25	0.053817	61675	3319	299990	0.011064	2.4743	2288017	0.0059	37.098	0.011064	25
30	0.050201	58356	2930	284343	0.010303	2.4621	1988027	0.0000	34.068	0.010303	30
35	0.050264	55426	2786	270216	0.010310	2.5181	1703684	0.0000	30.738	0.010310	35
40	0.060246	52640	3171	255401	0.012417	2.5407	1433469	0.0007	27.232	0.012417	40
45	0.068838	49469	3405	239007	0.014248	2.5517	1178068	0.0026	23.814	0.014245	45
50	0.087205	46063	4017	220530	0.018215	2.5636	939061	0.0028	20.386	0.018210	50
55	0.110151	42046	4631	199042	0.023269	2.5837	718531	0.0031	17.089	0.023259	55
60	0.157124	37415	5879	172915	0.033998	2.5913	519489	0.0231	13.885	0.033871	60
65	0.228528	31536	7207	140174	0.051414	2.5708	346575	0.0231	10.990	0.051203	65
70	0.342234	24329	8326	100858	0.082554	2.5033	206401	0.0231	8.484	0.082236	70
75	0.458648	16003	7340	60991	0.120342	2.4080	105543	0.0231	6.595	0.119920	75
80	0.587154	8663	5087	29575	0.171994	2.3459	44552	0.0231	5.143	0.171394	80
85+	1.000000	3577	3577	14977	0.238802	4.1876	14977	0.0231	4.188	0.236250	85+

TABLE 3 — FEMALE LIFE TABLE

x	$n q_x$	l_x	$n d_x$	$n L_x$	$n m_x$	$n a_x$	T_x	r_x	$\mathring{e}_x$	$n M_x$	x
0	0.169333	100000	16933	89329	0.189560	0.3698	4240245	0.0000	42.402	0.189560	0
1	0.114841	83067	9539	306112	0.031163	1.2582	4150916	0.0000	49.971	0.031163	1
5	0.039695	73527	2919	360340	0.008100	2.5000	3844804	0.0000	52.291	0.008100	5
10	0.025620	70609	1809	348391	0.005192	2.4286	3484465	0.0000	49.349	0.005192	10
15	0.033414	68800	2299	338407	0.006793	2.5682	3136074	0.0000	45.583	0.006793	15
20	0.038520	66501	2562	326270	0.007851	2.5665	2797666	0.0065	42.070	0.007847	20
25	0.048739	63939	3116	312003	0.009988	2.5314	2471396	0.0177	38.652	0.009979	25
30	0.049841	60823	3031	296485	0.010225	2.4833	2159394	0.0000	35.503	0.010225	30
35	0.049714	57791	2873	281750	0.010197	2.4915	1862909	0.0000	32.235	0.010197	35
40	0.053059	54918	2914	267339	0.010900	2.5110	1581159	0.0009	28.791	0.010899	40
45	0.058196	52004	3026	252583	0.011982	2.5419	1313821	0.0034	25.264	0.011979	45
50	0.071936	48978	3523	236359	0.014906	2.5788	1061238	0.0050	21.668	0.014898	50
55	0.095915	45455	4360	216826	0.020107	2.6038	824879	0.0062	18.147	0.020089	55
60	0.138601	41095	5696	191803	0.029696	2.5997	608053	0.0163	14.796	0.029618	60
65	0.200148	35399	7085	159900	0.044309	2.5871	416250	0.0163	11.759	0.044179	65
70	0.305819	28314	8659	120194	0.072042	2.5313	256350	0.0163	9.054	0.071836	70
75	0.426763	19655	8388	76886	0.109097	2.4501	136156	0.0163	6.927	0.108793	75
80	0.590135	11267	6649	38631	0.172115	2.3819	59270	0.0163	5.260	0.171620	80
85+	1.000000	4618	4618	20638	0.223755	4.4692	20638	0.0163	4.469	0.230472	85+

TABLE 4 — OBSERVED AND PROJECTED VITAL RATES

RATES PER THOUSAND	OBSERVED POPULATION BOTH SEXES	MALES	FEMALES	PROJECTED POPULATION 1877 MALES	FEMALES	1882 MALES	FEMALES	1887 MALES	FEMALES	STABLE POPULATION MALES	FEMALES
Birth	26.75	27.50	26.02	27.50	25.97	27.06	25.52	26.54	25.00	26.38	24.94
Death	21.96	22.79	21.15	23.89	22.20	24.19	22.50	24.25	22.63	24.67	23.23
Increase	4.79	4.71	4.87	3.61	3.77	2.87	3.03	2.29	2.37		1.7086
PERCENTAGE											
under 15	27.06	27.57	26.55	27.68	26.78	27.82	27.03	28.50	27.74	27.84	27.20
15-64	65.52	65.35	65.69	64.75	65.00	64.27	64.37	63.43	63.40	64.09	63.64
65 and over	7.42	7.08	7.76	7.57	8.22	7.91	8.61	8.06	8.86	8.07	9.16
DEP. RATIO X 100	52.63	53.02	52.23	54.43	53.84	55.60	55.35	57.64	57.73	56.03	57.14

Excluding L'Alsace-Lorraine

TABLE 1 — DATA

AGE AT LAST BIRTHDAY	POPULATION BOTH SEXES	MALES Number	MALES %	FEMALES Number	FEMALES %	BIRTHS BY AGE OF MOTHER	DEATHS BOTH SEXES	DEATHS MALES	DEATHS FEMALES	AGE AT LAST BIRTHDAY
0	778599	394470	2.2	384129	2.1	0	156225	86488	69737	0
1-4	2796945	1412769	7.7	1384176	7.5	0	78254	39891	38363	1-4
5-9	3208318	1621635	8.8	1586683	8.6	0	21033	10421	10612	5-9
10-14	3201992	1625589	8.9	1576403	8.5	0	13339	6183	7156	10-14
15-19	3154919	1585266	8.6	1569653	8.5	53956	18609	8510	10099	15-19
20-24	3223677	1552396	8.5	1671281	9.0	266298	26849	14546	12303	20-24
25-29	2615254	1303251	7.1	1312003	7.1	256365	24943	12303	12640	25-29
30-34	2602434	1306702	7.1	1295732	7.0	201771	25435	12698	12737	30-34
35-39	2515702	1267631	6.9	1248071	6.7	125717	25359	13122	12237	35-39
40-44	2361429	1190052	6.5	1171377	6.3	46733	26520	14356	12164	40-44
45-49	2223918	1105389	6.0	1118529	6.0	0	28750	15529	13221	45-49
50-54	2012170	997219	5.4	1014951	5.5	0	34127	18698	15429	50-54
55-59	1784107	872803	4.8	911304	4.9	0	39858	21399	18459	55-59
60-64	1530132	755059	4.1	775073	4.2	0	51205	26795	24410	60-64
65-69	1168020	572335	3.1	595685	3.2	0	57992	29923	28069	65-69
70-74	821229	395611	2.2	425618	2.3		65602	33324	32278	70-74
75-79	512997	242542	1.3	270455	1.5		63110	31709	31401	75-79
80-84	226263	100412	0.5	125851	0.7	486676 M.	41474	18605	22869	80-84
85+	85483	32278	0.2	53205	0.3	464164 F.	21810	8823	12987	85+
TOTAL	36823588	18333409		18490179		950840	820494	423323	397171	TOTAL

TABLE 2 — MALE LIFE TABLE

x	nq_x	l_x	nd_x	nL_x	nm_x	na_x	T_x	r_x	$\mathring{e}_x$	nM_x	x
0	0.191708	100000	19171	87438	0.219251	0.3447	4133376	0.0000	41.334	0.219251	
1	0.104700	80829	8463	299717	0.028236	1.2113	4045938	0.0000	50.055	0.028236	
5	0.031623	72366	2288	356111	0.006426	2.5000	3746221	0.0000	51.767	0.006426	
10	0.018833	70078	1320	346993	0.003804	2.4265	3390111	0.0000	48.376	0.003804	1
15	0.026514	68758	1823	339597	0.005368	2.6999	3043118	0.0000	44.258	0.005368	1
20	0.045856	66935	3069	327236	0.009380	2.5761	2703520	0.0111	40.390	0.009370	2
25	0.046110	63866	2945	311929	0.009441	2.4873	2376285	0.0077	37.208	0.009440	2
30	0.047435	60921	2890	297376	0.009718	2.4988	2064356	0.0000	33.886	0.009718	3
35	0.050465	58031	2929	282904	0.010352	2.5241	1766980	0.0000	30.449	0.010352	3
40	0.058583	55103	3228	267567	0.012065	2.5385	1484075	0.0016	26.933	0.012063	4
45	0.067939	51874	3524	250793	0.014053	2.5656	1216509	0.0031	23.451	0.014048	4
50	0.089721	48350	4338	231233	0.018760	2.5754	965716	0.0048	19.973	0.018750	5
55	0.115764	44012	5095	207746	0.024525	2.5831	734483	0.0023	16.688	0.024518	5
60	0.163672	38917	6370	179175	0.035550	2.5806	526737	0.0114	13.535	0.035487	6
65	0.232295	32547	7561	144324	0.052386	2.5646	347562	0.0114	10.679	0.052282	6
70	0.348721	24987	8713	103233	0.084406	2.5094	203238	0.0114	8.134	0.084234	7
75	0.488857	16273	7955	60736	0.130984	2.4066	100005	0.0114	6.145	0.130736	7
80	0.618822	8318	5147	27725	0.185659	2.3063	39269	0.0114	4.721	0.185287	8
85+	*1.000000	3171	3171	11545	0.274643	3.6411	11545	0.0114	3.641	0.273344	8

TABLE 3 — FEMALE LIFE TABLE

x	nq_x	l_x	nd_x	nL_x	nm_x	na_x	T_x	r_x	$\mathring{e}_x$	nM_x	x
0	0.162745	100000	16274	89644	0.181546	0.3637	4372158	0.0000	43.722	0.181546	
1	0.102999	83726	8624	311150	0.027715	1.2456	4282514	0.0000	51.149	0.027715	
5	0.032881	75102	2469	369336	0.006686	2.5000	3971365	0.0005	52.880	0.006688	
10	0.022440	72632	1630	359042	0.004539	2.4718	3602029	0.0000	49.593	0.004539	1
15	0.031676	71003	2249	349569	0.006434	2.5795	3242987	0.0000	45.674	0.006434	1
20	0.036193	68754	2488	337728	0.007368	2.5730	2893418	0.0102	42.084	0.007361	2
25	0.047095	66265	3121	323636	0.009643	2.5361	2555690	0.0163	38.568	0.009634	2
30	0.047963	63144	3029	308099	0.009830	2.4832	2232054	0.0000	35.348	0.009830	3
35	0.047846	60116	2876	293361	0.009805	2.4905	1923954	0.0002	32.004	0.009805	3
40	0.050618	57239	2897	279005	0.010385	2.5177	1630594	0.0004	28.487	0.010384	4
45	0.057451	54342	3122	264084	0.011822	2.5574	1351589	0.0022	24.872	0.011820	4
50	0.073354	51220	3757	247013	0.015210	2.5814	1087505	0.0051	21.232	0.015202	5
55	0.096691	47463	4589	226368	0.020273	2.6148	840492	0.0055	17.708	0.020256	5
60	0.146599	42874	6285	199313	0.031535	2.6047	614124	0.0076	14.324	0.031494	6
65	0.211734	36588	7747	164185	0.047184	2.5789	414811	0.0076	11.337	0.047121	6
70	0.319595	28841	9218	121380	0.075940	2.5236	250625	0.0076	8.690	0.075838	7
75	0.447935	19624	8790	75610	0.116258	2.4393	129245	0.0076	6.586	0.116104	7
80	0.614281	10834	6655	36570	0.181976	2.3556	53635	0.0076	4.951	0.181714	8
85+	*1.000000	4179	4179	17065	0.244869	4.0838	17065	0.0076	4.084	0.244094	8

TABLE 4 — OBSERVED AND PROJECTED VITAL RATES

	OBSERVED POPULATION BOTH SEXES	MALES	FEMALES	PROJECTED POPULATION 1881 MALES	1881 FEMALES	1886 MALES	1886 FEMALES	1891 MALES	1891 FEMALES	STABLE POPULATION MALES	FEMAL
RATES PER THOUSAND											
Birth	25.82	26.55	25.10	26.76	25.28	26.45	24.96	25.94	24.46	25.88	24.
Death	22.28	23.09	21.48	23.55	21.90	23.62	22.01	23.56	22.05	23.77	22-
Increase	3.54	3.46	3.62	3.22	3.38	2.83	2.95	2.38	2.41		2.10
PERCENTAGE											
under 15	27.12	27.57	26.67	27.66	26.89	28.09	27.38	28.31	27.65	27.78	27-
15-64	65.24	65.10	65.38	64.81	64.95	64.31	64.25	64.02	63.81	64.50	64-
65 and over	7.64	7.33	7.95	7.53	8.16	7.60	8.37	7.67	8.53	7.72	8-
DEP. RATIO X 100	53.28	53.60	52.96	54.30	53.96	55.49	55.63	56.21	56.71	55.04	56-

Excluding L'Alsace-Lorraine

AGE LAST BIRTHDAY	1881 BOTH SEXES	MALES	FEMALES	1886 BOTH SEXES	MALES	FEMALES	1891 BOTH SEXES	MALES	FEMALES	AGE AT LAST BIRTHDAY	
0-4	3789	1907	1882	3838	1931	1907	3829	1927	1902	0-4	
5-9	3292	1662	1630	3489	1754	1735	3534	1777	1757	5-9	
10-14	3122	1580	1542	3204	1620	1584	3395	1709	1686	10-14	TABLE 5
15-19	3126	1591	1535	3048	1546	1502	3127	1585	1542	15-19	POPULATION
20-24	3044	1528	1516	3016	1533	1483	2941	1490	1451	20-24	PROJECTED
25-29	3082	1480	1602	2909	1456	1453	2882	1461	1421	25-29	WITH
30-34	2491	1242	1249	2936	1411	1525	2771	1388	1383	30-34	FIXED
35-39	2477	1243	1234	2371	1182	1189	2794	1342	1452	35-39	AGE—
40-44	2386	1199	1187	2349	1176	1173	2249	1118	1131	40-44	SPECIFIC
45-49	2224	1115	1109	2248	1124	1124	2213	1102	1111	45-49	BIRTH
50-54	2065	1019	1046	2065	1028	1037	2087	1036	1051	50-54	AND
55-59	1826	896	930	1875	916	959	1874	924	950	55-59	DEATH
60-64	1555	753	802	1592	773	819	1634	790	844	60-64	RATES
65-69	1246	608	638	1267	606	661	1297	622	675	65-69	(IN 1000's)
70-74	849	409	440	907	435	472	923	434	489	70-74	
75-79	498	233	265	515	241	274	550	256	294	75-79	
80-84	242	111	131	234	106	128	243	110	133	80-84	
85+	101	42	59	107	46	61	104	44	60	85+	
TOTAL	37415	18618	18797	37970	18884	19086	38447	19115	19332	TOTAL	

STANDARD COUNTRIES:	ENGLAND AND WALES 1961			UNITED STATES 1960			MEXICO 1960			
STANDARDIZED RATES PER THOUSAND	BOTH SEXES	MALES	FEMALES	BOTH SEXES	MALES	FEMALES	BOTH SEXES	MALES	FEMALES	TABLE 6
Birth	21.93	24.23*	20.75	22.33	22.46*	21.48	24.38	21.94*	23.75	STANDARDIZED
Death	26.48	29.79*	27.52	24.74	25.76*	24.24	20.93	20.45*	19.86	RATES
Increase	-4.55	-5.57*	-6.77	-2.42	-3.30*	-2.76	3.46	1.49*	3.88	

	OBSERVED POP. MALES	FEMALES	STATIONARY POP. MALES	FEMALES	STABLE POP. MALES	FEMALES	OBSERVED BIRTHS	NET MATERNITY FUNCTION	BIRTHS IN STABLE POP.	
μ	31.38894	31.91541	32.39654	33.15584	31.44962	32.16964	28.65263	28.93816	28.85349	TABLE 7
σ^2	437.2503	447.4815	452.8166	471.5004	444.8044	463.3463	38.84963	38.13032	37.97362	MOMENTS
κ_3	3769.280	3907.616	3621.116	3665.445	3969.328	4059.077	89.7933	73.2499	75.3019	AND
κ_4	-154040.	-159765.	-172951.	-195114.	-157000.	-177848.	-1077.897	-981.428	-953.469	CUMULANTS
β_1	0.169952	0.170411	0.141227	0.128176	0.179030	0.165629	0.137508	0.096784	0.103554	
β_2	2.194302	2.202132	2.156511	2.122346	2.206473	2.171603	2.285827	2.324979	2.338785	
κ	-0.065368	-0.065949	-0.054227	-0.048480	-0.068909	-0.062790	-0.059761	-0.046422	-0.049957	

VITAL STATISTICS		THOMPSON AGE RANGE	NRR	1000r	INTERVAL	BOURGEOIS-PICHAT AGE RANGE	NRR	1000b	1000d	1000r	COALE		TABLE 8
GRR	1.673										IBR	23.21	RATES FROM AGE DISTRIBUTIONS
NRR	1.063	0-4	1.01	0.34	26.90	5-29	1.00	23.91	23.98	-0.07	IDR	24.20	AND VITAL
TFR	3.427	5-9	0.99	-0.28	26.78	30-54	1.03	23.72	22.70	1.02	IRI	-0.99	STATISTICS
GENERATION	28.896	10-14	1.05	1.88	26.73	55-79	1.30	38.10	28.43	9.67	K1	-4.32	(Females)
SEX RATIO	104.850	15-19	1.07	2.68	26.63	*35-59	1.07	25.53	22.89	2.64	K2	0.	

Start Age Interval	ORIGINAL MATRIX SUBDIAGONAL	ALTERNATIVE FIRST ROWS Projection	Integral	FIRST STABLE MATRIX % IN STABLE POPULATION	FISHER VALUES	REPRODUCTIVE VALUES	SECOND STABLE MATRIX Z₂ FIRST COLUMN	FIRST ROW	
0	0.92151	0.00000	0.00000	9.769	1.254	2217391	0.1424+0.0655	0.1424+0.0655	TABLE 9
5	0.97213	0.00000	0.00000	8.908	1.375	2182008	0.1435-0.0990	0.0148+0.1402	LESLIE
10	0.97362	0.03274	0.00000	8.569	1.430	2253678	-0.0139-0.2041	-0.0963+0.0719	MATRIX
15	0.96613	0.18422	0.06761	8.255	1.442	2263093	-0.2145-0.1085	-0.0992-0.0414	AND ITS
20	0.95827	0.33905	0.31340	7.892	1.269	2120942	-0.2365+0.1504	-0.0401-0.1038	SPECTRAL
25	0.95199	0.33617	0.38433	7.483	0.895	1173832	0.0099+0.3240	0.0091-0.0988	COMPONENTS
30	0.95216	0.24616	0.30628	7.049	0.507	656890	0.3259+0.1804	0.0277-0.0603	(Females)
35	0.95106	0.13566	0.19812	6.642	0.214	266960	0.3695-0.2161	0.0206-0.0230	
40	0.94652	0.03903	0.07847	6.250	0.048	56728	0.0034-0.4913	0.0061-0.0042	
45	0.93536	0.00000	0.00000	5.854	0.000	4	-0.4805-0.2900	0.0000-0.0000	
50	0.91642	0.00000	0.00000	5.418	0.000	1	-0.5585+0.2992	0.0000-0.0000	
55+	0.73336			17.909					

Start Age Interval	OBSERVED POPUL. (IN 100's)	CONTRIBUTIONS OF ROOTS (IN 100's) r_1	r_2, r_3	r_4-r_{11}	AGE-SP. BIRTH RATES	NET MATERNITY FUNCTION	COEFF. OF MATRIX EQUATION	PARAMETERS	INTEGRAL	MATRIX	EXP. INCREASE x	$e^{(x+2\frac{1}{2})r}$	
0	17683	18238	-374	-181	0.0000	0.0000	0.0000	L(1)	1.01060	1.01061	0	1.0053	TABLE 10
5	15867	16630	-754	-10	0.0000	0.0000	0.0000	L(2)	0.41834	0.42318	50	1.1171	AGE
10	15764	15997	-416	183	0.0000	0.0000	0.0293		0.73132	0.71235	55	1.1290	ANALYSIS
15	15697	15412	540	-255	0.0168	0.0587	0.1607	R(1)	0.00211	0.00211	60	1.1409	AND
20	16713	14733	1213	766	0.0778	0.2627	0.2857	R(2)	-0.03427	-0.03761	65	1.1530	MISCELLANEOUS
25	13120	13970	705	-1555	0.0954	0.3087	0.2715		0.21024	0.20695	70	1.1653	RESULTS
30	12957	13160	-785	582	0.0760	0.2342	0.1892	C(1)		186686	75	1.1776	(Females)
35	12481	12399	-1852	1934	0.0492	0.1443	0.0993	C(2)		-183765	80	1.1901	
40	11714	11669	-1136	1181	0.0195	0.0543	0.0272			-114335	85	1.2027	
45	11185	10929	1103	-846	0.0000	0.0000	0.0000	2P/Y	29.8859	30.3607	90	1.2155	
50	10150	10115	2737	-2702	0.0000	0.0000	0.0000	DELTA	1.8557		95	1.2284	
55+	31572	33434									100	1.2414	

Excluding L'Alsace-Lorraine

TABLE 1 — DATA

AGE AT LAST BIRTHDAY	POPULATION BOTH SEXES	MALES Number	MALES %	FEMALES Number	FEMALES %	BIRTHS BY AGE OF MOTHER	DEATHS BOTH SEXES	DEATHS MALES	DEATHS FEMALES	AGE AT LAST BIRTHDAY
0	698891	355216	1.9	343675	1.8	0	155535	86330	69205	0
1-4	2768746	1394027	7.5	1374719	7.3	0	80174	40717	39457	1-4
5-9	3566463	1706880	9.2	1859583	9.8	0	22818	11187	11631	5-9
10-14	3149075	1593525	8.6	1555550	8.2	0	13665	6323	7342	10-14
15-19	3237851	1627666	8.7	1610185	8.5	54429	19665	9178	10487	15-19
20-24	3366888	1625423	8.7	1741465	9.2	265508	27438	14989	12449	20-24
25-29	2557391	1296374	7.0	1261017	6.7	243751	24902	12489	12413	25-29
30-34	2608919	1315487	7.1	1293432	6.8	197920	25614	12953	12661	30-34
35-39	2535095	1281115	6.9	1253980	6.6	124924	26209	13667	12542	35-39
40-44	2391534	1203629	6.5	1187905	6.3	46923	27920	15332	12588	40-44
45-49	2228677	1107120	5.9	1121557	5.9	0	29783	16033	13750	45-49
50-54	2042036	1007691	5.4	1034345	5.5	0	35260	19372	15888	50-54
55-59	1806128	889831	4.8	916297	4.8	0	40982	22203	18779	55-59
60-64	1571079	779478	4.2	791601	4.2	0	52551	27553	24998	60-64
65-69	1234466	602221	3.2	632245	3.3	0	61403	31796	29607	65-69
70-74	873144	424919	2.3	448225	2.4		67549	34326	33223	70-74
75-79	526024	249939	1.3	276085	1.5		59861	29747	30114	75-79
80-84	263674	121722	0.7	141952	0.8	473249 M.	45835	21909	23926	80-84
85+	115090	48325	0.3	66765	0.4	460206 F.	24149	9947	14202	85+
TOTAL	37541171	18630588		18910583		933455	841313	436051	405262	TOTAL

TABLE 2 — MALE LIFE TABLE

x	$_nq_x$	l_x	$_nd_x$	$_nL_x$	$_nm_x$	$_na_x$	T_x	r_x	$\dot{e}_x$	$_nM_x$	x
0	0.209281	100000	20928	86111	0.243035	0.3364	4021813	0.0000	40.218	0.243035	0
1	0.107994	79072	8539	292360	0.029208	1.1979	3935702	0.0000	49.774	0.029208	1
5	0.032242	70533	2274	346978	0.006554	2.5000	3643342	0.0000	51.655	0.006554	5
10	0.019640	68258	1341	337855	0.003968	2.4360	3296364	0.0000	48.292	0.003968	10
15	0.027829	66918	1862	330266	0.005639	2.6787	2958509	0.0000	44.211	0.005639	15
20	0.045158	65056	2938	318154	0.009234	2.5752	2628243	0.0142	40.400	0.009222	20
25	0.047040	62118	2922	303265	0.009635	2.4933	2310088	0.0115	37.189	0.009634	25
30	0.048050	59196	2844	288869	0.009847	2.5005	2006824	0.0000	33.901	0.009847	30
35	0.051972	56351	2929	274530	0.010668	2.5324	1717954	0.0000	30.486	0.010668	35
40	0.061760	53423	3299	258985	0.012740	2.5365	1443424	0.0020	27.019	0.012738	40
45	0.069952	50123	3506	242056	0.014485	2.5584	1184439	0.0027	23.630	0.014482	45
50	0.091859	46617	4282	222687	0.019230	2.5717	942383	0.0026	20.215	0.019224	50
55	0.117643	42335	4980	199599	0.024952	2.5754	719696	0.0000	17.000	0.024952	55
60	0.162920	37355	6086	172045	0.035373	2.5800	520097	0.0047	13.923	0.035348	60
65	0.233978	31269	7316	138463	0.052839	2.5560	348052	0.0047	11.131	0.052798	65
70	0.336212	23953	8053	99614	0.080843	2.4981	209589	0.0047	8.750	0.080782	70
75	0.455515	15899	7242	60806	0.119106	2.4193	109975	0.0047	6.917	0.119017	75
80	0.606086	8657	5247	29129	0.180128	2.3478	49168	0.0047	5.680	0.179992	80
85+	1.000000	3410	3410	20040	0.170166	5.8766	20040	0.0047	5.877	0.205835	85

TABLE 3 — FEMALE LIFE TABLE

x	$_nq_x$	l_x	$_nd_x$	$_nL_x$	$_nm_x$	$_na_x$	T_x	r_x	$\dot{e}_x$	$_nM_x$	x
0	0.178242	100000	17824	88516	0.201368	0.3557	4284840	0.0000	42.848	0.201368	0
1	0.106353	82176	8740	304498	0.028702	1.2305	4196324	0.0000	51.065	0.028702	1
5	0.030792	73436	2261	361527	0.006255	2.5000	3891826	0.0000	52.996	0.006255	5
10	0.023325	71175	1660	351717	0.004720	2.4959	3530298	0.0089	49.600	0.004720	10
15	0.032056	69515	2228	342150	0.006513	2.5662	3178581	0.0000	45.725	0.006513	15
20	0.035190	67286	2368	330699	0.007160	2.5787	2836431	0.0168	42.155	0.007149	20
25	0.048110	64919	3123	316906	0.009855	2.5390	2505733	0.0205	38.598	0.009844	25
30	0.047766	61795	2952	301545	0.009789	2.4822	2188826	0.0000	35.421	0.009789	30
35	0.048787	58844	2871	287028	0.010002	2.4955	1887282	0.0000	32.073	0.010002	35
40	0.051629	55973	2890	272700	0.010597	2.5208	1600254	0.0004	28.590	0.010597	40
45	0.059520	53083	3159	257685	0.012261	2.5533	1327554	0.0013	25.009	0.012260	45
50	0.074081	49924	3698	240655	0.015368	2.5766	1069870	0.0046	21.430	0.015360	50
55	0.097765	46225	4519	220333	0.020511	2.6119	829215	0.0051	17.939	0.020494	55
60	0.146875	41706	6126	193834	0.031602	2.6009	608882	0.0044	14.599	0.031579	60
65	0.210403	35580	7486	159743	0.046864	2.5744	415048	0.0044	11.665	0.046828	65
70	0.313206	28094	8799	118628	0.074176	2.5176	255305	0.0044	9.087	0.074121	70
75	0.426576	19295	8231	75405	0.109153	2.4402	136677	0.0044	7.084	0.109075	75
80	0.581729	11064	6436	38158	0.168674	2.3834	61272	0.0044	5.538	0.168550	80
85+	1.000000	4628	4628	23114	0.200218	4.9945	23114	0.0044	4.995	0.212715	85

TABLE 4 — OBSERVED AND PROJECTED VITAL RATES

	OBSERVED POPULATION BOTH SEXES	MALES	FEMALES	PROJECTED POPULATION 1886 MALES	1886 FEMALES	1891 MALES	1891 FEMALES	1896 MALES	1896 FEMALES	STABLE POPULATION MALES	FEMALES
RATES PER THOUSAND											
Birth	24.86	25.40	24.34	26.02	24.83	26.07	24.79	26.34	24.97	25.67	24.1?
Death	22.41	23.41	21.43	24.04	22.03	24.19	22.22	24.29	22.35	24.68	23.1?
Increase	2.45	2.00	2.91	1.98	2.80	1.88	2.57	2.05	2.62		0.992?
PERCENTAGE											
under 15	27.13	27.10	27.15	27.07	27.31	26.88	26.37	27.33	26.95	27.10	26.4?
15-64	64.85	65.13	64.58	64.83	64.16	64.99	64.97	64.51	64.23	64.59	64.2?
65 and over	8.02	7.77	8.28	8.11	8.53	8.13	8.66	8.17	8.82	8.31	9.3?
DEP. RATIO X 100	54.20	53.54	54.86	54.26	55.85	53.88	53.92	55.02	55.69	54.83	55.7?

France 1884–88
Excluding L'Alsace-Lorraine

TABLE 1 — DATA

AGE AT LAST BIRTHDAY	POPULATION BOTH SEXES	MALES Number	MALES %	FEMALES Number	FEMALES %	BIRTHS BY AGE OF MOTHER	DEATHS BOTH SEXES	DEATHS MALES	FEMALES	AGE AT LAST BIRTHDAY
0	699777	354847	1.9	344930	1.8	0	152916	84690	68226	0
1-4	2787584	1402341	7.4	1385243	7.3	0	80723	41295	39428	1-4
5-9	3397346	1701743	9.0	1695603	8.9	0	21149	10386	10763	5-9
10-14	3340856	1682662	8.9	1658194	8.7	0	13698	6395	7303	10-14
15-19	3216123	1603744	8.5	1612379	8.5	51057	19442	9166	10276	15-19
20-24	3579607	1740010	9.2	1839597	9.7	258814	27248	14927	12321	20-24
25-29	2712069	1384560	7.3	1327509	7.0	244709	25116	12613	12503	25-29
30-34	2589492	1304802	6.9	1284690	6.7	190418	25220	13008	12212	30-34
35-39	2542862	1276134	6.8	1266728	6.7	121330	26195	13772	12423	35-39
40-44	2370058	1193008	6.3	1177050	6.2	45097	29120	15970	13150	40-44
45-49	2236847	1117739	5.9	1119108	5.9	0	30491	16927	13564	45-49
50-54	2035483	1004030	5.3	1031453	5.4	0	35387	19355	16032	50-54
55-59	1803992	895069	4.7	908923	4.8	0	41339	22338	19001	55-59
60-64	1571825	768389	4.1	803436	4.2	0	53578	28290	25288	60-64
65-69	1242307	604726	3.2	637581	3.3	0	62360	32221	30139	65-69
70-74	892406	434947	2.3	457459	2.4		71056	35994	35062	70-74
75-79	546564	263871	1.4	282693	1.5		61921	30629	31292	75-79
80-84	250756	116532	0.6	134224	0.7	465962 M.	43713	20705	23008	80-84
85+	118271	51706	0.3	66565	0.3	445463 F.	26645	11335	15310	85+
TOTAL	37934225	18900860		19033365		911425	847317	440016	407301	TOTAL

TABLE 2 — MALE LIFE TABLE

x	$_nq_x$	l_x	$_nd_x$	$_nL_x$	$_nm_x$	$_na_x$	T_x	r_x	$\dot{e}_x$	$_nM_x$	x
0	0.206154	100000	20615	86378	0.238666	0.3392	4040378	0.0000	40.404	0.238666	0
1	0.108824	79385	8639	293370	0.029447	1.2024	3954001	0.0000	49.808	0.029447	1
5	0.030057	70746	2126	348412	0.006103	2.5000	3660631	0.0000	51.744	0.006103	5
10	0.018821	68619	1291	339820	0.003800	2.4633	3312219	0.0012	48.270	0.003801	10
15	0.028200	67328	1899	332196	0.005715	2.6601	2972398	0.0000	44.148	0.005715	15
20	0.042040	65429	2751	320456	0.008583	2.5678	2640202	0.0066	40.352	0.008587	20
25	0.044566	62679	2793	306443	0.009115	2.5121	2319746	0.0195	37.010	0.009110	25
30	0.048641	59885	2913	292186	0.009969	2.5144	2013303	0.0000	33.619	0.009969	30
35	0.052565	56972	2995	277497	0.010792	2.5407	1721117	0.0000	30.210	0.010792	35
40	0.064799	53978	3498	261288	0.013386	2.5412	1443621	0.0001	26.745	0.013386	40
45	0.073015	50480	3686	243354	0.015146	2.5459	1182333	0.0016	23.422	0.015144	45
50	0.092088	46794	4309	223471	0.019283	2.5636	938979	0.0028	20.066	0.019277	50
55	0.117699	42485	5000	200347	0.024959	2.5846	715508	0.0006	16.841	0.024957	55
60	0.169145	37484	6340	172060	0.036849	2.5771	515161	0.0057	13.743	0.036817	60
65	0.235859	31144	7346	137736	0.053331	2.5516	343101	0.0057	11.017	0.053282	65
70	0.342877	23799	8160	98518	0.082828	2.4908	205365	0.0057	8.629	0.082755	70
75	0.446601	15639	6984	60118	0.116176	2.4120	106848	0.0057	6.832	0.116076	75
80	0.601899	8654	5209	29289	0.177848	2.3585	46730	0.0057	5.400	0.177676	80
85+	1.000000	3445	3445	17441	0.197545	5.0621	17441	0.0057	5.062	0.219221	85+

TABLE 3 — FEMALE LIFE TABLE

x	$_nq_x$	l_x	$_nd_x$	$_nL_x$	$_nm_x$	$_na_x$	T_x	r_x	$\dot{e}_x$	$_nM_x$	x
0	0.175475	100000	17547	88715	0.197797	0.3569	4311940	0.0000	43.119	0.197797	0
1	0.105539	82453	8702	305729	0.028463	1.2326	4223225	0.0000	51.220	0.028463	1
5	0.031242	73751	2304	362993	0.006348	2.5000	3917497	0.0000	53.118	0.006348	5
10	0.021780	71446	1556	353319	0.004404	2.4851	3554504	0.0000	49.751	0.004404	10
15	0.031379	69890	2193	344110	0.006373	2.5643	3201185	0.0000	45.803	0.006373	15
20	0.032990	67697	2233	333075	0.006705	2.5770	2857075	0.0121	42.204	0.006698	20
25	0.046106	65464	3018	319913	0.009435	2.5459	2523999	0.0271	38.556	0.009418	25
30	0.046420	62446	2899	304946	0.009506	2.4879	2204087	0.0000	35.296	0.009506	30
35	0.047868	59547	2850	290647	0.009807	2.5134	1899140	0.0000	31.893	0.009807	35
40	0.054358	56696	3082	275841	0.011173	2.5206	1608493	0.0014	28.370	0.011172	40
45	0.058854	53615	3155	260330	0.012121	2.5462	1332652	0.0006	24.856	0.012120	45
50	0.074942	50459	3782	243153	0.015552	2.5823	1072322	0.0050	21.251	0.015543	50
55	0.099588	46678	4649	222261	0.020915	2.6064	829169	0.0031	17.764	0.020905	55
60	0.146438	42029	6155	195377	0.031501	2.6004	606908	0.0051	14.440	0.031475	60
65	0.212273	35874	7615	160949	0.047314	2.5807	411531	0.0051	11.471	0.047271	65
70	0.322138	28259	9103	118672	0.076710	2.5148	250582	0.0051	8.867	0.076645	70
75	0.431236	19156	8261	74567	0.110783	2.4321	131910	0.0051	6.886	0.110693	75
80	0.588475	10895	6412	37371	0.171566	2.3773	57343	0.0051	5.263	0.171415	80
85+	1.000000	4484	4484	19972	0.224495	4.4544	19972	0.0051	4.454	0.230000	85+

TABLE 4 — OBSERVED AND PROJECTED TOTAL RATES

RATES PER THOUSAND	OBSERVED POPULATION BOTH SEXES	OBSERVED MALES	OBSERVED FEMALES	PROJECTED 1891 MALES	PROJECTED 1891 FEMALES	PROJECTED 1896 MALES	PROJECTED 1896 FEMALES	PROJECTED 1901 MALES	PROJECTED 1901 FEMALES	STABLE POPULATION MALES	STABLE POPULATION FEMALES
Birth	24.03	24.65	23.40	25.48	24.12	25.57	24.14	25.33	23.85	24.17	22.64
Death	22.34	23.28	21.40	23.71	21.78	23.92	22.01	23.92	22.08	24.90	23.36
Increase	1.69	1.37	2.01	1.76	2.33	1.65	2.13	1.41	1.77	-0.7239	
PERCENTAGE											
under 15	26.96	27.20	26.71	26.70	26.22	26.54	25.98	26.85	26.30	25.95	25.28
15-64	65.00	65.01	65.00	65.35	65.27	65.49	65.44	65.18	65.00	65.30	64.90
65 and over	8.04	7.79	8.29	7.95	8.50	7.97	8.58	7.97	8.71	8.74	9.82
DEP. RATIO X 100	53.84	53.82	53.86	53.02	53.20	52.69	52.81	53.42	53.86	53.13	54.09

TABLE 1 — DATA

AGE AT LAST BIRTHDAY	POPULATION BOTH SEXES	MALES Number	%	FEMALES Number	%	BIRTHS BY AGE OF MOTHER	DEATHS BOTH SEXES	MALES	FEMALES	AGE AT LAST BIRTHDAY
0	671859	338213	1.8	333646	1.7	0	146082	81304	64778	0
1-4	2650856	1329120	7.0	1321736	6.9	0	70329	35839	34490	1-4
5-9	3353519	1677146	8.9	1676373	8.7	0	18736	9063	9673	5-9
10-14	3326692	1670612	8.8	1656080	8.6	389	11985	5557	6428	10-14
15-19	3342341	1670595	8.8	1671746	8.7	44780	20006	9614	10392	15-19
20-24	3283377	1588355	8.4	1695022	8.8	221433	25066	13766	11300	20-24
25-29	2920258	1477129	7.8	1443129	7.5	249011	23731	11940	11791	25-29
30-34	2719756	1373947	7.3	1345809	7.0	186442	24607	12786	11821	30-34
35-39	2550390	1282872	6.8	1267518	6.6	113472	24871	13532	11339	35-39
40-44	2401764	1190859	6.3	1210905	6.3	44524	27801	15367	12434	40-44
45-49	2296491	1146233	6.1	1150258	6.0	2616	29893	16826	13067	45-49
50-54	2050155	1018323	5.4	1031832	5.4	413	35271	19566	15705	50-54
55-59	1799550	882192	4.7	917358	4.8	0	41671	22756	18915	55-59
60-64	1610692	787981	4.2	822711	4.3	0	57846	30221	27625	60-64
65-69	1269797	612958	3.2	656839	3.4	0	67871	34667	33204	65-69
70-74	935624	449882	2.4	485742	2.5		79086	39651	39435	70-74
75-79	577913	270286	1.4	307627	1.6		73947	36026	37921	75-79
80-84	265707	118931	0.6	146776	0.8	441281 M.	50436	23538	26898	80-84
85+	112345	46314	0.2	66031	0.3	421799 F.	29112	12376	16736	85+
TOTAL	38139086	18931948		19207138		863080	858347	444395	413952	TOTAL

TABLE 2 — MALE LIFE TABLE

x	$_nq_x$	l_x	$_nd_x$	$_nL_x$	$_nm_x$	$_na_x$	T_x	r_x	$\dot{e}_x$	$_nM_x$	x
0	0.207039	100000	20704	86125	0.240393	0.3298	4090052	0.0000	40.901	0.240393	0
1	0.100256	79296	7950	294830	0.026964	1.1881	4003927	0.0000	50.493	0.026964	1
5	0.026659	71346	1902	351976	0.005404	2.5000	3709097	0.0000	51.987	0.005404	5
10	0.016495	69444	1145	344365	0.003326	2.5068	3357121	0.0000	48.343	0.003326	10
15	0.028395	68299	1939	336993	0.005755	2.6795	3012756	0.0000	44.111	0.005755	15
20	0.042441	66359	2816	324876	0.008669	2.5428	2675763	0.0044	40.322	0.008667	20
25	0.039618	63543	2517	311413	0.008084	2.4967	2350887	0.0060	36.997	0.008083	25
30	0.045499	61026	2777	298286	0.009309	2.5359	2039474	0.0048	33.420	0.009306	30
35	0.051423	58249	2995	283898	0.010551	2.5472	1741188	0.0035	29.892	0.010548	35
40	0.062536	55254	3455	267770	0.012904	2.5407	1457291	0.0000	26.375	0.012904	40
45	0.070856	51798	3670	250017	0.014680	2.5548	1189521	0.0004	22.965	0.014679	45
50	0.091865	48128	4421	229928	0.019229	2.5771	939504	0.0067	19.521	0.019214	50
55	0.121429	43707	5307	205748	0.025795	2.5910	709576	0.0000	16.235	0.025795	55
60	0.175497	38399	6739	175683	0.038359	2.5791	503828	0.0011	13.121	0.038352	60
65	0.248396	31660	7864	139027	0.056567	2.5490	328145	0.0011	10.365	0.056557	65
70	0.360954	23796	8589	97437	0.088152	2.4918	189118	0.0011	7.947	0.088136	70
75	0.494959	15207	7527	56460	0.133312	2.3993	91681	0.0011	6.029	0.133288	75
80	0.644862	7680	4953	25019	0.197953	2.2981	35221	0.0011	4.586	0.197914	80
85+	*1.000000	2727	2727	10202	0.267339	3.7406	10202	0.0011	3.741	0.267219	85

TABLE 3 — FEMALE LIFE TABLE

x	$_nq_x$	l_x	$_nd_x$	$_nL_x$	$_nm_x$	$_na_x$	T_x	r_x	$\dot{e}_x$	$_nM_x$	x
0	0.172416	100000	17242	88804	0.194152	0.3507	4408843	0.0000	44.088	0.194152	0
1	0.097322	82758	8054	308655	0.026094	1.2215	4320038	0.0000	52.201	0.026094	1
5	0.028441	74704	2125	368210	0.005770	2.5000	4011383	0.0000	53.697	0.005770	5
10	0.019221	72580	1395	359422	0.003881	2.5082	3643174	0.0000	50.196	0.003881	10
15	0.030621	71185	2180	350654	0.006216	2.5831	3283752	0.0000	46.130	0.006216	15
20	0.032811	69005	2264	339467	0.006670	2.5456	2933097	0.0078	42.506	0.006667	20
25	0.040079	66741	2675	327118	0.008177	2.5381	2593631	0.0151	38.861	0.008170	25
30	0.042978	64066	2753	313447	0.008784	2.5006	2266513	0.0043	35.378	0.008784	30
35	0.043758	61312	2683	299892	0.008946	2.5142	1953066	0.0014	31.854	0.008946	35
40	0.050071	58629	2936	285891	0.010268	2.5281	1653174	0.0000	28.197	0.010268	40
45	0.055289	55694	3079	270965	0.011364	2.5629	1367283	0.0041	24.550	0.011360	45
50	0.073476	52615	3866	253765	0.015234	2.5923	1096318	0.0073	20.837	0.015221	50
55	0.098299	48749	4792	232381	0.020621	2.6289	842554	0.0005	17.284	0.020619	55
60	0.155412	43957	6831	203448	0.033578	2.6087	610173	0.0000	13.881	0.033578	60
65	0.225123	37125	8358	165333	0.050551	2.5719	406725	0.0000	10.955	0.050551	65
70	0.337707	28768	9715	119665	0.081185	2.5118	241392	0.0000	8.391	0.081185	70
75	0.467574	19053	8908	72268	0.123269	2.4188	121727	0.0000	6.389	0.123269	75
80	0.615469	10144	6243	34069	0.183258	2.3329	49459	0.0000	4.876	0.183258	80
85+	*1.000000	3901	3901	15390	0.253457	3.9454	15390	0.0000	3.945	0.253457	85

TABLE 4 — OBSERVED AND PROJECTED VITAL RATES

	OBSERVED POPULATION BOTH SEXES	MALES	FEMALES	PROJECTED POPULATION 1896 MALES	FEMALES	1901 MALES	FEMALES	1906 MALES	FEMALES	STABLE POPULATION MALES	FEMALES
RATES PER THOUSAND											
Birth	22.63	23.31	21.96	24.11	22.64	24.33	22.77	24.10	22.50	22.74	21.─
Death	22.51	23.47	21.55	23.57	21.59	23.63	21.63	23.59	21.60	24.95	23.─
Increase	0.12	-0.16	0.41	0.53	1.05	0.70	1.15	0.50	0.89	-2.21	
PERCENTAGE											
under 15	26.23	26.49	25.97	25.87	25.33	25.54	24.93	25.90	25.25	24.90	24.─
15-64	65.48	65.60	65.37	66.29	66.10	66.82	66.64	66.47	66.31	66.34	65.─
65 and over	8.29	7.91	8.66	7.84	8.57	7.65	8.43	7.63	8.44	8.76	10.─
DEP. RATIO X 100	52.71	52.45	52.97	50.85	51.28	49.67	50.06	50.43	50.80	50.74	51.─

France 1894–98
Excluding L'Alsace-Lorraine

TABLE 1 / DATA

AGE AT LAST BIRTHDAY	POPULATION BOTH SEXES	MALES Number	%	FEMALES Number	%	BIRTHS BY AGE OF MOTHER	DEATHS BOTH SEXES	MALES	FEMALES	AGE AT LAST BIRTHDAY
0	656340	331524	1.8	324816	1.7	0	136975	76225	60750	0
1-4	2657661	1327093	7.0	1330568	6.9	0	54617	27880	26737	1-4
5-9	3299354	1650024	8.7	1649330	8.5	0	14817	7163	7654	5-9
10-14	3334432	1670326	8.8	1664106	8.6	408	10396	4746	5650	10-14
15-19	3351391	1673176	8.8	1678215	8.7	42255	17546	8535	9011	15-19
20-24	3337484	1621331	8.6	1716153	8.9	217281	24448	13447	11001	20-24
25-29	2879311	1437397	7.6	1441914	7.4	242520	21927	11074	10853	25-29
30-34	2789897	1397594	7.4	1392303	7.2	184114	23366	12208	11158	30-34
35-39	2642486	1324916	7.0	1317570	6.8	115126	24380	13365	11015	35-39
40-44	2389239	1194843	6.3	1194396	6.2	43141	25487	14455	11032	40-44
45-49	2272070	1119401	5.9	1152669	6.0	6068	29070	16396	12674	45-49
50-54	2070748	1016612	5.4	1054136	5.4	724	33782	19058	14724	50-54
55-59	1817840	892004	4.7	925836	4.8	0	40900	22585	18315	55-59
60-64	1587273	767903	4.1	819370	4.2	0	52700	27963	24737	60-64
65-69	1284966	613816	3.2	671150	3.5	0	64339	33294	31045	65-69
70-74	933951	442543	2.3	491408	2.5		75026	37935	37091	70-74
75-79	580081	269984	1.4	310097	1.6		71367	34848	36519	75-79
80-84	281501	124786	0.7	156715	0.8	434348 M.	50897	23602	27295	80-84
85+	112076	47092	0.2	64984	0.3	417289 F.	28076	11710	16366	85+
TOTAL	38278101	18922365		19355736		851637	800116	416489	383627	TOTAL

TABLE 2 / MALE / FEMALE / ...BLE

x	$_nq_x$	l_x	$_nd_x$	$_nL_x$	$_nm_x$	$_na_x$	T_x	r_x	$\overset{\circ}{e}_x$	$_nM_x$	x
0	0.198446	100000	19845	86310	0.229923	0.3101	4303467	0.0000	43.035	0.229923	0
1	0.079304	80155	6357	302579	0.021008	1.1616	4217157	0.0000	52.612	0.021008	1
5	0.021473	73799	1585	365032	0.004341	2.5000	3914578	0.0000	53.044	0.004341	5
10	0.014108	72214	1019	358567	0.002841	2.5430	3549546	0.0000	49.153	0.002841	10
15	0.025211	71195	1795	351865	0.005101	2.7093	3190979	0.0000	44.820	0.005101	15
20	0.040665	69400	2822	340097	0.008298	2.5532	2839114	0.0077	40.909	0.008294	20
25	0.037794	66578	2516	326583	0.007705	2.4931	2499017	0.0067	37.535	0.007704	25
30	0.042756	64062	2739	313567	0.008735	2.5383	2172434	0.0000	33.911	0.008735	30
35	0.049237	61323	3019	299209	0.010091	2.5474	1858867	0.0055	30.313	0.010087	35
40	0.058770	58304	3427	283131	0.012102	2.5524	1559668	0.0047	26.751	0.012098	40
45	0.070718	54877	3881	264922	0.014649	2.5616	1276527	0.0012	23.262	0.014647	45
50	0.089693	50996	4574	243892	0.018754	2.5756	1011604	0.0036	19.837	0.018747	50
55	0.119334	46422	5540	218735	0.025326	2.5854	767713	0.0019	16.538	0.025319	55
60	0.167407	40883	6844	187848	0.036434	2.5796	548978	0.0034	13.428	0.036415	60
65	0.239614	34038	8156	150280	0.054273	2.5586	361130	0.0034	10.609	0.054241	65
70	0.353097	25882	9139	106552	0.085770	2.4987	210850	0.0034	8.146	0.085720	70
75	0.483616	16743	8097	62699	0.129146	2.4044	104298	0.0034	6.229	0.129074	75
80	0.627259	8646	5423	28656	0.189253	2.3127	41598	0.0034	4.811	0.189141	80
85+	*1.000000	3223	3223	12942	0.249014	4.0158	12942	0.0034	4.016	0.248662	85+

TABLE 3 / MALE / FEMALE / BLE

x	$_nq_x$	l_x	$_nd_x$	$_nL_x$	$_nm_x$	$_na_x$	T_x	r_x	$\overset{\circ}{e}_x$	$_nM_x$	x
0	0.166180	100000	16618	88853	0.187029	0.3292	4659241	0.0000	46.592	0.187029	0
1	0.076078	83382	6344	315685	0.020094	1.1872	4570388	0.0000	54.813	0.020094	1
5	0.022937	77038	1767	380775	0.004641	2.5000	4254703	0.0000	55.228	0.004641	5
10	0.016835	75271	1267	373230	0.003395	2.5320	3873928	0.0000	51.466	0.003395	10
15	0.026540	74004	1962	365327	0.005369	2.6070	3500699	0.0000	47.304	0.005369	15
20	0.031576	72043	2275	354655	0.006414	2.5566	3135372	0.0087	43.521	0.006410	20
25	0.036969	69768	2579	342467	0.007531	2.5295	2780717	0.0135	39.857	0.007527	25
30	0.039286	67189	2640	329357	0.008014	2.5051	2438250	0.0010	36.290	0.008014	30
35	0.040957	64549	2644	316168	0.008362	2.5123	2108893	0.0069	32.671	0.008360	35
40	0.045166	61905	2796	302645	0.009239	2.5389	1792725	0.0040	28.959	0.009236	40
45	0.053549	59109	3165	287839	0.010997	2.5650	1490080	0.0013	25.209	0.010995	45
50	0.067633	55944	3784	270629	0.013981	2.5972	1202241	0.0074	21.490	0.013968	50
55	0.094533	52160	4931	249072	0.019797	2.6212	931612	0.0046	17.861	0.019782	55
60	0.140849	47229	6652	220249	0.030203	2.6101	682540	0.0025	14.452	0.030190	60
65	0.208154	40577	8446	182515	0.046277	2.5881	462291	0.0025	11.393	0.046256	65
70	0.318208	32131	10224	135399	0.075513	2.5298	279777	0.0025	8.707	0.075479	70
75	0.452388	21907	9910	84117	0.117815	2.4354	144378	0.0025	6.591	0.117766	75
80	0.596196	11996	7152	41046	0.174248	2.3524	60261	0.0025	5.023	0.174170	80
85+	*1.000000	4844	4844	19215	0.252104	3.9666	19215	0.0025	3.967	0.251847	85+

TABLE 4 / OBSERVED AND PROJECTED TOTALS / RATES

	OBSERVED POPULATION BOTH SEXES	MALES	FEMALES	PROJECTED POPULATION 1901 MALES	FEMALES	1906 MALES	FEMALES	1911 MALES	FEMALES	STABLE POPULATION MALES	FEMALES
RATES PER THOUSAND											
Birth	22.25	22.95	21.56	23.60	22.08	23.67	22.06	23.33	21.68	22.16	20.43
Death	20.90	22.01	19.82	22.21	20.01	22.24	20.07	22.21	20.10	23.60	21.87
Increase	1.35	0.94	1.74	1.39	2.07	1.42	1.99	1.12	1.58		-1.4417
PERCENTAGE											
under 15	25.99	26.31	25.67	25.77	25.07	25.63	24.87	25.95	25.11	24.92	23.92
15-64	65.67	65.77	65.58	66.39	66.18	66.62	66.43	66.29	66.06	66.20	65.58
65 and over	8.34	7.92	8.75	7.84	8.75	7.75	8.70	7.77	8.82	8.89	10.49
DEP. RATIO X 100	52.27	52.05	52.50	50.63	51.10	50.11	50.53	50.86	51.37	51.06	52.48

Excluding L'Alsace-Lorraine

TABLE 1 — DATA

AGE AT LAST BIRTHDAY	POPULATION BOTH SEXES	MALES Number	%	FEMALES Number	%	BIRTHS BY AGE OF MOTHER	DEATHS BOTH SEXES	MALES	FEMALES	AGE AT LAST BIRTHDAY
0	719281	362618	1.9	356663	1.8	0	124135	68880	55255	0
1-4	2866454	1429137	7.6	1437317	7.4	0	48387	24706	23681	1-4
5-9	3227856	1612027	8.5	1615829	8.3	0	15182	7447	7735	5-9
10-14	3236017	1622301	8.6	1613716	8.3	290	10557	4840	5717	10-14
15-19	3272045	1631893	8.6	1640152	8.4	42934	16891	8247	8644	15-19
20-24	3181855	1564584	8.3	1617271	8.3	219755	23681	12625	11056	20-24
25-29	3015888	1501284	7.9	1514604	7.7	248512	22994	11479	11515	25-29
30-34	2790803	1382334	7.3	1408469	7.2	171632	22781	11827	10954	30-34
35-39	2683803	1335575	7.1	1348228	6.9	110173	25387	13791	11596	35-39
40-44	2469740	1228347	6.5	1241393	6.4	41694	26753	15133	11620	40-44
45-49	2244211	1112797	5.9	1131414	5.8	5339	29242	16745	12497	45-49
50-54	2088815	1001757	5.3	1087058	5.6	530	34638	19429	15209	50-54
55-59	1888670	918214	4.9	970456	5.0	0	42441	23609	18832	55-59
60-64	1633665	781715	4.1	851950	4.4	0	53654	28789	24865	60-64
65-69	1280084	601860	3.2	678224	3.5	0	65058	33460	31598	65-69
70-74	965692	445441	2.4	520251	2.7		76336	38325	38011	70-74
75-79	558034	251895	1.3	306139	1.6		72859	35399	37460	75-79
80-84	257939	109056	0.6	148883	0.8	428734 M.	52700	24295	28405	80-84
85+	91942	34269	0.2	57673	0.3	412125 F.	30208	12393	17815	85+
TOTAL	38472794	18927104		19545690		840859	793884	411419	382465	TOTAL

TABLE 2 — MALE LIFE TABLE

x	nq_x	l_x	nd_x	nL_x	nm_x	na_x	T_x	r_x	$\mathring{e}_x$	nM_x
0	0.168002	100000	16800	88445	0.189952	0.3122	4501977	0.0000	45.020	0.189952
1	0.065918	83200	5484	317247	0.017287	1.1642	4413532	0.0000	53.047	0.017287
5	0.022803	77715	1772	384147	0.004613	2.5000	4096285	0.0026	52.709	0.004620
10	0.014807	75943	1125	376925	0.002983	2.5179	3712139	0.0000	48.880	0.002983
15	0.024977	74819	1869	369789	0.005054	2.6964	3335214	0.0000	44.577	0.005054
20	0.039568	72950	2887	357692	0.008070	2.5548	2965425	0.0010	40.650	0.008069
25	0.037514	70063	2628	343734	0.007647	2.4952	2607733	0.0044	37.220	0.007646
30	0.041907	67435	2826	330241	0.008557	2.5461	2263999	0.0030	33.573	0.008556
35	0.050363	64609	3254	315086	0.010327	2.5541	1933759	0.0015	29.930	0.010326
40	0.059823	61355	3670	297794	0.012325	2.5531	1618672	0.0058	26.382	0.012320
45	0.072612	57685	4189	278220	0.015055	2.5639	1320878	0.0051	22.898	0.015048
50	0.092612	53496	4954	255446	0.019395	2.5709	1042658	0.0000	19.490	0.019395
55	0.121029	48542	5875	228492	0.025712	2.5802	787212	0.0000	16.217	0.025712
60	0.169097	42667	7215	195881	0.036833	2.5809	558720	0.0008	13.095	0.036828
65	0.244733	35452	8676	156042	0.055602	2.5545	362839	0.0008	10.235	0.055594
70	0.354213	26776	9484	110217	0.086051	2.5052	206797	0.0008	7.723	0.086038
75	0.515424	17291	8912	63410	0.140553	2.4140	96580	0.0008	5.585	0.140531
80	0.692956	8379	5806	26059	0.222817	2.2725	33170	0.0008	3.959	0.222776
85+	*1.000000	2573	2573	7112	0.361762	2.7642	7112	0.0008	2.764	0.361639

TABLE 3 — FEMALE LIFE TABLE

x	nq_x	l_x	nd_x	nL_x	nm_x	na_x	T_x	r_x	$\mathring{e}_x$	nM_x
0	0.140361	100000	14036	90601	0.154922	0.3303	4852944	0.0000	48.529	0.154922
1	0.062986	85964	5415	328635	0.016476	1.1889	4762343	0.0000	55.399	0.016476
5	0.023615	80549	1902	397992	0.004780	2.5000	4433709	0.0033	55.043	0.004787
10	0.017559	78647	1381	389806	0.003543	2.5164	4035717	0.0000	51.314	0.003543
15	0.026025	77266	2011	381543	0.005270	2.6191	3645911	0.0000	47.186	0.005270
20	0.033623	75255	2530	370098	0.006837	2.5579	3264367	0.0013	43.377	0.006836
25	0.037313	72725	2714	356871	0.007604	2.5108	2894270	0.0063	39.797	0.007603
30	0.038151	70011	2671	343405	0.007778	2.5095	2537399	0.0037	36.243	0.007777
35	0.042113	67340	2836	329671	0.008602	2.5206	2193994	0.0041	32.581	0.008601
40	0.045765	64505	2952	315242	0.009364	2.5335	1864323	0.0080	28.902	0.009360
45	0.053788	61552	3311	299692	0.011047	2.5623	1549081	0.0020	25.167	0.011045
50	0.067682	58242	3942	281714	0.013993	2.5913	1249389	0.0009	21.452	0.013991
55	0.092793	54300	5039	259482	0.019418	2.6150	967676	0.0042	17.821	0.019405
60	0.136496	49261	6724	230302	0.029196	2.6200	708194	0.0019	14.376	0.029186
65	0.209466	42537	8910	191180	0.046606	2.5863	477892	0.0019	11.235	0.046589
70	0.309722	33627	10415	142497	0.073090	2.5384	286712	0.0019	8.526	0.073063
75	0.466456	23212	10827	88454	0.122408	2.4503	144215	0.0019	6.213	0.122363
80	0.632414	12385	7832	41035	0.190865	2.3331	55761	0.0019	4.502	0.190788
85+	*1.000000	4552	4552	14726	0.309146	3.2347	14726	0.0019	3.235	0.308897

TABLE 4 — OBSERVED AND PROJECTED VITAL RATES

	OBSERVED POPULATION BOTH SEXES	MALES	FEMALES	PROJECTED POPULATION 1906 MALES	FEMALES	1911 MALES	FEMALES	1916 MALES	FEMALES	STABLE POPULATION MALES	FEMALES
RATES PER THOUSAND											
Birth	21.86	22.65	21.09	22.82	21.19	22.61	20.95	22.27	20.61	21.70	20.1
Death	20.63	21.74	19.57	21.45	19.39	21.39	19.43	21.37	19.51	22.42	20.8
Increase	1.22	0.91	1.52	1.37	1.80	1.22	1.52	0.91	1.10		-0.715
PERCENTAGE											
under 15	26.12	26.55	25.70	26.44	25.52	26.57	25.53	26.23	25.10	25.45	24.4
15-64	65.68	65.82	65.54	66.00	65.69	65.87	65.61	66.29	65.89	66.26	65.4
65 and over	8.20	7.62	8.75	7.56	8.79	7.56	8.86	7.49	9.01	8.29	10.1
DEP. RATIO X 100	52.25	51.92	52.57	51.52	52.22	51.82	52.42	50.86	51.77	50.93	52.7

Excluding L'Alsace-Lorraine

TABLE 5 — POPULATION PROJECTED WITH FIXED AGE-SPECIFIC BIRTH AND DEATH RATES (IN 1000's)

AGE AT LAST BIRTHDAY	1906 BOTH SEXES	MALES	FEMALES	1911 BOTH SEXES	MALES	FEMALES	1916 BOTH SEXES	MALES	FEMALES	AGE AT LAST BIRTHDAY
0-4	3488	1750	1738	3502	1757	1745	3476	1744	1732	0-4
5-9	3400	1697	1703	3307	1657	1650	3321	1664	1657	5-9
10-14	3165	1582	1583	3333	1665	1668	3242	1626	1616	10-14
15-19	3172	1592	1580	3101	1552	1549	3266	1633	1633	15-19
20-24	3170	1579	1591	3072	1540	1532	3004	1501	1503	20-24
25-29	3063	1504	1559	3051	1517	1534	2956	1479	1477	25-29
30-34	2899	1442	1457	2946	1445	1501	2933	1457	1476	30-34
35-39	2671	1319	1352	2775	1376	1399	2819	1378	1441	35-39
40-44	2551	1262	1289	2540	1247	1293	2639	1301	1338	40-44
45-49	2328	1148	1180	2405	1179	1226	2394	1165	1229	45-49
50-54	2086	1022	1064	2163	1054	1109	2235	1083	1152	50-54
55-59	1897	896	1001	1894	914	980	1964	942	1022	55-59
60-64	1648	787	861	1657	768	889	1652	783	869	60-64
65-69	1330	623	707	1342	627	715	1350	612	738	65-69
70-74	931	425	506	967	440	527	976	443	533	70-74
75-79	579	256	323	559	245	314	580	253	327	75-79
80-84	246	104	142	255	105	150	247	101	146	80-84
85+	83	30	53	79	28	51	83	29	54	85+
TOTAL	38707	19018	19689	38948	19116	19832	39137	19194	19943	TOTAL

TABLE 6 — STANDARDIZED RATES

STANDARD COUNTRIES: STANDARDIZED RATES PER THOUSAND	ENGLAND AND WALES 1961 BOTH SEXES	MALES	FEMALES	UNITED STATES 1960 BOTH SEXES	MALES	FEMALES	MEXICO 1960 BOTH SEXES	MALES	FEMALES
Birth	18.20	19.89*	17.28	18.48	18.55*	17.85	20.19	18.15*	19.74
Death	25.56	27.56*	26.16	23.13	23.95*	22.12	17.93	19.38*	16.59
Increase	-7.37	-7.67*	-8.87	-4.65	-5.40*	-4.28	2.26	-1.24*	3.15

TABLE 7 — MOMENTS AND CUMULANTS

	OBSERVED POP. MALES	FEMALES	STATIONARY POP. MALES	FEMALES	STABLE POP. MALES	FEMALES	OBSERVED BIRTHS	NET MATERNITY FUNCTION	BIRTHS IN STABLE POP.
μ	31.73444	32.59186	32.42634	33.73873	32.74327	34.07648	28.89484	29.08534	29.11596
σ^2	435.4943	454.8440	441.8395	470.9600	444.1594	473.2518	39.98396	40.67098	40.75468
κ_3	3706.867	3787.681	3303.480	3276.932	3181.668	3129.647	120.8951	117.2272	116.7645
κ_4	-149985.	-170358.	-167955.	-203373.	-172555.	-208346.	-571.557	-635.901	-646.980
β_1	0.166367	0.152461	0.126517	0.102798	0.115530	0.092409	0.228644	0.204269	0.201414
β_2	2.209182	2.176548	2.139670	2.083094	2.125319	2.069747	2.642490	2.615567	2.610474
κ	-0.065055	-0.058841	-0.048640	-0.038630	-0.044390	-0.034713	-0.131427	-0.118335	-0.116472

TABLE 8 — RATES FROM AGE DISTRIBUTIONS AND VITAL STATISTICS (Females)

VITAL STATISTICS		THOMPSON AGE RANGE	NRR	1000r	INTERVAL	BOURGEOIS-PICHAT AGE RANGE	NRR	1000b	1000d	1000r	COALE
GRR	1.394										IBR
NRR	0.979	0-4	1.02	0.85	26.98	5-29	0.93	20.54	23.40	-2.86	IDR
TFR	2.843	5-9	0.99	-0.36	26.89	30-54	1.12	24.00	19.96	4.04	IRI
GENERATION	29.100	10-14	1.03	1.16	26.82	55-79	1.06	21.71	19.43	2.28	K1
SEX RATIO	104.030	15-19	1.09	3.33	26.71	*20-44	1.14	24.88	19.97	4.90	K2

TABLE 9 — LESLIE MATRIX AND ITS SPECTRAL COMPONENTS (Females)

ORIGINAL MATRIX SUB-DIAGONAL	ALTERNATIVE FIRST ROWS Projection	Integral	FIRST STABLE MATRIX % IN STABLE POPULATION	FISHER VALUES	REPRODUCTIVE VALUES	SECOND STABLE MATRIX Z₂ FIRST COLUMN	FIRST ROW
0.94933	0.00000	0.00000	8.447	1.191	2135823	0.1441+0.0713	0.1441+0.0713
0.97943	0.00018	0.00000	8.048	1.250	2019175	0.1586-0.1022	0.0109+0.1365
0.97880	0.02651	0.00037	7.910	1.271	2051173	-0.0075-0.2283	-0.0921+0.0656
0.97000	0.16231	0.05369	7.770	1.262	2069436	-0.2418-0.1341	-0.0895-0.0394
0.96426	0.30215	0.27870	7.564	1.097	1773985	-0.2869+0.1663	-0.0342-0.0928
0.96227	0.28904	0.33654	7.320	0.760	1151764	-0.0056+0.3953	0.0069-0.0869
0.96001	0.20579	0.24994	7.069	0.430	605394	0.4002+0.2472	0.0224-0.0539
0.95623	0.11695	0.16761	6.811	0.191	257404	0.4957-0.2570	0.0178-0.0224
0.95067	0.03912	0.06889	6.536	0.053	66213	0.0403-0.6589	0.0064-0.0055
0.94001	0.00532	0.00968	6.236	0.007	7829	-0.6403-0.4383	0.0009-0.0007
0.92108	0.00050	0.00100	5.883	0.001	651	-0.8193+0.3770	0.0001-0.0001
0.73090			20.406				

TABLE 10 — AGE ANALYSIS AND MISCELLANEOUS RESULTS (Females)

OBSERVED POPUL. (IN 100's)	CONTRIBUTIONS OF ROOTS (IN 100's) r_1	r_2, r_3	$r_4 \cdot r_{11}$	AGE-SP. BIRTH RATES	NET MATERNITY FUNCTION	COEFF. OF MATRIX EQUATION	PARAMETERS INTEGRAL	MATRIX	EXP. INCREASE x	$e^{(x+2\frac{1}{2})r}$
17940	17507	8	425	0.0000	0.0000	0.0000	L(1) 0.99643	0.99643	0	0.9982
16158	16679	-117	-404	0.0000	0.0000	0.0002	L(2) 0.40903	0.41531	50	0.9631
16137	16395	-157	-101	0.0001	0.0003	0.0246	0.71268	0.69400	55	0.9597
16402	16105	-23	320	0.0128	0.0490	0.1477	R(1) -0.00072	-0.00072	60	0.9563
16173	15677	199	297	0.0666	0.2465	0.2667	R(2) -0.03927	-0.04245	65	0.9529
15146	15171	277	-302	0.0804	0.2870	0.2460	0.20995	0.20631	70	0.9495
14085	14651	56	-623	0.0597	0.2051	0.1686	C(1)	207256	75	0.9461
13482	14116	-322	-311	0.0401	0.1320	0.0920	C(2)	-14451	80	0.9427
12414	13546	-470	-662	0.0165	0.0519	0.0294		-34789	85	0.9393
11314	12924	-120	-1490	0.0023	0.0069	0.0038	2P/Y 29.9265	30.4556	90	0.9360
10871	12192	499	-1821	0.0002	0.0007	0.0003	DELTA 3.2811		95	0.9326
35336	42294								100	0.9293

Excluding L'Alsace-Lorraine

TABLE 1 — DATA

AGE AT LAST BIRTHDAY	POPULATION BOTH SEXES	MALES Number	%	FEMALES Number	%	BIRTHS BY AGE OF MOTHER	DEATHS BOTH SEXES	MALES	FEMALES	AGE AT LAST BIRTHDAY
0	863193	434732	2.3	428461	2.2	0	109137	60610	48527	0
1-4	2711262	1359392	7.1	1351870	6.8	0	40590	20826	19764	1-4
5-9	3311259	1660024	8.7	1651235	8.4	0	13132	6394	6738	5-9
10-14	3221792	1618905	8.5	1602887	8.1	136	9207	4207	5000	10-14
15-19	3190909	1589055	8.3	1601854	8.1	34231	15641	7588	8053	15-19
20-24	3152595	1556143	8.1	1596452	8.1	179181	21988	11563	10425	20-24
25-29	3080989	1524401	8.0	1556588	7.9	230732	22288	11228	11060	25-29
30-34	2876404	1437376	7.5	1439028	7.3	180226	22979	11983	10996	30-34
35-39	2709457	1337548	7.0	1371909	6.9	111883	23929	13158	10771	35-39
40-44	2535142	1261870	6.6	1273272	6.4	50011	27274	15473	11801	40-44
45-49	2351063	1157663	6.1	1193400	6.0	11356	30246	17583	12663	45-49
50-54	2092161	1019404	5.3	1072757	5.4	1495	34355	19814	14541	50-54
55-59	1882113	898213	4.7	983900	5.0	193	42052	23604	18448	55-59
60-64	1650220	790930	4.1	859290	4.3	0	53958	29467	24491	60-64
65-69	1344144	624884	3.3	719260	3.6	0	66018	34806	31212	65-69
70-74	943180	431748	2.3	511432	2.6		75798	37958	37840	70-74
75-79	589122	260785	1.4	328337	1.7		73985	35704	38281	75-79
80-84	298297	124703	0.7	173594	0.9	408103 M.	54121	24662	29459	80-84
85+	64515	22261	0.1	42254	0.2	391341 F.	32793	13226	19567	85+
TOTAL	38867817	19110037		19757780		799444	769491	399854	369637	TOTAL

TABLE 2 — MALE LIFE TABLE

x	$_nq_x$	l_x	$_nd_x$	$_nL_x$	$_nm_x$	$_na_x$	T_x	r_x	$\mathring{e}_x$	$_nM_x$	x
0	0.126353	100000	12635	91596	0.137947	0.3349	4806706	0.0157	48.067	0.139419	
1	0.058186	87365	5083	335203	0.015165	1.1956	4715110	0.0157	53.970	0.015320	
5	0.019031	82281	1566	407492	0.003843	2.5000	4379907	0.0041	53.231	0.003852	
10	0.012912	80715	1042	401037	0.002599	2.5631	3972416	0.0010	49.215	0.002599	10
15	0.023616	79673	1882	394036	0.004775	2.6989	3571379	0.0000	44.825	0.004775	15
20	0.036491	77792	2839	382034	0.007431	2.5608	3177343	0.0000	40.844	0.007431	20
25	0.036164	74953	2711	368011	0.007366	2.5087	2795309	0.0003	37.294	0.007366	25
30	0.040859	72242	2952	353961	0.008339	2.5437	2427298	0.0047	33.599	0.008337	30
35	0.048046	69290	3329	338333	0.009840	2.5611	2073338	0.0030	29.922	0.009837	35
40	0.059543	65961	3928	320241	0.012264	2.5645	1735005	0.0021	26.303	0.012262	40
45	0.073273	62034	4545	299099	0.015197	2.5647	1414763	0.0059	22.806	0.015188	45
50	0.092864	57488	5339	274491	0.019449	2.5740	1115664	0.0055	19.407	0.019437	50
55	0.123538	52150	6442	245158	0.026279	2.5799	841173	0.0000	16.130	0.026279	55
60	0.170863	45707	7810	209606	0.037259	2.5760	596016	0.0005	13.040	0.037256	60
65	0.245149	37898	9291	166783	0.055705	2.5561	386410	0.0005	10.196	0.055700	65
70	0.360374	28607	10309	117251	0.087925	2.4989	219627	0.0005	7.677	0.087917	70
75	0.504821	18298	9237	67463	0.136921	2.3990	102376	0.0005	5.595	0.136910	75
80	0.643455	9061	5830	29477	0.197788	2.2854	34913	0.0005	3.853	0.197766	80
85+	*1.000000	3231	3231	5436	0.594254	1.6828	5436	0.0005	1.683	0.594133	85

TABLE 3 — FEMALE LIFE TABLE

x	$_nq_x$	l_x	$_nd_x$	$_nL_x$	$_nm_x$	$_na_x$	T_x	r_x	$\mathring{e}_x$	$_nM_x$	x
0	0.104498	100000	10450	93239	0.112076	0.3530	5160826	0.0157	51.608	0.113259	
1	0.055726	89550	4990	344355	0.014492	1.2255	5067587	0.0157	56.589	0.014620	
5	0.020155	84560	1704	418539	0.004072	2.5000	4723232	0.0043	55.857	0.004081	
10	0.015479	82856	1282	411139	0.003119	2.5523	4304693	0.0000	51.954	0.003119	
15	0.024841	81573	2026	403065	0.005027	2.6310	3893555	0.0000	47.731	0.005027	
20	0.032137	79547	2556	391481	0.006530	2.5539	3490490	0.0000	43.880	0.006530	
25	0.034914	76990	2688	378279	0.007106	2.5178	3099009	0.0033	40.252	0.007105	
30	0.037495	74302	2786	364560	0.007642	2.5050	2720730	0.0051	36.617	0.007641	
35	0.038514	71516	2754	350764	0.007852	2.5250	2356170	0.0041	32.946	0.007851	
40	0.045322	68762	3116	336152	0.009271	2.5429	2005405	0.0047	29.164	0.009268	
45	0.051741	65645	3397	319938	0.010616	2.5596	1669253	0.0062	25.428	0.010611	
50	0.065674	62249	4088	301404	0.013564	2.5930	1349315	0.0054	21.676	0.013555	
55	0.089778	58161	5222	278370	0.018758	2.6188	1047911	0.0026	18.017	0.018750	
60	0.133470	52939	7066	247822	0.028512	2.6120	769540	0.0021	14.536	0.028501	
65	0.196605	45873	9019	207752	0.043412	2.6034	521718	0.0021	11.373	0.043395	
70	0.313127	36854	11540	155911	0.074017	2.5424	313966	0.0021	8.519	0.073988	
75	0.449005	25314	11366	97455	0.116631	2.4383	158056	0.0021	6.244	0.116591	
80	0.585992	13948	8173	48142	0.169779	2.3575	60601	0.0021	4.345	0.169700	
85+	*1.000000	5775	5775	12459	0.463479	2.1576	12459	0.0021	2.158	0.463080	

TABLE 4 — OBSERVED AND PROJECTED VITAL RATES

		OBSERVED POPULATION BOTH SEXES	MALES	FEMALES	PROJECTED POPULATION 1911 MALES	FEMALES	1916 MALES	FEMALES	1921 MALES	FEMALES	STABLE POPULATION MALES	FEMA
RATES PER THOUSAND	Birth	20.57	21.36	19.81	21.34	19.75	21.11	19.50	20.90	19.29	20.29	18.
	Death	19.80	20.92	18.71	20.64	18.58	20.53	18.58	20.51	18.67	21.06	19.
	Increase	0.77	0.43	1.10	0.70	1.16	0.58	0.92	0.39	0.62		-0.76
PERCENTAGE	under 15	26.00	26.55	25.48	26.52	25.33	26.41	25.10	26.00	24.62	25.21	24.
	15-64	65.66	65.79	65.54	65.91	65.69	66.15	65.85	66.60	66.26	66.51	65.
	65 and over	8.33	7.66	8.98	7.57	8.98	7.44	9.05	7.40	9.12	8.29	10.
	DEP. RATIO X 100	52.30	52.00	52.59	51.72	52.23	51.16	51.86	50.15	50.91	50.36	52.

Excluding L'Alsace-Lorraine

AGE AT LAST BIRTHDAY	BOTH SEXES	POPULATION MALES Number	%	FEMALES Number	%	BIRTHS BY AGE OF MOTHER	DEATHS BOTH SEXES	MALES	FEMALES	AGE AT LAST BIRTHDAY
0	717207	362926	1.9	354281	1.8	0	91012	50713	40299	0
1-4	2746315	1380811	7.2	1365504	6.8	0	34233	17488	16745	1-4
5-9	3325899	1670987	8.7	1654912	8.3	0	11803	5764	6039	5-9
10-14	3303686	1663159	8.6	1640527	8.2	124	8187	3770	4417	10-14
15-19	3184996	1591419	8.3	1593577	8.0	43271	13680	6728	6952	15-19
20-24	3097676	1531834	8.0	1565842	7.8	208464	19493	10437	9056	20-24
25-29	3071890	1520743	7.9	1551147	7.8	221741	20426	10520	9906	25-29
30-34	2984423	1482809	7.7	1501614	7.5	153876	21550	11503	10047	30-34
35-39	2807744	1401894	7.3	1405850	7.0	93664	23811	13317	10494	35-39
40-44	2569977	1268094	6.6	1301883	6.5	32464	25017	14459	10558	40-44
45-49	2418264	1192537	6.2	1225727	6.1	2902	29508	17283	12225	45-49
50-54	2170698	1058611	5.5	1112087	5.6	51	34363	20069	14294	50-54
55-59	1886050	912068	4.7	973982	4.9	0	40005	23104	16901	55-59
60-64	1648193	760912	3.9	887281	4.4	0	51002	27880	23122	60-64
65-69	1357648	630986	3.3	726662	3.6	0	64281	33682	30599	65-69
70-74	983434	441037	2.3	542397	2.7		74932	37841	37091	70-74
75-79	568887	247783	1.3	321104	1.6		73024	34799	38225	75-79
80-84	274981	111594	0.6	163387	0.8	386586 M.	54866	24645	30221	80-84
85+	97330	34556	0.2	62774	0.3	369971 F.	34599	13739	20860	85+
TOTAL	39215298	19264760		19950538		756557	725792	377741	348051	TOTAL

x	$_nq_x$	l_x	$_nd_x$	$_nL_x$	$_nm_x$	$_na_x$	T_x	r_x	$\dot{e}_x$	$_nM_x$	x
0	0.127525	100000	12753	91263	0.139734	0.3149	4918096	0.0000	49.181	0.139734	0
1	0.048906	87247	4267	336904	0.012665	1.1676	4826833	0.0000	55.323	0.012665	1
5	0.017100	82981	1419	411355	0.003449	2.5000	4489929	0.0000	54.108	0.003449	5
10	0.011273	81562	919	405566	0.002267	2.5614	4078573	0.0019	50.006	0.002267	10
15	0.020954	80642	1690	399346	0.004231	2.7129	3673008	0.0039	45.547	0.004228	15
20	0.033512	78952	2646	388336	0.006813	2.5713	3273661	0.0000	41.464	0.006813	20
25	0.034003	76307	2595	375079	0.006918	2.5128	2885326	0.0000	37.812	0.006918	25
30	0.038065	73712	2806	361690	0.007758	2.5519	2510246	0.0002	34.055	0.007758	30
35	0.046443	70906	3293	346494	0.009504	2.5599	2148557	0.0061	30.301	0.009499	35
40	0.055493	67613	3752	328930	0.011407	2.5655	1802062	0.0045	26.653	0.011402	40
45	0.070028	63861	4472	308465	0.014498	2.5762	1473132	0.0033	23.068	0.014493	45
50	0.090702	59389	5387	283890	0.018975	2.5765	1164668	0.0076	19.611	0.018958	50
55	0.119459	54002	6451	254428	0.025355	2.5844	880778	0.0068	16.310	0.025331	55
60	0.168272	47551	8002	218534	0.036645	2.5752	626350	0.0008	13.172	0.036640	60
65	0.236170	39550	9340	174955	0.053388	2.5598	407997	0.0008	10.316	0.053380	65
70	0.353628	30209	10683	124488	0.085813	2.5140	233041	0.0008	7.714	0.085800	70
75	0.515177	19526	10060	71617	0.140464	2.4139	108553	0.0008	5.559	0.140441	75
80	0.689232	9467	6525	29539	0.220887	2.2727	36936	0.0008	3.902	0.220846	80
85+	*1.000000	2942	2942	7397	0.397724	2.5143	7397	0.0008	2.514	0.397587	85+

x	$_nq_x$	l_x	$_nd_x$	$_nL_x$	$_nm_x$	$_na_x$	T_x	r_x	$\dot{e}_x$	$_nM_x$	x
0	0.105744	100000	10574	92963	0.113749	0.3345	5313596	0.0000	53.136	0.113749	0
1	0.047420	89426	4241	345808	0.012263	1.1951	5220634	0.0000	58.380	0.012263	1
5	0.018081	85185	1540	422074	0.003649	2.5000	4874826	0.0000	57.226	0.003649	5
10	0.013374	83645	1119	415478	0.002692	2.5450	4452751	0.0005	53.234	0.002692	10
15	0.021591	82526	1782	408423	0.004363	2.6384	4037274	0.0004	48.921	0.004363	15
20	0.028515	80744	2302	398108	0.005783	2.5619	3628851	0.0000	44.943	0.005783	20
25	0.031433	78442	2466	386086	0.006386	2.5167	3230743	0.0000	41.186	0.006386	25
30	0.032911	75976	2500	373677	0.006691	2.5190	2844657	0.0030	37.441	0.006691	30
35	0.036655	73476	2693	360711	0.007467	2.5243	2470980	0.0069	33.630	0.007465	35
40	0.039771	70782	2815	347003	0.008113	2.5457	2110269	0.0054	29.813	0.008110	40
45	0.048718	67967	3311	331813	0.009979	2.5767	1763266	0.0056	25.943	0.009974	45
50	0.062406	64656	4035	313557	0.012868	2.5900	1431453	0.0099	22.139	0.012853	50
55	0.083369	60621	5054	291052	0.017364	2.6149	1117896	0.0045	18.441	0.017352	55
60	0.122790	55567	6823	261669	0.026075	2.6305	826844	0.0033	14.880	0.026059	60
65	0.191371	48744	9328	221387	0.042136	2.6057	565174	0.0033	11.595	0.042109	65
70	0.293218	39416	11557	168898	0.068429	2.5616	343788	0.0033	8.722	0.068383	70
75	0.457429	27859	12743	106980	0.119118	2.4644	174890	0.0033	6.278	0.119042	75
80	0.620477	15115	9379	50670	0.185094	2.3444	67909	0.0033	4.493	0.184965	80
85+	*1.000000	5737	5737	17240	0.332755	3.0052	17240	0.0033	3.005	0.332303	85+

	OBSERVED POPULATION BOTH SEXES	MALES	FEMALES	PROJECTED POPULATION 1916 MALES	FEMALES	1921 MALES	FEMALES	1926 MALES	FEMALES	STABLE POPULATION MALES	FEMALES
RATES PER THOUSAND											
Birth	19.29	20.07	18.54	19.97	18.40	19.87	18.28	19.79	18.18	18.79	17.32
Death	18.51	19.61	17.45	19.31	17.29	19.38	17.45	19.54	17.71	21.16	19.69
Increase	0.78	0.46	1.10	0.66	1.11	0.49	0.83	0.25	0.47	-2.3694	
PERCENTAGE											
under 15	25.74	26.36	25.14	25.76	24.45	25.25	23.85	24.73	23.28	23.81	22.50
15-64	65.89	66.03	65.76	66.78	66.30	67.27	66.82	67.64	67.14	67.09	65.87
65 and over	8.37	7.61	9.10	7.47	9.25	7.48	9.33	7.63	9.57	9.10	11.63
DEP. RATIO X 100	51.76	51.44	52.07	49.75	50.84	48.65	49.65	47.84	48.93	49.05	51.82

TABLE 1 — DATA

AGE AT LAST BIRTHDAY	POPULATION BOTH SEXES	MALES Number	%	FEMALES Number	%	BIRTHS BY AGE OF MOTHER	DEATHS BOTH SEXES	MALES	FEMALES	AGE AT LAST BIRTHDAY
0	743786	376434	1.9	367352	1.8	0	81139	45642	35497	0
1-4	2917920	1468923	7.6	1448997	6.9	0	19355	10061	9294	1-4
5-9	2284548	1155810	6.0	1128738	5.4	0	8067	4011	4056	5-9
10-14	3097119	1558642	8.1	1538477	7.4	105	7472	3512	3960	10-14
15-19	3431137	1728851	9.0	1702286	8.1	40924	13937	6664	7273	15-19
20-24	3366909	1659822	8.6	1707087	8.2	216061	19715	10305	9410	20-24
25-29	3283952	1628514	8.4	1655438	7.9	242165	18170	8492	9678	25-29
30-34	2811963	1270354	6.6	1541609	7.4	165096	17985	8510	9475	30-34
35-39	2786164	1275194	6.6	1510970	7.2	98424	20158	10232	9926	35-39
40-44	2698817	1248115	6.5	1450702	6.9	35758	22854	12356	10498	40-44
45-49	2657720	1264083	6.5	1393637	6.7	3078	27999	15676	12323	45-49
50-54	2443923	1185081	6.1	1258842	6.0	55	32315	18491	13824	50-54
55-59	2152401	1024729	5.3	1127672	5.4	0	41399	23667	17732	55-59
60-64	1874336	879778	4.6	994558	4.8	0	51330	28374	22956	60-64
65-69	1505634	682601	3.5	823033	3.9	0	60559	31968	28591	65-69
70-74	1094234	471603	2.4	622631	3.0		73504	36059	37445	70-74
75-79	638556	266776	1.4	371780	1.8		74911	34637	40274	75-79
80-84	323997	125197	0.6	198800	1.0	411279 M.	56282	24409	31873	80-84
85+	115369	39061	0.2	76308	0.4	390387 F.	36792	13904	22888	85+
TOTAL	40228485	19309568		20918917		801666	683943	346970	336973	TOT.

TABLE 2 — MALE LIFE TABLE

x	$_nq_x$	l_x	$_nd_x$	$_nL_x$	$_nm_x$	$_na_x$	T_x	r_x	$\overset{\circ}{e}_x$	$_nM_x$
0	0.111338	100000	11134	91827	0.121248	0.2659	5288316	0.0000	52.883	0.121248
1	0.026866	88866	2387	348578	0.006849	1.1153	5196490	0.0000	58.475	0.006849
5	0.017151	86479	1483	428686	0.003460	2.5000	4847912	0.0128	56.059	0.003470
10	0.011204	84996	952	422622	0.002253	2.5268	4419227	0.0000	51.994	0.002253
15	0.019104	84043	1606	416529	0.003855	2.7035	3996604	0.0000	47.554	0.003855
20	0.030576	82438	2521	405981	0.006209	2.5374	3580075	0.0005	43.428	0.006208
25	0.025747	79917	2058	394452	0.005216	2.5050	3174094	0.0209	39.717	0.005215
30	0.033009	77859	2570	383061	0.006709	2.5734	2779643	0.0179	35.701	0.006699
35	0.039351	75289	2963	369233	0.008024	2.5651	2396582	0.0000	31.832	0.008024
40	0.048336	72327	3496	353139	0.009900	2.5703	2027349	0.0000	28.030	0.009900
45	0.060191	68831	4143	334082	0.012401	2.5690	1674209	0.0000	24.324	0.012401
50	0.075248	64688	4868	311771	0.015613	2.6031	1340128	0.0045	20.717	0.015603
55	0.109511	59820	6551	283371	0.023118	2.5988	1028356	0.0065	17.191	0.023096
60	0.149716	53269	7975	247030	0.032285	2.5780	744986	0.0071	13.985	0.032251
65	0.210540	45294	9536	203368	0.046891	2.5775	497956	0.0071	10.994	0.046833
70	0.322184	35758	11521	150462	0.076568	2.5413	294589	0.0071	8.238	0.076460
75	0.487580	24237	11818	90897	0.130010	2.4370	144126	0.0071	5.946	0.129836
80	0.639868	12420	7947	40701	0.195253	2.3074	53229	0.0071	4.286	0.194964
85+	*1.000000	4473	4473	12528	0.357010	2.8010	12528	0.0071	2.801	0.355956

TABLE 3 — FEMALE LIFE TABLE

x	$_nq_x$	l_x	$_nd_x$	$_nL_x$	$_nm_x$	$_na_x$	T_x	r_x	$\overset{\circ}{e}_x$	$_nM_x$
0	0.090379	100000	9038	93532	0.096629	0.2844	5660752	0.0000	56.608	0.096629
1	0.025193	90962	2292	357278	0.006414	1.1328	5567220	0.0000	61.204	0.006414
5	0.017765	88670	1575	439414	0.003585	2.5000	5209943	0.0125	58.756	0.003593
10	0.012789	87095	1114	432742	0.002574	2.5455	4770529	0.0000	54.774	0.002574
15	0.021149	85981	1818	425606	0.004272	2.6346	4337786	0.0000	50.450	0.004272
20	0.027194	84163	2289	415206	0.005512	2.5492	3912181	0.0000	46.483	0.005512
25	0.028814	81874	2359	403498	0.005847	2.5104	3496975	0.0043	42.712	0.005846
30	0.030270	79515	2407	391586	0.006147	2.5115	3093477	0.0030	38.904	0.006146
35	0.032320	77108	2492	379362	0.006569	2.5206	2701892	0.0000	35.040	0.006569
40	0.035553	74616	2653	366578	0.007237	2.5490	2322530	0.0007	31.126	0.007236
45	0.043301	71963	3116	352241	0.008846	2.5692	1955952	0.0053	27.180	0.008842
50	0.053564	68847	3688	335397	0.010995	2.6033	1603711	0.0097	23.294	0.010982
55	0.075873	65159	4944	314043	0.015743	2.6225	1268314	0.0074	19.465	0.015724
60	0.109533	60216	6596	285354	0.023114	2.6160	954271	0.0084	15.848	0.023082
65	0.160716	53620	8618	247049	0.034798	2.6269	668917	0.0084	12.475	0.034739
70	0.263160	45002	11843	196553	0.060252	2.5970	421269	0.0084	9.361	0.060140
75	0.426173	33160	14132	130243	0.108502	2.4841	224715	0.0084	6.777	0.108327
80	0.565613	19028	10762	67011	0.160606	2.3864	94472	0.0084	4.965	0.160328
85+	*1.000000	8265	8265	27460	0.300995	3.3223	27460	0.0084	3.322	0.299942

TABLE 4 — OBSERVED AND PROJECTED VITAL RATES

	OBSERVED POPULATION BOTH SEXES	MALES	FEMALES	PROJECTED POPULATION 1926 MALES	FEMALES	1931 MALES	FEMALES	1936 MALES	FEMALES	STABLE POPULATION MALES	FEMA
RATES PER THOUSAND											
Birth	19.93	21.30	18.66	20.88	18.36	19.72	17.42	17.95	15.91	18.15	16.
Death	17.00	17.97	16.11	18.05	16.37	18.13	16.59	18.21	16.92	19.36	18.
Increase	2.93	3.33	2.55	2.83	2.00	1.59	0.82	-0.26	-1.01		-1.21
PERCENTAGE											
under 15	22.48	23.61	21.43	24.19	21.92	26.70	24.26	25.62	23.27	23.65	22.
15-64	68.38	68.18	68.56	67.28	67.67	64.52	64.96	65.24	65.47	66.48	65.
65 and over	9.14	8.21	10.00	8.53	10.41	8.78	10.79	9.14	11.27	9.87	12.
DEP. RATIO X 100	46.25	46.68	45.85	48.63	47.77	55.00	53.95	53.28	52.75	50.42	53.

TABLE 1 — A

AGE AT LAST BIRTHDAY	POPULATION BOTH SEXES	MALES Number	MALES %	FEMALES Number	FEMALES %	BIRTHS BY AGE OF MOTHER	DEATHS BOTH SEXES	DEATHS MALES	DEATHS FEMALES	AGE AT LAST BIRTHDAY
0	743212	376080	1.9	367132	1.8	0	67508	38240	29268	0
1-4	2914086	1467461	7.6	1446625	6.9	0	24264	12657	11607	1-4
5-9	2367966	1198038	6.2	1169928	5.6	0	7001	3564	3437	5-9
10-14	3046144	1533741	7.9	1512403	7.2	154	5378	2536	2842	10-14
15-19	3406135	1716177	8.9	1689958	8.1	45087	13326	6214	7112	15-19
20-24	3368039	1663748	8.6	1704291	8.1	219531	19321	9846	9475	20-24
25-29	3297912	1639688	8.5	1658224	7.9	221850	18728	9577	9151	25-29
30-34	2842343	1293786	6.7	1548557	7.4	152543	17333	8705	8628	30-34
35-39	2786378	1273979	6.6	1512399	7.2	84921	18781	9997	8784	35-39
40-44	2697693	1246530	6.4	1451163	6.9	30073	22679	12623	10056	40-44
45-49	2652649	1258515	6.5	1394134	6.7	2635	27659	15890	11769	45-49
50-54	2447031	1184109	6.1	1262922	6.0	54	35018	20340	14678	50-54
55-59	2159211	1027902	5.3	1131309	5.4	0	41694	24450	17244	55-59
60-64	1876863	880312	4.5	996551	4.8	0	53711	30244	23467	60-64
65-69	1510233	684581	3.5	825652	3.9	0	64988	34875	30113	65-69
70-74	1097464	473167	2.4	624297	3.0		73986	37398	36588	70-74
75-79	641439	267727	1.4	373712	1.8		77580	35937	41643	75-79
80-84	324338	124980	0.6	199358	1.0	387017 M.	60676	26306	34370	80-84
85+	116014	39189	0.2	76825	0.4	369831 F.	40751	15345	25406	85+
TOTAL	40295150	19349710		20945440		756848	690382	354744	335638	TOTAL

TABLE 2 — MALE

x	$_nq_x$	l_x	$_nd_x$	$_nL_x$	$_nm_x$	$_na_x$	T_x	r_x	$\dot{e}_x$	$_nM_x$	x
0	0.095017	100000	9502	93446	0.101680	0.3103	5337271	0.0000	53.373	0.101680	0
1	0.033676	90498	3048	353344	0.008625	1.1618	5243824	0.0000	57.944	0.008625	1
5	0.014677	87451	1284	434045	0.002957	2.5000	4890481	0.0144	55.923	0.002975	5
10	0.008234	86167	710	429114	0.001653	2.5737	4456436	0.0000	51.719	0.001653	10
15	0.017957	85458	1535	423814	0.003621	2.7360	4027322	0.0000	47.127	0.003621	15
20	0.029170	83923	2448	413664	0.005918	2.5691	3603508	0.0000	42.938	0.005918	20
25	0.028801	81475	2347	401545	0.005844	2.5154	3189844	0.0191	39.151	0.005841	25
30	0.033133	79128	2622	389213	0.006736	2.5476	2788299	0.0185	35.238	0.006728	30
35	0.038502	76507	2946	375381	0.007847	2.5717	2399087	0.0000	31.358	0.007847	35
40	0.049420	73561	3635	358996	0.010127	2.5767	2023706	0.0000	27.511	0.010127	40
45	0.061263	69926	4284	339290	0.012626	2.5866	1664711	0.0000	23.807	0.012626	45
50	0.082510	65642	5416	315189	0.017184	2.5960	1325421	0.0027	20.192	0.017177	50
55	0.112574	60226	6780	284818	0.023804	2.5942	1010232	0.0052	16.774	0.023786	55
60	0.158726	53446	8483	246733	0.034382	2.5839	725414	0.0049	13.573	0.034356	60
65	0.226739	44963	10195	199955	0.050985	2.5617	478681	0.0049	10.646	0.050944	65
70	0.330805	34768	11501	145383	0.079111	2.5259	278726	0.0049	8.017	0.079038	70
75	0.499554	23266	11623	86506	0.134358	2.4338	133343	0.0049	5.731	0.134230	75
80	0.670820	11644	7811	37068	0.210713	2.2922	46837	0.0049	4.023	0.210482	80
85+	*1.000000	3833	3833	9769	0.392365	2.5486	9769	0.0049	2.549	0.391564	85+

TABLE 3 — FEMALE

x	$_nq_x$	l_x	$_nd_x$	$_nL_x$	$_nm_x$	$_na_x$	T_x	r_x	$\dot{e}_x$	$_nM_x$	x
0	0.075677	100000	7568	94927	0.079721	0.3297	5766896	0.0000	57.669	0.079721	0
1	0.031386	92432	2901	361571	0.008024	1.1879	5671969	0.0000	61.363	0.008024	1
5	0.014506	89531	1299	444410	0.002922	2.5000	5310397	0.0143	59.313	0.002938	5
10	0.009354	88233	825	439208	0.001879	2.6319	4865988	0.0000	55.150	0.001879	10
15	0.020838	87407	1821	432800	0.004208	2.6740	4426779	0.0000	50.645	0.004208	15
20	0.027422	85586	2347	422154	0.005559	2.5394	3993980	0.0040	46.666	0.005559	20
25	0.027216	83239	2265	410505	0.005519	2.4888	3571826	0.0036	42.911	0.005519	25
30	0.027476	80973	2225	399303	0.005572	2.4990	3161320	0.0005	39.041	0.005572	30
35	0.028631	78749	2255	388186	0.005808	2.5353	2762017	0.0005	35.074	0.005808	35
40	0.034076	76494	2607	376121	0.006930	2.5642	2373831	0.0012	31.033	0.006930	40
45	0.041393	73887	3058	362083	0.008447	2.5955	1997710	0.0051	27.037	0.008442	45
50	0.056594	70829	4008	344511	0.011635	2.5968	1635628	0.0093	23.093	0.011622	50
55	0.073631	66820	4920	322407	0.015260	2.6229	1291116	0.0075	19.322	0.015243	55
60	0.111646	61900	6911	293123	0.023577	2.6301	968709	0.0068	15.649	0.023548	60
65	0.167929	54989	9234	252874	0.036518	2.6096	675586	0.0068	12.286	0.036472	65
70	0.257225	45755	11769	200516	0.058695	2.5989	422712	0.0068	9.239	0.058607	70
75	0.436027	33986	14819	132801	0.111586	2.4945	222197	0.0068	6.538	0.111431	75
80	0.593783	19167	11381	65917	0.172656	2.3713	89395	0.0068	4.664	0.172404	80
85+	*1.000000	7786	7786	23478	0.331630	3.0154	23478	0.0068	3.015	0.330700	85+

TABLE 4 — OBSERVED AND PROJECTED RATES

	OBSERVED POPULATION BOTH SEXES	MALES	FEMALES	PROJECTED 1931 MALES	1931 FEMALES	1936 MALES	1936 FEMALES	1941 MALES	1941 FEMALES	STABLE POPULATION MALES	FEMALES
RATES PER THOUSAND											
Birth	18.78	20.00	17.66	19.67	17.38	18.58	16.43	17.10	15.14	17.20	15.84
Death	17.13	18.33	16.02	18.15	16.04	18.18	16.25	18.27	16.64	19.72	18.36
Increase	1.65	1.67	1.63	1.52	1.34	0.40	0.18	-1.17	-1.50	-2.5217	
PERCENTAGE											
under 15	22.51	23.65	21.47	24.08	21.81	26.10	23.67	24.73	22.40	22.95	21.63
15-64	68.33	68.14	68.51	67.51	67.83	65.29	65.59	66.36	66.37	67.17	65.50
65 and over	9.16	8.22	10.03	8.41	10.35	8.61	10.74	8.91	11.23	9.88	12.87
DEP. RATIO X 100	46.35	46.76	45.97	48.13	47.42	53.16	52.46	50.70	50.68	48.88	52.67

TABLE 1 — DATA

AGE AT LAST BIRTHDAY	POPULATION BOTH SEXES	MALES Number	MALES %	FEMALES Number	FEMALES %	BIRTHS BY AGE OF MOTHER	DEATHS BOTH SEXES	MALES	FEMALES	AGE AT LAST BIRTHDAY
0	728413	367624	1.8	360789	1.7	0	58159	32997	25162	0
1-4	2847686	1440048	7.2	1407638	6.6	0	19671	10392	9279	1-4
5-9	3525078	1783044	9.0	1742034	8.2	0	8040	4136	3904	5-9
10-14	2410523	1223968	6.1	1186555	5.6	113	4532	2254	2278	10-14
15-19	3003631	1512575	7.6	1491056	7.0	44728	9714	4743	4971	15-19
20-24	3355370	1703011	8.6	1652359	7.7	212988	16711	8744	7967	20-24
25-29	3481409	1787886	9.0	1693523	7.9	214615	17628	9496	8132	25-29
30-34	3274475	1627873	8.2	1646602	7.7	142839	18248	10279	7969	30-34
35-39	2813961	1276718	6.4	1537243	7.2	79192	18253	9958	8295	35-39
40-44	2679467	1221344	6.1	1458123	6.8	26191	21269	11842	9427	40-44
45-49	2578592	1177892	5.9	1400700	6.6	2278	26530	15034	11496	45-49
50-54	2485039	1164821	5.9	1320218	6.2	54	33833	19649	14184	50-54
55-59	2256854	1071053	5.4	1185801	5.6	0	43710	25552	18158	55-59
60-64	1918138	890368	4.5	1027770	4.8	0	52622	29910	22712	60-64
65-69	1576596	712756	3.6	863840	4.1	0	67342	36296	31046	65-69
70-74	1147229	496802	2.5	650427	3.1		78273	39685	38588	70-74
75-79	686074	282505	1.4	403569	1.9		77474	36625	40849	75-79
80-84	330614	122530	0.6	208084	1.0	368918 M.	62419	26482	35937	80-84
85+	126304	41243	0.2	85061	0.4	354080 F.	42943	15783	27160	85+
TOTAL	41225453	19904061		21321392		722998	677371	349857	327514	TOTAL

TABLE 2 — MALE LIFE TABLE

x	$_nq_x$	l_x	$_nd_x$	$_nL_x$	$_nm_x$	$_na_x$	T_x	r_x	$\overset{\circ}{e}_x$	$_nM_x$
0	0.084489	100000	8449	94130	0.089757	0.3053	5484607	0.0000	54.846	0.089757
1	0.028285	91551	2590	358839	0.007216	1.1557	5390477	0.0000	58.879	0.007216
5	0.011369	88962	1011	442279	0.002287	2.5000	5031638	0.0356	56.560	0.002320
10	0.009179	87950	807	437805	0.001844	2.5891	4589359	0.0142	52.181	0.001842
15	0.015567	87143	1357	432608	0.003136	2.7101	4151554	0.0000	47.641	0.003136
20	0.025357	85786	2175	423667	0.005134	2.5800	3718946	0.0000	43.351	0.005134
25	0.026213	83611	2192	412651	0.005311	2.5344	3295279	0.0000	39.412	0.005311
30	0.031163	81419	2537	400927	0.006328	2.5684	2882627	0.0273	35.405	0.006314
35	0.038344	78882	3025	387069	0.007814	2.5727	2481700	0.0209	31.461	0.007800
40	0.047370	75857	3593	370606	0.009696	2.5840	2094631	0.0000	27.613	0.009696
45	0.061912	72264	4474	350532	0.012763	2.5885	1724026	0.0000	23.857	0.012763
50	0.081058	67790	5495	325746	0.016869	2.5969	1373494	0.0000	20.261	0.016869
55	0.112843	62295	7030	294547	0.023866	2.5918	1047748	0.0026	16.819	0.023857
60	0.155480	55266	8593	255586	0.033620	2.5861	753201	0.0051	13.629	0.033593
65	0.226734	46673	10582	207627	0.050968	2.5679	497615	0.0051	10.662	0.050923
70	0.333608	36091	12040	150587	0.079954	2.5195	289988	0.0051	8.035	0.079881
75	0.486854	24050	11709	90229	0.129771	2.4359	139400	0.0051	5.796	0.129644
80	0.683606	12341	8437	38989	0.216383	2.3073	49172	0.0051	3.984	0.216126
85+	*1.000000	3905	3905	10182	0.383489	2.6076	10182	0.0051	2.608	0.382683

TABLE 3 — FEMALE LIFE TABLE

x	$_nq_x$	l_x	$_nd_x$	$_nL_x$	$_nm_x$	$_na_x$	T_x	r_x	$\overset{\circ}{e}_x$	$_nM_x$
0	0.066600	100000	6660	95496	0.069742	0.3237	5963923	0.0000	59.639	0.069742
1	0.025886	93340	2416	366545	0.006592	1.1794	5868428	0.0000	62.872	0.006592
5	0.010998	90924	1000	452119	0.002212	2.5000	5501883	0.0367	60.511	0.002241
10	0.009571	89924	861	447566	0.001923	2.6146	5049764	0.0133	56.156	0.001920
15	0.016541	89063	1473	441888	0.003334	2.6734	4602198	0.0000	51.673	0.003334
20	0.023827	87590	2087	432848	0.004822	2.5554	4160310	0.0000	47.498	0.004822
25	0.023723	85503	2028	422425	0.004802	2.4907	3727462	0.0000	43.595	0.004802
30	0.023914	83475	1996	412412	0.004840	2.5148	3305037	0.0047	39.593	0.004840
35	0.026639	81478	2171	402076	0.005398	2.5507	2892625	0.0067	35.502	0.005396
40	0.031835	79308	2525	390419	0.006467	2.5759	2490550	0.0027	31.404	0.006465
45	0.040248	76783	3090	376468	0.008209	2.5902	2100131	0.0016	27.351	0.008207
50	0.052413	73693	3862	359240	0.010752	2.6119	1723662	0.0055	23.390	0.010744
55	0.073971	69830	5165	336850	0.015335	2.6184	1364422	0.0094	19.539	0.015313
60	0.105146	64665	6799	307249	0.022129	2.6357	1027572	0.0077	15.891	0.022098
65	0.165798	57866	9594	266539	0.035995	2.6246	720323	0.0077	12.448	0.035940
70	0.259758	48272	12539	211023	0.059420	2.5807	453784	0.0077	9.401	0.059327
75	0.404473	35733	14453	142565	0.101378	2.5024	242761	0.0077	6.794	0.101219
80	0.596923	21280	12702	73419	0.173013	2.4036	100196	0.0077	4.709	0.172705
85+	*1.000000	8577	8577	26777	0.320321	3.1219	26777	0.0077	3.122	0.319300

TABLE 4 — OBSERVED AND PROJECTED VITAL RATES

	OBSERVED POPULATION BOTH SEXES	MALES	FEMALES	PROJECTED POPULATION 1936 MALES	1936 FEMALES	1941 MALES	1941 FEMALES	1946 MALES	1946 FEMALES	STABLE POPULATION MALES	FEMALES
RATES PER THOUSAND											
Birth	17.54	18.53	16.61	17.47	15.63	16.15	14.45	16.47	14.74	16.35	14.
Death	16.43	17.58	15.36	17.36	15.38	17.49	15.75	17.74	16.27	19.53	18.
Increase	1.11	0.96	1.25	0.10	0.25	-1.34	-1.30	-1.27	-1.53		-3.18
PERCENTAGE											
under 15	23.07	24.19	22.03	25.83	23.58	24.38	22.28	22.85	20.90	22.31	20.
15-64	67.55	67.49	67.60	65.70	65.68	66.83	66.44	68.18	67.22	67.44	65.
65 and over	9.38	8.32	10.37	8.48	10.74	8.79	11.28	8.96	11.89	10.24	13.
DEP. RATIO X 100	48.04	48.17	47.93	52.22	52.24	49.64	50.51	46.66	48.77	48.27	52.

AGE LAST BIRTHDAY	1936 BOTH SEXES	MALES	FEMALES	1941 BOTH SEXES	MALES	FEMALES	1946 BOTH SEXES	MALES	FEMALES	AGE AT LAST BIRTHDAY	
0-4	3216	1625	1591	3003	1517	1486	2900	1465	1435	0-4	**TABLE 5**
5-9	3495	1765	1730	3144	1587	1557	2936	1482	1454	5-9	POPULATION
10-14	3489	1765	1724	3460	1747	1713	3112	1571	1541	10-14	PROJECTED
15-19	2381	1209	1172	3447	1744	1703	3417	1726	1691	15-19	WITH
20-24	2942	1481	1461	2332	1184	1148	3376	1708	1668	20-24	FIXED
25-29	3272	1659	1613	2868	1443	1425	2274	1154	1120	25-29	AGE—
30-34	3390	1737	1653	3186	1612	1574	2794	1402	1392	30-34	SPECIFIC
35-39	3177	1572	1605	3289	1677	1612	3091	1556	1535	35-39	BIRTH
40-44	2715	1222	1493	3064	1505	1559	3171	1606	1565	40-44	AND
45-49	2561	1155	1406	2595	1156	1439	2926	1423	1503	45-49	DEATH
50-54	2432	1095	1337	2416	1074	1342	2447	1074	1373	50-54	RATES
55-59	2291	1053	1238	2243	990	1253	2229	971	1258	55-59	(IN 1000's)
60-64	2011	929	1082	2043	914	1129	2002	859	1143	60-64	
65-69	1615	723	892	1693	755	938	1722	742	980	65-69	
70-74	1201	517	684	1231	525	706	1291	548	743	70-74	
75-79	737	298	439	772	310	462	791	314	477	75-79	
80-84	330	122	208	355	129	226	372	134	238	80-84	
85+	108	32	76	108	32	76	117	34	83	85+	
TOTAL	41363	19959	21404	41249	19901	21348	40968	19769	21199	TOTAL	

STANDARD COUNTRIES: STANDARDIZED RATES PER THOUSAND	ENGLAND AND WALES 1961 BOTH SEXES	MALES	FEMALES	UNITED STATES 1960 BOTH SEXES	MALES	FEMALES	MEXICO 1960 BOTH SEXES	MALES	FEMALES	
Birth	14.14	15.28*	13.42	14.38	14.31*	13.87	16.41	14.17*	16.04	**TABLE 6** STANDARDIZED RATES
Death	20.00	20.81*	19.93	17.20	18.17*	15.81	11.28	15.08*	10.00	
Increase	-5.87	-5.54*	-6.52	-2.82	-3.86*	-1.94	5.13	-0.90*	6.04	

	OBSERVED POP. MALES	FEMALES	STATIONARY POP. MALES	FEMALES	STABLE POP. MALES	FEMALES	OBSERVED BIRTHS	NET MATERNITY FUNCTION	BIRTHS IN STABLE POP.	
μ	32.85251	34.93631	33.61325	35.60565	35.06569	37.19572	28.09748	27.99076	28.11885	**TABLE 7**
μ_2	442.7943	467.2108	452.1261	495.6573	460.5035	503.3817	36.49620	37.98388	38.36569	MOMENTS
μ_3	3150.408	2538.996	2936.628	2820.268	2320.093	2025.575	114.2824	120.8473	119.1172	AND
μ_4	-165684.	-194605.	-184905.	-240344.	-201974.	-258161.	-419.118	-512.903	-564.247	CUMULANTS
κ_1	0.114321	0.063210	0.093308	0.065319	0.055120	0.032167	0.268668	0.266487	0.251258	
κ_2	2.154962	2.108488	2.095457	2.021704	2.047579	1.981184	2.685340	2.644503	2.616661	
κ	-0.045134	-0.025357	-0.035785	-0.024244	-0.021133	-0.011943	-0.152242	-0.143709	-0.134183	

VITAL STATISTICS		THOMPSON AGE RANGE	NRR	1000r	INTERVAL	BOURGEOIS-PICHAT AGE RANGE	NRR	1000b	1000d	1000r	COALE	
GR	1.086										IBR	**TABLE 8** RATES FROM AGE DISTRIBUTIONS AND VITAL STATISTICS (Females)
RR	0.915	0-4	1.01	0.38	27.16	5-29	0.79	14.07	22.94	-8.88	IDR	
NRR	2.218	5-9	1.00	-0.00	27.10	30-54	1.11	20.93	17.07	3.86	IRI	
GENERATION	28.055	10-14	0.69	-13.78	27.04	55-79	1.26	27.02	18.42	8.60	K1	
SEX RATIO	104.191	15-19	0.90	-4.01	26.93	*50-74	1.26	27.18	18.49	8.69	K2	

	ORIGINAL MATRIX SUB-DIAGONAL	ALTERNATIVE FIRST ROWS Projection	Integral	FIRST STABLE MATRIX % IN STABLE POPULATION	FISHER VALUES	REPRODUCTIVE VALUES	SECOND STABLE MATRIX Z₂ FIRST COLUMN	FIRST ROW	
	0.97853	0.00000	0.00000	6.955	1.074	1898648	0.1491+0.0796	0.1491+0.0796	**TABLE 9**
	0.98993	0.00011	0.00000	6.915	1.080	1881199	0.1762-0.1151	0.0016+0.1357	LESLIE
	0.98731	0.03362	0.00021	6.955	1.074	1273819	-0.0204-0.2643	-0.0939+0.0529	MATRIX
	0.97954	0.17679	0.06734	6.977	1.034	1541195	-0.3034-0.1372	-0.0780-0.0480	AND ITS
	0.97592	0.28576	0.28936	6.944	0.845	1395899	-0.3319+0.2493	-0.0233-0.0877	SPECTRAL
	0.97630	0.23920	0.28448	6.885	0.538	910445	0.0731+0.5102	0.0092-0.0737	COMPONENTS
	0.97494	0.15497	0.19474	6.830	0.279	459273	0.5994+0.2252	0.0191-0.0415	(Females)
	0.97101	0.07802	0.11565	6.765	0.111	170510	0.6026-0.5175	0.0130-0.0153	
	0.96427	0.02210	0.04032	6.675	0.026	38153	-0.2024-0.9603	0.0039-0.0031	
	0.95424	0.00188	0.00365	6.539	0.002	2947	-1.1525-0.3491	0.0003-0.0002	
	0.93767	0.00005	0.00009	6.340	0.000	67	-1.0447+1.0229	0.0000-0.0000	
+	0.74849			25.219					

	OBSERVED POPUL. (IN 100's)	CONTRIBUTIONS OF ROOTS (IN 100's) r_1	r_2, r_3	r_4-r_{11}	AGE-SP. BIRTH RATES	NET MATERNITY FUNCTION	COEFF. OF MATRIX EQUATION	PARAMETERS INTEGRAL	MATRIX	EXP. INCREASE x	$e^{(x+8\frac{1}{2})/r}$	
	17684	15842	1473	369	0.0000	0.0000	0.0000	L(1) 0.98422	0.98422	0	0.9921	**TABLE 10**
	17420	15751	926	743	0.0000	0.0000	0.0001	L(2) 0.36874	0.37803	50	0.8462	AGE
	11866	15842	-1187	-2789	0.0000	0.0002	0.0326	0.70900	0.68900	55	0.8328	ANALYSIS
	14911	15892	-2901	1919	0.0147	0.0649	0.1691	R(1) -0.00318	-0.00318	60	0.8197	AND
	16524	15816	-1620	2327	0.0631	0.2732	0.2677	R(2) -0.04484	-0.04819	65	0.8067	MISCELLANEOUS
	16935	15683	2555	-1302	0.0621	0.2622	0.2187	0.21824	0.21379	70	0.7940	RESULTS
	16666	15556	5552	-4642	0.0425	0.1752	0.1383	C(1)	227771	75	0.7815	(Females)
	15372	15410	2689	-2726	0.0252	0.1014	0.0679	C(2)	390047	80	0.7691	
	14581	15203	-5314	4692	0.0088	0.0343	0.0187		-194446	85	0.7570	
	14007	14895	-10348	9460	0.0008	0.0030	0.0015	2P/Y 28.7901	29.3889	90	0.7450	
	13202	14441	-4172	2933	0.0000	0.0001	0.0000	DELTA 6.0061		95	0.7333	
+	44246	57441								100	0.7217	

TABLE 1 — DATA

AGE AT LAST BIRTHDAY	BOTH SEXES	POPULATION MALES Number	%	FEMALES Number	%	BIRTHS BY AGE OF MOTHER	DEATHS BOTH SEXES	MALES	FEMALES	AGE AT LAST BIRTHDAY
0	626397	315159	1.6	311238	1.5	0	42803	24477	18326	0
1-4	2613784	1314839	6.7	1298945	6.1	0	14241	7608	6633	1-
5-9	3345414	1681718	8.6	1663696	7.8	0	6218	3271	2947	5-
10-14	3478920	1755249	8.9	1723671	8.1	121	4842	2427	2415	10-
15-19	2343891	1183959	6.0	1159932	5.4	33063	6798	3489	3309	15-
20-24	2886342	1443448	7.3	1442894	6.8	176045	11439	6125	5314	20-
25-29	3251027	1629125	8.3	1621902	7.6	197241	14613	8019	6594	25-
30-34	3329482	1681670	8.6	1647812	7.7	132720	17093	10242	6851	30-
35-39	3141622	1541155	7.8	1600467	7.5	71606	19726	12166	7560	35-
40-44	2659807	1192638	6.1	1467169	6.9	23239	20864	12209	8655	40-
45-49	2525289	1132850	5.8	1392439	6.5	1835	25053	14391	10662	45-
50-54	2398719	1078712	5.5	1320007	6.2	38	32429	18684	13745	50-
55-59	2278042	1044826	5.3	1233216	5.8	0	41759	24497	17262	55-
60-64	2000537	924048	4.7	1076489	5.1	0	54996	31706	23290	60-
65-69	1609208	721064	3.7	888144	4.2	0	64630	35647	28983	65-
70-74	1216526	523419	2.7	693107	3.3		78324	40331	37993	70-
75-79	749213	304130	1.5	445083	2.1		79726	37906	41820	75-
80-84	357040	132585	0.7	224455	1.1	324021 M.	63511	28647	34864	80-
85+	145760	45559	0.2	100201	0.5	311887 F.	45291	16322	28969	85-
TOTAL	40957020	19646153		21310867		635908	644356	338164	306192	TOT

TABLE 2 — MALE LIFE TABLE

x	nq_x	l_x	nd_x	nL_x	nm_x	na_x	T_x	r_x	$\mathring{e}_x$	nM_x
0	0.073649	100000	7365	94828	0.077666	0.2978	5626965	0.0000	56.270	0.077666
1	0.022769	92635	2109	364523	0.005786	1.1471	5532136	0.0000	59.720	0.005786
5	0.009678	90526	876	450439	0.001945	2.5000	5167613	0.0000	57.084	0.001945
10	0.006925	89650	621	446787	0.001390	2.6447	4717174	0.0332	52.618	0.001383
15	0.014684	89029	1307	442131	0.002957	2.6947	4270388	0.0167	47.966	0.002947
20	0.021002	87722	1842	434165	0.004243	2.5884	3828257	0.0000	43.641	0.004243
25	0.024320	85879	2089	424315	0.004922	2.5671	3394092	0.0000	39.522	0.004922
30	0.030011	83791	2515	412890	0.006090	2.5885	2969777	0.0000	35.443	0.006090
35	0.038843	81276	3157	398778	0.007917	2.5920	2556887	0.0264	31.459	0.007894
40	0.050042	78119	3909	381117	0.010257	2.5755	2158109	0.0206	27.626	0.010237
45	0.061627	74210	4573	360007	0.012703	2.5856	1776992	0.0000	23.946	0.012703
50	0.083134	69636	5789	334233	0.017321	2.5904	1416984	0.0000	20.348	0.017321
55	0.110971	63847	7085	302192	0.023446	2.5943	1082751	0.0000	16.958	0.023446
60	0.158492	56762	8996	262040	0.034332	2.5801	780559	0.0039	13.751	0.034312
65	0.220704	47766	10542	213110	0.049468	2.5603	518519	0.0039	10.855	0.049437
70	0.323721	37224	12050	156278	0.077107	2.5236	305409	0.0039	8.205	0.077053
75	0.473079	25174	11909	95477	0.124732	2.4481	149131	0.0039	5.924	0.124638
80	0.684815	13264	9084	42003	0.216263	2.3228	53654	0.0039	4.045	0.216064
85+	*1.000000	4181	4181	11651	0.358836	2.7868	11651	0.0039	2.787	0.358261

TABLE 3 — FEMALE LIFE TABLE

x	nq_x	l_x	nd_x	nL_x	nm_x	na_x	T_x	r_x	$\mathring{e}_x$	nM_x
0	0.056599	100000	5660	96124	0.058881	0.3152	6213672	0.0000	62.137	0.058881
1	0.020135	94340	1900	371981	0.005106	1.1681	6117548	0.0000	64.846	0.005106
5	0.008818	92441	815	460165	0.001771	2.5000	5745567	0.0000	62.154	0.001771
10	0.007020	91625	643	456619	0.001409	2.6546	5285402	0.0343	57.685	0.001401
15	0.014204	90982	1292	451887	0.002860	2.6602	4828783	0.0151	53.074	0.002853
20	0.018250	89690	1637	444457	0.003683	2.5611	4376896	0.0000	48.800	0.003683
25	0.020125	88053	1772	435864	0.004066	2.5163	3932439	0.0000	44.660	0.004066
30	0.020576	86281	1775	427009	0.004158	2.5237	3496575	0.0000	40.525	0.004158
35	0.023362	84506	1974	417723	0.004726	2.5661	3069566	0.0068	36.324	0.004724
40	0.029105	82531	2402	406868	0.005904	2.5901	2651843	0.0079	32.131	0.005899
45	0.037608	80129	3014	393429	0.007660	2.6048	2244975	0.0027	28.017	0.007657
50	0.050807	77116	3918	376190	0.010415	2.6037	1851546	0.0016	24.010	0.010413
55	0.067801	73198	4963	354231	0.014010	2.6308	1475356	0.0056	20.156	0.013998
60	0.103069	68235	7033	324493	0.021673	2.6280	1121126	0.0102	16.430	0.021635
65	0.151709	61202	9285	283957	0.032698	2.6248	796633	0.0102	13.016	0.032633
70	0.242603	51917	12595	229288	0.054932	2.5945	512676	0.0102	9.875	0.054815
75	0.381441	39322	14999	159307	0.094151	2.5130	283388	0.0102	7.207	0.093960
80	0.556309	24323	13531	86911	0.155690	2.4352	124080	0.0102	5.101	0.155328
85+	*1.000000	10792	10792	37170	0.290339	3.4443	37170	0.0102	3.444	0.289109

TABLE 4 — OBSERVED AND PROJECTED VITAL RATES

	OBSERVED POPULATION BOTH SEXES	MALES	FEMALES	PROJECTED POPULATION 1941 MALES	FEMALES	1946 MALES	FEMALES	1951 MALES	FEMALES	STABLE POPULATION MALES	FEMA
RATES PER THOUSAND											
Birth	15.53	16.49	14.64	15.32	13.53	15.69	13.83	16.34	14.40	15.24	13.
Death	15.73	17.21	14.37	17.13	14.70	17.38	15.29	17.62	15.88	19.66	18.
Increase	-0.21	-0.72	0.27	-1.82	-1.16	-1.69	-1.46	-1.27	-1.47		-4.41
PERCENTAGE											
under 15	24.57	25.79	23.45	24.06	21.81	22.60	20.40	21.71	19.53	21.37	19.
15-64	65.47	65.42	65.52	66.87	66.53	68.15	67.23	69.20	67.55	67.74	65.
65 and over	9.96	8.79	11.03	9.07	11.66	9.25	12.38	9.10	12.92	10.89	15.
DEP. RATIO X 100	52.74	52.86	52.63	49.55	50.32	46.73	48.75	44.52	48.03	47.63	52.

TABLE 1 — DATA

AGE AT LAST BIRTHDAY	POPULATION BOTH SEXES	MALES Number	%	FEMALES Number	%	BIRTHS BY AGE OF MOTHER	DEATHS BOTH SEXES	MALES	FEMALES	AGE AT LAST BIRTHDAY
0	570894	290421	1.5	280473	1.3	0	60768	34544	26224	0
1-4	2329254	1184495	6.2	1144759	5.4	0	10575	5757	4818	1-4
5-9	2698276	1359914	7.1	1338362	6.3	0	3911	2154	1757	5-9
10-14	3058063	1541017	8.0	1517046	7.2	27	3318	1903	1415	10-14
15-19	3240310	1629252	8.5	1611058	7.6	32696	6067	3460	2607	15-19
20-24	3260777	1627483	8.5	1633294	7.7	222413	9645	5620	4025	20-24
25-29	2296043	1135895	5.9	1160148	5.5	213215	8118	4635	3483	25-29
30-34	2662126	1314124	6.8	1348002	6.4	152790	8766	4902	3864	30-34
35-39	3100737	1544073	8.0	1556664	7.4	113038	11938	6859	5079	35-39
40-44	3125952	1562677	8.1	1563275	7.4	39087	15225	9250	5975	40-44
45-49	2875498	1390620	7.2	1484878	7.0	3293	19621	11999	7622	45-49
50-54	2391542	1027631	5.4	1363911	6.5	51	22788	12711	10077	50-54
55-59	2193131	940235	4.9	1252896	5.9	0	29663	16456	13207	55-59
60-64	2001009	845103	4.4	1155906	5.5	0	41288	22303	18985	60-64
65-69	1731444	733524	3.8	997920	4.7	0	56287	29435	26852	65-69
70-74	1356898	565179	2.9	791719	3.8		73133	36624	36509	70-74
75-79	811320	316959	1.7	494361	2.3		73511	33857	39654	75-79
80-84	412632	145933	0.8	266699	1.3	398944 M.	62954	25833	37121	80-84
85+	165846	50390	0.3	115456	0.5	377666 F.	45480	15681	29799	85+
TOTAL	40281752	19204925		21076827		776610	563056	283983	279073	TOTAL

TABLE 2 — MALE LIFE TABLE

x	$_nq_x$	l_x	$_nd_x$	$_nL_x$	$_nm_x$	$_na_x$	T_x	r_x	$\mathring{e}_x$	$_nM_x$	x
0	0.108988	100000	10899	91630	0.118945	0.2320	5790476	0.0000	57.905	0.118945	0
1	0.019170	89101	1708	351432	0.004860	1.0888	5698847	0.0000	63.959	0.004860	1
5	0.007888	87393	689	435242	0.001584	2.5000	5347414	0.0000	61.188	0.001584	5
10	0.006156	86704	534	432230	0.001235	2.5863	4912172	0.0000	56.655	0.001235	10
15	0.010567	86170	911	428767	0.002124	2.7132	4479942	0.0000	51.990	0.002124	15
20	0.017191	85259	1466	422796	0.003467	2.6112	4051175	0.0327	47.516	0.003453	20
25	0.020202	83794	1693	414747	0.004082	2.5063	3628379	0.0175	43.301	0.004080	25
30	0.018480	82101	1517	406728	0.003730	2.5107	3213632	0.0000	39.142	0.003730	30
35	0.021976	80584	1771	398655	0.004442	2.5923	2806904	0.0000	34.832	0.004442	35
40	0.029206	78813	2302	388618	0.005923	2.6340	2408249	0.0043	30.557	0.005919	40
45	0.042492	76511	3251	374868	0.008673	2.6356	2019631	0.0331	26.397	0.008629	45
50	0.060303	73260	4418	355783	0.012417	2.6195	1644763	0.0265	22.451	0.012369	50
55	0.084033	68842	5785	330461	0.017506	2.6233	1288980	0.0014	18.724	0.017502	55
60	0.124365	63057	7842	296584	0.026441	2.6153	958518	0.0112	15.201	0.026391	60
65	0.183350	55215	10124	251765	0.040211	2.5987	661934	0.0112	11.988	0.040128	65
70	0.280267	45091	12638	194604	0.064940	2.5586	410169	0.0112	9.096	0.064801	70
75	0.421566	32454	13681	127802	0.107051	2.4808	215565	0.0112	6.642	0.106818	75
80	0.606055	18772	11377	64109	0.177463	2.3849	87763	0.0112	4.675	0.177019	80
85+	*1.000000	7395	7395	23654	0.312648	3.1985	23654	0.0112	3.198	0.311193	85+

TABLE 3 — FEMALE LIFE TABLE

x	$_nq_x$	l_x	$_nd_x$	$_nL_x$	$_nm_x$	$_na_x$	T_x	r_x	$\mathring{e}_x$	$_nM_x$	x
0	0.087319	100000	8732	93390	0.093499	0.2431	6369256	0.0000	63.693	0.093499	0
1	0.016632	91268	1518	360665	0.004209	1.0968	6275866	0.0000	68.763	0.004209	1
5	0.006543	89750	587	447283	0.001313	2.5000	5915200	0.0000	65.907	0.001313	5
10	0.004653	89163	415	444804	0.000933	2.5644	5467918	0.0000	61.325	0.000933	10
15	0.008061	88748	715	442091	0.001618	2.6943	5023114	0.0000	56.600	0.001618	15
20	0.012293	88033	1082	437579	0.002473	2.6118	4581023	0.0304	52.038	0.002464	20
25	0.014907	86950	1296	431540	0.003004	2.5220	4143444	0.0163	47.653	0.003002	25
30	0.014231	85654	1219	425239	0.002866	2.5120	3711904	0.0000	43.336	0.002866	30
35	0.016185	84435	1367	418834	0.003263	2.5540	3286665	0.0000	38.925	0.003263	35
40	0.018938	83069	1573	411558	0.003822	2.5930	2867831	0.0008	34.524	0.003822	40
45	0.025387	81496	2069	402580	0.005139	2.6324	2456273	0.0083	30.140	0.005133	45
50	0.036358	79427	2888	390304	0.007399	2.6350	2053694	0.0095	25.856	0.007388	50
55	0.051481	76539	3940	373442	0.010551	2.6519	1663390	0.0055	21.733	0.010541	55
60	0.079348	72599	5761	349539	0.016480	2.6645	1289947	0.0170	17.768	0.016424	60
65	0.126998	66838	8488	314303	0.027007	2.6572	940408	0.0170	14.070	0.026908	65
70	0.208464	58350	12164	262805	0.046285	2.6206	626105	0.0170	10.730	0.046114	70
75	0.336192	46186	15527	192881	0.080502	2.5496	363299	0.0170	7.866	0.080213	75
80	0.517339	30659	15861	113489	0.139757	2.4904	170418	0.0170	5.559	0.139187	80
85+	*1.000000	14798	14798	56929	0.259931	3.8472	56929	0.0170	3.847	0.258098	85+

TABLE 4 — OBSERVED AND PROJECTED VITAL RATES

	OBSERVED POPULATION BOTH SEXES	MALES	FEMALES	PROJECTED POPULATION 1951 MALES	FEMALES	1956 MALES	FEMALES	1961 MALES	FEMALES	STABLE POPULATION MALES	FEMALES
RATES PER THOUSAND											
Birth	19.28	20.77	17.92	21.12	18.33	20.71	18.11	19.76	17.42	20.52	18.84
Death	13.98	14.79	13.24	15.49	14.19	15.69	14.71	15.74	15.09	15.49	13.81
Increase	5.30	5.99	4.68	5.62	4.14	5.03	3.41	4.02	2.33		5.0307
PERCENTAGE											
under 15	21.49	22.79	20.31	23.34	20.85	25.02	22.44	26.17	23.69	25.90	24.43
15-64	67.39	67.78	67.04	67.20	65.78	65.66	63.77	64.65	62.15	64.69	63.35
65 and over	11.12	9.44	12.65	9.47	13.38	9.32	13.79	9.18	14.16	9.41	12.22
DEP. RATIO X 100	48.38	47.54	49.16	48.81	52.03	52.29	56.82	54.67	60.91	54.58	57.84

TABLE 1 — DATA

AGE AT LAST BIRTHDAY	POPULATION BOTH SEXES	MALES Number	%	FEMALES Number	%	BIRTHS BY AGE OF MOTHER	DEATHS BOTH SEXES	MALES	FEMALES	AGE AT LAST BIRTHDAY
0	796352	406144	2.0	390208	1.8	0	38177	21929	16248	0
1-4	3276897	1669337	8.3	1607560	7.4	0	7527	4099	3428	1-4
5-9	2910829	1481719	7.3	1429110	6.5	0	1789	1018	771	5-9
10-14	2738715	1381049	6.8	1357666	6.2	0	1503	861	642	10-14
15-19	3051304	1541246	7.6	1510058	6.9	34731	2939	1770	1169	15-19
20-24	3196477	1618637	8.0	1577840	7.2	249908	4695	2828	1867	20-24
25-29	3218745	1610527	8.0	1608218	7.4	279145	5937	3494	2443	25-29
30-34	2288736	1138310	5.6	1150426	5.3	148363	5364	3108	2256	30-34
35-39	2633528	1305764	6.5	1327764	6.1	83463	7403	4320	3083	35-39
40-44	3046395	1514946	7.5	1531449	7.0	35085	12716	7787	4929	40-44
45-49	3038694	1511416	7.5	1527278	7.0	3140	19207	12128	7079	45-49
50-54	2755953	1319415	6.5	1436538	6.6	0	26442	16529	9913	50-54
55-59	2267211	954133	4.7	1313078	6.0	0	30947	17910	13037	55-59
60-64	2022712	842692	4.2	1180020	5.4	0	40316	22440	17876	60-64
65-69	1766987	717716	3.6	1049271	4.8	0	55216	29276	25940	65-69
70-74	1406221	567671	2.8	838550	3.8		73293	36830	36463	70-74
75-79	967947	379169	1.9	588778	2.7		85391	40337	45054	75-79
80-84	460386	164731	0.8	295655	1.4	427161 M.	70269	29871	40398	80-84
85+	211456	63941	0.3	147515	0.7	406674 F.	58128	20301	37827	85+
TOTAL	42055545	20188563		21866982		833835	547259	276836	270423	TOTAL

TABLE 2 — MALE LIFE TABLE

x	$_nq_x$	l_x	$_nd_x$	$_nL_x$	$_nm_x$	$_na_x$	T_x	r_x	$\dot{e}_x$	$_nM_x$
0	0.051880	100000	5188	96087	0.053993	0.2457	6388473	0.0000	63.885	0.053993
1	0.009752	94812	925	376565	0.002455	1.0988	6292386	0.0000	66.367	0.002455
5	0.003368	93887	316	468646	0.000675	2.5000	5915821	0.0396	63.010	0.000687
10	0.003113	93571	291	467173	0.000623	2.6559	5447170	0.0000	58.214	0.000623
15	0.005727	93280	534	465171	0.001148	2.7011	4980003	0.0000	53.388	0.001148
20	0.008700	92746	807	461807	0.001747	2.6190	4514832	0.0000	48.680	0.001747
25	0.010824	91939	995	457295	0.002176	2.5897	4053025	0.0330	44.084	0.002169
30	0.013583	90944	1235	451729	0.002735	2.5805	3595730	0.0183	39.538	0.002730
35	0.016414	89708	1472	445070	0.003308	2.6423	3144001	0.0000	35.047	0.003308
40	0.025397	88236	2241	435976	0.005140	2.6783	2698931	0.0000	30.588	0.005140
45	0.039426	85995	3390	422084	0.008033	2.6729	2262955	0.0055	26.315	0.008024
50	0.061190	82604	5055	401136	0.012601	2.6485	1840871	0.0331	22.285	0.012528
55	0.090167	77550	6992	371056	0.018845	2.6127	1439736	0.0258	18.565	0.018771
60	0.125235	70557	8836	331629	0.026645	2.6056	1068680	0.0037	15.146	0.026629
65	0.185846	61721	11471	281021	0.040818	2.5952	737051	0.0037	11.942	0.040790
70	0.280150	50250	14078	216832	0.064924	2.5550	456030	0.0037	9.075	0.064879
75	0.419846	36173	15187	142654	0.106460	2.4840	239197	0.0037	6.613	0.106383
80	0.615392	20986	12915	71160	0.181485	2.3852	96543	0.0037	4.600	0.181331
85+	*1.000000	8071	8071	25383	0.317985	3.1448	25383	0.0037	3.145	0.317496

TABLE 3 — FEMALE LIFE TABLE

x	$_nq_x$	l_x	$_nd_x$	$_nL_x$	$_nm_x$	$_na_x$	T_x	r_x	$\dot{e}_x$	$_nM_x$
0	0.040393	100000	4039	97007	0.041639	0.2590	6962580	0.0000	69.626	0.041639
1	0.008477	95961	814	381491	0.002132	1.1094	6865573	0.0000	71.546	0.002132
5	0.002641	95147	251	475108	0.000529	2.5000	6484082	0.0377	68.148	0.000539
10	0.002362	94896	224	473943	0.000473	2.6064	6008974	0.0000	63.322	0.000473
15	0.003864	94672	366	472514	0.000774	2.6892	5535031	0.0000	58.465	0.000774
20	0.005900	94306	556	470211	0.001183	2.6295	5062518	0.0000	53.682	0.001183
25	0.007592	93750	712	467042	0.001524	2.6033	4592307	0.0300	48.985	0.001519
30	0.009773	93038	909	462989	0.001964	2.5806	4125265	0.0172	44.340	0.001961
35	0.011546	92129	1064	458097	0.002322	2.6068	3662275	0.0000	39.752	0.002322
40	0.015971	91065	1454	451895	0.003219	2.6420	3204178	0.0000	35.186	0.003219
45	0.022932	89610	2055	443232	0.004636	2.6543	2752283	0.0016	30.714	0.004635
50	0.033994	87556	2976	430765	0.006909	2.6438	2309051	0.0081	26.372	0.006901
55	0.048586	84579	4109	413233	0.009944	2.6485	1878286	0.0094	22.207	0.009929
60	0.073378	80470	5905	388553	0.015197	2.6635	1465053	0.0161	18.206	0.015149
65	0.117272	74565	8744	352446	0.024811	2.6695	1076501	0.0161	14.437	0.024722
70	0.197776	65821	13018	298295	0.043640	2.6334	724054	0.0161	11.000	0.043483
75	0.323408	52803	17077	222385	0.076790	2.5622	425759	0.0161	8.063	0.076521
80	0.507130	35726	18118	132176	0.137073	2.5061	203374	0.0161	5.693	0.136639
85+	1.000000	17608	17608	71198	0.247314	4.0434	71198	0.0161	4.043	0.256429

TABLE 4 — OBSERVED AND PROJECTED VITAL RATES

	OBSERVED POPULATION BOTH SEXES	MALES	FEMALES	PROJECTED POPULATION 1956 MALES	FEMALES	1961 MALES	FEMALES	1966 MALES	FEMALES	STABLE POPULATION MALES	FEMAL
RATES PER THOUSAND											
Birth	19.83	21.16	18.60	20.83	18.43	19.70	17.57	18.99	17.08	21.32	19.9
Death	13.01	13.71	12.37	13.53	12.76	13.45	13.12	13.38	13.24	12.13	10.7
Increase	6.81	7.45	6.23	7.30	5.67	6.25	4.45	5.61	3.84		9.195
PERCENTAGE											
under 15	23.12	24.46	21.88	26.62	23.86	28.23	25.50	27.12	24.71	28.05	26.6
15-64	65.44	66.16	64.77	64.35	62.42	63.04	60.45	63.50	60.92	63.91	62.5
65 and over	11.44	9.38	13.35	9.02	13.73	8.73	14.05	9.38	14.36	8.04	10.8
DEP. RATIO X 100	52.82	51.14	54.40	55.39	60.21	58.64	65.42	57.48	64.14	56.48	59.9

TABLE 1 — DATA

AGE AT LAST BIRTHDAY	POPULATION BOTH SEXES	MALES Number	%	FEMALES Number	%	BIRTHS BY AGE OF MOTHER	DEATHS BOTH SEXES	MALES	FEMALES	AGE AT LAST BIRTHDAY
0	787972	401808	1.9	386164	1.7	0	25587	14703	10884	0
1-4	3129062	1593378	7.5	1535684	6.8	0	5188	2842	2346	1-4
5-9	4086074	2080102	9.8	2005972	8.9	0	1632	945	687	5-9
10-14	2935656	1496472	7.1	1439184	6.4	0	1163	699	464	10-14
15-19	2759656	1399605	6.6	1360051	6.0	28986	2102	1418	684	15-19
20-24	3075025	1562927	7.4	1512098	6.7	233497	3376	2287	1089	20-24
25-29	3226717	1645503	7.8	1581214	7.0	269418	4611	3065	1546	25-29
30-34	3239299	1629994	7.7	1609305	7.1	173738	5835	3705	2130	30-34
35-39	2300151	1151925	5.4	1148226	5.1	75264	5925	3654	2271	35-39
40-44	2619744	1299900	6.1	1319844	5.8	23330	9104	5702	3402	40-44
45-49	2988642	1480044	7.0	1508598	6.7	2519	16824	10786	6038	45-49
50-54	2933878	1443172	6.8	1490706	6.6	0	25730	16867	8863	50-54
55-59	2607578	1224408	5.8	1383170	6.1	0	34016	22028	11988	55-59
60-64	2093586	855397	4.0	1238189	5.5	0	39706	23103	16603	60-64
65-69	1790602	716214	3.4	1074388	4.7	0	51410	27890	23520	65-69
70-74	1453441	557567	2.6	895874	4.0		68063	34209	33854	70-74
75-79	1013664	378591	1.8	635073	2.8		81278	37727	43551	75-79
80-84	561866	198654	0.9	363212	1.6	412753 M.	76360	32459	43901	80-84
85+	240472	71295	0.3	169177	0.7	393999 F.	63114	21935	41179	85+
TOTAL	43843085	21186956		22656129		806752	521024	266024	255000	TOTAL

TABLE 2 — MALE LIFE TABLE

x	nq_x	l_x	nd_x	nL_x	nm_x	na_x	T_x	r_x	$\dot{e}_x$	nM_x	x
0	0.035620	100000	3562	97342	0.036592	0.2539	6603156	0.0000	66.032	0.036592	0
1	0.007098	96438	685	383771	0.001784	1.1052	6505813	0.0000	67.461	0.001784	1
5	0.002238	95754	214	478232	0.000448	2.5000	6122043	0.0279	63.935	0.000454	5
10	0.002356	95539	225	477189	0.000472	2.7475	5643811	0.0390	59.073	0.000467	10
15	0.005054	95314	482	475463	0.001013	2.7017	5166622	0.0000	54.206	0.001013	15
20	0.007291	94832	691	472515	0.001463	2.6179	4691159	0.0000	49.468	0.001463	20
25	0.009272	94141	873	468599	0.001863	2.5876	4218644	0.0000	44.812	0.001863	25
30	0.011349	93268	1058	463816	0.002282	2.6147	3750044	0.0333	40.207	0.002273	30
35	0.015784	92210	1455	457600	0.003181	2.6305	3286229	0.0194	35.639	0.003172	35
40	0.021712	90754	1970	449205	0.004386	2.6825	2828629	0.0000	31.168	0.004386	40
45	0.035835	88784	3182	436570	0.007288	2.6902	2379424	0.0000	26.800	0.007288	45
50	0.056956	85602	4876	416619	0.011703	2.6633	1942854	0.0069	22.696	0.011687	50
55	0.086762	80727	7004	387058	0.018095	2.6334	1526235	0.0338	18.906	0.017991	55
60	0.126960	73723	9360	346144	0.027040	2.5994	1139178	0.0076	15.452	0.027009	60
65	0.178187	64363	11469	294137	0.038991	2.5867	793034	0.0076	12.321	0.038941	65
70	0.267136	52894	14130	229980	0.061440	2.5590	498897	0.0076	9.432	0.061354	70
75	0.399025	38764	15468	154998	0.099794	2.4901	268917	0.0076	6.937	0.099651	75
80	0.574959	23296	13394	81836	0.163674	2.4134	113919	0.0076	4.890	0.163394	80
85+	*1.000000	9902	9902	32083	0.308636	3.2401	32083	0.0076	3.240	0.307665	85+

TABLE 3 — FEMALE LIFE TABLE

x	nq_x	l_x	nd_x	nL_x	nm_x	na_x	T_x	r_x	$\dot{e}_x$	nM_x	x
0	0.027613	100000	2761	97973	0.028185	0.2658	7242687	0.0000	72.427	0.028185	0
1	0.006084	97239	592	387248	0.001528	1.1152	7144714	0.0000	73.476	0.001528	1
5	0.001682	96647	163	482829	0.000337	2.5000	6757466	0.0283	69.919	0.000342	5
10	0.001617	96484	156	482049	0.000324	2.6059	6274637	0.0385	65.033	0.000322	10
15	0.002512	96328	242	481077	0.000503	2.6631	5792588	0.0000	60.134	0.000503	15
20	0.003595	96086	345	479616	0.000720	2.6357	5311512	0.0000	55.278	0.000720	20
25	0.004877	95741	467	477597	0.000978	2.6277	4831896	0.0000	50.468	0.000978	25
30	0.006629	95274	632	474889	0.001330	2.6540	4354299	0.0306	45.703	0.001324	30
35	0.009866	94643	934	470997	0.001982	2.6269	3879410	0.0179	40.990	0.001978	35
40	0.012810	93709	1200	465730	0.002578	2.6563	3408414	0.0000	36.372	0.002578	40
45	0.019827	92508	1834	458260	0.004002	2.6657	2942683	0.0000	31.810	0.004002	45
50	0.029330	90674	2659	447120	0.005948	2.6496	2484423	0.0026	27.399	0.005946	50
55	0.042543	88015	3744	431303	0.008682	2.6578	2037303	0.0095	23.147	0.008667	55
60	0.065224	84270	5496	408545	0.013454	2.6701	1606000	0.0167	19.058	0.013409	60
65	0.104512	78774	8233	374701	0.021972	2.6718	1197454	0.0167	15.201	0.021892	65
70	0.174164	70541	12286	323856	0.037936	2.6519	822753	0.0167	11.663	0.037789	70
75	0.295040	58255	17188	249712	0.068830	2.5818	498897	0.0167	8.564	0.068576	75
80	0.463387	41068	19030	156949	0.121251	2.5531	249184	0.0167	6.068	0.120869	80
85+	1.000000	22037	22037	92235	0.238926	4.1854	92235	0.0167	4.185	0.243409	85+

TABLE 4 — OBSERVED AND PROJECTED VITAL RATES

	OBSERVED POPULATION BOTH SEXES	MALES	FEMALES	PROJECTED POPULATION 1961 MALES	FEMALES	1966 MALES	FEMALES	1971 MALES	FEMALES	STABLE POPULATION MALES	FEMALES
RATES PER THOUSAND											
Birth	18.40	19.48	17.39	18.55	16.63	17.90	16.14	19.08	17.31	19.92	18.52
Death	11.88	12.56	11.26	12.59	11.90	12.65	12.23	12.80	12.46	11.90	10.50
Increase	6.52	6.93	6.14	5.95	4.73	5.26	3.92	6.27	4.85		8.0184
PERCENTAGE											
under 15	24.95	26.30	23.69	27.55	24.94	26.14	23.80	25.56	23.41	26.97	25.30
15-64	63.51	64.63	62.46	63.58	60.61	64.29	61.22	64.05	61.19	64.24	62.47
65 and over	11.54	9.07	13.85	8.87	14.45	9.57	14.98	10.39	15.40	8.79	12.22
DEP. RATIO X 100	57.46	54.73	60.10	57.28	65.00	55.54	63.34	56.14	63.42	55.66	60.07

TABLE 1 — DATA

AGE AT LAST BIRTHDAY	POPULATION BOTH SEXES	MALES Number	%	FEMALES Number	%	BIRTHS BY AGE OF MOTHER	DEATHS BOTH SEXES	MALES	FEMALES	AGE AT LAST BIRTHDAY
0	813094	414769	1.9	398325	1.7	0	18885	10922	7963	0
1-4	3216575	1638440	7.3	1578135	6.6	0	3849	2127	1722	1-4
5-9	4010281	2041015	9.1	1969266	8.3	0	1535	901	634	5-9
10-14	4162096	2120395	9.5	2041701	8.6	0	1393	853	540	10-14
15-19	2984354	1522271	6.8	1462083	6.2	35130	2241	1551	690	15-19
20-24	2802146	1439991	6.4	1362155	5.7	230770	2877	1958	919	20-24
25-29	3137328	1608845	7.2	1528483	6.4	275218	3941	2717	1224	25-29
30-34	3284971	1670798	7.5	1614173	6.8	176655	5304	3541	1763	30-34
35-39	3276121	1642291	7.3	1633830	6.9	90341	7192	4652	2540	35-39
40-44	2311147	1152520	5.1	1158627	4.9	24450	7878	5049	2829	40-44
45-49	2607830	1282271	5.7	1325559	5.6	1719	12508	8080	4428	45-49
50-54	2914793	1425910	6.4	1488883	6.3	0	23041	15326	7715	50-54
55-59	2803005	1350886	6.0	1452119	6.1	0	33924	22941	10983	55-59
60-64	2430910	1106681	4.9	1324229	5.6	0	44744	28868	15876	60-64
65-69	1878962	738671	3.3	1140291	4.8	0	51537	28953	22584	65-69
70-74	1503110	568645	2.5	934465	3.9		65182	33183	31999	70-74
75-79	1085390	386716	1.7	698674	2.9		80081	36444	43637	75-79
80-84	624575	210438	0.9	414137	1.7	426539 M.	79284	32504	46780	80-84
85+	316151	93705	0.4	222446	0.9	407744 F.	76964	26323	50641	85+
TOTAL	46162839	22415258		23747581		834283	522360	266893	255467	TOTAL

TABLE 2 — MALE LIFE TABLE

x	nq_x	l_x	nd_x	nL_x	nm_x	na_x	T_x	r_x	$\overset{\circ}{e}_x$	nM_x	x
0	0.025822	100000	2582	98078	0.026329	0.2556	6745878	0.0002	67.459	0.026333	0
1	0.005172	97418	504	388213	0.001298	1.1065	6647801	0.0002	68.240	0.001298	1
5	0.002205	96914	214	484035	0.000441	2.5000	6259587	0.0000	64.589	0.000441	5
10	0.002027	96700	196	483069	0.000406	2.7980	5775552	0.0288	59.726	0.000402	10
15	0.005120	96504	494	481381	0.001026	2.6917	5292483	0.0377	54.842	0.001019	15
20	0.006777	96010	651	478488	0.001360	2.5986	4811102	0.0000	50.110	0.001360	20
25	0.008410	95360	802	474865	0.001689	2.5900	4332614	0.0000	45.435	0.001689	25
30	0.010543	94558	997	470404	0.002119	2.6091	3857749	0.0000	40.798	0.002119	30
35	0.014149	93561	1324	464704	0.002849	2.6589	3387345	0.0341	36.205	0.002833	35
40	0.021753	92237	2006	456476	0.004395	2.6535	2922641	0.0203	31.686	0.004381	40
45	0.031055	90230	2802	444684	0.006301	2.6917	2466165	0.0000	27.332	0.006301	45
50	0.052434	87428	4584	426509	0.010748	2.6805	2021481	0.0000	23.122	0.010748	50
55	0.081761	82844	6773	398282	0.017007	2.6469	1594972	0.0078	19.253	0.016982	55
60	0.123044	76071	9360	358035	0.026143	2.6155	1196690	0.0130	15.731	0.026085	60
65	0.179351	66711	11965	304610	0.039279	2.5809	838655	0.0130	12.572	0.039196	65
70	0.255832	54746	14006	239466	0.058487	2.5536	534046	0.0130	9.755	0.058355	70
75	0.382087	40740	15566	164775	0.094470	2.4993	294580	0.0130	7.231	0.094240	75
80	0.554306	25174	13954	90079	0.154909	2.4351	129805	0.0130	5.156	0.154459	80
85+	*1.000000	11220	11220	39726	0.282432	3.5407	39726	0.0130	3.541	0.280914	85

TABLE 3 — FEMALE LIFE TABLE

x	nq_x	l_x	nd_x	nL_x	nm_x	na_x	T_x	r_x	$\overset{\circ}{e}_x$	nM_x	x
0	0.019701	100000	1970	98556	0.019990	0.2669	7423348	0.0001	74.233	0.019991	0
1	0.004350	98030	426	390890	0.001091	1.1162	7324793	0.0001	74.720	0.001091	1
5	0.001608	97603	157	487625	0.000322	2.5000	6933903	0.0000	71.042	0.000322	5
10	0.001326	97446	129	486925	0.000265	2.6194	6446278	0.0295	66.152	0.000264	10
15	0.002374	97317	231	486050	0.000475	2.6783	5959354	0.0400	61.236	0.000472	15
20	0.003368	97086	327	484646	0.000675	2.5992	5473304	0.0000	56.376	0.000675	20
25	0.003996	96759	387	482871	0.000801	2.6067	4988658	0.0000	51.557	0.000801	25
30	0.005447	96373	525	480625	0.001092	2.6428	4505788	0.0000	46.754	0.001092	30
35	0.007789	95848	747	477503	0.001563	2.6765	4025163	0.0315	41.995	0.001555	35
40	0.012172	95101	1158	472780	0.002449	2.6458	3547659	0.0185	37.304	0.002442	40
45	0.016573	93943	1557	466076	0.003340	2.6616	3074880	0.0000	32.731	0.003340	45
50	0.025598	92386	2365	456393	0.005182	2.6578	2608803	0.0000	28.238	0.005182	50
55	0.037187	90022	3348	442302	0.007569	2.6684	2152410	0.0038	23.910	0.007563	55
60	0.058507	86674	5071	421609	0.012028	2.6809	1710108	0.0156	19.730	0.011989	60
65	0.094991	81603	7752	390026	0.019874	2.6794	1288498	0.0156	15.790	0.019805	65
70	0.159070	73851	11748	341798	0.034370	2.6626	898472	0.0156	12.166	0.034243	70
75	0.272473	62104	16922	269958	0.062682	2.6030	556674	0.0156	8.964	0.062457	75
80	0.445204	45182	20115	177320	0.113441	2.5844	286716	0.0156	6.346	0.112958	80
85+	*1.000000	25067	25067	109396	0.229138	4.3642	109396	0.0156	4.364	0.227655	85

TABLE 4 — OBSERVED AND PROJECTED VITAL RATES

	OBSERVED POPULATION BOTH SEXES	MALES	FEMALES	PROJECTED POPULATION 1966 MALES	FEMALES	1971 MALES	FEMALES	1976 MALES	FEMALES	STABLE POPULATION MALES	FEMALES
RATES PER THOUSAND											
Birth	18.07	19.03	17.17	18.33	16.60	19.60	17.84	20.67	18.92	20.81	19.39
Death	11.32	11.91	10.76	11.98	11.23	12.10	11.52	12.22	11.61	10.83	9.42
Increase	6.76	7.12	6.41	6.36	5.38	7.50	6.32	8.45	7.31		9.9733
PERCENTAGE											
under 15	26.43	27.72	25.21	26.54	24.23	26.16	23.99	26.52	24.45	28.09	26.37
15-64	61.85	63.36	60.43	63.90	60.75	63.50	60.49	62.85	59.98	63.51	61.74
65 and over	11.72	8.91	14.36	9.57	15.03	10.34	15.52	10.63	15.57	8.40	11.89
DEP. RATIO X 100	61.68	57.83	65.49	56.50	64.62	57.47	65.31	59.10	66.73	57.46	61.96

AGE AT LAST BIRTHDAY	1966 BOTH SEXES	1966 MALES	1966 FEMALES	1971 BOTH SEXES	1971 MALES	1971 FEMALES	1976 BOTH SEXES	1976 MALES	1976 FEMALES	AGE AT LAST BIRTHDAY	
0-4	4062	2070	1992	4271	2177	2094	4706	2398	2308	0-4	
5-9	4013	2044	1969	4045	2061	1984	4254	2167	2087	5-9	
10-14	4003	2037	1966	4006	2040	1966	4039	2057	1982	10-14	TABLE 5
15-19	4151	2113	2038	3993	2030	1963	3995	2032	1963	15-19	POPULATION
20-24	2971	1513	1458	4132	2100	2032	3975	2018	1957	20-24	PROJECTED
25-29	2786	1429	1357	2955	1502	1453	4109	2084	2025	25-29	WITH
30-34	3115	1594	1521	2767	1416	1351	2934	1488	1446	30-34	FIXED
35-39	3255	1651	1604	3085	1574	1511	2741	1399	1342	35-39	AGE—
40-44	3231	1613	1618	3209	1621	1588	3044	1547	1497	40-44	SPECIFIC
45-49	2265	1123	1142	3167	1572	1595	3144	1579	1565	45-49	BIRTH
50-54	2528	1230	1298	2195	1077	1118	3069	1507	1562	50-54	AND
55-59	2775	1332	1443	2406	1148	1258	2090	1006	1084	55-59	DEATH
60-64	2598	1214	1384	2572	1197	1375	2231	1032	1199	60-64	RATES
65-69	2167	942	1225	2313	1033	1280	2290	1018	1272	65-69	(IN 1000's)
70-74	1580	581	999	1814	740	1074	1934	812	1122	70-74	
75-79	1129	391	738	1189	400	789	1357	509	848	75-79	
80-84	670	211	459	699	214	485	736	218	518	80-84	
85+	348	93	255	376	93	283	393	94	299	85+	
TOTAL	47647	23181	24466	49194	23995	25199	51041	24965	26076	TOTAL	

STANDARD COUNTRIES: STANDARDIZED RATES PER THOUSAND	ENGLAND AND WALES 1961 BOTH SEXES	MALES	FEMALES	UNITED STATES 1960 BOTH SEXES	MALES	FEMALES	MEXICO 1960 BOTH SEXES	MALES	FEMALES	
Birth	17.76	18.21*	16.82	18.03	17.30*	17.36	20.73	16.32*	20.21	TABLE 6
Death	11.46	12.34*	10.63	9.39	11.02*	7.82	4.90	9.30*	3.80	STANDARDIZED RATES
Increase	6.30	5.87*	6.19	8.64	6.28*	9.54	15.84	7.02*	16.42	

	OBSERVED POP. MALES	OBSERVED POP. FEMALES	STATIONARY POP. MALES	STATIONARY POP. FEMALES	STABLE POP. MALES	STABLE POP. FEMALES	OBSERVED BIRTHS	NET MATERNITY FUNCTION	BIRTHS IN STABLE POP.	
μ	33.20580	36.48165	36.41314	39.25277	31.64192	33.86816	28.31827	28.09728	27.75032	TABLE 7
σ^2	479.7085	552.5022	494.1043	555.0185	459.3272	520.0363	31.91349	33.30485	32.10504	MOMENTS
κ_3	3534.052	3029.721	2413.908	2006.859	4435.358	4855.865	89.4600	119.6580	120.7381	AND
κ_4	-212946.	-328453.	-236783.	-325361.	-162317.	-234547.	-269.499	-167.027	-41.394	CUMULANTS
β_1	0.113139	0.054426	0.048304	0.023557	0.202998	0.167661	0.246227	0.387580	0.440523	
β_2	2.074630	1.924018	2.030130	1.943790	2.230657	2.132712	2.735388	2.849418	2.959840	
κ	-0.041785	-0.018916	-0.018377	-0.008558	-0.077765	-0.061474	-0.156528	-0.221273	-0.265302	

VITAL STATISTICS		THOMPSON AGE RANGE	NRR	1000r	INTERVAL	BOURGEOIS-PICHAT AGE RANGE	NRR	1000b	1000d	1000r	COALE	
GRR	1.370										IBR	TABLE 8
NRR	1.321	0-4	1.33	10.53	27.43	5-29	1.61	19.52	1.78	17.74	IDR	RATES FROM AGE DISTRIBUTIONS
TFR	2.803	5-9	1.34	10.81	27.39	30-54	1.14	15.76	10.90	4.86	IRI	AND VITAL
GENERATION	27.923	10-14	1.36	11.12	27.34	55-79	1.40	28.44	16.02	12.42	K1	STATISTICS
SEX RATIO	104.610	15-19	0.97	-1.14	27.27	*50-74	1.29	23.18	13.79	9.39	K2	(Females)

Start of Age Interval	ORIGINAL MATRIX SUB-DIAGONAL	ALTERNATIVE FIRST ROWS Projection	Integral	FIRST STABLE MATRIX % IN STABLE POPULATION	FISHER VALUES	REPRODUCTIVE VALUES	SECOND STABLE MATRIX Z2 FIRST COLUMN	FIRST ROW	
0	0.99628	0.00000	0.00000	9.261	1.047	2069939	0.1732+0.0743	0.1732+0.0743	
5	0.99856	0.00000	0.00000	8.777	1.105	2176074	0.1662-0.1433	0.0079+0.1616	TABLE 9
10	0.99820	0.02869	0.00000	8.338	1.163	2375016	-0.0651-0.2477	-0.1215+0.0668	LESLIE
15	0.99711	0.23078	0.05893	7.918	1.195	1747049	-0.2931-0.0585	-0.1021-0.0706	MATRIX
20	0.99634	0.41720	0.41549	7.510	1.017	1385737	-0.2111+0.2771	-0.0241-0.1225	AND ITS
25	0.99535	0.34565	0.44159	7.118	0.635	970253	0.1821+0.3624	0.0130-0.0958	SPECTRAL
30	0.99350	0.19660	0.26840	6.740	0.307	495080	0.4719-0.0055	0.0188-0.0519	COMPONENTS
35	0.99011	0.09112	0.13561	6.370	0.117	191601	0.2346-0.4952	0.0130-0.0198	(Females)
40	0.98582	0.02677	0.05175	6.000	0.028	32579	-0.3959-0.4954	0.0044-0.0042	
45	0.97922	0.00155	0.00318	5.627	0.002	2049	-0.7131+0.1596	0.0003-0.0002	
50	0.96913	0.00000	0.00000	5.242	0.000	1	-0.1939+0.8136	0.0000-0.0000	
65+	0.81040			21.097					

Start of Age Interval	OBSERVED POPUL. (IN 100's)	CONTRIBUTIONS OF ROOTS (IN 100's) r_1	r_2, r_3	$r_4 \cdot r_{11}$	AGE-SP. BIRTH RATES	NET MATERNITY FUNCTION	COEFF. OF MATRIX EQUATION	PARAMETERS INTEGRAL	MATRIX	EXP. INCREASE x	$e^{(x+8\frac{1}{2})r}$	
0	19765	19735	89	-59	0.0000	0.0000	0.0000	L(1) 1.05113	1.05119	0	1.0252	TABLE 10
5	19693	18705	1377	-389	0.0000	0.0000	0.0000	L(2) 0.36959	0.37528	50	1.6881	
10	20417	17768	1290	1359	0.0000	0.0000	0.0285	0.79681	0.76885	55	1.7744	AGE
15	14621	16872	-555	-1696	0.0117	0.0571	0.2292	R(1) 0.00997	0.00998	60	1.8651	ANALYSIS
20	13622	16004	-2322	-61	0.0828	0.4013	0.4131	R(2) -0.02594	-0.03120	65	1.9605	AND
25	15285	15169	-1619	1734	0.0880	0.4249	0.3410	0.22730	0.22334	70	2.0607	MISCELLANEOUS
30	16142	14364	1494	284	0.0535	0.2571	0.1931	C(1)	213100	75	2.1661	RESULTS
35	16338	13575	3708	-945	0.0270	0.1290	0.0889	C(2)	154786	80	2.2769	(Females)
40	11586	12787	1758	-2958	0.0103	0.0488	0.0259		301086	85	2.3933	
45	13256	11991	-3168	4433	0.0006	0.0030	0.0015	2P/Y 27.6427	28.1326	90	2.5156	
50	14889	11170	-5499	9218	0.0000	0.0000	0.0000	DELTA 6.7999		95	2.6443	
65+	61864	44959								100	2.7795	

TABLE 1 — DATA

AGE AT LAST BIRTHDAY	POPULATION BOTH SEXES	MALES Number	%	FEMALES Number	%	BIRTHS BY AGE OF MOTHER	DEATHS BOTH SEXES	MALES	FEMALES	AGE AT LAST BIRTHDAY
0	856724	437595	1.8	419129	1.7	0	15635	8988	6647	0
1-4	3350306	1707736	7.1	1642570	6.6	0	3077	1745	1332	1-4
5-9	3704788	1887244	7.9	1817544	7.3	0	1465	896	569	5-9
10-14	4111699	2090958	8.8	2020741	8.1	80	1370	843	527	10-14
15-19	4291885	2195984	9.2	2095901	8.4	58137	3097	2156	941	15-19
20-24	3013419	1568628	6.6	1444790	5.8	254664	3245	2285	960	20-24
25-29	3049120	1605569	6.7	1443551	5.8	259956	3525	2452	1073	25-29
30-34	3300286	1702133	7.1	1598153	6.4	171861	4985	3366	1619	30-34
35-39	3380284	1717592	7.2	1662692	6.6	88156	7512	4990	2522	35-39
40-44	3337319	1665019	7.0	1672300	6.7	27327	10686	7090	3596	40-44
45-49	2152398	1065079	4.5	1087319	4.3	2096	10470	6809	3661	45-49
50-54	2718127	1321165	5.5	1396962	5.6	56	20835	13977	6858	50-54
55-59	2853207	1369604	5.7	1483603	5.9	0	33603	22860	10743	55-59
60-64	2658283	1243069	5.2	1415214	5.7	0	47718	32006	15712	60-64
65-69	2204921	954523	4.0	1250398	5.0	0	59245	36449	22796	65-69
70-74	1614974	595823	2.5	1019151	4.1		66399	34057	32342	70-74
75-79	1183064	414730	1.7	768334	3.1		79836	36745	43091	75-79
80-84	719601	231558	1.0	488043	2.0	441588 M.	81550	32452	49098	80-84
85+	418293	120855	0.5	297438	1.2	420745 F.	86088	28594	57494	85+
TOTAL	48918697	23894864		25023833		862333	540341	278760	261581	TOTAL

TABLE 2 — MALE LIFE TABLE

x	nq_x	l_x	nd_x	nL_x	nm_x	na_x	T_x	r_x	$\mathring{e}_x$	nM_x	x
0	0.020205	100000	2021	98498	0.020513	0.2568	6826804	0.0016	68.268	0.020540	0
1	0.004068	97979	399	390765	0.001020	1.1075	6728306	0.0016	68.671	0.001022	1
5	0.002370	97581	231	487327	0.000475	2.5000	6337540	0.0020	64.946	0.000475	5
10	0.002014	97350	196	486310	0.000403	2.7630	5850214	0.0000	60.095	0.000403	10
15	0.004928	97154	479	484677	0.000988	2.7207	5363904	0.0278	55.211	0.000982	15
20	0.007275	96675	703	481668	0.001460	2.5744	4879227	0.0299	50.471	0.001457	20
25	0.007608	95972	730	478081	0.001527	2.5668	4397559	0.0000	45.821	0.001527	25
30	0.009842	95241	937	473995	0.001978	2.6401	3919478	0.0000	41.153	0.001978	30
35	0.014428	94304	1361	468335	0.002905	2.6587	3445483	0.0000	36.536	0.002905	35
40	0.021235	92943	1974	460099	0.004290	2.6598	2977148	0.0434	32.032	0.004258	40
45	0.031601	90970	2875	448199	0.006414	2.6866	2517050	0.0163	27.669	0.006393	45
50	0.051627	88095	4548	429904	0.010579	2.6756	2068851	0.0000	23.484	0.010579	50
55	0.080303	83547	6709	401961	0.016691	2.6489	1638947	0.0000	19.617	0.016691	55
60	0.121595	76838	9343	361897	0.025817	2.6141	1236986	0.0160	16.099	0.025748	60
65	0.175203	67495	11825	308878	0.038285	2.5818	875089	0.0160	12.965	0.038186	65
70	0.251277	55669	13988	244068	0.057314	2.5495	566210	0.0160	10.171	0.057160	70
75	0.363379	41681	15146	170469	0.088849	2.4953	322142	0.0160	7.729	0.088600	75
80	0.514269	26535	13646	97107	0.140527	2.4655	151673	0.0160	5.716	0.140146	80
85+	1.000000	12889	12889	54567	0.236204	4.2336	54567	0.0160	4.234	0.236599	85

TABLE 3 — FEMALE LIFE TABLE

x	nq_x	l_x	nd_x	nL_x	nm_x	na_x	T_x	r_x	$\mathring{e}_x$	nM_x	x
0	0.015658	100000	1566	98841	0.015842	0.2600	7547713	0.0014	75.477	0.015859	0
1	0.003231	98434	318	392818	0.000810	1.1102	7448872	0.0014	75.674	0.000811	1
5	0.001563	98116	153	490197	0.000313	2.5000	7056054	0.0016	71.915	0.000313	5
10	0.001303	97963	128	489509	0.000261	2.6099	6565857	0.0000	67.024	0.000261	10
15	0.002256	97835	221	488665	0.000452	2.6861	6076349	0.0331	62.108	0.000449	15
20	0.003328	97614	325	487289	0.000667	2.5899	5587684	0.0367	57.242	0.000664	20
25	0.003710	97289	361	485579	0.000743	2.5952	5100395	0.0000	52.425	0.000743	25
30	0.005053	96929	490	483495	0.001013	2.6565	4614816	0.0000	47.611	0.001013	30
35	0.007557	96439	729	480484	0.001517	2.6548	4131321	0.0000	42.839	0.001517	35
40	0.010775	95710	1031	476150	0.002166	2.6730	3650837	0.0402	38.145	0.002150	40
45	0.016744	94679	1585	469686	0.003375	2.6613	3174687	0.0146	33.531	0.003367	45
50	0.024266	93093	2259	460163	0.004909	2.6520	2705001	0.0000	29.057	0.004909	50
55	0.035603	90834	3234	446606	0.007241	2.6607	2244839	0.0000	24.714	0.007241	55
60	0.054266	87600	4754	426958	0.011134	2.6768	1798232	0.0142	20.528	0.011102	60
65	0.087731	82847	7268	397405	0.018289	2.6847	1371274	0.0142	16.552	0.018231	65
70	0.148159	75578	11198	351709	0.031838	2.6618	973869	0.0142	12.886	0.031734	70
75	0.247951	64381	15963	283725	0.056263	2.6083	622160	0.0142	9.664	0.056084	75
80	0.402721	48418	19499	193293	0.100876	2.6384	338435	0.0142	6.990	0.100602	80
85+	1.000000	28919	28919	145141	0.199246	5.0189	145141	0.0142	5.019	0.193298	85

TABLE 4 — OBSERVED AND PROJECTED VITAL RATES

	OBSERVED POPULATION BOTH SEXES	MALES	FEMALES	PROJECTED POPULATION 1970 MALES	FEMALES	1975 MALES	FEMALES	1980 MALES	FEMALES	STABLE POPULATION MALES	FEMALES
RATES PER THOUSAND											
Birth	17.63	18.48	16.81	19.68	17.95	20.59	18.87	20.17	18.56	20.87	19.42
Death	11.05	11.67	10.45	11.86	11.02	11.93	11.17	11.92	11.18	10.48	9.03
Increase	6.58	6.81	6.36	7.82	6.93	8.66	7.71	8.25	7.39		10.3859
PERCENTAGE											
under 15	24.58	25.63	23.58	25.39	23.36	26.68	24.62	27.38	25.34	28.27	26.46
15-64	62.87	64.67	61.14	64.13	60.67	62.53	59.25	62.23	59.08	63.22	61.31
65 and over	12.55	9.70	15.28	10.48	15.97	10.79	16.13	10.39	15.58	8.51	12.24
DEP. RATIO X 100	59.06	54.62	63.55	55.93	64.82	59.93	68.77	60.69	69.26	58.17	63.11

TABLE 5 — POPULATION PROJECTED WITH FIXED AGE-SPECIFIC BIRTH AND DEATH RATES (IN 1000's)

AGE AT LAST BIRTHDAY	1970 BOTH SEXES	1970 MALES	1970 FEMALES	1975 BOTH SEXES	1975 MALES	1975 FEMALES	1980 BOTH SEXES	1980 MALES	1980 FEMALES	AGE AT LAST BIRTHDAY
0-4	4451	2274	2177	4884	2495	2389	5150	2631	2519	0-4
5-9	4193	2137	2056	4435	2265	2170	4866	2485	2381	5-9
10-14	3698	1883	1815	4185	2132	2053	4427	2260	2167	10-14
15-19	4101	2084	2017	3689	1877	1812	4174	2125	2049	15-19
20-24	4272	2182	2090	4083	2071	2012	3672	1865	1807	20-24
25-29	2997	1557	1440	4249	2166	2083	4061	2056	2005	25-29
30-34	3029	1592	1437	2978	1544	1434	4222	2148	2074	30-34
35-39	3270	1682	1588	3001	1573	1428	2950	1525	1425	35-39
40-44	3335	1687	1648	3226	1652	1574	2961	1545	1416	40-44
45-49	3272	1622	1650	3269	1644	1625	3162	1609	1553	45-49
50-54	2087	1022	1065	3172	1556	1616	3169	1577	1592	50-54
55-59	2591	1235	1356	1989	955	1034	3024	1455	1569	55-59
60-64	2651	1233	1418	2408	1112	1296	1848	860	988	60-64
65-69	2378	1061	1317	2372	1052	1320	2155	949	1206	65-69
70-74	1861	754	1107	2004	838	1166	2000	832	1168	70-74
75-79	1238	416	822	1420	527	893	1526	586	940	75-79
80-84	759	236	523	797	237	560	908	300	608	80-84
85+	496	130	366	526	133	393	554	133	421	85+
TOTAL	50679	24787	25892	52687	25829	26858	54829	26941	27888	TOTAL

TABLE 6 — STANDARDIZED RATES

STANDARD COUNTRIES:
STANDARDIZED RATES PER THOUSAND

	ENGLAND AND WALES 1961 BOTH SEXES	MALES	FEMALES	UNITED STATES 1960 BOTH SEXES	MALES	FEMALES	MEXICO 1960 BOTH SEXES	MALES	FEMALES
Birth	17.82	17.97*	16.86	18.10	16.95*	17.40	21.03	15.95*	20.47
Death	10.59	11.62*	9.56	8.66	10.44*	7.02	4.48	8.85*	3.38
Increase	7.24	6.35*	7.29	9.44	6.50*	10.38	16.55	7.10*	17.09

TABLE 7 — MOMENTS AND CUMULANTS

	OBSERVED POP. MALES	OBSERVED POP. FEMALES	STATIONARY POP. MALES	STATIONARY POP. FEMALES	STABLE POP. MALES	STABLE POP. FEMALES	OBSERVED BIRTHS	NET MATERNITY FUNCTION	BIRTHS IN STABLE POP.
μ	33.47357	36.81080	36.63145	39.70113	31.60385	33.97776	27.89219	27.81019	27.45712
σ^2	480.3479	561.1175	501.2663	567.5638	463.2160	529.2212	35.25695	32.53102	31.29202
κ_3	3757.535	3384.821	2534.080	2061.762	4650.472	5143.292	105.9136	119.3962	119.0240
κ_4	-207862.	-335790.	-241292.	-341214.	-159563.	-239212.	-349.456	-9.688	89.637
β_1	0.127391	0.064850	0.050984	0.023251	0.217592	0.178472	0.255958	0.414083	0.462347
β_2	2.099128	1.933502	2.039701	1.940752	2.256355	2.145901	2.718872	2.990845	3.091542
κ	-0.047311	-0.022487	-0.019501	-0.008429	-0.083881	-0.065432	-0.155664	-0.274916	-0.324477

TABLE 8 — RATES FROM AGE DISTRIBUTIONS AND VITAL STATISTICS (Females)

VITAL STATISTICS

		THOMPSON AGE RANGE	NRR	1000r	INTERVAL	BOURGEOIS-PICHAT AGE RANGE	NRR	1000b	1000d	1000r	COALE
GRR	1.373										
NRR	1.332	0-4	1.23	7.53	27.43	5-29	1.52	18.69	3.23	15.46	IBR
TFR	2.815	5-9	1.20	6.68	27.40	30-54	1.36	20.09	8.65	11.44	IDR
GENERATION	27.633	10-14	1.33	10.35	27.35	55-79	1.28	23.06	13.82	9.24	IRI
SEX RATIO	104.954	15-19	1.36	10.80	27.28	*20-44	0.77	9.40	19.21	-9.81	K1
											K2

TABLE 9 — LESLIE MATRIX AND ITS SPECTRAL COMPONENTS (Females)

Start of Age Interval	ORIGINAL MATRIX SUB-DIAGONAL	ALTERNATIVE FIRST ROWS Projection	Integral	FIRST STABLE MATRIX % IN STABLE POPULATION	FISHER VALUES	REPRODUCTIVE VALUES	SECOND STABLE MATRIX Z2 FIRST COLUMN	FIRST ROW
0	0.99703	0.00000	0.00000	9.306	1.044	2151720	0.1752+0.0719	0.1752+0.0719
5	0.99860	0.00005	0.00000	8.808	1.103	2004093	0.1624-0.1483	0.0085+0.1628
10	0.99828	0.03326	0.00010	8.350	1.163	2350255	-0.0753-0.2446	-0.1234+0.0664
15	0.99718	0.24409	0.06829	7.913	1.192	2499315	-0.2946-0.0423	-0.1028-0.0739
20	0.99649	0.42666	0.43936	7.491	1.004	1450848	-0.1907+0.2884	-0.0231-0.1248
25	0.99571	0.34443	0.44336	7.087	0.615	887285	0.2081+0.3432	0.0137-0.0947
30	0.99377	0.19218	0.26475	6.699	0.289	462238	0.4630-0.0482	0.0182-0.0491
35	0.99098	0.08302	0.13053	6.320	0.105	174161	0.1785-0.5086	0.0112-0.0178
40	0.98642	0.02188	0.04023	5.946	0.024	39984	-0.4428-0.4372	0.0034-0.0038
45	0.97972	0.00236	0.00475	5.568	0.002	2590	-0.6717+0.2454	0.0004-0.0004
50	0.97054	0.00005	0.00010	5.179	0.000	67	-0.0743+0.8128	0.0000-0.0000
55+	0.81776			21.333				

TABLE 10 — AGE ANALYSIS AND MISCELLANEOUS RESULTS (Females)

Start of Age Interval	OBSERVED POPUL. (IN 100's)	CONTRIBUTIONS OF ROOTS (IN 100's) r_1	r_2, r_3	r_4-r_{11}	AGE-SP. BIRTH RATES	NET MATERNITY FUNCTION	COEFF. OF MATRIX EQUATION	PARAMETERS	PARAMETERS INTEGRAL	MATRIX	EXP. INCREASE x	$e^{(x+2\frac{1}{2})r}$
0	20617	21027	-961	550	0.0000	0.0000	0.0000	L(1)	1.05330	1.05337	0	1.0263
5	18175	19903	-657	-1071	0.0000	0.0000	0.0000	L(2)	0.36125	0.36672	50	1.7251
10	20207	18868	645	694	0.0000	0.0001	0.0331		0.80497	0.77609	55	1.8170
15	20959	17881	1530	1548	0.0135	0.0661	0.2426	R(1)	0.01039	0.01040	60	1.9139
20	14448	16927	647	-3126	0.0860	0.4191	0.4229	R(2)	-0.02504	-0.03054	65	2.0159
25	14436	16013	-1422	-156	0.0879	0.4267	0.3402		0.22979	0.22587	70	2.1233
30	15982	15137	-2280	3125	0.0525	0.2537	0.1890	C(1)		225958	75	2.2365
35	16627	14281	-346	2692	0.0259	0.1243	0.0811	C(2)		-251862	80	2.3557
40	16723	13435	2706	582	0.0080	0.0380	0.0212			54415	85	2.4813
45	10873	12581	3116	-4824	0.0009	0.0044	0.0023	2P/Y	27.3430	27.8173	90	2.6135
50	13970	11701	-510	2779	0.0000	0.0001	0.0000	DELTA	7.4489		95	2.7528
55+	67222	48203									100	2.8995

Including East Berlin

TABLE 1 — DATA

AGE AT LAST BIRTHDAY	POPULATION BOTH SEXES	MALES Number	%	FEMALES Number	%	BIRTHS BY AGE OF MOTHER	DEATHS BOTH SEXES	MALES	FEMALES	AGE AT LAST BIRTHDAY
0	292854	150417	1.8	142437	1.4	0	18086	10300	7786	0
1-4	1004136	512847	6.3	491289	4.8	0	2529	1403	1126	1-4
5-9	1095869	556827	6.8	539042	5.3	0	888	540	348	5-9
10-14	1670154	847832	10.4	822322	8.1	25	1132	717	415	10-14
15-19	1489567	751488	9.2	738079	7.3	27277	1677	1006	671	15-19
20-24	1185348	554149	6.8	631199	6.2	102884	1958	1099	859	20-24
25-29	1051102	418072	5.1	633030	6.2	86890	1727	778	949	25-29
30-34	992821	376371	4.6	616450	6.1	52678	1907	763	1144	30-34
35-39	963598	368598	4.5	595000	5.8	24695	2646	1124	1522	35-39
40-44	1394183	560269	6.9	833914	8.2	10345	4907	2253	2654	40-44
45-49	1474282	645515	7.9	828767	8.1	1210	7867	4043	3824	45-49
50-54	1410071	619644	7.6	790427	7.8	0	11508	6388	5120	50-54
55-59	1191880	487796	6.0	704084	6.9	0	14230	7521	6709	55-59
60-64	1035619	426915	5.2	608704	6.0	0	19640	10337	9303	60-64
65-69	843910	357812	4.4	486098	4.8	0	26179	13022	13157	65-69
70-74	619967	266094	3.3	353873	3.5		32788	15691	17097	70-74
75-79	396960	170184	2.1	226776	2.2		35713	16350	19363	75-79
80-84	162173	66452	0.8	95721	0.9	158109 M.	23721	10385	13336	80-84
85+	53751	19639	0.2	34112	0.3	147895 F.	12573	4889	7684	85+
TOTAL	18328245	8156921		10171324		306004	221676	108609	113067	TOTAL

TABLE 2 — MALE LIFE TABLE

x	nq_x	l_x	nd_x	nL_x	nm_x	na_x	T_x	r_x	$\mathring{e}_x$	nM_x	x
0	0.064398	100000	6440	95045	0.067755	0.2306	6428333	0.0136	64.283	0.068476	
1	0.010646	93560	996	371340	0.002682	1.0879	6333288	0.0136	67.692	0.002736	
5	0.004837	92564	448	461701	0.000970	2.5000	5961947	0.0000	64.409	0.000970	
10	0.004220	92116	389	459645	0.000846	2.5905	5500246	0.0000	59.710	0.000846	10
15	0.006721	91728	617	457204	0.001348	2.6734	5040601	0.0411	54.952	0.001339	15
20	0.009899	91111	902	453347	0.001989	2.5506	4583397	0.0568	50.306	0.001983	20
25	0.009263	90209	836	448958	0.001861	2.5002	4130050	0.0368	45.783	0.001861	25
30	0.010100	89374	903	444717	0.002030	2.6162	3681093	0.0104	41.188	0.002027	30
35	0.015138	88471	1339	439180	0.003049	2.6296	3236376	0.0000	36.581	0.003049	35
40	0.019919	87132	1736	431590	0.004021	2.6557	2797196	0.0000	32.103	0.004021	40
45	0.030870	85396	2636	420900	0.006263	2.6931	2365606	0.0000	27.702	0.006263	45
50	0.050490	82760	4179	404027	0.010342	2.6611	1944706	0.0176	23.498	0.010309	50
55	0.074671	78581	5868	379110	0.015478	2.6487	1540679	0.0211	19.606	0.015418	55
60	0.115050	72714	8366	343687	0.024341	2.6235	1161569	0.0302	15.975	0.024213	60
65	0.168240	64348	10826	295822	0.036596	2.6060	817882	0.0302	12.710	0.036393	65
70	0.259177	53522	13872	233889	0.059309	2.5691	522060	0.0302	9.754	0.058968	70
75	0.388992	39650	15424	159629	0.096622	2.4958	288171	0.0302	7.268	0.096072	75
80	0.559813	24227	13562	86236	0.157271	2.4269	128542	0.0302	5.306	0.156279	80
85+	*1.000000	10664	10664	42306	0.252075	3.9671	42306	0.0302	3.967	0.248943	85

TABLE 3 — FEMALE LIFE TABLE

x	nq_x	l_x	nd_x	nL_x	nm_x	na_x	T_x	r_x	$\mathring{e}_x$	nM_x	x
0	0.051969	100000	5197	96031	0.054117	0.2363	6832254	0.0129	68.323	0.054663	
1	0.008946	94803	848	376746	0.002251	1.0918	6736223	0.0129	71.055	0.002292	
5	0.003223	93955	303	469018	0.000646	2.5000	6359477	0.0000	67.686	0.000646	5
10	0.002520	93652	236	467697	0.000505	2.6086	5890459	0.0000	62.897	0.000505	10
15	0.004559	93416	426	466099	0.000914	2.6935	5422762	0.0255	58.050	0.000909	15
20	0.006791	92990	631	463428	0.001363	2.5871	4956664	0.0141	53.303	0.001361	20
25	0.007469	92359	690	460115	0.001499	2.5652	4493236	0.0008	48.650	0.001499	25
30	0.009243	91669	847	456324	0.001857	2.6143	4033121	0.0043	43.997	0.001856	30
35	0.012712	90822	1155	451341	0.002558	2.6027	3576798	0.0000	39.383	0.002558	35
40	0.015794	89667	1416	444975	0.003183	2.6265	3125457	0.0000	34.856	0.003183	40
45	0.022824	88251	2014	436499	0.004615	2.6385	2680482	0.0007	30.373	0.004614	45
50	0.031948	86237	2755	424690	0.006487	2.6428	2243983	0.0096	26.021	0.006478	50
55	0.046748	83482	3903	408312	0.009558	2.6691	1819294	0.0161	21.793	0.009529	55
60	0.074419	79579	5922	384247	0.015412	2.6954	1410982	0.0366	17.731	0.015283	60
65	0.128376	73657	9456	346331	0.027303	2.6783	1026735	0.0366	13.939	0.027067	65
70	0.218308	64201	14016	287706	0.048715	2.6241	680403	0.0366	10.598	0.048314	70
75	0.354737	50186	17803	206969	0.086016	2.5308	392698	0.0366	7.825	0.085384	75
80	0.514029	32383	16646	118700	0.140234	2.4741	185729	0.0366	5.735	0.139322	80
85+	1.000000	15737	15737	67029	0.234780	4.2593	67029	0.0366	4.259	0.225259	85

TABLE 4 — OBSERVED AND PROJECTED VITAL RATES

	OBSERVED POPULATION BOTH SEXES	MALES	FEMALES	PROJECTED POPULATION 1957 MALES	FEMALES	1962 MALES	FEMALES	1967 MALES	FEMALES	STABLE POPULATION MALES	FEMALES
RATES PER THOUSAND											
Birth	16.70	19.38	14.54	19.89	15.13	20.32	15.72	18.50	14.59	16.86	15.91
Death	12.09	13.31	11.12	14.40	12.67	14.86	13.86	14.84	14.75	14.62	13.68
Increase	4.60	6.07	3.42	5.48	2.47	5.46	1.86	3.66	-0.16		2.231
PERCENTAGE											
under 15	22.17	25.35	19.61	23.44	18.25	25.50	20.08	26.34	21.09	23.01	22.05
15-64	66.50	63.86	68.62	65.17	68.28	62.84	64.95	61.16	62.53	65.29	64.10
65 and over	11.33	10.79	11.76	11.39	13.47	11.66	14.96	12.50	16.37	11.70	13.85
DEP. RATIO X 100	50.37	56.60	45.73	53.44	46.47	59.14	53.96	63.50	59.92	53.16	56.01

TABLE 5 — POPULATION PROJECTED WITH FIXED AGE—SPECIFIC BIRTH AND DEATH RATES (IN 1000's)

AGE AT LAST BIRTHDAY	1957 BOTH SEXES	1957 MALES	1957 FEMALES	1962 BOTH SEXES	1962 MALES	1962 FEMALES	1967 BOTH SEXES	1967 MALES	1967 FEMALES	AGE AT LAST BIRTHDAY
0-4	1477	758	719	1557	799	758	1541	791	750	0-4
5-9	1286	657	629	1464	751	713	1543	791	752	5-9
10-14	1092	554	538	1281	654	627	1458	747	711	10-14
15-19	1663	843	820	1087	551	536	1275	650	625	15-19
20-24	1479	745	734	1651	836	815	1080	547	533	20-24
25-29	1176	549	627	1467	738	729	1637	828	809	25-29
30-34	1042	414	628	1166	544	622	1454	731	723	30-34
35-39	982	372	610	1030	409	621	1152	537	615	35-39
40-44	949	362	587	966	365	601	1014	402	612	40-44
45-49	1364	546	818	928	353	575	946	356	590	45-49
50-54	1426	620	806	1320	524	796	899	339	560	50-54
55-59	1341	581	760	1356	581	775	1257	492	765	55-59
60-64	1105	442	663	1242	527	715	1257	527	730	60-64
65-69	916	367	549	978	381	597	1099	454	645	65-69
70-74	687	283	404	747	291	456	797	301	496	70-74
75-79	437	182	255	483	193	290	526	198	328	75-79
80-84	222	92	130	244	98	146	271	104	167	80-84
85+	87	33	54	118	45	73	130	48	82	85+
TOTAL	18731	8400	10331	19085	8640	10445	19336	8843	10493	TOTAL

TABLE 6 — STANDARDIZED RATES

STANDARD COUNTRIES: STANDARDIZED RATES PER THOUSAND	ENGLAND AND WALES 1961 BOTH SEXES	MALES	FEMALES	UNITED STATES 1960 BOTH SEXES	MALES	FEMALES	MEXICO 1960 BOTH SEXES	MALES	FEMALES
Birth	15.17	23.50*	14.21	15.42	21.39*	14.68	18.24	20.11*	17.59
Death	13.52	12.80*	14.06	11.34	11.40*	10.75	6.92	10.31*	6.13
Increase	1.65	10.70*	0.14	4.08	9.99*	3.93	11.32	9.80*	11.45

TABLE 7 — MOMENTS AND CUMULANTS

	OBSERVED POP. MALES	OBSERVED POP. FEMALES	STATIONARY POP. MALES	STATIONARY POP. FEMALES	STABLE POP. MALES	STABLE POP. FEMALES	OBSERVED BIRTHS	NET MATERNITY FUNCTION	BIRTHS IN STABLE POP.
μ	34.95534	37.80226	36.52246	37.89430	35.41539	36.72519	27.18023	27.17104	27.09082
σ^2	497.1146	467.0446	499.1118	526.6811	493.0909	521.1014	36.71423	34.01687	33.72788
κ_3	2407.007	658.390	2431.660	2188.184	2960.582	2808.517	153.7604	129.4661	129.5766
κ_4	-276933.	-224050.	-243561.	-284534.	-230127.	-270955.	26.724	-57.659	-31.054
β_1	0.047161	0.004255	0.047557	0.032774	0.073109	0.055743	0.477733	0.425823	0.437609
β_2	1.879372	1.972863	2.022286	1.974256	2.053516	2.002179	3.019826	2.950171	2.972701
κ	-0.015972	-0.001615	-0.017987	-0.012092	-0.027640	-0.020560	-0.291730	-0.260079	-0.269812

TABLE 8 — RATES FROM AGE DISTRIBUTIONS AND VITAL STATISTICS (Females)

VITAL STATISTICS		THOMPSON AGE RANGE	NRR	1000r	INTERVAL	BOURGEOIS-PICHAT AGE RANGE	NRR	1000b	1000d	1000r	COALE
GRR	1.155										IBR
NRR	1.062	0-4	0.91	-3.50	27.38	5-29	0.95	13.56	15.65	-2.09	IDR
TFR	2.390	5-9	0.75	-10.29	27.33	30-54	0.58	6.85	26.96	-20.11	IRI
GENERATION	27.131	10-14	1.09	3.28	27.27	55-79	1.85	63.33	40.64	22.69	K1
SEX RATIO	106.906	15-19	0.95	-1.88	27.19	*50-74	1.75	55.31	34.62	20.69	K2

TABLE 9 — LESLIE MATRIX AND ITS SPECTRAL COMPONENTS (Females)

Start of Age Interval	ORIGINAL MATRIX SUB-DIAGONAL	ALTERNATIVE FIRST ROWS Projection	Integral	FIRST STABLE MATRIX % IN STABLE POPULATION	FISHER VALUES	REPRODUCTIVE VALUES	SECOND STABLE MATRIX Z_2 FIRST COLUMN	FIRST ROW
0	0.99205	0.00000	0.00000	7.479	1.063	673953	0.1715+0.0835	0.1715+0.0835
5	0.99718	0.00003	0.00000	7.337	1.084	584337	0.1830-0.1481	-0.0025+0.1545
10	0.99658	0.04211	0.00007	7.235	1.099	903940	-0.0704-0.2835	-0.1137+0.0509
15	0.99427	0.22738	0.08492	7.130	1.070	790083	-0.3555-0.3698	-0.0832-0.0692
20	0.99285	0.34192	0.37453	7.011	0.846	533680	-0.2644+0.3619	-0.0170-0.1037
25	0.99176	0.25364	0.31539	6.883	0.495	313288	0.2668+0.4851	0.0112-0.0768
30	0.98908	0.14453	0.19635	6.751	0.233	143403	0.6817-0.0448	0.0164-0.0395
35	0.98590	0.06139	0.09537	6.603	0.082	49047	0.3052-0.7835	0.0096-0.0137
40	0.98095	0.01581	0.02850	6.438	0.018	15284	-0.7123-0.7460	0.0028-0.0028
45	0.97295	0.00167	0.00335	6.245	0.002	1455	-1.1930+0.4022	0.0003-0.0002
50	0.96144	0.00000	0.00000	6.009	0.000	1	-0.1702+1.5146	0.0000-0.0000
55+	0.77901			24.878				

TABLE 10 — AGE ANALYSIS AND MISCELLANEOUS RESULTS (Females)

Start of Age Interval	OBSERVED POPUL. (IN 100's)	r_1	r_2, r_3	$r_4 \cdot r_{11}$	AGE-SP. BIRTH RATES	NET MATERNITY FUNCTION	COEFF. OF MATRIX EQUATION	PARAMETERS	INTEGRAL	MATRIX	EXP. INCREASE x	$e^{(x+2\frac{1}{2})r}$
0	6337	6960	-657	34	0.0000	0.0000	0.0000	L(1)	1.01122	1.01122	0	1.0056
5	5390	6828	-839	-598	0.0000	0.0000	0.0000	L(2)	0.32947	0.34020	50	1.1243
10	8223	6733	124	1366	0.0000	0.0000	0.0417		0.75476	0.72812	55	1.1369
15	7381	6636	1421	-677	0.0179	0.0833	0.2242	R(1)	0.00223	0.00223	60	1.1496
20	6312	6525	1299	-1512	0.0788	0.3651	0.3352	R(2)	-0.03883	-0.04371	65	1.1625
25	6330	6406	-814	738	0.0663	0.3052	0.2469		0.23184	0.22674	70	1.1756
30	6165	6283	-2831	2712	0.0413	0.1885	0.1395	C(1)		93066	75	1.1888
35	5950	6145	-1713	1518	0.0201	0.0905	0.0586	C(2)		-205679	80	1.2021
40	8339	5991	2494	-146	0.0060	0.0267	0.0149			-29233	85	1.2156
45	8288	5812	5143	-2667	0.0007	0.0031	0.0015	2P/Y	27.1012	27.7109	90	1.2292
50	7904	5592	1586	726	0.0000	0.0000	0.0000	DELTA	8.3193		95	1.2430
55+	25094	23153									100	1.2569

Including East Berlin

TABLE 1 — DATA

AGE AT LAST BIRTHDAY	POPULATION BOTH SEXES	MALES Number	MALES %	FEMALES Number	FEMALES %	BIRTHS BY AGE OF MOTHER	DEATHS BOTH SEXES	DEATHS MALES	DEATHS FEMALES	AGE AT LAST BIRTHDAY
0	285139	146584	1.8	138555	1.4	0	15036	8684	6352	0
1-4	1102700	565148	7.0	537552	5.4	0	2358	1308	1050	1-4
5-9	986150	500755	6.2	485395	4.9	0	676	400	276	5-9
10-14	1503624	764385	9.5	739239	7.4	34	771	478	293	10-14
15-19	1589756	805286	10.0	784470	7.8	31903	1421	885	536	15-19
20-24	1179708	571776	7.1	607932	6.1	100506	1573	957	616	20-24
25-29	1069394	454696	5.6	614698	6.1	81676	1559	786	773	25-29
30-34	1066723	403626	5.0	663097	6.6	52676	1738	718	1020	30-34
35-39	736428	278907	3.5	457521	4.6	18823	1697	692	1005	35-39
40-44	1289237	505728	6.3	783509	7.8	8947	4013	1797	2216	40-44
45-49	1426774	604480	7.5	822294	8.2	744	6571	3306	3265	45-49
50-54	1408882	625982	7.8	782900	7.8	0	10477	5824	4653	50-54
55-59	1222113	507147	6.3	714966	7.1	0	14027	7642	6385	55-59
60-64	1034442	418239	5.2	616203	6.2	0	18533	9646	8887	60-64
65-69	873012	363807	4.5	509205	5.1	0	25929	13181	12748	65-69
70-74	625467	264946	3.3	360521	3.6		31829	15324	16505	70-74
75-79	416784	176236	2.2	240548	2.4		36625	16811	19814	75-79
80-84	181678	76117	0.9	105561	1.1	152760 M.	26097	11515	14582	80-84
85+	60925	22436	0.3	38489	0.4	142549 F.	14578	5720	8858	85+
TOTAL	18058936	8056281		10002655		295309	215508	105674	109834	TOTAL

TABLE 2 — MALE LIFE TABLE

x	nq_x	l_x	nd_x	nL_x	nm_x	na_x	T_x	r_x	$\mathring{e}_x$	nM_x	x
0	0.056586	100000	5659	95639	0.059166	0.2294	6567868	0.0016	65.679	0.059242	0
1	0.009174	94341	865	374844	0.002309	1.0871	6472228	0.0016	68.604	0.002314	1
5	0.003986	93476	373	466448	0.000799	2.5000	6097384	0.0000	65.229	0.000799	5
10	0.003122	93103	291	464819	0.000625	2.5996	5630936	0.0000	60.480	0.000625	10
15	0.005512	92813	512	462885	0.001105	2.6963	5166117	0.0279	55.662	0.001099	15
20	0.008371	92301	773	459632	0.001681	2.5746	4703232	0.0556	50.955	0.001674	20
25	0.008610	91528	788	455679	0.001729	2.5091	4243601	0.0331	46.364	0.001729	25
30	0.008892	90740	807	451752	0.001786	2.5829	3787921	0.0470	41.745	0.001779	30
35	0.012333	89934	1109	447053	0.002481	2.6424	3336169	0.0000	37.096	0.002481	35
40	0.017620	88824	1565	440469	0.003553	2.6660	2889117	0.0000	32.526	0.003553	40
45	0.027007	87259	2357	430886	0.005469	2.7040	2448648	0.0000	28.062	0.005469	45
50	0.045616	84903	3873	415574	0.009319	2.6918	2017762	0.0079	23.766	0.009304	50
55	0.073096	81030	5923	391253	0.015138	2.6540	1602188	0.0249	19.773	0.015069	55
60	0.109843	75107	8250	356008	0.023174	2.6332	1210935	0.0261	16.123	0.023063	60
65	0.167468	66857	11196	307528	0.036408	2.6103	854927	0.0261	12.787	0.036231	65
70	0.254682	55660	14176	243871	0.058168	2.5711	547400	0.0261	9.835	0.057838	70
75	0.386529	41485	16035	167283	0.095856	2.4967	303529	0.0261	7.317	0.095389	75
80	0.546963	25450	13920	91510	0.152115	2.4326	136246	0.0261	5.354	0.151279	80
85+	*1.000000	11530	11530	44737	0.257721	3.8802	44737	0.0261	3.880	0.254947	85+

TABLE 3 — FEMALE LIFE TABLE

x	nq_x	l_x	nd_x	nL_x	nm_x	na_x	T_x	r_x	$\mathring{e}_x$	nM_x	x
0	0.044253	100000	4425	96633	0.045795	0.2391	6982575	0.0014	69.826	0.045845	0
1	0.007754	95575	741	380145	0.001950	1.0938	6885942	0.0014	72.048	0.001953	1
5	0.002839	94834	269	473495	0.000569	2.5000	6505797	0.0000	68.602	0.000569	5
10	0.001980	94564	187	472365	0.000396	2.5599	6032302	0.0000	63.790	0.000396	10
15	0.003423	94377	323	471138	0.000686	2.6867	5559937	0.0189	58.912	0.000683	15
20	0.005068	94054	477	469134	0.001016	2.6152	5088799	0.0234	54.105	0.001013	20
25	0.006269	93577	587	466470	0.001258	2.5847	4619665	0.0000	49.367	0.001258	25
30	0.007690	92991	715	463254	0.001544	2.6228	4153195	0.0279	44.662	0.001538	30
35	0.010926	92276	1008	458976	0.002197	2.6172	3689940	0.0000	39.988	0.002197	35
40	0.014047	91268	1282	453291	0.002828	2.6238	3230964	0.0000	35.401	0.002828	40
45	0.019670	89985	1770	445775	0.003971	2.6538	2777673	0.0000	30.868	0.003971	45
50	0.029348	88215	2589	435019	0.005951	2.6598	2331898	0.0079	26.434	0.005943	50
55	0.043867	85627	3756	419402	0.008956	2.6757	1896880	0.0146	22.153	0.008930	55
60	0.070316	81870	5757	396069	0.014535	2.6926	1477478	0.0346	18.047	0.014422	60
65	0.119262	76114	9078	359579	0.025247	2.6680	1081409	0.0346	14.208	0.025035	65
70	0.208082	67035	13949	302224	0.046154	2.6376	721830	0.0346	10.768	0.045781	70
75	0.344614	53086	18294	220497	0.082969	2.5437	419606	0.0346	7.904	0.082370	75
80	0.511340	34792	17791	127967	0.139025	2.4849	199109	0.0346	5.723	0.138138	80
85+	1.000000	17002	17002	71142	0.238981	4.1844	71142	0.0346	4.184	0.230143	85+

TABLE 4 — OBSERVED AND PROJECTED VITAL RATES

	OBSERVED POPULATION BOTH SEXES	MALES	FEMALES	PROJECTED POPULATION 1959 MALES	1959 FEMALES	1964 MALES	1964 FEMALES	1969 MALES	1969 FEMALES	STABLE POPULATION MALES	FEMALES
RATES PER THOUSAND											
Birth	16.35	18.96	14.25	19.99	15.25	19.66	15.25	17.60	13.92	16.51	15.58
Death	11.93	13.12	10.98	13.99	12.44	14.31	13.62	14.25	14.50	14.28	13.34
Increase	4.42	5.84	3.27	6.00	2.80	5.35	1.64	3.35	-0.58		2.2317
PERCENTAGE											
under 15	21.47	24.54	19.00	23.54	18.36	26.14	20.61	26.08	20.93	22.76	21.79
15-64	66.58	64.25	68.46	64.83	67.38	61.81	63.57	60.94	61.86	65.27	63.93
65 and over	11.95	11.22	12.54	11.63	14.26	12.06	15.82	12.98	17.20	11.98	14.28
DEP. RATIO X 100	50.20	55.65	46.08	54.25	48.41	61.79	57.31	64.10	61.65	53.22	56.43

Including East Berlin

TABLE 1 — DATA

AGE AT LAST BIRTHDAY	POPULATION BOTH SEXES	MALES Number	%	FEMALES Number	%	BIRTHS BY AGE OF MOTHER	DEATHS BOTH SEXES	MALES	FEMALES	AGE AT LAST BIRTHDAY
0	267752	137502	1.8	130250	1.3	0	12503	7202	5301	0
1-4	1094197	561721	7.2	532476	5.5	0	2126	1219	907	1-4
5-9	1203025	614531	7.8	588494	6.1	0	735	465	270	5-9
10-14	1035966	525831	6.7	510135	5.3	26	504	305	199	10-14
15-19	1522834	771968	9.8	750866	7.8	32262	1353	898	455	15-19
20-24	1278385	644778	8.2	633607	6.5	101986	1586	1049	537	20-24
25-29	1075876	504106	6.4	571770	5.9	72803	1420	848	572	25-29
30-34	961193	380411	4.9	580782	6.0	42532	1496	689	807	30-34
35-39	884999	335534	4.3	549465	5.7	20415	1800	768	1032	35-39
40-44	918835	349099	4.5	569736	5.9	4868	2764	1195	1569	40-44
45-49	1293762	517723	6.6	776039	8.0	445	5634	2671	2963	45-49
50-54	1364208	593383	7.6	770825	8.0	0	9566	5240	4326	50-54
55-59	1279950	553029	7.1	726921	7.5	0	14582	8392	6190	55-59
60-64	1061068	424707	5.4	636361	6.6	0	19074	10157	8917	60-64
65-69	891195	358743	4.6	532452	5.5	0	26226	13372	12854	65-69
70-74	665181	273591	3.5	391590	4.0		33279	16035	17244	70-74
75-79	427738	177503	2.3	250235	2.6		36799	16920	19879	75-79
80-84	216347	89090	1.1	127257	1.3	142155 M.	30496	13548	16948	80-84
85+	74830	27685	0.4	47145	0.5	133182 F.	17722	7198	10524	85+
TOTAL	17517341	7840935		9676406		275337	219665	108171	111494	TOTAL

TABLE 2 — MALE LIFE TABLE

x	nq_x	l_x	nd_x	nL_x	nm_x	na_x	T_x	r_x	$\dot{e}_x$	nM_x	x
0	0.050362	100000	5036	96152	0.052377	0.2359	6619335	0.0000	66.193	0.052377	0
1	0.008626	94964	819	377473	0.002170	1.0916	6523183	0.0000	68.691	0.002170	1
5	0.003739	94145	352	469843	0.000749	2.5000	6145711	0.0274	65.279	0.000757	5
10	0.002896	93793	272	468324	0.000580	2.6641	5675867	0.0000	60.515	0.000580	10
15	0.005801	93521	542	466350	0.001163	2.6858	5207544	0.0000	55.683	0.001163	15
20	0.008125	92979	755	463052	0.001631	2.5637	4741194	0.0411	50.992	0.001627	20
25	0.008386	92223	773	459197	0.001684	2.5192	4278142	0.0511	46.389	0.001682	25
30	0.009040	91450	827	455236	0.001816	2.5653	3818945	0.0388	41.760	0.001811	30
35	0.011393	90623	1032	450678	0.002291	2.6401	3363710	0.0062	37.118	0.002289	35
40	0.016980	89591	1521	444402	0.003423	2.6661	2913031	0.0000	32.515	0.003423	40
45	0.025494	88069	2245	435100	0.005159	2.7035	2468629	0.0000	28.031	0.005159	45
50	0.043279	85824	3714	420625	0.008831	2.7127	2033439	0.0000	23.693	0.008831	50
55	0.073538	82110	6038	396479	0.015229	2.6699	1612814	0.0179	19.642	0.015175	55
60	0.113565	76071	8639	359913	0.024003	2.6335	1216336	0.0199	15.989	0.023915	60
65	0.171655	67432	11575	309419	0.037409	2.6032	856422	0.0199	12.700	0.037275	65
70	0.257269	55857	14370	244285	0.058826	2.5643	547004	0.0199	9.793	0.058609	70
75	0.385884	41487	16009	167330	0.095674	2.4949	302719	0.0199	7.297	0.095322	75
80	0.548531	25478	13975	91512	0.152717	2.4328	135389	0.0199	5.314	0.152070	80
85+	*1.000000	11502	11502	43877	0.262150	3.8146	43877	0.0199	3.815	0.259996	85+

TABLE 3 — FEMALE LIFE TABLE

x	nq_x	l_x	nd_x	nL_x	nm_x	na_x	T_x	r_x	$\dot{e}_x$	nM_x	x
0	0.039474	100000	3947	96990	0.040699	0.2374	7079164	0.0000	70.792	0.040699	0
1	0.006780	96053	651	382317	0.001703	1.0927	6982174	0.0000	72.691	0.001703	1
5	0.002263	95401	216	476467	0.000453	2.5000	6599857	0.0254	69.180	0.000459	5
10	0.001949	95185	185	475479	0.000390	2.5803	6123390	0.0000	64.331	0.000390	10
15	0.003026	95000	287	474327	0.000606	2.6566	5647911	0.0000	59.452	0.000606	15
20	0.004240	94713	402	472597	0.000850	2.5952	5173585	0.0264	54.624	0.000848	20
25	0.004994	94311	471	470429	0.001001	2.6099	4700987	0.0077	49.846	0.001000	25
30	0.006927	93840	650	467658	0.001390	2.6283	4230558	0.0026	45.083	0.001390	30
35	0.009350	93190	871	463899	0.001878	2.6466	3762900	0.0000	40.379	0.001878	35
40	0.013681	92319	1263	458613	0.002754	2.6405	3299001	0.0000	35.735	0.002754	40
45	0.018921	91056	1723	451224	0.003818	2.6465	2840387	0.0000	31.194	0.003818	45
50	0.027701	89333	2475	440876	0.005613	2.6609	2389164	0.0008	26.745	0.005612	50
55	0.041838	86858	3634	425875	0.008533	2.6840	1948288	0.0102	22.431	0.008515	55
60	0.068303	83224	5684	403012	0.014105	2.6939	1522412	0.0292	18.293	0.014012	60
65	0.115096	77540	8925	367073	0.024313	2.6888	1119400	0.0292	14.436	0.024141	65
70	0.200717	68615	13772	310605	0.044340	2.6423	752327	0.0292	10.964	0.044036	70
75	0.334202	54843	18329	229311	0.079930	2.5500	441722	0.0292	8.054	0.079641	75
80	0.497718	36514	18174	135734	0.133893	2.5001	212412	0.0292	5.817	0.133179	80
85+	1.000000	18341	18341	76677	0.239191	4.1808	76677	0.0292	4.181	0.223225	85+

TABLE 4 — OBSERVED AND PROJECTED VITAL RATES

	OBSERVED POPULATION BOTH SEXES	MALES	FEMALES	PROJECTED POPULATION 1962 MALES	FEMALES	1967 MALES	FEMALES	1972 MALES	FEMALES	STABLE POPULATION MALES	FEMALES
RATES PER THOUSAND											
Birth	15.72	18.13	13.76	18.72	14.39	17.33	13.53	16.81	13.37	15.64	14.65
Death	12.54	13.80	11.52	14.43	12.96	14.55	14.06	14.49	15.04	14.69	13.70
Increase	3.18	4.33	2.24	4.29	1.43	2.78	-0.53	2.32	-1.67		0.9493
PERCENTAGE											
under 15	20.56	23.46	18.20	24.93	19.47	25.36	20.07	24.61	19.84	21.92	20.82
15-64	66.45	64.72	67.86	62.89	64.77	61.61	62.51	61.71	61.37	65.58	63.90
65 and over	12.99	11.82	13.94	12.17	15.76	13.03	17.42	13.68	18.79	12.49	15.28
DEP. RATIO X 100	50.48	54.51	47.36	59.00	54.39	62.32	59.97	62.06	62.95	52.48	56.49

TABLE 1 — DATA

AGE AT LAST BIRTHDAY	POPULATION BOTH SEXES	MALES Number	%	FEMALES Number	%	BIRTHS BY AGE OF MOTHER	DEATHS BOTH SEXES	MALES	FEMALES	AGE AT LAST BIRTHDAY
0	283922	145625	1.9	138297	1.5	0	11134	6391	4743	0
1-4	1053549	540612	7.0	512937	5.4	0	1772	1015	757	1-4
5-9	1336463	685389	8.8	651074	6.9	0	735	438	297	5-9
10-14	960243	488187	6.3	472056	5.0	35	414	249	165	10-14
15-19	1250048	633443	8.2	616605	6.5	35189	1100	776	324	15-19
20-24	1401108	709037	9.1	692071	7.3	117961	1701	1185	516	20-24
25-29	1118814	557472	7.2	561342	5.9	75836	1422	890	532	25-29
30-34	1017611	451924	5.8	565687	6.0	41303	1539	851	688	30-34
35-39	967898	369751	4.8	598147	6.3	20281	1902	853	1049	35-39
40-44	678647	256943	3.3	421704	4.4	4325	1919	843	1076	40-44
45-49	1110665	428536	5.5	682129	7.2	332	4831	2255	2576	45-49
50-54	1293897	533882	6.9	760015	8.0	0	8817	4662	4155	50-54
55-59	1291091	567315	7.3	723776	7.6	0	14671	8642	6029	55-59
60-64	1117915	461275	5.9	656640	6.9	0	20507	11605	8902	60-64
65-69	892502	348263	4.5	544239	5.7	0	26424	13482	12942	65-69
70-74	701916	278606	3.6	423310	4.5		35128	16745	18383	70-74
75-79	439617	176697	2.3	262920	2·8		38249	17134	21115	75-79
80-84	233924	94103	1.2	139821	1.5	152054 M.	34126	14772	19354	80-84
85+	90696	34096	0.4	56600	0.6	143208 F.	22405	9070	13335	85+
TOTAL	17240526	7761156		9479370		295262	228796	111858	116938	TOTAL

TABLE 2 — MALE LIFE TABLE

x	nq_x	l_x	nd_x	nL_x	nm_x	na_x	T_x	r_x	$\mathring{e}_x$	nM_x	x
0	0.042280	100000	4228	96784	0.043685	0.2393	6669285	0.0059	66.693	0.043887	0
1	0.007410	95772	710	381025	0.001863	1.0940	6572502	0.0059	68.627	0.001878	1
5	0.003152	95062	300	474562	0.000631	2.5000	6191476	0.0331	65.131	0.000639	5
10	0.002552	94763	242	473266	0.000511	2.7392	5716914	0.0072	60.329	0.000510	10
15	0.006108	94521	577	471273	0.001225	2.6950	5243648	0.0000	55.476	0.001225	15
20	0.008327	93943	782	467796	0.001672	2.5438	4772374	0.0112	50.800	0.001671	20
25	0.007961	93161	742	463970	0.001598	2.5243	4304578	0.0434	46.206	0.001596	25
30	0.009402	92420	869	459992	0.001889	2.5757	3840608	0.0392	41·556	0.001883	30
35	0.011549	91551	1057	455236	0.002323	2.6191	3380616	0.0541	36.926	0.002307	35
40	0.016280	90493	1473	449046	0.003281	2.6777	2925380	0.0000	32.327	0.003281	40
45	0.025996	89020	2314	439782	0.005262	2.7015	2476334	0.0000	27.818	0.005262	45
50	0.042806	86706	3712	425041	0.008732	2.7128	2036553	0.0000	23.488	0.008732	50
55	0.073572	82994	6106	400840	0.015233	2.6856	1611512	0.0000	19.417	0.015233	55
60	0.119032	76888	9152	362694	0.025227	2.6347	1210672	0.0145	15.746	0.025159	60
65	0.177488	67736	12022	309767	0.038811	2.5950	847878	0.0145	12.517	0.038712	65
70	0.262648	55714	14633	242827	0.060262	2.5574	538111	0.0145	9·658	0.060103	70
75	0.390845	41081	16056	165135	0.097231	2.4920	295285	0.0145	7.188	0.096968	75
80	0.560189	25024	14018	89024	0.157468	2.4249	130150	0.0145	5.201	0.156978	80
85+	*1.000000	11006	11006	41125	0.267622	3.7366	41125	0.0145	3.737	0.266014	85+

TABLE 3 — FEMALE LIFE TABLE

x	nq_x	l_x	nd_x	nL_x	nm_x	na_x	T_x	r_x	$\mathring{e}_x$	nM_x	x
0	0.033264	100000	3326	97473	0.034126	0.2403	7151196	0.0063	71.512	0.034296	0
1	0.005828	96674	563	385057	0.001463	1.0947	7053723	0.0063	72.964	0.001476	1
5	0.002248	96110	216	480011	0.000450	2.5000	6668666	0.0315	69.386	0.000456	5
10	0.001747	95894	167	479059	0.000350	2.5437	6188655	0.0050	64.536	0.000350	10
15	0.002624	95727	251	478044	0.000525	2.6561	5709597	0.0000	59.645	0.000525	15
20	0.003725	95475	356	476529	0.000746	2.6168	5231552	0.0086	54.795	0.000746	20
25	0.004737	95120	451	474518	0.000950	2.6010	4755023	0.0192	49.990	0.000948	25
30	0.006064	94669	574	471989	0.001216	2.6360	4280505	0.0000	45.215	0.001216	30
35	0.008771	94095	825	468539	0.001761	2.6537	3808517	0.0276	40.475	0.001754	35
40	0.012682	93270	1183	463579	0.002552	2.6582	3339978	0.0000	35.810	0.002552	40
45	0.018716	92087	1724	456388	0.003776	2.6518	2876399	0.0000	31.236	0.003776	45
50	0.026990	90363	2439	446110	0.005467	2.6600	2420011	0.0000	26.781	0.005467	50
55	0.040908	87925	3597	431284	0.008340	2.6815	1973901	0.0059	22.450	0.008330	55
60	0.066080	84328	5572	408818	0.013630	2.6992	1542617	0.0236	18.293	0.013557	60
65	0.113334	78755	8926	373183	0.023918	2.6927	1133799	0.0236	14.396	0.023780	65
70	0.198034	69830	13830	316648	0.043675	2.6499	760616	0.0236	10.892	0.043427	70
75	0.337131	56000	18879	233878	0.080723	2.5570	443967	0.0236	7.928	0.080310	75
80	0.511723	37121	18996	136622	0.139037	2.4917	210089	0.0236	5.660	0.138420	80
85+	1.000000	18125	18125	73468	0.246710	4.0533	73468	0.0236	4.053	0.235602	85+

TABLE 4 — OBSERVED AND PROJECTED VITAL RATES

	OBSERVED POPULATION BOTH SEXES	MALES	FEMALES	PROJECTED POPULATION 1965 MALES	FEMALES	1970 MALES	FEMALES	1975 MALES	FEMALES	STABLE POPULATION MALES	FEMALES
RATES PER THOUSAND											
Birth	17.13	19.59	15.11	18.85	14.73	17.48	13.89	17.77	14.41	17.19	16.14
Death	13.27	14.41	12.34	14.68	13.56	14.54	14.50	14.29	15.34	13.36	12.31
Increase	3.86	5.18	2.77	4.17	1.17	2.94	-0.60	3.48	-0.93		3.8297
PERCENTAGE											
under 15	21.08	23.96	18.72	26.25	20.71	25.86	20.76	25.45	20.86	23.82	22.61
15-64	65.24	64.03	66.23	61.23	62.55	60.81	61.07	61.29	59.86	65.17	63.61
65 and over	13.68	12.01	15.05	12.52	16.74	13.34	18.16	13.26	19.27	11.01	13.78
DEP. RATIO X 100	53.28	56.17	50.99	63.33	59.88	64.46	63.74	63.15	67.04	53.44	57.22

Including East Berlin

AGE AT LAST BIRTHDAY	1965 BOTH SEXES	MALES	FEMALES	1970 BOTH SEXES	MALES	FEMALES	1975 BOTH SEXES	MALES	FEMALES	AGE AT LAST BIRTHDAY	
0-4	1407	721	686	1358	696	662	1340	687	653	0-4	**TABLE 5**
5-9	1330	682	648	1398	716	682	1349	691	658	5-9	POPULATION
10-14	1334	684	650	1327	680	647	1395	714	681	10-14	PROJECTED
15-19	957	486	471	1329	681	648	1322	677	645	15-19	WITH
20-24	1244	629	615	953	483	470	1322	676	646	20-24	FIXED
25-29	1392	703	689	1236	624	612	947	479	468	25-29	AGE—
30-34	1111	553	558	1382	697	685	1227	618	609	30-34	SPECIFIC
35-39	1009	447	562	1101	547	554	1370	690	680	35-39	BIRTH
40-44	957	365	592	997	441	556	1088	540	548	40-44	AND
45-49	667	252	415	940	357	583	979	432	547	45-49	DEATH
50-54	1081	414	667	649	243	406	915	345	570	50-54	RATES
55-59	1238	503	735	1036	391	645	621	229	392	55-59	(IN 1000's)
60-64	1199	513	686	1152	456	696	965	354	611	60-64	
65-69	993	394	599	1064	438	626	1025	389	636	65-69	
70-74	735	273	462	818	309	509	875	344	531	70-74	
75-79	502	189	313	527	186	341	586	210	376	75-79	
80-84	249	95	154	285	102	183	299	100	199	80-84	
85+	118	43	75	127	44	83	145	47	98	85+	
TOTAL	17523	7946	9577	17679	8091	9588	17770	8222	9548	TOTAL	

STANDARD COUNTRIES: STANDARDIZED RATES PER THOUSAND	ENGLAND AND WALES 1961 BOTH SEXES	MALES	FEMALES	UNITED STATES 1960 BOTH SEXES	MALES	FEMALES	MEXICO 1960 BOTH SEXES	MALES	FEMALES	
Birth	15.25	19.65*	14.33	15.53	17.79*	14.84	18.89	18.83*	18.28	**TABLE 6** STANDAR-DIZED RATES
Death	12.50	12.16*	12.70	10.27	11.08*	9.43	5.69	10.10*	4.84	
Increase	2.75	7.49*	1.63	5.26	6.71*	5.42	13.20	8.73*	13.44	

	OBSERVED POP. MALES	FEMALES	STATIONARY POP. MALES	FEMALES	STABLE POP. MALES	FEMALES	OBSERVED BIRTHS	NET MATERNITY FUNCTION	BIRTHS IN STABLE POP.	
μ	35.14449	39.26186	36.65853	38.44984	34.77251	36.42214	25.93739	26.30455	26.17027	**TABLE 7**
σ^2	528.2140	519.8036	497.4033	533.9432	486.9648	524.2804	31.51883	33.22694	32.72781	MOMENTS
κ_3	3194.081	191.701	2272.123	1966.679	3164.438	3064.154	136.4252	130.3763	130.2596	AND
κ_4	-311521.	-301405.	-243893.	-297702.	-220814.	-273614.	115.618	13.716	57.251	CUMULANTS
β_1	0.069225	0.000262	0.041951	0.025409	0.086716	0.065152	0.594400	0.463368	0.484026	
β_2	1.883478	1.884494	2.014217	1.955781	2.068824	2.004569	3.116382	3.012424	3.053450	
κ	-0.023081	-0.000093	-0.015851	-0.009303	-0.032741	-0.023852	-0.335651	-0.287747	-0.306304	

VITAL STATISTICS		THOMPSON AGE RANGE	NRR	1000r	INTERVAL	BOURGEOIS-PICHAT AGE RANGE	NRR	1000b	1000d	1000r	COALE	
GRR	1.165										IBR	**TABLE 8** RATES FROM AGE DISTRI-BUTIONS AND VITAL STATISTICS (Females)
NRR	1.106	0-4	1.11	3.71	27.42	5-29	0.94	12.59	14.88	-2.29	IDR	
TFR	2.402	5-9	1.08	2.92	27.38	30-54	0.63	6.54	23.76	-17.22	IRI	
GENERATION	26.237	10-14	0.76	-9.95	27.33	55-79	1.52	43.96	28.38	15.58	K1	
SEX RATIO	106.177	15-19	0.94	-2.23	27.25	*50-74	1.40	35.73	23.23	12.51	K2	

Start of Age Interval	ORIGINAL MATRIX SUB-DIAGONAL	ALTERNATIVE FIRST ROWS Projection	Integral	FIRST STABLE MATRIX % IN STABLE POPULATION	FISHER VALUES	REPRODUCTIVE VALUES	SECOND STABLE MATRIX Z₂ FIRST COLUMN	FIRST ROW	
0	0.99478	0.00000	0.00000	7.714	1.046	681288	0.1819+0.0911	0.1819+0.0911	**TABLE 9**
5	0.99802	0.00000	0.00000	7.528	1.072	697940	0.1928-0.1664	-0.0113+0.1621	LESLIE
10	0.99788	0.06673	0.00018	7.371	1.095	516805	-0.1000-0.3039	-0.1226+0.0412	MATRIX
15	0.99683	0.26560	0.13485	7.215	1.048	646440	-0.4006-0.0307	-0.0800-0.0836	AND ITS
20	0.99578	0.35688	0.40275	7.056	0.793	549033	-0.2287+0.4492	-0.0114-0.1087	SPECTRAL
25	0.99467	0.24307	0.31922	6.893	0.437	245398	0.4096+0.4810	0.0114-0.0744	COMPO-NENTS
30	0.99269	0.12483	0.17252	6.726	0.192	108811	0.7529-0.2421	0.0139-0.0367	(Females)
35	0.98941	0.05155	0.08012	6.550	0.066	39459	0.0822-0.9847	0.0085-0.0124	
40	0.98449	0.01256	0.02423	6.358	0.013	5675	-1.0927-0.5657	0.0024-0.0023	
45	0.97748	0.00057	0.00115	6.140	0.001	400	-1.1673+0.9807	0.0001-0.0001	
50	0.96676	0.00000	0.00000	5.888	0.000	1	0.5621+1.7894	0.0000-0.0000	
55+	0.78756			24.560					

Start of Age Interval	OBSERVED POPUL. (IN 100's)	CONTRIBUTIONS OF ROOTS (IN 100's) r_1	r_2, r_3	$r_4 \cdot r_{11}$	AGE-SP. BIRTH RATES	NET MATERNITY FUNCTION	COEFF. OF MATRIX EQUATION	PARAMETERS	INTEGRAL	MATRIX	EXP. INCREASE x	$e^{(x+2\frac{1}{2})r}$	
0	6512	6382	328	-198	0.0000	0.0000	0.0000	L(1)	1.01933	1.01934	0	1.0096	**TABLE 10**
5	6511	6228	-154	437	0.0000	0.0000	0.0001	L(2)	0.29130	0.30529	50	1.2227	AGE
10	4721	6098	-665	-713	0.0000	0.0000	0.0002		0.76351	0.73355	55	1.2463	ANALYSIS
15	6166	5969	-399	595	0.0277	0.1323	0.2631	R(1)	0.00383	0.00383	60	1.2704	AND
20	6921	5838	663	420	0.0827	0.3939	0.3524	R(2)	-0.04038	-0.04600	65	1.2950	MISCEL-LANEOUS
25	5613	5703	1265	-1354	0.0655	0.3109	0.2390		0.24126	0.23528	70	1.3200	RESULTS
30	5657	5565	177	-85	0.0354	0.1671	0.1221	C(1)		82732	75	1.3456	(Females)
35	5981	5419	-1809	2371	0.0164	0.0771	0.0501	C(2)		42428	80	1.3716	
40	4217	5260	-2006	963	0.0050	0.0231	0.0121			-95384	85	1.3981	
45	6821	5080	880	861	0.0002	0.0011	0.0005	2P/Y	26.0428	26.7047	90	1.4251	
50	7600	4872	3891	-1162	0.0000	0.0000	0.0000	DELTA	8.8980		95	1.4527	
55+	28073	20319									100	1.4807	

TABLE 1 — DATA

AGE AT LAST BIRTHDAY	POPULATION BOTH SEXES	MALES Number	MALES %	FEMALES Number	FEMALES %	BIRTHS BY AGE OF MOTHER	DEATHS BOTH SEXES	DEATHS MALES	FEMALES	AGE AT LAST BIRTHDAY
0	292172	149921	1.9	142251	1.5	0	9411	5500	3911	0
1-4	1084293	555785	7.2	528508	5.6	0	1639	934	705	1-4
5-9	1310828	672293	8.7	638535	6.8	0	658	425	233	5-9
10-14	1155785	589851	7.6	565934	6.0	45	467	274	193	10-14
15-19	973049	491937	6.4	481112	5.1	31953	889	621	268	15-19
20-24	1384313	698569	9.0	685744	7.3	123120	1717	1253	464	20-24
25-29	1208802	612293	7.9	596509	6.4	79905	1382	882	500	25-29
30-34	1030062	484184	6.3	545878	5.8	39285	1512	868	644	30-34
35-39	914777	362665	4.7	552112	5.9	18338	1747	803	944	35-39
40-44	837145	317709	4.1	519436	5.5	5155	2272	981	1291	40-44
45-49	860675	326771	4.2	533904	5.7	181	3777	1690	2087	45-49
50-54	1209517	482785	6.3	726732	7.7	0	8204	4200	4004	50-54
55-59	1262986	544774	7.1	718212	7.7	0	13955	7923	6032	55-59
60-64	1155863	489831	6.3	666032	7.1	0	21026	12184	8842	60-64
65-69	914932	355259	4.6	559673	6.0	0	27214	13875	13339	65-69
70-74	709012	274246	3.6	434766	4.6		35741	16765	18976	70-74
75-79	461970	181579	2.4	280391	3.0		40419	17890	22529	75-79
80-84	234802	92793	1.2	142009	1.5	153482 M.	35598	15381	20217	80-84
85+	100864	37523	0.5	63341	0.7	144500 F.	26367	10600	15767	85+
TOTAL	17101847	7720768		9381079		297982	233995	113049	120946	TOTAL

TABLE 2 — MALE LIFE TABLE

x	nq_x	l_x	nd_x	nL_x	nm_x	na_x	T_x	r_x	$\dot{e}_x$	nM_x	x
0	0.035531	100000	3553	97324	0.036508	0.2469	6725249	0.0062	67.252	0.036686	0
1	0.006637	96447	640	383931	0.001667	1.0997	6627925	0.0062	68.721	0.001681	1
5	0.003138	95807	301	478282	0.000629	2.5000	6243994	0.0171	65.173	0.000632	5
10	0.002340	95506	224	477034	0.000469	2.7787	5765713	0.0306	60.370	0.000465	10
15	0.006294	95283	600	475043	0.001262	2.7160	5288679	0.0000	55.505	0.001262	15
20	0.008929	94683	845	471316	0.001794	2.5182	4813636	0.0000	50.840	0.001794	20
25	0.007177	93837	673	467502	0.001440	2.4969	4342320	0.0351	46.275	0.001440	25
30	0.008966	93164	835	463805	0.001801	2.5869	3874818	0.0506	41.591	0.001793	30
35	0.011065	92329	1022	459208	0.002225	2.6155	3411013	0.0398	36.944	0.002214	35
40	0.015351	91307	1402	453297	0.003092	2.6897	2951806	0.0071	32.328	0.003088	40
45	0.025557	89905	2298	444270	0.005172	2.7117	2498508	0.0000	27.790	0.005172	45
50	0.042645	87608	3736	429450	0.008700	2.7009	2054239	0.0000	23.448	0.008700	50
55	0.070357	83872	5901	405740	0.014544	2.6921	1624789	0.0000	19.372	0.014544	55
60	0.117712	77971	9178	368243	0.024924	2.6453	1219049	0.0102	15.635	0.024874	60
65	0.178843	68793	12303	314429	0.039128	2.5994	850806	0.0102	12.368	0.039056	65
70	0.266369	56490	15047	245684	0.061246	2.5567	536378	0.0102	9.495	0.061131	70
75	0.395693	41443	16399	166114	0.098719	2.4937	290694	0.0102	7.014	0.098525	75
80	0.581136	25044	14554	87604	0.166133	2.4154	124580	0.0102	4.974	0.165755	80
85+	*1.000000	10490	10490	36976	0.283699	3.5249	36976	0.0102	3.525	0.282493	85

TABLE 3 — FEMALE LIFE TABLE

x	nq_x	l_x	nd_x	nL_x	nm_x	na_x	T_x	r_x	$\dot{e}_x$	nM_x	x
0	0.026811	100000	2681	97999	0.027358	0.2535	7206594	0.0063	72.066	0.027494	0
1	0.005275	97319	513	387790	0.001324	1.1049	7108596	0.0063	73.044	0.001334	1
5	0.001809	96806	175	483590	0.000362	2.5000	6720806	0.0164	69.426	0.000365	5
10	0.001709	96630	165	482759	0.000342	2.6175	6237216	0.0279	64.547	0.000341	10
15	0.002782	96465	268	481689	0.000557	2.6240	5754457	0.0000	59.653	0.000557	15
20	0.003473	96197	325	480200	0.000677	2.5858	5272769	0.0000	54.812	0.000677	20
25	0.004194	95872	402	478404	0.000841	2.6229	4792569	0.0219	49.989	0.000838	25
30	0.005888	95470	562	476029	0.001181	2.6506	4314164	0.0065	45.189	0.001180	30
35	0.008519	94908	809	472643	0.001711	2.6548	3838136	0.0032	40.441	0.001710	35
40	0.012357	94099	1163	467799	0.002486	2.6776	3365493	0.0007	35.765	0.002485	40
45	0.019367	92936	1800	460456	0.003909	2.6523	2897697	0.0000	31.179	0.003909	45
50	0.027197	91137	2479	449872	0.005510	2.6556	2437241	0.0000	26.743	0.005510	50
55	0.041188	88658	3652	434790	0.008399	2.6725	1987369	0.0000	22.416	0.008399	55
60	0.064726	85006	5502	412396	0.013342	2.7035	1552579	0.0213	18.264	0.013276	60
65	0.113534	79504	9026	376728	0.023960	2.6965	1140184	0.0213	14.341	0.023834	65
70	0.198847	70478	14014	319439	0.043871	2.6489	763456	0.0213	10.833	0.043646	70
75	0.337236	56463	19042	235866	0.080730	2.5605	444016	0.0213	7.864	0.080349	75
80	0.522378	37422	19548	136739	0.142961	2.4876	208150	0.0213	5.562	0.142364	80
85+	1.000000	17874	17874	71411	0.250292	3.9953	71411	0.0213	3.995	0.248922	85+

TABLE 4 — OBSERVED AND PROJECTED VITAL RATES

	OBSERVED POPULATION BOTH SEXES	MALES	FEMALES	PROJECTED 1967 MALES	FEMALES	PROJECTED 1972 MALES	FEMALES	PROJECTED 1977 MALES	FEMALES	STABLE POPULATION MALES	FEMALES
RATES PER THOUSAND											
Birth	17.42	19.88	15.40	18.36	14.44	18.01	14.43	18.55	15.19	17.98	16.93
Death	13.68	14.64	12.89	14.56	13.94	14.34	14.84	13.93	15.48	12.60	11.55
Increase	3.74	5.24	2.51	3.80	0.50	3.67	-0.42	4.62	-0.29		5.3803
PERCENTAGE											
under 15	22.47	25.49	19.99	26.47	21.02	26.23	21.24	25.81	21.37	24.82	23.63
15-64	63.37	62.32	64.23	60.67	61.62	60.41	60.16	61.47	59.38	64.86	63.40
65 and over	14.16	12.19	15.78	12.87	17.35	13.36	18.60	12.72	19.25	10.32	12.97
DEP. RATIO X 100	57.81	60.46	55.69	64.84	62.28	65.54	66.23	62.68	68.39	54.17	57.72

TABLE 1 — DATA

AGE AT LAST BIRTHDAY	POPULATION Both Sexes	Males Number	Males %	Females Number	Females %	BIRTHS By Age of Mother	DEATHS Both Sexes	DEATHS Males	DEATHS Females	AGE AT LAST BIRTHDAY
0	292780	150233	1.9	142547	1.5	0	9396	5430	3966	0
1-4	1118879	573504	7.4	545375	5.8	0	1618	935	683	1-4
5-9	1300520	666911	8.6	633609	6.7	0	588	366	222	5-9
10-14	1232834	630393	8.1	602441	6.4	47	472	290	182	10-14
15-19	926804	468729	6.0	458075	4.9	31216	848	592	256	15-19
20-24	1352886	682206	8.8	670680	7.1	121768	1521	1078	443	20-24
25-29	1270299	644278	8.3	626021	6.7	84891	1396	880	516	25-29
30-34	1032712	495953	6.4	536759	5.7	39459	1477	900	577	30-34
35-39	930699	382531	4.9	548168	5.8	18617	1696	855	841	35-39
40-44	916172	347528	4.5	568644	6.1	5333	2491	1102	1389	40-44
45-49	731013	275861	3.6	455152	4.8	141	3096	1402	1694	45-49
50-54	1176394	463183	6.0	713211	7.6	0	7607	3829	3778	50-54
55-59	1251426	532045	6.9	719381	7.7	0	13446	7656	5790	55-59
60-64	1170132	501188	6.5	668944	7.1	0	20881	12295	8586	60-64
65-69	931115	363677	4.7	567438	6.0	0	26617	13665	12952	65-69
70-74	706368	269800	3.5	436568	4.6		33734	15823	17911	70-74
75-79	472906	183865	2.4	289041	3.1		38319	16859	21460	75-79
80-84	236083	92081	1.2	144002	1.5	155174 M.	32497	13651	18846	80-84
85+	104903	38870	0.5	66033	0.7	146298 F.	24301	9803	14498	85+
TOTAL	17154925	7762836		9392089		301472	222001	107411	114590	TOTAL

TABLE 2 — MALE LIFE TABLE

x	$_nq_x$	l_x	$_nd_x$	$_nL_x$	$_nm_x$	$_na_x$	T_x	r_x	$\mathring{e}_x$	$_nM_x$	x
0	0.035095	100000	3510	97352	0.036050	0.2454	6773181	0.0033	67.732	0.036144	0
1	0.006463	96490	624	384152	0.001623	1.0985	6675829	0.0033	69.186	0.001630	1
5	0.002727	95867	261	478680	0.000546	2.5000	6291677	0.0130	65.629	0.000549	5
10	0.002323	95605	222	477542	0.000465	2.8180	5812996	0.0346	60.802	0.000460	10
15	0.006297	95383	601	475524	0.001263	2.6817	5335454	0.0000	55.937	0.001263	15
20	0.007870	94783	746	472057	0.001580	2.5112	4859931	0.0000	51.274	0.001580	20
25	0.006814	94037	641	468603	0.001367	2.5332	4387874	0.0304	46.661	0.001366	25
30	0.009080	93396	848	464941	0.001824	2.5964	3919271	0.0503	41.964	0.001815	30
35	0.011163	92548	1033	460282	0.002244	2.6210	3454330	0.0332	37.325	0.002235	35
40	0.015824	91515	1448	454210	0.003188	2.6768	2994048	0.0293	32.717	0.003171	40
45	0.025117	90067	2262	445119	0.005082	2.6947	2539838	0.0000	28.200	0.005082	45
50	0.040566	87805	3562	430869	0.008267	2.7108	2094719	0.0000	23.857	0.008267	50
55	0.069641	84243	5867	407703	0.014390	2.6972	1663850	0.0000	19.751	0.014390	55
60	0.116294	78376	9115	370364	0.024610	2.6394	1256147	0.0167	16.027	0.024532	60
65	0.172787	69261	11967	317558	0.037686	2.5978	885783	0.0167	12.789	0.037575	65
70	0.257133	57294	14732	250459	0.058820	2.5557	568225	0.0167	9.918	0.058647	70
75	0.373715	42562	15906	172948	0.091969	2.4940	317766	0.0167	7.466	0.091692	75
80	0.535481	26656	14274	95994	0.148693	2.4486	144817	0.0167	5.433	0.148250	80
85+	1.000000	12382	12382	48823	0.253610	3.9431	48823	0.0167	3.943	0.252200	85+

TABLE 3 — FEMALE LIFE TABLE

x	$_nq_x$	l_x	$_nd_x$	$_nL_x$	$_nm_x$	$_na_x$	T_x	r_x	$\mathring{e}_x$	$_nM_x$	x
0	0.027179	100000	2718	97949	0.027748	0.2455	7264758	0.0034	72.648	0.027822	0
1	0.004969	97282	483	387726	0.001247	1.0985	7166809	0.0034	73.670	0.001252	1
5	0.001740	96799	168	483572	0.000348	2.5000	6779083	0.0127	70.033	0.000350	5
10	0.001516	96630	147	482806	0.000303	2.6433	6295511	0.0321	65.151	0.000302	10
15	0.002791	96484	269	481781	0.000559	2.6321	5812705	0.0000	60.245	0.000559	15
20	0.003297	96214	317	480305	0.000661	2.5828	5330924	0.0000	55.407	0.000661	20
25	0.004122	95897	395	478538	0.000826	2.6031	4850619	0.0214	50.581	0.000824	25
30	0.005370	95502	513	476296	0.001077	2.6344	4372080	0.0122	45.780	0.001075	30
35	0.007644	94989	726	473262	0.001534	2.6823	3895784	0.0000	41.013	0.001534	35
40	0.012181	94263	1148	468651	0.002450	2.6799	3422522	0.0161	36.308	0.002443	40
45	0.018448	93115	1718	461538	0.003722	2.6507	2953871	0.0000	31.723	0.003722	45
50	0.026161	91397	2391	451382	0.005297	2.6567	2492333	0.0000	27.269	0.005297	50
55	0.039504	89006	3516	436858	0.008049	2.6759	2040951	0.0000	22.931	0.008049	55
60	0.062692	85490	5360	415138	0.012910	2.7030	1604093	0.0251	18.764	0.012835	60
65	0.109046	80130	8738	380488	0.022965	2.6924	1188955	0.0251	14.838	0.022825	65
70	0.188100	71392	13429	325385	0.041271	2.6486	808467	0.0251	11.324	0.041027	70
75	0.315949	57964	18314	245300	0.074658	2.5691	483082	0.0251	8.334	0.074246	75
80	0.491965	39650	19506	148327	0.131510	2.5195	237782	0.0251	5.997	0.130873	80
85+	1.000000	20144	20144	89455	0.225183	4.4408	89455	0.0251	4.441	0.219556	85+

TABLE 4 — OBSERVED AND PROJECTED VITAL RATES

	OBSERVED POPULATION Both Sexes	Males	Females	PROJECTED POPULATION 1968 Males	1968 Females	1973 Males	1973 Females	1978 Males	1978 Females	STABLE POPULATION Males	STABLE Females
RATES PER THOUSAND											
Birth	17.57	19.99	15.58	18.33	14.49	18.25	14.69	18.74	15.42	18.24	17.19
Death	12.94	13.84	12.20	14.06	13.49	13.96	14.48	13.53	15.09	12.26	11.21
Increase	4.63	6.15	3.38	4.26	1.00	4.29	0.21	5.21	0.34		5.9808
PERCENTAGE											
under 15	23.00	26.03	20.49	26.48	21.13	26.38	21.45	25.89	21.52	25.09	23.87
15-64	62.71	61.75	63.51	60.32	61.09	60.03	59.45	61.34	58.85	64.50	63.01
65 and over	14.29	12.22	16.00	13.20	17.78	13.59	19.10	12.77	19.63	10.41	13.11
DEP. RATIO X 100	59.45	61.94	57.45	65.77	63.68	66.60	68.22	63.03	69.92	55.05	58.69

Including East Berlin

TABLE 1 — DATA

AGE AT LAST BIRTHDAY	POPULATION BOTH SEXES	MALES Number	%	FEMALES Number	%	BIRTHS BY AGE OF MOTHER	DEATHS BOTH SEXES	MALES	FEMALES	AGE AT LAST BIRTHDAY
0	288696	147782	1.9	140914	1.5	0	8341	4845	3496	0
1-4	1143587	585100	7.6	558487	6.0	0	1412	791	621	1-4
5-9	1302556	667742	8.6	634814	6.9	0	633	379	254	5-9
10-14	1277271	654831	8.5	622440	6.7	41	447	293	154	10-14
15-19	880197	447206	5.8	432991	4.7	27214	718	511	207	15-19
20-24	1272792	640402	8.3	632390	6.8	114889	1450	1058	392	20-24
25-29	1278736	644352	8.3	634384	6.9	86157	1459	946	513	25-29
30-34	1039155	520658	6.7	518497	5.6	39711	1472	882	590	30-34
35-39	961807	423436	5.5	538371	5.8	18510	1769	911	858	35-39
40-44	939107	359312	4.6	579795	6.3	5139	2620	1195	1425	40-44
45-49	630999	239078	3.1	391921	4.2	206	2629	1206	1423	45-49
50-54	1122772	438463	5.7	684309	7.4	0	7235	3657	3578	50-54
55-59	1230078	515691	6.7	714387	7.7	0	13237	7512	5725	55-59
60-64	1169040	506014	6.5	663026	7.2	0	21513	12587	8926	60-64
65-69	935972	369302	4.8	566670	6.1	0	27499	14533	12966	65-69
70-74	697171	261694	3.4	435477	4.7		34401	16127	18274	70-74
75-79	475381	180932	2.3	294449	3.2		39776	17430	22346	75-79
80-84	238736	91679	1.2	147057	1.6	150067 M.	33475	13965	19510	80-84
85+	107508	40483	0.5	67025	0.7	141800 F.	26105	10407	15698	85+
TOTAL	16991561	7734157		9257404		291867	226191	109235	116956	TOTAL

TABLE 2 — MALE LIFE TABLE

x	nq_x	l_x	nd_x	nL_x	nm_x	na_x	T_x	r_x	$\dot{e}_x$	nM_x	x
0	0.031984	100000	3198	97557	0.032785	0.2362	6779452	0.0000	67.795	0.032785	0
1	0.005386	96802	521	385690	0.001352	1.0918	6681895	0.0000	69.027	0.001352	1
5	0.002826	96280	272	480721	0.000566	2.5000	6296205	0.0105	65.395	0.000568	5
10	0.002259	96008	217	479556	0.000452	2.7632	5815484	0.0395	60.573	0.000447	10
15	0.005700	95791	546	477710	0.001143	2.7163	5335929	0.0011	55.704	0.001143	15
20	0.008227	95245	784	474298	0.001652	2.5385	4858219	0.0000	51.007	0.001652	20
25	0.007315	94461	691	470583	0.001468	2.5031	4383921	0.0191	46.410	0.001468	25
30	0.008464	93771	794	466934	0.001700	2.5813	3913338	0.0403	41.733	0.001694	30
35	0.010762	92977	1001	462537	0.002163	2.6538	3446404	0.0348	37.067	0.002151	35
40	0.016659	91976	1532	456313	0.003358	2.6705	2983867	0.0537	32.442	0.003326	40
45	0.024932	90444	2255	447016	0.005044	2.6919	2527554	0.0000	27.946	0.005044	45
50	0.040922	88189	3609	432696	0.008340	2.7139	2080538	0.0000	23.592	0.008340	50
55	0.070471	84580	5960	409178	0.014567	2.6975	1647842	0.0000	19.483	0.014567	55
60	0.117790	78620	9261	371310	0.024940	2.6471	1238664	0.0132	15.755	0.024875	60
65	0.180179	69359	12497	316802	0.039448	2.5999	867354	0.0132	12.505	0.039353	65
70	0.268252	56862	15253	246941	0.061769	2.5500	550552	0.0132	9.682	0.061625	70
75	0.388376	41609	16160	167355	0.096560	2.4821	303611	0.0132	7.297	0.096335	75
80	0.544848	25449	13866	90819	0.152675	2.4312	136256	0.0132	5.354	0.152325	80
85+	1.000000	11583	11583	45437	0.254928	3.9227	45437	0.0132	3.923	0.257070	85+

TABLE 3 — FEMALE LIFE TABLE

x	nq_x	l_x	nd_x	nL_x	nm_x	na_x	T_x	r_x	$\dot{e}_x$	nM_x	x
0	0.024354	100000	2435	98162	0.024809	0.2454	7276979	0.0000	72.770	0.024809	0
1	0.004433	97565	433	389004	0.001112	1.0985	7178817	0.0000	73.580	0.001112	1
5	0.001990	97132	193	485177	0.000398	2.5000	6789813	0.0111	69.903	0.000400	5
10	0.001239	96939	120	484401	0.000248	2.5656	6304636	0.0379	65.037	0.000247	10
15	0.002388	96819	231	483552	0.000478	2.6611	5820235	0.0000	60.115	0.000478	15
20	0.003095	96587	299	482223	0.000620	2.6104	5336682	0.0000	55.252	0.000620	20
25	0.004046	96289	390	480520	0.000811	2.6318	4854459	0.0190	50.416	0.000809	25
30	0.005687	95899	545	478208	0.001140	2.6404	4373939	0.0153	45.610	0.001138	30
35	0.007939	95354	757	475004	0.001594	2.6696	3895731	0.0000	40.856	0.001594	35
40	0.012280	94597	1162	470272	0.002470	2.6659	3420727	0.0292	36.161	0.002458	40
45	0.018001	93435	1682	463222	0.003631	2.6496	2950456	0.0000	31.578	0.003631	45
50	0.025827	91753	2370	453223	0.005229	2.6613	2487234	0.0000	27.108	0.005229	50
55	0.039342	89383	3517	438806	0.008014	2.6934	2034010	0.0000	22.756	0.008014	55
60	0.065614	85867	5634	416342	0.013532	2.6941	1595205	0.0231	18.578	0.013463	60
65	0.109248	80233	8765	380935	0.023010	2.6921	1178862	0.0231	14.693	0.022881	65
70	0.191933	71468	13717	325089	0.042194	2.6490	797927	0.0231	11.165	0.041963	70
75	0.321623	57751	18574	243514	0.076275	2.5644	472839	0.0231	8.188	0.075891	75
80	0.496612	39177	19456	145997	0.133260	2.5123	229325	0.0231	5.854	0.132670	80
85+	1.000000	19721	19721	83328	0.236668	4.2253	83328	0.0231	4.225	0.234210	85+

TABLE 4 — OBSERVED AND PROJECTED VITAL RATES

	OBSERVED POPULATION BOTH SEXES	MALES	FEMALES	PROJECTED POPULATION 1969 MALES	FEMALES	1974 MALES	FEMALES	1979 MALES	FEMALES	STABLE POPULATION MALES	FEMALES
RATES PER THOUSAND											
Birth	17.18	19.40	15.32	17.82	14.27	18.18	14.82	18.81	15.67	18.23	17.17
Death	13.31	14.12	12.63	14.17	13.80	13.96	14.71	13.45	15.17	12.22	11.16
Increase	3.87	5.28	2.68	3.66	0.47	4.21	0.11	5.36	0.50		6.0057
PERCENTAGE											
under 15	23.61	26.58	21.14	26.53	21.43	26.30	21.65	25.65	21.57	25.17	23.92
15-64	61.94	61.22	62.55	60.31	60.61	60.36	59.14	62.07	58.98	64.66	63.12
65 and over	14.45	12.21	16.32	13.16	17.96	13.34	19.21	12.28	19.44	10.18	12.97
DEP. RATIO X 100	61.44	63.35	59.88	65.81	65.00	65.68	69.09	61.10	69.54	54.66	58.44

Including East Berlin

AGE AT LAST BIRTHDAY	1969 BOTH SEXES	MALES	FEMALES	1974 BOTH SEXES	MALES	FEMALES	1979 BOTH SEXES	MALES	FEMALES	AGE AT LAST BIRTHDAY	
0-4	1373	703	670	1357	695	662	1425	730	695	0-4	
5-9	1426	729	697	1367	700	667	1350	691	659	5-9	
10-14	1300	666	634	1422	727	695	1364	698	666	10-14	
15-19	1273	652	621	1297	664	633	1418	724	694	15-19	**TABLE 5**
20-24	876	444	432	1268	648	620	1290	659	631	20-24	POPULATION
25-29	1265	635	630	871	441	430	1260	643	617	25-29	PROJECTED
30-34	1270	639	631	1257	630	627	865	437	428	30-34	WITH
35-39	1031	516	515	1260	633	627	1248	625	623	35-39	FIXED
40-44	951	418	533	1019	509	510	1246	625	621	40-44	AGE—
45-49	923	352	571	934	409	525	1000	498	502	45-49	SPECIFIC
50-54	614	231	383	900	341	559	910	396	514	50-54	BIRTH
55-59	1078	415	663	590	219	371	863	322	541	55-59	AND
60-64	1146	468	678	1005	376	629	551	199	352	60-64	DEATH
65-69	1039	432	607	1019	399	620	896	321	575	65-69	RATES
70-74	772	288	484	855	337	518	840	311	529	70-74	(IN 1000's)
75-79	503	177	326	557	195	362	616	228	388	75-79	
80-84	275	98	177	292	96	196	323	106	217	80-84	
85+	130	46	84	150	49	101	160	48	112	85+	
TOTAL	17245	7909	9336	17420	8068	9352	17625	8261	9364	TOTAL	

STANDARD COUNTRIES: STANDARDIZED RATES PER THOUSAND	ENGLAND AND WALES 1961 BOTH SEXES	MALES	FEMALES	UNITED STATES 1960 BOTH SEXES	MALES	FEMALES	MEXICO 1960 BOTH SEXES	MALES	FEMALES	
Birth	15.90	18.06*	14.97	16.21	16.78*	15.52	19.80	17.27*	19.19	**TABLE 6**
Death	11.99	11.83*	12.09	9.76	10.85*	8.86	5.15	9.74*	4.32	STANDAR-
Increase	3.91	6.23*	2.89	6.45	5.94*	6.65	14.65	7.54*	14.87	DIZED RATES

	OBSERVED POP. MALES	FEMALES	STATIONARY POP. MALES	FEMALES	STABLE POP. MALES	FEMALES	OBSERVED BIRTHS	NET MATERNITY FUNCTION	BIRTHS IN STABLE POP.	
μ	34.61667	39.20304	36.74371	38.65858	33.79899	35.46999	26.19002	26.13458	25.92794	**TABLE 7**
σ^2	533.7967	547.7539	498.5282	538.6050	480.7552	521.5442	29.38457	32.70385	31.94566	MOMENTS
κ_3	3834.519	459.763	2259.011	1966.565	3620.477	3671.887	128.4932	126.2389	126.1906	AND
κ_4	-306881.	-348791.	-244770.	-303258.	-205656.	-260323.	289.942	-18.865	44.500	CUMULANTS
β_1	0.096671	0.001286	0.041188	0.024752	0.117967	0.095040	0.650732	0.455606	0.488449	
β_2	1.922995	1.837498	2.015132	1.954626	2.110196	2.042959	3.335794	2.982361	3.043605	
κ	-0.032377	-0.000440	-0.015588	-0.009060	-0.044637	-0.034838	-0.447679	-0.275249	-0.302209	

VITAL STATISTICS		THOMPSON AGE RANGE	NRR	1000r	INTERVAL	BOURGEOIS-PICHAT AGE RANGE	NRR	1000b	1000d	1000r	COALE	
GRR	1.216										IBR	**TABLE 8** RATES FROM AGE
NRR	1.169	0-4	1.23	7.77	27.43	5-29	0.98	12.91	13.68	-0.77	IDR	DISTRI-BUTIONS
TFR	2.504	5-9	1.13	4.52	27.39	30-54	0.82	9.00	16.40	-7.40	IRI	AND VITAL
GENERATION	26.031	10-14	1.08	2.90	27.33	55-79	1.42	38.07	25.01	13.06	K1	STATISTICS
SEX RATIO	105.830	15-19	0.73	-12.19	27.26	*50-74	1.19	24.60	18.00	6.59	K2	(Females)

Start Age Interval	ORIGINAL MATRIX SUB-DIAGONAL	ALTERNATIVE FIRST ROWS Projection	Integral	FIRST STABLE MATRIX % IN STABLE POPULATION	FISHER VALUES	REPRODUCTIVE VALUES	SECOND STABLE MATRIX Z2 FIRST COLUMN	FIRST ROW	
0	0.99592	0.00000	0.00000	8.240	1.042	728664	0.1812+0.0920	0.1812+0.0920	
5	0.99840	0.00008	0.00000	7.963	1.078	684344	0.1906-0.1658	-0.0139+0.1628	**TABLE 9**
10	0.99825	0.07433	0.00016	7.715	1.113	692531	-0.1023-0.2977	-0.1253+0.0387	LESLIE
15	0.99725	0.28878	0.15101	7.474	1.071	463728	-0.3918-0.0211	-0.0801-0.0884	MATRIX
20	0.99647	0.37515	0.43650	7.232	0.805	509078	-0.2075+0.4421	-0.0108-0.1129	AND ITS
25	0.99519	0.25092	0.32631	6.994	0.440	279301	0.4128+0.4458	0.0126-0.0768	SPECTRAL
30	0.99330	0.13105	0.18401	6.754	0.193	100179	0.7058-0.2674	0.0154-0.0370	COMPO-NENTS
35	0.99004	0.05107	0.08261	6.510	0.063	33913	0.0214-0.9356	0.0084-0.0118	(Females)
40	0.98501	0.01110	0.02130	6.254	0.012	6855	-1.0618-0.4587	0.0021-0.0020	
45	0.97842	0.00062	0.00126	5.978	0.001	247	-1.0130+0.9983	0.0001-0.0001	
50	0.96819	0.00000	0.00000	5.676	0.000	1	0.6655+1.6046	0.0000-0.0000	
55+	0.79372			23.209					

Start Age Interval	OBSERVED POPUL. (IN 100's)	r_1	r_2, r_3	$r_4 \cdot r_{11}$	AGE-SP. BIRTH RATES	NET MATERNITY FUNCTION	COEFF. OF MATRIX EQUATION	PARAMETERS	INTEGRAL	MATRIX	EXP. INCREASE x	$e^{(x+2\frac{1}{2})r}$	
0	6994	6486	404	104	0.0000	0.0000	0.0000	L(1)	1.03048	1.03051	0	1.0151	**TABLE 10**
5	6348	6268	344	-264	0.0000	0.0000	0.0001	L(2)	0.28652	0.30080	50	1.3707	AGE
10	6224	6073	-304	456	0.0000	0.0002	0.0739			0.77309	0.74245	55	1.4124	ANALYSIS
15	4330	5883	-818	-734	0.0305	0.1477	0.2866	R(1)	0.00601	0.00601	60	1.4555	AND
20	6324	5693	-293	924	0.0883	0.4256	0.3713	R(2)	-0.03860	-0.04436	65	1.4999	MISCEL-LANEOUS
25	6344	5505	993	-154	0.0660	0.3171	0.2475			0.24317	0.23717	70	1.5456	RESULTS
30	5185	5316	1380	-1511	0.0372	0.1779	0.1286	C(1)		78712	75	1.5927	(Females)
35	5384	5124	-245	505	0.0167	0.0793	0.0498	C(2)		103606	80	1.6413	
40	5798	4923	-2342	3217	0.0043	0.0203	0.0107			-15463	85	1.6913	
45	3919	4706	-1790	1004	0.0003	0.0012	0.0006	2P/Y	25.8382	26.4920	90	1.7429	
50+	6843	4468	1875	500	0.0000	0.0000	0.0000	DELTA	9.8310		95	1.7960	
	28881	18268									100	1.8507	

Including West Berlin

TABLE 1 — DATA

AGE AT LAST BIRTHDAY	POPULATION BOTH SEXES	MALES Number	%	FEMALES Number	%	BIRTHS BY AGE OF MOTHER	DEATHS BOTH SEXES	MALES	FEMALES	AGE AT LAST BIRTHDAY
0	932745	478694	1.8	454051	1.5	0	32724	18761	13963	0
1-4	3428109	1760202	6.7	1667907	5.7	0	4518	2552	1966	1-4
5-9	3918577	2008641	7.7	1909936	6.5	0	2068	1294	774	5-9
10-14	3579364	1830031	7.0	1749333	5.9	35	1355	873	482	10-1
15-19	4066962	2075896	8.0	1991066	6.8	32810	3650	2603	1047	15-1
20-24	4780803	2446490	9.4	2334313	7.9	277372	5777	4333	1444	20-2
25-29	3730763	1905462	7.3	1825301	6.2	301506	5010	3378	1632	25-2
30-34	3802856	1865422	7.1	1937434	6.6	203581	5600	3363	2237	30-3
35-39	3806525	1617795	6.2	2188730	7.4	116142	7814	3991	3823	35-3
40-44	2644173	1114231	4.3	1529942	5.2	34107	7404	3847	3557	40-4
45-49	3891881	1669215	6.4	2222666	7.5	3076	17527	9244	8283	45-4
50-54	4105113	1826858	7.0	2278255	7.7	0	29531	17525	12006	50-5
55-59	3795992	1759250	6.7	2036742	6.9	0	46018	28991	17027	55-5
60-64	3072453	1317486	5.0	1754967	6.0	0	60359	35747	24612	60-6
65-69	2329712	926480	3.5	1403232	4.8	0	73113	38495	34618	65-6
70-74	1747912	704119	2.7	1043793	3.5		91582	45052	46530	70-7
75-79	1131741	466542	1.8	665199	2.3		101291	47299	53992	75-7
80-84	593381	246407	0.9	346974	1.2	498182 M.	88509	40089	48420	80-8
85+	225824	90688	0.3	135136	0.5	470447 F.	59112	25066	34046	85+
TOTAL	55584886	26109909		29474977		968629	642962	332503	310459	TOT

TABLE 2 — MALE LIFE TABLE

x	$_nq_x$	l_x	$_nd_x$	$_nL_x$	$_nm_x$	$_na_x$	T_x	r_x	$\dot{e}_x$	$_nM_x$
0	0.037828	100000	3783	97065	0.038972	0.2240	6646862	0.0071	66.469	0.039192
1	0.005713	96217	550	383266	0.001434	1.0835	6549797	0.0071	68.073	0.001450
5	0.003200	95667	306	477572	0.000641	2.5000	6166532	0.0193	64.458	0.000644
10	0.002383	95361	227	476299	0.000477	2.7646	5688960	0.0000	59.657	0.000477
15	0.006252	95134	595	474310	0.001254	2.7125	5212661	0.0000	54.793	0.001254
20	0.008821	94539	834	470661	0.001772	2.5580	4738351	0.0069	50.120	0.001771
25	0.008826	93705	827	466460	0.001773	2.5002	4267690	0.0253	45.544	0.001773
30	0.008985	92878	835	462370	0.001805	2.5772	3801230	0.0144	40.927	0.001803
35	0.012346	92044	1136	457529	0.002484	2.6324	3338860	0.0490	36.275	0.002467
40	0.017126	90908	1557	450918	0.003453	2.6749	2881331	0.0000	31.695	0.003453
45	0.027344	89351	2443	441171	0.005538	2.7151	2430413	0.0000	27.201	0.005538
50	0.046935	86908	4079	425205	0.009593	2.7120	1989243	0.0000	22.889	0.009593
55	0.079615	82829	6594	398837	0.016534	2.6789	1564038	0.0155	18.883	0.016479
60	0.127793	76234	9742	358063	0.027208	2.6281	1165201	0.0150	15.285	0.027133
65	0.189257	66492	12584	302082	0.041658	2.5860	807138	0.0150	12.139	0.041550
70	0.277111	53908	14938	232856	0.064153	2.5444	505056	0.0150	9.369	0.063983
75	0.404586	38969	15767	155091	0.101660	2.4784	272200	0.0150	6.985	0.101382
80	0.573477	23203	13306	81526	0.163216	2.4081	117109	0.0150	5.047	0.162694
85+	*1.000000	9897	9897	35583	0.278129	3.5955	35583	0.0150	3.595	0.276398

TABLE 3 — FEMALE LIFE TABLE

x	$_nq_x$	l_x	$_nd_x$	$_nL_x$	$_nm_x$	$_na_x$	T_x	r_x	$\dot{e}_x$	$_nM_x$
0	0.029866	100000	2987	97694	0.030571	0.2280	7184499	0.0075	71.845	0.030752
1	0.004647	97013	451	386740	0.001166	1.0861	7086805	0.0075	73.050	0.001179
5	0.002010	96563	194	482328	0.000402	2.5000	6700065	0.0187	69.386	0.000405
10	0.001377	96369	133	481523	0.000276	2.5921	6217737	0.0000	64.520	0.000276
15	0.002626	96236	253	480582	0.000526	2.6352	5736214	0.0000	59.606	0.000526
20	0.003092	95983	297	479210	0.000619	2.6229	5255632	0.0080	54.756	0.000619
25	0.004471	95686	428	477415	0.000896	2.6226	4776422	0.0178	49.917	0.000894
30	0.005757	95259	548	475005	0.001155	2.6514	4299007	0.0000	45.130	0.001155
35	0.008724	94710	826	471597	0.001752	2.6354	3824002	0.0219	40.376	0.001747
40	0.011562	93884	1085	466891	0.002325	2.6704	3352405	0.0000	35.708	0.002325
45	0.018472	92798	1714	459975	0.003727	2.6564	2885515	0.0000	31.094	0.003727
50	0.026044	91084	2372	449894	0.005273	2.6701	2425540	0.0032	26.630	0.005270
55	0.041160	88712	3651	435149	0.008391	2.6964	1975645	0.0173	22.270	0.008360
60	0.068365	85061	5815	411944	0.014116	2.7026	1540496	0.0280	18.111	0.014024
65	0.117443	79246	9307	374706	0.024838	2.6875	1128552	0.0280	14.241	0.024670
70	0.202900	69939	14191	316231	0.044874	2.6419	753847	0.0280	10.779	0.044578
75	0.340317	55748	18972	232331	0.081660	2.5538	437616	0.0280	7.850	0.081167
80	0.519058	36776	19089	135891	0.140473	2.4860	205285	0.0280	5.582	0.139550
85+	*1.000000	17687	17687	69394	0.254879	3.9234	69394	0.0280	3.923	0.251939

TABLE 4 — OBSERVED AND PROJECTED VITAL RATES

	OBSERVED POPULATION BOTH SEXES	MALES	FEMALES	PROJECTED POPULATION 1965 MALES	FEMALES	1970 MALES	FEMALES	1975 MALES	FEMALES	STABLE POPULATION MALES	FEMAL
RATES PER THOUSAND											
Birth	17.43	19.08	15.96	18.95	15.95	17.66	14.99	16.74	14.36	17.22	16.0
Death	11.57	12.73	10.53	13.03	11.56	13.15	12.42	13.31	13.27	13.41	12.2
Increase	5.86	6.35	5.43	5.92	4.39	4.51	2.57	3.44	1.09		3.806
PERCENTAGE											
under 15	21.33	23.28	19.61	24.70	20.94	25.42	21.76	25.15	21.79	24.00	22.5
15-64	67.82	67.40	68.19	65.47	65.45	63.66	63.22	63.31	61.76	65.48	63.7
65 and over	10.85	9.32	12.19	9.83	13.61	10.92	15.02	11.54	16.45	10.52	13.6
DEP. RATIO X 100	47.45	48.37	46.65	52.75	52.79	57.09	58.17	57.96	61.92	52.71	56.8

Including West Berlin

AGE AT LAST BIRTHDAY	1965 BOTH SEXES	MALES	FEMALES	1970 BOTH SEXES	MALES	FEMALES	1975 BOTH SEXES	MALES	FEMALES	AGE AT LAST BIRTHDAY
0-4	4729	2422	2307	4682	2398	2284	4502	2306	2196	0-4
5-9	4339	2226	2113	4705	2408	2297	4658	2384	2274	5-9
10-14	3910	2003	1907	4329	2220	2109	4695	2402	2293	10-14
15-19	3568	1822	1746	3898	1995	1903	4316	2211	2105	15-19
20-24	4045	2060	1985	3549	1808	1741	3878	1980	1898	20-24
25-29	4751	2425	2326	4020	2042	1978	3526	1792	1734	25-29
30-34	3705	1889	1816	4717	2403	2314	3992	2024	1968	30-34
35-39	3770	1846	1924	3672	1869	1803	4675	2378	2297	35-39
40-44	3761	1594	2167	3723	1819	1904	3627	1842	1785	40-44
45-49	2597	1090	1507	3695	1560	2135	3656	1780	1876	45-49
50-54	3783	1609	2174	2525	1051	1474	3591	1503	2088	50-54
55-59	3918	1714	2204	3612	1509	2103	2412	986	1426	55-59
60-64	3507	1579	1928	3624	1538	2086	3346	1355	1991	60-64
65-69	2708	1112	1596	3086	1332	1754	3196	1298	1898	65-69
70-74	1898	714	1184	2204	857	1347	2507	1027	1480	70-74
75-79	1236	469	767	1346	476	870	1561	571	990	75-79
80-84	634	245	389	696	247	449	759	250	509	80-84
85+	285	108	177	306	107	199	337	108	229	85+
TOTAL	57144	26927	30217	58389	27639	30750	59234	28197	31037	TOTAL

TABLE 5 POPULATION PROJECTED WITH FIXED AGE— SPECIFIC BIRTH AND DEATH RATES (IN 1000's)

STANDARD COUNTRIES: STANDARDIZED RATES PER THOUSAND	ENGLAND AND WALES 1961 BOTH SEXES	MALES	FEMALES	UNITED STATES 1960 BOTH SEXES	MALES	FEMALES	MEXICO 1960 BOTH SEXES	MALES	FEMALES
Birth	15.30	17.38*	14.40	15.55	15.94*	14.88	17.38	16.20*	16.84
Death	12.86	12.85*	12.88	10.51	11.44*	9.48	5.64	9.92*	4.70
Increase	2.44	4.52*	1.53	5.04	4.50*	5.40	11.74	6.28*	12.14

TABLE 6 STANDARDIZED RATES

	OBSERVED POP. MALES	FEMALES	STATIONARY POP. MALES	FEMALES	STABLE POP. MALES	FEMALES	OBSERVED BIRTHS	NET MATERNITY FUNCTION	BIRTHS IN STABLE POP.
μ	34.18576	37.43612	36.33634	38.39879	34.49098	36.39255	28.57055	28.82609	28.69162
σ^2	472.4127	485.2455	489.7187	531.4787	479.4030	522.0390	33.76244	33.44138	33.05178
κ_3	3014.909	1154.082	2277.149	1932.010	3129.223	3013.346	104.2796	101.9306	102.7614
κ_4	-212950.	-240502.	-234404.	-294892.	-212135.	-271533.	-403.291	-235.185	-191.189
β_1	0.086215	0.011657	0.044151	0.024863	0.088873	0.063825	0.282552	0.277816	0.292466
β_2	2.045811	1.978600	2.022601	1.956023	2.076982	2.003640	2.646206	2.789699	2.824986
κ	-0.031955	-0.004412	-0.016763	-0.009110	-0.033711	-0.023379	-0.148703	-0.179800	-0.193926

TABLE 7 MOMENTS AND CUMULANTS

VITAL STATISTICS		THOMPSON AGE RANGE	NRR	1000r	INTERVAL	BOURGEOIS-PICHAT AGE RANGE	NRR	1000b	1000d	1000r	COALE
GRR	1.171										IBR
NRR	1.116	0-4	1.06	2.05	27.42	5-29	0.89	12.76	17.22	-4.46	IDR
TFR	2.412	5-9	0.93	-2.61	27.38	30-54	0.77	9.82	19.28	-9.46	IRI
GENERATION	28.759	10-14	0.85	-6.01	27.33	55-79	1.89	62.07	38.53	23.53	K1
SEX RATIO	105.895	15-19	0.94	-2.40	27.25	*50-74	1.79	54.40	32.82	21.58	K2

TABLE 8 RATES FROM AGE DISTRIBUTIONS AND VITAL STATISTICS (Females)

Start Age Interval	ORIGINAL MATRIX SUB-DIAGONAL	ALTERNATIVE FIRST ROWS Projection	Integral	FIRST STABLE MATRIX % IN STABLE POPULATION	FISHER VALUES	REPRODUCTIVE VALUES	SECOND STABLE MATRIX Z2 FIRST COLUMN	FIRST ROW
	0.99565	0.00000	0.00000	7.701	1.042	2211036	0.1635+0.0644	0.1635+0.0644
	0.99833	0.00002	0.00000	7.523	1.067	2037225	0.1583-0.1326	0.0184+0.1484
	0.99804	0.01937	0.00005	7.369	1.089	1904919	-0.0482-0.2385	-0.1032+0.0738
	0.99715	0.15877	0.03914	7.216	1.092	2173888	-0.2740-0.0844	-0.1001-0.0482
	0.99625	0.33338	0.28224	7.059	0.950	2217787	-0.2413+0.2358	-0.0307-0.1045
	0.99495	0.31731	0.39236	6.900	0.623	1137719	0.1080+0.3818	0.0109-0.0869
	0.99283	0.18559	0.24959	6.736	0.306	593241	0.4545+0.1029	0.0173-0.0477
	0.99002	0.08839	0.12604	6.561	0.120	261686	0.3604-0.4103	0.0123-0.0185
	0.98519	0.02783	0.05295	6.373	0.030	45990	-0.2200-0.5991	0.0043-0.0041
	0.97808	0.00163	0.00329	6.161	0.002	3701	-0.7343-0.1082	0.0003-0.0002
	0.96722	0.00000	0.00000	5.912	0.000	1	-0.5148+0.6850	0.0000-0.0000
5+	0.78573			24.490				

TABLE 9 LESLIE MATRIX AND ITS SPECTRAL COMPONENTS (Females)

Start Age Interval	OBSERVED POPUL. (IN 100's)	r_1	r_2, r_3	$r_4 \cdot r_{11}$	AGE-SP. BIRTH RATES	NET MATERNITY FUNCTION	COEFF. OF MATRIX EQUATION	PARAMETERS	INTEGRAL	MATRIX	EXP. INCREASE x	$e^{(x+2\frac{1}{2})r}$
	21220	21069	364	-213	0.0000	0.0000	0.0000	L(1)	1.01921	1.01922	0	1.0096
	19099	20582	-1639	156	0.0000	0.0000	0.0000	L(2)	0.40090	0.40480	50	1.2212
	17493	20160	-2349	-317	0.0000	0.0000	0.0193		0.76798	0.74420	55	1.2447
	19911	19741	-370	539	0.0080	0.0385	0.1575	R(1)	0.00381	0.00381	60	1.2686
	23343	19314	2842	1188	0.0577	0.2766	0.3298	R(2)	-0.02870	-0.03317	65	1.2929
	18253	18878	3705	-4331	0.0802	0.3830	0.3127		0.21794	0.21452	70	1.3178
	19374	18429	234	711	0.0510	0.2424	0.1820	C(1)		273593	75	1.3431
	21887	17952	-4838	8773	0.0258	0.1215	0.0860	C(2)		-89774	80	1.3689
	15299	17437	-5724	3586	0.0108	0.0506	0.0268			-510627	85	1.3952
	22227	16855	214	5158	0.0007	0.0031	0.0015	2P/Y	28.8301	29.2889	90	1.4220
	22783	16175	7920	-1312	0.0000	0.0000	0.0000	DELTA	7.0748		95	1.4493
5+	73860	67002									100	1.4772

TABLE 10 AGE ANALYSIS AND MISCELLANEOUS RESULTS (Females)

TABLE 1 — DATA

AGE AT LAST BIRTHDAY	POPULATION BOTH SEXES	MALES Number	MALES %	FEMALES Number	FEMALES %	BIRTHS BY AGE OF MOTHER	DEATHS BOTH SEXES	MALES	FEMALES	AGE AT LAST BIRTHDAY
0	958913	490722	1.9	468191	1.6	0	32109	18435	13674	0
1-4	3518544	1804796	6.8	1713748	5.8	0	4762	2730	2032	1-4
5-9	3915383	2005641	7.6	1909742	6.4	0	2139	1337	802	5-9
10-14	3799567	1947078	7.4	1852489	6.2	40	1516	939	577	10-14
15-19	3684518	1883770	7.1	1800748	6.1	34088	3399	2479	920	15-19
20-24	4760979	2438857	9.2	2322122	7.8	293974	6023	4463	1560	20-24
25-29	3896283	2003429	7.6	1892854	6.4	327181	4824	3294	1530	25-29
30-34	3884835	1957682	7.4	1927153	6.5	202230	5650	3545	2105	30-34
35-39	3804900	1647713	6.2	2157187	7.2	114853	7406	3914	3492	35-39
40-44	2918408	1225760	4.6	1692648	5.7	37752	8067	4083	3984	40-44
45-49	3670228	1563980	5.9	2106248	7.1	2569	16169	8678	7491	45-49
50-54	4092073	1796313	6.8	2295760	7.7	0	29051	16808	12243	50-54
55-59	3851394	1772661	6.7	2078733	7.0	0	45406	28599	16807	55-59
60-64	3195305	1390915	5.3	1804390	6.1	0	61155	36775	24380	60-64
65-69	2405821	949743	3.6	1456078	4.9	0	72821	38456	34365	65-69
70-74	1789479	710937	2.7	1078542	3.6		87376	42646	44730	70-74
75-79	1165664	473410	1.8	692254	2.3		96969	44944	52025	75-79
80-84	611645	250042	0.9	361603	1.2	520590 M.	84332	37749	46583	80-84
85+	250887	99913	0.4	150974	0.5	492097 F.	58387	24426	33961	85+
TOTAL	56174826	26413362		29761464		1012687	627561	324300	303261	TOTAL

TABLE 2 — MALE LIFE TABLE

x	$_nq_x$	l_x	$_nd_x$	$_nL_x$	$_nm_x$	$_na_x$	T_x	r_x	$\mathring{e}_x$	$_nM_x$
0	0.036317	100000	3632	97215	0.037358	0.2330	6691058	0.0071	66.911	0.037567
1	0.005965	96368	575	383800	0.001498	1.0895	6593844	0.0071	68.423	0.001513
5	0.003314	95793	317	478174	0.000664	2.5000	6210044	0.0156	64.827	0.000667
10	0.002412	95476	230	476868	0.000483	2.7780	5731870	0.0056	60.035	0.000482
15	0.006560	95246	625	474798	0.001316	2.7106	5255002	0.0000	55.173	0.001316
20	0.009109	94621	862	470979	0.001830	2.5345	4780204	0.0000	50.520	0.001830
25	0.008187	93759	768	466871	0.001644	2.4939	4309225	0.0203	45.961	0.001644
30	0.009028	92991	840	462926	0.001814	2.5812	3842354	0.0177	41.319	0.001811
35	0.011880	92152	1095	458161	0.002389	2.6267	3379427	0.0444	36.672	0.002375
40	0.016533	91057	1505	451805	0.003332	2.6880	2921266	0.0017	32.082	0.003331
45	0.027395	89552	2453	442143	0.005549	2.7109	2469461	0.0000	27.576	0.005549
50	0.045803	87098	3989	426356	0.009357	2.7100	2027319	0.0000	23.276	0.009357
55	0.077897	83109	6474	400522	0.016164	2.6794	1600963	0.0088	19.263	0.016133
60	0.124813	76635	9565	360498	0.026533	2.6291	1200441	0.0191	15.664	0.026439
65	0.184915	67070	12402	305337	0.040618	2.5801	839943	0.0191	12.523	0.040491
70	0.262173	54668	14332	238154	0.060181	2.5451	534606	0.0191	9.779	0.059986
75	0.384353	40335	15503	162737	0.095264	2.4883	296452	0.0191	7.350	0.094937
80	0.542027	24832	13460	88857	0.151476	2.4361	133715	0.0191	5.385	0.150971
85+	1.000000	11373	11373	44858	0.253525	3.9444	44858	0.0191	3.944	0.244474

TABLE 3 — FEMALE LIFE TABLE

x	$_nq_x$	l_x	$_nd_x$	$_nL_x$	$_nm_x$	$_na_x$	T_x	r_x	$\mathring{e}_x$	$_nM_x$
0	0.028394	100000	2839	97825	0.029026	0.2342	7242954	0.0079	72.430	0.029206
1	0.004675	97161	454	387321	0.001173	1.0903	7145129	0.0079	73.539	0.001186
5	0.002086	96706	202	483027	0.000418	2.5000	6757808	0.0158	69.880	0.000420
10	0.001557	96505	150	482157	0.000312	2.5612	6274781	0.0055	65.021	0.000311
15	0.002551	96354	246	481193	0.000511	2.6458	5792624	0.0000	60.118	0.000511
20	0.003354	96109	322	479766	0.000672	2.5913	5311431	0.0000	55.265	0.000672
25	0.004041	95786	387	478005	0.000810	2.6062	4831664	0.0178	50.442	0.000808
30	0.005447	95399	520	475776	0.001092	2.6521	4353660	0.0000	45.636	0.001092
35	0.008078	94879	766	472602	0.001622	2.6582	3877884	0.0113	40.872	0.001619
40	0.011704	94113	1102	467993	0.002354	2.6653	3405282	0.0000	36.183	0.002354
45	0.017636	93011	1640	461228	0.003557	2.6657	2937288	0.0000	31.580	0.003557
50	0.026336	91371	2406	451236	0.005333	2.6646	2476060	0.0000	27.099	0.005333
55	0.039811	88965	3542	436642	0.008111	2.6899	2024824	0.0155	22.760	0.008085
60	0.065966	85423	5635	414162	0.013606	2.7013	1588183	0.0300	18.592	0.013511
65	0.112627	79788	8986	378105	0.023767	2.6814	1174021	0.0300	14.714	0.023601
70	0.190116	70802	13461	322300	0.041764	2.6443	795916	0.0300	11.241	0.041473
75	0.319328	57341	18311	242079	0.075639	2.5628	473617	0.0300	8.260	0.075153
80	0.486242	39031	18978	146497	0.129547	2.5191	231538	0.0300	5.932	0.128824
85+	1.000000	20052	20052	85040	0.235797	4.2409	85040	0.0300	4.241	0.224947

TABLE 4 — OBSERVED AND PROJECTED VITAL RATES

	OBSERVED POPULATION BOTH SEXES	MALES	FEMALES	PROJECTED 1966 MALES	1966 FEMALES	1971 MALES	1971 FEMALES	1976 MALES	1976 FEMALES	STABLE POPULATION MALES	FEMALES
RATES PER THOUSAND											
Birth	18.03	19.71	16.53	19.02	16.06	17.65	15.03	17.02	14.66	17.94	16.
Death	11.17	12.28	10.19	12.71	11.33	12.89	12.23	13.06	13.09	12.76	11.
Increase	6.86	7.43	6.34	6.31	4.73	4.75	2.80	3.96	1.56		5.17
PERCENTAGE											
under 15	21.70	23.66	19.97	24.82	21.12	25.65	22.04	25.35	22.04	24.79	23.
15-64	67.22	66.94	67.46	64.98	64.74	63.07	62.34	62.89	60.95	64.91	63.
65 and over	11.08	9.40	12.56	10.20	14.14	11.29	15.62	11.77	17.01	10.30	13.
DEP. RATIO X 100	48.77	49.39	48.23	53.90	54.47	58.56	60.40	59.01	64.06	54.07	58.

Including West Berlin

TABLE 1 — DATA

AGE AT LAST BIRTHDAY	POPULATION BOTH SEXES	MALES Number	%	FEMALES Number	%	BIRTHS BY AGE OF MOTHER	DEATHS BOTH SEXES	MALES	FEMALES	AGE AT LAST BIRTHDAY
0	989000	507000	1.9	482000	1.6	0	29808	17140	12668	0
1-4	3650900	1872700	7.0	1778200	5.9	0	4377	2431	1946	1-4
5-9	3998400	2049900	7.6	1948500	6.5	0	2118	1269	849	5-9
10-14	3854200	1977200	7.4	1877000	6.2	35	1493	961	532	10-14
15-19	3550700	1819400	6.8	1731300	5.8	35137	3097	2165	932	15-19
20-24	4818900	2482300	9.2	2336600	7.8	293217	5735	4336	1399	20-24
25-29	4157200	2150600	8.0	2006600	6.7	345426	5077	3454	1623	25-29
30-34	3871000	1985000	7.4	1886000	6.3	195261	5725	3652	2073	30-34
35-39	3784100	1691100	6.3	2093000	7.0	108872	7198	3975	3223	35-39
40-44	3309600	1394400	5.2	1915200	6.4	38373	8967	4657	4310	40-44
45-49	3265500	1385100	5.2	1880400	6.3	2231	14563	7869	6694	45-49
50-54	4067200	1770900	6.6	2296300	7.6	0	28578	16549	12029	50-54
55-59	3887900	1771800	6.6	2116100	7.0	0	46205	29157	17048	55-59
60-64	3317900	1466800	5.5	1851100	6.2	0	63972	39305	24667	60-64
65-69	2491600	983000	3.7	1508600	5.0	0	75188	40517	34671	65-69
70-74	1830600	714900	2.7	1115700	3.7		90883	44555	46328	70-74
75-79	1194600	476200	1.8	718400	2.4		100162	46635	53527	75-79
80-84	629100	253600	0.9	375500	1.2	523801 M.	87539	39052	48487	80-84
85+	269400	106400	0.4	163000	0.5	494751 F.	64134	27403	36731	85+
TOTAL	56937800	26858300		30079500		1018552	644819	335082	309737	TOTAL

TABLE 2 — MALE LIFE TABLE

x	$_nq_x$	l_x	$_nd_x$	$_nL_x$	$_nm_x$	$_na_x$	T_x	r_x	$\mathring{e}_x$	$_nM_x$	x
0	0.032774	100000	3277	97470	0.033625	0.2282	6710168	0.0068	67.102	0.033807	0
1	0.005122	96723	495	385447	0.001285	1.0862	6612698	0.0068	68.368	0.001298	1
5	0.003078	96227	296	480395	0.000617	2.5000	6227251	0.0177	64.714	0.000619	5
10	0.002434	95931	234	479127	0.000487	2.7423	5746856	0.0113	59.906	0.000486	10
15	0.005934	95697	568	477191	0.001190	2.7179	5267728	0.0000	55.046	0.001190	15
20	0.008697	95130	827	473619	0.001747	2.5470	4790537	0.0000	50.358	0.001747	20
25	0.008000	94302	754	469632	0.001606	2.5086	4316919	0.0207	45.777	0.001606	25
30	0.009175	93548	858	465663	0.001843	2.5810	3847287	0.0222	41.126	0.001840	30
35	0.011738	92689	1088	460866	0.002361	2.6273	3381624	0.0329	36.483	0.002351	35
40	0.016627	91601	1523	454499	0.003351	2.6967	2920758	0.0164	31.885	0.003340	40
45	0.028040	90078	2526	444595	0.005681	2.7047	2466259	0.0000	27.379	0.005681	45
50	0.045747	87553	4005	428604	0.009345	2.7132	2021664	0.0000	23.091	0.009345	50
55	0.079285	83547	6624	402367	0.016463	2.6797	1593060	0.0018	19.068	0.016456	55
60	0.126353	76923	9719	361569	0.026881	2.6287	1190693	0.0171	15.479	0.026796	60
65	0.187916	67204	12629	305503	0.041337	2.5836	829124	0.0171	12.337	0.041218	65
70	0.270923	54555	14786	236544	0.062507	2.5428	523621	0.0171	9.594	0.062323	70
75	0.393675	39790	15664	159466	0.098229	2.4795	287077	0.0171	7.215	0.097932	75
80	0.549030	24125	13246	85762	0.154446	2.4247	127611	0.0171	5.289	0.153991	80
85+	1.000000	10880	10880	41849	0.259980	3.8465	41849	0.0171	3.846	0.257548	85+

TABLE 3 — FEMALE LIFE TABLE

x	$_nq_x$	l_x	$_nd_x$	$_nL_x$	$_nm_x$	$_na_x$	T_x	r_x	$\mathring{e}_x$	$_nM_x$	x
0	0.025623	100000	2562	98045	0.026134	0.2370	7277436	0.0072	72.774	0.026282	0
1	0.004321	97438	421	388526	0.001084	1.0924	7179391	0.0072	73.682	0.001094	1
5	0.002164	97017	210	484558	0.000433	2.5000	6790864	0.0180	69.997	0.000436	5
10	0.001417	96807	137	483701	0.000284	2.5758	6306306	0.0114	65.143	0.000283	10
15	0.002688	96669	260	482729	0.000538	2.6210	5822605	0.0000	60.232	0.000538	15
20	0.002989	96410	288	481354	0.000599	2.5934	5339876	0.0000	55.387	0.000599	20
25	0.004047	96121	389	479684	0.000811	2.6267	4858522	0.0206	50.546	0.000809	25
30	0.005482	95732	525	477421	0.001099	2.6355	4378838	0.0000	45.740	0.001099	30
35	0.007672	95208	730	474323	0.001540	2.6524	3901417	0.0000	40.978	0.001540	35
40	0.011211	94477	1059	469930	0.002254	2.6807	3427094	0.0083	36.274	0.002250	40
45	0.017653	93418	1649	463242	0.003560	2.6662	2957164	0.0000	31.655	0.003560	45
50	0.025876	91769	2375	453303	0.005238	2.6663	2493922	0.0000	27.176	0.005238	50
55	0.039650	89394	3544	438779	0.008078	2.6887	2040619	0.0131	22.827	0.008056	55
60	0.065058	85850	5585	416385	0.013414	2.6966	1601840	0.0291	18.659	0.013326	60
65	0.109842	80265	8816	380951	0.023143	2.6893	1185455	0.0291	14.769	0.022982	65
70	0.190307	71448	13597	325232	0.041807	2.6459	804504	0.0291	11.260	0.041524	70
75	0.316994	57851	18338	244587	0.074977	2.5642	479271	0.0291	8.285	0.074509	75
80	0.487188	39513	19250	148263	0.129838	2.5208	234684	0.0291	5.939	0.129127	80
85+	1.000000	20263	20263	86422	0.234462	4.2651	86422	0.0291	4.265	0.225343	85+

TABLE 4 — OBSERVED AND PROJECTED VITAL RATES

RATES PER THOUSAND	OBSERVED POPULATION BOTH SEXES	MALES	FEMALES	PROJECTED POPULATION 1967 MALES	FEMALES	1972 MALES	FEMALES	1977 MALES	FEMALES	STABLE POPULATION MALES	FEMALES
Birth	17.89	19.50	16.45	18.60	15.78	17.22	14.73	16.78	14.51	17.73	16.52
Death	11.32	12.48	10.30	12.76	11.40	12.90	12.31	13.05	13.14	12.80	11.59
Increase	6.56	7.03	6.15	5.85	4.38	4.32	2.42	3.74	1.36		4.9269
PERCENTAGE											
under 15	21.94	23.85	20.23	24.96	21.32	25.61	22.08	25.03	21.83	24.65	23.17
15-64	66.79	66.71	66.86	64.73	64.20	63.13	61.96	63.42	60.93	65.10	63.24
65 and over	11.27	9.44	12.90	10.32	14.49	11.25	15.96	11.55	17.24	10.24	13.59
DEP. RATIO X 100	49.72	49.90	49.56	54.50	55.77	58.40	61.39	57.68	64.12	53.60	58.12

TABLE 4 OBSERVED AND PROJECTED VITAL RATES

354 Germany (West) 1963
Including West Berlin

TABLE 1 — DATA

AGE AT LAST BIRTHDAY	POPULATION BOTH SEXES	MALES Number	%	FEMALES Number	%	BIRTHS BY AGE OF MOTHER	DEATHS BOTH SEXES	MALES	FEMALES	AGE AT LAST BIRTHDAY
0	1012123	519157	1.9	492966	1.6	0	28474	16293	12181	0
1-4	3773033	1934568	7.1	1838465	6.1	0	4586	2595	1991	1-4
5-9	4095812	2101065	7.7	1994747	6.6	0	2139	1317	822	5-9
10-14	3898807	2000063	7.3	1898744	6.3	39	1456	931	525	10-14
15-19	3523004	1807251	6.6	1715753	5.7	35971	3062	2198	864	15-19
20-24	4715843	2437911	9.0	2277932	7.5	293069	5456	4135	1321	20-24
25-29	4435934	2303308	8.5	2132626	7.0	373784	5210	3602	1608	25-29
30-34	3810023	1969408	7.2	1840615	6.1	201233	5462	3581	1881	30-34
35-39	3827520	1777099	6.5	2050421	6.8	108769	7253	4119	3134	35-39
40-44	3647376	1541347	5.7	2106029	6.9	38827	10393	5374	5019	40-44
45-49	2874877	1214866	4.5	1660011	5.5	2431	12939	6845	6094	45-49
50-54	4039225	1746649	6.4	2292576	7.6	0	28474	16419	12055	50-54
55-59	3923120	1767393	6.5	2155727	7.1	0	46657	29120	17537	55-59
60-64	3414417	1522947	5.6	1891470	6.2	0	67736	41994	25742	60-64
65-69	2576731	1020894	3.7	1555837	5.1	0	80290	43692	36598	65-69
70-74	1870825	718155	2.6	1152670	3.8		95293	46496	48797	70-74
75-79	1226429	479591	1.8	746491	2.5		106101	48630	57471	75-79
80-84	639602	253651	0.9	385951	1.3	541812 M.	91708	40687	51021	80-84
85+	282691	109984	0.4	172707	0.6	512311 F.	70380	29689	40691	85+
TOTAL	57587392	27225654		30361738		1054123	673069	347717	325352	TOTAL

TABLE 2 — MALE LIFE TABLE

x	nq_x	l_x	nd_x	nL_x	nm_x	na_x	T_x	r_x	$\mathring{e}_x$	nM_x
0	0.030512	100000	3051	97680	0.031237	0.2397	6704213	0.0059	67.042	0.031384
1	0.005303	96949	514	386301	0.001331	1.0943	6606532	0.0059	68.145	0.001341
5	0.003114	96435	300	481422	0.000624	2.5000	6220231	0.0197	64.502	0.000627
10	0.002334	96134	224	480169	0.000467	2.7612	5738809	0.0144	59.696	0.000465
15	0.006064	95910	582	478217	0.001216	2.7080	5258640	0.0000	54.829	0.001216
20	0.008445	95328	805	474661	0.001696	2.5401	4780423	0.0000	50.147	0.001696
25	0.007791	94523	736	470784	0.001564	2.5129	4305762	0.0197	45.552	0.001564
30	0.009071	93787	851	466877	0.001822	2.5828	3834978	0.0241	40.890	0.001818
35	0.011564	92936	1075	462149	0.002326	2.6451	3368100	0.0221	36.241	0.002318
40	0.017409	91861	1599	455608	0.003510	2.6870	2905951	0.0344	31.634	0.003487
45	0.027812	90262	2510	445543	0.005634	2.7024	2450343	0.0000	27.147	0.005634
50	0.046012	87752	4038	429526	0.009400	2.7132	2004801	0.0000	22.846	0.009400
55	0.079357	83714	6643	403204	0.016476	2.6870	1575275	0.0000	18.817	0.016476
60	0.129750	77071	10000	361686	0.027648	2.6332	1172071	0.0141	15.208	0.027574
65	0.194341	67071	13035	303834	0.042900	2.5818	810385	0.0141	12.083	0.042798
70	0.279778	54036	15118	232947	0.064899	2.5371	506551	0.0141	9.374	0.064744
75	0.404191	38918	15730	154858	0.101579	2.4741	273604	0.0141	7.030	0.101326
80	0.567786	23188	13166	81835	0.160880	2.4097	118746	0.0141	5.121	0.160406
85+	*1.000000	10022	10022	36911	0.271522	3.6829	36911	0.0141	3.683	0.269939

TABLE 3 — FEMALE LIFE TABLE

x	nq_x	l_x	nd_x	nL_x	nm_x	na_x	T_x	r_x	$\mathring{e}_x$	nM_x
0	0.024142	100000	2414	98172	0.024591	0.2426	7274352	0.0061	72.744	0.024710
1	0.004284	97586	418	389129	0.001074	1.0965	7176180	0.0061	73.537	0.001083
5	0.002044	97168	199	485342	0.000409	2.5000	6787051	0.0200	69.849	0.000412
10	0.001383	96969	134	484520	0.000277	2.5697	6301709	0.0147	64.987	0.000276
15	0.002515	96835	244	483596	0.000504	2.6245	5817189	0.0000	60.073	0.000504
20	0.002896	96591	280	482283	0.000580	2.5893	5333593	0.0000	55.218	0.000580
25	0.003773	96312	363	480694	0.000756	2.6202	4851309	0.0205	50.371	0.000754
30	0.005100	95948	489	478595	0.001022	2.6548	4370615	0.0029	45.552	0.001022
35	0.007615	95459	727	475611	0.001528	2.6826	3892021	0.0000	40.772	0.001528
40	0.011891	94732	1126	471048	0.002391	2.6806	3416410	0.0187	36.064	0.002383
45	0.018199	93606	1703	464032	0.003671	2.6541	2945362	0.0000	31.466	0.003671
50	0.025972	91902	2387	453935	0.005258	2.6639	2481329	0.0000	27.000	0.005258
55	0.040014	89515	3582	439313	0.008153	2.6929	2027395	0.0106	23.649	0.008135
60	0.066378	85933	5704	416537	0.013694	2.6981	1588082	0.0271	18.480	0.013610
65	0.112233	80229	9004	380320	0.023676	2.6871	1171545	0.0271	14.602	0.023523
70	0.193618	71225	13790	323669	0.042606	2.6465	791225	0.0271	11.109	0.042334
75	0.325663	57435	18704	241535	0.077439	2.5601	467555	0.0271	8.141	0.076988
80	0.495272	38730	19182	144369	0.132868	2.5092	226020	0.0271	5.836	0.132196
85+	1.000000	19548	19548	81651	0.239411	4.1769	81651	0.0271	4.177	0.235606

TABLE 4 — OBSERVED AND PROJECTED VITAL RATES

	OBSERVED POPULATION BOTH SEXES	MALES	FEMALES	PROJECTED POPULATION 1968 MALES	FEMALES	1973 MALES	FEMALES	1978 MALES	FEMALES	STABLE POPULATION MALES	FEMALES
RATES PER THOUSAND											
Birth	18.30	19.90	16.87	18.78	16.02	17.44	15.01	17.07	14.86	18.33	17.1
Death	11.69	12.77	10.72	12.87	11.72	12.94	12.56	12.99	13.30	12.42	11.2
Increase	6.62	7.13	6.16	5.90	4.30	4.50	2.44	4.08	1.56		5.908
PERCENTAGE											
under 15	22.19	24.08	20.50	25.33	21.74	26.00	22.55	25.39	22.28	25.36	23.8
15-64	66.35	66.44	66.28	64.33	63.58	62.91	61.40	63.43	60.59	65.00	63.2
65 and over	11.45	9.49	13.22	10.34	14.68	11.08	16.05	11.18	17.13	9.64	12.9
DEP. RATIO X 100	50.71	50.52	50.88	55.45	57.28	58.95	62.86	57.66	65.04	53.85	58.2

TABLE 1 DATA

AGE AT LAST BIRTHDAY	POPULATION BOTH SEXES	MALES Number	%	FEMALES Number	%	BIRTHS BY AGE OF MOTHER	DEATHS BOTH SEXES	MALES	FEMALES	AGE AT LAST BIRTHDAY
0	1036293	531615	1.9	504678	1.6	0	26949	15430	11519	0
1-4	3885886	1991239	7.2	1894647	6.2	0	4145	2411	1734	1-4
5-9	4218300	2164650	7.8	2053650	6.7	0	2166	1323	843	5-9
10-14	3910755	2004705	7.3	1906050	6.2	45	1619	1047	572	10-14
15-19	3531913	1813274	6.6	1718639	5.6	37776	3026	2231	795	15-19
20-24	4550574	2356545	8.5	2194029	7.2	279138	5512	4206	1306	20-24
25-29	4700529	2448442	8.9	2252087	7.3	389606	5533	3927	1606	25-29
30-34	3810262	1979083	7.2	1831179	6.0	210011	5453	3576	1877	30-34
35-39	3908616	1887264	6.8	2021352	6.6	107590	7589	4503	3086	35-39
40-44	3853992	1634399	5.9	2219593	7.2	38275	10927	5778	5149	40-44
45-49	2617785	1104471	4.0	1513314	4.9	2996	11315	6065	5250	45-49
50-54	3982258	1708629	6.2	2273629	7.4	0	27309	15665	11644	50-54
55-59	3956472	1756909	6.4	2199563	7.2	0	45441	28055	17386	55-59
60-64	3493764	1564406	5.7	1929358	6.3	0	67091	41844	25247	60-64
65-69	2674483	1071313	3.9	1603170	5.2	0	79611	43986	35625	65-69
70-74	1918812	724442	2.6	1194370	3.9		91327	44479	46848	70-74
75-79	1262843	484386	1.8	778457	2.5		99601	45537	54064	75-79
80-84	654627	255378	0.9	399249	1.3	547979 M.	84313	36810	47503	80-84
85+	298168	114101	0.4	184067	0.6	517458 F.	65201	27006	38195	85+
TOTAL	58266332	27595251		30671081		1065437	644128	333879	310249	TOTAL

TABLE 2 MALE LIFE TABLE

x	nq_x	l_x	nd_x	nL_x	nm_x	na_x	T_x	r_x	$\dot{e}_x$	nM_x	x
0	0.028275	100000	2828	97843	0.028898	0.2372	6759169	0.0055	67.592	0.029025	0
1	0.004791	97172	466	387336	0.001202	1.0925	6661326	0.0055	68.552	0.001211	1
5	0.003038	96707	294	482800	0.000609	2.5000	6273990	0.0222	64.876	0.000611	5
10	0.002619	96413	253	481496	0.000524	2.7443	5791189	0.0170	60.066	0.000522	10
15	0.006135	96161	590	479453	0.001230	2.7107	5309693	0.0000	55.217	0.001230	15
20	0.008885	95571	849	475765	0.001785	2.5409	4830241	0.0000	50.541	0.001785	20
25	0.007988	94722	757	471716	0.001604	2.4994	4354476	0.0158	45.971	0.001604	25
30	0.009015	93965	847	467780	0.001811	2.5863	3882760	0.0242	41.321	0.001807	30
35	0.011893	93118	1107	462983	0.002392	2.6468	3414980	0.0166	36.674	0.002386	35
40	0.017689	92010	1628	456263	0.003567	2.6719	2951997	0.0499	32.083	0.003535	40
45	0.027114	90383	2451	446271	0.005491	2.6973	2495734	0.0000	27.613	0.005491	45
50	0.044899	87932	3948	430627	0.009168	2.7119	2049463	0.0000	23.307	0.009168	50
55	0.076999	83984	6467	404970	0.015968	2.6880	1618836	0.0000	19.276	0.015968	55
60	0.126228	77517	9785	364421	0.026850	2.6325	1213866	0.0204	15.659	0.026748	60
65	0.187320	67733	12688	307972	0.041197	2.5811	849445	0.0204	12.541	0.041058	65
70	0.267453	55045	14722	238977	0.061604	2.5379	541473	0.0204	9.837	0.061398	70
75	0.381009	40323	15363	162865	0.094332	2.4778	302496	0.0204	7.502	0.094010	75
80	0.524197	24960	13084	90470	0.144619	2.4445	139631	0.0204	5.594	0.144139	80
85+	1.000000	11876	11876	49160	0.241574	4.1395	49160	0.0204	4.140	0.236686	85+

TABLE 3 FEMALE LIFE TABLE

x	nq_x	l_x	nd_x	nL_x	nm_x	na_x	T_x	r_x	$\dot{e}_x$	nM_x	x
0	0.022335	100000	2234	98287	0.022724	0.2332	7357517	0.0055	73.575	0.022824	0
1	0.003623	97766	354	390035	0.000908	1.0897	7259230	0.0055	74.251	0.000915	1
5	0.002038	97412	199	486565	0.000408	2.5000	6869195	0.0225	70.517	0.000410	5
10	0.001500	97214	146	485709	0.000300	2.5367	6382630	0.0174	65.656	0.000300	10
15	0.002310	97068	224	484808	0.000463	2.6319	5896921	0.0000	60.751	0.000463	15
20	0.002972	96844	288	483523	0.000595	2.5870	5412113	0.0000	55.885	0.000595	20
25	0.003567	96556	344	481960	0.000715	2.6239	4928589	0.0173	51.044	0.000713	25
30	0.005121	96211	493	479905	0.001027	2.6622	4446629	0.0098	46.217	0.001025	30
35	0.007606	95719	728	476900	0.001527	2.6740	3966724	0.0000	41.442	0.001527	35
40	0.011589	94991	1101	472385	0.002330	2.6679	3489825	0.0266	36.739	0.002320	40
45	0.017206	93890	1615	465667	0.003469	2.6591	3017439	0.0000	32.138	0.003469	45
50	0.025304	92274	2335	455925	0.005121	2.6678	2551773	0.0000	27.654	0.005121	50
55	0.038877	89939	3497	441620	0.007918	2.6904	2095848	0.0081	23.303	0.007904	55
60	0.063972	86443	5530	419454	0.013184	2.6928	1654227	0.0336	19.137	0.013086	60
65	0.106451	80913	8613	384602	0.022395	2.6824	1234773	0.0336	15.261	0.022222	65
70	0.180803	72299	13072	330712	0.039527	2.6450	850171	0.0336	11.759	0.039224	70
75	0.298985	59228	17708	253153	0.069950	2.5726	519459	0.0336	8.771	0.069450	75
80	0.463488	41519	19244	160439	0.119944	2.5494	266306	0.0336	6.414	0.118982	80
85+	*1.000000	22276	22276	105867	0.210412	4.7526	105867	0.0336	4.753	0.207506	85+

TABLE 4 OBSERVED AND PROJECTED VITAL RATES

	OBSERVED POPULATION BOTH SEXES	MALES	FEMALES	1969 PROJECTED MALES	FEMALES	1974 MALES	FEMALES	1979 MALES	FEMALES	STABLE POPULATION MALES	FEMALES
RATES PER THOUSAND											
Birth	18.29	19.86	16.87	18.56	15.86	17.27	14.88	16.99	14.80	18.34	17.08
Death	11.05	12.10	10.12	12.46	11.36	12.63	12.33	12.71	13.10	12.22	10.96
Increase	7.23	7.76	6.76	6.10	4.50	4.64	2.55	4.28	1.71		6.1220
PERCENTAGE											
under 15	22.40	24.25	20.73	25.50	21.94	25.98	22.56	25.22	22.14	25.40	23.84
15-64	65.91	66.15	65.71	63.81	62.80	62.61	60.65	63.38	60.08	64.67	62.79
65 and over	11.69	9.60	13.56	10.69	15.26	11.41	16.78	11.40	17.78	9.93	13.37
DEP. RATIO X 100	51.71	51.18	52.19	56.72	59.23	59.71	64.87	57.78	66.45	54.64	59.26

TABLE 1 — DATA

AGE AT LAST BIRTHDAY	POPULATION BOTH SEXES	MALES Number	%	FEMALES Number	%	BIRTHS BY AGE OF MOTHER	DEATHS BOTH SEXES	MALES	FEMALES	AGE AT LAST BIRTHDAY
0	1032300	529900	1.9	502400	1.6	0	24947	14304	10643	0
1-4	3993000	2046700	7.3	1946300	6.3	0	4278	2413	1865	1-4
5-9	4365400	2241100	8.0	2124300	6.9	0	2165	1376	789	5-9
10-14	3921300	2010400	7.2	1910900	6.2	38	1522	948	574	10-14
15-19	3677600	1891600	6.7	1786000	5.8	42650	3067	2247	820	15-19
20-24	4244000	2200900	7.9	2043100	6.6	257864	4597	3425	1172	20-24
25-29	4917100	2575600	9.2	2341500	7.6	389003	5494	3840	1654	25-29
30-34	3930600	2054600	7.3	1876000	6.1	213256	5580	3684	1896	30-34
35-39	3975100	1986000	7.1	1989100	6.4	102083	7526	4605	2921	35-39
40-44	3893600	1672500	6.0	2221100	7.2	36079	10989	5914	5075	40-44
45-49	2655600	1121400	4.0	1534200	5.0	3355	11192	5991	5201	45-49
50-54	3844100	1639000	5.8	2205100	7.1	0	27096	15371	11725	50-54
55-59	3964400	1733900	6.2	2230500	7.2	0	45587	27877	17710	55-59
60-64	3563600	1596300	5.7	1967300	6.4	0	69713	43063	26650	60-64
65-69	2777300	1131900	4.0	1645400	5.3	0	86149	48420	37729	65-69
70-74	1970200	734600	2.6	1235600	4.0		97573	47177	50396	70-74
75-79	1294900	487200	1.7	807700	2.6		105744	47690	58054	75-79
80-84	675700	259200	0.9	416500	1.3	536930 M.	91259	39475	51784	80-84
85+	315800	119300	0.4	196500	0.6	507398 F.	73150	30148	43002	85+
TOTAL	59011600	28032100		30979500		1044328	677628	347968	329660	TOTAL

TABLE 2 — MALE LIFE TABLE

x	$_nq_x$	l_x	$_nd_x$	$_nL_x$	$_nm_x$	$_na_x$	T_x	r_x	$\overset{\circ}{e}_x$	$_nM_x$
0	0.026402	100000	2640	98000	0.026941	0.2424	6761197	0.0025	67.612	0.026994
1	0.004685	97360	456	388115	0.001175	1.0963	6663197	0.0025	68.439	0.001179
5	0.003050	96904	296	483780	0.000611	2.5000	6275082	0.0241	64.756	0.000614
10	0.002365	96608	228	482527	0.000473	2.7510	5791302	0.0163	59.946	0.000472
15	0.005923	96380	571	480578	0.001188	2.6876	5308776	0.0000	55.082	0.001188
20	0.007751	95809	743	477215	0.001556	2.5380	4828198	0.0000	50.394	0.001556
25	0.007429	95066	706	473586	0.001491	2.5300	4350982	0.0053	45.768	0.001491
30	0.008947	94360	844	469767	0.001797	2.5926	3877396	0.0242	41.092	0.001793
35	0.011564	93516	1081	465040	0.002325	2.6525	3407629	0.0181	36.439	0.002319
40	0.017700	92434	1636	458555	0.003569	2.6674	2942589	0.0535	31.834	0.003536
45	0.026389	90798	2396	448505	0.005342	2.7106	2484234	0.0000	27.360	0.005342
50	0.045907	88402	4058	432727	0.009378	2.7126	2035729	0.0000	23.028	0.009378
55	0.077505	84344	6537	406593	0.016078	2.6861	1603002	0.0000	19.006	0.016078
60	0.127189	77807	9896	365681	0.027062	2.6402	1196409	0.0161	15.377	0.026977
65	0.194336	67911	13198	307664	0.042896	2.5837	830728	0.0161	12.233	0.042778
70	0.277807	54713	15200	236054	0.064391	2.5320	523063	0.0161	9.560	0.064221
75	0.393178	39513	15536	158282	0.098153	2.4713	287010	0.0161	7.264	0.097886
80	0.544592	23978	13058	85509	0.152709	2.4264	128728	0.0161	5.369	0.152296
85+	1.000000	10920	10920	43219	0.252658	3.9579	43219	0.0161	3.958	0.252707

TABLE 3 — FEMALE LIFE TABLE

x	$_nq_x$	l_x	$_nd_x$	$_nL_x$	$_nm_x$	$_na_x$	T_x	r_x	$\overset{\circ}{e}_x$	$_nM_x$
0	0.020813	100000	2081	98432	0.021144	0.2464	7344219	0.0024	73.442	0.021184
1	0.003811	97919	373	390593	0.000955	1.0993	7245787	0.0024	73.998	0.000958
5	0.001842	97546	180	487279	0.000369	2.5000	6855195	0.0243	70.277	0.000371
10	0.001502	97366	146	486473	0.000301	2.5616	6367916	0.0170	65.402	0.000300
15	0.002293	97220	223	485568	0.000459	2.6229	5881443	0.0000	60.496	0.000459
20	0.002864	96997	278	484314	0.000574	2.5888	5395875	0.0000	55.629	0.000574
25	0.003530	96719	341	482785	0.000707	2.6277	4911561	0.0078	50.782	0.000706
30	0.005053	96378	487	480745	0.001013	2.6541	4428776	0.0153	45.952	0.001011
35	0.007318	95890	702	477823	0.001469	2.6779	3948031	0.0000	41.172	0.001469
40	0.011411	95189	1086	473412	0.002294	2.6690	3470208	0.0236	36.456	0.002285
45	0.016818	94103	1583	466837	0.003390	2.6768	2996796	0.0000	31.846	0.003390
50	0.026260	92520	2430	456929	0.005317	2.6657	2529959	0.0000	27.345	0.005317
55	0.039010	90090	3514	442352	0.007945	2.6952	2073031	0.0029	23.011	0.007940
60	0.066101	86576	5723	419687	0.013636	2.6946	1630679	0.0293	18.835	0.013546
65	0.109571	80853	8859	383734	0.023087	2.6823	1210992	0.0293	14.978	0.022930
70	0.187169	71994	13475	328187	0.041059	2.6413	827258	0.0293	11.491	0.040787
75	0.307549	58519	17997	248832	0.072328	2.5684	499071	0.0293	8.528	0.071876
80	0.478326	40522	19383	154806	0.125205	2.5338	250239	0.0293	6.175	0.124331
85+	*1.000000	21139	21139	95433	0.221508	4.5145	95433	0.0293	4.515	0.218840

TABLE 4 — OBSERVED AND PROJECTED VITAL RATES

	OBSERVED POPULATION BOTH SEXES	MALES	FEMALES	PROJECTED POPULATION 1970 MALES	FEMALES	1975 MALES	FEMALES	1980 MALES	FEMALES	STABLE POPULATION MALES	FEMALES
RATES PER THOUSAND											
Birth	17.70	19.15	16.38	17.91	15.41	16.85	14.63	16.79	14.74	17.96	16.7
Death	11.48	12.41	10.64	12.61	11.74	12.72	12.66	12.77	13.35	12.43	11.2
Increase	6.21	6.74	5.74	5.30	3.67	4.13	1.97	4.02	1.39		5.535
PERCENTAGE											
under 15	22.56	24.36	20.93	25.48	22.05	25.62	22.39	24.66	21.81	25.04	23.5
15-64	65.52	65.90	65.18	63.79	62.50	63.14	60.73	64.36	60.65	65.02	63.0
65 and over	11.92	9.75	13.89	10.72	15.45	11.24	16.87	10.97	17.54	9.94	13.4
DEP. RATIO X 100	52.62	51.76	53.41	56.76	59.99	58.37	64.66	55.37	64.88	53.80	58.5

AGE LAST BIRTHDAY	1970			1975			1980			AGE AT LAST BIRTHDAY	
	BOTH SEXES	MALES	FEMALES	BOTH SEXES	MALES	FEMALES	BOTH SEXES	MALES	FEMALES		
0-4	4999	2563	2436	4816	2469	2347	4765	2443	2322	0-4	
5-9	5004	2564	2440	4977	2550	2427	4796	2457	2339	5-9	
10-14	4356	2235	2121	4994	2558	2436	4967	2544	2423	10-14	
15-19	3909	2002	1907	4343	2226	2117	4978	2547	2431	15-19	**TABLE 5**
20-24	3659	1878	1781	3890	1988	1902	4322	2211	2111	20-24	POPULATION
25-29	4221	2184	2037	3640	1864	1776	3869	1973	1896	25-29	PROJECTED
30-34	4887	2555	2332	4195	2167	2028	3617	1849	1768	30-34	WITH
35-39	3899	2034	1865	4846	2529	2317	4161	2145	2016	35-39	FIXED
40-44	3928	1957	1971	3852	2005	1847	4789	2493	2296	40-44	AGE—
45-49	3827	1637	2190	3858	1915	1943	3784	1962	1822	45-49	SPECIFIC
50-54	2584	1082	1502	3723	1579	2144	3750	1848	1902	50-54	BIRTH
55-59	3675	1540	2135	2471	1017	1454	3559	1484	2075	55-59	AND
60-64	3675	1559	2116	3410	1385	2025	2293	914	1379	60-64	DEATH
65-69	3142	1343	1799	3247	1312	1935	3017	1165	1852	65-69	RATES
70-74	2275	868	1407	2568	1030	1538	2662	1007	1655	70-74	(IN 1000's)
75-79	1430	493	937	1649	582	1067	1857	691	1166	75-79	
80-84	765	263	502	849	266	583	979	315	664	80-84	
85+	388	131	257	443	133	310	493	134	359	85+	
TOTAL	60623	28888	31735	61771	29575	32196	62658	30182	32476	TOTAL	

STANDARD COUNTRIES:	ENGLAND AND WALES 1961			UNITED STATES 1960			MEXICO 1960			
STANDARDIZED RATES PER THOUSAND	BOTH SEXES	MALES	FEMALES	BOTH SEXES	MALES	FEMALES	BOTH SEXES	MALES	FEMALES	**TABLE 6**
Birth	15.85	16.29*	14.93	16.13	15.34*	15.44	18.23	15.17*	17.67	STANDAR-DIZED
Death	11.91	12.31*	11.54	9.69	11.03*	8.44	5.02	9.42*	4.05	RATES
Increase	3.94	3.98*	3.39	6.44	4.31*	7.01	13.21	5.75*	13.62	

	OBSERVED POP.		STATIONARY POP.		STABLE POP.		OBSERVED BIRTHS	NET MATERNITY FUNCTION	BIRTHS IN STABLE POP.	
	MALES	FEMALES	MALES	FEMALES	MALES	FEMALES				**TABLE 7**
	33.96644	37.83573	36.45382	38.83616	33.76938	35.86713	28.43745	28.46548	28.27324	MOMENTS
	477.3451	516.8100	492.4841	543.3925	476.2197	527.7653	31.24131	32.89069	32.39272	AND
	3293.667	1193.617	2315.106	2001.332	3528.527	3607.694	99.2026	89.6670	90.2052	CUMULANTS
	-208987.	-285978.	-235469.	-308100.	-200522.	-268437.	57.810	-109.963	-74.403	
	0.099738	0.010321	0.044871	0.024963	0.115283	0.088539	0.322744	0.225967	0.239398	
	2.082821	1.929292	2.029155	1.956568	2.115808	2.036259	3.059230	2.898352	2.929092	
	-0.037590	-0.003755	-0.017120	-0.009150	-0.043951	-0.032489	-0.309355	-0.204329	-0.222440	

VITAL STATISTICS		THOMPSON				BOURGEOIS-PICHAT				COALE	
		AGE RANGE	NRR	1000r	INTERVAL	AGE RANGE	NRR	1000b	1000d	1000r	
R	1.214										IBR	**TABLE 8**
R	1.170	0-4	1.18	6.03	27.43	5-29	0.86	12.24	17.93	-5.69	IDR	RATES FROM AGE DISTRIBUTIONS AND VITAL STATISTICS (Females)
R	2.498	5-9	1.04	1.46	27.40	30-54	0.90	11.37	15.14	-3.77	IRI	
GENERATION	28.369	10-14	0.92	-3.20	27.35	55-79	1.68	50.06	30.74	19.31	K1	
SEX RATIO	105.820	15-19	0.85	-5.91	27.27	*50-74	1.43	33.08	19.90	13.17	K2	

	ORIGINAL MATRIX			FIRST STABLE MATRIX			SECOND STABLE MATRIX Z2		
SUB-DIAGONAL	ALTERNATIVE FIRST ROWS		% IN STABLE POPULATION	FISHER VALUES	REPRODUCTIVE VALUES	FIRST COLUMN	FIRST ROW		
	Projection	Integral							
0.99643	0.00000	0.00000	8.076	1.037	2538488	0.1633+0.0600	0.1633+0.0600		**TABLE 9**
0.99835	0.00002	0.00000	7.828	1.070	2272148	0.1506-0.1352	0.0201+0.1481		LESLIE MATRIX AND ITS SPECTRAL COMPONENTS (Females)
0.99814	0.02834	0.00005	7.601	1.101	2104730	-0.0572-0.2290	-0.1042+0.0746		
0.99742	0.17792	0.05753	7.380	1.105	1973604	-0.2671-0.0659	-0.1031-0.0508		
0.99684	0.34668	0.30406	7.160	0.954	1949314	-0.2134+0.2390	-0.0320-0.1093		
0.99578	0.33184	0.40023	6.942	0.623	1459847	0.1297+0.3498	0.0133-0.0891		
0.99392	0.19564	0.27386	6.724	0.298	559475	0.4301+0.0570	0.0187-0.0457		
0.99077	0.08009	0.12364	6.500	0.104	207701	0.2920-0.4103	0.0102-0.0160		
0.98611	0.02186	0.03913	6.265	0.025	54537	-0.2615-0.5207	0.0032-0.0036		
0.97878	0.00260	0.00527	6.009	0.003	4019	-0.6709-0.0144	0.0004-0.0004		
0.96810	0.00000	0.00000	5.721	0.000	1	-0.3733+0.6701	0.0000-0.0000		
0.79534			23.795						

OBSERVED POPUL. (IN 100's)	CONTRIBUTIONS OF ROOTS (IN 100's)			AGE-SP. BIRTH RATES	NET MATERNITY FUNCTION	COEFF. OF MATRIX EQUATION	PARAMETERS		EXP. INCREASE		
	r_1	r_2, r_3	r_4-r_{11}				INTEGRAL	MATRIX	x	$e^{(x+2\frac{1}{2})r}$	
24487	22416	1758	314	0.0000	0.0000	0.0000	L(1) 1.02807	1.02808	0	1.0139	**TABLE 10**
21243	21725	44	-527	0.0000	0.0000	0.0000	L(2) 0.39749	0.40060	50	1.3373	AGE ANALYSIS AND MISCELLANEOUS RESULTS (Females)
19109	21097	-2336	348	0.0000	0.0000	0.0282	0.78108	0.75678	55	1.3748	
17860	20483	-2608	-14	0.0116	0.0563	0.1767	R(1) 0.00554	0.00554	60	1.4134	
20431	19872	330	230	0.0613	0.2970	0.3433	R(2) -0.02639	-0.03103	65	1.4531	
23415	19268	3896	251	0.0807	0.3897	0.3276	0.22001	0.21679	70	1.4938	
18760	18662	3794	-3696	0.0552	0.2655	0.1923	C(1)	277550	75	1.5358	
19891	18042	-1139	2988	0.0249	0.1191	0.0783	C(2)	386195	80	1.5789	
22211	17387	-6329	11152	0.0079	0.0374	0.0212		-413738	85	1.6232	
15342	16677	-5301	3966	0.0011	0.0050	0.0025	2P/Y 28.5585	28.9829	90	1.6687	
22051	15878	2661	3513	0.0000	0.0000	0.0000	DELTA 7.3094		95	1.7156	
84995	66044								100	1.7637	

TABLE 1 — DATA

AGE AT LAST BIRTHDAY	POPULATION BOTH SEXES	MALES Number	%	FEMALES Number	%	BIRTHS BY AGE OF MOTHER	DEATHS BOTH SEXES	MALES	FEMALES	AGE AT LAST BIRTH
0	158549	81936	2.0	76613	1.8	0	6290	3351	2939	0
1-4	592354	307013	7.6	285341	6.7	0	1152	628	524	1-
5-9	705813	366521	9.0	339292	8.0	0	438	262	176	5-
10-14	717376	368214	9.1	349162	8.2	33	331	201	130	10-
15-19	633002	324905	8.0	308097	7.2	5311	447	280	167	15-
20-24	741491	372932	9.2	368559	8.6	38155	594	368	226	20-
25-29	734213	356428	8.8	377785	8.9	56679	705	417	288	25-
30-34	670169	316C08	7.8	354161	8.3	38165	849	468	381	30-
35-39	554002	259930	6.4	294072	6.9	13845	817	448	369	35-
40-44	482705	227304	5.6	255401	6.0	3347	1015	564	451	40-
45-49	491364	233767	5.8	257597	6.0	458	1716	1011	705	45-
50-54	464199	224404	5.5	239795	5.6	60	2462	1488	974	50-
55-59	396037	190079	4.7	205958	4.8	0	3413	2100	1313	55-
60-64	309824	143363	3.5	166461	3.9	0	4371	2507	1864	60-
65-69	243356	106795	2.6	136561	3.2	0	5196	2834	2362	65-
70-74	189310	80729	2.0	108581	2.5		7070	3492	3578	70-
75-79	135483	57278	1.4	78205	1.8		8054	3847	4207	75-
80-84	76729	32635	0.8	44094	1.0	80731 M.	7874	3614	4260	80-
85+	31429	14348	0.4	17081	0.4	75322 F.	8999	3564	5435	85
TOTAL	8327405	4064589		4262816		156053	61793	31444	30349	TO

TABLE 2 — MALE LIFE TABLE

x	nq_x	l_x	nd_x	nL_x	nm_x	na_x	T_x	r_x	$\dot{e}_x$	nM_x
0	0.039544	100000	3954	97059	0.040742	0.2563	7009237	0.0049	70.092	0.040898
1	0.C08088	96046	777	381935	0.002034	1.1071	6912178	0.0049	71.968	0.002046
5	0.003562	95269	339	475496	0.000714	2.5000	6530243	0.0044	68.545	0.000715
10	0.002727	94929	259	474014	0.000546	2.5545	6054748	0.0114	63.782	0.000546
15	0.004300	94671	407	472378	0.000862	2.6049	5580734	0.0000	58.949	0.000862
20	0.004922	94263	464	470187	0.000987	2.5632	5108356	0.0000	54.192	0.000987
25	0.005841	93799	548	467675	0.001172	2.5858	4638170	0.0154	49.448	0.001170
30	0.007396	93252	690	464586	0.001484	2.5754	4170495	0.0301	44.723	0.001481
35	0.008614	92562	797	460909	0.001730	2.6161	3705909	0.0311	40.037	0.001724
40	0.012357	91765	1134	456226	0.002485	2.7100	3245001	0.0079	35.362	0.002481
45	0.021410	90631	1940	448671	0.004325	2.6901	2788775	0.0000	30.771	0.004325
50	0.032747	88690	2904	436750	0.006650	2.6944	2340104	0.0136	26.385	0.006631
55	0.054211	85786	4651	418124	0.011122	2.6767	1903350	0.0334	22.187	0.011048
60	0.084400	81135	6848	389530	0.017580	2.6422	1485225	0.0294	18.306	0.017487
65	0.125501	74287	9323	349360	0.026686	2.6328	1095695	0.0294	14.749	0.026537
70	0.196857	64964	12789	294056	0.043491	2.5994	746328	0.0294	11.488	0.043256
75	0.289698	52176	15115	223817	0.067534	2.5481	452271	0.0294	8.668	0.067164
80	0.439169	37060	16276	145794	0.111636	2.5726	228455	0.0294	6.164	0.110739
85+	*1.C00000	20785	20785	82661	0.251444	3.9770	82661	0.0294	3.977	0.248397

TABLE 3 — FEMALE LIFE TABLE

x	nq_x	l_x	nd_x	nL_x	nm_x	na_x	T_x	r_x	$\dot{e}_x$	nM_x
0	0.037132	100000	3713	97221	0.038193	0.2516	7333270	0.0056	73.333	0.038362
1	0.007256	96287	699	383123	0.001824	1.1034	7236049	0.0056	75.151	0.001836
5	0.002587	95588	247	477323	0.000518	2.5000	6852926	0.0027	71.692	0.000519
10	0.001860	95341	177	476263	0.000372	2.5121	6375603	0.0092	66.872	0.000372
15	0.002707	95164	258	475197	0.000542	2.5916	5899340	0.0000	61.992	0.000542
20	0.003061	94906	291	473825	0.000613	2.5735	5424143	0.0000	57.153	0.000613
25	0.003806	94615	360	472222	0.000763	2.6251	4950318	0.0032	52.320	0.000762
30	0.005377	94255	507	470057	0.001078	2.5939	4478096	0.0240	47.510	0.001076
35	0.006278	93748	589	467336	0.001259	2.6111	4008040	0.0314	42.753	0.001255
40	0.008810	93160	821	463887	0.001769	2.6695	3540703	0.0114	38.007	0.001766
45	0.013606	92339	1256	458767	0.002739	2.6688	3076817	0.0035	33.321	0.002737
50	0.020187	91083	1839	451144	0.004076	2.6775	2618050	0.0181	28.744	0.004062
55	0.031629	89244	2823	439769	0.006419	2.7144	2166906	0.0296	24.281	0.006375
60	0.054886	86421	4743	421086	0.011264	2.6765	1727137	0.0296	19.985	0.011198
65	0.083766	81678	6842	392696	0.017423	2.7061	1306051	0.0296	15.990	0.017296
70	0.153846	74836	11513	347134	0.033167	2.6508	913355	0.0296	12.205	0.032952
75	0.239630	63323	15174	280264	0.054142	2.6044	566220	0.0296	8.942	0.053794
80	0.397085	48149	19119	195833	0.097630	2.6510	285956	0.0296	5.939	0.096613
85+	*1.C00000	29030	29030	90123	0.322113	3.1045	90123	0.0296	3.104	0.318190

TABLE 4 — OBSERVED AND PROJECTED VITAL RATES

	OBSERVED POPULATION BOTH SEXES	MALES	FEMALES	PROJECTED POPULATION 1965 MALES	FEMALES	1970 MALES	FEMALES	1975 MALES	FEMALES	STABLE POPULATION MALES	FEM
RATES PER THOUSAND											
Birth	18.74	19.86	17.67	18.57	16.65	17.20	15.52	16.37	14.87	14.32	13.
Death	7.42	7.74	7.12	8.20	7.66	8.63	8.27	9.12	8.82	14.22	13.
Increase	11.32	12.13	10.55	10.37	8.98	8.56	7.25	7.25	6.06		0.10
PERCENTAGE											
under 15	26.11	27.65	24.64	26.42	23.64	25.36	22.93	23.97	21.85	20.45	19.
15-64	65.77	65.18	66.34	65.78	66.57	65.85	66.24	66.17	66.15	63.98	62.
65 and over	8.12	7.18	9.02	7.81	9.80	8.79	10.83	9.86	12.00	15.57	17.
DEP. RATIO X 100	52.04	53.43	50.74	52.02	50.23	51.87	50.98	51.13	51.17	56.30	59.

TABLE 5 — POPULATION PROJECTED WITH FIXED AGE-SPECIFIC BIRTH AND DEATH RATES (IN 1000's)

AGE AT LAST BIRTHDAY	1965 BOTH SEXES	MALES	FEMALES	1970 BOTH SEXES	MALES	FEMALES	1975 BOTH SEXES	MALES	FEMALES	AGE AT LAST BIRTHDAY
0-4	745	385	360	730	377	353	716	370	346	0-4
5-9	746	386	360	740	382	358	725	374	351	5-9
10-14	704	365	339	744	385	359	738	381	357	10-14
15-19	715	367	348	702	364	338	742	384	358	15-19
20-24	630	323	307	712	365	347	699	362	337	20-24
25-29	738	371	367	628	322	306	709	363	346	25-29
30-34	730	354	376	734	368	366	625	320	305	30-34
35-39	666	314	352	725	351	374	730	366	364	35-39
40-44	549	257	292	660	310	350	719	348	371	40-44
45-49	477	224	253	542	253	289	651	305	346	45-49
50-54	481	228	253	466	218	248	530	246	284	50-54
55-59	449	215	234	465	218	247	450	208	242	55-59
60-64	374	177	197	424	200	224	439	203	236	60-64
65-69	284	129	155	343	159	184	389	180	209	65-69
70-74	211	90	121	245	108	137	297	134	163	70-74
75-79	149	61	88	165	68	97	193	82	111	75-79
80-84	92	37	55	101	40	61	113	45	68	80-84
85+	39	19	20	46	21	25	51	23	28	85+
TOTAL	8779	4302	4477	9172	4509	4663	9516	4694	4822	TOTAL

TABLE 6 — STANDARDIZED RATES

STANDARD COUNTRIES:

STANDARDIZED RATES PER THOUSAND	ENGLAND AND WALES 1961 BOTH SEXES	MALES	FEMALES	UNITED STATES 1960 BOTH SEXES	MALES	FEMALES	MEXICO 1960 BOTH SEXES	MALES	FEMALES
Birth	13.98	16.55*	13.08	14.24	15.37*	13.54	15.93	15.53*	15.33
Death	10.03	9.60*	10.76	8.35	8.43*	8.18	4.78	6.64*	4.35
Increase	3.95	6.96*	2.32	5.89	6.94*	5.36	11.14	8.89*	10.99

TABLE 7 — MOMENTS AND CUMULANTS

	OBSERVED POP. MALES	FEMALES	STATIONARY POP. MALES	FEMALES	STABLE POP. MALES	FEMALES	OBSERVED BIRTHS	NET MATERNITY FUNCTION	BIRTHS IN STABLE POP.
μ	31.02244	32.98854	38.27842	39.50887	38.22268	39.45093	28.43404	28.73081	28.72733
σ^2	432.5795	450.3342	536.4984	557.6582	536.2615	557.4715	27.83377	31.46814	31.45987
κ_3	4470.281	3959.001	2264.537	1779.248	2295.053	1814.050	71.2078	79.5680	79.5671
κ_4	-117821.	-145439.	-293928.	-335118.	-293343.	-334622.	146.172	14.252	14.541
β_1	0.246872	0.171619	0.033209	0.018254	0.034155	0.018995	0.235146	0.203172	0.203328
β_2	2.370360	2.282850	1.978814	1.922391	1.979947	1.923265	3.188678	3.014393	3.014692
κ	-0.101826	-0.071296	-0.012293	-0.006554	-0.012643	-0.006819	-0.569546	-0.276364	-0.276648

TABLE 8 — RATES FROM AGE DISTRIBUTIONS AND VITAL STATISTICS (Females)

VITAL STATISTICS		THOMPSON AGE RANGE	NRR	1000r	INTERVAL	BOURGEOIS-PICHAT AGE RANGE	NRR	1000b	1000d	1000r	COALE
GRR	1.064										
NRR	1.003	0-4	1.09	3.03	27.44	5-29	0.85	15.49	21.40	-5.91	IBR
TFR	2.204	5-9	1.05	1.63	27.41	30-54	1.55	28.07	11.84	16.23	IDR
GENERATION	28.729	10-14	1.15	5.00	27.37	55-79	2.06	50.39	23.61	26.78	IRI
SEX RATIO	107.181	15-19	1.11	3.77	27.31	*50-74	2.08	51.70	24.54	27.16	K1
											K2

TABLE 9 — LESLIE MATRIX AND ITS SPECTRAL COMPONENTS (Females)

Part ORIGINAL MATRIX SUB-DIAGONAL	ALTERNATIVE FIRST ROWS Projection	Integral	FIRST STABLE MATRIX % IN STABLE POPULATION	FISHER VALUES	REPRODUCTIVE VALUES	SECOND STABLE MATRIX Z₂ FIRST COLUMN	FIRST ROW
0.99371	0.00000	0.00000	6.575	1.041	376863	0.1607+0.0531	0.1607+0.0531
0.99778	0.00011	0.00000	6.531	1.048	355689	0.1456-0.1349	0.0266+0.1419
0.99776	0.02005	0.00022	6.513	1.051	367001	-0.0563-0.2269	-0.0946+0.0780
0.99711	0.13965	0.03998	6.495	1.033	318287	-0.2660-0.0711	-0.1000-0.0394
0.99662	0.29334	0.24008	6.473	0.891	328307	-0.2245+0.2336	-0.0342-0.0980
0.99542	0.29827	0.34793	6.447	0.588	222067	0.1130+0.3640	0.0116-0.0814
0.99421	0.17918	0.24991	6.415	0.279	98755	0.4385+0.0904	0.0173-0.0408
0.99262	0.06966	0.10918	6.374	0.093	27338	0.3415-0.3992	0.0086-0.0135
0.98896	0.01723	0.03039	6.324	0.021	5271	-0.2162-0.5762	0.0023-0.0029
0.98338	0.00235	0.00412	6.251	0.003	705	-0.7107-0.1041	0.0003-0.0004
0.97479	0.00029	0.00058	6.144	0.000	72	-0.5043+0.6638	0.0000-0.0000
0.79723			29.459				

TABLE 10 — AGE ANALYSIS AND MISCELLANEOUS RESULTS (Females)

CONTRIBUTIONS OF ROOTS (IN 100's)

OBSERVED POPUL. (IN 100's)	r_1	r_2, r_3	r_4-r_{11}	AGE-SP. BIRTH RATES	NET MATERNITY FUNCTION	COEFF. OF MATRIX EQUATION	PARAMETERS INTEGRAL	MATRIX	EXP. INCREASE x	$e^{(x+2\frac{1}{2})r}$
3620	3511	88	20	0.0000	0.0000	0.0000	L(1) 1.00052	1.00052	0	1.0003
3393	3487	-26	-69	0.0000	0.0000	0.0001	L(2) 0.40706	0.40941	50	1.0055
3492	3478	-151	165	0.0000	0.0000	0.0002	0.76451	0.74184	55	1.0060
3081	3468	-137	-251	0.0083	0.0395	0.1381	R(1) 0.00010	0.00010	60	1.0065
3686	3456	54	175	0.0500	0.2368	0.2894	R(2) -0.02875	-0.03314	65	1.0070
3778	3443	251	84	0.0724	0.3420	0.2932	0.21631	0.21330	70	1.0076
3542	3425	210	-93	0.0520	0.2445	0.1753	C(1)	53398	75	1.0081
2941	3404	-108	-355	0.0227	0.1062	0.0678	C(2)	17966	80	1.0086
2554	3377	-410	-413	0.0063	0.0293	0.0166		-28851	85	1.0091
2576	3338	-315	-446	0.0009	0.0039	0.0022	2P/Y 29.0477	29.4567	90	1.0097
2398	3281	202	-1084	0.0001	0.0005	0.0003	DELTA 12.7610		95	1.0102
7569	15731								100	1.0107

TABLE 1 DATA

AGE AT LAST BIRTHDAY	POPULATION BOTH SEXES	MALES Number	%	FEMALES Number	%	BIRTHS BY AGE OF MOTHER	DEATHS BOTH SEXES	MALES	FEMALES	AGE AT LAST BIRTHDAY
0	151206	77923	1.9	73283	1.7	0	5829	3096	2733	0
1-4	594898	305054	7.4	289054	6.6	0	913	481	432	1-4
5-9	728148	374358	9.1	353790	8.1	0	400	241	159	5-9
10-14	700177	359084	8.7	341093	7.8	37	303	194	109	10-14
15-19	726008	367435	8.9	358573	8.2	6441	458	290	168	15-19
20-24	623082	308385	7.5	314697	7.2	34918	531	342	189	20-24
25-29	706239	333938	8.1	372301	8.6	52613	655	400	255	25-29
30-34	690096	328891	8.0	361205	8.3	36407	788	451	337	30-34
35-39	618486	295262	7.2	323224	7.4	14547	875	486	389	35-39
40-44	466604	222226	5.4	244378	5.6	2898	1028	583	445	40-44
45-49	468081	223366	5.4	244715	5.6	334	1616	937	679	45-49
50-54	490130	237311	5.7	252819	5.8	54	2499	1514	985	50-54
55-59	428479	210221	5.1	218258	5.0	0	3681	2300	1381	55-59
60-64	351434	164746	4.0	186688	4.3	0	4940	2946	1994	60-64
65-69	267007	119438	2.9	147569	3.4	0	6252	3361	2891	65-69
70-74	200842	85972	2.1	114870	2.6		7822	3815	4007	70-74
75-79	137523	59815	1.4	77708	1.8		9031	4221	4810	75-79
80-84	84867	36901	0.9	47966	1.1	76740 M.	9106	4210	4896	80-84
85+	46318	18192	0.4	28126	0.6	71509 F.	10086	4265	5821	85+
TOTAL	8479625	4129308		4350317		148249	66813	34133	32680	TOTAL

TABLE 2 MALE LIFE TABLE

x	$_nq_x$	l_x	$_nd_x$	$_nL_x$	$_nm_x$	$_na_x$	T_x	r_x	$\mathring{e}_x$	$_nM_x$
0	0.038539	100000	3854	97039	0.039715	0.2316	7020417	0.0005	70.204	0.039732
1	0.006258	96146	602	382833	0.001572	1.0885	6923378	0.0005	72.009	0.001573
5	0.003209	95544	307	476956	0.000643	2.5000	6540546	0.0057	68.456	0.000644
10	0.002698	95238	257	475561	0.000540	2.5554	6063590	0.0012	63.668	0.000540
15	0.003947	94981	375	474023	0.000791	2.6481	5588029	0.0144	58.833	0.000789
20	0.005534	94606	524	471760	0.001110	2.5744	5114006	0.0085	54.056	0.001109
25	0.005972	94082	562	469032	0.001198	2.5430	4642246	0.0000	49.342	0.001198
30	0.006839	93521	640	466047	0.001372	2.5665	4173214	0.0109	44.623	0.001371
35	0.008247	92881	766	462609	0.001656	2.6543	3707167	0.0374	39.913	0.001646
40	0.013104	92115	1207	457792	0.002637	2.6937	3244559	0.0252	35.223	0.002623
45	0.020772	90908	1888	450151	0.004195	2.6756	2786767	0.0000	30.655	0.004195
50	0.031438	89020	2799	438672	0.006380	2.7037	2336616	0.0000	26.248	0.006380
55	0.053638	86221	4625	420426	0.011000	2.6909	1897944	0.0251	22.013	0.010941
60	0.086235	81596	7036	391485	0.017974	2.6556	1477518	0.0264	18.108	0.017882
65	0.132499	74560	9879	349349	0.028279	2.6262	1086033	0.0264	14.566	0.028140
70	0.201334	64681	13022	292039	0.044591	2.5915	736684	0.0264	11.390	0.044375
75	0.301942	51658	15598	219953	0.070914	2.5420	444645	0.0264	8.607	0.070568
80	0.448404	36060	16170	140773	0.114864	2.5553	224692	0.0264	6.231	0.114089
85+	*1.000000	19891	19891	83920	0.237023	4.2190	83920	0.0264	4.219	0.234444

TABLE 3 FEMALE LIFE TABLE

x	$_nq_x$	l_x	$_nd_x$	$_nL_x$	$_nm_x$	$_na_x$	T_x	r_x	$\mathring{e}_x$	$_nM_x$
0	0.036254	100000	3625	97219	0.037291	0.2330	7371813	0.0001	73.718	0.037294
1	0.005951	96375	574	383829	0.001494	1.0895	7274593	0.0001	75.482	0.001495
5	0.002239	95801	215	478469	0.000448	2.5000	6890764	0.0053	71.928	0.000449
10	0.001597	95587	153	477553	0.000320	2.5123	6412296	0.0000	67.084	0.000320
15	0.002342	95434	224	476638	0.000469	2.6238	5934743	0.0076	62.187	0.000469
20	0.002999	95210	285	475359	0.000601	2.5737	5458104	0.0000	57.327	0.000601
25	0.003419	94925	325	473845	0.000685	2.5998	4982745	0.0000	52.491	0.000685
30	0.004662	94600	441	471950	0.000934	2.6151	4508900	0.0132	47.663	0.000933
35	0.006035	94159	568	469462	0.001211	2.6508	4036950	0.0378	42.874	0.001203
40	0.009108	93591	852	465972	0.001829	2.6735	3567488	0.0259	38.118	0.001821
45	0.013783	92739	1278	460688	0.002775	2.6492	3101516	0.0000	33.444	0.002775
50	0.019332	91460	1768	453201	0.003901	2.6807	2640828	0.0073	28.874	0.003896
55	0.031346	89692	2811	442014	0.006361	2.7068	2187628	0.0237	24.390	0.006327
60	0.052477	86881	4559	424037	0.010752	2.7263	1745614	0.0264	20.092	0.010681
65	0.094317	82321	7764	393765	0.019718	2.7021	1321576	0.0264	16.054	0.019591
70	0.162155	74557	12090	344463	0.035098	2.6573	927811	0.0264	12.444	0.034883
75	0.270443	62467	16894	271449	0.062236	2.5797	583348	0.0264	9.338	0.061898
80	0.407104	45573	18553	180944	0.102535	2.6137	311899	0.0264	6.844	0.102072
85+	1.000000	27020	27020	130955	0.206333	4.8465	130955	0.0264	4.847	0.206961

TABLE 4 OBSERVED AND PROJECTED VITAL RATES

	OBSERVED POPULATION BOTH SEXES	MALES	FEMALES	PROJECTED POPULATION 1968 MALES	FEMALES	1973 MALES	FEMALES	1978 MALES	FEMALES	STABLE POPULATION MALES	FEMA
RATES PER THOUSAND											
Birth	17.48	18.58	16.44	17.66	15.72	16.86	15.10	16.35	14.72	13.87	13.
Death	7.88	8.27	7.51	8.69	8.07	9.11	8.59	9.66	9.26	14.56	13.
Increase	9.60	10.32	8.93	8.98	7.65	7.75	6.51	6.69	5.46		-0.69
PERCENTAGE											
under 15	25.64	27.06	24.30	25.90	23.30	24.62	22.20	23.38	21.13	19.97	19.
15-64	65.67	65.19	66.13	65.52	66.14	65.71	66.20	65.94	66.07	64.17	62.
65 and over	8.69	7.76	9.57	8.58	10.57	9.67	11.60	10.68	12.81	15.86	18.
DEP. RATIO X 100	52.27	53.40	51.22	52.62	51.20	52.18	51.07	51.66	51.36	55.84	59.

TABLE 1 — DATA

AGE AT LAST BIRTHDAY	POPULATION BOTH SEXES	MALES Number	%	FEMALES Number	%	BIRTHS BY AGE OF MOTHER	DEATHS BOTH SEXES	MALES	FEMALES	AGE AT LAST BIRTHDAY
0	151241	78028	1.9	73213	1.7	0	5493	3008	2485	0
1-4	593360	305074	7.4	288286	6.6	0	874	476	398	1-4
5-9	730952	375769	9.1	355183	8.1	0	393	241	152	5-9
10-14	703821	361288	8.7	342533	7.8	42	258	159	99	10-14
15-19	734606	372809	9.0	361797	8.3	7883	491	337	154	15-19
20-24	593201	295213	7.1	297988	6.8	36144	511	354	157	20-24
25-29	689944	325754	7.9	364190	8.3	53593	628	363	265	25-29
30-34	687496	324275	7.8	363221	8.3	37158	770	438	332	30-34
35-39	644563	306823	7.4	337740	7.7	15034	1041	594	447	35-39
40-44	485236	230447	5.6	254789	5.8	2918	1039	588	451	40-44
45-49	448710	213143	5.1	235567	5.4	287	1570	936	634	45-49
50-54	490933	236386	5.7	254547	5.8	50	2630	1649	981	50-54
55-59	435721	213772	5.2	221949	5.1	0	3820	2358	1462	55-59
60-64	365166	173120	4.2	192046	4.4	0	5545	3276	2269	60-64
65-69	281850	126176	3.0	155674	3.6	0	6588	3600	2988	65-69
70-74	197354	84828	2.0	112526	2.6		8151	3978	4173	70-74
75-79	144495	61932	1.5	82563	1.9		9767	4568	5199	75-79
80-84	87748	38120	0.9	49628	1.1	78970 M.	9558	4354	5204	80-84
85+	44032	16861	0.4	27171	0.6	74139 F.	10302	4402	5900	85+
TOTAL	8510429	4139818		4370611		153109	69429	35679	33750	TOTAL

TABLE 2 — MALE, FEMALE, TABLE

x	nq_x	l_x	nd_x	nL_x	nm_x	na_x	T_x	r_x	$\dot{e}_x$	nM_x	x
0	0.037418	100000	3742	97134	0.038522	0.2339	6986566	0.0009	69.866	0.038550	0
1	0.006205	96258	597	383295	0.001558	1.0902	6889433	0.0009	71.572	0.001560	1
5	0.003197	95661	306	477540	0.000640	2.5000	6506138	0.0050	68.012	0.000641	5
10	0.002198	95355	210	476278	0.000440	2.6240	6028598	0.0002	63.223	0.000440	10
15	0.004525	95146	431	474725	0.000907	2.6727	5552320	0.0193	58.356	0.000904	15
20	0.005981	94715	566	472178	0.001200	2.5340	5077595	0.0124	53.609	0.001199	20
25	0.005556	94148	523	469448	0.001114	2.5256	4605417	0.0000	48.917	0.001114	25
30	0.006736	93625	631	466629	0.001351	2.6244	4135969	0.0046	44.176	0.001351	30
35	0.009676	92995	900	462838	0.001944	2.6262	3669341	0.0322	39.458	0.001936	35
40	0.012767	92095	1176	457759	0.002569	2.6907	3206503	0.0336	34.817	0.002552	40
45	0.021737	90919	1976	450046	0.004391	2.6979	2748744	0.0000	30.233	0.004391	45
50	0.034324	88943	3053	437636	0.006976	2.6817	2298698	0.0000	25.845	0.006976	50
55	0.054008	85890	4639	418757	0.011077	2.6949	1861062	0.0193	21.668	0.011030	55
60	0.090995	81251	7393	388871	0.019013	2.6486	1442305	0.0250	17.751	0.018923	60
65	0.134217	73858	9913	345784	0.028668	2.6289	1053434	0.0250	14.263	0.028532	65
70	0.211557	63945	13528	287127	0.047115	2.5904	707650	0.0250	11.067	0.046895	70
75	0.313047	50417	15783	213043	0.074083	2.5264	420524	0.0250	8.341	0.073758	75
80	0.448291	34634	15526	135047	0.114968	2.5446	207481	0.0250	5.991	0.114219	80
85+	*1.000000	19108	19108	72434	0.263798	3.7908	72434	0.0250	3.791	0.261076	85+

TABLE 3 — MALE, FEMALE, TABLE

x	nq_x	l_x	nd_x	nL_x	nm_x	na_x	T_x	r_x	$\dot{e}_x$	nM_x	x
0	0.033073	100000	3307	97469	0.033932	0.2347	7374703	0.0004	73.747	0.033942	0
1	0.005497	96693	532	385224	0.001380	1.0907	7277234	0.0004	75.261	0.001381	1
5	0.002133	96161	205	480293	0.000427	2.5000	6892010	0.0047	71.671	0.000428	5
10	0.001444	95956	139	479433	0.000289	2.4984	6411717	0.0000	66.819	0.000289	10
15	0.002129	95817	204	478601	0.000426	2.6154	5932283	0.0135	61.912	0.000426	15
20	0.002631	95613	252	477468	0.000527	2.6179	5453683	0.0000	57.039	0.000527	20
25	0.003632	95362	346	475981	0.000728	2.6096	4976215	0.0000	52.182	0.000728	25
30	0.004564	95015	434	474052	0.000915	2.6347	4500234	0.0066	47.363	0.000914	30
35	0.006627	94582	627	471425	0.001330	2.6326	4026182	0.0341	42.568	0.001323	35
40	0.008862	93955	833	467822	0.001780	2.6547	3554757	0.0342	37.835	0.001770	40
45	0.013372	93122	1245	462691	0.002691	2.6544	3086935	0.0000	33.149	0.002691	45
50	0.019108	91877	1756	455350	0.003855	2.7011	2624244	0.0018	28.563	0.003854	50
55	0.032619	90122	2940	443943	0.006622	2.7328	2168894	0.0211	24.066	0.006587	55
60	0.057819	87182	5041	424278	0.011881	2.6926	1724951	0.0255	19.786	0.011815	60
65	0.092511	82141	7599	393321	0.019320	2.7123	1300673	0.0255	15.835	0.019194	65
70	0.171494	74542	12784	342699	0.037303	2.6523	907352	0.0255	12.172	0.037085	70
75	0.274370	61759	16945	267701	0.063297	2.5749	564653	0.0255	9.143	0.062970	75
80	0.421192	44814	18875	178755	0.105593	2.5993	296952	0.0255	6.626	0.104860	80
85+	*1.000000	25939	25939	118197	0.219453	4.5568	118197	0.0255	4.557	0.217143	85+

TABLE 4 — OBSERVED, PROJECTED

	OBSERVED POPULATION BOTH SEXES	MALES	FEMALES	PROJECTED POPULATION 1969 MALES	FEMALES	1974 MALES	FEMALES	1979 MALES	FEMALES	STABLE POPULATION MALES	FEMALES
RATES PER THOUSAND											
Birth	17.99	19.08	16.96	18.08	16.17	17.39	15.64	16.98	15.35	15.00	14.24
Death	8.16	8.62	7.72	9.03	8.25	9.41	8.76	9.88	9.29	13.75	12.99
Increase	9.83	10.46	9.24	9.05	7.91	7.98	6.88	7.10	6.06		1.2523
PERCENTAGE											
under 15	25.61	27.06	24.23	26.09	23.47	25.01	22.61	24.06	21.86	21.32	20.35
15-64	65.51	65.02	65.98	65.14	65.80	65.22	65.71	65.35	65.42	64.28	62.78
65 and over	8.88	7.92	9.78	8.77	10.73	9.77	11.67	10.59	12.71	14.40	16.87
DEP. RATIO X 100	52.64	53.80	51.56	53.51	51.97	53.32	52.17	53.02	52.85	55.58	59.28

TABLE 1 — DATA

AGE AT LAST BIRTHDAY	POPULATION BOTH SEXES	MALES Number	%	FEMALES Number	%	BIRTHS BY AGE OF MOTHER	DEATHS BOTH SEXES	MALES	FEMALES	AGE AT LAST BIRTH
0	152691	78874	1.9	73817	1.7	0	5197	2831	2366	0
1-4	586359	301792	7.3	284567	6.5	0	748	408	340	1-
5-9	733905	376916	9.1	356989	8.1	0	382	227	155	5-
10-14	712619	366095	8.8	346524	7.9	28	327	204	123	10-
15-19	727456	370246	8.9	357210	8.1	9123	448	293	155	15-
20-24	587488	294332	7.1	293156	6.7	35187	524	353	171	20-
25-29	673277	319454	7.7	353823	8.1	52226	548	348	200	25-
30-34	684394	319752	7.7	364642	8.3	36212	709	414	295	30-
35-39	664953	315519	7.6	349434	8.0	15460	978	537	441	35-
40-44	500568	237131	5.7	263437	6.0	2832	1067	608	459	40-
45-49	437321	206652	5.0	230669	5.3	312	1396	817	579	45-
50-54	496130	237893	5.7	258237	5.9	68	2562	1566	996	50-
55-59	441265	215923	5.2	225342	5.1	0	3810	2388	1422	55-
60-64	379606	181324	4.4	198282	4.5	0	5297	3164	2133	60-
65-69	290490	130696	3.1	159794	3.6	0	6779	3717	3062	65-
70-74	200239	86006	2.1	114233	2.6		7588	3813	3775	70-
75-79	148466	63013	1.5	85453	1.9		9361	4323	5038	75-
80-84	91271	39462	0.9	51809	1.2	78112 M.	9091	4193	4898	80-
85+	41835	16211	0.4	25624	0.6	73336 F.	10457	4237	6220	85
TOTAL	8550333	4157291		4393042		151448	67269	34441	32828	TOT

TABLE 2 — MALE LIFE TABLE

x	$_nq_x$	l_x	$_nd_x$	$_nL_x$	$_nm_x$	$_na_x$	T_x	r_x	$\dot{e}_x$	$_nM_x$
0	0.034836	100000	3484	97305	0.035801	0.2263	7057204	0.0032	70.572	0.035893
1	0.005351	96516	517	384557	0.001345	1.0850	6959899	0.0032	72.111	0.001352
5	0.003005	95999	288	479274	0.000602	2.5000	6575342	0.0031	68.494	0.000602
10	0.002783	95711	266	477906	0.000557	2.5703	6096068	0.0012	63.693	0.000557
15	0.003964	95444	378	476338	0.000794	2.6666	5618162	0.0210	58.863	0.000791
20	0.005983	95066	569	473936	0.001200	2.5495	5141824	0.0137	54.087	0.001199
25	0.005432	94497	513	471210	0.001089	2.5153	4667888	0.0000	49.397	0.001089
30	0.006454	93984	607	468461	0.001295	2.5967	4196678	0.0000	44.653	0.001295
35	0.008513	93377	795	465020	0.001709	2.6525	3728216	0.0281	39.926	0.001702
40	0.012835	92582	1188	460148	0.002582	2.6745	3263196	0.0397	35.246	0.002564
45	0.019589	91394	1790	452852	0.003954	2.6998	2803048	0.0000	30.670	0.003954
50	0.032425	89604	2905	441359	0.006583	2.7078	2350196	0.0000	26.229	0.006583
55	0.054081	86699	4689	422605	0.011095	2.6781	1908837	0.0158	22.017	0.011059
60	0.084298	82010	6913	393883	0.017552	2.6617	1486232	0.0292	18.123	0.017449
65	0.133899	75096	10055	351629	0.028597	2.6278	1092349	0.0292	14.546	0.028440
70	0.201154	65041	13083	293591	0.044563	2.5837	740721	0.0292	11.389	0.044334
75	0.294664	51958	15310	222034	0.068954	2.5340	447129	0.0292	8.606	0.068605
80	0.425253	36648	15585	145475	0.107128	2.5769	225095	0.0292	6.142	0.106253
85+	*1.000000	21063	21063	79619	0.264548	3.7800	79619	0.0292	3.780	0.261366

TABLE 3 — FEMALE LIFE TABLE

x	$_nq_x$	l_x	$_nd_x$	$_nL_x$	$_nm_x$	$_na_x$	T_x	r_x	$\dot{e}_x$	$_nM_x$
0	0.031212	100000	3121	97582	0.031986	0.2254	7432462	0.0026	74.325	0.032052
1	0.004744	96879	460	386175	0.001190	1.0844	7334880	0.0026	75.712	0.001195
5	0.002167	96419	209	481574	0.000434	2.5000	6948705	0.0027	72.068	0.000434
10	0.001773	96210	171	480625	0.000355	2.4995	6467131	0.0000	67.219	0.000355
15	0.002171	96040	209	479700	0.000435	2.6084	5986506	0.0163	62.334	0.000434
20	0.002912	95831	279	478471	0.000583	2.5457	5506807	0.0004	57.464	0.000583
25	0.002822	95552	270	477108	0.000565	2.5816	5028336	0.0000	52.624	0.000565
30	0.004038	95282	385	475519	0.000809	2.6788	4551228	0.0004	47.766	0.000809
35	0.006322	94898	600	473080	0.001268	2.6522	4075709	0.0312	42.948	0.001262
40	0.008727	94298	823	469549	0.001753	2.6434	3602629	0.0397	38.205	0.001742
45	0.012477	93475	1166	464654	0.002510	2.6682	3133080	0.0000	33.518	0.002510
50	0.019115	92308	1764	457477	0.003857	2.6963	2668426	0.0000	28.908	0.003857
55	0.031240	90544	2829	446247	0.006339	2.7114	2210948	0.0198	24.418	0.006310
60	0.052845	87715	4635	427997	0.010830	2.7176	1764702	0.0279	20.118	0.010757
65	0.092320	83080	7670	397684	0.019287	2.6901	1336704	0.0279	16.089	0.019162
70	0.154284	75410	11635	349812	0.033260	2.6588	939021	0.0279	12.452	0.033046
75	0.259324	63776	16539	278938	0.059291	2.5850	589209	0.0279	9.239	0.058956
80	0.389234	47237	18386	192784	0.095372	2.6395	310271	0.0279	6.568	0.094540
85+	*1.000000	28851	28851	117487	0.245564	4.0723	117487	0.0279	4.072	0.242741

TABLE 4 — OBSERVED AND PROJECTED VITAL RATES

	OBSERVED POPULATION BOTH SEXES	MALES	FEMALES	PROJECTED POPULATION 1970 MALES	FEMALES	1975 MALES	FEMALES	1980 MALES	FEMALES	STABLE POPULATION MALES	FEM
RATES PER THOUSAND											
Birth	17.71	18.79	16.69	17.72	15.84	17.20	15.46	16.89	15.26	14.88	14
Death	7.87	8.28	7.47	8.85	8.08	9.28	8.65	9.78	9.22	13.59	12
Increase	9.85	10.50	9.22	8.87	7.76	7.93	6.80	7.11	6.04		1.2
PERCENTAGE											
under 15	25.56	27.03	24.17	25.87	23.25	24.72	22.31	23.82	21.62	21.20	20
15-64	65.41	64.90	65.88	64.99	65.70	65.12	65.62	65.20	65.22	64.03	62
65 and over	9.03	8.07	9.95	9.14	11.05	10.16	12.07	10.99	13.16	14.77	17
DEP. RATIO X 100	52.89	54.07	51.79	53.86	52.20	53.56	52.38	53.38	53.32	56.19	59

AGE AT LAST BIRTHDAY	1970 BOTH SEXES	MALES	FEMALES	1975 BOTH SEXES	MALES	FEMALES	1980 BOTH SEXES	MALES	FEMALES	AGE AT LAST BIRTHDAY	
0-4	728	375	353	728	375	353	740	381	359	0-4	
5-9	736	379	357	724	373	351	725	373	352	5-9	
10-14	732	376	356	734	378	356	723	372	351	10-14	
15-19	711	365	346	731	375	356	731	376	355	15-19	TABLE 5
20-24	724	368	356	708	363	345	728	373	355	20-24	POPULATION
25-29	585	293	292	721	366	355	705	361	344	25-29	PROJECTED
30-34	671	318	353	582	291	291	718	364	354	30-34	WITH
35-39	680	317	363	666	315	351	579	289	290	35-39	FIXED
40-44	659	312	347	674	314	360	660	312	348	40-44	AGE—
45-49	494	233	261	650	307	343	665	309	356	45-49	SPECIFIC
50-54	428	201	227	484	227	257	637	299	338	50-54	BIRTH
55-59	480	228	252	415	193	222	468	218	250	55-59	AND
60-64	417	201	216	454	212	242	392	180	212	60-64	DEATH
65-69	346	162	184	381	180	201	414	190	224	65-69	RATES
70-74	250	109	141	297	135	162	327	150	177	70-74	(IN 1000's)
75-79	156	65	91	195	83	112	231	102	129	75-79	
80-84	100	41	59	106	43	63	131	54	77	80-84	
85+	54	22	32	59	23	36	61	23	38	85+	
TOTAL	8951	4365	4586	9309	4553	4756	9635	4726	4909	TOTAL	

STANDARD COUNTRIES: STANDARDIZED RATES PER THOUSAND	ENGLAND AND WALES 1961 BOTH SEXES	MALES	FEMALES	UNITED STATES 1960 BOTH SEXES	MALES	FEMALES	MEXICO 1960 BOTH SEXES	MALES	FEMALES	
Birth	14.24	16.95*	13.37	14.50	16.00*	13.84	16.61	15.39*	16.04	TABLE 6
Death	9.66	9.36*	10.08	7.99	8.31*	7.56	4.44	6.80*	3.92	STANDARDIZED RATES
Increase	4.58	7.59*	3.29	6.51	7.69*	6.27	12.17	8.59*	12.12	

	OBSERVED POP. MALES	FEMALES	STATIONARY POP. MALES	FEMALES	STABLE POP. MALES	FEMALES	OBSERVED BIRTHS	NET MATERNITY FUNCTION	BIRTHS IN STABLE POP.	
μ	32.04136	33.84865	38.22246	39.65894	37.53831	38.93898	28.28241	28.09073	28.04681	TABLE 7
σ^2	454.5430	469.7585	534.1502	561.7934	531.0372	559.1416	30.67618	32.15848	32.04936	MOMENTS
κ_3	4207.749	3809.810	2238.196	1849.342	2607.290	2278.135	51.2986	84.9279	84.9797	AND
κ_4	-157833.	-174516.	-291078.	-337231.	-283420.	-330161.	-116.719	-37.140	-33.094	CUMULANTS
β_1	0.188528	0.140018	0.032870	0.019289	0.045395	0.029689	0.091161	0.216877	0.219368	
β_2	2.236079	2.209165	1.979807	1.931501	1.994965	1.943954	2.875967	2.964087	2.967781	
κ	-0.073670	-0.056379	-0.012182	-0.006968	-0.016819	-0.010722	-0.134344	-0.238226	-0.241075	

VITAL STATISTICS		THOMPSON AGE RANGE	NRR	1000r	INTERVAL	BOURGEOIS-PICHAT AGE RANGE	NRR	1000b	1000d	1000r	COALE	
GRR	1.088										IBR	TABLE 8
NRR	1.037	0-4	1.07	2.36	27.44	5-29	1.09	17.11	13.87	3.24	IDR	RATES FROM AGE DISTRIBUTIONS
TFR	2.246	5-9	1.13	4.61	27.42	30-54	1.73	33.12	12.91	20.20	IRI	AND VITAL STATISTICS
GENERATION	28.069	10-14	1.12	3.99	27.38	55-79	2.19	62.76	33.76	29.00	K1	(Females)
SEX RATIO	106.512	15-19	1.23	7.29	27.32	*50-74	2.04	52.88	26.41	26.46	K2	

Start Age Interval	ORIGINAL MATRIX SUB-DIAGONAL	ALTERNATIVE FIRST ROWS Projection	Integral	FIRST STABLE MATRIX % IN STABLE POPULATION	FISHER VALUES	REPRODUCTIVE VALUES	SECOND STABLE MATRIX Z₂ FIRST COLUMN	FIRST ROW	
0	0.99549	0.00000	0.00000	6.824	1.037	371606	0.1618+0.0589	0.1618+0.0589	TABLE 9
5	0.99803	0.00009	0.00000	6.749	1.048	374234	0.1511-0.1377	0.0193+0.1437	LESLIE
10	0.99808	0.02995	0.00019	6.693	1.057	366292	-0.0616-0.2355	-0.0994+0.0704	MATRIX
15	0.99744	0.17014	0.06002	6.637	1.035	369639	-0.2823-0.0651	-0.0960-0.0483	AND ITS
20	0.99715	0.31297	0.28207	6.578	0.867	254246	-0.2246+0.2615	-0.0292-0.1004	SPECTRAL
25	0.99667	0.28881	0.34688	6.517	0.550	194569	0.1515+0.3810	0.0126-0.0794	COMPONENTS
30	0.99487	0.16787	0.23338	6.454	0.255	92922	0.4847+0.0508	0.0172-0.0387	(Females)
35	0.99254	0.06432	0.10397	6.380	0.083	28946	0.3205-0.4815	0.0083-0.0123	
40	0.98958	0.01416	0.02526	6.292	0.017	4427	-0.3287-0.6007	0.0019-0.0024	
45	0.98455	0.00189	0.00318	6.186	0.002	520	-0.8080+0.0144	0.0003-0.0003	
50	0.97545	0.00031	0.00062	6.052	0.000	82	-0.4256+0.8483	0.0000-0.0000	
+	0.80032			28.638					

Start Age Interval	OBSERVED POPUL. (IN 100's)	CONTRIBUTIONS OF ROOTS (IN 100's) r_1	r_2, r_3	$r_4 \cdot r_{11}$	AGE-SP. BIRTH RATES	NET MATERNITY FUNCTION	COEFF. OF MATRIX EQUATION	PARAMETERS	INTEGRAL	MATRIX	EXP. INCREASE x	$e^{(x+2\frac{1}{2})r}$	
	3584	3538	36	10	0.0000	0.0000	0.0000	L(1)	1.00644	1.00644	0	1.0032	TABLE 10
	3570	3500	82	-12	0.0000	0.0000	0.0001	L(2)	0.38520	0.38926	50	1.0698	AGE
	3465	3471	40	-45	0.0000	0.0002	0.0298		0.76627	0.74255	55	1.0767	ANALYSIS
	3572	3442	-72	202	0.0124	0.0593	0.1687	R(1)	0.00128	0.00128	60	1.0836	AND
	2932	3411	-136	-343	0.0581	0.2781	0.3096	R(2)	-0.03071	-0.03525	65	1.0906	MISCELLANEOUS
	3538	3380	-48	207	0.0715	0.3410	0.2848		0.22100	0.21759	70	1.0976	RESULTS
	3646	3347	139	161	0.0481	0.2287	0.1650	C(1)		51855	75	1.1047	(Females)
	3494	3308	221	-35	0.0214	0.1014	0.0629	C(2)		15635	80	1.1118	
	2634	3262	48	-676	0.0052	0.0244	0.0137			12568	85	1.1190	
	2307	3208	-256	-645	0.0007	0.0030	0.0018	2P/Y	28.4308	28.8759	90	1.1262	
	2582	3138	-346	-209	0.0001	0.0006	0.0003	DELTA	10.4529		95	1.1334	
+	8605	14850									100	1.1407	

TABLE 1 — DATA

AGE AT LAST BIRTHDAY	POPULATION BOTH SEXES	MALES Number	%	FEMALES Number	%	BIRTHS BY AGE OF MOTHER	DEATHS BOTH SEXES	MALES	FEMALES	AGE AT LAST BIRTHDAY
0	182000	93000	2.0	89000	1.8	0	15260	8657	6603	0
1-4	674000	344000	7.6	330000	6.8	0	2295	1218	1077	1-4
5-9	763000	388000	8.6	375000	7.7	0	777	451	326	5-9
10-14	737000	372000	8.2	365000	7.5	55	671	397	274	10-14
15-19	747000	375000	8.3	372000	7.6	18742	1242	707	535	15-19
20-24	778000	386000	8.5	392000	8.0	66072	1890	1134	756	20-24
25-29	789000	380000	8.4	409000	8.4	56382	2000	1111	889	25-29
30-34	560000	263000	5.8	297000	6.1	25935	1515	830	685	30-34
35-39	668000	315000	6.9	353000	7.2	16500	2145	1175	970	35-39
40-44	716000	342000	7.5	374000	7.7	6500	3078	1756	1322	40-44
45-49	636000	307000	6.8	329000	6.7	463	4129	2375	1754	45-49
50-54	584000	276000	6.1	308000	6.3	24	5660	3281	2379	50-54
55-59	467000	207000	4.6	260000	5.3	4	6606	3592	3014	55-59
60-64	374000	164000	3.6	210000	4.3	0	8583	4497	4086	60-64
65-69	316000	138000	3.0	178000	3.6	0	11238	5714	5524	65-69
70-74	217000	95000	2.1	122000	2.5		12620	6129	6491	70-74
75-79	129000	56000	1.2	73000	1.5		12321	5893	6428	75-79
80-84	61000	27000	0.6	34000	0.7	98425 M.	9542	4482	5060	80-84
85+	25000	10000	0.2	15000	0.3	92252 F.	6542	2834	3708	85+
TOTAL	9423000	4538000		4885000		190677	108114	56233	51881	TOTAL

TABLE 2 — MALE LIFE TABLE

x	$_nq_x$	l_x	$_nd_x$	$_nL_x$	$_nm_x$	$_na_x$	T_x	r_x	$\overset{\circ}{e}_x$	$_nM_x$
0	0.086529	100000	8653	93296	0.092748	0.2252	6057880	0.0047	60.579	0.093086
1	0.013919	91347	1271	361681	0.003515	1.0842	5964584	0.0047	65.296	0.003541
5	0.005766	90076	519	449080	0.001156	2.5000	5602903	0.0143	62.202	0.001162
10	0.005324	89556	477	446655	0.001068	2.6384	5153824	0.0022	57.548	0.001067
15	0.009386	89079	836	443476	0.001885	2.7019	4707168	0.0000	52.842	0.001885
20	0.014585	88243	1287	438088	0.002938	2.5690	4263693	0.0000	48.317	0.002938
25	0.014521	86956	1263	431637	0.002925	2.5092	3825604	0.0354	43.995	0.002924
30	0.015671	85694	1343	425173	0.003158	2.5460	3393968	0.0156	39.606	0.003156
35	0.018485	84351	1559	418014	0.003730	2.6012	2968795	0.0000	35.196	0.003730
40	0.025366	82792	2100	409023	0.005135	2.6502	2550781	0.0000	30.810	0.005135
45	0.038084	80691	3073	396276	0.007755	2.6632	2141759	0.0134	26.543	0.007736
50	0.058074	77618	4508	377459	0.011942	2.6413	1745483	0.0273	22.488	0.011888
55	0.083835	73111	6129	351093	0.017458	2.6406	1368023	0.0337	18.712	0.017353
60	0.129053	66982	8644	314314	0.027502	2.6176	1016931	0.0169	15.182	0.027421
65	0.188721	58337	11009	265116	0.041527	2.5866	702617	0.0169	12.044	0.041406
70	0.279306	47328	13219	204260	0.064716	2.5505	437501	0.0169	9.244	0.064516
75	0.416749	34109	14215	134661	0.105561	2.4756	233241	0.0169	6.838	0.105232
80	0.580808	19894	11555	69360	0.166590	2.3941	98580	0.0169	4.955	0.165999
85+	*1.000000	8339	8339	29221	0.285393	3.5039	29221	0.0169	3.504	0.283400

TABLE 3 — FEMALE LIFE TABLE

x	$_nq_x$	l_x	$_nd_x$	$_nL_x$	$_nm_x$	$_na_x$	T_x	r_x	$\overset{\circ}{e}_x$	$_nM_x$
0	0.069988	100000	6999	94689	0.073913	0.2411	6509458	0.0048	65.095	0.074191
1	0.012848	93001	1195	368534	0.003242	1.0953	6414769	0.0048	68.975	0.003264
5	0.004311	91806	396	458042	0.000864	2.5000	6046235	0.0123	65.859	0.000869
10	0.003747	91411	342	456250	0.000751	2.6562	5588193	0.0000	61.133	0.000751
15	0.007167	91068	653	453818	0.001438	2.6677	5131943	0.0000	56.353	0.001438
20	0.009598	90415	868	449973	0.001929	2.5759	4678125	0.0000	51.740	0.001929
25	0.010820	89548	969	445346	0.002176	2.5319	4228152	0.0256	47.217	0.002174
30	0.011474	88579	1016	440399	0.002308	2.5464	3782806	0.0124	42.706	0.002306
35	0.013649	87562	1195	434927	0.002748	2.5868	3342406	0.0000	38.172	0.002748
40	0.017537	86367	1515	428267	0.003537	2.6436	2907479	0.0033	33.664	0.003535
45	0.026386	84853	2239	419004	0.005343	2.6514	2479212	0.0140	29.218	0.005331
50	0.038029	82614	3142	405687	0.007744	2.6505	2060208	0.0156	24.938	0.007724
55	0.056735	79472	4509	386894	0.011654	2.6789	1654521	0.0259	20.819	0.011592
60	0.093556	74963	7013	358401	0.019568	2.6595	1267627	0.0283	16.910	0.019457
65	0.145391	67950	9879	316458	0.031218	2.6424	909226	0.0283	13.381	0.031034
70	0.237041	58071	13765	257232	0.053512	2.5939	592768	0.0283	10.208	0.053205
75	0.362986	44305	16082	181621	0.088549	2.5186	335536	0.0283	7.573	0.088055
80	0.538565	28223	15200	101590	0.149621	2.4581	153916	0.0283	5.454	0.148823
85+	1.000000	13023	13023	52325	0.248890	4.0178	52325	0.0283	4.018	0.247201

TABLE 4 — OBSERVED AND PROJECTED VITAL RATES

	OBSERVED POPULATION BOTH SEXES	MALES	FEMALES	PROJECTED 1956 MALES	FEMALES	1961 MALES	FEMALES	1966 MALES	FEMALES	STABLE MALES	FEMA
RATES PER THOUSAND											
Birth	20.24	21.69	18.88	20.66	18.08	19.69	17.34	19.19	17.01	18.63	17.4
Death	11.47	12.39	10.62	12.75	11.32	13.08	12.01	13.48	12.66	15.16	13.
Increase	8.76	9.30	8.26	7.91	6.76	6.61	5.34	5.70	4.35		3.47
PERCENTAGE											
under 15	25.00	26.38	23.73	26.67	23.93	26.71	24.03	25.98	23.49	24.52	23.
15-64	67.06	66.44	67.64	65.99	66.71	65.61	65.75	65.46	65.29	65.32	64.
65 and over	7.94	7.18	8.64	7.33	9.36	7.68	10.22	8.57	11.22	10.16	12.
DEP. RATIO X 100	49.12	50.51	47.85	51.53	49.90	52.41	52.09	52.77	53.16	53.09	55.

AGE AT LAST BIRTHDAY	1956 BOTH SEXES	MALES	FEMALES	1961 BOTH SEXES	MALES	FEMALES	1966 BOTH SEXES	MALES	FEMALES	AGE AT LAST BIRTHDAY	
0-4	873	447	426	866	443	423	862	441	421	0-4	
5-9	845	431	414	862	441	421	855	437	418	5-9	
10-14	760	386	374	842	429	413	858	438	420	10-14	**TABLE 5**
15-19	732	369	363	755	383	372	836	426	410	15-19	POPULATION
20-24	739	370	369	725	365	360	747	379	368	20-24	PROJECTED
25-29	768	380	388	730	365	365	715	359	356	25-29	WITH
30-34	778	374	404	759	375	384	721	360	361	30-34	FIXED
35-39	552	259	293	767	368	399	747	368	379	35-39	AGE—
40-44	656	308	348	542	253	289	753	360	393	40-44	SPECIFIC
45-49	697	331	366	639	299	340	528	245	283	45-49	BIRTH
50-54	611	292	319	670	316	354	613	284	329	50-54	AND
55-59	551	257	294	576	272	304	632	294	338	55-59	DEATH
60-64	426	185	241	502	230	272	525	244	281	60-64	RATES
65-69	323	138	185	369	156	213	434	194	240	65-69	(IN 1000's)
70-74	251	106	145	258	107	151	293	120	173	70-74	
75-79	149	63	86	172	70	102	176	70	106	75-79	
80-84	70	29	41	80	32	48	93	36	57	80-84	
85+	29	11	18	33	12	21	39	14	25	85+	
TOTAL	9810	4736	5074	10147	4916	5231	10427	5069	5358	TOTAL	

STANDARD COUNTRIES:

STANDARDIZED RATES PER THOUSAND	ENGLAND AND WALES 1961 BOTH SEXES	MALES	FEMALES	UNITED STATES 1960 BOTH SEXES	MALES	FEMALES	MEXICO 1960 BOTH SEXES	MALES	FEMALES	
Birth	16.23	19.33*	15.22	16.52	17.87*	15.75	19.51	17.43*	18.83	**TABLE 6**
Death	15.53	16.10*	15.96	13.23	13.88*	12.44	8.54	10.94*	7.55	STANDARDIZED RATES
Increase	0.71	3.23*	-0.74	3.29	3.99*	3.31	10.97	6.49*	11.28	

	OBSERVED POP. MALES	FEMALES	STATIONARY POP. MALES	FEMALES	STABLE POP. MALES	FEMALES	OBSERVED BIRTHS	NET MATERNITY FUNCTION	BIRTHS IN STABLE POP.	
μ	31.75430	33.62938	35.71207	37.22613	34.04405	35.45435	26.88928	27.10841	26.97031	**TABLE 7**
σ^2	428.9499	444.6239	485.5463	515.1260	475.3072	505.4486	36.89322	37.97034	37.45317	MOMENTS
κ_3	3342.135	2728.815	2569.707	2336.872	3318.384	3227.065	169.6043	148.6551	149.3611	AND
κ_4	-144734.	-170475.	-226345.	-267314.	-204215.	-244482.	119.520	-228.160	-168.649	CUMULANTS
β_1	0.141523	0.084717	0.057687	0.039951	0.102549	0.080646	0.572841	0.403670	0.424629	
β_2	2.213391	2.137666	2.039917	1.992616	2.096063	2.043043	3.087811	2.841747	2.879772	
κ	-0.057106	-0.034052	-0.021912	-0.014856	-0.038967	-0.029992	-0.323529	-0.221996	-0.236551	

VITAL STATISTICS

		THOMPSON AGE RANGE	NRR	1000r	INTERVAL	BOURGEOIS-PICHAT AGE RANGE	NRR	1000b	1000d	1000r	COALE	
GRR	1.233										IBR	**TABLE 8**
NRR	1.098	0-4	1.09	3.24	27.34	5-29	0.84	15.48	21.78	-6.30	IDR	RATES FROM AGE DISTRIBUTIONS
TFR	2.549	5-9	1.00	-0.18	27.30	30-54	0.90	13.39	17.47	-4.08	IRI	AND VITAL
GENERATION	27.039	10-14	0.99	-0.20	27.24	55-79	1.80	47.84	26.11	21.73	K1	STATISTICS
SEX RATIO	106.691	15-19	1.07	2.58	27.14	*40-69	1.64	39.04	20.76	18.28	K2	(Females)

	ORIGINAL MATRIX SUB-DIAGONAL	ALTERNATIVE FIRST ROWS Projection	Integral	FIRST STABLE MATRIX % IN STABLE POPULATION	FISHER VALUES	REPRODUCTIVE VALUES	SECOND STABLE MATRIX Z_2 FIRST COLUMN	FIRST ROW	
Start of Age interval									
0	0.98882	0.00000	0.00000	8.004	1.089	456190	0.1629+0.1019	0.1629+0.1019	**TABLE 9**
5	0.99609	0.00017	0.00000	7.778	1.120	420137	0.2046-0.1307	-0.0175+0.1510	LESLIE
10	0.99467	0.05632	0.00034	7.614	1.144	417664	-0.0385-0.3067	-0.1131+0.0384	MATRIX
15	0.99153	0.24373	0.11390	7.443	1.109	412520	-0.3731-0.1231	-0.0747-0.0732	AND ITS
20	0.98972	0.34176	0.38104	7.253	0.870	341185	-0.3437+0.3601	-0.0132-0.1031	SPECTRAL
25	0.98889	0.25124	0.31164	7.055	0.519	212215	0.2250+0.5880	0.0129-0.0796	COMPONENTS
30	0.98757	0.14958	0.19741	6.856	0.257	76410	0.7933+0.3620	0.0199-0.0437	(Females)
35	0.98469	0.07155	0.10567	6.655	0.100	35359	0.5003-0.8708	0.0133-0.0161	
40	0.97837	0.02102	0.03929	6.440	0.024	9123	-0.7197-1.0388	0.0042-0.0033	
45	0.96822	0.00168	0.00318	6.192	0.002	652	-1.5593+0.2555	0.0003-0.0003	
50	0.95368	0.00012	0.00021	5.892	0.000	61	-0.5422+1.8784	0.0000-0.0000	
55+	0.77127			22.818					

Start Age interval	OBSERVED POPUL. (IN 100's)	r_1	r_2, r_3	r_4-r_{11}	AGE-SP. BIRTH RATES	NET MATERNITY FUNCTION	COEFF. OF MATRIX EQUATION	PARAMETERS INTEGRAL	MATRIX	EXP. INCREASE x	$e^{(x+2\frac{1}{2})r}$	
0	4190	4058	100	31	0.0000	0.0000	0.0000	L(1) 1.01750	1.01751	0	1.0087	**TABLE 10**
5	3750	3944	-100	-93	0.0000	0.0000	0.0002	L(2) 0.32108	0.33572	50	1.1998	AGE
10	3650	3861	-271	60	0.0001	0.0000	0.0555	0.73117	0.70682	55	1.2208	ANALYSIS
15	3720	3774	-133	79	0.0244	0.1106	0.2388	R(1) 0.00347	0.00347	60	1.2422	AND
20	3920	3678	291	-49	0.0815	0.3669	0.3320	R(2) -0.04499	-0.04905	65	1.2640	MISCELLANEOUS
25	4090	3577	530	-17	0.0667	0.2970	0.2415	0.23140	0.22547	70	1.2861	RESULTS
30	2970	3476	109	-615	0.0422	0.1861	0.1422	C(1)		75	1.3086	(Females)
35	3530	3374	-728	883	0.0226	0.0984	0.0672		50703	80	1.3315	
40	3740	3265	-959	1433	0.0084	0.0360	0.0194	C(2)	3443	85	1.3548	
45	3290	3140	116	34	0.0007	0.0029	0.0015		-43751	90	1.3785	
50	3080	2987	1606	-1514	0.0000	0.0002	0.0001	2P/Y 27.1525	27.8667	95	1.4026	
55+	8920	11570						DELTA 5.5796		100	1.4272	

TABLE 1 — DATA

AGE AT LAST BIRTHDAY	POPULATION BOTH SEXES	MALES Number	%	FEMALES Number	%	BIRTHS BY AGE OF MOTHER	DEATHS BOTH SEXES	MALES	FEMALES	AGE AT LAST BIRTHDAY
0	205000	105000	2.2	100000	2.0	0	13618	7781	5837	0
1-4	710000	362000	7.7	348000	6.9	0	1802	958	844	1-4
5-9	795000	405000	8.6	390000	7.8	0	563	330	233	5-9
10-14	764000	388000	8.3	376000	7.5	75	476	288	188	10-14
15-19	726000	365000	7.8	361000	7.2	18818	770	487	283	15-19
20-24	762000	381000	8.1	381000	7.6	71912	1127	704	423	20-24
25-29	777000	381000	8.1	396000	7.9	61669	1299	760	539	25-29
30-34	771000	366000	7.8	405000	8.1	40193	1445	772	673	30-34
35-39	473000	222000	4.7	251000	5.0	13675	1205	627	578	35-39
40-44	738000	350000	7.5	388000	7.7	6754	2533	1371	1162	40-44
45-49	667000	320000	6.8	347000	6.9	448	3574	1999	1575	45-49
50-54	612000	295000	6.3	317000	6.3	22	5168	2999	2169	50-54
55-59	518000	235000	5.0	283000	5.6	1	6887	3827	3060	55-59
60-64	393000	172000	3.7	221000	4.4	0	8438	4442	3996	60-64
65-69	328000	141000	3.0	187000	3.7	0	11454	5678	5776	65-69
70-74	239000	103000	2.2	136000	2.7		13851	6589	7262	70-74
75-79	140000	60000	1.3	80000	1.6		14023	6410	7613	75-79
80-84	63000	27000	0.6	36000	0.7	110557 M.	10452	4732	5720	80-84
85+	25000	10000	0.2	15000	0.3	103010 F.	6837	2910	3927	85+
TOTAL	9706000	4688000		5018000		213567	105522	53664	51858	TOTAL

TABLE 2 — MALE LIFE TABLE

x	$_nq_x$	l_x	$_nd_x$	$_nL_x$	$_nm_x$	$_na_x$	T_x	r_x	$\mathring{e}_x$	$_nM_x$	x
0	0.069406	100000	6941	94577	0.073385	0.2187	6351980	0.0125	63.520	0.074105	0
1	0.010296	93059	958	369440	0.002593	1.0800	6257403	0.0125	67.241	0.002646	1
5	0.004039	92101	372	459576	0.000809	2.5000	5887963	0.0172	63.929	0.000815	5
10	0.003710	91729	340	457845	0.000743	2.6444	5428387	0.0095	59.178	0.000742	10
15	0.006651	91389	608	455528	0.001334	2.6695	4970542	0.0005	54.389	0.001334	15
20	0.009198	90781	835	451878	0.001848	2.5711	4515014	0.0000	49.735	0.001848	20
25	0.009925	89946	893	447521	0.001999	2.5241	4063136	0.0020	45.173	0.001995	25
30	0.010537	89053	938	442993	0.002118	2.5763	3615616	0.0518	40.601	0.002109	30
35	0.014031	88115	1236	437641	0.002825	2.6260	3172623	0.0016	36.005	0.002824	35
40	0.019409	86879	1686	430469	0.003917	2.6720	2734982	0.0000	31.480	0.003917	40
45	0.030857	85193	2629	419897	0.006261	2.6926	2304514	0.0106	27.051	0.006247	45
50	0.049859	82564	4117	403271	0.010208	2.6805	1884616	0.0203	22.826	0.010166	50
55	0.078977	78447	6196	377727	0.016402	2.6582	1481346	0.0370	18.883	0.016285	55
60	0.122074	72252	8820	340351	0.025914	2.6296	1103619	0.0187	15.275	0.025826	60
65	0.184168	63432	11682	289108	0.040407	2.5988	763267	0.0187	12.033	0.040270	65
70	0.277520	51750	14362	223698	0.064200	2.5595	474160	0.0187	9.163	0.063971	70
75	0.422148	37388	15783	147202	0.107222	2.4823	250461	0.0187	6.699	0.106833	75
80	0.602558	21605	13018	73979	0.175970	2.3848	103259	0.0187	4.779	0.175260	80
85+	*1.000000	8587	8587	29280	0.293262	3.4099	29280		3.410	0.291000	85

TABLE 3 — FEMALE LIFE TABLE

x	$_nq_x$	l_x	$_nd_x$	$_nL_x$	$_nm_x$	$_na_x$	T_x	r_x	$\mathring{e}_x$	$_nM_x$	x
0	0.055383	100000	5538	95764	0.057833	0.2352	6742662	0.0119	67.427	0.058370	0
1	0.009473	94462	895	375244	0.002385	1.0911	6646898	0.0119	70.366	0.002425	1
5	0.002957	93567	277	467142	0.000592	2.5000	6271654	0.0164	67.029	0.000597	5
10	0.002498	93290	233	465886	0.000500	2.5782	5804512	0.0071	62.220	0.000500	10
15	0.003912	93057	364	464433	0.000784	2.6603	5338626	0.0000	57.369	0.000784	15
20	0.005536	92693	513	462236	0.001110	2.6060	4874193	0.0000	52.584	0.001110	20
25	0.006783	92180	625	459387	0.001361	2.5828	4411956	0.0000	47.863	0.001361	25
30	0.008318	91555	762	455955	0.001670	2.6134	3952569	0.0439	43.172	0.001662	30
35	0.011454	90793	1040	451484	0.002303	2.6148	3496614	0.0020	38.512	0.002303	35
40	0.014870	89753	1335	445627	0.002995	2.6485	3045130	0.0000	33.928	0.002995	40
45	0.022517	88418	1991	437445	0.004551	2.6657	2599530	0.0156	29.400	0.004539	45
50	0.033758	86427	2918	425351	0.006859	2.6740	2162058	0.0133	25.016	0.006842	50
55	0.053014	83510	4427	407311	0.010869	2.6874	1736708	0.0246	20.796	0.010813	55
60	0.087259	79083	6901	379417	0.018188	2.6819	1329397	0.0264	16.810	0.018081	60
65	0.144797	72182	10452	336404	0.031069	2.6553	949980	0.0264	13.161	0.030888	65
70	0.237999	61730	14692	273533	0.053711	2.6097	613576	0.0264	9.940	0.053397	70
75	0.386597	47038	18185	190052	0.095684	2.5177	340044	0.0264	7.229	0.095162	75
80	0.562770	28854	16238	101690	0.159681	2.4285	149991	0.0264	5.198	0.158889	80
85+	1.000000	12616	12616	48302	0.261183	3.8287	48302	0.0264	3.829	0.261801	85

TABLE 4 — OBSERVED AND PROJECTED VITAL RATES

	OBSERVED POPULATION BOTH SEXES	MALES	FEMALES	PROJECTED POPULATION 1959 MALES	FEMALES	1964 MALES	FEMALES	1969 MALES	FEMALES	STABLE POPULATION MALES	FEMALES
RATES PER THOUSAND											
Birth	22.00	23.58	20.53	22.13	19.45	21.07	18.69	20.58	18.42	21.08	20.0
Death	10.87	11.45	10.33	11.81	10.98	12.06	11.51	12.37	12.01	12.52	11.5
Increase	11.13	12.14	10.19	10.32	8.47	9.01	7.18	8.21	6.42		8.557
PERCENTAGE											
under 15	25.49	26.88	24.19	27.76	25.04	28.34	25.67	27.99	25.47	27.34	26.4
15-64	66.32	65.85	66.76	64.90	65.41	63.77	63.93	63.29	63.37	64.05	63.4
65 and over	8.19	7.27	9.05	7.33	9.55	7.88	10.41	8.72	11.16	8.62	10.1
DEP. RATIO X 100	50.78	51.86	49.79	54.08	52.88	56.80	56.43	58.01	57.80	56.14	57.7

TABLE 1 — DATA

AGE AT LAST BIRTHDAY	POPULATION BOTH SEXES	MALES Number	%	FEMALES Number	%	BIRTHS BY AGE OF MOTHER	DEATHS BOTH SEXES	MALES	FEMALES	AGE AT LAST BIRTHDAY
0	172000	88000	1.9	84000	1.6	0	10371	5964	4407	0
1-4	769000	394000	8.3	375000	7.4	0	1564	839	725	1-4
5-9	857000	436000	9.2	421000	8.3	0	495	304	191	5-9
10-14	754000	382000	8.1	372000	7.3	89	438	258	180	10-14
15-19	713000	353000	7.5	360000	7.1	19884	827	566	261	15-19
20-24	695000	339000	7.2	356000	7.0	63195	1120	771	349	20-24
25-29	745000	366000	7.7	379000	7.4	46155	1240	799	441	25-29
30-34	761000	367000	7.7	394000	7.7	27871	1429	815	614	30-34
35-39	624000	293000	6.2	331000	6.5	12222	1453	804	649	35-39
40-44	578000	271000	5.7	307000	6.0	3080	1989	1119	870	40-44
45-49	707000	337000	7.1	370000	7.3	307	3496	1955	1541	45-49
50-54	618000	296000	6.2	322000	6.3	11	4893	2877	2016	50-54
55-59	563000	266000	5.6	297000	5.8	0	7049	4174	2875	55-59
60-64	445000	194000	4.1	251000	4.9	0	8962	4860	4102	60-64
65-69	329000	141000	3.0	188000	3.7	0	10913	5464	5449	65-69
70-74	256000	108000	2.3	148000	2.9		14134	6666	7468	70-74
75-79	153000	65000	1.4	88000	1.7		14056	6348	7708	75-79
80-84	71000	30000	0.6	41000	0.8	89531 M.	10601	4644	5957	80-84
85+	29000	12000	0.3	17000	0.3	83283 F.	6883	2913	3970	85+
TOTAL	9839000	4738000		5101000		172814	101913	52140	49773	TOTAL

TABLE 2 — MALE LIFE TABLE

x	$_nq_x$	l_x	$_nd_x$	$_nL_x$	$_nm_x$	$_na_x$	T_x	r_x	$\mathring{e}_x$	$_nM_x$	x
0	0.064316	100000	6432	94899	0.067773	0.2070	6426459	0.0000	64.265	0.067773	0
1	0.008465	93568	792	371955	0.002129	1.0730	6331560	0.0000	67.668	0.002129	1
5	0.003453	92776	320	463081	0.000692	2.5000	5959605	0.0221	64.236	0.000697	5
10	0.003391	92456	314	461583	0.000679	2.7772	5496524	0.0202	59.450	0.000675	10
15	0.008005	92142	738	459018	0.001607	2.7034	5034941	0.0104	54.643	0.001603	15
20	0.011309	91405	1034	454491	0.002274	2.5491	4575923	0.0000	50.062	0.002274	20
25	0.010856	90371	981	449394	0.002183	2.4903	4121432	0.0000	45.606	0.002183	25
30	0.011055	89390	988	444528	0.002223	2.5482	3672038	0.0199	41.079	0.002221	30
35	0.013685	88402	1210	439151	0.002755	2.6368	3227510	0.0274	36.509	0.002744	35
40	0.020447	87192	1783	431761	0.004129	2.6443	2788359	0.0000	31.979	0.004129	40
45	0.028622	85409	2445	421388	0.005801	2.6851	2356599	0.0000	27.592	0.005801	45
50	0.047662	82965	3954	405681	0.009747	2.6878	1935211	0.0136	23.326	0.009720	50
55	0.076058	79011	6009	381012	0.015772	2.6635	1529530	0.0259	19.359	0.015692	55
60	0.118777	73001	8671	344463	0.025172	2.6308	1148518	0.0261	15.733	0.025052	60
65	0.178056	64330	11454	294175	0.038937	2.6012	804055	0.0261	12.499	0.038752	65
70	0.269249	52876	14237	229568	0.062016	2.5548	509880	0.0261	9.643	0.061722	70
75	0.393408	38639	15201	154921	0.098120	2.4821	280312	0.0261	7.255	0.097662	75
80	0.551774	23438	12933	83163	0.155509	2.4244	125391	0.0261	5.350	0.154800	80
85+	1.000000	10506	10506	42228	0.248783	4.0196	42228	0.0261	4.020	0.242751	85+

TABLE 3 — FEMALE LIFE TABLE

x	$_nq_x$	l_x	$_nd_x$	$_nL_x$	$_nm_x$	$_na_x$	T_x	r_x	$\mathring{e}_x$	$_nM_x$	x
0	0.050411	100000	5041	96087	0.052464	0.2237	6879284	0.0000	68.793	0.052464	0
1	0.007690	94959	730	377706	0.001933	1.0833	6783197	0.0000	71.433	0.001933	1
5	0.002242	94229	211	470615	0.000449	2.5000	6405491	0.0201	67.978	0.000454	5
10	0.002421	94017	228	469545	0.000485	2.6175	5934876	0.0151	63.125	0.000484	10
15	0.003621	93790	340	468148	0.000725	2.6407	5465331	0.0037	58.272	0.000725	15
20	0.004890	93450	457	466150	0.000980	2.5911	4997184	0.0000	53.474	0.000980	20
25	0.005802	92993	540	463672	0.001164	2.6010	4531033	0.0000	48.724	0.001164	25
30	0.007713	92454	719	460547	0.001560	2.6039	4067361	0.0120	43.993	0.001558	30
35	0.009788	91735	898	456547	0.001967	2.6299	3606815	0.0229	39.318	0.001961	35
40	0.014076	90837	1279	451187	0.002834	2.6546	3150267	0.0000	34.680	0.002834	40
45	0.020623	89559	1847	443474	0.004165	2.6619	2699080	0.0000	30.138	0.004165	45
50	0.030940	87712	2714	432229	0.006279	2.6681	2255606	0.0155	25.716	0.006261	50
55	0.047487	84998	4036	415670	0.009710	2.6913	1823376	0.0146	21.452	0.009680	55
60	0.079295	80961	6420	390039	0.016459	2.6995	1407706	0.0302	17.387	0.016343	60
65	0.136623	74542	10184	348947	0.029185	2.6669	1017668	0.0302	13.652	0.028984	65
70	0.226486	64358	14576	286978	0.050792	2.6118	668720	0.0302	10.391	0.050459	70
75	0.361756	49781	18009	204352	0.088126	2.5259	381742	0.0302	7.668	0.087591	75
80	0.529304	31773	16817	115113	0.146095	2.4622	177390	0.0302	5.583	0.145293	80
85+	1.000000	14955	14955	62277	0.240140	4.1642	62277	0.0302	4.164	0.233528	85+

TABLE 4 — OBSERVED AND PROJECTED VITAL RATES

	OBSERVED POPULATION BOTH SEXES	MALES	FEMALES	PROJECTED POPULATION 1962 MALES	FEMALES	1967 MALES	FEMALES	1972 MALES	FEMALES	STABLE POPULATION MALES	FEMALES
RATES PER THOUSAND											
Birth	17.56	18.90	16.33	18.13	15.77	17.90	15.68	18.46	16.29	16.81	15.75
Death	10.36	11.00	9.76	11.43	10.49	11.99	11.27	12.54	11.99	14.66	13.60
Increase	7.21	7.89	6.57	6.70	5.28	5.91	4.41	5.92	4.30		2.1469
PERCENTAGE											
under 15	25.94	27.44	24.54	27.06	24.16	25.85	23.08	24.26	21.75	23.02	21.91
15-64	65.55	65.05	66.01	64.82	65.25	64.96	65.21	65.74	65.69	65.44	64.41
65 and over	8.52	7.51	9.45	8.12	10.59	9.19	11.71	10.01	12.56	11.54	13.68
DEP. RATIO X 100	52.57	53.73	51.50	54.27	53.26	53.94	53.36	52.12	52.24	52.81	55.26

TABLE 1 — DATA

AGE AT LAST BIRTHDAY	POPULATION BOTH SEXES	MALES Number	%	FEMALES Number	%	BIRTHS BY AGE OF MOTHER	DEATHS BOTH SEXES	MALES	FEMALES	AGE AT LAST BIRTHDAY
0	143000	73000	1.5	70000	1.4	0	7031	4010	3021	0
1-4	657000	337000	7.0	320000	6.2	0	1025	559	466	1-4
5-9	924000	472000	9.8	452000	8.7	0	454	278	176	5-9
10-14	804000	409000	8.5	395000	7.6	87	384	250	134	10-14
15-19	750000	377000	7.8	373000	7.2	19537	667	449	218	15-19
20-24	684000	333000	6.9	351000	6.8	55793	800	529	271	20-24
25-29	714000	350000	7.3	364000	7.0	38062	905	565	340	25-29
30-34	751000	367000	7.6	384000	7.4	20398	1206	726	480	30-34
35-39	757000	361000	7.5	396000	7.7	9958	1622	906	716	35-39
40-44	476000	223000	4.6	253000	4.9	1990	1420	763	657	40-44
45-49	692000	326000	6.8	366000	7.1	176	3138	1762	1376	45-49
50-54	659000	313000	6.5	346000	6.7	7	4798	2791	2007	50-54
55-59	579000	275000	5.7	304000	5.9	0	7069	4264	2805	55-59
60-64	492000	223000	4.6	269000	5.2	0	9593	5490	4103	60-64
65-69	358000	152000	3.2	206000	4.0	0	11418	5869	5549	65-69
70-74	262000	109000	2.3	153000	3.0		14092	6751	7341	70-74
75-79	170000	70000	1.5	100000	1.9		15428	7007	8421	75-79
80-84	80000	33000	0.7	47000	0.9	75598 M.	11848	5201	6647	80-84
85+	32000	13000	0.3	19000	0.4	70410 F.	7705	3285	4420	85+
TOTAL	9984000	4816000		5168000		146008	100603	51455	49148	TOTAL

TABLE 2 — MALE LIFE TABLE

x	nq_x	l_x	nd_x	nL_x	nm_x	na_x	T_x	r_x	$\mathring{e}_x$	nM_x	x
0	0.052628	100000	5263	95807	0.054931	0.2034	6587258	0.0000	65.873	0.054931	0
1	0.006603	94737	626	377116	0.001659	1.0709	6491451	0.0000	68.521	0.001659	1
5	0.002941	94112	277	469866	0.000589	2.5000	6114335	0.0000	64.969	0.000589	5
10	0.003066	93835	288	468514	0.000614	2.7032	5644468	0.0217	60.153	0.000611	10
15	0.005958	93547	557	466436	0.001195	2.6676	5175955	0.0194	55.330	0.001191	15
20	0.007915	92990	736	463148	0.001589	2.5522	4709519	0.0059	50.646	0.001589	20
25	0.008040	92254	742	459449	0.001614	2.5463	4246371	0.0000	46.029	0.001614	25
30	0.009844	91512	901	455391	0.001978	2.5913	3786922	0.0000	41.382	0.001978	30
35	0.012544	90611	1137	450344	0.002524	2.6135	3331531	0.0472	36.767	0.002510	35
40	0.016991	89475	1520	443825	0.003425	2.6660	2881187	0.0066	32.201	0.003422	40
45	0.026692	87954	2348	434367	0.005405	2.6976	2437362	0.0000	27.712	0.005405	45
50	0.043767	85607	3747	419458	0.008932	2.7113	2002995	0.0075	23.398	0.008917	50
55	0.075095	81860	6147	394994	0.015563	2.6728	1583537	0.0180	19.344	0.015505	55
60	0.116835	75713	8846	357640	0.024734	2.6347	1188543	0.0250	15.698	0.024619	60
65	0.177476	66867	11867	305918	0.038792	2.6055	830903	0.0250	12.426	0.038612	65
70	0.270108	55000	14856	238741	0.062226	2.5594	524985	0.0250	9.545	0.061936	70
75	0.401178	40144	16105	160158	0.100556	2.4814	286244	0.0250	7.130	0.100100	75
80	0.558289	24039	13421	84784	0.158293	2.4148	126086	0.0250	5.245	0.157606	80
85+	1.000000	10618	10618	41302	0.257087	3.8897	41302	0.0250	3.890	0.252691	85+

TABLE 3 — FEMALE LIFE TABLE

x	nq_x	l_x	nd_x	nL_x	nm_x	na_x	T_x	r_x	$\mathring{e}_x$	nM_x	x
0	0.041743	100000	4174	96723	0.043157	0.2149	7030239	0.0000	70.302	0.043157	0
1	0.005800	95826	556	381679	0.001456	1.0777	6933516	0.0000	72.355	0.001456	1
5	0.001945	95270	185	475886	0.000389	2.5000	6551837	0.0000	68.771	0.000389	5
10	0.001699	95085	162	475038	0.000340	2.6189	6075951	0.0188	63.900	0.000339	10
15	0.002923	94923	277	473964	0.000585	2.6526	5600913	0.0112	59.005	0.000584	15
20	0.003854	94646	365	472350	0.000772	2.5924	5126949	0.0017	54.170	0.000772	20
25	0.004660	94281	439	470352	0.000934	2.6043	4654599	0.0000	49.370	0.000934	25
30	0.006232	93841	585	467830	0.001250	2.6444	4184247	0.0000	44.588	0.001250	30
35	0.009058	93257	845	464299	0.001819	2.6502	3716417	0.0399	39.851	0.001808	35
40	0.012916	92412	1194	459254	0.002599	2.6693	3252119	0.0052	35.192	0.002597	40
45	0.018634	91218	1700	452129	0.003760	2.6685	2792864	0.0000	30.617	0.003760	45
50	0.028687	89519	2568	441640	0.005815	2.6818	2340735	0.0125	26.148	0.005801	50
55	0.045316	86951	3940	425650	0.009257	2.6897	1899095	0.0155	21.841	0.009227	55
60	0.074168	83010	6157	400882	0.015358	2.6985	1473445	0.0295	17.750	0.015253	60
65	0.127591	76854	9806	361497	0.027126	2.6778	1072563	0.0295	13.956	0.026937	65
70	0.216629	67048	14524	300720	0.048299	2.6234	711066	0.0295	10.605	0.047980	70
75	0.350462	52523	18407	217265	0.084723	2.5362	410347	0.0295	7.813	0.084210	75
80	0.519595	34116	17726	124657	0.142201	2.4763	193081	0.0295	5.660	0.141426	80
85+	1.000000	16389	16389	68424	0.239527	4.1749	68424	0.0295	4.175	0.232631	85+

TABLE 4 — OBSERVED AND PROJECTED VITAL RATES

	OBSERVED POPULATION BOTH SEXES	MALES	FEMALES	PROJECTED POPULATION 1965 MALES	FEMALES	1970 MALES	FEMALES	1975 MALES	FEMALES	STABLE POPULATION MALES	FEMALES
RATES PER THOUSAND											
Birth	14.62	15.70	13.62	15.59	13.60	16.00	14.04	16.54	14.61	13.33	12.42
Death	10.08	10.68	9.51	11.28	10.45	11.96	11.34	12.57	12.12	16.80	15.89
Increase	4.55	5.01	4.11	4.31	3.15	4.05	2.70	3.97	2.48	-3.4745	
PERCENTAGE											
under 15	25.32	26.81	23.94	25.13	22.40	22.59	20.15	21.80	19.50	19.31	18.22
15-64	65.65	65.37	65.91	66.03	66.06	67.50	67.14	67.37	66.63	66.40	64.55
65 and over	9.03	7.83	10.16	8.84	11.55	9.91	12.71	10.83	13.87	14.29	17.23
DEP. RATIO X 100	52.33	52.99	51.73	51.44	51.38	48.15	48.94	48.43	50.08	50.61	54.91

TABLE 5 — POPULATION PROJECTED WITH FIXED AGE-SPECIFIC BIRTH AND DEATH RATES (IN 1000's)

AGE LAST BIRTHDAY	1965 BOTH SEXES	1965 MALES	1965 FEMALES	1970 BOTH SEXES	1970 MALES	1970 FEMALES	1975 BOTH SEXES	1975 MALES	1975 FEMALES	AGE AT LAST BIRTHDAY
0-4	700	360	340	723	372	351	759	391	368	0-4
5-9	795	407	388	696	358	338	719	370	349	5-9
10-14	922	471	451	793	406	387	694	357	337	10-14
15-19	801	407	394	919	469	450	790	404	386	15-19
20-24	746	374	372	797	404	393	914	465	449	20-24
25-29	680	330	350	741	371	370	792	401	391	25-29
30-34	709	347	362	675	327	348	736	368	368	30-34
35-39	744	363	381	702	343	359	669	324	345	35-39
40-44	748	356	392	735	358	377	693	338	355	40-44
45-49	467	218	249	734	348	386	721	350	371	45-49
50-54	673	315	358	454	211	243	713	336	377	50-54
55-59	628	295	333	641	296	345	432	198	234	55-59
60-64	535	249	286	581	267	314	593	268	325	60-64
65-69	434	191	243	471	213	258	511	228	283	65-69
70-74	290	119	171	351	149	202	381	166	215	70-74
75-79	184	73	111	204	80	124	246	100	146	75-79
80-84	94	37	57	102	39	63	113	42	71	80-84
85+	42	16	26	49	18	31	54	19	35	85+
TOTAL	10192	4928	5264	10368	5029	5339	10530	5125	5405	TOTAL

TABLE 6 — STANDARDIZED RATES

STANDARD COUNTRIES: — STANDARDIZED RATES PER THOUSAND

	ENGLAND AND WALES 1961 BOTH SEXES	MALES	FEMALES	UNITED STATES 1960 BOTH SEXES	MALES	FEMALES	MEXICO 1960 BOTH SEXES	MALES	FEMALES
Birth	12.79	14.62*	11.95	13.02	13.81*	12.37	16.12	13.16*	15.51
Death	13.05	12.61*	13.50	10.76	11.05*	10.09	6.12	9.30*	5.32
Increase	-0.26	2.01*	-1.55	2.25	2.76*	2.28	10.00	3.87*	10.19

TABLE 7 — MOMENTS AND CUMULANTS

	OBSERVED POP. MALES	OBSERVED POP. FEMALES	STATIONARY POP. MALES	STATIONARY POP. FEMALES	STABLE POP. MALES	STABLE POP. FEMALES	OBSERVED BIRTHS	NET MATERNITY FUNCTION	BIRTHS IN STABLE POP.
μ	32.69778	34.82392	36.58978	38.14896	38.32547	39.99030	25.85266	25.78304	25.90344
γ^2	452.6449	474.7581	496.0775	527.0456	502.5293	532.2871	32.16238	32.30397	32.83420
κ_3	3263.419	2618.893	2286.208	2015.026	1419.717	995.170	132.1859	152.0569	153.1320
κ_4	-185312.	-218667.	-241929.	-286750.	-255602.	-298689.	70.940	334.765	293.994
β_1	0.114835	0.064094	0.042814	0.027734	0.015883	0.006567	0.525201	0.685874	0.662449
β_2	2.095542	2.029849	2.016919	1.967699	1.987859	1.945791	3.068579	3.320796	3.272701
κ	-0.043066	-0.023980	-0.016200	-0.010230	-0.006032	-0.002431	-0.314206	-0.430970	-0.407000

TABLE 8 — RATES FROM AGE DISTRIBUTIONS AND VITAL STATISTICS (Females)

VITAL STATISTICS		THOMPSON AGE RANGE	NRR	1000r	INTERVAL	BOURGEOIS-PICHAT AGE RANGE	NRR	1000b	1000d	1000r	COALE	
GRR	0.971										IBR	
NRR	0.914	0-4	1.08	2.79	27.42	5-29	1.33	18.91	8.47	10.44	IDR	
TFR	2.014	5-9	1.25	8.25	27.38	30-54	1.08	16.52	13.61	2.91	IRI	
GENERATION	25.843	10-14	1.09	3.03	27.32	55-79	1.89	54.84	31.22	23.62	K1	
SEX RATIO	107.368	15-19	1.04	1.47	27.24	*50-74	1.80	48.45	26.67	21.78	K2	

TABLE 9 — LESLIE MATRIX AND ITS SPECTRAL COMPONENTS (Females)

Start Age Interval	ORIGINAL MATRIX SUB-DIAGONAL	ALTERNATIVE FIRST ROWS Projection	ALTERNATIVE FIRST ROWS Integral	FIRST STABLE MATRIX % IN STABLE POPULATION	FISHER VALUES	REPRODUCTIVE VALUES	SECOND STABLE MATRIX Z_2 FIRST COLUMN	FIRST ROW
	0.99474	0.00000	0.00000	5.993	1.036	404089	0.2003+0.0996	0.2003+0.0996
	0.99822	0.00025	0.00000	6.066	1.024	462699	0.2169-0.1993	-0.0162+0.1692
	0.99774	0.06054	0.00050	6.161	1.008	397994	-0.1432-0.3617	-0.1240+0.0344
	0.99659	0.24315	0.11979	6.255	0.930	346746	-0.5136+0.0056	-0.0701-0.0844
	0.99577	0.30346	0.36354	6.343	0.664	233043	-0.2355+0.6351	-0.0081-0.0969
	0.99464	0.18156	0.23915	6.427	0.340	123585	0.6703+0.5894	0.0054-0.0624
	0.99245	0.09006	0.12149	6.504	0.146	56194	1.0401-0.5461	0.0092-0.0313
	0.98914	0.03798	0.05751	6.568	0.051	20152	-0.1807-1.5322	0.0066-0.0111
	0.98449	0.00962	0.01799	6.611	0.011	2726	-1.9573-0.4971	0.0020-0.0021
	0.97680	0.00058	0.00110	6.622	0.001	232	-1.5175+2.1490	0.0001-0.0001
	0.96379	0.00002	0.00005	6.582	0.000	9	1.8916+2.8259	0.0000-0.0000
85+	0.77038			29.866				

TABLE 10 — AGE ANALYSIS AND MISCELLANEOUS RESULTS (Females)

Start Age Interval	OBSERVED POPUL. (IN 100's)	CONTRIBUTIONS OF ROOTS (IN 100's) r_1	r_2, r_3	$r_4 \cdot r_{11}$	AGE-SP. BIRTH RATES	NET MATERNITY FUNCTION	COEFF. OF MATRIX EQUATION	PARAMETERS INTEGRAL	PARAMETERS MATRIX	EXP. INCREASE x	$e^{(x+2\frac{1}{2})r}$
	3900	3811	29	59	0.0000	0.0000	0.0000	L(1) 0.98278	0.98278	0	0.9914
	4520	3858	596	66	0.0000	0.0000	0.0003	L(2) 0.25174	0.27052	50	0.8333
	3950	3918	513	-481	0.0001	0.0005	0.0601	0.73783	0.70561	55	0.8189
	3730	3978	-555	308	0.0253	0.1197	0.2409	R(1) -0.00347	-0.00347	60	0.8048
	3510	4034	-1417	893	0.0767	0.3621	0.2996	R(2) -0.04980	-0.05602	65	0.7909
	3640	4087	-372	-75	0.0504	0.2372	0.1785	0.24840	0.24094	70	0.7773
	3840	4136	2107	-2403	0.0256	0.1198	0.0881	C(1)	63590	75	0.7639
	3960	4177	2624	-2840	0.0121	0.0563	0.0369	C(2)	53050	80	0.7508
	2530	4204	-1163	-511	0.0038	0.0174	0.0092		91871	85	0.7378
	3660	4211	-5559	5008	0.0002	0.0010	0.0005	2P/Y 25.2947	26.0778	90	0.7251
	3460	4185	-3185	2460	0.0000	0.0000	0.0000	DELTA 10.3361		95	0.7127
85+	10980	18991								100	0.7004

TABLE 1 — DATA

AGE AT LAST BIRTHDAY	POPULATION BOTH SEXES	MALES Number	%	FEMALES Number	%	BIRTHS BY AGE OF MOTHER	DEATHS BOTH SEXES	MALES	FEMALES	AGE AT LAST BIRTHDAY
0	126000	65000	1.3	61000	1.2	0	5678	3197	2481	0
1-4	553000	284000	5.8	269000	5.2	0	794	416	378	1-4
5-9	907000	465000	9.5	442000	8.5	0	365	223	142	5-9
10-14	867000	442000	9.1	425000	8.1	98	386	246	140	10-14
15-19	766000	388000	8.0	378000	7.2	16352	685	453	232	15-19
20-24	722000	359000	7.4	363000	7.0	52224	808	566	242	20-24
25-29	679000	329000	6.8	350000	6.7	35240	821	535	286	25-29
30-34	732000	359000	7.4	373000	7.2	18054	1130	727	403	30-34
35-39	746000	362000	7.4	384000	7.4	8096	1562	958	604	35-39
40-44	694000	326000	6.7	368000	7.1	2201	2017	1100	917	40-44
45-49	492000	230000	4.7	262000	5.0	60	2296	1256	1040	45-49
50-54	693000	328000	6.7	365000	7.0	9	4774	2780	1994	50-54
55-59	597000	281000	5.8	316000	6.1	1	6774	4169	2605	55-59
60-64	529000	247000	5.1	282000	5.4	0	9992	5918	4074	60-64
65-69	406000	174000	3.6	232000	4.4	0	12298	6463	5835	65-69
70-74	272000	112000	2.3	160000	3.1		13703	6633	7070	70-74
75-79	182000	73000	1.5	109000	2.1		15450	7028	8422	75-79
80-84	89000	35000	0.7	54000	1.0	68276 M.	12091	5253	6838	80-84
85+	36000	13000	0.3	23000	0.4	64059 F.	8247	3368	4879	85+
TOTAL	10088000	4872000		5216000		132335	99871	51289	48582	TOTAL

TABLE 2 — MALE LIFE TABLE

x	nq_x	l_x	nd_x	nL_x	nm_x	na_x	T_x	r_x	$\overset{\circ}{e}_x$	nM_x
0	0.047327	100000	4733	96224	0.049185	0.2022	6660199	0.0000	66.602	0.049185
1	0.005834	95267	556	379441	0.001465	1.0702	6563975	0.0000	68.901	0.001465
5	0.002395	94711	227	472990	0.000480	2.5000	6184534	0.0000	65.299	0.000480
10	0.002792	94485	264	471831	0.000559	2.7556	5711544	0.0174	60.449	0.000557
15	0.005843	94221	550	469826	0.001172	2.6788	5239713	0.0197	55.611	0.001168
20	0.007860	93670	736	466553	0.001578	2.5572	4769887	0.0150	50.922	0.001577
25	0.008098	92934	753	462829	0.001626	2.5533	4303333	0.0000	46.305	0.001626
30	0.010076	92181	929	458679	0.002025	2.6005	3840504	0.0000	41.662	0.002025
35	0.013158	91253	1201	453384	0.002648	2.6022	3381826	0.0070	37.060	0.002646
40	0.016858	90052	1518	446711	0.003398	2.6628	2928442	0.0417	32.519	0.003374
45	0.026963	88534	2387	437131	0.005461	2.6800	2481730	0.0000	28.031	0.005461
50	0.041570	86147	3581	422520	0.008476	2.7065	2044600	0.0000	23.734	0.008476
55	0.071906	82566	5937	399059	0.014877	2.6808	1622079	0.0130	19.646	0.014836
60	0.113964	76629	8733	362498	0.024091	2.6360	1223021	0.0293	15.960	0.023960
65	0.171396	67896	11637	311614	0.037344	2.6056	860523	0.0293	12.674	0.037144
70	0.260043	56259	14630	245671	0.059550	2.5651	548908	0.0293	9.757	0.059223
75	0.389343	41629	16208	167458	0.096788	2.4897	303237	0.0293	7.284	0.096274
80	0.543978	25421	13829	91572	0.151012	2.4305	135779	0.0293	5.341	0.150085
85+	*1.000000	11593	11593	44206	0.262236	3.8134	44206	0.0293	3.813	0.259077

TABLE 3 — FEMALE LIFE TABLE

x	nq_x	l_x	nd_x	nL_x	nm_x	na_x	T_x	r_x	$\overset{\circ}{e}_x$	nM_x
0	0.039418	100000	3942	96915	0.040672	0.2174	7128334	0.0000	71.283	0.040672
1	0.005598	96058	538	382662	0.001405	1.0793	7031419	0.0000	73.200	0.001405
5	0.001605	95521	153	477219	0.000321	2.5000	6648756	0.0000	69.606	0.000321
10	0.001650	95367	157	476472	0.000330	2.6839	6171537	0.0152	64.713	0.000329
15	0.003070	95210	292	475351	0.000615	2.6131	5695065	0.0152	59.816	0.000614
20	0.003329	94918	316	473817	0.000667	2.5616	5219714	0.0070	54.992	0.000667
25	0.004078	94602	386	472083	0.000817	2.6035	4745897	0.0000	50.167	0.000817
30	0.005388	94216	508	469882	0.001080	2.6430	4273814	0.0000	45.362	0.001080
35	0.007836	93708	734	466841	0.001573	2.6850	3803931	0.0000	40.593	0.001573
40	0.012475	92974	1160	462192	0.002510	2.6924	3337091	0.0356	35.893	0.002492
45	0.019664	91814	1805	454820	0.003969	2.6663	2874898	0.0000	31.312	0.003969
50	0.026969	90009	2427	444339	0.005463	2.6503	2420078	0.0000	26.887	0.005463
55	0.040603	87581	3556	429743	0.008275	2.7046	1975740	0.0169	22.559	0.008244
60	0.070442	84025	5919	406534	0.014559	2.7038	1545997	0.0329	18.399	0.014447
65	0.119670	78106	9347	368814	0.025343	2.6766	1139463	0.0329	14.589	0.025151
70	0.201318	68759	13842	310979	0.044513	2.6293	770648	0.0329	11.208	0.044187
75	0.326598	54917	17936	230591	0.077781	2.5472	459669	0.0329	8.370	0.077266
80	0.484209	36981	17907	140376	0.127561	2.5132	229078	0.0329	6.194	0.126629
85+	*1.000000	19074	19074	88702	0.215039	4.6503	88702	0.0329	4.650	0.212130

TABLE 4 — OBSERVED AND PROJECTED VITAL RATES

	OBSERVED POPULATION BOTH SEXES	MALES	FEMALES	PROJECTED POPULATION 1968 MALES	FEMALES	1973 MALES	FEMALES	1978 MALES	FEMALES	STABLE POPULATION MALES	FEMALES
RATES PER THOUSAND											
Birth	13.12	14.01	12.28	14.19	12.47	14.89	13.14	15.01	13.32	11.42	10.5
Death	9.90	10.53	9.31	11.40	10.53	12.21	11.56	12.89	12.38	18.52	17.6
Increase	3.22	3.49	2.97	2.79	1.94	2.68	1.58	2.12	0.94		-7.105
PERCENTAGE											
under 15	24.32	25.78	22.95	23.04	20.47	20.31	18.08	20.27	18.15	17.11	15.9
15-64	65.92	65.87	65.97	67.20	66.84	68.90	67.92	67.90	66.46	66.31	63.7
65 and over	9.76	8.35	11.08	9.75	12.69	10.80	14.00	11.84	15.39	16.58	20.3
DEP. RATIO X 100	51.70	51.82	51.58	48.80	49.60	45.15	47.23	47.28	50.47	50.81	56.8

TABLE 1 — DATA

AGE AT LAST BIRTHDAY	POPULATION BOTH SEXES	MALES Number	%	FEMALES Number	%	BIRTHS BY AGE OF MOTHER	DEATHS BOTH SEXES	MALES	FEMALES	AGE AT LAST BIRTHDAY
0	128000	66000	1.3	62000	1.2	0	5286	3029	2257	0
1-4	531000	273000	5.6	258000	4.9	0	661	342	319	1-4
5-9	855000	438000	9.0	417000	8.0	0	351	199	152	5-9
10-14	895000	456000	9.3	439000	8.4	101	295	193	102	10-14
15-19	780000	396000	8.1	384000	7.3	16048	586	425	161	15-19
20-24	738000	369000	7.5	369000	7.1	53529	813	591	222	20-24
25-29	676000	327000	6.7	349000	6.7	35323	797	548	249	25-29
30-34	722000	354000	7.2	368000	7.0	17669	1038	669	369	30-34
35-39	746000	363000	7.4	383000	7.3	7337	1506	918	588	35-39
40-44	739000	349000	7.1	390000	7.5	2052	2028	1168	860	40-44
45-49	450000	211000	4.3	239000	4.6	75	1962	1103	859	45-49
50-54	695000	327000	6.7	368000	7.0	7	4661	2722	1939	50-54
55-59	612000	288000	5.9	324000	6.2	0	6794	4093	2701	55-59
60-64	536000	250000	5.1	286000	5.5	0	9998	6046	3952	60-64
65-69	420000	182000	3.7	238000	4.5	0	12829	7017	5812	65-69
70-74	281000	115000	2.4	166000	3.2		14209	6865	7344	70-74
75-79	186000	74000	1.5	112000	2.1		15406	6911	8495	75-79
80-84	93000	37000	0.8	56000	1.1	68380 M.	12896	5490	7406	80-84
85+	37000	14000	0.3	23000	0.4	63761 F.	8714	3573	5141	85+
TOTAL	10120000	4889000		5231000		132141	100830	51902	48928	TOTAL

TABLE 2 — MALE LIFE TABLE

x	$_nq_x$	l_x	$_nd_x$	$_nL_x$	$_nm_x$	$_na_x$	T_x	r_x	$\dot{e}_x$	$_nM_x$	x
0	0.044256	100000	4426	96432	0.045894	0.1937	6702963	0.0000	67.030	0.045894	0
1	0.004993	95574	477	380897	0.001253	1.0656	6606531	0.0000	69.125	0.001253	1
5	0.002269	95097	216	474947	0.000454	2.5000	6225634	0.0000	65.466	0.000454	5
10	0.002120	94881	201	473965	0.000424	2.8038	5750687	0.0095	60.609	0.000423	10
15	0.005378	94680	509	472243	0.001078	2.7255	5276722	0.0201	55.732	0.001073	15
20	0.007988	94171	752	469031	0.001604	2.5749	4804479	0.0176	51.019	0.001602	20
25	0.008345	93419	780	465170	0.001676	2.5318	4335448	0.0024	46.409	0.001676	25
30	0.009406	92639	871	461095	0.001890	2.5894	3870278	0.0000	41.778	0.001890	30
35	0.012569	91768	1153	456090	0.002529	2.6166	3409183	0.0000	37.150	0.002529	35
40	0.016742	90614	1517	449518	0.003375	2.6576	2953093	0.0507	32.590	0.003347	40
45	0.025830	89097	2301	440155	0.005229	2.6835	2503574	0.0011	28.099	0.005227	45
50	0.040840	86796	3545	425835	0.008324	2.7023	2063419	0.0000	23.773	0.008324	50
55	0.068984	83251	5743	403017	0.014250	2.6949	1637584	0.0119	19.670	0.014212	55
60	0.115033	77508	8916	366588	0.024322	2.6499	1234567	0.0282	15.928	0.024184	60
65	0.177273	68592	12160	313779	0.038752	2.6001	867979	0.0282	12.654	0.038555	65
70	0.261543	56433	14760	246029	0.059991	2.5518	554200	0.0282	9.821	0.059696	70
75	0.379813	41673	15828	168629	0.093863	2.4895	308171	0.0282	7.395	0.093392	75
80	0.540081	25845	13958	93508	0.149275	2.4412	139542	0.0282	5.399	0.148378	80
85+	*1.000000	11887	11887	46034	0.258214	3.8728	46034	0.0282	3.873	0.255214	85+

TABLE 3 — FEMALE LIFE TABLE

x	$_nq_x$	l_x	$_nd_x$	$_nL_x$	$_nm_x$	$_na_x$	T_x	r_x	$\dot{e}_x$	$_nM_x$	x
0	0.035393	100000	3539	97225	0.036403	0.2158	7185689	0.0000	71.857	0.036403	0
1	0.004928	96461	475	384454	0.001236	1.0783	7088465	0.0000	73.486	0.001236	1
5	0.001821	95985	175	479490	0.000365	2.5000	6704011	0.0000	69.844	0.000365	5
10	0.001162	95811	111	478780	0.000232	2.5492	6224521	0.0079	64.967	0.000232	10
15	0.002101	95699	201	478030	0.000421	2.6822	5745741	0.0170	60.040	0.000419	15
20	0.003007	95498	287	476802	0.000602	2.6002	5267710	0.0090	55.160	0.000602	20
25	0.003561	95211	339	475247	0.000713	2.6152	4790908	0.0000	50.319	0.000713	25
30	0.005002	94872	475	473254	0.001003	2.6681	4315661	0.0000	45.489	0.001003	30
35	0.007649	94398	722	470300	0.001535	2.6621	3842408	0.0000	40.705	0.001535	35
40	0.011064	93675	1036	465980	0.002224	2.6868	3372108	0.0448	35.998	0.002205	40
45	0.017828	92639	1652	459344	0.003596	2.6680	2906128	0.0022	31.370	0.003594	45
50	0.026026	90987	2368	449431	0.005269	2.6746	2446784	0.0000	26.891	0.005269	50
55	0.041035	88619	3636	434706	0.008365	2.6926	1997354	0.0165	22.539	0.008336	55
60	0.067414	84983	5729	411756	0.013914	2.7031	1562648	0.0294	18.388	0.013818	60
65	0.116363	79254	9222	374958	0.024595	2.6892	1150892	0.0294	14.522	0.024420	65
70	0.201394	70032	14104	316724	0.044531	2.6294	775934	0.0294	11.080	0.044241	70
75	0.321578	55928	17985	235657	0.076319	2.5546	459210	0.0294	8.211	0.075848	75
80	0.495922	37943	18817	141477	0.133001	2.5126	223553	0.0294	5.892	0.132250	80
85+	1.000000	19126	19126	82076	0.233027	4.2913	82076	0.0294	4.291	0.223521	85+

TABLE 4 — OBSERVED AND PROJECTED VITAL RATES

	OBSERVED POPULATION BOTH SEXES	MALES	FEMALES	PROJECTED POPULATION 1969 MALES	FEMALES	1974 MALES	FEMALES	1979 MALES	FEMALES	STABLE POPULATION MALES	FEMALES
RATES PER THOUSAND											
Birth	13.06	13.99	12.19	14.28	12.48	14.99	13.16	14.73	13.00	11.26	10.36
Death	9.96	10.62	9.35	11.51	10.53	12.29	11.52	12.92	12.35	18.54	17.64
Increase	3.09	3.37	2.84	2.77	1.96	2.70	1.64	1.81	0.65		−7.2818
PERCENTAGE											
under 15	23.80	25.22	22.48	22.29	19.79	20.21	17.93	20.37	18.16	16.97	15.76
15-64	66.15	66.15	66.14	67.74	67.28	68.79	67.80	67.68	66.20	66.32	63.76
65 and over	10.05	8.63	11.37	9.97	12.93	11.01	14.27	11.94	15.63	16.71	20.48
DEP. RATIO X 100	51.18	51.18	51.18	47.62	48.62	45.37	47.49	47.75	51.05	50.78	56.84

TABLE 1 — DATA

AGE AT LAST BIRTHDAY	POPULATION BOTH SEXES	MALES Number	%	FEMALES Number	%	BIRTHS BY AGE OF MOTHER	DEATHS BOTH SEXES	MALES	FEMALES	AGE AT LAST BIRTHDAY
0	128000	66000	1.3	62000	1.2	0	5167	2970	2197	0
1-4	516000	265000	5.4	251000	4.8	0	689	384	305	1-4
5-9	796000	408000	8.3	388000	7.4	0	337	207	130	5-9
10-14	922000	471000	9.6	451000	8.6	92	338	213	125	10-14
15-19	801000	407000	8.3	394000	7.5	16530	565	357	208	15-19
20-24	746000	374000	7.6	372000	7.1	54956	722	517	205	20-24
25-29	680000	330000	6.7	350000	6.7	35213	742	481	261	25-29
30-34	709000	347000	7.1	362000	6.9	17302	1047	701	346	30-34
35-39	745000	363000	7.4	382000	7.3	6958	1529	946	583	35-39
40-44	748000	356000	7.3	392000	7.5	1851	2175	1259	916	40-44
45-49	467000	219000	4.5	248000	4.7	101	1982	1103	879	45-49
50-54	673000	315000	6.4	358000	6.8	6	4599	2729	1870	50-54
55-59	630000	296000	6.0	334000	6.4	0	7223	4315	2908	55-59
60-64	537000	250000	5.1	287000	5.5	0	10190	6100	4090	60-64
65-69	435000	191000	3.9	244000	4.7	0	13663	7462	6201	65-69
70-74	292000	119000	2.4	173000	3.3		15631	7747	7884	70-74
75-79	187000	74000	1.5	113000	2.2		16949	7686	9263	75-79
80-84	97000	38000	0.8	59000	1.1	68603 M.	14646	6288	8358	80-84
85+	39000	14000	0.3	25000	0.5	64406 F.	9925	4018	5907	85+
TOTAL	10148000	4903000		5245000		133009	108119	55483	52636	TOTAL

TABLE 2 — MALE LIFE TABLE

x	nq_x	l_x	nd_x	nL_x	nm_x	na_x	T_x	r_x	$\overset{\circ}{e}_x$	nM_x
0	0.043455	100000	4346	96568	0.045000	0.2101	6670886	0.0000	66.709	0.045000
1	0.005772	95654	552	381003	0.001449	1.0748	6574319	0.0000	68.730	0.001449
5	0.002534	95102	241	474909	0.000507	2.5000	6193316	0.0000	65.123	0.000507
10	0.002259	94861	214	473808	0.000452	2.6705	5718407	0.0000	60.282	0.000452
15	0.004398	94647	416	472286	0.000881	2.7182	5244599	0.0222	55.412	0.000877
20	0.006901	94231	650	469584	0.001385	2.5845	4772313	0.0197	50.645	0.001382
25	0.007266	93581	680	466262	0.001458	2.5869	4302729	0.0059	45.979	0.001458
30	0.010052	92901	934	462275	0.002020	2.6140	3836467	0.0000	41.296	0.002020
35	0.012950	91967	1191	456996	0.002606	2.6169	3374192	0.0000	36.689	0.002606
40	0.017652	90776	1602	450088	0.003560	2.6342	2917197	0.0469	32.136	0.003537
45	0.024928	89173	2223	440745	0.005044	2.6959	2467109	0.0068	27.666	0.005037
50	0.042473	86950	3693	426281	0.008663	2.7063	2026363	0.0000	23.305	0.008663
55	0.070627	83257	5880	402684	0.014603	2.6867	1600082	0.0078	19.219	0.014578
60	0.115816	77377	8961	365813	0.024497	2.6486	1197398	0.0199	15.475	0.024400
65	0.179349	68416	12270	312831	0.039223	2.6164	831585	0.0199	12.155	0.039068
70	0.281764	56145	15820	242087	0.065347	2.5575	518754	0.0199	9.239	0.065101
75	0.412575	40326	16637	159602	0.104243	2.4740	276666	0.0199	6.861	0.103865
80	0.580111	23688	13742	82693	0.166179	2.3986	117064	0.0199	4.942	0.165473
85+	*1.000000	9946	9946	34372	0.289381	3.4557	34372	0.0199	3.456	0.287000

TABLE 3 — FEMALE LIFE TABLE

x	nq_x	l_x	nd_x	nL_x	nm_x	na_x	T_x	r_x	$\overset{\circ}{e}_x$	nM_x
0	0.034479	100000	3448	97300	0.035435	0.2168	7156387	0.0000	71.564	0.035435
1	0.004843	96552	468	384843	0.001215	1.0789	7059087	0.0000	73.112	0.001215
5	0.001674	96084	161	480020	0.000335	2.5000	6674245	0.0000	69.462	0.000335
10	0.001385	95924	133	479305	0.000277	2.6446	6194224	0.0000	64.575	0.000277
15	0.002642	95791	253	478349	0.000529	2.6073	5714919	0.0188	59.660	0.000528
20	0.002754	95538	263	477052	0.000552	2.5805	5236570	0.0112	54.812	0.000551
25	0.003723	95275	355	475526	0.000746	2.6113	4759518	0.0020	49.956	0.000746
30	0.004768	94920	453	473544	0.000956	2.6674	4283992	0.0000	45.133	0.000956
35	0.007604	94467	718	470675	0.001526	2.6870	3810448	0.0000	40.336	0.001526
40	0.011705	93749	1097	466192	0.002354	2.6731	3339773	0.0408	35.625	0.002337
45	0.017592	92652	1630	459444	0.003548	2.6600	2873581	0.0055	31.015	0.003544
50	0.025806	91022	2349	449687	0.005223	2.6920	2414137	0.0000	26.523	0.005223
55	0.042793	88673	3795	434615	0.008731	2.6943	1964450	0.0131	22.154	0.008707
60	0.069369	84878	5888	410866	0.014330	2.7030	1529835	0.0237	18.024	0.014251
65	0.120657	78990	9531	372890	0.025559	2.6852	1118968	0.0237	14.166	0.025414
70	0.206721	69460	14359	313350	0.045823	2.6357	746079	0.0237	10.741	0.045572
75	0.342753	55101	18886	229223	0.082391	2.5495	432729	0.0237	7.853	0.081973
80	0.520284	36215	18842	132408	0.142303	2.4833	203505	0.0237	5.619	0.141661
85+	1.000000	17373	17373	71098	0.244352	4.0925	71098	0.0237	4.092	0.236281

TABLE 4 — OBSERVED AND PROJECTED VITAL RATES

	OBSERVED POPULATION BOTH SEXES	MALES	FEMALES	PROJECTED POPULATION 1970 MALES	FEMALES	1975 MALES	FEMALES	1980 MALES	FEMALES	STABLE POPULATION MALES	FEMALES
RATES PER THOUSAND											
Birth	13.11	13.99	12.28	14.49	12.75	15.17	13.41	14.46	12.85	11.43	10.5
Death	10.65	11.32	10.04	12.00	11.04	12.66	11.90	13.24	12.69	18.51	17.5
Increase	2.45	2.68	2.24	2.49	1.71	2.50	1.51	1.21	0.15		-7.081
PERCENTAGE											
under 15	23.28	24.68	21.96	21.58	19.20	20.21	18.04	20.54	18.45	17.20	15.9
15-64	66.38	66.43	66.33	68.47	67.79	68.86	67.66	67.91	66.19	66.83	64.1
65 and over	10.35	8.89	11.71	9.95	13.01	10.93	14.30	11.54	15.37	15.97	19.8
DEP. RATIO X 100	50.65	50.54	50.76	46.06	47.51	45.22	47.81	47.24	51.09	49.63	55.8

AGE AT LAST BIRTHDAY	1970 BOTH SEXES	1970 MALES	1970 FEMALES	1975 BOTH SEXES	1975 MALES	1975 FEMALES	1980 BOTH SEXES	1980 MALES	1980 FEMALES	AGE AT LAST BIRTHDAY	
0-4	654	336	318	689	354	335	695	357	338	0-4	
5-9	641	329	312	651	334	317	686	352	334	5-9	
10-14	794	407	387	639	328	311	649	333	316	10-14	
15-19	919	469	450	793	406	387	638	327	311	15-19	**TABLE 5**
20-24	798	405	393	916	467	449	789	403	386	20-24	POPULATION
25-29	742	371	371	794	402	392	910	463	447	25-29	PROJECTED
30-34	676	327	349	737	368	369	788	398	390	30-34	WITH
35-39	703	343	360	669	323	346	731	364	367	35-39	FIXED
40-44	736	358	378	694	338	356	662	319	343	40-44	AGE—
45-49	735	349	386	723	350	373	682	331	351	45-49	SPECIFIC
50-54	455	212	243	715	337	378	704	339	365	50-54	BIRTH
55-59	644	298	346	435	200	235	684	319	365	55-59	AND
60-64	585	269	316	597	270	327	404	182	222	60-64	DEATH
65-69	474	214	260	517	230	287	528	231	297	65-69	RATES
70-74	353	148	205	384	165	219	419	178	241	70-74	(IN 1000's)
75-79	205	78	127	247	97	150	269	109	160	75-79	
80-84	103	38	65	114	41	73	137	50	87	80-84	
85+	48	16	32	51	16	35	56	17	39	85+	
TOTAL	10265	4967	5298	10365	5026	5339	10431	5072	5359	TOTAL	

STANDARD COUNTRIES:	ENGLAND AND WALES 1961			UNITED STATES 1960			MEXICO 1960				
STANDARDIZED RATES PER THOUSAND	BOTH SEXES	MALES	FEMALES	BOTH SEXES	MALES	FEMALES	BOTH SEXES	MALES	FEMALES		**TABLE 6**
Birth	11.44	13.15*	10.73	11.63	12.30*	11.10	14.52	11.69*	14.03		STANDAR-
Death	12.77	12.47*	12.93	10.47	11.02*	9.55	5.69	9.70*	4.82		DIZED
Increase	-1.33	0.68*	-2.20	1.16	1.28*	1.55	8.83	1.99*	9.20		RATES

	OBSERVED POP. MALES	OBSERVED POP. FEMALES	STATIONARY POP. MALES	STATIONARY POP. FEMALES	STABLE POP. MALES	STABLE POP. FEMALES	OBSERVED BIRTHS	NET MATERNITY FUNCTION	BIRTHS IN STABLE POP.	
μ	33.77687	36.13232	36.54951	38.38936	40.07497	42.17676	25.57957	25.64812	25.86516	**TABLE 7**
σ^2	451.2250	479.0600	492.2528	530.5402	501.3617	536.6326	29.08771	28.12595	29.00886	MOMENTS
κ_3	3116.560	2469.081	2168.345	1924.191	383.345	-217.508	130.7296	123.2678	126.0584	AND
κ_4	-187969.	-226802.	-240534.	-292967.	-258261.	-304814.	375.249	417.137	380.253	CUMULANTS
β_1	0.105723	0.055450	0.039418	0.024794	0.001166	0.000306	0.694415	0.682933	0.650955	
β_2	2.076790	2.011749	2.007343	1.959166	1.972561	1.941525	3.443507	3.527309	3.451868	
κ	-0.039407	-0.020619	-0.014847	-0.009109	-0.000444	-0.000114	-0.515401	-0.606677	-0.544685	

VITAL STATISTICS		THOMPSON				BOURGEOIS-PICHAT					COALE	**TABLE 8**
		AGE RANGE	NRR	1000r	INTERVAL	AGE RANGE	NRR	1000b	1000d	1000r		RATES
GRR	0.876										IBR	FROM AGE
NRR	0.833	0-4	0.82	-7.21	27.43	5-29	1.22	17.72	10.22	7.50	IDR	DISTRI- BUTIONS
TFR	1.808	5-9	1.08	2.93	27.39	30-54	1.19	18.66	12.13	6.53	IRI	AND VITAL
GENERATION	25.756	10-14	1.26	8.31	27.34	55-79	1.77	50.03	28.88	21.15	K1	STATISTICS
SEX RATIO	106.516	15-19	1.09	3.22	27.26	*20-44	0.87	12.75	17.72	-4.97	K2	(Females)

Start of Age Interval	ORIGINAL MATRIX SUB-DIAGONAL	ORIGINAL MATRIX ALTERNATIVE FIRST ROWS Projection	ORIGINAL MATRIX ALTERNATIVE FIRST ROWS Integral	FIRST STABLE MATRIX % IN STABLE POPULATION	FIRST STABLE MATRIX FISHER VALUES	FIRST STABLE MATRIX REPRODUCTIVE VALUES	SECOND STABLE MATRIX Z_2 FIRST COLUMN	SECOND STABLE MATRIX Z_2 FIRST ROW	
0	0.99560	0.00000	0.00000	5.157	1.019	318904	0.1929+0.0762	0.1929+0.0762	**TABLE 9**
5	0.99851	0.00024	0.00000	5.319	0.988	383266	0.1812-0.1970	-0.0014+0.1607	LESLIE
10	0.99800	0.04911	0.00047	5.503	0.955	430545	-0.1537-0.3105	-0.1163+0.0436	MATRIX
15	0.99729	0.22096	0.09623	5.689	0.873	344027	-0.4463+0.0413	-0.0732-0.0755	AND ITS
20	0.99680	0.28952	0.33885	5.878	0.619	230406	-0.1575+0.5576	-0.0086-0.0907	SPECTRAL
25	0.99583	0.17300	0.23076	6.070	0.304	106343	0.5992+0.4488	0.0071-0.0535	COMPO-
30	0.99394	0.07693	0.10963	6.263	0.118	42535	0.8187-0.5137	0.0072-0.0230	NENTS
35	0.99047	0.02672	0.04178	6.449	0.035	13467	-0.2387-1.2222	0.0037-0.0071	(Females)
40	0.98553	0.00598	0.01083	6.618	0.007	2692	-1.5746-0.2778	0.0010-0.0013	
45	0.97876	0.00049	0.00093	6.757	0.001	135	-1.0540+1.7497	0.0001-0.0001	
50	0.96648	0.00002	0.00004	6.851	0.000	7	1.5913+2.0457	0.0000-0.0000	
55+	0.76726			33.446					

Start of Age Interval	OBSERVED POPUL. (IN 100's)	CONTRIBUTIONS OF ROOTS (IN 100's) r_1	r_2, r_3	$r_4 \cdot r_{11}$	AGE-SP. BIRTH RATES	NET MATERNITY FUNCTION	COEFF. OF MATRIX EQUATION	PARAMETERS INTEGRAL	PARAMETERS MATRIX	EXP. INCREASE x	$e^{(x+8\frac{1}{4})r}$	
0	3130	3546	-354	-62	0.0000	0.0000	0.0000	L(1) 0.96521	0.96524	0	0.9825	**TABLE 10**
5	3880	3658	125	97	0.0000	0.0000	0.0002	L(2) 0.26337	0.27718	50	0.6895	
10	4510	3784	708	18	0.0001	0.0005	0.0488	0.75139	0.71990	55	0.6655	AGE
15	3940	3912	449	-421	0.0203	0.0972	0.2192	R(1) -0.00708	-0.00708	60	0.6424	ANALYSIS
20	3720	4042	-767	445	0.0715	0.3413	0.2865	R(2) -0.04558	-0.05190	65	0.6200	AND
25	3500	4174	-1462	788	0.0487	0.2317	0.1706	0.24673	0.24065	70	0.5985	MISCEL-
30	3620	4307	-77	-610	0.0231	0.1096	0.0756	C(1)	68767	75	0.5776	LANEOUS
35	3820	4435	2361	-2976	0.0088	0.0415	0.0261	C(2)	-58172	80	0.5576	RESULTS
40	3920	4551	2306	-2936	0.0023	0.0107	0.0058		85248	85	0.5382	(Females)
45	2480	4646	-1757	-409	0.0002	0.0009	0.0005			90	0.5194	
50	3580	4711	-5339	4208	0.0000	0.0000	0.0000	2P/Y 25.4654	26.1088	95	0.5014	
55+	12350	23000						DELTA 11.9597		100	0.4839	

AGE AT LAST BIRTHDAY	POPULATION BOTH SEXES	MALES Number	%	FEMALES Number	%	BIRTHS BY AGE OF MOTHER	DEATHS BOTH SEXES	MALES	FEMALES	AGE AT LAST BIRTHDAY
0	2473	1283	2.8	1190	2.5	0	219	114	105	0
1-4	8685	4463	9.7	4222	8.7	0	116	58	58	1-4
5-9	10383	5237	11.4	5146	10.7	0	30	16	14	5-9
10-14	9684	5001	10.9	4683	9.7	0	20	9	11	10-14
15-19	8970	4623	10.1	4347	9.0	65	47	23	24	15-19
20-24	8235	4107	9.0	4128	8.6	520	64	34	30	20-24
25-29	7696	3790	8.3	3906	8.1	807	64	36	28	25-29
30-34	5961	2912	6.3	3049	6.3	597	53	29	24	30-34
35-39	5096	2463	5.4	2633	5.5	418	32	18	14	35-39
40-44	4852	2290	5.0	2562	5.3	204	31	18	13	40-44
45-49	4347	2021	4.4	2326	4.8	16	39	26	13	45-49
50-54	4039	1824	4.0	2215	4.6	0	50	28	22	50-54
55-59	4059	1857	4.0	2202	4.6	0	60	32	28	55-59
60-64	3133	1392	3.0	1741	3.6	0	67	38	29	60-64
65-69	2728	1180	2.6	1548	3.2	0	88	42	46	65-69
70-74	1745	712	1.6	1033	2.1		88	37	51	70-74
75-79	1136	413	0.9	723	1.5		109	53	56	75-79
80-84	582	203	0.4	379	0.8	1376 M.	83	32	51	80-84
85+	355	109	0.2	246	0.5	1251 F.	100	35	65	85+
TOTAL	94159	45880		48279		2627	1360	678	682	TOTAL

TABLE 1 DATA

TABLE 2 — MALE LIFE TABLE

x	nq_x	l_x	nd_x	nL_x	nm_x	na_x	T_x	r_x	$\dot{e}_x$	nM_x
0	0.083744	100000	8374	94698	0.088433	0.3669	5330986	0.0072	53.310	0.088854
1	0.050011	91626	4582	353911	0.012947	1.2522	5236288	0.0072	57.149	0.012996
5	0.015075	87043	1312	431936	0.003038	2.5000	4882377	0.0089	56.091	0.003055
10	0.008980	85731	770	426895	0.001803	2.7127	4450441	0.0097	51.912	0.001800
15	0.024698	84961	2098	420102	0.004995	2.7579	4023546	0.0147	47.357	0.004975
20	0.040641	82863	3368	406228	0.008290	2.5986	3603444	0.0120	43.487	0.008279
25	0.046441	79495	3692	388311	0.009507	2.5174	3197216	0.0249	40.219	0.009499
30	0.048485	75803	3675	369598	0.009944	2.4372	2808905	0.0338	37.055	0.009959
35	0.035829	72128	2584	353974	0.007301	2.4203	2439307	0.0161	33.819	0.007308
40	0.038640	69544	2687	341333	0.007873	2.6235	2085333	0.0110	29.986	0.007860
45	0.062474	66857	4177	324247	0.012881	2.5972	1744000	0.0105	26.086	0.012865
50	0.073949	62680	4635	301943	0.015351	2.5283	1419753	0.0000	22.651	0.015351
55	0.082818	58045	4807	278665	0.017251	2.5954	1117810	0.0080	19.258	0.017232
60	0.128404	53238	6836	249684	0.027378	2.5857	839145	0.0207	15.762	0.027299
65	0.164168	46402	7618	213422	0.035693	2.5600	589461	0.0207	12.703	0.035593
70	0.232851	38784	9031	172774	0.052270	2.6585	376039	0.0207	9.696	0.051966
75	0.486981	29753	14489	112409	0.128897	2.4908	203265	0.0207	6.832	0.128329
80	0.549660	15264	8390	53129	0.157918	2.3109	90856	0.0207	5.952	0.157636
85+	1.000000	6874	6874	37727	0.182200	5.4885	37727	0.0207	5.488	0.321101

TABLE 3 — FEMALE LIFE TABLE

x	nq_x	l_x	nd_x	nL_x	nm_x	na_x	T_x	r_x	$\dot{e}_x$	nM_x
0	0.083351	100000	8335	94773	0.087948	0.3729	5671539	0.0050	56.715	0.088235
1	0.052832	91665	4843	353413	0.013703	1.2648	5576766	0.0050	60.839	0.013738
5	0.013421	86822	1165	431197	0.002702	2.5000	5223352	0.0094	60.162	0.002721
10	0.011722	85657	1004	426013	0.002357	2.7376	4792155	0.0137	55.946	0.002349
15	0.027292	84653	2310	417891	0.005529	2.6746	4366142	0.0074	51.577	0.005521
20	0.035704	82342	2940	404464	0.007269	2.5345	3948251	0.0038	47.949	0.007267
25	0.035224	79402	2797	390022	0.007171	2.5008	3543787	0.0229	44.631	0.007168
30	0.038523	76606	2951	375469	0.007860	2.4387	3153764	0.0323	41.169	0.007871
35	0.026186	73655	1929	363210	0.005310	2.3754	2778295	0.0116	37.721	0.005317
40	0.025055	71726	1797	354137	0.005075	2.5003	2415085	0.0073	33.671	0.005074
45	0.027623	69929	1932	345127	0.005597	2.6620	2060948	0.0081	29.472	0.005589
50	0.048519	67997	3299	332167	0.009932	2.6303	1715821	0.0000	25.234	0.009932
55	0.061756	64698	3995	313831	0.012731	2.5826	1383654	0.0112	21.386	0.012716
60	0.080461	60702	4884	292091	0.016721	2.6616	1069823	0.0193	17.624	0.016657
65	0.139438	55818	7783	260830	0.029840	2.6538	777732	0.0193	13.933	0.029716
70	0.221288	48035	10630	214522	0.049550	2.5866	516902	0.0193	10.761	0.049371
75	0.326203	37405	12202	156941	0.077747	2.5343	302380	0.0193	8.084	0.077455
80	0.501406	25204	12637	93567	0.135061	2.5060	145439	0.0193	5.771	0.134565
85+	1.000000	12566	12566	51872	0.242258	4.1278	51872	0.0193	4.128	0.264227

TABLE 4 — OBSERVED AND PROJECTED VITAL RATES

	OBSERVED POPULATION BOTH SEXES	MALES	FEMALES	PROJECTED POPULATION 1925 MALES	FEMALES	1930 MALES	FEMALES	1935 MALES	FEMALES	STABLE POPULATION MALES	FEMALES
RATES PER THOUSAND											
Birth	27.90	29.99	25.91	30.08	26.43	29.84	26.58	29.33	26.45	26.96	25.84
Death	14.44	14.78	14.13	15.17	14.09	15.25	14.30	15.24	14.36	15.47	14.35
Increase	13.46	15.21	11.79	14.91	12.34	14.59	12.28	14.08	12.09		11.4854
PERCENTAGE											
under 15	33.16	34.84	31.57	34.57	31.45	34.75	31.24	35.00	31.52	32.41	31.01
15-64	59.89	59.46	60.29	59.49	60.31	58.96	60.09	58.89	59.89	60.75	60.38
65 and over	6.95	5.70	8.14	5.95	8.24	6.29	8.66	6.11	8.59	6.85	8.61
DEP. RATIO X 100	66.98	68.19	65.86	68.11	65.80	69.61	66.41	69.80	66.96	64.62	65.62

TABLE 5 — POPULATION PROJECTED WITH FIXED AGE-SPECIFIC BIRTH AND DEATH RATES (IN 1000's)

AGE AT LAST BIRTHDAY	1925 BOTH SEXES	1925 MALES	1925 FEMALES	1930 BOTH SEXES	1930 MALES	1930 FEMALES	1935 BOTH SEXES	1935 MALES	1935 FEMALES	AGE AT LAST BIRTHDAY
0-4	12	6	6	13	7	6	14	7	7	0-4
5-9	11	6	5	12	6	6	13	7	6	5-9
10-14	10	5	5	10	5	5	12	6	6	10-14
15-19	10	5	5	10	5	5	10	5	6	15-19
20-24	8	4	4	9	5	4	10	5	5	20-24
25-29	8	4	4	8	4	4	9	5	4	25-29
30-34	8	4	4	8	4	4	8	4	4	30-34
35-39	6	3	3	7	3	4	8	4	4	35-39
40-44	5	2	3	6	3	3	7	3	4	40-44
45-49	4	2	2	5	2	3	6	3	3	45-49
50-54	4	2	2	4	2	2	4	2	2	50-54
55-59	4	2	2	4	2	2	4	2	2	55-59
60-64	4	2	2	4	2	2	4	2	2	60-64
65-69	3	1	2	3	1	2	3	1	2	65-69
70-74	2	1	1	2	1	1	3	1	2	70-74
75-79	1	0	1	2	1	1	2	1	1	75-79
80-84	0	0	0	0	0	0	1	0	1	80-84
85+	0	0	0	0	0	0	0	0	0	85+
TOTAL	100	49	51	107	53	54	118	58	60	TOTAL

TABLE 6 — STANDARDIZED RATES

STANDARD COUNTRIES:

STANDARDIZED RATES PER THOUSAND

	ENGLAND AND WALES 1961 BOTH SEXES	MALES	FEMALES	UNITED STATES 1960 BOTH SEXES	MALES	FEMALES	MEXICO 1960 BOTH SEXES	MALES	FEMALES
Birth	25.47	27.59*	23.51	25.87	25.23*	24.27	26.04	26.53*	24.73
Death	18.13	22.84*	18.02	16.29	19.53*	15.25	12.36	13.52*	11.52
Increase	7.34	4.74*	5.49	9.58	5.70*	9.02	13.68	13.00*	13.21

TABLE 7 — MOMENTS AND CUMULANTS

	OBSERVED POP. MALES	OBSERVED POP. FEMALES	STATIONARY POP. MALES	STATIONARY POP. FEMALES	STABLE POP. MALES	STABLE POP. FEMALES	OBSERVED BIRTHS	NET MATERNITY FUNCTION	BIRTHS IN STABLE POP.
μ	27.30559	29.90707	34.30100	36.21469	28.94811	30.42785	30.27693	31.16380	30.67713
σ^2	412.5003	466.5690	491.7091	528.2339	436.8603	474.6596	39.12994	40.57070	39.98013
κ_3	5898.640	5966.694	3740.539	3294.824	5592.483	5790.056	84.0952	44.1887	58.4394
κ_4	-70210.	-137988.	-215960.	-276494.	-103174.	-150366.	-980.691	-1288.609	-1178.249
β_1	0.495714	0.350526	0.117691	0.073652	0.375130	0.313486	0.118036	0.029241	0.053442
β_2	2.587380	2.366118	2.106782	2.009091	2.459387	2.332601	2.359508	2.217119	2.262862
κ	-0.188789	-0.129321	-0.044419	-0.026836	-0.145397	-0.116747	-0.057068	-0.013704	-0.025462

TABLE 8 — RATES FROM AGE DISTRIBUTIONS AND VITAL STATISTICS (Females)

VITAL STATISTICS		THOMPSON AGE RANGE	NRR	1000r	INTERVAL	BOURGEOIS-PICHAT AGE RANGE	NRR	1000b	1000d	1000r	COALE	
GRR	1.878											
NRR	1.426	0-4	1.35	11.25	27.03	5-29	1.26	25.69	17.19	8.50	IBR	26.88
TFR	3.943	5-9	1.43	13.41	27.03	30-54	1.29	22.13	12.79	9.34	IDR	14.21
GENERATION	30.922	10-14	1.42	12.90	27.05	55-79	1.84	53.17	30.50	22.67	IRI	12.66
SEX RATIO	109.992	15-19	1.45	13.07	27.01	* 5-29	1.26	25.69	17.19	8.50	K1	0.
											K2	0.

TABLE 9 — LESLIE MATRIX AND ITS SPECTRAL COMPONENTS (Females)

Start of Age Interval	ORIGINAL MATRIX SUB-DIAGONAL	ALTERNATIVE FIRST ROWS Projection	ALTERNATIVE FIRST ROWS Integral	FIRST STABLE MATRIX % IN STABLE POPULATION	FISHER VALUES	REPRODUCTIVE VALUES	SECOND STABLE MATRIX Z2 FIRST COLUMN	SECOND STABLE MATRIX Z2 FIRST ROW
0	0.96209	0.00000	0.00000	11.257	1.148	6211	0.1364+0.0542	0.1364+0.0542
5	0.98798	0.00000	0.00000	10.225	1.263	6502	0.1304-0.0892	0.0291+0.1332
10	0.98094	0.01565	0.00000	9.538	1.355	6343	-0.0012-0.1747	-0.0852+0.0892
15	0.96787	0.14607	0.03284	8.833	1.444	6278	-0.1597-0.1061	-0.1129-0.0198
20	0.96430	0.34703	0.27669	8.072	1.407	5810	-0.1919+0.0792	-0.0637-0.1049
25	0.96269	0.42163	0.45380	7.349	1.133	4425	-0.0449+0.2195	-0.0015-0.1227
30	0.96735	0.37283	0.43007	6.679	0.744	2267	0.1691+0.1722	0.0340-0.0885
35	0.97502	0.25226	0.34870	6.100	0.372	979	0.2569-0.0476	0.0328-0.0406
40	0.97456	0.09168	0.17489	5.615	0.107	274	0.1136-0.2614	0.0123-0.0099
45	0.96245	0.00735	0.01416	5.167	0.008	20	-0.1672-0.2620	0.0010-0.0008
50	0.94480	0.00048	0.00099	4.695	0.001	1	-0.3346-0.0084	0.0001-0.0000
55+	0.78987			16.470				

TABLE 10 — AGE ANALYSIS AND MISCELLANEOUS RESULTS (Females)

Start of Age Interval	OBSERVED POPUL. (IN 100's)	CONTRIBUTIONS OF ROOTS (IN 100's) r_1	r_2, r_3	r_4-r_{11}	AGE-SP. BIRTH RATES	NET MATERNITY FUNCTION	COEFF. OF MATRIX EQUATION	PARAMETERS	INTEGRAL	MATRIX	EXP. INCREASE x	$e^{(x+2\frac{1}{2})r}$
0	54	56	-1	-1	0.0000	0.0000	0.0000	L(1)	1.05911	1.05918	0	1.0291
5	51	51	-1	2	0.0000	0.0000	0.0000	L(2)	0.49949	0.49947	50	1.8276
10	47	47	0	-1	0.0000	0.0000	0.0149		0.75814	0.74107	55	1.9356
15	43	44	1	-1	0.0071	0.0298	0.1362	R(1)	0.01149	0.01150	60	2.0500
20	41	40	1	0	0.0600	0.2426	0.3132	R(2)	-0.01933	-0.02248	65	2.1712
25	39	36	-0	3	0.0984	0.3837	0.3669			0.19765	0.19555	70	2.2995
30	30	33	-1	-1	0.0932	0.3501	0.3123	C(1)		495	75	2.4354
35	26	30	-2	-2	0.0756	0.2746	0.2044	C(2)		-310	80	2.5794
40	26	28	-0	-2	0.0379	0.1343	0.0728			76	85	2.7318
45	23	26	1	-4	0.0033	0.0113	0.0057	2P/Y	31.7901	32.1309	90	2.8933
50	22	23	2	-3	0.0000	0.0000	0.0000	DELTA	2.5205		95	3.0643
55+	79	81									100	3.2454

TABLE 1 — DATA

AGE AT LAST BIRTHDAY	POPULATION BOTH SEXES	MALES Number	MALES %	FEMALES Number	FEMALES %	BIRTHS BY AGE OF MOTHER	DEATHS BOTH SEXES	DEATHS MALES	FEMALES	AGE AT LAST BIRTHDAY
0	3974	2111	2.9	1863	2.6	0	89	44	45	0
1-4	14110	7259	10.1	6851	9.6	0	19	11	8	1-4
5-9	14270	7250	10.1	7020	9.9	0	13	10	3	5-9
10-14	11257	5724	8.0	5533	7.8	0	8	6	2	10-14
15-19	12229	6204	8.7	6025	8.5	409	11	8	3	15-19
20-24	12322	6252	8.7	6070	8.5	1143	17	15	2	20-24
25-29	11068	5693	8.0	5375	7.6	1088	25	19	6	25-29
30-34	9901	5068	7.1	4833	6.8	786	22	15	7	30-34
35-39	9122	4576	6.4	4546	6.4	472	29	15	14	35-39
40-44	8280	4258	5.9	4022	5.7	186	35	21	14	40-44
45-49	7577	3843	5.4	3734	5.3	9	42	25	17	45-49
50-54	6897	3426	4.8	3471	4.9	0	44	23	21	50-54
55-59	6378	3106	4.3	3272	4.6	0	56	32	24	55-59
60-64	4532	2163	3.0	2369	3.3	0	80	51	29	60-64
65-69	3587	1647	2.3	1940	2.7	0	81	46	35	65-69
70-74	2924	1285	1.8	1639	2.3		125	66	59	70-74
75-79	2111	911	1.3	1200	1.7		135	62	73	75-79
80-84	1255	503	0.7	752	1.1	2152 M.	143	59	84	80-84
85+	890	299	0.4	591	0.8	1941 F.	148	57	91	85+
TOTAL	142684	71578		71106		4093	1122	585	537	TOTAL

TABLE 2 — MALE LIFE TABLE

x	nq_x	l_x	nd_x	nL_x	nm_x	na_x	T_x	r_x	$\mathring{e}_x$	nM_x	x
0	0.020327	100000	2033	98574	0.020621	0.2984	6871262	0.0141	68.713	0.020843	0
1	0.005977	97967	586	390199	0.001501	1.1478	6772688	0.0141	69.132	0.001515	1
5	0.006852	97382	667	485240	0.001375	2.5000	6382489	0.0480	65.541	0.001379	5
10	0.005226	96714	505	482299	0.001048	2.4799	5897248	0.0144	60.976	0.001048	10
15	0.006429	96209	618	479632	0.001289	2.7143	5414950	0.0000	56.283	0.001289	15
20	0.011943	95591	1142	475296	0.002402	2.6726	4935318	0.0062	51.630	0.002399	20
25	0.016561	94449	1564	468381	0.003340	2.5297	4460023	0.0179	47.222	0.003337	25
30	0.014688	92885	1364	460998	0.002959	2.4888	3991642	0.0187	42.974	0.002960	30
35	0.016291	91520	1491	454049	0.003284	2.6165	3530644	0.0139	38.578	0.003278	35
40	0.024415	90030	2198	444928	0.004940	2.6254	3076596	0.0125	34.173	0.004932	40
45	0.032044	87831	2814	432249	0.006511	2.5455	2631668	0.0156	29.963	0.006505	45
50	0.033088	85017	2813	418338	0.006724	2.6015	2199419	0.0140	25.870	0.006713	50
55	0.050904	82204	4185	401794	0.010415	2.7952	1781081	0.0335	21.667	0.010303	55
60	0.112057	78019	8743	369267	0.023676	2.6174	1379287	0.0255	17.679	0.023578	60
65	0.131496	69277	9110	324661	0.028059	2.6154	1010021	0.0255	14.579	0.027930	65
70	0.229144	60167	13787	267294	0.051580	2.5671	685360	0.0255	11.391	0.051362	70
75	0.292191	46380	13552	198281	0.068347	2.5192	418066	0.0255	9.014	0.068057	75
80	0.458021	32828	15036	127435	0.117990	2.5588	219784	0.0255	6.695	0.117297	80
85+	*1.000000	17792	17792	92350	0.192662	5.1904	92350	0.0255	5.190	0.190635	85+

TABLE 3 — FEMALE LIFE TABLE

x	nq_x	l_x	nd_x	nL_x	nm_x	na_x	T_x	r_x	$\mathring{e}_x$	nM_x	x
0	0.023591	100000	2359	98238	0.024014	0.2532	7383516	0.0075	73.835	0.024155	0
1	0.004614	97641	450	389259	0.001157	1.1046	7285278	0.0075	74.613	0.001168	1
5	0.002104	97190	205	485441	0.000421	2.5000	6896018	0.0448	70.954	0.000427	5
10	0.001807	96986	175	484499	0.000362	2.5430	6410577	0.0149	66.098	0.000361	10
15	0.002487	96811	241	483448	0.000498	2.4865	5926078	0.0000	61.213	0.000498	15
20	0.001653	96570	160	482513	0.000331	2.8894	5442630	0.0109	56.359	0.000329	20
25	0.005593	96410	539	480815	0.001121	2.7068	4960117	0.0218	51.448	0.001116	25
30	0.007249	95871	695	477810	0.001454	2.7755	4479302	0.0150	46.722	0.001448	30
35	0.015319	95176	1458	472428	0.003086	2.6321	4001493	0.0156	42.043	0.003080	35
40	0.017283	93718	1620	464670	0.003486	2.5795	3529064	0.0160	37.656	0.003481	40
45	0.022545	92098	2076	455523	0.004558	2.6070	3064394	0.0101	33.273	0.004553	45
50	0.029836	90022	2686	443622	0.006054	2.5844	2608871	0.0073	28.980	0.006050	50
55	0.036237	87336	3165	429256	0.007373	2.6538	2165249	0.0301	24.792	0.007335	55
60	0.059672	84171	5023	409075	0.012278	2.6543	1735993	0.0166	20.624	0.012241	60
65	0.086983	79149	6885	379994	0.018118	2.7123	1326917	0.0166	16.765	0.018041	65
70	0.166587	72264	12038	333131	0.036137	2.6583	946924	0.0166	13.104	0.035998	70
75	0.266194	60226	16032	262564	0.061059	2.5944	613793	0.0166	10.192	0.060833	75
80	0.436794	44194	19304	172270	0.112055	2.5956	351229	0.0166	7.947	0.111702	80
85+	1.000000	24890	24890	178959	0.139085	7.1899	178959	0.0166	7.190	0.153976	85+

TABLE 4 — OBSERVED AND PROJECTED VITAL RATES

	OBSERVED POPULATION BOTH SEXES	MALES	FEMALES	PROJECTED 1955 MALES	FEMALES	1960 MALES	FEMALES	1965 MALES	FEMALES	STABLE POP. MALES	FEMALES
RATES PER THOUSAND											
Birth	28.69	30.07	27.30	28.50	26.09	26.86	24.77	26.52	24.59	27.81	26.72
Death	7.86	8.17	7.55	8.30	7.72	8.31	7.63	8.37	7.67	7.86	6.77
Increase	20.82	21.89	19.75	20.20	18.37	18.54	17.14	18.15	16.92		19.9463
PERCENTAGE											
under 15	30.56	31.22	29.91	34.33	32.40	35.66	33.23	35.22	32.68	35.00	33.65
15-64	61.89	62.29	61.48	59.18	58.97	57.36	57.64	57.52	57.91	58.59	58.39
65 and over	7.55	6.49	8.61	6.49	8.63	6.98	9.13	7.26	9.40	6.41	7.96
DEP. RATIO X 100	61.58	60.53	62.65	68.97	69.57	74.33	73.50	73.85	72.67	70.67	71.25

TABLE 1 DATA

AGE AT LAST BIRTHDAY	POPULATION BOTH SEXES	MALES Number	%	FEMALES Number	%	BIRTHS BY AGE OF MOTHER	DEATHS BOTH SEXES	MALES	FEMALES	AGE AT LAST BIRTHDAY
0	4740	2452	2.8	2288	2.6	0	64	41	23	0
1-4	18230	9358	10.5	8872	10.2	0	23	14	9	1-4
5-9	20433	10521	11.8	9912	11.4	0	10	10	0	5-9
10-14	17850	9226	10.4	8624	9.9	2	8	5	3	10-14
15-19	14266	7177	8.1	7089	8.1	609	7	4	3	15-19
20-24	11671	5923	6.7	5748	6.6	1383	12	7	5	20-24
25-29	12087	6167	6.9	5920	6.8	1235	11	6	5	25-29
30-34	11813	6045	6.8	5768	6.6	918	14	10	4	30-34
35-39	10898	5606	6.3	5292	6.1	556	15	11	4	35-39
40-44	9622	4908	5.5	4714	5.4	199	24	19	5	40-44
45-49	8849	4432	5.0	4417	5.1	14	40	22	18	45-49
50-54	7973	4038	4.5	3935	4.5	0	53	34	19	50-54
55-59	7095	3590	4.0	3505	4.0	0	64	34	30	55-59
60-64	6292	3059	3.4	3233	3.7	0	86	50	36	60-64
65-69	5489	2624	3.0	2865	3.3	0	102	55	47	65-69
70-74	3727	1731	1.9	1996	2.3		117	49	68	70-74
75-79	2416	1066	1.2	1350	1.5		146	63	83	75-79
80-84	1563	631	0.7	932	1.1	2547 M.	186	75	111	80-84
85+	994	348	0.4	646	0.7	2369 F.	185	76	109	85+
TOTAL	176008	88902		87106		4916	1167	585	582	TOTAL

TABLE 2 MALE LIFE TABLE

x	nq_x	l_x	nd_x	nL_x	nm_x	na_x	T_x	r_x	$\dot{e}_x$	nM_x	x
0	0.016488	100000	1649	98881	0.016674	0.3212	7252686	0.0037	72.527	0.016721	0
1	0.005945	98351	585	391754	0.001493	1.1760	7153805	0.0037	72.737	0.001496	1
5	0.004720	97767	461	487679	0.000946	2.5000	6762051	0.0237	69.165	0.000950	5
10	0.002691	97305	262	485831	0.000539	2.3499	6274372	0.0376	64.481	0.000542	10
15	0.002812	97043	273	484598	0.000563	2.7358	5788541	0.0436	59.649	0.000557	15
20	0.005898	96770	571	482465	0.001183	2.5708	5303943	0.0142	54.810	0.001182	20
25	0.004853	96200	467	479876	0.000973	2.5976	4821478	0.0000	50.120	0.000973	25
30	0.008247	95733	790	476786	0.001656	2.6226	4341602	0.0080	45.351	0.001654	30
35	0.009809	94943	931	472600	0.001971	2.7281	3864816	0.0185	40.707	0.001962	35
40	0.019243	94012	1809	465815	0.003884	2.6539	3392216	0.0199	36.083	0.003871	40
45	0.024600	92203	2268	455740	0.004977	2.6752	2926401	0.0140	31.739	0.004964	45
50	0.041326	89935	3717	440743	0.008433	2.5973	2470661	0.0133	27.472	0.008420	50
55	0.046449	86218	4005	421657	0.009498	2.6447	2029918	0.0170	23.544	0.009471	55
60	0.079037	82213	6498	395566	0.016427	2.6146	1608261	0.0338	19.562	0.016345	60
65	0.100100	75715	7579	360175	0.021043	2.5721	1212696	0.0338	16.017	0.020960	65
70	0.133854	68136	9120	319517	0.028544	2.6795	852521	0.0338	12.512	0.028307	70
75	0.261572	59016	15437	258808	0.059646	2.6503	533004	0.0338	9.032	0.059099	75
80	0.464860	43579	20258	168892	0.119947	2.5811	274196	0.0338	6.292	0.118860	80
85+	*1.000000	23321	23321	105304	0.221462	4.5154	105304	0.0338	4.515	0.218391	85+

TABLE 3 FEMALE LIFE TABLE

x	nq_x	l_x	nd_x	nL_x	nm_x	na_x	T_x	r_x	$\dot{e}_x$	nM_x	x
0	0.009967	100000	997	99337	0.010034	0.3346	7593499	0.0025	75.935	0.010052	0
1	0.004039	99003	400	394892	0.001013	1.1951	7494163	0.0025	75.696	0.001014	1
5	0.	98603	0	493017	0.	-0.	7099271	0.0255	71.998	0.	5
10	0.001753	98603	173	492629	0.000351	2.7534	6606254	0.0332	66.998	0.000348	10
15	0.002136	98431	210	491680	0.000428	2.7519	6113626	0.0401	62.111	0.000423	15
20	0.004348	98220	427	490076	0.000871	2.5985	5621945	0.0173	57.238	0.000870	20
25	0.004214	97793	412	487918	0.000845	2.4545	5131869	0.0000	52.477	0.000845	25
30	0.003460	97381	337	486054	0.000693	2.4720	4643951	0.0105	47.688	0.000693	30
35	0.003780	97044	367	484342	0.000757	2.6023	4157897	0.0194	42.845	0.000756	35
40	0.005349	96677	517	482423	0.001072	3.1364	3673555	0.0164	37.998	0.001061	40
45	0.020242	96160	1946	476298	0.004087	2.6862	3191132	0.0146	33.186	0.004075	45
50	0.023953	94214	2257	465827	0.004845	2.6770	2714834	0.0176	28.816	0.004828	50
55	0.042020	91957	3864	450654	0.008574	2.6366	2249007	0.0114	24.457	0.008559	55
60	0.054388	88093	4791	429062	0.011167	2.6199	1798354	0.0196	20.414	0.011135	60
65	0.079488	83302	6622	401492	0.016492	2.7319	1369292	0.0196	16.438	0.016405	65
70	0.158618	76680	12163	355234	0.034239	2.6841	967800	0.0196	12.621	0.034068	70
75	0.269238	64517	17371	281181	0.061777	2.6163	612566	0.0196	9.495	0.061481	75
80	0.463657	47147	21860	182734	0.119627	2.5754	331385	0.0196	7.029	0.119099	80
85+	*1.000000	25287	25287	148651	0.170109	5.8786	148651	0.0196	5.879	0.168731	85+

TABLE 4 OBSERVED AND PROJECTED VITAL RATES

	OBSERVED POPULATION BOTH SEXES	MALES	FEMALES	PROJECTED POPULATION 1965 MALES	FEMALES	1970 MALES	FEMALES	1975 MALES	FEMALES	STABLE POPULATION MALES	FEMALES
RATES PER THOUSAND											
Birth	27.93	28.65	27.20	28.30	27.03	28.89	27.75	29.70	28.61	30.88	30.04
Death	6.63	6.58	6.68	6.74	6.65	6.95	6.57	7.17	6.63	5.89	5.05
Increase	21.30	22.07	20.52	21.56	20.38	21.94	21.18	22.53	21.98	24.9931	
PERCENTAGE											
under 15	34.80	35.50	34.09	35.65	34.53	35.69	34.72	35.98	35.02	37.70	37.06
15-64	57.14	57.30	56.97	56.68	56.38	56.37	56.36	56.08	56.26	56.45	56.55
65 and over	8.06	7.20	8.94	7.67	9.09	7.93	8.91	7.94	8.72	5.85	6.39
DEP. RATIO X 100	75.02	74.51	75.54	76.43	77.38	77.39	77.43	78.32	77.74	77.16	76.85

TABLE 1 — DATA

AGE AT LAST BIRTHDAY	POPULATION BOTH SEXES	MALES Number	%	FEMALES Number	%	BIRTHS BY AGE OF MOTHER	DEATHS BOTH SEXES	MALES	FEMALES	AGE AT LAST BIRTHDAY
0	4640	2380	2.6	2260	2.5	0	80	50	30	0
1-4	18689	9599	10.4	9090	10.1	0	21	13	8	1-4
5-9	21533	11105	12.0	10428	11.6	0	6	2	4	5-9
10-14	18951	9716	10.5	9235	10.2	2	5	3	2	10-14
15-19	15759	8079	8.8	7680	8.5	611	8	5	3	15-19
20-24	11908	6044	6.6	5864	6.5	1322	11	9	2	20-24
25-29	11619	5876	6.4	5743	6.4	1167	15	12	3	25-29
30-34	12142	6235	6.8	5907	6.5	869	20	13	7	30-34
35-39	11020	5628	6.1	5392	6.0	531	30	22	8	35-39
40-44	10158	5193	5.6	4965	5.5	194	30	20	10	40-44
45-49	9067	4574	5.0	4493	5.0	15	32	18	14	45-49
50-54	8170	4085	4.4	4085	4.5	0	54	35	19	50-54
55-59	7461	3800	4.1	3661	4.1	0	74	48	26	55-59
60-64	6276	3069	3.3	3207	3.6	0	66	44	22	60-64
65-69	5703	2732	3.0	2971	3.3	0	114	65	49	65-69
70-74	4164	1950	2.1	2214	2.5		135	67	68	70-74
75-79	2694	1192	1.3	1502	1.7		174	80	94	75-79
80-84	1487	626	0.7	861	1.0	2410 M.	151	71	80	80-84
85+	1044	366	0.4	678	0.8	2301 F.	210	71	139	85+
TOTAL	182485	92249		90236		4711	1236	648	588	TOTAL

TABLE 2 — MALE LIFE TABLE

x	$_nq_x$	l_x	$_nd_x$	$_nL_x$	$_nm_x$	$_na_x$	T_x	r_x	$\overset{\circ}{e}_x$	$_nM_x$	x
0	0.020698	100000	2070	98520	0.021008	0.2851	7144729	0.0000	71.447	0.021008	0
1	0.005396	97930	528	390206	0.001354	1.1335	7046209	0.0000	71.951	0.001354	1
5	0.000883	97402	86	486794	0.000177	2.5000	6656003	0.0204	68.336	0.000180	5
10	0.001558	97316	152	486246	0.000312	2.8022	6169209	0.0315	63.394	0.000309	10
15	0.003148	97164	306	485175	0.000630	2.8892	5682963	0.0467	58.488	0.000619	15
20	0.007464	96858	723	482624	0.001498	2.6933	5197788	0.0304	53.664	0.001489	20
25	0.010160	96135	977	478290	0.002042	2.5564	4715164	0.0000	49.047	0.002042	25
30	0.010378	95159	988	473501	0.002086	2.6791	4236874	0.0018	44.524	0.002085	30
35	0.019390	94171	1826	466451	0.003915	2.5883	3763373	0.0148	39.963	0.003909	35
40	0.019073	92345	1761	457311	0.003851	2.4939	3296922	0.0169	35.702	0.003851	40
45	0.019592	90584	1775	448894	0.003954	2.7321	2839610	0.0191	31.348	0.003935	45
50	0.042096	88809	3739	435417	0.008586	2.6921	2390716	0.0101	26.920	0.008568	50
55	0.061375	85070	5221	412679	0.012652	2.5728	1955300	0.0166	22.984	0.012632	55
60	0.069657	79849	5562	386005	0.014409	2.6194	1542621	0.0329	19.319	0.014337	60
65	0.113200	74287	8409	351451	0.023927	2.6235	1156615	0.0329	15.570	0.023792	65
70	0.160087	65878	10546	304622	0.034620	2.6516	805165	0.0329	12.222	0.034359	70
75	0.290647	55332	16082	237871	0.067608	2.5881	500542	0.0329	9.046	0.067114	75
80	0.442057	39250	17351	152092	0.114080	2.5698	262671	0.0329	6.692	0.113419	80
85+	1.000000	21899	21899	110579	0.198040	5.0495	110579	0.0329	5.049	0.193988	85+

TABLE 3 — FEMALE LIFE TABLE

x	$_nq_x$	l_x	$_nd_x$	$_nL_x$	$_nm_x$	$_na_x$	T_x	r_x	$\overset{\circ}{e}_x$	$_nM_x$	x
0	0.013150	100000	1315	99065	0.013274	0.2886	7652833	0.0000	76.528	0.013274	0
1	0.003512	98685	347	393748	0.000880	1.1371	7553768	0.0000	76.544	0.000880	1
5	0.001904	98338	187	491224	0.000381	2.5000	7160021	0.0201	72.810	0.000384	5
10	0.001083	98151	106	490491	0.000217	2.5091	6668797	0.0303	67.944	0.000217	10
15	0.001957	98045	192	489758	0.000392	2.5661	6178305	0.0451	63.015	0.000391	15
20	0.001708	97853	167	488861	0.000342	2.5785	5688548	0.0287	58.134	0.000341	20
25	0.002609	97686	255	487878	0.000522	2.8344	5199687	0.0000	53.229	0.000522	25
30	0.005914	97431	576	485811	0.001186	2.6672	4711810	0.0052	48.360	0.001185	30
35	0.007406	96855	717	482562	0.001486	2.6133	4225998	0.0158	43.632	0.001484	35
40	0.010050	96138	966	478430	0.002020	2.6636	3743436	0.0161	38.938	0.002014	40
45	0.015511	95171	1476	472415	0.003125	2.6687	3265006	0.0163	34.307	0.003116	45
50	0.023069	93695	2161	463431	0.004664	2.6660	2792591	0.0156	29.805	0.004651	50
55	0.034945	91534	3199	449847	0.007111	2.5550	2329160	0.0178	25.446	0.007102	55
60	0.034020	88335	3005	434920	0.006910	2.7522	1879312	0.0266	21.275	0.006860	60
65	0.080112	85330	6836	411296	0.016620	2.7541	1444393	0.0266	16.927	0.016493	65
70	0.144486	78494	11341	366512	0.030944	2.7112	1033097	0.0266	13.161	0.030714	70
75	0.273029	67153	18335	291395	0.062920	2.5801	666585	0.0266	9.926	0.062583	75
80	0.376738	48818	18392	197216	0.093256	2.6370	375190	0.0266	7.685	0.092916	80
85+	1.000000	30426	30426	177974	0.170960	5.8493	177974	0.0266	5.849	0.205015	85+

TABLE 4 — OBSERVED AND PROJECTED VITAL RATES

	OBSERVED POPULATION BOTH SEXES	MALES	FEMALES	PROJECTED POPULATION 1967 MALES	FEMALES	1972 MALES	FEMALES	1977 MALES	FEMALES	STABLE POPULATION MALES	FEMALES
RATES PER THOUSAND											
Birth	25.82	26.12	25.50	26.68	26.01	27.90	27.16	28.89	28.08	29.70	28.61
Death	6.77	7.02	6.52	7.30	6.69	7.55	6.86	7.66	6.90	6.48	5.39
Increase	19.04	19.10	18.98	19.38	19.31	20.35	20.29	21.23	21.18	23.2193	
PERCENTAGE											
under 15	34.97	35.56	34.37	34.98	33.94	34.44	33.65	34.61	33.93	36.65	35.6
15-64	56.76	57.00	56.52	57.24	56.77	57.51	57.03	57.46	56.88	57.23	57.1
65 and over	8.27	7.44	9.12	7.78	9.28	8.05	9.32	7.93	9.20	6.12	7.2
DEP. RATIO X 100	76.18	75.44	76.94	74.69	76.13	73.89	75.36	74.03	75.82	74.74	75.0

TABLE 5 — POPULATION PROJECTED WITH FIXED AGE-SPECIFIC BIRTH AND DEATH RATES (IN 1000's)

AGE AT LAST BIRTHDAY	1967 BOTH SEXES	1967 MALES	1967 FEMALES	1972 BOTH SEXES	1972 MALES	1972 FEMALES	1977 BOTH SEXES	1977 MALES	1977 FEMALES	AGE AT LAST BIRTHDAY
0-4	25	13	12	28	14	14	32	16	16	0-4
5-9	23	12	11	24	12	12	28	14	14	5-9
10-14	21	11	10	23	12	11	24	12	12	10-14
15-19	19	10	9	21	11	10	23	12	11	15-19
20-24	16	8	8	19	10	9	21	11	10	20-24
25-29	12	6	6	16	8	8	19	10	9	25-29
30-34	12	6	6	12	6	6	16	8	8	30-34
35-39	12	6	6	12	6	6	12	6	6	35-39
40-44	11	6	5	12	6	6	12	6	6	40-44
45-49	10	5	5	12	6	6	12	6	6	45-49
50-54	8	4	4	10	5	5	12	6	6	50-54
55-59	8	4	4	10	5	5	10	5	5	55-59
60-64	8	4	4	8	4	4	10	5	5	60-64
65-69	6	3	3	8	4	4	8	4	4	65-69
70-74	5	2	3	6	3	3	7	3	4	70-74
75-79	4	2	2	5	2	2	6	3	3	75-79
80-84	2	1	1	4	2	2	4	2	2	80-84
85+	1	0	1	2	1	1	2	1	1	85+
TOTAL	203	103	100	222	112	110	248	125	123	TOTAL

TABLE 6 — STANDARDIZED RATES

STANDARD COUNTRIES:

STANDARDIZED RATES PER THOUSAND	ENGLAND AND WALES 1961 BOTH SEXES	MALES	FEMALES	UNITED STATES 1960 BOTH SEXES	MALES	FEMALES	MEXICO 1960 BOTH SEXES	MALES	FEMALES
Birth	25.51	27.15*	24.15	25.99	25.44*	25.01	29.67	24.55*	28.91
Death	8.96	8.84*	9.24	7.25	7.81*	6.75	3.80	5.77*	3.15
Increase	16.55	18.31*	14.91	18.74	17.63*	18.27	25.86	18.77*	25.75

TABLE 7 — MOMENTS AND CUMULANTS

	OBSERVED POP. MALES	OBSERVED POP. FEMALES	STATIONARY POP. MALES	STATIONARY POP. FEMALES	STABLE POP. MALES	STABLE POP. FEMALES	OBSERVED BIRTHS	NET MATERNITY FUNCTION	BIRTHS IN STABLE POP.
μ	28.74776	29.90109	38.38780	40.09370	26.88966	27.87338	27.52441	28.02167	26.98435
σ^2	465.0548	500.4912	547.6964	576.6745	426.2431	455.4067	44.41893	44.20723	40.89694
κ_3	6114.334	6656.044	2594.090	2022.002	6811.124	7256.550	130.6160	131.3614	151.6598
κ_4	-138185.	-169689.	-304556.	-354401.	6811.124	7256.550	-1164.618	-1143.345	-599.283
β_1	0.371694	0.353381	0.040959	0.021319	-43203.	-67264.	0.194665	0.199736	0.336255
β_2	2.361070	2.322575	1.984716	1.934305	0.599054	0.557522	2.409735	2.414953	2.641697
κ	-0.133996	-0.125922	-0.015117	-0.007703	2.762205	2.675672	-0.089139	-0.091333	-0.162247
					-0.236489	-0.214203			

TABLE 8 — RATES FROM AGE DISTRIBUTIONS AND VITAL STATISTICS (Females)

VITAL STATISTICS

		THOMPSON AGE RANGE	NRR	1000r	INTERVAL	BOURGEOIS-PICHAT AGE RANGE	NRR	1000b	1000d	1000r	COALE
GRR	1.945										
NRR	1.894	0-4	1.89	23.84	27.44	5-29	2.41	30.33	-2.28	32.60	IBR
TFR	3.982	5-9	1.90	23.79	27.40	30-54	1.54	22.70	6.62	16.09	IDR
GENERATION	27.497	10-14	1.77	20.47	27.35	55-79	1.64	26.04	7.74	18.30	IRI
SEX RATIO	104.737	15-19	1.56	15.42	27.29	*30-59	1.54	22.66	6.62	16.03	K1
											K2

TABLE 9 — LESLIE MATRIX AND ITS SPECTRAL COMPONENTS (Females)

Start of Age Interval	ORIGINAL MATRIX SUB-DIAGONAL	ALTERNATIVE FIRST ROWS Projection	Integral	FIRST STABLE MATRIX % IN STABLE POPULATION	FISHER VALUES	REPRODUCTIVE VALUES	SECOND STABLE MATRIX Z_2 FIRST COLUMN	FIRST ROW
0	0.99678	0.00000	0.00000	13.324	1.075	12202	0.1363+0.1062	0.1363+0.1062
5	0.99851	0.00026	0.00000	11.821	1.212	12635	0.1848-0.0868	-0.0279+0.1435
10	0.99850	0.09587	0.00055	10.507	1.363	12587	0.0074-0.2417	-0.1188+0.0338
15	0.99817	0.36658	0.20294	9.338	1.430	10985	-0.2512-0.1373	-0.0839-0.0868
20	0.99799	0.51540	0.57509	8.297	1.215	7125	-0.2794+0.1916	-0.0168-0.1354
25	0.99576	0.42087	0.51835	7.370	0.813	4667	0.0526+0.3975	0.0252-0.1193
30	0.99331	0.29478	0.37527	6.532	0.462	2732	0.4466+0.1570	0.0422-0.0715
35	0.99144	0.16515	0.25121	5.776	0.204	1100	0.4030-0.3854	0.0299-0.0271
40	0.98743	0.05073	0.09967	5.097	0.052	259	-0.1896-0.6275	0.0094-0.0054
45	0.98098	0.00404	0.00795	4.480	0.004	18	-0.7556-0.1345	0.0008-0.0004
50	0.97069	0.00029	0.00062	3.912	0.000	1	-0.5373+0.7129	0.0001-0.0000
55+	0.84315			13.546				

TABLE 10 — AGE ANALYSIS AND MISCELLANEOUS RESULTS (Females)

Start of Age Interval	OBSERVED POPUL. (IN 100's)	CONTRIBUTIONS OF ROOTS (IN 100's) r_1	r_2, r_3	r_4-r_{11}	AGE-SP. BIRTH RATES	NET MATERNITY FUNCTION	COEFF. OF MATRIX EQUATION	PARAMETERS INTEGRAL	PARAMETERS MATRIX	EXP. INCREASE x	$e^{(x+2\frac{1}{2})r}$
0	114	111	0	2	0.0000	0.0000	0.0000	L(1) 1.12310	1.12346	0	1.0598
5	104	99	6	-1	0.0000	0.0000	0.0003	L(2) 0.36928	0.38166	50	3.3839
10	92	88	6	-1	0.0001	0.0005	0.0954	0.77440	0.75205	55	3.8004
15	77	78	-2	1	0.0389	0.1903	0.3643	R(1) 0.02322	0.02328	60	4.2683
20	59	69	-10	-0	0.1101	0.5383	0.5113	R(2) -0.03064	-0.03407	65	4.7937
25	57	62	-8	4	0.0993	0.4842	0.4167	0.22517	0.22023	70	5.3838
30	59	55	6	-1	0.0719	0.3491	0.2906	C(1)	837	75	6.0466
35	54	48	17	-12	0.0481	0.2321	0.1617	C(2)	1058	80	6.7910
40	50	43	11	-4	0.0191	0.0913	0.0495		1162	85	7.6270
45	45	37	-13	20	0.0016	0.0077	0.0039	2P/Y 27.9046	28.5296	90	8.5659
50	41	33	-28	36	0.0000	0.0000	0.0000	DELTA 4.8607		95	9.6204
55+	151	113								100	10.8047

TABLE 1 — DATA

AGE AT LAST BIRTHDAY	POPULATION BOTH SEXES	MALES Number	%	FEMALES Number	%	BIRTHS BY AGE OF MOTHER	DEATHS BOTH SEXES	MALES	FEMALES	AGE AT LAST BIRTHDAY
0	55474	28129	1.9	27345	1.9	0	4552	2538	2014	0
1-4	232666	118276	7.8	114390	7.8	0	2229	1138	1091	1-4
5-9	285056	144994	9.6	140062	9.5	0	784	363	421	5-9
10-14	295971	151053	10.0	144918	9.9	0	570	239	331	10-14
15-19	286612	146279	9.7	140333	9.6	655	963	452	511	15-19
20-24	240587	124715	8.3	115872	7.9	8254	1077	534	543	20-24
25-29	215720	106815	7.1	108905	7.4	17998	1098	520	578	25-29
30-34	183572	92649	6.1	90923	6.2	16744	1030	473	557	30-34
35-39	176020	87488	5.8	88532	6.0	11998	1135	518	617	35-39
40-44	169335	86186	5.7	83149	5.7	5527	1322	659	663	40-44
45-49	169144	87148	5.8	81996	5.6	0	1567	804	763	45-49
50-54	162960	85784	5.7	77176	5.3	0	2115	1079	1036	50-54
55-59	125900	67227	4.5	58673	4.0	0	2260	1189	1071	55-59
60-64	105302	53756	3.6	51546	3.5	0	2987	1535	1452	60-64
65-69	101362	51581	3.4	49781	3.4	0	3508	1795	1713	65-69
70-74	77340	35417	2.3	41923	2.9		4109	2019	2090	70-74
75-79	52290	23599	1.6	28691	2.0		4199	2034	2165	75-79
80-84	29334	13040	0.9	16294	1.1	31382 M.	3704	1767	1937	80-84
85+	11754	5143	0.3	6611	0.5	29794 F.	2531	1188	1343	85+
TOTAL	2976399	1509279		1467120		61176	41740	20844	20896	TOTAL

TABLE 2 — MALE LIFE TABLE

x	nq_x	l_x	nd_x	nL_x	nm_x	na_x	T_x	r_x	$\mathring{e}_x$	nM_x	x
0	0.085120	100000	8512	94339	0.090227	0.3350	5746954	0.0000	57.470	0.090227	0
1	0.037475	91488	3429	356338	0.009622	1.1958	5652615	0.0000	61.785	0.009622	1
5	0.012440	88059	1095	437559	0.002504	2.5000	5296277	0.0000	60.144	0.002504	5
10	0.007881	86964	685	433155	0.001582	2.5705	4858718	0.0000	55.870	0.001582	10
15	0.015385	86279	1327	428308	0.003099	2.6756	4425563	0.0162	51.294	0.003090	15
20	0.021239	84951	1804	420386	0.004292	2.5778	3997255	0.0273	47.053	0.004282	20
25	0.024072	83147	2002	410782	0.004873	2.5252	3576869	0.0249	43.019	0.004868	25
30	0.025224	81146	2047	400675	0.005108	2.5313	3166087	0.0147	39.017	0.005105	30
35	0.029188	79099	2309	389896	0.005921	2.5754	2765412	0.0011	34.962	0.005921	35
40	0.037535	76790	2882	376958	0.007646	2.5742	2375516	0.0000	30.935	0.007646	40
45	0.045125	73908	3335	361499	0.009226	2.5896	1998558	0.0000	27.041	0.009226	45
50	0.061164	70573	4317	342554	0.012601	2.6118	1637059	0.0131	23.197	0.012578	50
55	0.085294	66256	5651	317941	0.017774	2.6396	1294505	0.0278	19.538	0.017686	55
60	0.133729	60605	8105	283344	0.028603	2.5717	976563	0.0133	16.114	0.028555	60
65	0.160742	52500	8439	242017	0.034869	2.5727	693220	0.0133	13.204	0.034800	65
70	0.250768	44061	11049	193367	0.057141	2.5619	451203	0.0133	10.240	0.057007	70
75	0.355050	33012	11721	135683	0.086385	2.4936	257836	0.0133	7.810	0.086190	75
80	0.501934	21291	10687	78689	0.135811	2.4782	122153	0.0133	5.737	0.135506	80
85+	1.000000	10604	10604	43464	0.243981	4.0987	43464	0.0133	4.099	0.230993	85

TABLE 3 — FEMALE LIFE TABLE

x	nq_x	l_x	nd_x	nL_x	nm_x	na_x	T_x	r_x	$\mathring{e}_x$	nM_x	x
0	0.070316	100000	7032	95471	0.073651	0.3559	5785951	0.0000	57.860	0.073651	0
1	0.037169	92968	3456	362305	0.009538	1.2309	5690480	0.0000	61.209	0.009538	1
5	0.014917	89513	1335	444226	0.003006	2.5000	5328175	0.0000	59.524	0.003006	5
10	0.011357	88178	1001	438435	0.002284	2.5504	4883949	0.0000	55.388	0.002284	10
15	0.018097	87176	1578	432142	0.003651	2.6300	4445514	0.0188	50.995	0.003641	15
20	0.023202	85599	1986	423156	0.004693	2.5645	4013371	0.0207	46.886	0.004686	20
25	0.026223	83613	2193	412680	0.005313	2.5449	3590216	0.0189	42.939	0.005307	25
30	0.030201	81420	2459	401059	0.006131	2.5434	3177536	0.0146	39.026	0.006126	30
35	0.034262	78961	2705	388151	0.006970	2.5403	2776477	0.0019	35.163	0.006969	35
40	0.039102	76256	2982	373955	0.007974	2.5440	2388326	0.0000	31.320	0.007974	40
45	0.045510	73274	3335	358361	0.009305	2.5986	2014371	0.0000	27.491	0.009305	45
50	0.065206	69939	4560	338795	0.013461	2.6097	1656010	0.0200	23.678	0.013424	50
55	0.087751	65379	5737	313241	0.018315	2.6204	1317215	0.0210	20.147	0.018254	55
60	0.132055	59642	7876	279037	0.028226	2.5659	1003973	0.0165	16.833	0.028169	60
65	0.158947	51766	8228	238637	0.034479	2.5461	724936	0.0165	14.004	0.034411	65
70	0.222700	43538	9696	193980	0.049984	2.5548	486299	0.0165	11.170	0.049853	70
75	0.318539	33842	10780	142453	0.075673	2.5180	292319	0.0165	8.638	0.075459	75
80	0.460886	23062	10629	89081	0.119317	2.5324	149866	0.0165	6.498	0.118879	80
85+	*1.000000	12433	12433	60784	0.204543	4.8890	60784	0.0165	4.889	0.203146	85

TABLE 4 — OBSERVED AND PROJECTED VITAL RATES

	OBSERVED POPULATION BOTH SEXES	MALES	FEMALES	PROJECTED POPULATION 1931 MALES	FEMALES	1936 MALES	FEMALES	1941 MALES	FEMALES	STABLE POPULATION MALES	FEMALES
RATES PER THOUSAND											
Birth	20.55	20.79	20.31	21.71	21.28	22.87	22.49	23.47	23.15	21.63	21.49
Death	14.02	13.81	14.24	14.19	14.75	14.40	14.81	14.48	14.70	15.22	15.08
Increase	6.53	6.98	6.06	7.53	6.53	8.47	7.68	8.99	8.45		6.4110
PERCENTAGE											
under 15	29.20	29.32	29.09	27.68	27.57	27.31	27.28	27.75	27.76	27.26	27.48
15-64	61.66	62.15	61.15	63.83	62.90	64.16	63.69	63.29	63.13	63.39	62.84
65 and over	9.14	8.53	9.77	8.49	9.53	8.53	9.03	8.96	9.11	9.35	9.68
DEP. RATIO X 100	62.19	60.90	63.54	56.67	58.98	55.86	57.02	58.00	58.41	57.75	59.14

TABLE 5 — POPULATION PROJECTED WITH FIXED AGE-SPECIFIC BIRTH AND DEATH RATES (IN 1000's)

AGE AT LAST BIRTHDAY	1931 BOTH SEXES	1931 MALES	1931 FEMALES	1936 BOTH SEXES	1936 MALES	1936 FEMALES	1941 BOTH SEXES	1941 MALES	1941 FEMALES	AGE AT LAST BIRTHDAY
0-4	289	147	142	315	160	155	341	174	167	0-4
5-9	280	142	138	281	143	138	306	156	150	5-9
10-14	282	144	138	277	141	136	278	142	136	10-14
15-19	292	149	143	278	142	136	273	139	134	15-19
20-24	281	144	137	287	147	140	272	139	133	20-24
25-29	235	122	113	274	140	134	279	143	136	25-29
30-34	210	104	106	229	119	110	267	137	130	30-34
35-39	178	90	88	203	101	102	222	116	106	35-39
40-44	170	85	85	172	87	85	197	98	99	40-44
45-49	163	83	80	163	81	82	165	84	81	45-49
50-54	161	83	78	153	78	75	154	77	77	50-54
55-59	151	80	71	149	77	72	143	73	70	55-59
60-64	112	60	52	135	71	64	132	68	64	60-64
65-69	90	46	44	96	51	45	115	61	54	65-69
70-74	81	41	40	73	37	36	77	41	36	70-74
75-79	56	25	31	59	29	30	52	26	26	75-79
80-84	32	14	18	33	14	19	36	17	19	80-84
85+	18	7	11	20	8	12	21	8	13	85+
TOTAL	3081	1566	1515	3197	1626	1571	3330	1699	1631	TOTAL

TABLE 6 — STANDARDIZED RATES

STANDARD COUNTRIES:
STANDARDIZED RATES PER THOUSAND

	ENGLAND AND WALES 1961 BOTH SEXES	MALES	FEMALES	UNITED STATES 1960 BOTH SEXES	MALES	FEMALES	MEXICO 1960 BOTH SEXES	MALES	FEMALES
Birth	20.28	20.31*	19.14	20.66	18.63*	19.83	20.16	18.68*	19.59
Death	16.82	15.96*	18.27	14.82	14.19*	15.12	10.74	11.64*	10.59
Increase	3.46	4.35*	0.87	5.85	4.43*	4.71	9.42	7.04*	9.00

TABLE 7 — MOMENTS AND CUMULANTS

	OBSERVED POP. MALES	OBSERVED POP. FEMALES	STATIONARY POP. MALES	STATIONARY POP. FEMALES	STABLE POP. MALES	STABLE POP. FEMALES	OBSERVED BIRTHS	NET MATERNITY FUNCTION	BIRTHS IN STABLE POP.
μ	31.05812	31.47198	35.50370	35.60379	32.36874	32.39954	31.40325	31.85988	31.63420
σ^2	462.8816	482.0261	500.8934	512.9839	475.6855	485.1915	33.90771	33.16330	33.06724
κ_3	5072.836	5633.079	3242.385	3633.766	4561.847	4969.260	26.7677	12.1508	17.7893
κ_4	-161559.	-168734.	-232422.	-238478.	-176737.	-175832.	-923.465	-886.423	-861.372
β_1	0.259473	0.283322	0.083655	0.097814	0.193340	0.216194	0.018379	0.004048	0.008752
β_2	2.245963	2.273789	2.073627	2.093765	2.218933	2.253085	2.196801	2.194017	2.212238
κ	-0.095150	-0.103774	-0.031815	-0.037281	-0.074083	-0.083235	-0.008553	-0.001918	-0.004206

TABLE 8 — RATES FROM AGE DISTRIBUTIONS AND VITAL STATISTICS (Females)

VITAL STATISTICS

		THOMPSON AGE RANGE	NRR	1000r	INTERVAL	BOURGEOIS-PICHAT AGE RANGE	NRR	1000b	1000d	1000r	COALE	
GRR	1.528										IBR	22.76
NRR	1.226	0-4	1.20	6.76	27.10	5-29	1.34	24.77	13.89	10.88	IDR	14.65
TFR	3.137	5-9	1.31	9.93	27.02	30-54	0.99	15.29	15.54	-0.25	IRI	8.11
GENERATION	31.747	10-14	1.42	12.77	26.94	55-79	0.74	6.62	17.64	-11.02	K1	0.
SEX RATIO	105.330	15-19	1.47	13.68	26.81	*30-54	0.99	15.29	15.54	-0.25	K2	0.

TABLE 9 — LESLIE MATRIX AND ITS SPECTRAL COMPONENTS (Females)

ORIGINAL MATRIX SUB-DIAGONAL	ALTERNATIVE FIRST ROWS Projection	ALTERNATIVE FIRST ROWS Integral	FIRST STABLE MATRIX % IN STABLE POPULATION	FISHER VALUES	REPRODUCTIVE VALUES	SECOND STABLE MATRIX Z2 FIRST COLUMN	SECOND STABLE MATRIX Z2 FIRST ROW
0.97040	0.00000	0.00000	9.683	1.110	157286	0.1408+0.0413	0.1408+0.0413
0.98696	0.00000	0.00000	9.100	1.181	165391	0.1226-0.0982	0.0437+0.1299
0.98565	0.00513	0.00000	8.698	1.235	179037	-0.0111-0.1706	-0.0748+0.1013
0.97921	0.08296	0.01057	8.302	1.289	180821	-0.1590-0.0964	-0.1165-0.0032
0.97524	0.25907	0.16138	7.873	1.265	146549	-0.1837+0.0811	-0.0713-0.0936
0.97184	0.38373	0.37440	7.436	1.044	113733	-0.0417+0.2119	-0.0041-0.1151
0.96781	0.35149	0.41720	6.998	0.671	61050	0.1606+0.1668	0.0303-0.0810
0.96343	0.22243	0.30702	6.559	0.313	27743	0.2442-0.0384	0.0273-0.0352
0.95830	0.07408	0.15053	6.120	0.080	6623	0.1152-0.2361	0.0094-0.0075
0.94540	0.00003	0.00003	5.679	0.000	4	-0.1348-0.2428	0.0000-0.0000
0.92457	0.00001	0.00003	5.200	0.000	1	-0.2881-0.0299	0.0000-0.0000
0.77065			18.353				

TABLE 10 — AGE ANALYSIS AND MISCELLANEOUS RESULTS (Females)

CONTRIBUTIONS OF ROOTS (IN 100's)

OBSERVED POPUL. (IN 100's)	r_1	r_2, r_3	$r_4 \cdot r_{11}$	AGE-SP. BIRTH RATES	NET MATERNITY FUNCTION	COEFF. OF MATRIX EQUATION	PARAMETERS	INTEGRAL	MATRIX	x	$e^{(x+8\frac{1}{2})r}$ EXP. INCREASE
1417	1481	-77	14	0.0000	0.0000	0.0000	L(1)	1.03257	1.03260	0	1.0162
1401	1391	19	-10	0.0000	0.0000	0.0000	L(2)	0.52178	0.51943	50	1.4001
1449	1330	114	5	0.0000	0.0000	0.0049		0.75938	0.74300	55	1.4458
1403	1269	119	15	0.0023	0.0098	0.0783	R(1)	0.00641	0.00642	60	1.4929
1159	1204	14	-59	0.0347	0.1468	0.2395	R(2)	-0.01638	-0.01962	65	1.5415
1089	1137	-122	74	0.0805	0.3322	0.3459		0.19375	0.19213	70	1.5917
909	1070	-165	4	0.0897	0.3597	0.3079	C(1)		15291	75	1.6435
885	1003	-63	-54	0.0660	0.2562	0.1886	C(2)		-18003	80	1.6971
831	936	111	-215	0.0324	0.1211	0.0605			32214	85	1.7524
820	868	205	-253	0.0000	0.0000	0.0000	2P/Y	32.4286	32.7020	90	1.8094
772	795	123	-146	0.0000	0.0000	0.0000	DELTA	3.5349		95	1.8684
2535	2806									100	1.9292

TABLE 1 — DATA

AGE AT LAST BIRTHDAY	POPULATION BOTH SEXES	MALES Number	MALES %	FEMALES Number	FEMALES %	BIRTHS BY AGE OF MOTHER	DEATHS BOTH SEXES	MALES	FEMALES	AGE AT LAST BIRTHDAY
0	53670	27183	1.8	26487	1.8	0	4309	2414	1895	0
1-4	214915	109338	7.2	105577	7.3	0	1527	796	731	1-4
5-9	269665	136504	9.0	133161	9.2	0	606	283	323	5-9
10-14	283119	143885	9.5	139234	9.6	0	447	235	212	10-1
15-19	268644	138270	9.1	130374	9.0	784	665	318	347	15-1
20-24	254814	134834	8.9	119980	8.3	8649	1055	541	514	20-2
25-29	217042	113455	7.5	103587	7.1	15589	994	455	539	25-2
30-34	183502	94186	6.2	89316	6.2	15333	855	394	461	30-3
35-39	192649	96894	6.4	95755	6.6	12632	1053	512	541	35-3
40-44	163098	83837	5.5	79261	5.5	5128	1127	592	535	40-4
45-49	156769	80599	5.3	76170	5.3	0	1282	661	621	45-4
50-54	152888	78771	5.2	74117	5.1	0	2020	1085	935	50-5
55-59	143611	75175	4.9	68436	4.7	0	2569	1399	1170	55-5
60-64	130533	68188	4.5	62345	4.3	0	3732	2027	1705	60-6
65-69	113135	60125	3.9	53010	3.7	0	4480	2414	2066	65-6
70-74	79221	36921	2.4	42300	2.9		4665	2304	2361	70-7
75-79	53403	24866	1.6	28537	2.0		4647	2287	2360	75-7
80-84	29624	13769	0.9	15855	1.1	29602 M.	3962	1941	2021	80-8
85+	11641	5395	0.4	6246	0.4	28513 F.	2591	1262	1329	85+
TOTAL	2971943	1522195		1449748		58115	42586	21920	20666	TOTA

TABLE 2 — MALE LIFE TABLE

x	$_nq_x$	l_x	$_nd_x$	$_nL_x$	$_nm_x$	$_na_x$	T_x	r_x	$\mathring{e}_x$	$_nM_x$
0	0.083660	100000	8366	94206	0.088805	0.3074	5841756	0.0000	58.418	0.088805
1	0.028530	91634	2614	359107	0.007280	1.1583	5747550	0.0000	62.723	0.007280
5	0.010313	89020	918	442803	0.002073	2.5000	5388444	0.0000	60.531	0.002073
10	0.008133	88102	717	438734	0.001633	2.5240	4945640	0.0000	56.136	0.001633
15	0.011449	87385	1000	434633	0.002302	2.7087	4506906	0.0000	51.575	0.002300
20	0.019898	86385	1719	427768	0.004018	2.5825	4072273	0.0040	47.141	0.004012
25	0.019858	84666	1681	419126	0.004011	2.5001	3644506	0.0161	43.046	0.004010
30	0.020719	82984	1719	410716	0.004186	2.5534	3225380	0.0318	38.867	0.004183
35	0.026108	81265	2122	401236	0.005288	2.6012	2814664	0.0114	34.636	0.005284
40	0.034746	79143	2750	389041	0.007068	2.5721	2413428	0.0062	30.494	0.007061
45	0.040229	76394	3073	374731	0.008201	2.6451	2024387	0.0000	26.499	0.008201
50	0.066692	73320	4890	355007	0.013774	2.6289	1649657	0.0000	22.499	0.013774
55	0.089117	68430	6098	327693	0.018610	2.6289	1294649	0.0000	18.919	0.018610
60	0.138984	62332	8663	290781	0.029793	2.5899	966957	0.0148	15.513	0.029727
65	0.183272	53669	9836	244425	0.040242	2.5681	676176	0.0148	12.599	0.040150
70	0.271017	43833	11879	189906	0.062555	2.5370	431751	0.0148	9.850	0.062404
75	0.373858	31953	11946	129577	0.092193	2.4728	241845	0.0148	7.569	0.091973
80	0.515840	20007	10321	73035	0.141311	2.4544	112268	0.0148	5.611	0.140969
85+	1.000000	9687	9687	39233	0.246905	4.0501	39233	0.0148	4.050	0.233919

TABLE 3 — FEMALE LIFE TABLE

x	$_nq_x$	l_x	$_nd_x$	$_nL_x$	$_nm_x$	$_na_x$	T_x	r_x	$\mathring{e}_x$	$_nM_x$
0	0.068254	100000	6825	95400	0.071545	0.3261	5954987	0.0000	59.550	0.071545
1	0.027166	93175	2531	365568	0.006924	1.1827	5859587	0.0000	62.888	0.006924
5	0.012055	90643	1093	450486	0.002426	2.5000	5494019	0.0000	60.611	0.002426
10	0.007585	89551	679	446074	0.001523	2.5263	5043534	0.0001	56.320	0.001523
15	0.013262	88872	1179	441658	0.002669	2.7094	4597460	0.0121	51.732	0.002662
20	0.021253	87693	1864	434020	0.004294	2.6149	4155802	0.0188	47.390	0.004284
25	0.025708	85829	2207	423686	0.005208	2.5252	3721782	0.0245	43.363	0.005203
30	0.025480	83623	2131	412801	0.005162	2.5063	3298096	0.0026	39.440	0.005161
35	0.027873	81492	2271	401886	0.005652	2.5461	2885296	0.0062	35.406	0.005650
40	0.033243	79221	2634	389684	0.006758	2.5626	2483409	0.0161	31.348	0.006750
45	0.039990	76587	3063	375668	0.008153	2.6271	2093725	0.0000	27.338	0.008153
50	0.061238	73524	4502	356909	0.012615	2.6207	1718058	0.0000	23.367	0.012615
55	0.082158	69022	5671	331692	0.017096	2.6340	1361149	0.0000	19.721	0.017096
60	0.128628	63351	8149	297253	0.027413	2.6067	1029457	0.0147	16.250	0.027348
65	0.178316	55202	9843	252029	0.039057	2.5635	732204	0.0147	13.264	0.038974
70	0.245811	45359	11150	199316	0.055940	2.5355	480175	0.0147	10.586	0.055816
75	0.343227	34209	11742	141636	0.082899	2.4952	280859	0.0147	8.210	0.082700
80	0.484317	22468	10882	85102	0.127864	2.4970	139223	0.0147	6.197	0.127467
85+	1.000000	11586	11586	54120	0.214082	4.6711	54120	0.0147	4.671	0.212776

TABLE 4 — OBSERVED AND PROJECTED VITAL RATES

	OBSERVED POPULATION BOTH SEXES	MALES	FEMALES	PROJECTED 1941 MALES	FEMALES	1946 MALES	FEMALES	1951 MALES	FEMALES	STABLE POPULATION MALES	FEMAL
RATES PER THOUSAND											
Birth	19.55	19.45	19.67	20.37	20.55	21.33	21.48	21.95	22.05	21.00	20.6
Death	14.33	14.40	14.25	14.77	14.74	14.87	14.72	14.86	14.55	14.98	14.6
Increase	5.23	5.05	5.41	5.60	5.81	6.46	6.76	7.09	7.49		6.023
PERCENTAGE											
under 15	27.64	27.39	27.90	26.10	26.63	25.98	26.50	26.56	27.14	26.81	26.8
15-64	62.70	63.34	62.03	64.27	63.18	64.44	63.59	64.19	63.30	64.06	63.5
65 and over	9.66	9.27	10.07	9.64	10.19	9.58	9.91	9.25	9.57	9.12	9.6
DEP. RATIO X 100	59.48	57.87	61.20	55.60	58.27	55.19	57.26	55.79	57.99	56.09	57.4

TABLE 1 — DATA

AGE AT LAST BIRTHDAY	POPULATION BOTH SEXES	MALES Number	%	FEMALES Number	%	BIRTHS BY AGE OF MOTHER	DEATHS BOTH SEXES	MALES	FEMALES	AGE AT LAST BIRTHDAY
0	66215	33866	2.3	32349	2.2	0	4390	2491	1899	0
1-4	229148	116986	7.8	112162	7.7	0	860	461	399	1-4
5-9	266454	135388	9.0	131066	9.0	0	326	170	156	5-9
10-14	262860	133587	8.9	129273	8.8	269	269	144	125	10-14
15-19	251998	128050	8.5	123948	8.5	1274	569	269	300	15-19
20-24	231759	118297	7.9	113462	7.8	10584	758	376	382	20-24
25-29	208610	104348	7.0	104262	7.1	18719	736	333	403	25-29
30-34	205112	104025	6.9	101087	6.9	19226	778	362	416	30-34
35-39	192271	97732	6.5	94539	6.5	12797	813	387	426	35-39
40-44	165933	84479	5.6	81454	5.6	5322	934	477	457	40-44
45-49	173413	87171	5.8	86242	5.9	0	1251	646	605	45-49
50-54	137771	70082	4.7	67689	4.6	0	1621	852	769	50-54
55-59	135132	67921	4.5	67211	4.6	0	2029	1118	911	55-59
60-64	119467	60053	4.0	59414	4.1	0	2970	1619	1351	60-64
65-69	114764	58585	3.9	56179	3.8	0	4407	2484	1923	65-69
70-74	100112	50024	3.3	50088	3.4		6087	3280	2807	70-74
75-79	60625	29795	2.0	30830	2.1		5570	2947	2623	75-79
80-84	26195	11957	0.8	14238	1.0	35120 M.	4417	2204	2213	80-84
85+	13264	5536	0.4	7728	0.5	32802 F.	2672	1243	1429	85+
TOTAL	2961103	1497882		1463221		67922	41457	21863	19594	TOTAL

TABLE 2 — MALE LIFE TABLE

x	nq_x	l_x	nd_x	nL_x	nm_x	na_x	T_x	r_x	$\mathring{e}_x$	nM_x	x
0	0.069184	100000	6918	94894	0.072906	0.2620	6143484	0.0116	61.435	0.073555	0
1	0.015386	93082	1432	368190	0.003890	1.1120	6048589	0.0116	64.982	0.003941	1
5	0.006234	91649	571	456819	0.001251	2.5000	5680399	0.0102	61.980	0.001256	5
10	0.005380	91078	490	454244	0.001079	2.6605	5223580	0.0042	57.353	0.001078	10
15	0.010475	90588	949	450761	0.002105	2.7032	4769334	0.0100	52.649	0.002101	15
20	0.015790	89639	1415	444751	0.003182	2.5659	4318575	0.0175	48.177	0.003178	20
25	0.015833	88224	1397	437644	0.003192	2.5123	3873824	0.0096	43.909	0.003191	25
30	0.017254	86827	1498	430447	0.003480	2.5389	3436181	0.0031	39.575	0.003480	30
35	0.019649	85329	1677	422626	0.003967	2.6036	3005733	0.0166	35.225	0.003960	35
40	0.027877	83652	2332	412700	0.005651	2.6153	2583107	0.0058	30.879	0.005646	40
45	0.036491	81320	2967	399663	0.007425	2.6619	2170408	0.0106	26.690	0.007411	45
50	0.059198	78353	4638	380766	0.012182	2.6290	1770745	0.0130	22.600	0.012157	50
55	0.079227	73714	5840	354801	0.016460	2.6421	1389979	0.0000	18.856	0.016460	55
60	0.127019	67874	8621	318981	0.027028	2.6349	1035178	0.0132	15.251	0.026960	60
65	0.192750	59253	11421	268734	0.042499	2.5894	716197	0.0132	12.087	0.042400	65
70	0.282746	47832	13524	205807	0.065713	2.5339	447464	0.0132	9.355	0.065569	70
75	0.397039	34308	13621	137359	0.099167	2.4908	241656	0.0132	7.044	0.098909	75
80	0.624658	20686	12922	69906	0.184845	2.4056	104297	0.0132	5.042	0.184328	80
85+	*1.000000	7764	7764	34391	0.225766	4.4294	34391	0.0132	4.429	0.224530	85+

TABLE 3 — FEMALE LIFE TABLE

x	nq_x	l_x	nd_x	nL_x	nm_x	na_x	T_x	r_x	$\mathring{e}_x$	nM_x	x
0	0.055834	100000	5583	95959	0.058186	0.2762	6363483	0.0117	63.635	0.058704	0
1	0.013924	94417	1315	373886	0.003516	1.1247	6267524	0.0117	66.382	0.003557	1
5	0.005913	93102	551	464133	0.001186	2.5000	5893638	0.0094	63.303	0.001190	5
10	0.004830	92551	447	461756	0.000968	2.7612	5429505	0.0042	58.665	0.000967	10
15	0.012061	92104	1111	457968	0.002426	2.7015	4967749	0.0108	53.936	0.002420	15
20	0.016719	90993	1521	451290	0.003371	2.5825	4509780	0.0140	49.562	0.003367	20
25	0.019150	89472	1713	443133	0.003866	2.5324	4058491	0.0077	45.360	0.003865	25
30	0.020372	87759	1788	434367	0.004116	2.5239	3615358	0.0057	41.197	0.004115	30
35	0.022311	85971	1918	425172	0.004511	2.5586	3180991	0.0169	37.001	0.004506	35
40	0.027686	84053	2327	414636	0.005612	2.5812	2755819	0.0036	32.787	0.005611	40
45	0.034568	81726	2825	401992	0.007028	2.6507	2341183	0.0108	28.647	0.007015	45
50	0.055388	78901	4370	384009	0.011380	2.5986	1939192	0.0142	24.578	0.011361	50
55	0.065666	74531	4894	361075	0.013554	2.6345	1555183	0.0000	20.866	0.013554	55
60	0.108118	69636	7529	330391	0.022788	2.6371	1194107	0.0118	17.148	0.022739	60
65	0.158548	62107	9847	287040	0.034305	2.6138	863716	0.0118	13.907	0.034230	65
70	0.247010	52260	12909	229864	0.056159	2.5646	576676	0.0118	11.035	0.056041	70
75	0.351919	39352	13849	162395	0.085277	2.5187	346812	0.0118	8.813	0.085079	75
80	0.554875	25503	14151	90831	0.155794	2.4632	184416	0.0118	7.231	0.155429	80
85+	1.000000	11352	11352	93585	0.121302	8.2439	93585	0.0118	8.244	0.184911	85+

TABLE 4 — OBSERVED, PROJECTED, STABLE RATES

	OBSERVED POPULATION BOTH SEXES	MALES	FEMALES	PROJECTED POPULATION 1951 MALES	FEMALES	1956 MALES	FEMALES	1961 MALES	FEMALES	STABLE POPULATION MALES	FEMALES
RATES PER THOUSAND											
Birth	22.94	23.45	22.42	23.61	22.49	23.68	22.56	23.59	22.51	23.57	22.96
Death	14.00	14.60	13.39	14.55	14.18	14.14	14.08	13.52	13.74	12.37	11.75
Increase	8.94	8.85	9.03	9.07	8.31	9.54	8.48	10.07	8.77		11.2069
PERCENTAGE											
under 15	27.85	28.03	27.67	28.74	28.07	29.73	28.86	30.20	29.27	29.82	29.51
15-64	61.51	61.56	61.46	61.69	61.27	61.47	60.95	61.79	61.22	62.73	61.86
65 and over	10.64	10.41	10.87	9.57	10.66	8.80	10.19	8.01	9.51	7.44	8.63
DEP. RATIO X 100	62.57	62.43	62.71	62.10	63.22	62.67	64.07	61.84	63.34	59.40	61.65

TABLE 1 — DATA

AGE AT LAST BIRTHDAY	POPULATION BOTH SEXES	MALES Number	MALES %	FEMALES Number	FEMALES %	BIRTHS BY AGE OF MOTHER	DEATHS BOTH SEXES	DEATHS MALES	DEATHS FEMALES	AGE AT LAST BIRTHDAY
0	63385	32530	2.2	3C855	2.1	0	2876	1679	1197	0
1-4	248771	127292	8.5	121479	8.4	0	644	351	293	1-4
5-9	281733	143862	9.6	137871	9.5	0	228	133	95	5-9
10-14	261652	133072	8.8	128580	8.8	0	170	79	91	10-14
15-19	240767	125515	8.3	115252	7.9	782	311	167	144	15-19
20-24	201113	104748	7.0	96365	6.6	8500	413	209	204	20-24
25-29	197106	98878	6.6	98228	6.8	17695	492	252	240	25-29
30-34	190815	95975	6.4	94840	6.5	17471	514	268	246	30-34
35-39	200045	101674	6.8	98371	6.8	13089	746	370	376	35-39
40-44	180523	94004	6.2	86519	6.0	5341	805	441	364	40-44
45-49	161439	82663	5.5	78776	5.4	0	1037	614	423	45-49
50-54	162262	82596	5.5	79666	5.5	0	1737	973	764	50-54
55-59	129901	65565	4.4	64336	4.4	0	2026	1152	874	55-59
60-64	121823	61181	4.1	60642	4.2	0	3069	1715	1354	60-64
65-69	107610	54195	3.6	53415	3.7	0	4262	2335	1927	65-69
70-74	99790	48940	3.3	50850	3.5		6576	3500	3076	70-74
75-79	64619	31673	2.1	32946	2.3		7194	3752	3442	75-79
80-84	30963	14674	1.0	16289	1.1	32303 M.	5660	2872	2788	80-84
85+	13420	5559	0.4	7861	0.5	30575 F.	3622	1614	2008	85+
TOTAL	2957737	1504596		1453141		62878	42382	22476	19906	TOTAL

TABLE 2 — MALE LIFE TABLE

x	$_nq_x$	l_x	$_nd_x$	$_nL_x$	$_nm_x$	$_na_x$	T_x	r_x	$\mathring{e}_x$	$_nM_x$	x
0	0.C49721	100000	4972	96336	0.051612	0.2631	6358060	0.0000	63.581	0.051614	0
1	0.010942	95028	1040	377109	0.002757	1.1129	6261723	0.0000	65.894	0.002757	1
5	0.004580	93988	430	468864	0.000918	2.5000	5884614	0.0170	62.610	0.000924	5
10	0.002970	93558	278	467133	0.000595	2.6434	5415750	0.0128	57.887	0.000594	10
15	0.006665	93280	622	464979	0.001337	2.7160	4948617	0.0226	53.051	0.001331	15
20	0.009957	92658	923	461096	0.002001	2.6221	4483638	0.0219	48.389	0.001995	20
25	0.012669	91735	1162	455841	0.002550	2.5598	4022542	0.0063	43.849	0.002549	25
30	0.013868	90573	1256	449819	0.002792	2.5745	3566701	0.0000	39.379	0.002792	30
35	0.018038	89317	1611	442721	0.003639	2.6014	3116882	0.0000	34.897	0.003639	35
40	0.023261	87706	2040	433746	0.004703	2.6552	2674161	0.0157	30.490	0.004691	40
45	0.036546	85666	3131	421065	0.007435	2.6796	2240414	0.0052	26.153	0.007428	45
50	0.057426	82535	4740	401544	0.011803	2.6515	1819349	0.0112	22.043	0.011780	50
55	0.084535	77796	6576	373499	0.017608	2.6463	1417805	0.0115	18.225	0.017570	55
60	0.131401	71219	9358	333846	0.028032	2.6225	1044306	0.0000	14.663	0.028032	60
65	0.195236	61861	12077	280317	0.043085	2.5999	710461	0.0000	11.485	0.043085	65
70	0.304283	49783	15148	211815	0.071516	2.5508	430144	0.0000	8.640	0.071516	70
75	0.455321	34635	15770	133125	0.118461	2.4604	218329	0.0000	6.304	0.118461	75
80	0.643948	18865	12148	62069	0.195720	2.3447	85204	0.0000	4.516	0.195720	80
85+	*1.C00000	6717	6717	23135	0.290340	3.4442	23135	0.0000	3.444	0.290340	85

TABLE 3 — FEMALE LIFE TABLE

x	$_nq_x$	l_x	$_nd_x$	$_nL_x$	$_nm_x$	$_na_x$	T_x	r_x	$\mathring{e}_x$	$_nM_x$	x
0	0.C37741	100000	3774	97284	0.038794	0.2802	6618066	0.0000	66.181	0.038794	0
1	0.009581	96226	922	382256	0.002412	1.1287	6520783	0.0000	67.765	0.002412	1
5	0.003417	95304	326	475706	0.000685	2.5000	6138526	0.0158	64.410	0.000689	5
10	0.003543	94978	337	474106	0.000710	2.6657	5662821	0.0171	59.622	0.000708	10
15	0.006270	94642	593	471862	0.001257	2.7302	5188714	0.0275	54.825	0.001249	15
20	0.010549	94048	992	467874	0.002120	2.6127	4716852	0.0140	50.153	0.002117	20
25	0.012143	93056	1130	462497	0.002443	2.5355	4248979	0.0000	45.660	0.002443	25
30	0.012889	91926	1185	456792	0.002594	2.6036	3786482	0.0000	41.190	0.002594	30
35	0.018946	90741	1719	449819	0.003824	2.5814	3329689	0.0056	36.694	0.003822	35
40	0.020851	89022	1856	440595	0.004213	2.5666	2880140	0.0179	32.353	0.004207	40
45	0.026532	87166	2313	430493	0.005372	2.6919	2439545	0.0023	27.987	0.005370	45
50	0.C46985	84854	3987	414930	0.009609	2.6580	2009052	0.0108	23.677	0.009590	50
55	0.065982	80867	5336	391833	0.013617	2.6673	1594122	0.0128	19.713	0.013585	55
60	0.106107	75531	8014	358845	0.022334	2.6530	1202289	0.0014	15.918	0.022828	60
65	0.166198	67517	11221	310956	0.036086	2.6271	843444	0.0014	12.492	0.036076	65
70	0.263945	56295	14859	245566	0.060509	2.5832	532488	0.0014	9.459	0.060492	70
75	0.414046	41437	17157	164175	0.104502	2.4932	286922	0.0014	6.924	0.104474	75
80	0.588987	24280	14301	83530	0.171202	2.3954	122747	0.0014	5.056	0.171158	80
85+	1.000000	9979	9979	39217	0.254465	3.9298	39217	0.0014	3.930	0.255437	85

TABLE 4 — OBSERVED AND PROJECTED VITAL RATES

	OBSERVED POPULATION BOTH SEXES	MALES	FEMALES	1956 MALES	1956 FEMALES	1961 MALES	1961 FEMALES	1966 MALES	1966 FEMALES	STABLE POPULATION MALES	STABLE POPULATION FEMALES
RATES PER THOUSAND											
Birth	21.26	21.47	21.04	21.23	20.74	21.62	21.08	22.50	21.91	23.30	22.
Death	14.33	14.94	13.70	14.02	13.02	13.23	12.40	12.60	11.86	11.33	10.
Increase	6.93	6.53	7.34	7.21	7.72	8.39	8.68	9.90	10.05		11.96
PERCENTAGE											
under 15	28.93	29.03	28.82	29.30	28.95	29.15	28.77	28.64	28.28	30.06	29.
15-64	60.38	60.67	60.08	61.49	60.90	62.59	61.95	63.30	62.60	63.00	62.
65 and over	10.70	10.30	11.10	9.20	10.15	8.25	9.28	8.06	9.12	6.94	7.
DEP. RATIO X 100	65.63	64.83	66.45	62.62	64.21	59.76	61.42	57.97	59.74	58.73	60.

TABLE 1 — DATA

AGE AT LAST BIRTHDAY	POPULATION BOTH SEXES	MALES Number	MALES %	FEMALES Number	FEMALES %	BIRTHS BY AGE OF MOTHER	DEATHS BOTH SEXES	DEATHS MALES	DEATHS FEMALES	AGE AT LAST BIRTHDAY
0	59946	30523	2.1	29423	2.1	0	2151	1240	911	0
1-4	238258	120877	8.3	117381	8.2	0	363	204	159	1-4
5-9	295703	151396	10.4	144307	10.1	0	165	89	76	5-9
10-14	277151	140650	9.6	136501	9.5	2	117	68	49	10-14
15-19	232209	120775	8.3	111434	7.8	1088	133	81	52	15-19
20-24	178095	91080	6.2	87015	6.1	8083	188	108	80	20-24
25-29	168611	83418	5.7	85193	5.9	15789	220	123	97	25-29
30-34	174139	85761	5.9	88378	6.2	17787	307	157	150	30-34
35-39	181228	88763	6.1	92465	6.4	13070	425	215	210	35-39
40-44	183967	93552	6.4	90415	6.3	5047	613	325	288	40-44
45-49	172449	88688	6.1	83761	5.8	331	863	492	371	45-49
50-54	147640	76069	5.2	71571	5.0	3	1340	774	566	50-54
55-59	151103	76366	5.2	74737	5.2	0	1872	1127	745	55-59
60-64	117545	58056	4.0	59489	4.1	0	2585	1480	1105	60-64
65-69	108654	55049	3.8	53605	3.7	0	3432	2014	1418	65-69
70-74	93006	45129	3.1	47877	3.3	0	5147	2736	2411	70-74
75-79	65826	32191	2.2	33635	2.3		5865	3088	2777	75-79
80-84	32750	15260	1.0	17490	1.2	31357 M.	5287	2686	2601	80-84
85+	16322	7198	0.5	9124	0.6	29843 F.	3922	1793	2129	85+
TOTAL	2894602	1460801		1433801		61200	34995	18800	16195	TOTAL

TABLE 2 — MALE LIFE TABLE

x	nq_x	l_x	nd_x	nL_x	nm_x	na_x	T_x	r_x	$\mathring{e}_x$	nM_x	x
0	0.039403	100000	3940	96992	0.040625	0.2367	6711261	0.0000	67.113	0.040625	0
1	0.006718	96060	645	382362	0.001688	1.0921	6614269	0.0000	68.856	0.001688	1
5	0.002928	95414	279	476373	0.000587	2.5000	6231907	0.0065	65.314	0.000588	5
10	0.002417	95135	230	475109	0.000484	2.5375	5755534	0.0221	60.499	0.000483	10
15	0.003380	94905	321	473793	0.000677	2.7157	5280425	0.0427	55.639	0.000671	15
20	0.005942	94584	562	471594	0.001192	2.6373	4806632	0.0359	50.818	0.001186	20
25	0.007349	94022	691	468444	0.001475	2.5870	4335038	0.0045	46.106	0.001474	25
30	0.009113	93331	851	464618	0.001831	2.6035	3866594	0.0000	41.429	0.001831	30
35	0.012042	92481	1114	459770	0.002422	2.6354	3401976	0.0000	36.786	0.002422	35
40	0.017231	91367	1574	453182	0.003474	2.6793	2942206	0.0000	32.202	0.003474	40
45	0.027491	89793	2468	443369	0.005568	2.7337	2489024	0.0146	27.720	0.005548	45
50	0.049740	87324	4343	426484	0.010184	2.6662	2045654	0.0049	23.426	0.010175	50
55	0.071495	82981	5933	401097	0.014791	2.6728	1619170	0.0110	19.513	0.014758	55
60	0.120247	77048	9265	363219	0.025508	2.6231	1218073	0.0034	15.809	0.025493	60
65	0.168273	67783	11406	311575	0.036608	2.6029	854854	0.0034	12.612	0.036586	65
70	0.264284	56377	14900	245607	0.060664	2.5651	543279	0.0034	9.637	0.060626	70
75	0.387238	41478	16062	167321	0.095993	2.5055	297673	0.0034	7.177	0.095927	75
80	0.602829	25416	15321	86983	0.176143	2.4189	130351	0.0034	5.129	0.176016	80
85+	1.000000	10094	10094	43368	0.232761	4.2963	43368	0.0034	4.296	0.249098	85+

TABLE 3 — FEMALE LIFE TABLE

x	nq_x	l_x	nd_x	nL_x	nm_x	na_x	T_x	r_x	$\mathring{e}_x$	nM_x	x
0	0.030253	100000	3025	97708	0.030962	0.2425	7022312	0.0000	70.223	0.030962	0
1	0.005397	96975	523	386379	0.001355	1.0964	6924603	0.0000	71.406	0.001355	1
5	0.002624	96451	253	481624	0.000526	2.5000	6538224	0.0065	67.788	0.000527	5
10	0.001792	96198	172	480555	0.000359	2.4676	6056600	0.0254	62.960	0.000359	10
15	0.002357	96026	226	479620	0.000472	2.7474	5576045	0.0445	58.068	0.000467	15
20	0.004605	95800	441	477961	0.000923	2.6688	5096426	0.0260	53.199	0.000919	20
25	0.005678	95358	541	475514	0.001139	2.6386	4618465	0.0000	48.433	0.001139	25
30	0.008452	94817	801	472190	0.001697	2.6353	4142952	0.0000	43.694	0.001697	30
35	0.011295	94016	1062	467563	0.002271	2.6313	3670762	0.0000	39.044	0.002271	35
40	0.015822	92954	1471	461290	0.003188	2.6348	3203199	0.0067	34.460	0.003185	40
45	0.022011	91483	2014	452798	0.004447	2.7073	2741909	0.0184	29.972	0.004429	45
50	0.038836	89469	3475	439114	0.007913	2.6308	2289111	0.0039	25.585	0.007908	50
55	0.048791	85995	4196	420278	0.009983	2.6894	1849997	0.0071	21.513	0.009968	55
60	0.089106	81799	7289	391835	0.018602	2.6458	1429718	0.0079	17.478	0.018575	60
65	0.124780	74510	9297	350847	0.026500	2.6656	1037883	0.0079	13.929	0.026453	65
70	0.225127	65213	14681	291040	0.050444	2.6144	687036	0.0079	10.535	0.050358	70
75	0.343544	50532	17360	209917	0.082698	2.5380	395996	0.0079	7.837	0.082563	75
80	0.537958	33172	17845	119805	0.148950	2.4763	186078	0.0079	5.610	0.148714	80
85+	1.000000	15327	15327	66273	0.231267	4.3240	66273	0.0079	4.324	0.233340	85+

TABLE 4 — OBSERVED AND PROJECTED VITAL RATES

RATES PER THOUSAND	OBSERVED BOTH SEXES	OBSERVED MALES	OBSERVED FEMALES	1961 MALES	1961 FEMALES	1966 MALES	1966 FEMALES	1971 MALES	1971 FEMALES	STABLE MALES	STABLE FEMALES
Birth	21.14	21.47	20.81	21.01	20.29	22.06	21.26	23.89	23.00	24.36	23.61
Death	12.09	12.87	11.30	12.51	11.12	12.06	10.87	11.58	10.56	9.51	8.76
Increase	9.05	8.60	9.52	8.50	9.17	10.00	10.39	12.31	12.44	14.8538	
PERCENTAGE											
under 15	30.09	30.36	29.82	29.73	29.02	28.93	28.26	29.12	28.33	31.25	30.61
15-64	58.97	59.04	58.90	60.55	60.25	61.53	61.03	61.87	61.49	61.73	61.18
65 and over	10.94	10.60	11.28	9.72	10.72	9.54	10.71	9.02	10.17	7.02	8.20
DEP. RATIO X 100	69.57	69.36	69.79	65.15	65.97	62.51	63.85	61.64	62.62	61.99	63.44

TABLE 1 — DATA

AGE AT LAST BIRTHDAY	POPULATION BOTH SEXES	MALES Number	%	FEMALES Number	%	BIRTHS BY AGE OF MOTHER	DEATHS BOTH SEXES	MALES	FEMALES	AGE AT LAST BIRTHDAY
0	62908	32215	2.3	30693	2.2	0	1802	1035	767	0
1-4	238007	121313	8.6	116694	8.3	0	294	161	133	1-4
5-9	287282	146779	10.4	140503	10.0	0	140	78	62	5-9
10-14	289360	148687	10.5	140673	10.0	5	101	60	41	10-1
15-19	233910	120326	8.5	113584	8.1	1120	124	85	39	15-1
20-24	157042	79908	5.6	77134	5.5	8597	134	82	52	20-2
25-29	144261	71754	5.1	72507	5.2	16029	146	89	57	25-2
30-34	151762	74736	5.3	77026	5.5	16548	218	116	102	30-3
35-39	166099	81283	5.7	84816	6.1	13175	344	183	161	35-3
40-44	169636	84374	6.0	85262	6.1	4939	490	273	217	40-4
45-49	174730	89053	6.3	85677	6.1	364	819	468	351	45-4
50-54	157578	81958	5.8	75620	5.4	2	1311	769	542	50-5
55-59	135404	68247	4.8	67157	4.8	0	1676	1035	641	55-5
60-64	131709	64741	4.6	66968	4.8	0	2625	1573	1052	60-6
65-69	103240	50953	3.6	52287	3.7	0	3343	1986	1357	65-6
70-74	92780	44061	3.1	48719	3.5		4741	2562	2179	70-7
75-79	63084	29574	2.1	33510	2.4		5364	2789	2575	75-7
80-84	37246	16742	1.2	20504	1.5	31158 M.	5360	2678	2682	80-8
85+	18641	7718	0.5	10923	0.8	29621 F.	4723	2175	2548	85-
TOTAL	2814679	1414422		1400257		60779	33755	18197	15558	TOT

TABLE 2 — MALE LIFE TABLE

x	$_nq_x$	l_x	$_nd_x$	$_nL_x$	$_nm_x$	$_na_x$	T_x	r_x	$\mathring{e}_x$	$_nM_x$
0	0.031240	100000	3124	97614	0.032004	0.2361	6811985	0.0049	68.120	0.032128
1	0.005253	96876	509	386024	0.001318	1.0917	6714371	0.0049	69.309	0.001327
5	0.002652	96367	256	481197	0.000531	2.5000	6328347	0.0025	65.669	0.000531
10	0.002019	96112	194	480091	0.000404	2.5929	5847151	0.0194	60.837	0.000404
15	0.003566	95917	342	478794	0.000714	2.6813	5367060	0.0614	55.955	0.000706
20	0.005146	95575	492	476699	0.001032	2.6043	4888266	0.0507	51.146	0.001026
25	0.006186	95084	588	473997	0.001241	2.5846	4411567	0.0054	46.397	0.001240
30	0.007732	94495	731	470746	0.001552	2.6317	3937570	0.0000	41.669	0.001552
35	0.011198	93765	1050	466357	0.002251	2.6504	3466823	0.0000	36.974	0.002251
40	0.016058	92715	1489	460127	0.003236	2.6846	3000467	0.0000	32.362	0.003236
45	0.025967	91226	2369	450751	0.005255	2.7292	2540340	0.0000	27.847	0.005255
50	0.046086	88857	4095	434850	0.009417	2.6958	2089589	0.0170	23.516	0.009383
55	0.073344	84762	6217	409296	0.015189	2.6653	1654740	0.0078	19.522	0.015166
60	0.114919	78545	9026	371446	0.024300	2.6424	1245444	0.0008	15.856	0.024297
65	0.178191	69519	12388	317775	0.038982	2.5928	873998	0.0008	12.572	0.038977
70	0.254581	57131	14545	250101	0.058155	2.5554	556223	0.0008	9.736	0.058147
75	0.381759	42587	16258	172369	0.094320	2.5049	306121	0.0008	7.188	0.094306
80	0.567001	26329	14928	93311	0.159986	2.4322	133752	0.0008	5.080	0.159958
85+	*1.000000	11400	11400	40441	0.281901	3.5473	40441	0.0008	3.547	0.281809

TABLE 3 — FEMALE LIFE TABLE

x	$_nq_x$	l_x	$_nd_x$	$_nL_x$	$_nm_x$	$_na_x$	T_x	r_x	$\mathring{e}_x$	$_nM_x$
0	0.024450	100000	2445	98159	0.024908	0.2470	7187926	0.0041	71.879	0.024989
1	0.004520	97555	441	388941	0.001134	1.0998	7089767	0.0041	72.675	0.001140
5	0.002201	97114	214	485036	0.000441	2.5000	6700826	0.0041	69.000	0.000441
10	0.001454	96900	141	484140	0.000291	2.4328	6215791	0.0209	64.146	0.000291
15	0.001739	96759	168	483415	0.000348	2.7304	5731651	0.0597	59.236	0.000343
20	0.003386	96591	327	482181	0.000678	2.6334	5248236	0.0443	54.335	0.000674
25	0.003923	96264	378	480440	0.000786	2.6687	4766055	0.0000	49.510	0.000786
30	0.006601	95886	633	477958	0.001324	2.6719	4285615	0.0000	44.695	0.001324
35	0.009449	95253	900	474134	0.001898	2.6298	3807657	0.0000	39.974	0.001898
40	0.012651	94353	1194	468990	0.002545	2.6735	3333523	0.0000	35.330	0.002545
45	0.020330	93160	1894	461487	0.004104	2.7235	2864532	0.0076	30.749	0.004097
50	0.035337	91266	3225	448728	0.007187	2.6432	2403045	0.0174	26.330	0.007167
55	0.046696	88041	4111	430580	0.009548	2.6592	1954317	0.0019	22.198	0.009545
60	0.075893	83930	6367	404854	0.015725	2.6763	1523736	0.0050	18.155	0.015709
65	0.122468	77563	9499	365611	0.025981	2.6624	1118882	0.0050	14.425	0.025953
70	0.202328	68064	13771	307574	0.044774	2.6221	753272	0.0050	11.067	0.044726
75	0.323619	54293	17570	228417	0.076921	2.5500	445698	0.0050	8.209	0.076843
80	0.489849	36723	17989	137398	0.130923	2.5135	217281	0.0050	5.917	0.130804
85+	1.000000	18734	18734	79883	0.234519	4.2641	79883	0.0050	4.264	0.233270

TABLE 4 — OBSERVED AND PROJECTED VITAL RATES

	OBSERVED POPULATION BOTH SEXES	MALES	FEMALES	PROJECTED POPULATION 1966 MALES	FEMALES	1971 MALES	FEMALES	1976 MALES	FEMALES	STABLE POPULATION MALES	FEMA
RATES PER THOUSAND											
Birth	21.59	22.03	21.15	21.98	21.04	24.26	23.19	26.85	25.67	27.17	26.
Death	11.99	12.87	11.11	12.19	10.86	11.65	10.49	11.13	10.15	8.06	7.
Increase	9.60	9.16	10.04	9.79	10.17	12.61	12.70	15.72	15.52		19.10
PERCENTAGE											
under 15	31.18	31.74	30.61	30.57	29.50	30.38	29.30	31.14	30.00	34.13	33.
15-64	57.63	57.72	57.54	59.38	58.78	60.21	59.54	59.74	59.27	60.00	59.
65 and over	11.19	10.54	11.85	10.05	11.72	9.41	11.16	9.13	10.73	5.87	7.
DEP. RATIO X 100	73.52	73.26	73.78	68.41	70.14	66.09	67.94	67.40	68.72	66.68	68.

TABLE 5 — POPULATION PROJECTED WITH FIXED AGE-SPECIFIC BIRTH AND DEATH RATES (IN 1000's)

AGE AT LAST BIRTHDAY	1966 BOTH SEXES	1966 MALES	1966 FEMALES	1971 BOTH SEXES	1971 MALES	1971 FEMALES	1976 BOTH SEXES	1976 MALES	1976 FEMALES	AGE AT LAST BIRTHDAY
0-4	302	154	148	335	171	164	394	201	193	0-4
5-9	300	153	147	300	153	147	333	170	163	5-9
10-14	286	146	140	298	152	146	300	153	147	10-14
15-19	288	148	140	286	146	140	298	152	146	15-19
20-24	233	120	113	288	148	140	285	145	140	20-24
25-29	156	79	77	232	119	113	287	147	140	25-29
30-34	143	71	72	155	79	76	230	118	112	30-34
35-39	150	74	76	143	71	72	154	78	76	35-39
40-44	164	80	84	149	73	76	141	70	71	40-44
45-49	167	83	84	162	79	83	146	72	74	45-49
50-54	169	86	83	162	80	82	156	76	80	50-54
55-59	150	77	73	161	81	80	153	75	78	55-59
60-64	125	62	63	138	70	68	148	73	75	60-64
65-69	115	55	60	110	53	57	122	60	62	65-69
70-74	84	40	44	95	44	51	90	42	48	70-74
75-79	66	30	36	61	28	33	68	30	38	75-79
80-84	36	16	20	38	16	22	35	15	20	80-84
85+	19	7	12	19	7	12	20	7	13	85+
TOTAL	2953	1481	1472	3132	1570	1562	3360	1684	1676	TOTAL

TABLE 6 — STANDARDIZED RATES

STANDARD COUNTRIES: STANDARDIZED RATES PER THOUSAND	ENGLAND AND WALES 1961 BOTH SEXES	MALES	FEMALES	UNITED STATES 1960 BOTH SEXES	MALES	FEMALES	MEXICO 1960 BOTH SEXES	MALES	FEMALES
Birth	24.95	26.84*	23.56	25.40	25.01*	24.39	25.68	23.13*	24.96
Death	12.35	11.96*	12.77	10.02	10.90*	9.39	5.23	9.18*	4.59
Increase	12.60	14.88*	10.79	15.38	14.11*	15.00	20.45	13.95*	20.38

TABLE 7 — MOMENTS AND CUMULANTS

	OBSERVED POP. MALES	OBSERVED POP. FEMALES	STATIONARY POP. MALES	STATIONARY POP. FEMALES	STABLE POP. MALES	STABLE POP. FEMALES	OBSERVED BIRTHS	NET MATERNITY FUNCTION	BIRTHS IN STABLE POP.
μ	32.35589	33.27602	36.76862	38.28892	27.91381	28.79865	31.47580	31.22844	30.53773
σ^2	529.4150	548.3875	497.5118	532.4412	418.6654	448.0937	36.69064	34.42075	33.65920
κ_3	5031.905	5042.655	2220.186	2126.876	5510.757	6082.071	11.7819	32.8339	46.5469
κ_4	-274439.	-297766.	-244458.	-291058.	-85423.	-102749.	-920.030	-760.519	-659.300
β_1	0.170638	0.154190	0.040028	0.029969	0.413829	0.411146	0.002810	0.026435	0.056816
β_2	2.020842	2.009851	2.012363	1.973316	2.512652	2.488273	2.316574	2.358097	2.418064
κ	-0.057498	-0.052271	-0.015132	-0.011080	-0.161044	-0.157325	-0.001560	-0.014882	-0.032888

TABLE 8 — RATES FROM AGE DISTRIBUTIONS AND VITAL STATISTICS (Females)

VITAL STATISTICS		THOMPSON AGE RANGE	NRR	1000r	INTERVAL	BOURGEOIS-PICHAT AGE RANGE	NRR	1000b	1000d	1000r	COALE
GRR	1.888.										
NRR	1.804	0-4	1.70	19.83	27.42	5-29	2.79	30.10	-7.92	38.02	IBR
TFR	3.874	5-9	1.71	19.83	27.38	30-54	0.93	11.22	13.75	-2.53	IDR
GENERATION	30.882	10-14	1.70	19.11	27.31	55-79	1.06	12.63	10.65	1.98	IRI
SEX RATIO	105.189	15-19	1.36	11.00	27.21	*25-49	0.75	8.18	18.88	-10.70	K1
											K2

TABLE 9 — LESLIE MATRIX AND ITS SPECTRAL COMPONENTS (Females)

Start Age Interval	ORIGINAL MATRIX SUB-DIAGONAL	ALTERNATIVE FIRST ROWS Projection	Integral	FIRST STABLE MATRIX % IN STABLE POPULATION	FISHER VALUES	REPRODUCTIVE VALUES	SECOND STABLE MATRIX Z₂ FIRST COLUMN	FIRST ROW
0	0.99576	0.00000	0.00000	12.245	1.077	158667	0.1461+0.0482	0.1461+0.0482
5	0.99815	0.00004	0.00000	11.080	1.190	167161	0.1258-0.1016	0.0368+0.1417
10	0.99850	0.01173	0.00009	10.050	1.312	184512	-0.0182-0.1694	-0.0942+0.1023
15	0.99745	0.14366	0.02455	9.119	1.433	162759	-0.1604-0.0806	-0.1317-0.0231
20	0.99639	0.39374	0.27753	8.265	1.426	109984	-0.1628+0.0960	-0.0704-0.1240
25	0.99484	0.51608	0.55048	7.483	1.149	83340	-0.0079+0.1986	0.0051-0.1392
30	0.99200	0.43790	0.53496	6.765	0.713	54919	0.1707+0.1200	0.0382-0.0928
35	0.98915	0.25239	0.38680	6.098	0.316	26779	0.2024-0.0822	0.0297-0.0386
40	0.98400	0.07372	0.14424	5.481	0.077	6529	0.0424-0.2241	0.0092-0.0084
45	0.97235	0.00507	0.01058	4.901	0.005	428	-0.1717-0.1631	0.0006-0.0005
50	0.95956	0.00003	0.00007	4.331	0.000	2	-0.2361+0.0575	0.0000-0.0000
55+	0.80743			14.181				

TABLE 10 — AGE ANALYSIS AND MISCELLANEOUS RESULTS (Females)

Start Age Interval	OBSERVED POPUL. (IN 100's)	CONTRIBUTIONS OF ROOTS (IN 100's) r_1	r_2, r_3	$r_4 \cdot r_{11}$	AGE-SP. BIRTH RATES	NET MATERNITY FUNCTION	COEFF. OF MATRIX EQUATION	PARAMETERS			EXP. INCREASE	
									INTEGRAL	MATRIX	x	$e^{(x+2\frac{1}{2})r}$
	1474	1458	-5	20	0.0000	0.0000	0.0000	L(1)	1.10026	1.10047	0	1.0489
	1405	1320	138	-52	0.0000	0.0000	0.0000	L(2)	0.51678	0.51337	50	2.7271
	1407	1197	163	47	0.0000	0.0001	0.0117		0.81568	0.79641	55	3.0005
	1136	1086	33	17	0.0048	0.0232	0.1426	R(1)	0.01911	0.01915	60	3.3014
	771	984	-143	-70	0.0543	0.2619	0.3898	R(2)	-0.00700	-0.01078	65	3.6324
	725	891	-199	33	0.1077	0.5176	0.5090		0.20121	0.19964	70	3.9966
	770	806	-69	33	0.1047	0.5004	0.4297	C(1)		11910	75	4.3973
	848	726	141	-19	0.0757	0.3589	0.2457	C(2)		14646	80	4.8381
	853	653	234	-35	0.0282	0.1324	0.0710			49544	85	5.3232
	857	584	111	162	0.0021	0.0096	0.0048	2P/Y	31.2265	31.4720	90	5.8569
	756	516	-126	367	0.0000	0.0001	0.0000	DELTA	10.1165		95	6.4441
+	3001	1689									100	7.0902

TABLE 1 — DATA

AGE AT LAST BIRTHDAY	POPULATION BOTH SEXES	MALES Number	%	FEMALES Number	%	BIRTHS BY AGE OF MOTHER	DEATHS BOTH SEXES	MALES	FEMALES	AGE AT LAST BIRTHD
0	1005425	512013	2.5	493412	2.3	0	115879	62601	53278	0
1-4	3561325	1812151	9.0	1749174	8.3	0	58996	29974	29022	1-4
5-9	4479009	2275751	11.3	2203258	10.5	0	11678	5987	5691	5-9
10-14	3234148	1643417	8.2	1590731	7.5	85	6249	3167	3082	10-14
15-19	4010411	2014688	10.0	1995723	9.5	66981	12749	6356	6393	15-19
20-24	3820875	1904759	9.5	1916116	9.1	206652	16007	8087	7920	20-24
25-29	3228546	1570810	7.8	1657736	7.9	284422	14273	6895	7378	25-29
30-34	2878439	1355629	6.7	1522810	7.2	232796	13518	6589	6929	30-34
35-39	2519726	1145219	5.7	1374507	6.5	157170	13454	6598	6856	35-39
40-44	2346943	1072014	5.3	1274929	6.0	67891	14891	7448	7443	40-44
45-49	2128061	993223	4.9	1134838	5.4	7210	16889	8938	7951	45-49
50-54	1890142	905793	4.5	984349	4.7	283	20538	11197	9341	50-54
55-59	1668742	810404	4.0	858338	4.1	0	25923	14016	11907	55-59
60-64	1440043	695575	3.5	744468	3.5	0	34378	18289	16089	60-64
65-69	1230919	596928	3.0	633991	3.0	0	47563	24663	22900	65-69
70-74	901325	431794	2.1	469531	2.2		58091	29606	28485	70-74
75-79	540685	256959	1.3	283726	1.3		58818	29275	29543	75-79
80-84	251795	115684	0.6	136111	0.6	525949 M.	43918	21065	22853	80-84
85+	88879	38380	0.2	50499	0.2	497541 F.	25593	11706	13887	85+
TOTAL	41225438	20151191		21074247		1023490	609405	312457	296948	TOTA

TABLE 2 — MALE LIFE TABLE

x	nq_x	l_x	nd_x	nL_x	nm_x	na_x	T_x	r_x	$\mathring{e}_x$	nM_x
0	0.113120	100000	11312	92723	0.121997	0.3567	5380024	0.0033	53.800	0.122264
1	0.063150	88688	5601	339251	0.016509	1.2323	5287301	0.0033	59.617	0.016541
5	0.012707	83087	1056	412797	0.002558	2.5000	4948050	0.0290	59.552	0.002631
10	0.009596	82032	787	408235	0.001928	2.5572	4535253	0.0098	55.287	0.001927
15	0.015658	81244	1272	403228	0.003155	2.6466	4127018	0.0000	50.798	0.003155
20	0.021037	79972	1682	395745	0.004251	2.5531	3723790	0.0208	46.564	0.004246
25	0.021729	78290	1701	387230	0.004393	2.5196	3328045	0.0295	42.509	0.004389
30	0.024053	76589	1842	378427	0.004868	2.5481	2940815	0.0267	38.398	0.004860
35	0.028445	74746	2126	368551	0.005769	2.5628	2562389	0.0177	34.281	0.005761
40	0.034187	72620	2483	357096	0.006952	2.5811	2193838	0.0071	30.210	0.006948
45	0.044086	70138	3092	343280	0.009007	2.6042	1836742	0.0076	26.188	0.008999
50	0.060097	67046	4029	325603	0.012375	2.6111	1493462	0.0077	22.275	0.012362
55	0.083171	63016	5241	302632	0.017318	2.6245	1167859	0.0084	18.533	0.017295
60	0.123965	57775	7162	271865	0.026344	2.6249	865228	0.0108	14.976	0.026293
65	0.188358	50613	9533	230257	0.041403	2.6076	593363	0.0108	11.724	0.041317
70	0.294171	41080	12084	175876	0.068710	2.5569	363105	0.0108	8.839	0.068565
75	0.442711	28995	12837	112441	0.114162	2.4654	187230	0.0108	6.457	0.113922
80	0.615916	16159	9952	54531	0.182508	2.3612	74789	0.0108	4.628	0.182090
85+	*1.000000	6206	6206	20258	0.306370	3.2640	20258	0.0108	3.264	0.305003

TABLE 3 — FEMALE LIFE TABLE

x	nq_x	l_x	nd_x	nL_x	nm_x	na_x	T_x	r_x	$\mathring{e}_x$	nM_x
0	0.100884	100000	10088	93645	0.107730	0.3701	5592347	0.0036	55.923	0.107979
1	0.063366	89912	5697	344029	0.016561	1.2588	5498702	0.0036	61.157	0.016592
5	0.012474	84214	1050	418445	0.002510	2.5000	5154673	0.0288	61.209	0.002583
10	0.009647	83164	802	413867	0.001939	2.5672	4736228	0.0075	56.951	0.001937
15	0.015896	82362	1309	408713	0.003203	2.6365	4322361	0.0000	52.480	0.003203
20	0.020479	81052	1660	401203	0.004137	2.5551	3913648	0.0145	48.285	0.004133
25	0.022017	79392	1748	392610	0.004452	2.5104	3512445	0.0186	44.242	0.004451
30	0.022504	77644	1747	383879	0.004552	2.5147	3119835	0.0141	40.181	0.004550
35	0.024654	75897	1871	374888	0.004991	2.5429	2735956	0.0127	36.048	0.004988
40	0.028807	74026	2132	364925	0.005844	2.5596	2361068	0.0133	31.895	0.005838
45	0.034518	71893	2482	353492	0.007020	2.5921	1996143	0.0186	27.765	0.007006
50	0.046524	69412	3229	339397	0.009515	2.6273	1642651	0.0181	23.665	0.009490
55	0.067323	66182	4456	320427	0.013905	2.6467	1303254	0.0135	19.692	0.013872
60	0.103133	61727	6366	293715	0.021674	2.6564	982827	0.0143	15.922	0.021611
65	0.166831	55361	9236	254937	0.036228	2.6323	689112	0.0143	12.448	0.036120
70	0.265206	46125	12233	201040	0.060847	2.5815	434176	0.0143	9.413	0.060667
75	0.413707	33892	14021	134283	0.104418	2.4911	233136	0.0143	6.879	0.104125
80	0.585373	19871	11632	69070	0.168407	2.3964	98853	0.0143	4.975	0.167899
85+	*1.000000	8239	8239	29783	0.276634	3.6149	29783	0.0143	3.615	0.274996

TABLE 4 — OBSERVED AND PROJECTED VITAL RATES

	OBSERVED POPULATION BOTH SEXES	MALES	FEMALES	PROJECTED POPULATION 1936 MALES	FEMALES	1941 MALES	FEMALES	1946 MALES	FEMALES	STABLE POPULATION MALES	FEMA
RATES PER THOUSAND											
Birth	24.83	26.10	23.61	26.17	23.80	25.53	23.36	24.82	22.85	22.84	22.
Death	14.78	15.51	14.09	15.29	14.10	15.19	14.22	15.04	14.31	16.69	15.
Increase	10.04	10.59	9.52	10.87	9.70	10.35	9.15	9.78	8.55		6.14
PERCENTAGE											
under 15	29.79	30.98	28.64	32.02	29.68	30.63	28.47	29.85	27.85	27.36	26.
15-64	62.90	61.87	63.89	60.99	62.80	62.52	63.98	63.41	64.48	63.98	63.
65 and over	7.31	7.14	7.47	7.00	7.52	6.86	7.55	6.74	7.67	8.66	9.
DEP. RATIO X 100	58.98	61.62	56.53	63.97	59.23	59.96	56.29	57.71	55.10	56.30	57.

E AST DAY	1936 BOTH SEXES	1936 MALES	FEMALES	1941 BOTH SEXES	1941 MALES	FEMALES	1946 BOTH SEXES	1946 MALES	FEMALES	AGE AT LAST BIRTHDAY	
4	4579	2338	2241	4777	2439	2338	4900	2502	2398	0-4	**TABLE 5**
9	4365	2221	2144	4377	2234	2143	4566	2331	2235	5-9	
14	4430	2251	2179	4317	2196	2121	4329	2210	2119	10-14	POPULATION
19	3194	1623	1571	4375	2223	2152	4263	2169	2094	15-19	PROJECTED
24	3936	1977	1959	3135	1593	1542	4294	2182	2112	20-24	WITH
29	3739	1864	1875	3852	1935	1917	3068	1559	1509	25-29	FIXED
34	3156	1535	1621	3654	1821	1833	3765	1891	1874	30-34	AGE—
39	2807	1320	1487	3078	1495	1583	3564	1774	1790	35-39	SPECIFIC
44	2448	1110	1338	2727	1279	1448	2990	1449	1541	40-44	BIRTH
49	2266	1031	1235	2363	1067	1296	2632	1230	1402	45-49	AND
54	2032	942	1090	2163	977	1186	2256	1012	1244	50-54	DEATH
59	1771	842	929	1905	876	1029	2028	909	1119	55-59	RATES
64	1515	728	787	1608	756	852	1730	787	943	60-64	(IN 1000's)
69	1235	589	646	1300	617	683	1380	641	739	65-69	
74	956	456	500	960	450	510	1010	471	539	70-74	
79	590	276	314	625	291	334	628	288	340	75-79	
84	271	125	146	295	134	161	313	141	172	80-84	
+	102	43	59	109	46	63	120	50	70	85+	
AL	43392	21271	22121	45620	22429	23191	47836	23596	24240	TOTAL	

STANDARD COUNTRIES: DARDIZED RATES PER THOUSAND	ENGLAND AND WALES 1961 BOTH SEXES	MALES	FEMALES	UNITED STATES 1960 BOTH SEXES	MALES	FEMALES	MEXICO 1960 BOTH SEXES	MALES	FEMALES	
h	20.65	23.63*	19.45	21.02	21.57*	20.13	21.85	22.45*	21.19	**TABLE 6**
th	19.16	20.91*	20.39	17.13	18.19*	16.95	12.85	13.73*	12.25	STANDAR-DIZED
ease	1.49	2.71*	-0.94	3.89	3.37*	3.18	8.99	8.72*	8.93	RATES

OBSERVED POP. MALES	FEMALES	STATIONARY POP. MALES	FEMALES	STABLE POP. MALES	FEMALES	OBSERVED BIRTHS	NET MATERNITY FUNCTION	BIRTHS IN STABLE POP.	
29.09987	30.21161	34.98877	35.81615	32.08667	32.80177	29.65046	30.35463	30.06950	**TABLE 7**
438.3376	437.7580	481.9912	500.1796	460.8167	479.0057	43.86109	44.44696	44.13538	MOMENTS
5495.066	4824.314	2803.744	2730.231	4037.495	4108.110	69.2319	46.8859	54.4254	AND
-115427.	-123389.	-222351.	-246843.	-176642.	-198507.	-1163.331	-1244.363	-1196.783	CUMULANTS
0.358525	0.277440	0.070204	0.059569	0.166586	0.153554	0.056803	0.025036	0.034454	
2.399253	2.356113	2.042892	2.013338	2.168164	2.134845	2.395294	2.370113	2.385613	
-0.134660	-0.109233	-0.026386	-0.022087	-0.062912	-0.057184	-0.031834	-0.014376	-0.019869	

TAL STATISTICS		THOMPSON AGE RANGE	NRR	1000r	INTERVAL	BOURGEOIS-PICHAT AGE RANGE	NRR	1000b	1000d	1000r	COALE		**TABLE 8**
	1.556												RATES
	1.204	0-4	1.22	7.49	27.21	5-29	1.13	23.46	18.97	4.49	IBR	24.88	FROM AGE DISTRI-
	3.201	5-9	1.35	11.05	27.14	30-54	1.51	31.01	15.83	15.18	IDR	16.10	BUTIONS
ERATION	30.212	10-14	1.07	2.43	27.08	55-79	1.26	20.81	12.20	8.61	IRI	8.78	AND VITAL
RATIO	105.710	15-19	1.46	13.38	26.99	*25-49	1.44	29.09	15.59	13.50	K1	-3.53	STATISTICS
											K2	0.	(Females)

ORIGINAL MATRIX SUB-DIAGONAL	ALTERNATIVE FIRST ROWS Projection	Integral	FIRST STABLE MATRIX % IN STABLE POPULATION	FISHER VALUES	REPRODUCTIVE VALUES	SECOND STABLE MATRIX Z2 FIRST COLUMN	FIRST ROW	
0.95607	0.00000	0.00000	9.517	1.160	2601034	0.1337+0.0559	0.1337+0.0559	**TABLE 9**
0.98906	0.00006	0.00000	8.824	1.251	2756342	0.1347+0.0895	0.0248+0.1274	LESLIE
0.98755	0.03532	0.00012	8.463	1.304	2074813	0.0003-0.1868	-0.0799+0.0790	MATRIX
0.98163	0.14833	0.07251	8.104	1.321	2635437	-0.1790-0.1198	-0.1003-0.0216	AND ITS
0.97858	0.29334	0.23302	7.714	1.212	2322387	-0.2281+0.0945	-0.0530-0.0917	SPECTRAL
0.97776	0.34153	0.37070	7.320	0.930	1540977	-0.0548-0.2767	0.0009-0.0999	COMPO-
0.97658	0.28142	0.33029	6.941	0.575	876035	0.2281+0.2273	0.0266-0.0674	NENTS
0.97343	0.17679	0.24705	6.573	0.273	375573	0.3599-0.0726	0.0236-0.0295	(Females)
0.96867	0.06320	0.11505	6.204	0.079	100500	-0.1583-0.3861	0.0089-0.0073	
0.96013	0.00705	0.01373	5.828	0.008	9365	-0.2640-0.3913	0.0010-0.0007	
0.94411	0.00031	0.00062	5.426	0.000	339	-0.5292+0.0028	0.0000-0.0000	
0.76281			19.085					

OBSERVED POPUL. (IN 100's)	CONTRIBUTIONS OF ROOTS (IN 100's) r1	r2,r3	r4-r11	AGE-SP. BIRTH RATES	NET MATERNITY FUNCTION	COEFF. OF MATRIX EQUATION	PARAMETERS	INTEGRAL	MATRIX	EXP. INCREASE x	e(x+2½)r	
22426	21953	247	225	0.0000	0.0000	0.0000	L(1)	1.03122	1.03124	0	1.0155	**TABLE 10**
22033	20353	43	1637	0.0000	0.0000	0.0001	L(2)	0.47333	0.47518	50	1.3809	AGE
15907	19520	-264	-3349	0.0000	0.0000	0.0334		0.72893	0.71253	55	1.4241	ANALYSIS
19957	18693	-395	1659	0.0163	0.0667	0.1385	R(1)	0.00615	0.00615	60	1.4685	AND
19161	17794	-153	1520	0.0524	0.2103	0.2689	R(2)	-0.02805	-0.03099	65	1.5144	MISCEL-
16577	16885	323	-631	0.0834	0.3275	0.3064		0.19898	0.19653	70	1.5616	LANEOUS
15228	16010	609	-1391	0.0743	0.2853	0.2468	C(1)		230660	75	1.6104	RESULTS
13745	15161	350	-1766	0.0556	0.2084	0.1514	C(2)		62929	80	1.6607	(Females)
12745	14311	-348	-1214	0.0259	0.0945	0.0527			-70869	85	1.7125	
11348	13443	-887	-1208	0.0031	0.0109	0.0057	2P/Y	31.5777	31.9712	90	1.7660	
9843	12516	-662	-2010	0.0001	0.0005	0.0002	DELTA	6.3312		95	1.8211	
31767	44021									100	1.8779	

TABLE 1 — DATA

AGE AT LAST BIRTHDAY	POPULATION BOTH SEXES	MALES Number	MALES %	FEMALES Number	FEMALES %	BIRTHS BY AGE OF MOTHER	DEATHS BOTH SEXES	DEATHS MALES	FEMALES	AT BIRTH
0	946131	482451	2.3	463680	2.1	0	96690	53192	43498	
1-4	3403852	1731494	8.4	1672358	7.6	0	47466	24503	22963	1
5-9	4353829	2207551	10.7	2146278	9.8	0	9817	4970	4847	5
10-14	4459738	2256522	10.9	2203216	10.1	131	7428	3853	3575	10
15-19	3052065	1541397	7.5	1510668	6.9	25373	8571	4475	4096	15
20-24	3706767	1750330	8.5	1956437	8.9	208314	13842	6919	6923	20
25-29	3561361	1712946	8.3	1848415	8.4	292305	13634	6717	6917	25
30-34	3074793	1488083	7.2	1586710	7.3	220734	13084	6689	6395	30
35-39	2767182	1293305	6.3	1473877	6.7	149738	13897	7272	6625	35
40-44	2415970	1092578	5.3	1323392	6.0	60441	14567	7618	6949	40
45-49	2243997	1023304	5.0	1220693	5.6	5501	16941	9026	7915	45
50-54	2029651	947187	4.6	1082464	4.9	149	21045	11345	9700	50
55-59	1760045	842552	4.1	917493	4.2	0	26788	14692	12096	55
60-64	1515870	731137	3.5	784733	3.6	0	35660	19036	16624	60
65-69	1229199	587985	2.9	641214	2.9	0	46827	24246	22581	65
70-74	969488	463895	2.3	505593	2.3		61198	31048	30150	70
75-79	605727	283034	1.4	322693	1.5		62910	31098	31812	75
80-84	286924	130286	0.6	156638	0.7	493466 M.	48715	23479	25236	80
85+	110769	46302	0.2	64467	0.3	469220 F.	30556	13543	17013	85
TOTAL	42493358	20612339		21881019		962686	589636	303721	285915	TO

TABLE 2 — MALE LIFE TABLE

x	$_nq_x$	l_x	$_nd_x$	$_nL_x$	$_nm_x$	$_na_x$	T_x	r_x	$\mathring{e}_x$	$_nM_x$
0	0.102710	100000	10271	93349	0.110029	0.3524	5539473	0.0030	55.395	0.110254
1	0.054371	89729	4879	345375	0.014126	1.2245	5446125	0.0030	60.695	0.014151
5	0.011194	84850	950	421877	0.002251	2.5000	5100749	0.0000	60.115	0.002251
10	0.008525	83901	715	417767	0.001712	2.5739	4678872	0.0338	55.767	0.001707
15	0.014470	83185	1204	413103	0.002914	2.6540	4261105	0.0225	51.224	0.002903
20	0.019575	81982	1605	405971	0.003953	2.5464	3848003	0.0000	46.937	0.003953
25	0.019424	80377	1561	398012	0.003923	2.5201	3442032	0.0122	42.824	0.003921
30	0.022273	78816	1755	389010	0.004503	2.5689	3044020	0.0235	38.622	0.004495
35	0.027800	77060	2142	380115	0.005636	2.5794	2654210	0.0252	34.443	0.005623
40	0.034336	74918	2572	368363	0.006983	2.5797	2274095	0.0164	30.355	0.006972
45	0.043213	72345	3126	354216	0.008826	2.5974	1905731	0.0052	26.342	0.008820
50	0.058287	69219	4035	336497	0.011990	2.6207	1551515	0.0070	22.415	0.011978
55	0.083825	65185	5464	312950	0.017460	2.6257	1215018	0.0079	18.640	0.017437
60	0.122781	59721	7333	281184	0.026077	2.6245	902068	0.0088	15.105	0.026036
65	0.187926	52388	9845	238352	0.041305	2.6041	620884	0.0088	11.852	0.041236
70	0.287989	42543	12252	182751	0.067041	2.5544	382532	0.0088	8.992	0.066929
75	0.430552	30291	13042	118499	0.110059	2.4730	199781	0.0088	6.595	0.109874
80	0.612450	17249	10564	58511	0.180552	2.3746	81282	0.0088	4.712	0.180211
85+	*1.000000	6685	6685	22772	0.293564	3.4064	22772	0.0088	3.406	0.292493

TABLE 3 — FEMALE LIFE TABLE

x	$_nq_x$	l_x	$_nd_x$	$_nL_x$	$_nm_x$	$_na_x$	T_x	r_x	$\mathring{e}_x$	$_nM_x$
0	0.088374	100000	8837	94402	0.093615	0.3665	5827939	0.0032	58.279	0.093810
1	0.052839	91163	4817	351410	0.013708	1.2514	5733537	0.0032	62.894	0.013731
5	0.011228	86346	970	429304	0.002258	2.5000	5382127	0.0000	62.332	0.002258
10	0.008096	85376	691	425189	0.001626	2.5521	4952822	0.0331	58.012	0.001623
15	0.013489	84685	1142	420730	0.002715	2.6412	4527633	0.0092	53.464	0.002711
20	0.017541	83543	1465	414129	0.003539	2.5540	4106903	0.0000	49.159	0.003539
25	0.018547	82077	1522	406610	0.003744	2.5196	3692775	0.0172	44.991	0.003742
30	0.019967	80555	1608	398802	0.004033	2.5303	3286165	0.0186	40.794	0.004030
35	0.022246	78946	1756	390424	0.004498	2.5468	2887363	0.0136	36.574	0.004495
40	0.025951	77190	2003	381078	0.005256	2.5674	2496939	0.0135	32.348	0.005251
45	0.031974	75187	2404	370175	0.006494	2.6039	2115861	0.0134	28.141	0.006484
50	0.044002	72783	3203	356338	0.008988	2.6340	1745687	0.0193	23.985	0.008961
55	0.064157	69580	4464	337447	0.013229	2.6580	1389349	0.0183	19.968	0.013184
60	0.101168	65116	6588	310169	0.021239	2.6604	1051902	0.0125	16.154	0.021184
65	0.162941	58529	9537	270094	0.035309	2.6355	741733	0.0125	12.673	0.035216
70	0.261110	48992	12792	213979	0.059783	2.5782	471639	0.0125	9.627	0.059633
75	0.396065	36200	14337	145086	0.098820	2.4952	257660	0.0125	7.118	0.098583
80	0.569942	21862	12460	77132	0.161543	2.4175	112574	0.0125	5.149	0.161111
85+	*1.000000	9402	9402	35442	0.265281	3.7696	35442	0.0125	3.770	0.263902

TABLE 4 — OBSERVED AND PROJECTED VITAL RATES

	OBSERVED POPULATION BOTH SEXES	MALES	FEMALES	PROJECTED POPULATION 1941 MALES	1941 FEMALES	1946 MALES	1946 FEMALES	1951 MALES	1951 FEMALES	STABLE POPULATION MALES	FEMA
RATES PER THOUSAND											
Birth	22.65	23.94	21.44	23.30	20.97	23.05	20.84	23.11	21.00	20.51	19.
Death	13.88	14.73	13.07	14.54	13.12	14.49	13.28	14.47	13.49	16.78	15.
Increase	8.78	9.21	8.38	8.76	7.85	8.56	7.56	8.64	7.51		3.72
PERCENTAGE											
under 15	30.98	32.40	29.64	30.14	27.61	28.64	26.32	27.93	25.82	25.51	24.
15-64	61.49	60.27	62.63	62.62	64.59	64.20	65.74	64.96	65.91	64.79	64.
65 and over	7.54	7.33	7.73	7.24	7.80	7.16	7.94	7.12	8.28	9.70	11.
DEP. RATIO X 100	62.64	65.92	59.66	59.70	54.83	55.76	52.12	53.95	51.73	54.35	55.

1   Italy 1950–52

AGE AT LAST BIRTHDAY	POPULATION BOTH SEXES	MALES Number	%	FEMALES Number	%	BIRTHS BY AGE OF MOTHER	DEATHS BOTH SEXES	MALES	FEMALES	AGE AT LAST BIRTHDAY
0	825729	422729	1.8	403000	1.7	0	56328	30879	25449	0
1-4	3507479	1796829	7.8	1710650	7.1	0	15531	8014	7517	1-4
5-9	3864780	1976760	8.6	1888020	7.8	0	3540	1989	1551	5-9
10-14	4211476	2138691	9.3	2072785	8.6	102	3067	1734	1333	10-14
15-19	4012193	2015100	8.8	1997093	8.3	32078	4452	2602	1850	15-19
20-24	4030403	2011910	8.8	2018493	8.4	206211	6000	3460	2540	20-24
25-29	3900287	1885359	8.2	2014928	8.3	286402	6704	3666	3038	25-29
30-34	2782227	1324726	5.8	1457501	6.0	168088	6225	3643	2582	30-34
35-39	3378386	1629527	7.1	1748859	7.2	126892	7795	3964	3831	35-39
40-44	3363656	1642561	7.2	1721095	7.1	50462	11621	6678	4943	40-44
45-49	2853155	1383782	6.0	1469373	6.1	4033	15157	9072	6085	45-49
50-54	2476839	1160088	5.1	1316751	5.5	66	19744	11632	8112	50-54
55-59	2106532	934164	4.1	1172368	4.9	0	25167	14125	11042	55-59
60-64	1865050	828980	3.6	1036070	4.3	0	33798	18078	15720	60-64
65-69	1523798	686349	3.0	837449	3.5	0	45309	23061	22248	65-69
70-74	1111470	512964	2.2	598506	2.5		57767	28969	28798	70-74
75-79	724981	331733	1.4	393248	1.6		62951	30734	32217	75-79
80-84	346003	152877	0.7	193126	0.8	448990 M.	50704	23984	26720	80-84
85+	158350	64982	0.3	93368	0.4	425344 F.	37649	16653	20996	85+
TOTAL	47042794	22900111		24142683		874334	469509	242937	226572	TOTAL

x	$_nq_x$	l_x	$_nd_x$	$_nL_x$	$_nm_x$	$_na_x$	T_x	r_x	$\mathring{e}_x$	$_nM_x$	x
0	0.069380	100000	6938	94981	0.073047	0.2766	6383166	0.0000	63.832	0.073047	0
1	0.017614	93062	1639	367535	0.004460	1.1251	6288185	0.0000	67.570	0.004460	1
5	0.005013	91423	458	455968	0.001005	2.5000	5920650	0.0018	64.761	0.001006	5
10	0.004046	90964	368	453928	0.000811	2.5709	5464682	0.0000	60.075	0.000811	10
15	0.006441	90596	584	451607	0.001292	2.6439	5010754	0.0048	55.309	0.001291	15
20	0.008567	90013	771	448196	0.001720	2.5767	4559147	0.0050	50.650	0.001720	20
25	0.009719	89242	867	444131	0.001953	2.6048	4110951	0.0397	46.065	0.001944	25
30	0.013663	88374	1208	438892	0.002751	2.5322	3666820	0.0121	41.492	0.002750	30
35	0.012093	87167	1054	433310	0.002433	2.6050	3227928	0.0000	37.032	0.002433	35
40	0.020191	86113	1739	426568	0.004076	2.7018	2794618	0.0121	32.453	0.004066	40
45	0.032455	84374	2738	415500	0.006591	2.6734	2368049	0.0280	28.066	0.006556	45
50	0.049223	81636	4018	398746	0.010098	2.6525	1952550	0.0289	23.918	0.010027	50
55	0.073188	77617	5681	374606	0.015164	2.6269	1553804	0.0182	20.019	0.015120	55
60	0.103957	71937	7478	341901	0.021873	2.6220	1179198	0.0177	16.392	0.021808	60
65	0.156092	64458	10061	298405	0.033712	2.6259	837297	0.0177	12.990	0.033600	65
70	0.249214	54397	13556	239209	0.056672	2.5823	538892	0.0177	9.907	0.056474	70
75	0.377421	40841	15414	165798	0.092969	2.5084	299683	0.0177	7.338	0.092647	75
80	0.557750	25426	14182	90089	0.157418	2.4388	133886	0.0177	5.266	0.156884	80
85+	1.000000	11245	11245	43797	0.256750	3.8948	43797	0.0177	3.895	0.256270	85+

x	$_nq_x$	l_x	$_nd_x$	$_nL_x$	$_nm_x$	$_na_x$	T_x	r_x	$\mathring{e}_x$	$_nM_x$	x
0	0.060444	100000	6044	95716	0.063149	0.2912	6742403	0.0000	67.424	0.063149	0
1	0.017359	93956	1631	371158	0.004394	1.1399	6646687	0.0000	70.743	0.004394	1
5	0.004098	92325	378	460678	0.000821	2.5000	6275529	0.0003	67.972	0.000821	5
10	0.003210	91946	295	459003	0.000643	2.5320	5814852	0.0000	63.242	0.000643	10
15	0.004623	91651	424	457254	0.000927	2.6362	5355849	0.0017	58.437	0.000926	15
20	0.006273	91227	572	454761	0.001258	2.5942	4898595	0.0000	53.696	0.001258	20
25	0.007528	90655	682	451616	0.001511	2.5678	4443834	0.0311	49.019	0.001508	25
30	0.008828	89973	794	447938	0.001773	2.5759	3992218	0.0124	44.371	0.001772	30
35	0.010896	89178	972	443560	0.002191	2.6000	3544280	0.0000	39.744	0.002191	35
40	0.014292	88207	1261	438053	0.002878	2.6352	3100719	0.0144	35.153	0.002872	40
45	0.020582	86946	1790	430534	0.004157	2.6551	2662667	0.0225	30.624	0.004141	45
50	0.030451	85157	2593	419722	0.006178	2.6627	2232132	0.0162	26.212	0.006161	50
55	0.046209	82563	3815	403949	0.009445	2.6754	1812410	0.0141	21.952	0.009419	55
60	0.073713	78748	5805	380347	0.015262	2.6926	1408462	0.0259	17.886	0.015173	60
65	0.125862	72944	9181	343438	0.026732	2.6822	1028114	0.0259	14.095	0.026566	65
70	0.216953	63763	13833	285878	0.048390	2.6191	684676	0.0259	10.738	0.048116	70
75	0.342315	49929	17092	207534	0.082355	2.5361	398798	0.0259	7.987	0.081925	75
80	0.511394	32838	16793	120797	0.139019	2.4870	191264	0.0259	5.825	0.138355	80
85+	1.000000	16045	16045	70467	0.227691	4.3919	70467	0.0259	4.392	0.224874	85+

	OBSERVED POPULATION BOTH SEXES	MALES	FEMALES	PROJECTED POPULATION 1956 MALES	FEMALES	1961 MALES	FEMALES	1966 MALES	FEMALES	STABLE POPULATION MALES	FEMALES
RATES PER THOUSAND											
Birth	18.59	19.61	17.62	19.57	17.65	19.35	17.54	18.70	17.05	16.63	15.78
Death	9.98	10.61	9.38	10.88	9.92	11.21	10.50	11.48	11.02	14.98	14.13
Increase	8.61	9.00	8.23	8.68	7.74	8.14	7.04	7.22	6.03		1.6515
PERCENTAGE											
under 15	26.38	27.66	25.16	26.23	23.86	25.93	23.72	25.04	23.06	22.55	21.61
15-64	65.41	64.70	66.08	65.89	66.55	66.11	66.04	66.60	66.11	65.12	64.03
65 and over	8.22	7.64	8.76	7.87	9.59	7.96	10.24	8.37	10.83	12.33	14.36
DEP. RATIO X 100	52.89	54.56	51.34	51.76	50.26	51.27	51.42	50.16	51.26	53.57	56.18

TABLE 1 — DATA

AGE AT LAST BIRTHDAY	BOTH SEXES	POPULATION MALES Number	%	FEMALES Number	%	BIRTHS BY AGE OF MOTHER	DEATHS BOTH SEXES	MALES	FEMALES
0	895649	457773	1.9	437876	1.7	0	38998	21823	17175
1-4	3408790	1744111	7.1	1664679	6.5	0	6429	3411	3018
5-9	4040228	2064608	8.3	1975620	7.7	0	2340	1356	984
10-14	4172928	2138033	8.6	2034895	7.9	254	2116	1306	810
15-19	3791057	1935005	7.8	1856052	7.2	34939	3119	2220	899
20-24	4063353	2057710	8.3	2005643	7.8	222417	4065	2775	1290
25-29	3834300	1919303	7.8	1914997	7.4	296940	4376	2766	1610
30-34	3811535	1902130	7.7	1909405	7.4	217272	5479	3337	2142
35-39	3742780	1827120	7.4	1915660	7.4	118830	7241	4324	2917
40-44	2783984	1335360	5.4	1448624	5.6	32184	7532	4471	3061
45-49	3221579	1559228	6.3	1662351	6.4	2752	14318	8789	5529
50-54	3153183	1532385	6.2	1620798	6.3	112	22224	14136	8088
55-59	2633644	1253055	5.1	1380589	5.4	0	29978	19256	10722
60-64	2202146	1000428	4.0	1201718	4.7	0	39175	23841	15334
65-69	1764943	748874	3.0	1016069	3.9	0	49187	26966	22221
70-74	1388165	585379	2.4	802786	3.1		63080	31842	31238
75-79	924047	389130	1.6	534917	2.1		72076	34528	37548
80-84	470762	199661	0.8	271101	1.1	475107 M.	63390	29721	33669
85+	218017	84999	0.3	133018	0.5	450593 F.	51066	21839	29227
TOTAL	50521090	24734292		25786798		925700	486189	258707	227482

TABLE 2 — MALE LIFE TABLE

x	nq_x	l_x	nd_x	nL_x	nm_x	na_x	T_x	r_x	$\overset{\circ}{e}_x$	nM_x
0	0.045884	100000	4588	96489	0.047553	0.2349	6683244	0.0032	66.832	0.047672
1	0.007744	95412	739	379497	0.001947	1.0908	6586754	0.0032	69.035	0.001956
5	0.003276	94673	310	472588	0.000656	2.5000	6207257	0.0019	65.565	0.000657
10	0.003053	94363	288	471140	0.000611	2.6650	5734669	0.0057	60.773	0.000611
15	0.005723	94074	538	469097	0.001148	2.6318	5263529	0.0028	55.951	0.001147
20	0.006721	93536	629	466136	0.001349	2.5427	4794432	0.0000	51.258	0.001349
25	0.007183	92907	667	462906	0.001442	2.5554	4328296	0.0064	46.587	0.001441
30	0.008738	92240	806	459272	0.001755	2.6069	3865390	0.0031	41.906	0.001754
35	0.011821	91434	1081	454614	0.002378	2.6347	3406118	0.0330	37.252	0.002367
40	0.016653	90353	1505	448294	0.003356	2.6926	2951504	0.0123	32.666	0.003348
45	0.027824	88849	2472	438564	0.005637	2.7028	2503210	0.0000	28.174	0.005637
50	0.045280	86377	3911	422870	0.009249	2.6958	2064646	0.0121	23.903	0.009225
55	0.074541	82465	6147	397943	0.015447	2.6600	1641775	0.0268	19.909	0.015367
60	0.113100	76318	8632	361075	0.023905	2.6231	1243833	0.0180	16.298	0.023831
65	0.166138	67687	11245	311354	0.036117	2.5920	882758	0.0180	13.042	0.036009
70	0.240883	56441	13596	249129	0.054573	2.5670	571403	0.0180	10.124	0.054396
75	0.364557	42846	15620	175417	0.089043	2.5153	322275	0.0180	7.522	0.088731
80	0.541414	27226	14741	98625	0.149459	2.4557	146857	0.0180	5.394	0.148857
85+	*1.000000	12485	12485	48232	0.258863	3.8630	48232	0.0180	3.863	0.256932

TABLE 3 — FEMALE LIFE TABLE

x	nq_x	l_x	nd_x	nL_x	nm_x	na_x	T_x	r_x	$\overset{\circ}{e}_x$	nM_x
0	0.037996	100000	3800	97142	0.039114	0.2479	7204757	0.0036	72.048	0.039223
1	0.007181	96200	691	382799	0.001805	1.1005	7107615	0.0036	73.883	0.001813
5	0.002484	95510	237	476955	0.000497	2.5000	6724816	0.0024	70.410	0.000498
10	0.001988	95272	189	475887	0.000398	2.4920	6247862	0.0058	65.579	0.000398
15	0.002419	95083	230	474863	0.000484	2.6043	5771975	0.0010	60.705	0.000484
20	0.003211	94853	305	473538	0.000643	2.6141	5297112	0.0000	55.846	0.000643
25	0.004197	94548	397	471796	0.000841	2.6166	4823574	0.0041	51.017	0.000841
30	0.005594	94151	527	469506	0.001122	2.6250	4351779	0.0000	46.221	0.001122
35	0.007613	93625	713	466436	0.001528	2.6322	3882272	0.0261	41.466	0.001523
40	0.010535	92912	979	462280	0.002117	2.6712	3415836	0.0119	36.764	0.002113
45	0.016502	91933	1517	456135	0.003326	2.6726	2953556	0.0000	32.127	0.003326
50	0.024725	90416	2236	446879	0.005002	2.6735	2497422	0.0134	27.621	0.004990
55	0.038314	88180	3379	433092	0.007801	2.6882	2050543	0.0217	23.254	0.007766
60	0.062345	84802	5287	411823	0.012838	2.6950	1617451	0.0272	19.073	0.012760
65	0.104719	79515	8327	378316	0.022010	2.6871	1205628	0.0272	15.162	0.021870
70	0.179316	71188	12765	325964	0.039161	2.6516	827312	0.0272	11.621	0.038912
75	0.301558	58423	17618	249475	0.070620	2.5797	501348	0.0272	8.581	0.070194
80	0.478039	40805	19506	156026	0.125020	2.5393	251873	0.0272	6.173	0.124193
85+	*1.000000	21299	21299	95847	0.222215	4.5002	95847	0.0272	4.500	0.219722

TABLE 4 — OBSERVED AND PROJECTED VITAL RATES

	OBSERVED POPULATION BOTH SEXES	MALES	FEMALES	PROJECTED POPULATION 1966 MALES	FEMALES	1971 MALES	FEMALES	1976 MALES	FEMALES	STABLE POPULATION MALES	FE...
RATES PER THOUSAND											
Birth	18.32	19.21	17.47	18.57	16.91	17.98	16.41	17.58	16.10	17.03	1...
Death	9.62	10.46	8.82	10.82	9.57	11.14	10.21	11.49	10.71	13.43	1...
Increase	8.70	8.75	8.65	7.75	7.34	6.83	6.20	6.09	5.38		3..
PERCENTAGE											
under 15	24.78	25.89	23.71	25.27	23.21	25.12	23.13	24.67	22.79	23.54	2...
15-64	65.79	65.99	65.60	66.23	65.26	65.79	64.58	65.37	63.94	64.92	6...
65 and over	9.43	8.12	10.69	8.50	11.53	9.09	12.30	9.96	13.26	11.54	1...
DEP. RATIO X 100	52.00	51.54	52.44	50.99	53.23	52.01	54.85	52.97	56.39	54.03	5...

AGE LAST BIRTHDAY	1966 BOTH SEXES	1966 MALES	1966 FEMALES	1971 BOTH SEXES	1971 MALES	1971 FEMALES	1976 BOTH SEXES	1976 MALES	1976 FEMALES	AGE AT LAST BIRTHDAY	
0-4	4441	2270	2171	4466	2283	2183	4498	2299	2199	0-4	**TABLE 5**
5-9	4275	2186	2089	4411	2254	2157	4437	2267	2170	5-9	POPULATION
10-14	4029	2058	1971	4264	2179	2085	4399	2247	2152	10-14	PROJECTED
15-19	4160	2129	2031	4016	2049	1967	4250	2170	2080	15-19	WITH
20-24	3774	1923	1851	4140	2115	2025	3997	2036	1961	20-24	FIXED
25-29	4041	2043	1998	3753	1909	1844	4118	2101	2017	25-29	AGE—
30-34	3810	1904	1906	4016	2027	1989	3729	1894	1835	30-34	SPECIFIC
35-39	3780	1883	1897	3778	1885	1893	3983	2007	1976	35-39	BIRTH
40-44	3701	1802	1899	3737	1857	1880	3735	1859	1876	40-44	AND
45-49	2735	1306	1429	3636	1763	1873	3671	1816	1855	45-49	DEATH
50-54	3132	1503	1629	2660	1260	1400	3535	1700	1835	50-54	RATES
55-59	3013	1442	1571	2993	1415	1578	2542	1185	1357	55-59	(IN 1000's)
60-64	2450	1137	1313	2802	1308	1494	2785	1284	1501	60-64	
65-69	1967	863	1104	2186	980	1206	2500	1128	1372	65-69	
70-74	1474	599	875	1641	690	951	1823	784	1039	70-74	
75-79	1026	412	614	1092	422	670	1214	486	728	75-79	
80-84	554	219	335	616	232	384	656	237	419	80-84	
85+	265	98	167	313	107	206	349	113	236	85+	
TOTAL	52627	25777	26850	54520	26735	27785	56221	27613	28608	TOTAL	

STANDARD COUNTRIES: STANDARDIZED RATES PER THOUSAND	ENGLAND AND WALES 1961 BOTH SEXES	MALES	FEMALES	UNITED STATES 1960 BOTH SEXES	MALES	FEMALES	MEXICO 1960 BOTH SEXES	MALES	FEMALES	
Birth	15.43	16.80*	14.56	15.71	15.70*	15.06	17.29	15.34*	16.79	**TABLE 6** STANDARDIZED RATES
Death	11.74	11.99*	11.66	9.75	10.58*	8.77	5.59	8.71*	4.72	
Increase	3.69	4.81*	2.90	5.96	5.11*	6.30	11.70	6.63*	12.07	

	OBSERVED POP. MALES	OBSERVED POP. FEMALES	STATIONARY POP. MALES	STATIONARY POP. FEMALES	STABLE POP. MALES	STABLE POP. FEMALES	OBSERVED BIRTHS	NET MATERNITY FUNCTION	BIRTHS IN STABLE POP.	
	32.49937	34.59090	36.89613	38.94510	35.09818	36.99425	28.95833	29.13775	29.00473	**TABLE 7** MOMENTS AND CUMULANTS
	446.5894	478.9701	504.6742	546.6567	494.6217	537.5355	33.42468	35.04998	34.75577	
	3713.861	3239.477	2356.805	1984.764	3219.657	3073.359	73.5679	81.0204	82.5638	
	-155558.	-204809.	-250667.	-313519.	-227972.	-290088.	-409.134	-440.845	-407.030	
	0.154855	0.095505	0.043213	0.024114	0.085664	0.060814	0.144936	0.152449	0.162367	
	2.220034	2.107244	2.015818	1.950859	2.068172	1.996041	2.633790	2.641152	2.663045	
	-0.061917	-0.036914	-0.016329	-0.008805	-0.032362	-0.022207	-0.097549	-0.102121	-0.110304	

VITAL STATISTICS		THOMPSON AGE RANGE	NRR	1000r	INTERVAL	BOURGEOIS-PICHAT AGE RANGE	NRR	1000b	1000d	1000r	COALE	
R	1.180										IBR	**TABLE 8** RATES FROM AGE DISTRIBUTIONS AND VITAL STATISTICS (Females)
R	1.110	0-4	1.12	4.07	27.43	5-29	1.03	16.27	15.27	1.00	IDR	
R	2.423	5-9	1.07	2.41	27.39	30-54	1.21	19.29	12.32	6.97	IRI	
GENERATION	29.071	10-14	1.13	4.53	27.35	55-79	1.59	33.09	15.95	17.14	K1	
X RATIO	105.440	15-19	1.08	2.64	27.27	*50-74	1.67	37.29	18.38	18.91	K2	

ORIGINAL MATRIX SUB-DIAGONAL	ALTERNATIVE FIRST ROWS Projection	Integral	FIRST STABLE MATRIX % IN STABLE POPULATION	FISHER VALUES	REPRODUCTIVE VALUES	SECOND STABLE MATRIX Z2 FIRST COLUMN	FIRST ROW	
0.99378	0.00000	0.00000	7.568	1.051	2210160	0.1541+0.0604	0.1541+0.0604	**TABLE 9** LESLIE MATRIX AND ITS SPECTRAL COMPONENTS (Females)
0.99776	0.00015	0.00000	7.387	1.077	2127665	0.1512-0.1209	0.0209+0.1399	
0.99785	0.02209	0.00029	7.239	1.099	2235980	-0.0345-0.2248	-0.0944+0.0748	
0.99721	0.15116	0.04437	7.095	1.098	2037775	-0.2490-0.0965	-0.0987-0.0392	
0.99632	0.30999	0.26141	6.949	0.962	1928677	-0.2441+0.1969	-0.0364-0.0987	
0.99515	0.31339	0.36552	6.800	0.656	1255543	0.0573+0.3633	0.0095-0.0876	
0.99346	0.20490	0.26823	6.646	0.340	648729	0.4023+0.1541	0.0204-0.0493	
0.99109	0.09818	0.14622	6.485	0.131	251710	0.3909-0.3179	0.0135-0.0184	
0.98671	0.02786	0.05237	6.313	0.031	44697	-0.0940-0.5802	0.0041-0.0038	
0.97971	0.00201	0.00390	6.118	0.002	3588	-0.6386-0.2416	0.0003-0.0003	
0.96915	0.00008	0.00016	5.887	0.000	135	-0.6088+0.4993	0.0000-0.0000	
0.79456			25.515					

OBSERVED POPUL. (IN 100's)	CONTRIBUTIONS OF ROOTS (IN 100's) r_1	r_2, r_3	r_4-r_{11}	AGE-SP. BIRTH RATES	NET MATERNITY FUNCTION	COEFF. OF MATRIX EQUATION	PARAMETERS INTEGRAL	MATRIX	EXP. INCREASE x	$e^{(x+2\frac{1}{2})r}$	
21026	20917	131	-22	0.0000	0.0000	0.0000	L(1) 1.01815	1.01815	0	1.0090	**TABLE 10** AGE ANALYSIS AND MISCELLANEOUS RESULTS (Females)
19756	20416	-291	-368	0.0000	0.0000	0.0001	L(2) 0.42064	0.42374	50	1.2078	
20349	20007	-522	864	0.0001	0.0003	0.0219	0.75763	0.73625	55	1.2297	
18561	19608	-209	-838	0.0092	0.0435	0.1496	R(1) 0.00360	0.00360	60	1.2521	
20056	19205	474	378	0.0540	0.2556	0.3059	R(2) -0.02864	-0.03262	65	1.2748	
19150	18793	843	-486	0.0755	0.3561	0.3081	0.21279	0.20971	70	1.2979	
19094	18368	334	392	0.0554	0.2601	0.2004	C(1)	276377	75	1.3215	
19157	17923	-765	1999	0.0302	0.1408	0.0954	C(2)	-3147	80	1.3454	
14486	17446	-1346	-1614	0.0108	0.0500	0.0268		-116525	85	1.3698	
16624	16908	-523	239	0.0008	0.0037	0.0019	2P/Y 29.5272	29.9610	90	1.3947	
16269	16269	1202	-1263	0.0000	0.0002	0.0001	DELTA 5.5021		95	1.4200	
53402	70518								100	1.4458	

TABLE 1 — DATA

AGE AT LAST BIRTHDAY	POPULATION BOTH SEXES	MALES Number	%	FEMALES Number	%	BIRTHS BY AGE OF MOTHER	DEATHS BOTH SEXES	MALES	FEMALES	AGE AT LAST BIRTH
0	954000	488000	1.9	466000	1.8	0	36671	20474	16197	0
1-4	3535000	1809000	7.1	1726000	6.5	0	5255	2809	2446	1-
5-9	4117000	2100000	8.2	2017000	7.6	0	2085	1288	797	5-
10-14	4028000	2055000	8.0	1973000	7.4	65	1754	1076	678	10-
15-19	4114000	2092000	8.2	2022000	7.6	27041	3220	2334	886	15-
20-24	3981000	2011000	7.9	1970000	7.4	197798	3702	2592	1110	20-
25-29	3917000	1969000	7.7	1948000	7.3	338925	4013	2598	1415	25-
30-34	3867000	1928000	7.5	1939000	7.3	252537	5052	3202	1850	30-
35-39	3829000	1892000	7.4	1937000	7.3	142595	7050	4367	2683	35-
40-44	3520000	1698000	6.6	1822000	6.9	52655	10082	6198	3884	40-
45-49	2659000	1284000	5.0	1375000	5.2	4347	10939	6723	4216	45-
50-54	3349000	1633000	6.4	1716000	6.5	157	22409	14183	8226	50-
55-59	2853000	1371000	5.4	1482000	5.6	0	31677	20608	11069	55-
60-64	2338000	1085000	4.2	1253000	4.7	0	41444	26243	15201	60-
65-69	1859000	795000	3.1	1064000	4.0	0	50944	28867	22077	65-
70-74	1438000	604000	2.4	834000	3.1		63446	32639	30807	70-
75-79	988000	410000	1.6	578000	2.2		72833	34476	38357	75-
80-84	522000	217000	0.8	305000	1.1	521377 M.	63993	29043	34950	80-
85+	262000	104000	0.4	158000	0.6	494743 F.	53481	22562	30919	85
TOTAL	52130000	25545000		26585000		1016120	490050	262282	227768	TOT

TABLE 2 — MALE LIFE TABLE

x	$_nq_x$	l_x	$_nd_x$	$_nL_x$	$_nm_x$	$_na_x$	T_x	r_x	$\overset{\circ}{e}_x$	$_nM_x$
0	0.040439	100000	4044	96862	0.041749	0.2240	6771220	0.0062	67.712	0.041955
1	0.006125	95956	588	382110	0.001538	1.0835	6674358	0.0062	69.556	0.001553
5	0.003053	95368	291	476114	0.000612	2.5000	6292248	0.0103	65.978	0.000613
10	0.002615	95077	249	474814	0.000524	2.6982	5816134	0.0000	61.173	0.000524
15	0.005565	94829	528	472898	0.001116	2.6411	5341320	0.0011	56.326	0.001116
20	0.006425	94301	606	470008	0.001289	2.5304	4868422	0.0048	51.626	0.001289
25	0.006577	93695	616	466969	0.001320	2.5555	4398414	0.0028	46.944	0.001319
30	0.008274	93079	770	463561	0.001661	2.6205	3931446	0.0023	42.238	0.001661
35	0.011500	92309	1062	459075	0.002312	2.6748	3467885	0.0103	37.568	0.002308
40	0.018201	91247	1661	452345	0.003671	2.6575	3008810	0.0351	32.974	0.003650
45	0.025866	89586	2317	442567	0.005236	2.6848	2556465	0.0000	28.536	0.005236
50	0.042580	87269	3716	427843	0.008685	2.7120	2113898	0.0000	24.223	0.008685
55	0.072993	83553	6099	403597	0.015111	2.6768	1686055	0.0253	20.179	0.015031
60	0.114797	77454	8892	366164	0.024283	2.6262	1282458	0.0223	16.558	0.024187
65	0.167483	68563	11483	315101	0.036443	2.5867	916294	0.0223	13.364	0.036311
70	0.239460	57080	13668	251989	0.054242	2.5557	601192	0.0223	10.533	0.054038
75	0.348728	43411	15139	179322	0.084422	2.5074	349203	0.0223	8.044	0.084088
80	0.502393	28273	14204	105630	0.134469	2.4843	169882	0.0223	6.009	0.133838
85+	*1.000000	14069	14069	64252	0.218961	4.5670	64252	0.0223	4.567	0.216942

TABLE 3 — FEMALE LIFE TABLE

x	$_nq_x$	l_x	$_nd_x$	$_nL_x$	$_nm_x$	$_na_x$	T_x	r_x	$\overset{\circ}{e}_x$	$_nM_x$
0	0.033689	100000	3369	97421	0.034581	0.2345	7316597	0.0065	73.166	0.034758
1	0.005594	96631	541	384952	0.001404	1.0906	7219176	0.0065	74.709	0.001417
5	0.001965	96091	189	479981	0.000393	2.5000	6834224	0.0098	71.123	0.000395
10	0.001717	95902	165	479102	0.000344	2.5262	6354243	0.0000	66.258	0.000344
15	0.002189	95737	210	478184	0.000438	2.6036	5875142	0.0000	61.367	0.000438
20	0.002814	95528	269	476994	0.000564	2.6053	5396958	0.0032	56.496	0.000563
25	0.003626	95259	345	475468	0.000726	2.6103	4919964	0.0009	51.648	0.000726
30	0.004760	94913	452	473501	0.000954	2.6417	4444496	0.0000	46.827	0.000954
35	0.006909	94462	653	470790	0.001386	2.6750	3970995	0.0048	42.038	0.001385
40	0.010661	93809	1000	466703	0.002143	2.6685	3500204	0.0321	37.312	0.002132
45	0.015230	92809	1413	460753	0.003068	2.6719	3033502	0.0028	32.685	0.003066
50	0.023705	91395	2167	451952	0.004794	2.6805	2572748	0.0000	28.150	0.004794
55	0.036883	89229	3291	438528	0.007505	2.6857	2120797	0.0236	23.768	0.007469
60	0.059351	85938	5100	417929	0.012204	2.6944	1682269	0.0269	19.575	0.012132
65	0.099601	80837	8051	385588	0.020881	2.6900	1264340	0.0269	15.641	0.020749
70	0.170963	72786	12444	334755	0.037173	2.6555	878752	0.0269	12.073	0.036939
75	0.287343	60342	17339	259763	0.066749	2.5807	543997	0.0269	9.015	0.066362
80	0.445585	43003	19162	166388	0.115162	2.5707	284235	0.0269	6.610	0.114590
85+	1.000000	23842	23842	117846	0.202311	4.9429	117846	0.0269	4.943	0.195689

TABLE 4 — OBSERVED AND PROJECTED VITAL RATES

	OBSERVED POPULATION BOTH SEXES	MALES	FEMALES	PROJECTED POPULATION 1969 MALES	FEMALES	1974 MALES	FEMALES	1979 MALES	FEMALES	STABLE POPULATION MALES	FEMA
RATES PER THOUSAND											
Birth	19.49	20.41	18.61	19.65	17.93	18.94	17.32	18.32	16.80	18.53	17.
Death	9.40	10.27	8.57	10.75	9.38	11.04	9.93	11.32	10.36	12.14	10.
Increase	10.09	10.14	10.04	8.90	8.56	7.90	7.39	7.00	6.44		6.38
PERCENTAGE											
under 15	24.24	25.26	23.25	25.70	23.66	26.12	24.06	26.00	24.02	25.26	23.
15-64	66.04	66.40	65.69	65.45	64.45	64.33	63.19	63.63	62.24	64.14	62.
65 and over	9.72	8.34	11.06	8.85	11.89	9.55	12.75	10.37	13.74	10.59	13.
DEP. RATIO X 100	51.42	50.59	52.23	52.80	55.15	55.44	58.26	57.16	60.66	55.90	60.

Table 5 — Population projected with fixed age-specific birth and death rates (in 1000's)

AGE AT LAST BIRTHDAY	1969 BOTH SEXES	1969 MALES	1969 FEMALES	1974 BOTH SEXES	1974 MALES	1974 FEMALES	1979 BOTH SEXES	1979 MALES	1979 FEMALES
0-4	4909	2510	2399	4947	2530	2417	4971	2542	2429
5-9	4464	2283	2181	4882	2495	2387	4919	2514	2405
10-14	4107	2094	2013	4454	2277	2177	4870	2488	2382
15-19	4016	2047	1969	4095	2086	2009	4441	2268	2173
20-24	4096	2079	2017	3998	2034	1964	4077	2073	2004
25-29	3962	1998	1964	4077	2066	2011	3979	2021	1958
30-34	3895	1955	1940	3939	1983	1956	4053	2051	2002
35-39	3837	1909	1928	3865	1936	1929	3908	1964	1944
40-44	3784	1864	1920	3792	1881	1911	3819	1907	1912
45-49	3460	1661	1799	3720	1824	1896	3728	1841	1887
50-54	2590	1241	1349	3370	1606	1764	3622	1763	1859
55-59	3205	1540	1665	2480	1171	1309	3227	1515	1712
60-64	2656	1244	1412	2985	1398	1587	2309	1062	1247
65-69	2090	934	1156	2373	1070	1303	2667	1203	1464
70-74	1560	636	924	1751	747	1004	1987	856	1131
75-79	1077	430	647	1169	452	717	1310	531	779
80-84	612	242	370	668	253	415	726	267	459
85+	348	132	216	409	147	262	448	154	294
TOTAL	54668	26799	27869	56974	27956	29018	59061	29020	30041

Table 6 — Standardized rates

STANDARD COUNTRIES: STANDARDIZED RATES PER THOUSAND

	ENGLAND AND WALES 1961 BOTH SEXES	MALES	FEMALES	UNITED STATES 1960 BOTH SEXES	MALES	FEMALES	MEXICO 1960 BOTH SEXES	MALES	FEMALES
	16.70	18.03*	15.76	16.99	16.91*	16.30	18.22	16.30*	17.70
	11.02	11.35*	10.82	9.12	10.06*	8.10	5.16	8.28*	4.29
	5.68	6.68*	4.94	7.87	6.85*	8.20	13.07	8.02*	13.41

Table 7 — Moments and cumulants

OBSERVED POP. MALES	FEMALES	STATIONARY POP. MALES	FEMALES	STABLE POP. MALES	FEMALES	OBSERVED BIRTHS	NET MATERNITY FUNCTION	BIRTHS IN STABLE POP.
32.82388	34.85306	37.10517	39.26179	33.90150	35.77325	29.77232	29.85062	29.61775
452.0274	485.6709	511.0832	554.7081	490.4446	535.5551	34.00908	34.63590	34.10860
3615.468	3238.236	2462.254	2011.227	3950.307	3932.443	73.9951	81.4235	83.6209
-162079.	-211335.	-254520.	-323108.	-208005.	-273147.	-402.275	-368.117	-309.735
0.141526	0.091536	0.045414	0.023699	0.132279	0.100673	0.139194	0.159559	0.176213
2.206772	2.104042	2.025598	1.949927	2.135242	2.047667	2.652197	2.693145	2.733766
-0.056765	-0.035433	-0.017264	-0.008651	-0.050359	-0.036838	-0.097994	-0.114976	-0.131159

Table 8 — Rates from age distributions and vital statistics (Females)

VITAL STATISTICS:

	1.275
	1.209
	2.619
ERATION	29.734
RATIO	105.383

THOMPSON:

AGE RANGE	NRR	1000r	INTERVAL
0-4	1.11	3.81	27.44
5-9	1.08	2.81	27.40
10-14	1.07	2.59	27.36
15-19	1.14	4.64	27.29

BOURGEOIS-PICHAT:

AGE RANGE	NRR	1000b	1000d	1000r
5-29	1.03	15.89	14.94	0.96
30-54	1.29	21.10	11.65	9.45
55-79	1.71	39.75	19.80	19.95
*15-39	1.03	16.10	14.83	1.26

COALE: IBR, IDR, IRI, K1, K2

Table 9 — Leslie matrix and its spectral components (Females)

ORIGINAL MATRIX SUB-DIAGONAL	ALTERNATIVE FIRST ROWS Projection	Integral	FIRST STABLE MATRIX % IN STABLE POPULATION	FISHER VALUES	REPRODUCTIVE VALUES	SECOND STABLE MATRIX Z2 FIRST COLUMN	FIRST ROW
0.99504	0.00000	0.00000	8.246	1.053	2308581	0.1548+0.0561	0.1548+0.0561
0.99817	0.00000	0.00000	7.947	1.093	2204186	0.1452-0.1189	0.0272+0.1419
0.99808	0.01571	0.00008	7.683	1.130	2230127	-0.0319-0.2122	-0.0945+0.0839
0.99751	0.13332	0.03191	7.427	1.153	2330749	-0.2272-0.0927	-0.1078-0.0344
0.99680	0.32157	0.23961	7.176	1.052	2073103	-0.2238+0.1688	-0.0431-0.1039
0.99586	0.35663	0.41521	6.928	0.750	1461458	0.0349+0.3182	-0.0090-0.0971
0.99427	0.23890	0.31081	6.682	0.401	776881	0.3323+0.1514	0.0217-0.0569
0.99132	0.12009	0.17568	6.435	0.163	315730	0.3418-0.2370	0.0154-0.0226
0.98725	0.03760	0.06897	6.178	0.042	76848	-0.0328-0.4712	0.0053-0.0053
0.98090	0.00382	0.00754	5.908	0.004	5494	-0.4769-0.2407	0.0006-0.0005
0.97030	0.00011	0.00022	5.613	0.000	188	-0.5065+0.3221	0.0000-0.0000
0.80344			23.778				

Table 10 — Age analysis and miscellaneous results (Females)

OBSERVED POPUL. (IN 100's)	CONTRIBUTIONS OF ROOTS (IN 100's) r_1	r_2, r_3	r_4-r_{11}	AGE-SP. BIRTH RATES	NET MATERNITY FUNCTION	COEFF. OF MATRIX EQUATION	PARAMETERS	INTEGRAL	MATRIX	EXP. INCREASE x	$e^{(x+2\frac{1}{2})r}$
21920	22124	99	-303	0.0000	0.0000	0.0000	L(1)	1.03245	1.03247	0	1.0161
20170	21322	-982	-169	0.0000	0.0000	0.0000	L(2)	0.44544	0.44651	50	1.3984
19730	20613	-1278	395	0.0000	0.0001	0.0156		0.77135	0.75014	55	1.4438
20220	19926	-211	504	0.0065	0.0311	0.1322	R(1)	0.00639	0.00639	60	1.4907
19700	19252	1423	-975	0.0489	0.2332	0.3180	R(2)	-0.02314	-0.02717	65	1.5390
19480	18586	1938	-1044	0.0847	0.4028	0.3515		0.20942	0.20678	70	1.5890
19390	17927	407	1056	0.0634	0.3003	0.2345	C(1)		268292	75	1.6405
19370	17264	-2043	4149	0.0358	0.1687	0.1172	C(2)		-81542	80	1.6938
18220	16576	-2900	4544	0.0141	0.0657	0.0364			-313386	85	1.7487
13750	15850	-731	-1369	0.0015	0.0071	0.0036	2P/Y	30.0028	30.3861	90	1.8055
17160	15058	2845	-743	0.0000	0.0002	0.0001	DELTA	4.1597		95	1.8641
56740	63793									100	1.9246

TABLE 1 — DATA

AGE AT LAST BIRTHDAY	POPULATION BOTH SEXES	MALES Number	%	FEMALES Number	%	BIRTHS BY AGE OF MOTHER	DEATHS BOTH SEXES	MALES	FEMALES	AGE AT LAST BIRTH
0	4922	2499	1.6	2423	1.5	0	163	94	69	0
1-4	19184	9836	6.2	9348	5.9	0	29	15	14	1-4
5-9	21918	11185	7.1	10733	6.7	0	14	9	5	5-9
10-14	19902	10181	6.4	9721	6.1	1	8	5	3	10-14
15-19	19849	9996	6.3	9853	6.2	219	15	11	4	15-1
20-24	21798	11280	7.1	10518	6.6	1495	27	22	5	20-2
25-29	24065	12574	7.9	11491	7.2	1669	32	23	9	25-2
30-34	25886	13611	8.6	12275	7.7	1075	37	23	14	30-3
35-39	22426	10762	6.8	11664	7.3	454	42	22	20	35-3
40-44	18694	9335	5.9	9359	5.9	101	57	32	25	40-4
45-49	23047	11638	7.3	11409	7.2	8	121	81	40	45-4
50-54	23519	11867	7.5	11652	7.3	0	201	138	63	50-5
55-59	21373	10495	6.6	10878	6.8	0	270	176	94	55-5
60-64	17298	8106	5.1	9192	5.8	0	347	212	135	60-6
65-69	13092	5988	3.8	7104	4.5	0	424	238	186	65-6
70-74	9497	4226	2.7	5271	3.3		516	266	250	70-7
75-79	6367	2737	1.7	3630	2.3		555	270	285	75-7
80-84	3431	1458	0.9	1973	1.2	2576 M.	492	231	261	80-8
85+	1570	645	0.4	925	0.6	2446 F.	348	148	200	85+
TOTAL	317838	158419		159419		5022	3698	2016	1682	TOT

TABLE 2 — MALE LIFE TABLE

x	nq_x	l_x	nd_x	nL_x	nm_x	na_x	T_x	r_x	$\mathring{e}_x$	nM_x
0	0.036554	100000	3655	97201	0.037607	0.2342	6643809	0.0003	66.438	0.037615
1	0.006071	96345	585	383677	0.001524	1.0904	6546609	0.0003	67.950	0.001525
5	0.003998	95760	383	477841	0.000801	2.5000	6162932	0.0182	64.358	0.000805
10	0.002456	95377	234	476328	0.000492	2.6239	5685090	0.0105	59.607	0.000491
15	0.005489	95143	522	474550	0.001100	2.7729	5208763	0.0000	54.747	0.001100
20	0.009706	94620	918	470875	0.001950	2.5750	4734213	0.0000	50.034	0.001950
25	0.009104	93702	853	466349	0.001829	2.4666	4263338	0.0000	45.499	0.001829
30	0.008417	92849	782	462310	0.001690	2.5238	3796989	0.0138	40.894	0.001690
35	0.010236	92067	942	458142	0.002057	2.6699	3334679	0.0355	36.220	0.002044
40	0.017011	91125	1550	452193	0.003428	2.7858	2876537	0.0000	31.567	0.003428
45	0.034258	89575	3069	440900	0.006960	2.7272	2424344	0.0000	27.065	0.006960
50	0.056598	86506	4896	421028	0.011629	2.6505	1983444	0.0000	22.928	0.011629
55	0.080931	81610	6605	392448	0.016830	2.6376	1562416	0.0205	19.145	0.016770
60	0.123420	75005	9257	352999	0.026224	2.6204	1169968	0.0154	15.598	0.026153
65	0.181847	65748	11956	299986	0.039856	2.5949	816969	0.0154	12.426	0.039746
70	0.273319	53792	14702	232938	0.063117	2.5499	516983	0.0154	9.611	0.062944
75	0.395918	39090	15476	156450	0.098922	2.4801	284045	0.0154	7.266	0.098648
80	0.560010	23613	13224	83237	0.158869	2.4199	127595	0.0154	5.404	0.158436
85+	1.000000	10390	10390	44359	0.234220	4.2695	44359	0.0154	4.269	0.229458

TABLE 3 — FEMALE LIFE TABLE

x	nq_x	l_x	nd_x	nL_x	nm_x	na_x	T_x	r_x	$\mathring{e}_x$	nM_x
0	0.027839	100000	2784	97947	0.028423	0.2624	7190610	0.0024	71.906	0.028477
1	0.005948	97216	578	387194	0.001494	1.1123	7092663	0.0024	72.958	0.001498
5	0.002308	96638	223	482631	0.000462	2.5000	6705469	0.0184	69.388	0.000466
10	0.001541	96415	149	481696	0.000309	2.4610	6222838	0.0082	64.542	0.000309
15	0.002028	96266	195	480859	0.000406	2.5848	5741141	0.0000	59.638	0.000406
20	0.002374	96071	228	479822	0.000475	2.6639	5260282	0.0000	54.754	0.000475
25	0.003909	95843	375	478343	0.000783	2.6751	4780460	0.0000	49.878	0.000783
30	0.005688	95468	543	476075	0.001141	2.6687	4302117	0.0000	45.063	0.001141
35	0.008579	94925	814	472737	0.001723	2.6806	3826042	0.0253	40.306	0.001715
40	0.013272	94111	1249	467598	0.002671	2.6335	3353305	0.0000	35.631	0.002671
45	0.017387	92862	1615	460520	0.003506	2.6532	2885707	0.0000	31.075	0.003506
50	0.026700	91247	2436	450595	0.005407	2.6847	2425187	0.0000	26.578	0.005407
55	0.042498	88811	3774	435376	0.008669	2.7008	1974592	0.0146	22.234	0.008641
60	0.071420	85037	6073	411254	0.014768	2.7066	1539216	0.0230	18.101	0.014687
65	0.124084	78963	9798	372139	0.026329	2.6856	1127962	0.0230	14.285	0.026182
70	0.213983	69165	14800	310524	0.047662	2.6148	755823	0.0230	10.928	0.047429
75	0.330218	54365	17952	227616	0.078871	2.5374	445299	0.0230	8.191	0.078512
80	0.494966	36413	18023	135671	0.132844	2.5051	217683	0.0230	5.978	0.132286
85+	1.000000	18390	18390	82012	0.224230	4.4597	82012	0.0230	4.460	0.216216

TABLE 4 — OBSERVED AND PROJECTED VITAL RATES

	OBSERVED POPULATION BOTH SEXES	MALES	FEMALES	PROJECTED POPULATION 1965 MALES	FEMALES	1970 MALES	FEMALES	1975 MALES	FEMALES	STABLE POPULATION MALES	FEMAL
RATES PER THOUSAND											
Birth	15.80	16.26	15.34	15.15	14.22	14.40	13.45	14.49	13.50	15.88	14.
Death	11.63	12.73	10.55	13.31	11.44	13.90	12.22	14.62	13.05	14.40	13.
Increase	4.17	3.53	4.79	1.84	2.78	0.50	1.23	-0.13	0.45		1.480
PERCENTAGE											
under 15	20.74	21.27	20.21	22.08	20.90	22.06	20.79	21.36	20.09	22.53	21.
15-64	68.57	69.22	67.93	67.58	65.90	66.31	64.47	65.81	63.86	65.83	64.
65 and over	10.68	9.50	11.86	10.34	13.21	11.63	14.74	12.83	16.05	11.63	14.
DEP. RATIO X 100	45.83	44.46	47.21	47.97	51.75	50.81	55.11	51.96	56.60	51.90	56.

TABLE 5 — POPULATION PROJECTED WITH FIXED AGE—SPECIFIC BIRTH AND DEATH RATES (IN 1000's)

AGE AT LAST BIRTHDAY	1965 BOTH SEXES	1965 MALES	1965 FEMALES	1970 BOTH SEXES	1970 MALES	1970 FEMALES	1975 BOTH SEXES	1975 MALES	1975 FEMALES	AGE AT LAST BIRTHDAY
0-4	24	12	12	22	11	11	22	11	11	0-4
5-9	24	12	12	23	12	11	22	11	11	5-9
10-14	22	11	11	24	12	12	23	12	11	10-14
15-19	20	10	10	22	11	11	24	12	12	15-19
20-24	20	10	10	20	10	10	22	11	11	20-24
25-29	21	11	10	20	10	10	20	10	10	25-29
30-34	23	12	11	21	11	10	20	10	10	30-34
35-39	25	13	12	23	12	11	21	11	10	35-39
40-44	23	11	12	25	13	12	23	12	11	40-44
45-49	18	9	9	21	10	11	25	13	12	45-49
50-54	22	11	11	18	9	9	21	10	11	50-54
55-59	22	11	11	21	10	11	17	8	9	55-59
60-64	19	9	10	21	10	11	19	9	10	60-64
65-69	15	7	8	17	8	9	18	8	10	65-69
70-74	11	5	6	12	5	7	14	6	8	70-74
75-79	7	3	4	7	3	4	9	4	5	75-79
80-84	3	1	2	4	2	2	5	2	3	80-84
85+	2	1	1	2	1	1	2	1	1	85+
TOTAL	321	159	162	323	160	163	327	161	166	TOTAL

TABLE 6 — STANDARDIZED RATES

STANDARD COUNTRIES: STANDARDIZED RATES PER THOUSAND	ENGLAND AND WALES 1961 BOTH SEXES	MALES	FEMALES	UNITED STATES 1960 BOTH SEXES	MALES	FEMALES	MEXICO 1960 BOTH SEXES	MALES	FEMALES
Birth	14.15	14.18*	13.36	14.38	13.49*	13.80	16.81	12.69*	16.34
Death	12.62	12.64*	12.59	10.30	11.22*	9.29	5.58	9.79*	4.63
Increase	1.54	1.54*	0.77	4.08	2.27*	4.51	11.24	2.90*	11.70

TABLE 7 — MOMENTS AND CUMULANTS

	OBSERVED POP. MALES	OBSERVED POP. FEMALES	STATIONARY POP. MALES	STATIONARY POP. FEMALES	STABLE POP. MALES	STABLE POP. FEMALES	OBSERVED BIRTHS	NET MATERNITY FUNCTION	BIRTHS IN STABLE POP.
μ	35.62967	37.20253	36.36021	38.41119	35.63322	37.62438	27.88033	27.62154	27.57370
σ^2	454.3625	482.9265	493.0403	533.1983	489.2042	529.8777	29.17385	30.31250	30.16489
κ_3	1742.428	1387.377	2420.422	2028.112	2760.970	2456.775	80.5695	99.6802	99.7760
κ_4	-188269.	-225440.	-234124.	-293521.	-225850.	-285425.	-132.495	-65.665	-53.340
β_1	0.032367	0.017090	0.048880	0.027134	0.065111	0.040570	0.261433	0.356741	0.362699
β_2	2.088044	2.033351	2.036880	1.967567	2.056287	1.983423	2.844327	2.928536	2.941379
κ	-0.013210	-0.006749	-0.018693	-0.010014	-0.024884	-0.014963	-0.192345	-0.242757	-0.248706

TABLE 8 — RATES FROM AGE DISTRIBUTIONS AND VITAL STATISTICS (Females)

VITAL STATISTICS		THOMPSON AGE RANGE	NRR	1000r	INTERVAL	BOURGEOIS-PICHAT AGE RANGE	NRR	1000b	1000d	1000r	COALE	
GRR	1.090										IBR	14.44
NRR	1.042	0-4	1.06	2.24	27.43	5-29	0.88	12.54	17.28	-4.74	IDR	13.59
TFR	2.239	5-9	0.95	-2.06	27.38	30-54	0.99	15.00	15.20	-0.20	IRI	0.85
GENERATION	27.604	10-14	0.83	-6.65	27.33	55-79	2.04	71.72	45.37	26.35	K1	38.07
SEX RATIO	105.315	15-19	0.84	-6.44	27.25	*10-34	0.70	10.48	23.46	-12.98	K2	0.63

TABLE 9 — LESLIE MATRIX AND ITS SPECTRAL COMPONENTS (Females)

Start of Age Interval	ORIGINAL MATRIX SUB-DIAGONAL	ALTERNATIVE FIRST ROWS Projection	ALTERNATIVE FIRST ROWS Integral	FIRST STABLE MATRIX % IN STABLE POPULATION	FISHER VALUES	REPRODUCTIVE VALUES	SECOND STABLE MATRIX Z_2 FIRST COLUMN	SECOND STABLE MATRIX Z_2 FIRST ROW
0	0.99483	0.00000	0.00000	7.111	1.034	12176	0.1706+0.0664	0.1706+0.0664
5	0.99806	0.00012	0.00000	7.022	1.048	11243	0.1609-0.1489	0.0126+0.1524
10	0.99826	0.02634	0.00024	6.957	1.057	10278	-0.0761-0.2521	-0.1095+0.0649
15	0.99784	0.19383	0.05271	6.894	1.040	10244	-0.3124-0.0505	-0.0930-0.0600
20	0.99692	0.33900	0.33710	6.828	0.849	8927	-0.2188+0.3107	-0.0221-0.1044
25	0.99526	0.27458	0.34447	6.757	0.506	5813	0.2202+0.3993	0.0121-0.0773
30	0.99299	0.14913	0.20770	6.675	0.227	2783	0.5455-0.0277	0.0153-0.0375
35	0.98913	0.05860	0.09231	6.579	0.075	871	0.2558-0.6006	0.0082-0.0122
40	0.98486	0.01346	0.02559	6.460	0.015	138	-0.5095-0.5869	0.0021-0.0022
45	0.97845	0.00082	0.00146	6.315	0.001	11	-0.8899+0.2383	0.0001-0.0001
50	0.96623	0.00010	0.00020	6.134	0.000	1	-0.2067+1.0650	0.0000-0.0000
55+	0.78182			26.269				

TABLE 10 — AGE ANALYSIS AND MISCELLANEOUS RESULTS (Females)

Start of Age Interval	OBSERVED POPUL. (IN 100's)	CONTRIBUTIONS OF ROOTS (IN 100's) r_1	r_2, r_3	$r_4 \cdot r_{11}$	AGE-SP. BIRTH RATES	NET MATERNITY FUNCTION	COEFF. OF MATRIX EQUATION	PARAMETERS	INTEGRAL	MATRIX	EXP. INCREASE x	$e^{(x+2\frac{1}{2})r}$
0	118	110	7	1	0.0000	0.0000	0.0000	L(1)	1.00743	1.00743	0	1.0037
5	107	108	1	-1	0.0000	0.0000	0.0001	L(2)	0.35780	0.36386	50	1.0808
10	97	107	-10	0	0.0001	0.0002	0.0261		0.77331	0.74693	55	1.0888
15	99	106	-12	4	0.0108	0.0521	0.1921	R(1)	0.00148	0.00148	60	1.0969
20	105	105	2	-2	0.0692	0.3322	0.3353	R(2)	-0.03202	-0.03706	65	1.1051
25	115	104	19	-8	0.0707	0.3384	0.2707		0.22749	0.22350	70	1.1133
30	123	103	17	3	0.0427	0.2031	0.1463	C(1)		1541	75	1.1215
35	117	101	-10	25	0.0190	0.0896	0.0571	C(2)		1599	80	1.1299
40	94	100	-34	28	0.0053	0.0246	0.0131			-1520	85	1.1383
45	114	97	-21	38	0.0003	0.0016	0.0008	2P/Y	27.6198	28.1128	90	1.1467
50	117	95	26	-4	0.0000	0.0000	0.0000	DELTA	5.6938		95	1.1552
55+	390	405									100	1.1638

TABLE 1 — DATA

AGE AT LAST BIRTHDAY	POPULATION BOTH SEXES	MALES Number	%	FEMALES Number	%	BIRTHS BY AGE OF MOTHER	DEATHS BOTH SEXES	MALES	FEMALES	AGE AT LAST BIRTHDAY
0	5076	2628	1.6	2448	1.5	0	146	89	57	0
1-4	19890	10110	6.1	9780	6.0	0	29	13	16	1-4
5-9	24014	12247	7.4	11767	7.2	0	14	10	4	5-9
10-14	21305	10902	6.6	10403	6.4	0	7	3	4	10-14
15-19	20824	10749	6.5	10075	6.2	248	27	23	4	15-19
20-24	22483	11914	7.2	10569	6.5	1592	37	30	7	20-24
25-29	23255	12378	7.5	10877	6.6	1659	29	19	10	25-29
30-34	25467	13418	8.1	12049	7.4	1048	25	15	10	30-34
35-39	23740	11759	7.1	11981	7.3	442	46	30	16	35-39
40-44	20791	9791	5.9	11000	6.7	117	68	36	32	40-44
45-49	19230	9588	5.8	9642	5.9	6	99	58	41	45-49
50-54	22912	11388	6.9	11524	7.0	0	206	122	84	50-54
55-59	25973	14702	8.9	11271	6.9	0	292	193	99	55-59
60-64	18900	8855	5.3	10045	6.1	0	425	277	148	60-64
65-69	14195	6339	3.8	7856	4.8	0	462	270	192	65-69
70-74	9919	4351	2.6	5568	3.4		559	293	266	70-74
75-79	6567	2779	1.7	3788	2.3		580	272	308	75-79
80-84	3535	1456	0.9	2079	1.3	2681 M.	531	251	280	80-84
85+	1699	663	0.4	1036	0.6	2431 F.	347	127	220	85+
TOTAL	329775	166017		163758		5112	3929	2131	1798	TOTAL

TABLE 2 — MALE LIFE TABLE

x	$_nq_x$	l_x	$_nd_x$	$_nL_x$	$_nm_x$	$_na_x$	T_x	r_x	$\dot{e}_x$	$_nM_x$	x
0	0.032932	100000	3293	97455	0.033792	0.2273	6687139	0.0028	66.871	0.033866	
1	0.005104	96707	494	385389	0.001281	1.0856	6589684	0.0028	68.141	0.001286	
5	0.004060	96213	391	480089	0.000814	2.5000	6204296	0.0147	64.485	0.000817	5
10	0.001392	95822	133	478910	0.000279	3.4810	5724207	0.0122	59.738	0.000275	10
15	0.010647	95689	1019	476118	0.002140	2.7149	5245297	0.0000	54.816	0.002140	15
20	0.012510	94670	1184	470328	0.002518	2.4465	4769179	0.0000	50.377	0.002518	20
25	0.007643	93486	715	465505	0.001535	2.3056	4298852	0.0000	45.984	0.001535	25
30	0.005579	92771	518	462660	0.001119	2.6862	3833347	0.0036	41.320	0.001118	30
35	0.012759	92254	1177	458566	0.002567	2.7032	3370687	0.0291	36.537	0.002551	35
40	0.018287	91077	1666	451531	0.003689	2.6864	2912121	0.0165	31.974	0.003677	40
45	0.029835	85411	2668	440985	0.006049	2.7238	2460590	0.0000	27.520	0.006049	45
50	0.052233	86744	4531	422931	0.010713	2.6190	2019605	0.0000	23.282	0.010713	50
55	0.063927	82213	5256	399325	0.013161	2.7663	1596675	0.0086	19.421	0.013127	55
60	0.146174	76957	11249	358218	0.031403	2.6382	1197350	0.0196	15.559	0.031282	60
65	0.193515	65708	12716	297604	0.042726	2.5670	839132	0.0196	12.771	0.042593	65
70	0.289455	52993	15339	227053	0.067557	2.5286	541528	0.0196	10.219	0.067341	70
75	0.393524	37654	14818	150856	0.098224	2.4751	314475	0.0196	8.352	0.097877	75
80	0.594273	22836	13571	78428	0.173034	2.4148	163619	0.0196	7.165	0.172390	80
85+	1.000000	9265	9265	85191	0.108758	9.1947	85191	0.0196	9.195	0.191554	85

TABLE 3 — FEMALE LIFE TABLE

x	$_nq_x$	l_x	$_nd_x$	$_nL_x$	$_nm_x$	$_na_x$	T_x	r_x	$\dot{e}_x$	$_nM_x$	x
0	0.022908	100000	2291	98384	0.023284	0.2944	7199441	0.0000	71.994	0.023284	0
1	0.006514	97709	636	389109	0.001636	1.1434	7101058	0.0000	72.675	0.001636	1
5	0.001682	97073	163	484956	0.000337	2.5000	6712039	0.0155	69.144	0.000340	5
10	0.001922	96909	186	484088	0.000385	2.5319	6227083	0.0152	64.257	0.000385	10
15	0.001983	96723	192	483164	0.000397	2.6444	5742996	0.0000	59.376	0.000397	15
20	0.003306	96531	319	481911	0.000662	2.6628	5259831	0.0000	54.488	0.000662	20
25	0.004586	96212	441	479974	0.000919	2.5366	4777920	0.0000	49.660	0.000919	25
30	0.004141	95771	397	477904	0.000830	2.6026	4297946	0.0000	44.877	0.000830	30
35	0.006674	95374	637	475484	0.001339	2.8200	3820042	0.0076	40.053	0.001335	35
40	0.014505	94738	1374	470530	0.002921	2.7015	3344558	0.0189	35.303	0.002909	40
45	0.021055	93364	1966	462299	0.004252	2.7014	2874028	0.0000	30.783	0.004252	45
50	0.035823	91398	3274	449185	0.007289	2.6164	2411729	0.0000	26.387	0.007289	50
55	0.043060	88124	3795	431707	0.008790	2.6517	1962544	0.0040	22.270	0.008784	55
60	0.071595	84329	6038	407659	0.014810	2.6835	1530837	0.0241	18.153	0.014734	60
65	0.116387	78292	9112	370527	0.024592	2.7030	1123177	0.0241	14.346	0.024440	65
70	0.215635	69179	14918	310549	0.048036	2.6304	752650	0.0241	10.880	0.047773	70
75	0.340045	54262	18451	225843	0.081701	2.5359	442101	0.0241	8.148	0.081309	75
80	0.505290	35810	18095	133662	0.135376	2.4915	216259	0.0241	6.039	0.134681	80
85+	*1.000000	17716	17716	82597	0.214484	4.6623	82597	0.0241	4.662	0.212355	85

TABLE 4 — OBSERVED AND PROJECTED VITAL RATES

	OBSERVED POPULATION BOTH SEXES	MALES	FEMALES	PROJECTED POPULATION 1968 MALES	FEMALES	1973 MALES	FEMALES	1978 MALES	FEMALES	STABLE POPULATION MALES	FEMALES
RATES PER THOUSAND											
Birth	15.50	16.15	14.85	15.20	13.99	14.90	13.67	15.45	14.14	16.07	14.98
Death	11.91	12.84	10.98	14.56	11.83	15.19	12.66	15.85	13.46	14.08	12.98
Increase	3.59	3.31	3.87	0.64	2.16	-0.28	1.01	-0.40	0.68		1.9932
PERCENTAGE											
under 15	21.31	21.62	21.01	22.25	21.35	22.13	20.84	21.90	20.25	22.83	21.49
15-64	67.80	68.99	66.58	67.02	64.65	64.39	63.72	64.32	63.42	65.54	64.00
65 and over	10.89	9.39	12.41	10.73	14.00	13.48	15.45	13.77	16.33	11.63	14.51
DEP. RATIO X 100	47.50	44.94	50.19	49.20	54.68	55.30	56.95	55.47	57.69	52.58	56.25

TABLE 5 — POPULATION PROJECTED WITH FIXED AGE-SPECIFIC BIRTH AND DEATH RATES (IN 1000's)

AGE AT LAST BIRTHDAY	1968 BOTH SEXES	1968 MALES	1968 FEMALES	1973 BOTH SEXES	1973 MALES	1973 FEMALES	1978 BOTH SEXES	1978 MALES	1978 FEMALES	AGE AT LAST BIRTHDAY
0-4	25	13	12	23	12	11	23	12	11	0-4
5-9	25	13	12	25	13	12	23	12	11	5-9
10-14	24	12	12	25	13	12	23	12	11	10-14
15-19	21	11	10	24	12	12	25	13	12	15-19
20-24	21	11	10	21	11	10	24	12	12	20-24
25-29	23	12	11	21	11	10	21	11	10	25-29
30-34	23	12	11	22	12	10	20	10	10	30-34
35-39	25	13	12	23	12	11	22	12	10	35-39
40-44	24	12	12	25	13	12	23	12	11	40-44
45-49	21	10	11	23	11	12	25	13	12	45-49
50-54	18	9	9	20	9	11	22	11	11	50-54
55-59	22	11	11	18	9	9	19	9	10	55-59
60-64	24	13	11	20	10	10	17	8	9	60-64
65-69	16	7	9	21	11	10	18	8	10	65-69
70-74	12	5	7	14	6	8	16	8	8	70-74
75-79	7	3	4	8	3	5	10	4	6	75-79
80-84	3	1	2	4	2	2	5	2	3	80-84
85+	3	2	1	3	2	1	3	2	1	85+
TOTAL	337	170	167	340	172	168	341	172	169	TOTAL

TABLE 6 — STANDARDIZED RATES

STANDARD COUNTRIES:

STANDARDIZED RATES PER THOUSAND	ENGLAND AND WALES 1961 BOTH SEXES	MALES	FEMALES	UNITED STATES 1960 BOTH SEXES	MALES	FEMALES	MEXICO 1960 BOTH SEXES	MALES	FEMALES
Birth	14.62	14.60*	13.47	14.85	13.84*	13.91	17.50	13.11*	16.60
Death	12.72	12.62*	12.71	10.33	11.19*	9.32	5.54	9.82*	4.56
Increase	1.90	1.99*	0.76	4.51	2.65*	4.59	11.97	3.29*	12.04

TABLE 7 — MOMENTS AND CUMULANTS

	OBSERVED POP. MALES	OBSERVED POP. FEMALES	STATIONARY POP. MALES	STATIONARY POP. FEMALES	STABLE POP. MALES	STABLE POP. FEMALES	OBSERVED BIRTHS	NET MATERNITY FUNCTION	BIRTHS IN STABLE POP.
μ	35.77008	37.24437	36.57713	38.32076	35.57966	37.26424	27.71420	27.41982	27.35687
σ^2	462.5569	496.1039	503.2833	532.3267	497.4197	527.5886	29.89837	29.60227	29.39898
κ_3	1603.371	1447.547	2711.683	2090.489	3167.692	2659.861	90.7208	102.0098	101.9662
κ_4	-209839.	-247741.	-234817.	-291194.	-222405.	-279617.	-130.816	19.428	34.688
β_1	0.025976	0.017161	0.057682	0.028971	0.081530	0.048176	0.307944	0.401152	0.409182
β_2	2.019256	1.993408	2.072947	1.972395	2.101128	1.995447	2.853659	3.022171	3.040134
κ	-0.010029	-0.006540	-0.022549	-0.010714	-0.031826	-0.017807	-0.206700	-0.288265	-0.297538

TABLE 8 — RATES FROM AGE DISTRIBUTIONS AND VITAL STATISTICS (Females)

VITAL STATISTICS		THOMPSON AGE RANGE	NRR	1000r	INTERVAL	BOURGEOIS-PICHAT AGE RANGE	NRR	1000b	1000d	1000r	COALE	
GRR	1.101										IBR	16.81
NRR	1.056	0-4	1.08	2.87	27.43	5-29	1.06	14.13	11.80	2.33	IDR	8.88
TFR	2.314	5-9	1.05	1.62	27.39	30-54	1.09	16.70	13.62	3.08	IRI	7.93
GENERATION	27.409	10-14	0.90	-3.79	27.32	55-79	1.99	71.49	45.94	25.55	K1	53.57
SEX RATIO	110.284	15-19	0.86	-5.85	27.21	*15-39	0.76	10.61	20.97	-10.36	K2	0.76

TABLE 9 — LESLIE MATRIX AND ITS SPECTRAL COMPONENTS (Females)

Start of Age Interval	ORIGINAL MATRIX SUB-DIAGONAL	ALTERNATIVE FIRST ROWS Projection	ALTERNATIVE FIRST ROWS Integral	FIRST STABLE MATRIX % IN STABLE POPULATION	FISHER VALUES	REPRODUCTIVE VALUES	SECOND STABLE MATRIX Z_2 FIRST COLUMN	SECOND STABLE MATRIX Z_2 FIRST ROW
0	0.99498	0.00000	0.00000	7.264	1.031	12607	0.1745+0.0660	0.1745+0.0660
5	0.99821	0.00000	0.00000	7.155	1.047	12315	0.1603-0.1549	0.0123+0.1557
10	0.99809	0.02847	0.00000	7.072	1.059	11016	-0.0859-0.2529	-0.1131+0.0647
15	0.99741	0.20264	0.05734	6.988	1.042	10500	-0.3180-0.0362	-0.0941-0.0642
20	0.99598	0.35062	0.35088	6.901	0.846	8940	-0.2017+0.3260	-0.0205-0.1074
25	0.99569	0.27713	0.35529	6.805	0.495	5383	0.2496+0.3844	0.0125-0.0770
30	0.99494	0.14334	0.20261	6.708	0.215	2591	0.5429-0.0739	0.0142-0.0364
35	0.98958	0.05495	0.08594	6.608	0.070	836	0.1969-0.6242	0.0075-0.0118
40	0.98251	0.01292	0.02478	6.475	0.014	154	-0.5710-0.5279	0.0020-0.0022
45	0.97163	0.00070	0.00121	6.298	0.001	8	-0.8506+0.3435	0.0001-0.0001
50	0.96109	0.00010	0.00020	6.059	0.000	1	-0.0609+1.0683	0.0000-0.0000
55+	0.78314			25.667				

TABLE 10 — AGE ANALYSIS AND MISCELLANEOUS RESULTS (Females)

Start of Age Interval	OBSERVED POPUL. (IN 100's)	CONTRIBUTIONS OF ROOTS (IN 100's) r_1	r_2, r_3	$r_4 \cdot r_{11}$	AGE-SP. BIRTH RATES	NET MATERNITY FUNCTION	COEFF. OF MATRIX EQUATION	PARAMETERS	INTEGRAL	MATRIX	EXP. INCREASE x	$e^{(x+2\frac{1}{2})r}$
0	122	114	7	1	0.0000	0.0000	0.0000	L(1)	1.01002	1.01002	0	1.0050
5	118	112	6	-0	0.0000	0.0000	0.0000	L(2)	0.34920	0.35533	50	1.1103
10	104	111	-5	-3	0.0000	0.0000	0.0283			0.78093	0.75331	55	1.1214
15	101	110	-13	4	0.0117	0.0566	0.2009	R(1)	0.00199	0.00199	60	1.1327
20	106	108	-6	4	0.0716	0.3452	0.3467	R(2)	-0.03123	-0.03657	65	1.1440
25	109	107	12	-10	0.0725	0.3481	0.2729			0.23006	0.22601	70	1.1555
30	120	105	21	-6	0.0414	0.1977	0.1405	C(1)		1571	75	1.1670
35	120	104	5	11	0.0175	0.0834	0.0536	C(2)		1955	80	1.1787
40	110	102	-25	33	0.0051	0.0238	0.0126			-240	85	1.1905
45	96	99	-32	29	0.0003	0.0014	0.0007	2P/Y	27.3110	27.8005	90	1.2025
50	115	95	3	17	0.0000	0.0000	0.0000	DELTA	4.6734		95	1.2145
55+	416	403									100	1.2267

TABLE 1 — DATA

AGE AT LAST BIRTHDAY	POPULATION BOTH SEXES	MALES Number	MALES %	FEMALES Number	FEMALES %	BIRTHS BY AGE OF MOTHER	DEATHS BOTH SEXES	DEATHS MALES	DEATHS FEMALES	AGE AT LAST BIRTHDAY
0	8422	4335	2.8	4087	2.4	0	290	165	125	0
1-4	31198	15965	10.2	15233	8.9	0	33	19	14	1-4
5-9	38523	19727	12.6	18796	10.9	0	13	6	7	5-9
10-14	42277	21542	13.7	20735	12.1	1	17	12	5	10-14
15-19	28859	14166	9.0	14693	8.6	315	14	9	5	15-19
20-24	22947	10072	6.4	12875	7.5	2435	15	10	5	20-24
25-29	21336	8698	5.5	12638	7.4	2429	22	12	10	25-29
30-34	19676	8572	5.5	11104	6.5	1604	25	15	10	30-34
35-39	19137	8809	5.6	10328	6.0	1086	31	20	11	35-39
40-44	15835	7457	4.8	8378	4.9	340	41	24	17	40-44
45-49	15286	7358	4.7	7928	4.6	35	71	42	29	45-49
50-54	16306	7800	5.0	8506	5.0	1	128	73	55	50-54
55-59	13330	6368	4.1	6962	4.1	0	194	112	82	55-59
60-64	11665	5335	3.4	6330	3.7	0	290	165	125	60-64
65-69	10422	4657	3.0	5765	3.4	0	366	190	176	65-69
70-74	6407	2931	1.9	3476	2.0		408	209	199	70-74
75-79	4041	1820	1.2	2221	1.3		377	195	182	75-79
80-84	1845	826	0.5	1019	0.6	4228 M.	300	144	156	80-84
85+	1005	414	0.3	591	0.3	4018 F.	229	104	125	85+
TOTAL	328517	156852		171665		8246	2864	1526	1338	TOTAL

TABLE 2 — MALE LIFE TABLE

x	$_nq_x$	l_x	$_nd_x$	$_nL_x$	$_nm_x$	$_na_x$	T_x	r_x	$\dot{e}_x$	$_nM_x$	x
0	0.036743	100000	3674	97085	0.037847	0.2066	6674201	0.0071	66.742	0.038062	0
1	0.004683	96326	451	383982	0.001175	1.0728	6577116	0.0071	68.280	0.001190	1
5	0.001520	95875	146	479009	0.000304	2.5000	6193134	0.0000	64.596	0.000304	5
10	0.002793	95729	267	478009	0.000559	2.6250	5714125	0.0326	59.691	0.000557	10
15	0.003206	95462	306	476586	0.000642	2.6412	5236116	0.0753	54.851	0.000635	15
20	0.004989	95155	475	474662	0.001000	2.6518	4759530	0.0478	50.018	0.000993	20
25	0.006887	94681	652	471845	0.001382	2.6101	4284868	0.0148	45.256	0.001380	25
30	0.008713	94029	819	468179	0.001750	2.6022	3813023	0.0000	40.552	0.001750	30
35	0.011309	93209	1054	463549	0.002274	2.6300	3344844	0.0116	35.885	0.002270	35
40	0.016025	92155	1477	457397	0.003229	2.7117	2881295	0.0145	31.266	0.003218	40
45	0.028172	90678	2555	447540	0.005708	2.7092	2423898	0.0000	26.731	0.005708	45
50	0.045873	88124	4042	431468	0.009369	2.7363	1976358	0.0042	22.427	0.009359	50
55	0.084913	84081	7140	404027	0.017761	2.7058	1544889	0.0193	18.374	0.017588	55
60	0.144189	76942	11094	358039	0.030986	2.5960	1140862	0.0120	14.828	0.030928	60
65	0.186083	65848	12253	299688	0.040886	2.5884	782824	0.0120	11.888	0.040799	65
70	0.303978	53594	16292	227967	0.071464	2.5444	483136	0.0120	9.015	0.071307	70
75	0.421617	37303	15728	146485	0.107367	2.4548	255168	0.0120	6.840	0.107143	75
80	0.596868	21575	12878	73702	0.174726	2.3863	108684	0.0120	5.037	0.174334	80
85+	1.000000	8698	8698	34982	0.248636	4.0219	34982	0.0120	4.022	0.251207	85+

TABLE 3 — FEMALE LIFE TABLE

x	$_nq_x$	l_x	$_nd_x$	$_nL_x$	$_nm_x$	$_na_x$	T_x	r_x	$\dot{e}_x$	$_nM_x$	x
0	0.029713	100000	2971	97632	0.030434	0.2030	7102533	0.0062	71.025	0.030585	0
1	0.003625	97029	352	387084	0.000909	1.0707	7004901	0.0062	72.194	0.000919	1
5	0.001860	96677	180	482935	0.000372	2.5000	6617817	0.0000	68.453	0.000372	5
10	0.001204	96497	116	482192	0.000241	2.4726	6134882	0.0243	63.576	0.000241	10
15	0.001707	96381	165	481508	0.000342	2.5900	5652690	0.0473	58.649	0.000340	15
20	0.001947	96216	187	480658	0.000390	2.7395	5171182	0.0146	53.745	0.000388	20
25	0.003956	96029	380	479246	0.000793	2.6332	4690524	0.0141	48.845	0.000791	25
30	0.004499	95649	430	477197	0.000902	2.5624	4211278	0.0193	44.028	0.000901	30
35	0.005344	95219	509	474933	0.001071	2.7180	3734082	0.0269	39.216	0.001065	35
40	0.010164	94710	963	471391	0.002042	2.7579	3259149	0.0243	34.412	0.002029	40
45	0.018140	93747	1701	464897	0.003658	2.7419	2787757	0.0000	29.737	0.003658	45
50	0.031914	92047	2938	453604	0.006476	2.7432	2322861	0.0061	25.236	0.006466	50
55	0.057562	89109	5129	433768	0.011825	2.7039	1869257	0.0173	20.977	0.011778	55
60	0.094770	83980	7959	401202	0.019837	2.6507	1435488	0.0237	17.093	0.019747	60
65	0.143205	76021	10887	354654	0.030696	2.6622	1034287	0.0237	13.605	0.030529	65
70	0.252294	65134	16433	285789	0.057501	2.5730	679633	0.0237	10.434	0.057250	70
75	0.341705	48701	16642	202160	0.082319	2.5154	393844	0.0237	8.087	0.081945	75
80	0.550914	32060	17662	114793	0.153862	2.4735	191684	0.0237	5.979	0.153091	80
85+	1.000000	14398	14398	76891	0.187246	5.3406	76891	0.0237	5.341	0.211507	85+

TABLE 4 — OBSERVED AND PROJECTED VITAL RATES

	OBSERVED POPULATION BOTH SEXES	MALES	FEMALES	PROJECTED POPULATION 1965 MALES	1965 FEMALES	1970 MALES	1970 FEMALES	1975 MALES	1975 FEMALES	STABLE POPULATION MALES	FEMALES
RATES PER THOUSAND											
Birth	25.10	26.96	23.41	27.30	23.91	29.33	25.96	29.29	26.22	25.73	24.74
Death	8.72	9.73	7.79	9.46	8.10	9.25	8.27	8.89	8.26	8.99	8.00
Increase	16.38	17.23	15.61	17.84	15.81	20.09	17.69	20.39	17.96		16.7403
PERCENTAGE											
under 15	36.66	39.25	34.28	35.80	31.49	35.06	31.22	35.35	31.90	32.72	31.72
15-64	56.12	53.96	58.10	57.66	60.63	58.69	61.01	58.51	60.31	61.33	60.82
65 and over	7.22	6.79	7.61	6.54	7.88	6.25	7.78	6.14	7.79	5.95	7.46
DEP. RATIO X 100	78.18	85.33	72.11	73.44	64.94	70.39	63.92	70.90	65.81	63.04	64.41

AGE AT LAST BIRTHDAY	1965 BOTH SEXES	1965 MALES	1965 FEMALES	1970 BOTH SEXES	1970 MALES	1970 FEMALES	1975 BOTH SEXES	1975 MALES	1975 FEMALES	AGE AT LAST BIRTHDAY	
0-4	42	21	21	48	25	23	55	28	27	0-4	
5-9	39	20	19	41	21	20	47	24	23	5-9	
10-14	39	20	19	39	20	19	41	21	20	10-14	
15-19	42	21	21	39	20	19	39	20	19	15-19	**TABLE 5**
20-24	29	14	15	42	21	21	39	20	19	20-24	POPULATION
25-29	23	10	13	29	14	15	42	21	21	25-29	PROJECTED
30-34	22	9	13	23	10	13	29	14	15	30-34	WITH
35-39	19	8	11	22	9	13	23	10	13	35-39	FIXED
40-44	19	9	10	19	8	11	20	8	12	40-44	AGE—
45-49	15	7	8	19	9	10	19	8	11	45-49	SPECIFIC
50-54	15	7	8	15	7	8	18	8	10	50-54	BIRTH
55-59	15	7	8	14	7	7	15	7	8	55-59	AND
60-64	12	6	6	14	6	8	13	6	7	60-64	DEATH
65-69	10	4	6	11	5	6	12	5	7	65-69	RATES
70-74	9	4	5	8	3	5	9	4	5	70-74	(IN 1000's)
75-79	4	2	2	5	2	3	5	2	3	75-79	
80-84	2	1	1	2	1	1	3	1	2	80-84	
85+	1	0	1	1	0	1	1	0	1	85+	
TOTAL	357	170	187	391	188	203	430	207	223	TOTAL	

STANDARD COUNTRIES:	ENGLAND AND WALES 1961 BOTH SEXES	MALES	FEMALES	UNITED STATES 1960 BOTH SEXES	MALES	FEMALES	MEXICO 1960 BOTH SEXES	MALES	FEMALES	
STANDARDIZED RATES PER THOUSAND										**TABLE 6**
Birth	22.30	31.60*	21.06	22.61	29.19*	21.71	24.80	28.60*	24.10	STANDAR-
Death	13.62	13.37*	14.06	11.00	11.63*	10.26	5.75	8.46*	4.99	DIZED
Increase	8.67	18.23*	7.00	11.61	17.56*	11.45	19.05	20.14*	19.12	RATES

	OBSERVED POP. MALES	OBSERVED POP. FEMALES	STATIONARY POP. MALES	STATIONARY POP. FEMALES	STABLE POP. MALES	STABLE POP. FEMALES	OBSERVED BIRTHS	NET MATERNITY FUNCTION	BIRTHS IN STABLE POP.	
μ	27.65491	29.21181	36.19490	37.88383	28.57579	29.66700	28.63570	29.34511	28.65675	**TABLE 7**
σ^2	458.5782	456.2571	482.9749	519.8102	419.3255	452.1678	36.94033	40.05169	37.98283	MOMENTS
κ_3	6607.912	5895.341	2205.542	2105.435	5041.921	5554.816	121.0800	116.1673	130.0973	AND
κ_4	-134255.	-136903.	-226083.	-271347.	-100909.	-123972.	-591.896	-988.830	-664.187	CUMULANTS
β_1	0.452781	0.365922	0.043177	0.031561	0.344777	0.333765	0.290832	0.210042	0.308869	
β_2	2.361585	2.342352	2.030788	1.995765	2.426111	2.393648	2.566245	2.383576	2.539621	
κ	-0.152674	-0.130808	-0.016527	-0.011870	-0.134139	-0.127885	-0.137840	-0.091746	-0.138942	

VITAL STATISTICS		THOMPSON AGE RANGE	NRR	1000r	INTERVAL	BOURGEOIS-PICHAT AGE RANGE	NRR	1000b	1000d	1000r	COALE		**TABLE 8**
GRR	1.699												RATES FROM AGE DISTRI-
NRR	1.625	0-4	1.63	18.23	27.44	5-29	1.97	29.31	4.27	25.04	IBR	24.76	BUTIONS
TFR	3.488	5-9	1.75	20.76	27.41	30-54	1.44	20.24	6.74	13.50	IDR	7.97	AND VITAL
GENERATION	28.998	10-14	2.06	25.88	27.35	55-79	1.54	24.72	8.68	16.04	IRI	16.78	STATISTICS
SEX RATIO	105.226	15-19	1.59	16.15	27.24	*15-39	1.56	23.35	6.99	16.37	K1	0.	(Females)
											K2	0.	

Start Age Interval	ORIGINAL MATRIX SUB-DIAGONAL	ALTERNATIVE FIRST ROWS Projection	ALTERNATIVE FIRST ROWS Integral	FIRST STABLE MATRIX % IN STABLE POPULATION	FISHER VALUES	REPRODUCTIVE VALUES	SECOND STABLE MATRIX Z2 FIRST COLUMN	FIRST ROW	
0	0.99633	0.00000	0.00000	11.512	1.075	20778	0.1466+0.0818	0.1466+0.0818	
5	0.99846	0.00006	0.00000	10.547	1.174	22064	0.1638-0.1003	0.0005+0.1467	
10	0.99858	0.02534	0.00012	9.683	1.278	26509	-0.0081-0.2201	-0.1113+0.0632	
15	0.99824	0.24827	0.05280	8.892	1.365	20055	-0.2245-0.1157	-0.0993-0.0596	**TABLE 9**
20	0.99706	0.44965	0.46578	8.162	1.220	15701	-0.2419+0.1593	-0.0336-0.1214	LESLIE
25	0.99572	0.39683	0.47335	7.484	0.845	10680	0.0231+0.3308	0.0118-0.1144	MATRIX
30	0.99526	0.29418	0.35576	6.852	0.494	5489	0.3426+0.1625	0.0339-0.0727	AND ITS
35	0.99254	0.17174	0.25897	6.271	0.222	2295	0.3539-0.2502	0.0266-0.0295	SPECTRAL
40	0.98622	0.05307	0.09995	5.724	0.057	481	-0.0507-0.4914	0.0087-0.0065	COMPO-
45	0.97571	0.00535	0.01087	5.191	0.005	43	-0.5132-0.2229	0.0009-0.0006	NENTS
50	0.95627	0.00014	0.00029	4.657	0.000	1	-0.4998+0.3787	0.0000-0.0000	(Females)
55+	0.79105			15.025					

Start Age Interval	OBSERVED POPUL. (IN 100's)	CONTRIBUTIONS OF ROOTS (IN 100's) r_1	r_2, r_3	$r_4 \cdot r_{11}$	AGE-SP. BIRTH RATES	NET MATERNITY FUNCTION	COEFF. OF MATRIX EQUATION	PARAMETERS INTEGRAL	MATRIX	EXP. INCREASE x	$e^{(x+2\frac{1}{2})r}$	
	193	202	-10	1	0.0000	0.0000	0.0000	L(1) 1.08730	1.08747	0	1.0427	**TABLE 10**
	188	185	6	-4	0.0000	0.0000	0.0001	L(2) 0.42148	0.42705	50	2.4082	AGE
	207	170	20	18	0.0000	0.0001	0.0252	0.78117	0.75884	55	2.6184	ANALYSIS
	147	156	14	-23	0.0104	0.0503	0.2466	R(1) 0.01674	0.01677	60	2.8470	AND
	129	143	-11	-4	0.0922	0.4430	0.4459	R(2) -0.02384	-0.02768	65	3.0956	MISCEL-
	126	131	-30	25	0.0937	0.4488	0.3924	0.21520	0.21164	70	3.3658	LANEOUS
	111	120	-20	10	0.0704	0.3359	0.2896	C(1)	1755	75	3.6597	RESULTS
	103	110	17	-24	0.0512	0.2433	0.1683	C(2)	-763	80	3.9792	(Females)
	84	100	45	-61	0.0198	0.0932	0.0516		4462	85	4.3266	
	79	91	28	-40	0.0022	0.0100	0.0051	2P/Y 29.1967	29.6879	90	4.7043	
	85	82	-26	29	0.0001	0.0003	0.0001	DELTA 3.8293		95	5.1150	
+	264	264								100	5.5616	

TABLE 1 — DATA

AGE AT LAST BIRTHDAY	POPULATION BOTH SEXES	MALES Number	MALES %	FEMALES Number	FEMALES %	BIRTHS BY AGE OF MOTHER	DEATHS BOTH SEXES	MALES	FEMALES	AGE AT LAST BIRTHDAY
0	6786	3576	2.3	3210	1.9	0	228	135	93	0
1-4	30354	15569	9.9	14785	8.6	0	27	11	16	1-4
5-9	37212	19265	12.3	17947	10.5	0	14	11	3	5-9
10-14	38521	19740	12.6	18781	11.0	19	6	3	3	10-14
15-19	38319	19205	12.2	19114	11.2	310	21	17	4	15-19
20-24	19824	8905	5.7	10919	6.4	1853	19	15	4	20-24
25-29	20951	8629	5.5	12322	7.2	2015	17	9	8	25-29
30-34	19152	7778	5.0	11374	6.6	1327	25	10	15	30-34
35-39	19065	8556	5.5	1C509	6.1	823	24	13	11	35-39
40-44	17387	8079	5.2	9308	5.4	304	44	25	19	40-44
45-49	14657	6906	4.4	7751	4.5	21	80	49	31	45-49
50-54	14999	7250	4.6	7749	4.5	0	104	68	36	50-54
55-59	14718	7033	4.5	7685	4.5	0	205	120	85	55-59
60-64	11463	5398	3.4	6065	3.5	0	278	160	118	60-64
65-69	10065	4459	2.8	5606	3.3	0	375	208	167	65-69
70-74	7477	3334	2.1	4143	2.4		455	216	239	70-74
75-79	4092	1795	1.1	2297	1.3		421	205	216	75-79
80-84	2076	906	0.6	1170	0.7	3481 M.	350	157	193	80-84
85+	998	428	0.3	570	0.3	3191 F.	288	108	180	85+
TOTAL	328116	156811		171305		6672	2981	1540	1441	TOTAL

TABLE 2 — MALE LIFE TABLE

x	nq_x	l_x	nd_x	nL_x	nm_x	na_x	T_x	r_x	$\dot{e}_x$	nM_x	x
0	0.036590	1CCCCO	3659	96922	0.037752	0.1589	6678094	0.0000	66.781	0.037752	0
1	0.002820	96341	272	384562	0.000707	1.0493	6581172	0.0000	68.311	0.000707	1
5	0.002851	96069	274	479662	0.000571	2.5000	6196609	0.0000	64.501	0.000571	5
10	0.000760	95795	73	478829	0.000152	2.9608	5716948	0.0000	59.679	0.000152	10
15	0.004543	95723	435	477678	0.000910	2.8486	5238119	0.0787	54.722	0.000885	15
20	0.008399	95288	800	474450	0.001687	2.5146	4760441	0.0786	49.959	0.001684	20
25	0.005196	94488	491	471169	0.001042	2.4160	4285991	0.0123	45.360	0.001043	25
30	0.006408	93997	602	468522	0.001286	2.5748	3814822	0.0000	40.585	0.001286	30
35	0.007571	93394	707	465377	0.001519	2.7450	3346300	0.0000	35.830	0.001519	35
40	0.015471	92687	1434	460367	0.003115	2.8603	2880923	0.0178	31.082	0.003094	40
45	0.034926	91253	3187	448841	0.007101	2.6705	2420556	0.0042	26.526	0.007095	45
50	0.045903	88066	4042	431001	0.009379	2.6922	1971714	0.0000	22.389	0.009379	50
55	0.082308	84024	6916	404215	0.017109	2.7006	1540713	0.0116	18.337	0.017062	55
60	0.138768	77108	10700	360249	0.029702	2.6365	1136498	0.0104	14.739	0.029641	60
65	0.209700	66408	13926	298055	0.046722	2.5597	776250	0.0104	11.689	0.046647	65
70	0.279864	52482	14688	226283	0.064909	2.5404	478195	0.0104	9.112	0.064787	70
75	0.443798	37794	16773	146572	0.114435	2.4722	251912	0.0104	6.665	0.114206	75
80	0.592134	21021	12447	71705	0.173590	2.3628	105340	0.0104	5.011	0.173289	80
85+	1.000000	8574	8574	33635	0.254908	3.9230	33635	0.0104	3.923	0.252336	85

TABLE 3 — FEMALE LIFE TABLE

x	nq_x	l_x	nd_x	nL_x	nm_x	na_x	T_x	r_x	$\dot{e}_x$	nM_x	x
0	0.028336	1CCCCO	2834	97807	0.028972	0.2259	7089249	0.0000	70.892	0.028972	
1	0.004315	97166	419	387443	0.001082	1.0847	6991443	0.0000	71.953	0.001082	
5	0.000835	96747	81	483533	0.000167	2.4999	6604000	0.0000	68.260	0.000167	
10	0.000798	96666	77	483143	0.000160	2.5576	6120466	0.0000	63.315	0.000160	10
15	0.001058	96589	102	482711	0.000212	2.7066	5637324	0.0540	58.364	0.000209	15
20	0.001850	96487	178	482032	0.000370	2.7451	5154613	0.0435	53.423	0.000366	20
25	0.003242	96308	312	480856	0.000649	2.8023	4672581	0.0000	48.517	0.000649	25
30	0.006579	95996	632	478441	0.001320	2.5617	4191725	0.0148	43.666	0.001319	30
35	0.005235	95365	499	475646	0.001050	2.6421	3713284	0.0187	38.938	0.001047	35
40	0.010246	94865	972	472181	0.002058	2.7925	3237638	0.0282	34.129	0.002041	40
45	0.019849	93893	1864	465046	0.004007	2.6279	2765456	0.0147	29.453	0.003999	45
50	0.022993	92030	2116	455485	0.004646	2.7959	2300410	0.0000	24.996	0.004646	50
55	0.054148	89914	4869	438609	0.011100	2.7490	1844925	0.0132	20.519	0.011061	55
60	0.093292	85045	7934	406621	0.019512	2.6551	1406316	0.0147	16.536	0.019456	60
65	0.139750	77111	10776	360473	0.029895	2.6724	999695	0.0147	12.964	0.029790	65
70	0.254072	66335	16854	291231	0.057871	2.6004	639022	0.0147	9.636	0.057688	70
75	0.381891	49481	18896	200352	0.094316	2.5100	347992	0.0147	7.033	0.094036	75
80	0.580583	30585	17757	107267	0.165540	2.4288	147640	0.0147	4.827	0.164957	80
85+	*1.000000	12828	12828	40373	0.317729	3.1473	40373	0.0147	3.147	0.315789	85

TABLE 4 — OBSERVED AND PROJECTED VITAL RATES

	OBSERVED POPULATION BOTH SEXES	MALES	FEMALES	PROJECTED POPULATION 1968 MALES	1968 FEMALES	1973 MALES	1973 FEMALES	1978 MALES	1978 FEMALES	STABLE POPULATION MALES	FEMALES
RATES PER THOUSAND											
Birth	20.33	22.20	18.63	24.91	21.15	26.41	22.71	26.02	22.67	20.97	20.0
Death	9.09	9.82	8.41	9.62	8.27	9.39	8.39	9.06	8.43	11.01	10.0
Increase	11.25	12.38	10.22	15.30	12.88	17.01	14.32	16.96	14.24		9.959
PERCENTAGE											
under 15	34.40	37.08	31.94	33.78	29.17	32.45	28.29	32.26	28.35	28.05	27.0
15-64	58.07	55.95	60.01	59.49	62.88	60.83	63.59	61.32	63.75	64.08	63.3
65 and over	7.53	6.97	8.05	6.73	7.95	6.72	8.12	6.42	7.90	7.87	9.6
DEP. RATIO X 100	72.21	78.72	66.65	68.11	59.03	64.40	57.26	63.08	56.86	56.05	57.8

TABLE 1 A

AGE AT LAST BIRTHDAY	POPULATION BOTH SEXES	MALES Number	%	FEMALES Number	%	BIRTHS BY AGE OF MOTHER	DEATHS BOTH SEXES	MALES	FEMALES	AGE AT LAST BIRTHDAY
0	6326	3293	2.1	3033	1.8	0	219	119	100	0
1-4	28621	14825	9.6	13796	8.2	0	22	14	8	1-4
5-9	36666	18969	12.3	17697	10.5	0	10	7	3	5-9
10-14	37111	19109	12.4	18002	10.6	8	10	4	6	10-14
15-19	38180	19075	12.4	19105	11.3	303	14	9	5	15-19
20-24	20653	9320	6.0	11333	6.7	1792	11	6	5	20-24
25-29	20003	8250	5.3	11753	6.9	1865	13	5	8	25-29
30-34	19144	7644	5.0	11500	6.8	1320	14	8	6	30-34
35-39	18660	8270	5.4	10390	6.1	788	34	16	18	35-39
40-44	17519	8073	5.2	9446	5.6	294	45	23	22	40-44
45-49	14614	6857	4.4	7757	4.6	24	60	35	25	45-49
50-54	14520	6988	4.5	7532	4.5	0	106	63	43	50-54
55-59	14888	7113	4.6	7775	4.6	0	195	110	85	55-59
60-64	11602	5478	3.5	6124	3.6	0	301	168	133	60-64
65-69	9865	4407	2.9	5458	3.2	0	362	190	172	65-69
70-74	8037	3555	2.3	4482	2.6		399	211	188	70-74
75-79	3988	1736	1.1	2252	1.3		399	206	193	75-79
80-84	2212	977	0.6	1235	0.7	3287 M.	308	137	171	80-84
85+	982	432	0.3	550	0.3	3107 F.	234	97	137	85+
TOTAL	323591	154371		169220		6394	2756	1428	1328	TOTAL

TABLE 2 (MALE)

x	nq_x	l_x	nd_x	nL_x	nm_x	na_x	T_x	r_x	$\mathring{e}_x$	nM_x	x
0	0.035109	100000	3511	97155	0.036137	0.1897	6797198	0.0000	67.972	0.036137	0
1	0.003767	96489	363	384889	0.000944	1.0635	6700043	0.0000	69.438	0.000944	1
5	0.001843	96126	177	480185	0.000369	2.5000	6315154	0.0000	65.697	0.000369	5
10	0.001046	95948	100	479502	0.000209	2.6075	5834969	0.0000	60.814	0.000209	10
15	0.002389	95848	229	478711	0.000478	2.6893	5355467	0.0713	55.875	0.000472	15
20	0.003225	95619	308	477337	0.000646	2.5407	4876756	0.0832	51.002	0.000644	20
25	0.003034	95311	289	475870	0.000608	2.6352	4399419	0.0191	46.159	0.000606	25
30	0.005221	95022	496	473997	0.001047	2.7609	3923549	0.0000	41.291	0.001047	30
35	0.009630	94525	910	470525	0.001935	2.6908	3449553	0.0000	36.493	0.001935	35
40	0.014204	93615	1330	465048	0.002859	2.7230	2979027	0.0156	31.822	0.002849	40
45	0.025286	92285	2334	456144	0.005116	2.7360	2513980	0.0091	27.241	0.005104	45
50	0.044167	89952	3973	440682	0.009015	2.7151	2057835	0.0000	22.877	0.009015	50
55	0.074853	85979	6436	415353	0.015495	2.7405	1617154	0.0070	18.809	0.015465	55
60	0.143349	79543	11402	370642	0.030764	2.6256	1201800	0.0167	15.109	0.030668	60
65	0.195328	68141	13310	308027	0.043210	2.5449	831158	0.0167	12.198	0.043113	65
70	0.260241	54831	14269	239573	0.059561	2.5764	523131	0.0167	9.541	0.059353	70
75	0.457228	40562	18546	155821	0.119021	2.4664	283559	0.0167	6.991	0.118664	75
80	0.512330	22016	11279	80253	0.140547	2.3558	127738	0.0167	5.802	0.140226	80
85+	*1.000000	10736	10736	47484	0.226104	4.4227	47484	0.0167	4.423	0.224537	85+

TABLE 3 (FEMALE)

x	nq_x	l_x	nd_x	nL_x	nm_x	na_x	T_x	r_x	$\mathring{e}_x$	nM_x	x
0	0.032076	100000	3208	97285	0.032971	0.1536	7121126	0.0000	71.211	0.032971	0
1	0.002316	96792	224	386508	0.000580	1.0471	7023841	0.0000	72.566	0.000580	1
5	0.000847	96568	82	482637	0.000170	2.5000	6637333	0.0000	68.732	0.000170	5
10	0.001665	96486	161	482040	0.000333	2.5579	6154696	0.0000	63.788	0.000333	10
15	0.001313	96326	126	481324	0.000263	2.5879	5672656	0.0460	58.890	0.000262	15
20	0.002225	96199	214	480503	0.000445	2.6944	5191332	0.0481	53.964	0.000441	20
25	0.003398	95985	326	479119	0.000681	2.5233	4710829	0.0000	49.079	0.000681	25
30	0.002618	95659	250	477774	0.000524	2.9161	4231710	0.0115	44.237	0.000522	30
35	0.008662	95409	826	475154	0.001739	2.7140	3753935	0.0181	39.346	0.001732	35
40	0.011622	94582	1099	470304	0.002337	2.6279	3278781	0.0268	34.666	0.002329	40
45	0.016062	93483	1501	463973	0.003236	2.7072	2808477	0.0191	30.043	0.003223	45
50	0.028185	91982	2593	454110	0.005709	2.7636	2344504	0.0000	25.489	0.005709	50
55	0.053493	89389	4782	436280	0.010960	2.7696	1890395	0.0086	21.148	0.010932	55
60	0.103772	84607	8780	402409	0.021818	2.6506	1454115	0.0237	17.187	0.021718	60
65	0.146775	75827	11130	352067	0.031612	2.5678	1051705	0.0237	13.870	0.031513	65
70	0.191649	64698	12399	294049	0.042167	2.6257	699638	0.0237	10.814	0.041946	70
75	0.355808	52299	18608	216003	0.086148	2.5554	405589	0.0237	7.755	0.085702	75
80	0.514879	33690	17346	124614	0.139202	2.4728	189586	0.0237	5.627	0.138462	80
85+	*1.000000	16344	16344	64973	0.251550	3.9754	64973	0.0237	3.975	0.249091	85+

TABLE 4 (OBSERVED AND PROJECTED RATES)

	OBSERVED POPULATION BOTH SEXES	MALES	FEMALES	PROJECTED POPULATION 1969 MALES	FEMALES	1974 MALES	FEMALES	1979 MALES	FEMALES	STABLE POPULATION MALES	FEMALES
RATES PER THOUSAND											
Birth	19.76	21.29	18.36	23.87	20.78	25.14	22.11	24.84	22.12	20.04	19.35
Death	8.52	9.25	7.85	9.32	8.24	9.06	8.49	8.84	8.60	11.06	10.37
Increase	11.24	12.04	10.51	14.55	12.54	16.07	13.63	16.01	13.53		8.9823
PERCENTAGE											
under 15	33.60	36.40	31.04	32.97	28.45	31.26	27.45	31.04	27.77	27.03	26.22
15-64	58.65	56.40	60.70	59.90	63.10	61.57	63.84	62.14	63.78	64.34	63.29
65 and over	7.75	7.20	8.26	7.13	8.45	7.17	8.72	6.82	8.45	8.63	10.49
DEP. RATIO X 100	70.51	77.30	64.75	66.95	58.47	62.43	56.65	60.92	56.78	55.43	57.99

TABLE 1 — DATA

AGE AT LAST BIRTHDAY	POPULATION BOTH SEXES	MALES Number	%	FEMALES Number	%	BIRTHS BY AGE OF MOTHER	DEATHS BOTH SEXES	MALES	FEMALES	AGE AT LAST BIRTH
0	5798	2958	1.9	2840	1.7	0	196	116	80	0
1-4	26525	13831	9.1	12694	7.6	0	26	14	12	1-4
5-9	36694	19050	12.5	17644	10.6	0	5	2	3	5-9
10-14	36013	18684	12.3	17329	10.4	10	8	7	1	10-1
15-19	33842	15446	10.1	18396	11.0	236	25	19	6	15-1
20-24	22269	10161	6.7	12108	7.3	1511	9	4	5	20-2
25-29	19039	7911	5.2	11128	6.7	1755	14	4	10	25-2
30-34	19063	7555	5.0	11508	6.9	974	24	7	17	30-3
35-39	18206	7898	5.2	10308	6.2	862	30	16	14	35-3
40-44	17651	8117	5.3	9534	5.7	264	50	32	18	40-4
45-49	14742	6934	4.5	7808	4.7	16	57	38	19	45-4
50-54	14229	6848	4.5	7381	4.4	0	101	59	42	50-5
55-59	14974	7170	4.7	7804	4.7	0	207	126	81	55-5
60-64	11745	5610	3.7	6135	3.7	0	295	174	121	60-6
65-69	9742	4394	2.9	5348	3.2	0	386	212	174	65-6
70-74	8323	3647	2.4	4676	2.8		436	225	211	70-74
75-79	7079	4757	3.1	2322	1.4		478	242	236	75-7
80-84	2252	1012	0.7	1240	0.7	2893 M.	358	154	204	80-8
85+	978	439	0.3	539	0.3	2735 F.	296	118	178	85+
TOTAL	319164	152422		166742		5628	3001	1569	1432	TOT

TABLE 2 — MALE LIFE TABLE

x	$_nq_x$	l_x	$_nd_x$	$_nL_x$	$_nm_x$	$_na_x$	T_x	r_x	$\overset{\circ}{e}_x$	$_nM_x$
0	0.038006	100000	3801	96916	0.039216	0.1884	6771307	0.0000	67.713	0.039216
1	0.004037	96159	388	383657	0.001012	1.0629	6674392	0.0000	69.381	0.001012
5	0.000525	95811	50	478930	0.000105	2.5000	6290735	0.0000	65.658	0.000105
10	0.001896	95761	182	478462	0.000379	3.1149	5811805	0.0204	60.691	0.000375
15	0.006132	95579	586	476431	0.001230	2.5002	5333344	0.0601	55.800	0.001230
20	0.001916	94993	182	474439	0.000384	2.1049	4856913	0.0663	51.129	0.000394
25	0.002542	94811	241	473506	0.000509	2.7207	4382474	0.0291	46.223	0.000506
30	0.004623	94570	437	471905	0.000927	2.8375	3908968	0.0000	41.334	0.000927
35	0.010084	94133	949	468580	0.002026	2.8042	3437063	0.0000	36.513	0.002026
40	0.019565	93184	1823	461678	0.003949	2.6745	2968483	0.0092	31.856	0.003942
45	0.027107	91360	2477	451014	0.005491	2.6626	2506805	0.0113	27.439	0.005480
50	0.042263	88884	3757	436011	0.008616	2.7616	2055791	0.0000	23.129	0.008616
55	0.084513	85127	7194	409230	0.017580	2.7195	1619780	0.0016	19.028	0.017573
60	0.145456	77933	11336	362831	0.031243	2.6328	1210550	0.0368	15.533	0.031016
65	0.216567	66597	14423	297462	0.048486	2.5370	847719	0.0368	12.729	0.048248
70	0.266312	52174	13895	224948	0.061768	2.4145	550257	0.0368	10.546	0.061695
75	0.227845	38280	8722	170141	0.051262	2.5627	325309	0.0368	8.498	0.050872
80	0.558866	29558	16519	107392	0.153819	2.5544	155168	0.0368	5.250	0.152174
85+	*1.000000	13039	13039	47776	0.272917	3.6641	47776	0.0368	3.664	0.268793

TABLE 3 — FEMALE LIFE TABLE

x	$_nq_x$	l_x	$_nd_x$	$_nL_x$	$_nm_x$	$_na_x$	T_x	r_x	$\overset{\circ}{e}_x$	$_nM_x$
0	0.027559	100000	2756	97836	0.028169	0.2149	7107372	0.0000	71.074	0.028169
1	0.003771	97244	367	387905	0.000945	1.0777	7009536	0.0000	72.082	0.000945
5	0.000850	96877	82	484181	0.000170	2.5000	6621632	0.0000	68.351	0.000170
10	0.000289	96795	28	483921	0.000058	3.0719	6137451	0.0000	63.407	0.000058
15	0.001643	96767	159	483474	0.000329	2.7283	5653529	0.0356	58.424	0.000326
20	0.002092	96608	202	482592	0.000419	2.7821	5170055	0.0498	53.516	0.000413
25	0.004489	96406	433	481053	0.000900	2.7429	4687463	0.0042	48.622	0.000899
30	0.007363	95973	707	478144	0.001478	2.5627	4206410	0.0063	43.829	0.001477
35	0.006776	95267	646	474758	0.001360	2.5598	3728266	0.0173	39.135	0.001358
40	0.009427	94621	892	470979	0.001894	2.6161	3253508	0.0259	34.385	0.001888
45	0.012190	93729	1143	466146	0.002451	2.8117	2782529	0.0226	29.687	0.002433
50	0.028096	92587	2601	457144	0.005690	2.7747	2316383	0.0000	25.019	0.005690
55	0.050810	89985	4572	439638	0.010400	2.7497	1859239	0.0072	20.662	0.010379
60	0.094626	85413	8082	408344	0.019793	2.6836	1419601	0.0157	16.620	0.019723
65	0.151227	77331	11695	358534	0.032618	2.5954	1011256	0.0157	13.077	0.032536
70	0.204717	65636	13437	296588	0.045305	2.6488	652723	0.0157	9.945	0.045124
75	0.407834	52199	21289	208697	0.102008	2.5433	356134	0.0157	6.823	0.101637
80	0.577860	30911	17862	108182	0.165112	2.4039	147437	0.0157	4.770	0.164516
85+	*1.000000	13049	13049	39255	0.332404	3.0084	39255	0.0157	3.008	0.330241

TABLE 4 — OBSERVED AND PROJECTED VITAL RATES

	OBSERVED POPULATION BOTH SEXES	MALES	FEMALES	PROJECTED POPULATION 1970 MALES	FEMALES	1975 MALES	FEMALES	1980 MALES	FEMALES	STABLE POPULATION MALES	FEMA
RATES PER THOUSAND											
Birth	17.63	18.98	16.40	21.31	18.47	22.96	19.98	22.83	19.99	17.50	16.
Death	9.40	10.29	8.59	11.08	8.63	10.94	8.82	9.53	8.91	12.72	11.
Increase	8.23	8.69	7.81	10.23	9.84	12.01	11.16	13.29	11.07		4.78
PERCENTAGE											
under 15	32.91	35.77	30.29	31.86	27.31	29.17	25.40	28.76	25.46	24.29	23.
15-64	58.20	54.88	61.24	59.29	64.22	62.38	65.85	63.67	66.07	65.29	64.
65 and over	8.89	9.35	8.47	8.85	8.47	8.45	8.76	7.57	8.47	10.42	11.
DEP. RATIO X 100	71.82	82.21	63.30	68.66	55.70	60.31	51.87	57.07	51.36	53.17	54.

TABLE 5 — POPULATION PROJECTED WITH FIXED AGE-SPECIFIC BIRTH AND DEATH RATES (IN 1000's)

AGE AT LAST BIRTHDAY	1970 BOTH SEXES	MALES	FEMALES	1975 BOTH SEXES	MALES	FEMALES	1980 BOTH SEXES	MALES	FEMALES	AGE AT LAST BIRTHDAY
0-4	29	15	14	34	17	17	37	19	18	0-4
5-9	32	17	15	29	15	14	34	17	17	5-9
10-14	37	19	18	32	17	15	29	15	14	10-14
15-19	36	19	17	37	19	18	32	17	15	15-19
20-24	33	15	18	36	19	17	37	19	18	20-24
25-29	22	10	12	33	15	18	35	18	17	25-29
30-34	19	8	11	22	10	12	33	15	18	30-34
35-39	19	8	11	19	8	11	22	10	12	35-39
40-44	18	8	10	18	7	11	19	8	11	40-44
45-49	17	8	9	18	8	10	18	7	11	45-49
50-54	15	7	8	17	8	9	17	7	10	50-54
55-59	13	6	7	13	6	7	16	7	9	55-59
60-64	13	6	7	13	6	7	13	6	7	60-64
65-69	10	5	5	11	5	6	11	5	6	65-69
70-74	7	3	4	7	3	4	9	4	5	70-74
75-79	6	3	3	6	3	3	6	3	3	75-79
80-84	4	3	1	4	2	2	4	2	2	80-84
85+	0	0	0	1	1	0	2	1	1	85+
TOTAL	330	160	170	350	169	181	374	180	194	TOTAL

TABLE 6 — STANDARDIZED RATES

STANDARD COUNTRIES:

STANDARDIZED RATES PER THOUSAND	ENGLAND AND WALES 1961 BOTH SEXES	MALES	FEMALES	UNITED STATES 1960 BOTH SEXES	MALES	FEMALES	MEXICO 1960 BOTH SEXES	MALES	FEMALES
Birth	15.78	23.10*	14.86	15.99	21.09*	15.31	17.56	20.88*	17.02
Death	13.61	11.05*	15.22	10.83	10.06*	11.01	5.50	8.53*	5.06
Increase	2.17	12.05*	-0.36	5.16	11.02*	4.31	12.06	12.35*	11.97

TABLE 7 — MOMENTS AND CUMULANTS

	OBSERVED POP. MALES	FEMALES	STATIONARY POP. MALES	FEMALES	STABLE POP. MALES	FEMALES	OBSERVED BIRTHS	NET MATERNITY FUNCTION	BIRTHS IN STABLE POP.
μ	29.69335	30.43353	36.69468	37.70466	34.34543	35.28909	28.86905	29.38709	29.19339
σ^2	508.3342	459.4823	497.5549	510.0379	483.3876	498.4806	38.68185	38.65304	38.12561
κ_3	7209.991	5614.792	2418.154	1787.139	3478.267	3021.180	104.3704	107.9509	112.3912
κ_4	-196434.	-147688.	-235834.	-270190.	-205406.	-243115.	-867.216	-972.111	-872.938
β_1	0.395750	0.324983	0.047473	0.024072	0.107112	0.073690	0.188206	0.201791	0.227937
β_2	2.239818	2.300469	2.047368	1.961360	2.120932	2.021601	2.420421	2.349348	2.399449
κ	-0.129084	-0.116872	-0.018349	-0.008866	-0.041372	-0.027120	-0.087964	-0.086115	-0.098876

TABLE 8 — RATES FROM AGE DISTRIBUTIONS AND VITAL STATISTICS (Females)

VITAL STATISTICS		THOMPSON AGE RANGE	NRR	1000r	INTERVAL	BOURGEOIS-PICHAT AGE RANGE	NRR	1000b	1000d	1000r	COALE
GRR	1.200										
NRR	1.150	0-4	1.26	8.46	27.43	5-29	1.98	28.98	3.69	25.29	IBR
TFR	2.470	5-9	1.67	18.89	27.40	30-54	1.77	28.83	7.67	21.16	IDR
GENERATION	29.289	10-14	1.76	20.25	27.36	55-79	1.22	15.21	7.95	7.26	IRI
SEX RATIO	105.777	15-19	1.95	24.51	27.28	*30-54	1.77	28.83	7.67	21.16	K1
											K2

TABLE 9 — LESLIE MATRIX AND ITS SPECTRAL COMPONENTS (Females)

Start Age Interval	ORIGINAL MATRIX SUB-DIAGONAL	ALTERNATIVE FIRST ROWS Projection	Integral	FIRST STABLE MATRIX % IN STABLE POPULATION	FISHER VALUES	REPRODUCTIVE VALUES	SECOND STABLE MATRIX Z₂ FIRST COLUMN	FIRST ROW
0	0.99679	0.00000	0.00000	8.042	1.042	16182	0.1424+0.0754	0.1424+0.0754
5	0.99946	0.00068	0.00000	7.827	1.070	18886	0.1648-0.1003	0.0067+0.1344
10	0.99908	0.01581	0.00138	7.638	1.096	18996	-0.0023-0.2317	-0.0934+0.0620
15	0.99818	0.16216	0.03065	7.450	1.107	20370	-0.2403-0.1400	-0.0864-0.0416
20	0.99681	0.33283	0.29812	7.261	0.967	11708	-0.2917+0.1618	-0.0302-0.0919
25	0.99395	0.28543	0.37676	7.066	0.646	7186	-0.0123+0.3993	0.0055-0.0861
30	0.99292	0.19789	0.20219	6.857	0.366	4215	0.4022+0.2565	0.0234-0.0546
35	0.99204	0.13112	0.19977	6.648	0.170	1755	0.5084-0.2557	0.0210-0.0216
40	0.98974	0.03493	0.06615	6.439	0.038	363	0.0482-0.6766	0.0057-0.0041
45	0.98069	0.00242	0.00459	6.222	0.003	20	-0.6620-0.4608	0.0004-0.0003
50	0.96171	0.00016	0.00032	5.957	0.000	1	-0.8656+0.3924	0.0000-0.0000
55+	0.77065			22.594				

TABLE 10 — AGE ANALYSIS AND MISCELLANEOUS RESULTS (Females)

Start Age Interval	OBSERVED POPUL. (IN 100's)	CONTRIBUTIONS OF ROOTS (IN 100's) r_1	r_2, r_3	$r_4 \cdot r_{11}$	AGE-SP. BIRTH RATES	NET MATERNITY FUNCTION	COEFF. OF MATRIX EQUATION	PARAMETERS	INTEGRAL	MATRIX	EXP. INCREASE x	$e^{(x+2\frac{1}{2})r}$
0	155	164	-13	4	0.0000	0.0000	0.0000	L(1)	1.02422	1.02423	0	1.0120
5	176	160	10	6	0.0000	0.0000	0.0007	L(2)	0.41986	0.42583	50	1.2856
10	173	156	31	-14	0.0003	0.0014	0.0157		0.73453	0.71514	55	1.3168
15	184	152	23	9	0.0062	0.0301	0.1614	R(1)	0.00479	0.00479	60	1.3486
20	121	148	-16	-11	0.0606	0.2927	0.3307	R(2)	-0.03343	-0.03671	65	1.3813
25	111	144	-53	21	0.0766	0.3687	0.2827		0.21030	0.20675	70	1.4148
30	115	140	-42	17	0.0411	0.1967	0.1948	C(1)		2040	75	1.4490
35	103	136	25	-58	0.0406	0.1929	0.1282	C(2)		-920	80	1.4841
40	95	131	90	-126	0.0135	0.0634	0.0340			6726	85	1.5201
45	78	127	74	-123	0.0010	0.0046	0.0023	2P/Y	29.8767	30.3907	90	1.5569
50	74	122	-37	-11	0.0000	0.0000	0.0000	DELTA	10.4139		95	1.5946
55+	281	461									100	1.6332

TABLE 1 DATA

AGE AT LAST BIRTHDAY	POPULATION BOTH SEXES	MALES Number	%	FEMALES Number	%	BIRTHS BY AGE OF MOTHER	DEATHS BOTH SEXES	MALES	FEMALES	AGE AT LAST BIRTHDAY
0	146991	74577	2.9	72414	2.8	0	17024	9668	7356	0
1-4	520897	262543	10.3	258354	9.9	0	18560	10003	8557	1-4
5-9	587515	295407	11.6	292108	11.2	0	2887	1478	1409	5-9
10-14	538931	270951	10.6	267980	10.2	0	1396	667	729	10-14
15-19	493356	247115	9.7	246241	9.4	2408	1894	957	937	15-19
20-24	450586	221945	8.7	228641	8.7	27035	2271	1298	973	20-24
25-29	393055	190807	7.5	202248	7.7	48494	2111	1017	1094	25-29
30-34	344151	167650	6.6	176501	6.8	44074	2009	907	1102	30-34
35-39	312426	153731	6.0	158695	6.1	30143	2089	978	1111	35-39
40-44	261251	129499	5.1	131752	5.0	16226	2072	1049	1023	40-44
45-49	238610	118142	4.6	120468	4.6	0	2292	1236	1056	45-49
50-54	207551	101727	4.0	105824	4.0	0	2648	1392	1256	50-54
55-59	192153	93755	3.7	98398	3.8	0	3368	1859	1509	55-59
60-64	168048	80697	3.2	87351	3.3	0	4471	2335	2136	60-64
65-69	125576	59316	2.3	66260	2.5	0	5352	2733	2619	65-69
70-74	90049	41481	1.6	48568	1.9		6056	2953	3103	70-74
75-79	58680	26420	1.0	32260	1.2		6140	2882	3258	75-79
80-84	25646	11233	0.4	14413	0.6	86333 M.	4407	2059	2348	80-84
85+	10049	3990	0.2	6059	0.2	82047 F.	2920	1226	1694	85+
TOTAL	5165521	2550986		2614535		168380	89967	46697	43270	TOTAL

TABLE 2 MALE LIFE TABLE

x	nq_x	l_x	nd_x	nL_x	nm_x	na_x	T_x	r_x	$\mathring{e}_x$	nM_x	x
0	0.120618	100000	12062	93042	0.129638	0.4232	4740125	0.0000	47.401	0.129638	0
1	0.138710	87938	12198	320150	0.038100	1.4092	4647083	0.0000	52.845	0.038100	1
5	0.024393	75740	1848	374083	0.004939	2.5000	4326933	0.0100	57.129	0.005003	5
10	0.012213	73893	902	367115	0.002458	2.3978	3952850	0.0145	53.494	0.002462	10
15	0.019246	72990	1405	361682	0.003884	2.6725	3585734	0.0160	49.126	0.003873	15
20	0.028859	71586	2066	352851	0.005855	2.5426	3224052	0.0205	45.038	0.005848	20
25	0.026285	69520	1827	342977	0.005328	2.4706	2871201	0.0226	41.301	0.005330	25
30	0.026710	67692	1808	333992	0.005413	2.5276	2528225	0.0160	37.349	0.005410	30
35	0.031377	65884	2067	324406	0.006372	2.5738	2194233	0.0193	33.304	0.006362	35
40	0.039800	63817	2540	312957	0.008116	2.5873	1869827	0.0181	29.300	0.008100	40
45	0.051096	61277	3131	298833	0.010478	2.5876	1556870	0.0135	25.407	0.010462	45
50	0.066329	58146	3857	281507	0.013700	2.6086	1258038	0.0089	21.636	0.013684	50
55	0.094703	54289	5141	259179	0.019837	2.6139	976530	0.0029	17.988	0.019828	55
60	0.135676	49148	6668	229837	0.029013	2.6152	717351	0.0151	14.596	0.028935	60
65	0.207798	42480	8827	191068	0.046199	2.5835	487514	0.0151	11.476	0.046075	65
70	0.303278	33653	10206	142999	0.071371	2.5247	296446	0.0151	8.809	0.071189	70
75	0.428039	23446	10036	91749	0.109385	2.4608	153447	0.0151	6.545	0.109084	75
80	0.620261	13410	8318	45228	0.183915	2.3762	61698	0.0151	4.601	0.183298	80
85+	*1.000000	5092	5092	16470	0.309197	3.2342	16470	0.0151	3.234	0.307268	85

TABLE 3 FEMALE LIFE TABLE

x	nq_x	l_x	nd_x	nL_x	nm_x	na_x	T_x	r_x	$\mathring{e}_x$	nM_x	x
0	0.096053	100000	9605	94556	0.101583	0.4332	5066141	0.0000	50.661	0.101583	0
1	0.122168	90395	11043	333422	0.033121	1.4503	4971585	0.0000	54.999	0.033121	1
5	0.023554	79351	1869	392084	0.004767	2.5000	4638163	0.0104	58.451	0.004824	5
10	0.013493	77482	1045	384709	0.002717	2.4150	4246079	0.0136	54.801	0.002720	10
15	0.018872	76437	1442	378690	0.003809	2.5774	3861370	0.0123	50.517	0.003805	15
20	0.021085	74994	1581	371127	0.004261	2.5685	3482680	0.0153	46.439	0.004256	20
25	0.026736	73413	1963	362288	0.005418	2.5656	3111553	0.0205	42.384	0.005409	25
30	0.030775	71450	2199	351843	0.006250	2.5400	2749265	0.0180	38.478	0.006244	30
35	0.034443	69252	2385	340367	0.007008	2.5306	2397422	0.0222	34.619	0.007001	35
40	0.038127	66866	2549	328036	0.007772	2.5309	2057055	0.0198	30.764	0.007765	40
45	0.042968	64317	2764	314885	0.008776	2.5758	1729018	0.0127	26.883	0.008766	45
50	0.057747	61553	3555	299199	0.011880	2.5896	1414134	0.0084	22.974	0.011869	50
55	0.074021	57999	4293	279817	0.015343	2.6296	1114935	0.0028	19.223	0.015336	55
60	0.115921	53706	6226	253860	0.024524	2.6440	835118	0.0147	15.550	0.024453	60
65	0.181041	47480	8596	216857	0.039638	2.6101	581257	0.0147	12.242	0.039526	65
70	0.276906	38884	10767	168075	0.064062	2.5531	364401	0.0147	9.371	0.063890	70
75	0.403352	28117	11341	111995	0.101263	2.4791	196326	0.0147	6.982	0.100992	75
80	0.574066	16776	9630	58929	0.163424	2.4092	84331	0.0147	5.027	0.162908	80
85+	*1.000000	7145	7145	25402	0.281298	3.5549	25402	0.0147	3.555	0.279584	85

TABLE 4 OBSERVED AND PROJECTED VITAL RATES

	OBSERVED POPULATION BOTH SEXES	MALES	FEMALES	PROJECTED POPULATION 1906 MALES	FEMALES	1911 MALES	FEMALES	1916 MALES	FEMALES	STABLE POPULATION MALES	FEMALES
RATES PER THOUSAND											
Birth	32.60	33.84	31.38	34.39	31.99	34.42	32.10	34.23	32.00	33.27	31.41
Death	17.42	18.31	16.55	18.42	16.68	18.41	16.68	18.27	16.55	18.49	16.63
Increase	15.18	15.54	14.83	15.97	15.31	16.01	15.42	15.96	15.45		14.7804
PERCENTAGE											
under 15	34.74	35.42	34.07	35.16	34.01	35.07	34.09	35.38	34.51	34.56	34.04
15-64	59.26	59.00	59.52	59.21	59.55	59.38	59.57	59.30	59.41	59.90	59.76
65 and over	6.00	5.58	6.41	5.63	6.44	5.55	6.34	5.32	6.08	5.54	6.21
DEP. RATIO X 100	68.74	69.49	68.02	68.89	67.93	68.42	67.86	68.64	68.33	66.94	67.35

TABLE 5 — POPULATION PROJECTED WITH FIXED AGE-SPECIFIC BIRTH AND DEATH RATES (IN 1000's)

AGE AT LAST BIRTHDAY	1906 BOTH SEXES	1906 MALES	1906 FEMALES	1911 BOTH SEXES	1911 MALES	1911 FEMALES	1916 BOTH SEXES	1916 MALES	1916 FEMALES	AGE AT LAST BIRTHDAY
0-4	742	374	368	810	408	402	875	441	434	0-4
5-9	608	305	303	677	339	338	737	369	368	5-9
10-14	577	290	287	597	300	297	664	333	331	10-14
15-19	531	267	264	568	286	282	588	295	293	15-19
20-24	482	241	241	519	260	259	555	279	276	20-24
25-29	439	216	223	470	234	236	505	253	252	25-29
30-34	382	186	196	427	210	217	457	228	229	30-34
35-39	334	163	171	370	180	190	414	204	210	35-39
40-44	301	148	153	322	157	165	357	174	183	40-44
45-49	250	124	126	289	142	147	308	150	158	45-49
50-54	225	111	114	236	116	120	273	133	140	50-54
55-59	193	94	99	209	102	107	219	107	112	55-59
60-64	172	83	89	173	83	90	188	91	97	60-64
65-69	142	67	75	145	69	76	146	69	77	65-69
70-74	95	44	51	108	50	58	111	52	59	70-74
75-79	59	27	32	62	28	34	71	32	39	75-79
80-84	30	13	17	30	13	17	32	14	18	80-84
85+	10	4	6	12	5	7	12	5	7	85+
TOTAL	5572	2757	2815	6024	2982	3042	6512	3229	3283	TOTAL

TABLE 6 — STANDARDIZED RATES

STANDARD COUNTRIES: STANDARDIZED RATES PER THOUSAND	ENGLAND AND WALES 1961 BOTH SEXES	MALES	FEMALES	UNITED STATES 1960 BOTH SEXES	MALES	FEMALES	MEXICO 1960 BOTH SEXES	MALES	FEMALES
Birth	30.10	31.80*	28.42	30.61	29.19*	29.39	29.89	30.05*	29.05
Death	21.69	28.65*	22.64	20.14	24.43*	19.59	16.53	16.86*	15.35
Increase	8.41	3.15*	5.78	10.46	4.76*	9.79	13.36	13.18*	13.70

TABLE 7 — MOMENTS AND CUMULANTS

	OBSERVED POP. MALES	OBSERVED POP. FEMALES	STATIONARY POP. MALES	STATIONARY POP. FEMALES	STABLE POP. MALES	STABLE POP. FEMALES	OBSERVED BIRTHS	NET MATERNITY FUNCTION	BIRTHS IN STABLE POP.
μ	27.21754	28.02124	34.22091	34.95471	27.59239	28.08894	31.09862	31.88457	31.30340
σ^2	414.4323	430.2408	477.9115	494.9516	413.4477	427.9541	36.53852	37.40025	37.02873
κ_3	5786.589	5947.515	3076.265	3120.448	5330.722	5599.105	39.0412	15.8277	34.1827
κ_4	-76437.	-88390.	-212723.	-233297.	-86515.	-95103.	-1124.712	-1286.000	-1180.184
β_1	0.470419	0.444157	0.086697	0.080306	0.402078	0.399987	0.031246	0.004789	0.023014
β_2	2.554965	2.522491	2.068637	2.047676	2.493885	2.480723	2.157559	2.080626	2.139260
κ	-0.179020	-0.169047	-0.032730	-0.029990	-0.155952	-0.153829	-0.013685	-0.002007	-0.009999

TABLE 8 — RATES FROM AGE DISTRIBUTIONS AND VITAL STATISTICS (Females)

VITAL STATISTICS		THOMPSON AGE RANGE	NRR	1000r	INTERVAL	BOURGEOIS-PICHAT AGE RANGE	NRR	1000b	1000d	1000r	COALE	
GRR	2.267											
NRR	1.595	0-4	1.44	13.69	27.13	5-29	1.46	31.76	17.76	14.00	IBR	31.48
TFR	4.653	5-9	1.51	15.50	27.02	30-54	1.62	34.23	16.30	17.93	IDR	16.77
GENERATION	31.594	10-14	1.55	16.12	26.95	55-79	1.47	30.86	16.70	14.16	IRI	14.71
SEX RATIO	105.224	15-19	1.57	15.94	26.85	* 5-29	1.46	31.76	17.76	14.00	K1	-12.13
											K2	-0.19

TABLE 9 — LESLIE MATRIX AND ITS SPECTRAL COMPONENTS (Females)

Start of Age Interval	ORIGINAL MATRIX SUB-DIAGONAL	ALTERNATIVE FIRST ROWS Projection	ALTERNATIVE FIRST ROWS Integral	FIRST STABLE MATRIX % IN STABLE POPULATION	FISHER VALUES	REPRODUCTIVE VALUES	SECOND STABLE MATRIX Z₂ FIRST COLUMN	FIRST ROW
0	0.91613	0.00000	0.00000	12.966	1.211	400641	0.1373+0.0482	0.1373+0.0482
5	0.98119	0.00000	0.00000	11.031	1.424	415872	0.1165-0.0843	0.0390+0.1419
10	0.98435	0.01004	0.00000	10.051	1.562	418705	-0.0031-0.1523	-0.0891+0.1067
15	0.98003	0.13103	0.02116	9.188	1.697	417839	-0.1348-0.0896	-0.1317-0.0122
20	0.97618	0.36735	0.25587	8.362	1.703	389265	-0.1591+0.0632	-0.0798-0.1153
25	0.97117	0.50288	0.51885	7.581	1.422	287641	-0.0408+0.1757	-0.0049-0.1428
30	0.96739	0.45197	0.54035	6.837	0.950	167630	0.1269+0.1401	0.0382-0.1065
35	0.96377	0.32180	0.41102	6.142	0.491	77963	0.1957-0.0255	0.0405-0.0506
40	0.95991	0.12841	0.26647	5.497	0.144	19034	0.0942-0.1824	0.0163-0.0118
45	0.95019	0.00002	0.00002	4.901	0.000	4	-0.0996-0.1879	0.0000-0.0000
50	0.93522	0.00001	0.00002	4.324	0.000	1	-0.2166-0.0259	0.0000-0.0000
55+	0.76857			13.119				

TABLE 10 — AGE ANALYSIS AND MISCELLANEOUS RESULTS (Females)

Start of Age Interval	OBSERVED POPUL. (IN 100's)	CONTRIBUTIONS OF ROOTS (IN 100's) r_1	r_2, r_3	r_4-r_{11}	AGE-SP. BIRTH RATES	NET MATERNITY FUNCTION	COEFF. OF MATRIX EQUATION	PARAMETERS	INTEGRAL	MATRIX	EXP. INCREASE x	$e^{(x+2\frac{1}{2})r}$
0	3308	3432	-68	-56	0.0000	0.0000	0.0000	L(1)	1.07670	1.07682	0	1.0376
5	2921	2920	-49	50	0.0000	0.0000	0.0000	L(2)	0.53028	0.52806	50	2.1727
10	2680	2660	12	7	0.0000	0.0000	0.0090		0.77808	0.76135	55	2.3394
15	2462	2432	70	-40	0.0048	0.0180	0.1159	R(1)	0.01478	0.01480	60	2.5188
20	2286	2213	71	2	0.0576	0.2138	0.3186	R(2)	-0.01204	-0.01526	65	2.7120
25	2022	2006	7	9	0.1168	0.4233	0.4257			0.19451	0.19288	70	2.9200
30	1765	1810	-70	25	0.1217	0.4281	0.3716	C(1)		26468	75	3.1440
35	1587	1626	-91	52	0.0926	0.3150	0.2559	C(2)		-23618	80	3.3851
40	1318	1455	-31	-106	0.0600	0.1969	0.0984			3596	85	3.6447
45	1205	1297	61	-153	0.0000	0.0000	0.0000	2P/Y	32.3019	32.5760	90	3.9243
50	1058	1145	104	-190	0.0000	0.0000	0.0000	DELTA	1.5087		95	4.2253
55+	3533	3472									100	4.5494

TABLE 1 — DATA

AGE AT LAST BIRTHDAY	POPULATION BOTH SEXES	MALES Number	MALES %	FEMALES Number	FEMALES %	BIRTHS BY AGE OF MOTHER	DEATHS BOTH SEXES	DEATHS MALES	FEMALES	AGE AT LAST BIRTHDAY
0	155129	78816	2.9	76313	2.8	0	14917	8376	6541	0
1-4	547196	276652	10.3	270544	9.8	0	15325	8181	7144	1-4
5-9	624900	314871	11.7	310029	11.2	0	2252	1175	1077	5-9
10-14	565773	284220	10.5	281553	10.2	0	1278	617	661	10-14
15-19	516968	258239	9.6	258729	9.4	2290	1764	862	902	15-19
20-24	464142	229474	8.5	234668	8.5	26953	2131	1169	962	20-24
25-29	427414	209018	7.7	218396	7.9	48941	2020	998	1022	25-29
30-34	370527	180076	6.7	190451	6.9	45145	1921	871	1050	30-34
35-39	330589	161660	6.0	168929	6.1	30753	1966	919	1047	35-39
40-44	292653	144525	5.4	148128	5.4	16884	2145	1050	1095	40-44
45-49	244882	121110	4.5	123772	4.5	0	2201	1197	1004	45-49
50-54	226590	111580	4.1	115010	4.2	0	2702	1453	1249	50-54
55-59	187374	91003	3.4	96371	3.5	0	3240	1744	1496	55-59
60-64	172665	83402	3.1	89263	3.2	0	4397	2283	2114	60-64
65-69	139428	66084	2.4	73344	2.7	0	5707	2887	2820	65-69
70-74	94441	43802	1.6	50639	1.8		6186	3022	3164	70-74
75-79	58655	26397	1.0	32258	1.2		6083	2889	3194	75-79
80-84	30078	13198	0.5	16880	0.6	87553 M.	4960	2280	2680	80-84
85+	11327	4626	0.2	6701	0.2	83413 F.	3322	1420	1902	85+
TOTAL	5460731	2698753		2761978		170966	84517	43393	41124	TOTAL

TABLE 2 — MALE LIFE TABLE

x	nq_x	l_x	nd_x	nL_x	nm_x	na_x	T_x	r_x	$\dot{e}_x$	nM_x	x
0	0.100060	100000	10006	94209	0.106211	0.4212	5118202	0.0011	51.182	0.106273	0
1	0.109805	89994	9882	334302	0.029560	1.4019	5023993	0.0011	55.826	0.029571	1
5	0.018171	80112	1456	396922	0.003667	2.5000	4689691	0.0132	58.539	0.003732	5
10	0.010788	78656	849	391127	0.002170	2.4600	4292770	0.0170	54.576	0.002171	10
15	0.016615	77808	1293	386032	0.003349	2.6738	3901643	0.0179	50.145	0.003338	15
20	0.025182	76515	1927	377856	0.005099	2.5504	3515611	0.0165	45.947	0.005094	20
25	0.023584	74588	1759	368505	0.004774	2.4781	3137755	0.0194	42.068	0.004775	25
30	0.023917	72829	1742	359841	0.004841	2.5283	2769250	0.0207	38.024	0.004837	30
35	0.028077	71087	1996	350599	0.005693	2.5763	2409409	0.0162	33.894	0.005685	35
40	0.035794	69091	2473	339540	0.007284	2.6033	2058810	0.0214	29.798	0.007265	40
45	0.048363	66618	3222	325358	0.009903	2.5995	1719281	0.0159	25.808	0.009884	45
50	0.063281	63396	4012	307417	0.013050	2.6157	1393923	0.0150	21.987	0.013022	50
55	0.091757	59385	5449	283912	0.019192	2.6121	1086506	0.0097	18.296	0.019164	55
60	0.128730	53936	6943	253124	0.027430	2.6158	802595	0.0118	14.881	0.027373	60
65	0.198045	46993	9307	212569	0.043782	2.5938	549470	0.0118	11.693	0.043687	65
70	0.295426	37686	11133	161030	0.069139	2.5390	336901	0.0118	8.940	0.068992	70
75	0.428957	26553	11390	103850	0.109677	2.4615	175871	0.0118	6.624	0.109444	75
80	0.595572	15163	9030	52142	0.173190	2.3787	72021	0.0118	4.750	0.172754	80
85+	*1.000000	6132	6132	19880	0.308467	3.2418	19880	0.0118	3.242	0.306961	85+

TABLE 3 — FEMALE LIFE TABLE

x	nq_x	l_x	nd_x	nL_x	nm_x	na_x	T_x	r_x	$\dot{e}_x$	nM_x	x
0	0.081653	100000	8165	95351	0.085634	0.4307	5380751	0.0018	53.808	0.085713	0
1	0.098878	91835	9080	344087	0.026390	1.4393	5285399	0.0018	57.553	0.026406	1
5	0.016959	82754	1403	410263	0.003421	2.5000	4941312	0.0125	59.711	0.003474	5
10	0.011671	81351	949	404378	0.002348	2.4975	4531049	0.0152	55.698	0.002348	10
15	0.017313	80401	1392	398664	0.003492	2.5981	4126671	0.0149	51.326	0.003486	15
20	0.020309	79009	1605	391119	0.004103	2.5520	3728007	0.0128	47.184	0.004099	20
25	0.023156	77405	1792	382638	0.004684	2.5528	3336888	0.0161	43.110	0.004680	25
30	0.027229	75612	2059	373010	0.005520	2.5461	2954250	0.0202	39.071	0.005513	30
35	0.030561	73554	2248	362259	0.006205	2.5494	2581240	0.0188	35.093	0.006198	35
40	0.036347	71306	2592	350151	0.007402	2.5393	2218981	0.0239	31.119	0.007392	40
45	0.039831	68714	2737	336916	0.008124	2.5690	1868830	0.0168	27.197	0.008112	45
50	0.053029	65977	3499	321544	0.010881	2.6160	1531914	0.0139	23.219	0.010860	50
55	0.074977	62478	4684	301304	0.015547	2.6332	1210370	0.0092	19.373	0.015523	55
60	0.112369	57794	6494	273643	0.023732	2.6401	909066	0.0110	15.729	0.023683	60
65	0.176439	51300	9051	234907	0.038531	2.6146	635422	0.0110	12.386	0.038449	65
70	0.271520	42248	11471	183223	0.062608	2.5575	400515	0.0110	9.480	0.062481	70
75	0.396933	30777	12216	123135	0.099212	2.4829	217292	0.0110	7.060	0.099014	75
80	0.563982	18561	10468	65774	0.159148	2.4179	94157	0.0110	5.073	0.158769	80
85+	*1.000000	8093	8093	28382	0.285134	3.5071	28382	0.0110	3.507	0.283838	85+

TABLE 4 — OBSERVED AND PROJECTED VITAL RATES

	OBSERVED POPULATION BOTH SEXES	MALES	FEMALES	PROJECTED POPULATION 1910 MALES	1910 FEMALES	1915 MALES	1915 FEMALES	1920 MALES	1920 FEMALES	STABLE POPULATION MALES	FEMALES
RATES PER THOUSAND											
Birth	31.31	32.44	30.20	32.50	30.40	32.35	30.38	32.13	30.28	31.13	29.85
Death	15.48	16.08	14.89	16.07	14.89	15.97	14.81	15.87	14.72	16.20	14.92
Increase	15.83	16.36	15.31	16.43	15.50	16.38	15.57	16.26	15.57		14.9291
PERCENTAGE											
under 15	34.67	35.37	33.98	35.21	33.93	34.97	33.84	35.04	34.04	34.02	33.61
15-64	59.22	58.92	59.51	59.10	59.62	59.59	59.98	59.60	59.89	60.21	60.02
65 and over	6.12	5.71	6.51	5.69	6.45	5.44	6.17	5.36	6.06	5.77	6.37
DEP. RATIO X 100	68.86	69.72	68.03	69.22	67.73	67.82	66.71	67.78	66.96	66.08	66.62

TABLE 1 — DATA

AGE AT LAST BIRTHDAY	POPULATION BOTH SEXES	MALES Number	%	FEMALES Number	%	BIRTHS BY AGE OF MOTHER	DEATHS BOTH SEXES	MALES	FEMALES	AGE AT LAST BIRTHDAY
0	158632	80617	2.8	78015	2.6	0	16235	9130	7105	0
1-4	578096	291886	10.1	286210	9.7	0	10059	5287	4772	1-4
5-9	669406	338124	11.7	331282	11.2	0	1972	1041	931	5-9
10-14	616199	310558	10.7	305641	10.3	0	1198	578	620	10-14
15-19	555804	279057	9.6	276747	9.3	2306	1685	844	841	15-19
20-24	496770	245823	8.5	250947	8.5	26685	1941	1031	910	20-24
25-29	444385	217429	7.5	226956	7.7	48334	1826	892	934	25-29
30-34	412128	201159	6.9	210969	7.1	44728	1850	832	1018	30-34
35-39	359295	175251	6.0	184044	6.2	30496	1952	881	1071	35-39
40-44	319445	156585	5.4	162860	5.5	17116	2047	977	1070	40-44
45-49	280953	138644	4.8	142309	4.8	0	2331	1199	1132	45-49
50-54	232019	114269	3.9	117750	4.0	0	2714	1440	1274	50-54
55-59	210503	103008	3.6	107495	3.6	0	3496	1877	1619	55-59
60-64	167581	80683	2.8	86898	2.9	0	4327	2255	2072	60-64
65-69	145805	69541	2.4	76264	2.6	0	5912	2969	2943	65-69
70-74	107081	50050	1.7	57031	1.9		6970	3452	3518	70-74
75-79	62140	28383	1.0	33757	1.1		6544	3103	3441	75-79
80-84	30162	13160	0.5	17002	0.6	87059 M.	4945	2250	2695	80-84
85+	13329	5551	0.2	7778	0.3	82606 F.	3722	1606	2116	85+
TOTAL	5859733	2899778		2959955		169665	81726	41644	40082	TOTAL

TABLE 2 — MALE LIFE TABLE

x	$_nq_x$	l_x	$_nd_x$	$_nL_x$	$_nm_x$	$_na_x$	T_x	r_x	$\mathring{e}_x$	$_nM_x$	x
0	0.105696	100000	10570	93377	0.113193	0.3734	5409038	0.0008	54.090	0.113252	0
1	0.069007	89430	6171	340848	0.018106	1.2659	5315661	0.0008	59.439	0.018113	1
5	0.015109	83259	1258	413151	0.003045	2.5000	4974813	0.0120	59.751	0.003079	5
10	0.009262	82001	759	408100	0.001861	2.4906	4561662	0.0168	55.629	0.001861	10
15	0.015065	81242	1224	403337	0.003034	2.6538	4153563	0.0204	51.126	0.003024	15
20	0.020780	80018	1663	396008	0.004199	2.5460	3750226	0.0210	46.867	0.004194	20
25	0.020302	78355	1591	387779	0.004102	2.4882	3354218	0.0159	42.808	0.004102	25
30	0.020488	76764	1573	379947	0.004139	2.5370	2966438	0.0173	38.644	0.004136	30
35	0.024875	75191	1870	371424	0.005036	2.5764	2586491	0.0200	34.399	0.005027	35
40	0.030800	73321	2258	361199	0.006252	2.6062	2215067	0.0170	30.211	0.006239	40
45	0.042514	71063	3021	348160	0.008678	2.6321	1853867	0.0226	26.088	0.008648	45
50	0.061336	68042	4173	330310	0.012635	2.6283	1505707	0.0168	22.129	0.012602	50
55	0.087560	63868	5592	306085	0.018270	2.6295	1175397	0.0158	18.403	0.018222	55
60	0.131261	58276	7649	273137	0.028005	2.6151	869313	0.0116	14.917	0.027949	60
65	0.193957	50627	9819	229502	0.042785	2.5935	596176	0.0116	11.776	0.042694	65
70	0.295426	40807	12056	174418	0.069118	2.5432	366673	0.0116	8.985	0.068971	70
75	0.428541	28752	12321	112468	0.109554	2.4604	192255	0.0116	6.687	0.109326	75
80	0.591370	16430	9716	56693	0.171388	2.3798	79787	0.0116	4.856	0.170973	80
85+	*1.000000	6714	6714	23094	0.290721	3.4397	23094	0.0116	3.440	0.289317	85+

TABLE 3 — FEMALE LIFE TABLE

x	$_nq_x$	l_x	$_nd_x$	$_nL_x$	$_nm_x$	$_na_x$	T_x	r_x	$\mathring{e}_x$	$_nM_x$	x
0	0.086228	100000	8623	94720	0.091035	0.3876	5629729	0.0007	56.297	0.091072	0
1	0.063800	91377	5830	349763	0.016668	1.2992	5535010	0.0007	60.573	0.016673	1
5	0.013806	85547	1181	424784	0.002780	2.5000	5185246	0.0118	60.613	0.002810	5
10	0.010096	84366	852	419719	0.002029	2.5198	4760462	0.0155	56.426	0.002029	10
15	0.015112	83515	1262	414548	0.003044	2.6037	4340743	0.0168	51.976	0.003039	15
20	0.017990	82252	1480	407643	0.003630	2.5542	3926195	0.0162	47.733	0.003626	20
25	0.020388	80773	1647	399832	0.004119	2.5518	3518552	0.0132	43.561	0.004115	25
30	0.023874	79126	1889	391026	0.004831	2.5631	3118720	0.0161	39.415	0.004825	30
35	0.028723	77237	2218	380751	0.005827	2.5507	2727694	0.0201	35.316	0.005819	35
40	0.032371	75018	2428	369151	0.006578	2.5533	2346943	0.0190	31.285	0.006570	40
45	0.039127	72590	2840	356112	0.007976	2.5923	1977792	0.0242	27.246	0.007955	45
50	0.052853	69750	3686	339944	0.010844	2.6116	1621681	0.0170	23.250	0.010820	50
55	0.072897	66063	4816	318952	0.015099	2.6402	1281737	0.0145	19.402	0.015061	55
60	0.113086	61247	6926	289921	0.023890	2.6443	962785	0.0099	15.720	0.023844	60
65	0.176961	54321	9613	248633	0.038662	2.6101	672864	0.0099	12.387	0.038590	65
70	0.268573	44708	12007	194288	0.061802	2.5637	424231	0.0099	9.489	0.061686	70
75	0.406195	32701	13283	130072	0.102120	2.4830	229942	0.0099	7.032	0.101934	75
80	0.562617	19418	10925	68780	0.158839	2.4087	99871	0.0099	5.143	0.158511	80
85+	*1.000000	8493	8493	31091	0.273171	3.6607	31091	0.0099	3.661	0.272049	85+

TABLE 4 — OBSERVED AND PROJECTED VITAL RATES

	OBSERVED POPULATION BOTH SEXES	MALES	FEMALES	PROJECTED POPULATION 1915 MALES	FEMALES	1920 MALES	FEMALES	1925 MALES	FEMALES	STABLE POPULATION MALES	FEMALES
RATES PER THOUSAND											
Birth	28.95	30.02	27.91	30.05	28.10	30.06	28.26	30.00	28.33	28.62	27.66
Death	13.95	14.36	13.54	14.18	13.37	14.14	13.34	14.11	13.32	14.90	13.94
Increase	15.01	15.66	14.37	15.88	14.74	15.92	14.92	15.89	15.01		13.7197
PERCENTAGE											
under 15	34.51	35.22	33.82	34.50	33.24	33.90	32.78	33.65	32.62	32.52	32.26
15-64	59.37	59.04	59.70	60.00	60.55	60.65	61.08	61.04	61.40	61.19	60.91
65 and over	6.12	5.75	6.48	5.50	6.22	5.45	6.13	5.31	5.98	6.28	6.83
DEP. RATIO X 100	68.44	69.39	67.52	66.67	65.16	64.88	63.71	63.83	62.87	63.42	64.17

TABLE 1 — DATA

AGE AT LAST BIRTHDAY	POPULATION BOTH SEXES	MALES Number	%	FEMALES Number	%	BIRTHS BY AGE OF MOTHER	DEATHS BOTH SEXES	MALES	FEMALES	AGE AT LAST BIRTHDAY
0	163761	83337	2.7	80424	2.5	0	15367	8700	6667	0
1-4	596807	302425	9.6	294382	9.2	0	7030	3673	3357	1-4
5-9	715699	361390	11.5	354309	11.1	0	1803	951	852	5-9
10-14	667097	336374	10.7	330723	10.3	0	1269	597	672	10-14
15-19	607186	304040	9.7	303146	9.5	2700	1969	1000	969	15-19
20-24	541975	269292	8.6	272683	8.5	28179	2093	1132	961	20-24
25-29	486475	239395	7.6	247080	7.7	49325	1921	922	999	25-29
30-34	436125	214104	6.8	222021	6.9	44240	1880	857	1023	30-34
35-39	404985	198312	6.3	206673	6.5	30646	2035	905	1130	35-39
40-44	351391	171907	5.5	179484	5.6	17606	2143	999	1144	40-44
45-49	309473	151828	4.8	157645	4.9	0	2438	1226	1212	45-49
50-54	269863	132471	4.2	137392	4.3	0	2986	1569	1417	50-54
55-59	217797	106381	3.4	111416	3.5	0	3532	1869	1663	55-59
60-64	190756	92499	2.9	98257	3.1	0	4768	2516	2252	60-64
65-69	143699	68467	2.2	75232	2.4	0	5793	2941	2852	65-69
70-74	113815	53555	1.7	60260	1.9		7236	3550	3686	70-74
75-79	72191	33117	1.1	39074	1.2		7408	3526	3882	75-79
80-84	33452	14880	0.5	18572	0.6	88626 M.	5371	2481	2890	80-84
85+	14363	5889	0.2	8474	0.3	84070 F.	3862	1647	2215	85+
TOTAL	6336910	3139663		3197247		172696	80904	41061	39843	TOTAL

TABLE 2 — MALE LIFE TABLE

x	$_nq_x$	l_x	$_nd_x$	$_nL_x$	$_nm_x$	$_na_x$	T_x	r_x	$\mathring{e}_x$	$_nM_x$	x
0	0.097521	100000	9752	93592	0.104197	0.3430	5629235	0.0028	56.292	0.104395	0
1	0.046909	90248	4233	349174	0.012124	1.2084	5535643	0.0028	61.338	0.012145	1
5	0.012991	86014	1117	427279	0.002615	2.5000	5186469	0.0091	60.298	0.002632	5
10	0.008846	84897	751	422662	0.001777	2.5720	4759191	0.0150	56.058	0.001775	10
15	0.016367	84146	1377	417489	0.003299	2.6470	4336529	0.0191	51.536	0.003289	15
20	0.020813	82769	1723	409572	0.004206	2.5203	3919040	0.0200	47.349	0.004204	20
25	0.019068	81046	1545	401337	0.003851	2.4803	3509467	0.0190	43.302	0.003851	25
30	0.019828	79501	1576	393608	0.004005	2.5285	3108130	0.0148	39.096	0.004003	30
35	0.022599	77924	1761	385347	0.004570	2.5724	2714523	0.0173	34.835	0.004564	35
40	0.028732	76163	2188	375591	0.005826	2.6121	2329176	0.0207	30.581	0.005811	40
45	0.039724	73975	2939	362929	0.008097	2.6361	1953584	0.0177	26.409	0.008075	45
50	0.057824	71036	4108	345481	0.011889	2.6381	1590656	0.0234	22.392	0.011844	50
55	0.084594	66929	5662	321269	0.017623	2.6376	1245175	0.0176	18.604	0.017569	55
60	0.128061	61267	7846	287712	0.027270	2.6263	923906	0.0139	15.080	0.027200	60
65	0.195053	53421	10420	241980	0.043061	2.5887	636194	0.0139	11.909	0.042955	65
70	0.285613	43001	12282	184820	0.066452	2.5422	394214	0.0139	9.168	0.066287	70
75	0.420185	30720	12908	120929	0.106739	2.4691	209394	0.0139	6.816	0.106471	75
80	0.582064	17812	10368	62001	0.167215	2.3902	88465	0.0139	4.967	0.166733	80
85+	*1.000000	7444	7444	26464	0.281295	3.5550	26464	0.0139	3.555	0.279674	85+

TABLE 3 — FEMALE LIFE TABLE

x	$_nq_x$	l_x	$_nd_x$	$_nL_x$	$_nm_x$	$_na_x$	T_x	r_x	$\mathring{e}_x$	$_nM_x$	x
0	0.078591	100000	7859	94980	0.082745	0.3613	5829381	0.0027	58.294	0.082898	0
1	0.044158	92141	4069	357338	0.011386	1.2410	5734401	0.0027	62.235	0.011404	1
5	0.011887	88072	1047	437743	0.002392	2.5000	5377063	0.0081	61.053	0.002405	5
10	0.010121	87025	881	432991	0.002034	2.5761	4939320	0.0132	56.757	0.002032	10
15	0.015885	86144	1368	427426	0.003202	2.5916	4506329	0.0163	52.311	0.003196	15
20	0.017484	84776	1482	420237	0.003527	2.5422	4078903	0.0169	48.114	0.003524	20
25	0.020036	83294	1669	412375	0.004047	2.5473	3658666	0.0165	43.925	0.004043	25
30	0.022801	81625	1861	403573	0.004612	2.5543	3246290	0.0132	39.771	0.004608	30
35	0.027006	79764	2154	393554	0.005473	2.5559	2842718	0.0158	35.639	0.005468	35
40	0.031427	77610	2439	382094	0.006383	2.5588	2449163	0.0206	31.557	0.006374	40
45	0.037815	75171	2843	369000	0.007703	2.5890	2067069	0.0188	27.498	0.007688	45
50	0.050502	72328	3653	352951	0.010349	2.6211	1698069	0.0240	23.477	0.010314	50
55	0.072303	68675	4965	331649	0.014972	2.6381	1345118	0.0180	19.587	0.014926	55
60	0.109004	63710	6945	302214	0.022979	2.6478	1013469	0.0132	15.908	0.022919	60
65	0.174256	56765	9892	260255	0.038008	2.6171	711255	0.0132	12.530	0.037909	65
70	0.266746	46874	12503	203900	0.061321	2.5632	451000	0.0132	9.622	0.061168	70
75	0.398164	34370	13685	137415	0.099589	2.4837	247100	0.0132	7.189	0.099350	75
80	0.552552	20685	11430	73285	0.155962	2.4193	109685	0.0132	5.303	0.155611	80
85+	1.000000	9256	9256	36400	0.254274	3.9328	36400	0.0132	3.933	0.261387	85+

TABLE 4 — OBSERVED AND PROJECTED VITAL RATES

RATES PER THOUSAND	OBSERVED POPULATION BOTH SEXES	MALES	FEMALES	PROJECTED POPULATION 1920 MALES	FEMALES	1925 MALES	FEMALES	1930 MALES	FEMALES	STABLE POPULATION MALES	FEMALES
Birth	27.25	28.23	26.29	28.34	26.56	28.39	26.76	28.39	26.88	26.73	25.94
Death	12.77	13.08	12.46	13.00	12.41	13.01	12.43	13.03	12.45	14.09	13.29
Increase	14.49	15.15	13.83	15.33	14.14	15.38	14.33	15.37	14.43		
										12.6427	
PERCENTAGE under 15	33.82	34.51	33.15	33.60	32.35	32.95	31.80	32.80	31.78	31.51	31.29
15-64	60.22	59.89	60.55	60.83	61.41	61.61	62.08	61.68	61.99	61.73	61.40
65 and over	5.96	5.60	6.31	5.56	6.25	5.44	6.12	5.52	6.23	6.76	7.31
DEP. RATIO X 100	66.06	66.98	65.16	64.38	62.85	62.30	61.08	62.13	61.31	61.99	62.86

TABLE 1 — DATA

AGE AT LAST BIRTHDAY	POPULATION BOTH SEXES	MALES Number	%	FEMALES Number	%	BIRTHS BY AGE OF MOTHER	DEATHS BOTH SEXES	MALES	FEMALES	AGE AT LAST BIRTHDAY
0	169833	86916	2.6	82917	2.4	0	14766	8444	6322	0
1-4	597631	303851	9.0	293780	8.6	0	7915	4181	3734	1-4
5-9	740665	375220	11.1	365445	10.7	0	2169	1108	1061	5-9
10-14	713297	360575	10.7	352722	10.3	0	1563	735	828	10-14
15-19	663712	334726	9.9	328986	9.6	3037	2538	1268	1270	15-19
20-24	592481	294423	8.7	298058	8.7	29933	2924	1530	1394	20-24
25-29	525820	258642	7.7	267178	7.8	51459	2820	1357	1463	25-29
30-34	472056	231814	6.9	240242	7.0	45010	2671	1264	1407	30-34
35-39	427869	210054	6.2	217815	6.4	31511	2576	1166	1410	35-39
40-44	395574	194244	5.8	201330	5.9	18350	2606	1232	1374	40-44
45-49	342077	167509	5.0	174568	5.1	0	2774	1360	1414	45-49
50-54	296477	145250	4.3	151227	4.4	0	3323	1705	1618	50-54
55-59	254463	124219	3.7	130244	3.8	0	4194	2173	2021	55-59
60-64	196745	95622	2.8	101123	3.0	0	5020	2580	2440	60-64
65-69	162082	77590	2.3	84492	2.5	0	6508	3282	3226	65-69
70-74	111748	52512	1.6	59236	1.7		7300	3557	3743	70-74
75-79	74780	34539	1.0	40241	1.2		7756	3732	4024	75-79
80-84	37516	16691	0.5	20825	0.6	92307 M.	6116	2831	3285	80-84
85+	15001	6332	0.2	8669	0.3	86993 F.	4011	1755	2256	85+
TOTAL	6789827	3370729		3419098		179300	89550	45260	44290	TOTAL

TABLE 2 — MALE LIFE TABLE

x	$_nq_x$	l_x	$_nd_x$	$_nL_x$	$_nm_x$	$_na_x$	T_x	r_x	$\mathring{e}_x$	$_nM_x$	x
0	0.091138	100000	9114	94196	0.096753	0.3631	5530659	0.0062	55.307	0.097151	0
1	0.052860	90886	4804	350307	0.013714	1.2446	5436463	0.0062	59.816	0.013760	1
5	0.014628	86082	1259	427262	0.002947	2.5000	5086156	0.0029	59.085	0.002953	5
10	0.010149	84823	861	422029	0.002040	2.5778	4658894	0.0088	54.925	0.002038	10
15	0.018828	83962	1581	416119	0.003799	2.6654	4236865	0.0166	50.462	0.003788	15
20	0.025688	82381	2116	406718	0.005203	2.5490	3820746	0.0209	46.379	0.005197	20
25	0.025898	80265	2079	396125	0.005248	2.4987	3414028	0.0186	42.535	0.005247	25
30	0.026901	78186	2103	385674	0.005454	2.5005	3017903	0.0154	38.599	0.005453	30
35	0.027389	76083	2084	375249	0.005553	2.5211	2632230	0.0120	34.597	0.005551	35
40	0.031273	73999	2314	364372	0.006351	2.5701	2256981	0.0161	30.500	0.006343	40
45	0.039935	71685	2863	351607	0.008142	2.6184	1892609	0.0206	26.402	0.008119	45
50	0.057270	68822	3941	334801	0.011772	2.6379	1541002	0.0178	22.391	0.011738	50
55	0.084329	64881	5471	311477	0.017566	2.6374	1206202	0.0236	18.591	0.017493	55
60	0.127066	59409	7549	279114	0.027046	2.6244	894725	0.0132	15.060	0.026981	60
65	0.192408	51860	9978	235323	0.042403	2.5968	615611	0.0132	11.871	0.042299	65
70	0.290999	41882	12188	179491	0.067901	2.5451	380288	0.0132	9.080	0.067737	70
75	0.424878	29694	12617	116486	0.108310	2.4647	200797	0.0132	6.762	0.108052	75
80	0.588538	17078	10051	59098	0.170075	2.3841	84312	0.0132	4.937	0.169613	80
85+	*1.000000	7027	7027	25214	0.278691	3.5882	25214	0.0132	3.588	0.277164	85+

TABLE 3 — FEMALE LIFE TABLE

x	$_nq_x$	l_x	$_nd_x$	$_nL_x$	$_nm_x$	$_na_x$	T_x	r_x	$\mathring{e}_x$	$_nM_x$	x
0	0.072543	100000	7254	95505	0.075957	0.3803	5700452	0.0058	57.005	0.076245	0
1	0.049012	92746	4546	358625	0.012675	1.2815	5604948	0.0058	60.433	0.012710	1
5	0.014398	88200	1270	437825	0.002900	2.5000	5246322	0.0016	59.482	0.002903	5
10	0.011678	86930	1015	432191	0.002349	2.5772	4808497	0.0077	55.314	0.002347	10
15	0.019157	85915	1646	425655	0.003867	2.6184	4376306	0.0132	50.938	0.003860	15
20	0.023147	84269	1951	416589	0.004682	2.5619	3950651	0.0161	46.881	0.004677	20
25	0.027033	82318	2225	406104	0.005480	2.5339	3534062	0.0162	42.932	0.005476	25
30	0.028879	80093	2313	394736	0.005860	2.5228	3127957	0.0145	39.054	0.005857	30
35	0.031866	77780	2479	382749	0.006476	2.5181	2733222	0.0113	35.140	0.006473	35
40	0.033583	75302	2529	370273	0.006830	2.5344	2350473	0.0151	31.214	0.006825	40
45	0.039799	72773	2896	356857	0.008116	2.5810	1980200	0.0203	27.211	0.008100	45
50	0.052298	69876	3654	340679	0.010727	2.6186	1623343	0.0182	23.232	0.010699	50
55	0.075147	66222	4976	319367	0.015582	2.6402	1282664	0.0240	19.369	0.015517	55
60	0.114366	61246	7004	289662	0.024181	2.6349	963297	0.0117	15.728	0.024129	60
65	0.175340	54241	9511	248526	0.038268	2.6153	673635	0.0117	12.419	0.038181	65
70	0.274238	44731	12267	193709	0.063326	2.5590	425110	0.0117	9.504	0.063188	70
75	0.399974	32464	12985	129579	0.100206	2.4786	231400	0.0117	7.128	0.099997	75
80	0.561250	19479	10933	69139	0.158125	2.4154	101821	0.0117	5.227	0.157744	80
85+	*1.000000	8546	8546	32682	0.261501	3.8241	32682	0.0117	3.824	0.260238	85+

TABLE 4 — OBSERVED AND PROJECTED VITAL RATES

	OBSERVED POPULATION BOTH SEXES	MALES	FEMALES	PROJECTED 1925 MALES	FEMALES	1930 MALES	FEMALES	1935 MALES	FEMALES	STABLE POPULATION MALES	FEMALES
RATES PER THOUSAND											
Birth	26.41	27.38	25.44	27.49	25.72	27.59	25.97	27.38	25.91	25.48	24.79
Death	13.19	13.43	12.95	13.53	13.06	13.61	13.13	13.70	13.24	14.93	14.24
Increase	13.22	13.96	12.49	13.97	12.67	13.98	12.84	13.68	12.68	10.5492	
PERCENTAGE											
under 15	32.72	33.42	32.02	32.43	31.14	31.96	30.80	32.15	31.14	30.52	30.39
15-64	61.38	61.01	61.73	62.08	62.72	62.40	62.91	62.06	62.38	62.22	61.89
65 and over	5.91	5.57	6.24	5.49	6.14	5.64	6.29	5.79	6.48	7.27	7.72
DEP. RATIO X 100	62.93	63.91	61.98	61.08	59.45	60.25	58.97	61.12	60.30	60.73	61.56

TABLE 1 — DATA

AGE AT LAST BIRTHDAY	POPULATION BOTH SEXES	MALES Number	%	FEMALES Number	%	BIRTHS BY AGE OF MOTHER	DEATHS BOTH SEXES	MALES	FEMALES	AGE AT LAST BIRTHDAY
0	175065	89463	2.5	85602	2.3	0	8446	4720	3726	0
1-4	680368	346550	9.5	333818	9.1	0	6406	3697	2709	1-4
5-9	741723	376880	10.4	364843	9.9	0	1301	718	583	5-9
10-14	741031	373528	10.3	367503	10.0	0	949	478	471	10-14
15-19	708313	354237	9.8	354076	9.6	2923	1561	787	774	15-19
20-24	648252	322828	8.9	325424	8.8	29292	1825	950	875	20-24
25-29	578856	285425	7.9	293431	8.0	52397	1690	825	865	25-29
30-34	512471	251361	6.9	261110	7.1	45753	1595	719	876	30-34
35-39	461039	226579	6.2	234460	6.4	31575	1727	767	960	35-39
40-44	415709	204302	5.6	211407	5.7	17907	1937	866	1071	40-44
45-49	382670	188197	5.2	194473	5.3	0	2412	1163	1249	45-49
50-54	325798	159563	4.4	166235	4.5	0	3028	1493	1535	50-54
55-59	277836	135832	3.7	142004	3.9	0	3839	1936	1903	55-59
60-64	228762	111619	3.1	117143	3.2	0	5030	2557	2473	60-64
65-69	168749	81438	2.2	87311	2.4	0	6014	2982	3032	65-69
70-74	127687	60581	1.7	67106	1.8		7401	3630	3771	70-74
75-79	75189	34966	1.0	40223	1.1		7208	3446	3762	75-79
80-84	40183	18083	0.5	22100	0.6	92508 M.	5896	2765	3131	80-84
85+	17619	7384	0.2	10235	0.3	87339 F.	4419	1945	2474	85+
TOTAL	7307320	3628816		3678504		179847	72684	36444	36240	TOTAL

TABLE 2 — MALE LIFE TABLE

x	$_nq_x$	l_x	$_nd_x$	$_nL_x$	$_nm_x$	$_na_x$	T_x	r_x	$\overset{\circ}{e}_x$	$_nM_x$	x
0	0.051140	100000	5114	96930	0.052759	0.3997	6222443	0.0000	62.224	0.052759	0
1	0.041491	94886	3937	369039	0.010668	1.3316	6125513	0.0000	64.557	0.010668	1
5	0.009386	90949	854	452612	0.001886	2.5000	5756474	0.0118	63.293	0.001905	5
10	0.006380	90095	575	449069	0.001280	2.5498	5303863	0.0046	58.869	0.001280	10
15	0.011072	89521	991	445275	0.002226	2.6512	4854794	0.0124	54.231	0.002222	15
20	0.014621	88529	1294	439466	0.002945	2.5419	4409519	0.0188	49.808	0.002943	20
25	0.014346	87235	1251	433032	0.002890	2.4879	3970053	0.0221	45.510	0.002890	25
30	0.014212	85984	1222	426899	0.002862	2.5296	3537021	0.0201	41.136	0.002860	30
35	0.016812	84762	1425	420356	0.003390	2.5775	3110122	0.0173	36.693	0.003385	35
40	0.021023	83337	1752	412525	0.004247	2.6269	2689766	0.0141	32.276	0.004239	40
45	0.030552	81585	2493	402084	0.006199	2.6574	2277241	0.0183	27.913	0.006180	45
50	0.045962	79092	3635	386941	0.009395	2.6565	1875157	0.0229	23.709	0.009357	50
55	0.069231	75457	5224	365063	0.014310	2.6607	1488216	0.0208	19.723	0.014253	55
60	0.109129	70233	7664	333119	0.023008	2.6455	1123153	0.0224	15.992	0.022908	60
65	0.169073	62568	10579	287642	0.036777	2.6178	790034	0.0224	12.627	0.036617	65
70	0.262519	51990	13648	226789	0.060180	2.5704	502392	0.0224	9.663	0.059920	70
75	0.396263	38341	15193	153534	0.098957	2.4875	275603	0.0224	7.188	0.098553	75
80	0.550191	23148	12736	82905	0.153621	2.4218	122069	0.0224	5.273	0.152905	80
85+	*1.000000	10412	10412	39164	0.265862	3.7613	39164	0.0224	3.761	0.263407	85+

TABLE 3 — FEMALE LIFE TABLE

x	$_nq_x$	l_x	$_nd_x$	$_nL_x$	$_nm_x$	$_na_x$	T_x	r_x	$\overset{\circ}{e}_x$	$_nM_x$	x
0	0.042407	100000	4241	97427	0.043527	0.3932	6365946	0.0000	63.659	0.043527	0
1	0.031768	95759	3042	374865	0.008115	1.3136	6268519	0.0000	65.461	0.008115	1
5	0.007899	92717	732	461755	0.001586	2.5000	5893654	0.0103	63.566	0.001598	5
10	0.006389	91985	588	458510	0.001282	2.5932	5431899	0.0014	59.052	0.001282	10
15	0.010808	91397	995	454627	0.002189	2.6300	4973390	0.0101	54.415	0.002186	15
20	0.013369	90402	1209	449053	0.002691	2.5536	4518762	0.0161	49.985	0.002689	20
25	0.014646	89193	1306	442755	0.002951	2.5408	4069709	0.0190	45.628	0.002948	25
30	0.016661	87887	1464	435868	0.003359	2.5638	3626954	0.0190	41.268	0.003355	30
35	0.020301	86423	1754	427865	0.004101	2.5780	3191086	0.0170	36.924	0.004095	35
40	0.025056	84668	2121	418218	0.005073	2.5847	2763222	0.0136	32.636	0.005066	40
45	0.031701	82547	2617	406505	0.006437	2.6196	2345004	0.0173	28.408	0.006422	45
50	0.045334	79930	3624	391082	0.009266	2.6356	1938499	0.0220	24.252	0.009234	50
55	0.065196	76306	4975	369840	0.013451	2.6498	1547417	0.0209	20.279	0.013401	55
60	0.100947	71332	7201	339770	0.021193	2.6547	1177576	0.0193	16.508	0.021111	60
65	0.160963	64131	10323	296129	0.034859	2.6242	837806	0.0193	13.064	0.034726	65
70	0.248166	53808	13352	236712	0.056407	2.5788	541677	0.0193	10.067	0.056195	70
75	0.379944	40456	15371	163774	0.093855	2.4949	304965	0.0193	7.538	0.093529	75
80	0.517428	25085	12980	91340	0.142103	2.4476	141190	0.0193	5.628	0.141674	80
85+	1.000000	12105	12105	49851	0.242831	4.1181	49851	0.0193	4.118	0.241719	85+

TABLE 4 — OBSERVED AND PROJECTED VITAL RATES

	OBSERVED POPULATION BOTH SEXES	MALES	FEMALES	PROJECTED POPULATION 1930 MALES	FEMALES	1935 MALES	FEMALES	1940 MALES	FEMALES	STABLE POPULATION MALES	FEMALES
RATES PER THOUSAND											
Birth	24.61	25.49	23.74	25.75	24.16	25.71	24.28	25.17	23.91	23.37	22.89
Death	9.95	10.04	9.85	10.15	9.99	10.34	10.15	10.54	10.38	12.23	11.75
Increase	14.67	15.45	13.89	15.60	14.17	15.37	14.13	14.63	13.53	11.1420	
PERCENTAGE											
under 15	32.00	32.69	31.31	31.83	30.50	31.80	30.63	31.35	30.31	29.46	29.37
15-64	62.13	61.73	62.52	62.33	63.09	62.12	62.72	62.33	62.76	62.38	62.18
65 and over	5.88	5.58	6.17	5.84	6.41	6.08	6.65	6.32	6.93	8.16	8.46
DEP. RATIO X 100	60.96	62.00	59.95	60.44	58.51	60.99	59.44	60.43	59.33	60.31	60.83

TABLE 1 / A

AGE AT LAST BIRTHDAY	POPULATION BOTH SEXES	MALES Number	MALES %	FEMALES Number	FEMALES %	BIRTHS BY AGE OF MOTHER	DEATHS BOTH SEXES	DEATHS MALES	FEMALES	AGE AT LAST BIRTHDAY
0	173027	88593	2.3	84434	2.1	0	9234	5361	3873	0
1-4	661650	337167	8.6	324483	8.2	0	3578	1980	1598	1-4
5-9	838735	426632	10.9	412103	10.4	0	1363	759	604	5-9
10-14	745292	378460	9.7	366832	9.3	0	868	465	403	10-14
15-19	741398	371998	9.5	369400	9.3	2862	1403	725	678	15-19
20-24	703303	347474	8.9	355829	9.0	28165	1708	894	814	20-24
25-29	640518	314912	8.1	325606	8.2	52764	1636	773	863	25-29
30-34	571078	279858	7.2	291220	7.4	45302	1621	740	881	30-34
35-39	506361	247976	6.4	258385	6.5	32666	1745	781	964	35-39
40-44	452121	222360	5.7	229761	5.8	17135	1965	896	1069	40-44
45-49	406498	199811	5.1	206587	5.2	0	2447	1162	1285	45-49
50-54	369181	181571	4.7	187610	4.7	0	3334	1616	1718	50-54
55-59	309261	151343	3.9	157918	4.0	0	4272	2162	2110	55-59
60-64	255013	124368	3.2	130645	3.3	0	5642	2831	2811	60-64
65-69	200523	97209	2.5	103314	2.6	0	7190	3632	3558	65-69
70-74	134279	64475	1.7	69804	1.8		7985	3937	4048	70-74
75-79	87113	40853	1.0	46260	1.2		8432	4086	4346	75-79
80-84	41198	18821	0.5	22377	0.6	92131 M.	6391	3026	3365	80-84
85+	19415	8289	0.2	11126	0.3	86763 F.	4952	2171	2781	85+
TOTAL	7855964	3902270		3953694		178894	75766	37997	37769	TOTAL

TABLE 2 / LE / E / BLE

x	nq_x	l_x	nd_x	nL_x	nm_x	na_x	T_x	r_x	$\mathring{e}_x$	nM_x	x
0	0.058091	100000	5809	96091	0.060454	0.3271	6327741	0.0013	63.277	0.060513	0
1	0.023087	94191	2175	370640	0.005867	1.1842	6231650	0.0013	66.160	0.005872	1
5	0.008819	92016	812	458053	0.001772	2.5000	5861009	0.0092	63.695	0.001779	5
10	0.006127	91205	559	454641	0.001229	2.5256	5402956	0.0122	59.240	0.001229	10
15	0.009709	90646	880	451153	0.001951	2.6395	4948315	0.0066	54.589	0.001949	15
20	0.012791	89766	1148	446001	0.002574	2.5365	4497163	0.0142	50.099	0.002573	20
25	0.012200	88618	1081	440386	0.002455	2.5006	4051162	0.0191	45.715	0.002455	25
30	0.013151	87537	1151	434862	0.002647	2.5491	3610775	0.0212	41.249	0.002644	30
35	0.015657	86385	1353	428660	0.003155	2.5847	3175914	0.0198	36.764	0.003149	35
40	0.020004	85033	1701	421129	0.004039	2.6277	2747253	0.0174	32.308	0.004029	40
45	0.028743	83332	2395	411055	0.005827	2.6601	2326124	0.0142	27.914	0.005813	45
50	0.043753	80937	3541	396451	0.008932	2.6752	1915069	0.0185	23.661	0.008900	50
55	0.069425	77396	5373	374435	0.014350	2.6657	1518618	0.0230	19.622	0.014285	55
60	0.108510	72022	7815	341759	0.022867	2.6516	1144182	0.0228	15.886	0.022763	60
65	0.172272	64207	11061	294710	0.037532	2.6199	802424	0.0228	12.497	0.037363	65
70	0.266840	53146	14182	231228	0.061331	2.5670	507714	0.0228	9.553	0.061062	70
75	0.401009	38965	15625	155559	0.100446	2.4871	276486	0.0228	7.096	0.100017	75
80	0.566172	23339	13214	81852	0.161439	2.4133	120928	0.0228	5.181	0.160778	80
85+	1.000000	10125	10125	39075	0.259122	3.8592	39075	0.0228	3.859	0.261914	85+

TABLE 3 / MALE / E / BLE

x	nq_x	l_x	nd_x	nL_x	nm_x	na_x	T_x	r_x	$\mathring{e}_x$	nM_x	x
0	0.044486	100000	4449	97058	0.045835	0.3387	6471360	0.0011	64.714	0.045870	0
1	0.019418	95551	1855	377013	0.004921	1.2016	6374301	0.0011	66.711	0.004925	1
5	0.007273	93696	681	466776	0.001460	2.5000	5997288	0.0087	64.008	0.001466	5
10	0.005482	93014	510	463832	0.001099	2.5670	5530512	0.0096	59.459	0.001099	10
15	0.009139	92505	845	460520	0.001836	2.6315	5066681	0.0013	54.772	0.001835	15
20	0.011384	91659	1043	455760	0.002289	2.5697	4606161	0.0103	50.253	0.002288	20
25	0.013180	90616	1194	450156	0.002653	2.5526	4150401	0.0174	45.802	0.002650	25
30	0.015038	89421	1345	443836	0.003030	2.5677	3700245	0.0200	41.380	0.003025	30
35	0.018521	88077	1631	436441	0.003738	2.5828	3256409	0.0199	36.972	0.003731	35
40	0.023051	86445	1993	427446	0.004662	2.6006	2819968	0.0176	32.621	0.004653	40
45	0.030712	84453	2594	416131	0.006233	2.6354	2392522	0.0138	28.330	0.006220	45
50	0.044942	81859	3679	400617	0.009183	2.6411	1976391	0.0175	24.144	0.009157	50
55	0.065038	78180	5085	378988	0.013416	2.6572	1575773	0.0221	20.156	0.013361	55
60	0.102805	73096	7515	347816	0.021605	2.6496	1196785	0.0211	16.373	0.021516	60
65	0.159832	65581	10482	303063	0.034587	2.6301	848969	0.0211	12.945	0.034439	65
70	0.255146	55099	14058	241427	0.058230	2.5767	545906	0.0211	9.908	0.057991	70
75	0.381466	41041	15656	165996	0.094314	2.4956	304479	0.0211	7.419	0.093947	75
80	0.540767	25385	13727	90950	0.150934	2.4393	138483	0.0211	5.455	0.150378	80
85+	1.000000	11658	11658	47533	0.245252	4.0774	47533	0.0211	4.077	0.249954	85+

TABLE 4 / SERVED / D / OJEC- / D / AL / TES

	OBSERVED POPULATION BOTH SEXES	MALES	FEMALES	PROJECTED POPULATION 1935 MALES	FEMALES	1940 MALES	FEMALES	1945 MALES	FEMALES	STABLE POPULATION MALES	FEMALES
RATES PER THOUSAND											
Birth	22.77	23.61	21.94	23.85	22.33	23.57	22.20	23.08	21.86	21.07	20.63
Death	9.64	9.74	9.55	9.94	9.76	10.20	10.04	10.43	10.30	12.70	12.26
Increase	13.13	13.87	12.39	13.92	12.57	13.37	12.16	12.65	11.56		8.3660
PERCENTAGE											
under 15	30.79	31.54	30.04	30.82	29.48	29.78	28.60	29.51	28.47	27.32	27.24
15-64	63.07	62.57	63.56	63.03	63.84	63.80	64.41	63.73	64.17	63.52	63.29
65 and over	6.14	5.88	6.40	6.15	6.68	6.42	6.99	6.76	7.36	9.16	9.47
DEP. RATIO X 100	58.55	59.81	57.33	58.66	56.64	56.74	55.25	56.91	55.83	57.44	58.01

TABLE 1 — DATA

AGE AT LAST BIRTHDAY	POPULATION BOTH SEXES	MALES Number	%	FEMALES Number	%	BIRTHS BY AGE OF MOTHER	DEATHS BOTH SEXES	MALES	FEMALES	AGE AT LAST BIRTHDAY
0	166073	85209	2.0	80864	1.9	0	6966	4030	2936	0
1-4	667506	341631	8.2	325875	7.7	0	2314	1277	1037	1-4
5-9	820686	417821	10.0	402865	9.6	0	994	567	427	5-9
10-14	836693	425369	10.2	411324	9.8	0	754	411	343	10-14
15-19	734191	372658	8.9	361533	8.6	3099	1086	592	494	15-19
20-24	749148	371308	8.9	377840	9.0	27839	1372	745	627	20-24
25-29	708614	349696	8.4	358918	8.5	49422	1417	704	713	25-29
30-34	636869	312932	7.5	323937	7.7	43607	1492	710	782	30-34
35-39	565797	276975	6.6	288822	6.9	30174	1682	785	897	35-39
40-44	495857	242913	5.8	252944	6.0	17025	1898	909	989	40-44
45-49	442064	217482	5.2	224582	5.3	0	2384	1174	1210	45-49
50-54	390584	192156	4.6	198424	4.7	0	3214	1578	1636	50-54
55-59	348557	171432	4.1	177125	4.2	0	4497	2265	2232	55-59
60-64	282473	137866	3.3	144607	3.4	0	5865	2938	2927	60-64
65-69	221821	107644	2.6	114177	2.7	0	7427	3779	3648	65-69
70-74	159260	76686	1.8	82574	2.0		8929	4406	4523	70-74
75-79	92499	43942	1.1	48557	1.2		8603	4208	4395	75-79
80-84	48042	22124	0.5	25918	0.6	88147 M.	7003	3334	3669	80-84
85+	20509	8905	0.2	11604	0.3	83019 F.	5175	2304	2871	85+
TOTAL	8387243	4174749		4212494		171166	73072	36716	36356	TOTAL

TABLE 2 — MALE LIFE TABLE

x	$_nq_x$	l_x	$_nd_x$	$_nL_x$	$_nm_x$	$_na_x$	T_x	r_x	$\mathring{e}_x$	$_nM_x$	x
0	0.045792	100000	4579	96822	0.047295	0.3059	6575695	0.0000	65.757	0.047295	0
1	0.014795	95421	1412	377669	0.003738	1.1565	6478873	0.0000	67.898	0.003738	1
5	0.006762	94009	636	468456	0.001357	2.5000	6101204	0.0000	64.900	0.001357	5
10	0.004822	93373	450	465762	0.000967	2.5466	5632748	0.0102	60.325	0.000966	10
15	0.007926	92923	737	462872	0.001591	2.6330	5166986	0.0121	55.605	0.001589	15
20	0.009985	92187	920	458669	0.002007	2.5403	4704114	0.0044	51.028	0.002006	20
25	0.010020	91266	914	454065	0.002014	2.5229	4245445	0.0150	46.517	0.002013	25
30	0.011300	90352	1021	449278	0.002272	2.5706	3791380	0.0210	41.963	0.002269	30
35	0.014109	89331	1260	443631	0.002841	2.6020	3342102	0.0224	37.413	0.002834	35
40	0.018599	88070	1638	436475	0.003753	2.6336	2898471	0.0203	32.911	0.003742	40
45	0.026734	86432	2311	426751	0.005415	2.6588	2461996	0.0178	28.485	0.005398	45
50	0.040409	84122	3399	412710	0.008236	2.6767	2035245	0.0152	24.194	0.008212	50
55	0.064334	80722	5193	391525	0.013264	2.6727	1622535	0.0194	20.100	0.013212	55
60	0.101998	75529	7704	359604	0.021423	2.6582	1231010	0.0258	16.298	0.021311	60
65	0.162802	67825	11042	312913	0.035288	2.6260	871405	0.0258	12.848	0.035106	65
70	0.253315	56783	14384	249080	0.057748	2.5782	558493	0.0258	9.836	0.057455	70
75	0.387747	42399	16440	170848	0.096227	2.4971	309412	0.0258	7.298	0.095763	75
80	0.545372	25959	14157	93435	0.151520	2.4317	138564	0.0258	5.338	0.150695	80
85+	*1.000000	11802	11802	45129	0.261512	3.8239	45129	0.0258	3.824	0.258731	85+

TABLE 3 — FEMALE LIFE TABLE

x	$_nq_x$	l_x	$_nd_x$	$_nL_x$	$_nm_x$	$_na_x$	T_x	r_x	$\mathring{e}_x$	$_nM_x$	x
0	0.035430	100000	3543	97583	0.036308	0.3177	6719371	0.0000	67.194	0.036308	0
1	0.012615	96457	1217	382386	0.003182	1.1714	6621789	0.0000	68.650	0.003182	1
5	0.005286	95240	503	474942	0.001060	2.5000	6239403	0.0000	65.512	0.001060	5
10	0.004164	94737	394	472727	0.000835	2.5737	5764460	0.0098	60.847	0.000834	10
15	0.006816	94342	643	470183	0.001368	2.6231	5291734	0.0072	56.091	0.001366	15
20	0.008264	93699	774	466618	0.001659	2.5744	4821551	0.0000	51.458	0.001659	20
25	0.009895	92925	920	462395	0.001989	2.5752	4354933	0.0134	46.865	0.001987	25
30	0.012023	92005	1106	457362	0.002419	2.5913	3892539	0.0193	42.308	0.002414	30
35	0.015447	90899	1404	451117	0.003112	2.5937	3435176	0.0216	37.791	0.003106	35
40	0.019418	89495	1738	443326	0.003920	2.6124	2984059	0.0211	33.343	0.003910	40
45	0.026684	87757	2342	433292	0.005404	2.6536	2540733	0.0186	28.952	0.005388	45
50	0.040553	85416	3464	418979	0.008267	2.6619	2107441	0.0152	24.673	0.008245	50
55	0.061417	81952	5033	398009	0.012646	2.6655	1688462	0.0184	20.603	0.012601	55
60	0.097026	76918	7463	367045	0.020333	2.6488	1290453	0.0236	16.777	0.020241	60
65	0.149223	69455	10364	322802	0.032107	2.6386	923408	0.0236	13.295	0.031950	65
70	0.242964	59091	14357	260856	0.055038	2.5901	600606	0.0236	10.164	0.054775	70
75	0.370442	44734	16571	182290	0.090906	2.5029	339750	0.0236	7.595	0.090512	75
80	0.518089	28163	14591	102668	0.142116	2.4572	157460	0.0236	5.591	0.141562	80
85+	1.000000	13572	13572	54792	0.247699	4.0372	54792	0.0236	4.037	0.247414	85+

TABLE 4 — OBSERVED AND PROJECTED VITAL RATES

	OBSERVED POPULATION BOTH SEXES	MALES	FEMALES	PROJECTED POPULATION 1940 MALES	FEMALES	1945 MALES	FEMALES	1950 MALES	FEMALES	STABLE POPULATION MALES	FEMALES
RATES PER THOUSAND											
Birth	20.41	21.11	19.71	21.10	19.81	20.80	19.64	20.40	19.36	18.10	17.7
Death	8.71	8.79	8.63	9.13	9.01	9.49	9.38	9.85	9.80	13.21	12.8
Increase	11.70	12.32	11.08	11.97	10.81	11.32	10.26	10.55	9.56		4.886
PERCENTAGE											
under 15	29.70	30.42	28.98	28.59	27.29	27.63	26.44	27.07	26.03	24.59	24.4
15-64	63.84	63.37	64.30	64.81	65.56	65.31	65.93	65.55	65.96	64.40	64.1
65 and over	6.46	6.21	6.71	6.60	7.15	7.06	7.63	7.38	8.01	11.01	11.4
DEP. RATIO X 100	56.65	57.81	55.52	54.30	52.54	53.11	51.68	52.56	51.60	55.28	55.8

AGE LAST BIRTHDAY	1940 BOTH SEXES	MALES	FEMALES	1945 BOTH SEXES	MALES	FEMALES	1950 BOTH SEXES	MALES	FEMALES	AGE AT LAST BIRTHDAY	
0-4	842	431	411	887	454	433	922	472	450	0-4	**TABLE 5**
5-9	823	421	402	833	426	407	876	448	428	5-9	POPULATION
10-14	816	415	401	820	419	401	828	423	405	10-14	PROJECTED
15-19	832	423	409	812	413	399	814	416	398	15-19	WITH
20-24	728	369	359	825	419	406	805	409	396	20-24	FIXED
25-29	742	368	374	722	366	356	817	415	402	25-29	AGE—
30-34	701	346	355	734	364	370	714	362	352	30-34	SPECIFIC
35-39	629	309	320	692	342	350	724	359	365	35-39	BIRTH
40-44	557	273	284	618	304	314	680	336	344	40-44	AND
45-49	485	238	247	543	266	277	604	297	307	45-49	DEATH
50-54	427	210	217	469	230	239	526	258	268	50-54	RATES
55-59	370	182	188	406	200	206	445	218	227	55-59	(IN 1000's)
60-64	320	157	163	341	167	174	373	183	190	60-64	
65-69	247	120	127	281	137	144	299	146	153	65-69	
70-74	178	86	92	198	95	103	225	109	116	70-74	
75-79	111	53	58	123	59	64	138	66	72	75-79	
80-84	51	24	27	61	29	32	68	32	36	80-84	
85+	25	11	14	27	12	15	31	14	17	85+	
TOTAL	8884	4436	4448	9392	4702	4690	9889	4963	4926	TOTAL	

STANDARD COUNTRIES: STANDARDIZED RATES PER THOUSAND	ENGLAND AND WALES 1961 BOTH SEXES	MALES	FEMALES	UNITED STATES 1960 BOTH SEXES	MALES	FEMALES	MEXICO 1960 BOTH SEXES	MALES	FEMALES	
Birth	17.01	18.08*	15.99	17.29	16.77*	16.52	17.11	16.92*	16.56	**TABLE 6** STANDARDIZED RATES
Death	13.90	12.87*	15.60	11.48	11.07*	11.81	6.71	8.32*	6.43	
Increase	3.11	5.21*	0.39	5.81	5.70*	4.72	10.40	8.59*	10.13	

	OBSERVED POP. MALES	FEMALES	STATIONARY POP. MALES	FEMALES	STABLE POP. MALES	FEMALES	OBSERVED BIRTHS	NET MATERNITY FUNCTION	BIRTHS IN STABLE POP.	
μ_1	29.37175	30.12622	36.83499	37.09115	34.39574	34.61953	31.03438	31.71631	31.51443	**TABLE 7**
μ_2	411.6988	417.9376	505.9238	512.7185	491.5640	497.9966	37.67866	39.27260	39.18856	MOMENTS
μ_3	4746.441	4612.830	2339.232	2397.295	3511.798	3600.753	39.6365	13.7159	20.6571	AND
μ_4	−94194.	−100494.	−255318.	−262322.	−222480.	−228045.	−1194.253	−1430.809	−1398.959	CUMULANTS
β_1	0.322848	0.291475	0.042256	0.042639	0.103829	0.104980	0.029370	0.003106	0.007090	
β_2	2.444268	2.424672	2.002505	2.002124	2.079273	2.080467	2.158788	2.072311	2.089067	
κ	−0.130571	−0.119996	−0.015805	−0.015937	−0.038854	−0.039277	−0.012913	−0.001294	−0.002988	

VITAL STATISTICS		THOMPSON AGE RANGE	NRR	1000r	INTERVAL	BOURGEOIS-PICHAT AGE RANGE	NRR	1000b	1000d	1000r	COALE	
GRR	1.276										IBR	**TABLE 8** RATES FROM AGE DISTRIBUTIONS AND VITAL STATISTICS (Females)
NRR	1.167	0-4	1.19	6.32	27.34	5-29	1.14	21.08	16.09	4.99	IDR	
TFR	2.632	5-9	1.26	8.52	27.29	30-54	1.73	32.45	12.12	20.32	IRI	
GENERATION	31.615	10-14	1.41	12.45	27.22	55-79	1.84	38.60	16.00	22.60	K1	
SEX RATIO	106.177	15-19	1.36	11.05	27.11	*25-49	1.74	32.54	12.06	20.48	K2	

First Age Interval ORIGINAL MATRIX SUBDIAGONAL	ALTERNATIVE FIRST ROWS Projection	Integral	FIRST STABLE MATRIX % IN STABLE POPULATION	FISHER VALUES	REPRODUCTIVE VALUES	SECOND STABLE MATRIX Z₂ FIRST COLUMN	FIRST ROW	
0.98953	0.00000	0.00000	8.408	1.054	428902	0.1329+0.0468	0.1329+0.0468	**TABLE 9** LESLIE MATRIX AND ITS SPECTRAL COMPONENTS (Females)
0.99533	0.00000	0.00000	8.119	1.092	439935	0.1295-0.0908	0.0351+0.1206	
0.99462	0.00992	0.00000	7.886	1.124	462444	0.0018-0.1785	-0.0688+0.0874	
0.99242	0.09509	0.02020	7.654	1.148	414972	-0.1626-0.1188	-0.0998-0.0049	
0.99095	0.24459	0.17363	7.413	1.084	409641	-0.2153+0.0709	-0.0608-0.0792	
0.98912	0.31526	0.32449	7.168	0.861	308981	-0.0760+0.2431	-0.0070-0.0965	
0.98635	0.27663	0.31723	6.919	0.556	180038	0.1722+0.2281	-0.0240-0.0701	
0.98273	0.19859	0.24620	6.660	0.282	81354	0.3196-0.0081	0.0261-0.0322	
0.97737	0.07834	0.15860	6.387	0.081	20395	0.2000-0.2949	0.0103-0.0072	
0.96697	0.00001	0.00001	6.091	0.000	4	-0.1368-0.3705	0.0000-0.0000	
0.94995	0.00001	0.00001	5.748	0.000	1	-0.4177-0.1145	0.0000-0.0000	
+ 0.77134			21.547					

First Age Interval OBSERVED POPUL. (IN 100's)	CONTRIBUTIONS OF ROOTS (IN 100's) r_1	r_2, r_3	$r_4 \text{-} r_{11}$	AGE-SP. BIRTH RATES	NET MATERNITY FUNCTION	COEFF. OF MATRIX EQUATION	PARAMETERS INTEGRAL	MATRIX	EXP. INCREASE x	$e^{(x+8\frac{1}{2})r}$	
4067	4137	−76	6	0.0000	0.0000	0.0000	L(1) 1.02473	1.02474	0	1.0123	**TABLE 10** AGE ANALYSIS AND MISCELLANEOUS RESULTS (Females)
4029	3994	13	21	0.0000	0.0000	0.0000	L(2) 0.51371	0.51322	50	1.2924	
4113	3880	113	121	0.0000	0.0000	0.0098	0.73218	0.71698	55	1.3424	
3615	3766	132	−282	0.0042	0.0195	0.0931	R(1) 0.00489	0.00489	60	1.3571	
3778	3647	30	102	0.0357	0.1668	0.2378	R(2) −0.02232	−0.02517	65	1.3907	
3589	3527	−128	190	0.0668	0.3088	0.3037	0.19180	0.18991	70	1.4251	
3239	3404	−204	40	0.0653	0.2986	0.2636	C(1)	49199	75	1.4603	
2888	3277	−106	−283	0.0507	0.2286	0.1867	C(2)	−17316	80	1.4965	
2529	3142	118	−730	0.0326	0.1447	0.0724		31701	85	1.5335	
2246	2997	282	−1033	0.0000	0.0000	0.0000	2P/Y 32.7596	33.0854	90	1.5714	
1984	2828	217	−1061	0.0000	0.0000	0.0000	DELTA 9.3775		95	1.6103	
+ 6046	10601								100	1.6501	

TABLE 1 — DATA

AGE AT LAST BIRTHDAY	POPULATION BOTH SEXES	MALES Number	%	FEMALES Number	%	BIRTHS BY AGE OF MOTHER	DEATHS BOTH SEXES	MALES	FEMALES	AGE AT LAST BIRTH
0	176898	90337	2.0	86561	2.0	0	7057	4092	2965	0
1-4	662152	339032	7.7	323120	7.3	0	2265	1257	1008	1-4
5-9	823377	421252	9.5	402125	9.1	0	1023	595	428	5-9
10-14	816341	415464	9.4	400877	9.0	0	766	425	341	10-14
15-19	837346	425421	9.6	411925	9.3	4023	1297	772	525	15-19
20-24	724410	366468	8.3	357942	8.1	31164	1678	1108	570	20-24
25-29	725865	361478	8.2	364387	8.2	56170	1619	979	640	25-29
30-34	687325	337721	7.6	349604	7.9	49117	1710	960	750	30-34
35-39	623430	305733	6.9	317697	7.2	30488	1860	993	867	35-39
40-44	553738	271398	6.1	282340	6.4	11333	2126	1113	1013	40-44
45-49	485963	237931	5.4	248032	5.6	930	2689	1409	1280	45-49
50-54	427556	210398	4.8	217158	4.9	0	3557	1847	1710	50-54
55-59	372514	182998	4.1	189516	4.3	0	4748	2500	2248	55-59
60-64	323379	158628	3.6	164751	3.7	0	6548	3397	3151	60-64
65-69	249569	121243	2.7	128326	2.9	0	8514	4353	4161	65-69
70-74	179115	86061	1.9	93054	2.1		10196	5135	5061	70-74
75-79	112111	53341	1.2	58770	1.3		10654	5321	5333	75-79
80-84	51552	24032	0.5	27520	0.6	94385 M.	8078	3967	4111	80-84
85+	23663	10292	0.2	13371	0.3	88840 F.	6283	2863	3420	85+
TOTAL	8856304	4419228		4437076		183225	82668	43086	39582	TOT

TABLE 2 — MALE LIFE TABLE

x	nq_x	l_x	nd_x	nL_x	nm_x	na_x	T_x	r_x	$\dot{e}_x$	nM_x
0	0.043800	100000	4380	96977	0.045165	0.3098	6490030	0.0039	64.900	0.045297
1	0.014633	95620	1399	378508	0.003697	1.1612	6393053	0.0039	66.859	0.003708
5	0.007034	94221	663	469447	0.001412	2.5000	6014544	0.0014	63.835	0.001412
10	0.005102	93558	477	466635	0.001023	2.5787	5545097	0.0000	59.269	0.001023
15	0.009058	93081	843	463485	0.001819	2.7244	5078463	0.0106	54.560	0.001815
20	0.015019	92238	1385	457804	0.003026	2.5570	4614978	0.0136	50.034	0.003023
25	0.013449	90852	1222	451182	0.002708	2.4796	4157174	0.0053	45.758	0.002708
30	0.014122	89630	1266	445030	0.002844	2.5336	3705992	0.0139	41.347	0.002843
35	0.016137	88365	1426	438364	0.003253	2.5737	3260962	0.0185	36.903	0.003248
40	0.020364	86939	1770	430491	0.004112	2.6258	2822598	0.0208	32.466	0.004101
45	0.029294	85168	2495	419979	0.005941	2.6500	2392107	0.0194	28.087	0.005922
50	0.043140	82673	3567	405025	0.008806	2.6609	1972128	0.0171	23.854	0.008779
55	0.066359	79107	5249	383243	0.013698	2.6585	1567104	0.0141	19.810	0.013661
60	0.102367	73857	7561	351586	0.021504	2.6587	1183860	0.0203	16.029	0.021415
65	0.166080	66297	11011	305396	0.036054	2.6306	832274	0.0203	12.554	0.035903
70	0.261575	55286	14461	241389	0.059909	2.5769	526879	0.0203	9.530	0.059667
75	0.400377	40825	16345	163206	0.100151	2.4967	285490	0.0203	6.993	0.099754
80	0.580034	24479	14199	85637	0.165804	2.4110	122284	0.0203	4.995	0.165071
85+	*1.000000	10281	10281	36647	0.280528	3.5647	36647	0.0203	3.565	0.278177

TABLE 3 — FEMALE LIFE TABLE

x	nq_x	l_x	nd_x	nL_x	nm_x	na_x	T_x	r_x	$\dot{e}_x$	nM_x
0	0.033356	100000	3336	97739	0.034128	0.3220	6771882	0.0049	67.719	0.034253
1	0.012327	96664	1192	383294	0.003109	1.1771	6674143	0.0049	69.045	0.003120
5	0.005306	95473	507	476097	0.001064	2.5000	6290850	0.0007	65.892	0.001064
10	0.004244	94966	403	473843	0.000851	2.5491	5814752	0.0000	61.230	0.000851
15	0.006361	94563	602	471383	0.001276	2.6187	5340910	0.0101	56.480	0.001275
20	0.007937	93962	746	467988	0.001594	2.5597	4869527	0.0107	51.825	0.001592
25	0.008745	93216	815	464091	0.001756	2.5617	4401539	0.0006	47.219	0.001756
30	0.010683	92401	987	459624	0.002148	2.5900	3937447	0.0115	42.613	0.002145
35	0.013584	91414	1242	454093	0.002735	2.6043	3477823	0.0186	38.045	0.002729
40	0.017840	90172	1609	447051	0.003598	2.6326	3023730	0.0210	33.533	0.003588
45	0.025585	88563	2266	437513	0.005179	2.6598	2576679	0.0209	29.094	0.005161
50	0.038784	86297	3347	423646	0.007900	2.6578	2139167	0.0188	24.788	0.007874
55	0.057876	82950	4801	403549	0.011896	2.6668	1715520	0.0152	20.681	0.011862
60	0.091969	78149	7190	374009	0.019223	2.6720	1311971	0.0238	16.788	0.019126
65	0.151318	70960	10737	329486	0.032589	2.6426	937962	0.0238	13.218	0.032425
70	0.241440	60222	14540	266060	0.054650	2.5893	608476	0.0238	10.104	0.054388
75	0.371532	45682	16972	186175	0.091164	2.5115	342416	0.0238	7.496	0.090744
80	0.539063	28710	15476	103155	0.150030	2.4497	156241	0.0238	5.442	0.149382
85+	1.000000	13233	13233	53086	0.249282	4.0115	53086	0.0238	4.012	0.255778

TABLE 4 — OBSERVED AND PROJECTED VITAL RATES

	OBSERVED POPULATION BOTH SEXES	MALES	FEMALES	PROJECTED POPULATION 1945 MALES	FEMALES	1950 MALES	FEMALES	1955 MALES	FEMALES	STABLE POPULATION MALES	FEMA
RATES PER THOUSAND											
Birth	20.69	21.36	20.02	21.11	19.84	20.80	19.59	20.25	19.12	18.73	18.
Death	9.33	9.75	8.92	10.03	9.29	10.35	9.68	10.63	10.03	13.17	12.
Increase	11.35	11.61	11.10	11.08	10.55	10.45	9.91	9.61	9.09		5.55
PERCENTAGE											
under 15	27.99	28.65	27.33	27.84	26.53	27.42	26.20	27.31	26.14	25.37	24.
15-64	65.06	64.68	65.43	65.11	65.77	65.24	65.74	65.09	65.46	64.26	64.4
65 and over	6.96	6.67	7.24	7.06	7.70	7.34	8.06	7.60	8.40	10.37	11.
DEP. RATIO X 100	53.71	54.62	52.83	53.60	52.05	53.28	52.11	53.64	52.78	55.63	56.

AGE AT LAST BIRTHDAY	POPULATION BOTH SEXES	MALES Number	%	FEMALES Number	%	BIRTHS BY AGE OF MOTHER	DEATHS BOTH SEXES	MALES	FEMALES	AGE AT LAST BIRTHDAY
0	205930	105973	2.3	99957	2.2	0	11051	6361	4690	0
1-4	724836	371877	8.1	352959	7.6	0	3864	2135	1729	1-4
5-9	819064	418497	9.1	400567	8.7	0	1713	993	720	5-9
10-14	812990	415484	9.0	397506	8.6	0	1254	727	527	10-14
15-19	802537	407748	8.9	394789	8.5	4686	2121	1371	750	15-19
20-24	804866	405647	8.8	399219	8.5	39123	3522	2571	951	20-24
25-29	700620	351991	7.7	348629	7.5	68888	2605	1753	852	25-29
30-34	700514	346968	7.5	353546	7.7	65275	2478	1559	919	30-34
35-39	661786	323831	7.0	337955	7.3	43401	2603	1576	1027	35-39
40-44	597513	292126	6.4	305387	6.6	15665	2882	1708	1174	40-44
45-49	527529	257332	5.6	270197	5.8	1109	3398	1975	1423	45-49
50-54	457153	223066	4.8	234087	5.1	0	4080	2305	1775	50-54
55-59	395872	193854	4.2	202018	4.4	0	5220	2855	2365	55-59
60-64	335848	163921	3.6	171927	3.7	0	6868	3713	3155	60-64
65-69	276285	134405	2.9	141880	3.1	0	9154	4798	4356	65-69
70-74	194905	93641	2.0	101264	2.2		10841	5516	5325	70-74
75-79	119969	56676	1.2	63293	1.4		11239	5602	5637	75-79
80-84	58165	26848	0.6	31317	0.7	122981 M.	8973	4342	4631	80-84
85+	21995	9686	0.2	12309	0.3	115166 F.	5880	2667	3213	85+
TOTAL	9218377	4599571		4618806		238147	99746	54527	45219	TOTAL

TABLE 1

x	$_nq_x$	l_x	$_nd_x$	$_nL_x$	$_nm_x$	$_na_x$	T_x	r_x	$\mathring{e}_x$	$_nM_x$	x
0	0.057308	100000	5731	96136	0.059611	0.3257	6048377	0.0095	60.484	0.060025	0
1	0.022460	94269	2117	371111	0.005705	1.1822	5952241	0.0095	63.141	0.005741	1
5	0.011756	92152	1083	458051	0.002365	2.5000	5581131	0.0110	60.564	0.002373	5
10	0.008713	91069	793	453447	0.001750	2.6111	5123079	0.0004	56.255	0.001750	10
15	0.016687	90275	1506	448022	0.003362	2.7735	4669632	0.0000	51.727	0.003362	15
20	0.031221	88769	2771	437041	0.006341	2.5456	4221610	0.0093	47.557	0.006338	20
25	0.024564	85997	2112	424516	0.004976	2.4105	3784569	0.0104	44.008	0.004980	25
30	0.022214	83885	1863	414736	0.004493	2.4845	3360053	0.0037	40.056	0.004493	30
35	0.024063	82021	1974	405266	0.004870	2.5473	2945317	0.0122	35.909	0.004867	35
40	0.028875	80048	2311	394660	0.005857	2.5867	2540051	0.0170	31.732	0.005847	40
45	0.037767	77736	2936	381648	0.007693	2.6043	2145391	0.0192	27.598	0.007675	45
50	0.050546	74800	3781	364993	0.010359	2.6174	1763743	0.0177	23.579	0.010333	50
55	0.071341	71019	5067	343126	0.014766	2.6372	1398750	0.0154	19.695	0.014728	55
60	0.107914	65953	7117	312940	0.022743	2.6361	1055624	0.0219	16.006	0.022651	60
65	0.165165	58836	9718	271049	0.035852	2.6199	742684	0.0219	12.623	0.035698	65
70	0.258746	49118	12709	214809	0.059165	2.5780	471635	0.0219	9.602	0.058906	70
75	0.397574	36409	14475	145824	0.099266	2.4977	256826	0.0219	7.054	0.098842	75
80	0.572188	21934	12550	77232	0.162500	2.4155	111002	0.0219	5.061	0.161726	80
85+	*1.000000	9383	9383	33770	0.277863	3.5989	33770	0.0219	3.599	0.275346	85+

TABLE 2 / MALE / LIFE TABLE

x	$_nq_x$	l_x	$_nd_x$	$_nL_x$	$_nm_x$	$_na_x$	T_x	r_x	$\mathring{e}_x$	$_nM_x$	x
0	0.045199	100000	4520	96998	0.046598	0.3358	6563642	0.0095	65.636	0.046920	0
1	0.019216	95480	1835	376778	0.004870	1.1971	6466644	0.0095	67.728	0.004899	1
5	0.008915	93645	835	466139	0.001791	2.5000	6089866	0.0106	65.031	0.001797	5
10	0.006607	92810	613	462527	0.001326	2.5126	5623727	0.0000	60.594	0.001326	10
15	0.009456	92197	872	458904	0.001900	2.6120	5161200	0.0000	55.980	0.001900	15
20	0.011847	91325	1082	453969	0.002383	2.5432	4702295	0.0101	51.489	0.002382	20
25	0.012148	90244	1096	448491	0.002444	2.5132	4248326	0.0097	47.076	0.002444	25
30	0.012915	89147	1151	442906	0.002599	2.5420	3799835	0.0005	42.624	0.002599	30
35	0.015098	87996	1329	436763	0.003042	2.5789	3356928	0.0115	38.149	0.003039	35
40	0.019089	86667	1654	429386	0.003853	2.6120	2920165	0.0184	33.694	0.003844	40
45	0.026089	85013	2218	419821	0.005283	2.6354	2490779	0.0212	29.299	0.005267	45
50	0.037387	82795	3095	406724	0.007611	2.6574	2070958	0.0212	25.013	0.007583	50
55	0.057170	79700	4556	387847	0.011748	2.6622	1664234	0.0187	20.881	0.011707	55
60	0.088407	75143	6643	360212	0.018442	2.6662	1276387	0.0241	16.986	0.018351	60
65	0.143879	68500	9856	319342	0.030863	2.6503	916175	0.0241	13.375	0.030702	65
70	0.234506	58644	13752	260212	0.052851	2.5997	596832	0.0241	10.177	0.052585	70
75	0.366187	44892	16439	183694	0.089490	2.5202	336620	0.0241	7.498	0.089062	75
80	0.539309	28453	15345	103209	0.148679	2.4548	152926	0.0241	5.375	0.147874	80
85+	*1.000000	13108	13108	49717	0.263653	3.7929	49717	0.0241	3.793	0.261029	85+

TABLE 3 / FEMALE / LIFE TABLE

	OBSERVED POPULATION			PROJECTED POPULATION 1950		1955		1960		STABLE POPULATION	
	BOTH SEXES	MALES	FEMALES	MALES	FEMALES	MALES	FEMALES	MALES	FEMALES	MALES	FEMALES
RATES PER THOUSAND											
Birth	25.83	26.74	24.93	25.88	24.10	24.84	23.11	23.78	22.12	24.59	23.01
Death	10.82	11.85	9.79	12.29	10.28	12.37	10.49	12.44	10.69	12.49	10.91
Increase	15.01	14.88	15.14	13.60	13.83	12.47	12.63	11.34	11.43		12.1000
PERCENTAGE											
under 15	27.80	28.52	27.08	29.74	28.18	31.16	29.47	31.77	30.05	31.02	29.53
15-64	64.92	64.49	65.34	63.09	63.96	61.55	62.44	60.80	61.57	61.45	61.81
65 and over	7.28	6.98	7.58	7.17	7.86	7.30	8.09	7.44	8.38	7.53	8.66
DEP. RATIO X 100	54.04	55.05	53.05	58.49	56.35	62.48	60.15	64.48	62.41	62.74	61.79

TABLE 4 / OBSERVED / PROJECTED / TOTAL RATES

TABLE 1 — DATA

AGE AT LAST BIRTHDAY	POPULATION BOTH SEXES	MALES Number	%	FEMALES Number	%	BIRTHS BY AGE OF MOTHER	DEATHS BOTH SEXES	MALES	FEMALES	AGE AT LAST BIRTHDAY
0	227959	117226	2.3	11C733	2.2	0	6065	3491	2574	0
1-4	978962	502883	10.0	476079	9.4	0	1642	918	724	1-4
5-9	931820	477640	9.5	454180	9.0	0	622	387	235	5-9
10-14	824472	420698	8.3	4C3774	8.0	10	381	234	147	10-
15-19	810845	413561	8.2	397284	7.8	5105	547	347	200	15-
20-24	8C0208	404416	8.0	395792	7.8	38685	977	709	268	20-
25-29	795993	394778	7.8	401215	7.9	73411	879	523	356	25-
30-34	689295	341C59	6.8	348236	6.9	59966	901	487	414	30-
35-39	683061	335570	6.7	347491	6.9	40617	1151	594	557	35-
40-44	649627	317245	6.3	332382	6.6	15858	1621	862	759	40-
45-49	593114	288762	5.7	304352	6.0	1285	2287	1232	1055	45-
50-54	520495	252148	5.0	268347	5.3	4	3267	1818	1449	50-
55-59	448581	217781	4.3	230800	4.6	0	4299	2374	1925	55-
60-64	376552	183262	3.6	193290	3.8	0	5902	3177	2725	60-
65-69	304741	147711	2.9	157030	3.1	0	8152	4225	3927	65-
70-74	231312	111479	2.2	119833	2.4		10506	5266	5240	70-
75-79	144669	68528	1.4	76141	1.5		11241	5460	5781	75-
80-84	70990	32704	0.6	38286	0.8	121243 M.	9205	4385	4820	80-
85+	30831	13554	0.3	17277	0.3	113698 F.	6813	3082	3731	85-
TOTAL	1C113527	5041005		5C72522		234941	76458	39571	36887	TOT

TABLE 2 — MALE LIFE TABLE

x	$_nq_x$	l_x	$_nd_x$	$_nL_x$	$_nm_x$	$_na_x$	T_x	r_x	$\mathring{e}_x$	$_nM_x$
0	0.029154	10CCC0	2915	97898	0.029780	0.2792	7007086	0.0000	70.071	0.029780
1	0.007264	97085	705	386313	0.001825	1.1276	6909188	0.0000	71.167	0.001825
5	0.C04001	96379	386	480933	0.000802	2.5000	6522875	0.0378	67.679	0.000810
10	0.0C2778	95994	267	479305	0.000556	2.5122	6041943	0.0137	62.941	0.000556
15	0.004191	95727	401	477750	0.000840	2.7937	5562637	0.0030	58.109	0.000839
20	C.008730	95326	832	474595	0.001753	2.5556	5084887	0.0032	53.342	0.001753
25	0.006596	94494	623	470876	0.001324	2.4453	4610292	0.0156	48.789	0.001325
30	0.007122	93870	669	467722	0.001429	2.5620	4139416	0.0148	44.097	0.001428
35	0.008821	93202	822	464075	0.001772	2.6474	3671694	0.0054	39.395	0.001770
40	0.013532	92380	1250	459005	0.002723	2.6851	3207619	0.0122	34.722	0.002717
45	0.C21210	91130	1933	451217	0.004284	2.7075	2748614	0.0184	30.162	0.004266
50	0.035594	89197	3175	438600	0.007239	2.6743	2297397	0.0209	25.756	0.007210
55	0.053353	86022	4590	419396	0.010943	2.6657	1858797	0.0205	21.608	0.010901
60	0.083819	81432	6826	391237	0.017446	2.6668	1439400	0.0310	17.676	0.017336
65	0.134787	746C7	10056	349341	0.028786	2.6440	1048164	0.0310	14.049	0.028603
70	C.213393	64551	13775	289763	0.047538	2.6050	698822	0.0310	10.826	0.047238
75	C.334787	5C776	16999	212034	0.080172	2.5383	409059	0.0310	8.056	0.079675
80	0.5C0367	33777	16901	125331	0.134850	2.4985	197025	0.0310	5.833	0.134081
85+	1.C00000	16876	16876	71694	0.235389	4.2483	71694	0.0310	4.248	0.227386

TABLE 3 — FEMALE LIFE TABLE

x	$_nq_x$	l_x	$_nd_x$	$_nL_x$	$_nm_x$	$_na_x$	T_x	r_x	$\mathring{e}_x$	$_nM_x$
0	C.022866	100000	2287	98369	0.023245	0.2866	7254492	0.0000	72.545	0.023245
1	C.C6057	97713	592	389158	0.001521	1.1351	7156123	0.0000	73.236	0.001521
5	0.C02547	97122	247	484989	0.000510	2.5000	6766965	0.0366	69.675	0.000517
10	0.001819	96874	176	483930	0.000364	2.4950	6281976	0.0130	64.847	0.000364
15	0.002515	96698	243	482913	0.000504	2.6284	5798046	0.0015	59.960	0.000503
20	0.C03380	96455	326	481497	0.000677	2.6170	5315133	0.0000	55.105	0.000677
25	0.C04433	96129	426	479629	0.000889	2.6184	4833635	0.0119	50.283	0.000887
30	0.005937	95703	568	477162	0.001191	2.6224	4354006	0.0132	45.495	0.001189
35	0.007988	95134	760	473878	0.001604	2.6386	3876844	0.0030	40.751	0.001603
40	0.C11378	94375	1074	469365	0.002288	2.6648	3402966	0.0109	36.058	0.002284
45	C.C17250	93301	1609	462768	C.003478	2.6788	2933601	0.0178	31.442	0.003466
50	0.026773	91691	2455	452748	0.005422	2.6748	2470834	0.0221	26.947	0.005400
55	0.041122	89236	3670	437723	0.008383	2.6948	2018085	0.0239	22.615	0.008341
60	0.C68784	85567	5886	414331	0.014205	2.7058	1580362	0.0319	18.469	0.014098
65	0.119008	79681	9483	376389	0.025194	2.6782	1166031	0.0319	14.634	0.025008
70	0.199358	70198	13995	317799	0.044036	2.6281	789642	0.0319	11.249	0.043728
75	0.321849	56204	18089	236711	0.076419	2.5505	471843	0.0319	8.395	0.075925
80	0.482302	38115	18383	144959	0.126814	2.5186	235132	0.0319	6.169	0.125894
85+	*1.C00000	19732	19732	90174	0.218821	4.5699	90174	0.0319	4.570	0.215952

TABLE 4 — OBSERVED AND PROJECTED VITAL RATES

	OBSERVED POPULATION BOTH SEXES	MALES	FEMALES	PROJECTED POPULATION 1955 MALES	FEMALES	1960 MALES	FEMALES	1965 MALES	FEMALES	STABLE POPULATION MALES	FEMA...
RATES PER THOUSAND											
Birth	23.23	24.05	22.41	23.02	21.56	21.99	20.68	21.36	20.18	21.99	21...
Death	7.56	7.85	7.27	8.23	7.74	8.54	8.13	8.80	8.47	9.53	8...
Increase	15.67	16.20	15.14	14.79	13.82	13.44	12.55	12.56	11.70		12.46
PERCENTAGE											
under 15	29.30	30.12	28.48	31.01	29.35	31.17	29.59	29.43	28.03	28.98	28...
15-64	62.96	62.46	63.46	61.15	62.07	60.64	61.33	62.04	62.35	61.84	61...
65 and over	7.74	7.42	8.05	7.84	8.58	8.18	9.08	8.52	9.62	9.19	9...
DEP. RATIO X 100	58.82	60.10	57.57	63.53	61.10	64.90	63.05	61.17	60.39	61.71	62...

TABLE 1 - DATA

AGE AT LAST BIRTHDAY	POPULATION BOTH SEXES	MALES Number	MALES %	FEMALES Number	FEMALES %	BIRTHS BY AGE OF MOTHER	DEATHS BOTH SEXES	DEATHS MALES	DEATHS FEMALES	AGE AT LAST BIRTHDAY
0	224134	114990	2.1	109144	2.0	0	4577	2661	1916	0
1-4	886051	455370	8.5	430681	8.0	0	1193	664	529	1-4
5-9	1185946	608528	11.4	577418	10.7	0	675	415	260	5-9
10-14	918479	470434	8.8	448045	8.3	4	406	248	158	10-14
15-19	817649	416666	7.8	400983	7.4	5504	476	312	164	15-19
20-24	789870	400579	7.5	389291	7.2	40582	589	394	195	20-24
25-29	766959	382794	7.1	384165	7.1	73799	642	396	246	25-29
30-34	773162	380476	7.1	392686	7.3	61092	819	455	364	30-34
35-39	675325	333132	6.2	342193	6.3	34909	994	525	469	35-39
40-44	669900	328104	6.1	341796	6.3	13447	1481	811	670	40-44
45-49	636803	309840	5.8	326963	6.1	1099	2296	1288	1008	45-49
50-54	579280	280905	5.2	298375	5.5	8	3382	1970	1412	50-54
55-59	502322	241671	4.5	260651	4.8	0	4748	2792	1956	55-59
60-64	423728	203711	3.8	220017	4.1	0	6455	3698	2757	60-64
65-69	342132	164530	3.1	177602	3.3	0	8629	4674	3955	65-69
70-74	258211	123477	2.3	134734	2.5		11263	5820	5443	70-74
75-79	173265	82239	1.5	91026	1.7		12985	6495	6490	75-79
80-84	88013	40946	0.8	47067	0.9	118590 M.	11134	5397	5737	80-84
85+	39613	17363	0.3	22250	0.4	111854 F.	8939	4099	4840	85+
TOTAL	10750842	5355755		5395087		230444	81683	43114	38569	TOTAL

TABLE 2 - MALE LIFE TABLE

x	$_nq_x$	l_x	$_nd_x$	$_nL_x$	$_nm_x$	$_na_x$	T_x	r_x	$\mathring{e}_x$	$_nM_x$	x
0	0.022763	100000	2276	98367	0.023141	0.2825	7103010	0.0000	71.030	0.023141	0
1	0.005808	97724	568	389266	0.001458	1.1309	7004643	0.0000	71.678	0.001458	1
5	0.003389	97156	329	484957	0.000679	2.5000	6615377	0.0184	68.090	0.000682	5
10	0.002635	96827	255	483503	0.000528	2.5264	6130420	0.0373	63.313	0.000527	10
15	0.003745	96572	362	481999	0.000750	2.6251	5646917	0.0153	58.474	0.000749	15
20	0.004908	96210	472	479897	0.000984	2.5584	5164918	0.0075	53.684	0.000984	20
25	0.005160	95738	494	477474	0.001035	2.5406	4685021	0.0041	48.936	0.001034	25
30	0.005969	95244	569	474850	0.001197	2.5919	4207547	0.0127	44.177	0.001196	30
35	0.007868	94675	745	471636	0.001579	2.6642	3732698	0.0131	39.426	0.001576	35
40	0.012302	93930	1155	467006	0.002474	2.7110	3261062	0.0046	34.718	0.002472	40
45	0.020641	92775	1915	459501	0.004167	2.7167	2794055	0.0112	30.117	0.004157	45
50	0.034638	90860	3147	447064	0.007040	2.7011	2334554	0.0175	25.694	0.007013	50
55	0.056470	87713	4953	427033	0.011599	2.6721	1887490	0.0202	21.519	0.011553	55
60	0.087463	82759	7238	396774	0.018243	2.6482	1460457	0.0264	17.647	0.018153	60
65	0.133766	75521	10102	353742	0.028558	2.6378	1063683	0.0264	14.085	0.028408	65
70	0.212788	65419	13920	293752	0.047388	2.6047	709941	0.0264	10.852	0.047134	70
75	0.332038	51499	17099	215383	0.079391	2.5374	416189	0.0264	8.082	0.078977	75
80	0.493799	34399	16986	128254	0.132443	2.5038	200806	0.0264	5.838	0.131808	80
85+	1.000000	17413	17413	72552	0.240006	4.1666	72552	0.0264	4.167	0.236078	85+

TABLE 3 - FEMALE LIFE TABLE

x	$_nq_x$	l_x	$_nd_x$	$_nL_x$	$_nm_x$	$_na_x$	T_x	r_x	$\mathring{e}_x$	$_nM_x$	x
0	0.017334	100000	1733	98777	0.017548	0.2943	7402237	0.0005	74.022	0.017555	0
1	0.004894	98267	481	391693	0.001228	1.1432	7303460	0.0005	74.323	0.001228	1
5	0.002235	97786	219	488382	0.000448	2.5000	6911767	0.0180	70.683	0.000450	5
10	0.001760	97567	172	487402	0.000352	2.4765	6423385	0.0361	65.836	0.000353	10
15	0.002045	97395	199	486494	0.000409	2.5748	5935983	0.0136	60.947	0.000409	15
20	0.002502	97196	243	485396	0.000501	2.5949	5449489	0.0038	56.067	0.000501	20
25	0.003197	96953	310	484033	0.000640	2.6375	4964093	0.0000	51.201	0.000640	25
30	0.004633	96643	448	482169	0.000929	2.6621	4480060	0.0106	46.357	0.000927	30
35	0.006844	96195	658	479432	0.001373	2.6534	3997892	0.0125	41.560	0.001371	35
40	0.009761	95537	933	475518	0.001961	2.6770	3518460	0.0025	36.828	0.001960	40
45	0.015335	94604	1451	469657	0.003089	2.6802	3042941	0.0104	32.165	0.003083	45
50	0.023484	93154	2188	460699	0.004749	2.6829	2573285	0.0177	27.624	0.004732	50
55	0.037059	90966	3371	447066	0.007541	2.6969	2112586	0.0226	23.224	0.007504	55
60	0.061339	87595	5373	425667	0.012623	2.7094	1665520	0.0307	19.014	0.012531	60
65	0.106672	82222	8771	390904	0.022437	2.6963	1239853	0.0307	15.079	0.022269	65
70	0.185639	73451	13635	335147	0.040685	2.6452	848949	0.0307	11.558	0.040398	70
75	0.305497	59816	18274	254635	0.071764	2.5679	513802	0.0307	8.590	0.071298	75
80	0.471496	41542	19587	159510	0.122794	2.5392	259168	0.0307	6.239	0.121891	80
85+	*1.000000	21955	21955	99657	0.220307	4.5391	99657	0.0307	4.539	0.217528	85+

TABLE 4 - OBSERVED, PROJECTED, STABLE

	OBSERVED POPULATION BOTH SEXES	MALES	FEMALES	PROJECTED 1960 MALES	1960 FEMALES	1965 MALES	1965 FEMALES	1970 MALES	1970 FEMALES	STABLE MALES	STABLE FEMALES
RATES PER THOUSAND											
Birth	21.43	22.14	20.73	21.23	19.92	20.80	19.58	21.43	20.23	21.28	20.64
Death	7.60	8.05	7.15	8.46	7.69	8.75	8.13	8.96	8.49	9.45	8.81
Increase	13.84	14.09	13.58	12.77	12.23	12.06	11.45	12.47	11.74	11.8340	
PERCENTAGE											
under 15	29.90	30.80	29.01	30.72	29.00	28.77	27.24	28.25	26.86	28.40	27.74
15-64	61.72	61.20	62.23	60.89	61.57	62.49	62.66	62.66	62.44	62.16	61.63
65 and over	8.38	8.00	8.76	8.40	9.43	8.74	10.09	9.09	10.70	9.45	10.64
DEP. RATIO X 100	62.03	63.39	60.71	64.23	62.43	60.02	59.58	59.60	60.15	60.89	62.27

AGE AT LAST BIRTHDAY	POPULATION BOTH SEXES	MALES Number	%	FEMALES Number	%	BIRTHS BY AGE OF MOTHER	DEATHS BOTH SEXES	MALES	FEMALES	AGE AT LAST BIRTHDAY
0	235324	120509	2.1	114815	2.0	0	3934	2273	1661	0
1-4	918719	470705	8.2	448014	7.8	0	1068	631	437	1-4
5-9	1106969	567851	9.9	539118	9.3	0	566	358	208	5-9
10-14	1184144	606704	10.6	577440	10.0	0	402	253	149	10-1
15-19	912922	466477	8.2	446445	7.7	7554	513	358	155	15-1
20-24	806988	410549	7.2	396439	6.9	48777	579	414	165	20-2
25-29	769321	389018	6.8	380303	6.6	79939	609	397	212	25-2
30-34	758114	377259	6.6	380855	6.6	59146	703	423	280	30-3
35-39	761567	374396	6.5	387171	6.7	34311	988	559	429	35-3
40-44	675397	332199	5.8	343198	6.0	11368	1429	814	615	40-4
45-49	661396	323050	5.6	338346	5.9	956	2209	1293	916	45-4
50-54	625306	303132	5.3	322174	5.6	5	3508	2158	1350	50-5
55-59	561359	269743	4.7	291616	5.1	0	5205	3280	1925	55-5
60-64	474988	225008	3.9	249980	4.3	0	7074	4339	2735	60-6
65-69	387119	182399	3.2	204720	3.6	0	9376	5398	3978	65-6
70-74	293032	137960	2.4	155072	2.7		11905	6358	5547	70-7
75-79	196216	91613	1.6	104603	1.8		13832	7010	6822	75-7
80-84	107507	49629	0.9	57878	1.0	124137 M.	12935	6355	6580	80-8
85+	50163	22068	0.4	28095	0.5	117919 F.	10943	5012	5931	85+
TOTAL	11486551	5720269		5766282		242056	87778	47683	40095	TOTA

TABLE 1 DATA

x	nq_x	l_x	nd_x	nL_x	nm_x	na_x	T_x	r_x	$\dot{e}_x$	nM_x
0	0.018594	100000	1859	98691	0.018841	0.2959	7138509	0.0014	71.385	0.018862
1	0.005335	98141	524	391067	0.001339	1.1450	7039818	0.0014	71.732	0.001341
5	0.003147	97617	307	487317	0.000630	2.5000	6648751	0.0000	68.111	0.000630
10	0.002086	97310	203	486055	0.000418	2.5688	6161434	0.0191	63.318	0.000417
15	0.003854	97107	374	484657	0.000772	2.6581	5675379	0.0383	58.445	0.000767
20	0.005034	96733	487	482469	0.001009	2.5495	5190722	0.0172	53.661	0.001008
25	0.005091	96246	490	480013	0.001021	2.5206	4708252	0.0074	48.919	0.001021
30	0.005592	95756	536	477485	0.001122	2.5856	4228239	0.0027	44.157	0.001121
35	0.007455	95220	710	474455	0.001496	2.6816	3750754	0.0111	39.390	0.001493
40	0.012215	94510	1154	469904	0.002457	2.7064	3276299	0.0122	34.666	0.002450
45	0.019855	93356	1854	462574	0.004007	2.7314	2806396	0.0049	30.061	0.004002
50	0.035112	91502	3213	450184	0.007137	2.7195	2343822	0.0106	25.615	0.007119
55	0.059332	88289	5238	429284	0.012203	2.6781	1893637	0.0173	21.448	0.012160
60	0.092592	83051	7690	397117	0.019364	2.6414	1464354	0.0228	17.632	0.019284
65	0.138748	75361	10456	351879	0.029715	2.6161	1067236	0.0228	14.162	0.029594
70	0.208256	64905	13517	292015	0.046288	2.5948	715357	0.0228	11.022	0.046086
75	0.323229	51388	16610	216101	0.076863	2.5413	423342	0.0228	8.238	0.076518
80	0.483314	34778	16809	130724	0.128581	2.5168	207241	0.0228	5.959	0.128050
85+	1.000000	17969	17969	76517	0.234840	4.2582	76517	0.0228	4.258	0.227115

TABLE 2 MALE LIFE TABLE

x	nq_x	l_x	nd_x	nL_x	nm_x	na_x	T_x	r_x	$\dot{e}_x$	nM_x
0	0.014300	100000	1430	98985	0.014447	0.2904	7543167	0.0018	75.432	0.014467
1	0.003885	98570	383	393184	0.000974	1.1390	7444182	0.0018	75.522	0.000975
5	0.001927	98187	189	490462	0.000386	2.5000	7050997	0.0000	71.812	0.000386
10	0.001289	97998	126	489669	0.000258	2.4689	6560535	0.0186	66.946	0.000258
15	0.001741	97872	170	488948	0.000348	2.5944	6070866	0.0373	62.029	0.000347
20	0.002082	97701	203	488018	0.000417	2.6036	5581918	0.0156	57.133	0.000416
25	0.002785	97498	272	486842	0.000558	2.6177	5093899	0.0035	52.246	0.000557
30	0.003670	97226	357	485294	0.000735	2.6546	4607058	0.0000	47.385	0.000735
35	0.005536	96869	536	483112	0.001110	2.6960	4121763	0.0092	42.550	0.001108
40	0.008942	96333	861	479668	0.001796	2.6811	3638662	0.0117	37.772	0.001792
45	0.013461	95472	1285	474375	0.002709	2.6778	3158983	0.0035	33.088	0.002707
50	0.020792	94187	1958	466397	0.004199	2.6835	2684609	0.0105	28.503	0.004190
55	0.032636	92228	3010	454208	0.006627	2.6964	2218212	0.0184	24.051	0.006601
60	0.053761	89218	4796	435122	0.011023	2.7129	1764004	0.0316	19.772	0.010941
65	0.093726	84422	7913	403979	0.019587	2.7086	1328882	0.0316	15.741	0.019431
70	0.166249	76509	12720	352867	0.036046	2.6666	924903	0.0316	12.089	0.035770
75	0.283501	63790	18084	275357	0.065676	2.5895	572036	0.0316	8.968	0.065218
80	0.448311	45705	20490	178787	0.114607	2.5725	296680	0.0316	6.491	0.113688
85+	*1.000000	25215	25215	117893	0.213881	4.6755	117893	0.0316	4.676	0.211105

TABLE 3 FEMALE LIFE TABLE

	OBSERVED POPULATION			PROJECTED POPULATION 1965		1970		1975		STABLE POPULATION	
RATES PER THOUSAND	BOTH SEXES	MALES	FEMALES	MALES	FEMALES	MALES	FEMALES	MALES	FEMALES	MALES	FEMAL
Birth	21.07	21.70	20.45	21.33	20.09	22.17	20.90	23.04	21.76	22.35	21.5
Death	7.64	8.34	6.95	8.71	7.57	8.89	7.99	9.00	8.33	8.81	7.9
Increase	13.43	13.37	13.50	12.62	12.52	13.27	12.91	14.03	13.43		13.53
PERCENTAGE											
under 15	29.99	30.87	29.12	29.11	27.51	28.85	27.34	29.17	27.73	29.59	28.6
15-64	61.00	60.68	61.33	62.09	62.13	62.05	61.61	61.55	60.77	61.64	60.8
65 and over	9.00	8.46	9.54	8.80	10.36	9.10	11.05	9.28	11.50	8.77	10.
DEP. RATIO X 100	63.92	64.81	63.05	61.07	60.95	61.16	62.30	62.46	64.54	62.24	64.

TABLE 4 OBSERVED AND PROJECTED VITAL RATES

TABLE 5 — POPULATION PROJECTED WITH FIXED AGE-SPECIFIC BIRTH AND DEATH RATES (IN 1000's)

AGE LAST BIRTHDAY	1965 BOTH SEXES	MALES	FEMALES	1970 BOTH SEXES	MALES	FEMALES	1975 BOTH SEXES	MALES	FEMALES	AGE AT LAST BIRTHDAY
0-4	1218	623	595	1314	672	642	1460	747	713	0-4
5-9	1149	588	561	1212	620	592	1309	669	640	5-9
10-14	1104	566	538	1147	587	560	1210	618	592	10-14
15-19	1182	605	577	1102	565	537	1144	585	559	15-19
20-24	910	464	446	1177	602	575	1098	562	536	20-24
25-29	803	408	395	907	462	445	1173	599	574	25-29
30-34	766	387	379	800	406	394	903	460	443	30-34
35-39	754	375	379	762	385	377	796	404	392	35-39
40-44	755	371	384	747	371	376	756	381	375	40-44
45-49	666	327	339	745	365	380	737	365	372	45-49
50-54	647	314	333	652	318	334	729	355	374	50-54
55-59	603	289	314	624	300	324	628	303	325	55-59
60-64	529	250	279	568	267	301	587	277	310	60-64
65-69	431	199	232	480	221	259	516	237	279	65-69
70-74	330	151	179	368	165	203	410	183	227	70-74
75-79	223	102	121	252	112	140	280	122	158	75-79
80-84	123	55	68	141	62	79	159	68	91	80-84
85+	67	29	38	77	32	45	88	36	52	85+
TOTAL	12260	6103	6157	13075	6512	6563	13983	6971	7012	TOTAL

TABLE 6 — STANDARDIZED RATES

STANDARD COUNTRIES:
STANDARDIZED RATES PER THOUSAND

	ENGLAND AND WALES 1961 BOTH SEXES	MALES	FEMALES	UNITED STATES 1960 BOTH SEXES	MALES	FEMALES	MEXICO 1960 BOTH SEXES	MALES	FEMALES
birth	20.08	21.53*	18.96	20.43	20.10*	19.61	22.01	19.42*	21.39
death	9.76	9.40*	10.16	7.85	8.37*	7.36	3.96	6.76*	3.40
increase	10.32	12.13*	8.80	12.59	11.73*	12.25	18.05	12.66*	17.98

TABLE 7 — MOMENTS AND CUMULANTS

OBSERVED POP. MALES	FEMALES	STATIONARY POP. MALES	FEMALES	STABLE POP. MALES	FEMALES	OBSERVED BIRTHS	NET MATERNITY FUNCTION	BIRTHS IN STABLE POP.
31.13575	32.44985	37.96774	39.48156	31.14784	32.24187	29.60356	29.74565	29.26315
472.6782	489.3284	526.5986	556.6271	473.8539	504.4290	34.09345	34.07221	33.02365
4955.257	4461.550	2224.187	1862.730	5289.448	5543.285	68.7100	74.8118	79.8050
-176437.	-209282.	-280227.	-328730.	-159192.	-196207.	-453.503	-424.280	-303.819
0.232507	0.169891	0.033877	0.020119	0.262959	0.239406	0.119131	0.141494	0.176842
2.210305	2.125959	1.989467	1.939011	2.291021	2.228893	2.609844	2.634530	2.721410
-0.085101	-0.061832	-0.012643	-0.007306	-0.099573	-0.088314	-0.081713	-0.096105	-0.128489

TABLE 8 — RATES FROM AGE DISTRIBUTIONS AND VITAL STATISTICS (Females)

VITAL STATISTICS

		THOMPSON AGE RANGE	NRR	1000r	INTERVAL	BOURGEOIS-PICHAT AGE RANGE	NRR	1000b	1000d	1000r	COALE	
	1.535										IBR	20.90
	1.491	0-4	1.43	13.16	27.45	5-29	1.77	23.70	2.58	21.12	IDR	8.57
	3.150	5-9	1.43	13.18	27.42	30-54	1.22	17.60	10.16	7.44	IRI	12.33
GENERATION	29.503	10-14	1.58	16.39	27.38	55-79	1.98	47.94	22.68	25.25	K1	0.
RATIO	105.273	15-19	1.26	8.18	27.31	*50-74	1.85	40.68	17.86	22.82	K2	0.

TABLE 9 — LESLIE MATRIX AND ITS SPECTRAL COMPONENTS (Females)

SUB-DIAGONAL	ORIGINAL MATRIX ALTERNATIVE FIRST ROWS Projection	Integral	FIRST STABLE MATRIX % IN STABLE POPULATION	FISHER VALUES	REPRODUCTIVE VALUES	SECOND STABLE MATRIX Z₂ FIRST COLUMN	FIRST ROW
0.99653	0.00000	0.00000	10.248	1.051	591421	0.1569+0.0571	0.1569+0.0571
0.99838	0.00000	0.00000	9.543	1.128	608354	0.1411-0.1187	0.0262+0.1489
0.99853	0.02025	0.00000	8.903	1.210	698433	-0.0358-0.2009	-0.1048+0.0877
0.99810	0.16750	0.04197	8.307	1.275	569206	-0.2124-0.0767	-0.1192-0.0437
0.99759	0.39888	0.30516	7.748	1.191	472024	-0.1907+0.1612	-0.0459-0.1226
0.99682	0.43757	0.52133	7.223	0.857	325959	0.0491+0.2717	0.0126-0.1142
0.99550	0.29193	0.38517	6.728	0.459	174768	0.2871+0.1028	0.0264-0.0668
0.99287	0.14567	0.21979	6.259	0.185	71681	0.2564-0.2177	0.0184-0.0262
0.98896	0.04306	0.08215	5.807	0.045	15577	-0.0667-0.3641	0.0060-0.0058
0.98318	0.00341	0.00701	5.366	0.003	1137	-0.3822-0.1359	0.0005-0.0004
0.97387	0.00002	0.00004	4.930	0.000	6	-0.3362+0.2869	0.0000-0.0000
0.81663			18.939				

TABLE 10 — AGE ANALYSIS AND MISCELLANEOUS RESULTS (Females)

CONTRIBUTIONS OF ROOTS (IN 100's)

OBSERVED POPUL. (IN 100's)	r₁	r₂, r₃	r₄-r₁₁	AGE-SP. BIRTH RATES	NET MATERNITY FUNCTION	COEFF. OF MATRIX EQUATION	PARAMETERS	INTEGRAL	MATRIX	EXP. INCREASE x	e^{(x+8½)r}
5628	5754	-106	-20	0.0000	0.0000	0.0000	L(1)	1.07004	1.07015	0	1.0344
5391	5359	205	-173	0.0000	0.0000	0.0000	L(2)	0.45071	0.45057	50	2.0357
5774	4999	357	418	0.0000	0.0000	0.0202			0.80459	0.78186	55	2.1782
4464	4665	143	-343	0.0082	0.0403	0.1664	R(1)	0.01354	0.01356	60	2.3308
3964	4351	-279	-107	0.0599	0.2925	0.3955	R(2)	-0.01619	-0.02054	65	2.4941
3803	4056	-483	230	0.1024	0.4985	0.4328			0.21204	-0.20960	70	2.6688
3809	3778	-192	223	0.0757	0.3671	0.2879	C(1)		56151	75	2.8557
3872	3514	377	-19	0.0432	0.2086	0.1430	C(2)		-1690	80	3.0557
3432	3260	647	-476	0.0161	0.0774	0.0420			88560	85	3.2697
3383	3013	254	117	0.0014	0.0065	0.0033	2P/Y	29.6327	29.9770	90	3.4987
3222	2768	-497	950	0.0000	0.0000	0.0000	DELTA	3.8180		95	3.7438
10920	10634									100	4.0060

TABLE 1 — DATA

AGE AT LAST BIRTHDAY	POPULATION BOTH SEXES	MALES Number	MALES %	FEMALES Number	FEMALES %	BIRTHS BY AGE OF MOTHER	DEATHS BOTH SEXES	DEATHS MALES	DEATHS FEMALES	AGE AT LAST BIRTHDAY
0	244300	125109	2.1	119191	2.0	0	3941	2285	1656	0
1-4	951681	486634	8.2	465047	7.7	0	924	563	361	1-4
5-9	1126294	577316	9.7	548978	9.1	0	576	366	210	5-9
10-14	1117627	573203	9.6	544424	9.1	19	382	229	153	10-14
15-19	1118065	571438	9.6	546627	9.1	10280	590	409	181	15-19
20-24	857587	438549	7.4	419038	7.0	57229	566	419	147	20-24
25-29	774546	395929	6.6	378617	6.3	81195	590	408	182	25-29
30-34	772876	389760	6.5	383116	6.4	58270	701	419	282	30-34
35-39	753266	372458	6.2	380808	6.3	31192	994	587	407	35-39
40-44	733435	360628	6.0	372807	6.2	10862	1501	887	614	40-44
45-49	661355	324265	5.4	337090	5.6	829	2324	1415	909	45-49
50-54	640234	310631	5.2	329603	5.5	3	3681	2325	1356	50-54
55-59	589563	282738	4.7	306825	5.1	0	5500	3609	1891	55-59
60-64	505067	238031	4.0	267036	4.4	0	7707	4898	2809	60-64
65-69	417365	193755	3.2	223610	3.7	0	10637	6270	4367	65-69
70-74	313390	144998	2.4	168392	2.8		13009	7140	5869	70-74
75-79	214217	98606	1.7	115611	1.9		15145	7853	7292	75-79
80-84	116710	52938	0.9	63772	1.1	128459 M.	14102	6968	7134	80-84
85+	58388	25607	0.4	32781	0.5	121420 F.	12864	6004	6860	85+
TOTAL	11965966	5962593		6003373		249879	95734	53054	42680	TOTAL

TABLE 2 — MALE LIFE TABLE

x	$_nq_x$	l_x	$_nd_x$	$_nL_x$	$_nm_x$	$_na_x$	T_x	r_x	$\mathring{e}_x$	$_nM_x$
0	0.018001	100000	1800	98710	0.018237	0.2833	7101257	0.0019	71.013	0.018264
1	0.004604	98200	452	391503	0.001155	1.1317	7002547	0.0019	71.309	0.001157
5	0.003161	97748	309	487966	0.000633	2.5000	6611044	0.0058	67.634	0.000634
10	0.001996	97439	194	486716	0.000400	2.5428	6123078	0.0005	62.840	0.000400
15	0.003588	97244	349	485405	0.000719	2.6603	5636362	0.0261	57.961	0.000716
20	0.004778	96895	463	483350	0.000958	2.5661	5150957	0.0358	53.160	0.000955
25	0.005141	96432	496	480934	0.001031	2.5217	4667607	0.0108	48.403	0.001030
30	0.005364	95937	515	478450	0.001076	2.6030	4186673	0.0049	43.640	0.001075
35	0.007860	95422	750	475370	0.001578	2.6795	3708223	0.0061	38.861	0.001576
40	0.012262	94672	1161	470724	0.002466	2.7288	3232853	0.0112	34.148	0.002460
45	0.021657	93511	2025	462954	0.004374	2.7273	2762129	0.0104	29.538	0.004364
50	0.036843	91486	3371	449723	0.007495	2.7134	2299175	0.0058	25.131	0.007485
55	0.062156	88116	5477	427878	0.012800	2.6813	1849452	0.0134	20.989	0.012764
60	0.098469	82639	8137	394046	0.020651	2.6471	1421574	0.0187	17.202	0.020577
65	0.150637	74501	11223	345663	0.032467	2.6081	1027527	0.0187	13.792	0.032360
70	0.220644	63279	13962	282578	0.049409	2.5781	681864	0.0187	10.776	0.049242
75	0.333697	49317	16457	205904	0.079924	2.5282	399286	0.0187	8.096	0.079640
80	0.492625	32860	16188	122571	0.132067	2.5028	193382	0.0187	5.885	0.131626
85+	1.000000	16672	16672	70811	0.235448	4.2472	70811	0.0187	4.247	0.234466

TABLE 3 — FEMALE LIFE TABLE

x	$_nq_x$	l_x	$_nd_x$	$_nL_x$	$_nm_x$	$_na_x$	T_x	r_x	$\mathring{e}_x$	$_nM_x$
0	0.013734	100000	1373	98997	0.013873	0.2697	7579655	0.0019	75.797	0.013894
1	0.003092	98627	305	393628	0.000775	1.1187	7480658	0.0019	75.848	0.000776
5	0.001908	98322	188	491139	0.000382	2.5000	7087030	0.0066	72.080	0.000383
10	0.001404	98134	138	490320	0.000281	2.4618	6595891	0.0001	67.213	0.000281
15	0.001656	97996	162	489583	0.000331	2.5439	6105571	0.0259	62.304	0.000331
20	0.001758	97834	172	488755	0.000352	2.5878	5615988	0.0364	57.403	0.000351
25	0.002404	97662	235	487761	0.000481	2.6650	5127234	0.0085	52.500	0.000481
30	0.003674	97427	358	486300	0.000736	2.6646	4639472	0.0000	47.620	0.000736
35	0.005332	97069	518	484143	0.001069	2.6754	4153173	0.0016	42.786	0.001069
40	0.008221	96552	794	480933	0.001651	2.7015	3669030	0.0105	38.001	0.001647
45	0.013423	95758	1285	475811	0.002701	2.6836	3188097	0.0096	33.293	0.002697
50	0.020393	94472	1927	467865	0.004118	2.6660	2712285	0.0052	28.710	0.004114
55	0.030478	92546	2821	456244	0.006182	2.7007	2244420	0.0145	24.252	0.006163
60	0.051760	89725	4644	438096	0.010601	2.7327	1788176	0.0300	19.929	0.010519
65	0.094124	85081	8008	407022	0.019675	2.7044	1350080	0.0300	15.868	0.019530
70	0.162209	77073	12502	356147	0.035103	2.6630	943058	0.0300	12.236	0.034853
75	0.275462	64571	17787	280101	0.063502	2.5963	586911	0.0300	9.089	0.063074
80	0.443013	46784	20726	183829	0.112746	2.5831	306810	0.0300	6.558	0.111868
85+	*1.000000	26058	26058	122982	0.211886	4.7195	122982	0.0300	4.720	0.209268

TABLE 4 — OBSERVED AND PROJECTED VITAL RATES

	OBSERVED POPULATION BOTH SEXES	MALES	FEMALES	PROJECTED 1968 MALES	1968 FEMALES	1973 MALES	1973 FEMALES	1978 MALES	1978 FEMALES	STABLE POPULATION MALES	FEMALES
RATES PER THOUSAND											
Birth	20.88	21.54	20.23	22.23	20.83	23.21	21.77	23.23	21.83	22.73	21.
Death	8.00	8.90	7.11	9.11	7.69	9.17	8.08	9.15	8.35	8.72	7.
Increase	12.88	12.65	13.12	13.12	13.15	14.04	13.68	14.08	13.48		14.00
PERCENTAGE											
under 15	28.75	29.56	27.94	29.02	27.42	29.37	27.76	29.99	28.36	30.03	28.
15-64	61.89	61.79	61.99	62.14	61.75	61.65	60.84	61.05	59.99	61.66	60.
65 and over	9.36	8.65	10.06	8.84	10.83	8.98	11.40	8.97	11.65	8.31	10.
DEP. RATIO X 100	61.57	61.83	61.31	60.93	61.94	62.20	64.37	63.81	66.70	62.18	64.

TABLE 1 — DATA

AGE AT LAST BIRTHDAY	POPULATION BOTH SEXES	MALES Number	%	FEMALES Number	%	BIRTHS BY AGE OF MOTHER	DEATHS BOTH SEXES	MALES	FEMALES	AGE AT LAST BIRTHDAY
0	246756	126612	2.1	120144	2.0	0	3719	2154	1565	0
1-4	960174	491067	8.1	469107	7.7	0	959	555	404	1-4
5-9	1138941	583279	9.6	555662	9.1	0	562	345	217	5-9
10-14	1107613	568079	9.4	539534	8.9	28	432	277	155	10-14
15-19	1154043	590310	9.8	563733	9.3	11001	677	501	176	15-19
20-24	886787	454686	7.5	432101	7.1	60135	622	465	157	20-24
25-29	789153	405144	6.7	384009	6.3	81979	598	414	184	25-29
30-34	773349	392131	6.5	381218	6.3	56716	703	439	264	30-34
35-39	751768	373361	6.2	378407	6.2	30038	992	599	393	35-39
40-44	756175	371636	6.1	384539	6.3	10269	1549	923	626	40-44
45-49	653947	320881	5.3	333066	5.5	741	2349	1457	892	45-49
50-54	646055	313705	5.2	332350	5.5	7	3616	2233	1383	50-54
55-59	597990	286498	4.7	311492	5.1	0	5620	3692	1928	55-59
60-64	516749	243332	4.0	273417	4.5	0	7924	5044	2880	60-64
65-69	424001	195954	3.2	228047	3.8	0	10524	6432	4092	65-69
70-74	321903	147605	2.4	174298	2.9		12817	7021	5796	70-74
75-79	220129	100772	1.7	119357	2.0		14615	7630	6985	75-79
80-84	120320	54163	0.9	66157	1.1	129035 M.	13072	6317	6755	80-84
85+	61267	26738	0.4	34529	0.6	121879 F.	12087	5492	6595	85+
TOTAL	12127120	6045953		6081167		250914	93437	51990	41447	TOTAL

TABLE 2 — MALE LIFE TABLE

x	$_nq_x$	l_x	$_nd_x$	$_nL_x$	$_nm_x$	$_na_x$	T_x	r_x	$\mathring{e}_x$	$_nM_x$	x
0	0.016780	100000	1678	98806	0.016983	0.2886	7131146	0.0023	71.311	0.017013	0
1	0.004497	98322	442	392022	0.001128	1.1371	7032340	0.0023	71.524	0.001130	1
5	0.002949	97880	289	488677	0.000591	2.5000	6640318	0.0077	67.842	0.000591	5
10	0.002435	97591	238	487388	0.000488	2.6094	6151640	0.0000	63.035	0.000488	10
15	0.004247	97354	413	485788	0.000851	2.6297	5664253	0.0215	58.182	0.000849	15
20	0.005107	96940	495	483479	0.001024	2.5329	5178465	0.0367	53.419	0.001023	20
25	0.005098	96445	492	481004	0.001022	2.5174	4694986	0.0138	48.680	0.001022	25
30	0.005587	95953	536	478483	0.001120	2.6055	4213982	0.0070	43.917	0.001120	30
35	0.007997	95417	763	475311	0.001605	2.6737	3735499	0.0037	39.149	0.001604	35
40	0.012386	94654	1172	470620	0.002491	2.7386	3260188	0.0124	34.443	0.002484	40
45	0.022527	93482	2106	462567	0.004552	2.7009	2789568	0.0124	29.841	0.004541	45
50	0.035053	91376	3203	449586	0.007124	2.7228	2327001	0.0036	25.466	0.007118	50
55	0.062729	88173	5531	428079	0.012921	2.6884	1877415	0.0122	21.292	0.012887	55
60	0.099265	82642	8203	393917	0.020825	2.6482	1449336	0.0241	17.538	0.020729	60
65	0.152682	74438	11365	344881	0.032955	2.5970	1055419	0.0241	14.178	0.032824	65
70	0.213970	63073	13496	282563	0.047762	2.5694	710538	0.0241	11.265	0.047566	70
75	0.319955	49577	15862	208613	0.076038	2.5241	427975	0.0241	8.632	0.075715	75
80	0.454811	33715	15334	130764	0.117264	2.5342	219362	0.0241	6.506	0.116630	80
85+	*1.000000	18381	18381	88598	0.207465	4.8201	88598	0.0241	4.820	0.205401	85+

TABLE 3 — FEMALE LIFE TABLE

x	$_nq_x$	l_x	$_nd_x$	$_nL_x$	$_nm_x$	$_na_x$	T_x	r_x	$\mathring{e}_x$	$_nM_x$	x
0	0.012889	100000	1289	99083	0.013008	0.2883	7627864	0.0018	76.279	0.013026	0
1	0.003431	98711	339	393875	0.000860	1.1368	7528782	0.0018	76.271	0.000861	1
5	0.001947	98372	191	491384	0.000390	2.5000	7134907	0.0083	72.530	0.000391	5
10	0.001435	98181	141	490545	0.000287	2.4432	6643523	0.0000	67.666	0.000287	10
15	0.001562	98040	153	489825	0.000313	2.5509	6152979	0.0219	62.760	0.000312	15
20	0.001822	97887	178	489006	0.000365	2.5948	5663154	0.0380	57.854	0.000363	20
25	0.002397	97709	234	487991	0.000480	2.6411	5174148	0.0120	52.955	0.000479	25
30	0.003457	97474	337	486585	0.000693	2.6663	4686157	0.0008	48.076	0.000693	30
35	0.005180	97137	503	484522	0.001039	2.6857	4199572	0.0000	43.233	0.001039	35
40	0.008128	96634	785	481369	0.001632	2.7056	3715049	0.0110	38.444	0.001628	40
45	0.013339	95849	1279	476290	0.002684	2.6897	3233681	0.0118	33.737	0.002678	45
50	0.020615	94570	1950	468301	0.004163	2.6662	2757391	0.0025	29.157	0.004161	50
55	0.030596	92621	2834	456581	0.006207	2.6985	2289090	0.0129	24.715	0.006190	55
60	0.051785	89787	4650	438260	0.010609	2.7043	1832509	0.0316	20.410	0.010533	60
65	0.086831	85137	7393	408752	0.018086	2.7093	1394249	0.0316	16.376	0.017944	65
70	0.155354	77745	12078	360519	0.033502	2.6648	985497	0.0316	12.676	0.033253	70
75	0.258069	65667	16947	287594	0.058925	2.5960	624978	0.0316	9.517	0.058522	75
80	0.408240	48720	19890	193643	0.102712	2.6245	337384	0.0316	6.925	0.102106	80
85+	1.000000	28831	28831	143741	0.200573	4.9857	143741	0.0316	4.986	0.190999	85+

TABLE 4 — OBSERVED, PROJECTED, STABLE

	OBSERVED POPULATION BOTH SEXES	MALES	FEMALES	PROJECTED POPULATION 1969 MALES	FEMALES	1974 MALES	FEMALES	1979 MALES	FEMALES	STABLE POPULATION MALES	FEMALES
RATES PER THOUSAND											
Birth	20.69	21.34	20.04	22.22	20.83	23.12	21.68	22.98	21.60	22.49	21.52
Death	7.70	8.60	6.82	9.00	7.52	9.12	7.95	9.10	8.23	8.75	7.77
Increase	12.99	12.74	13.23	13.22	13.32	14.00	13.73	13.89	13.37	13.7464	
PERCENTAGE											
under 15	28.48	29.26	27.70	28.90	27.32	29.27	27.65	29.89	28.24	29.82	28.68
15-64	62.06	62.05	62.07	62.08	61.54	61.54	60.60	60.95	59.77	61.61	60.58
65 and over	9.46	8.69	10.23	9.02	11.14	9.19	11.75	9.16	11.99	8.58	10.74
DEP. RATIO X 100	61.14	61.15	61.12	61.08	62.49	62.49	65.01	64.07	67.30	62.32	65.07

TABLE 1 — DATA

AGE AT LAST BIRTHDAY	POPULATION BOTH SEXES	MALES Number	MALES %	FEMALES Number	FEMALES %	BIRTHS BY AGE OF MOTHER	DEATHS BOTH SEXES	DEATHS MALES	DEATHS FEMALES	AGE AT LAST BIRTHDAY
0	244556	125521	2.0	119035	1.9	0	3541	2029	1512	0
1-4	970356	496597	8.1	473759	7.7	0	894	536	358	1-4
5-9	1152440	589866	9.6	562574	9.1	0	548	329	219	5-9
10-14	1107109	567710	9.3	539399	8.8	17	367	233	134	10-14
15-19	1183947	606216	9.9	577731	9.4	12092	693	482	211	15-19
20-24	911870	468602	7.6	443268	7.2	62193	697	494	203	20-24
25-29	808046	417111	6.8	390935	6.3	81001	589	408	181	25-29
30-34	773702	394857	6.4	378845	6.1	52339	652	411	241	30-34
35-39	757325	378495	6.2	378830	6.1	27607	1025	629	396	35-39
40-44	762800	374932	6.1	387868	6.3	9262	1612	978	634	40-44
45-49	663158	325482	5.3	337676	5.5	705	2341	1411	930	45-49
50-54	649649	315745	5.1	333904	5.4	0	3822	2480	1342	50-54
55-59	604411	289515	4.7	314896	5.1	0	5735	3789	1946	55-59
60-64	529272	249058	4.1	280214	4.5	0	8179	5234	2945	60-64
65-69	431085	198220	3.2	232865	3.8	0	10807	6457	4350	65-69
70-74	330575	150355	2.5	180220	2.9		13506	7504	6002	70-74
75-79	224921	102180	1.7	122741	2.0		15452	7933	7519	75-79
80-84	124834	55842	0.9	68992	1.1	126105 M.	14077	6929	7148	80-84
85+	64676	28102	0.5	36574	0.6	119111 F.	13489	6218	7271	85+
TOTAL	12294732	6134406		6160326		245216	98026	54484	43542	TOTAL

TABLE 2 — MALE LIFE TABLE

x	nq_x	l_x	nd_x	nL_x	nm_x	na_x	T_x	r_x	$\mathring{e}_x$	nM_x
0	0.015977	100000	1598	98864	0.016161	0.2892	7114310	0.0003	71.143	0.016165
1	0.004303	98402	423	392397	0.001079	1.1378	7015446	0.0003	71.294	0.001079
5	0.002780	97979	272	489213	0.000557	2.5000	6623049	0.0085	67.597	0.000558
10	0.002050	97707	200	488056	0.000410	2.6204	6133835	0.0000	62.778	0.000410
15	0.003980	97506	388	486625	0.000798	2.6669	5645780	0.0184	57.902	0.000795
20	0.005264	97118	511	484330	0.001056	2.5339	5159154	0.0364	53.122	0.001054
25	0.004879	96607	471	481853	0.000978	2.4949	4674825	0.0161	48.390	0.000978
30	0.005198	96136	500	479495	0.001042	2.6338	4192971	0.0086	43.615	0.001041
35	0.008283	95636	792	476352	0.001663	2.6928	3713476	0.0035	38.829	0.001662
40	0.012999	94844	1233	471391	0.002615	2.7067	3237124	0.0124	34.131	0.002608
45	0.021531	93611	2016	463495	0.004349	2.7381	2765733	0.0125	29.545	0.004335
50	0.038610	91595	3536	449883	0.007861	2.7114	2302238	0.0036	25.135	0.007854
55	0.063634	88059	5604	427274	0.013115	2.6765	1852355	0.0101	21.035	0.013087
60	0.100466	82455	8284	392741	0.021093	2.6418	1425081	0.0197	17.283	0.021015
65	0.151581	74171	11243	343950	0.032688	2.6068	1032340	0.0197	13.918	0.032575
70	0.223233	62928	14048	280505	0.050080	2.5700	688390	0.0197	10.939	0.049909
75	0.326503	48881	15960	204842	0.077912	2.5212	407884	0.0197	8.344	0.077638
80	0.475927	32921	15668	125704	0.124642	2.5172	203042	0.0197	6.168	0.124082
85+	*1.000000	17253	17253	77338	0.223086	4.4826	77338	0.0197	4.483	0.221265

TABLE 3 — FEMALE LIFE TABLE

x	nq_x	l_x	nd_x	nL_x	nm_x	na_x	T_x	r_x	$\mathring{e}_x$	nM_x
0	0.012587	100000	1259	99090	0.012702	0.2767	7617365	0.0000	76.174	0.012702
1	0.003016	98741	298	394109	0.000756	1.1252	7518275	0.0000	76.141	0.000756
5	0.001940	98444	191	491740	0.000388	2.5000	7124166	0.0090	72.368	0.000389
10	0.001241	98253	122	490955	0.000248	2.4802	6632426	0.0000	67.504	0.000248
15	0.001829	98131	179	490225	0.000366	2.6189	6141471	0.0193	62.585	0.000365
20	0.002291	97951	224	489204	0.000459	2.5434	5651245	0.0386	57.695	0.000458
25	0.002315	97727	226	488085	0.000464	2.5786	5162041	0.0152	52.821	0.000463
30	0.003178	97500	310	486786	0.000636	2.6886	4673956	0.0025	47.938	0.000636
35	0.005214	97191	507	484786	0.001045	2.6970	4187170	0.0000	43.082	0.001045
40	0.008160	96684	789	481615	0.001638	2.7134	3702384	0.0098	38.294	0.001635
45	0.013713	95895	1315	476415	0.002760	2.6735	3220769	0.0122	33.586	0.002754
50	0.019919	94580	1884	468506	0.004021	2.6676	2744353	0.0028	29.016	0.004019
55	0.030538	92696	2831	456978	0.006195	2.7031	2275848	0.0110	24.552	0.006180
60	0.051676	89865	4644	438728	0.010585	2.7177	1818869	0.0294	20.240	0.010510
65	0.090170	85221	7684	408441	0.018814	2.7011	1380142	0.0294	16.195	0.018680
70	0.155561	77537	12062	359591	0.033543	2.6708	971700	0.0294	12.532	0.033304
75	0.268392	65475	17573	285046	0.061650	2.5912	612110	0.0294	9.349	0.061259
80	0.412360	47902	19753	189653	0.104153	2.6115	327064	0.0294	6.828	0.103606
85+	1.000000	28149	28149	137411	0.204854	4.8815	137411	0.0294	4.882	0.198803

TABLE 4 — OBSERVED AND PROJECTED VITAL RATES

	OBSERVED POPULATION BOTH SEXES	OBSERVED POPULATION MALES	OBSERVED POPULATION FEMALES	PROJECTED 1970 MALES	PROJECTED 1970 FEMALES	PROJECTED 1975 MALES	PROJECTED 1975 FEMALES	PROJECTED 1980 MALES	PROJECTED 1980 FEMALES	STABLE POPULATION MALES	STABLE POPULATION FEM.
RATES PER THOUSAND											
Birth	19.94	20.56	19.34	21.69	20.36	22.57	21.19	22.36	21.04	21.66	20.
Death	7.97	8.88	7.07	9.14	7.73	9.22	8.13	9.20	8.41	9.14	8.
Increase	11.97	11.68	12.27	12.55	12.63	13.35	13.06	13.17	12.63		12.52
PERCENTAGE											
under 15	28.26	29.01	27.51	28.61	27.07	28.83	27.24	29.28	27.68	29.01	27.
15-64	62.17	62.27	62.08	62.40	61.65	62.05	60.93	61.63	60.29	62.13	60.
65 and over	9.57	8.72	10.41	9.00	11.29	9.13	11.83	9.08	12.03	8.86	11.
DEP. RATIO X 100	60.84	60.59	61.09	60.27	62.21	61.17	64.13	62.25	65.87	60.95	64.

Table 5

AGE LAST BIRTHDAY	1970 BOTH SEXES	1970 MALES	1970 FEMALES	1975 BOTH SEXES	1975 MALES	1975 FEMALES	1980 BOTH SEXES	1980 MALES	1980 FEMALES	AGE AT LAST BIRTHDAY	
0-4	1280	657	623	1428	733	695	1547	794	753	0-4	**TABLE 5**
5-9	1211	620	591	1275	654	621	1423	730	693	5-9	POPULATION
10-14	1150	588	562	1208	618	590	1273	653	620	10-14	PROJECTED
15-19	1105	566	539	1148	587	561	1205	616	589	15-19	WITH
20-24	1180	603	577	1100	563	537	1144	584	560	20-24	FIXED
25-29	908	466	442	1175	600	575	1096	560	536	25-29	AGE—
30-34	805	415	390	905	464	441	1171	597	574	30-34	SPECIFIC
35-39	769	392	377	800	412	388	900	461	439	35-39	BIRTH
40-44	751	375	376	763	388	375	794	408	386	40-44	AND
45-49	753	369	384	740	368	372	753	382	371	45-49	DEATH
50-54	648	316	332	735	358	377	723	357	366	50-54	RATES
55-59	626	300	326	624	300	324	708	340	368	55-59	(IN 1000's)
60-64	568	266	302	589	276	313	587	276	311	60-64	
65-69	479	218	261	514	233	281	532	241	291	65-69	
70-74	367	162	205	408	178	230	438	190	248	70-74	
75-79	253	110	143	281	118	163	312	130	182	75-79	
80-84	145	63	82	162	67	95	180	72	108	80-84	
85+	84	34	50	98	39	59	110	41	69	85+	
TOTAL	13082	6520	6562	13953	6956	6997	14896	7432	7464	TOTAL	

Table 6

STANDARD COUNTRIES: STANDARDIZED RATES PER THOUSAND	ENGLAND AND WALES 1961 BOTH SEXES	MALES	FEMALES	UNITED STATES 1960 BOTH SEXES	MALES	FEMALES	MEXICO 1960 BOTH SEXES	MALES	FEMALES	
Birth	19.23	20.30*	18.10	19.56	18.77*	18.72	21.72	18.46*	21.05	**TABLE 6** STANDARDIZED RATES
Death	9.59	9.69*	9.52	7.73	8.69*	6.89	3.85	7.05*	3.16	
Increase	9.64	10.61*	8.59	11.83	10.08*	11.83	17.87	11.41*	17.89	

Table 7

OBSERVED POP. MALES	FEMALES	STATIONARY POP. MALES	FEMALES	STABLE POP. MALES	FEMALES	OBSERVED BIRTHS	NET MATERNITY FUNCTION	BIRTHS IN STABLE POP.	
31.32699	32.89735	37.73483	39.75888	31.45861	32.94721	28.55480	28.97709	28.54675	**TABLE 7**
474.0793	502.6914	522.2820	564.0089	474.3424	516.4887	34.33413	32.82194	31.74217	MOMENTS
5125.219	4681.862	2318.981	1877.399	5108.876	5450.722	92.0767	84.7649	87.4821	AND
−171934.	−225749.	−271393.	−338419.	−163005.	−214792.	−319.813	−265.159	−159.947	CUMULANTS
0.246531	0.172557	0.037747	0.019645	0.244554	0.215638	0.209470	0.203207	0.239292	
2.235003	2.106647	2.005078	1.936145	2.275537	2.194815	2.728704	2.753862	2.841253	
−0.090753	−0.061727	−0.014216	−0.007121	−0.093160	−0.079251	−0.142677	−0.146683	−0.185162	

Table 8

VITAL STATISTICS		THOMPSON AGE RANGE	NRR	1000r	INTERVAL	BOURGEOIS-PICHAT AGE RANGE	NRR	1000b	1000d	1000r	COALE		
R	1.470										iBR	20.19	**TABLE 8**
R	1.434	0-4	1.37	11.71	27.45	5-29	1.63	22.61	4.50	18.12	IDR	8.67	RATES FROM AGE
ACCELERATION	3.027	5-9	1.44	13.29	27.43	30-54	1.16	15.49	10.02	5.47	IRI	11.52	DISTRIBUTIONS
	28.761	10-14	1.44	13.08	27.39	55-79	1.78	38.79	17.41	21.37	K1	0.	AND VITAL
RATIO	105.872	15-19	1.58	15.82	27.32	*40-64	1.30	19.29	9.45	9.84	K2	0.	STATISTICS (Females)

Table 9

ORIGINAL MATRIX SUB-DIAGONAL	ALTERNATIVE FIRST ROWS Projection	Integral	FIRST STABLE MATRIX % IN STABLE POPULATION	FISHER VALUES	REPRODUCTIVE VALUES	SECOND STABLE MATRIX Z₂ FIRST COLUMN	FIRST ROW	
0.99704	0.00000	0.00000	9.892	1.046	620038	0.1629+0.0601	0.1629+0.0601	**TABLE 9**
0.99840	0.00004	0.00000	9.263	1.117	628359	0.1457−0.1288	0.0216+0.1536	LESLIE
0.99851	0.02507	0.00008	8.686	1.191	642459	−0.0498−0.2122	−0.1115+0.0819	MATRIX
0.99792	0.19278	0.05174	8.146	1.244	718554	−0.2360−0.0635	−0.1155−0.0545	AND ITS
0.99771	0.41568	0.34681	7.635	1.125	498643	−0.1879+0.1992	−0.0374−0.1254	SPECTRAL
0.99734	0.41323	0.51216	7.155	0.765	298935	0.0969+0.2911	0.0149−0.1075	COMPONENTS
0.99589	0.25242	0.34149	6.702	0.383	145074	0.3385+0.0589	0.0233−0.0586	(Females)
0.99346	0.11571	0.18013	6.269	0.144	54660	0.2373−0.3022	0.0148−0.0217	
0.98920	0.03107	0.05903	5.850	0.033	12727	−0.1716−0.3928	0.0044−0.0045	
0.98340	0.00250	0.00515	5.435	0.002	831	−0.4746−0.0388	0.0004−0.0003	
0.97540	0.00000	0.00001	5.020	0.000	1	−0.2859+0.4413	0.0000−0.0000	
0.91923			19.946					

Table 10

OBSERVED POPUL. (IN 100's)	CONTRIBUTIONS OF ROOTS (IN 100's) r₁	r₂,r₃	r₄-r₁₁	AGE-SP. BIRTH RATES	NET MATERNITY FUNCTION	COEFF. OF MATRIX EQUATION	PARAMETERS INTEGRAL	MATRIX	EXP. INCREASE x	$e^{(x+2\frac{1}{2})r}$	
5928	6079	−253	101	0.0000	0.0000	0.0000	L(1) 1.06461	1.06470	0	1.0318	**TABLE 10**
5626	5693	−40	−27	0.0000	0.0000	0.0000	L(2) 0.42062	0.42176	50	1.9297	AGE
5394	5338	275	−219	0.0000	0.0001	0.0250	0.80918	0.78433	55	2.0544	ANALYSIS
5777	5007	342	429	0.0102	0.0498	0.1916	R(1) 0.01252	0.01254	60	2.1871	AND
4433	4692	18	−278	0.0682	0.3334	0.4123	R(2) −0.01843	−0.02319	65	2.3284	MISCELLANEOUS
3909	4397	−410	−78	0.1006	0.4912	0.4089	0.21828	0.21548	70	2.4789	RESULTS
3788	4119	−458	127	0.0671	0.3267	0.2491	C(1)	61457	75	2.6390	(Females)
3788	3853	29	−94	0.0354	0.1716	0.1137	C(2)	−58728	80	2.8095	
3879	3595	602	−318	0.0116	0.0559	0.0303		50914	85	2.9911	
3377	3340	597	−560	0.0010	0.0048	0.0024	2P/Y 28.7844	29.1585	90	3.1843	
3339	3085	−114	368	0.0000	0.0000	0.0000	DELTA 3.2595		95	3.3900	
12365	12259								100	3.6091	

TABLE 1 — DATA

AGE AT LAST BIRTHDAY	POPULATION BOTH SEXES	MALES Number	%	FEMALES Number	%	BIRTHS BY AGE OF MOTHER	DEATHS BOTH SEXES	MALES	FEMALES	AGE AT LAST BIRTHDAY
0	60175	31028	1.9	29147	1.8	0	1599	927	672	0
1-4	255107	131370	8.0	123737	7.4	0	374	209	165	1-4
5-9	280629	143939	8.8	136690	8.2	0	208	133	75	5-9
10-14	214951	109476	6.7	105475	6.4	0	110	70	40	10-14
15-19	202673	103197	6.3	99476	6.0	1859	151	101	50	15-19
20-24	226704	115841	7.1	110863	6.7	12735	271	188	83	20-24
25-29	258659	131396	8.0	127263	7.7	18239	320	198	122	25-29
30-34	265764	133133	8.1	132631	8.0	15666	372	233	139	30-34
35-39	250695	126041	7.7	124654	7.5	9382	450	277	173	35-39
40-44	235320	117200	7.2	118120	7.1	3604	570	328	242	40-44
45-49	216912	105675	6.5	111237	6.7	352	806	462	344	45-49
50-54	200787	97105	5.9	103682	6.2	6	1145	671	474	50-54
55-59	170584	82238	5.0	88346	5.3	0	1494	851	643	55-59
60-64	138319	64935	4.0	73384	4.4	0	1890	1015	875	60-64
65-69	111182	50700	3.1	60482	3.6	0	2499	1306	1193	65-69
70-74	89560	40726	2.5	48834	2.9		3434	1697	1737	70-74
75-79	62084	27754	1.7	34330	2.1		4155	1972	2183	75-79
80-84	34460	14604	0.9	19856	1.2	31976 M.	3980	1774	2206	80-84
85+	21307	8606	0.5	12701	0.8	29867 F.	4786	1969	2817	85+
TOTAL	3295872	1634964		1660908		61843	28614	14381	14233	TOTAL

TABLE 2 — MALE LIFE TABLE

x	nq_x	l_x	nd_x	nL_x	nm_x	na_x	T_x	r_x	$\mathring{e}_x$	nM_x
0	0.029233	100000	2923	97848	0.029876	0.2638	7058561	0.0000	70.586	0.029876
1	0.006335	97077	615	386532	0.001591	1.1135	6960713	0.0000	71.703	0.001591
5	0.004577	96462	441	481205	0.000917	2.5000	6574182	0.0384	68.153	0.000924
10	0.003194	96020	307	479340	0.000640	2.5176	6092977	0.0325	63.455	0.000639
15	0.004883	95714	467	477496	0.000979	2.7065	5613637	0.0000	58.650	0.000979
20	0.008083	95246	770	474357	0.001623	2.5654	5136141	0.0000	53.925	0.001623
25	0.007506	94476	709	470619	0.001507	2.5139	4661784	0.0000	49.343	0.001507
30	0.008715	93767	817	466857	0.001750	2.5785	4191165	0.0024	44.698	0.001750
35	0.010942	92950	1017	462304	0.002200	2.5950	3724308	0.0105	40.068	0.002198
40	0.013934	91933	1281	456660	0.002805	2.6545	3262004	0.0146	35.482	0.002799
45	0.021700	90652	1967	448705	0.004384	2.6847	2805345	0.0143	30.946	0.004372
50	0.034109	88685	3025	436357	0.006932	2.6640	2356640	0.0180	26.573	0.006910
55	0.050764	85660	4348	418080	0.010401	2.6501	1920282	0.0296	22.418	0.010348
60	0.075735	81311	6158	392165	0.015703	2.6630	1502202	0.0232	18.475	0.015631
65	0.121965	75153	9166	354185	0.025879	2.6455	1110037	0.0232	14.770	0.025759
70	0.190353	65987	12561	300008	0.041868	2.6174	755852	0.0232	11.455	0.041669
75	0.304070	53426	16245	227540	0.071395	2.5629	455843	0.0232	8.532	0.071053
80	0.469769	37181	17466	142961	0.122176	2.5414	228303	0.0232	6.140	0.121474
85+	*1.000000	19715	19715	85342	0.231007	4.3289	85342	0.0232	4.329	0.228794

TABLE 3 — FEMALE LIFE TABLE

x	nq_x	l_x	nd_x	nL_x	nm_x	na_x	T_x	r_x	$\mathring{e}_x$	nM_x
0	0.022676	100000	2268	98352	0.023056	0.2731	7397938	0.0000	73.979	0.023056
1	0.005314	97732	519	389435	0.001333	1.1218	7299587	0.0000	74.689	0.001333
5	0.002710	97213	263	485407	0.000543	2.5000	6910152	0.0364	71.082	0.000549
10	0.001893	96950	184	484286	0.000379	2.4767	6424744	0.0313	66.269	0.000379
15	0.002510	96766	243	483261	0.000503	2.6519	5940459	0.0000	61.390	0.000503
20	0.003737	96523	361	481760	0.000749	2.6253	5457198	0.0000	56.538	0.000749
25	0.004782	96163	460	479693	0.000959	2.5632	4975438	0.0000	51.740	0.000959
30	0.005227	95703	500	477305	0.001048	2.5831	4495746	0.0010	46.976	0.001048
35	0.006927	95203	659	474461	0.001390	2.6469	4018441	0.0101	42.209	0.001388
40	0.010211	94543	965	470464	0.002052	2.6682	3543980	0.0093	37.485	0.002049
45	0.015377	93578	1439	464525	0.003098	2.6630	3073516	0.0099	32.845	0.003092
50	0.022696	92139	2091	455841	0.004588	2.6795	2608991	0.0182	28.316	0.004572
55	0.035986	90047	3240	442754	0.007319	2.6907	2153150	0.0269	23.911	0.007278
60	0.058258	86807	5057	422331	0.011974	2.6856	1710396	0.0201	19.703	0.011924
65	0.094759	81750	7747	390872	0.019819	2.6922	1288065	0.0201	15.756	0.019725
70	0.164899	74003	12203	341458	0.035738	2.6598	897194	0.0201	12.124	0.035569
75	0.276765	61800	17104	267794	0.063871	2.5908	555735	0.0201	8.992	0.063589
80	0.439811	44696	19658	175989	0.111699	2.5841	287941	0.0201	6.442	0.111099
85+	*1.000000	25038	25038	111952	0.223651	4.4713	111952	0.0201	4.471	0.221794

TABLE 4 — OBSERVED AND PROJECTED VITAL RATES

RATES PER THOUSAND	OBSERVED POPULATION BOTH SEXES	MALES	FEMALES	PROJECTED POPULATION 1956 MALES	FEMALES	1961 MALES	FEMALES	1966 MALES	FEMALES	STABLE POPULATION MALES	FEMALES
Birth	18.76	19.56	17.98	17.55	16.23	16.14	15.00	16.17	15.09	17.13	16.
Death	8.68	8.80	8.57	9.09	8.82	9.64	9.36	10.23	9.96	11.98	11.
Increase	10.08	10.76	9.41	8.46	7.41	6.50	5.64	5.94	5.12		5.14
PERCENTAGE											
under 15	24.60	25.43	23.79	26.53	24.82	25.42	23.83	23.51	22.13	23.82	23.
15-64	65.73	65.86	65.61	64.22	63.96	64.38	63.97	65.19	64.45	63.21	62.
65 and over	9.67	8.71	10.61	9.25	11.22	10.21	12.20	11.30	13.42	12.97	14.
DEP. RATIO X 100	52.13	51.84	52.42	55.72	56.35	55.33	56.33	53.40	55.16	58.21	59.

AGE LAST BIRTHDAY	1956 BOTH SEXES	MALES	FEMALES	1961 BOTH SEXES	MALES	FEMALES	1966 BOTH SEXES	MALES	FEMALES	AGE AT LAST BIRTHDAY	
0-4	291	150	141	276	142	134	275	142	133	0-4	**TABLE 5**
5-9	313	161	152	290	149	141	275	142	133	5-9	POPULATION
10-14	279	143	136	313	161	152	289	149	140	10-14	PROJECTED
15-19	214	109	105	279	143	136	311	160	151	15-19	WITH
20-24	202	103	99	213	108	105	278	142	136	20-24	FIXED
25-29	225	115	110	201	102	99	211	107	104	25-29	AGE—
30-34	257	130	127	224	114	110	199	101	98	30-34	SPECIFIC
35-39	264	132	132	255	129	126	222	113	109	35-39	BIRTH
40-44	249	125	124	261	130	131	252	127	125	40-44	AND
45-49	232	115	117	244	122	122	257	128	129	45-49	DEATH
50-54	212	103	109	226	112	114	239	119	120	50-54	RATES
55-59	194	93	101	204	98	106	218	107	111	55-59	(IN 1000's)
60-64	161	77	84	183	87	96	193	92	101	60-64	
65-69	127	59	68	148	70	78	168	79	89	65-69	
70-74	96	43	53	109	50	59	127	59	68	70-74	
75-79	69	31	38	74	33	41	85	38	47	75-79	
80-84	40	17	23	44	19	25	47	20	27	80-84	
85+	22	9	13	24	10	14	28	12	16	85+	
TOTAL	3447	1715	1732	3568	1779	1789	3674	1837	1837	TOTAL	

STANDARD COUNTRIES:	ENGLAND AND WALES 1961 BOTH SEXES	MALES	FEMALES	UNITED STATES 1960 BOTH SEXES	MALES	FEMALES	MEXICO 1960 BOTH SEXES	MALES	FEMALES	
STANDARDIZED RATES PER THOUSAND										**TABLE 6**
Birth	16.13	16.88*	15.10	16.40	16.08*	15.60	17.70	14.99*	17.05	STANDAR-
Death	9.88	9.34*	10.61	8.07	8.33*	7.86	4.44	6.75*	3.94	DIZED
Increase	6.25	7.54*	4.48	8.32	7.74*	7.75	13.26	8.24*	13.11	RATES

	OBSERVED POP. MALES	FEMALES	STATIONARY POP. MALES	FEMALES	STABLE POP. MALES	FEMALES	OBSERVED BIRTHS	NET MATERNITY FUNCTION	BIRTHS IN STABLE POP.	
1	33.21548	34.85804	38.25485	39.30262	35.52196	36.47553	29.94385	29.64616	29.43402	**TABLE 7**
2	458.9980	484.7105	538.2300	555.8188	522.5882	541.4725	37.05163	39.36293	38.90928	MOMENTS
3	3220.379	2921.105	2304.589	1974.664	3740.395	3567.993	69.7896	85.9416	90.2960	AND
4	-163591.	-197641.	-297080.	-326721.	-257867.	-288824.	-706.158	-873.881	-807.631	CUMULANTS
1	0.107246	0.074928	0.034063	0.022708	0.098029	0.080190	0.095755	0.121100	0.138413	
2	2.223505	2.158776	1.974494	1.942426	2.055774	2.014900	2.485616	2.436002	2.466534	
k	-0.045521	-0.031079	-0.012554	-0.008247	-0.036198	-0.029167	-0.056692	-0.063951	-0.073819	

VITAL STATISTICS		AGE RANGE	THOMPSON NRR	1000r	INTERVAL	AGE RANGE	BOURGEOIS-PICHAT NRR	1000b	1000d	1000r	COALE	
GRR	1.217					5-29	1.04	14.68	13.40	1.28	IBR	**TABLE 8**
NRR	1.164	0-4	1.26	8.53	27.43	30-54	1.31	22.99	13.13	9.86	IDR	RATES FROM AGE
R	2.520	5-9	1.11	3.71	27.40	55-79	1.83	42.70	20.40	22.30	IRI	DISTRI- BUTIONS
GENERATION	29.540	10-14	0.86	-5.68	27.36	*30-54	1.31	22.99	13.13	9.86	K1	AND VITAL STATISTICS
SEX RATIO	107.061	15-19	0.84	-6.30	27.29						K2	(Females)

	ORIGINAL MATRIX SUB-DIAGONAL	ALTERNATIVE FIRST ROWS Projection	Integral	FIRST STABLE MATRIX % IN STABLE POPULATION	FISHER VALUES	REPRODUCTIVE VALUES	SECOND STABLE MATRIX Z2 FIRST COLUMN	FIRST ROW	
	0.99512	0.00000	0.00000	7.911	1.038	158737	0.1434+0.0638	0.1434+0.0638	**TABLE 9**
	0.99769	0.00000	0.00000	7.673	1.071	146338	0.1520-0.1046	0.0174+0.1325	LESLIE
	0.99788	0.02197	0.00000	7.460	1.101	116133	-0.0116-0.2171	-0.0882+0.0713	MATRIX
	0.99689	0.15690	0.04459	7.255	1.109	110349	-0.2254-0.1219	-0.0938-0.0337	AND ITS
	0.99571	0.30339	0.27411	7.049	0.978	108465	-0.2609+0.1514	-0.0398-0.0929	SPECTRAL
	0.99502	0.30725	0.34199	6.840	0.692	88047	-0.0083+0.3546	0.0060-0.0896	COMPO-
	0.99404	0.22725	0.28186	6.633	0.393	52103	0.3503+0.2258	0.0234-0.0551	NENTS
	0.99158	0.12429	0.17960	6.426	0.168	20959	0.4408-0.2124	0.0177-0.0221	(Females)
	0.98738	0.03962	0.07281	6.210	0.044	5179	0.0573-0.5701	0.0060-0.0050	
	0.98130	0.00379	0.00755	5.976	0.004	434	-0.5321-0.4040	0.0006-0.0004	
	0.97129	0.00007	0.00014	5.715	0.000	7	-0.7213+0.2815	0.0000-0.0000	
	0.80272			24.852					

	OBSERVED POPUL. (IN 100's)	CONTRIBUTIONS OF ROOTS (IN 100's) r1	r2, r3	r4·r11	AGE-SP. BIRTH RATES	NET MATERNITY FUNCTION	COEFF. OF MATRIX EQUATION	PARAMETERS	INTEGRAL	MATRIX	EXP. INCREASE x	e(x+2½)r	
	1529	1321	162	45	0.0000	0.0000	0.0000	L(1)	1.02607	1.02608	0	1.0129	**TABLE 10**
	1367	1281	92	-7	0.0000	0.0000	0.0000	L(2)	0.43851	0.44204	50	1.3102	AGE
	1055	1246	-111	-80	0.0000	0.0000	0.0218		0.74126	0.72222	55	1.3444	ANALYSIS
	995	1212	-265	48	0.0090	0.0436	0.1554	R(1)	0.00515	0.00515	60	1.3794	AND
	1109	1177	-171	102	0.0555	0.2673	0.2996	R(2)	-0.02987	-0.03327	65	1.4154	MISCEL-
	1273	1142	156	-26	0.0692	0.3320	0.3021		0.20732	0.20431	70	1.4523	LANEOUS
	1326	1108	428	-210	0.0570	0.2723	0.2224	C(1)		16702	75	1.4901	RESULTS
	1247	1073	309	-136	0.0363	0.1725	0.1209	C(2)		46235	80	1.5289	(Females)
	1181	1037	-211	355	0.0147	0.0693	0.0382			-23141	85	1.5688	
	1112	998	-679	793	0.0015	0.0071	0.0036	2P/Y	30.3069	30.7527	90	1.6097	
	1037	955	-537	619	0.0000	0.0001	0.0001	DELTA	7.2561		95	1.6517	
	3379	4151									100	1.6947	

AGE AT LAST BIRTHDAY	POPULATION BOTH SEXES	MALES Number	%	FEMALES Number	%	BIRTHS BY AGE OF MOTHER	DEATHS BOTH SEXES	MALES	FEMALES	AGE AT LAST BIRTH
0	61638	31466	1.9	3C172	1.8	0	1345	776	569	0
1-4	241298	124242	7.4	117056	6.9	0	302	178	124	1-
5-9	318409	163796	9.7	154613	9.1	0	175	115	60	5-
10-14	242653	124126	7.4	118527	6.9	0	108	72	36	10-
15-19	204749	104271	6.2	10C478	5.9	2369	148	103	45	15-
20-24	211140	108112	6.4	103028	6.0	14257	184	139	45	20-
25-29	234344	119780	7.1	114564	6.7	18168	235	156	79	25-
30-34	268960	135704	8.0	133256	7.8	15534	325	203	122	30-
35-39	253275	126971	7.5	126304	7.4	9064	394	236	158	35-
40-44	245835	123483	7.3	122352	7.2	3386	555	338	217	40-
45-49	224354	110525	6.5	113829	6.7	310	766	449	317	45-
50-54	208589	101209	6.0	107380	6.3	3	1147	673	474	50-
55-59	186544	89989	5.3	96555	5.7	0	1620	960	660	55-
60-64	151212	71786	4.3	79426	4.7	0	2050	1184	866	60-
65-69	121237	55745	3.3	65492	3.8	0	2727	1481	1246	65-
70-74	91817	41137	2.4	50680	3.0		3487	1756	1731	70-
75-79	68288	30628	1.8	37660	2.2		4406	2120	2286	75-
80-84	37534	16232	1.0	21302	1.2	32397 M.	4117	1837	2280	80-
85+	22270	8976	0.5	13294	0.8	30694 F.	4798	1955	2843	85
TOTAL	3394146	1688178		1705968		63091	28889	14731	14158	TOT

TABLE 1 DATA

TABLE 2 MALE LIFE TABLE

x	nq_x	l_x	nd_x	nL_x	nm_x	na_x	T_x	r_x	$\dot{e}_x$	nM_x
0	0.024224	100000	2422	98240	0.024658	0.2735	7137847	0.0002	71.378	0.024662
1	0.005706	97578	557	388708	0.001432	1.1222	7039606	0.0002	72.144	0.001433
5	0.003488	97021	338	484258	0.000699	2.5000	6650898	0.0218	68.551	0.000702
10	0.002910	96682	281	482737	0.000583	2.6018	6166640	0.0445	63.782	0.000580
15	0.004937	96401	476	480885	0.000990	2.6459	5683903	0.0129	58.961	0.000988
20	0.006408	95925	615	478119	0.001286	2.5484	5203017	0.0000	54.240	0.001286
25	0.006491	95310	619	475025	0.001302	2.5306	4724899	0.0000	49.574	0.001302
30	0.007452	94692	706	471747	0.001496	2.5744	4249874	0.0000	44.881	0.001496
35	0.009262	93986	871	467871	0.001861	2.6347	3778127	0.0075	40.199	0.001859
40	0.013624	93116	1269	462611	0.002742	2.6615	3310256	0.0111	35.550	0.002737
45	0.020185	91847	1854	454951	0.004075	2.6895	2847645	0.0156	31.004	0.004062
50	0.032835	89993	2955	443139	0.006668	2.6900	2392693	0.0136	26.588	0.006650
55	0.052269	87038	4549	424572	0.010715	2.6661	1949554	0.0234	22.399	0.010668
60	0.079788	82489	6582	397028	0.016577	2.6578	1524982	0.0262	18.487	0.016493
65	0.125595	75907	9534	357020	0.026703	2.6383	1127954	0.0262	14.860	0.026567
70	0.194503	66374	12910	300917	0.042902	2.6026	770934	0.0262	11.615	0.042687
75	0.297181	53464	15888	228397	0.069565	2.5503	470017	0.0262	8.791	0.069218
80	0.445751	37575	16749	147032	0.113915	2.5614	241620	0.0262	6.430	0.113172
85+	*1.000000	20826	20826	94588	0.220177	4.5418	94588	0.0262	4.542	0.217803

TABLE 3 FEMALE LIFE TABLE

x	nq_x	l_x	nd_x	nL_x	nm_x	na_x	T_x	r_x	$\dot{e}_x$	nM_x
0	0.018570	100000	1857	98644	0.018826	0.2701	7512734	0.0022	75.127	0.018859
1	0.004215	98143	414	391380	0.001057	1.1190	7414090	0.0022	75.544	0.001059
5	0.001925	97729	188	488176	0.000385	2.5000	7022710	0.0211	71.859	0.000388
10	0.001520	97541	148	487342	0.000304	2.5420	6534534	0.0427	66.993	0.000304
15	0.002239	97393	218	486433	0.000448	2.5609	6047192	0.0136	62.091	0.000448
20	0.002182	97175	212	485369	0.000437	2.6137	5560759	0.0000	57.224	0.000437
25	0.003442	96963	334	484028	0.000690	2.6432	5075391	0.0000	52.344	0.000690
30	0.004568	96629	441	482098	0.000916	2.6259	4591363	0.0000	47.515	0.000916
35	0.006243	96188	600	479522	0.001252	2.6402	4109265	0.0073	42.721	0.001251
40	0.008845	95587	845	475971	0.001776	2.6757	3629744	0.0085	37.973	0.001774
45	0.013863	94742	1313	470676	0.002790	2.6904	3153773	0.0102	33.288	0.002785
50	0.021897	93428	2046	462397	0.004424	2.6807	2683097	0.0119	28.718	0.004414
55	0.033794	91383	3088	449750	0.006866	2.6804	2220700	0.0230	24.301	0.006835
60	0.053462	88294	4720	430624	0.010962	2.7017	1770950	0.0237	20.057	0.010903
65	0.091638	83574	7659	400255	0.019134	2.6999	1340326	0.0237	16.038	0.019025
70	0.158956	75916	12067	351353	0.034345	2.6611	940071	0.0237	12.383	0.034155
75	0.266101	63848	16990	278431	0.061021	2.5980	588718	0.0237	9.221	0.060701
80	0.428054	46858	20058	186190	0.107728	2.6019	310287	0.0237	6.622	0.107032
85+	*1.000000	26800	26800	124097	0.215963	4.6304	124097	0.0237	4.630	0.213856

TABLE 4 OBSERVED AND PROJECTED VITAL RATES

	OBSERVED POPULATION BOTH SEXES	MALES	FEMALES	PROJECTED POPULATION 1959 MALES	FEMALES	1964 MALES	FEMALES	1969 MALES	FEMALES	STABLE POPULATION MALES	FEMA
RATES PER THOUSAND											
Birth	18.59	19.19	17.99	17.30	16.27	16.74	15.79	17.74	16.77	18.85	18.
Death	8.51	8.73	8.30	9.23	8.73	9.82	9.33	10.32	9.86	10.65	9.
Increase	10.08	10.46	9.69	8.06	7.55	6.92	6.46	7.43	6.91		8.20
PERCENTAGE											
under 15	25.46	26.28	24.64	26.66	25.11	24.84	23.54	24.04	22.90	25.79	24.
15-64	64.49	64.68	64.31	63.56	63.05	64.35	63.46	64.27	63.05	62.65	61.
65 and over	10.05	9.05	11.05	9.78	11.84	10.81	13.00	11.69	14.05	11.56	13.
DEP. RATIO X 100	55.05	54.62	55.49	57.33	58.60	55.40	57.59	55.60	58.60	59.61	61.

TABLE 1 — DATA

AGE AT LAST BIRTHDAY	POPULATION BOTH SEXES	MALES Number	%	FEMALES Number	%	BIRTHS BY AGE OF MOTHER	DEATHS BOTH SEXES	MALES	FEMALES	AGE AT LAST BIRTHDAY
0	62288	31767	1.8	30521	1.7	0	1304	748	556	0
1-4	246272	126095	7.3	120177	6.9	0	279	160	119	1-4
5-9	305590	157320	9.0	148270	8.5	0	159	105	54	5-9
10-14	299068	153546	8.8	145522	8.3	0	112	77	35	10-14
15-19	219971	112023	6.4	107948	6.2	2962	143	106	37	15-19
20-24	198367	101475	5.8	96892	5.5	15423	180	137	43	20-24
25-29	218786	111757	6.4	107029	6.1	18180	205	143	62	25-29
30-34	247242	125923	7.2	121319	6.9	14313	272	174	98	30-34
35-39	264662	132923	7.6	131739	7.5	9114	368	221	147	35-39
40-44	249047	124938	7.2	124109	7.1	3125	533	335	198	40-44
45-49	236364	118046	6.8	118318	6.7	286	802	481	321	45-49
50-54	213983	104163	6.0	109820	6.3	2	1159	717	442	50-54
55-59	197114	94864	5.5	102250	5.8	0	1687	1040	647	55-59
60-64	167149	79893	4.6	87256	5.0	0	2328	1411	917	60-64
65-69	130686	60575	3.5	70111	4.0	0	2926	1637	1289	65-69
70-74	99904	44837	2.6	55067	3.1		3885	1977	1908	70-74
75-79	70027	30969	1.8	39058	2.2		4659	2230	2429	75-79
80-84	42097	18440	1.1	23657	1.3	32519 M.	4694	2142	2552	80-84
85+	23320	9474	0.5	13846	0.8	30886 F.	5032	2088	2944	85+
TOTAL	3491937	1739028		1752909		63405	30727	15929	14798	TOTAL

TABLE 2 — MALE LIFE TABLE

x	nq_x	l_x	nd_x	nL_x	nm_x	na_x	T_x	r_x	$\mathring{e}_x$	nM_x	x
0	0.023146	100000	2315	98300	0.023546	0.2654	7132991	0.0000	71.330	0.023546	0
1	0.005057	97685	494	389316	0.001269	1.1148	7034691	0.0000	72.014	0.001269	1
5	0.003330	97191	324	485148	0.000667	2.5000	6645375	0.0020	68.374	0.000667	5
10	0.002514	96868	244	483758	0.000503	2.6163	6160227	0.0333	63.594	0.000501	10
15	0.004756	96624	460	482056	0.000953	2.6829	5676469	0.0405	58.748	0.000946	15
20	0.006728	96165	647	479237	0.001350	2.5482	5194413	0.0000	54.016	0.001350	20
25	0.006377	95518	609	476066	0.001280	2.5022	4715177	0.0000	49.364	0.001280	25
30	0.006886	94908	654	472944	0.001382	2.5546	4239110	0.0000	44.665	0.001382	30
35	0.008281	94255	781	469447	0.001663	2.6586	3766166	0.0000	39.957	0.001663	35
40	0.013347	93474	1248	464479	0.002686	2.6814	3296719	0.0091	35.269	0.002681	40
45	0.020243	92227	1867	456847	0.004087	2.7034	2832240	0.0138	30.709	0.004075	45
50	0.033980	90360	3070	444709	0.006904	2.6908	2375393	0.0148	26.288	0.006883	50
55	0.053611	87289	4680	425573	0.010996	2.6764	1930684	0.0151	22.118	0.010963	55
60	0.085142	82610	7034	396498	0.017739	2.6469	1505111	0.0239	18.220	0.017661	60
65	0.127547	75576	9640	355068	0.027148	2.6333	1108613	0.0239	14.669	0.027024	65
70	0.200240	65937	13203	298041	0.044300	2.6034	753545	0.0239	11.428	0.044093	70
75	0.307103	52734	16195	223887	0.072334	2.5436	455504	0.0239	8.638	0.072007	75
80	0.454065	36539	16591	141999	0.116839	2.5471	231617	0.0239	6.339	0.116161	80
85+	*1.000000	19948	19948	89618	0.222588	4.4926	89618	0.0239	4.493	0.220393	85+

TABLE 3 — FEMALE LIFE TABLE

x	nq_x	l_x	nd_x	nL_x	nm_x	na_x	T_x	r_x	$\mathring{e}_x$	nM_x	x
0	0.017966	100000	1797	98682	0.018206	0.2665	7548040	0.0008	75.480	0.018217	0
1	0.003946	98203	388	391696	0.000989	1.1159	7449358	0.0008	75.856	0.000990	1
5	0.001817	97816	178	488635	0.000364	2.5000	7057662	0.0030	72.152	0.000364	5
10	0.001201	97638	117	487895	0.000240	2.4823	6569027	0.0314	67.279	0.000241	10
15	0.001721	97521	168	487205	0.000344	2.6223	6081131	0.0403	62.357	0.000343	15
20	0.002217	97353	216	486249	0.000444	2.6092	5593926	0.0004	57.460	0.000444	20
25	0.002892	97137	281	485020	0.000579	2.6295	5107677	0.0000	52.582	0.000579	25
30	0.004031	96856	390	483358	0.000808	2.6365	4622657	0.0000	47.727	0.000808	30
35	0.005565	96466	537	481065	0.001116	2.6449	4139298	0.0000	42.909	0.001116	35
40	0.007963	95929	764	477891	0.001598	2.7041	3658233	0.0090	38.135	0.001595	40
45	0.013504	95165	1285	472845	0.002718	2.6802	3180342	0.0095	33.419	0.002713	45
50	0.019976	93880	1875	465044	0.004033	2.6770	2707497	0.0104	28.840	0.004025	50
55	0.031290	92005	2879	453394	0.006349	2.6970	2242453	0.0163	24.373	0.006328	55
60	0.051587	89126	4598	435098	0.010567	2.7094	1789060	0.0236	20.073	0.010509	60
65	0.088740	84528	7501	405516	0.018497	2.7170	1353961	0.0236	16.018	0.018385	65
70	0.161145	77027	12413	356199	0.034847	2.6687	948445	0.0236	12.313	0.034649	70
75	0.271682	64615	17555	280821	0.062512	2.5931	592246	0.0236	9.166	0.062190	75
80	0.430426	47060	20256	186587	0.108560	2.5951	311425	0.0236	6.618	0.107874	80
85+	*1.000000	26804	26804	124838	0.214712	4.6574	124838	0.0236	4.657	0.212625	85+

TABLE 4 — OBSERVED AND PROJECTED VITAL RATES

	OBSERVED POPULATION BOTH SEXES	MALES	FEMALES	PROJECTED POPULATION 1962 MALES	FEMALES	1967 MALES	FEMALES	1972 MALES	FEMALES	STABLE POPULATION MALES	FEMALES
RATES PER THOUSAND											
Birth	18.16	18.70	17.62	17.53	16.54	18.29	17.28	19.34	18.30	20.35	19.49
Death	8.80	9.16	8.44	9.70	8.94	10.16	9.45	10.65	9.99	9.84	8.98
Increase	9.36	9.54	9.18	7.83	7.60	8.13	7.83	8.69	8.32	10.5107	
PERCENTAGE											
under 15	26.15	26.95	25.36	25.92	24.51	25.11	23.88	25.06	23.88	27.43	26.46
15-64	63.37	63.60	63.13	63.77	63.02	63.73	62.56	63.16	61.78	62.23	61.49
65 and over	10.48	9.45	11.51	10.31	12.47	11.17	13.55	11.79	14.34	10.35	12.05
DEP. RATIO X 100	57.81	57.24	58.39	56.81	58.68	56.92	59.84	58.34	61.87	60.71	62.63

TABLE 4 — OBSERVED AND PROJECTED VITAL RATES

TABLE 1 — DATA

AGE AT LAST BIRTHDAY	POPULATION BOTH SEXES	MALES Number	%	FEMALES Number	%	BIRTHS BY AGE OF MOTHER	DEATHS BOTH SEXES	MALES	FEMALES	AGE AT LAST BIRTHDAY
0	61135	31305	1.8	29830	1.7	0	1153	672	481	0
1-4	247573	126817	7.1	120756	6.7	0	250	145	105	1-4
5-9	302383	155151	8.7	147232	8.2	0	153	99	54	5-9
10-14	317332	162958	9.1	154374	8.6	3	113	73	40	10-14
15-19	258612	132354	7.4	126258	7.0	3801	174	134	40	15-19
20-24	207690	106067	5.9	101623	5.7	17073	179	136	43	20-24
25-29	201102	102426	5.7	98676	5.5	17310	179	133	46	25-29
30-34	224978	114509	6.4	110469	6.1	12979	253	176	77	30-34
35-39	260400	131562	7.4	128838	7.2	8178	376	234	142	35-39
40-44	253997	127179	7.1	126818	7.1	2893	555	346	209	40-44
45-49	243411	122084	6.8	121327	6.8	242	786	486	300	45-49
50-54	223618	110286	6.2	113332	6.3	2	1156	736	420	50-54
55-59	203611	98123	5.5	105488	5.9	0	1762	1094	668	55-59
60-64	180346	85639	4.8	94707	5.3	0	2614	1599	1015	60-64
65-69	143968	67531	3.8	76437	4.3	0	3342	1896	1446	65-69
70-74	107265	48428	2.7	58837	3.3		4158	2205	1953	70-74
75-79	73288	31980	1.8	41308	2.3		4829	2341	2488	75-79
80-84	45080	19569	1.1	25511	1.4	32125 M.	5044	2333	2711	80-84
85+	25461	10483	0.6	14978	0.8	30356 F.	5461	2319	3142	85+
TOTAL	3581250	1784451		1796799		62481	32537	17157	15380	TOTAL

TABLE 2 — MALE LIFE TABLE

x	$_nq_x$	l_x	$_nd_x$	$_nL_x$	$_nm_x$	$_na_x$	T_x	r_x	$\dot{e}_x$	$_nM_x$	x
0	0.021132	100000	2113	98445	0.021466	0.2642	7129355	0.0000	71.294	0.021466	
1	0.004558	97887	446	390259	0.001143	1.1138	7030910	0.0000	71.827	0.001143	
5	0.003185	97441	310	486427	0.000638	2.5000	6640651	0.0000	68.151	0.000638	5
10	0.002244	97130	218	485144	0.000449	2.6745	6154224	0.0153	63.361	0.000448	10
15	0.005087	96912	493	483412	0.001020	2.6686	5669080	0.0420	58.497	0.001012	15
20	0.006398	96419	617	480581	0.001284	2.5429	5185668	0.0244	53.782	0.001282	20
25	0.006472	95802	620	477485	0.001298	2.5376	4705087	0.0000	49.112	0.001298	25
30	0.007656	95182	729	474135	0.001537	2.5619	4227602	0.0000	44.416	0.001537	30
35	0.008856	94454	836	470289	0.001779	2.6339	3753467	0.0000	39.739	0.001779	35
40	0.013528	93617	1266	465126	0.002723	2.6626	3283178	0.0047	35.070	0.002721	40
45	0.019764	92351	1825	457549	0.003989	2.6961	2818052	0.0100	30.515	0.003981	45
50	0.032971	90526	2985	445780	0.006695	2.7057	2360504	0.0149	26.076	0.006674	50
55	0.054506	87541	4772	426702	0.011182	2.6941	1914724	0.0135	21.872	0.011149	55
60	0.089763	82769	7430	396352	0.018745	2.6453	1488022	0.0213	17.978	0.018671	60
65	0.132102	75340	9953	353075	0.028188	2.6264	1091670	0.0213	14.490	0.028076	65
70	0.205950	65387	13467	294563	0.045717	2.5960	738595	0.0213	11.296	0.045532	70
75	0.311210	51921	16158	219850	0.073497	2.5397	444032	0.0213	8.552	0.073202	75
80	0.462681	35762	16547	138083	0.119831	2.5385	224183	0.0213	6.269	0.119220	80
85+	*1.000000	19216	19216	86100	0.223181	4.4807	86100	0.0213	4.481	0.221215	85

TABLE 3 — FEMALE LIFE TABLE

x	$_nq_x$	l_x	$_nd_x$	$_nL_x$	$_nm_x$	$_na_x$	T_x	r_x	$\dot{e}_x$	$_nM_x$	x
0	0.015936	100000	1594	98830	0.016125	0.2658	7588635	0.0000	75.886	0.016125	
1	0.003469	98406	341	392641	0.000870	1.1152	7489805	0.0000	76.111	0.000870	
5	0.001832	98065	180	489876	0.000367	2.5000	7097164	0.0000	72.372	0.000367	5
10	0.001294	97885	127	489105	0.000259	2.4601	6607288	0.0151	67.500	0.000259	10
15	0.001590	97759	155	488421	0.000318	2.6072	6118184	0.0415	62.585	0.000317	15
20	0.002117	97603	207	487514	0.000424	2.5719	5629762	0.0242	57.680	0.000423	20
25	0.002328	97397	227	486443	0.000466	2.6208	5142248	0.0000	52.797	0.000466	25
30	0.003480	97170	338	485067	0.000697	2.6882	4655805	0.0000	47.914	0.000697	30
35	0.005497	96832	532	482922	0.001102	2.6773	4170737	0.0000	43.072	0.001102	35
40	0.008215	96299	791	479654	0.001649	2.6695	3687815	0.0043	38.295	0.001648	40
45	0.012311	95508	1176	474799	0.002476	2.6676	3208161	0.0087	33.590	0.002473	45
50	0.018413	94333	1737	467679	0.003714	2.7065	2733362	0.0100	28.976	0.003706	50
55	0.031290	92596	2897	456356	0.006349	2.7143	2265683	0.0113	24.469	0.006332	55
60	0.052595	89698	4718	437707	0.010778	2.7140	1809327	0.0238	20.171	0.010717	60
65	0.091125	84981	7744	407052	0.019024	2.6948	1371620	0.0238	16.140	0.018918	65
70	0.154842	77237	11960	358267	0.033382	2.6657	964568	0.0238	12.488	0.033193	70
75	0.264387	65277	17258	285008	0.060554	2.6024	606300	0.0238	9.288	0.060231	75
80	0.425748	48019	20444	191134	0.106961	2.6051	321293	0.0238	6.691	0.106267	80
85+	*1.000000	27575	27575	130159	0.211855	4.7202	130159	0.0238	4.720	0.209774	85

TABLE 4 — OBSERVED AND PROJECTED VITAL RATES

RATES PER THOUSAND	OBSERVED POPULATION BOTH SEXES	MALES	FEMALES	PROJECTED POPULATION 1965 MALES	FEMALES	1970 MALES	FEMALES	1975 MALES	FEMALES	STABLE POPULATION MALES	FEMALES
Birth	17.45	18.00	16.89	18.06	16.96	19.40	18.23	20.18	18.98	20.77	19.8
Death	9.09	9.61	8.56	10.11	9.13	10.52	9.63	10.96	10.14	9.62	8.6
Increase	8.36	8.39	8.33	7.95	7.83	8.88	8.60	9.22	8.84		11.154
PERCENTAGE											
under 15	25.92	26.69	25.17	25.42	24.03	25.31	23.96	25.85	24.49	27.93	26.8
15-64	63.04	63.34	62.75	63.76	62.76	63.23	61.92	62.16	60.77	62.15	61.3
65 and over	11.03	9.97	12.08	10.81	13.21	11.46	14.12	11.99	14.74	9.92	11.8
DEP. RATIO X 100	58.62	57.88	59.36	56.83	59.32	58.15	61.49	60.87	64.55	60.91	63.1

AGE AT LAST BIRTHDAY	1965 BOTH SEXES	1965 MALES	1965 FEMALES	1970 BOTH SEXES	1970 MALES	1970 FEMALES	1975 BOTH SEXES	1975 MALES	1975 FEMALES	AGE AT LAST BIRTHDAY	
0-4	314	161	153	339	174	165	374	192	182	0-4	
5-9	307	157	150	312	160	152	338	173	165	5-9	
10-14	302	155	147	307	157	150	311	159	152	10-14	
15-19	316	162	154	301	154	147	306	156	150	15-19	**TABLE 5**
20-24	258	132	126	315	161	154	300	153	147	20-24	POPULATION
25-29	206	105	101	257	131	126	314	160	154	25-29	PROJECTED
30-34	200	102	98	206	105	101	255	130	125	30-34	WITH
35-39	224	114	110	199	101	98	205	104	101	35-39	FIXED
40-44	258	130	128	221	112	109	197	100	97	40-44	AGE—
45-49	251	125	126	255	128	127	219	111	108	45-49	SPECIFIC
50-54	239	119	120	246	122	124	250	125	125	50-54	BIRTH
55-59	217	106	111	231	114	117	238	117	121	55-59	AND
60-64	192	91	101	204	98	106	218	106	112	60-64	DEATH
65-69	164	76	88	175	81	94	186	87	99	65-69	RATEŠ
70-74	123	56	67	142	64	78	151	68	83	70-74	(IN 1000's)
75-79	83	36	47	96	42	54	110	48	62	75-79	
80-84	48	20	28	54	23	31	62	26	36	80-84	
85+	29	12	17	32	13	19	35	14	21	85+	
TOTAL	3731	1859	1872	3892	1940	1952	4069	2029	2040	TOTAL	

STANDARD COUNTRIES:	ENGLAND AND WALES 1961 BOTH SEXES	MALES	FEMALES	UNITED STATES 1960 BOTH SEXES	MALES	FEMALES	MEXICO 1960 BOTH SEXES	MALES	FEMALES	
STANDARDIZED RATES PER THOUSAND										**TABLE 6**
Birth	18.41	19.01*	17.34	18.71	17.99*	17.91	21.33	16.17*	20.67	STANDARDIZED
Death	9.41	9.20*	9.68	7.61	8.29*	7.04	3.93	7.06*	3.29	RATES
Increase	9.00	9.81*	7.66	11.10	9.69*	10.87	17.40	9.11*	17.38	

	OBSERVED POP. MALES	OBSERVED POP. FEMALES	STATIONARY POP. MALES	STATIONARY POP. FEMALES	STABLE POP. MALES	STABLE POP. FEMALES	OBSERVED BIRTHS	NET MATERNITY FUNCTION	BIRTHS IN STABLE POP.	
μ	34.09418	35.71443	38.11647	39.73938	32.37619	33.64903	28.64499	28.27467	27.85841	**TABLE 7**
σ^2	490.1109	518.7474	533.0050	562.8786	491.1233	522.9821	39.80040	35.88308	34.57593	MOMENTS
κ_3	3148.120	2755.494	2303.660	1845.149	5018.431	5110.793	104.0856	115.3486	118.7338	AND
κ_4	-226488.	-269931.	-287829.	-337722.	-188359.	-232953.	-868.896	-374.595	-223.851	CUMULANTS
β_1	0.084182	0.054392	0.035046	0.019091	0.212601	0.182606	0.171838	0.287976	0.341057	
β_2	2.057119	1.996906	1.986854	1.934067	2.219082	2.148285	2.451479	2.709074	2.812755	
κ	-0.031558	-0.020003	-0.013035	-0.006912	-0.079890	-0.066806	-0.085219	-0.162752	-0.201532	

VITAL STATISTICS		THOMPSON AGE RANGE	NRR	1000r	INTERVAL	BOURGEOIS-PICHAT AGE RANGE	NRR	1000b	1000d	1000r	COALE	
GRR	1.407										IBR	**TABLE 8**
NRR	1.368	0-4	1.29	9.31	27.45	5-29	1.91	21.44	-2.58	24.02	IDR	RATES FROM AGE DISTRIBUTIONS AND VITAL STATISTICS (Females)
TFR	2.897	5-9	1.27	8.64	27.43	30-54	0.96	13.04	14.66	-1.62	IRI	
GENERATION	28.065	10-14	1.30	9.45	27.39	55-79	1.88	50.30	26.95	23.34	K1	
SEX RATIO	105.828	15-19	1.04	1.49	27.33	*40-64	1.31	22.73	12.71	10.02	K2	

Start Age Interval	ORIGINAL MATRIX SUB-DIAGONAL	ALTERNATIVE FIRST ROWS Projection	ALTERNATIVE FIRST ROWS Integral	FIRST STABLE MATRIX % IN STABLE POPULATION	FISHER VALUES	REPRODUCTIVE VALUES	SECOND STABLE MATRIX Z₂ FIRST COLUMN	SECOND STABLE MATRIX Z₂ FIRST ROW	
0	0.99675	0.00000	0.00000	9.484	1.046	157523	0.1636+0.0774	0.1636+0.0774	**TABLE 9**
5	0.99843	0.00002	0.00000	8.940	1.110	163390	0.1675-0.1294	0.0044+0.1547	LESLIE
10	0.99860	0.03592	0.00005	8.441	1.175	181437	-0.0461-0.2436	-0.1160+0.0633	MATRIX
15	0.99814	0.23615	0.07392	7.971	1.207	152384	-0.2788-0.0813	-0.0990-0.0666	AND ITS
20	0.99780	0.40955	0.41250	7.525	1.031	104787	-0.2329+0.2477	-0.0264-0.1194	SPECTRAL
25	0.99717	0.34931	0.43072	7.100	0.663	65461	0.1348+0.3744	0.0136-0.0982	COMPONENTS
30	0.99558	0.21572	0.28847	6.696	0.337	37233	0.4619+0.0581	0.0227-0.0549	(Females)
35	0.99323	0.10283	0.15585	6.304	0.131	16920	0.3052-0.4499	0.0152-0.0207	
40	0.98988	0.02959	0.05601	5.921	0.032	3997	-0.3059-0.5546	0.0049-0.0044	
45	0.98500	0.00240	0.00490	5.543	0.002	291	-0.7351+0.0245	0.0004-0.0003	
50	0.97579	0.00002	0.00004	5.163	0.000	2	-0.3601+0.7698	0.0000-0.0000	
55+	0.81651			20.912					

Start Age Interval	OBSERVED POPUL. (IN 100's)	CONTRIBUTIONS OF ROOTS (IN 100's) r_1	r_2, r_3	$r_4 \cdot r_{11}$	AGE-SP. BIRTH RATES	NET MATERNITY FUNCTION	COEFF. OF MATRIX EQUATION	PARAMETERS	PARAMETERS INTEGRAL	PARAMETERS MATRIX	EXP. INCREASE x	EXP. INCREASE $e^{(x+2\frac{1}{2})r}$	
0	1506	1520	-26	13	0.0000	0.0000	0.0000	L(1)	1.05736	1.05743	0	1.0283	**TABLE 10**
5	1472	1432	83	-43	0.0000	0.0000	0.0000	L(2)	0.38040	0.38667	50	1.7961	AGE
10	1544	1352	124	67	0.0000	0.0000	0.0357		0.78548	0.75974	55	1.8991	ANALYSIS
15	1263	1277	18	-33	0.0146	0.0714	0.2347	R(1)	0.01115	0.01117	60	2.0081	AND
20	1016	1206	-151	-38	0.0816	0.3979	0.4063	R(2)	-0.02722	-0.03192	65	2.1233	MISCELLANEOUS
25	987	1138	-186	35	0.0852	0.4146	0.3457		0.22396	0.22000	70	2.2450	RESULTS
30	1105	1073	10	22	0.0571	0.2769	0.2129	C(1)		16022	75	2.3738	(Females)
35	1288	1010	264	14	0.0308	0.1489	0.1010	C(2)		4415	80	2.5100	
40	1268	949	266	54	0.0111	0.0532	0.0289			26386	85	2.6540	
45	1213	888	-78	403	0.0010	0.0046	0.0023	2P/Y	28.0549	28.5595	90	2.8062	
50	1133	827	-438	744	0.0000	0.0000	0.0000	DELTA	7.1200		95	2.9671	
55+	4173	3351									00	3.1373	

TABLE 1 — DATA

AGE AT LAST BIRTHDAY	POPULATION BOTH SEXES	MALES Number	%	FEMALES Number	%	BIRTHS BY AGE OF MOTHER	DEATHS BOTH SEXES	MALES	FEMALES	AGE AT LAST BIRTHDAY
0	61852	31650	1.7	30202	1.6	0	1068	605	463	0
1-4	244713	125589	6.9	119124	6.5	0	240	159	81	1-4
5-9	307911	157466	8.6	150445	8.2	0	144	98	46	5-9
10-14	301976	155249	8.5	146727	8.0	0	114	68	46	10-14
15-19	312034	160128	8.8	151906	8.3	5662	202	146	56	15-19
20-24	227594	116373	6.4	111221	6.0	19660	163	128	35	20-24
25-29	195769	99635	5.5	96134	5.2	16944	159	122	37	25-29
30-34	210561	106998	5.9	103563	5.6	11699	197	130	67	30-34
35-39	236580	120184	6.6	116396	6.3	6763	337	219	118	35-39
40-44	262302	131597	7.2	130705	7.1	2405	586	378	208	40-44
45-49	246968	123362	6.8	123606	6.7	157	839	518	321	45-49
50-54	235123	117118	6.4	118005	6.4	0	1277	817	460	50-54
55-59	208774	100876	5.5	107898	5.9	0	1962	1295	667	55-59
60-64	188860	89504	4.9	99356	5.4	0	2790	1714	1076	60-64
65-69	157528	73458	4.0	84070	4.6	0	3894	2328	1566	65-69
70-74	115653	52351	2.9	63302	3.4		5014	2611	2403	70-74
75-79	79665	34771	1.9	44894	2.4		5857	2787	3070	75-79
80-84	45409	19312	1.1	26097	1.4	32368 M.	5674	2539	3135	80-84
85+	27267	11270	0.6	15997	0.9	30922 F.	6333	2656	3677	85+
TOTAL	3666539	1826891		1839648		63290	36850	19318	17532	TOTAL

TABLE 2 — MALE LIFE TABLE

x	nq_x	l_x	nd_x	nL_x	nm_x	na_x	T_x	r_x	$\overset{\circ}{e}_x$	nM_x	x
0	0.018859	100000	1886	98658	0.019115	0.2882	7083040	0.0000	70.830	0.019115	
1	0.005046	98114	495	391039	0.001266	1.1367	6984383	0.0000	71.186	0.001266	
5	0.003107	97619	303	487337	0.000622	2.5000	6593344	0.0005	67.542	0.000622	
10	0.002188	97316	213	486076	0.000438	2.6373	6106007	0.0000	62.744	0.000438	10
15	0.004568	97103	444	484472	0.000916	2.6497	5619931	0.0280	57.876	0.000912	15
20	0.005500	96659	532	481997	0.001103	2.5561	5135459	0.0463	53.129	0.001100	20
25	0.006105	96128	587	479181	0.001225	2.5167	4653462	0.0072	48.409	0.001224	25
30	0.006057	95541	579	476315	0.001215	2.5989	4174281	0.0000	43.691	0.001215	30
35	0.009073	94962	862	472816	0.001822	2.6847	3697966	0.0000	38.941	0.001822	35
40	0.014266	94101	1342	467370	0.002872	2.6660	3225150	0.0000	34.273	0.002872	40
45	0.020824	92758	1932	459334	0.004205	2.6926	2757780	0.0072	29.731	0.004199	45
50	0.034444	90827	3128	447051	0.006998	2.7363	2298446	0.0125	25.306	0.006976	50
55	0.062489	87698	5480	425713	0.012873	2.6684	1851395	0.0141	21.111	0.012838	55
60	0.091919	82218	7557	393354	0.019213	2.6531	1425683	0.0168	17.340	0.019150	60
65	0.147808	74661	11035	347098	0.031793	2.6254	1032329	0.0168	13.827	0.031692	65
70	0.223146	63625	14198	283785	0.050030	2.5813	685231	0.0168	10.770	0.049875	70
75	0.335296	49427	16573	206114	0.080406	2.5247	401446	0.0168	8.122	0.080153	75
80	0.491908	32855	16161	122565	0.131860	2.5016	195332	0.0168	5.945	0.131473	80
85+	1.000000	16693	16693	72767	0.229405	4.3591	72767	0.0168	4.359	0.235669	85

TABLE 3 — FEMALE LIFE TABLE

x	nq_x	l_x	nd_x	nL_x	nm_x	na_x	T_x	r_x	$\overset{\circ}{e}_x$	nM_x	x
0	0.015145	100000	1514	98856	0.015320	0.2446	7546991	0.0008	75.470	0.015330	
1	0.002712	98486	267	393167	0.000679	1.0979	7448135	0.0008	75.627	0.000680	
5	0.001527	98218	150	490717	0.000306	2.5000	7054968	0.0013	71.829	0.000306	5
10	0.001566	98068	154	489965	0.000314	2.5411	6564251	0.0000	66.935	0.000314	10
15	0.001842	97915	180	489124	0.000369	2.5001	6074286	0.0274	62.036	0.000369	15
20	0.001573	97735	154	488290	0.000315	2.5102	5585162	0.0454	57.146	0.000315	20
25	0.001925	97581	188	487468	0.000385	2.6784	5096873	0.0067	52.232	0.000385	25
30	0.003230	97393	315	486241	0.000647	2.7007	4609405	0.0000	47.328	0.000647	30
35	0.005057	97078	491	484259	0.001014	2.6915	4123163	0.0000	42.473	0.001014	35
40	0.007928	96587	766	481179	0.001591	2.7034	3638905	0.0000	37.675	0.001591	40
45	0.012925	95822	1238	476234	0.002601	2.6791	3157726	0.0076	32.954	0.002597	45
50	0.019351	94583	1830	468673	0.003905	2.6816	2681492	0.0095	28.351	0.003898	50
55	0.030552	92753	2834	457293	0.006197	2.7161	2212819	0.0106	23.857	0.006182	55
60	0.053044	89919	4770	438674	0.010873	2.7102	1755526	0.0170	19.523	0.010830	60
65	0.089787	85150	7645	408468	0.018717	2.7398	1316852	0.0170	15.465	0.018627	65
70	0.175074	77504	13569	355927	0.038123	2.6716	908384	0.0170	11.720	0.037961	70
75	0.294355	63935	18820	274178	0.068640	2.5824	552458	0.0170	8.641	0.068383	75
80	0.465727	45116	21012	174150	0.120652	2.5524	278280	0.0170	6.168	0.120129	80
85+	*1.000000	24104	24104	104129	0.231482	4.3200	104129	0.0170	4.320	0.229856	85

TABLE 4 — OBSERVED AND PROJECTED VITAL RATES

	OBSERVED POPULATION BOTH SEXES	MALES	FEMALES	PROJECTED POPULATION 1968 MALES	FEMALES	1973 MALES	FEMALES	1978 MALES	FEMALES	STABLE POPULATION MALES	FEMALES
RATES PER THOUSAND											
Birth	17.26	17.72	16.81	19.11	18.12	20.17	19.13	20.48	19.43	21.23	20.2
Death	10.05	10.57	9.53	10.88	9.76	11.20	10.17	11.43	10.50	9.49	8.5
Increase	7.21	7.14	7.28	8.23	8.36	8.97	8.96	9.05	8.92		11.740
PERCENTAGE											
under 15	25.00	25.72	24.27	25.37	24.08	25.73	24.48	26.74	25.53	28.48	27.3
15-64	63.40	63.81	62.99	63.62	62.40	62.90	61.44	61.48	59.95	62.31	61.4
65 and over	11.61	10.46	12.74	11.02	13.52	11.36	14.09	11.78	14.52	9.21	11.1
DEP. RATIO X 100	57.73	56.71	58.76	57.19	60.26	58.97	62.77	62.66	66.80	60.49	62.7

TABLE 5 — POPULATION PROJECTED WITH FIXED AGE-SPECIFIC BIRTH AND DEATH RATES (IN 1000's)

AGE AT LAST BIRTHDAY	1968 BOTH SEXES	1968 MALES	1968 FEMALES	1973 BOTH SEXES	1973 MALES	1973 FEMALES	1978 BOTH SEXES	1978 MALES	1978 FEMALES	AGE AT LAST BIRTHDAY
0-4	329	168	161	366	187	179	396	202	194	0-4
5-9	305	156	149	328	167	161	365	186	179	5-9
10-14	307	157	150	305	156	149	328	167	161	10-14
15-19	301	155	146	307	157	150	304	156	148	15-19
20-24	311	159	152	300	154	146	306	156	150	20-24
25-29	227	116	111	309	158	151	299	153	146	25-29
30-34	195	99	96	226	115	111	308	157	151	30-34
35-39	209	106	103	194	98	96	224	114	110	35-39
40-44	235	119	116	207	105	102	192	97	95	40-44
45-49	258	129	129	231	117	114	204	103	101	45-49
50-54	242	120	122	253	126	127	227	114	113	50-54
55-59	227	112	115	233	114	119	244	120	124	55-59
60-64	197	93	104	213	103	110	220	106	114	60-64
65-69	172	79	93	178	82	96	194	91	103	65-69
70-74	133	60	73	146	65	81	151	67	84	70-74
75-79	87	38	49	100	44	56	109	47	62	75-79
80-84	50	21	29	54	23	31	62	26	36	80-84
85+	27	11	16	29	12	17	32	13	19	85+
TOTAL	3812	1898	1914	3979	1983	1996	4165	2075	2090	TOTAL

TABLE 6 — STANDARDIZED RATES

STANDARD COUNTRIES: STANDARDIZED RATES PER THOUSAND	ENGLAND AND WALES 1961 BOTH SEXES	MALES	FEMALES	UNITED STATES 1960 BOTH SEXES	MALES	FEMALES	MEXICO 1960 BOTH SEXES	MALES	FEMALES
Birth	18.45	19.42*	17.47	18.76	18.11*	18.06	21.73	16.59*	21.18
Death	10.13	9.84*	10.47	8.13	8.90*	7.54	4.06	7.65*	3.41
Increase	8.32	9.58*	7.00	10.62	9.22*	10.52	17.66	8.94*	17.77

TABLE 7 — MOMENTS AND CUMULANTS

	OBSERVED POP. MALES	OBSERVED POP. FEMALES	STATIONARY POP. MALES	STATIONARY POP. FEMALES	STABLE POP. MALES	STABLE POP. FEMALES	OBSERVED BIRTHS	NET MATERNITY FUNCTION	BIRTHS IN STABLE POP.
μ	34.31116	35.98601	37.74309	39.41170	31.83678	33.13207	27.66464	27.80758	27.38481
σ^2	496.6269	526.9078	522.2047	552.2065	478.6820	511.0991	39.45063	34.57972	33.27035
κ_3	3216.807	2784.194	2262.682	1753.352	4954.034	5040.910	129.2482	109.9760	112.8107
κ_4	-240448.	-288465.	-273844.	-324926.	-174061.	-219754.	-668.376	-307.069	-167.557
β_1	0.084481	0.052990	0.035952	0.018257	0.223757	0.190328	0.272074	0.292504	0.345564
β_2	2.025098	1.960979	1.995797	1.934432	2.240359	2.158748	2.570550	2.743201	2.848627
κ	-0.030848	-0.018965	-0.013460	-0.006617	-0.084591	-0.069683	-0.133110	-0.171751	-0.213003

TABLE 8 — RATES FROM AGE DISTRIBUTIONS AND VITAL STATISTICS (Females)

VITAL STATISTICS		THOMPSON AGE RANGE	NRR	1000r	INTERVAL	BOURGEOIS-PICHAT AGE RANGE	NRR	1000b	1000d	1000r	COALE	
GRR	1.419					5-29	1.87	21.50	-1.62	23.12	IBR	
NRR	1.383	0-4	1.25	8.12	27.46	30-54	0.80	9.44	17.67	-8.23	IDR	
TFR	2.905	5-9	1.31	9.80	27.43	55-79	1.66	38.99	20.11	18.87	IRI	
GENERATION	27.595	10-14	1.25	8.23	27.39	*40-64	1.28	21.87	12.70	9.18	K1	
SEX RATIO	104.676	15-19	1.27	8.39	27.33						K2	

TABLE 9 — LESLIE MATRIX AND ITS SPECTRAL COMPONENTS (Females)

ORIGINAL MATRIX SUB-DIAGONAL	ALTERNATIVE FIRST ROWS Projection	ALTERNATIVE FIRST ROWS Integral	% IN STABLE POPULATION	FISHER VALUES	REPRODUCTIVE VALUES	SECOND STABLE MATRIX Z2 FIRST COLUMN	FIRST ROW
0.99735	0.00000	0.00000	9.692	1.046	156258	0.1672+0.0777	0.1672+0.0777
0.99847	0.00000	0.00000	9.114	1.113	167404	0.1671-0.1364	0.0026+0.1576
0.99828	0.04472	0.00000	8.581	1.182	173417	-0.0584-0.2458	-0.1201+0.0606
0.99830	0.25690	0.09227	8.077	1.209	183614	-0.2889-0.0640	-0.0988-0.0732
0.99832	0.42396	0.43758	7.603	1.015	112869	-0.2149+0.2717	-0.0236-0.1232
0.99748	0.34729	0.43632	7.157	0.634	60918	0.1766+0.3652	0.0149-0.0970
0.99592	0.20533	0.27965	6.732	0.309	32044	0.4747+0.0004	0.0219-0.0517
0.99364	0.09181	0.14384	6.321	0.114	13240	0.2422-0.4989	0.0136-0.0184
0.98972	0.02362	0.04555	5.923	0.025	3231	-0.4001-0.5077	0.0039-0.0036
0.98412	0.00153	0.00312	5.527	0.002	187	-0.7330+0.1610	0.0003-0.0002
0.97572	0.00001	0.00002	5.129	0.000	1	-0.2017+0.8425	0.0000-0.0000
0.81211			20.144				

TABLE 10 — AGE ANALYSIS AND MISCELLANEOUS RESULTS (Females)

OBSERVED POPUL. (IN 100's)	CONTRIBUTIONS OF ROOTS (IN 100's) r1	r2, r3	r4-r11	AGE-SP. BIRTH RATES	NET MATERNITY FUNCTION	COEFF. OF MATRIX EQUATION	PARAMETERS	INTEGRAL	MATRIX	EXP. INCREASE x	e(x+2½)r
1493	1580	-82	-5	0.0000	0.0000	0.0000	L(1)	1.06046	1.06054	0	1.0298
1504	1486	2	17	0.0000	0.0000	0.0000	L(2)	0.36497	0.37175	50	1.8522
1467	1399	114	-45	0.0000	0.0000	0.0445		0.79437	0.76717	55	1.9641
1519	1317	114	88	0.0182	0.0891	0.2554	R(1)	0.01174	0.01176	60	2.0829
1112	1240	-40	-88	0.0864	0.4217	0.4207	R(2)	-0.02689	-0.03192	65	2.2088
961	1167	-196	-9	0.0861	0.4198	0.3441			0.22802	0.22802	70	2.3424
1036	1098	-146	84	0.0552	0.2684	0.2029	C(1)		16304	75	2.4840
1164	1031	119	14	0.0284	0.1375	0.0904	C(2)		-15398	80	2.6341
1307	966	321	21	0.0090	0.0433	0.0231			19452	85	2.7934
1236	901	163	172	0.0006	0.0030	0.0015	2P/Y	27.5550	28.0608	90	2.9623
1180	836	-266	609	0.0000	0.0000	0.0000	DELTA	7.6945		95	3.1414
4416	3284									100	3.3313

TABLE 1 — DATA

AGE AT LAST BIRTHDAY	POPULATION BOTH SEXES	MALES Number	%	FEMALES Number	%	BIRTHS BY AGE OF MOTHER	DEATHS BOTH SEXES	MALES	FEMALES	AGE AT LAST BIRTHDAY
0	63507	32639	1.8	30868	1.7	0	1078	612	466	0
1-4	244631	125459	6.8	119172	6.4	0	268	147	121	1-4
5-9	308305	157775	8.6	150530	8.1	0	150	107	43	5-9
10-14	301299	154577	8.4	146722	7.9	0	82	56	26	10-14
15-19	317114	162782	8.8	154332	8.3	6106	198	151	47	15-19
20-24	240513	123350	6.7	117163	6.3	21079	181	142	39	20-24
25-29	199633	101493	5.5	98140	5.3	17883	162	120	42	25-29
30-34	204967	104202	5.7	100765	5.4	11464	207	138	69	30-34
35-39	228991	116240	6.3	112751	6.1	6467	331	223	108	35-39
40-44	262967	132212	7.2	130755	7.1	2415	563	354	209	40-44
45-49	247153	123284	6.7	123869	6.7	156	813	535	278	45-49
50-54	237193	118262	6.4	118931	6.4	0	1266	830	436	50-54
55-59	212132	102951	5.6	109181	5.9	0	1842	1200	642	55-59
60-64	190807	90427	4.9	100380	5.4	0	2791	1746	1045	60-64
65-69	161296	74874	4.1	86422	4.7	0	3933	2297	1636	65-69
70-74	119414	54157	2.9	65257	3.5		4692	2498	2194	70-74
75-79	80882	35323	1.9	45559	2.5		5502	2654	2848	75-79
80-84	45710	19265	1.0	26445	1.4	33969 M.	5312	2377	2935	80-84
85+	27825	11553	0.6	16272	0.9	31601 F.	5800	2477	3323	85+
TOTAL	3694339	1840825		1853514		65570	35171	18664	16507	TOTA

TABLE 2 — MALE LIFE TABLE

x	$_nq_x$	l_x	$_nd_x$	$_nL_x$	$_nm_x$	$_na_x$	T_x	r_x	$\mathring{e}_x$	$_nM_x$
0	0.018457	100000	1846	98674	0.018705	0.2818	7126599	0.0031	71.266	0.018751
1	0.004658	98154	457	391305	0.001168	1.1302	7027925	0.0031	71.601	0.001172
5	0.003384	97697	331	487659	0.000678	2.5000	6636620	0.0015	67.931	0.000678
10	0.001810	97366	176	486417	0.000362	2.6430	6148962	0.0000	63.153	0.000362
15	0.004646	97190	452	484901	0.000931	2.6754	5662545	0.0217	58.262	0.000928
20	0.005752	96739	556	482326	0.001154	2.5433	5177643	0.0461	53.522	0.001151
25	0.005897	96182	567	479509	0.001183	2.5274	4695317	0.0157	48.817	0.001182
30	0.006601	95615	631	476568	0.001324	2.6122	4215808	0.0000	44.091	0.001324
35	0.009549	94984	907	472781	0.001918	2.6425	3739240	0.0000	39.367	0.001918
40	0.013305	94077	1252	467482	0.002678	2.6814	3266459	0.0000	34.721	0.002678
45	0.021512	92825	1997	459528	0.004346	2.6974	2798977	0.0066	30.153	0.004340
50	0.034611	90828	3144	446906	0.007034	2.6984	2339449	0.0107	25.757	0.007018
55	0.056925	87685	4991	426887	0.011693	2.6888	1892543	0.0146	21.584	0.011656
60	0.092723	82693	7668	395498	0.019387	2.6567	1465656	0.0206	17.724	0.019308
65	0.143394	75026	10758	349423	0.030789	2.6106	1070157	0.0206	14.264	0.030678
70	0.208207	64267	13381	289016	0.046298	2.5845	720735	0.0206	11.215	0.046125
75	0.318120	50886	16188	214604	0.075432	2.5396	431719	0.0206	8.484	0.075135
80	0.474361	34698	16460	132771	0.123970	2.5260	217115	0.0206	6.257	0.123385
85+	*1.000000	18239	18239	84345	0.216242	4.6245	84345	0.0206	4.624	0.214403

TABLE 3 — FEMALE LIFE TABLE

x	$_nq_x$	l_x	$_nd_x$	$_nL_x$	$_nm_x$	$_na_x$	T_x	r_x	$\mathring{e}_x$	$_nM_x$
0	0.014904	100000	1490	98942	0.015064	0.2900	7608098	0.0028	76.081	0.015097
1	0.004039	98510	398	392900	0.001013	1.1386	7509157	0.0028	76.228	0.001015
5	0.001426	98112	140	490209	0.000285	2.5000	7116257	0.0018	72.532	0.000286
10	0.000886	97972	87	489644	0.000177	2.5225	6626048	0.0000	67.632	0.000177
15	0.001525	97885	149	489068	0.000305	2.6065	6136405	0.0222	62.690	0.000305
20	0.001669	97736	163	488283	0.000334	2.5764	5647337	0.0449	57.782	0.000333
25	0.002143	97573	209	487376	0.000429	2.6691	5159054	0.0146	52.874	0.000428
30	0.003418	97363	333	486038	0.000685	2.6594	4671679	0.0000	47.982	0.000685
35	0.004779	97031	464	484085	0.000958	2.6959	4185640	0.0000	43.137	0.000958
40	0.007962	96567	769	481039	0.001598	2.6645	3701555	0.0000	38.331	0.001598
45	0.011179	95798	1071	476512	0.002247	2.6860	3220516	0.0071	33.618	0.002244
50	0.018209	94727	1725	469640	0.003673	2.6974	2744004	0.0088	28.967	0.003666
55	0.029084	93002	2705	458852	0.005895	2.7228	2274340	0.0107	24.455	0.005880
60	0.051137	90297	4618	441007	0.010470	2.7305	1815488	0.0226	20.106	0.010410
65	0.091187	85680	7813	410447	0.019035	2.7023	1374481	0.0226	16.042	0.018930
70	0.156711	77867	12203	360936	0.033804	2.6727	964033	0.0226	12.381	0.033621
75	0.273044	65664	17929	285330	0.062837	2.6021	603097	0.0226	9.185	0.062512
80	0.439749	47735	20991	188033	0.111637	2.5875	317768	0.0226	6.657	0.110984
85+	*1.000000	26744	26744	129735	0.206141	4.8511	129735	0.0226	4.851	0.204216

TABLE 4 — OBSERVED AND PROJECTED VITAL RATES

	OBSERVED POPULATION BOTH SEXES	MALES	FEMALES	PROJECTED POPULATION 1969 MALES	FEMALES	1974 MALES	FEMALES	1979 MALES	FEMALES	STABLE POPULATION MALES	FEMALES
RATES PER THOUSAND											
Birth	17.75	18.45	17.05	19.91	18.42	20.82	19.30	20.89	19.42	21.31	20.3
Death	9.52	10.14	8.91	10.57	9.47	10.96	9.99	11.19	10.38	9.33	8.3
Increase	8.23	8.31	8.14	9.34	8.95	9.86	9.31	9.70	9.04	11.985	
PERCENTAGE											
under 15	24.84	25.56	24.13	25.56	24.04	26.25	24.58	27.50	25.70	28.56	27.4
15-64	63.38	63.84	62.92	63.20	62.04	62.10	60.88	60.45	59.33	62.05	61.1
65 and over	11.78	10.60	12.95	11.23	13.92	11.64	14.54	12.05	14.98	9.39	11.4
DEP. RATIO X 100	57.78	56.64	58.93	58.22	61.18	61.02	64.24	65.42	68.55	61.16	63.5

TABLE 5 — POPULATION PROJECTED WITH FIXED AGE-SPECIFIC BIRTH AND DEATH RATES (IN 1000's)

AGE LAST BIRTHDAY	1969 BOTH SEXES	1969 MALES	1969 FEMALES	1974 BOTH SEXES	1974 MALES	1974 FEMALES	1979 BOTH SEXES	1979 MALES	1979 FEMALES	AGE AT LAST BIRTHDAY
0-4	342	177	165	381	197	184	410	212	198	0-4
5-9	307	157	150	341	176	165	379	196	183	5-9
10-14	307	157	150	306	157	149	341	176	165	10-14
15-19	301	154	147	307	157	150	305	156	149	15-19
20-24	316	162	154	299	153	146	306	156	150	20-24
25-29	240	123	117	315	161	154	298	152	146	25-29
30-34	199	101	98	239	122	117	313	160	153	30-34
35-39	203	103	100	197	100	97	237	121	116	35-39
40-44	227	115	112	202	102	100	196	99	97	40-44
45-49	260	130	130	224	113	111	199	100	99	45-49
50-54	242	120	122	254	126	128	219	110	109	50-54
55-59	229	113	116	234	115	119	246	121	125	55-59
60-64	200	95	105	217	105	112	221	106	115	60-64
65-69	173	80	93	182	84	98	196	92	104	65-69
70-74	138	62	76	148	66	82	156	70	86	70-74
75-79	92	40	52	106	46	60	114	49	65	75-79
80-84	52	22	30	59	25	34	68	28	40	80-84
85+	30	12	18	35	14	21	39	16	23	85+
TOTAL	3858	1923	1935	4046	2019	2027	4243	2120	2123	TOTAL

TABLE 6 — STANDARDIZED RATES

STANDARD COUNTRIES:	ENGLAND AND WALES 1961 BOTH SEXES	MALES	FEMALES	UNITED STATES 1960 BOTH SEXES	MALES	FEMALES	MEXICO 1960 BOTH SEXES	MALES	FEMALES
STANDARDIZED RATES PER THOUSAND									
Birth	18.80	20.23*	17.56	19.12	18.76*	18.16	22.21	17.40*	21.36
Death	9.51	9.35*	9.69	7.66	8.46*	7.01	3.89	7.28*	3.23
Increase	9.30	10.88*	7.88	11.46	10.30*	11.15	18.33	10.12*	18.12

TABLE 7 — MOMENTS AND CUMULANTS

	OBSERVED POP. MALES	FEMALES	STATIONARY POP. MALES	FEMALES	STABLE POP. MALES	FEMALES	OBSERVED BIRTHS	NET MATERNITY FUNCTION	BIRTHS IN STABLE POP.
μ	34.35535	36.04621	37.97481	39.75448	31.87249	33.23897	27.42192	27.73106	27.30235
μ_2	498.7522	529.5139	529.3169	561.9968	483.3610	518.3127	38.73183	34.35286	33.01481
K_3	3251.117	2808.568	2325.047	1801.588	5127.329	5257.302	140.0748	110.3505	112.6599
K_4	−244460.	−294014.	−281658.	−336948.	−174746.	−223103.	−477.256	−256.885	−120.512
β_1	0.085194	0.053130	0.036452	0.018286	0.232792	0.198495	0.337688	0.300372	0.352706
β_2	2.017262	1.951390	1.994711	1.933169	2.252063	2.169535	2.681862	2.782323	2.889436
K	−0.030894	−0.018873	−0.013627	−0.006621	−0.088041	−0.072714	−0.170103	−0.183674	−0.227705

TABLE 8 — RATES FROM AGE DISTRIBUTIONS AND VITAL STATISTICS (Females)

VITAL STATISTICS		THOMPSON AGE RANGE	NRR	1000r	INTERVAL	BOURGEOIS-PICHAT AGE RANGE	NRR	1000b	1000d	1000r	COALE	
RR	1.428										IBR	
RR	1.391	0-4	1.25	8.09	27.46	5-29	1.78	21.06	−0.26	21.32	IDR	
FR	2.963	5-9	1.30	9.76	27.43	30-54	0.76	8.53	18.73	−10.20	IRI	
GENERATION	27.515	10-14	1.26	8.42	27.40	55-79	1.63	37.13	19.09	18.04	K1	
SEX RATIO	107.493	15-19	1.29	9.16	27.34	*40-64	1.27	21.45	12.58	8.87	K2	

TABLE 9 — LESLIE MATRIX AND ITS SPECTRAL COMPONENTS (Females)

t age ival	ORIGINAL MATRIX SUB-DIAGONAL	ALTERNATIVE FIRST ROWS Projection	Integral	FIRST STABLE MATRIX % IN STABLE POPULATION	FISHER VALUES	REPRODUCTIVE VALUES	SECOND STABLE MATRIX Z_2 FIRST COLUMN	FIRST ROW
	0.99668	0.00000	0.00000	9.716	1.047	157158	0.1691+0.0771	0.1691+0.0771
	0.99885	0.00000	0.00000	9.120	1.116	167980	0.1664−0.1392	0.0029+0.1592
	0.99882	0.04684	0.00000	8.579	1.186	174057	−0.0628−0.2458	−0.1217+0.0610
	0.99840	0.25978	0.09664	8.070	1.212	187057	−0.2911−0.0579	−0.0999−0.0749
	0.99814	0.42880	0.43943	7.588	1.017	119100	−0.2080+0.2778	−0.0231−0.1248
	0.99726	0.35044	0.44507	7.132	0.631	61969	0.1880+0.3595	0.0151−0.0970
	0.99598	0.20255	0.27788	6.699	0.304	30659	0.4735−0.0168	0.0211−0.0513
	0.99371	0.08973	0.14009	6.283	0.111	12557	0.2208−0.5067	0.0131−0.0183
	0.99059	0.02336	0.04511	5.880	0.024	3194	−0.4209−0.4863	0.0038−0.0036
	0.98563	0.00149	0.00306	5.485	0.001	184	−0.7197+0.1969	0.0002−0.0002
	0.97698	0.00001	0.00002	5.092	0.000	1	−0.1536+0.8475	0.0000−0.0000
+	0.81749			20.357				

TABLE 10 — AGE ANALYSIS AND MISCELLANEOUS RESULTS (Females)

t age ival	OBSERVED POPUL. (IN 100's)	CONTRIBUTIONS OF ROOTS (IN 100's) r_1	r_2, r_3	$r_4 \cdot r_{11}$	AGE-SP. BIRTH RATES	NET MATERNITY FUNCTION	COEFF. OF MATRIX EQUATION	PARAMETERS	INTEGRAL	MATRIX	EXP. INCREASE x	$e^{(x+2\frac{1}{2})r}$
	1500	1602	−91	−11	0.0000	0.0000	0.0000	L(1)	1.06176	1.06185	0	1.0304
	1505	1504	−24	25	0.0000	0.0000	0.0000	L(2)	0.36194	0.36862	50	1.8762
	1467	1415	100	−48	0.0000	0.0000	0.0466		0.79795	0.77020	55	1.9920
	1543	1331	134	79	0.0191	0.0933	0.2583	R(1)	0.01199	0.01200	60	2.1151
	1172	1251	−2	−78	0.0867	0.4234	0.4257	R(2)	−0.02643	−0.03159	65	2.2457
	981	1176	−185	−10	0.0878	0.4280	0.3473		0.22899	0.22488	70	2.3844
	1008	1105	−183	86	0.0548	0.2665	0.2002	C(1)		16491	75	2.5316
	1128	1036	67	25	0.0276	0.1338	0.0883	C(2)		−19904	80	2.6880
	1308	970	316	22	0.0089	0.0428	0.0229			15268	85	2.8540
	1239	905	226	108	0.0006	0.0029	0.0014	2P/Y	27.4383	27.9399	90	3.0302
	1189	840	−198	547	0.0000	0.0000	0.0000	DELTA	7.8833		95	3.2174
+	4495	3357									100	3.4161

TABLE 1 — DATA

AGE AT LAST BIRTHDAY	POPULATION BOTH SEXES	MALES Number	MALES %	FEMALES Number	FEMALES %	BIRTHS BY AGE OF MOTHER	DEATHS BOTH SEXES	DEATHS MALES	FEMALES	AGE AT LAST BIRTHDAY
.0	617207	318728	2.2	298479	2.0	0	37571	21586	15985	0
1-4	2831871	1461922	10.2	1369949	9.0	0	4769	2557	2212	1-4
5-9	3526304	1816605	12.7	1709699	11.2	0	1932	1181	751	5-9
10-14	2963465	1522214	10.6	1441251	9.4	299	1379	880	499	10-14
15-19	1980262	1006037	7.0	974225	6.4	43474	1687	1152	535	15-19
20-24	2024645	923800	6.5	1100845	7.2	222077	2939	2027	912	20-24
25-29	2322157	1162812	8.1	1159345	7.6	192556	3631	2349	1282	25-29
30-34	2326839	1139862	8.0	1186977	7.8	121441	4306	2706	1600	30-34
35-39	2014147	941866	6.6	1072281	7.0	63453	4687	2737	1950	35-39
40-44	1382458	644054	4.5	738404	4.8	15594	4229	2466	1763	40-44
45-49	1659157	770910	5.4	888247	5.8	1858	8160	4659	3501	45-49
50-54	1697732	804722	5.6	893010	5.8	188	12509	7638	4871	50-54
55-59	1408495	649973	4.5	758522	5.0	0	16485	10023	6462	55-59
60-64	1077829	464844	3.3	612985	4.0	0	20205	11527	8678	60-64
65-69	729226	298067	2.1	431159	2.8	0	21807	11464	10343	65-69
70-74	510857	195539	1.4	315318	2.1		24582	11429	13153	70-74
75-79	290930	106826	0.7	184104	1.2		22466	9598	12868	75-79
80-84	140854	48077	0.3	92777	0.6	342388 M.	17740	6906	10834	80-84
85+	72467	21922	0.2	50545	0.3	318552 F.	13083	4404	8679	85+
TOTAL	29576902	14298780		15278122		660940	224167	117289	106878	TOTAL

TABLE 2 — MALE LIFE TABLE

x	$_nq_x$	l_x	$_nd_x$	$_nL_x$	$_nm_x$	$_na_x$	T_x	r_x	$\dot{e}_x$	$_nM_x$	x
0	0.064194	100000	6419	94786	0.067725	0.1878	6485434	0.0000	64.854	0.067725	0
1	0.006961	93581	651	372409	0.001749	1.0626	6390648	0.0000	68.290	0.001749	1
5	0.003231	92929	300	463895	0.000647	2.5000	6018239	0.0147	64.762	0.000650	5
10	0.002918	92629	270	462518	0.000584	2.6809	5554344	0.0584	59.963	0.000578	10
15	0.005792	92359	535	460609	0.001161	2.7850	5091826	0.0487	55.131	0.001145	15
20	0.010913	91824	1002	456692	0.002194	2.5786	4631217	0.0000	50.436	0.002194	20
25	0.010050	90822	913	451839	0.002020	2.5138	4174525	0.0000	45.964	0.002020	25
30	0.011819	89909	1063	446967	0.002377	2.5738	3722686	0.0187	41.405	0.002374	30
35	0.014510	88846	1289	441134	0.002922	2.5975	3275719	0.0541	36.870	0.002906	35
40	0.019025	87557	1666	433886	0.003839	2.6589	2834585	0.0160	32.374	0.003829	40
45	0.029800	85891	2560	423519	0.006044	2.6798	2400699	0.0000	27.950	0.006044	45
50	0.046502	83332	3875	407680	0.009505	2.6827	1977180	0.0071	23.727	0.009491	50
55	0.074991	79457	5959	383389	0.015542	2.6681	1569501	0.0387	19.753	0.015421	55
60	0.118122	73498	8682	346941	0.025024	2.6329	1186112	0.0488	16.138	0.024798	60
65	0.177362	64816	11496	296394	0.038786	2.5914	839171	0.0488	12.947	0.038461	65
70	0.257453	53321	13727	232934	0.058933	2.5474	542777	0.0488	10.180	0.058449	70
75	0.369233	39593	14619	161313	0.090625	2.4928	309843	0.0488	7.826	0.089847	75
80	0.529532	24974	13225	91211	0.144988	2.4548	148530	0.0488	5.947	0.143645	80
85+	*1.000000	11749	11749	57319	0.204982	4.8785	57319	0.0488	4.878	0.200894	85

TABLE 3 — FEMALE LIFE TABLE

x	$_nq_x$	l_x	$_nd_x$	$_nL_x$	$_nm_x$	$_na_x$	T_x	r_x	$\dot{e}_x$	$_nM_x$	x
0	0.051363	100000	5136	95908	0.053555	0.2033	7069293	0.0000	70.693	0.053555	0
1	0.006428	94864	610	377669	0.001615	1.0709	6973385	0.0000	73.510	0.001615	1
5	0.002179	94254	205	470756	0.000436	2.5000	6595717	0.0138	69.978	0.000439	5
10	0.001736	94048	163	469845	0.000348	2.5680	6124961	0.0558	65.126	0.000346	10
15	0.002755	93885	259	468826	0.000552	2.6802	5655116	0.0264	60.234	0.000549	15
20	0.004134	93626	387	467218	0.000828	2.6375	5186290	0.0000	55.393	0.000828	20
25	0.005514	93239	514	464961	0.001106	2.5958	4719072	0.0000	50.612	0.001106	25
30	0.006723	92725	623	462135	0.001349	2.6084	4254111	0.0064	45.879	0.001348	30
35	0.009103	92102	838	458510	0.001828	2.6151	3791975	0.0456	41.172	0.001819	35
40	0.011907	91264	1087	453793	0.002395	2.6769	3333465	0.0162	36.526	0.002388	40
45	0.019527	90177	1761	446752	0.003941	2.6536	2879672	0.0000	31.934	0.003941	45
50	0.026976	88416	2385	436503	0.005464	2.6620	2432920	0.0100	27.517	0.005455	50
55	0.042022	86031	3615	421807	0.008571	2.6911	1996417	0.0286	23.206	0.008519	55
60	0.069178	82416	5701	398904	0.014293	2.6893	1574609	0.0431	19.106	0.014157	60
65	0.114654	76714	8796	363102	0.024223	2.6728	1175705	0.0431	15.326	0.023989	65
70	0.191340	67919	12996	308713	0.042096	2.6237	812603	0.0431	11.964	0.041713	70
75	0.300672	54923	16514	234243	0.070499	2.5552	503890	0.0431	9.174	0.069895	75
80	0.452323	38409	17373	147666	0.117653	2.5542	269647	0.0431	7.020	0.116775	80
85+	1.000000	21036	21036	121981	0.172453	5.7987	121981	0.0431	5.799	0.171709	85

TABLE 4 — OBSERVED AND PROJECTED VITAL RATES

	OBSERVED POPULATION BOTH SEXES	MALES	FEMALES	PROJECTED POPULATION 1965 MALES	1965 FEMALES	1970 MALES	1970 FEMALES	1975 MALES	1975 FEMALES	STABLE POPULATION MALES	FEMALES
RATES PER THOUSAND											
Birth	22.35	23.95	20.85	22.04	19.35	23.06	20.40	24.71	22.04	22.17	20.7
Death	7.58	8.20	7.00	8.59	7.61	9.22	8.31	9.80	9.01	11.50	10.1
Increase	14.77	15.74	13.85	13.45	11.74	13.84	12.09	14.91	13.03		10.670
PERCENTAGE											
under 15	33.60	35.80	31.54	33.63	29.86	30.53	27.35	29.15	26.38	28.56	27.1
15-64	60.50	59.51	61.43	60.79	61.81	62.83	63.10	63.28	62.98	62.96	61.8
65 and over	5.90	4.69	7.03	5.58	8.33	6.64	9.56	7.57	10.63	8.48	11.0
DEP. RATIO X 100	65.29	68.05	62.80	64.51	61.78	59.15	58.49	58.04	58.78	58.84	61.7

TABLE 5 — POPULATION PROJECTED WITH FIXED AGE-SPECIFIC BIRTH AND DEATH RATES (IN 1000's)

AGE LAST BIRTHDAY	1965 BOTH SEXES	1965 MALES	1965 FEMALES	1970 BOTH SEXES	1970 MALES	1970 FEMALES	1975 BOTH SEXES	1975 MALES	1975 FEMALES	AGE AT LAST BIRTHDAY
0-4	3092	1591	1501	3259	1677	1582	3701	1905	1796	0-4
5-9	3426	1768	1658	3072	1580	1492	3237	1665	1572	5-9
10-14	3517	1811	1706	3418	1763	1655	3064	1575	1489	10-14
15-19	2954	1516	1438	3507	1804	1703	3408	1756	1652	15-19
20-24	1968	997	971	2936	1503	1433	3485	1788	1697	20-24
25-29	2010	914	1096	1953	987	966	2913	1487	1426	25-29
30-34	2302	1150	1152	1993	904	1089	1936	976	960	30-34
35-39	2303	1125	1178	2278	1135	1143	1972	892	1080	35-39
40-44	1987	926	1061	2273	1107	1166	2248	1117	1131	40-44
45-49	1356	629	727	1949	904	1045	2227	1080	1147	45-49
50-54	1610	742	868	1315	605	710	1891	870	1021	50-54
55-59	1620	757	863	1537	698	839	1255	569	686	55-59
60-64	1305	588	717	1501	685	816	1425	632	793	60-64
65-69	955	397	558	1155	502	653	1328	585	743	65-69
70-74	601	234	367	786	312	474	950	395	555	70-74
75-79	374	135	239	440	162	278	576	216	360	75-79
80-84	176	60	116	228	77	151	267	92	175	80-84
85+	107	30	77	134	38	96	173	48	125	85+
TOTAL	31663	15370	16293	33734	16443	17291	36056	17648	18408	TOTAL

TABLE 6 — STANDARDIZED RATES

STANDARD COUNTRIES:	ENGLAND AND WALES 1961 BOTH SEXES	MALES	FEMALES	UNITED STATES 1960 BOTH SEXES	MALES	FEMALES	MEXICO 1960 BOTH SEXES	MALES	FEMALES
STANDARDIZED RATES PER THOUSAND									
Birth	19.00	21.98*	17.75	19.30	20.93*	18.32	22.62	20.26*	21.75
Death	12.11	13.88*	11.82	10.22	11.58*	9.07	6.30	8.05*	5.26
Increase	6.89	8.11*	5.93	9.07	9.36*	9.26	16.33	12.20*	16.49

TABLE 7 — MOMENTS AND CUMULANTS

	OBSERVED POP. MALES	OBSERVED POP. FEMALES	STATIONARY POP. MALES	STATIONARY POP. FEMALES	STABLE POP. MALES	STABLE POP. FEMALES	OBSERVED BIRTHS	NET MATERNITY FUNCTION	BIRTHS IN STABLE POP.
μ	28.04824	30.65016	36.67936	38.87390	31.48803	33.18797	27.45143	27.46589	27.05350
σ^2	412.3445	453.1114	504.5015	550.4811	464.6328	510.1957	33.79846	37.38336	35.74758
κ_3	4489.642	4297.149	2561.296	2262.273	4756.998	5108.291	121.4598	152.7373	153.5502
κ_4	-119553.	-164714.	-245258.	-311242.	-159148.	-210872.	-113.344	-162.723	17.206
β_1	0.287503	0.198493	0.051090	0.030681	0.225599	0.196490	0.382098	0.446535	0.516133
β_2	2.296860	2.197728	2.036395	1.972897	2.262805	2.189888	2.900779	2.883563	3.013465
κ	-0.106769	-0.074356	-0.019484	-0.011331	-0.086712	-0.073289	-0.236536	-0.241057	-0.291926

TABLE 8 — RATES FROM AGE DISTRIBUTIONS AND VITAL STATISTICS (Females)

VITAL STATISTICS		THOMPSON AGE RANGE	NRR	1000r	INTERVAL	BOURGEOIS-PICHAT AGE RANGE	NRR	1000b	1000d	1000r	COALE
GRR	1.440					5-29	1.73	24.95	4.63	20.32	IBR
NRR	1.338	0-4	1.57	16.78	27.41	30-54	1.40	23.10	10.76	12.35	IDR
TFR	2.988	5-9	1.63	18.00	27.37	55-79	2.87	112.43	73.33	39.10	IRI
GENERATION	27.258	10-14	1.41	12.36	27.32	*50-74	2.65	91.76	55.67	36.09	K1
SEX RATIO	107.483	15-19	1.01	0.20	27.24						K2

TABLE 9 — LESLIE MATRIX AND ITS SPECTRAL COMPONENTS (Females)

Start Age Interval	ORIGINAL MATRIX SUB-DIAGONAL	ALTERNATIVE FIRST ROWS Projection	ALTERNATIVE FIRST ROWS Integral	FIRST STABLE MATRIX % IN STABLE POPULATION	FISHER VALUES	REPRODUCTIVE VALUES	SECOND STABLE MATRIX Z_2 FIRST COLUMN	FIRST ROW
0	0.99404	0.00000	0.00000	9.581	1.084	1808975	0.1741+0.1010	0.1741+0.1010
5	0.99807	0.00024	0.00000	9.029	1.151	1967504	0.1997-0.1411	-0.0158+0.1648
10	0.99783	0.05105	0.00049	8.542	1.216	1752287	-0.0549-0.2933	-0.1282+0.0445
15	0.99657	0.28036	0.10461	8.080	1.230	1198136	-0.3532-0.0883	-0.0859-0.0855
20	0.99517	0.41886	0.47290	7.634	0.997	1097269	-0.2773+0.3462	-0.0146-0.1217
25	0.99392	0.30560	0.38935	7.202	0.600	695836	0.2422+0.4823	0.0127-0.0951
30	0.99216	0.18377	0.23984	6.786	0.304	360401	0.6554-0.0232	0.0220-0.0542
35	0.98971	0.09139	0.13872	6.382	0.122	130819	0.3060-0.7343	0.0159-0.0209
40	0.98449	0.02645	0.04951	5.988	0.030	22091	-0.6532-0.7070	0.0051-0.0045
45	0.97706	0.00262	0.00490	5.589	0.003	2597	-1.1013+0.3598	0.0005-0.0004
50	0.96633	0.00024	0.00049	5.176	0.000	221	-0.1579+1.3750	0.0000-0.0000
55+	0.80490			20.011				

TABLE 10 — AGE ANALYSIS AND MISCELLANEOUS RESULTS (Females)

Start Age Interval	OBSERVED POPUL. (IN 100's)	CONTRIBUTIONS OF ROOTS (IN 100's) r_1	r_2, r_3	$r_4\text{-}r_{11}$	AGE-SP. BIRTH RATES	NET MATERNITY FUNCTION	COEFF. OF MATRIX EQUATION	PARAMETERS	INTEGRAL	MATRIX	EXP. INCREASE x	$e^{(x+2\frac{1}{2})r}$
0	16684	15441	820	424	0.0000	0.0000	0.0000	L(1)	1.05480	1.05487	0	1.0270
5	17097	14550	2545	2	0.0000	0.0000	0.0002	L(2)	0.32809	0.34106	50	1.7510
10	14413	13767	1373	-728	0.0001	0.0005	0.0507		0.77212	0.74343	55	1.8470
15	9742	13022	-2391	-890	0.0215	0.1008	0.2776	R(1)	0.01067	0.01068	60	1.9482
20	11008	12303	-4471	3176	0.0972	0.4543	0.4132	R(2)	-0.03513	-0.04020	65	2.0549
25	11593	11607	-992	979	0.0801	0.3722	0.3000			0.23380	0.22814	70	2.1675
30	11870	10936	5604	-4671	0.0493	0.2279	0.1793	C(1)		161160	75	2.2863
35	10723	10286	7132	-6695	0.0285	0.1308	0.0885	C(2)		416536	80	2.4116
40	7384	9650	-1029	-1237	0.0102	0.0462	0.0253			312069	85	2.5438
45	8882	9007	-11420	11296	0.0010	0.0045	0.0025	2P/Y	26.8744	27.5414	90	2.6832
50	8930	8342	-9897	10485	0.0001	0.0004	0.0002	DELTA	7.5480		95	2.8302
55+	24454	32249									100	2.9853

TABLE 1 — DATA

AGE AT LAST BIRTHDAY	POPULATION BOTH SEXES	MALES Number	%	FEMALES Number	%	BIRTHS BY AGE OF MOTHER	DEATHS BOTH SEXES	MALES	FEMALES	AGE AT LAST BIRTHDAY
0	599600	309700	2.1	289900	1.9	0	32887	18976	13911	0
1-4	2643800	1359200	9.3	1284600	8.2	0	4053	2200	1853	1-4
5-9	3546499	1815099	12.4	1731400	11.1	0	1919	1151	768	5-9
10-14	3256000	1664100	11.3	1591900	10.2	0	1551	985	566	10-14
15-19	2164400	1093900	7.4	1070500	6.8	39199	1827	1267	560	15-19
20-24	2110500	1059000	7.2	1051500	6.7	202722	2860	2035	825	20-24
25-29	2296000	1150500	7.8	1145500	7.3	174123	3628	2459	1169	25-29
30-34	2384800	1181800	8.0	1203000	7.7	110060	4593	3010	1583	30-34
35-39	2150300	998900	6.8	1151400	7.4	56644	5115	3146	1969	35-39
40-44	1550300	719000	4.9	831300	5.3	15400	4947	2863	2084	40-44
45-49	1440600	656000	4.5	784600	5.0	1176	7103	4079	3024	45-49
50-54	1694500	789800	5.4	904700	5.8	181	12884	7784	5100	50-54
55-59	1470500	676600	4.6	793900	5.1	0	17498	10813	6685	55-59
60-64	1159200	504600	3.4	654600	4.2	0	22522	13213	9309	60-64
65-69	802200	327000	2.2	475200	3.0	0	25471	13561	11910	65-69
70-74	493565	194689	1.3	298876	1.9		27083	12777	14306	70-74
75-79	318858	113448	0.8	205410	1.3		26635	11332	15303	75-79
80-84	173535	54246	0.4	119289	0.8	311002 M.	20299	7880	12419	80-84
85+	68743	18318	0.1	50425	0.3	288503 F.	16324	5408	10916	85+
TOTAL	30323900	14685900		15638000		599505	239199	124939	114260	TOTAL

TABLE 2 — MALE LIFE TABLE

x	nq_x	l_x	nd_x	nL_x	nm_x	na_x	T_x	r_x	$\dot{e}_x$	nM_x
0	0.058375	100000	5838	95272	0.061272	0.1901	6456377	0.0000	64.564	0.061272
1	0.006444	94162	607	374868	0.001619	1.0637	6361105	0.0000	67.555	0.001619
5	0.003166	93556	296	467038	0.000634	2.5000	5986237	0.0000	63.986	0.000634
10	0.002983	93260	278	465654	0.000597	2.6846	5519199	0.0499	59.181	0.000592
15	0.005836	92981	543	463676	0.001170	2.7326	5053546	0.0440	54.350	0.001158
20	0.009564	92439	884	460073	0.001922	2.6015	4589869	0.0000	49.653	0.001922
25	0.010631	91555	973	455394	0.002137	2.5564	4129797	0.0000	45.107	0.002137
30	0.012669	90581	1148	450127	0.002549	2.5782	3674402	0.0115	40.565	0.002547
35	0.015698	89434	1404	443783	0.003164	2.5889	3224275	0.0465	36.052	0.003149
40	0.019841	88030	1747	436041	0.004006	2.6480	2780492	0.0378	31.586	0.003982
45	0.030648	86283	2644	425280	0.006218	2.6799	2344451	0.0000	27.172	0.006218
50	0.048178	83639	4030	408854	0.009856	2.6822	1919171	0.0000	22.946	0.009856
55	0.077472	79609	6168	383688	0.016074	2.6720	1510317	0.0280	18.972	0.015981
60	0.124207	73442	9122	345662	0.026390	2.6380	1126628	0.0402	15.340	0.026185
65	0.189838	64320	12210	292257	0.041779	2.5970	780966	0.0402	12.142	0.041471
70	0.284190	52109	14809	224092	0.066084	2.5383	488708	0.0402	9.379	0.065628
75	0.400394	37300	14935	148557	0.100533	2.4593	264616	0.0402	7.094	0.099887
80	0.531716	22366	11892	81168	0.146513	2.4218	116059	0.0402	5.189	0.145264
85+	*1.000000	10473	10473	34891	0.300173	3.3314	34891	0.0402	3.331	0.295229

TABLE 3 — FEMALE LIFE TABLE

x	nq_x	l_x	nd_x	nL_x	nm_x	na_x	T_x	r_x	$\dot{e}_x$	nM_x
0	0.046218	100000	4622	96317	0.047986	0.2031	7067973	0.0000	70.680	0.047986
1	0.005746	95378	548	379907	0.001442	1.0708	6971657	0.0000	73.095	0.001442
5	0.002215	94830	210	473626	0.000444	2.5000	6591749	0.0000	69.511	0.000444
10	0.001780	94620	168	472687	0.000356	2.5475	6118123	0.0477	64.660	0.000356
15	0.002631	94452	248	471679	0.000527	2.6680	5645436	0.0409	59.771	0.000523
20	0.003916	94203	369	470141	0.000785	2.6294	5173758	0.0000	54.921	0.000785
25	0.005090	93834	478	468028	0.001021	2.6062	4703616	0.0000	50.127	0.001021
30	0.006519	93357	612	465318	0.001316	2.6076	4235588	0.0000	45.370	0.001316
35	0.008560	92744	794	461850	0.001719	2.6419	3770270	0.0352	40.652	0.001710
40	0.012540	91950	1153	457066	0.002523	2.6699	3308420	0.0357	35.980	0.002507
45	0.019099	90797	1734	449928	0.003854	2.6591	2851354	0.0000	31.403	0.003854
50	0.027819	89063	2478	439510	0.005637	2.6563	2401426	0.0000	26.963	0.005637
55	0.041498	86586	3593	424631	0.008462	2.6907	1961916	0.0234	22.659	0.008420
60	0.069480	82993	5766	401723	0.014354	2.7040	1537286	0.0395	18.523	0.014221
65	0.119637	77226	9239	364896	0.025320	2.7016	1135562	0.0395	14.704	0.025063
70	0.216297	67987	14705	304752	0.048254	2.6075	770667	0.0395	11.335	0.047866
75	0.315776	53282	16825	224459	0.074958	2.5067	465915	0.0395	8.744	0.074500
80	0.418272	36457	15249	145074	0.105110	2.5599	241456	0.0395	6.623	0.104108
85+	*1.000000	21208	21208	96381	0.220041	4.5446	96381	0.0395	4.545	0.216480

TABLE 4 — OBSERVED AND PROJECTED VITAL RATES

	OBSERVED POPULATION BOTH SEXES	MALES	FEMALES	PROJECTED POPULATION 1967 MALES	FEMALES	1972 MALES	FEMALES	1977 MALES	FEMALES	STABLE POPULATION MALES	FEMALES
RATES PER THOUSAND											
Birth	19.77	21.18	18.45	20.25	17.76	22.10	19.53	23.49	20.93	19.93	18.56
Death	7.89	8.51	7.31	8.91	7.95	9.53	8.59	10.07	9.19	12.61	11.18
Increase	11.88	12.67	11.14	11.34	9.81	12.57	10.94	13.42	11.73		7.3215
PERCENTAGE											
under 15	33.13	35.05	31.32	31.69	28.38	28.53	25.60	27.69	25.02	26.48	24.92
15-64	60.75	60.13	61.33	62.59	62.99	64.79	64.59	64.95	64.25	64.41	62.88
65 and over	6.12	4.82	7.35	5.72	8.64	6.69	9.80	7.36	10.73	9.11	12.20
DEP. RATIO X 100	64.62	66.32	63.05	59.78	58.76	54.35	54.81	53.97	55.64	55.26	59.03

TABLE 5 — POPULATION PROJECTED WITH FIXED AGE—SPECIFIC BIRTH AND DEATH RATES (IN 1000's)

AGE AT LAST BIRTHDAY	1967 BOTH SEXES	1967 MALES	1967 FEMALES	1972 BOTH SEXES	1972 MALES	1972 FEMALES	1977 BOTH SEXES	1977 MALES	1977 FEMALES	AGE AT LAST BIRTHDAY
0-4	2857	1473	1384	3105	1601	1504	3554	1832	1722	0-4
5-9	3224	1658	1566	2840	1463	1377	3086	1590	1496	5-9
10-14	3538	1810	1728	3216	1653	1563	2833	1459	1374	10-14
15-19	3246	1657	1589	3526	1802	1724	3205	1646	1559	15-19
20-24	2152	1085	1067	3227	1644	1583	3507	1788	1719	20-24
25-29	2095	1048	1047	2136	1074	1062	3203	1627	1576	25-29
30-34	2276	1137	1139	2077	1036	1041	2118	1062	1056	30-34
35-39	2359	1165	1194	2251	1121	1130	2055	1022	1033	35-39
40-44	2120	981	1139	2327	1145	1182	2221	1102	1119	40-44
45-49	1519	701	818	2079	957	1122	2280	1117	1163	45-49
50-54	1397	631	766	1473	674	799	2016	920	1096	50-54
55-59	1615	741	874	1332	592	740	1405	633	772	55-59
60-64	1361	610	751	1495	668	827	1234	533	701	60-64
65-69	1022	427	595	1197	515	682	1316	565	751	65-69
70-74	648	251	397	824	327	497	965	395	570	70-74
75-79	349	129	220	458	166	292	583	217	366	75-79
80-84	195	62	133	213	71	142	280	91	189	80-84
85+	102	23	79	115	27	88	125	30	95	85+
TOTAL	32075	15589	16486	33891	16536	17355	35986	17629	18357	TOTAL

TABLE 6 — STANDARDIZED RATES

STANDARD COUNTRIES: STANDARDIZED RATES PER THOUSAND	ENGLAND AND WALES 1961 BOTH SEXES	MALES	FEMALES	UNITED STATES 1960 BOTH SEXES	MALES	FEMALES	MEXICO 1960 BOTH SEXES	MALES	FEMALES
Birth	17.21	19.18*	16.05	17.46	18.12*	16.55	20.61	17.75*	19.79
Death	12.82	14.35*	12.32	10.78	12.01*	9.37	6.32	8.56*	5.18
Increase	4.39	4.82*	3.73	6.68	6.11*	7.18	14.29	9.19*	14.61

TABLE 7 — MOMENTS AND CUMULANTS

	OBSERVED POP. MALES	OBSERVED POP. FEMALES	STATIONARY POP. MALES	STATIONARY POP. FEMALES	STABLE POP. MALES	STABLE POP. FEMALES	OBSERVED BIRTHS	NET MATERNITY FUNCTION	BIRTHS IN STABLE POP.
μ	28.17706	30.92635	36.22092	38.58417	32.71026	34.70159	27.45027	27.32981	27.05820
σ^2	406.9645	456.0866	490.2073	540.7697	466.9057	517.3645	33.69767	35.58593	34.44174
κ_3	4582.949	4419.906	2381.182	2155.656	3922.608	4166.526	122.2240	156.4219	155.9931
κ_4	-109685.	-165951.	-233706.	-300767.	-183573.	-242609.	-154.821	5.105	120.571
β_1	0.311616	0.205913	0.048133	0.029385	0.151169	0.125360	0.390403	0.542951	0.595601
β_2	2.337731	2.202215	2.027455	1.971496	2.157927	2.093613	2.863658	3.004031	3.101642
κ	-0.116728	-0.076845	-0.018274	-0.010854	-0.057512	-0.046444	-0.226005	-0.290642	-0.329648

TABLE 8 — RATES FROM AGE DISTRIBUTIONS AND VITAL STATISTICS (Females)

VITAL STATISTICS		THOMPSON AGE RANGE	NRR	1000r	INTERVAL	BOURGEOIS-PICHAT AGE RANGE	NRR	1000b	1000d	1000r	COALE	
GRR	1.305											
NRR	1.220	0-4	1.43	13.31	27.42	5-29	1.92	26.72	2.49	24.23	IBR	
TFR	2.712	5-9	1.64	18.37	27.38	30-54	1.55	26.97	10.70	16.26	IDR	
GENERATION	27.193	10-14	1.53	15.46	27.32	55-79	3.21	148.83	105.64	43.20	IRI	
SEX RATIO	107.799	15-19	1.08	2.81	27.24	*15-39	0.84	12.79	19.45	-6.65	K1	
											K2	

TABLE 9 — LESLIE MATRIX AND ITS SPECTRAL COMPONENTS (Females)

Start of Age Interval	ORIGINAL MATRIX SUB-DIAGONAL	ALTERNATIVE FIRST ROWS Projection	ALTERNATIVE FIRST ROWS Integral	FIRST STABLE MATRIX % IN STABLE POPULATION	FISHER VALUES	REPRODUCTIVE VALUES	SECOND STABLE MATRIX Z_2 FIRST COLUMN	SECOND STABLE MATRIX Z_2 FIRST ROW
0	0.99454	0.00000	0.00000	8.652	1.069	1683555	0.1822+0.0977	0.1822+0.0977
5	0.99802	0.00000	0.00000	8.295	1.115	1930947	0.2008-0.1550	-0.0119+0.1681
10	0.99787	0.04187	0.00000	7.981	1.159	1845279	-0.0731-0.3036	-0.1285+0.0470
15	0.99674	0.26216	0.08547	7.678	1.160	1241920	-0.3778-0.0707	-0.0852-0.0838
20	0.99551	0.39432	0.45000	7.377	0.926	973824	-0.2693+0.3884	-0.0140-0.1168
25	0.99421	0.27841	0.35480	7.080	0.541	620285	0.3001+0.4968	0.0099-0.0880
30	0.99255	0.16079	0.21354	6.786	0.266	319457	0.7066-0.0867	0.0178-0.0493
35	0.98964	0.07738	0.11483	6.493	0.104	120108	0.2568-0.8329	0.0132-0.0190
40	0.98438	0.02292	0.04324	6.194	0.026	21393	-0.7998-0.7019	0.0044-0.0042
45	0.97685	0.00194	0.00350	5.878	0.002	1745	-1.1750+0.5378	0.0004-0.0004
50	0.96615	0.00023	0.00047	5.536	0.000	214	0.0125+1.5571	0.0000-0.0000
55+	0.79477			22.050				

TABLE 10 — AGE ANALYSIS AND MISCELLANEOUS RESULTS (Females)

Start Age Interval	OBSERVED POPUL. (IN 100's)	CONTRIBUTIONS OF ROOTS (IN 100's) r_1	r_2, r_3	r_4-r_{11}	AGE-SP. BIRTH RATES	NET MATERNITY FUNCTION	COEFF. OF MATRIX EQUATION	PARAMETERS INTEGRAL	PARAMETERS MATRIX	EXP. INCREASE x	$e^{(x+2\frac{1}{2})r}$
0	15745	15162	150	432	0.0000	0.0000	0.0000	L(1) 1.03729	1.03732	0	1.0185
5	17314	14537	2790	-13	0.0000	0.0000	0.0000	L(2) 0.31852	0.33144	50	1.4687
10	15919	13986	2582	-649	0.0000	0.0000	0.0416	0.76971	0.73976	55	1.5235
15	10705	13454	-1630	-1120	0.0176	0.0831	0.2597	R(1) 0.00732	0.00733	60	1.5803
20	10515	12928	-5547	3134	0.0928	0.4362	0.3893	R(2) -0.03654	-0.04199	65	1.6392
25	11455	12407	-3110	2157	0.0732	0.3424	0.2736	0.23569	0.22991	70	1.7003
30	12030	11891	5236	-5097	0.0440	0.2049	0.1571	C(1)	175244	75	1.7637
35	11514	11378	9912	-9777	0.0237	0.1093	0.0750	C(2)	309218	80	1.8295
40	8313	10855	2069	-4611	0.0089	0.0407	0.0220		499692	85	1.8977
45	7846	10301	-12641	10186	0.0007	0.0032	0.0018	2P/Y 26.6590	27.3283	90	1.9684
50	9047	9701	-15485	14831	0.0001	0.0004	0.0002	DELTA 8.6670		95	2.0418
55+	25977	38641								100	2.1180

TABLE 1 — DATA

AGE AT LAST BIRTHDAY	POPULATION BOTH SEXES	MALES Number	%	FEMALES Number	%	BIRTHS BY AGE OF MOTHER	DEATHS BOTH SEXES	MALES	FEMALES	AGE AT LAST BIRTHD
0	175300	90300	2.2	85000	1.9	0	19277	10620	8657	0
1-4	714500	364300	9.0	350200	8.0	0	9426	4918	4508	1-4
5-9	801200	407200	10.0	394000	9.0	0	1528	818	710	5-9
10-14	800700	406700	10.0	394000	9.0	8	928	510	418	10-14
15-19	807700	402200	9.9	405500	9.2	7472	1551	819	732	15-19
20-24	758400	377700	9.3	380700	8.7	50512	2279	1311	968	20-24
25-29	680600	333900	8.2	346700	7.9	60642	2256	1285	971	25-29
30-34	545400	265000	6.5	280400	6.4	40528	1905	1085	820	30-34
35-39	568200	273600	6.7	294600	6.7	32140	2301	1329	972	35-39
40-44	523400	247500	6.1	275900	6.3	14755	2721	1640	1081	40-44
45-49	462200	212400	5.2	249800	5.7	1954	3148	1902	1246	45-49
50-54	394800	178000	4.4	216800	4.9	71	3628	2159	1469	50-54
55-59	335300	147900	3.6	187400	4.3	0	4412	2562	1850	55-59
60-64	296200	126400	3.1	169800	3.9	0	5985	3245	2740	60-64
65-69	231400	95700	2.4	135700	3.1	0	7408	3845	3563	65-69
70-74	170400	69400	1.7	101000	2.3		9507	4627	4880	70-74
75-79	115098	43338	1.1	71760	1.6		9736	4351	5385	75-79
80-84	57505	19546	0.5	37959	0.9	107787 M.	7871	3044	4827	80-84
85+	20397	6116	0.2	14281	0.3	100295 F.	7048	2132	4916	85+
TOTAL	8458700	4067200		4391500		208082	102915	52202	50713	TOTAL

TABLE 2 — MALE LIFE TABLE

x	$_nq_x$	l_x	$_nd_x$	$_nL_x$	$_nm_x$	$_na_x$	T_x	r_x	$\mathring{e}_x$	$_nM_x$	x
0	0.109144	100000	10914	92803	0.117608	0.3406	5586203	0.0000	55.862	0.117608	
1	0.052036	89086	4636	343384	0.013500	1.2046	5493400	0.0000	61.664	0.013500	
5	0.009925	84450	838	420154	0.001995	2.5000	5150016	0.0066	60.983	0.002009	
10	0.006250	83612	523	416753	0.001254	2.5019	4729862	0.0000	56.569	0.001254	10
15	0.010146	83089	843	413525	0.002039	2.7213	4313108	0.0052	51.909	0.002036	15
20	0.017241	82246	1418	407831	0.003477	2.6027	3899584	0.0154	47.414	0.003471	20
25	0.019081	80828	1542	400325	0.003853	2.5257	3491753	0.0316	43.200	0.003848	25
30	0.020284	79286	1608	392476	0.004098	2.5418	3091428	0.0157	38.991	0.004094	30
35	0.024012	77678	1865	383907	0.004858	2.5972	2698952	0.0018	34.746	0.004857	35
40	0.032692	75812	2478	373149	0.006642	2.6142	2315046	0.0186	30.536	0.006626	40
45	0.043965	73334	3224	358957	0.008982	2.6077	1941897	0.0239	26.480	0.008955	45
50	0.059131	70110	4146	340659	0.012170	2.6144	1582940	0.0237	22.578	0.012129	50
55	0.083391	65964	5501	316734	0.017367	2.6209	1242280	0.0163	18.833	0.017323	55
60	0.121371	60463	7339	284860	0.025762	2.6212	925546	0.0198	15.308	0.025672	60
65	0.183925	53125	9771	242263	0.040332	2.6091	640686	0.0198	12.060	0.040178	65
70	0.287315	43354	12456	186175	0.066906	2.5439	398424	0.0198	9.190	0.066671	70
75	0.401166	30898	12395	123052	0.100730	2.4639	212248	0.0198	6.869	0.100397	75
80	0.556989	18503	10306	65874	0.156446	2.4151	89196	0.0198	4.821	0.155736	80
85+	*1.000000	8197	8197	23322	0.351463	2.8453	23322	0.0198	2.845	0.348594	85

TABLE 3 — FEMALE LIFE TABLE

x	$_nq_x$	l_x	$_nd_x$	$_nL_x$	$_nm_x$	$_na_x$	T_x	r_x	$\mathring{e}_x$	$_nM_x$	x
0	0.095537	100000	9554	93804	0.101847	0.3514	6094896	0.0000	60.949	0.101847	0
1	0.049713	90446	4496	349298	0.012873	1.2228	6001092	0.0000	66.350	0.012873	1
5	0.008912	85950	766	427835	0.001790	2.5000	5651794	0.0057	65.757	0.001802	5
10	0.005291	85184	451	424792	0.001061	2.4981	5223959	0.0000	61.326	0.001061	10
15	0.008991	84733	762	421889	0.001806	2.6672	4799167	0.0017	56.638	0.001805	15
20	0.012649	83972	1062	417284	0.002545	2.5769	4377277	0.0132	52.128	0.002543	20
25	0.013918	82909	1154	411688	0.002803	2.5226	3959994	0.0278	47.763	0.002801	25
30	0.014524	81755	1187	405843	0.002926	2.5289	3548306	0.0133	43.401	0.002924	30
35	0.016365	80568	1318	399617	0.003299	2.5557	3142463	0.0000	39.004	0.003299	35
40	0.019428	79250	1540	392524	0.003922	2.5813	2742846	0.0125	34.610	0.003918	40
45	0.024701	77710	1920	383958	0.004999	2.6081	2350322	0.0190	30.245	0.004988	45
50	0.033450	75790	2535	372952	0.006798	2.6335	1966364	0.0217	25.945	0.006776	50
55	0.048377	73255	3544	358021	0.009899	2.6708	1593412	0.0140	21.752	0.009872	55
60	0.078042	69711	5440	335880	0.016197	2.6701	1235391	0.0184	17.722	0.016137	60
65	0.124240	64271	7985	302805	0.026370	2.6770	899511	0.0184	13.996	0.026256	65
70	0.217215	56286	12226	252115	0.048494	2.6024	596705	0.0184	10.601	0.048317	70
75	0.317577	44060	13992	185811	0.075305	2.5532	344590	0.0184	7.821	0.075042	75
80	0.485316	30067	14592	114165	0.127816	2.5212	158779	0.0184	5.281	0.127163	80
85+	*1.000000	15475	15475	44614	0.346868	2.8829	44614	0.0184	2.883	0.344234	85

TABLE 4 — OBSERVED AND PROJECTED VITAL RATES

	OBSERVED POPULATION BOTH SEXES	MALES	FEMALES	PROJECTED POPULATION 1956 MALES	FEMALES	1961 MALES	FEMALES	1966 MALES	FEMALES	STABLE POPULATION MALES	FEMALES
RATES PER THOUSAND											
Birth	24.60	26.50	22.84	26.61	23.18	26.21	23.07	25.35	22.51	23.15	21.54
Death	12.17	12.83	11.55	13.05	11.76	13.21	12.04	13.30	12.19	15.49	13.87
Increase	12.43	13.67	11.29	13.56	11.43	13.00	11.03	12.05	10.32		7.6665
PERCENTAGE											
under 15	29.46	31.19	27.85	30.57	27.40	30.63	27.54	30.44	27.52	27.86	26.38
15-64	63.51	63.06	63.93	63.52	64.00	63.40	63.65	63.42	63.37	63.66	62.62
65 and over	7.03	5.76	8.21	5.91	8.60	5.97	8.81	6.14	9.11	8.47	11.01
DEP. RATIO X 100	57.45	58.59	56.41	57.44	56.25	57.73	57.11	57.68	57.79	57.07	59.70

TABLE 5 — POPULATION PROJECTED WITH FIXED AGE-SPECIFIC BIRTH AND DEATH RATES (IN 1000's)

AGE AT LAST BIRTHDAY	1956 BOTH SEXES	1956 MALES	1956 FEMALES	1961 BOTH SEXES	1961 MALES	1961 FEMALES	1966 BOTH SEXES	1966 MALES	1966 FEMALES	AGE AT LAST BIRTHDAY
0-4	948	487	461	1007	518	489	1047	538	509	0-4
5-9	858	438	420	914	469	445	970	498	472	5-9
10-14	795	404	391	851	434	417	908	466	442	10-14
15-19	795	404	391	790	401	389	845	431	414	15-19
20-24	798	397	401	785	398	387	779	395	384	20-24
25-29	747	371	376	785	389	396	773	391	382	25-29
30-34	669	327	342	733	363	370	772	382	390	30-34
35-39	535	259	276	657	320	337	721	356	365	35-39
40-44	555	266	289	523	252	271	642	311	331	40-44
45-49	508	238	270	539	256	283	507	242	265	45-49
50-54	445	202	243	488	226	262	518	243	275	50-54
55-59	373	165	208	420	187	233	462	210	252	55-59
60-64	309	133	176	344	149	195	388	169	219	60-64
65-69	260	107	153	271	113	158	303	127	176	65-69
70-74	187	74	113	210	83	127	219	87	132	70-74
75-79	120	46	74	132	49	83	149	55	94	75-79
80-84	67	23	44	71	25	46	77	26	51	80-84
85+	22	7	15	25	8	17	27	9	18	85+
TOTAL	8991	4348	4643	9545	4640	4905	10107	4936	5171	TOTAL

TABLE 6 — STANDARDIZED RATES

STANDARD COUNTRIES:

STANDARDIZED RATES PER THOUSAND	ENGLAND AND WALES 1961 BOTH SEXES	MALES	FEMALES	UNITED STATES 1960 BOTH SEXES	MALES	FEMALES	MEXICO 1960 BOTH SEXES	MALES	FEMALES
Birth	20.62	23.23*	19.26	20.91	21.32*	19.86	21.93	21.75*	21.08
Death	16.62	19.97*	16.53	14.94	17.04*	13.76	11.00	12.43*	9.80
Increase	4.00	3.27*	2.73	5.97	4.28*	6.09	10.93	9.32*	11.28

TABLE 7 — MOMENTS AND CUMULANTS

	OBSERVED POP. MALES	OBSERVED POP. FEMALES	STATIONARY POP. MALES	STATIONARY POP. FEMALES	STABLE POP. MALES	STABLE POP. FEMALES	OBSERVED BIRTHS	NET MATERNITY FUNCTION	BIRTHS IN STABLE POP.
μ	28.57542	31.22303	35.38773	37.47427	31.75463	33.51980	29.70500	30.37754	30.03377
σ^2	403.4281	452.1313	486.5113	527.5416	459.3196	501.5419	42.96215	43.13121	42.37346
κ_3	4907.829	4801.093	2746.068	2359.305	4272.390	4340.989	123.5014	94.3548	103.1600
κ_4	−80372.	−142017.	−226593.	−287670.	−168045.	−223541.	−1104.430	−1207.077	−1078.272
β_1	0.366843	0.249394	0.065485	0.037914	0.188364	0.149367	0.192347	0.110957	0.139875
β_2	2.506175	2.305279	2.042671	1.966334	2.203480	2.111323	2.401635	2.351139	2.399462
κ	−0.149205	−0.096890	−0.024729	−0.013828	−0.071623	−0.054816	−0.087602	−0.053697	−0.068536

TABLE 8 — RATES FROM AGE DISTRIBUTIONS AND VITAL STATISTICS (Females)

VITAL STATISTICS

		THOMPSON AGE RANGE	NRR	1000r	INTERVAL	BOURGEOIS-PICHAT AGE RANGE	NRR	1000b	1000d	1000r	COALE
GRR	1.546										
NRR	1.261	)−4	1.21	7.11	27.32	5−29	1.11	22.24	18.33	3.91	IBR
TFR	3.207	5−9	1.21	7.16	27.26	30−54	1.29	22.77	13.36	9.41	IDR
GENERATION	30.205	10−14	1.32	10.09	27.22	55−79	1.65	35.28	16.83	18.46	K1
SEX RATIO	107.470	15−19	1.48	13.71	27.15	*40−69	1.62	34.04	16.25	17.78	K2

TABLE 9 — LESLIE MATRIX AND ITS SPECTRAL COMPONENTS (Females)

Start of Age Interval	ORIGINAL MATRIX SUB-DIAGONAL	ALTERNATIVE FIRST ROWS Projection	ALTERNATIVE FIRST ROWS Integral	FIRST STABLE MATRIX % IN STABLE POPULATION	FISHER VALUES	REPRODUCTIVE VALUES	SECOND STABLE MATRIX Z_2 FIRST COLUMN	SECOND STABLE MATRIX Z_2 FIRST ROW
0	0.96554	0.00000	0.00000	9.364	1.150	500466	0.1360+0.0654	0.1360+0.0654
5	0.99289	0.00002	0.00000	8.701	1.238	487608	0.1457−0.0888	0.0168+0.1324
10	0.99317	0.01956	0.00004	8.314	1.295	510297	0.0054−0.1984	−0.0877+0.0740
15	0.98908	0.15982	0.04012	7.946	1.332	540299	−0.1903−0.1308	−0.0971−0.0299
20	0.98659	0.32597	0.28886	7.564	1.214	462172	−0.2470+0.1026	−0.0458−0.0949
25	0.98580	0.33894	0.38080	7.181	0.899	311574	−0.0557−0.3040	0.0024−0.0996
30	0.98466	0.26906	0.31467	6.813	0.552	154752	0.2597+0.2448	0.0268−0.0676
35	0.98225	0.17260	0.23751	6.456	0.268	79007	0.3998−0.0978	0.0247−0.0303
40	0.97818	0.06528	0.11643	6.103	0.082	22525	0.1556−0.4473	0.0098−0.0078
45	0.97134	0.00869	0.01703	5.745	0.010	2494	−0.3331−0.4283	0.0013−0.0009
50	0.95997	0.00035	0.00071	5.370	0.000	84	−0.6150+0.0532	0.0001−0.0000
55+	0.78697			20.445				

TABLE 10 — AGE ANALYSIS AND MISCELLANEOUS RESULTS (Females)

Start Age Interval	OBSERVED POPUL. (IN 100's)	CONTRIBUTIONS OF ROOTS (IN 100's) r_1	r_2, r_3	$r_4 \cdot r_{11}$	AGE-SP. BIRTH RATES	NET MATERNITY FUNCTION	COEFF. OF MATRIX EQUATION	PARAMETERS INTEGRAL	PARAMETERS MATRIX	EXP. INCREASE x	$e^{(x+2\frac{1}{2})r}$
0	4352	4453	−137	36	0.0000	0.0000	0.0000	L(1) 1.03908	1.03911	0	1.0194
5	3940	4138	−146	−52	0.0000	0.0000	0.0000	L(2) 0.46099	0.46420	50	1.4955
10	3940	3954	−4	−10	0.0000	0.0000	0.0188	0.73398	0.71653	55	1.5540
15	4055	3779	192	84	0.0089	0.0375	0.1522	R(1) 0.00767	0.00767	60	1.6147
20	3807	3597	248	−38	0.0640	0.2669	0.3070	R(2) −0.02860	−0.03162	65	1.6778
25	3467	3415	55	−3	0.0843	0.3471	0.3149	0.20200	0.19919	70	1.7434
30	2804	3240	−263	−174	0.0697	0.2827	0.2464	C(1)	47561	75	1.8115
35	2946	3070	−402	278	0.0526	0.2101	0.1557	C(2)	−50347	80	1.8823
40	2759	2902	−154	11	0.0258	0.1012	0.0578		252	85	1.9558
45	2498	2732	338	−572	0.0038	0.0145	0.0075	2P/Y 31.1051	31.5440	90	2.0323
50	2168	2554	619	−1005	0.0002	0.0006	0.0003	DELTA 5.0966		95	2.1117
55+	7179	9724								100	2.1942

TABLE 1 — DATA

AGE AT LAST BIRTHDAY	POPULATION BOTH SEXES	MALES Number	%	FEMALES Number	%	BIRTHS BY AGE OF MOTHER	DEATHS BOTH SEXES	MALES	FEMALES	AGE AT LAST BIRTHDAY
0	178600	92200	2.2	86400	1.9	0	18405	10206	8199	0
1-4	712700	363700	8.8	349000	7.8	0	7745	4066	3679	1-4
5-9	814801	414401	10.1	400400	9.0	0	1276	682	594	5-9
10-14	810000	410800	10.0	399200	9.0	10	661	365	296	10-14
15-19	787600	390100	9.5	397500	8.9	7555	926	533	393	15-19
20-24	740300	364200	8.9	376100	8.4	50185	1314	757	557	20-24
25-29	676600	330000	8.0	346600	7.8	59142	1452	843	609	25-29
30-34	572200	276800	6.7	295400	6.6	42363	1458	857	601	30-34
35-39	573800	276400	6.7	297400	6.7	28254	1651	970	681	35-39
40-44	515000	244500	5.9	270500	6.1	13776	2276	1373	903	40-44
45-49	475800	221400	5.4	254400	5.7	1809	2820	1700	1120	45-49
50-54	420400	191600	4.7	228800	5.1	59	3560	2104	1456	50-54
55-59	356900	158600	3.9	198300	4.5	0	4340	2573	1767	55-59
60-64	307200	131900	3.2	175300	3.9	0	5871	3282	2589	60-64
65-69	240600	100400	2.4	140200	3.1	0	7625	3991	3634	65-69
70-74	181000	73600	1.8	107400	2.4		9421	4625	4796	70-74
75-79	119469	45252	1.1	74217	1.7		10541	4747	5794	75-79
80-84	62995	21441	0.5	41554	0.9	104789 M.	8527	3367	5160	80-84
85+	23835	7106	0.2	16729	0.4	98364 F.	7468	2253	5215	85+
TOTAL	8569800	4114400		4455400		203153	97337	49294	48043	TOTAL

TABLE 2 — MALE LIFE TABLE

x	nq_x	l_x	nd_x	nL_x	nm_x	na_x	T_x	r_x	$\mathring{e}_x$	nM_x	x
0	0.103030	100000	10303	93076	0.110694	0.3280	5834049	0.0000	58.340	0.110694	0
1	0.043354	89697	3889	347843	0.011180	1.1855	5740973	0.0000	64.004	0.011180	1
5	0.008137	85808	698	427296	0.001634	2.5000	5393130	0.0066	62.851	0.001646	5
10	0.004431	85110	377	424583	0.000888	2.4337	4965834	0.0049	58.346	0.000889	10
15	0.006823	84733	578	422322	0.001369	2.6783	4541252	0.0106	53.595	0.001366	15
20	0.010359	84155	872	418695	0.002082	2.6150	4118929	0.0147	48.945	0.002079	20
25	0.012720	83283	1059	413848	0.002560	2.5772	3700234	0.0249	44.430	0.002555	25
30	0.015379	82224	1264	408030	0.003099	2.5579	3286386	0.0147	39.969	0.003096	30
35	0.017425	80959	1411	401466	0.003514	2.6396	2878356	0.0085	35.553	0.003509	35
40	0.027781	79548	2210	392532	0.005630	2.6426	2476890	0.0166	31.137	0.005616	40
45	0.037793	77339	2923	379758	0.007697	2.6273	2084357	0.0165	26.951	0.007678	45
50	0.053699	74416	3996	362629	0.011020	2.6354	1704600	0.0220	22.906	0.010981	50
55	0.078389	70420	5520	339059	0.016281	2.6379	1341970	0.0205	19.057	0.016223	55
60	0.117886	64899	7651	306392	0.024971	2.6335	1002911	0.0189	15.453	0.024882	60
65	0.182047	57249	10422	261261	0.039891	2.6029	696520	0.0189	12.167	0.039751	65
70	0.273294	46827	12797	202917	0.063067	2.5607	435259	0.0189	9.295	0.062840	70
75	0.415801	34020	14149	134422	0.105261	2.4752	232342	0.0189	6.828	0.104901	75
80	0.559096	19880	11115	70491	0.157677	2.3991	97920	0.0189	4.926	0.157036	80
85+	*1.000000	8765	8765	27429	0.319556	3.1293	27429	0.0189	3.129	0.317056	85+

TABLE 3 — FEMALE LIFE TABLE

x	nq_x	l_x	nd_x	nL_x	nm_x	na_x	T_x	r_x	$\mathring{e}_x$	nM_x	x
0	0.089294	100000	8929	94097	0.094896	0.3389	6347263	0.0000	63.473	0.094896	0
1	0.040958	91071	3730	353845	0.010542	1.2018	6253166	0.0000	68.663	0.010542	1
5	0.007347	87341	642	435099	0.001475	2.5000	5899321	0.0052	67.544	0.001484	5
10	0.003700	86699	321	432648	0.000741	2.3602	5464223	0.0000	63.025	0.000741	10
15	0.004936	86378	426	430890	0.000989	2.6536	5031575	0.0049	58.251	0.000989	15
20	0.007389	85952	635	428238	0.001483	2.6053	4600685	0.0123	53.526	0.001481	20
25	0.008761	85317	747	424761	0.001760	2.5618	4172447	0.0224	48.905	0.001757	25
30	0.010129	84569	857	420748	0.002036	2.5502	3747686	0.0133	44.315	0.002035	30
35	0.011395	83713	954	416286	0.002292	2.6127	3326938	0.0063	39.742	0.002290	35
40	0.016587	82759	1373	410533	0.003344	2.6248	2910652	0.0123	35.170	0.003338	40
45	0.021823	81386	1776	402725	0.004410	2.6325	2500119	0.0122	30.719	0.004403	45
50	0.031430	79610	2502	392128	0.006381	2.6333	2097394	0.0185	26.346	0.006364	50
55	0.043789	77108	3376	377678	0.008940	2.6718	1705267	0.0171	22.115	0.008911	55
60	0.071704	73731	5287	356486	0.014830	2.6979	1327589	0.0180	18.006	0.014769	60
65	0.122692	68444	8398	322662	0.026026	2.6706	971103	0.0180	14.188	0.025920	65
70	0.202596	60047	12165	271348	0.044833	2.6255	648442	0.0180	10.799	0.044655	70
75	0.328464	47882	15727	200745	0.078345	2.5417	377093	0.0180	7.876	0.078068	75
80	0.476208	32154	15312	122723	0.124770	2.5152	176348	0.0180	5.484	0.124175	80
85+	*1.000000	16842	16842	53624	0.314075	3.1839	53624	0.0180	3.184	0.311734	85+

TABLE 4 — OBSERVED AND PROJECTED VITAL RATES

	OBSERVED POPULATION BOTH SEXES	MALES	FEMALES	PROJECTED POPULATION 1959 MALES	FEMALES	1964 MALES	FEMALES	1969 MALES	FEMALES	STABLE POPULATION MALES	FEMALES
RATES PER THOUSAND											
Birth	23.71	25.47	22.08	25.55	22.38	25.19	22.28	24.49	21.85	22.40	20.90
Death	11.36	11.98	10.78	12.12	10.97	12.27	11.21	12.41	11.43	14.53	13.03
Increase	12.35	13.49	11.29	13.43	11.41	12.92	11.07	12.08	10.42		7.8734
PERCENTAGE											
under 15	29.36	31.14	27.72	30.30	27.11	30.08	27.08	29.73	26.99	27.33	25.95
15-64	63.31	62.84	63.75	63.53	63.98	63.62	63.72	63.70	63.42	63.89	62.70
65 and over	7.33	6.02	8.53	6.17	8.90	6.31	9.20	6.57	9.60	8.78	11.35
DEP. RATIO X 100	57.95	59.13	56.86	57.40	56.29	57.19	56.94	56.98	57.69	56.52	59.48

TABLE 1 — DATA

AGE AT LAST BIRTHDAY	POPULATION BOTH SEXES	MALES Number	%	FEMALES Number	%	BIRTHS BY AGE OF MOTHER	DEATHS BOTH SEXES	MALES	FEMALES	AGE AT LAST BIRTHDAY
0	182000	94000	2.3	88000	1.9	0	18098	10008	8090	0
1-4	710400	362800	8.7	347600	7.7	0	6953	3602	3351	1-4
5-9	828199	421400	10.1	406799	9.0	0	1150	620	530	5-9
10-14	820000	415000	10.0	405000	9.0	33	645	368	277	10-14
15-19	766400	377700	9.1	388700	8.6	9868	791	460	331	15-19
20-24	721500	350200	8.4	371300	8.2	53947	1100	647	453	20-24
25-29	672300	326000	7.8	346300	7.7	59912	1318	776	542	25-29
30-34	599300	288500	6.9	310800	6.9	43876	1481	874	607	30-34
35-39	579400	279000	6.7	300400	6.6	27593	1612	974	638	35-39
40-44	506100	241200	5.8	264900	5.9	12108	2154	1328	826	40-44
45-49	489400	230400	5.5	259000	5.7	1512	2940	1818	1122	45-49
50-54	446500	205600	4.9	240900	5.3	26	3752	2298	1454	50-54
55-59	379000	169500	4.1	209500	4.6	0	4826	2860	1966	55-59
60-64	318200	137500	3.3	180700	4.0	0	6051	3448	2603	60-64
65-69	250200	105200	2.5	145000	3.2	0	8119	4302	3817	65-69
70-74	191600	77900	1.9	113700	2.5		10280	5041	5239	70-74
75-79	128396	48429	1.2	79967	1.8		11324	5080	6244	75-79
80-84	66664	22725	0.5	43939	1.0	107288 M.	9687	3790	5897	80-84
85+	24741	7446	0.2	17295	0.4	101587 F.	7914	2397	5517	85+
TOTAL	8680300	4160500		4519800		208875	100195	50691	49504	TOTAL

TABLE 2 — MALE LIFE TABLE

x	$_nq_x$	l_x	$_nd_x$	$_nL_x$	$_nm_x$	$_na_x$	T_x	r_x	$\mathring{e}_x$	$_nM_x$	x
0	0.099280	100000	9928	93248	0.106468	0.3200	5886823	0.0000	58.868	0.106468	0
1	0.038630	90072	3479	350456	0.009928	1.1743	5793575	0.0000	64.322	0.009928	1
5	0.007282	86593	631	431386	0.001462	2.5000	5443119	0.0062	62.859	0.001471	5
10	0.004421	85962	380	428837	0.000886	2.4400	5011732	0.0099	58.302	0.000887	10
15	0.006088	85582	521	426691	0.001221	2.6614	4582895	0.0157	53.550	0.001218	15
20	0.009213	85061	784	423445	0.001851	2.6271	4156204	0.0129	48.861	0.001848	20
25	0.011855	84277	999	418987	0.002385	2.5980	3732759	0.0170	44.291	0.002380	25
30	0.015051	83278	1253	413346	0.003032	2.5705	3313772	0.0126	39.792	0.003029	30
35	0.017348	82025	1423	406763	0.003498	2.6379	2900426	0.0141	35.360	0.003491	35
40	0.027238	80602	2195	397838	0.005518	2.6535	2493663	0.0136	30.938	0.005506	40
45	0.038774	78406	3040	384832	0.007900	2.6316	2095806	0.0079	26.730	0.007891	45
50	0.054615	75366	4116	367116	0.011212	2.6398	1710974	0.0190	22.702	0.011177	50
55	0.081423	71250	5801	342508	0.016938	2.6312	1343858	0.0230	18.861	0.016873	55
60	0.118705	65449	7769	308857	0.025154	2.6333	1001350	0.0166	15.300	0.025076	60
65	0.186750	57680	10772	262587	0.041021	2.6038	692493	0.0166	12.006	0.040894	65
70	0.280046	46908	13136	202380	0.064910	2.5518	429906	0.0166	9.165	0.064711	70
75	0.415682	33772	14038	133422	0.105217	2.4757	227526	0.0166	6.737	0.104896	75
80	0.582804	19733	11501	68706	0.167391	2.3948	94104	0.0166	4.769	0.166776	80
85+	*1.000000	8233	8233	25399	0.324138	3.0851	25399	0.0166	3.085	0.321918	85+

TABLE 3 — FEMALE LIFE TABLE

x	$_nq_x$	l_x	$_nd_x$	$_nL_x$	$_nm_x$	$_na_x$	T_x	r_x	$\mathring{e}_x$	$_nM_x$	x
0	0.086621	100000	8662	94224	0.091932	0.3331	6405320	0.0000	64.053	0.091932	0
1	0.037546	91338	3429	355725	0.009640	1.1930	6311096	0.0000	69.096	0.009640	1
5	0.006462	87909	568	438123	0.001297	2.5000	5955371	0.0041	67.745	0.001303	5
10	0.003412	87340	298	435916	0.000684	2.3617	5517248	0.0037	63.169	0.000684	10
15	0.004254	87042	370	434335	0.000852	2.6293	5081332	0.0078	58.378	0.000852	15
20	0.006090	86672	528	432105	0.001222	2.6194	4646997	0.0103	53.616	0.001220	20
25	0.007808	86144	673	429104	0.001568	2.5940	4214893	0.0162	48.928	0.001565	25
30	0.009726	85472	831	425327	0.001954	2.5559	3785789	0.0123	44.293	0.001953	30
35	0.010582	84640	896	421060	0.002127	2.6086	3360462	0.0137	39.703	0.002124	35
40	0.015503	83745	1298	415660	0.003124	2.6401	2939402	0.0117	35.100	0.003118	40
45	0.021455	82446	1769	408041	0.004335	2.6306	2523742	0.0051	30.611	0.004332	45
50	0.029833	80678	2407	397753	0.006051	2.6590	2115700	0.0149	26.224	0.006036	50
55	0.046072	78271	3606	382925	0.009417	2.6627	1717947	0.0191	21.949	0.009384	55
60	0.069964	74665	5224	361313	0.014458	2.7009	1335022	0.0157	17.880	0.014405	60
65	0.124474	69441	8644	327144	0.026421	2.6792	973709	0.0157	14.022	0.026324	65
70	0.208228	60797	12660	273831	0.046232	2.6180	646564	0.0157	10.635	0.046077	70
75	0.328560	48138	15816	201905	0.078334	2.5479	372733	0.0157	7.743	0.078082	75
80	0.504155	32321	16295	120913	0.134766	2.5027	170828	0.0157	5.285	0.134209	80
85+	*1.000000	16026	16026	49915	0.321074	3.1145	49915	0.0157	3.115	0.318994	85+

TABLE 4 — OBSERVED AND PROJECTED VITAL RATES

	OBSERVED POPULATION BOTH SEXES	MALES	FEMALES	PROJECTED POPULATION 1962 MALES	FEMALES	1967 MALES	FEMALES	1972 MALES	FEMALES	STABLE POPULATION MALES	FEMALES
RATES PER THOUSAND											
Birth	24.06	25.79	22.48	25.65	22.58	25.27	22.44	24.63	22.05	23.01	21.51
Death	11.54	12.18	10.95	12.32	11.12	12.41	11.28	12.50	11.43	14.00	12.51
Increase	12.52	13.60	11.52	13.33	11.46	12.86	11.16	12.13	10.62		9.0046
PERCENTAGE											
under 15	29.27	31.08	27.60	30.45	27.18	30.30	27.27	30.13	27.39	28.08	26.65
15-64	63.11	62.63	63.55	63.20	63.73	63.18	63.33	63.06	62.81	63.66	62.56
65 and over	7.62	6.29	8.85	6.36	9.09	6.52	9.40	6.81	9.80	8.26	10.79
DEP. RATIO X 100	58.45	59.68	57.35	58.24	56.92	58.28	57.89	58.59	59.21	57.07	59.85

TABLE 1 — DATA

AGE AT LAST BIRTHDAY	POPULATION BOTH SEXES	MALES Number	%	FEMALES Number	%	BIRTHS BY AGE OF MOTHER	DEATHS BOTH SEXES	MALES	FEMALES	AGE AT LAST BIRTHDAY
0	187000	96700	2.3	90300	2.0	0	18265	10092	8173	0
1-4	713800	365000	8.6	348800	7.5	0	6176	3241	2935	1-4
5-9	848600	432500	10.2	416100	9.0	0	1006	557	449	5-9
10-14	837200	422800	10.0	414400	9.0	32	599	357	242	10-14
15-19	750600	368200	8.7	382400	8.3	10000	710	442	268	15-19
20-24	708000	339000	8.0	365000	8.0	55568	932	578	354	20-24
25-29	673400	324900	7.7	348500	7.5	62720	1120	673	447	25-29
30-34	632400	303300	7.1	329100	7.1	44799	1337	814	523	30-34
35-39	589900	284100	6.7	305800	6.6	29324	1599	971	628	35-39
40-44	500800	240000	5.7	260800	5.6	11213	1752	1079	673	40-44
45-49	507800	241800	5.7	266000	5.8	1158	2562	1624	938	45-49
50-54	476800	221700	5.2	255100	5.5	10	3560	2172	1388	50-54
55-59	404900	182400	4.3	222500	4.8	0	4585	2799	1786	55-59
60-64	332000	144400	3.4	187600	4.1	0	5913	3473	2440	60-64
65-69	262300	111000	2.6	151300	3.3	0	7748	4201	3547	65-69
70-74	204300	83000	2.0	121300	2.6		10205	5060	5145	70-74
75-79	135486	51449	1.2	84037	1.8		11258	5068	6190	75-79
80-84	72315	24545	0.6	47770	1.0	110697 M.	9887	3877	6010	80-84
85+	27799	8206	0.2	19593	0.4	104127 F.	8231	2520	5711	85+
TOTAL	8865400	4245000		4620400		214824	97445	49598	47847	TOTAL

TABLE 2 — MALE LIFE TABLE

x	$_nq_x$	l_x	$_nd_x$	$_nL_x$	$_nm_x$	$_na_x$	T_x	r_x	$\mathring{e}_x$	$_nM_x$	x
0	0.097356	100000	9736	93287	0.104363	0.3104	6016199	0.0000	60.162	0.104364	0
1	0.034644	90264	3127	352183	0.008879	1.1620	5922912	0.0000	65.617	0.008879	1
5	0.006380	87137	556	434296	0.001280	2.5000	5570730	0.0057	63.931	0.001288	5
10	0.004212	86581	365	431987	0.000844	2.4781	5136433	0.0151	59.325	0.000844	10
15	0.006004	86217	518	429865	0.001204	2.6464	4704446	0.0209	54.565	0.001200	15
20	0.008500	85699	728	426749	0.001707	2.6026	4274581	0.0108	49.879	0.001705	20
25	0.010315	84971	876	422744	0.002073	2.5937	3847832	0.0090	45.284	0.002071	25
30	0.013348	84094	1122	417776	0.002687	2.5989	3425088	0.0107	40.729	0.002684	30
35	0.016987	82972	1409	411479	0.003425	2.6027	3007312	0.0199	36.245	0.003418	35
40	0.022281	81562	1817	403524	0.004504	2.6407	2595833	0.0114	31.826	0.004496	40
45	0.033065	79745	2637	392526	0.006717	2.6491	2192310	0.0011	27.492	0.006716	45
50	0.048038	77108	3704	376869	0.009829	2.6590	1799784	0.0179	23.341	0.009797	50
55	0.074424	73404	5463	354207	0.015423	2.6546	1422915	0.0269	19.385	0.015345	55
60	0.114198	67941	7759	321353	0.024144	2.6347	1068708	0.0207	15.730	0.024051	60
65	0.174152	60182	10481	275850	0.037995	2.6088	747354	0.0207	12.418	0.037847	65
70	0.266280	49701	13235	216246	0.061201	2.5624	471504	0.0207	9.487	0.060964	70
75	0.396041	36467	14442	146054	0.098884	2.4879	255258	0.0207	7.000	0.098505	75
80	0.562914	22025	12398	78125	0.158694	2.4191	109204	0.0207	4.958	0.157955	80
85+	*1.000000	9627	9627	31080	0.309740	3.2285	31080	0.0207	3.229	0.307092	85+

TABLE 3 — FEMALE LIFE TABLE

x	$_nq_x$	l_x	$_nd_x$	$_nL_x$	$_nm_x$	$_na_x$	T_x	r_x	$\mathring{e}_x$	$_nM_x$	x
0	0.085267	100000	8527	94207	0.090509	0.3206	6556719	0.0000	65.567	0.090509	0
1	0.032877	91473	3007	357398	0.008415	1.1752	6462512	0.0000	70.649	0.008415	1
5	0.005361	88466	474	441144	0.001075	2.5000	6105114	0.0030	69.011	0.001079	5
10	0.002912	87992	256	439283	0.000583	2.3643	5663970	0.0077	64.369	0.000584	10
15	0.003503	87735	307	437943	0.000702	2.6102	5224686	0.0109	59.550	0.000701	15
20	0.004791	87428	419	436146	0.000960	2.6241	4786743	0.0083	54.751	0.000959	20
25	0.006400	87009	557	433710	0.001284	2.5996	4350597	0.0102	50.002	0.001283	25
30	0.007925	86452	685	430616	0.001591	2.5977	3916887	0.0114	45.307	0.001589	30
35	0.010239	85767	878	426726	0.002058	2.5961	3486271	0.0212	40.648	0.002054	35
40	0.012841	84889	1090	421843	0.002584	2.6122	3059546	0.0113	36.042	0.002581	40
45	0.017487	83799	1465	415567	0.003526	2.6601	2637703	0.0000	31.476	0.003526	45
50	0.026919	82334	2216	406483	0.005453	2.6602	2222136	0.0123	26.989	0.005441	50
55	0.039566	80117	3170	393217	0.008062	2.6751	1815653	0.0223	22.662	0.008027	55
60	0.063427	76947	4881	373552	0.013065	2.7083	1422436	0.0190	18.486	0.013006	60
65	0.111699	72067	8050	341774	0.023553	2.6943	1048884	0.0190	14.554	0.023443	65
70	0.193506	64017	12388	290808	0.042597	2.6366	707111	0.0190	11.046	0.042415	70
75	0.313244	51629	16173	218692	0.073951	2.5604	416302	0.0190	8.063	0.073658	75
80	0.481640	35457	17077	135050	0.126452	2.5269	197610	0.0190	5.573	0.125811	80
85+	*1.000000	18379	18379	62560	0.293789	3.4038	62560	0.0190	3.404	0.291482	85+

TABLE 4 — OBSERVED AND PROJECTED VITAL RATES

	OBSERVED POPULATION BOTH SEXES	MALES	FEMALES	PROJECTED 1965 MALES	FEMALES	1970 MALES	FEMALES	1975 MALES	FEMALES	STABLE MALES	FEMALE
RATES PER THOUSAND											
Birth	24.23	26.08	22.54	25.67	22.41	25.27	22.27	24.69	21.95	23.14	21.64
Death	10.99	11.68	10.36	11.96	10.67	12.08	10.85	12.20	11.06	13.39	11.88
Increase	13.24	14.39	12.18	13.71	11.75	13.18	11.41	12.49	10.88		9.755
PERCENTAGE											
under 15	29.18	31.02	27.48	30.48	27.06	30.33	27.12	30.29	27.34	28.25	26.8
15-64	62.90	62.42	63.35	62.84	63.45	62.71	62.93	62.33	62.19	63.27	62.1
65 and over	7.92	6.55	9.18	6.69	9.50	6.97	9.95	7.38	10.47	8.47	11.0
DEP. RATIO X 100	58.98	60.20	57.87	59.14	57.61	59.48	58.91	60.44	60.80	58.05	60.9

TABLE 5 — POPULATION PROJECTED WITH FIXED AGE-SPECIFIC BIRTH AND DEATH RATES (IN 1000's)

AGE AT LAST BIRTHDAY	1965 BOTH SEXES	1965 MALES	1965 FEMALES	1970 BOTH SEXES	1970 MALES	1970 FEMALES	1975 BOTH SEXES	1975 MALES	1975 FEMALES	AGE AT LAST BIRTHDAY
0-4	990	507	483	1043	534	509	1092	559	533	0-4
5-9	879	450	429	966	494	472	1018	521	497	5-9
10-14	844	430	414	875	448	427	961	491	470	10-14
15-19	834	421	413	841	428	413	872	446	426	15-19
20-24	747	366	381	829	418	411	836	425	411	20-24
25-29	703	336	367	741	362	379	823	414	409	25-29
30-34	667	321	346	696	332	364	734	358	376	30-34
35-39	625	299	326	659	316	343	688	327	361	35-39
40-44	581	279	302	615	293	322	649	310	339	40-44
45-49	490	233	257	569	271	298	603	285	318	45-49
50-54	492	232	260	475	224	251	551	260	291	50-54
55-59	455	208	247	470	218	252	454	211	243	55-59
60-64	376	165	211	423	189	234	437	198	239	60-64
65-69	296	124	172	335	142	193	376	162	214	65-69
70-74	216	87	129	243	97	146	276	111	165	70-74
75-79	147	56	91	156	59	97	176	66	110	75-79
80-84	80	28	52	86	30	56	91	31	60	80-84
85+	32	10	22	35	11	24	38	12	26	85+
TOTAL	9454	4552	4902	10057	4866	5191	10675	5187	5488	TOTAL

TABLE 6 — STANDARDIZED RATES

STANDARD COUNTRIES: STANDARDIZED RATES PER THOUSAND

	ENGLAND AND WALES 1961 BOTH SEXES	MALES	FEMALES	UNITED STATES 1960 BOTH SEXES	MALES	FEMALES	MEXICO 1960 BOTH SEXES	MALES	FEMALES
Birth	20.37	23.80*	19.14	20.69	22.17*	19.76	22.42	21.87*	21.68
Death	14.30	16.21*	14.11	12.64	13.99*	11.46	8.86	10.60*	7.72
Increase	6.08	7.60*	5.03	8.05	8.18*	8.30	13.56	11.26*	13.95

TABLE 7 — MOMENTS AND CUMULANTS

OBSERVED POP. MALES	FEMALES	STATIONARY POP. MALES	FEMALES	STABLE POP. MALES	FEMALES	OBSERVED BIRTHS	NET MATERNITY FUNCTION	BIRTHS IN STABLE POP.
29.74485	32.23521	36.29067	38.43433	31.60896	33.32795	29.03856	29.56570	29.14471
430.1604	472.8963	495.1727	537.7088	461.2949	504.8501	39.49779	41.57716	40.54693
4637.685	4592.844	2400.562	1993.125	4423.509	4608.150	107.6296	100.6542	110.2594
-124672.	-175591.	-241126.	-304160.	-167310.	-221968.	-787.166	-1067.273	-890.517
0.270216	0.199465	0.047463	0.025552	0.199342	0.165031	0.187994	0.140961	0.182372
2.326234	2.214816	2.016598	1.948018	2.213741	2.129105	2.495431	2.382601	2.458341
-0.104539	-0.075691	-0.017867	-0.009296	-0.075587	-0.060492	-0.095803	-0.067627	-0.089717

TABLE 8 — RATES FROM AGE DISTRIBUTIONS AND VITAL STATISTICS (Females)

VITAL STATISTICS

		THOMPSON AGE RANGE	NRR	1000r	INTERVAL	BOURGEOIS-PICHAT AGE RANGE	NRR	1000b	1000d	1000r	COALE	
R	1.542											
R	1.332	0-4	1.26	8.54	27.41	5-29	1.26	22.14	13.55	8.59	IBR	21.45
R	3.181	5-9	1.29	9.29	27.36	30-54	1.31	22.35	12.21	10.14	IDR	13.92
NERATION	29.354	10-14	1.35	11.01	27.32	55-79	1.75	40.09	19.27	20.82	IRI	7.53
X RATIO	106.310	15-19	1.33	10.08	27.25	*15-39	1.31	22.72	12.78	9.94	K1	-5.15
											K2	0.

TABLE 9 — LESLIE MATRIX AND ITS SPECTRAL COMPONENTS (Females)

ORIGINAL MATRIX SUB-DIAGONAL	ALTERNATIVE FIRST ROWS Projection	Integral	FIRST STABLE MATRIX % IN STABLE POPULATION	FISHER VALUES	REPRODUCTIVE VALUES	SECOND STABLE MATRIX Z_2 FIRST COLUMN	FIRST ROW
0.97684	0.00000	0.00000	9.540	1.134	498041	0.1405+0.0729	0.1405+0.0729
0.99578	0.00008	0.00000	8.875	1.219	507323	0.1551-0.0950	0.0087+0.1374
0.99695	0.02862	0.00017	8.416	1.286	532742	-0.0016-0.2132	-0.0966+0.0669
0.99590	0.19276	0.05866	7.991	1.321	505334	-0.2152-0.1275	-0.0953-0.0432
0.99442	0.36070	0.33778	7.579	1.174	433128	-0.2581+0.1390	-0.0376-0.1029
0.99287	0.34490	0.40368	7.177	0.828	288572	-0.0165+0.3426	0.0078-0.0993
0.99096	0.25299	0.30533	6.786	0.482	158533	0.3329+0.2231	0.0274-0.0635
0.98856	0.15147	0.21509	6.404	0.221	67567	0.4232-0.1983	0.0229-0.0266
0.98512	0.05175	0.09644	6.029	0.061	15860	0.0564-0.5408	0.0082-0.0061
0.97814	0.00481	0.00976	5.657	0.005	1393	-0.5033-0.3795	0.0008-0.0005
0.96736	0.00004	0.00009	5.269	0.000	12	-0.6731+0.2708	0.0000-0.0000
0.79866			20.277				

TABLE 10 — AGE ANALYSIS AND MISCELLANEOUS RESULTS (Females)

OBSERVED POPUL. (IN 100's)	CONTRIBUTIONS OF ROOTS (IN 100's) r_1	r_2, r_3	r_4-r_{11}	AGE-SP. BIRTH RATES	NET MATERNITY FUNCTION	COEFF. OF MATRIX EQUATION	PARAMETERS	INTEGRAL	MATRIX	x	EXP. INCREASE $e^{(x+2\frac{1}{2})r}$
4391	4560	-80	-90	0.0000	0.0000	0.0000	L(1)	1.04999	1.05004	0	1.0247
4161	4242	-105	23	0.0000	0.0000	0.0001	L(2)	0.43366	0.43848	50	1.6689
4144	4023	-19	140	0.0000	0.0002	0.0278		0.74726	0.72791	55	1.7524
3824	3820	120	-116	0.0127	0.0555	0.1869	R(1)	0.00976	0.00977	60	1.8400
3690	3623	172	-105	0.0730	0.3184	0.3483	R(2)	-0.02924	-0.03256	65	1.9319
3485	3431	43	12	0.0872	0.3783	0.3312			0.20899	0.20573	70	2.0285
3291	3244	-184	231	0.0660	0.2841	0.2412	C(1)		47800	75	2.1299
3058	3061	-279	276	0.0465	0.1983	0.1431	C(2)		-30774	80	2.2364
2608	2882	-86	-188	0.0208	0.0879	0.0483			-4760	85	2.3482
2660	2704	274	-318	0.0021	0.0088	0.0044	2P/Y	30.0640	30.5416	90	2.4656
2551	2519	440	-408	0.0000	0.0001	0.0000	DELTA	2.6906		95	2.5888
8341	9693									100	2.7182

446   Portugal 1963

TABLE 1 — DATA

AGE AT LAST BIRTHDAY	POPULATION BOTH SEXES	MALES Number	%	FEMALES Number	%	BIRTHS BY AGE OF MOTHER	DEATHS BOTH SEXES	MALES	FEMALES	AGE AT LAST BIRTHDAY
0	192400	99500	2.3	92900	2.0	0	15522	8583	6939	0
1-4	718700	368000	8.5	350700	7.4	0	4738	2518	2220	1-4
5-9	871799	444600	10.2	427199	9.0	0	1027	573	454	5-9
10-14	856200	431800	10.0	424400	9.0	41	550	332	218	10-14
15-19	735900	359100	8.3	376800	8.0	10556	707	460	247	15-19
20-24	694800	327400	7.5	367400	7.8	51377	751	464	287	20-24
25-29	675600	323800	7.5	351800	7.4	62439	970	586	384	25-29
30-34	667900	319100	7.4	348800	7.4	45576	1236	811	425	30-34
35-39	601800	289800	6.7	312000	6.6	29426	1496	955	541	35-39
40-44	496400	239100	5.5	257300	5.4	11825	1776	1122	654	40-44
45-49	527400	253800	5.8	273600	5.8	897	2447	1549	898	45-49
50-54	509800	238800	5.5	271000	5.7	15	3729	2297	1432	50-54
55-59	432600	195800	4.5	236800	5.0	0	4925	3037	1888	55-59
60-64	347400	152000	3.5	195400	4.1	0	6390	3788	2602	60-64
65-69	275200	117200	2.7	158000	3.3	0	8094	4574	3520	65-69
70-74	217800	88500	2.0	129300	2.7		11143	5689	5454	70-74
75-79	145419	55518	1.3	89901	1.9		12291	5487	6804	75-79
80-84	77486	26103	0.6	51383	1.1	109457 M.	10852	4402	6450	80-84
85+	29796	8579	0.2	21217	0.4	102695 F.	9367	2930	6437	85+
TOTAL	9074400	4338500		4735900		212152	98011	50157	47854	TOTAL

TABLE 2 — MALE LIFE TABLE

x	nq_x	l_x	nd_x	nL_x	nm_x	na_x	T_x	r_x	$\mathring{e}_x$	nM_x
0	0.081193	100000	8119	94349	0.086056	0.3040	6170886	0.0033	61.709	0.086261
1	0.026775	91881	2460	360522	0.006824	1.1542	6076537	0.0033	66.135	0.006842
5	0.006395	89421	572	445674	0.001283	2.5000	5716015	0.0054	63.923	0.001289
10	0.003837	88849	341	443391	0.000769	2.4968	5270342	0.0203	59.318	0.000769
15	0.006403	88508	567	441181	0.001285	2.6031	4826951	0.0265	54.537	0.001281
20	0.007067	87941	621	438198	0.001418	2.5738	4385770	0.0089	49.872	0.001417
25	0.009011	87320	787	434730	0.001810	2.6252	3947572	0.0007	45.208	0.001810
30	0.012644	86533	1094	430057	0.002544	2.6171	3512842	0.0086	40.595	0.002542
35	0.016405	85439	1402	423868	0.003307	2.6275	3082785	0.0254	36.082	0.003295
40	0.023228	84037	1952	415528	0.004698	2.6140	2658917	0.0086	31.640	0.004693
45	0.030085	82085	2470	404628	0.006103	2.6523	2243389	0.0000	27.330	0.006103
50	0.047192	79616	3757	389360	0.009650	2.6796	1838761	0.0159	23.095	0.009619
55	0.075260	75858	5709	365961	0.015600	2.6650	1449401	0.0290	19.107	0.015511
60	0.118008	70149	8278	331169	0.024997	2.6350	1083440	0.0162	15.445	0.024921
65	0.179000	61871	11075	282890	0.039149	2.6103	752271	0.0162	12.159	0.039027
70	0.278399	50796	14142	219349	0.064471	2.5511	469381	0.0162	9.240	0.064282
75	0.396708	36655	14541	146686	0.099132	2.4839	250032	0.0162	6.821	0.098833
80	0.588642	22113	13017	76891	0.169291	2.4129	103347	0.0162	4.673	0.168639
85+	*1.000000	9097	9097	26456	0.343834	2.9084	26456	0.0162	2.908	0.341532

TABLE 3 — FEMALE LIFE TABLE

x	nq_x	l_x	nd_x	nL_x	nm_x	na_x	T_x	r_x	$\mathring{e}_x$	nM_x
0	0.070959	100000	7096	95116	0.074603	0.3118	6740971	0.0017	67.410	0.074693
1	0.024842	92904	2308	365070	0.006322	1.1637	6645855	0.0017	71.535	0.006330
5	0.005289	90596	479	451783	0.001061	2.5000	6280784	0.0022	69.327	0.001063
10	0.002560	90117	231	449970	0.000513	2.3332	5829001	0.0119	64.683	0.000514
15	0.003276	89886	294	448720	0.000656	2.5841	5379032	0.0138	59.843	0.000656
20	0.003901	89592	350	447125	0.000782	2.6141	4930311	0.0060	55.031	0.000781
25	0.005445	89242	486	445036	0.001092	2.5816	4483186	0.0042	50.236	0.001092
30	0.006082	88756	540	442491	0.001220	2.6078	4038150	0.0107	45.497	0.001218
35	0.008674	88217	765	439288	0.001742	2.6542	3595659	0.0286	40.759	0.001734
40	0.012649	87451	1106	434625	0.002545	2.6207	3156372	0.0106	36.093	0.002542
45	0.016286	86345	1406	428443	0.003282	2.6651	2721747	0.0000	31.522	0.003282
50	0.026143	84939	2221	419528	0.005293	2.6733	2293304	0.0091	26.999	0.005284
55	0.039335	82718	3254	406068	0.008013	2.6877	1873776	0.0242	22.652	0.007973
60	0.064826	79465	5151	385414	0.013366	2.6882	1467707	0.0171	18.470	0.013316
65	0.106399	74313	7907	353391	0.022374	2.7013	1082293	0.0171	14.564	0.022278
70	0.192606	66406	12790	301987	0.042354	2.6510	728902	0.0171	10.976	0.042181
75	0.320330	53616	17175	226126	0.075953	2.5572	426915	0.0171	7.962	0.075683
80	0.480348	36441	17505	138812	0.126102	2.5210	200789	0.0171	5.510	0.125527
85+	*1.000000	18937	18937	61976	0.305549	3.2728	61976	0.0171	3.273	0.303389

TABLE 4 — OBSERVED AND PROJECTED VITAL RATES

RATES PER THOUSAND	OBSERVED POPULATION BOTH SEXES	MALES	FEMALES	1968 MALES	FEMALES	1973 MALES	FEMALES	1978 MALES	FEMALES	STABLE POPULATION MALES	FEMALES
Birth	23.38	25.23	21.68	24.78	21.51	24.44	21.41	24.06	21.25	22.50	21.6
Death	10.80	11.56	10.10	11.70	10.31	11.80	10.48	11.90	10.69	12.81	11.3
Increase	12.58	13.67	11.58	13.07	11.19	12.64	10.93	12.16	10.56		9.68
PERCENTAGE											
under 15	29.08	30.98	27.35	30.42	26.84	30.17	26.78	30.14	26.97	28.16	26.6
15-64	62.70	62.20	63.15	62.72	63.40	62.68	62.95	62.25	62.15	63.49	62.2
65 and over	8.22	6.82	9.50	6.86	9.76	7.16	10.28	7.62	10.87	8.35	11.1
DEP. RATIO X 100	59.49	60.76	58.34	59.43	57.73	59.55	58.86	60.65	60.89	57.49	60.

TABLE 1 / DATA

AGE AT LAST BIRTHDAY	POPULATION BOTH SEXES	MALES Number	%	FEMALES Number	%	BIRTHS BY AGE OF MOTHER	DEATHS BOTH SEXES	MALES	FEMALES	AGE AT LAST BIRTHDAY
0	194200	100600	2.3	93600	2.0	0	14986	8312	6674	0
1-4	720100	369300	8.4	350800	7.4	0	4665	2471	2194	1-4
5-9	879500	449300	10.3	430200	9.0	0	1034	553	481	5-9
10-14	862400	435000	9.9	427400	9.0	54	576	334	242	10-14
15-19	730600	356200	8.1	374400	7.9	10826	770	519	251	15-19
20-24	690200	323800	7.4	366400	7.7	52557	745	459	286	20-24
25-29	676200	323900	7.4	352300	7.4	63906	1006	654	352	25-29
30-34	679900	324800	7.4	355100	7.4	46232	1155	705	450	30-34
35-39	605800	292100	6.7	313700	6.6	30358	1571	976	595	35-39
40-44	494600	239000	5.5	255600	5.4	12329	2015	1289	726	40-44
45-49	534100	258200	5.9	275900	5.8	856	2382	1537	845	45-49
50-54	520900	245000	5.6	275900	5.8	18	3805	2365	1440	50-54
55-59	442000	200600	4.6	241400	5.1	0	5011	3152	1859	55-59
60-64	352400	154700	3.5	197700	4.1	0	6610	3844	2766	60-64
65-69	279600	119500	2.7	160100	3.4	0	8072	4418	3654	65-69
70-74	222400	90500	2.1	131900	2.8		10785	5465	5320	70-74
75-79	146799	55948	1.3	90851	1.9		12211	5512	6699	75-79
80-84	80035	27176	0.6	52859	1.1	112434 M.	10465	4085	6380	80-84
85+	31566	9276	0.2	22290	0.5	104702 F.	9014	2790	6224	85+
TOTAL	9143300	4374900		4768400		217136	96878	49440	47438	TOTAL

TABLE 2 / MALE / LIFE TABLE

x	nq_x	l_x	nd_x	nL_x	nm_x	na_x	T_x	r_x	$\mathring{e}_x$	nM_x	x
0	0.077922	100000	7792	94596	0.082374	0.3064	6210128	0.0041	62.101	0.082624	0
1	0.026176	92208	2414	361969	0.006668	1.1571	6115532	0.0041	66.323	0.006691	1
5	0.006109	89794	549	447599	0.001226	2.5000	5753563	0.0052	64.075	0.001231	5
10	0.003837	89246	342	445392	0.000769	2.5600	5305964	0.0222	59.454	0.000768	10
15	0.007279	88903	647	442957	0.001461	2.5906	4860571	0.0283	54.673	0.001457	15
20	0.007068	88256	624	439769	0.001418	2.5779	4417615	0.0079	50.055	0.001418	20
25	0.010046	87632	880	436026	0.002019	2.5743	3977845	0.0000	45.392	0.002019	25
30	0.010808	86752	938	431530	0.002173	2.6222	3541820	0.0080	40.827	0.002171	30
35	0.016668	85814	1430	425768	0.003359	2.6909	3110290	0.0271	36.244	0.003341	35
40	0.026640	84384	2248	416504	0.005397	2.5909	2684522	0.0073	31.813	0.005393	40
45	0.029350	82136	2411	404971	0.005953	2.6320	2268018	0.0000	27.613	0.005953	45
50	0.047357	79725	3776	389891	0.009683	2.6863	1863047	0.0152	23.368	0.009653	50
55	0.076204	75950	5788	366213	0.015804	2.6614	1473156	0.0296	19.396	0.015713	55
60	0.117708	70162	8259	331156	0.024939	2.6201	1106943	0.0212	15.777	0.024848	60
65	0.170426	61903	10550	284248	0.037115	2.6048	775787	0.0212	12.532	0.036971	65
70	0.264202	51353	13568	223767	0.060633	2.5677	491539	0.0212	9.572	0.060387	70
75	0.395950	37786	14961	151284	0.098895	2.4838	267772	0.0212	7.087	0.098520	75
80	0.543597	22824	12407	82157	0.151019	2.4237	116488	0.0212	5.104	0.150316	80
85+	*1.000000	10417	10417	34331	0.303435	3.2956	34331	0.0212	3.296	0.300776	85+

TABLE 3 / FEMALE / LIFE TABLE

x	nq_x	l_x	nd_x	nL_x	nm_x	na_x	T_x	r_x	$\mathring{e}_x$	nM_x	x
0	0.067869	100000	6787	95356	0.071174	0.3157	6771344	0.0025	67.713	0.071303	0
1	0.024535	93213	2287	366377	0.006242	1.1686	6675989	0.0025	71.621	0.006254	1
5	0.005567	90926	506	453365	0.001116	2.5000	6309612	0.0016	69.393	0.001118	5
10	0.002821	90420	255	451420	0.000565	2.3333	5856246	0.0132	64.767	0.000566	10
15	0.003350	90165	302	450089	0.000671	2.5656	5404827	0.0147	59.944	0.000670	15
20	0.003897	89863	350	448469	0.000781	2.5858	4954737	0.0053	55.137	0.000781	20
25	0.004985	89513	446	446492	0.000999	2.5996	4506269	0.0021	50.342	0.000999	25
30	0.006327	89066	564	444005	0.001269	2.6456	4059777	0.0103	45.581	0.001267	30
35	0.009492	88503	840	440555	0.001907	2.6672	3615771	0.0309	40.855	0.001897	35
40	0.014117	87663	1238	435319	0.002843	2.5798	3175216	0.0102	36.221	0.002840	40
45	0.015204	86425	1314	429042	0.003063	2.6522	2739897	0.0000	31.702	0.003063	45
50	0.025822	85111	2198	420446	0.005227	2.6745	2310856	0.0082	27.151	0.005219	50
55	0.038053	82914	3155	407353	0.007745	2.7132	1890410	0.0248	22.800	0.007701	55
60	0.068039	79758	5427	386253	0.014050	2.6894	1483057	0.0191	18.594	0.013991	60
65	0.108812	74332	8088	352860	0.022922	2.6758	1096804	0.0191	14.756	0.022823	65
70	0.184971	66244	12253	302427	0.040516	2.6503	743944	0.0191	11.230	0.040334	70
75	0.313560	53990	16929	228681	0.074030	2.5622	441517	0.0191	8.178	0.073736	75
80	0.466892	37061	17304	142636	0.121313	2.5341	212836	0.0191	5.743	0.120699	80
85+	*1.000000	19758	19758	70199	0.281450	3.5530	70199	0.0191	3.553	0.279228	85+

TABLE 4 / OBSERVED AND PROJECTED / PROJECTIONAL RATES

	OBSERVED POPULATION BOTH SEXES	MALES	FEMALES	PROJECTED POPULATION 1969 MALES	FEMALES	1974 MALES	FEMALES	1979 MALES	FEMALES	STABLE POPULATION MALES	FEMALES
RATES PER THOUSAND											
Birth	23.75	25.70	21.96	25.12	21.70	24.73	21.58	24.33	21.42	22.86	21.40
Death	10.60	11.30	9.95	11.64	10.31	11.75	10.47	11.85	10.68	12.51	11.05
Increase	13.15	14.40	12.01	13.49	11.40	12.98	11.11	12.48	10.74		10.3481
PERCENTAGE											
under 15	29.05	30.95	27.30	30.56	26.90	30.45	26.93	30.58	27.27	28.58	27.10
15-64	62.63	62.13	63.09	62.40	63.21	62.18	62.64	61.55	61.70	63.10	61.99
65 and over	8.32	6.91	9.60	7.03	9.90	7.38	10.43	7.87	11.03	8.31	10.91
DEP. RATIO X 100	59.66	60.94	58.50	60.25	58.21	60.83	59.65	62.48	62.08	58.47	61.31

TABLE 1 — DATA

AGE AT LAST BIRTHDAY	POPULATION BOTH SEXES	MALES Number	MALES %	FEMALES Number	FEMALES %	BIRTHS BY AGE OF MOTHER	DEATHS BOTH SEXES	DEATHS MALES	FEMALES	AGE AT LAST BIRTHDAY
0	196600	102200	2.3	94400	2.0	0	13664	7698	5966	0
1-4	723300	372100	8.4	351200	7.3	0	3733	1978	1755	1-4
5-9	889301	455900	10.3	433401	9.0	0	852	480	372	5-9
10-14	870800	440200	9.9	43C600	9.0	54	481	289	192	10-1
15-19	726700	354600	8.0	372100	7.7	10470	684	448	236	15-1
20-24	687000	321200	7.3	365600	7.6	51382	701	477	224	20-2
25-29	678200	325100	7.3	353100	7.3	61716	866	527	339	25-2
30-34	693700	332000	7.5	361700	7.5	44975	1158	720	438	30-3
35-39	611200	295600	6.7	315600	6.6	28838	1497	960	537	35-3
40-44	494000	239800	5.4	254200	5.3	11931	1972	1252	720	40-4
45-49	542100	263700	6.0	278400	5.8	915	2371	1513	858	45-4
50-54	533400	252200	5.7	281200	5.9	18	3619	2351	1268	50-5
55-59	452600	206400	4.7	246200	5.1	0	5100	3199	1901	55-5
60-64	358400	158100	3.6	200300	4.2	0	6634	4001	2633	60-6
65-69	284600	122300	2.8	162300	3.4	0	8335	4651	3684	65-6
70-74	227600	92800	2.1	134800	2.8		10928	5474	5454	70-7
75-79	150211	57112	1.3	93099	1.9		12444	5670	6774	75-7
80-84	82189	28132	0.6	54057	1.1	108574 M.	10853	4281	6572	80-8
85+	32499	9756	0.2	22743	0.5	101725 F.	9295	2959	6336	85+
TOTAL	9234400	4429400		4805C00		210299	95187	48928	46259	TOTA

TABLE 2 — MALE LIFE TABLE

x	$_nq_x$	l_x	$_nd_x$	$_nL_x$	$_nm_x$	$_na_x$	T_x	r_x	$\dot{e}_x$	$_nM_x$
0	0.071222	10CCCO	7122	94957	0.075004	0.2920	6312214	0.0057	63.122	0.075323
1	0.020837	92878	1935	365977	0.005288	1.1407	6217257	0.0057	66.940	0.005316
5	0.005229	90942	476	453523	0.001049	2.5000	5851279	0.0054	64.340	0.001053
10	0.003283	90467	297	451612	0.000658	2.5664	5397756	0.0242	59.666	0.000657
15	0.006324	90170	570	449500	0.001269	2.6336	4946144	0.0303	54.854	0.001263
20	0.007396	89600	663	446372	0.001485	2.5465	4496644	0.0072	50.186	0.001484
25	0.008074	88937	718	442950	0.001621	2.5842	4050272	0.0000	45.541	0.001621
30	0.010801	88219	953	438858	0.002171	2.6522	3607321	0.0073	40.891	0.002169
35	0.016207	87266	1414	433058	0.003266	2.6859	3168464	0.0291	36.308	0.003248
40	0.025797	85852	2215	423920	0.005224	2.5896	2735406	0.0066	31.862	0.005221
45	0.028303	83637	2367	412581	0.005738	2.6325	2311486	0.0000	27.637	0.005738
50	0.045771	81270	3720	397772	0.009351	2.6943	1898906	0.0147	23.365	0.009322
55	0.075257	77550	5836	374174	0.015597	2.6738	1501133	0.0305	19.357	0.015499
60	0.119764	71714	8589	338180	0.025397	2.6260	1126959	0.0199	15.715	0.025307
65	0.174746	63125	11031	289068	0.038160	2.5924	788780	0.0199	12.495	0.038029
70	0.258783	52094	13481	227676	0.059212	2.5673	499712	0.0199	9.592	0.058987
75	0.398540	38613	15389	154437	0.099645	2.4898	272036	0.0199	7.045	0.099279
80	0.548081	23224	12729	83280	0.152843	2.4199	117599	0.0199	5.064	0.152175
85+	*1.000000	10495	10495	34319	0.305818	3.2699	34319	0.0199	3.270	0.303301

TABLE 3 — FEMALE LIFE TABLE

x	$_nq_x$	l_x	$_nd_x$	$_nL_x$	$_nm_x$	$_na_x$	T_x	r_x	$\dot{e}_x$	$_nM_x$
0	0.060373	10CCCO	6037	95804	0.063017	0.3050	6894611	0.0039	68.946	0.063199
1	0.019645	93963	1846	370600	0.004981	1.1554	6798807	0.0039	72.356	0.004997
5	0.004276	92117	394	459599	0.000857	2.5000	6428207	0.0016	69.783	0.000858
10	0.002223	91723	204	458083	0.000445	2.3939	5968607	0.0147	65.072	0.000446
15	0.003169	91519	290	456886	0.000635	2.5541	5510524	0.0158	60.212	0.000634
20	0.003060	91229	279	455477	0.000613	2.6086	5053639	0.0045	55.395	0.000613
25	0.004790	90950	436	453716	0.000960	2.6282	4598161	0.0001	50.557	0.000960
30	0.006045	90514	547	451272	0.001213	2.6263	4144446	0.0100	45.788	0.001211
35	0.008530	89967	767	448064	0.001713	2.6924	3693174	0.0334	41.050	0.001702
40	0.014080	89200	1256	442978	0.002835	2.5958	3245110	0.0099	36.380	0.002832
45	0.015297	87944	1345	436496	0.003082	2.6052	2802132	0.0000	31.863	0.003082
50	0.022350	86598	1935	428546	0.004516	2.7029	2365635	0.0075	27.317	0.004509
55	0.038158	84663	3231	415922	0.007767	2.7116	1937089	0.0258	22.880	0.007721
60	0.064071	81432	5217	395165	0.013203	2.7006	1521167	0.0191	18.680	0.013145
65	0.108295	76215	8254	361979	0.022801	2.6865	1126003	0.0191	14.774	0.022699
70	0.185451	67961	12605	310151	0.040641	2.6473	764023	0.0191	11.242	0.040460
75	0.310101	55356	17166	234977	0.073054	2.5647	453872	0.0191	8.199	0.072761
80	0.469595	38190	17934	146761	0.122199	2.5359	218895	0.0191	5.732	0.121576
85+	*1.000000	20256	20256	72135	0.280813	3.5611	72135	0.0191	3.561	0.278591

TABLE 4 — OBSERVED AND PROJECTED VITAL RATES

	OBSERVED POPULATION BOTH SEXES	MALES	FEMALES	PROJECTED POPULATION 1970 MALES	FEMALES	1975 MALES	FEMALES	1980 MALES	FEMALES	STABLE POPULATION MALES	FEMAL
RATES PER THOUSAND											
Birth	22.77	24.51	21.17	24.01	20.92	23.74	20.87	23.47	20.79	22.09	20.6
Death	10.31	11.05	9.63	11.31	9.96	11.45	10.15	11.59	10.38	12.32	10.8
Increase	12.47	13.47	11.54	12.70	10.97	12.29	10.72	11.89	10.41		9.774
PERCENTAGE											
under 15	29.02	30.94	27.25	30.29	26.68	29.90	26.55	29.82	26.76	28.08	26.5
15-64	62.56	62.06	63.03	62.59	63.30	62.59	62.84	62.14	61.98	63.40	62.1
65 and over	8.42	7.00	9.72	7.12	10.02	7.51	10.61	8.04	11.26	8.52	11.2
DEP. RATIO X 100	59.84	61.13	58.66	59.78	57.99	59.77	59.13	60.93	61.34	57.74	60.9

TABLE 5 — POPULATION PROJECTED WITH FIXED AGE—SPECIFIC BIRTH AND DEATH RATES (IN 1000's)

AGE LAST DAY	1970 BOTH SEXES	1970 MALES	FEMALES	1975 BOTH SEXES	1975 MALES	FEMALES	1980 BOTH SEXES	1980 MALES	FEMALES	AGE AT LAST BIRTHDAY
4	997	512	485	1046	537	509	1100	565	535	0-4
9	906	467	439	982	504	478	1031	529	502	5-9
14	886	454	432	903	465	438	979	502	477	10-14
19	867	438	429	883	452	431	900	463	437	15-19
24	723	352	371	863	435	428	879	449	430	20-24
29	683	319	364	719	349	370	858	432	426	25-29
34	673	322	351	678	316	362	714	346	368	30-34
39	687	328	359	667	318	349	672	312	360	35-39
44	601	289	312	676	321	355	656	311	345	40-44
49	483	233	250	589	282	307	662	312	350	45-49
54	527	254	273	471	225	246	574	272	302	50-54
59	510	237	273	504	239	265	451	212	239	55-59
64	421	187	234	473	214	259	468	216	252	60-64
69	318	135	183	373	159	214	421	183	238	65-69
74	235	96	139	263	106	157	310	126	184	70-74
79	165	63	102	170	65	105	191	72	119	75-79
84	89	31	58	98	34	64	101	35	66	80-84
+	39	12	27	42	13	29	45	14	31	85+
AL	9810	4729	5081	10400	5034	5366	11012	5351	5661	TOTAL

TABLE 6 — STANDARDIZED RATES

STANDARD COUNTRIES:

DARDIZED RATES PER THOUSAND	ENGLAND AND WALES 1961 BOTH SEXES	MALES	FEMALES	UNITED STATES 1960 BOTH SEXES	MALES	FEMALES	MEXICO 1960 BOTH SEXES	MALES	FEMALES
h	19.53	22.91*	18.31	19.84	21.53*	18.91	21.47	20.82*	20.71
th	13.23	14.44*	12.94	11.37	12.53*	10.13	7.24	9.68*	6.13
ease	6.30	8.47*	5.37	8.46	9.00*	8.77	14.22	11.14*	14.58

TABLE 7 — MOMENTS AND CUMULANTS

OBSERVED POP. MALES	FEMALES	STATIONARY POP. MALES	FEMALES	STABLE POP. MALES	FEMALES	OBSERVED BIRTHS	NET MATERNITY FUNCTION	BIRTHS IN STABLE POP.
30.39517	32.80561	36.40477	38.68881	31.71104	33.54125	29.15740	29.61132	29.17512
443.9840	483.5821	495.3805	540.7194	461.7175	508.1989	39.93262	43.05274	42.01625
4415.649	4417.503	2369.541	1927.962	4398.344	4591.670	96.8231	100.2220	111.5278
−149653.	−194743.	−240960.	−308282.	−167827.	−226434.	−862.523	−1252.570	−1049.091
0.222786	0.172561	0.046186	0.023512	0.196539	0.160635	0.147223	0.125870	0.167693
2.240811	2.167237	2.018098	1.945601	2.212756	2.123252	2.459102	2.324228	2.405737
−0.084337	−0.064726	−0.017432	−0.008554	−0.074678	−0.058860	−0.076637	−0.057838	−0.079410

TABLE 8 — RATES FROM AGE DISTRIBUTIONS AND VITAL STATISTICS (Females)

VITAL STATISTICS

	THOMPSON AGE RANGE	NRR	1000r	INTERVAL	BOURGEOIS-PICHAT AGE RANGE	NRR	1000b	1000d	1000r	COALE	
1.474										IBR	20.30
1.333	0-4	1.28	9.09	27.43	5-29	1.34	21.45	10.61	10.84	IDR	12.53
3.048	5-9	1.31	10.05	27.38	30-54	1.31	21.34	11.35	9.99	IRI	7.77
ERATION 29.392	10-14	1.36	11.05	27.34	55-79	1.76	40.04	19.05	20.99	K1	−3.89
RATIO 106.733	15-19	1.23	7.40	27.27	*50-74	1.81	42.97	20.94	22.03	K2	0.

TABLE 9 — LESLIE MATRIX AND ITS SPECTRAL COMPONENTS (Females)

ORIGINAL MATRIX SUB-DIAGONAL	ALTERNATIVE FIRST ROWS Projection	Integral	FIRST STABLE MATRIX % IN STABLE POPULATION	FISHER VALUES	REPRODUCTIVE VALUES	SECOND STABLE MATRIX Z₂ FIRST COLUMN	FIRST ROW
0.98541	0.00000	0.00000	9.397	1.098	489438	0.1358+0.0752	0.1358+0.0752
0.99670	0.00014	0.00000	8.818	1.171	507309	0.1576−0.0893	0.0058+0.1329
0.99673	0.03180	0.00029	8.369	1.233	530987	0.0072−0.2137	−0.0935+0.0629
0.99692	0.18979	0.06505	7.948	1.263	470088	−0.2109−0.1390	−0.0911−0.0421
0.99613	0.35494	0.32492	7.546	1.122	410086	−0.2700+0.1267	−0.0357−0.0987
0.99461	0.33667	0.40408	7.158	0.791	279347	−0.0389+0.3497	0.0072−0.0963
0.99289	0.24261	0.28747	6.779	0.463	167648	0.3274+0.2541	0.0270−0.0630
0.98865	0.15542	0.21125	6.410	0.222	70014	0.4559−0.1724	0.0245−0.0268
0.98537	0.05660	0.10851	6.034	0.063	16008	0.1066−0.5606	0.0091−0.0060
0.98179	0.00378	0.00760	5.662	0.004	1120	−0.4931−0.4476	0.0006−0.0004
0.97054	0.00007	0.00015	5.294	0.000	21	−0.7433+0.2173	0.0000−0.0000
0.80058			20.587				

TABLE 10 — AGE ANALYSIS AND MISCELLANEOUS RESULTS (Females)

CONTRIBUTIONS OF ROOTS (IN 100's)

OBSERVED POPUL. (IN 100's)	r₁	r₂, r₃	r₄-r₁₁	AGE-SP. BIRTH RATES	NET MATERNITY FUNCTION	COEFF. OF MATRIX EQUATION	PARAMETERS INTEGRAL	MATRIX	EXP. INCREASE x	e^{(x+2½)r}
4456	4600	−34	−110	0.0000	0.0000	0.0000	L(1) 1.05009	1.05014	0	1.0247
4334	4317	−29	46	0.0000	0.0000	0.0001	L(2) 0.43548	0.44083	50	1.6706
4306	4097	12	197	0.0001	0.0003	0.0312	0.73859	0.72014	55	1.7542
3721	3891	55	−225	0.0136	0.0622	0.1859	R(1) 0.00977	0.00978	60	1.8421
3656	3694	51	−89	0.0680	0.3096	0.3466	R(2) −0.03077	−0.03384	65	1.9344
3531	3504	−14	41	0.0845	0.3836	0.3275	0.20761	0.20430	70	2.0312
3617	3319	−88	386	0.0601	0.2714	0.2347	C(1)	48955	75	2.1330
3156	3138	−89	107	0.0442	0.1980	0.1493	C(2)	−10914	80	2.2398
2542	2954	12	−424	0.0227	0.1006	0.0538		3173	85	2.3520
2784	2772	136	−124	0.0016	0.0069	0.0035	2P/Y 30.2644	30.7549	90	2.4698
2812	2591	148	72	0.0000	0.0001	0.0001	DELTA 2.8814		95	2.5935
9135	10078								100	2.7234

TABLE 1 — DATA

AGE AT LAST BIRTHDAY	POPULATION BOTH SEXES	MALES Number	%	FEMALES Number	%	BIRTHS BY AGE OF MOTHER	DEATHS BOTH SEXES	MALES	FEMALES
0	341776	175668	2.0	166108	1.8	0	26099	14474	11625
1-4	1463129	748755	8.3	714374	7.6	0	5505	2854	2651
5-9	1805685	921592	10.3	884093	9.4	0	1632	939	693
10-14	1558515	792442	8.8	766073	8.1	153	981	585	396
15-19	1345222	681932	7.6	663290	7.0	40567	1318	823	495
20-24	1585153	784405	8.7	800748	8.5	129018	2156	1300	856
25-29	1582363	795804	8.9	786559	8.3	94065	2448	1402	1046
30-34	1530604	767379	8.5	763225	8.1	51039	2788	1592	1196
35-39	1325285	631217	7.0	694068	7.4	26378	3138	1652	1486
40-44	814467	367956	4.1	446511	4.7	6325	2690	1383	1307
45-49	1135839	531096	5.9	604743	6.4	776	5701	3090	2611
50-54	1051344	511606	5.7	539738	5.7	48	8355	4904	3451
55-59	878984	430115	4.8	448864	4.2	0	11549	6969	4580
60-64	715772	321610	3.6	394162	4.2	0	14627	8097	6530
65-69	525357	222697	2.5	302660	3.2	0	17642	8891	8751
70-74	380458	153657	1.7	226801	2.4		22015	10182	11833
75-79	217086	90116	1.0	126970	1.3		20901	8948	11953
80-84	109986	41532	0.5	68454	0.7	179828 M.	12674	5164	7510
85+	39897	13466	0.1	26431	0.3	168541 F.	7587	2791	4796
TOTAL	18406917	8983045		9423872		348369	169806	86040	83766

TABLE 2 — MALE LIFE TABLE

x	$_nq_x$	l_x	$_nd_x$	$_nL_x$	$_nm_x$	$_na_x$	T_x	r_x	$\dot{e}_x$	$_nM_x$
0	0.077577	100000	7758	94154	0.082394	0.2464	6325918	0.0000	63.259	0.082394
1	0.015080	92242	1391	364934	0.003812	1.0993	6231764	0.0000	67.559	0.003812
5	0.005046	90851	458	453110	0.001012	2.5000	5866830	0.0137	64.576	0.001019
10	0.003690	90393	334	451148	0.000739	2.5522	5413720	0.0292	59.891	0.000738
15	0.006017	90059	542	449026	0.001207	2.6558	4962572	0.0000	55.103	0.001207
20	0.008253	89517	739	445789	0.001657	2.5668	4513546	0.0000	50.421	0.001657
25	0.008771	88779	779	441982	0.001762	2.5458	4067757	0.0004	45.819	0.001762
30	0.010340	88000	910	437801	0.002078	2.5835	3625775	0.0211	41.202	0.002075
35	0.013127	87090	1143	432736	0.002642	2.6266	3187974	0.0708	36.606	0.002617
40	0.018673	85947	1605	425988	0.003767	2.6659	2755238	0.0134	32.058	0.003759
45	0.028706	84342	2421	416124	0.005818	2.6933	2329250	0.0000	27.617	0.005818
50	0.047005	81921	3851	400749	0.009609	2.7006	1913126	0.0110	23.353	0.009585
55	0.078498	78070	6128	376022	0.016298	2.6619	1512376	0.0298	19.372	0.016203
60	0.119738	71942	8614	339320	0.025387	2.6331	1136355	0.0443	15.795	0.025176
65	0.183698	63328	11633	288850	0.040274	2.6113	797034	0.0443	12.586	0.039924
70	0.286848	51694	14828	222032	0.066785	2.5426	508185	0.0443	9.831	0.066264
75	0.397710	36866	14662	146780	0.099891	2.4389	286153	0.0443	7.762	0.099294
80	0.474253	22204	10530	84072	0.125254	2.4409	139373	0.0443	6.277	0.124337
85+	*1.000000	11674	11674	55302	0.211092	4.7373	55302	0.0443	4.737	0.207263

TABLE 3 — FEMALE LIFE TABLE

x	$_nq_x$	l_x	$_nd_x$	$_nL_x$	$_nm_x$	$_na_x$	T_x	r_x	$\dot{e}_x$	$_nM_x$
0	0.066545	100000	6655	95086	0.069985	0.2615	6706381	0.0000	67.064	0.069985
1	0.014686	93345	1371	369422	0.003711	1.1115	6611295	0.0000	70.826	0.003711
5	0.003878	91975	357	458981	0.000777	2.5000	6241873	0.0124	67.865	0.000784
10	0.002580	91618	236	457495	0.000517	2.4857	5782892	0.0281	63.120	0.000517
15	0.003725	91381	340	456108	0.000746	2.6524	5325397	0.0000	58.277	0.000746
20	0.005331	91041	485	454046	0.001069	2.6116	4869289	0.0000	53.485	0.001069
25	0.006630	90556	600	451323	0.001330	2.5755	4415243	0.0035	48.757	0.001330
30	0.007815	89955	703	448094	0.001569	2.6057	3963919	0.0109	44.065	0.001567
35	0.010723	89252	957	443991	0.002156	2.6268	3515826	0.0514	39.392	0.002141
40	0.014559	88295	1286	438451	0.002932	2.6463	3071835	0.0107	34.790	0.002927
45	0.021372	87010	1860	430694	0.004318	2.6578	2633384	0.0000	30.265	0.004318
50	0.031643	85150	2694	419489	0.006422	2.6753	2202691	0.0231	25.868	0.006394
55	0.050046	82456	4127	402716	0.010247	2.6818	1783202	0.0208	21.626	0.010204
60	0.080369	78330	6295	377099	0.016694	2.6888	1380486	0.0339	17.624	0.016567
65	0.136486	72034	9832	337310	0.029147	2.6746	1003387	0.0339	13.929	0.028914
70	0.233667	62203	14535	276422	0.052582	2.6200	666077	0.0339	10.708	0.052173
75	0.381958	47668	18207	192403	0.094630	2.4770	389655	0.0339	8.174	0.094140
80	0.425004	29461	12521	113877	0.109952	2.4789	197253	0.0339	6.695	0.109709
85+	1.000000	16940	16940	83375	0.203177	4.9218	83375	0.0339	4.922	0.181453

TABLE 4 — OBSERVED AND PROJECTED VITAL RATES

	OBSERVED POPULATION BOTH SEXES	MALES	FEMALES	PROJECTED POPULATION 1965 MALES	FEMALES	1970 MALES	FEMALES	1975 MALES	FEMALES	STABLE POPULATION MALES	FEM.
RATES PER THOUSAND											
Birth	18.93	20.02	17.88	18.61	16.74	18.35	16.62	18.75	17.07	16.03	15.
Death	9.23	9.58	8.89	10.11	9.59	10.71	10.14	11.30	10.80	15.65	14.
Increase	9.70	10.44	9.00	8.50	7.16	7.65	6.48	7.45	6.27		0.3
PERCENTAGE											
under 15	28.08	29.37	26.85	28.08	25.72	25.79	23.70	24.15	22.28	21.79	20.
15-64	65.00	64.82	65.17	65.28	65.28	66.60	66.59	67.35	67.08	65.79	64.
65 and over	6.91	5.81	7.97	6.64	9.00	7.61	9.72	8.50	10.64	12.42	14.
DEP. RATIO X 100	53.84	54.27	53.44	53.18	53.18	50.15	50.18	48.48	49.08	52.00	55.

AGE AT LAST BIRTHDAY	1965 BOTH SEXES	MALES	FEMALES	1970 BOTH SEXES	MALES	FEMALES	1975 BOTH SEXES	MALES	FEMALES	AGE AT LAST BIRTHDAY	
0-4	1588	815	773	1589	816	773	1658	851	807	0-4	TABLE 5
5-9	1782	912	870	1569	805	764	1569	805	764	5-9	
10-14	1799	918	881	1775	908	867	1563	801	762	10-14	
15-19	1553	789	764	1792	913	879	1769	904	865	15-19	POPULATION
20-24	1337	677	660	1543	783	760	1782	907	875	20-24	PROJECTED
25-29	1574	778	796	1327	671	656	1532	776	756	25-29	WITH FIXED
30-34	1569	788	781	1560	770	790	1317	665	652	30-34	AGE—
35-39	1515	759	756	1553	779	774	1544	761	783	35-39	SPECIFIC
40-44	1306	621	685	1494	747	747	1531	767	764	40-44	BIRTH
45-49	798	359	439	1280	607	673	1463	729	734	45-49	AND
50-54	1100	511	589	773	346	427	1241	585	656	50-54	DEATH
55-59	998	480	518	1045	480	565	735	325	410	55-59	RATES
60-64	808	388	420	918	433	485	962	433	529	60-64	(IN 1000's)
65-69	627	274	353	706	330	376	803	369	434	65-69	
70-74	419	171	248	499	210	289	562	254	308	70-74	
75-79	260	102	158	286	113	173	340	139	201	75-79	
80-84	127	52	75	151	58	93	167	65	102	80-84	
85+	77	27	50	89	34	55	106	38	68	85+	
TOTAL	19237	9421	9816	19949	9803	10146	20644	10174	10470	TOTAL	

STANDARD COUNTRIES: STANDARDIZED RATES PER THOUSAND	ENGLAND AND WALES 1961 BOTH SEXES	MALES	FEMALES	UNITED STATES 1960 BOTH SEXES	MALES	FEMALES	MEXICO 1960 BOTH SEXES	MALES	FEMALES	TABLE 6
Birth	14.74	16.43*	13.82	15.02	15.39*	14.32	18.14	15.50*	17.50	STANDAR-DIZED RATES
Death	13.58	14.32*	14.01	11.58	12.16*	10.95	7.47	9.20*	6.71	
Increase	1.16	2.11*	-0.19	3.44	3.23*	3.37	10.67	6.30*	10.79	

	OBSERVED POP. MALES	FEMALES	STATIONARY POP. MALES	FEMALES	STABLE POP. MALES	FEMALES	OBSERVED BIRTHS	NET MATERNITY FUNCTION	BIRTHS IN STABLE POP.	TABLE 7
μ	30.00621	32.01189	36.54201	37.93244	36.35452	37.73429	26.28725	26.43466	26.41942	MOMENTS AND CUMULANTS
σ^2	412.C045	444.4663	499.9261	528.2800	498.9668	527.4052	33.74507	38.54007	38.47427	
κ_3	3972.702	3802.673	2510.507	2277.601	2599.914	2382.802	143.1941	175.2880	175.2891	
κ_4	-117432.	-154317.	-239185.	-281261.	-237112.	-279189.	126.800	-1.515	5.905	
β_1	0.225666	0.164688	0.050444	0.035185	0.054413	0.038703	0.533605	0.536744	0.539509	
β_2	2.308197	2.218846	2.042975	1.992186	2.047619	1.996286	3.111352	2.998980	3.003989	
κ	-0.090167	-0.065063	-0.019360	-0.013143	-0.020878	-0.014454	-0.333378	-0.288395	-0.290348	

VITAL STATISTICS		THOMPSON AGE RANGE	NRR	1000r	INTERVAL	BOURGEOIS-PICHAT AGE RANGE	NRR	1000b	1000d	1000r	COALE	TABLE 8
GRR	1.119										IBR	RATES FROM AGE DISTRI-BUTIONS AND VITAL STATISTICS (Females)
NRR	1.010	0-4	1.23	7.58	27.40	5-29	1.08	19.06	16.09	2.97	IDR	
TFR	2.312	5-9	1.25	8.32	27.35	30-54	1.43	25.73	12.37	13.37	IRI	
GENERATION	26.427	10-14	1.15	5.08	27.29	55-79	1.78	41.13	19.70	21.43	K1	
SEX RATIO	106.697	15-19	1.07	2.61	27.20	*45-74	1.81	42.47	20.57	21.90	K2	

Start Age Interval	ORIGINAL MATRIX SUB-DIAGONAL	ALTERNATIVE FIRST ROWS Projection	Integral	FIRST STABLE MATRIX % IN STABLE POPULATION	FISHER VALUES	REPRODUCTIVE VALUES	SECOND STABLE MATRIX Z_2 FIRST COLUMN	FIRST ROW	TABLE 9
	0.98810	0.00000	0.00000	7.019	1.077	948644	0.1719+0.1315	0.1719+0.1315	LESLIE MATRIX AND ITS SPECTRAL COMPO-NENTS (Females)
	0.99676	0.00022	0.00000	6.922	1.092	965815	0.2522-0.1392	-0.0385+0.1580	
	0.99697	0.06874	0.00045	6.887	1.098	840997	-0.0351-0.3851	-0.1193+0.0210	
	0.99548	0.24895	0.13757	6.853	1.029	682475	-0.4925-0.1647	-0.0619-0.0842	
	0.99400	0.31461	0.36243	6.809	0.766	613454	-0.4676+0.5159	-0.0041-0.1003	
	0.99284	0.20898	0.26901	6.756	0.431	339129	0.3809+0.8509	0.0130-0.0745	
	0.99084	0.11745	0.15042	6.695	0.208	158977	1.2467-0.0092	0.0187-0.0412	
	0.98752	0.05842	0.08549	6.621	0.083	57539	0.6575-1.5286	0.0135-0.0151	
	0.98231	0.01733	0.03186	6.526	0.020	9093	-1.5104-1.6179	0.0043-0.0030	
	0.97398	0.00154	0.00289	6.399	0.002	1064	-2.7634+0.9697	0.0004-0.0003	
	0.96001	0.0001C	0.00020	6.221	0.000	58	-0.2920+3.8310	0.0000-0.0000	
+	0.77473			26.291					

Start Age Interval	OBSERVED POPUL. (IN 100's)	CONTRIBUTIONS OF ROOTS (IN 100's) r_1	r_2, r_3	$r_4 \cdot r_{11}$	AGE-SP. BIRTH RATES	NET MATERNITY FUNCTION	COEFF. OF MATRIX EQUATION	PARAMETERS INTEGRAL	MATRIX	EXP. INCREASE x	$e^{(x+2\frac{1}{2})r}$	TABLE 10
	8805	8111	353	340	0.0000	0.0000	0.0000	L(1)	1.00188	1.00188	0	1.0009	AGE ANALYSIS AND MISCEL-LANEOUS RESULTS (Females)
	8841	8000	1000	-159	0.000C	0.0000	0.0002	L(2)	0.27534	0.29835	50	1.0199	
	7661	7959	448	-746	0.0001	0.0004	0.0677		0.70469	0.67982	55	1.0218	
	6633	7920	-1320	33	0.0296	0.1350	0.2444	R(1)	0.00038	0.00038	60	1.0237	
	8007	7869	-2228	2367	0.0780	0.3539	0.3075	R(2)	-0.05579	-0.05957	65	1.0257	
	7866	7807	-28	87	0.0579	0.2611	0.2030		0.23966	-0.23145	70	1.0276	
	7632	7737	3960	-4064	0.0324	0.1450	0.1133	C(1)		115563	75	1.0295	
	6941	7652	4298	-5009	0.0184	0.0816	0.0558	C(2)		158268	80	1.0315	
	4465	7542	-2434	-643	0.0069	0.0300	0.0164			72514	85	1.0334	
	6047	7395	-10153	8806	0.0006	0.0027	0.0014	2P/Y	26.2169	27.1473	90	1.0353	
	5397	7189	-6480	4689	0.0000	0.0002	0.0001	DELTA	11.6546		95	1.0373	
	15943	30383									100	1.0392	

TABLE 1 — DATA

AGE AT LAST BIRTHDAY	POPULATION BOTH SEXES	MALES Number	%	FEMALES Number	%	BIRTHS BY AGE OF MOTHER	DEATHS BOTH SEXES	MALES	FEMALES	AGE AT LAST BIRTHDAY
0	290960	149409	1.6	141551	1.5	0	16288	9001	7287	0
1-4	1281791	657266	7.1	624525	6.5	0	3161	1688	1473	1-4
5-9	1827764	933914	10.2	893850	9.3	0	1312	758	554	5-9
10-14	1794404	914393	9.9	880011	9.2	212	997	611	386	10-14
15-19	1346724	683206	7.4	663518	6.9	40787	1298	877	421	15-19
20-24	1447781	726084	7.9	721697	7.5	103904	1746	1154	592	20-24
25-29	1566164	783925	8.5	782239	8.1	80489	2173	1333	840	25-29
30-34	1583339	792333	8.6	791006	8.2	42037	2642	1631	1011	30-34
35-39	1439146	713544	7.8	725602	7.5	20450	3151	1853	1298	35-39
40-44	1156642	534204	5.8	622438	6.5	6684	3326	1763	1563	40-44
45-49	824828	373853	4.1	450975	4.7	309	3979	2151	1828	45-49
50-54	1133682	537784	5.8	595898	6.2	14	7834	4547	3287	50-54
55-59	938501	457831	5.0	480670	5.0	0	10737	6452	4285	55-59
60-64	801879	375868	4.1	426011	4.4	0	14323	8269	6054	60-64
65-69	559458	240016	2.6	319442	3.3	0	17389	8728	8661	65-69
70-74	413895	168944	1.8	244951	2.5		20224	9357	10867	70-74
75-79	236976	97068	1.1	139908	1.5		22049	9388	12661	75-79
80-84	123146	45957	0.5	77189	0.8	151785 M.	14855	5912	8943	80-84
85+	46051	15398	0.2	30653	0.3	143101 F.	8283	2993	5290	85+
TOTAL	18813131	9200997		9612134		294886	155767	78466	77301	TOTAL

TABLE 2 — MALE LIFE TABLE

x	$_nq_x$	l_x	$_nd_x$	$_nL_x$	$_nm_x$	$_na_x$	T_x	r_x	$\dot{e}_x$	$_nM_x$	x
0	0.057602	100000	5760	95614	0.060244	0.2386	6590630	0.0000	65.906	0.060244	0
1	0.010197	94240	961	374166	0.002568	1.0935	6495015	0.0000	68.920	0.002568	1
5	0.004050	93279	378	465450	0.000812	2.5000	6120849	0.0000	65.619	0.000812	5
10	0.003351	92901	311	463772	0.000671	2.6450	5655399	0.0304	60.875	0.000668	10
15	0.006420	92590	594	461550	0.001288	2.6461	5191627	0.0218	56.071	0.001284	15
20	0.007916	91995	728	458194	0.001589	2.5510	4730077	0.0000	51.416	0.001589	20
25	0.008467	91267	773	454445	0.001700	2.5537	4271884	0.0000	46.806	0.001700	25
30	0.010248	90494	927	450234	0.002060	2.5870	3817438	0.0073	42.184	0.002058	30
35	0.012952	89567	1160	445047	0.002607	2.5965	3367204	0.0368	37.594	0.002597	35
40	0.016570	88407	1465	438645	0.003340	2.6860	2922157	0.0610	33.053	0.003300	40
45	0.028388	86942	2468	428964	0.005754	2.6720	2483512	0.0000	28.565	0.005754	45
50	0.041463	84474	3503	414254	0.008455	2.6831	2054548	0.0000	24.322	0.008455	50
55	0.068499	80971	5546	391920	0.014152	2.6675	1640294	0.0213	20.258	0.014093	55
60	0.105573	75425	7963	358432	0.022216	2.6525	1248374	0.0486	16.551	0.022000	60
65	0.168638	67462	11377	310087	0.036689	2.6071	889942	0.0486	13.192	0.036364	65
70	0.246245	56085	13811	246978	0.055919	2.5781	579855	0.0486	10.339	0.055385	70
75	0.391508	42275	16551	169728	0.097514	2.4838	332878	0.0486	7.874	0.096716	75
80	0.486976	25724	12527	96603	0.129674	2.4442	163149	0.0486	6.342	0.128641	80
85+	*1.000000	13197	13197	66546	0.198311	5.0426	66546	0.0486	5.043	0.194376	85

TABLE 3 — FEMALE LIFE TABLE

x	$_nq_x$	l_x	$_nd_x$	$_nL_x$	$_nm_x$	$_na_x$	T_x	r_x	$\dot{e}_x$	$_nM_x$	x
0	0.049558	100000	4956	96267	0.051480	0.2466	6972693	0.0000	69.727	0.051480	0
1	0.009370	95044	891	377594	0.002359	1.0995	6876427	0.0000	72.350	0.002359	1
5	0.003094	94154	291	470040	0.000620	2.5000	6498833	0.0000	69.024	0.000620	5
10	0.002191	93862	206	468799	0.000439	2.5061	6028793	0.0293	64.230	0.000439	10
15	0.003175	93657	297	467576	0.000636	2.6236	5559995	0.0192	59.366	0.000634	15
20	0.004093	93359	382	465883	0.000820	2.6093	5092418	0.0000	54.546	0.000820	20
25	0.005355	92977	498	463684	0.001074	2.5868	4626536	0.0000	49.760	0.001074	25
30	0.006376	92479	590	460989	0.001279	2.6142	4162852	0.0062	45.014	0.001278	30
35	0.008935	91890	821	457511	0.001795	2.6412	3701863	0.0221	40.286	0.001789	35
40	0.012586	91068	1146	452682	0.002532	2.6789	3244352	0.0449	35.625	0.002511	40
45	0.020077	89922	1805	445359	0.004054	2.6446	2791670	0.0004	31.045	0.004053	45
50	0.027230	88117	2399	434994	0.005516	2.6698	2346311	0.0000	26.627	0.005516	50
55	0.043881	85717	3761	419869	0.008959	2.6821	1911317	0.0244	22.298	0.008915	55
60	0.069387	81956	5687	396820	0.014331	2.7209	1491449	0.0330	18.198	0.014211	60
65	0.128376	76269	9791	358488	0.027312	2.6653	1094629	0.0330	14.352	0.027113	65
70	0.202427	66478	13457	300809	0.044736	2.6531	736141	0.0330	11.073	0.044364	70
75	0.371205	53021	19682	216186	0.091041	2.5144	435332	0.0330	8.211	0.090495	75
80	0.444536	33339	14821	127505	0.116235	2.4837	219146	0.0330	6.573	0.115858	80
85+	1.000000	18519	18519	91641	0.202081	4.9485	91641	0.0330	4.949	0.172578	85

TABLE 4 — OBSERVED AND PROJECTED VITAL RATES

	OBSERVED POPULATION BOTH SEXES	MALES	FEMALES	PROJECTED POPULATION 1968 MALES	FEMALES	1973 MALES	FEMALES	1978 MALES	FEMALES	STABLE POPULATION MALES	FEMA.
RATES PER THOUSAND											
Birth	15.67	16.50	14.89	15.90	14.43	16.56	15.11	16.59	15.21	13.08	12.
Death	8.28	8.53	8.04	9.38	8.93	10.16	9.61	10.93	10.42	16.98	16.
Increase	7.39	7.97	6.85	6.53	5.50	6.40	5.50	5.66	4.79		-3.89
PERCENTAGE											
under 15	27.61	28.86	26.42	25.59	23.49	22.76	20.96	21.83	20.21	18.85	17.
15-64	65.05	64.98	65.13	66.87	66.76	68.55	68.34	68.42	67.76	65.62	64.
65 and over	7.33	6.17	8.45	7.54	9.75	8.69	10.70	9.75	12.03	15.53	17.
DEP. RATIO X 100	53.72	53.90	53.55	49.54	49.79	45.89	46.32	46.15	47.58	52.39	55.

TABLE 1 — A

AGE AT LAST BIRTHDAY	POPULATION BOTH SEXES	MALES Number	%	FEMALES Number	%	BIRTHS BY AGE OF MOTHER	DEATHS BOTH SEXES	MALES	FEMALES	AGE AT LAST BIRTHDAY
0	283038	145518	1.6	137520	1.4	0	13988	7785	6203	0
1-4	1217899	624680	6.7	593219	6.1	0	2973	1565	1408	1-4
5-9	1810571	925263	10.0	885308	9.2	0	1173	711	462	5-9
10-14	1811207	923440	10.0	887767	9.2	172	936	561	375	10-14
15-19	1424133	722719	7.8	701414	7.3	39824	1264	866	398	15-19
20-24	1387362	699738	7.6	687624	7.1	99081	1540	1010	530	20-24
25-29	1576224	784795	8.5	791429	8.2	81257	2122	1320	802	25-29
30-34	1575698	788940	8.5	786758	8.1	41061	2553	1596	957	30-34
35-39	1470801	733552	7.9	737249	7.6	19333	3177	1882	1295	35-39
40-44	1253809	586855	6.3	666954	6.9	6318	3656	2031	1625	40-44
45-49	764336	343476	3.7	420860	4.4	317	3349	1858	1491	45-49
50-54	1140479	537398	5.8	603081	6.2	20	7739	4424	3315	50-54
55-59	960011	464506	5.0	495505	5.1	0	10658	6342	4316	55-59
60-64	819933	391021	4.2	428912	4.4	0	14525	8572	5953	60-64
65-69	587345	252141	2.7	335204	3.5	0	17063	8829	8234	65-69
70-74	417790	172089	1.9	245701	2.5		19603	9047	10556	70-74
75-79	246569	100170	1.1	146399	1.5		21828	9328	12500	75-79
80-84	130261	48625	0.5	81636	0.8	148078 M.	15646	6318	9328	80-84
85+	49615	16772	0.2	32843	0.3	139305 F.	8683	3200	5483	85+
TOTAL	18927081	9261698		9665383		287383	152476	77245	75231	TOTAL

TABLE 2 — A, LE, LE

x	nq_x	l_x	nd_x	nL_x	nm_x	na_x	T_x	r_x	$\mathring{e}_x$	nM_x	x
0	0.051432	100000	5143	96137	0.053499	0.2489	6669438	0.0000	66.694	0.053499	0
1	0.009949	94857	944	376692	0.002505	1.1012	6573301	0.0000	69.297	0.002505	1
5	0.003835	93913	360	468665	0.000768	2.5000	6196610	0.0000	65.982	0.000768	5
10	0.003044	93553	285	467094	0.000610	2.6458	5727945	0.0239	61.227	0.000608	10
15	0.005997	93268	559	465022	0.001203	2.6423	5260850	0.0266	56.406	0.001198	15
20	0.007192	92709	667	461921	0.001443	2.5661	4795828	0.0000	51.730	0.001443	20
25	0.008376	92042	771	458336	0.001682	2.5682	4333907	0.0000	47.086	0.001682	25
30	0.010070	91271	919	454138	0.002024	2.5872	3875571	0.0047	42.462	0.002023	30
35	0.012791	90352	1156	449003	0.002574	2.6137	3421433	0.0270	37.868	0.002566	35
40	0.017373	89196	1550	442355	0.003503	2.6595	2972430	0.0722	33.325	0.003461	40
45	0.026726	87647	2342	432773	0.005413	2.6686	2530075	0.0033	28.867	0.005409	45
50	0.040392	85304	3446	418552	0.008232	2.6870	2097302	0.0000	24.586	0.008232	50
55	0.066399	81859	5435	396662	0.013703	2.6760	1678750	0.0176	20.508	0.013653	55
60	0.105181	76423	8038	363208	0.022131	2.6476	1282088	0.0486	16.776	0.021922	60
65	0.162787	68385	11132	315227	0.035315	2.6016	918880	0.0486	13.437	0.035016	65
70	0.235266	57253	13470	253740	0.053084	2.5853	603654	0.0486	10.544	0.052572	70
75	0.380287	43783	16650	177262	0.093930	2.4983	349914	0.0486	7.992	0.093122	75
80	0.491301	27133	13331	101746	0.131018	2.4555	172652	0.0486	6.363	0.129933	80
85+	*1.000000	13803	13803	70906	0.194660	5.1371	70906	0.0486	5.137	0.190794	85+

TABLE 3 — ALE, LE

x	nq_x	l_x	nd_x	nL_x	nm_x	na_x	T_x	r_x	$\mathring{e}_x$	nM_x	x
0	0.043653	100000	4365	96778	0.045106	0.2618	7065686	0.0000	70.657	0.045106	0
1	0.009429	95635	902	379934	0.002373	1.1118	6968909	0.0000	72.870	0.002373	1
5	0.002606	94733	247	473048	0.000522	2.5000	6588974	0.0000	69.553	0.000522	5
10	0.002111	94486	199	471936	0.000423	2.5221	6115927	0.0228	64.728	0.000422	10
15	0.002842	94287	268	470797	0.000569	2.6261	5643990	0.0250	59.860	0.000567	15
20	0.003847	94019	362	469232	0.000771	2.6183	5173193	0.0000	55.023	0.000771	20
25	0.005054	93657	473	467144	0.001013	2.5897	4703961	0.0000	50.225	0.001013	25
30	0.006069	93184	566	464575	0.001217	2.6247	4236818	0.0058	45.467	0.001216	30
35	0.008765	92618	812	461177	0.001760	2.6426	3772243	0.0147	40.729	0.001757	35
40	0.012211	91806	1121	456392	0.002456	2.6455	3311066	0.0535	36.066	0.002436	40
45	0.017588	90685	1595	449709	0.003547	2.6694	2854674	0.0064	31.479	0.003543	45
50	0.027138	89090	2418	439849	0.005497	2.6829	2404966	0.0000	26.995	0.005497	50
55	0.042897	86672	3718	424734	0.008754	2.6794	1965117	0.0250	22.673	0.008710	55
60	0.067749	82954	5620	401834	0.013986	2.6977	1540382	0.0334	18.569	0.013879	60
65	0.117057	77334	9053	365668	0.024756	2.6798	1138549	0.0334	14.722	0.024564	65
70	0.196719	68282	13432	309990	0.043332	2.6609	772880	0.0334	11.319	0.042963	70
75	0.354192	54849	19427	226134	0.085910	2.5234	462891	0.0334	8.439	0.085383	75
80	0.440834	35422	15615	136147	0.114695	2.5051	236757	0.0334	6.684	0.114263	80
85+	1.000000	19807	19807	100610	0.196869	5.0795	100610	0.0334	5.080	0.166946	85+

TABLE 4 — OBSERVED, PROJECTED

	OBSERVED POPULATION BOTH SEXES	MALES	FEMALES	PROJECTED POPULATION 1969 MALES	FEMALES	1974 MALES	FEMALES	1979 MALES	FEMALES	STABLE POPULATION MALES	FEMALES
RATES PER THOUSAND											
Birth	15.18	15.99	14.41	15.60	14.13	16.28	14.82	16.17	14.79	12.60	11.82
Death	8.06	8.34	7.78	9.26	8.73	10.06	9.45	10.84	10.25	17.13	16.34
Increase	7.13	7.65	6.63	6.33	5.40	6.22	5.37	5.33	4.54	−4.5241	
PERCENTAGE											
under 15	27.07	28.28	25.90	24.90	22.84	22.16	20.37	21.54	19.89	18.37	17.38
15-64	65.37	65.36	65.39	67.24	67.10	68.82	68.50	68.42	67.61	65.44	63.77
65 and over	7.56	6.37	8.71	7.86	10.06	9.02	11.13	10.04	12.50	16.19	18.85
DEP. RATIO X 100	52.97	53.01	52.94	48.71	49.02	45.31	45.98	46.15	47.90	52.82	56.82

TABLE 1 — DATA

AGE AT LAST BIRTHDAY	POPULATION BOTH SEXES	MALES Number	%	FEMALES Number	%	BIRTHS BY AGE OF MOTHER	DEATHS BOTH SEXES	MALES	FEMALES	AGE AT L. BIRT
0	275110	140761	1.5	134349	1.4	0	12275	6880	5395	0
1-4	1163733	597017	6.4	566716	5.8	0	2439	1266	1173	1-
5-9	1776668	908787	9.8	867881	8.9	0	1128	673	455	5-
10-14	1794202	914688	9.8	879514	9.1	193	960	600	360	10-
15-19	1546322	785427	8.4	760895	7.8	39846	1417	964	453	15-
20-24	1330193	673496	7.2	656697	6.8	92420	1577	1062	515	20-
25-29	1565258	773493	8.3	791765	8.2	79034	2015	1258	757	25-
30-34	1560057	783766	8.4	776291	8.0	41561	2610	1624	986	30-
35-39	1506450	754210	8.1	752240	7.7	18853	3148	1875	1273	35-
40-44	1300043	618133	6.6	681910	7.0	6096	3832	2126	1706	40-
45-49	794339	357899	3.8	436440	4.5	346	3367	1764	1603	45-
50-54	1097307	510586	5.5	586721	6.0	13	7681	4279	3402	50-
55-59	998938	481486	5.2	517452	5.3	0	11177	6588	4589	55-
60-64	810930	390060	4.2	420870	4.3	0	15375	9091	6284	60-
65-69	632762	276683	3.0	356079	3.7	0	19227	10154	9073	65-
70-74	427765	175776	1.9	251989	2.6		21874	10141	11733	70-
75-79	261832	106325	1.1	155507	1.6		24466	10505	13961	75-
80-84	135323	50200	0.5	85123	0.9	139566 M.	18584	7578	11006	80-
85+	50135	16717	0.2	33418	0.3	138796 F.	10241	3683	6558	85
TOTAL	19027367	9315510		9711857		278362	163393	82111	81282	TO

TABLE 2 — MALE LIFE TABLE

x	$_nq_x$	l_x	$_nd_x$	$_nL_x$	$_nm_x$	$_na_x$	T_x	r_x	$\dot{e}_x$	$_nM_x$
0	0.047129	100000	4713	96423	0.048877	0.2409	6657391	0.0000	66.574	0.048877
1	0.008430	95287	803	378815	0.002121	1.0952	6560969	0.0000	68.855	0.002121
5	0.003696	94484	349	471546	0.000741	2.5000	6182154	0.0000	65.431	0.000741
10	0.003282	94135	309	469948	0.000657	2.6535	5710607	0.0138	60.664	0.000656
15	0.006147	93826	577	467775	0.001233	2.6530	5240659	0.0294	55.855	0.001227
20	0.007854	93249	732	464450	0.001577	2.5491	4772884	0.0000	51.184	0.001577
25	0.008100	92517	749	460754	0.001626	2.5594	4308435	0.0000	46.569	0.001626
30	0.010309	91767	946	456549	0.002072	2.5827	3847681	0.0005	41.929	0.002072
35	0.012387	90821	1125	451418	0.002492	2.6111	3391132	0.0211	37.339	0.002486
40	0.017236	89696	1546	444830	0.003475	2.6387	2939713	0.0710	32.774	0.003439
45	0.024435	88150	2154	435781	0.004943	2.6924	2494883	0.0138	28.303	0.004929
50	0.041109	85996	3535	421837	0.008381	2.6962	2059103	0.0000	23.944	0.008381
55	0.066494	82461	5483	399645	0.013720	2.6910	1637266	0.0124	19.855	0.013683
60	0.111229	76978	8562	364760	0.023473	2.6491	1237621	0.0359	16.078	0.023307
65	0.169698	68416	11610	314283	0.036941	2.6059	872861	0.0359	12.758	0.036699
70	0.254643	56806	14465	248958	0.058103	2.5755	558577	0.0359	9.833	0.057693
75	0.398032	42341	16853	169435	0.099466	2.4919	309620	0.0359	7.313	0.098801
80	0.541963	25488	13813	90972	0.151843	2.4219	140185	0.0359	5.500	0.150956
85+	1.000000	11674	11674	49214	0.237217	4.2156	49214	0.0359	4.216	0.220315

TABLE 3 — FEMALE LIFE TABLE

x	$_nq_x$	l_x	$_nd_x$	$_nL_x$	$_nm_x$	$_na_x$	T_x	r_x	$\dot{e}_x$	$_nM_x$
0	0.038997	100000	3900	97113	0.040157	0.2598	7060021	0.0000	70.600	0.040157
1	0.008230	96100	791	382115	0.002070	1.1100	6962908	0.0000	72.455	0.002070
5	0.002618	95309	250	475923	0.000524	2.5000	6580793	0.0000	69.047	0.000524
10	0.002045	95060	194	474820	0.000410	2.5359	6104870	0.0127	64.221	0.000409
15	0.002984	94865	283	473656	0.000598	2.6293	5630050	0.0286	59.348	0.000595
20	0.003914	94582	370	472021	0.000784	2.5936	5156394	0.0000	54.518	0.000784
25	0.004770	94212	449	469984	0.000956	2.6037	4684373	0.0000	49.722	0.000956
30	0.006334	93763	594	467399	0.001271	2.6183	4214389	0.0038	44.947	0.001270
35	0.008442	93169	787	463996	0.001695	2.6496	3746989	0.0112	40.217	0.001692
40	0.012542	92382	1159	459198	0.002523	2.6579	3282994	0.0519	35.537	0.002502
45	0.018246	91224	1664	452250	0.003680	2.6756	2823796	0.0112	30.955	0.003673
50	0.028606	89559	2562	441836	0.005798	2.6736	2371546	0.0000	26.480	0.005798
55	0.043667	86997	3799	426215	0.008913	2.6911	1929710	0.0238	22.181	0.008868
60	0.072671	83198	6046	402033	0.015039	2.6913	1503495	0.0321	18.071	0.014931
65	0.121186	77152	9350	364113	0.025678	2.6846	1101462	0.0321	14.276	0.025480
70	0.211386	67803	14333	305345	0.046939	2.6510	737349	0.0321	10.875	0.046562
75	0.369093	53470	19735	218464	0.090337	2.5229	432003	0.0321	8.079	0.089777
80	0.489214	33735	16503	126893	0.130058	2.4684	213540	0.0321	6.330	0.129295
85+	*1.000000	17231	17231	86647	0.198866	5.0285	86647	0.0321	5.029	0.196242

TABLE 4 — OBSERVED AND PROJECTED VITAL RATES

	OBSERVED POPULATION BOTH SEXES	MALES	FEMALES	PROJECTED POPULATION 1970 MALES	FEMALES	1975 MALES	FEMALES	1980 MALES	FEMALES	STABLE POPULATION MALES	FEMA
RATES PER THOUSAND											
Birth	14.63	14.98	14.29	15.00	14.31	15.57	14.89	15.36	14.69	12.77	11.
Death	8.59	8.81	8.37	9.62	9.32	10.39	10.00	11.09	10.69	17.05	16.
Increase	6.04	6.17	5.92	5.38	5.00	5.19	4.89	4.27	4.00		−4.28
PERCENTAGE											
under 15	26.33	27.49	25.21	24.10	22.40	21.38	20.25	20.83	20.12	18.68	17.
15-64	65.75	65.79	65.71	67.98	67.51	69.59	68.60	69.47	67.67	66.04	64.
65 and over	7.92	6.72	9.08	7.92	10.10	9.04	11.15	9.70	12.22	15.28	18.
DEP. RATIO X 100	52.10	52.00	52.19	47.10	48.13	43.71	45.78	43.95	47.78	51.42	55.

TABLE 5 — POPULATION PROJECTED WITH FIXED AGE-SPECIFIC BIRTH AND DEATH RATES (IN 1000's)

AGE LAST BIRTHDAY	1970 BOTH SEXES	MALES	FEMALES	1975 BOTH SEXES	MALES	FEMALES	1980 BOTH SEXES	MALES	FEMALES	AGE AT LAST BIRTHDAY
0-4	1348	673	675	1414	706	708	1465	731	734	0-4
5-9	1428	732	696	1339	668	671	1403	700	703	5-9
10-14	1772	906	866	1425	730	695	1335	666	669	10-14
15-19	1787	910	877	1766	902	864	1419	726	693	15-19
20-24	1538	780	758	1778	904	874	1756	895	861	20-24
25-29	1322	668	654	1529	774	755	1768	897	871	25-29
30-34	1553	766	787	1312	662	650	1518	767	751	30-34
35-39	1546	775	771	1540	758	782	1301	655	646	35-39
40-44	1487	743	744	1527	764	763	1521	747	774	40-44
45-49	1278	606	672	1461	728	733	1499	748	751	45-49
50-54	772	346	426	1242	586	656	1421	705	716	50-54
55-59	1050	484	566	739	328	411	1188	555	633	55-59
60-64	927	439	488	976	442	534	688	300	388	60-64
65-69	717	336	381	821	379	442	864	380	484	65-69
70-74	518	219	299	586	266	320	671	300	371	70-74
75-79	300	120	180	363	149	214	410	181	229	75-79
80-84	147	57	90	169	64	105	204	80	124	80-84
85+	85	27	58	93	31	62	107	35	72	85+
TOTAL	19575	9587	9988	20080	9841	10239	20538	10068	10470	TOTAL

TABLE 6 — STANDARDIZED RATES

STANDARD COUNTRIES — STANDARDIZED RATES PER THOUSAND

	ENGLAND AND WALES 1961 BOTH SEXES	MALES	FEMALES	UNITED STATES 1960 BOTH SEXES	MALES	FEMALES	MEXICO 1960 BOTH SEXES	MALES	FEMALES
Birth	12.13	12.66*	11.72	12.36	12.03*	12.15	15.17	11.52*	15.09
Death	12.43	12.12*	12.96	10.26	10.46*	9.71	5.90	8.49*	5.21
Increase	-0.30	0.54*	-1.24	2.11	1.57*	2.44	9.27	3.03*	9.88

TABLE 7 — MOMENTS AND CUMULANTS

OBSERVED POP. MALES	FEMALES	STATIONARY POP. MALES	FEMALES	STABLE POP. MALES	FEMALES	OBSERVED BIRTHS	NET MATERNITY FUNCTION	BIRTHS IN STABLE POP.
31.28556	33.30460	36.86174	38.33542	39.03440	40.63376	26.17642	25.98725	26.14662
416.1015	449.5144	503.3510	533.2872	510.8566	539.5057	34.89485	34.79834	35.48832
3776.359	3577.265	2303.150	2090.739	1191.799	804.339	133.1396	160.6561	161.6402
-126203.	-164685.	-250568.	-292195.	-266603.	-306224.	-13.381	263.727	205.629
0.197947	0.140887	0.041594	0.028821	0.010654	0.004120	0.417187	0.612519	0.584578
2.271096	2.184984	2.011028	1.972574	1.978432	1.947924	2.989011	3.217790	3.163273
-0.078932	-0.055463	-0.015680	-0.010662	-0.004036	-0.001531	-0.274412	-0.382713	-0.356881

TABLE 8 — RATES FROM AGE DISTRIBUTIONS AND VITAL STATISTICS (Females)

VITAL STATISTICS

	THOMPSON AGE RANGE	NRR	$1000r$	INTERVAL	BOURGEOIS-PICHAT AGE RANGE	NRR	$1000b$	$1000d$	$1000r$	COALE
0.951										IBR
0.894	0-4	0.93	-2.68	27.42	5-29	1.27	20.01	11.11	8.89	IDR
1.907	5-9	1.24	7.90	27.38	30-54	1.68	32.46	13.13	19.32	IRI
ERATION 26.067	10-14	1.27	8.62	27.33	55-79	1.94	51.02	26.50	24.52	K1
RATIO 100.555	15-19	1.16	5.38	27.24	*50-74	1.88	47.14	23.79	23.35	K2

TABLE 9 — LESLIE MATRIX AND ITS SPECTRAL COMPONENTS (Females)

ORIGINAL MATRIX SUB-DIAGONAL	ALTERNATIVE FIRST ROWS Projection	Integral	FIRST STABLE MATRIX % IN STABLE POPULATION	FISHER VALUES	REPRODUCTIVE VALUES	SECOND STABLE MATRIX Z_2 FIRST COLUMN	FIRST ROW
0.99310	0.00000	0.00000	5.794	1.032	723682	0.1901+0.1069	0.1901+0.1069
0.99768	0.00026	0.00000	5.879	1.017	883008	0.2281-0.1808	-0.0202+0.1622
0.99755	0.06267	0.00052	5.992	0.998	877698	-0.1085-0.3748	-0.1177+0.0319
0.99655	0.23013	0.12380	6.107	0.914	695730	-0.5201-0.0556	-0.0672-0.0790
0.99568	0.28689	0.33271	6.217	0.660	433240	-0.3327+0.6164	-0.0083-0.0935
0.99450	0.18287	0.23598	6.324	0.351	278013	0.5947+0.7244	0.0075-0.0630
0.99272	0.09369	0.12657	6.426	0.156	120932	1.1969-0.3689	0.0108-0.0323
0.98966	0.04051	0.05925	6.517	0.056	42261	0.1493-1.6641	0.0075-0.0118
0.98487	0.01161	0.02113	6.589	0.013	9075	-1.9730-1.0219	0.0025-0.0025
0.97697	0.00097	0.00187	6.629	0.001	460	-2.2406+1.9044	0.0002-0.0002
0.96465	0.00003	0.00005	6.617	0.000	16	1.1999+3.6693	0.0000-0.0000
0.77233			30.909				

TABLE 10 — AGE ANALYSIS AND MISCELLANEOUS RESULTS (Females)

OBSERVED POPUL. (IN 100's)	CONTRIBUTIONS OF ROOTS (IN 100's) r_1	r_2, r_3	r_4-r_{11}	AGE-SP. BIRTH RATES	NET MATERNITY FUNCTION	COEFF. OF MATRIX EQUATION	PARAMETERS	INTEGRAL	MATRIX	EXP. INCREASE x	$e^{(x+2\frac{1}{2})r}$
7011	7521	-450	-61	0.0000	0.0000	0.0000	L(1)	0.97882	0.97883	0	0.9894
8679	7631	678	370	0.0000	0.0000	0.0003	L(2)	0.26220	0.28184	50	0.7987
8795	7778	1493	-476	0.0001	0.0005	0.0621		0.71749	0.68874	55	0.7818
7609	7927	298	-615	0.0261	0.1237	0.2275	R(1)	-0.00428	-0.00428	60	0.7652
6567	8070	-2379	875	0.0702	0.3312	0.2826	R(2)	-0.05386	-0.05910	65	0.7490
7918	8209	-2944	2653	0.0498	0.2339	0.1793		0.24409	0.23647	70	0.7332
7763	8340	1272	-1850	0.0267	0.1248	0.0914	C(1)		129800	75	0.7176
7522	8459	6535	-7471	0.0125	0.0580	0.0392	C(2)		-7563	80	0.7024
6819	8552	4325	-6058	0.0045	0.0205	0.0111			197021	85	0.6876
4364	8605	-7165	2925	0.0004	0.0018	0.0009	2P/Y	25.7417	26.5703	90	0.6730
5867	8589	-14640	11919	0.0000	0.0000	0.0000	DELTA	14.8779		95	0.6588
18204	40120									100	0.6448

TABLE 1 — DATA

AGE AT LAST BIRTHDAY	POPULATION BOTH SEXES	MALES Number	%	FEMALES Number	%	BIRTHS BY AGE OF MOTHER	DEATHS BOTH SEXES	MALES	FEMALES	AGE AT LAST BIRTHDAY
0	448248	232502	1.7	215746	1.5	0	39392	21607	17785	0
1-4	2113638	1079497	8.1	1034141	7.2	0	15709	8116	7593	1-4
5-9	2424674	1245130	9.3	1179544	8.2	0	4480	2369	2111	5-9
10-14	2317242	1174259	8.8	1142983	7.9	32	3016	1660	1356	10-1
15-19	2676877	1319056	9.8	1357821	9.4	10439	5710	3079	2631	15-1
20-24	2660148	1318772	9.8	1341376	9.3	110143	8050	4544	3506	20-2
25-29	2368899	1155232	8.6	1213667	8.4	187932	8155	4640	3515	25-2
30-34	1934250	901452	6.7	1032798	7.1	129020	6819	3764	3055	30-3
35-39	1855195	852494	6.4	1002701	6.9	85345	7359	4067	3292	35-3
40-44	1818205	877356	6.5	940849	6.5	31313	8840	5073	3767	40-4
45-49	1637951	777948	5.8	860003	6.0	3826	10583	6318	4265	45-4
50-54	1409847	658521	4.9	751326	5.2	915	13059	7808	5251	50-5
55-59	1141228	527207	3.9	614021	4.3	0	15486	9311	6175	55-5
60-64	1028419	460160	3.4	568259	3.9	0	21275	12067	9208	60-6
65-69	800596	345819	2.6	454777	3.1	0	26052	13827	12225	65-6
70-74	587100	246122	1.8	340978	2.4		32638	15861	16777	70-7
75-79	355271	139032	1.0	216239	1.5		31321	14430	16891	75-7
80-84	179819	65002	0.5	114817	0.8	286806 M.	24874	10285	14589	80-8
85+	91576	28636	0.2	62940	0.4	272159 F.	21582	7322	14260	85+
TOTAL	27849183	13404197		14444986		558965	304400	156148	148252	TOTA

TABLE 2 — MALE LIFE TABLE

x	$n q_x$	l_x	$n d_x$	$n L_x$	$n m_x$	$n a_x$	T_x	r_x	$\dot{e}_x$	$n M_x$
0	0.087300	100000	8730	93939	0.092933	0.3057	5868207	0.0000	58.682	0.092933
1	0.029444	91270	2687	357438	0.007518	1.1563	5774268	0.0000	63.266	0.007518
5	0.009427	88583	835	440826	0.001894	2.5000	5416830	0.0079	61.150	0.001903
10	0.007044	87748	618	437229	0.001414	2.5594	4976004	0.0000	56.708	0.001414
15	0.011608	87130	1011	433297	0.002334	2.6761	4538775	0.0000	52.092	0.002334
20	0.017104	86118	1473	427048	0.003449	2.5953	4105478	0.0099	47.673	0.003446
25	0.019911	84645	1685	419063	0.004022	2.5300	3678429	0.0341	43.457	0.004017
30	0.020684	82960	1716	410557	0.004180	2.5280	3259366	0.0261	39.289	0.004175
35	0.023579	81244	1916	401544	0.004771	2.5595	2848809	0.0000	35.065	0.004771
40	0.028527	79328	2263	391226	0.005784	2.6072	2447265	0.0031	30.850	0.005782
45	0.039965	77065	3080	378048	0.008147	2.6368	2056039	0.0203	26.679	0.008121
50	0.057915	73985	4285	359807	0.011909	2.6383	1677992	0.0267	22.680	0.011857
55	0.084990	69700	5924	334445	0.017712	2.6270	1318185	0.0177	18.912	0.017661
60	0.123829	63777	7897	300037	0.026321	2.6136	983739	0.0220	15.425	0.026223
65	0.183079	55879	10230	254832	0.040145	2.5989	683703	0.0220	12.235	0.039983
70	0.279341	45649	12752	197060	0.064709	2.5545	428871	0.0220	9.395	0.064444
75	0.412291	32897	13563	130172	0.104195	2.4700	231811	0.0220	7.047	0.103789
80	0.558685	19334	10802	68020	0.158801	2.4030	101639	0.0220	5.257	0.158226
85+	1.000000	8532	8532	33619	0.253795	3.9402	33619	0.0220	3.940	0.255691

TABLE 3 — FEMALE LIFE TABLE

x	$n q_x$	l_x	$n d_x$	$n L_x$	$n m_x$	$n a_x$	T_x	r_x	$\dot{e}_x$	$n M_x$
0	0.078039	100000	7804	94667	0.082435	0.3166	6344192	0.0000	63.442	0.082435
1	0.028771	92196	2653	361277	0.007342	1.1699	6249525	0.0000	67.785	0.007342
5	0.008877	89544	795	445730	0.001783	2.5000	5888248	0.0059	65.759	0.001790
10	0.005914	88749	525	442442	0.001186	2.5222	5442517	0.0000	61.325	0.001186
15	0.009644	88224	851	439119	0.001938	2.6495	5000075	0.0000	56.675	0.001938
20	0.012995	87373	1135	434107	0.002615	2.5715	4560956	0.0087	52.201	0.002614
25	0.014386	86237	1241	428109	0.002898	2.5190	4126849	0.0233	47.854	0.002896
30	0.014689	84997	1248	421889	0.002959	2.5207	3698740	0.0161	43.516	0.002958
35	0.016292	83748	1364	415411	0.003284	2.5590	3276851	0.0060	39.127	0.003283
40	0.019846	82384	1635	407961	0.004008	2.5788	2861440	0.0113	34.733	0.004004
45	0.024559	80749	1983	399013	0.004970	2.6138	2453479	0.0173	30.384	0.004959
50	0.034512	78766	2718	387401	0.007017	2.6353	2054466	0.0265	26.083	0.006989
55	0.049284	76047	3748	371483	0.010089	2.6641	1667065	0.0173	21.921	0.010057
60	0.078420	72300	5670	348307	0.016278	2.6735	1295582	0.0219	17.920	0.016204
65	0.127121	66630	8470	313470	0.027020	2.6766	947275	0.0219	14.217	0.026881
70	0.220946	58160	12850	260009	0.049422	2.6039	633805	0.0219	10.898	0.049203
75	0.328435	45310	14881	189739	0.078430	2.5265	373796	0.0219	8.250	0.078113
80	0.484523	30428	14743	115451	0.127701	2.5114	184056	0.0219	6.049	0.127063
85+	*1.000000	15685	15685	68605	0.228628	4.3739	68605	0.0219	4.374	0.226565

TABLE 4 — OBSERVED AND PROJECTED VITAL RATES

	OBSERVED POPULATION BOTH SEXES	MALES	FEMALES	PROJECTED POPULATION 1955 MALES	FEMALES	1960 MALES	FEMALES	1965 MALES	FEMALES	STABLE POPULATION MALES	FEMA
RATES PER THOUSAND											
Birth	20.07	21.40	18.84	21.82	19.32	21.21	18.88	19.85	17.75	17.41	16.
Death	10.93	11.65	10.26	12.02	10.68	12.41	11.16	12.75	11.57	16.81	15.
Increase	9.14	9.75	8.58	9.80	8.64	8.79	7.72	7.10	6.18		0.60
PERCENTAGE											
under 15	26.23	27.84	24.73	27.43	24.41	27.03	24.28	26.50	23.96	23.04	21.
15-64	66.54	66.01	67.03	65.99	66.71	66.16	66.48	66.23	66.14	65.57	63.
65 and over	7.23	6.15	8.24	6.58	8.88	6.81	9.23	7.27	9.90	11.39	14.
DEP. RATIO X 100	50.28	51.49	49.18	51.55	49.90	51.16	50.41	50.98	51.19	52.50	56

TABLE 5 — POPULATION PROJECTED WITH FIXED AGE-SPECIFIC BIRTH AND DEATH RATES (IN 1000's)

AGE LAST BIRTHDAY	1955 BOTH SEXES	1955 MALES	1955 FEMALES	1960 BOTH SEXES	1960 MALES	1960 FEMALES	1965 BOTH SEXES	1965 MALES	1965 FEMALES	AGE AT LAST BIRTHDAY
0-4	2623	1339	1284	2734	1396	1338	2719	1388	1331	0-4
5-9	2503	1281	1222	2563	1308	1255	2671	1363	1308	5-9
10-14	2406	1235	1171	2484	1271	1213	2543	1297	1246	10-14
15-19	2298	1164	1134	2386	1224	1162	2463	1259	1204	15-19
20-24	2642	1300	1342	2268	1147	1121	2355	1206	1149	20-24
25-29	2617	1294	1323	2600	1276	1324	2231	1125	1106	25-29
30-34	2328	1132	1196	2572	1268	1304	2555	1250	1305	30-34
35-39	1899	882	1017	2285	1107	1178	2524	1240	1284	35-39
40-44	1816	831	985	1858	859	999	2235	1078	1157	40-44
45-49	1768	848	920	1766	803	963	1807	830	977	45-49
50-54	1575	740	835	1700	807	893	1699	764	935	50-54
55-59	1332	612	720	1489	688	801	1607	750	857	55-59
60-64	1049	473	576	1225	549	676	1368	617	751	60-64
65-69	902	391	511	920	402	518	1074	466	608	65-69
70-74	644	267	377	726	302	424	741	311	430	70-74
75-79	412	163	249	452	177	275	510	200	310	75-79
80-84	205	73	132	236	85	151	259	92	167	80-84
85+	100	32	68	114	36	78	132	42	90	85+
TOTAL	29119	14057	15062	30378	14705	15673	31493	15278	16215	TOTAL

TABLE 6 — STANDARDIZED RATES

STANDARD COUNTRIES: STANDARDIZED RATES PER THOUSAND	ENGLAND AND WALES 1961 BOTH SEXES	MALES	FEMALES	UNITED STATES 1960 BOTH SEXES	MALES	FEMALES	MEXICO 1960 BOTH SEXES	MALES	FEMALES
Birth	15.83	18.07*	14.94	16.07	16.55*	15.42	16.69	16.93*	16.21
Death	15.27	17.20*	15.10	13.41	14.75*	12.28	9.40	11.27*	8.37
Increase	0.56	0.87*	-0.16	2.66	1.80*	3.15	7.28	5.66*	7.83

TABLE 7 — MOMENTS AND CUMULANTS

	OBSERVED POP. MALES	OBSERVED POP. FEMALES	STATIONARY POP. MALES	STATIONARY POP. FEMALES	STABLE POP. MALES	STABLE POP. FEMALES	OBSERVED BIRTHS	NET MATERNITY FUNCTION	BIRTHS IN STABLE POP.
μ	29.90696	32.05886	35.54649	37.59672	35.25160	37.27611	30.02620	30.63504	30.61174
μ_2	405.2519	436.7493	489.7389	532.2952	488.0115	530.7213	35.74595	36.57886	36.52416
μ_3	4332.352	4281.635	2795.458	2522.860	2931.753	2695.476	104.6247	90.5757	90.7882
μ_4	-95870.	-125917.	-227840.	-288101.	-224045.	-284191.	-279.868	-349.098	-344.918
κ_1	0.282015	0.220051	0.066529	0.042202	0.073954	0.048604	0.239656	0.167623	0.169168
κ_2	2.416243	2.339886	2.050050	1.983190	2.059250	1.991032	2.780972	2.739092	2.741444
κ	-0.116474	-0.091052	-0.025253	-0.015536	-0.028071	-0.017893	-0.166322	-0.128857	-0.130101

TABLE 8 — RATES FROM AGE DISTRIBUTIONS AND VITAL STATISTICS (Females)

VITAL STATISTICS		THOMPSON AGE RANGE	NRR	1000r	INTERVAL	BOURGEOIS-PICHAT AGE RANGE	NRR	1000b	1000d	1000r	COALE
GRR	1.202										IBR
NRR	1.019	0-4	1.01	0.49	27.30	5-29	0.84	17.61	23.94	-6.34	IDR
R	2.468	5-9	1.04	1.36	27.26	30-54	1.37	25.42	13.84	11.58	IRI
GENERATION	30.623	10-14	1.10	3.34	27.22	55-79	1.55	29.93	13.69	16.23	K1
SEX RATIO	105.382	15-19	1.43	12.59	27.14	*40-74	1.67	36.01	17.03	18.99	K2

TABLE 9 — LESLIE MATRIX AND ITS SPECTRAL COMPONENTS (Females)

ORIGINAL MATRIX SUB-DIAGONAL	ALTERNATIVE FIRST ROWS Projection	ALTERNATIVE FIRST ROWS Integral	FIRST STABLE MATRIX % IN STABLE POPULATION	FISHER VALUES	REPRODUCTIVE VALUES	SECOND STABLE MATRIX Z₂ FIRST COLUMN	SECOND STABLE MATRIX Z₂ FIRST ROW
0.97760	0.00000	0.00000	7.340	1.098	1372710	0.1479+0.0523	0.1479+0.0523
0.99262	0.00003	0.00000	7.154	1.127	1329143	0.1419-0.1095	0.0317+0.1336
0.99249	0.00850	0.00006	7.080	1.139	1301396	-0.0175-0.2072	-0.0819+0.0854
0.98859	0.09864	0.01709	7.005	1.141	1549645	-0.2130-0.1133	-0.1014-0.0198
0.98618	0.26065	0.18256	6.905	1.048	1406240	-0.2435+0.1357	-0.0479-0.0883
0.98547	0.30853	0.34428	6.789	0.776	941785	-0.0208+0.3206	0.0027-0.0903
0.98465	0.23169	0.27775	6.670	0.446	460589	0.2973+0.2205	0.0208-0.0569
0.98207	0.13076	0.18924	6.548	0.196	196388	0.3987-0.1498	0.0166-0.0239
0.97807	0.04177	0.07400	6.411	0.054	50627	0.1037-0.4778	0.0057-0.0061
0.97090	0.00625	0.00989	6.251	0.008	7118	-0.3946-0.3959	0.0009-0.0010
0.95891	0.00135	0.00271	6.051	0.001	1112	-0.6203+0.1325	0.0002-0.0002
0.77809			25.797				

TABLE 10 — AGE ANALYSIS AND MISCELLANEOUS RESULTS (Females)

OBSERVED POPUL. (IN 100's)	CONTRIBUTIONS OF ROOTS (IN 100's) r_1	r_2, r_3	$r_4 \cdot r_{11}$	AGE-SP. BIRTH RATES	NET MATERNITY FUNCTION	COEFF. OF MATRIX EQUATION	PARAMETERS	INTEGRAL	MATRIX	EXP. INCREASE x	$e^{(x+2\frac{1}{2})r}$
12499	12817	-514	196	0.0000	0.0000	0.0000	L(1)	1.00302	1.00302	0	1.0015
11795	12492	-777	81	0.0000	0.0000	0.0000	L(2)	0.46289	0.46403	50	1.0322
11430	12362	-297	-636	0.0000	0.0001	0.0082		0.73721	0.71879	55	1.0353
13578	12232	673	673	0.0037	0.0164	0.0950	R(1)	0.00060	0.00060	60	1.0384
13414	12056	1241	116	0.0400	0.1736	0.2482	R(2)	-0.02774	-0.03120	65	1.0416
12137	11854	655	-373	0.0754	0.3228	0.2897		0.20202	0.19951	70	1.0447
10328	11647	-829	-490	0.0608	0.2566	0.2144	C(1)		174615	75	1.0479
10027	11433	-1903	497	0.0414	0.1722	0.1191	C(2)		-205278	80	1.0510
9408	11194	-1275	-511	0.0162	0.0661	0.0374			-88874	85	1.0542
8600	10916	916	-3232	0.0022	0.0086	0.0055	2P/Y	31.1013	31.4933	90	1.0574
7513	10566	2782	-5835	0.0006	0.0023	0.0011	DELTA	10.5559		95	1.0606
23720	45046									100	1.0638

TABLE 1 — DATA

AGE AT LAST BIRTHDAY	POPULATION BOTH SEXES	MALES Number	%	FEMALES Number	%	BIRTHS BY AGE OF MOTHER	DEATHS BOTH SEXES	MALES	FEMALES	AGE AT LAST BIRTHDAY
0	631047	321788	2.2	309259	2.0	0	23345	13276	10069	0
1-4	2373938	1210537	8.2	1163401	7.4	0	4771	2595	2176	1-4
5-9	2671970	1392058	9.4	1279912	8.2	0	1733	1007	726	5-9
10-14	2636887	1331364	9.0	1305523	8.3	68	1355	779	576	10-14
15-19	2396820	1172274	7.9	1224546	7.8	11343	1803	1169	634	15-19
20-24	2232548	1138477	7.7	1094071	7.0	116789	2142	1332	810	20-24
25-29	2482565	1211424	8.2	1271141	8.1	234787	3217	1873	1344	25-29
30-34	2367101	1187382	8.0	1179719	7.5	167989	3644	2178	1466	30-34
35-39	2234981	1076920	7.3	1158061	7.4	92299	4590	2629	1961	35-39
40-44	1781479	833411	5.6	948068	6.1	28062	5222	2905	2317	40-44
45-49	1748645	821539	5.6	927106	5.9	2882	7605	4364	3241	45-49
50-54	1658789	781971	5.3	876818	5.6	318	11185	6713	4472	50-54
55-59	1450963	687461	4.7	763502	4.9	0	15615	9469	6146	55-59
60-64	1247467	567735	3.8	679732	4.3	0	16894	9500	7394	60-64
65-69	932303	404200	2.7	528103	3.4	0	22873	12261	10612	65-69
70-74	738974	312345	2.1	426629	2.7		29635	15002	14633	70-74
75-79	420412	167117	1.1	253295	1.6		35744	16878	18866	75-79
80-84	268636	101274	0.7	167362	1.1	337126 M.	38198	16551	21647	80-84
85+	125758	44267	0.3	81491	0.5	317411 F.	32689	12720	19969	85+
TOTAL	30401283	14763544		15637739		654537	262260	133201	129059	TOTAL

TABLE 2 — MALE LIFE TABLE

x	$_nq_x$	l_x	$_nd_x$	$_nL_x$	$_nm_x$	$_na_x$	T_x	r_x	$\dot{e}_x$	$_nM_x$
0	0.039902	100000	3990	97049	0.041115	0.2604	6790649	0.0044	67.906	0.041257
1	0.008479	96010	814	381687	0.002133	1.1106	6693600	0.0044	69.718	0.002144
5	0.003593	95196	342	475124	0.000720	2.5000	6311913	0.0130	66.305	0.000723
10	0.002926	94854	278	473601	0.000586	2.5970	5836790	0.0165	61.535	0.000585
15	0.004983	94576	471	471759	0.000999	2.6200	5363188	0.0147	56.708	0.000997
20	0.005833	94105	549	469204	0.001170	2.5946	4891429	0.0000	51.979	0.001170
25	0.007702	93556	721	466040	0.001546	2.5866	4422226	0.0000	47.268	0.001546
30	0.009140	92835	849	462139	0.001836	2.5984	3956185	0.0099	42.615	0.001834
35	0.012192	91987	1122	457282	0.002453	2.6353	3494047	0.0329	37.984	0.002441
40	0.017356	90865	1577	450638	0.003500	2.6614	3036765	0.0234	33.421	0.003486
45	0.026241	89288	2343	441019	0.005313	2.6857	2586127	0.0008	28.964	0.005312
50	0.042160	86945	3666	426233	0.008600	2.6831	2145108	0.0088	24.672	0.008585
55	0.066817	83280	5564	403032	0.013806	2.5979	1718875	0.0189	20.640	0.013774
60	0.080823	77715	6281	373829	0.016802	2.6522	1315844	0.0216	16.932	0.016733
65	0.142140	71434	10154	333245	0.030469	2.6437	942015	0.0216	13.187	0.030334
70	0.216822	61280	13287	275127	0.048294	2.6462	608770	0.0216	9.934	0.048030
75	0.405836	47993	19477	191926	0.101484	2.5335	333643	0.0216	6.952	0.100995
80	0.575791	28516	16419	99994	0.164202	2.4064	141717	0.0216	4.970	0.163429
85+	*1.000000	12097	12097	41723	0.289927	3.4491	41723	0.0216	3.449	0.287347

TABLE 3 — FEMALE LIFE TABLE

x	$_nq_x$	l_x	$_nd_x$	$_nL_x$	$_nm_x$	$_na_x$	T_x	r_x	$\dot{e}_x$	$_nM_x$
0	0.031691	100000	3169	97692	0.032440	0.2718	7238076	0.0047	72.381	0.032558
1	0.007405	96831	717	385259	0.001861	1.1206	7140384	0.0047	73.741	0.001870
5	0.002819	96114	271	479892	0.000565	2.5000	6755125	0.0112	70.283	0.000567
10	0.002203	95843	211	478682	0.000441	2.4772	6275233	0.0039	65.474	0.000441
15	0.002591	95632	248	477569	0.000519	2.6188	5796551	0.0171	60.613	0.000518
20	0.003695	95384	352	476091	0.000740	2.6497	5318983	0.0000	55.764	0.000740
25	0.005273	95032	501	473953	0.001057	2.5971	4842891	0.0000	50.961	0.001057
30	0.006200	94530	586	471248	0.001244	2.6043	4368938	0.0080	46.217	0.001243
35	0.008458	93944	795	467849	0.001698	2.6440	3897690	0.0201	41.489	0.001693
40	0.012186	93150	1135	463078	0.002451	2.6471	3429841	0.0197	36.821	0.002444
45	0.017348	92015	1596	456321	0.003498	2.6500	2966763	0.0042	32.242	0.003496
50	0.025267	90418	2285	446774	0.005113	2.6727	2510442	0.0140	27.765	0.005100
55	0.039598	88134	3490	432408	0.008071	2.6330	2063667	0.0176	23.415	0.008050
60	0.053302	84644	4512	412823	0.010929	2.6958	1631260	0.0212	19.272	0.010878
65	0.096471	80132	7730	382806	0.020194	2.6904	1218437	0.0212	15.205	0.020095
70	0.159894	72402	11577	335476	0.034508	2.7081	835631	0.0212	11.542	0.034299
75	0.317210	60825	19294	257730	0.074862	2.5954	500155	0.0212	8.223	0.074482
80	0.491521	41531	20413	157000	0.130020	2.5186	242424	0.0212	5.837	0.129342
85+	*1.000000	21118	21118	85424	0.247208	4.0452	85424	0.0212	4.045	0.245045

TABLE 4 — OBSERVED AND PROJECTED VITAL RATES

	OBSERVED POPULATION BOTH SEXES	MALES	FEMALES	PROJECTED POPULATION 1965 MALES	FEMALES	1970 MALES	FEMALES	1975 MALES	FEMALES	STABLE POPULATION MALES	FEMALES
RATES PER THOUSAND											
Birth	21.53	22.84	20.30	21.38	19.16	20.57	18.58	20.06	18.24	19.58	18.
Death	8.63	9.02	8.25	9.11	8.52	9.37	8.81	9.87	9.41	11.48	10.5
Increase	12.90	13.81	12.04	12.27	10.64	11.20	9.77	10.19	8.83		8.09
PERCENTAGE											
under 15	27.35	28.83	25.95	28.70	25.81	28.41	26.01	27.70	25.43	26.32	25.
15-64	64.48	64.20	64.73	63.77	64.12	63.39	63.27	63.56	63.10	63.50	62.
65 and over	8.18	6.97	9.32	7.53	10.07	8.19	10.72	8.74	11.47	10.19	12.
DEP. RATIO X 100	55.10	55.76	54.48	56.82	55.96	57.74	58.07	57.33	58.48	57.49	60.

TABLE 1 — DATA

AGE AT LAST BIRTHDAY	POPULATION BOTH SEXES	MALES Number	%	FEMALES Number	%	BIRTHS BY AGE OF MOTHER	DEATHS BOTH SEXES	MALES	FEMALES	AGE AT LAST BIRTHDAY
0	646182	329821	2.2	316361	2.0	0	21236	12064	9172	0
1-4	2430874	1240755	8.3	1190119	7.5	0	4199	2320	1879	1-4
5-9	2784350	1438849	9.6	1345501	8.4	0	1729	988	741	5-9
10-14	2656441	1355598	9.1	1300843	8.2	553	1385	775	610	10-14
15-19	2458276	1213206	8.1	1245070	7.8	15046	1823	1202	621	15-19
20-24	2255568	1126316	7.5	1129252	7.1	114236	1960	1220	740	20-24
25-29	2332523	1135481	7.6	1197042	7.5	227508	3039	1775	1264	25-29
30-34	2340882	1144451	7.7	1196431	7.5	170171	3696	2149	1547	30-34
35-39	2241124	1081006	7.2	1160118	7.3	90574	4427	2532	1895	35-39
40-44	1911483	897142	6.0	1014341	6.4	28837	5559	3233	2326	40-44
45-49	1757755	822733	5.5	935022	5.9	2410	7345	4267	3078	45-49
50-54	1672209	784134	5.2	888075	5.6	345	11317	6710	4607	50-54
55-59	1500865	706206	4.7	794659	5.0	0	15912	9718	6194	55-59
60-64	1290313	591507	4.0	698806	4.4	0	18159	10423	7736	60-64
65-69	999273	436638	2.9	562635	3.5	0	24484	13353	11131	65-69
70-74	756228	317764	2.1	438464	2.8		31616	16219	15397	70-74
75-79	444476	177160	1.2	267316	1.7		38049	18115	19934	75-79
80-84	283388	106550	0.7	176838	1.1	334138 M.	40629	17635	22994	80-84
85+	132546	46225	0.3	86321	0.5	315542 F.	34809	13455	21354	85+
TOTAL	30894756	14951542		15943214		649680	271373	138153	133220	TOTAL

TABLE 2 — MALE LIFE TABLE

x	nq_x	l_x	nd_x	nL_x	nm_x	na_x	T_x	r_x	$\mathring{e}_x$	nM_x	x
0	0.035487	100000	3549	97370	0.036445	0.2589	6817798	0.0047	68.178	0.036577	0
1	0.007400	96451	714	383742	0.001860	1.1093	6720428	0.0047	69.677	0.001870	1
5	0.003412	95738	327	477871	0.000684	2.5000	6336686	0.0137	66.188	0.000687	5
10	0.002860	95411	273	476402	0.000573	2.6102	5858815	0.0164	61.406	0.000572	10
15	0.004951	95138	471	474562	0.000993	2.6056	5382412	0.0176	56.575	0.000991	15
20	0.005405	94667	512	472110	0.001084	2.6067	4907850	0.0054	51.843	0.001083	20
25	0.007787	94155	733	469019	0.001563	2.6028	4435740	0.0000	47.111	0.001563	25
30	0.009349	93422	873	465000	0.001878	2.5831	3966721	0.0030	42.460	0.001878	30
35	0.011686	92549	1082	460200	0.002350	2.6478	3501721	0.0218	37.837	0.002342	35
40	0.017936	91467	1641	453490	0.003618	2.6554	3041522	0.0237	33.253	0.003604	40
45	0.025663	89827	2305	443794	0.005194	2.6840	2588032	0.0079	28.811	0.005186	45
50	0.042009	87521	3677	429101	0.008568	2.6865	2144238	0.0063	24.500	0.008557	50
55	0.066746	83845	5596	405851	0.013789	2.6104	1715137	0.0149	20.456	0.013761	55
60	0.084895	78248	6643	375605	0.017686	2.6461	1309286	0.0197	16.732	0.017621	60
65	0.143217	71606	10255	333929	0.030710	2.6501	933681	0.0197	13.039	0.030581	65
70	0.228707	61350	14031	273573	0.051289	2.6353	599752	0.0197	9.776	0.051041	70
75	0.409357	47319	19370	188626	0.102692	2.5236	326179	0.0197	6.893	0.102252	75
80	0.580437	27949	16222	97595	0.166223	2.4018	137553	0.0197	4.922	0.165509	80
85+	*1.000000	11726	11726	39958	0.293461	3.4076	39958	0.0197	3.408	0.291076	85+

TABLE 3 — FEMALE LIFE TABLE

x	nq_x	l_x	nd_x	nL_x	nm_x	na_x	T_x	r_x	$\mathring{e}_x$	nM_x	x
0	0.028282	100000	2828	97924	0.028882	0.2661	7276989	0.0049	72.770	0.028992	0
1	0.006253	97172	608	386934	0.001570	1.1155	7179065	0.0049	73.880	0.001571	1
5	0.002737	96564	264	482160	0.000548	2.5000	6792131	0.0139	70.338	0.000551	5
10	0.002341	96300	225	480930	0.000469	2.4772	6309971	0.0073	65.524	0.000469	10
15	0.002493	96074	240	479791	0.000499	2.5767	5829041	0.0136	60.672	0.000499	15
20	0.003273	95835	314	478445	0.000656	2.6750	5349250	0.0032	55.817	0.000655	20
25	0.005266	95521	503	476410	0.001056	2.6237	4870805	0.0000	50.992	0.001056	25
30	0.006446	95018	612	473614	0.001293	2.5906	4394395	0.0018	46.248	0.001293	30
35	0.008151	94406	770	470199	0.001637	2.6241	3920781	0.0148	41.531	0.001633	35
40	0.011437	93636	1071	465658	0.002300	2.6650	3450581	0.0192	36.851	0.002293	40
45	0.016363	92565	1515	459303	0.003298	2.6743	2984923	0.0098	32.247	0.003292	45
50	0.025678	91050	2338	449801	0.005198	2.6683	2525620	0.0110	27.739	0.005188	50
55	0.038364	88712	3403	435530	0.007814	2.6399	2075820	0.0161	23.399	0.007795	55
60	0.054201	85309	4624	415875	0.011118	2.6922	1640290	0.0199	19.228	0.011070	60
65	0.095045	80685	7669	385776	0.019879	2.6984	1224415	0.0199	15.175	0.019784	65
70	0.163333	73017	11926	337710	0.035314	2.7047	838639	0.0199	11.486	0.035116	70
75	0.317385	61091	19389	258781	0.074925	2.5929	500929	0.0199	8.200	0.074571	75
80	0.493326	41701	20572	157438	0.130669	2.5176	242148	0.0199	5.807	0.130028	80
85+	*1.000000	21129	21129	84710	0.249427	4.0092	84710	0.0199	4.009	0.247379	85+

TABLE 4 — OBSERVED AND PROJECTED TOTAL RATES

	OBSERVED POPULATION BOTH SEXES	MALES	FEMALES	PROJECTED POPULATION 1967 MALES	FEMALES	1972 MALES	FEMALES	1977 MALES	FEMALES	STABLE POPULATION MALES	FEMALES
RATES PER THOUSAND											
Birth	21.03	22.35	19.79	21.11	18.84	20.48	18.42	20.18	18.27	19.63	18.64
Death	8.78	9.24	8.36	9.26	8.58	9.51	8.87	9.97	9.45	11.32	10.33
Increase	12.25	13.11	11.44	11.85	10.26	10.97	9.55	10.21	8.82		8.3115
PERCENTAGE											
under 15	27.57	29.19	26.05	28.95	25.98	28.46	25.89	27.67	25.28	26.49	25.38
15-64	63.96	63.55	64.35	63.27	63.71	63.17	63.14	63.56	63.10	63.54	62.29
65 and over	8.47	7.25	9.61	7.78	10.30	8.37	10.97	8.77	11.62	9.97	12.33
DEP. RATIO X 100	56.34	57.35	55.41	58.04	56.96	58.30	58.39	57.33	58.47	57.38	60.53

TABLE 1 — DATA

AGE AT LAST BIRTHDAY	POPULATION BOTH SEXES	MALES Number	%	FEMALES Number	%	BIRTHS BY AGE OF MOTHER	DEATHS BOTH SEXES	MALES	FEMALES	AGE AT LAST BIRTH
0	653825	333879	2.2	319946	2.0	0	21219	12418	8801	0
1-4	2459627	1256021	8.3	1203606	7.5	0	4041	2204	1837	1-4
5-9	2841487	1462556	9.7	1378931	8.6	0	1793	1060	733	5-9
10-14	2666338	1367815	9.1	1298523	8.1	63	1290	733	557	10-1
15-19	2490734	1234942	8.2	1255792	7.8	12920	1763	1176	587	15-1
20-24	2269309	1121531	7.4	1147778	7.1	115447	1954	1273	681	20-2
25-29	2260868	1099819	7.3	1161049	7.2	226371	2782	1664	1118	25-2
30-34	2330202	1124990	7.5	1205212	7.5	180693	3592	2131	1461	30-3
35-39	2245918	1084560	7.2	1161358	7.2	93432	4429	2611	1818	35-3
40-44	1979607	931086	6.2	1048521	6.5	30792	5708	3324	2384	40-4
45-49	1762470	823446	5.5	939024	5.8	2551	7303	4208	3095	45-4
50-54	1679088	785328	5.2	893760	5.6	248	11417	6914	4503	50-5
55-59	1526155	715680	4.8	810475	5.0	0	16112	9876	6236	55-5
60-64	1312027	603582	4.0	708445	4.4	0	18721	10802	7919	60-6
65-69	1033649	453334	3.0	580315	3.6	0	25162	13768	11394	65-6
70-74	764938	320494	2.1	444444	2.8		32398	16633	15765	70-7
75-79	457018	182388	1.2	274630	1.7		38894	18477	20417	75-7
80-84	290907	109222	0.7	181685	1.1	340645 M.	41457	17886	23571	80-8
85+	135911	47175	0.3	88736	0.6	321872 F.	35484	13565	21919	85+
TOTAL	31160078	15057848		16102230		662517	275519	140723	134796	TOTA

TABLE 2 — MALE LIFE TABLE

x	nq_x	l_x	nd_x	nL_x	nm_x	na_x	T_x	r_x	$\dot{e}_x$	nM_x
0	0.036055	100000	3605	97296	0.037057	0.2502	6814479	0.0047	68.145	0.037193
1	0.006944	96395	669	383638	0.001745	1.1022	6717182	0.0047	69.684	0.001755
5	0.003603	95725	345	477764	0.000722	2.5000	6333544	0.0141	66.164	0.000725
10	0.002680	95380	256	476285	0.000537	2.5882	5855780	0.0162	61.394	0.000536
15	0.004762	95125	453	474549	0.000955	2.6291	5379495	0.0190	56.552	0.000952
20	0.005666	94672	536	472071	0.001136	2.5996	4904946	0.0104	51.810	0.001135
25	0.007538	94135	710	468974	0.001513	2.6011	4432875	0.0000	47.090	0.001513
30	0.009428	93426	881	465010	0.001894	2.5948	3963901	0.0000	42.428	0.001894
35	0.011997	92545	1110	460104	0.002413	2.6396	3498891	0.0164	37.807	0.002407
40	0.017768	91435	1625	453354	0.003583	2.6492	3038787	0.0239	33.235	0.003570
45	0.025314	89810	2273	443815	0.005123	2.6975	2585433	0.0115	28.788	0.005110
50	0.043183	87537	3780	428926	0.008813	2.6836	2141618	0.0050	24.465	0.008804
55	0.066909	83757	5604	405388	0.013824	2.6098	1712691	0.0129	20.448	0.013799
60	0.086147	78152	6733	374881	0.017959	2.6411	1307304	0.0193	16.728	0.017896
65	0.142307	71420	10164	333249	0.030494	2.6534	932423	0.0193	13.056	0.030371
70	0.232046	61256	14214	272609	0.052142	2.6311	599174	0.0193	9.781	0.051898
75	0.406184	47042	19108	187834	0.101727	2.5206	326565	0.0193	6.942	0.101306
80	0.576371	27934	16101	97905	0.164451	2.4059	138731	0.0193	4.966	0.163759
85+	*1.000000	11834	11834	40826	0.289858	3.4500	40826	0.0193	3.450	0.287546

TABLE 3 — FEMALE LIFE TABLE

x	nq_x	l_x	nd_x	nL_x	nm_x	na_x	T_x	r_x	$\dot{e}_x$	nM_x
0	0.026863	100000	2686	98034	0.027402	0.2682	7301045	0.0050	73.010	0.027508
1	0.006046	97314	588	387559	0.001518	1.1174	7203011	0.0050	74.018	0.001526
5	0.002640	96725	255	482988	0.000529	2.5000	6815452	0.0152	70.462	0.000532
10	0.002142	96470	207	481827	0.000429	2.4693	6332464	0.0089	65.642	0.000429
15	0.002337	96263	225	480770	0.000468	2.5725	5850638	0.0119	60.777	0.000467
20	0.002966	96038	285	479529	0.000594	2.6719	5369868	0.0072	55.914	0.000593
25	0.004804	95753	460	477678	0.000963	2.6318	4890339	0.0000	51.072	0.000963
30	0.006044	95294	576	475086	0.001212	2.6013	4412661	0.0000	46.306	0.001212
35	0.007812	94718	740	471840	0.001568	2.6380	3937575	0.0123	41.572	0.001565
40	0.011342	93978	1066	467387	0.002280	2.6530	3465735	0.0189	36.878	0.002274
45	0.016389	92912	1523	461005	0.003303	2.6660	2998348	0.0125	32.271	0.003296
50	0.024941	91389	2279	451633	0.005047	2.6694	2537343	0.0095	27.764	0.005038
55	0.037882	89110	3376	437611	0.007714	2.6488	2085710	0.0155	23.406	0.007694
60	0.054706	85734	4690	417834	0.011225	2.6897	1648099	0.0195	19.223	0.011178
65	0.094362	81044	7647	387643	0.019728	2.7018	1230264	0.0195	15.180	0.019634
70	0.164827	73396	12098	339186	0.035667	2.7024	842621	0.0195	11.480	0.035471
75	0.316512	61299	19402	259767	0.074689	2.5917	503435	0.0195	8.213	0.074344
80	0.492513	41897	20635	158285	0.130364	2.5188	243667	0.0195	5.816	0.129735
85+	*1.000000	21262	21262	85382	0.249023	4.0157	85382	0.0195	4.016	0.247014

TABLE 4 — OBSERVED AND PROJECTED VITAL RATES

	OBSERVED POPULATION BOTH SEXES	MALES	FEMALES	PROJECTED POPULATION 1968 MALES	FEMALES	1973 MALES	FEMALES	1978 MALES	FEMALES	STABLE POPULATION MALES	FEMAL
RATES PER THOUSAND											
Birth	21.26	22.62	19.99	21.43	19.08	20.82	18.68	20.57	18.58	20.20	19.1
Death	8.84	9.35	8.37	9.37	8.59	9.61	8.86	10.03	9.41	11.03	9.9
Increase	12.42	13.28	11.62	12.06	10.50	11.21	9.82	10.54	9.17		9.167
PERCENTAGE											
under 15	27.67	29.36	26.09	29.19	26.21	28.75	26.11	28.05	25.61	27.08	25.
15-64	63.72	63.26	64.16	62.90	63.38	62.80	62.83	63.17	62.76	63.30	62.
65 and over	8.61	7.39	9.75	7.91	10.40	8.46	11.06	8.77	11.63	9.62	11.
DEP. RATIO X 100	56.93	58.09	55.86	58.99	57.77	59.25	59.15	58.29	59.34	57.98	60.

TABLE 5 — POPULATION PROJECTED WITH FIXED AGE-SPECIFIC BIRTH AND DEATH RATES (IN 1000's)

AGE AT LAST BIRTHDAY	1968 BOTH SEXES	1968 MALES	1968 FEMALES	1973 BOTH SEXES	1973 MALES	1973 FEMALES	1978 BOTH SEXES	1978 MALES	1978 FEMALES	AGE AT LAST BIRTHDAY
0-4	3216	1646	1570	3279	1678	1601	3398	1739	1659	0-4
5-9	3094	1579	1515	3197	1635	1562	3259	1667	1592	5-9
10-14	2834	1458	1376	3087	1575	1512	3188	1630	1558	10-14
15-19	2659	1363	1296	2826	1453	1373	3077	1569	1508	15-19
20-24	2481	1228	1253	2648	1356	1292	2814	1445	1369	20-24
25-29	2257	1114	1143	2468	1220	1248	2634	1347	1287	25-29
30-34	2246	1091	1155	2242	1105	1137	2451	1210	1241	30-34
35-39	2310	1113	1197	2226	1079	1147	2222	1093	1129	35-39
40-44	2219	1069	1150	2283	1097	1186	2199	1063	1136	40-44
45-49	1945	911	1034	2181	1046	1135	2243	1074	1169	45-49
50-54	1716	796	920	1894	881	1013	2123	1011	1112	50-54
55-59	1608	742	866	1643	752	891	1815	833	982	55-59
60-64	1436	662	774	1513	686	827	1547	696	851	60-64
65-69	1194	537	657	1306	588	718	1377	610	767	65-69
70-74	879	371	508	1014	439	575	1109	481	628	70-74
75-79	561	221	340	645	256	389	742	302	440	75-79
80-84	262	95	167	322	115	207	370	133	237	80-84
85+	144	46	98	130	40	90	160	48	112	85+
TOTAL	33061	16042	17019	34904	17001	17903	36728	17951	18777	TOTAL

TABLE 6 — STANDARDIZED RATES

STANDARD COUNTRIES:	ENGLAND AND WALES 1961 BOTH SEXES	MALES	FEMALES	UNITED STATES 1960 BOTH SEXES	MALES	FEMALES	MEXICO 1960 BOTH SEXES	MALES	FEMALES
STANDARDIZED RATES PER THOUSAND									
Birth	18.12	20.78*	17.06	18.44	19.52*	17.65	19.64	18.78*	19.04
Death	11.49	11.60*	11.59	9.44	10.14*	8.57	5.13	7.90*	4.32
Increase	6.63	9.19*	5.47	9.00	9.38*	9.08	14.51	10.88*	14.72

TABLE 7 — MOMENTS AND CUMULANTS

	OBSERVED POP. MALES	OBSERVED POP. FEMALES	STATIONARY POP. MALES	STATIONARY POP. FEMALES	STABLE POP. MALES	STABLE POP. FEMALES	OBSERVED BIRTHS	NET MATERNITY FUNCTION	BIRTHS IN STABLE POP.
μ	30.96230	33.23725	37.12659	38.96679	32.60161	34.08105	29.98975	30.00836	29.69828
σ^2	447.7031	479.5291	506.9360	545.8200	477.0042	516.0784	31.19824	32.08630	31.39144
κ_3	4278.422	3924.724	2158.749	1889.304	4265.510	4481.503	63.0047	74.8398	76.6605
κ_4	-151369.	-191024.	-260713.	-316063.	-192078.	-239731.	-216.857	-223.270	-163.933
β_1	0.203984	0.139693	0.035772	0.021951	0.167639	0.146117	0.130724	0.169553	0.189981
β_2	2.244808	2.169275	1.585490	1.939098	2.155822	2.099895	2.777201	2.783134	2.833642
κ	-0.078995	-0.054315	-0.013280	-0.007957	-0.062609	-0.053311	-0.121492	-0.141598	-0.166344

TABLE 8 — RATES FROM AGE DISTRIBUTIONS AND VITAL STATISTICS (Females)

VITAL STATISTICS		THOMPSON AGE RANGE	NRR	1000r	INTERVAL	BOURGEOIS-PICHAT AGE RANGE	NRR	1000b	1000d	1000r	COALE	
GRR	1.381										IBR	18.91
NRR	1.315	0-4	1.28	9.17	27.42	5-29	1.27	18.78	9.97	8.81	IDR	11.29
TFR	2.843	5-9	1.21	7.11	27.39	30-54	1.45	24.93	11.21	13.72	IRI	7.62
GENERATION	29.853	10-14	1.18	6.00	27.34	55-79	1.87	44.35	21.10	23.25	K1	15.57
SEX RATIO	105.832	15-19	1.19	6.30	27.27	*40-64	1.42	24.13	11.02	13.10	K2	0.31

TABLE 9 — LESLIE MATRIX AND ITS SPECTRAL COMPONENTS (Females)

Start Age Interval	ORIGINAL MATRIX SUB-DIAGONAL	ALTERNATIVE FIRST ROWS Projection	ALTERNATIVE FIRST ROWS Integral	FIRST STABLE MATRIX % IN STABLE POPULATION	FISHER VALUES	REPRODUCTIVE VALUES	SECOND STABLE MATRIX Z₂ FIRST COLUMN	FIRST ROW
0	0.99464	0.00000	0.00000	9.086	1.053	1605022	0.1575+0.0511	0.1575+0.0511
5	0.99760	0.00006	0.00000	8.632	1.109	1529074	0.1377-0.1215	0.0325+0.1457
5	0.99781	0.01217	0.00012	8.225	1.164	1511072	-0.0384-0.2006	-0.0979+0.0918
5	0.99742	0.13048	0.02483	7.839	1.208	1517189	-0.2139-0.0767	-0.1177-0.0344
0	0.99614	0.34774	0.24279	7.468	1.130	1297384	-0.1945+0.1614	-0.0478-0.1135
5	0.99457	0.40588	0.47063	7.106	0.820	952341	0.0444+0.2772	0.0111-0.1069
0	0.99317	0.27110	0.36190	6.750	0.434	522492	0.2897+0.1140	0.0239-0.0613
5	0.99056	0.12921	0.19420	6.404	0.169	196783	0.2719-0.2120	0.0156-0.0236
0	0.98635	0.03780	0.07089	6.059	0.042	43691	-0.0488-0.3776	0.0050-0.0053
5	0.97967	0.00353	0.00656	5.708	0.004	3620	-0.3849-0.1651	0.0005-0.0005
0	0.96895	0.00033	0.00067	5.341	0.000	294	-0.3692+0.2702	0.0000-0.0000
5+	0.80490			21.381				

TABLE 10 — AGE ANALYSIS AND MISCELLANEOUS RESULTS (Females)

Start Age Interval	OBSERVED POPUL. (IN 100's)	CONTRIBUTIONS OF ROOTS (IN 100's) r_1	r_2, r_3	$r_4 \cdot r_{11}$	AGE-SP. BIRTH RATES	NET MATERNITY FUNCTION	COEFF. OF MATRIX EQUATION	PARAMETERS		INTEGRAL	MATRIX	x	EXP. INCREASE $e^{(x+2\frac{1}{2})r}$
0	15236	14698	410	128	0.0000	0.0000	0.0000	L(1)	1.04690	1.04695	0	1.0232
5	13789	13963	98	-272	0.0000	0.0000	0.0001	L(2)	0.45710	0.45627	50	1.6182
5	12985	13305	-395	75	0.0000	0.0001	0.0121		0.79395	0.77208	55	1.6941
5	12558	12681	-568	446	0.0050	0.0240	0.1292	R(1)	0.00917	0.00918	60	1.7735
0	11478	12081	-155	-448	0.0489	0.2343	0.3434	R(2)	-0.01752	-0.02178	65	1.8567
5	11610	11494	527	-411	0.0947	0.4525	0.3993			0.20968	0.20741	70	1.9438
0	12052	10919	786	347	0.0728	0.3460	0.2652	C(1)		161758	75	2.0350
5	11614	10358	238	1017	0.0391	0.1844	0.1256	C(2)		104792	80	2.1304
0	10485	9800	-694	1379	0.0143	0.0667	0.0364			-78333	85	2.2304
5	9390	9233	-1065	1222	0.0013	0.0061	0.0033	2P/Y	29.9653	30.2936	90	2.3350
0	8938	8640	-351	648	0.0001	0.0006	0.0003	DELTA	2.8989		95	2.4445
5+	30887	34586									100	2.5592

TABLE 1 — DATA

AGE AT LAST BIRTHDAY	BOTH SEXES	POPULATION MALES Number	%	FEMALES Number	%	BIRTHS BY AGE OF MOTHER	DEATHS BOTH SEXES	MALES	FEMALES	AGE AT LAST BIRTHDAY
0	66582	33519	3.3	33063	3.0	0	14090	7538	6552	0
1-4	213486	106153	10.5	107333	9.8	0	9624	4869	4755	1-4
5-9	190176	94567	9.4	95609	8.7	0	2635	1360	1275	5-9
10-14	201303	99604	9.9	101699	9.3	0	1295	676	619	10-14
15-19	189825	92923	9.2	96902	8.9	1653	1195	620	575	15-19
20-24	187694	90080	8.9	97614	8.9	10245	1489	770	719	20-24
25-29	175159	83882	8.3	91277	8.3	18829	1594	805	789	25-29
30-34	155990	74985	7.4	81005	7.4	19237	1638	791	847	30-34
35-39	133137	64245	6.4	68892	6.3	14000	1433	699	734	35-39
40-44	123239	58938	5.8	64301	5.9	7020	1676	843	833	40-44
45-49	111053	51753	5.1	59300	5.4	1621	1593	836	757	45-49
50-54	101092	47386	4.7	53706	4.9	0	1849	985	864	50-54
55-59	83089	38337	3.8	44752	4.1	0	1889	986	903	55-59
60-64	68676	30594	3.0	38082	3.5	0	2421	1155	1266	60-64
65-69	45233	19689	1.9	25544	2.3	0	3039	1419	1620	65-69
70-74	29661	12487	1.2	17174	1.6		2697	1146	1551	70-74
75-79	17267	7218	0.7	10049	0.9		2091	886	1205	75-79
80-84	8240	3186	0.3	5054	0.5	37154 M.	1370	535	835	80-84
85+	3051	1040	0.1	2011	0.2	35451 F.	908	323	585	85+
TOTAL	2103953	1010586		1093367		72605	54526	27242	27284	TOTAL

TABLE 2 — MALE LIFE TABLE

x	nq_x	l_x	nd_x	nL_x	nm_x	na_x	T_x	r_x	$\dot{e}_x$	nM_x	x
0	0.197351	100000	19735	87879	0.224572	0.3858	3599944	0.0026	35.999	0.224887	
1	0.163061	80265	13088	285651	0.045818	1.2946	3512066	0.0026	43.756	0.045868	
5	0.068931	67177	4631	324308	0.014278	2.5000	3226415	0.0142	48.029	0.014381	
10	0.033309	62546	2083	306972	0.006787	2.2354	2902107	0.0000	46.399	0.006787	10
15	0.032827	60463	1985	297428	0.006673	2.5383	2595135	0.0031	42.921	0.006672	15
20	0.041870	58478	2448	286403	0.008549	2.5546	2297707	0.0019	39.292	0.008548	20
25	0.046888	56030	2627	273642	0.009600	2.5236	2011304	0.0087	35.897	0.009597	25
30	0.051412	53402	2746	260161	0.010553	2.5045	1737662	0.0163	32.539	0.010549	30
35	0.053030	50657	2686	246688	0.010890	2.5443	1477501	0.0125	29.167	0.010880	35
40	0.069134	47971	3316	231725	0.014312	2.5493	1230814	0.0078	25.658	0.014303	40
45	0.077718	44654	3470	214753	0.016160	2.5456	999088	0.0050	22.374	0.016154	45
50	0.098986	41184	4077	195942	0.020805	2.5527	784335	0.0093	19.045	0.020787	50
55	0.121291	37107	4501	174616	0.025775	2.5738	588393	0.0168	15.857	0.025719	55
60	0.173955	32606	5672	149635	0.037906	2.6381	413777	0.0182	12.690	0.037752	60
65	0.306727	26934	8261	114282	0.072291	2.5319	264142	0.0182	9.807	0.072071	65
70	0.371504	18673	6937	75437	0.091958	2.4158	149860	0.0182	8.026	0.091775	70
75	0.464974	11736	5457	44353	0.123033	2.3746	74423	0.0182	6.342	0.122749	75
80	0.581617	6279	3652	21675	0.168484	2.3386	30070	0.0182	4.789	0.167921	80
85+	*1.000000	2627	2627	8395	0.312932	3.1956	8395	0.0182	3.196	0.310577	85

TABLE 3 — FEMALE LIFE TABLE

x	nq_x	l_x	nd_x	nL_x	nm_x	na_x	T_x	r_x	$\dot{e}_x$	nM_x	x
0	0.176847	100000	17685	89313	0.198008	0.3957	3852280	0.0015	38.523	0.198167	0
1	0.158319	82315	13032	294340	0.044276	1.3204	3762967	0.0015	45.714	0.044301	1
5	0.064070	69283	4439	335319	0.013238	2.5000	3468627	0.0137	50.064	0.013336	5
10	0.029927	64844	1941	318828	0.006087	2.2209	3133308	0.0000	48.321	0.006087	10
15	0.029241	62904	1839	309976	0.005934	2.5304	2814480	0.0000	44.743	0.005934	15
20	0.036179	61064	2209	299935	0.007366	2.5616	2504504	0.0000	41.014	0.007366	20
25	0.042356	58855	2493	288182	0.008650	2.5556	2204570	0.0099	37.458	0.008644	25
30	0.050997	56362	2874	274685	0.010464	2.5206	1916388	0.0181	34.001	0.010456	30
35	0.051930	53488	2778	260560	0.010660	2.5231	1641703	0.0119	30.693	0.010654	35
40	0.062756	50710	3182	245629	0.012956	2.5107	1381144	0.0027	27.236	0.012955	40
45	0.061881	47528	2941	230344	0.012768	2.5193	1135514	0.0045	23.892	0.012766	45
50	0.077488	44587	3455	214511	0.016106	2.5619	905171	0.0121	20.301	0.016088	50
55	0.096457	41132	3967	196218	0.020220	2.6202	690660	0.0125	16.791	0.020178	55
60	0.154570	37164	5745	172435	0.033314	2.6695	494443	0.0087	13.304	0.033244	60
65	0.275039	31420	8642	136042	0.063522	2.5632	322008	0.0087	10.249	0.063420	65
70	0.367335	22778	8367	92543	0.090414	2.4486	185966	0.0087	8.164	0.090311	70
75	0.456512	14411	6579	54803	0.120044	2.3777	93423	0.0087	6.483	0.119912	75
80	0.575140	7832	4505	27222	0.165476	2.3496	38620	0.0087	4.931	0.165215	80
85+	*1.000000	3328	3328	11398	0.291953	3.4252	11398	0.0087	3.425	0.290900	85

TABLE 4 — OBSERVED AND PROJECTED VITAL RATES

RATES PER THOUSAND	OBSERVED POPULATION BOTH SEXES	MALES	FEMALES	PROJECTED POPULATION 1785 MALES	FEMALES	1790 MALES	FEMALES	1795 MALES	FEMALES	STABLE POPULATION MALES	FEMALES
Birth	34.51	36.76	32.42	36.59	32.60	35.78	32.15	34.40	31.12	33.17	31.16
Death	25.92	26.96	24.95	26.96	24.76	27.00	24.83	26.86	24.80	27.27	25.26
Increase	8.59	9.81	7.47	9.63	7.84	8.78	7.32	7.54	6.32		5.8987
PERCENTAGE											
under 15	31.92	33.03	30.89	33.23	31.03	34.63	32.37	33.92	31.69	31.97	31.01
15-64	63.16	62.65	63.64	62.20	63.28	60.60	61.79	61.04	62.21	62.31	62.45
65 and over	4.92	4.32	5.47	4.57	5.69	4.78	5.84	5.04	6.10	5.72	6.54
DEP. RATIO X 100	58.32	59.62	57.13	60.77	58.04	65.03	61.84	63.83	60.75	60.48	60.12

TABLE 5 — POPULATION PROJECTED WITH FIXED AGE—SPECIFIC BIRTH AND DEATH RATES (IN 1000's)

AGE LAST BIRTHDAY	1785 BOTH SEXES	1785 MALES	1785 FEMALES	1790 BOTH SEXES	1790 MALES	1790 FEMALES	1795 BOTH SEXES	1795 MALES	1795 FEMALES	AGE AT LAST BIRTHDAY
0-4	281	142	139	291	147	144	295	149	146	0-4
5-9	244	121	123	245	123	122	253	127	126	5-9
10-14	181	90	91	232	115	117	233	117	116	10-14
15-19	196	97	99	175	87	88	224	111	113	15-19
20-24	183	89	94	189	93	96	170	84	86	20-24
25-29	180	86	94	175	85	90	181	89	92	25-29
30-34	167	80	87	171	82	89	167	81	86	30-34
35-39	148	71	77	159	76	83	163	78	85	35-39
40-44	125	60	65	139	67	72	149	71	78	40-44
45-49	115	55	60	117	56	61	130	62	68	45-49
50-54	102	47	55	106	50	56	108	51	57	50-54
55-59	91	42	49	93	42	51	95	44	51	55-59
60-64	72	33	39	79	36	43	80	36	44	60-64
65-69	53	23	30	56	25	31	62	28	34	65-69
70-74	30	13	17	35	15	20	38	17	21	70-74
75-79	17	7	10	18	8	10	21	9	12	75-79
80-84	9	4	5	9	4	5	9	4	5	80-84
85+	3	1	2	3	1	2	3	1	2	85+
TOTAL	2197	1061	1136	2292	1112	1180	2381	1159	1222	TOTAL

TABLE 6 — STANDARDIZED RATES

STANDARD COUNTRIES:

STANDARDIZED RATES PER THOUSAND

	ENGLAND AND WALES 1961 BOTH SEXES	MALES	FEMALES	UNITED STATES 1960 BOTH SEXES	MALES	FEMALES	MEXICO 1960 BOTH SEXES	MALES	FEMALES
Birth	29.49	31.77*	27.91	29.88	29.42*	28.75	28.63	29.78*	27.88
Death	30.22	47.53*	31.32	29.00	39.05*	28.41	25.60	25.14*	24.30
Increase	-0.73	-15.76*	-3.41	0.88	-9.63*	0.33	3.03	4.65*	3.59

TABLE 7 — MOMENTS AND CUMULANTS

	OBSERVED POP. MALES	OBSERVED POP. FEMALES	STATIONARY POP. MALES	STATIONARY POP. FEMALES	STABLE POP. MALES	STABLE POP. FEMALES	OBSERVED BIRTHS	NET MATERNITY FUNCTION	BIRTHS IN STABLE POP.
μ	27.51907	28.90950	31.36787	32.26891	28.83013	29.63393	31.71665	32.24149	31.97437
σ^2	387.9028	412.0369	442.1678	458.4854	417.4806	434.0114	42.53235	43.28642	43.10814
κ_3	4342.586	4415.122	3763.966	3663.094	4561.680	4587.480	51.1098	26.8386	33.5793
κ_4	-81656.	-103313.	-157539.	-180230.	-112191.	-132075.	-1027.583	-1151.937	-1122.210
β_1	0.323093	0.278662	0.163882	0.139226	0.285983	0.257422	0.033951	0.008881	0.014076
β_2	2.457319	2.391472	2.194226	2.142614	2.356295	2.298839	2.431961	2.385212	2.396113
κ	-0.132147	-0.112986	-0.063435	-0.052947	-0.111601	-0.098650	-0.021017	-0.005387	-0.008590

TABLE 8 — RATES FROM AGE DISTRIBUTIONS AND VITAL STATISTICS (Females)

VITAL STATISTICS		THOMPSON AGE RANGE	NRR	1000r	INTERVAL	BOURGEOIS-PICHAT AGE RANGE	NRR	1000b	1000d	1000r	COALE	
RR	2.211										IBR	33.10
NRR	1.209	0-4	1.23	7.74	26.91	5-29	0.88	26.28	30.89	-4.61	IDR	24.92
GFR	4.528	5-9	0.99	-0.52	26.73	30-54	1.21	32.79	25.71	7.08	IRI	8.19
GENERATION	32.108	10-14	1.15	5.35	26.65	55-79	1.52	51.66	36.04	15.62	K1	0.
SEX RATIO	104.804	15-19	1.20	6.57	26.54	*40-64	1.28	36.09	26.87	9.22	K2	0.

TABLE 9 — LESLIE MATRIX AND ITS SPECTRAL COMPONENTS (Females)

Part Age Interval	ORIGINAL MATRIX SUB-DIAGONAL	ALTERNATIVE FIRST ROWS Projection	ALTERNATIVE FIRST ROWS Integral	FIRST STABLE MATRIX % IN STABLE POPULATION	FISHER VALUES	REPRODUCTIVE VALUES	SECOND STABLE MATRIX Z₂ FIRST COLUMN	SECOND STABLE MATRIX Z₂ FIRST ROW
	0.87402	0.00000	0.00000	11.780	1.322	185599	0.1329+0.0462	0.1329+0.0462
	0.95082	0.00000	0.00000	9.996	1.558	148942	0.1145-0.0788	0.0421+0.1361
	0.97224	0.01553	0.00000	9.228	1.687	171614	0.0046-0.1492	-0.0789-0.1066
	0.96761	0.11110	0.03243	8.711	1.767	171179	-0.1291-0.1012	-0.1229-0.0012
	0.96082	0.28395	0.19953	8.184	1.729	168731	-0.1727+0.0482	-0.0810-0.0965
	0.95316	0.40523	0.39217	7.635	1.462	133471	-0.0689+0.1820	-0.0118-0.1264
	0.94858	0.40298	0.45147	7.065	1.018	82466	0.1140-0.1759	0.0315-0.0980
	0.94270	0.28674	0.38634	6.507	0.544	37461	0.2243+0.0132	0.0346-0.0500
	0.93777	0.12625	0.20755	5.956	0.192	12345	0.1528-0.1842	0.0167-0.0157
	0.93126	0.02560	0.05194	5.423	0.033	1950	-0.0614-0.2460	0.0034-0.0023
	0.91472	0.00002	0.00004	4.903	0.000	1	-0.2468-0.1013	0.0000-0.0000
85+	0.72297			14.610				

TABLE 10 — AGE ANALYSIS AND MISCELLANEOUS RESULTS (Females)

Part Age Interval	OBSERVED POPUL. (IN 100's)	CONTRIBUTIONS OF ROOTS (IN 100's) r_1	r_2, r_3	$r_4 \cdot r_{11}$	AGE-SP. BIRTH RATES	NET MATERNITY FUNCTION	COEFF. OF MATRIX EQUATION	PARAMETERS	PARAMETERS INTEGRAL	PARAMETERS MATRIX	EXP. INCREASE x	EXP. INCREASE $e^{(x+2\frac{1}{2})r}$
	1404	1319	-0	85	0.0000	0.0000	0.0000	L(1)	1.02993	1.02995	0	1.0149
	956	1119	-52	-111	0.0000	0.0000	0.0000	L(2)	0.52497	0.52416	50	1.3630
	1017	1033	-66	50	0.0000	0.0000	0.0129		0.72792	0.71314	55	1.4038
	969	975	-24	18	0.0083	0.0258	0.0898	R(1)	0.00590	0.00590	60	1.4458
	976	916	48	12	0.0512	0.1537	0.2220	R(2)	-0.02163	-0.02442	65	1.4891
	913	855	90	-32	0.1007	0.2903	0.3044		0.18920	0.18739	70	1.5337
	810	791	59	-40	0.1160	0.3185	0.2885	C(1)		11197	75	1.5796
	689	729	-29	-11	0.0992	0.2585	0.1947	C(2)		-7759	80	1.6268
	643	667	-104	80	0.0533	0.1309	0.0808			-21813	85	1.6755
	593	607	-98	84	0.0133	0.0307	0.0154	2P/Y	33.2094	33.5294	90	1.7257
	537	549	-6	-6	0.0000	0.0000	0.0000	DELTA	3.0946		95	1.7774
85+	1427	1636									100	1.8306

TABLE 1 — DATA

AGE AT LAST BIRTHDAY	POPULATION BOTH SEXES	MALES Number	%	FEMALES Number	%	BIRTHS BY AGE OF MOTHER	DEATHS BOTH SEXES	MALES	FEMALES	AGE AT LAST BIRTHDAY
0	57412	28830	2.8	28582	2.6	0	13288	7093	6195	0
1-4	211788	105304	10.2	106484	9.6	0	9651	4917	4734	1-4
5-9	209068	104488	10.1	104580	9.4	0	3127	1638	1489	5-9
10-14	194963	97617	9.5	97346	8.7	0	1620	824	796	10-14
15-19	188682	92732	9.0	95950	8.6	1543	1439	718	721	15-19
20-24	191933	91645	8.9	100288	9.0	9596	1595	848	747	20-24
25-29	174273	83293	8.1	90980	8.2	17431	1786	939	847	25-29
30-34	166172	80068	7.8	86104	7.7	18528	1908	966	942	30-34
35-39	142274	68999	6.7	73275	6.6	13225	1666	846	820	35-39
40-44	127689	61533	6.0	66156	5.9	6305	1937	1000	937	40-44
45-49	108225	51176	5.0	57049	5.1	1240	1854	998	856	45-49
50-54	103214	47843	4.6	55371	5.0	0	2204	1172	1032	50-54
55-59	85680	39133	3.8	46547	4.2	0	2291	1201	1090	55-59
60-64	74090	32841	3.2	41249	3.7	0	3064	1497	1567	60-64
65-69	50206	21995	2.1	28211	2.5	0	3325	1554	1771	65-69
70-74	33399	14090	1.4	19309	1.7		3074	1365	1709	70-74
75-79	16839	6779	0.7	10060	0.9		2236	946	1290	75-79
80-84	7964	3023	0.3	4941	0.4	34603 M.	1550	626	924	80-84
85+	3622	1310	0.1	2312	0.2	33265 F.	928	354	574	85+
TOTAL	2147493	1032699		1114794		67868	58543	29502	29041	TOTAL

TABLE 2 — MALE LIFE TABLE

x	$n q_x$	l_x	$n d_x$	$n L_x$	$n m_x$	$n a_x$	T_x	r_x	$\mathring{e}_x$	$n M_x$
0	0.213369	100000	21337	86725	0.246028	0.3778	3358279	0.0000	33.583	0.246028
1	0.165696	78663	13034	279144	0.046693	1.2758	3271554	0.0000	41.589	0.046693
5	0.075069	65629	4927	315828	0.015599	2.5000	2992410	0.0108	45.596	0.015676
10	0.041241	60702	2503	296687	0.008438	2.2739	2676582	0.0018	44.094	0.008441
15	0.037979	58199	2210	285474	0.007743	2.5028	2379895	0.0000	40.893	0.007743
20	0.045249	55988	2533	273759	0.009254	2.5593	2094421	0.0014	37.408	0.009253
25	0.054847	53455	2932	260034	0.011275	2.5302	1820662	0.0025	34.060	0.011273
30	0.058560	50523	2959	245199	0.012066	2.4930	1560628	0.0069	30.889	0.012065
35	0.059561	47565	2833	230853	0.012272	2.5398	1315429	0.0132	27.656	0.012261
40	0.078255	44732	3500	215116	0.016272	2.5598	1084576	0.0139	24.246	0.016251
45	0.093091	41231	3838	196731	0.019510	2.5445	869460	0.0053	21.088	0.019501
50	0.115553	37393	4321	176347	0.024502	2.5428	672730	0.0023	17.991	0.024497
55	0.142879	33072	4725	153860	0.030712	2.5664	496383	0.0053	15.009	0.030690
60	0.205541	28347	5826	127594	0.045663	2.5733	342523	0.0104	12.083	0.045583
65	0.300792	22520	6774	95727	0.070763	2.5089	214928	0.0104	9.544	0.070652
70	0.388481	15746	6117	63053	0.097016	2.4369	119201	0.0104	7.570	0.096877
75	0.511166	9629	4922	35214	0.139778	2.3727	56148	0.0104	5.831	0.139549
80	0.660410	4707	3109	14984	0.207462	2.2773	20934	0.0104	4.447	0.207079
85+	1.000000	1598	1598	5950	0.268647	3.7224	5950	0.0104	3.722	0.270230

TABLE 3 — FEMALE LIFE TABLE

x	$n q_x$	l_x	$n d_x$	$n L_x$	$n m_x$	$n a_x$	T_x	r_x	$\mathring{e}_x$	$n M_x$
0	0.191321	100000	19132	88270	0.216745	0.3869	3656455	0.0000	36.565	0.216745
1	0.158755	80868	12838	288775	0.044457	1.2974	3568184	0.0000	44.124	0.044457
5	0.068329	68030	4648	328527	0.014149	2.5000	3279410	0.0132	48.206	0.014238
10	0.040003	63381	2535	310067	0.008177	2.3024	2950882	0.0000	46.558	0.008177
15	0.036869	60846	2243	298539	0.007514	2.4636	2640815	0.0000	43.402	0.007514
20	0.036570	58603	2143	287723	0.007449	2.5318	2342276	0.0000	39.969	0.007449
25	0.045535	56459	2571	276021	0.009314	2.5590	2054553	0.0060	36.390	0.009310
30	0.053275	53889	2871	262309	0.010945	2.5152	1778531	0.0110	33.004	0.010940
35	0.054494	51018	2780	248228	0.011200	2.5324	1516223	0.0145	29.720	0.011191
40	0.068467	48237	3303	233029	0.014173	2.5297	1267995	0.0114	26.287	0.014163
45	0.072347	44935	3251	216633	0.015007	2.5265	1034966	0.0022	23.033	0.015005
50	0.089140	41684	3716	199330	0.018641	2.5539	818333	0.0017	19.632	0.018638
55	0.110943	37968	4212	179763	0.023433	2.6075	619003	0.0041	16.303	0.023417
60	0.174451	33756	5889	154760	0.038051	2.6193	439240	0.0082	13.012	0.037989
65	0.272208	27867	7586	120673	0.062861	2.5397	284480	0.0082	10.208	0.062777
70	0.361696	20281	7336	82785	0.088612	2.4614	163807	0.0082	8.077	0.088508
75	0.481048	12946	6228	48504	0.128393	2.3946	81022	0.0082	6.259	0.128231
80	0.623152	6718	4186	22355	0.187272	2.3161	32518	0.0082	4.840	0.187007
85+	*1.000000	2532	2532	10163	0.249116	4.0142	10163	0.0082	4.014	0.248270

TABLE 4 — OBSERVED AND PROJECTED VITAL RATES

	OBSERVED POPULATION BOTH SEXES	MALES	FEMALES	PROJECTED POPULATION 1790 MALES	FEMALES	1795 MALES	FEMALES	1800 MALES	FEMALES	STABLE POPULATION MALES	FEMALES
RATES PER THOUSAND											
Birth	31.60	33.51	29.84	33.73	30.18	33.09	29.74	32.18	29.03	31.06	28.5
Death	27.26	28.57	26.05	28.12	25.61	28.20	25.74	28.17	25.77	29.66	27.1
Increase	4.34	4.94	3.79	5.61	4.57	4.89	4.01	4.01	3.26		1.400
PERCENTAGE											
under 15	31.35	32.56	30.23	32.37	30.25	32.38	30.36	31.49	29.48	30.09	28.7
15-64	63.43	62.87	63.96	62.80	63.62	62.71	63.43	63.45	64.10	63.88	63.9
65 and over	5.22	4.57	5.82	4.83	6.13	4.91	6.21	5.06	6.41	6.03	7.3
DEP. RATIO X 100	57.65	59.06	56.36	59.24	57.18	59.45	57.67	57.60	56.00	56.54	56.4

TABLE 1 (DATA)

AGE AT LAST BIRTHDAY	POPULATION BOTH SEXES	MALES Number	%	FEMALES Number	%	BIRTHS BY AGE OF MOTHER	DEATHS BOTH SEXES	MALES	FEMALES	AGE AT LAST BIRTHDAY
0	57952	29204	2.8	28748	2.6	0	14795	7977	6818	0
1-4	213889	106589	10.3	107300	9.6	0	7960	4030	3930	1-4
5-9	209907	106124	10.2	103783	9.3	0	2461	1280	1181	5-9
10-14	208573	104557	10.1	104016	9.3	0	1411	779	632	10-14
15-19	181527	89299	8.6	92228	8.2	1499	1292	716	576	15-19
20-24	181646	85731	8.2	95915	8.6	9737	1704	976	728	20-24
25-29	174095	81677	7.9	92418	8.2	18102	1961	1097	864	25-29
30-34	162099	77671	7.5	84428	7.5	19708	2131	1166	965	30-34
35-39	148800	71410	6.9	77390	6.9	15073	2105	1143	962	35-39
40-44	133655	64367	6.2	69288	6.2	7169	2341	1244	1097	40-44
45-49	110915	53079	5.1	57836	5.2	1417	2176	1190	986	45-49
50-54	98972	46202	4.4	52770	4.7	1	2334	1243	1091	50-54
55-59	88315	40364	3.9	47951	4.3	0	2549	1294	1255	55-59
60-64	72884	33012	3.2	39872	3.6	0	3156	1526	1630	60-64
65-69	54136	24148	2.3	29988	2.7	0	3264	1528	1736	65-69
70-74	34061	14449	1.4	19612	1.7		3272	1415	1857	70-74
75-79	18117	7324	0.7	10793	1.0		2482	1060	1422	75-79
80-84	7846	3016	0.3	4830	0.4	37291 M.	1540	612	928	80-84
85+	3609	1257	0.1	2352	0.2	35415 F.	947	348	599	85+
TOTAL	2160998	1039480		1121518		72706	59881	30624	29257	TOTAL

TABLE 2 (MALE / FEMALE / BLE)

x	nq_x	l_x	nd_x	nL_x	nm_x	na_x	T_x	r_x	$\dot{e}_x$	nM_x	x
0	0.231831	100000	23183	84874	0.273148	0.3475	3333790	0.0000	33.338	0.273148	0
1	0.136832	76817	10511	278005	0.037809	1.2160	3248916	0.0000	42.294	0.037809	1
5	0.058302	66306	3866	321865	0.012011	2.5000	2970911	0.0092	44.806	0.012061	5
10	0.036498	62440	2279	306191	0.007443	2.3631	2649046	0.0086	42.425	0.007450	10
15	0.039371	60161	2369	295076	0.008027	2.5811	2342855	0.0113	38.943	0.008018	15
20	0.055394	57793	3201	281205	0.011384	2.5768	2047779	0.0000	35.433	0.011384	20
25	0.064998	54591	3548	264188	0.013431	2.5289	1766574	0.0000	32.360	0.013431	25
30	0.072351	51043	3693	246002	0.015012	2.5055	1502386	0.0000	29.434	0.015012	30
35	0.076984	47350	3645	227708	0.016008	2.5195	1256384	0.0023	26.534	0.016006	35
40	0.092293	43705	4034	208558	0.019341	2.5295	1028677	0.0105	23.537	0.019327	40
45	0.106268	39671	4216	187907	0.022435	2.5216	820118	0.0104	20.673	0.022419	45
50	0.126103	35455	4471	166180	0.026905	2.5181	632211	0.0005	17.831	0.026904	50
55	0.148600	30984	4604	143621	0.032058	2.5457	466032	0.0000	15.041	0.032058	55
60	0.207807	26380	5482	118428	0.046289	2.5425	322410	0.0101	12.222	0.046226	60
65	0.273790	20898	5722	90286	0.063373	2.5175	203982	0.0101	9.761	0.063276	65
70	0.392913	15176	5963	60789	0.098093	2.4689	113696	0.0101	7.492	0.097931	70
75	0.524509	9213	4832	33337	0.144961	2.3657	52907	0.0101	5.742	0.144730	75
80	0.649953	4381	2847	14010	0.203242	2.2586	19570	0.0101	4.467	0.202918	80
85+	1.000000	1534	1534	5560	0.275798	3.6258	5560	0.0101	3.626	0.276849	85+

TABLE 3 (MALE / FEMALE / BLE)

x	nq_x	l_x	nd_x	nL_x	nm_x	na_x	T_x	r_x	$\dot{e}_x$	nM_x	x
0	0.205926	100000	20593	86828	0.237164	0.3604	3731541	0.0000	37.315	0.237164	0
1	0.133051	79407	10565	288461	0.036626	1.2392	3644713	0.0000	45.899	0.036626	1
5	0.055035	68842	3789	334739	0.011319	2.5000	3356252	0.0109	48.753	0.011380	5
10	0.029866	65053	1943	320025	0.006071	2.3019	3021513	0.0044	46.447	0.006076	10
15	0.030756	63111	1941	310770	0.006246	2.5361	2701488	0.0017	42.806	0.006245	15
20	0.037263	61169	2279	300305	0.007590	2.5687	2390718	0.0000	39.084	0.007590	20
25	0.045717	58890	2692	287896	0.009351	2.5654	2090412	0.0033	35.497	0.009349	25
30	0.055603	56198	3125	273284	0.011434	2.5340	1802516	0.0066	32.074	0.011430	30
35	0.060340	53073	3202	257501	0.012437	2.5441	1529233	0.0068	28.814	0.012431	35
40	0.076248	49871	3803	239965	0.015846	2.5311	1271732	0.0138	25.501	0.015832	40
45	0.081826	46068	3770	220992	0.017057	2.5198	1031767	0.0097	22.397	0.017048	45
50	0.098382	42299	4161	201282	0.020675	2.5463	810775	0.0000	19.168	0.020675	50
55	0.123103	38137	4695	179378	0.026173	2.5915	609493	0.0000	15.982	0.026173	55
60	0.186108	33442	6224	152112	0.040916	2.5740	430115	0.0056	12.861	0.040881	60
65	0.253662	27218	6904	119154	0.057944	2.5467	278002	0.0056	10.214	0.057890	65
70	0.382499	20314	7770	81987	0.094773	2.4796	158849	0.0056	7.820	0.094687	70
75	0.489722	12544	6143	46588	0.131859	2.3740	76862	0.0056	6.127	0.131752	75
80	0.633328	6401	4054	21079	0.192318	2.3049	30274	0.0056	4.730	0.192132	80
85+	*1.000000	2347	2347	9194	0.255266	3.9175	9194	0.0056	3.917	0.254677	85+

TABLE 4 (OBSERVED AND PROJECTED TOTAL RATES)

	OBSERVED POPULATION BOTH SEXES	MALES	FEMALES	PROJECTED POPULATION 1795 MALES	FEMALES	1800 MALES	FEMALES	1805 MALES	FEMALES	STABLE POPULATION MALES	FEMALES
RATES PER THOUSAND											
Birth	33.64	35.87	31.58	35.35	31.21	34.59	30.61	33.91	30.05	34.03	30.61
Death	27.71	29.46	26.09	29.31	25.76	29.20	25.64	29.03	25.51	29.66	26.25
Increase	5.93	6.41	5.49	6.05	5.45	5.39	4.96	4.88	4.54		4.3638
PERCENTAGE											
under 15	31.94	33.33	30.66	33.45	30.81	33.99	31.45	33.39	30.75	32.68	30.56
15-64	62.61	61.84	63.32	61.53	63.10	60.92	62.41	61.57	63.19	62.25	63.23
65 and over	5.45	4.83	6.03	5.02	6.09	5.09	6.14	5.04	6.06	5.07	6.21
DEP. RATIO X 100	59.73	61.71	57.94	62.51	58.48	64.15	60.23	62.43	58.26	60.64	58.14

TABLE 1 — DATA

AGE AT LAST BIRTHDAY	POPULATION BOTH SEXES	MALES Number	%	FEMALES Number	%	BIRTHS BY AGE OF MOTHER	DEATHS BOTH SEXES	MALES	FEMALES	AGE AT LAST BIRTHDAY
0	62936	31822	2.9	31114	2.6	0	15009	8103	6906	0
1-4	235677	117231	10.7	118446	10.1	0	8098	4160	3938	1-4
5-9	223608	113054	10.3	110554	9.4	0	2333	1213	1120	5-9
10-14	216865	109584	10.0	107281	9.1	0	1080	557	523	10-14
15-19	199337	98772	9.0	100565	8.6	1509	1051	544	507	15-19
20-24	182973	86929	7.9	96044	8.2	10043	1204	630	574	20-24
25-29	175375	82688	7.5	92687	7.9	19317	1434	696	738	25-29
30-34	168792	80874	7.4	87918	7.5	21259	1585	759	826	30-34
35-39	153258	73727	6.7	79531	6.8	15652	1566	767	799	35-39
40-44	145830	70834	6.4	74996	6.4	7995	2007	1010	997	40-44
45-49	120535	57745	5.3	62790	5.3	1471	1921	1040	881	45-49
50-54	103226	48943	4.5	54283	4.6	0	2047	1095	952	50-54
55-59	84715	38828	3.5	45887	3.9	0	2178	1110	1068	55-59
60-64	76981	34590	3.1	42391	3.6	0	3080	1493	1587	60-64
65-69	55895	24858	2.3	31037	2.6	0	3183	1471	1712	65-69
70-74	38394	16692	1.5	21702	1.8		3542	1604	1938	70-74
75-79	18991	7714	0.7	11277	1.0		2657	1123	1534	75-79
80-84	7926	3092	0.3	4834	0.4	39432 M.	1707	694	1013	80-84
85+	2750	923	0.1	1827	0.2	37814 F.	894	336	558	85+
TOTAL	2274064	1098900		1175164		77246	56576	28405	28171	TOTAL

TABLE 2 — MALE LIFE TABLE

x	nq_x	l_x	nd_x	nL_x	nm_x	na_x	T_x	r_x	$\mathring{e}_x$	nM_x
0	0.218454	100000	21845	85791	0.254635	0.3496	3744763	0.0000	37.448	0.254635
1	0.129195	78155	10097	284544	0.035485	1.2195	3658972	0.0000	46.817	0.035485
5	0.051834	68057	3528	331468	0.010643	2.5000	3374428	0.0156	49.582	0.010729
10	0.025028	64530	1615	318233	0.005075	2.2658	3042960	0.0069	47.156	0.005083
15	0.027212	62915	1712	310411	0.005515	2.5689	2724727	0.0175	43.308	0.005508
20	0.035640	61203	2181	300710	0.007254	2.5689	2414316	0.0107	39.448	0.007247
25	0.041231	59021	2433	289109	0.008417	2.5354	2113606	0.0000	35.811	0.008417
30	0.045864	56588	2595	276515	0.009386	2.5246	1824497	0.0021	32.242	0.009385
35	0.050745	53993	2740	263309	0.010405	2.5715	1547982	0.0023	28.670	0.010403
40	0.068993	51253	3536	247711	0.014275	2.5815	1284673	0.0103	25.065	0.014259
45	0.086398	47717	4123	228505	0.018042	2.5553	1036961	0.0188	21.732	0.018010
50	0.106214	43594	4630	206621	0.022410	2.5490	808457	0.0170	18.545	0.022373
55	0.133762	38964	5212	182199	0.028605	2.5786	601836	0.0044	15.446	0.028588
60	0.195477	33752	6598	152642	0.043223	2.5571	419637	0.0097	12.433	0.043163
65	0.258580	27154	7022	118468	0.059269	2.5357	266995	0.0097	9.833	0.059176
70	0.387524	20133	7802	81051	0.096259	2.4862	148527	0.0097	7.377	0.096094
75	0.527562	12331	6505	44609	0.145827	2.3799	67476	0.0097	5.472	0.145579
80	0.695483	5826	4052	18013	0.224923	2.2567	22866	0.0097	3.925	0.224450
85+	*1.000000	1774	1774	4853	0.365507	2.7359	4853	0.0097	2.736	0.364030

TABLE 3 — FEMALE LIFE TABLE

x	nq_x	l_x	nd_x	nL_x	nm_x	na_x	T_x	r_x	$\mathring{e}_x$	nM_x
0	0.194303	100000	19430	87540	0.221958	0.3587	4018413	0.0000	40.184	0.221958
1	0.121797	80570	9813	295157	0.033247	1.2362	3930873	0.0000	48.788	0.033247
5	0.048935	70757	3462	345127	0.010032	2.5000	3635716	0.0190	51.383	0.010131
10	0.024037	67294	1618	332046	0.004872	2.2647	3290589	0.0033	48.899	0.004875
15	0.024905	65677	1636	324350	0.005043	2.5343	2958543	0.0060	45.047	0.005042
20	0.029463	64041	1887	315652	0.005978	2.5875	2634193	0.0020	41.133	0.005976
25	0.039060	62154	2428	304879	0.007963	2.5734	2318541	0.0010	37.303	0.007962
30	0.045922	59726	2743	291851	0.009398	2.5279	2013662	0.0061	33.715	0.009395
35	0.049048	56984	2795	278086	0.010050	2.5557	1721811	0.0052	30.216	0.010046
40	0.064408	54189	3490	262352	0.013303	2.5386	1443725	0.0110	26.643	0.013294
45	0.067874	50698	3441	244991	0.014046	2.5297	1181372	0.0177	23.302	0.014031
50	0.084220	47257	3980	226614	0.017563	2.5696	936381	0.0135	19.815	0.017538
55	0.110253	43277	4771	205008	0.023275	2.6152	709767	0.0000	16.400	0.023275
60	0.171881	38506	6618	176605	0.037476	2.5940	504760	0.0060	13.109	0.037437
65	0.243297	31887	7758	140499	0.055218	2.5590	328154	0.0060	10.291	0.055160
70	0.365294	24129	8814	98599	0.089396	2.4986	187655	0.0060	7.777	0.089301
75	0.502795	15315	7700	56549	0.136171	2.3993	89056	0.0060	5.815	0.136029
80	0.668633	7615	5091	24266	0.209815	2.2882	32507	0.0060	4.269	0.209558
85+	*1.000000	2523	2523	8241	0.306187	3.2660	8241	0.0060	3.266	0.305419

TABLE 4 — OBSERVED AND PROJECTED VITAL RATES

	OBSERVED POPULATION BOTH SEXES	MALES	FEMALES	PROJECTED POPULATION 1800 MALES	FEMALES	1805 MALES	FEMALES	1810 MALES	FEMALES	STABLE POPULATION MALES	FEMALES
RATES PER THOUSAND											
Birth	33.97	35.88	32.18	34.91	31.55	34.02	30.94	33.35	30.49	33.49	31.4
Death	24.88	25.85	23.97	25.34	23.45	25.13	23.25	24.95	23.11	25.91	23.8
Increase	9.09	10.03	8.21	9.56	8.10	8.89	7.69	8.40	7.38		7.582
PERCENTAGE											
under 15	32.50	33.82	31.26	33.82	31.71	34.12	32.37	33.08	31.43	32.36	31.5
15-64	62.05	61.33	62.72	61.23	62.20	61.09	61.74	62.11	62.75	62.46	62.5
65 and over	5.45	4.85	6.01	4.95	6.09	4.79	5.89	4.81	5.83	5.18	5.9
DEP. RATIO X 100	61.16	63.06	59.43	63.33	60.78	63.68	61.97	61.01	59.37	60.11	59.9

TABLE 1 DATA

AGE AT LAST BIRTHDAY	POPULATION BOTH SEXES	MALES Number	MALES %	FEMALES Number	FEMALES %	BIRTHS BY AGE OF MOTHER	DEATHS BOTH SEXES	DEATHS MALES	DEATHS FEMALES	AGE AT LAST BIRTHDAY
0	58703	29730	2.6	28973	2.4	0	14615	7912	6703	0
1-4	239452	118985	10.5	120467	9.9	0	8726	4419	4307	1-4
5-9	242778	121542	10.8	121236	9.9	0	2520	1317	1203	5-9
10-14	225851	113932	10.1	111919	9.2	0	1128	575	553	10-14
15-19	203960	100478	8.9	103482	8.5	1465	1165	579	586	15-19
20-24	197805	94213	8.3	103592	8.5	10173	1472	787	685	20-24
25-29	173220	81558	7.2	91662	7.5	17564	1434	724	710	25-29
30-34	169280	80487	7.1	88793	7.3	19757	1685	802	883	30-34
35-39	156972	74452	6.6	82520	6.7	15404	1707	850	857	35-39
40-44	147349	70543	6.2	76806	6.3	7534	2139	1060	1079	40-44
45-49	131993	62381	5.5	69612	5.7	1506	2226	1204	1022	45-49
50-54	113454	53231	4.7	60223	4.9	0	2531	1359	1172	50-54
55-59	88296	40551	3.6	47745	3.9	0	2540	1312	1228	55-59
60-64	73873	32936	2.9	40937	3.3	0	3177	1556	1621	60-64
65-69	57927	25219	2.2	32708	2.7	0	3493	1643	1850	65-69
70-74	38984	16468	1.5	22516	1.8		3926	1757	2169	70-74
75-79	20805	8519	0.8	12286	1.0		3256	1427	1829	75-79
80-84	8498	3266	0.3	5232	0.4	37674 M.	2080	838	1242	80-84
85+	2948	1002	0.1	1946	0.2	35729 F.	1049	383	666	85+
TOTAL	2352148	1129493		1222655		73403	60869	30504	30365	TOTAL

TABLE 2 MALE LIFE TABLE

x	$_nq_x$	l_x	$_nd_x$	$_nL_x$	$_nm_x$	$_na_x$	T_x	r_x	$\mathring{e}_x$	$_nM_x$	x
0	0.226821	100000	22682	85230	0.266128	0.3488	3598984	0.0000	35.990	0.266128	0
1	0.134646	77318	10411	280312	0.037139	1.2182	3513755	0.0000	45.446	0.037139	1
5	0.052443	66907	3509	325765	0.010771	2.5000	3233443	0.0110	48.327	0.010836	5
10	0.024825	63399	1574	312694	0.005033	2.2685	2907678	0.0124	45.863	0.005047	10
15	0.028463	61825	1760	304909	0.005771	2.6050	2594984	0.0130	41.973	0.005762	15
20	0.040975	60065	2461	294327	0.008362	2.5629	2290075	0.0130	38.127	0.008353	20
25	0.043439	57604	2502	281809	0.008879	2.5182	1995749	0.0067	34.646	0.008877	25
30	0.048626	55102	2679	268895	0.009964	2.5318	1713940	0.0000	31.105	0.009964	30
35	0.055546	52422	2912	255021	0.011418	2.5652	1445045	0.0013	27.566	0.011417	35
40	0.072512	49510	3590	238852	0.015031	2.5769	1190025	0.0026	24.036	0.015026	40
45	0.092263	45920	4237	219307	0.019319	2.5702	951172	0.0085	20.714	0.019301	45
50	0.120354	41683	5017	196140	0.025577	2.5527	731866	0.0175	17.558	0.025530	50
55	0.150185	36667	5507	169895	0.032413	2.5597	535726	0.0140	14.611	0.032354	55
60	0.211655	31160	6595	139600	0.047243	2.5437	365830	0.0000	11.740	0.047243	60
65	0.280518	24565	6891	105770	0.065150	2.5251	226230	0.0000	9.210	0.065149	65
70	0.420194	17674	7426	69606	0.106692	2.4735	120460	0.0000	6.816	0.106692	70
75	0.580195	10247	5946	35494	0.167509	2.3521	50854	0.0000	4.963	0.167508	75
80	0.744875	4302	3204	12489	0.256585	2.1848	15360	0.0000	3.570	0.256584	80
85+	*1.000000	1098	1098	2871	0.382239	2.6162	2871	0.0000	2.616	0.382236	85+

TABLE 3 FEMALE LIFE TABLE

x	$_nq_x$	l_x	$_nd_x$	$_nL_x$	$_nm_x$	$_na_x$	T_x	r_x	$\mathring{e}_x$	$_nM_x$	x
0	0.201551	100000	20155	87118	0.231353	0.3609	3888536	0.0000	38.885	0.231353	0
1	0.130167	79845	10393	290697	0.035753	1.2402	3801418	0.0000	47.610	0.035753	1
5	0.048032	69452	3336	338919	0.009843	2.5000	3510721	0.0142	50.549	0.009923	5
10	0.024338	66116	1609	326236	0.004932	2.3014	3171803	0.0095	47.973	0.004941	10
15	0.027930	64507	1802	318119	0.005664	2.5499	2845566	0.0022	44.113	0.005663	15
20	0.032547	62705	2041	308528	0.006615	2.5516	2527447	0.0055	40.307	0.006612	20
25	0.038039	60664	2308	297716	0.007751	2.5715	2218919	0.0074	36.577	0.007746	25
30	0.048536	58357	2832	284807	0.009945	2.5371	1921203	0.0010	32.922	0.009944	30
35	0.050654	55524	2813	270745	0.010388	2.5554	1636396	0.0033	29.472	0.010385	35
40	0.067911	52712	3580	254748	0.014052	2.5390	1365651	0.0037	25.908	0.014048	40
45	0.070891	49132	3483	237092	0.014691	2.5401	1110903	0.0087	22.611	0.014681	45
50	0.093107	45649	4250	217939	0.019502	2.5754	873811	0.0181	19.142	0.019461	50
55	0.121309	41399	5022	194922	0.025764	2.5963	655872	0.0113	15.843	0.025720	55
60	0.180647	36377	6571	165952	0.039598	2.5756	460950	0.0001	12.672	0.039597	60
65	0.248507	29805	7407	130951	0.056562	2.5597	294999	0.0001	9.898	0.056561	65
70	0.388130	22398	8694	90245	0.096332	2.4984	164047	0.0001	7.324	0.096331	70
75	0.535656	13705	7341	49312	0.148870	2.3829	73802	0.0001	5.385	0.148869	75
80	0.717833	6364	4568	19243	0.237389	2.2471	24490	0.0001	3.848	0.237386	80
85+	*1.000000	1796	1796	5247	0.342248	2.9219	5247	0.0001	2.922	0.342240	85+

TABLE 4 OBSERVED AND PROJECTED VITAL RATES

RATES PER THOUSAND	OBSERVED POPULATION BOTH SEXES	MALES	FEMALES	PROJECTED 1805 MALES	1805 FEMALES	1810 MALES	1810 FEMALES	1815 MALES	1815 FEMALES	STABLE POPULATION MALES	FEMALES
Birth	31.21	33.35	29.22	33.06	29.21	32.81	29.20	32.78	29.36	31.60	29.38
Death	25.88	27.01	24.84	25.86	23.69	25.69	23.57	25.68	23.63	27.30	25.08
Increase	5.33	6.35	4.39	7.19	5.52	7.12	5.62	7.10	5.73		4.3060
PERCENTAGE											
under 15	32.60	34.01	31.29	33.36	30.98	32.78	30.55	31.67	29.46	30.77	29.71
15-64	61.91	61.16	62.60	62.03	63.15	62.74	63.76	63.70	64.70	63.98	63.93
65 and over	5.49	4.82	6.11	4.61	5.87	4.48	5.69	4.63	5.84	5.25	6.36
DEP. RATIO X 100	61.53	63.50	59.75	61.22	58.36	59.38	56.83	56.99	54.57	56.30	56.42

TABLE 1 — DATA

AGE AT LAST BIRTHDAY	POPULATION BOTH SEXES	MALES Number	%	FEMALES Number	%	BIRTHS BY AGE OF MOTHER	DEATHS BOTH SEXES	MALES	FEMALES	AGE AT LAST BIRTHDAY
0	65199	32916	2.8	32283	2.6	0	14544	7895	6649	0
1-4	236834	118073	10.1	118761	9.5	0	7140	3679	3461	1-4
5-9	247334	124516	10.7	122818	9.8	0	2158	1089	1069	5-9
10-14	242264	122242	10.5	120022	9.6	0	1336	693	643	10-1
15-19	213009	105494	9.1	107515	8.6	1379	1351	672	679	15-1
20-24	201370	96834	8.3	104536	8.3	10538	1628	858	770	20-2
25-29	188772	91168	7.8	97604	7.8	19392	1682	849	833	25-2
30-34	163268	77689	6.7	85579	6.8	19310	1607	789	818	30-3
35-39	155360	73317	6.3	82043	6.6	15196	1831	865	966	35-3
40-44	149334	70702	6.1	78632	6.3	8209	2114	1049	1065	40-4
45-49	131858	62476	5.4	69382	5.5	1565	2150	1144	1006	45-4
50-54	121513	57137	4.9	64376	5.1	24	2810	1483	1327	50-5
55-59	94971	43746	3.8	51225	4.1	0	2895	1487	1408	55-5
60-64	75332	34208	2.9	41124	3.3	0	3281	1609	1672	60-6
65-69	55644	23778	2.0	31866	2.5	0	3402	1547	1855	65-6
70-74	40296	16689	1.4	23607	1.9		3820	1707	2113	70-7
75-79	22056	9068	0.8	12988	1.0		3184	1355	1829	75-7
80-84	9968	3906	0.3	6062	0.5	38645 M.	2130	833	1297	80-8
85+	3376	1260	0.1	2116	0.2	36968 F.	1110	403	707	85+
TOTAL	2417758	1165219		1252539		75613	60173	30006	30167	TOTA

TABLE 2 — MALE LIFE TABLE

x	nq_x	l_x	nd_x	nL_x	nm_x	na_x	T_x	r_x	$\mathring{e}_x$	nM_x
0	0.207247	100000	20725	86406	0.239853	0.3440	3780774	0.0000	37.808	0.239853
1	0.114667	79275	9090	291741	0.031159	1.2102	3694368	0.0000	46.602	0.031159
5	0.042622	70185	2991	343447	0.008710	2.5000	3402627	0.0078	48.481	0.008746
10	0.027908	67194	1875	331085	0.005664	2.3957	3059180	0.0100	45.528	0.005669
15	0.031421	65318	2052	321642	0.006381	2.5882	2728095	0.0166	41.766	0.006370
20	0.043381	63266	2745	309615	0.008864	2.5533	2406453	0.0062	38.037	0.008861
25	0.045523	60522	2755	295744	0.009316	2.5090	2096838	0.0126	34.646	0.009312
30	0.049564	57766	2863	281756	0.010162	2.5286	1801093	0.0115	31.179	0.010156
35	0.057337	54903	3148	266822	0.011798	2.5558	1519337	0.0000	27.673	0.011798
40	0.071600	51755	3706	249734	0.014839	2.5599	1252515	0.0012	24.201	0.014837
45	0.087695	48050	4214	230058	0.018316	2.5817	1002781	0.0021	20.870	0.018311
50	0.122220	43836	5358	206168	0.025987	2.5713	772723	0.0097	17.628	0.025955
55	0.157187	38478	6048	177579	0.034060	2.5510	566555	0.0163	14.724	0.033992
60	0.210818	32430	6837	145292	0.047056	2.5342	388976	0.0033	11.994	0.047036
65	0.280209	25593	7171	110172	0.065093	2.5188	243684	0.0033	9.521	0.065060
70	0.406239	18422	7484	73126	0.102338	2.4635	133512	0.0033	7.248	0.102283
75	0.535702	10938	5860	39193	0.149504	2.3552	60386	0.0033	5.521	0.149426
80	0.671843	5079	3412	15989	0.213393	2.2440	21193	0.0033	4.173	0.213263
85+	*1.000000	1667	1667	5203	0.320277	3.1223	5203	0.0033	3.122	0.319841

TABLE 3 — FEMALE LIFE TABLE

x	nq_x	l_x	nd_x	nL_x	nm_x	na_x	T_x	r_x	$\mathring{e}_x$	nM_x
0	0.181797	100000	18180	88268	0.205960	0.3547	4059180	0.0000	40.592	0.205960
1	0.107859	81820	8825	302823	0.029143	1.2286	3970912	0.0000	48.532	0.029143
5	0.042380	72995	3094	357243	0.008660	2.5000	3668088	0.0104	50.251	0.008704
10	0.026400	69902	1845	344692	0.005354	2.3898	3310846	0.0069	47.364	0.005357
15	0.031112	68056	2117	335101	0.006319	2.5532	2966154	0.0076	43.584	0.006315
20	0.036181	65939	2386	323843	0.007367	2.5472	2631053	0.0023	39.901	0.007366
25	0.041819	63553	2658	311218	0.008540	2.5360	2307210	0.0115	36.304	0.008534
30	0.046722	60896	2845	297503	0.009563	2.5486	1995993	0.0075	32.777	0.009558
35	0.057219	58050	3322	282102	0.011774	2.5465	1698490	0.0000	29.259	0.011774
40	0.065525	54729	3586	264733	0.013546	2.5152	1416387	0.0035	25.880	0.013544
45	0.070052	51143	3583	246984	0.014506	2.5633	1151654	0.0044	22.518	0.014499
50	0.098301	47560	4675	226520	0.020639	2.5872	904670	0.0098	19.022	0.020613
55	0.129152	42885	5539	201043	0.027550	2.5840	678151	0.0161	15.813	0.027487
60	0.185018	37346	6910	169917	0.040665	2.5667	477108	0.0012	12.775	0.040658
65	0.254610	30436	7749	133097	0.058224	2.5372	307191	0.0012	10.093	0.058213
70	0.365546	22687	8293	92633	0.089542	2.4917	174094	0.0012	7.674	0.089507
75	0.515457	14394	7419	52675	0.140854	2.3994	81460	0.0012	5.659	0.140822
80	0.675616	6974	4712	22018	0.214012	2.2720	28785	0.0012	4.127	0.213957
85+	*1.000000	2262	2262	6768	0.334294	2.9914	6768	0.0012	2.991	0.334121

TABLE 4 — OBSERVED AND PROJECTED VITAL RATES

	OBSERVED POPULATION BOTH SEXES	MALES	FEMALES	PROJECTED POPULATION 1810 MALES	FEMALES	1815 MALES	FEMALES	1820 MALES	FEMALES	STABLE POPULATION MALES	FEMA
RATES PER THOUSAND											
Birth	31.27	33.17	29.51	32.86	29.50	32.73	29.60	32.64	29.71	32.00	29.
Death	24.89	25.75	24.08	25.11	23.40	24.98	23.26	24.95	23.26	25.55	23.
Increase	6.39	7.41	5.43	7.75	6.11	7.75	6.35	7.69	6.45		6.44
PERCENTAGE											
under 15	32.74	34.13	31.45	33.53	31.29	33.44	31.52	32.77	30.96	32.16	31.
15-64	61.83	61.17	62.43	61.87	62.88	61.96	62.74	62.44	63.10	62.94	62.
65 and over	5.43	4.69	6.12	4.60	5.83	4.60	5.75	4.80	5.93	4.91	5.
DEP. RATIO X 100	61.75	63.48	60.17	61.63	59.04	61.40	59.39	60.16	58.48	58.89	58.

TABLE 5 — POPULATION PROJECTED WITH FIXED AGE—SPECIFIC BIRTH AND DEATH RATES (IN 1000's)

AGE LAST BIRTHDAY	1810 BOTH SEXES	1810 MALES	1810 FEMALES	1815 BOTH SEXES	1815 MALES	1815 FEMALES	1820 BOTH SEXES	1820 MALES	1820 FEMALES	AGE AT LAST BIRTHDAY
0-4	295	148	147	304	153	151	314	158	156	0-4
5-9	275	137	138	269	135	134	277	139	138	5-9
10-14	239	120	119	265	132	133	259	130	129	10-14
15-19	236	119	117	232	117	115	257	128	129	15-19
20-24	206	102	104	227	114	113	223	112	111	20-24
25-29	192	92	100	197	97	100	217	109	108	25-29
30-34	180	87	93	184	88	96	187	92	95	30-34
35-39	155	74	81	170	82	88	174	83	91	35-39
40-44	146	69	77	145	69	76	160	77	83	40-44
45-49	138	65	73	135	63	72	134	63	71	45-49
50-54	120	56	64	125	58	67	123	57	66	50-54
55-59	106	49	57	104	48	56	110	50	60	55-59
60-64	79	36	43	88	40	48	87	39	48	60-64
65-69	58	26	32	61	27	34	69	31	38	65-69
70-74	38	16	22	39	17	22	42	18	24	70-74
75-79	22	9	13	21	8	13	22	9	13	75-79
80-84	9	4	5	10	4	6	8	3	5	80-84
85+	3	1	2	3	1	2	3	1	2	85+
TOTAL	2497	1210	1287	2579	1253	1326	2666	1299	1367	TOTAL

TABLE 6 — STANDARDIZED RATES

STANDARD COUNTRIES: STANDARDIZED RATES PER THOUSAND	ENGLAND AND WALES 1961 BOTH SEXES	MALES	FEMALES	UNITED STATES 1960 BOTH SEXES	MALES	FEMALES	MEXICO 1960 BOTH SEXES	MALES	FEMALES
Birth	27.66	30.41*	26.21	28.03	28.14*	27.00	26.92	28.12*	26.25
Death	31.76	44.46*	33.11	29.31	36.89*	28.75	24.04	24.77*	22.69
Increase	-4.10	-14.05*	-6.90	-1.29	-8.75*	-1.75	2.87	3.36*	3.56

TABLE 7 — MOMENTS AND CUMULANTS

	OBSERVED POP. MALES	OBSERVED POP. FEMALES	STATIONARY POP. MALES	STATIONARY POP. FEMALES	STABLE POP. MALES	STABLE POP. FEMALES	OBSERVED BIRTHS	NET MATERNITY FUNCTION	BIRTHS IN STABLE POP.
μ	27.64686	29.26590	30.87483	31.81513	28.25235	29.06819	31.95777	32.19295	31.90905
σ^2	397.4753	423.2442	419.1896	438.6238	394.0998	413.1507	42.73923	42.10471	41.85098
κ_3	4587.547	4502.496	3496.913	3485.371	4245.742	4371.394	46.1757	35.8254	42.8954
κ_4	-91578.	-119214.	-137241.	-160615.	-94577.	-113435.	-1213.877	-1111.836	-1071.455
β_1	0.335143	0.267383	0.166012	0.143953	0.294502	0.270966	-0.027312	0.017195	0.025102
β_2	2.420345	2.334507	2.218980	2.165162	2.391060	2.335449	2.335460	2.372839	2.388266
κ	-0.131069	-0.104471	-0.065499	-0.055521	-0.117304	-0.105556	-0.014876	-0.010066	-0.014801

TABLE 8 — RATES FROM AGE DISTRIBUTIONS AND VITAL STATISTICS (Females)

VITAL STATISTICS		THOMPSON AGE RANGE	NRR	1000r	INTERVAL	BOURGEOIS-PICHAT AGE RANGE	NRR	1000b	1000d	1000r	COALE	
GRR	2.079										IBR	28.92
NRR	1.229	0-4	1.26	8.71	26.89	5-29	1.15	28.81	23.62	5.19	IDR	23.32
GFR	4.253	5-9	1.15	5.13	26.72	30-54	1.03	24.18	23.00	1.18	IRI	5.60
GENERATION	32.051	10-14	1.19	6.43	26.59	55-79	1.01	20.04	19.83	0.21	K1	0.
SEX RATIO	104.536	15-19	1.13	4.56	26.40	*30-54	1.03	24.18	23.00	1.18	K2	0.

TABLE 9 — LESLIE MATRIX AND ITS SPECTRAL COMPONENTS (Females)

ORIGINAL MATRIX SUB-DIAGONAL	ALTERNATIVE FIRST ROWS Projection	ALTERNATIVE FIRST ROWS Integral	FIRST STABLE MATRIX % IN STABLE POPULATION	FISHER VALUES	REPRODUCTIVE VALUES	SECOND STABLE MATRIX Z₂ FIRST COLUMN	SECOND STABLE MATRIX Z₂ FIRST ROW
0.91345	0.00000	0.00000	11.536	1.299	196157	0.1343+0.0470	0.1343+0.0470
0.96487	0.00000	0.00000	10.203	1.468	180334	0.1204-0.0834	0.0399+0.1324
0.97218	0.01192	0.00000	9.533	1.572	188629	0.0036-0.1591	-0.0770+0.1013
0.96641	0.10540	0.02492	8.973	1.654	177790	-0.1386-0.1057	-0.1178-0.0030
0.96101	0.27892	0.19588	8.397	1.626	169927	-0.1818+0.0544	-0.0760-0.0943
0.95593	0.39616	0.38606	7.813	1.370	133714	-0.0681+0.1938	-0.0098-0.1217
0.94823	0.38363	0.43845	7.232	0.942	80604	0.1257+0.1820	0.0303-0.0933
0.93843	0.27074	0.35991	6.640	0.500	41055	0.2362+0.0057	0.0330-0.0474
0.93295	0.11993	0.20286	6.034	0.176	13842	0.1518-0.1984	0.0158-0.0147
0.91714	0.02189	0.04383	5.451	0.028	1938	-0.0749-0.2516	0.0029-0.0021
0.88753	0.00036	0.00072	4.840	0.000	29	-0.2558-0.0903	0.0000-0.0000
0.71089			13.347				

TABLE 10 — AGE ANALYSIS AND MISCELLANEOUS RESULTS (Females)

OBSERVED POPUL. (IN 100's)	CONTRIBUTIONS OF ROOTS (IN 100's) r_1	r_2, r_3	$r_4 \cdot r_{11}$	AGE-SP. BIRTH RATES	NET MATERNITY FUNCTION	COEFF. OF MATRIX EQUATION	PARAMETERS	INTEGRAL	MATRIX	EXP. INCREASE x	$e^{(x+2\frac{1}{2})r}$
1510	1430	22	58	0.0000	0.0000	0.0000	L(1)	1.03274	1.03276	0	1.0162
1228	1265	18	-55	0.0000	0.0000	0.0000	L(2)	0.52285	0.52200	50	1.4025
1200	1182	-2	20	0.0000	0.0000	0.0105		0.73318	0.71802	55	1.4484
1075	1113	-24	-14	0.0063	0.0210	0.0903	R(1)	0.00644	0.00645	60	1.4958
1045	1041	-29	33	0.0493	0.1596	0.2310	R(2)	-0.02096	-0.02382	65	1.5448
976	969	-8	16	0.0971	0.3023	0.3153			0.19026	0.18844	70	1.5954
856	897	23	-64	0.1103	0.3282	0.2918	C(1)		12400	75	1.6476
820	823	38	-41	0.0906	0.2555	0.1953	C(2)		8119	80	1.7015
786	748	22	16	0.0510	0.1351	0.0812			-670	85	1.7572
694	676	-16	33	0.0110	0.0272	0.0138	2P/Y	33.0236	33.3440	90	1.8148
644	600	-43	86	0.0002	0.0004	0.0002	DELTA	1.6347		95	1.8742
1690	1655									100	1.9355

TABLE 1 — DATA

AGE AT LAST BIRTHDAY	POPULATION BOTH SEXES	MALES Number	%	FEMALES Number	%	BIRTHS BY AGE OF MOTHER	DEATHS BOTH SEXES	MALES	FEMALES	AGE AT LAST BIRTHD
0	61007	30750	2.7	30257	2.4	0	15867	8636	7231	0
1-4	220943	110328	9.7	110615	8.9	0	10318	5319	4999	1-4
5-9	240913	120476	10.6	120437	9.7	0	3816	2018	1798	5-9
10-14	237145	119013	10.5	118132	9.5	0	2244	1198	1046	10-14
15-19	225355	111491	9.8	113864	9.2	1459	2080	1066	1014	15-19
20-24	198695	92875	8.2	105820	8.5	10836	2393	1326	1067	20-24
25-29	182810	85684	7.5	97126	7.8	19838	2379	1272	1107	25-29
30-34	172885	82020	7.2	90865	7.3	20840	2620	1366	1254	30-34
35-39	145831	68846	6.1	76985	6.2	14630	2616	1365	1251	35-39
40-44	141873	65885	5.8	75988	6.1	7527	2945	1513	1432	40-44
45-49	130905	61121	5.4	69784	5.6	1494	3236	1759	1477	45-49
50-54	117699	54443	4.8	63256	5.1	0	3826	2007	1819	50-54
55-59	101924	46687	4.1	55237	4.4	0	4127	2107	2020	55-59
60-64	78939	35100	3.1	43839	3.5	0	4710	2266	2444	60-64
65-69	54135	23637	2.1	30498	2.5	0	4307	2003	2304	65-69
70-74	35862	15166	1.3	20696	1.7		4198	1862	2336	70-74
75-79	20907	8534	0.8	12373	1.0		3585	1497	2088	75-79
80-84	8897	3453	0.3	5444	0.4	39136 M.	2243	916	1327	80-84
85+	3238	1157	0.1	2081	0.2	37488 F.	1250	465	785	85+
TOTAL	2379963	1136666		1243297		76624	78760	39961	38799	TOTA

TABLE 2 — MALE LIFE TABLE

x	$_nq_x$	l_x	$_nd_x$	$_nL_x$	$_nm_x$	$_na_x$	T_x	r_x	$\dot{e}_x$	$_nM_x$	
0	0.238415	100000	23841	84892	0.280846	0.3663	2898986	0.0000	28.990	0.280846	
1	0.170276	76159	12968	268985	0.048211	1.2510	2814094	0.0000	36.950	0.048211	
5	0.080385	63191	5080	303254	0.016750	2.5000	2545109	0.0000	40.277	0.016750	
10	0.049007	58111	2848	282916	0.010066	2.3175	2241855	0.0000	38.579	0.010066	
15	0.046774	55263	2585	270018	0.009573	2.5636	1958940	0.0142	35.447	0.009561	
20	0.069046	52678	3637	254491	0.014292	2.5530	1688922	0.0130	32.061	0.014277	
25	0.071570	49041	3510	236431	0.014845	2.5003	1434431	0.0050	29.250	0.014845	
30	0.080000	45531	3642	218643	0.016659	2.5257	1197999	0.0022	26.312	0.016654	
35	0.094510	41889	3959	199646	0.019830	2.5252	979356	0.0000	23.380	0.019827	
40	0.108657	37930	4121	179467	0.022964	2.5295	779711	0.0000	20.557	0.022964	
45	0.134373	33808	4543	157856	0.028779	2.5376	600244	0.0000	17.754	0.028779	
50	0.168862	29265	4942	134055	0.036864	2.5166	442388	0.0000	15.116	0.036864	
55	0.202929	24324	4936	109371	0.045130	2.5188	308333	0.0000	12.676	0.045130	
60	0.277924	19388	5388	83456	0.064565	2.4978	198962	0.0008	10.262	0.064558	
65	0.348471	13999	4878	57563	0.084748	2.4512	115506	0.0008	8.251	0.084740	
70	0.465506	9121	4246	34579	0.122789	2.4031	57943	0.0008	6.353	0.122775	
75	0.595408	4875	2903	16545	0.175439	2.3024	23365	0.0008	4.793	0.175416	
80	0.756755	1972	1493	5626	0.265323	2.1618	6819	0.0008	3.457	0.265276	
85+	*1.000000	480	480	1193	0.402031	2.4874	1193	0.0008	2.487	0.401901	

TABLE 3 — FEMALE LIFE TABLE

x	$_nq_x$	l_x	$_nd_x$	$_nL_x$	$_nm_x$	$_na_x$	T_x	r_x	$\dot{e}_x$	$_nM_x$	x
0	0.208064	100000	20806	87061	0.238986	0.3781	3276150	0.0000	32.761	0.238986	
1	0.160959	79194	12747	282057	0.045193	1.2764	3189089	0.0000	40.270	0.045193	
5	0.071959	66447	4781	320280	0.014929	2.5000	2907032	0.0000	43.750	0.014929	
10	0.043249	61665	2667	301198	0.008855	2.3273	2586752	0.0000	41.948	0.008855	1
15	0.043563	58998	2570	288589	0.008906	2.5089	2285554	0.0020	38.739	0.008905	1
20	0.049205	56428	2777	275284	0.010086	2.5304	1996965	0.0058	35.390	0.010083	2
25	0.055448	53652	2975	260947	0.011400	2.5426	1721682	0.0036	32.090	0.011398	2
30	0.066786	50677	3384	245072	0.013810	2.5443	1460735	0.0095	28.825	0.013801	3
35	0.078123	47292	3695	227337	0.016252	2.5304	1215662	0.0016	25.705	0.016250	3
40	0.090011	43598	3924	208239	0.018845	2.5157	988326	0.0000	22.669	0.018845	4
45	0.100600	39673	3991	188570	0.021165	2.5453	780086	0.0000	19.663	0.021165	4
50	0.134325	35682	4793	166677	0.028756	2.5519	591517	0.0000	16.577	0.028756	5
55	0.167872	30889	5185	141796	0.036570	2.5605	424839	0.0000	13.754	0.036570	5
60	0.245061	25704	6299	112974	0.055756	2.5322	283043	0.0008	11.012	0.055749	6
65	0.317411	19405	6159	81521	0.075555	2.4830	170069	0.0008	8.764	0.075546	6
70	0.437672	13245	5797	51354	0.112887	2.4344	88548	0.0008	6.685	0.112872	7
75	0.581700	7448	4333	25671	0.168778	2.3294	37194	0.0008	4.994	0.168754	7
80	0.722251	3116	2250	9230	0.243796	2.1790	11523	0.0008	3.699	0.243755	8
85+	*1.000000	865	865	2293	0.377350	2.6501	2293	0.0008	2.650	0.377222	8

TABLE 4 — OBSERVED AND PROJECTED VITAL RATES

	OBSERVED POPULATION BOTH SEXES	MALES	FEMALES	PROJECTED POPULATION 1815 MALES	FEMALES	1820 MALES	FEMALES	1825 MALES	FEMALES	STABLE POPULATION MALES	FEMALE
RATES PER THOUSAND											
Birth	32.20	34.43	30.15	35.35	30.98	36.03	31.60	36.15	31.74	35.20	31.1
Death	33.09	35.16	31.21	34.52	30.46	34.39	30.31	34.23	30.23	34.46	30.4
Increase	-0.90	-0.73	-1.05	0.83	0.52	1.64	1.29	1.92	1.51		0.737
PERCENTAGE											
under 15	31.93	33.48	30.52	32.94	30.31	33.10	30.59	33.29	30.80	32.92	30.7
15-64	62.90	61.95	63.76	62.71	64.28	62.58	64.09	62.51	63.97	63.22	64.2
65 and over	5.17	4.57	5.72	4.35	5.41	4.31	5.33	4.19	5.24	3.86	5.0
DEP. RATIO X 100	58.99	61.42	56.83	59.47	55.56	59.78	56.04	59.97	56.33	58.17	55.6

TABLE 1 — DATA

AGE AT LAST BIRTHDAY	POPULATION BOTH SEXES	MALES Number	MALES %	FEMALES Number	FEMALES %	BIRTHS BY AGE OF MOTHER	DEATHS BOTH SEXES	DEATHS MALES	DEATHS FEMALES	AGE AT LAST BIRTHDAY
0	68790	34837	3.0	33953	2.7	0	14926	8181	6745	0
1-4	236028	117662	10.1	118366	9.2	0	8062	4179	3883	1-4
5-9	233542	116595	10.0	116947	9.1	0	2139	1099	1040	5-9
10-14	236067	117945	10.1	118122	9.2	0	1236	645	591	10-14
15-19	229319	114115	9.8	115204	9.0	1401	1321	650	671	15-19
20-24	218607	104632	8.9	113975	8.9	11468	1689	896	793	20-24
25-29	190701	89911	7.7	100790	7.9	20517	1633	840	793	25-29
30-34	175370	82539	7.1	92831	7.3	21542	1768	883	885	30-34
35-39	163346	77752	6.6	85594	6.7	16909	1948	956	992	35-39
40-44	136402	63144	5.4	73258	5.7	7745	1931	987	944	40-44
45-49	128140	59374	5.1	68766	5.4	1329	2145	1141	1004	45-49
50-54	119131	54384	4.7	64747	5.1	2	2607	1371	1236	50-54
55-59	101442	45443	3.9	55999	4.4	0	2899	1455	1444	55-59
60-64	86172	38040	3.3	48132	3.8	0	3620	1770	1850	60-64
65-69	59795	25820	2.2	33975	2.7	0	3662	1682	1980	65-69
70-74	36306	15307	1.3	20999	1.6		3421	1528	1893	70-74
75-79	19027	7588	0.6	11439	0.9		2586	1099	1487	75-79
80-84	8565	3262	0.3	5303	0.4	41318 M.	1828	739	1089	80-84
85+	3054	1132	0.1	1922	0.2	39595 F.	1009	368	641	85+
TOTAL	2449804	1169482		1280322		80913	60430	30469	29961	TOTAL

TABLE 2 — MALE LIFE TABLE

x	$_nq_x$	l_x	$_nd_x$	$_nL_x$	$_nm_x$	$_na_x$	T_x	r_x	$\mathring{e}_x$	$_nM_x$	x
0	0.204096	100000	20410	86910	0.234837	0.3586	3732671	0.0000	37.327	0.234837	0
1	0.129368	79590	10296	289902	0.035517	1.2359	3645761	0.0000	45.807	0.035517	1
5	0.045753	69294	3170	338544	0.009365	2.5000	3355860	0.0112	48.429	0.009426	5
10	0.026951	66123	1782	325878	0.005469	2.3408	3017316	0.0000	45.632	0.005469	10
15	0.028113	64341	1809	317361	0.005700	2.5973	2691438	0.0058	41.831	0.005696	15
20	0.042004	62533	2627	306290	0.008576	2.5736	2374077	0.0158	37.965	0.008563	20
25	0.045688	59906	2737	292761	0.009349	2.5269	2067788	0.0142	34.517	0.009343	25
30	0.052127	57169	2980	278499	0.010700	2.5350	1775027	0.0038	31.049	0.010698	30
35	0.059750	54189	3238	263029	0.012310	2.5553	1496528	0.0141	27.617	0.012295	35
40	0.075357	50951	3840	245383	0.015647	2.5589	1233498	0.0114	24.209	0.015631	40
45	0.091782	47112	4324	225007	0.019217	2.5598	988115	0.0000	20.974	0.019217	45
50	0.118740	42788	5081	201502	0.025214	2.5524	763109	0.0015	17.835	0.025210	50
55	0.148532	37707	5601	174874	0.032027	2.5608	561606	0.0022	14.894	0.032018	55
60	0.209125	32106	6714	144064	0.046606	2.5474	386733	0.0114	12.045	0.046530	60
65	0.280782	25392	7130	109255	0.065257	2.5166	242668	0.0114	9.557	0.065143	65
70	0.398775	18262	7283	72821	0.100006	2.4610	133414	0.0114	7.305	0.099824	70
75	0.525066	10980	5765	39730	0.145110	2.3687	60592	0.0114	5.519	0.144834	75
80	0.699975	5215	3650	16073	0.227099	2.2602	20863	0.0114	4.001	0.226547	80
85+	*1.000000	1565	1565	4790	0.326635	3.0615	4790	0.0114	3.062	0.325088	85+

TABLE 3 — FEMALE LIFE TABLE

x	$_nq_x$	l_x	$_nd_x$	$_nL_x$	$_nm_x$	$_na_x$	T_x	r_x	$\mathring{e}_x$	$_nM_x$	x
0	0.176544	100000	17654	88869	0.198657	0.3695	4076197	0.0000	40.762	0.198657	0
1	0.120389	82346	9914	302195	0.032805	1.2576	3987328	0.0000	48.422	0.032805	1
5	0.043208	72432	3130	354336	0.008832	2.5000	3685133	0.0120	50.877	0.008893	5
10	0.024690	69302	1711	341987	0.005003	2.3552	3330797	0.0000	48.062	0.005003	10
15	0.028714	67591	1941	333216	0.005824	2.5575	2988810	0.0000	44.219	0.005824	15
20	0.034218	65651	2246	322742	0.006960	2.5471	2655594	0.0065	40.450	0.006958	20
25	0.038627	63404	2449	311021	0.007874	2.5506	2332852	0.0125	36.793	0.007868	25
30	0.046609	60955	2841	297845	0.009539	2.5607	2021830	0.0067	33.169	0.009533	30
35	0.056381	58114	3277	282500	0.011598	2.5371	1723986	0.0123	29.666	0.011590	35
40	0.062461	54837	3425	265696	0.012892	2.5211	1441486	0.0089	26.287	0.012886	40
45	0.070484	51412	3624	248196	0.014600	2.5538	1175789	0.0000	22.870	0.014600	45
50	0.091244	47788	4360	228385	0.019092	2.5789	927593	0.0011	19.410	0.019090	50
55	0.121444	43428	5274	204447	0.025797	2.5932	699208	0.0028	16.100	0.025786	55
60	0.176136	38154	6720	174543	0.038502	2.5853	494761	0.0104	12.967	0.038436	60
65	0.255364	31434	8027	137494	0.058381	2.5490	320218	0.0104	10.187	0.058278	65
70	0.367791	23407	8609	95338	0.090297	2.4799	182724	0.0104	7.806	0.090147	70
75	0.486238	14798	7195	55257	0.130216	2.3965	87386	0.0104	5.905	0.129994	75
80	0.662228	7603	5035	24462	0.205812	2.3085	32129	0.0104	4.226	0.205355	80
85+	*1.000000	2568	2568	7667	0.334954	2.9855	7667	0.0104	2.985	0.333507	85+

TABLE 4 — OBSERVED AND PROJECTED VITAL RATES

	OBSERVED POPULATION BOTH SEXES	MALES	FEMALES	PROJECTED 1820 MALES	FEMALES	1825 MALES	FEMALES	1830 MALES	FEMALES	STABLE POPULATION MALES	FEMALES
RATES PER THOUSAND											
Birth	33.03	35.33	30.93	35.31	31.16	34.79	30.94	33.85	30.30	33.12	30.58
Death	24.67	26.05	23.40	26.05	23.47	25.98	23.53	25.75	23.47	25.90	23.35
Increase	8.36	9.28	7.52	9.26	7.70	8.81	7.40	8.10	6.83		7.2266
PERCENTAGE											
under 15	31.61	33.09	30.26	33.38	30.80	34.42	32.00	34.13	31.90	32.75	31.57
15-64	63.21	62.36	63.99	61.84	63.15	60.79	61.87	61.09	61.93	62.47	62.62
65 and over	5.17	4.54	5.75	4.78	6.05	4.79	6.14	4.78	6.17	4.78	5.81
DEP. RATIO X 100	58.19	60.35	56.27	61.71	58.36	64.51	61.64	63.69	61.48	60.08	59.69

TABLE 1 — DATA

AGE AT LAST BIRTHDAY	POPULATION BOTH SEXES	MALES Number	%	FEMALES Number	%	BIRTHS BY AGE OF MOTHER	BIRTHS BOTH SEXES	DEATHS MALES	FEMALES	AGE AT LAST BIRTHDAY
0	72803	36910	3.0	35893	2.7	0	15048	8233	6815	0
1-4	261912	130728	10.6	131184	9.8	0	8695	4511	4184	1-4
5-9	259084	128989	10.5	130095	9.7	0	2500	1276	1224	5-9
10-14	231451	115506	9.4	115945	8.7	0	1291	649	642	10-14
15-19	232136	115364	9.4	116772	8.7	1319	1373	689	684	15-19
20-24	225136	110306	8.9	114830	8.6	11917	1752	927	825	20-24
25-29	214187	103866	8.4	110321	8.2	22828	1834	953	881	25-29
30-34	184865	87593	7.1	97272	7.3	23484	1862	931	931	30-34
35-39	165547	78097	6.3	87450	6.5	17825	2069	1039	1030	35-39
40-44	154478	72420	5.9	82058	6.1	9360	2366	1248	1118	40-44
45-49	125060	58034	4.7	67026	5.0	1491	2155	1183	972	45-49
50-54	117683	53582	4.3	64101	4.8	12	2721	1437	1284	50-54
55-59	103897	46319	3.8	57578	4.3	0	3133	1618	1515	55-59
60-64	85605	37520	3.0	48085	3.6	0	3728	1801	1927	60-64
65-69	66053	28211	2.3	37842	2.8	0	4053	1895	2158	65-69
70-74	41374	17263	1.4	24111	1.8		3890	1734	2156	70-74
75-79	20420	8253	0.7	12167	0.9		2800	1229	1571	75-79
80-84	8335	3168	0.3	5167	0.4	45209 M.	1746	693	1053	80-84
85+	3209	1106	0.1	2103	0.2	43027 F.	1059	382	677	85+
TOTAL	2573235	1233235		1340000		88236	64075	32428	31647	TOTAL

TABLE 2 — MALE LIFE TABLE

x	nq_x	l_x	nd_x	nL_x	nm_x	na_x	T_x	r_x	$\dot{e}_x$	nM_x	x
0	0.195253	100000	19525	87536	0.223056	0.3616	3741626	0.0000	37.416	0.223056	0
1	0.126031	80475	10142	293923	0.034507	1.2417	3654091	0.0000	45.407	0.034507	1
5	0.047700	70332	3355	343275	0.009773	2.5000	3360168	0.0227	47.776	0.009892	5
10	0.027662	66978	1853	329956	0.005615	2.3383	3016893	0.0045	45.043	0.005619	10
15	0.029437	65125	1917	320988	0.005972	2.5816	2686937	0.0000	41.258	0.005972	15
20	0.041185	63208	2603	309698	0.008406	2.5643	2365950	0.0025	37.431	0.008404	20
25	0.044890	60605	2721	296304	0.009182	2.5306	2056252	0.0137	33.929	0.009175	25
30	0.051869	57884	3002	282084	0.010644	2.5568	1759947	0.0177	30.405	0.010629	30
35	0.064474	54882	3538	265822	0.013311	2.5734	1477863	0.0055	26.928	0.013304	35
40	0.082761	51343	4249	246309	0.017252	2.5508	1212042	0.0127	23.607	0.017233	40
45	0.097154	47094	4575	224261	0.020402	2.5501	965733	0.0091	20.507	0.020385	45
50	0.125841	42519	5351	199509	0.026819	2.5547	741472	0.0000	17.439	0.026819	50
55	0.160874	37168	5979	171173	0.034932	2.5470	541964	0.0000	14.581	0.034932	55
60	0.214831	31189	6700	139416	0.048060	2.5334	370791	0.0092	11.889	0.048001	60
65	0.288042	24488	7054	104866	0.067263	2.5083	231374	0.0092	9.448	0.067172	65
70	0.400492	17435	6982	69413	0.100592	2.4565	126508	0.0092	7.256	0.100446	70
75	0.535248	10452	5595	37512	0.149141	2.3636	57095	0.0092	5.462	0.148916	75
80	0.683281	4858	3319	15146	0.219152	2.2454	19583	0.0092	4.031	0.218749	80
85+	*1.000000	1539	1539	4437	0.346710	2.8843	4437	0.0092	2.884	0.345389	85

TABLE 3 — FEMALE LIFE TABLE

x	nq_x	l_x	nd_x	nL_x	nm_x	na_x	T_x	r_x	$\dot{e}_x$	nM_x	x
0	0.169635	100000	16964	89343	0.189870	0.3718	4090275	0.0000	40.903	0.189870	0
1	0.117332	83036	9743	305473	0.031894	1.2623	4000933	0.0000	48.183	0.031894	1
5	0.045438	73294	3330	358143	0.009299	2.5000	3695459	0.0230	50.420	0.009409	5
10	0.027270	69963	1908	344763	0.005534	2.3509	3337317	0.0043	47.701	0.005537	10
15	0.028873	68055	1965	335453	0.005858	2.5451	2992554	0.0000	43.972	0.005858	15
20	0.035301	66091	2333	324731	0.007185	2.5476	2657101	0.0000	40.204	0.007185	20
25	0.039181	63757	2498	312654	0.007990	2.5446	2332370	0.0084	36.582	0.007986	25
30	0.046815	61259	2868	299303	0.009582	2.5614	2019716	0.0135	32.970	0.009571	30
35	0.057259	58392	3343	283758	0.011783	2.5474	1720413	0.0053	29.463	0.011778	35
40	0.065928	55048	3629	266222	0.013632	2.5149	1436655	0.0132	26.098	0.013625	40
45	0.070079	51419	3603	248282	0.014513	2.5542	1170433	0.0092	22.763	0.014502	45
50	0.095523	47816	4568	228023	0.020031	2.5797	922151	0.0000	19.286	0.020031	50
55	0.123738	43248	5351	203354	0.026316	2.5920	694128	0.0009	16.050	0.026312	55
60	0.182879	37897	6930	172658	0.040140	2.5723	490774	0.0106	12.950	0.040075	60
65	0.250450	30966	7755	135766	0.057124	2.5417	318117	0.0106	10.273	0.057027	65
70	0.365510	23211	8484	94713	0.089573	2.4845	182351	0.0106	7.856	0.089420	70
75	0.483892	14727	7126	55096	0.129343	2.3985	87638	0.0106	5.951	0.129120	75
80	0.659232	7601	5011	24532	0.204249	2.3114	32542	0.0106	4.281	0.203794	80
85+	*1.000000	2590	2590	8010	0.323337	3.0927	8010	0.0106	3.093	0.321921	85

TABLE 4 — OBSERVED AND PROJECTED VITAL RATES

	OBSERVED POPULATION BOTH SEXES	MALES	FEMALES	PROJECTED POPULATION 1825 MALES	FEMALES	1830 MALES	FEMALES	1835 MALES	FEMALES	STABLE POPULATION MALES	FEMALES
RATES PER THOUSAND											
Birth	34.29	36.66	32.11	36.10	31.89	35.04	31.19	33.91	30.39	34.01	31.4
Death	24.90	26.30	23.62	26.14	23.54	25.79	23.42	25.38	23.17	25.66	23.1
Increase	9.39	10.36	8.49	9.96	8.35	9.25	7.77	8.53	7.22		8.344
PERCENTAGE											
under 15	32.07	33.42	30.83	34.77	32.22	35.58	33.07	35.01	32.65	33.79	32.5
15-64	62.51	61.88	63.10	60.56	61.66	59.86	60.85	60.60	61.42	61.90	62.0
65 and over	5.42	4.70	6.07	4.67	6.12	4.56	6.08	4.39	5.93	4.32	5.4
DEP. RATIO X 100	59.97	61.61	58.49	65.12	62.17	67.07	64.35	65.02	62.82	61.56	61.2

TABLE 1 — DATA

AGE AT LAST BIRTHDAY	POPULATION BOTH SEXES	MALES Number	MALES %	FEMALES Number	FEMALES %	BIRTHS BY AGE OF MOTHER	DEATHS BOTH SEXES	DEATHS MALES	FEMALES	AGE AT LAST BIRTHDAY
0	84490	42518	3.2	41972	2.9	0	15069	8228	6841	0
1-4	304882	153065	11.6	151817	10.6	0	6530	3404	3126	1-4
5-9	290315	145361	11.0	144954	10.2	0	1750	917	833	5-9
10-14	258459	128901	9.7	129598	9.1	0	1002	513	489	10-14
15-19	234668	116283	8.8	118385	8.3	1395	1079	535	544	15-19
20-24	225142	110728	8.4	114414	8.0	12843	1550	849	701	20-24
25-29	216249	106414	8.0	109835	7.7	24283	1720	946	774	25-29
30-34	206826	100246	7.6	106580	7.5	26277	1908	1043	865	30-34
35-39	173874	82089	6.2	91785	6.4	19333	1943	1019	924	35-39
40-44	155709	72967	5.5	82742	5.8	9693	2154	1186	968	40-44
45-49	141575	65627	5.0	75948	5.3	1653	2290	1298	992	45-49
50-54	113938	51722	3.9	62216	4.4	6	2370	1297	1073	50-54
55-59	102473	45166	3.4	57307	4.0	0	2777	1474	1303	55-59
60-64	88731	38558	2.9	50173	3.5	0	3535	1736	1799	60-64
65-69	66654	28405	2.1	38249	2.7	0	3648	1728	1920	65-69
70-74	47434	19664	1.5	27770	1.9		3962	1811	2151	70-74
75-79	24576	9750	0.7	14826	1.0		3113	1329	1784	75-79
80-84	9613	3643	0.3	5970	0.4	48745 M.	1906	797	1109	80-84
85+	3417	1122	0.1	2295	0.2	46738 F.	1044	373	671	85+
TOTAL	2749065	1322229		1426836		95483	59350	30483	28867	TOTAL

TABLE 2 — MALE LIFE TABLE

x	nq_x	l_x	nd_x	nL_x	nm_x	na_x	T_x	r_x	$\mathring{e}_x$	nM_x	x
0	0.171467	100000	17147	88605	0.193518	0.3355	4196352	0.0000	41.964	0.193518	0
1	0.083735	82853	6938	311963	0.022239	1.1965	4107747	0.0000	49.579	0.022239	1
5	0.030547	75916	2319	373780	0.006204	2.5000	3795783	0.0322	50.000	0.006308	5
10	0.019665	73597	1447	364224	0.003974	2.4029	3422003	0.0177	46.497	0.003980	10
15	0.022796	72149	1645	356886	0.004608	2.6529	3057779	0.0101	42.381	0.004601	15
20	0.037652	70505	2655	346158	0.007669	2.6026	2700893	0.0016	38.308	0.007667	20
25	0.043502	67850	2952	332004	0.008890	2.5452	2354735	0.0010	34.705	0.008890	25
30	0.050782	64898	3296	316412	0.010416	2.5484	2022731	0.0155	31.168	0.010404	30
35	0.060355	61603	3718	298975	0.012436	2.5690	1706319	0.0190	27.699	0.012413	35
40	0.078215	57885	4527	278380	0.016263	2.5608	1407345	0.0063	24.313	0.016254	40
45	0.094437	53357	5039	254436	0.019804	2.5491	1128965	0.0143	21.159	0.019778	45
50	0.118265	48318	5714	227597	0.025107	2.5510	874529	0.0119	18.099	0.025076	50
55	0.151106	42604	6438	197263	0.032635	2.5525	646932	0.0000	15.185	0.032635	55
60	0.202861	36166	7337	162737	0.045083	2.5338	449669	0.0106	12.433	0.045023	60
65	0.264595	28830	7628	125201	0.060927	2.5163	286931	0.0106	9.953	0.060834	65
70	0.374124	21201	7932	85980	0.092253	2.4752	161730	0.0106	7.628	0.092097	70
75	0.503570	13269	6682	48933	0.136556	2.3939	75750	0.0106	5.709	0.136308	75
80	0.687474	6587	4529	20652	0.219284	2.2873	26817	0.0106	4.071	0.218777	80
85+	*1.000000	2059	2059	6166	0.333908	2.9948	6166	0.0106	2.995	0.332442	85+

TABLE 3 — FEMALE LIFE TABLE

x	nq_x	l_x	nd_x	nL_x	nm_x	na_x	T_x	r_x	$\mathring{e}_x$	nM_x	x
0	0.147310	100000	14731	90380	0.162990	0.3470	4640204	0.0000	46.402	0.162990	0
1	0.077896	85269	6642	322578	0.020591	1.2151	4549824	0.0000	53.358	0.020591	1
5	0.027871	78627	2191	387656	0.005653	2.5000	4227246	0.0315	53.763	0.005747	5
10	0.018667	76436	1427	378509	0.003770	2.4291	3839590	0.0158	50.233	0.003773	10
15	0.022743	75009	1706	370943	0.004599	2.5960	3461080	0.0078	46.142	0.004595	15
20	0.030189	73303	2213	361139	0.006128	2.5712	3090138	0.0015	42.156	0.006127	20
25	0.034635	71090	2462	349402	0.007047	2.5440	2728998	0.0000	38.388	0.007047	25
30	0.039820	68628	2733	336468	0.008122	2.5593	2379596	0.0096	34.674	0.008116	30
35	0.049180	65895	3241	321546	0.010078	2.5534	2043128	0.0153	31.006	0.010067	35
40	0.056874	62654	3563	304467	0.011704	2.5294	1721583	0.0073	27.478	0.011699	40
45	0.063366	59091	3744	286306	0.013078	2.5569	1417115	0.0149	23.982	0.013062	45
50	0.082873	55346	4587	265626	0.017268	2.5785	1130809	0.0108	20.431	0.017246	50
55	0.107827	50760	5473	240719	0.022737	2.6104	865183	0.0000	17.045	0.022737	55
60	0.165325	45286	7487	208338	0.035937	2.5833	624464	0.0144	13.789	0.035856	60
65	0.223957	37799	8465	168263	0.050311	2.5507	416126	0.0144	11.009	0.050197	65
70	0.325431	29334	9546	122940	0.077649	2.5142	247863	0.0144	8.450	0.077458	70
75	0.460580	19788	9114	75551	0.120632	2.4338	124924	0.0144	6.313	0.120329	75
80	0.622894	10674	6649	35688	0.186303	2.3406	49373	0.0144	4.626	0.185763	80
85+	*1.000000	4025	4025	13685	0.294131	3.3998	13685	0.0144	3.400	0.292375	85+

TABLE 4 — OBSERVED AND PROJECTED VITAL RATES

	OBSERVED POPULATION BOTH SEXES	MALES	FEMALES	PROJECTED POPULATION 1830 MALES	FEMALES	1835 MALES	FEMALES	1840 MALES	FEMALES	STABLE POPULATION MALES	FEMALES
RATES PER THOUSAND											
Birth	34.73	36.87	32.76	35.52	31.75	34.21	30.75	33.49	30.26	35.03	32.37
Death	21.59	23.05	20.23	22.42	19.88	21.92	19.59	21.51	19.32	21.52	18.85
Increase	13.14	13.81	12.52	13.10	11.87	12.29	11.16	11.98	10.94		13.5113
PERCENTAGE											
under 15	34.13	35.53	32.82	36.96	34.26	37.64	35.07	36.34	33.99	36.18	34.62
15-64	60.35	59.73	60.93	58.40	59.49	57.96	58.85	59.54	60.22	60.02	60.33
65 and over	5.52	4.73	6.25	4.64	6.26	4.39	6.08	4.12	5.79	3.80	5.05
DEP. RATIO X 100	65.69	67.41	64.12	71.23	68.11	72.52	69.91	67.95	66.06	66.61	65.76

TABLE 1 — DATA

AGE AT LAST BIRTHDAY	BOTH SEXES	POPULATION MALES Number	%	FEMALES Number	%	BIRTHS BY AGE OF MOTHER	DEATHS BOTH SEXES	MALES	FEMALES	AGE AT LAST BIRTHDAY
0	83373	42086	3.0	41287	2.8	0	17007	9338	7669	0
1-4	302513	151316	10.9	151197	10.1	0	9268	4819	4449	1-4
5-9	335970	168468	12.2	167502	11.2	0	2876	1493	1383	5-9
10-14	287474	143659	10.4	143815	9.6	0	1400	720	680	10-14
15-19	260418	128949	9.3	131469	8.8	1189	1352	686	666	15-19
20-24	218419	107469	7.8	110950	7.4	11616	1692	934	758	20-24
25-29	216545	106358	7.7	110187	7.4	23240	2067	1165	902	25-29
30-34	208262	102041	7.4	106221	7.1	25580	2455	1382	1073	30-34
35-39	192340	92534	6.7	99806	6.7	20422	2704	1512	1192	35-39
40-44	162873	76079	5.5	86794	5.8	9942	2759	1516	1243	40-44
45-49	141487	64926	4.7	76561	5.1	1527	2886	1604	1282	45-49
50-54	128075	58157	4.2	69918	4.7	1	3394	1856	1538	50-54
55-59	98364	43650	3.2	54714	3.7	0	3284	1678	1606	55-59
60-64	85812	36715	2.7	49097	3.3	0	4107	1993	2114	60-64
65-69	67261	28257	2.0	39004	2.6	0	4629	2122	2507	65-69
70-74	45995	18876	1.4	27119	1.8		4674	2069	2605	70-74
75-79	26338	10402	0.8	15936	1.1		4028	1702	2326	75-79
80-84	10632	3919	0.3	6713	0.5	47871 M.	2468	970	1498	80-84
85+	3456	1194	0.1	2262	0.2	45646 F.	1188	421	767	85+
TOTAL	2875607	1385055		1490552		93517	74238	37980	36258	TOTAL

TABLE 2 — MALE LIFE TABLE

x	nq_x	l_x	nd_x	nL_x	nm_x	na_x	T_x	r_x	$\mathring{e}_x$	nM_x	x
0	0.194093	100000	19409	87477	0.221879	0.3548	3676735	0.0000	36.767	0.221879	
1	0.117058	80591	9434	296220	0.031847	1.2288	3589258	0.0000	44.537	0.031847	
5	0.042968	71157	3057	348141	0.008782	2.5000	3293038	0.0165	46.279	0.008862	
10	0.024654	68099	1679	336027	0.004996	2.3378	2944897	0.0208	43.244	0.005012	10
15	0.026353	66420	1750	327951	0.005337	2.6283	2608870	0.0231	39.278	0.005320	15
20	0.042634	64670	2757	316781	0.008704	2.6173	2280919	0.0109	35.270	0.008691	20
25	0.053347	61913	3303	301534	0.010954	2.5684	1964138	0.0000	31.724	0.010954	25
30	0.065549	58610	3842	283655	0.013544	2.5544	1662604	0.0004	28.367	0.013544	30
35	0.078629	54768	4306	263275	0.016357	2.5463	1378949	0.0129	25.178	0.016340	35
40	0.095103	50462	4799	240523	0.019953	2.5440	1115674	0.0153	22.109	0.019927	40
45	0.116482	45663	5319	215261	0.024709	2.5459	875151	0.0017	19.165	0.024705	45
50	0.147987	40344	5970	186943	0.031937	2.5251	659890	0.0081	16.357	0.031914	50
55	0.175630	34374	6037	156944	0.038466	2.5279	472947	0.0057	13.759	0.038442	55
60	0.239254	28337	6780	124894	0.054283	2.5237	316003	0.0000	11.152	0.054283	60
65	0.315843	21557	6809	90665	0.075096	2.4856	191109	0.0000	8.865	0.075096	65
70	0.427746	14748	6309	57554	0.109610	2.4341	100444	0.0000	6.811	0.109610	70
75	0.570127	8440	4812	29408	0.163622	2.3417	42890	0.0000	5.082	0.163622	75
80	0.730827	3628	2651	10712	0.247511	2.1987	13482	0.0000	3.716	0.247511	80
85+	*1.000000	977	977	2770	0.352596	2.8361	2770	0.0000	2.836	0.352596	85

TABLE 3 — FEMALE LIFE TABLE

x	nq_x	l_x	nd_x	nL_x	nm_x	na_x	T_x	r_x	$\mathring{e}_x$	nM_x	x
0	0.166199	100000	16620	89475	0.185749	0.3667	4127320	0.0000	41.273	0.185749	
1	0.108895	83380	9080	308568	0.029425	1.2519	4037845	0.0000	48.427	0.029425	
5	0.040087	74300	2978	364056	0.008181	2.5000	3729277	0.0169	50.192	0.008257	5
10	0.023287	71322	1661	352201	0.004716	2.3454	3365221	0.0186	47.184	0.004728	10
15	0.025065	69661	1746	344070	0.005075	2.5744	3013021	0.0207	43.253	0.005066	15
20	0.033639	67915	2285	334048	0.006839	2.5810	2668951	0.0109	39.298	0.006832	20
25	0.040130	65630	2634	321738	0.008186	2.5649	2334902	0.0000	35.577	0.008186	25
30	0.049291	62997	3105	307396	0.010102	2.5566	2013164	0.0000	31.957	0.010102	30
35	0.058050	59891	3477	290932	0.011950	2.5479	1705768	0.0081	28.481	0.011943	35
40	0.069226	56415	3905	272466	0.014333	2.5399	1414836	0.0122	25.079	0.014321	40
45	0.080464	52509	4225	252222	0.016751	2.5563	1142370	0.0043	21.756	0.016745	45
50	0.104536	48284	5047	229157	0.022026	2.5703	890148	0.0113	18.436	0.021997	50
55	0.137109	43237	5928	201827	0.029373	2.5781	660991	0.0048	15.288	0.029353	55
60	0.194887	37309	7271	168866	0.043058	2.5688	459164	0.0000	12.307	0.043058	60
65	0.277313	30038	8330	129596	0.064275	2.5279	290298	0.0000	9.664	0.064275	65
70	0.386322	21708	8386	87303	0.096058	2.4678	160702	0.0000	7.403	0.096058	70
75	0.527941	13322	7033	48185	0.145959	2.3805	73399	0.0000	5.510	0.145959	75
80	0.692016	6289	4352	19502	0.223150	2.2560	25214	0.0000	4.009	0.223150	80
85+	*1.000000	1937	1937	5712	0.339080	2.9492	5712	0.0000	2.949	0.339080	85

TABLE 4 — OBSERVED AND PROJECTED VITAL RATES

RATES PER THOUSAND	OBSERVED POPULATION BOTH SEXES	MALES	FEMALES	PROJECTED POPULATION 1835 MALES	FEMALES	1840 MALES	FEMALES	1845 MALES	FEMALES	STABLE POPULATION MALES	FEMALES
Birth	32.52	34.56	30.62	33.98	30.23	33.97	30.32	34.76	31.12	35.18	31.85
Death	25.82	27.42	24.33	26.15	23.19	25.66	22.73	25.52	22.56	25.93	22.61
Increase	6.70	7.14	6.30	7.84	7.04	8.30	7.59	9.24	8.56		9.2483
PERCENTAGE											
under 15	35.10	36.50	33.80	36.44	33.86	35.40	33.03	34.48	32.20	35.16	33.21
15-64	59.56	58.98	60.09	59.45	60.47	60.87	61.77	61.86	62.69	61.37	62.04
65 and over	5.34	4.52	6.11	4.11	5.67	3.73	5.20	3.67	5.11	3.47	4.75
DEP. RATIO X 100	67.91	69.55	66.41	68.20	65.37	64.29	61.89	61.66	59.52	62.93	61.20

AGE AT LAST BIRTHDAY	BOTH SEXES	1835 MALES	FEMALES	BOTH SEXES	1840 MALES	FEMALES	BOTH SEXES	1845 MALES	FEMALES	AGE AT LAST BIRTHDAY	
0-4	370	186	184	380	191	189	400	201	199	0-4	
5-9	351	175	176	336	168	168	346	173	173	5-9	**TABLE 5**
10-14	325	163	162	339	169	170	324	162	162	10-14	
15-19	280	140	140	317	159	158	331	165	166	15-19	POPULATION
20-24	253	125	128	271	135	136	307	153	154	20-24	PROJECTED
25-29	209	102	1C7	242	119	123	260	129	131	25-29	WITH
30-34	205	10C	105	198	96	102	229	112	117	30-34	FIXED
35-39	196	95	101	193	93	100	186	89	97	35-39	AGE—
40-44	178	85	93	181	87	94	178	85	93	40-44	SPECIFIC
45-49	148	68	80	163	76	87	164	77	87	45-49	BIRTH
50-54	126	56	70	132	59	73	145	66	79	50-54	AND
55-59	111	49	62	108	47	61	114	50	64	55-59	DEATH
60-64	81	35	46	91	39	52	89	38	51	60-64	RATES
65-69	65	27	38	60	25	35	68	28	40	65-69	(IN 1000's)
70-74	44	18	26	42	17	25	40	16	24	70-74	
75-79	25	10	15	24	9	15	23	9	14	75-79	
80-84	10	4	6	10	4	6	9	3	6	80-84	
85+	3	1	2	3	1	2	3	1	2	85+	
TOTAL	2980	1439	1541	3090	1494	1596	3216	1557	1659	TOTAL	

STANDARD COUNTRIES:	ENGLAND AND WALES 1961 BOTH SEXES	MALES	FEMALES	UNITED STATES 1960 BOTH SEXES	MALES	FEMALES	MEXICO 1960 BOTH SEXES	MALES	FEMALES	
STANDARDIZED RATES PER THOUSAND										**TABLE 6**
Birth	29.43	31.62*	27.84	29.83	29.52*	28.69	28.49	29.35*	27.74	STANDAR-
Death	33.90	50.39*	34.09	30.91	41.66*	29.20	24.40	26.71*	22.24	DIZED
Increase	-4.48	-18.78*	-6.26	-1.08	-12.15*	-0.51	4.09	2.64*	5.50	RATES

	OBSERVED POP. MALES	FEMALES	STATIONARY POP. MALES	FEMALES	STABLE POP. MALES	FEMALES	OBSERVED BIRTHS	NET MATERNITY FUNCTION	BIRTHS IN STABLE POP.	
μ	26.42859	28.41009	29.58708	31.51181	26.12024	27.71607	32.22476	32.31710	31.92854	**TABLE 7**
σ^2	387.2087	426.9467	392.5683	428.0028	356.0168	391.1603	39.10543	40.08316	39.76431	
κ_3	5038.396	5040.213	3539.556	3385.938	4281.489	4482.462	24.6477	29.2993	39.5777	MOMENTS
κ_4	-64848.	-113599.	-107179.	-149883.	-53274.	-85963.	-1006.643	-1130.170	-1079.804	AND
β_1	0.437270	0.326420	0.207087	0.146224	0.406236	0.335714	0.010159	0.013330	0.024913	CUMULANTS
β_2	2.567482	2.376800	2.304530	2.181800	2.579685	2.438170	2.341704	2.296572	2.317098	
κ	-0.173765	-0.124297	-0.084212	-0.05707C	-0.168720	-0.133194	-0.005762	-0.007065	-0.013295	

VITAL STATISTICS		THOMPSON AGE RANGE	NRR	1000r	INTERVAL	BOURGEOIS-PICHAT AGE RANGE	NRR	1000b	1000d	1000r	COALE	
GRR	2.208										IBR	**TABLE 8**
NRR	1.346	0-4	1.40	12.76	26.89	5-29	1.54	33.90	17.96	15.94	IDR	RATES FROM AGE DISTRI-
TFR	4.523	5-9	1.39	12.34	26.69	30-54	1.22	29.68	22.25	7.43	IRI	BUTIONS
GENERATION	32.123	10-14	1.24	8.17	26.53	55-79	0.79	11.05	19.91	-8.86	K1	AND VITAL
SEX RATIO	104.874	15-19	1.20	6.83	26.32	*30-54	1.22	29.68	22.25	7.43	K2	STATISTICS (Females)

Start of Age Interval	ORIGINAL MATRIX SUB-DIAGONAL	ALTERNATIVE FIRST ROWS Projection	Integral	FIRST STABLE MATRIX % IN STABLE POPULATION	FISHER VALUES	REPRODUCTIVE VALUES	SECOND STABLE MATRIX Z₂ FIRST COLUMN	FIRST ROW	
0	0.91461	0.00000	C.C0000	12.393	1.285	247295	0.1353+0.0458	0.1353+0.0458	**TABLE 9**
5	0.96744	0.00000	0.00000	10.822	1.471	246436	0.1177-0.0837	0.0417+0.1350	
10	0.97691	0.00858	0.00000	9.996	1.593	229069	0.0012-0.1545	-0.0795+0.1056	LESLIE
15	0.97087	0.10753	0.01798	9.324	1.696	223023	-0.1344-0.0988	-0.1236-0.0027	MATRIX
20	0.96315	0.29904	0.20817	8.643	1.688	187257	-0.1704+0.0548	-0.0804-0.0999	AND ITS
25	0.95542	0.42840	0.41936	7.948	1.436	158278	-0.0591+0.1812	-0.0102-0.1304	SPECTRAL
30	0.94644	0.42206	0.47882	7.250	0.999	106075	0.1185+0.1627	0.0337-0.1007	COMPO-
35	0.93653	0.30298	0.40684	6.551	0.532	53115	0.2106-0.0007	0.0365-0.0508	NENTS
40	0.92570	0.12921	0.22775	5.858	0.180	15582	0.1271-0.1771	0.0167-0.0150	(Females)
45	0.90855	0.01939	0.03966	5.178	0.024	1822	-0.0706-0.2116	0.0025-0.0018	
50	0.88073	0.00001	C.00003	4.491	0.000	1	-0.2137-0.0670	0.0000-0.0000	
55+	0.70478			11.546					

Start of Age Interval	OBSERVED POPUL. (IN 100's)	CONTRIBUTIONS OF ROOTS (IN 100's) r_1	r_2, r_3	$r_4 \cdot r_{11}$	AGE-SP. BIRTH RATES	NET MATERNITY FUNCTION	COEFF. OF MATRIX EQUATION	PARAMETERS INTEGRAL	MATRIX	EXP. INCREASE x	$e^{(x+2\frac{1}{2})r}$	
0	1925	1793	84	49	0.0000C	0.0000	0.0000	L(1) 1.04733	1.04737	0	1.0234	**TABLE 10**
5	1675	1565	109	1	0.0000	0.0000	0.0000	L(2) 0.53175	0.53010	50	1.6250	
10	1438	1446	46	-54	0.0000	0.0000	0.0076	0.74856	0.73310	55	1.7020	AGE
15	1315	1349	-67	33	0.0044	0.0152	0.0929	R(1) 0.00925	0.00926	60	1.7825	ANALYSIS
20	1110	1250	-138	-3	0.0511	0.1707	0.2510	R(2) -0.01707	-0.02003	65	1.8669	AND
25	1102	1150	-95	47	0.1029	0.3312	0.3463	0.19063	-0.18895	70	1.9552	MISCEL-
30	1062	1049	37	-24	0.1175	0.3613	0.3259			75	2.0477	LANEOUS
35	998	948	151	-101	0.0999	0.2906	0.2215	C(1)	14464	80	2.1447	RESULTS
40	868	847	143	-122	0.0559	0.1523	0.0884	C(2)	35796	85	2.2462	(Females)
45	766	749	11	6	0.0097	0.0246	0.0123		14590	90	2.3525	
50	699	650	-133	183	0.0000	0.0000	0.0000	2P/Y 32.9600	33.2536	95	2.4638	
55+	1948	1670						DELTA 2.9749		100	2.5804	

TABLE 1 — DATA

AGE AT LAST BIRTHDAY	POPULATION BOTH SEXES	MALES Number	MALES %	FEMALES Number	FEMALES %	BIRTHS BY AGE OF MOTHER	DEATHS BOTH SEXES	DEATHS MALES	FEMALES	AGE AT LAST BIRTHDAY
0	86637	43793	3.0	42844	2.8	0	16114	8829	7285	0
1-4	307161	154219	10.6	152942	9.8	0	7222	3788	3434	1-4
5-9	334071	167258	11.5	166813	10.7	0	2298	1196	1102	5-9
10-14	330013	165166	11.4	164847	10.6	0	1434	737	697	10-14
15-19	289570	144045	9.9	145525	9.4	1222	1387	710	677	15-19
20-24	242417	119663	8.2	122754	7.9	12707	1694	937	757	20-24
25-29	209600	103126	7.1	106474	6.9	23497	1830	1017	813	25-29
30-34	206955	101180	7.0	105775	6.8	26274	2224	1238	986	30-34
35-39	194566	94640	6.5	99926	6.4	21292	2480	1387	1093	35-39
40-44	180463	85806	5.9	94657	6.1	11387	2718	1490	1228	40-44
45-49	148177	68184	4.7	79993	5.2	1652	2635	1442	1193	45-49
50-54	127174	57158	3.9	70016	4.5	0	2911	1575	1336	50-54
55-59	110213	48878	3.4	61335	3.9	0	3192	1637	1555	55-59
60-64	82758	35702	2.5	47056	3.0	0	3317	1618	1699	60-64
65-69	66187	27571	1.9	38616	2.5	0	3782	1707	2075	65-69
70-74	46538	18906	1.3	27632	1.8		4164	1809	2355	70-74
75-79	26117	10231	0.7	15886	1.0		3435	1441	1994	75-79
80-84	11681	4296	0.3	7385	0.5	50123 M.	2401	961	1440	80-84
85+	3949	1358	0.1	2591	0.2	47908 F.	1231	444	787	85+
TOTAL	3004247	1451180		1553067		98031	66469	33963	32506	TOTAL

TABLE 2 — MALE LIFE TABLE

x	nq_x	l_x	nd_x	nL_x	nm_x	na_x	T_x	r_x	$\mathring{e}_x$	nM_x	x
0	0.177952	100000	17795	88266	0.201608	0.3406	4025377	0.0000	40.254	0.201608	0
1	0.091937	82205	7558	307693	0.024562	1.2046	3937110	0.0000	47.894	0.024562	1
5	0.034995	74647	2612	366705	0.007124	2.5000	3629418	0.0075	48.621	0.007151	5
10	0.022031	72035	1587	356021	0.004458	2.3832	3262713	0.0098	45.294	0.004462	10
15	0.024451	70448	1723	348154	0.004948	2.6286	2906691	0.0268	41.260	0.004929	15
20	0.038561	68725	2650	337306	0.007857	2.6149	2558537	0.0258	37.228	0.007830	20
25	0.048185	66075	3184	322643	0.009868	2.5710	2221232	0.0068	33.617	0.009862	25
30	0.059402	62891	3736	305326	0.012236	2.5558	1898589	0.0000	30.188	0.012236	30
35	0.070739	59156	4185	285492	0.014657	2.5421	1593263	0.0018	26.933	0.014656	35
40	0.083361	54971	4582	263584	0.017385	2.5405	1307771	0.0152	23.790	0.017365	40
45	0.100714	50388	5075	239519	0.021187	2.5520	1044187	0.0189	20.723	0.021149	45
50	0.129086	45314	5849	212161	0.027570	2.5369	804667	0.0060	17.758	0.027555	50
55	0.154858	39464	6111	182241	0.033534	2.5324	592507	0.0124	15.014	0.033542	55
60	0.203863	33353	6799	149978	0.045336	2.5312	410265	0.0029	12.301	0.045320	60
65	0.268462	26554	7129	115089	0.061940	2.5201	260287	0.0029	9.802	0.061913	65
70	0.385402	19425	7486	78204	0.095729	2.4726	145198	0.0029	7.475	0.095684	70
75	0.514737	11939	6145	43609	0.140917	2.3827	66995	0.0029	5.612	0.140846	75
80	0.695016	5793	4026	17988	0.223837	2.2735	23386	0.0029	4.037	0.223696	80
85+	*1.000000	1767	1767	5397	0.327349	3.0548	5397	0.0029	3.055	0.326951	85-

TABLE 3 — FEMALE LIFE TABLE

x	nq_x	l_x	nd_x	nL_x	nm_x	na_x	T_x	r_x	$\mathring{e}_x$	nM_x	x
0	0.153131	100000	15313	90058	0.170035	0.3508	4466610	0.0000	44.666	0.170035	0
1	0.084538	84687	7159	318856	0.022453	1.2216	4376552	0.0000	51.679	0.022453	1
5	0.032377	77528	2510	381363	0.006582	2.5000	4057696	0.0075	52.339	0.006606	5
10	0.020892	75018	1567	370999	0.004225	2.3914	3676333	0.0088	49.006	0.004228	10
15	0.023050	73450	1693	363148	0.004662	2.5761	3305334	0.0247	45.001	0.004652	15
20	0.030457	71757	2186	353513	0.006182	2.5873	2942186	0.0251	41.002	0.006167	20
25	0.037505	69572	2609	341516	0.007640	2.5691	2588673	0.0072	37.209	0.007636	25
30	0.045569	66962	3051	327349	0.009322	2.5543	2247157	0.0000	33.558	0.009322	30
35	0.053261	63911	3404	311202	0.010938	2.5462	1919808	0.0001	30.039	0.010938	35
40	0.062894	60507	3806	293163	0.012981	2.5372	1608606	0.0093	26.585	0.012973	40
45	0.072026	56701	4084	273505	0.014932	2.5508	1315443	0.0148	23.199	0.014914	45
50	0.091250	52617	4801	251425	0.019096	2.5710	1041939	0.0071	19.802	0.019081	50
55	0.119638	47816	5721	225235	0.025399	2.5798	790514	0.0136	16.532	0.025353	55
60	0.166080	42096	6991	193546	0.036122	2.5781	565278	0.0029	13.428	0.036106	60
65	0.237635	35104	8342	155169	0.053761	2.5602	371733	0.0029	10.589	0.053734	65
70	0.351363	26762	9403	110279	0.085268	2.4974	216564	0.0029	8.092	0.085227	70
75	0.473799	17359	8225	65494	0.125579	2.4101	106285	0.0029	6.123	0.125519	75
80	0.640907	9134	5854	30006	0.195104	2.3240	40792	0.0029	4.466	0.194989	80
85+	*1.000000	3280	3280	10786	0.304109	3.2883	10786	0.0029	3.288	0.303744	85

TABLE 4 — OBSERVED AND PROJECTED VITAL RATES

RATES PER THOUSAND	OBSERVED POPULATION BOTH SEXES	MALES	FEMALES	PROJECTED POPULATION 1840 MALES	1840 FEMALES	1845 MALES	1845 FEMALES	1850 MALES	1850 FEMALES	STABLE POPULATION MALES	FEMALES
Birth	32.63	34.54	30.85	34.05	30.58	34.64	31.26	35.44	32.11	35.13	32.2
Death	22.13	23.40	20.93	22.94	20.53	22.82	20.38	22.86	20.38	22.88	20.0
Increase	10.51	11.14	9.92	11.11	10.05	11.82	10.88	12.58	11.73	12.2549	
PERCENTAGE											
under 15	35.21	36.55	33.96	35.76	33.39	35.77	33.52	35.60	33.47	35.99	34.3
15-64	59.65	59.15	60.11	60.18	61.01	60.19	60.92	60.46	61.06	60.23	60.7
65 and over	5.14	4.30	5.93	4.06	5.61	4.04	5.56	3.95	5.47	3.79	4.9
DEP. RATIO X 100	67.66	69.06	66.37	66.16	63.92	66.14	64.14	65.41	63.77	66.03	64.6

TABLE 1 — DATA

AGE AT LAST BIRTHDAY	POPULATION BOTH SEXES	MALES Number	%	FEMALES Number	%	BIRTHS BY AGE OF MOTHER	DEATHS BOTH SEXES	MALES	FEMALES	AGE AT LAST BIRTHDAY
0	83211	42226	2.8	40985	2.5	0	15362	8455	6907	0
1-4	303719	152151	10.1	151568	9.4	0	7439	3852	3587	1-4
5-9	343720	172545	11.4	171175	10.6	0	2609	1351	1258	5-9
10-14	326820	163086	10.8	163734	10.1	0	1543	802	741	10-14
15-19	331462	165258	11.0	166204	10.3	1001	1716	841	875	15-19
20-24	270215	132900	8.8	137315	8.5	12288	1966	1081	885	20-24
25-29	234120	114725	7.6	119395	7.4	24381	1954	1076	878	25-29
30-34	199245	97353	6.5	101892	6.3	24796	2092	1166	926	30-34
35-39	193420	93718	6.2	99702	6.2	20476	2422	1347	1075	35-39
40-44	181955	87246	5.8	94709	5.9	10756	2780	1551	1229	40-44
45-49	164532	77012	5.1	87520	5.4	1660	2849	1581	1268	45-49
50-54	134387	60524	4.0	73863	4.6	0	3038	1603	1435	50-54
55-59	110338	48731	3.2	61607	3.8	0	3258	1676	1582	55-59
60-64	98373	42372	2.8	56001	3.5	0	3885	1899	1986	60-64
65-69	62287	25831	1.7	36456	2.3	0	3767	1739	2028	65-69
70-74	44467	17964	1.2	26503	1.6		4108	1778	2330	70-74
75-79	25571	9844	0.7	15727	1.0		3514	1460	2054	75-79
80-84	10688	3871	0.3	6817	0.4	48671 M.	2275	891	1384	80-84
85+	4143	1288	0.1	2855	0.2	46687 F.	1285	439	846	85+
TOTAL	3122673	1508645		1614028		95358	67862	34588	33274	TOTAL

TABLE 2 — MALE LIFE TABLE

x	nq_x	l_x	nd_x	nL_x	nm_x	na_x	T_x	r_x	$\mathring{e}_x$	nM_x	x
0	0.176995	100000	17700	88395	0.200232	0.3443	3997157	0.0000	39.972	0.200232	0
1	0.094588	82300	7785	307488	0.025317	1.2107	3908762	0.0000	47.494	0.025317	1
5	0.038287	74516	2853	365447	0.007807	2.5000	3601274	0.0063	48.329	0.007830	5
10	0.024274	71663	1740	353738	0.004918	2.3692	3235827	0.0000	45.154	0.004918	10
15	0.025188	69923	1761	345419	0.005099	2.6169	2882090	0.0148	41.218	0.005089	15
20	0.040015	68162	2727	334251	0.008160	2.5950	2536671	0.0288	37.215	0.008134	20
25	0.045927	65435	3005	319849	0.009396	2.5629	2202420	0.0214	33.658	0.009379	25
30	0.058227	62429	3635	303284	0.011986	2.5617	1882571	0.0083	30.155	0.011977	30
35	0.069422	58794	4082	283981	0.014373	2.5523	1579287	0.0000	26.861	0.014373	35
40	0.085169	54713	4660	262084	0.017780	2.5365	1295306	0.0021	23.675	0.017777	40
45	0.097835	50053	4897	238223	0.020556	2.5411	1033223	0.0154	20.643	0.020529	45
50	0.124594	45156	5626	212000	0.026539	2.5507	794999	0.0190	17.606	0.026485	50
55	0.158546	39530	6267	182208	0.034396	2.5364	583000	0.0009	14.748	0.034393	55
60	0.202030	33262	6720	149803	0.044859	2.5433	400791	0.0067	12.049	0.044817	60
65	0.288718	26542	7663	113710	0.067393	2.5204	250988	0.0067	9.456	0.067322	65
70	0.395676	18879	7470	75394	0.099080	2.4562	137278	0.0067	7.271	0.098976	70
75	0.534082	11409	6093	41037	0.148486	2.3728	61885	0.0067	5.424	0.148314	75
80	0.705237	5316	3749	16263	0.230507	2.2484	20848	0.0067	3.922	0.230174	80
85+	*1.000000	1567	1567	4584	0.341792	2.9258	4584	0.0067	2.926	0.340839	85+

TABLE 3 — FEMALE LIFE TABLE

x	nq_x	l_x	nd_x	nL_x	nm_x	na_x	T_x	r_x	$\mathring{e}_x$	nM_x	x
0	0.152044	100000	15204	90220	0.168525	0.3568	4420631	0.0000	44.206	0.168525	0
1	0.088845	84796	7534	318333	0.023666	1.2325	4330411	0.0000	51.069	0.023666	1
5	0.035988	77262	2780	379359	0.007329	2.5000	4012078	0.0058	51.928	0.007349	5
10	0.022364	74481	1666	368059	0.004526	2.3892	3632719	0.0000	48.773	0.004526	10
15	0.026014	72816	1894	359466	0.005270	2.5647	3264661	0.0123	44.835	0.005265	15
20	0.031782	70922	2254	349096	0.006457	2.5545	2905195	0.0267	40.963	0.006445	20
25	0.036178	68668	2484	337271	0.007366	2.5579	2556099	0.0223	37.224	0.007354	25
30	0.044485	66183	2944	323730	0.009094	2.5592	2218828	0.0090	33.526	0.009088	30
35	0.052524	63239	3322	308063	0.010782	2.5516	1895098	0.0000	29.967	0.010782	35
40	0.062872	59918	3767	290297	0.012977	2.5337	1587035	0.0003	26.487	0.012977	40
45	0.070023	56150	3932	271149	0.014501	2.5575	1296738	0.0096	23.094	0.014488	45
50	0.092934	52219	4853	249335	0.019463	2.5770	1025589	0.0155	19.640	0.019428	50
55	0.120877	47366	5725	222922	0.025683	2.5711	776254	0.0014	16.389	0.025679	55
60	0.163495	41640	6808	191768	0.035501	2.5862	553332	0.0065	13.288	0.035464	60
65	0.245216	34832	8541	153364	0.055694	2.5651	361564	0.0065	10.380	0.055629	65
70	0.360500	26291	9478	107690	0.088011	2.4926	208199	0.0065	7.919	0.087915	70
75	0.488020	16813	8205	62756	0.130747	2.4029	100510	0.0065	5.978	0.130603	75
80	0.656809	8608	5654	27811	0.203290	2.3065	37754	0.0065	4.386	0.203023	80
85+	*1.000000	2954	2954	9942	0.297127	3.3656	9942	0.0065	3.366	0.296322	85+

TABLE 4 — OBSERVED AND PROJECTED TOTAL RATES

	OBSERVED POPULATION BOTH SEXES	MALES	FEMALES	PROJECTED POPULATION 1845 MALES	FEMALES	1850 MALES	FEMALES	1855 MALES	FEMALES	STABLE POPULATION MALES	FEMALES
RATES PER THOUSAND											
Birth	30.54	32.26	28.93	33.09	29.81	34.29	31.03	34.80	31.61	33.31	30.60
Death	21.73	22.93	20.62	22.71	20.37	22.88	20.50	23.05	20.61	23.32	20.61
Increase	8.81	9.33	8.31	10.38	9.44	11.41	10.53	11.75	11.00		9.9976
PERCENTAGE											
under 15	33.86	35.13	32.68	34.52	32.21	34.47	32.34	34.78	32.74	34.56	32.91
15-64	61.42	60.97	61.85	61.44	62.14	61.57	62.12	61.31	61.75	61.36	61.71
65 and over	4.71	3.90	5.47	4.05	5.65	3.96	5.54	3.91	5.50	4.08	5.37
DEP. RATIO X 100	62.80	64.01	61.69	62.77	60.92	62.41	60.98	63.10	61.93	62.98	62.04

TABLE 1 — DATA

AGE AT LAST BIRTHDAY	POPULATION BOTH SEXES	MALES Number	%	FEMALES Number	%	BIRTHS BY AGE OF MOTHER	DEATHS BOTH SEXES	MALES	FEMALES	AGE AT LAST BIRTHDAY
0	91180	45877	2.9	45303	2.7	0	15880	8698	7182	0
1-4	325031	162917	10.2	162114	9.5	0	8413	4401	4012	1-4
5-9	343852	171553	10.8	172299	10.1	0	2875	1543	1332	5-9
10-14	337773	169444	10.6	168329	9.9	0	1539	797	742	10-1
15-19	329786	163844	10.3	165942	9.8	949	1635	810	825	15-1
20-24	313000	154687	9.7	158313	9.3	13100	2008	1093	915	20-2
25-29	260257	127860	8.0	132397	7.8	26471	1926	1045	881	25-2
30-34	225038	109919	6.9	115119	6.8	27532	1983	1071	912	30-3
35-39	189245	92163	5.8	97082	5.7	20463	2113	1165	948	35-3
40-44	183221	87976	5.5	95245	5.6	11145	2518	1400	1118	40-4
45-49	168308	79576	5.0	88732	5.2	1619	2705	1550	1155	45-4
50-54	151483	69746	4.4	81737	4.8	0	3228	1796	1432	50-5
55-59	118373	52232	3.3	66141	3.9	0	3332	1731	1601	55-5
60-64	100011	43013	2.7	56998	3.4	0	3845	1891	1954	60-6
65-69	72001	29945	1.9	42056	2.5	0	4344	2046	2298	65-6
70-74	44927	18106	1.1	26821	1.6		4064	1747	2317	70-7
75-79	26247	10069	0.6	16178	1.0		3620	1480	2140	75-7
80-84	11684	4172	0.3	7512	0.4	51794 M.	2468	966	1502	80-8
85+	4418	1385	0.1	3033	0.2	49485 F.	1361	458	903	85+
TOTAL	3295835	1594484		1701351		101279	69857	35688	34169	TOTA

TABLE 2 — MALE LIFE TABLE

x	nq_x	l_x	nd_x	nL_x	nm_x	na_x	T_x	r_x	$\mathring{e}_x$	nM_x
0	0.168980	100000	16898	89127	0.189594	0.3566	4078053	0.0000	40.781	0.189594
1	0.100538	83102	8355	309282	0.027014	1.2321	3988926	0.0000	48.000	0.027014
5	0.043814	74747	3275	365548	0.008959	2.5000	3679643	0.0087	49.228	0.008994
10	0.023223	71472	1660	352885	0.004704	2.3031	3314095	0.0000	46.369	0.004704
15	0.024436	69812	1706	344945	0.004946	2.5867	2961210	0.0039	42.417	0.004944
20	0.034795	68106	2370	334802	0.007078	2.5820	2616265	0.0180	38.414	0.007066
25	0.040132	65737	2638	322221	0.008187	2.5505	2281464	0.0259	34.706	0.008173
30	0.047691	63099	3009	308188	0.009764	2.5727	1959242	0.0227	31.051	0.009744
35	0.061380	60089	3688	291499	0.012653	2.5740	1651054	0.0096	27.477	0.012641
40	0.076588	56401	4320	271447	0.015913	2.5557	1359556	0.0032	24.105	0.015913
45	0.093003	52081	4844	248592	0.019485	2.5607	1088109	0.0032	20.892	0.019478
50	0.121329	47238	5731	222178	0.025796	2.5554	839517	0.0162	17.772	0.025751
55	0.153445	41506	6369	191870	0.033194	2.5409	617340	0.0146	14.873	0.033141
60	0.198677	35137	6981	158623	0.044010	2.5556	425470	0.0071	12.109	0.043963
65	0.292380	28156	8232	120356	0.068400	2.5188	266847	0.0071	9.477	0.068325
70	0.387593	19924	7722	79949	0.096591	2.4528	146491	0.0071	7.352	0.096487
75	0.531191	12202	6481	44040	0.147171	2.3820	66542	0.0071	5.454	0.146986
80	0.708252	5720	4051	17470	0.231902	2.2525	22502	0.0071	3.934	0.231544
85+	*1.000000	1669	1669	5032	0.331663	3.0151	5032	0.0071	3.015	0.330686

TABLE 3 — FEMALE LIFE TABLE

x	nq_x	l_x	nd_x	nL_x	nm_x	na_x	T_x	r_x	$\mathring{e}_x$	nM_x
0	0.144086	100000	14409	90887	0.158533	0.3675	4519708	0.0000	45.197	0.158533
1	0.092692	85591	7934	320576	0.024748	1.2535	4428821	0.0000	51.744	0.024748
5	0.037744	77658	2931	380961	0.007694	2.5000	4108246	0.0101	52.902	0.007731
10	0.021786	74727	1628	369327	0.004408	2.3547	3727284	0.0000	49.879	0.004408
15	0.024560	73099	1795	361090	0.004972	2.5471	3357957	0.0012	45.937	0.004972
20	0.028523	71303	2034	351532	0.005786	2.5488	2996867	0.0168	42.030	0.005780
25	0.032792	69270	2271	340789	0.006665	2.5527	2645336	0.0251	38.189	0.006654
30	0.038932	66998	2608	328636	0.007937	2.5640	2304547	0.0230	34.397	0.007922
35	0.047723	64390	3073	314452	0.009772	2.5603	1975911	0.0092	30.687	0.009765
40	0.057040	61317	3498	297960	0.011738	2.5342	1661459	0.0000	27.096	0.011738
45	0.063089	57819	3648	280199	0.013019	2.5607	1363499	0.0016	23.582	0.013017
50	0.084174	54172	4560	259882	0.017546	2.5929	1083300	0.0115	19.998	0.017520
55	0.114523	49612	5682	234355	0.024244	2.5882	823418	0.0113	16.597	0.024206
60	0.158537	43930	6965	202915	0.034323	2.5970	589063	0.0070	13.409	0.034282
65	0.241455	36965	8926	163140	0.054711	2.5702	386149	0.0070	10.446	0.054641
70	0.355563	28040	9970	115271	0.086492	2.4996	223009	0.0070	7.953	0.086388
75	0.492867	18070	8906	67248	0.132436	2.4061	107738	0.0070	5.962	0.132278
80	0.649874	9164	5955	29744	0.200221	2.3007	40490	0.0070	4.418	0.199947
85+	*1.000000	3209	3209	10746	0.298588	3.3491	10746	0.0070	3.349	0.297725

TABLE 4 — OBSERVED AND PROJECTED VITAL RATES

RATES PER THOUSAND	OBSERVED POPULATION BOTH SEXES	MALES	FEMALES	PROJECTED POPULATION 1850 MALES	FEMALES	1855 MALES	FEMALES	1860 MALES	FEMALES	STABLE POPULATION MALES	FEMALE
Birth	30.73	32.48	29.09	33.79	30.41	34.56	31.23	34.24	31.06	32.83	30.1
Death	21.20	22.38	20.08	22.20	19.83	22.38	19.96	22.43	19.99	22.78	20.0
Increase	9.53	10.10	9.00	11.59	10.57	12.18	11.27	11.81	11.07		10.054
PERCENTAGE											
under 15	33.31	34.48	32.21	34.10	32.06	34.75	32.73	34.91	32.93	34.11	32.5
15-64	61.86	61.53	62.17	61.87	62.28	61.29	61.69	61.02	61.40	61.64	61.8
65 and over	4.83	3.99	5.62	4.02	5.66	3.96	5.59	4.07	5.67	4.25	5.6
DEP. RATIO X 100	61.66	62.53	60.85	61.62	60.57	63.16	62.11	63.88	62.86	62.24	61.6

TABLE 1 — DATA

AGE AT LAST BIRTHDAY	POPULATION BOTH SEXES	MALES Number	%	FEMALES Number	%	BIRTHS BY AGE OF MOTHER	DEATHS BOTH SEXES	MALES	FEMALES	AGE AT LAST BIRTHDAY
0	97831	49449	2.9	48382	2.7	0	16201	8967	7234	0
1-4	337591	169658	10.1	167933	9.4	0	8230	4335	3895	1-4
5-9	368189	184203	11.0	183986	10.3	0	2980	1532	1448	5-9
10-14	335675	167646	10.0	168029	9.4	0	1477	766	711	10-14
15-19	338762	169127	10.1	169635	9.5	872	1571	811	760	15-19
20-24	311103	153522	9.2	157581	8.8	12515	1936	1082	854	20-24
25-29	300987	148355	8.8	152632	8.6	29167	2190	1227	963	25-29
30-34	251555	123103	7.3	128452	7.2	30657	2276	1241	1035	30-34
35-39	213796	103737	6.2	110059	6.2	22918	2381	1326	1055	35-39
40-44	179170	86292	5.1	92878	5.2	11079	2440	1395	1045	40-44
45-49	168790	79646	4.7	89144	5.0	1713	2692	1590	1102	45-49
50-54	154382	71564	4.3	82818	4.6	0	3190	1786	1404	50-54
55-59	133242	59847	3.6	73395	4.1	0	3596	1917	1679	55-59
60-64	104871	45100	2.7	59771	3.3	0	3922	1912	2010	60-64
65-69	72885	30258	1.8	42627	2.4	0	4346	2005	2341	65-69
70-74	50980	20352	1.2	30628	1.7		4489	1970	2519	70-74
75-79	26036	9972	0.6	16064	0.9		3477	1432	2045	75-79
80-84	11648	4176	0.2	7472	0.4	55767 M.	2351	900	1451	80-84
85+	4421	1393	0.1	3028	0.2	53154 F.	1346	443	903	85+
TOTAL	3461914	1677400		1784514		108921	71091	36637	34454	TOTAL

TABLE 2 — MALE LIFE TABLE

x	$_nq_x$	l_x	$_nd_x$	$_nL_x$	$_nm_x$	$_na_x$	T_x	r_x	$\mathring{e}_x$	$_nM_x$	x
0	0.162212	100000	16221	89556	0.181129	0.3562	4153884	0.0018	41.539	0.181338	0
1	0.095366	83779	7990	312995	0.025526	1.2313	4064328	0.0018	48.513	0.025551	1
5	0.040459	75789	3066	371280	0.008259	2.5000	3751333	0.0154	49.497	0.008317	5
10	0.022559	72723	1641	359225	0.004567	2.3246	3380053	0.0030	46.479	0.004569	10
15	0.023712	71082	1685	351357	0.004797	2.5946	3020828	0.0036	42.498	0.004795	15
20	0.034673	69397	2406	341184	0.007052	2.5894	2669471	0.0063	38.467	0.007048	20
25	0.040576	66991	2718	328316	0.008279	2.5585	2328288	0.0137	34.755	0.008271	25
30	0.049313	64272	3169	313663	0.010105	2.5708	1999971	0.0255	31.117	0.010081	30
35	0.062120	61103	3796	296294	0.012811	2.5708	1686308	0.0226	27.598	0.012782	35
40	0.077830	57307	4460	275642	0.016181	2.5576	1390014	0.0102	24.255	0.016166	40
45	0.095159	52847	5029	251905	0.019963	2.5482	1114372	0.0000	21.087	0.019963	45
50	0.117618	47818	5624	225289	0.024965	2.5461	862467	0.0033	18.036	0.024957	50
55	0.148678	42194	6273	195554	0.032080	2.5427	637177	0.0136	15.101	0.032032	55
60	0.192408	35921	6911	162741	0.042469	2.5603	441623	0.0116	12.294	0.042395	60
65	0.285161	29010	8272	124606	0.066388	2.5291	278882	0.0116	9.614	0.066263	65
70	0.388944	20737	8065	83176	0.096969	2.4572	154277	0.0116	7.440	0.096796	70
75	0.522200	12671	6617	45990	0.143878	2.3755	71101	0.0116	5.611	0.143602	75
80	0.678780	6054	4110	19025	0.216015	2.2631	25111	0.0116	4.148	0.215517	80
85+	*1.000000	1945	1945	6086	0.319550	3.1294	6086	0.0116	3.129	0.318019	85+

TABLE 3 — FEMALE LIFE TABLE

x	$_nq_x$	l_x	$_nd_x$	$_nL_x$	$_nm_x$	$_na_x$	T_x	r_x	$\mathring{e}_x$	$_nM_x$	x
0	0.136419	100000	13642	91374	0.149297	0.3677	4627662	0.0024	46.277	0.149518	0
1	0.087126	86358	7524	324770	0.023167	1.2538	4536288	0.0024	52.529	0.023194	1
5	0.038349	78834	3023	386612	0.007820	2.5000	4211518	0.0148	53.423	0.007870	5
10	0.020909	75811	1585	374804	0.004229	2.3188	3824906	0.0029	50.453	0.004231	10
15	0.022160	74226	1645	367091	0.004481	2.5452	3450101	0.0019	46.481	0.004480	15
20	0.026753	72581	1942	358165	0.005421	2.5593	3083010	0.0052	42.477	0.005419	20
25	0.031108	70639	2197	347862	0.006317	2.5728	2724845	0.0139	38.574	0.006309	25
30	0.039594	68442	2710	335618	0.008074	2.5681	2376983	0.0247	34.730	0.008057	30
35	0.046960	65732	3083	321102	0.009601	2.5487	2041364	0.0228	31.056	0.009586	35
40	0.054762	62649	3431	304766	0.011257	2.5286	1720262	0.0100	27.459	0.011251	40
45	0.060004	59218	3553	287438	0.012362	2.5647	1415496	0.0000	23.903	0.012362	45
50	0.081463	55665	4535	267404	0.016958	2.5917	1128058	0.0024	20.265	0.016953	50
55	0.108553	51130	5550	242311	0.022906	2.5965	860654	0.0089	16.833	0.022876	55
60	0.155915	45580	7107	210921	0.033693	2.6109	618343	0.0105	13.566	0.033628	60
65	0.242577	38473	9333	169628	0.055019	2.5635	407422	0.0105	10.590	0.054918	65
70	0.341524	29141	9952	120796	0.082388	2.4973	237794	0.0105	8.160	0.082245	70
75	0.479766	19188	9206	72183	0.127536	2.4192	116998	0.0105	6.097	0.127303	75
80	0.639242	9982	6381	32792	0.194598	2.3170	44815	0.0105	4.489	0.194191	80
85+	*1.000000	3601	3601	12023	0.299525	3.3386	12023	0.0105	3.339	0.298217	85+

TABLE 4 — OBSERVED, PROJECTED, STABLE RATES

	OBSERVED POPULATION BOTH SEXES	MALES	FEMALES	PROJECTED POPULATION 1855 MALES	FEMALES	1860 MALES	FEMALES	1865 MALES	FEMALES	STABLE POPULATION MALES	FEMALES
RATES PER THOUSAND											
Birth	31.46	33.25	29.79	34.01	30.60	33.85	30.56	33.01	29.89	32.33	29.53
Death	20.54	21.84	19.31	21.91	19.32	22.00	19.37	21.94	19.31	22.20	19.39
Increase	10.93	11.40	10.48	12.10	11.28	11.85	11.19	11.08	10.58	10.1355	
PERCENTAGE											
under 15	32.91	34.04	31.85	34.54	32.37	35.06	32.91	35.08	33.01	34.05	32.32
15-64	62.30	62.02	62.56	61.44	61.96	60.79	61.33	60.72	61.25	61.60	61.91
65 and over	4.79	3.94	5.59	4.02	5.67	4.15	5.76	4.20	5.75	4.35	5.77
DEP. RATIO X 100	60.52	61.24	59.85	62.77	61.40	64.51	63.06	64.70	63.27	62.34	61.52

Left margin labels: TABLE 1 / DATA; TABLE 2 / MALE / LIFE / TABLE; TABLE 3 / FEMALE / LIFE / TABLE; TABLE 4 / OBSERVED / PROJECTED / TOTAL RATES

TABLE 1 — DATA

AGE AT LAST BIRTHDAY	BOTH SEXES	POPULATION MALES Number	%	FEMALES Number	%	BIRTHS BY AGE OF MOTHER	DEATHS BOTH SEXES	MALES	FEMALES	AGE AT LAST BIRTH
0	104578	53192	3.0	51386	2.7	0	17234	9516	7718	0
1-4	359796	180698	10.3	179098	9.6	0	11993	6242	5751	1-
5-9	380958	188804	10.8	192154	10.3	0	4870	2564	2306	5-
10-14	358255	179397	10.2	178858	9.6	0	2243	1172	1071	10-
15-19	338185	167605	9.6	170580	9.1	835	1957	1019	938	15-
20-24	316668	156520	8.9	160148	8.6	12483	2212	1250	962	20-
25-29	295760	144633	8.2	151127	8.1	28308	2370	1289	1081	25-
30-34	289393	141587	8.1	147806	7.9	34257	2775	1475	1300	30-
35-39	238145	115923	6.6	122222	6.5	25928	2767	1449	1318	35-
40-44	200707	96244	5.5	104463	5.6	12657	2828	1526	1302	40-
45-49	164104	77359	4.4	86745	4.6	1704	2796	1545	1251	45-
50-54	152830	70845	4.0	81985	4.4	30	3306	1764	1542	50-
55-59	134850	61308	3.5	73542	3.9	0	3824	1946	1878	55-
60-64	113375	49721	2.8	63654	3.4	0	4566	2182	2384	60-
65-69	78600	32748	1.9	45852	2.5	0	4643	2047	2596	65-
70-74	51449	20598	1.2	30851	1.6		4690	1996	2694	70-
75-79	30355	11560	0.7	18795	1.0		4073	1674	2399	75-
80-84	11904	4286	0.2	7618	0.4	59473 M.	2283	871	1412	80-
85+	4656	1490	0.1	3166	0.2	56729 F.	1314	441	873	85
TOTAL	3624568	1754518		1870050		116202	82744	41968	40776	TOT

TABLE 2 — MALE LIFE TABLE

x	nq_x	l_x	nd_x	nL_x	nm_x	na_x	T_x	r_x	$\mathring{e}_x$	nM_x
0	0.161145	100000	16115	90090	0.178872	0.3850	3874825	0.0003	38.748	0.178899
1	0.126346	83885	10599	306848	0.034540	1.2926	3784736	0.0003	45.118	0.034544
5	0.065430	73287	4795	354447	0.013529	2.5000	3477888	0.0100	47.456	0.013580
10	0.032056	68492	2196	336385	0.006527	2.2335	3123442	0.0037	45.603	0.006533
15	0.029960	66296	1986	326583	0.006082	2.5340	2787057	0.0072	42.039	0.006080
20	0.039187	64310	2520	315397	0.007990	2.5585	2460474	0.0070	38.260	0.007986
25	0.043606	61790	2694	302314	0.008913	2.5374	2145077	0.0010	34.716	0.008912
30	0.050833	59095	3004	288116	0.010426	2.5496	1842764	0.0116	31.183	0.010418
35	0.060787	56091	3410	272147	0.012529	2.5627	1554648	0.0258	27.716	0.012500
40	0.076502	52682	4030	253589	0.015893	2.5634	1282501	0.0244	24.344	0.015856
45	0.095291	48652	4636	231904	0.019991	2.5509	1028912	0.0105	21.149	0.019972
50	0.117322	44015	5164	207394	0.024899	2.5439	797009	0.0000	18.107	0.024899
55	0.147305	38851	5723	180244	0.031751	2.5514	589615	0.0027	15.176	0.031741
60	0.198462	33128	6575	149514	0.043974	2.5469	409371	0.0147	12.357	0.043885
65	0.271258	26554	7203	114964	0.062654	2.5281	259858	0.0147	9.786	0.062508
70	0.389953	19351	7546	77680	0.097140	2.4723	144894	0.0147	7.488	0.096903
75	0.525225	11805	6200	42715	0.145153	2.3695	67213	0.0147	5.694	0.144810
80	0.653579	5605	3663	17978	0.203750	2.2578	24498	0.0147	4.371	0.203219
85+	*1.000000	1942	1942	6520	0.297790	3.3581	6520	0.0147	3.358	0.295973

TABLE 3 — FEMALE LIFE TABLE

x	nq_x	l_x	nd_x	nL_x	nm_x	na_x	T_x	r_x	$\mathring{e}_x$	nM_x
0	0.137707	100000	13771	91685	0.150197	0.3961	4260112	0.0000	42.601	0.150197
1	0.118272	86229	10198	317602	0.032111	1.3216	4168428	0.0000	48.341	0.032111
5	0.058022	76031	4411	369125	0.011951	2.5000	3850826	0.0104	50.648	0.012001
10	0.029424	71619	2107	352302	0.005982	2.2503	3481701	0.0045	48.614	0.005988
15	0.027120	69512	1885	342825	0.005499	2.4884	3129398	0.0055	45.020	0.005499
20	0.029608	67627	2002	333217	0.006009	2.5439	2786573	0.0060	41.205	0.006007
25	0.035155	65625	2307	322507	0.007153	2.5656	2453357	0.0008	37.385	0.007153
30	0.043100	63318	2729	309949	0.008805	2.5673	2130850	0.0124	33.653	0.008795
35	0.052617	60589	3188	295128	0.010802	2.5487	1820901	0.0240	30.054	0.010784
40	0.060538	57401	3475	278435	0.012480	2.5342	1525773	0.0218	26.581	0.012464
45	0.069710	53926	3759	260447	0.014433	2.5575	1247338	0.0093	23.131	0.014422
50	0.089947	50167	4512	239913	0.018808	2.5800	986891	0.0000	19.672	0.018808
55	0.120282	45654	5491	215041	0.025536	2.5908	746979	0.0000	16.362	0.025536
60	0.171955	40163	6906	184129	0.037507	2.5841	531937	0.0090	13.245	0.037452
65	0.248951	33257	8279	146011	0.056703	2.5515	347808	0.0090	10.458	0.056617
70	0.358450	24977	8953	102380	0.087450	2.4862	201797	0.0090	8.079	0.087323
75	0.479564	16024	7685	60121	0.127820	2.3974	99417	0.0090	6.204	0.127640
80	0.619713	8340	5168	27837	0.185656	2.3181	39296	0.0090	4.712	0.185351
85+	*1.000000	3171	3171	11458	0.276778	3.6130	11458	0.0090	3.613	0.275742

TABLE 4 — OBSERVED AND PROJECTED VITAL RATES

	OBSERVED POPULATION BOTH SEXES	MALES	FEMALES	PROJECTED POPULATION 1860 MALES	FEMALES	1865 MALES	FEMALES	1870 MALES	FEMALES	STABLE POPULATION MALES	FEMA
RATES PER THOUSAND											
Birth	32.06	33.90	30.34	33.94	30.57	33.40	30.23	32.69	29.70	32.08	29.
Death	22.83	23.92	21.80	23.93	21.72	23.99	21.68	23.94	21.53	24.66	22.
Increase	9.23	9.98	8.53	10.00	8.85	9.41	8.56	8.75	8.17		7.41
PERCENTAGE											
under 15	33.21	34.32	32.16	34.19	32.24	34.48	32.45	34.11	32.21	33.10	31.
15-64	61.91	61.65	62.15	61.58	61.99	61.20	61.85	61.60	62.25	62.02	62.
65 and over	4.88	4.03	5.68	4.24	5.77	4.32	5.70	4.29	5.55	4.88	5.
DEP. RATIO X 100	61.52	62.19	60.90	62.39	61.32	63.40	61.69	62.33	60.65	61.25	60.

AGE LAST DAY	1860 BOTH SEXES	MALES	FEMALES	1865 BOTH SEXES	MALES	FEMALES	1870 BOTH SEXES	MALES	FEMALES	AGE AT LAST BIRTHDAY	
4	480	242	238	500	252	248	515	260	255	0-4	
9	417	209	208	431	216	215	449	225	224	5-9	
14	362	179	183	396	198	198	410	205	205	10-14	
19	348	174	174	352	174	178	385	192	193	15-19	**TABLE 5**
24	328	162	166	337	168	169	341	168	173	20-24	POPULATION
29	305	150	155	315	155	160	325	161	164	25-29	PROJECTED
34	283	138	145	292	143	149	302	148	154	30-34	WITH
39	275	134	141	268	130	138	277	135	142	35-39	FIXED
44	223	108	115	258	125	133	251	121	130	40-44	AGE—
49	186	88	98	207	99	108	238	114	124	45-49	SPECIFIC
54	149	69	80	169	79	90	187	88	99	50-54	BIRTH
59	135	62	73	132	60	72	149	68	81	55-59	AND
64	114	51	63	114	51	63	111	50	61	60-64	DEATH
69	88	38	50	89	39	50	89	39	50	65-69	RATES
74	54	22	32	61	26	35	61	26	35	70-74	(IN 1000's)
79	29	11	18	31	12	19	35	14	21	75-79	
84	14	5	9	13	5	8	14	5	9	80-84	
+	5	2	3	6	2	4	5	2	3	85+	
AL	3795	1844	1951	3971	1934	2037	4144	2021	2123	TOTAL	

STANDARD COUNTRIES:	ENGLAND AND WALES 1961 BOTH SEXES	MALES	FEMALES	UNITED STATES 1960 BOTH SEXES	MALES	FEMALES	MEXICO 1960 BOTH SEXES	MALES	FEMALES	
ARDIZED RATES PER THOUSAND										**TABLE 6**
h	27.93	28.78*	26.43	28.31	26.74*	27.23	26.27	27.18*	25.59	STANDAR-DIZED
h	29.74	45.79*	30.28	27.57	37.45*	26.40	22.63	23.71*	20.91	RATES
ease	-1.80	-17.01*	-3.85	0.74	-10.71*	0.83	3.65	3.47*	4.68	

OBSERVED POP. MALES	FEMALES	STATIONARY POP. MALES	FEMALES	STABLE POP. MALES	FEMALES	OBSERVED BIRTHS	NET MATERNITY FUNCTION	BIRTHS IN STABLE POP.	
26.67903	28.41448	30.88372	32.29661	27.83699	29.06305	32.52990	33.04293	32.74446	**TABLE 7**
371.6398	410.8748	425.4706	450.4159	394.9008	420.0598	36.23848	38.20462	38.08743	MOMENTS
4573.140	4889.394	3665.640	3525.406	4511.433	4588.041	22.8040	12.0301	19.5460	AND
-56602.	-91580.	-139787.	-171050.	-87592.	-114029.	-800.765	-1014.392	-1000.116	CUMULANTS
0.407439	0.344652	0.174458	0.136012	0.330495	0.284002	0.010927	0.002595	0.006915	
2.590185	2.457525	2.227806	2.156869	2.438323	2.353763	2.390231	2.305017	2.310575	
-0.170584	-0.137692	-0.068726	-0.052530	-0.131875	-0.110823	-0.006652	-0.001418	-0.003777	

TAL STATISTICS		AGE RANGE	THOMPSON NRR	1000r	INTERVAL	AGE RANGE	BOURGEOIS-PICHAT NRR	1000b	1000d	1000r	COALE		
	2.088												**TABLE 8**
	1.276	0-4	1.24	7.99	26.96	5-29	1.15	29.02	23.72	5.30	IBR	30.93	RATES FROM AGE DISTRI-
	4.276	5-9	1.21	7.24	26.79	30-54	1.61	43.63	25.94	17.69	IDR	21.78	BUTIONS
ERATION	32.894	10-14	1.25	8.25	26.65	55-79	1.29	32.28	22.76	9.51	IRI	9.14	AND VITAL
RATIO	104.837	15-19	1.29	9.31	26.47	* 5-29	1.15	29.02	23.72	5.30	K1	0.	STATISTICS
											K2	0.	(Females)

ORIGINAL MATRIX SUB-DIAGONAL	ALTERNATIVE FIRST ROWS Projection	Integral	FIRST STABLE MATRIX % IN STABLE POPULATION	FISHER VALUES	REPRODUCTIVE VALUES	SECOND STABLE MATRIX Z₂ FIRST COLUMN	FIRST ROW	
0.90188	0.00000	0.00000	11.842	1.244	286706	0.1344+0.0400	0.1344+0.0400	**TABLE 9**
0.95442	0.00000	0.00000	10.291	1.431	275054	0.1116-0.0823	0.0495+0.1329	LESLIE
0.97310	0.00476	0.00000	9.464	1.556	278392	0.0015-0.1451	-0.0729+0.1142	MATRIX
0.97197	0.08058	0.00996	8.874	1.654	282126	-0.1227-0.0945	-0.1272+0.0097	AND ITS
0.96786	0.25899	0.15866	8.311	1.663	266300	-0.1592+0.0437	-0.0903-0.0931	SPECTRAL
0.96106	0.40967	0.38128	7.750	1.450	219158	-0.0646+0.1629	-0.0171-0.1314	COMPO-NENTS
0.95218	0.43335	0.47177	7.177	1.036	153086	0.0960+0.1577	0.0325-0.1051	(Females)
0.94344	0.32614	0.43181	6.585	0.563	68778	0.1919+0.0191	0.0380-0.0539	
0.93540	0.13941	0.24663	5.986	0.189	19744	0.1353-0.1466	0.0172-0.0159	
0.92116	0.01996	0.03999	5.395	0.024	2109	-0.0365-0.2013	0.0025-0.0019	
0.89633	0.00037	0.00074	4.789	0.000	36	-0.1846-0.0930	0.0000-0.0000	
0.72069			13.536					

OBSERVED POPUL. (IN 100's)	CONTRIBUTIONS OF ROOTS (IN 100's) r₁	r₂, r₃	r₄·r₁₁	AGE-SP. BIRTH RATES	NET MATERNITY FUNCTION	COEFF. OF MATRIX EQUATION	PARAMETERS	INTEGRAL	MATRIX	EXP. INCREASE x	e^{(x+8½)r}	
2305	2276	4	25	0.0000	0.0000	0.0000	L(1)	1.03779	1.03781	0	1.0187	**TABLE 10**
1922	1978	-28	-28	0.0000	0.0000	0.0000	L(2)	0.55158	0.54900	50	1.4762	AGE
1789	1819	-39	9	0.0000	0.0000	0.0041		0.74256	0.72814	55	1.5320	ANALYSIS
1706	1706	-19	19	0.0024	0.0082	0.0675	R(1)	0.00742	0.00742	60	1.5898	AND
1601	1597	20	-16	0.0381	0.1268	0.2109	R(2)	-0.01559	-0.01844	65	1.6499	MISCEL-
1511	1490	47	-25	0.0914	0.2949	0.3228		0.18638	0.18495	70	1.7123	LANEOUS
1478	1379	37	61	0.1131	0.3507	0.3282	C(1)		19220	75	1.7770	RESULTS
1222	1266	-5	-38	0.1036	0.3056	0.2352	C(2)		-2623	80	1.8441	(Females)
1045	1151	-46	-60	0.0592	0.1647	0.0948			-13384	85	1.9138	
867	1037	-52	-118	0.0096	0.0250	0.0127	2P/Y	33.7111	33.9721	90	1.9861	
820	920	-15	-85	0.0002	0.0004	0.0002	DELTA	2.1511		95	2.0612	
2435	2602									100	2.1391	

TABLE 1 — DATA

AGE AT LAST BIRTHDAY	POPULATION BOTH SEXES	MALES Number	%	FEMALES Number	%	BIRTHS BY AGE OF MOTHER	DEATHS BOTH SEXES	MALES	FEMALES	AGE AT LAST BIRTHDAY
0	118656	60210	3.2	58446	3.0	0	17889	9849	8040	0
1-4	388464	195335	10.5	193129	9.8	0	11546	5993	5553	1-4
5-9	403848	202936	10.9	200912	10.2	0	3750	1920	1830	5-9
10-14	369153	184903	10.0	184250	9.4	0	1730	889	841	10-14
15-19	351246	175256	9.4	175990	9.0	1001	1671	863	808	15-19
20-24	312548	154062	8.3	158486	8.1	13581	1943	1091	852	20-24
25-29	304254	149409	8.0	154845	7.9	30500	2055	1099	956	25-29
30-34	284489	138418	7.5	146071	7.4	35549	2210	1140	1070	30-34
35-39	278140	135578	7.3	142562	7.3	31700	2544	1303	1241	35-39
40-44	226590	109442	5.9	117148	6.0	15952	2483	1299	1184	40-44
45-49	187607	88729	4.8	98878	5.0	2123	2481	1351	1130	45-49
50-54	149629	69415	3.7	80214	4.1	0	2631	1428	1203	50-54
55-59	135654	61603	3.3	74051	3.8	0	3150	1641	1509	55-59
60-64	115352	51266	2.8	64086	3.3	0	3899	1914	1985	60-64
65-69	91460	39290	2.1	52170	2.7	0	4421	2056	2365	65-69
70-74	56788	23101	1.2	33687	1.7		4250	1840	2410	70-74
75-79	30867	11929	0.6	18938	1.0		3594	1479	2115	75-79
80-84	14241	5074	0.3	9167	0.5	66668 M.	2454	941	1513	80-84
85+	4746	1487	0.1	3259	0.2	63738 F.	1275	430	845	85+
TOTAL	3823732	1857443		1966289		130406	75976	38526	37450	TOTAL

TABLE 2 — MALE LIFE TABLE

x	$_nq_x$	l_x	$_nd_x$	$_nL_x$	$_nm_x$	$_na_x$	T_x	r_x	$\mathring{e}_x$	$_nM_x$
0	0.148088	100000	14809	90876	0.162955	0.3839	4307206	0.0065	43.072	0.163577
1	0.113010	85191	9627	314674	0.030595	1.2899	4216330	0.0065	49.493	0.030681
5	0.045781	75564	3459	369171	0.009371	2.5000	3901656	0.0193	51.634	0.009461
10	0.023689	72104	1708	355888	0.004800	2.2872	3532486	0.0087	48.991	0.004808
15	0.024361	70396	1715	347837	0.004930	2.5831	3176597	0.0130	45.124	0.004924
20	0.034829	68681	2392	337568	0.007086	2.5592	2828760	0.0093	41.187	0.007082
25	0.036122	66289	2395	325499	0.007356	2.5163	2491192	0.0032	37.581	0.007356
30	0.040365	63895	2579	313128	0.008237	2.5394	2165693	0.0014	33.895	0.008236
35	0.047001	61316	2882	299541	0.009621	2.5579	1852565	0.0137	30.214	0.009611
40	0.057850	58434	3380	283963	0.011904	2.5724	1553025	0.0303	26.578	0.011869
45	0.073675	55053	4056	265465	0.015279	2.5834	1269062	0.0299	23.051	0.015226
50	0.098132	50997	5004	242830	0.020609	2.5707	1003597	0.0159	19.679	0.020572
55	0.125131	45993	5755	215973	0.026647	2.5689	760768	0.0027	16.541	0.026638
60	0.171659	40238	6907	184338	0.037470	2.5603	544795	0.0263	13.539	0.037335
65	0.232673	33331	7755	147603	0.052541	2.5436	360457	0.0263	10.815	0.052329
70	0.333507	25575	8530	106612	0.080006	2.5069	212854	0.0263	8.323	0.079650
75	0.471472	17046	8037	64528	0.124544	2.4242	106242	0.0263	6.233	0.123984
80	0.622130	9009	5605	30069	0.186403	2.3278	41714	0.0263	4.630	0.185456
85+	*1.000000	3404	3404	11645	0.292340	3.4207	11645	0.0263	3.421	0.289173

TABLE 3 — FEMALE LIFE TABLE

x	$_nq_x$	l_x	$_nd_x$	$_nL_x$	$_nm_x$	$_na_x$	T_x	r_x	$\mathring{e}_x$	$_nM_x$
0	0.126587	100000	12659	92347	0.137077	0.3955	4654263	0.0061	46.543	0.137563
1	0.106545	87341	9306	324424	0.028684	1.3198	4561916	0.0061	52.231	0.028753
5	0.044135	78036	3444	381568	0.009026	2.5000	4237492	0.0188	54.302	0.009108
10	0.022507	74591	1679	368388	0.004557	2.2781	3855925	0.0076	51.694	0.004564
15	0.022707	72913	1656	360469	0.004593	2.5267	3487537	0.0104	47.832	0.004591
20	0.026542	71257	1891	351652	0.005378	2.5500	3127069	0.0074	43.884	0.005376
25	0.030414	69366	2110	341665	0.006175	2.5522	2775417	0.0019	40.011	0.006174
30	0.035984	67256	2420	330367	0.007326	2.5564	2433752	0.0009	36.186	0.007325
35	0.042653	64836	2765	317400	0.008713	2.5486	2103385	0.0134	32.442	0.008705
40	0.049378	62071	3065	302799	0.010122	2.5355	1785985	0.0265	28.773	0.010107
45	0.055714	59006	3287	287012	0.011454	2.5617	1483186	0.0260	25.136	0.011428
50	0.072486	55718	4039	268855	0.015022	2.5895	1196174	0.0137	21.468	0.014997
55	0.097177	51679	5022	246405	0.020381	2.6123	927319	0.0011	17.944	0.020378
60	0.144561	46657	6745	217081	0.031070	2.5974	680913	0.0192	14.594	0.030974
65	0.204815	39913	8175	179737	0.045481	2.5747	463832	0.0192	11.621	0.045333
70	0.304882	31738	9676	134797	0.071784	2.5309	284095	0.0192	8.951	0.071541
75	0.435572	22062	9609	85766	0.112043	2.4460	149298	0.0192	6.767	0.111680
80	0.577179	12452	7187	43388	0.165648	2.3741	63533	0.0192	5.102	0.165048
85+	*1.000000	5265	5265	20145	0.261360	3.8261	20145	0.0192	3.826	0.259282

TABLE 4 — OBSERVED AND PROJECTED VITAL RATES

	OBSERVED POPULATION BOTH SEXES	MALES	FEMALES	PROJECTED POPULATION 1865 MALES	FEMALES	1870 MALES	FEMALES	1875 MALES	FEMALES	STABLE POPULATION MALES	FEMALES
RATES PER THOUSAND											
Birth	34.10	35.89	32.42	34.48	31.39	33.18	30.39	32.37	29.79	32.69	30.
Death	19.87	20.74	19.05	21.00	19.28	20.91	19.17	20.83	19.07	21.27	19.
Increase	14.23	15.15	13.37	13.48	12.10	12.27	11.22	11.54	10.72	11.41	
PERCENTAGE											
under 15	33.48	34.64	32.38	35.22	33.12	35.55	33.62	34.94	33.18	34.06	32.
15-64	61.34	61.01	61.66	60.22	60.80	59.87	60.35	60.59	60.98	60.79	60.
65 and over	5.18	4.35	5.96	4.56	6.08	4.58	6.03	4.47	5.83	5.15	6.
DEP. RATIO X 100	63.02	63.91	62.19	66.06	64.47	67.03	65.69	65.03	63.98	64.49	64.

TABLE 1

AGE AT LAST BIRTHDAY	POPULATION BOTH SEXES	MALES Number	%	FEMALES Number	%	BIRTHS BY AGE OF MOTHER	DEATHS BOTH SEXES	MALES	FEMALES	AGE AT LAST BIRTHDAY
0	121553	61536	3.1	60017	2.9	0	17995	9901	8094	0
1-4	421623	212595	10.7	209028	10.0	0	12328	6455	5873	1-4
5-9	455144	228736	11.5	226408	10.8	0	4073	2129	1944	5-9
10-14	393836	197603	9.9	196233	9.3	0	1673	869	804	10-14
15-19	361147	180435	9.1	180712	8.6	1202	1685	896	789	15-19
20-24	341717	169455	8.5	172262	8.2	15299	2058	1163	895	20-24
25-29	300635	146617	7.4	154018	7.3	30548	2032	1100	932	25-29
30-34	292266	142641	7.2	149625	7.1	35794	2193	1144	1049	30-34
35-39	275175	133166	6.7	142009	6.8	30675	2476	1289	1187	35-39
40-44	265650	128836	6.5	136814	6.5	18205	2783	1483	1300	40-44
45-49	216430	103578	5.2	112852	5.4	2354	2738	1520	1218	45-49
50-54	175159	81760	4.1	93399	4.4	0	2882	1553	1329	50-54
55-59	134406	61254	3.1	73152	3.5	0	3187	1641	1546	55-59
60-64	117211	52140	2.6	65071	3.1	0	3903	1942	1961	60-64
65-69	95865	41548	2.1	54317	2.6	0	4706	2216	2490	65-69
70-74	68453	28366	1.4	40087	1.9		5133	2345	2788	70-74
75-79	35452	13965	0.7	21487	1.0		4261	1812	2449	75-79
80-84	14907	5381	0.3	9526	0.5	68673 M.	2819	1123	1696	80-84
85+	5472	1716	0.1	3756	0.2	65404 F.	1700	578	1122	85+
TOTAL	4092101	1591328		2100773		134077	80625	41159	39466	TOTAL

TABLE 2 — MALE

x	$_nq_x$	l_x	$_nd_x$	$_nL_x$	$_nm_x$	$_na_x$	T_x	r_x	$\mathring{e}_x$	$_nM_x$	x
0	0.146371	100000	14637	90991	0.160863	0.3845	4334733	0.0004	43.347	0.160898	0
1	0.112206	85363	9578	315508	0.030358	1.2915	4243742	0.0004	49.714	0.030363	1
5	0.045031	75785	3413	370392	0.009214	2.5000	3928234	0.0199	51.834	0.009308	5
10	0.021647	72372	1567	357595	0.004381	2.2774	3557842	0.0180	49.160	0.004398	10
15	0.024561	70805	1739	349839	0.004971	2.5919	3200248	0.0102	45.198	0.004966	15
20	0.033788	69066	2334	339647	0.006871	2.5642	2850409	0.0142	41.271	0.006863	20
25	0.036838	66733	2458	327558	0.007505	2.5164	2510762	0.0097	37.624	0.007503	25
30	0.039327	64274	2528	315149	0.008021	2.5380	2183204	0.0014	33.967	0.008020	30
35	0.047281	61747	2919	301595	0.009680	2.5549	1868055	0.0005	30.254	0.009680	35
40	0.056050	58827	3297	286107	0.011524	2.5649	1566460	0.0133	26.628	0.011511	40
45	0.071073	55530	3947	268076	0.014722	2.5742	1280353	0.0306	23.057	0.014675	45
50	0.091176	51583	4703	246568	0.019074	2.5870	1012277	0.0328	19.624	0.018995	50
55	0.126086	46880	5911	220103	0.026855	2.5812	765709	0.0177	16.333	0.026790	55
60	0.171038	40969	7007	187768	0.037319	2.5629	545606	0.0139	13.317	0.037246	60
65	0.236318	33962	8026	150141	0.053455	2.5493	357837	0.0139	10.536	0.053336	65
70	0.343387	25936	8906	107471	0.082870	2.5063	207697	0.0139	8.008	0.082669	70
75	0.487131	17030	8296	63773	0.130084	2.4232	100225	0.0139	5.885	0.129753	75
80	0.669368	8734	5846	27928	0.209336	2.3073	36452	0.0139	4.174	0.208698	80
85+	*1.000000	2888	2888	8524	0.338781	2.9518	8524	0.0139	2.952	0.336830	85+

TABLE 3 — FEMALE

x	$_nq_x$	l_x	$_nd_x$	$_nL_x$	$_nm_x$	$_na_x$	T_x	r_x	$\mathring{e}_x$	$_nM_x$	x
0	0.124619	100000	12462	92464	0.134775	0.3953	4717695	0.0011	47.177	0.134862	0
1	0.104472	87538	9145	325637	0.028084	1.3193	4625231	0.0011	52.837	0.028097	1
5	0.041617	78393	3262	383808	0.008500	2.5000	4299594	0.0197	54.847	0.008586	5
10	0.020184	75130	1516	371512	0.004082	2.2703	3915786	0.0173	52.120	0.004097	10
15	0.021608	73614	1591	364162	0.004368	2.5435	3544274	0.0087	48.147	0.004366	15
20	0.025671	72023	1849	355599	0.005199	2.5566	3180112	0.0108	44.154	0.005196	20
25	0.029829	70174	2093	345742	0.006054	2.5495	2824513	0.0080	40.250	0.006051	25
30	0.034465	68081	2346	334664	0.007011	2.5532	2478771	0.0010	36.409	0.007011	30
35	0.040954	65735	2692	322064	0.008359	2.5451	2144106	0.0006	32.618	0.008359	35
40	0.046455	63043	2929	307991	0.009509	2.5339	1822042	0.0135	28.902	0.009502	40
45	0.052707	60114	3168	292858	0.010819	2.5661	1514051	0.0270	25.186	0.010793	45
50	0.069089	56946	3934	275345	0.014289	2.6152	1221193	0.0284	21.445	0.014229	50
55	0.100800	53011	5344	252275	0.021181	2.6082	945848	0.0147	17.842	0.021134	55
60	0.140742	47668	6709	222216	0.030191	2.5969	693573	0.0112	14.550	0.030136	60
65	0.206607	40959	8462	184254	0.045928	2.5727	471357	0.0112	11.508	0.045842	65
70	0.297369	32496	9663	138666	0.069668	2.5355	287103	0.0112	8.835	0.069549	70
75	0.442645	22833	10107	88493	0.114212	2.4600	148436	0.0112	6.501	0.113976	75
80	0.606695	12726	7721	43265	0.178453	2.3623	59943	0.0112	4.710	0.178038	80
85+	*1.000000	5005	5005	16678	0.300114	3.3321	16678	0.0112	3.332	0.298722	85+

TABLE 4 — OBSERVED AND PROJECTED

	OBSERVED POPULATION BOTH SEXES	MALES	FEMALES	PROJECTED POPULATION 1870 MALES	FEMALES	1875 MALES	FEMALES	1880 MALES	FEMALES	STABLE POPULATION MALES	FEMALES
RATES PER THOUSAND											
Birth	32.76	34.49	31.13	33.17	30.14	32.38	29.57	32.22	29.54	32.60	30.38
Death	19.70	20.67	18.79	20.53	18.65	20.42	18.56	20.44	18.56	21.06	18.83
Increase	13.06	13.82	12.35	12.64	11.48	11.96	11.01	11.77	10.98	11.5470	
PERCENTAGE											
under 15	34.02	35.18	32.93	35.43	33.34	34.99	33.07	34.24	32.46	34.05	32.81
15-64	60.60	60.26	60.93	60.05	60.62	60.65	61.14	61.29	61.67	60.88	61.01
65 and over	5.38	4.57	6.15	4.52	6.04	4.36	5.80	4.48	5.87	5.06	6.18
DEP. RATIO X 100	65.02	65.96	64.13	66.53	64.96	64.89	63.57	63.17	62.16	64.25	63.92

TABLE 1 — DATA

AGE AT LAST BIRTHDAY	POPULATION BOTH SEXES	MALES Number	MALES %	FEMALES Number	FEMALES %	BIRTHS BY AGE OF MOTHER	DEATHS BOTH SEXES	MALES	FEMALES	AGE AT L. BIRTH
0	105355	53455	2.7	51900	2.4	0	16615	9166	7449	0
1-4	392700	197974	9.8	194726	9.1	0	10729	5571	5158	1-
5-9	483845	242731	12.0	241114	11.2	0	3887	2009	1878	5-
10-14	434692	217713	10.8	216979	10.1	0	1751	887	864	10-
15-19	375613	187798	9.3	187815	8.7	1094	1730	884	846	15-
20-24	329080	161272	8.0	167808	7.8	13723	2085	1150	935	20-
25-29	307641	148039	7.3	159602	7.4	28669	2139	1108	1031	25-
30-34	275714	131564	6.5	144150	6.7	31835	2200	1137	1063	30-
35-39	270403	129933	6.4	140470	6.5	28347	2469	1281	1188	35-
40-44	253750	121234	6.0	132516	6.2	15394	2836	1489	1347	40-
45-49	243690	116388	5.8	127302	5.9	2296	3213	1769	1444	45-
50-54	196186	92096	4.6	104090	4.8	0	3381	1860	1521	50-
55-59	155487	71116	3.5	84371	3.9	0	3635	1926	1709	55-
60-64	114652	51181	2.5	63471	3.0	0	4044	2055	1989	60-
65-69	93685	40529	2.0	53156	2.5	0	4842	2331	2511	65-
70-74	68337	28638	1.4	39699	1.8		5464	2544	2920	70-
75-79	41237	16168	0.8	25069	1.2		4974	2190	2784	75-
80-84	16134	6061	0.3	10073	0.5	62249 M.	3048	1211	1837	80-
85+	5440	1702	0.1	3738	0.2	59109 F.	1734	571	1163	85
TOTAL	4163641	2015592		2148049		121358	80776	41139	39637	TOT

TABLE 2 — MALE LIFE TABLE

x	$_nq_x$	l_x	$_nd_x$	$_nL_x$	$_nm_x$	$_na_x$	T_x	r_x	$\mathring{e}_x$	$_nM_x$
0	0.154781	100000	15478	90266	0.171471	0.3711	4311453	0.0000	43.115	0.171471
1	0.104505	84522	8833	313894	0.028140	1.2610	4221187	0.0000	49.942	0.028140
5	0.040490	75689	3065	370783	0.008265	2.5000	3907293	0.0026	51.623	0.008277
10	0.020072	72624	1458	359185	0.004058	2.2995	3536510	0.0204	48.696	0.004074
15	0.023353	71167	1662	351882	0.004723	2.6230	3177325	0.0250	44.646	0.004707
20	0.035095	69505	2439	341592	0.007141	2.5686	2825442	0.0171	40.651	0.007131
25	0.036761	67065	2465	329225	0.007488	2.5249	2483850	0.0127	37.036	0.007485
30	0.042321	64600	2734	316272	0.008644	2.5391	2154625	0.0044	33.353	0.008642
35	0.048134	61866	2978	302047	0.009859	2.5544	1838353	0.0000	29.715	0.009859
40	0.059627	58888	3511	285889	0.012282	2.5644	1536306	0.0000	26.089	0.012282
45	0.073383	55377	4064	267026	0.015218	2.5741	1250417	0.0119	22.580	0.015199
50	0.096590	51313	4956	244561	0.020266	2.5779	983391	0.0287	19.164	0.020196
55	0.127629	46357	5916	217504	0.027202	2.5864	738830	0.0304	15.938	0.027083
60	0.183213	40440	7409	184183	0.040227	2.5680	521326	0.0125	12.891	0.040152
65	0.252361	33031	8336	144644	0.057629	2.5394	337143	0.0125	10.207	0.057514
70	0.363796	24695	8984	100922	0.089020	2.4894	192499	0.0125	7.795	0.088833
75	0.501492	15711	7879	58046	0.135738	2.3969	91577	0.0125	5.829	0.135453
80	0.649122	7832	5084	25382	0.200302	2.2897	33531	0.0125	4.281	0.199803
85+	*1.000000	2748	2748	8149	0.337238	2.9653	8149	0.0125	2.965	0.335488

TABLE 3 — FEMALE LIFE TABLE

x	$_nq_x$	l_x	$_nd_x$	$_nL_x$	$_nm_x$	$_na_x$	T_x	r_x	$\mathring{e}_x$	$_nM_x$
0	0.131867	100000	13187	91877	0.143526	0.3840	4687094	0.0000	46.871	0.143526
1	0.098858	86813	8582	323997	0.026488	1.2902	4595217	0.0000	52.932	0.026488
5	0.038167	78231	2986	383691	0.007782	2.5000	4271220	0.0017	54.597	0.007789
10	0.019630	75245	1477	372255	0.003968	2.3110	3887529	0.0199	51.665	0.003982
15	0.022312	73768	1646	364832	0.004511	2.5642	3515275	0.0212	47.653	0.004504
20	0.027507	72122	1984	355774	0.005576	2.5615	3150443	0.0108	43.682	0.005572
25	0.031811	70138	2231	345213	0.006463	2.5445	2794669	0.0087	39.845	0.006460
30	0.036225	67907	2460	333487	0.007376	2.5407	2449456	0.0054	36.071	0.007374
35	0.041428	65447	2711	320594	0.008457	2.5500	2115969	0.0000	32.331	0.008457
40	0.049584	62736	3111	306024	0.010165	2.5390	1795375	0.0000	28.618	0.010165
45	0.055239	59625	3294	290075	0.011354	2.5555	1489351	0.0124	24.979	0.011343
50	0.070802	56332	3988	272059	0.014660	2.5933	1199276	0.0261	21.290	0.014612
55	0.097044	52343	5080	249624	0.020349	2.6194	927216	0.0281	17.714	0.020256
60	0.145993	47264	6900	219794	0.031394	2.6053	677592	0.0106	14.336	0.031337
65	0.212243	40364	8567	181026	0.047324	2.5731	457798	0.0106	11.342	0.047238
70	0.311486	31797	9904	134414	0.073684	2.5194	276772	0.0106	8.704	0.073553
75	0.433382	21892	9488	85275	0.111261	2.4507	142357	0.0106	6.503	0.111054
80	0.617308	12405	7657	41892	0.182791	2.3710	57083	0.0106	4.602	0.182368
85+	*1.000000	4747	4747	15191	0.312499	3.2000	15191	0.0106	3.200	0.311129

TABLE 4 — OBSERVED AND PROJECTED VITAL RATES

	OBSERVED POPULATION BOTH SEXES	MALES	FEMALES	PROJECTED POPULATION 1875 MALES	FEMALES	1880 MALES	FEMALES	1885 MALES	FEMALES	STABLE POPULATION MALES	FEM
RATES PER THOUSAND											
Birth	29.15	30.88	27.52	30.33	27.20	30.53	27.53	31.28	28.34	30.13	28.
Death	19.40	20.41	18.45	20.26	18.34	20.34	18.47	20.59	18.70	21.51	19.
Increase	9.75	10.47	9.06	10.08	8.86	10.19	9.06	10.69	9.65		8.62
PERCENTAGE											
under 15	34.02	35.32	32.81	34.04	31.69	32.58	30.38	32.36	30.29	32.11	30.
15-64	60.58	60.06	61.06	61.52	62.39	62.88	63.57	62.81	63.35	62.44	62.
65 and over	5.40	4.62	6.13	4.43	5.92	4.54	6.05	4.83	6.36	5.45	6.
DEP. RATIO X 100	65.08	66.49	63.77	62.54	60.29	59.03	57.31	59.21	57.86	60.16	60.

TABLE 1

AGE AT LAST BIRTHDAY	POPULATION BOTH SEXES	MALES Number	%	FEMALES Number	%	BIRTHS BY AGE OF MOTHER	DEATHS BOTH SEXES	MALES	FEMALES	AGE AT LAST BIRTHDAY
0	119957	60935	2.9	59022	2.6	0	18637	10275	8362	0
1-4	420589	213126	10.1	207463	9.2	0	11330	5866	5464	1-4
5-9	458842	231349	10.9	227493	10.1	0	4087	2096	1991	5-9
10-14	469168	235597	11.1	233571	10.4	1	1995	992	1003	10-14
15-19	424650	213112	10.1	211538	9.4	1751	1973	1003	970	15-19
20-24	353196	175340	8.3	177856	7.9	17865	2398	1344	1054	20-24
25-29	302286	145481	6.9	156805	7.0	32718	2343	1202	1141	25-29
30-34	285432	135178	6.4	150254	6.7	33529	2335	1188	1147	30-34
35-39	259566	122856	5.8	136710	6.1	29492	2487	1254	1233	35-39
40-44	254341	121227	5.7	133114	5.9	17297	2697	1445	1252	40-44
45-49	237774	112455	5.3	125299	5.6	2381	2876	1609	1267	45-49
50-54	225960	106673	5.0	119287	5.3	10	3458	1892	1566	50-54
55-59	178159	82499	3.9	95660	4.3	0	3703	1982	1721	55-59
60-64	136430	61389	2.9	75041	3.3	0	4054	2050	2004	60-64
65-69	94784	41643	2.0	53141	2.4	0	4403	2138	2265	65-69
70-74	70679	29875	1.4	40804	1.8		4903	2275	2628	70-74
75-79	43332	17548	0.8	25784	1.1		4779	2120	2659	75-79
80-84	20678	7650	0.4	13028	0.6	69272 M.	3445	1406	2039	80-84
85+	6602	2035	0.1	4567	0.2	65772 F.	1944	671	1273	85+
TOTAL	4362425	2115988		2246437		135044	83847	42808	41039	TOTAL

TABLE 2 (MALE)

x	nq_x	l_x	nd_x	nL_x	nm_x	na_x	T_x	r_x	$\mathring{e}_x$	nM_x	x
0	0.152449	100000	15245	90409	0.168622	0.3709	4364013	0.0000	43.640	0.168622	0
1	0.102375	84755	8677	315249	0.027524	1.2604	4273604	0.0000	50.423	0.027524	1
5	0.044235	76078	3365	371978	0.009047	2.5000	3958355	0.0030	52.030	0.009060	5
10	0.020801	72713	1512	359429	0.004208	2.2655	3586377	0.0027	49.322	0.004211	10
15	0.023358	71200	1663	352076	0.004724	2.6393	3226948	0.0244	45.322	0.004706	15
20	0.037741	69537	2624	341344	0.007688	2.5831	2874872	0.0310	41.343	0.007665	20
25	0.040498	66913	2710	327819	0.008266	2.5106	2533528	0.0177	37.863	0.008262	25
30	0.043022	64203	2762	314183	0.008792	2.5263	2205709	0.0079	34.355	0.008788	30
35	0.049788	61441	3059	299686	0.010207	2.5421	1891527	0.0007	30.786	0.010207	35
40	0.057905	58382	3381	283612	0.011920	2.5457	1591841	0.0000	27.266	0.011920	40
45	0.069108	55001	3801	265708	0.014305	2.5536	1308228	0.0000	23.785	0.014305	45
50	0.085138	51200	4359	245424	0.017762	2.5735	1042521	0.0127	20.362	0.017736	50
55	0.113959	46841	5338	221293	0.024122	2.5809	797097	0.0307	17.017	0.024025	55
60	0.154999	41503	6433	191993	0.033506	2.5870	575805	0.0212	13.874	0.033394	60
65	0.228816	35070	8025	155758	0.051520	2.5584	383811	0.0212	10.944	0.051341	65
70	0.321055	27046	8683	113618	0.076424	2.5113	228053	0.0212	8.432	0.076151	70
75	0.462555	18362	8494	70042	0.121265	2.4368	114435	0.0212	6.232	0.120811	75
80	0.618935	9869	6108	33088	0.184605	2.3386	44393	0.0212	4.498	0.183791	80
85+	*1.000000	3761	3761	11305	0.332645	3.0062	11305	0.0212	3.006	0.329730	85+

TABLE 3 (FEMALE)

x	nq_x	l_x	nd_x	nL_x	nm_x	na_x	T_x	r_x	$\mathring{e}_x$	nM_x	x
0	0.130287	100000	13029	91985	0.141639	0.3848	4722288	0.0004	47.223	0.141676	0
1	0.098319	86971	8551	324731	0.026332	1.2922	4630303	0.0004	53.239	0.026337	1
5	0.042793	78420	3356	383712	0.008746	2.5000	4305573	0.0016	54.904	0.008752	5
10	0.021215	75065	1593	370990	0.004293	2.2793	3921860	0.0018	52.246	0.004294	10
15	0.022711	73472	1669	363295	0.004593	2.5636	3550870	0.0225	48.330	0.004585	15
20	0.029277	71803	2102	353933	0.005940	2.5816	3187575	0.0240	44.393	0.005926	20
25	0.035759	69701	2492	342362	0.007280	2.5348	2833642	0.0098	40.654	0.007277	25
30	0.037472	67209	2518	329823	0.007636	2.5299	2491280	0.0058	37.068	0.007634	30
35	0.044116	64690	2854	316384	0.009020	2.5236	2161457	0.0033	33.412	0.009019	35
40	0.045949	61836	2841	302091	0.009405	2.5042	1845073	0.0000	29.838	0.009405	40
45	0.049339	58995	2911	287851	0.010112	2.5525	1542982	0.0004	26.154	0.010112	45
50	0.063734	56084	3575	271826	0.013150	2.5954	1255130	0.0136	22.379	0.013128	50
55	0.086598	52510	4547	251695	0.018066	2.6130	983304	0.0276	18.726	0.017991	55
60	0.125945	47963	6041	225457	0.026793	2.6234	731609	0.0181	15.254	0.026705	60
65	0.193791	41922	8124	190004	0.042757	2.5867	506152	0.0181	12.074	0.042622	65
70	0.278768	33798	9422	145825	0.064610	2.5414	316149	0.0181	9.354	0.064405	70
75	0.409999	24376	9994	96604	0.103455	2.4709	170324	0.0181	6.987	0.103126	75
80	0.558043	14382	8026	51087	0.157098	2.4056	73720	0.0181	5.126	0.156510	80
85+	*1.000000	6356	6356	22632	0.280846	3.5607	22632	0.0181	3.561	0.278739	85+

TABLE 4 (OBSERVED, PROJECTED)

	OBSERVED POPULATION BOTH SEXES	MALES	FEMALES	PROJECTED POPULATION 1880 MALES	FEMALES	1885 MALES	FEMALES	1890 MALES	FEMALES	STABLE POPULATION MALES	FEMALES
RATES PER THOUSAND											
Birth	30.96	32.74	29.28	32.54	29.30	33.11	30.00	33.42	30.45	32.27	30.25
Death	19.22	20.23	18.27	20.40	18.50	20.60	18.73	20.82	19.01	20.93	18.92
Increase	11.74	12.51	11.01	12.15	10.80	12.51	11.27	12.60	11.44	11.3335	
PERCENTAGE											
under 15	33.66	35.02	32.39	33.96	31.51	34.17	31.86	34.31	32.20	33.82	32.66
15-64	60.92	60.31	61.50	61.17	62.15	60.61	61.42	60.02	60.57	60.73	60.65
65 and over	5.41	4.67	6.11	4.87	6.34	5.22	6.71	5.68	7.23	5.44	6.69
DEP. RATIO X 100	64.14	65.80	62.60	63.48	60.90	64.99	62.80	66.61	65.09	64.66	64.89

TABLE 1 — DATA

AGE AT LAST BIRTHDAY	POPULATION BOTH SEXES	MALES Number	MALES %	FEMALES Number	FEMALES %	BIRTHS BY AGE OF MOTHER	DEATHS BOTH SEXES	DEATHS MALES	DEATHS FEMALES	AGE AT LAST BIRTHDAY
0	124044	62933	2.8	61111	2.6	0	16291	9021	7270	0
1-4	441326	223391	10.1	217935	9.3	0	11416	5893	5523	1-
5-9	484981	245334	11.0	239647	10.2	0	4512	2280	2232	5-
10-14	442830	223321	10.1	219509	9.3	1	2031	984	1047	10-
15-19	453549	228036	10.3	225513	9.6	2171	2041	1011	1030	15-
20-24	395162	195926	8.8	199236	8.5	20286	2292	1276	1016	20-
25-29	327559	159821	7.2	167738	7.1	33564	2105	1081	1024	25-
30-34	287187	137202	6.2	149985	6.4	33772	2001	985	1016	30-
35-39	273223	129269	5.8	143954	6.1	27898	2094	1036	1058	35-
40-44	247375	116782	5.3	130593	5.6	14885	2243	1135	1108	40-
45-49	240886	114079	5.1	126807	5.4	2310	2515	1339	1176	45-
50-54	222819	104449	4.7	118370	5.0	88	2969	1584	1385	50-
55-59	207515	96778	4.4	110737	4.7	0	3688	1960	1728	55-
60-64	158423	72479	3.3	85944	3.7	0	4146	2080	2066	60-
65-69	114800	50809	2.3	63991	2.7	0	4564	2225	2339	65-
70-74	72388	30966	1.4	41422	1.8		4720	2212	2508	70-
75-79	46769	19123	0.9	27646	1.2		4710	2101	2609	75-
80-84	22647	8534	0.4	14113	0.6	69225 M.	3599	1497	2102	80-
85+	8802	2817	0.1	5985	0.3	65750 F.	2366	831	1535	85
TOTAL	4572285	2222049		2350236		134975	80303	40531	39772	TO

TABLE 2 — MALE LIFE TABLE

x	$_nq_x$	l_x	$_nd_x$	$_nL_x$	$_nm_x$	$_na_x$	T_x	r_x	$\mathring{e}_x$	$_nM_x$
0	0.131709	100000	13171	91884	0.143343	0.3838	4657834	0.0000	46.578	0.143343
1	0.098478	86829	8551	324141	0.026380	1.2896	4565951	0.0000	52.585	0.026380
5	0.045165	78278	3535	382553	0.009242	2.5000	4241810	0.0129	54.189	0.009293
10	0.021759	74743	1626	369247	0.004404	2.2527	3859257	0.0017	51.634	0.004406
15	0.021950	73111	1605	361710	0.004437	2.5871	3490010	0.0083	47.732	0.004434
20	0.032125	71512	2297	351960	0.006527	2.5633	3128300	0.0295	43.745	0.006513
25	0.033277	69214	2303	340327	0.006768	2.5058	2776339	0.0288	40.112	0.006764
30	0.035286	66911	2361	328702	0.007183	2.5207	2436013	0.0140	36.407	0.007179
35	0.039319	64550	2538	316527	0.008018	2.5479	2107311	0.0079	32.646	0.008014
40	0.047479	62012	2944	302873	0.009721	2.5589	1790784	0.0028	28.878	0.009719
45	0.057060	59068	3370	287148	0.011737	2.5699	1487911	0.0000	25.190	0.011737
50	0.073154	55697	4074	268639	0.015167	2.5830	1200763	0.0010	21.559	0.015165
55	0.096750	51623	4995	246089	0.020296	2.5923	932124	0.0157	18.056	0.020253
60	0.134819	46628	6286	218058	0.028829	2.6005	686035	0.0281	14.713	0.028698
65	0.199012	40342	8029	182382	0.044020	2.5926	467976	0.0281	11.600	0.043791
70	0.304992	32313	9855	137273	0.071794	2.5349	285594	0.0281	8.838	0.071433
75	0.430924	22458	9678	87649	0.110415	2.4538	148322	0.0281	6.604	0.109868
80	0.603047	12780	7707	43675	0.176468	2.3755	60673	0.0281	4.747	0.175417
85+	*1.000000	5073	5073	16998	0.298454	3.3506	16998	0.0281	3.351	0.294995

TABLE 3 — FEMALE LIFE TABLE

x	$_nq_x$	l_x	$_nd_x$	$_nL_x$	$_nm_x$	$_na_x$	T_x	r_x	$\mathring{e}_x$	$_nM_x$
0	0.111016	100000	11102	93323	0.118959	0.3985	4952647	0.0001	49.526	0.118964
1	0.094939	88898	8440	333045	0.025342	1.3283	4859324	0.0001	54.662	0.025342
5	0.045290	80458	3644	393182	0.009268	2.5000	4526279	0.0123	56.256	0.009314
10	0.023542	76815	1808	379145	0.004770	2.2753	4133096	0.0002	53.806	0.004770
15	0.022581	75006	1694	370805	0.004568	2.5050	3753951	0.0051	50.049	0.004567
20	0.025221	73312	1849	362035	0.005107	2.5516	3383146	0.0244	46.147	0.005099
25	0.030111	71463	2152	352034	0.006113	2.5446	3021111	0.0224	42.275	0.006105
30	0.033322	69312	2310	340840	0.006776	2.5241	2669077	0.0085	38.508	0.006774
35	0.036104	67002	2419	329040	0.007352	2.5322	2328238	0.0064	34.749	0.007350
40	0.041559	64583	2684	316285	0.008486	2.5301	1999197	0.0043	30.955	0.008484
45	0.045340	61899	2807	302620	0.009274	2.5504	1682912	0.0002	27.188	0.009274
50	0.056906	59092	3363	287346	0.011703	2.5865	1380292	0.0017	23.358	0.011701
55	0.075413	55730	4203	268666	0.015643	2.6249	1092946	0.0155	19.612	0.015605
60	0.114154	51527	5882	243659	0.024140	2.6240	824280	0.0241	15.997	0.024039
65	0.168804	45645	7705	209830	0.036720	2.6126	580621	0.0241	12.720	0.036552
70	0.264814	37940	10047	165200	0.060817	2.5615	370791	0.0241	9.773	0.060548
75	0.382638	27893	10673	112616	0.094772	2.4844	205591	0.0241	7.371	0.094372
80	0.537145	17220	9250	61846	0.149559	2.4391	92975	0.0241	5.399	0.148941
85+	1.000000	7970	7970	31129	0.256046	3.9055	31129	0.0241	3.906	0.256474

TABLE 4 — OBSERVED AND PROJECTED VITAL RATES

	OBSERVED POPULATION BOTH SEXES	MALES	FEMALES	PROJECTED POPULATION 1885 MALES	1885 FEMALES	1890 MALES	1890 FEMALES	1895 MALES	1895 FEMALES	STABLE POPULATION MALES	FEM
RATES PER THOUSAND											
Birth	29.52	31.15	27.98	31.59	28.61	31.90	29.12	31.77	29.21	30.31	28
Death	17.56	18.24	16.92	18.43	17.18	18.74	17.53	18.95	17.81	19.25	17
Increase	11.96	12.91	11.05	13.16	11.43	13.16	11.60	12.81	11.40		11.0
PERCENTAGE											
under 15	32.66	33.98	31.41	33.74	31.39	33.74	31.62	33.73	31.83	32.69	31
15-64	61.54	60.97	62.07	60.71	61.58	60.12	60.69	59.96	60.24	60.96	60
65 and over	5.80	5.05	6.52	5.55	7.04	6.14	7.68	6.30	7.93	6.34	7
DEP. RATIO X 100	62.50	64.01	61.10	64.71	62.40	66.33	64.77	66.77	66.01	64.03	64

TABLE 5 — POPULATION PROJECTED WITH FIXED AGE—SPECIFIC BIRTH AND DEATH RATES (IN 1000's)

AGE AT LAST BIRTHDAY	1885 BOTH SEXES	MALES	FEMALES	1890 BOTH SEXES	MALES	FEMALES	1895 BOTH SEXES	MALES	FEMALES	AGE AT LAST BIRTHDAY
0-4	592	300	292	639	324	315	683	346	337	0-4
5-9	520	263	257	545	276	269	589	298	291	5-9
10-14	468	237	231	502	254	248	525	266	259	10-14
15-19	434	219	215	458	232	226	492	249	243	15-19
20-24	442	222	220	423	213	210	447	226	221	20-24
25-29	383	189	194	429	215	214	410	206	204	25-29
30-34	316	154	162	371	183	188	414	207	207	30-34
35-39	277	132	145	306	149	157	357	176	181	35-39
40-44	262	124	138	265	126	139	293	142	151	40-44
45-49	236	111	125	249	117	132	253	120	133	45-49
50-54	227	107	120	223	104	119	236	110	126	50-54
55-59	207	96	111	211	98	113	206	95	111	55-59
60-64	186	86	100	185	85	100	189	87	102	60-64
65-69	135	61	74	158	72	86	157	71	86	65-69
70-74	88	38	50	104	46	58	122	54	68	70-74
75-79	48	20	28	58	24	34	69	29	40	75-79
80-84	25	10	15	26	10	16	31	12	19	80-84
85+	10	3	7	12	4	8	12	4	8	85+
TOTAL	4856	2372	2484	5164	2532	2632	5485	2698	2787	TOTAL

TABLE 6 — STANDARDIZED RATES

STANDARD COUNTRIES:

STANDARDIZED RATES PER THOUSAND	ENGLAND AND WALES 1961 BOTH SEXES	MALES	FEMALES	UNITED STATES 1960 BOTH SEXES	MALES	FEMALES	MEXICO 1960 BOTH SEXES	MALES	FEMALES
Birth	28.09	29.95*	26.52	28.47	27.31*	27.32	27.19	28.09*	26.42
Death	21.74	29.74*	22.28	20.34	24.94*	19.60	16.95	17.17*	15.90
Increase	6.35	0.21*	4.24	8.13	2.38*	7.72	10.24	10.92*	10.52

TABLE 7 — MOMENTS AND CUMULANTS

OBSERVED POP. MALES	FEMALES	STATIONARY POP. MALES	FEMALES	STABLE POP. MALES	FEMALES	OBSERVED BIRTHS	NET MATERNITY FUNCTION	BIRTHS IN STABLE POP.
27.67774	29.45251	33.75045	34.87825	28.72535	29.57352	31.91830	32.47236	31.99245
410.9620	440.7988	477.0982	503.0635	428.7238	452.7992	42.75314	41.49587	41.13225
5093.593	4981.079	3402.534	3414.415	5167.856	5475.920	41.8111	26.1500	39.5315
-100134.	-134368.	-206511.	-238424.	-109193.	-129379.	-1343.049	-1230.425	-1175.788
0.373804	0.289685	0.106606	0.091572	0.338913	0.322996	0.022371	0.009570	0.022456
2.407106	2.308464	2.092747	2.057883	2.405927	2.368965	2.265223	2.285429	2.305033
-0.139204	-0.108332	-0.040226	-0.034093	-0.130476	-0.122642	-0.011218	-0.005031	-0.011846

TABLE 8 — RATES FROM AGE DISTRIBUTIONS AND VITAL STATISTICS (Females)

VITAL STATISTICS

		THOMPSON AGE RANGE	NRR	1000r	INTERVAL	BOURGEOIS-PICHAT AGE RANGE	NRR	1000b	1000d	1000r	COALE	
	2.103										IBR	29.45
	1.428	0-4	1.33	10.75	27.09	5-29	1.34	28.94	18.08	10.86	IDR	17.82
	4.317	5-9	1.33	10.63	26.98	30-54	1.10	20.94	17.44	3.50	IRI	11.63
ERATION	32.232	10-14	1.33	10.59	26.92	55-79	2.42	115.98	83.25	32.73	K1	0.
RATIO	105.285	15-19	1.44	12.94	26.82	*30-54	1.10	20.94	17.44	3.50	K2	0.

TABLE 9 — LESLIE MATRIX AND ITS SPECTRAL COMPONENTS (Females)

ORIGINAL MATRIX SUB-DIAGONAL	ALTERNATIVE FIRST ROWS Projection	Integral	FIRST STABLE MATRIX % IN STABLE POPULATION	FISHER VALUES	REPRODUCTIVE VALUES	SECOND STABLE MATRIX Z₂ FIRST COLUMN	FIRST ROW
0.92217	0.00000	0.00000	11.957	1.205	336219	0.1335+0.0463	0.1335+0.0463
0.96430	0.00000	0.00000	10.433	1.381	330934	0.1176-0.0816	0.0408+0.1334
0.97800	0.00978	0.00001	9.519	1.514	332231	0.0037-0.1516	-0.0790+0.1053
0.97635	0.11323	0.02056	8.808	1.624	366134	-0.1292-0.0992	-0.1239-0.0021
0.97237	0.30779	0.21740	8.137	1.618	322317	-0.1676+0.0492	-0.0820-0.0998
0.96820	0.43419	0.42724	7.486	1.377	230974	-0.0631+0.1756	-0.0121-0.1318
0.96538	0.42812	0.48077	6.858	0.963	144405	0.1112+0.1643	0.0336-0.1030
0.96124	0.31503	0.41379	6.264	0.520	74818	0.2103+0.0074	0.0379-0.0522
0.95679	0.13647	0.24337	5.697	0.177	23059	0.1372-0.1747	0.0174-0.0154
0.94953	0.01965	0.03890	5.157	0.023	2941	-0.0633-0.2247	0.0025-0.0019
0.93499	0.00077	0.00159	4.634	0.001	104	-0.2282-0.0849	0.0001-0.0001
0.76905			15.051				

TABLE 10 — AGE ANALYSIS AND MISCELLANEOUS RESULTS (Females)

OBSERVED POPUL. (IN 100's)	CONTRIBUTIONS OF ROOTS (IN 100's) r₁	r₂,r₃	r₄-r₁₁	AGE-SP. BIRTH RATES	NET MATERNITY FUNCTION	COEFF. OF MATRIX EQUATION	PARAMETERS INTEGRAL	MATRIX	EXP. INCREASE x	e^{(x+2½)r}
2790	2813	-71	48	0.0000	0.0000	0.0000	L(1) 1.05683	1.05690	0	1.0280
2396	2455	-37	-21	0.0000	0.0000	0.0000	L(2) 0.53851	0.53675	50	1.7868
2195	2240	30	-75	0.0000	0.0000	0.0087	0.75051	0.73532	55	1.8883
2255	2072	80	103	0.0047	0.0174	0.0985	R(1) 0.01106	0.01107	60	1.9956
1992	1914	67	11	0.0496	0.1796	0.2614	R(2) -0.01587	-0.01878	65	2.1090
1677	1761	-8	-76	0.0975	0.3431	0.3585	0.18968	0.18805	70	2.2289
1500	1614	-85	-28	0.1097	0.3739	0.3422	C(1)	23528	75	2.3556
1440	1474	-98	64	0.0944	0.3106	0.2431	C(2)	-22955	80	2.4895
1306	1340	-26	-8	0.0555	0.1756	0.1012		10463	85	2.6309
1268	1213	76	-21	0.0089	0.0269	0.0139	2P/Y 33.1249	33.4123	90	2.7805
1184	1090	123	-29	0.0004	0.0010	0.0005	DELTA 2.5199		95	2.9385
3498	3541								100	3.1055

TABLE 1 — DATA

AGE AT LAST BIRTHDAY	POPULATION BOTH SEXES	MALES Number	%	FEMALES Number	%	BIRTHS BY AGE OF MOTHER	DEATHS BOTH SEXES	MALES	FEMALES
0	126261	64326	2.8	61935	2.6	0	15365	8603	6762
1-4	442020	224160	9.9	217860	9.1	0	10304	5357	4947
5-9	503826	254353	11.2	249473	10.4	0	4068	2084	1984
10-14	458477	231754	10.2	226723	9.4	1	1871	920	951
15-19	420423	212286	9.4	208137	8.7	2226	1927	978	949
20-24	403584	199806	8.8	203778	8.5	21487	2377	1295	1082
25-29	344185	165971	7.3	178214	7.4	35496	2174	1111	1063
30-34	294639	140725	6.2	153914	6.4	34153	1994	960	1034
35-39	267089	126488	5.6	140601	5.9	27298	2030	967	1063
40-44	256228	120598	5.3	135630	5.7	14922	2222	1135	1087
45-49	231553	108409	4.8	123144	5.1	2022	2391	1270	1121
50-54	223721	104909	4.6	118812	5.0	190	2864	1544	1320
55-59	203389	94255	4.2	109134	4.5	0	3518	1851	1667
60-64	184149	84731	3.7	99418	4.1	0	4565	2304	2261
65-69	133058	59968	2.6	73090	3.0	0	5095	2491	2604
70-74	88441	38232	1.7	50209	2.1		5303	2466	2837
75-79	47789	19656	0.9	28133	1.2		4868	2168	2700
80-84	24803	9509	0.4	15294	0.6	70758 M.	3879	1651	2228
85+	9974	3264	0.1	6710	0.3	67037 F.	2707	966	1741
TOTAL	4663609	2263400		2400209		137795	79522	40121	39401

TABLE 2 — MALE LIFE TABLE

x	nq_x	l_x	nd_x	nL_x	nm_x	na_x	T_x	r_x	$\dot{e}_x$	nM_x
0	0.123372	100000	12337	92375	0.133555	0.3820	4808321	0.0023	48.083	0.133741
1	0.089686	87663	7862	329308	0.023875	1.2853	4715946	0.0023	53.796	0.023898
5	0.039950	79801	3188	391033	0.008153	2.5000	4386638	0.0112	54.970	0.008193
10	0.019589	76613	1501	379004	0.003960	2.2953	3995605	0.0129	52.153	0.003970
15	0.022809	75112	1713	371452	0.004612	2.6026	3616601	0.0100	48.150	0.004607
20	0.031941	73399	2344	361263	0.006489	2.5557	3245149	0.0185	44.213	0.006481
25	0.032928	71054	2340	349416	0.006696	2.4966	2883886	0.0284	40.587	0.006694
30	0.033559	68715	2306	337840	0.006826	2.5139	2534473	0.0202	36.884	0.006822
35	0.037543	66409	2493	325942	0.007649	2.5531	2196633	0.0076	33.078	0.007645
40	0.046029	63915	2942	312426	0.009416	2.5694	1870690	0.0059	29.268	0.009411
45	0.056963	60973	3473	296423	0.011717	2.5686	1558264	0.0021	25.556	0.011715
50	0.071055	57500	4086	277607	0.014718	2.5783	1261841	0.0000	21.945	0.014718
55	0.093766	53415	5008	254993	0.019642	2.5881	984234	0.0013	18.426	0.019638
60	0.128163	48406	6204	227144	0.027313	2.6005	729241	0.0278	15.065	0.027192
65	0.189614	42202	8002	191708	0.041741	2.5877	502097	0.0278	11.897	0.041539
70	0.279918	34200	9573	147623	0.064849	2.5580	310389	0.0278	9.076	0.064501
75	0.433214	24627	10669	96209	0.110891	2.4762	162766	0.0278	6.609	0.110297
80	0.598650	13958	8356	47845	0.174648	2.3737	66557	0.0278	4.768	0.173626
85+	*1.000000	5602	5602	18712	0.299389	3.3401	18712	0.0278	3.340	0.295956

TABLE 3 — FEMALE LIFE TABLE

x	nq_x	l_x	nd_x	nL_x	nm_x	na_x	T_x	r_x	$\dot{e}_x$	nM_x
0	0.102295	100000	10229	93836	0.109015	0.3974	5113156	0.0025	51.132	0.109179
1	0.085550	89771	7680	338539	0.022685	1.3251	5019320	0.0025	55.913	0.022707
5	0.038816	82091	3186	402487	0.007917	2.5000	4680781	0.0108	57.020	0.007953
10	0.020693	78904	1633	390138	0.004185	2.3158	4278294	0.0129	54.221	0.004195
15	0.022552	77271	1743	382073	0.004561	2.5416	3888156	0.0061	50.318	0.004559
20	0.026221	75529	1980	372781	0.005313	2.5443	3506082	0.0102	46.420	0.005310
25	0.029423	73548	2164	362411	0.005971	2.5366	3133302	0.0221	42.602	0.005965
30	0.033070	71384	2361	351103	0.006724	2.5351	2770891	0.0170	38.817	0.006718
35	0.037113	69024	2562	338766	0.007562	2.5204	2419788	0.0052	35.057	0.007560
40	0.039300	66462	2612	325839	0.008016	2.5225	2081022	0.0051	31.311	0.008014
45	0.044535	63850	2844	312285	0.009106	2.5505	1755183	0.0040	27.489	0.009103
50	0.054104	61006	3301	297074	0.011111	2.5890	1442899	0.0006	23.652	0.011110
55	0.073716	57706	4254	278412	0.015279	2.6219	1145825	0.0020	19.856	0.015275
60	0.108330	53452	5790	253533	0.022839	2.6296	867412	0.0237	16.228	0.022742
65	0.164823	47661	7856	219530	0.035784	2.6099	613880	0.0237	12.880	0.035627
70	0.249541	39806	9933	174975	0.056769	2.5785	394349	0.0237	9.907	0.056504
75	0.388265	29872	11598	120323	0.096394	2.4963	219374	0.0237	7.344	0.095973
80	0.532154	18274	9725	66423	0.146403	2.4347	99051	0.0237	5.420	0.145678
85+	*1.000000	8549	8549	32628	0.262031	3.8163	32628	0.0237	3.816	0.259463

TABLE 4 — OBSERVED AND PROJECTED VITAL RATES

	OBSERVED POPULATION BOTH SEXES	MALES	FEMALES	PROJECTED POPULATION 1890 MALES	FEMALES	1895 MALES	FEMALES	1900 MALES	FEMALES	STABLE POPULATION MALES	FEMALES
RATES PER THOUSAND											
Birth	29.55	31.26	27.93	31.32	28.25	31.33	28.50	31.19	28.60	30.13	28.
Death	17.05	17.73	16.42	18.01	16.77	18.24	17.06	18.36	17.29	18.27	16.
Increase	12.50	13.54	11.51	13.31	11.48	13.10	11.45	12.83	11.31		11.85
PERCENTAGE											
under 15	32.82	34.22	31.50	34.01	31.57	33.91	31.70	33.97	32.01	32.96	32.
15-64	60.66	60.01	61.28	59.54	60.49	59.42	60.08	59.40	59.74	60.66	60.
65 and over	6.52	5.77	7.23	6.45	7.94	6.67	8.23	6.63	8.25	6.38	7.
DEP. RATIO X 100	64.85	66.65	63.19	67.97	65.32	68.30	66.45	68.34	67.39	64.86	65.

TABLE 1 / A

AGE AT LAST BIRTHDAY	POPULATION BOTH SEXES	MALES Number	MALES %	FEMALES Number	FEMALES %	BIRTHS BY AGE OF MOTHER	DEATHS BOTH SEXES	DEATHS MALES	DEATHS FEMALES	AGE AT LAST BIRTHDAY
0	121578	61756	2.7	59822	2.4	0	14087	7887	6200	0
1-4	464107	234853	10.1	229254	9.3	0	8894	4588	4306	1-4
5-9	520507	263625	11.4	256882	10.4	0	3351	1694	1657	5-9
10-14	484848	244870	10.6	239978	9.7	1	1772	870	902	10-14
15-19	429103	217031	9.4	212072	8.6	2255	1962	978	984	15-19
20-24	356486	174358	7.5	182128	7.4	19346	2166	1159	1007	20-24
25-29	352160	170190	7.3	181970	7.4	34889	2243	1111	1132	25-29
30-34	314346	148745	6.4	165601	6.7	34567	2079	993	1086	30-34
35-39	276181	130895	5.7	145286	5.9	26447	2070	988	1082	35-39
40-44	251916	118566	5.1	133350	5.4	13850	2176	1071	1105	40-44
45-49	241713	112913	4.9	128800	5.2	1938	2422	1251	1171	45-49
50-54	217018	100715	4.3	116303	4.7	157	2757	1446	1311	50-54
55-59	206579	96090	4.1	110489	4.5	0	3575	1883	1692	55-59
60-64	182320	83607	3.6	98713	4.0	0	4524	2285	2239	60-64
65-69	157698	71732	3.1	85966	3.5	0	5986	2899	3087	65-69
70-74	104843	46640	2.0	58203	2.4		6476	3035	3441	70-74
75-79	60800	25599	1.1	35201	1.4		6013	2716	3297	75-79
80-84	25956	10175	0.4	15781	0.6	68351 M.	4331	1854	2477	80-84
85+	11536	3918	0.2	7618	0.3	65099 F.	3171	1136	2035	85+
TOTAL	4779695	2316278		2463417		133450	80055	39844	40211	TOTAL

TABLE 2 / MALE / FEMALE

x	$_nq_x$	l_x	$_nd_x$	$_nL_x$	$_nm_x$	$_na_x$	T_x	r_x	$\mathring{e}_x$	$_nM_x$	x
0	0.118175	100000	11817	92532	0.127712	0.3680	4978265	0.0000	49.783	0.127712	0
1	0.074165	88183	6540	334775	0.019536	1.2545	4885733	0.0000	55.405	0.019536	1
5	0.031476	81643	2570	401788	0.006396	2.5000	4550958	0.0105	55.743	0.006426	5
10	0.017570	79073	1389	391717	0.003547	2.3754	4149170	0.0150	52.473	0.003553	10
15	0.022385	77683	1739	384298	0.004525	2.6315	3757453	0.0292	48.369	0.004506	15
20	0.032742	75944	2487	373635	0.006655	2.5519	3373155	0.0182	44.416	0.006647	20
25	0.032113	73458	2359	361361	0.006528	2.4867	2999520	0.0093	40.833	0.006528	25
30	0.032855	71099	2336	349695	0.006680	2.5171	2638159	0.0194	37.105	0.006676	30
35	0.037090	68763	2550	337562	0.007555	2.5483	2288464	0.0150	33.280	0.007548	35
40	0.044211	66213	2927	323925	0.009037	2.5616	1950902	0.0057	29.464	0.009033	40
45	0.053973	63285	3416	308143	0.011085	2.5749	1626977	0.0050	25.709	0.011079	45
50	0.069398	59870	4155	289335	0.014360	2.5901	1318834	0.0014	22.028	0.014357	50
55	0.093569	55715	5213	266029	0.019596	2.5936	1029499	0.0000	18.478	0.019596	55
60	0.128640	50502	6497	236875	0.027426	2.5937	763470	0.0231	15.118	0.027330	60
65	0.184845	44005	8134	200442	0.040581	2.5925	526595	0.0231	11.967	0.040414	65
70	0.281769	35871	10107	154647	0.065357	2.5555	326153	0.0231	9.092	0.065073	70
75	0.420206	25764	10826	101574	0.106582	2.4835	171505	0.0231	6.657	0.106098	75
80	0.619140	14938	9248	50497	0.183150	2.3843	69931	0.0231	4.682	0.182210	80
85+	*1.000000	5689	5689	19435	0.292730	3.4161	19435	0.0231	3.416	0.289944	85+

TABLE 3 / MALE / FEMALE

x	$_nq_x$	l_x	$_nd_x$	$_nL_x$	$_nm_x$	$_na_x$	T_x	r_x	$\mathring{e}_x$	$_nM_x$	x
0	0.097437	100000	9744	94014	0.103641	0.3857	5243945	0.0000	52.439	0.103641	0
1	0.071497	90256	6453	343565	0.018783	1.2943	5149931	0.0000	57.059	0.018783	1
5	0.031609	83803	2649	412394	0.006423	2.5000	4806366	0.0101	57.353	0.006450	5
10	0.018583	81154	1508	401831	0.003753	2.3869	4393972	0.0146	54.143	0.003759	10
15	0.022983	79646	1830	393783	0.004648	2.5701	3992141	0.0230	50.123	0.004640	15
20	0.027291	77816	2124	383871	0.005532	2.5479	3598358	0.0098	46.242	0.005529	20
25	0.030635	75692	2319	372714	0.006222	2.5220	3214487	0.0034	42.468	0.006221	25
30	0.032285	73373	2369	361002	0.006562	2.5246	2841772	0.0158	38.730	0.006558	30
35	0.036590	71004	2598	348612	0.007452	2.5328	2480771	0.0142	34.938	0.007447	35
40	0.040606	68406	2778	335154	0.008288	2.5241	2132159	0.0038	31.169	0.008286	40
45	0.044479	65629	2919	320984	0.009094	2.5474	1797005	0.0043	27.381	0.009092	45
50	0.054892	62710	3442	305246	0.011277	2.5883	1476021	0.0038	23.537	0.011272	50
55	0.073880	59267	4379	285908	0.015315	2.6183	1170775	0.0005	19.754	0.015314	55
60	0.108011	54889	5929	260403	0.022767	2.6318	884867	0.0208	16.121	0.022682	60
65	0.166027	48960	8129	225449	0.036056	2.6194	624465	0.0208	12.755	0.035910	65
70	0.259304	40831	10588	178392	0.059351	2.5665	399016	0.0208	9.772	0.059121	70
75	0.380592	30244	11510	122413	0.094030	2.4975	220624	0.0208	7.295	0.093662	75
80	0.557943	18733	10452	66328	0.157579	2.4356	98211	0.0208	5.243	0.156961	80
85+	1.000000	8281	8281	31882	0.259741	3.8500	31882	0.0208	3.850	0.267131	85+

TABLE 4 / OBSERVED / PROJECTED / RATES

	OBSERVED POPULATION BOTH SEXES	MALES	FEMALES	PROJECTED POPULATION 1895 MALES	1895 FEMALES	1900 MALES	1900 FEMALES	1905 MALES	1905 FEMALES	STABLE POPULATION MALES	FEMALES
RATES PER THOUSAND											
Birth	27.92	29.51	26.43	29.33	26.53	29.48	26.92	29.72	27.36	28.79	27.57
Death	16.75	17.20	16.32	17.20	16.42	17.34	16.64	17.31	16.69	17.37	16.15
Increase	11.17	12.31	10.10	12.12	10.11	12.15	10.28	12.40	10.67	11.4158	
PERCENTAGE											
under 15	33.29	34.76	31.90	33.98	31.49	33.42	31.28	33.00	31.16	32.36	31.77
15-64	59.16	58.42	59.86	58.97	60.01	59.55	60.19	60.31	60.58	61.05	60.77
65 and over	7.55	6.82	8.23	7.05	8.50	7.03	8.53	6.68	8.26	6.60	7.46
DEP. RATIO X 100	69.02	71.18	67.04	69.58	66.63	67.92	66.14	65.81	65.07	63.81	64.54

490   Sweden 1893–97

TABLE 1 — DATA

AGE AT LAST BIRTHDAY	POPULATION BOTH SEXES	MALES Number	MALES %	FEMALES Number	FEMALES %	BIRTHS BY AGE OF MOTHER	DEATHS BOTH SEXES	DEATHS MALES	DEATHS FEMALES	AGE AT LAST BIRTHDAY
0	124099	63251	2.7	60848	2.4	0	13270	7397	5873	0
1-4	450598	228578	9.6	222020	8.8	0	7485	3840	3645	1-
5-9	538419	271876	11.4	266543	10.6	0	3253	1628	1625	5-
10-14	500444	253369	10.7	247075	9.8	1	1800	881	919	10-
15-19	460012	233543	9.8	226469	9.0	2813	2094	1044	1050	15-
20-24	373374	185201	7.8	188173	7.5	20513	2285	1219	1066	20
25-29	318734	154326	6.5	164408	6.5	31702	1980	1002	978	25-
30-34	323422	153791	6.5	169631	6.7	34814	2117	1012	1105	30-
35-39	296807	139333	5.9	157474	6.3	27526	2158	1031	1127	35-
40-44	262378	123921	5.2	138457	5.5	13846	2121	1057	1064	40-
45-49	238884	111831	4.7	127053	5.0	1723	2219	1152	1067	45-
50-54	227286	105490	4.4	121796	4.8	71	2683	1412	1271	50-
55-59	200757	92402	3.9	108355	4.3	0	3223	1693	1530	55-
60-64	185749	85520	3.6	100229	4.0	0	4243	2164	2079	60-
65-69	155793	70535	3.0	85258	3.4	0	5454	2699	2755	65-
70-74	124208	55588	2.3	68620	2.7		6799	3287	3512	70-
75-79	70805	30839	1.3	39966	1.6		6546	3033	3513	75-
80-84	32526	13194	0.6	19332	0.8	68376 M.	4826	2094	2732	80-
85+	11926	4124	0.2	7802	0.3	64633 F.	3177	1200	1977	85
TOTAL	4896221	2376712		2519509		133009	77733	38845	38888	TOT

TABLE 2 — MALE LIFE TABLE

x	nq_x	l_x	nd_x	nL_x	nm_x	na_x	T_x	r_x	$\dot{e}_x$	nM_x
0	0.108752	100000	10875	93072	0.116848	0.3629	5151430	0.0013	51.514	0.116947
1	0.064185	89125	5720	340735	0.016789	1.2442	5058358	0.0013	56.756	0.016800
5	0.029426	83404	2454	410886	0.005973	2.5000	4717624	0.0063	56.563	0.005988
10	0.017212	80950	1393	401124	0.003474	2.3971	4306738	0.0109	53.202	0.003477
15	0.022201	79557	1766	393604	0.004487	2.6335	3905614	0.0267	49.092	0.004470
20	0.032462	77790	2525	382772	0.006597	2.5526	3512010	0.0353	45.147	0.006582
25	0.031942	75265	2404	370281	0.006493	2.4856	3129238	0.0120	41.576	0.006493
30	0.032375	72861	2359	358442	0.006581	2.5141	2758956	0.0035	37.866	0.006580
35	0.036364	70502	2564	346202	0.007405	2.5392	2400515	0.0142	34.049	0.007400
40	0.041814	67939	2841	332738	0.008538	2.5520	2054313	0.0133	30.238	0.008530
45	0.050277	65098	3273	317550	0.010307	2.5745	1721574	0.0056	26.446	0.010301
50	0.064978	61825	4011	299471	0.013394	2.5936	1404024	0.0054	22.710	0.013385
55	0.087770	57814	5074	276862	0.018328	2.5945	1104553	0.0024	19.105	0.018322
60	0.119699	52739	6313	248558	0.025398	2.6020	827691	0.0237	15.694	0.025304
65	0.175840	46427	8164	212476	0.038421	2.5922	579132	0.0237	12.474	0.038265
70	0.259442	38263	9927	167134	0.059395	2.5642	366656	0.0237	9.583	0.059131
75	0.395989	28336	11221	113574	0.098796	2.4952	199522	0.0237	7.041	0.098349
80	0.565026	17115	9671	60613	0.159546	2.4187	85947	0.0237	5.022	0.158709
85+	*1.000000	7445	7445	25335	0.293855	3.4030	25335	0.0237	3.403	0.290980

TABLE 3 — FEMALE LIFE TABLE

x	nq_x	l_x	nd_x	nL_x	nm_x	na_x	T_x	r_x	$\dot{e}_x$	nM_x
0	0.091014	100000	9101	94361	0.096452	0.3805	5408973	0.0011	54.090	0.096519
1	0.062836	90899	5712	348069	0.016410	1.2818	5314612	0.0011	58.467	0.016417
5	0.029962	85187	2552	419554	0.006084	2.5000	4966543	0.0057	58.302	0.006097
10	0.018402	82635	1521	409227	0.003716	2.4056	4546989	0.0118	55.025	0.003720
15	0.022969	81114	1863	401057	0.004646	2.5778	4137762	0.0226	51.012	0.004636
20	0.027971	79251	2217	390794	0.005672	2.5371	3736705	0.0265	47.150	0.005665
25	0.029314	77034	2258	379562	0.005949	2.5166	3345911	0.0043	43.434	0.005949
30	0.032054	74776	2397	367947	0.006514	2.5250	2966348	0.0000	39.670	0.006514
35	0.035175	72379	2546	355580	0.007160	2.5194	2598401	0.0132	35.900	0.007157
40	0.037721	69833	2634	342626	0.007688	2.5174	2242821	0.0138	32.117	0.007685
45	0.041155	67199	2766	329216	0.008400	2.5488	1900195	0.0042	28.277	0.008398
50	0.050926	64433	3281	314258	0.010442	2.5898	1570980	0.0052	24.381	0.010435
55	0.068352	61152	4180	295804	0.014130	2.6182	1256722	0.0049	20.551	0.014120
60	0.099204	56972	5652	271470	0.020820	2.6307	960917	0.0212	16.866	0.020742
65	0.150559	51320	7727	238184	0.032440	2.6164	689447	0.0212	13.434	0.032314
70	0.228698	43594	9970	193970	0.051399	2.5929	451263	0.0212	10.352	0.051180
75	0.362046	33624	12173	137923	0.088262	2.5195	257293	0.0212	7.652	0.087900
80	0.517873	21450	11109	78319	0.141838	2.4657	119370	0.0212	5.565	0.141320
85+	1.000000	10342	10342	41052	0.251923	3.9695	41052	0.0212	3.969	0.253398

TABLE 4 — OBSERVED AND PROJECTED VITAL RATES

	OBSERVED POPULATION BOTH SEXES	MALES	FEMALES	PROJECTED POPULATION 1900 MALES	FEMALES	1905 MALES	FEMALES	1910 MALES	FEMALES	STABLE POPULATION MALES	FEM
RATES PER THOUSAND											
Birth	27.17	28.77	25.65	28.63	25.80	28.98	26.37	29.49	27.08	28.08	27.
Death	15.88	16.34	15.43	16.57	15.79	16.63	15.99	16.56	16.05	16.49	15.
Increase	11.29	12.43	10.22	12.07	10.00	12.35	10.38	12.93	11.03		11.5
PERCENTAGE											
under 15	32.96	34.38	31.61	33.53	31.03	32.95	30.64	32.96	30.89	32.16	31.
15-64	58.97	58.29	59.62	59.02	59.95	59.85	60.47	60.10	60.38	60.87	60.
65 and over	8.07	7.33	8.77	7.45	9.02	7.20	8.89	6.93	8.73	6.97	7.
DEP. RATIO X 100	69.57	71.56	67.74	69.44	66.80	67.07	65.37	66.38	65.62	64.28	65.

AGE AT LAST BIRTHDAY	BOTH SEXES	POPULATION MALES Number	%	FEMALES Number	%	BIRTHS BY AGE OF MOTHER	DEATHS BOTH SEXES	MALES	FEMALES	AGE AT LAST BIRTHDAY
0	125730	63971	2.6	61759	2.4	0	13433	7531	5902	0
1-4	463975	236167	9.5	227808	8.7	0	7318	3814	3504	1-4
5-9	544621	276482	11.1	268139	10.2	0	2905	1466	1439	5-9
10-14	527934	266965	10.7	260969	10.0	1	1912	886	1026	10-14
15-19	481862	245652	9.8	236210	9.0	3623	2359	1176	1183	15-19
20-24	424150	214860	8.6	209290	8.0	24443	2649	1452	1197	20-24
25-29	351122	173509	7.0	177613	6.8	34422	2301	1176	1125	25-29
30-34	305197	146762	5.9	158435	6.0	31472	2002	969	1033	30-34
35-39	310748	146891	5.9	163857	6.3	27484	2247	1090	1157	35-39
40-44	285066	133556	5.3	151510	5.8	13974	2339	1167	1172	40-44
45-49	250629	117813	4.7	132816	5.1	1596	2409	1283	1126	45-49
50-54	226215	105214	4.2	121001	4.6	42	2782	1446	1336	50-54
55-59	211827	97558	3.9	114269	4.4	0	3317	1733	1584	55-59
60-64	182104	82876	3.3	99228	3.8	0	4223	2174	2049	60-64
65-69	161058	73221	2.9	87837	3.4	0	5624	2797	2827	65-69
70-74	124458	55471	2.2	68987	2.6		7041	3351	3690	70-74
75-79	86584	37861	1.5	48723	1.9		7942	3706	4236	75-79
80-84	38921	16237	0.7	22684	0.9	70406 M.	6069	2754	3315	80-84
85+	14721	5376	0.2	9345	0.4	66651 F.	3979	1533	2446	85+
TOTAL	5116922	2496442		2620480		137057	82851	41504	41347	TOTAL

TABLE 1 — A

TABLE 2 — MALE AND FEMALE

x	nq_x	l_x	nd_x	nL_x	nm_x	na_x	T_x	r_x	$\mathring{e}_x$	nM_x	x
0	0.109457	100000	10946	92977	0.117725	0.3584	5152802	0.0000	51.528	0.117725	0
1	0.061838	89054	5507	340993	0.016150	1.2354	5059825	0.0000	56.817	0.016150	1
5	0.026116	83547	2182	412282	0.005292	2.5000	4718832	0.0044	56.481	0.005302	5
10	0.016451	81365	1339	403422	0.003318	2.4559	4306550	0.0077	52.928	0.003319	10
15	0.023727	80027	1899	395651	0.004799	2.6386	3903128	0.0168	48.773	0.004787	15
20	0.033297	78128	2601	384266	0.006770	2.5494	3507477	0.0284	44.894	0.006758	20
25	0.033315	75527	2516	371295	0.006777	2.4810	3123211	0.0314	41.352	0.006778	25
30	0.032484	73011	2372	359136	0.006604	2.5051	2751916	0.0098	37.692	0.006603	30
35	0.036442	70639	2574	346872	0.007421	2.5440	2392781	0.0019	33.873	0.007420	35
40	0.042824	68065	2915	333221	0.008747	2.5633	2045909	0.0132	30.058	0.008738	40
45	0.053111	65150	3460	317347	0.010903	2.5716	1712688	0.0128	26.288	0.010890	45
50	0.066532	61690	4104	298489	0.013750	2.5736	1395342	0.0050	22.619	0.013743	50
55	0.085251	57585	4909	276155	0.017777	2.6022	1096852	0.0052	19.047	0.017764	55
60	0.123639	52676	6513	247762	0.026287	2.6018	820697	0.0133	15.580	0.026232	60
65	0.175269	46163	8091	211325	0.038287	2.5909	572935	0.0133	12.411	0.038199	65
70	0.263832	38072	10045	165865	0.060559	2.5612	361610	0.0133	9.498	0.060410	70
75	0.394028	28028	11044	112527	0.098143	2.4998	195745	0.0133	6.984	0.097884	75
80	0.590807	16984	10034	58981	0.170126	2.4150	83218	0.0133	4.900	0.169613	80
85+	*1.000000	6950	6950	24237	0.286738	3.4875	24237	0.0133	3.488	0.285156	85+

TABLE 3 — MALE AND FEMALE

x	nq_x	l_x	nd_x	nL_x	nm_x	na_x	T_x	r_x	$\mathring{e}_x$	nM_x	x
0	0.090163	100000	9016	94368	0.095544	0.3754	5425679	0.0003	54.257	0.095565	0
1	0.059038	90984	5371	349272	0.015379	1.2702	5331311	0.0003	58.596	0.015381	1
5	0.026447	85612	2264	422401	0.005360	2.5000	4982039	0.0032	58.193	0.005367	5
10	0.019460	83348	1622	412635	0.003931	2.4692	4559639	0.0082	54.706	0.003932	10
15	0.024771	81726	2024	403700	0.005015	2.5646	4147003	0.0172	50.743	0.005008	15
20	0.028230	79702	2250	392965	0.005726	2.5363	3743303	0.0228	46.966	0.005719	20
25	0.031197	77452	2416	381250	0.006338	2.5136	3350339	0.0216	43.257	0.006334	25
30	0.032080	75035	2407	369181	0.006520	2.5090	2969088	0.0015	39.569	0.006520	30
35	0.034698	72628	2520	356894	0.007061	2.5211	2599908	0.0000	35.797	0.007061	35
40	0.037969	70108	2662	343945	0.007739	2.5222	2243013	0.0133	31.994	0.007735	40
45	0.041574	67446	2804	330391	0.008487	2.5606	1899068	0.0136	28.157	0.008478	45
50	0.053790	64642	3477	314790	0.011046	2.5780	1568677	0.0041	24.267	0.011041	50
55	0.067134	61165	4106	296009	0.013872	2.6093	1253887	0.0052	20.500	0.013862	55
60	0.098680	57059	5631	271969	0.020703	2.6333	957878	0.0146	16.788	0.020649	60
65	0.149912	51428	7710	238857	0.032278	2.6284	685909	0.0146	13.337	0.032185	65
70	0.237456	43719	10381	193524	0.053641	2.5850	447052	0.0146	10.226	0.053488	70
75	0.358356	33338	11947	137025	0.087187	2.5170	253529	0.0146	7.605	0.086940	75
80	0.530783	21391	11354	77481	0.146540	2.4650	116504	0.0146	5.446	0.146138	80
85+	1.000000	10037	10037	39023	0.257206	3.8879	39023	0.0146	3.888	0.261745	85+

TABLE 4 — OBSERVED AND PROJECTED AL [RA]TES

RATES PER THOUSAND	OBSERVED POPULATION BOTH SEXES	MALES	FEMALES	PROJECTED POPULATION 1905 MALES	FEMALES	1910 MALES	FEMALES	1915 MALES	FEMALES	STABLE POPULATION MALES	FEMALES
Birth	26.79	28.20	25.43	28.42	25.86	29.01	26.63	29.40	27.22	27.96	26.81
Death	16.19	16.63	15.78	16.66	15.99	16.57	16.03	16.36	15.88	16.48	15.33
Increase	10.59	11.58	9.66	11.76	9.87	12.44	10.60	13.04	11.34		11.4832
PERCENTAGE											
under 15	32.49	33.79	31.24	32.95	30.65	32.72	30.71	32.90	31.17	32.15	31.54
15-64	59.19	58.67	59.69	59.78	60.41	60.27	60.50	60.44	60.37	60.94	60.56
65 and over	8.32	7.54	9.07	7.27	8.94	7.01	8.79	6.66	8.46	6.92	7.90
DEP. RATIO X 100	68.94	70.44	67.53	67.27	65.54	65.92	65.29	65.44	65.65	64.11	65.14

TABLE 1 — DATA

AGE AT LAST BIRTHDAY	POPULATION BOTH SEXES	MALES Number	%	FEMALES Number	%	BIRTHS BY AGE OF MOTHER	DEATHS BOTH SEXES	MALES	FEMALES	AGE AT LAST BIRTHDAY
0	127215	64944	2.5	62271	2.3	0	11470	6463	5007	0
1-4	477194	242386	9.4	234808	8.7	0	5647	2953	2694	1-4
5-9	556430	282861	11.0	273569	10.1	0	2348	1188	1160	5-9
10-14	531697	270124	10.5	261573	9.7	0	1743	811	932	10-14
15-19	499832	253175	9.8	246657	9.1	4107	2402	1202	1200	15-19
20-24	426233	212691	8.3	213542	7.9	25206	2615	1402	1213	20-24
25-29	385084	191384	7.4	193700	7.2	36198	2361	1192	1169	25-29
30-34	330424	161593	6.3	168831	6.2	31778	2027	976	1051	30-34
35-39	289982	137649	5.3	152333	5.6	23447	2007	952	1055	35-39
40-44	296873	139307	5.4	157566	5.8	13252	2296	1142	1154	40-44
45-49	272252	126989	4.9	145263	5.4	1539	2487	1267	1220	45-49
50-54	237538	111105	4.3	126433	4.7	7	2702	1434	1268	50-54
55-59	211176	97688	3.8	113488	4.2	0	3240	1689	1551	55-59
60-64	192598	88118	3.4	104480	3.9	0	4187	2139	2048	60-64
65-69	158685	71419	2.8	87266	3.2	0	5303	2640	2663	65-69
70-74	130032	58232	2.3	71800	2.7		6930	3350	3580	70-74
75-79	87478	38319	1.5	49159	1.8		7705	3578	4127	75-79
80-84	48663	20694	0.8	27969	1.0	69689 M.	6990	3139	3851	80-84
85+	18462	7071	0.3	11391	0.4	65845 F.	4683	1902	2781	85+
TOTAL	5277848	2575749		2702099		135534	79143	39419	39724	TOTAL

TABLE 2 — MALE LIFE TABLE

x	nq_x	l_x	nd_x	nL_x	nm_x	na_x	T_x	r_x	$\mathring{e}_x$	nM_x
0	0.093453	100000	9345	93911	0.099512	0.3484	5427812	0.0001	54.278	0.099517
1	0.047133	90655	4273	350730	0.012183	1.2176	5333901	0.0001	58.838	0.012183
5	0.020725	86382	1790	427434	0.004188	2.5000	4983171	0.0072	57.688	0.004200
10	0.014905	84592	1261	419842	0.003003	2.5284	4555737	0.0074	53.856	0.003002
15	0.023546	83331	1962	412037	0.004762	2.6466	4135895	0.0191	49.632	0.004748
20	0.032465	81369	2642	400333	0.006599	2.5355	3723858	0.0218	45.765	0.006592
25	0.030646	78727	2413	387527	0.006226	2.4681	3323525	0.0212	42.216	0.006228
30	0.029770	76314	2272	375914	0.006044	2.5098	2935999	0.0267	38.472	0.006040
35	0.034021	74043	2519	364041	0.006920	2.5498	2560084	0.0079	34.576	0.006916
40	0.040185	71523	2874	350605	0.008198	2.5601	2196044	0.0000	30.704	0.008198
45	0.048766	68649	3348	335131	0.009989	2.5758	1845439	0.0124	26.882	0.009977
50	0.062677	65302	4093	316637	0.012926	2.5884	1510308	0.0131	23.128	0.012907
55	0.083057	61209	5084	293825	0.017302	2.5965	1193670	0.0055	19.502	0.017290
60	0.114892	56125	6448	265204	0.024314	2.6086	899846	0.0103	16.033	0.024274
65	0.170034	49677	8447	228093	0.037032	2.5979	634642	0.0103	12.775	0.036965
70	0.252715	41230	10419	180775	0.057638	2.5647	406548	0.0103	9.861	0.057528
75	0.379131	30810	11681	124859	0.093555	2.5009	225774	0.0103	7.328	0.093374
80	0.547183	19129	10467	68849	0.152031	2.4399	100914	0.0103	5.275	0.151686
85+	*1.000000	8662	8662	32065	0.270141	3.7018	32065	0.0103	3.702	0.268986

TABLE 3 — FEMALE LIFE TABLE

x	nq_x	l_x	nd_x	nL_x	nm_x	na_x	T_x	r_x	$\mathring{e}_x$	nM_x
0	0.076501	100000	7650	95142	0.080407	0.3650	5676951	0.0000	56.770	0.080407
1	0.044488	92350	4108	358095	0.011473	1.2484	5581808	0.0000	60.442	0.011473
5	0.020931	88241	1847	436590	0.004231	2.5000	5223714	0.0070	59.198	0.004240
10	0.017664	86394	1526	428198	0.003564	2.5268	4787124	0.0063	55.410	0.003563
15	0.024076	84868	2043	419399	0.004872	2.5811	4358927	0.0156	51.361	0.004865
20	0.028031	82825	2322	408394	0.005685	2.5315	3939527	0.0186	47.564	0.005680
25	0.029738	80503	2394	396547	0.006037	2.5064	3531133	0.0175	43.863	0.006035
30	0.030667	78109	2395	384597	0.006228	2.5160	3134586	0.0177	40.131	0.006225
35	0.034043	75714	2578	372175	0.006926	2.5190	2749989	0.0001	36.321	0.006926
40	0.035968	73136	2631	359174	0.007324	2.5258	2377814	0.0000	32.512	0.007324
45	0.041182	70506	2904	345413	0.008406	2.5491	2018640	0.0135	28.631	0.008399
50	0.049032	67602	3315	330007	0.010044	2.5851	1673227	0.0143	24.751	0.010029
55	0.066221	64288	4257	311278	0.013676	2.6134	1343221	0.0050	20.894	0.013667
60	0.093807	60030	5631	286802	0.019635	2.6294	1031943	0.0097	17.190	0.019602
65	0.142531	54399	7754	253606	0.030573	2.6282	745141	0.0097	13.698	0.030516
70	0.223023	46646	10403	208234	0.049959	2.5974	491535	0.0097	10.538	0.049861
75	0.348128	36243	12617	150004	0.084112	2.5264	283301	0.0097	7.817	0.083952
80	0.508089	23625	12004	87031	0.137927	2.4827	133298	0.0097	5.642	0.137688
85+	1.000000	11622	11622	46267	0.251188	3.9811	46267	0.0097	3.981	0.244139

TABLE 4 — OBSERVED AND PROJECTED VITAL RATES

	OBSERVED POPULATION BOTH SEXES	MALES	FEMALES	PROJECTED POPULATION 1910 MALES	FEMALES	1915 MALES	FEMALES	1920 MALES	FEMALES	STABLE POPULATION MALES	FEMALES
RATES PER THOUSAND											
Birth	25.68	27.06	24.37	27.43	24.95	27.93	25.66	28.00	25.96	26.53	25.
Death	15.00	15.30	14.70	15.28	14.82	15.11	14.73	14.94	14.63	15.22	14.
Increase	10.68	11.75	9.67	12.14	10.14	12.81	10.93	13.06	11.33		11.30
PERCENTAGE											
under 15	32.07	33.40	30.80	32.73	30.44	32.54	30.54	32.60	30.83	31.56	31.
15-64	59.53	59.00	60.04	59.83	60.44	60.34	60.60	60.52	60.51	61.09	60.
65 and over	8.40	7.60	9.16	7.44	9.13	7.12	8.86	6.88	8.65	7.35	8.
DEP. RATIO X 100	67.98	69.49	66.56	67.13	65.46	65.72	65.02	65.24	65.26	63.69	64.

AGE LAST BIRTHDAY	1910 BOTH SEXES	1910 MALES	FEMALES	1915 BOTH SEXES	1915 MALES	FEMALES	1920 BOTH SEXES	1920 MALES	FEMALES	AGE AT LAST BIRTHDAY	
0-4	632	322	310	682	347	335	734	374	360	0-4	
5-9	581	295	286	607	309	298	656	334	322	5-9	
10-14	546	278	268	571	290	281	597	304	293	10-14	
15-19	521	265	256	536	273	263	560	285	275	15-19	**TABLE 5**
20-24	486	246	240	507	258	249	521	265	256	20-24	POPULATION
25-29	413	206	207	471	238	233	491	249	242	25-29	PROJECTED
30-34	374	186	188	401	200	201	457	231	226	30-34	WITH
35-39	319	156	163	362	180	182	388	193	195	35-39	FIXED
40-44	280	133	147	309	151	158	348	173	175	40-44	AGE—
45-49	285	133	152	268	127	141	296	144	152	45-49	SPECIFIC
50-54	259	120	139	271	126	145	255	120	135	50-54	BIRTH
55-59	222	103	119	242	111	131	254	117	137	55-59	AND
60-64	193	88	105	203	93	110	221	100	121	60-64	DEATH
65-69	168	76	92	168	76	92	177	80	97	65-69	RATES
70-74	129	57	72	136	60	76	136	60	76	70-74	(IN 1000's)
75-79	92	40	52	91	39	52	96	41	55	75-79	
80-84	50	21	29	52	22	30	52	22	30	80-84	
85+	25	10	15	25	10	15	26	10	16	85+	
TOTAL	5575	2735	2840	5902	2910	2992	6265	3102	3163	TOTAL	

STANDARD COUNTRIES:	ENGLAND AND WALES 1961 BOTH SEXES	MALES	FEMALES	UNITED STATES 1960 BOTH SEXES	MALES	FEMALES	MEXICO 1960 BOTH SEXES	MALES	FEMALES	
STANDARDIZED RATES PER THOUSAND										**TABLE 6**
Birth	24.55	26.28*	23.12	24.92	24.12*	23.85	24.83	24.70*	24.06	STANDARDIZED
Death	17.63	19.16*	18.46	15.82	16.97*	15.49	12.03	13.01*	11.37	RATES
Increase	6.92	7.12*	4.66	9.10	7.15*	8.36	12.80	11.68*	12.70	

	OBSERVED POP. MALES	FEMALES	STATIONARY POP. MALES	FEMALES	STABLE POP. MALES	FEMALES	OBSERVED BIRTHS	NET MATERNITY FUNCTION	BIRTHS IN STABLE POP.	
	28.88429	30.79243	34.98180	35.85165	29.61188	30.25045	30.86443	31.42926	30.92265	**TABLE 7**
	455.6923	485.1877	498.2905	519.1688	447.4565	466.9440	44.01219	42.96391	42.42832	MOMENTS
	6310.602	5811.683	3371.797	3344.152	5410.653	5663.551	67.0592	39.4878	55.0361	AND
	-116062.	-171643.	-232107.	-261524.	-123455.	-142094.	-1447.740	-1416.882	-1317.241	CUMULANTS
	0.420849	0.295716	0.091891	0.079918	0.326774	0.315053	0.052747	0.019661	0.039658	
	2.441086	2.270868	2.065192	2.029726	2.383394	2.348303	2.252614	2.232416	2.268266	
	-0.153915	-0.106842	-0.034407	-0.029422	-0.125049	-0.118603	-0.024863	-0.009516	-0.019420	

VITAL STATISTICS		THOMPSON AGE RANGE	NRR	1000r	INTERVAL	BOURGEOIS-PICHAT AGE RANGE	NRR	1000b	1000d	1000r	COALE		
R	1.842										I BR	27.07	**TABLE 8**
R	1.423	0-4	1.35	11.37	27.07	5-29	1.42	26.28	13.20	13.07	I DR	12.45	RATES FROM AGE DISTRIBUTIONS
R	3.792	5-9	1.38	11.94	27.02	30-54	1.14	19.03	14.13	4.90	I RI	14.62	AND VITAL
GENERATION	31.175	10-14	1.42	12.75	26.97	55-79	1.13	17.55	13.07	4.49	K1	4.96	STATISTICS
X RATIO	105.838	15-19	1.43	12.76	26.90	*15-39	1.63	29.48	11.48	18.00	K2	0.	(Females)

ORIGINAL MATRIX SUB-DIAGONAL	ALTERNATIVE FIRST ROWS Projection	Integral	FIRST STABLE MATRIX % IN STABLE POPULATION	FISHER VALUES	REPRODUCTIVE VALUES	SECOND STABLE MATRIX Z₂ FIRST COLUMN	FIRST ROW	
0.96327	0.00000	0.00000	11.277	1.134	337023	0.1329+0.0533	0.1329+0.0533	**TABLE 9**
0.98078	0.00000	0.00000	10.265	1.246	340952	0.1291-0.0852	0.0296+0.1292	LESLIE
0.97945	0.01795	0.00000	9.514	1.345	351751	0.0039-0.1700	-0.0812+0.0890	MATRIX
0.97376	0.14488	0.03771	8.805	1.432	353247	-0.1510-0.1099	-0.1111-0.0155	AND ITS
0.97099	0.32973	0.26736	8.102	1.388	296314	-0.1926+0.0672	-0.0661-0.0997	SPECTRAL
0.96986	0.40672	0.42329	7.434	1.127	218314	-0.0594+0.2140	-0.0045-0.1201	COMPONENTS
0.96770	0.37121	0.42634	6.813	0.754	127304	0.1545+0.1858	0.0327-0.0886	(Females)
0.96507	0.25882	0.34864	6.230	0.389	59320	0.2612-0.0229	0.0333-0.0422	
0.96169	0.10381	0.19050	5.682	0.123	19343	0.1407-0.2464	0.0139-0.0112	
0.95540	0.01172	0.02400	5.163	0.013	1834	-0.1320-0.2761	0.0016-0.0010	
0.94325	0.00006	0.00013	4.662	0.000	8	-0.3237-0.0524	0.0000-0.0000	
0.78433			16.052					

OBSERVED POPUL. (IN 100's)	CONTRIBUTIONS OF ROOTS (IN 100's) r_1	r_2, r_3	$r_4 \cdot r_{11}$	AGE-SP. BIRTH RATES	NET MATERNITY FUNCTION	COEFF. OF MATRIX EQUATION	PARAMETERS INTEGRAL	MATRIX	EXP. INCREASE x	$e^{(x+2\frac{1}{2})r}$	
2971	3008	-61	24	0.0000	0.0000	0.0000	L(1) 1.05818	1.05825	0	1.0287	**TABLE 10**
2736	2738	11	-13	0.0000	0.0000	0.0000	L(2) 0.50812	0.50809	50	1.8108	AGE
2616	2537	86	-8	0.0000	0.0000	0.0170	0.74893	0.73280	55	1.9161	ANALYSIS
2467	2348	95	24	0.0081	0.0339	0.1341	R(1) 0.01131	0.01132	60	2.0276	AND
2135	2161	14	-40	0.0573	0.2342	0.2971	R(2) -0.01996	-0.02292	65	2.1456	MISCELLANEOUS
1937	1983	-95	49	0.0908	0.3600	0.3559	0.19493	0.19291	70	2.2704	RESULTS
1688	1817	-134	6	0.0914	0.3517	0.3150	C(1)	26671	75	2.4025	(Females)
1523	1662	-54	-84	0.0748	0.2783	0.2125	C(2)	-12601	80	2.5423	
1576	1515	91	-31	0.0409	0.1468	0.0823		25706	85	2.6902	
1453	1377	175	-100	0.0051	0.0178	0.0089	2P/Y 32.2323	32.5706	90	2.8467	
1264	1243	109	-87	0.0000	0.0001	0.0000	DELTA 2.0597		95	3.0123	
4656	4281								100	3.1876	

TABLE 1 — DATA

AGE AT LAST BIRTHDAY	POPULATION BOTH SEXES	MALES Number	MALES %	FEMALES Number	FEMALES %	BIRTHS BY AGE OF MOTHER	DEATHS BOTH SEXES	MALES	FEMALES	AGE AT LAST BIRTHDAY
0	129599	66468	2.5	63131	2.2	0	9044	5126	3918	0
1-4	491307	250456	9.3	240851	8.6	0	5720	3046	2674	1-4
5-9	580674	294887	11.0	285787	10.2	0	1927	985	942	5-9
10-14	547422	278309	10.4	269113	9.6	0	1477	717	760	10-14
15-19	509447	258540	9.6	250907	8.9	4840	2169	1098	1071	15-19
20-24	454494	225370	8.4	229124	8.2	27318	2624	1418	1206	20-24
25-29	400266	197407	7.3	202859	7.2	36056	2324	1178	1146	25-29
30-34	367512	180900	6.7	186612	6.6	32223	2133	1079	1054	30-34
35-39	317117	154069	5.7	163048	5.8	23159	2008	982	1026	35-39
40-44	279022	132033	4.9	146989	5.2	10946	2054	1009	1045	40-44
45-49	284791	133207	5.0	151584	5.4	1421	2447	1268	1179	45-49
50-54	258973	120313	4.5	138660	4.9	7	2824	1464	1360	50-54
55-59	222431	103372	3.8	119059	4.2	0	3284	1708	1576	55-59
60-64	192960	88415	3.3	104545	3.7	0	4068	2087	1981	60-64
65-69	168379	76112	2.8	92267	3.3	0	5408	2669	2739	65-69
70-74	128721	57093	2.1	71628	2.5		6796	3246	3550	70-74
75-79	92931	40831	1.5	52100	1.9		8026	3733	4293	75-79
80-84	49659	21065	0.8	28594	1.0	70014 M.	7152	3171	3981	80-84
85+	23717	9299	0.3	14418	0.5	65956 F.	6119	2535	3584	85+
TOTAL	5499422	2688146		2811276		135970	77604	38519	39085	TOT

TABLE 2 — MALE LIFE TABLE

x	nq_x	l_x	nd_x	nL_x	nm_x	na_x	T_x	r_x	$\mathring{e}_x$	nM_x
0	0.073573	100000	7357	95401	0.077120	0.3749	5634999	0.0000	56.350	0.077120
1	0.047084	92643	4362	358659	0.012162	1.2692	5539598	0.0000	59.795	0.012162
5	0.016499	88281	1457	437762	0.003327	2.5000	5180939	0.0079	58.687	0.003340
10	0.012810	86824	1112	431414	0.002578	2.5658	4743177	0.0100	54.630	0.002576
15	0.021090	85712	1808	424351	0.004260	2.6718	4311763	0.0168	50.305	0.004247
20	0.031019	83904	2603	413136	0.006300	2.5466	3887412	0.0212	46.331	0.006292
25	0.029388	81302	2389	400476	0.005966	2.4753	3474276	0.0159	42.733	0.005967
30	0.029393	78912	2319	388767	0.005966	2.5015	3073800	0.0188	38.952	0.005965
35	0.031418	76593	2406	377045	0.006382	2.5403	2685033	0.0250	35.056	0.006374
40	0.037534	74186	2785	364162	0.007646	2.5685	2307988	0.0068	31.111	0.007642
45	0.046523	71402	3322	348965	0.009519	2.5781	1943826	0.0000	27.224	0.009519
50	0.059196	68080	4030	330696	0.012187	2.5919	1594862	0.0129	23.426	0.012168
55	0.079617	64050	5099	308035	0.016555	2.6047	1264166	0.0138	19.737	0.016523
60	0.111823	58951	6592	278977	0.023629	2.6068	956131	0.0067	16.219	0.023605
65	0.161945	52359	8479	241507	0.035109	2.6076	677154	0.0067	12.933	0.035067
70	0.250065	43879	10973	192753	0.056926	2.5718	435646	0.0067	9.928	0.056855
75	0.372590	32907	12261	133937	0.091541	2.5045	242894	0.0067	7.381	0.091426
80	0.544310	20646	11238	74541	0.150760	2.4471	108957	0.0067	5.277	0.150533
85+	*1.000000	9408	9408	34416	0.273369	3.6581	34416	0.0067	3.658	0.272610

TABLE 3 — FEMALE LIFE TABLE

x	nq_x	l_x	nd_x	nL_x	nm_x	na_x	T_x	r_x	$\mathring{e}_x$	nM_x
0	0.059790	100000	5979	96340	0.062061	0.3879	5895299	0.0000	58.953	0.062061
1	0.043117	94021	4054	365138	0.011102	1.2999	5798958	0.0000	61.677	0.011102
5	0.016295	89967	1466	446171	0.003286	2.5000	5433821	0.0073	60.398	0.003296
10	0.014034	88501	1242	439480	0.002826	2.5638	4987650	0.0098	56.357	0.002824
15	0.021157	87259	1846	431884	0.004275	2.6105	4548170	0.0119	52.123	0.004269
20	0.026004	85413	2221	421610	0.005268	2.5442	4116286	0.0161	48.193	0.005264
25	0.027859	83192	2318	410172	0.005650	2.5029	3694676	0.0150	44.411	0.005649
30	0.027859	80874	2253	398763	0.005650	2.5111	3284504	0.0161	40.612	0.005648
35	0.031008	78621	2438	387096	0.006298	2.5349	2885740	0.0175	36.704	0.006293
40	0.034934	76183	2661	374339	0.007109	2.5288	2498644	0.0002	32.798	0.007109
45	0.038163	73522	2806	360747	0.007778	2.5544	2124305	0.0000	28.894	0.007778
50	0.047986	70716	3393	345414	0.009824	2.5934	1763558	0.0141	24.939	0.009808
55	0.064285	67323	4328	326278	0.013264	2.6120	1418144	0.0146	21.065	0.013237
60	0.090792	62995	5719	301431	0.018974	2.6321	1091866	0.0078	17.333	0.018949
65	0.138899	57275	7955	267575	0.029732	2.6366	790434	0.0078	13.801	0.029686
70	0.221767	49320	10938	220339	0.049639	2.5991	522859	0.0078	10.601	0.049562
75	0.342799	38382	13157	159433	0.082526	2.5315	302520	0.0078	7.882	0.082399
80	0.512488	25225	12927	92720	0.139425	2.4861	143087	0.0078	5.672	0.139225
85+	1.000000	12297	12297	50367	0.244158	4.0957	50367	0.0078	4.096	0.248579

TABLE 4 — OBSERVED AND PROJECTED VITAL RATES

	OBSERVED POPULATION BOTH SEXES	MALES	FEMALES	PROJECTED POPULATION 1915 MALES	1915 FEMALES	1920 MALES	1920 FEMALES	1925 MALES	1925 FEMALES	STABLE POPULATION MALES	FEMALES
RATES PER THOUSAND											
Birth	24.72	26.05	23.46	26.48	24.10	26.71	24.54	26.66	24.72	25.14	24.3
Death	14.11	14.33	13.90	14.15	13.84	14.03	13.78	13.88	13.66	14.48	13.9
Increase	10.61	11.72	9.56	12.33	10.26	12.68	10.77	12.79	11.06		10.662
PERCENTAGE											
under 15	31.80	33.11	30.55	32.47	30.19	32.11	30.06	32.05	30.25	30.77	30.1
15-64	59.77	59.28	60.24	60.20	60.79	60.74	61.09	60.89	60.89	61.45	61.4
65 and over	8.43	7.60	9.21	7.34	9.02	7.14	8.85	7.07	8.86	7.78	8.
DEP. RATIO X 100	67.31	68.68	66.01	66.12	64.49	64.62	63.71	64.24	64.24	62.74	63.

TABLE 1 (A)

AGE AT LAST BIRTHDAY	POPULATION BOTH SEXES	MALES Number	%	FEMALES Number	%	BIRTHS BY AGE OF MOTHER	DEATHS BOTH SEXES	MALES	FEMALES	AGE AT LAST BIRTHDAY
0	119735	61093	2.2	58642	2.0	0	6154	3509	2645	0
1-4	478591	244134	8.8	234457	8.1	0	6429	3453	2976	1-4
5-9	598532	305176	11.0	293356	10.1	0	1971	1023	948	5-9
10-14	571067	290094	10.4	280973	9.7	0	1488	716	772	10-14
15-19	530716	269761	9.7	260955	9.0	4740	2333	1166	1167	15-19
20-24	471080	234595	8.4	236085	8.1	25218	2918	1650	1268	20-24
25-29	428823	210136	7.5	218687	7.5	33427	2550	1305	1245	25-29
30-34	381521	185594	6.7	195927	6.7	28963	2248	1103	1145	30-34
35-39	351486	170763	6.1	180723	6.2	21479	2156	1049	1107	35-39
40-44	304209	146670	5.3	157539	5.4	10138	2143	1043	1100	40-44
45-49	268004	126300	4.5	141704	4.9	1066	2202	1117	1085	45-49
50-54	271205	126112	4.5	145093	5.0	7	2845	1475	1370	50-54
55-59	243053	112056	4.0	130997	4.5	0	3489	1830	1659	55-59
60-64	203506	93633	3.4	109873	3.8	0	4210	2159	2051	60-64
65-69	168879	76568	2.7	92311	3.2	0	5468	2727	2741	65-69
70-74	136433	60630	2.2	75803	2.6		7080	3389	3691	70-74
75-79	91382	39717	1.4	51665	1.8		8035	3724	4311	75-79
80-84	52905	22670	0.8	30235	1.0	64255 M.	7858	3567	4291	80-84
85+	25047	9898	0.4	15149	0.5	60783 F.	7179	3037	4142	85+
TOTAL	5696174	2786000		2910174		125038	78756	39042	39714	TOTAL

TABLE 2 (MALE LIFE TABLE)

x	nq_x	l_x	nd_x	nL_x	nm_x	na_x	T_x	r_x	$\mathring{e}_x$	nM_x	x
0	0.055573	100000	5557	96754	0.057437	0.4160	5697905	0.0000	56.979	0.057437	0
1	0.054556	94443	5152	364287	0.014144	1.3831	5601151	0.0000	59.307	0.014144	1
5	0.016622	89290	1484	442741	0.003352	2.5000	5236864	0.0000	58.650	0.003352	5
10	0.012276	87806	1078	436415	0.002470	2.5731	4794123	0.0093	54.599	0.002468	10
15	0.021476	86728	1863	429371	0.004338	2.7074	4357708	0.0165	50.246	0.004322	15
20	0.034550	84866	2932	417131	0.007029	2.5455	3928337	0.0187	46.289	0.007021	20
25	0.030548	81934	2503	403284	0.006206	2.4495	3511206	0.0172	42.854	0.006210	25
30	0.029277	79431	2325	391305	0.005943	2.4849	3107922	0.0147	39.127	0.005943	30
35	0.030275	77105	2334	379751	0.006147	2.5261	2716617	0.0173	35.233	0.006143	35
40	0.035012	74771	2618	367474	0.007124	2.5630	2336866	0.0229	31.254	0.007111	40
45	0.043324	72153	3126	353223	0.008850	2.5872	1969392	0.0061	27.295	0.008844	45
50	0.056887	69027	3927	335735	0.011696	2.6061	1616169	0.0000	23.414	0.011696	50
55	0.078725	65100	5125	313237	0.016361	2.6070	1280435	0.0131	19.669	0.016331	55
60	0.109379	59975	6560	284236	0.023080	2.6158	967197	0.0056	16.127	0.023058	60
65	0.164236	53415	8773	246069	0.035651	2.6054	682961	0.0056	12.786	0.035615	65
70	0.246371	44643	10999	196555	0.055957	2.5763	436892	0.0056	9.786	0.055896	70
75	0.380461	33644	12800	136364	0.093868	2.5113	240337	0.0056	7.144	0.093763	75
80	0.561033	20844	11694	74223	0.157552	2.4350	103973	0.0056	4.988	0.157345	80
85+	*1.000000	9150	9150	29750	0.307549	3.2515	29750	0.0056	3.252	0.306830	85+

TABLE 3 (FEMALE LIFE TABLE)

x	nq_x	l_x	nd_x	nL_x	nm_x	na_x	T_x	r_x	$\mathring{e}_x$	nM_x	x
0	0.043969	100000	4397	97483	0.045104	0.4276	5958241	0.0000	59.582	0.045104	0
1	0.049167	95603	4700	370316	0.012693	1.4266	5860758	0.0000	61.303	0.012693	1
5	0.016028	90903	1457	450871	0.003232	2.5000	5490442	0.0000	60.399	0.003232	5
10	0.013658	89446	1222	444278	0.002750	2.5849	5039571	0.0085	56.342	0.002748	10
15	0.022159	88224	1955	436454	0.004479	2.6136	4595294	0.0131	52.087	0.004472	15
20	0.026520	86269	2288	425709	0.005374	2.5367	4158839	0.0124	48.208	0.005371	20
25	0.028073	83981	2358	414025	0.005694	2.5056	3733130	0.0130	44.452	0.005693	25
30	0.028806	81624	2351	402247	0.005845	2.5031	3319105	0.0132	40.664	0.005844	30
35	0.030187	79272	2393	390439	0.006129	2.5252	2916858	0.0156	36.795	0.006125	35
40	0.034347	76879	2641	377878	0.006988	2.5313	2526419	0.0174	32.862	0.006982	40
45	0.037580	74239	2790	364356	0.007657	2.5491	2148541	0.0004	28.941	0.007657	45
50	0.046160	71449	3298	349292	0.009442	2.5889	1784185	0.0000	24.971	0.009442	50
55	0.061599	68151	4198	330764	0.012692	2.6204	1434893	0.0147	21.055	0.012664	55
60	0.089503	63953	5724	306264	0.018690	2.6416	1104128	0.0066	17.265	0.018667	60
65	0.138892	58229	8088	272013	0.029732	2.6345	797864	0.0066	13.702	0.029693	65
70	0.218297	50141	10946	224487	0.048759	2.6046	525851	0.0066	10.487	0.048692	70
75	0.346488	39196	13581	162538	0.083555	2.5377	301364	0.0066	7.689	0.083441	75
80	0.523221	25615	13402	94283	0.142148	2.4787	138827	0.0066	5.420	0.141922	80
85+	*1.000000	12213	12213	44543	0.274174	3.6473	44543	0.0066	3.647	0.273417	85+

TABLE 4 (OBSERVED PROJECTED NATIONAL RATES)

	OBSERVED POPULATION BOTH SEXES	MALES	FEMALES	PROJECTED POPULATION 1920 MALES	FEMALES	1925 MALES	FEMALES	1930 MALES	FEMALES	STABLE POPULATION MALES	FEMALES
RATES PER THOUSAND											
Birth	21.95	23.06	20.89	23.53	21.50	23.85	21.97	23.90	22.19	21.68	20.84
Death	13.83	14.01	13.65	13.72	13.46	13.68	13.48	13.71	13.54	15.41	14.57
Increase	8.13	9.05	7.24	9.82	8.05	10.16	8.49	10.19	8.65		6.2702
PERCENTAGE											
under 15	31.04	32.32	29.81	30.84	28.64	29.67	27.81	29.46	27.82	27.75	27.12
15-64	60.63	60.16	61.08	61.80	62.33	62.94	63.00	63.10	62.83	62.90	62.41
65 and over	8.33	7.52	9.11	7.36	9.03	7.39	9.19	7.44	9.35	9.35	10.47
DEP. RATIO X 100	64.93	66.23	63.72	61.82	60.43	58.89	58.72	58.47	59.16	58.97	60.24

TABLE 1 — DATA

AGE AT LAST BIRTHDAY	POPULATION BOTH SEXES	MALES Number	MALES %	FEMALES Number	FEMALES %	BIRTHS BY AGE OF MOTHER	DEATHS BOTH SEXES	DEATHS MALES	FEMALES	AGE AT LAST BIRTHDAY
0	120488	61749	2.1	58739	2.0	0	5593	3223	2370	0
1-4	436842	222803	7.7	214039	7.2	0	5886	3207	2679	1-4
5-9	578723	294929	10.2	283794	9.5	0	2137	1094	1043	5-9
10-14	590552	301164	10.4	289388	9.7	0	1688	827	861	10-14
15-19	557219	283355	9.8	273864	9.2	4892	2744	1390	1354	15-19
20-24	505005	255146	8.8	249859	8.3	26459	3835	2193	1642	20-24
25-29	447999	220783	7.7	227216	7.6	33050	3619	1953	1666	25-29
30-34	410691	199448	6.9	211243	7.1	28264	3120	1619	1501	30-34
35-39	368003	178473	6.2	189530	6.3	20114	2659	1335	1324	35-39
40-44	339778	165167	5.7	174611	5.8	9489	2478	1243	1235	40-44
45-49	293133	141393	4.9	151740	5.1	1043	2441	1233	1208	45-49
50-54	256205	120573	4.2	135632	4.5	4	2717	1368	1349	50-54
55-59	255378	118320	4.1	137058	4.6	0	3655	1847	1808	55-59
60-64	222847	102042	3.5	120805	4.0	0	4569	2277	2292	60-64
65-69	178887	81482	2.8	97405	3.3	0	5660	2762	2898	65-69
70-74	137346	61475	2.1	75871	2.5		7148	3377	3771	70-74
75-79	97115	42351	1.5	54764	1.8		8259	3762	4497	75-79
80-84	52329	21923	0.8	30406	1.0	63457 M.	7675	3379	4296	80-84
85+	27223	10750	0.4	16473	0.6	59858 F.	7496	3100	4396	85+
TOTAL	5875763	2883326		2992437		123315	83379	41189	42190	TOTAL

TABLE 2 — MALE LIFE TABLE

x	$_nq_x$	l_x	$_nd_x$	$_nL_x$	$_nm_x$	$_na_x$	T_x	r_x	$\mathring{e}_x$	$_nM_x$
0	0.050552	100000	5055	97096	0.052064	0.4255	5595675	0.0044	55.957	0.052195
1	0.055434	94945	5263	366191	0.014373	1.4182	5498579	0.0044	57.913	0.014394
5	0.018376	89682	1648	444288	0.003709	2.5000	5132388	0.0000	57.229	0.003709
10	0.013640	88034	1201	437263	0.002746	2.5805	4688100	0.0006	53.254	0.002746
15	0.024325	86833	2112	429378	0.004919	2.7339	4250837	0.0113	48.954	0.004906
20	0.042169	84721	3573	414963	0.008609	2.5815	3821460	0.0171	45.107	0.008595
25	0.043254	81148	3510	396864	0.008844	2.4711	3406497	0.0159	41.979	0.008846
30	0.039745	77638	3086	380315	0.008114	2.4477	3009633	0.0131	38.765	0.008117
35	0.036698	74552	2736	365832	0.007479	2.4671	2629319	0.0113	35.268	0.007480
40	0.036957	71816	2654	352493	0.007530	2.5175	2263487	0.0156	31.518	0.007526
45	0.042582	69162	2959	338623	0.008738	2.5707	1910994	0.0225	27.631	0.008720
50	0.055266	66203	3659	322234	0.011355	2.5995	1572371	0.0062	23.751	0.011346
55	0.075250	62545	4707	301472	0.015612	2.6097	1250137	0.0007	19.988	0.015610
60	0.106090	57838	6136	274561	0.022349	2.6159	948665	0.0094	16.402	0.022314
65	0.157056	51702	8120	239136	0.033956	2.6140	674103	0.0094	13.038	0.033897
70	0.242780	43582	10581	192271	0.055031	2.5769	434968	0.0094	9.980	0.054933
75	0.364470	33001	12028	135153	0.088995	2.5181	242696	0.0094	7.354	0.088829
80	0.554220	20973	11624	75248	0.154472	2.4520	107544	0.0094	5.128	0.154129
85+	*1.000000	9349	9349	32295	0.289498	3.4543	32295	0.0094	3.454	0.288372

TABLE 3 — FEMALE LIFE TABLE

x	$_nq_x$	l_x	$_nd_x$	$_nL_x$	$_nm_x$	$_na_x$	T_x	r_x	$\mathring{e}_x$	$_nM_x$
0	0.039356	100000	3936	97778	0.040250	0.4354	5871177	0.0044	58.712	0.040348
1	0.048460	96064	4655	372432	0.012500	1.4598	5773399	0.0044	60.099	0.012516
5	0.018209	91409	1664	452884	0.003675	2.5000	5400967	0.0000	59.086	0.003675
10	0.014770	89745	1326	445513	0.002975	2.5785	4948083	0.0000	55.135	0.002975
15	0.024471	88419	2164	436992	0.004951	2.6412	4502570	0.0098	50.923	0.004944
20	0.032370	86255	2792	424472	0.006578	2.5628	4065578	0.0123	47.134	0.006572
25	0.036007	83463	3005	409806	0.007333	2.5011	3641106	0.0096	43.625	0.007332
30	0.034898	80458	2808	395200	0.007105	2.4748	3231299	0.0110	40.161	0.007106
35	0.034325	77650	2665	381546	0.006986	2.4843	2836100	0.0120	36.524	0.006986
40	0.034767	74985	2607	368441	0.007076	2.5131	2454554	0.0150	32.734	0.007073
45	0.039094	72378	2830	354976	0.007971	2.5567	2086113	0.0171	28.823	0.007961
50	0.048565	69548	3378	339590	0.009946	2.5865	1731137	0.0000	24.891	0.009946
55	0.063942	66171	4231	320746	0.013191	2.6110	1391547	0.0000	21.030	0.013191
60	0.090934	61940	5632	296369	0.019005	2.6335	1070801	0.0097	17.288	0.018973
65	0.139240	56307	7840	263007	0.029810	2.6367	774432	0.0097	13.754	0.029752
70	0.222390	48467	10779	216440	0.049799	2.5976	511425	0.0097	10.552	0.049703
75	0.341982	37688	12889	156652	0.082276	2.5335	294985	0.0097	7.827	0.082116
80	0.518278	24800	12853	90805	0.141547	2.4847	138333	0.0097	5.578	0.141288
85+	1.000000	11947	11947	47528	0.251357	3.9784	47528	0.0097	3.978	0.266862

TABLE 4 — OBSERVED AND PROJECTED VITAL RATES

	OBSERVED POPULATION BOTH SEXES	MALES	FEMALES	PROJECTED POPULATION 1925 MALES	1925 FEMALES	1930 MALES	1930 FEMALES	1935 MALES	1935 FEMALES	STABLE POPULATION MALES	FEMALES
RATES PER THOUSAND											
Birth	20.99	22.01	20.00	22.37	20.51	22.57	20.84	22.30	20.73	20.04	19.1
Death	14.19	14.29	14.10	14.31	14.14	14.49	14.26	14.57	14.33	16.69	15.8
Increase	6.80	7.72	5.90	8.06	6.37	8.08	6.58	7.73	6.40		3.34
PERCENTAGE											
under 15	29.39	30.54	28.27	28.86	26.94	28.09	26.41	28.39	26.85	26.29	25.1
15-64	62.23	61.90	62.54	63.45	63.67	64.04	63.96	63.88	63.69	63.15	62.
65 and over	8.39	7.56	9.19	7.69	9.39	7.86	9.63	7.73	9.46	10.56	11.5
DEP. RATIO X 100	60.70	61.56	59.89	57.61	57.06	56.15	56.34	56.54	57.01	58.35	59.

TABLE 1 — DATA

AGE AT LAST BIRTHDAY	POPULATION BOTH SEXES	MALES Number	%	FEMALES Number	%	BIRTHS BY AGE OF MOTHER	DEATHS BOTH SEXES	MALES	FEMALES	AGE AT LAST BIRTHDAY
0	103187	52755	1.8	50432	1.6	0	4335	2504	1831	0
1-4	444368	226614	7.6	217754	7.1	0	3903	2162	1741	1-4
5-9	542738	276725	9.3	266013	8.6	0	1100	583	517	5-9
10-14	571579	291288	9.8	280291	9.1	0	994	501	493	10-14
15-19	578057	294229	9.9	283828	9.2	4788	1789	916	873	15-19
20-24	528459	265016	8.9	263443	8.6	23093	2352	1271	1081	20-24
25-29	476521	235660	7.9	240861	7.8	28573	2108	1080	1028	25-29
30-34	429557	208630	7.0	220927	7.2	23732	1870	914	956	30-34
35-39	398179	192230	6.5	205949	6.7	16937	1848	917	931	35-39
40-44	357099	173038	5.8	184061	6.0	7760	1956	960	996	40-44
45-49	328682	159730	5.4	168952	5.5	869	2295	1166	1129	45-49
50-54	281228	135531	4.6	145697	4.7	5	2642	1333	1309	50-54
55-59	241915	113521	3.8	128394	4.2	0	3155	1609	1546	55-59
60-64	235369	108436	3.7	126933	4.1	0	4565	2297	2268	60-64
65-69	196792	89333	3.0	107459	3.5	0	5998	2946	3052	65-69
70-74	147211	66475	2.2	80736	2.6		7214	3452	3762	70-74
75-79	99158	43766	1.5	55392	1.8		8315	3849	4466	75-79
80-84	56625	24288	0.8	32337	1.1	54382 M.	7846	3502	4344	80-84
85+	28116	11127	0.4	16989	0.6	51375 F.	7698	3215	4483	85+
TOTAL	6044840	2968392		3076448		105757	71983	35177	36806	TOTAL

TABLE 2 — MALE LIFE TABLE

x	$_nq_x$	l_x	$_nd_x$	$_nL_x$	$_nm_x$	$_na_x$	T_x	r_x	$\mathring{e}_x$	$_nM_x$	x
0	0.046150	100000	4615	97229	0.047465	0.3996	6145998	0.0000	61.460	0.047465	0
1	0.037214	95385	3550	372067	0.009540	1.3314	6048768	0.0000	63.414	0.009540	1
5	0.010479	91835	962	456771	0.002107	2.5000	5676701	0.0000	61.814	0.002107	5
10	0.008565	90873	778	452509	0.001720	2.6156	5219930	0.0000	57.442	0.001720	10
15	0.015475	90095	1394	447264	0.003117	2.6982	4767421	0.0063	52.916	0.003113	15
20	0.023729	88701	2105	438359	0.004802	2.5561	4320156	0.0178	48.705	0.004796	20
25	0.022644	86596	1961	428020	0.004581	2.4712	3881798	0.0193	44.827	0.004583	25
30	0.021670	84635	1834	418588	0.004382	2.4992	3453778	0.0159	40.808	0.004381	30
35	0.023591	82801	1953	409200	0.004774	2.5407	3035190	0.0139	36.657	0.004770	35
40	0.027405	80847	2216	398880	0.005555	2.5821	2625990	0.0128	32.481	0.005548	40
45	0.035945	78632	2826	386393	0.007315	2.6061	2227110	0.0170	28.323	0.007300	45
50	0.048213	75805	3655	370333	0.009869	2.6212	1840717	0.0240	24.282	0.009835	50
55	0.068649	72151	4953	349023	0.014191	2.6317	1470384	0.0077	20.379	0.014174	55
60	0.101002	67197	6787	319914	0.021215	2.6318	1121361	0.0086	16.688	0.021183	60
65	0.153081	60410	9248	279982	0.033030	2.6135	801447	0.0086	13.267	0.032978	65
70	0.231089	51163	11823	227292	0.052017	2.5877	521465	0.0086	10.192	0.051929	70
75	0.361527	39340	14222	161445	0.088094	2.5213	294173	0.0086	7.478	0.087945	75
80	0.528613	25117	13277	91897	0.144481	2.4626	132728	0.0086	5.284	0.144187	80
85+	*1.000000	11840	11840	40831	0.289974	3.4486	40831	0.0086	3.449	0.288937	85+

TABLE 3 — FEMALE LIFE TABLE

x	$_nq_x$	l_x	$_nd_x$	$_nL_x$	$_nm_x$	$_na_x$	T_x	r_x	$\mathring{e}_x$	$_nM_x$	x
0	0.035543	100000	3554	97898	0.036306	0.4085	6376629	0.0000	63.766	0.036306	0
1	0.031320	96446	3021	377803	0.007995	1.3582	6278731	0.0000	65.101	0.007995	1
5	0.009671	93425	903	464867	0.001944	2.5000	5900928	0.0000	63.162	0.001944	5
10	0.008758	92522	810	460686	0.001759	2.6279	5436061	0.0000	58.755	0.001759	10
15	0.015276	91711	1401	455268	0.003077	2.6525	4975376	0.0032	54.250	0.003076	15
20	0.020328	90310	1836	447059	0.004106	2.5530	4520108	0.0125	50.051	0.004103	20
25	0.021118	88474	1868	437705	0.004269	2.5020	4073049	0.0133	46.036	0.004268	25
30	0.021408	86606	1854	428401	0.004328	2.5031	3635344	0.0113	41.976	0.004327	30
35	0.022369	84752	1896	419096	0.004524	2.5397	3206943	0.0136	37.839	0.004521	35
40	0.026737	82856	2215	408901	0.005418	2.5715	2787848	0.0143	33.647	0.005411	40
45	0.032942	80641	2657	396818	0.006695	2.5958	2378947	0.0165	29.501	0.006682	45
50	0.044072	77984	3437	381685	0.009005	2.6035	1982129	0.0184	25.417	0.008984	50
55	0.058541	74547	4364	362367	0.012043	2.6237	1600444	0.0013	21.469	0.012041	55
60	0.085882	70183	6027	336721	0.017901	2.6448	1238077	0.0100	17.641	0.017868	60
65	0.133326	64156	8554	300573	0.028458	2.6376	901357	0.0100	14.049	0.028402	65
70	0.210044	55602	11679	250115	0.046694	2.6114	600784	0.0100	10.805	0.046596	70
75	0.336980	43923	14801	183209	0.080789	2.5403	350669	0.0100	7.984	0.080625	75
80	0.499323	29122	14541	108054	0.134574	2.4968	167459	0.0100	5.750	0.134335	80
85+	1.000000	14581	14581	59405	0.245445	4.0742	59405	0.0100	4.074	0.263876	85+

TABLE 4 — OBSERVED AND PROJECTED VITAL RATES

	OBSERVED POPULATION BOTH SEXES	MALES	FEMALES	PROJECTED POPULATION 1930 MALES	FEMALES	1935 MALES	FEMALES	1940 MALES	FEMALES	STABLE POPULATION MALES	FEMALES
RATES PER THOUSAND											
Birth	17.50	18.32	16.70	18.80	17.27	18.89	17.49	18.50	17.25	15.59	15.01
Death	11.91	11.85	11.96	11.87	12.10	12.10	12.33	12.35	12.59	16.76	16.19
Increase	5.59	6.47	4.74	6.93	5.17	6.78	5.16	6.15	4.66	-1.1786	
PERCENTAGE											
under 15	27.49	28.55	26.48	26.36	24.64	25.25	23.78	24.57	23.29	21.68	21.22
15-64	63.77	63.54	64.00	65.48	65.46	66.64	66.36	67.12	66.77	64.70	64.02
65 and over	8.73	7.92	9.52	8.16	9.90	8.11	9.85	8.31	9.95	13.62	14.76
DEP. RATIO X 100	56.80	57.39	56.24	52.72	52.77	50.06	50.69	48.98	49.78	54.56	56.21

TABLE 1 — DATA

AGE AT LAST BIRTHDAY	POPULATION BOTH SEXES	MALES Number	%	FEMALES Number	%	BIRTHS BY AGE OF MOTHER	DEATHS BOTH SEXES	MALES	FEMALES	AGE AT LAST BIRTHDAY
0	89616	45697	1.5	43919	1.4	0	3813	2213	1600	0
1-4	369815	188374	6.2	181441	5.8	0	2908	1600	1308	1-4
5-9	537505	273935	9.1	263570	8.5	0	944	511	433	5-9
10-14	538080	274348	9.1	263732	8.5	0	852	433	419	10-14
15-19	563118	287132	9.5	275986	8.9	4965	1599	799	800	15-19
20-24	553472	278836	9.2	274636	8.8	21844	2195	1134	1061	20-24
25-29	504341	249689	8.3	254652	8.2	25340	2056	1037	1019	25-29
30-34	459992	226108	7.5	233884	7.5	20582	1926	958	968	30-34
35-39	417083	201925	6.7	215158	6.9	13647	1872	919	953	35-39
40-44	386969	186442	6.2	200527	6.4	6124	2060	1036	1024	40-44
45-49	345509	167125	5.5	178384	5.7	654	2429	1242	1187	45-49
50-54	315272	153011	5.1	162261	5.2	4	2956	1507	1449	50-54
55-59	266068	127977	4.2	138091	4.4	0	3489	1796	1693	55-59
60-64	223085	104011	3.4	119074	3.8	0	4406	2245	2161	60-64
65-69	207857	94977	3.1	112880	3.6	0	6448	3145	3303	65-69
70-74	161267	72577	2.4	88690	2.8		8172	3853	4319	70-74
75-79	105526	47035	1.6	58491	1.9		9149	4210	4939	75-79
80-84	57111	24738	0.8	32373	1.0	47796 M.	8334	3739	4595	80-84
85+	29140	11769	0.4	17371	0.6	45364 F.	8026	3363	4663	85+
TOTAL	6130826	3015706		3115120		93160	73634	35740	37894	TOTAL

TABLE 2 — MALE LIFE TABLE

x	$_nq_x$	l_x	$_nd_x$	$_nL_x$	$_nm_x$	$_na_x$	T_x	r_x	$\mathring{e}_x$	$_nM_x$	x
0	0.047032	100000	4703	97118	0.048428	0.3872	6201766	0.0000	62.018	0.048428	0
1	0.033213	95297	3165	372635	0.008494	1.2981	6104649	0.0000	64.059	0.008494	1
5	0.009284	92132	855	458520	0.001865	2.5000	5732013	0.0000	62.215	0.001865	5
10	0.007862	91276	718	454671	0.001578	2.6151	5273493	0.0000	57.775	0.001578	10
15	0.013824	90559	1252	449890	0.002783	2.6800	4818822	0.0000	53.212	0.002783	15
20	0.020149	89307	1799	442150	0.004070	2.5633	4368933	0.0102	48.920	0.004067	20
25	0.020555	87507	1799	433040	0.004154	2.4998	3926783	0.0168	44.874	0.004153	25
30	0.020970	85709	1797	424069	0.004238	2.5106	3493743	0.0170	40.763	0.004237	30
35	0.022525	83911	1890	414926	0.004555	2.5501	3069674	0.0146	36.582	0.004551	35
40	0.027455	82021	2252	404690	0.005565	2.5949	2654748	0.0132	32.367	0.005557	40
45	0.036560	79769	2916	391859	0.007442	2.6039	2250057	0.0123	28.207	0.007432	45
50	0.048222	76853	3706	375431	0.009871	2.6164	1858199	0.0165	24.179	0.009849	50
55	0.068183	73147	4987	353954	0.014090	2.6379	1482767	0.0239	20.271	0.014034	55
60	0.102802	68160	7007	324199	0.021613	2.6311	1128813	0.0075	16.561	0.021584	60
65	0.153647	61153	9396	283354	0.033160	2.6150	804614	0.0075	13.157	0.033113	65
70	0.235615	51757	12195	229362	0.053168	2.5873	521260	0.0075	10.071	0.053088	70
75	0.366733	39562	14509	161849	0.089643	2.5214	291898	0.0075	7.378	0.089508	75
80	0.546305	25053	13687	90395	0.151410	2.4522	130048	0.0075	5.191	0.151143	80
85+	*1.000000	11367	11367	39653	0.286649	3.4886	39653	0.0075	3.489	0.285751	85-

TABLE 3 — FEMALE LIFE TABLE

x	$_nq_x$	l_x	$_nd_x$	$_nL_x$	$_nm_x$	$_na_x$	T_x	r_x	$\mathring{e}_x$	$_nM_x$	x
0	0.035650	100000	3565	97858	0.036431	0.3991	6411292	0.0000	64.113	0.036431	0
1	0.028291	96435	2728	378456	0.007209	1.3301	6313434	0.0000	65.468	0.007209	1
5	0.008181	93707	767	466617	0.001643	2.5000	5934978	0.0000	63.336	0.001643	5
10	0.007914	92940	736	462979	0.001589	2.6588	5468361	0.0000	58.837	0.001589	10
15	0.014396	92205	1327	457914	0.002899	2.6576	5005383	0.0000	54.286	0.002899	15
20	0.019141	90877	1739	450129	0.003864	2.5526	4547469	0.0043	50.040	0.003863	20
25	0.019813	89138	1766	441284	0.004002	2.5060	4097340	0.0120	45.966	0.004002	25
30	0.020489	87372	1790	432406	0.004140	2.5128	3656056	0.0127	41.845	0.004139	30
35	0.021918	85582	1876	423286	0.004431	2.5359	3223650	0.0109	37.668	0.004429	35
40	0.025251	83706	2114	413411	0.005107	2.5789	2800365	0.0135	33.455	0.005107	40
45	0.032804	81592	2677	401549	0.006666	2.6046	2386953	0.0144	29.255	0.006654	45
50	0.043809	78916	3457	386316	0.008949	2.6103	1985404	0.0165	25.159	0.008930	50
55	0.059728	75458	4507	366592	0.012294	2.6260	1599088	0.0182	21.192	0.012260	55
60	0.087139	70951	6183	340211	0.018173	2.6472	1232496	0.0073	17.371	0.018148	60
65	0.137050	64769	8877	302907	0.029304	2.6414	892285	0.0073	13.776	0.029261	65
70	0.218398	55892	12207	250279	0.048773	2.6094	589378	0.0073	10.545	0.048698	70
75	0.349883	43685	15285	180745	0.084566	2.5346	339099	0.0073	7.762	0.084440	75
80	0.519310	28401	14749	103771	0.142127	2.4769	158354	0.0073	5.576	0.141939	80
85+	1.000000	13652	13652	54582	0.250116	3.9981	54582	0.0073	3.998	0.268437	85

TABLE 4 — OBSERVED AND PROJECTED VITAL RATES

	OBSERVED POPULATION BOTH SEXES	MALES	FEMALES	PROJECTED POPULATION 1935 MALES	FEMALES	1940 MALES	FEMALES	1945 MALES	FEMALES	STABLE POPULATION MALES	FEMALES
RATES PER THOUSAND											
Birth	15.20	15.85	14.56	16.12	14.92	16.00	14.91	15.55	14.57	12.42	11.97
Death	12.01	11.85	12.16	12.02	12.38	12.39	12.71	12.77	13.06	19.29	18.83
Increase	3.18	4.00	2.40	4.10	2.54	3.61	2.20	2.78	1.51	-6.865	
PERCENTAGE											
under 15	25.04	25.94	24.16	23.69	22.27	21.82	20.67	21.48	20.47	18.09	17.71
15-64	65.81	65.73	65.89	67.98	67.78	69.56	69.20	69.32	68.90	65.33	64.54
65 and over	9.15	8.33	9.95	8.32	9.95	8.62	10.13	9.20	10.63	16.58	17.75
DEP. RATIO X 100	51.94	52.14	51.76	47.09	47.53	43.77	44.51	44.27	45.14	53.06	54.9

AGE AT LAST BIRTHDAY	1935			1940			1945			AGE AT LAST BIRTHDAY	
	BOTH SEXES	MALES	FEMALES	BOTH SEXES	MALES	FEMALES	BOTH SEXES	MALES	FEMALES		
0-4	449	229	220	460	234	226	459	234	225	0-4	
5-9	449	228	221	439	223	216	450	229	221	5-9	
10-14	534	272	262	446	227	219	435	221	214	10-14	
15-19	532	271	261	528	269	259	441	224	217	15-19	TABLE 5
20-24	553	282	271	523	267	256	518	264	254	20-24	POPULATION
25-29	542	273	269	542	276	266	512	261	251	25-29	PROJECTED
30-34	495	245	250	531	267	264	532	271	261	30-34	WITH
35-39	450	221	229	483	239	244	520	262	258	35-39	FIXED
40-44	407	197	210	440	216	224	472	233	239	40-44	AGE—
45-49	376	181	195	395	191	204	426	209	217	45-49	SPECIFIC
50-54	332	160	172	360	173	187	379	183	196	50-54	BIRTH
55-59	298	144	154	314	151	163	341	163	178	55-59	AND
60-64	245	117	128	275	132	143	289	138	151	60-64	DEATH
65-69	197	91	106	216	102	114	242	115	127	65-69	RATES
70-74	170	77	93	162	74	88	177	83	94	70-74	(IN 1000's)
75-79	115	51	64	121	54	67	115	52	63	75-79	
80-84	60	26	34	66	29	37	69	30	39	80-84	
85+	28	11	17	30	12	18	32	13	19	85+	
TOTAL	6232	3076	3156	6331	3136	3195	6409	3185	3224	TOTAL	

STANDARD COUNTRIES:	ENGLAND AND WALES 1961			UNITED STATES 1960			MEXICO 1960			TABLE 6
STANDARDIZED RATES PER THOUSAND	BOTH SEXES	MALES	FEMALES	BOTH SEXES	MALES	FEMALES	BOTH SEXES	MALES	FEMALES	STANDAR-
Birth	12.31	13.42*	11.62	12.52	12.40*	12.01	13.24	12.49*	12.86	DIZED
Death	14.83	13.96*	16.19	12.62	12.44*	12.71	8.19	10.31*	7.77	RATES
Increase	-2.52	-0.54*	-4.57	-0.10	-0.03*	-0.70	5.04	2.18*	5.09	

	OBSERVED POP.		STATIONARY POP.		STABLE POP.		OBSERVED BIRTHS	NET MATERNITY FUNCTION	BIRTHS IN STABLE POP.	TABLE 7
	MALES	FEMALES	MALES	FEMALES	MALES	FEMALES				
μ	31.60153	33.12594	36.23550	36.79102	39.77627	40.41980	29.49173	29.99410	30.31460	MOMENTS
σ^2	434.1366	457.0785	508.2199	521.2016	521.1140	533.6339	42.93903	44.34673	44.84160	AND
κ_3	4743.418	4508.696	2794.349	2786.175	927.916	801.818	93.2747	76.8797	67.1787	CUMULANTS
κ_4	-115545.	-147782.	-254318.	-271323.	-283860.	-300639.	-1155.918	-1361.361	-1452.546	
β_1	0.274982	0.212877	0.059485	0.054828	0.006084	0.004231	0.109893	0.067770	0.050052	
β_2	2.386946	2.292639	2.015367	2.001207	1.954705	1.944257	2.373065	2.307771	2.277617	
κ	-0.111505	-0.085095	-0.022094	-0.020225	-0.002270	-0.001568	-0.054665	-0.033299	-0.024388	

VITAL STATISTICS		THOMPSON				BOURGEOIS-PICHAT					COALE	TABLE 8
		AGE RANGE	NRR	1000r	INTERVAL	AGE RANGE	NRR	1000b	1000d	1000r		RATES FROM AGE DISTRI-
GRR	0.932					5-29	0.94	18.05	20.28	-2.23	IBR	BUTIONS
NRR	0.813	0-4	0.85	-5.86	27.22	30-54	1.41	26.43	13.62	12.81	IDR	AND VITAL
TFR	1.913	5-9	1.07	2.37	27.17	55-79	1.07	13.64	11.23	2.41	IRI	STATISTICS
GENERATION	30.154	10-14	1.14	4.91	27.12	*20-44	1.37	25.48	13.77	11.71	K1	(Females)
SEX RATIO	105.361	15-19	1.29	9.26	27.03						K2	

Start of Age interval	ORIGINAL MATRIX			FIRST STABLE MATRIX			SECOND STABLE MATRIX Z_2		TABLE 9
	SUB-DIAGONAL	ALTERNATIVE FIRST ROWS		% IN STABLE POPULATION	FISHER VALUES	REPRODUCTIVE VALUES	FIRST COLUMN	FIRST ROW	LESLIE MATRIX
		Projection	Integral						AND ITS
0	0.97964	0.00000	0.00000	5.800	1.032	232560	0.1300+0.0573	0.1300+0.0573	SPECTRAL
5	0.99220	0.00000	0.00000	5.880	1.018	268280	0.1475-0.0917	0.0213+0.1142	COMPO-
10	0.98906	0.02063	0.00000	6.037	0.991	261432	0.0093-0.2148	-0.0665+0.0662	NENTS
15	0.98300	0.11153	0.04102	6.180	0.947	261335	-0.2124-0.1591	-0.0774-0.0154	(Females)
20	0.98035	0.20537	0.18134	6.287	0.814	223477	-0.3082+0.1050	-0.0400-0.0657	
25	0.97988	0.21540	0.22687	6.378	0.586	149190	-0.1067+0.3838	-0.0014-0.0693	
30	0.97891	0.17406	0.20064	6.468	0.351	82065	0.3138+0.3726	0.0176-0.0455	
35	0.97667	0.10815	0.14461	6.553	0.163	35041	0.5921-0.0597	0.0157-0.0193	
40	0.97131	0.03955	0.06963	6.623	0.047	9396	0.3471-0.6369	0.0060-0.0046	
45	0.96206	0.00428	0.00836	6.658	0.005	821	-0.4000-0.7830	0.0006-0.0004	
50	0.94894	0.00003	0.00006	6.629	0.000	5	-1.0471-0.1340	0.0000-0.0000	
55+	0.76010			30.508					

Start Age interval	OBSERVED POPUL. (IN 100's)	CONTRIBUTIONS OF ROOTS (IN 100's)			AGE-SP. BIRTH RATES	NET MATERNITY FUNCTION	COEFF. OF MATRIX EQUATION	PARAMETERS		EXP. INCREASE		TABLE 10
		r_1	r_2, r_3	$r_4\text{-}r_{11}$					INTEGRAL	MATRIX	x	$e^{(x+2\frac{1}{2})r}$
0	2254	2432	-130	-48	0.0000	0.0000	0.0000	L(1)	0.96626	0.96628	0	0.9830
5	2636	2465	7	164	0.0000	0.0000	0.0000	L(2)	0.44813	0.45213	50	0.6974
10	2637	2532	206	-101	0.0000	0.0000	0.0201		0.67619	0.66156	55	0.6738
15	2760	2591	277	-109	0.0088	0.0401	0.1072	R(1)	-0.00687	-0.00686	60	0.6511
20	2746	2636	71	39	0.0387	0.1743	0.1941	R(2)	-0.04185	-0.04430	65	0.6291
25	2547	2674	-317	190	0.0485	0.2138	0.1996		0.19710	0.19426	70	0.6079
30	2339	2712	-545	172	0.0429	0.1853	0.1580	C(1)		41930	75	0.5874
35	2152	2748	-277	-319	0.0309	0.1307	0.0961	C(2)		-28354	80	0.5676
40	2005	2777	430	-1202	0.0149	0.0615	0.0343			49245	85	0.5484
45	1784	2792	998	-2006	0.0018	0.0072	0.0036	2P/Y	31.8776	32.3450	90	0.5299
50	1623	2779	726	-1882	0.0000	0.0000	0.0000	DELTA	14.8495		95	0.5120
55-	5670	12792									100	0.4947

AGE ANALYSIS AND MISCEL- LANEOUS RESULTS (Females)

TABLE 1 — DATA

AGE AT LAST BIRTHDAY	POPULATION BOTH SEXES	MALES Number	MALES %	FEMALES Number	FEMALES %	BIRTHS BY AGE OF MOTHER	DEATHS BOTH SEXES	DEATHS MALES	DEATHS FEMALES	AGE AT LAST BIRTHDAY
0	82068	42111	1.4	39957	1.3	0	3058	1777	1281	0
1-4	334154	170284	5.5	163870	5.2	0	2024	1163	861	1-4
5-9	453659	230708	7.5	222951	7.1	0	686	383	303	5-9
10-14	536219	272950	8.8	263269	8.3	0	695	374	321	10-14
15-19	535053	272742	8.8	262311	8.3	4599	1223	644	579	15-19
20-24	553977	282090	9.1	271887	8.6	20406	1791	971	820	20-24
25-29	546393	275221	8.9	271172	8.6	24712	1751	905	846	25-29
30-34	500874	248517	8.1	252357	8.0	19753	1657	831	826	30-34
35-39	455347	224292	7.3	231055	7.3	12189	1742	900	842	35-39
40-44	410656	199316	6.5	211340	6.7	4902	1934	992	942	40-44
45-49	377804	182340	5.9	195464	6.2	502	2399	1219	1180	45-49
50-54	334116	161781	5.2	172335	5.5	3	2956	1525	1431	50-54
55-59	299716	145294	4.7	154422	4.9	0	3845	2009	1836	55-59
60-64	246708	118165	3.8	128543	4.1	0	4764	2476	2288	60-64
65-69	197277	91354	3.0	105923	3.4	0	6164	3061	3103	65-69
70-74	170475	77117	2.5	93358	3.0		8665	4126	4539	70-74
75-79	116170	51737	1.7	64433	2.0		10028	4629	5399	75-79
80-84	61188	26689	0.9	34499	1.1	44831 M.	8786	4005	4781	80-84
85+	29944	12362	0.4	17582	0.6	42235 F.	8347	3556	4791	85+
TOTAL	6241798	3085070		3156728		87066	72515	35546	36969	TOTAL

TABLE 2 — MALE LIFE TABLE

x	$_nq_x$	l_x	$_nd_x$	$_nL_x$	$_nm_x$	$_na_x$	T_x	r_x	$\mathring{e}_x$	$_nM_x$	x
0	0.041122	100000	4112	97451	0.042198	0.3801	6374601	0.0000	63.746	0.042198	0
1	0.026821	95888	2572	376558	0.006830	1.2810	6277150	0.0000	65.464	0.006830	1
5	0.008266	93316	771	464651	0.001660	2.5000	5900591	0.0000	63.232	0.001660	5
10	0.006829	92545	632	461207	0.001370	2.6015	5435940	0.0000	58.739	0.001370	10
15	0.011742	91913	1079	457056	0.002361	2.6773	4974733	0.0000	54.125	0.002361	15
20	0.017067	90833	1550	450370	0.003442	2.5506	4517676	0.0000	49.736	0.003442	20
25	0.016306	89283	1456	442757	0.003288	2.4867	4067306	0.0093	45.555	0.003288	25
30	0.016595	87827	1458	435548	0.003346	2.5376	3624549	0.0170	41.269	0.003344	30
35	0.019900	86370	1719	427683	0.004019	2.5761	3189002	0.0180	36.923	0.004013	35
40	0.024633	84651	2085	418251	0.004986	2.6002	2761319	0.0156	32.620	0.004977	40
45	0.032966	82566	2722	406359	0.006698	2.6227	2343067	0.0140	28.378	0.006685	45
50	0.046195	79844	3688	390497	0.009445	2.6351	1936709	0.0130	24.256	0.009426	50
55	0.067138	76156	5113	368708	0.013867	2.6392	1546211	0.0171	20.303	0.013827	55
60	0.100008	71043	7105	338457	0.020992	2.6415	1177504	0.0097	16.575	0.020954	60
65	0.155426	63938	9938	296035	0.033569	2.6197	839047	0.0097	13.123	0.033507	65
70	0.237293	54000	12814	239043	0.053605	2.5840	543013	0.0097	10.056	0.053503	70
75	0.366669	41186	15102	168463	0.089644	2.5189	303970	0.0097	7.380	0.089472	75
80	0.543727	26085	14183	94299	0.150403	2.4530	135507	0.0097	5.195	0.150061	80
85+	*1.000000	11902	11902	41208	0.288822	3.4623	41208	0.0097	3.462	0.287656	85+

TABLE 3 — FEMALE LIFE TABLE

x	$_nq_x$	l_x	$_nd_x$	$_nL_x$	$_nm_x$	$_na_x$	T_x	r_x	$\mathring{e}_x$	$_nM_x$	x
0	0.031437	100000	3144	98058	0.032059	0.3821	6615008	0.0000	66.150	0.032059	0
1	0.020721	96856	2007	381978	0.005254	1.2857	6516951	0.0000	67.285	0.005254	1
5	0.006772	94849	642	472641	0.001359	2.5000	6134973	0.0000	64.681	0.001359	5
10	0.006079	94207	573	469684	0.001219	2.6403	5662332	0.0000	60.105	0.001219	10
15	0.010980	93634	1028	465771	0.002207	2.6649	5192648	0.0000	55.457	0.002207	15
20	0.014970	92606	1386	459645	0.003016	2.5577	4726877	0.0000	51.043	0.003016	20
25	0.015480	91220	1412	452585	0.003120	2.5107	4267232	0.0043	46.780	0.003120	25
30	0.016241	89808	1459	445432	0.003275	2.5264	3814647	0.0127	42.476	0.003273	30
35	0.018077	88349	1597	437849	0.003648	2.5596	3369216	0.0140	38.135	0.003644	35
40	0.022080	86752	1915	429166	0.004463	2.6014	2931367	0.0121	33.790	0.004457	40
45	0.029812	84837	2529	418161	0.006048	2.6189	2502200	0.0143	29.494	0.006037	45
50	0.040803	82308	3358	403569	0.008322	2.6271	2084039	0.0150	25.320	0.008304	50
55	0.057979	78949	4577	383929	0.011922	2.6369	1680471	0.0170	21.285	0.011889	55
60	0.085600	74372	6366	356935	0.017836	2.6557	1296541	0.0105	17.433	0.017799	60
65	0.137293	68006	9337	318027	0.029358	2.6436	939606	0.0105	13.817	0.029295	65
70	0.218197	58669	12801	262719	0.048726	2.6077	621580	0.0105	10.595	0.048619	70
75	0.347780	45867	15952	189973	0.083969	2.5323	358861	0.0105	7.824	0.083792	75
80	0.510514	29916	15272	109998	0.138842	2.4822	168888	0.0105	5.645	0.138584	80
85+	1.000000	14643	14643	58890	0.248656	4.0216	58890	0.0105	4.022	0.272496	85+

TABLE 4 — OBSERVED AND PROJECTED VITAL RATES

RATES PER THOUSAND	OBSERVED POPULATION BOTH SEXES	OBSERVED MALES	OBSERVED FEMALES	PROJECTED 1940 MALES	1940 FEMALES	1945 MALES	1945 FEMALES	1950 MALES	1950 FEMALES	STABLE MALES	STABLE FEMALES
Birth	13.95	14.53	13.38	14.51	13.44	14.17	13.19	13.37	12.52	10.61	10.15
Death	11.62	11.52	11.71	11.79	12.08	12.23	12.48	12.73	12.92	20.62	20.17
Increase	2.33	3.01	1.67	2.72	1.36	1.94	0.71	0.64	-0.40	-10.01	-10.014
PERCENTAGE											
under 15	22.53	23.21	21.86	20.81	19.68	19.91	18.88	19.62	18.66	16.01	15.57
15-64	68.26	68.39	68.14	70.50	70.10	70.77	70.35	70.40	69.89	65.35	64.39
65 and over	9.21	8.40	10.00	8.70	10.22	9.33	10.77	9.98	11.46	18.63	20.04
DEP. RATIO X 100	46.50	46.23	46.76	41.85	42.65	41.31	42.14	42.05	43.09	53.01	55.29

TABLE 1

AGE AT LAST BIRTHDAY	POPULATION BOTH SEXES	MALES Number	%	FEMALES Number	%	BIRTHS BY AGE OF MOTHER	DEATHS BOTH SEXES	MALES	FEMALES	AGE AT LAST BIRTHDAY
0	93431	47772	1.5	45659	1.4	0	2925	1693	1232	0
1-4	346606	176889	5.6	169717	5.3	0	1594	914	680	1-4
5-9	412390	210139	6.7	202251	6.3	0	463	267	196	5-9
10-14	452094	229809	7.3	222285	6.9	0	390	218	172	10-14
15-19	533200	271229	8.6	261971	8.2	5436	881	490	391	15-19
20-24	529235	268793	8.5	260442	8.1	23456	1374	821	553	20-24
25-29	548043	278141	8.8	269902	8.4	29012	1397	770	627	25-29
30-34	541137	272360	8.6	268777	8.4	23267	1426	750	676	30-34
35-39	495334	245918	7.8	249416	7.8	13718	1529	816	713	35-39
40-44	448318	220759	7.0	227559	7.1	4837	1829	997	832	40-44
45-49	401290	194639	6.2	206651	6.4	430	2252	1194	1058	45-49
50-54	365046	175929	5.6	189117	5.9	2	2977	1579	1398	50-54
55-59	317487	153008	4.9	164479	5.1	0	3789	2045	1744	55-59
60-64	277442	133607	4.2	143835	4.5	0	5078	2702	2376	60-64
65-69	218002	103492	3.3	114510	3.6	0	6485	3336	3149	65-69
70-74	160646	73599	2.3	87047	2.7		8075	3918	4157	70-74
75-79	120820	53882	1.7	66938	2.1		10308	4850	5458	75-79
80-84	65284	28574	0.9	36710	1.1	51438 M.	9555	4336	5219	80-84
85+	30563	12703	0.4	17860	0.6	48720 F.	8470	3653	4817	85+
TOTAL	6356368	3151242		3205126		100158	70797	35349	35448	TOTAL

TABLE 2 — MALE LIFE TABLE

x	$_nq_x$	l_x	$_nd_x$	$_nL_x$	$_nm_x$	$_na_x$	T_x	r_x	$\mathring{e}_x$	$_nM_x$	x
0	0.034549	100000	3455	97826	0.035317	0.3707	6561832	0.0050	65.618	0.035439	0
1	0.020329	96545	1963	380803	0.005154	1.2600	6464006	0.0050	66.953	0.005167	1
5	0.006333	94582	599	471415	0.001271	2.5000	6083203	0.0000	64.316	0.001271	5
10	0.004732	93983	445	468856	0.000949	2.6136	5611788	0.0000	59.710	0.000949	10
15	0.008996	93539	841	465790	0.001807	2.7378	5142933	0.0000	54.982	0.001807	15
20	0.015159	92697	1405	460059	0.003054	2.5613	4677143	0.0000	50.456	0.003054	20
25	0.013746	91292	1255	453287	0.002768	2.4712	4217083	0.0000	46.193	0.002768	25
30	0.013681	90037	1232	447150	0.002755	2.5355	3763797	0.0095	41.803	0.002754	30
35	0.016492	88805	1465	440516	0.003325	2.6030	3316647	0.0176	37.347	0.003318	35
40	0.022395	87341	1956	432048	0.004527	2.6196	2876131	0.0188	32.930	0.004516	40
45	0.030307	85385	2588	420807	0.006149	2.6362	2444083	0.0163	28.624	0.006134	45
50	0.044053	82797	3647	405398	0.008997	2.6457	2023276	0.0148	24.437	0.008975	50
55	0.064933	79150	5139	383631	0.013397	2.6423	1617877	0.0137	20.441	0.013365	55
60	0.096710	74010	7158	353176	0.020266	2.6424	1234246	0.0114	16.677	0.020223	60
65	0.150049	66853	10031	310493	0.032307	2.6303	881070	0.0114	13.179	0.032234	65
70	0.236417	56822	13434	251766	0.053357	2.5925	570577	0.0114	10.042	0.053234	70
75	0.368629	43388	15994	177284	0.090217	2.5206	318811	0.0114	7.348	0.090012	75
80	0.548086	27394	15014	98681	0.152149	2.4498	141527	0.0114	5.166	0.151745	80
85+	*1.000000	12380	12380	42846	0.288933	3.4610	42846	0.0114	3.461	0.287570	85+

TABLE 3 — FEMALE LIFE TABLE

x	$_nq_x$	l_x	$_nd_x$	$_nL_x$	$_nm_x$	$_na_x$	T_x	r_x	$\mathring{e}_x$	$_nM_x$	x
0	0.026439	100000	2644	98343	0.026885	0.3731	6841739	0.0052	68.417	0.026983	0
1	0.015812	97356	1539	385214	0.003996	1.2652	6743397	0.0052	69.265	0.004007	1
5	0.004834	95817	463	477926	0.000969	2.5000	6358182	0.0000	66.358	0.000969	5
10	0.003862	95354	368	475898	0.000774	2.6376	5880257	0.0000	61.668	0.000774	10
15	0.007437	94985	706	473291	0.001493	2.6851	5404359	0.0000	56.897	0.001493	15
20	0.010562	94279	996	468982	0.002123	2.5776	4931068	0.0000	52.303	0.002123	20
25	0.011549	93283	1077	463755	0.002323	2.5303	4462085	0.0000	47.834	0.002323	25
30	0.012501	92206	1153	458192	0.002516	2.5392	3998331	0.0054	43.363	0.002515	30
35	0.014211	91053	1294	452130	0.002862	2.5768	3540138	0.0137	38.880	0.002859	35
40	0.018158	89759	1630	444917	0.003663	2.6201	3088008	0.0150	34.403	0.003656	40
45	0.025343	88129	2233	435375	0.005130	2.6397	2643092	0.0132	29.991	0.005120	45
50	0.036410	85896	3127	422090	0.007410	2.6372	2207717	0.0153	25.702	0.007392	50
55	0.051872	82768	4293	403760	0.010633	2.6517	1785627	0.0163	21.574	0.010603	55
60	0.079684	78475	6253	377795	0.016552	2.6684	1381868	0.0098	17.609	0.016519	60
65	0.129452	72222	9349	339246	0.027559	2.6615	1004073	0.0098	13.903	0.027500	65
70	0.214765	62873	13503	282157	0.047846	2.6149	664827	0.0098	10.574	0.047756	70
75	0.340426	49370	16798	205599	0.081705	2.5444	382669	0.0098	7.751	0.081538	75
80	0.524478	32571	17083	119877	0.142505	2.4840	177070	0.0098	5.436	0.142169	80
85+	*1.000000	15488	15488	57194	0.270805	3.6927	57194	0.0098	3.693	0.269709	85+

TABLE 4 — OBSERVED AND PROJECTED TOTAL RATES

	OBSERVED POPULATION BOTH SEXES	MALES	FEMALES	PROJECTED POPULATION 1945 MALES	FEMALES	1950 MALES	FEMALES	1955 MALES	FEMALES	STABLE POPULATION MALES	FEMALES
RATES PER THOUSAND											
Birth	15.76	16.32	15.20	15.76	14.74	14.71	13.81	13.53	12.74	12.53	11.96
Death	11.14	11.22	11.06	11.51	11.29	11.92	11.66	12.48	12.17	17.67	17.11
Increase	4.62	5.11	4.14	4.25	3.46	2.79	2.14	1.05	0.57	-5.1470	
PERCENTAGE											
under 15	20.52	21.09	19.97	20.93	19.85	21.27	20.24	21.01	20.04	18.47	17.87
15-64	70.11	70.27	69.96	69.91	69.60	68.98	68.57	68.50	67.87	65.40	64.55
65 and over	9.37	8.64	10.08	9.16	10.54	9.75	11.19	10.49	12.09	16.13	17.58
DEP. RATIO X 100	42.63	42.31	42.95	43.05	43.67	44.97	45.83	45.98	47.34	52.91	54.92

TABLE 1 — DATA

AGE AT LAST BIRTHDAY	POPULATION BOTH SEXES	MALES Number	%	FEMALES Number	%	BIRTHS BY AGE OF MOTHER	DEATHS BOTH SEXES	MALES	FEMALES	AGE AT LAST BIRTHDAY
0	130986	67679	2.1	63307	1.9	0	3106	1807	1299	0
1-4	439288	224895	6.8	214393	6.4	0	1439	821	618	1-4
5-9	442466	225107	6.8	217359	6.5	0	465	278	187	5-9
10-14	414436	211101	6.4	203335	6.1	0	319	184	135	10-14
15-19	451268	228979	6.9	222289	6.7	6886	668	374	294	15-19
20-24	529658	269097	8.2	260561	7.8	31650	1239	753	486	20-24
25-29	524603	264582	8.0	260021	7.8	37682	1194	679	515	25-29
30-34	547964	277992	8.4	269972	8.1	30344	1248	683	565	30-34
35-39	538216	270571	8.2	267645	8.0	18423	1419	768	651	35-39
40-44	491077	243637	7.4	247440	7.4	6002	1672	873	799	40-44
45-49	442443	217501	6.6	224942	6.7	438	2144	1126	1018	45-49
50-54	389139	188982	5.7	200157	6.0	2	2807	1503	1304	50-54
55-59	347284	167025	5.1	180259	5.4	0	3823	2070	1753	55-59
60-64	294260	140845	4.3	153415	4.6	0	5124	2719	2405	60-64
65-69	248494	118907	3.6	129587	3.9	0	6908	3580	3328	65-69
70-74	182609	86336	2.6	96273	2.9		8541	4239	4302	70-74
75-79	116068	52510	1.6	63558	1.9		9564	4498	5066	75-79
80-84	70061	30598	0.9	39463	1.2	67691 M.	9941	4531	5410	80-84
85+	35228	14793	0.4	20435	0.6	63736 F.	9281	3995	5286	85+
TOTAL	6635548	3301137		3334411		131427	70902	35481	35421	TOTAL

TABLE 2 — MALE LIFE TABLE

x	$_nq_x$	l_x	$_nd_x$	$_nL_x$	$_nm_x$	$_na_x$	T_x	r_x	$\mathring{e}_x$	$_nM_x$
0	0.025956	100000	2596	98352	0.026391	0.3652	6762916	0.0166	67.629	0.026700
1	0.014338	97404	1397	385775	0.003620	1.2487	6664563	0.0166	68.422	0.003651
5	0.006083	96008	584	478579	0.001220	2.5000	6278788	0.0310	65.399	0.001235
10	0.004349	95424	415	476121	0.000872	2.5949	5800209	0.0000	60.784	0.000872
15	0.008137	95009	773	473298	0.001633	2.7411	5324089	0.0000	56.038	0.001633
20	0.013897	94236	1310	467991	0.002798	2.5655	4850791	0.0000	51.475	0.002798
25	0.012749	92926	1185	461630	0.002566	2.4667	4382800	0.0000	47.164	0.002566
30	0.012210	91742	1120	455927	0.002457	2.5174	3921171	0.0000	42.742	0.002457
35	0.014107	90621	1278	450009	0.002841	2.5767	3465244	0.0103	38.239	0.002838
40	0.017808	89343	1591	442940	0.003592	2.6275	3015235	0.0181	33.749	0.003583
45	0.025664	87752	2252	433496	0.005195	2.6626	2572295	0.0200	29.313	0.005177
50	0.039171	85500	3349	419691	0.007980	2.6686	2138800	0.0181	25.015	0.007953
55	0.060400	82151	4962	399140	0.012432	2.6594	1719109	0.0166	20.926	0.012393
60	0.092568	77189	7145	369103	0.019358	2.6431	1319969	0.0150	17.101	0.019305
65	0.140888	70044	9868	326820	0.030195	2.6290	950866	0.0150	13.575	0.030108
70	0.220297	60175	13256	269146	0.049254	2.6064	624046	0.0150	10.370	0.049099
75	0.354643	46919	16639	193639	0.085960	2.5386	354900	0.0150	7.564	0.085660
80	0.539738	30279	16343	109977	0.148604	2.4655	161261	0.0150	5.326	0.148081
85+	*1.000000	13936	13936	51285	0.271747	3.6799	51285	0.0150	3.680	0.270060

TABLE 3 — FEMALE LIFE TABLE

x	$_nq_x$	l_x	$_nd_x$	$_nL_x$	$_nm_x$	$_na_x$	T_x	r_x	$\mathring{e}_x$	$_nM_x$
0	0.020046	100000	2005	98734	0.020303	0.3683	7015937	0.0151	70.159	0.020519
1	0.011354	97995	1113	388928	0.002861	1.2551	6917203	0.0151	70.587	0.002883
5	0.004236	96883	410	483388	0.000849	2.5000	6528276	0.0299	67.383	0.000860
10	0.003314	96472	320	481609	0.000664	2.6456	6044888	0.0000	62.659	0.000664
15	0.006593	96153	634	479296	0.001323	2.6864	5563279	0.0000	57.859	0.001323
20	0.009284	95519	887	475439	0.001865	2.5702	5083982	0.0000	53.225	0.001865
25	0.009855	94632	933	470847	0.001981	2.5198	4608544	0.0000	48.700	0.001981
30	0.010410	93699	975	466098	0.002093	2.5404	4137697	0.0000	44.159	0.002093
35	0.012098	92724	1122	460918	0.002434	2.5919	3671600	0.0062	39.597	0.002432
40	0.016053	91602	1470	454522	0.003235	2.6277	3210681	0.0141	35.050	0.003229
45	0.022444	90132	2023	445885	0.004537	2.6404	2756159	0.0166	30.579	0.004526
50	0.032164	88109	2834	433885	0.006531	2.6503	2310274	0.0154	26.221	0.006515
55	0.047693	85275	4067	416899	0.009755	2.6702	1876390	0.0164	22.004	0.009725
60	0.075818	81208	6157	391698	0.015719	2.6709	1459491	0.0132	17.972	0.015676
65	0.121474	75051	9117	353962	0.025756	2.6645	1067792	0.0132	14.228	0.025682
70	0.202592	65934	13358	298039	0.044819	2.6319	713830	0.0132	10.826	0.044685
75	0.334292	52576	17576	219889	0.079931	2.5538	415791	0.0132	7.908	0.079707
80	0.511413	35001	17900	130154	0.137527	2.4945	195903	0.0132	5.597	0.137091
85+	*1.000000	17101	17101	65749	0.260094	3.8448	65749	0.0132	3.845	0.258674

TABLE 4 — OBSERVED AND PROJECTED VITAL RATES

	OBSERVED POPULATION BOTH SEXES	MALES	FEMALES	PROJECTED POPULATION 1950 MALES	FEMALES	1955 MALES	FEMALES	1960 MALES	FEMALES	STABLE POPULATION MALES	FEMA...
RATES PER THOUSAND											
Birth	19.81	20.51	19.11	18.62	17.45	16.74	15.76	15.74	14.87	17.58	17.0
Death	10.69	10.75	10.62	10.94	10.73	11.29	11.04	11.87	11.63	12.77	12.1
Increase	9.12	·9.76	8.49	7.68	6.72	5.45	4.73	3.87	3.24		4.814
PERCENTAGE											
under 15	21.51	22.08	20.95	24.14	22.94	25.34	24.09	24.49	23.36	24.41	23.8
15-64	68.66	68.74	68.58	66.32	66.19	64.58	64.37	64.82	64.34	63.87	63.4
65 and over	9.83	9.18	10.48	9.54	10.87	10.08	11.54	10.69	12.30	11.73	12.7
DEP. RATIO X 100	45.65	45.48	45.82	50.78	51.08	54.84	55.36	54.28	55.42	56.58	57.6

TABLE 5 — POPULATION PROJECTED WITH FIXED AGE-SPECIFIC BIRTH AND DEATH RATES (IN 1000's)

AGE AT LAST BIRTHDAY	1950 BOTH SEXES	MALES	FEMALES	1955 BOTH SEXES	MALES	FEMALES	1960 BOTH SEXES	MALES	FEMALES	AGE AT LAST BIRTHDAY
0-4	622	319	303	584	300	284	552	283	269	0-4
5-9	564	289	275	616	316	300	578	296	282	5-9
10-14	441	224	217	562	288	274	613	314	299	10-14
15-19	412	210	202	439	223	216	559	286	273	15-19
20-24	446	226	220	408	207	201	434	220	214	20-24
25-29	523	265	258	441	223	218	404	205	199	25-29
30-34	518	261	257	517	262	255	437	221	216	30-34
35-39	541	274	267	513	258	255	512	259	253	35-39
40-44	530	266	264	533	270	263	505	254	251	40-44
45-49	481	238	243	520	261	259	522	264	258	45-49
50-54	430	211	219	467	231	236	504	252	252	50-54
55-59	372	180	192	410	200	210	447	220	227	55-59
60-64	323	154	169	347	166	181	383	185	198	60-64
65-69	264	125	139	290	137	153	310	147	163	65-69
70-74	207	98	109	220	103	117	242	113	129	70-74
75-79	133	62	71	151	70	81	160	74	86	75-79
80-84	68	30	38	77	35	42	88	40	48	80-84
85+	34	14	20	33	14	19	37	16	21	85+
TOTAL	6909	3446	3463	7128	3564	3564	7287	3649	3638	TOTAL

TABLE 6 — STANDARDIZED RATES

STANDARD COUNTRIES: STANDARDIZED RATES PER THOUSAND	ENGLAND AND WALES 1961 BOTH SEXES	MALES	FEMALES	UNITED STATES 1960 BOTH SEXES	MALES	FEMALES	MEXICO 1960 BOTH SEXES	MALES	FEMALES
Birth	16.14	16.93*	15.17	16.43	15.99*	15.70	18.19	15.11*	17.60
Death	12.34	11.25*	13.58	10.10	9.99*	10.13	5.66	8.24*	5.25
Increase	3.79	5.68*	1.59	6.34	6.00*	5.57	12.53	6.87*	12.34

TABLE 7 — MOMENTS AND CUMULANTS

	OBSERVED POP. MALES	FEMALES	STATIONARY POP. MALES	FEMALES	STABLE POP. MALES	FEMALES	OBSERVED BIRTHS	NET MATERNITY FUNCTION	BIRTHS IN STABLE POP.
μ	34.15265	35.36447	37.19664	37.92629	34.73923	35.40521	29.08019	28.87147	28.67329
σ^2	443.5937	461.4313	517.1501	530.0593	502.6228	516.0848	38.08707	39.27716	38.87081
κ_3	2751.481	2548.346	2390.831	2228.719	3615.600	3548.095	73.1920	82.4001	86.3412
κ_4	−148678.	−170069.	−270576.	−290051.	−235878.	−255380.	−834.848	−841.887	−784.592
β_1	0.086731	0.066099	0.041328	0.033353	0.102952	0.091586	0.096960	0.112056	0.126930
β_2	2.244430	2.201250	1.988291	1.967655	2.066308	2.041164	2.424491	2.454275	2.480726
κ	−0.038621	−0.028924	−0.015292	−0.012233	−0.038154	−0.033638	−0.052585	−0.061572	−0.070380

TABLE 8 — RATES FROM AGE DISTRIBUTIONS AND VITAL STATISTICS (Females)

VITAL STATISTICS		THOMPSON AGE RANGE	NRR	1000r	INTERVAL	BOURGEOIS-PICHAT AGE RANGE	NRR	1000b	1000d	1000r	COALE
GRR	1.224					5-29	0.70	11.48	24.92	−13.44	IBR
RRR	1.149	0-4	1.05	1.65	27.35	30-54	1.38	26.48	14.56	11.92	IDR
TFR	2.524	5-9	0.81	−7.46	27.32	55-79	1.66	38.40	19.56	18.84	IRI
GENERATION	28.772	10-14	0.78	−8.96	27.27	*35-59	1.50	30.84	15.73	15.11	K1
SEX RATIO	106.205	15-19	0.89	−4.20	27.19						K2

TABLE 9 — LESLIE MATRIX AND ITS SPECTRAL COMPONENTS (Females)

Start Age Interval	ORIGINAL MATRIX SUB-DIAGONAL	ALTERNATIVE FIRST ROWS Projection	Integral	% IN STABLE POPULATION	FISHER VALUES	REPRODUCTIVE VALUES	SECOND STABLE MATRIX Z_2 FIRST COLUMN	FIRST ROW
0	0.99124	0.00000	0.00000	8.194	1.038	288164	0.1442+0.0669	0.1442+0.0669
5	0.99632	0.00000	0.00000	7.929	1.072	233091	0.1549−0.1078	0.0126+0.1333
10	0.99520	0.03645	0.00000	7.712	1.103	224193	−0.0179−0.2246	−0.0911+0.0654
15	0.99195	0.17911	0.07415	7.492	1.097	243828	−0.2419−0.1166	−0.0912−0.0407
20	0.99034	0.31334	0.29074	7.255	0.945	246333	−0.2647+0.1783	−0.0351−0.0956
25	0.98991	0.30293	0.34687	7.014	0.650	168902	0.0243+0.3778	0.0090−0.0874
30	0.98889	0.21339	0.26903	6.778	0.355	95743	0.4014+0.2011	0.0234−0.0510
35	0.98612	0.10968	0.16476	6.543	0.143	38393	0.4455−0.2905	0.0160−0.0191
40	0.98100	0.03094	0.05806	6.299	0.034	8314	−0.0309−0.6275	0.0048−0.0039
45	0.97309	0.00231	0.00466	6.032	0.002	530	−0.6551−0.3405	0.0004−0.0003
50	0.96085	0.00001	0.00002	5.730	0.000	2	−0.7280+0.4593	0.0000−0.0000
55+	0.78524			23.023				

TABLE 10 — AGE ANALYSIS AND MISCELLANEOUS RESULTS (Females)

Start Age Interval	OBSERVED POPUL. (IN 100's)	CONTRIBUTIONS OF ROOTS (IN 100's) r_1	r_2, r_3	$r_4 \cdot r_{11}$	AGE-SP. BIRTH RATES	NET MATERNITY FUNCTION	COEFF. OF MATRIX EQUATION	PARAMETERS	INTEGRAL	MATRIX	EXP. INCREASE x	$e^{(x+2\frac{1}{2})r}$
0	2777	2603	181	−7	0.0000	0.0000	0.0000	L(1)	1.02437	1.02438	0	1.0121
5	2174	2519	−215	−130	0.0000	0.0000	0.0000	L(2)	0.41615	0.42101	50	1.2876
10	2033	2450	−516	99	0.0000	0.0000	0.0360			0.74050	0.72083	55	1.3190
15	2223	2380	−314	157	0.0150	0.0720	0.1760	R(1)	0.00481	0.00482	60	1.3511
20	2606	2305	354	−53	0.0589	0.2801	0.3055	R(2)	−0.03264	−0.03612	65	1.3840
25	2600	2228	866	−494	0.0703	0.3309	0.2925			0.21176	0.20844	70	1.4178
30	2700	2153	538	8	0.0545	0.2541	0.2040	C(1)		31770	75	1.4523
35	2676	2079	−574	1172	0.0334	0.1539	0.1037	C(2)		9910	80	1.4877
40	2474	2001	−1437	1910	0.0118	0.0535	0.0288			−114019	85	1.5239
45	2249	1916	−906	1240	0.0009	0.0042	0.0021	2P/Y	29.6714	30.1444	90	1.5611
50	2002	1820	903	−722	0.0000	0.0000	0.0000	DELTA	6.5098		95	1.5991
55+	6830	7314									100	1.6381

TABLE 1 — DATA

AGE AT LAST BIRTHDAY	POPULATION BOTH SEXES	MALES Number	MALES %	FEMALES Number	FEMALES %	BIRTHS BY AGE OF MOTHER	DEATHS BOTH SEXES	DEATHS MALES	DEATHS FEMALES	AGE AT LAST BIRTHDAY
0	116091	59761	1.7	56330	1.6	0	2197	128	910	0
1-4	502832	257704	7.4	245128	7.0	0	930	528	402	1-4
5-9	571204	292219	8.4	278985	7.9	0	366	238	128	5-9
10-14	444983	226477	6.5	218506	6.2	0	216	129	87	10-14
15-19	418138	211896	6.1	206242	5.9	7814	330	217	113	15-19
20-24	463733	233107	6.7	230626	6.6	29060	545	358	187	20-24
25-29	545359	275703	7.9	269656	7.7	34695	656	404	252	25-29
30-34	533000	269715	7.7	263285	7.5	24946	798	460	338	30-34
35-39	548031	277636	7.9	270395	7.7	14768	1027	566	461	35-39
40-44	536906	269766	7.7	267140	7.6	5071	1363	754	609	40-44
45-49	485899	240726	6.9	245173	7.0	391	1981	1092	889	45-49
50-54	431480	211605	6.1	219875	6.2	2	2783	1535	1248	50-54
55-59	376126	181051	5.2	195075	5.5	0	3804	2081	1723	55-59
60-64	328210	156155	4.5	172055	4.9	0	5328	2884	2444	60-64
65-69	267086	126458	3.6	140628	4.0	0	7181	3781	3400	65-69
70-74	207555	97836	2.8	109719	3.1		9417	4726	4691	70-74
75-79	133152	61696	1.8	71456	2.0		10625	5163	5462	75-79
80-84	68627	30412	0.9	38215	1.1	60161 M.	9507	4370	5137	80-84
85+	38139	15901	0.5	22238	0.6	56586 F.	10065	4390	5675	85+
TOTAL	7016551	3495824		3520727		116747	69119	34963	34156	TOTAL

TABLE 2 — MALE LIFE TABLE

x	nq_x	l_x	nd_x	nL_x	nm_x	na_x	T_x	r_x	$\dot{e}_x$	nM_x
0	0.021228	100000	2123	98572	0.021536	0.3275	7004060	0.0000	70.041	0.021536
1	0.008148	97877	798	389263	0.002049	1.1847	6905488	0.0000	70.553	0.002049
5	0.004022	97080	390	484422	0.000806	2.5000	6516224	0.0327	67.122	0.000814
10	0.002851	96689	276	482778	0.000571	2.5771	6031802	0.0314	62.383	0.000570
15	0.005108	96413	493	480932	0.001024	2.6938	5549025	0.0000	57.554	0.001024
20	0.007650	95921	734	477812	0.001536	2.5575	5068093	0.0000	52.836	0.001536
25	0.007300	95187	695	474213	0.001465	2.5206	4590281	0.0000	48.224	0.001465
30	0.008492	94492	802	470508	0.001705	2.5663	4116068	0.0000	43.560	0.001705
35	0.010144	93690	950	466175	0.002039	2.6070	3645560	0.0000	38.911	0.002039
40	0.013914	92739	1290	460703	0.002801	2.6793	3179385	0.0113	34.283	0.002795
45	0.022535	91449	2061	452491	0.004554	2.6932	2718682	0.0196	29.729	0.004536
50	0.035815	89388	3201	439517	0.007284	2.6809	2266191	0.0210	25.352	0.007254
55	0.056172	86187	4841	419670	0.011536	2.6733	1826674	0.0184	21.194	0.011494
60	0.088875	81345	7230	389809	0.018546	2.6598	1407004	0.0210	17.297	0.018469
65	0.140133	74116	10388	345990	0.030023	2.6328	1017195	0.0210	13.724	0.029899
70	0.217328	63728	13850	285471	0.048516	2.6050	671205	0.0210	10.532	0.048305
75	0.348215	49878	17368	206643	0.084051	2.5387	385734	0.0210	7.733	0.083685
80	0.525203	32510	17074	118354	0.144264	2.4764	179092	0.0210	5.509	0.143693
85+	1.000000	15436	15436	60737	0.254137	3.9349	60737	0.0210	3.935	0.276084

TABLE 3 — FEMALE LIFE TABLE

x	nq_x	l_x	nd_x	nL_x	nm_x	na_x	T_x	r_x	$\dot{e}_x$	nM_x
0	0.015983	100000	1598	98937	0.016155	0.3348	7276235	0.0000	72.762	0.016155
1	0.006530	98402	643	391805	0.001640	1.1955	7177298	0.0000	72.939	0.001640
5	0.002258	97759	221	488244	0.000452	2.5000	6785494	0.0315	69.410	0.000459
10	0.001992	97538	194	487216	0.000399	2.5488	6297250	0.0298	64.562	0.000398
15	0.002736	97344	266	486096	0.000548	2.6553	5810034	0.0000	59.686	0.000548
20	0.004046	97078	393	484445	0.000811	2.5978	5323938	0.0000	54.842	0.000811
25	0.004662	96685	451	482344	0.000935	2.6031	4839493	0.0000	50.054	0.000935
30	0.006399	96234	616	479707	0.001284	2.6221	4357149	0.0000	45.277	0.001284
35	0.008490	95618	812	476158	0.001705	2.6182	3877443	0.0000	40.551	0.001705
40	0.011353	94807	1076	471525	0.002283	2.6700	3401284	0.0074	35.876	0.002280
45	0.018034	93730	1690	464740	0.003637	2.6861	2929760	0.0157	31.257	0.003626
50	0.028099	92040	2586	454191	0.005694	2.6766	2465020	0.0170	26.782	0.005676
55	0.043403	89454	3883	438254	0.008859	2.6783	2010829	0.0153	22.479	0.008832
60	0.069052	85571	5909	414182	0.014266	2.6860	1572575	0.0199	18.377	0.014205
65	0.114961	79662	9158	377049	0.024289	2.6783	1158393	0.0199	14.541	0.024177
70	0.194984	70504	13747	320068	0.042951	2.6393	781344	0.0199	11.082	0.042755
75	0.323345	56757	18352	239050	0.076771	2.5624	461276	0.0199	8.127	0.076439
80	0.501132	38405	19246	142628	0.134938	2.5087	222076	0.0199	5.786	0.134424
85+	1.000000	19159	19159	79598	0.240696	4.1546	79598	0.0199	4.155	0.255193

TABLE 4 — OBSERVED AND PROJECTED VITAL RATES

	OBSERVED POPULATION BOTH SEXES	MALES	FEMALES	PROJECTED POPULATION 1955 MALES	FEMALES	1960 MALES	FEMALES	1965 MALES	FEMALES	STABLE POPULATION MALES	FEMALES
RATES PER THOUSAND											
Birth	16.64	17.21	16.07	15.56	14.59	14.77	13.89	15.23	14.37	15.78	15.2
Death	9.85	10.00	9.70	10.41	10.07	11.07	10.76	11.75	11.49	13.07	12.5
Increase	6.79	7.21	6.37	5.15	4.51	3.70	3.13	3.49	2.87		2.714
PERCENTAGE											
under 15	23.30	23.92	22.69	24.68	23.40	23.46	22.26	21.85	20.76	22.51	21.8
15-64	66.51	66.58	66.45	65.21	64.94	65.75	65.20	66.53	65.77	64.36	63.7
65 and over	10.18	9.51	10.86	10.11	11.66	10.78	12.54	11.62	13.47	13.14	14.4
DEP. RATIO X 100	50.35	50.21	50.49	53.36	53.99	52.09	53.37	50.30	52.04	55.39	56.9

TABLE 1

AGE AT LAST BIRTHDAY	POPULATION BOTH SEXES	MALES Number	%	FEMALES Number	%	BIRTHS BY AGE OF MOTHER	DEATHS BOTH SEXES	MALES	FEMALES	AGE AT LAST BIRTHDAY
0	104591	53754	1.5	50837	1.4	0	1702	988	714	0
1-4	431324	222036	6.1	209288	5.7	0	630	367	263	1-4
5-9	618188	316917	8.8	301271	8.3	0	327	207	120	5-9
10-14	571075	292098	8.1	278977	7.7	0	226	141	85	10-14
15-19	448324	227406	6.3	220918	6.1	8419	317	219	98	15-19
20-24	430756	215458	6.0	215298	5.9	28513	389	271	118	20-24
25-29	472952	237408	6.6	235544	6.5	31197	456	298	158	25-29
30-34	546528	275509	7.6	271019	7.4	23030	647	405	242	30-34
35-39	530307	267774	7.4	262533	7.2	12159	839	495	344	35-39
40-44	543283	274472	7.6	268811	7.4	3916	1218	700	518	40-44
45-49	529376	265198	7.3	264178	7.3	298	1876	1081	795	45-49
50-54	474481	234134	6.5	240347	6.6	1	2690	1529	1161	50-54
55-59	415061	202183	5.6	212878	5.8	0	3877	2242	1635	55-59
60-64	353281	168249	4.6	185032	5.1	0	5385	3054	2331	60-64
65-69	296167	138898	3.8	157269	4.3	0	7526	4049	3477	65-69
70-74	224266	104352	2.9	119914	3.3		9882	5038	4844	70-74
75-79	154322	71394	2.0	82928	2.3		11574	5743	5831	75-79
80-84	79653	36152	1.0	43501	1.2	55425 M.	10572	5032	5540	80-84
85+	38453	16106	0.4	22347	0.6	52108 F.	9976	4369	5607	85+
TOTAL	7262388	3619498		3642890		107533	70109	36228	33881	TOTAL

TABLE 2 — MALE LIFE TABLE

x	nq_x	l_x	nd_x	nL_x	nm_x	na_x	T_x	r_x	$\mathring{e}_x$	nM_x	x
0	0.018154	100000	1815	98769	0.018380	0.3216	7093783	0.0000	70.938	0.018380	0
1	0.006581	98185	646	390914	0.001653	1.1766	6995015	0.0000	71.243	0.001653	1
5	0.003261	97538	318	486897	0.000653	2.5000	6604101	0.0000	67.708	0.000653	5
10	0.002421	97220	235	485545	0.000485	2.6329	6117203	0.0326	62.921	0.000483	10
15	0.004828	96985	468	483832	0.000968	2.6645	5631658	0.0295	58.067	0.000963	15
20	0.006270	96517	605	481099	0.001258	2.5454	5147826	0.0000	53.336	0.001258	20
25	0.006257	95912	600	478078	0.001255	2.5323	4666728	0.0000	48.657	0.001255	25
30	0.007324	95312	698	474869	0.001470	2.5808	4188650	0.0000	43.947	0.001470	30
35	0.009202	94614	871	470993	0.001849	2.6173	3713781	0.0000	39.252	0.001849	35
40	0.012677	93743	1188	465952	0.002550	2.6758	3242788	0.0000	34.592	0.002550	40
45	0.020239	92555	1873	458543	0.004086	2.6937	2776836	0.0117	30.002	0.004076	45
50	0.032312	90681	2930	446684	0.006560	2.7056	2318383	0.0202	25.566	0.006530	50
55	0.054301	87751	4765	427744	0.011140	2.6889	1871699	0.0215	21.330	0.011089	55
60	0.087381	82986	7251	397969	0.018221	2.6609	1443955	0.0191	17.400	0.018152	60
65	0.136864	75735	10365	354206	0.029264	2.6395	1045985	0.0191	13.811	0.029151	65
70	0.217086	65369	14191	292803	0.048465	2.6009	691779	0.0191	10.583	0.048279	70
75	0.336876	51179	17241	213494	0.080756	2.5408	398976	0.0191	7.796	0.080441	75
80	0.517535	33938	17564	125598	0.139843	2.4897	185482	0.0191	5.465	0.139191	80
85+	*1.000000	16374	16374	59884	0.273427	3.6573	59884	0.0191	3.657	0.271265	85+

TABLE 3 — FEMALE LIFE TABLE

x	nq_x	l_x	nd_x	nL_x	nm_x	na_x	T_x	r_x	$\mathring{e}_x$	nM_x	x
0	0.013912	100000	1391	99056	0.014045	0.3214	7417655	0.0000	74.177	0.014045	0
1	0.005009	98609	494	393040	0.001257	1.1762	7318599	0.0000	74.219	0.001257	1
5	0.001990	98115	195	490086	0.000398	2.5000	6925558	0.0000	70.586	0.000398	5
10	0.001524	97920	149	489230	0.000305	2.5308	6435472	0.0307	65.722	0.000305	10
15	0.002222	97770	217	488334	0.000445	2.6129	5946242	0.0255	60.818	0.000444	15
20	0.002737	97553	267	487121	0.000548	2.5847	5457909	0.0000	55.948	0.000548	20
25	0.003349	97286	326	485651	0.000671	2.6055	4970788	0.0000	51.094	0.000671	25
30	0.004455	96960	432	483786	0.000893	2.6470	4485137	0.0000	46.257	0.000893	30
35	0.006532	96528	630	481168	0.001310	2.6612	4001351	0.0000	41.453	0.001310	35
40	0.009592	95898	920	477355	0.001927	2.6792	3520183	0.0000	36.708	0.001927	40
45	0.014967	94978	1422	471612	0.003014	2.6938	3042828	0.0081	32.037	0.003009	45
50	0.023964	93557	2242	462602	0.004847	2.6893	2571216	0.0166	27.483	0.004831	50
55	0.037873	91315	3458	448586	0.007709	2.6906	2108614	0.0181	23.092	0.007680	55
60	0.061537	87856	5406	426861	0.012666	2.7028	1660028	0.0232	18.895	0.012598	60
65	0.105761	82450	8720	392169	0.022235	2.6973	1233167	0.0232	14.957	0.022109	65
70	0.185315	73730	13663	336449	0.040610	2.6433	840998	0.0232	11.406	0.040396	70
75	0.301687	60067	18121	256400	0.070676	2.5756	504548	0.0232	8.400	0.070314	75
80	0.482568	41945	20241	158208	0.127942	2.5369	248148	0.0232	5.916	0.127353	80
85+	1.000000	21704	21704	89940	0.241313	4.1440	89940	0.0232	4.144	0.250907	85+

TABLE 4 — OBSERVED AND PROJECTED VITAL RATES

	OBSERVED POPULATION BOTH SEXES	MALES	FEMALES	PROJECTED POPULATION 1960 MALES	FEMALES	1965 MALES	FEMALES	1970 MALES	FEMALES	STABLE POPULATION MALES	FEMALES
RATES PER THOUSAND											
Birth	14.81	15.31	14.30	14.58	13.63	15.08	14.12	15.84	14.87	15.21	14.58
Death	9.65	10.01	9.30	10.60	10.03	11.28	10.83	11.89	11.53	13.17	12.54
Increase	5.15	5.30	5.00	3.98	3.60	3.80	3.29	3.95	3.34		2.0401
PERCENTAGE											
under 15	23.75	24.45	23.07	23.17	21.83	21.48	20.24	21.41	20.23	21.90	21.13
15-64	65.33	65.42	65.24	66.04	65.49	66.87	66.03	65.99	64.99	64.41	63.42
65 and over	10.92	10.14	11.69	10.80	12.68	11.64	13.72	12.59	14.78	13.69	15.45
DEP. RATIO X 100	53.07	52.86	53.28	51.43	52.70	49.54	51.44	51.53	53.87	55.25	57.67

TABLE 1 — DATA

AGE AT LAST BIRTHDAY	POPULATION Both Sexes	Males Number	%	Females Number	%	BIRTHS by age of mother	DEATHS Both Sexes	Males	Females	AGE AT LAST BIRTHDAY
0	101856	52234	1.4	49622	1.3	0	1586	934	652	0
1-4	419684	216070	5.8	203614	5.4	0	430	246	184	1-
5-9	535813	275406	7.4	260407	6.9	0	248	153	95	5-
10-14	617662	316164	8.5	301498	8.0	0	203	121	82	10-
15-19	574843	293028	7.9	281815	7.5	10288	366	260	106	15-
20-24	459882	232165	6.2	227717	6.1	30125	357	258	99	20-
25-29	438708	221026	5.9	217682	5.8	30419	379	247	132	25-
30-34	475331	239093	6.4	236238	6.3	19980	487	313	174	30-
35-39	545568	275160	7.4	270408	7.2	10672	759	458	301	35-
40-44	526755	265943	7.1	260812	7.0	3138	1102	638	464	40-
45-49	536655	270794	7.3	265861	7.1	227	1759	1017	742	45-
50-54	518617	259033	6.9	259584	6.9	1	2749	1618	1131	50-
55-59	458379	224719	6.0	233660	6.2	0	3945	2371	1574	55-
60-64	391224	188182	5.0	203042	5.4	0	5632	3353	2279	60-
65-69	320458	149666	4.0	170792	4.6	0	7800	4401	3399	65-
70-74	250529	114734	3.1	135795	3.6		10582	5578	5004	70-
75-79	168501	76442	2.0	92059	2.5		12391	6172	6219	75-
80-84	94823	42503	1.1	52320	1.4	54015 M.	11861	5664	6197	80-
85+	45107	19131	0.5	25976	0.7	50835 F.	10845	4838	6007	85-
TOTAL	7480395	3731493		3748902		104850	73481	38640	34841	TOT

TABLE 2 — MALE LIFE TABLE

x	$_nq_x$	l_x	$_nd_x$	$_nL_x$	$_nm_x$	$_na_x$	T_x	r_x	$\mathring{e}_x$	$_nM_x$
0	0.017655	100000	1766	98736	0.017881	0.2839	7154560	0.0000	71.546	0.017881
1	0.004539	98234	446	391659	0.001139	1.1323	7055824	0.0000	71.826	0.001139
5	0.002774	97789	271	488265	0.000556	2.5000	6664165	0.0000	68.149	0.000556
10	0.001912	97517	186	487154	0.000383	2.6809	6175900	0.0000	63.331	0.000383
15	0.004450	97331	433	485645	0.000892	2.6689	5688746	0.0301	58.447	0.000887
20	0.005548	96898	538	483167	0.001113	2.5402	5203101	0.0271	53.697	0.001111
25	0.005572	96360	537	480477	0.001118	2.5340	4719935	0.0000	48.982	0.001118
30	0.006525	95823	625	477606	0.001309	2.5840	4239458	0.0000	44.242	0.001309
35	0.008290	95198	789	474122	0.001664	2.6322	3761852	0.0000	39.516	0.001664
40	0.011929	94409	1126	469426	0.002399	2.6753	3287731	0.0000	34.824	0.002399
45	0.018618	93283	1737	462426	0.003756	2.7040	2818304	0.0000	30.213	0.003756
50	0.030874	91546	2826	451259	0.006263	2.7103	2355878	0.0121	25.734	0.006246
55	0.051592	88720	4590	433039	0.010600	2.6996	1904620	0.0209	21.468	0.010551
60	0.085875	84129	7225	403840	0.017890	2.6737	1471581	0.0190	17.492	0.017818
65	0.137997	76905	10613	359504	0.029520	2.6424	1067741	0.0190	13.884	0.029405
70	0.218418	66292	14479	296696	0.048802	2.5990	708237	0.0190	10.684	0.048617
75	0.337677	51813	17496	215891	0.081041	2.5324	411541	0.0190	7.943	0.080741
80	0.501248	34317	17201	128501	0.133860	2.4954	195650	0.0190	5.701	0.133260
85+	*1.000000	17116	17116	67149	0.254891	3.9233	67149	0.0190	3.923	0.252888

TABLE 3 — FEMALE LIFE TABLE

x	$_nq_x$	l_x	$_nd_x$	$_nL_x$	$_nm_x$	$_na_x$	T_x	r_x	$\mathring{e}_x$	$_nM_x$
0	0.013018	100000	1302	99079	0.013139	0.2927	7521657	0.0000	75.217	0.013139
1	0.003605	98698	356	393775	0.000904	1.1414	7422578	0.0000	75.205	0.000904
5	0.001822	98342	179	491264	0.000365	2.5000	7028803	0.0000	71.473	0.000365
10	0.001359	98163	133	490483	0.000272	2.5085	6537539	0.0000	66.599	0.000272
15	0.001884	98030	185	489703	0.000377	2.5899	6047056	0.0277	61.686	0.000376
20	0.002178	97845	213	488716	0.000436	2.6085	5557353	0.0254	56.797	0.000435
25	0.003028	97632	296	487451	0.000606	2.6020	5068637	0.0000	51.916	0.000606
30	0.003676	97336	358	485838	0.000737	2.6413	4581186	0.0000	47.065	0.000737
35	0.005551	96979	538	483650	0.001113	2.6921	4095348	0.0000	42.229	0.001113
40	0.008859	96440	854	480229	0.001779	2.6919	3611698	0.0000	37.450	0.001779
45	0.013865	95586	1325	474862	0.002791	2.6858	3131469	0.0000	32.761	0.002791
50	0.021601	94261	2036	466576	0.004364	2.6785	2656607	0.0084	28.184	0.004357
55	0.033286	92224	3070	454045	0.006761	2.6947	2190031	0.0175	23.747	0.006736
60	0.055011	89155	4905	434552	0.011286	2.7121	1735986	0.0232	19.472	0.011224
65	0.095705	84250	8063	402778	0.020019	2.7090	1301434	0.0232	15.447	0.019901
70	0.170550	76187	12994	350611	0.037060	2.6663	898656	0.0232	11.795	0.036820
75	0.291720	63193	18435	271476	0.067906	2.5866	548044	0.0232	8.673	0.067554
80	0.461471	44759	20655	173337	0.119160	2.5572	276569	0.0232	6.179	0.118445
85+	*1.000000	24104	24104	103232	0.233491	4.2828	103232	0.0232	4.283	0.231252

TABLE 4 — OBSERVED AND PROJECTED VITAL RATES

	OBSERVED POPULATION Both Sexes	Males	Females	PROJECTED POPULATION 1965 Males	Females	1970 Males	Females	1975 Males	Females	STABLE POPULATION Males	Females
RATES PER THOUSAND											
Birth	14.02	14.48	13.56	15.02	14.06	15.79	14.80	15.69	14.72	14.98	14.2
Death	9.82	10.36	9.29	11.03	10.15	11.63	10.90	12.23	11.61	13.13	12.4
Increase	4.19	4.12	4.27	3.99	3.91	4.16	3.90	3.46	3.11		1.853
PERCENTAGE											
under 15	22.39	23.04	21.74	21.39	20.13	21.32	20.09	21.79	20.57	21.66	20.7
15-64	65.85	66.17	65.53	67.00	65.98	66.11	64.84	64.56	63.20	64.39	63.0
65 and over	11.76	10.79	12.72	11.61	13.90	12.56	15.07	13.64	16.23	13.95	16.1
DEP. RATIO X 100	51.86	51.13	52.59	49.26	51.57	51.25	54.22	54.89	58.22	55.30	58.6

AGE AT LAST BIRTHDAY	1965 BOTH SEXES	MALES	FEMALES	1970 BOTH SEXES	MALES	FEMALES	1975 BOTH SEXES	MALES	FEMALES	AGE AT LAST BIRTHDAY	
0-4	531	273	258	566	291	275	589	303	286	0-4	
5-9	519	267	252	528	271	257	563	289	274	5-9	
10-14	535	275	260	519	267	252	528	271	257	10-14	
15-19	616	315	301	534	274	260	518	266	252	15-19	**TABLE 5**
20-24	573	292	281	614	314	300	532	273	259	20-24	POPULATION
25-29	458	231	227	571	290	281	612	312	300	25-29	PROJECTED
30-34	437	220	217	455	229	226	568	288	280	30-34	WITH
35-39	472	237	235	434	218	216	453	228	225	35-39	FIXED
40-44	540	272	268	469	235	234	430	216	214	40-44	AGE—
45-49	520	262	258	533	268	265	462	231	231	45-49	SPECIFIC
50-54	525	264	261	509	256	253	523	262	261	50-54	BIRTH
55-59	502	249	253	508	254	254	492	245	247	55-59	AND
60-64	434	210	224	474	232	242	479	236	243	60-64	DEATH
65-69	356	168	188	394	187	207	430	206	224	65-69	RATES
70-74	273	124	149	302	138	164	334	154	180	70-74	(IN 1000's)
75-79	188	83	105	205	90	115	228	101	127	75-79	
80-84	104	45	59	117	50	67	127	53	74	80-84	
85+	53	22	31	59	24	35	66	26	40	85+	
TOTAL	7636	3809	3827	7791	3888	3903	7934	3960	3974	TOTAL	

STANDARD COUNTRIES: STANDARDIZED RATES PER THOUSAND	ENGLAND AND WALES 1961 BOTH SEXES	MALES	FEMALES	UNITED STATES 1960 BOTH SEXES	MALES	FEMALES	MEXICO 1960 BOTH SEXES	MALES	FEMALES	
Birth	14.13	14.97*	13.28	14.39	14.11*	13.75	16.85	12.74*	16.30	**TABLE 6** STANDAR-DIZED RATES
Death	9.99	9.45*	10.57	8.01	8.54*	7.63	3.97	7.67*	3.45	
Increase	4.14	5.52*	2.71	6.38	5.58*	6.12	12.88	5.08*	12.85	

	OBSERVED POP. MALES	FEMALES	STATIONARY POP. MALES	FEMALES	STABLE POP. MALES	FEMALES	OBSERVED BIRTHS	NET MATERNITY FUNCTION	BIRTHS IN STABLE POP.	
μ	35.69174	37.01917	37.96078	39.30664	36.99238	38.28767	27.54530	27.44985	27.38336	**TABLE 7**
σ^2	479.8198	499.7817	524.4677	551.5186	520.0919	547.5793	37.45777	33.87299	33.68291	MOMENTS
κ_3	2276.567	1966.771	2102.610	1828.500	2614.883	2418.107	104.6713	102.3532	102.7090	AND
κ_4	-222702.	-251334.	-281353.	-322881.	-270886.	-312683.	-541.772	-195.368	-178.112	CUMULANTS
β_1	0.046917	0.030969	0.030645	0.019930	0.048603	0.035613	0.208463	0.269552	0.276051	
β_2	2.032684	1.994156	1.977145	1.938493	1.998558	1.957179	2.613871	2.829726	2.843009	
κ	-0.017915	-0.011638	-0.011358	-0.007235	-0.018003	-0.012923	-0.119547	-0.189613	-0.195652	

VITAL STATISTICS		THOMPSON AGE RANGE	NRR	1000r	INTERVAL	BOURGEOIS-PICHAT AGE RANGE	NRR	1000b	1000d	1000r	COALE	
GRR	1.080										I BR	**TABLE 8** RATES
NRR	1.052	0-4	1.00	0.08	27.45	5-29	1.40	17.32	4.92	12.40	I DR	FROM AGE DISTRI-BUTIONS
TFR	2.227	5-9	1.04	1.43	27.42	30-54	0.86	11.45	16.86	-5.42	I RI	AND VITAL
GENERATION	27.417	10-14	1.17	5.75	27.38	55-79	1.67	40.87	21.87	18.99	K1	STATISTICS
SEX RATIO	106.256	15-19	1.07	2.54	27.31	*50-74	1.64	39.16	20.80	18.36	K2	(Females)

Part Age Interval	ORIGINAL MATRIX SUB-DIAGONAL	ALTERNATIVE FIRST ROWS Projection	Integral	FIRST STABLE MATRIX % IN STABLE POPULATION	FISHER VALUES	REPRODUCTIVE VALUES	SECOND STABLE MATRIX Z₂ FIRST COLUMN	FIRST ROW	
0	0.99677	0.00000	0.00000	7.009	1.019	258099	0.1648+0.0723	0.1648+0.0723	**TABLE 9**
5	0.99841	0.00000	0.00000	6.922	1.032	268748	0.1684-0.1414	0.0067+0.1472	LESLIE
10	0.99841	0.04355	0.00000	6.847	1.043	314553	-0.0639-0.2612	-0.1055+0.0582	MATRIX
15	0.99798	0.20135	0.08764	6.773	1.010	284701	-0.3211-0.0714	-0.0880-0.0594	AND ITS
20	0.99741	0.32458	0.31758	6.697	0.816	185834	-0.2522+0.3134	-0.0216-0.1007	SPECTRAL
25	0.99669	0.26767	0.33547	6.618	0.494	107565	0.2069+0.4460	0.0124-0.0758	COMPO-NENTS
30	0.99550	0.14799	0.20304	6.535	0.227	53550	0.6002+0.0146	0.0159-0.0378	(Females)
35	0.99293	0.06143	0.09474	6.446	0.078	21176	0.3401-0.6485	0.0091-0.0128	
40	0.98882	0.01538	0.02888	6.341	0.017	4317	-0.5242-0.7204	0.0025-0.0024	
45	0.98255	0.00102	0.00205	6.212	0.001	276	-1.0637+0.1830	0.0002-0.0001	
50	0.97314	0.00000	0.00001	6.047	0.000	1	-0.3696+1.2458	0.0000-0.0000	
55+	0.79573			27.554					

Part Age Interval	OBSERVED POPUL. (IN 100's)	CONTRIBUTIONS OF ROOTS (IN 100's) r_1	r_2, r_3	r_4-r_{11}	AGE-SP. BIRTH RATES	NET MATERNITY FUNCTION	COEFF. OF MATRIX EQUATION	PARAMETERS INTEGRAL	MATRIX	EXP. INCREASE x	$e^{(x+8\frac{1}{3})r}$	
0	2532	2686	-169	15	0.0000	0.0000	0.0000	L(1) 1.00931	1.00931	0	1.0046	**TABLE 10**
5	2604	2653	17	-66	0.0000	0.0000	0.0000	L(2) 0.35364	0.36140	50	1.1022	AGE
10	3015	2624	271	120	0.0000	0.0000	0.0433	0.75667	0.73178	55	1.1125	ANALYSIS
15	2818	2596	267	-45	0.0177	0.0867	0.2001	R(1) 0.00185	0.00185	60	1.1228	AND
20	2277	2567	-115	-174	0.0641	0.3135	0.3219	R(2) -0.03601	-0.04063	65	1.1333	MISCEL-LANEOUS
25	2177	2537	-525	165	0.0678	0.3303	0.2647	0.22672	0.22241	70	1.1439	RESULTS
30	2362	2505	-395	253	0.0410	0.1992	0.1459	C(1)	38328	75	1.1545	(Females)
35	2704	2470	354	-121	0.0191	0.0925	0.0603	C(2)	-31851	80	1.1653	
40	2608	2430	968	-791	0.0058	0.0280	0.0150		44031	85	1.1761	
45	2659	2381	517	-239	0.0004	0.0020	0.0010	2P/Y 27.7135	28.2499	90	1.1871	
50	2596	2318	-862	1140	0.0000	0.0000	0.0000	DELTA 5.5066		95	1.1981	
55+	9136	10561								100	1.2093	

TABLE 1 — DATA

AGE AT LAST BIRTHDAY	POPULATION BOTH SEXES	MALES Number	%	FEMALES Number	%	BIRTHS BY AGE OF MOTHER	DEATHS BOTH SEXES	MALES	FEMALES	AGE AT LAST BIRTHDAY
0	121309	62214	1.6	59095	1.5	0	1639	926	713	0
1-4	433740	222673	5.8	211067	5.5	0	282	167	115	1-4
5-9	525373	270289	7.0	255084	6.6	0	226	145	81	5-9
10-14	539205	277081	7.2	262124	6.8	23	173	107	66	10-14
15-19	625825	319744	8.3	306081	7.9	14881	433	299	134	15-19
20-24	593793	304858	7.9	288935	7.5	40711	456	330	126	20-24
25-29	473903	243019	6.3	230884	6.0	35552	391	274	117	25-29
30-34	442353	223899	5.8	218454	5.6	19515	479	311	168	30-34
35-39	474979	238919	6.2	236060	6.1	9273	745	473	272	35-39
40-44	542494	272960	7.1	269534	7.0	2666	1172	681	491	40-44
45-49	520718	262081	6.8	258637	6.7	185	1683	984	699	45-49
50-54	525770	264020	6.8	261750	6.8	0	2879	1784	1095	50-54
55-59	501073	248114	6.4	252959	6.5	0	4187	2581	1606	55-59
60-64	432905	208898	5.4	224007	5.8	0	6162	3820	2342	60-64
65-69	356495	167632	4.3	188863	4.9	0	8473	4970	3503	65-69
70-74	273547	123545	3.2	150002	3.9		11168	6166	5002	70-74
75-79	189797	83386	2.2	106411	2.7		13293	6744	6549	75-79
80-84	104989	45247	1.2	59742	1.5	62954 M.	12393	5985	6408	80-84
85+	55585	23106	0.6	32479	0.8	59852 F.	11960	5284	6676	85+
TOTAL	7733853	3861685		3872168		122806	78194	42031	36163	TOTAL

TABLE 2 — MALE LIFE TABLE

x	nq_x	l_x	nd_x	nL_x	nm_x	na_x	T_x	r_x	$\mathring{e}_x$	nM_x
0	0.014602	100000	1460	98917	0.014762	0.2581	7174592	0.0105	71.746	0.014884
1	0.002960	98540	292	393316	0.000742	1.1086	7075675	0.0105	71.805	0.000750
5	0.002678	98248	263	490583	0.000536	2.5000	6682359	0.0022	68.015	0.000536
10	0.001929	97985	189	489493	0.000386	2.7129	6191777	0.0000	63.191	0.000386
15	0.004665	97796	456	487909	0.000935	2.6538	5702284	0.0000	58.308	0.000935
20	0.005403	97340	526	485402	0.001084	2.5352	5214375	0.0264	53.569	0.001082
25	0.005631	96814	545	482735	0.001129	2.5537	4728973	0.0297	48.846	0.001127
30	0.006922	96269	666	479759	0.001389	2.6240	4246238	0.0002	44.108	0.001389
35	0.009852	95602	942	475762	0.001980	2.6123	3766479	0.0000	39.397	0.001980
40	0.012401	94660	1174	470533	0.002495	2.6417	3290717	0.0000	34.763	0.002495
45	0.018614	93486	1740	463473	0.003755	2.7249	2820184	0.0000	30.167	0.003755
50	0.033266	91746	3052	451679	0.006757	2.6896	2356712	0.0000	25.687	0.006757
55	0.050933	88694	4517	433085	0.010431	2.7011	1905032	0.0122	21.479	0.010402
60	0.088050	84177	7412	403637	0.018362	2.6731	1471947	0.0196	17.486	0.018286
65	0.139088	76765	10677	358666	0.029769	2.6437	1068310	0.0196	13.917	0.029648
70	0.223559	66088	14775	294891	0.050102	2.5940	709644	0.0196	10.738	0.049909
75	0.337960	51313	17342	213632	0.081176	2.5242	414753	0.0196	8.083	0.080877
80	0.494232	33971	16790	126496	0.132730	2.4980	201121	0.0196	5.920	0.132274
85+	1.000000	17182	17182	74626	0.230239	4.3433	74626	0.0196	4.343	0.228684

TABLE 3 — FEMALE LIFE TABLE

x	nq_x	l_x	nd_x	nL_x	nm_x	na_x	T_x	r_x	$\mathring{e}_x$	nM_x
0	0.011855	100000	1186	99106	0.011962	0.2462	7613650	0.0109	76.136	0.012065
1	0.002148	98814	212	394642	0.000538	1.0991	7514543	0.0109	76.047	0.000545
5	0.001586	98602	156	492620	0.000317	2.5000	7119901	0.0027	72.208	0.000318
10	0.001258	98446	124	491932	0.000252	2.5986	6627281	0.0000	67.319	0.000252
15	0.002187	98322	215	491091	0.000438	2.5872	6135349	0.0000	62.401	0.000438
20	0.002180	98107	214	490007	0.000436	2.5328	5644257	0.0277	57.532	0.000436
25	0.002540	97893	249	488878	0.000509	2.6348	5154250	0.0274	52.652	0.000507
30	0.003838	97644	375	487350	0.000769	2.6725	4665372	0.0000	47.779	0.000769
35	0.005746	97270	559	485056	0.001152	2.6873	4178022	0.0000	42.953	0.001152
40	0.009070	96711	877	481513	0.001822	2.6729	3692967	0.0000	38.186	0.001822
45	0.013429	95834	1287	476176	0.002703	2.6751	3211454	0.0001	33.511	0.002703
50	0.020715	94547	1959	468173	0.004183	2.6718	2735278	0.0000	28.930	0.004183
55	0.031341	92588	2902	456238	0.006360	2.6901	2267104	0.0089	24.486	0.006349
60	0.051363	89686	4607	437897	0.010520	2.7131	1810867	0.0261	20.191	0.010455
65	0.089497	85080	7614	407915	0.018667	2.7039	1372970	0.0261	16.137	0.018548
70	0.155645	77465	12057	359270	0.033560	2.6730	965055	0.0261	12.458	0.033346
75	0.269484	65408	17626	284732	0.061905	2.5997	605786	0.0261	9.262	0.061544
80	0.428803	47782	20489	189700	0.108007	2.5983	321054	0.0261	6.719	0.107261
85+	*1.000000	27293	27293	131354	0.207781	4.8128	131354	0.0261	4.813	0.205548

TABLE 4 — OBSERVED AND PROJECTED VITAL RATES

	OBSERVED POPULATION BOTH SEXES	MALES	FEMALES	PROJECTED POPULATION 1970 MALES	FEMALES	1975 MALES	FEMALES	1980 MALES	FEMALES	STABLE POPULATION MALES	FEMAL
RATES PER THOUSAND											
Birth	15.88	16.30	15.46	17.02	16.09	16.75	15.81	15.99	15.09	16.84	16.
Death	10.11	10.88	9.34	11.50	10.30	12.00	11.04	12.44	11.61	11.67	10.
Increase	5.77	5.42	6.12	5.52	5.79	4.75	4.77	3.55	3.48		5.17
PERCENTAGE											
under 15	20.94	21.55	20.33	22.04	20.80	23.02	21.78	23.66	22.42	23.86	22.
15-64	66.38	66.98	65.78	65.64	64.02	63.73	61.89	62.41	60.50	63.87	62.
65 and over	12.68	11.47	13.88	12.32	15.18	13.26	16.33	13.93	17.08	12.27	14.
DEP. RATIO X 100	50.65	49.30	52.01	52.33	56.21	56.92	61.58	60.23	65.29	56.58	60.

TABLE 5 — POPULATION PROJECTED WITH FIXED AGE—SPECIFIC BIRTH AND DEATH RATES (IN 1000's)

AGE LAST BIRTHDAY	1970 BOTH SEXES	MALES	FEMALES	1975 BOTH SEXES	MALES	FEMALES	1980 BOTH SEXES	MALES	FEMALES	AGE AT LAST BIRTHDAY
0-4	627	321	306	653	334	319	648	332	316	0-4
5-9	554	284	270	626	320	306	651	333	318	5-9
10-14	525	270	255	552	283	269	624	319	305	10-14
15-19	538	276	262	523	269	254	551	282	269	15-19
20-24	623	318	305	536	275	261	521	267	254	20-24
25-29	591	303	288	621	316	305	533	273	260	25-29
30-34	472	242	230	588	301	287	618	314	304	30-34
35-39	439	222	217	469	240	229	585	299	286	35-39
40-44	470	236	234	436	220	216	464	237	227	40-44
45-49	536	269	267	465	233	232	429	216	213	45-49
50-54	509	255	254	524	262	262	455	227	228	50-54
55-59	508	253	255	493	245	248	506	251	255	55-59
60-64	474	231	243	481	236	245	466	228	238	60-64
65-69	395	186	209	431	205	226	438	210	228	65-69
70-74	304	138	166	337	153	184	368	169	199	70-74
75-79	209	90	119	232	100	132	257	111	146	75-79
80-84	120	49	71	132	53	79	147	59	88	80-84
85+	68	27	41	78	29	49	86	31	55	85+
TOTAL	7962	3970	3992	8177	4074	4103	8347	4158	4189	TOTAL

TABLE 6 — STANDARDIZED RATES

STANDARD COUNTRIES:

STANDARDIZED RATES PER THOUSAND

	ENGLAND AND WALES 1961 BOTH SEXES	MALES	FEMALES	UNITED STATES 1960 BOTH SEXES	MALES	FEMALES	MEXICO 1960 BOTH SEXES	MALES	FEMALES
Birth	15.32	16.55*	14.47	15.63	15.23*	15.00	18.49	14.57*	17.98
Death	9.49	9.38*	9.66	7.63	8.52*	6.97	3.76	7.64*	3.16
Increase	5.83	7.16*	4.81	7.99	6.71*	8.03	14.73	6.93*	14.82

TABLE 7 — MOMENTS AND CUMULANTS

	OBSERVED POP. MALES	FEMALES	STATIONARY POP. MALES	FEMALES	STABLE POP. MALES	FEMALES	OBSERVED BIRTHS	NET MATERNITY FUNCTION	BIRTHS IN STABLE POP.
μ	36.06883	37.62233	37.93428	39.69513	35.25266	36.81715	26.53331	27.08403	26.90358
σ^2	490.0415	516.5857	525.2043	562.6460	510.3297	548.5497	34.44024	33.02913	32.56608
κ_3	2321.147	1932.964	2177.644	1880.622	3542.127	3536.274	124.2712	89.0013	89.9841
κ_4	-239159.	-278025.	-280121.	-337002.	-244547.	-299167.	-98.955	-201.837	-167.963
β_1	0.045783	0.027103	0.032733	0.019856	0.094401	0.075761	0.378044	0.219837	0.234442
β_2	2.004087	1.958163	1.984478	1.93546C	2.061011	2.005783	2.916573	2.814985	2.841626
κ	-0.017085	-0.009926	-0.012180	-0.007192	-0.035135	-0.027476	-0.241453	-0.170283	-0.183876

TABLE 8 — RATES FROM AGE DISTRIBUTIONS AND VITAL STATISTICS (Females)

VITAL STATISTICS		THOMPSON AGE RANGE	NRR	1000r	INTERVAL	BOURGEOIS-PICHAT AGE RANGE	NRR	1000b	1000d	1000r	COALE	
GRR	1.177					5-29	1.05	14.48	12.82	1.66	IBR	16.53
NRR	1.150	0-4	1.03	1.16	27.45	30-54	0.74	8.36	19.39	-11.03	IDR	8.67
TFR	2.414	5-9	1.00	0.09	27.42	55-79	1.67	43.00	23.99	19.01	IRI	7.86
GENERATION	26.994	10-14	1.04	1.53	27.38	*40-64	1.09	16.65	13.46	3.19	K1	36.28
SEX RATIO	1C5.183	15-19	1.19	6.18	27.31						K2	0.51

TABLE 9 — LESLIE MATRIX AND ITS SPECTRAL COMPONENTS (Females)

Part age interval	ORIGINAL MATRIX SUB-DIAGONAL	ALTERNATIVE FIRST ROWS Projection	Integral	FIRST STABLE MATRIX % IN STABLE POPULATION	FISHER VALUES	REPRODUCTIVE VALUES	SECOND STABLE MATRIX Z2 FIRST COLUMN	FIRST ROW
	0.99771	0.00000	0.00000	7.803	1.026	277140	0.1656+0.0699	0.1656+0.0699
	0.99860	0.00011	C.CC000	7.587	1.055	269148	0.1614-0.1440	0.0065+0.1492
	0.99829	0.05850	0.00021	7.382	1.084	284197	-0.0734-0.2499	-0.1097+0.0580
	0.99779	0.22765	0.11852	7.182	1.054	322739	-0.3097-0.0491	-0.0922-0.0658
	0.99769	0.35437	0.34347	6.983	0.850	245715	-0.2131+0.3114	-0.0212-0.1086
	0.99688	0.29242	C.37536	6.788	0.510	117835	0.2287+0.3922	0.0152-0.0795
	0.99529	0.15453	0.21777	6.594	0.224	49038	0.5439-0.0464	0.0166-0.0374
	0.99270	0.05908	0.09576	6.396	0.072	17041	0.2294-0.6137	-0.0084-0.0117
	0.98892	0.01275	0.02411	6.187	0.014	3659	-0.5462-0.5630	0.0020-0.0021
	0.98319	0.00086	C.00173	5.962	0.001	224	-0.8858+0.3008	0.0001-0.0001
	0.97451	0.00000	0.00001	5.712	0.000	1	-0.1278+1.1019	0.0000-0.0000
+	0.80729			25.425				

TABLE 10 — AGE ANALYSIS AND MISCELLANEOUS RESULTS (Females)

Part age interval	OBSERVED POPUL. (IN 100's)	CONTRIBUTIONS OF ROOTS (IN 100's) r_1	r_2, r_3	$r_4 \cdot r_{11}$	AGE-SP. BIRTH RATES	NET MATERNITY FUNCTION	COEFF. OF MATRIX EQUATION	PARAMETERS INTEGRAL	MATRIX	EXP. INCREASE x	$e^{(x+2\frac{1}{2})r}$
	2702	2878	-141	-35	0.0000	0.0000	0.0000	L(1) 1.02620	1.02622	0	1.0130
	2551	2798	-274	27	0.0000	0.0000	0.0001	L(2) 0.34812	0.35531	50	1.3121
	2621	2723	-78	-23	0.0000	0.0002	0.0583	0.77530	0.74921	55	1.3464
	3061	2649	316	96	0.0237	0.1164	0.2264	R(1) 0.00517	0.00518	60	1.3817
	2889	2575	440	-126	0.0687	0.3365	0.3517	R(2) -0.03254	-0.03746	65	1.4179
	2309	2504	-5	-190	0.0750	0.3669	0.2895	0.22975	0.22559	70	1.4551
	2185	2432	-641	393	0.0435	0.2122	0.1525	C(1)	36884	75	1.4932
	2361	2359	-652	654	0.0191	0.0929	0.0580	C(2)	-56164	80	1.5323
	2695	2282	251	162	0.0048	0.0232	0.0124		-32159	85	1.5725
	2586	2199	1189	-801	0.0003	0.0017	0.0008	2P/Y 27.3476	27.8520	90	1.6137
+	2618	2107	852	-341	0.0000	0.0000	0.0000	DELTA 5.8344		95	1.6560
	10145	9378								100	1.6994

TABLE 1 DATA

AGE AT LAST BIRTHDAY	POPULATION BOTH SEXES	MALES Number	%	FEMALES Number	%	BIRTHS BY AGE OF MOTHER	DEATHS BOTH SEXES	MALES	FEMALES	AGE AT LAST BIRTHDAY
0	81153	41657	1.8	39496	1.6	0	2514	1459	1055	0
1-4	333772	170652	7.4	163120	6.7	0	617	350	267	1-4
5-9	397421	202616	8.8	194805	8.0	0	262	152	110	5-9
10-14	305764	155174	6.7	150590	6.2	4	174	109	65	10-1
15-19	319926	160855	6.9	159071	6.5	2105	292	200	92	15-1
20-24	341556	169484	7.3	172072	7.1	18494	457	304	153	20-2
25-29	362858	180693	7.8	182165	7.5	28380	536	331	205	25-2
30-34	337512	170175	7.3	167337	6.9	19388	580	338	242	30-3
35-39	349039	174705	7.5	174334	7.2	10928	767	451	316	35-3
40-44	362935	178396	7.7	184539	7.6	3793	1129	650	479	40-4
45-49	339533	163966	7.1	175567	7.2	314	1688	970	718	45-4
50-54	302026	141734	6.1	160292	6.6	2	2394	1379	1015	50-5
55-59	253059	116430	5.0	136629	5.6	0	3154	1806	1348	55-5
60-64	210065	95142	4.1	114923	4.7	0	4104	2288	1816	60-6
65-69	176691	79189	3.4	97502	4.0	0	5608	3015	2593	65-6
70-74	135771	58588	2.5	77183	3.2		7232	3633	3599	70-7
75-79	84773	35202	1.5	49571	2.0		7345	3437	3908	75-7
80-84	38617	15159	0.7	23458	1.0	42922 M.	5533	2346	3187	80-8
85+	16177	5665	0.2	10512	0.4	40486 F.	3932	1480	2452	85+
TOTAL	4748648	2315482		2433166		83408	48318	24698	23620	TOT

TABLE 2 MALE LIFE TABLE

x	$_nq_x$	l_x	$_nd_x$	$_nL_x$	$_nm_x$	$_na_x$	T_x	r_x	$\mathring{e}_x$	$_nM_x$
0	0.034156	100000	3416	97520	0.035024	0.2739	6677852	0.0000	66.779	0.035024
1	0.008156	96584	788	384071	0.002051	1.1226	6580332	0.0000	68.130	0.002051
5	0.003710	95797	355	478095	0.000743	2.5000	6196261	0.0303	64.681	0.000750
10	0.003518	95441	336	476416	0.000705	2.6453	5718165	0.0223	59.913	0.000702
15	0.006199	95106	590	474160	0.001243	2.6796	5241749	0.0000	55.115	0.001243
20	0.008929	94516	844	470525	0.001794	2.5653	4767589	0.0000	50.442	0.001794
25	0.009118	93672	854	466241	0.001832	2.5179	4297064	0.0000	45.873	0.001832
30	0.009884	92818	917	461864	0.001986	2.5738	3830823	0.0013	41.272	0.001986
35	0.012829	91901	1179	456706	0.002581	2.6276	3368959	0.0000	36.659	0.002581
40	0.018074	90722	1640	449807	0.003645	2.6817	2912253	0.0025	32.101	0.003644
45	0.029285	89082	2609	439407	0.005937	2.6992	2462447	0.0168	27.643	0.005916
50	0.047801	86473	4133	422778	0.009777	2.6804	2023040	0.0241	23.395	0.009729
55	0.075156	82340	6188	397179	0.015581	2.6538	1600262	0.0238	19.435	0.015511
60	0.114258	76151	8701	360178	0.024157	2.6639	1203083	0.0243	15.799	0.024048
65	0.175247	67450	11820	309021	0.038251	2.6117	842906	0.0243	12.497	0.038073
70	0.270307	55630	15037	241419	0.062287	2.5574	533885	0.0243	9.597	0.062009
75	0.393183	40593	15960	162761	0.098060	2.4811	292465	0.0243	7.205	0.097636
80	0.551602	24632	13587	87423	0.155421	2.4246	129704	0.0243	5.266	0.154760
85+	1.000000	11045	11045	42282	0.261227	3.8281	42282	0.0243	3.828	0.261252

TABLE 3 FEMALE LIFE TABLE

x	$_nq_x$	l_x	$_nd_x$	$_nL_x$	$_nm_x$	$_na_x$	T_x	r_x	$\mathring{e}_x$	$_nM_x$
0	0.026207	100000	2621	98111	0.026712	0.2793	7119648	0.0000	71.196	0.026712
1	0.006517	97379	635	387694	0.001637	1.1277	7021537	0.0000	72.105	0.001637
5	0.002790	96745	270	483049	0.000559	2.5000	6633842	0.0289	68.571	0.000565
10	0.002156	96475	208	481856	0.000432	2.5081	6150793	0.0198	63.755	0.000432
15	0.002888	96267	278	480684	0.000578	2.6632	5668938	0.0000	58.888	0.000578
20	0.004436	95989	426	478933	0.000889	2.6264	5188253	0.0000	54.051	0.000889
25	0.005613	95563	536	476528	0.001126	2.6006	4709320	0.0016	49.280	0.001125
30	0.007208	95027	685	473486	0.001447	2.5958	4232793	0.0029	44.543	0.001446
35	0.009024	94342	851	469688	0.001813	2.6275	3759306	0.0000	39.848	0.001813
40	0.012900	93490	1206	464649	0.002596	2.6764	3289618	0.0000	35.187	0.002596
45	0.020294	92284	1873	457078	0.004097	2.6807	2824969	0.0099	30.612	0.004090
50	0.031309	90411	2831	445474	0.006354	2.6744	2367892	0.0185	26.190	0.006332
55	0.048437	87581	4242	428039	0.009911	2.6745	1922417	0.0230	21.950	0.009866
60	0.076612	83339	6385	401866	0.015888	2.6777	1494379	0.0255	17.931	0.015802
65	0.125885	76954	9687	362176	0.026748	2.6677	1092513	0.0255	14.197	0.026594
70	0.210855	67267	14183	302524	0.046884	2.6163	730337	0.0255	10.857	0.046629
75	0.331697	53083	17607	222175	0.079250	2.5442	427814	0.0255	8.059	0.078836
80	0.505176	35476	17921	131272	0.136521	2.4994	205638	0.0255	5.797	0.135860
85+	1.000000	17554	17554	74366	0.236052	4.2364	74366	0.0255	4.236	0.233256

TABLE 4 OBSERVED AND PROJECTED VITAL RATES

	OBSERVED POPULATION BOTH SEXES	MALES	FEMALES	PROJECTED POPULATION 1956 MALES	FEMALES	1961 MALES	FEMALES	1966 MALES	FEMALES	STABLE POPULATION MALES	FEMA
RATES PER THOUSAND											
Birth	17.56	18.54	16.64	17.37	15.67	16.28	14.74	16.24	14.77	16.84	15.
Death	10.18	10.67	9.71	11.28	10.51	11.85	11.24	12.38	11.85	13.56	12.
Increase	7.39	7.87	6.93	6.09	5.15	4.43	3.51	3.86	2.92		3.28
PERCENTAGE											
under 15	23.55	24.62	22.52	25.71	23.51	24.74	22.66	23.54	21.64	23.60	22.
15-64	66.94	67.01	66.86	65.57	65.16	66.06	65.17	66.51	65.13	65.25	63.
65 and over	9.52	8.37	10.61	8.73	11.33	9.20	12.17	9.95	13.23	11.16	13.
DEP. RATIO X 100	49.40	49.23	49.56	52.51	53.47	51.37	53.45	50.36	53.54	53.26	56.

AGE LAST BIRTHDAY	1956 BOTH SEXES	1956 MALES	1956 FEMALES	1961 BOTH SEXES	1961 MALES	1961 FEMALES	1966 BOTH SEXES	1966 MALES	1966 FEMALES	AGE AT LAST BIRTHDAY	
0-4	398	204	194	384	197	187	380	195	185	0-4	**TABLE 5**
5-9	412	211	201	395	202	193	381	195	186	5-9	POPULATION
10-14	396	202	194	411	210	201	393	201	192	10-14	PROJECTED
15-19	304	154	150	395	201	194	409	209	200	15-19	WITH
20-24	318	160	158	303	153	150	392	199	193	20-24	FIXED
25-29	339	168	171	316	158	158	301	152	149	25-29	AGE—
30-34	360	179	181	336	166	170	314	157	157	30-34	SPECIFIC
35-39	334	168	166	357	177	180	334	165	169	35-39	BIRTH
40-44	344	172	172	330	166	164	352	174	178	40-44	AND
45-49	356	174	182	338	168	170	324	162	162	45-49	DEATH
50-54	329	158	171	345	168	177	327	162	165	50-54	RATES
55-59	287	133	154	312	148	164	328	158	170	55-59	(IN 1000's)
60-64	234	106	128	266	121	145	288	134	154	60-64	
65-69	186	82	104	207	91	116	234	104	130	65-69	
70-74	143	62	81	151	64	87	168	71	97	70-74	
75-79	96	39	57	102	42	60	107	43	64	75-79	
80-84	48	19	29	54	21	33	57	22	35	80-84	
85+	20	7	13	26	9	17	29	10	19	85+	
TOTAL	4904	2398	2506	5028	2462	2566	5118	2513	2605	TOTAL	

STANDARD COUNTRIES:	ENGLAND AND WALES 1961 BOTH SEXES	MALES	FEMALES	UNITED STATES 1960 BOTH SEXES	MALES	FEMALES	MEXICO 1960 BOTH SEXES	MALES	FEMALES	
STANDARDIZED RATES PER THOUSAND										**TABLE 6**
Birth	15.19	16.40*	14.29	15.45	15.50*	14.78	16.92	14.44*	16.39	STANDARDIZED
Death	12.73	12.45*	13.12	10.39	10.87*	9.69	5.63	9.00*	4.86	RATES
Increase	2.46	3.96*	1.17	5.06	4.62*	5.09	11.29	5.44*	11.53	

	OBSERVED POP. MALES	FEMALES	STATIONARY POP. MALES	FEMALES	STABLE POP. MALES	FEMALES	OBSERVED BIRTHS	NET MATERNITY FUNCTION	BIRTHS IN STABLE POP.	
m_1	33.33704	35.34650	36.53964	38.15676	34.92344	36.43134	29.36871	29.29608	29.18089	**TABLE 7**
m_2	443.6062	473.1444	496.7973	529.7779	487.8200	521.3193	33.16819	33.14869	32.88676	MOMENTS
m_3	2589.792	2173.355	2348.889	2114.774	3111.681	3029.242	86.7800	79.1925	80.4327	AND
k_4	-168150.	-206517.	-241896.	-288373.	-222066.	-267700.	-359.524	-386.650	-358.847	CUMULANTS
β_1	0.076833	0.044594	0.044997	0.030078	0.083409	0.064767	0.206383	0.172175	0.181887	
β_2	2.145519	2.077495	2.019901	1.972534	2.066824	2.014991	2.673198	2.648127	2.668207	
κ	-0.031397	-0.017765	-0.017030	-0.011112	-0.031548	-0.023921	-0.129521	-0.111680	-0.119297	

VITAL STATISTICS		THOMPSON AGE RANGE	NRR	1000r	INTERVAL	BOURGEOIS-PICHAT AGE RANGE	NRR	1000b	1000d	1000r	COALE		
GRR	1.159										IBR	15.89	**TABLE 8**
NRR	1.101	0-4	1.14	4.84	27.41	5-29	0.98	14.47	15.12	-0.65	IDR	13.22	RATES FROM AGE DISTRI-BUTIONS AND VITAL STATISTICS (Females)
R	2.387	5-9	1.08	2.72	27.37	30-54	0.96	14.43	15.84	-1.40	IRI	2.68	
GENERATION	29.238	10-14	0.83	-6.68	27.31	55-79	1.49	29.97	15.32	14.65	K1	30.10	
SEX RATIO	106.017	15-19	0.91	-3.61	27.22	*45-69	1.66	38.89	20.07	18.81	K2	0.53	

	ORIGINAL MATRIX SUB-DIAGONAL	ALTERNATIVE FIRST ROWS Projection	Integral	FIRST STABLE MATRIX % IN STABLE POPULATION	FISHER VALUES	REPRODUCTIVE VALUES	SECOND STABLE MATRIX Z_2 FIRST COLUMN	FIRST ROW	
	0.99433	0.00000	0.00000	7.649	1.038	210250	0.1558+0.0572	0.1558+0.0572	**TABLE 9**
	0.99753	0.00003	0.00000	7.482	1.061	206663	0.1479-0.1234	0.0244+0.1409	LESLIE
	0.99757	0.01560	0.00006	7.342	1.081	162774	-0.0384-0.2209	-0.0944+0.0787	MATRIX
	0.99636	0.14186	0.03146	7.205	1.085	172657	-0.2451-0.0898	-0.1015-0.0373	AND ITS
	0.99498	0.30949	0.25553	7.062	0.960	165131	-0.2330+0.1947	-0.0380-0.0998	SPECTRAL
	0.99362	0.31942	0.37040	6.912	0.658	119810	0.0606+0.3473	0.0096-0.0891	COMPO-NENTS
	0.99198	0.20992	0.27546	6.756	0.339	56776	0.3839+0.1404	0.0206-0.0496	(Females)
	0.98927	0.09788	0.14903	6.593	0.128	22333	0.3630-0.3037	0.0130-0.0181	
	0.98371	0.02631	0.04887	6.416	0.029	5345	-0.0942-0.5383	0.0038-0.0037	
	0.97461	0.00212	0.00425	6.208	0.002	383	-0.5893-0.2152	0.0003-0.0003	
	0.96086	0.00001	0.00003	5.952	0.000	2	-0.5470+0.4583	0.0000-0.0000	
+	0.78239			24.425					

	OBSERVED POPUL. (IN 100's)	CONTRIBUTIONS OF ROOTS (IN 100's) r_1	r_2, r_3	r_4-r_{11}	AGE-SP. BIRTH RATES	NET MATERNITY FUNCTION	COEFF. OF MATRIX EQUATION	PARAMETERS INTEGRAL	MATRIX	EXP. INCREASE x	$e^{(x+2\frac{1}{2})r}$	
	2026	1854	153	19	0.0000	0.0000	0.0000	L(1) 1.01654	1.01655	0	1.0082	**TABLE 10**
	1948	1814	76	58	0.0000	0.0000	0.0000	L(2) 0.42605	0.42827	50	1.1880	AGE ANALYSIS
	1506	1780	-119	-155	0.0000	0.0001	0.0155	0.76372	0.74212	55	1.2077	AND MISCEL-LANEOUS
	1591	1747	-241	85	0.0064	0.0309	0.1404	R(1) 0.00328	0.00328	60	1.2276	RESULTS
	1721	1712	-120	128	0.0522	0.2499	0.3051	R(2) -0.02681	-0.03090	65	1.2479	(Females)
	1822	1676	187	-40	0.0756	0.3604	0.3133	0.21239	0.20948	70	1.2686	
	1673	1638	377	-342	0.0562	0.2663	0.2046	C(1)	24242	75	1.2896	
	1743	1598	186	-41	0.0304	0.1429	0.0946	C(2)	41994	80	1.3109	
	1845	1555	-289	580	0.0100	0.0464	0.0252		-19534	85	1.3326	
	1756	1505	-579	830	0.0009	0.0040	0.0020	2P/Y 29.5834	29.9943	90	1.3546	
	1603	1443	-280	440	0.0000	0.0000	0.0000	DELTA 5.2936		95	1.3771	
+	5098	5921								100	1.3998	

TABLE 1 — DATA

AGE AT LAST BIRTHDAY	POPULATION BOTH SEXES	MALES Number	%	FEMALES Number	%	BIRTHS BY AGE OF MOTHER	DEATHS BOTH SEXES	MALES	FEMALES	AGE AT LAST BIRTHDAY
0	81323	41465	1.7	39858	1.6	0	2338	1327	1011	0
1-4	323034	165438	7.0	157596	6.2	0	511	287	224	1-4
5-9	419510	214482	9.0	205028	8.0	0	264	163	101	5-9
10-14	363828	185038	7.8	178790	7.0	5	170	107	63	10-14
15-19	323497	163485	6.9	160012	6.3	2191	273	186	87	15-19
20-24	353180	171000	7.2	182180	7.2	19554	438	317	121	20-24
25-29	362145	170928	7.2	191217	7.5	28649	455	291	164	25-29
30-34	362156	176293	7.4	185863	7.3	20346	547	335	212	30-34
35-39	319684	158393	6.7	161291	6.3	9546	631	368	263	35-39
40-44	360740	176953	7.4	183787	7.2	3456	1039	606	433	40-44
45-49	354378	171633	7.2	182745	7.2	286	1626	954	672	45-49
50-54	323045	153120	6.4	169925	6.7	1	2439	1456	983	50-54
55-59	275134	126757	5.3	148377	5.8	0	3228	1899	1329	55-59
60-64	223868	100456	4.2	123412	4.8	0	4173	2395	1778	60-64
65-69	182492	80637	3.4	101855	4.0	0	5643	3074	2569	65-69
70-74	141500	61070	2.6	80430	3.2		7090	3572	3518	70-74
75-79	94877	38979	1.6	55898	2.2		8103	3763	4340	75-79
80-84	44419	17391	0.7	27028	1.1	43032 M.	6213	2703	3510	80-84
85+	18351	6401	0.3	11950	0.5	41002 F.	4539	1687	2852	85+
TOTAL	4927161	2375919		2547242		84034	49720	25490	24230	TOTAL

TABLE 2 — MALE LIFE TABLE

x	$_nq_x$	l_x	$_nd_x$	$_nL_x$	$_nm_x$	$_na_x$	T_x	r_x	$\dot{e}_x$	$_nM_x$	x
0	0.031268	100000	3127	97704	0.032003	0.2656	6740072	0.0000	67.401	0.032003	0
1	0.006905	96873	669	385563	0.001735	1.1151	6642368	0.0000	68.568	0.001735	1
5	0.003782	96204	364	480112	0.000758	2.5000	6256805	0.0102	65.037	0.000760	5
10	0.002898	95840	278	478545	0.000580	2.6344	5776693	0.0264	60.274	0.000578	10
15	0.005683	95563	543	476581	0.001139	2.7298	5298148	0.0067	55.442	0.001138	15
20	0.009227	95020	877	472959	0.001854	2.5606	4821567	0.0000	50.743	0.001854	20
25	0.008476	94143	798	468721	0.001702	2.5017	4348608	0.0000	46.192	0.001702	25
30	0.009461	93345	883	464573	0.001901	2.5637	3879887	0.0057	41.565	0.001900	30
35	0.011553	92462	1068	459778	0.002323	2.6306	3415314	0.0000	36.938	0.002323	35
40	0.016989	91394	1553	453378	0.003425	2.6881	2955536	0.0000	32.339	0.003425	40
45	0.027495	89841	2470	443556	0.005569	2.7132	2502158	0.0086	27.851	0.005558	45
50	0.046710	87371	4081	427398	0.009549	2.6831	2058603	0.0205	23.562	0.009509	50
55	0.072730	83290	6058	402277	0.015058	2.6606	1631205	0.0265	19.585	0.014981	55
60	0.113321	77232	8752	365518	0.023944	2.6415	1228928	0.0223	15.912	0.023841	60
65	0.175271	68480	12003	313593	0.038274	2.5999	863410	0.0223	12.608	0.038121	65
70	0.256890	56477	14509	247026	0.058733	2.5627	549817	0.0223	9.735	0.058490	70
75	0.390078	41969	16371	168865	0.096948	2.4968	302791	0.0223	7.215	0.096539	75
80	0.556995	25598	14258	91296	0.156171	2.4265	133927	0.0223	5.232	0.155426	80
85+	*1.000000	11340	11340	42630	0.266006	3.7593	42630	0.0223	3.759	0.263553	85-

TABLE 3 — FEMALE LIFE TABLE

x	$_nq_x$	l_x	$_nd_x$	$_nL_x$	$_nm_x$	$_na_x$	T_x	r_x	$\dot{e}_x$	$_nM_x$	x
0	0.024902	100000	2490	98181	0.025364	0.2696	7214782	0.0001	72.148	0.025365	0
1	0.005662	97510	552	388448	0.001421	1.1186	7116601	0.0001	72.983	0.001421	1
5	0.002452	96958	238	484194	0.000491	2.5000	6728153	0.0092	69.393	0.000493	5
10	0.001762	96720	170	483179	0.000353	2.5299	6243959	0.0244	64.557	0.000352	10
15	0.002715	96550	262	482124	0.000544	2.6183	5760780	0.0000	59.667	0.000544	15
20	0.003316	96287	319	480670	0.000664	2.5970	5278656	0.0000	54.822	0.000664	20
25	0.004280	95968	411	478861	0.000858	2.6144	4797986	0.0000	49.996	0.000858	25
30	0.005700	95557	545	476501	0.001143	2.6381	4319125	0.0158	45.199	0.001141	30
35	0.008122	95013	772	473251	0.001631	2.6510	3842624	0.0000	40.443	0.001631	35
40	0.011716	94241	1104	468638	0.002356	2.6750	3369373	0.0000	35.753	0.002356	40
45	0.018245	93137	1699	461752	0.003680	2.6855	2900735	0.0040	31.145	0.003677	45
50	0.028620	91438	2617	451107	0.005801	2.6763	2438983	0.0149	26.674	0.005785	50
55	0.044064	88821	3914	435014	0.008997	2.6776	1987876	0.0226	22.381	0.008957	55
60	0.070115	84907	5953	410806	0.014492	2.6940	1552861	0.0259	18.289	0.014407	60
65	0.119787	78954	9458	372768	0.025371	2.6738	1142055	0.0259	14.465	0.025222	65
70	0.199220	69496	13845	314696	0.043995	2.6321	769287	0.0259	11.070	0.043740	70
75	0.327646	55651	18234	233594	0.078058	2.5506	454591	0.0259	8.169	0.077641	75
80	0.488455	37417	18277	140077	0.130475	2.5103	220997	0.0259	5.906	0.129665	80
85+	1.000000	19141	19141	80920	0.236536	4.2277	80920	0.0259	4.228	0.238660	85

TABLE 4 — OBSERVED AND PROJECTED VITAL RATES

	OBSERVED POPULATION BOTH SEXES	MALES	FEMALES	PROJECTED POPULATION 1959 MALES	FEMALES	1964 MALES	FEMALES	1969 MALES	FEMALES	STABLE POPULATION MALES	FEMALES
RATES PER THOUSAND											
Birth	17.06	18.08	16.10	17.04	15.22	16.31	14.63	16.46	14.82	16.17	15.1
Death	10.09	10.71	9.51	11.32	10.35	11.86	11.05	12.36	11.63	13.79	12.7
Increase	6.96	7.37	6.58	5.72	4.87	4.45	3.57	4.10	3.19		2.380
PERCENTAGE											
under 15	24.11	25.48	22.82	25.40	22.80	24.16	21.81	23.46	21.31	22.90	21.6
15-64	66.12	65.93	66.30	65.63	65.50	66.23	65.48	66.04	64.87	65.38	63.8
65 and over	9.78	8.59	10.88	8.97	11.70	9.62	12.71	10.50	13.83	11.72	14.5
DEP. RATIO X 100	51.24	51.68	50.83	52.37	52.68	51.00	52.73	51.43	54.16	52.96	56.7

TABLE 1

AGE AT LAST BIRTHDAY	POPULATION BOTH SEXES	MALES Number	MALES %	FEMALES Number	FEMALES %	BIRTHS BY AGE OF MOTHER	DEATHS BOTH SEXES	DEATHS MALES	DEATHS FEMALES	AGE AT LAST BIRTHDAY
0	87469	44832	1.8	42637	1.6	0	2128	1225	903	0
1-4	327330	167170	6.8	160160	6.1	0	465	279	186	1-4
5-9	408165	208771	8.4	199394	7.6	0	242	159	83	5-9
10-14	415083	214042	8.6	201041	7.6	3	189	120	69	10-14
15-19	340864	173870	7.0	166994	6.3	2571	278	199	79	15-19
20-24	362326	170392	6.9	191934	7.3	22191	443	345	98	20-24
25-29	380485	173886	7.0	206599	7.8	31116	449	315	134	25-29
30-34	370580	176678	7.1	193902	7.3	20864	502	314	188	30-34
35-39	343714	172159	7.0	171555	6.5	10008	611	372	239	35-39
40-44	336832	170173	6.9	166659	6.3	3042	913	551	362	40-44
45-49	359823	177899	7.2	181924	6.9	254	1564	943	621	45-49
50-54	336112	163342	6.6	172770	6.5	3	2345	1439	906	50-54
55-59	298085	139593	5.6	158492	6.0	0	3331	2012	1319	55-59
60-64	242702	110070	4.4	132632	5.0	0	4381	2525	1856	60-64
65-69	190303	83231	3.4	107072	4.1	0	5627	3079	2548	65-69
70-74	146633	62786	2.5	83847	3.2		7169	3663	3506	70-74
75-79	98825	40351	1.6	58474	2.2		8227	3852	4375	75-79
80-84	51279	19914	0.8	31365	1.2	46255 M.	6880	2942	3938	80-84
85+	20548	7163	0.3	13385	0.5	43797 F.	4895	1858	3037	85+
TOTAL	5117158	2476322		2640836		90052	50639	26192	24447	TOTAL

TABLE 2

x	$_nq_x$	l_x	$_nd_x$	$_nL_x$	$_nm_x$	$_na_x$	T_x	r_x	$\overset{\circ}{e}_x$	$_nM_x$	x
0	0.026679	100000	2668	98076	0.027203	0.2788	6803321	0.0058	68.033	0.027324	0
1	0.006608	97332	643	387481	0.001660	1.1272	6705245	0.0058	68.890	0.001669	1
5	0.003801	96689	367	482526	0.000762	2.5000	6317765	0.0000	65.341	0.000762	5
10	0.002807	96321	270	480970	0.000562	2.6417	5835239	0.0176	60.581	0.000561	10
15	0.005741	96051	551	479021	0.001151	2.7614	5354269	0.0216	55.744	0.001145	15
20	0.010074	95500	962	475156	0.002025	2.5652	4875248	0.0000	51.050	0.002025	20
25	0.009016	94538	852	470529	0.001812	2.4674	4400092	0.0000	46.543	0.001812	25
30	0.008847	93685	829	466384	0.001777	2.5367	3929563	0.0000	41.944	0.001777	30
35	0.010751	92856	998	461921	0.002161	2.6351	3463178	0.0015	37.296	0.002161	35
40	0.016069	91858	1476	455885	0.003238	2.6931	3001257	0.0000	32.673	0.003238	40
45	0.026185	90382	2367	446480	0.005301	2.7056	2545372	0.0000	28.162	0.005301	45
50	0.043307	88015	3812	431283	0.008838	2.6930	2098893	0.0151	23.847	0.008810	50
55	0.070052	84204	5899	407260	0.014484	2.6676	1667609	0.0245	19.804	0.014413	55
60	0.109294	78305	8558	371380	0.023044	2.6461	1260349	0.0233	16.095	0.022940	60
65	0.170622	69747	11900	320290	0.037155	2.6098	888970	0.0233	12.746	0.036993	65
70	0.256416	57846	14833	253134	0.058596	2.5663	568680	0.0233	9.831	0.058341	70
75	0.386422	43014	16621	173380	0.095867	2.4919	315546	0.0233	7.336	0.095462	75
80	0.537600	26392	14188	95570	0.148462	2.4351	142166	0.0233	5.387	0.147735	80
85+	*1.000000	12204	12204	46596	0.261904	3.8182	46596	0.0233	3.818	0.259389	85+

TABLE 3

x	$_nq_x$	l_x	$_nd_x$	$_nL_x$	$_nm_x$	$_na_x$	T_x	r_x	$\overset{\circ}{e}_x$	$_nM_x$	x
0	0.020769	100000	2077	98478	0.021090	0.2672	7317171	0.0054	73.172	0.021179	0
1	0.004603	97923	451	390393	0.001155	1.1165	7218693	0.0054	73.718	0.001161	1
5	0.002079	97472	203	486855	0.000416	2.5000	6828301	0.0003	70.054	0.000416	5
10	0.001716	97270	167	485937	0.000343	2.5335	6341446	0.0173	65.194	0.000343	10
15	0.002363	97103	229	484957	0.000473	2.5727	5855509	0.0042	60.302	0.000473	15
20	0.002550	96873	247	483766	0.000511	2.5703	5370552	0.0000	55.439	0.000511	20
25	0.003238	96626	313	482395	0.000649	2.6466	4886786	0.0000	50.574	0.000649	25
30	0.004850	96313	467	480473	0.000972	2.6580	4404391	0.0176	45.730	0.000970	30
35	0.006960	95846	667	477680	0.001397	2.6753	3923918	0.0137	40.940	0.001393	35
40	0.010806	95179	1029	473518	0.002172	2.6878	3446237	0.0000	36.208	0.002172	40
45	0.016933	94151	1594	467053	0.003414	2.6794	2972720	0.0000	31.574	0.003414	45
50	0.025946	92556	2401	457215	0.005252	2.6822	2505666	0.0083	27.072	0.005244	50
55	0.040981	90155	3695	442265	0.008354	2.6968	2048451	0.0176	22.721	0.008322	55
60	0.068140	86460	5891	418706	0.014070	2.6923	1606186	0.0245	18.577	0.013994	60
65	0.113356	80569	9133	381631	0.023931	2.6773	1187481	0.0245	14.739	0.023797	65
70	0.191275	71436	13664	324941	0.042050	2.6406	805850	0.0245	11.281	0.041814	70
75	0.317682	57772	18353	244044	0.075204	2.5581	480909	0.0245	8.324	0.074820	75
80	0.476503	39419	18783	148940	0.126113	2.5253	236865	0.0245	6.009	0.125554	80
85+	1.000000	20636	20636	87925	0.234695	4.2608	87925	0.0245	4.261	0.226895	85+

TABLE 4

	OBSERVED POPULATION BOTH SEXES	MALES	FEMALES	PROJECTED POPULATION 1962 MALES	1962 FEMALES	1967 MALES	1967 FEMALES	1972 MALES	1972 FEMALES	STABLE POPULATION MALES	FEMALES
RATES PER THOUSAND											
Birth	17.60	18.68	16.58	17.58	15.67	16.98	15.19	16.85	15.13	16.44	15.37
Death	9.90	10.58	9.26	11.21	10.08	11.71	10.65	12.22	11.21	13.33	12.27
Increase	7.70	8.10	7.33	6.37	5.59	5.27	4.53	4.63	3.92		3.1077
PERCENTAGE											
under 15	24.19	25.64	22.84	24.95	22.45	24.55	22.18	24.24	21.95	23.28	21.96
15-64	65.89	65.75	66.02	65.87	65.49	65.45	64.69	64.85	63.97	65.09	63.55
65 and over	9.92	8.62	11.14	9.18	12.07	10.00	13.14	10.92	14.08	11.63	14.50
DEP. RATIO X 100	51.78	52.10	51.47	51.80	52.70	52.79	54.59	54.21	56.33	53.63	57.36

TABLE 1 — DATA

AGE AT LAST BIRTHDAY	POPULATION BOTH SEXES	MALES Number	%	FEMALES Number	%	BIRTHS BY AGE OF MOTHER	DEATHS BOTH SEXES	MALES	FEMALES	AGE AT BIRTH
0	85583	43510	1.6	42073	1.5	0	2046	1199	847	
1-4	353809	181185	6.8	172624	6.2	0	435	252	183	1
5-9	410771	209748	7.9	201023	7.3	0	196	115	81	5
10-14	424853	216761	8.1	208092	7.5	4	174	111	63	10
15-19	427051	217712	8.2	209339	7.6	3275	317	235	82	15
20-24	405546	207895	7.8	197651	7.1	24704	449	337	112	20
25-29	406775	209806	7.9	196969	7.1	33135	419	288	131	25
30-34	386157	193966	7.3	192191	6.9	21135	461	300	161	30
35-39	375586	185996	7.0	189590	6.9	10191	622	369	253	35
40-44	323917	161175	6.1	162742	5.9	2832	809	496	313	40
45-49	344977	170018	6.4	174959	6.3	251	1403	865	538	45
50-54	349092	168489	6.3	180603	6.5	1	2311	1439	872	50
55-59	315139	147600	5.5	167539	6.1	0	3330	2094	1236	55
60-64	265565	119060	4.5	146505	5.3	0	4552	2742	1810	60
65-69	208410	90361	3.4	118049	4.3	0	5605	3153	2452	65
70-74	154867	64960	2.4	89907	3.3		6971	3635	3336	70
75-79	106807	43708	1.6	63099	2.3		8089	3864	4225	75
80-84	58191	22332	0.8	35859	1.3	48857 M.	7288	3095	4193	80
85+	25965	9150	0.3	16815	0.6	46671 F.	5580	2075	3505	85
TOTAL	5429061	2663432		2765629		95528	51057	26664	24393	TO

TABLE 2 — MALE LIFE TABLE

x	$_nq_x$	l_x	$_nd_x$	$_nL_x$	$_nm_x$	$_na_x$	T_x	r_x	$\overset{\circ}{e}_x$	$_nM_x$
0	0.027005	100000	2700	97996	0.027557	0.2581	6883408	0.0000	68.834	0.027557
1	0.005541	97300	539	387639	0.001391	1.1086	6785412	0.0000	69.737	0.001391
5	0.002736	96760	265	483140	0.000548	2.5000	6397773	0.0028	66.120	0.000548
10	0.002557	96496	247	481914	0.000512	2.7143	5914632	0.0000	61.294	0.000512
15	0.005387	96249	519	480058	0.001080	2.7114	5432718	0.0031	56.444	0.001079
20	0.008073	95730	773	476747	0.001621	2.5353	4952660	0.0023	51.736	0.001621
25	0.006839	94958	649	473154	0.001373	2.4854	4475913	0.0055	47.136	0.001373
30	0.007711	94308	727	469780	0.001548	2.5793	4002759	0.0105	42.443	0.001547
35	0.009899	93581	926	465732	0.001989	2.6552	3532979	0.0164	37.753	0.001984
40	0.015297	92654	1417	460014	0.003081	2.7011	3067247	0.0058	33.104	0.003077
45	0.025146	91237	2294	450932	0.005088	2.7099	2607234	0.0000	28.576	0.005088
50	0.041927	88943	3729	436138	0.008550	2.7001	2156302	0.0052	24.244	0.008541
55	0.068946	85214	5875	412416	0.014246	2.6762	1720164	0.0199	20.186	0.014187
60	0.109636	79339	8698	376102	0.023128	2.6328	1307748	0.0232	16.483	0.023030
65	0.161661	70640	11420	325890	0.035042	2.6084	931646	0.0232	13.189	0.034893
70	0.247196	59221	14639	260499	0.056196	2.5679	605756	0.0232	10.229	0.055958
75	0.363187	44581	16191	182399	0.088770	2.4981	345257	0.0232	7.744	0.088405
80	0.510536	28390	14494	104175	0.139133	2.4670	162858	0.0232	5.736	0.138590
85+	1.000000	13896	13896	58683	0.236794	4.2231	58683	0.0232	4.223	0.226777

TABLE 3 — FEMALE LIFE TABLE

x	$_nq_x$	l_x	$_nd_x$	$_nL_x$	$_nm_x$	$_na_x$	T_x	r_x	$\overset{\circ}{e}_x$	$_nM_x$
0	0.019837	100000	1984	98538	0.020132	0.2630	7431939	0.0000	74.319	0.020132
1	0.004227	98016	414	390869	0.001060	1.1128	7333401	0.0000	74.818	0.001060
5	0.002011	97602	196	487519	0.000403	2.5000	6942532	0.0026	71.131	0.000403
10	0.001513	97406	147	486659	0.000303	2.4917	6455013	0.0000	66.269	0.000303
15	0.001958	97258	190	485842	0.000392	2.6394	5968355	0.0047	61.366	0.000392
20	0.002831	97068	275	484680	0.000567	2.5993	5482513	0.0055	56.481	0.000567
25	0.003321	96793	321	483189	0.000665	2.5834	4997834	0.0021	51.634	0.000665
30	0.004182	96472	403	481416	0.000838	2.6648	4514645	0.0029	46.798	0.000838
35	0.006669	96068	641	478846	0.001338	2.6662	4033229	0.0153	41.983	0.001334
40	0.009584	95427	915	475018	0.001925	2.6827	3554384	0.0060	37.247	0.001923
45	0.015267	94513	1443	469229	0.003075	2.6888	3079365	0.0000	32.581	0.003075
50	0.023873	93070	2222	460183	0.004828	2.6745	2610136	0.0000	28.045	0.004828
55	0.036368	90848	3304	446620	0.007398	2.6935	2149953	0.0131	23.665	0.007377
60	0.060425	87544	5290	425517	0.012432	2.6929	1703333	0.0283	19.457	0.012355
65	0.099727	82254	8203	392311	0.020909	2.6886	1277817	0.0283	15.535	0.020771
70	0.171736	74051	12717	340457	0.037354	2.6567	885505	0.0283	11.958	0.037105
75	0.289731	61334	17770	263746	0.067377	2.5845	545049	0.0283	8.887	0.066958
80	0.457408	43564	19926	169225	0.117751	2.5613	281303	0.0283	6.457	0.116931
85+	*1.000000	23637	23637	112078	0.210900	4.7416	112078	0.0283	4.742	0.208445

TABLE 4 — OBSERVED AND PROJECTED VITAL RATES

	OBSERVED POPULATION BOTH SEXES	MALES	FEMALES	PROJECTED POPULATION 1965 MALES	FEMALES	1970 MALES	FEMALES	1975 MALES	FEMALES	STABLE POPULATION MALES	FEM.
RATES PER THOUSAND											
Birth	17.60	18.34	16.88	18.07	16.64	17.77	16.41	17.28	16.00	17.47	16
Death	9.40	10.01	8.82	10.63	9.71	11.06	10.30	11.44	10.85	12.33	11
Increase	8.19	8.33	8.06	7.43	6.93	6.72	6.11	5.84	5.15		5.1
PERCENTAGE											
under 15	23.49	24.45	22.56	24.29	22.47	24.65	22.90	24.68	23.05	24.39	23
15-64	66.31	66.90	65.74	66.38	64.60	65.25	63.11	64.49	62.12	64.47	62
65 and over	10.21	8.65	11.71	9.33	12.93	10.10	13.99	10.83	14.83	11.14	14
DEP. RATIO X 100	50.82	49.49	52.12	50.64	54.79	53.25	58.45	55.06	60.99	55.10	59

TABLE 5 — POPULATION PROJECTED WITH FIXED AGE-SPECIFIC BIRTH AND DEATH RATES (IN 1000's)

AGE AT LAST BIRTHDAY	1965 BOTH SEXES	MALES	FEMALES	1970 BOTH SEXES	MALES	FEMALES	1975 BOTH SEXES	MALES	FEMALES	AGE AT LAST BIRTHDAY
0-4	471	240	231	481	245	236	487	248	239	0-4
5-9	438	224	214	469	239	230	479	244	235	5-9
10-14	410	209	201	436	223	213	468	238	230	10-14
15-19	424	216	208	408	208	200	435	222	213	15-19
20-24	425	216	209	421	214	207	407	207	200	20-24
25-29	403	206	197	423	215	208	420	213	207	25-29
30-34	404	208	196	401	205	196	420	213	207	30-34
35-39	383	192	191	402	207	195	398	203	195	35-39
40-44	372	184	188	380	190	190	398	204	194	40-44
45-49	319	158	161	366	180	186	373	186	187	45-49
50-54	336	164	172	311	153	158	356	174	182	50-54
55-59	334	159	175	322	155	167	297	144	153	55-59
60-64	295	135	160	312	145	167	301	142	159	60-64
65-69	238	103	135	264	117	147	280	126	154	65-69
70-74	174	72	102	199	82	117	221	93	128	70-74
75-79	115	45	70	130	51	79	149	58	91	75-79
80-84	65	25	40	71	26	45	80	29	51	80-84
85+	37	13	24	41	14	27	45	15	30	85+
TOTAL	5643	2769	2874	5837	2869	2968	6014	2959	3055	TOTAL

TABLE 6 — STANDARDIZED RATES

STANDARD COUNTRIES:
STANDARDIZED RATES PER THOUSAND

	ENGLAND AND WALES 1961 BOTH SEXES	MALES	FEMALES	UNITED STATES 1960 BOTH SEXES	MALES	FEMALES	MEXICO 1960 BOTH SEXES	MALES	FEMALES
Birth	15.57	16.40*	14.75	15.83	15.35*	15.24	17.80	14.86*	17.34
Death	10.82	10.98*	10.71	8.80	9.72*	7.84	4.63	8.25*	3.78
Increase	4.75	5.41*	4.03	7.03	5.62*	7.40	13.16	6.61*	13.56

TABLE 7 — MOMENTS AND CUMULANTS

OBSERVED POP. MALES	FEMALES	STATIONARY POP. MALES	FEMALES	STABLE POP. MALES	FEMALES	OBSERVED BIRTHS	NET MATERNITY FUNCTION	BIRTHS IN STABLE POP.
33.38663	35.73726	37.12812	39.22845	34.54681	36.42127	28.53404	28.68338	28.51174
452.5815	495.7024	509.2875	552.5533	494.0216	538.3547	30.67729	31.54378	31.06944
3262.633	2779.704	2338.925	1963.968	3571.233	3528.867	86.0909	91.8541	92.6716
-174457.	-237830.	-255854.	-321153.	-221251.	-284183.	-145.002	-175.525	-132.436
0.114827	0.063436	0.041414	0.022864	0.105779	0.079811	0.256722	0.268817	0.286348
2.148286	2.032112	2.013572	1.948125	2.093448	2.019468	2.845922	2.823595	2.862805
-0.045042	-0.023794	-0.015649	-0.008341	-0.039971	-0.029145	-0.191647	-0.187460	-0.204957

TABLE 8 — RATES FROM AGE DISTRIBUTIONS AND VITAL STATISTICS (Females)

VITAL STATISTICS
1.200
1.158
2.457
GENERATION 28.597
SEX RATIO 104.684

THOMPSON AGE RANGE	NRR	1000r	INTERVAL	BOURGEOIS-PICHAT AGE RANGE	NRR	1000b	1000d	1000r	COALE	
0-4	1.10	3.61	27.44	5-29	1.04	15.46	14.05	1.41	IBR	16.94
5-9	1.06	2.24	27.41	30-54	1.05	14.89	13.00	1.88	IDR	11.19
10-14	1.11	3.80	27.36	55-79	1.90	53.90	30.15	23.76	IRI	5.75
15-19	1.13	4.56	27.29	*10-39	1.10	16.24	12.73	3.51	K1	22.20
									K2	0.37

TABLE 9 — LESLIE MATRIX AND ITS SPECTRAL COMPONENTS (Females)

SUB-DIAGONAL	ALTERNATIVE FIRST ROWS Projection	Integral	% IN STABLE POPULATION	FISHER VALUES	REPRODUCTIVE VALUES	SECOND STABLE MATRIX Z2 FIRST COLUMN	FIRST ROW
0.99614	0.00000	0.00000	7.897	1.035	222176	0.1644+0.0601	0.1644+0.0601
0.99824	0.00002	0.00000	7.667	1.066	214271	0.1512-0.1352	0.0211+0.1496
0.99832	0.01869	0.00005	7.459	1.096	227981	-0.0558-0.2289	-0.1051+0.0767
0.99761	0.16777	0.03789	7.257	1.107	231660	-0.2650-0.0681	-0.1039-0.0498
0.99692	0.34992	0.30272	7.056	0.964	190564	-0.2146+0.2340	-0.0320-0.1093
0.99633	0.33210	0.40743	6.856	0.629	123910	0.1221+0.3474	0.0124-0.0898
0.99466	0.19539	0.26634	6.657	0.303	58216	0.4219+0.0648	0.0186-0.0471
0.99201	0.08490	0.13019	6.454	0.109	20701	0.2961-0.3952	0.0112-0.0168
0.98781	0.02250	0.04215	6.240	0.024	3966	-0.2413-0.5164	0.0033-0.0034
0.98072	0.00172	0.00347	6.007	0.002	305	-0.6540-0.0350	0.0003-0.0002
0.97053	0.00001	0.00001	5.742	0.000	1	-0.3868+0.6394	0.0000-0.0000
0.80053			24.709				

TABLE 10 — AGE ANALYSIS AND MISCELLANEOUS RESULTS (Females)

OBSERVED POPUL. (IN 100's)	CONTRIBUTIONS OF ROOTS (IN 100's) r1	r2, r3	r4-r11	AGE-SP. BIRTH RATES	NET MATERNITY FUNCTION	COEFF. OF MATRIX EQUATION	PARAMETERS	INTEGRAL	MATRIX	EXP. INCREASE x	$e^{(x+2\frac{1}{2})r}$
2147	2195	-33	-15	0.0000	0.0000	0.0000	L(1)	1.02603	1.02605	0	1.0129
2010	2131	-92	-28	0.0000	0.0000	0.0000	L(2)	0.40218	0.40498	50	1.3098
2081	2073	-56	64	0.0000	0.0000	0.0186		0.78261	0.75821	55	1.3439
2093	2017	63	13	0.0076	0.0371	0.1665	R(1)	0.00514	0.00514	60	1.3789
1977	1961	145	-130	0.0611	0.2960	0.3465	R(2)	-0.02559	-0.03026	65	1.4148
1970	1906	73	-9	0.0822	0.3971	0.3279		0.21922	0.21604	70	1.4516
1922	1850	-115	186	0.0537	0.2586	0.1922	C(1)		27795	75	1.4894
1896	1794	-223	325	0.0263	0.1258	0.0831	C(2)		-16090	80	1.5282
1627	1734	-90	-17	0.0085	0.0404	0.0218			-16199	85	1.5679
1750	1670	199	-119	0.0007	0.0033	0.0017	2P/Y	28.6617	29.0830	90	1.6088
1806	1596	332	-121	0.0000	0.0000	0.0000	DELTA	3.4172		95	1.6506
6378	6868									100	1.6936

TABLE 1 — DATA

AGE AT LAST BIRTHDAY	POPULATION BOTH SEXES	MALES Number	%	FEMALES Number	%	BIRTHS BY AGE OF MOTHER	DEATHS BOTH SEXES	MALES	FEMALES	AGE AT LAST BIRTHDAY
0	89295	45477	1.7	43818	1.5	0	2211	1258	953	0
1-4	369157	189374	6.9	179783	6.3	0	441	246	195	1-4
5-9	415550	214050	7.8	201500	7.1	0	234	144	90	5-9
10-14	412950	209450	7.6	203500	7.2	6	172	108	64	10-14
15-19	453800	234250	8.5	219550	7.8	4124	387	287	100	15-19
20-24	438950	226250	8.2	212700	7.5	29295	445	337	108	20-24
25-29	423350	220650	8.0	202700	7.2	35660	421	290	131	25-29
30-34	399100	199050	7.2	200050	7.1	21663	496	322	174	30-34
35-39	378600	190150	6.9	188450	6.7	10320	629	407	222	35-39
40-44	339000	167800	6.1	171200	6.0	3046	894	539	355	40-44
45-49	337750	166250	6.0	171500	6.1	201	1379	887	492	45-49
50-54	352350	173150	6.3	179200	6.3	7	2285	1432	853	50-54
55-59	319050	149700	5.4	169350	6.0	-0	3535	2243	1292	55-59
60-64	270450	122950	4.5	147500	5.2	-0	4816	2935	1881	60-64
65-69	219550	95500	3.5	124050	4.4	-0	6140	3477	2663	65-69
70-74	162400	68500	2.5	93900	3.3		7428	3906	3522	70-74
75-79	111500	45200	1.6	66300	2.3		8597	4108	4489	75-79
80-84	67603	26482	1.0	41121	1.5	53452 M.	7989	3391	4598	80-84
85+	23599	7869	0.3	15730	0.6	50870 F.	6626	2494	4132	85+
TOTAL	5584004	2752102		2831902		104322	55125	28811	26314	TOT

TABLE 2 — MALE LIFE TABLE

x	nq_x	l_x	nd_x	nL_x	nm_x	na_x	T_x	r_x	$\overset{\circ}{e}_x$	nM_x
0	0.027100	100000	2710	97968	0.027662	0.2503	6844484	0.0000	68.445	0.027662
1	0.005177	97290	504	387701	0.001299	1.1023	6746516	0.0000	69.344	0.001299
5	0.003351	96786	324	483121	0.000671	2.5000	6358815	0.0106	65.700	0.000673
10	0.002575	96462	248	481744	0.000516	2.7209	5875694	0.0000	60.912	0.000516
15	0.006108	96214	588	479695	0.001225	2.6635	5393950	0.0000	56.062	0.001225
20	0.007420	95626	710	476363	0.001490	2.5100	4914256	0.0046	51.390	0.001489
25	0.006552	94916	622	473038	0.001315	2.5172	4437893	0.0114	46.756	0.001314
30	0.008069	94294	761	469649	0.001620	2.6031	3964855	0.0132	42.048	0.001618
35	0.010673	93534	998	465322	0.002145	2.6497	3495207	0.0148	37.368	0.002140
40	0.015975	92535	1478	459273	0.003219	2.6975	3029885	0.0100	32.743	0.003212
45	0.026351	91057	2399	449729	0.005335	2.6842	2570612	0.0000	28.231	0.005335
50	0.040600	88658	3599	435078	0.008273	2.7189	2120883	0.0015	23.922	0.008270
55	0.072680	85058	6182	410948	0.015043	2.6800	1685805	0.0189	19.819	0.014983
60	0.113341	78876	8940	373190	0.023955	2.6297	1274857	0.0195	16.163	0.023871
65	0.167950	69936	11746	321498	0.036535	2.6006	901667	0.0195	12.893	0.036408
70	0.251100	58190	14612	255342	0.057224	2.5629	580169	0.0195	9.970	0.057022
75	0.370781	43579	16158	177226	0.091173	2.4831	324827	0.0195	7.454	0.090885
80	0.485171	27421	13304	103419	0.128639	2.4680	147601	0.0195	5.383	0.128049
85+	*1.000000	14117	14117	44182	0.319517	3.1297	44182	0.0195	3.130	0.316940

TABLE 3 — FEMALE LIFE TABLE

x	nq_x	l_x	nd_x	nL_x	nm_x	na_x	T_x	r_x	$\overset{\circ}{e}_x$	nM_x
0	0.021403	100000	2140	98410	0.021749	0.2570	7391425	0.0000	73.914	0.021749
1	0.004325	97860	423	390215	0.001085	1.1077	7293015	0.0000	74.525	0.001085
5	0.002225	97436	217	486640	0.000445	2.5000	6902801	0.0088	70.844	0.000447
10	0.001571	97220	153	485717	0.000314	2.5055	6416160	0.0000	65.997	0.000314
15	0.002275	97067	221	484802	0.000455	2.5877	5930443	0.0000	61.096	0.000455
20	0.002537	96846	246	483635	0.000508	2.5772	5445642	0.0075	56.230	0.000508
25	0.003228	96600	312	482258	0.000647	2.6152	4962006	0.0055	51.366	0.000646
30	0.004344	96288	418	480450	0.000870	2.6260	4479748	0.0064	46.524	0.000870
35	0.005892	95870	565	478057	0.001182	2.7089	3999299	0.0143	41.716	0.001178
40	0.010331	95305	985	474228	0.002076	2.6649	3521242	0.0074	36.947	0.002074
45	0.014249	94321	1344	468495	0.002869	2.6867	3047014	0.0000	32.305	0.002869
50	0.023542	92977	2189	459842	0.004760	2.6968	2578519	0.0000	27.733	0.004760
55	0.037578	90788	3412	446087	0.007648	2.6984	2118677	0.0114	23.337	0.007629
60	0.062244	87376	5439	424298	0.012817	2.6918	1672589	0.0230	19.142	0.012753
65	0.102754	81938	8419	390159	0.021580	2.6805	1248261	0.0230	15.234	0.021467
70	0.173213	73518	12734	337698	0.037709	2.6526	858102	0.0230	11.672	0.037508
75	0.291970	60784	17747	260860	0.068033	2.5737	520404	0.0230	8.562	0.067707
80	0.441797	43037	19013	168958	0.112534	2.5688	259544	0.0230	6.031	0.111817
85+	*1.000000	24023	24023	90587	0.265196	3.7708	90587	0.0230	3.771	0.262683

TABLE 4 — OBSERVED AND PROJECTED VITAL RATES

	OBSERVED POPULATION BOTH SEXES	MALES	FEMALES	PROJECTED POPULATION 1967 MALES	FEMALES	1972 MALES	FEMALES	1977 MALES	FEMALES	STABLE POPULATION MALES	FEMA
RATES PER THOUSAND											
Birth	18.68	19.42	17.96	19.19	17.78	18.49	17.17	17.63	16.41	18.49	17
Death	9.87	10.47	9.29	11.00	10.07	11.20	10.41	11.47	10.82	11.81	10
Increase	8.81	8.95	8.67	8.19	7.71	7.30	6.76	6.15	5.58		6.6
PERCENTAGE											
under 15	23.05	23.92	22.20	24.75	22.91	25.57	23.87	25.74	24.13	25.52	24
15-64	66.48	67.23	65.76	65.96	64.19	64.62	62.45	63.83	61.62	64.27	62
65 and over	10.47	8.85	12.04	9.30	12.89	9.81	13.68	10.43	14.26	10.21	13
DEP. RATIO X 100	50.41	48.75	52.07	51.61	55.78	54.76	60.12	56.66	62.30	55.59	59

TABLE 1

AGE AT LAST BIRTHDAY	POPULATION BOTH SEXES	MALES Number	%	FEMALES Number	%	BIRTHS BY AGE OF MOTHER	DEATHS BOTH SEXES	MALES	FEMALES	AGE AT LAST BIRTHDAY
0	89432	45457	1.6	43975	1.5	0	2252	1307	945	0
1-4	369719	189293	6.8	180426	6.3	0	431	267	164	1-4
5-9	423750	217300	7.8	206450	7.2	0	234	135	99	5-9
10-14	412900	210150	7.5	202750	7.1	7	161	104	57	10-14
15-19	468400	239850	8.6	228550	8.0	4707	356	265	91	15-19
20-24	466350	242300	8.7	224050	7.8	32070	442	342	100	20-24
25-29	421200	221050	7.9	200150	7.0	37268	422	291	131	25-29
30-34	397400	200050	7.2	197350	6.9	22382	495	329	166	30-34
35-39	377800	187700	6.7	190100	6.6	10332	629	411	218	35-39
40-44	350350	173000	6.2	177350	6.2	3045	937	592	345	40-44
45-49	330000	164100	5.9	165900	5.8	180	1362	864	498	45-49
50-54	354100	172900	6.2	181200	6.3	2	2303	1456	847	50-54
55-59	324700	152950	5.5	171750	6.0	-0	3587	2307	1280	55-59
60-64	280700	127250	4.6	153450	5.3	-0	4940	3026	1914	60-64
65-69	224800	97150	3.5	127650	4.4	-0	6328	3677	2651	65-69
70-74	166000	69150	2.5	96850	3.4		7684	3980	3704	70-74
75-79	112950	45250	1.6	67700	2.4		9092	4417	4675	75-79
80-84	68106	26454	0.9	41652	1.4	56247 M.	8279	3556	4723	80-84
85+	24345	8096	0.3	16249	0.6	53746 F.	7055	2699	4356	85+
TOTAL	5663002	2789450		2873552		109993	56989	30025	26964	TOTAL

TABLE 2 (MALE)

x	nq_x	l_x	nd_x	nL_x	nm_x	na_x	T_x	r_x	$\mathring{e}_x$	nM_x	x
0	0.028149	100000	2815	97903	0.028752	0.2549	6817883	0.0000	68.179	0.028752	0
1	0.005619	97185	546	387160	0.001411	1.1060	6719980	0.0000	69.146	0.001411	1
5	0.003093	96639	299	482447	0.000620	2.5000	6332820	0.0103	65.531	0.000621	5
10	0.002472	96340	238	481153	0.000495	2.7017	5850373	0.0000	60.726	0.000495	10
15	0.005510	96102	530	479276	0.001105	2.6708	5369220	0.0000	55.870	0.001105	15
20	0.007034	95572	672	476201	0.001412	2.5290	4889944	0.0068	51.165	0.001411	20
25	0.006565	94900	623	472964	0.001317	2.5338	4413743	0.0178	46.509	0.001316	25
30	0.008204	94277	773	469534	0.001647	2.6071	3940779	0.0147	41.800	0.001645	30
35	0.010915	93504	1021	465133	0.002194	2.6632	3471245	0.0122	37.124	0.002190	35
40	0.017006	92483	1573	458763	0.003428	2.6780	3006112	0.0099	32.504	0.003422	40
45	0.026008	90910	2364	449075	0.005265	2.6837	2547349	0.0000	28.020	0.005265	45
50	0.041312	88546	3658	434384	0.008421	2.7187	2098274	0.0000	23.697	0.008421	50
55	0.073085	84888	6204	410018	0.015131	2.6755	1663890	0.0153	19.601	0.015083	55
60	0.112911	78684	8884	372445	0.023854	2.6392	1253872	0.0163	15.936	0.023780	60
65	0.173931	69800	12140	319837	0.037958	2.5980	881427	0.0163	12.628	0.037849	65
70	0.253131	57659	14595	252801	0.057735	2.5681	561590	0.0163	9.740	0.057556	70
75	0.392636	43064	16908	172740	0.097884	2.4817	308789	0.0163	7.170	0.097613	75
80	0.501338	26155	13113	97190	0.134918	2.4386	136049	0.0163	5.202	0.134422	80
85+	*1.000000	13043	13043	38859	0.335643	2.9794	38859	0.0163	2.979	0.333375	85+

TABLE 3 (FEMALE)

x	nq_x	l_x	nd_x	nL_x	nm_x	na_x	T_x	r_x	$\mathring{e}_x$	nM_x	x
0	0.021144	100000	2114	98392	0.021489	0.2393	7403085	0.0000	74.031	0.021489	0
1	0.003626	97886	355	390511	0.000909	1.0940	7304694	0.0000	74.625	0.000909	1
5	0.002389	97531	233	487071	0.000478	2.5000	6914183	0.0096	70.892	0.000480	5
10	0.001405	97298	137	486138	0.000281	2.4393	6427112	0.0000	66.056	0.000281	10
15	0.001989	97161	193	485338	0.000398	2.5861	5940974	0.0000	61.146	0.000398	15
20	0.002233	96968	216	484323	0.000447	2.6187	5455636	0.0128	56.262	0.000446	20
25	0.003272	96751	317	483004	0.000655	2.6240	4971313	0.0120	51.382	0.000655	25
30	0.004200	96435	405	481209	0.000842	2.6202	4488309	0.0043	46.543	0.000841	30
35	0.005730	96030	550	478881	0.001149	2.6975	4007100	0.0094	41.728	0.001147	35
40	0.009705	95479	927	475259	0.001950	2.6932	3528219	0.0116	36.953	0.001945	40
45	0.014905	94553	1409	469496	0.003002	2.6814	3052960	0.0000	32.288	0.003002	45
50	0.023122	93143	2154	460735	0.004674	2.6867	2583464	0.0000	27.736	0.004674	50
55	0.036703	90990	3340	447263	0.007467	2.6987	2122729	0.0088	23.329	0.007453	55
60	0.060904	87650	5338	425918	0.012533	2.6896	1675465	0.0223	19.115	0.012473	60
65	0.099610	82312	8199	392673	0.020880	2.6965	1249548	0.0223	15.181	0.020768	65
70	0.176364	74113	13071	339954	0.038449	2.6581	856875	0.0223	11.562	0.038245	70
75	0.296832	61042	18119	261180	0.069375	2.5700	516921	0.0223	8.468	0.069055	75
80	0.446291	42923	19156	167900	0.114092	2.5614	255742	0.0223	5.958	0.113392	80
85+	*1.000000	23767	23767	87841	0.270564	3.6960	87841	0.0223	3.696	0.268078	85+

TABLE 4

	OBSERVED POPULATION BOTH SEXES	MALES	FEMALES	PROJECTED POPULATION 1968 MALES	FEMALES	1973 MALES	FEMALES	1978 MALES	FEMALES	STABLE POPULATION MALES	FEMALES
RATES PER THOUSAND											
Birth	19.42	20.16	18.70	20.16	18.72	19.32	17.97	18.25	17.02	19.56	18.33
Death	10.06	10.76	9.38	11.15	10.08	11.25	10.38	11.47	10.75	11.28	10.04
Increase	9.36	9.40	9.32	9.02	8.64	8.07	7.58	6.78	6.26		8.2865
PERCENTAGE											
under 15	22.88	23.74	22.05	24.98	23.24	26.13	24.48	26.69	25.11	26.65	25.20
15-64	66.59	67.44	65.77	65.80	63.73	64.19	61.82	63.16	60.73	63.95	62.42
65 and over	10.53	8.82	12.18	9.22	13.03	9.68	13.70	10.15	14.16	9.39	12.38
DEP. RATIO X 100	50.17	48.28	52.05	51.99	56.91	55.80	61.75	58.33	64.67	56.36	60.21

TABLE 1 — DATA

AGE AT LAST BIRTHDAY	POPULATION BOTH SEXES	MALES Number	%	FEMALES Number	%	BIRTHS BY AGE OF MOTHER	DEATHS BOTH SEXES	MALES	FEMALES	AGE AT LAST BIRTH
0	90623	45825	1.6	44798	1.5	0	2142	1248	894	0
1-4	374628	190825	6.7	183803	6.3	0	409	232	177	1-4
5-9	430050	219100	7.7	210950	7.2	0	215	142	73	5-9
10-14	415900	212650	7.5	203250	6.9	8	150	100	50	10-
15-19	474200	238350	8.4	235850	8.0	5038	343	259	84	15-
20-24	506450	260900	9.2	245550	8.4	33907	471	359	112	20-
25-29	432200	225550	8.0	206650	7.0	37548	439	308	131	25-
30-34	406400	208150	7.3	198250	6.7	22694	469	308	161	30-
35-39	381800	187900	6.6	193900	6.6	10497	605	379	226	35-
40-44	359850	177600	6.3	182250	6.2	3022	945	611	334	40-
45-49	324400	163300	5.8	161100	5.5	175	1223	762	461	45-
50-54	347900	168500	5.9	179400	6.1	1	2177	1437	740	50-
55-59	334100	157250	5.6	176850	6.0	0	3431	2165	1266	55-
60-64	291700	130750	4.6	160950	5.5	0	4816	3003	1813	60-
65-69	229000	97650	3.4	131350	4.5	0	6208	3573	2635	65-
70-74	169400	69450	2.5	99950	3.4		7347	3827	3520	70-
75-79	112650	44750	1.6	67900	2.3		8131	3802	4329	75-
80-84	66353	25292	0.9	41061	1.4	57856 M.	7628	3286	4342	80-
85+	25398	8758	0.3	16640	0.6	55034 F.	6460	2508	3952	85-
TOTAL	5773002	2832550		2940452		112890	53609	28309	25300	TOT

TABLE 2 — MALE LIFE TABLE

x	nq_x	l_x	nd_x	nL_x	nm_x	na_x	T_x	r_x	$\dot{e}_x$	nM_x
0	0.026685	100000	2669	97985	0.027234	0.2449	6892086	0.0000	68.921	0.027234
1	0.004846	97331	472	387957	0.001216	1.0981	6794101	0.0000	69.804	0.001216
5	0.003229	96860	313	483517	0.000647	2.5000	6406144	0.0099	66.138	0.000648
10	0.002349	96547	227	482212	0.000470	2.6923	5922627	0.0000	61.344	0.000470
15	0.005419	96320	522	480386	0.001087	2.6717	5440415	0.0000	56.483	0.001087
20	0.006858	95798	657	477375	0.001376	2.5398	4960029	0.0042	51.776	0.001376
25	0.006807	95141	648	474096	0.001366	2.5131	4482654	0.0212	47.116	0.001366
30	0.007383	94494	698	470786	0.001482	2.5885	4008558	0.0167	42.421	0.001480
35	0.010066	93796	944	466805	0.002023	2.6963	3537772	0.0137	37.718	0.002017
40	0.017093	92852	1587	460534	0.003446	2.6526	3070967	0.0107	33.074	0.003440
45	0.023085	91265	2107	451503	0.004666	2.7118	2610433	0.0001	28.603	0.004666
50	0.041821	89158	3729	437219	0.008528	2.7014	2158930	0.0000	24.215	0.008528
55	0.066859	85429	5712	413908	0.013800	2.6822	1721712	0.0108	20.154	0.013768
60	0.109450	79717	8725	378082	0.023077	2.6498	1307804	0.0240	16.405	0.022967
65	0.168817	70992	11985	326178	0.036743	2.5983	929723	0.0240	13.096	0.036590
70	0.243656	59008	14378	259866	0.055327	2.5537	603545	0.0240	10.228	0.055104
75	0.351511	44630	15688	183900	0.085307	2.4981	343679	0.0240	7.701	0.084961
80	0.491782	28942	14233	108923	0.130672	2.4857	159779	0.0240	5.521	0.129922
85+	*1.000000	14709	14709	50855	0.289229	3.4575	50855	0.0240	3.457	0.286367

TABLE 3 — FEMALE LIFE TABLE

x	nq_x	l_x	nd_x	nL_x	nm_x	na_x	T_x	r_x	$\dot{e}_x$	nM_x
0	0.019663	100000	1966	98532	0.019956	0.2535	7485086	0.0000	74.851	0.019956
1	0.003841	98034	377	391044	0.000963	1.1049	7386554	0.0000	75.347	0.000963
5	0.001722	97657	168	487865	0.000345	2.5000	6995510	0.0113	71.633	0.000346
10	0.001229	97489	120	487146	0.000246	2.5089	6507645	0.0000	66.753	0.000246
15	0.001779	97369	173	486434	0.000356	2.6226	6020498	0.0000	61.832	0.000356
20	0.002282	97196	222	485453	0.000457	2.6263	5534065	0.0127	56.937	0.000456
25	0.003172	96974	308	484137	0.000635	2.6153	5048612	0.0208	52.061	0.000634
30	0.004056	96666	392	482405	0.000813	2.6342	4564475	0.0055	47.219	0.000812
35	0.005820	96274	560	480072	0.001167	2.6800	4082071	0.0072	42.400	0.001166
40	0.009154	95714	876	476544	0.001838	2.6873	3601999	0.0166	37.633	0.001833
45	0.014213	94838	1348	471035	0.002862	2.6598	3125455	0.0000	32.956	0.002862
50	0.020431	93490	1910	463067	0.004125	2.7050	2654419	0.0000	28.393	0.004125
55	0.035237	91580	3227	450452	0.007164	2.6919	2191353	0.0036	23.928	0.007159
60	0.055266	88353	4883	430564	0.011341	2.7060	1740901	0.0292	19.704	0.011264
65	0.096503	83470	8055	398767	0.020200	2.6930	1310338	0.0292	15.698	0.020061
70	0.163716	75415	12347	348179	0.035461	2.6596	911570	0.0292	12.087	0.035218
75	0.277691	63068	17514	273012	0.064149	2.5830	563392	0.0292	8.933	0.063756
80	0.424255	45555	19327	181272	0.106618	2.5939	290380	0.0292	6.374	0.105745
85+	*1.000000	26228	26228	109107	0.240387	4.1600	109107	0.0292	4.160	0.237500

TABLE 4 — OBSERVED AND PROJECTED VITAL RATES

	OBSERVED POPULATION BOTH SEXES	MALES	FEMALES	PROJECTED POPULATION 1969 MALES	FEMALES	1974 MALES	FEMALES	1979 MALES	FEMALES	STABLE POPULATION MALES	FEMA
RATES PER THOUSAND											
Birth	19.55	20.43	18.72	20.46	18.78	19.32	17.79	18.03	16.66	19.03	17.
Death	9.29	9.99	8.60	10.55	9.55	10.80	10.01	11.08	10.49	11.32	10.
Increase	10.27	10.43	10.11	9.92	9.23	8.52	7.79	6.95	6.17		7.70
PERCENTAGE											
under 15	22.71	23.60	21.86	24.93	23.16	26.18	24.38	26.78	24.97	26.09	24.
15-64	66.85	67.72	66.00	65.74	63.50	63.87	61.47	62.91	60.52	63.88	62.
65 and over	10.44	8.68	12.14	9.33	13.34	9.95	14.15	10.31	14.51	10.03	13.
DEP. RATIO X 100	49.60	47.66	51.51	52.11	57.48	56.57	62.68	58.96	65.24	56.55	60.

AGE LAST BIRTHDAY	1969 BOTH SEXES	MALES	FEMALES	1974 BOTH SEXES	MALES	FEMALES	1979 BOTH SEXES	MALES	FEMALES	AGE AT LAST BIRTHDAY	
0-4	566	289	277	577	295	282	564	288	276	0-4	
5-9	463	235	228	563	287	276	574	293	281	5-9	**TABLE 5**
10-14	430	219	211	462	235	227	562	287	275	10-14	POPULATION
15-19	415	212	203	428	218	210	461	234	227	15-19	PROJECTED
20-24	472	237	235	414	211	203	426	216	210	20-24	WITH
25-29	504	259	245	470	235	235	411	209	202	25-29	FIXED
30-34	430	224	206	501	257	244	468	234	234	30-34	AGE—
35-39	403	206	197	427	222	205	498	255	243	35-39	SPECIFIC
40-44	377	185	192	400	204	196	422	219	203	40-44	BIRTH
45-49	354	174	180	372	182	190	394	200	194	45-49	AND
50-54	316	158	158	346	169	177	363	176	187	50-54	DEATH
55-59	335	160	175	304	150	154	332	160	172	55-59	RATES
60-64	313	144	169	313	146	167	284	137	147	60-64	(IN 1000's)
65-69	262	113	149	281	124	157	280	126	154	65-69	
70-74	193	78	115	220	90	130	236	99	137	70-74	
75-79	127	49	78	145	55	90	166	64	102	75-79	
80-84	72	27	45	81	29	52	93	33	60	80-84	
85+	37	12	25	39	12	27	45	14	31	85+	
TOTAL	6069	2981	3088	6343	3121	3222	6579	3244	3335	TOTAL	

STANDARD COUNTRIES:	ENGLAND AND WALES 1961 BOTH SEXES	MALES	FEMALES	UNITED STATES 1960 BOTH SEXES	MALES	FEMALES	MEXICO 1960 BOTH SEXES	MALES	FEMALES	
STANDARDIZED RATES PER THOUSAND										**TABLE 6**
Birth	16.71	17.63*	15.78	16.99	16.29*	16.32	19.30	16.26*	18.77	STANDARDIZED RATES
Death	10.69	11.00*	10.39	8.74	9.75*	7.61	4.53	8.32*	3.61	
Increase	6.01	6.63*	5.40	8.25	6.54*	8.71	14.77	7.94*	15.16	

OBSERVED POP. MALES	FEMALES	STATIONARY POP. MALES	FEMALES	STABLE POP. MALES	FEMALES	OBSERVED BIRTHS	NET MATERNITY FUNCTION	BIRTHS IN STABLE POP.	
33.27891	35.71184	37.11595	39.40771	33.28757	35.20856	27.91864	28.38403	28.13025	**TABLE 7**
449.1592	499.6515	507.9635	555.1669	483.2080	531.5260	30.70181	31.18072	30.50614	MOMENTS
3467.737	3054.367	2287.740	1871.435	4064.076	4183.155	97.3398	86.9846	87.9922	AND
-166666.	-243063.	-255985.	-327137.	-200090.	-265002.	-117.134	-155.119	-96.586	CUMULANTS
0.132706	0.074790	0.039932	0.020468	0.146393	0.116529	0.327408	0.249589	0.272726	
2.173875	2.026390	2.007912	1.938593	2.143046	2.061688	2.875733	2.840451	2.896214	
-0.052202	-0.027601	-0.015040	-0.007427	-0.055283	-0.042455	-0.218241	-0.187803	-0.214629	

VITAL STATISTICS		THOMPSON AGE RANGE	NRR	1000r	INTERVAL	BOURGEOIS-PICHAT AGE RANGE	NRR	1000b	1000d	1000r	COALE	
R	1.286										IBR	**TABLE 8**
R	1.243	0-4	1.07	2.50	27.45	5-29	0.91	14.50	17.84	-3.33	IDR	RATES FROM AGE
R	2.637	5-9	1.05	1.72	27.42	30-54	1.17	16.65	10.97	5.69	IRI	DISTRIBUTIONS
GENERATION	28.257	10-14	1.06	2.23	27.37	55-79	1.78	46.65	25.34	21.32	K1	AND VITAL STATISTICS
K RATIO	105.128	15-19	1.25	8.07	27.31	*25-49	1.32	19.62	9.32	10.30	K2	(Females)

	ORIGINAL MATRIX			FIRST STABLE MATRIX			SECOND STABLE MATRIX Z₂		
SUB-DIAGONAL	ALTERNATIVE FIRST ROWS Projection	Integral	% IN STABLE POPULATION	FISHER VALUES	REPRODUCTIVE VALUES	FIRST COLUMN		FIRST ROW	
0.99650	0.00000	0.00000	8.554	1.041	238001	0.1664+0.0607		0.1664+0.0607	**TABLE 9**
0.99853	0.00000	0.00000	8.202	1.086	229061	0.1496-0.1379		0.0195+0.1530	LESLIE MATRIX
0.99854	0.02550	0.00010	7.880	1.130	229707	-0.0620-0.2257		-0.1104+0.0760	AND ITS
0.99798	0.18994	0.05197	7.571	1.150	271167	-0.2636-0.0557		-0.1070-0.0565	SPECTRAL
0.99729	0.38103	0.33598	7.269	0.999	245358	-0.1959+0.2400		-0.0307-0.1167	COMPONENTS
0.99642	0.35294	0.44210	6.975	0.644	132991	0.1418+0.3266		0.0144-0.0935	(Females)
0.99516	0.20089	0.27852	6.688	0.302	59969	0.4080+0.0273		0.0192-0.0477	
0.99265	0.08425	0.13172	6.403	0.106	20503	0.2424-0.4014		0.0110-0.0165	
0.98844	0.02107	0.04035	6.116	0.022	4074	-0.2809-0.4570		0.0031-0.0032	
0.98308	0.00130	0.00264	5.816	0.001	211	-0.6094+0.0456		0.0002-0.0002	
0.97276	0.00001	0.00001	5.502	0.000	1	-0.2707+0.6372		0.0000-0.0000	
0.80687			23.024						

OBSERVED POPUL. (IN 100's)	CONTRIBUTIONS OF ROOTS (IN 100's) r₁	r₂, r₃	r₄-r₁₁	AGE-SP. BIRTH RATES	NET MATERNITY FUNCTION	COEFF. OF MATRIX EQUATION	PARAMETERS	INTEGRAL	MATRIX	EXP. INCREASE x	e^((x+2½)r)	
2286	2447	-71	-91	0.0000	0.0000	0.0000	L(1)	1.03929	1.03932	0	1.0195	**TABLE 10**
2110	2347	-302	65	0.0000	0.0000	0.0000	L(2)	0.39527	0.39796	50	1.4987	AGE ANALYSIS
2033	2254	-225	3	0.0000	0.0001	0.0254		0.79668	0.77109	55	1.5576	AND
2359	2166	162	31	0.0104	0.0507	0.1887	R(1)	0.00771	0.00771	60	1.6188	MISCELLANEOUS
2456	2080	469	-93	0.0673	0.3268	0.3778	R(2)	-0.02345	-0.02838	65	1.6824	RESULTS
2067	1996	280	-209	0.0886	0.4288	0.3490			0.22205	0.21887	70	1.7485	(Females)
1983	1913	-324	393	0.0558	0.2692	0.1980	C(1)		28610	75	1.8172	
1939	1832	-709	816	0.0264	0.1267	0.0826	C(2)		-43812	80	1.8886	
1823	1750	-319	392	0.0081	0.0385	0.0205			-61880	85	1.9628	
1611	1664	590	-643	0.0005	0.0025	0.0013	2P/Y	28.2965	28.7074	90	2.0399	
1794	1574	1026	-806	0.0000	0.0000	0.0000	DELTA	4.3594		95	2.1201	
6947	6587									100	2.2034	

TABLE 1 — DATA

AGE AT LAST BIRTHDAY	POPULATION BOTH SEXES	MALES Number	%	FEMALES Number	%	BIRTHS BY AGE OF MOTHER	DEATHS BOTH SEXES	MALES	FEMALES	AGE AT LAST BIRTHDAY
0	597505	299770	3.1	297735	2.9	0	106428	59673	46755	0
1-4	2112458	1059668	10.8	1052790	10.2	0	74701	37804	36897	1-4
5-9	2353158	1177445	12.0	1175713	11.4	0	15890	7926	7964	5-9
10-14	2113178	1063923	10.8	1049255	10.2	0	9180	4606	4574	10-1
15-19	1938795	961070	9.8	977725	9.5	26661	13048	6191	6857	15-1
20-24	1833881	862493	8.8	971388	9.4	150087	14955	7117	7838	20-2
25-29	1574485	737025	7.5	837460	8.1	187837	13863	6399	7464	25-2
30-34	1391130	663815	6.8	727315	7.0	157822	13854	6488	7366	30-3
35-39	1227518	591563	6.0	635955	6.2	115441	13945	6883	7062	35-3
40-44	1136590	552075	5.6	584515	5.7	58558	13992	7139	6853	40-4
45-49	933855	454640	4.6	479215	4.6	0	13676	7249	6427	45-4
50-54	810053	393790	4.0	416263	4.0	0	14414	7682	6732	50-5
55-59	616606	300173	3.1	316433	3.1	0	16161	8427	7734	55-5
60-64	557863	266230	2.7	291633	2.8	0	17686	9054	8632	60-6
65-69	378121	176248	1.8	201873	2.0	0	20183	10094	10089	65-6
70-74	282368	128938	1.3	153430	1.5		20107	9855	10252	70-7
75-79	161233	72058	0.7	89175	0.9		18530	8779	9751	75-7
80-84	79956	34408	0.4	45548	0.4	355972 M.	14715	6799	7916	80-8
85+	33703	13038	0.1	20665	0.2	340434 F.	9786	4116	5670	85+
TOTAL	20132456	9808370		10324086		696406	435114	222281	212833	TOT

TABLE 2 — MALE LIFE TABLE

x	nq_x	l_x	nd_x	nL_x	nm_x	na_x	T_x	r_x	$\dot{e}_x$	nM_x
0	0.177093	100000	17709	88963	0.199063	0.3768	4050559	0.0000	40.506	0.199063
1	0.130051	82291	10702	299983	0.035675	1.2734	3961596	0.0000	48.141	0.035675
5	0.032780	71589	2347	352077	0.006665	2.5000	3661613	0.0118	51.148	0.006732
10	0.021407	69242	1482	342464	0.004328	2.4728	3309536	0.0149	47.797	0.004329
15	0.031779	67760	2153	333660	0.006454	2.6135	2967072	0.0147	43.788	0.006442
20	0.040480	65606	2656	321502	0.008260	2.5411	2633412	0.0186	40.140	0.008252
25	0.042521	62951	2677	308108	0.008688	2.5173	2311910	0.0173	36.726	0.008682
30	0.047757	60274	2879	294292	0.009781	2.5413	2003802	0.0120	33.245	0.009774
35	0.056575	57395	3247	278967	0.011640	2.5332	1709510	0.0070	29.785	0.011635
40	0.062716	54148	3396	262387	0.012943	2.5400	1430543	0.0130	26.419	0.012931
45	0.076600	50752	3900	244216	0.015969	2.5523	1168155	0.0178	23.017	0.015944
50	0.093371	46852	4375	223677	0.019558	2.5803	923940	0.0209	19.720	0.019508
55	0.131508	42478	5586	198721	0.028110	2.5533	700263	0.0119	16.485	0.028074
60	0.157320	36892	5804	170413	0.034057	2.5800	501541	0.0092	13.595	0.034008
65	0.251368	31088	7814	136250	0.057354	2.5444	331128	0.0092	10.651	0.057272
70	0.320956	23273	7470	97596	0.076537	2.4871	194878	0.0092	8.373	0.076432
75	0.465097	15804	7350	60227	0.122041	2.4435	97282	0.0092	6.156	0.121832
80	0.647916	8453	5477	27663	0.197993	2.3336	37055	0.0092	4.383	0.197598
85+	*1.000000	2976	2976	9392	0.316906	3.1555	9392	0.0092	3.156	0.315693

TABLE 3 — FEMALE LIFE TABLE

x	nq_x	l_x	nd_x	nL_x	nm_x	na_x	T_x	r_x	$\dot{e}_x$	nM_x
0	0.143496	100000	14350	91378	0.157036	0.3991	4303371	0.0000	43.034	0.157036
1	0.128192	85650	10980	313286	0.035047	1.3300	4211993	0.0000	49.177	0.035047
5	0.032965	74671	2462	367200	0.006703	2.5000	3898707	0.0128	52.212	0.006774
10	0.021563	72209	1557	357148	0.004360	2.4967	3531507	0.0129	48.907	0.004359
15	0.034489	70652	2437	347407	0.007014	2.5977	3174359	0.0011	44.929	0.007013
20	0.039571	68215	2699	334417	0.008072	2.5326	2826952	0.0074	41.442	0.008069
25	0.043644	65516	2859	320515	0.008921	2.5290	2492535	0.0199	38.045	0.008913
30	0.049438	62657	3098	305614	0.010136	2.5242	2172021	0.0174	34.665	0.010128
35	0.054045	59559	3219	289772	0.011108	2.5074	1866406	0.0108	31.337	0.011105
40	0.056998	56340	3211	273722	0.011732	2.5152	1576634	0.0164	27.984	0.011724
45	0.065004	53129	3454	257150	0.013430	2.5403	1302913	0.0204	24.524	0.013412
50	0.078083	49675	3879	239062	0.016225	2.5986	1045763	0.0241	21.052	0.016172
55	0.115503	45797	5290	216118	0.024476	2.5679	806700	0.0121	17.615	0.024441
60	0.138343	40507	5604	189045	0.029643	2.5927	590582	0.0094	14.580	0.029599
65	0.222997	34903	7783	155510	0.050050	2.5582	401538	0.0094	11.504	0.049977
70	0.286858	27120	7780	116257	0.066917	2.5137	246027	0.0094	9.072	0.066819
75	0.428859	19340	8294	75721	0.109537	2.4704	129771	0.0094	6.710	0.109347
80	0.597776	11046	6603	37920	0.174130	2.3785	54050	0.0094	4.893	0.173795
85+	*1.000000	4443	4443	16130	0.275447	3.6305	16130	0.0094	3.630	0.274377

TABLE 4 — OBSERVED AND PROJECTED VITAL RATES

	OBSERVED POPULATION BOTH SEXES	MALES	FEMALES	PROJECTED POPULATION 1866 MALES	FEMALES	1871 MALES	FEMALES	1876 MALES	FEMALES	STABLE POPULATION MALES	FEMA
RATES PER THOUSAND											
Birth	34.59	36.29	32.97	36.11	32.99	35.60	32.69	35.11	32.38	33.49	31.
Death	21.61	22.66	20.62	22.44	20.52	22.36	20.53	22.34	20.60	23.29	21.
Increase	12.98	13.63	12.36	13.68	12.47	13.25	12.17	12.77	11.79		10.20
PERCENTAGE											
under 15	35.65	36.71	34.63	36.29	34.54	35.75	34.18	35.34	33.96	33.72	33.
15-64	59.71	58.96	60.42	59.29	60.41	59.93	60.89	60.22	60.96	60.98	60.
65 and over	4.65	4.33	4.95	4.42	5.06	4.32	4.93	4.44	5.08	5.29	6.
DEP. RATIO X 100	67.48	69.61	65.51	68.66	65.54	66.86	64.23	66.06	64.05	63.98	64.

AGE LAST BIRTHDAY	1866 BOTH SEXES	1866 MALES	FEMALES	1871 BOTH SEXES	1871 MALES	FEMALES	1876 BOTH SEXES	1876 MALES	FEMALES	AGE AT LAST BIRTHDAY	
0-4	2850	1429	1421	3015	1511	1504	3172	1590	1582	0-4	**TABLE 5**
5-9	2456	1231	1225	2583	1293	1290	2733	1368	1365	5-9	POPULATION
10-14	2289	1145	1144	2389	1197	1192	2513	1258	1255	10-14	PROJECTED
15-19	2058	1037	1021	2228	1116	1112	2325	1166	1159	15-19	WITH
20-24	1867	926	941	1981	999	982	2146	1075	1071	20-24	FIXED
25-29	1758	827	931	1789	887	902	1899	957	942	25-29	AGE—
30-34	1503	704	799	1677	789	888	1708	848	860	30-34	SPECIFIC
35-39	1319	629	690	1424	667	757	1590	748	842	35-39	BIRTH
40-44	1157	556	601	1243	592	651	1343	628	715	40-44	AND
45-49	1063	514	549	1082	518	564	1163	551	612	45-49	DEATH
50-54	862	416	446	982	471	511	999	474	525	50-54	RATES
55-59	726	350	376	773	370	403	880	418	462	55-59	(IN 1000's)
60-64	534	257	277	629	300	329	669	317	352	60-64	
65-69	453	213	240	434	206	228	511	240	271	65-69	
70-74	277	126	151	331	152	179	317	147	170	70-74	
75-79	180	80	100	176	78	98	211	94	117	75-79	
80-84	78	33	45	87	37	50	85	36	49	80-84	
85+	31	12	19	30	11	19	33	12	21	85+	
TOTAL	21461	10485	10976	22853	11194	11659	24297	11927	12370	TOTAL	

STANDARD COUNTRIES: STANDARDIZED RATES PER THOUSAND	ENGLAND AND WALES 1961 BOTH SEXES	MALES	FEMALES	UNITED STATES 1960 BOTH SEXES	MALES	FEMALES	MEXICO 1960 BOTH SEXES	MALES	FEMALES	
Birth	29.24	33.56*	27.70	29.74	30.84*	28.64	30.14	31.54*	29.40	**TABLE 6**
Death	27.01	41.29*	27.84	25.35	34.33*	24.67	21.47	21.93	20.28	STANDARDIZED RATES
Increase	2.23	-7.72*	-0.13	4.39	-3.49*	3.97	8.68	9.61*	9.12	

	OBSERVED POP. MALES	FEMALES	STATIONARY POP. MALES	FEMALES	STABLE POP. MALES	FEMALES	OBSERVED BIRTHS	NET MATERNITY FUNCTION	BIRTHS IN STABLE POP.	
1	26.11545	26.91093	32.10757	32.85687	27.73991	28.28912	30.09166	30.77820	30.32969	**TABLE 7**
2	383.5824	392.2691	449.6386	470.4203	404.5436	422.7072	41.57789	42.03252	41.71251	MOMENTS
3	5354.086	5418.853	3706.785	3870.625	4994.250	5325.559	55.7898	23.1125	39.4828	AND
4	-48003.	-48021.	-166659.	-188146.	-84413.	-95310.	-1523.019	-1641.517	-1552.681	CUMULANTS
μ_1	0.507919	0.486477	0.151149	0.143914	0.376742	0.375501	0.043303	0.007193	0.021479	
μ_2	2.673750	2.687924	2.175669	2.149796	2.484204	2.466595	2.118991	2.070874	2.107620	
κ	-0.204803	-0.203225	-0.058373	-0.054792	-0.148794	-0.146345	-0.017966	-0.002977	-0.009055	

VITAL STATISTICS		THOMPSON AGE RANGE	NRR	1000r	INTERVAL	BOURGEOIS-PICHAT AGE RANGE	NRR	1000b	1000d	1000r	COALE		
CBR	2.211										IBR	33.75	**TABLE 8**
GRR	1.366	0-4	1.32	10.45	26.87	5-29	1.25	32.38	24.02	8.36	IDR	22.24	RATES FROM AGE DISTRIBUTIONS AND VITAL STATISTICS (Females)
NRR	4.524	5-9	1.35	11.21	26.74	30-54	1.53	38.81	23.04	15.77	IRI	11.50	
GENERATION	30.554	10-14	1.35	11.03	26.66	55-79	1.30	25.49	15.81	9.68	K1	-3.28	
SEX RATIO	104.564	15-19	1.41	12.37	26.53	*25-54	1.54	39.12	23.18	15.94	K2	0.	

ORIGINAL MATRIX SUB-DIAGONAL	ALTERNATIVE FIRST ROWS Projection	Integral	FIRST STABLE MATRIX % IN STABLE POPULATION	FISHER VALUES	REPRODUCTIVE VALUES	SECOND STABLE MATRIX Z_2 FIRST COLUMN	FIRST ROW	
0.90742	0.00000	0.00000	12.521	1.267	1710621	0.1308+0.0541	0.1308+0.0541	**TABLE 9**
0.97263	0.00000	0.00000	10.796	1.469	1727101	0.1217-0.0803	0.0279+0.1346	LESLIE MATRIX AND ITS SPECTRAL COMPONENTS (Females)
0.97272	0.02624	0.00000	9.978	1.589	1667726	0.0020-0.1609	-0.0868+0.0893	
0.96261	0.17408	0.05533	9.223	1.685	1647893	-0.1457-0.1015	-0.1146-0.0211	
0.95843	0.36545	0.31354	8.436	1.614	1567395	-0.1811+0.0695	-0.0665-0.1075	
0.95351	0.42649	0.45515	7.683	1.289	1079295	-0.0480+0.2055	-0.0024-0.1267	
0.94816	0.38486	0.44034	6.961	0.856	622478	0.1549+0.1677	0.0371-0.0917	
0.94461	0.27314	0.36836	6.272	0.436	277151	0.2429-0.0367	0.0368-0.0412	
0.93946	0.09909	0.20329	5.629	0.119	69714	0.1136-0.2376	0.0133-0.0088	
0.92966	0.00000	0.00000	5.025	0.000	4	-0.1417-0.2424	0.0000-0.0000	
0.90402	0.00000	0.00000	4.439	0.000	1	-0.2956-0.0198	0.0000-0.0000	
+ 0.74457			13.038					

OBSERVED POPUL. (IN 100's)	CONTRIBUTIONS OF ROOTS (IN 100's) r_1	r_2, r_3	$r_4 \cdot r_{11}$	AGE-SP. BIRTH RATES	NET MATERNITY FUNCTION	COEFF. OF MATRIX EQUATION	PARAMETERS INTEGRAL	MATRIX	EXP. INCREASE x	$e^{(x+2\frac{1}{2})r}$	
13505	13525	-43	24	0.0000	0.0000	0.0000	L(1) 1.05232	1.05238	0	1.0258	**TABLE 10**
11757	11662	-97	193	0.0000	0.0000	0.0000	L(2) 0.49381	0.49451	50	1.7083	AGE ANALYSIS AND MISCELLANEOUS RESULTS (Females)
10493	10778	-71	-214	0.0000	0.0000	0.0232	0.74551	0.72936	55	1.7977	
9777	9962	30	-215	0.0133	0.0463	0.1494	R(1) 0.01020	0.01021	60	1.8918	
9714	9112	123	479	0.0755	0.2526	0.3020	R(2) -0.02236	-0.02530	65	1.9908	
8375	8299	114	-38	0.1096	0.3514	0.3378	0.19715	0.19500	70	2.0949	
7273	7519	-6	-240	0.1061	0.3242	0.2907	C(1)	108018	75	2.2046	
6360	6774	-140	-275	0.0887	0.2571	0.1956	C(2)	-25581	80	2.3199	
5845	6081	-162	-74	0.0490	0.1341	0.0670		-21773	85	2.4413	
4792	5428	-33	-603	0.0000	0.0000	0.0000	2P/Y 31.8694	32.2221	90	2.5690	
4163	4795	143	-775	0.0000	0.0000	0.0000	DELTA 3.1103		95	2.7035	
+ 11188	14083								100	2.8449	

TABLE 1 — DATA

AGE AT LAST BIRTHDAY	POPULATION BOTH SEXES	MALES Number	MALES %	FEMALES Number	FEMALES %	BIRTHS BY AGE OF MOTHER	DEATHS BOTH SEXES	DEATHS MALES	DEATHS FEMALES	AGE AT LAST BIRTH
0	689938	346680	3.1	343258	2.9	0	125868	69699	56169	0
1-4	2392500	1195250	10.8	1197250	10.2	0	80745	40824	39921	1-4
5-9	2717423	1356245	12.2	1361178	11.6	0	21445	11206	10239	5-9
10-14	2433698	1225333	11.0	1208365	10.3	0	10825	5421	5404	10-1
15-19	2189573	1089290	9.8	11CC283	9.4	29488	14261	6951	7310	15-1
20-24	2012791	955913	8.6	1056878	9.0	168019	17448	8772	8676	20-2
25-29	1787285	846750	7.6	94C535	8.0	217492	16927	8696	8231	25-2
30-34	1564638	748650	6.7	815988	7.0	183479	17798	8959	8839	30-3
35-39	1346303	643403	5.8	702900	6.0	132240	17080	8809	8271	35-3
40-44	1234041	592173	5.3	641868	5.5	66710	17218	9014	8204	40-4
45-49	1055460	507915	4.6	547545	4.7	0	17449	9405	8044	45-4
50-54	946635	456550	4.1	49C085	4.2	0	18387	9900	8487	50-5
55-59	720408	346803	3.1	373605	3.2	0	20087	10598	9489	55-5
60-64	625326	295848	2.7	329478	2.8	0	21714	11188	10526	60-6
65-69	442828	206053	1.9	236775	2.0	0	24679	12279	12400	65-6
70-74	324648	150110	1.4	174538	1.5		24180	11750	12430	70-7
75-79	182508	82293	0.7	100215	0.9		21275	9997	11278	75-7
80-84	90048	38665	0.3	51383	0.4	405605 M.	16537	7560	8977	80-8
85+	37713	14505	0.1	23208	0.2	391823 F.	10956	4535	6421	85+
TOTAL	22793764	11098429		11695335		797428	514879	265563	249316	TOT/

TABLE 2 — MALE LIFE TABLE

x	$_nq_x$	l_x	$_nd_x$	$_nL_x$	$_nm_x$	$_na_x$	T_x	r_x	$\mathring{e}_x$	$_nM_x$
0	0.178505	1CCCC0	17850	88788	0.201047	0.3719	3921976	0.0000	39.220	0.201047
1	0.124939	82150	10264	300502	0.034155	1.2626	3833189	0.0000	46.661	0.034155
5	0.040225	71886	2892	352200	0.008210	2.5000	3532687	0.0098	49.143	0.008263
10	0.021836	68994	1507	341045	0.004417	2.3943	3180487	0.0161	46.098	0.004424
15	0.031520	67488	2127	332418	0.006399	2.6402	2839442	0.0184	42.073	0.006381
20	0.044947	65360	2938	319666	0.009190	2.5710	2507023	0.0164	38.357	0.009177
25	0.050119	62423	3129	304399	0.010278	2.5341	2187357	0.0140	35.041	0.010270
30	0.058171	59294	3449	287966	0.011978	2.5345	1882958	0.0155	31.756	0.011967
35	0.066241	55845	3699	270055	0.013698	2.5213	1594992	0.0098	28.561	0.013691
40	0.073390	52146	3827	251282	0.015230	2.5316	1324936	0.0080	25.408	0.015222
45	0.088590	48319	4281	231041	0.018527	2.5348	1073654	0.0076	22.220	0.018517
50	0.103139	44038	4542	209115	0.021720	2.5615	842613	0.0152	19.134	0.021684
55	0.142347	39496	5622	183702	0.030605	2.5492	633497	0.0135	16.039	0.030559
60	0.173279	33874	5870	155041	0.037859	2.5588	449795	0.0078	13.278	0.037817
65	0.259928	28004	7279	122013	0.059658	2.5260	294754	0.0078	10.525	0.059591
70	0.327092	20725	6779	86509	0.078362	2.4750	172741	0.0078	8.335	0.078276
75	0.463669	13946	6466	53155	0.121651	2.4367	86232	0.0078	6.183	0.121481
80	0.643472	7480	4813	24575	0.195853	2.3355	33076	0.0078	4.422	0.195525
85+	*1.000000	2667	2667	8502	0.313670	3.1881	8502	0.0078	3.188	0.312651

TABLE 3 — FEMALE LIFE TABLE

x	$_nq_x$	l_x	$_nd_x$	$_nL_x$	$_nm_x$	$_na_x$	T_x	r_x	$\mathring{e}_x$	$_nM_x$
0	0.148804	1CCCC0	14880	90937	0.163635	0.3909	4242665	0.0000	42.427	0.163635
1	0.122388	85120	10418	312430	0.033344	1.3076	4151729	0.0000	48.775	0.033344
5	0.036623	74702	2736	366670	0.007461	2.5000	3839299	0.0117	51.395	0.007522
10	0.022093	71966	1590	355766	0.004469	2.4433	3472628	0.0156	48.254	0.004472
15	0.032725	70376	2303	346363	0.006649	2.6040	3116863	0.0070	44.289	0.006644
20	0.040249	68073	2740	333620	0.008213	2.5379	2770500	0.0077	40.699	0.008209
25	0.042878	65333	2801	319780	0.008760	2.5418	2436880	0.0167	37.299	0.008751
30	0.052810	62532	3302	304526	0.010844	2.5369	2117099	0.0186	33.856	0.010832
35	0.057183	59230	3387	287714	0.011772	2.5098	1812573	0.0122	30.602	0.011767
40	0.061977	55843	3461	270630	0.012789	2.5198	1524859	0.0120	27.306	0.012781
45	0.070940	52382	3716	252742	0.014703	2.5332	1254230	0.0122	23.944	0.014691
50	0.083302	48666	4054	233533	0.017359	2.5837	1001488	0.0197	20.579	0.017317
55	0.119810	44612	5345	210067	0.025444	2.5692	767954	0.0149	17.214	0.025398
60	0.148478	39267	5830	182264	0.031988	2.5866	557887	0.0081	14.208	0.031948
65	0.232353	33437	7769	148164	0.052436	2.5519	375624	0.0081	11.234	0.052370
70	0.302615	25668	7767	108933	0.071304	2.5018	227460	0.0081	8.862	0.071217
75	0.437849	17900	7838	69544	0.112669	2.4538	118526	0.0081	6.622	0.112538
80	0.599089	10063	6028	34450	0.174991	2.3686	48982	0.0081	4.868	0.174708
85+	*1.000000	4034	4034	14532	0.277600	3.6023	14532	0.0081	3.602	0.276672

TABLE 4 — OBSERVED AND PROJECTED VITAL RATES

		OBSERVED POPULATION BOTH SEXES	MALES	FEMALES	PROJECTED POPULATION 1876 MALES	1876 FEMALES	1881 MALES	1881 FEMALES	1886 MALES	1886 FEMALES	STABLE POPULATION MALES	FEMA
RATES PER THOUSAND	Birth	34.98	36.55	33.50	36.57	33.59	36.44	33.53	36.30	33.46	35.33	33.
	Death	22.59	23.93	21.32	23.75	21.21	23.69	21.21	23.66	21.26	24.08	21.
	Increase	12.40	12.62	12.18	12.82	12.38	12.75	12.32	12.64	12.20		11.24
PERCENTAGE	under 15	36.12	37.15	35.14	36.73	35.03	36.25	34.66	36.11	34.62	35.28	34.
	15-64	59.15	58.42	59.85	58.85	59.94	59.45	60.43	59.50	60.33	60.11	60.
	65 and over	4.73	4.43	5.01	4.42	5.03	4.30	4.91	4.39	5.05	4.61	5.
	DEP. RATIO X 100	69.06	71.19	67.10	69.93	66.84	68.21	65.47	68.07	65.75	66.37	66.

TABLE 1

AGE AT LAST BIRTHDAY	POPULATION BOTH SEXES	MALES Number	%	FEMALES Number	%	BIRTHS BY AGE OF MOTHER	DEATHS BOTH SEXES	MALES	FEMALES	AGE AT LAST BIRTHDAY
0	788371	396273	3.1	392098	2.9	0	114976	64165	50811	0
1-4	2733148	1361765	10.7	1371383	10.3	0	69206	35265	33941	1-4
5-9	3153498	1571720	12.4	1581778	11.8	0	18084	9108	8976	5-9
10-14	2810785	1407320	11.1	1403465	10.5	0	9102	4557	4545	10-14
15-19	2557391	1273223	10.0	1284168	9.6	28914	11806	5766	6040	15-19
20-24	2336253	1115773	8.8	1220480	9.1	190363	14103	6759	7344	20-24
25-29	2055555	984545	7.8	1071010	8.0	243366	14743	7158	7585	25-29
30-34	1752550	843740	6.7	908810	6.8	203199	15938	7934	8004	30-34
35-39	1547410	747915	5.9	799495	6.0	146497	17213	8932	8281	35-39
40-44	1403091	674813	5.3	728278	5.4	71303	18009	9544	8465	40-44
45-49	1156036	549868	4.3	606168	4.5	0	17777	9615	8162	45-49
50-54	1025550	487395	3.8	538155	4.0	0	19290	10380	8910	50-54
55-59	808443	382783	3.0	425660	3.2	0	22636	11893	10743	55-59
60-64	728831	341008	2.7	387823	2.9	0	24701	12704	11997	60-64
65-69	504140	232205	1.8	271935	2.0	0	27248	13595	13653	65-69
70-74	351601	158973	1.3	192628	1.4		26359	12899	13460	70-74
75-79	203076	90098	0.7	112978	0.8		22800	10897	11903	75-79
80-84	96046	41263	0.3	54783	0.4	450180 M.	17414	8123	9291	80-84
85+	38338	14738	0.1	23600	0.2	433462 F.	10530	4311	6219	85+
TOTAL	26050113	12675418		13374695		883642	491935	253605	238330	TOTAL

TABLE 2 — MALE — LIFE TABLE

x	nq_x	l_x	nd_x	nL_x	nm_x	na_x	T_x	r_x	$\mathring{e}_x$	nM_x	x
0	0.146745	100000	14675	90749	0.161705	0.3696	4418464	0.0022	44.185	0.161921	0
1	0.096619	85325	8244	318694	0.025868	1.2577	4327715	0.0022	50.720	0.025897	1
5	0.028316	77081	2183	379950	0.005745	2.5000	4009021	0.0125	52.010	0.005795	5
10	0.016033	74899	1201	371382	0.003234	2.4084	3629071	0.0169	48.453	0.003238	10
15	0.022456	73698	1655	364551	0.004540	2.6201	3257689	0.0187	44.203	0.004529	15
20	0.029906	72043	2155	355005	0.006069	2.5818	2893139	0.0197	40.159	0.006058	20
25	0.035791	69888	2501	343386	0.007284	2.5790	2538134	0.0205	36.317	0.007270	25
30	0.046055	67387	3103	329433	0.009421	2.5827	2194747	0.0180	32.569	0.009403	30
35	0.058069	64284	3733	312302	0.011953	2.5581	1865314	0.0105	29.017	0.011943	35
40	0.068435	60551	4144	292603	0.014162	2.5504	1553012	0.0164	25.648	0.014143	40
45	0.083938	56407	4735	270426	0.017508	2.5483	1260409	0.0151	22.345	0.017486	45
50	0.101426	51672	5241	245669	0.021333	2.5784	989983	0.0136	19.159	0.021297	50
55	0.144437	46431	6706	215713	0.031089	2.5481	744314	0.0057	16.030	0.031070	55
60	0.170923	39725	6790	182010	0.037305	2.5531	528601	0.0101	13.307	0.037254	60
65	0.256178	32935	8437	143888	0.058637	2.5363	346590	0.0101	10.523	0.058547	65
70	0.337150	24498	8259	101645	0.081258	2.4763	202702	0.0101	8.274	0.081140	70
75	0.461842	16238	7500	61900	0.121157	2.4275	101057	0.0101	6.223	0.120946	75
80	0.646693	8739	5651	28647	0.197278	2.3374	39158	0.0101	4.481	0.196860	80
85+	*1.000000	3087	3087	10511	0.293734	3.4044	10511	0.0101	3.404	0.292509	85+

TABLE 3 — MALE — LIFE TABLE

x	nq_x	l_x	nd_x	nL_x	nm_x	na_x	T_x	r_x	$\mathring{e}_x$	nM_x	x
0	0.119948	100000	11995	92662	0.129447	0.3882	4738049	0.0018	47.380	0.129587	0
1	0.092729	88005	8161	329992	0.024730	1.3007	4645387	0.0018	52.785	0.024749	1
5	0.027726	79845	2214	393688	0.005623	2.5000	4315395	0.0135	54.047	0.005675	5
10	0.016041	77631	1245	384950	0.003235	2.4272	3921706	0.0167	50.517	0.003238	10
15	0.023283	76385	1778	377683	0.004709	2.6135	3536756	0.0094	46.301	0.004703	15
20	0.029682	74607	2215	367654	0.006023	2.5702	3159073	0.0122	42.343	0.006017	20
25	0.034872	72393	2525	355818	0.007095	2.5662	2791419	0.0222	38.559	0.007082	25
30	0.043176	69868	3017	341976	0.008821	2.5590	2435601	0.0205	34.860	0.008807	30
35	0.050533	66851	3378	325931	0.010365	2.5353	2093624	0.0118	31.318	0.010358	35
40	0.056543	63473	3589	308504	0.011634	2.5307	1767693	0.0159	27.849	0.011623	40
45	0.065251	59884	3907	289836	0.013482	2.5468	1459189	0.0166	24.367	0.013465	45
50	0.079813	55977	4468	269178	0.016597	2.6037	1169354	0.0176	20.890	0.016557	50
55	0.119016	51509	6130	242652	0.025264	2.5705	900176	0.0084	17.476	0.025238	55
60	0.144197	45379	6543	211071	0.031001	2.5819	657524	0.0144	14.490	0.030934	60
65	0.224075	38835	8702	172929	0.050321	2.5583	446454	0.0144	11.496	0.050207	65
70	0.298005	30133	8980	128239	0.070024	2.5025	273525	0.0144	9.077	0.069876	70
75	0.416380	21153	8808	83392	0.105620	2.4597	145287	0.0144	6.868	0.105357	75
80	0.589211	12346	7274	42764	0.170099	2.3930	61895	0.0144	5.014	0.169597	80
85+	*1.000000	5071	5071	19131	0.265095	3.7722	19131	0.0144	3.772	0.263517	85+

TABLE 4 — OBSERVED POPULATION AND PROJECTED POPULATION / STABLE POPULATION

	OBSERVED POPULATION BOTH SEXES	MALES	FEMALES	PROJECTED 1886 MALES	FEMALES	1891 MALES	FEMALES	1896 MALES	FEMALES	STABLE POPULATION MALES	FEMALES
RATES PER THOUSAND											
Birth	33.92	35.52	32.41	35.61	32.64	35.52	32.69	35.34	32.66	34.06	32.20
Death	18.88	20.01	17.82	19.96	17.86	19.85	17.89	19.76	17.91	20.04	18.18
Increase	15.04	15.51	14.59	15.66	14.78	15.67	14.80	15.58	14.75		14.0267
PERCENTAGE											
under 15	36.41	37.37	35.51	37.15	35.43	36.82	35.17	36.88	35.27	35.74	34.97
15-64	59.01	58.39	59.59	58.56	59.52	59.08	59.92	59.09	59.81	59.98	59.86
65 and over	4.58	4.24	4.90	4.29	5.05	4.09	4.91	4.03	4.92	4.28	5.17
DEP. RATIO X 100	69.47	71.26	67.81	70.76	68.02	69.25	66.88	69.23	67.21	66.73	67.06

TABLE 1 DATA

AGE AT LAST BIRTHDAY	POPULATION BOTH SEXES	MALES Number	MALES %	FEMALES Number	FEMALES %	BIRTHS BY AGE OF MOTHER	DEATHS BOTH SEXES	MALES	FEMALES	AGE AT LAST BIRTHDAY
0	768433	383913	2.7	384520	2.6	0	135801	76257	59544	0
1-4	2789051	1393193	9.9	1395858	9.3	0	74477	38016	36461	1-4
5-9	3397501	1694538	12.0	1702963	11.4	0	16000	7959	8041	5-9
10-14	3226556	1612403	11.4	1614153	10.8	0	8872	4243	4629	10-14
15-19	2958281	1468758	10.4	1489523	9.9	26049	12496	6157	6339	15-19
20-24	2658263	1252933	8.9	1405330	9.4	192374	14333	7077	7256	20-24
25-29	2362058	1116530	7.9	1245528	8.3	264136	15490	7714	7776	25-29
30-34	2037598	982395	7.0	1055203	7.0	214486	17243	8779	8464	30-34
35-39	1790890	869725	6.2	921165	6.1	149477	19402	10238	9164	35-39
40-44	1554590	749300	5.3	805290	5.4	67635	21459	11523	9936	40-44
45-49	1342710	645145	4.6	697565	4.7	0	23320	12758	10562	45-49
50-54	1164323	551768	3.9	612555	4.1	0	25893	14004	11889	50-54
55-59	888410	415405	2.9	473005	3.2	0	29120	15271	13849	55-59
60-64	775843	358238	2.5	417605	2.8	0	32317	16453	15864	60-64
65-69	573443	260268	1.8	313175	2.1	0	37910	18561	19349	65-69
70-74	418613	185458	1.3	233155	1.6		36890	17658	19232	70-74
75-79	234080	101985	0.7	132095	0.9		30470	14184	16286	75-79
80-84	106178	43910	0.3	62268	0.4	465660 M.	22821	10322	12499	80-84
85+	43820	16245	0.1	27575	0.2	448497 F.	13611	5320	8291	85+
TOTAL	29090641	14102110		14988531		914157	587925	302494	285431	TOTAL

TABLE 2 MALE LIFE TABLE

x	$_nq_x$	l_x	$_nd_x$	$_nL_x$	$_nm_x$	$_na_x$	T_x	r_x	$\mathring{e}_x$	$_nM_x$
0	0.175993	100000	17599	88603	0.198631	0.3524	4193880	0.0000	41.939	0.198631
1	0.101464	82401	8361	306398	0.027287	1.2245	4105277	0.0000	49.821	0.027287
5	0.023207	74040	1718	365905	0.004696	2.5000	3798879	0.0002	51.308	0.004697
10	0.013063	72322	945	359199	0.002630	2.4488	3432975	0.0108	47.468	0.002631
15	0.020820	71377	1486	353380	0.004205	2.6411	3073776	0.0211	43.064	0.004192
20	0.027922	69891	1952	344748	0.005661	2.5882	2720396	0.0218	38.923	0.005648
25	0.034034	67939	2312	334109	0.006921	2.5833	2375648	0.0173	34.967	0.006909
30	0.043817	65627	2876	321215	0.008952	2.5931	2041539	0.0159	31.108	0.008936
35	0.057328	62752	3597	305080	0.011792	2.5878	1720324	0.0152	27.415	0.011772
40	0.074237	59154	4391	285120	0.015402	2.5747	1415244	0.0143	23.925	0.015378
45	0.094429	54763	5171	261209	0.019797	2.5624	1130123	0.0107	20.637	0.019775
50	0.119807	49592	5941	233561	0.025448	2.5769	868915	0.0174	17.521	0.025380
55	0.168717	43650	7365	200161	0.036793	2.5437	635353	0.0072	14.556	0.036762
60	0.206307	36286	7486	162995	0.045928	2.5377	435192	0.0000	11.993	0.045928
65	0.302708	28800	8718	122245	0.071315	2.5047	272197	0.0000	9.451	0.071315
70	0.382625	20082	7684	80701	0.095213	2.4351	149952	0.0000	7.467	0.095213
75	0.510213	12398	6326	45482	0.139079	2.3903	69251	0.0000	5.586	0.139079
80	0.716898	6072	4353	18519	0.235071	2.2795	23768	0.0000	3.914	0.235071
85+	*1.000000	1719	1719	5249	0.327485	3.0536	5249	0.0000	3.054	0.327485

TABLE 3 FEMALE LIFE TABLE

x	$_nq_x$	l_x	$_nd_x$	$_nL_x$	$_nm_x$	$_na_x$	T_x	r_x	$\mathring{e}_x$	$_nM_x$
0	0.141188	100000	14119	91175	0.154853	0.3750	4563658	0.0000	45.637	0.154853
1	0.097527	85881	8376	320653	0.026121	1.2693	4472483	0.0000	52.078	0.026121
5	0.023321	77506	1807	383009	0.004719	2.5000	4151830	0.0006	53.568	0.004722
10	0.014230	75698	1077	375748	0.002867	2.4547	3768821	0.0098	49.788	0.002868
15	0.021087	74621	1574	369334	0.004260	2.6042	3393073	0.0098	45.471	0.004256
20	0.025522	73047	1864	360705	0.005168	2.5693	3023738	0.0127	41.394	0.005163
25	0.030815	71183	2194	350610	0.006256	2.5813	2663033	0.0223	37.411	0.006243
30	0.039424	68990	2720	338363	0.008038	2.5789	2312423	0.0221	33.518	0.008021
35	0.048639	66270	3223	323511	0.009963	2.5686	1974061	0.0170	29.788	0.009948
40	0.059968	63046	3781	306011	0.012355	2.5611	1650549	0.0154	26.180	0.012338
45	0.073094	59266	4332	285775	0.015159	2.5638	1344538	0.0120	22.687	0.015141
50	0.092960	54934	5107	262420	0.019460	2.6014	1058763	0.0183	19.273	0.019409
55	0.136840	49827	6818	232584	0.029316	2.5725	796343	0.0096	15.982	0.029279
60	0.173938	43009	7481	196905	0.037992	2.5753	563759	0.0007	13.108	0.037988
65	0.268046	35528	9523	154121	0.061790	2.5304	366854	0.0007	10.326	0.061783
70	0.341122	26005	8871	107533	0.082494	2.4646	212733	0.0007	8.181	0.082486
75	0.467915	17134	8017	65020	0.123305	2.4243	105200	0.0007	6.140	0.123290
80	0.653510	9117	5958	29677	0.200759	2.3301	40180	0.0007	4.407	0.200730
85+	*1.000000	3159	3159	10503	0.300756	3.3250	10503	0.0007	3.325	0.300671

TABLE 4 OBSERVED AND PROJECTED VITAL RATES

		OBSERVED POPULATION BOTH SEXES	MALES	FEMALES	PROJECTED POPULATION 1896 MALES	1896 FEMALES	1901 MALES	1901 FEMALES	1906 MALES	1906 FEMALES	STABLE POPULATION MALES	FEMALES
RATES PER THOUSAND	Birth	31.42	33.02	29.92	33.98	30.88	34.37	31.34	34.17	31.25	31.97	29.7
	Death	20.21	21.45	19.04	21.19	18.88	21.10	18.85	21.00	18.81	21.96	19.7
	Increase	11.21	11.57	10.88	12.78	12.00	13.27	12.49	13.17	12.44		10.012
PERCENTAGE	under 15	35.00	36.05	34.01	34.98	33.17	34.41	32.76	34.78	33.23	33.31	32.3
	15-64	60.27	59.64	60.86	61.01	61.98	61.94	62.73	61.65	62.30	62.46	62.3
	65 and over	4.73	4.31	5.13	4.00	4.85	3.65	4.51	3.58	4.47	4.24	5.2
	DEP. RATIO X 100	65.92	67.68	64.30	63.90	61.34	61.46	59.42	62.21	60.52	60.11	60.3

TABLE 1 — DATA

AGE AT LAST BIRTHDAY	POPULATION BOTH SEXES	MALES Number	%	FEMALES Number	%	BIRTHS BY AGE OF MOTHER	DEATHS BOTH SEXES	MALES	FEMALES	AGE AT LAST BIRTHDAY
0	796618	399878	2.5	396740	2.4	0	140648	78493	62155	0
1-4	2923523	1457440	9.2	1466083	8.7	0	61099	31088	30011	1-4
5-9	3492440	1741610	11.0	175C830	10.4	0	14162	7014	7148	5-9
10-14	3345748	1672915	10.6	1672833	9.9	0	7829	3834	3995	10-14
15-19	3248363	1608685	10.2	1639678	9.7	13685	10850	5557	5293	15-19
20-24	3122273	1473353	9.3	1648920	9.8	198078	13243	6918	6325	20-24
25-29	2830866	1331488	8.4	1499378	8.9	285619	14251	7271	6980	25-29
30-34	2442545	1163155	7.4	1279390	7.6	223932	16066	8279	7787	30-34
35-39	2157096	1040173	6.6	1116923	6.6	147369	18316	9665	8651	35-39
40-44	1860150	901940	5.7	958210	5.7	61124	20302	10880	9422	40-44
45-49	1582011	764153	4.8	817858	4.9	0	21900	12022	9878	45-49
50-54	1335841	639598	4.1	696243	4.1	0	24338	13273	11065	50-54
55-59	1058246	500263	3.2	557983	3.3	0	27694	14823	12871	55-59
60-64	893835	412070	2.6	481765	2.9	0	30441	15737	14704	60-64
65-69	634128	284488	1.8	349640	2.1	0	33638	16767	16871	65-69
70-74	449080	196535	1.2	252545	1.5		32968	15836	17132	70-74
75-79	265638	113460	0.7	152178	0.9		28991	13305	15686	75-79
80-84	129088	52208	0.3	76880	0.5	473944 M.	22242	9856	12386	80-84
85+	48888	18118	0.1	3C770	0.2	455863 F.	12607	5000	7607	85+
TOTAL	32616377	15771530		16844847		929807	551585	285618	265967	TOTAL

TABLE 2 — MALE LIFE TABLE

x	nq_x	l_x	nd_x	nL_x	nm_x	na_x	T_x	r_x	$\mathring{e}_x$	nM_x	x
0	0.173469	1CCCCO	17347	88373	0.196292	0.3297	4539987	0.0000	45.4C0	0.196292	0
1	0.C80494	82653	6653	311904	C.021331	1.1880	4451614	0.0000	53.859	0.021331	1
5	0.019892	76000	1512	376221	C.004018	2.5000	4139710	0.0027	54.470	0.004027	5
10	0.011389	74488	848	370268	C.002291	2.4390	3763490	0.0050	50.525	0.002292	10
15	0.C17155	73640	1263	365215	0.003459	2.6375	3393221	0.0093	46.079	0.003454	15
20	0.C23243	72377	1682	357812	0.004701	2.5799	3028006	0.0143	41.837	0.004695	20
25	0.026992	7C694	1908	348853	0.005470	2.5796	2670195	0.0180	37.771	0.005461	25
30	0.C35057	68786	2411	338134	0.007132	2.5962	2321341	0.0175	33.747	0.007118	30
35	0.045519	66375	3021	324593	0.009308	2.5903	1983207	0.0160	29.879	0.009292	35
40	0.058723	63353	3720	3C7780	C.012088	2.5844	1658614	0.0186	26.180	0.012063	40
45	0.075929	59633	4528	287208	0.015765	2.5800	1350834	0.0184	22.652	0.015732	45
50	0.099079	55105	5460	262365	C.02081C	2.5894	1063625	0.0208	19.302	0.020752	50
55	0.138398	49645	6871	231472	C.029683	2.5614	801261	0.0146	16.140	0.029630	55
60	0.174996	42775	7485	195623	C.038265	2.5619	569789	0.0135	13.321	0.038190	60
65	0.257681	35289	9093	153982	C.059055	2.5297	374166	0.0135	10.603	0.058937	65
70	0.335189	26196	8781	108770	C.080726	2.4707	220184	0.0135	8.405	0.080576	70
75	0.451201	17415	7858	66858	0.117530	2.4269	111413	0.0135	6.397	0.117266	75
80	0.630355	9558	6025	31825	0.189305	2.3504	44555	0.0135	4.662	0.188784	80
85+	*1.000000	3533	3533	12730	C.277517	3.6034	12730	0.0135	3.603	0.275969	85+

TABLE 3 — FEMALE LIFE TABLE

x	nq_x	l_x	nd_x	nL_x	nm_x	na_x	T_x	r_x	$\mathring{e}_x$	nM_x	x
0	0.142200	1CCCCO	14220	90767	C.156664	0.3507	4939037	0.0000	49.390	0.156664	0
1	0.C77474	85780	6646	324655	0.020470	1.2215	4848270	0.0000	56.520	0.020470	1
5	0.C2C157	79134	1595	391684	0.004072	2.5000	4523615	0.0032	57.164	0.004083	5
10	0.C11864	77539	920	385319	0.002388	2.4167	4131931	0.0036	53.288	0.002388	10
15	0.C16016	76619	1227	380135	0.003228	2.5871	3746612	0.0000	48.899	0.003228	15
20	0.019009	75392	1433	373478	0.003837	2.5696	3366476	0.0051	44.653	0.003836	20
25	0.023065	73959	1706	365684	0.004665	2.5903	2992999	0.0206	40.468	0.004655	25
30	0.030066	72253	2172	356035	C.0C6101	2.5924	2627315	0.0233	36.363	0.006086	30
35	0.038094	7C081	2670	343953	0.007762	2.5836	2271279	0.0211	32.409	0.007745	35
40	0.048109	67411	3243	329177	0.009852	2.5708	1927327	0.0213	28.591	0.009833	40
45	0.058787	64168	3772	311700	0.012102	2.5770	1598149	0.0196	24.906	0.012078	45
50	0.C76770	6C396	4637	290873	0.015940	2.6047	1286449	0.0216	21.3C0	0.015892	50
55	0.109433	55759	6102	264049	0.023109	2.5833	995577	0.0139	17.855	0.023067	55
60	0.142492	49657	7076	231245	0.030599	2.5916	731527	0.0161	14.732	0.030521	60
65	0.216329	42582	9212	190426	0.048374	2.5594	500282	0.0161	11.749	0.048252	65
70	0.290781	33370	9703	142691	0.068003	2.5103	309857	0.0161	9.286	0.067837	70
75	0.409414	23667	9689	93745	0.103359	2.4624	167166	0.0161	7.063	0.103077	75
80	0.569259	13977	7957	49230	C.161622	2.4039	73421	0.0161	5.253	0.161109	80
85+	*1.C00000	6021	6021	24191	0.248875	4.0181	24191	0.0161	4.018	0.247221	85+

TABLE 4 — OBSERVED, PROJECTED, STABLE RATES

	OBSERVED POPULATION BOTH SEXES	MALES	FEMALES	PROJECTED POPULATION 1906 MALES	FEMALES	1911 MALES	FEMALES	1916 MALES	FEMALES	STABLE POPULATION MALES	FEMALES
RATES PER THOUSAND											
Birth	28.51	30.05	27.06	30.51	27.56	30.06	27.23	29.18	26.50	26.73	24.76
Death	16.91	18.11	15.79	18.26	16.02	18.43	16.23	18.52	16.40	20.58	18.61
Increase	11.60	11.94	11.27	12.25	11.54	11.63	11.00	10.66	10.11		6.1501
PERCENTAGE											
under 15	32.37	33.43	31.38	32.45	30.56	31.90	30.09	31.74	29.98	29.30	28.23
15-64	62.95	62.36	63.50	63.24	64.15	63.79	64.61	63.81	64.55	64.30	63.87
65 and over	4.68	4.22	5.12	4.31	5.29	4.31	5.30	4.45	5.47	6.40	7.90
DEP. RATIO X 100	58.86	60.36	57.48	58.12	55.88	56.77	54.78	56.71	54.93	55.53	56.56

TABLE 1 — DATA

AGE AT LAST BIRTHDAY	POPULATION BOTH SEXES	MALES Number	%	FEMALES Number	%	BIRTHS BY AGE OF MOTHER	DEATHS BOTH SEXES	MALES	FEMALES	AGE AT LAST BIRTHDAY
0	782045	395335	2.3	386710	2.1	0	114600	63874	50726	0
1-4	3058943	1534303	8.8	1524640	8.2	0	54470	27983	26487	1-4
5-9	3692353	1845280	10.6	1847073	9.9	0	12668	6411	6257	5-9
10-14	3503703	1749838	10.0	1753865	9.4	0	7210	3574	3636	10-14
15-19	3340761	1656723	9.5	1684038	9.0	20024	9632	5038	4594	15-19
20-24	3175193	1501343	8.6	1673850	9.0	178644	11184	5802	5382	20-24
25-29	3076130	1452905	8.3	1623225	8.7	271873	12582	6504	6078	25-29
30-34	2875293	1373535	7.9	1501758	8.1	221548	14491	7623	6868	30-34
35-39	2616501	1261698	7.2	1354803	7.3	137873	16995	8994	8001	35-39
40-44	2241815	1078800	6.2	1163015	6.2	51176	18592	9989	8603	40-44
45-49	1937616	932003	5.3	1005613	5.4	0	21474	11596	9878	45-49
50-54	1612888	773270	4.4	839618	4.5	0	24479	13407	11072	50-54
55-59	1287208	612340	3.5	674868	3.6	0	27803	14971	12832	55-59
60-64	1026550	480300	2.8	546250	2.9	0	32346	17255	15091	60-64
65-69	811283	367988	2.1	443295	2.4	0	36550	19106	17444	65-69
70-74	556180	237990	1.4	318190	1.7		40388	19209	21179	70-74
75-79	312063	128275	0.7	183788	1.0		33490	15287	18203	75-79
80-84	145093	56665	0.3	88428	0.5	448933 M.	23058	9724	13334	80-84
85+	64296	22753	0.1	41543	0.2	432205 F.	15798	6165	9633	85+
TOTAL	36115914	17461344		18654570		881138	527810	272512	255298	TOTAL

TABLE 2 — MALE LIFE TABLE

x	nq_x	l_x	nd_x	nL_x	nm_x	na_x	T_x	r_x	$\mathring{e}_x$	nM_x
0	0.145913	100000	14591	90310	0.161569	0.3359	4935964	0.0000	49.360	0.161569
1	0.069405	85409	5928	325020	0.018238	1.1972	4845654	0.0000	56.735	0.018238
5	0.017178	79481	1365	393991	0.003465	2.5000	4520634	0.0031	56.877	0.003474
10	0.010156	78116	793	388553	0.002042	2.4484	4126643	0.0082	52.827	0.002042
15	0.015119	77322	1169	383827	0.003046	2.6186	3738089	0.0124	48.344	0.003041
20	0.019157	76153	1459	377220	0.003867	2.5693	3354262	0.0093	44.046	0.003865
25	0.022149	74694	1654	369449	0.004478	2.5684	2977042	0.0043	39.856	0.004477
30	0.027406	73040	2002	360370	0.005555	2.5874	2607593	0.0085	35.701	0.005550
35	0.035104	71038	2494	349188	0.007142	2.5927	2247222	0.0169	31.634	0.007128
40	0.045399	68545	3112	335249	0.009282	2.5984	1898034	0.0208	27.691	0.009259
45	0.060571	65433	3963	317676	0.012476	2.6062	1562785	0.0205	23.884	0.012442
50	0.083506	61469	5133	295048	0.017397	2.6040	1245108	0.0243	20.256	0.017338
55	0.115837	56336	6526	266017	0.024532	2.5996	950060	0.0223	16.864	0.024449
60	0.165684	49810	8253	229061	0.036029	2.5776	684043	0.0189	13.733	0.035925
65	0.230984	41558	9599	184313	0.052081	2.5544	454983	0.0189	10.948	0.051920
70	0.336708	31959	10761	132907	0.080964	2.5015	270670	0.0189	8.469	0.080713
75	0.456556	21198	9678	80971	0.119524	2.4149	137762	0.0189	6.499	0.119174
80	0.591077	11520	6809	39542	0.172202	2.3480	56791	0.0189	4.930	0.171606
85+	*1.000000	4711	4711	17250	0.273088	3.6618	17250	0.0189	3.662	0.270953

TABLE 3 — FEMALE LIFE TABLE

x	nq_x	l_x	nd_x	nL_x	nm_x	na_x	T_x	r_x	$\mathring{e}_x$	nM_x
0	0.120925	100000	12092	92187	0.131173	0.3539	5332736	0.0000	53.327	0.131173
1	0.066297	87908	5828	335470	0.017373	1.2272	5240548	0.0000	59.614	0.017373
5	0.016766	82080	1376	406957	0.003381	2.5000	4905078	0.0023	59.760	0.003388
10	0.010306	80703	832	401376	0.002072	2.4264	4498121	0.0067	55.736	0.002073
15	0.013553	79872	1082	396741	0.002728	2.5818	4096745	0.0020	51.292	0.002728
20	0.015952	78789	1257	390878	0.003215	2.5591	3700004	0.0005	46.961	0.003215
25	0.018563	77532	1439	384161	0.003746	2.5675	3309126	0.0071	42.681	0.003744
30	0.022646	76093	1723	376310	0.004579	2.5883	2924965	0.0134	38.439	0.004573
35	0.029170	74370	2169	366615	0.005917	2.5871	2548656	0.0196	34.270	0.005906
40	0.036426	72201	2630	354673	0.007415	2.5933	2182041	0.0222	30.222	0.007397
45	0.048112	69571	3347	339822	0.009850	2.6007	1827368	0.0226	26.266	0.009823
50	0.064153	66223	4248	320977	0.013236	2.6132	1487546	0.0262	22.463	0.013187
55	0.091256	61975	5656	296374	0.019082	2.6129	1166569	0.0234	18.823	0.019014
60	0.129856	56319	7313	263976	0.027705	2.5907	870195	0.0191	15.451	0.027627
65	0.180351	49006	8838	223811	0.039490	2.5993	606218	0.0191	12.370	0.039351
70	0.286907	40168	11524	172553	0.066788	2.5456	382407	0.0191	9.520	0.066561
75	0.396656	28643	11362	114358	0.099351	2.4600	209854	0.0191	7.326	0.099043
80	0.540578	17282	9342	61763	0.151258	2.4237	95496	0.0191	5.526	0.150789
85+	1.000000	7940	7940	33733	0.235366	4.2487	33733	0.0191	4.249	0.231881

TABLE 4 — OBSERVED AND PROJECTED VITAL RATES

	OBSERVED POPULATION BOTH SEXES	MALES	FEMALES	PROJECTED POPULATION 1916 MALES	FEMALES	1921 MALES	FEMALES	1926 MALES	FEMALES	STABLE POPULATION MALES	FEMALES
RATES PER THOUSAND											
Birth	24.40	25.71	23.17	25.41	22.97	24.82	22.49	24.30	22.07	21.93	20.
Death	14.61	15.61	13.69	15.66	13.86	15.98	14.21	16.32	14.59	19.54	17.
Increase	9.78	10.10	9.48	9.75	9.10	8.84	8.28	7.98	7.49		2.39
PERCENTAGE											
under 15	30.56	31.64	29.55	30.27	28.28	29.01	27.11	28.18	26.41	25.82	24.
15-64	64.21	63.70	64.69	64.90	65.76	65.98	66.70	66.48	66.99	65.80	64.
65 and over	5.23	4.66	5.76	4.82	5.96	5.02	6.19	5.35	6.61	8.39	10.
DEP. RATIO X 100	55.74	56.99	54.59	54.07	52.07	51.57	49.93	50.43	49.28	51.98	54.

AGE LAST BIRTHDAY	1916 BOTH SEXES	1916 MALES	FEMALES	1921 BOTH SEXES	1921 MALES	FEMALES	1926 BOTH SEXES	1926 MALES	FEMALES	AGE AT LAST BIRTHDAY	
0-4	3783	1900	1883	3895	1956	1939	3977	1997	1980	0-4	
5-9	3649	1830	1819	3594	1802	1792	3701	1856	1845	5-9	
10-14	3642	1820	1822	3599	1805	1794	3544	1777	1767	10-14	
15-19	3463	1729	1734	3599	1798	1801	3556	1783	1773	15-19	TABLE 5
20-24	3287	1628	1659	3407	1699	1708	3541	1767	1774	20-24	POPULATION
25-29	3115	1470	1645	3226	1595	1631	3343	1664	1679	25-29	PROJECTED
30-34	3007	1417	1590	3045	1434	1611	3152	1555	1597	30-34	WITH
35-39	2794	1331	1463	2922	1373	1549	2960	1390	1570	35-39	FIXED
40-44	2522	1211	1311	2693	1278	1415	2817	1318	1499	40-44	AGE—
45-49	2136	1022	1114	2404	1148	1256	2567	1211	1356	45-49	SPECIFIC
50-54	1816	866	950	2002	949	1053	2252	1066	1186	50-54	BIRTH
55-59	1472	697	775	1657	780	877	1828	856	972	55-59	AND
60-64	1128	527	601	1291	600	691	1453	672	781	60-64	DEATH
65-69	849	386	463	934	424	510	1068	483	585	65-69	RATES
70-74	607	265	342	636	279	357	699	306	393	70-74	(IN 1000's)
75-79	356	145	211	389	162	227	407	170	237	75-79	
80-84	162	63	99	185	71	114	201	79	122	80-84	
85+	73	25	48	81	27	54	93	31	62	85+	
TOTAL	37861	18332	19529	39559	19180	20379	41159	19981	21178	TOTAL	

STANDARD COUNTRIES:	ENGLAND AND WALES 1961 BOTH SEXES	MALES	FEMALES	UNITED STATES 1960 BOTH SEXES	MALES	FEMALES	MEXICO 1960 BOTH SEXES	MALES	FEMALES	
STANDARDIZED RATES PER THOUSAND										TABLE 6
Birth	18.59	21.66*	17.67	18.92	20.20*	18.28	19.72	20.06*	19.29	STANDARDIZED
Death	21.38	28.00*	21.62	19.34	23.24*	18.26	14.88	15.95*	13.57	RATES
Increase	-2.79	-6.34*	-3.95	-0.43	-3.05*	0.02	4.84	4.12*	5.72	

	OBSERVED POP. MALES	FEMALES	STATIONARY POP. MALES	FEMALES	STABLE POP. MALES	FEMALES	OBSERVED BIRTHS	NET MATERNITY FUNCTION	BIRTHS IN STABLE POP.	
μ_1	28.05277	29.17849	33.74552	35.16690	32.65925	34.00454	29.95211	30.36945	30.27857	TABLE 7
μ_2	376.9691	394.3587	457.9160	489.7760	450.1280	481.8516	34.24576	35.96286	35.85068	MOMENTS
μ_3	4213.737	4424.872	3041.033	3054.304	3464.237	3564.323	53.8576	45.6905	48.0942	AND
μ_4	-67892.	-72937.	-184432.	-221618.	-169109.	-204394.	-813.166	-1010.436	-988.719	CUMULANTS
κ_1	0.331450	0.319247	0.096313	0.079402	0.131585	0.113557	0.072223	0.044884	0.050199	
κ_2	2.522240	2.531009	2.120441	2.076130	2.165370	2.119676	2.306629	2.218732	2.230732	
κ	-0.142495	-0.140510	-0.037624	-0.030399	-0.051440	-0.043514	-0.035196	-0.020602	-0.023173	

VITAL STATISTICS		THOMPSON AGE RANGE	NRR	1000r	INTERVAL	BOURGEOIS-PICHAT AGE RANGE	NRR	1000b	1000d	1000r	COALE	TABLE 8
GRR	1.421										IBR	RATES
NRR	1.075	0-4	1.13	4.41	27.22	5-29	1.09	24.58	21.31	3.27	IDR	FROM AGE
TFR	2.897	5-9	1.21	6.96	27.10	30-54	1.78	43.43	22.09	21.34	IRI	DISTRIBUTIONS
GENERATION	30.324	10-14	1.25	8.22	26.99	55-79	1.44	26.31	12.78	13.53	K1	AND VITAL
SEX RATIO	103.870	15-19	1.33	10.36	26.83	*35-64	1.89	47.97	24.44	23.52	K2	STATISTICS (Females)

Age Interval	ORIGINAL MATRIX SUB-DIAGONAL	ALTERNATIVE FIRST ROWS Projection	Integral	% IN STABLE POPULATION	FISHER VALUES	REPRODUCTIVE VALUES	SECOND STABLE MATRIX Z_2 FIRST COLUMN	FIRST ROW	
	0.95160	0.00000	0.00000	8.659	1.176	2247865	0.1418+0.0525	0.1418+0.0525	TABLE 9
	0.98629	0.00000	0.00000	8.142	1.251	2310740	0.1339-0.0999	0.0300+0.1334	LESLIE
	0.98845	0.01233	0.00000	7.935	1.283	2250929	-0.0125-0.1910	-0.0834+0.0854	MATRIX
	0.98522	0.12276	0.02509	7.750	1.299	2188183	-0.1918-0.1074	-0.1037-0.0211	AND ITS
	0.98281	0.28459	0.22522	7.545	1.188	1988857	-0.2225+0.1172	-0.0515-0.0926	SPECTRAL
	0.97956	0.32724	0.35345	7.327	0.883	1433260	-0.0260+0.2859	0.0025-0.0972	COMPONENTS
	0.97424	0.25872	0.31132	7.092	0.519	779948	0.2568+0.2019	0.0255-0.0622	(Females)
	0.96743	0.15138	0.21475	6.827	0.227	307799	0.3499-0.1194	0.0207-0.0250	
	0.95813	0.04615	0.09285	6.526	0.054	62379	0.1014-0.4029	0.0065-0.0048	
	0.94454	0.00000	0.00000	6.179	0.000	4	-0.3147-0.3388	0.0000-0.0000	
	0.92335	0.00000	0.00000	5.766	0.000	1	-0.4997+0.0873	0.0000-0.0000	
+	0.74911			20.251					

Age Interval	OBSERVED POPUL. (IN 100's)	CONTRIBUTIONS OF ROOTS (IN 100's) r_1	r_2, r_3	$r_4 \cdot r_{11}$	AGE-SP. BIRTH RATES	NET MATERNITY FUNCTION	COEFF. OF MATRIX EQUATION	PARAMETERS	INTEGRAL	MATRIX	EXP. INCREASE x	$e^{(x+2\frac{1}{2})r}$	
	19114	19063	-59	110	0.0000	0.0000	0.0000	L(1)	1.01203	1.01204	0	1.0060	TABLE 10
	18471	17924	246	301	0.0000	0.0000	0.0000	L(2)	0.46747	0.46862	50	1.1338	AGE
	17539	17468	381	-310	0.0000	0.0000	0.0116		0.73992	0.72220	55	1.1475	ANALYSIS
	16840	17061	153	-373	0.0058	0.0231	0.1139	R(1)	0.00239	0.00239	60	1.1613	AND
	16739	16609	-310	439	0.0524	0.2046	0.2601	R(2)	-0.02665	-0.02995	65	1.1752	MISCELLANEOUS
	16232	16129	-585	688	0.0822	0.3156	0.2940		0.20147	0.19904	70	1.1894	RESULTS
	15018	15612	-322	-272	0.0724	0.2723	0.2277	C(1)		220137	75	1.2037	(Females)
	13548	15029	357	-1837	0.0499	0.1830	0.1298	C(2)		16557	80	1.2182	
	11630	14366	845	-3582	0.0216	0.0766	0.0383			100758	85	1.2328	
	10056	13601	578	-4123	0.0000	0.0000	0.0000	2P/Y	31.1873	31.5671	90	1.2477	
	8396	12694	-341	-3957	0.0000	0.0000	0.0000	DELTA	10.2863		95	1.2627	
+	22964	44580									100	1.2779	

TABLE 1 — DATA

AGE AT LAST BIRTHDAY	POPULATION BOTH SEXES	MALES Number	%	FEMALES Number	%	BIRTHS BY AGE OF MOTHER	DEATHS BOTH SEXES	MALES	FEMALES	AGE AT LAST BIRTHDAY
0	794710	404094	2.2	390616	2.0	0	70250	40381	29869	0
1-4	2525737	1276707	7.1	1249030	6.3	0	26391	13913	12478	1-4
5-9	3518099	1766138	9.8	1751961	8.8	0	9707	4967	4740	5-9
10-14	3657953	1836216	10.2	1821737	9.2	0	6558	3234	3324	10-1
15-19	3502721	1727726	9.6	1774995	9.0	24852	9692	4914	4778	15-1
20-24	3152900	1449423	8.0	1703477	8.6	195510	10689	5171	5518	20-2
25-29	2961920	1341180	7.4	1620740	8.2	262947	10951	5190	5761	25-2
30-34	2801938	1281920	7.1	1520018	7.7	199974	11686	5834	5852	30-3
35-39	2745436	1273340	7.0	1472096	7.4	122316	14323	7405	6918	35-3
40-44	2601454	1223125	6.8	1378329	7.0	43215	16803	8901	7902	40-4
45-49	2406804	1162300	6.4	1244504	6.3	0	20352	11124	9228	45-4
50-54	2015600	971593	5.4	1044007	5.3	0	24027	13231	10796	50-5
55-59	1632487	782440	4.3	850047	4.3	0	28373	15767	12606	55-5
60-64	1283531	601922	3.3	681609	3.4	0	33154	17979	15175	60-6
65-69	987262	449925	2.5	537337	2.7	0	39033	20483	18550	65-6
70-74	657674	280892	1.6	376782	1.9		41462	20243	21219	70-7
75-79	392939	158687	0.9	234252	1.2		39044	17663	21381	75-7
80-84	180088	67068	0.4	113020	0.6	434895 M.	27767	11363	16404	80-8
85+	75883	24824	0.1	51059	0.3	413919 F.	18367	6528	11839	85+
TOTAL	37895136	18079520		19815616		848814	458629	234291	224338	TOT

TABLE 2 — MALE LIFE TABLE

x	nq_x	l_x	nd_x	nL_x	nm_x	na_x	T_x	r_x	$\dot{e}_x$	nM_x
0	0.092675	100000	9268	93854	0.098744	0.3368	5597630	0.0172	55.976	0.099930
1	0.041850	90732	3797	352293	0.010778	1.1986	5503776	0.0172	60.659	0.010898
5	0.013964	86935	1214	431642	0.002812	2.5000	5151483	0.0000	59.257	0.002812
10	0.008768	85721	752	426726	0.001761	2.4971	4719842	0.0000	55.060	0.001761
15	0.014165	84970	1204	421993	0.002852	2.6266	4293116	0.0209	50.525	0.002844
20	0.017707	83766	1483	415201	0.003572	2.5526	3871123	0.0218	46.213	0.003568
25	0.019175	82283	1578	407540	0.003877	2.5440	3455922	0.0083	42.000	0.003870
30	0.022508	80705	1817	399128	0.004551	2.5785	3048382	0.0005	37.772	0.004551
35	0.028674	78889	2262	388981	0.005815	2.5851	2649254	0.0000	33.582	0.005815
40	0.035766	76627	2741	376532	0.007279	2.5913	2260273	0.0017	29.497	0.007277
45	0.046868	73886	3463	361174	0.009588	2.6157	1883741	0.0131	25.495	0.009571
50	0.066218	70423	4663	341059	0.013673	2.6289	1522567	0.0255	21.620	0.013618
55	0.096550	65760	6349	313689	0.020240	2.6200	1181508	0.0271	17.967	0.020151
60	0.140026	59411	8319	277127	0.030019	2.6046	867819	0.0298	14.607	0.029869
65	0.206034	51092	10527	230005	0.045767	2.5820	590692	0.0298	11.561	0.045525
70	0.307212	40565	12462	172025	0.072444	2.5284	360687	0.0298	8.892	0.072067
75	0.435096	28103	12228	109297	0.111874	2.4469	188662	0.0298	6.713	0.111307
80	0.588563	15876	9344	54832	0.170408	2.3730	79366	0.0298	4.999	0.169424
85+	*1.000000	6532	6532	24534	0.266234	3.7561	24534	0.0298	3.756	0.262971

TABLE 3 — FEMALE LIFE TABLE

x	nq_x	l_x	nd_x	nL_x	nm_x	na_x	T_x	r_x	$\dot{e}_x$	nM_x
0	0.072083	100000	7208	95364	0.075587	0.3569	5994302	0.0170	59.943	0.076466
1	0.038536	92792	3576	361271	0.009898	1.2327	5898937	0.0170	63.572	0.009990
5	0.013437	89216	1199	443082	0.002706	2.5000	5537666	0.0000	62.070	0.002706
10	0.009082	88017	799	438080	0.001825	2.4917	5094584	0.0000	57.882	0.001825
15	0.013379	87218	1167	433293	0.002693	2.6042	4656503	0.0041	53.389	0.002692
20	0.016074	86051	1383	426864	0.003240	2.5490	4223210	0.0059	49.078	0.003239
25	0.017623	84668	1492	419651	0.003556	2.5284	3796346	0.0078	44.838	0.003555
30	0.019077	83176	1587	411995	0.003851	2.5531	3376695	0.0057	40.597	0.003850
35	0.023242	81589	1896	403343	0.004701	2.5735	2964700	0.0051	36.337	0.004699
40	0.028304	79693	2256	393018	0.005739	2.5861	2561356	0.0109	32.140	0.005733
45	0.036523	77437	2828	380432	0.007434	2.6123	2168338	0.0201	28.001	0.007415
50	0.050665	74609	3780	364066	0.010383	2.6250	1787906	0.0275	23.964	0.010341
55	0.071940	70829	5095	342072	0.014896	2.6308	1423840	0.0272	20.103	0.014830
60	0.106189	65733	6980	312116	0.022364	2.6289	1081768	0.0255	16.457	0.022263
65	0.160210	58753	9413	271337	0.034691	2.6172	769652	0.0255	13.100	0.034522
70	0.248812	49340	12276	216930	0.056592	2.5749	498315	0.0255	10.100	0.056316
75	0.372996	37064	13825	150755	0.091703	2.4998	281385	0.0255	7.592	0.091273
80	0.527774	23239	12265	84133	0.145782	2.4516	130630	0.0255	5.621	0.145142
85+	1.000000	10974	10974	46497	0.236020	4.2369	46497	0.0255	4.237	0.231870

TABLE 4 — OBSERVED AND PROJECTED VITAL RATES

	OBSERVED POPULATION BOTH SEXES	MALES	FEMALES	PROJECTED POPULATION 1926 MALES	FEMALES	1931 MALES	FEMALES	1936 MALES	FEMALES	STABLE POPULATION MALES	FEMA
RATES PER THOUSAND											
Birth	22.40	24.05	20.89	23.54	20.59	23.02	20.26	22.18	19.63	19.69	18.
Death	12.10	12.96	11.32	13.82	12.10	14.30	12.61	14.71	13.11	16.84	15.
Increase	10.30	11.10	9.57	9.72	8.49	8.72	7.65	7.48	6.52		2.85
PERCENTAGE											
under 15	27.70	29.22	26.31	28.04	25.28	27.73	25.03	28.34	25.71	25.15	24.
15-64	66.25	65.35	67.07	66.06	67.60	65.83	67.27	64.61	65.84	65.40	64.
65 and over	6.05	5.43	6.62	5.90	7.12	6.44	7.70	7.05	8.45	9.44	11.
DEP. RATIO X 100	50.95	53.02	49.10	51.37	47.93	51.91	48.67	54.77	51.88	52.90	55.

TABLE 1 — DATA

AGE AT LAST BIRTHDAY	POPULATION BOTH SEXES	MALES Number	%	FEMALES Number	%	BIRTHS BY AGE OF MOTHER	DEATHS BOTH SEXES	MALES	FEMALES	AGE AT LAST BIRTHDAY
0	598179	303035	1.6	295144	1.4	0	41939	24332	17607	0
1-4	2385575	1203782	6.3	1181793	5.7	0	18038	9705	8333	1-4
5-9	3318723	1676048	8.8	1642675	7.9	0	7073	3820	3253	5-9
10-14	3198261	1616120	8.4	1582141	7.6	0	4740	2387	2353	10-14
15-19	3433250	1709241	8.9	1724009	8.3	25272	8518	4415	4103	15-19
20-24	3501274	1704051	8.9	1797223	8.6	160475	10830	5650	5180	20-24
25-29	3364936	1634707	8.5	1730229	8.3	202546	10873	5409	5464	25-29
30-34	3060324	1436302	7.5	1624002	7.8	141045	10756	5268	5488	30-34
35-39	2804142	1283192	6.7	1520950	7.3	76742	12337	6247	6090	35-39
40-44	2664730	1229422	6.4	1435308	6.9	26001	15492	8238	7254	40-44
45-49	2556919	1187082	6.2	1369837	6.6	0	20808	11416	9392	45-49
50-54	2388858	1119150	5.8	1269688	6.1	0	27349	15023	12326	50-54
55-59	2077044	991464	5.2	1085580	5.2	0	34699	19295	15404	55-59
60-64	1664406	781594	4.1	882812	4.2	0	42342	22979	19363	60-64
65-69	1276321	580540	3.0	695781	3.3	0	51741	27626	24115	65-69
70-74	875026	378396	2.0	496630	2.4		56990	28481	28509	70-74
75-79	502022	205103	1.1	296919	1.4		53399	24709	28690	75-79
80-84	226707	83928	0.4	142779	0.7	323565 M.	37667	15632	22035	80-84
85+	96501	30715	0.2	65786	0.3	308516 F.	26039	9085	16954	85+
TOTAL	39993198	19153892		20839306		632081	491630	249717	241913	TOTAL

TABLE 2 — MALE LIFE TABLE

x	nq_x	l_x	nd_x	nL_x	nm_x	na_x	T_x	r_x	$\mathring{e}_x$	nM_x	x
0	0.076192	100000	7619	94890	0.080294	0.3294	5815056	0.0000	58.151	0.080294	0
1	0.031533	92381	2913	361330	0.008062	1.1875	5720165	0.0000	61.919	0.008062	1
5	0.011331	89468	1014	444804	0.002279	2.5000	5358835	0.0000	59.897	0.002279	5
10	0.007358	88454	651	440666	0.001477	2.5363	4914031	0.0000	55.555	0.001477	10
15	0.012837	87803	1127	436359	0.002583	2.6432	4473365	0.0000	50.948	0.002583	15
20	0.016445	86676	1425	429873	0.003316	2.5398	4037006	0.0013	46.576	0.003316	20
25	0.016414	85251	1399	422776	0.003310	2.5151	3607132	0.0137	42.312	0.003309	25
30	0.018210	83851	1527	415561	0.003674	2.5797	3184357	0.0204	37.976	0.003668	30
35	0.024095	82324	1984	406897	0.004875	2.6180	2768796	0.0106	33.633	0.004868	35
40	0.032984	80341	2650	395427	0.006702	2.6312	2361899	0.0009	29.399	0.006701	40
45	0.047010	77691	3652	379775	0.009617	2.6237	1966472	0.0000	25.312	0.009617	45
50	0.065079	74039	4818	358730	0.013432	2.6211	1586697	0.0042	21.431	0.013423	50
55	0.093237	69220	6454	330766	0.019512	2.6240	1227967	0.0157	17.740	0.019461	55
60	0.137959	62766	8659	293254	0.029528	2.6236	897201	0.0232	14.294	0.029400	60
65	0.214261	54107	11593	242569	0.047793	2.5877	603947	0.0232	11.162	0.047587	65
70	0.318420	42514	13537	179100	0.075585	2.5276	361377	0.0232	8.500	0.075268	70
75	0.461887	28977	13384	110632	0.120977	2.4409	182277	0.0232	6.290	0.120471	75
80	0.624624	15593	9740	52046	0.187135	2.3389	71645	0.0232	4.595	0.186256	80
85+	*1.000000	5853	5853	19599	0.298644	3.3485	19599	0.0232	3.348	0.295784	85+

TABLE 3 — FEMALE LIFE TABLE

x	nq_x	l_x	nd_x	nL_x	nm_x	na_x	T_x	r_x	$\mathring{e}_x$	nM_x	x
0	0.057421	100000	5742	96254	0.059656	0.3477	6233719	0.0000	62.337	0.059656	0
1	0.027662	94258	2607	369774	0.007051	1.2163	6137464	0.0000	65.114	0.007051	1
5	0.009853	91651	903	455995	0.001980	2.5000	5767691	0.0000	62.931	0.001980	5
10	0.007409	90748	672	452091	0.001487	2.5504	5311695	0.0000	58.533	0.001487	10
15	0.011832	90075	1066	447837	0.002380	2.6175	4859605	0.0000	53.951	0.002380	15
20	0.014310	89009	1274	441927	0.002882	2.5506	4411768	0.0000	49.565	0.002882	20
25	0.015671	87736	1375	435277	0.003159	2.5264	3969841	0.0070	45.248	0.003158	25
30	0.016765	86361	1448	428249	0.003381	2.5446	3534564	0.0094	40.928	0.003379	30
35	0.019842	84913	1685	420484	0.004007	2.5781	3106316	0.0083	36.582	0.004004	35
40	0.024983	83228	2079	411161	0.005057	2.6057	2685832	0.0053	32.271	0.005054	40
45	0.033757	81149	2739	399239	0.006861	2.6254	2274671	0.0052	28.031	0.006856	45
50	0.047545	78409	3728	383228	0.009728	2.6345	1875432	0.0133	23.918	0.009708	50
55	0.068903	74681	5146	361283	0.014243	2.6438	1492203	0.0215	19.981	0.014190	55
60	0.104690	69536	7280	330492	0.022027	2.6392	1130921	0.0229	16.264	0.021933	60
65	0.160777	62256	10009	287049	0.034816	2.6237	800429	0.0229	12.857	0.034659	65
70	0.253066	52247	13222	229268	0.057670	2.5824	512934	0.0229	9.818	0.057405	70
75	0.390445	39025	15237	157005	0.097048	2.4983	283667	0.0229	7.269	0.096626	75
80	0.550481	23788	13095	84510	0.154949	2.4277	126662	0.0229	5.325	0.154329	80
85+	1.000000	10693	10693	42152	0.253676	3.9420	42152	0.0229	3.942	0.257715	85+

TABLE 4 — OBSERVED AND PROJECTED VITAL RATES

	OBSERVED POPULATION BOTH SEXES	MALES	FEMALES	PROJECTED POPULATION 1936 MALES	FEMALES	1941 MALES	FEMALES	1946 MALES	FEMALES	STABLE POPULATION MALES	FEMALES
RATES PER THOUSAND											
Birth	15.80	16.89	14.80	16.75	14.72	16.15	14.23	15.51	13.71	12.88	11.86
Death	12.29	13.04	11.61	13.68	12.30	14.39	13.10	15.04	13.92	20.75	19.74
Increase	3.51	3.86	3.20	3.07	2.42	1.76	1.14	0.47	-0.21	-7.8754	
PERCENTAGE											
under 15	23.76	25.05	22.56	23.67	21.38	22.17	20.06	21.66	19.61	18.33	17.29
15-64	68.80	68.27	69.29	68.95	69.66	69.63	70.00	69.49	69.36	67.86	65.75
65 and over	7.44	6.68	8.15	7.38	8.96	8.20	9.94	8.85	11.03	13.81	16.96
DEP. RATIO X 100	45.35	46.48	44.32	45.03	43.55	43.61	42.86	43.91	44.18	47.36	52.09

TABLE 1 — DATA

AGE AT LAST BIRTHDAY	POPULATION BOTH SEXES	MALES Number	%	FEMALES Number	%	BIRTHS BY AGE OF MOTHER	DEATHS BOTH SEXES	MALES	FEMALES	AGE AT LAST BIRTHDAY
0	548000	280000	1.6	268000	1.2	0	34550	19912	14638	0
1-4	2294000	1169000	6.8	1125000	5.2	0	12149	6523	5626	1-4
5-9	2757000	1399000	8.1	1358000	6.3	0	5677	3148	2529	5-9
10-14	2943000	1482000	8.6	1461000	6.8	48	4031	2219	1812	10-14
15-19	3061000	1444000	8.4	1617000	7.5	24424	7925	4243	3682	15-19
20-24	2154000	580000	3.4	1574000	7.3	147548	7649	3228	4421	20-24
25-29	2583000	879000	5.1	1704000	7.9	180494	9073	4244	4829	25-29
30-34	3001000	1241000	7.2	1760000	8.2	127283	10651	5600	5051	30-34
35-39	3122000	1431000	8.3	1691000	7.9	73035	12701	7162	5539	35-39
40-44	2900000	1333000	7.7	1567000	7.3	24298	15147	8420	6727	40-44
45-49	2664000	1202000	7.0	1462000	6.8	1935	19527	10624	8903	45-49
50-54	2523000	1161000	6.7	1362000	6.3	26	27017	15430	11587	50-54
55-59	2303000	1052000	6.1	1251000	5.8	0	36925	21561	15364	55-59
60-64	2027000	924000	5.4	1103000	5.1	0	48929	28083	20846	60-64
65-69	1610000	728000	4.2	882000	4.1	0	60725	33300	27425	65-69
70-74	1141000	500000	2.9	641000	3.0		67206	34497	32709	70-74
75-79	669000	268000	1.6	401000	1.9		65080	31015	34065	75-79
80-84	312000	113000	0.7	199000	0.9	297054 M.	47092	20267	26825	80-84
85+	131000	42000	0.2	89000	0.4	282037 F.	32380	10868	21512	85+
TOTAL	38743000	17228000		21515000		579091	524434	270344	254090	TOTAL

TABLE 2 — MALE LIFE TABLE

x	$_nq_x$	l_x	$_nd_x$	$_nL_x$	$_nm_x$	$_na_x$	T_x	r_x	$\dot{e}_x$	$_nM_x$
0	0.067759	100000	6776	95282	0.071114	0.3037	5854409	0.0000	58.544	0.071114
1	0.021971	93224	2048	367067	0.005580	1.1539	5759126	0.0000	61.777	0.005580
5	0.011188	91176	1020	453329	0.002250	2.5000	5392060	0.0000	59.139	0.002250
10	0.007460	90156	673	449164	0.001497	2.5991	4938731	0.0000	54.780	0.001497
15	0.014973	89483	1340	444432	0.003015	2.7729	4489566	0.0906	50.172	0.002938
20	0.027541	88143	2428	434795	0.005583	2.5604	4045134	0.0448	45.893	0.005566
25	0.023847	85716	2044	423352	0.004828	2.4428	3610339	0.0000	42.120	0.004828
30	0.022311	83672	1867	413688	0.004512	2.4976	3186987	0.0000	38.089	0.004512
35	0.024723	81805	2022	404098	0.005005	2.5638	2773299	0.0000	33.901	0.005005
40	0.031155	79783	2486	392975	0.006325	2.6112	2369201	0.0109	29.696	0.006317
45	0.043322	77297	3349	378588	0.008845	2.6618	1976226	0.0046	25.567	0.008839
50	0.064438	73948	4765	358540	0.013290	2.6493	1597638	0.0000	21.605	0.013290
55	0.097752	69183	6763	329864	0.020502	2.6265	1239098	0.0019	17.910	0.020495
60	0.142111	62420	8871	290820	0.030502	2.6009	909234	0.0217	14.566	0.030393
65	0.206492	53550	11058	240876	0.045906	2.5698	618414	0.0217	11.548	0.045742
70	0.295908	42492	12574	181519	0.069270	2.5392	377537	0.0217	8.885	0.068994
75	0.448643	29918	13423	115512	0.116202	2.4610	196018	0.0217	6.552	0.115728
80	0.609990	16496	10062	55867	0.180110	2.3553	80506	0.0217	4.880	0.179353
85+	*1.000000	6433	6433	24639	0.261106	3.8299	24639	0.0217	3.830	0.258762

TABLE 3 — FEMALE LIFE TABLE

x	$_nq_x$	l_x	$_nd_x$	$_nL_x$	$_nm_x$	$_na_x$	T_x	r_x	$\dot{e}_x$	$_nM_x$
0	0.052667	100000	5267	96425	0.054619	0.3213	6462742	0.0000	64.627	0.054619
1	0.019725	94733	1869	373656	0.005001	1.1761	6366317	0.0000	67.203	0.005001
5	0.009268	92865	861	462172	0.001862	2.5000	5992660	0.0000	64.531	0.001862
10	0.006183	92004	569	458634	0.001240	2.5640	5530489	0.0000	60.111	0.001240
15	0.011324	91435	1035	454741	0.002277	2.6392	5071586	0.0000	55.469	0.002277
20	0.013947	90400	1261	448892	0.002809	2.5361	4617123	0.0000	51.075	0.002809
25	0.014070	89139	1254	442557	0.002834	2.4986	4168231	0.0000	46.761	0.002834
30	0.014248	87885	1252	436325	0.002870	2.5257	3725674	0.0000	42.393	0.002870
35	0.016261	86633	1409	429758	0.003278	2.5830	3289349	0.0082	37.969	0.003276
40	0.021277	85224	1813	421814	0.004299	2.6261	2859591	0.0101	33.554	0.004293
45	0.030048	83410	2506	411112	0.006096	2.6300	2437777	0.0078	29.226	0.006090
50	0.041738	80904	3377	396522	0.008516	2.6312	2026665	0.0069	25.050	0.008507
55	0.059765	77527	4633	376731	0.012299	2.6462	1630143	0.0083	21.027	0.012281
60	0.090940	72894	6629	348941	0.018997	2.6575	1253412	0.0260	17.195	0.018899
65	0.145536	66265	9644	308527	0.031258	2.6360	904471	0.0260	13.649	0.031094
70	0.228278	56621	12925	251988	0.051293	2.5926	595945	0.0260	10.525	0.051028
75	0.352180	43696	15389	180267	0.085366	2.5169	343956	0.0260	7.872	0.084950
80	0.500843	28307	14177	104713	0.135392	2.4815	163689	0.0260	5.783	0.134799
85+	1.000000	14130	14130	58976	0.239582	4.1739	58976	0.0260	4.174	0.241707

TABLE 4 — OBSERVED AND PROJECTED VITAL RATES

	OBSERVED POPULATION BOTH SEXES	MALES	FEMALES	PROJECTED 1946 MALES	FEMALES	1951 MALES	FEMALES	1956 MALES	FEMALES	STABLE POPULATION MALES	FEMALES
RATES PER THOUSAND											
Birth	14.95	17.24	13.11	16.61	12.64	15.83	12.05	14.99	11.44	11.68	10.3
Death	13.54	15.69	11.81	16.53	12.82	17.26	13.79	17.79	14.75	21.88	20.5
Increase	1.41	1.55	1.30	0.08	-0.18	-1.43	-1.74	-2.80	-3.31	-10.192	
PERCENTAGE											
under 15	22.05	25.13	19.58	24.04	18.63	23.37	18.11	22.31	17.35	17.22	15.5
15-64	67.98	65.28	70.14	65.48	69.79	65.57	69.16	66.17	68.91	67.55	64.6
65 and over	9.97	9.58	10.28	10.48	11.58	11.06	12.73	11.52	13.74	15.23	19.8
DEP. RATIO X 100	47.10	53.18	42.57	52.71	43.30	52.51	44.60	51.12	45.12	48.03	54.7

AGE AT LAST BIRTHDAY	1946 BOTH SEXES	1946 MALES	1946 FEMALES	1951 BOTH SEXES	1951 MALES	1951 FEMALES	1956 BOTH SEXES	1956 MALES	1956 FEMALES	AGE AT LAST BIRTHDAY	
0-4	2655	1351	1304	2545	1295	1250	2400	1221	1179	0-4	
5-9	2791	1421	1370	2607	1325	1282	2498	1269	1229	5-9	**TABLE 5**
10-14	2734	1386	1348	2767	1408	1359	2584	1312	1272	10-14	POPULATION
15-19	2915	1466	1449	2708	1372	1336	2741	1393	1348	15-19	PROJECTED
20-24	3009	1413	1596	2865	1435	1430	2661	1342	1319	20-24	WITH
25-29	2117	565	1552	2950	1376	1574	2807	1397	1410	25-29	FIXED
30-34	2539	859	1680	2082	552	1530	2896	1344	1552	30-34	AGE—
35-39	2946	1212	1734	2494	839	1655	2046	539	1507	35-39	SPECIFIC
40-44	3052	1392	1660	2880	1179	1701	2440	816	1624	40-44	BIRTH
45-49	2811	1284	1527	2959	1341	1618	2794	1136	1658	45-49	AND
50-54	2548	1138	1410	2689	1216	1473	2830	1270	1560	50-54	DEATH
55-59	2362	1068	1294	2387	1047	1340	2519	1119	1400	55-59	RATES
60-64	2086	927	1159	2141	942	1199	2164	923	1241	60-64	(IN 1000's)
65-69	1740	765	975	1793	768	1025	1840	780	1060	65-69	
70-74	1269	549	720	1374	577	797	1416	579	837	70-74	
75-79	777	318	459	864	349	515	937	367	570	75-79	
80-84	363	130	233	420	154	266	468	169	299	80-84	
85+	162	50	112	188	57	131	218	68	150	85+	
TOTAL	38876	17294	21582	38713	17232	21481	38259	17044	21215	TOTAL	

STANDARD COUNTRIES:	ENGLAND AND WALES 1961 BOTH SEXES	MALES	FEMALES	UNITED STATES 1960 BOTH SEXES	MALES	FEMALES	MEXICO 1960 BOTH SEXES	MALES	FEMALES	
STANDARDIZED RATES PER THOUSAND										**TABLE 6**
Birth	11.05	19.17*	10.43	11.23	18.80*	10.77	12.59	15.49*	12.23	STANDAR-
Death	16.16	16.55*	15.78	13.82	14.55*	12.39	8.97	12.71*	7.61	DIZED
Increase	-5.11	2.63*	-5.35	-2.59	4.25*	-1.61	3.62	2.77*	4.62	RATES

	OBSERVED POP. MALES	OBSERVED POP. FEMALES	STATIONARY POP. MALES	STATIONARY POP. FEMALES	STABLE POP. MALES	STABLE POP. FEMALES	OBSERVED BIRTHS	NET MATERNITY FUNCTION	BIRTHS IN STABLE POP.	
μ	34.89955	35.92140	34.80320	37.05871	39.75543	42.44279	28.86055	28.63207	29.02954	**TABLE 7**
σ^2	470.9758	442.9785	475.2877	519.9149	492.4555	531.6027	35.58400	36.36921	37.44997	MOMENTS
K_3	1618.114	2114.747	2842.607	2596.371	467.975	-343.998	92.0699	108.8757	102.9520	AND
K_4	-231525.	-167650.	-211122.	-269677.	-245144.	-293673.	-514.008	-502.045	-650.378	CUMULANTS
β_1	0.025062	0.051448	0.075260	0.047966	0.001834	0.000788	0.188136	0.246411	0.201797	
β_2	1.956240	2.145645	2.065411	2.002349	1.989150	1.960822	2.594062	2.620445	2.536273	
K	-0.009183	-0.021688	-0.028676	-0.017834	-0.000708	-0.000297	-0.108995	-0.133308	-0.105744	

VITAL STATISTICS		THOMPSON AGE RANGE	NRR	1000r	INTERVAL	BOURGEOIS-PICHAT AGE RANGE	NRR	1000b	1000d	1000r	COALE	
GRR	0.845										IBR	**TABLE 8**
NRR	0.745	0-4	0.79	-8.66	27.30	5-29	0.71	12.62	25.35	-12.73	IDR	RATES FROM AGE
TFR	1.736	5-9	0.78	-9.06	27.25	30-54	1.26	24.82	16.37	8.45	IRI	DISTRI- BUTIONS
GENERATION	28.830	10-14	0.85	-6.14	27.19	55-79	1.63	44.27	26.27	18.00	K1	AND VITAL STATISTICS
SEX RATIO	105.324	15-19	0.97	-1.25	27.09	*40-64	1.24	24.06	16.23	7.83	K2	(Females)

Start Age Interval	ORIGINAL MATRIX SUB-DIAGONAL	ALTERNATIVE FIRST ROWS Projection	ALTERNATIVE FIRST ROWS Integral	FIRST STABLE MATRIX % IN STABLE POPULATION	FISHER VALUES	REPRODUCTIVE VALUES	SECOND STABLE MATRIX Z₂ FIRST COLUMN	FIRST ROW	
0	0.98317	0.00000	0.00000	4.979	1.037	1444534	0.1483+0.0682	0.1483+0.0682	**TABLE 9**
5	0.99235	0.00004	0.00000	5.150	1.002	1361254	0.1688-0.1175	0.0130+0.1289	LESLIE
10	0.99149	0.01718	0.00007	5.378	0.960	1402496	-0.0200-0.2607	-0.0822+0.0602	MATRIX
15	0.98716	0.12322	0.03371	5.611	0.902	1458816	-0.2983-0.1460	-0.0762-0.0330	AND ITS
20	0.98589	0.22685	0.20922	5.828	0.739	1163361	-0.3504+0.2316	-0.0266-0.0737	SPECTRAL
25	0.98592	0.20287	0.23641	6.046	0.474	807481	0.0278+0.5299	0.0055-0.0634	COMPO-
30	0.98495	0.13148	0.16141	6.272	0.243	428389	0.5948+0.3091	0.0150-0.0357	NENTS
35	0.98152	0.06686	0.09639	6.500	0.096	163056	0.7167-0.4493	0.0106-0.0132	(Females)
40	0.97463	0.01923	0.03461	6.713	0.023	35607	-0.0302-1.0633	0.0033-0.0027	
45	0.96451	0.00154	0.00295	6.884	0.002	2486	-1.1637-0.6407	0.0003-0.0002	
50	0.95009	0.00002	0.00004	6.987	0.000	32	-1.4115+0.8383	0.0000-0.0000	
55+	0.75312			33.653					

Start Age Interval	OBSERVED POPUL. (IN 100's)	CONTRIBUTIONS OF ROOTS (IN 100's) r_1	r_2, r_3	$r_4 \cdot r_{11}$	AGE-SP. BIRTH RATES	NET MATERNITY FUNCTION	COEFF. OF MATRIX EQUATION	PARAMETERS	INTEGRAL	MATRIX	EXP. INCREASE x	$e^{(x+2\frac{1}{2})r}$	
0	13930	13702	-38	266	0.0000	0.0000	0.0000	L(1)	0.95032	0.95037	0	0.9748	**TABLE 10**
5	13580	14175	-222	-373	0.0000	0.0000	0.0000	L(2)	0.38845	0.39564	50	0.5856	AGE
10	14610	14801	-224	33	0.0000	0.0001	0.0168		0.69132	0.67277	55	0.5565	ANALYSIS
15	16170	15441	69	659	0.0074	0.0335	0.1192	R(1)	-0.01019	-0.01018	60	0.5289	AND
20	15740	16039	449	-749	0.0457	0.2049	0.2166	R(2)	-0.04639	-0.04957	65	0.5026	MISCEL-
25	17040	16639	465	-63	0.0516	0.2283	0.1910		0.21177	0.20784	70	0.4776	LANEOUS
30	17600	17261	-122	461	0.0352	0.1537	0.1220	C(1)		275217	75	0.4539	RESULTS
35	16910	17889	-897	-82	0.0210	0.0904	0.0611	C(2)		-33965	80	0.4313	(Females)
40	15670	18475	-950	-1856	0.0076	0.0319	0.0173			-45618	85	0.4099	
45	14620	18947	206	-4533	0.0006	0.0027	0.0013	2P/Y	29.6696	30.2312	90	0.3896	
50	13620	19229	1724	-7332	0.0000	0.0000	0.0000	DELTA	13.1871		95	0.3702	
55+	45660	92619									100	0.3518	

TABLE 1 — DATA

AGE AT LAST BIRTHDAY	POPULATION BOTH SEXES	MALES Number	MALES %	FEMALES Number	FEMALES %	BIRTHS BY AGE OF MOTHER	DEATHS BOTH SEXES	DEATHS MALES	DEATHS FEMALES	AGE AT LAST BIRTHDAY
0	701000	360000	1.9	341000	1.6	0	34116	19690	14426	0
1-4	2562000	1311000	7.0	1251000	5.7	0	5846	3244	2602	1-4
5-9	2822000	1435000	7.7	1387000	6.3	0	2779	1616	1163	5-9
10-14	2707000	1371000	7.4	1336000	6.1	41	2175	1241	934	10-14
15-19	2646000	1184000	6.4	1462000	6.7	25942	3686	1877	1809	15-19
20-24	2322000	762000	4.1	1560000	7.1	199217	5061	2163	2898	20-24
25-29	2808000	1215000	6.5	1593000	7.2	237269	5737	2631	3106	25-29
30-34	3169000	1457000	7.8	1712000	7.8	187158	6882	3378	3504	30-34
35-39	3342000	1592000	8.6	1750000	8.0	110495	8791	4533	4258	35-39
40-44	3203000	1550000	8.3	1653000	7.5	31596	11872	6546	5326	40-44
45-49	2878000	1334000	7.2	1544000	7.0	2155	16807	9445	7362	45-49
50-54	2571000	1168000	6.3	1403000	6.4	20	22927	13115	9812	50-54
55-59	2340000	1064000	5.7	1276000	5.8	0	32189	18926	13263	55-59
60-64	2079000	928000	5.0	1151000	5.2	0	45077	26049	19028	60-64
65-69	1751000	774000	4.2	977000	4.4	0	58042	32058	25984	65-69
70-74	1317000	575000	3.1	742000	3.4		70412	36411	34001	70-74
75-79	803000	331000	1.8	472000	2.1		70135	33758	36377	75-79
80-84	393000	147000	0.8	246000	1.1	408653 M.	53802	23210	30592	80-84
85+	181000	58000	0.3	123000	0.6	385240 F.	38968	13650	25318	85+
TOTAL	40595000	18616000		21979000		793893	495304	253541	241763	TOTAL

TABLE 2 — MALE LIFE TABLE

x	nq_x	l_x	nd_x	nL_x	nm_x	na_x	T_x	r_x	$\mathring{e}_x$	nM_x
0	0.052238	100000	5224	96055	0.054383	0.2448	6397004	0.0073	63.970	0.054694
1	0.009737	94776	923	376427	0.002452	1.0981	6300949	0.0073	66.482	0.002474
5	0.005590	93853	525	467955	0.001121	2.5000	5924523	0.0183	63.125	0.001126
10	0.004525	93329	422	465633	0.000907	2.6083	5456568	0.0181	58.466	0.000905
15	0.008012	92906	744	462853	0.001608	2.7454	4990935	0.0570	53.720	0.001585
20	0.014094	92162	1299	457611	0.002839	2.5375	4528081	0.0000	49.132	0.002839
25	0.010768	90863	978	451814	0.002165	2.4440	4070470	0.0000	44.798	0.002165
30	0.011527	89885	1036	446891	0.002318	2.5559	3618656	0.0000	40.259	0.002318
35	0.014141	88849	1256	441268	0.002847	2.6328	3171765	0.0000	35.699	0.002847
40	0.020969	87592	1837	433732	0.004235	2.6977	2730497	0.0132	31.173	0.004223
45	0.034977	85755	2999	421841	0.007110	2.6876	2296765	0.0210	26.783	0.007080
50	0.054824	82756	4537	403204	0.011252	2.6692	1874924	0.0110	22.656	0.011229
55	0.085444	78219	6683	375407	0.017803	2.6528	1471720	0.0045	18.815	0.017788
60	0.131933	71536	9438	335132	0.028162	2.6112	1096313	0.0192	15.325	0.028070
65	0.188759	62098	11721	282103	0.041550	2.5784	761181	0.0192	12.258	0.041419
70	0.274866	50376	13847	217917	0.063541	2.5471	479078	0.0192	9.510	0.063323
75	0.406639	36529	14854	145147	0.102339	2.4755	261161	0.0192	7.149	0.101988
80	0.558119	21675	12097	76370	0.158405	2.4091	116014	0.0192	5.352	0.157891
85+	1.000000	9578	9578	39644	0.241594	4.1392	39644	0.0192	4.139	0.235346

TABLE 3 — FEMALE LIFE TABLE

x	nq_x	l_x	nd_x	nL_x	nm_x	na_x	T_x	r_x	$\mathring{e}_x$	nM_x
0	0.040796	100000	4080	96958	0.042076	0.2543	6894377	0.0070	68.944	0.042305
1	0.008203	95920	787	381404	0.002063	1.1055	6797419	0.0070	70.865	0.002080
5	0.004165	95134	396	474677	0.000835	2.5000	6416015	0.0164	67.442	0.000838
10	0.003490	94737	331	472899	0.000699	2.6173	5941338	0.0000	62.714	0.000699
15	0.006169	94407	582	470690	0.001237	2.6921	5468439	0.0000	57.924	0.001237
20	0.009247	93824	868	467019	0.001858	2.5767	4997749	0.0000	53.267	0.001858
25	0.009702	92957	902	462544	0.001950	2.5161	4530730	0.0000	48.740	0.001950
30	0.010182	92055	937	457973	0.002047	2.5445	4068186	0.0000	44.193	0.002047
35	0.012096	91118	1102	452937	0.002433	2.5952	3610213	0.0010	39.621	0.002433
40	0.016011	90015	1441	446680	0.003226	2.6431	3157276	0.0092	35.075	0.003222
45	0.023621	88574	2092	437961	0.004777	2.6533	2710595	0.0115	30.603	0.004768
50	0.034469	86482	2981	425406	0.007007	2.6504	2272634	0.0119	26.279	0.006994
55	0.050822	83501	4244	407595	0.010412	2.6648	1847228	0.0089	22.122	0.010394
60	0.079965	79257	6338	381469	0.016614	2.6621	1439633	0.0251	18.164	0.016532
65	0.125813	72920	9174	343098	0.026739	2.6565	1058164	0.0251	14.511	0.026596
70	0.207522	63745	13229	287167	0.046066	2.6143	715066	0.0251	11.218	0.045823
75	0.325228	50517	16429	212143	0.077445	2.5385	427899	0.0251	8.470	0.077070
80	0.477135	34087	16264	130066	0.125046	2.5179	215756	0.0251	6.330	0.124357
85+	*1.000000	17823	17823	85690	0.207994	4.8078	85690	0.0251	4.808	0.205837

TABLE 4 — OBSERVED AND PROJECTED VITAL RATES

	OBSERVED POPULATION BOTH SEXES	MALES	FEMALES	1951 MALES	1951 FEMALES	1956 MALES	1956 FEMALES	1961 MALES	1961 FEMALES	STABLE POPULATION MALES	FEMALES
RATES PER THOUSAND											
Birth	19.56	21.95	17.53	20.11	16.19	18.41	14.93	17.40	14.23	17.39	16.2
Death	12.20	13.62	11.00	14.27	11.96	14.57	12.65	14.79	13.29	14.37	13.2
Increase	7.36	8.33	6.53	5.84	4.22	3.84	2.28	2.61	0.94	3.01	
PERCENTAGE											
under 15	21.66	24.05	19.63	25.74	21.06	26.74	21.99	26.37	21.86	23.90	22.6
15-64	67.39	65.83	68.72	63.83	66.31	62.67	64.65	62.93	64.06	65.49	63.6
65 and over	10.95	10.13	11.65	10.43	12.63	10.59	13.37	10.70	14.08	10.61	13.7
DEP. RATIO X 100	48.38	51.92	45.52	56.68	50.80	59.57	54.69	58.92	56.11	52.70	57.

AGE AT LAST BIRTHDAY	1951 BOTH SEXES	MALES	FEMALES	1956 BOTH SEXES	MALES	FEMALES	1961 BOTH SEXES	MALES	FEMALES	AGE AT LAST BIRTHDAY	
0-4	3678	1882	1796	3471	1776	1695	3295	1686	1609	0-4	
5-9	3235	1655	1580	3646	1864	1782	3441	1759	1682	5-9	
10-14	2810	1428	1382	3221	1647	1574	3631	1855	1776	10-14	**TABLE 5**
15-19	2693	1363	1330	2794	1419	1375	3203	1637	1566	15-19	POPULATION
20-24	2622	1171	1451	2666	1347	1319	2768	1403	1365	20-24	PROJECTED
25-29	2297	752	1545	2593	1156	1437	2637	1330	1307	25-29	WITH
30-34	2779	1202	1577	2274	744	1530	2566	1143	1423	30-34	FIXED
35-39	3132	1439	1693	2747	1187	1560	2248	735	1513	35-39	AGE—
40-44	3291	1565	1726	3084	1414	1670	2704	1166	1538	40-44	SPECIFIC
45-49	3129	1508	1621	3214	1522	1692	3012	1375	1637	45-49	BIRTH
50-54	2775	1275	1500	3015	1441	1574	3099	1455	1644	50-54	AND
55-59	2431	1087	1344	2624	1187	1437	2850	1342	1508	55-59	DEATH
60-64	2144	950	1194	2229	971	1258	2405	1060	1345	60-64	RATES
65-69	1816	781	1035	1874	800	1074	1949	817	1132	65-69	(IN 1000's)
70-74	1416	598	818	1469	603	866	1517	618	899	70-74	
75-79	931	383	548	1002	398	604	1042	402	640	75-79	
80-84	463	174	289	538	202	336	580	210	370	80-84	
85+	238	76	162	281	90	191	326	105	221	85+	
TOTAL	41880	19289	22591	42742	19768	22974	43273	20098	23175	TOTAL	

STANDARD COUNTRIES:	ENGLAND AND WALES 1961 BOTH SEXES	MALES	FEMALES	UNITED STATES 1960 BOTH SEXES	MALES	FEMALES	MEXICO 1960 BOTH SEXES	MALES	FEMALES	
STANDARDIZED RATES PER THOUSAND										**TABLE 6**
Birth	15.51	21.55*	14.59	15.77	21.15*	15.08	17.57	17.85*	17.01	STANDAR-
Death	13.49	13.65*	13.36	11.28	12.10*	10.20	6.73	10.41*	5.77	DIZED
Increase	2.02	7.90*	1.23	4.49	9.05*	4.88	10.84	7.45*	11.24	RATES

	OBSERVED POP. MALES	FEMALES	STATIONARY POP. MALES	FEMALES	STABLE POP. MALES	FEMALES	OBSERVED BIRTHS	NET MATERNITY FUNCTION	BIRTHS IN STABLE POP.	
μ	35.28526	36.70417	36.02156	38.00862	34.55941	36.40968	29.14022	28.81197	28.70217	**TABLE 7**
σ^2	468.7954	466.5083	489.6668	534.9996	481.0428	526.4614	34.64714	34.51117	34.24172	MOMENTS
κ_3	1524.058	1802.892	2527.181	2407.531	3190.911	3252.258	75.7106	88.6748	90.2568	AND
κ_4	-209498.	-193101.	-229301.	-290545.	-210778.	-269389.	-654.699	-536.625	-503.609	CUMULANTS
β_1	0.022545	0.032016	0.054396	0.037852	0.091470	0.072489	0.137820	0.191303	0.202905	
β_2	2.046734	2.112711	2.043677	1.984906	2.089127	2.028043	2.454611	2.549441	2.570481	
κ	-0.008956	-0.013387	-0.020802	-0.014016	-0.034959	-0.026850	-0.072461	-0.103756	-0.110865	

VITAL STATISTICS		THOMPSON AGE RANGE	NRR	1000r	INTERVAL	BOURGEOIS-PICHAT AGE RANGE	NRR	1000b	1000d	1000r	COALE	
RR	1.183											**TABLE 8**
RR	1.090	0-4	0.94	-2.13	27.36	5-29	0.76	11.93	21.85	-9.93	IBR	RATES FROM AGE DISTRIBUTIONS
FR	2.437	5-9	0.81	-7.60	27.32	30-54	1.20	22.03	15.19	6.84	IDR	AND VITAL STATISTICS
GENERATION	28.757	10-14	0.79	-8.93	27.27	55-79	1.41	29.94	17.27	12.67	K1	(Females)
SEX RATIO	106.078	15-19	0.87	-5.02	27.17	*35-59	1.34	26.45	15.73	10.72	K2	

ORIGINAL MATRIX SUB-DIAGONAL	ALTERNATIVE FIRST ROWS Projection	Integral	FIRST STABLE MATRIX % IN STABLE POPULATION	FISHER VALUES	REPRODUCTIVE VALUES	SECOND STABLE MATRIX Z_2 FIRST COLUMN	FIRST ROW	
0.99230	0.00000	0.00000	7.703	1.053	1676550	0.1537+0.0648	0.1537+0.0648	
0.99625	0.00004	0.00000	7.530	1.077	1494340	0.1557-0.1208	0.0160+0.1403	**TABLE 9**
0.99533	0.02053	0.00007	7.389	1.098	1466683	-0.0344-0.2311	-0.0965+0.0697	LESLIE
0.99220	0.16766	0.04150	7.245	1.098	1605251	-0.2587-0.0986	-0.0944-0.0435	MATRIX
0.99042	0.31943	0.29867	7.081	0.945	1474916	-0.2513+0.2093	-0.0330-0.0987	AND ITS
0.99012	0.29850	0.34835	6.908	0.629	1002705	0.0700+0.3792	0.0097-0.0863	SPECTRAL
0.98900	0.19936	0.25568	6.738	0.328	561340	0.4300+0.1471	0.0215-0.0483	COMPO-
0.98619	0.09516	0.14767	6.564	0.124	217493	0.3990-0.3564	0.0137-0.0172	NENTS
0.98048	0.02377	0.04470	6.376	0.026	43501	-0.1352-0.6133	0.0037-0.0033	(Females)
0.97133	0.00164	0.00326	6.158	0.002	2646	-0.7014-0.2132	0.0003-0.0002	
0.95813	0.00002	0.00003	5.893	0.000	24	-0.6122+0.5862	0.0000-0.0000	
0.78394			24.416					

OBSERVED POPUL. (IN 100's)	CONTRIBUTIONS OF ROOTS (IN 100's) r_1	r_2, r_3	r_4-r_{11}	AGE-SP. BIRTH RATES	NET MATERNITY FUNCTION	COEFF. OF MATRIX EQUATION	PARAMETERS INTEGRAL	MATRIX	EXP. INCREASE x	$e^{(x+2\frac{1}{2})r}$	
15920	15800	621	-501	0.0000	0.0000	0.0000	L(1) 1.01517	1.01518	0	1.0076	**TABLE 10**
13870	15444	-1343	-231	0.0000	0.0000	0.0000	L(2) 0.40724	0.41163	50	1.1713	AGE
13360	15156	-2431	635	0.0000	0.0001	0.0203	0.75397	0.73230	55	1.1891	ANALYSIS
14620	14860	-935	695	0.0086	0.0405	0.1650	R(1) 0.00301	0.00301	60	1.2071	AND
15600	14524	2319	-1243	0.0620	0.2894	0.3119	R(2) -0.03088	-0.03486	65	1.2254	MISCEL-
15930	14169	3982	-2221	0.0723	0.3343	0.2886	0.21511	0.21174	70	1.2440	LANEOUS
17120	13820	1376	1924	0.0530	0.2429	0.1909	C(1)	205113	75	1.2629	RESULTS
17500	13463	-3937	7974	0.0306	0.1388	0.0901	C(2)	-20913	80	1.2820	(Females)
16530	13079	-6432	9883	0.0093	0.0414	0.0222		-528950	85	1.3015	
15440	12632	-1962	4770	0.0007	0.0030	0.0015	2P/Y 29.2089	29.6737	90	1.3212	
14030	12086	6457	-4513	0.0000	0.0000	0.0000	DELTA 5.6619		95	1.3413	
49870	50080								100	1.3616	

TABLE 1 — DATA

AGE AT LAST BIRTHDAY	POPULATION BOTH SEXES	MALES Number	%	FEMALES Number	%	BIRTHS BY AGE OF MOTHER	DEATHS BOTH SEXES	MALES	FEMALES	AGE AT LAST BIRTHDAY
0	674000	346000	1.6	328000	1.4	0	19865	11498	8367	0
1-4	3048000	1559000	7.4	1489000	6.5	0	3858	2131	1727	1-4
5-9	3187000	1631000	7.7	1556000	6.8	0	1819	1087	732	5-9
10-14	2829000	1438000	6.8	1391000	6.1	38	1298	778	520	10-14
15-19	2715000	1331000	6.3	1384000	6.1	29658	2141	1248	893	15-19
20-24	2879000	1393000	6.6	1486000	6.5	189166	3312	1947	1365	20-24
25-29	3235000	1603000	7.6	1632000	7.2	220817	4289	2370	1919	25-29
30-34	3106000	1531000	7.3	1575000	6.9	140795	4832	2619	2213	30-34
35-39	3314000	1627000	7.7	1687000	7.4	77543	6812	3708	3104	35-39
40-44	3394000	1683000	8.0	1711000	7.5	23131	10264	5782	4482	40-44
45-49	3197000	1568000	7.4	1629000	7.2	1618	16347	9615	6732	45-49
50-54	2817000	1326000	6.3	1491000	6.6	22	23628	14199	9429	50-54
55-59	2435000	1095000	5.2	1340000	5.9	0	32546	19537	13009	55-59
60-64	2157000	950000	4.5	1207000	5.3	0	46277	27412	18865	60
65-69	1821000	779000	3.7	1042000	4.6	0	62552	35100	27452	65-69
70-74	1429000	587000	2.8	842000	3.7		78309	40674	37635	70-74
75-79	927000	373000	1.8	554000	2.4		84530	40863	43667	75-79
80-84	445000	170000	0.8	275000	1.2	351067 M.	66119	28632	37487	80-84
85+	191000	59000	0.3	132000	0.6	331721 F.	50256	17677	32579	85+
TOTAL	43800000	21049000		22751000		682788	519054	266877	252177	TOTAL

TABLE 2 — MALE LIFE TABLE

x	nq_x	l_x	nd_x	nL_x	nm_x	na_x	T_x	r_x	$\dot{e}_x$	nM_x
0	0.032408	100000	3241	97524	0.033231	0.2359	6644347	0.0000	66.443	0.033231
1	0.005446	96759	527	385504	0.001367	1.0915	6546824	0.0000	67.661	0.001367
5	0.003307	96232	318	480365	0.000663	2.5000	6161320	0.0273	64.026	0.000666
10	0.002707	95914	260	478948	0.000542	2.6038	5680954	0.0197	59.230	0.000541
15	0.004680	95654	448	477236	0.000938	2.6878	5202007	0.0022	54.383	0.000938
20	0.006965	95207	663	474427	0.001398	2.5781	4724770	0.0000	49.626	0.001398
25	0.007366	94544	696	471005	0.001478	2.5408	4250343	0.0000	44.956	0.001478
30	0.008518	93847	799	467312	0.001711	2.5934	3779338	0.0000	40.271	0.001711
35	0.011335	93048	1055	462762	0.002279	2.6518	3312026	0.0000	35.595	0.002279
40	0.017044	91993	1568	456398	0.003436	2.7247	2849264	0.0000	30.973	0.003436
45	0.030366	90425	2746	445894	0.006158	2.7305	2392867	0.0174	26.462	0.006132
50	0.052534	87679	4606	427795	0.010767	2.6985	1946973	0.0247	22.206	0.010708
55	0.085890	83073	7135	398708	0.017896	2.6654	1519177	0.0148	18.287	0.017842
60	0.135233	75938	10269	355313	0.028902	2.6263	1120470	0.0088	14.755	0.028855
65	0.203433	65669	13359	296034	0.045127	2.5815	765157	0.0088	11.652	0.045058
70	0.296262	52309	15497	223311	0.069398	2.5327	469122	0.0088	8.968	0.069291
75	0.428958	36812	15791	143917	0.109722	2.4578	245812	0.0088	6.677	0.109552
80	0.585050	21021	12298	72888	0.168732	2.3803	101895	0.0088	4.847	0.168423
85+	*1.000000	8723	8723	29007	0.300710	3.3255	29007	0.0088	3.325	0.299610

TABLE 3 — FEMALE LIFE TABLE

x	nq_x	l_x	nd_x	nL_x	nm_x	na_x	T_x	r_x	$\dot{e}_x$	nM_x
0	0.025028	100000	2503	98115	0.025509	0.2469	7149768	0.0000	71.498	0.025509
1	0.004624	97497	451	388681	0.001160	1.0997	7051653	0.0000	72.327	0.001160
5	0.002332	97046	226	484666	0.000467	2.5000	6662972	0.0261	68.658	0.000470
10	0.001870	96820	181	483665	0.000374	2.5978	6178306	0.0113	63.812	0.000374
15	0.003221	96639	311	482471	0.000645	2.6743	5694641	0.0000	58.927	0.000645
20	0.004583	96328	441	480587	0.000919	2.6184	5212169	0.0000	54.109	0.000919
25	0.005863	95886	562	478073	0.001176	2.5837	4731582	0.0000	49.346	0.001176
30	0.007002	95324	667	475016	0.001405	2.5952	4253509	0.0000	44.622	0.001405
35	0.009160	94657	867	471231	0.001840	2.6330	3778493	0.0000	39.918	0.001840
40	0.013020	93790	1221	466110	0.002620	2.6759	3307262	0.0007	35.263	0.002620
45	0.020502	92569	1898	458433	0.004140	2.6768	2841152	0.0095	30.692	0.004133
50	0.031233	90671	2832	446749	0.006339	2.6678	2382718	0.0130	26.279	0.006324
55	0.047569	87839	4178	429477	0.009729	2.6746	1935970	0.0110	22.040	0.009708
60	0.075712	83660	6334	403603	0.015694	2.6794	1506493	0.0192	18.007	0.015630
65	0.124564	77326	9632	364092	0.026455	2.6600	1102890	0.0192	14.263	0.026345
70	0.202812	67694	13729	305869	0.044886	2.6253	738798	0.0192	10.914	0.044697
75	0.331504	53965	17890	226044	0.079142	2.5527	432930	0.0192	8.022	0.078821
80	0.505951	36075	18252	133411	0.136813	2.4992	206886	0.0192	5.735	0.136316
85+	1.000000	17823	17823	73475	0.242572	4.1225	73475	0.0192	4.122	0.246810

TABLE 4 — OBSERVED AND PROJECTED VITAL RATES

	OBSERVED POPULATION BOTH SEXES	MALES	FEMALES	PROJECTED POPULATION 1956 MALES	FEMALES	1961 MALES	FEMALES	1966 MALES	FEMALES	STABLE POPULATION MALES	FEMALES
RATES PER THOUSAND											
Birth	15.59	16.68	14.58	15.53	13.62	14.81	13.04	14.96	13.24	15.17	14.1
Death	11.85	12.68	11.08	12.96	11.84	13.30	12.59	13.71	13.20	14.95	13.8
Increase	3.74	4.00	3.50	2.58	1.78	1.51	0.45	1.24	0.04		0.219
PERCENTAGE											
under 15	22.23	23.63	20.94	24.17	21.40	23.63	21.00	21.89	19.54	21.84	20.4
15-64	66.78	67.02	66.56	66.42	65.31	66.86	65.01	68.07	65.69	66.73	64.2
65 and over	10.99	9.35	12.50	9.41	13.29	9.51	13.99	10.04	14.76	11.42	15.3
DEP. RATIO X 100	49.75	49.21	50.25	50.56	53.11	49.56	53.82	46.91	52.23	49.85	55.7

TABLE 1 — A

AGE AT LAST BIRTHDAY	POPULATION BOTH SEXES	MALES Number	%	FEMALES Number	%	BIRTHS BY AGE OF MOTHER	DEATHS BOTH SEXES	MALES	FEMALES	AGE AT LAST BIRTHDAY
0	677000	348000	1.6	329000	1.4	0	16629	9624	7005	0
1-4	2614000	1339000	6.2	1275000	5.5	0	2523	1372	1151	1-4
5-9	3682000	1883000	8.8	1799000	7.8	0	1487	878	609	5-9
10-14	3192000	1633000	7.6	1559000	6.7	53	1190	718	472	10-14
15-19	2755000	1366000	6.3	1389000	6.0	37318	1747	1187	560	15-19
20-24	2755000	1366000	6.3	1389000	6.0	202701	2298	1544	754	20-24
25-29	2961000	1482000	6.9	1479000	6.4	221824	2744	1644	1100	25-29
30-34	3228000	1607000	7.5	1621000	7.0	142751	3799	2125	1674	30-34
35-39	3077000	1516000	7.0	1561000	6.7	70852	5233	2903	2330	35-39
40-44	3258000	1603000	7.4	1655000	7.1	20340	8716	4897	3819	40-44
45-49	3296000	1626000	7.6	1670000	7.2	1327	14867	8770	6097	45-49
50-54	3096000	1503000	7.0	1593000	6.9	10	23658	14792	8866	50-54
55-59	2661000	1225000	5.7	1436000	6.2	0	33723	21318	12405	55-59
60-64	2242000	975000	4.5	1267000	5.5	0	45497	27485	18012	60-64
65-69	1883000	790000	3.7	1093000	4.7	0	60786	34753	26033	65-69
70-74	1485000	596000	2.8	889000	3.8		77234	40390	36844	70-74
75-79	1017000	386000	1.8	631000	2.7		85733	41141	44592	75-79
80-84	535000	193000	0.9	342000	1.5	358618 M.	73032	31559	41473	80-84
85+	253000	80000	0.4	173000	0.7	338558 F.	57455	19994	37461	85+
TOTAL	44667000	21517000		23150000		697176	518351	267094	251257	TOTAL

TABLE 2 — MALE LIFE TABLE

x	nq_x	l_x	nd_x	nL_x	nm_x	na_x	T_x	r_x	$\dot{e}_x$	nM_x	x
0	0.027013	100000	2701	97906	0.027590	0.2249	6770642	0.0030	67.706	0.027655	0
1	0.004068	97259	396	388041	0.001020	1.0840	6672736	0.0030	68.580	0.001025	1
5	0.002327	96903	226	483951	0.000466	2.5000	6284695	0.0026	64.856	0.000466	5
10	0.002209	96677	214	482893	0.000442	2.6891	5800744	0.0316	60.001	0.000440	10
15	0.004348	96464	419	481339	0.000871	2.6628	5317851	0.0170	55.128	0.000869	15
20	0.005636	96044	541	478891	0.001130	2.5419	4836512	0.0000	50.357	0.001130	20
25	0.005531	95503	528	476212	0.001109	2.5334	4357621	0.0000	45.628	0.001109	25
30	0.006591	94975	626	473386	0.001322	2.6235	3881409	0.0000	40.868	0.001322	30
35	0.009532	94349	899	469661	0.001915	2.6834	3408023	0.0000	36.122	0.001915	35
40	0.015169	93449	1418	464027	0.003055	2.7283	2938362	0.0000	31.443	0.003055	40
45	0.026649	92032	2453	454635	0.005395	2.7474	2474336	0.0007	26.886	0.005394	45
50	0.048341	89579	4330	438053	0.009886	2.7268	2019701	0.0179	22.547	0.009842	50
55	0.084059	85249	7166	409580	0.017496	2.6745	1581648	0.0253	18.553	0.017402	55
60	0.132312	78083	10331	365904	0.028235	2.6275	1172068	0.0086	15.011	0.028190	60
65	0.199095	67752	13489	306170	0.044057	2.5841	806164	0.0086	11.899	0.043991	65
70	0.290719	54263	15775	232432	0.067870	2.5353	499994	0.0086	9.214	0.067768	70
75	0.419937	38487	16162	151414	0.106743	2.4618	267561	0.0086	6.952	0.106583	75
80	0.573824	22325	12811	78214	0.163790	2.3919	116147	0.0086	5.203	0.163518	80
85+	*1.000000	9514	9514	37933	0.250820	3.9869	37933	0.0086	3.987	0.249925	85+

TABLE 3 — FEMALE LIFE TABLE

x	nq_x	l_x	nd_x	nL_x	nm_x	na_x	T_x	r_x	$\dot{e}_x$	nM_x	x
0	0.020913	100000	2091	98409	0.021252	0.2394	7329487	0.0024	73.295	0.021292	0
1	0.003590	97909	351	390613	0.000900	1.0941	7231078	0.0024	73.855	0.000903	1
5	0.001690	97557	165	487374	0.000338	2.5000	6840465	0.0023	70.118	0.000339	5
10	0.001514	97392	147	486599	0.000303	2.5441	6353091	0.0255	65.232	0.000303	10
15	0.002017	97245	196	485758	0.000404	2.6228	5866492	0.0111	60.327	0.000403	15
20	0.002711	97049	263	484620	0.000543	2.6292	5380734	0.0000	55.444	0.000543	20
25	0.003712	96786	359	483079	0.000744	2.6355	4896114	0.0000	50.587	0.000744	25
30	0.005151	96426	497	480964	0.001033	2.6486	4413036	0.0000	45.766	0.001033	30
35	0.007437	95930	713	477989	0.001493	2.6741	3932072	0.0000	40.989	0.001493	35
40	0.011477	95216	1093	473555	0.002308	2.6888	3454083	0.0000	36.276	0.002308	40
45	0.018101	94123	1704	466660	0.003651	2.6774	2980528	0.0001	31.666	0.003651	45
50	0.027519	92420	2543	456180	0.005575	2.6731	2513868	0.0093	27.201	0.005566	50
55	0.042464	89876	3816	440549	0.008663	2.6857	2057688	0.0138	22.895	0.008639	55
60	0.069085	86060	5945	416531	0.014274	2.6843	1617139	0.0187	18.791	0.014216	60
65	0.113284	80114	9076	379447	0.023918	2.6723	1200607	0.0187	14.986	0.023818	65
70	0.189379	71039	13453	323298	0.041612	2.6292	821160	0.0187	11.559	0.041444	70
75	0.302459	57586	17417	245505	0.070945	2.5643	497862	0.0187	8.646	0.070669	75
80	0.468797	40168	18831	154581	0.121818	2.5434	252357	0.0187	6.282	0.121267	80
85+	*1.000000	21337	21337	97776	0.218229	4.5824	97776	0.0187	4.582	0.216538	85+

TABLE 4 — OBSERVED AND PROJECTED VITAL RATES

	OBSERVED POPULATION BOTH SEXES	MALES	FEMALES	PROJECTED POPULATION 1961 MALES	FEMALES	1966 MALES	FEMALES	1971 MALES	FEMALES	STABLE POPULATION MALES	FEMALES
RATES PER THOUSAND											
Birth	15.61	16.67	14.62	15.84	13.94	15.97	14.12	16.81	14.95	16.69	15.54
Death	11.60	12.41	10.85	12.77	11.73	13.11	12.38	13.49	12.84	13.24	12.10
Increase	4.00	4.25	3.77	3.07	2.21	2.86	1.74	3.33	2.11		3.4466
PERCENTAGE											
under 15	22.76	24.18	21.43	24.06	21.37	22.88	20.38	22.97	20.56	23.63	22.16
15-64	65.66	66.32	65.05	66.37	64.29	67.12	64.46	66.19	63.43	65.91	63.39
65 and over	11.58	9.50	13.51	9.57	14.35	9.99	15.17	10.84	16.00	10.46	14.44
DEP. RATIO X 100	52.30	50.80	53.72	50.67	55.56	48.98	55.14	51.08	57.65	51.72	57.74

TABLE 1 — DATA

AGE AT LAST BIRTHDAY	POPULATION BOTH SEXES	MALES Number	%	FEMALES Number	%	BIRTHS BY AGE OF MOTHER	DEATHS BOTH SEXES	MALES	FEMALES	AGE AT LAST BIRTHDAY
0	785000	403000	1.8	382000	1.6	0	17566	10157	7409	0
1-4	2880000	1479000	6.6	1401000	5.9	0	2547	1444	1103	1-4
5-9	3254000	1668000	7.5	1586000	6.7	0	1339	812	527	5-9
10-14	3667000	1876000	8.4	1791000	7.5	158	1186	742	444	10-1
15-19	3208000	1631000	7.3	1577000	6.6	59430	2114	1523	591	15-1
20-24	2879000	1441000	6.4	1438000	6.0	250280	2324	1624	700	20-2
25-29	2843000	1443000	6.5	1400000	5.9	249288	2304	1457	847	25-2
30-34	2967000	1489000	6.7	1478000	6.2	152311	3121	1821	1300	30-3
35-39	3218000	1597000	7.1	1621000	6.8	77113	5228	3013	2215	35-3
40-44	3072000	1518000	6.8	1554000	6.5	21717	7871	4510	3361	40-4
45-49	3235000	1594000	7.1	1641000	6.9	1362	13927	8277	5650	45-4
50-54	3210000	1571000	7.0	1639000	6.9	15	23275	14536	8739	50-5
55-59	2962000	1415000	6.3	1547000	6.5	0	36270	23753	12517	55-5
60-64	2465000	1101000	4.9	1364000	5.7	0	49720	31155	18565	60-6
65-69	1996000	830000	3.7	1166000	4.9	0	62535	36147	26388	65-6
70-74	1540000	601000	2.7	939000	3.9		78008	40853	37155	70-7
75-79	1087000	397000	1.8	690000	2.9		87756	40771	46985	75-7
80-84	601000	200000	0.9	401000	1.7	417850 M.	78972	32409	46563	80-8
85+	297000	92000	0.4	205000	0.9	393824 F.	69153	23364	45789	85+
TOTAL	46166000	22346000		23820000		811674	545216	278368	266848	TOTAL

TABLE 2 — MALE LIFE TABLE

x	$_nq_x$	l_x	$_nd_x$	$_nL_x$	$_nm_x$	$_na_x$	T_x	r_x	$\mathring{e}_x$	$_nM_x$
0	0.024575	100000	2457	98106	0.025049	0.2293	6809669	0.0078	68.097	0.025203
1	0.003851	97543	376	389076	0.000966	1.0870	6711563	0.0078	68.807	0.000976
5	0.002431	97167	236	485244	0.000487	2.5000	6322487	0.0000	65.068	0.000487
10	0.001977	96931	192	484219	0.000396	2.7352	5837243	0.0017	60.221	0.000396
15	0.004678	96739	453	482637	0.000938	2.6609	5353024	0.0255	55.335	0.000934
20	0.005620	96286	541	480086	0.001127	2.5114	4870388	0.0112	50.582	0.001127
25	0.005036	95745	482	477530	0.001010	2.5172	4390302	0.0000	45.854	0.001010
30	0.006097	95263	581	474949	0.001223	2.6460	3912773	0.0000	41.073	0.001223
35	0.009392	94682	889	471356	0.001887	2.6881	3437824	0.0000	36.309	0.001887
40	0.014755	93793	1384	465814	0.002971	2.7231	2966468	0.0000	31.628	0.002971
45	0.025661	92409	2371	456679	0.005193	2.7370	2500654	0.0000	27.061	0.005193
50	0.045337	90038	4082	440942	0.009257	2.7348	2043975	0.0020	22.701	0.009253
55	0.081122	85956	6973	413682	0.016856	2.6916	1603033	0.0180	18.650	0.016787
60	0.132855	78983	10493	370045	0.028357	2.6300	1189351	0.0112	15.058	0.028297
65	0.197383	68490	13519	309803	0.043636	2.5852	819306	0.0112	11.962	0.043551
70	0.291498	54971	16024	235288	0.068103	2.5308	509503	0.0112	9.269	0.067975
75	0.407925	38947	15887	154407	0.102894	2.4616	274215	0.0112	7.041	0.102698
80	0.567976	23060	13097	80666	0.162364	2.4058	119808	0.0112	5.196	0.162045
85+	1.000000	9962	9962	39142	0.254517	3.9290	39142	0.0112	3.929	0.253956

TABLE 3 — FEMALE LIFE TABLE

x	$_nq_x$	l_x	$_nd_x$	$_nL_x$	$_nm_x$	$_na_x$	T_x	r_x	$\mathring{e}_x$	$_nM_x$
0	0.018993	100000	1899	98546	0.019273	0.2345	7396680	0.0080	73.967	0.019395
1	0.003107	98101	305	391516	0.000779	1.0905	7298134	0.0080	74.394	0.000787
5	0.001660	97796	162	488574	0.000332	2.5000	6906618	0.0000	70.623	0.000332
10	0.001239	97634	121	487870	0.000248	2.5357	6418044	0.0003	65.736	0.000248
15	0.001878	97513	183	487129	0.000376	2.6319	5930174	0.0216	60.814	0.000375
20	0.002434	97330	237	486078	0.000487	2.5969	5443045	0.0114	55.924	0.000487
25	0.003021	97093	293	484769	0.000605	2.6335	4956967	0.0000	51.054	0.000605
30	0.004389	96759	425	483010	0.000880	2.6781	4472197	0.0000	46.201	0.000880
35	0.006811	96375	656	480358	0.001366	2.6921	3989187	0.0000	41.393	0.001366
40	0.010760	95718	1030	476216	0.002163	2.6943	3508829	0.0000	36.658	0.002163
45	0.017079	94688	1617	469694	0.003443	2.6831	3032614	0.0000	32.027	0.003443
50	0.026334	93071	2451	459642	0.005332	2.6691	2562920	0.0004	27.537	0.005332
55	0.039794	90620	3606	444774	0.008108	2.6912	2103278	0.0098	23.210	0.008091
60	0.066206	87014	5761	421743	0.013660	2.6866	1658503	0.0166	19.060	0.013611
65	0.107883	81253	8766	385892	0.022716	2.6758	1236761	0.0166	15.221	0.022631
70	0.181526	72487	13158	331336	0.039713	2.6364	850869	0.0166	11.738	0.039569
75	0.293008	59329	17384	254410	0.068330	2.5705	519533	0.0166	8.757	0.068094
80	0.453917	41945	19040	163277	0.116609	2.5604	265122	0.0166	6.321	0.116118
85+	*1.000000	22906	22906	101846	0.224904	4.4463	101846	0.0166	4.446	0.223361

TABLE 4 — OBSERVED AND PROJECTED VITAL RATES

	OBSERVED POPULATION BOTH SEXES	MALES	FEMALES	PROJECTED 1966 MALES	FEMALES	1971 MALES	FEMALES	1976 MALES	FEMALES	STABLE POPULATION MALES	FEMALES
RATES PER THOUSAND											
Birth	17.58	18.70	16.53	18.64	16.56	19.18	17.14	19.08	17.17	20.49	19.2
Death	11.81	12.46	11.20	12.71	11.87	12.93	12.24	13.10	12.46	10.72	9.5
Increase	5.77	6.24	5.33	5.93	4.69	6.25	4.90	5.98	4.71		9.772
PERCENTAGE											
under 15	22.93	24.28	21.66	24.32	21.76	25.61	23.04	26.32	23.84	27.76	26.3
15-64	65.11	66.23	64.06	65.91	63.25	63.95	61.30	62.72	60.04	64.02	62.1
65 and over	11.96	9.49	14.28	9.77	14.99	10.44	15.66	10.96	16.11	8.22	11.5
DEP. RATIO X 100	53.58	50.99	56.10	51.73	58.10	56.37	63.13	59.45	66.54	56.20	60.8

AGE LAST BIRTHDAY	BOTH SEXES	1966 MALES	FEMALES	BOTH SEXES	1971 MALES	FEMALES	BOTH SEXES	1976 MALES	FEMALES	AGE AT LAST BIRTHDAY	
0-4	4021	2064	1957	4200	2156	2044	4379	2248	2131	0-4	
5-9	3653	1875	1778	4007	2056	1951	4184	2147	2037	5-9	
10-14	3248	1664	1584	3646	1871	1775	3999	2051	1948	10-14	
15-19	3658	1870	1788	3240	1659	1581	3636	1864	1772	15-19	TABLE 5
20-24	3196	1622	1574	3644	1860	1784	3228	1650	1578	20-24	POPULATION
25-29	2867	1433	1434	3183	1614	1569	3630	1850	1780	25-29	PROJECTED
30-34	2830	1435	1395	2855	1426	1429	3169	1605	1564	30-34	WITH
35-39	2948	1478	1470	2811	1424	1387	2836	1415	1421	35-39	FIXED
40-44	3185	1578	1607	2917	1460	1457	2783	1408	1375	40-44	AGE—
45-49	3021	1488	1533	3132	1547	1585	2869	1432	1437	45-49	SPECIFIC
50-54	3145	1539	1606	2937	1437	1500	3045	1494	1551	50-54	BIRTH
55-59	3060	1474	1586	2998	1444	1554	2799	1348	1451	55-59	AND
60-64	2733	1266	1467	2822	1318	1504	2765	1292	1473	60-64	DEATH
65-69	2170	922	1248	2402	1060	1342	2480	1104	1376	65-69	RATES
70-74	1631	630	1001	1772	700	1072	1957	805	1152	70-74	(IN 1000's)
75-79	1115	394	721	1183	414	769	1282	459	823	75-79	
80-84	650	207	443	669	206	463	709	216	493	80-84	
85+	347	97	250	377	101	276	389	100	289	85+	
TOTAL	47478	23036	24442	48795	23753	25042	50139	24488	25651	TOTAL	

STANDARD COUNTRIES:	ENGLAND AND WALES 1961			UNITED STATES 1960			MEXICO 1960			
STANDARDIZED RATES PER THOUSAND	BOTH SEXES	MALES	FEMALES	BOTH SEXES	MALES	FEMALES	BOTH SEXES	MALES	FEMALES	TABLE 6
Birth	17.58	18.70*	16.53	17.88	17.65*	17.09	21.02	16.16*	20.35	STANDAR-
Death	11.81	12.46*	11.20	9.59	11.07*	8.17	4.85	9.53*	3.86	DIZED
Increase	5.77	6.24*	5.33	8.28	6.57*	8.92	16.17	6.64*	16.49	RATES

	OBSERVED POP. MALES	FEMALES	STATIONARY POP. MALES	FEMALES	STABLE POP. MALES	FEMALES	OBSERVED BIRTHS	NET MATERNITY FUNCTION	BIRTHS IN STABLE POP.	
μ	34.78580	37.84515	36.41439	38.97328	31.79076	33.77304	27.54680	27.41781	27.09057	TABLE 7
σ^2	471.5694	526.3207	487.2509	546.6711	455.7950	513.2018	33.88350	31.91011	30.89372	MOMENTS
κ_3	2243.607	1654.105	2181.529	2012.214	4148.499	4698.782	105.0055	103.7013	104.1711	AND
κ_4	-215169.	-289986.	-230934.	-311924.	-165374.	-227539.	-263.452	-86.004	-1.323	CUMULANTS
β_1	0.048002	0.018766	0.041140	0.024784	0.181750	0.163345	0.283438	0.330966	0.368030	
β_2	2.032414	1.953169	2.027292	1.956250	2.203971	2.136070	2.770531	2.915538	2.998614	
κ	-0.018304	-0.006902	-0.015734	-0.009083	-0.069611	-0.060303	-0.176138	-0.233581	-0.274656	

VITAL STATISTICS		THOMPSON AGE RANGE	NRR	1000r	INTERVAL	BOURGEOIS-PICHAT AGE RANGE	NRR	1000b	1000d	1000r	COALE	TABLE 8
RR	1.347										IBR	RATES
IRR	1.305	0-4	1.16	5.53	27.44	5-29	1.27	15.67	6.67	8.99	IDR	FROM AGE DISTRI-
FR	2.777	5-9	1.02	0.86	27.40	30-54	0.83	10.52	17.33	-6.81	IRI	BUTIONS
GENERATION	27.253	10-14	1.12	4.21	27.35	55-79	1.45	31.94	18.29	13.65	K1	AND VITAL STATISTICS
SEX RATIO	106.101	15-19	0.96	-1.47	27.27	*50-74	1.38	28.58	16.58	12.00	K2	(Females)

Start Age Interval	ORIGINAL MATRIX SUB-DIAGONAL	ALTERNATIVE FIRST ROWS Projection	Integral	% IN STABLE POPULATION	FIRST STABLE MATRIX FISHER VALUES	REPRODUCTIVE VALUES	SECOND STABLE MATRIX Z_2 FIRST COLUMN	FIRST ROW	
0	0.99696	0.00000	0.00000	9.226	1.045	1864060	0.1738+0.0715	0.1738+0.0715	TABLE 9
5	0.99856	0.00010	0.00000	8.759	1.101	1746536	0.1611-0.1493	0.0069+0.1607	LESLIE
10	0.99848	0.04484	0.00021	8.329	1.158	2073957	-0.0794-0.2445	-0.1222+0.0630	MATRIX
15	0.99784	0.25128	0.09182	7.919	1.171	1846572	-0.2987-0.0358	-0.1005-0.0754	AND ITS
20	0.99731	0.41805	0.42408	7.525	0.969	1393465	-0.1847+0.2995	-0.0214-0.1231	SPECTRAL
25	0.99637	0.33377	0.43387	7.146	0.582	814972	0.2271+0.3428	0.0150-0.0908	COMPO-
30	0.99451	0.17876	0.25110	6.780	0.263	389184	0.4747-0.0726	0.0177-0.0449	NENTS
35	0.99138	0.07303	0.11591	6.421	0.090	146089	0.1555-0.5377	0.0101-0.0152	(Females)
40	0.98630	0.01759	0.03405	6.062	0.018	28674	-0.4912-0.4263	0.0028-0.0029	
45	0.97860	0.00100	0.00202	5.693	0.001	1646	-0.6857+0.3084	0.0002-0.0002	
50	0.96765	0.00001	0.00002	5.306	0.000	18	-0.0091+0.8623	0.0000-0.0000	
55+	0.80371			20.834					

Start Age Interval	OBSERVED POPUL. (IN 100's)	CONTRIBUTIONS OF ROOTS (IN 100's) r_1	r_2, r_3	$r_4 \cdot r_{11}$	AGE-SP. BIRTH RATES	NET MATERNITY FUNCTION	COEFF. OF MATRIX EQUATION	PARAMETERS	INTEGRAL	MATRIX	EXP. INCREASE x	$e^{(x+8\frac{1}{2})r}$	
0	17830	18234	-380	-24	0.0000	0.0000	0.0000	L(1)	1.05008	1.05013	0	1.0247	TABLE 10
5	15860	17311	-684	-767	0.0000	0.0000	0.0001	L(2)	0.35215	0.35822	50	1.6704	AGE
10	17910	16461	-153	1602	0.0000	0.0000	0.0002		0.80322	0.77437	55	1.7540	ANALYSIS
15	15770	15651	787	-668	0.0183	0.0891	0.2498	R(1)	0.00977	0.00978	60	1.8419	AND
20	14380	14872	982	-1473	0.0844	0.4105	0.1447	R(2)	-0.02624	-0.03175	65	1.9341	MISCEL-
25	14000	14124	-112	-12	0.0864	0.4188	0.3302			0.22750	70	2.0309	LANEOUS
30	14780	13401	-1450	2829	0.0500	0.2415	0.1762	C(1)		197639	75	2.1326	RESULTS
35	16210	12691	-1267	4786	0.0231	0.1109	0.0716	C(2)		-140948	80	2.2394	(Females)
40	15540	11981	728	2831	0.0068	0.0323	0.0171			-77009	85	2.3516	
45	16410	11252	2408	2750	0.0004	0.0019	0.0010	2P/Y	27.1386	27.6178	90	2.4693	
50	16390	10486	1354	4550	0.0000	0.0000	0.0000	DELTA	9.2713		95	2.5930	
55+	63120	41176									100	2.7228	

TABLE 1 — DATA

AGE AT LAST BIRTHDAY	POPULATION BOTH SEXES	MALES Number	%	FEMALES Number	%	BIRTHS BY AGE OF MOTHER	DEATHS BOTH SEXES	MALES	FEMALES	AGE AT LAST BIRTHDAY
0	832200	426900	1.9	405300	1.7	0	18046	10404	7642	0
1-4	3068100	1575000	6.9	1493100	6.2	0	2780	1547	1233	1-4
5-9	3370400	1727900	7.6	1642500	6.8	0	1365	843	522	5-9
10-14	3378700	1731700	7.6	1647000	6.8	195	1072	685	387	10-14
15-19	3653800	1861800	8.2	1792000	7.4	71445	2294	1662	632	15-19
20-24	2997400	1496800	6.6	1500600	6.2	267559	2308	1656	652	20-24
25-29	2935200	1495700	6.6	1439500	5.9	263241	2334	1477	857	25-29
30-34	2974600	1517200	6.6	1457400	6.0	153696	3115	1827	1288	30-34
35-39	3093100	1557500	6.8	1535600	6.3	74401	4945	2808	2137	35-39
40-44	3330700	1663500	7.3	1667200	6.9	22312	8702	5114	3588	40-44
45-49	2989700	1467000	6.4	1522700	6.3	1205	13453	7917	5536	45-49
50-54	3190500	1551900	6.8	1638600	6.8	1	23424	14721	8703	50-54
55-59	3007600	1443000	6.3	1564600	6.5	0	37608	24630	12978	55-59
60-64	2588100	1192400	5.2	1395700	5.8	0	53564	34375	19189	60-64
65-69	2024800	835400	3.7	1189400	4.9	0	65489	38099	27390	65-69
70-74	1569100	607400	2.7	961700	4.0		81384	42762	38622	70-74
75-79	1087300	387100	1.7	700200	2.9		91049	42238	48811	75-79
80-84	612500	201500	0.9	411000	1.7	438476 M.	83676	33927	49749	80-84
85+	323900	94300	0.4	229600	0.9	415579 F.	76274	25724	50550	85+
TOTAL	47027700	22834000		24193700		854055	572882	292416	280466	TOTAL

TABLE 2 — MALE LIFE TABLE

x	nq_x	l_x	nd_x	nL_x	nm_x	na_x	T_x	r_x	$\overset{\circ}{e}_x$	nM_x
0	0.023790	100000	2379	98177	0.024232	0.2336	6786887	0.0072	67.869	0.024371
1	0.003879	97621	379	389382	0.000972	1.0900	6688710	0.0072	68.517	0.000982
5	0.002429	97242	236	485621	0.000486	2.5000	6299328	0.0139	64.780	0.000488
10	0.001976	97006	192	484592	0.000396	2.7130	5813707	0.0000	59.931	0.000396
15	0.004464	96814	432	483062	0.000895	2.6640	5329115	0.0137	55.045	0.000893
20	0.005519	96382	532	480589	0.001107	2.5156	4846053	0.0209	50.280	0.001106
25	0.004925	95850	472	478080	0.000987	2.5180	4365464	0.0000	45.545	0.000987
30	0.006004	95378	573	475538	0.001204	2.6379	3887384	0.0000	40.758	0.001204
35	0.008977	94806	851	472080	0.001803	2.7111	3411846	0.0000	35.988	0.001803
40	0.015275	93954	1435	466521	0.003076	2.7346	2939767	0.0027	31.289	0.003074
45	0.026665	92519	2467	457001	0.005398	2.7319	2473246	0.0013	26.732	0.005397
50	0.046429	90052	4181	440766	0.009486	2.7290	2016245	0.0000	22.390	0.009486
55	0.082260	85871	7064	413045	0.017102	2.6909	1575479	0.0085	18.347	0.017069
60	0.135191	78807	10654	368851	0.028884	2.6360	1162434	0.0099	14.750	0.028828
65	0.205715	68153	14020	306883	0.045686	2.5832	793583	0.0099	11.644	0.045606
70	0.300260	54133	16254	230484	0.070521	2.5279	486700	0.0099	8.991	0.070402
75	0.427534	37879	16195	148166	0.109301	2.4541	256216	0.0099	6.764	0.109114
80	0.585095	21684	12687	75204	0.168707	2.3818	108050	0.0099	4.983	0.168372
85+	*1.000000	8997	8997	32846	0.273914	3.6508	32846	0.0099	3.651	0.272789

TABLE 3 — FEMALE LIFE TABLE

x	nq_x	l_x	nd_x	nL_x	nm_x	na_x	T_x	r_x	$\overset{\circ}{e}_x$	nM_x
0	0.018481	100000	1848	98600	0.018743	0.2427	7387420	0.0075	73.874	0.018855
1	0.003263	98152	320	391678	0.000818	1.0965	7288819	0.0075	74.261	0.000826
5	0.001581	97832	155	488771	0.000316	2.5000	6897142	0.0138	70.500	0.000318
10	0.001174	97677	115	488102	0.000235	2.5316	6408370	0.0000	65.608	0.000235
15	0.001764	97562	172	487401	0.000353	2.6177	5920269	0.0090	60.682	0.000353
20	0.002176	97390	212	486446	0.000436	2.6149	5432867	0.0215	55.785	0.000434
25	0.002974	97178	289	485214	0.000596	2.6553	4946422	0.0023	50.900	0.000595
30	0.004410	96889	427	483458	0.000884	2.6853	4461208	0.0000	46.044	0.000884
35	0.006936	96462	669	480762	0.001392	2.6864	3977751	0.0000	41.236	0.001392
40	0.010708	95793	1026	476617	0.002152	2.7111	3496988	0.0000	36.506	0.002152
45	0.018026	94767	1708	469861	0.003636	2.6726	3020371	0.0000	31.871	0.003636
50	0.026231	93059	2441	459606	0.005311	2.6694	2550510	0.0000	27.407	0.005311
55	0.040755	90618	3693	444558	0.008307	2.6899	2090904	0.0073	23.074	0.008295
60	0.066813	86925	5808	421188	0.013789	2.6865	1646346	0.0135	18.940	0.013749
65	0.109607	81117	8891	384915	0.023099	2.6751	1225158	0.0135	15.104	0.023028
70	0.183897	72226	13282	329742	0.040280	2.6368	840243	0.0135	11.634	0.040160
75	0.298823	58944	17614	251947	0.069911	2.5716	510501	0.0135	8.661	0.069710
80	0.467869	41330	19337	159220	0.121449	2.5472	258554	0.0135	6.256	0.121045
85+	*1.000000	21993	21993	99334	0.221405	4.5166	99334	0.0135	4.517	0.220165

TABLE 4 — OBSERVED AND PROJECTED VITAL RATES

	OBSERVED POPULATION BOTH SEXES	MALES	FEMALES	PROJECTED POPULATION 1968 MALES	FEMALES	1973 MALES	FEMALES	1978 MALES	FEMALES	STABLE POPULATION MALES	FEMALES
RATES PER THOUSAND											
Birth	18.16	19.20	17.18	19.61	17.62	19.59	17.70	19.26	17.50	21.23	20.0
Death	12.18	12.81	11.59	12.81	11.99	12.91	12.23	13.01	12.36	10.38	9.
Increase	5.98	6.40	5.58	6.80	5.63	6.68	5.47	6.25	5.14		10.84
PERCENTAGE											
under 15	22.64	23.92	21.44	25.07	22.61	26.52	24.08	27.05	24.74	28.57	27.0
15-64	65.41	66.77	64.12	65.21	62.42	63.22	60.43	62.42	59.48	63.79	61.
65 and over	11.95	9.31	14.43	9.72	14.98	10.26	15.49	10.54	15.78	7.64	10.9
DEP. RATIO X 100	52.88	49.76	55.95	53.35	60.21	58.18	65.49	60.21	68.12	56.76	61.3

TABLE 5 — POPULATION PROJECTED WITH FIXED AGE—SPECIFIC BIRTH AND DEATH RATES (IN 1000's)

AGE AT LAST BIRTHDAY	1968 BOTH SEXES	MALES	FEMALES	1973 BOTH SEXES	MALES	FEMALES	1978 BOTH SEXES	MALES	FEMALES	AGE AT LAST BIRTHDAY
0-4	4291	2197	2094	4480	2294	2186	4588	2349	2239	0-4
5-9	3887	1994	1893	4277	2189	2088	4464	2285	2179	5-9
10-14	3364	1724	1640	3880	1990	1890	4269	2184	2085	10-14
15-19	3371	1726	1645	3357	1719	1638	3870	1983	1887	15-19
20-24	3640	1852	1788	3358	1717	1641	3345	1710	1635	20-24
25-29	2986	1489	1497	3627	1843	1784	3345	1708	1637	25-29
30-34	2922	1488	1434	2972	1481	1491	3611	1833	1778	30-34
35-39	2955	1506	1449	2903	1477	1426	2953	1470	1483	35-39
40-44	3061	1539	1522	2925	1488	1437	2874	1460	1414	40-44
45-49	3274	1630	1644	3009	1508	1501	2874	1458	1416	45-49
50-54	2904	1415	1489	3180	1572	1608	2922	1454	1468	50-54
55-59	3039	1454	1585	2767	1326	1441	3028	1473	1555	55-59
60-64	2771	1289	1482	2801	1299	1502	2549	1184	1365	60-64
65-69	2268	992	1276	2427	1072	1355	2453	1081	1372	65-69
70-74	1646	627	1019	1838	745	1093	1966	805	1161	70-74
75-79	1125	390	735	1182	403	779	1314	479	835	75-79
80-84	638	196	442	662	198	464	697	205	492	80-84
85+	344	88	256	362	86	276	377	87	290	85+
TOTAL	48486	23596	24890	50007	24407	25600	51499	25208	26291	TOTAL

TABLE 6 — STANDARDIZED RATES

STANDARD COUNTRIES: STANDARDIZED RATES PER THOUSAND	ENGLAND AND WALES 1961 BOTH SEXES	MALES	FEMALES	UNITED STATES 1960 BOTH SEXES	MALES	FEMALES	MEXICO 1960 BOTH SEXES	MALES	FEMALES
Birth	18.02	19.12*	17.00	18.33	17.99*	17.57	21.59	16.62*	20.95
Death	12.11	12.90*	11.37	9.84	11.45*	8.28	4.93	9.79*	3.88
Increase	5.91	6.23*	5.63	8.49	6.54*	9.30	16.66	6.83*	17.07

TABLE 7 — MOMENTS AND CUMULANTS

	OBSERVED POP. MALES	FEMALES	STATIONARY POP. MALES	FEMALES	STABLE POP. MALES	FEMALES	OBSERVED BIRTHS	NET MATERNITY FUNCTION	BIRTHS IN STABLE POP.
μ	34.56710	37.69269	36.23942	38.90152	31.18231	33.17284	27.28470	27.36275	27.00282
σ^2	472.4561	533.5889	481.8639	544.7437	446.7399	506.2361	33.77277	31.64111	30.55444
κ_3	2385.258	1880.208	2120.419	2012.894	4224.054	4911.635	108.6713	99.7778	100.4186
κ_4	-215795.	-300168.	-226390.	-309190.	-154286.	-213245.	-191.867	-99.237	-10.292
β_1	0.053949	0.023270	0.040186	0.025065	0.200122	0.185949	0.306570	0.314277	0.353513
β_2	2.033239	1.945731	2.024989	1.958064	2.226934	2.167904	2.831784	2.900878	2.988976
κ	-0.020457	-0.008469	-0.015354	-0.009197	-0.076654	-0.068863	-0.199384	-0.224899	-0.268748

TABLE 8 — RATES FROM AGE DISTRIBUTIONS AND VITAL STATISTICS (Females)

VITAL STATISTICS		THOMPSON AGE RANGE	NRR	1000r	INTERVAL	BOURGEOIS-PICHAT AGE RANGE	NRR	1000b	1000d	1000r	COALE
GRR	1.385					5-29	1.20	15.28	8.50	6.78	IBR
NRR	1.343	0-4	1.20	6.56	27.44	30-54	0.83	10.12	17.12	-7.00	IDR
TFR	2.846	5-9	1.06	2.19	27.40	55-79	1.41	30.16	17.49	12.67	IRI
GENERATION	27.182	10-14	1.04	1.45	27.35	*50-74	1.33	26.29	15.65	10.64	K1
SEX RATIO	105.510	15-19	1.10	3.54	27.26						K2

TABLE 9 — LESLIE MATRIX AND ITS SPECTRAL COMPONENTS (Females)

Start Age Interval	ORIGINAL MATRIX SUB-DIAGONAL	ALTERNATIVE FIRST ROWS Projection	Integral	FIRST STABLE MATRIX % IN STABLE POPULATION	FISHER VALUES	REPRODUCTIVE VALUES	SECOND STABLE MATRIX Z2 FIRST COLUMN	FIRST ROW
0	0.99693	0.00000	0.00000	9.549	1.048	1989154	0.1737+0.0709	0.1737+0.0709
5	0.99863	0.00014	0.00000	9.017	1.110	1822665	0.1591-0.1490	0.0069+0.1614
10	0.99857	0.04763	0.00029	8.528	1.173	1932058	-0.0804-0.2406	-0.1236+0.0633
15	0.99804	0.25982	0.09773	8.066	1.190	2133094	-0.2934-0.0318	-0.1020-0.0772
20	0.99747	0.43027	0.43706	7.625	0.986	1480283	-0.1760+0.2947	-0.0215-0.1259
25	0.99638	0.34347	0.44826	7.203	0.592	852439	0.2259+0.3288	0.0158-0.0926
30	0.99442	0.18327	0.25851	6.798	0.266	388098	0.4563-0.0791	0.0183-0.0453
35	0.99138	0.07362	0.11876	6.403	0.090	137632	0.1373-0.5188	0.0101-0.0151
40	0.98582	0.01689	0.03280	6.012	0.018	29413	-0.4784-0.3941	0.0026-0.0028
45	0.97818	0.00094	0.00194	5.613	0.001	1429	-0.6407+0.3106	0.0002-0.0001
50	0.96726	0.00000	0.00000	5.201	0.000	1	0.0170+0.8114	0.0000-0.0000
55+	0.80411			19.986				

TABLE 10 — AGE ANALYSIS AND MISCELLANEOUS RESULTS (Females)

Start Age Interval	OBSERVED POPUL. (IN 100's)	CONTRIBUTIONS OF ROOTS (IN 100's) r_1	r_2, r_3	r_4-r_{11}	AGE-SP. BIRTH RATES	NET MATERNITY FUNCTION	COEFF. OF MATRIX EQUATION	PARAMETERS	INTEGRAL	MATRIX	EXP. INCREASE x	$e^{(x+2\frac{1}{2})r}$
0	18984	19074	-159	69	0.0000	0.0000	0.0000	L(1)	1.05573	1.05581	0	1.0275
5	16425	18010	-1148	-437	0.0000	0.0000	0.0001	L(2)	0.35229	0.35806	50	1.7674
10	16470	17035	-900	335	0.0001	0.0003	0.0474			0.80910	0.77996	55	1.8659
15	17920	16112	680	1128	0.0194	0.0946	0.2583	R(1)	0.01085	0.01086	60	1.9698
20	15006	15230	1878	-2102	0.0868	0.4220	0.4269	R(2)	-0.02501	-0.03058	65	2.0796
25	14395	14388	902	-896	0.0890	0.4318	0.3399				70	2.1955
30	14574	13579	-1661	2656	0.0513	0.2481	0.1807	C(1)		199749	75	2.3179
35	15356	12789	-2819	5386	0.0236	0.1133	0.0722	C(2)		-141353	80	2.4471
40	16672	12009	-494	5158	0.0065	0.0310	0.0164			-234329	85	2.5835
45	15227	11213	3267	747	0.0004	0.0018	0.0009	2P/Y	27.0792	27.5478	90	2.7275
50	16386	10388	3754	2243	0.0000	0.0000	0.0000	DELTA	9.8024		95	2.8795
55+	64522	39921									100	3.0400

TABLE 1 — DATA

AGE AT LAST BIRTHDAY	POPULATION BOTH SEXES	MALES Number	%	FEMALES Number	%	BIRTHS BY AGE OF MOTHER	DEATHS BOTH SEXES	MALES	FEMALES	AGE AT LAST BIRTHDAY
0	87254	44768	1.8	42486	1.6	0	3381	1949	1432	0
1-4	379684	194184	8.0	185500	7.0	0	633	349	284	1-4
5-9	403573	205334	8.4	198239	7.4	0	290	175	115	5-9
10-14	385992	195303	8.0	190689	7.2	5	189	105	84	10-14
15-19	362561	173927	7.1	188634	7.1	3789	385	200	185	15-19
20-24	361157	170163	7.0	190994	7.2	24806	558	265	293	20-24
25-29	379183	185405	7.6	193778	7.3	28587	693	339	354	25-29
30-34	347070	168039	6.9	179031	6.7	19199	712	353	359	30-34
35-39	364210	175905	7.2	188305	7.1	11326	969	493	476	35-39
40-44	371441	180385	7.4	191056	7.2	3280	1425	774	651	40-44
45-49	351138	169239	6.9	181899	6.8	204	2199	1283	916	45-49
50-54	310171	142983	5.9	167188	6.3	1	3141	1868	1273	50-54
55-59	261559	116040	4.8	145519	5.5	0	4176	2410	1766	55-59
60-64	225532	98522	4.0	127010	4.8	0	5602	3164	2438	60-64
65-69	193051	83352	3.4	109699	4.1	0	7399	3887	3512	65-69
70-74	151674	66071	2.7	85603	3.2		9302	4657	4645	70-74
75-79	98548	41799	1.7	56749	2.1		9901	4798	5103	75-79
80-84	46116	17973	0.7	28143	1.1	46930 M.	7503	3296	4207	80-84
85+	19869	6420	0.3	13449	0.5	44267 F.	5302	1871	3431	85+
TOTAL	5099783	2435812		2663971		91197	63760	32236	31524	TOTAL

TABLE 2 — MALE LIFE TABLE

x	$_nq_x$	l_x	$_nd_x$	$_nL_x$	$_nm_x$	$_na_x$	T_x	r_x	$\mathring{e}_x$	$_nM_x$	x
0	0.042134	100000	4213	96781	0.043536	0.2359	6439222	0.0000	64.392	0.043536	0
1	0.007152	95787	685	381154	0.001797	1.0916	6342442	0.0000	66.214	0.001797	1
5	0.004231	95102	402	474502	0.000848	2.5000	5961288	0.0191	62.683	0.000852	5
10	0.002690	94699	255	472888	0.000539	2.6149	5486786	0.0159	57.939	0.000538	10
15	0.005748	94444	543	470964	0.001153	2.6818	5013897	0.0127	53.088	0.001150	15
20	0.007757	93902	728	467751	0.001557	2.5873	4542933	0.0000	48.330	0.001557	20
25	0.009102	93173	848	463795	0.001828	2.5582	4075183	0.0000	43.738	0.001828	25
30	0.010454	92325	965	459301	0.002101	2.5915	3611387	0.0031	39.116	0.002101	30
35	0.013922	91360	1272	453818	0.002803	2.6554	3152086	0.0000	34.502	0.002803	35
40	0.021246	90088	1914	446078	0.004291	2.7204	2698268	0.0000	29.951	0.004291	40
45	0.037394	88174	3297	433355	0.007609	2.7207	2252190	0.0152	25.543	0.007581	45
50	0.063705	84877	5407	411823	0.013130	2.6769	1818835	0.0243	21.429	0.013064	50
55	0.099263	79470	7888	378727	0.020829	2.6393	1407012	0.0158	17.705	0.020769	55
60	0.149207	71581	10680	332221	0.032149	2.5951	1028285	0.0066	14.365	0.032115	60
65	0.209559	60901	12762	273388	0.046682	2.5618	696064	0.0066	11.429	0.046634	65
70	0.300498	48139	14466	204991	0.070567	2.5319	422676	0.0066	8.780	0.070485	70
75	0.444780	33673	14977	130317	0.114928	2.4596	217685	0.0066	6.465	0.114787	75
80	0.618292	18696	11560	62948	0.183638	2.3587	87368	0.0066	4.673	0.183387	80
85+	*1.000000	7136	7136	24421	0.292229	3.4220	24421	0.0066	3.422	0.291433	85

TABLE 3 — FEMALE LIFE TABLE

x	$_nq_x$	l_x	$_nd_x$	$_nL_x$	$_nm_x$	$_na_x$	T_x	r_x	$\mathring{e}_x$	$_nM_x$	x
0	0.032870	100000	3287	97523	0.033705	0.2464	6864721	0.0000	68.647	0.033705	0
1	0.006097	96713	590	385141	0.001531	1.0993	6767198	0.0000	69.972	0.001531	1
5	0.002880	96123	277	479924	0.000577	2.5000	6382057	0.0170	66.394	0.000580	5
10	0.002202	95846	211	478744	0.000441	2.6886	5902132	0.0044	61.579	0.000441	10
15	0.004893	95635	468	477115	0.000981	2.7298	5423388	0.0000	56.709	0.000981	15
20	0.007642	95167	727	474100	0.001534	2.6120	4946274	0.0000	51.974	0.001534	20
25	0.009090	94440	859	470096	0.001827	2.5501	4472173	0.0047	47.355	0.001827	25
30	0.009978	93581	934	465635	0.002005	2.5680	4002077	0.0008	42.766	0.002005	30
35	0.012563	92647	1164	460455	0.002528	2.6096	3536442	0.0000	38.171	0.002528	35
40	0.016901	91483	1546	453776	0.003407	2.6452	3075988	0.0000	33.623	0.003407	40
45	0.024921	89937	2241	444446	0.005043	2.6620	2622211	0.0082	29.156	0.005036	45
50	0.037509	87696	3289	430830	0.007635	2.6744	2177765	0.0143	24.833	0.007614	50
55	0.059176	84407	4995	410384	0.012171	2.6678	1746935	0.0149	20.697	0.012136	55
60	0.092084	79412	7313	379978	0.019245	2.6642	1336552	0.0125	16.831	0.019195	60
65	0.149213	72059	10758	335150	0.032099	2.6640	956573	0.0125	13.267	0.032015	65
70	0.240472	61341	14751	271161	0.054399	2.5903	621423	0.0125	10.131	0.054262	70
75	0.368180	46590	17154	190298	0.090141	2.5135	350262	0.0125	7.518	0.089922	75
80	0.538762	29437	15859	105849	0.149830	2.4530	159964	0.0125	5.434	0.149487	80
85+	1.000000	13577	13577	54115	0.250898	3.9857	54115	0.0125	3.986	0.255111	85

TABLE 4 — OBSERVED AND PROJECTED VITAL RATES

	OBSERVED POPULATION BOTH SEXES	MALES	FEMALES	PROJECTED POPULATION 1956 MALES	FEMALES	1961 MALES	FEMALES	1966 MALES	FEMALES	STABLE POPULATION MALES	FEMALES
RATES PER THOUSAND											
Birth	17.88	19.27	16.62	18.63	16.17	18.14	15.86	17.95	15.83	17.42	16.4
Death	12.50	13.23	11.83	13.18	12.16	13.16	12.51	13.18	12.80	14.11	13.1
Increase	5.38	6.03	4.78	5.45	4.02	4.98	3.35	4.77	3.02		3.312
PERCENTAGE											
under 15	24.64	26.26	23.16	26.56	23.41	26.50	23.45	25.33	22.58	24.23	23.1
15-64	65.38	64.89	65.82	64.95	65.32	65.24	64.97	66.19	65.30	66.25	64.5
65 and over	9.99	8.85	11.02	8.49	11.27	8.26	11.58	8.48	12.12	9.53	12.3
DEP. RATIO X 100	52.96	54.11	51.93	53.96	53.09	53.29	53.92	51.09	53.14	50.95	54.8

TABLE 5 — POPULATION PROJECTED WITH FIXED AGE—SPECIFIC BIRTH AND DEATH RATES (IN 1000's)

AGE LAST BHDAY	1956 BOTH SEXES	1956 MALES	1956 FEMALES	1961 BOTH SEXES	1961 MALES	1961 FEMALES	1966 BOTH SEXES	1966 MALES	1966 FEMALES	AGE AT LAST BIRTHDAY
0-4	437	224	213	435	223	212	438	224	214	0-4
5-9	464	237	227	434	222	212	432	221	211	5-9
10-14	403	205	198	462	236	226	432	221	211	10-14
15-19	385	195	190	401	204	197	460	235	225	15-19
20-24	360	173	187	382	193	189	398	202	196	20-24
25-29	358	169	189	357	171	186	379	192	187	25-29
30-34	376	184	192	355	167	188	354	170	184	30-34
35-39	343	166	177	371	181	190	350	165	185	35-39
40-44	359	173	186	337	163	174	365	178	187	40-44
45-49	362	175	187	350	168	182	330	159	171	45-49
50-54	337	161	176	348	167	181	336	160	176	50-54
55-59	290	131	159	316	148	168	326	153	173	55-59
60-64	237	102	135	262	115	147	286	130	156	60-64
65-69	193	81	112	203	84	119	225	95	130	65-69
70-74	151	62	89	152	61	91	159	63	96	70-74
75-79	102	42	60	102	40	62	103	39	64	75-79
80-84	52	20	32	53	20	33	54	19	35	80-84
85+	21	7	14	24	8	16	25	8	17	85+
TOTAL	5230	2507	2723	5344	2571	2773	5452	2634	2818	TOTAL

TABLE 6 — STANDARDIZED RATES

STANDARD COUNTRIES:

STANDARDIZED RATES PER THOUSAND	ENGLAND AND WALES 1961 BOTH SEXES	MALES	FEMALES	UNITED STATES 1960 BOTH SEXES	MALES	FEMALES	MEXICO 1960 BOTH SEXES	MALES	FEMALES
Birth	15.37	17.76*	14.46	15.63	16.76*	14.95	17.55	15.65*	16.99
Death	15.05	14.87*	15.27	12.30	13.13*	11.36	6.69	10.94*	5.84
Increase	0.32	2.89*	-0.81	3.33	3.64*	3.59	10.86	4.71*	11.15

TABLE 7 — MOMENTS AND CUMULANTS

	OBSERVED POP. MALES	OBSERVED POP. FEMALES	STATIONARY POP. MALES	STATIONARY POP. FEMALES	STABLE POP. MALES	STABLE POP. FEMALES	OBSERVED BIRTHS	NET MATERNITY FUNCTION	BIRTHS IN STABLE POP.
	32.98984	35.13773	35.49759	37.29081	33.95059	35.60580	28.60272	28.60230	28.48287
	458.6582	483.1663	471.3159	512.9445	462.4415	504.0425	34.34418	34.11607	33.82770
	3149.380	2670.489	2338.864	2259.468	3009.721	3104.336	92.3779	86.2201	87.8903
	-181709.	-216569.	-211213.	-264919.	-193105.	-244119.	-505.675	-516.381	-481.726
	0.102798	0.063225	0.052249	0.037827	0.091597	0.075255	0.210658	0.187215	0.199556
	2.136230	2.072312	2.049186	1.993132	2.097018	2.039125	2.571288	2.556338	2.579026
	-0.040430	-0.024551	-0.020122	-0.014103	-0.035240	-0.028050	-0.113697	-0.103194	-0.110923

TABLE 8 — RATES FROM AGE DISTRIBUTIONS AND VITAL STATISTICS (Females)

VITAL STATISTICS

		AGE RANGE	THOMPSON NRR	1000r	INTERVAL	AGE RANGE	BOURGEOIS-PICHAT NRR	1000b	1000d	1000r	COALE	
R	1.173										IBR	15.30
R	1.099	0-4	1.17	5.75	27.36	5-29	1.00	15.14	15.28	-0.14	IDR	15.13
R	2.416	5-9	1.02	0.60	27.32	30-54	0.99	14.85	15.23	-0.39	IRI	0.17
GENERATION	28.543	10-14	0.99	-0.53	27.26	55-79	1.22	20.19	12.80	7.39	K1	7.36
SEX RATIO	106.016	15-19	1.00	0.03	27.15	*40-64	1.39	26.93	14.83	12.10	K2	0.18

TABLE 9 — LESLIE MATRIX AND ITS SPECTRAL COMPONENTS (Females)

	ORIGINAL MATRIX SUB-DIAGONAL	ALTERNATIVE FIRST ROWS Projection	ALTERNATIVE FIRST ROWS Integral	FIRST STABLE MATRIX % IN STABLE POPULATION	FISHER VALUES	REPRODUCTIVE VALUES	SECOND STABLE MATRIX Z₂ FIRST COLUMN	SECOND STABLE MATRIX Z₂ FIRST ROW
	0.99432	0.00000	0.00000	7.868	1.045	238133	0.1548+0.0652	0.1548+0.0652
	0.99754	0.00003	0.00000	7.695	1.068	211723	0.1562-0.1231	0.0150+0.1410
	0.99660	0.02348	0.00006	7.550	1.089	207566	-0.0384-0.2331	-0.0978+0.0684
	0.99368	0.17471	0.04745	7.401	1.086	204830	-0.2642-0.0938	-0.0939-0.0459
	0.99155	0.32350	0.30682	7.233	0.927	177122	-0.2484+0.2201	-0.0317-0.0997
	0.99051	0.29724	0.34850	7.054	0.610	118228	0.0857+0.3823	0.0105-0.0855
	0.98887	0.19530	0.25333	6.872	0.313	56002	0.4437+0.1294	0.0213-0.0469
	0.98550	0.09028	0.14209	6.684	0.115	21717	0.3860-0.3838	0.0130-0.0163
	0.97944	0.02140	0.04056	6.479	0.023	4451	-0.1754-0.6143	0.0033-0.0030
	0.96936	0.00132	0.00265	6.242	0.001	248	-0.7262-0.1672	0.0002-0.0002
	0.95254	0.00001	0.00001	5.951	0.000	1	-0.5742+0.6406	0.0000-0.0000
+	0.76995			22.972				

TABLE 10 — AGE ANALYSIS AND MISCELLANEOUS RESULTS (Females)

OBSERVED POPUL. (IN 100's)	CONTRIBUTIONS OF ROOTS (IN 100's) r₁	r₂, r₃	r₄-r₁₁	AGE-SP. BIRTH RATES	NET MATERNITY FUNCTION	COEFF. OF MATRIX EQUATION	PARAMETERS	INTEGRAL	MATRIX	EXP. INCREASE x	$e^{(x+2\frac{1}{2})r}$
2280	2086	96	98	0.0000	0.0000	0.0000	L(1)	1.01670	1.01670	0	1.0083
1982	2040	46	-103	0.0000	0.0000	0.0000	L(2)	0.40123	0.40584	50	1.1899
1907	2001	-82	-12	0.0000	0.0001	0.0233		0.75721	0.73510	55	1.2098
1886	1962	-159	84	0.0097	0.0465	0.1727	R(1)	0.00331	0.00331	60	1.2300
1910	1917	-66	59	0.0630	0.2989	0.3178	R(2)	-0.03088	-0.03494	65	1.2505
1938	1870	147	-79	0.0716	0.3366	0.2895		0.21671	0.21327	70	1.2714
1790	1822	259	-290	0.0521	0.2424	0.1884	C(1)		26506	75	1.2927
1883	1772	91	20	0.0292	0.1344	0.0861	C(2)		25264	80	1.3142
1911	1717	-255	448	0.0083	0.0378	0.0201			-13513	85	1.3362
1819	1654	-412	577	0.0005	0.0024	0.0012	2P/Y	28.9938	29.4611	90	1.3585
1672	1577	-117	212	0.0000	0.0000	0.0000	DELTA	2.9043		95	1.3812
+ 5662	6089									100	1.4042

TABLE 1 — DATA

AGE AT LAST BIRTHDAY	POPULATION BOTH SEXES	MALES Number	MALES %	FEMALES Number	FEMALES %	BIRTHS BY AGE OF MOTHER	DEATHS BOTH SEXES	DEATHS MALES	FEMALES	AGE AT LAST BIRTH
0	91700	46900	1.9	44800	1.7	0	2780	1604	1176	0
1-4	343300	175500	7.1	167800	6.3	0	382	225	157	1-4
5-9	461100	236200	9.6	224900	8.4	0	225	134	91	5-9
10-14	392700	199800	8.1	192900	7.2	7	174	104	70	10-14
15-19	360700	174200	7.1	186500	7.0	4715	231	150	81	15-1
20-24	342500	161800	6.6	180700	6.7	28016	297	179	118	20-2
25-29	358800	176800	7.2	182000	6.8	30106	425	245	180	25-2
30-34	360600	177500	7.2	183100	6.8	19507	544	310	234	30-3
35-39	335300	161900	6.6	173400	6.5	9963	727	395	332	35-3
40-44	355000	171200	7.0	183800	6.9	2797	1172	663	509	40-4
45-49	357400	173800	7.1	183600	6.8	164	2000	1188	812	45-4
50-54	332700	159400	6.5	173300	6.5	0	3105	1938	1167	50-5
55-59	289800	131400	5.3	158400	5.9	0	4335	2657	1678	55-5
60-64	236600	101900	4.1	134700	5.0	0	5622	3236	2386	60-6
65-69	193200	80600	3.3	112600	4.2	0	7205	3886	3319	65-6
70-74	152400	62500	2.5	89900	3.4		8811	4439	4372	70-7
75-79	103400	42100	1.7	61300	2.3		9674	4572	5102	75-7
80-84	54700	21600	0.9	33100	1.2	48941 M.	7998	3533	4465	80-8
85+	22900	7800	0.3	15100	0.6	46334 F.	5818	2076	3742	85-+
TOTAL	5144800	2462900		2681900		95275	61525	31534	29991	TOT.

TABLE 2 — MALE LIFE TABLE

x	$_nq_x$	l_x	$_nd_x$	$_nL_x$	$_nm_x$	$_na_x$	T_x	r_x	$\mathring{e}_x$	$_nM_x$
0	0.033176	100000	3318	97431	0.034051	0.2257	6591484	0.0055	65.915	0.034200
1	0.005067	96682	490	385301	0.001271	1.0846	6494053	0.0055	67.169	0.001282
5	0.002826	96192	272	480283	0.000566	2.5000	6108752	0.0099	63.506	0.000567
10	0.002609	95921	250	479007	0.000522	2.6169	5628469	0.0298	58.678	0.000521
15	0.004309	95670	412	477379	0.000864	2.6391	5149463	0.0203	53.825	0.000861
20	0.005517	95258	526	475027	0.001106	2.5959	4672084	0.0000	49.047	0.001106
25	0.006906	94733	654	472089	0.001386	2.5934	4197057	0.0000	44.304	0.001386
30	0.008704	94078	819	468444	0.001748	2.6214	3724968	0.0070	39.594	0.001746
35	0.012132	93260	1131	463667	0.002440	2.6748	3256524	0.0011	34.919	0.002440
40	0.019194	92128	1768	456618	0.003873	2.7250	2792857	0.0000	30.315	0.003873
45	0.033656	90360	3041	444907	0.006835	2.7338	2336240	0.0000	25.855	0.006835
50	0.059333	87319	5181	424666	0.012200	2.6979	1891333	0.0153	21.660	0.012158
55	0.096947	82138	7963	391985	0.020315	2.6512	1466666	0.0239	17.856	0.020221
60	0.147765	74175	10960	344658	0.031801	2.6081	1074681	0.0080	14.489	0.031757
65	0.215953	63214	13651	282780	0.048275	2.5613	730024	0.0080	11.548	0.048213
70	0.302174	49563	14977	210596	0.071116	2.5149	447244	0.0080	9.024	0.071024
75	0.425652	34586	14722	135380	0.108743	2.4493	236648	0.0080	6.842	0.108599
80	0.573494	19865	11392	69540	0.163821	2.3857	101267	0.0080	5.098	0.163564
85+	*1.000000	8472	8472	31727	0.267042	3.7447	31727	0.0080	3.745	0.266154

TABLE 3 — FEMALE LIFE TABLE

x	$_nq_x$	l_x	$_nd_x$	$_nL_x$	$_nm_x$	$_na_x$	T_x	r_x	$\mathring{e}_x$	$_nM_x$
0	0.025609	100000	2561	98004	0.026131	0.2207	7109978	0.0057	71.100	0.026250
1	0.003699	97439	360	388704	0.000927	1.0813	7011974	0.0057	71.963	0.000936
5	0.002017	97079	196	484904	0.000404	2.5000	6623270	0.0092	68.226	0.000405
10	0.001813	96883	176	483978	0.000363	2.5168	6138366	0.0183	63.359	0.000363
15	0.002171	96707	210	483040	0.000435	2.6379	5654388	0.0061	58.469	0.000434
20	0.003261	96497	315	481754	0.000653	2.6751	5171348	0.0018	53.591	0.000653
25	0.004933	96183	475	479788	0.000989	2.6297	4689594	0.0000	48.757	0.000989
30	0.006374	95708	610	477105	0.001279	2.6475	4209806	0.0035	43.986	0.001278
35	0.009530	95098	906	473367	0.001915	2.6577	3732701	0.0000	39.251	0.001915
40	0.013758	94192	1296	467953	0.002769	2.6813	3259335	0.0000	34.603	0.002769
45	0.021894	92896	2034	459752	0.004424	2.6762	2791382	0.0014	30.049	0.004423
50	0.033199	90862	3016	447293	0.006744	2.6741	2331629	0.0078	25.661	0.006734
55	0.051849	87845	4555	428692	0.010625	2.6871	1884336	0.0140	21.451	0.010593
60	0.085330	83291	7107	399930	0.017771	2.6571	1455644	0.0152	17.477	0.017713
65	0.138210	76183	10529	356101	0.029568	2.6431	1055714	0.0152	13.858	0.029476
70	0.218408	65654	14339	293928	0.048785	2.6050	699613	0.0152	10.656	0.048632
75	0.346015	51315	17756	212699	0.083478	2.5289	405685	0.0152	7.906	0.083230
80	0.500780	33559	16806	124257	0.135250	2.4876	192987	0.0152	5.751	0.134894
85+	1.000000	16753	16753	68730	0.243756	4.1025	68730	0.0152	4.102	0.247815

TABLE 4 — OBSERVED AND PROJECTED VITAL RATES

	OBSERVED POPULATION BOTH SEXES	MALES	FEMALES	PROJECTED POPULATION 1961 MALES	1961 FEMALES	1966 MALES	1966 FEMALES	1971 MALES	1971 FEMALES	STABLE POPULATION MALES	FEMALES
RATES PER THOUSAND											
Birth	18.52	19.87	17.28	19.34	16.91	19.19	16.89	19.69	17.46	19.42	18.2
Death	11.96	12.80	11.18	12.85	11.68	12.78	11.97	12.80	12.21	12.17	11.0
Increase	6.56	7.07	6.09	6.49	5.23	6.41	4.92	6.89	5.24		7.253
PERCENTAGE											
under 15	25.05	26.73	23.51	27.23	24.01	26.50	23.55	26.69	23.88	26.54	25.2
15-64	64.71	64.55	64.86	64.32	63.97	64.91	63.90	64.27	63.09	65.11	63.5
65 and over	10.24	8.71	11.63	8.45	12.03	8.59	12.56	9.04	13.03	8.35	11.2
DEP. RATIO X 100	54.53	54.91	54.18	55.47	56.34	54.06	56.50	55.60	58.50	53.59	57.4

TABLE 1 / A

AGE AT LAST BIRTHDAY	POPULATION BOTH SEXES	MALES Number	%	FEMALES Number	%	BIRTHS BY AGE OF MOTHER	DEATHS BOTH SEXES	MALES	FEMALES	AGE AT LAST BIRTHDAY
0	96900	49100	2.0	47800	1.8	0	2685	1578	1107	0
1-4	372300	190500	7.7	181800	6.7	0	392	222	170	1-4
5-9	419000	213800	8.6	205200	7.6	0	201	121	80	5-9
10-14	445000	227800	9.2	217200	8.1	13	165	102	63	10-14
15-19	373800	187300	7.5	186500	6.9	6436	218	146	72	15-19
20-24	340700	163600	6.6	177100	6.6	31741	272	185	87	20-24
25-29	333400	164500	6.6	168900	6.3	31768	317	199	118	25-29
30-34	337800	165200	6.6	172600	6.4	19502	426	257	169	30-34
35-39	343300	167900	6.8	175400	6.5	9963	719	414	305	35-39
40-44	321700	154800	6.2	166900	6.2	2674	1056	599	457	40-44
45-49	341800	164100	6.6	177700	6.6	167	1797	1049	748	45-49
50-54	340300	164000	6.6	176300	6.5	0	3086	1937	1149	50-54
55-59	310400	146000	5.9	164400	6.1	0	4645	2959	1686	55-59
60-64	261800	115200	4.6	146600	5.4	0	6152	3723	2429	60-64
65-69	201900	82600	3.3	119300	4.4	0	7461	4092	3369	65-69
70-74	152600	59400	2.4	93200	3.5		8795	4412	4383	70-74
75-79	106000	40100	1.6	65900	2.4		9529	4336	5193	75-79
80-84	57300	21300	0.9	36000	1.3	52614 M.	8441	3644	4797	80-84
85+	27800	10100	0.4	17700	0.7	49650 F.	6602	2425	4177	85+
TOTAL	5183800	2487300		2696500		102264	62959	32400	30559	TOTAL

TABLE 2 / MALE

x	$_nq_x$	l_x	$_nd_x$	$_nL_x$	$_nm_x$	$_na_x$	T_x	r_x	$\mathring{e}_x$	$_nM_x$	x
0	0.031307	100000	3131	97566	0.032088	0.2226	6614360	0.0020	66.144	0.032138	0
1	0.004631	96869	449	386168	0.001162	1.0825	6516794	0.0020	67.274	0.001165	1
5	0.002823	96421	272	481423	0.000565	2.5000	6130626	0.0043	63.582	0.000566	5
10	0.002239	96148	215	480226	0.000448	2.5999	5649203	0.0127	58.755	0.000448	10
15	0.003913	95933	375	478795	0.000784	2.6798	5168977	0.0323	53.881	0.000779	15
20	0.005644	95558	539	476482	0.001132	2.5763	4690182	0.0119	49.082	0.001131	20
25	0.006031	95018	573	473700	0.001210	2.5700	4213701	0.0000	44.346	0.001210	25
30	0.007750	94445	732	470517	0.001556	2.6641	3740001	0.0000	39.600	0.001556	30
35	0.012268	93713	1150	465910	0.002468	2.6890	3269484	0.0040	34.888	0.002466	35
40	0.019177	92564	1775	458737	0.003870	2.7008	2803574	0.0000	30.288	0.003870	40
45	0.031507	90789	2860	447475	0.006392	2.7390	2344836	0.0000	25.827	0.006392	45
50	0.057502	87928	5056	428080	0.011811	2.7134	1897361	0.0000	21.579	0.011811	50
55	0.097019	82872	8040	395549	0.020327	2.6602	1469281	0.0144	17.729	0.020267	55
60	0.150206	74832	11240	347316	0.032363	2.6118	1073733	0.0078	14.349	0.032318	60
65	0.221277	63592	14071	283674	0.049604	2.5635	726417	0.0078	11.423	0.049540	65
70	0.313628	49520	15531	208845	0.074366	2.5045	442742	0.0078	8.941	0.074276	70
75	0.423967	33989	14410	133099	0.108269	2.4429	233897	0.0078	6.881	0.108130	75
80	0.591587	19579	11583	67602	0.171336	2.3846	100798	0.0078	5.148	0.171079	80
85+	*1.000000	7996	7996	33196	0.240881	4.1514	33196	0.0078	4.151	0.240099	85+

TABLE 3 / FEMALE

x	$_nq_x$	l_x	$_nd_x$	$_nL_x$	$_nm_x$	$_na_x$	T_x	r_x	$\mathring{e}_x$	$_nM_x$	x
0	0.022681	100000	2268	98263	0.023082	0.2340	7190700	0.0042	71.907	0.023159	0
1	0.003708	97732	362	389873	0.000930	1.0902	7092437	0.0042	72.570	0.000935	1
5	0.001945	97370	189	486374	0.000389	2.5000	6702564	0.0050	68.836	0.000390	5
10	0.001449	97180	141	485548	0.000290	2.4973	6216189	0.0092	63.966	0.000290	10
15	0.001933	97039	188	484748	0.000387	2.6078	5730641	0.0200	59.055	0.000386	15
20	0.002456	96852	238	483695	0.000492	2.6309	5245893	0.0094	54.164	0.000491	20
25	0.003488	96614	337	482275	0.000699	2.6436	4762198	0.0019	49.291	0.000699	25
30	0.004885	96277	470	480311	0.000979	2.7184	4279923	0.0000	44.454	0.000979	30
35	0.008663	95807	830	477129	0.001739	2.7063	3799611	0.0016	39.659	0.001739	35
40	0.013604	94977	1292	471887	0.002738	2.6810	3322482	0.0000	34.982	0.002738	40
45	0.020843	93685	1953	463885	0.004209	2.6764	2850596	0.0000	30.428	0.004209	45
50	0.032107	91732	2945	451817	0.006519	2.6769	2386710	0.0010	26.018	0.006517	50
55	0.050161	88787	4454	433592	0.010271	2.6780	1934893	0.0078	21.793	0.010255	55
60	0.080032	84333	6749	406011	0.016624	2.6806	1501301	0.0152	17.802	0.016569	60
65	0.132817	77584	10304	363722	0.028331	2.6518	1095291	0.0152	14.118	0.028240	65
70	0.211932	67279	14259	302258	0.047174	2.6058	731569	0.0152	10.874	0.047028	70
75	0.330874	53021	17543	221949	0.079041	2.5401	429311	0.0152	8.097	0.078801	75
80	0.497128	35478	17637	131990	0.133623	2.5035	207362	0.0152	5.845	0.133250	80
85+	1.000000	17841	17841	75372	0.236701	4.2247	75372	0.0152	4.225	0.235988	85+

TABLE 4 / OBSERVED AND PROJECTED TOTAL RATES

	OBSERVED POPULATION			PROJECTED POPULATION 1966		1971		1976		STABLE POPULATION	
	BOTH SEXES	MALES	FEMALES	MALES	FEMALES	MALES	FEMALES	MALES	FEMALES	MALES	FEMALES
RATES PER THOUSAND											
Birth	19.73	21.15	18.41	21.00	18.39	21.52	18.98	21.61	19.23	22.19	20.92
Death	12.15	13.03	11.33	12.88	11.71	12.73	11.90	12.60	11.98	10.58	9.31
Increase	7.58	8.13	7.08	8.12	6.68	8.78	7.08	9.01	7.25	11.6102	
PERCENTAGE											
under 15	25.72	27.39	24.18	27.43	24.36	28.41	25.37	28.90	25.97	29.44	28.03
15-64	63.76	64.03	63.50	63.94	62.79	62.63	61.38	61.93	60.57	63.64	62.26
65 and over	10.53	8.58	12.32	8.63	12.85	8.96	13.25	9.17	13.46	6.92	9.72
DEP. RATIO X 100	56.85	56.18	57.47	56.40	59.26	59.66	62.92	61.47	65.10	57.13	60.63

TABLE 1 — DATA

AGE AT LAST BIRTHDAY	POPULATION BOTH SEXES	MALES Number	%	FEMALES Number	%	BIRTHS BY AGE OF MOTHER	DEATHS BOTH SEXES	MALES	FEMALES	AGE AT LAST BIRTHDAY
0	99700	51200	2.0	48500	1.8	0	2624	1512	1112	0
1-4	382100	195600	7.8	186500	6.9	0	408	236	172	1-
5-9	435200	222500	8.9	212700	7.9	0	199	135	64	5-
10-14	414400	212200	8.5	202200	7.5	13	150	100	50	10-
15-19	414000	208700	8.3	205300	7.6	7355	235	169	66	15-
20-24	339400	165600	6.6	173800	6.4	31888	266	180	86	20-
25-29	322800	158900	6.4	163900	6.1	32051	328	197	131	25-
30-34	324800	159700	6.4	165100	6.1	19306	419	232	187	30-
35-39	330600	161800	6.5	168800	6.2	9290	722	428	294	35-
40-44	345100	167300	6.7	177800	6.6	2647	1143	641	502	40-
45-49	309700	147100	5.9	162600	6.0	141	1774	1066	708	45-
50-54	340100	163200	6.5	176900	6.5	0	3100	1934	1166	50-
55-59	315500	148900	6.0	166600	6.2	0	4832	3124	1708	55-
60-64	274200	123200	4.9	151000	5.6	0	6814	4184	2630	60-
65-69	206700	83400	3.3	123300	4.6	0	7919	4430	3489	65-
70-74	157200	60500	2.4	96700	3.6		9083	4649	4434	70-
75-79	106300	39400	1.6	66900	2.5		9752	4496	5256	75-
80-84	58100	20800	0.8	37300	1.4	52669 M.	8752	3743	5009	80-
85+	28900	9500	0.4	19400	0.7	50022 F.	7001	2637	4364	85-
TOTAL	5204800	2499500		2705300		102691	65521	34093	31428	TOT

TABLE 2 — MALE LIFE TABLE

x	nq_x	l_x	nd_x	nL_x	nm_x	na_x	T_x	r_x	$\dot{e}_x$	nM_x
0	0.028800	100000	2880	97797	0.029448	0.2351	6581550	0.0036	65.815	0.029531
1	0.004786	97120	465	387128	0.001201	1.0910	6483752	0.0036	66.760	0.001207
5	0.003020	96655	292	482546	0.000605	2.5000	6096625	0.0143	63.076	0.000607
10	0.002355	96363	227	481270	0.000472	2.5901	5614078	0.0058	58.260	0.000471
15	0.004057	96136	390	479768	0.000813	2.6566	5132809	0.0240	53.391	0.000810
20	0.005432	95746	520	477473	0.001089	2.5796	4653041	0.0262	48.598	0.001087
25	0.006181	95226	589	474694	0.001242	2.5584	4175568	0.0024	43.849	0.001240
30	0.007239	94638	685	471610	0.001453	2.6966	3700874	0.0000	39.106	0.001453
35	0.013146	93953	1235	466900	0.002645	2.6819	3229263	0.0000	34.371	0.002645
40	0.019017	92717	1763	459598	0.003836	2.7371	2762364	0.0052	29.793	0.003831
45	0.035643	90954	3242	447354	0.007247	2.7118	2302766	0.0000	25.318	0.007247
50	0.057685	87712	5060	426962	0.011850	2.7073	1855413	0.0000	21.153	0.011850
55	0.100139	82653	8277	393955	0.021009	2.6671	1428451	0.0065	17.283	0.020981
60	0.157301	74376	11699	343980	0.034012	2.6152	1034496	0.0080	13.909	0.033961
65	0.235307	62677	14748	277295	0.053186	2.5531	690516	0.0080	11.017	0.053117
70	0.322517	47928	15458	200914	0.076937	2.4946	413221	0.0080	8.622	0.076843
75	0.441882	32471	14348	125569	0.114266	2.4363	212307	0.0080	6.538	0.114112
80	0.610853	18122	11070	61417	0.180246	2.3627	86738	0.0080	4.786	0.179953
85+	*1.000000	7052	7052	25322	0.278509	3.5906	25322	0.0080	3.591	0.277579

TABLE 3 — FEMALE LIFE TABLE

x	nq_x	l_x	nd_x	nL_x	nm_x	na_x	T_x	r_x	$\dot{e}_x$	nM_x
0	0.022477	100000	2248	98278	0.022871	0.2337	7189271	0.0031	71.893	0.022928
1	0.003663	97752	358	389967	0.000918	1.0900	7090994	0.0031	72.540	0.000922
5	0.001495	97394	146	486607	0.000299	2.5000	6701027	0.0146	68.803	0.000301
10	0.001236	97249	120	485945	0.000247	2.5187	6214419	0.0033	63.902	0.000247
15	0.001610	97128	156	485277	0.000322	2.6606	5728474	0.0148	58.978	0.000321
20	0.002482	96972	241	484307	0.000497	2.6988	5243198	0.0220	54.069	0.000495
25	0.003992	96731	386	482755	0.000800	2.6637	4758891	0.0043	49.197	0.000799
30	0.005648	96345	544	480459	0.001133	2.6703	4276136	0.0000	44.383	0.001133
35	0.008674	95801	831	477092	0.001742	2.6976	3795678	0.0000	39.620	0.001742
40	0.014028	94970	1332	471767	0.002824	2.6857	3318586	0.0008	34.943	0.002823
45	0.021553	93638	2018	463486	0.004354	2.6695	2846818	0.0000	30.402	0.004354
50	0.032458	91620	2974	451170	0.006591	2.6699	2383332	0.0000	26.013	0.006591
55	0.050127	88646	4444	432974	0.010263	2.6919	1932162	0.0049	21.796	0.010252
60	0.083922	84202	7066	404557	0.017467	2.6714	1499188	0.0137	17.805	0.017417
65	0.132957	77136	10256	361454	0.028374	2.6379	1094632	0.0137	14.191	0.028297
70	0.207140	66880	13854	301277	0.045983	2.6090	733177	0.0137	10.963	0.045853
75	0.330120	53027	17505	222184	0.078787	2.5465	431900	0.0137	8.145	0.078565
80	0.499939	35521	17759	131904	0.134632	2.5030	209716	0.0137	5.904	0.134290
85+	1.000000	17763	17763	77811	0.228281	4.3806	77811	0.0137	4.381	0.224947

TABLE 4 — OBSERVED AND PROJECTED VITAL RATES

	OBSERVED POPULATION BOTH SEXES	MALES	FEMALES	PROJECTED POPULATION 1968 MALES	FEMALES	1973 MALES	FEMALES	1978 MALES	FEMALES	STABLE POPULATION MALES	FEMA
RATES PER THOUSAND											
Birth	19.73	21.07	18.49	21.59	19.03	21.95	19.47	22.06	19.73	22.96	21.
Death	12.59	13.64	11.62	13.26	11.93	12.99	12.05	12.72	12.07	10.30	8.
Increase	7.14	7.43	6.87	8.33	7.10	8.96	7.42	9.34	7.67	12.66	
PERCENTAGE											
under 15	25.58	27.27	24.02	28.13	24.94	29.03	25.94	29.48	26.58	30.30	28.
15-64	63.71	64.19	63.28	63.20	61.83	62.09	60.54	61.62	59.82	63.38	61.
65 and over	10.71	8.55	12.70	8.67	13.23	8.88	13.53	8.91	13.61	6.32	9.
DEP. RATIO X 100	56.95	55.79	58.04	58.23	61.74	61.06	65.19	62.29	67.18	57.77	61.

TABLE 5 — POPULATION PROJECTED WITH FIXED AGE—SPECIFIC BIRTH AND DEATH RATES (IN 1000's)

AGE LAST BIRTHDAY	1968 BOTH SEXES	1968 MALES	1968 FEMALES	1973 BOTH SEXES	1973 MALES	1973 FEMALES	1978 BOTH SEXES	1978 MALES	1978 FEMALES	AGE AT LAST BIRTHDAY
0-4	516	264	252	549	281	268	579	296	283	0-4
5-9	480	246	234	514	263	251	546	279	267	5-9
10-14	434	222	212	479	245	234	513	262	251	10-14
15-19	414	212	202	433	221	212	478	244	234	15-19
20-24	413	208	205	413	211	202	432	220	212	20-24
25-29	338	165	173	410	206	204	410	209	201	25-29
30-34	321	158	163	336	164	172	408	205	203	30-34
35-39	322	158	164	318	156	162	333	162	171	35-39
40-44	326	159	167	318	156	162	314	154	160	40-44
45-49	338	163	175	319	155	164	310	151	159	45-49
50-54	298	140	158	325	155	170	308	148	160	50-54
55-59	321	151	170	282	130	152	306	143	163	55-59
60-64	286	130	156	290	131	159	255	113	142	60-64
65-69	234	99	135	244	105	139	248	106	142	65-69
70-74	163	60	103	184	72	112	192	76	116	70-74
75-79	109	38	71	114	38	76	128	45	83	75-79
80-84	59	19	40	60	18	42	63	18	45	80-84
85+	31	9	22	31	8	23	33	8	25	85+
TOTAL	5403	2601	2802	5619	2715	2904	5856	2839	3017	TOTAL

TABLE 6 — STANDARDIZED RATES

STANDARD COUNTRIES:

STANDARDIZED RATES PER THOUSAND

	ENGLAND AND WALES 1961 BOTH SEXES	MALES	FEMALES	UNITED STATES 1960 BOTH SEXES	MALES	FEMALES	MEXICO 1960 BOTH SEXES	MALES	FEMALES
Birth	19.08	21.66*	18.01	19.40	20.28*	18.62	22.64	19.02*	22.00
Death	13.79	14.62*	13.01	11.20	12.93*	9.51	5.71	10.72*	4.54
Increase	5.29	7.04*	5.00	8.20	7.35*	9.11	16.93	8.30*	17.46

TABLE 7 — MOMENTS AND CUMULANTS

	OBSERVED POP. MALES	OBSERVED POP. FEMALES	STATIONARY POP. MALES	STATIONARY POP. FEMALES	STABLE POP. MALES	STABLE POP. FEMALES	OBSERVED BIRTHS	NET MATERNITY FUNCTION	BIRTHS IN STABLE POP.
μ	32.99986	35.96274	35.48117	38.13979	29.81442	31.70947	27.48802	27.63168	27.21508
κ_2	478.5117	526.2096	466.5545	528.2848	423.7321	480.7820	32.96584	31.41694	30.19736
κ_3	3322.312	2661.014	2224.482	2141.894	4361.678	5121.406	102.3394	95.5295	96.8303
κ_4	-219456.	-290779.	-206158.	-284328.	-123904.	-173347.	-211.768	-150.747	-46.357
β_1	0.100740	0.048598	0.048725	0.031117	0.250054	0.236012	0.292343	0.294295	0.340499
β_2	2.041568	1.949864	2.052899	1.981214	2.309913	2.250072	2.805136	2.847271	2.949163
κ	-0.036682	-0.017316	-0.018899	-0.011566	-0.097458	-0.088829	-0.187973	-0.201485	-0.248942

TABLE 8 — RATES FROM AGE DISTRIBUTIONS AND VITAL STATISTICS (Females)

VITAL STATISTICS		THOMPSON AGE RANGE	NRR	1000r	INTERVAL	BOURGEOIS-PICHAT AGE RANGE	NRR	1000b	1000d	1000r	COALE	
GRR	1.468										IBR	
NRR	1.415	0-4	1.32	10.12	27.42	5-29	1.42	18.26	5.19	13.07	IDR	
GFR	3.013	5-9	1.24	7.76	27.38	30-54	0.87	10.80	15.91	-5.11	IRI	
GENERATION	27.422	10-14	1.16	5.37	27.31	55-79	1.41	29.85	17.17	12.68	K1	
SEX RATIO	105.292	15-19	1.15	5.18	27.21	*50-74	1.32	25.61	15.20	10.42	K2	

TABLE 9 — LESLIE MATRIX AND ITS SPECTRAL COMPONENTS (Females)

Start Age Interval	ORIGINAL MATRIX SUB-DIAGONAL	ALTERNATIVE FIRST ROWS Projection	Integral	FIRST STABLE MATRIX % IN STABLE POPULATION	FISHER VALUES	REPRODUCTIVE VALUES	SECOND STABLE MATRIX Z₂ FIRST COLUMN	FIRST ROW
	0.99665	0.00000	0.00000	10.239	1.057	248381	0.1722+0.0689	0.1722+0.0689
	0.99864	0.00008	0.00000	9.578	1.130	240337	0.1550-0.1449	0.0094+0.1619
	0.99862	0.04262	0.00016	8.977	1.205	243747	-0.0749-0.2313	-0.1245+0.0674
	0.99800	0.26035	0.08795	8.414	1.241	254791	-0.2765-0.0349	-0.1067-0.0763
	0.99680	0.44598	0.45040	7.881	1.049	182360	-0.1706+0.2697	-0.0241-0.1306
	0.99524	0.37093	0.48004	7.373	0.644	105621	0.1965+0.3077	0.0167-0.0987
	0.99299	0.20404	0.28705	6.887	0.296	48864	0.4135-0.0540	0.0203-0.0492
	0.98884	0.08295	0.13510	6.418	0.100	16946	0.1444-0.4527	0.0112-0.0164
	0.98245	0.01871	0.03655	5.957	0.020	3468	-0.3956-0.3665	0.0028-0.0030
	0.97343	0.00103	0.00211	5.493	0.001	167	-0.5635+0.2284	0.0002-0.0002
	0.95967	0.00001	0.00001	5.018	0.000	1	-0.0362+0.6782	0.0000-0.0000
85+	0.79439			17.765				

TABLE 10 — AGE ANALYSIS AND MISCELLANEOUS RESULTS (Females)

Start Age Interval	OBSERVED POPUL. (IN 100's)	CONTRIBUTIONS OF ROOTS (IN 100's) r_1	r_2, r_3	$r_4 \cdot r_{11}$	AGE-SP. BIRTH RATES	NET MATERNITY FUNCTION	COEFF. OF MATRIX EQUATION	PARAMETERS	INTEGRAL	MATRIX	EXP. INCREASE x	$e^{(x+8\frac{1}{2})r}$
	2350	2344	-6	12	0.0000	0.0000	0.0000	L(1)	1.06538	1.06548	0	1.0322
	2127	2193	-39	-27	0.0000	0.0000	0.0001	L(2)	0.36547	0.36997	50	1.9444
	2022	2055	-30	-4	0.0000	0.0002	0.0424			0.81781	0.78894	55	2.0715
	2053	1926	22	105	0.0175	0.0847	0.2588	R(1)	0.01267	0.01268	60	2.2069
	1738	1804	60	-126	0.0894	0.4328	0.4463	R(2)	-0.02202	-0.02754	65	2.3512
	1639	1688	30	-79	0.0953	0.4599	0.3668			0.23011	0.22646	70	2.5049
	1651	1577	-50	124	0.0570	0.2737	0.2008	C(1)		22895	75	2.6687
	1688	1469	-87	305	0.0268	0.1279	0.0811	C(2)		-4957	80	2.8432
	1778	1364	-19	434	0.0073	0.0342	0.0181			-7992	85	3.0291
	1626	1258	92	276	0.0004	0.0020	0.0010	2P/Y	27.3055	27.7452	90	3.2271
	1769	1149	112	508	0.0000	0.0000	0.0000	DELTA	9.3143		95	3.4381
85+	6612	4067									100	3.6628

TABLE 1 — DATA

AGE AT LAST BIRTHDAY	POPULATION BOTH SEXES	MALES Number	%	FEMALES Number	%	BIRTHS BY AGE OF MOTHER	DEATHS BOTH SEXES	MALES	FEMALES	AGE AT L. BIRTH
0	497894	255477	3.2	242417	2.8	0	58590	32006	26584	0
1-4	1409065	712060	8.9	697005	8.2	0	17393	8628	8765	1-4
5-9	1441633	735439	9.2	706194	8.3	0	3136	1657	1479	5-9
10-14	1731870	883544	11.1	848326	10.0	28	2536	1314	1222	10-1
15-19	1786214	907426	11.4	878788	10.3	33274	4548	2277	2271	15-1
20-24	1643372	816329	10.2	827043	9.7	160467	6580	3401	3179	20-2
25-29	1355745	610032	7.7	745713	8.8	144762	5434	2550	2884	25-2
30-34	827002	375594	4.7	451408	5.3	66904	3624	1677	1947	30-3
35-39	944618	436927	5.5	507691	6.0	44619	4335	2151	2184	35-3
40-44	1088430	529555	6.6	558875	6.6	23297	6115	3377	2738	40-4
45-49	949832	465577	5.8	484057	5.7	4608	7093	4128	2965	45-4
50-54	787019	369992	4.6	417027	4.9	1181	8641	4864	3777	50-5
55-59	589076	259358	3.3	329718	3.9	0	8918	4791	4127	55-5
60-64	491991	209938	2.6	282053	3.3	0	12475	6184	6291	60-6
65-69	409500	175381	2.2	234119	2.8	0	14783	7229	7554	65-6
70-74	270616	116037	1.5	154579	1.8		15975	7493	8482	70-7
75-79	149526	64140	0.8	85386	1.0		13846	6407	7439	75-7
80-84	68673	30224	0.4	38449	0.5	247876 M.	10737	4923	5814	80-8
85+	35259	14549	0.2	20710	0.2	231264 F.	9369	4073	5296	85+
TOTAL	16477335	7967777		8509558		479140	214128	109130	104998	TOT

TABLE 2 — MALE LIFE TABLE

x	nq_x	l_x	nd_x	nL_x	nm_x	na_x	T_x	r_x	$\dot{e}_x$	nM_x
0	0.113375	100000	11337	92320	0.122806	0.3226	5528217	0.0288	55.282	0.125279
1	0.045931	88663	4072	343158	0.011867	1.1779	5435896	0.0288	61.310	0.012117
5	0.011161	84590	944	420591	0.002245	2.5000	5092739	0.0047	60.205	0.002253
10	0.007409	83646	620	416700	0.001487	2.5312	4672148	0.0000	55.856	0.001487
15	0.012489	83026	1037	412764	0.002512	2.7162	4255448	0.0053	51.254	0.002509
20	0.020685	81989	1696	405837	0.004179	2.5769	3842684	0.0359	46.868	0.004166
25	0.020706	80293	1663	397320	0.004184	2.5053	3436847	0.0734	42.804	0.004180
30	0.022102	78631	1738	388853	0.004469	2.5249	3039527	0.0289	38.656	0.004465
35	0.024324	76893	1870	379918	0.004923	2.5689	2650674	0.0000	34.472	0.004923
40	0.031408	75023	2356	369493	0.006377	2.6147	2270756	0.0000	30.268	0.006377
45	0.043584	72666	3167	355852	0.008900	2.6383	1901264	0.0266	26.164	0.008863
50	0.064161	69499	4459	336895	0.013236	2.6226	1545412	0.0452	22.236	0.013146
55	0.089042	65040	5791	311496	0.018592	2.6335	1208517	0.0370	18.581	0.018473
60	0.137911	59249	8171	276609	0.029540	2.5970	897021	0.0181	15.140	0.029456
65	0.187860	51078	9595	232112	0.041340	2.5742	620412	0.0181	12.146	0.041219
70	0.279408	41482	11590	178927	0.064778	2.5424	388300	0.0181	9.361	0.064574
75	0.399976	29892	11956	119301	0.100217	2.4776	209373	0.0181	7.004	0.099891
80	0.574532	17936	10305	63016	0.163524	2.4126	90071	0.0181	5.022	0.162883
85+	*1.000000	7631	7631	27055	0.282059	3.5454	27055	0.0181	3.545	0.279951

TABLE 3 — FEMALE LIFE TABLE

x	nq_x	l_x	nd_x	nL_x	nm_x	na_x	T_x	r_x	$\dot{e}_x$	nM_x
0	0.100608	100000	10061	93373	0.107748	0.3413	5819335	0.0259	58.193	0.109662
1	0.047824	89939	4301	347738	0.012369	1.2058	5725962	0.0259	63.665	0.012575
5	0.010363	85638	887	425971	0.002083	2.5000	5378224	0.0058	62.802	0.002094
10	0.007177	84751	608	422272	0.001440	2.5662	4952253	0.0000	58.433	0.001440
15	0.012844	84142	1081	418212	0.002584	2.6879	4529981	0.0000	53.837	0.002584
20	0.019058	83061	1583	411450	0.003847	2.5634	4111768	0.0128	49.503	0.003844
25	0.019180	81478	1563	403511	0.003873	2.5165	3700318	0.0566	45.415	0.003867
30	0.021352	79916	1706	395334	0.004316	2.5124	3296807	0.0342	41.254	0.004313
35	0.021282	78209	1664	386916	0.004302	2.5183	2901473	0.0000	37.099	0.004302
40	0.024207	76545	1853	378217	0.004899	2.5672	2514557	0.0000	32.851	0.004899
45	0.030283	74692	2262	368091	0.006145	2.6263	2136340	0.0228	28.602	0.006125
50	0.044519	72430	3224	354499	0.009096	2.6272	1768249	0.0293	24.413	0.009057
55	0.061134	69206	4231	336221	0.012584	2.6820	1413749	0.0252	20.428	0.012517
60	0.106497	64975	6920	308515	0.022429	2.6359	1077529	0.0307	16.584	0.022304
65	0.150650	58055	8746	269470	0.032456	2.6212	769013	0.0307	13.246	0.032266
70	0.243481	49309	12006	217506	0.055198	2.5812	499543	0.0307	10.131	0.054872
75	0.359876	37303	13425	153167	0.087647	2.5158	282037	0.0307	7.561	0.087122
80	0.545317	23879	13021	85596	0.152126	2.4589	128871	0.0307	5.397	0.151213
85+	1.000000	10857	10857	43274	0.250894	3.9857	43274	0.0307	3.986	0.255723

TABLE 4 — OBSERVED AND PROJECTED VITAL RATES

	OBSERVED POPULATION BOTH SEXES	MALES	FEMALES	PROJECTED POPULATION 1956 MALES	FEMALES	1961 MALES	FEMALES	1966 MALES	FEMALES	STABLE POPULATION MALES	FEMAL
RATES PER THOUSAND											
Birth	29.08	31.11	27.18	31.54	27.92	30.26	27.11	27.67	25.07	26.17	25.1
Death	13.00	13.70	12.34	14.19	12.92	14.30	13.30	14.16	13.41	14.81	13.8
Increase	16.08	17.41	14.84	17.34	14.99	15.96	13.81	13.51	11.66		11.357
PERCENTAGE											
under 15	30.83	32.46	29.31	32.14	29.20	34.19	31.27	34.24	31.42	30.65	29.8
15-64	63.50	62.51	64.43	62.86	64.14	60.82	61.84	60.31	61.25	62.27	61.7
65 and over	5.67	5.02	6.27	5.00	6.65	4.99	6.88	5.45	7.33	7.08	8.4
DEP. RATIO X 100	57.48	59.97	55.22	59.08	55.90	64.42	61.70	65.81	63.28	60.59	61.9

TABLE 5 — POPULATION PROJECTED WITH FIXED AGE-SPECIFIC BIRTH AND DEATH RATES (IN 1000's)

AGE LAST BIRTHDAY	1956 BOTH SEXES	MALES	FEMALES	1961 BOTH SEXES	MALES	FEMALES	1966 BOTH SEXES	MALES	FEMALES	AGE AT LAST BIRTHDAY
0-4	2214	1138	1076	2382	1225	1157	2422	1245	1177	0-4
5-9	1841	934	907	2138	1099	1039	2301	1183	1118	5-9
10-14	1429	729	700	1825	926	899	2119	1089	1030	10-14
15-19	1715	875	840	1415	722	693	1808	917	891	15-19
20-24	1757	892	865	1688	861	827	1392	710	682	20-24
25-29	1610	799	811	1721	873	848	1653	842	811	25-29
30-34	1328	597	731	1577	782	795	1686	855	831	30-34
35-39	809	367	442	1298	583	715	1542	764	778	35-39
40-44	921	425	496	789	357	432	1266	567	699	40-44
45-49	1054	510	544	892	409	483	764	344	420	45-49
50-54	907	441	466	1007	483	524	852	387	465	50-54
55-59	738	342	396	850	408	442	943	446	497	55-59
60-64	533	230	303	667	304	363	768	362	406	60-64
65-69	422	176	246	457	193	264	572	255	317	65-69
70-74	324	135	189	335	136	199	362	149	213	70-74
75-79	186	77	109	223	90	133	231	91	140	75-79
80-84	82	34	48	102	41	61	122	48	74	80-84
85+	32	13	19	39	15	24	49	18	31	85+
TOTAL	17902	8714	9188	19405	9507	9898	20852	10272	10580	TOTAL

TABLE 6 — STANDARDIZED RATES

STANDARD COUNTRIES: STANDARDIZED RATES PER THOUSAND	ENGLAND AND WALES 1961 BOTH SEXES	MALES	FEMALES	UNITED STATES 1960 BOTH SEXES	MALES	FEMALES	MEXICO 1960 BOTH SEXES	MALES	FEMALES
Birth	22.90	29.33*	21.42	23.21	26.18*	22.07	25.72	27.57*	24.77
Death	17.72	22.69*	18.40	15.81	18.96*	15.29	11.80	12.66*	11.05
Increase	5.18	6.65*	3.02	7.40	7.23*	6.78	13.93	14.91*	13.72

TABLE 7 — MOMENTS AND CUMULANTS

	OBSERVED POP. MALES	FEMALES	STATIONARY POP. MALES	FEMALES	STABLE POP. MALES	FEMALES	OBSERVED BIRTHS	NET MATERNITY FUNCTION	BIRTHS IN STABLE POP.
μ	27.55050	29.39680	35.19195	36.43980	29.91560	30.85535	27.74284	28.91857	28.39844
κ_2	391.3114	413.9648	485.2449	512.3372	440.0396	466.4517	42.31865	44.78874	42.63552
κ_3	5010.373	4680.319	2883.600	2737.357	4898.766	5144.386	246.2612	189.4573	189.3190
κ_4	-67473.	-100647.	-221085.	-259660.	-128088.	-156099.	724.002	-86.090	116.300
β_1	0.418960	0.308788	0.072776	0.055718	0.281642	0.260764	0.800196	0.399499	0.462459
β_2	2.559359	2.412684	2.061063	2.010781	2.338506	2.282559	3.404274	2.957084	3.063979
κ	-0.168585	-0.123386	-0.027700	-0.020696	-0.108781	-0.098287	-0.459478	-0.259609	-0.310590

TABLE 8 — RATES FROM AGE DISTRIBUTIONS AND VITAL STATISTICS (Females)

VITAL STATISTICS		THOMPSON AGE RANGE	NRR	1000r	INTERVAL	BOURGEOIS-PICHAT AGE RANGE	NRR	1000b	1000d	1000r	COALE	
GRR	1.728										IBR	
NRR	1.385	0-4	1.28	9.29	27.23	5-29	0.89	20.89	25.25	-4.36	IDR	
GFR	3.581	5-9	1.09	3.07	27.18	30-54	0.97	14.26	15.50	-1.24	IRI	
GENERATION	28.656	10-14	1.45	13.58	27.13	55-79	1.73	38.02	17.68	20.34	K1	
SEX RATIO	107.183	15-19	1.70	16.32	27.05	*40-64	1.97	50.59	25.52	25.07	K2	

TABLE 9 — LESLIE MATRIX AND ITS SPECTRAL COMPONENTS (Females)

Sort age val	ORIGINAL MATRIX SUB-DIAGONAL	ALTERNATIVE FIRST ROWS Projection	Integral	FIRST STABLE MATRIX % IN STABLE POPULATION	FISHER VALUES	REPRODUCTIVE VALUES	SECOND STABLE MATRIX Z_2 FIRST COLUMN	FIRST ROW
	0.96568	0.00000	0.00000	10.797	1.166	1095105	0.1582+0.0911	0.1582+0.0911
	0.99132	0.00003	0.00000	9.850	1.278	902363	0.1811-0.1122	-0.0045+0.1563
	0.99039	0.03596	0.00007	9.225	1.364	1157414	-0.0156-0.2548	-0.1167+0.0585
	0.98383	0.24352	0.08294	8.631	1.411	1240117	-0.2774-0.1280	-0.0956-0.0664
	0.98070	0.40922	0.42499	8.022	1.230	1017051	-0.2903+0.2183	-0.0281-0.1198
	0.97973	0.36124	0.42521	7.432	0.841	627060	0.0649+0.4256	0.0118-0.1068
	0.97871	0.24934	0.32464	6.879	0.479	216082	0.4802+0.1711	0.0258-0.0676
	0.97752	0.13694	0.19251	6.361	0.221	112060	0.4474-0.4043	0.0203-0.0311
	0.97323	0.05424	0.09131	5.874	0.076	42313	-0.1702-0.6918	0.0091-0.0101
	0.96308	0.01304	0.02085	5.401	0.017	8412	-0.8114-0.2093	0.0024-0.0023
	0.94844	0.00301	0.00620	4.914	0.003	1385	-0.6620+0.7163	0.0006-0.0004
+	0.77801			16.615				

TABLE 10 — AGE ANALYSIS AND MISCELLANEOUS RESULTS (Females)

Sort age val	OBSERVED POPUL. (IN 100's)	CONTRIBUTIONS OF ROOTS (IN 100's) r_1	r_2, r_3	r_4-r_{11}	AGE-SP. BIRTH RATES	NET MATERNITY FUNCTION	COEFF. OF MATRIX EQUATION	PARAMETERS	INTEGRAL	MATRIX	EXP. INCREASE x	$e^{(x+2\frac{1}{2})r}$
	9394	9720	-472	146	0.0000	0.0000	0.0000	L(1)	1.05843	1.05851	0	1.0288
	7062	8868	-1177	-628	0.0000	0.0000	0.0000	L(2)	0.38304	0.39204	50	1.8154
	8483	8305	-676	855	0.0000	0.0001	0.0382		0.75219	0.72865	55	1.9214
	8788	7770	921	97	0.0183	0.0764	0.2309	R(1)	0.01136	0.01137	60	2.0337
	8270	7222	2000	-952	0.0936	0.3853	0.3817	R(2)	-0.03390	-0.03789	65	2.1526
	7457	6691	949	-183	0.0937	0.3781	0.3304		0.21996	0.21544	70	2.2783
	4514	6193	-1743	63	0.0715	0.2828	0.2235	C(1)		90028	75	2.4115
	5077	5726	-3282	2633	0.0424	0.1641	0.1201	C(2)		-233886	80	2.5524
	5589	5288	-1239	1540	0.0201	0.0761	0.0465			-147122	85	2.7015
	4841	4862	3180	-3201	0.0046	0.0169	0.0109	2P/Y	28.5655	29.1648	90	2.8594
	4170	4424	5204	-5458	0.0014	0.0048	0.0024	DELTA	6.9665		95	3.0264
+	11450	14958									100	3.2033

TABLE 1 — DATA

AGE AT LAST BIRTHDAY	POPULATION BOTH SEXES	MALES Number	%	FEMALES Number	%	BIRTHS BY AGE OF MOTHER	DEATHS BOTH SEXES	MALES	FEMALES	AGE AT LAST BIRTHDAY
0	482199	249081	3.0	233118	2.6	0	52858	28492	24366	0
1-4	1729540	884941	10.5	844599	9.5	0	16021	7838	8183	1-4
5-9	1680508	858547	10.2	821961	9.3	0	2678	1384	1294	5-9
10-14	1627495	830019	9.9	797476	9.0	58	1491	834	657	10-1
15-19	1757325	893019	10.6	864306	9.7	34884	2478	1264	1214	15-1
20-24	1724054	865312	10.3	858742	9.7	165112	3457	1712	1745	20-2
25-29	1471409	694246	8.3	777163	8.8	146755	3532	1697	1835	25-2
30-34	1154177	534722	6.4	619455	7.0	80829	3079	1386	1693	30-3
35-39	682105	306122	3.6	375983	4.2	31636	2347	1068	1279	35-3
40-44	1020146	482375	5.7	537771	6.1	18865	4394	2260	2134	40-4
45-49	950972	462844	5.5	488128	5.5	3836	5967	3403	2564	45-4
50-54	822338	392824	4.7	429514	4.8	696	8314	4707	3607	50-5
55-59	642801	291361	3.5	351440	4.0	0	9793	5274	4519	55-5
60-64	501764	219598	2.6	282166	3.2	0	11489	5759	5730	60-6
65-69	418907	178350	2.1	240557	2.7	0	15664	7457	8207	65-6
70-74	295660	125159	1.5	170501	1.9		17496	8115	9381	70-7
75-79	167514	69617	0.8	97897	1.1		15865	7144	8721	75-7
80-84	86405	36511	0.4	49894	0.6	249398 M.	11596	5180	6416	80-8
85+	51681	20352	0.2	31329	0.4	233273 F.	10457	4827	5630	85+
TOTAL	17267000	8395000		8872000		482671	198976	99801	99175	TOTA

TABLE 2 — MALE LIFE TABLE

x	nq_x	l_x	nd_x	nL_x	nm_x	na_x	T_x	r_x	$\dot{e}_x$	nM_x
0	0.105488	100000	10549	92613	0.113902	0.2998	5876341	0.0059	58.763	0.114388
1	0.034384	89451	3076	349037	0.008812	1.1493	5783727	0.0059	64.658	0.008857
5	0.007842	86376	677	430184	0.001575	2.5000	5434690	0.0279	62.919	0.001612
10	0.005011	85698	429	427401	0.001005	2.4632	5004506	0.0000	58.397	0.001005
15	0.007054	85269	601	424925	0.001415	2.6407	4577105	0.0000	53.679	0.001415
20	0.009870	84667	836	421334	0.001983	2.6046	4152180	0.0232	49.041	0.001978
25	0.012179	83832	1021	416655	0.002450	2.5485	3730846	0.0458	44.504	0.002444
30	0.012963	82811	1073	411451	0.002609	2.5765	3314191	0.0791	40.021	0.002592
35	0.017315	81737	1415	405312	0.003492	2.6160	2902740	0.0068	35.513	0.003489
40	0.023172	80322	1861	397254	0.004685	2.6599	2497428	0.0000	31.093	0.004685
45	0.036241	78461	2843	385731	0.007372	2.6885	2100174	0.0128	26.767	0.007352
50	0.058633	75617	4434	367704	0.012058	2.6584	1714443	0.0340	22.673	0.011982
55	0.087297	71184	6214	341134	0.018216	2.6210	1346739	0.0397	18.919	0.018101
60	0.123774	64969	8042	305708	0.026305	2.6199	1005605	0.0171	15.478	0.026225
65	0.190479	56928	10844	258547	0.041940	2.5937	699898	0.0171	12.294	0.041811
70	0.280374	46084	12921	198678	0.065034	2.5432	441351	0.0171	9.577	0.064838
75	0.407835	33163	13525	131441	0.102900	2.4584	242672	0.0171	7.317	0.102619
80	0.520287	19638	10218	71792	0.142321	2.4163	111231	0.0171	5.664	0.141876
85+	*1.000000	9421	9421	39439	0.238868	4.1864	39439	0.0171	4.186	0.237176

TABLE 3 — FEMALE LIFE TABLE

x	nq_x	l_x	nd_x	nL_x	nm_x	na_x	T_x	r_x	$\dot{e}_x$	nM_x
0	0.097334	100000	9733	93376	0.104239	0.3194	6113212	0.0038	61.132	0.104522
1	0.037616	90267	3395	351470	0.009661	1.1736	6019836	0.0038	66.690	0.009689
5	0.007638	86871	664	432697	0.001534	2.5000	5668367	0.0268	65.250	0.001574
10	0.004111	86208	354	430139	0.000824	2.4632	5235670	0.0000	60.733	0.000824
15	0.007000	85853	601	427870	0.001405	2.6762	4805531	0.0000	55.974	0.001405
20	0.010119	85252	863	424186	0.002034	2.5945	4377661	0.0087	51.350	0.002032
25	0.011760	84390	992	419524	0.002366	2.5579	3953476	0.0303	46.848	0.002361
30	0.013649	83397	1138	414222	0.002748	2.5725	3533952	0.0698	42.375	0.002733
35	0.016883	82259	1389	407916	0.003404	2.5677	3119729	0.0108	37.926	0.003402
40	0.019653	80870	1589	400517	0.003968	2.5884	2711814	0.0000	33.533	0.003968
45	0.026020	79281	2063	391580	0.005268	2.6621	2311296	0.0169	29.153	0.005253
50	0.041366	77218	3194	378641	0.008436	2.6684	1919716	0.0242	24.861	0.008398
55	0.062741	74024	4644	359249	0.012928	2.6598	1541075	0.0286	20.819	0.012859
60	0.097398	69379	6757	331103	0.020409	2.6628	1181825	0.0241	17.034	0.020307
65	0.158513	62622	9926	289561	0.034281	2.6277	850722	0.0241	13.585	0.034117
70	0.243696	52695	12842	232338	0.055272	2.5751	561161	0.0241	10.649	0.055020
75	0.365243	39854	14556	162743	0.089444	2.4907	328824	0.0241	8.251	0.089083
80	0.482004	25297	12193	94511	0.129017	2.4752	166081	0.0241	6.565	0.128593
85+	1.000000	13104	13104	71570	0.183094	5.4617	71570	0.0241	5.462	0.179705

TABLE 4 — OBSERVED AND PROJECTED VITAL RATES

RATES PER THOUSAND	OBSERVED POPULATION BOTH SEXES	MALES	FEMALES	PROJECTED POPULATION 1959 MALES	FEMALES	1964 MALES	FEMALES	1969 MALES	FEMALES	STABLE POPULATION MALES	FEMAL
Birth	27.95	29.71	26.29	29.61	26.56	27.96	25.40	26.42	24.27	24.69	24.0
Death	11.52	11.89	11.18	11.65	11.26	11.64	11.45	11.62	11.55	13.50	12.8
Increase	16.43	17.82	15.11	17.96	15.30	16.33	13.96	14.80	12.72		11.184
PERCENTAGE											
under 15	31.97	33.62	30.40	33.84	30.80	34.34	31.49	32.80	30.33	29.55	28.9
15-64	62.12	61.26	62.95	61.11	62.38	60.46	61.44	61.52	62.18	62.84	62.1
65 and over	5.91	5.12	6.65	5.05	6.83	5.20	7.07	5.68	7.49	7.61	8.9
DEP. RATIO X 100	60.97	63.25	58.86	63.64	60.32	65.40	62.76	62.55	60.82	59.14	60.9

TABLE 1 A

AGE AT LAST BIRTHDAY	POPULATION BOTH SEXES	MALES Number	%	FEMALES Number	%	BIRTHS BY AGE OF MOTHER	DEATHS BOTH SEXES	MALES	FEMALES	AGE AT LAST BIRTHDAY
0	407000	209000	2.4	198000	2.1	0	42021	22576	19445	0
1-4	1673000	860000	9.8	813000	8.8	0	12813	6202	6611	1-4
5-9	1913000	978000	11.1	935000	10.1	0	2289	1222	1067	5-9
10-14	1447000	738000	8.4	709000	7.7	61	1140	624	516	10-14
15-19	1617000	823000	9.4	794000	8.6	33665	1938	1047	891	15-19
20-24	1750000	888000	10.1	862000	9.3	151426	2867	1446	1421	20-24
25-29	1669000	841000	9.6	828000	9.0	133163	3320	1715	1605	25-29
30-34	1363000	619000	7.1	744000	8.1	74100	3068	1471	1597	30-34
35-39	948000	433000	4.9	515000	5.6	32807	2609	1223	1386	35-39
40-44	824000	374000	4.3	450000	4.9	11180	3082	1553	1529	40-44
45-49	1043000	503000	5.7	540000	5.8	2999	5584	3033	2551	45-49
50-54	924000	451000	5.1	473000	5.1	377	7926	4564	3362	50-54
55-59	773000	363000	4.1	410000	4.4	0	10733	5947	4786	55-59
60-64	551000	239000	2.7	312000	3.4	0	12135	6300	5835	60-64
65-69	425000	177000	2.0	248000	2.7	0	15505	7459	8046	65-69
70-74	329000	135000	1.5	194000	2.1		18480	8508	9972	70-74
75-79	198000	81000	0.9	117000	1.3		17142	7581	9561	75-79
80-84	97000	39000	0.4	58000	0.6	227069 M.	12379	5363	7016	80-84
85+	54000	21000	0.2	33000	0.4	212709 F.	10182	4258	5924	85+
TOTAL	18005000	8772000		9233000		439778	185213	92092	93121	TOTAL

TABLE 2 — MALE

x	$_nq_x$	l_x	$_nd_x$	$_nL_x$	$_nm_x$	$_na_x$	T_x	r_x	$\overset{\circ}{e}_x$	$_nM_x$	x
0	0.100268	100000	10027	92825	0.108019	0.2844	6053086	0.0000	60.531	0.108019	0
1	0.028262	89973	2543	352602	0.007212	1.1328	5960261	0.0000	66.245	0.007212	1
5	0.006042	87430	528	435831	0.001212	2.5000	5607660	0.0344	64.139	0.001249	5
10	0.004220	86902	367	433598	0.000846	2.5116	5171829	0.0162	59.513	0.000846	10
15	0.006342	86535	549	431374	0.001272	2.6255	4738231	0.0000	54.755	0.001272	15
20	0.008110	85987	697	428256	0.001628	2.5952	4306857	0.0000	50.088	0.001628	20
25	0.010173	85289	868	424340	0.002045	2.5731	3878601	0.0341	45.476	0.002039	25
30	0.011866	84422	1002	419668	0.002387	2.5644	3454261	0.0640	40.917	0.002376	30
35	0.014113	83420	1177	414299	0.002842	2.6220	3034593	0.0474	36.377	0.002824	35
40	0.020561	82242	1691	407239	0.004152	2.6500	2620294	0.0000	31.861	0.004152	40
45	0.029735	80551	2395	397226	0.006030	2.6906	2213055	0.0000	27.474	0.006030	45
50	0.049668	78156	3882	381809	0.010167	2.6888	1815829	0.0221	23.233	0.010120	50
55	0.079601	74274	5912	357558	0.016535	2.6636	1434020	0.0464	19.307	0.016383	55
60	0.124683	68362	8524	321664	0.026498	2.6364	1076461	0.0272	15.746	0.026360	60
65	0.192060	59839	11493	271442	0.042339	2.5853	754797	0.0272	12.614	0.042141	65
70	0.273669	48346	13231	209035	0.063295	2.5289	483355	0.0272	9.998	0.063022	70
75	0.379590	35115	13329	141815	0.093991	2.4672	274320	0.0272	7.812	0.093593	75
80	0.510919	21786	11131	80545	0.138193	2.4499	132505	0.0272	6.082	0.137513	80
85+	*1.000000	10655	10655	51960	0.205061	4.8766	51960	0.0272	4.877	0.202762	85+

TABLE 3 — FEMALE

x	$_nq_x$	l_x	$_nd_x$	$_nL_x$	$_nm_x$	$_na_x$	T_x	r_x	$\overset{\circ}{e}_x$	$_nM_x$	x
0	0.091957	100000	9196	93636	0.098207	0.3079	6313532	0.0000	63.135	0.098207	0
1	0.031792	90804	2887	355015	0.008132	1.1589	6219896	0.0000	68.498	0.008132	1
5	0.005484	87917	482	438382	0.001100	2.5000	5864880	0.0327	66.709	0.001141	5
10	0.003633	87435	318	436384	0.000728	2.5035	5426499	0.0154	62.063	0.000728	10
15	0.005596	87118	488	434452	0.001122	2.6682	4990115	0.0000	57.280	0.001122	15
20	0.008210	86630	711	431444	0.001648	2.6001	4555663	0.0000	52.587	0.001648	20
25	0.009653	85919	829	427563	0.001940	2.5503	4124220	0.0128	48.001	0.001938	25
30	0.010712	85090	912	423232	0.002154	2.5688	3696657	0.0453	43.444	0.002147	30
35	0.013430	84178	1131	418166	0.002704	2.5899	3273425	0.0476	38.887	0.002691	35
40	0.016852	83048	1400	411901	0.003398	2.6156	2855259	0.0000	34.381	0.003398	40
45	0.023361	81648	1907	403763	0.004724	2.6529	2443359	0.0000	29.926	0.004724	45
50	0.035103	79741	2799	392224	0.007137	2.6854	2039596	0.0200	25.578	0.007108	50
55	0.057157	76941	4398	374492	0.011743	2.6773	1647372	0.0295	21.411	0.011673	55
60	0.090163	72544	6541	347533	0.018820	2.6783	1272879	0.0287	17.546	0.018702	60
65	0.151447	66003	9996	306342	0.032630	2.6317	925346	0.0287	14.020	0.032444	65
70	0.229610	56007	12860	248866	0.051674	2.5762	619005	0.0287	11.052	0.051402	70
75	0.340730	43147	14702	179039	0.082114	2.5039	370139	0.0287	8.578	0.081718	75
80	0.461668	28446	13132	108114	0.121469	2.5097	191099	0.0287	6.718	0.120966	80
85+	1.000000	15313	15313	82986	0.184528	5.4192	82986	0.0287	5.419	0.179515	85+

TABLE 4 — OBSERVED, PROJECTED, STABLE

	OBSERVED POPULATION BOTH SEXES	MALES	FEMALES	PROJECTED POPULATION 1962 MALES	FEMALES	1967 MALES	FEMALES	1972 MALES	FEMALES	STABLE POPULATION MALES	FEMALES
RATES PER THOUSAND											
Birth	24.43	25.89	23.04	24.61	22.15	22.81	20.75	22.68	20.82	20.39	19.69
Death	10.29	10.50	10.09	10.48	10.31	10.67	10.62	10.94	10.96	14.36	13.66
Increase	14.14	15.39	12.95	14.13	11.84	12.14	10.13	11.74	9.86		6.0334
PERCENTAGE											
under 15	30.21	31.75	28.76	32.23	29.36	30.48	27.93	28.59	26.42	25.65	24.92
15-64	63.66	63.09	64.20	62.47	63.20	63.51	63.95	64.64	64.83	64.48	63.44
65 and over	6.13	5.16	7.04	5.30	7.44	6.01	8.12	6.78	8.76	9.87	11.64
DEP. RATIO X 100	57.08	58.51	55.75	60.08	58.23	57.46	56.37	54.71	54.26	55.08	57.64

TABLE 1 — DATA

AGE AT LAST BIRTHDAY	POPULATION BOTH SEXES	MALES Number	%	FEMALES Number	%	BIRTHS BY AGE OF MOTHER	DEATHS BOTH SEXES	MALES	FEMALES	AGE AT LAST BIRTHDAY
0	413900	210450	2.3	203450	2.1	0	34649	18558	16091	0
1-4	1517159	776009	8.6	741150	7.8	0	6714	3326	3388	1-4
5-9	2005938	1025665	11.3	980273	10.3	0	1432	794	638	5-9
10-14	1864379	951744	10.5	912635	9.6	124	981	574	407	10-14
15-19	1362178	685728	7.6	676450	7.1	35484	1336	771	565	15-19
20-24	1570876	791266	8.7	779610	8.2	140494	2086	1153	933	20-24
25-29	1644723	822394	9.1	822329	8.6	127381	2737	1464	1273	25-29
30-34	1572220	776917	8.6	795303	8.4	71967	2945	1600	1345	30-34
35-39	1262087	570512	6.3	691575	7.3	33501	2804	1413	1391	35-39
40-44	761106	344838	3.8	416268	4.4	10486	2504	1300	1204	40-44
45-49	903653	416574	4.6	487079	5.1	2079	4151	2279	1872	45-49
50-54	1004366	486010	5.4	518356	5.4	664	7429	4263	3166	50-54
55-59	856536	412418	4.6	444118	4.7	0	10143	6029	4114	55-59
60-64	694165	316657	3.5	377508	4.0	0	13501	7493	6008	60-64
65-69	431523	185109	2.0	246414	2.6	0	14457	7283	7174	65-69
70-74	338652	136329	1.5	202323	2.1		17703	8010	9693	70-74
75-79	211970	86418	1.0	125552	1.3		17554	7746	9808	75-79
80-84	108398	41848	0.5	66550	0.7	216952 M.	13618	5730	7888	80-84
85+	58218	22123	0.2	36095	0.4	205228 F.	10703	4327	6376	85+
TOTAL	18582047	9059009		9523038		422180	167447	84113	83334	TOTAL

TABLE 2 — MALE LIFE TABLE

x	nq_x	l_x	nd_x	nL_x	nm_x	na_x	T_x	r_x	$\dot{e}_x$	nM_x
0	0.082443	100000	8244	93826	0.087868	0.2512	6354858	0.0047	63.549	0.088182
1	0.016835	91756	1545	362548	0.004261	1.1030	6261032	0.0047	68.236	0.004286
5	0.003857	90211	348	450185	0.000773	2.5000	5898484	0.0019	65.385	0.000774
10	0.003026	89863	272	448668	0.000606	2.6193	5448299	0.0395	60.629	0.000603
15	0.005622	89591	504	446774	0.001127	2.6551	4999631	0.0174	55.805	0.001124
20	0.007260	89087	647	443878	0.001457	2.5902	4552857	0.0000	51.105	0.001457
25	0.008863	88441	784	440296	0.001780	2.5674	4108978	0.0001	46.460	0.001780
30	0.010271	87657	900	436095	0.002065	2.5686	3668682	0.0345	41.853	0.002059
35	0.012450	86756	1080	431229	0.002505	2.6365	3232587	0.0786	37.260	0.002477
40	0.018768	85676	1608	424610	0.003787	2.6543	2801358	0.0276	32.697	0.003770
45	0.027011	84068	2271	415063	0.005471	2.6751	2376748	0.0000	28.272	0.005471
50	0.042988	81798	3516	400884	0.008771	2.6952	1961685	0.0000	23.982	0.008771
55	0.071084	78281	5565	378473	0.014703	2.6757	1560801	0.0276	19.938	0.014619
60	0.112894	72717	8209	344331	0.023841	2.6548	1182328	0.0364	16.259	0.023663
65	0.180795	64508	11663	294512	0.039600	2.5969	837997	0.0364	12.991	0.039344
70	0.258045	52845	13636	230706	0.059107	2.5420	543485	0.0364	10.285	0.058755
75	0.367572	39209	14412	159810	0.090182	2.4859	312779	0.0364	7.977	0.089634
80	0.510632	24797	12662	91854	0.137849	2.4625	152969	0.0364	6.169	0.136925
85+	*1.000000	12135	12135	61115	0.198554	5.0364	61115	0.0364	5.036	0.195588

TABLE 3 — FEMALE LIFE TABLE

x	nq_x	l_x	nd_x	nL_x	nm_x	na_x	T_x	r_x	$\dot{e}_x$	nM_x
0	0.074459	100000	7446	94566	0.078738	0.2702	6681974	0.0059	66.820	0.079091
1	0.017932	92554	1660	365435	0.004542	1.1191	6587408	0.0059	71.174	0.004571
5	0.003243	90894	295	453735	0.000650	2.5000	6221973	0.0018	68.453	0.000651
10	0.002234	90600	202	452509	0.000447	2.5855	5768238	0.0365	63.667	0.000446
15	0.004180	90397	378	451111	0.000838	2.6845	5315729	0.0149	58.804	0.000835
20	0.005967	90019	537	448819	0.001197	2.6211	4864618	0.0000	54.040	0.001197
25	0.007711	89482	690	445730	0.001548	2.5638	4415799	0.0000	49.348	0.001548
30	0.008429	88792	748	442131	0.001693	2.5551	3970069	0.0156	44.712	0.001691
35	0.010087	88044	888	438105	0.002027	2.6193	3527938	0.0626	40.070	0.002011
40	0.014423	87156	1257	432792	0.002905	2.6240	3089833	0.0322	35.452	0.002892
45	0.019046	85899	1636	425670	0.003843	2.6632	2657041	0.0000	30.932	0.003843
50	0.030127	84263	2539	415402	0.006111	2.6713	2231371	0.0030	26.481	0.006108
55	0.045558	81724	3723	400041	0.009307	2.6956	1815969	0.0218	22.221	0.009263
60	0.077361	78001	6034	376199	0.016040	2.7122	1415928	0.0315	18.153	0.015915
65	0.137143	71967	9870	336696	0.029314	2.6557	1039729	0.0315	14.447	0.029114
70	0.215986	62097	13412	278232	0.048205	2.5953	703033	0.0315	11.322	0.047909
75	0.328712	48685	16003	203722	0.078555	2.5191	424801	0.0315	8.726	0.078119
80	0.455269	32682	14879	124937	0.119091	2.5252	221079	0.0315	6.765	0.118527
85+	1.000000	17803	17803	96142	0.185170	5.4004	96142	0.0315	5.400	0.176646

TABLE 4 — OBSERVED AND PROJECTED VITAL RATES

	OBSERVED POPULATION BOTH SEXES	MALES	FEMALES	PROJECTED POPULATION 1966 MALES	FEMALES	1971 MALES	FEMALES	1976 MALES	FEMALES	STABLE POPULATION MALES	FEMA
RATES PER THOUSAND											
Birth	22.72	23.95	21.55	22.28	20.21	22.36	20.45	22.63	20.85	20.04	19.
Death	9.01	9.29	8.75	9.61	9.22	10.01	9.65	10.42	10.14	13.16	12.
Increase	13.71	14.66	12.80	12.66	10.99	12.35	10.81	12.21	10.71		6.87
PERCENTAGE											
under 15	31.22	32.72	29.80	30.75	28.19	28.70	26.50	27.97	25.98	25.81	24.
15-64	62.60	62.07	63.10	63.19	63.72	64.33	64.59	64.30	64.31	64.08	63.
65 and over	6.18	5.21	7.11	6.06	8.09	6.98	8.91	7.73	9.71	10.11	11.
DEP. RATIO X 100	59.75	61.10	58.49	58.24	56.93	55.46	54.82	55.51	55.49	56.06	58.

TABLE 5 — POPULATION PROJECTED WITH FIXED AGE-SPECIFIC BIRTH AND DEATH RATES (IN 1000's)

AGE AT LAST BIRTHDAY	1966 BOTH SEXES	MALES	FEMALES	1971 BOTH SEXES	MALES	FEMALES	1976 BOTH SEXES	MALES	FEMALES	AGE AT LAST BIRTHDAY
0-4	1930	988	942	1993	1020	973	2138	1094	1044	0-4
5-9	1905	973	932	1904	975	929	1967	1007	960	5-9
10-14	2000	1022	978	1899	970	929	1899	972	927	10-14
15-19	1858	948	910	1993	1018	975	1892	966	926	15-19
20-24	1354	681	673	1847	942	905	1981	1011	970	20-24
25-29	1559	785	774	1344	676	668	1833	934	899	25-29
30-34	1631	815	816	1545	777	768	1332	669	663	30-34
35-39	1556	768	788	1613	805	808	1530	769	761	35-39
40-44	1245	562	683	1535	756	779	1591	793	798	40-44
45-49	746	337	409	1221	549	672	1505	739	766	45-49
50-54	877	402	475	726	326	400	1186	530	656	50-54
55-59	958	459	499	838	380	458	692	307	385	55-59
60-64	793	375	418	886	417	469	776	346	430	60-64
65-69	609	271	338	695	321	374	777	357	420	65-69
70-74	349	145	204	491	212	279	560	251	309	70-74
75-79	242	94	148	249	100	149	351	147	204	75-79
80-84	127	50	77	145	54	91	149	58	91	80-84
85+	79	28	51	92	33	59	106	36	70	85+
TOTAL	19818	9703	10115	21016	10331	10685	22265	10986	11279	TOTAL

TABLE 6 — STANDARDIZED RATES

STANDARD COUNTRIES: STANDARDIZED RATES PER THOUSAND	ENGLAND AND WALES 1961 BOTH SEXES	MALES	FEMALES	UNITED STATES 1960 BOTH SEXES	MALES	FEMALES	MEXICO 1960 BOTH SEXES	MALES	FEMALES
Birth	17.75	19.82*	16.72	18.03	18.55*	17.27	21.14	19.04*	20.50
Death	13.10	14.26*	13.55	11.29	12.15*	10.76	7.55	8.73*	6.93
Increase	4.66	5.56*	3.17	6.73	6.40*	6.50	13.58	10.30*	13.57

TABLE 7 — MOMENTS AND CUMULANTS

	OBSERVED POP. MALES	FEMALES	STATIONARY POP. MALES	FEMALES	STABLE POP. MALES	FEMALES	OBSERVED BIRTHS	NET MATERNITY FUNCTION	BIRTHS IN STABLE POP.
μ	28.59186	30.63228	36.88276	38.25142	33.46433	34.62534	27.14741	27.43340	27.13287
σ^2	408.3480	440.7317	507.9151	537.8713	485.1626	515.3086	27.14741	27.43340	27.13287
κ_3	4900.951	4705.034	2504.476	2330.783	4059.134	4172.171	35.32107	42.39237	40.90664
κ_4	-89298.	-127715.	-249579.	-293031.	-199140.	-237884.	161.4285	217.9945	214.2593
β_1	0.352752	0.258585	0.047870	0.034911	0.144280	0.127210	630.805	487.369	606.977
β_2	2.464472	2.342502	2.032554	1.987122	2.153975	2.104159	0.591370	0.623775	0.670653
κ	-0.140541	-0.102689	-0.018258	-0.012990	-0.055103	-0.047446	3.505623	3.271196	3.362731
							-0.669657	-0.411553	-0.461243

TABLE 8 — RATES FROM AGE DISTRIBUTIONS AND VITAL STATISTICS (Females)

VITAL STATISTICS		THOMPSON AGE RANGE	NRR	1000r	INTERVAL	BOURGEOIS-PICHAT AGE RANGE	NRR	1000b	1000d	1000r	COALE
GRR	1.355										
NRR	1.206	0-4	1.31	9.86	27.39	5-29	1.29	22.70	13.40	9.30	IBR
TFR	2.787	5-9	1.43	13.07	27.35	30-54	1.77	33.74	12.68	21.06	IDR
GENERATION	27.282	10-14	1.41	12.34	27.30	55-79	2.35	72.33	40.63	31.70	IRI
SEX RATIO	105.713	15-19	1.14	4.81	27.22	*50-74	2.24	64.20	34.27	29.93	K1
											K2

TABLE 9 — LESLIE MATRIX AND ITS SPECTRAL COMPONENTS (Females)

Start Age Interval	ORIGINAL MATRIX SUB-DIAGONAL	ALTERNATIVE FIRST ROWS Projection	Integral	FIRST STABLE MATRIX % IN STABLE POPULATION	FISHER VALUES	REPRODUCTIVE VALUES	SECOND STABLE MATRIX Z₂ FIRST COLUMN	FIRST ROW
0	0.98638	0.00000	0.00000	8.693	1.106	1044419	0.1956+0.1126	0.1956+0.1126
5	0.99730	0.00015	0.00000	8.285	1.160	1137272	0.2302-0.1682	-0.0187+0.1777
10	0.99691	0.05862	0.00031	7.983	1.204	1098660	-0.0773-0.3558	-0.1332+0.0430
15	0.99492	0.25911	0.11933	7.690	1.185	801456	-0.4552-0.0939	-0.0846-0.0884
20	0.99312	0.37349	0.40996	7.392	0.945	736383	-0.3444+0.6486	-0.0144-0.1181
25	0.99193	0.27355	0.35239	7.093	0.569	467542	0.3824+0.6486	0.0067-0.0904
30	0.99089	0.15484	0.20585	6.798	0.288	229304	0.9500-0.1102	0.0133-0.0550
35	0.98787	0.08198	0.11020	6.508	0.128	88781	0.3607-1.1586	0.0133-0.0256
40	0.98355	0.03286	0.05731	6.212	0.043	17790	-1.1549-1.0111	0.0066-0.0079
45	0.97588	0.00617	0.00971	5.903	0.008	3913	-1.7537+0.8135	0.0013-0.0016
50	0.96302	0.00143	0.00291	5.566	0.002	793	0.0412+2.4154	0.0003-0.0002
55+	0.78996			21.876				

TABLE 10 — AGE ANALYSIS AND MISCELLANEOUS RESULTS (Females)

Start Age Interval	OBSERVED POPUL. (IN 100's)	CONTRIBUTIONS OF ROOTS (IN 100's) r_1	r_2, r_3	r_4-r_{11}	AGE-SP. BIRTH RATES	NET MATERNITY FUNCTION	COEFF. OF MATRIX EQUATION	PARAMETERS	INTEGRAL	MATRIX	EXP. INCREASE x	$e^{(x+2\frac{1}{2})r}$
	9446	9392	105	-51	0.0000	0.0000	0.0000	L(1)	1.03496	1.03499	0	1.0173
	9803	8951	699	153	0.0000	0.0000	0.0001	L(2)	0.29980	0.31652	50	1.4345
	9126	8625	554	-53	0.0001	0.0003	0.0577		0.74492	0.71393	55	1.4846
	6765	8308	-566	-978	0.0255	0.1150	0.2541	R(1)	0.00687	0.00688	60	1.5365
	7796	7986	-1486	1296	0.0876	0.3932	0.3644	R(2)	-0.04388	-0.04945	65	1.5902
	8223	7663	-615	1175	0.0753	0.3356	0.2651		0.23763	0.23070	70	1.6458
	7953	7344	1767	-1158	0.0440	0.1945	0.1488	C(1)		108038	75	1.7033
	6916	7031	2808	-2924	0.0235	0.1032	0.0781	C(2)		81877	80	1.7629
	4163	6711	44	-2593	0.0122	0.0530	0.0309			95694	85	1.8245
	4871	6378	-4429	2922	0.0021	0.0088	0.0057	2P/Y	26.4406	27.2354	90	1.8883
	5184	6014	-4555	3725	0.0006	0.0026	0.0013	DELTA	9.4826		95	1.9543
+	14986	23635									100	2.0226

TABLE 1 — DATA

AGE AT LAST BIRTHDAY	POPULATION BOTH SEXES	MALES Number	%	FEMALES Number	%	BIRTHS BY AGE OF MOTHER	DEATHS BOTH SEXES	MALES	FEMALES	AGE AT LAST BIRTH
0	116451	59470	2.6	56981	2.6	0	8380	4754	3626	0
1-4	412658	209607	9.0	203051	9.4	0	2632	1384	1248	1-
5-9	456251	231021	10.0	225230	10.5	0	973	515	458	5-
10-14	430997	217155	9.4	213842	9.9	25	679	357	322	10-
15-19	453342	229185	9.9	224157	10.4	6020	1047	556	491	15-
20-24	451060	230563	9.9	220497	10.2	28958	1619	852	767	20-
25-29	392552	202017	8.7	190535	8.9	35413	1674	867	807	25-
30-34	334534	172921	7.4	161613	7.5	26599	1672	900	772	30-
35-39	294584	153476	6.6	141108	6.6	17469	1825	988	837	35-
40-44	272429	146394	6.3	126035	5.9	6965	2059	1260	799	40-
45-49	244219	134478	5.8	109741	5.1	736	2364	1471	893	45-
50-54	194993	109267	4.7	85726	4.0	8	2595	1676	919	50-
55-59	130365	72813	3.1	57552	2.7	0	2447	1576	871	55-
60-64	96417	51953	2.2	44464	2.1	0	2590	1628	962	60-
65-69	77511	40643	1.8	36868	1.7	0	3278	1957	1321	65-
70-74	55661	29365	1.3	26296	1.2		3633	2115	1518	70-
75-79	35707	19022	0.8	16685	0.8		3786	2155	1631	75-
80-84	16671	8896	0.4	7775	0.4	62508 M.	2714	1571	1143	80-
85+	7052	3456	0.1	3596	0.2	59685 F.	1902	1009	893	85
TOTAL	4473454	2321702		2151752		122193	47869	27591	20278	TOT

TABLE 2 — MALE LIFE TABLE

x	nq_x	l_x	nd_x	nL_x	nm_x	na_x	T_x	r_x	$\dot{e}_x$	nM_x
0	0.075318	100000	7532	94793	0.079455	0.3087	5734615	0.0083	57.346	0.079939
1	0.025762	92468	2382	363107	0.006561	1.1599	5639821	0.0083	60.992	0.006603
5	0.011007	90086	992	447951	0.002214	2.5000	5276714	0.0183	58.574	0.002229
10	0.008187	89094	729	443664	0.001644	2.5212	4828764	0.0000	54.198	0.001644
15	0.012062	88365	1066	439342	0.002426	2.6702	4385100	0.0000	49.625	0.002426
20	0.018331	87299	1600	432653	0.003699	2.5986	3945758	0.0091	45.198	0.003695
25	0.021274	85699	1823	424053	0.004299	2.5639	3513105	0.0244	40.994	0.004292
30	0.025747	83876	2160	414140	0.005215	2.5743	3089053	0.0222	36.829	0.005205
35	0.031731	81716	2593	402344	0.006444	2.5946	2674913	0.0100	32.734	0.006437
40	0.042181	79123	3338	387575	0.008611	2.5908	2272569	0.0046	28.722	0.008607
45	0.053413	75786	4048	369226	0.010963	2.6031	1884994	0.0179	24.873	0.010939
50	0.074449	71738	5341	345927	0.015439	2.6105	1515768	0.0456	21.129	0.015339
55	0.103634	66397	6881	315479	0.021811	2.6012	1169841	0.0520	17.619	0.021644
60	0.145913	59516	8684	276721	0.031382	2.5981	854362	0.0090	14.355	0.031336
65	0.215792	50832	10969	227468	0.048223	2.5667	577641	0.0090	11.364	0.048151
70	0.305950	39863	12196	169075	0.072134	2.5206	350174	0.0090	8.784	0.072025
75	0.440078	27667	12175	107301	0.113470	2.4513	181099	0.0090	6.546	0.113290
80	0.603382	15491	9347	52832	0.176923	2.3656	73798	0.0090	4.764	0.176596
85+	*1.000000	6144	6144	20966	0.293049	3.4124	20966	0.0090	3.412	0.291956

TABLE 3 — FEMALE LIFE TABLE

x	nq_x	l_x	nd_x	nL_x	nm_x	na_x	T_x	r_x	$\dot{e}_x$	nM_x
0	0.060692	100000	6069	95912	0.063279	0.3264	6111476	0.0078	61.115	0.063635
1	0.024042	93931	2258	369362	0.006114	1.1833	6015564	0.0078	64.043	0.006146
5	0.010050	91672	921	456059	0.002020	2.5000	5646202	0.0167	61.591	0.002033
10	0.007501	90751	681	452066	0.001506	2.5184	5190143	0.0000	57.191	0.001506
15	0.010897	90070	981	448077	0.002190	2.6822	4738077	0.0000	52.604	0.002190
20	0.017277	89089	1539	441775	0.003484	2.6160	4290000	0.0129	48.154	0.003479
25	0.020996	87550	1838	433255	0.004243	2.5553	3848224	0.0269	43.955	0.004235
30	0.023652	85712	2027	423617	0.004786	2.5628	3414969	0.0251	39.843	0.004777
35	0.029263	83684	2449	412406	0.005938	2.5435	2991352	0.0191	35.746	0.005932
40	0.031255	81235	2539	399976	0.006348	2.5576	2578946	0.0185	31.747	0.006340
45	0.040039	78696	3151	385904	0.008165	2.5950	2178970	0.0303	27.688	0.008137
50	0.052629	75546	3976	368228	0.010797	2.6107	1793066	0.0534	23.735	0.010720
55	0.073552	71570	5264	345287	0.015246	2.6138	1424838	0.0501	19.908	0.015134
60	0.103334	66306	6852	315355	0.021727	2.6396	1079551	0.0225	16.281	0.021635
65	0.165758	59454	9855	273832	0.035989	2.6217	764195	0.0225	12.854	0.035831
70	0.254221	49599	12609	217453	0.057985	2.5778	490364	0.0225	9.887	0.057727
75	0.393758	36990	14565	148390	0.098154	2.4900	272910	0.0225	7.378	0.097752
80	0.530965	22425	11907	80709	0.147528	2.4292	124520	0.0225	5.553	0.147010
85+	1.000000	10518	10518	43812	0.240074	4.1654	43812	0.0225	4.165	0.248332

TABLE 4 — OBSERVED AND PROJECTED VITAL RATES

	OBSERVED POPULATION BOTH SEXES	MALES	FEMALES	PROJECTED POPULATION 1916 MALES	FEMALES	1921 MALES	FEMALES	1926 MALES	FEMALES	STABLE POPULATION MALES	FEMA
RATES PER THOUSAND											
Birth	27.32	26.92	27.74	27.26	27.66	26.60	26.65	25.58	25.34	25.72	24.
Death	10.70	11.88	9.42	12.03	9.68	12.20	9.87	12.43	10.09	13.44	12.
Increase	16.61	15.04	18.31	15.22	17.98	14.40	16.78	13.15	15.26		12.28
PERCENTAGE											
under 15	31.66	30.89	32.49	31.60	32.61	32.40	32.99	32.42	32.68	31.72	30.
15-64	64.03	64.74	63.27	64.23	63.18	63.29	62.69	62.60	62.40	62.20	61.
65 and over	4.31	4.37	4.24	4.17	4.21	4.31	4.32	4.98	4.92	6.08	7.
DEP. RATIO X 100	56.17	54.46	58.05	55.69	58.28	58.01	59.51	59.75	60.26	60.78	62.

AGE LAST BIRTHDAY	1916 BOTH SEXES	1916 MALES	FEMALES	1921 BOTH SEXES	1921 MALES	FEMALES	1926 BOTH SEXES	1926 MALES	FEMALES	AGE AT LAST BIRTHDAY	
0-4	590	299	291	632	321	311	658	334	324	0-4	
5-9	518	263	255	578	293	285	619	314	305	5-9	
10-14	452	229	223	514	261	253	572	290	282	10-14	
15-19	427	215	212	448	227	221	508	258	250	15-19	TABLE 5
20-24	447	226	221	421	212	209	441	223	218	20-24	POPULATION
25-29	442	226	216	438	221	217	413	208	205	25-29	PROJECTED
30-34	383	197	186	432	221	211	428	216	212	30-34	WITH
35-39	325	168	157	373	192	181	420	214	206	35-39	FIXED
40-44	285	148	137	315	162	153	361	185	176	40-44	AGE—
45-49	261	139	122	273	141	132	301	154	147	45-49	SPECIFIC
50-54	231	126	105	247	131	116	258	132	126	50-54	BIRTH
55-59	180	100	80	213	115	98	228	119	109	55-59	AND
60-64	117	64	53	160	87	73	191	101	90	60-64	DEATH
65-69	82	43	39	98	52	46	136	72	64	65-69	RATES
70-74	59	30	29	63	32	31	75	39	36	70-74	(IN 1000's)
75-79	37	19	18	39	19	20	41	20	21	75-79	
80-84	18	9	9	19	9	10	20	9	11	80-84	
85+	8	4	4	9	4	5	9	4	5	85+	
TOTAL	4862	2505	2357	5272	2700	2572	5679	2892	2787	TOTAL	

STANDARD COUNTRIES:	ENGLAND AND WALES 1961 BOTH SEXES	MALES	FEMALES	UNITED STATES 1960 BOTH SEXES	MALES	FEMALES	MEXICO 1960 BOTH SEXES	MALES	FEMALES	
STANDARDIZED RATES PER THOUSAND										TABLE 6
Birth	22.37	22.07*	21.17	22.74	20.30*	21.88	23.73	20.73*	23.13	STANDAR-
Death	17.96	21.54*	18.34	15.40	17.85*	14.55	10.08	11.88*	9.14	DIZED
Increase	4.40	0.53*	2.83	7.33	2.45*	7.33	13.66	8.85*	13.98	RATES

OBSERVED POP. MALES	FEMALES	STATIONARY POP. MALES	FEMALES	STABLE POP. MALES	FEMALES	OBSERVED BIRTHS	NET MATERNITY FUNCTION	BIRTHS IN STABLE POP.	
27.73718	26.70836	34.42282	35.93604	28.95568	30.04875	29.31447	30.30993	29.76694	TABLE 7
367.9442	357.3235	467.4164	502.5625	418.4975	450.8073	40.53515	42.51208	41.66723	MOMENTS
4232.705	4703.245	2937.930	2926.076	4828.704	5266.025	94.2133	61.6371	75.5796	AND
-49668.	-21307.	-198587.	-242546.	-104357.	-131001.	-888.566	-1197.379	-1057.668	CUMULANTS
0.359658	0.484853	0.084522	0.067453	0.318114	0.302687	0.133269	0.049448	0.078963	
2.633132	2.833121	2.091044	2.039685	2.404150	2.355395	2.459213	2.337468	2.390800	
-0.166497	-0.233476	-0.032598	-0.025356	-0.124942	-0.116017	-0.071027	-0.025976	-0.042268	

VITAL STATISTICS		THOMPSON AGE RANGE	NRR	1000r	INTERVAL	BOURGEOIS-PICHAT AGE RANGE	NRR	1000b	1000d	1000r	COALE	
R	1.696										IBR	TABLE 8
R	1.446	0-4	1.34	11.04	27.18	5-29	1.10	23.78	20.21	3.57	IDR	RATES FROM AGE
R	3.473	5-9	1.30	9.71	27.11	30-54	1.88	38.65	15.20	23.46	IRI	DISTRI- BUTIONS
GENERATION	30.038	10-14	1.41	12.50	27.04	55-79	1.72	24.12	3.95	20.18	K1	AND VITAL STATISTICS
SEX RATIO	104.730	15-19	1.71	16.63	26.92	*25-49	1.78	35.96	14.69	21.26	K2	(Females)

ORIGINAL MATRIX SUB-DIAGONAL	ALTERNATIVE FIRST ROWS Projection	Integral	FIRST STABLE MATRIX % IN STABLE POPULATION	FISHER VALUES	REPRODUCTIVE VALUES	SECOND STABLE MATRIX Z2 FIRST COLUMN	FIRST ROW	
0.98019	0.00000	0.00000	11.072	1.108	288092	0.1371+0.0609	0.1371+0.0609	TABLE 9
0.99125	0.00013	0.00000	10.205	1.202	270731	0.1397-0.0922	0.0203+0.1328	LESLIE
0.99118	0.03038	0.00027	9.512	1.289	275735	-0.0027-0.1890	-0.0894+0.0786	MATRIX
0.98594	0.17765	0.06294	8.865	1.350	302500	-0.1813-0.1125	-0.1055-0.0310	AND ITS
0.98071	0.35636	0.30778	8.219	1.256	276939	-0.2162+0.1033	-0.0521-0.1050	SPECTRAL
0.97775	0.39405	0.43557	7.580	0.959	182793	-0.0330+0.2655	0.0042-0.1121	COMPO-
0.97354	0.32397	0.38571	6.969	0.597	96474	0.2292+0.1904	0.0316-0.0756	NENTS
0.96986	0.20158	0.29013	6.380	0.283	39989	0.3148-0.1002	0.0272-0.0330	(Females)
0.96482	0.07015	0.12951	5.818	0.080	10142	0.0942-0.3525	0.0100-0.0081	
0.95420	0.00772	0.01572	5.279	0.008	894	-0.2704-0.2961	0.0011-0.0007	
0.93770	0.00011	0.00022	4.736	0.000	9	-0.4294+0.0740	0.0000-0.0000	
0.77441			15.365					

OBSERVED POPUL. (IN 100's)	CONTRIBUTIONS OF ROOTS (IN 100's) r1	r2, r3	r4-r11	AGE-SP. BIRTH RATES	NET MATERNITY FUNCTION	COEFF. OF MATRIX EQUATION	PARAMETERS		INTEGRAL	MATRIX	EXP. INCREASE x	e(x+2½)r	
2600	2651	-58	7	0.0000	0.0000	0.0000	L(1)		1.06337	1.06345	0	1.0312	TABLE 10
2252	2444	-165	-26	0.0000	0.0000	0.0001	L(2)		0.47173	0.47344	50	1.9063	AGE
2138	2278	-127	-12	0.0001	0.0003	0.0295			0.75755	0.73948	55	2.0271	ANALYSIS
2242	2123	55	63	0.0131	0.0588	0.1711	R(1)		0.01229	0.01230	60	2.1555	AND
2205	1968	228	8	0.0641	0.2834	0.3384	R(2)		-0.02276	-0.02601	65	2.2921	MISCEL-
1905	1815	206	-116	0.0908	0.3933	0.3669			0.20277	-0.20026	70	2.4374	LANEOUS
1616	1669	-37	-16	0.0804	0.3406	0.2950	C(1)			23948	75	2.5918	RESULTS
1411	1528	-298	182	0.0605	0.2494	0.1787	C(2)			-36501	80	2.7561	(Females)
1260	1393	-310	177	0.0270	0.1080	0.0603				-34201	85	2.9307	
1097	1264	-5	-162	0.0033	0.0126	0.0064	2P/Y		30.9870	31.3746	90	3.1164	
857	1134	364	-641	0.0000	0.0002	0.0001	DELTA		7.3270		95	3.3139	
1932	3680										100	3.5239	

TABLE 1 — DATA

AGE AT LAST BIRTHDAY	POPULATION BOTH SEXES	MALES Number	MALES %	FEMALES Number	FEMALES %	BIRTHS BY AGE OF MOTHER	DEATHS BOTH SEXES	DEATHS MALES	DEATHS FEMALES	AGE AT LAST BIRTHDAY
0	133952	68381	2.5	65571	2.4	0	8967	5125	3842	0
1-4	468505	238222	8.6	230283	8.6	0	3100	1695	1405	1-4
5-9	597994	302640	10.9	295354	11.0	0	1173	606	567	5-9
10-14	531025	268951	9.7	262074	9.8	36	799	464	335	10-1
15-19	465959	235768	8.5	230191	8.6	6154	999	521	478	15-1
20-24	455735	221525	8.0	234210	8.7	31263	1375	708	667	20-2
25-29	464189	226247	8.2	237942	8.9	40105	1734	840	894	25-2
30-34	451008	228636	8.2	222372	8.3	31499	1948	1006	942	30-3
35-39	388585	197886	7.1	190699	7.1	19488	2188	1164	1024	35-3
40-44	332760	170898	6.2	161862	6.0	7063	2160	1249	911	40-4
45-49	281528	145331	5.2	136197	5.1	588	2405	1458	947	45-4
50-54	257024	136632	4.9	120392	4.5	2	2892	1759	1133	50-5
55-59	216721	116780	4.2	99941	3.7	0	3526	2231	1295	55-5
60-64	169976	90976	3.3	79000	2.9	0	4136	2626	1510	60-6
65-69	105391	56311	2.0	49080	1.8	0	3969	2412	1557	65-6
70-74	65434	33489	1.2	31945	1.2		3706	2089	1617	70-7
75-79	40168	19672	0.7	20496	0.8		3718	2000	1718	75-7
80-84	20022	9619	0.3	10403	0.4	70039 M.	2817	1464	1353	80-8
85+	10152	4682	0.2	5470	0.2	66159 F.	2464	1235	1229	85-
TOTAL	5456128	2772646		2683482		136198	54076	30652	23424	TOT

TABLE 2 — MALE LIFE TABLE

x	$_nq_x$	l_x	$_nd_x$	$_nL_x$	$_nm_x$	$_na_x$	T_x	r_x	$\dot{e}_x$	$_nM_x$
0	0.070875	100000	7088	95208	0.074443	0.3239	5905034	0.0094	59.050	0.074948
1	0.027721	92912	2576	364386	0.007068	1.1797	5809826	0.0094	62.530	0.007115
5	0.009917	90337	896	449444	0.001993	2.5000	5445440	0.0099	60.279	0.002002
10	0.008594	89441	769	445300	0.001726	2.5220	4995096	0.0231	55.858	0.001725
15	0.011017	88672	977	441049	0.002215	2.6327	4550696	0.0171	51.320	0.002210
20	0.015860	87695	1391	435127	0.003196	2.5915	4109648	0.0010	46.863	0.003196
25	0.018397	86305	1588	427648	0.003713	2.5597	3674521	0.0000	42.576	0.003713
30	0.021789	84717	1846	419140	0.004404	2.5927	3246873	0.0088	38.326	0.004400
35	0.029069	82871	2409	408551	0.005896	2.5909	2827733	0.0233	34.122	0.005882
40	0.036008	80462	2897	395357	0.007328	2.6003	2419182	0.0233	30.066	0.007308
45	0.049047	77565	3804	378670	0.010047	2.5939	2023825	0.0124	26.092	0.010032
50	0.062524	73760	4612	357800	0.012889	2.6146	1645155	0.0083	22.304	0.012874
55	0.091691	69149	6340	330707	0.019172	2.6286	1287355	0.0209	18.617	0.019104
60	0.135727	62808	8525	293612	0.029034	2.6036	956648	0.0356	15.231	0.028865
65	0.194919	54283	10581	245664	0.043070	2.5661	663035	0.0356	12.214	0.042834
70	0.271866	43703	11881	189300	0.062764	2.5413	417371	0.0356	9.550	0.062379
75	0.406493	31821	12935	126436	0.102306	2.4742	228071	0.0356	7.167	0.101667
80	0.544423	18886	10282	67182	0.153048	2.4122	101635	0.0356	5.381	0.152199
85+	1.000000	8604	8604	34453	0.249734	4.0043	34453	0.0356	4.004	0.263777

TABLE 3 — FEMALE LIFE TABLE

x	$_nq_x$	l_x	$_nd_x$	$_nL_x$	$_nm_x$	$_na_x$	T_x	r_x	$\dot{e}_x$	$_nM_x$
0	0.056032	100000	5603	96272	0.058201	0.3347	6305595	0.0094	63.056	0.058593
1	0.023854	94397	2252	371272	0.006065	1.1954	6209323	0.0094	65.779	0.006101
5	0.009514	92145	877	458534	0.001912	2.5000	5838050	0.0094	63.357	0.001920
10	0.006375	91268	582	454901	0.001279	2.5221	5379516	0.0233	58.942	0.001278
15	0.010347	90687	938	451230	0.002080	2.6526	4924616	0.0092	54.304	0.002077
20	0.014143	89748	1269	445716	0.002848	2.6164	4473385	0.0000	49.844	0.002848
25	0.018618	88479	1647	438392	0.003758	2.5700	4027670	0.0015	45.521	0.003757
30	0.020994	86832	1823	429727	0.004242	2.5696	3589278	0.0177	41.336	0.004236
35	0.026537	85009	2256	419503	0.005378	2.5441	3159550	0.0266	37.167	0.005370
40	0.027802	82753	2301	408117	0.005637	2.5455	2740047	0.0278	33.111	0.005628
45	0.034279	80452	2758	395634	0.006971	2.5970	2331931	0.0224	28.985	0.006953
50	0.046147	77694	3585	379908	0.009437	2.6116	1936297	0.0214	24.922	0.009411
55	0.063123	74109	4678	359436	0.013015	2.6252	1556389	0.0287	21.001	0.012958
60	0.092142	69431	6398	332138	0.019262	2.6527	1196954	0.0394	17.239	0.019114
65	0.148585	63033	9366	292959	0.031970	2.6288	864816	0.0394	13.720	0.031724
70	0.227090	53668	12187	238934	0.051007	2.5873	571857	0.0394	10.656	0.050618
75	0.348977	41480	14476	171448	0.084432	2.5163	332923	0.0394	8.026	0.083821
80	0.493280	27005	13321	101556	0.131167	2.4876	161474	0.0394	5.980	0.130058
85+	*1.000000	13684	13684	59918	0.228373	4.3788	59918	0.0394	4.379	0.224680

TABLE 4 — OBSERVED AND PROJECTED VITAL RATES

	OBSERVED POPULATION BOTH SEXES	MALES	FEMALES	PROJECTED POPULATION 1926 MALES	1926 FEMALES	1931 MALES	1931 FEMALES	1936 MALES	1936 FEMALES	STABLE POPULATION MALES	FEM
RATES PER THOUSAND											
Birth	24.96	25.26	24.65	24.29	23.52	23.63	22.71	23.50	22.43	22.81	21
Death	9.91	11.06	8.73	11.51	9.13	11.98	9.60	12.49	10.14	13.80	12
Increase	15.05	14.21	15.93	12.78	14.39	11.65	13.11	11.01	12.29		9.0
PERCENTAGE											
under 15	31.73	31.67	31.80	31.22	30.98	30.21	29.64	29.86	29.06	28.91	27
15-64	63.85	63.86	63.83	63.48	63.81	63.71	64.31	63.51	64.13	63.27	62
65 and over	4.42	4.46	4.37	5.30	5.21	6.07	6.05	6.62	6.81	7.82	9
DEP. RATIO X 100	56.63	56.59	56.67	57.52	56.72	56.95	55.49	57.45	55.93	58.06	60

AGE AT LAST BIRTHDAY	POPULATION BOTH SEXES	MALES Number	%	FEMALES Number	%	BIRTHS BY AGE OF MOTHER	DEATHS BOTH SEXES	MALES	FEMALES	AGE AT LAST BIRTHDAY
0	105390	53890	1.6	51500	1.6	0	4399	2502	1897	0
1-4	463575	236571	7.0	227004	7.0	0	1726	928	798	1-4
5-9	627380	318937	9.5	308443	9.5	0	827	467	360	5-9
10-14	625222	317526	9.4	307696	9.4	28	631	367	264	10-14
15-19	615410	311792	9.3	303618	9.3	7755	930	525	405	15-19
20-24	584618	298001	8.9	286617	8.8	28415	1252	679	573	20-24
25-29	533970	277462	8.2	256508	7.9	31441	1352	689	663	25-29
30-34	489179	251515	7.5	237664	7.3	23068	1450	747	703	30-34
35-39	466153	228660	6.8	237493	7.3	14439	1789	881	908	35-39
40-44	456291	229822	6.8	226469	6.9	5604	2199	1219	980	40-44
45-49	408713	209325	6.2	199388	6.1	519	2852	1683	1169	45-49
50-54	334462	171688	5.1	162774	5.0	0	3360	1993	1367	50-54
55-59	261171	132314	3.9	128857	3.9	0	3870	2379	1491	55-59
60-64	228605	114859	3.4	113746	3.5	0	5024	3033	1991	60-64
65-69	183445	92946	2.8	90499	2.8	0	6373	3758	2615	65-69
70-74	130300	66018	2.0	64282	2.0		7228	4241	2987	70-74
75-79	72175	35920	1.1	36255	1.1		6301	3478	2823	75-79
80-84	29598	13862	0.4	15736	0.5	57160 M.	4136	2186	1950	80-84
85+	14182	6003	0.2	8179	0.3	54109 F.	3418	1495	1923	85+
TOTAL	6629839	3367111		3262728		111269	59117	33250	25867	TOTAL

TABLE 1 ... TA

x	nq_x	l_x	nd_x	nL_x	nm_x	na_x	T_x	r_x	$\mathring{e}_x$	nM_x	x
0	0.044993	100000	4499	96910	0.046428	0.3132	6354771	0.0000	63.548	0.046428	0
1	0.015518	95501	1482	377802	0.003923	1.1655	6257861	0.0000	65.527	0.003923	1
5	0.007294	94019	686	468379	0.001464	2.5000	5880060	0.0000	62.541	0.001464	5
10	0.005763	93333	538	465339	0.001156	2.5360	5411681	0.0009	57.983	0.001156	10
15	0.008391	92795	779	462134	0.001685	2.6352	4946342	0.0047	53.304	0.001684	15
20	0.011338	92016	1043	457545	0.002280	2.5689	4484208	0.0095	48.733	0.002279	20
25	0.012351	90973	1124	452115	0.002485	2.5526	4026663	0.0144	44.262	0.002483	25
30	0.014767	89849	1327	446048	0.002975	2.5891	3574547	0.0163	39.784	0.002970	30
35	0.019101	88523	1691	438584	0.003855	2.6169	3128499	0.0051	35.341	0.003853	35
40	0.026208	86832	2276	428814	0.005307	2.6516	2689916	0.0033	30.978	0.005304	40
45	0.039586	84556	3347	414899	0.008068	2.6456	2261101	0.0210	26.741	0.008040	45
50	0.056821	81209	4614	395191	0.011676	2.6481	1846202	0.0337	22.734	0.011608	50
55	0.086528	76594	6628	367261	0.018046	2.6295	1451011	0.0219	18.944	0.017980	55
60	0.124822	69967	8733	328988	0.026547	2.6124	1083749	0.0314	15.489	0.026406	60
65	0.185198	61233	11340	278894	0.040662	2.5950	754767	0.0314	12.326	0.040432	65
70	0.278671	49893	13904	215274	0.064587	2.5408	475873	0.0314	9.538	0.064240	70
75	0.390771	35989	14064	144449	0.097360	2.4759	260600	0.0314	7.241	0.096826	75
80	0.559886	21926	12276	77396	0.158611	2.4251	116151	0.0314	5.297	0.157697	80
85+	1.000000	9650	9650	38755	0.248999	4.0161	38755	0.0314	4.016	0.249041	85+

TABLE 2 ... MALE ... E ... BLE

x	nq_x	l_x	nd_x	nL_x	nm_x	na_x	T_x	r_x	$\mathring{e}_x$	nM_x	x
0	0.035944	100000	3594	97580	0.036835	0.3268	6732840	0.0000	67.328	0.036835	0
1	0.013924	96406	1342	381842	0.003515	1.1838	6635259	0.0000	68.826	0.003515	1
5	0.005819	95063	553	473934	0.001167	2.5000	6253417	0.0000	65.782	0.001167	5
10	0.004281	94510	405	471555	0.000858	2.5377	5779483	0.0005	61.152	0.000858	10
15	0.006656	94106	626	469072	0.001335	2.6754	5307929	0.0057	56.404	0.001334	15
20	0.009968	93479	932	465184	0.002003	2.6260	4838857	0.0149	51.764	0.001999	20
25	0.012859	92547	1190	459847	0.002588	2.5718	4373673	0.0162	47.259	0.002585	25
30	0.014690	91357	1342	453539	0.002959	2.5799	3913826	0.0046	42.841	0.002958	30
35	0.018942	90015	1705	445929	0.003824	2.5674	3460287	0.0011	38.441	0.003823	35
40	0.021440	88310	1893	436985	0.004333	2.5884	3014358	0.0130	34.134	0.004327	40
45	0.029024	86417	2508	426143	0.005886	2.6311	2577373	0.0270	29.825	0.005863	45
50	0.041368	83909	3471	411290	0.008440	2.6223	2151230	0.0352	25.638	0.008398	50
55	0.056524	80438	4547	391437	0.011615	2.6355	1739940	0.0237	21.631	0.011571	55
60	0.084693	75891	6427	364410	0.017638	2.6593	1348503	0.0385	17.769	0.017504	60
65	0.136209	69464	9462	324956	0.029116	2.6366	984093	0.0385	14.167	0.028895	65
70	0.210478	60002	12629	269709	0.046825	2.6007	659137	0.0385	10.985	0.046467	70
75	0.328625	47373	15568	198474	0.078438	2.5340	389428	0.0385	8.220	0.077865	75
80	0.476988	31805	15171	121320	0.125045	2.5146	190954	0.0385	6.004	0.123919	80
85+	*1.000000	16634	16634	69633	0.238885	4.1861	69633	0.0385	4.186	0.235114	85+

TABLE 3 ... FEMALE ... FE ... BLE

	OBSERVED POPULATION			PROJECTED POPULATION 1938		1943		1948		STABLE POPULATION	
	BOTH SEXES	MALES	FEMALES	MALES	FEMALES	MALES	FEMALES	MALES	FEMALES	MALES	FEMALES
RATES PER THOUSAND											
Birth	16.78	16.98	16.58	17.32	16.80	17.54	16.90	17.40	16.68	14.97	14.10
Death	8.92	9.87	7.93	10.53	8.62	11.21	9.46	11.77	10.19	16.35	15.47
Increase	7.87	7.10	8.66	6.79	8.18	6.32	7.44	5.63	6.49	−1.3734	
PERCENTAGE											
under 15	27.48	27.53	27.42	25.32	24.95	23.70	23.12	23.35	22.64	21.31	20.30
15-64	66.04	66.09	65.99	67.80	67.55	69.16	68.73	68.92	68.36	66.19	64.33
65 and over	6.48	6.38	6.59	6.88	7.50	7.14	8.14	7.74	9.00	12.50	15.37
DEP. RATIO X 100	51.42	51.30	51.53	47.48	48.04	44.59	45.49	45.10	46.29	51.07	55.44

TABLE 4 ... OBSERVED ... AND ... PROJEC- D ... TAL ... ATES

AGE AT LAST BIRTHDAY	POPULATION BOTH SEXES	MALES Number	%	FEMALES Number	%	BIRTHS BY AGE OF MOTHER	DEATHS BOTH SEXES	MALES	FEMALES	AGE AT LAST BIRTH
0	190701	97642	2.3	93059	2.2	0	4781	2729	2052	0
1-4	738632	377547	8.9	361085	8.7	0	1204	676	528	1-4
5-9	742099	378489	8.9	363610	8.7	0	517	308	209	5-9
10-14	607000	309272	7.3	297728	7.1	36	372	223	149	10-1
15-19	552990	282957	6.7	270033	6.5	10328	614	439	175	15-1
20-24	641361	330955	7.8	310406	7.4	55656	954	692	262	20-2
25-29	698184	360891	8.5	337293	8.1	63051	975	630	345	25-2
30-34	642253	326016	7.7	316237	7.6	39086	1052	615	437	30-3
35-39	633412	322980	7.6	310432	7.4	20885	1465	847	618	35-3
40-44	580768	300989	7.1	279779	6.7	5752	1978	1168	810	40-4
45-49	491877	257092	6.0	234785	5.6	384	2784	1698	1086	45-4
50-54	458255	228085	5.4	230170	5.5	2	4039	2485	1554	50-5
55-59	398953	193218	4.5	205735	4.9	0	5650	3538	2112	55-5
60-64	369921	180652	4.2	189269	4.5	0	7943	5023	2920	60-6
65-69	273272	130190	3.1	143082	3.4	0	9344	5648	3696	65-6
70-74	191740	86899	2.0	104841	2.5		10102	5674	4428	70-7
75-79	115476	50151	1.2	65325	1.6		10110	5223	4887	75-7
80-84	64943	27742	0.7	37201	0.9	100204 M.	8799	4205	4594	80-8
85+	29938	11975	0.3	17963	0.4	94976 F.	7839	3353	4486	85-
TOTAL	8421775	4253742		4168033		195180	80522	45174	35348	TOT

TABLE 1 DATA

TABLE 2 — MALE LIFE TABLE

x	nq_x	l_x	nd_x	nL_x	nm_x	na_x	T_x	r_x	$\mathring{e}_x$	nM_x
0	0.027358	100000	2736	98041	0.027904	0.2840	6627923	0.0021	66.279	0.027949
1	0.007112	97264	692	387073	0.001787	1.1324	6529881	0.0021	67.135	0.001791
5	0.004023	96572	388	481891	0.000806	2.5000	6142808	0.0419	63.608	0.000814
10	0.003621	96184	348	480123	0.000725	2.7107	5660917	0.0282	58.855	0.000721
15	0.007730	95836	741	477460	0.001551	2.6802	5180794	0.0000	54.059	0.001551
20	0.010401	95095	989	473018	0.002091	2.5162	4703334	0.0000	49.459	0.002091
25	0.008690	94106	818	468462	0.001746	2.4714	4230316	0.0000	44.953	0.001746
30	0.009398	93288	877	464330	0.001888	2.5921	3761854	0.0091	40.325	0.001886
35	0.013043	92411	1205	459228	0.002625	2.6528	3297525	0.0053	35.683	0.002622
40	0.019307	91206	1761	451986	0.003896	2.7032	2838297	0.0187	31.120	0.003881
45	0.032676	89445	2923	440514	0.006635	2.7034	2386311	0.0209	26.679	0.006605
50	0.053332	86523	4614	421967	0.010935	2.6929	1945797	0.0171	22.489	0.010895
55	0.087850	81908	7196	392625	0.018327	2.6492	1523830	0.0047	18.604	0.018311
60	0.130727	74712	9767	350308	0.027881	2.6191	1131205	0.0153	15.141	0.027805
65	0.196772	64946	12779	293808	0.043496	2.5805	780897	0.0153	12.024	0.043383
70	0.281903	52166	14706	224625	0.065468	2.5380	487089	0.0153	9.337	0.065294
75	0.412756	37460	15462	148081	0.104415	2.4634	262464	0.0153	7.006	0.104146
80	0.545151	21998	11992	78874	0.152045	2.4052	114382	0.0153	5.200	0.151574
85+	*1.000000	10006	10006	35508	0.281790	3.5487	35508	0.0153	3.549	0.280000

TABLE 3 — FEMALE LIFE TABLE

x	nq_x	l_x	nd_x	nL_x	nm_x	na_x	T_x	r_x	$\mathring{e}_x$	nM_x
0	0.021677	100000	2168	98457	0.022017	0.2881	7168436	0.0020	71.684	0.022051
1	0.005814	97832	569	389700	0.001460	1.1366	7069979	0.0020	72.266	0.001462
5	0.002836	97263	276	485628	0.000568	2.5000	6680279	0.0414	68.682	0.000575
10	0.002502	96988	243	484339	0.000501	2.5319	6194651	0.0292	63.871	0.000500
15	0.003235	96745	313	482976	0.000648	2.6088	5710312	0.0000	59.024	0.000648
20	0.004212	96432	406	481181	0.000844	2.5907	5227336	0.0000	54.207	0.000844
25	0.005102	96026	490	478957	0.001023	2.6074	4746154	0.0000	49.426	0.001023
30	0.006894	95536	659	476127	0.001383	2.6429	4267197	0.0069	44.666	0.001382
35	0.009924	94877	942	472178	0.001994	2.6545	3791070	0.0102	39.958	0.001991
40	0.014446	93936	1357	466533	0.002909	2.6815	3318892	0.0249	35.331	0.002895
45	0.022938	92579	2124	457929	0.004637	2.6621	2852359	0.0148	30.810	0.004626
50	0.033267	90455	3009	445225	0.006759	2.6569	2394430	0.0062	26.471	0.006752
55	0.050197	87446	4390	426925	0.010282	2.6523	1949205	0.0090	22.290	0.010266
60	0.074865	83056	6218	400783	0.015515	2.6681	1522280	0.0278	18.328	0.015428
65	0.122424	76838	9407	362091	0.025979	2.6505	1121497	0.0278	14.596	0.025831
70	0.192987	67432	13013	306267	0.042491	2.6262	759406	0.0278	11.262	0.042235
75	0.317707	54418	17289	229796	0.075236	2.5537	453140	0.0278	8.327	0.074811
80	0.470489	37129	17469	140782	0.124084	2.5283	223343	0.0278	6.015	0.123491
85+	1.000000	19660	19660	82561	0.238131	4.1994	82561	0.0278	4.199	0.249737

TABLE 4 — OBSERVED AND PROJECTED VITAL RATES

	OBSERVED POPULATION BOTH SEXES	MALES	FEMALES	PROJECTED POPULATION 1956 MALES	FEMALES	1961 MALES	FEMALES	1966 MALES	FEMALES	STABLE POPULATION MALES	FEMA
RATES PER THOUSAND											
Birth	23.18	23.56	22.79	21.25	20.42	19.97	19.10	20.46	19.49	23.20	21.
Death	9.56	10.62	8.48	10.72	8.90	10.93	9.29	11.26	9.77	10.15	8.
Increase	13.61	12.94	14.31	10.53	11.52	9.04	9.81	9.20	9.72		13.04
PERCENTAGE											
under 15	27.05	27.34	26.76	29.37	28.51	29.66	28.60	28.34	27.21	30.50	29.
15-64	64.93	65.44	64.40	62.92	61.77	62.56	61.13	63.70	62.10	62.52	61.
65 and over	8.02	7.22	8.84	7.71	9.72	7.78	10.26	7.96	10.69	6.98	9.
DEP. RATIO X 100	54.02	52.80	55.28	58.92	61.90	59.85	63.57	56.98	61.04	59.95	62.

AGE AT LAST BIRTHDAY	1956 BOTH SEXES	1956 MALES	1956 FEMALES	1961 BOTH SEXES	1961 MALES	1961 FEMALES	1966 BOTH SEXES	1966 MALES	1966 FEMALES	AGE AT LAST BIRTHDAY	
0-4	930	476	454	902	462	440	928	475	453	0-4	
5-9	924	472	452	923	472	451	897	459	438	5-9	
10-14	740	377	363	921	470	451	921	471	450	10-14	
15-19	605	308	297	737	375	362	917	468	449	15-19	**TABLE 5**
20-24	549	280	269	601	305	296	732	372	360	20-24	POPULATION
25-29	637	328	309	546	278	268	596	302	294	25-29	PROJECTED
30-34	693	358	335	632	325	307	541	275	266	30-34	WITH
35-39	636	322	314	687	354	333	626	321	305	35-39	FIXED
40-44	625	318	307	627	317	310	677	348	329	40-44	AGE—
45-49	568	293	275	611	310	301	613	309	304	45-49	SPECIFIC
50-54	474	246	228	548	281	267	590	297	293	50-54	BIRTH
55-59	433	212	221	448	229	219	517	261	256	55-59	AND
60-64	365	172	193	396	189	207	409	204	205	60-64	DEATH
65-69	323	152	171	319	145	174	346	159	187	65-69	RATES
70-74	221	100	121	261	116	145	259	111	148	70-74	(IN 1000's)
75-79	136	57	79	157	66	91	185	76	109	75-79	
80-84	67	27	40	79	31	48	91	35	56	80-84	
85+	34	12	22	35	12	23	42	14	28	85+	
TOTAL	8960	4510	4450	9430	4737	4693	9887	4957	4930	TOTAL	

STANDARD COUNTRIES:	ENGLAND AND WALES 1961 BOTH SEXES	MALES	FEMALES	UNITED STATES 1960 BOTH SEXES	MALES	FEMALES	MEXICO 1960 BOTH SEXES	MALES	FEMALES	
STANDARDIZED RATES PER THOUSAND										**TABLE 6**
Birth	19.63	20.00*	18.52	19.97	18.88*	19.15	22.92	18.05*	22.25	STANDARDIZED
Death	12.95	13.37*	12.74	10.57	11.58*	9.42	5.59	8.91*	4.64	RATES
Increase	6.69	6.63*	5.78	9.40	7.30*	9.73	17.33	9.15*	17.61	

	OBSERVED POP. MALES	OBSERVED POP. FEMALES	STATIONARY POP. MALES	STATIONARY POP. FEMALES	STABLE POP. MALES	STABLE POP. FEMALES	OBSERVED BIRTHS	NET MATERNITY FUNCTION	BIRTHS IN STABLE POP.	
μ	31.64424	32.68474	36.05713	38.27747	29.99356	31.58494	28.09530	28.02107	27.54198	**TABLE 7**
σ^2	439.0806	469.8059	486.1373	534.9057	437.9624	483.9526	33.15507	35.31985	33.92975	MOMENTS
κ_3	3359.492	3594.369	2391.877	2206.552	4774.962	5334.653	95.0726	104.2464	108.4659	AND
κ_4	-149298.	-182439.	-227428.	-293462.	-129235.	-172199.	-298.837	-396.322	-241.868	CUMULANTS
β_1	0.133326	0.124592	0.049797	0.031812	0.271412	0.251075	0.248005	0.246641	0.301193	
β_2	2.225597	2.173428	2.037665	1.974355	2.326237	2.264767	2.728146	2.682305	2.789905	
κ	-0.054931	-0.049434	-0.019038	-0.011750	-0.104872	-0.094198	-0.155363	-0.144917	-0.185924	

VITAL STATISTICS		THOMPSON AGE RANGE	NRR	1000r	INTERVAL	BOURGEOIS-PICHAT AGE RANGE	NRR	1000b	1000d	1000r	COALE	
GRR	1.503										IBR	**TABLE 8** RATES FROM AGE DISTRIBUTIONS
NRR	1.437	0-4	1.46	13.99	27.41	5-29	1.04	16.03	14.54	1.49	IDR	AND VITAL
TFR	3.088	5-9	1.19	6.25	27.36	30-54	1.50	26.62	11.62	15.00	IRI	STATISTICS
GENERATION	27.780	10-14	1.01	0.23	27.30	55-79	1.92	48.09	24.00	24.08	K1	(Females)
SEX RATIO	105.505	15-19	0.97	-1.01	27.19	*25-59	1.44	24.91	11.43	13.48	K2	

Start Age Interval	ORIGINAL MATRIX SUB-DIAGONAL	ALTERNATIVE FIRST ROWS Projection	ALTERNATIVE FIRST ROWS Integral	FIRST STABLE MATRIX % IN STABLE POPULATION	FISHER VALUES	REPRODUCTIVE VALUES	SECOND STABLE MATRIX Z₂ FIRST COLUMN	FIRST ROW	
0	0.99482	0.00000	0.00000	10.396	1.058	480542	0.1633+0.0764	0.1633+0.0764	**TABLE 9**
5	0.99735	0.00014	0.00000	9.688	1.135	412866	0.1634-0.1298	0.0037+0.1557	LESLIE
10	0.99719	0.04544	0.00030	9.051	1.215	361803	-0.0504-0.2369	-0.1187+0.0626	MATRIX
15	0.99628	0.25759	0.09387	8.455	1.253	338274	-0.2721-0.0701	-0.1013-0.0710	AND ITS
20	0.99538	0.43395	0.44004	7.890	1.069	331735	-0.2133+0.2462	-0.0263-0.1253	SPECTRAL
25	0.99409	0.36795	0.45877	7.357	0.685	231003	0.1452+0.3483	0.0156-0.1019	COMPONENTS
30	0.99171	0.22604	0.30333	6.851	0.344	108727	0.4355+0.0291	0.0244-0.0555	(Females)
35	0.98804	0.10403	0.16511	6.364	0.129	40021	0.2539-0.4350	0.0152-0.0199	
40	0.98156	0.02632	0.05046	5.891	0.028	7801	-0.3177-0.4842	0.0042-0.0039	
45	0.97226	0.00195	0.00401	5.416	0.002	457	-0.6568+0.0785	0.0003-0.0003	
50	0.95890	0.00001	0.00002	4.933	0.000	2	-0.2516+0.7048	0.0000-0.0000	
55+	0.80040			17.707					

Start Age Interval	OBSERVED POPUL. (IN 100's)	CONTRIBUTIONS OF ROOTS (IN 100's) r_1	r_2, r_3	r_4-r_{11}	AGE-SP. BIRTH RATES	NET MATERNITY FUNCTION	COEFF. OF MATRIX EQUATION	PARAMETERS INTEGRAL	PARAMETERS MATRIX	EXP. INCREASE x	$e^{(x+8\frac{1}{2})r}$	
0	4541	3981	472	89	0.0000	0.0000	0.0000	L(1) 1.06742	1.06753	0	1.0332	**TABLE 10**
5	3636	3710	91	-165	0.0000	0.0000	0.0001	L(2) 0.37681	0.38287	50	1.9840	AGE
10	2977	3466	-539	51	0.0001	0.0003	0.0451	0.79568	0.76938	55	2.1178	ANALYSIS
15	2700	3237	-680	143	0.0186	0.0899	0.2549	R(1) 0.01305	0.01307	60	2.2605	AND
20	3104	3021	23	60	0.0872	0.4198	0.4277	R(2) -0.02548	-0.03031	65	2.4130	MISCELLANEOUS
25	3373	2817	937	-381	0.0910	0.4357	0.3610		0.22570	0.22181	70	2.5756	RESULTS
30	3162	2623	935	-396	0.0601	0.2864	0.2205	C(1)	38290	75	2.7493	(Females)
35	3104	2437	-289	957	0.0327	0.1546	0.1006	C(2)	101221	80	2.9347	
40	2798	2256	-1537	2080	0.0100	0.0467	0.0252		-92341	85	3.1325	
45	2348	2074	-1185	1459	0.0008	0.0036	0.0018	2P/Y 27.8383	28.3269	90	3.3438	
50	2302	1889	792	-379	0.0000	0.0000	0.0000	DELTA 5.9606		95	3.5692	
55+	7634	6780								100	3.8099	

TABLE 1 — DATA

AGE AT LAST BIRTHDAY	POPULATION BOTH SEXES	MALES Number	%	FEMALES Number	%	BIRTHS BY AGE OF MOTHER	DEATHS BOTH SEXES	MALES	FEMALES	AGE AT LAST BIRTHDAY
0	194752	99421	2.2	95331	2.1	0	4611	2632	1979	0
1-4	771665	394261	8.7	377404	8.5	0	1188	672	516	1-4
5-9	902737	461903	10.2	440834	9.9	0	528	308	220	5-9
10-14	694180	354075	7.8	340105	7.7	35	350	224	126	10-14
15-19	591771	302287	6.6	289484	6.5	11554	625	457	168	15-19
20-24	600166	311979	6.9	288187	6.5	57566	760	568	192	20-24
25-29	704817	368639	8.1	336178	7.6	65503	893	616	277	25-29
30-34	707843	364238	8.0	343605	7.7	42292	1036	655	381	30-34
35-39	643123	325768	7.2	317355	7.1	20548	1324	775	549	35-39
40-44	628428	323418	7.1	305010	6.9	6184	1956	1180	776	40-44
45-49	546929	286705	6.3	260224	5.9	371	2787	1710	1077	45-49
50-54	479201	246061	5.4	233140	5.3	2	3971	2507	1464	50-54
55-59	397270	193148	4.2	204122	4.6	0	5367	3406	1961	55-59
60-64	377642	178947	3.9	198695	4.5	0	7692	4779	2913	60-64
65-69	303312	143140	3.1	160172	3.6	0	9786	5929	3857	65-69
70-74	210390	94961	2.1	115429	2.6		10865	6165	4700	70-74
75-79	127842	55104	1.2	72738	1.6		10506	5395	5111	75-79
80-84	68442	27972	0.6	40470	0.9	104500 M.	8825	4130	4695	80-84
85+	36020	14091	0.3	21929	0.5	99555 F.	8273	3492	4781	85+
TOTAL	8986530	4546118		4440412		204055	81343	45600	35743	TOTAL

TABLE 2 — MALE LIFE TABLE

x	$_nq_x$	l_x	$_nd_x$	$_nL_x$	$_nm_x$	$_na_x$	T_x	r_x	$\mathring{e}_x$	$_nM_x$
0	0.025981	100000	2598	98142	0.026473	0.2847	6705927	0.0000	67.059	0.026473
1	0.006785	97402	661	387713	0.001704	1.1331	6607785	0.0000	67.840	0.001704
5	0.003300	96741	319	482907	0.000661	2.5000	6220072	0.0323	64.296	0.000667
10	0.003195	96422	308	481423	0.000640	2.7746	5737165	0.0416	59.501	0.000633
15	0.007546	96114	725	478871	0.001515	2.6598	5255742	0.0113	54.683	0.001512
20	0.009062	95388	864	474794	0.001821	2.5147	4776870	0.0000	50.078	0.001821
25	0.008320	94524	786	470649	0.001671	2.4935	4302077	0.0000	45.513	0.001671
30	0.008960	93738	840	466653	0.001800	2.5779	3831428	0.0105	40.874	0.001798
35	0.011847	92898	1101	461908	0.002383	2.6559	3364775	0.0094	36.220	0.002379
40	0.018123	91797	1664	455152	0.003655	2.6958	2902866	0.0089	31.623	0.003649
45	0.029559	90133	2664	444573	0.005993	2.7126	2447714	0.0210	27.157	0.005964
50	0.050104	87469	4383	427304	0.010256	2.7086	2003141	0.0287	22.901	0.010189
55	0.084883	83087	7053	398883	0.017681	2.6534	1575837	0.0140	18.966	0.017634
60	0.125919	76034	9574	357380	0.026790	2.6197	1176904	0.0177	15.479	0.026706
65	0.188864	66460	12552	302076	0.041552	2.5921	819574	0.0177	12.332	0.041421
70	0.280581	53908	15126	232287	0.065116	2.5371	517498	0.0177	9.600	0.064921
75	0.393083	38782	15245	155260	0.098188	2.4646	285211	0.0177	7.354	0.097906
80	0.532458	23538	12533	84646	0.148061	2.4295	129951	0.0177	5.521	0.147648
85+	1.000000	11005	11005	45305	0.242908	4.1168	45305	0.0177	4.117	0.247819

TABLE 3 — FEMALE LIFE TABLE

x	$_nq_x$	l_x	$_nd_x$	$_nL_x$	$_nm_x$	$_na_x$	T_x	r_x	$\mathring{e}_x$	$_nM_x$
0	0.020456	100000	2046	98542	0.020759	0.2875	7269971	0.0000	72.700	0.020759
1	0.005447	97954	534	390289	0.001367	1.1360	7171429	0.0000	73.212	0.001367
5	0.002465	97421	240	486504	0.000494	2.5000	6781139	0.0322	69.607	0.000499
10	0.001854	97181	180	485462	0.000371	2.5479	6294636	0.0416	64.772	0.000370
15	0.002903	97000	282	484328	0.000581	2.6047	5809174	0.0160	59.888	0.000580
20	0.003326	96719	322	482814	0.000666	2.5744	5324846	0.0000	55.055	0.000666
25	0.004112	96397	396	481039	0.000824	2.6102	4842032	0.0000	50.230	0.000824
30	0.005534	96001	531	478765	0.001110	2.6677	4360993	0.0046	45.427	0.001109
35	0.008630	95470	824	475428	0.001733	2.6693	3882227	0.0102	40.665	0.001730
40	0.012689	94646	1201	470455	0.002553	2.6907	3406800	0.0171	35.995	0.002544
45	0.020583	93445	1923	462757	0.004156	2.6776	2936344	0.0226	31.423	0.004139
50	0.031041	91521	2841	450973	0.006299	2.6648	2473587	0.0178	27.027	0.006279
55	0.047029	88681	4171	433639	0.009618	2.6589	2022614	0.0061	22.808	0.009607
60	0.071253	84510	6022	408501	0.014741	2.6669	1588976	0.0273	18.802	0.014661
65	0.114611	78488	8996	371401	0.024221	2.6610	1180474	0.0273	15.040	0.024080
70	0.186663	69493	12972	316709	0.040958	2.6291	809073	0.0273	11.643	0.040718
75	0.301339	56521	17032	241059	0.070655	2.5607	492365	0.0273	8.711	0.070266
80	0.454155	39489	17934	153552	0.116795	2.5525	251306	0.0273	6.364	0.116012
85+	*1.000000	21555	21555	97754	0.220502	4.5351	97754	0.0273	4.535	0.218022

TABLE 4 — OBSERVED AND PROJECTED VITAL RATES

RATES PER THOUSAND	OBSERVED POPULATION BOTH SEXES	MALES	FEMALES	PROJECTED POPULATION 1959 MALES	FEMALES	1964 MALES	FEMALES	1969 MALES	FEMALES	STABLE POPULATION MALES	FEMAL
Birth	22.71	22.99	22.42	20.95	20.30	20.67	19.93	22.20	21.32	24.37	23.1
Death	9.05	10.03	8.05	10.24	8.48	10.51	8.90	10.80	9.28	9.38	8.1
Increase	13.66	12.96	14.37	10.71	11.82	10.16	11.04	11.41	12.04		14.983
PERCENTAGE											
under 15	28.52	28.81	28.23	30.08	29.30	29.25	28.39	28.65	27.72	31.65	30.2
15-64	63.17	63.82	62.52	62.26	60.64	63.14	61.28	63.46	61.75	61.68	60.7
65 and over	8.30	7.37	9.25	7.67	10.07	7.61	10.32	7.88	10.53	6.67	8.9
DEP. RATIO X 100	58.29	56.70	59.96	60.63	64.91	58.38	63.18	57.57	61.93	62.12	64.6

AGE AT LAST BIRTHDAY	POPULATION BOTH SEXES	MALES Number	%	FEMALES Number	%	BIRTHS BY AGE OF MOTHER	DEATHS BOTH SEXES	MALES	FEMALES	AGE AT LAST BIRTHDAY
0	211185	108327	2.2	102858	2.2	0	4630	2623	2007	0
1-4	807460	412785	8.5	394675	8.3	0	1050	590	460	1-4
5-9	977924	499936	10.2	477988	10.0	0	468	287	181	5-9
10-14	851976	435835	8.9	416141	8.7	50	378	229	149	10-14
15-19	665797	341388	7.0	324409	6.8	14118	626	456	170	15-19
20-24	611876	319027	6.5	292849	6.2	62803	779	592	187	20-24
25-29	690009	363947	7.5	326062	6.9	68001	826	579	247	25-29
30-34	744097	387731	7.9	356366	7.5	44865	1084	713	371	30-34
35-39	690328	352129	7.2	338199	7.1	21818	1351	819	532	35-39
40-44	661210	336577	6.9	324633	6.8	6254	1956	1175	781	40-44
45-49	600677	311003	6.4	289674	6.1	421	2930	1837	1093	45-49
50-54	500017	260269	5.3	239748	5.0	1	3980	2607	1373	50-54
55-59	440346	219515	4.5	220831	4.6	0	5522	3608	1914	55-59
60-64	372425	173971	3.6	198454	4.2	0	7561	4752	2809	60-64
65-69	332558	153924	3.2	178634	3.8	0	10356	6295	4061	65-69
70-74	227978	102135	2.1	125843	2.6		11702	6638	5064	70-74
75-79	145947	61487	1.3	84460	1.8		11459	5887	5572	75-79
80-84	70270	28011	0.6	42259	0.9	112260 M.	9326	4267	5059	80-84
85+	38058	14277	0.3	23781	0.5	106071 F.	8937	3679	5258	85+
TOTAL	9640138	4882274		4757864		218331	84921	47633	37288	TOTAL

TABLE 1 — DATA

TABLE 2 — MALE LIFE TABLE

x	nq_x	l_x	nd_x	nL_x	nm_x	na_x	T_x	r_x	$\mathring{e}_x$	nM_x	x
0	0.023728	100000	2373	98280	0.024143	0.2752	6749552	0.0038	67.496	0.024214	0
1	0.005673	97627	554	388916	0.001424	1.1238	6651272	0.0038	68.129	0.001429	1
5	0.002853	97073	277	484675	0.000571	2.5000	6262356	0.0171	64.512	0.000574	5
10	0.002654	96796	257	483417	0.000531	2.7998	5777681	0.0374	59.689	0.000525	10
15	0.006699	96540	647	481212	0.001344	2.7025	5294264	0.0299	54.840	0.001336	15
20	0.009236	95893	886	477272	0.001856	2.5249	4813053	0.0000	50.192	0.001856	20
25	0.007923	95007	753	473149	0.001591	2.4937	4335781	0.0000	45.636	0.001591	25
30	0.009155	94254	863	469183	0.001839	2.5795	3862632	0.0014	40.981	0.001839	30
35	0.011586	93392	1082	464406	0.002330	2.6422	3393448	0.0117	36.336	0.002326	35
40	0.017348	92310	1601	457872	0.003497	2.7046	2929042	0.0087	31.731	0.003491	40
45	0.029268	90708	2655	447472	0.005933	2.7143	2471170	0.0195	27.243	0.005907	45
50	0.049202	88053	4332	430269	0.010069	2.6925	2023697	0.0244	22.983	0.010017	50
55	0.079525	83721	6658	403123	0.016516	2.6747	1593428	0.0229	19.033	0.016436	55
60	0.128683	77063	9917	361748	0.027413	2.6235	1190305	0.0200	15.446	0.027315	60
65	0.186737	67146	12539	305514	0.041041	2.5901	828557	0.0200	12.340	0.040897	65
70	0.280906	54608	15340	235238	0.065209	2.5358	523043	0.0200	9.578	0.064992	70
75	0.386400	39268	15173	157949	0.096063	2.4699	287805	0.0200	7.329	0.095744	75
80	0.545502	24095	13144	85981	0.152867	2.4331	129856	0.0200	5.389	0.152333	80
85+	1.000000	10951	10951	43875	0.249598	4.0064	43875	0.0200	4.006	0.257686	85+

TABLE 3 — FEMALE LIFE TABLE

x	nq_x	l_x	nd_x	nL_x	nm_x	na_x	T_x	r_x	$\mathring{e}_x$	nM_x	x
0	0.019193	100000	1919	98612	0.019463	0.2768	7334881	0.0033	73.349	0.019512	0
1	0.004631	98081	454	391017	0.001162	1.1253	7236269	0.0033	73.779	0.001166	1
5	0.001880	97627	184	487674	0.000376	2.5000	6845252	0.0173	70.117	0.000379	5
10	0.001795	97443	175	486793	0.000359	2.5858	6357578	0.0384	65.244	0.000358	10
15	0.002627	97268	256	485730	0.000526	2.6096	5870785	0.0346	60.357	0.000524	15
20	0.003188	97013	309	484313	0.000639	2.5742	5385056	0.0000	55.509	0.000639	20
25	0.003781	96703	366	482642	0.000758	2.6088	4900743	0.0000	50.678	0.000758	25
30	0.005193	96338	500	480518	0.001041	2.6609	4418101	0.0000	45.861	0.001041	30
35	0.007847	95837	752	477440	0.001575	2.6773	3937583	0.0077	41.086	0.001573	35
40	0.011992	95085	1140	472787	0.002412	2.6851	3460142	0.0130	36.390	0.002406	40
45	0.018791	93945	1765	465619	0.003791	2.6739	2987355	0.0264	31.799	0.003773	45
50	0.028360	92180	2614	454790	0.005748	2.6631	2521736	0.0212	27.357	0.005727	50
55	0.042563	89566	3812	438983	0.008684	2.6799	2066946	0.0098	23.077	0.008667	55
60	0.068875	85753	5906	415013	0.014232	2.6713	1627963	0.0269	18.984	0.014154	60
65	0.108579	79847	8670	379068	0.022871	2.6738	1212950	0.0269	15.191	0.022734	65
70	0.184600	71177	13139	324688	0.040468	2.6256	833882	0.0269	11.716	0.040241	70
75	0.285828	58038	16589	250002	0.066355	2.5774	509194	0.0269	8.773	0.065972	75
80	0.465726	41449	19304	160143	0.120542	2.5600	259192	0.0269	6.253	0.119715	80
85+	*1.000000	22145	22145	99048	0.223580	4.4727	99048	0.0269	4.473	0.221101	85+

TABLE 4 — OBSERVED AND PROJECTED VITAL RATES

	OBSERVED POPULATION BOTH SEXES	MALES	FEMALES	PROJECTED POPULATION 1962 MALES	FEMALES	1967 MALES	FEMALES	1972 MALES	FEMALES	STABLE POPULATION MALES	FEMALES
RATES PER THOUSAND											
Birth	22.65	22.99	22.29	21.67	20.90	22.49	21.60	24.02	23.00	25.64	24.40
Death	8.81	9.76	7.84	9.97	8.25	10.24	8.69	10.41	8.92	8.70	7.46
Increase	13.84	13.24	14.46	11.70	12.65	12.26	12.91	13.61	14.08		16.9374
PERCENTAGE											
under 15	29.55	29.84	29.25	30.12	29.32	29.70	28.74	29.96	28.86	32.95	31.55
15-64	62.00	62.79	61.19	62.54	60.63	62.81	60.96	62.38	60.87	60.90	60.03
65 and over	8.45	7.37	9.56	7.35	10.04	7.49	10.30	7.66	10.27	6.15	8.43
DEP. RATIO X 100	61.29	59.26	63.43	59.91	64.92	59.21	64.03	60.32	64.28	64.22	66.59

TABLE 1 — DATA

AGE AT LAST BIRTHDAY	BOTH SEXES	MALES Number	%	FEMALES Number	%	BIRTHS BY AGE OF MOTHER	DEATHS BOTH SEXES	MALES	FEMALES	AGE AT LAST BIRTHDAY
0	224723	115252	2.2	109471	2.2	0	4742	2713	2029	0
1-4	867262	444243	8.6	423019	8.3	0	987	547	440	1-4
5-9	1021307	521685	10.0	499622	9.8	0	483	284	199	5-9
10-14	980655	502358	9.7	478297	9.4	62	400	254	146	10-14
15-19	770342	394145	7.6	376197	7.4	17028	702	520	182	15-19
20-24	670558	346782	6.7	323776	6.4	71999	751	562	189	20-24
25-29	654897	342049	6.6	312848	6.2	68128	729	502	227	25-29
30-34	747164	391960	7.5	355204	7.0	45437	1030	682	348	30-34
35-39	755117	387703	7.5	367414	7.2	23206	1450	891	559	35-39
40-44	660616	334503	6.4	326113	6.4	6125	1990	1234	756	40-44
45-49	651414	332760	6.4	318654	6.3	442	3145	1945	1200	45-49
50-54	553491	286411	5.5	267080	5.3	2	4280	2830	1450	50-54
55-59	459890	234027	4.5	225863	4.4	0	5764	3891	1873	55-59
60-64	388767	184346	3.6	204421	4.0	0	7619	4871	2748	60-64
65-69	331734	148581	2.9	183153	3.6	0	10462	6367	4095	65-69
70-74	261279	115856	2.2	145423	2.9		12593	7251	5342	70-74
75-79	155029	63994	1.2	91035	1.8		12304	6420	5884	75-79
80-84	83117	32090	0.6	51027	1.0	119038 M.	10001	4565	5436	80-84
85+	37658	13540	0.3	24118	0.5	113391 F.	9447	3729	5718	85+
TOTAL	10275020	5192285		5082735		232429	88879	50058	38821	TOTAL

TABLE 2 — MALE LIFE TABLE

x	nq_x	l_x	nd_x	nL_x	nm_x	na_x	T_x	r_x	$\dot{e}_x$	nM_x	x
0	0.023089	100000	2309	98296	0.023490	0.2620	6767056	0.0027	67.671	0.023540	0
1	0.004893	97691	478	389384	0.001228	1.1119	6668760	0.0027	68.264	0.001231	1
5	0.002712	97213	264	485406	0.000543	2.5000	6279377	0.0101	64.594	0.000544	5
10	0.002547	96949	247	484208	0.000510	2.8174	5793970	0.0273	59.763	0.000506	10
15	0.006618	96702	640	482022	0.001328	2.6720	5309763	0.0359	54.908	0.001319	15
20	0.008072	96062	775	478386	0.001621	2.5152	4827740	0.0126	50.256	0.001621	20
25	0.007311	95287	697	474703	0.001468	2.5132	4349355	0.0000	45.645	0.001468	25
30	0.008664	94590	819	470982	0.001740	2.5960	3874652	0.0000	40.962	0.001740	30
35	0.011456	93771	1074	466352	0.002304	2.6706	3403671	0.0134	36.298	0.002298	35
40	0.018331	92697	1699	459559	0.003697	2.6907	2937319	0.0115	31.687	0.003689	40
45	0.028897	90997	2630	448953	0.005857	2.7054	2477760	0.0093	27.229	0.005845	45
50	0.048568	88368	4292	431971	0.009936	2.7007	2028807	0.0248	22.959	0.009881	50
55	0.080441	84076	6763	404587	0.016716	2.6649	1596836	0.0269	18.993	0.016626	55
60	0.124760	77313	9646	363786	0.026514	2.6384	1192249	0.0177	15.421	0.026423	60
65	0.194667	67667	13173	306482	0.042980	2.5818	828464	0.0177	12.243	0.042852	65
70	0.271863	54495	14815	236006	0.062774	2.5385	521982	0.0177	9.579	0.062586	70
75	0.400948	39680	15909	158122	0.100615	2.4684	285976	0.0177	7.207	0.100322	75
80	0.521891	23770	12405	86890	0.142771	2.4237	127854	0.0177	5.379	0.142257	80
85+	*1.000000	11365	11365	40964	0.277433	3.6045	40964	0.0177	3.604	0.275406	85+

TABLE 3 — FEMALE LIFE TABLE

x	nq_x	l_x	nd_x	nL_x	nm_x	na_x	T_x	r_x	$\dot{e}_x$	nM_x	x
0	0.018250	100000	1825	98668	0.018496	0.2700	7386749	0.0027	73.867	0.018535	0
1	0.004137	98175	406	391530	0.001037	1.1189	7288081	0.0027	74.236	0.001040	1
5	0.001983	97769	194	488360	0.000397	2.5000	6896551	0.0102	70.539	0.000398	5
10	0.001528	97575	149	487511	0.000306	2.5595	6408192	0.0280	65.675	0.000305	10
15	0.002427	97426	236	486567	0.000486	2.6186	5920680	0.0386	60.771	0.000484	15
20	0.002919	97189	284	485262	0.000585	2.5841	5434114	0.0178	55.913	0.000584	20
25	0.003622	96906	351	483691	0.000726	2.6117	4948852	0.0000	51.069	0.000726	25
30	0.004887	96555	472	481673	0.000980	2.6670	4465162	0.0000	46.245	0.000980	30
35	0.007590	96083	729	478722	0.001523	2.6800	3983489	0.0070	41.459	0.001521	35
40	0.011557	95354	1102	474229	0.002324	2.6956	3504766	0.0118	36.755	0.002318	40
45	0.018717	94252	1764	467137	0.003776	2.6641	3030537	0.0162	32.154	0.003766	45
50	0.026936	92488	2491	456608	0.005456	2.6597	2563400	0.0288	27.716	0.005429	50
55	0.040823	89996	3674	441456	0.008322	2.6795	2106793	0.0180	23.410	0.008293	55
60	0.065527	86322	5656	418500	0.013516	2.6819	1665336	0.0257	19.292	0.013443	60
65	0.106771	80666	8613	383169	0.022478	2.6593	1246837	0.0257	15.457	0.022358	65
70	0.169888	72053	12241	331366	0.036941	2.6391	863667	0.0257	11.987	0.036734	70
75	0.280672	59812	16788	258363	0.064977	2.5757	532301	0.0257	8.900	0.064635	75
80	0.426250	43025	18339	170920	0.107297	2.5897	273938	0.0257	6.367	0.106531	80
85+	*1.000000	24685	24685	103018	0.239623	4.1732	103018	0.0257	4.173	0.237084	85+

TABLE 4 — OBSERVED AND PROJECTED VITAL RATES

	OBSERVED POPULATION BOTH SEXES	MALES	FEMALES	PROJECTED POPULATION 1965 MALES	FEMALES	1970 MALES	FEMALES	1975 MALES	FEMALES	STABLE POPULATION MALES	FEMALES
RATES PER THOUSAND											
Birth	22.62	22.93	22.31	22.63	21.88	24.00	23.10	25.07	24.05	26.55	25.28
Death	8.65	9.64	7.64	9.85	8.12	10.01	8.43	10.12	8.62	8.29	7.01
Increase	13.97	13.29	14.67	12.77	13.76	13.99	14.67	14.95	15.43		18.265
PERCENTAGE											
under 15	30.11	30.50	29.72	30.20	29.31	30.40	29.39	31.04	29.96	33.85	32.4
15-64	61.43	62.30	60.55	62.63	60.62	62.30	60.50	61.39	59.81	60.36	59.4
65 and over	8.46	7.20	9.73	7.18	10.07	7.30	10.11	7.57	10.23	5.79	8.1
DEP. RATIO X 100	62.78	60.52	65.15	59.67	64.97	60.52	65.28	62.89	67.20	65.67	68.1

AGE LAST BHDAY	1965 BOTH SEXES	1965 MALES	1965 FEMALES	1970 BOTH SEXES	1970 MALES	1970 FEMALES	1975 BOTH SEXES	1975 MALES	1975 FEMALES	AGE AT LAST BIRTHDAY	
0-4	1167	596	571	1277	652	625	1441	736	705	0-4	**TABLE 5**
5-9	1087	557	530	1162	593	569	1271	649	622	5-9	POPULATION
10-14	1019	520	499	1086	556	530	1160	592	568	10-14	PROJECTED
15-19	977	500	477	1016	518	498	1082	553	529	15-19	WITH
20-24	766	391	375	972	496	476	1010	514	496	20-24	FIXED
25-29	667	344	323	762	388	374	967	492	475	25-29	AGE-
30-34	651	339	312	662	341	321	757	385	372	30-34	SPECIFIC
35-39	741	388	353	646	336	310	657	338	319	35-39	BIRTH
40-44	746	382	364	732	382	350	638	331	307	40-44	AND
45-49	648	327	321	732	373	359	718	374	344	45-49	DEATH
50-54	631	320	311	628	314	314	709	359	350	50-54	RATES
55-59	526	268	258	601	300	301	598	294	304	55-59	(IN 1000's)
60-64	424	210	214	486	241	245	555	270	285	60-64	
65-69	342	155	187	373	177	196	427	203	224	65-69	
70-74	272	114	158	282	120	162	307	137	170	70-74	
75-79	191	78	113	200	77	123	206	80	126	75-79	
80-84	95	35	60	118	43	75	124	42	82	80-84	
85+	46	15	31	53	17	36	65	20	45	85+	
TOTAL	10996	5539	5457	11788	5924	5864	12692	6369	6323	TOTAL	

STANDARD COUNTRIES:

STANDARDIZED RATES PER THOUSAND

	ENGLAND AND WALES 1961 BOTH SEXES	MALES	FEMALES	UNITED STATES 1960 BOTH SEXES	MALES	FEMALES	MEXICO 1960 BOTH SEXES	MALES	FEMALES	
Birth	22.08	21.95*	20.87	22.44	20.78*	21.57	26.32	19.30*	25.62	**TABLE 6** STANDARDIZED RATES
Death	11.66	12.43*	11.02	9.52	10.79*	8.10	4.89	8.33*	3.87	
Increase	10.41	9.52*	9.85	12.91	9.99*	13.47	21.43	10.97*	21.75	

	OBSERVED POP. MALES	FEMALES	STATIONARY POP. MALES	FEMALES	STABLE POP. MALES	FEMALES	OBSERVED BIRTHS	NET MATERNITY FUNCTION	BIRTHS IN STABLE POP.	
	30.85813	32.24756	36.39683	39.01628	28.01128	29.60526	27.62393	27.48917	26.87102	**TABLE 7** MOMENTS AND CUMULANTS
	445.3610	491.0173	491.8030	549.6081	417.0514	467.9356	34.59821	32.79148	30.72717	
	3977.780	4457.542	2337.180	2062.168	5386.526	6274.464	102.0413	112.5265	112.9677	
	-156558.	-206357.	-234547.	-315867.	-86769.	-122619.	-383.349	-111.699	67.298	
	0.179120	0.167842	0.045921	0.025615	0.399990	0.384233	0.251415	0.359109	0.439887	
	2.210684	2.144096	2.030278	1.954322	2.501134	2.440003	2.679752	2.896121	3.071278	
	-0.069183	-0.062086	-0.017517	-0.009366	-0.156393	-0.145320	-0.145891	-0.231144	-0.314051	

VITAL STATISTICS

		THOMPSON AGE RANGE	NRR	1000r	INTERVAL	BOURGEOIS-PICHAT AGE RANGE	NRR	1000b	1000d	1000r	COALE	
R	1.700		1.52	15.64	27.43	5-29	2.02	24.94	-1.11	26.05	IBR	**TABLE 8** RATES FROM AGE DISTRIBUTIONS AND VITAL STATISTICS (Females)
R	1.643	0-4	1.52	15.64	27.43	5-29	2.02	24.94	-1.11	26.05	IDR	
R	3.484	5-9	1.47	14.09	27.39	30-54	1.37	22.22	10.59	11.63	IRI	
GENERATION	27.177	10-14	1.43	12.99	27.34	55-79	1.30	17.62	7.98	9.64	K1	
X RATIO	104.980	15-19	1.16	5.46	27.25	*50-74	1.41	21.88	9.03	12.85	K2	

ORIGINAL MATRIX SUB-DIAGONAL	ALTERNATIVE FIRST ROWS Projection	Integral	FIRST STABLE MATRIX % IN STABLE POPULATION	FISHER VALUES	REPRODUCTIVE VALUES	SECOND STABLE MATRIX Z₂ FIRST COLUMN	FIRST ROW	
0.99625	0.00000	0.00000	11.850	1.068	568440	0.1783+0.0759	0.1783+0.0759	**TABLE 9** LESLIE MATRIX AND ITS SPECTRAL COMPONENTS (Females)
0.99826	0.00015	0.00000	10.773	1.174	586668	0.1599-0.1492	0.0026+0.1717	
0.99806	0.05417	0.00032	9.814	1.289	616446	-0.0809-0.2337	-0.1380+0.0636	
0.99732	0.31931	0.11330	8.938	1.357	510558	-0.2786-0.0235	-0.1106-0.0928	
0.99676	0.52544	0.55664	8.135	1.149	372162	-0.1518+0.2770	-0.0221-0.1471	
0.99583	0.41270	0.54511	7.399	0.701	219294	0.2164+0.2835	0.0173-0.1104	
0.99387	0.22801	0.32020	6.724	0.329	116842	0.3913-0.0935	0.0218-0.0571	
0.99061	0.09777	0.15810	6.098	0.118	43275	0.0824-0.4453	0.0133-0.0203	
0.98505	0.02409	0.04701	5.513	0.025	8132	-0.4193-0.2871	0.0037-0.0040	
0.97746	0.00167	0.00347	4.955	0.002	520	-0.4825+0.2978	0.0003-0.0003	
0.96682	0.00001	0.00002	4.420	0.000	2	0.0848+0.6220	0.0000-0.0000	
0.81798			15.380					

OBSERVED POPUL. (IN 100's)	CONTRIBUTIONS OF ROOTS (IN 100's) r₁	r₂, r₃	r₄-r₁₁	AGE-SP. BIRTH RATES	NET MATERNITY FUNCTION	COEFF. OF MATRIX EQUATION	PARAMETERS		INTEGRAL	MATRIX	EXP. INCREASE x	e^{(x+2½)r}	
5325	5326	20	-21	0.0000	0.0000	0.0000	L(1)		1.09563	1.09584	0	1.0467	**TABLE 10** AGE ANALYSIS AND MISCELLANEOUS RESULTS (Females)
4996	4842	225	-70	0.0000	0.0000	0.0002	L(2)		0.35265	0.35792	50	2.6089	
4783	4411	181	191	0.0001	0.0003	0.0539			0.83882	0.80703	55	2.8583	
3762	4017	-122	-134	0.0221	0.1074	0.3169	R(1)		0.01827	0.01830	60	3.1317	
3238	3656	-342	-76	0.1085	0.5264	0.5202	R(2)		-0.01888	-0.02492	65	3.4311	
3128	3325	-158	-39	0.1062	0.5139	0.4072			0.23456	-0.23067	70	3.7592	
3552	3022	291	239	0.0624	0.3006	0.2240	C(1)			44944	75	4.1187	
3674	2741	467	467	0.0308	0.1475	0.0955	C(2)			25817	80	4.5126	
3261	2478	57	727	0.0092	0.0435	0.0233				47624	85	4.9441	
3187	2227	-533	1492	0.0007	0.0032	0.0016	2P/Y		26.7867	27.2386	90	5.4169	
2671	1987	-549	1233	0.0000	0.0000	0.0000	DELTA	7.2845			95	5.9349	
9250	6912										100	6.5024	

TABLE 1 — DATA

AGE AT LAST BIRTHDAY	POPULATION BOTH SEXES	MALES Number	MALES %	FEMALES Number	FEMALES %	BIRTHS BY AGE OF MOTHER	DEATHS BOTH SEXES	DEATHS MALES	DEATHS FEMALES	AGE AT LAST BIRTHDAY
0	230853	118559	2.2	112294	2.1	0	4607	2636	1971	0
1-4	913391	467246	8.5	446145	8.2	0	875	467	408	1-4
5-9	1081223	553627	10.1	527596	9.8	0	466	276	190	5-9
10-14	1033164	528450	9.6	504714	9.3	87	398	265	133	10-14
15-19	936848	480709	8.7	456139	8.4	20914	781	562	219	15-19
20-24	738566	379196	6.9	359370	6.6	74400	842	618	224	20-24
25-29	678978	350476	6.4	328502	6.1	69266	751	511	240	25-29
30-34	711735	371086	6.7	340649	6.3	41971	946	613	333	30-34
35-39	765250	396193	7.2	369057	6.8	22075	1490	921	569	35-39
40-44	731983	372550	6.6	359433	6.6	6617	2161	1312	849	40-44
45-49	654895	331267	6.0	323628	6.0	359	3296	2106	1190	45-49
50-54	603730	309618	5.6	294112	5.4	0	4771	3132	1639	50-54
55-59	492535	252388	4.6	240147	4.4	0	6237	4198	2039	55-59
60-64	417139	202895	3.7	214244	4.0	0	8442	5480	2962	60-64
65-69	333975	148063	2.7	185912	3.4	0	10399	6421	3978	65-69
70-74	273045	118447	2.2	154598	2.9		13244	7496	5748	70-74
75-79	180008	74549	1.4	105459	1.9		13792	7220	6572	75-79
80-84	91032	34707	0.6	56325	1.0	120710 M.	11080	5014	6066	80-84
85+	47899	16440	0.3	31459	0.6	114979 F.	10316	3964	6352	85+
TOTAL	10916249	5506466		5409783		235689	94894	53212	41682	TOTAL

TABLE 2 — MALE LIFE TABLE

x	nq_x	l_x	nd_x	nL_x	nm_x	na_x	T_x	r_x	$\overset{\circ}{e}_x$	nM_x
0	0.021856	100000	2186	98352	0.022222	0.2458	6785977	0.0006	67.860	0.022234
1	0.003983	97814	390	390127	0.000999	1.0988	6687625	0.0006	68.371	0.000999
5	0.002486	97425	242	486519	0.000498	2.5000	6297498	0.0097	64.640	0.000499
10	0.002514	97183	244	485370	0.000503	2.7785	5810979	0.0135	59.794	0.000501
15	0.005867	96938	569	483382	0.001177	2.6973	5325609	0.0321	54.938	0.001169
20	0.008125	96370	783	479916	0.001632	2.5334	4842227	0.0301	50.246	0.001630
25	0.007264	95587	694	476196	0.001458	2.4993	4362311	0.0006	45.637	0.001458
30	0.008227	94892	781	472591	0.001652	2.6051	3886114	0.0000	40.953	0.001652
35	0.011560	94112	1088	468015	0.002325	2.6627	3413523	0.0000	36.271	0.002325
40	0.017526	93024	1630	461413	0.003533	2.7278	2945508	0.0141	31.664	0.003522
45	0.031409	91393	2871	450365	0.006374	2.7003	2484094	0.0120	27.180	0.006357
50	0.049587	88523	4390	432452	0.010150	2.6850	2033730	0.0165	22.974	0.010116
55	0.080453	84133	6769	404883	0.016718	2.6683	1601278	0.0249	19.033	0.016633
60	0.127399	77364	9856	363539	0.027112	2.6378	1196395	0.0194	15.464	0.027009
65	0.196807	67508	13286	305372	0.043508	2.5787	832856	0.0194	12.337	0.043367
70	0.274371	54222	14877	234346	0.063483	2.5288	527484	0.0194	9.728	0.063286
75	0.389905	39345	15341	157896	0.097158	2.4689	293138	0.0194	7.450	0.096849
80	0.524337	24004	12586	86861	0.144902	2.4351	135242	0.0194	5.634	0.144466
85+	1.000000	11418	11418	48381	0.235999	4.2373	48381	0.0194	4.237	0.241120

TABLE 3 — FEMALE LIFE TABLE

x	nq_x	l_x	nd_x	nL_x	nm_x	na_x	T_x	r_x	$\overset{\circ}{e}_x$	nM_x
0	0.017328	100000	1733	98721	0.017552	0.2620	7417194	0.0000	74.172	0.017552
1	0.003648	98267	359	392033	0.000914	1.1119	7318473	0.0000	74.475	0.000914
5	0.001794	97909	176	489105	0.000359	2.5000	6926440	0.0096	70.744	0.000360
10	0.001319	97733	129	488356	0.000264	2.5965	6437335	0.0142	65.866	0.000264
15	0.002410	97604	235	487469	0.000480	2.6549	5948979	0.0335	60.950	0.000480
20	0.003120	97369	304	486110	0.000625	2.5815	5461510	0.0322	56.091	0.000623
25	0.003648	97065	354	484475	0.000731	2.5987	4975400	0.0046	51.258	0.000731
30	0.004877	96711	472	482456	0.000978	2.6701	4490924	0.0000	46.437	0.000978
35	0.007681	96239	739	479485	0.001542	2.6838	4008468	0.0000	41.651	0.001542
40	0.011769	95500	1124	474896	0.002367	2.6828	3528983	0.0107	36.953	0.002362
45	0.018283	94376	1725	467866	0.003688	2.6733	3054087	0.0163	32.361	0.003677
50	0.027623	92651	2559	457281	0.005597	2.6662	2586221	0.0241	27.914	0.005573
55	0.041817	90091	3767	441715	0.008529	2.6795	2128940	0.0227	23.631	0.008491
60	0.067253	86324	5806	418039	0.013888	2.6607	1687225	0.0236	19.545	0.013825
65	0.102390	80519	8244	383357	0.021506	2.6668	1269186	0.0236	15.763	0.021397
70	0.171666	72274	12407	332027	0.037368	2.6349	885829	0.0236	12.256	0.037180
75	0.271886	59867	16277	259917	0.062624	2.5782	553802	0.0236	9.251	0.062318
80	0.424880	43590	18521	171216	0.108171	2.5989	293885	0.0236	6.742	0.107696
85+	1.000000	25070	25070	122669	0.204368	4.8931	122669	0.0236	4.893	0.201915

TABLE 4 — OBSERVED AND PROJECTED VITAL RATES

	OBSERVED POPULATION BOTH SEXES	MALES	FEMALES	PROJECTED POPULATION 1968 MALES	FEMALES	1973 MALES	FEMALES	1978 MALES	FEMALES	STABLE POPULATION MALES	FEMAL
RATES PER THOUSAND											
Birth	21.59	21.92	21.25	22.75	21.93	23.98	23.02	24.54	23.49	25.32	24.0
Death	8.69	9.66	7.70	9.88	8.17	10.03	8.44	10.06	8.51	8.65	7.3
Increase	12.90	12.26	13.55	12.87	13.76	13.96	14.58	14.49	14.98		16.670
PERCENTAGE											
under 15	29.85	30.29	29.41	29.95	28.94	30.19	29.10	30.86	29.69	32.71	31.2
15-64	61.67	62.59	60.73	62.82	60.91	62.41	60.71	61.43	59.86	61.07	59.9
65 and over	8.48	7.12	9.87	7.23	10.15	7.40	10.19	7.71	10.45	6.22	8.8
DEP. RATIO X 100	62.16	59.78	64.67	59.20	64.19	60.24	64.71	62.79	67.05	63.74	66.7

TABLE 1 — DATA

AGE AT LAST BIRTHDAY	POPULATION BOTH SEXES	MALES Number	%	FEMALES Number	%	BIRTHS BY AGE OF MOTHER	DEATHS BOTH SEXES	MALES	FEMALES	AGE AT LAST BIRTHDAY
0	228993	117737	2.1	111256	2.0	0	4368	2509	1859	0
1-4	922819	472776	8.4	450043	8.2	0	923	509	414	1-4
5-9	1109294	567793	10.1	541501	9.8	0	512	302	210	5-9
10-14	1049057	536587	9.6	512470	9.3	94	449	285	164	10-14
15-19	978392	502242	8.9	476150	8.6	22163	852	587	265	15-19
20-24	776261	398801	7.1	377460	6.8	71691	919	683	236	20-24
25-29	701030	360541	6.4	340489	6.2	67379	719	483	236	25-29
30-34	700566	364549	6.5	336017	6.1	39799	997	671	326	30-34
35-39	767992	398627	7.1	369365	6.7	21566	1511	921	590	35-39
40-44	753604	384966	6.9	368638	6.7	6082	2416	1533	883	40-44
45-49	651330	328073	5.8	323257	5.9	373	3319	2043	1276	45-49
50-54	621976	317691	5.7	304285	5.5	2	4991	3267	1724	50-54
55-59	509986	260358	4.6	249628	4.5	0	6695	4543	2152	55-59
60-64	426196	209305	3.7	216891	3.9	0	8918	5903	3015	60-64
65-69	334452	148487	2.6	185965	3.4	0	10683	6573	4110	65-69
70-74	273856	117171	2.1	156685	2.8		14082	7978	6104	70-74
75-79	187732	77291	1.4	110441	2.0		14871	7643	7228	75-79
80-84	93276	35517	0.6	57759	1.0	118062 M.	12216	5510	6706	80-84
85+	48697	16508	0.3	32189	0.6	111087 F.	11153	4303	6850	85+
TOTAL	11135509	5615020		5520489		229149	100594	56246	44348	TOTAL

TABLE 2 — MALE LIFE TABLE

x	$_nq_x$	l_x	$_nd_x$	$_nL_x$	$_nm_x$	$_na_x$	T_x	r_x	$\mathring{e}_x$	$_nM_x$	x
0	0.020979	100000	2098	98444	0.021310	0.2585	6746079	0.0000	67.461	0.021310	0
1	0.004293	97902	420	390393	0.001077	1.1089	6647635	0.0000	67.901	0.001077	1
5	0.002652	97482	259	486763	0.000531	2.5000	6257241	0.0089	64.189	0.000532	5
10	0.002660	97223	259	485535	0.000533	2.7497	5770479	0.0116	59.353	0.000531	10
15	0.005863	96965	569	483520	0.001176	2.7066	5284944	0.0285	54.504	0.001169	15
20	0.008533	96396	823	479939	0.001714	2.5176	4801424	0.0316	49.809	0.001713	20
25	0.006677	95574	638	476283	0.001340	2.5155	4321485	0.0074	45.216	0.001340	25
30	0.009163	94936	870	472595	0.001841	2.6060	3845203	0.0000	40.503	0.001841	30
35	0.011491	94066	1081	467828	0.002310	2.6870	3372607	0.0154	35.854	0.002310	35
40	0.019791	92985	1840	460682	0.003995	2.6952	2904779	0.0127	31.239	0.003982	40
45	0.030775	91144	2805	449253	0.006244	2.6938	2444097	0.0122	26.816	0.006227	45
50	0.050363	88339	4449	431462	0.010312	2.6995	1994844	0.0236	22.582	0.010284	50
55	0.084229	83890	7066	402982	0.017534	2.6691	1563381	0.0167	18.636	0.017449	55
60	0.132566	76824	10184	359972	0.028292	2.6287	1160399	0.0167	15.105	0.028203	60
65	0.200478	66640	13360	300920	0.044397	2.5837	800427	0.0167	12.011	0.044266	65
70	0.291943	53280	15555	227843	0.068270	2.5211	499507	0.0167	9.375	0.068089	70
75	0.395982	37725	14939	150660	0.099155	2.4584	271664	0.0167	7.201	0.098886	75
80	0.551837	22787	12575	80820	0.155587	2.4217	121004	0.0167	5.310	0.155137	80
85+	1.000000	10212	10212	40184	0.254139	3.9349	40184	0.0167	3.935	0.260661	85+

TABLE 3 — FEMALE LIFE TABLE

x	$_nq_x$	l_x	$_nd_x$	$_nL_x$	$_nm_x$	$_na_x$	T_x	r_x	$\mathring{e}_x$	$_nM_x$	x
0	0.016507	100000	1651	98792	0.016709	0.2680	7382099	0.0000	73.821	0.016709	0
1	0.003670	98349	361	392357	0.000920	1.1172	7283308	0.0000	74.056	0.000920	1
5	0.001933	97988	189	489468	0.000387	2.5000	6890951	0.0086	70.324	0.000388	5
10	0.001601	97799	157	488621	0.000320	2.6103	6401483	0.0125	65.456	0.000320	10
15	0.002789	97642	272	487562	0.000558	2.6131	5912862	0.0301	60.556	0.000557	15
20	0.003126	97370	304	486103	0.000626	2.5438	5425300	0.0329	55.718	0.000625	20
25	0.003464	97066	336	484522	0.000694	2.6015	4939198	0.0109	50.885	0.000693	25
30	0.004840	96729	468	482566	0.000970	2.6912	4454676	0.0000	46.053	0.000970	30
35	0.007957	96261	766	479532	0.001597	2.6827	3972109	0.0000	41.264	0.001597	35
40	0.011937	95495	1140	474853	0.002401	2.6981	3492578	0.0108	36.573	0.002395	40
45	0.019607	94355	1850	467455	0.003958	2.6638	3017725	0.0152	31.983	0.003947	45
50	0.028052	92505	2595	456449	0.005685	2.6580	2550270	0.0199	27.569	0.005666	50
55	0.042458	89910	3817	440680	0.008663	2.6759	2093821	0.0248	23.288	0.008621	55
60	0.067588	86093	5819	416888	0.013958	2.6667	1653140	0.0207	19.202	0.013901	60
65	0.105560	80274	8474	381653	0.022203	2.6730	1236253	0.0207	15.400	0.022101	65
70	0.179073	71800	12857	328575	0.039131	2.6335	854600	0.0207	11.902	0.038957	70
75	0.283560	58943	16714	254250	0.065738	2.5790	526025	0.0207	8.924	0.065447	75
80	0.454582	42229	19197	164470	0.116718	2.5686	271775	0.0207	6.436	0.116104	80
85+	*1.000000	23032	23032	107305	0.214645	4.6589	107305	0.0207	4.659	0.212806	85+

TABLE 4 — OBSERVED AND PROJECTED VITAL RATES

	OBSERVED POPULATION BOTH SEXES	MALES	FEMALES	PROJECTED POPULATION 1969 MALES	FEMALES	1974 MALES	FEMALES	1979 MALES	FEMALES	STABLE POPULATION MALES	FEMALES
RATES PER THOUSAND											
Birth	20.58	21.03	20.12	22.06	21.01	23.24	22.07	23.78	22.53	23.69	22.38
Death	9.03	10.02	8.03	10.12	8.38	10.24	8.63	10.25	8.65	9.40	8.09
Increase	11.54	11.01	12.09	11.94	12.64	13.01	13.44	13.52	13.88	14.2869	
PERCENTAGE											
under 15	29.73	30.18	29.26	29.65	28.53	29.59	28.30	30.09	28.66	31.16	29.59
15-64	61.85	62.78	60.90	63.22	61.44	63.09	61.56	62.27	60.85	62.17	60.84
65 and over	8.42	7.03	9.84	7.13	10.03	7.32	10.14	7.64	10.48	6.67	9.57
DEP. RATIO X 100	61.68	59.28	64.19	58.19	62.75	58.51	62.45	60.59	64.33	60.85	64.35

TABLE 1 — DATA

AGE AT LAST BIRTHDAY	POPULATION BOTH SEXES	MALES Number	%	FEMALES Number	%	BIRTHS BY AGE OF MOTHER	DEATHS BOTH SEXES	MALES	FEMALES	AGE AT LAST BIRTHDAY
0	221113	113508	2.0	107605	1.9	0	4118	2358	1760	0
1-4	937865	480503	8.4	457362	8.1	0	919	515	404	1-4
5-9	1128888	578911	10.1	549977	9.8	0	433	249	184	5-9
10-14	1066993	545311	9.5	521682	9.3	105	429	276	153	10-14
15-19	1018110	523157	9.1	494953	8.8	23328	950	686	264	15-19
20-24	818727	420443	7.3	398284	7.1	71334	925	681	244	20-24
25-29	725444	374019	6.5	351425	6.2	66031	812	548	264	25-29
30-34	696554	361271	6.3	335283	6.0	36578	917	589	328	30-34
35-39	763586	397510	6.9	366076	6.5	19461	1582	998	584	35-39
40-44	777857	396880	6.9	380977	6.8	5657	2331	1465	866	40-44
45-49	652080	329732	5.8	322348	5.7	358	3286	2000	1286	45-49
50-54	642818	325561	5.7	317257	5.6	2	5241	3481	1760	50-54
55-59	520125	265587	4.6	254538	4.5	0	6692	4508	2184	55-59
60-64	432385	213144	3.7	219241	3.9	0	8644	5750	2894	60-64
65-69	345509	155400	2.7	190109	3.4	0	10890	6733	4157	65-69
70-74	276136	115858	2.0	160278	2.8		13650	7662	5988	70-74
75-79	188252	77395	1.4	110857	2.0		14705	7716	6989	75-79
80-84	98601	37302	0.7	61299	1.1	114466 M.	11942	5291	6651	80-84
85+	48467	16132	0.3	32335	0.6	108388 F.	11249	4264	6985	85+
TOTAL	11359510	5727624		5631886		222854	99715	55770	43945	TOTAL

TABLE 2 — MALE LIFE TABLE

x	nq_x	l_x	nd_x	nL_x	nm_x	na_x	T_x	r_x	$\mathring{e}_x$	nM_x	x
0	0.020460	100000	2046	98488	0.020774	0.2608	6774628	0.0000	67.746	0.020774	0
1	0.004274	97954	419	390607	0.001072	1.1109	6676140	0.0000	68.156	0.001072	1
5	0.002145	97535	209	487154	0.000429	2.5000	6285534	0.0079	64.444	0.000430	5
10	0.002537	97326	247	486103	0.000508	2.8613	5798380	0.0095	59.577	0.000506	10
15	0.006565	97079	637	483914	0.001317	2.6737	5312277	0.0248	54.721	0.001311	15
20	0.008071	96442	778	480277	0.001621	2.5163	4828363	0.0320	50.065	0.001620	20
25	0.007299	95664	698	476571	0.001465	2.4978	4348086	0.0136	45.452	0.001465	25
30	0.008120	94965	771	472998	0.001630	2.6289	3871516	0.0000	40.768	0.001630	30
35	0.012480	94194	1176	468227	0.002511	2.6659	3398517	0.0000	36.080	0.002511	35
40	0.018354	93019	1707	461151	0.003702	2.6909	2930290	0.0148	31.502	0.003691	40
45	0.030007	91311	2740	450316	0.006085	2.7223	2469140	0.0133	27.041	0.006066	45
50	0.052285	88571	4631	432143	0.010716	2.6864	2018824	0.0107	22.793	0.010692	50
55	0.081997	83940	6883	403573	0.017055	2.6566	1586681	0.0247	18.902	0.016974	55
60	0.127233	77058	9804	362100	0.027076	2.6349	1183109	0.0191	15.354	0.026977	60
65	0.196739	67253	13231	304353	0.043474	2.5880	821009	0.0191	12.208	0.043327	65
70	0.284989	54022	15396	232071	0.066340	2.5292	516656	0.0191	9.564	0.066133	70
75	0.398502	38626	15393	153943	0.099990	2.4541	284585	0.0191	7.368	0.099696	75
80	0.516540	23234	12001	84385	0.142219	2.4278	130642	0.0191	5.623	0.141842	80
85+	1.000000	11233	11233	46257	0.242826	4.1182	46257	0.0191	4.118	0.264320	85

TABLE 3 — FEMALE LIFE TABLE

x	nq_x	l_x	nd_x	nL_x	nm_x	na_x	T_x	r_x	$\mathring{e}_x$	nM_x	x
0	0.016162	100000	1616	98814	0.016356	0.2659	7412982	0.0000	74.130	0.016356	
1	0.003524	98384	347	392535	0.000883	1.1153	7314168	0.0000	74.343	0.000883	
5	0.001668	98037	163	489777	0.000334	2.5000	6921633	0.0075	70.602	0.000335	
10	0.001468	97874	144	489029	0.000294	2.6417	6431857	0.0102	65.716	0.000293	
15	0.002672	97730	261	488029	0.000535	2.6238	5942828	0.0265	60.809	0.000533	
20	0.003066	97469	299	486618	0.000614	2.5723	5454799	0.0336	55.965	0.000613	
25	0.003756	97170	365	484973	0.000752	2.5991	4968180	0.0165	51.129	0.000751	
30	0.004880	96805	472	482927	0.000978	2.6767	4483207	0.0000	46.312	0.000978	
35	0.007947	96333	766	479876	0.001595	2.6661	4000280	0.0000	41.526	0.001595	
40	0.011332	95567	1083	475358	0.002278	2.7128	3520404	0.0102	36.837	0.002273	
45	0.019811	94484	1872	468045	0.003999	2.6626	3045046	0.0144	32.228	0.003989	
50	0.027464	92612	2544	457105	0.005564	2.6585	2577001	0.0178	27.826	0.005548	
55	0.042271	90069	3807	441451	0.008625	2.6644	2119896	0.0281	23.536	0.008580	
60	0.064311	86261	5548	418402	0.013259	2.6738	1678445	0.0219	19.458	0.013200	
65	0.104502	80714	8435	383921	0.021971	2.6707	1260043	0.0219	15.611	0.021866	
70	0.172361	72279	12458	331913	0.037534	2.6336	876122	0.0219	12.121	0.037360	
75	0.274583	59821	16426	259350	0.063334	2.5798	544209	0.0219	9.097	0.063045	
80	0.432103	43395	18751	171809	0.109139	2.5913	284859	0.0219	6.564	0.108500	
85+	*1.000000	24644	24644	113050	0.217990	4.5874	113050	0.0219	4.587	0.216020	

TABLE 4 — OBSERVED AND PROJECTED VITAL RATES

	OBSERVED POPULATION BOTH SEXES	MALES	FEMALES	PROJECTED POPULATION 1970 MALES	FEMALES	1975 MALES	FEMALES	1980 MALES	FEMALES	STABLE POPULATION MALES	FEMALES
RATES PER THOUSAND											
Birth	19.62	19.98	19.25	21.18	20.29	22.30	21.28	22.72	21.61	22.25	20.
Death	8.78	9.74	7.80	10.01	8.24	10.20	8.52	10.29	8.64	9.96	8.
Increase	10.84	10.25	11.44	11.17	12.05	12.10	12.75	12.43	12.98		12.29
PERCENTAGE											
under 15	29.53	30.00	29.06	29.15	28.06	28.76	27.60	29.01	27.75	29.72	28.
15-64	62.04	62.98	61.09	63.61	61.83	63.73	62.11	63.08	61.44	62.86	61.
65 and over	8.42	7.02	9.85	7.23	10.12	7.50	10.30	7.91	10.81	7.42	10.
DEP. RATIO X 100	61.18	58.78	63.70	57.20	61.74	56.90	61.02	58.53	62.77	59.08	63.

TABLE 5 — POPULATION PROJECTED WITH FIXED AGE-SPECIFIC BIRTH AND DEATH RATES (IN 1000's)

AGE AT LAST BIRTHDAY	1970 BOTH SEXES	1970 MALES	1970 FEMALES	1975 BOTH SEXES	1975 MALES	1975 FEMALES	1980 BOTH SEXES	1980 MALES	1980 FEMALES	AGE AT LAST BIRTHDAY
0-4	1157	593	564	1293	663	630	1421	728	693	0-4
5-9	1155	592	563	1153	591	562	1288	660	628	5-9
10-14	1127	578	549	1152	590	562	1151	589	562	10-14
15-19	1064	543	521	1123	575	548	1149	588	561	15-19
20-24	1013	519	494	1058	539	519	1117	571	546	20-24
25-29	814	417	397	1007	515	492	1052	535	517	25-29
30-34	721	371	350	809	414	395	1001	511	490	30-34
35-39	691	358	333	715	367	348	803	410	393	35-39
40-44	755	392	363	682	352	330	706	362	344	40-44
45-49	763	388	375	739	382	357	669	344	325	45-49
50-54	631	316	315	738	372	366	716	367	349	50-54
55-59	610	304	306	600	296	304	701	347	354	55-59
60-64	479	238	241	563	273	290	553	265	288	60-64
65-69	380	179	201	421	200	221	495	229	266	65-69
70-74	282	118	164	311	137	174	344	153	191	70-74
75-79	202	77	125	207	79	128	227	91	136	75-79
80-84	115	42	73	125	42	83	128	43	85	80-84
85+	60	20	40	71	23	48	78	23	55	85+
TOTAL	12019	6045	5974	12767	6410	6357	13599	6816	6783	TOTAL

TABLE 6 — STANDARDIZED RATES

STANDARD COUNTRIES: STANDARDIZED RATES PER THOUSAND

	ENGLAND AND WALES 1961 BOTH SEXES	MALES	FEMALES	UNITED STATES 1960 BOTH SEXES	MALES	FEMALES	MEXICO 1960 BOTH SEXES	MALES	FEMALES
Birth	18.79	19.78*	17.72	19.13	18.40*	18.33	22.46	17.53*	21.80
Death	11.61	12.52*	10.82	9.46	10.91*	7.92	4.81	8.56*	3.76
Increase	7.18	7.26*	6.90	9.67	7.48*	10.41	17.65	8.97*	18.04

TABLE 7 — MOMENTS AND CUMULANTS

	OBSERVED POP. MALES	OBSERVED POP. FEMALES	STATIONARY POP. MALES	STATIONARY POP. FEMALES	STABLE POP. MALES	STABLE POP. FEMALES	OBSERVED BIRTHS	NET MATERNITY FUNCTION	BIRTHS IN STABLE POP.
μ	30.69262	32.21150	36.32439	39.07205	30.53527	32.53532	26.95274	27.38721	26.95983
σ^2	445.4041	495.0532	490.9964	552.1561	446.0003	504.5164	35.38898	33.31067	32.04510
κ_3	4315.219	4930.532	2403.375	2118.999	4724.746	5382.370	121.9123	102.1514	103.5103
κ_4	-152883.	-203486.	-230970.	-317883.	-138470.	-198285.	-215.711	-160.552	-52.394
β_1	0.210738	0.200370	0.048799	0.026673	0.251624	0.225901	0.335344	0.282318	0.325598
β_2	2.229361	2.169707	2.041927	1.957336	2.303879	2.220998	2.827759	2.855307	2.948978
κ	-0.080005	-0.073279	-0.018745	-0.009766	-0.097414	-0.083818	-0.204591	-0.201381	-0.246808

TABLE 8 — RATES FROM AGE DISTRIBUTIONS AND VITAL STATISTICS (Females)

VITAL STATISTICS		THOMPSON AGE RANGE	NRR	1000r	INTERVAL	BOURGEOIS-PICHAT AGE RANGE	NRR	1000b	1000d	1000r	COALE	
GRR	1.441										IBR	20.99
NRR	1.397	0-4	1.43	13.31	27.43	5-29	1.85	24.79	1.97	22.82	IDR	8.68
GFR	2.963	5-9	1.50	14.95	27.39	30-54	1.06	14.09	12.03	2.06	IRI	12.31
GENERATION	27.172	10-14	1.47	13.83	27.33	55-79	1.37	19.79	8.01	11.77	K1	0.
SEX RATIO	105.608	15-19	1.44	12.79	27.25	*40-69	1.69	32.23	12.73	19.50	K2	0.

TABLE 9 — LESLIE MATRIX AND ITS SPECTRAL COMPONENTS (Females)

Age Interval	ORIGINAL MATRIX SUB-DIAGONAL	ALTERNATIVE FIRST ROWS Projection	Integral	FIRST STABLE MATRIX % IN STABLE POPULATION	FISHER VALUES	REPRODUCTIVE VALUES	SECOND STABLE MATRIX Z₂ FIRST COLUMN	FIRST ROW
	0.99680	0.00000	0.00000	9.981	1.049	592820	0.1712+0.0740	0.1712+0.0740
	0.99847	0.00024	0.00000	9.355	1.120	615701	0.1617-0.1446	0.0041+0.1603
	0.99796	0.05644	0.00050	8.783	1.192	621924	-0.0738-0.2418	-0.1234+0.0609
	0.99711	0.26970	0.11615	8.242	1.211	599436	-0.2917-0.0402	-0.1016-0.0784
	0.99662	0.43776	0.44137	7.728	1.008	401433	-0.1851+0.2884	-0.0219-0.1275
	0.99578	0.35432	0.46303	7.242	0.615	216000	0.2141+0.3362	0.0164-0.0956
	0.99368	0.19347	0.26885	6.781	0.283	94911	0.4591-0.0618	0.0197-0.0480
	0.99059	0.08110	0.13101	6.336	0.099	36117	0.1586-0.5133	0.0114-0.0164
	0.98462	0.01905	0.03659	5.901	0.020	7627	-0.4616-0.4156	0.0030-0.0031
	0.97663	0.00133	0.00274	5.464	0.001	427	-0.6562+0.2809	0.0002-0.0002
	0.96575	0.00001	0.00002	5.017	0.000	2	-0.0235+0.8132	0.0000-0.0000
+	0.81074			19.170				

TABLE 10 — AGE ANALYSIS AND MISCELLANEOUS RESULTS (Females)

Age Interval	OBSERVED POPUL. (IN 100's)	CONTRIBUTIONS OF ROOTS (IN 100's) r_1	r_2, r_3	$r_4 \cdot r_{11}$	AGE-SP BIRTH RATES	NET MATERNITY FUNCTION	COEFF. OF MATRIX EQUATION	PARAMETERS		INTEGRAL	MATRIX	EXP. INCREASE x	$e^{(x+2\frac{1}{2})r}$
	5650	5648	-133	135	0.0000	0.0000	0.0000	L(1)		1.06340	1.06349	0	1.0312
	5500	5294	255	-50	0.0000	0.0000	0.0002	L(2)		0.35342	0.35978	50	1.9068
	5217	4970	431	-184	0.0001	0.0005	0.0562			0.80630	0.77763	55	2.0277
	4950	4664	74	211	0.0229	0.1119	0.2679	R(1)		0.01229	0.01231	60	2.1563
	3983	4373	-511	121	0.0871	0.4239	0.4335	R(2)		-0.02549	-0.03090	65	2.2930
	3514	4098	-600	16	0.0914	0.4432	0.3497			0.23154	0.22749	70	2.4383
	3353	3837	105	-589	0.0531	0.2562	0.1902	C(1)			56587	75	2.5929
	3661	3585	911	-835	0.0259	0.1241	0.0792	C(2)			-504	80	2.7573
	3810	3339	744	-273	0.0072	0.0343	0.0184				88893	85	2.9321
	3223	3092	-493	625	0.0005	0.0025	0.0013	2P/Y		27.1365	27.6193	90	3.1180
	3173	2839	-1446	1779	0.0000	0.0000	0.0000	DELTA		3.5453		95	3.3157
+	10287	10848										100	3.5259

TABLE 1 — DATA

AGE AT LAST BIRTHDAY	POPULATION BOTH SEXES	MALES Number	%	FEMALES Number	%	BIRTHS BY AGE OF MOTHER	DEATHS BOTH SEXES	MALES	FEMALES	AGE AT LAST BIRTHDAY
0	14193	7151	4.0	7042	4.2	0	653	366	287	0
1-4	47939	24298	13.7	23641	14.3	0	228	117	111	1-4
5-9	52095	26494	15.0	25601	15.4	0	54	19	35	5-9
10-14	43776	22297	12.6	21479	13.0	1	52	29	23	10-14
15-19	36212	18186	10.3	18026	10.9	1925	62	25	37	15-19
20-24	29694	15029	8.5	14665	8.8	4445	70	27	43	20-24
25-29	24593	12580	7.1	12013	7.2	3624	53	22	31	25-29
30-34	19781	10097	5.7	9684	5.8	2136	65	22	43	30-34
35-39	17918	9235	5.2	8683	5.2	1368	54	24	30	35-39
40-44	14446	7722	4.4	6724	4.1	465	76	40	36	40-44
45-49	10780	5919	3.3	4861	2.9	112	99	64	35	45-49
50-54	7959	4255	2.4	3704	2.2	0	86	52	34	50-54
55-59	6296	3443	1.9	2853	1.7	0	92	67	25	55-59
60-64	6299	3684	2.1	2615	1.6	0	196	104	92	60-64
65-69	4318	2660	1.5	1658	1.0	0	131	87	44	65-69
70-74	2843	1717	1.0	1126	0.7		231	152	79	70-74
75-79	2003	1223	0.7	780	0.5		148	98	50	75-79
80-84	1181	726	0.4	455	0.3	7205 M.	141	93	48	80-84
85+	501	308	0.2	193	0.1	6871 F.	104	68	36	85+
TOTAL	342827	177024		165803		14076	2595	1476	1119	TOTAL

TABLE 2 — MALE LIFE TABLE

x	$_nq_x$	l_x	$_nd_x$	$_nL_x$	$_nm_x$	$_na_x$	T_x	r_x	$\mathring{e}_x$	$_nM_x$	x
0	0.049009	100000	4901	96689	0.050687	0.3244	6349057	0.0133	63.491	0.051182	0
1	0.018820	95099	1790	375350	0.004768	1.1804	6252368	0.0133	65.746	0.004815	1
5	0.003489	93309	326	465733	0.000699	2.5000	5877018	0.0326	62.984	0.000717	5
10	0.006509	92984	605	463470	0.001306	2.6064	5411286	0.0365	58.196	0.001301	10
15	0.006870	92379	635	460351	0.001379	2.5711	4947815	0.0380	53.560	0.001375	15
20	0.008957	91744	822	456698	0.001799	2.5401	4487464	0.0352	48.913	0.001797	20
25	0.008721	90922	793	452661	0.001752	2.5413	4030766	0.0379	44.332	0.001749	25
30	0.010863	90129	979	448275	0.002184	2.5777	3578104	0.0288	39.700	0.002179	30
35	0.012992	89150	1158	443127	0.002614	2.7343	3129830	0.0238	35.107	0.002599	35
40	0.025928	87992	2281	434962	0.005245	2.8095	2686703	0.0386	30.534	0.005180	40
45	0.053060	85711	4548	417717	0.010887	2.6174	2251740	0.0498	26.271	0.010813	45
50	0.059695	81163	4845	394232	0.012290	2.6096	1834023	0.0406	22.597	0.012221	50
55	0.093003	76318	7098	364741	0.019460	2.6263	1439791	0.0000	18.866	0.019460	55
60	0.132165	69220	9148	323661	0.028266	2.5472	1075050	0.0123	15.531	0.028230	60
65	0.152670	60072	9171	279378	0.032827	2.7125	751389	0.0123	12.508	0.032707	65
70	0.363474	50900	18501	208570	0.088704	2.5173	472011	0.0123	9.273	0.088526	70
75	0.330482	32399	10707	133556	0.080172	2.3438	263442	0.0123	8.131	0.080131	75
80	0.482727	21692	10471	81564	0.128382	2.5102	129886	0.0123	5.988	0.128099	80
85+	1.000000	11221	11221	48322	0.232206	4.3065	48322	0.0123	4.307	0.220780	85

TABLE 3 — FEMALE LIFE TABLE

x	$_nq_x$	l_x	$_nd_x$	$_nL_x$	$_nm_x$	$_na_x$	T_x	r_x	$\mathring{e}_x$	$_nM_x$	x
0	0.039291	100000	3929	97433	0.040326	0.3466	6491202	0.0148	64.912	0.040755	0
1	0.018379	96071	1766	379365	0.004654	1.2145	6393769	0.0148	66.553	0.004695	1
5	0.006710	94305	633	469944	0.001347	2.5000	6014404	0.0336	63.776	0.001367	5
10	0.005365	93672	503	467173	0.001076	2.6349	5544460	0.0337	59.190	0.001071	10
15	0.010284	93170	958	463629	0.002067	2.6830	5077287	0.0361	54.495	0.002053	15
20	0.014577	92212	1344	457742	0.002936	2.5329	4613658	0.0379	50.033	0.002932	20
25	0.012882	90868	1171	451542	0.002592	2.6118	4155915	0.0384	45.736	0.002581	25
30	0.021988	89697	1972	443624	0.004446	2.5354	3704373	0.0287	41.299	0.004440	30
35	0.017159	87725	1505	434928	0.003461	2.5449	3260749	0.0323	37.170	0.003455	35
40	0.026636	86219	2297	425664	0.005395	2.6344	2825821	0.0527	32.775	0.005354	40
45	0.035587	83923	2987	412428	0.007241	2.5936	2400156	0.0523	28.600	0.007200	45
50	0.044952	80936	3638	395605	0.009195	2.5217	1987729	0.0451	24.559	0.009179	50
55	0.043532	77298	3365	379826	0.008859	3.0194	1592064	0.0198	20.596	0.008763	55
60	0.162689	73933	12028	340513	0.035324	2.5763	1212238	0.0308	16.396	0.035182	60
65	0.125483	61905	7768	290985	0.026696	2.6133	871725	0.0308	14.082	0.026538	65
70	0.300243	54137	16254	230603	0.070486	2.5341	580740	0.0308	10.727	0.070160	70
75	0.275248	37883	10427	162354	0.064225	2.4049	350137	0.0308	9.243	0.064103	75
80	0.418632	27456	11494	108324	0.106106	2.6003	187783	0.0308	6.839	0.105494	80
85+	1.000000	15962	15962	79458	0.200883	4.9780	79458	0.0308	4.978	0.186529	85

TABLE 4 — OBSERVED AND PROJECTED VITAL RATES

	OBSERVED POPULATION BOTH SEXES	MALES	FEMALES	PROJECTED POPULATION 1961 MALES	FEMALES	1966 MALES	FEMALES	1971 MALES	FEMALES	STABLE POPULATION MALES	FEMALES
RATES PER THOUSAND											
Birth	41.06	40.70	41.44	41.36	41.69	41.76	41.79	41.87	41.72	41.48	41.18
Death	7.57	8.34	6.75	8.09	6.73	7.83	6.74	7.51	6.69	7.32	7.0
Increase	33.49	32.36	34.69	33.27	34.96	33.92	35.05	34.36	35.03		34.160
PERCENTAGE											
under 15	46.09	45.33	46.90	45.39	46.42	45.52	46.13	45.75	45.99	45.49	45.5
15-64	50.75	50.93	50.56	51.04	50.95	51.49	51.41	51.64	51.62	51.93	51.5
65 and over	3.16	3.75	2.54	3.56	2.63	2.99	2.46	2.62	2.39	2.58	2.9
DEP. RATIO X 100	97.05	96.37	97.79	95.91	96.26	94.22	94.53	93.66	93.73	92.56	94.0

TABLE 1 — DATA

AGE AT LAST BIRTHDAY	POPULATION BOTH SEXES	MALES Number	%	FEMALES Number	%	BIRTHS BY AGE OF MOTHER	DEATHS BOTH SEXES	MALES	FEMALES	AGE AT LAST BIRTHDAY
0	16119	8365	3.8	7754	3.7	0	465	234	231	0
1-4	60828	31311	14.1	29517	13.9	0	187	102	85	1-4
5-9	63456	32291	14.5	31165	14.7	0	58	23	35	5-9
10-14	54244	27502	12.3	26742	12.6	0	46	16	30	10-14
15-19	45794	23099	10.4	22695	10.7	2142	63	37	26	15-19
20-24	38393	19215	8.6	19178	9.1	5795	56	22	34	20-24
25-29	32079	16215	7.3	15864	7.5	4314	63	30	33	25-29
30-34	26489	13441	6.0	13048	6.2	2314	70	36	34	30-34
35-39	22367	11517	5.2	10850	5.1	1384	70	40	30	35-39
40-44	18654	9672	4.3	8982	4.2	420	107	54	53	40-44
45-49	15100	7825	3.5	7275	3.4	150	114	83	31	45-49
50-54	11718	6243	2.8	5475	2.6	0	135	81	54	50-54
55-59	8728	4623	2.1	4105	1.9	0	105	72	33	55-59
60-64	6612	3494	1.6	3118	1.5	0	204	130	74	60-64
65-69	5314	2914	1.3	2400	1.1	0	133	81	52	65-69
70-74	3874	2265	1.0	1609	0.8		159	108	51	70-74
75-79	2644	1538	0.7	1106	0.5		176	116	60	75-79
80-84	1527	879	0.4	648	0.3	8565 M.	169	109	60	80-84
85+	643	364	0.2	279	0.1	7954 F.	130	81	49	85+
TOTAL	434583	222773		211810		16519	2510	1455	1055	TOTAL

TABLE 2 — MALE LIFE TABLE

x	$_nq_x$	l_x	$_nd_x$	$_nL_x$	$_nm_x$	$_na_x$	T_x	r_x	$\overset{\circ}{e}_x$	$_nM_x$	x
0	0.027380	100000	2738	98216	0.027878	0.3485	6613625	0.0048	66.136	0.027974	0
1	0.012877	97262	1252	385563	0.003248	1.2176	6515409	0.0048	66.988	0.003258	1
5	0.003476	96010	334	479213	0.000696	2.5000	6129846	0.0354	63.846	0.000712	5
10	0.002936	95676	281	477766	0.000588	2.8184	5650633	0.0326	59.060	0.000582	10
15	0.007998	95395	763	475121	0.001606	2.5710	5172866	0.0346	54.226	0.001602	15
20	0.005717	94632	541	471830	0.001147	2.5419	4697745	0.0340	49.642	0.001145	20
25	0.009265	94091	872	468422	0.001861	2.6683	4225915	0.0339	44.913	0.001850	25
30	0.013360	93219	1245	463133	0.002689	2.6205	3757493	0.0316	40.308	0.002678	30
35	0.017313	91974	1592	456152	0.003491	2.6658	3294360	0.0292	35.818	0.003473	35
40	0.027800	90381	2513	446246	0.005630	2.7467	2838208	0.0324	31.403	0.005583	40
45	0.051981	87869	4568	428497	0.010659	2.6250	2391963	0.0337	27.222	0.010607	45
50	0.063074	83301	5254	403656	0.013016	2.5542	1963466	0.0398	23.571	0.012975	50
55	0.076036	78047	5934	376869	0.015747	2.7476	1559810	0.0379	19.985	0.015574	55
60	0.170649	72113	12306	330182	0.037270	2.5311	1182941	0.0184	16.404	0.037207	60
65	0.129944	59807	7772	279368	0.027818	2.4695	852759	0.0184	14.259	0.027797	65
70	0.214600	52035	11167	233355	0.047853	2.5981	573391	0.0184	11.019	0.047682	70
75	0.318842	40869	13031	172175	0.075682	2.5314	340036	0.0184	8.320	0.075423	75
80	0.471578	27838	13128	105519	0.124411	2.5267	167861	0.0184	6.030	0.124005	80
85+	1.000000	14710	14710	62342	0.235960	4.2380	62342	0.0184	4.238	0.222527	85+

TABLE 3 — FEMALE LIFE TABLE

x	$_nq_x$	l_x	$_nd_x$	$_nL_x$	$_nm_x$	$_na_x$	T_x	r_x	$\overset{\circ}{e}_x$	$_nM_x$	x
0	0.029140	100000	2914	98044	0.029721	0.3287	6964557	0.0032	69.646	0.029791	0
1	0.011403	97086	1107	385229	0.002874	1.1865	6866514	0.0032	70.726	0.002880	1
5	0.005553	95979	533	478562	0.001114	2.5000	6481284	0.0317	67.528	0.001123	5
10	0.005595	95446	534	475897	0.001122	2.5044	6002722	0.0306	62.891	0.001122	10
15	0.005734	94912	544	473262	0.001150	2.6156	5526825	0.0320	58.231	0.001146	15
20	0.008860	94368	836	469837	0.001780	2.6063	5053563	0.0341	53.552	0.001773	20
25	0.010380	93532	971	465307	0.002086	2.5782	4583726	0.0364	49.007	0.002080	25
30	0.012972	92561	1201	459864	0.002611	2.5511	4118419	0.0355	44.494	0.002606	30
35	0.013851	91360	1265	453934	0.002788	2.7345	3658556	0.0338	40.045	0.002765	35
40	0.029140	90095	2625	444033	0.005913	2.5472	3204622	0.0353	35.570	0.005901	40
45	0.021263	87469	1860	433012	0.004295	2.6697	2760589	0.0435	31.561	0.004261	45
50	0.048364	85609	4140	417988	0.009906	2.5706	2327577	0.0493	27.188	0.009863	50
55	0.040058	81469	3263	400162	0.008155	2.7991	1909588	0.0440	23.439	0.008039	55
60	0.112852	78205	8826	369773	0.023868	2.5917	1509426	0.0428	19.301	0.023733	60
65	0.103057	69380	7150	329111	0.021725	2.5122	1139653	0.0428	16.426	0.021667	65
70	0.148559	62230	9245	289217	0.031965	2.6277	810542	0.0428	13.025	0.031697	70
75	0.241879	52985	12816	234126	0.054740	2.5968	521325	0.0428	9.839	0.054250	75
80	0.378437	40169	15201	162877	0.093331	2.6665	287199	0.0428	7.150	0.092593	80
85+	1.000000	24968	24968	124321	0.200831	4.9793	124321	0.0428	4.979	0.175626	85+

TABLE 4 — OBSERVED AND PROJECTED VITAL RATES

	OBSERVED POPULATION			PROJECTED POPULATION 1968		1973		1978		STABLE POPULATION	
	BOTH SEXES	MALES	FEMALES	MALES	FEMALES	MALES	FEMALES	MALES	FEMALES	MALES	FEMALES
RATES PER THOUSAND											
Birth	38.01	38.45	37.55	38.79	37.80	38.83	37.81	38.69	37.68	37.21	36.77
Death	5.78	6.53	4.98	6.42	5.11	6.28	5.21	6.17	5.31	6.50	6.06
Increase	32.24	31.92	32.57	32.38	32.68	32.55	32.60	32.52	32.38		30.7110
PERCENTAGE											
under 15	44.79	44.65	44.94	44.61	44.06	44.66	43.56	44.30	43.07	42.96	42.36
15-64	51.99	51.78	52.21	52.13	52.96	52.32	53.38	52.74	53.71	53.74	53.39
65 and over	3.22	3.57	2.85	3.26	2.99	3.01	3.07	2.96	3.22	3.31	4.25
DEP. RATIO X 100	92.35	93.14	91.53	91.83	88.83	91.11	87.35	89.61	86.18	86.09	87.32

TABLE 1 — DATA

AGE AT LAST BIRTHDAY	BOTH SEXES	MALES Number	%	FEMALES Number	%	BIRTHS BY AGE OF MOTHER	DEATHS BOTH SEXES	MALES	FEMALES	AGE AT LAST BIRTHDAY
0	16279	8360	3.6	7919	3.6	0	518	283	235	0
1-4	62282	32109	14.0	30173	13.8	0	247	139	108	1-4
5-9	65137	33242	14.5	31895	14.6	0	77	42	35	5-9
10-14	56044	28443	12.4	27601	12.6	0	54	30	24	10-14
15-19	47449	23961	10.4	23488	10.7	1511	42	25	17	15-19
20-24	39837	19977	8.7	19860	9.1	6000	61	37	24	20-24
25-29	33396	16897	7.3	16499	7.5	4637	66	37	29	25-29
30-34	27452	13872	6.0	13580	6.2	2624	78	40	38	30-34
35-39	23132	11871	5.2	11261	5.1	1517	65	36	29	35-39
40-44	19310	9995	4.3	9315	4.3	550	75	45	30	40-44
45-49	15702	8119	3.5	7583	3.5	150	115	77	38	45-49
50-54	12257	6476	2.8	5781	2.6	0	139	90	49	50-54
55-59	9213	4871	2.1	4342	2.0	0	124	84	40	55-59
60-64	6833	3597	1.6	3236	1.5	0	204	119	85	60-64
65-69	5442	2945	1.3	2497	1.1	0	134	91	43	65-69
70-74	4075	2421	1.1	1654	0.8		186	132	54	70-74
75-79	2757	1579	0.7	1178	0.5		200	133	67	75-79
80-84	1582	860	0.4	722	0.3	8756 M.	190	117	73	80-84
85+	666	337	0.1	329	0.2	8233 F.	145	80	65	85+
TOTAL	448845	229932		218913		16989	2720	1637	1083	TOTAL

TABLE 2 — MALE LIFE TABLE

x	$_nq_x$	l_x	$_nd_x$	$_nL_x$	$_nm_x$	$_na_x$	T_x	r_x	$\mathring{e}_x$	$_nM_x$
0	0.033093	100000	3309	97874	0.033812	0.3576	6496647	0.0017	64.966	0.033852
1	0.017096	96691	1653	382191	0.004325	1.2340	6398773	0.0017	66.178	0.004329
5	0.006205	95038	590	473714	0.001245	2.5000	6016583	0.0334	63.307	0.001263
10	0.005253	94448	496	470979	0.001053	2.4588	5542869	0.0317	58.687	0.001055
15	0.005232	93952	492	468607	0.001049	2.6565	5071890	0.0341	53.984	0.001043
20	0.009260	93460	865	465246	0.001860	2.6252	4603283	0.0332	49.254	0.001852
25	0.010927	92595	1012	460538	0.002197	2.5923	4138037	0.0342	44.690	0.002190
30	0.014345	91583	1314	454704	0.002889	2.5557	3677499	0.0326	40.155	0.002884
35	0.015103	90269	1363	448081	0.003043	2.6049	3222795	0.0295	35.702	0.003033
40	0.022501	88906	2000	440090	0.004546	2.7808	2774714	0.0327	31.210	0.004502
45	0.046717	86905	4060	425126	0.009550	2.6844	2334624	0.0340	26.864	0.009484
50	0.067522	82845	5594	400741	0.013959	2.5892	1909498	0.0375	23.049	0.013897
55	0.083546	77252	6454	371217	0.017386	2.6696	1508757	0.0386	19.530	0.017245
60	0.153206	70797	10847	327322	0.033137	2.5416	1137541	0.0162	16.068	0.033083
65	0.143819	59951	8622	278522	0.030957	2.5375	810218	0.0162	13.515	0.030900
70	0.241540	51329	12398	226682	0.054693	2.5833	531696	0.0162	10.359	0.054523
75	0.348869	38931	13582	160779	0.084475	2.5058	305014	0.0162	7.835	0.084231
80	0.504011	25349	12776	93643	0.136435	2.4835	144235	0.0162	5.690	0.136047
85+	1.000000	12573	12573	50592	0.248517	4.0239	50592	0.0162	4.024	0.237388

TABLE 3 — FEMALE LIFE TABLE

x	$_nq_x$	l_x	$_nd_x$	$_nL_x$	$_nm_x$	$_na_x$	T_x	r_x	$\mathring{e}_x$	$_nM_x$
0	0.029058	100000	2906	98117	0.029615	0.3520	7010195	0.0028	70.102	0.029675
1	0.014154	97094	1374	384562	0.003574	1.2237	6912078	0.0028	71.189	0.003579
5	0.005401	95720	517	477307	0.001083	2.5000	6527516	0.0306	68.194	0.001097
10	0.004327	95203	412	474949	0.000867	2.4123	6050209	0.0297	63.551	0.000870
15	0.003624	94791	344	473130	0.000726	2.5974	5575260	0.0321	58.816	0.000724
20	0.006062	94447	573	470907	0.001216	2.6760	5102131	0.0341	54.021	0.001208
25	0.008812	93875	827	467457	0.001770	2.6822	4631224	0.0361	49.334	0.001758
30	0.013926	93048	1296	462072	0.002804	2.5560	4163767	0.0357	44.749	0.002798
35	0.012810	91752	1175	455854	0.002578	2.5284	3701695	0.0349	40.345	0.002575
40	0.016073	90577	1456	449462	0.003239	2.6506	3245841	0.0361	35.835	0.003221
45	0.024995	89121	2228	440487	0.005057	2.7031	2796378	0.0423	31.377	0.005011
50	0.041744	86893	3627	425730	0.008520	2.5916	2355891	0.0481	27.113	0.008476
55	0.045899	83266	3822	408068	0.009366	2.8382	1930162	0.0448	23.181	0.009212
60	0.123756	79444	9832	373044	0.026355	2.5410	1522094	0.0406	19.159	0.026267
65	0.082694	69612	5757	333659	0.017253	2.4979	1149050	0.0406	16.506	0.017221
70	0.153052	63856	9773	296490	0.032963	2.6681	815091	0.0406	12.769	0.032648
75	0.252287	54083	13644	237732	0.057394	2.6048	518902	0.0406	9.595	0.056876
80	0.411457	40438	16639	162710	0.102259	2.6272	281169	0.0406	6.953	0.101108
85+	*1.000000	23800	23800	118459	0.200911	4.9773	118459	0.0406	4.977	0.197568

TABLE 4 — OBSERVED AND PROJECTED VITAL RATES

	OBSERVED POPULATION BOTH SEXES	MALES	FEMALES	PROJECTED POPULATION 1969 MALES	FEMALES	1974 MALES	FEMALES	1979 MALES	FEMALES	STABLE POPULATION MALES	FEMALES
RATES PER THOUSAND											
Birth	37.85	38.08	37.61	38.64	37.88	38.81	37.87	38.66	37.60	37.83	36.76
Death	6.06	7.12	4.95	6.96	5.06	6.81	5.13	6.69	5.21	6.99	5.9
Increase	31.79	30.96	32.66	31.68	32.82	32.01	32.74	31.97	32.39	30.838	
PERCENTAGE											
under 15	44.50	44.43	44.58	44.22	43.74	44.19	43.36	43.89	42.99	43.17	42.2
15-64	52.26	52.03	52.51	52.60	53.24	52.84	53.55	53.20	53.76	53.64	53.5
65 and over	3.24	3.54	2.91	3.18	3.01	2.96	3.09	2.91	3.25	3.20	4.2
DEP. RATIO X 100	91.34	92.19	90.45	90.12	87.82	89.24	86.75	87.98	86.00	86.44	86.9

AGE LAST BIRTHDAY	BOTH SEXES	1969 MALES	FEMALES	BOTH SEXES	1974 MALES	FEMALES	BOTH SEXES	1979 MALES	FEMALES	AGE AT LAST BIRTHDAY	
0-4	89	46	43	105	54	51	124	64	60	0-4	
5-9	78	40	38	88	45	43	105	54	51	5-9	
10-14	65	33	32	77	40	37	88	45	43	10-14	
15-19	55	28	27	65	33	32	77	40	37	15-19	TABLE 5
20-24	47	24	23	55	28	27	64	33	31	20-24	POPULATION
25-29	40	20	20	47	24	23	55	28	27	25-29	PROJECTED
30-34	33	17	16	39	20	19	46	23	23	30-34	WITH
35-39	27	14	13	32	16	16	38	19	19	35-39	FIXED
40-44	23	12	11	26	13	13	32	16	16	40-44	AGE—
45-49	19	10	9	22	11	11	26	13	13	45-49	SPECIFIC
50-54	15	8	7	18	9	9	22	11	11	50-54	BIRTH
55-59	12	6	6	14	7	7	16	8	8	55-59	AND
60-64	8	4	4	10	5	5	12	6	6	60-64	DEATH
65-69	6	3	3	8	4	4	10	5	5	65-69	RATES
70-74	4	2	2	5	2	3	6	3	3	70-74	(IN 1000's)
75-79	3	2	1	4	2	2	4	2	2	75-79	
80-84	2	1	1	2	1	1	2	1	1	80-84	
85+	1	0	1	1	0	1	2	1	1	85+	
TOTAL	527	270	257	618	314	304	729	372	357	TOTAL	

STANDARD COUNTRIES:	ENGLAND AND WALES 1961			UNITED STATES 1960			MEXICO 1960			
STANDARDIZED RATES PER THOUSAND	BOTH SEXES	MALES	FEMALES	BOTH SEXES	MALES	FEMALES	BOTH SEXES	MALES	FEMALES	TABLE 6
Birth	33.74	37.72*	31.69	34.18	34.32*	32.64	38.25	36.66*	36.98	STANDAR-
Death	12.30	14.93*	11.82	10.31	12.39*	9.12	6.17	6.91*	5.28	DIZED RATES
Increase	21.44	22.79*	19.87	23.87	21.92*	23.52	32.08	29.75*	31.70	

	OBSERVED POP.		STATIONARY POP.		STABLE POP		OBSERVED BIRTHS	NET MATERNITY FUNCTION	BIRTHS IN STABLE POP.	
	MALES	FEMALES	MALES	FEMALES	MALES	FEMALES				
μ_1	22.56004	22.07983	36.19347	38.50781	22.96103	23.83551	27.17214	28.75941	27.36350	TABLE 7
μ_2	346.1615	324.3491	499.7200	553.7368	342.5680	375.9996	39.13886	46.18462	40.14808	MOMENTS
μ_3	6539.794	6010.949	2832.987	2693.791	5951.606	6956.682	195.9899	190.3542	196.8486	AND
μ_4	50736.	56673.	-233737.	-310167.	25205.	31547.	289.033	-648.656	185.288	CUMULANTS
β_1	1.031079	1.058883	0.064314	0.042738	0.881106	0.910421	0.640682	0.367818	0.598784	
β_2	3.423406	3.538704	2.064005	1.988448	3.214777	3.223141	3.188682	2.695898	3.114952	
κ	-0.446631	-0.491110	-0.024765	-0.015793	-0.376198	-0.379638	-0.366610	-0.180052	-0.335106	

VITAL STATISTICS		THOMPSON				BOURGEOIS-PICHAT					COALE		TABLE 8
		AGE RANGE	NRR	1000r	INTERVAL	AGE RANGE	NRR	1000b	1000d	1000r			RATES FROM AGE DISTRI-
GRR	2.555					5-29	2.37	39.27	7.33	31.94	IBR	37.97	BUTIONS
NRR	2.375	0-4	2.33	30.97	27.36	30-54	2.80	47.03	8.92	38.11	IDR	7.04	AND VITAL
TFR	5.271	5-9	2.35	31.96	27.31	55-79	3.08	54.11	12.41	41.70	IRI	30.93	STATISTICS
GENERATION	28.046	10-14	2.45	32.09	27.24	*20-44	2.61	42.82	7.26	35.56	K1	-7.32	(Females)
SEX RATIO	106.352	15-19	2.53	34.17	27.15						K2	0.	

ORIGINAL MATRIX			FIRST STABLE MATRIX			SECOND STABLE MATRIX Z₂			
SUB- DIAGONAL	ALTERNATIVE FIRST ROWS Projection	Integral	% IN STABLE POPULATION	FISHER VALUES	REPRODUCTIVE VALUES	FIRST COLUMN	FIRST ROW		TABLE 9
0.98887	0.00000	0.00000	16.469	1.118	42601	0.1820+0.1237	0.1820+0.1237		LESLIE
0.99506	0.00000	0.00000	13.951	1.320	42109	0.2124-0.1282	-0.0323+0.1925		MATRIX
0.99617	0.07495	0.00000	11.892	1.549	42749	-0.0316-0.2796	-0.1661+0.0450		AND ITS
0.99530	0.42692	0.16254	10.148	1.731	40654	-0.3035-0.1000	-0.1108-0.1257		SPECTRAL
0.99267	0.67963	0.76331	8.652	1.550	30789	-0.2469+0.2656	-0.0182-0.1880		COMPO-
0.98848	0.55208	0.71008	7.358	1.057	17446	0.1565+0.3793	0.0197-0.1687		NENTS
0.98655	0.38142	0.48820	6.230	0.624	8476	0.4620+0.0182	0.0416-0.1157		(Females)
0.98598	0.22564	0.34036	5.265	0.306	3447	0.2355-0.4635	0.0386-0.0572		
0.98003	0.09158	0.14918	4.447	0.107	992	-0.3629-0.4581	0.0189-0.0183		
0.96650	0.02318	0.04964	3.734	0.022	170	-0.6343+0.1547	0.0050-0.0031		
0.95851	0.00020	0.00044	3.091	0.000	1	-0.1368+0.7062	0.0000-0.0000		
+ 0.82921			8.763						

OBSERVED POPUL. (IN 100's)	CONTRIBUTIONS OF ROOTS (IN 100's)				AGE-SP. BIRTH RATES	NET MATERNITY FUNCTION	COEFF. OF MATRIX EQUATION	PARAMETERS				EXP. INCREASE		
	r_1	r_2, r_3	$r_4 \cdot r_{11}$						INTEGRAL	MATRIX	x	$e^{(x+2\frac{1}{2})r}$		TABLE 10
381	378	-2	5		0.0000	0.0000	0.0000	L(1)	1.16671	1.16735	0	1.0801		AGE
319	320	3	-4		0.0000	0.0000	0.0000	L(2)	0.35378	0.36624	50	5.0480		ANALYSIS
276	273	6	-3		0.0000	0.0000	0.0737		0.83158	0.79712	55	5.8896		AND
235	233	1	1		0.0312	0.1475	0.4185	R(1)	0.03084	0.03095	60	6.8715		MISCEL-
199	198	-7	7		0.1464	0.6894	0.6631	R(2)	-0.02025	-0.02620	65	8.0170		LANEOUS
165	169	-8	4		0.1362	0.6367	0.5347			0.23371	0.22802	70	9.3536	RESULTS
136	143	1	-8		0.0936	0.4327	0.3651	C(1)			2293	75	10.9129	(Females)
113	121	11	-19		0.0653	0.2976	0.2131	C(2)			152	80	12.7322	
93	102	9	-18		0.0286	0.1286	0.0854				1085	85	14.8548	
76	86	-5	-4		0.0096	0.0422	0.0211	2P/Y	26.8844	27.5552	90	17.3313	
58	71	-16	3		0.0000	0.0000	0.0000	DELTA	3.5262		95	20.2207	
+ 140	201										100	23.5917	

European Population

TABLE 1 — DATA

AGE AT LAST BIRTHDAY	BOTH SEXES	MALES Number	%	FEMALES Number	%	BIRTHS BY AGE OF MOTHER	DEATHS BOTH SEXES	MALES	FEMALES	AGE AT LAST BIRTHDAY
0	42870	21812	2.4	21058	2.3	0	1017	611	406	0
1-4	170898	87146	9.5	83752	9.2	0	223	123	100	1-4
5-9	167648	85604	9.3	82044	9.0	0	95	60	35	5-9
10-14	140612	71375	7.8	69237	7.6	4	60	40	20	10-14
15-19	118909	60926	6.6	57983	6.3	1745	115	78	37	15-19
20-24	130184	66498	7.2	63686	7.0	12118	170	118	52	20-24
25-29	138423	70297	7.6	68126	7.5	14953	196	123	73	25-29
30-34	131005	64628	7.0	66377	7.3	9444	203	119	84	30-34
35-39	132438	66208	7.2	66230	7.3	4933	268	159	109	35-39
40-44	123565	62948	6.8	60617	6.6	1358	372	221	151	40-44
45-49	108634	55833	6.1	52801	5.8	96	542	325	217	45-49
50-54	94829	47175	5.1	47654	5.2	0	733	417	316	50-54
55-59	80575	38361	4.2	42214	4.6	0	1042	598	444	55-59
60-64	76730	37088	4.0	39642	4.3	0	1568	921	647	60-64
65-69	69341	33532	3.6	35809	3.9	0	2153	1281	872	65-69
70-74	53341	25634	2.8	27707	3.0		2673	1491	1182	70-74
75-79	30907	14592	1.6	16315	1.8		2495	1292	1203	75-79
80-84	15110	6851	0.7	8259	0.9	23068 M.	1982	985	997	80-84
85+	6767	2815	0.3	3952	0.4	21583 F.	1605	677	928	85+
TOTAL	1832786	919323		913463		44651	17512	9639	7873	TOTAL

TABLE 2 — MALE LIFE TABLE

x	$_nq_x$	l_x	$_nd_x$	$_nL_x$	$_nm_x$	$_na_x$	T_x	r_x	$\dot{e}_x$	$_nM_x$
0	0.027442	100000	2744	97963	0.028012	0.2579	6784873	0.0000	67.849	0.028012
1	0.005623	97256	547	387442	0.001411	1.1084	6686909	0.0000	68.756	0.001411
5	0.003468	96709	335	482706	0.000695	2.5000	6299467	0.0414	65.138	0.000701
10	0.002819	96374	272	481247	0.000564	2.7137	5816761	0.0333	60.356	0.000560
15	0.006390	96102	614	479094	0.001282	2.6940	5335514	0.0058	55.519	0.001280
20	0.008834	95488	844	475374	0.001774	2.5520	4856420	0.0000	50.859	0.001774
25	0.008711	94644	824	471164	0.001750	2.5042	4381046	0.0011	46.290	0.001750
30	0.009168	93820	860	467009	0.001842	2.5692	3909882	0.0041	41.674	0.001841
35	0.011940	92960	1110	462179	0.002402	2.6396	3442873	0.0001	37.036	0.002402
40	0.017460	91850	1604	455551	0.003520	2.6939	2980694	0.0133	32.452	0.003511
45	0.028840	90246	2603	445186	0.005846	2.6774	2525143	0.0229	27.981	0.005821
50	0.043583	87643	3820	429441	0.008895	2.7025	2079958	0.0279	23.732	0.008839
55	0.075339	83824	6315	404435	0.015615	2.6749	1650517	0.0081	19.690	0.015589
60	0.117680	77509	9121	365924	0.024927	2.6299	1246082	0.0207	16.077	0.024833
65	0.175485	68387	12001	313033	0.038338	2.5915	880157	0.0207	12.870	0.038202
70	0.255283	56386	14394	246625	0.058366	2.5472	567125	0.0207	10.058	0.058165
75	0.363523	41992	15261	171729	0.088865	2.4949	320500	0.0207	7.632	0.088542
80	0.524525	26731	14021	97162	0.144307	2.4621	148771	0.0207	5.565	0.143775
85+	1.000000	12710	12710	51609	0.246273	4.0605	51609	0.0207	4.061	0.240496

TABLE 3 — FEMALE LIFE TABLE

x	$_nq_x$	l_x	$_nd_x$	$_nL_x$	$_nm_x$	$_na_x$	T_x	r_x	$\dot{e}_x$	$_nM_x$
0	0.019016	100000	1902	98632	0.019280	0.2808	7231508	0.0000	72.315	0.019280
1	0.004760	98098	467	391053	0.001194	1.1292	7132875	0.0000	72.711	0.001194
5	0.002099	97631	205	487645	0.000420	2.5000	6741822	0.0409	69.054	0.000427
10	0.001451	97427	141	486801	0.000290	2.6554	6254178	0.0343	64.194	0.000289
15	0.003190	97285	310	485703	0.000639	2.6703	5767376	0.0078	59.283	0.000638
20	0.004075	96975	395	483929	0.000817	2.6085	5281674	0.0000	54.464	0.000817
25	0.005344	96580	516	481652	0.001072	2.5852	4797745	0.0000	49.677	0.001072
30	0.006309	96064	606	478858	0.001266	2.5919	4316093	0.0015	44.930	0.001265
35	0.008207	95457	783	475448	0.001648	2.6519	3837234	0.0074	40.198	0.001646
40	0.012435	94674	1177	470662	0.002501	2.6996	3361787	0.0200	35.509	0.002491
45	0.020439	93497	1911	463086	0.004127	2.6987	2891124	0.0198	30.922	0.004110
50	0.032753	91586	3000	450980	0.006652	2.6835	2428038	0.0155	26.511	0.006631
55	0.051400	88586	4553	432304	0.010533	2.6662	1977058	0.0075	22.318	0.010518
60	0.078918	84033	6632	404503	0.016395	2.6385	1544754	0.0260	18.383	0.016321
65	0.115777	77401	8961	365997	0.024484	2.6557	1140252	0.0260	14.732	0.024351
70	0.194726	68440	13327	310616	0.042905	2.6302	774255	0.0260	11.313	0.042661
75	0.313695	55113	17289	233249	0.074121	2.5524	463638	0.0260	8.413	0.073736
80	0.467402	37824	17679	145518	0.121490	2.5337	230389	0.0260	6.091	0.120718
85+	*1.000000	20145	20145	84871	0.237361	4.2130	84871	0.0260	4.213	0.234818

TABLE 4 — OBSERVED AND PROJECTED VITAL RATES

	OBSERVED POPULATION BOTH SEXES	MALES	FEMALES	PROJECTED POPULATION 1956 MALES	FEMALES	1961 MALES	FEMALES	1966 MALES	FEMALES	STABLE POPULATION MALES	FEMALES
RATES PER THOUSAND											
Birth	24.36	25.09	23.63	22.67	21.31	21.71	20.40	22.53	21.18	25.22	24.1
Death	9.55	10.48	8.62	10.66	9.06	10.69	9.43	10.65	9.65	8.84	7.8
Increase	14.81	14.61	15.01	12.01	12.25	11.02	10.97	11.88	11.53		16.380
PERCENTAGE											
under 15	28.48	28.93	28.04	30.92	29.67	31.36	29.95	30.17	28.65	32.41	31.4
15-64	61.94	62.00	61.89	60.14	59.89	60.23	59.64	61.58	60.99	60.92	60.3
65 and over	9.57	9.07	10.08	8.95	10.44	8.41	10.41	8.25	10.36	6.67	8.2
DEP. RATIO X 100	61.44	61.30	61.58	66.29	66.97	66.04	67.67	62.40	63.97	64.15	65.5

European Population

AGE AT LAST BIRTHDAY	1956 BOTH SEXES	1956 MALES	1956 FEMALES	1961 BOTH SEXES	1961 MALES	1961 FEMALES	1966 BOTH SEXES	1966 MALES	1966 FEMALES	AGE AT LAST BIRTHDAY	
0-4	214	11C	104	212	109	103	224	115	109	0-4	
5-9	212	108	104	212	109	103	210	108	102	5-9	**TABLE 5**
10-14	167	85	82	212	108	104	212	109	103	10-14	POPULATION
15-19	140	71	69	167	85	82	212	108	1C4	15-19	PROJECTED
20-24	118	6C	58	14C	71	69	165	84	81	20-24	WITH
25-29	129	66	63	117	60	57	139	70	69	25-29	FIXED
30-34	138	70	68	128	65	63	116	59	57	30-34	AGE—
35-39	130	64	66	136	69	67	128	65	63	35-39	SPECIFIC
40-44	131	65	66	128	63	65	135	68	67	40-44	BIRTH
45-49	122	62	60	129	64	65	126	62	64	45-49	AND
50-54	105	54	51	117	59	58	125	62	63	50-54	DEATH
55-59	90	44	46	100	51	49	112	56	56	55-59	RATES
60-64	74	35	39	83	40	43	92	46	46	60-64	(IN 1000's)
65-69	68	32	36	66	30	36	73	34	39	65-69	
70-74	56	26	30	55	25	30	53	23	30	70-74	
75-79	39	18	21	41	18	23	40	17	23	75-79	
80-84	18	8	10	23	10	13	24	10	14	80-84	
85+	9	4	5	1C	4	6	13	5	8	85+	
TOTAL	1960	982	978	2076	1040	1036	2199	1101	1098	TOTAL	

STANDARD COUNTRIES:	ENGLAND AND WALES 1961 BOTH SEXES	MALES	FEMALES	UNITED STATES 1960 BOTH SEXES	MALES	FEMALES	MEXICO 1960 BOTH SEXES	MALES	FEMALES	
STANDARDIZED RATES PER THOUSAND										**TABLE 6**
Birth	21.60	23.07*	20.24	21.96	21.75*	20.91	25.00	20.64*	24.11	STANDAR-DIZED
Death	12.01	11.72*	12.36	9.73	10.38*	9.07	5.11	8.28*	4.37	RATES
Increase	9.60	11.35*	7.88	12.23	11.37*	11.85	19.89	12.36*	19.74	

	OBSERVED POP. MALES	FEMALES	STATIONARY POP. MALES	FEMALES	STABLE POP. MALES	FEMALES	OBSERVED BIRTHS	NET MATERNITY FUNCTION	BIRTHS IN STABLE POP.	
μ	31.84672	32.74685	36.76157	38.37906	29.00915	30.08298	28.41241	28.30271	27.74000	**TABLE 7**
μ_2	474.2294	491.5813	502.8191	536.0649	435.4914	466.7706	31.83592	33.08412	31.44586	MOMENTS
κ_3	4007.006	3904.908	2416.454	2171.648	5415.110	5840.493	89.9518	98.1608	101.4279	AND
κ_4	-189041.	-213213.	-246631.	-295144.	-107168.	-134732.	-258.743	-276.109	-115.579	CUMULANTS
β_1	0.150548	0.128362	0.045933	0.030614	0.355039	0.335420	0.250208	0.266083	0.330845	
β_2	2.159419	2.117686	2.024505	1.972931	2.434927	2.381606	2.744710	2.747744	2.883116	
κ	-0.057384	-0.048353	-0.017435	-0.011308	-0.137679	-0.127077	-0.160027	-0.165500	-0.221485	

VITAL STATISTICS		THOMPSON AGE RANGE	NRR	1000r	INTERVAL	BOURGEOIS-PICHAT AGE RANGE	NRR	1000b	1000d	1000r	COALE	
GRR	1.646										IBR	**TABLE 8**
NRR	1.582	0-4	1.61	17.70	27.41	5-29	1.26	17.74	9.25	8.49	IDR	RATES FROM AGE DISTRI-
TFR	3.405	5-9	1.27	8.80	27.38	30-54	1.49	25.64	10.78	14.86	IRI	BUTIONS
GENERATION	28.019	10-14	1.11	3.77	27.32	55-79	1.16	14.93	9.46	5.46	K1	AND VITAL
SEX RATIO	106.880	15-19	0.98	-0.56	27.22	*35-59	1.63	30.13	11.96	18.17	K2	STATISTICS (Females)

ORIGINAL MATRIX SUB-DIAGONAL	ALTERNATIVE FIRST ROWS Projection	Integral	FIRST STABLE MATRIX % IN STABLE POPULATION	FISHER VALUES	REPRODUCTIVE VALUES	SECOND STABLE MATRIX Z_2 FIRST COLUMN	FIRST ROW	
0.99583	0.00000	C.00000	11.379	1.064	111478	0.1682+0.0690	0.1682+0.0690	
0.99827	0.00007	0.00000	10.439	1.159	95122	0.1526-0.1344	0.0115+0.1621	**TABLE 9**
0.99774	0.03561	C.00014	9.600	1.261	87284	-0.0592-0.2203	-0.1250+0.0733	LESLIE
0.99635	0.25999	0.07421	8.824	1.334	77326	-0.2507-0.0501	-0.1140-0.0734	MATRIX
0.99529	0.48374	0.46921	8.099	1.175	74857	-0.1748+0.2266	-0.0303-0.1384	AND ITS
0.99420	0.42718	0.54125	7.426	0.765	52117	0.1404+0.2875	0.0171-0.1127	SPECTRAL
0.99288	0.25591	0.35085	6.801	0.378	25108	0.3574+0.0019	0.0250-0.0606	COMPO-
0.98993	0.11440	0.18367	6.221	0.139	9234	0.1788-0.3563	0.0153-0.0218	NENTS
0.98390	0.02861	0.05524	5.673	0.030	1816	-0.2669-0.3540	0.0043-0.0043	(Females)
0.97386	0.00215	C.00444	5.142	0.002	113	-0.4816+0.0908	0.0003-0.0003	
0.95859	0.00002	0.00005	4.613	0.000	1	-0.1447+0.5163	0.0000-0.0000	
+ 0.80532			15.782					

OBSERVED POPUL. (IN 100's)	CONTRIBUTIONS OF ROOTS (IN 100's) r_1	r_2, r_3	$r_4 \cdot r_{11}$	AGE-SP. BIRTH RATES	NET MATERNITY FUNCTION	COEFF. OF MATRIX EQUATION	PARAMETERS INTEGRAL	MATRIX	EXP. INCREASE x	$e^{(x+8\frac{1}{2})r}$	
1048	909	110	29	0.0000	0.0000	0.0000	L(1) 1.08535	1.08551	0	1.0418	**TABLE 10**
820	834	36	-50	0.0000	0.0000	0.0001	L(2) 0.39189	0.39488	50	2.3631	AGE
692	767	-101	27	0.0000	0.0001	0.0354	0.82549	0.79771	55	2.5648	ANALYSIS
580	705	-147	22	0.0145	0.0707	0.2579	R(1) 0.01638	0.01641	60	2.7837	AND
637	647	-18	8	0.0920	0.4451	0.4781	R(2) -0.01803	-0.02328	65	3.0213	MISCEL-
681	593	165	-77	0.1061	0.5110	0.4202	0.22551	0.22223	70	3.2791	LANEOUS
664	543	187	-66	0.0688	0.3293	0.2503	C(1)	7989	75	3.5590	RESULTS
662	497	-21	186	0.0360	0.1712	0.1111	C(2)	26045	80	3.8627	(Females)
606	453	-253	406	0.0108	0.0510	0.0275		-16034	85	4.1924	
528	411	-222	339	0.0009	0.0041	0.0020	2P/Y 27.8618	28.2736	90	4.5502	
477	369	90	18	0.0000	0.0000	0.0000	DELTA 7.1882		95	4.9386	
+ 1739	1261								100	5.3601	

European Population

TABLE 1 — DATA

AGE AT LAST BIRTHDAY	BOTH SEXES	MALES Number	%	FEMALES Number	%	BIRTHS BY AGE OF MOTHER	DEATHS BOTH SEXES	MALES	FEMALES	AGE AT LAST BIRTHDAY
0	46554	23893	2.4	22661	2.3	0	967	568	399	0
1-4	176850	90460	9.2	86390	8.8	0	234	127	107	1-4
5-9	204030	104060	10.5	99970	10.2	0	93	53	40	5-9
10-14	160570	82060	8.3	78510	8.0	11	70	40	30	10-14
15-19	128080	65000	6.6	63080	6.4	1885	119	86	33	15-19
20-24	127890	65590	6.6	62300	6.4	13346	158	113	45	20-24
25-29	143020	74390	7.5	68630	7.0	15830	163	110	53	25-29
30-34	142710	71890	7.3	70820	7.2	10459	179	111	68	30-34
35-39	133630	66090	6.7	67540	6.9	5123	227	133	94	35-39
40-44	132740	66950	6.8	65790	6.7	1466	340	194	146	40-44
45-49	118710	60550	6.1	58160	5.9	115	528	308	220	45-49
50-54	102880	52310	5.3	50570	5.2	3	758	455	303	50-54
55-59	85620	41280	4.2	44340	4.5	0	1012	609	403	55-59
60-64	76010	35830	3.6	40180	4.1	0	1432	867	565	60-64
65-69	69400	32840	3.3	36560	3.7	0	2067	1215	852	65-69
70-74	56310	26570	2.7	29740	3.0		2659	1498	1161	70-74
75-79	36100	16780	1.7	19320	2.0		2774	1478	1296	75-79
80-84	17340	7800	0.8	9540	1.0	24820 M.	2091	1047	1044	80-84
85+	8010	3370	0.3	4640	0.5	23418 F.	1673	737	936	85+
TOTAL	1966454	987713		978741		48238	17544	9749	7795	TOTAL

TABLE 2 — MALE LIFE TABLE

x	nq_x	l_x	nd_x	nL_x	nm_x	na_x	T_x	r_x	$\mathring{e}_x$	nM_x
0	0.023291	100000	2329	98312	0.023691	0.2753	6887976	0.0044	68.880	0.023773
1	0.005568	97671	544	389119	0.001398	1.1239	6789664	0.0044	69.516	0.001404
5	0.002519	97127	245	485023	0.000504	2.5000	6400545	0.0325	65.899	0.000509
10	0.002474	96882	240	483895	0.000495	2.8436	5915521	0.0464	61.059	0.000487
15	0.006622	96643	640	481735	0.001328	2.6900	5431626	0.0212	56.203	0.001323
20	0.008577	96003	823	477967	0.001723	2.5155	4949891	0.0000	51.560	0.001723
25	0.007366	95179	701	474123	0.001479	2.4714	4471924	0.0000	46.984	0.001479
30	0.007697	94478	727	470622	0.001545	2.5683	3997801	0.0102	42.315	0.001544
35	0.010021	93751	940	466533	0.002014	2.6353	3527178	0.0051	37.623	0.002012
40	0.014411	92811	1337	460999	0.002901	2.7135	3060645	0.0056	32.977	0.002898
45	0.025256	91474	2310	452113	0.005110	2.7245	2599646	0.0193	28.420	0.005087
50	0.042917	89164	3827	437044	0.008756	2.7071	2147534	0.0291	24.085	0.008698
55	0.071651	85337	6114	412497	0.014823	2.6796	1710489	0.0224	20.044	0.014753
60	0.114827	79223	9097	374586	0.024285	2.6336	1297993	0.0196	16.384	0.024198
65	0.170387	70126	11948	321874	0.037122	2.5935	923407	0.0196	13.168	0.036998
70	0.248492	58177	14457	255550	0.056570	2.5557	601533	0.0196	10.340	0.056379
75	0.361771	43721	15817	178970	0.088377	2.4943	345983	0.0196	7.914	0.088081
80	0.502558	27904	14023	104057	0.134765	2.4712	167013	0.0196	5.985	0.134230
85+	*1.000000	13880	13880	62956	0.220481	4.5355	62956	0.0196	4.536	0.218694

TABLE 3 — FEMALE LIFE TABLE

x	nq_x	l_x	nd_x	nL_x	nm_x	na_x	T_x	r_x	$\mathring{e}_x$	nM_x
0	0.017340	100000	1734	98777	0.017554	0.2948	7360551	0.0039	73.606	0.017607
1	0.004920	98266	483	391683	0.001234	1.1438	7261774	0.0039	73.899	0.001239
5	0.001976	97783	193	488430	0.000396	2.5000	6870091	0.0323	70.259	0.000400
10	0.001915	97589	187	487493	0.000383	2.5692	6381661	0.0456	65.393	0.000382
15	0.002620	97403	255	486408	0.000525	2.6333	5894169	0.0226	60.514	0.000523
20	0.003605	97147	350	484885	0.000722	2.5701	5407760	0.0000	55.666	0.000722
25	0.003854	96797	373	483076	0.000772	2.5624	4922875	0.0000	50.858	0.000772
30	0.004790	96424	462	481026	0.000960	2.6323	4439799	0.0006	46.045	0.000960
35	0.006944	95962	666	478268	0.001393	2.6854	3958773	0.0059	41.254	0.001392
40	0.011071	95296	1055	474072	0.002225	2.7189	3480505	0.0126	36.523	0.002219
45	0.018836	94241	1775	467117	0.003800	2.6980	3006433	0.0224	31.902	0.003783
50	0.029657	92466	2742	455936	0.006015	2.6692	2539316	0.0210	27.462	0.005992
55	0.044607	89723	4002	439261	0.009111	2.6627	2083381	0.0136	23.220	0.009089
60	0.068450	85721	5868	414950	0.014140	2.6729	1644119	0.0274	19.180	0.014062
65	0.111109	79853	8872	378519	0.023440	2.6616	1229169	0.0274	15.393	0.023304
70	0.179625	70981	12750	324695	0.039267	2.6306	850650	0.0274	11.984	0.039038
75	0.289610	58231	16864	250040	0.067446	2.5620	525955	0.0274	9.032	0.067081
80	0.429616	41367	17772	161634	0.109951	2.5789	275914	0.0274	6.670	0.109434
85+	1.000000	23595	23595	114280	0.206465	4.8434	114280	0.0274	4.843	0.201725

TABLE 4 — OBSERVED AND PROJECTED VITAL RATES

	OBSERVED POPULATION BOTH SEXES	MALES	FEMALES	PROJECTED POPULATION 1959 MALES	FEMALES	1964 MALES	FEMALES	1969 MALES	FEMALES	STABLE POPULATION MALES	FEMALES
RATES PER THOUSAND											
Birth	24.53	25.13	23.93	22.91	21.75	22.82	21.64	24.63	23.37	26.82	25.8
Death	8.92	9.87	7.96	10.06	8.56	10.07	8.89	9.95	8.97	7.91	6.9
Increase	15.61	15.26	15.96	12.85	13.20	12.76	12.75	14.68	14.40		18.912
PERCENTAGE											
under 15	29.90	30.42	29.38	31.82	30.57	31.37	30.00	31.03	29.65	34.01	32.9
15-64	60.58	60.73	60.43	59.69	58.97	60.52	59.56	60.84	59.97	59.83	59.2
65 and over	9.52	8.84	10.20	8.49	10.46	8.11	10.44	8.12	10.38	6.17	7.7
DEP. RATIO X 100	65.07	64.65	65.49	67.52	69.57	65.23	67.91	64.36	66.76	67.15	68.

European Population

TABLE 1

AGE AT LAST BIRTHDAY	POPULATION BOTH SEXES	MALES Number	%	FEMALES Number	%	BIRTHS BY AGE OF MOTHER	DEATHS BOTH SEXES	MALES	FEMALES	AGE AT LAST BIRTHDAY
0	50237	25701	2.4	24536	2.4	0	1019	585	434	0
1-4	186800	95100	9.1	91700	8.8	0	211	117	94	1-4
5-9	221200	113100	10.8	108100	10.4	0	102	62	40	5-9
10-14	182900	93600	8.9	89300	8.6	9	77	43	34	10-14
15-19	151800	77200	7.4	74600	7.2	2743	123	93	30	15-19
20-24	127100	65000	6.2	62100	6.0	14836	138	108	30	20-24
25-29	140400	72900	6.9	67500	6.5	16938	159	109	50	25-29
30-34	147400	76100	7.3	71300	6.9	10593	184	122	62	30-34
35-39	140000	69700	6.6	70300	6.8	5346	246	133	113	35-39
40-44	135700	67700	6.5	68000	6.5	1455	338	196	142	40-44
45-49	127700	64900	6.2	62800	6.0	98	539	320	219	45-49
50-54	110300	56300	5.4	54000	5.2	1	761	468	293	50-54
55-59	93900	46800	4.5	47100	4.5	0	1070	671	399	55-59
60-64	77100	35900	3.4	41200	4.0	0	1416	844	572	60-64
65-69	69200	31800	3.0	37400	3.6	0	2043	1202	841	65-69
70-74	57220	26350	2.5	30870	3.0		2728	1569	1159	70-74
75-79	40250	18300	1.7	21950	2.1		3141	1703	1438	75-79
80-84	21954	9906	0.9	12048	1.2	26745 M.	2513	1241	1272	80-84
85+	8146	3114	0.3	5032	0.5	25274 F.	2136	941	1195	85+
TOTAL	2089307	1049471		1039836		52019	18944	10527	8417	TOTAL

TABLE 2 (MALE)

x	nq_x	l_x	nd_x	nL_x	nm_x	na_x	T_x	r_x	$\overset{\circ}{e}_x$	nM_x	x
0	0.022271	100000	2227	98364	0.022641	0.2655	6888089	0.0068	68.881	0.022762	0
1	0.004868	97773	476	389719	0.001221	1.1150	6789725	0.0068	69.444	0.001230	1
5	0.002721	97297	265	485823	0.000545	2.5000	6400006	0.0248	65.778	0.000548	5
10	0.002321	97032	225	484665	0.000465	2.7970	5914184	0.0375	60.951	0.000459	10
15	0.006050	96807	586	482690	0.001213	2.7031	5429519	0.0353	56.086	0.001205	15
20	0.008275	96221	796	479142	0.001662	2.5327	4946829	0.0042	51.411	0.001662	20
25	0.007448	95425	711	475340	0.001495	2.4883	4467687	0.0000	46.819	0.001495	25
30	0.007986	94714	756	471719	0.001603	2.5504	3992347	0.0029	42.151	0.001603	30
35	0.009511	93958	894	467677	0.001911	2.6359	3520629	0.0097	37.470	0.001908	35
40	0.014393	93064	1339	462254	0.002898	2.7099	3052951	0.0041	32.805	0.002895	40
45	0.024452	91725	2243	453503	0.004946	2.7164	2590697	0.0133	28.244	0.004931	45
50	0.041009	89482	3670	439017	0.008359	2.7128	2137194	0.0239	23.884	0.008313	50
55	0.069815	85812	5991	415177	0.014430	2.6823	1698177	0.0301	19.789	0.014338	55
60	0.111662	79821	8913	378143	0.023571	2.6479	1283000	0.0131	16.073	0.023510	60
65	0.173706	70908	12317	325071	0.037891	2.6073	904858	0.0131	12.761	0.037799	65
70	0.260413	58591	15258	255650	0.059683	2.5550	579787	0.0131	9.895	0.059545	70
75	0.377216	43333	16346	175301	0.093245	2.4694	324137	0.0131	7.480	0.093060	75
80	0.476434	26987	12858	102331	0.125648	2.4641	148835	0.0131	5.515	0.125277	80
85+	*1.000000	14130	14130	46505	0.303830	3.2913	46505	0.0131	3.291	0.302184	85+

TABLE 3 (FEMALE)

x	nq_x	l_x	nd_x	nL_x	nm_x	na_x	T_x	r_x	$\overset{\circ}{e}_x$	nM_x	x
0	0.017383	100000	1738	98737	0.017606	0.2735	7396688	0.0060	73.967	0.017688	0
1	0.004063	98262	399	391898	0.001019	1.1221	7297951	0.0060	74.271	0.001025	1
5	0.001835	97862	180	488863	0.000367	2.5000	6906053	0.0258	70.569	0.000370	5
10	0.001903	97683	186	487953	0.000380	2.5187	6417190	0.0367	65.694	0.000381	10
15	0.002013	97497	196	487004	0.000403	2.5522	5929237	0.0359	60.815	0.000402	15
20	0.002416	97301	235	485950	0.000484	2.6441	5442233	0.0095	55.932	0.000483	20
25	0.003697	97066	359	484469	0.000741	2.6071	4956284	0.0000	51.061	0.000741	25
30	0.004339	96707	420	482571	0.000870	2.7048	4471814	0.0000	46.241	0.000870	30
35	0.008011	96287	771	479627	0.001608	2.6552	3989244	0.0032	41.431	0.001607	35
40	0.010408	95516	994	475275	0.002092	2.6823	3509617	0.0090	36.744	0.002088	40
45	0.017364	94522	1641	468819	0.003501	2.6911	3034342	0.0195	32.102	0.003487	45
50	0.026908	92880	2499	458597	0.005450	2.6773	2565524	0.0231	27.622	0.005426	50
55	0.041693	90381	3768	443183	0.008503	2.6853	2106927	0.0181	23.312	0.008471	55
60	0.067543	86613	5850	419459	0.013947	2.6744	1663744	0.0222	19.209	0.013883	60
65	0.107282	80763	8664	383536	0.022591	2.6596	1244285	0.0222	15.407	0.022487	65
70	0.173196	72098	12487	330991	0.037727	2.6375	860749	0.0222	11.939	0.037545	70
75	0.283639	59611	16908	256946	0.065804	2.5686	529758	0.0222	8.887	0.065513	75
80	0.422862	42703	18058	169984	0.106231	2.5893	272811	0.0222	6.389	0.105577	80
85+	*1.000000	24646	24646	102828	0.239679	4.1722	102828	0.0222	4.172	0.237480	85+

TABLE 4

	OBSERVED POPULATION BOTH SEXES	MALES	FEMALES	PROJECTED POPULATION 1962 MALES	FEMALES	1967 MALES	FEMALES	1972 MALES	FEMALES	STABLE POPULATION MALES	FEMALES
RATES PER THOUSAND											
Birth	24.90	25.48	24.31	24.36	23.17	25.19	23.94	26.95	25.64	28.99	27.94
Death	9.07	10.03	8.09	10.02	8.55	9.75	8.65	9.51	8.52	7.19	6.15
Increase	15.83	15.45	16.21	14.34	14.61	15.43	15.29	17.44	17.11	21.7963	
PERCENTAGE											
under 15	30.69	31.21	30.16	32.33	31.11	32.33	31.03	32.88	31.46	36.06	34.97
15-64	59.90	60.27	59.52	59.79	58.60	60.00	58.82	59.42	58.51	58.62	58.13
65 and over	9.42	8.53	10.32	7.88	10.30	7.67	10.15	7.71	10.02	5.32	6.90
DEP. RATIO X 100	66.96	65.92	68.01	67.25	70.66	66.68	70.02	68.30	70.90	70.59	72.04

TABLE 1 — DATA

AGE AT LAST BIRTHDAY	POPULATION BOTH SEXES	MALES Number	%	FEMALES Number	%	BIRTHS BY AGE OF MOTHER	DEATHS BOTH SEXES	MALES	FEMALES	AGE AT LAST BIRTHDAY
0	60900	31005	2.5	29895	2.5	0	1490	867	623	0
1-4	232774	118841	9.7	113933	9.4	0	294	161	133	1-4
5-9	263305	134685	11.0	128620	10.6	0	110	60	50	5-9
10-14	245839	125698	10.3	120141	9.9	23	104	67	37	10-14
15-19	189214	96832	7.9	92382	7.6	3959	153	105	48	15-19
20-24	159799	81020	6.6	78779	6.5	18455	169	125	44	20-24
25-29	144340	73870	6.1	70470	5.8	17118	162	119	43	25-29
30-34	157699	81781	6.7	75918	6.3	10946	195	111	84	30-34
35-39	159100	81267	6.7	77833	6.4	5538	309	185	124	35-39
40-44	144949	71799	5.9	73150	6.1	1565	391	223	168	40-44
45-49	141499	71111	5.8	70388	5.8	102	658	395	263	45-49
50-54	126858	64613	5.3	62245	5.2	0	946	601	345	50-54
55-59	105492	53781	4.4	51711	4.3	0	1268	805	463	55-59
60-64	86915	41989	3.4	44926	3.7	0	1722	1088	634	60-64
65-69	71061	31526	2.6	39535	3.3	0	2086	1218	868	65-69
70-74	58461	25854	2.1	32607	2.7		2783	1511	1272	70-74
75-79	43006	19020	1.6	23986	2.0		3372	1736	1636	75-79
80-84	24516	10360	0.8	14156	1.2	29703 M.	2939	1393	1546	80-84
85+	12078	4771	0.4	7307	0.6	28003 F.	2631	1129	1502	85+
TOTAL	2427805	1219823		1207982		57706	21782	11899	9883	TOTAL

TABLE 2 — MALE LIFE TABLE

x	$_nq_x$	l_x	$_nd_x$	$_nL_x$	$_nm_x$	$_na_x$	T_x	r_x	$\dot{e}_x$	$_nM_x$
0	0.027325	100000	2732	97960	0.027894	0.2535	6825341	0.0032	68.253	0.027963
1	0.005377	97268	523	387556	0.001350	1.1049	6727381	0.0032	69.164	0.001355
5	0.002214	96744	214	483187	0.000443	2.5000	6339825	0.0169	65.532	0.000445
10	0.002684	96530	259	482069	0.000537	2.7499	5856638	0.0324	60.672	0.000533
15	0.005453	96271	525	480143	0.001093	2.6897	5374570	0.0428	55.827	0.001084
20	0.007699	95746	737	476938	0.001546	2.5670	4894426	0.0256	51.119	0.001543
25	0.008022	95009	762	473119	0.001611	2.4728	4417488	0.0000	46.495	0.001611
30	0.006764	94247	638	469703	0.001357	2.5979	3944369	0.0000	41.851	0.001357
35	0.011341	93609	1062	465558	0.002280	2.6555	3474666	0.0108	37.119	0.002276
40	0.015453	92548	1430	459464	0.003113	2.7098	3009108	0.0099	32.514	0.003106
45	0.027456	91118	2502	449880	0.005561	2.7181	2549644	0.0048	27.982	0.005555
50	0.045699	88616	4050	433716	0.009337	2.6878	2099765	0.0183	23.695	0.009302
55	0.072756	84566	6153	408605	0.015058	2.6877	1666048	0.0270	19.701	0.014968
60	0.122331	78414	9592	369343	0.025972	2.6310	1257444	0.0126	16.036	0.025912
65	0.177017	68821	12183	314673	0.038715	2.5840	888101	0.0126	12.904	0.038635
70	0.256097	56639	14505	247656	0.058569	2.5500	573428	0.0126	10.124	0.058444
75	0.371714	42134	15662	171238	0.091462	2.4823	325772	0.0126	7.732	0.091272
80	0.497807	26472	13178	97824	0.134711	2.4626	154535	0.0126	5.838	0.134459
85+	1.000000	13294	13294	56711	0.234418	4.2659	56711	0.0126	4.266	0.236639

TABLE 3 — FEMALE LIFE TABLE

x	$_nq_x$	l_x	$_nd_x$	$_nL_x$	$_nm_x$	$_na_x$	T_x	r_x	$\dot{e}_x$	$_nM_x$
0	0.020465	100000	2047	98505	0.020776	0.2696	7355270	0.0039	73.553	0.020840
1	0.004634	97953	454	390506	0.001162	1.1186	7256765	0.0039	74.084	0.001167
5	0.001929	97500	188	487027	0.000386	2.5000	6866259	0.0174	70.424	0.000389
10	0.001543	97311	150	486195	0.000309	2.5903	6379232	0.0327	65.555	0.000308
15	0.002606	97161	253	485198	0.000522	2.5990	5893036	0.0417	60.652	0.000520
20	0.002791	96908	270	483873	0.000559	2.5319	5407838	0.0265	55.804	0.000559
25	0.003048	96638	295	482506	0.000611	2.6847	4923965	0.0030	50.953	0.000610
30	0.005518	96343	532	480483	0.001106	2.6826	4441459	0.0000	46.100	0.001106
35	0.007939	95811	761	477271	0.001594	2.6522	3960976	0.0021	41.341	0.001593
40	0.011439	95051	1087	472740	0.002300	2.6885	3483705	0.0076	36.651	0.002297
45	0.018562	93963	1744	465758	0.003745	2.6730	3010965	0.0124	32.044	0.003736
50	0.027493	92219	2535	455218	0.005570	2.6813	2545206	0.0250	27.600	0.005543
55	0.044052	89684	3951	439238	0.008995	2.6760	2089989	0.0233	23.304	0.008954
60	0.068509	85733	5873	414903	0.014156	2.6567	1650751	0.0167	19.255	0.014112
65	0.104808	79860	8370	379820	0.022037	2.6728	1235848	0.0167	15.475	0.021955
70	0.179249	71490	12814	327253	0.039158	2.6437	856028	0.0167	11.974	0.039010
75	0.293245	58675	17206	251432	0.068433	2.5623	528775	0.0167	9.012	0.068207
80	0.433067	41469	17959	163761	0.109665	2.5731	277343	0.0167	6.688	0.109211
85+	*1.000000	23510	23510	113581	0.206989	4.8312	113581	0.0167	4.831	0.205556

TABLE 4 — OBSERVED AND PROJECTED VITAL RATES

	OBSERVED POPULATION BOTH SEXES	MALES	FEMALES	PROJECTED POPULATION 1966 MALES	FEMALES	1971 MALES	FEMALES	1976 MALES	FEMALES	STABLE POPULATION MALES	FEM
RATES PER THOUSAND											
Birth	23.77	24.35	23.18	24.70	23.48	26.65	25.34	28.16	26.80	28.54	27
Death	8.97	9.75	8.18	9.64	8.38	9.45	8.31	9.25	8.13	7.59	6
Increase	14.80	14.60	15.00	15.06	15.09	17.20	17.03	18.91	18.66		20.9
PERCENTAGE											
under 15	33.07	33.63	32.50	33.05	31.83	32.98	31.71	33.26	31.90	35.53	34
15-64	58.32	58.87	57.77	59.70	58.53	59.78	58.85	59.38	58.65	59.02	58
65 and over	8.61	7.50	9.73	7.25	9.64	7.24	9.44	7.35	9.45	5.45	7
DEP. RATIO X 100	71.47	69.88	73.11	67.51	70.85	67.28	69.92	68.39	70.50	69.43	71

TABLE 5 — POPULATION PROJECTED WITH FIXED AGE-SPECIFIC BIRTH AND DEATH RATES (IN 1000's)

AGE AT LAST BIRTHDAY	1966 BOTH SEXES	MALES	FEMALES	1971 BOTH SEXES	MALES	FEMALES	1976 BOTH SEXES	MALES	FEMALES	AGE AT LAST BIRTHDAY
0-4	294	151	143	333	171	162	388	199	189	0-4
5-9	292	149	143	293	150	143	332	170	162	5-9
10-14	262	134	128	292	149	143	292	150	142	10-14
15-19	245	125	120	262	134	128	291	148	143	15-19
20-24	188	96	92	244	124	120	261	133	128	20-24
25-29	159	80	79	187	95	92	242	123	119	25-29
30-34	143	73	70	158	80	78	186	95	91	30-34
35-39	156	81	75	143	73	70	157	79	78	35-39
40-44	157	80	77	155	80	75	141	72	69	40-44
45-49	142	70	72	155	79	76	152	78	74	45-49
50-54	138	69	69	138	68	70	150	76	74	50-54
55-59	121	61	60	131	65	66	132	64	68	55-59
60-64	98	49	49	112	55	57	121	58	63	60-64
65-69	77	36	41	86	41	45	99	47	52	65-69
70-74	59	25	34	63	28	35	72	33	39	70-74
75-79	43	18	25	43	17	26	46	19	27	75-79
80-84	27	11	16	26	10	16	27	10	17	80-84
85+	16	6	10	17	6	11	17	6	11	85+
TOTAL	2617	1314	1303	2838	1425	1413	3106	1560	1546	TOTAL

TABLE 6 — STANDARDIZED RATES

STANDARD COUNTRIES — STANDARDIZED RATES PER THOUSAND

	ENGLAND AND WALES 1961 BOTH SEXES	MALES	FEMALES	UNITED STATES 1960 BOTH SEXES	MALES	FEMALES	MEXICO 1960 BOTH SEXES	MALES	FEMALES
Birth	24.02	25.27*	22.59	24.41	23.70*	23.34	28.43	22.39*	27.52
Death	11.30	11.61*	11.11	9.21	10.28*	8.18	4.85	7.84*	4.00
Increase	12.72	13.66*	11.48	15.20	13.42*	15.16	23.58	14.55*	23.52

TABLE 7 — MOMENTS AND CUMULANTS

	OBSERVED POP. MALES	FEMALES	STATIONARY POP. MALES	FEMALES	STABLE POP. MALES	FEMALES	OBSERVED BIRTHS	NET MATERNITY FUNCTION	BIRTHS IN STABLE POP
μ	29.91785	31.23934	36.84415	38.98038	27.14587	28.34184	27.55918	27.70546	27.00733
σ^2	470.9897	510.0475	503.3917	549.9943	410.6333	450.0781	34.00690	32.37111	30.11427
κ_3	5343.987	5670.700	2404.598	2139.611	5794.570	6576.035	109.0159	107.0176	107.7713
κ_4	-161397.	-210354.	-246041.	-313723.	-63962.	-86563.	-288.727	-132.992	63.560
β_1	0.273336	0.242349	0.045328	0.027517	0.484931	0.474313	0.302189	0.337627	0.425294
β_2	2.272433	2.191408	2.029054	1.962877	2.620674	2.572678	2.750338	2.873086	3.070087
κ	-0.100962	-0.086651	-0.017284	-0.010112	-0.191664	-0.182324	-0.176018	-0.219328	-0.313461

TABLE 8 — RATES FROM AGE DISTRIBUTIONS AND VITAL STATISTICS (Females)

VITAL STATISTICS

		THOMPSON AGE RANGE	NRR	1000r	INTERVAL	BOURGEOIS-PICHAT AGE RANGE	NRR	1000b	1000d	1000r	COALE
GRR	1.840										
NRR	1.774	0-4	1.81	22.21	27.43	5-29	2.38	28.55	-3.49	32.04	IBR
GFR	3.792	5-9	1.69	19.48	27.39	30-54	1.22	17.22	9.91	7.30	IDR
GENERATION	27.352	10-14	1.63	17.59	27.34	55-79	1.34	17.91	7.11	10.80	IRI
SEX RATIO	106.071	15-19	1.29	9.12	27.25	*45-69	1.70	31.23	11.65	19.58	K1
											K2

TABLE 9 — LESLIE MATRIX AND ITS SPECTRAL COMPONENTS (Females)

ORIGINAL MATRIX SUB-DIAGONAL	ALTERNATIVE FIRST ROWS Projection	Integral	FIRST STABLE MATRIX % IN STABLE POPULATION	FISHER VALUES	REPRODUCTIVE VALUES	SECOND STABLE MATRIX Z₂ FIRST COLUMN	FIRST ROW
0.99594	0.00000	0.00000	12.740	1.077	154940	0.1778+0.0727	0.1778+0.0727
0.99829	0.00023	0.00000	11.424	1.201	154522	0.1537-0.1464	0.0059+0.1738
0.99795	0.05097	0.00048	10.268	1.336	160559	-0.0782-0.2216	-0.1410+0.0691
0.99727	0.32804	0.10716	9.225	1.432	132328	-0.2593-0.0214	-0.1182-0.0944
0.99718	0.56536	0.58580	8.283	1.241	97762	-0.1391+0.2520	-0.0244-0.1563
0.99581	0.45857	0.60743	7.437	0.771	54367	0.1913+0.2545	0.0191-0.1191
0.99332	0.25493	0.36054	6.667	0.364	27666	0.3430-0.0777	0.0236-0.0619
0.99051	0.10957	0.17792	5.963	0.131	10197	0.0766-0.3799	0.0144-0.0221
0.98523	0.02706	0.05350	5.317	0.028	2029	-0.3463-0.2476	0.0040-0.0044
0.97737	0.00172	0.00359	4.717	0.002	119	-0.4019+0.2345	0.0003-0.0003
0.96490	0.00002	0.00004	4.151	0.000	1	0.0536+0.5017	0.0000-0.0000
0.82067			13.808				

TABLE 10 — AGE ANALYSIS AND MISCELLANEOUS RESULTS (Females)

CONTRIBUTIONS OF ROOTS (IN 100's)

OBSERVED POPUL. (IN 100's)	r_1	r_2, r_3	$r_4 \cdot r_{11}$	AGE-SP. BIRTH RATES	NET MATERNITY FUNCTION	COEFF. OF MATRIX EQUATION	PARAMETERS	INTEGRAL	MATRIX	EXP. INCREASE x	$e^{(x+2\frac{1}{2})r}$
1438	1372	22	44	0.0000	0.0000	0.0000	L(1)	1.11042	1.11070	0	1.0538
1286	1230	109	-53	0.0000	0.0000	0.0002	L(2)	0.36564	0.36906	50	3.0034
1201	1106	72	24	0.0001	0.0005	0.0507		0.85441	0.82246	55	3.3350
924	994	-69	-1	0.0208	0.1009	0.3255	R(1)	0.02095	0.02100	60	3.7033
788	892	-150	46	0.1137	0.5501	0.5594	R(2)	-0.01465	-0.02075	65	4.1122
705	801	-52	-45	0.1179	0.5688	0.4525		0.23329	0.22980	70	4.5663
759	718	137	-96	0.0700	0.3362	0.2505	C(1)		10770	75	5.0705
778	642	2	157	0.0345	0.1648	0.1069	C(2)		15071	80	5.6304
732	573	-222	418	0.0104	0.0491	0.0262			21492	85	6.2520
704	508	-199	375	0.0007	0.0033	0.0016	2P/Y	26.9333	27.3420	90	6.9424
622	447			0.0000	0.0000	0.0000	DELTA	7.2151		95	7.7090
2142	1487									100	8.5602

TABLE 1 — DATA

AGE AT LAST BIRTHDAY	POPULATION BOTH SEXES	MALES Number	%	FEMALES Number	%	BIRTHS BY AGE OF MOTHER	DEATHS BOTH SEXES	MALES	FEMALES	AGE AT LAST BIRTHDAY
0	65640	33600	2.5	32040	2.4	0	1174	698	476	0
1-4	246930	126398	9.5	120532	9.1	0	268	146	122	1-4
5-9	293125	149665	11.2	143460	10.9	0	111	71	40	5-9
10-14	262265	134350	10.1	127915	9.7	160	107	61	46	10-14
15-19	241585	123485	9.3	118100	8.9	6756	201	150	51	15-19
20-24	186115	95615	7.2	90500	6.9	20920	188	136	52	20-24
25-29	161495	82105	6.2	79390	6.0	17002	186	126	60	25-29
30-34	153315	78875	5.9	74440	5.6	8882	209	141	68	30-34
35-39	162425	84275	6.3	78150	5.9	4815	284	186	98	35-39
40-44	161060	81765	6.1	79295	6.0	1543	482	281	201	40-44
45-49	142090	70210	5.3	71880	5.4	98	651	386	265	45-49
50-54	138950	69695	5.2	69255	5.2	2	1052	654	398	50-54
55-59	119595	60160	4.5	59435	4.5	0	1502	964	538	55-59
60-64	98220	48575	3.6	49645	3.8	0	1934	1252	682	60-64
65-69	76670	35110	2.6	41560	3.1	0	2341	1402	939	65-69
70-74	59803	25208	1.9	34595	2.6		2695	1490	1205	70-74
75-79	43538	18040	1.4	25498	1.9		3336	1743	1593	75-79
80-84	26219	10677	0.8	15542	1.2	30869 M.	3098	1495	1603	80-84
85+	13303	4948	0.4	8355	0.6	29309 F.	3157	1277	1880	85+
TOTAL	2652343	1332756		1319587		60178	22976	12659	10317	TOTAL

TABLE 2 — MALE LIFE TABLE

x	$_nq_x$	l_x	$_nd_x$	$_nL_x$	$_nm_x$	$_na_x$	T_x	r_x	$\dot{e}_x$	$_nM_x$
0	0.020381	100000	2038	98510	0.020689	0.2688	6843802	0.0053	68.438	0.020774
1	0.004580	97962	449	390555	0.001149	1.1179	6745292	0.0053	68.856	0.001155
5	0.002359	97513	230	486991	0.000472	2.5000	6354738	0.0168	65.168	0.000474
10	0.002282	97283	222	485936	0.000457	2.8387	5867747	0.0186	60.316	0.000454
15	0.006089	97061	591	483925	0.001221	2.6632	5381811	0.0329	55.448	0.001215
20	0.007100	96470	685	480668	0.001425	2.5431	4897886	0.0394	50.771	0.001422
25	0.007651	95785	733	477127	0.001536	2.5458	4417218	0.0177	46.116	0.001535
30	0.008900	95052	846	473210	0.001788	2.5742	3940091	0.0000	41.452	0.001788
35	0.010978	94206	1034	468602	0.002207	2.6505	3466882	0.0000	36.801	0.002207
40	0.017097	93172	1593	462182	0.003447	2.6906	2998280	0.0147	32.180	0.003437
45	0.027207	91579	2492	452188	0.005510	2.7094	2536098	0.0102	27.693	0.005498
50	0.045988	89088	4097	436049	0.009396	2.7084	2083909	0.0056	23.392	0.009384
55	0.077539	84991	6590	409612	0.016089	2.6721	1647860	0.0195	19.389	0.016024
60	0.121708	78400	9542	369391	0.025832	2.6304	1238248	0.0120	15.794	0.025775
65	0.182415	68858	12561	313936	0.040011	2.5833	868857	0.0120	12.618	0.039932
70	0.258669	56298	14562	245849	0.059233	2.5527	554921	0.0120	9.857	0.059108
75	0.389202	41735	16243	167775	0.096817	2.4820	309072	0.0120	7.406	0.096619
80	0.516199	25492	13159	93747	0.140365	2.4381	141297	0.0120	5.543	0.140021
85+	*1.000000	12333	12333	47549	0.259371	3.8555	47549	0.0120	3.855	0.258084

TABLE 3 — FEMALE LIFE TABLE

x	$_nq_x$	l_x	$_nd_x$	$_nL_x$	$_nm_x$	$_na_x$	T_x	r_x	$\dot{e}_x$	$_nM_x$
0	0.014641	100000	1464	98963	0.014795	0.2914	7429138	0.0054	74.291	0.014856
1	0.004017	98536	396	393011	0.001007	1.1401	7330176	0.0054	74.391	0.001012
5	0.001384	98140	136	490361	0.000277	2.5000	6937164	0.0171	70.686	0.000279
10	0.001800	98004	176	489596	0.000360	2.5897	6446804	0.0191	65.781	0.000360
15	0.002165	97828	212	488632	0.000433	2.6033	5957208	0.0342	60.895	0.000432
20	0.002882	97616	281	487409	0.000577	2.6155	5468577	0.0391	56.021	0.000575
25	0.003779	97335	368	485788	0.000757	2.5910	4981167	0.0188	51.176	0.000756
30	0.004558	96967	442	483779	0.000914	2.6111	4495380	0.0006	46.360	0.000913
35	0.006252	96525	604	481276	0.001254	2.7652	4011601	0.0000	41.560	0.001254
40	0.012615	95921	1210	476818	0.002538	2.6946	3530325	0.0059	36.804	0.002535
45	0.018308	94711	1734	469520	0.003693	2.6722	3053507	0.0097	32.240	0.003687
50	0.028427	92977	2643	458756	0.005761	2.6803	2583987	0.0130	27.792	0.005747
55	0.044511	90334	4021	442270	0.009091	2.6617	2125231	0.0240	23.526	0.009052
60	0.066786	86313	5765	418124	0.013787	2.6679	1682962	0.0180	19.498	0.013738
65	0.107596	80549	8667	382295	0.022670	2.6405	1264838	0.0180	15.703	0.022594
70	0.161501	71882	11609	332002	0.034967	2.6390	882542	0.0180	12.278	0.034832
75	0.272296	60273	16412	261711	0.062711	2.5838	550541	0.0180	9.134	0.062476
80	0.415250	43861	18213	175696	0.103664	2.6056	288829	0.0180	6.585	0.103139
85+	*1.000000	25648	25648	113133	0.226703	4.4110	113133	0.0180	4.411	0.225015

TABLE 4 — OBSERVED AND PROJECTED VITAL RATES

	OBSERVED POPULATION BOTH SEXES	MALES	FEMALES	PROJECTED POPULATION 1970 MALES	FEMALES	1975 MALES	FEMALES	1980 MALES	FEMALES	STABLE POPULATION MALES	FEMALES
RATES PER THOUSAND											
Birth	22.69	23.16	22.21	24.90	23.82	26.37	25.19	27.17	25.94	26.97	25
Death	8.66	9.50	7.82	9.31	7.95	9.15	7.93	9.04	7.82	7.88	6
Increase	14.03	13.66	14.39	15.59	15.86	17.22	17.26	18.13	18.12		19.0
PERCENTAGE											
under 15	32.72	33.32	32.13	32.87	31.66	32.68	31.41	33.05	31.77	34.28	32
15-64	59.00	59.63	58.36	60.06	58.80	60.13	58.99	59.68	58.51	59.93	59
65 and over	8.28	7.05	9.51	7.07	9.54	7.19	9.60	7.27	9.71	5.79	7
DEP. RATIO X 100	69.50	67.69	71.35	66.51	70.06	66.31	69.53	67.57	70.90	66.87	69

TABLE 5 — POPULATION PROJECTED WITH FIXED AGE-SPECIFIC BIRTH AND DEATH RATES (IN 1000's)

AGE LAST BIRTHDAY	1970 BOTH SEXES	MALES	FEMALES	1975 BOTH SEXES	MALES	FEMALES	1980 BOTH SEXES	MALES	FEMALES	AGE AT LAST BIRTHDAY
0-4	319	163	156	367	188	179	417	213	204	0-4
5-9	311	159	152	317	162	155	366	187	179	5-9
10-14	292	149	143	311	159	152	317	162	155	10-14
15-19	262	134	128	292	149	143	310	158	152	15-19
20-24	241	123	118	260	133	127	291	148	143	20-24
25-29	185	95	90	239	122	117	259	132	127	25-29
30-34	160	81	79	184	94	90	238	121	117	30-34
35-39	152	78	74	160	81	79	182	93	89	35-39
40-44	160	83	77	150	77	73	158	80	78	40-44
45-49	158	80	78	157	81	76	147	75	72	45-49
50-54	138	68	70	153	77	76	152	78	74	50-54
55-59	132	65	67	132	64	68	146	72	74	55-59
60-64	110	54	56	122	59	63	121	57	64	60-64
65-69	86	41	45	97	46	51	108	50	58	65-69
70-74	63	27	36	71	32	39	81	36	45	70-74
75-79	44	17	27	47	19	28	53	22	31	75-79
80-84	27	10	17	28	10	18	29	10	19	80-84
85+	15	5	10	16	5	11	17	5	12	85+
TOTAL	2855	1432	1423	3103	1558	1545	3392	1699	1693	TOTAL

TABLE 6 — STANDARDIZED RATES

STANDARD COUNTRIES / STANDARDIZED RATES PER THOUSAND

	ENGLAND AND WALES 1961 BOTH SEXES	MALES	FEMALES	UNITED STATES 1960 BOTH SEXES	MALES	FEMALES	MEXICO 1960 BOTH SEXES	MALES	FEMALES
Birth	22.39	24.35*	21.13	22.77	22.52*	21.85	26.97	21.82*	26.20
Death	11.23	11.79*	10.74	9.13	10.37*	7.86	4.63	7.84*	3.69
Increase	11.15	12.56*	10.39	13.63	12.15*	13.99	22.34	13.98*	22.52

TABLE 7 — MOMENTS AND CUMULANTS

	OBSERVED POP. MALES	FEMALES	STATIONARY POP. MALES	FEMALES	STABLE POP MALES	FEMALES	OBSERVED BIRTHS	NET MATERNITY FUNCTION	BIRTHS IN STABLE POP.
	29.53679	31.01881	36.65654	39.09476	27.82217	29.25762	26.55539	27.16545	26.49302
	462.3431	508.3814	498.0524	552.6796	417.5459	464.4285	35.67263	34.32230	31.98745
	5469.283	5974.768	2352.729	2125.614	5560.339	6442.156	141.6890	122.4175	121.6086
	-150847.	-203766.	-241547.	-318317.	-81228.	-110998.	-0.384	-63.450	149.306
β_1	0.302669	0.271690	0.044804	0.026764	0.424707	0.414291	0.442249	0.370645	0.451845
β_2	2.294321	2.211591	2.026242	1.957891	2.534094	2.485390	2.999699	2.946138	3.145921
κ	-0.110584	-0.096035	-0.017053	-0.009803	-0.166336	-0.157682	-0.280952	-0.251686	-0.357255

TABLE 8 — RATES FROM AGE DISTRIBUTIONS AND VITAL STATISTICS (Females)

VITAL STATISTICS

GR	1.718
NRR	1.668
R	3.528
GENERATION	26.826
SEX RATIO	105.323

THOMPSON

AGE RANGE	NRR	1000r	INTERVAL
0-4	1.73	20.54	27.43
5-9	1.78	21.39	27.40
10-14	1.65	18.03	27.34
15-19	1.57	15.72	27.25

BOURGEOIS-PICHAT

AGE RANGE	NRR	1000b	1000d	1000r
5-29	2.26	28.72	-1.40	30.12
30-54	1.05	12.94	11.00	1.94
55-79	1.58	26.58	9.55	17.03
*50-74	1.67	30.50	11.43	19.07

COALE: IBR, IDR, IRI, K1, K2

TABLE 9 — LESLIE MATRIX AND ITS SPECTRAL COMPONENTS (Females)

ORIGINAL MATRIX SUB-DIAGONAL	ALTERNATIVE FIRST ROWS Projection	Integral	FIRST STABLE MATRIX % IN STABLE POPULATION	FISHER VALUES	REPRODUCTIVE VALUES	SECOND STABLE MATRIX Z₂ FIRST COLUMN	FIRST ROW
0.99672	0.00000	0.00000	12.102	1.066	162616	0.1829+0.0830	0.1829+0.0830
0.99844	0.00150	0.00000	10.962	1.177	168803	0.1691-0.1556	-0.0044+0.1755
0.99803	0.06990	0.00314	9.947	1.295	165670	-0.0886-0.2479	-0.1428+0.0560
0.99750	0.34478	0.14377	9.022	1.353	159824	-0.3011-0.0173	-0.1065-0.1015
0.99667	0.53266	0.58095	8.179	1.124	101761	-0.1528+0.3097	-0.0179-0.1489
0.99587	0.39893	0.53822	7.408	0.672	53333	0.2581+0.2991	0.0160-0.1095
0.99483	0.21638	0.29987	6.705	0.315	23472	0.4299-0.1382	0.0204-0.0577
0.99074	0.09691	0.15484	6.062	0.117	9138	0.0461-0.5136	0.0137-0.0213
0.98470	0.02492	0.04890	5.458	0.026	2031	-0.5173-0.2761	0.0041-0.0043
0.97707	0.00167	0.00343	4.884	0.002	118	-0.5154+0.4166	0.0003-0.0003
0.96406	0.00003	0.00007	4.337	0.000	2	0.2047+0.7145	0.0000-0.0000
0.82041			14.935				

TABLE 10 — AGE ANALYSIS AND MISCELLANEOUS RESULTS (Females)

CONTRIBUTIONS OF ROOTS (IN 100's)

OBSERVED POPUL. (IN 100's)	r_1	r_2, r_3	$r_4 \cdot r_{11}$	AGE-SP BIRTH RATES	NET MATERNITY FUNCTION	COEFF. OF MATRIX EQUATION	PARAMETERS	INTEGRAL	MATRIX	x	$e^{(x+8\frac{1}{2})r}$
1526	1506	-20	39	0.0000	0.0000	0.0000	L(1)	1.10012	1.10035	0	1.0489
1435	1364	87	-16	0.0000	0.0000	0.0015	L(2)	0.33232	0.33986	50	2.7234
1279	1238	103	-62	0.0006	0.0030	0.0696		0.83560	0.80221	55	2.9960
1181	1123	-21	80	0.0279	0.1361	0.3424	R(1)	0.01908	0.01913	60	3.2960
905	1018	-155	42	0.1126	0.5487	0.5277	R(2)	-0.02124	-0.02757	65	3.6259
794	922	-110	-18	0.1043	0.5067	0.3939		0.23846	0.23401	70	3.9889
744	834	104	-194	0.0581	0.2811	0.2128	C(1)		12446	75	4.3883
782	754	236	-209	0.0300	0.1444	0.0948	C(2)		4868	80	4.8276
793	679	74	39	0.0095	0.0452	0.0242			22558	85	5.3110
719	608	-238	349	0.0007	0.0031	0.0016	2P/Y	26.3495	26.8498	90	5.8427
693	540	-302	455	0.0000	0.0001	0.0000	DELTA	4.8363		95	6.4276
2346	1859									100	7.0711

Pooled Data

States of the United States by Mortality Levels
Aggregates for Europe and Regions, 1961

AGGREGATES FOR REGIONS AND TYPES OF POPULATION

As among a number of countries with similar conditions affecting mortality and fertility, the differences in vital rates may be insignificant, either because they arise from variations in statistical reporting or because they are due to chance variation in numbers which are, in a statistical sense, samples from a single population. Aside from this there is an interest in certain groups of countries which may be incipient political units, such as the European Common Market.

For grouped populations the computer was instructed to add corresponding items in the data of Table 1, so that an aggregate was assembled showing the same breakdowns by age and sex as the individual countries.' The pooled data was then put through the standard program. This was done for three areas of Europe whose comparison might be of interest, listed in Table E: the Common Market Six, the Outer Seven, the socialist countries of Eastern Europe. These, along with most of the remainder of Europe without the USSR, were then put together as a grand total. The only omissions were Albania and Northern Ireland, for which we lack 1961 information, containing about 3 million people, less than 1 per cent of Europe. Data was divided by 100 to economize space in the printout.

The tables for Europe 1961 permit a comparison with the United States, if we take for the latter 1959–61. The expectation of life at birth for males in Europe is 66.89, almost identical with the United States at 66.84. European women, on the other hand, at 72.22 are below United States women at 73.40. The difference is increased by one year if on the United States side we confine the calculation to white women. Standardizing both sexes together by the United States 1960 population gives 9.71 per thou-

TABLE E

GROUPING OF COUNTRIES TO FORM THE THREE DIVISIONS OF
EUROPE, AND EUROPE AS A WHOLE, ALL FOR 1961

COMMON MARKET (The Six)	EUROPEAN FREE TRADE ASSOCIATION (The Outer Seven)
Belgium	Austria
Federal Republic of Germany	Denmark
France	Norway
Italy	Portugal
Luxemburg	Sweden
Netherlands	Switzerland
	United Kingdom
	England and Wales
	Scotland

SOCIALIST COUNTRIES OF EASTERN EUROPE (COMECON)	OTHER, INCLUDED IN EUROPE
Bulgaria	Finland
Czechoslovakia	Greece
Democratic Republic of Germany	Iceland
Hungary	Ireland
Poland	Malta and Gozo
Roumania	Yugoslavia

sand for Europe against 9.39 for the United States; the United States also shows lower on standardization by England and Wales 1961.

Europe increases far more slowly; its intrinsic rate was 6.42 per thousand, against 20.70 for the United States, though since 1960 the difference has narrowed. As among groups of European countries, the male $\overset{\circ}{e}_0$ for the Common Market Six was 67.55 years; for the Outer Seven, 67.26; for the Comecon countries, 65.99.

The states of the United States were grouped by standardized death rates: over ten per thousand; over nine and under ten per thousand; under nine per thousand. Which states are in each group may be ascertained from the Summary Table.

States with Low Mortality Rates

TABLE 1 — DATA

AGE AT LAST BIRTHDAY	POPULATION BOTH SEXES	MALES Number	%	FEMALES Number	%	BIRTHS BY AGE OF MOTHER	DEATHS BOTH SEXES	MALES	FEMALES	AGE AT LAST BIRTHDAY
0	1362998	694261	2.4	668737	2.3	0	34872	20210	14662	0
1-4	5350529	2721129	9.4	2629400	8.9	0	5688	3183	2505	1-4
5-9	6224568	3166492	10.9	3058076	10.4	0	2937	1741	1196	5-9
10-14	5506124	2798562	9.6	2707562	9.2	2083	2457	1587	870	10-14
15-19	4311566	2186716	7.5	2124850	7.2	205653	4163	2948	1215	15-19
20-24	3582298	1786118	6.1	1796180	6.1	490724	4527	3286	1241	20-24
25-29	3574528	1779713	6.1	1794815	6.1	355436	4488	3004	1484	25-29
30-34	3844475	1900426	6.5	1944049	6.6	214864	5875	3676	2199	30-34
35-39	4012737	1976758	6.8	2035979	6.9	111919	8559	5257	3302	35-39
40-44	3686841	1828576	6.3	1858265	6.3	29041	12419	7790	4629	40-44
45-49	3463800	1725679	5.9	1738121	5.9	1642	18441	11802	6639	45-49
50-54	3051846	1523423	5.2	1528423	5.2	29	25883	17104	8779	50-54
55-59	2686490	1327375	4.6	1359115	4.6	0	33138	22185	10953	55-59
60-64	2295994	1104861	3.8	1191133	4.0	0	43379	28493	14886	60-64
65-69	2057325	978219	3.4	1079106	3.7	0	56764	36135	20629	65-69
70-74	1594430	752761	2.6	841669	2.9		66337	39925	26412	70-74
75-79	1039840	475064	1.6	564776	1.9		67882	37583	30299	75-79
80-84	542058	235484	0.8	306574	1.0	723086 M.	58456	29299	29157	80-84
85+	318447	129205	0.4	189242	0.6	688305 F.	60202	26254	33948	85+
TOTAL	58506894	29090822		29416072		1411391	516467	301462	215005	TOTAL

TABLE 2 — MALE LIFE TABLE

x	$_nq_x$	l_x	$_nd_x$	$_nL_x$	$_nm_x$	$_na_x$	T_x	r_x	$\dot{e}_x$	$_nM_x$
0	0.028452	100000	2845	97819	0.029087	0.2335	6772986	0.0010	67.730	0.029110
1	0.004657	97155	452	387302	0.001168	1.0899	6675167	0.0010	68.707	0.001170
5	0.002736	96702	265	482850	0.000548	2.5000	6287865	0.0192	65.023	0.000550
10	0.002862	96438	276	481579	0.000573	2.7922	5805014	0.0363	60.194	0.000567
15	0.006777	96162	652	479304	0.001360	2.6915	5323435	0.0436	55.359	0.001348
20	0.009164	95510	875	475392	0.001841	2.5342	4844131	0.0189	50.719	0.001840
25	0.008404	94635	795	471192	0.001688	2.5074	4368738	0.0000	46.164	0.001688
30	0.009627	93840	903	467029	0.001934	2.5999	3897547	0.0000	41.534	0.001934
35	0.013218	92936	1228	461825	0.002660	2.6755	3430518	0.0010	36.913	0.002659
40	0.021132	91708	1938	454069	0.004268	2.6936	2968692	0.0092	32.371	0.004260
45	0.033741	89770	3029	441864	0.006855	2.6939	2514624	0.0111	28.012	0.006839
50	0.054841	86741	4757	422557	0.011257	2.6567	2072760	0.0149	23.896	0.011227
55	0.080595	81984	6607	394322	0.016757	2.6395	1650203	0.0147	20.128	0.016713
60	0.121801	75376	9181	354896	0.025869	2.6053	1255881	0.0197	16.661	0.025789
65	0.169929	66195	11249	303636	0.037046	2.5694	900984	0.0197	13.611	0.036940
70	0.235244	54947	12926	242977	0.053198	2.5431	597348	0.0197	10.871	0.053038
75	0.331310	42021	13922	175397	0.079374	2.5070	354371	0.0197	8.433	0.079111
80	0.476576	28099	13391	107181	0.124942	2.5122	178974	0.0197	6.369	0.124420
85+	*1.000000	14708	14708	71794	0.204861	4.8814	71794	0.0197	4.881	0.203196

TABLE 3 — FEMALE LIFE TABLE

x	$_nq_x$	l_x	$_nd_x$	$_nL_x$	$_nm_x$	$_na_x$	T_x	r_x	$\dot{e}_x$	$_nM_x$
0	0.021551	100000	2155	98367	0.021909	0.2421	7460203	0.0009	74.602	0.021925
1	0.003796	97845	371	390301	0.000952	1.0961	7361837	0.0009	75.240	0.000953
5	0.001943	97473	189	486894	0.000389	2.5000	6971536	0.0192	71.522	0.000391
10	0.001612	97284	157	486047	0.000323	2.6188	6484642	0.0360	66.657	0.000321
15	0.002871	97127	279	484976	0.000575	2.6327	5998595	0.0405	61.760	0.000572
20	0.003453	96848	334	483431	0.000692	2.5744	5513619	0.0162	56.930	0.000691
25	0.004126	96514	398	481618	0.000827	2.6087	5030189	0.0000	52.119	0.000827
30	0.005641	96116	542	479301	0.001131	2.6438	4548571	0.0000	47.324	0.001131
35	0.008083	95574	772	476069	0.001623	2.6712	4069270	0.0028	42.577	0.001622
40	0.012413	94801	1177	471273	0.002497	2.6779	3593202	0.0132	37.903	0.002491
45	0.018981	93624	1777	463977	0.003830	2.6680	3121928	0.0156	33.345	0.003820
50	0.028416	91847	2610	453078	0.005760	2.6406	2657951	0.0188	28.939	0.005744
55	0.039657	89237	3539	437885	0.008082	2.6542	2204873	0.0164	24.708	0.008059
60	0.061063	85698	5230	416223	0.012565	2.6639	1766988	0.0298	20.619	0.012497
65	0.091998	80469	7403	384983	0.019229	2.6550	1350765	0.0298	16.786	0.019117
70	0.146973	73066	10739	340044	0.031580	2.6455	965782	0.0298	13.218	0.031381
75	0.239085	62327	14901	275959	0.053999	2.6059	625738	0.0298	10.040	0.053648
80	0.386124	47426	18312	191449	0.095651	2.6617	349778	0.0298	7.375	0.095106
85+	1.000000	29113	29113	158330	0.183878	5.4384	158330	0.0298	5.438	0.179389

TABLE 4 — OBSERVED AND PROJECTED VITAL RATES

	OBSERVED POPULATION BOTH SEXES	MALES	FEMALES	PROJECTED POPULATION 1965 MALES	FEMALES	1970 MALES	FEMALES	1975 MALES	FEMALES	STABLE POPULATION MALES	FEMA
RATES PER THOUSAND											
Birth	24.12	24.86	23.40	25.11	23.47	26.91	25.05	28.32	26.33	29.58	28.
Death	8.83	10.36	7.31	10.51	7.86	10.50	8.23	10.24	8.35	7.54	6.
Increase	15.30	14.49	16.09	14.59	15.61	16.41	16.82	18.08	17.98		22.03
PERCENTAGE											
under 15	31.52	32.25	30.81	32.65	30.90	32.95	31.00	33.81	31.69	36.50	35.
15-64	58.99	58.92	59.05	58.66	58.48	58.57	58.19	57.99	57.52	58.25	57.
65 and over	9.49	8.84	10.14	8.69	10.62	8.48	10.81	8.20	10.78	5.25	7.
DEP. RATIO X 100	69.53	69.73	69.34	70.47	70.99	70.74	71.84	72.44	73.84	71.68	73.

33 United States 1959–61
States with Medium Mortality Rates

TABLE 1

AGE AT LAST BIRTHDAY	POPULATION BOTH SEXES	MALES Number	%	FEMALES Number	%	BIRTHS BY AGE OF MOTHER	DEATHS BOTH SEXES	MALES	FEMALES	AGE AT LAST BIRTHDAY
0	1947493	989860	2.3	957633	2.2	0	50467	29052	21415	0
1-4	7701214	3915680	9.2	3785534	8.6	0	7612	4215	3397	1-4
5-9	8803360	4478617	10.5	4324743	9.8	0	4132	2433	1699	5-9
10-14	7919713	4026008	9.5	3893705	8.8	2653	3341	2116	1225	10-14
15-19	6210859	3089265	7.3	3121594	7.1	248492	5308	3747	1561	15-19
20-24	5072592	2429330	5.7	2643262	6.0	659556	5936	4203	1733	20-24
25-29	5223403	2544867	6.0	2678536	6.1	530838	6309	4070	2239	25-29
30-34	5836150	2848235	6.7	2987915	6.8	342252	9008	5492	3516	30-34
35-39	6096508	2960582	7.0	3135926	7.1	177893	13621	8140	5481	35-39
40-44	5698379	2768320	6.5	2930059	6.6	44592	20356	12425	7931	40-44
45-49	5352656	2619820	6.2	2732836	6.2	2387	30890	19430	11460	45-49
50-54	4764950	2336615	5.5	2428335	5.5	51	44137	28715	15422	50-54
55-59	4219494	2063289	4.9	2156205	4.9	0	57992	37963	20029	55-59
60-64	3602849	1719053	4.0	1883796	4.3	0	77136	48972	28164	60-64
65-69	3111748	1452369	3.4	1659379	3.8	0	99806	61048	38758	65-69
70-74	2344677	1073101	2.5	1271576	2.9		113139	64585	48554	70-74
75-79	1497091	659476	1.6	837615	1.9		110865	57910	52955	75-79
80-84	775188	321648	0.8	453540	1.0	1028717 M.	93247	43869	49378	80-84
85+	455347	173495	0.4	281852	0.6	979997 F.	92478	37558	54920	85+
TOTAL	86633671	42469630		44164041		2008714	845780	475943	369837	TOTAL

TABLE 2

x	$_nq_x$	l_x	$_nd_x$	$_nL_x$	$_nm_x$	$_na_x$	T_x	r_x	$\mathring{e}_x$	$_nM_x$	x
0	0.028693	100000	2869	97773	0.029346	0.2240	6682168	0.0001	66.822	0.029350	0
1	0.004291	97131	417	387307	0.001076	1.0834	6584395	0.0001	67.789	0.001076	1
5	0.002704	96714	262	482916	0.000542	2.5000	6197088	0.0191	64.077	0.000543	5
10	0.002651	96452	256	481691	0.000531	2.7658	5714172	0.0365	59.243	0.000526	10
15	0.006109	96197	588	479633	0.001225	2.7016	5232482	0.0493	54.394	0.001213	15
20	0.008621	95609	824	476020	0.001732	2.5423	4752849	0.0178	49.711	0.001730	20
25	0.007965	94785	755	472053	0.001599	2.5216	4276829	0.0000	45.121	0.001599	25
30	0.009597	94030	902	468001	0.001928	2.6194	3804776	0.0000	40.463	0.001928	30
35	0.013660	93127	1272	462695	0.002749	2.6869	3336775	0.0000	35.830	0.002749	35
40	0.022248	91855	2044	454586	0.004496	2.7048	2874081	0.0075	31.289	0.004488	40
45	0.036531	89812	3281	441509	0.007431	2.6991	2419495	0.0092	26.940	0.007417	45
50	0.059847	86531	5179	420521	0.012315	2.6571	1977986	0.0114	22.859	0.012289	50
55	0.088336	81352	7186	389782	0.018437	2.6374	1557465	0.0115	19.145	0.018399	55
60	0.133707	74166	9916	347098	0.028570	2.6070	1167683	0.0173	15.744	0.028488	60
65	0.191088	64249	12277	291329	0.042142	2.5632	820585	0.0173	12.772	0.042033	65
70	0.262472	51972	13641	226077	0.060339	2.5234	529255	0.0173	10.183	0.060185	70
75	0.360344	38331	13812	156857	0.088057	2.4807	303178	0.0173	7.910	0.087812	75
80	0.504220	24519	12363	90387	0.136776	2.4721	146321	0.0173	5.968	0.136388	80
85+	1.000000	12156	12156	55934	0.217322	4.6015	55934	0.0173	4.601	0.216478	85+

TABLE 3

x	$_nq_x$	l_x	$_nd_x$	$_nL_x$	$_nm_x$	$_na_x$	T_x	r_x	e_x	$_nM_x$	x
0	0.021979	100000	2198	98316	0.022355	0.2337	7318598	0.0004	73.186	0.022362	0
1	0.003578	97802	350	390190	0.000897	1.0900	7220282	0.0004	73.825	0.000897	1
5	0.001953	97452	190	486785	0.000393	2.5000	6830092	0.0192	70.087	0.000393	5
10	0.001576	97262	153	485937	0.000315	2.5728	6343307	0.0322	65.219	0.000315	10
15	0.002511	97109	244	484968	0.000503	2.6404	5857370	0.0382	60.318	0.000500	15
20	0.003278	96865	318	483563	0.000657	2.6042	5372402	0.0146	55.463	0.000656	20
25	0.004171	96547	403	481781	0.000836	2.6276	4888839	0.0000	50.637	0.000836	25
30	0.005868	96145	564	479402	0.001177	2.6585	4407058	0.0000	45.838	0.001177	30
35	0.008704	95580	832	475971	0.001748	2.6785	3927656	0.0001	41.093	0.001748	35
40	0.013477	94748	1277	470782	0.002712	2.6817	3451686	0.0110	36.430	0.002707	40
45	0.020818	93472	1946	462825	0.004204	2.6707	2980903	0.0145	31.891	0.004193	45
50	0.031376	91526	2872	450886	0.006369	2.6521	2518078	0.0172	27.512	0.006351	50
55	0.045592	88654	4042	433846	0.009316	2.6684	2067193	0.0156	23.318	0.009289	55
60	0.072561	84612	6140	408688	0.015022	2.6690	1633347	0.0251	19.304	0.014951	60
65	0.111217	78473	8727	371820	0.023472	2.6462	1224659	0.0251	15.606	0.023357	65
70	0.175830	69745	12263	319546	0.038377	2.6206	852839	0.0251	12.228	0.038184	70
75	0.275286	57482	15824	249013	0.063547	2.5735	533293	0.0251	9.278	0.063221	75
80	0.428448	41658	17848	163180	0.109378	2.5932	284280	0.0251	6.824	0.108872	80
85+	1.000000	23810	23810	121100	0.196611	5.0862	121100	0.0251	5.086	0.194853	85+

TABLE 4

	OBSERVED POPULATION BOTH SEXES	MALES	FEMALES	PROJECTED POPULATION 1965 MALES	FEMALES	1970 MALES	FEMALES	1975 MALES	FEMALES	STABLE POPULATION MALES	FEMALES
RATES PER THOUSAND											
Birth	23.19	24.22	22.19	24.12	22.03	25.60	23.35	26.99	24.65	28.02	26.66
Death	9.76	11.21	8.37	11.28	8.79	11.23	9.12	10.99	9.25	8.18	6.81
Increase	13.42	13.02	13.82	12.84	13.24	14.37	14.24	16.00	15.41	19.8407	
PERCENTAGE											
under 15	30.44	31.58	29.35	32.00	29.57	32.28	29.75	32.84	30.23	35.13	33.68
15-64	60.11	59.76	60.45	59.41	59.81	59.25	59.42	58.93	58.87	59.51	58.86
65 and over	9.45	8.67	10.20	8.59	10.61	8.47	10.83	8.23	10.90	5.36	7.46
DEP. RATIO X 100	66.35	67.34	65.42	68.32	67.18	68.76	68.30	69.68	69.86	68.04	69.91

States with High Mortality Rates

TABLE 1 — DATA

AGE AT LAST BIRTHDAY	POPULATION BOTH SEXES	MALES Number	MALES %	FEMALES Number	FEMALES %	BIRTHS BY AGE OF MOTHER	DEATHS BOTH SEXES	DEATHS MALES	FEMALES	AGE AT LAST BIRTHDAY
0	816144	412953	2.4	403191	2.3	0	25124	14298	10826	0
1-4	3215030	1631226	9.6	1583804	8.9	0	3862	2108	1754	1-4
5-9	3730533	1891799	11.1	1838734	10.4	0	1937	1098	839	5-9
10-14	3407322	1728822	10.1	1678500	9.5	2273	1622	1053	569	10-1
15-19	2743850	1380366	8.1	1363484	7.7	133136	2588	1826	762	15-1
20-24	2184397	1074987	6.3	1109410	6.3	277819	2941	2045	896	20-2
25-29	2109780	1026674	6.0	1083106	6.1	207011	3170	2038	1132	25-2
30-34	2310745	1117375	6.5	1193370	6.7	132681	4334	2563	1771	30-3
35-39	2415807	1162718	6.8	1253089	7.1	70298	6605	3952	2653	35-3
40-44	2255714	1098110	6.4	1157604	6.5	18235	9600	5839	3761	40-4
45-49	2101090	1030437	6.0	1070653	6.0	1088	13950	8874	5076	45-4
50-54	1822644	890651	5.2	931993	5.3	37	19448	12506	6942	50-5
55-59	1553187	750364	4.4	802823	4.5	0	24293	15475	8818	55-5
60-64	1268329	596721	3.5	671608	3.8	0	30586	18782	11804	60-6
65-69	1110511	510224	3.0	600287	3.4	0	37968	22680	15288	65-6
70-74	816371	366707	2.1	449664	2.5		40415	22734	17681	70-7
75-79	527235	229391	1.3	297844	1.7		38654	20089	18565	75-7
80-84	268177	110166	0.6	158011	0.9	430991 M.	31653	14808	16845	80-8
85+	158556	60683	0.4	97873	0.6	411587 F.	30187	12365	17822	85+
TOTAL	34815422	17070374		17745048		842578	328937	185133	143804	TOTA

TABLE 2 — MALE LIFE TABLE

x	nq_x	l_x	nd_x	nL_x	nm_x	na_x	T_x	r_x	$\mathring{e}_x$	nM_x
0	0.033717	100000	3372	97389	0.034621	0.2256	6533695	0.0001	65.337	0.034624
1	0.005149	96628	498	385063	0.001292	1.0845	6436306	0.0001	66.609	0.001292
5	0.002889	96131	278	479959	0.000579	2.5000	6051243	0.0160	62.948	0.000580
10	0.003065	95853	294	478605	0.000614	2.7541	5571284	0.0308	58.123	0.000609
15	0.006656	95559	636	476332	0.001335	2.6987	5092678	0.0462	53.293	0.001323
20	0.009487	94923	901	472426	0.001906	2.5677	4616346	0.0278	48.632	0.001902
25	0.009877	94023	929	467825	0.001985	2.5362	4143921	0.0000	44.074	0.001985
30	0.011407	93094	1062	462945	0.002294	2.6223	3676095	0.0000	39.488	0.002294
35	0.016862	92032	1552	456556	0.003399	2.6769	3213150	0.0000	34.913	0.003399
40	0.026298	90480	2379	446906	0.005324	2.6906	2756595	0.0065	30.466	0.005317
45	0.042321	88101	3729	431885	0.008633	2.6884	2309688	0.0119	26.216	0.008612
50	0.068163	84372	5751	408322	0.014085	2.6457	1877803	0.0175	22.256	0.014041
55	0.098595	78621	7752	374694	0.020688	2.6248	1469481	0.0185	18.691	0.020623
60	0.146658	70870	10394	329279	0.031565	2.5881	1094787	0.0186	15.448	0.031475
65	0.200845	60476	12146	272558	0.044564	2.5448	765507	0.0186	12.658	0.044451
70	0.269095	48330	13005	209249	0.062152	2.5088	492949	0.0186	10.200	0.061995
75	0.359380	35324	12695	144547	0.087825	2.4734	283700	0.0186	8.031	0.087575
80	0.503051	22630	11384	84386	0.134901	2.4735	139153	0.0186	6.149	0.134416
85+	*1.000000	11246	11246	54767	0.205339	4.8700	54767	0.0186	4.870	0.203764

TABLE 3 — FEMALE LIFE TABLE

x	nq_x	l_x	nd_x	nL_x	nm_x	na_x	T_x	r_x	$\mathring{e}_x$	nM_x
0	0.026294	100000	2629	97992	0.026833	0.2364	7189147	0.0009	71.891	0.026851
1	0.004410	97371	429	388234	0.001106	1.0919	7091155	0.0009	72.826	0.001107
5	0.002268	96941	220	484156	0.000454	2.5000	6702922	0.0162	69.144	0.000456
10	0.001697	96721	164	483207	0.000340	2.5654	6218765	0.0295	64.296	0.000339
15	0.002811	96557	271	482154	0.000563	2.6727	5735559	0.0408	59.401	0.000559
20	0.004042	96286	389	480504	0.000810	2.6223	5253404	0.0222	54.561	0.000808
25	0.005213	95897	500	478299	0.001045	2.6318	4772901	0.0000	49.771	0.001045
30	0.007394	95397	705	475324	0.001484	2.6470	4294601	0.0000	45.018	0.001484
35	0.010535	94691	998	471131	0.002117	2.6688	3819278	0.0008	40.334	0.002117
40	0.016156	93694	1514	464928	0.003256	2.6611	3348146	0.0124	35.735	0.003249
45	0.023517	92180	2168	455854	0.004756	2.6723	2883218	0.0167	31.278	0.004741
50	0.036736	90012	3307	442314	0.007476	2.6570	2427364	0.0212	26.967	0.007449
55	0.053751	86706	4661	422636	0.011027	2.6629	1985050	0.0211	22.894	0.010984
60	0.084731	82045	6952	393761	0.017655	2.6316	1562415	0.0267	19.043	0.017576
65	0.120556	75093	9053	353868	0.025583	2.6142	1168654	0.0267	15.563	0.025468
70	0.180439	66040	11916	301590	0.039511	2.5990	814786	0.0267	12.338	0.039320
75	0.271847	54124	14713	234816	0.062660	2.5665	513196	0.0267	9.482	0.062331
80	0.421611	39411	16616	155102	0.107129	2.6013	278380	0.0267	7.064	0.106606
85+	1.000000	22795	22795	123278	0.184904	5.4082	123278	0.0267	5.408	0.182094

TABLE 4 — OBSERVED AND PROJECTED VITAL RATES

	OBSERVED POPULATION BOTH SEXES	MALES	FEMALES	PROJECTED POPULATION 1965 MALES	1965 FEMALES	1970 MALES	1970 FEMALES	1975 MALES	1975 FEMALES	STABLE POPULATION MALES	FEMA
RATES PER THOUSAND											
Birth	24.20	25.25	23.19	25.74	23.58	27.28	24.99	28.33	25.99	28.85	27.
Death	9.45	10.85	8.10	10.91	8.53	10.86	8.82	10.63	8.92	8.50	7.
Increase	14.75	14.40	15.09	14.83	15.05	16.42	16.16	17.70	17.07		20.34
PERCENTAGE											
under 15	32.08	33.18	31.02	33.21	30.88	33.45	30.99	34.13	31.58	35.82	34.
15-64	59.64	59.33	59.94	59.47	59.79	59.35	59.48	58.80	58.80	59.22	58.
65 and over	8.27	7.48	9.04	7.32	9.34	7.20	9.52	7.07	9.62	4.95	7.
DEP. RATIO X 100	67.66	68.54	66.82	68.16	67.27	68.49	68.11	70.07	70.07	68.85	70.

Europe 1961

Excluding Albania, Northern Ireland, and European Russia
Data in Hundreds

AGE AT LAST BIRTHDAY	POPULATION BOTH SEXES	MALES Number	%	FEMALES Number	%	BIRTHS BY AGE OF MOTHER	DEATHS BOTH SEXES	MALES	FEMALES	AGE AT LAST BIRTHDAY
0	76429	39144	1.9	37285	1.7	0	2991	1685	1306	0
1-4	297826	152521	7.4	145305	6.6	0	549	297	252	1-4
5-9	362534	185662	9.0	176872	8.0	0	200	119	81	5-9
10-14	360288	183831	8.9	176457	8.0	19	156	96	60	10-14
15-19	305498	154906	7.5	150592	6.9	4773	244	168	76	15-19
20-24	310735	156379	7.6	154356	7.0	23018	338	234	104	20-24
25-29	304182	153000	7.4	151182	6.9	24448	370	239	131	25-29
30-34	307058	152815	7.4	154243	7.0	15840	456	283	173	30-34
35-39	298479	142136	6.9	156343	7.1	8376	584	338	246	35-39
40-44	230767	108555	5.3	122212	5.6	2462	643	368	275	40-44
45-49	259747	122074	5.9	137673	6.3	214	1140	664	476	45-49
50-54	270902	128209	6.2	142693	6.5	0	1912	1168	744	50-54
55-59	244647	115571	5.6	129076	5.9	0	2798	1773	1025	55-59
60-64	205582	92228	4.5	113354	5.2	0	4043	2429	1614	60-64
65-69	157289	65548	3.2	91741	4.2	0	4618	2508	2110	65-69
70-74	119585	48414	2.4	71171	3.2		5626	2785	2841	70-74
75-79	79622	31560	1.5	48062	2.2		6202	2853	3349	75-79
80-84	43269	16536	0.8	26733	1.2	40700 M.	5389	2316	3073	80-84
85+	19622	6937	0.3	12685	0.6	38450 F.	4324	1657	2667	85+
TOTAL	4254061	2056026		2198035		79150	42583	21980	20603	TOTAL

x	nq_x	l_x	nd_x	nL_x	nm_x	na_x	T_x	r_x	$\dot{e}_x$	nM_x	x
0	0.041661	100000	4166	96857	0.043013	0.2456	6688970	0.0010	66.890	0.043046	0
1	0.007735	95834	741	381185	0.001945	1.0987	6592113	0.0010	68.787	0.001947	1
5	0.003196	95093	304	474703	0.000640	2.5000	6210929	0.0032	65.315	0.000641	5
10	0.002616	94789	248	473367	0.000524	2.6755	5736225	0.0174	60.516	0.000522	10
15	0.005424	94541	513	471516	0.001088	2.6840	5262858	0.0151	55.668	0.001085	15
20	0.007455	94028	701	468432	0.001496	2.5634	4791342	0.0000	50.957	0.001496	20
25	0.007781	93327	726	464851	0.001562	2.5439	4322910	0.0007	46.320	0.001562	25
30	0.009223	92601	854	460945	0.001853	2.5886	3858059	0.0055	41.663	0.001852	30
35	0.011874	91747	1089	456151	0.002388	2.6289	3397114	0.0317	37.027	0.002378	35
40	0.016854	90657	1528	449739	0.003397	2.6779	2940963	0.0116	32.440	0.003390	40
45	0.026861	89129	2394	440150	0.005439	2.7038	2491224	0.0000	27.951	0.005439	45
50	0.044617	86735	3870	424787	0.009110	2.7028	2051074	0.0000	23.647	0.009110	50
55	0.074351	82866	6161	400106	0.015399	2.6918	1626287	0.0166	19.626	0.015341	55
60	0.124393	76704	9542	360842	0.026442	2.6231	1226181	0.0226	15.986	0.026337	60
65	0.175667	67163	11798	307248	0.038400	2.5788	865339	0.0226	12.884	0.038262	65
70	0.252975	55365	14006	242535	0.057748	2.5519	558090	0.0226	10.080	0.057525	70
75	0.369635	41359	15288	168449	0.090755	2.4918	315555	0.0226	7.630	0.090399	75
80	0.514068	26071	13402	95336	0.140580	2.4593	147106	0.0226	5.643	0.140058	80
85+	1.000000	12669	12669	51771	0.244710	4.0865	51771	0.0226	4.086	0.238863	85+

x	nq_x	l_x	nd_x	nL_x	nm_x	na_x	T_x	r_x	$\dot{e}_x$	nM_x	x
0	0.034106	100000	3411	97461	0.034995	0.2556	7221947	0.0012	72.219	0.035027	0
1	0.006893	96589	666	384431	0.001732	1.1066	7124485	0.0012	73.761	0.001734	1
5	0.002284	95924	219	479070	0.000457	2.5000	6740054	0.0026	70.265	0.000458	5
10	0.001699	95705	163	478121	0.000340	2.5283	6260984	0.0157	65.420	0.000340	10
15	0.002525	95542	241	477139	0.000506	2.6364	5782863	0.0129	60.527	0.000505	15
20	0.003363	95301	321	475737	0.000674	2.6101	5305724	0.0000	55.674	0.000674	20
25	0.004324	94980	411	473917	0.000867	2.6057	4829986	0.0000	50.853	0.000867	25
30	0.005593	94569	529	471594	0.001122	2.6295	4356069	0.0000	46.062	0.001122	30
35	0.007864	94041	739	468462	0.001579	2.6457	3884475	0.0217	41.306	0.001573	35
40	0.011212	93301	1046	464066	0.002254	2.6678	3416014	0.0104	36.613	0.002250	40
45	0.017149	92255	1582	457588	0.003457	2.6698	2951948	0.0000	31.998	0.003457	45
50	0.025762	90673	2336	447915	0.005215	2.6671	2494360	0.0011	27.509	0.005214	50
55	0.039125	88337	3456	433783	0.007968	2.7139	2046445	0.0144	23.166	0.007941	55
60	0.069319	84881	5884	410781	0.014324	2.6847	1612662	0.0277	18.999	0.014239	60
65	0.109775	78997	8672	374766	0.023139	2.6685	1201881	0.0277	15.214	0.023000	65
70	0.183417	70325	12899	321152	0.040164	2.6375	827115	0.0277	11.761	0.039918	70
75	0.299280	57426	17187	245259	0.070075	2.5637	505963	0.0277	8.811	0.069681	75
80	0.451075	40240	18151	156842	0.115729	2.5563	260704	0.0277	6.479	0.114952	80
85+	*1.000000	22089	22089	103862	0.212673	4.7021	103862	0.0277	4.702	0.210248	85+

	OBSERVED POPULATION			PROJECTED POPULATION 1966		1971		1976		STABLE POPULATION	
	BOTH SEXES	MALES	FEMALES	MALES	FEMALES	MALES	FEMALES	MALES	FEMALES	MALES	FEMALES
RATES PER THOUSAND											
Birth	18.61	19.80	17.49	19.13	16.98	19.13	17.09	19.28	17.34	18.74	17.58
Death	10.01	10.69	9.37	11.16	10.22	11.47	10.79	11.74	11.27	12.32	11.16
Increase	8.60	9.10	8.12	7.97	6.77	7.66	6.30	7.54	6.06		6.4245
PERCENTAGE											
under 15	25.79	27.29	24.38	26.60	23.83	26.17	23.59	25.94	23.54	25.48	24.12
15-64	64.35	64.49	64.23	64.51	63.69	64.17	63.04	63.85	62.33	64.41	62.78
65 and over	9.86	8.22	11.39	8.89	12.47	9.65	13.36	10.21	14.13	10.11	13.10
DEP. RATIO X 100	55.39	55.07	55.70	55.02	57.00	55.83	58.62	56.61	60.44	55.26	59.28

TABLE 1 — DATA

AGE AT LAST BIRTHDAY	POPULATION BOTH SEXES	MALES Number	MALES %	FEMALES Number	FEMALES %	BIRTHS BY AGE OF MOTHER	DEATHS BOTH SEXES	MALES	FEMALES	AGE AT LAST BIRTHDAY
0	3061050	1564755	1.9	1496295	1.7	0	96451	54980	41471	0
1-4	11641496	5952837	7.1	5688659	6.3	0	16162	8975	7187	1-4
5-9	13784023	7040311	8.4	6743712	7.5	0	6839	4132	2707	5-9
10-14	14082111	7199144	8.6	6882967	7.7	478	5748	3544	2204	10-1
15-19	11960347	6105441	7.3	5854906	6.5	119620	9659	6938	2721	15-1
20-24	13038823	6649282	7.9	6389541	7.1	843920	14150	10174	3976	20-2
25-29	12310003	6263205	7.5	6046798	6.7	1034586	14451	9756	4695	25-2
30-34	12511400	6300411	7.5	6210989	6.9	693487	18013	11538	6475	30-3
35-39	12323574	5862097	7.0	6461477	7.2	376176	23998	14219	9779	35-3
40-44	9105830	4258012	5.1	4847818	5.4	111692	25749	15052	10697	40-4
45-49	10856288	5076301	6.0	5779987	6.4	8177	47579	28462	19117	45-4
50-54	11422683	5371562	6.4	6051121	6.7	0	81386	50867	30519	50-5
55-59	10459983	4943599	5.9	5516384	6.1	0	120069	77866	42203	55-5
60-64	8839282	3964199	4.7	4875083	5.4	0	160179	99005	61174	60-6
65-69	6853633	2803417	3.3	4050216	4.5	0	191058	104379	86679	65-6
70-74	5283068	2133537	2.5	3149531	3.5		236556	118904	117652	70-7
75-79	3590367	1434672	1.7	2155695	2.4		273179	128345	144834	75-7
80-84	1929955	756672	0.9	1173283	1.3	1635302 M.	247176	109908	137268	80-8
85+	887103	319649	0.4	567454	0.6	1552834 F.	203034	80358	122676	85+
TOTAL	173941019	83999103		89941916		3188136	1791436	937402	854034	TOT

TABLE 2 — MALE LIFE TABLE

x	$_nq_x$	l_x	$_nd_x$	$_nL_x$	$_nm_x$	$_na_x$	T_x	r_x	$\dot{e}_x$	$_nM_x$
0	0.034125	100000	3412	97407	0.035033	0.2401	6754773	0.0037	67.548	0.035136
1	0.005975	96588	577	384673	0.001500	1.0946	6657366	0.0037	68.926	0.001508
5	0.002927	96010	281	479349	0.000586	2.5000	6272693	0.0035	65.333	0.000587
10	0.002466	95729	236	478111	0.000494	2.7301	5793343	0.0136	60.518	0.000492
15	0.005674	95493	542	476213	0.001138	2.6875	5315232	0.0069	55.661	0.001136
20	0.007622	94951	724	472987	0.001530	2.5545	4839019	0.0000	50.963	0.001530
25	0.007760	94228	731	469337	0.001558	2.5368	4366032	0.0038	46.335	0.001558
30	0.009121	93497	853	465432	0.001832	2.5958	3896695	0.0047	41.677	0.001831
35	0.012123	92644	1123	460568	0.002439	2.6400	3431262	0.0367	37.037	0.002426
40	0.017565	91521	1608	453869	0.003542	2.6770	2970694	0.0107	32.459	0.003535
45	0.027678	89913	2489	443853	0.005607	2.7046	2516825	0.0000	27.992	0.005607
50	0.046339	87424	4051	427799	0.009470	2.6986	2072973	0.0000	23.712	0.009470
55	0.076168	83373	6350	402044	0.015795	2.6659	1645174	0.0141	19.733	0.015751
60	0.118249	77023	9108	363446	0.025060	2.6209	1243130	0.0196	16.140	0.024975
65	0.171306	67915	11634	311477	0.037352	2.5849	879684	0.0196	12.953	0.037233
70	0.246033	56281	13847	247605	0.055923	2.5591	568207	0.0196	10.096	0.055731
75	0.366758	42434	15563	173334	0.089786	2.5046	320602	0.0196	7.555	0.089459
80	0.528152	26871	14192	97365	0.145761	2.4577	147268	0.0196	5.481	0.145252
85+	1.000000	12679	12679	49903	0.254072	3.9359	49903	0.0196	3.936	0.251394

TABLE 3 — FEMALE LIFE TABLE

x	$_nq_x$	l_x	$_nd_x$	$_nL_x$	$_nm_x$	$_na_x$	T_x	r_x	$\dot{e}_x$	$_nM_x$
0	0.027065	100000	2706	97962	0.027628	0.2469	7334390	0.0040	73.344	0.027716
1	0.005009	97294	487	387760	0.001257	1.0996	7236428	0.0040	74.377	0.001263
5	0.002002	96806	194	483546	0.000401	2.5000	6848668	0.0037	70.746	0.000401
10	0.001601	96612	155	482681	0.000320	2.5408	6365122	0.0138	65.883	0.000320
15	0.002323	96458	224	481758	0.000465	2.6342	5882440	0.0070	60.985	0.000465
20	0.003107	96234	299	480451	0.000622	2.6029	5400682	0.0000	56.121	0.000622
25	0.003876	95935	372	478785	0.000777	2.6109	4920231	0.0020	51.287	0.000776
30	0.005200	95563	497	476644	0.001043	2.6458	4441447	0.0000	46.477	0.001043
35	0.007568	95066	719	473643	0.001519	2.6564	3964803	0.0232	41.706	0.001513
40	0.010992	94346	1037	469308	0.002210	2.6631	3491160	0.0089	37.004	0.002207
45	0.016411	93309	1531	462979	0.003307	2.6701	3021852	0.0000	32.385	0.003307
50	0.024924	91778	2288	453555	0.005044	2.6677	2558873	0.0000	27.881	0.005044
55	0.037688	89490	3373	439644	0.007671	2.6850	2105318	0.0135	23.526	0.007650
60	0.061335	86118	5282	418408	0.012624	2.6939	1665674	0.0271	19.342	0.012548
65	0.102553	80836	8290	384964	0.021534	2.6821	1247266	0.0271	15.430	0.021401
70	0.172713	72546	12530	333310	0.037591	2.6520	862302	0.0271	11.886	0.037355
75	0.290486	60016	17434	257945	0.067588	2.5831	528992	0.0271	8.814	0.067187
80	0.457515	42582	19482	165387	0.117797	2.5606	271047	0.0271	6.365	0.116995
85+	*1.000000	23100	23100	105659	0.218630	4.5739	105659	0.0271	4.574	0.216187

TABLE 4 — OBSERVED AND PROJECTED VITAL RATES

	OBSERVED POPULATION BOTH SEXES	MALES	FEMALES	PROJECTED POPULATION 1966 MALES	1966 FEMALES	1971 MALES	1971 FEMALES	1976 MALES	1976 FEMALES	STABLE POPULATION MALES	FEMA
RATES PER THOUSAND											
Birth	18.33	19.47	17.26	18.72	16.65	18.41	16.45	18.45	16.59	18.63	17.
Death	10.30	11.16	9.50	11.56	10.38	11.81	11.03	12.04	11.55	12.09	10.
Increase	8.03	8.31	7.77	7.16	6.28	6.60	5.43	6.41	5.04		6.53
PERCENTAGE											
under 15	24.47	25.90	23.14	25.63	22.98	25.72	23.18	25.59	23.20	25.55	24.
15-64	64.87	65.23	64.52	64.85	63.54	63.94	62.38	63.54	61.52	64.32	62.
65 and over	10.66	8.87	12.34	9.52	13.48	10.34	14.45	10.87	15.28	10.13	13.
DEP. RATIO X 100	54.16	53.30	54.98	54.20	57.38	56.39	60.32	57.38	62.55	55.48	59.

TABLE 1 — DATA

AGE AT LAST BIRTHDAY	POPULATION BOTH SEXES	MALES Number	MALES %	FEMALES Number	FEMALES %	BIRTHS BY AGE OF MOTHER	DEATHS BOTH SEXES	DEATHS MALES	DEATHS FEMALES	AGE AT LAST BIRTHDAY
0	1523741	781697	1.8	742044	1.6	0	50138	28452	21686	0
1-4	5754452	2951407	6.9	2803045	6.1	0	11708	6379	5329	1-4
5-9	6637688	3399501	7.9	3238187	7.1	0	3570	2116	1454	5-9
10-14	7164118	3641231	8.5	3522887	7.7	273	2718	1680	1038	10-14
15-19	6564504	3329730	7.8	3234774	7.1	117025	4730	3310	1420	15-19
20-24	5865017	2929047	6.8	2935970	6.4	479891	5411	3768	1643	20-24
25-29	5593337	2815807	6.6	2777530	6.1	479739	5404	3552	1852	25-29
30-34	5775894	2876717	6.7	2899177	6.3	306912	7168	4404	2764	30-34
35-39	6108654	2994854	7.0	3113800	6.8	166739	10700	6245	4455	35-39
40-44	5681152	2778910	6.5	2902242	6.4	50120	14972	8646	6326	40-44
45-49	5951565	2901900	6.8	3049665	6.7	3563	25326	15003	10323	45-49
50-54	5938290	2878063	6.7	3060227	6.7	0	42123	25922	16201	50-54
55-59	5424582	2573115	6.0	2851467	6.2	0	63663	40879	22784	55-59
60-64	4568384	2057320	4.8	2511064	5.5	0	87697	54192	33505	60-64
65-69	3672210	1560431	3.6	2111779	4.6	0	110226	62825	47401	65-69
70-74	2811917	1137308	2.6	1674609	3.7		138666	71363	67303	70-74
75-79	1953965	752925	1.8	1201040	2.6		156065	72916	83149	75-79
80-84	1101630	399527	0.9	702103	1.5	825066 M.	141049	59394	81655	80-84
85+	490775	163033	0.4	327742	0.7	779196 F.	120791	43615	77176	85+
TOTAL	88581875	42922523		45659352		1604262	1002125	514661	487464	TOTAL

TABLE 2 — MALE LIFE TABLE

x	nq_x	l_x	nd_x	nL_x	nm_x	na_x	T_x	r_x	$\dot{e}_x$	nM_x	x
0	0.035352	100000	3535	97438	0.036282	0.2752	6725526	0.0042	67.255	0.036398	0
1	0.008556	96465	825	383485	0.002152	1.1238	6628089	0.0042	68.710	0.002161	1
5	0.003105	95639	297	477455	0.000622	2.5000	6244603	0.0015	65.293	0.000622	5
10	0.002305	95342	220	476200	0.000461	2.6672	5767148	0.0015	60.489	0.000461	10
15	0.004977	95123	473	474511	0.000998	2.6705	5290949	0.0208	55.622	0.000994	15
20	0.006416	94649	607	471753	0.001287	2.5405	4816438	0.0155	50.887	0.001286	20
25	0.006288	94042	591	468754	0.001261	2.5371	4344685	0.0005	46.199	0.001261	25
30	0.007627	93451	713	465549	0.001531	2.6085	3875931	0.0000	41.476	0.001531	30
35	0.010378	92738	962	461431	0.002086	2.6526	3410382	0.0013	36.774	0.002085	35
40	0.015446	91776	1418	455615	0.003111	2.6978	2948951	0.0000	32.132	0.003111	40
45	0.025550	90358	2309	446533	0.005170	2.7229	2493336	0.0000	27.594	0.005170	45
50	0.044155	88049	3888	431395	0.009012	2.7231	2046803	0.0025	23.246	0.009007	50
55	0.076895	84162	6472	405831	0.015947	2.6857	1615408	0.0170	19.194	0.015887	55
60	0.124283	77690	9656	365570	0.026412	2.6304	1209577	0.0146	15.569	0.026341	60
65	0.183937	68035	12514	310027	0.040364	2.5911	844007	0.0146	12.406	0.040261	65
70	0.272445	55520	15126	240461	0.062906	2.5445	533979	0.0146	9.618	0.062747	70
75	0.389874	40394	15749	162216	0.097084	2.4757	293519	0.0146	7.266	0.096844	75
80	0.539091	24646	13286	89098	0.149119	2.4312	131303	0.0146	5.328	0.148660	80
85+	*1.000000	11359	11359	42205	0.269147	3.7154	42205	0.0146	3.715	0.267523	85+

TABLE 3 — FEMALE LIFE TABLE

x	nq_x	l_x	nd_x	nL_x	nm_x	na_x	T_x	r_x	$\dot{e}_x$	nM_x	x
0	0.028534	100000	2853	97962	0.029127	0.2856	7275223	0.0043	72.752	0.029225	0
1	0.007532	97147	732	386489	0.001893	1.1340	7177261	0.0043	73.881	0.001901	1
5	0.002243	96415	216	481534	0.000449	2.5000	6790772	0.0000	70.433	0.000449	5
10	0.001472	96199	142	480638	0.000295	2.4925	6309238	0.0000	65.585	0.000295	10
15	0.002198	96057	211	479784	0.000440	2.6249	5828600	0.0178	60.679	0.000439	15
20	0.002797	95846	268	478582	0.000560	2.5832	5348816	0.0147	55.806	0.000560	20
25	0.003329	95578	318	477132	0.000667	2.6211	4870234	0.0006	50.956	0.000667	25
30	0.004756	95260	453	475240	0.000953	2.6645	4393102	0.0000	46.117	0.000953	30
35	0.007130	94807	676	472461	0.001431	2.6749	3917862	0.0000	41.325	0.001431	35
40	0.010844	94131	1021	468286	0.002180	2.6812	3445400	0.0000	36.602	0.002180	40
45	0.016793	93110	1564	461927	0.003385	2.6830	2977114	0.0000	31.974	0.003385	45
50	0.026154	91546	2394	452150	0.005295	2.6689	2515187	0.0013	27.474	0.005294	50
55	0.039317	89152	3505	437658	0.008009	2.6885	2063037	0.0113	23.141	0.007990	55
60	0.064982	85647	5566	415378	0.013399	2.6900	1625379	0.0190	18.978	0.013343	60
65	0.107138	80081	8580	380542	0.022546	2.6847	1210002	0.0190	15.110	0.022446	65
70	0.184244	71502	13174	326398	0.040361	2.6385	829459	0.0190	11.601	0.040190	70
75	0.297222	58328	17336	249435	0.069502	2.5656	503062	0.0190	8.625	0.069231	75
80	0.454547	40991	18633	159422	0.116875	2.5562	253626	0.0190	6.187	0.116301	80
85+	*1.000000	22359	22359	94204	0.237346	4.2133	94204	0.0190	4.213	0.235478	85+

TABLE 4 — OBSERVED AND PROJECTED TOTAL RATES

	OBSERVED POPULATION BOTH SEXES	MALES	FEMALES	PROJECTED POPULATION 1966 MALES	1966 FEMALES	1971 MALES	1971 FEMALES	1976 MALES	1976 FEMALES	STABLE POPULATION MALES	FEMALES
RATES PER THOUSAND											
Birth	18.11	19.22	17.07	19.25	17.16	19.60	17.58	19.45	17.55	20.12	18.94
Death	11.31	11.99	10.68	12.34	11.38	12.55	11.76	12.72	12.06	11.35	10.17
Increase	6.80	7.23	6.39	6.91	5.78	7.05	5.81	6.73	5.49		8.7647
PERCENTAGE											
under 15	23.80	25.10	22.57	25.05	22.51	25.92	23.43	26.44	24.05	27.05	25.67
15-64	64.88	65.55	64.25	65.23	63.53	63.75	61.91	62.75	60.76	64.02	62.38
65 and over	11.32	9.35	13.18	9.73	13.96	10.32	14.66	10.81	15.19	8.93	11.95
DEP. RATIO X 100	54.13	52.56	55.64	53.31	57.40	56.85	61.52	59.36	64.59	56.20	60.31

TABLE 1 — DATA

AGE AT LAST BIRTHDAY	POPULATION BOTH SEXES	MALES Number	MALES %	FEMALES Number	FEMALES %	BIRTHS BY AGE OF MOTHER	DEATHS BOTH SEXES	DEATHS MALES	DEATHS FEMALES	AGE AT LAST BIRTHDAY
0	1695640	872382	1.9	823258	1.6	0	83676	47464	36212	0
1-4	7260707	3727866	8.0	3532841	7.0	0	13844	7491	6353	1-4
5-9	9603150	4918346	10.5	4684804	9.3	0	5644	3388	2256	5-9
10-14	8720091	4452532	9.5	4267559	8.4	876	4211	2635	1576	10-14
15-19	6915636	3503499	7.5	3412137	6.7	181382	6016	4100	1916	15-19
20-24	7138521	3522616	7.5	3615905	7.1	650337	9078	6302	2776	20-24
25-29	7272728	3641348	7.8	3631380	7.2	479230	10091	6595	3496	25-29
30-34	7306923	3587621	7.7	3719302	7.3	268950	12244	7694	4550	30-34
35-39	6860564	3203392	6.8	3657172	7.2	133120	14508	8228	6280	35-39
40-44	4756804	2171339	4.6	2585465	5.1	33067	13394	7288	6106	40-44
45-49	5552958	2530876	5.4	3022082	6.0	2943	25576	13915	11661	45-49
50-54	6131855	2851783	6.1	3280072	6.5	0	42882	25171	17711	50-54
55-59	5456683	2550998	5.4	2905685	5.7	0	62389	37932	24457	55-59
60-64	4524934	2001307	4.3	2523627	5.0	0	83972	48697	35275	60-64
65-69	3309067	1365209	2.9	1943858	3.8	0	98450	51354	47096	65-69
70-74	2383187	951465	2.0	1431722	2.8		119062	56268	62794	70-74
75-79	1506445	597561	1.3	908884	1.8		125945	55517	70428	75-79
80-84	757810	288551	0.6	469259	0.9	903441 M.	97631	40773	56858	80-84
85+	321322	113679	0.2	207643	0.4	846464 F.	69169	26911	42258	85+
TOTAL	97475025	46852370		50622655		1749905	897782	457723	440059	TOTAL

TABLE 2 — MALE LIFE TABLE

x	nq_x	l_x	nd_x	nL_x	nm_x	na_x	T_x	r_x	e_x	nM_x	x
0	0.052203	100000	5220	95948	0.054407	0.2239	6599041	0.0000	65.990	0.054407	0
1	0.007991	94780	757	376910	0.002009	1.0834	6503093	0.0000	68.613	0.002009	1
5	0.003436	94022	323	469304	0.000688	2.5000	6126183	0.0022	65.157	0.000689	5
10	0.002972	93699	278	467847	0.000595	2.6681	5656879	0.0332	60.373	0.000592	10
15	0.005863	93421	548	465849	0.001176	2.7087	5189032	0.0222	55.545	0.001170	15
20	0.008906	92873	827	462356	0.001789	2.5711	4723183	0.0000	50.856	0.001789	20
25	0.009015	92046	830	458186	0.001811	2.5368	4260827	0.0000	46.290	0.001811	25
30	0.010676	91216	974	453714	0.002146	2.5700	3802641	0.0107	41.688	0.002145	30
35	0.012823	90242	1157	448426	0.002581	2.5927	3348927	0.0476	37.110	0.002569	35
40	0.016711	89085	1489	441958	0.003368	2.6708	2900501	0.0199	32.559	0.003356	40
45	0.027146	87596	2378	432495	0.005498	2.6925	2458543	0.0000	28.067	0.005498	45
50	0.043253	85218	3686	417608	0.008826	2.6981	2026048	0.0000	23.775	0.008826	50
55	0.072160	81533	5883	394010	0.014932	2.6794	1608440	0.0199	19.728	0.014869	55
60	0.115704	75649	8753	357555	0.024480	2.6361	1214431	0.0322	16.053	0.024333	60
65	0.173430	66896	11602	306644	0.037835	2.6006	856876	0.0322	12.809	0.037616	65
70	0.259654	55294	14357	241387	0.059479	2.5563	550232	0.0322	9.951	0.059138	70
75	0.378206	40937	15483	165731	0.093420	2.4840	308845	0.0322	7.544	0.092906	75
80	0.517476	25454	13172	92737	0.142036	2.4494	143114	0.0322	5.622	0.141303	80
85+	1.000000	12282	12282	50377	0.243809	4.1016	50377	0.0322	4.102	0.236729	85

TABLE 3 — FEMALE LIFE TABLE

x	nq_x	l_x	nd_x	nL_x	nm_x	na_x	T_x	r_x	e_x	nM_x	x
0	0.042554	100000	4255	96744	0.043986	0.2348	7096807	0.0000	70.968	0.043986	0
1	0.007156	95745	685	380985	0.001798	1.0908	7000063	0.0000	73.112	0.001798	1
5	0.002403	95059	228	474726	0.000481	2.5000	6619078	0.0012	69.631	0.000482	5
10	0.001847	94831	175	473725	0.000370	2.5447	6144352	0.0313	64.793	0.000369	10
15	0.002811	94656	266	472653	0.000563	2.6460	5670627	0.0160	59.908	0.000562	15
20	0.003832	94390	362	471083	0.000768	2.6069	5197974	0.0000	55.069	0.000768	20
25	0.004802	94028	452	469055	0.000963	2.5965	4726891	0.0000	50.271	0.000963	25
30	0.006099	93577	571	466528	0.001223	2.6269	4257836	0.0000	45.501	0.001223	30
35	0.008592	93006	799	463139	0.001725	2.6344	3791307	0.0346	40.764	0.001717	35
40	0.011780	92207	1086	458515	0.002369	2.6809	3328168	0.0165	36.095	0.002362	40
45	0.019120	91121	1742	451517	0.003859	2.6551	2869654	0.0000	31.493	0.003859	45
50	0.026661	89378	2383	441322	0.005400	2.6628	2418137	0.0000	27.055	0.005400	50
55	0.041430	86995	3604	426655	0.008448	2.6912	1976815	0.0173	22.723	0.008417	55
60	0.068248	83391	5691	403849	0.014093	2.6970	1550159	0.0358	18.589	0.013978	60
65	0.115650	77700	8986	367714	0.024437	2.6870	1146311	0.0358	14.753	0.024228	65
70	0.200178	68714	13755	311058	0.044220	2.6364	778597	0.0358	11.331	0.043859	70
75	0.327350	54959	17991	230561	0.078030	2.5413	467539	0.0358	8.507	0.077498	75
80	0.468636	36968	17325	141873	0.122113	2.5199	236978	0.0358	6.410	0.121166	80
85+	*1.000000	19644	19644	95105	0.206546	4.8415	95105	0.0358	4.842	0.203513	85

TABLE 4 — OBSERVED AND PROJECTED VITAL RATES

	OBSERVED POPULATION BOTH SEXES	MALES	FEMALES	PROJECTED 1966 MALES	FEMALES	1971 MALES	FEMALES	1976 MALES	FEMALES	STABLE POPULATION MALES	FEMALES
RATES PER THOUSAND											
Birth	17.95	19.28	16.72	18.54	16.19	19.21	16.92	19.86	17.64	17.39	16.2
Death	9.21	9.77	8.69	10.31	9.59	10.85	10.35	11.29	11.02	13.55	12.4
Increase	8.74	9.51	8.03	8.22	6.60	8.36	6.56	8.57	6.62		3.837
PERCENTAGE											
under 15	27.99	29.82	26.29	28.08	24.85	26.00	23.16	25.35	22.77	23.82	22.5
15-64	63.52	63.10	63.91	63.88	63.96	64.94	64.51	64.88	63.90	64.94	63.4
65 and over	8.49	7.08	9.80	8.04	11.19	9.06	12.33	9.77	13.33	11.23	14.0
DEP. RATIO X 100	57.43	58.47	56.47	56.53	56.34	53.99	55.01	54.12	56.50	53.98	57.7

Cohort Arrangement of Period Data

for the United States and Sweden;
Female Dominant

The preceding materials suffer from the disadvantage of being period cross sections of what is essentially a generational or cohort process (Ryder 1964). For each five-year interval the population was taken at mid-point, and births and deaths were centered on the point at which population was known. For instance, the 1780 tables for Sweden are based on population estimates for July 1, 1780, and births and deaths averaged over the calendar years 1778–82. This simplified Lexis diagram (Fig. 1) shows the vertical strips which our period data represent, a distribution of population by age being available for each mid-point shown by a dotted line.

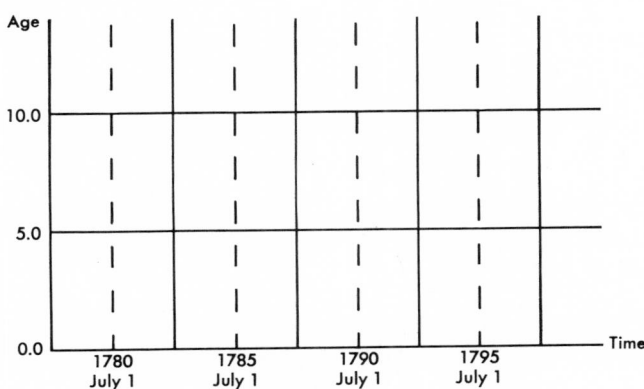

FIG. 1—PERIODS

But our material extends from 1778–82 to 1958–62, and a long series such as this lends itself to a calculation by cohorts. In terms of the diagram we would constitute a cohort by selecting data referring to a diagonal rather than a vertical strip (Fig. 2). The question is how that portion of the Lexis

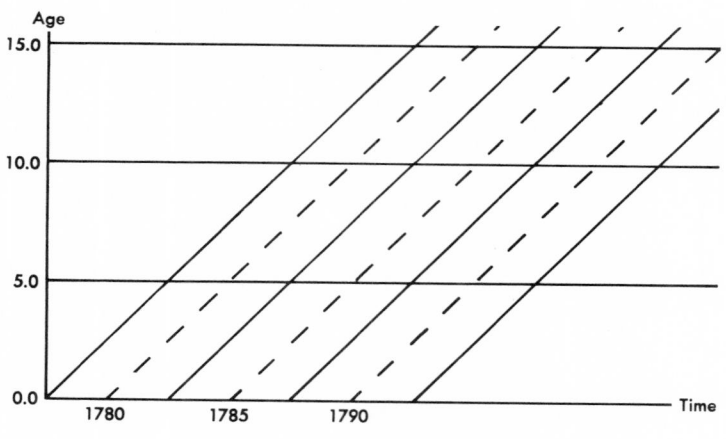

FIG. 2.—COHORTS

diagram relating to a given cohort may be approximated. Lacking statistics covering births and deaths among those individuals born exactly in the years 1778–82, we have recourse to the squares in Figure 3 as an estimate of the cohort.

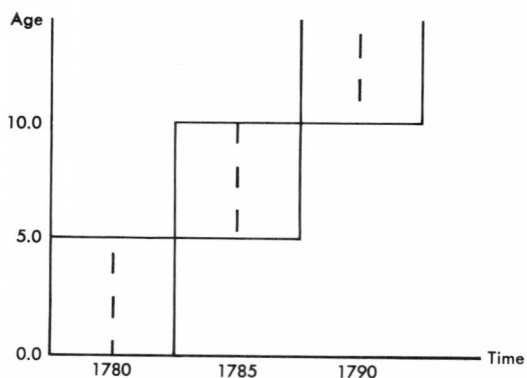

FIG. 3.—COHORTS MADE FROM PERIODS

How considerable is the discrepancy between this set of squares and the diagonal strip? If the squares are divided into triangles as in Figure 4, and the triangles lettered with P's and C's as shown, then P_2 and C_1 make up the first age group in the first period; P_4 and C_3 the second age group in the

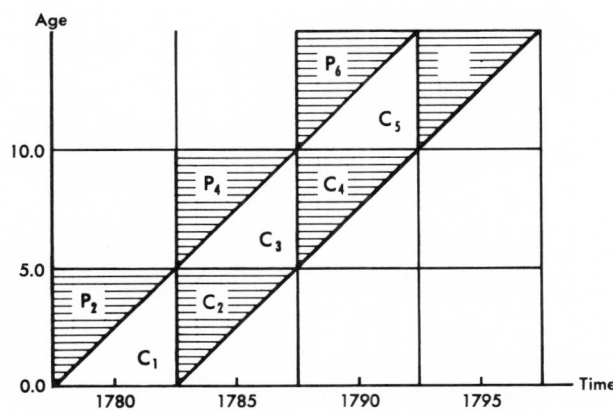

FIG. 4—REPLACEMENTS IN ASSEMBLING COHORTS FROM PERIODS

second period, etc. The true cohort would cover $C_1, C_2, C_3, \ldots$; our approximation replaces C_2 by P_2, C_4 by P_4, etc. The P's cover half the total number of events and are five years earlier than the events they replace. Hence we can say that our approximate cohort based on $C_1, P_2, C_3, P_4, C_5,$ $\ldots$ is about half a period or 2½ years earlier than it professes to be. It averages in a certain fashion the information on the cohort born in 1778–82 with that on the cohort born in 1773–77. In a sense we are dealing with a 50 per cent sample of the events occurring to those born between 1772 and 1782; we will refer to it as the cohort born about 1778, or the cohort under five years of age in 1780.

The "sample" may be thought of as covering 50 per cent of the experience of the cohorts born in a ten-year range, for example 1773–82, but it does not give equal weight to all the birth years of the range. For the cohorts of birth years 1777 and 1778 practically all exposure is included. For the birth years 1772 and 1782 only a minimal amount is included. Three quarters of the exposure in the group designated as about the years 1778 is of the individuals who were 0–4 in 1870. An overlap of one quarter exists with the next older cohort, and an overlap of one quarter with the next younger cohort. The result is a light smoothing, as by a moving average, which seems safe enough to use in establishing trends and turning points.

TABLE 1 — DATA

AGE AT LAST BIRTHDAY	POPULATION BOTH SEXES	MALES Number	%	FEMALES Number	%	BIRTHS BY AGE OF MOTHER	DEATHS BOTH SEXES	MALES	FEMALES	AGE AT LAST BIRTHDAY
0	2225229	1128247	1.5	1096982	1.4	-0	265052	148108	116944	0
1-4	8453455	4279445	5.8	4174010	5.2	-0	108073	56904	51169	1-4
5-9	10673999	5385000	7.2	5288999	6.5	-0	26468	14191	12277	5-9
10-14	10735265	5415431	7.3	5319834	6.6	1589	23668	12673	10995	10-14
15-19	10784000	5357000	7.2	5427000	6.7	254746	33736	16974	16762	15-19
20-24	10899558	5353542	7.2	5546016	6.9	694916	43215	22142	21073	20-24
25-29	10558000	5207000	7.0	5351000	6.6	565763	39486	20644	18842	25-29
30-34	10245043	5051936	6.8	5193107	6.4	400952	34620	18901	15719	30-34
35-39	9766381	4634766	6.2	5131615	6.3	280641	37778	20881	16897	35-39
40-44	10251022	5089590	6.8	5161432	6.4	74921	45069	26942	18127	40-44
45-49	10085000	4980000	6.7	5105000	6.3	5019	59936	37788	22148	45-49
50-54	9650000	4754000	6.4	4896000	6.1	140	90593	59316	31277	50-54
55-59	9156000	4420000	5.9	4736000	5.9	0	126870	83438	43432	55-59
60-64	8410825	3935392	5.3	4475433	5.5	0	172163	110383	61780	60-64
65-69	7394248	3301078	4.4	4093170	5.1	0	232877	141499	91378	65-69
70-74	6116283	2555144	3.4	3561139	4.4		274635	153448	121187	70-74
75-79	4642161	1786523	2.4	2855638	3.5		310385	150944	159441	75-79
80-84	3047924	1076512	1.4	1971412	2.4	1167128 M.	320559	133722	186837	80-84
85+	2208546	692726	0.9	1515820	1.9	1111559 F.	443516	147454	296062	85+
TOTAL	155302939	74403332		80899607		2278687	2688699	1376352	1312347	TOTAL

TABLE 2 — MALE LIFE TABLE

x	$_nq_x$	l_x	$_nd_x$	$_nL_x$	$_nm_x$	$_na_x$	T_x	r_x	$\dot{e}_x$	$_nM_x$	x
0	0.120616	100000	12062	91882	0.131273	0.3269	5503792	0.0000	55.038	0.131273	0
1	0.051268	87938	4508	339058	0.013297	1.1840	5411910	0.0000	61.542	0.013297	1
5	0.013090	83430	1092	414419	0.002635	2.5000	5072853	0.0000	60.804	0.002635	5
10	0.011634	82338	958	409334	0.002340	2.5408	4658433	0.0000	56.577	0.002340	10
15	0.015724	81380	1280	403843	0.003169	2.6110	4249100	0.0000	52.213	0.003169	15
20	0.020471	80100	1640	396457	0.004136	2.5331	3845257	0.0000	48.006	0.004136	20
25	0.019626	78461	1540	388409	0.003965	2.4711	3448800	0.0018	43.956	0.003965	25
30	0.018539	76921	1426	381068	0.003742	2.5208	3060392	0.0077	39.786	0.003741	30
35	0.022282	75495	1682	373373	0.004505	2.5623	2679323	0.0000	35.490	0.004505	35
40	0.026137	73813	1929	364448	0.005294	2.6078	2305950	0.0000	31.241	0.005294	40
45	0.037282	71883	2680	353189	0.007588	2.6761	1941503	0.0000	27.009	0.007588	45
50	0.060615	69203	4195	336195	0.012477	2.6586	1588314	0.0000	22.951	0.012477	50
55	0.090340	65009	5873	311106	0.018877	2.6269	1252119	0.0000	19.261	0.018877	55
60	0.131438	59136	7773	277100	0.028050	2.6098	941012	0.0003	15.913	0.028049	60
65	0.194063	51363	9968	232530	0.042866	2.5636	663912	0.0003	12.926	0.042864	65
70	0.261262	41395	10815	180081	0.060057	2.5131	431382	0.0003	10.421	0.060055	70
75	0.348140	30580	10646	126000	0.084494	2.4732	251301	0.0003	8.218	0.084490	75
80	0.473781	19934	9444	76027	0.124224	2.4965	125301	0.0003	6.286	0.124217	80
85+	*1.000000	10490	10490	49274	0.212885	4.6974	49274	0.0003	4.697	0.212860	85-

TABLE 3 — FEMALE LIFE TABLE

x	$_nq_x$	l_x	$_nd_x$	$_nL_x$	$_nm_x$	$_na_x$	T_x	r_x	$\dot{e}_x$	$_nM_x$	x
0	0.099613	100000	9961	93441	0.106605	0.3416	6155800	0.0000	61.558	0.106605	0
1	0.047412	90039	4269	348228	0.012259	1.2062	6062359	0.0000	67.331	0.012259	1
5	0.011539	85770	990	426374	0.002321	2.5000	5714131	0.0000	66.622	0.002321	5
10	0.010282	84780	872	421783	0.002067	2.5709	5287756	0.0000	62.370	0.002067	10
15	0.015330	83908	1286	416468	0.003089	2.6107	4865974	0.0000	57.992	0.003089	15
20	0.018821	82622	1555	409249	0.003800	2.5172	4449506	0.0000	53.854	0.003800	20
25	0.017447	81067	1414	401724	0.003521	2.4472	4040257	0.0031	49.839	0.003521	25
30	0.015020	79653	1196	395244	0.003027	2.4768	3638533	0.0010	45.680	0.003027	30
35	0.016330	78456	1281	389109	0.003293	2.5240	3243288	0.0000	41.339	0.003293	35
40	0.017410	77175	1344	382588	0.003512	2.5538	2854179	0.0000	36.983	0.003512	40
45	0.021473	75831	1628	375293	0.004339	2.6269	2471591	0.0007	32.593	0.004338	45
50	0.031472	74203	2335	365510	0.006389	2.6425	2096298	0.0010	28.251	0.006388	50
55	0.044884	71868	3226	351744	0.009171	2.6457	1730789	0.0000	24.083	0.009171	55
60	0.066881	68642	4591	332476	0.013808	2.6619	1379045	0.0015	20.090	0.013804	60
65	0.106053	64051	6793	304195	0.022330	2.6357	1046569	0.0015	16.340	0.022325	65
70	0.157431	57258	9014	264814	0.034040	2.6174	742374	0.0015	12.965	0.034030	70
75	0.246078	48244	11872	212565	0.055850	2.5863	477560	0.0015	9.899	0.055834	75
80	0.383007	36372	13931	146953	0.094798	2.6581	264994	0.0015	7.286	0.094773	80
85+	1.000000	22441	22441	118041	0.190116	5.2600	118041	0.0015	5.260	0.195314	85-

TABLE 4 — OBSERVED AND PROJECTED VITAL RATES

	OBSERVED POPULATION BOTH SEXES	MALES	FEMALES	PROJECTED POPULATION 1915 MALES	FEMALES	1920 MALES	FEMALES	1925 MALES	FEMALES	STABLE POPULATION MALES	FEMALES
RATES PER THOUSAND											
Birth	14.67	15.69	13.74	15.75	13.77	15.72	13.72	15.62	13.62	14.24	12.48
Death	17.31	18.50	16.22	18.52	16.41	18.69	16.58	18.82	16.75	20.76	19.00
Increase	-2.64	-2.81	-2.48	-2.77	-2.64	-2.97	-2.86	-3.20	-3.12	-6.5229	
PERCENTAGE											
under 15	20.66	21.78	19.63	21.15	19.02	20.59	18.47	20.15	18.07	18.76	16.90
15-64	64.27	65.57	63.07	66.01	63.38	66.38	63.68	66.63	63.85	65.92	61.76
65 and over	15.07	12.65	17.30	12.84	17.60	13.03	17.85	13.22	18.09	15.33	21.34
DEP. RATIO X 100	55.61	52.52	58.56	51.50	57.78	50.65	57.03	50.09	56.63	51.70	61.91

TABLE 5 — POPULATION PROJECTED WITH FIXED AGE-SPECIFIC BIRTH AND DEATH RATES (IN 1000's)

AGE AT LAST BIRTHDAY	1915 BOTH SEXES	1915 MALES	1915 FEMALES	1920 BOTH SEXES	1920 MALES	1920 FEMALES	1925 BOTH SEXES	1925 MALES	1925 FEMALES	AGE AT LAST BIRTHDAY
0-4	9890	5005	4885	9760	4939	4821	9576	4846	4730	0-4
5-9	10288	5200	5088	9529	4813	4716	9404	4750	4654	5-9
10-14	10551	5319	5232	10171	5137	5034	9419	4754	4665	10-14
15-19	10596	5343	5253	10414	5248	5166	10038	5068	4970	15-19
20-24	10592	5259	5333	10407	5245	5162	10229	5152	5077	20-24
25-29	10689	5245	5444	10387	5152	5235	10206	5139	5067	25-29
30-34	10374	5109	5265	10502	5146	5356	10205	5055	5150	30-34
35-39	10062	4950	5112	10188	5005	5183	10315	5042	5273	35-39
40-44	9570	4524	5046	9859	4832	5027	9982	4886	5096	40-44
45-49	9995	4932	5063	9333	4384	4949	9613	4682	4931	45-49
50-54	9712	4740	4972	9626	4695	4931	8993	4173	4820	50-54
55-59	9111	4399	4712	9172	4387	4785	9090	4345	4745	55-59
60-64	8414	3937	4477	8372	3918	4454	8430	3907	4523	60-64
65-69	7397	3302	4095	7400	3304	4096	7363	3288	4075	65-69
70-74	6119	2556	3563	6123	2558	3565	6124	2558	3566	70-74
75-79	4647	1788	2859	4649	1789	2860	4650	1789	2861	75-79
80-84	3052	1078	1974	3055	1079	1976	3056	1079	1977	80-84
85+	2282	698	1584	2285	699	1586	2286	699	1587	85+
TOTAL	153341	73384	79957	151232	72330	78902	148979	71212	77767	TOTAL

TABLE 6 — STANDARDIZED RATES

STANDARD COUNTRIES: STANDARDIZED RATES PER THOUSAND	ENGLAND AND WALES 1961 BOTH SEXES	MALES	FEMALES	UNITED STATES 1960 BOTH SEXES	MALES	FEMALES	MEXICO 1960 BOTH SEXES	MALES	FEMALES
Birth	13.64	15.20*	12.90	13.91	14.24*	13.37	16.07	13.47*	15.64
Death	14.71	14.40*	13.47	13.67	13.32*	11.80	11.09	11.86*	9.58
Increase	-1.06	0.80*	-0.58	0.25	0.92*	1.58	4.99	1.61*	6.06

TABLE 7 — MOMENTS AND CUMULANTS

	OBSERVED POP. MALES	OBSERVED POP. FEMALES	STATIONARY POP. MALES	STATIONARY POP. FEMALES	STABLE POP. MALES	STABLE POP. FEMALES	OBSERVED BIRTHS	NET MATERNITY FUNCTION	BIRTHS IN STABLE POP.
μ	36.49535	39.17621	35.71472	38.57844	39.04809	42.33125	27.49692	27.51487	27.80544
σ^2	505.1157	559.2211	502.5710	568.5861	517.6909	579.5606	41.90920	42.08502	42.83112
κ_3	2686.868	2426.080	3121.717	2818.875	1478.275	514.364	122.8382	118.1999	110.4215
κ_4	-244250.	-322684.	-233307.	-335043.	-266264.	-364040.	-1072.980	-1121.619	-1252.124
β_1	0.056017	0.033656	0.076771	0.043228	0.015751	0.001359	0.204993	0.187436	0.155177
β_2	2.042690	1.968166	2.076296	1.963645	2.006494	1.916195	2.389096	2.366728	2.317459
κ	-0.021366	-0.012345	-0.029479	-0.015650	-0.006081	-0.000494	-0.090625	-0.082874	-0.068059

TABLE 8 — RATES FROM AGE DISTRIBUTIONS AND VITAL STATISTICS (Females)

VITAL STATISTICS		THOMPSON AGE RANGE	NRR	1000r	INTERVAL	BOURGEOIS-PICHAT AGE RANGE	NRR	1000b	1000d	1000r	COALE	
GRR	1.038										IBR	14.59
NRR	0.835	0-4	0.90	-3.91	27.28	5-29	0.89	14.88	19.17	-4.28	IDR	19.00
TFR	2.128	5-9	0.93	-2.77	27.25	30-54	0.96	15.57	16.96	-1.39	IRI	-4.41
GENERATION	27.660	10-14	0.94	-2.10	27.23	55-79	1.00	16.72	16.64	0.08	K1	-8.45
SEX RATIO	104.999	15-19	0.97	-0.96	27.17	*50-74	1.00	16.47	16.61	-0.14	K2	-0.08

TABLE 9 — LESLIE MATRIX AND ITS SPECTRAL COMPONENTS (Females)

Start Age Interval	ORIGINAL MATRIX SUB-DIAGONAL	ALTERNATIVE FIRST ROWS Projection	ALTERNATIVE FIRST ROWS Integral	FIRST STABLE MATRIX % IN STABLE POPULATION	FISHER VALUES	REPRODUCTIVE VALUES	SECOND STABLE MATRIX Z2 FIRST COLUMN	SECOND STABLE MATRIX Z2 FIRST ROW
0	0.96537	0.00000	0.00000	5.603	1.114	5871652	0.1270+0.0766	0.1270+0.0766
5	0.98923	0.00032	0.00000	5.588	1.117	5907363	0.1658-0.0906	-0.0017+0.1163
5	0.98740	0.05025	0.00063	5.711	1.093	5811983	0.0069-0.2466	-0.0776+0.0438
0	0.98267	0.18321	0.09950	5.826	1.014	5504515	-0.2731-0.1698	-0.0655-0.0384
0	0.98161	0.24678	0.26559	5.914	0.791	4389088	-0.3688+0.1950	-0.0235-0.0728
5	0.98387	0.19573	0.22411	5.998	0.500	2677174	-0.0225+0.5401	0.0075-0.0632
5	0.98448	0.14117	0.16365	6.096	0.271	1405264	0.5912+0.3788	0.0197-0.0348
5	0.98324	0.07429	0.11592	6.201	0.106	545577	0.8123-0.4155	0.0126-0.0114
0	0.98093	0.01668	0.03077	6.299	0.020	105798	0.0655-1.1824	0.0029-0.0018
5	0.97393	0.00109	0.00208	6.383	0.001	6581	-1.2798-0.8448	0.0002-0.0001
5	0.96234	0.00003	0.00006	6.423	0.000	174	-1.7673+0.8738	0.0000-0.0000
5+	0.78593			33.960				

TABLE 10 — AGE ANALYSIS AND MISCELLANEOUS RESULTS (Females)

Start Age Interval	OBSERVED POPUL. (IN 100's)	CONTRIBUTIONS OF ROOTS (IN 100's) r_1	r_2, r_3	r_4-r_{11}	AGE-SP. BIRTH RATES	NET MATERNITY FUNCTION	COEFF. OF MATRIX EQUATION	PARAMETERS INTEGRAL	PARAMETERS MATRIX	x	EXP. INCREASE $e^{(x+2\frac{1}{2})r}$
0	52710	51944	-321	1087	0.0000	0.0000	0.0000	L(1) 0.96791	0.96793	0	0.9838
5	52890	51806	931	153	0.0000	0.0000	0.0003	L(2) 0.37235	0.38175	50	0.7100
0	53198	52946	1759	-1507	0.0001	0.0006	0.0480	0.66943	0.65432	55	0.6872
5	54270	54011	727	-468	0.0229	0.0954	0.1728	R(1) -0.00652	-0.00652	60	0.6652
0	55460	54833	-2024	2652	0.0611	0.2501	0.2287	R(2) -0.05331	-0.05554	65	0.6438
5	53510	55608	-3865	1767	0.0516	0.2072	0.1780	0.21264	0.20853	70	0.6232
0	51931	56523	-1653	-2940	0.0377	0.1489	0.1263	C(1)	927145	75	0.6032
5	51316	57489	4359	-10532	0.0267	0.1038	0.0654	C(2)	87147	80	0.5838
0	51614	58398	8490	-15274	0.0071	0.0271	0.0144		354176	85	0.5651
5	51050	59182	3754	-11886	0.0005	0.0018	0.0009	2P/Y 29.5486	30.1309	90	0.5470
0	48960	59549	-9270	-1319	0.0000	0.0001	0.0000	DELTA 5.7207		95	0.5294
5+	232086	314854								100	0.5124

TABLE 1 — DATA

AGE AT LAST BIRTHDAY	POPULATION BOTH SEXES	MALES Number	%	FEMALES Number	%	BIRTHS BY AGE OF MOTHER	DEATHS BOTH SEXES	MALES	FEMALES	AGE AT LAST BIRTHDAY
0	2317000	1179000	1.5	1138000	1.3	-0	221683	125461	96222	0
1-4	9030000	4566000	5.8	4464000	5.1	-0	81565	43241	38324	1-4
5-9	11475275	5794759	7.3	5680516	6.5	0	32917	17600	15317	5-9
10-14	11527000	5784000	7.3	5743000	6.5	2195	20619	11407	9212	10-14
15-19	11572958	5768600	7.3	5804358	6.6	285598	32259	16844	15415	15-19
20-24	11317000	5599000	7.1	5718000	6.5	661946	36458	19408	17050	20-24
25-29	10997943	5341558	6.7	5656385	6.4	647039	30731	16751	13980	25-29
30-34	10298147	4684922	5.9	5613725	6.4	532239	28780	15488	13292	30-34
35-39	11260606	5522804	7.0	5737802	6.5	293900	31936	18504	13432	35-39
40-44	11192000	5476000	6.9	5716000	6.5	87587	41725	25371	16354	40-44
45-49	10912000	5371000	6.8	5541000	6.3	5042	64283	40824	23459	45-49
50-54	10570000	5146000	6.5	5424000	6.2	0	96589	62553	34036	50-54
55-59	9985786	4765155	6.0	5220631	5.9	0	137873	89984	47889	55-59
60-64	9176105	4242705	5.3	4933400	5.6	0	187104	119002	68102	60-64
65-69	8070879	3558858	4.5	4512021	5.1	0	253277	152549	100728	65-69
70-74	6680222	2754674	3.5	3925548	4.5		299019	165431	133588	70-74
75-79	5073885	1926032	2.4	3147853	3.6		338488	162731	175757	75-79
80-84	3333721	1160576	1.5	2173145	2.5	1288284 M.	350121	144165	205956	80-84
85+	2417753	746820	0.9	1670933	1.9	1227262 F.	485326	158968	326358	85+
TOTAL	167208280	79387963		87820317		2515546	2770753	1406282	1364471	TOTAL

TABLE 2 — MALE LIFE TABLE

x	$_nq_x$	l_x	$_nd_x$	$_nL_x$	$_nm_x$	$_na_x$	T_x	r_x	$\mathring{e}_x$	$_nM_x$	x
0	0.099184	100000	9918	93206	0.106413	0.3150	5781199	0.0000	57.812	0.106413	0
1	0.036891	90082	3323	350915	0.009470	1.1678	5687993	0.0000	63.143	0.009470	1
5	0.015072	86758	1308	430523	0.003037	2.5000	5337078	0.0000	61.517	0.003037	5
10	0.009812	85451	838	425141	0.001972	2.4799	4906555	0.0000	57.420	0.001972	10
15	0.014499	84612	1227	420119	0.002920	2.6010	4481414	0.0004	52.964	0.002920	15
20	0.017184	83386	1433	413356	0.003467	2.5070	4061296	0.0044	48.705	0.003466	20
25	0.015555	81953	1275	406553	0.003135	2.4820	3647940	0.0146	44.513	0.003136	25
30	0.016396	80678	1323	400092	0.003306	2.5069	3241387	0.0000	40.177	0.003306	30
35	0.016617	79355	1319	393576	0.003350	2.5736	2841295	0.0000	35.805	0.003350	35
40	0.022919	78036	1789	386029	0.004633	2.6781	2447719	0.0000	31.366	0.004633	40
45	0.037347	76248	2848	374652	0.007601	2.6865	2061690	0.0000	27.039	0.007601	45
50	0.059099	73400	4338	356864	0.012156	2.6630	1687038	0.0000	22.984	0.012156	50
55	0.090376	69062	6242	330524	0.018884	2.6308	1330175	0.0000	19.260	0.018884	55
60	0.131437	62821	8257	294367	0.028050	2.6097	999650	0.0003	15.913	0.028049	60
65	0.194064	54564	10589	247020	0.042866	2.5636	705283	0.0003	12.926	0.042865	65
70	0.261263	43975	11489	191302	0.060057	2.5131	458263	0.0003	10.421	0.060055	70
75	0.348140	32486	11310	133852	0.084494	2.4732	266961	0.0003	8.218	0.084490	75
80	0.473783	21176	10033	80764	0.124225	2.4965	133109	0.0003	6.286	0.124218	80
85+	*1.000000	11143	11143	52345	0.212884	4.6974	52345	0.0003	4.697	0.212860	85+

TABLE 3 — FEMALE LIFE TABLE

x	$_nq_x$	l_x	$_nd_x$	$_nL_x$	$_nm_x$	$_na_x$	T_x	r_x	$\mathring{e}_x$	$_nM_x$
0	0.080022	100000	8002	94641	0.084554	0.3303	6467397	0.0000	64.674	0.084554
1	0.033531	91998	3085	359319	0.008585	1.1888	6372756	0.0000	69.271	0.008585
5	0.013392	88913	1191	441588	0.002696	2.5000	6013437	0.0000	67.633	0.002696
10	0.007988	87722	701	436851	0.001604	2.4874	5571849	0.0000	63.517	0.001604
15	0.013195	87022	1148	432356	0.002656	2.6034	5134998	0.0000	59.008	0.002656
20	0.014798	85873	1271	426167	0.002982	2.4821	4702642	0.0000	54.763	0.002982
25	0.012280	84603	1039	420356	0.002472	2.4424	4276475	0.0000	50.548	0.002472
30	0.011769	83564	983	415343	0.002368	2.4835	3856120	0.0000	46.146	0.002368
35	0.011638	82580	961	410535	0.002341	2.5382	3440776	0.0000	41.666	0.002341
40	0.014210	81619	1160	405347	0.002861	2.6304	3030241	0.0005	37.127	0.002861
45	0.020964	80459	1687	398346	0.004234	2.6576	2624894	0.0009	32.624	0.004234
50	0.030919	78773	2436	388137	0.006275	2.6489	2226548	0.0000	28.266	0.006275
55	0.044897	76337	3427	373625	0.009173	2.6484	1838411	0.0015	24.083	0.009173
60	0.066881	72910	4876	353147	0.013808	2.6618	1464786	0.0015	20.090	0.013804
65	0.106052	68033	7215	323108	0.022330	2.6357	1111639	0.0015	16.340	0.022324
70	0.157431	60818	9575	281279	0.034040	2.6174	788531	0.0015	12.965	0.034030
75	0.246078	51244	12610	225781	0.055850	2.5863	507252	0.0015	9.899	0.055834
80	0.383007	38634	14797	156090	0.094798	2.6581	281470	0.0015	7.286	0.094773
85+	1.000000	23837	23837	125380	0.190116	5.2600	125380	0.0015	5.260	0.195314

TABLE 4 — OBSERVED AND PROJECTED VITAL RATES

	OBSERVED POPULATION BOTH SEXES	MALES	FEMALES	PROJECTED 1920 MALES	FEMALES	1925 MALES	FEMALES	1930 MALES	FEMALES	STABLE POPULATION MALES	FEMA...
RATES PER THOUSAND											
Birth	15.04	16.23	13.97	16.22	13.97	16.20	13.95	16.08	13.87	15.19	13.
Death	16.57	17.71	15.54	17.83	15.80	17.91	15.92	17.97	16.03	18.72	16.
Increase	-1.53	-1.49	-1.56	-1.60	-1.83	-1.72	-1.96	-1.88	-2.17		-3.52
PERCENTAGE											
under 15	20.54	21.82	19.39	21.57	19.07	21.34	18.86	21.32	18.84	20.27	18.
15-64	64.16	65.40	63.04	65.53	63.13	65.65	63.17	65.54	63.00	65.82	62.
65 and over	15.30	12.78	17.57	12.90	17.80	13.01	17.97	13.14	18.16	13.91	19.
DEP. RATIO X 100	55.86	52.91	58.62	52.59	58.40	52.33	58.31	52.57	58.74	51.93	60.

TABLE 1 — DATA

AGE AT LAST BIRTHDAY	POPULATION BOTH SEXES	MALES Number	%	FEMALES Number	%	BIRTHS BY AGE OF MOTHER	DEATHS BOTH SEXES	MALES	FEMALES	AGE AT LAST BIRTHDAY
0	2278571	1153736	1.4	1124835	1.2	0	212598	120782	91816	0
1-4	9376978	4749510	5.9	4627468	5.0	0	89708	47265	42443	1-4
5-9	12086998	6112999	7.6	5973999	6.5	0	25162	13905	11257	5-9
10-14	12033597	6082707	7.6	5950890	6.5	3016	18375	10305	8070	10-14
15-19	11813000	5888000	7.3	5925000	6.5	270929	26897	14761	12136	15-19
20-24	11465777	5560455	6.9	5905322	6.4	739776	27865	15464	12401	20-24
25-29	9024061	3159487	3.9	5864574	6.4	755365	23610	12884	10726	25-29
30-34	11554959	5642117	7.0	5912842	6.4	598758	22981	13350	9631	30-34
35-39	11545000	5628000	7.0	5917000	6.4	345305	28017	16685	11332	35-39
40-44	11641000	5693000	7.1	5948000	6.5	91564	42942	26234	16708	40-44
45-49	11449000	5570000	6.9	5879000	6.4	4829	66259	41408	24851	45-49
50-54	11035399	5307422	6.6	5727977	6.2	1	100490	64537	35953	50-54
55-59	10427840	4914630	6.1	5513210	6.0	0	143379	92806	50573	55-59
60-64	9585674	4375792	5.4	5209882	5.7	0	194654	122735	71919	60-64
65-69	8435381	3670493	4.6	4764888	5.2	0	263707	157334	106373	65-69
70-74	6986630	2841083	3.5	4145547	4.5		311695	170620	141075	70-74
75-79	5310716	1986448	2.5	3324268	3.6		353443	167836	185607	75-79
80-84	3491916	1196982	1.5	2294934	2.5	1438688 M.	366186	148687	217499	80-84
85+	2534824	770247	1.0	1764577	1.9	1370855 F.	508603	163955	344648	85+
TOTAL	172077321	80303108		91774213		2809543	2826571	1421553	1405018	TOTAL

TABLE 2 — MALE LIFE TABLE

x	$_nq_x$	l_x	$_nd_x$	$_nL_x$	$_nm_x$	$_na_x$	T_x	r_x	$\dot{e}_x$	$_nM_x$	x
0	0.097750	100000	9775	93373	0.104688	0.3221	5832865	0.0000	58.329	0.104688	0
1	0.038719	90225	3493	351039	0.009952	1.1772	5739491	0.0000	63.613	0.009952	1
5	0.011309	86732	981	431206	0.002275	2.5000	5388453	0.0000	62.128	0.002275	5
10	0.008436	85751	723	426962	0.001694	2.5228	4957247	0.0017	57.810	0.001694	10
15	0.012467	85027	1060	422579	0.002508	2.5873	4530285	0.0066	53.280	0.002507	15
20	0.013908	83967	1168	417044	0.002800	2.6090	4107706	0.0592	48.920	0.002781	20
25	0.020181	82800	1671	409776	0.004078	2.4733	3690661	0.0000	44.573	0.004078	25
30	0.011758	81129	954	403156	0.002366	2.3928	3280886	0.0000	40.441	0.002366	30
35	0.014721	80175	1180	398099	0.002965	2.6495	2877730	0.0000	35.893	0.002965	35
40	0.022798	78994	1801	390811	0.004608	2.6898	2479632	0.0000	31.390	0.004608	40
45	0.036543	77193	2821	379456	0.007434	2.6917	2088820	0.0000	27.060	0.007434	45
50	0.059121	74373	4397	361600	0.012160	2.6660	1709364	0.0000	22.984	0.012160	50
55	0.090375	69976	6324	334895	0.018884	2.6308	1347764	0.0000	19.261	0.018884	55
60	0.131437	63651	8366	298260	0.028050	2.6097	1012870	0.0000	15.913	0.028049	60
65	0.194063	55285	10729	250287	0.042866	2.5636	714610	0.0003	12.926	0.042865	65
70	0.261263	44556	11641	193832	0.060057	2.5131	464323	0.0003	10.421	0.060055	70
75	0.348141	32916	11459	135622	0.084494	2.4732	270491	0.0003	8.218	0.084491	75
80	0.473782	21456	10166	81832	0.124225	2.4965	134869	0.0003	6.286	0.124218	80
85+	*1.000000	11291	11291	53037	0.212884	4.6974	53037	0.0003	4.697	0.212860	85+

TABLE 3 — FEMALE LIFE TABLE

x	$_nq_x$	l_x	$_nd_x$	$_nL_x$	$_nm_x$	$_na_x$	T_x	r_x	$\dot{e}_x$	$_nM_x$	x
0	0.077459	100000	7746	94895	0.081626	0.3410	6571142	0.0000	65.711	0.081626	0
1	0.035771	92254	3300	359793	0.009172	1.2052	6476246	0.0000	70.200	0.009172	1
5	0.009377	88954	834	442685	0.001884	2.5000	6116453	0.0000	68.760	0.001884	5
10	0.006758	88120	595	439123	0.001356	2.5202	5673768	0.0000	64.387	0.001356	10
15	0.010191	87524	892	435457	0.002048	2.5723	5234646	0.0000	59.808	0.002048	15
20	0.010444	86632	905	430877	0.002100	2.4743	4799189	0.0000	55.397	0.002100	20
25	0.009102	85728	780	426642	0.001829	2.4424	4368312	0.0000	50.956	0.001829	25
30	0.008111	84947	689	423019	0.001629	2.5069	3941670	0.0000	46.401	0.001629	30
35	0.009532	84258	803	419383	0.001915	2.6233	3518651	0.0000	41.760	0.001915	35
40	0.013954	83455	1164	414556	0.002809	2.6644	3099268	0.0000	37.137	0.002809	40
45	0.020928	82291	1722	407424	0.004227	2.6606	2684713	0.0000	32.625	0.004227	45
50	0.030927	80568	2492	396984	0.006277	2.6491	2277289	0.0000	28.265	0.006277	50
55	0.044897	78077	3505	382140	0.009173	2.6483	1880304	0.0000	24.083	0.009173	55
60	0.066882	74571	4987	361195	0.013808	2.6618	1498165	0.0015	20.090	0.013804	60
65	0.106052	69584	7380	330471	0.022330	2.6357	1136970	0.0015	16.340	0.022324	65
70	0.157431	62204	9793	287689	0.034040	2.6174	806499	0.0015	12.965	0.034030	70
75	0.246078	52411	12897	230027	0.055850	2.5863	518810	0.0015	9.899	0.055834	75
80	0.383008	39514	15134	159647	0.094798	2.6581	287884	0.0015	7.286	0.094774	80
85+	1.000000	24380	24380	128237	0.190116	5.2600	128237	0.0015	5.260	0.195314	85+

TABLE 4 — OBSERVED, PROJECTED, STABLE

RATES PER THOUSAND	OBSERVED POPULATION BOTH SEXES	MALES	FEMALES	PROJECTED POPULATION 1925 MALES	FEMALES	1930 MALES	FEMALES	1935 MALES	FEMALES	STABLE POPULATION MALES	FEMALES
Birth	16.33	17.92	14.94	17.78	14.85	17.69	14.81	17.53	14.72	16.94	15.03
Death	16.43	17.70	15.31	17.93	15.62	17.92	15.67	17.85	15.71	17.27	15.35
Increase	-0.10	0.21	-0.37	-0.15	-0.77	-0.23	-0.86	-0.31	-1.00		-0.3258
PERCENTAGE											
under 15	20.79	22.54	19.26	22.61	19.37	22.67	19.47	23.15	19.94	22.12	20.13
15-64	63.66	64.43	62.98	64.33	62.73	64.25	62.55	63.74	62.00	65.47	62.36
65 and over	15.55	13.03	17.75	13.05	17.90	13.08	17.98	13.11	18.06	12.40	17.51
DEP. RATIO X 100	57.09	55.21	58.77	55.44	59.40	55.65	59.87	56.89	61.28	52.74	60.35

TABLE 1 — DATA

AGE AT LAST BIRTHDAY	POPULATION BOTH SEXES	MALES Number	MALES %	FEMALES Number	FEMALES %	BIRTHS BY AGE OF MOTHER	DEATHS BOTH SEXES	DEATHS MALES	FEMALES	AGE AT LAST BIRTHDAY
0	2460000	1252000	1.5	1208000	1.2	0	181017	103169	77848	0
1-4	9856000	5008000	5.9	4848000	5.0	0	62961	33661	29300	1-4
5-9	12577837	6368321	7.6	6209516	6.4	0	23896	13352	10544	5-9
10-14	12424000	6260000	7.4	6164000	6.3	3160	17284	9899	7385	10-14
15-19	12261267	6126813	7.3	6134454	6.3	301293	21194	11751	9443	15-19
20-24	9024615	2921712	3.5	6102903	6.3	796849	22274	12630	9644	20-24
25-29	12211629	5957170	7.1	6254459	6.4	1023504	19523	11785	7738	25-29
30-34	12314000	5990000	7.1	6324000	6.5	722277	20058	12133	7925	30-34
35-39	12481000	6079000	7.2	6402000	6.6	359908	29161	17594	11567	35-39
40-44	12411000	6033000	7.2	6378000	6.6	83255	45847	28045	17802	40-44
45-49	12125252	5856903	7.0	6268349	6.4	5148	70059	43555	26504	45-49
50-54	11688123	5580799	6.6	6107324	6.3	1	106195	67861	38334	50-54
55-59	11046110	5167776	6.1	5878334	6.0	0	151509	97587	53922	55-59
60-64	10156099	4601182	5.5	5554917	5.7	0	205738	129057	76681	60-64
65-69	8940008	3859555	4.6	5080453	5.2	0	278856	165438	113418	65-69
70-74	7407518	2987424	3.5	4420094	4.5		329827	179409	150418	70-74
75-79	5633191	2088767	2.5	3544424	3.6		374380	176481	197899	75-79
80-84	3705558	1258637	1.5	2446921	2.5	1687129 M.	388249	156346	231903	80-84
85+	2691360	809921	1.0	1881439	1.9	1608266 F.	539873	172400	367473	85+
TOTAL	181414567	84206980		97207587		3295395	2887901	1442153	1445748	TOTAL

TABLE 2 — MALE LIFE TABLE

x	nq_x	l_x	nd_x	nL_x	nm_x	na_x	T_x	r_x	$\dot{e}_x$	nM_x	x
0	0.077953	100000	7795	94600	0.082403	0.3072	6066880	0.0000	60.669	0.082403	0
1	0.026382	92205	2433	361906	0.006721	1.1581	5972280	0.0000	64.772	0.006721	1
5	0.010428	89772	936	446520	0.002097	2.5000	5610375	0.0000	62.496	0.002097	5
10	0.007875	88836	700	442415	0.001581	2.4773	5163855	0.0021	58.128	0.001581	10
15	0.009755	88136	860	438775	0.001960	2.7827	4721440	0.0738	53.570	0.001918	15
20	0.021383	87277	1866	431713	0.004323	2.4978	4282664	0.0000	49.070	0.004323	20
25	0.009838	85410	840	424740	0.001978	2.2486	3850951	0.0000	45.088	0.001978	25
30	0.010078	84570	852	420795	0.002026	2.5888	3426211	0.0000	40.513	0.002026	30
35	0.014375	83718	1203	415798	0.002894	2.6809	3005416	0.0000	35.899	0.002894	35
40	0.022996	82514	1898	408191	0.004649	2.6914	2589618	0.0000	31.384	0.004649	40
45	0.036555	80617	2947	396278	0.007437	2.6905	2181427	0.0000	27.059	0.007437	45
50	0.059121	77670	4592	377632	0.012160	2.6659	1785149	0.0000	22.984	0.012160	50
55	0.090376	73078	6604	349742	0.018884	2.6308	1407517	0.0000	19.260	0.018884	55
60	0.131437	66473	8737	311483	0.028050	2.6097	1057775	0.0003	15.913	0.028049	60
65	0.194063	57736	11205	261383	0.042866	2.5636	746292	0.0003	12.926	0.042865	65
70	0.261263	46532	12157	202426	0.060057	2.5131	484909	0.0003	10.421	0.060055	70
75	0.348141	34375	11967	141635	0.084494	2.4732	282483	0.0003	8.218	0.084491	75
80	0.473783	22408	10616	85460	0.124225	2.4965	140848	0.0003	6.286	0.124218	80
85+	*1.000000	11791	11791	55388	0.212884	4.6974	55388	0.0003	4.697	0.212860	85+

TABLE 3 — FEMALE LIFE TABLE

x	nq_x	l_x	nd_x	nL_x	nm_x	na_x	T_x	r_x	$\dot{e}_x$	nM_x	x
0	0.061750	100000	6175	95821	0.064444	0.3232	6820681	0.0000	68.207	0.064444	0
1	0.023770	93825	2230	369008	0.006044	1.1787	6724860	0.0000	71.675	0.006044	1
5	0.008454	91595	774	456038	0.001698	2.5000	6355852	0.0000	69.391	0.001698	5
10	0.005972	90820	542	452729	0.001198	2.4685	5899814	0.0000	64.961	0.001198	10
15	0.007668	90278	692	449693	0.001539	2.5489	5447085	0.0000	60.337	0.001539	15
20	0.007870	89586	705	446136	0.001580	2.4574	4997392	0.0000	55.783	0.001580	20
25	0.006166	88881	548	443002	0.001237	2.4418	4551256	0.0000	51.206	0.001237	25
30	0.006247	88333	552	440334	0.001253	2.5912	4108254	0.0000	46.509	0.001253	30
35	0.008996	87781	790	437066	0.001807	2.6726	3667920	0.0000	41.785	0.001807	35
40	0.013866	86991	1206	432150	0.002791	2.6738	3230854	0.0000	37.140	0.002791	40
45	0.020934	85785	1796	424725	0.004228	2.6614	2798704	0.0000	32.625	0.004228	45
50	0.030927	83989	2598	413839	0.006277	2.6490	2373978	0.0000	28.265	0.006277	50
55	0.044897	81392	3654	398364	0.009173	2.6483	1960139	0.0000	24.083	0.009173	55
60	0.066881	77737	5199	376530	0.013808	2.6618	1561775	0.0015	20.090	0.013804	60
65	0.106052	72538	7693	344503	0.022330	2.6357	1185245	0.0015	16.340	0.022324	65
70	0.157431	64845	10209	299904	0.034040	2.6174	840742	0.0015	12.965	0.034030	70
75	0.246078	54637	13445	240731	0.055850	2.5863	540838	0.0015	9.899	0.055834	75
80	0.383007	41192	15777	166425	0.094798	2.6581	300107	0.0015	7.286	0.094773	80
85+	1.000000	25415	25415	133682	0.190116	5.2600	133682	0.0015	5.260	0.195314	85+

TABLE 4 — OBSERVED AND PROJECTED VITAL RATES

	OBSERVED POPULATION BOTH SEXES	MALES	FEMALES	PROJECTED POPULATION 1930 MALES	1930 FEMALES	1935 MALES	1935 FEMALES	1940 MALES	1940 FEMALES	STABLE POPULATION MALES	FEMA
RATES PER THOUSAND											
Birth	18.16	20.04	16.54	19.48	16.16	19.08	15.91	18.75	15.70	19.48	17.
Death	15.92	17.13	14.87	17.37	15.18	17.20	15.10	17.00	15.03	14.70	12.
Increase	2.25	2.91	1.67	2.10	0.98	1.88	0.81	1.75	0.67		4.77
PERCENTAGE											
under 15	20.57	22.43	18.96	23.56	19.94	24.49	20.82	25.62	21.91	25.29	23.
15-64	63.79	64.50	63.17	63.51	62.21	62.69	61.41	61.68	60.39	64.49	62.
65 and over	15.64	13.07	17.87	12.93	17.85	12.81	17.77	12.70	17.70	10.21	14.
DEP. RATIO X 100	56.77	55.04	58.31	57.45	60.73	59.51	62.85	62.13	65.59	55.06	60.

TABLE 5 — POPULATION PROJECTED WITH FIXED AGE-SPECIFIC BIRTH AND DEATH RATES (IN 1000's)

AGE LAST BIRTHDAY	BOTH SEXES	1930 MALES	FEMALES	BOTH SEXES	1935 MALES	FEMALES	BOTH SEXES	1940 MALES	FEMALES	AGE AT LAST BIRTHDAY
0-4	15052	7638	7414	14848	7535	7313	14705	7462	7243	0-4
5-9	12064	6123	5941	14745	7471	7274	14545	7370	7175	5-9
10-14	12474	6310	6164	11965	6067	5898	14623	7402	7221	10-14
15-19	12332	6209	6123	12381	6258	6123	11876	6017	5859	15-19
20-24	12114	6028	6086	12183	6109	6074	12232	6157	6075	20-24
25-29	8935	2875	6060	11974	5931	6043	12042	6010	6032	25-29
30-34	12119	5902	6217	8872	2848	6024	11883	5876	6007	30-34
35-39	12196	5919	6277	12003	5832	6171	8793	2814	5979	35-39
40-44	12298	5968	6330	12017	5811	6206	11826	5725	6101	40-44
45-49	12125	5857	6268	12015	5794	6221	11741	5641	6100	45-49
50-54	11689	5581	6108	11689	5581	6108	11583	5521	6062	50-54
55-59	11048	5169	5879	11048	5169	5879	11048	5169	5879	55-59
60-64	10158	4602	5556	10160	4603	5557	10161	4604	5557	60-64
65-69	8943	3861	5082	8946	3862	5084	8947	3863	5084	65-69
70-74	7412	2989	4423	7414	2990	4424	7416	2991	4425	70-74
75-79	5638	2090	3548	5641	2091	3550	5643	2092	3551	75-79
80-84	3710	1260	2450	3714	1261	2453	3716	1262	2454	80-84
85+	2782	816	1966	2785	817	1968	2787	817	1970	85+
TOTAL	183089	85197	97892	184400	86030	98370	185567	86793	98774	TOTAL

TABLE 6 — STANDARDIZED RATES

STANDARD COUNTRIES: STANDARDIZED RATES PER THOUSAND	ENGLAND AND WALES 1961 BOTH SEXES	MALES	FEMALES	UNITED STATES 1960 BOTH SEXES	MALES	FEMALES	MEXICO 1960 BOTH SEXES	MALES	FEMALES
Birth	16.83	20.75*	15.92	17.19	20.35*	16.53	19.72	17.50*	19.20
Death	12.84	12.94*	11.68	11.33	11.98*	9.51	7.92	10.72*	6.46
Increase	3.98	7.81*	4.23	5.86	8.37*	7.02	11.80	6.78*	12.74

TABLE 7 — MOMENTS AND CUMULANTS

	OBSERVED POP. MALES	FEMALES	STATIONARY POP. MALES	FEMALES	STABLE POP. MALES	FEMALES	OBSERVED BIRTHS	NET MATERNITY FUNCTION	BIRTHS IN STABLE POP.
μ	37.13577	39.91715	36.11750	39.11820	33.75820	36.45112	27.96055	27.81274	27.63339
σ^2	512.3680	557.6518	501.6448	565.3942	485.3402	550.0929	35.81879	35.61158	35.31409
κ_3	1939.690	1828.773	2879.742	2440.144	3918.589	3933.544	57.0250	60.9455	63.5887
κ_4	-258049.	-321810.	-234342.	-331644.	-198950.	-290523.	-585.678	-561.460	-534.704
β_1	0.027972	0.019285	0.065693	0.032944	0.134314	0.092952	0.070762	0.082245	0.091815
β_2	2.017036	1.965160	2.068768	1.962546	2.155381	2.039917	2.543504	2.557273	2.571237
κ	-0.010755	-0.007160	-0.025362	-0.012038	-0.051902	-0.034060	-0.048497	-0.056185	-0.062824

TABLE 8 — RATES FROM AGE DISTRIBUTIONS AND VITAL STATISTICS (Females)

VITAL STATISTICS		THOMPSON AGE RANGE	NRR	1000r	INTERVAL	BOURGEOIS-PICHAT AGE RANGE	NRR	1000b	1000d	1000r	COALE	
GRR	1.289										IBR	13.37
NRR	1.142	0-4	0.92	-3.12	27.40	5-29	0.96	13.75	15.29	-1.54	IDR	16.58
GFR	2.641	5-9	0.95	-2.00	27.36	30-54	0.97	14.30	15.54	-1.24	IRI	-3.22
GENERATION	27.723	10-14	0.93	-2.47	27.31	55-79	1.00	15.25	15.17	0.08	K1	-1.73
SEX RATIO	104.904	15-19	0.93	-2.70	27.22	*40-64	1.00	15.20	15.18	0.02	K2	0.

TABLE 9 — LESLIE MATRIX AND ITS SPECTRAL COMPONENTS (Females)

ORIGINAL MATRIX SUB-DIAGONAL	ALTERNATIVE FIRST ROWS Projection	Integral	FIRST STABLE MATRIX % IN STABLE POPULATION	FISHER VALUES	REPRODUCTIVE VALUES	SECOND STABLE MATRIX Z₂ FIRST COLUMN	FIRST ROW
0.98109	0.00000	0.00000	8.067	1.089	6591969	0.1522+0.0630	0.1522+0.0630
0.99274	0.00058	0.00000	7.727	1.136	7055980	0.1492-0.1228	0.0136+0.1398
0.99329	0.05592	0.00118	7.490	1.172	7222188	-0.0454-0.2248	-0.0986+0.0654
0.99209	0.20264	0.11276	7.264	1.147	7035193	-0.2610-0.0779	-0.0962-0.0510
0.99297	0.33241	0.29976	7.036	0.962	5868576	-0.2271+0.2298	-0.0313-0.1047
0.99398	0.31438	0.37569	6.822	0.627	3924295	0.1140+0.3662	0.0145-0.0858
0.99258	0.19284	0.26221	6.621	0.302	1911297	0.4479+0.0850	0.0213-0.0431
0.98875	0.07841	0.12906	6.417	0.100	642617	0.3389-0.4217	0.0110-0.0135
0.98282	0.01572	0.02997	6.195	0.018	112631	-0.2516-0.5880	0.0023-0.0022
0.97437	0.00093	0.00189	5.944	0.001	6208	-0.7489-0.0638	0.0001-0.0001
0.96261	0.00000	0.00000	5.655	0.000	1	-0.4757+0.7351	0.0000-0.0000
0.80434			24.762				

TABLE 10 — AGE ANALYSIS AND MISCELLANEOUS RESULTS (Females)

OBSERVED POPUL. (IN 100's)	CONTRIBUTIONS OF ROOTS (IN 100's) r_1	r_2, r_3	$r_4 \cdot r_{11}$	AGE-SP. BIRTH RATES	NET MATERNITY FUNCTION	COEFF. OF MATRIX EQUATION	PARAMETERS	INTEGRAL	MATRIX	EXP. INCREASE x	$e^{(x+z\frac{1}{2})r}$
60560	67181	-1441	-5180	0.0000	0.0000	0.0000	L(1)	1.02417	1.02418	0	1.0120
62095	64354	-5123	2864	0.0000	0.0000	0.0006	L(2)	0.38825	0.39318	50	1.2850
61640	62379	-3710	2972	0.0003	0.0011	0.0545		0.76033	0.73819	55	1.3161
61345	60497	3079	-2232	0.0240	0.1078	0.1960	R(1)	0.00478	0.00478	60	1.3479
61029	58601	8661	-6233	0.0637	0.2843	0.3190	R(2)	-0.03163	-0.03574	65	1.3805
62545	56816	5331	398	0.0799	0.3538	0.2996		0.21974	0.21628	70	1.4139
63240	55140	-6263	14363	0.0557	0.2454	0.1827	C(1)		832825	75	1.4480
64020	53438	-14508	25089	0.0274	0.1199	0.0737	C(2)		-889926	80	1.4830
63780	51590	-7339	19529	0.0064	0.0275	0.0146			-1004928	85	1.5189
62683	49506	12046	1132	0.0004	0.0017	0.0009	2P/Y	28.5943	29.0515	90	1.5556
61073	47098	23241	-9266	0.0000	0.0000	0.0000	DELTA	6.5374		95	1.5932
288066	206225									100	1.6317

TABLE 1 — DATA

AGE AT LAST BIRTHDAY	POPULATION BOTH SEXES	MALES Number	%	FEMALES Number	%	BIRTHS BY AGE OF MOTHER	DEATHS BOTH SEXES	MALES	FEMALES	AGE AT LAST BIRTHDAY
0	2225229	1128247	1.5	1096982	1.4	-0	265052	148108	116944	0
1-4	8453455	4279445	5.8	4174010	5.2	-0	108073	56904	51169	1-4
5-9	10673999	5385000	7.2	5288999	6.5	-0	26468	14191	12277	5-9
10-14	10735265	5415431	7.3	5319834	6.6	3245	23668	12673	10995	10-14
15-19	10784000	5357000	7.2	5427000	6.7	341920	33736	16974	16762	15-19
20-24	10899558	5353542	7.2	5546016	6.9	775318	43215	22142	21073	20-24
25-29	10558000	5207000	7.0	5351000	6.6	617062	39486	20644	18842	25-29
30-34	10245043	5051936	6.8	5193107	6.4	431452	34620	18901	15719	30-34
35-39	9766381	4634766	6.2	5131615	6.3	296806	37778	20881	16897	35-39
40-44	10251022	5089590	6.8	5161432	6.4	77745	45069	26942	18127	40-44
45-49	10085000	4980000	6.7	5105000	6.3	5438	59936	37788	22148	45-49
50-54	9650000	4754000	6.4	4896000	6.1	0	90593	59316	31277	50-54
55-59	9156000	4420000	5.9	4736000	5.9	0	126870	83438	43432	55-59
60-64	8410825	3935392	5.3	4475433	5.5	0	172163	110383	61780	60-64
65-69	7394248	3301078	4.4	4093170	5.1	0	232877	141499	91378	65-69
70-74	6116283	2555144	3.4	3561139	4.4		274635	153448	121187	70-74
75-79	4642161	1786523	2.4	2855638	3.5		310385	150944	159441	75-79
80-84	3047924	1076512	1.4	1971412	2.4	1305689 M.	320559	133722	186837	80-84
85+	2208546	692726	0.9	1515820	1.9	1243297 F.	443516	147454	296062	85+
TOTAL	155302939	74403332		80899607		2548986	2688699	1376352	1312347	TOTAL

TABLE 2 — MALE LIFE TABLE

x	$_nq_x$	l_x	$_nd_x$	$_nL_x$	$_nm_x$	$_na_x$	T_x	r_x	$\dot{e}_x$	$_nM_x$	x
0	0.120616	100000	12062	91882	0.131273	0.3269	5503792	0.0000	55.038	0.131273	0
1	0.051268	87938	4508	339058	0.013297	1.1840	5411910	0.0000	61.542	0.013297	1
5	0.013090	83430	1092	414419	0.002635	2.5000	5072853	0.0000	60.804	0.002635	5
10	0.011634	82338	958	409334	0.002340	2.5408	4658433	0.0000	56.577	0.002340	10
15	0.015724	81380	1280	403843	0.003169	2.6110	4249100	0.0000	52.213	0.003169	15
20	0.020471	80100	1640	396457	0.004136	2.5331	3845257	0.0000	48.006	0.004136	20
25	0.019626	78461	1540	388409	0.003965	2.4711	3448800	0.0018	43.956	0.003965	25
30	0.018539	76921	1426	381068	0.003742	2.5208	3060392	0.0077	39.786	0.003741	30
35	0.022282	75495	1682	373373	0.004505	2.5623	2679323	0.0000	35.490	0.004505	35
40	0.026137	73813	1929	364448	0.005294	2.6078	2305950	0.0000	31.241	0.005294	40
45	0.037282	71883	2680	353189	0.007588	2.6761	1941503	0.0000	27.009	0.007588	45
50	0.060615	69203	4195	336195	0.012477	2.6586	1588314	0.0000	22.951	0.012477	50
55	0.090340	65009	5873	311106	0.018877	2.6269	1252119	0.0000	19.261	0.018877	55
60	0.131438	59136	7773	277100	0.028050	2.6098	941012	0.0003	15.913	0.028049	60
65	0.194063	51363	9968	232530	0.042866	2.5636	663912	0.0003	12.926	0.042864	65
70	0.261262	41395	10815	180081	0.060057	2.5131	431382	0.0003	10.421	0.060055	70
75	0.348140	30580	10646	126000	0.084494	2.4732	251301	0.0003	8.218	0.084490	75
80	0.473781	19934	9444	76027	0.124224	2.4965	125301	0.0003	6.286	0.124217	80
85+	*1.000000	10490	10490	49274	0.212885	4.6974	49274	0.0003	4.697	0.212860	85+

TABLE 3 — FEMALE LIFE TABLE

x	$_nq_x$	l_x	$_nd_x$	$_nL_x$	$_nm_x$	$_na_x$	T_x	r_x	$\dot{e}_x$	$_nM_x$	x
0	0.099613	100000	9961	93441	0.106605	0.3416	6155800	0.0000	61.558	0.106605	0
1	0.047412	90039	4269	348228	0.012259	1.2062	6062359	0.0000	67.331	0.012259	1
5	0.011539	85770	990	426374	0.002321	2.5000	5714131	0.0000	66.622	0.002321	5
10	0.010282	84780	872	421783	0.002067	2.5709	5287756	0.0000	62.370	0.002067	10
15	0.015330	83908	1286	416468	0.003089	2.6107	4865974	0.0000	57.992	0.003089	15
20	0.018821	82622	1555	409249	0.003800	2.5172	4449506	0.0000	53.854	0.003800	20
25	0.017447	81067	1414	401724	0.003521	2.4472	4040257	0.0031	49.839	0.003521	25
30	0.015020	79653	1196	395244	0.003027	2.4768	3638533	0.0010	45.680	0.003027	30
35	0.016330	78456	1281	389109	0.003293	2.5240	3243288	0.0000	41.339	0.003293	35
40	0.017410	77175	1344	382588	0.003512	2.5538	2854179	0.0000	36.983	0.003512	40
45	0.021473	75831	1628	375293	0.004339	2.6269	2471591	-0.0007	32.593	0.004338	45
50	0.031472	74203	2335	365510	0.006389	2.6425	2096298	-0.0010	28.251	0.006388	50
55	0.044884	71868	3226	351744	0.009171	2.6457	1730789	0.0000	24.083	0.009171	55
60	0.066881	68642	4591	332476	0.013808	2.6619	1379045	0.0015	20.090	0.013804	60
65	0.106053	64051	6793	304195	0.022330	2.6357	1046569	0.0015	16.340	0.022325	65
70	0.157431	57258	9014	264814	0.034040	2.6174	742374	0.0015	12.965	0.034030	70
75	0.246078	48244	11872	212565	0.055850	2.5863	477560	0.0015	9.899	0.055834	75
80	0.383007	36372	13931	146953	0.094798	2.6581	264994	0.0015	7.286	0.094773	80
85+	1.000000	22441	22441	118041	0.190116	5.2600	118041	0.0015	5.260	0.195314	85

TABLE 4 — OBSERVED AND PROJECTED VITAL RATES

	OBSERVED POPULATION BOTH SEXES	MALES	FEMALES	PROJECTED POPULATION 1915 MALES	FEMALES	1920 MALES	FEMALES	1925 MALES	FEMALES	STABLE POPULATION MALES	FEMALES
RATES PER THOUSAND											
Birth	16.41	17.55	15.37	17.46	15.27	17.29	15.11	17.04	14.89	16.59	14.72
Death	17.31	18.50	16.22	18.68	16.52	18.72	16.58	18.72	16.65	19.09	17.23
Increase	-0.90	-0.95	-0.85	-1.22	-1.25	-1.43	-1.47	-1.68	-1.76	-2.5004	
PERCENTAGE											
under 15	20.66	21.78	19.63	21.79	19.60	21.83	19.61	22.00	19.77	21.21	19.35
15-64	64.27	65.57	63.07	65.48	62.93	65.34	62.79	65.09	62.52	65.54	62.05
65 and over	15.07	12.65	17.30	12.74	17.48	12.83	17.60	12.91	17.71	13.25	18.60
DEP. RATIO X 100	55.61	52.52	58.56	52.72	58.92	53.04	59.26	53.64	59.95	52.58	61.15

United States, Cohort 0–4 Years of Age in 1910
With Adjusted Births

TABLE 5 POPULATION PROJECTED WITH FIXED AGE—SPECIFIC BIRTH AND DEATH RATES (IN 1000's)

AGE AT LAST BIRTHDAY	1915 BOTH SEXES	1915 MALES	1915 FEMALES	1920 BOTH SEXES	1920 MALES	1920 FEMALES	1925 BOTH SEXES	1925 MALES	1925 FEMALES	AGE AT LAST BIRTHDAY
0-4	11059	5597	5462	10907	5520	5387	10697	5414	5283	0-4
5-9	10288	5200	5088	10655	5382	5273	10510	5309	5201	5-9
10-14	10551	5319	5232	10171	5137	5034	10532	5316	5216	10-14
15-19	10596	5343	5253	10414	5248	5166	10038	5068	4970	15-19
20-24	10592	5259	5333	10407	5245	5162	10229	5152	5077	20-24
25-29	10689	5245	5444	10387	5152	5235	10206	5139	5067	25-29
30-34	10374	5109	5265	10502	5146	5356	10205	5055	5150	30-34
35-39	10062	4950	5112	10188	5005	5183	10315	5042	5273	35-39
40-44	9570	4524	5046	9859	4832	5027	9982	4886	5096	40-44
45-49	9995	4932	5063	9333	4384	4949	9613	4682	4931	45-49
50-54	9712	4740	4972	9626	4695	4931	8993	4173	4820	50-54
55-59	9111	4399	4712	9172	4387	4785	9090	4345	4745	55-59
60-64	8414	3937	4477	8372	3918	4454	8430	3907	4523	60-64
65-69	7397	3302	4095	7400	3304	4096	7363	3288	4075	65-69
70-74	6119	2556	3563	6123	2558	3565	6124	2558	3566	70-74
75-79	4647	1788	2859	4649	1789	2860	4650	1789	2861	75-79
80-84	3052	1078	1974	3055	1079	1976	3056	1079	1977	80-84
85+	2282	698	1584	2285	699	1586	2286	699	1587	85+
TOTAL	154510	73976	80534	153505	73480	80025	152319	72901	79418	TOTAL

TABLE 6 STANDARDIZED RATES

STANDARD COUNTRIES: STANDARDIZED RATES PER THOUSAND	ENGLAND AND WALES 1961 BOTH SEXES	MALES	FEMALES	UNITED STATES 1960 BOTH SEXES	MALES	FEMALES	MEXICO 1960 BOTH SEXES	MALES	FEMALES
Birth	15.26	17.01*	14.43	15.59	15.93*	14.99	18.20	15.07*	17.71
Death	14.71	14.40*	13.47	13.67	13.32*	11.80	11.09	11.86*	9.58
Increase	0.56	2.60*	0.95	1.93	2.61*	3.19	7.11	3.21*	8.13

TABLE 7 MOMENTS AND CUMULANTS

	OBSERVED POP. MALES	OBSERVED POP. FEMALES	STATIONARY POP. MALES	STATIONARY POP. FEMALES	STABLE POP. MALES	STABLE POP. FEMALES	OBSERVED BIRTHS	NET MATERNITY FUNCTION	BIRTHS IN STABLE POP.
μ	36.49535	39.17621	35.71472	38.57844	36.98047	40.00804	27.12957	27.14171	27.25457
σ^2	505.1157	559.2211	502.5710	568.5861	509.6299	574.5683	42.67566	42.89708	43.21020
κ_3	2686.868	2426.080	3121.717	2818.875	2518.056	1959.341	130.9382	126.7029	123.7359
κ_4	-244250.	-322684.	-233307.	-335043.	-248976.	-351450.	-1096.178	-1153.777	-1208.970
β_1	0.056017	0.033656	0.076771	0.043228	0.047903	0.020239	0.220593	0.203371	0.189772
β_2	2.042690	1.968166	2.076296	1.963645	2.041375	1.935417	2.398105	2.373001	2.352495
κ	-0.021366	-0.012345	-0.029479	-0.015650	-0.018410	-0.007327	-0.096454	-0.088652	-0.082467

TABLE 8 RATES FROM AGE DISTRIBUTIONS AND VITAL STATISTICS (Females)

VITAL STATISTICS		THOMPSON AGE RANGE	NRR	1000r	INTERVAL	BOURGEOIS-PICHAT AGE RANGE	NRR	1000b	1000d	1000r	COALE	
GRR	1.160											
NRR	0.934	0-4	0.90	-3.91	27.28	5-29	0.89	14.88	19.17	-4.28	IBR	14.59
TFR	2.379	5-9	0.93	-2.77	27.25	30-54	0.96	15.57	16.96	-1.39	IDR	19.00
GENERATION	27.198	10-14	0.94	-2.10	27.23	55-79	1.00	16.72	16.64	0.08	IRI	-4.41
SEX RATIO	105.018	15-19	0.97	-0.96	27.17	*50-74	1.00	16.47	16.61	-0.14	K1	-8.45
											K2	-0.08

TABLE 9 LESLIE MATRIX AND ITS SPECTRAL COMPONENTS (Females)

Start of Age Interval	ORIGINAL MATRIX SUB-DIAGONAL	ALTERNATIVE FIRST ROWS Projection	Integral	FIRST STABLE MATRIX % IN STABLE POPULATION	FISHER VALUES	REPRODUCTIVE VALUES	SECOND STABLE MATRIX Z_2 FIRST COLUMN	FIRST ROW
0	0.96537	0.00000	0.00000	6.544	1.125	5930360	0.1232+0.0826	0.1232+0.0826
5	0.98923	0.00065	0.00000	6.397	1.151	6087520	0.1690-0.0850	-0.0089+0.1160
10	0.98740	0.06767	0.00131	6.408	1.148	6108859	0.0119-0.2468	-0.0808+0.0377
15	0.98267	0.21584	0.13488	6.407	1.071	5814622	-0.2727-0.1717	-0.0640-0.0454
20	0.98161	0.27251	0.29929	6.375	0.830	4601323	-0.3680+0.1986	-0.0209-0.0783
25	0.98387	0.21226	0.24688	6.336	0.522	2795156	-0.0104+0.5420	0.0105-0.0667
30	0.98448	0.15082	0.17787	6.313	0.282	1462390	0.6066+0.3579	0.0221-0.0360
35	0.98324	0.07825	0.12383	6.293	0.110	565103	0.7930-0.4579	0.0136-0.0115
40	0.98093	0.01735	0.03225	6.265	0.021	108723	-0.0116-1.1890	0.0031-0.0018
45	0.97393	0.00115	0.00228	6.223	0.001	6674	-1.3486-0.7442	0.0002-0.0001
50	0.96234	0.00000	0.00000	6.137	0.000	1	-1.6863+1.0399	0.0000-0.0000
55+	0.79268			30.302				

TABLE 10 AGE ANALYSIS AND MISCELLANEOUS RESULTS (Females)

Start of Age Interval	OBSERVED POPUL. (IN 100's)	CONTRIBUTIONS OF ROOTS (IN 100's) r_1	r_2, r_3	r_4-r_{11}	AGE-SP. BIRTH RATES	NET MATERNITY FUNCTION	COEFF. OF MATRIX EQUATION
0	52710	54562	-670	-1182	0.0000	0.0000	0.0000
5	52890	53335	-1395	950	0.0000	0.0000	0.0006
10	53198	53424	-676	450	0.0003	0.0013	0.0646
15	54270	53414	1509	-653	0.0307	0.1280	0.2035
20	55460	53148	3070	-758	0.0682	0.2791	0.252[illegible]
25	53510	52827	1374	-691	0.0562	0.2260	0.1931
30	51931	52629	-3415	2718	0.0405	0.1602	0.1350
35	51316	52464	-6687	5540	0.0282	0.1098	0.0689
40	51614	52233	-2772	2153	0.0073	0.0281	0.0150
45	51050	51881	7718	-8549	0.0005	0.0019	0.0010
50	48960	51165	14379	-16583	0.0000	0.0000	0.0000
55+	232086	252634					

PARAMETERS	INTEGRAL	MATRIX
L(1)	0.98758	0.98758
L(2)	0.36166	0.37228
	0.67431	0.65938
R(1)	-0.00250	-0.00250
R(2)	-0.05353	-0.05562
	0.21570	0.21136
C(1)		833716
C(2)		-352344
		-120001
2P/Y	29.1294	29.7269
DELTA	1.7282	

EXP. INCREASE x	$e^{(x+2\frac{1}{2})r}$
0	0.9938
50	0.8770
55	0.8661
60	0.8553
65	0.8447
70	0.8342
75	0.8238
80	0.8136
85	0.8035
90	0.7935
95	0.7837
100	0.7739

United States, Cohort 0–4 Years of Age in 1915
With Adjusted Births

TABLE 1 DATA

AGE AT LAST BIRTHDAY	POPULATION BOTH SEXES	MALES Number	MALES %	FEMALES Number	FEMALES %	BIRTHS BY AGE OF MOTHER	DEATHS BOTH SEXES	MALES	FEMALES	AGE AT LAST BIRTHDAY
0	2317000	1179000	1.5	1138000	1.3	-0	221683	125461	96222	0
1-4	9030000	4566000	5.8	4464000	5.1	-0	81565	43241	38324	1-4
5-9	11475275	5794759	7.3	5680516	6.5	0	32917	17600	15317	5-9
10-14	11527000	5784000	7.3	5743000	6.5	3778	20619	11407	9212	10-14
15-19	11572958	5768600	7.3	5804358	6.6	325622	32259	16844	15415	15-19
20-24	11317000	5599000	7.1	5718000	6.5	725929	36458	19408	17050	20-24
25-29	10997943	5341558	6.7	5656385	6.4	693245	30731	16751	13980	25-29
30-34	10298147	4684422	5.9	5613725	6.4	554839	28780	15488	13292	30-34
35-39	11260606	5522804	7.0	5737802	6.5	302769	31936	18504	13432	35-39
40-44	11192000	5476000	6.9	5716000	6.5	89775	41725	25371	16354	40-44
45-49	10912000	5371000	6.8	5541000	6.3	5445	64283	40824	23459	45-49
50-54	10570000	5146000	6.5	5424000	6.2	0	96589	62553	34036	50-54
55-59	9985786	4765155	6.0	5220631	5.9	0	137873	89984	47889	55-59
60-64	9176105	4242705	5.3	4933400	5.6	0	187104	119002	68102	60-64
65-69	8070879	3558858	4.5	4512021	5.1	0	253277	152549	100728	65-69
70-74	6680222	2754674	3.5	3925548	4.5		299019	165431	133588	70-74
75-79	5073885	1926032	2.4	3147853	3.6		338488	162731	175757	75-79
80-84	3333721	1160576	1.5	2173145	2.5	1383581 M.	350121	144165	205956	80-84
85+	2417753	746820	0.9	1670933	1.9	1317821 F.	485326	158968	326358	85+
TOTAL	167208280	79387963		87820317		2701402	2770753	1406282	1364471	TOTAL

TABLE 2 MALE LIFE TABLE

x	nq_x	l_x	nd_x	nL_x	nm_x	na_x	T_x	r_x	$\dot{e}_x$	nM_x
0	0.099184	100000	9918	93206	0.106413	0.3150	5781199	0.0000	57.812	0.106413
1	0.036891	90082	3323	350915	0.009470	1.1678	5687993	0.0000	63.143	0.009470
5	0.015072	86758	1308	430523	0.003037	2.5000	5337078	0.0000	61.517	0.003037
10	0.009812	85451	838	425141	0.001972	2.4799	4906555	0.0000	57.420	0.001972
15	0.014499	84612	1227	420119	0.002920	2.6010	4481414	0.0004	52.964	0.002920
20	0.017184	83386	1433	413356	0.003467	2.5070	4061296	0.0044	48.705	0.003466
25	0.015555	81953	1275	406553	0.003135	2.4820	3647940	0.0146	44.513	0.003136
30	0.016396	80678	1323	400092	0.003306	2.5069	3241387	0.0000	40.177	0.003306
35	0.016617	79355	1319	393576	0.003350	2.5736	2841295	0.0000	35.805	0.003350
40	0.022919	78036	1789	386029	0.004633	2.6781	2447719	0.0000	31.366	0.004633
45	0.037347	76248	2848	374652	0.007601	2.6865	2061690	0.0000	27.039	0.007601
50	0.059099	73400	4338	356864	0.012156	2.6630	1687038	0.0000	22.984	0.012156
55	0.090376	69062	6242	330524	0.018884	2.6308	1330175	0.0000	19.260	0.018884
60	0.131437	62821	8257	294367	0.028050	2.6097	999650	0.0003	15.913	0.028049
65	0.194064	54564	10589	247020	0.042866	2.5636	705283	0.0003	12.926	0.042865
70	0.261263	43975	11489	191302	0.060057	2.5131	458263	0.0003	10.421	0.060055
75	0.348140	32486	11310	133852	0.084494	2.4732	266961	0.0003	8.218	0.084490
80	0.473783	21176	10033	80764	0.124225	2.4965	133109	0.0003	6.286	0.124218
85+	*1.000000	11143	11143	52345	0.212884	4.6974	52345	0.0003	4.697	0.212860

TABLE 3 FEMALE LIFE TABLE

x	nq_x	l_x	nd_x	nL_x	nm_x	na_x	T_x	r_x	$\dot{e}_x$	nM_x
0	0.080022	100000	8002	94641	0.084554	0.3303	6467397	0.0000	64.674	0.084554
1	0.033531	91998	3085	359319	0.008585	1.1888	6372756	0.0000	69.271	0.008585
5	0.013392	88913	1191	441588	0.002696	2.5000	6013437	0.0000	67.633	0.002696
10	0.007988	87722	701	436851	0.001604	2.4874	5571849	0.0000	63.517	0.001604
15	0.013195	87022	1148	432356	0.002656	2.6034	5134998	0.0000	59.008	0.002656
20	0.014798	85873	1271	426167	0.002982	2.4821	4702642	0.0000	54.763	0.002982
25	0.012280	84603	1039	420356	0.002472	2.4424	4276475	0.0000	50.548	0.002472
30	0.011769	83564	983	415343	0.002368	2.4835	3856120	0.0000	46.146	0.002368
35	0.011638	82580	961	410535	0.002341	2.5382	3440776	0.0000	41.666	0.002341
40	0.014210	81619	1160	405347	0.002861	2.6304	3030241	0.0005	37.127	0.002861
45	0.020964	80459	1687	398346	0.004234	2.6576	2624894	0.0009	32.624	0.004234
50	0.030919	78773	2436	388137	0.006275	2.6489	2226548	0.0000	28.266	0.006275
55	0.044897	76337	3427	373625	0.009173	2.6484	1838411	0.0000	24.083	0.009173
60	0.066881	72910	4876	353147	0.013808	2.6618	1464786	0.0015	20.090	0.013804
65	0.106052	68033	7215	323108	0.022330	2.6357	1111639	0.0015	16.340	0.022324
70	0.157431	60818	9575	281279	0.034040	2.6174	788531	0.0015	12.965	0.034030
75	0.246078	51244	12610	225781	0.055850	2.5863	507252	0.0015	9.899	0.055834
80	0.383007	38634	14797	156090	0.094798	2.6581	281470	0.0015	7.286	0.094773
85+	1.000000	23837	23837	125380	0.190116	5.2600	125380	0.0015	5.260	0.195314

TABLE 4 OBSERVED AND PROJECTED VITAL RATES

	OBSERVED POPULATION BOTH SEXES	MALES	FEMALES	PROJECTED POPULATION 1920 MALES	1920 FEMALES	1925 MALES	1925 FEMALES	1930 MALES	1930 FEMALES	STABLE POPULATION MALES	FEMALES
RATES PER THOUSAND											
Birth	16.16	17.43	15.01	17.33	14.93	17.21	14.84	17.00	14.68	16.71	14.89
Death	16.57	17.71	15.54	17.89	15.84	17.90	15.89	17.87	15.94	17.67	15.85
Increase	-0.41	-0.29	-0.53	-0.56	-0.91	-0.69	-1.05	-0.87	-1.26	-0.9602	
PERCENTAGE											
under 15	20.54	21.82	19.39	21.99	19.45	22.17	19.61	22.54	19.96	21.87	19.98
15-64	64.16	65.40	63.04	65.19	62.84	64.96	62.59	64.53	62.13	65.48	62.22
65 and over	15.30	12.78	17.57	12.83	17.72	12.88	17.81	12.93	17.91	12.65	17.79
DEP. RATIO X 100	55.86	52.91	58.62	53.41	59.15	53.95	59.78	54.97	60.94	52.72	60.72

With Adjusted Births

TABLE 1 — DATA

AGE AT LAST BIRTHDAY	POPULATION BOTH SEXES	MALES Number	%	FEMALES Number	%	BIRTHS BY AGE OF MOTHER	DEATHS BOTH SEXES	MALES	FEMALES	AGE AT LAST BIRTHDAY
0	2278571	1153736	1.4	1124835	1.2	0	212598	120782	91816	0
1-4	9376978	4749510	5.9	4627468	5.0	0	89708	47265	42443	1-4
5-9	12086998	6112999	7.6	5973999	6.5	0	25162	13905	11257	5-9
10-14	12033597	6082707	7.6	5950890	6.5	3717	18375	10305	8070	10-14
15-19	11813000	5888000	7.3	5925000	6.5	302616	26897	14761	12136	15-19
20-24	11465777	5560455	6.9	5905322	6.4	800029	27865	15464	12401	20-24
25-29	9024061	3159487	3.9	5864574	6.4	785254	23610	12884	10726	25-29
30-34	11554959	5642117	7.0	5912842	6.4	610802	22981	13350	9631	30-34
35-39	11545000	5628000	7.0	5917000	6.4	352322	28017	16685	11332	35-39
40-44	11641000	5693000	7.1	5948000	6.5	93360	42942	26234	16708	40-44
45-49	11449000	5570000	6.9	5879000	6.4	4829	66259	41408	24851	45-49
50-54	11035399	5307422	6.6	5727977	6.2	1	100490	64537	35953	50-54
55-59	10427840	4914630	6.1	5513210	6.0	0	143379	92806	50573	55-59
60-64	9585674	4375792	5.4	5209882	5.7	0	194654	122735	71919	60-64
65-69	8435381	3670493	4.6	4764488	5.2	0	263707	157334	106373	65-69
70-74	6986630	2841083	3.5	4145547	4.5		311695	170620	141075	70-74
75-79	5310716	1986448	2.5	3324268	3.6		353443	167836	185607	75-79
80-84	3491916	1196982	1.5	2294934	2.5	1512231 M.	366186	148687	217499	80-84
85+	2534824	770247	1.0	1764577	1.9	1440699 F.	508603	163955	344648	85+
TOTAL	172077321	80303108		91774213		2952930	2826571	1421553	1405018	TOTAL

TABLE 2 — MALE LIFE TABLE

x	nq_x	l_x	nd_x	nL_x	nm_x	na_x	T_x	r_x	$\mathring{e}_x$	nM_x	x
0	0.097750	100000	9775	93373	0.104688	0.3221	5832865	0.0000	58.329	0.104688	0
1	0.038719	90225	3493	351039	0.009952	1.1772	5739491	0.0000	63.613	0.009952	1
5	0.011309	86732	981	431206	0.002275	2.5000	5388453	0.0000	62.128	0.002275	5
10	0.008436	85751	723	426962	0.001694	2.5228	4957247	0.0017	57.810	0.001694	10
15	0.012467	85027	1060	422579	0.002508	2.5873	4530285	0.0066	53.280	0.002507	15
20	0.013908	83967	1168	417044	0.002800	2.6090	4107706	0.0592	48.920	0.002781	20
25	0.020181	82800	1671	409776	0.004078	2.4733	3690661	0.0000	44.573	0.004078	25
30	0.011758	81129	954	403156	0.002366	2.3928	3280886	0.0000	40.441	0.002366	30
35	0.014721	80175	1180	398099	0.002965	2.6495	2877730	0.0000	35.893	0.002965	35
40	0.022798	78994	1801	390811	0.004608	2.6898	2479632	0.0000	31.390	0.004608	40
45	0.036543	77193	2821	379456	0.007434	2.6917	2088820	0.0000	27.060	0.007434	45
50	0.059121	74373	4397	361600	0.012160	2.6660	1709364	0.0000	22.984	0.012160	50
55	0.090375	69976	6324	334895	0.018884	2.6308	1347764	0.0000	19.261	0.018884	55
60	0.131437	63651	8366	298260	0.028050	2.6097	1012870	0.0003	15.913	0.028049	60
65	0.194063	55285	10729	250287	0.042866	2.5636	714610	0.0003	12.926	0.042865	65
70	0.261263	44556	11641	193832	0.060057	2.5131	464323	0.0003	10.421	0.060055	70
75	0.348141	32916	11459	135622	0.084494	2.4732	270491	0.0003	8.218	0.084491	75
80	0.473782	21456	10166	81832	0.124225	2.4965	134869	0.0003	6.286	0.124218	80
85+	*1.000000	11291	11291	53037	0.212884	4.6974	53037	0.0003	4.697	0.212860	85+

TABLE 3 — FEMALE LIFE TABLE

x	nq_x	l_x	nd_x	nL_x	nm_x	na_x	T_x	r_x	$\mathring{e}_x$	nM_x	x
0	0.077459	100000	7746	94895	0.081626	0.3410	6571142	0.0000	65.711	0.081626	0
1	0.035771	92254	3300	359793	0.009172	1.2052	6476246	0.0000	70.200	0.009172	1
5	0.009377	88954	834	442685	0.001884	2.5000	6116453	0.0000	68.760	0.001884	5
10	0.006758	88120	595	439123	0.001356	2.5202	5673768	0.0000	64.387	0.001356	10
15	0.010191	87524	892	435457	0.002048	2.5723	5234646	0.0000	59.808	0.002048	15
20	0.010444	86632	905	430877	0.002100	2.4743	4799189	0.0000	55.397	0.002100	20
25	0.009102	85728	780	426642	0.001829	2.4424	4368312	0.0000	50.956	0.001829	25
30	0.008111	84947	689	423019	0.001629	2.5069	3941670	0.0000	46.401	0.001629	30
35	0.009532	84258	803	419383	0.001915	2.6233	3518651	0.0000	41.760	0.001915	35
40	0.013954	83455	1164	414556	0.002809	2.6644	3099268	0.0000	37.137	0.002809	40
45	0.020928	82291	1722	407424	0.004227	2.6606	2684713	0.0000	32.625	0.004227	45
50	0.030927	80568	2492	396984	0.006277	2.6491	2277289	0.0000	28.265	0.006277	50
55	0.044897	78077	3505	382140	0.009173	2.6483	1880304	0.0000	24.083	0.009173	55
60	0.066882	74571	4987	361195	0.013808	2.6618	1498165	0.0015	20.090	0.013804	60
65	0.106052	69584	7380	330471	0.022330	2.6357	1136970	0.0015	16.340	0.022324	65
70	0.157431	62204	9793	287689	0.034040	2.6174	806499	0.0015	12.965	0.034030	70
75	0.246078	52411	12897	230927	0.055850	2.5863	518810	0.0015	9.899	0.055834	75
80	0.383008	39514	15134	159647	0.094798	2.6581	287884	0.0015	7.286	0.094774	80
85+	1.000000	24380	24380	128237	0.190116	5.2600	128237	0.0015	5.260	0.195314	85+

TABLE 4 — OBSERVED AND PROJECTED VITAL RATES

RATES PER THOUSAND	OBSERVED POPULATION BOTH SEXES	MALES	FEMALES	PROJECTED POPULATION 1925 MALES	FEMALES	1930 MALES	FEMALES	1935 MALES	FEMALES	STABLE POPULATION MALES	FEMALES
Birth	17.16	18.83	15.70	18.61	15.55	18.45	15.46	18.21	15.31	18.07	16.11
Death	16.43	17.70	15.31	17.97	15.65	17.90	15.65	17.77	15.64	16.59	14.63
Increase	0.73	1.13	0.39	0.64	-0.09	0.55	-0.19	0.45	-0.33		1.4761
PERCENTAGE											
under 15	20.79	22.54	19.26	22.93	19.65	23.29	20.02	24.05	20.74	23.28	21.30
15-64	63.66	64.43	62.98	64.07	62.52	63.74	62.13	62.99	61.38	65.14	62.31
65 and over	15.55	13.03	17.75	13.00	17.83	12.98	17.85	12.96	17.88	11.58	16.39
DEP. RATIO X 100	57.09	55.21	58.77	56.08	59.95	56.90	60.96	58.74	62.92	53.52	60.49

With Adjusted Births

TABLE 1 — DATA

AGE AT LAST BIRTHDAY	BOTH SEXES	MALES Number	MALES %	FEMALES Number	FEMALES %	BIRTHS BY AGE OF MOTHER	DEATHS BOTH SEXES	DEATHS MALES	DEATHS FEMALES	AGE AT LAST BIRTHDAY
0	2460000	1252000	1.5	1208000	1.2	0	181017	103169	77848	0
1-4	9856000	5008000	5.9	4848000	5.0	0	62961	33661	29300	1-4
5-9	12577837	6368321	7.6	6209516	6.4	0	23896	13352	10544	5-9
10-14	12424000	6260000	7.4	6164000	6.3	3760	17284	9899	7385	10-14
15-19	12261267	6126813	7.3	6134454	6.3	332249	21194	11751	9443	15-19
20-24	9024615	2921712	3.5	6102903	6.3	833233	22274	12630	9644	20-24
25-29	12211629	5957170	7.1	6254459	6.4	1041327	19523	11785	7738	25-29
30-34	12314000	5990000	7.1	6324000	6.5	732540	20058	12133	7925	30-34
35-39	12481000	6079000	7.2	6402000	6.6	365667	29161	17594	11567	35-39
40-44	12411000	6033000	7.2	6378000	6.6	83255	45847	28045	17802	40-44
45-49	12125252	5856903	7.0	6268349	6.4	5148	70059	43555	26504	45-49
50-54	11688123	5580799	6.6	6107324	6.3	1	106195	67861	38334	50-54
55-59	11046110	5167776	6.1	5878334	6.0	0	151509	97587	53922	55-59
60-64	10156099	4601182	5.5	5554917	5.7	0	205738	129057	76681	60-64
65-69	8940008	3859555	4.6	5080453	5.2	0	278856	165438	113418	65-69
70-74	7407518	2987424	3.5	4420094	4.5		329827	179409	150418	70-74
75-79	5633191	2088767	2.5	3544424	3.6		374380	176481	197899	75-79
80-84	3705558	1258637	1.5	2446921	2.5	1739344 M.	388249	156346	231903	80-84
85+	2691360	809921	1.0	1881439	1.9	1657836 F.	539873	172400	367473	85+
TOTAL	181414567	84206980		97207587		3397180	2887901	1442153	1445748	TOTAL

TABLE 2 — MALE LIFE TABLE

x	nq_x	l_x	nd_x	nL_x	nm_x	na_x	T_x	r_x	$\mathring{e}_x$	nM_x
0	0.077953	100000	7795	94600	0.082403	0.3072	6066880	0.0000	60.669	0.082403
1	0.026382	92205	2433	361906	0.006721	1.1581	5972280	0.0000	64.772	0.006721
5	0.010428	89772	936	446520	0.002097	2.5000	5610375	0.0000	62.496	0.002097
10	0.007875	88836	700	442415	0.001581	2.4773	5163855	0.0021	58.128	0.001581
15	0.009755	88136	860	438775	0.001960	2.7827	4721440	0.0738	53.570	0.001918
20	0.021383	87277	1866	431713	0.004323	2.4978	4282664	0.0000	49.070	0.004323
25	0.009838	85410	840	424740	0.001978	2.2486	3850951	0.0000	45.088	0.001978
30	0.010078	84570	852	420795	0.002026	2.5888	3426211	0.0000	40.513	0.002026
35	0.014375	83718	1203	415798	0.002894	2.6809	3005416	0.0000	35.899	0.002894
40	0.022996	82514	1898	408191	0.004649	2.6914	2589618	0.0000	31.384	0.004649
45	0.036555	80617	2947	396278	0.007437	2.6905	2181427	0.0000	27.059	0.007437
50	0.059121	77670	4592	377632	0.012160	2.6659	1785149	0.0000	22.984	0.012160
55	0.090376	73078	6604	349742	0.018884	2.6308	1407517	0.0000	19.260	0.018884
60	0.131437	66473	8737	311483	0.028050	2.6097	1057775	0.0003	15.913	0.028049
65	0.194063	57736	11205	261383	0.042866	2.5636	746292	0.0003	12.926	0.042865
70	0.261263	46532	12157	202426	0.060057	2.5131	484909	0.0003	10.421	0.060055
75	0.348141	34375	11967	141635	0.084494	2.4732	282483	0.0003	8.218	0.084491
80	0.473783	22408	10616	85460	0.124225	2.4965	140848	0.0003	6.286	0.124218
85+	*1.000000	11791	11791	55388	0.212884	4.6974	55388	0.0003	4.697	0.212860

TABLE 3 — FEMALE LIFE TABLE

x	nq_x	l_x	nd_x	nL_x	nm_x	na_x	T_x	r_x	$\mathring{e}_x$	nM_x
0	0.061750	100000	6175	95821	0.064444	0.3232	6820681	0.0000	68.207	0.064444
1	0.023770	93825	2230	369008	0.006044	1.1787	6724860	0.0000	71.675	0.006044
5	0.008454	91595	774	456038	0.001698	2.5000	6355852	0.0000	69.391	0.001698
10	0.005972	90820	542	452729	0.001198	2.4685	5899814	0.0000	64.961	0.001198
15	0.007668	90278	692	449693	0.001539	2.5489	5447085	0.0000	60.337	0.001539
20	0.007870	89586	705	446136	0.001580	2.4574	4997392	0.0000	55.783	0.001580
25	0.006166	88881	548	443002	0.001237	2.4418	4551256	0.0000	51.206	0.001237
30	0.006247	88333	552	440334	0.001253	2.5912	4108254	0.0000	46.509	0.001253
35	0.008996	87781	790	437066	0.001807	2.6726	3667920	0.0000	41.785	0.001807
40	0.013866	86991	1206	432150	0.002791	2.6738	3230854	0.0000	37.140	0.002791
45	0.020934	85785	1796	424725	0.004228	2.6614	2798704	0.0000	32.625	0.004228
50	0.030927	83989	2598	413839	0.006277	2.6490	2373978	0.0000	28.265	0.006277
55	0.044897	81392	3654	398364	0.009173	2.6483	1960139	0.0000	24.083	0.009173
60	0.066881	77737	5199	376530	0.013808	2.6618	1561775	0.0015	20.090	0.013804
65	0.106052	72538	7693	344503	0.022330	2.6357	1185245	0.0015	16.340	0.022324
70	0.157431	64845	10209	299904	0.034040	2.6174	840742	0.0015	12.965	0.034030
75	0.246078	54637	13445	240731	0.055862	2.5863	540838	0.0015	9.899	0.055834
80	0.383007	41192	15777	166425	0.094798	2.6581	300107	0.0015	7.286	0.094773
85+	1.000000	25415	25415	133682	0.190116	5.2600	133682	0.0015	5.260	0.195314

TABLE 4 — OBSERVED AND PROJECTED VITAL RATES

	OBSERVED POPULATION BOTH SEXES	MALES	FEMALES	PROJECTED POPULATION 1930 MALES	1930 FEMALES	1935 MALES	1935 FEMALES	1940 MALES	1940 FEMALES	STABLE POPULATION MALES	FEMALES
RATES PER THOUSAND											
Birth	18.73	20.66	17.05	20.03	16.62	19.58	16.33	19.18	16.08	20.24	18.3
Death	15.92	17.13	14.87	17.39	15.18	17.17	15.08	16.93	14.98	14.32	12.3
Increase	2.81	3.53	2.18	2.64	1.44	2.40	1.25	2.25	1.11		5.922
PERCENTAGE											
under 15	20.57	22.43	18.96	23.77	20.13	24.90	21.19	26.21	22.43	26.06	24.0
15-64	63.79	64.50	63.17	63.33	62.07	62.35	61.13	61.19	59.98	64.18	62.0
65 and over	15.64	13.07	17.87	12.89	17.80	12.74	17.69	12.60	17.58	9.75	13.9
DEP. RATIO X 100	56.77	55.04	58.31	57.89	61.11	60.37	63.60	63.42	66.72	55.80	61.2

TABLE 5 — POPULATION PROJECTED WITH FIXED AGE-SPECIFIC BIRTH AND DEATH RATES (IN 1000's)

AGE AT LAST BIRTHDAY	1930 BOTH SEXES	MALES	FEMALES	1935 BOTH SEXES	MALES	FEMALES	1940 BOTH SEXES	MALES	FEMALES	AGE AT LAST BIRTHDAY
0-4	15518	7875	7643	15311	7770	7541	15163	7695	7468	0-4
5-9	12064	6123	5941	15202	7703	7499	14998	7600	7398	5-9
10-14	12474	6310	6164	11965	6067	5898	15076	7632	7444	10-14
15-19	12332	6209	6123	12381	6258	6123	11876	6017	5859	15-19
20-24	12114	6028	6086	12183	6109	6074	12232	6157	6075	20-24
25-29	8935	2875	6060	11974	5931	6043	12042	6010	6032	25-29
30-34	12119	5902	6217	8872	2848	6024	11883	5876	6007	30-34
35-39	12196	5919	6277	12003	5832	6171	8793	2814	5979	35-39
40-44	12298	5968	6330	12017	5811	6206	11826	5725	6101	40-44
45-49	12125	5857	6268	12015	5794	6221	11741	5641	6100	45-49
50-54	11689	5581	6108	11689	5581	6108	11583	5521	6062	50-54
55-59	11048	5169	5879	11048	5169	5879	11048	5169	5879	55-59
60-64	10158	4602	5556	10160	4603	5557	10161	4604	5557	60-64
65-69	8943	3861	5082	8946	3862	5084	8947	3863	5084	65-69
70-74	7412	2989	4423	7414	2990	4424	7416	2991	4425	70-74
75-79	5638	2090	3548	5641	2091	3550	5643	2092	3551	75-79
80-84	3710	1260	2450	3714	1261	2453	3716	1262	2454	80-84
85+	2782	816	1966	2785	817	1968	2787	817	1970	85+
TOTAL	183555	85434	98121	185320	86497	98823	186931	87486	99445	TOTAL

TABLE 6 — STANDARDIZED RATES

STANDARD COUNTRIES:

STANDARDIZED RATES PER THOUSAND	ENGLAND AND WALES 1961 BOTH SEXES	MALES	FEMALES	UNITED STATES 1960 BOTH SEXES	MALES	FEMALES	MEXICO 1960 BOTH SEXES	MALES	FEMALES
Birth	17.36	21.39*	16.42	17.74	20.98*	17.06	20.44	18.05*	19.89
Death	12.84	12.94*	11.68	11.33	11.98*	9.51	7.92	10.72*	6.46
Increase	4.51	8.45*	4.74	6.41	9.00*	7.55	12.51	7.32*	13.43

TABLE 7 — MOMENTS AND CUMULANTS

	OBSERVED POP. MALES	FEMALES	STATIONARY POP. MALES	FEMALES	STABLE POP. MALES	FEMALES	OBSERVED BIRTHS	NET MATERNITY FUNCTION	BIRTHS IN STABLE POP.
μ	37.13577	39.91715	36.11750	39.11820	33.20493	35.82372	27.83149	27.68241	27.45788
σ^2	512.3680	557.6518	501.6448	565.3942	480.7236	545.3997	36.24281	36.02012	35.63577
κ_3	1939.690	1828.773	2879.742	2440.144	4140.888	4259.277	59.0852	63.1523	66.6136
κ_4	-258049.	-321810.	-234342.	-331644.	-189148.	-278125.	-623.356	-596.823	-561.466
β_1	0.027972	0.019285	0.065693	0.032944	0.154348	0.111822	0.073332	0.085338	0.098054
β_2	2.017036	1.965160	2.068768	1.962546	2.181515	2.065003	2.525439	2.540003	2.557869
κ	-0.010755	-0.007160	-0.025362	-0.012038	-0.059703	-0.041035	-0.048448	-0.056219	-0.064662

TABLE 8 — RATES FROM AGE DISTRIBUTIONS AND VITAL STATISTICS (Females)

VITAL STATISTICS:

GRR	1.329
NRR	1.177
TFR	2.723
GENERATION	27.570
SEX RATIO	104.917

THOMPSON:

AGE RANGE	NRR	1000r	INTERVAL
0-4	0.92	-3.12	27.40
5-9	0.95	-2.00	27.36
10-14	0.93	-2.47	27.31
15-19	0.93	-2.70	27.22

BOURGEOIS-PICHAT:

AGE RANGE	NRR	1000b	1000d	1000r
5-29	0.96	13.75	15.29	-1.54
30-54	0.97	14.30	15.54	-1.24
55-79	1.00	15.25	15.17	0.08
*40-64	1.00	15.20	15.18	0.02

COALE:

IBR	13.37
IDR	16.58
IRI	-3.22
K1	-1.73
K2	0.

TABLE 9 — LESLIE MATRIX AND ITS SPECTRAL COMPONENTS (Females)

Start Age Interval	ORIGINAL MATRIX SUB-DIAGONAL	ALTERNATIVE FIRST ROWS Projection	Integral	FIRST STABLE MATRIX % IN STABLE POPULATION	FISHER VALUES	REPRODUCTIVE VALUES	SECOND STABLE MATRIX Z2 FIRST COLUMN	FIRST ROW
0	0.98109	0.00000	0.00000	8.384	1.092	6610736	0.1516+0.0648	0.1516+0.0648
5	0.99274	0.00069	0.00000	7.985	1.146	7116759	0.1502-0.1219	0.0113+0.1401
10	0.99329	0.06171	0.00140	7.696	1.188	7325589	-0.0450-0.2253	-0.1001+0.0634
15	0.99209	0.21506	0.12469	7.421	1.165	7144408	-0.2617-0.0774	-0.0959-0.0537
20	0.99297	0.34236	0.31432	7.147	0.973	5935682	-0.2259+0.2319	-0.0305-0.1066
25	0.99398	0.31942	0.38330	6.890	0.633	3956405	0.1187+0.3657	0.0152-0.0869
30	0.99258	0.19568	0.26668	6.649	0.305	1927240	0.4504+0.0778	0.0219-0.0436
35	0.98875	0.07942	0.13150	6.406	0.101	646988	0.3308-0.4300	0.0112-0.0135
40	0.98282	0.01572	0.03005	6.149	0.018	112264	-0.2676-0.5830	0.0024-0.0022
45	0.97437	0.00093	0.00189	5.867	0.001	6190	-0.7529-0.0410	0.0001-0.0001
50	0.96261	0.00000	0.00000	5.550	0.000	1	-0.4511+0.7540	0.0000-0.0000
85+	0.80611			23.855				

TABLE 10 — AGE ANALYSIS AND MISCELLANEOUS RESULTS (Females)

Start Age Interval	OBSERVED POPUL. (IN 100's)	CONTRIBUTIONS OF ROOTS (IN 100's) r_1	r_2, r_3	r_4-r_{11}	AGE-SP. BIRTH RATES	NET MATERNITY FUNCTION	COEFF. OF MATRIX EQUATION
0	60560	68124	-1617	-5947	0.0000	0.0000	0.0000
5	62095	64884	-6021	3232	0.0000	0.0000	0.0007
10	61640	62533	-4410	3517	0.0003	0.0013	0.0601
15	61345	60300	3609	-2565	0.0264	0.1189	0.2081
20	61029	58076	10206	-7253	0.0666	0.2972	0.3286
25	62545	55985	6210	350	0.0812	0.3599	0.3044
30	63240	54023	-7528	16745	0.0565	0.2489	0.1854
35	64020	52056	-17090	29054	0.0279	0.1218	0.0747
40	63780	49968	-8267	22079	0.0064	0.0275	0.0146
45	62683	47676	14697	311	0.0004	0.0017	0.0009
50	61073	45097	27283	-11307	0.0000	0.0000	0.0000
85+	288066	193834			0.0000	0.0000	0.0000

PARAMETERS:

	INTEGRAL	MATRIX
L(1)	1.03005	1.03007
L(2)	0.38430	0.38964
	0.76215	0.73985
R(1)	0.00592	0.00593
R(2)	-0.03167	-0.03578
	0.22075	0.21721
C(1)		812556
C(2)		-1040681
		-1186699
2P/Y	28.4624	28.9265
DELTA	7.6806	

EXP. INCREASE:

x	$e^{(x+2\frac{1}{2})r}$
0	1.0149
50	1.3647
55	1.4057
60	1.4479
65	1.4914
70	1.5363
75	1.5824
80	1.6300
85	1.6790
90	1.7294
95	1.7814
100	1.8350

TABLE 1 DATA

AGE AT LAST BIRTHDAY	POPULATION BOTH SEXES	MALES Number	%	FEMALES Number	%	BIRTHS BY AGE OF MOTHER	DEATHS BOTH SEXES	MALES	FEMALES	AGE AT LAST BIRTHDAY
0	66582	33519	2.9	33063	2.6	0	14090	7538	6552	0
1-4	213486	106153	9.2	107333	8.4	0	9624	4869	4755	1-4
5-9	209068	104488	9.1	104580	8.2	0	3127	1638	1489	5-9
10-14	208573	104557	9.1	104016	8.1	0	1411	779	632	10-1
15-19	199337	98772	8.6	100565	7.9	1509	1051	544	507	15-1
20-24	197805	94213	8.2	103592	8.1	10173	1472	787	685	20-2
25-29	188772	91168	7.9	97604	7.6	19392	1682	849	833	25-2
30-34	172885	82020	7.1	90865	7.1	20840	2620	1366	1254	30-3
35-39	163346	77752	6.8	85594	6.7	16909	1948	956	992	35-3
40-44	154478	72420	6.3	82058	6.4	9360	2366	1248	1118	40-4
45-49	141575	65627	5.7	75948	5.9	1653	2290	1298	992	45-4
50-54	128075	58157	5.1	69918	5.5	1	3394	1856	1538	50-5
55-59	110213	48878	4.3	61335	4.8	0	3192	1637	1555	55-5
60-64	98373	42372	3.7	56001	4.4	0	3885	1899	1986	60-6
65-69	72001	29945	2.6	42056	3.3	0	4344	2046	2298	65-6
70-74	50980	20352	1.8	30628	2.4		4489	1970	2519	70-7
75-79	30355	11560	1.0	18795	1.5		4073	1674	2399	75-7
80-84	14241	5074	0.4	9167	0.7	40833 M.	2454	941	1513	80-8
85+	5472	1716	0.1	3756	0.3	39004 F.	1700	578	1122	85+
TOTAL	2425617	1148743		1276874		79837	69212	34473	34739	TOTA

TABLE 2 MALE LIFE TABLE

x	$_nq_x$	l_x	$_nd_x$	$_nL_x$	$_nm_x$	$_na_x$	T_x	r_x	$\mathring{e}_x$	$_nM_x$
0	0.197351	100000	19735	87879	0.224572	0.3858	3435904	0.0026	34.359	0.224887
1	0.163064	80265	13088	285651	0.045819	1.2946	3348025	0.0026	41.712	0.045868
5	0.075146	67177	5048	323263	0.015616	2.5000	3062374	0.0084	45.587	0.015676
10	0.036487	62129	2267	304262	0.007450	2.1855	2739112	0.0000	44.088	0.007450
15	0.027169	59862	1626	295267	0.005508	2.5150	2434849	0.0040	40.675	0.005508
20	0.040941	58235	2384	285407	0.008354	2.5804	2139583	0.0003	36.740	0.008353
25	0.045590	55851	2546	273281	0.009317	2.6537	1854176	0.0030	33.199	0.009312
30	0.079975	53305	4263	255945	0.016656	2.5185	1580895	0.0020	29.658	0.016654
35	0.059621	49042	2924	237805	0.012295	2.4680	1324950	0.0000	27.017	0.012295
40	0.082689	46118	3813	221278	0.017234	2.5584	1087145	0.0006	23.573	0.017233
45	0.094405	42304	3994	201924	0.019778	2.5967	865866	0.0000	20.468	0.019778
50	0.147968	38311	5668	177602	0.031914	2.5386	663943	0.0001	17.331	0.031914
55	0.154501	32643	5043	150585	0.033492	2.4961	486341	0.0000	14.899	0.033492
60	0.201974	27599	5574	124350	0.044828	2.5520	335756	0.0016	12.165	0.044817
65	0.292110	22025	6434	94140	0.068342	2.5155	211405	0.0016	9.598	0.068325
70	0.388262	15591	6053	62524	0.096819	2.4506	117265	0.0016	7.521	0.096796
75	0.524111	9538	4999	34512	0.144844	2.3640	54741	0.0016	5.739	0.144810
80	0.614750	4539	2790	15042	0.185504	2.2573	20230	0.0016	4.457	0.185456
85+	*1.000000	1749	1749	5188	0.337052	2.9669	5188	0.0016	2.967	0.336830

TABLE 3 FEMALE LIFE TABLE

x	$_nq_x$	l_x	$_nd_x$	$_nL_x$	$_nm_x$	$_na_x$	T_x	r_x	$\mathring{e}_x$	$_nM_x$
0	0.176847	100000	17685	89313	0.198008	0.3957	3789344	0.0015	37.893	0.198167
1	0.158320	82315	13032	294340	0.044276	1.3204	3700031	0.0015	44.949	0.044301
5	0.068378	69283	4737	334572	0.014160	2.5000	3405691	0.0110	49.156	0.014238
10	0.029864	64546	1928	317247	0.006076	2.1565	3071119	0.0000	47.581	0.006076
15	0.024895	62618	1559	309206	0.005042	2.5080	2753872	0.0000	43.979	0.005042
20	0.032545	61059	1987	300519	0.006612	2.5958	2444667	0.0000	40.038	0.006612
25	0.041860	59072	2473	289551	0.008540	2.6508	2144148	0.0037	36.297	0.008534
30	0.066730	56599	3777	273659	0.013801	2.5276	1854597	0.0010	32.767	0.013801
35	0.056294	52822	2974	256575	0.011590	2.4655	1580938	0.0000	29.929	0.011590
40	0.065877	49849	3284	241029	0.013625	2.4984	1324363	0.0000	26.568	0.013625
45	0.063321	46565	2949	225718	0.013063	2.5898	1083334	0.0008	23.265	0.013062
50	0.104434	43616	4555	207051	0.021999	2.5784	857616	0.0009	19.663	0.021997
55	0.119343	39061	4662	183874	0.025353	2.5476	650564	0.0000	16.655	0.025353
60	0.163351	34400	5619	158424	0.035549	2.5844	466690	0.0010	13.567	0.035464
65	0.241045	28780	6937	126940	0.054651	2.5550	308266	0.0010	10.711	0.054641
70	0.341116	21843	7451	90580	0.082259	2.4990	181325	0.0010	8.301	0.082245
75	0.479442	14392	6900	54051	0.127660	2.4045	90745	0.0010	6.305	0.127640
80	0.572254	7492	4287	25971	0.165076	2.3204	36695	0.0010	4.898	0.165048
85+	*1.000000	3205	3205	10723	0.298850	3.3462	10723	0.0010	3.346	0.298722

TABLE 4 OBSERVED AND PROJECTED VITAL RATES

RATES PER THOUSAND	OBSERVED POPULATION BOTH SEXES	MALES	FEMALES	PROJECTED POPULATION 1785 MALES	FEMALES	1790 MALES	FEMALES	1795 MALES	FEMALES	STABLE POPULATION MALES	FEMAL
Birth	32.91	35.55	30.55	34.69	30.09	33.79	29.54	32.86	28.93	33.31	30.4
Death	28.53	30.01	27.21	30.48	27.49	30.05	27.22	29.54	26.85	28.68	25.8
Increase	4.38	5.54	3.34	4.21	2.59	3.74	2.32	3.32	2.08		4.624
PERCENTAGE											
under 15	28.76	30.36	27.33	31.60	28.65	33.12	30.16	33.25	30.28	32.27	30.4
15-64	64.10	63.67	64.49	62.45	63.16	61.09	61.85	61.08	61.85	62.69	62.8
65 and over	7.13	5.98	8.18	5.95	8.18	5.79	7.99	5.67	7.87	5.04	6.7
DEP. RATIO X 100	56.00	57.07	55.06	60.13	58.32	63.69	61.68	63.71	61.67	59.52	59.2

AGE LAST BHDAY	1785 BOTH SEXES	1785 MALES	1785 FEMALES	1790 BOTH SEXES	1790 MALES	1790 FEMALES	1795 BOTH SEXES	1795 MALES	1795 FEMALES	AGE AT LAST BIRTHDAY	
0-4	302	152	150	301	152	149	299	151	148	0-4	**TABLE 5**
5-9	243	121	122	262	132	130	262	132	130	5-9	POPULATION
10-14	197	98	99	230	114	116	248	124	124	10-14	PROJECTED
15-19	202	101	101	192	95	97	223	110	113	15-19	WITH
20-24	193	95	98	197	98	99	186	92	94	20-24	FIXED
25-29	190	90	100	185	91	94	189	94	95	25-29	AGE—
30-34	177	85	92	178	84	94	175	86	89	30-34	SPECIFIC
35-39	161	76	85	165	79	86	166	78	88	35-39	BIRTH
40-44	152	72	80	151	71	80	155	74	81	40-44	AND
45-49	143	66	77	141	66	75	140	65	75	45-49	DEATH
50-54	128	58	70	128	58	70	127	58	69	50-54	RATES
55-59	111	49	62	111	49	62	112	49	63	55-59	(IN 1000's)
60-64	93	40	53	94	41	53	93	40	53	60-64	
65-69	77	32	45	73	31	42	74	31	43	65-69	
70-74	50	20	30	53	21	32	50	20	30	70-74	
75-79	29	11	18	29	11	18	31	12	19	75-79	
80-84	14	5	9	14	5	9	14	5	9	80-84	
85+	6	2	4	6	2	4	6	2	4	85+	
TOTAL	2468	1173	1295	2510	1200	1310	2550	1223	1327	TOTAL	

STANDARD COUNTRIES: STANDARDIZED RATES PER THOUSAND	ENGLAND AND WALES 1961 BOTH SEXES	MALES	FEMALES	UNITED STATES 1960 BOTH SEXES	MALES	FEMALES	MEXICO 1960 BOTH SEXES	MALES	FEMALES	
Birth	28.49	31.66*	26.98	28.88	29.49*	27.80	27.54	29.03*	26.84	**TABLE 6**
Death	32.17	43.71*	32.01	30.70	37.02*	29.03	26.69	26.55*	24.77	STANDARDIZED RATES
Increase	-3.68	-12.05*	-5.04	-1.82	-7.53*	-1.24	0.84	2.48*	2.07	

	OBSERVED POP. MALES	FEMALES	STATIONARY POP. MALES	FEMALES	STABLE POP. MALES	FEMALES	OBSERVED BIRTHS	NET MATERNITY FUNCTION	BIRTHS IN STABLE POP.	
	29.62472	31.91713	30.11607	31.87060	28.22972	29.81820	32.26997	32.28849	32.08343	**TABLE 7**
	421.9282	459.1084	417.2764	453.3369	398.1809	433.7954	42.61337	42.31240	42.20703	MOMENTS
	4102.547	3830.191	3863.846	3866.897	4370.262	4555.663	22.9739	20.0601	25.4972	AND
	-126811.	-173938.	-125408.	-167547.	-93405.	-129775.	-1243.398	-1180.300	-1160.168	CUMULANTS
	0.224074	0.151599	0.205479	0.160495	0.302534	0.254243	0.006821	0.005312	0.008646	
	2.287673	2.174792	2.279759	2.184744	2.410875	2.310362	2.315271	2.340740	2.348745	
	-0.088099	-0.058475	-0.081878	-0.061846	-0.121523	-0.098693	-0.003751	-0.003037	-0.004969	

VITAL STATISTICS		THOMPSON AGE RANGE	NRR	1000r	INTERVAL	BOURGEOIS-PICHAT AGE RANGE	NRR	1000b	1000d	1000r	COALE		
R	2.136										IBR	25.41	**TABLE 8**
R	1.160	0-4	1.09	3.26	26.85	5-29	0.90	24.04	28.06	-4.02	IDR	26.17	RATES FROM AGE
R	4.373	5-9	0.93	-2.87	26.65	30-54	0.98	25.39	26.23	-0.85	IRI	-0.76	DISTRIBUTIONS
GENERATION	32.186	10-14	0.98	-0.93	26.54	55-79	1.01	27.39	26.91	0.48	K1	0.	AND VITAL
SEX RATIO	104.689	15-19	0.97	-1.19	26.40	*30-54	0.98	25.39	26.23	-0.85	K2	0.	STATISTICS (Females)

ORIGINAL MATRIX SUB-DIAGONAL	ALTERNATIVE FIRST ROWS Projection	Integral	FIRST STABLE MATRIX % IN STABLE POPULATION	FISHER VALUES	REPRODUCTIVE VALUES	SECOND STABLE MATRIX Z2 FIRST COLUMN	FIRST ROW	
0.87207	0.00000	0.00000	11.543	1.318	185029	0.1326+0.0449	0.1326+0.0449	**TABLE 9**
0.94822	0.00000	0.00000	9.836	1.547	161744	0.1135-0.0789	0.0433+0.1350	LESLIE
0.97465	0.01371	0.00000	9.114	1.669	173627	0.0043-0.1483	-0.0771+0.1072	MATRIX
0.97191	0.10351	0.02845	8.680	1.734	174399	-0.1288-0.1012	-0.1215+0.0009	AND ITS
0.96351	0.27143	0.18620	8.243	1.686	174627	-0.1738+0.0478	-0.0804-0.0930	SPECTRAL
0.94511	0.38934	0.37672	7.760	1.419	138524	-0.0708+0.1835	-0.0126-0.1226	COMPONENTS
0.93757	0.38852	0.43488	7.167	0.994	90310	0.1128+0.1777	0.0305-0.0961	(Females)
0.93941	0.28556	0.37457	6.566	0.539	46115	0.2229+0.0159	0.0349-0.0493	
0.93648	0.12600	0.21628	6.027	0.186	15289	0.1546-0.1806	0.0165-0.0148	
0.91730	0.02041	0.04127	5.515	0.026	1997	-0.0565-0.2456	0.0027-0.0018	
0.88806	0.00001	0.00003	4.943	0.000	1	-0.2400-0.1045	0.0000-0.0000	
0.72286			14.606					

OBSERVED POPUL. (IN 100's)	CONTRIBUTIONS OF ROOTS (IN 100's) r_1	r_2, r_3	r_4-r_{11}	AGE-SP. BIRTH RATES	NET MATERNITY FUNCTION	COEFF. OF MATRIX EQUATION	PARAMETERS INTEGRAL	MATRIX	EXP. INCREASE x	$e^{(x+8\frac{1}{2})r}$	
1404	1375	13	16	0.0000	0.0000	0.0000	L(1) 1.02339	1.02340	0	1.0116	**TABLE 10**
1046	1172	-60	-66	0.0000	0.0000	0.0000	L(2) 0.52596	0.52508	50	1.2748	AGE
1040	1086	-90	45	0.0000	0.0000	0.0113	0.72463	0.71006	55	1.3046	ANALYSIS
1006	1034	-48	19	0.0073	0.0227	0.0834	R(1) 0.00462	0.00463	60	1.3351	AND
1036	982	47	7	0.0480	0.1442	0.2126	R(2) -0.02210	-0.02486	65	1.3663	MISCELLANEOUS
976	924	119	-67	0.0971	0.2811	0.2938	0.18859	0.18681	70	1.3983	RESULTS
909	854	96	-41	0.1120	0.3066	0.2771	C(1)	11911	75	1.4310	(Females)
856	782	-14	88	0.0965	0.2476	0.1910	C(2)	-5326	80	1.4645	
821	718	-126	229	0.0557	0.1343	0.0792		-30315	85	1.4987	
759	657	-143	246	0.0106	0.0240	0.0120	2P/Y 33.3167	33.6340	90	1.5338	
699	589	-38	148	0.0000	0.0000	0.0000	DELTA 4.2620		95	1.5697	
2217	1740								100	1.6064	

TABLE 1 — DATA

AGE AT LAST BIRTHDAY	POPULATION BOTH SEXES	MALES Number	%	FEMALES Number	%	BIRTHS BY AGE OF MOTHER	DEATHS BOTH SEXES	MALES	FEMALES	AGE AT LAST BIRTHDAY
0	57412	28830	2.5	28582	2.2	0	13288	7093	6195	0
1-4	211788	105304	9.2	106484	8.3	0	9651	4917	4734	1-
5-9	209907	106124	9.2	103783	8.1	0	2461	1280	1181	5-
10-14	216865	109584	9.5	107281	8.3	0	1080	557	523	10-
15-19	203960	100478	8.7	103482	8.1	1465	1165	579	586	15-
20-24	201370	96834	8.4	104536	8.1	10538	1628	858	770	20-
25-29	182810	85684	7.4	97126	7.6	19838	2379	1272	1107	25-
30-34	175370	82539	7.2	92831	7.2	21542	1768	883	885	30-
35-39	165547	78097	6.8	87450	6.8	17825	2069	1039	1030	35-
40-44	155709	72967	6.3	82742	6.4	9693	2154	1186	968	40-
45-49	141487	64926	5.6	76561	6.0	1527	2886	1604	1282	45-
50-54	127174	57158	5.0	70016	5.4	0	2911	1575	1336	50-
55-59	110338	48731	4.2	61607	4.8	0	3258	1676	1582	55-
60-64	100011	43013	3.7	56998	4.4	0	3845	1891	1954	60-
65-69	72885	30258	2.6	42627	3.3	0	4346	2005	2341	65-
70-74	51449	20598	1.8	30851	2.4		4690	1996	2694	70-
75-79	30867	11929	1.0	18938	1.5		3594	1479	2115	75-
80-84	14907	5381	0.5	9526	0.7	42166 M.	2819	1123	1696	80-
85+	5440	1702	0.1	3738	0.3	40262 F.	1734	571	1163	85
TOTAL	2435296	1150137		1285159		82428	67726	33584	34142	TOT

TABLE 2 — MALE LIFE TABLE

x	nq_x	l_x	nd_x	nL_x	nm_x	na_x	T_x	r_x	$\mathring{e}_x$	nM_x
0	0.213369	100000	21337	86725	0.246028	0.3778	3423033	0.0000	34.230	0.246028
1	0.165696	78663	13034	279144	0.046693	1.2758	3336307	0.0000	42.413	0.046693
5	0.058472	65629	3837	318551	0.012047	2.5000	3057163	0.0019	46.583	0.012061
10	0.025059	61791	1548	304644	0.005083	2.2143	2738612	0.0000	44.320	0.005083
15	0.028446	60243	1714	297138	0.005767	2.6211	2433969	0.0063	40.403	0.005762
20	0.043469	58529	2544	286764	0.008872	2.6879	2136830	0.0063	36.509	0.008861
25	0.071587	55985	4008	269940	0.014847	2.5084	1850067	0.0034	33.046	0.014845
30	0.052062	51977	2706	252948	0.010698	2.4358	1580127	0.0000	30.400	0.010698
35	0.064428	49271	3174	238608	0.013304	2.5591	1327179	0.0000	26.936	0.013304
40	0.078232	46097	3606	221838	0.016256	2.6026	1088572	0.0010	23.615	0.016254
45	0.116492	42491	4950	200335	0.024708	2.5519	866733	0.0011	20.398	0.024705
50	0.128932	37541	4840	175652	0.027556	2.5100	666398	0.0002	17.751	0.027555
55	0.158474	32701	5182	150676	0.034393	2.5249	490746	0.0000	15.007	0.034393
60	0.198414	27518	5460	124170	0.043972	2.5418	340070	0.0015	12.358	0.043963
65	0.284646	22058	6279	94733	0.066279	2.5221	215900	0.0015	9.788	0.066263
70	0.388272	15780	6127	63213	0.096921	2.4401	121166	0.0015	7.679	0.096903
75	0.467827	9653	4516	36415	0.124010	2.3762	57953	0.0015	6.004	0.123984
80	0.670169	5137	3443	16490	0.208766	2.3293	21538	0.0015	4.193	0.208696
85+	*1.000000	1694	1694	5047	0.335694	2.9789	5047	0.0015	2.979	0.335488

TABLE 3 — FEMALE LIFE TABLE

x	nq_x	l_x	nd_x	nL_x	nm_x	na_x	T_x	r_x	$\mathring{e}_x$	nM_x
0	0.191321	100000	19132	88270	0.216745	0.3869	3779400	0.0000	37.794	0.216745
1	0.158755	80868	12838	288775	0.044457	1.2974	3691130	0.0000	45.644	0.044457
5	0.055126	68030	3750	330773	0.011338	2.5000	3402355	0.0057	50.013	0.011380
10	0.024051	64279	1546	317116	0.004875	2.2308	3071582	0.0000	47.785	0.004875
15	0.027931	62734	1752	309425	0.005663	2.5787	2754466	0.0000	43.907	0.005663
20	0.036201	60981	2208	299701	0.007366	2.6421	2445041	0.0000	40.095	0.007366
25	0.055428	58774	3258	285803	0.011399	2.5241	2145093	0.0018	36.502	0.011398
30	0.046550	55516	2584	271072	0.009533	2.4815	1859537	0.0000	33.495	0.009533
35	0.057219	52932	3029	257140	0.011778	2.5175	1588465	0.0004	30.010	0.011778
40	0.056871	49903	2838	242578	0.011699	2.5556	1331325	0.0004	26.678	0.011699
45	0.080444	47065	3786	226091	0.016746	2.5609	1088747	0.0007	23.133	0.016745
50	0.091161	43279	3945	206733	0.019084	2.5511	862656	0.0017	19.932	0.019081
55	0.120845	39334	4753	185104	0.025679	2.5671	655923	0.0000	16.676	0.025679
60	0.158338	34580	5475	159692	0.034287	2.5875	470820	0.0009	13.615	0.034282
65	0.242314	29105	7053	128397	0.054928	2.5713	311127	0.0009	10.690	0.054918
70	0.357792	22052	7890	90344	0.087335	2.4756	182731	0.0009	8.286	0.087323
75	0.432693	14162	6128	54863	0.111694	2.3974	92387	0.0009	6.523	0.111680
80	0.606617	8034	4874	27369	0.178075	2.3732	37524	0.0009	4.670	0.178040
85+	*1.000000	3161	3161	10154	0.311250	3.2129	10154	0.0009	3.213	0.311129

TABLE 4 — OBSERVED AND PROJECTED VITAL RATES

	OBSERVED POPULATION BOTH SEXES	MALES	FEMALES	PROJECTED POPULATION 1790 MALES	FEMALES	1795 MALES	FEMALES	1800 MALES	FEMALES	STABLE POPULATION MALES	FEM.
RATES PER THOUSAND											
Birth	33.85	36.66	31.33	35.69	30.81	34.70	30.22	33.62	29.51	33.90	30-
Death	27.81	29.20	26.57	30.09	27.18	29.61	26.87	29.04	26.47	28.80	25-
Increase	6.04	7.46	4.76	5.60	3.63	5.09	3.35	4.59	3.04		5.09
PERCENTAGE											
under 15	28.58	30.42	26.93	31.51	28.28	33.04	30.01	33.59	30.55	32.33	30-
15-64	64.21	63.51	64.84	62.40	63.49	61.08	62.01	60.69	61.60	62.60	62-
65 and over	7.21	6.07	8.22	6.08	8.22	5.88	7.99	5.72	7.85	5.07	6-
DEP. RATIO X 100	55.73	57.46	54.22	60.25	57.50	63.73	61.28	64.78	62.33	59.74	59-

TABLE 1 — DATA

AGE AT LAST BIRTHDAY	POPULATION BOTH SEXES	MALES Number	%	FEMALES Number	%	BIRTHS BY AGE OF MOTHER	DEATHS BOTH SEXES	MALES	FEMALES	AGE AT LAST BIRTHDAY
0	57952	29204	2.4	28748	2.1	0	14795	7977	6818	0
1-4	213889	106589	8.9	107300	8.0	0	7960	4030	3930	1-4
5-9	223608	113054	9.4	110554	8.2	0	2333	1213	1120	5-9
10-14	225851	113932	9.5	111919	8.3	0	1128	575	553	10-14
15-19	213009	105494	8.8	107515	8.0	1379	1351	672	679	15-19
20-24	198695	92875	7.7	105820	7.9	10836	2393	1326	1067	20-24
25-29	190701	89911	7.5	100790	7.5	20517	1633	840	793	25-29
30-34	184865	87593	7.3	97272	7.2	23484	1862	931	931	30-34
35-39	173874	82089	6.8	91785	6.8	19333	1943	1019	924	35-39
40-44	162873	76079	6.3	86794	6.5	9942	2759	1516	1243	40-44
45-49	148177	68184	5.7	79993	6.0	1652	2635	1442	1193	45-49
50-54	134387	60524	5.0	73863	5.5	0	3038	1603	1435	50-54
55-59	118373	52232	4.3	66141	4.9	0	3332	1731	1601	55-59
60-64	104871	45100	3.8	59771	4.4	0	3922	1912	2010	60-64
65-69	78600	32748	2.7	45852	3.4	0	4643	2047	2596	65-69
70-74	56788	23101	1.9	33687	2.5		4250	1840	2410	70-74
75-79	35452	13965	1.2	21487	1.6		4261	1812	2449	75-79
80-84	16134	6061	0.5	10073	0.7	44593 M.	3048	1211	1837	80-84
85+	6602	2035	0.2	4567	0.3	42550 F.	1944	671	1273	85+
TOTAL	2544701	1200770		1343931		87143	69230	34368	34862	TOTAL

TABLE 2 — MALE LIFE TABLE

x	$_nq_x$	l_x	$_nd_x$	$_nL_x$	$_nm_x$	$_na_x$	T_x	r_x	$\dot{e}_x$	$_nM_x$	x
0	0.231831	100000	23183	84874	0.273148	0.3475	3478232	0.0000	34.782	0.273148	0
1	0.136832	76817	10511	278005	0.037809	1.2160	3393358	0.0000	44.175	0.037809	1
5	0.052194	66306	3461	322877	0.010719	2.5000	3115352	0.0018	46.985	0.010729	5
10	0.024893	62845	1564	309996	0.005047	2.2963	2792475	0.0003	44.434	0.005047	10
15	0.031518	61281	1931	302102	0.006393	2.7728	2482479	0.0126	40.510	0.006370	15
20	0.068971	59349	4093	286635	0.014281	2.5299	2180378	0.0046	36.738	0.014277	20
25	0.045600	55256	2520	269696	0.009343	2.3874	1893743	0.0000	34.272	0.009343	25
30	0.051788	52736	2731	256956	0.010629	2.5378	1624046	0.0000	30.796	0.010629	30
35	0.060289	50005	3015	242850	0.012414	2.6198	1367090	0.0004	27.339	0.012413	35
40	0.095013	46990	4465	224052	0.019927	2.5587	1124241	0.0001	23.925	0.019927	40
45	0.100466	42526	4272	202008	0.021150	2.5142	900189	0.0007	21.168	0.021149	45
50	0.124319	38253	4756	179556	0.026485	2.5376	698181	0.0000	18.252	0.026485	50
55	0.153156	33498	5130	154806	0.033141	2.5281	518625	0.0000	15.482	0.033141	55
60	0.192005	28367	5447	128442	0.042406	2.5408	363819	0.0020	12.825	0.042395	60
65	0.270406	22921	6198	99129	0.062523	2.5033	235377	0.0020	10.269	0.062508	65
70	0.331569	16723	5545	69594	0.079673	2.4715	136248	0.0020	8.147	0.079650	70
75	0.486679	11178	5440	41911	0.129800	2.4304	66654	0.0020	5.963	0.129753	75
80	0.649809	5738	3729	18653	0.199885	2.3083	24742	0.0020	4.312	0.199803	80
85+	*1.000000	2009	2009	6089	0.330001	3.0303	6089	0.0020	3.030	0.329730	85+

TABLE 3 — FEMALE LIFE TABLE

x	$_nq_x$	l_x	$_nd_x$	$_nL_x$	$_nm_x$	$_na_x$	T_x	r_x	$\dot{e}_x$	$_nM_x$	x
0	0.205926	100000	20593	86828	0.237164	0.3604	3851856	0.0000	38.519	0.237164	0
1	0.133051	79407	10565	288461	0.036626	1.2392	3765028	0.0000	47.414	0.036626	1
5	0.049279	68842	3392	335730	0.010105	2.5000	3476566	0.0045	50.501	0.010131	5
10	0.024382	65450	1596	322966	0.004941	2.3165	3140837	0.0000	47.989	0.004941	10
15	0.031116	63854	1987	314604	0.006315	2.6517	2817871	0.0000	44.130	0.006315	15
20	0.049186	61867	3043	301787	0.010083	2.5193	2503267	0.0000	40.462	0.010083	20
25	0.038569	58824	2269	288365	0.007868	2.4634	2201480	0.0000	37.425	0.007868	25
30	0.046736	56555	2644	276246	0.009571	2.5300	1913115	0.0002	33.827	0.009571	30
35	0.049136	53911	2649	263122	0.010067	2.5710	1636869	0.0005	30.362	0.010067	35
40	0.069177	51262	3546	247609	0.014322	2.5460	1373747	0.0003	26.798	0.014321	40
45	0.071925	47716	3432	230118	0.014914	2.5340	1126138	0.0003	23.601	0.014914	45
50	0.092741	44284	4107	211395	0.019428	2.5588	896021	0.0000	20.233	0.019428	50
55	0.114293	40177	4592	189704	0.024206	2.5650	684626	0.0000	17.040	0.024206	55
60	0.155660	35585	5539	164677	0.033637	2.6081	494921	0.0014	13.908	0.033628	60
65	0.248477	30046	7466	131838	0.056628	2.5365	330244	0.0014	10.991	0.056617	65
70	0.303196	22580	6846	95679	0.071555	2.4844	198406	0.0014	8.787	0.071541	70
75	0.441903	15734	6953	60988	0.114004	2.4569	102727	0.0014	6.529	0.113976	75
80	0.615781	8781	5407	29642	0.182419	2.3621	41739	0.0014	4.753	0.182368	80
85+	*1.000000	3374	3374	12097	0.278898	3.5855	12097	0.0014	3.586	0.278739	85+

TABLE 4 — OBSERVED AND PROJECTED POPULATION / STABLE POPULATION

RATES PER THOUSAND	OBSERVED BOTH SEXES	MALES	FEMALES	1795 MALES	1795 FEMALES	1800 MALES	1800 FEMALES	1805 MALES	1805 FEMALES	STABLE MALES	STABLE FEMALES
Birth	34.24	37.14	31.66	35.92	30.95	34.81	30.26	33.71	29.53	34.32	31.30
Death	27.21	28.62	25.94	29.77	26.78	29.26	26.45	28.63	26.04	28.28	25.25
Increase	7.04	8.52	5.72	6.15	4.17	5.55	3.80	5.08	3.50	6.0439	
PERCENTAGE											
under 15	28.35	30.21	26.68	31.57	28.26	33.10	29.99	33.89	30.83	32.73	30.99
15-64	64.05	63.30	64.72	61.97	63.20	60.61	61.65	59.98	60.99	62.06	62.35
65 and over	7.61	6.49	8.61	6.45	8.54	6.29	8.35	6.13	8.19	5.22	6.66
DEP. RATIO X 100	56.13	57.98	54.52	61.36	58.23	64.98	62.20	66.71	63.97	61.15	60.37

TABLE 1 — DATA

AGE AT LAST BIRTHDAY	POPULATION BOTH SEXES	MALES Number	MALES %	FEMALES Number	FEMALES %	BIRTHS BY AGE OF MOTHER	DEATHS BOTH SEXES	DEATHS MALES	FEMALES	AGE AT LAST BIRTHDAY
0	62936	31822	2.4	31114	2.1	0	15009	8103	6906	0
1-4	235677	117231	8.7	118446	8.0	0	8098	4160	3938	1-4
5-9	242778	121542	9.1	121236	8.2	0	2520	1317	1203	5-9
10-14	242264	122242	9.1	120022	8.1	0	1336	693	643	10-14
15-19	225355	111491	8.3	113864	7.7	1459	2080	1066	1014	15-19
20-24	218607	104632	7.8	113975	7.7	11468	1689	896	793	20-24
25-29	214187	103866	7.7	110321	7.5	22828	1834	953	881	25-29
30-34	206826	100246	7.5	106580	7.2	26277	1908	1043	865	30-34
35-39	192340	92534	6.9	99806	6.8	20422	2704	1512	1192	35-39
40-44	180463	85806	6.4	94657	6.4	11387	2718	1490	1228	40-44
45-49	164532	77012	5.7	87520	5.9	1660	2849	1581	1268	45-49
50-54	151483	69746	5.2	81737	5.6	0	3228	1796	1432	50-54
55-59	133242	59847	4.5	73395	5.0	0	3596	1917	1679	55-59
60-64	113375	49721	3.7	63654	4.3	0	4566	2182	2384	60-64
65-69	91460	39290	2.9	52170	3.5	0	4421	2056	2365	65-69
70-74	68453	28366	2.1	40087	2.7		5133	2345	2788	70-74
75-79	41237	16168	1.2	25069	1.7		4974	2190	2784	75-79
80-84	20678	7650	0.6	13028	0.9	48874 M.	3445	1406	2039	80-84
85+	8802	2817	0.2	5985	0.4	46627 F.	2366	831	1535	85+
TOTAL	2814695	1342029		1472666		95501	74474	37537	36937	TOTAL

TABLE 2 — MALE LIFE TABLE

x	nq_x	l_x	nd_x	nL_x	nm_x	na_x	T_x	r_x	$\dot{e}_x$	nM_x
0	0.218454	100000	21845	85791	0.254635	0.3496	3585521	0.0000	35.855	0.254635
1	0.129195	78155	10097	284544	0.035485	1.2195	3499730	0.0000	44.780	0.035485
5	0.052633	68057	3582	331332	0.010811	2.5000	3215186	0.0045	47.242	0.010836
10	0.027936	64475	1801	317738	0.005669	2.4245	2883854	0.0007	44.728	0.005669
15	0.046735	62674	2929	306195	0.009566	2.5500	2566116	0.0072	40.944	0.009561
20	0.041909	59745	2504	292391	0.008563	2.4699	2259922	0.0000	37.826	0.008563
25	0.044857	57241	2568	279844	0.009175	2.5220	1967531	0.0000	34.373	0.009175
30	0.050762	54674	2775	266744	0.010405	2.6134	1687687	0.0001	30.868	0.010404
35	0.078572	51898	4078	249548	0.016341	2.5615	1420943	0.0004	27.379	0.016340
40	0.083228	47821	3980	229196	0.017365	2.5108	1171395	0.0005	24.496	0.017365
45	0.097710	43841	4284	208662	0.020529	2.5394	942200	0.0000	21.492	0.020529
50	0.121078	39557	4789	185994	0.025751	2.5382	733538	0.0000	18.544	0.025751
55	0.148484	34767	5162	161153	0.032034	2.5431	547544	0.0006	15.749	0.032032
60	0.197838	29605	5857	133453	0.043888	2.5120	386391	0.0008	13.052	0.043885
65	0.231559	23748	5499	105076	0.052334	2.5152	252938	0.0008	10.651	0.052329
70	0.342993	18249	6259	75703	0.082661	2.5171	147862	0.0008	8.102	0.082669
75	0.501430	11990	6012	44378	0.135471	2.4102	72158	0.0008	6.018	0.135453
80	0.613459	5978	3667	19950	0.183816	2.2897	27780	0.0008	4.647	0.183791
85+	*1.000000	2311	2311	7830	0.295090	3.3888	7830	0.0008	3.389	0.294995

TABLE 3 — FEMALE LIFE TABLE

x	nq_x	l_x	nd_x	nL_x	nm_x	na_x	T_x	r_x	$\dot{e}_x$	nM_x
0	0.194303	100000	19430	87540	0.221958	0.3587	3991780	0.0000	39.918	0.221958
1	0.121797	80570	9813	295157	0.033247	1.2362	3904239	0.0000	48.458	0.033247
5	0.048224	70757	3412	345253	0.009883	2.5000	3609083	0.0078	51.007	0.009923
10	0.026424	67344	1779	332158	0.005357	2.4349	3263830	0.0000	48.465	0.005357
15	0.043567	65565	2856	320759	0.008905	2.5266	2931672	0.0000	44.714	0.008905
20	0.034183	62708	2144	308082	0.006958	2.4528	2610913	0.0000	41.636	0.006958
25	0.039152	60565	2371	296933	0.007986	2.5152	2302831	0.0000	38.023	0.007986
30	0.039802	58194	2316	285359	0.008117	2.5784	2005898	0.0011	34.469	0.008116
35	0.058030	55877	3243	271487	0.011944	2.5637	1720539	0.0006	30.791	0.011943
40	0.062838	52635	3307	254949	0.012973	2.5131	1449051	0.0000	27.530	0.012973
45	0.069941	49327	3450	238126	0.014488	2.5330	1194102	0.0000	24.208	0.014488
50	0.084007	45877	3854	219983	0.017520	2.5599	955977	0.0000	20.838	0.017520
55	0.108473	42023	4558	199258	0.022877	2.6177	735994	0.0002	17.514	0.022876
60	0.171618	37465	6430	171619	0.037465	2.5573	536736	0.0025	14.326	0.037452
65	0.203897	31035	6328	139545	0.045347	2.5299	365117	0.0025	11.765	0.045333
70	0.296943	24707	7337	105443	0.069580	2.5338	225571	0.0025	9.130	0.069549
75	0.432763	17371	7517	67663	0.111100	2.4472	120129	0.0025	6.916	0.111053
80	0.551402	9853	5433	34702	0.156564	2.3812	52465	0.0025	5.325	0.156509
85+	1.000000	4420	4420	17763	0.248835	4.0187	17763	0.0025	4.019	0.256474

TABLE 4 — OBSERVED AND PROJECTED VITAL RATES

	OBSERVED POPULATION BOTH SEXES	MALES	FEMALES	PROJECTED POPULATION 1800 MALES	1800 FEMALES	1805 MALES	1805 FEMALES	1810 MALES	1810 FEMALES	STABLE POPULATION MALES	FEMALES
RATES PER THOUSAND											
Birth	33.93	36.42	31.66	35.16	30.76	33.95	29.88	32.83	29.03	34.35	31.
Death	26.46	27.97	25.08	29.12	26.02	28.53	25.58	27.93	25.15	27.24	24.
Increase	7.47	8.45	6.58	6.03	4.74	5.42	4.29	4.91	3.89		7.11
PERCENTAGE											
under 15	27.84	29.27	26.54	31.11	28.47	33.01	30.34	33.91	31.18	33.28	31.
15-64	63.96	63.70	64.20	62.07	62.49	60.37	60.86	59.59	60.18	61.53	61.
65 and over	8.19	7.03	9.26	6.82	9.04	6.63	8.80	6.49	8.64	5.19	6.
DEP. RATIO X 100	56.34	56.98	55.75	61.10	60.04	65.66	64.32	67.80	66.17	62.52	61.

TABLE 1 — DATA

AGE AT LAST BIRTHDAY	POPULATION BOTH SEXES	MALES Number	MALES %	FEMALES Number	FEMALES %	BIRTHS BY AGE OF MOTHER	DEATHS BOTH SEXES	MALES	FEMALES	AGE AT LAST BIRTHDAY
0	58703	29730	2.2	28973	2.0	0	14615	7912	6703	0
1-4	239452	118985	8.7	120467	8.1	0	8726	4419	4307	1-4
5-9	247334	124516	9.1	122818	8.3	0	2158	1089	1069	5-9
10-14	237145	119013	8.7	118132	8.0	0	2244	1198	1046	10-14
15-19	229319	114115	8.3	115204	7.8	1401	1321	650	671	15-19
20-24	225136	110306	8.1	114830	7.8	11917	1752	927	825	20-24
25-29	216249	106414	7.8	109835	7.4	24283	1720	946	774	25-29
30-34	208262	102041	7.4	106221	7.2	25580	2455	1382	1073	30-34
35-39	194566	94640	6.9	99926	6.7	21292	2480	1387	1093	35-39
40-44	181955	87246	6.4	94709	6.4	10756	2780	1551	1229	40-44
45-49	168308	79576	5.8	88732	6.0	1619	2705	1550	1155	45-49
50-54	154382	71564	5.2	82818	5.6	0	3190	1786	1404	50-54
55-59	134850	61308	4.5	73542	5.0	0	3824	1946	1878	55-59
60-64	115352	51266	3.7	64086	4.3	0	3899	1914	1985	60-64
65-69	95865	41548	3.0	54317	3.7	0	4706	2216	2490	65-69
70-74	68337	28638	2.1	39699	2.7		5464	2544	2920	70-74
75-79	43332	17548	1.3	25784	1.7		4779	2120	2659	75-79
80-84	22647	8534	0.6	14113	1.0	49580 M.	3599	1497	2102	80-84
85+	9974	3264	0.2	6710	0.5	47268 F.	2707	966	1741	85+
TOTAL	2851168	1370252		1480916		96848	75124	38000	37124	TOTAL

TABLE 2 — MALE LIFE TABLE

x	nq_x	l_x	nd_x	nL_x	nm_x	na_x	T_x	r_x	$\overset{\circ}{e}_x$	nM_x	x
0	0.226821	100000	22682	85230	0.266128	0.3488	3551522	0.0000	35.515	0.266128	0
1	0.134646	77318	10411	280312	0.037139	1.2182	3466292	0.0000	44.832	0.037139	1
5	0.042644	66907	2853	327404	0.008715	2.5000	3185980	0.0065	47.618	0.008746	5
10	0.049059	64054	3142	312176	0.010066	2.4242	2858577	0.0000	44.628	0.010066	10
15	0.028066	60912	1710	300138	0.005696	2.4141	2546400	0.0003	41.805	0.005696	15
20	0.041177	59202	2438	290075	0.008404	2.5650	2246262	0.0000	37.942	0.008404	20
25	0.043518	56764	2470	277880	0.008890	2.5946	1956187	0.0000	34.462	0.008890	25
30	0.065556	54294	3559	262805	0.013544	2.5654	1678307	0.0000	30.911	0.013544	30
35	0.070716	50735	3588	244799	0.014656	2.5264	1415307	0.0005	27.900	0.014656	35
40	0.085136	47147	4014	225788	0.017777	2.5218	1170703	0.0000	24.831	0.017777	40
45	0.092922	43133	4008	205768	0.019478	2.5305	944915	0.0000	21.907	0.019478	45
50	0.117600	39125	4601	184346	0.024959	2.5485	739147	0.0009	18.892	0.024957	50
55	0.147138	34524	5080	160011	0.031747	2.5177	554801	0.0020	16.070	0.031741	55
60	0.170919	29444	5033	134782	0.037339	2.5282	394791	0.0010	13.408	0.037335	60
65	0.236040	24412	5762	108016	0.053345	2.5630	260009	0.0010	10.651	0.053336	65
70	0.363247	18650	6774	76247	0.088847	2.4905	151993	0.0010	8.150	0.088833	70
75	0.459213	11875	5453	45132	0.120828	2.3880	75746	0.0010	6.379	0.120811	75
80	0.598413	6422	3843	21903	0.175450	2.3442	30614	0.0010	4.767	0.175417	80
85+	*1.000000	2579	2579	8710	0.296079	3.3775	8710	0.0010	3.377	0.295956	85+

TABLE 3 — FEMALE LIFE TABLE

x	nq_x	l_x	nd_x	nL_x	nm_x	na_x	T_x	r_x	$\overset{\circ}{e}_x$	nM_x	x
0	0.201551	100000	20155	87118	0.231353	0.3609	3943112	0.0000	39.431	0.231353	0
1	0.130167	79845	10393	290697	0.035753	1.2402	3855993	0.0000	48.294	0.035753	1
5	0.042398	69452	2945	339897	0.008663	2.5000	3565296	0.0085	51.335	0.008704	5
10	0.043283	66507	2879	325106	0.008855	2.4190	3225399	0.0000	48.497	0.008855	10
15	0.028691	63628	1826	313433	0.005824	2.4204	2900294	0.0000	45.582	0.005824	15
20	0.035295	61803	2181	303611	0.007185	2.5229	2586861	0.0000	41.857	0.007185	20
25	0.034641	59622	2065	293081	0.007047	2.5662	2283250	0.0000	38.296	0.007047	25
30	0.049294	57556	2837	280865	0.010102	2.5623	1990169	0.0000	34.578	0.010102	30
35	0.053252	54719	2914	266398	0.010938	2.5299	1709304	0.0002	31.238	0.010938	35
40	0.062852	51805	3256	250916	0.012977	2.5094	1442906	0.0000	27.853	0.012977	40
45	0.063057	48549	3061	235186	0.013017	2.5306	1191990	0.0000	24.552	0.013017	45
50	0.081474	45488	3706	218582	0.016955	2.6103	956804	0.0009	21.034	0.016953	50
55	0.120223	41782	5023	196681	0.025539	2.5658	738222	0.0010	17.669	0.025536	55
60	0.144014	36759	5294	170865	0.030982	2.5579	541541	0.0021	14.732	0.030974	60
65	0.206382	31465	6494	141605	0.045859	2.5793	370676	0.0021	11.781	0.045842	65
70	0.311001	24971	7766	105549	0.073578	2.5140	229071	0.0021	9.173	0.073553	70
75	0.407727	17205	7015	68003	0.103156	2.4309	123522	0.0021	7.179	0.103126	75
80	0.533881	10190	5440	36515	0.148986	2.4133	55519	0.0021	5.448	0.148941	80
85+	1.000000	4750	4750	19004	0.249939	4.0010	19004	0.0021	4.001	0.259463	85+

TABLE 4 — OBSERVED AND PROJECTED TOTAL RATES

	OBSERVED POPULATION BOTH SEXES	MALES	FEMALES	PROJECTED POPULATION 1805 MALES	1805 FEMALES	1810 MALES	1810 FEMALES	1815 MALES	1815 FEMALES	STABLE POPULATION MALES	FEMALES
RATES PER THOUSAND											
Birth	33.97	36.18	31.92	35.07	31.08	33.96	30.23	32.94	29.43	34.70	31.64
Death	26.35	27.73	25.07	28.91	26.00	28.37	25.59	27.88	25.19	27.60	24.55
Increase	7.62	8.45	6.85	6.16	5.08	5.59	4.64	5.06	4.24		7.0948
PERCENTAGE											
under 15	27.45	28.63	26.36	30.70	28.37	32.47	30.14	33.47	31.02	33.15	31.36
15-64	64.13	64.11	64.14	62.26	62.38	60.66	60.85	59.76	60.11	61.45	61.66
65 and over	8.42	7.26	9.50	7.04	9.25	6.87	9.02	6.77	8.86	5.39	6.98
DEP. RATIO X 100	55.94	55.98	55.90	60.62	60.31	64.85	64.34	67.34	66.36	62.72	62.19

TABLE 1 — DATA

AGE AT LAST BIRTHDAY	POPULATION Both Sexes	MALES Number	MALES %	FEMALES Number	FEMALES %	BIRTHS By Age of Mother	DEATHS Both Sexes	DEATHS Males	DEATHS Females	AGE AT LAST BIRTHDAY
0	65199	32916	2.4	32283	2.2	0	14544	7895	6649	0
1-4	236834	118073	8.6	118761	8.0	0	7140	3679	3461	1-4
5-9	240913	120476	8.8	120437	8.1	0	3816	2018	1798	5-9
10-14	236067	117945	8.6	118122	7.9	0	1236	645	591	10-14
15-19	232136	115364	8.4	116772	7.9	1319	1373	689	684	15-19
20-24	225142	110728	8.1	114414	7.7	12843	1550	849	701	20-24
25-29	216545	106358	7.8	110187	7.4	23240	2067	1165	902	25-29
30-34	206955	101180	7.4	105775	7.1	26274	2224	1238	986	30-34
35-39	193420	93718	6.8	99702	6.7	20476	2422	1347	1075	35-39
40-44	183221	87976	6.4	95245	6.4	11145	2518	1400	1118	40-44
45-49	168790	79646	5.8	89144	6.0	1713	2692	1590	1102	45-49
50-54	152830	70845	5.2	81985	5.5	30	3306	1764	1542	50-54
55-59	135654	61603	4.5	74051	5.0	0	3150	1641	1509	55-59
60-64	117211	52140	3.8	65071	4.4	0	3903	1942	1961	60-64
65-69	93685	40529	3.0	53156	3.6	0	4842	2331	2511	65-69
70-74	70679	29875	2.2	40804	2.7		4903	2275	2628	70-74
75-79	46769	19123	1.4	27646	1.9		4710	2101	2609	75-79
80-84	24803	9509	0.7	15294	1.0	49676 M.	3879	1651	2228	80-84
85+	11536	3918	0.3	7618	0.5	47364 F.	3171	1136	2035	85+
TOTAL	2858389	1371922		1486467		97040	73446	37356	36090	TOTAL

TABLE 2 — MALE LIFE TABLE

x	$_nq_x$	l_x	$_nd_x$	$_nL_x$	$_nm_x$	$_na_x$	T_x	r_x	$\dot{e}_x$	$_nM_x$	x
0	0.207247	100000	20725	86406	0.239853	0.3440	3684249	0.0000	36.842	0.239853	0
1	0.114667	79275	9090	291741	0.031159	1.2102	3597844	0.0000	45.384	0.031159	1
5	0.080224	70185	5631	336849	0.016715	2.5000	3306102	0.0073	47.105	0.016750	5
10	0.026909	64555	1737	317642	0.005469	2.0465	2969253	0.0000	45.996	0.005469	10
15	0.029434	62817	1849	309581	0.005973	2.5629	2651611	0.0004	42.211	0.005972	15
20	0.037650	60968	2295	299371	0.007668	2.6163	2342030	0.0001	38.414	0.007667	20
25	0.053346	58673	3130	285749	0.010954	2.5668	2042659	0.0000	34.814	0.010954	25
30	0.059385	55543	3298	269573	0.012236	2.5313	1756910	0.0002	31.631	0.012236	30
35	0.069395	52245	3626	252248	0.014373	2.5244	1487337	0.0000	28.469	0.014373	35
40	0.076565	48619	3723	233924	0.015913	2.5362	1235090	0.0000	25.403	0.015913	40
45	0.095176	44897	4273	214017	0.019966	2.5507	1001166	0.0015	22.299	0.019963	45
50	0.117237	40623	4763	191255	0.024902	2.5091	787149	0.0016	19.377	0.024899	50
55	0.124985	35861	4482	168224	0.026643	2.5278	595894	0.0022	16.617	0.026638	55
60	0.170849	31379	5361	143923	0.037249	2.5804	427670	0.0006	13.629	0.037246	60
65	0.251784	26018	6551	113890	0.057519	2.5272	283748	0.0006	10.906	0.057514	65
70	0.319285	19467	6215	81615	0.076157	2.4708	169858	0.0006	8.725	0.076151	70
75	0.428697	13251	5681	51701	0.109878	2.4377	88243	0.0006	6.659	0.109868	75
80	0.596661	7571	4517	26013	0.173647	2.3788	36542	0.0006	4.827	0.173626	80
85+	*1.000000	3054	3054	10529	0.290016	3.4481	10529	0.0006	3.448	0.289944	85

TABLE 3 — FEMALE LIFE TABLE

x	$_nq_x$	l_x	$_nd_x$	$_nL_x$	$_nm_x$	$_na_x$	T_x	r_x	$\dot{e}_x$	$_nM_x$	x
0	0.181797	100000	18180	88268	0.205960	0.3547	4131953	0.0000	41.320	0.205960	
1	0.107859	81820	8825	302823	0.029143	1.2286	4043685	0.0000	49.422	0.029143	
5	0.071775	72995	5239	351878	0.014889	2.5000	3740862	0.0088	51.248	0.014929	
10	0.024657	67756	1671	333910	0.005003	2.0846	3388983	0.0000	50.017	0.005003	1
15	0.028870	66085	1908	325713	0.005858	2.5291	3055074	0.0000	46.229	0.005858	1
20	0.030184	64178	1937	316168	0.006127	2.5634	2729361	0.0000	42.528	0.006127	2
25	0.040131	62240	2498	305121	0.008186	2.5655	2413193	0.0000	38.772	0.008186	2
30	0.045564	59743	2722	292011	0.009322	2.5380	2108072	0.0006	35.286	0.009322	3
35	0.052509	57021	2994	277692	0.010782	2.5249	1816061	0.0000	31.849	0.010782	3
40	0.057020	54026	3081	262444	0.011738	2.5043	1538369	0.0000	28.474	0.011738	4
45	0.060026	50946	3058	247339	0.012364	2.5835	1275925	0.0013	25.045	0.012362	4
50	0.089918	47888	4306	228918	0.018810	2.5567	1028586	0.0010	21.479	0.018808	5
55	0.097074	43582	4231	207588	0.020380	2.5604	799668	0.0010	18.349	0.020378	5
60	0.140571	39351	5532	183537	0.030139	2.6104	592081	0.0005	15.046	0.030136	6
65	0.211745	33819	7161	151583	0.047242	2.5543	408544	0.0005	12.080	0.047238	6
70	0.277461	26658	7397	114837	0.064410	2.5050	256961	0.0005	9.639	0.064405	7
75	0.380928	19262	7337	77743	0.094380	2.4697	142124	0.0005	7.379	0.094372	7
80	0.530728	11924	6329	43438	0.145694	2.4427	64381	0.0005	5.399	0.145678	8
85+	*1.000000	5596	5596	20943	0.267189	3.7427	20943	0.0005	3.743	0.267130	8

TABLE 4 — OBSERVED AND PROJECTED VITAL RATES

	OBSERVED POPULATION Both Sexes	Males	Females	PROJECTED 1810 Males	1810 Females	1815 Males	1815 Females	1820 Males	1820 Females	STABLE POPULATION Males	Females
RATES PER THOUSAND											
Birth	33.95	36.21	31.86	34.96	30.90	33.83	30.00	32.69	29.07	34.80	31.5
Death	25.69	27.23	24.28	28.46	25.18	28.04	24.86	27.42	24.38	26.35	23.
Increase	8.25	8.98	7.58	6.51	5.73	5.79	5.14	5.27	4.70		8.44
PERCENTAGE											
under 15	27.25	28.38	26.21	30.71	28.43	32.94	30.56	34.04	31.58	33.84	31.
15-64	64.09	64.11	64.07	62.06	62.13	60.01	60.21	59.03	59.38	60.82	61.
65 and over	8.66	7.50	9.72	7.24	9.43	7.05	9.22	6.93	9.04	5.34	6.
DEP. RATIO X 100	56.03	55.98	56.08	61.14	60.94	66.64	66.08	69.40	68.41	64.43	63.

TABLE 5 — POPULATION PROJECTED WITH FIXED—SPECIFIC BIRTH AND DEATH RATES (IN 1000's)

AGE AT LAST BIRTHDAY	BOTH SEXES	1810 MALES	FEMALES	BOTH SEXES	1815 MALES	FEMALES	BOTH SEXES	1820 MALES	FEMALES	AGE AT LAST BIRTHDAY
0-4	373	188	185	372	187	185	370	186	184	0-4
5-9	270	134	136	334	167	167	333	167	166	5-9
10-14	228	114	114	256	127	129	316	158	158	10-14
15-19	230	115	115	222	111	111	250	124	126	15-19
20-24	225	112	113	223	111	112	215	107	108	20-24
25-29	216	106	110	215	106	109	214	106	108	25-29
30-34	205	100	105	206	100	106	205	100	105	30-34
35-39	196	95	101	194	94	100	193	93	100	35-39
40-44	181	87	94	183	88	95	182	87	95	40-44
45-49	170	80	90	169	80	89	170	80	90	45-49
50-54	154	71	83	155	72	83	153	71	82	50-54
55-59	136	62	74	138	63	75	138	63	75	55-59
60-64	118	53	65	119	53	66	120	54	66	60-64
65-69	95	41	54	96	42	54	96	42	54	65-69
70-74	69	29	40	71	30	41	71	30	41	70-74
75-79	47	19	28	45	18	27	47	19	28	75-79
80-84	25	10	15	25	10	15	24	9	15	80-84
85+	11	4	7	11	4	7	11	4	7	85+
TOTAL	2949	1420	1529	3034	1463	1571	3108	1500	1608	TOTAL

TABLE 6 — STANDARDIZED RATES

STANDARD COUNTRIES: STANDARDIZED RATES PER THOUSAND	ENGLAND AND WALES 1961 BOTH SEXES	MALES	FEMALES	UNITED STATES 1960 BOTH SEXES	MALES	FEMALES	MEXICO 1960 BOTH SEXES	MALES	FEMALES
Birth	30.08	32.30*	28.45	30.50	30.16*	29.33	29.23	29.45*	28.46
Death	27.72	33.66*	27.24	26.69	29.43*	24.93	23.70	22.79*	21.65
Increase	2.36	-1.35*	1.22	3.81	0.73*	4.40	5.53	6.66*	6.81

TABLE 7 — MOMENTS AND CUMULANTS

	OBSERVED POP. MALES	FEMALES	STATIONARY POP. MALES	FEMALES	STABLE POP. MALES	FEMALES	OBSERVED BIRTHS	NET MATERNITY FUNCTION	BIRTHS IN STABLE POP.
μ	31.00750	33.03488	31.25267	33.20480	27.65165	29.29264	32.24969	32.25192	31.88920
σ^2	444.7705	481.9180	445.5886	482.1012	405.6277	442.2347	40.98983	40.98171	40.71369
κ_3	4246.477	4010.738	4206.571	3994.847	5154.820	5329.449	27.4785	26.8479	36.5505
κ_4	-143655.	-194844.	-147311.	-197449.	-76976.	-116763.	-1164.604	-1162.209	-1122.320
β_1	0.204951	0.143724	0.200011	0.142425	0.398148	0.328402	0.010964	0.010472	0.019795
β_2	2.273814	2.161042	2.258063	2.150471	2.532155	2.402964	2.306852	2.308003	2.322927
κ	-0.081290	-0.055252	-0.078673	-0.054340	-0.160071	-0.127484	-0.005916	-0.005664	-0.010745

TABLE 8 — RATES FROM AGE DISTRIBUTIONS AND VITAL STATISTICS (Females)

VITAL STATISTICS		THOMPSON AGE RANGE	NRR	1000r	INTERVAL	BOURGEOIS-PICHAT AGE RANGE	NRR	1000b	1000d	1000r	COALE	
GRR	2.257										IBR	23.95
NRR	1.311	0-4	1.07	2.52	26.94	5-29	0.93	22.85	25.45	-2.60	IDR	24.01
TFR	4.624	5-9	0.95	-2.02	26.78	30-54	1.01	24.65	24.27	0.38	IRI	-0.06
GENERATION	32.070	10-14	0.98	-0.73	26.68	55-79	1.01	24.55	24.10	0.46	K1	0.
SEX RATIO	104.881	15-19	1.00	-0.17	26.54	*40-64	1.03	25.61	24.47	1.14	K2	0.

TABLE 9 — LESLIE MATRIX AND ITS SPECTRAL COMPONENTS (Females)

Start Age Interval	ORIGINAL MATRIX SUB-DIAGONAL	ALTERNATIVE FIRST ROWS Projection	Integral	FIRST STABLE MATRIX % IN STABLE POPULATION	FISHER VALUES	REPRODUCTIVE VALUES	SECOND STABLE MATRIX Z_2 FIRST COLUMN	FIRST ROW
0	0.89973	0.00000	0.00000	12.067	1.305	197116	0.1343+0.0459	0.1343+0.0459
5	0.94893	0.00000	0.00000	10.408	1.513	182231	0.1161-0.0818	0.0417+0.1356
10	0.97545	0.01052	0.00000	9.468	1.663	196479	0.0021-0.1498	-0.0808+0.1074
15	0.97069	0.11478	0.02202	8.853	1.765	206077	-0.1302-0.0973	-0.1254-0.0026
20	0.96506	0.30141	0.21884	8.238	1.742	199338	-0.1676+0.0521	-0.0821-0.1008
25	0.95703	0.42819	0.41120	7.621	1.476	162603	-0.0603+0.1784	-0.0108-0.1314
30	0.95096	0.42348	0.48427	6.992	1.025	108381	0.1160+0.1634	0.0339-0.1013
35	0.94509	0.30156	0.40040	6.373	0.543	54124	0.2119+0.0022	0.0365-0.0507
40	0.94245	0.12897	0.22813	5.774	0.183	17409	0.1327-0.1789	0.0166-0.0148
45	0.92552	0.01866	0.03746	5.217	0.024	2116	-0.0701-0.2227	0.0024-0.0018
50	0.90682	0.00035	0.00071	4.628	0.000	36	-0.2279-0.0762	0.0000-0.0000
55+	0.75095			14.362				

TABLE 10 — AGE ANALYSIS AND MISCELLANEOUS RESULTS (Females)

Start Age Interval	OBSERVED POPUL. (IN 100's)	CONTRIBUTIONS OF ROOTS (IN 100's) r_1	r_2, r_3	$r_4 \cdot r_{11}$	AGE-SP. BIRTH RATES	NET MATERNITY FUNCTION	COEFF. OF MATRIX EQUATION	PARAMETERS INTEGRAL	MATRIX	EXP. INCREASE x	$e^{(x+2\frac{1}{2})r}$
0	1510	1596	-9	-77	0.0000	0.0000	0.0000	L(1) 1.04314	1.04318	0	1.0213
5	1204	1376	-130	-42	0.0000	0.0000	0.0000	L(2) 0.52946	0.52807	50	1.5582
10	1181	1252	-152	81	0.0000	0.0000	0.0090	0.74311	0.72785	55	1.6254
15	1168	1171	-45	42	0.0055	0.0180	0.0956	R(1) 0.00845	0.00845	60	1.6955
20	1144	1089	121	-66	0.0548	0.1732	0.2437	R(2) -0.01833	-0.02124	65	1.7686
25	1102	1008	205	-111	0.1029	0.3141	0.3341	0.19035	0.18863	70	1.8450
30	1058	925	118	16	0.1212	0.3540	0.3162	C(1)	13223	75	1.9245
35	997	843	-84	239	0.1002	0.2784	0.2141	C(2)	-20432	80	2.0076
40	952	764	-235	424	0.0571	0.1499	0.0865		-50495	85	2.0942
45	891	690	-196	398	0.0094	0.0232	0.0118	2P/Y 33.0089	33.3095	90	2.1845
50	820	612	16	192	0.0002	0.0004	0.0002	DELTA 7.4753		95	2.2788
55+	2836	1899								100	2.3771

TABLE 1 — DATA

AGE AT LAST BIRTHDAY	POPULATION Both Sexes	Males Number	%	Females Number	%	BIRTHS By Age of Mother	DEATHS Both Sexes	Males	Females	AGE AT LAST BIRTHDAY
0	61007	30750	2.3	30257	2.1	0	15867	8636	7231	0
1-4	220943	110328	8.2	110615	7.6	0	10318	5319	4999	1-4
5-9	233542	116595	8.7	116947	8.1	0	2139	1099	1040	5-9
10-14	231451	115506	8.6	115945	8.0	0	1291	649	642	10-14
15-19	234668	116283	8.7	118385	8.2	1395	1079	535	544	15-19
20-24	218419	107469	8.0	110950	7.6	11616	1692	934	758	20-24
25-29	209600	103126	7.7	106474	7.3	23497	1830	1017	813	25-29
30-34	199245	97353	7.3	101892	7.0	24796	2092	1166	926	30-34
35-39	189245	92163	6.9	97082	6.7	20463	2113	1165	948	35-39
40-44	179170	86292	6.4	92878	6.4	11079	2440	1395	1045	40-44
45-49	164104	77359	5.8	86745	6.0	1704	2796	1545	1251	45-49
50-54	149629	69415	5.2	80214	5.5	0	2631	1428	1203	50-54
55-59	134406	61254	4.6	73152	5.0	0	3187	1641	1546	55-59
60-64	114652	51181	3.8	63471	4.4	0	4044	2055	1989	60-64
65-69	94784	41643	3.1	53141	3.7	0	4403	2138	2265	65-69
70-74	72388	30966	2.3	41422	2.9		4720	2212	2508	70-74
75-79	47789	19656	1.5	28133	1.9		4868	2168	2700	75-79
80-84	25956	10175	0.8	15781	1.1	48417 M.	4331	1854	2477	80-84
85+	11926	4124	0.3	7802	0.5	46133 F.	3177	1200	1977	85+
TOTAL	2792924	1341638		1451286		94550	75018	38156	36862	TOTAL

TABLE 2 — MALE LIFE TABLE

x	nq_x	l_x	nd_x	nL_x	nm_x	na_x	T_x	r_x	$\dot{e}_x$	nM_x
0	0.238415	100000	23841	84892	0.280846	0.3663	3478394	0.0000	34.784	0.280846
1	0.170276	76159	12968	268985	0.048211	1.2510	3393502	0.0000	44.558	0.048211
5	0.045952	63191	2904	308693	0.009407	2.5000	3124517	0.0025	49.446	0.009426
10	0.027675	60287	1668	296936	0.005619	2.3040	2815824	0.0000	46.707	0.005619
15	0.022760	58618	1334	289917	0.004602	2.6205	2518888	0.0016	42.971	0.004601
20	0.042592	57284	2440	280594	0.008695	2.6115	2228971	0.0041	38.911	0.008691
25	0.048144	54844	2640	267745	0.009862	2.5471	1948377	0.0000	35.526	0.009862
30	0.058161	52204	3036	253507	0.011977	2.5256	1680632	0.0000	32.194	0.011977
35	0.061296	49168	3014	238419	0.012641	2.5382	1427125	0.0000	29.026	0.012641
40	0.077772	46154	3589	222012	0.016168	2.5601	1188706	0.0013	25.755	0.016166
45	0.095138	42564	4050	202736	0.019974	2.5093	966694	0.0026	22.711	0.019972
50	0.097872	38515	3770	183218	0.020574	2.5179	763958	0.0016	19.835	0.020572
55	0.125849	34745	4373	163166	0.026799	2.5849	580740	0.0023	16.714	0.026790
60	0.182766	30373	5551	138252	0.040152	2.5479	417574	0.0001	13.748	0.040152
65	0.227607	24822	5650	110038	0.051342	2.5096	279322	0.0001	11.253	0.051341
70	0.303120	19172	5811	81354	0.071434	2.5038	169283	0.0001	8.830	0.071433
75	0.430775	13361	5755	52180	0.110299	2.4593	87930	0.0001	6.581	0.110297
80	0.616208	7605	4686	25719	0.182214	2.3739	35750	0.0001	4.701	0.182211
85+	*1.000000	2919	2919	10031	0.290991	3.4365	10031	0.0001	3.437	0.290980

TABLE 3 — FEMALE LIFE TABLE

x	nq_x	l_x	nd_x	nL_x	nm_x	na_x	T_x	r_x	$\dot{e}_x$	nM_x
0	0.208064	100000	20806	87061	0.238986	0.3781	3902499	0.0000	39.025	0.238986
1	0.160959	79194	12747	282057	0.045193	1.2764	3815438	0.0000	48.179	0.045193
5	0.043392	66447	2883	325025	0.008871	2.5000	3533381	0.0030	53.176	0.008893
10	0.027281	63563	1734	313174	0.005537	2.3224	3208356	0.0000	50.475	0.005537
15	0.022719	61829	1405	305697	0.004595	2.5441	2895182	0.0000	46.825	0.004595
20	0.033617	60425	2031	297208	0.006835	2.5804	2589486	0.0042	42.855	0.006832
25	0.037477	58393	2188	286593	0.007636	2.5444	2292278	0.0007	39.256	0.007636
30	0.044444	56205	2498	274857	0.009088	2.5310	2005685	0.0003	35.685	0.009088
35	0.047672	53707	2560	262197	0.009765	2.5246	1730828	0.0000	32.227	0.009765
40	0.054753	51147	2800	248900	0.011251	2.5600	1468632	0.0000	28.714	0.011251
45	0.069629	48346	3366	233409	0.014422	2.5281	1219732	0.0009	25.229	0.014422
50	0.072338	44980	3254	216938	0.014999	2.5533	986323	0.0009	21.928	0.014997
55	0.100612	41726	4198	198596	0.021139	2.6097	769385	0.0016	18.439	0.021134
60	0.145625	37528	5465	174391	0.031338	2.5758	570789	0.0001	15.210	0.031337
65	0.192932	32063	6186	145131	0.042623	2.5455	396398	0.0001	12.363	0.042622
70	0.263443	25877	6817	112589	0.060549	2.5362	251267	0.0001	9.710	0.060548
75	0.386744	19060	7371	76804	0.095975	2.4910	138678	0.0001	7.276	0.095973
80	0.555889	11689	6498	41395	0.156964	2.4301	61873	0.0001	5.294	0.156961
85+	1.000000	5191	5191	20478	0.253487	3.9450	20478	0.0001	3.945	0.253396

TABLE 4 — OBSERVED AND PROJECTED VITAL RATES

	OBSERVED POPULATION Both Sexes	Males	Females	PROJECTED POPULATION 1815 Males	Females	1820 Males	Females	1825 Males	Females	STABLE POPULATION Males	Females
RATES PER THOUSAND											
Birth	33.85	36.09	31.79	35.33	31.23	34.69	30.75	33.83	30.07	35.19	31.7
Death	26.86	28.44	25.40	29.88	26.56	29.43	26.20	28.94	25.82	28.48	25.0
Increase	6.99	7.65	6.39	5.45	4.67	5.25	4.55	4.89	4.24		6.71
PERCENTAGE											
under 15	26.74	27.82	25.75	29.55	27.44	31.27	29.12	32.43	30.26	32.19	30.4
15-64	64.20	64.24	64.17	62.82	62.78	61.31	61.29	60.28	60.31	61.78	61.
65 and over	9.05	7.94	10.08	7.63	9.78	7.43	9.59	7.29	9.43	6.03	7.
DEP. RATIO X 100	55.76	55.66	55.84	59.17	59.30	63.12	63.16	65.90	65.81	61.86	61.

TABLE 1 DATA

AGE AT LAST BIRTHDAY	POPULATION BOTH SEXES	MALES Number	%	FEMALES Number	%	BIRTHS BY AGE OF MOTHER	DEATHS BOTH SEXES	MALES	FEMALES	AGE AT LAST BIRTHDAY
0	68790	34837	2.3	33953	2.1	0	14926	8181	6745	0
1-4	236028	117662	7.7	118366	7.2	0	8062	4179	3883	1-4
5-9	259084	128989	8.5	130095	7.9	0	2500	1276	1224	5-9
10-14	258499	128901	8.5	129598	7.9	0	1002	513	489	10-14
15-19	260418	128949	8.5	131469	8.0	1189	1352	686	666	15-19
20-24	242417	119663	7.9	122754	7.5	12707	1694	937	757	20-24
25-29	234120	114725	7.5	119395	7.3	24381	1954	1076	878	25-29
30-34	225038	109919	7.2	115119	7.0	27532	1983	1071	912	30-34
35-39	213796	103737	6.8	110059	6.7	22918	2381	1326	1055	35-39
40-44	200707	96244	6.3	104463	6.4	12657	2828	1526	1302	40-44
45-49	187607	88729	5.8	98878	6.0	2123	2481	1351	1130	45-49
50-54	175159	81760	5.4	93399	5.7	0	2882	1553	1329	50-54
55-59	155487	71116	4.7	84371	5.1	0	3635	1926	1709	55-59
60-64	136430	61389	4.0	75041	4.6	0	4054	2050	2004	60-64
65-69	114800	50809	3.3	63991	3.9	0	4564	2225	2339	65-69
70-74	88441	38232	2.5	50209	3.1		5303	2466	2837	70-74
75-79	60800	25599	1.7	35201	2.1		6013	2716	3297	75-79
80-84	32526	13194	0.9	19332	1.2	53020 M.	4826	2094	2732	80-84
85+	14721	5376	0.4	9345	0.6	50487 F.	3979	1533	2446	85+
TOTAL	3164868	1519830		1645038		103507	76419	38685	37734	TOTAL

TABLE 2 MALE FEMALE BLE

x	nq_x	l_x	nd_x	nL_x	nm_x	na_x	T_x	r_x	$\mathring{e}_x$	nM_x	x
0	0.204096	100000	20410	86910	0.234837	0.3586	3908038	0.0000	39.080	0.234837	0
1	0.129368	79590	10296	289902	0.035517	1.2359	3821128	0.0000	48.010	0.035517	1
5	0.048202	69294	3340	338119	0.009879	2.5000	3531226	0.0024	50.960	0.009892	5
10	0.019683	65954	1298	326182	0.003980	2.2366	3193107	0.0000	48.414	0.003980	10
15	0.026277	64656	1699	319265	0.005322	2.6376	2866925	0.0020	44.341	0.005320	15
20	0.038444	62957	2420	308957	0.007834	2.5926	2547660	0.0041	40.467	0.007830	20
25	0.045831	60536	2774	295814	0.009379	2.5246	2238704	0.0000	36.981	0.009379	25
30	0.047581	57762	2748	282071	0.009744	2.5482	1942890	0.0000	33.636	0.009744	30
35	0.061991	55014	3410	266789	0.012783	2.5725	1660818	0.0005	30.189	0.012782	35
40	0.076262	51603	3935	248196	0.015856	2.5045	1394029	0.0006	27.014	0.015856	40
45	0.073344	47668	3496	229615	0.015226	2.5046	1145833	0.0002	24.038	0.015226	45
50	0.090830	44172	4012	211163	0.019000	2.5834	916219	0.0023	20.742	0.018995	50
55	0.127037	40160	5102	188334	0.027089	2.5570	705056	0.0021	17.556	0.027083	55
60	0.154270	35058	5408	161927	0.033400	2.5293	516721	0.0020	14.739	0.033394	60
65	0.197736	29649	5863	133843	0.043803	2.5432	354795	0.0020	11.966	0.043791	65
70	0.278445	23787	6623	102650	0.064523	2.5414	220951	0.0020	9.289	0.064501	70
75	0.418359	17163	7180	67654	0.106135	2.4705	118301	0.0020	6.893	0.106098	75
80	0.561640	9983	5607	35313	0.158773	2.3958	50647	0.0020	5.073	0.158709	80
85+	*1.000000	4376	4376	15334	0.285389	3.5040	15334	0.0020	3.504	0.285156	85+

TABLE 3 MALE FEMALE BLE

x	nq_x	l_x	nd_x	nL_x	nm_x	na_x	T_x	r_x	$\mathring{e}_x$	nM_x	x
0	0.176544	100000	17654	88869	0.198657	0.3695	4332356	0.0000	43.324	0.198657	0
1	0.120389	82346	9914	302195	0.032805	1.2576	4243487	0.0000	51.533	0.032805	1
5	0.045892	72432	3324	353850	0.009394	2.5000	3941292	0.0027	54.414	0.009409	5
10	0.018671	69108	1290	341975	0.003773	2.2373	3587442	0.0000	51.911	0.003773	10
15	0.025025	67818	1697	334995	0.005066	2.5882	3245467	0.0006	47.856	0.005066	15
20	0.030386	66121	2009	325709	0.006168	2.5641	2910472	0.0034	44.018	0.006167	20
25	0.036114	64111	2315	314850	0.007354	2.5353	2584763	0.0000	40.317	0.007354	25
30	0.038854	61796	2401	303075	0.007922	2.5405	2269913	0.0000	36.732	0.007922	30
35	0.046841	59395	2782	290233	0.009586	2.5764	1966838	0.0000	33.115	0.009586	35
40	0.060443	56613	3422	274546	0.012464	2.5105	1676606	0.0000	29.615	0.012464	40
45	0.055555	53191	2955	258575	0.011428	2.5024	1402060	0.0000	26.359	0.011428	45
50	0.068800	50236	3456	242865	0.014231	2.5942	1143485	0.0011	22.762	0.014229	50
55	0.096575	46780	4518	222989	0.020260	2.5851	900620	0.0017	19.252	0.020256	55
60	0.125435	42262	5301	198410	0.026718	2.5665	677631	0.0039	16.034	0.026705	60
65	0.167994	36961	6209	169769	0.036574	2.5786	479222	0.0039	12.966	0.036552	65
70	0.248569	30752	7644	135182	0.056545	2.5698	309452	0.0039	10.063	0.056504	70
75	0.379501	23108	8769	93563	0.093728	2.4940	174270	0.0039	7.542	0.093662	75
80	0.515543	14338	7392	52275	0.141405	2.4486	80708	0.0039	5.629	0.141320	80
85+	1.000000	6946	6946	28432	0.244311	4.0931	28432	0.0039	4.093	0.261743	85+

TABLE 4 OBSERVED AND PROJECTED TOTAL RATES

	OBSERVED POPULATION BOTH SEXES	MALES	FEMALES	PROJECTED POPULATION 1820 MALES	FEMALES	1825 MALES	FEMALES	1830 MALES	FEMALES	STABLE POPULATION MALES	FEMALES
RATES PER THOUSAND											
Birth	32.70	34.89	30.69	33.74	29.84	32.80	29.15	31.79	28.38	33.48	30.60
Death	24.15	25.45	22.94	27.17	24.37	26.68	24.03	26.07	23.56	24.65	21.78
Increase	8.56	9.43	7.75	6.58	5.47	6.12	5.12	5.72	4.82		8.8239
PERCENTAGE											
under 15	25.99	27.00	25.05	29.28	27.19	31.50	29.30	33.09	30.84	32.72	31.22
15-64	64.18	64.23	64.13	62.21	62.19	60.25	60.32	58.82	58.97	61.04	61.12
65 and over	9.84	8.76	10.83	8.51	10.62	8.25	10.38	8.09	10.20	6.23	7.66
DEP. RATIO X 100	55.81	55.68	55.94	60.74	60.80	65.98	65.77	70.00	69.58	63.81	63.62

TABLE 1 — DATA

AGE AT LAST BIRTHDAY	BOTH SEXES	POPULATION MALES Number	%	FEMALES Number	%	BIRTHS BY AGE OF MOTHER	DEATHS BOTH SEXES	MALES	FEMALES	AGE AT LAST BIRTHDAY
0	72803	36910	2.1	35893	1.9	0	15048	8233	6815	0
1-4	261912	130728	7.6	131184	7.1	0	8695	4511	4184	1-4
5-9	290315	145361	8.4	144954	7.9	0	1750	917	833	5-9
10-14	287474	143659	8.3	143815	7.8	0	1400	720	680	10-14
15-19	289570	144045	8.4	145525	7.9	1222	1387	710	677	15-19
20-24	270215	132900	7.7	137315	7.5	12288	1966	1081	885	20-24
25-29	260257	127860	7.4	132397	7.2	26471	1926	1045	881	25-29
30-34	251555	123103	7.2	128452	7.0	30657	2276	1241	1035	30-34
35-39	238145	115923	6.7	122222	6.6	25928	2767	1449	1318	35-39
40-44	226590	109442	6.4	117148	6.4	15952	2483	1299	1184	40-44
45-49	216430	103578	6.0	112852	6.1	2354	2738	1520	1218	45-49
50-54	196186	92096	5.4	104090	5.6	0	3381	1860	1521	50-54
55-59	178159	82499	4.8	95660	5.2	0	3703	1982	1721	55-59
60-64	158423	72479	4.2	85944	4.7	0	4146	2080	2066	60-64
65-69	133058	59968	3.5	73090	4.0	0	5095	2491	2604	65-69
70-74	104843	46640	2.7	58203	3.2		6476	3035	3441	70-74
75-79	70805	30839	1.8	39966	2.2		6546	3033	3513	75-79
80-84	38921	16237	0.9	22684	1.2	58863 M.	6069	2754	3315	80-84
85+	18462	7071	0.4	11391	0.6	56009 F.	4683	1902	2781	85+
TOTAL	3564123	1721338		1842785		114872	82535	41863	40672	TOTAL

TABLE 2 — MALE LIFE TABLE

x	nq_x	l_x	nd_x	nL_x	nm_x	na_x	T_x	r_x	$\dot{e}_x$	nM_x	x
0	0.195253	100000	19525	87536	0.223056	0.3616	4076001	0.0000	40.760	0.223056	0
1	0.126031	80475	10142	293923	0.034507	1.2417	3988465	0.0000	49.562	0.034507	1
5	0.030979	70332	2179	346215	0.006293	2.5000	3694542	0.0029	52.530	0.006308	5
10	0.024741	68153	1686	336435	0.005012	2.4309	3348328	0.0000	49.129	0.005012	10
15	0.024365	66467	1620	328476	0.004930	2.6159	3011892	0.0021	45.314	0.004929	15
20	0.039897	64848	2587	317953	0.008137	2.5704	2683417	0.0046	41.380	0.008134	20
25	0.040056	62261	2494	305142	0.008173	2.5295	2365464	0.0000	37.993	0.008173	25
30	0.049198	59767	2940	291680	0.010081	2.5673	2060322	0.0000	34.473	0.010081	30
35	0.060611	56826	3444	275549	0.012500	2.5083	1768642	0.0000	31.124	0.012500	35
40	0.057642	53382	3077	259243	0.011869	2.5082	1493093	0.0000	27.970	0.011869	40
45	0.070878	50305	3565	242907	0.014678	2.5831	1233850	0.0021	24.527	0.014675	45
50	0.096260	46739	4499	222704	0.020202	2.5567	990943	0.0030	21.201	0.020196	50
55	0.113375	42240	4789	199338	0.024025	2.5227	768238	0.0000	18.187	0.024025	55
60	0.134095	37451	5022	174979	0.028701	2.5553	568900	0.0008	15.190	0.028698	60
65	0.188748	32429	6121	147335	0.041544	2.5802	393921	0.0008	12.147	0.041539	65
70	0.280467	26308	7379	113375	0.065082	2.5379	246586	0.0008	9.373	0.065073	70
75	0.394212	18930	7462	75864	0.098364	2.4828	133211	0.0008	7.037	0.098350	75
80	0.589643	11467	6762	39859	0.169642	2.4151	57347	0.0008	5.001	0.169612	80
85+	*1.000000	4706	4706	17488	0.269076	3.7164	17488	0.0008	3.716	0.268986	85

TABLE 3 — FEMALE LIFE TABLE

x	nq_x	l_x	nd_x	nL_x	nm_x	na_x	T_x	r_x	$\dot{e}_x$	nM_x	x
0	0.169635	100000	16964	89343	0.189870	0.3718	4474771	0.0000	44.748	0.189870	
1	0.117332	83036	9743	305473	0.031894	1.2623	4385428	0.0000	52.813	0.031894	
5	0.028245	73294	2070	361293	0.005730	2.5000	4079955	0.0035	55.666	0.005747	10
10	0.023359	71223	1664	351860	0.004728	2.4411	3718662	0.0000	52.211	0.004728	15
15	0.023000	69560	1600	343902	0.004652	2.5642	3366802	0.0000	48.402	0.004652	20
20	0.031732	67960	2157	334524	0.006446	2.5535	3022900	0.0034	44.481	0.006445	25
25	0.032734	65803	2154	323707	0.006654	2.5347	2688376	0.0000	40.855	0.006654	30
30	0.039519	63649	2515	312179	0.008057	2.5875	2364670	0.0000	37.151	0.008057	35
35	0.052515	61134	3210	297715	0.010784	2.5220	2052491	0.0000	33.574	0.010784	40
40	0.049278	57924	2854	282416	0.010107	2.4770	1754776	0.0004	30.295	0.010107	4!
45	0.052581	55069	2896	268280	0.010793	2.5596	1472360	0.0021	26.737	0.010793	50
50	0.070574	52174	3682	251930	0.014616	2.5726	1204081	0.0007	23.078	0.014612	5!
55	0.086188	48492	4179	232291	0.017992	2.5675	952150	0.0018	19.635	0.017991	6!
60	0.113650	44312	5036	209443	0.024045	2.5939	719859	0.0018	16.245	0.024039	6!
65	0.164216	39276	6450	180974	0.035639	2.6113	510416	0.0018	12.996	0.035627	7!
70	0.258367	32826	8481	143412	0.059139	2.5570	329442	0.0018	10.036	0.059121	7!
75	0.360268	24345	8771	99750	0.087927	2.4945	186030	0.0018	7.641	0.087900	8
80	0.529678	15574	8249	56431	0.146186	2.4635	86280	0.0018	5.540	0.146138	8
85+	1.000000	7325	7325	29849	0.245397	4.0750	29849	0.0018	4.075	0.244141	

TABLE 4 — OBSERVED AND PROJECTED VITAL RATES

	OBSERVED POPULATION BOTH SEXES	MALES	FEMALES	PROJECTED POPULATION 1825 MALES	FEMALES	1830 MALES	FEMALES	1835 MALES	FEMALES	STABLE POPULATION MALES	FEMAL
RATES PER THOUSAND											
Birth	32.23	34.20	30.39	32.97	29.46	31.99	28.71	30.98	27.91	32.80	30.2
Death	23.16	24.32	22.07	25.94	23.38	25.35	22.93	24.78	22.50	23.37	20.8
Increase	9.07	9.88	8.32	7.04	6.08	6.64	5.78	6.20	5.41	9.433	
PERCENTAGE											
under 15	25.60	26.53	24.74	28.99	27.08	31.23	29.26	32.95	30.91	32.62	31.3
15-64	64.13	64.13	64.12	61.96	62.03	59.98	60.09	58.52	58.66	60.90	60.9
65 and over	10.27	9.34	11.14	9.05	10.89	8.79	10.65	8.54	10.42	6.48	7.7
DEP. RATIO X 100	55.94	55.93	55.96	61.40	61.20	66.72	66.42	70.90	70.46	64.21	64.

TABLE 1 — DATA

AGE AT LAST BIRTHDAY	POPULATION BOTH SEXES	MALES Number	%	FEMALES Number	%	BIRTHS BY AGE OF MOTHER	DEATHS BOTH SEXES	MALES	FEMALES	AGE AT LAST BIRTHDAY
0	84490	42518	2.1	41972	2.0	0	15069	8228	6841	0
1-4	304882	153065	7.6	151817	7.1	0	6530	3404	3126	1-4
5-9	335970	168468	8.4	167502	7.9	0	2876	1493	1383	5-9
10-14	330013	165166	8.2	164847	7.7	0	1434	737	697	10-14
15-19	331462	165258	8.2	166204	7.8	1001	1716	841	875	15-19
20-24	313000	154687	7.7	158313	7.4	13100	2008	1093	915	20-24
25-29	300987	148355	7.4	152632	7.2	29167	2190	1227	963	25-29
30-34	289393	141587	7.1	147806	6.9	34257	2775	1475	1300	30-34
35-39	278140	135578	6.8	142562	6.7	31700	2544	1303	1241	35-39
40-44	265650	128836	6.4	136814	6.4	18205	2783	1483	1300	40-44
45-49	243690	116388	5.8	127302	6.0	2296	3213	1769	1444	45-49
50-54	225960	106673	5.3	119287	5.6	10	3458	1892	1566	50-54
55-59	207515	96778	4.8	110737	5.2	0	3688	1960	1728	55-59
60-64	184149	84731	4.2	99418	4.7	0	4565	2304	2261	60-64
65-69	157698	71732	3.6	85966	4.0	0	5986	2899	3087	65-69
70-74	124208	55588	2.8	68620	3.2		6799	3287	3512	70-74
75-79	86584	37861	1.9	48723	2.3		7942	3706	4236	75-79
80-84	48663	20694	1.0	27969	1.3	66500 M.	6990	3139	3851	80-84
85+	23717	9299	0.5	14418	0.7	63236 F.	6119	2535	3584	85+
TOTAL	4136171	2003262		2132909		129736	88685	44775	43910	TOTAL

TABLE 2 — MALE LIFE TABLE

x	$_nq_x$	l_x	$_nd_x$	$_nL_x$	$_nm_x$	$_na_x$	T_x	r_x	$\overset{\circ}{e}_x$	$_nM_x$	x
0	0.171467	100000	17147	88605	0.193518	0.3355	4423599	0.0000	44.236	0.193518	0
1	0.083735	82853	6938	311963	0.022239	1.1965	4334994	0.0000	52.321	0.022239	1
5	0.043259	75916	3284	371367	0.008843	2.5000	4023030	0.0059	52.994	0.008862	5
10	0.022046	72631	1601	358842	0.004462	2.3051	3651663	0.0000	50.277	0.004462	10
15	0.025141	71030	1786	350855	0.005090	2.5939	3292821	0.0013	46.358	0.005089	15
20	0.034748	69244	2406	340400	0.007068	2.5800	2941966	0.0039	42.487	0.007066	20
25	0.040538	66838	2710	327595	0.008271	2.5653	2601567	0.0003	38.923	0.008271	25
30	0.050771	64129	3256	312535	0.010418	2.5094	2273971	0.0000	35.459	0.010418	30
35	0.046926	60873	2857	297222	0.009611	2.4995	1961436	0.0000	32.222	0.009611	35
40	0.056009	58016	3249	282200	0.011515	2.5742	1664214	0.0034	28.685	0.011511	40
45	0.073297	54767	4014	264021	0.015204	2.5551	1382014	0.0040	25.234	0.015199	45
50	0.084953	50753	4312	243082	0.017737	2.5226	1117993	0.0008	22.028	0.017736	50
55	0.096489	46441	4481	221220	0.020256	2.5485	874911	0.0020	18.839	0.020253	55
60	0.127613	41960	5355	196884	0.027197	2.5878	653690	0.0013	15.579	0.027192	60
65	0.184055	36605	6737	166676	0.040422	2.5730	456806	0.0013	12.479	0.040414	65
70	0.258337	29868	7716	130460	0.059145	2.5531	290131	0.0013	9.714	0.059131	70
75	0.392993	22152	8706	88917	0.097907	2.4909	159670	0.0013	7.208	0.097884	75
80	0.545583	13446	7336	48351	0.151726	2.4263	70753	0.0013	5.262	0.151686	80
85+	*1.000000	6110	6110	22402	0.272753	3.6663	22402	0.0013	3.666	0.272610	85+

TABLE 3 — FEMALE LIFE TABLE

x	$_nq_x$	l_x	$_nd_x$	$_nL_x$	$_nm_x$	$_na_x$	T_x	r_x	$\overset{\circ}{e}_x$	$_nM_x$	x
0	0.147310	100000	14731	90380	0.162990	0.3470	4803439	0.0000	48.034	0.162990	0
1	0.077896	85269	6642	322578	0.020591	1.2151	4713059	0.0000	55.273	0.020591	1
5	0.040363	78627	3174	385201	0.008239	2.5000	4390481	0.0060	55.839	0.008257	5
10	0.020905	75453	1577	373062	0.004228	2.3344	4005280	0.0000	53.083	0.004228	10
15	0.025988	73876	1920	364679	0.005265	2.5513	3632218	0.0000	49.166	0.005265	15
20	0.028494	71956	2050	354707	0.005780	2.5256	3267539	0.0028	45.410	0.005780	20
25	0.031073	69906	2172	344279	0.006309	2.5830	2912832	0.0001	41.668	0.006309	25
30	0.043046	67734	2916	331501	0.008795	2.5421	2568554	0.0000	37.921	0.008795	30
35	0.042597	64818	2761	317180	0.008705	2.4974	2237052	0.0000	34.513	0.008705	35
40	0.046427	62057	2881	303187	0.009503	2.5365	1919872	0.0016	30.937	0.009502	40
45	0.055186	59176	3266	287855	0.011345	2.5430	1616686	0.0024	27.320	0.011343	45
50	0.063589	55910	3555	270802	0.013129	2.5394	1328831	0.0007	23.767	0.013128	50
55	0.075209	52355	3938	252278	0.015608	2.5884	1058029	0.0018	20.209	0.015605	55
60	0.107946	48417	5226	229687	0.022755	2.6276	805750	0.0031	16.642	0.022742	60
65	0.165305	43191	7140	198726	0.035927	2.5871	576063	0.0031	13.338	0.035910	65
70	0.227725	36051	8210	160319	0.051209	2.5716	377337	0.0031	10.467	0.051180	70
75	0.357717	27841	9959	114487	0.086991	2.5179	217018	0.0031	7.795	0.086940	75
80	0.506981	17882	9066	65810	0.137758	2.4737	102531	0.0031	5.734	0.137688	80
85+	1.000000	8816	8816	36721	0.240086	4.1652	36721	0.0031	4.165	0.248579	85+

TABLE 4 — OBSERVED AND PROJECTED VITAL RATES

	OBSERVED POPULATION BOTH SEXES	MALES	FEMALES	PROJECTED 1830 MALES	FEMALES	1835 MALES	FEMALES	1840 MALES	FEMALES	STABLE MALES	FEMALES
RATES PER THOUSAND											
Birth	31.37	33.20	29.65	31.77	28.54	30.58	27.63	29.44	26.74	31.36	29.24
Death	21.44	22.35	20.59	23.56	21.62	23.03	21.22	22.45	20.76	20.81	18.70
Increase	9.92	10.84	9.06	8.20	6.92	7.55	6.41	7.00	5.97	10.5459	
PERCENTAGE											
under 15	25.52	26.42	24.67	29.17	27.28	31.64	29.68	33.33	31.35	32.87	31.74
15-64	63.83	63.84	63.81	61.47	61.53	59.28	59.40	57.85	58.00	60.52	60.52
65 and over	10.66	9.74	11.52	9.36	11.20	9.08	10.91	8.82	10.65	6.62	7.75
DEP. RATIO X 100	56.68	56.64	56.71	62.68	62.53	68.69	68.35	72.86	72.42	65.24	65.24

TABLE 1 — DATA

AGE AT LAST BIRTHDAY	POPULATION BOTH SEXES	MALES Number	MALES %	FEMALES Number	FEMALES %	BIRTHS BY AGE OF MOTHER	DEATHS BOTH SEXES	DEATHS MALES	DEATHS FEMALES	AGE AT LAST BIRTHDAY
0	83373	42086	2.1	41287	2.0	0	17007	9338	7669	0
1-4	302513	151316	7.7	151197	7.1	0	9268	4819	4449	1-4
5-9	334071	167258	8.5	166813	7.9	0	2298	1196	1102	5-9
10-14	326820	163086	8.3	163734	7.7	0	1543	802	741	10-14
15-19	329786	163844	8.3	165942	7.8	949	1635	810	825	15-19
20-24	311103	153522	7.8	157581	7.4	12515	1936	1082	854	20-24
25-29	295760	144633	7.3	151127	7.1	28308	2370	1289	1081	25-29
30-34	284489	138418	7.0	146071	6.9	35549	2210	1140	1070	30-34
35-39	275175	133166	6.8	142009	6.7	30675	2476	1289	1187	35-39
40-44	253750	121234	6.2	132516	6.3	15394	2836	1489	1347	40-44
45-49	237774	112475	5.7	125299	5.9	2381	2876	1609	1267	45-49
50-54	222819	104449	5.3	118370	5.6	88	2969	1584	1385	50-54
55-59	203389	94255	4.8	109134	5.2	0	3518	1851	1667	55-59
60-64	182320	83607	4.2	98713	4.7	0	4524	2285	2239	60-64
65-69	155793	70535	3.6	85258	4.0	0	5454	2699	2755	65-69
70-74	124458	55471	2.8	68987	3.3		7041	3351	3690	70-74
75-79	87478	38319	1.9	49159	2.3		7705	3578	4127	75-79
80-84	49659	21065	1.1	28594	1.4	64533 M.	7152	3171	3981	80-84
85+	25047	9898	0.5	15149	0.7	61326 F.	7179	3037	4142	85+
TOTAL	4085577	1968637		2116940		125859	91997	46419	45578	TOTAL

TABLE 2 — MALE LIFE TABLE

x	nq_x	l_x	nd_x	nL_x	nm_x	na_x	T_x	r_x	$\mathring{e}_x$	nM_x	x
0	0.194093	100000	19409	87477	0.221879	0.3548	4210956	0.0000	42.110	0.221879	
1	0.117058	80591	9434	296220	0.031847	1.2288	4123479	0.0000	51.166	0.031847	
5	0.035017	71157	2492	349555	0.007128	2.5000	3827259	0.0047	53.786	0.007151	
10	0.024277	68665	1667	338980	0.004918	2.3931	3477703	0.0000	50.647	0.004918	10
15	0.024427	66998	1637	331024	0.004944	2.5763	3138723	0.0007	46.848	0.004944	15
20	0.034675	65362	2266	321374	0.007052	2.6024	2807699	0.0055	42.956	0.007048	20
25	0.043597	63095	2751	308634	0.008913	2.5128	2486325	0.0020	39.406	0.008912	25
30	0.040349	60344	2435	295632	0.008236	2.4990	2177691	0.0000	36.088	0.008236	30
35	0.047297	57910	2739	282879	0.009682	2.5651	1882058	0.0034	32.500	0.009680	35
40	0.059640	55171	3290	267803	0.012287	2.5535	1599180	0.0047	28.986	0.012282	40
45	0.069073	51880	3584	250492	0.014306	2.5140	1331377	0.0009	25.663	0.014305	45
50	0.073104	48297	3531	232785	0.015167	2.5362	1080884	0.0018	22.380	0.015165	50
55	0.093765	44766	4197	213684	0.019643	2.5829	848100	0.0021	18.945	0.019638	55
60	0.128180	40569	5200	190259	0.027332	2.5800	634415	0.0004	15.638	0.027330	60
65	0.175139	35368	6194	161872	0.038267	2.5833	444157	0.0004	12.558	0.038265	65
70	0.263159	29174	7677	127080	0.060414	2.5525	282284	0.0004	9.676	0.060410	70
75	0.378229	21497	8131	87070	0.093380	2.4894	155204	0.0004	7.220	0.093374	75
80	0.543441	13366	7264	48248	0.150547	2.4418	68134	0.0004	5.098	0.150533	80
85+	*1.000000	6102	6102	19885	0.306878	3.2586	19885	0.0004	3.259	0.306830	85

TABLE 3 — FEMALE LIFE TABLE

x	nq_x	l_x	nd_x	nL_x	nm_x	na_x	T_x	r_x	$\mathring{e}_x$	nM_x	x
0	0.166199	100000	16620	89475	0.185749	0.3667	4609653	0.0000	46.097	0.185749	
1	0.108895	83380	9080	308568	0.029425	1.2519	4520178	0.0000	54.212	0.029425	
5	0.032391	74300	2407	365485	0.006585	2.5000	4211610	0.0048	56.684	0.006606	
10	0.022366	71894	1608	355307	0.004526	2.4118	3846124	0.0000	53.497	0.004526	10
15	0.024556	70286	1726	347161	0.004972	2.5273	3490817	0.0000	49.666	0.004972	15
20	0.026753	68560	1834	338343	0.005421	2.5703	3143656	0.0036	45.853	0.005419	20
25	0.035148	66726	2345	327865	0.007153	2.5428	2805314	0.0008	42.043	0.007153	25
30	0.035972	64380	2316	316153	0.007325	2.5177	2477448	0.0000	38.481	0.007325	30
35	0.040958	62064	2542	304099	0.008359	2.5521	2161296	0.0012	34.823	0.008359	35
40	0.049578	59522	2951	290286	0.010166	2.5175	1857196	0.0028	31.202	0.010165	40
45	0.049318	56571	2790	275905	0.010112	2.5081	1566910	0.0008	27.698	0.010112	45
50	0.056891	53781	3060	261455	0.011702	2.5646	1291006	0.0018	24.005	0.011701	50
55	0.073707	50722	3739	244678	0.015280	2.6112	1029550	0.0022	20.298	0.015275	55
60	0.107579	46983	5054	222811	0.022685	2.6052	784872	0.0008	16.705	0.022682	60
65	0.150014	41929	6290	194624	0.032318	2.6121	562061	0.0008	13.405	0.032314	65
70	0.236798	35639	8439	157754	0.053496	2.5780	367437	0.0008	10.310	0.053488	70
75	0.347363	27200	9448	112526	0.083964	2.5157	209683	0.0008	7.709	0.083952	75
80	0.515435	17751	9150	65707	0.139251	2.4807	97157	0.0008	5.473	0.139226	80
85+	*1.000000	8602	8602	31450	0.273505	3.6562	31450	0.0008	3.656	0.273417	85

TABLE 4 — OBSERVED AND PROJECTED VITAL RATES

	OBSERVED POPULATION BOTH SEXES	OBSERVED MALES	OBSERVED FEMALES	PROJECTED 1835 MALES	PROJECTED 1835 FEMALES	PROJECTED 1840 MALES	PROJECTED 1840 FEMALES	PROJECTED 1845 MALES	PROJECTED 1845 FEMALES	STABLE POPULATION MALES	STABLE POPULATION FEMALES
RATES PER THOUSAND											
Birth	30.81	32.78	28.97	31.75	28.23	30.82	27.56	29.89	26.86	31.15	28.7
Death	22.52	23.58	21.53	24.63	22.30	24.13	21.94	23.61	21.56	22.57	20.1
Increase	8.29	9.20	7.44	7.12	5.93	6.70	5.62	6.29	5.30		8.580
PERCENTAGE											
under 15	25.62	26.60	24.71	28.73	26.75	30.61	28.62	31.96	29.96	31.40	30.2
15-64	63.55	63.48	63.62	61.75	61.93	60.15	60.30	59.01	59.15	61.22	61.1
65 and over	10.83	9.92	11.67	9.52	11.32	9.24	11.08	9.03	10.89	7.38	8.5
DEP. RATIO X 100	57.36	57.54	57.19	61.96	61.47	66.25	65.83	69.45	69.06	63.35	63.4

AGE AT LAST BIRTHDAY	1835 BOTH SEXES	MALES	FEMALES	1840 BOTH SEXES	MALES	FEMALES	1845 BOTH SEXES	MALES	FEMALES	AGE AT LAST BIRTHDAY	
0-4	493	248	245	495	249	246	496	250	246	0-4	
5-9	353	176	177	451	226	225	453	227	226	5-9	
10-14	324	162	162	343	171	172	437	219	218	10-14	
15-19	319	159	160	316	158	158	335	167	168	15-19	TABLE 5
20-24	321	159	162	311	155	156	308	154	154	20-24	POPULATION
25-29	300	147	153	310	153	157	299	148	151	25-29	PROJECTED
30-34	285	139	146	288	141	147	297	146	151	30-34	WITH
35-39	273	132	141	273	133	140	277	135	142	35-39	FIXED
40-44	262	126	136	259	125	134	259	125	134	40-44	AGE—
45-49	239	113	126	247	118	129	244	117	127	45-49	SPECIFIC
50-54	224	105	119	224	105	119	232	110	122	50-54	BIRTH
55-59	207	96	111	207	96	111	209	97	112	55-59	AND
60-64	183	84	99	186	85	101	186	85	101	60-64	DEATH
65-69	157	71	86	158	71	87	161	73	88	65-69	RATES
70-74	124	55	69	126	56	70	126	56	70	70-74	(IN 1000's)
75-79	87	38	49	87	38	49	88	38	50	75-79	
80-84	50	21	29	50	21	29	50	21	29	80-84	
85+	23	9	14	23	9	14	23	9	14	85+	
TOTAL	4224	2040	2184	4354	2110	2244	4480	2177	2303	TOTAL	

STANDARD COUNTRIES:	ENGLAND AND WALES 1961 BOTH SEXES	MALES	FEMALES	UNITED STATES 1960 BOTH SEXES	MALES	FEMALES	MEXICO 1960 BOTH SEXES	MALES	FEMALES	
STANDARDIZED RATES PER THOUSAND										TABLE 6
Birth	28.34	30.45*	26.76	28.74	28.40*	27.59	26.73	27.65*	25.98	STANDARDIZED RATES
Death	22.69	23.31*	22.86	21.96	21.08*	20.90	19.78	17.56*	18.23	
Increase	5.64	7.14*	3.90	6.78	7.32*	6.69	6.96	10.09*	7.76	

	OBSERVED POP. MALES	FEMALES	STATIONARY POP. MALES	FEMALES	STABLE POP. MALES	FEMALES	OBSERVED BIRTHS	NET MATERNITY FUNCTION	BIRTHS IN STABLE POP.	
μ	32.78377	34.45722	33.67547	34.96302	29.64838	30.73294	33.00743	33.02426	32.68204	TABLE 7
σ^2	483.7242	507.0730	488.4324	511.4741	448.1946	472.0487	37.78285	37.85717	37.73585	MOMENTS
κ_3	4425.476	3934.630	3906.959	3662.464	5350.645	5398.188	8.4005	10.3099	17.9565	AND
κ_4	-191369.	-231880.	-209460.	-245360.	-124886.	-155579.	-879.736	-889.535	-880.850	CUMULANTS
β_1	0.173032	0.118740	0.130998	0.100248	0.317989	0.277036	0.001308	0.001959	0.006000	
β_2	2.182144	2.098174	2.122007	2.062101	2.378299	2.301805	2.383741	2.379321	2.381423	
κ	-0.065669	-0.044450	-0.049389	-0.037125	-0.122266	-0.104343	-0.000804	-0.001195	-0.003640	

VITAL STATISTICS		THOMPSON AGE RANGE	NRR	1000r	INTERVAL	BOURGEOIS-PICHAT AGE RANGE	NRR	1000b	1000d	1000r	COALE		
GRR	2.114										IBR	22.39	TABLE 8
NRR	1.326	0-4	1.04	1.43	27.04	5-29	0.98	21.70	22.31	-0.61	IDR	21.39	RATES FROM AGE DISTRIBUTIONS
TFR	4.339	5-9	0.99	-0.39	26.91	30-54	1.04	22.95	21.58	1.37	IRI	1.00	AND VITAL
GENERATION	32.853	10-14	1.00	0.13	26.84	55-79	1.04	22.84	21.43	1.41	K1	0.	STATISTICS
SEX RATIO	105.229	15-19	1.05	1.67	26.76	*45-69	1.05	23.51	21.63	1.87	K2	0.	(Females)

Start Age Interval	ORIGINAL MATRIX SUB-DIAGONAL	ALTERNATIVE FIRST ROWS Projection	Integral	FIRST STABLE MATRIX % IN STABLE POPULATION	FISHER VALUES	REPRODUCTIVE VALUES	SECOND STABLE MATRIX Z₂ FIRST COLUMN	FIRST ROW	
0	0.91820	0.00000	0.00000	11.204	1.283	246893	0.1353+0.0394	0.1353+0.0394	TABLE 9
5	0.97215	0.00000	0.00000	9.855	1.458	243568	0.1127-0.0846	0.0497+0.1319	LESLIE
10	0.97707	0.00542	0.00000	9.178	1.566	256374	-0.0001-0.1492	-0.0716+0.1123	MATRIX
15	0.97460	0.08061	0.01133	8.590	1.666	276414	-0.1271-0.0951	-0.1255+0.0093	AND ITS
20	0.96903	0.25304	0.15737	8.020	1.678	264427	-0.1617+0.0474	-0.0891-0.0927	SPECTRAL
25	0.96428	0.40922	0.37117	7.445	1.473	222564	-0.0624+0.1665	-0.0158-0.1305	COMPONENTS
30	0.96187	0.43749	0.48225	6.878	1.050	153362	0.1006+0.1573	0.0330-0.1033	(Females)
35	0.95458	0.31701	0.42803	6.337	0.556	78959	0.1951+0.0145	0.0362-0.0518	
40	0.95046	0.13017	0.23019	5.795	0.182	24126	0.1337-0.1532	0.0159-0.0151	
45	0.94763	0.01911	0.03765	5.277	0.024	3043	-0.0439-0.2058	0.0023-0.0019	
50	0.93583	0.00072	0.00147	4.790	0.001	105	-0.1971-0.0912	0.0001-0.0001	
55+	0.77431			16.630					

Start Age Interval	OBSERVED POPUL. (IN 100's)	CONTRIBUTIONS OF ROOTS (IN 100's) r_1	r_2, r_3	r_4-r_{11}	AGE-SP. BIRTH RATES	NET MATERNITY FUNCTION	COEFF. OF MATRIX EQUATION	PARAMETERS INTEGRAL	MATRIX	EXP. INCREASE x	$e^{(x+2\frac{1}{2})r}$	
0	1925	2114	-45	-144	0.0000	0.0000	0.0000	L(1) 1.04383	1.04387	0	1.0217	TABLE 10
5	1668	1860	-179	-12	0.0000	0.0000	0.0000	L(2) 0.55375	0.55083	50	1.5690	AGE
10	1637	1732	-180	85	0.0000	0.0000	0.0048	0.74931	0.73471	55	1.6378	ANALYSIS
15	1659	1621	-28	66	0.0028	0.0097	0.0703	R(1) 0.00858	0.00859	60	1.7096	AND
20	1576	1513	168	-105	0.0387	0.1309	0.2151	R(2) -0.01414	-0.01705	65	1.7845	MISCELLANEOUS
25	1511	1405	244	-137	0.0913	0.2992	0.3371	0.18687	0.18549	70	1.8628	RESULTS
30	1461	1298	121	42	0.1186	0.3749	0.3475	C(1)	18870	75	1.9444	(Females)
35	1420	1196	-116	340	0.1053	0.3201	0.2422	C(2)	-34253	80	2.0297	
40	1325	1094	-276	508	0.0566	0.1643	0.0949		-60283	85	2.1186	
45	1253	996	-218	475	0.0093	0.0255	0.0132	2P/Y 33.6227	33.8727	90	2.2115	
50	1184	904	25	255	0.0004	0.0009	0.0005	DELTA 7.1605		95	2.3084	
55+	4550	3138								100	2.4096	

TABLE 1 — DATA

AGE AT LAST BIRTHDAY	POPULATION BOTH SEXES	MALES Number	%	FEMALES Number	%	BIRTHS BY AGE OF MOTHER	DEATHS BOTH SEXES	MALES	FEMALES	AGE AT LAST BIRTHDAY
0	86637	43793	2.2	42844	2.0	0	16114	8829	7285	0
1-4	307161	154219	7.7	152942	7.1	0	7222	3788	3434	1-4
5-9	343720	172545	8.6	171175	7.9	0	2609	1351	1258	5-9
10-14	337773	169444	8.4	168329	7.8	0	1539	797	742	10-14
15-19	338762	169127	8.4	169635	7.9	872	1571	811	760	15-19
20-24	316668	156520	7.8	160148	7.4	12483	2212	1250	962	20-24
25-29	304254	149409	7.4	154845	7.2	30500	2055	1099	956	25-29
30-34	292266	142641	7.1	149625	6.9	35794	2193	1144	1049	30-34
35-39	270403	129933	6.4	140470	6.5	28347	2469	1281	1188	35-39
40-44	254341	121227	6.0	133114	6.2	17297	2697	1445	1252	40-44
45-49	240886	114079	5.7	126807	5.9	2310	2515	1339	1176	45-49
50-54	223721	104909	5.2	118812	5.5	190	2864	1544	1320	50-54
55-59	206579	96090	4.8	110489	5.1	0	3575	1883	1692	55-59
60-64	185749	85520	4.2	100229	4.6	0	4243	2164	2079	60-64
65-69	161058	73221	3.6	87837	4.1	0	5624	2797	2827	65-69
70-74	130032	58232	2.9	71800	3.3		6930	3350	3580	70-74
75-79	92931	40831	2.0	52100	2.4		8026	3733	4293	75-79
80-84	52905	22670	1.1	30235	1.4	65543 M.	7858	3567	4291	80-84
85+	27223	10750	0.5	16473	0.8	62250 F.	7496	3100	4396	85+
TOTAL	4173069	2015160		2157909		127793	89812	45272	44540	TOTAL

TABLE 2 — MALE LIFE TABLE

x	nq_x	l_x	nd_x	nL_x	nm_x	na_x	T_x	r_x	$\mathring{e}_x$	nM_x	x
0	0.177952	100000	17795	88266	0.201608	0.3406	4442502	0.0000	44.425	0.201608	0
1	0.091937	82205	7558	307693	0.024562	1.2046	4354236	0.0000	52.968	0.024562	1
5	0.038320	74647	2860	366084	0.007814	2.5000	4046543	0.0045	54.209	0.007830	5
10	0.023229	71787	1668	354515	0.004704	2.3504	3680459	0.0000	51.269	0.004704	10
15	0.023714	70119	1663	346650	0.004797	2.6271	3325944	0.0025	47.433	0.004795	15
20	0.039181	68456	2682	335724	0.007989	2.5553	2979294	0.0053	43.521	0.007986	20
25	0.036110	65774	2375	322894	0.007356	2.4835	2643569	0.0016	40.192	0.007356	25
30	0.039341	63399	2494	310876	0.008023	2.5466	2320675	0.0057	36.604	0.008020	30
35	0.048162	60905	2933	297371	0.009864	2.5612	2009799	0.0063	32.999	0.009859	35
40	0.057885	57972	3356	281507	0.011920	2.5113	1712429	0.0016	29.539	0.011920	40
45	0.057033	54616	3115	265356	0.011739	2.5204	1430922	0.0020	26.200	0.011737	45
50	0.071070	51501	3660	248638	0.014721	2.5774	1165567	0.0021	22.632	0.014718	50
55	0.093536	47841	4475	228332	0.019598	2.5703	916929	0.0008	19.166	0.019596	55
60	0.119246	43366	5171	204361	0.025304	2.5888	688597	0.0001	15.879	0.025304	60
65	0.174878	38195	6679	174854	0.038200	2.5866	484236	0.0001	12.678	0.038199	65
70	0.252176	31515	7947	138145	0.057529	2.5549	309382	0.0001	9.817	0.057529	70
75	0.372320	23568	8775	95976	0.091427	2.5083	171238	0.0001	7.266	0.091426	75
80	0.561005	14793	8299	52743	0.157349	2.4427	75262	0.0001	5.088	0.157345	80
85+	*1.000000	6494	6494	22519	0.288384	3.4676	22519	0.0001	3.468	0.288372	85+

TABLE 3 — FEMALE LIFE TABLE

x	nq_x	l_x	nd_x	nL_x	nm_x	na_x	T_x	r_x	$\mathring{e}_x$	nM_x	x
0	0.153131	100000	15313	90058	0.170035	0.3508	4837982	0.0000	48.380	0.170035	0
1	0.084538	84687	7159	318856	0.022453	1.2216	4747924	0.0000	56.064	0.022453	1
5	0.036006	77528	2791	380660	0.007333	2.5000	4429067	0.0049	57.129	0.007349	5
10	0.021786	74736	1628	369366	0.004408	2.3501	4048407	0.0000	54.169	0.004408	10
15	0.022159	73108	1620	361592	0.004480	2.5628	3679041	0.0002	50.323	0.004480	15
20	0.029605	71488	2116	352251	0.006008	2.5482	3317449	0.0034	46.406	0.006007	20
25	0.030405	69372	2109	341627	0.006174	2.5200	2965199	0.0005	42.744	0.006174	25
30	0.034469	67262	2318	330637	0.007012	2.5523	2623572	0.0026	39.005	0.007011	30
35	0.041433	64544	2691	318105	0.008459	2.5420	2292935	0.0033	35.306	0.008457	35
40	0.045948	62253	2860	304115	0.009406	2.5001	1974829	0.0011	31.723	0.009405	40
45	0.045328	59393	2692	290276	0.009275	2.5161	1670715	0.0017	28.130	0.009274	45
50	0.054112	56701	3068	276097	0.011113	2.5862	1380438	0.0022	24.346	0.011110	50
55	0.073865	53632	3962	258641	0.015317	2.5968	1104342	0.0016	20.591	0.015314	55
60	0.098835	49671	4909	236649	0.020745	2.6158	845701	0.0006	17.026	0.020742	60
65	0.149449	44762	6690	207826	0.032188	2.6110	609052	0.0006	13.607	0.032185	65
70	0.222532	38072	8472	169897	0.049867	2.5848	401226	0.0006	10.539	0.049861	70
75	0.342445	29600	10136	122999	0.082410	2.5336	231328	0.0006	7.815	0.082399	75
80	0.519288	19463	10107	71208	0.141939	2.4839	108330	0.0006	5.566	0.141922	80
85+	1.000000	9356	9356	37122	0.252044	3.9676	37122	0.0006	3.968	0.266862	85+

TABLE 4 — OBSERVED AND PROJECTED VITAL RATES

	OBSERVED POPULATION BOTH SEXES	MALES	FEMALES	PROJECTED POPULATION 1840 MALES	FEMALES	1845 MALES	FEMALES	1850 MALES	FEMALES	STABLE POPULATION MALES	FEMALES
RATES PER THOUSAND											
Birth	30.62	32.52	28.85	31.53	28.15	30.59	27.48	29.54	26.68	30.87	28.68
Death	21.52	22.47	20.64	23.38	21.39	22.83	20.98	22.25	20.54	20.88	18.68
Increase	9.10	10.06	8.21	8.14	6.76	7.76	6.49	7.29	6.14		9.9942
PERCENTAGE											
under 15	25.77	26.80	24.81	29.08	27.03	31.20	29.14	32.72	30.67	32.07	30.92
15-64	63.11	63.00	63.22	61.23	61.44	59.49	59.67	58.31	58.44	60.74	60.72
65 and over	11.12	10.21	11.98	9.69	11.53	9.30	11.18	8.98	10.89	7.18	8.36
DEP. RATIO X 100	58.45	58.74	58.18	63.31	62.76	68.09	67.58	71.50	71.11	64.63	64.70

TABLE 1 — DATA

AGE AT LAST BIRTHDAY	POPULATION BOTH SEXES	MALES Number	%	FEMALES Number	%	BIRTHS BY AGE OF MOTHER	DEATHS BOTH SEXES	MALES	FEMALES	AGE AT LAST BIRTHDAY
0	83211	42226	2.2	40985	1.9	0	15362	8455	6907	0
1-4	303719	152151	7.8	151568	7.1	0	7439	3852	3587	1-4
5-9	343852	171553	8.8	172299	8.1	0	2875	1543	1332	5-9
10-14	335675	167646	8.6	168029	7.9	0	1477	766	711	10-14
15-19	338185	167605	8.6	170580	8.0	835	1957	1019	938	15-19
20-24	312548	154062	7.9	158486	7.4	13581	1943	1091	852	20-24
25-29	300635	146617	7.5	154018	7.2	30548	2032	1100	932	25-29
30-34	275714	131564	6.7	144150	6.8	31835	2200	1137	1063	30-34
35-39	259566	122856	6.3	136710	6.4	29492	2487	1254	1233	35-39
40-44	247375	116782	6.0	130593	6.1	14885	2243	1135	1108	40-44
45-49	231553	108409	5.5	123144	5.8	2022	2391	1270	1121	45-49
50-54	217018	100715	5.1	116303	5.5	157	2757	1446	1311	50-54
55-59	200757	92402	4.7	108355	5.1	0	3223	1693	1530	55-59
60-64	182104	82876	4.2	99228	4.7	0	4223	2174	2049	60-64
65-69	158685	71419	3.6	87266	4.1	0	5303	2640	2663	65-69
70-74	128721	57093	2.9	71628	3.4		6796	3246	3550	70-74
75-79	91382	39717	2.0	51665	2.4		8035	3724	4311	75-79
80-84	52329	21923	1.1	30406	1.4	63283 M.	7675	3379	4296	80-84
85+	28116	11127	0.6	16989	0.8	60072 F.	7698	3215	4483	85+
TOTAL	4091145	1958743		2132402		123355	88116	44139	43977	TOTAL

TABLE 2 — MALE LIFE TABLE

x	nq_x	l_x	nd_x	nL_x	nm_x	na_x	T_x	r_x	$\overset{\circ}{e}_x$	nM_x	x
0	0.176995	100000	17700	88395	0.200232	0.3443	4420051	0.0000	44.201	0.200232	0
1	0.094588	82300	7785	307488	0.025317	1.2107	4331656	0.0000	52.632	0.025317	1
5	0.043928	74516	3273	364396	0.008983	2.5000	4024168	0.0030	54.004	0.008994	5
10	0.022572	71242	1608	351945	0.004569	2.3462	3659772	0.0000	51.371	0.004569	10
15	0.029964	69634	2087	343110	0.006081	2.5742	3307827	0.0026	47.503	0.006080	15
20	0.034808	67548	2351	331927	0.007083	2.5280	2964717	0.0064	43.891	0.007082	20
25	0.036842	65197	2402	320043	0.007505	2.5267	2632790	0.0081	40.382	0.007503	25
30	0.042337	62795	2659	307450	0.008647	2.5463	2312747	0.0089	36.830	0.008642	30
35	0.049770	60136	2993	293209	0.010208	2.5037	2005297	0.0022	33.346	0.010207	35
40	0.047449	57143	2711	278960	0.009720	2.5083	1712088	0.0022	29.961	0.009719	40
45	0.056958	54432	3100	264585	0.011718	2.5571	1433128	0.0030	26.329	0.011715	45
50	0.069370	51331	3561	247982	0.014359	2.5638	1168543	0.0014	22.765	0.014357	50
55	0.087741	47771	4191	228752	0.018323	2.5902	920561	0.0004	19.270	0.018322	55
60	0.123357	43579	5376	204933	0.026232	2.5888	691808	0.0000	15.875	0.026232	60
65	0.169659	38203	6482	175343	0.036965	2.5818	486875	0.0000	12.744	0.036965	65
70	0.249733	31722	7922	139338	0.056855	2.5674	311532	0.0000	9.821	0.056855	70
75	0.379944	23800	9043	96441	0.093763	2.5053	172194	0.0000	7.235	0.093763	75
80	0.552464	14757	8153	52896	0.154130	2.4377	75753	0.0000	5.133	0.154130	80
85+	*1.000000	6604	6604	22857	0.288937	3.4610	22857	0.0000	3.461	0.288937	85+

TABLE 3 — FEMALE LIFE TABLE

x	nq_x	l_x	nd_x	nL_x	nm_x	na_x	T_x	r_x	$\overset{\circ}{e}_x$	nM_x	x
0	0.152044	100000	15204	90220	0.168525	0.3568	4820429	0.0000	48.204	0.168525	0
1	0.088845	84796	7534	318333	0.023666	1.2325	4730208	0.0000	55.784	0.023666	1
5	0.037869	77262	2926	378995	0.007720	2.5000	4411875	0.0031	57.103	0.007731	5
10	0.020924	74336	1555	367594	0.004231	2.3726	4032880	0.0000	54.252	0.004231	10
15	0.027127	72781	1974	359035	0.005499	2.5341	3665287	0.0008	50.361	0.005499	15
20	0.026527	70806	1878	349353	0.005376	2.5090	3306252	0.0047	46.694	0.005376	20
25	0.029822	68928	2056	339615	0.006053	2.5552	2956899	0.0033	42.898	0.006051	25
30	0.036235	66872	2423	328469	0.007377	2.5677	2617284	0.0045	39.138	0.007374	30
35	0.044107	64449	2843	315169	0.009019	2.5099	2288816	0.0013	35.513	0.009019	35
40	0.041535	61607	2559	301592	0.008484	2.4826	1973647	0.0017	32.036	0.008484	40
45	0.044526	59048	2629	288778	0.009104	2.5425	1672055	0.0022	28.317	0.009103	45
50	0.054865	56419	3095	274566	0.011274	2.5682	1383276	0.0015	24.518	0.011272	50
55	0.068299	53323	3642	257886	0.014122	2.6026	1108710	0.0011	20.792	0.014120	55
60	0.098407	49681	4889	236753	0.020650	2.6163	850825	0.0003	17.126	0.020649	60
65	0.142248	44792	6372	208787	0.030517	2.6183	614071	0.0003	13.709	0.030516	65
70	0.221450	38421	8508	171662	0.049564	2.5974	405284	0.0003	10.549	0.049562	70
75	0.345988	29912	10349	124025	0.083446	2.5324	233622	0.0003	7.810	0.083441	75
80	0.517312	19563	10120	71625	0.141295	2.4813	109598	0.0003	5.602	0.141288	80
85+	1.000000	9443	9443	37972	0.248678	4.0213	37972	0.0003	4.021	0.263876	85+

TABLE 4 — OBSERVED AND PROJECTED VITAL RATES

	OBSERVED POPULATION BOTH SEXES	MALES	FEMALES	PROJECTED POPULATION 1845 MALES	FEMALES	1850 MALES	FEMALES	1855 MALES	FEMALES	STABLE POPULATION MALES	FEMALES
RATES PER THOUSAND											
Birth	30.15	32.31	28.17	31.53	27.73	30.81	27.30	29.85	26.64	30.50	28.27
Death	21.54	22.53	20.62	23.29	21.25	22.81	20.90	22.25	20.51	21.11	18.88
Increase	8.61	9.77	7.55	8.24	6.47	8.00	6.41	7.59	6.13		9.3914
PERCENTAGE											
under 15	26.07	27.24	24.99	29.26	26.93	31.18	28.77	32.67	30.29	31.70	30.52
15-64	62.71	62.48	62.91	61.02	61.41	59.52	59.92	58.38	58.70	60.84	60.79
65 and over	11.23	10.28	12.10	9.72	11.66	9.30	11.31	8.95	11.01	7.46	8.69
DEP. RATIO X 100	59.47	60.04	58.95	63.89	62.83	68.02	66.89	71.29	70.35	64.36	64.49

TABLE 1 — DATA

AGE AT LAST BIRTHDAY	POPULATION BOTH SEXES	MALES Number	%	FEMALES Number	%	BIRTHS BY AGE OF MOTHER	DEATHS BOTH SEXES	MALES	FEMALES	AGE AT LAST BIRTHDAY
0	91180	45877	2.2	45303	2.0	0	15880	8698	7182	0
1-4	325031	162917	7.9	162114	7.2	0	8413	4401	4012	1-4
5-9	368189	184203	8.9	183986	8.2	0	2980	1532	1448	5-9
10-14	358255	179397	8.7	178858	7.9	0	2243	1172	1071	10-14
15-19	351246	175256	8.5	175990	7.8	1001	1671	863	808	15-19
20-24	341717	169455	8.2	172262	7.7	15299	2058	1163	895	20-24
25-29	307641	148039	7.2	159602	7.1	28669	2139	1108	1031	25-29
30-34	285432	135178	6.5	150254	6.7	33529	2335	1188	1147	30-34
35-39	273223	129269	6.2	143954	6.4	27898	2094	1036	1058	35-39
40-44	256228	120598	5.8	135630	6.0	14922	2222	1135	1087	40-44
45-49	241713	112913	5.5	128800	5.7	1938	2422	1251	1171	45-49
50-54	227286	105490	5.1	121796	5.4	71	2683	1412	1271	50-54
55-59	211827	97558	4.7	114269	5.1	0	3317	1733	1584	55-59
60-64	192598	88118	4.3	104480	4.6	0	4187	2139	2048	60-64
65-69	168379	76112	3.7	92267	4.1	0	5408	2669	2739	65-69
70-74	136433	60630	2.9	75803	3.4		7080	3389	3691	70-74
75-79	97115	42351	2.0	54764	2.4		8259	3762	4497	75-79
80-84	56625	24288	1.2	32337	1.4	63282 M.	7846	3502	4344	80-84
85+	29140	11769	0.6	17371	0.8	60045 F.	8026	3363	4663	85+
TOTAL	4319258	2069418		2249840		123327	91263	45516	45747	TOTAL

TABLE 2 — MALE LIFE TABLE

x	nq_x	l_x	nd_x	nL_x	nm_x	na_x	T_x	r_x	$\dot{e}_x$	nM_x	x
0	0.168980	100000	16898	89127	0.189594	0.3566	4485235	0.0000	44.852	0.189594	0
1	0.100538	83102	8355	309282	0.027014	1.2321	4396108	0.0000	52.900	0.027014	1
5	0.040686	74747	3041	366133	0.008306	2.5000	4086826	0.0029	54.675	0.008317	5
10	0.032115	71706	2303	352491	0.006533	2.3776	3720693	0.0000	51.888	0.006533	10
15	0.024321	69403	1688	342793	0.004924	2.4981	3368202	0.0000	48.531	0.004924	15
20	0.033779	67715	2287	333007	0.006869	2.5654	3025410	0.0104	44.678	0.006863	20
25	0.036773	65428	2406	321212	0.007490	2.5366	2692403	0.0149	41.151	0.007485	25
30	0.043000	63022	2710	308327	0.008789	2.4972	2371191	0.0053	37.625	0.008788	30
35	0.039285	60312	2369	295627	0.008015	2.4561	2062864	0.0029	34.203	0.008014	35
40	0.046008	57943	2666	283176	0.009414	2.5479	1767237	0.0041	30.500	0.009411	40
45	0.053942	55277	2982	269080	0.011081	2.5506	1484062	0.0022	26.848	0.011079	45
50	0.064825	52295	3390	253246	0.013386	2.5727	1214981	0.0009	23.233	0.013385	50
55	0.085168	48905	4165	234475	0.017764	2.5870	961735	0.0000	19.665	0.017764	55
60	0.114670	44740	5130	211340	0.024275	2.5910	727260	0.0003	16.255	0.024274	60
65	0.161724	39609	6406	182666	0.035068	2.5989	515920	0.0003	13.025	0.035067	65
70	0.246056	33204	8170	146155	0.055899	2.5688	333254	0.0003	10.037	0.055896	70
75	0.363594	25034	9102	102463	0.088833	2.5054	187099	0.0003	7.474	0.088829	75
80	0.527754	15932	8408	58309	0.144196	2.4609	84636	0.0003	5.312	0.144187	80
85+	*1.000000	7524	7524	26327	0.285782	3.4992	26327	0.0003	3.499	0.285751	85+

TABLE 3 — FEMALE LIFE TABLE

x	nq_x	l_x	nd_x	nL_x	nm_x	na_x	T_x	r_x	$\dot{e}_x$	nM_x	x
0	0.144086	100000	14409	90887	0.158533	0.3675	4859271	0.0000	48.593	0.158533	0
1	0.092692	85591	7934	320576	0.024748	1.2535	4768384	0.0000	55.711	0.024748	1
5	0.038535	77658	2993	380808	0.007858	2.5000	4447808	0.0035	57.274	0.007870	5
10	0.029476	74665	2201	367543	0.005988	2.3724	4067000	0.0000	54.470	0.005988	10
15	0.022690	72464	1644	358132	0.004591	2.4514	3699457	0.0000	51.052	0.004591	15
20	0.025662	70820	1817	349672	0.005197	2.5632	3341325	0.0045	47.180	0.005196	20
25	0.031817	69003	2195	339668	0.006463	2.5650	2991653	0.0072	43.356	0.006460	25
30	0.037460	66807	2503	327807	0.007634	2.5104	2651984	0.0030	39.696	0.007634	30
35	0.036084	64305	2320	315709	0.007350	2.4940	2324178	0.0027	36.143	0.007350	35
40	0.039299	61984	2436	303901	0.008016	2.5280	2008469	0.0030	32.403	0.008014	40
45	0.044466	59548	2648	291219	0.009092	2.5362	1704568	0.0017	28.625	0.009092	45
50	0.050892	56901	2896	277467	0.010437	2.5702	1413349	0.0011	24.839	0.010435	50
55	0.067093	54005	3623	261346	0.013864	2.6048	1135883	0.0011	21.033	0.013862	55
60	0.093672	50381	4719	240674	0.019609	2.6197	874537	0.0022	17.358	0.019602	60
65	0.138715	45662	6334	213279	0.029698	2.6269	633863	0.0022	13.882	0.029686	65
70	0.218086	39328	8577	176066	0.048714	2.6012	420584	0.0022	10.694	0.048692	70
75	0.341472	30751	10501	127821	0.082152	2.5301	244518	0.0022	7.951	0.082116	75
80	0.498547	20251	10096	75125	0.134387	2.4929	116697	0.0022	5.763	0.134335	80
85+	1.000000	10155	10155	41572	0.244269	4.0938	41572	0.0022	4.094	0.268435	85+

TABLE 4 — OBSERVED AND PROJECTED VITAL RATES

	OBSERVED POPULATION BOTH SEXES	MALES	FEMALES	PROJECTED POPULATION 1850 MALES	FEMALES	1855 MALES	FEMALES	1860 MALES	FEMALES	STABLE POPULATION MALES	FEMALES
RATES PER THOUSAND											
Birth	28.55	30.58	26.69	30.09	26.48	29.53	26.20	28.80	25.75	28.89	26.89
Death	21.13	21.99	20.33	22.55	20.89	22.18	20.64	21.77	20.37	20.90	18.90
Increase	7.42	8.59	6.36	7.53	5.59	7.35	5.56	7.03	5.38		7.9870
PERCENTAGE											
under 15	26.45	27.66	25.35	29.04	26.73	30.46	28.16	31.52	29.26	30.47	29.44
15-64	62.25	61.94	62.54	60.97	61.44	59.91	60.30	59.18	59.46	61.24	61.11
65 and over	11.29	10.40	12.11	9.99	11.82	9.63	11.54	9.30	11.28	8.29	9.45
DEP. RATIO X 100	60.63	61.44	59.90	64.01	62.75	66.91	65.84	68.99	68.18	63.28	63.64

TABLE 1 — DATA

AGE AT LAST BIRTHDAY	POPULATION BOTH SEXES	MALES Number	%	FEMALES Number	%	BIRTHS BY AGE OF MOTHER	DEATHS BOTH SEXES	MALES	FEMALES	AGE AT LAST BIRTHDAY
0	97831	49449	2.4	48382	2.1	0	16201	8967	7234	0
1-4	337591	169658	8.1	167933	7.4	0	8230	4335	3895	1-4
5-9	380958	188804	9.1	192154	8.5	0	4870	2564	2306	5-9
10-14	369153	184903	8.9	184250	8.1	0	1730	889	841	10-14
15-19	361147	180435	8.7	180712	8.0	1202	1685	896	789	15-19
20-24	329080	161272	7.7	167808	7.4	13723	2085	1150	935	20-24
25-29	302286	145481	7.0	156805	6.9	32718	2343	1202	1141	25-29
30-34	287187	137202	6.6	149985	6.6	33772	2001	985	1016	30-34
35-39	267089	126488	6.1	140601	6.2	27298	2030	967	1063	35-39
40-44	251916	118566	5.7	133350	5.9	13850	2176	1071	1105	40-44
45-49	238884	111831	5.4	127053	5.6	1723	2219	1152	1067	45-49
50-54	226215	105214	5.0	121001	5.4	42	2782	1446	1336	50-54
55-59	211176	97688	4.7	113488	5.0	0	3240	1689	1551	55-59
60-64	192960	88415	4.2	104545	4.6	0	4068	2087	1981	60-64
65-69	168879	76568	3.7	92311	4.1	0	5468	2727	2741	65-69
70-74	137346	61475	2.9	75871	3.4		7148	3377	3771	70-74
75-79	99158	43766	2.1	55392	2.4		8315	3849	4466	75-79
80-84	57111	24738	1.2	32373	1.4	63814 M.	8334	3739	4595	80-84
85+	29944	12362	0.6	17582	0.8	60514 F.	8347	3556	4791	85+
TOTAL	4345911	2084315		2261596		124328	93272	46648	46624	TOTAL

TABLE 2 — MALE LIFE TABLE

x	$_nq_x$	l_x	$_nd_x$	$_nL_x$	$_nm_x$	$_na_x$	T_x	r_x	$\mathring{e}_x$	$_nM_x$	x
0	0.162213	100000	16221	89556	0.181129	0.3562	4489799	0.0018	44.898	0.181338	0
1	0.095374	83779	7990	312993	0.025529	1.2314	4400242	0.0018	52.522	0.025551	1
5	0.065622	75788	4973	366509	0.013570	2.5000	4087250	0.0028	53.930	0.013580	5
10	0.023708	70815	1679	349195	0.004808	2.0935	3720741	0.0000	52.542	0.004808	10
15	0.024554	69136	1698	341580	0.004970	2.5844	3371546	0.0085	48.767	0.004966	15
20	0.035099	67439	2367	331470	0.007141	2.5824	3029966	0.0146	44.929	0.007131	20
25	0.040472	65072	2634	318739	0.008262	2.4869	2698496	0.0084	41.470	0.008262	25
30	0.035250	62438	2201	306610	0.007178	2.4647	2379757	0.0065	38.114	0.007179	30
35	0.037530	60237	2261	295609	0.007648	2.5333	2073147	0.0068	34.416	0.007645	35
40	0.044193	57976	2562	283586	0.009035	2.5426	1777538	0.0034	30.660	0.009033	40
45	0.050254	55414	2785	270304	0.010302	2.5702	1493953	0.0012	26.960	0.010301	45
50	0.066502	52629	3500	254666	0.013743	2.5769	1223648	0.0000	23.250	0.013743	50
55	0.082975	49129	4076	235775	0.017290	2.5783	968982	0.0000	19.723	0.017290	55
60	0.111703	45053	5033	213202	0.023605	2.6030	733207	0.0000	16.274	0.023605	60
65	0.164041	40020	6565	184330	0.035615	2.5975	520005	0.0000	12.993	0.035615	65
70	0.242276	33455	8105	147552	0.054933	2.5664	335675	0.0000	10.034	0.054933	70
75	0.360909	25350	9149	104031	0.087945	2.5168	188123	0.0000	7.421	0.087945	75
80	0.545943	16201	8845	58519	0.151143	2.4578	84092	0.0000	5.191	0.151143	80
85+	*1.000000	7356	7356	25573	0.287656	3.4764	25573	0.0000	3.476	0.287656	85+

TABLE 3 — FEMALE LIFE TABLE

x	$_nq_x$	l_x	$_nd_x$	$_nL_x$	$_nm_x$	$_na_x$	T_x	r_x	$\mathring{e}_x$	$_nM_x$	x
0	0.136419	100000	13642	91374	0.149297	0.3677	4860763	0.0024	48.608	0.149518	0
1	0.087135	86358	7525	324768	0.023170	1.2538	4769389	0.0024	55.228	0.023194	1
5	0.058202	78833	4588	382696	0.011989	2.5000	4444621	0.0033	56.380	0.012001	5
10	0.022527	74245	1672	366415	0.004564	2.1238	4061925	0.0000	54.710	0.004564	10
15	0.021603	72573	1568	359002	0.004367	2.5374	3695510	0.0049	50.922	0.004366	15
20	0.027516	71005	1954	350327	0.005577	2.5960	3336509	0.0085	46.990	0.005572	20
25	0.035744	69051	2468	339140	0.007278	2.5223	2986182	0.0044	43.246	0.007277	25
30	0.033305	66583	2218	327354	0.006774	2.4926	2647042	0.0038	39.756	0.006774	30
35	0.037114	64365	2389	315916	0.007562	2.5260	2319688	0.0042	36.039	0.007560	35
40	0.040595	61976	2516	303604	0.008287	2.5048	2003772	0.0020	32.331	0.008286	40
45	0.041145	59460	2446	291301	0.008398	2.5468	1700168	0.0008	28.593	0.008398	45
50	0.053769	57014	3066	277640	0.011042	2.5763	1408867	0.0004	24.711	0.011041	50
55	0.066156	53948	3569	261132	0.013667	2.5877	1131227	0.0005	20.969	0.013667	55
60	0.090672	50379	4568	241058	0.018950	2.6271	870095	0.0003	17.271	0.018949	60
65	0.138741	45811	6356	214040	0.029695	2.6374	629037	0.0003	13.731	0.029693	65
70	0.221986	39456	8759	176208	0.049706	2.5944	414997	0.0003	10.518	0.049703	70
75	0.336384	30697	10326	128066	0.080630	2.5383	238789	0.0003	7.779	0.080625	75
80	0.523193	20371	10658	75082	0.141950	2.4880	110723	0.0003	5.435	0.141940	80
85+	*1.000000	9713	9713	35640	0.272528	3.6693	35640	0.0003	3.669	0.272495	85+

TABLE 4 — OBSERVED AND PROJECTED VITAL RATES

	OBSERVED POPULATION BOTH SEXES	MALES	FEMALES	PROJECTED POPULATION 1855 MALES	FEMALES	1860 MALES	FEMALES	1865 MALES	FEMALES	STABLE POPULATION MALES	FEMALES
RATES PER THOUSAND											
Birth	28.61	30.62	26.76	30.23	26.66	29.93	26.61	29.47	26.39	29.52	27.49
Death	21.46	22.38	20.62	22.65	20.73	22.32	20.54	21.89	20.24	20.80	18.77
Increase	7.15	8.24	6.14	7.59	5.93	7.61	6.07	7.58	6.15		8.7207
PERCENTAGE											
under 15	27.28	28.44	26.21	29.54	27.40	30.87	28.64	31.81	29.68	31.02	30.08
15-64	61.39	61.06	61.70	60.46	60.92	59.53	60.01	58.97	59.28	60.89	60.83
65 and over	11.33	10.50	12.09	10.00	11.68	9.60	11.36	9.22	11.04	8.09	9.09
DEP. RATIO X 100	62.89	63.79	62.08	65.41	64.15	67.99	66.64	69.58	68.69	64.22	64.40

TABLE 1 — DATA

AGE AT LAST BIRTHDAY	POPULATION BOTH SEXES	MALES Number	%	FEMALES Number	%	BIRTHS BY AGE OF MOTHER	DEATHS BOTH SEXES	DEATHS MALES	DEATHS FEMALES	AGE AT LAST BIRTHDAY
0	104578	53192	2.4	51386	2.2	0	17234	9516	7718	0
1-4	359796	180698	8.2	179098	7.5	0	11993	6242	5751	1-4
5-9	403848	202936	9.2	200912	8.5	0	3750	1920	1830	5-9
10-14	393836	197603	8.9	196233	8.3	0	1673	869	804	10-14
15-19	375613	187798	8.5	187815	7.9	1094	1730	884	846	15-19
20-24	353196	175340	7.9	177856	7.5	17865	2398	1344	1054	20-24
25-29	327559	159821	7.2	167738	7.1	33564	2105	1081	1024	25-29
30-34	294639	140725	6.4	153914	6.5	34153	1994	960	1034	30-34
35-39	276181	130895	5.9	145286	6.1	26447	2070	988	1082	35-39
40-44	262378	123921	5.6	138457	5.8	13846	2121	1057	1064	40-44
45-49	250629	117813	5.3	132816	5.6	1596	2409	1283	1126	45-49
50-54	237538	111105	5.0	126433	5.3	7	2702	1434	1268	50-54
55-59	222431	103372	4.7	119059	5.0	0	3284	1708	1576	55-59
60-64	203506	93633	4.2	109873	4.6	0	4210	2159	2051	60-64
65-69	178887	81482	3.7	97405	4.1	0	5660	2762	2898	65-69
70-74	147211	66475	3.0	80736	3.4		7214	3452	3762	70-74
75-79	105526	47035	2.1	58491	2.5		9149	4210	4939	75-79
80-84	61188	26689	1.2	34499	1.5	66002 M.	8786	4005	4781	80-84
85+	30563	12703	0.6	17860	0.8	62570 F.	8470	3653	4817	85+
TOTAL	4589103	2213236		2375867		128572	98952	49527	49425	TOTAL

TABLE 2 — MALE LIFE TABLE

x	nq_x	l_x	nd_x	nL_x	nm_x	na_x	T_x	r_x	$\overset{\circ}{e}_x$	nM_x	x
0	0.161145	100000	16115	90090	0.178872	0.3850	4472317	0.0003	44.723	0.178899	0
1	0.126345	83885	10599	306848	0.034540	1.2926	4382227	0.0003	52.241	0.034544	1
5	0.046135	73287	3381	357982	0.009445	2.5000	4075379	0.0029	55.608	0.009461	5
10	0.021716	69906	1518	345362	0.004396	2.2546	3717397	0.0021	53.177	0.004398	10
15	0.023298	68388	1593	338163	0.004712	2.6302	3372035	0.0067	49.308	0.004707	15
20	0.037638	66794	2514	327800	0.007669	2.5450	3033872	0.0093	45.421	0.007665	20
25	0.033234	64280	2136	315972	0.006761	2.4582	2706072	0.0150	42.098	0.006764	25
30	0.033549	62144	2085	305527	0.006824	2.5089	2390100	0.0130	38.461	0.006822	30
35	0.037058	60059	2226	294801	0.007550	2.5310	2084572	0.0052	34.709	0.007548	35
40	0.041785	57834	2417	283275	0.008531	2.5615	1789771	0.0017	30.947	0.008530	40
45	0.053043	55417	2939	269917	0.010890	2.5614	1506496	0.0002	27.185	0.010890	45
50	0.062564	52478	3283	254381	0.012907	2.5615	1236579	0.0000	23.564	0.012907	50
55	0.079450	49194	3908	236547	0.016523	2.5887	982198	0.0001	19.966	0.016523	55
60	0.109249	45286	4947	214563	0.023058	2.6016	745651	0.0000	16.465	0.023058	60
65	0.156713	40338	6322	186493	0.033897	2.5956	531088	0.0000	13.166	0.033897	65
70	0.230731	34017	7849	151143	0.051929	2.5867	344595	0.0000	10.130	0.051929	70
75	0.366377	26168	9587	107112	0.089508	2.5250	193452	0.0000	7.393	0.089508	75
80	0.542864	16581	9001	59983	0.150061	2.4535	86340	0.0000	5.207	0.150061	80
85+	*1.000000	7580	7580	26358	0.287570	3.4774	26358	0.0000	3.477	0.287570	85+

TABLE 3 — FEMALE LIFE TABLE

x	nq_x	l_x	nd_x	nL_x	nm_x	na_x	T_x	r_x	$\overset{\circ}{e}_x$	nM_x	x
0	0.137707	100000	13771	91685	0.150197	0.3961	4792578	0.0000	47.926	0.150197	0
1	0.118272	86229	10198	317602	0.032111	1.3216	4700893	0.0000	54.516	0.032111	1
5	0.044454	76031	3380	371704	0.009093	2.5000	4383291	0.0030	57.652	0.009108	5
10	0.020251	72651	1471	359203	0.004096	2.2460	4011587	0.0013	55.217	0.004097	10
15	0.022288	71180	1586	352049	0.004506	2.5738	3652384	0.0052	51.312	0.004504	15
20	0.029215	69593	2033	342976	0.005928	2.5456	3300335	0.0057	47.423	0.005926	20
25	0.030074	67560	2032	332748	0.006106	2.5136	2957359	0.0082	43.774	0.006105	25
30	0.033052	65528	2166	322286	0.006720	2.5274	2624611	0.0076	40.053	0.006718	30
35	0.036563	63362	2317	311049	0.007448	2.5122	2302325	0.0033	36.336	0.007447	35
40	0.037704	61046	2302	299500	0.007685	2.5111	1991277	0.0012	32.619	0.007685	40
45	0.041524	58744	2439	287717	0.008478	2.5389	1691777	0.0005	28.799	0.008478	45
50	0.048958	56305	2757	274840	0.010030	2.5753	1404060	0.0006	24.937	0.010029	50
55	0.064155	53548	3435	259512	0.013238	2.6045	1129220	0.0005	21.088	0.013237	55
60	0.089392	50113	4480	239970	0.018668	2.6351	869708	0.0002	17.355	0.018667	60
65	0.138942	45633	6340	213098	0.029753	2.6235	629738	0.0002	13.800	0.029752	65
70	0.209681	39293	8239	176807	0.046599	2.6142	416641	0.0002	10.603	0.046596	70
75	0.349621	31054	10857	128571	0.084444	2.5409	239833	0.0002	7.723	0.084440	75
80	0.513548	20197	10372	74839	0.138591	2.4793	111263	0.0002	5.509	0.138584	80
85+	*1.000000	9825	9825	36424	0.269734	3.7074	36424	0.0002	3.707	0.269709	85+

TABLE 4 — OBSERVED AND PROJECTED VITAL RATES

	OBSERVED POPULATION BOTH SEXES	MALES	FEMALES	PROJECTED 1860 MALES	1860 FEMALES	1865 MALES	1865 FEMALES	1870 MALES	1870 FEMALES	STABLE MALES	STABLE FEMALES
RATES PER THOUSAND											
Birth	28.02	29.82	26.34	29.72	26.47	29.59	26.57	29.24	26.45	28.95	27.20
Death	21.56	22.38	20.80	22.56	20.94	22.23	20.73	21.86	20.48	21.06	19.31
Increase	6.45	7.44	5.53	7.16	5.53	7.36	5.84	7.38	5.97		7.8910
PERCENTAGE											
under 15	27.50	28.67	26.42	29.36	27.20	30.23	28.18	30.92	28.98	30.11	29.30
15-64	61.09	60.74	61.42	60.50	60.99	60.00	60.33	59.67	59.84	61.28	61.13
65 and over	11.40	10.59	12.16	10.15	11.80	9.77	11.49	9.41	11.18	8.61	9.57
DEP. RATIO X 100	63.68	64.62	62.81	65.29	63.95	66.67	65.76	67.59	67.10	63.17	63.60

AGE AT LAST BIRTHDAY	BOTH SEXES	1860 MALES	FEMALES	BOTH SEXES	1865 MALES	FEMALES	BOTH SEXES	1870 MALES	FEMALES	AGE AT LAST BIRTHDAY	
0-4	526	266	260	544	275	269	559	283	276	0-4	
5-9	420	211	209	476	240	236	492	248	244	5-9	**TABLE 5**
10-14	390	196	194	405	203	202	460	232	228	10-14	
15-19	385	193	192	382	192	190	397	199	198	15-19	POPULATION
20-24	365	182	183	375	188	187	371	186	185	20-24	PROJECTED
25-29	342	169	173	353	175	178	363	181	182	25-29	WITH
30-34	317	155	162	330	163	167	342	170	172	30-34	FIXED
35-39	285	136	149	306	149	157	319	158	161	35-39	AGE—
40-44	266	126	140	273	130	143	294	143	151	40-44	SPECIFIC
45-49	251	118	133	254	120	134	261	124	137	45-49	BIRTH
50-54	238	111	127	238	111	127	241	113	128	50-54	AND
55-59	222	103	119	223	103	120	223	103	120	55-59	DEATH
60-64	204	94	110	204	94	110	205	94	111	60-64	RATES
65-69	179	81	98	179	81	98	179	81	98	65-69	(IN 1000's)
70-74	147	66	81	147	66	81	147	66	81	70-74	
75-79	106	47	59	106	47	59	106	47	59	75-79	
80-84	60	26	34	60	26	34	60	26	34	80-84	
85+	29	12	17	29	12	17	29	12	17	85+	
TOTAL	4732	2292	2440	4884	2375	2509	5048	2466	2582	TOTAL	

STANDARD COUNTRIES:	ENGLAND AND WALES 1961			UNITED STATES 1960			MEXICO 1960			
STANDARDIZED RATES PER THOUSAND	BOTH SEXES	MALES	FEMALES	BOTH SEXES	MALES	FEMALES	BOTH SEXES	MALES	FEMALES	**TABLE 6**
Birth	26.69	29.08*	25.17	27.08	26.88*	25.97	26.11	26.82*	25.35	STANDAR-
Death	20.68	20.92*	21.25	20.11	19.11*	19.48	18.33	15.89*	17.14	DIZED RATES
Increase	6.01	8.15*	3.92	6.98	7.76*	6.49	7.78	10.92*	8.21	

	OBSERVED POP.		STATIONARY POP.		STABLE POP.		OBSERVED BIRTHS	NET MATERNITY FUNCTION	BIRTHS IN STABLE POP.	
	MALES	FEMALES	MALES	FEMALES	MALES	FEMALES				
μ	32.27822	34.00381	34.71664	35.62092	30.83923	31.61026	31.97030	32.22265	31.90330	**TABLE 7**
σ^2	507.5529	526.0632	508.0059	524.4690	472.6222	489.6688	38.69809	38.51962	38.24379	
κ_3	5348.839	4600.496	3625.961	3449.834	5235.753	5259.732	40.3898	30.4962	39.3569	MOMENTS
κ_4	-214960.	-256224.	-242643.	-269094.	-162118.	-185383.	-1141.309	-1138.149	-1095.354	AND
β_1	0.218814	0.145377	0.100286	0.082497	0.259667	0.235624	0.028150	0.016272	0.027692	CUMULANTS
β_2	2.165560	2.074142	2.059780	2.021717	2.274225	2.226850	2.237878	2.232929	2.251085	
κ	-0.078408	-0.052034	-0.037068	-0.030101	-0.097330	-0.087097	-0.013535	-0.007922	-0.013535	

VITAL STATISTICS		THOMPSON				BOURGEOIS-PICHAT				COALE		**TABLE 8**
		AGE RANGE	NRR	1000r	INTERVAL	AGE RANGE	NRR	1000b	1000d	1000r			RATES FROM AGE DISTRI-
GRR	2.001										IBR	24.02	BUTIONS
NRR	1.288	0-4	1.14	4.77	27.09	5-29	1.11	23.78	19.95	3.83	IDR	19.16	AND VITAL
TFR	4.112	5-9	1.12	4.17	26.99	30-54	1.05	21.10	19.37	1.73	IRI	4.87	STATISTICS
GENERATION	32.063	10-14	1.16	5.33	26.95	55-79	1.01	19.66	19.34	0.32	K1	-3.00	(Females)
SEX RATIO	105.485	15-19	1.15	5.03	26.88	*40-64	1.01	19.89	19.38	0.51	K2	-0.08	

Start of Age Interval	ORIGINAL MATRIX			FIRST STABLE MATRIX			SECOND STABLE MATRIX Z2		
	SUB-DIAGONAL	ALTERNATIVE FIRST ROWS Projection	Integral	% IN STABLE POPULATION	FISHER VALUES	REPRODUCTIVE VALUES	FIRST COLUMN	FIRST ROW	
0	0.90818	0.00000	0.00000	10.917	1.245	287036	0.1361+0.0453	0.1361+0.0453	
5	0.96637	0.00000	0.00000	9.531	1.427	286603	0.1172-0.0847	0.0423+0.1359	**TABLE 9**
10	0.98008	0.00569	0.00000	8.854	1.536	301337	-0.0003-0.1550	-0.0798+0.1061	
15	0.97423	0.10326	0.01183	8.342	1.623	304766	-0.1371-0.0982	-0.1228-0.0029	LESLIE
20	0.97018	0.29337	0.20406	7.812	1.601	284695	-0.1727+0.0583	-0.0786-0.0986	MATRIX
25	0.96856	0.41332	0.40650	7.286	1.340	224731	-0.0576+0.1876	-0.0094-0.1265	AND ITS
30	0.96513	0.39595	0.45078	6.783	0.908	139683	0.1275+0.1679	0.0323-0.0952	SPECTRAL
35	0.96287	0.27718	0.36980	6.293	0.467	67889	0.2257-0.0058	0.0339-0.0460	COMPO-
40	0.96066	0.11109	0.20315	5.825	0.146	20261	0.1358-0.1994	0.0143-0.0124	NENTS
45	0.95524	0.01202	0.02441	5.379	0.014	1919	-0.0880-0.2416	0.0016-0.0011	(Females)
50	0.94423	0.00006	0.00011	4.940	0.000	8	-0.2624-0.0738	0.0000-0.0000	
55+	0.78172			18.039					

Start of Age Interval	OBSERVED POPUL. (IN 100's)	CONTRIBUTIONS OF ROOTS (IN 100's)			AGE-SP. BIRTH RATES	NET MATERNITY FUNCTION	COEFF. OF MATRIX EQUATION	PARAMETERS			EXP. INCREASE		
		r_1	r_2, r_3	$r_4 \cdot r_{11}$					INTEGRAL	MATRIX	x	$e^{(x+2\frac{1}{2})r}$	
0	2305	2419	-46	-67	0.0000	0.0000	0.0000	L(1)	1.04024	1.04028	0	1.0199	**TABLE 10**
5	2009	2112	-92	-11	0.0000	0.0000	0.0000	L(2)	0.52784	0.52626	50	1.5133	
10	1962	1962	-65	65	0.0000	0.0000	0.0050		0.74717	0.73159	55	1.5742	AGE ANALYSIS
15	1878	1848	25	5	0.0028	0.0100	0.0888	R(1)	0.00789	0.00790	60	1.6375	AND
20	1779	1731	107	-59	0.0489	0.1677	0.2458	R(2)	-0.01781	-0.02080	65	1.7034	MISCEL-
25	1677	1614	106	-43	0.0974	0.3240	0.3360		0.19115	0.18944	70	1.7720	LANEOUS
30	1539	1503	9	28	0.1080	0.3480	0.3118	C(1)		22154	75	1.8433	RESULTS
35	1453	1394	-111	169	0.0886	0.2756	0.2107	C(2)		-24018	80	1.9175	(Females)
40	1385	1290	-148	243	0.0487	0.1458	0.0813			-20864	85	1.9946	
45	1328	1192	-59	195	0.0058	0.0168	0.0084	2P/Y	32.8703	33.1667	90	2.0749	
50	1264	1094	95	75	0.0000	0.0001	0.0000	DELTA	4.3527		95	2.1584	
55+	5179	3996									100	2.2453	

TABLE 1 — DATA

AGE AT LAST BIRTHDAY	POPULATION BOTH SEXES	MALES Number	MALES %	FEMALES Number	FEMALES %	BIRTHS BY AGE OF MOTHER	DEATHS BOTH SEXES	DEATHS MALES	DEATHS FEMALES	AGE AT LAST BIRTHDAY
0	118656	60210	2.5	58446	2.2	0	17889	9849	8040	0
1-4	388464	195335	8.1	193129	7.4	0	11546	5993	5553	1-4
5-9	455144	228736	9.5	226408	8.7	0	4073	2129	1944	5-9
10-14	434692	217713	9.0	216979	8.3	0	1751	887	864	10-14
15-19	424650	213112	8.8	211538	8.1	1751	1973	1003	970	15-19
20-24	395162	195926	8.1	199236	7.6	20286	2292	1276	1016	20-24
25-29	344185	165971	6.9	178214	6.8	35496	2174	1111	1063	25-29
30-34	314346	148745	6.2	165601	6.3	34567	2079	993	1086	30-34
35-39	296807	139333	5.8	157474	6.0	27526	2158	1031	1127	35-39
40-44	285066	133556	5.5	151510	5.8	13974	2339	1167	1172	40-44
45-49	272252	126989	5.3	145263	5.6	1539	2487	1267	1220	45-49
50-54	258973	120313	5.0	138660	5.3	7	2824	1464	1360	50-54
55-59	243053	112056	4.6	130997	5.0	0	3489	1830	1659	55-59
60-64	222847	102042	4.2	120805	4.6	0	4569	2277	2292	60-64
65-69	196792	89333	3.7	107459	4.1	0	5998	2946	3052	65-69
70-74	161267	72577	3.0	88690	3.4		8172	3853	4319	70-74
75-79	116170	51737	2.1	64433	2.5		10028	4629	5399	75-79
80-84	65284	28574	1.2	36710	1.4	69401 M.	9555	4336	5219	80-84
85+	35228	14793	0.6	20435	0.8	65745 F.	9281	3995	5286	85+
TOTAL	5029038	2417051		2611987		135146	104677	52036	52641	TOTAL

TABLE 2 — MALE LIFE TABLE

x	$_nq_x$	l_x	$_nd_x$	$_nL_x$	$_nm_x$	$_na_x$	T_x	r_x	$\mathring{e}_x$	$_nM_x$	x
0	0.148087	100000	14809	90876	0.162955	0.3839	4651959	0.0065	46.520	0.163577	0
1	0.113009	85191	9627	314674	0.030595	1.2899	4561083	0.0065	53.539	0.030681	1
5	0.045407	75564	3431	369241	0.009292	2.5000	4246409	0.0032	56.196	0.009308	5
10	0.020137	72133	1453	356660	0.004073	2.2439	3877167	0.0016	53.750	0.004074	10
15	0.023283	70680	1646	349446	0.004709	2.5966	3520507	0.0057	49.809	0.004706	15
20	0.032091	69035	2215	339750	0.006521	2.5521	3171061	0.0188	45.934	0.006513	20
25	0.032920	66819	2200	328577	0.006695	2.4912	2831311	0.0209	42.373	0.006694	25
30	0.032840	64619	2122	317807	0.006677	2.5070	2502734	0.0107	38.730	0.006676	30
35	0.036343	62497	2271	306903	0.007401	2.5416	2184927	0.0033	34.960	0.007400	35
40	0.042773	60226	2576	294801	0.008738	2.5433	1878025	0.0006	31.183	0.008738	40
45	0.048697	57650	2807	281370	0.009977	2.5494	1583223	0.0003	27.463	0.009977	45
50	0.059101	54843	3241	266370	0.012168	2.5801	1301853	0.0000	23.738	0.012168	50
55	0.078566	51601	4054	248245	0.016331	2.5922	1035484	0.0000	20.067	0.016331	55
60	0.105903	47547	5035	225657	0.022314	2.6011	787238	0.0000	16.557	0.022314	60
65	0.152844	42512	6498	197031	0.032978	2.6103	561582	0.0000	13.210	0.032978	65
70	0.235314	36014	8475	159631	0.053089	2.5882	364550	0.0000	10.122	0.053088	70
75	0.366182	27539	10084	112711	0.089472	2.5222	204919	0.0000	7.441	0.089472	75
80	0.547196	17455	9551	62942	0.151747	2.4524	92209	0.0000	5.283	0.151746	80
85+	*1.000000	7904	7904	29266	0.270064	3.7028	29266	0.0000	3.703	0.270060	85+

TABLE 3 — FEMALE LIFE TABLE

x	$_nq_x$	l_x	$_nd_x$	$_nL_x$	$_nm_x$	$_na_x$	T_x	r_x	$\mathring{e}_x$	$_nM_x$	x
0	0.126587	100000	12659	92347	0.137077	0.3955	4954301	0.0061	49.543	0.137563	0
1	0.106542	87341	9306	324424	0.028683	1.3197	4861954	0.0061	55.666	0.028753	1
5	0.041968	78036	3275	381991	0.008574	2.5000	4537530	0.0028	58.147	0.008586	5
10	0.019689	74761	1472	369788	0.003981	2.2717	4155538	0.0015	55.584	0.003982	10
15	0.022676	73289	1662	362358	0.004586	2.5417	3785751	0.0041	51.655	0.004585	15
20	0.025199	71627	1805	353703	0.005103	2.5452	3423393	0.0120	47.795	0.005099	20
25	0.029411	69822	2054	344055	0.005969	2.5388	3069689	0.0126	43.965	0.005965	25
30	0.032273	67768	2187	333427	0.006559	2.5240	2725634	0.0058	40.220	0.006558	30
35	0.035162	65581	2306	322186	0.007157	2.5193	2392207	0.0017	36.477	0.007157	35
40	0.037949	63275	2401	310415	0.007736	2.5172	2070021	0.0003	32.714	0.007735	40
45	0.041141	60874	2504	298192	0.008399	2.5328	1759605	0.0003	28.906	0.008399	45
50	0.047900	58370	2796	285049	0.009808	2.5679	1461414	0.0003	25.037	0.009808	50
55	0.061472	55574	3416	269733	0.012665	2.6183	1176365	0.0005	21.168	0.012664	55
60	0.090791	52158	4735	249553	0.018976	2.6274	906632	0.0009	17.383	0.018973	60
65	0.133110	47422	6312	222212	0.028407	2.6397	657079	0.0009	13.856	0.028402	65
70	0.218169	41110	8969	184137	0.048707	2.6127	434867	0.0009	10.578	0.048698	70
75	0.347321	32141	11163	133199	0.083809	2.5361	250730	0.0009	7.801	0.083792	75
80	0.519678	20978	10902	76668	0.142193	2.4792	117531	0.0009	5.603	0.142168	80
85+	1.000000	10076	10076	40863	0.246583	4.0554	40863	0.0009	4.055	0.258673	85+

TABLE 4 — OBSERVED AND PROJECTED VITAL RATES

	OBSERVED POPULATION BOTH SEXES	OBSERVED MALES	OBSERVED FEMALES	PROJECTED POPULATION 1865 MALES	1865 FEMALES	1870 MALES	1870 FEMALES	1875 MALES	1875 FEMALES	STABLE POPULATION MALES	STABLE FEMALES
RATES PER THOUSAND											
Birth	26.87	28.71	25.17	28.89	25.57	29.01	25.92	28.84	26.00	27.98	26.44
Death	20.81	21.53	20.15	21.55	20.24	21.27	20.09	20.92	19.87	19.97	18.43
Increase	6.06	7.18	5.02	7.34	5.34	7.73	5.83	7.91	6.14		8.0085
PERCENTAGE											
under 15	27.78	29.04	26.61	29.58	27.21	30.20	27.96	30.91	28.79	29.89	29.16
15-64	60.79	60.32	61.23	60.25	60.95	60.03	60.51	59.72	60.01	61.39	61.22
65 and over	11.43	10.63	12.16	10.17	11.84	9.77	11.53	9.37	11.20	8.72	9.62
DEP. RATIO X 100	64.49	65.77	63.32	65.97	64.07	66.59	65.27	67.45	66.63	62.90	63.35

TABLE 1 DATA

AGE AT LAST BIRTHDAY	BOTH SEXES	POPULATION MALES Number	%	FEMALES Number	%	BIRTHS BY AGE OF MOTHER	DEATHS BOTH SEXES	MALES	FEMALES	AGE AT LAST BIRTHDAY
0	121553	61536	2.4	60017	2.2	0	17995	9901	8094	0
1-4	421623	212595	8.3	209028	7.6	0	12328	6455	5873	1-4
5-9	483845	242731	9.5	241114	8.8	0	3887	2009	1878	5-9
10-14	469168	235597	9.2	233571	8.5	1	1995	992	1003	10-14
15-19	453549	228036	8.9	225513	8.2	2171	2041	1011	1030	15-19
20-24	403584	199806	7.8	203778	7.4	21487	2377	1295	1082	20-24
25-29	352160	170190	6.7	181970	6.6	34889	2243	1111	1132	25-29
30-34	323422	153791	6.0	169631	6.2	34814	2117	1012	1105	30-34
35-39	310748	146891	5.8	163857	6.0	27484	2247	1090	1157	35-39
40-44	296873	139307	5.5	157566	5.7	13252	2296	1142	1154	40-44
45-49	284791	133207	5.2	151584	5.5	1421	2447	1268	1179	45-49
50-54	271205	126112	4.9	145093	5.3	7	2845	1475	1370	50-54
55-59	255378	118320	4.6	137058	5.0	0	3655	1847	1808	55-59
60-64	235369	108436	4.3	126933	4.6	0	4565	2297	2268	60-64
65-69	207857	94977	3.7	112880	4.1	0	6448	3145	3303	65-69
70-74	170475	77117	3.0	93358	3.4		8665	4126	4539	70-74
75-79	120820	53882	2.1	66938	2.4		10308	4850	5458	75-79
80-84	70061	30598	1.2	39463	1.4	69628 M.	9941	4531	5410	80-84
85+	38139	15901	0.6	22238	0.8	65898 F.	10065	4390	5675	85+
TOTAL	5290620	2549030		2741590		135526	108465	53947	54518	TOTAL

TABLE 2 MALE LIFE TABLE

x	nq_x	l_x	nd_x	nL_x	nm_x	na_x	T_x	r_x	$\dot{e}_x$	nM_x	x
0	0.146371	100000	14637	90991	0.160863	0.3845	4709168	0.0004	47.092	0.160898	0
1	0.112206	85363	9578	315509	0.030358	1.2915	4618177	0.0004	54.101	0.030363	1
5	0.040479	75785	3068	371254	0.008263	2.5000	4302668	0.0029	56.775	0.008277	5
10	0.020812	72717	1513	359488	0.004210	2.2929	3931414	0.0010	54.065	0.004211	10
15	0.021940	71204	1564	352257	0.004439	2.5948	3571927	0.0117	50.165	0.004434	15
20	0.031951	69640	2225	342762	0.006492	2.5563	3219669	0.0232	46.233	0.006481	20
25	0.032115	67415	2165	331638	0.006528	2.4892	2876907	0.0196	42.675	0.006528	25
30	0.032379	65250	2113	320995	0.006582	2.5134	2545269	0.0080	39.008	0.006580	30
35	0.036439	63137	2301	310003	0.007421	2.5300	2224274	0.0025	35.229	0.007420	35
40	0.040180	60836	2444	298158	0.008198	2.5354	1914271	0.0015	31.466	0.008198	40
45	0.046514	58392	2716	285320	0.009519	2.5554	1616114	0.0003	27.677	0.009519	45
50	0.056871	55676	3166	270721	0.011696	2.5812	1330793	0.0000	23.902	0.011696	50
55	0.075223	52510	3950	253034	0.015610	2.5912	1060072	0.0000	20.188	0.015610	55
60	0.100827	48560	4896	231132	0.021183	2.6171	807038	0.0001	16.619	0.021183	60
65	0.153474	43664	6701	202369	0.033114	2.6201	575907	0.0001	13.190	0.033113	65
70	0.236935	36962	8758	163683	0.053504	2.5874	373537	0.0001	10.106	0.053503	70
75	0.367840	28205	10375	115259	0.090013	2.5166	209854	0.0001	7.440	0.090012	75
80	0.537677	17830	9587	64739	0.148084	2.4537	94595	0.0001	5.305	0.148081	80
85+	*1.000000	8243	8243	29857	0.276092	3.6220	29857	0.0001	3.622	0.276083	85+

TABLE 3 FEMALE LIFE TABLE

x	nq_x	l_x	nd_x	nL_x	nm_x	na_x	T_x	r_x	$\dot{e}_x$	nM_x	x
0	0.124619	100000	12462	92464	0.134775	0.3953	4997822	0.0011	49.978	0.134862	0
1	0.104471	87538	9145	325637	0.028084	1.3193	4905357	0.0011	56.037	0.028097	1
5	0.038146	78393	2990	384489	0.007777	2.5000	4579720	0.0027	58.420	0.007789	5
10	0.021222	75403	1600	372737	0.004293	2.3278	4195232	0.0015	55.638	0.004294	10
15	0.022592	73802	1667	364904	0.004569	2.5365	3822495	0.0091	51.794	0.004567	15
20	0.026235	72135	1892	356045	0.005315	2.5534	3457591	0.0161	47.932	0.005310	20
25	0.030648	70243	2153	345891	0.006224	2.5281	3101546	0.0123	44.155	0.006221	25
30	0.032055	68090	2183	335020	0.006515	2.5128	2755655	0.0039	40.471	0.006514	30
35	0.034695	65907	2287	323841	0.007061	2.5096	2420635	0.0004	36.728	0.007061	35
40	0.035963	63620	2288	312394	0.007324	2.5049	2096794	0.0004	32.958	0.007324	40
45	0.038159	61332	2340	300902	0.007778	2.5388	1784401	0.0003	29.094	0.007778	45
50	0.046165	58992	2723	288414	0.009442	2.5962	1483499	0.0002	25.147	0.009442	50
55	0.063938	56269	3598	272723	0.013192	2.6038	1195085	0.0001	21.239	0.013191	55
60	0.085736	52671	4516	252609	0.017871	2.6381	922362	0.0010	17.512	0.017868	60
65	0.136894	48155	6592	225241	0.029267	2.6433	669672	0.0010	13.907	0.029261	65
70	0.217756	41563	9051	186115	0.048629	2.6023	444432	0.0010	10.693	0.048619	70
75	0.339504	32512	11038	135346	0.081554	2.5344	258316	0.0010	7.945	0.081538	75
80	0.506272	21474	10872	79290	0.137115	2.4917	122970	0.0010	5.726	0.137090	80
85+	1.000000	10603	10603	43680	0.242731	4.1198	43680	0.0010	4.120	0.255193	85+

TABLE 4 OBSERVED AND PROJECTED VITAL RATES

RATES PER THOUSAND	OBSERVED POPULATION BOTH SEXES	MALES	FEMALES	PROJECTED POPULATION 1870 MALES	FEMALES	1875 MALES	FEMALES	1880 MALES	FEMALES	STABLE POPULATION MALES	FEMALES
Birth	25.62	27.32	24.04	27.67	24.58	28.14	25.23	28.32	25.61	27.11	25.69
Death	20.50	21.16	19.89	20.82	19.76	20.60	19.65	20.36	19.52	19.76	18.33
Increase	5.11	6.15	4.15	6.85	4.82	7.54	5.58	7.96	6.09		7.3554
PERCENTAGE											
under 15	28.28	29.52	27.13	29.45	27.21	29.73	27.61	30.09	28.13	29.24	28.63
15-64	60.24	59.79	60.66	60.28	60.84	60.37	60.72	60.40	60.53	61.66	61.38
65 and over	11.48	10.69	12.21	10.28	11.95	9.90	11.67	9.50	11.35	9.09	9.99
DEP. RATIO X 100	66.00	67.25	64.86	65.90	64.37	65.66	64.69	65.56	65.22	62.17	62.92

AGE AT LAST BIRTHDAY	POPULATION BOTH SEXES	MALES Number	%	FEMALES Number	%	BIRTHS BY AGE OF MOTHER	DEATHS BOTH SEXES	MALES	FEMALES	AGE AT LAST BIRTHDAY
0	105355	53455	2.2	51900	2.0	0	16615	9166	7449	0
1-4	392700	197974	8.3	194726	7.6	0	10729	5571	5158	1-4
5-9	458842	231349	9.7	227493	8.9	0	4087	2096	1991	5-9
10-14	442830	223321	9.3	219509	8.6	1	2031	984	1047	10-14
15-19	420423	212286	8.9	208137	8.2	2226	1927	978	949	15-19
20-24	356486	174358	7.3	182128	7.1	19346	2166	1159	1007	20-24
25-29	318734	154326	6.5	164408	6.5	31702	1980	1002	978	25-29
30-34	305197	146762	6.1	158435	6.2	31472	2002	969	1033	30-34
35-39	289982	137649	5.8	152333	6.0	23447	2007	952	1055	35-39
40-44	279022	132033	5.5	146989	5.8	10946	2054	1009	1045	40-44
45-49	268004	126300	5.3	141704	5.6	1066	2202	1117	1085	45-49
50-54	256205	120573	5.0	135632	5.3	4	2717	1368	1349	50-54
55-59	241915	113521	4.7	128394	5.0	0	3155	1609	1546	55-59
60-64	223085	104011	4.3	119074	4.7	0	4406	2245	2161	60-64
65-69	197277	91354	3.8	105923	4.2	0	6164	3061	3103	65-69
70-74	160646	73599	3.1	87047	3.4		8075	3918	4157	70-74
75-79	116068	52510	2.2	63558	2.5		9564	4498	5066	75-79
80-84	68627	30412	1.3	38215	1.5	61780 M.	9507	4370	5137	80-84
85+	38453	16106	0.7	22347	0.9	58430 F.	9976	4369	5607	85+
TOTAL	4939851	2391899		2547952		120210	101364	50441	50923	TOTAL

TABLE 1 / DATA

x	nq_x	l_x	nd_x	nL_x	nm_x	na_x	T_x	r_x	$\mathring{e}_x$	nM_x	
0	0.154781	100000	15478	90266	0.171471	0.3711	4703192	0.0000	47.032	0.171471	
1	0.104505	84522	8833	313894	0.028140	1.2610	4612926	0.0000	54.577	0.028140	
5	0.044296	75689	3353	370063	0.009060	2.5000	4299032	0.0000	56.799	0.009060	
10	0.021755	72336	1574	357385	0.004403	2.2700	3928969	0.0030	54.315	0.004406	
15	0.022826	70763	1615	349918	0.004616	2.5891	3571585	0.0198	50.473	0.004607	
20	0.032754	69147	2265	340183	0.006658	2.5479	3221666	0.0257	46.591	0.006647	
25	0.031941	66882	2136	329038	0.006493	2.4842	2881483	0.0106	43.083	0.006493	
30	0.032478	64746	2103	318472	0.006603	2.4994	2552446	0.0048	39.422	0.006603	
35	0.034000	62643	2130	307926	0.006917	2.5163	2233973	0.0036	35.662	0.006916	
40	0.037506	60513	2270	296974	0.007642	2.5359	1926047	0.0009	31.828	0.007642	
45	0.043289	58244	2521	285084	0.008844	2.5667	1629072	0.0000	27.970	0.008844	
50	0.055209	55723	3076	271148	0.011346	2.5736	1343989	0.0000	24.119	0.011346	
55	0.068549	52646	3609	254616	0.014174	2.6131	1072841	0.0000	20.378	0.014174	
60	0.102676	49037	5035	233269	0.021584	2.6331	818224	0.0000	16.686	0.021584	
65	0.155132	44002	6826	203723	0.033507	2.6138	584955	0.0000	13.294	0.033507	
70	0.235754	37176	8764	164638	0.053235	2.5763	381232	0.0000	10.255	0.053234	
75	0.353233	28412	10036	117160	0.085660	2.5191	216593	0.0000	7.623	0.085660	
80	0.526975	18376	9684	67390	0.143694	2.4711	99433	0.0000	5.411	0.143694	
85+	*1.000000	8692	8692	32043	0.271267	3.6864	32043	0.0000	3.686	0.271265	

TABLE 2 / MALE LIFE TABLE

x	nq_x	l_x	nd_x	nL_x	nm_x	na_x	T_x	r_x	$\mathring{e}_x$	nM_x	
0	0.131867	100000	13187	91877	0.143526	0.3840	4966904	0.0000	49.669	0.143526	
1	0.098858	86813	8582	323997	0.026488	1.2902	4875027	0.0000	56.155	0.026488	
5	0.042823	78231	3350	382780	0.008752	2.5000	4551030	0.0000	58.174	0.008752	
10	0.023531	74881	1762	369646	0.004767	2.2989	4168250	0.0032	55.665	0.004770	
15	0.022553	73119	1649	361512	0.004562	2.5239	3798604	0.0139	51.951	0.004559	
20	0.027300	71470	1951	352553	0.005534	2.5415	3437092	0.0182	48.091	0.005529	
25	0.029319	69519	2038	342543	0.005950	2.5218	3084540	0.0079	44.370	0.005949	
30	0.032082	67481	2165	332029	0.006520	2.5178	2741997	0.0011	40.634	0.006520	
35	0.034040	65316	2223	321028	0.006926	2.5036	2409969	0.0006	36.897	0.006926	
40	0.034928	63092	2204	309966	0.007109	2.5061	2088941	0.0001	33.109	0.007109	
45	0.037582	60889	2288	298856	0.007657	2.5584	1778975	0.0000	29.217	0.007657	
50	0.048558	58600	2845	286091	0.009946	2.5714	1480119	0.0001	25.258	0.009946	
55	0.058523	55755	3263	270976	0.012041	2.6100	1194029	0.0002	21.416	0.012041	
60	0.087039	52492	4569	251725	0.018150	2.6506	923053	0.0005	17.585	0.018148	
65	0.137001	47923	6566	224095	0.029298	2.6362	671327	0.0005	14.008	0.029295	
70	0.214248	41357	8861	185523	0.047761	2.6002	447232	0.0005	10.814	0.047756	
75	0.333177	32497	10827	135824	0.079715	2.5377	261709	0.0005	8.053	0.079707	
80	0.499201	21670	10817	80465	0.134436	2.5005	125885	0.0005	5.809	0.134424	
85+	1.000000	10852	10852	45420	0.238930	4.1853	45420	0.0005	4.185	0.250905	

TABLE 3 / FEMALE LIFE TABLE

		OBSERVED POPULATION			PROJECTED POPULATION 1875		1880		1885		STABLE POPULATION	
		BOTH SEXES	MALES	FEMALES	MALES	FEMALES	MALES	FEMALES	MALES	FEMALES	MALES	FEMAL
RATES PER THOUSAND												
Birth		24.33	25.83	22.93	26.25	23.50	26.96	24.33	27.47	24.99	26.00	24.7
Death		20.52	21.09	19.99	20.60	19.69	20.45	19.61	20.30	19.56	20.03	18.7
Increase		3.82	4.74	2.95	5.64	3.81	6.51	4.72	7.16	5.43		5.966
PERCENTAGE												
under 15		28.34	29.52	27.22	28.90	26.82	28.65	26.76	28.85	27.10	28.18	27.6
15-64		59.90	59.44	60.33	60.43	60.96	61.00	61.25	61.15	61.18	62.02	61.6
65 and over		11.76	11.04	12.44	10.67	12.22	10.35	11.99	10.00	11.72	9.80	10.6
DEP. RATIO X 100		66.94	68.23	65.75	65.48	64.04	63.94	63.27	63.53	63.44	61.25	62.

TABLE 4 / OBSERVED AND PROJECTED VITAL RATES

TABLE 1

AGE AT LAST BIRTHDAY	POPULATION BOTH SEXES	MALES Number	%	FEMALES Number	%	BIRTHS BY AGE OF MOTHER	DEATHS BOTH SEXES	MALES	FEMALES	AGE AT LAST BIRTHDAY
0	119957	60935	2.3	59022	2.2	0	18637	10275	8362	0
1-4	420589	213126	8.1	207463	7.6	0	11330	5866	5464	1-4
5-9	484981	245334	9.4	239647	8.8	0	4512	2280	2232	5-9
10-14	458477	231754	8.8	226723	8.3	1	1871	920	951	10-14
15-19	429103	217031	8.3	212072	7.8	2255	1962	978	984	15-19
20-24	373374	185201	7.1	188173	6.9	20513	2285	1219	1066	20-24
25-29	351122	173509	6.6	177613	6.5	34422	2301	1176	1125	25-29
30-34	330424	161564	6.2	168831	6.2	31778	2027	976	1051	30-34
35-39	317117	154069	5.9	163048	6.0	23159	2008	982	1026	35-39
40-44	304209	146670	5.6	157539	5.8	10138	2143	1043	1100	40-44
45-49	293133	141393	5.4	151740	5.6	1043	2441	1233	1208	45-49
50-54	281228	135531	5.2	145697	5.4	5	2642	1333	1309	50-54
55-59	266068	127977	4.9	138091	5.1	0	3489	1796	1693	55-59
60-64	246708	118165	4.5	128543	4.7	0	4764	2476	2288	60-64
65-69	218002	103492	4.0	114510	4.2	0	6485	3336	3149	65-69
70-74	182609	86336	3.3	96273	3.5		8541	4239	4302	70-74
75-79	133152	61696	2.4	71456	2.6		10625	5163	5462	75-79
80-84	79653	36152	1.4	43501	1.6	63390 M.	10572	5032	5540	80-84
85+	45107	19131	0.7	25976	1.0	59924 F.	10845	4838	6007	85+
TOTAL	5335013	2619095		2715918		123314	109480	55161	54319	TOTAL

TABLE 2 (MALE, FEMALE)

x	nq_x	l_x	nd_x	nL_x	nm_x	na_x	T_x	r_x	$\dot{e}_x$	nM_x	x
0	0.152449	100000	15245	90409	0.168622	0.3709	4776089	0.0000	47.761	0.168622	0
1	0.102375	84755	8677	315249	0.027524	1.2604	4685680	0.0000	55.285	0.027524	1
5	0.045318	76078	3448	371772	0.009274	2.5000	4370431	0.0046	57.447	0.009293	5
10	0.019598	72631	1423	359207	0.003963	2.2282	3998659	0.0069	55.055	0.003970	10
15	0.022338	71207	1591	352233	0.004516	2.6092	3639451	0.0177	51.111	0.004506	15
20	0.032428	69617	2258	342575	0.006590	2.5603	3287218	0.0162	47.219	0.006582	20
25	0.033314	67359	2244	331118	0.006777	2.4702	2944643	0.0070	43.716	0.006778	25
30	0.029743	65115	1937	320679	0.006039	2.4719	2613525	0.0056	40.137	0.006040	30
35	0.031377	63178	1982	310978	0.006374	2.5212	2292846	0.0033	36.292	0.006374	35
40	0.034951	61196	2139	300745	0.007112	2.5525	1981868	0.0013	32.386	0.007111	40
45	0.042689	59057	2521	289103	0.008720	2.5477	1681123	0.0000	28.466	0.008720	45
50	0.048037	56536	2716	276127	0.009835	2.5870	1392019	0.0000	24.622	0.009835	50
55	0.067911	53820	3655	260441	0.014034	2.6306	1115892	0.0000	20.734	0.014034	55
60	0.099826	50165	5008	238953	0.020957	2.6291	855451	0.0009	17.053	0.020954	60
65	0.149646	45158	6758	209607	0.032240	2.6055	616497	0.0009	13.652	0.032234	65
70	0.219554	38400	8431	171680	0.049108	2.5899	406891	0.0009	10.596	0.049099	70
75	0.346845	29969	10395	124189	0.083700	2.5317	235211	0.0009	7.848	0.083685	75
80	0.511609	19574	10014	71936	0.139214	2.4826	111022	0.0009	5.672	0.139190	80
85+	1.000000	9560	9560	39086	0.244585	4.0886	39086	0.0009	4.089	0.252887	85+

TABLE 3 (MALE, FEMALE)

x	nq_x	l_x	nd_x	nL_x	nm_x	na_x	T_x	r_x	$\dot{e}_x$	nM_x	x
0	0.130287	100000	13029	91985	0.141639	0.3848	5005097	0.0004	50.051	0.141676	0
1	0.098319	86971	8551	324731	0.026332	1.2922	4913113	0.0004	56.491	0.026337	1
5	0.045426	78420	3562	383196	0.009296	2.5000	4588382	0.0043	58.510	0.009314	5
10	0.020701	74858	1550	370025	0.004188	2.2474	4205186	0.0067	56.175	0.004195	10
15	0.022960	73308	1683	362428	0.004644	2.5561	3835161	0.0140	52.315	0.004640	15
20	0.027958	71625	2003	353221	0.005669	2.5507	3472733	0.0121	48.485	0.005665	20
25	0.031180	69623	2171	342700	0.006335	2.5062	3119511	0.0047	44.806	0.006334	25
30	0.030646	67452	2067	332061	0.006225	2.4854	2776812	0.0023	41.167	0.006225	30
35	0.030978	65385	2026	321882	0.006293	2.5111	2444750	0.0005	37.390	0.006293	35
40	0.034321	63359	2175	311435	0.006982	2.5348	2122868	0.0002	33.505	0.006982	40
45	0.039039	61185	2389	300037	0.007961	2.5358	1811433	0.0000	29.606	0.007961	45
50	0.043965	58796	2585	287718	0.008984	2.5773	1511396	0.0000	25.706	0.008984	50
55	0.059562	56211	3348	273087	0.012260	2.6201	1223678	0.0000	21.769	0.012260	55
60	0.085414	52863	4515	253630	0.017803	2.6336	950591	0.0010	17.982	0.017799	60
65	0.129119	48348	6243	232600	0.027505	2.6330	696961	0.0010	14.416	0.027500	65
70	0.201923	42105	8502	190224	0.044695	2.6121	469998	0.0010	11.162	0.044685	70
75	0.321897	33603	10817	141480	0.076454	2.5468	279774	0.0010	8.326	0.076439	75
80	0.479838	22786	10934	85838	0.127376	2.5197	138294	0.0010	6.069	0.127353	80
85+	1.000000	11853	11853	52456	0.225955	4.4257	52456	0.0010	4.426	0.231253	85+

TABLE 4 — OBSERVED, PROJECTED, STABLE POPULATION

	OBSERVED POPULATION BOTH SEXES	MALES	FEMALES	PROJECTED POPULATION 1880 MALES	FEMALES	1885 MALES	FEMALES	1890 MALES	FEMALES	STABLE POPULATION MALES	FEMALES
RATES PER THOUSAND											
Birth	23.11	24.20	22.06	24.49	22.45	25.10	23.14	25.67	23.80	24.71	23.64
Death	20.52	21.06	20.00	20.55	19.65	20.40	19.57	20.29	19.54	19.88	18.82
Increase	2.59	3.14	2.06	3.94	2.80	4.70	3.56	5.38	4.26		4.8286
PERCENTAGE											
under 15	27.82	28.68	26.98	28.09	26.53	27.63	26.23	27.34	26.08	27.12	26.71
15-64	59.84	59.61	60.07	60.44	60.65	61.19	61.16	61.79	61.55	62.21	61.77
65 and over	12.34	11.71	12.95	11.48	12.81	11.18	12.61	10.87	12.37	10.67	11.52
DEP. RATIO X 100	67.11	67.77	66.48	65.47	64.88	63.44	63.50	61.83	62.48	60.74	61.90

TABLE 1 — DATA

AGE AT LAST BIRTHDAY	POPULATION BOTH SEXES	MALES Number	%	FEMALES Number	%	BIRTHS BY AGE OF MOTHER	DEATHS BOTH SEXES	MALES	FEMALES	AGE AT LAST BIRTHD
0	124044	62933	2.2	61111	2.1	0	16291	9021	7270	0
1-4	441326	223391	7.7	217935	7.3	0	11416	5893	5523	1-4
5-9	503826	254353	8.8	249473	8.4	0	4068	2084	1984	5-9
10-14	484848	244870	8.5	239978	8.1	1	1772	870	902	10-14
15-19	460012	233543	8.1	226469	7.6	2813	2094	1044	1050	15-19
20-24	424150	214860	7.4	209290	7.0	24443	2649	1452	1197	20-24
25-29	385084	191384	6.6	193700	6.5	36198	2361	1192	1169	25-29
30-34	367512	180900	6.3	186612	6.3	32223	2133	1079	1054	30-34
35-39	351486	170763	5.9	180723	6.1	21479	2156	1049	1107	35-39
40-44	339778	165167	5.7	174611	5.9	9489	2478	1243	1235	40-44
45-49	328682	159730	5.5	168952	5.7	869	2295	1166	1129	45-49
50-54	315272	153011	5.3	162261	5.5	4	2956	1507	1449	50-54
55-59	299716	145294	5.0	154422	5.2	0	3845	2009	1836	55-59
60-64	277442	133607	4.6	143835	4.8	0	5078	2702	2376	60-64
65-69	248494	118907	4.1	129587	4.4	0	6908	3580	3328	65-69
70-74	207555	97836	3.4	109719	3.7		9417	4726	4691	70-74
75-79	154322	71394	2.5	82928	2.8		11574	5743	5831	75-79
80-84	94823	42503	1.5	52320	1.8	65567 M.	11861	5664	6197	80-84
85+	53370	22210	0.8	31160	1.0	61952 F.	12823	5617	7206	85+
TOTAL	5861742	2886656		2975086		127519	114175	57641	56534	TOTAL

TABLE 2 — MALE LIFE TABLE

x	nq_x	l_x	nd_x	nL_x	nm_x	na_x	T_x	r_x	$\mathring{e}_x$	nM_x
0	0.131709	100000	13171	91884	0.143343	0.3838	4977988	0.0000	49.780	0.143343
1	0.098478	86829	8551	324141	0.026380	1.2896	4886105	0.0000	56.273	0.026380
5	0.040055	78278	3135	383553	0.008175	2.5000	4561964	0.0045	58.279	0.008193
10	0.017579	75143	1321	372100	0.003550	2.2633	4178411	0.0036	55.606	0.003553
15	0.022145	73822	1635	365248	0.004476	2.6377	3806311	0.0084	51.561	0.004470
20	0.033263	72187	2401	355038	0.006763	2.5437	3441063	0.0138	47.669	0.006758
25	0.030648	69786	2139	343497	0.006226	2.4597	3086025	0.0109	44.221	0.006228
30	0.029382	67647	1988	333236	0.005965	2.4841	2742528	0.0054	40.542	0.005965
35	0.030262	65660	1987	323407	0.006144	2.5382	2409292	0.0027	36.694	0.006143
40	0.036939	63673	2352	312528	0.007526	2.5188	2085885	0.0000	32.759	0.007526
45	0.035857	61321	2199	301209	0.007300	2.5467	1773358	0.0000	28.919	0.007300
50	0.048115	59122	2845	288825	0.009849	2.6148	1472149	0.0000	24.900	0.009849
55	0.066936	56277	3767	272432	0.013827	2.6229	1183324	0.0000	21.027	0.013827
60	0.096501	52510	5067	250487	0.020230	2.6192	910892	0.0019	17.347	0.020223
65	0.140508	47443	6666	221333	0.030118	2.6175	660404	0.0019	13.920	0.030108
70	0.216469	40777	8827	182663	0.048324	2.5958	439071	0.0019	10.768	0.048305
75	0.335710	31950	10726	133289	0.080471	2.5330	256408	0.0019	8.025	0.080441
80	0.495913	21224	10525	78956	0.133307	2.4995	123119	0.0019	5.801	0.133261
85+	1.000000	10699	10699	44164	0.242252	4.1279	44164	0.0019	4.128	0.252905

TABLE 3 — FEMALE LIFE TABLE

x	nq_x	l_x	nd_x	nL_x	nm_x	na_x	T_x	r_x	$\mathring{e}_x$	nM_x
0	0.111016	100000	11102	93323	0.118959	0.3985	5225397	0.0001	52.254	0.118964
1	0.094939	88898	8440	333045	0.025342	1.3283	5132074	0.0001	57.730	0.025342
5	0.038908	80458	3130	394466	0.007936	2.5000	4799029	0.0043	59.646	0.007953
10	0.018588	77328	1437	382757	0.003755	2.2986	4404563	0.0047	56.959	0.003759
15	0.022943	75891	1741	375237	0.004640	2.5783	4021806	0.0091	52.995	0.004636
20	0.028214	74149	2092	365601	0.005722	2.5399	3646570	0.0101	49.179	0.005719
25	0.029724	72057	2142	354902	0.006035	2.4859	3280969	0.0056	45.533	0.006035
30	0.027846	69916	1947	344692	0.005648	2.4903	2926067	0.0011	41.851	0.005648
35	0.030172	67969	2051	334788	0.006126	2.5349	2581375	0.0004	37.979	0.006125
40	0.034751	65918	2291	323871	0.007073	2.5037	2246587	0.0000	34.082	0.007073
45	0.032872	63627	2092	312991	0.006682	2.5398	1922716	0.0001	30.218	0.006682
50	0.043714	61536	2690	301227	0.008930	2.6014	1609725	0.0000	26.159	0.008930
55	0.057802	58846	3401	286083	0.011889	2.6052	1308499	0.0000	22.236	0.011889
60	0.079494	55444	4407	266782	0.016521	2.6314	1022416	0.0007	18.440	0.016519
65	0.121100	51037	6181	240628	0.025685	2.6448	755633	0.0007	14.806	0.025682
70	0.193993	44856	8702	203499	0.042761	2.6117	515006	0.0007	11.481	0.042755
75	0.300050	36155	10848	154260	0.070324	2.5560	311506	0.0007	8.616	0.070314
80	0.459123	25306	11619	98076	0.118466	2.5509	157247	0.0007	6.214	0.118445
85+	*1.000000	13688	13688	59170	0.231327	4.3229	59170	0.0007	4.323	0.231258

TABLE 4 — OBSERVED AND PROJECTED VITAL RATES

	OBSERVED POPULATION BOTH SEXES	MALES	FEMALES	PROJECTED POPULATION 1885 MALES	FEMALES	1890 MALES	FEMALES	1895 MALES	FEMALES	STABLE POPULATION MALES	FEMA
RATES PER THOUSAND											
Birth	21.75	22.71	20.82	22.98	21.17	23.41	21.67	23.76	22.10	23.04	22.
Death	19.48	19.97	19.00	19.72	18.76	19.59	18.72	19.47	18.66	19.10	18.
Increase	2.28	2.75	1.82	3.26	2.41	3.83	2.95	4.29	3.43		3.94
PERCENTAGE											
under 15	26.51	27.21	25.83	26.85	25.54	26.68	25.42	26.47	25.28	26.24	25.
15-64	60.55	60.56	60.53	61.10	60.94	61.49	61.21	61.98	61.56	62.40	61.
65 and over	12.94	12.22	13.64	12.06	13.53	11.82	13.37	11.55	13.16	11.37	12.
DEP. RATIO X 100	65.16	65.12	65.20	63.68	64.10	62.62	63.37	61.34	62.45	60.27	61.

AGE LAST BIRTHDAY	1885 BOTH SEXES	1885 MALES	1885 FEMALES	1890 BOTH SEXES	1890 MALES	1890 FEMALES	1895 BOTH SEXES	1895 MALES	1895 FEMALES	AGE AT LAST BIRTHDAY	
0-4	545	277	268	563	286	277	583	296	287	0-4	**TABLE 5**
5-9	522	264	258	503	255	248	519	263	256	5-9	POPULATION
10-14	489	247	242	507	256	251	487	247	240	10-14	PROJECTED
15-19	475	240	235	479	242	237	497	251	246	15-19	WITH
20-24	448	227	221	463	234	229	466	235	231	20-24	FIXED
25-29	411	208	203	434	220	214	449	226	223	25-29	AGE—
30-34	374	186	188	399	202	197	421	213	208	30-34	SPECIFIC
35-39	357	176	181	363	180	183	388	196	192	35-39	BIRTH
40-44	340	165	175	345	170	175	351	174	177	40-44	AND
45-49	328	159	169	328	159	169	333	164	169	45-49	DEATH
50-54	316	153	163	315	153	162	316	153	163	50-54	RATES
55-59	298	144	154	298	144	154	298	144	154	55-59	(IN 1000's)
60-64	278	134	144	277	133	144	277	133	144	60-64	
65-69	248	118	130	248	118	130	247	117	130	65-69	
70-74	208	98	110	207	97	110	207	97	110	70-74	
75-79	154	71	83	155	72	83	154	71	83	75-79	
80-84	95	42	53	95	42	53	95	42	53	80-84	
85+	56	24	32	56	24	32	56	24	32	85+	
TOTAL	5942	2933	3009	6035	2987	3048	6144	3046	3098	TOTAL	

STANDARD COUNTRIES: STANDARDIZED RATES PER THOUSAND	ENGLAND AND WALES 1961 BOTH SEXES	MALES	FEMALES	UNITED STATES 1960 BOTH SEXES	MALES	FEMALES	MEXICO 1960 BOTH SEXES	MALES	FEMALES	
Birth	21.44	23.15*	20.19	21.80	21.46*	20.87	22.44	21.02*	21.74	**TABLE 6** STANDARDIZED RATES
Death	17.58	16.37*	18.20	16.95	15.17*	16.55	15.19	13.06*	14.37	
Increase	3.86	6.78*	1.99	4.84	6.29*	4.32	7.25	7.95*	7.38	

	OBSERVED POP. MALES	FEMALES	STATIONARY POP. MALES	FEMALES	STABLE POP. MALES	FEMALES	OBSERVED BIRTHS	NET MATERNITY FUNCTION	BIRTHS IN STABLE POP.	
	33.80533	35.09194	35.81670	36.53077	33.77128	34.41872	30.52198	30.65126	30.49375	**TABLE 7**
μ_2	533.0964	550.9195	526.0923	543.0215	510.5661	527.3691	38.43337	37.98191	37.73016	MOMENTS
μ_3	4818.995	4373.429	3429.238	3414.594	4419.520	4496.687	65.2075	62.0193	65.6297	AND
μ_4	-267378.	-299365.	-269543.	-293851.	-231301.	-253327.	-958.475	-929.477	-890.813	CUMULANTS
	0.153284	0.114388	0.080762	0.072816	0.146755	0.137861	0.074898	0.070198	0.080193	
	2.059163	2.013664	2.026124	2.003465	2.112694	2.089139	2.351121	2.355705	2.374238	
	-0.053863	-0.040252	-0.029622	-0.026435	-0.054054	-0.050275	-0.038364	-0.036448	-0.041925	

VITAL STATISTICS		THOMPSON AGE RANGE	NRR	1000r	INTERVAL	BOURGEOIS-PICHAT AGE RANGE	NRR	1000b	1000d	1000r	COALE	**TABLE 8**
GRR	1.621					5-29	1.23	22.90	15.19	7.71	IBR	RATES FROM AGE
NRR	1.128	0-4	1.17	5.92	27.12	30-54	1.01	18.30	18.10	0.20	IDR	DISTRIBUTIONS
R	3.336	5-9	1.16	5.39	27.05	55-79	1.00	18.23	18.14	0.09	IRI	AND VITAL
GENERATION	30.572	10-14	1.16	5.44	27.03	*35-74	1.00	18.16	18.13	0.04	K1	STATISTICS
SEX RATIO	105.835	15-19	1.12	4.08	26.97						K2	(Females)

ORIGINAL MATRIX SUB-DIAGONAL	ALTERNATIVE FIRST ROWS Projection	Integral	FIRST STABLE MATRIX % IN STABLE POPULATION	FISHER VALUES	REPRODUCTIVE VALUES	SECOND STABLE MATRIX Z₂ FIRST COLUMN	FIRST ROW	
0.92518	0.00000	0.00000	9.293	1.184	330415	0.1417+0.0539	0.1417+0.0539	**TABLE 9**
0.97032	0.00000	0.00000	8.430	1.305	325649	0.1314-0.0951	0.0305+0.1383	LESLIE
0.98035	0.01262	0.00001	8.020	1.372	329268	-0.0083-0.1819	-0.0881-0.0903	MATRIX
0.97432	0.13072	0.02598	7.709	1.412	319824	-0.1777-0.1053	-0.1110-0.0219	AND ITS
0.97074	0.30884	0.24432	7.364	1.319	276149	-0.2092+0.1023	-0.0568-0.1002	SPECTRAL
0.97123	0.36724	0.39093	7.009	1.010	195557	-0.0328+0.2595	0.0018-0.1084	COMPONENTS
0.97127	0.29840	0.36122	6.674	0.612	114295	0.2235+0.1908	0.0280-0.0719	(Females)
0.96739	0.17754	0.24863	6.356	0.279	50490	0.3170-0.0924	0.0237-0.0309	
0.96640	0.06143	0.11368	6.029	0.077	13486	0.1082-0.3534	0.0087-0.0074	
0.96241	0.00535	0.01076	5.712	0.006	1054	-0.2639-0.3179	0.0008-0.0006	
0.94973	0.00003	0.00005	5.390	0.000	5	-0.4572+0.0515	0.0000-0.0000	
0.78738			22.014					

OBSERVED POPUL. (IN 100's)	CONTRIBUTIONS OF ROOTS (IN 100's) r_1	r_2, r_3	r_4-r_{11}	AGE-SP. BIRTH RATES	NET MATERNITY FUNCTION	COEFF. OF MATRIX EQUATION	PARAMETERS INTEGRAL	MATRIX	EXP. INCREASE x	$e^{(x+2\frac{1}{2})r}$	
2790	2711	10	70	0.0000	0.0000	0.0000	L(1) 1.01991	1.01992	0	1.0099	**TABLE 10**
2495	2459	75	-40	0.0000	0.0000	0.0000	L(2) 0.47314	0.47423	50	1.2300	AGE
2400	2340	81	-21	0.0000	0.0000	0.0113	0.74028	0.72264	55	1.2545	ANALYSIS
2265	2249	5	11	0.0060	0.0226	0.1150	R(1) 0.00394	0.00395	60	1.2795	AND
2093	2148	-97	42	0.0567	0.2074	0.2648	R(2) -0.02589	-0.02916	65	1.3050	MISCELLANEOUS
1937	2045	-126	19	0.0908	0.3222	0.3057	0.20042	0.19801	70	1.3310	RESULTS
1866	1947	-33	-48	0.0839	0.2892	0.2412	C(1)	29173	75	1.3575	(Females)
1807	1854	119	-166	0.0577	0.1933	0.1394	C(2)	12049	80	1.3845	
1746	1759	188	-200	0.0264	0.0855	0.0467		22842	85	1.4121	
1690	1666	82	-59	0.0025	0.0078	0.0039	2P/Y 31.3500	31.7318	90	1.4402	
1623	1572	-134	184	0.0000	0.0000	0.0000	DELTA 1.8429		95	1.4689	
7040	6422								100	1.4981	

TABLE 1 — DATA

AGE AT LAST BIRTHDAY	POPULATION BOTH SEXES	MALES Number	MALES %	FEMALES Number	FEMALES %	BIRTHS BY AGE OF MOTHER	DEATHS BOTH SEXES	DEATHS MALES	DEATHS FEMALES	AGE AT LAST BIRTHDAY
0	126261	64326	2.1	61935	2.0	0	15365	8603	6762	0
1-4	442020	224160	7.5	217860	7.0	0	10304	5357	4947	1-4
5-9	520507	263625	8.8	256882	8.2	0	3351	1694	1657	5-9
10-14	500444	253369	8.5	247075	7.9	1	1800	881	919	10-14
15-19	481862	245652	8.2	236210	7.6	3623	2359	1176	1183	15-19
20-24	426233	212691	7.1	213542	6.8	25206	2615	1402	1213	20-24
25-29	400266	197407	6.6	202859	6.5	36056	2324	1178	1146	25-29
30-34	381521	185594	6.2	195927	6.3	28963	2248	1103	1145	30-34
35-39	368003	178473	6.0	189530	6.1	20114	2659	1335	1324	35-39
40-44	357099	173038	5.8	184061	5.9	7760	1956	960	996	40-44
45-49	345509	167125	5.6	178384	5.7	654	2429	1242	1187	45-49
50-54	334116	161781	5.4	172335	5.5	3	2956	1525	1431	50-54
55-59	317487	153008	5.1	164459	5.3	0	3789	2045	1744	55-59
60-64	294260	140845	4.7	153415	4.9	0	5124	2719	2405	60-64
65-69	267086	126458	4.2	140628	4.5	0	7181	3781	3400	65-69
70-74	224266	104352	3.5	119914	3.8		9882	5038	4844	70-74
75-79	168501	76442	2.6	92059	2.9		12391	6172	6219	75-79
80-84	104279	45499	1.5	58780	1.9	62942 M.	13025	6063	6962	80-84
85+	58783	23776	0.8	35007	1.1	59438 F.	14108	6013	8095	85+
TOTAL	6118503	2997621		3120882		122380	115866	58287	57579	TOTAL

TABLE 2 — MALE LIFE TABLE

x	$_nq_x$	l_x	$_nd_x$	$_nL_x$	$_nm_x$	$_na_x$	T_x	r_x	$\dot{e}_x$	$_nM_x$
0	0.123372	100000	12337	92375	0.133555	0.3820	5127066	0.0023	51.271	0.133741
1	0.089682	87663	7862	329309	0.023874	1.2853	5034691	0.0023	57.432	0.023898
5	0.031562	79801	2519	392708	0.006414	2.5000	4705382	0.0033	58.964	0.006426
10	0.017225	77282	1331	382934	0.003476	2.3876	4312673	0.0026	55.804	0.003477
15	0.023707	75951	1801	375478	0.004795	2.6244	3929739	0.0126	51.740	0.004787
20	0.032450	74151	2406	364802	0.006596	2.5266	3554261	0.0158	47.933	0.006592
25	0.029387	71744	2108	353375	0.005966	2.4638	3189460	0.0075	44.456	0.005967
30	0.029292	69636	2040	343158	0.005944	2.5381	2836085	0.0038	40.727	0.005943
35	0.036708	67596	2481	331724	0.007480	2.4783	2492926	0.0004	36.880	0.007480
40	0.027357	65115	1781	321086	0.005548	2.4802	2161202	0.0002	33.191	0.005548
45	0.036505	63334	2312	311103	0.007432	2.5929	1840116	0.0000	29.054	0.007432
50	0.046092	61022	2813	298380	0.009426	2.6080	1529014	0.0000	25.057	0.009426
55	0.064770	58209	3770	282080	0.013366	2.6223	1230633	0.0002	21.142	0.013365
60	0.092329	54439	5026	260280	0.019311	2.6297	948553	0.0019	17.424	0.019305
65	0.139635	49412	6900	230682	0.029910	2.6260	688273	0.0019	13.929	0.029899
70	0.216381	42513	9199	190466	0.048297	2.5978	457591	0.0019	10.764	0.048279
75	0.336743	33314	11218	138890	0.080771	2.5326	267124	0.0019	8.018	0.080741
80	0.495834	22096	10956	82189	0.133300	2.4985	128235	0.0019	5.804	0.133256
85+	1.000000	11140	11140	46046	0.241929	4.1334	46046	0.0019	4.133	0.252901

TABLE 3 — FEMALE LIFE TABLE

x	$_nq_x$	l_x	$_nd_x$	$_nL_x$	$_nm_x$	$_na_x$	T_x	r_x	$\dot{e}_x$	$_nM_x$
0	0.102295	100000	10229	93836	0.109015	0.3974	5399019	0.0025	53.990	0.109179
1	0.085547	89771	7680	338540	0.022684	1.3251	5305183	0.0025	59.097	0.022707
5	0.031690	82091	2601	403951	0.006440	2.5000	4966643	0.0031	60.502	0.006450
10	0.018414	79489	1464	393649	0.003718	2.4047	4562692	0.0037	57.400	0.003720
15	0.024760	78026	1932	385548	0.005012	2.5720	4169044	0.0098	53.432	0.005008
20	0.028013	76094	2132	375167	0.005682	2.5125	3783605	0.0097	49.723	0.005680
25	0.027852	73962	2060	364649	0.005649	2.4939	3408438	0.0029	46.083	0.005649
30	0.028806	71902	2071	354403	0.005844	2.5339	3043790	0.0007	42.332	0.005844
35	0.034323	69831	2397	343106	0.006986	2.4764	2689387	0.0000	38.513	0.006986
40	0.026691	67434	1800	332620	0.005411	2.4713	2346280	0.0000	34.794	0.005411
45	0.032743	65634	2149	322962	0.006654	2.5760	2013661	0.0000	30.680	0.006654
50	0.040700	63485	2584	311175	0.008304	2.5807	1690698	0.0000	26.631	0.008304
55	0.051713	60901	3149	297005	0.010604	2.6179	1379523	0.0005	22.652	0.010603
60	0.075593	57752	4366	278462	0.015678	2.6411	1082519	0.0004	18.744	0.015676
65	0.114392	53386	6107	252570	0.024179	2.6483	804057	0.0004	15.061	0.024177
70	0.184289	47279	8713	215643	0.040399	2.6216	551487	0.0004	11.664	0.040396
75	0.290199	38566	11192	165657	0.067561	2.5719	335814	0.0004	8.707	0.067554
80	0.459463	27374	12578	106179	0.118456	2.5597	170157	0.0004	6.216	0.118442
85+	*1.000000	14797	14797	63978	0.231282	4.3237	63978	0.0004	4.324	0.231239

TABLE 4 — OBSERVED AND PROJECTED VITAL RATES

	OBSERVED POPULATION BOTH SEXES	MALES	FEMALES	PROJECTED POPULATION 1890 MALES	1890 FEMALES	1895 MALES	1895 FEMALES	1900 MALES	1900 FEMALES	STABLE POPULATION MALES	FEMALES
RATES PER THOUSAND											
Birth	20.00	21.00	19.05	21.29	19.42	21.75	19.94	22.12	20.38	20.98	19.
Death	18.94	19.44	18.45	19.14	18.19	19.04	18.18	18.95	18.16	18.92	17.
Increase	1.06	1.55	0.60	2.16	1.23	2.71	1.76	3.17	2.22		2.05.
PERCENTAGE											
under 15	25.97	26.87	25.11	26.22	24.61	25.71	24.23	25.29	23.94	24.74	24.
15-64	60.58	60.57	60.58	61.36	61.18	62.07	61.68	62.71	62.12	62.86	62.
65 and over	13.45	12.56	14.30	12.41	14.21	12.21	14.10	12.00	13.95	12.40	13.
DEP. RATIO X 100	65.08	65.10	65.06	62.96	63.45	61.10	62.14	59.46	60.99	59.09	61.

TABLE 1 — DATA

AGE AT LAST BIRTHDAY	POPULATION Both Sexes	Males Number	Males %	Females Number	Females %	BIRTHS By Age of Mother	DEATHS Both Sexes	Males	Females	AGE AT LAST BIRTHDAY
0	121578	61756	1.9	59822	1.8	0	14087	7887	6200	0
1-4	464107	234853	7.3	229254	6.8	0	8894	4588	4306	1-4
5-9	538419	271876	8.5	266543	7.9	0	3253	1628	1625	5-9
10-14	527934	266965	8.4	260969	7.7	1	1912	886	1026	10-14
15-19	499832	253175	7.9	246657	7.3	4107	2402	1202	1200	15-19
20-24	454494	225370	7.1	229124	6.8	27318	2624	1418	1206	20-24
25-29	428823	210136	6.6	218687	6.5	33427	2550	1305	1245	25-29
30-34	410691	199448	6.2	211243	6.3	28264	3120	1619	1501	30-34
35-39	398179	192230	6.0	205949	6.1	16937	1848	917	931	35-39
40-44	386969	186442	5.8	200527	5.9	6124	2060	1036	1024	40-44
45-49	377804	182340	5.7	195464	5.8	502	2399	1219	1180	45-49
50-54	365046	175929	5.5	189117	5.6	2	2977	1579	1398	50-54
55-59	347284	167025	5.2	180259	5.3	0	3823	2070	1753	55-59
60-64	328210	156155	4.9	172055	5.1	0	5328	2884	2444	60-64
65-69	296167	138898	4.3	157269	4.7	0	7526	4049	3477	65-69
70-74	250529	114734	3.6	135795	4.0		10582	5578	5004	70-74
75-79	188631	83486	2.6	105145	3.1		13844	6741	7103	75-79
80-84	116827	49692	1.6	67135	2.0	60023 M.	14574	6622	7952	80-84
85+	65950	25967	0.8	39983	1.2	56659 F.	15813	6567	9246	85+
TOTAL	6567474	3196477		3370997		116682	119616	59795	59821	TOTAL

TABLE 2 — MALE LIFE TABLE

x	$_nq_x$	l_x	$_nd_x$	$_nL_x$	$_nm_x$	$_na_x$	T_x	r_x	$\dot{e}_x$	$_nM_x$	x
0	0.118175	100000	11817	92532	0.127712	0.3680	5279664	0.0000	52.797	0.127712	0
1	0.074165	88183	6540	334775	0.019536	1.2545	5187132	0.0000	58.823	0.019536	1
5	0.029469	81643	2406	402198	0.005982	2.5000	4852358	0.0021	59.434	0.005988	5
10	0.016449	79237	1303	392805	0.003318	2.4083	4450160	0.0028	56.163	0.003319	10
15	0.023510	77933	1832	385306	0.004755	2.6200	4057355	0.0122	52.062	0.004748	15
20	0.030999	76101	2359	374696	0.006296	2.5374	3672049	0.0127	48.252	0.006292	20
25	0.030595	73742	2256	363170	0.006212	2.5446	3297353	0.0055	44.715	0.006210	25
30	0.039762	71486	2842	350190	0.008117	2.4531	2934183	0.0020	41.046	0.008117	30
35	0.023553	68643	1617	338966	0.004770	2.3705	2583993	0.0010	37.644	0.004770	35
40	0.027412	67027	1837	330650	0.005557	2.5598	2245027	0.0000	33.495	0.005557	40
45	0.032897	65189	2145	320780	0.006685	2.5906	1914377	0.0000	29.366	0.006685	45
50	0.043934	63045	2770	308609	0.008975	2.6116	1593597	0.0000	25.277	0.008975	50
55	0.060198	60275	3628	292772	0.012393	2.6289	1284989	0.0000	21.319	0.012393	55
60	0.088520	56647	5014	271409	0.018475	2.6419	992217	0.0019	17.516	0.018469	60
65	0.136418	51632	7044	241531	0.029162	2.6389	720809	0.0019	13.960	0.029151	65
70	0.217768	44589	9710	199648	0.048636	2.6009	479278	0.0019	10.749	0.048617	70
75	0.336724	34879	11744	145399	0.080774	2.5312	279630	0.0019	8.017	0.080744	75
80	0.495855	23134	11471	86052	0.133306	2.4985	134231	0.0019	5.802	0.133261	80
85+	1.000000	11663	11663	48179	0.242074	4.1310	48179	0.0019	4.131	0.252899	85+

TABLE 3 — FEMALE LIFE TABLE

x	$_nq_x$	l_x	$_nd_x$	$_nL_x$	$_nm_x$	$_na_x$	T_x	r_x	$\dot{e}_x$	$_nM_x$	x
0	0.097437	100000	9744	94014	0.103641	0.3857	5579958	0.0000	55.800	0.103641	0
1	0.071497	90256	6453	343565	0.018783	1.2943	5485944	0.0000	60.782	0.018783	1
5	0.030002	83803	2514	412731	0.006092	2.5000	5142379	0.0018	61.363	0.006097	5
10	0.019456	81289	1582	402367	0.003931	2.4213	4729649	0.0031	58.183	0.003932	10
15	0.024050	79707	1917	393836	0.004867	2.5478	4327282	0.0083	54.290	0.004865	15
20	0.025984	77790	2021	383943	0.005265	2.5217	3933446	0.0068	50.565	0.005264	20
25	0.028078	75769	2127	373641	0.005694	2.5537	3549503	0.0021	46.846	0.005693	25
30	0.034897	73642	2570	361671	0.007106	2.4562	3175862	0.0000	43.126	0.007106	30
35	0.022339	71072	1588	351219	0.004521	2.3927	2814191	0.0000	39.596	0.004521	35
40	0.025218	69484	1752	343129	0.005107	2.5508	2462971	0.0001	35.447	0.005107	40
45	0.029747	67732	2015	333754	0.006037	2.5656	2119842	0.0000	31.298	0.006037	45
50	0.036315	65717	2387	322826	0.007393	2.5869	1786088	0.0006	27.178	0.007392	50
55	0.047525	63330	3010	309494	0.009725	2.6218	1463262	0.0000	23.105	0.009725	55
60	0.068732	60321	4146	291841	0.014206	2.6454	1153768	0.0006	19.127	0.014205	60
65	0.105105	56175	5904	267025	0.022111	2.6545	861926	0.0006	15.344	0.022109	65
70	0.169597	50270	8526	231334	0.036854	2.6520	594901	0.0006	11.834	0.036850	70
75	0.290467	41745	12125	179469	0.067563	2.5873	363567	0.0006	8.709	0.067554	75
80	0.459483	29619	13610	114882	0.118466	2.5595	184097	0.0006	6.215	0.118448	80
85+	*1.000000	16010	16010	69215	0.231303	4.3233	69215	0.0006	4.323	0.231248	85+

TABLE 4 — OBSERVED AND PROJECTED TOTAL RATES

	OBSERVED POPULATION Both Sexes	Males	Females	PROJECTED POPULATION 1895 Males	Females	1900 Males	Females	1905 Males	Females	STABLE POPULATION Males	Females
RATES PER THOUSAND											
Birth	17.77	18.78	16.81	19.07	17.17	19.50	17.65	19.86	18.07	18.05	17.06
Death	18.21	18.71	17.75	18.38	17.46	18.37	17.53	18.39	17.60	19.37	18.37
Increase	-0.45	0.07	-0.94	0.69	-0.30	1.14	0.12	1.47	0.46	-1.3172	
PERCENTAGE											
under 15	25.15	26.14	24.22	25.07	23.28	24.26	22.56	23.41	21.83	22.28	21.57
15-64	60.87	60.95	60.79	62.00	61.64	62.91	62.39	63.86	63.14	63.38	62.21
65 and over	13.98	12.91	14.99	12.93	15.07	12.84	15.05	12.72	15.02	14.34	16.22
DEP. RATIO X 100	64.30	64.07	64.51	61.28	62.23	58.96	60.28	56.59	58.37	57.79	60.75

TABLE 1 — DATA

AGE AT LAST BIRTHDAY	POPULATION BOTH SEXES	MALES Number	%	FEMALES Number	%	BIRTHS BY AGE OF MOTHER	DEATHS BOTH SEXES	MALES	FEMALES	AGE AT LAST BIRTHDAY
0	124099	63251	1.9	60848	1.7	0	13270	7397	5873	0
1-4	450598	228578	6.8	222020	6.3	0	7485	3840	3645	1-4
5-9	544621	276482	8.3	268139	7.6	0	2905	1466	1439	5-9
10-14	531697	270124	8.1	261573	7.4	0	1743	811	932	10-14
15-19	509447	258540	7.7	250907	7.1	4840	2169	1098	1071	15-19
20-24	471080	234995	7.0	236085	6.7	25218	2918	1650	1268	20-24
25-29	447999	220783	6.6	227216	6.5	33050	3619	1953	1666	25-29
30-34	429557	208630	6.2	220927	6.3	23732	1870	914	956	30-34
35-39	417083	201925	6.0	215158	6.1	13647	1872	919	953	35-39
40-44	410656	199316	6.0	211340	6.0	4902	1934	992	942	40-44
45-49	401290	194639	5.8	206651	5.9	430	2252	1194	1058	45-49
50-54	389139	188982	5.7	200157	5.7	2	2807	1503	1304	50-54
55-59	376126	181051	5.4	195075	5.6	0	3804	2081	1723	55-59
60-64	353281	168249	5.0	185032	5.3	0	5385	3054	2331	60-64
65-69	320458	149666	4.5	170792	4.9	0	7800	4401	3399	65-69
70-74	272190	123518	3.7	148672	4.2		11483	6005	5478	70-74
75-79	204993	89878	2.7	115115	3.3		15034	7257	7777	75-79
80-84	126998	53497	1.6	73501	2.1	54455 M.	15835	7129	8706	80-84
85+	71729	27955	0.8	43774	1.2	51366 F.	17192	7069	10123	85+
TOTAL	6853041	3340059		3512982		105821	121377	60733	60644	TOTAL

TABLE 2 — MALE LIFE TABLE

x	$_nq_x$	l_x	$_nd_x$	$_nL_x$	$_nm_x$	$_na_x$	T_x	r_x	$\overset{\circ}{e}_x$	$_nM_x$	x
0	0.108752	100000	10875	93071	0.116848	0.3629	5449331	0.0013	54.493	0.116947	0
1	0.064184	89125	5720	340735	0.016788	1.2442	5356260	0.0013	60.098	0.016800	1
5	0.026161	83404	2182	411567	0.005301	2.5000	5015525	0.0004	60.135	0.005302	5
10	0.014893	81223	1210	402985	0.003002	2.4145	4603958	0.0029	56.683	0.003002	10
15	0.021066	80013	1686	396163	0.004255	2.6852	4200973	0.0094	52.504	0.004247	15
20	0.034572	78327	2708	385197	0.007030	2.6218	3804810	0.0089	48.576	0.007021	20
25	0.043234	75619	3269	369686	0.008844	2.4272	3419613	0.0044	45.221	0.008846	25
30	0.021631	72350	1565	357489	0.004378	2.2768	3049927	0.0034	42.155	0.004381	30
35	0.022502	70785	1593	349972	0.004551	2.5178	2692439	0.0001	38.037	0.004551	35
40	0.024586	69192	1701	341802	0.004977	2.5548	2342467	0.0000	33.854	0.004977	40
45	0.030225	67491	2040	332534	0.006134	2.5871	2000665	0.0000	29.643	0.006134	45
50	0.039027	65451	2554	321179	0.007953	2.6207	1668132	0.0000	25.487	0.007953	50
55	0.055962	62897	3520	306230	0.011494	2.6549	1346953	0.0000	21.415	0.011494	55
60	0.087090	59377	5171	284777	0.018159	2.6586	1040723	0.0019	17.527	0.018152	60
65	0.137537	54206	7455	253435	0.029417	2.6400	755946	0.0019	13.946	0.029405	65
70	0.217753	46751	10180	209315	0.048635	2.5994	502511	0.0019	10.749	0.048616	70
75	0.336721	36570	12314	152452	0.080773	2.5313	293196	0.0019	8.017	0.080743	75
80	0.495854	24256	12028	90226	0.133305	2.4985	140744	0.0019	5.802	0.133260	80
85+	1.000000	12229	12229	50518	0.242068	4.1311	50518	0.0019	4.131	0.252872	85

TABLE 3 — FEMALE LIFE TABLE

x	$_nq_x$	l_x	$_nd_x$	$_nL_x$	$_nm_x$	$_na_x$	T_x	r_x	$\overset{\circ}{e}_x$	$_nM_x$	x
0	0.091014	100000	9101	94361	0.096452	0.3805	5770274	0.0011	57.703	0.096519	0
1	0.062835	90899	5712	348069	0.016409	1.2818	5675913	0.0011	62.442	0.016417	1
5	0.026473	85187	2255	420297	0.005366	2.5000	5327843	0.0004	62.543	0.005367	5
10	0.017650	82932	1464	410889	0.003562	2.4241	4907547	0.0025	59.176	0.003563	10
15	0.021135	81468	1722	403171	0.004271	2.5788	4496658	0.0060	55.195	0.004269	15
20	0.026527	79746	2115	393666	0.005374	2.6056	4093487	0.0043	51.331	0.005371	20
25	0.035991	77631	2794	381062	0.007332	2.4616	3699821	0.0004	47.659	0.007332	25
30	0.021389	74837	1601	369934	0.004327	2.3451	3318759	0.0004	44.347	0.004327	30
35	0.021904	73236	1604	362165	0.004429	2.4972	2948825	0.0001	40.265	0.004429	35
40	0.022043	71632	1579	354247	0.004457	2.5221	2586660	0.0000	36.110	0.004457	40
45	0.025285	70053	1771	345964	0.005120	2.5719	2232413	0.0002	31.868	0.005120	45
50	0.032074	68282	2190	336160	0.006515	2.6034	1886449	0.0000	27.627	0.006515	50
55	0.043254	66092	2859	323661	0.008832	2.6223	1550289	0.0000	23.457	0.008832	55
60	0.061183	63233	3869	307074	0.012599	2.6502	1226628	0.0005	19.399	0.012598	60
65	0.095150	59364	5649	283792	0.019904	2.6934	919554	0.0005	15.490	0.019901	65
70	0.169667	53716	9114	247316	0.036851	2.6670	635762	0.0005	11.836	0.036846	70
75	0.290476	44602	12956	191750	0.067566	2.5873	388446	0.0005	8.709	0.067559	75
80	0.459474	31646	14541	122743	0.118463	2.5595	196696	0.0005	6.216	0.118448	80
85+	*1.000000	17106	17106	73953	0.231303	4.3233	73953	0.0005	4.323	0.231256	85

TABLE 4 — OBSERVED AND PROJECTED VITAL RATES

	OBSERVED POPULATION BOTH SEXES	MALES	FEMALES	PROJECTED POPULATION 1900 MALES	FEMALES	1905 MALES	FEMALES	1910 MALES	FEMALES	STABLE POPULATION MALES	FEMALES
RATES PER THOUSAND											
Birth	15.44	16.30	14.62	16.60	14.96	17.00	15.38	17.35	15.77	15.07	14.1
Death	17.71	18.18	17.26	17.87	16.99	17.97	17.15	18.10	17.31	20.29	19.3
Increase	-2.27	-1.88	-2.64	-1.27	-2.03	-0.98	-1.76	-0.75	-1.54	-5.221	
PERCENTAGE											
under 15	24.09	25.10	23.13	23.65	21.86	22.34	20.68	21.13	19.60	19.55	18.7
15-64	61.37	61.59	61.16	62.90	62.23	64.14	63.23	65.31	64.24	63.68	62.1
65 and over	14.54	13.31	15.71	13.45	15.92	13.52	16.08	13.56	16.17	16.77	19.1
DEP. RATIO X 100	62.95	62.37	63.50	58.99	60.70	55.92	58.15	53.12	55.68	57.04	61.0

TABLE 1 — DATA

AGE AT LAST BIRTHDAY	POPULATION BOTH SEXES	MALES Number	%	FEMALES Number	%	BIRTHS BY AGE OF MOTHER	DEATHS BOTH SEXES	MALES	FEMALES	AGE AT LAST BIRTHDAY
0	125730	63971	1.8	61759	1.6	0	13433	7531	5902	0
1-4	463975	236167	6.5	227808	6.1	0	7318	3814	3504	1-4
5-9	556430	282861	7.8	273569	7.3	0	2348	1188	1160	5-9
10-14	547422	278309	7.7	269113	7.2	0	1477	717	760	10-14
15-19	530716	269761	7.5	260955	7.0	4740	2333	1166	1167	15-19
20-24	505005	255146	7.1	249859	6.7	26459	3835	2193	1642	20-24
25-29	476521	235660	6.5	240861	6.4	28573	2108	1080	1028	25-29
30-34	459992	226108	6.3	233884	6.2	20582	1926	958	968	30-34
35-39	455347	224292	6.2	231055	6.2	12189	1742	900	842	35-39
40-44	448318	220759	6.1	227559	6.1	4837	1829	997	832	40-44
45-49	442443	217501	6.0	224942	6.0	438	2144	1126	1018	45-49
50-54	431480	211605	5.9	219875	5.9	2	2783	1535	1248	50-54
55-59	415061	202183	5.6	212878	5.7	0	3877	2242	1635	55-59
60-64	391224	188182	5.2	203042	5.4	0	5632	3353	2279	60-64
65-69	355718	167522	4.6	188196	5.0	0	8671	4926	3745	65-69
70-74	302076	138255	3.8	163821	4.4		12759	6722	6037	70-74
75-79	227446	100601	2.8	126845	3.4		16692	8123	8569	75-79
80-84	140870	59879	1.7	80991	2.2	50344 M.	17573	7980	9593	80-84
85+	79524	31290	0.9	48234	1.3	47476 F.	19067	7913	11154	85+
TOTAL	7355298	3610052		3745246		97820	127547	64464	63083	TOTAL

TABLE 2 — MALE LIFE TABLE

x	nq_x	l_x	nd_x	nL_x	nm_x	na_x	T_x	r_x	$\mathring{e}_x$	nM_x	x
0	0.109457	100000	10946	92977	0.117725	0.3584	5566909	0.0000	55.669	0.117725	0
1	0.061838	89054	5507	340993	0.016150	1.2354	5473932	0.0000	61.467	0.016150	1
5	0.020770	83547	1735	413399	0.004198	2.5000	5132939	0.0010	61.437	0.004200	5
10	0.012799	81812	1047	406442	0.002576	2.4991	4719541	0.0014	57.688	0.002576	10
15	0.021428	80765	1731	399973	0.004327	2.7742	4313099	0.0038	53.403	0.004322	15
20	0.042075	79034	3325	386854	0.008596	2.4988	3913126	0.0068	49.512	0.008595	20
25	0.022603	75709	1711	373897	0.004577	2.2840	3526271	0.0066	46.577	0.004583	25
30	0.020959	73998	1551	366055	0.004237	2.4634	3152374	0.0008	42.601	0.004237	30
35	0.019864	72447	1439	358644	0.004013	2.5051	2786319	0.0000	38.460	0.004013	35
40	0.022333	71008	1586	351144	0.004516	2.5441	2427675	0.0000	34.189	0.004516	40
45	0.025567	69422	1775	342845	0.005177	2.5970	2076531	0.0000	29.912	0.005177	45
50	0.035663	67647	2412	332569	0.007254	2.6512	1733687	0.0000	25.628	0.007254	50
55	0.054050	65235	3526	317955	0.011089	2.6694	1401118	0.0002	21.478	0.011089	55
60	0.085567	61709	5280	296225	0.017825	2.6671	1083163	0.0020	17.553	0.017818	60
65	0.137546	56428	7762	263846	0.029417	2.6627	786938	0.0020	13.946	0.029405	65
70	0.217769	48667	10598	217893	0.048639	2.5994	523091	0.0020	10.748	0.048620	70
75	0.336728	38069	12819	158697	0.080775	2.5312	305199	0.0020	8.017	0.080745	75
80	0.495879	25250	12521	93920	0.133315	2.4985	146501	0.0020	5.802	0.133269	80
85+	1.000000	12729	12729	52581	0.242083	4.1308	52581	0.0020	4.131	0.252893	85+

TABLE 3 — FEMALE LIFE TABLE

x	nq_x	l_x	nd_x	nL_x	nm_x	na_x	T_x	r_x	$\mathring{e}_x$	nM_x	x
0	0.090163	100000	9016	94368	0.095544	0.3754	5925351	0.0003	59.254	0.095565	0
1	0.059037	90984	5371	349272	0.015379	1.2702	5830983	0.0003	64.088	0.015381	1
5	0.020969	85612	1795	423573	0.004238	2.5000	5481711	0.0009	64.030	0.004240	5
10	0.014022	83817	1175	416154	0.002824	2.5061	5058138	0.0012	60.347	0.002824	10
15	0.022140	82642	1830	408934	0.004474	2.6636	4641984	0.0028	56.170	0.004472	15
20	0.032324	80812	2612	397949	0.006572	2.4857	4233050	0.0024	52.381	0.006572	20
25	0.021099	78200	1650	386657	0.004267	2.3681	3835557	0.0018	49.048	0.004268	25
30	0.020479	76550	1568	378769	0.004139	2.4606	3448900	0.0002	45.054	0.004139	30
35	0.018054	74982	1354	371479	0.003644	2.4640	3070130	0.0000	40.945	0.003644	35
40	0.018118	73629	1334	364863	0.003656	2.5413	2698651	0.0000	36.652	0.003656	40
45	0.022383	72295	1618	357562	0.004526	2.5830	2333788	0.0000	32.282	0.004526	45
50	0.027999	70676	1979	348638	0.005676	2.6024	1976226	0.0000	27.962	0.005676	50
55	0.037717	68698	2591	337352	0.007681	2.6317	1627588	0.0001	23.692	0.007680	55
60	0.054711	66107	3617	322190	0.011225	2.6933	1290237	0.0005	19.518	0.011224	60
65	0.095171	62490	5947	298827	0.019902	2.7094	968046	0.0005	15.491	0.019899	65
70	0.169687	56543	9595	260329	0.036855	2.6670	669220	0.0005	11.836	0.036851	70
75	0.290462	46948	13637	201839	0.067562	2.5872	408891	0.0005	8.709	0.067555	75
80	0.459467	33311	15306	129204	0.118460	2.5595	207053	0.0005	6.216	0.118446	80
85+	*1.000000	18006	18006	77849	0.231294	4.3235	77849	0.0005	4.324	0.231248	85+

TABLE 4 — OBSERVED AND PROJECTED TOTAL RATES

	OBSERVED POPULATION BOTH SEXES	MALES	FEMALES	PROJECTED POPULATION 1905 MALES	FEMALES	1910 MALES	FEMALES	1915 MALES	FEMALES	STABLE POPULATION MALES	FEMALES
RATES PER THOUSAND											
Birth	13.30	13.95	12.68	14.28	13.01	14.66	13.38	15.00	13.73	12.41	11.51
Death	17.34	17.86	16.84	17.47	16.52	17.68	16.77	17.93	17.03	21.83	20.93
Increase	-4.04	-3.91	-4.17	-3.18	-3.51	-3.03	-3.39	-2.94	-3.30	-9.4168	
PERCENTAGE											
under 15	23.02	23.86	22.22	22.05	20.58	20.33	19.01	18.55	17.38	16.70	15.85
15-64	61.94	62.36	61.54	63.89	62.86	65.39	64.12	66.95	65.46	63.65	61.62
65 and over	15.03	13.78	16.24	14.06	16.57	14.28	16.87	14.50	17.17	19.65	22.53
DEP. RATIO X 100	61.44	60.36	62.49	56.51	59.09	52.93	55.95	49.37	52.78	57.10	62.27

TABLE 1 — DATA

AGE AT LAST BIRTHDAY	POPULATION BOTH SEXES	MALES Number	%	FEMALES Number	%	BIRTHS BY AGE OF MOTHER	DEATHS BOTH SEXES	MALES	FEMALES	AGE AT LAST BIRTHDAY
0	127215	64944	1.7	62271	1.5	0	11470	6463	5007	0
1-4	477194	242386	6.2	234808	5.8	0	5647	2953	2694	1-4
5-9	580674	294887	7.6	285787	7.1	0	1927	985	942	5-9
10-14	571067	290094	7.5	280973	7.0	0	1488	716	772	10-14
15-19	557219	283355	7.3	273864	6.8	4892	2744	1390	1354	15-19
20-24	528459	265016	6.8	263443	6.6	23093	2352	1271	1081	20-24
25-29	504341	249689	6.4	254652	6.3	25340	2056	1037	1019	25-29
30-34	500874	248517	6.4	252357	6.3	19753	1657	831	826	30-34
35-39	495334	245918	6.3	249416	6.2	13718	1529	816	713	35-39
40-44	491077	243637	6.3	247440	6.2	6002	1672	873	799	40-44
45-49	485899	240726	6.2	245173	6.1	391	1981	1092	889	45-49
50-54	474481	234134	6.0	240347	6.0	1	2690	1529	1161	50-54
55-59	458379	224719	5.8	233660	5.8	0	3945	2371	1574	55-59
60-64	433195	209567	5.4	223628	5.6	0	6244	3734	2510	60-64
65-69	393836	186559	4.8	207277	5.2	0	9611	5486	4125	65-69
70-74	334397	153966	4.0	180431	4.5		14134	7485	6649	70-74
75-79	251739	112033	2.9	139706	3.5		18484	9046	9438	75-79
80-84	155886	66684	1.7	89202	2.2	47970 M.	19451	8886	10565	80-84
85+	87971	34846	0.9	53125	1.3	45220 F.	21097	8812	12285	85+
TOTAL	7909237	3891677		4017560		93190	130179	65776	64403	TOTAL

TABLE 2 — MALE LIFE TABLE

x	nq_x	l_x	nd_x	nL_x	nm_x	na_x	T_x	r_x	$\mathring{e}_x$	nM_x
0	0.093453	100000	9345	93911	0.099512	0.3484	5896418	0.0001	58.964	0.099517
1	0.047133	90655	4273	350730	0.012183	1.2176	5802508	0.0001	64.007	0.012183
5	0.016558	86382	1430	428334	0.003339	2.5000	5451777	0.0006	63.112	0.003340
10	0.012270	84952	1042	422278	0.002468	2.6209	5023444	0.0007	59.133	0.002468
15	0.024253	83909	2035	414646	0.004908	2.5918	4601165	0.0047	54.835	0.004906
20	0.023685	81874	1939	404442	0.004795	2.4578	4186519	0.0079	51.134	0.004796
25	0.020542	79935	1642	395437	0.004152	2.4186	3782078	0.0023	47.314	0.004153
30	0.016577	78293	1298	388142	0.003344	2.4398	3386641	0.0000	43.256	0.003344
35	0.016455	76995	1267	381818	0.003318	2.5077	2998499	0.0000	38.944	0.003318
40	0.017761	75728	1345	375362	0.003583	2.5623	2616680	0.0000	34.554	0.003583
45	0.022440	74383	1669	367950	0.004536	2.6240	2241318	0.0000	30.132	0.004536
50	0.032164	72714	2339	358131	0.006530	2.6742	1873368	0.0000	25.763	0.006530
55	0.051502	70375	3624	343518	0.010551	2.6939	1515237	0.0000	21.531	0.010551
60	0.085577	66751	5712	320468	0.017825	2.6740	1171718	0.0019	17.554	0.017818
65	0.137551	61039	8396	285401	0.029418	2.6427	851251	0.0019	13.946	0.029406
70	0.217746	52643	11463	235696	0.048633	2.5994	565850	0.0019	10.749	0.048615
75	0.336725	41180	13866	171667	0.080774	2.5313	330153	0.0019	8.017	0.080744
80	0.495840	27314	13543	101599	0.133301	2.4985	158486	0.0019	5.802	0.133255
85+	1.000000	13770	13770	56887	0.242065	4.1311	56887	0.0019	4.131	0.252885

TABLE 3 — FEMALE LIFE TABLE

x	nq_x	l_x	nd_x	nL_x	nm_x	na_x	T_x	r_x	$\mathring{e}_x$	nM_x
0	0.076501	100000	7650	95142	0.080407	0.3650	6235185	0.0000	62.352	0.080407
1	0.044488	92350	4108	358095	0.011473	1.2484	6140042	0.0000	66.487	0.011473
5	0.016342	88241	1442	437602	0.003295	2.5000	5781948	0.0006	65.524	0.003296
10	0.013650	86799	1185	431170	0.002748	2.6142	5344346	0.0009	61.571	0.002748
15	0.024428	85615	2091	422951	0.004945	2.5509	4913175	0.0022	57.387	0.004944
20	0.020301	83523	1696	413279	0.004103	2.4422	4490224	0.0029	53.760	0.004103
25	0.019805	81828	1621	405005	0.004001	2.4494	4076945	0.0005	49.824	0.004002
30	0.016229	80207	1302	397677	0.003273	2.4198	3671941	0.0000	45.781	0.003273
35	0.014192	78905	1120	391716	0.002859	2.4896	3274264	0.0000	41.496	0.002859
40	0.016018	77786	1246	385866	0.003229	2.5428	2882548	0.0000	37.058	0.003229
45	0.017973	76540	1376	379373	0.003626	2.5831	2496682	0.0000	32.619	0.003626
50	0.023878	75164	1795	371553	0.004831	2.6228	2117309	0.0000	28.169	0.004831
55	0.033163	73369	2433	361198	0.006736	2.6787	1745755	0.0000	23.794	0.006736
60	0.054720	70936	3882	345799	0.011225	2.7119	1384557	0.0000	19.518	0.011224
65	0.095177	67054	6382	320653	0.019903	2.7094	1038759	0.0004	15.491	0.019901
70	0.169684	60672	10295	279343	0.036855	2.6670	718106	0.0004	11.836	0.036851
75	0.290465	50377	14633	216581	0.067563	2.5872	438763	0.0004	8.710	0.067556
80	0.459447	35744	16423	138642	0.118453	2.5595	222182	0.0004	6.216	0.118440
85+	*1.000000	19322	19322	83539	0.231290	4.3236	83539	0.0004	4.324	0.231247

TABLE 4 — OBSERVED AND PROJECTED VITAL RATES

RATES PER THOUSAND	OBSERVED POPULATION BOTH SEXES	MALES	FEMALES	PROJECTED 1910 MALES	FEMALES	1915 MALES	FEMALES	1920 MALES	FEMALES	STABLE POPULATION MALES	FEMALES
Birth	11.78	12.33	11.26	12.63	11.56	12.98	11.90	13.32	12.24	10.69	9.9
Death	16.46	16.90	16.03	16.66	15.83	16.92	16.12	17.22	16.42	22.17	21.4
Increase	-4.68	-4.58	-4.77	-4.03	-4.27	-3.95	-4.23	-3.90	-4.19	-11.487	
PERCENTAGE											
under 15	22.20	22.93	21.50	20.98	19.69	19.05	17.87	17.08	16.01	15.09	14.3
15-64	62.32	62.83	61.83	64.44	63.25	66.08	64.68	67.76	66.16	63.56	61.2
65 and over	15.47	14.24	16.67	14.58	17.07	14.87	17.45	15.16	17.83	21.35	24.4
DEP. RATIO X 100	60.45	59.15	61.74	55.19	58.11	51.34	54.60	47.58	51.14	57.32	63.2

AGE AT LAST BIRTHDAY	1910 BOTH SEXES	MALES	FEMALES	1915 BOTH SEXES	MALES	FEMALES	1920 BOTH SEXES	MALES	FEMALES	AGE AT LAST BIRTHDAY	
0-4	419	214	205	422	215	207	425	217	208	0-4	TABLE 5
5-9	583	296	287	404	206	198	407	207	200	5-9	
10-14	573	291	282	575	292	283	398	203	195	10-14	POPULATION
15-19	561	285	276	561	285	276	564	287	277	15-19	PROJECTED
20-24	544	276	268	547	278	269	548	278	270	20-24	WITH
25-29	517	259	258	532	270	262	536	272	264	25-29	FIXED
30-34	495	245	250	507	254	253	522	265	257	30-34	AGE—
35-39	493	244	249	487	241	246	500	250	250	35-39	SPECIFIC
40-44	488	242	246	485	240	245	480	237	243	40-44	BIRTH
45-49	482	239	243	479	237	242	477	236	241	45-49	AND
50-54	474	234	240	470	232	238	468	231	237	50-54	DEATH
55-59	459	225	234	458	225	233	455	223	232	55-59	RATES
60-64	434	210	224	434	210	224	433	210	223	60-64	(IN 1000's)
65-69	394	187	207	394	187	207	394	187	207	65-69	
70-74	335	154	181	335	154	181	335	154	181	70-74	
75-79	252	112	140	252	112	140	252	112	140	75-79	
80-84	155	66	89	156	66	90	156	66	90	80-84	
85+	91	37	54	91	37	54	91	37	54	85+	
TOTAL	7749	3816	3933	7589	3741	3848	7441	3672	3769	TOTAL	

STANDARD COUNTRIES: STANDARDIZED RATES PER THOUSAND	ENGLAND AND WALES 1961 BOTH SEXES	MALES	FEMALES	UNITED STATES 1960 BOTH SEXES	MALES	FEMALES	MEXICO 1960 BOTH SEXES	MALES	FEMALES	
Birth	11.67	12.68*	10.97	11.86	11.87*	11.34	12.90	11.22*	12.49	TABLE 6
Death	13.48	12.17*	13.84	12.36	11.38*	11.79	9.90	10.39*	9.14	STANDARDIZED RATES
Increase	-1.81	0.51*	-2.87	-0.50	0.49*	-0.45	3.01	0.84*	3.35	

	OBSERVED POP. MALES	FEMALES	STATIONARY POP. MALES	FEMALES	STABLE POP. MALES	FEMALES	OBSERVED BIRTHS	NET MATERNITY FUNCTION	BIRTHS IN STABLE POP.	
μ	36.68672	38.27409	37.10455	38.32796	43.30952	44.82941	29.31817	29.31929	29.83068	TABLE 7
σ^2	536.3545	562.1070	531.3901	559.2183	542.C992	564.9810	42.25151	41.92583	42.91269	MOMENTS
κ_3	2900.995	2483.688	2682.196	2497.494	-858.465	-1512.032	93.4988	93.2347	78.2171	AND
κ_4	-297835.	-339297.	-288047.	-332708.	-309C67.	-341915.	-1241.377	-1205.039	-1395.523	CUMULANTS
β_1	0.054543	0.034733	0.047945	0.035667	0.004626	0.012677	0.115900	0.117953	0.077419	
β_2	1.964688	1.926155	1.979915	1.936101	1.948293	1.928850	2.304625	2.314452	2.242181	
κ	-0.019549	-0.012311	-0.017503	-0.012729	-0.001719	-0.004600	-0.052870	-0.054226	-0.034830	

VITAL STATISTICS		THOMPSON AGE RANGE	NRR	1000r	INTERVAL	BOURGEOIS-PICHAT AGE RANGE	NRR	1000b	1000d	1000r	COALE		
GRR	0.884					5-29	1.05	16.58	14.62	1.96	IBR	16.92	TABLE 8
NRR	0.712	0-4	1.03	1.00	27.26	30-54	0.97	15.25	16.32	-1.06	IDR	14.46	RATES FROM AGE DISTRIBUTIONS
TFR	1.821	5-9	1.02	0.89	27.25	55-79	1.00	16.20	16.10	0.10	IRI	2.46	AND VITAL STATISTICS
GENERATION	29.574	10-14	1.02	0.72	27.26	*50-74	1.00	16.17	16.09	0.07	K1	7.30	(Females)
SEX RATIO	1C6.081	15-19	1.01	0.32	27.23						K2	0.08	

Start of Age Interval	ORIGINAL MATRIX SUB-DIAGONAL	ALTERNATIVE FIRST ROWS Projection	Integral	FIRST STABLE MATRIX % IN STABLE POPULATION	FISHER VALUES	REPRODUCTIVE VALUES	SECOND STABLE MATRIX Z₂ FIRST COLUMN	FIRST ROW	
0	0.96550	0.00000	0.00000	4.643	1.072	318532	0.1314+0.0616	0.1314+0.0616	TABLE 9
5	0.98530	0.00000	0.00000	4.747	1.049	299678	0.1537-0.0942	0.0168+0.1156	LESLIE
10	0.98094	0.01927	0.00000	4.954	1.005	282354	0.0075-0.2283	-0.0689+0.0612	MATRIX
15	0.97713	0.11383	0.03817	5.146	0.946	259148	-0.2354-0.1664	-0.0731-0.0201	AND ITS
20	0.97998	0.20363	0.18733	5.326	0.790	207990	-0.3375+0.1320	-0.0340-0.0645	SPECTRAL
25	0.98191	0.19394	0.21265	5.527	0.538	136984	-0.0951+0.4469	0.0006-0.0635	COMPONENTS
30	0.98501	0.14565	0.16728	5.748	0.306	77099	0.4053+0.4109	0.0163-0.0394	(Females)
35	0.98507	0.08676	0.11754	5.996	0.134	33504	0.7173-0.1425	0.0136-0.0155	
40	0.98317	0.02840	0.05184	6.255	0.034	8495	0.3494-0.8584	0.0045-0.0032	
45	0.97939	0.00176	0.00341	6.513	0.002	491	-0.6636-0.9663	0.0003-0.0002	
50	0.97213	0.00000	0.00001	6.755	0.000	1	-1.4767+0.0283	0.0000-0.0000	
55+	0.77319			38.390					

Start of Age Interval	OBSERVED POPUL. (IN 100's)	CONTRIBUTIONS OF ROOTS (IN 100's) r_1	r_2, r_3	$r_4 \cdot r_{11}$	AGE-SP. BIRTH RATES	NET MATERNITY FUNCTION	COEFF. OF MATRIX EQUATION	PARAMETERS INTEGRAL	MATRIX	EXP. INCREASE x	$e^{(x+2\frac{1}{2})r}$	
0	2971	2533	87	351	0.0000	0.0000	0.0000	L(1) 0.94418	0.94425	0	0.9717	TABLE 10
5	2858	2590	376	-108	0.0000	0.0000	0.0000	L(2) 0.42203	0.42765	50	0.5471	
10	2810	2703	387	-280	0.0000	0.0000	0.0183	0.66388	0.64911	55	0.5166	AGE
15	2739	2808	-64	-6	0.0087	0.0367	0.1062	R(1) -0.01149	-0.01147	60	0.4877	ANALYSIS
20	2634	2906	-702	431	0.0425	0.1758	0.1857	R(2) -0.04799	-0.05038	65	0.4605	AND
25	2547	3016	-873	404	0.0483	0.1956	0.1733	0.20091	0.19765	70	0.4348	MISCELLANEOUS
30	2524	3136	-95	-517	0.0380	0.1510	0.1278	C(1)	54558	75	0.4105	RESULTS
35	2494	3271	1264	-2041	0.0267	0.1045	0.0750	C(2)	71740	80	0.3876	(Females)
40	2474	3413	1916	-2854	0.0118	0.0454	0.0242		82394	85	0.3660	
45	2452	3553	640	-1742	0.0008	0.0029	0.0015	2P/Y 31.2740	31.7898	90	0.3456	
50	2403	3685	-2165	883	0.0000	0.0000	0.0000	DELTA 11.6312		95	0.3263	
55+	11270	20945								100	0.3081	

TABLE 1 — DATA

AGE AT LAST BIRTHDAY	POPULATION BOTH SEXES	MALES Number	%	FEMALES Number	%	BIRTHS BY AGE OF MOTHER	DEATHS BOTH SEXES	MALES	FEMALES	AGE AT LAST BIRTHDAY
0	129599	66468	1.6	63131	1.5	0	9044	5126	3918	0
1-4	491307	250456	6.0	240851	5.7	0	5720	3046	2674	1-4
5-9	598532	305176	7.3	293356	6.9	0	1971	1023	948	5-9
10-14	590552	301164	7.2	289388	6.8	0	1688	827	861	10-14
15-19	578057	294229	7.0	283828	6.7	4788	1789	916	873	15-19
20-24	553472	278836	6.6	274636	6.4	21844	2195	1134	1061	20-24
25-29	546393	275221	6.6	271172	6.4	24712	1751	905	846	25-29
30-34	541137	272360	6.5	268777	6.3	23267	1426	750	676	30-34
35-39	538216	270571	6.4	267645	6.3	18423	1419	768	651	35-39
40-44	536906	269766	6.4	267140	6.3	5071	1363	754	609	40-44
45-49	529376	265198	6.3	264178	6.2	298	1876	1081	795	45-49
50-54	518617	259033	6.2	259584	6.1	1	2749	1618	1131	50-54
55-59	501187	248574	5.9	252613	5.9	0	4325	2623	1702	55-59
60-64	473581	231814	5.5	241767	5.7	0	6844	4130	2714	60-64
65-69	430453	206364	4.9	224089	5.3	0	10528	6068	4460	65-69
70-74	365377	170311	4.1	195066	4.6		15468	8280	7188	70-74
75-79	274964	123926	2.9	151038	3.5		20209	10006	10203	75-79
80-84	170201	73763	1.8	96438	2.3	50660 M.	21252	9830	11422	80-84
85+	95979	38545	0.9	57434	1.3	47744 F.	23030	9748	13282	85+
TOTAL	8463906	4201775		4262131		98404	134647	68633	66014	TOTAL

TABLE 2 — MALE LIFE TABLE

x	nq_x	l_x	nd_x	nL_x	nm_x	na_x	T_x	r_x	$\mathring{e}_x$	nM_x	x
0	0.073573	100000	7357	95401	0.077120	0.3749	6124153	0.0000	61.242	0.077120	0
1	0.047084	92643	4362	358659	0.012162	1.2692	6028752	0.0000	65.075	0.012162	1
5	0.016622	88281	1467	437735	0.003352	2.5000	5670093	0.0000	64.228	0.003352	5
10	0.013635	86813	1184	431078	0.002746	2.4747	5232358	0.0007	60.271	0.002746	10
15	0.015456	85630	1323	424947	0.003114	2.5808	4801280	0.0045	56.070	0.003113	15
20	0.020131	84306	1697	417293	0.004067	2.5029	4376333	0.0030	51.910	0.004067	20
25	0.016302	82609	1347	409556	0.003288	2.4093	3959041	0.0000	47.925	0.003288	25
30	0.013673	81262	1111	403489	0.002754	2.4593	3549484	0.0000	43.679	0.002754	30
35	0.014092	80151	1129	397929	0.002838	2.4974	3145996	0.0000	39.251	0.002838	35
40	0.013881	79022	1097	392459	0.002795	2.5843	2748066	0.0000	34.776	0.002795	40
45	0.020189	77925	1573	385952	0.004076	2.6660	2355608	0.0000	30.229	0.004076	45
50	0.030789	76352	2351	376347	0.006246	2.6984	1969656	0.0000	25.797	0.006246	50
55	0.051511	74001	3812	361236	0.010552	2.6998	1593308	0.0001	21.531	0.010552	55
60	0.085569	70189	6006	336975	0.017823	2.6740	1232073	0.0019	17.554	0.017816	60
65	0.137543	64183	8828	300105	0.029416	2.6427	895098	0.0019	13.946	0.029404	65
70	0.217755	55355	12054	247839	0.048636	2.5994	594993	0.0019	10.749	0.048617	70
75	0.336717	43301	14580	180511	0.080772	2.5313	347154	0.0019	8.017	0.080742	75
80	0.495867	28721	14242	106832	0.133310	2.4985	166643	0.0019	5.802	0.133265	80
85+	1.000000	14479	14479	59811	0.242082	4.1308	59811	0.0019	4.131	0.252900	85

TABLE 3 — FEMALE LIFE TABLE

x	nq_x	l_x	nd_x	nL_x	nm_x	na_x	T_x	r_x	$\mathring{e}_x$	nM_x	x
0	0.059790	100000	5979	96340	0.062061	0.3879	6466179	0.0000	64.662	0.062061	0
1	0.043117	94021	4054	365138	0.011102	1.2999	6369839	0.0000	67.749	0.011102	1
5	0.016028	89967	1442	446231	0.003232	2.5000	6004701	0.0000	66.743	0.003232	5
10	0.014766	88525	1307	439335	0.002975	2.4824	5558470	0.0003	62.790	0.002975	10
15	0.015266	87218	1331	432831	0.003076	2.5526	5119136	0.0020	58.694	0.003076	15
20	0.019132	85887	1643	425319	0.003863	2.4965	4686305	0.0010	54.564	0.003863	20
25	0.015474	84243	1304	417832	0.003120	2.4030	4260986	0.0000	50.579	0.003120	25
30	0.012495	82940	1036	412043	0.002515	2.4370	3843154	0.0000	46.337	0.002515	30
35	0.012087	81903	990	407018	0.002432	2.4749	3431111	0.0000	41.892	0.002432	35
40	0.011335	80913	917	402317	0.002280	2.5466	3024094	0.0000	37.374	0.002280	40
45	0.014940	79996	1195	397157	0.003009	2.6364	2621777	0.0000	32.774	0.003009	45
50	0.021566	78801	1699	390041	0.004357	2.6670	2224620	0.0000	28.231	0.004357	50
55	0.033173	77102	2558	379610	0.006738	2.6939	1834579	0.0000	23.794	0.006738	55
60	0.054728	74544	4080	363386	0.011227	2.7119	1454968	0.0004	19.518	0.011226	60
65	0.095185	70464	6707	336958	0.019905	2.7093	1091583	0.0004	15.491	0.019903	65
70	0.169677	63757	10818	293547	0.036853	2.6669	754625	0.0004	11.836	0.036849	70
75	0.290452	52939	15376	227597	0.067559	2.5873	461078	0.0004	8.710	0.067553	75
80	0.459446	37563	17258	145696	0.118453	2.5595	233481	0.0004	6.216	0.118439	80
85+	*1.000000	20305	20305	87785	0.231300	4.3234	87785	0.0004	4.323	0.231257	85

TABLE 4 — OBSERVED AND PROJECTED VITAL RATES

	OBSERVED POPULATION BOTH SEXES	MALES	FEMALES	PROJECTED POPULATION 1915 MALES	FEMALES	1920 MALES	FEMALES	1925 MALES	FEMALES	STABLE POPULATION MALES	FEMALES
RATES PER THOUSAND											
Birth	11.63	12.06	11.20	12.28	11.42	12.55	11.68	12.83	11.95	10.76	10.0
Death	15.91	16.33	15.49	16.27	15.42	16.52	15.68	16.79	15.95	21.15	20.4
Increase	-4.28	-4.28	-4.29	-3.99	-4.00	-3.97	-4.00	-3.96	-4.00	-10.384	
PERCENTAGE											
under 15	21.38	21.97	20.80	20.28	19.22	18.62	17.65	16.92	16.04	15.39	14.6
15-64	62.82	63.44	62.21	64.79	63.41	66.16	64.62	67.55	65.86	63.79	61.5
65 and over	15.80	14.59	16.99	14.93	17.37	15.23	17.73	15.53	18.10	20.82	23.8
DEP. RATIO X 100	59.19	57.63	60.75	54.36	57.70	51.16	54.75	48.03	51.83	56.77	62.5

TABLE 1 — DATA

AGE AT LAST BIRTHDAY	POPULATION BOTH SEXES	MALES Number	%	FEMALES Number	%	BIRTHS BY AGE OF MOTHER	DEATHS BOTH SEXES	MALES	FEMALES	AGE AT LAST BIRTHDAY
0	119735	61093	1.4	58642	1.4	0	6154	3509	2645	0
1-4	478591	244134	5.8	234457	5.5	0	6429	3453	2976	1-4
5-9	578723	294929	7.0	283794	6.7	0	2137	1094	1043	5-9
10-14	571579	291288	6.9	280291	6.6	0	994	501	493	10-14
15-19	563118	287132	6.8	275986	6.5	4965	1599	799	800	15-19
20-24	553977	282090	6.7	271887	6.4	20406	1791	971	820	20-24
25-29	548043	278141	6.6	269902	6.4	29012	1397	770	627	25-29
30-34	547964	277992	6.6	269972	6.4	30344	1248	683	565	30-34
35-39	548031	277636	6.6	270395	6.4	14768	1027	566	461	35-39
40-44	543283	274472	6.5	268811	6.3	3916	1218	700	518	40-44
45-49	536655	270794	6.4	265861	6.3	227	1759	1017	742	45-49
50-54	525476	264254	6.3	261222	6.2	1	2789	1651	1138	50-54
55-59	507791	253585	6.0	254206	6.0	0	4388	2676	1712	55-59
60-64	479779	236486	5.6	243293	5.7	0	6945	4214	2731	60-64
65-69	436026	210523	5.0	225503	5.3	0	10679	6191	4488	65-69
70-74	370041	173744	4.1	196297	4.6		15680	8447	7233	70-74
75-79	278415	126424	3.0	151991	3.6		20476	10208	10268	75-79
80-84	172296	75250	1.8	97046	2.3	53357 M.	21523	10028	11495	80-84
85+	97118	39322	0.9	57796	1.4	50282 F.	23310	9944	13366	85+
TOTAL	8456641	4219289		4237352		103639	131543	67422	64121	TOTAL

TABLE 2 — MALE LIFE TABLE

x	$_nq_x$	l_x	$_nd_x$	$_nL_x$	$_nm_x$	$_na_x$	T_x	r_x	$\mathring{e}_x$	$_nM_x$	x
0	0.055573	100000	5557	96754	0.057437	0.4160	6267076	0.0000	62.671	0.057437	0
1	0.054556	94443	5152	364287	0.014144	1.3831	6170322	0.0000	65.334	0.014144	1
5	0.018376	89290	1641	442349	0.003709	2.5000	5806035	0.0000	65.024	0.003709	5
10	0.008561	87649	750	436280	0.001720	2.3779	5363686	0.0002	61.195	0.001720	10
15	0.013823	86899	1201	431641	0.002783	2.6235	4927406	0.0005	56.703	0.002783	15
20	0.017064	85698	1462	424825	0.003442	2.4938	4495765	0.0000	52.461	0.003442	20
25	0.013744	84236	1158	418190	0.002768	2.4194	4070941	0.0000	48.328	0.002768	25
30	0.012208	83078	1014	412786	0.002457	2.4331	3652751	0.0000	43.968	0.002457	30
35	0.010142	82064	832	408241	0.002039	2.5039	3239965	0.0000	39.481	0.002039	35
40	0.012675	81231	1030	403721	0.002550	2.6337	2831724	0.0000	34.860	0.002550	40
45	0.018617	80202	1493	397567	0.003756	2.6946	2428003	0.0000	30.274	0.003756	45
50	0.030798	78709	2424	387991	0.006248	2.7094	2030436	0.0000	25.797	0.006248	50
55	0.051513	76285	3930	372384	0.010553	2.6698	1642446	0.0000	21.531	0.010553	55
60	0.085584	72355	6192	347371	0.017827	2.6740	1270062	0.0019	17.553	0.017819	60
65	0.137557	66162	9101	309358	0.029419	2.6427	922691	0.0019	13.946	0.029408	65
70	0.217757	57061	12426	255478	0.048636	2.5994	613333	0.0019	10.749	0.048618	70
75	0.336725	44636	15030	186074	0.080774	2.5313	357854	0.0019	8.017	0.080744	75
80	0.495860	29606	14680	110124	0.133308	2.4985	171780	0.0019	5.802	0.133262	80
85+	1.000000	14925	14925	61657	0.242074	4.1310	61657	0.0019	4.131	0.252887	85+

TABLE 3 — FEMALE LIFE TABLE

x	$_nq_x$	l_x	$_nd_x$	$_nL_x$	$_nm_x$	$_na_x$	T_x	r_x	$\mathring{e}_x$	$_nM_x$	x
0	0.043969	100000	4397	97483	0.045104	0.4276	6622872	0.0000	66.229	0.045104	0
1	0.049167	95603	4700	370316	0.012693	1.4266	6525389	0.0000	68.255	0.012693	1
5	0.018209	90903	1655	450375	0.003675	2.5000	6155073	0.0000	67.711	0.003675	5
10	0.008754	89247	781	444204	0.001759	2.3982	5704698	0.0003	63.920	0.001759	10
15	0.014393	88466	1273	439256	0.002899	2.5857	5260494	0.0004	59.463	0.002899	15
20	0.014965	87193	1305	432643	0.003016	2.4550	4821237	0.0000	55.294	0.003016	20
25	0.011546	85888	992	426873	0.002323	2.4115	4388594	0.0000	51.097	0.002323	25
30	0.010408	84896	884	422214	0.002093	2.4343	3961721	0.0000	46.665	0.002093	30
35	0.008488	84013	713	418263	0.001705	2.4753	3539507	0.0000	42.131	0.001705	35
40	0.009591	83300	799	414590	0.001927	2.6123	3121244	0.0000	37.470	0.001927	40
45	0.013865	82501	1144	409843	0.002791	2.6740	2706653	0.0000	32.808	0.002791	45
50	0.021564	81357	1754	402710	0.004356	2.6776	2296811	0.0000	28.231	0.004356	50
55	0.033159	79602	2640	391925	0.006735	2.6940	1894101	0.0000	23.795	0.006735	55
60	0.054726	76963	4212	375178	0.011226	2.7120	1502176	0.0004	19.518	0.011225	60
65	0.095182	72751	6925	347693	0.019904	2.7093	1126998	0.0004	15.491	0.019902	65
70	0.169669	65826	11169	303075	0.036851	2.6670	779105	0.0004	11.836	0.036847	70
75	0.290467	54658	15876	234984	0.067563	2.5873	476029	0.0004	8.709	0.067557	75
80	0.459475	38781	17819	150419	0.118463	2.5595	241046	0.0004	6.215	0.118450	80
85+	*1.000000	20962	20962	90627	0.231304	4.3233	90627	0.0004	4.323	0.231262	85+

TABLE 4 — OBSERVED AND PROJECTED VITAL RATES

	OBSERVED POPULATION BOTH SEXES	MALES	FEMALES	PROJECTED POPULATION 1920 MALES	FEMALES	1925 MALES	FEMALES	1930 MALES	FEMALES	STABLE POPULATION MALES	FEMALES
RATES PER THOUSAND											
Birth	12.26	12.65	11.87	12.76	11.98	12.93	12.13	13.13	12.32	11.65	10.91
Death	15.55	15.98	15.13	16.06	15.15	16.25	15.35	16.48	15.58	19.58	18.84
Increase	-3.30	-3.33	-3.27	-3.30	-3.17	-3.32	-3.21	-3.35	-3.25	-7.9336	
PERCENTAGE											
under 15	20.68	21.13	20.23	19.95	19.10	18.79	17.97	17.65	16.84	16.56	15.76
15-64	63.31	64.05	62.58	64.93	63.40	65.85	64.24	66.73	65.06	64.07	62.01
65 and over	16.01	14.82	17.20	15.12	17.50	15.36	17.80	15.62	18.10	19.36	22.23
DEP. RATIO X 100	57.95	56.12	59.81	54.01	57.73	51.87	55.68	49.85	53.70	56.07	61.28

TABLE 1 — DATA

AGE AT LAST BIRTHDAY	POPULATION BOTH SEXES	MALES Number	MALES %	FEMALES Number	FEMALES %	BIRTHS BY AGE OF MOTHER	DEATHS BOTH SEXES	DEATHS MALES	DEATHS FEMALES	AGE AT LAST BIRTHDAY
0	120488	61749	1.5	58739	1.4	0	5593	3223	2370	0
1-4	436842	222803	5.5	214039	5.3	0	5886	3207	2679	1-4
5-9	542738	276725	6.8	266013	6.5	0	1100	583	517	5-9
10-14	538080	274348	6.8	263732	6.5	0	852	433	419	10-14
15-19	535053	272742	6.7	262311	6.4	4599	1223	644	579	15-19
20-24	529235	268793	6.7	260442	6.4	23456	1374	821	553	20-24
25-29	524603	264582	6.5	260021	6.4	37682	1194	679	515	25-29
30-34	533000	269715	6.7	263285	6.5	24946	798	460	338	30-34
35-39	530307	267774	6.6	262533	6.4	12159	839	495	344	35-39
40-44	526755	265943	6.6	260812	6.4	3138	1102	638	464	40-44
45-49	519874	261977	6.5	257897	6.3	220	1704	984	720	45-49
50-54	509048	255651	6.3	253397	6.2	1	2701	1597	1104	50-54
55-59	491921	245329	6.1	246592	6.1	0	4249	2588	1661	55-59
60-64	464792	228787	5.7	236005	5.8	0	6725	4076	2649	60-64
65-69	422417	203669	5.0	218748	5.4	0	10342	5989	4353	65-69
70-74	358504	168087	4.2	190417	4.7		15189	8172	7017	70-74
75-79	269746	122308	3.0	147438	3.6		19835	9875	9960	75-79
80-84	166939	72800	1.8	94139	2.3	54684 M.	20851	9701	11150	80-84
85+	94107	38042	0.9	56065	1.4	51517 F.	22585	9620	12965	85+
TOTAL	8114449	4041824		4072625		106201	124142	63785	60357	TOTAL

TABLE 2 — MALE LIFE TABLE

x	nq_x	l_x	nd_x	nL_x	nm_x	na_x	T_x	r_x	$\dot{e}_x$	nM_x	x
0	0.050552	100000	5055	97096	0.052064	0.4255	6384512	0.0044	63.845	0.052195	0
1	0.055427	94945	5263	366192	0.014371	1.4182	6287416	0.0044	66.222	0.014394	1
5	0.010479	89682	940	446062	0.002107	2.5000	5921224	0.0000	66.024	0.002107	5
10	0.007861	88743	698	441988	0.001578	2.5280	5475162	0.0000	61.697	0.001578	10
15	0.011740	88045	1034	437770	0.002361	2.6252	5033174	0.0000	57.166	0.002361	15
20	0.015157	87011	1319	431772	0.003054	2.5093	4595404	0.0002	52.814	0.003054	20
25	0.012746	85692	1092	425607	0.002566	2.3855	4163632	0.0000	48.588	0.002566	25
30	0.008490	84600	718	421139	0.001705	2.4071	3738026	0.0000	44.185	0.001705	30
35	0.009202	83882	772	417537	0.001849	2.5737	3316887	0.0000	39.542	0.001849	35
40	0.011928	83110	991	413230	0.002399	2.6591	2899350	0.0000	34.886	0.002399	40
45	0.018620	82119	1529	407082	0.003756	2.7031	2486120	0.0000	30.275	0.003756	45
50	0.030793	80590	2482	397264	0.006247	2.7093	2079038	0.0000	25.798	0.006247	50
55	0.051496	78108	4022	381289	0.010549	2.6998	1681774	0.0000	21.531	0.010549	55
60	0.085568	74086	6339	355684	0.017823	2.6740	1300485	0.0019	17.554	0.017816	60
65	0.137548	67746	9318	316766	0.029417	2.6427	944801	0.0019	13.946	0.029406	65
70	0.217758	58428	12723	261597	0.048636	2.5994	628035	0.0019	10.749	0.048618	70
75	0.336642	45705	15389	190533	0.080769	2.5313	366438	0.0019	8.017	0.080739	75
80	0.495842	30316	15032	112766	0.133301	2.4985	175905	0.0019	5.802	0.133255	80
85+	1.000000	15284	15284	63139	0.242069	4.1311	63139	0.0019	4.131	0.252879	85

TABLE 3 — FEMALE LIFE TABLE

x	nq_x	l_x	nd_x	nL_x	nm_x	na_x	T_x	r_x	$\dot{e}_x$	nM_x	x
0	0.039356	100000	3936	97778	0.040250	0.4354	6786952	0.0044	67.870	0.040348	0
1	0.048453	96064	4655	372434	0.012498	1.4598	6689174	0.0044	69.632	0.012516	1
5	0.009671	91410	884	454839	0.001944	2.5000	6316740	0.0000	69.104	0.001944	5
10	0.007913	90526	716	450860	0.001589	2.5296	5861901	0.0000	64.754	0.001589	10
15	0.010977	89810	986	446629	0.002207	2.5468	5411042	0.0000	60.250	0.002207	15
20	0.010560	88824	938	441748	0.002123	2.4734	4964412	0.0000	55.891	0.002123	20
25	0.009852	87886	866	437184	0.001981	2.4083	4522664	0.0000	51.461	0.001981	25
30	0.006397	87020	557	433645	0.001284	2.3873	4085480	0.0000	46.949	0.001284	30
35	0.006531	86463	565	430946	0.001310	2.5754	3651835	0.0000	42.236	0.001310	35
40	0.008859	85898	761	427718	0.001779	2.6687	3220889	0.0000	37.496	0.001779	40
45	0.013869	85137	1181	422954	0.002792	2.6852	2793171	0.0000	32.808	0.002792	45
50	0.021566	83957	1811	415578	0.004357	2.6776	2370217	0.0000	28.231	0.004357	50
55	0.033164	82146	2724	404448	0.006736	2.6939	1954638	0.0000	23.795	0.006736	55
60	0.054722	79422	4346	387165	0.011226	2.7119	1550190	0.0004	19.518	0.011224	60
65	0.095171	75076	7145	359012	0.019902	2.7094	1163026	0.0004	15.491	0.019900	65
70	0.169684	67931	11527	312761	0.036855	2.6670	804014	0.0004	11.836	0.036851	70
75	0.290456	56404	16383	242492	0.067561	2.5873	491253	0.0004	8.710	0.067554	75
80	0.459455	40021	18388	155229	0.118456	2.5595	248761	0.0004	6.216	0.118442	80
85+	*1.000000	21633	21633	93532	0.231292	4.3235	93532	0.0004	4.324	0.231249	85

TABLE 4 — OBSERVED AND PROJECTED VITAL RATES

	OBSERVED POPULATION BOTH SEXES	OBSERVED POPULATION MALES	OBSERVED POPULATION FEMALES	PROJECTED POPULATION 1925 MALES	1925 FEMALES	1930 MALES	1930 FEMALES	1935 MALES	1935 FEMALES	STABLE POPULATION MALES	STABLE POPULATION FEMALES
RATES PER THOUSAND											
Birth	13.09	13.53	12.65	13.54	12.67	13.61	12.72	13.71	12.82	12.79	11.9
Death	15.30	15.78	14.82	15.92	14.88	16.06	15.03	16.23	15.19	17.98	17.1
Increase	-2.21	-2.25	-2.17	-2.38	-2.21	-2.45	-2.31	-2.52	-2.38	-5.193	
PERCENTAGE											
under 15	20.19	20.67	19.71	20.01	19.08	19.33	18.42	18.68	17.78	17.97	17.0
15-64	63.65	64.36	62.94	64.80	63.35	65.30	63.79	65.76	64.22	64.28	62.4
65 and over	16.17	14.97	17.36	15.19	17.57	15.37	17.79	15.55	18.00	17.76	20.4
DEP. RATIO X 100	57.12	55.38	58.88	54.32	57.86	53.13	56.76	52.06	55.73	55.58	60.1

TABLE 1 DATA

AGE AT LAST BIRTHDAY	POPULATION BOTH SEXES	MALES Number	%	FEMALES Number	%	BIRTHS BY AGE OF MOTHER	DEATHS BOTH SEXES	MALES	FEMALES	AGE AT LAST BIRTHDAY
0	103187	52755	1.3	50432	1.2	0	4335	2504	1831	0
1-4	444368	226614	5.5	217754	5.2	0	3903	2162	1741	1-4
5-9	537505	273935	6.7	263570	6.4	0	944	511	433	5-9
10-14	536219	272950	6.7	263269	6.3	0	695	374	321	10-14
15-19	533200	271229	6.6	261971	6.3	5436	881	490	391	15-19
20-24	529658	269097	6.6	260561	6.3	31650	1239	753	486	20-24
25-29	545359	275703	6.7	269656	6.5	34695	656	404	252	25-29
30-34	546528	275509	6.7	271019	6.5	23030	647	405	242	30-34
35-39	545568	275160	6.7	270408	6.5	10672	759	458	301	35-39
40-44	540930	272435	6.6	268495	6.5	3230	1132	654	478	40-44
45-49	533867	268372	6.5	265495	6.4	227	1749	1008	741	45-49
50-54	522753	261891	6.4	260862	6.3	1	2773	1636	1137	50-54
55-59	505173	251317	6.1	253856	6.1	0	4362	2652	1710	55-59
60-64	477329	234372	5.7	242957	5.9	0	6903	4176	2727	60-64
65-69	433833	208641	5.1	225192	5.4	0	10617	6135	4482	65-69
70-74	368216	172190	4.2	196026	4.7		15594	8371	7223	70-74
75-79	277075	125294	3.1	151781	3.7		20370	10116	10254	75-79
80-84	171489	74577	1.8	96912	2.3	56099 M.	21417	9938	11479	80-84
85+	96687	38970	1.0	57717	1.4	52842 F.	23202	9855	13347	85+
TOTAL	8248944	4101011		4147933		108941	122178	62602	59576	TOTAL

TABLE 2 MALE LIFE TABLE

x	nq_x	l_x	nd_x	nL_x	nm_x	na_x	T_x	r_x	$\mathring{e}_x$	nM_x	x
0	0.046150	100000	4615	97229	0.047465	0.3996	6594555	0.0000	65.946	0.047465	0
1	0.037214	95385	3550	372067	0.009540	1.3314	6497326	0.0000	68.117	0.009540	1
5	0.009284	91835	853	457045	0.001865	2.5000	6125259	0.0000	66.698	0.001865	5
10	0.006828	90983	621	453353	0.001370	2.4867	5668214	0.0000	62.300	0.001370	10
15	0.008995	90362	813	449906	0.001807	2.6597	5214861	0.0000	57.711	0.001807	15
20	0.013893	89549	1244	444599	0.002798	2.4718	4764955	0.0000	53.211	0.002798	20
25	0.007298	88305	644	439787	0.001465	2.3053	4320357	0.0000	48.926	0.001465	25
30	0.007323	87660	642	436712	0.001470	2.5250	3880570	0.0000	44.268	0.001470	30
35	0.008289	87018	721	433369	0.001664	2.6121	3443857	0.0000	39.576	0.001664	35
40	0.011936	86297	1030	429090	0.002401	2.6752	3010488	0.0000	34.885	0.002401	40
45	0.018619	85267	1588	422688	0.003756	2.7030	2581398	0.0000	30.274	0.003756	45
50	0.030794	83679	2577	412494	0.006247	2.7094	2158711	0.0000	25.797	0.006247	50
55	0.051512	81102	4178	395903	0.010553	2.6998	1746217	0.0000	21.531	0.010552	55
60	0.085577	76925	6583	369311	0.017825	2.6740	1350314	0.0019	17.554	0.017818	60
65	0.137543	70342	9675	328901	0.029416	2.6427	981003	0.0019	13.946	0.029405	65
70	0.217747	60667	13210	271622	0.048634	2.5994	652102	0.0019	10.749	0.048615	70
75	0.336705	47457	15979	197836	0.080768	2.5313	380480	0.0019	8.017	0.080738	75
80	0.495849	31478	15608	117088	0.133304	2.4985	182644	0.0019	5.802	0.133258	80
85+	1.000000	15870	15870	65556	0.242074	4.1310	65556	0.0019	4.131	0.252888	85+

TABLE 3 FEMALE LIFE TABLE

x	nq_x	l_x	nd_x	nL_x	nm_x	na_x	T_x	r_x	$\mathring{e}_x$	nM_x	x
0	0.035543	100000	3554	97898	0.036306	0.4085	7011703	0.0000	70.117	0.036306	0
1	0.031320	96446	3021	377803	0.007995	1.3582	6913805	0.0000	71.686	0.007995	1
5	0.008181	93425	764	465215	0.001643	2.5000	6536002	0.0000	69.960	0.001643	5
10	0.006078	92661	563	461880	0.001219	2.4706	6070788	0.0000	65.516	0.001219	10
15	0.007436	92098	685	458836	0.001493	2.5868	5608908	0.0000	60.902	0.001493	15
20	0.009282	91413	848	454888	0.001865	2.4355	5150073	0.0000	56.339	0.001865	20
25	0.004661	90564	422	451673	0.000935	2.2794	4695185	0.0000	51.844	0.000935	25
30	0.004455	90142	402	449723	0.000893	2.5395	4243511	0.0000	47.076	0.000893	30
35	0.005551	89741	498	447539	0.001113	2.6629	3793788	0.0000	42.275	0.001113	35
40	0.008865	89243	791	444386	0.001780	2.6918	3346249	0.0000	37.496	0.001780	40
45	0.013865	88451	1226	439418	0.002791	2.6853	2901863	0.0000	32.807	0.002791	45
50	0.021575	87225	1882	431754	0.004359	2.6776	2462445	0.0000	28.231	0.004359	50
55	0.033165	85343	2830	420188	0.006736	2.6938	2030690	0.0000	23.794	0.006736	55
60	0.054721	82513	4515	402232	0.011225	2.7120	1610502	0.0004	19.518	0.011224	60
65	0.095186	77997	7424	372980	0.019905	2.7093	1208270	0.0004	15.491	0.019903	65
70	0.169669	70573	11974	324930	0.036851	2.6670	835290	0.0004	11.836	0.036847	70
75	0.290471	58599	17021	251927	0.067565	2.5873	510360	0.0004	8.709	0.067558	75
80	0.459471	41578	19104	161265	0.118462	2.5595	258432	0.0004	6.216	0.118448	80
85+	*1.000000	22474	22474	97167	0.231292	4.3235	97167	0.0004	4.324	0.231249	85+

TABLE 4 OBSERVED AND PROJECTED TOTAL RATES

RATES PER THOUSAND	OBSERVED POPULATION BOTH SEXES	MALES	FEMALES	PROJECTED POPULATION 1930 MALES	FEMALES	1935 MALES	FEMALES	1940 MALES	FEMALES	STABLE POPULATION MALES	FEMALES
Birth	13.21	13.68	12.74	13.57	12.64	13.54	12.62	13.57	12.65	13.00	12.16
Death	14.81	15.27	14.36	15.47	14.47	15.58	14.60	15.72	14.74	16.96	16.12
Increase	-1.60	-1.59	-1.62	-1.90	-1.83	-2.04	-1.99	-2.14	-2.09		-3.9634
PERCENTAGE											
under 15	19.65	20.15	19.17	19.79	18.80	19.40	18.42	19.01	18.01	18.48	17.57
15-64	64.01	64.74	63.29	64.91	63.47	65.15	63.67	65.38	63.88	64.42	62.68
65 and over	16.33	15.11	17.54	15.30	17.73	15.45	17.91	15.61	18.11	17.11	19.75
DEP. RATIO X 100	56.22	54.46	58.00	54.05	57.56	53.49	57.06	52.94	56.54	55.24	59.54

Male Dominant Period Calculations

United States
Trinidad and Tobago
Chile
Cyprus
Hungary
Norway
England and Wales

MALE AND FEMALE DOMINANCE

Most of the tables of this volume have been compiled on the assumption of female dominance, which is to say the births by age of mother provided female age-specific birth rates, and these were applied to the female population for projections, direct standardization, intrinsic rates, and other purposes. The results may be thought of as essentially a one-sex calculation; the female population is first projected and then a number of male births introduced at each stage in the ratio of male to female births in the year of the data. The only point at which there is even a suggestion of relating births to fathers is in the indirect standardization. The results are a crude approximation to what would be obtained with a proper two-sex calculation.

Lack of information on births by age of father left for most populations no alternative to the assumption of female dominance. Fortunately, however, we do have information on births by age of father for the seven countries shown in Table F.

The comparison of male- and female-dominant results is affected at many points of our printout by any tendency for one of the sexes to increase even slightly more rapidly than the other. For the United States in 1964 the intrinsic rate is 15.70 for females and 17.48 for males, a difference of 1.70, all per 1000 population. At the end of 102.5 years the female rate would multiply the population by 5 times its starting value, and the male rate by 6 times. The issue is an important one on which Goodman (1953) and others have made contributions.

Because dominance does not affect mortality, life tables are not printed again in the present ·male-dominant section, which is confined to the right-

TABLE F

BIRTHS BY AGE OF FATHER FOR SEVEN COUNTRIES, SINGLE YEARS AND THREE-YEAR AVERAGES

	Chile 1964	Cyprus 1956–58	England & Wales 1960–62
−15	0	105	0
15–19	5,433	2,260	11,863
20–24	50,048	3,911	149,265
25–29	68,929	3,525	255,467
30–34	62,187	2,169	200,161
35–39	41,375	1,258	115,288
40–44	23,903	572	52,137
45–49	12,380	189	18,908
50+	11,068	109	8,585
Total	275,323	14,098	811,674

	Hungary 1964	Norway 1963	Trinidad & Tobago 1956–58
−15	0	0	0
15–19	1,975	756	408
20–24	29,495	10,541	5,153
25–29	46,445	17,291	6,995
30–34	30,895	15,207	6,575
35–39	14,338	10,634	4,527
40–44	6,158	5,854	2,950
45–49	1,486	2,178	1,358
50+	1,349	829	689
Total	132,141	63,290	28,655

	United States			
	1959–61	1962	1963	1964
−15	0	72	104	140
15–19	134,669	141,956	140,756	140,916
20–24	1,051,760	1,077,858	1,083,488	1,086,750
25–29	1,244,665	1,209,981	1,192,730	1,170,440
30–34	911,552	865,149	833,381	802,091
35–39	537,237	506,666	493,387	481,212
40–44	245,624	239,010	230,791	227,059
45–49	90,310	83,766	80,853	78,530
50+	41,174	42,904	42,531	40,352
Total	4,256,991	4,167,362	4,098,020	4,027,490

Source: United Nations *Demographic Yearbook*, 1965, Table 18. Special adjustment made for not stated based on illegitimate births.

hand page of the printout showing Tables 5–10. The projections of Table 5 were for the main part of this volume calculated with female age-specific rates applied to female population at the beginning of each period, to produce both the female and male births of the period; now the same program is applied with the sexes reversed, and the projections will be seen to come out differently. So also do standardized rates of birth. The moments and cumulants for the paternity function are very different from those for the maternity function shown earlier, and so is the length of generation.

AGE AT LAST BIRTHDAY	BOTH SEXES	1965 MALES	FEMALES	BOTH SEXES	1970 MALES	FEMALES	BOTH SEXES	1975 MALES	FEMALES	AGE AT LAST BIRTHDAY	
0-4	21168	10801	10367	23174	11825	11349	26669	13608	13061	0-4	
5-9	20279	10303	9976	21080	10751	10329	23076	11769	11307	5-9	
10-14	18785	9547	9238	20234	10276	9958	21033	10723	10310	10-14	
15-19	16853	8556	8297	18722	9504	9218	20167	10230	9937	15-19	TABLE 5
20-24	13278	6647	6631	16760	8489	8271	18620	9430	9190	20-24	POPULATION
25-29	10781	5248	5533	13194	6589	6605	16654	8415	8239	25-29	PROJECTED
30-34	10745	5264	5481	10706	5201	5505	13099	6529	6570	30-34	WITH
35-39	11786	5754	6032	10643	5202	5441	10603	5139	5464	35-39	FIXED
40-44	12301	5970	6331	11616	5651	5965	10489	5108	5381	40-44	AGE—
45-49	11374	5527	5847	12020	5796	6224	11350	5486	5864	45-49	SPECIFIC
50-54	10513	5115	5398	10960	5264	5696	11583	5520	6063	50-54	BIRTH
55-59	9120	4408	4712	9938	4743	5195	10364	4882	5482	55-59	AND
60-64	7768	3693	4075	8372	3930	4442	9127	4229	4898	60-64	DEATH
65-69	6296	2879	3417	6829	3110	3719	7364	3310	4054	65-69	RATES
70-74	5181	2292	2889	5212	2253	2959	5655	2434	3221	70-74	(IN 1000's)
75-79	3581	1545	2036	3898	1614	2284	3926	1586	2340	75-79	
80-84	1964	815	1149	2285	919	1366	2492	959	1533	80-84	
85+	1162	435	727	1427	526	901	1664	592	1072	85+	
TOTAL	192935	94799	98136	207070	101643	105427	223935	109949	113986	TOTAL	

STANDARD COUNTRIES: STANDARDIZED RATES PER THOUSAND	ENGLAND AND WALES 1961 BOTH SEXES	MALES	FEMALES	UNITED STATES 1960 BOTH SEXES	MALES	FEMALES	MEXICO 1960 BOTH SEXES	MALES	FEMALES	
Birth	24.63	26.06	22.00*	23.65	24.59	22.74*	25.31	25.99	25.10*	TABLE 6
Death	11.44	12.21	10.93*	9.39	10.85	7.97*	5.10	6.16	5.56*	STANDAR-DIZED
Increase	13.20	13.85	11.07*	14.26	13.74	14.77*	20.21	19.83	19.54*	RATES

	OBSERVED POP. MALES	FEMALES	STATIONARY POP. MALES	FEMALES	STABLE POP. MALES	FEMALES	OBSERVED BIRTHS	NET PATERNITY FUNCTION	BIRTHS IN STABLE POP.	
μ	31.06962	32.35280	36.40658	39.09770	26.83417	28.36217	29.81255	29.55257	28.60116	TABLE 7
σ^2	484.0616	504.3773	500.5406	557.4892	403.8885	453.3208	47.39521	46.23498	40.66034	MOMENTS
κ_3	4658.402	4568.530	2753.278	2330.219	5830.999	6765.555	250.3886	279.8511	252.1714	AND
κ_4	-201102.	-224021.	-233772.	-320384.	-51188.	-81859.	688.429	1164.886	1445.781	CUMULANTS
β_1	0.191325	0.162662	0.060448	0.031539	0.516062	0.491349	0.588879	0.792396	0.945973	
β_2	2.141749	2.119401	2.066930	1.969144	2.686206	2.601657	3.306471	3.544932	3.874502	
κ	-0.069071	-0.059308	-0.023434	-0.011531	-0.208470	-0.190029	-0.442886	-0.558508	-0.810718	

VITAL STATISTICS		THOMPSON AGE RANGE	NRR	1000r	INTERVAL	BOURGEOIS-PICHAT AGE RANGE	NRR	1000b	1000d	1000r	COALE	
GRR	1.963										IBR	TABLE 8 RATES FROM AGE DISTRI-BUTIONS AND VITAL STATISTICS (Males)
NRR	1.837	0-4	1.72	20.27	27.35	5-29	2.38	28.50	-3.54	32.04	IDR	
TFR	3.833	5-9	1.64	18.25	27.29	30-54	1.15	17.45	12.15	5.30	IRI	
GENERATION	29.067	10-14	1.47	13.91	27.18	55-79	1.17	16.57	10.72	5.85	K1	
SEX RATIO	104.947	15-19	1.15	5.21	26.99	*35-59	1.33	22.23	11.73	10.51	K2	

Start of Age Interval	ORIGINAL MATRIX SUB-DIAGONAL	ALTERNATIVE FIRST ROWS Projection	Integral	FIRST STABLE MATRIX % IN STABLE POPULATION	FISHER VALUES	REPRODUCTIVE VALUES	SECOND STABLE MATRIX Z2 FIRST COLUMN	FIRST ROW	
0	0.99533	0.00000	0.00000	13.300	1.087	10884917	0.1895+0.0688	0.1895+0.0688	TABLE 9
5	0.99739	0.00000	0.00000	11.920	1.213	11224099	0.1614+0.1570	0.0186+0.1796	LESLIE
10	0.99551	0.02482	0.00000	10.706	1.350	11227818	-0.0793-0.2392	-0.1372+0.0849	MATRIX
15	0.99215	0.26943	0.05255	9.597	1.479	9839355	-0.2791-0.3368	-0.1267-0.0791	AND ITS
20	0.99120	0.53456	0.51931	8.574	1.361	7558532	-0.1723+0.2617	-0.0372-0.1521	SPECTRAL
25	0.99091	0.48314	0.61259	7.653	0.938	5169510	0.1784+0.2994	0.0062-0.1268	COMPO⁹NENTS
30	0.98820	0.30256	0.40927	6.829	0.521	3168744	0.3861-0.0333	0.0127-0.0782	(Males)
35	0.98201	0.16220	0.23105	6.076	0.253	1620647	0.1535-0.4014	0.0104-0.0415	
40	0.97091	0.07378	0.11280	5.373	0.107	634758	-0.3242-0.3450	0.0067-0.0193	
45	0.95240	0.03109	0.04396	4.698	0.039	218630	-0.4923+0.1540	0.0042-0.0074	
50	0.92729	0.01074	0.02264	4.029	0.011	51495	-0.0813+0.5452	0.0017-0.0017	
55+	0.77830			11.245					

Start of Age Interval	OBSERVED POPUL. (IN 100's)	CONTRIBUTIONS OF ROOTS (IN 100's) r_1	r_2, r_3	r_4-r_{11}	AGE-SP. BIRTH RATES	NET MATERNITY FUNCTION	COEFF. OF MATRIX EQUATION	PARAMETERS	INTEGRAL	MATRIX	EXP. INCREASE x	$e^{(x+2\frac{1}{2})r}$	
0	103510	100194	3098	218	0.0000	0.0000	0.0000	L(1)	1.11026	1.11052	0	1.0537	TABLE 10
5	95720	89801	7277	-1358	0.0000	0.0000	0.0000	L(2)	0.38676	0.38864	50	2.9988	AGE
10	85950	80652	3231	2067	0.0000	0.0000	0.0246		0.83334	0.80202	55	3.3294	ANALYSIS
15	67000	72300	-5949	649	0.0103	0.0493	0.2663	R(1)	0.02092	0.02097	60	3.6965	AND
20	52950	64593	-9794	-1850	0.1017	0.4833	0.5241	R(2)	-0.01696	-0.02303	65	4.1041	MISCEL-LANEOUS
25	53120	57653	-2134	-2399	0.1200	0.5650	0.4696			0.22725	0.22391	70	4.5565	RESULTS
30	58230	51443	10041	-3255	0.0802	0.3741	0.2914	C(1)		753351	75	5.0589	(Males)
35	60790	45777	12341	2672	0.0453	0.2087	0.1544	C(2)		1207583	80	5.6167	
40	56930	40479	-408	16859	0.0221	0.1000	0.0690			1075697	85	6.2360	
45	53710	35390	-15202	33522	0.0086	0.0379	0.0282	2P/Y	27.6483	28.0610	90	6.9236	
50	47540	30351	-13694	30883	0.0044	0.0186	0.0093	DELTA	10.2761		95	7.6869	
55+	150970	84716									100	8.5344	

AGE AT LAST BIRTHDAY	1967 BOTH SEXES	1967 MALES	1967 FEMALES	1972 BOTH SEXES	1972 MALES	1972 FEMALES	1977 BOTH SEXES	1977 MALES	1977 FEMALES	AGE AT LAST BIRTHDAY	
0-4	21135	10779	10356	23682	12078	11604	27351	13949	13402	0-4	**TABLE 5**
5-9	20664	10515	10149	21052	10733	10319	23589	12026	11563	5-9	
10-14	19693	10005	9688	20621	10490	10131	21008	10706	10302	10-14	POPULATION
15-19	17652	8968	8684	19631	9962	9669	20555	10444	10111	15-19	PROJECTED
20-24	14779	7408	7371	17556	8899	8657	19524	9885	9639	20-24	WITH
25-29	11509	5603	5906	14686	7344	7342	17444	8821	8623	25-29	FIXED
30-34	10654	5231	5423	11428	5552	5876	14581	7277	7304	30-34	AGE—
35-39	11390	5572	5818	10551	5169	5382	11318	5486	5832	35-39	SPECIFIC
40-44	12226	5942	6284	11223	5471	5752	10396	5075	5321	40-44	BIRTH
45-49	11745	5685	6060	11948	5770	6178	10968	5313	5655	45-49	AND
50-54	10723	5195	5528	11319	5415	5904	11515	5496	6019	50-54	DEATH
55-59	9492	4564	4928	10137	4816	5321	10703	5020	5683	55-59	RATES
60-64	8024	3798	4226	8720	4071	4649	9317	4296	5021	60-64	(IN 1000's)
65-69	6481	2955	3526	7044	3188	3856	7660	3418	4242	65-69	
70-74	5175	2251	2924	5355	2299	3056	5823	2481	3342	70-74	
75-79	3764	1592	2172	3905	1583	2322	4043	1617	2426	75-79	
80-84	2125	871	1254	2424	953	1471	2519	947	1572	80-84	
85+	1225	452	773	1487	538	949	1702	589	1113	85+	
TOTAL	198456	97386	101070	212769	104331	108438	230016	112846	117170	TOTAL	

STANDARD COUNTRIES:	ENGLAND AND WALES 1961 BOTH SEXES	MALES	FEMALES	UNITED STATES 1960 BOTH SEXES	MALES	FEMALES	MEXICO 1960 BOTH SEXES	MALES	FEMALES	
STANDARDIZED RATES PER THOUSAND										**TABLE 6**
Birth	23.80	25.16	21.14*	22.85	23.75	21.63*	24.47	25.11	24.19*	STANDARDIZED
Death	11.44	12.25	10.85*	9.38	10.87	7.94*	5.04	6.10	5.59*	RATES
Increase	12.36	12.92	10.30*	13.47	12.87	13.69*	19.44	19.01	18.59*	

	OBSERVED POP. MALES	FEMALES	STATIONARY POP. MALES	FEMALES	STABLE POP. MALES	FEMALES	OBSERVED BIRTHS	NET PATERNITY FUNCTION	BIRTHS IN STABLE POP.	
μ	30.89496	32.33227	36.36526	39.10286	27.26745	28.87154	29.63937	29.52913	28.63706	**TABLE 7**
σ^2	485.5304	509.4157	499.0042	557.4212	409.3510	460.8364	47.94314	45.62053	40.35350	MOMENTS
κ_3	4921.490	4796.752	2731.323	2316.260	5736.732	6664.846	265.4418	279.6616	251.2886	AND
κ_4	-199490.	-229917.	-232436.	-320893.	-61228.	-96181.	820.826	1308.590	1525.125	CUMULANTS
β_1	0.211614	0.174051	0.060039	0.030976	0.479779	0.453879	0.639380	0.823729	0.960953	
β_2	2.153771	2.114015	2.066543	1.967254	2.634609	2.547107	3.357107	3.628757	3.936576	
κ	-0.075660	-0.062523	-0.023277	-0.011384	-0.192853	-0.174453	-0.466157	-0.619044	-0.889979	

VITAL STATISTICS		THOMPSON AGE RANGE	NRR	1000r	INTERVAL	BOURGEOIS-PICHAT AGE RANGE	NRR	1000b	1000d	1000r	COALE	
												TABLE 8
GRR	1.896										IBR	RATES FROM AGE DISTRIBUTIONS AND VITAL STATISTICS (Males)
NRR	1.779	0-4	1.70	19.95	27.35	5-29	2.49	29.96	-3.86	33.82	IDR	
TFR	3.705	5-9	1.70	19.63	27.29	30-54	1.06	14.93	12.70	2.23	IRI	
GENERATION	29.074	10-14	1.53	15.43	27.18	55-79	1.17	16.44	10.53	5.91	K1	
SEX RATIO	104.795	15-19	1.27	8.69	26.99	*40-64	1.39	23.88	11.79	12.10	K2	

Start of Age interval	ORIGINAL MATRIX SUB-DIAGONAL	ALTERNATIVE FIRST ROWS Projection	Integral	FIRST STABLE MATRIX % IN STABLE POPULATION	FISHER VALUES	REPRODUCTIVE VALUES	SECOND STABLE MATRIX Z₂ FIRST COLUMN	FIRST ROW	
0	0.99569	0.00000	0.00000	12.939	1.082	11022123	0.1878+0.0660	0.1878+0.0660	**TABLE 9**
5	0.99754	0.00001	0.00000	11.666	1.200	11649126	0.1582-0.1564	0.0205+0.1769	LESLIE
10	0.99570	0.02352	0.00002	10.537	1.329	11563853	-0.0798-0.2359	-0.1340+0.0857	MATRIX
15	0.99228	0.25862	0.04963	9.500	1.448	10709099	-0.2761-0.0352	-0.1259-0.0758	AND ITS
20	0.99126	0.51901	0.49773	8.536	1.330	7886385	-0.1699+0.2592	-0.0373-0.1486	SPECTRAL
25	0.99099	0.47348	0.59823	7.662	0.915	4987985	0.1765+0.2963	0.0071-0.1231	COMPONENTS
30	0.98803	0.29328	0.40043	6.875	0.503	2946871	0.3822-0.0322	0.0126-0.0743	(Males)
35	0.98192	0.15378	0.21854	6.151	0.241	1529694	0.1536-0.3967	0.0094-0.0387	
40	0.97112	0.06923	0.10656	5.469	0.101	623805	-0.3189-0.3436	0.0059-0.0180	
45	0.95251	0.02938	0.04009	4.809	0.038	215276	-0.4889+0.1485	0.0038-0.0071	
50	0.92702	0.01082	0.02275	4.148	0.011	54292	-0.0862+0.5394	0.0017-0.0017	
55+	0.77596			11.707					

Start of Age interval	OBSERVED POPUL. (IN 100's)	CONTRIBUTIONS OF ROOTS (IN 100's) r₁	r₂,r₃	r₄·r₁₁	AGE-SP. BIRTH RATES	NET PATERNITY FUNCTION	COEFF. OF MATRIX EQUATION	PARAMETERS INTEGRAL	MATRIX	EXP. INCREASE x	$e^{(x+2\frac{1}{2})r}$	
0	105610	103292	1222	1096	0.0000	0.0000	0.0000	L(1) 1.10414	1.10438	0	1.0508	**TABLE 10**
5	100300	93126	8266	-1092	0.0000	0.0000	0.0000	L(2) 0.38865	0.39018	50	2.8298	AGE
10	90070	84117	6576	-623	0.0000	0.0000	0.0234	0.83174	0.80097	55	3.1245	ANALYSIS
15	74660	75839	-3905	2726	0.0097	0.0467	0.2558	R(1) 0.01981	0.01986	60	3.4499	AND
20	56520	68141	-11995	374	0.0976	0.4648	0.5093	R(2) -0.01710	-0.02309	65	3.8092	MISCELLANEOUS
25	52790	61162	-6850	-1522	0.1173	0.5538	0.4606	0.22673	0.22350	70	4.2059	RESULTS
30	56390	54882	8171	-6662	0.0785	0.3674	0.2827	C(1)	798270	75	4.6439	(Males)
35	60510	49100	16386	-4976	0.0428	0.1981	0.1465	C(2)	925168	80	5.1275	
40	58540	43656	5831	9053	0.0209	0.0948	0.0647		1707228	85	5.6615	
45	54540	38388	-14117	30269	0.0079	0.0346	0.0267	2P/Y 27.7116	28.1129	90	6.2511	
50	49230	33109	-20014	36135	0.0045	0.0187	0.0094	DELTA 9.0141		95	6.9021	
55+	155020	93457								100	7.6208	

AGE AT LAST BIRTHDAY	1968 BOTH SEXES	1968 MALES	1968 FEMALES	1973 BOTH SEXES	1973 MALES	1973 FEMALES	1978 BOTH SEXES	1978 MALES	1978 FEMALES	AGE AT LAST BIRTHDAY	
0-4	20924	10695	10229	23575	12050	11525	27130	13867	13263	0-4	**TABLE 5**
5-9	20667	10526	10141	20841	10648	10193	23482	11997	11485	5-9	
10-14	20033	10178	9855	20624	10500	10124	20798	10622	10176	10-14	POPULATIO
15-19	17977	9130	8847	19968	10134	9834	20558	10455	10103	15-19	PROJECTED
20-24	15382	7729	7653	17878	9059	8819	19858	10055	9803	20-24	WITH
25-29	12225	5961	6264	15281	7659	7622	17761	8977	8784	25-29	FIXED
30-34	10761	5278	5483	12136	5905	6231	15171	7588	7583	30-34	AGE—
35-39	11173	5470	5703	10655	5214	5441	12017	5833	6184	35-39	SPECIFIC
40-44	12099	5886	6213	11008	5370	5638	10497	5118	5379	40-44	BIRTH
45-49	11931	5769	6162	11821	5714	6107	10754	5213	5541	45-49	AND
50-54	10802	5219	5583	11496	5493	6003	11389	5441	5948	50-54	DEATH
55-59	9666	4634	5032	10200	4830	5370	10857	5083	5774	55-59	RATES
60-64	8126	3830	4296	8867	4123	4744	9359	4297	5062	60-64	(IN 1000's)
65-69	6597	3002	3595	7123	3205	3918	7777	3450	4327	65-69	
70-74	5133	2210	2923	5427	2315	3112	5864	2473	3391	70-74	
75-79	3814	1588	2226	3857	1538	2319	4079	1611	2468	75-79	
80-84	2179	882	1297	2448	942	1506	2481	912	1569	80-84	
85+	1246	455	791	1490	529	961	1681	565	1116	85+	
TOTAL	200735	98442	102293	214695	105228	109467	231513	113557	117956	TOTAL	

STANDARD COUNTRIES:	ENGLAND AND WALES 1961 BOTH SEXES	MALES	FEMALES	UNITED STATES 1960 BOTH SEXES	MALES	FEMALES	MEXICO 1960 BOTH SEXES	MALES	FEMALES	
STANDARDIZED RATES PER THOUSAND										**TABLE 6**
Birth	23.03	24.40	20.31*	22.12	23.03	20.68*	23.64	24.31	23.36*	STANDAR-
Death	11.62	12.51	10.94*	9.54	11.11	8.01*	5.11	6.21	5.68*	DIZED
Increase	11.41	11.89	9.37*	12.58	11.93	12.67*	18.53	18.10	17.68*	RATES

	OBSERVED POP. MALES	OBSERVED POP. FEMALES	STATIONARY POP. MALES	STATIONARY POP. FEMALES	STABLE POP. MALES	STABLE POP. FEMALES	OBSERVED BIRTHS	NET PATERNITY FUNCTION	BIRTHS IN STABLE POP.	
μ	30.83302	32.35349	36.23137	39.05196	27.65882	29.36768	29.55378	29.57948	28.74202	**TABLE 7**
σ^2	484.6250	510.4885	495.5256	556.2088	413.1570	467.3023	47.92252	45.22312	40.34659	MOMENTS
κ_3	5025.263	4887.649	2713.646	2318.496	5599.773	6527.354	271.6425	274.0722	247.4127	AND
κ_4	-196345.	-230630.	-228634.	-319253.	-70692.	-110090.	891.529	1323.138	1506.544	CUMULANT!
β_1	0.221871	0.179573	0.060521	0.031239	0.444627	0.417523	0.670465	0.812173	0.932016	
β_2	2.163996	2.114999	2.068872	1.968048	2.585867	2.495860	3.388200	3.646970	3.925483	
κ	-0.079190	-0.064225	-0.023500	-0.011485	-0.178044	-0.159721	-0.479899	-0.646137	-0.916233	

VITAL STATISTICS		THOMPSON AGE RANGE	NRR	1000r	INTERVAL	BOURGEOIS-PICHAT AGE RANGE	NRR	1000b	1000d	1000r	COALE	**TABLE 8**
GRR	1.838											RATES FROM AGE
NRR	1.724	0-4	1.67	19.26	27.34	5-29	2.45	30.13	-3.10	33.23	IBR	DISTRI-
TFR	3.585	5-9	1.71	19.84	27.28	30-54	1.01	13.71	13.23	0.48	IDR	BUTIONS
GENERATION	29.153	10-14	1.55	15.93	27.17	55-79	1.17	16.30	10.56	5.74	IRI	AND VITAL
SEX RATIO	105.272	15-19	1.32	10.01	26.99	*45-69	1.38	23.75	11.88	11.88	K1	STATISTICS
											K2	(Males)

Start of Age Interval	ORIGINAL MATRIX SUB-DIAGONAL	ALTERNATIVE FIRST ROWS Projection	ALTERNATIVE FIRST ROWS Integral	FIRST STABLE MATRIX % IN STABLE POPULATION	FISHER VALUES	REPRODUCTIVE VALUES	SECOND STABLE MATRIX Z₂ FIRST COLUMN	FIRST ROW	
0	0.99561	0.00000	0.00000	12.602	1.079	10981940	0.1854+0.0648	0.1854+0.0648	**TABLE 9**
5	0.99758	0.00001	0.00000	11.425	1.190	11749606	0.1572-0.1538	0.0216+0.1740	LESLIE
10	0.99567	0.02241	0.00003	10.379	1.310	11615616	-0.0764-0.2347	-0.1304+0.0861	MATRIX
15	0.99216	0.24495	0.04713	9.411	1.421	10906327	-0.2735-0.3400	-0.1247-0.0717	AND ITS
20	0.99102	0.50036	0.46987	8.503	1.306	8213232	-0.1755+0.2537	-0.0378-0.1447	SPECTRAL
25	0.99066	0.46421	0.58394	7.674	0.902	4973382	0.1666+0.3008	0.0077-0.1207	COMPO-
30	0.98776	0.28849	0.39254	6.923	0.495	2841935	0.3828-0.0176	0.0133-0.0723	NENTS
35	0.98169	0.14988	0.21464	6.227	0.235	1474415	0.1712-0.3898	0.0095-0.0371	(Males)
40	0.97070	0.06616	0.10130	5.567	0.098	612379	-0.3018-0.3605	0.0056-0.0171	
45	0.95222	0.02843	0.03848	4.921	0.037	211731	-0.4990+0.1206	0.0037-0.0068	
50	0.92537	0.01057	0.02215	4.267	0.010	54339	-0.1214+0.5362	0.0017-0.0016	
55+	0.77186			12.102					

Start of Age Interval	OBSERVED POPUL. (IN 100's)	CONTRIBUTIONS OF ROOTS (IN 100's) r_1	r_2, r_3	$r_4 \cdot r_{11}$	AGE-SP. BIRTH RATES	NET PATERNITY FUNCTION	COEFF. OF MATRIX EQUATION	PARAMETERS	INTEGRAL	MATRIX	EXP. INCREASE x	$e^{(x+2\frac{1}{2})r}$	
0	105720	104048	363	1308	0.0000	0.0000	0.0000	L(1)	1.09791	1.09812	0	1.0478	**TABLE 10**
5	102030	94335	8373	-678	0.0000	0.0000	0.0000	L(2)	0.39311	0.39457	50	2.6666	AGE
1ᶜ	91700	85698	7883	-1881	0.0000	0.0000	0.0223		0.82659	0.79666	55	2.9277	ANALYSIS
15	77900	77703	-2686	2882	0.0093	0.0445	0.2422	R(1)	0.01868	0.01872	60	3.2144	AND
2ᶜ	60150	70205	-12513	2458	0.0924	0.4400	0.4909	R(2)	-0.01770	-0.02353	65	3.5291	MISCEL-
25	53280	63358	-9041	-1037	0.1148	0.5419	0.4514			0.22537	0.22219	70	3.8477	LANEOUS
30	55380	57158	6601	-8379	0.0772	0.3609	0.2779	C(1)		825662	75	4.2540	RESULTS
35	59960	51413	17704	-9157	0.0422	0.1949	0.1426	C(2)		773475	80	4.6706	(Males)
40	59430	45962	9254	4214	0.0199	0.0903	0.0618			1931172	85	5.1279	
45	54810	40628	-12376	26558	0.0076	0.0333	0.0258	2P/Y	27.8790	28.2789	90	5.6300	
50	50080	35231	-22590	37439	0.0044	0.0183	0.0091	DELTA	7.9794		95	6.1812	
55+	156710	99922									100	6.7864	

TABLE 5 — POPULATION PROJECTED WITH FIXED AGE-SPECIFIC BIRTH AND DEATH RATES (IN 1000's)

AGE AT LAST BIRTHDAY	1969 BOTH SEXES	MALES	FEMALES	1974 BOTH SEXES	MALES	FEMALES	1979 BOTH SEXES	MALES	FEMALES	AGE AT LAST BIRTHDAY
0-4	20736	10574	10162	23538	12003	11535	26998	13767	13231	0-4
5-9	20612	10510	10102	20656	10528	10128	23447	11951	11496	5-9
10-14	20305	10316	9989	20569	10484	10085	20614	10503	10111	10-14
15-19	18375	9329	9046	20237	10269	9968	20501	10437	10064	15-19
20-24	16141	8122	8019	18270	9253	9017	20123	10186	9937	20-24
25-29	12742	6222	6520	16035	8047	7988	18150	9168	8982	25-29
30-34	10963	5379	5584	12647	6161	6486	15915	7969	7946	30-34
35-39	10955	5366	5589	10853	5312	5541	12520	6084	6436	35-39
40-44	11929	5806	6123	10791	5266	5525	10691	5213	5478	40-44
45-49	12068	5831	6237	11655	5636	6019	10543	5111	5432	45-49
50-54	10904	5258	5646	11633	5557	6076	11234	5371	5863	50-54
55-59	9844	4710	5134	10304	4871	5433	10996	5149	5847	55-59
60-64	8265	3882	4383	9044	4196	4848	9469	4339	5130	60-64
65-69	6745	3068	3677	7267	3260	4007	7956	3524	4432	65-69
70-74	5169	2218	2951	5578	2382	3196	6015	2531	3484	70-74
75-79	3902	1608	2294	3920	1558	2362	4232	1673	2559	75-79
80-84	2286	920	1366	2551	973	1578	2569	943	1626	80-84
85+	1376	515	861	1649	599	1050	1847	634	1213	85+
TOTAL	203317	99634	103683	217197	106355	110842	233820	114553	119267	TOTAL

TABLE 6 — STANDARDIZED RATES

STANDARD COUNTRIES: STANDARDIZED RATES PER THOUSAND	ENGLAND AND WALES 1961 BOTH SEXES	MALES	FEMALES	UNITED STATES 1960 BOTH SEXES	MALES	FEMALES	MEXICO 1960 BOTH SEXES	MALES	FEMALES
Birth	22.32	23.59	19.65*	21.44	22.27	19.93*	22.88	23.46	22.71*
Death	11.31	12.23	10.59*	9.29	10.85	7.77*	5.00	6.09	5.54*
Increase	11.02	11.36	9.06*	12.15	11.42	12.16*	17.88	17.37	17.17*

TABLE 7 — MOMENTS AND CUMULANTS

	OBSERVED POP. MALES	FEMALES	STATIONARY POP. MALES	FEMALES	STABLE POP. MALES	FEMALES	OBSERVED BIRTHS	NET PATERNITY FUNCTION	BIRTHS IN STABLE POP.
μ	30.78450	32.38614	36.35730	39.19916	28.22133	30.01610	29.47712	29.62043	28.83684
σ^2	484.1064	511.8785	500.0401	560.4505	422.7917	478.3333	47.93342	45.01590	40.56012
κ_3	5141.085	4987.929	2785.039	2336.549	5605.025	6468.316	273.9543	266.2680	243.1433
κ_4	-193333.	-231648.	-232216.	-324940.	-81063.	-127040.	872.395	1225.027	1403.124
β_1	0.232963	0.185498	0.062037	0.031013	0.415696	0.382288	0.681461	0.777213	0.885987
β_2	2.175057	2.115913	2.071285	1.965506	2.546509	2.444762	3.379696	3.604524	3.852899
κ	-0.082995	-0.066031	-0.024099	-0.011381	-0.166039	-0.145402	-0.470274	-0.624658	-0.856586

TABLE 8 — RATES FROM AGE DISTRIBUTIONS AND VITAL STATISTICS (Males)

VITAL STATISTICS		THOMPSON AGE RANGE	NRR	1000r	INTERVAL	BOURGEOIS-PICHAT AGE RANGE	NRR	1000b	1000d	1000r	COALE
GRR	1.777										IBR
NRR	1.666	0-4	1.64	18.50	27.34	5-29	2.41	30.22	-2.32	32.54	IDR
TFR	3.473	5-9	1.71	19.99	27.28	30-54	0.97	12.55	13.84	-1.28	IRI
GENERATION	29.222	10-14	1.58	16.56	27.17	55-79	1.22	18.01	10.56	7.46	K1
SEX RATIO	104.719	15-19	1.39	11.65	26.99	*40-64	1.36	22.95	11.63	11.33	K2

TABLE 9 — LESLIE MATRIX AND ITS SPECTRAL COMPONENTS (Males)

Start of Age Interval	ORIGINAL MATRIX SUB-DIAGONAL	ALTERNATIVE FIRST ROWS Projection	Integral	FIRST STABLE MATRIX % IN STABLE POPULATION	FISHER VALUES	REPRODUCTIVE VALUES	SECOND STABLE MATRIX Z_2 FIRST COLUMN	FIRST ROW
0	0.99571	0.00000	0.00000	12.210	1.075	10895317	0.1834+0.0661	0.1834+0.0661
5	0.99757	0.00002	0.00000	11.138	1.178	11790200	0.1595-0.1511	0.0209+0.1717
10	0.99547	0.02131	0.00004	10.180	1.289	11686958	-0.0714-0.2376	-0.1275+0.0849
15	0.99190	0.23472	0.04468	9.284	1.391	11187288	-0.2753-0.0486	-0.1222-0.0686
20	0.99086	0.48038	0.44936	8.437	1.276	8351705	-0.1877+0.2515	-0.0378-0.1403
25	0.99031	0.44940	0.55943	7.659	0.884	4964445	0.1572+0.3149	0.0076-0.1184
30	0.98742	0.28323	0.38323	6.949	0.487	2741964	0.3945+0.0014	0.0142-0.0714
35	0.98138	0.14717	0.21118	6.286	0.230	1423432	0.1997-0.3930	0.0101-0.0364
40	0.97071	0.06414	0.09814	5.652	0.094	599180	-0.2900-0.3945	0.0058-0.0165
45	0.95305	0.02709	0.03696	5.027	0.035	203773	-0.5305+0.0896	0.0037-0.0064
50	0.92648	0.00986	0.02061	4.389	0.010	51829	-0.1711+0.5545	0.0016-0.0015
55+	0.77352			12.789				

TABLE 10 — AGE ANALYSIS AND MISCELLANEOUS RESULTS (Males)

Start of Age Interval	OBSERVED POPUL. (IN 100's)	CONTRIBUTIONS OF ROOTS (IN 100's) r_1	r_2, r_3	$r_4 \cdot r_{11}$	AGE-SP. BIRTH RATES	NET PATERNITY FUNCTION	COEFF. OF MATRIX EQUATION	PARAMETERS	INTEGRAL	MATRIX	EXP. INCREASE x	$e^{(x+2\frac{1}{2})r}$
0	105550	104652	-776	1675	0.0000	0.0000	0.0000	L(1)	1.09131	1.09149	0	1.0447
5	103410	95468	8433	-491	0.0000	0.0000	0.0000	L(2)	0.39555	0.39746	50	2.5030
10	93710	87253	9554	-3097	0.0000	0.0000	0.0212		-0.81826	0.78908	55	2.7316
15	81880	79577	-1042	3346	0.0088	0.0423	0.2321	R(1)	0.01748	0.01751	60	2.9810
20	62790	72316	-13138	3612	0.0885	0.4219	0.4711	R(2)	-0.01911	-0.02477	65	3.2532
25	54320	65649	-11944	615	0.1102	0.5204	0.4367			0.22410	0.22084	70	3.5503
30	54340	59563	4470	-9693	0.0755	0.3531	0.2726	C(1)		857133	75	3.8744
35	59160	53883	19456	-14179	0.0416	0.1921	0.1399	C(2)		574562	80	4.2282
40	60070	48448	13894	-2272	0.0193	0.0876	0.0598			2183336	85	4.6143
45	55170	43086	-10009	22093	0.0073	0.0320	0.0245	2P/Y	28.0371	28.4514	90	5.0357
50	50840	37621	-26180	39398	0.0041	0.0170	0.0085	DELTA	6.6746		95	5.4955
55+	158660	109617									100	5.9973

AGE AT LAST BIRTHDAY	BOTH SEXES	1969 MALES	FEMALES	BOTH SEXES	1974 MALES	FEMALES	BOTH SEXES	1979 MALES	FEMALES	AGE AT LAST BIRTHDAY	
0-4	1296	654	642	1483	748	735	1709	862	847	0-4	
5-9	1228	621	607	1267	639	628	1450	731	719	5-9	
10-14	1083	542	541	1221	617	604	1260	635	625	10-14	
15-19	975	488	487	1076	538	538	1214	613	601	15-19	TABLE 5
20-24	823	410	413	965	482	483	1066	532	534	20-24	POPULATION
25-29	710	344	366	813	404	409	953	475	478	25-29	PROJECTED
30-34	585	279	306	698	337	361	798	395	403	30-34	WITH
35-39	525	249	276	571	271	300	680	327	353	35-39	FIXED
40-44	472	226	246	509	239	270	553	260	293	40-44	AGE—
45-49	397	188	209	454	215	239	490	227	263	45-49	SPECIFIC
50-54	331	158	173	376	175	201	430	200	230	50-54	BIRTH
55-59	291	137	154	308	144	164	349	159	190	55-59	AND
60-64	225	107	118	262	120	142	276	126	150	60-64	DEATH
65-69	171	78	93	192	88	104	224	99	125	65-69	RATES
70-74	116	52	64	136	59	77	153	67	86	70-74	(IN 1000's)
75-79	76	32	44	84	35	49	98	40	58	75-79	
80-84	43	17	26	48	19	29	54	21	33	80-84	
85+	19	8	11	23	10	13	26	11	15	85+	
TOTAL	9366	4590	4776	10486	5140	5346	11783	5780	6003	TOTAL	

STANDARD COUNTRIES:	ENGLAND AND WALES 1961			UNITED STATES 1960			MEXICO 1960			
STANDARDIZED RATES PER THOUSAND	BOTH SEXES	MALES	FEMALES	BOTH SEXES	MALES	FEMALES	BOTH SEXES	MALES	FEMALES	TABLE 6
Birth	35.37	37.12	25.73*	33.54	34.60	25.98*	31.33	31.91	31.13*	STANDAR-
Death	16.49	17.01	24.26*	14.68	16.09	16.76*	10.61	11.91	9.40*	DIZED
Increase	18.88	20.11	1.46*	18.86	18.51	9.22*	20.72	20.01	21.74*	RATES

	OBSERVED POP. MALES	FEMALES	STATIONARY POP. MALES	FEMALES	STABLE POP. MALES	FEMALES	OBSERVED BIRTHS	NET PATERNITY FUNCTION	BIRTHS IN STABLE POP.	
μ	24.58431	25.62592	34.84345	37.22088	24.75457	26.06797	32.23248	33.66344	32.04508	TABLE 7
σ^2	374.8664	393.8508	481.4115	526.7484	365.7781	405.8839	65.35789	70.58361	62.58214	MOMENTS
κ_3	6019.962	6245.943	3287.880	2791.400	5747.807	6479.961	353.4333	321.3521	349.8806	AND
κ_4	-18260.	-26678.	-201832.	-273275.	-8331.	-30366.	-646.765	-2316.017	-203.781	CUMULANTS
β_1	0.687952	0.638558	0.096891	0.053313	0.675074	0.627970	0.447426	0.293664	0.499446	
β_2	2.870061	2.828015	2.129122	2.015096	2.937731	2.815673	2.848591	2.535127	2.947969	
κ	-0.270840	-0.255377	-0.038117	-0.019923	-0.284591	-0.251336	-0.231375	-0.134154	-0.267812	

VITAL STATISTICS			THOMPSON			BOURGEOIS-PICHAT					COALE		
		AGE RANGE	NRR	1000r	INTERVAL	AGE RANGE	NRR	1000b	1000d	1000r			
GRR	2.751										IBR	38.13	RATES FROM AGE DISTRI-
NRR	2.167	0-4	2.02	26.68	27.18	5-29	2.29	40.20	9.45	30.75	IDR	11.34	BUTIONS
TFR	5.416	5-9	2.01	26.19	27.04	30-54	1.64	28.42	10.04	18.38	IRI	26.79	AND VITAL
GENERATION	32.839	10-14	2.02	25.60	26.89	55-79	1.92	39.30	15.12	24.18	K1	4.31	STATISTICS
SEX RATIO	103.235	15-19	1.87	23.47	26.70	*50-74	1.92	39.16	15.03	24.13	K2	0.	(Males)

TABLE 8

Start of Age Interval	ORIGINAL MATRIX SUB-DIAGONAL	ALTERNATIVE FIRST ROWS Projection	Integral	FIRST STABLE MATRIX % IN STABLE POPULATION	FISHER VALUES	REPRODUCTIVE VALUES	SECOND STABLE MATRIX Z₂ FIRST COLUMN	FIRST ROW	
0	0.97772	0.00000	0.00000	14.893	1.210	750808	0.1399+0.1955	0.1399+0.1955	TABLE 9
5	0.99422	0.00000	0.00000	12.940	1.393	757375	0.2801-0.0049	-0.0700+0.1940	LESLIE
10	0.99336	0.01446	0.00000	11.433	1.576	771611	0.1837-0.2765	-0.1683+0.0443	MATRIX
15	0.98856	0.17196	0.03089	10.093	1.768	736350	-0.1462-0.3649	-0.1135-0.0987	AND ITS
20	0.98397	0.42371	0.33775	8.867	1.802	666222	-0.4519-0.1024	-0.0101-0.1608	SPECTRAL
25	0.97820	0.53223	0.57019	7.753	1.540	477357	-0.3996+0.3685	0.0478-0.1691	COMPO-
30	0.97049	0.45901	0.57127	6.740	1.113	313541	0.0894+0.6276	0.0666-0.1550	NENTS
35	0.96084	0.32477	0.41467	5.813	0.718	180577	0.6564+0.3261	0.0768-0.1211	(Males)
40	0.94931	0.21153	0.28544	4.964	0.432	92766	0.7342-0.4067	0.0779-0.0709	
45	0.93247	0.15732	0.17200	4.187	0.242	43636	0.0926-0.9446	0.0595-0.0225	
50	0.91003	0.08176	0.17343	3.470	0.088	14371	-0.8061-0.6808	0.0234-0.0004	
55+	0.76840			8.848					

Start of Age Interval	OBSERVED POPUL. (IN 100's)	CONTRIBUTIONS OF ROOTS (IN 100's) r_1	r_2, r_3	$r_4 \cdot r_{11}$	AGE-SP. BIRTH RATES	NET PATERNITY FUNCTION	COEFF. OF MATRIX EQUATION	PARAMETERS INTEGRAL	MATRIX	EXP. INCREASE x	$e^{(x+2\frac{1}{2})r}$	
0	6351	6088	-101	364	0.0000	0.0000	0.0000	L(1) 1.12496	1.12526	0	1.0606	TABLE 10
5	5452	5290	317	-154	0.0000	0.0000	0.0000	L(2) 0.45708	0.47609	50	3.4430	AGE
10	4912	4674	566	-327	0.0000	0.0000	0.0141	0.71493	0.69073	55	3.8732	ANALYSIS
15	4150	4126	315	-291	0.0067	0.0281	0.1660	R(1) 0.02355	0.02360	60	4.3572	AND
20	3496	3625	-367	239	0.0727	0.3040	0.4045	R(2) -0.03284	-0.03513	65	4.9017	MISCEL-
25	2852	3169	-926	608	0.1228	0.5049	0.4999	0.20039	0.19346	70	5.5142	LANEOUS
30	2568	2755	-722	535	0.1230	0.4949	0.4217	C(1)	40879	75	6.2033	RESULTS
35	2354	2376	301	-323	0.0893	0.3486	0.2896	C(2)	55450	80	6.9784	(Males)
40	1976	2029	1346	-1400	0.0615	0.2306	0.1812		65440	85	7.8504	
45	1698	1712	1339	-1353	0.0370	0.1319	0.1280	2P/Y 31.3548	32.4774	90	8.8314	
50	1506	1418	-3	90	0.0373	0.1240	0.0620	DELTA 2.0339		95	9.9350	
55+	3794	3617								100	11.1765	

TABLE 5 — POPULATION PROJECTED WITH FIXED AGE—SPECIFIC BIRTH AND DEATH RATES (IN 1000's)

AGE AT LAST BIRTHDAY	1962 BOTH SEXES	MALES	FEMALES	1967 BOTH SEXES	MALES	FEMALES	1972 BOTH SEXES	MALES	FEMALES	AGE AT LAST BIRTHDAY
0-4	140	71	69	158	80	78	184	93	91	0-4
5-9	126	64	62	138	70	68	156	79	77	5-9
10-14	106	53	53	126	64	62	138	70	68	10-14
15-19	89	45	44	106	53	53	125	63	62	15-19
20-24	67	34	33	88	44	44	105	53	52	20-24
25-29	55	27	28	67	34	33	87	44	43	25-29
30-34	51	25	26	54	27	27	65	33	32	30-34
35-39	48	24	24	51	25	26	54	27	27	35-39
40-44	45	23	22	47	23	24	49	24	25	40-44
45-49	40	20	20	44	22	22	45	22	23	45-49
50-54	34	17	17	38	19	19	41	20	21	50-54
55-59	27	14	13	32	16	16	34	17	17	55-59
60-64	20	10	10	24	12	12	28	14	14	60-64
65-69	12	6	6	15	7	8	18	9	9	65-69
70-74	7	3	4	8	4	4	11	5	6	70-74
75-79	5	2	3	5	2	3	6	3	3	75-79
80-84	3	1	2	3	1	2	3	1	2	80-84
85+	1	0	1	1	0	1	1	0	1	85+
TOTAL	876	439	437	1005	503	502	1150	577	573	TOTAL

TABLE 6 — STANDARDIZED RATES

STANDARD COUNTRIES:	ENGLAND AND WALES 1961 BOTH SEXES	MALES	FEMALES	UNITED STATES 1960 BOTH SEXES	MALES	FEMALES	MEXICO 1960 BOTH SEXES	MALES	FEMALES
STANDARDIZED RATES PER THOUSAND									
Birth	39.11	41.21	32.24*	37.30	38.64	32.87*	35.55	36.36	38.40*
Death	18.26	17.43	23.06*	15.35	15.95	15.77*	8.88	9.66	8.26*
Increase	20.85	23.78	9.17*	21.95	22.69	17.10*	26.67	26.70	30.14*

TABLE 7 — MOMENTS AND CUMULANTS

	OBSERVED POP. MALES	FEMALES	STATIONARY POP. MALES	FEMALES	STABLE POP. MALES	FEMALES	OBSERVED BIRTHS	NET PATERNITY FUNCTION	BIRTHS IN STABLE POP.
μ	24.17802	24.51790	34.54906	35.82799	22.51784	22.96924	32.27875	33.05208	31.17101
σ^2	369.7504	382.7220	453.3333	487.2460	320.8310	339.0817	59.68240	63.74544	55.10406
κ_3	5488.326	6111.948	2475.787	2666.649	5145.400	5740.915	257.6111	263.9189	292.7560
κ_4	-36017.	-17910.	-185972.	-222211.	10670.	18205.	-1183.726	-1879.369	-97.257
β_1	0.595873	0.666360	0.065792	0.061473	0.801696	0.845375	0.312169	0.268902	0.512225
β_2	2.736558	2.877728	2.095076	2.064016	3.103664	3.158339	2.667678	2.537498	2.967970
κ	-0.231265	-0.269683	-0.025996	-0.023744	-0.339418	-0.357659	-0.160845	-0.127405	-0.275687

TABLE 8 — RATES FROM AGE DISTRIBUTIONS AND VITAL STATISTICS (Males)

VITAL STATISTICS		THOMPSON AGE RANGE	NRR	1000r	INTERVAL	BOURGEOIS-PICHAT AGE RANGE	NRR	1000b	1000d	1000r	COALE	
GRR	3.063										IBR	43.23
NRR	2.665	0-4	2.37	31.60	27.31	5-29	2.82	40.26	1.92	38.34	IDR	6.52
TFR	6.006	5-9	2.18	29.23	27.22	30-54	1.59	26.13	8.88	17.26	IRI	36.71
GENERATION	32.090	10-14	1.96	24.37	27.08	55-79	1.73	25.01	4.63	20.38	K1	50.88
SEX RATIO	104.110	15-19	1.64	16.28	26.87	*20-44	1.30	19.81	9.97	9.84	K2	0.63

TABLE 9 — LESLIE MATRIX AND ITS SPECTRAL COMPONENTS (Males)

Start Age Interval	ORIGINAL MATRIX SUB-DIAGONAL	ALTERNATIVE FIRST ROWS Projection	Integral	FIRST STABLE MATRIX % IN STABLE POPULATION	FISHER VALUES	REPRODUCTIVE VALUES	SECOND STABLE MATRIX Z2 FIRST COLUMN	FIRST ROW
0	0.98687	0.00000	0.00000	16.935	1.163	73216	0.1524+0.1155	0.1524+0.1155
5	0.99523	0.00000	0.00000	14.339	1.374	72737	0.1972-0.0708	-0.0124+0.1740
10	0.99420	0.01396	0.00000	12.243	1.609	71269	0.0533-0.2253	-0.1381+0.0755
15	0.99206	0.23349	0.03032	10.443	1.870	62543	-0.1763-0.1851	-0.1285-0.0686
20	0.99030	0.54372	0.47750	8.889	1.923	54037	-0.2768+0.0514	-0.0473-0.1590
25	0.98863	0.64139	0.70306	7.552	1.625	43381	-0.1187+0.2859	0.0140-0.1784
30	0.98343	0.54676	0.68934	6.406	1.161	28675	0.1919+0.2805	0.0443-0.1530
35	0.97562	0.39412	0.49923	5.405	0.729	16665	0.3710-0.0084	0.0548-0.1067
40	0.96181	0.25133	0.36034	4.524	0.401	8149	0.2117-0.3417	0.0486-0.0580
45	0.94317	0.13899	0.18945	3.733	0.183	3204	-0.1824-0.3886	0.0306-0.0217
50	0.91314	0.05432	0.11726	3.021	0.054	764	-0.4453-0.0621	0.0109-0.0039
55+	0.74184			6.510				

TABLE 10 — AGE ANALYSIS AND MISCELLANEOUS RESULTS (Males)

Start Age Interval	OBSERVED POPUL. (IN 100's)	CONTRIBUTIONS OF ROOTS (IN 100's) r_1	r_2, r_3	$r_4 \cdot r_{11}$	AGE-SP BIRTH RATES	NET PATERNITY FUNCTION	COEFF. OF MATRIX EQUATION	PARAMETERS INTEGRAL	MATRIX	x	EXP. INCREASE $e^{(x+2\frac{1}{2})r}$
0	648	607	34	6	0.0000	0.0000	0.0000	L(1) 1.16501	1.16556	0	1.0794
5	538	514	42	-18	0.0000	0.0000	0.0000	L(2) 0.48566	0.49152	50	4.9713
10	449	439	8	1	0.0000	0.0000	0.0137	0.77794	0.75466	55	5.7917
15	344	375	-41	10	0.0061	0.0274	0.2280	R(1) 0.03055	0.03064	60	6.7474
20	276	319	-59	16	0.0954	0.4286	0.5267	R(2) -0.01731	-0.02093	65	7.8608
25	254	271	-22	5	0.1405	0.6249	0.6153	0.20254	0.19870	70	9.1579
30	244	230	45	-31	0.1377	0.6057	0.5186	C(1)	3586	75	10.6691
35	232	194	80	-42	0.0997	0.4314	0.3676	C(2)	10800	80	12.4296
40	209	162	41	6	0.0720	0.3038	0.2287		-673	85	14.4806
45	183	134	-45	94	0.0379	0.1536	0.1216	2P/Y 31.0217	31.6216	90	16.8701
50	150	108	-97	139	0.0234	0.0897	0.0448	DELTA 5.1173		95	19.6539
55+	314	233								100	22.8971

AGE AT LAST BIRTHDAY	1962 BOTH SEXES	MALES	FEMALES	1967 BOTH SEXES	MALES	FEMALES	1972 BOTH SEXES	MALES	FEMALES	AGE AT LAST BIRTHDAY	
0-4	72	37	35	82	42	40	94	48	46	0-4	
5-9	66	34	32	72	37	35	82	42	40	5-9	
10-14	65	34	31	65	34	31	72	37	35	10-14	
15-19	56	29	27	65	34	31	65	34	31	15-19	**TABLE 5**
20-24	49	25	24	56	29	27	65	34	31	20-24	POPULATION
25-29	42	21	21	48	24	24	55	28	27	25-29	PROJECTED
30-34	39	18	21	41	20	21	48	24	24	30-34	WITH
35-39	36	17	19	38	17	21	41	20	21	35-39	FIXED
40-44	32	15	17	35	16	19	38	17	21	40-44	AGE—
45-49	29	14	15	32	15	17	35	16	19	45-49	SPECIFIC
50-54	27	13	14	29	14	15	32	15	17	50-54	BIRTH
55-59	23	11	12	27	13	14	28	13	15	55-59	AND
60-64	21	10	11	23	11	12	26	12	14	60-64	DEATH
65-69	16	8	8	19	9	10	21	10	11	65-69	RATES
70-74	12	6	6	15	7	8	17	8	9	70-74	(IN 1000's)
75-79	10	5	5	10	5	5	12	6	6	75-79	
80-84	5	2	3	6	3	3	8	4	4	80-84	
85+	0	0	0	2	1	1	2	1	1	85+	
TOTAL	600	299	301	665	331	334	741	369	372	TOTAL	

STANDARD COUNTRIES:	ENGLAND AND WALES 1961 BOTH SEXES	MALES	FEMALES	UNITED STATES 1960 BOTH SEXES	MALES	FEMALES	MEXICO 1960 BOTH SEXES	MALES	FEMALES	
STANDARDIZED RATES PER THOUSAND										**TABLE 6**
Birth	24.35	25.74	20.57*	23.63	24.55	21.12*	26.15	26.82	24.56*	STANDARDIZED RATES
Death	11.15	9.71	11.13*	9.26	9.08	7.83*	4.93	5.32	5.12*	
Increase	13.20	16.03	9.44*	14.37	15.47	13.30*	21.22	21.50	19.44*	

	OBSERVED POP. MALES	FEMALES	STATIONARY POP. MALES	FEMALES	STABLE POP. MALES	FEMALES	OBSERVED BIRTHS	NET PATERNITY FUNCTION	BIRTHS IN STABLE POP.	
μ	27.99414	29.08202	38.33950	39.66975	27.89962	28.86355	27.12973	28.20071	27.02439	**TABLE 7**
σ^2	444.8809	439.6926	544.1142	555.7586	443.4657	464.2397	54.51457	57.62196	51.29177	MOMENTS
κ_3	6121.717	5379.387	2230.200	1415.988	6595.963	6553.858	316.2533	314.7903	291.7045	AND
κ_4	-114666.	-117911.	-315858.	-343336.	-82087.	-116148.	1178.190	853.196	1316.375	CUMULANTS
β_1	0.425613	0.340422	0.030876	0.011680	0.498857	0.429306	0.617351	0.517939	0.630585	
β_2	2.420642	2.390106	1.933130	1.888404	2.582600	2.461076	3.396452	3.256964	3.500362	
κ	-0.152716	-0.129207	-0.011044	-0.004110	-0.188725	-0.158125	-0.508108	-0.424857	-0.617352	

VITAL STATISTICS		THOMPSON AGE RANGE	NRR	1000r	INTERVAL	BOURGEOIS-PICHAT AGE RANGE	NRR	1000b	1000d	1000r	COALE		
GRR	1.916										IBR	27.24	**TABLE 8** RATES FROM AGE DISTRIBUTIONS AND VITAL STATISTICS (Males)
NRR	1.777	0-4	1.77	21.42	27.29	5-29	2.30	33.03	2.25	30.78	IDR	7.92	
TFR	3.746	5-9	1.96	25.06	27.26	30-54	1.44	21.12	7.73	13.40	IRI	19.33	
GENERATION	27.602	10-14	1.80	21.30	27.24	55-79	1.99	41.05	15.61	25.43	K1	0.	
SEX RATIO	104.734	15-19	1.65	16.37	27.19	* 5-29	2.30	33.03	2.25	30.78	K2	0.	

Start of Age Interval	ORIGINAL MATRIX SUB-DIAGONAL	ALTERNATIVE FIRST ROWS Projection	Integral	FIRST STABLE MATRIX % IN STABLE POPULATION	FISHER VALUES	REPRODUCTIVE VALUES	SECOND STABLE MATRIX Z2 FIRST COLUMN	FIRST ROW	
0	0.99213	0.00000	0.00000	13.037	1.088	34649	0.1886+0.1014	0.1886+0.1014	**TABLE 9**
5	0.99624	0.00445	0.00000	11.653	1.217	38351	0.2099-0.1606	-0.0119+0.1730	LESLIE
10	0.99606	0.11672	0.00942	10.459	1.351	36649	-0.0743-0.3191	-0.1320+0.0482	MATRIX
15	0.99164	0.34182	0.23743	9.385	1.378	32842	-0.3983-0.0789	-0.1014-0.0929	AND ITS
20	0.98493	0.46938	0.48680	8.385	1.168	24967	-0.2910+0.4078	-0.0302-0.1408	SPECTRAL
25	0.98319	0.39803	0.50981	7.440	0.798	16711	0.3086+0.5308	0.0047-0.1181	COMPONENTS
30	0.98500	0.25842	0.33440	6.590	0.460	8915	0.7472-0.0768	0.0132-0.0773	(Males)
35	0.98312	0.14937	0.21325	5.848	0.233	4054	0.2913-0.8733	0.0124-0.0427	
40	0.98300	0.06579	0.10320	5.180	0.098	1525	-0.8268-0.7646	0.0074-0.0205	
45	0.97677	0.02834	0.03603	4.587	0.038	551	-1.2686+0.5366	0.0051-0.0082	
50	0.96262	0.01150	0.02423	4.037	0.011	139	-0.0404+1.6736	0.0024-0.0019	
55+	0.82000			13.399					

Start of Age Interval	OBSERVED POPUL. (IN 100's)	CONTRIBUTIONS OF ROOTS (IN 100's) r_1	r_2, r_3	r_4-r_{11}	AGE-SP. BIRTH RATES	NET PATERNITY FUNCTION	COEFF. OF MATRIX EQUATION	PARAMETERS	INTEGRAL	MATRIX	EXP. INCREASE x	$e^{(x+8\frac{1}{2})r}$	
0	342	350	-5	-3	0.0000	0.0000	0.0000	L(1)	1.10971	1.10999	0	1.0534	**TABLE 10**
5	343	313	20	10	0.0000	0.0000	0.0044	L(2)	0.31737	0.33088	50	2.9833	AGE
10	291	281	28	-18	0.0018	0.0088	0.1154		0.76228	0.73240	55	3.3106	ANALYSIS
15	248	252	-2	-1	0.0466	0.2219	0.3365	R(1)	0.02082	0.02087	60	3.6738	AND
20	210	225	-46	30	0.0955	0.4511	0.4582	R(2)	-0.03830	-0.04371	65	4.0769	MISCELLANEOUS
25	180	200	-43	23	0.1000	0.4653	0.3827		0.23526	0.22929	70	4.5242	RESULTS
30	169	177	26	-34	0.0656	0.3001	0.2443	C(1)		2685	75	5.0205	(Males)
35	154	157	90	-93	0.0418	0.1885	0.1391	C(2)		1239	80	5.5713	
40	145	139	52	-46	0.0202	0.0897	0.0602			4743	85	6.1825	
45	137	123	-82	96	0.0071	0.0308	0.0255	2P/Y	26.7079	27.4024	90	6.8608	
50	117	108	-160	169	0.0048	0.0202	0.0101	DELTA	3.0677		95	7.6135	
55+	374	360									100	8.4488	

AGE AT LAST BIRTHDAY	BOTH SEXES	1969 MALES	FEMALES	BOTH SEXES	1974 MALES	FEMALES	BOTH SEXES	1979 MALES	FEMALES	AGE AT LAST BIRTHDAY	
0-4	646	333	313	683	352	331	731	377	354	0-4	
5-9	656	337	319	643	331	312	681	351	330	5-9	
10-14	853	437	416	655	337	318	642	331	311	10-14	
15-19	892	454	438	852	436	416	653	335	318	15-19	TABLE 5
20-24	776	393	383	888	451	437	848	433	415	20-24	POPULATION
25-29	734	366	368	772	390	382	884	448	436	25-29	PROJECTED
30-34	672	324	348	729	363	366	767	387	380	30-34	WITH
35-39	716	350	366	666	321	345	723	359	364	35-39	FIXED
40-44	737	358	379	707	345	362	658	316	342	40-44	AGE—
45-49	726	342	384	724	350	374	695	338	357	45-49	SPECIFIC
50-54	438	204	234	707	331	376	705	339	366	50-54	BIRTH
55-59	665	309	356	419	193	226	677	313	364	55-59	AND
60-64	569	262	307	619	282	337	390	176	214	60-64	DEATH
65-69	474	214	260	503	224	279	548	241	307	65-69	RATES
70-74	344	143	201	388	168	220	412	176	236	70-74	(IN 1000's)
75-79	203	79	124	248	98	150	279	115	164	75-79	
80-84	108	41	67	118	44	74	144	54	90	80-84	
85+	50	18	32	59	20	39	65	22	43	85+	
TOTAL	10259	4964	5295	10380	5036	5344	10502	5111	5391	TOTAL	

STANDARD COUNTRIES:	ENGLAND AND WALES 1961			UNITED STATES 1960			MEXICO 1960			
STANDARDIZED RATES PER THOUSAND	BOTH SEXES	MALES	FEMALES	BOTH SEXES	MALES	FEMALES	BOTH SEXES	MALES	FEMALES	TABLE 6
Birth	12.26	13.10	10.72*	11.76	12.36	11.10*	12.50	12.97	12.33*	STANDAR-
Death	12.14	11.93	12.35*	9.98	10.82	8.97*	5.53	6.35	7.05*	DIZED
Increase	0.11	1.17	-1.63*	1.78	1.54	2.13*	6.98	6.62	5.28*	RATES

	OBSERVED POP.		STATIONARY POP.		STABLE POP.		OBSERVED BIRTHS	NET PATERNITY FUNCTION	BIRTHS IN STABLE POP.	
	MALES	FEMALES	MALES	FEMALES	MALES	FEMALES				
μ	33.54919	35.84926	36.79835	38.59062	38.28738	40.18303	29.66772	29.73350	29.85516	TABLE 7
σ^2	451.8317	478.0268	500.9209	536.4682	506.6120	540.9629	38.35220	38.71713	39.47120	MOMENTS
κ_3	3163.269	2508.300	2298.241	1969.744	1547.912	1067.431	228.4961	252.4338	257.9816	AND
κ_4	-187728.	-225325.	-247335.	-299480.	-259628.	-310040.	1623.182	1885.171	1879.549	CUMULANTS
β_1	0.108478	0.057597	0.042023	0.025130	0.018427	0.007197	0.925522	1.097958	1.082272	
β_2	2.080447	2.013936	2.014292	1.959411	1.988417	1.940546	4.103537	4.257606	4.206405	
κ	-0.040442	-0.021409	-0.015879	-0.009231	-0.006983	-0.002651	-1.503318	-1.351717	-1.240745	

VITAL STATISTICS		THOMPSON				BOURGEOIS-PICHAT				COALE	
		AGE RANGE	NRR	1000r	INTERVAL	AGE RANGE	NRR	1000b	1000d	1000r	
GRR	0.990										IBR	TABLE 8
NRR	0.916	0-4	0.91	-3.33	27.36	5-29	1.49	22.22	7.34	14.88	IDR	RATES
TFR	1.913	5-9	1.28	9.13	27.32	30-54	1.31	22.19	12.06	10.13	IRI	FROM AGE
GENERATION	29.794	10-14	1.34	10.76	27.25	55-79	2.17	79.69	50.99	28.71	K1	DISTRI-
SEX RATIO	107.244	15-19	1.17	5.62	27.13	* 5-29	1.49	22.22	7.34	14.88	K2	BUTIONS

AND VITAL STATISTICS (Males)

Start of Age Interval	ORIGINAL MATRIX			FIRST STABLE MATRIX			SECOND STABLE MATRIX Z_2		
	SUB-DIAGONAL	ALTERNATIVE FIRST ROWS Projection	Integral	% IN STABLE POPULATION	FISHER VALUES	REPRODUCTIVE VALUES	FIRST COLUMN	FIRST ROW	
0	0.99501	0.00000	0.00000	6.421	1.040	332736	0.1806+0.0482	0.1806+0.0482	
5	0.99793	0.00000	0.00000	6.484	1.030	429383	0.1545-0.1629	0.0365+0.1512	
10	0.99637	0.00614	0.00000	6.567	1.017	446330	-0.0835-0.2574	-0.0958+0.0866	TABLE 9
15	0.99320	0.10421	0.01223	6.640	0.999	383632	-0.3200-0.0596	-0.1024-0.0359	LESLIE
20	0.99177	0.27269	0.19598	6.693	0.882	325474	-0.2460+0.3031	-0.0334-0.0944	MATRIX
25	0.99124	0.28226	0.34825	6.737	0.590	206059	0.1781+0.4322	0.0063-0.0754	AND ITS
30	0.98914	0.15604	0.21399	6.777	0.291	107023	0.5563+0.0597	0.0064-0.0392	SPECTRAL
35	0.98559	0.07026	0.09685	6.803	0.126	48133	0.3800-0.5496	0.0030-0.0186	COMPO-
40	0.97917	0.03031	0.04326	6.805	0.052	20094	-0.3587-0.7097	0.0020-0.0087	NENTS
45	0.96746	0.01363	0.01727	6.763	0.020	4698	-0.9397-0.0281	0.0017-0.0035	(Males)
50	0.94642	0.00509	0.01011	6.640	0.005	1980	-0.5531+0.9487	0.0008-0.0008	
55+	0.74971			26.669					

Start Age Interval	OBSERVED POPUL. (IN 100's)	CONTRIBUTIONS OF ROOTS (IN 100's)			AGE-SP. BIRTH RATES	NET PATERNITY FUNCTION	COEFF. OF MATRIX EQUATION	PARAMETERS		EXP. INCREASE		
		r_1	r_2, r_3	$r_4 \cdot r_{11}$					INTEGRAL	MATRIX	x	$e^{(x+8\frac{1}{2})r}$
0	3390	3789	-253	-146	0.0000	0.0000	0.0000	L(1)	0.98533	0.98534	0	0.9926
5	4380	3826	355	199	0.0000	0.0000	0.0000	L(2)	0.39344	0.39555	50	0.8563
10	4560	3875	774	-89	0.0000	0.0000	0.0061			0.75255	0.72765	55	0.8438
15	3960	3918	375	-333	0.0026	0.0122	0.1031	R(1)	-0.00295	-0.00295	60	0.8314
20	3690	3949	-688	428	0.0414	0.1940	0.2680	R(2)	-0.03269	-0.03770	65	0.8192
25	3270	3975	-1325	620	0.0735	0.3419	0.2751			0.21781	0.21458	70	0.8072
30	3540	3999	-529	71	0.0452	0.2082	0.1507	C(1)		59005	75	0.7953
35	3630	4014	1290	-1675	0.0204	0.0932	0.0671	C(2)		-32571	80	0.7837
40	3490	4015	2219	-2745	0.0091	0.0410	0.0285			139890	85	0.7722
45	2110	3990	691	-2571	0.0036	0.0160	0.0126	2P/Y	28.8465	29.2819	90	0.7609
50	3270	3918	-2294	1646	0.0021	0.0091	0.0045	DELTA	9.5293		95	0.7497
55+	9600	15736									100	0.7387

TABLE 10 AGE ANALYSIS AND MISCELLANEOUS RESULTS (Males)

AGE AT LAST BIRTHDAY	1968 BOTH SEXES	1968 MALES	1968 FEMALES	1973 BOTH SEXES	1973 MALES	1973 FEMALES	1978 BOTH SEXES	1978 MALES	1978 FEMALES	AGE AT LAST BIRTHDAY	
0-4	320	163	157	349	178	171	382	195	187	0-4	
5-9	305	156	149	319	163	156	347	177	170	5-9	
10-14	307	157	150	305	156	149	318	162	156	10-14	
15-19	301	155	146	307	157	150	304	156	148	15-19	TABLE 5
20-24	311	159	152	300	154	146	306	156	150	20-24	POPULATION
25-29	227	116	111	309	158	151	299	153	146	25-29	PROJECTED
30-34	195	99	96	226	115	111	308	157	151	30-34	WITH
35-39	209	106	103	194	98	96	224	114	110	35-39	FIXED
40-44	235	119	116	207	105	102	192	97	95	40-44	AGE—
45-49	258	129	129	231	117	114	204	103	101	45-49	SPECIFIC
50-54	242	120	122	253	126	127	227	114	113	50-54	BIRTH
55-59	227	112	115	233	114	119	244	120	124	55-59	AND
60-64	197	93	104	213	103	110	220	106	114	60-64	DEATH
65-69	172	79	93	178	82	96	194	91	103	65-69	RATES
70-74	133	60	73	146	65	81	151	67	84	70-74	(IN 1000's)
75-79	87	38	49	100	44	56	109	47	62	75-79	
80-84	50	21	29	54	23	31	62	26	36	80-84	
85+	27	11	16	29	12	17	32	13	19	85+	
TOTAL	3803	1893	1910	3953	1970	1983	4123	2054	2069	TOTAL	

STANDARD COUNTRIES:	ENGLAND AND WALES 1961 BOTH SEXES	MALES	FEMALES	UNITED STATES 1960 BOTH SEXES	MALES	FEMALES	MEXICO 1960 BOTH SEXES	MALES	FEMALES	
STANDARDIZED RATES PER THOUSAND										TABLE 6
Birth	18.38	19.42	17.46*	17.67	18.35	17.67*	17.69	18.14	19.78*	STANDAR-
Death	10.13	9.77	10.44*	8.13	8.74	7.74*	4.06	4.72	5.86*	DIZED
Increase	8.25	9.65	7.02*	9.54	9.61	9.94*	13.63	13.42	13.92*	RATES

	OBSERVED POP. MALES	OBSERVED POP. FEMALES	STATIONARY POP. MALES	STATIONARY POP. FEMALES	STABLE POP. MALES	STABLE POP. FEMALES	OBSERVED BIRTHS	NET PATERNITY FUNCTION	BIRTHS IN STABLE POP.	
μ	34.31116	35.98601	37.74309	39.41170	32.47080	33.80881	31.83252	31.44836	30.96410	TABLE 7
σ^2	496.6269	526.9078	522.2047	552.2065	485.0453	517.5366	50.07620	45.48028	43.27091	MOMENTS
κ_3	3216.807	2784.194	2262.682	1753.352	4715.867	4741.322	198.1575	213.7695	209.7686	AND
κ_4	-240448.	-288465.	-273844.	-324926.	-187915.	-235546.	-458.362	284.862	485.269	CUMULANTS
β_1	0.084481	0.052990	0.035952	0.018257	0.194884	0.162172	0.312699	0.485760	0.543117	
β_2	2.025098	1.960979	1.995797	1.934432	2.201276	2.120587	2.817213	3.137717	3.259174	
κ	-0.030848	-0.018965	-0.013460	-0.006617	-0.073479	-0.059212	-0.196425	-0.348933	-0.419727	

VITAL STATISTICS		THOMPSON AGE RANGE	NRR	1000r	INTERVAL	BOURGEOIS-PICHAT AGE RANGE	NRR	1000b	1000d	1000r	COALE	
GRR	1.454										IBR	TABLE 8
NRR	1.384	0-4	1.25	8.24	27.40	5-29	1.87	22.99	-0.24	23.23	IDR	RATES FROM AGE DISTRI-
TFR	2.843	5-9	1.31	10.02	27.37	30-54	0.82	10.35	17.61	-7.25	IRI	BUTIONS AND VITAL
GENERATION	31.204	10-14	1.28	8.99	27.31	55-79	1.56	34.20	17.73	16.47	K1	STATISTICS
SEX RATIO	104.676	15-19	1.30	9.28	27.19	*45-69	1.40	26.77	14.42	12.35	K2	(Males·)

Start of Age Interval	ORIGINAL MATRIX SUB-DIAGONAL	ALTERNATIVE FIRST ROWS Projection	ALTERNATIVE FIRST ROWS Integral	FIRST STABLE MATRIX % IN STABLE POPULATION	FISHER VALUES	REPRODUCTIVE VALUES	SECOND STABLE MATRIX Z2 FIRST COLUMN	FIRST ROW	
0	0.99518	0.00000	0.00000	9.712	1.048	156483	0.1622+0.0643	0.1622+0.0643	TABLE 9
5	0.99741	0.00000	0.00000	9.174	1.109	166905	0.1600-0.1175	0.0278+0.1508	LESLIE
10	0.99670	0.00589	0.00000	8.685	1.172	171943	-0.0166-0.2258	-0.0991+0.0909	MATRIX
15	0.99489	0.11876	0.01214	8.217	1.233	187227	-0.2281-0.1206	-0.1147-0.0317	AND ITS
20	0.99416	0.32947	0.23284	7.759	1.180	131254	-0.2541+0.1470	-0.0493-0.1079	SPECTRAL
25	0.99402	0.39422	0.44610	7.321	0.903	86842	-0.0117+0.3334	0.0037-0.1085	COMPO-
30	0.99265	0.28795	0.36534	6.908	0.542	56116	0.3140+0.2126	0.0183-0.0735	NENTS
35	0.98848	0.16586	0.22744	6.508	0.271	31557	0.3937-0.1739	0.0163-0.0394	(Males)
40	0.98281	0.07743	0.11435	6.106	0.113	14787	0.0698-0.4814	0.0100-0.0170	
45	0.97326	0.03073	0.04538	5.696	0.039	4785	-0.4168-0.3537	0.0048-0.0056	
50	0.95227	0.00886	0.01819	5.262	0.009	1040	-0.5798+0.1840	0.0014-0.0010	
55+	0.78489			18.650					

Start of Age Interval	OBSERVED POPUL. (IN 100's)	CONTRIBUTIONS OF ROOTS (IN 100's) r_1	r_2, r_3	$r_4 \cdot r_{11}$	AGE-SP. BIRTH RATES	NET PATERNITY FUNCTION	COEFF. OF MATRIX EQUATION	PARAMETERS INTEGRAL	MATRIX	EXP. INCREASE x	$e^{(x+2\frac{1}{2})r}$	
0	1572	1633	-65	5	0.0000	0.0000	0.0000	L(1) 1.05350	1.05356	0	1.0264	TABLE 10
5	1575	1542	35	-3	0.0000	0.0000	0.0000	L(2) 0.46329	0.46446	50	1.7285	AGE
10	1552	1460	127	-35	0.0000	0.0000	0.0058	0.76261	0.74109	55	1.8210	ANALYSIS
15	1601	1381	108	112	0.0024	0.0117	0.1175	R(1) 0.01042	0.01043	60	1.9185	AND
20	1164	1304	-34	-106	0.0463	0.2233	0.3243	R(2) -0.02279	-0.02680	65	2.0211	MISCEL-
25	996	1231	-181	-53	0.0888	0.4253	0.3858	0.20498	0.20219	70	2.1292	LANEOUS
30	1070	1161	-174	83	0.0727	0.3462	0.2801	C(1)	16811	75	2.2432	RESULTS
35	1202	1094	24	84	0.0453	0.2140	0.1601	C(2)	-9135	80	2.3632	(Males)
40	1316	1027	252	37	0.0228	0.1063	0.0739		27494	85	2.4896	
45	1234	958	271	5	0.0090	0.0415	0.0288	2P/Y 30.6534	31.0753	90	2.6228	
50	1171	885	5	282	0.0036	0.0162	0.0081	DELTA 6.1468		95	2.7632	
55+	3815	3135								100	2.9110	

TABLE 5 — POPULATION PROJECTED WITH FIXED AGE-SPECIFIC BIRTH AND DEATH RATES (IN 1000's)

AGE AT LAST BIRTHDAY	BOTH SEXES	1966 MALES	FEMALES	BOTH SEXES	1971 MALES	FEMALES	BOTH SEXES	1976 MALES	FEMALES	AGE AT LAST BIRTHDAY
0-4	3974	2040	1934	4095	2102	1993	4311	2213	2098	0-4
5-9	3653	1875	1778	3960	2032	1928	4081	2094	1987	5-9
10-14	3248	1664	1584	3646	1871	1775	3954	2028	1926	10-14
15-19	3658	1870	1788	3240	1659	1581	3636	1864	1772	15-19
20-24	3196	1622	1574	3644	1860	1784	3228	1650	1578	20-24
25-29	2867	1433	1434	3183	1614	1569	3630	1850	1780	25-29
30-34	2830	1435	1395	2855	1426	1429	3169	1605	1564	30-34
35-39	2948	1478	1470	2811	1424	1387	2836	1415	1421	35-39
40-44	3185	1578	1607	2917	1460	1457	2783	1408	1375	40-44
45-49	3021	1488	1533	3132	1547	1585	2869	1432	1437	45-49
50-54	3145	1539	1606	2937	1437	1500	3045	1494	1551	50-54
55-59	3060	1474	1586	2998	1444	1554	2799	1348	1451	55-59
60-64	2733	1266	1467	2822	1318	1504	2765	1292	1473	60-64
65-69	2170	922	1248	2402	1060	1342	2480	1104	1376	65-69
70-74	1631	630	1001	1772	700	1072	1957	805	1152	70-74
75-79	1115	394	721	1183	414	769	1282	459	823	75-79
80-84	650	207	443	669	206	463	709	216	493	80-84
85+	347	97	250	377	101	276	389	100	289	85+
TOTAL	47431	23012	24419	48643	23675	24968	49923	24377	25546	TOTAL

TABLE 6 — STANDARDIZED RATES

STANDARD COUNTRIES:	ENGLAND AND WALES 1961 BOTH SEXES	MALES	FEMALES	UNITED STATES 1960 BOTH SEXES	MALES	FEMALES	MEXICO 1960 BOTH SEXES	MALES	FEMALES
STANDARDIZED RATES PER THOUSAND									
Birth	17.58	18.70	16.53*	16.91	17.68	17.13*	17.47	18.04	18.91*
Death	11.81	12.46	11.20*	9.59	11.06	8.33*	4.85	5.85	6.56*
Increase	5.77	6.24	5.33*	7.32	6.62	8.80*	12.62	12.19	12.35*

TABLE 7 — MOMENTS AND CUMULANTS

	OBSERVED POP. MALES	FEMALES	STATIONARY POP. MALES	FEMALES	STABLE POP. MALES	FEMALES	OBSERVED BIRTHS	NET PATERNITY FUNCTION	BIRTHS IN STABLE POP.
μ	34.78580	37.84515	36.41439	38.97328	31.89181	33.88682	30.78158	30.52265	30.10923
σ^2	471.5694	526.3207	487.2509	546.6711	456.7098	514.2369	43.95694	42.21697	40.19924
κ_3	2243.607	1654.105	2181.529	2012.214	4111.667	4648.109	215.0817	215.2864	207.0730
κ_4	-215169.	-289986.	-230934.	-311924.	-167218.	-230052.	678.367	812.153	911.885
β_1	0.048002	0.018766	0.041140	0.024784	0.177466	0.158878	0.544659	0.615988	0.660075
β_2	2.032414	1.953169	2.027292	1.956250	2.198317	2.130041	3.351083	3.455684	3.564293
κ	-0.018304	-0.006902	-0.015734	-0.009083	-0.067952	-0.058630	-0.500775	-0.572239	-0.680084

TABLE 8 — RATES FROM AGE DISTRIBUTIONS AND VITAL STATISTICS (Males)

VITAL STATISTICS		THOMPSON AGE RANGE	NRR	1000r	INTERVAL	BOURGEOIS-PICHAT AGE RANGE	NRR	1000b	1000d	1000r	COALE	
GRR	1.406					5-29	1.32	17.82	7.56	10.26	IBR	
NRR	1.336	0-4	1.21	6.97	27.40	30-54	0.86	11.81	17.52	-5.71	IDR	
TFR	2.731	5-9	1.07	2.47	27.36	55-79	1.70	46.27	26.65	19.62	IRI	
GENERATION	30.314	10-14	1.17	5.80	27.28	*20-54	0.85	11.64	17.65	-6.01	K1	
SEX RATIO	106.101	15-19	1.00	0.08	27.13						K2	

TABLE 9 — LESLIE MATRIX AND ITS SPECTRAL COMPONENTS (Males)

Start of Age Interval	ORIGINAL MATRIX SUB-DIAGONAL	ALTERNATIVE FIRST ROWS Projection	Integral	% IN STABLE POPULATION	FISHER VALUES	REPRODUCTIVE VALUES	SECOND STABLE MATRIX Z2 FIRST COLUMN	FIRST ROW
0	0.99602	0.00000	0.00000	9.680	1.051	1874028	0.1695+0.0598	0.1695+0.0598
5	0.99789	0.00000	0.00000	9.192	1.107	1755575	0.1561-0.1332	0.0292+0.1548
10	0.99673	0.00909	0.00000	8.744	1.164	2083963	-0.0422-0.2308	-0.1043+0.0900
15	0.99471	0.13833	0.01868	8.309	1.215	1915997	-0.2522-0.0905	-0.1155-0.0400
20	0.99468	0.35072	0.26607	7.879	1.135	1632214	-0.2334+0.1970	-0.0440-0.1136
25	0.99460	0.38967	0.45475	7.471	0.826	1156972	0.0608+0.3428	0.0071-0.1045
30	0.99244	0.25841	0.34529	7.084	0.460	679577	0.3727+0.1360	0.0160-0.0640
35	0.98824	0.13309	0.18543	6.702	0.212	344149	0.3464-0.2891	0.0116-0.0316
40	0.98039	0.05765	0.08822	6.314	0.084	130228	-0.0865-0.5036	0.0065-0.0132
45	0.96554	0.02149	0.03047	5.901	0.028	45710	-0.5382-0.1997	0.0031-0.0044
50	0.93818	0.00685	0.01404	5.432	0.007	11254	-0.4899+0.4044	0.0011-0.0009
55+	0.75423			17.291				

TABLE 10 — AGE ANALYSIS AND MISCELLANEOUS RESULTS (Males)

Start of Age Interval	OBSERVED POPUL. (IN 100's)	CONTRIBUTIONS OF ROOTS (IN 100's) r_1	r_2, r_3	r_4-r_{11}	AGE-SP. BIRTH RATES	NET PATERNITY FUNCTION	COEFF. OF MATRIX EQUATION	PARAMETERS	INTEGRAL	MATRIX	EXP. INCREASE x	$e^{(x+2\frac{1}{2})r}$
0	18820	19034	-214	-0	0.0000	0.0000	0.0000	L(1)	1.04891	1.04896	0	1.0242
5	16680	18073	-411	-982	0.0000	0.0000	0.0000	L(2)	0.43667	0.43770	50	1.6511
10	18760	17193	-193	1759	0.0000	0.0000	0.0090		0.77867	0.75496	55	1.7318
15	16310	16337	316	-344	0.0037	0.0181	0.1370	R(1)	0.00955	0.00956	60	1.8165
20	14410	15492	613	-1695	0.0533	0.2560	0.3456	R(2)	-0.02269	-0.02724	65	1.9054
25	14430	14691	290	-550	0.0911	0.4352	0.3819			0.20908	70	1.9986
30	14890	13929	-465	1426	0.0692	0.3287	0.2519	C(1)		196629	75	2.0964
35	15970	13179	-906	3697	0.0372	0.1752	0.1288	C(2)		-83151	80	2.1989
40	15180	12416	-430	3194	0.0177	0.0824	0.0551			-56984	85	2.3065
45	15940	11604	667	3669	0.0061	0.0279	0.0201	2P/Y	29.6458	30.0518	90	2.4193
50	15710	10681	1275	3753	0.0028	0.0124	0.0062	DELTA	7.2004		95	2.5376
55+	46360	33999									100	2.6617

Hypothetical Materials

Relatively high-quality official data, on which the tables of the present volume have up to this point been based, cover about 30 per cent of world population. The following pages are a suggestion of the kind of interim treatment that might be of use for the remainder. Some 25 countries have over 20 million population; nine of these have registration systems and are included in the preceding sections. To eleven of those remaining have been assigned "data" which in the nature of the case can only be guessed, and the standard female dominant computations are made for them. We are indebted to M. K. Premi for the development of this section.

The hypothetical data are not given with the same confidence or lack of confidence for all countries. The USSR has had a number of censuses, and it reports crude birth and death rates along with some age-specific rates. India has a sample survey in which the crude birth rate appears to be estimated with an accuracy comparable with that attained by the average national registration system. Indonesia provides less information; Mainland China, less yet.

It may be said of the pages of this section, even more than of the volume as a whole, that it is a first attempt, whose aim is principally to invite challenge and improvement.

TABLE 1 — DATA

AGE AT LAST BIRTHDAY	BOTH SEXES	POPULATION MALES Number	%	FEMALES Number	%	BIRTHS BY AGE OF MOTHER	DEATHS BOTH SEXES	MALES	FEMALES	AGE AT LAST BIRTHDAY
0	752584	383366	2.9	369218	2.9	0	130564	79035	51529	0
1-4	3379648	1728125	13.2	1651523	12.8	0	81034	45400	35634	1-4
5-9	3799104	1971956	15.1	1827148	14.2	0	19861	11158	8703	5-9
10-14	3178708	1651445	12.6	1527263	11.9	0	12436	6772	5664	10-14
15-19	2124492	1114165	8.5	1010327	7.8	36431	11697	6517	5180	15-19
20-24	1795396	921134	7.0	874262	6.8	200961	13208	7676	5532	20-24
25-29	1914129	859819	6.6	1054310	8.2	399886	15428	7891	7537	25-29
30-34	1681013	836869	6.4	844144	6.6	336004	15379	8527	6852	30-34
35-39	1726672	847459	6.5	879213	6.8	186429	18606	10649	7957	35-39
40-44	1274911	660676	5.0	614235	4.8	37509	16447	10304	6143	40-44
45-49	1144339	567171	4.3	577168	4.5	12133	17453	10902	6551	45-49
50-54	997400	493806	3.8	503594	3.9	0	20265	12655	7610	50-54
55-59	638328	322941	2.5	315387	2.4	0	17268	10948	6320	55-59
60-64	674680	320801	2.4	353879	2.7	0	26141	15532	10609	60-64
65-69	333370	163878	1.3	169492	1.3	0	18490	11235	7255	65-69
70-74	301301	133533	1.0	167768	1.3		24362	13377	10985	70-74
75-79	176403	80579	0.6	95824	0.7		21508	12032	9476	75-79
80-84	75515	35667	0.3	39848	0.3	641590 M.	16462	9459	7003	80-84
85+	16108	4622	0.0	11486	0.1	567763 F.	4884	1790	3094	85+
TOTAL	25984101	13098012		12886089		1209353	501493	291859	209634	TOTAL

TABLE 2 — MALE LIFE TABLE

x	$_nq_x$	l_x	$_nd_x$	$_nL_x$	$_nm_x$	$_na_x$	T_x	r_x	$\dot{e}_x$	$_nM_x$	x
0	0.181623	100000	18162	88098	0.206161	0.3447	4041667	0.0000	40.417	0.206161	0
1	0.097912	81838	8013	305005	0.026271	1.2112	3953569	0.0000	48.310	0.026271	1
5	0.027622	73825	2039	364026	0.005602	2.5000	3648564	0.0145	49.422	0.005658	5
10	0.020307	71786	1458	355285	0.004103	2.5008	3284538	0.0522	45.755	0.004101	10
15	0.029070	70328	2044	346807	0.005895	2.6360	2929253	0.0524	41.651	0.005849	15
20	0.040898	68284	2793	334622	0.008346	2.5667	2582446	0.0179	37.819	0.008333	20
25	0.044868	65491	2938	320174	0.009178	2.5224	2247824	0.0004	34.323	0.009178	25
30	0.049703	62552	3109	305133	0.010189	2.5462	1927650	0.0000	30.817	0.010189	30
35	0.061020	59443	3627	288376	0.012578	2.5627	1622517	0.0110	27.295	0.012566	35
40	0.075273	55816	4201	268810	0.015630	2.5553	1334140	0.0245	23.902	0.015596	40
45	0.091897	51615	4743	246522	0.019241	2.5646	1065331	0.0093	20.640	0.019222	45
50	0.121007	46871	5672	220535	0.025718	2.5629	818809	0.0304	17.469	0.025627	50
55	0.156707	41200	6456	190245	0.033937	2.5599	598274	0.0080	14.521	0.033901	55
60	0.216694	34743	7529	155213	0.048506	2.5421	408029	0.0130	11.744	0.048416	60
65	0.293175	27215	7979	116160	0.068687	2.5042	252816	0.0130	9.290	0.068557	65
70	0.399677	19236	7688	76591	0.100380	2.4520	136656	0.0130	7.104	0.100177	70
75	0.537569	11548	6208	41473	0.149684	2.3796	60065	0.0130	5.201	0.149319	75
80	0.768040	5340	4101	15412	0.266122	2.2476	18593	0.0130	3.482	0.265204	80
85+	*1.000000	1239	1239	3181	0.389380	2.5682	3181	0.0130	2.568	0.387278	85+

TABLE 3 — FEMALE LIFE TABLE

x	$_nq_x$	l_x	$_nd_x$	$_nL_x$	$_nm_x$	$_na_x$	T_x	r_x	$\dot{e}_x$	$_nM_x$	x
0	0.128252	100000	12825	91896	0.139563	0.3681	4845907	0.0000	48.459	0.139563	0
1	0.081479	87175	7103	329199	0.021576	1.2547	4754011	0.0000	54.534	0.021576	1
5	0.023235	80072	1860	395708	0.004702	2.5000	4424812	0.0197	55.261	0.004763	5
10	0.018396	78211	1439	387479	0.003713	2.5136	4029104	0.0550	51.516	0.003709	10
15	0.025458	76773	1954	379162	0.005155	2.5951	3641625	0.0507	47.434	0.005127	15
20	0.031156	74818	2331	368386	0.006328	2.5529	3262462	0.0000	43.605	0.006328	20
25	0.035125	72487	2546	356165	0.007149	2.5371	2894076	0.0000	39.925	0.007149	25
30	0.039808	69941	2784	342834	0.008121	2.5321	2537912	0.0101	36.286	0.008117	30
35	0.044302	67157	2975	328419	0.009059	2.5247	2195078	0.0227	32.686	0.009050	35
40	0.048870	64182	3137	313149	0.010016	2.5265	1866659	0.0320	29.084	0.010001	40
45	0.055266	61045	3374	297018	0.011359	2.5673	1553509	0.0080	25.449	0.011350	45
50	0.073243	57671	4226	278156	0.015192	2.5861	1256492	0.0452	21.787	0.015111	50
55	0.095796	53446	5120	254962	0.020081	2.6042	978336	0.0142	18.305	0.020039	55
60	0.140438	48326	6787	225280	0.030126	2.5912	723374	0.0318	14.969	0.029979	60
65	0.194745	41539	8090	188030	0.043023	2.5691	498094	0.0318	11.991	0.042804	65
70	0.283123	33449	9470	143874	0.065824	2.5319	310064	0.0318	9.270	0.065477	70
75	0.397873	23979	9541	95896	0.099490	2.4845	166191	0.0318	6.931	0.098890	75
80	0.606682	14438	8760	49489	0.177000	2.4082	70295	0.0318	4.869	0.175744	80
85+	*1.000000	5679	5679	20806	0.272944	3.6638	20806	0.0318	3.664	0.269371	85+

TABLE 4 — OBSERVED AND PROJECTED VITAL RATES

	OBSERVED POPULATION BOTH SEXES	MALES	FEMALES	PROJECTED POPULATION 1965 MALES	FEMALES	1970 MALES	FEMALES	1975 MALES	FEMALES	STABLE POPULATION MALES	FEMALES
RATES PER THOUSAND											
Birth	46.54	48.98	44.06	44.83	39.96	44.00	38.97	46.38	40.93	48.92	43.24
Death	19.30	22.28	16.27	22.32	16.60	21.53	16.27	21.42	16.30	22.61	16.92
Increase	27.24	26.70	27.79	22.51	23.35	22.47	22.71	24.96	24.64		26.3146
PERCENTAGE											
under 15	42.76	43.78	41.71	43.87	41.96	42.82	41.14	43.30	41.34	45.17	43.18
15-64	53.77	53.02	54.53	53.00	53.90	54.44	55.03	53.93	54.61	52.94	53.65
65 and over	3.47	3.19	3.76	3.12	4.14	2.74	3.83	2.77	4.05	1.88	3.17
DEP. RATIO X 100	85.98	88.60	83.39	88.67	85.53	83.69	81.73	85.41	83.12	88.88	86.39

TABLE 1 — DATA

AGE AT LAST BIRTHDAY	POPULATION BOTH SEXES	MALES Number	MALES %	FEMALES Number	FEMALES %	BIRTHS BY AGE OF MOTHER	DEATHS BOTH SEXES	DEATHS MALES	DEATHS FEMALES	AGE AT LAST BIRTHDAY
0	1920067	971808	3.8	948259	3.6	0	352023	194444	157579	0
1-4	6469630	3272903	12.6	3196727	12.3	0	164031	83448	80583	1-4
5-9	7031293	3568277	13.8	3463016	13.3	0	39132	19595	19537	5-9
10-14	6322757	3171305	12.3	3151452	12.1	0	26475	12623	13852	10-14
15-19	5514730	2650047	10.2	2864683	11.0	263711	32029	15042	16987	15-19
20-24	5002404	2389433	9.2	2612971	10.0	605931	39099	19324	19775	20-24
25-29	4141580	2034547	7.9	2107033	8.1	600470	36182	18121	18061	25-29
30-34	3252348	1625122	6.3	1627226	6.2	403749	32493	16667	15826	30-34
35-39	3047847	1527155	5.9	1520692	5.8	290489	35167	18623	16544	35-39
40-44	2394029	1230112	4.8	1163917	4.5	102250	32718	18619	14099	40-44
45-49	1981130	1020679	3.9	960451	3.7	18953	32393	19041	13352	45-49
50-54	1588233	812583	3.1	775650	3.0	0	34638	20212	14426	50-54
55-59	1068032	550835	2.1	517197	2.0	0	30971	18125	12846	55-59
60-64	938276	474396	1.8	463880	1.8	0	39583	22292	17291	60-64
65-69	516456	255926	1.0	260530	1.0	0	31036	17027	14009	65-69
70-74	361206	165117	0.6	196089	0.8		32311	16052	16259	70-74
75-79	185199	83155	0.3	102044	0.4		24949	12051	12898	75-79
80-84	119099	48227	0.2	70872	0.3	1177060 M.	24915	10645	14270	80-84
85+	90081	33374	0.1	56707	0.2	1108493 F.	29855	11467	18388	85+
TOTAL	51944397	25885001		26059396		2285553	1070000	563418	506582	TOTAL

TABLE 2 — MALE LIFE TABLE

x	nq_x	l_x	nd_x	nL_x	nm_x	na_x	T_x	r_x	$\mathring{e}_x$	nM_x	x
0	0.176589	100000	17659	88436	0.199680	0.3451	4114590	0.0032	41.146	0.200085	0
1	0.095046	82341	7826	307545	0.025447	1.2120	4026154	0.0032	48.896	0.025447	1
5	0.026729	74515	1992	367596	0.005418	2.5000	3718609	0.0194	49.904	0.005491	5
10	0.019711	72523	1430	359044	0.003981	2.5009	3351013	0.0251	46.206	0.003980	10
15	0.028098	71094	1998	350749	0.005695	2.6371	2991970	0.0225	42.085	0.005676	15
20	0.039718	69096	2744	338807	0.008100	2.5682	2641221	0.0187	38.225	0.008087	20
25	0.043638	66352	2895	324611	0.008920	2.5312	2302414	0.0295	34.700	0.008907	25
30	0.050079	63456	3178	309478	0.010268	2.5444	1977804	0.0183	31.168	0.010256	30
35	0.059282	60279	3573	292661	0.012210	2.5565	1668325	0.0154	27.677	0.012195	35
40	0.073137	56705	4147	273392	0.015170	2.5566	1375664	0.0251	24.260	0.015136	40
45	0.089425	52558	4700	251349	0.018699	2.5659	1102272	0.0222	20.973	0.018655	45
50	0.117736	47858	5635	225567	0.024980	2.5646	850923	0.0365	17.780	0.024874	50
55	0.152670	42223	6446	195400	0.032990	2.5619	625356	0.0197	14.811	0.032905	55
60	0.211066	35777	7551	160345	0.047094	2.5448	429956	0.0156	12.018	0.046990	60
65	0.285906	28226	8070	121020	0.066682	2.5082	269611	0.0156	9.552	0.066531	65
70	0.390500	20156	7871	80767	0.097451	2.4574	148590	0.0156	7.372	0.097216	70
75	0.525958	12285	6461	44468	0.145306	2.3756	67824	0.0156	5.521	0.144922	75
80	0.688975	5824	4012	18118	0.221449	2.2586	23356	0.0156	4.011	0.220726	80
85+	*1.000000	1811	1811	5238	0.345824	2.8916	5238	0.0156	2.892	0.343591	85+

TABLE 3 — FEMALE LIFE TABLE

x	nq_x	l_x	nd_x	nL_x	nm_x	na_x	T_x	r_x	$\mathring{e}_x$	nM_x	x
0	0.149948	100000	14995	90468	0.165747	0.3643	4413308	0.0042	44.133	0.166177	0
1	0.094095	85005	7999	318000	0.025153	1.2470	4322839	0.0042	50.854	0.025208	1
5	0.027503	77007	2118	379738	0.005577	2.5000	4004839	0.0176	52.006	0.005642	5
10	0.021743	74889	1628	370378	0.004396	2.5034	3625101	0.0140	48.407	0.004395	10
15	0.029274	73260	2145	361153	0.005938	2.5989	3254722	0.0128	44.427	0.005930	15
20	0.037216	71116	2647	349115	0.007581	2.5578	2893570	0.0233	40.688	0.007568	20
25	0.042055	68469	2879	335245	0.008589	2.5341	2544455	0.0387	37.162	0.008572	25
30	0.047540	65590	3118	320243	0.009737	2.5289	2209209	0.0229	33.682	0.009726	30
35	0.053022	62472	3312	304153	0.010891	2.5231	1888966	0.0226	30.237	0.010879	35
40	0.058905	59159	3485	287176	0.012135	2.5263	1584812	0.0338	26.789	0.012113	40
45	0.067393	55674	3752	269233	0.013936	2.5643	1297637	0.0261	23.308	0.013902	45
50	0.089431	51922	4643	248380	0.018695	2.5811	1028403	0.0431	19.807	0.018599	50
55	0.117540	47279	5560	223016	0.024930	2.5938	780023	0.0253	16.498	0.024838	55
60	0.171275	41719	7145	191287	0.037354	2.5778	557007	0.0138	13.351	0.037275	60
65	0.238011	34574	8229	152695	0.053891	2.5486	365720	0.0138	10.578	0.053771	65
70	0.344072	26345	9064	109067	0.083109	2.5005	213025	0.0138	8.086	0.082916	70
75	0.477467	17280	8251	65118	0.126704	2.4205	103958	0.0138	6.016	0.126396	75
80	0.655076	9029	5915	29290	0.201947	2.3191	38840	0.0138	4.301	0.201350	80
85+	*1.000000	3114	3114	9550	0.326131	3.0663	9550	0.0138	3.066	0.324263	85+

TABLE 4 — OBSERVED AND PROJECTED VITAL RATES

	OBSERVED POPULATION BOTH SEXES	OBSERVED POPULATION MALES	OBSERVED POPULATION FEMALES	PROJECTED 1955 MALES	PROJECTED 1955 FEMALES	PROJECTED 1960 MALES	PROJECTED 1960 FEMALES	PROJECTED 1965 MALES	PROJECTED 1965 FEMALES	STABLE POPULATION MALES	STABLE POPULATION FEMALES
RATES PER THOUSAND											
Birth	44.00	45.47	42.54	45.69	42.81	45.07	42.27	44.07	41.36	42.83	40.76
Death	20.60	21.77	19.44	21.76	19.16	21.70	19.12	21.57	19.10	21.86	19.79
Increase	23.40	23.71	23.10	23.92	23.65	23.37	23.15	22.50	22.26		20.9689
PERCENTAGE											
under 15	41.86	42.43	41.29	42.56	41.20	42.80	41.49	43.01	41.66	41.40	40.67
15-64	55.69	55.30	56.08	55.15	56.27	54.99	56.09	54.68	55.74	56.04	56.05
65 and over	2.45	2.26	2.63	2.29	2.54	2.20	2.43	2.30	2.59	2.56	3.28
DEP. RATIO X 100	79.56	80.83	78.32	81.34	77.72	81.84	78.29	82.87	79.39	78.46	78.40

Data in Hundreds

TABLE 1 DATA

AGE AT LAST BIRTHDAY	POPULATION BOTH SEXES	MALES Number	%	FEMALES Number	%	BIRTHS BY AGE OF MOTHER	DEATHS BOTH SEXES	MALES	FEMALES	AGE AT LAST BIRTHDAY
0	192300	99000	3.3	93300	3.3	0	33945	18091	15854	0
1-4	716700	369000	12.2	347700	12.4	0	18027	8750	9277	1-4
5-9	638000	338000	11.2	300000	10.7	0	3435	1691	1744	5-9
10-14	548000	296000	9.8	252000	9.0	0	2211	1071	1140	10-14
15-19	530000	280000	9.3	250000	8.9	22628	2947	1435	1512	15-19
20-24	481000	250000	8.3	231000	8.2	57932	3595	1826	1769	20-24
25-29	451000	240000	7.9	211000	7.5	63438	3763	1938	1825	25-29
30-34	402000	214000	7.1	188000	6.7	47126	3834	1990	1844	30-34
35-39	373000	194000	6.4	179000	6.4	33706	4091	2140	1951	35-39
40-44	323000	167000	5.5	156000	5.6	14271	4144	2276	1868	40-44
45-49	292000	149000	4.9	143000	5.1	3261	4402	2478	1924	45-49
50-54	248000	127000	4.2	121000	4.3	0	4950	2792	2158	50-54
55-59	209000	106000	3.5	103000	3.7	0	5463	3043	2420	55-59
60-64	169000	82000	2.7	87000	3.1	0	6393	3341	3052	60-64
65-69	119000	55000	1.8	64000	2.3	0	6321	3147	3174	65-69
70-74	80000	34000	1.1	46000	1.6		6286	2822	3464	70-74
75-79	37000	15000	0.5	22000	0.8		4326	1846	2480	75-79
80-84	13000	5000	0.2	8000	0.3	124137 M.	2429	967	1462	80-84
85+	6000	2000	0.1	4000	0.1	118225 F.	1784	612	1172	85+
TOTAL	5828000	3022000		2806000		242362	122346	62256	60090	TOTAL

TABLE 2 MALE LIFE TABLE

x	$_nq_x$	l_x	$_nd_x$	$_nL_x$	$_nm_x$	$_na_x$	T_x	r_x	$\dot{e}_x$	$_nM_x$	x
0	0.163286	100000	16329	89356	0.182737	0.3481	4355394	0.0000	43.554	0.182737	0
1	0.088979	83671	7445	313966	0.023713	1.2171	4266038	0.0000	50.986	0.023713	1
5	0.024072	76226	1835	376544	0.004873	2.5000	3952072	0.0368	51.847	0.005003	5
10	0.017932	74391	1334	368626	0.003619	2.5028	3575528	0.0146	48.064	0.003618	10
15	0.025362	73057	1853	360910	0.005134	2.6375	3206902	0.0117	43.896	0.005125	15
20	0.035909	71205	2557	349811	0.007309	2.5705	2845992	0.0084	39.969	0.007304	20
25	0.039601	68648	2719	336534	0.008078	2.5339	2496181	0.0074	36.362	0.008075	25
30	0.045493	65929	2999	322286	0.009306	2.5462	2159647	0.0119	32.757	0.009299	30
35	0.053765	62930	3383	306385	0.011043	2.5574	1837361	0.0136	29.197	0.011031	35
40	0.066016	59546	3931	288127	0.013643	2.5565	1530976	0.0127	25.711	0.013629	40
45	0.080000	55615	4449	267249	0.016648	2.5662	1242849	0.0103	22.347	0.016631	45
50	0.104472	51166	5345	242823	0.022014	2.5666	975600	0.0119	19.067	0.021984	50
55	0.134401	45821	6158	214132	0.028760	2.5689	732777	0.0140	15.992	0.028708	55
60	0.186125	39662	7382	180266	0.040951	2.5555	518645	0.0363	13.076	0.040744	60
65	0.251736	32280	8126	141283	0.057516	2.5243	338378	0.0363	10.483	0.057218	65
70	0.344846	24154	8329	99801	0.083461	2.4824	197095	0.0363	8.160	0.083000	70
75	0.469097	15825	7423	59951	0.123822	2.4173	97295	0.0363	6.148	0.123067	75
80	0.640840	8401	5384	27629	0.194864	2.3295	37343	0.0363	4.445	0.193399	80
85+	*1.000000	3017	3017	9714	0.310626	3.2193	9714	0.0363	3.219	0.306000	85+

TABLE 3 FEMALE LIFE TABLE

x	$_nq_x$	l_x	$_nd_x$	$_nL_x$	$_nm_x$	$_na_x$	T_x	r_x	$\dot{e}_x$	$_nM_x$	x
0	0.153427	100000	15343	90291	0.169925	0.3672	4401017	0.0000	44.010	0.169925	0
1	0.099436	84657	8418	315503	0.026681	1.2527	4310726	0.0000	50.920	0.026681	1
5	0.027782	76239	2118	375902	0.005635	2.5000	3995223	0.0458	52.404	0.005813	5
10	0.022371	74121	1658	366470	0.004525	2.5053	3619321	0.0131	48.830	0.004524	10
15	0.029815	72463	2160	357120	0.006050	2.5951	3252851	0.0027	44.890	0.006048	15
20	0.037611	70303	2644	345050	0.007663	2.5556	2895732	0.0094	41.190	0.007658	20
25	0.042368	67658	2867	331222	0.008655	2.5334	2550682	0.0119	37.699	0.008649	25
30	0.047896	64792	3103	316286	0.009812	2.5274	2219460	0.0067	34.255	0.009809	30
35	0.053079	61689	3274	300319	0.010903	2.5188	1903174	0.0078	30.851	0.010899	35
40	0.058171	58414	3398	283641	0.011980	2.5192	1602855	0.0104	27.439	0.011974	40
45	0.065196	55016	3587	266324	0.013468	2.5584	1319214	0.0114	23.979	0.013455	45
50	0.085621	51429	4403	246482	0.017865	2.5780	1052890	0.0148	20.473	0.017835	50
55	0.111318	47026	5235	222537	0.023523	2.5945	806408	0.0083	17.148	0.023495	55
60	0.162174	41791	6777	192539	0.035200	2.5778	583871	0.0227	13.971	0.035080	60
65	0.221805	35014	7766	156046	0.049769	2.5507	391331	0.0227	11.177	0.049594	65
70	0.318041	27247	8666	114654	0.075583	2.5094	235285	0.0227	8.635	0.075304	70
75	0.438882	18582	8155	72059	0.113173	2.4434	120631	0.0227	6.492	0.112727	75
80	0.618764	10427	6452	35133	0.183633	2.3650	48572	0.0227	4.659	0.182749	80
85+	*1.000000	3975	3975	13439	0.295774	3.3810	13439	0.0227	3.381	0.293000	85+

TABLE 4 OBSERVED AND PROJECTED VITAL RATES

	OBSERVED POPULATION BOTH SEXES	MALES	FEMALES	PROJECTED POPULATION 1958 MALES	FEMALES	1963 MALES	FEMALES	1968 MALES	FEMALES	STABLE POPULATION MALES	FEMALES
RATES PER THOUSAND											
Birth	41.59	41.08	42.13	38.94	39.90	37.26	38.11	37.30	38.08	42.11	42.09
Death	20.99	20.60	21.41	20.68	21.38	20.41	20.94	20.27	20.63	20.11	20.09
Increase	20.59	20.48	20.72	18.26	18.52	16.85	17.18	17.03	17.45	22.0022	
PERCENTAGE											
under 15	35.95	36.47	35.39	38.52	38.58	39.73	40.44	38.98	39.79	41.33	41.32
15-64	59.68	59.86	59.48	57.50	56.22	56.11	54.46	56.83	55.25	55.76	55.34
65 and over	4.38	3.67	5.13	3.98	5.19	4.16	5.10	4.19	4.97	2.91	3.34
DEP. RATIO X 100	67.57	67.05	68.12	73.92	77.86	78.23	83.63	75.95	81.00	79.35	80.72

Data in Hundreds

TABLE 1 — DATA

AGE AT LAST BIRTHDAY	POPULATION BOTH SEXES	MALES Number	%	FEMALES Number	%	BIRTHS BY AGE OF MOTHER	DEATHS BOTH SEXES	MALES	FEMALES	AGE AT LAST BIRTHDAY
0	168970	84680	3.7	84290	4.0	0	27989	13743	14246	0
1-4	557340	282770	12.5	274570	12.9	0	12902	5681	7221	1-4
5-9	580580	295260	13.0	285320	13.4	0	2951	1305	1646	5-9
10-14	497770	255450	11.3	242320	11.4	259	1905	817	1088	10-14
15-19	430690	221740	9.8	208950	9.8	32148	2287	1029	1258	15-19
20-24	380370	195260	8.6	185110	8.7	52171	2707	1293	1414	20-24
25-29	343420	176200	7.8	167220	7.9	43676	2729	1286	1443	25-29
30-34	303890	157630	7.0	146260	6.9	29446	2752	1319	1433	30-34
35-39	257770	136340	6.0	121430	5.7	16605	2684	1359	1325	35-39
40-44	216650	115750	5.1	100900	4.7	5351	2649	1435	1214	40-44
45-49	180730	96810	4.3	83920	3.9	1579	2629	1488	1141	45-49
50-54	146520	78360	3.5	68160	3.2	168	2853	1612	1241	50-54
55-59	114470	60550	2.7	53920	2.5	0	2949	1661	1288	55-59
60-64	84830	43870	1.9	40960	1.9	0	3189	1726	1463	60-64
65-69	57340	29180	1.3	28160	1.3	0	3075	1634	1441	65-69
70-74	36360	17080	0.8	19280	0.9		2898	1405	1493	70-74
75-79	14160	6760	0.3	7400	0.3		1693	831	862	75-79
80-84	12950	5810	0.3	7140	0.3	93423 M.	2470	1117	1353	80-84
85+	7540	3430	0.2	4110	0.2	87980 F.	2259	1027	1232	85+
TOTAL	4392350	2262930		2129420		181403	85570	41768	43802	TOTAL

TABLE 2 — MALE LIFE TABLE

x	nq_x	l_x	nd_x	nL_x	nm_x	na_x	T_x	r_x	$\dot{e}_x$	nM_x	x
0	0.146107	100000	14611	90431	0.161567	0.3451	4602399	0.0069	46.024	0.162293	0
1	0.075798	85389	6472	323512	0.020007	1.2119	4511968	0.0069	52.840	0.020091	1
5	0.021446	78917	1692	390353	0.004336	2.5000	4188456	0.0286	53.074	0.004420	5
10	0.015872	77224	1226	383070	0.003200	2.5098	3798102	0.0249	49.183	0.003198	10
15	0.023029	75999	1750	375868	0.004656	2.6425	3415032	0.0221	44.935	0.004641	15
20	0.032631	74249	2423	365358	0.006631	2.5711	3039165	0.0166	40.932	0.006622	20
25	0.035872	71826	2577	352775	0.007304	2.5339	2673806	0.0140	37.226	0.007299	25
30	0.041043	69249	2842	339279	0.008377	2.5484	2321031	0.0172	33.517	0.008368	30
35	0.048738	66407	3237	324145	0.009985	2.5622	1981753	0.0207	29.842	0.009968	35
40	0.060285	63171	3808	306576	0.012422	2.5641	1657607	0.0218	26.240	0.012397	40
45	0.074269	59362	4409	286121	0.015409	2.5752	1351031	0.0232	22.759	0.015370	45
50	0.098266	54954	5400	261682	0.020636	2.5767	1064910	0.0261	19.378	0.020572	50
55	0.129096	49553	6397	232269	0.027542	2.5773	803228	0.0295	16.209	0.027432	55
60	0.180122	43156	7773	196835	0.039492	2.5626	570960	0.0261	13.230	0.039344	60
65	0.246828	35383	8733	155360	0.056215	2.5320	374125	0.0261	10.574	0.055997	65
70	0.342019	26649	9115	110351	0.082596	2.4880	218765	0.0261	8.209	0.082260	70
75	0.468195	17535	8210	66489	0.123474	2.4196	108414	0.0261	6.183	0.122929	75
80	0.637523	9325	5945	30757	0.193289	2.3308	41924	0.0261	4.496	0.192255	80
85+	*1.000000	3380	3380	11167	0.302676	3.3039	11167	0.0261	3.304	0.299417	85+

TABLE 3 — FEMALE LIFE TABLE

x	nq_x	l_x	nd_x	nL_x	nm_x	na_x	T_x	r_x	$\dot{e}_x$	nM_x	x
0	0.152057	100000	15206	90368	0.168264	0.3665	4403316	0.0072	44.033	0.169012	0
1	0.097765	84794	8290	316392	0.026201	1.2514	4312948	0.0072	50.864	0.026299	1
5	0.027892	76504	2134	377187	0.005657	2.5000	3996556	0.0292	52.240	0.005769	5
10	0.022209	74371	1652	367729	0.004492	2.5036	3619369	0.0260	48.667	0.004490	10
15	0.029740	72719	2163	358395	0.006034	2.5960	3251639	0.0209	44.715	0.006021	15
20	0.037532	70556	2648	346308	0.007647	2.5557	2893244	0.0148	41.006	0.007639	20
25	0.042280	67908	2871	332460	0.008636	2.5338	2546936	0.0149	37.506	0.008629	25
30	0.047880	65037	3114	317488	0.009808	2.5282	2214476	0.0222	34.050	0.009798	30
35	0.053178	61923	3293	301448	0.010924	2.5199	1896989	0.0262	30.635	0.010912	35
40	0.058482	58630	3429	284650	0.012046	2.5211	1595541	0.0249	27.214	0.012032	40
45	0.065946	55201	3640	267130	0.013627	2.5618	1310891	0.0250	23.747	0.013596	45
50	0.087443	51561	4509	246886	0.018262	2.5782	1043760	0.0259	20.243	0.018207	50
55	0.113339	47052	5333	222423	0.023976	2.5926	796875	0.0258	16.936	0.023887	55
60	0.164861	41719	6878	191947	0.035832	2.5791	574452	0.0210	13.769	0.035718	60
65	0.228009	34842	7944	154738	0.051340	2.5492	382505	0.0210	10.978	0.051172	65
70	0.325425	26897	8753	112649	0.077702	2.5052	227767	0.0210	8.468	0.077438	70
75	0.449826	18144	8162	69809	0.116915	2.4378	115118	0.0210	6.345	0.116486	75
80	0.632763	9983	6317	33185	0.190347	2.3517	45308	0.0210	4.539	0.189496	80
85+	*1.000000	3666	3666	12124	0.302374	3.3072	12124	0.0210	3.307	0.299757	85+

TABLE 4 — OBSERVED AND PROJECTED VITAL RATES

	OBSERVED POPULATION BOTH SEXES	MALES	FEMALES	PROJECTED POPULATION 1966 MALES	FEMALES	1971 MALES	FEMALES	1976 MALES	FEMALES	STABLE POPULATION MALES	FEMALES
RATES PER THOUSAND											
Birth	41.30	41.28	41.32	40.47	40.80	40.20	40.74	40.59	41.31	39.44	41.22
Death	19.48	18.46	20.57	18.13	19.66	18.09	19.59	18.24	19.77	18.22	20.00
Increase	21.82	22.83	20.75	22.35	21.15	22.11	21.16	22.35	21.54	21.2162	
PERCENTAGE											
under 15	41.09	40.57	41.63	41.12	41.67	41.33	41.30	41.04	40.55	40.22	40.81
15-64	55.99	56.67	55.27	56.09	55.31	55.73	55.61	55.88	56.27	56.60	55.80
65 and over	2.92	2.75	3.10	2.80	3.02	2.95	3.09	3.08	3.18	3.18	3.39
DEP. RATIO X 100	78.60	76.45	80.95	78.30	80.81	79.45	79.82	78.97	77.72	76.69	79.22

TABLE 1 — DATA

AGE AT LAST BIRTHDAY	POPULATION BOTH SEXES	MALES Number	%	FEMALES Number	%	BIRTHS BY AGE OF MOTHER	DEATHS BOTH SEXES	MALES	FEMALES	AGE AT LAST BIRTHDAY
0	3473159	1681282	3.5	1791877	3.7	0	661111	332041	329070	0
1-4	13174553	6563651	13.8	6610902	13.5	0	358847	168216	190631	1-4
5-9	14329979	7147825	15.0	7182154	14.7	0	83767	38646	45121	5-9
10-14	9868287	5024850	10.6	4843437	9.9	0	43318	19646	23672	10-14
15-19	8870033	4407430	9.3	4462603	9.1	536346	53585	24413	29172	15-19
20-24	8211289	3870749	8.1	4340540	8.9	1240764	66476	30544	35932	20-24
25-29	8014834	3737766	7.9	4277068	8.8	1221766	72595	32617	39978	25-29
30-34	6728070	3310322	7.0	3417748	7.0	738359	69495	33268	36227	30-34
35-39	5756671	2954118	6.2	2802553	5.7	419010	68240	35223	33017	35-39
40-44	4613006	2298702	4.8	2314304	4.7	148192	63819	33868	29951	40-44
45-49	3654035	1847511	3.9	1806524	3.7	29910	59470	33203	26267	45-49
50-54	3164673	1538801	3.2	1625872	3.3	0	67893	36554	31339	50-54
55-59	2003165	997371	2.1	1005794	2.1	0	56486	30944	25542	55-59
60-64	1926909	930880	2.0	996029	2.0	0	78752	40984	37768	60-64
65-69	1021512	484437	1.0	537075	1.1	0	58743	29956	28787	65-69
70-74	800112	370452	0.8	429660	0.9		68224	33227	34997	70-74
75-79	351763	166228	0.3	185535	0.4		44702	22101	22601	75-79
80-84	198308	87485	0.2	110823	0.2	2232189 M.	38002	16997	21005	80-84
85+	158471	73994	0.2	84477	0.2	2102158 F.	47698	22375	25323	85+
TOTAL	96318829	47493854		48824975		4334347	2061223	1014823	1046400	TOTAL

TABLE 2 — MALE LIFE TABLE

x	nq_x	l_x	nd_x	nL_x	nm_x	na_x	T_x	r_x	$\mathring{e}_x$	nM_x
0	0.174934	100000	17493	88578	0.197493	0.3471	4170430	0.0000	41.704	0.197493
1	0.095685	82507	7895	308041	0.025628	1.2152	4081852	0.0000	49.473	0.025628
5	0.025932	74612	1935	368223	0.005254	2.5000	3773811	0.0398	50.579	0.005407
10	0.019370	72677	1408	359870	0.003912	2.5029	3405588	0.0438	46.859	0.003910
15	0.027419	71269	1954	351728	0.005556	2.6362	3045718	0.0204	42.735	0.005539
20	0.038741	69315	2685	340049	0.007897	2.5693	2693990	0.0089	38.866	0.007891
25	0.042726	66630	2847	326125	0.008729	2.5326	2353942	0.0068	35.329	0.008726
30	0.049081	63783	3131	311229	0.010059	2.5448	2027817	0.0134	31.792	0.010050
35	0.058040	60652	3520	294658	0.011947	2.5558	1716588	0.0243	28.302	0.011923
40	0.071293	57132	4073	275698	0.014774	2.5541	1421930	0.0321	24.888	0.014734
45	0.086270	53059	4577	254142	0.018011	2.5633	1146232	0.0216	21.603	0.017972
50	0.112722	48482	5465	229088	0.023855	2.5625	892090	0.0377	18.401	0.023755
55	0.144532	43017	6217	199928	0.031098	2.5624	663002	0.0181	15.413	0.031026
60	0.199084	36799	7326	166035	0.044124	2.5483	463074	0.0158	12.584	0.044027
65	0.268526	29473	7914	127699	0.061977	2.5150	297038	0.0158	10.078	0.061837
70	0.366225	21559	7895	87815	0.089910	2.4695	169339	0.0158	7.855	0.089693
75	0.494574	13664	6758	50697	0.133294	2.3925	81524	0.0158	5.967	0.132956
80	0.638325	6906	4408	22621	0.194868	2.2987	30827	0.0158	4.464	0.194284
85+	*1.000000	2498	2498	8206	0.304383	3.2853	8206	0.0158	3.285	0.302389

TABLE 3 — FEMALE LIFE TABLE

x	nq_x	l_x	nd_x	nL_x	nm_x	na_x	T_x	r_x	$\mathring{e}_x$	nM_x
0	0.164496	100000	16450	89573	0.183645	0.3661	4209255	0.0000	42.093	0.183645
1	0.106870	83550	8929	309651	0.028836	1.2505	4119682	0.0000	49.308	0.028836
5	0.030021	74621	2240	367506	0.006096	2.5000	3810031	0.0441	51.058	0.006282
10	0.024158	72381	1749	357541	0.004891	2.5040	3442525	0.0420	47.561	0.004887
15	0.032194	70633	2274	347691	0.006540	2.5939	3084984	0.0045	43.677	0.006537
20	0.040570	68359	2773	335011	0.008278	2.5544	2737293	0.0000	40.043	0.008278
25	0.045715	65585	2998	320527	0.009354	2.5322	2402282	0.0145	36.628	0.009347
30	0.051720	62587	3237	304926	0.010616	2.5259	2081755	0.0317	33.262	0.010600
35	0.057294	59350	3400	288306	0.011794	2.5169	1776828	0.0272	29.938	0.011781
40	0.062777	55950	3512	271027	0.012959	2.5170	1488522	0.0309	26.605	0.012942
45	0.070326	52437	3688	253175	0.014566	2.5562	1217494	0.0201	23.218	0.014540
50	0.092470	48750	4508	232816	0.019362	2.5750	964320	0.0391	19.781	0.019275
55	0.120010	44242	5309	208407	0.025476	2.5889	731503	0.0223	16.534	0.025395
60	0.174007	38932	6775	178209	0.038014	2.5714	523096	0.0169	13.436	0.037919
65	0.237347	32158	7633	142029	0.053740	2.5421	344887	0.0169	10.725	0.053600
70	0.339074	24525	8316	101815	0.081676	2.4974	202858	0.0169	8.271	0.081453
75	0.464498	16209	7529	61633	0.122163	2.4215	101043	0.0169	6.234	0.121815
80	0.631123	8680	5478	28804	0.190193	2.3354	39410	0.0169	4.540	0.189537
85+	*1.000000	3202	3202	10607	0.301874	3.3126	10607	0.0169	3.313	0.299762

TABLE 4 — OBSERVED AND PROJECTED VITAL RATES

	OBSERVED POPULATION BOTH SEXES	MALES	FEMALES	PROJECTED POPULATION 1966 MALES	FEMALES	1971 MALES	FEMALES	1976 MALES	FEMALES	STABLE POPULATION MALES	FEMALES
RATES PER THOUSAND											
Birth	45.00	47.00	43.05	43.87	40.76	42.80	40.21	43.91	41.65	41.71	41.71
Death	21.40	21.37	21.43	20.77	20.37	20.38	20.18	20.48	20.43	21.55	21.54
Increase	23.60	25.63	21.62	23.11	20.39	22.42	20.03	23.43	21.23		20.1677
PERCENTAGE											
under 15	42.41	42.99	41.84	44.42	43.09	42.97	41.24	42.22	40.05	40.62	40.62
15-64	54.97	54.52	55.40	53.02	54.02	54.61	56.01	55.23	56.95	56.48	56.04
65 and over	2.63	2.49	2.76	2.56	2.89	2.42	2.75	2.56	3.00	2.89	3.34
DEP. RATIO X 100	81.93	83.42	80.51	88.61	85.13	83.13	78.54	81.06	75.58	77.05	78.45

AGE AT LAST BIRTHDAY	POPULATION BOTH SEXES	MALES Number	%	FEMALES Number	%	BIRTHS BY AGE OF MOTHER	DEATHS BOTH SEXES	MALES	FEMALES	AGE AT LAST BIRTHDAY
0	834764	421509	4.3	413255	4.3	0	193891	101516	92375	0
1-4	2677687	1345328	13.7	1332359	13.9	0	91030	43158	47872	1-4
5-9	2822975	1419050	14.4	1403925	14.6	0	20007	9281	10726	5-9
10-14	2214838	1110061	11.3	1104777	11.5	0	11790	5228	6562	10-14
15-19	1926525	964408	9.8	962117	10.0	154027	13918	6346	7572	15-19
20-24	1557318	788241	8.0	769077	8.0	290943	15039	7402	7637	20-24
25-29	1330958	676644	6.9	654314	6.8	235452	14379	7057	7322	25-29
30-34	1238376	626165	6.4	612211	6.4	168216	15308	7545	7763	30-34
35-39	1092111	555531	5.6	536580	5.6	101848	15434	7911	7523	35-39
40-44	930298	484852	4.9	445446	4.6	34535	15263	8470	6793	40-44
45-49	787867	414965	4.2	372902	3.9	6479	14965	8685	6280	45-49
50-54	653554	342151	3.5	311403	3.2	0	16231	9330	6901	50-54
55-59	537290	280448	2.8	256842	2.7	0	17183	9768	7415	55-59
60-64	436121	225042	2.3	211079	2.2	0	20066	10996	9070	60-64
65-69	193455	95955	1.0	97500	1.0	0	12306	6486	5820	65-69
70-74	117744	56386	0.6	61358	0.6		10940	5452	5488	70-74
75-79	60478	27698	0.3	32780	0.3		8240	3927	4313	75-79
80-84	13900	5977	0.1	7923	0.1	510622 M.	2678	1164	1514	80-84
85+	14930	6883	0.1	8047	0.1	480878 F.	4390	2023	2367	85+
TOTAL	19441189	9847294		9593895		991500	513058	261745	251313	TOTAL

TABLE 1 DATA

TABLE 2 MALE LIFE TABLE

x	$_nq_x$	l_x	$_nd_x$	$_nL_x$	$_nm_x$	$_na_x$	T_x	r_x	$\mathring{e}_x$	$_nM_x$	x
0	0.207501	100000	20750	86438	0.240057	0.3464	3735064	0.0054	37.351	0.240839	0
1	0.117446	79250	9308	291070	0.031977	1.2141	3648626	0.0054	46.039	0.032080	1
5	0.031366	69942	2194	344227	0.006373	2.5000	3357556	0.0345	48.005	0.006540	5
10	0.023278	67749	1577	334791	0.004711	2.4945	3013329	0.0331	44.478	0.004710	10
15	0.032525	66171	2152	325762	0.006607	2.6324	2678538	0.0275	40.479	0.006580	15
20	0.046007	64019	2945	312932	0.009412	2.5675	2352776	0.0264	36.751	0.009391	20
25	0.050870	61074	3107	297696	0.010436	2.5301	2039844	0.0124	33.400	0.010429	25
30	0.058541	57967	3393	281487	0.012055	2.5400	1742148	0.0076	30.054	0.012050	30
35	0.068858	54574	3758	263654	0.014253	2.5480	1460661	0.0111	26.765	0.014240	35
40	0.083826	50816	4260	243614	0.017485	2.5431	1197007	0.0117	23.556	0.017469	40
45	0.099661	46556	4640	221411	0.020956	2.5495	953393	0.0133	20.478	0.020929	45
50	0.127945	41916	5363	196430	0.027302	2.5477	731982	0.0118	17.463	0.027269	50
55	0.160553	36553	5869	168379	0.034854	2.5484	535552	0.0057	14.651	0.034830	55
60	0.219254	30685	6728	136832	0.049168	2.5339	367173	0.0463	11.966	0.048862	60
65	0.290640	23957	6963	102356	0.068025	2.4970	230342	0.0463	9.615	0.067594	65
70	0.389981	16994	6627	68072	0.097358	2.4502	127985	0.0463	7.531	0.096691	70
75	0.518864	10367	5379	37669	0.142793	2.3667	59913	0.0463	5.779	0.141779	75
80	0.638721	4988	3186	16229	0.196300	2.2661	22244	0.0463	4.460	0.194747	80
85+	*1.000000	1802	1802	6015	0.299580	3.3380	6015	0.0463	3.338	0.293913	85+

TABLE 3 FEMALE LIFE TABLE

x	$_nq_x$	l_x	$_nd_x$	$_nL_x$	$_nm_x$	$_na_x$	T_x	r_x	$\mathring{e}_x$	$_nM_x$	x
0	0.195385	100000	19538	87596	0.223053	0.3651	3754756	0.0037	37.548	0.223530	0
1	0.130566	80462	10506	292941	0.035862	1.2486	3667161	0.0037	45.577	0.035930	1
5	0.036656	69956	2564	343369	0.007468	2.5000	3374220	0.0321	48.233	0.007640	5
10	0.029273	67392	1973	332020	0.005942	2.4968	3030850	0.0310	44.974	0.005940	10
15	0.038731	65419	2534	320986	0.007894	2.5889	2698830	0.0284	41.255	0.007870	15
20	0.048566	62885	3054	306942	0.009950	2.5495	2377845	0.0288	37.812	0.009930	20
25	0.054476	59831	3259	291095	0.011197	2.5271	2070903	0.0115	34.612	0.011190	25
30	0.061489	56572	3479	274233	0.012685	2.5203	1779808	0.0072	31.461	0.012680	30
35	0.067781	53093	3599	256503	0.014030	2.5093	1505575	0.0178	28.357	0.014020	35
40	0.073514	49495	3639	238400	0.015262	2.5066	1249072	0.0211	25.237	0.015250	40
45	0.080976	45856	3713	220163	0.016866	2.5448	1010672	0.0182	22.040	0.016841	45
50	0.105297	42143	4438	199907	0.022198	2.5648	790509	0.0150	18.758	0.022161	50
55	0.135071	37705	5093	176198	0.028904	2.5793	590601	0.0085	15.664	0.028870	55
60	0.195479	32612	6375	147492	0.043223	2.5577	414404	0.0403	12.707	0.042970	60
65	0.261359	26237	6857	114196	0.060049	2.5223	266912	0.0403	10.173	0.059692	65
70	0.366742	19380	7107	78961	0.090012	2.4760	152716	0.0403	7.880	0.089442	70
75	0.492088	12273	6039	45607	0.132418	2.3911	73755	0.0403	6.010	0.131574	75
80	0.633560	6233	3949	20511	0.192536	2.3019	28148	0.0403	4.516	0.191090	80
85+	*1.000000	2284	2284	7637	0.299090	3.3435	7637	0.0403	3.343	0.294147	85+

TABLE 4 OBSERVED AND PROJECTED VITAL RATES

	OBSERVED POPULATION BOTH SEXES	MALES	FEMALES	PROJECTED POPULATION 1961 MALES	FEMALES	1966 MALES	FEMALES	1971 MALES	FEMALES	STABLE POPULATION MALES	FEMALES
RATES PER THOUSAND											
Birth	51.00	51.85	50.12	51.13	49.66	51.49	50.20	52.59	51.47	52.09	52.28
Death	26.39	26.58	26.20	26.78	25.98	26.73	26.09	26.77	26.31	26.03	26.22
Increase	24.61	25.27	23.93	24.35	23.68	24.76	24.11	25.82	25.16	26.0574	
PERCENTAGE											
under 15	43.98	43.63	44.34	45.18	45.09	45.48	44.84	45.85	44.88	45.80	45.98
15-64	53.96	54.42	53.49	52.33	52.28	51.85	52.36	51.53	52.34	52.35	51.88
65 and over	2.06	1.96	2.16	2.49	2.63	2.67	2.80	2.62	2.78	1.85	2.13
DEP. RATIO X 100	85.32	83.77	86.94	91.09	91.27	92.87	90.97	94.08	91.06	91.01	92.74

662 Pakistan 1961, Hypothetical Data

TABLE 1 — DATA

AGE AT LAST BIRTHDAY	POPULATION BOTH SEXES	MALES Number	%	FEMALES Number	%	BIRTHS BY AGE OF MOTHER	DEATHS BOTH SEXES	MALES	FEMALES	AGE AT LAST BIRTHDAY
0	3911833	2004563	4.1	1907270	4.3	0	695528	350184	345344	0
1-4	12899976	6680230	13.5	6219746	14.0	0	325543	148709	176834	1-4
5-9	13609122	7104842	14.4	6504280	14.6	0	74353	34065	40288	5-9
10-14	11604559	6082811	12.3	5521748	12.4	7089	47747	21139	26608	10-14
15-19	9899765	5213838	10.6	4685927	10.5	865628	56041	25839	30202	15-19
20-24	8372270	4428800	9.0	3943470	8.9	1334440	63458	31272	32186	20-24
25-29	7036394	3737572	7.6	3298822	7.4	1034563	59466	29064	30402	25-29
30-34	5878797	3140153	6.4	2738644	6.2	662005	56740	28119	28621	30-34
35-39	4879732	2616794	5.3	2262938	5.1	371551	54147	27862	26285	35-39
40-44	4020433	2157621	4.4	1862812	4.2	118611	52283	28514	23769	40-44
45-49	3278176	1757695	3.6	1520481	3.4	34353	50426	28629	21797	45-49
50-54	2629262	1402207	2.8	1227055	2.8	3623	53771	30452	23319	50-54
55-59	2037137	1081279	2.2	955858	2.1	0	54995	31063	23932	55-59
60-64	1520078	799850	1.6	720228	1.6	0	59741	32815	26926	60-64
65-69	1055364	552983	1.1	502381	1.1	0	58672	32123	26549	65-69
70-74	660778	340677	0.7	320101	0.7		54607	28918	25689	70-74
75-79	356070	182682	0.4	173388	0.4		43941	23116	20825	75-79
80-84	135613	67411	0.1	68202	0.2	2269978 M.	25800	13130	12670	80-84
85+	46623	21461	0.0	25162	0.1	2161885 F.	17061	7895	9166	85+
TOTAL	93831982	49373469		44458513		4431863	1904320	952908	951412	TOTAL

TABLE 2 — MALE LIFE TABLE

x	$_nq_x$	l_x	$_nd_x$	$_nL_x$	$_nm_x$	$_na_x$	T_x	r_x	$\dot{e}_x$	$_nM_x$	x
0	0.156262	100000	15626	89797	0.174018	0.3470	4437825	0.0060	44.378	0.174693	0
1	0.083561	84374	7050	317861	0.022181	1.2152	4348029	0.0060	51.533	0.022261	1
5	0.023255	77323	1798	382122	0.004706	2.5000	4030167	0.0271	52.121	0.004795	5
10	0.017232	75525	1301	374378	0.003476	2.5043	3648046	0.0269	48.302	0.003475	10
15	0.024589	74224	1825	366809	0.004976	2.6389	3273668	0.0267	44.105	0.004956	15
20	0.034786	72399	2518	355873	0.007077	2.5698	2906858	0.0265	40.151	0.007061	20
25	0.038199	69880	2669	342817	0.007786	2.5337	2550985	0.0265	36.505	0.007776	25
30	0.043887	67211	2950	328820	0.008970	2.5475	2208168	0.0266	32.854	0.008955	30
35	0.052000	64261	3342	313152	0.010671	2.5598	1879348	0.0267	29.245	0.010647	35
40	0.064159	60920	3909	295063	0.013246	2.5606	1566196	0.0265	25.709	0.013215	40
45	0.078550	57011	4478	274178	0.016333	2.5710	1271133	0.0263	22.296	0.016288	45
50	0.103451	52533	5435	249467	0.021785	2.5716	996955	0.0266	18.978	0.021717	50
55	0.134713	47098	6345	220085	0.028829	2.5718	747488	0.0263	15.871	0.028728	55
60	0.187020	40753	7622	185149	0.041165	2.5573	527403	0.0238	12.941	0.041026	60
65	0.254721	33132	8439	144777	0.058292	2.5256	342254	0.0238	10.330	0.058090	65
70	0.350723	24692	8660	101650	0.085196	2.4813	197477	0.0238	7.997	0.084884	70
75	0.477971	16032	7663	60319	0.127041	2.4106	95828	0.0238	5.977	0.126537	75
80	0.641943	8369	5373	27443	0.195775	2.3191	35509	0.0238	4.243	0.194774	80
85+	*1.000000	2997	2997	8066	0.371518	2.6917	8066	0.0238	2.692	0.367877	85+

TABLE 3 — FEMALE LIFE TABLE

x	$_nq_x$	l_x	$_nd_x$	$_nL_x$	$_nm_x$	$_na_x$	T_x	r_x	$\dot{e}_x$	$_nM_x$	x
0	0.161895	100000	16189	89742	0.180399	0.3664	4244676	0.0061	42.447	0.181067	0
1	0.105174	83811	8815	311012	0.028342	1.2512	4154934	0.0061	49.575	0.028431	1
5	0.029938	74996	2245	369366	0.006079	2.5000	3843922	0.0278	51.255	0.006194	5
10	0.023816	72751	1733	359425	0.004821	2.5018	3474555	0.0273	47.760	0.004819	10
15	0.031826	71018	2260	349653	0.006464	2.5944	3115131	0.0272	43.864	0.006445	15
20	0.040086	68758	2756	337048	0.008178	2.5542	2765478	0.0271	40.221	0.008162	20
25	0.045117	66002	2978	322659	0.009229	2.5320	2428430	0.0272	36.794	0.009216	25
30	0.051002	63024	3214	307167	0.010464	2.5261	2105771	0.0272	33.412	0.010451	30
35	0.056510	59809	3380	290656	0.011628	2.5172	1798605	0.0269	30.072	0.011615	35
40	0.061911	56430	3494	273475	0.012775	2.5176	1507949	0.0270	26.723	0.012760	40
45	0.069409	52936	3674	255701	0.014369	2.5564	1234474	0.0268	23.320	0.014336	45
50	0.091109	49262	4488	235428	0.019064	2.5757	978772	0.0272	19.869	0.019004	50
55	0.118496	44774	5305	211082	0.025135	2.5901	743344	0.0269	16.602	0.025037	55
60	0.171879	39468	6784	180873	0.037505	2.5725	532262	0.0215	13.486	0.037385	60
65	0.234559	32684	7666	144589	0.053022	2.5435	351389	0.0215	10.751	0.052846	65
70	0.335172	25018	8385	104123	0.080533	2.4996	206799	0.0215	8.266	0.080253	70
75	0.459906	16633	7649	63460	0.120540	2.4242	102676	0.0215	6.173	0.120106	75
80	0.623709	8983	5603	30019	0.186643	2.3413	39216	0.0215	4.366	0.185772	80
85+	*1.000000	3380	3380	9197	0.367540	2.7208	9197	0.0215	2.721	0.364279	85+

TABLE 4 — OBSERVED AND PROJECTED VITAL RATES

	OBSERVED POPULATION BOTH SEXES	MALES	FEMALES	PROJECTED POPULATION 1966 MALES	FEMALES	1971 MALES	FEMALES	1976 MALES	FEMALES	STABLE POPULATION MALES	FEMALES
RATES PER THOUSAND											
Birth	47.23	45.98	48.63	46.08	48.62	46.18	48.61	46.30	48.66	46.62	48.70
Death	20.29	19.30	21.40	19.27	21.32	19.27	21.31	19.27	21.30	19.36	21.44
Increase	26.94	26.68	27.23	26.82	27.30	26.91	27.31	27.03	27.36	27.2591	
PERCENTAGE											
under 15	44.79	44.30	45.33	44.36	45.38	44.41	45.41	44.46	45.38	44.72	45.38
15-64	52.81	53.34	52.22	53.30	52.20	53.27	52.18	53.23	52.21	53.04	52.23
65 and over	2.40	2.36	2.45	2.34	2.43	2.32	2.41	2.31	2.41	2.24	2.39
DEP. RATIO X 100	89.36	87.48	91.50	87.60	91.59	87.73	91.64	87.86	91.54	88.54	91.47

TABLE 1 — DATA

AGE AT LAST BIRTHDAY	POPULATION BOTH SEXES	MALES Number	%	FEMALES Number	%	BIRTHS BY AGE OF MOTHER	DEATHS BOTH SEXES	MALES	FEMALES	AGE AT LAST BIRTHDAY
0	796101	409376	3.0	386725	2.8	0	83078	47726	35352	0
1-4	3832346	1973682	14.3	1858664	13.7	0	54882	29298	25584	1-4
5-9	4422943	2282360	16.5	2140583	15.8	0	12730	7200	5530	5-9
10-14	3477526	1787763	12.9	1689763	12.4	985	5785	3402	2383	10-14
15-19	2848784	1401830	10.1	1446954	10.6	79329	5704	3320	2384	15-19
20-24	2488741	1208904	8.7	1279837	9.4	368017	7426	4211	3215	20-24
25-29	1977278	964109	7.0	1013169	7.5	318174	7712	4197	3515	25-29
30-34	1575519	774409	5.6	801110	5.9	220002	7866	4012	3854	30-34
35-39	1445974	711229	5.1	734745	5.4	142866	8715	4333	4382	35-39
40-44	1112443	553129	4.0	559314	4.1	51377	8157	4365	3792	40-44
45-49	1045337	531106	3.8	514231	3.8	11346	9439	5170	4269	45-49
50-54	718801	369858	2.7	348943	2.6	0	8740	4915	3825	50-54
55-59	493909	255505	1.8	238404	1.8	0	8771	4805	3966	55-59
60-64	436186	234643	1.7	201543	1.5	0	9940	5556	4384	60-64
65-69	228594	114091	0.8	114503	0.8	0	7711	4203	3508	65-69
70-74	211501	108116	0.8	103385	0.8		10668	5507	5161	70-74
75-79	111359	56418	0.4	54941	0.4		8450	4484	3966	75-79
80-84	100563	49082	0.4	51481	0.4	615593 M.	10457	5195	5262	80-84
85+	95680	45693	0.3	49987	0.4	576503 F.	21734	9910	11824	85+
TOTAL	27419585	13831303		13588282		1192096	297965	161809	136156	TOTAL

TABLE 2 — MALE LIFE TABLE

x	$_nq_x$	l_x	$_nd_x$	$_nL_x$	$_nm_x$	$_na_x$	T_x	r_x	$\mathring{e}_x$	$_nM_x$	x
0	0.108383	100000	10838	92967	0.116582	0.3511	5539756	0.0000	55.398	0.116582	0
1	0.057026	89162	5085	342523	0.014844	1.2222	5446789	0.0000	61.089	0.014844	1
5	0.015392	84077	1294	417150	0.003102	2.5000	5104266	0.0232	60.709	0.003155	5
10	0.009433	82783	781	411896	0.001896	2.4137	4687115	0.0465	56.619	0.001903	10
15	0.011836	82002	971	407714	0.002380	2.6340	4275220	0.0366	52.135	0.002368	15
20	0.017342	81032	1405	401801	0.003497	2.6112	3867505	0.0340	47.728	0.003483	20
25	0.021608	79626	1721	393953	0.004367	2.5716	3465704	0.0402	43.525	0.004353	25
30	0.025625	77906	1996	384656	0.005190	2.5588	3071751	0.0252	39.429	0.005181	30
35	0.030093	75909	2284	374016	0.006108	2.5784	2687095	0.0274	35.399	0.006092	35
40	0.038796	73625	2856	361213	0.007908	2.5797	2313079	0.0213	31.417	0.007891	40
45	0.047719	70769	3377	345718	0.009768	2.5937	1951867	0.0301	27.581	0.009734	45
50	0.064916	67392	4375	326503	0.013399	2.6099	1606149	0.0594	23.833	0.013289	50
55	0.090195	63017	5684	301306	0.018864	2.5758	1279664	0.0269	20.306	0.018806	55
60	0.112367	57333	6442	271174	0.023757	2.5953	978340	0.0225	17.064	0.023679	60
65	0.169623	50891	8632	233531	0.036964	2.5761	707166	0.0225	13.896	0.036839	65
70	0.227115	42259	9598	187761	0.051116	2.5481	473635	0.0225	11.208	0.050936	70
75	0.332206	32661	10850	136068	0.079741	2.4897	285874	0.0225	8.753	0.079478	75
80	0.415464	21811	9062	85410	0.106096	2.5437	149806	0.0225	6.868	0.105843	80
85+	1.000000	12749	12749	64396	0.197983	5.0510	64396	0.0225	5.051	0.216882	85+

TABLE 3 — FEMALE LIFE TABLE

x	$_nq_x$	l_x	$_nd_x$	$_nL_x$	$_nm_x$	$_na_x$	T_x	r_x	$\mathring{e}_x$	$_nM_x$	x
0	0.086431	100000	8643	94549	0.091414	0.3694	5867611	0.0000	58.676	0.091414	0
1	0.053056	91357	4847	352133	0.013765	1.2573	5773061	0.0000	63.192	0.013765	1
5	0.012584	86510	1089	429828	0.002533	2.5000	5420928	0.0236	62.663	0.002583	5
10	0.006991	85421	597	425532	0.001403	2.3639	4991100	0.0374	58.429	0.001410	10
15	0.008236	84824	699	422469	0.001654	2.6367	4565568	0.0260	53.824	0.001648	15
20	0.012549	84125	1056	418142	0.002525	2.6458	4143099	0.0331	49.249	0.002512	20
25	0.017306	83070	1438	411940	0.003490	2.6291	3724957	0.0433	44.841	0.003469	25
30	0.023848	81632	1947	403483	0.004825	2.5973	3313016	0.0273	40.585	0.004811	30
35	0.029452	79685	2347	392692	0.005976	2.5566	2909533	0.0300	36.513	0.005964	35
40	0.033414	77338	2584	380379	0.006794	2.5570	2516841	0.0288	32.543	0.006780	40
45	0.040857	74754	3054	366403	0.008336	2.5876	2136462	0.0387	28.580	0.008302	45
50	0.053945	71700	3868	349330	0.011072	2.6292	1770058	0.0652	24.687	0.010962	50
55	0.080379	67832	5452	326071	0.016721	2.5991	1420728	0.0384	20.945	0.016636	55
60	0.103601	62380	6463	296276	0.021813	2.5824	1094657	0.0216	17.548	0.021752	60
65	0.143242	55917	8010	260445	0.030754	2.6101	798381	0.0216	14.278	0.030637	65
70	0.223277	47908	10697	213504	0.050100	2.5662	537936	0.0216	11.229	0.049920	70
75	0.306536	37211	11407	157522	0.072412	2.4985	324432	0.0216	8.719	0.072187	75
80	0.411391	25804	10616	103271	0.102795	2.5742	166910	0.0216	6.468	0.102212	80
85+	*1.000000	15189	15189	63639	0.238670	4.1899	63639	0.0216	4.190	0.236541	85+

TABLE 4 — OBSERVED AND PROJECTED VITAL RATES

	OBSERVED POPULATION BOTH SEXES	MALES	FEMALES	PROJECTED POPULATION 1965 MALES	FEMALES	1970 MALES	FEMALES	1975 MALES	FEMALES	STABLE POPULATION MALES	FEMALES
RATES PER THOUSAND											
Birth	43.48	44.51	42.43	44.65	42.59	44.72	42.65	44.91	42.85	43.46	41.66
Death	10.87	11.70	10.02	11.63	9.82	11.53	9.77	11.65	9.91	12.91	11.10
Increase	32.61	32.81	32.41	33.02	32.77	33.19	32.88	33.26	32.94	30.5562	
PERCENTAGE											
under 15	45.69	46.66	44.71	45.96	44.48	44.54	43.50	45.08	44.27	44.20	43.60
15-64	51.58	50.64	52.53	51.30	52.92	52.82	53.95	52.14	52.99	52.58	52.90
65 and over	2.73	2.70	2.75	2.74	2.61	2.64	2.55	2.77	2.73	3.23	3.49
DEP. RATIO X 100	93.87	97.46	90.36	94.93	88.98	89.31	85.36	91.78	88.70	90.20	89.02

TABLE 1 — DATA

AGE AT LAST BIRTHDAY	POPULATION BOTH SEXES	MALES Number	MALES %	FEMALES Number	FEMALES %	BIRTHS BY AGE OF MOTHER	DEATHS BOTH SEXES	DEATHS MALES	DEATHS FEMALES	AGE AT LAST BIRTHDAY
0	884231	454476	3.6	429755	3.5	0	87750	46376	41374	0
1-4	3648947	1872356	14.9	1776591	14.3	0	42085	19886	22199	1-4
5-9	3413641	1773014	14.1	1640627	13.2	0	9789	4763	5026	5-9
10-14	2823493	1483536	11.8	1339957	10.8	0	6112	2939	3173	10-14
15-19	2367004	1229785	9.8	1137219	9.1	95797	7613	3755	3858	15-19
20-24	2181077	1110020	8.8	1071057	8.6	273874	9568	4817	4751	20-24
25-29	1825007	864423	6.9	960584	7.7	289700	8925	4051	4874	25-29
30-34	1489140	700402	5.6	788738	6.3	184118	8301	3750	4551	30-34
35-39	1403596	689073	5.5	714523	5.7	119422	9158	4469	4689	35-39
40-44	1136242	575808	4.6	560434	4.5	42298	9021	4802	4219	40-44
45-49	1009092	505110	4.0	503982	4.0	9354	10103	5545	4558	45-49
50-54	827095	416223	3.3	410872	3.3	0	11458	6383	5075	50-54
55-59	632263	297386	2.4	334877	2.7	0	12088	6415	5673	55-59
60-64	532148	239233	1.9	292915	2.4	0	15126	7602	7524	60-64
65-69	376157	158810	1.3	217347	1.7	0	15758	7406	8352	65-69
70-74	249276	101508	0.8	147768	1.2		16107	7130	8977	70-74
75-79	123724	48594	0.4	75130	0.6		12345	5202	7143	75-79
80-84	50450	18700	0.1	31750	0.3	522500 M.	8722	3414	5308	80-84
85+	16658	5511	0.0	11147	0.1	492063 F.	4840	1636	3204	85+
TOTAL	24989241	12543968		12445273		1014563	304869	150341	154528	TOTAL

TABLE 2 — MALE LIFE TABLE

x	nq_x	l_x	nd_x	nL_x	nm_x	na_x	T_x	r_x	$\mathring{e}_x$	nM_x	x
0	0.095528	100000	9553	93616	0.102043	0.3317	5479942	0.0000	54.799	0.102043	0
1	0.041253	90447	3731	351307	0.010621	1.1908	5386326	0.0000	59.552	0.010621	1
5	0.013044	86716	1131	430752	0.002626	2.5000	5035019	0.0406	58.063	0.002686	5
10	0.009872	85585	845	425845	0.001984	2.5391	4604266	0.0342	53.798	0.001981	10
15	0.015221	84740	1290	420674	0.003066	2.6536	4178421	0.0259	49.309	0.003053	15
20	0.021524	83450	1796	412887	0.004350	2.5702	3757747	0.0311	45.030	0.004340	20
25	0.023206	81654	1895	403598	0.004695	2.5345	3344861	0.0413	40.964	0.004686	25
30	0.026456	79759	2110	393643	0.005360	2.5580	2941262	0.0172	36.877	0.005354	30
35	0.031966	77649	2482	382242	0.006494	2.5814	2547619	0.0130	32.809	0.006486	35
40	0.040978	75167	3080	368422	0.008361	2.5936	2165377	0.0226	28.808	0.008340	40
45	0.053629	72087	3866	351184	0.011008	2.6073	1796955	0.0211	24.928	0.010978	45
50	0.074342	68221	5072	328975	0.015416	2.6085	1445771	0.0373	21.193	0.015336	50
55	0.103056	63149	6508	300172	0.021681	2.6070	1116796	0.0330	17.685	0.021571	55
60	0.148526	56641	8413	262936	0.031995	2.5905	816624	0.0436	14.417	0.031777	60
65	0.210688	48229	10161	216374	0.046961	2.5624	553688	0.0436	11.480	0.046634	65
70	0.300940	38067	11456	161929	0.070747	2.5202	337314	0.0436	8.861	0.070241	70
75	0.423661	26611	11274	104471	0.107911	2.4645	175385	0.0436	6.591	0.107050	75
80	0.621591	15337	9533	51713	0.184355	2.3805	70914	0.0436	4.624	0.182566	80
85+	*1.000000	5804	5804	19202	0.302253	3.3085	19202	0.0436	3.308	0.296861	85+

TABLE 3 — FEMALE LIFE TABLE

x	nq_x	l_x	nd_x	nL_x	nm_x	na_x	T_x	r_x	$\mathring{e}_x$	nM_x	x
0	0.090641	100000	9064	94149	0.096273	0.3545	5569064	0.0000	55.691	0.096273	0
1	0.048308	90936	4393	351568	0.012495	1.2283	5474915	0.0000	60.206	0.012495	1
5	0.014815	86543	1282	429510	0.002985	2.5000	5123347	0.0448	59.200	0.003063	5
10	0.011785	85261	1005	423821	0.002371	2.5288	4693838	0.0339	55.053	0.002368	10
15	0.016867	84256	1421	417897	0.003401	2.6194	4270016	0.0190	50.679	0.003392	15
20	0.021964	82835	1819	409754	0.004440	2.5700	3852119	0.0125	46.504	0.004436	20
25	0.025092	81016	2033	400085	0.005081	2.5441	3442365	0.0255	42.490	0.005074	25
30	0.028482	78983	2250	389383	0.005777	2.5416	3042280	0.0238	38.518	0.005770	30
35	0.032340	76733	2482	377566	0.006573	2.5420	2652897	0.0276	34.573	0.006562	35
40	0.037027	74252	2749	364528	0.007542	2.5523	2275331	0.0273	30.644	0.007528	40
45	0.044358	71502	3172	349846	0.009065	2.5896	1910803	0.0216	26.724	0.009044	45
50	0.060201	68331	4114	331800	0.012398	2.6048	1560937	0.0283	22.844	0.012352	50
55	0.081622	64217	5242	308620	0.016984	2.6218	1229137	0.0161	19.140	0.016941	55
60	0.121702	58976	7177	277751	0.025841	2.6138	920517	0.0357	15.608	0.025687	60
65	0.176895	51798	9163	236950	0.038670	2.5946	642766	0.0357	12.409	0.038427	65
70	0.265926	42635	11338	185441	0.061140	2.5537	405816	0.0357	9.518	0.060751	70
75	0.386228	31297	12088	126257	0.095741	2.4991	220375	0.0357	7.041	0.095075	75
80	0.587595	19209	11287	66961	0.168567	2.4231	94118	0.0357	4.900	0.167180	80
85+	*1.000000	7922	7922	27157	0.291710	3.4281	27157	0.0357	3.428	0.287432	85+

TABLE 4 — OBSERVED AND PROJECTED VITAL RATES

	OBSERVED POPULATION BOTH SEXES	MALES	FEMALES	PROJECTED POPULATION 1965 MALES	FEMALES	1970 MALES	FEMALES	1975 MALES	FEMALES	STABLE POPULATION MALES	FEMALES
RATES PER THOUSAND											
Birth	40.60	41.65	39.54	39.86	38.26	38.85	37.63	39.28	38.31	39.64	39.56
Death	12.20	11.99	12.42	11.69	12.12	11.67	12.07	11.73	12.09	12.38	12.30
Increase	28.40	29.67	27.12	28.17	26.14	27.19	25.56	27.55	26.23	27.2627	
PERCENTAGE											
under 15	43.10	44.51	41.68	44.58	42.63	44.08	42.69	42.48	41.37	42.42	42.27
15-64	53.63	52.83	54.44	52.57	53.33	53.02	53.35	54.47	54.75	54.55	54.25
65 and over	3.27	2.66	3.88	2.85	4.04	2.89	3.96	3.05	3.88	3.04	3.49
DEP. RATIO X 100	86.45	89.27	83.69	90.22	87.51	88.59	87.43	83.59	82.65	83.33	84.35

TABLE 1 — DATA

AGE AT LAST BIRTHDAY	POPULATION BOTH SEXES	MALES Number	%	FEMALES Number	%	BIRTHS BY AGE OF MOTHER	DEATHS BOTH SEXES	MALES	FEMALES	AGE AT LAST BIRTHDAY
0	804514	419040	3.0	385474	2.9	0	113409	60845	52564	0
1-4	3420762	1745285	12.4	1675477	12.4	0	64067	29939	34128	1-4
5-9	3968508	2057489	14.7	1911019	14.2	0	16851	8044	8807	5-9
10-14	3151089	1675424	11.9	1475665	11.0	0	10064	4771	5293	10-14
15-19	2288445	1238340	8.8	1050105	7.8	129060	10328	5215	5113	15-19
20-24	2285479	1167374	8.3	1118105	8.3	320334	13967	7010	6957	20-24
25-29	2313891	1146809	8.2	1167082	8.7	369167	15775	7543	8232	25-29
30-34	1996046	1018785	7.3	977261	7.3	248899	15525	7702	7823	30-34
35-39	1430556	742783	5.3	687773	5.1	129406	12877	6703	6174	35-39
40-44	1044965	501281	3.6	543684	4.0	48255	11106	5659	5447	40-44
45-49	1100482	604809	4.3	495673	3.7	12172	14322	8586	5736	45-49
50-54	1119564	543398	3.9	576166	4.3	0	19363	10416	8947	50-54
55-59	787029	420817	3.0	366212	2.7	0	18531	10910	7621	55-59
60-64	822909	365531	2.6	457378	3.4	0	27998	13691	14307	60-64
65-69	376866	164907	1.2	211959	1.6	0	18481	8865	9616	65-69
70-74	306858	112887	0.8	193971	1.4		22599	8975	13624	70-74
75-79	128548	50908	0.4	77640	0.6		14435	6085	8350	75-79
80-84	96700	33672	0.2	63028	0.5	647506 M.	17299	6228	11071	80-84
85+	62745	22896	0.2	39849	0.3	609787 F.	18182	6678	11504	85+
TOTAL	27505956	14032435		13473521		1257293	455179	223865	231314	TOTAL

TABLE 2 — MALE LIFE TABLE

x	$_nq_x$	l_x	$_nd_x$	$_nL_x$	$_nm_x$	$_na_x$	T_x	r_x	$\mathring{e}_x$	$_nM_x$	x
0	0.132531	100000	13253	91274	0.145201	0.3416	4827356	0.0000	48.274	0.145201	0
1	0.065479	86747	5680	331119	0.017154	1.2062	4736082	0.0000	54.597	0.017154	1
5	0.019129	81067	1551	401457	0.003863	2.5000	4404963	0.0188	54.337	0.003910	5
10	0.014154	79516	1125	394786	0.002851	2.5170	4003506	0.0474	50.348	0.002848	10
15	0.020952	78391	1642	388086	0.004232	2.6454	3608720	0.0318	46.035	0.004211	15
20	0.029598	76748	2272	378222	0.006006	2.5705	3220634	0.0019	41.964	0.006005	20
25	0.032373	74477	2411	366441	0.006580	2.5354	2842412	0.0069	38.165	0.006577	25
30	0.037202	72066	2681	353765	0.007578	2.5519	2475971	0.0358	34.357	0.007560	30
35	0.044377	69385	3079	339427	0.009071	2.5653	2122206	0.0617	30.586	0.009024	35
40	0.054984	66306	3646	322668	0.011299	2.5698	1782779	0.0092	26.887	0.011289	40
45	0.068626	62660	4300	302905	0.014196	2.5829	1460111	0.0000	23.302	0.014196	45
50	0.091784	58360	5357	278861	0.019209	2.5847	1157206	0.0168	19.829	0.019168	50
55	0.122199	53003	6477	249378	0.025972	2.5857	878345	0.0128	16.572	0.025926	55
60	0.172366	46526	8020	213145	0.037625	2.5702	628967	0.0305	13.519	0.037455	60
65	0.238359	38507	9178	169951	0.054006	2.5396	415821	0.0305	10.799	0.053758	65
70	0.332855	29328	9762	122194	0.079890	2.4957	245871	0.0305	8.383	0.079504	70
75	0.458854	19566	8978	74726	0.120147	2.4264	123676	0.0305	6.321	0.119529	75
80	0.622604	10588	6592	35422	0.186104	2.3426	48951	0.0305	4.623	0.184960	80
85+	*1.000000	3996	3996	13528	0.295375	3.3855	13528	0.0305	3.386	0.291667	85+

TABLE 3 — FEMALE LIFE TABLE

x	$_nq_x$	l_x	$_nd_x$	$_nL_x$	$_nm_x$	$_na_x$	T_x	r_x	$\mathring{e}_x$	$_nM_x$	x
0	0.125497	100000	12550	92032	0.136362	0.3651	4871998	0.0000	48.720	0.136362	0
1	0.077153	87450	6747	331237	0.020369	1.2486	4779966	0.0000	54.659	0.020369	1
5	0.022415	80703	1809	398994	0.004534	2.5000	4448729	0.0255	55.125	0.004609	5
10	0.017793	78894	1404	390975	0.003590	2.5090	4049735	0.0558	51.331	0.003587	10
15	0.024125	77491	1869	382969	0.004882	2.6018	3658761	0.0229	47.216	0.004869	15
20	0.030645	75621	2317	372452	0.006222	2.5605	3275791	0.0000	43.319	0.006222	20
25	0.034677	73304	2542	360260	0.007056	2.5382	2903340	0.0064	39.607	0.007053	25
30	0.039337	70762	2784	346943	0.008023	2.5337	2543079	0.0449	35.939	0.008005	30
35	0.044009	67978	2992	332494	0.008997	2.5276	2196136	0.0496	32.307	0.008977	35
40	0.048942	64986	3181	317082	0.010031	2.5319	1863642	0.0227	28.677	0.010019	40
45	0.056279	61806	3478	300582	0.011572	2.5714	1546560	0.0000	25.023	0.011572	45
50	0.074969	58328	4373	281095	0.015556	2.5891	1245978	0.0146	21.362	0.015529	50
55	0.099131	53955	5349	256968	0.020814	2.6058	964883	0.0013	17.883	0.020810	55
60	0.145831	48606	7088	225968	0.031369	2.5928	707915	0.0179	14.564	0.031280	60
65	0.204845	41518	8505	186914	0.045501	2.5690	481947	0.0179	11.608	0.045367	65
70	0.299987	33013	9904	140574	0.070451	2.5269	295033	0.0179	8.937	0.070237	70
75	0.423432	23110	9785	90696	0.107891	2.4603	154459	0.0179	6.684	0.107548	75
80	0.603290	13324	8038	45588	0.176327	2.3834	63763	0.0179	4.785	0.175653	80
85+	*1.000000	5286	5286	18175	0.290838	3.4383	18175	0.0179	3.438	0.288690	85+

TABLE 4 — OBSERVED AND PROJECTED VITAL RATES

	OBSERVED POPULATION BOTH SEXES	MALES	FEMALES	PROJECTED POPULATION 1965 MALES	FEMALES	1970 MALES	FEMALES	1975 MALES	FEMALES	STABLE POPULATION MALES	FEMALES
RATES PER THOUSAND											
Birth	45.71	46.14	45.26	43.11	42.64	42.35	42.12	42.47	42.38	44.44	44.59
Death	16.55	15.95	17.17	16.44	17.19	16.19	16.74	16.13	16.54	16.40	16.56
Increase	29.16	30.19	28.09	26.67	25.45	26.16	25.38	26.34	25.84	28.0384	
PERCENTAGE											
under 15	41.25	42.03	40.43	42.99	42.38	42.74	42.44	43.77	43.51	44.34	44.32
15-64	55.22	55.23	55.22	53.80	52.87	53.92	53.33	52.80	52.19	53.23	52.87
65 and over	3.53	2.75	4.35	3.21	4.75	3.34	4.23	3.43	4.31	2.43	2.81
DEP. RATIO X 100	81.09	81.07	81.11	85.88	89.15	85.46	87.52	89.39	91.61	87.88	89.15

TABLE 1 — DATA

AGE AT LAST BIRTHDAY	POPULATION BOTH SEXES	MALES Number	MALES %	FEMALES Number	FEMALES %	BIRTHS BY AGE OF MOTHER	DEATHS BOTH SEXES	DEATHS MALES	DEATHS FEMALES	AGE AT LAST BIRTHDAY
0	4942142	2521649	2.7	2420493	2.1	0	151795	87175	64620	0
1-4	19214649	9782326	10.4	9432323	8.2	0	17152	9553	7599	1-4
5-9	22207440	11305331	12.0	10902109	9.5	0	7757	4830	2927	5-9
10-14	16025661	8105819	8.6	7919842	6.9	0	5597	3760	1837	10-14
15-19	15784270	7961352	8.5	7822918	6.8	228429	10636	7581	3055	15-19
20-24	20343847	10056407	10.7	10287440	9.0	1668623	19525	13749	5776	20-24
25-29	18190861	8917349	9.5	9273512	8.1	1528275	18636	12410	6226	25-29
30-34	18999660	8611378	9.2	10388282	9.1	1143750	22271	13140	9131	30-34
35-39	11590970	4528533	4.8	7062437	6.2	470358	17668	8789	8879	35-39
40-44	10408508	3998409	4.3	6410099	5.6	154483	23970	11763	12207	40-44
45-49	12263982	4705965	5.0	7558017	6.6	37790	47793	23898	23895	45-49
50-54	10447149	4010285	4.3	6436864	5.6	0	69226	37010	32216	50-54
55-59	8699198	2905610	3.1	5793588	5.0	0	89955	44975	44980	55-59
60-64	6696520	2347664	2.5	4348856	3.8	0	115035	57488	57547	60-64
65-69	5040190	1751433	1.9	3288757	2.9	0	147020	67731	79289	65-69
70-74	3916792	1277330	1.4	2639462	2.3		203074	81861	121213	70-74
75-79	2251473	743275	0.8	1508198	1.3		205347	78239	127108	75-79
80-84	1127468	333904	0.4	793564	0.7	2694330 M.	159341	55040	104301	80-84
85+	675870	186284	0.2	489586	0.4	2537378 F.	192637	56651	135986	85+
TOTAL	208826650	94050303		114776347		5231708	1524435	675643	848792	TOTAL

TABLE 2 — MALE LIFE TABLE

x	nq_x	l_x	nd_x	nL_x	nm_x	na_x	T_x	r_x	$\mathring{e}_x$	nM_x	x
0	0.033582	100000	3358	97304	0.034513	0.1971	6773270	0.0021	67.733	0.034571	0
1	0.003879	96642	375	385468	0.000973	1.0674	6675966	0.0021	69.079	0.000977	1
5	0.002117	96267	204	480825	0.000424	2.5000	6290499	0.0411	65.344	0.000427	5
10	0.002336	96063	224	479807	0.000468	2.7335	5809674	0.0345	60.478	0.000464	10
15	0.004751	95839	455	478144	0.000952	2.6947	5329867	0.0000	55.613	0.000952	15
20	0.006813	95383	650	475334	0.001367	2.5647	4851723	0.0000	50.865	0.001367	20
25	0.006937	94734	657	472039	0.001392	2.5218	4376388	0.0141	46.197	0.001392	25
30	0.007640	94076	719	468638	0.001534	2.5738	3904349	0.0662	41.502	0.001526	30
35	0.009768	93358	912	464640	0.001963	2.6444	3435711	0.0747	36.802	0.001941	35
40	0.014611	92446	1351	459138	0.002942	2.7121	2971071	0.0000	32.139	0.002942	40
45	0.025104	91095	2287	450320	0.005078	2.7458	2511932	0.0000	27.575	0.005078	45
50	0.045586	88808	4048	434772	0.009311	2.7105	2061613	0.0386	23.214	0.009229	50
55	0.075233	84760	6377	408911	0.015595	2.6652	1626841	0.0375	19.194	0.015479	55
60	0.116164	78383	9105	370388	0.024583	2.6357	1217930	0.0208	15.538	0.024487	60
65	0.177687	69278	12310	317018	0.038830	2.6141	847542	0.0208	12.234	0.038672	65
70	0.278135	56968	15845	246237	0.064348	2.5637	530524	0.0208	9.313	0.064088	70
75	0.417055	41123	17151	162309	0.105667	2.4749	284287	0.0208	6.913	0.105263	75
80	0.574713	23973	13777	83282	0.165429	2.3948	121979	0.0208	5.088	0.164838	80
85+	1.000000	10195	10195	38696	0.263469	3.7955	38696	0.0208	3.796	0.304110	85

TABLE 3 — FEMALE LIFE TABLE

x	nq_x	l_x	nd_x	nL_x	nm_x	na_x	T_x	r_x	$\mathring{e}_x$	nM_x	x
0	0.026104	100000	2610	97922	0.026658	0.2039	7286891	0.0018	72.869	0.026697	0
1	0.003204	97390	312	388645	0.000803	1.0712	7188969	0.0018	73.817	0.000806	1
5	0.001322	97078	128	485067	0.000265	2.5000	6800324	0.0399	70.050	0.000268	5
10	0.001163	96949	113	484477	0.000233	2.6118	6315257	0.0329	65.140	0.000232	10
15	0.001951	96836	189	483743	0.000391	2.6744	5830781	0.0000	60.213	0.000391	15
20	0.002804	96648	271	482588	0.000561	2.6031	5347038	0.0000	55.325	0.000561	20
25	0.003351	96377	323	481107	0.000671	2.5980	4864450	0.0000	50.473	0.000671	25
30	0.004402	96054	423	479269	0.000882	2.6385	4383343	0.0263	45.634	0.000879	30
35	0.006317	95631	604	476743	0.001267	2.6649	3904074	0.0470	40.824	0.001257	35
40	0.009480	95027	901	473063	0.001904	2.7019	3427331	0.0000	36.067	0.001904	40
45	0.015693	94126	1477	467227	0.003162	2.6975	2954269	0.0000	31.386	0.003162	45
50	0.024838	92649	2301	457905	0.005025	2.6803	2487041	0.0214	26.844	0.005005	50
55	0.038390	90347	3468	443757	0.007816	2.6993	2029136	0.0309	22.459	0.007764	55
60	0.064680	86879	5619	421572	0.013329	2.7181	1585380	0.0294	18.248	0.013233	60
65	0.115073	81260	9351	384875	0.024296	2.7090	1163808	0.0294	14.322	0.024109	65
70	0.208571	71909	14998	324257	0.046254	2.6472	778933	0.0294	10.832	0.045923	70
75	0.350548	56911	19950	235338	0.084772	2.5330	454676	0.0294	7.989	0.084278	75
80	0.491360	36961	18161	137541	0.132041	2.4868	219338	0.0294	5.934	0.131434	80
85+	1.000000	18800	18800	81797	0.229834	4.3510	81797	0.0294	4.351	0.277756	85

TABLE 4 — OBSERVED AND PROJECTED VITAL RATES

	OBSERVED POPULATION BOTH SEXES	MALES	FEMALES	PROJECTED POPULATION 1964 MALES	FEMALES	1969 MALES	FEMALES	1974 MALES	FEMALES	STABLE POPULATION MALES	FEMALES
RATES PER THOUSAND											
Birth	25.05	28.65	22.11	25.26	20.09	22.35	18.25	22.02	18.41	20.47	19.35
Death	7.30	7.18	7.40	7.08	7.63	7.19	8.11	7.45	8.78	10.95	9.83
Increase	17.75	21.46	14.71	18.18	12.46	15.15	10.14	14.57	9.63		9.5228
PERCENTAGE											
under 15	29.88	33.72	26.73	35.03	28.38	33.16	27.45	30.98	26.13	27.53	26.26
15-64	63.89	61.71	65.68	60.40	63.48	62.13	63.32	63.79	63.71	63.82	62.60
65 and over	6.23	4.56	7.60	4.57	8.14	4.71	9.24	5.23	10.16	8.65	11.14
DEP. RATIO X 100	56.51	62.04	52.26	65.57	57.54	60.96	57.94	56.76	56.96	56.69	59.75

Bibliography and Acknowledgment

METHODS AND THEORY

Bogue, D. J., and Kitagawa, E. M. "Techniques of Demographic Research: A Laboratory Manual." Mimeographed. Community and Family Study Center, University of Chicago.

Bourgeois-Pichat, Jean. "Utilisation de la notion de population stable pour mesurer la mortalité et la fécondité des populations des pays sous-développés," *Bulletin de l'Institut International de Statistique* (Actes de la 30ᵉ Session), 1957).

Coale, Ansley J. "A New Method for Calculating Lotka's *r*—the Intrinsic Rate of Growth in a Stable Population," *Population Studies*, 11 (July, 1957): 92–94.

———. "Estimates of Various Demographic Measures Through the Quasi-Stable Age Distribution," *Emerging Techniques in Population Research*: Proceedings of the 1962 Annual Conference of the Milbank Memorial Fund. pp. 175–93.

Durand, J. D. "A Long-Range View of World Population Growth," *Annals of the American Academy of Political and Social Science*, 369 (January, 1967): 1–8.

Fisher, R. A. *The Genetical Theory of Natural Selection.* New York: Dover Publications, 1958. 1st ed. 1930.

Goodman, L. A. "Population Growth of the Sexes," *Biometrics*, 9 (1953): 212–25.

Hauser, P. M. *World Population Programs.* Headline Series, No. 174. New York: Foreign Policy Association, 1965.

———. *World Population Prospects and Implications.* Chicago: Population Research and Training Center, 1967.

———, and Duncan, O. D. *The Study of Population.* Chicago: University of Chicago Press, 1959.

Keyfitz, Nathan. "A Life Table that Agrees with the Data," *Journal of the American Statistical Association*, 61, pt. 1 (June, 1966): 305–12.

———. "Reconciliation of Population Models: Matrix, Integral Equation, and Partial Fraction," *Journal of the Royal Statistical Society,* 130, no. 1 (1967): 61–83.

————, Nagnur, D., and Sharma, D. "The Interpretation of Age Distributions," *Journal of the American Statistical Association*, vol. 62, pt. 2 (September, 1967).

Leslie, P. H. "On the Use of Matrices in Certain Population Mathematics," *Biometrika*, 33 (1945): 183–212.

————. "Some Further Notes on the Use of Matrices in Population Mathematics," *Biometrika*, 35 (1948): 213–45.

Lotka, A. J. *Théorie analytique des associations biologiques*. Pt. 2. Analyse démographique avec application particulière a l'espèce humaine. (Actualités Scientifiques et Industrielles, no. 780.) Paris: Hermann & Cie, 1939.

Myers, R. J. "The Validity and Significance of Male Net Reproduction Rates," *Journal of the American Statistical Association*, 36 (1941): 275-82.

Pressat, Roland. *L'Analyse démographique: méthodes, résultats, applications*. Paris: Presses Universitaires de France, 1961.

Ryder, Norman B. "The Process of Demographic Translation," *Demography*, 1, no. 1 (1964): 74–82.

Spiegelman, Mortimer. *Introduction to Demography*. Chicago: University of Chicago Press, 1955.

United Nations. *World Population Prospects as Assessed in 1963*. Population Studies, No. 41. New York: United Nations, 1966.

Whelpton, P. K. "An Empirical Method of Calculating Future Population," *Journal of the American Statistical Association*, 31 (1936): 457–73.

SOURCES

General

United Nations. *Demographic Yearbook*, 1948–65. New York: United Nations.

America

BARBADOS
    Central Statistical Office. *Population Census 1960*. Vol. 2, Summary Tables.
CANADA
    Dominion Bureau of Statistics. *Census* 1931, 1941, 1951, 1961.
    Dominion Bureau of Statistics. *Vital Statistics* 1930, 1931, 1932, 1940, 1941, 1942, 1950, 1951, 1952, 1960, 1961, 1962, 1963, 1964.
CHILE
    Dirección de Estadística y Censos. *Demografía* 1954, 1960, 1962.
DOMINICAN REPUBLIC
    Oficina Nacional de Estadística. *Cuarto Censo Nacional de Población 1960*. Resumen General.
HONDURAS
    Dirección General de Estadística y Censos. *Anuarios Estadísticas* 1952–64.
    ————. *Estadísticas Demográficas* 1926–51.
UNITED STATES
    Department of Commerce, Bureau of the Census. *Birth, Stillbirth, and Infant Mortality Statistics* 1919, 1920, 1921, 1924, 1925, 1926, 1929, 1930, 1931, 1934, 1935, 1936.
    ————. *Mortality Statistics* 1919, 1920, 1921, 1924, 1925, 1926, 1929, 1930, 1931, 1934, 1935, 1936.

————. *U.S. Census of Population* 1920, 1930, 1940, 1950, 1960.

————. "Population Estimates," *Current Population Reports*, ser. P-25, nos. 311, 321.

Bureau of the Census and the National Center for Health Statistics. *U.S. Vital Statistics* 1939–64

Asia

CEYLON

Report of the Registrar General of Ceylon On Vital Statistics, 1954–62.

CHINA (MAINLAND)

Roland Pressat. "La Population de la Chine," *Population*, vol. 16 (4).

ISRAEL

Central Bureau of Statistics. *Statistical Abstracts of Israel* 1950–65.

JAPAN

Bureau of Statistics, Office of the Prime Minister. *Japan Statistical Yearbook* 1951–64.

TURKEY

State Institute of Statistics. *Census of Population*. Pub. no. 452.

Europe

AUSTRIA

Österreichisches Statistisches Zentralamt. *Statistische Nachrichten*, 1960, vol. 9.

BELGIUM

Ministère des Affaires Économiques. *Bulletin de Statistique*. Vols. 31 (1945); 32 (1946).

Ministère de L'Intérieur et de L'Instruction Publique. *Annuaire Statistique de la Belgique*. Vol. 36 (1905).

Ministère de L'Intérieur. *Annuaire Statistique de la Belgique et du Congo Belge* 1912–59.

————. *Annuaire Statistique de la Belgique*. Vols. 81 (1960); 82 (1961).

————. *Statistique du Mouvement de la Population et de L'Etat Civil de 1901 à 1910*.

BULGARIA

Central Statistical Office, Sofia. *Vital Statistics of Bulgaria* 1947–59.

DENMARK

Det Statistiske Departement. *Statistisk Årbog 1966*. Vol. 70.

————. *Befolkningens Bevaegelser* 1963, 1965.

FINLAND

Statistiska Central-Byrau. Vaestolilastoa, Suomen Vaesto 1930.

————. Vaestolilastoa, Vaestosuhteet Vuonna 1931. Vol. 4, no. 74.

————. *Vital Statistics* 1950, 1952, 1955, 1956, 1959, 1960, 1961, 1962, 1963, 1964.

FRANCE

Bourgeois-Pichat, J. "Note sur l'évolution générale de la population française depuis le 18e siècle," *Population*, April–June, 1952.

Ministère de Commerce, Statistique Générale de la France. *Résultats Statistiques du Dénombrement de 1891*.

Ministère de Commerce, de L'Industrie, des Postes, et des Télégraphes, Statistique Générale de la France. *Statistique Annuelle.* N.s. Vols. 1 (1871)— 36 (1906).

Ministère du Travail et de la Prévoyance Sociale. *Annuaire Statistique de la France.* Vols. 27 (1907); 29 (1909); 34 (1914); 43 (1927).

————. *Statistique du Mouvement de la Population.* Vols. 1 (1907–10); 2 (1911–13); 3 (1914–19); 19 (1940–42); 21 (1944); 22 (1945); 23 (1946–47).

Bureau de la Statistique Générale. *Annuaire Statistique de la France.* Vols. 45 (1929)—54 (1938).

Institut National de la Statistique et des Etudes Economiques. *Annuaire Statistique de la France.* Vols. 56 (1940–45); 58 (1951)—70 (1964).

————. *Bulletin Mensuel de Statistique.* N.s. Vols. 1–3.

GERMANY—EAST

Staatliche Zentralverwaltung für Statistik. *Bevölkerungsstatistisches Jahrbuch der Deutschen Demokratischen Republik,* 1965, 1966.

GERMANY—WEST

Statistisches Bundesamt. Wiesbaden, Fachserie A, "Bevölkerung und Kultur," Reihe 2, *Natürliche Bevölkerungsbewegung im Jahre 1960,* 1961, 1962, 1963, 1964.

————. Wiesbaden, Fachserie A, "Bevölkerung und Kultur," Reihe 1, *Bevölkerungsstand und -entwicklung 1961 und 1962.*

IRELAND

Central Statistics Office. *Census of Population of Ireland.* Vol. 2, 1961.

————. *Annual Report on Vital Statistics* 1936, 1946, 1951, 1955, 1956, 1957, 1960, 1961, 1962.

ITALY

Istituto Centrale di Statistica. *VII Censimento generale della popolazione.* Vol. 4, pt. 2, 1931. "Movimento della popolazione, 1931."

LUXEMBOURG

Office de la Statistique. *Annuaire Statistique* 1960, 1964.

————. *La Population du Grand-Duché suivant l'âge. Période de 1880 à 1955.*

Aperçu Statistique, 1931. Extrait de l'Annuaire Officiel, 1931.

NETHERLANDS

Bevolking van Nederland, Leeftijd en Geslacht, 1900–1952. Utrecht, 1953.

Centraal Bureau voor de Statistiek. *Bijdragen tot de Statistiek van Nederland,* Nieuwe Volgreeks, "Statistiek van den Loop der Bevolking in Nederland over het jaar 1900–1931."

————. *Statistiek van den Loop der Bevolking in Nederland* 1938–54.

————. *Jaarcijfers voor het Koninkrijk der Nederlanden* 1910, 1919, 1922.

————. *Jaarcijfers voor Nederland* 1933, 1941–42, 1947–50.

NORWAY

Statistisk Sentral Byrå. *Statistik Arbok for Norge* 1953, 1963.

————. *Vital Statistics and Migration Statistics* 1963, 1964.

ROMANIA

Directia Centrala de Statistica. *Annuarul Statistic al R.P.R. 1965.*

SWEDEN

Kungl. Statistiska Centralbyrån. *Statistisk Tidskrift.* Vol. 135 (1905).

Statistiska Centralbyrån, Bidrag till Sveriges Officiella Statistik. *Befolknings-statistik*. Vols. 17 (1876); 23 (1881); 43 (1901)—52 (1910).
———. *Befolkningsstatistik för År 1905*, 1915.
Statistiska Centralbyrån, Sveriges Officiella Statistik. *Befolkningsrörelsen*, Översikt för Åren 1911–20; 1921–30; 1931–40; 1941–50; 1951–60.
———. *Befolkningsrörelsen* Åren 1918–1920, 1924–1925. År 1930, 1935, 1940, 1945, 1950, 1955, 1960.
———. *Folkmängdens Förandringar År 1962*.

SWITZERLAND
Eidgenössisches Statistisches Amt. *Statistisches Jahrbuch der Schweiz* 1961.

UNITED KINGDOM
Mitchell, B. R. *Abstract of British Historical Statistics*. Cambridge University Press, 1962.
Annual Report of the Registrar General. Nos. 57, 1894; 76, 1913.
Annual Abstract of Statistics. Nos. 89, 1952; 100, 1963; 102, 1965.
Statistical Abstract of the United Kingdom 1927, 1937.
Registrar General's Statistical Review of England and Wales 1940, pt. 2; 1941, pt. 1; 1942, pt. 2; 1945, pt. 2; 1946, pt. 1; 1947, pt. 1; 1950, pt. 2; 1951, pt. 2; 1952, pt. 2; 1956, pt. 2; 1960, pt. 2; 1961, pt. 2; 1962, pt. 2.
Annual Report of the Registrar General for Scotland 1950–63.

Oceania

AUSTRALIA
Commonwealth Bureau of Census and Statistics. *Census of the Commonwealth of Australia* 1911, vol. 2; 1921, vol. 2; 1933, vol. 1; 1947.
———. *Official Yearbook of the Commonwealth of Australia*. No. 6, 1913.
———. *Demographic Bulletin*. Nos. 29, 1911; 39, 1921; 51, 1933; 65, 1947; 68, 1950—82, 1964.
———. *Demographic Review*. No. 226, 1965.

CORRESPONDENTS

We have had help from many correspondents and wish to express particular appreciation to the following colleagues, none of whom is responsible for whatever errors remain in the volume.

ARGENTINA: Ricardo V. Brega, Direccion Nacional de Estadistica y Censos; CANADA: Walter E. Duffett, Fraser F. Harris, Harry G. Page, Dominion Bureau of Statistics; CHILE: Sergio Chaparro-Ruiz, Direccion de Estadística y Censos; DOMINICAN REPUBLIC: Manuel de Jesus Cordero C., Oficina Nacional de Estadística; MEXICO: Ruben Gleason Galicia, Direccion General de Estadística; PANAMA: Esperanza Espino, Luisa Quesada, Direccion de Estadística y Censo; HONDURAS: J. Trinidad Fiallos, Direccion General de Estadística y Censos; TRINIDAD: Jack Harewood, Central Statistical Office; UNITED STATES: James W. Brackett, Bureau of the Census; Arthur A. Campbell and Clara E. Councell, National Center for Health Statistics.

And CEYLON: A. R. Ratnavale, Bureau of Census and Statistics; CYPRUS: C. Memelaou, Department of Statistics and Research; JAPAN: Akira Noda, Bureau of Statistics; SINGAPORE: P.C.K. Tan, Department of Statistics; THAILAND: Bundhit Kantabutra, National Statistical Office.

And AUSTRIA: D. Hansluwka, Osterreichisches Statistisches Zentralamt; BELGIUM: A Dufrasne, Institut National de Statistique; BULGARIA: Stephan Stanev, Central Statistical Office; CZECHOSLOVAKIA: J. Kazimour, Lidove Kontroly a Statistiky; DENMARK: Kjeld Bjerke, Danmarks Statistik; ENGLAND AND WALES: Leslie V. Martin, Government Actuary's Department; FINLAND: Eino H. Laurila, Central Statistical Office of Finland; FRANCE: J. Dumontier, Institut National de la Statistique et des Etudes Economiques; EAST GERMANY: D. Poschbeck, Staatliche Zentralverwaltung für Statistik; WEST GERMANY: Karl Schwarz, Statistisches Bundesamt; GREECE: P. Couvelis, National Statistical Service; HUNGARY: George Peter, Hungarian Central Statistical Office; IRELAND: M. D. McCarthy, Central Statistics Office; ITALY: Nora Federici, Istituto de Demografia; NETHERLANDS: Ph. J. Idenburg, Centraal Bureau voor de Statistiek; NORWAY: Odd Aukrust, Central Bureau of Statistics; PORTUGAL: Amaro D. Guerreiro, National Statistical Institute; ROMANIA: C. Ionescu, Directia Centrala de Statistica; SPAIN: R. Bermejo, Instituto Nacional de Estadística; SWEDEN: Erland v. Hofsten, Statistica Centralbyran; SWITZERLAND: H. Gross, Eidgenössisches Statistisches Amt; AUSTRALIA: J. P. O'Neill, Commonwealth Bureau of Census and Statistics.

And at the UNITED NATIONS: P. J. Loftus, Director of the U.N. Statistical Office.